W9-DDC-145

THE HOLY QUR'ÃN

English Translation

By

ABDULLAH YUSUF ALI

&

Urdu Translation

By

MAULANA FATEH MOHAMMAD JALLENDHRI

New Delhi - 110002 (India)

KITAB BHAVAN
Publishers, Distributors, Exporters & Importers
1784, Kalan Mahal, Darya Ganj,
New Delhi - 1100 02 (India)

Phones : 91-11-23277392, 23274686
Fax : (91-11) 23263383
Mob. : 9910114484
Website : www.kitabbhavan.net
E-mail : info@kitabbhavan.net
:nasri@vsnl.com

Reprint : 2020

ISBN-10 : 81-7151-227-5
ISBN-13 : 978-81-7151-227-0

Book Code No. : H00076

Printed & Published in India by :
Moonis Ali Nasri for KITAB BHAVAN
1784, Kalan Mahal, Darya Ganj,
New Delhi - 1100 02 [India]

CONTENTS

LIST OF PARTS

FROM THE PREFACE TO FIRST EDITION, 1934

. . . It may be asked: Is there any need for a fresh English translation? To those who ask this question I commend a careful consideration of the facts which I have set out in my Note on Translation. After they have read it, I would invite them to take any particular passage, say 2: 74 or 2: 102, or 2: 164 and compare it with any previous version they choose. If they find that I have helped them even the least bit further in understanding its meanings, or appreciating its beauty or catching something of the grandeur of the original, I would claim that my humble attempt is justified.

It is the duty of every Muslim, man, woman, or child, to read the Qur-ãn and understand it according to his own capacity. If any one of us attains to some knowledge or understanding of it by study, contemplation, and the test of life, both outward and inward, it is his duty, according to his capacity, to instruct others, and share with them the joy and peace which result from contact with the spiritual world. The Qur-ãn—indeed every religious book—has to be read, not only with the tongue and voice and eyes, but with the best light that our intellect can supply, and even more, with the truest and purest light which our heart and conscience can give us. It is in this spirit that I would have my readers approach the Qur-ãn.

It was between the age of four and five that I first learned to read its Arabic words, to revel in its rhythm and music and wonder at its meaning. I have a dim recollection of the *Khatm* ceremony which closed that stage. It was called "completion": it really just *began* a spiritual awakening that has gone on ever since. My revered father taught me Arabic, but I must have imbibed from him into my innermost being something more,—something which told me that all the world's thoughts, all the world's most beautiful languages and literatures, are but vehicles for that ineffable message which comes to the heart in rare moments of ecstasy. The soul of mysticism and ecstasy is in the Qur-ãn, as well as that plain guidance for the plain man which a world in a hurry affects to consider as sufficient. It is good to make this personal confession, to an age in which it is in the highest degree unfashionable to speak of religion or spiritual peace or consolation, an age in which words like these draw forth only derision, pity, or contempt.

I have explored Western lands, Western manners, and the depths of Western thought and Western learning to an extent which has rarely fallen to the lot of an Eastern mortal. But I have never lost touch with my Eastern heritage. Through all my successes and failures I have learned to rely more and more upon the one true thing in all life—the voice that speaks in a tongue above that of mortal man. For me the embodiment of that voice has been in the noble words of the Arabic Qur-ãn, which I have tried to translate for myself and apply to my experience again and again. The service of the Qur-ãn has been the pride and the privilege of many Muslims. I felt that with such life-experience as has fallen to my lot, my service to the Qur-ãn should be to present it in a fitting garb in English. That ambition I have cherished in my mind for more than forty years.

I have collected books and materials for it. I have visited places, undertaken journeys, taken notes, sought the society of men, and tried to explore their thoughts and hearts, in order to equip myself for the task. Sometimes I have considered it too stupendous for me,—the double task of understanding the original, and reproducing its nobility, its beauty, its poetry, its grandeur, and its sweet, practical, reasonable application to everyday experience. Then I have blamed myself for lack of courage,—the spiritual courage of men who dared all in the Cause which was so dear to them.

Two sets of apparently accidental circumstances at last decided me. A man's life is subject to inner storms far more devastating than those in the physical world around him. In such a storm, in the bitter anguish of a personal sorrow which nearly unseated my reason and made life seem meaningless, a new hope was born out of a systematic pursuit of my long-cherished project. Watered by tears, my manuscript began to grow in depth and earnestness if not in bulk. I guarded it like a secret treasure. Wanderer that I am, I carried it about, thousands of miles, to all sorts of countries and among all sorts of people. At length, in the city of Lahore, I happened to mention the matter to some young people who held me in respect and affection. They showed an enthusiasm and an eagerness which surprised me. They almost took the matter out of my hands. They asked for immediate publication. I had various bits ready, but not even one complete *Sîpãra*. They made me promise to complete at least one *Sîpãra* before I left Lahore. As if by magic, a publisher, a *kãtib* (calligraphist, to write the Arabic Text), an engraver of blocks for such text, and a printer were found, all equally anxious to push forward the scheme. Blessed be youth, for its energy and determination! "Where others flinch, rash youth will dare!"

Gentle and discerning reader! what I wish to present to you is an English Interpretation, side by side with the Arabic Text. The English shall be, not a mere substitution of one word for another, but the best expression I can give to the fullest meaning which I can understand from the Arabic Text. The rhythm, music, and exalted tone of the original should be reflected in the English Interpretation. It may be but a faint reflection, but such beauty and power as my pen commands shall be brought to its service. I want to make English itself an Islamic language, if such a person as I can do it. And I must give you all the necessary aid which I can....

The Text in English is printed . . . in parallel columns with the Arabic Text. Each *Sûra* and the verse of each *Sûra* is separately numbered, and the numbers are shown page by page. The system of numbering the verses has not been uniform in previous translations. European editors and translators have allowed their numbering to diverge considerably from that accepted in the East. This causes confusion in giving and verifying references. The different *Qirãats* sometimes differ as to the punctuation stops and the numbering of the verses. This is not a vital matter, but it causes confusion in references. It is important that at least in Islamic countries one system of numbering should be adopted. I have adopted mainly that of the Egyptian edition published under the authority of the King of Egypt. This will probably be accepted in Egypt and in Arabic-speaking countries, as those countries generally look up to Egypt in matters of literature. I am glad to see that the text . . . published by the Anjuman-i-Himayat-i-Islam of Lahore is following the same system of numbering. I recommend to other publishers . . . the same good example.

If once this is done, we shall have a uniform system of numbering. I have retained the numbering of Sections as it is universally used in the Arabic copies, and marks a logical division of the *Sûras.* I have supplied a further aid to the reader in indicating sub-division of the Sections into paragraphs. They are not numbered, but are distinguished by the use of a flowery initial letter ....

. . . Every earnest and reverent student of the Qur-ãn, as he proceeds with his study, will find, with an inward joy difficult to describe, how this general meaning also enlarges as his own capacity for understanding increases. It is like a traveller climbing a mountain; the higher he goes, the farther he sees. From a literary point of view the poet Keats has described his feeling when he discovered Chapman's Homer:

Then felt I like some watcher of the skies
When a new planet swims into his ken,
Or like stout Cortez when with eagle eyes.
He stared at the Pacific,—and all his men
Looked at each other with a wild surmise,—
Silent, upon a peak in Darien.

How much greater is the joy and sense of wonder and miracle when the Qur-ãn opens our spiritual eyes ! The meaning which we thought we had grasped expands. New words are opened out. As we progress, still newer, and again newer worlds "swim into our ken". The miracle deepens and deepens, and almost completely absorbs us. And yet we know that the "face of God"—our final goal—has not yet been reached. We are in the *mulk* of Sulaiman (Q. 2: 102), which the evil ones denied, belied, and even turned into blasphemy. But we can ignore blasphemy, ridicule and contempt, for we are in the threshold of Realities and a little perfume from the garden of the Holy One has already gladdened our nostrils . . .

The Arabic Text I have had printed from photographic blocks, made for me by Master Muhammad Sharif. The calligraphy is from the pen of Pir 'Abdul Hamid, with whom I have been in touch and who has complied with my desire for a bold round hand, with the words clearly separated, the vowel points accurately placed over or under the letter to which they relate, and the verses duly numbered and placed in juxtaposition with their English equivalents. Calligraphy occupies an important place in Muslim Art, and it is my desire that my version should not in any way be deficient in this respect.

I have been fortunate in securing the co-operation of Professor Zafar Iqbal in looking over the proofs of the Arabic Text. In connection with the Anjuman's edition of the Arabic Qur-ãn he has devoted much time and thought to the correct punctuation of the Text, and he has also investigated its history and problems. I hope he will some day publish these valuable notes. I have been privileged to see the Anjuman's Text before its formal publication. I consider it the most carefully prepared Text of any produced in India and I have generally followed it in punctuation and the numbering of verses,—the only points on which my difficulties are likely to arise on the Qur'anic Text....

One final word to my readers. Read, study and digest the Holy Book. Read slowly, and let it sink into your heart and soul. Such study will, like virtue, be its own reward. If you find anything in this volume to criticise, please let it not spoil your enjoyment of the rest. If you write to me, quoting chapter and verse, I shall be glad to consider your criticism, but let it not vex you if I exercise my own judgment in deciding for myself. Any corrections accepted will be gratefully acknowledged. On the other hand, if there is something that specially pleases you or helps you, please do not hesitate to write to me. I have given up other interests to help you. It will be a pleasure to know that my labour has not been in vain. If you address me care of my Publisher at his Lahore address, he will always forward the letters to me.

LAHORE **A. YUSUF 'ALI**

4th April, 1934

= 18th of the month of Pilgrimage 1352 H.

LIST OF SÛRAS (CHAPTERS)

TRANSLITERATION OF ARABIC WORDS AND NAMES

Arabic		Transliteration	Arabic		Transliteration
ا ء	consonantal sound	a	ط	....	ṭ
			ظ	....	z̲
آ	Long vowel *	ã	ع	....	‘ (inverted apostrophe)
ب	....	b	غ	....	g̲
ت	....	t	ف	....	f
ث	....	th	ق	....	q
ج	....	j	ك	....	k
ح	....	ḥ	ل	....	l
خ	....	kh	م	....	m
د	....	d	ن	....	n
ذ	....	ẓ	ه ھ	....	h
ر	....	r	و	consonant	w
ز	....	z	و	long vowel *	û
س	....	s	و	diphthong	au
ش	....	sh	ي	consonant	y
ص	....	ṣ	ي	long vowel *	î
ض	....	dh	ي	diphthong	ai

Short vowels:		
(*fatḥa*)	ـَ	a
(*kasra*)	ـِ	i
(*dhamma*)	ـُ	u

1. For the *hamzã* (ء) I have used no distinctive sign. An apostrophe for it and an inverted apostrophe for the *'ain* (ع), or *vice versa*, is confusing to English readers. As a moved consonant, it is sufficiently shown in English by the long or short vowel which moves it, e.g. *ab, Raûf.* Where it is a hiatus preceded by a *fatḥa*, I have shown it by a second *a* : thus, *Iqraa*, the cave of *Ḥiraa*, In other cases it has not been possible to show it without using a distinctive sign. The name of the Holy Book is usually written Qurãn; but I prefer to write Qur-ãn. However a few words like juz have an apostrophe indicating Hamza.

2. The final *h* preceded by the short *a* is scarcely pronounced, and I have left it out. Hence Sûra, Fãtiḥa, Hijra, etc., where the Arabic spelling would require Sûrah, Fãtiḥah, Hijrah, etc.

---

* Where it is really *pronounced* long. Hence *khalaqnã-kum* but *khalaqnal-insãn; Abû Sufyãn* but *Abul-Qãsim; fin-nãr* but *fî-hi.*

3. In internationalised words and names I have used the spelling ordinarily current in English; e.g. Mecca, Medina, Maulvi, Urud, Islam, Israel, Abraham, Jacob. Here the boundary is thin and rather ill-defined, and possibly my practice and that of my proof-readers have not been absolutely uniform. But in place of Mecca and Madina, the more accurate form of Makkah and Madinah is adopted.

SÛRA–I

AL-FÃTIḤA

(INTRODUCTION)

First comes that beautiful Sûra,The Opening Chapter of Seven Verses, rightly called the Essence of the Book. It teaches us the perfect Prayer. For if we can pray aright, it means that we have some knowledge of Allah and His attributes, of His relations to us and His creation, which includes ourselves; that we glimpse the source from which we come, and that final goal which is our spiritual destiny under Allah's true judgement: then we offer oursleves to Allah and seek His light.

Prayer is the heart of Religion and Faith: but how shall we pray ? What words shall convey the yearnings of our miserable, ignorant hearts to the Knower of all ? Is it worth of Him or of our spiritual nature to ask for vanities, or even for such physical needs as our daily bread ? The Inspired One taught us a Prayer that sums up our faith, our hope, and our aspiration in things that matter. We think in devotion of Allah's name and His Nature; we praise Him for His creation and His cherishing care; we call to mind the Realities, seen and unseen; we offer Him worship and ask for His guidance; and we know the straight from the crooked path by the light of His grace that illumines the righteous.

Al-Fātiḥa, or the Opening Chapter

1. In the name of Allah, Most Gracious, Most Merciful.
2. Praise be to Allah, the Cherisher and Sustainer of the Worlds:
3. Most Gracious, Most Merciful;
4. Master of the Day of Judgment.
5. Thee do we worship, and Thine aid we seek.
6. Show us the straight way,
7. The way of those on whom Thou has bestowed Thy Grace, those whose (portion) is not wrath. And who go not astray.

سُوْرَةُ الْفَاتِحَةِ مَكِّيَّةٌ وَّهِيَ سَبْعُ اٰيَاتٍ	سُورہ فاتحہ مکی ہے اور اس میں سات آیتیں ہیں
بِسْمِ اللّٰهِ الرَّحْمٰنِ الرَّحِيْمِ ○	شروع خدا کا نام لیکر جو بڑا مہربان نہایت رحم والا ہے ○ وا
اَلْحَمْدُ لِلّٰهِ رَبِّ الْعٰلَمِيْنَ ۱	سب طرح کی تعریف خدا ہی کو (سزاوار) ہی جو تمام مخلوقات کا پروردگار ہے وا ۱
الرَّحْمٰنِ الرَّحِيْمِ ۲	بڑا مہربان نہایت رحم والا ۲
مٰلِكِ يَوْمِ الدِّيْنِ ۳	انصاف کے دن کا حاکم وس ۳
اِيَّاكَ نَعْبُدُ وَاِيَّاكَ نَسْتَعِيْنُ ۴	(اے پروردگار) ہم تیری ہی عبادت کرتے ہیں اور تجھی سے مدد مانگتے ہیں ۴
اِهْدِنَا الصِّرَاطَ الْمُسْتَقِيْمَ ۵	ہم کو سیدھے رستے چلا ۵
صِرَاطَ الَّذِيْنَ اَنْعَمْتَ عَلَيْهِمْ ۶	اُن لوگوں کے رستے جن پر تو اپنا فضل و کرم کرتا رہا ۶
غَيْرِ الْمَغْضُوْبِ عَلَيْهِمْ وَلَا الضَّآلِّيْنَ ۷ ع	نہ اُن کے جن پر غصّے ہوتا رہا اور نہ گمراہوں کے ۷

ع ۱ ۷

وا چونکہ حکم ہے کہ قرآن مجید خدا کا نام لیکر شروع کیا جائے اسلئے ہمیں بِسْمِ اللّٰهِ کے ترجمے کے شروع میں کہو کا لفظ جو مقدر ہی لکھ دینا چاہیے تھا
مگر پھر سب جگہ ترجمے میں یہ لفظ لکھنا پڑتا اور اس میں وہ لُطف نہ رہتا جو بِسْمِ اللّٰهِ الرَّحْمٰنِ الرَّحِيْمِ میں ہو اسلئے یہ لفظ مقدر ہی
رہنے دیا۔ و۲ یہ سُورت خدا نے بندوں کی زبان میں نازل فرمائی ہی مقصود اس بات کا سکھانا ہی کہ وہ اس طرح خدا سے دُعا
کیا کریں۔ حدیث شریف میں آیا ہی کہ سب سے افضل ذکر لَآ اِلٰهَ اِلَّا اللّٰهُ ہے اور سب سے افضل دُعا اَلْحَمْدُ لِلّٰهِ الخ۔
و۳ انصاف کے دن سے مُراد قیامت کا دن ہے کیونکہ دوسری جگہ ارشاد ہوا ہی مَآ اَدْرٰكَ مَا يَوْمُ الدِّيْنِ ○ يَوْمَ لَا تَمْلِكُ نَفْسٌ
لِّنَفْسٍ شَيْئًا ؕ وَالْاَمْرُ يَوْمَئِذٍ لِّلّٰهِ ○ "یعنی تم کو کیا معلوم ہی کہ انصاف کا دن کونسا ہے جس دن کوئی کسی کے کچھ کام نہ آئے گا
اور اس دن خدا ہی کا حکم ہوگا"۔ اگرچہ اور دنوں کا مالک بھی خدا ہی ہی مگر اس روز کی تخصیص اسلئے ہی کہ اس روز خدا کے سوا کسی کا حکم نہ چلے گا
خدا فرمائے گا:۔ لِمَنِ الْمُلْكُ الْيَوْمَ ؕ لِلّٰهِ الْوَاحِدِ الْقَهَّارِ ○

یادداشت: صرف اس صفحہ پر نوٹ درج کر دیئے ہیں بقایا ہر صفحہ کے نوٹ آخر میں یکجا چھاپ دیئے ہیں ف نمبر دیکھ کر آخر میں تشریح ملاحظہ فرمائیے

SÛRA–2

AL-BAQARAH

(INTRODUCTION)

As the Opening Sûra sums up in seven beautiful verses the essence of the Qur-ãn, so this Sûra sums up in 286 verses the whole teaching of the Qur-ãn. It is a closely reasoned argument.

This is the longest Sûra of the Qur-ãn and in it occurs the longest verse (2: 282). The name of the Sûra is from the Parable of the Heifer in 2: 67-71, which illustrates the insufficiency of carping obedience. When faith is lost, people put off obedience with various excuses: even when at last they obey in the letter, they fail in the spirit, which means that they get fossilised, and their self-sufficiency prevents them from seeing that spiritually they are not alive but dead. For life is movement, activity, striving, fighting, against baser things. And this is the burden of the Sûra.

This is in the main an early Madinah Sûra.

Al-Baqarah, or the Heifer (The Cow)

In the name of Allah, Most Gracious, Most Merciful.

1. A. L. M.

2. This is the Book; in it is guidance sure, without doubt, to those who fear Allah;

3. Who believe in the Unseen, are steadfast in prayer, and spend out of what We have provided for them;

4. And who believe in the Revelation sent to thee, and sent before thy time, and (in their hearts) have the assurance of the Hereafter.

5. They are on (true guidance), from their Lord, and it is these who will prosper.

6. As to those who reject Faith, it is the same to them whether thou warn them or do not warn them; they will not believe.

7. Allah hath set a seal on their hearts and on their hearing. And on their eyes is a veil; great is the chastisement they (incur).

8. Of the people there are some who say: "We believe in Allah and the Last day:" but they do not (really) believe.

9. Fain would they deceive Allah and those who believe, but they only deceive themselves, and realize (it) not !

10. In their hearts is a disease; and Allah has increased their disease: and grievous is the chastisement they (incur), because they lied (to themselves).

سورۂ بقرہ مدنی ہے اور اسمیں دو سو چھیاسی آیتیں اور چالیس رکوع ہیں

شروع خدا کا نام لیکر جو بڑا مہربان نہایت رحم والا ہے

الم (۱) یہ کتاب (قرآن مجید) اس میں کچھ شک نہیں
کہ کلامِ خدا ہے۔ خدا سے ڈرنے والوں
کی رہنما ہے (۲)
جو غیب پر ایمان لاتے اور آداب کے ساتھ
نماز پڑھتے اور جو کچھ ہم نے اُن کو عطا فرمایا ہے
اُس میں سے خرچ کرتے ہیں (۳)
اور جو کتاب (اے محمدؐ) تم پر نازل ہوئی
اور جو کتابیں تم سے پہلے (پیغمبروں پر)
نازل ہوئیں سب پر ایمان لاتے
اور آخرت کا یقین رکھتے ہیں (۴)
یہی لوگ اپنے پروردگار (کی طرف) سے ہدایت پر
ہیں اور یہی نجات پانے والے ہیں (۵)
جو لوگ کافر ہیں انہیں تم نصیحت کرو یا نہ کرو اُن کیلئے
برابر ہے۔ وہ ایمان نہیں لانے کے (۶)
خدا نے اُن کے دلوں اور کانوں پر مہر لگا رکھی
ہے۔ اور اُن کی آنکھوں پر پردہ (پڑا ہوا) ہے
اور اُن کے لئے بڑا عذاب (تیار) ہے (۷)
اور بعض لوگ ایسے ہیں جو کہتے ہیں کہ ہم خدا پر اور روزِ
آخرت پر ایمان رکھتے ہیں حالانکہ وہ ایمان نہیں رکھتے (۸)
یہ (اپنے پندار میں) خدا کو اور مومنوں کو چکما دیتے ہیں
مگر (حقیقت میں) اپنے سوا کسی کو چکما نہیں دیتے
اور اس سے بے خبر ہیں (۹)
اِن کے دلوں میں (کفر کا) مرض تھا خدا نے اُن کا
مرض اور زیادہ کر دیا اور اُن کے جھوٹ بولنے کے
سبب اُن کو دکھ دینے والا عذاب ہوگا (۱۰)

سُوْرَةُ الْبَقَرَةِ مَدَنِيَّةٌ وَهِيَ مِائَتَانِ وَسِتٌّ وَثَمَانُوْنَ آيَةً وَأَرْبَعُوْنَ رُكُوْعًا

بِسْمِ اللّٰهِ الرَّحْمٰنِ الرَّحِيْمِ ○

الٓمّٓ ﴿۱﴾ ذٰلِكَ الْكِتٰبُ
لَا رَيْبَ ۛ فِيْهِ ۛ هُدًى
لِّلْمُتَّقِيْنَ ﴿۲﴾
الَّذِيْنَ يُؤْمِنُوْنَ بِالْغَيْبِ
وَيُقِيْمُوْنَ الصَّلٰوةَ وَمِمَّا
رَزَقْنٰهُمْ يُنْفِقُوْنَ ﴿۳﴾
وَالَّذِيْنَ يُؤْمِنُوْنَ بِمَآ
اُنْزِلَ اِلَيْكَ وَمَآ اُنْزِلَ
مِنْ قَبْلِكَ ۚ وَبِالْاٰخِرَةِ
هُمْ يُوْقِنُوْنَ ﴿۴﴾
اُولٰٓئِكَ عَلٰى هُدًى مِّنْ رَّبِّهِمْ ۚ
وَاُولٰٓئِكَ هُمُ الْمُفْلِحُوْنَ ﴿۵﴾
اِنَّ الَّذِيْنَ كَفَرُوْا سَوَآءٌ عَلَيْهِمْ ءَاَنْذَرْتَهُمْ
اَمْ لَمْ تُنْذِرْهُمْ لَا يُؤْمِنُوْنَ ﴿۶﴾
خَتَمَ اللّٰهُ عَلٰى قُلُوْبِهِمْ وَعَلٰى
سَمْعِهِمْ ؕ وَعَلٰٓى اَبْصَارِهِمْ غِشَاوَةٌ ؗ
وَّلَهُمْ عَذَابٌ عَظِيْمٌ ﴿۷﴾
وَمِنَ النَّاسِ مَنْ يَّقُوْلُ اٰمَنَّا بِاللّٰهِ
وَبِالْيَوْمِ الْاٰخِرِ وَمَا هُمْ بِمُؤْمِنِيْنَ ﴿۸﴾
يُخٰدِعُوْنَ اللّٰهَ وَالَّذِيْنَ اٰمَنُوْا ۚ
وَمَا يَخْدَعُوْنَ اِلَّآ اَنْفُسَهُمْ
وَمَا يَشْعُرُوْنَ ﴿۹﴾
فِىْ قُلُوْبِهِمْ مَّرَضٌ ۙ فَزَادَهُمُ اللّٰهُ
مَرَضًا ۚ وَلَهُمْ عَذَابٌ اَلِيْمٌ ۢ ۙ
بِمَا كَانُوْا يَكْذِبُوْنَ ﴿۱۰﴾

11. When it is said to them: "Make not mischief on the earth," they say: "We are only ones that put things right."

اور جب اُن سے کہا جاتا ہے کہ زمین میں فساد نہ ڈالو
تو کہتے ہیں ہم تو اصلاح کرنے والے ہیں ⑪

وَإِذَا قِيلَ لَهُمْ لَا تُفْسِدُوا فِي الْأَرْضِ
قَالُوا إِنَّمَا نَحْنُ مُصْلِحُونَ ⑪

12. Of a surety, they are the ones who make mischief, but they realize (it) not.

دیکھو یہ بلاشبہ مُفسد ہیں لیکن خبر
نہیں رکھتے ⑫

أَلَا إِنَّهُمْ هُمُ الْمُفْسِدُونَ وَلَٰكِن
لَّا يَشْعُرُونَ ⑫

13. When it is said to them: "Believe as the others believe:" they say: "Shall we believe as the fools believe?"—Nay, of a surety they are the fools, but they do not know.

اور جب اُن سے کہا جاتا ہے کہ جس طرح اور لوگ
ایمان لے آئے تم بھی ایمان لے آؤ تو کہتے ہیں بھلا
جس طرح بیوقوف ایمان لے آئے ہیں اُسی طرح ہم بھی ایمان
لے آئیں؟ سُن لو کہ یہی بیوقوف ہیں لیکن نہیں جانتے ⑬

وَإِذَا قِيلَ لَهُمْ آمِنُوا كَمَا آمَنَ
النَّاسُ قَالُوا أَنُؤْمِنُ كَمَا آمَنَ
السُّفَهَاءُ ۗ أَلَا إِنَّهُمْ هُمُ السُّفَهَاءُ
وَلَٰكِن لَّا يَعْلَمُونَ ⑬

14. When they meet those who believe, they say: "We believe;" but when they are alone with their evil ones, they say: "We are really with you; we (were) only jesting."

اور یہ لوگ جب مومنوں سے ملتے ہیں تو کہتے ہیں کہ
ہم ایمان لے آئے ہیں اور جب اپنے شیطانوں میں جاتے
ہیں تو (اُن سے) کہتے ہیں کہ ہم تمہارے ساتھ ہیں اور
(پیروانِ محمدؐ سے) تو ہم ہنسی کیا کرتے ہیں ⑭

وَإِذَا لَقُوا الَّذِينَ آمَنُوا قَالُوا آمَنَّا
وَإِذَا خَلَوْا إِلَىٰ شَيَاطِينِهِمْ
قَالُوا إِنَّا مَعَكُمْ إِنَّمَا نَحْنُ
مُسْتَهْزِئُونَ ⑭

15. Allah will throw back their mockery on them, and give them rope in their trespasses; so they will wander like blind ones (to and fro).

اِن (منافقوں) سے خدا ہنسی کرتا ہے اور اُنہیں مہلت
دیئے جاتا ہے کہ شرارت و سرکشی میں پڑے بہک رہے ہیں ⑮

اللَّهُ يَسْتَهْزِئُ بِهِمْ وَيَمُدُّهُمْ
فِي طُغْيَانِهِمْ يَعْمَهُونَ ⑮

16. These are they who have bartered guidance for error: but their traffic is profitless, and they have lost true direction,

یہ وہ لوگ ہیں جنہوں نے ہدایت چھوڑ کر گمراہی خریدی
تو نہ تو اُن کی تجارت ہی نے کچھ نفع دیا اور نہ وہ
ہدایت یاب ہی ہوئے ⑯

أُولَٰئِكَ الَّذِينَ اشْتَرَوُا الضَّلَالَةَ
بِالْهُدَىٰ فَمَا رَبِحَت تِّجَارَتُهُمْ
وَمَا كَانُوا مُهْتَدِينَ ⑯

17. Their similitude is that of a man who kindled a fire; when it lighted all around him, Allah took away their light and left them in utter darkness, so they could not see.

اُن کی مثال اُس شخص کی سی ہے جس نے (شب تاریک
میں) آگ جلائی جب آگ نے اس کے اردگرد کی چیزیں
روشن کیں تو خدا نے اُن لوگوں کی روشنی زائل
کردی اور اُن کو اندھیروں میں چھوڑ دیا کہ کچھ نہیں دیکھتے ⑰

مَثَلُهُمْ كَمَثَلِ الَّذِي اسْتَوْقَدَ
نَارًا فَلَمَّا أَضَاءَتْ مَا حَوْلَهُ
ذَهَبَ اللَّهُ بِنُورِهِمْ وَتَرَكَهُمْ
فِي ظُلُمَاتٍ لَّا يُبْصِرُونَ ⑰

18. Deaf, dumb, and blind, they will not return (to the path).

(یہ) بہرے ہیں گونگے ہیں اندھے ہیں کہ (کسی طرح
سیدھے رستے کی طرف) لوٹ ہی نہیں سکتے ⑱

صُمٌّ بُكْمٌ عُمْيٌ فَهُمْ لَا
يَرْجِعُونَ ⑱

19. Or (another similitude) is that of a rain-laden cloud from the sky: in it are zones of darkness, and thunder and lightning: they press their fingers in their ears to keep out the stunning thunder-clap, the while they are in terror of death.

یا اُن کی مثال مینہ کی سی ہے کہ آسمان سے (برس رہا ہو
اور) اُس میں اندھیرے پر اندھیرا (چھا رہا) ہو اور (بادل)
گرج (رہا) ہو اور بجلی (کوند رہی) ہو تو یہ کڑک سے (ڈر کر)
موت کے خوف سے کانوں میں اُنگلیاں دے لیں اور خدا

أَوْ كَصَيِّبٍ مِّنَ السَّمَاءِ فِيهِ
ظُلُمَاتٌ وَرَعْدٌ وَبَرْقٌ يَجْعَلُونَ
أَصَابِعَهُمْ فِي آذَانِهِم مِّنَ
الصَّوَاعِقِ حَذَرَ الْمَوْتِ ۚ وَاللَّهُ

But Allah is ever round the rejecters of Faith !

20. The lightning all but snatches away their sight: every time the light (helps) them, they walk therein, and when the darkness grows on them, they stand still, and if Allah willed, He could take away their faculty of hearing and seeing; for Allah hath power over all things.

21. O ye people ! worship your Guardian Lord, Who created you and those who came before you, that ye may become righteous,

22. Who has made the earth your couch, and the heavens your canopy; and sent down rain from the heavens; and brought forth therewith fruits for your sustenance; then set not up rivals unto Allah when ye know (the truth).

23. And if ye are in doubt as to what We have revealed from time to time to Our servant, then produce a Sura like thereunto; and call your witnesses or helpers (if there are any) besides Allah, if ye are truthful.

24. But if ye cannot— and of a surety ye cannot—then fear the Fire whose fuel is Men and Stones,— which is prepared for those who reject Faith.

25. But give glad tidings to those who believe and work righteousness, that their portion is Gardens, beneath which rivers flow. Every time they are fed with fruits therefrom, they say: "Why, this is what we were fed with before," for they are given things in similitude; and they have therein spouses purified; and they abide therein (for ever).

مُحِيطٌ بِالْكٰفِرِينَ ﴿١٩﴾
يَكَادُ الْبَرْقُ يَخْطَفُ أَبْصَارَهُمْ
كُلَّمَا أَضَاءَ لَهُمْ مَشَوْا فِيهِ
وَإِذَا أَظْلَمَ عَلَيْهِمْ قَامُوا وَلَوْ
شَاءَ اللّٰهُ لَذَهَبَ بِسَمْعِهِمْ
وَأَبْصَارِهِمْ إِنَّ اللّٰهَ عَلٰى كُلِّ
شَيْءٍ قَدِيرٌ ﴿٢٠﴾
يٰأَيُّهَا النَّاسُ اعْبُدُوا رَبَّكُمُ الَّذِي خَلَقَكُمْ
وَالَّذِينَ مِنْ قَبْلِكُمْ لَعَلَّكُمْ تَتَّقُونَ ﴿٢١﴾
الَّذِي جَعَلَ لَكُمُ الْأَرْضَ فِرَاشًا وَ
السَّمَاءَ بِنَاءً وَأَنْزَلَ مِنَ السَّمَاءِ مَاءً
فَأَخْرَجَ بِهِ مِنَ الثَّمَرَاتِ رِزْقًا لَكُمْ فَلَا
تَجْعَلُوا لِلّٰهِ أَنْدَادًا وَأَنْتُمْ تَعْلَمُونَ ﴿٢٢﴾
وَإِنْ كُنْتُمْ فِي رَيْبٍ مِمَّا نَزَّلْنَا
عَلٰى عَبْدِنَا فَأْتُوا بِسُورَةٍ مِنْ
مِثْلِهِ وَادْعُوا شُهَدَاءَكُمْ مِنْ
دُونِ اللّٰهِ إِنْ كُنْتُمْ صٰدِقِينَ ﴿٢٣﴾
فَإِنْ لَمْ تَفْعَلُوا وَلَنْ تَفْعَلُوا فَاتَّقُوا
النَّارَ الَّتِي وَقُودُهَا النَّاسُ وَ
الْحِجَارَةُ أُعِدَّتْ لِلْكٰفِرِينَ ﴿٢٤﴾
وَبَشِّرِ الَّذِينَ آمَنُوا وَعَمِلُوا
الصّٰلِحٰتِ أَنَّ لَهُمْ جَنّٰتٍ تَجْرِي
مِنْ تَحْتِهَا الْأَنْهٰرُ كُلَّمَا رُزِقُوا
مِنْهَا مِنْ ثَمَرَةٍ رِزْقًا قَالُوا هٰذَا
الَّذِي رُزِقْنَا مِنْ قَبْلُ وَأُتُوا بِهِ
مُتَشٰبِهًا وَلَهُمْ فِيهَا أَزْوَاجٌ
مُطَهَّرَةٌ وَهُمْ فِيهَا خٰلِدُونَ ﴿٢٥﴾

کافروں کو (ہر طرف سے) گھیرے ہوئے ہے ﴿١٩﴾
قریب ہے کہ بجلی (کی چمک) اُن کی آنکھوں (کی بصارت)
کو اُچک لیجائے جب بجلی (چمکتی اور) اُن پر روشنی
ڈالتی ہے تو اُس میں چل پڑتے ہیں اور جب اندھیرا
ہو جاتا ہے تو کھڑے کے کھڑے رہ جاتے ہیں اور اگر خدا
چاہتا تو اُنکے کانوں (کی شنوائی) اور آنکھوں (کی بینائی
دونوں) کو زائل کر دیتا۔ بلاشبہ خدا ہر چیز پر قادر ہے ﴿٢٠﴾
لوگو! اپنے پروردگار کی عبادت کرو جس نے تمکو اور تم سے
پہلے لوگوں کو پیدا کیا تاکہ تم (اُسکے عذاب سے) بچو ﴿٢١﴾
جس نے تمہارے لئے زمین کو بچھونا اور آسمان کو چھت
بنایا اور آسمان سے مینہ برسا کر تمہارے کھانے کیلئے
انواع و اقسام کے میوے پیدا کئے پس کسی کو خدا
کا ہمسر نہ بناؤ۔ اور تم جانتے تو ہو ﴿٢٢﴾
اور اگر تم کو اس (کتاب) میں جو ہم نے اپنے بندے
(محمد عربی) پر نازل فرمائی ہے کچھ شک ہو تو اسی طرح کی
ایک سورت تم بھی بنا لاؤ اور خدا کے سوا جو تمہارے
مددگار ہوں اُن کو بھی بلا لو اگر تم سچے ہو ﴿٢٣﴾
لیکن اگر (ایسا) نہ کر سکو اور ہرگز نہیں کر سکو گے تو
اُس آگ سے ڈرو جس کا ایندھن آدمی اور پتھر ہونگے
(اور جو) کافروں کیلئے تیار کی گئی ہے ﴿٢٤﴾
اور جو لوگ ایمان لائے اور نیک عمل کرتے رہے اُنکو
خوشخبری سُنا دو کہ انکے لئے (نعمت کے) باغ ہیں جنکے
نیچے نہریں بہ رہی ہیں جب اُنہیں اُن میں سے
کسی قسم کا میوہ کھانے کو دیا جائیگا تو کہیں گے یہ تو
وہی ہے جو ہم کو پہلے دیا گیا تھا۔ اور اُن کو ایک دوسرے
کے ہمشکل میوے دیئے جائینگے اور وہاں اُنکے لئے
پاک بیویاں ہونگی اور وہ بہشتوں میں ہمیشہ رہیں گے ﴿٢٥﴾

26. Allah disdains not to use the similitude of things, even of a gnat as well as anything above it. Those who believe know that it is the truth from their Lord; but those who reject Faith say: "What means Allah by this similitude?" By it He causes many to stray, and many He leads into the right path; but He causes not to stray, except those who forsake (the path),—

27. Those who break Allah's Covenant after it is ratified, and who sunder what Allah has ordered to be joined, and do mischief on earth: these cause loss (only) to themselves.

28. How can ye reject the faith in Allah?—seeing that ye were without life, and He gave you life; then will He cause you to die, and will again bring you to life; and again to Him will ye return.

29. It is He Who hath created for you all things that are on earth; then He turned to the heaven and made them into seven firmaments; and of all things He hath perfect knowledge.

30. Behold, thy Lord said to the angels; "I will create a vicegerent on earth." They said: "Wilt Thou place therein one who will make mischief therein and shed blood?—whilst we do celebrate Thy praises and glorify Thy holy (name)?" He said: "I know what ye know not".

31. And He taught Adam the names of all things; then He placed them before the angels, and said: "Tell Me the names of these if ye are right."

32. They said: "Glory to Thee: of knowledge we have none, save

خدا اس بات سے عار نہیں کرتا کہ مچھر یا اُس سے
بڑھ کر کسی چیز (مثلاً مکھی مکڑی وغیرہ) کی مثال بیان
فرمائے۔ جو مومن ہیں وہ یقین کرتے ہیں کہ وہ اُن کے
پروردگار کی طرف سے سچ ہے اور جو کافر ہیں وہ کہتے
ہیں کہ اس مثال سے خدا کی مُراد ہی کیا ہے اس سے
(خدا) بہتوں کو گمراہ کرتا ہے اور بہتوں کو ہدایت بخشتا
ہے اور گمراہ بھی کرتا ہے تو نافرمانوں ہی کو ﴿۲۶﴾
جو خدا کے اقرار کو مضبوط کرنے کے بعد توڑ دیتے
ہیں اور جس چیز (یعنی رشتۂ قرابت) کے جوڑے رکھنے
کا خدا نے حکم دیا ہے اُسکو قطع کئے ڈالتے ہیں اور زمین میں
خرابی کرتے ہیں یہی لوگ نقصان اُٹھانے والے ہیں ﴿۲۷﴾
(کافرو) تم خدا سے کیونکر منکر ہو سکتے ہو جس حال میں کہ
تم بے جان تھے تو اُسنے تمکو جان بخشی پھر وہی تمکو مارتا ہے پھر
وہی تمکو زندہ کریگا پھر تم اُسی کیطرف لوٹ کر جاؤ گے ﴿۲۸﴾
وہی تو ہے جس نے سب چیزیں جو زمین میں ہیں تمہارے لئے
پیدا کیں پھر آسمانوں کیطرف متوجہ ہوا تو اُنکو ٹھیک
سات آسمان بنا دیا اور وہ ہر چیز سے خبردار ہے ﴿۲۹﴾
اور (وہ وقت یاد کرنیکے قابل ہے) جب تمہارے پروردگار
نے فرشتوں سے فرمایا کہ میں زمین میں (اپنا) نائب بنانیوالا
ہوں انہوں نے کہا کیا تو اس میں ایسے شخص کو نائب بنانا
چاہتا ہے جو خرابیاں کرے اور کشت و خون کرتا پھرے اور ہم تیری
تعریف کیساتھ تسبیح و تقدیس کرتے رہتے ہیں (خدا نے) فرمایا
میں وہ باتیں جانتا ہوں جو تم نہیں جانتے ﴿۳۰﴾
اور اُس نے آدم کو سب (چیزوں کے) نام سکھائے پھر
اُن کو فرشتوں کے سامنے کیا اور فرمایا کہ اگر سچے ہو تو
مجھے ان کے نام بتاؤ ﴿۳۱﴾
اُنہوں نے کہا تو پاک ہے جتنا علم تو نے ہمیں بخشا ہے اسکے سوا

إِنَّ اللَّهَ لَا يَسْتَحْيِي أَنْ يَضْرِبَ
مَثَلًا مَّا بَعُوضَةً فَمَا فَوْقَهَا ۚ فَأَمَّا
الَّذِينَ آمَنُوا فَيَعْلَمُونَ أَنَّهُ الْحَقُّ
مِن رَّبِّهِمْ ۖ وَأَمَّا الَّذِينَ كَفَرُوا
فَيَقُولُونَ مَاذَا أَرَادَ اللَّهُ بِهَٰذَا
مَثَلًا ۘ يُضِلُّ بِهِ كَثِيرًا وَيَهْدِي بِهِ
كَثِيرًا ۚ وَمَا يُضِلُّ بِهِ إِلَّا الْفَاسِقِينَ ﴿٢٦﴾
الَّذِينَ يَنقُضُونَ عَهْدَ اللَّهِ مِن
بَعْدِ مِيثَاقِهِ وَيَقْطَعُونَ مَا أَمَرَ اللَّهُ
بِهِ أَن يُوصَلَ وَيُفْسِدُونَ فِي
الْأَرْضِ ۚ أُولَٰئِكَ هُمُ الْخَاسِرُونَ ﴿٢٧﴾
كَيْفَ تَكْفُرُونَ بِاللَّهِ وَكُنتُمْ أَمْوَاتًا
فَأَحْيَاكُمْ ۖ ثُمَّ يُمِيتُكُمْ ثُمَّ يُحْيِيكُمْ
ثُمَّ إِلَيْهِ تُرْجَعُونَ ﴿٢٨﴾
هُوَ الَّذِي خَلَقَ لَكُم مَّا فِي الْأَرْضِ
جَمِيعًا ثُمَّ اسْتَوَىٰ إِلَى السَّمَاءِ فَسَوَّاهُنَّ
سَبْعَ سَمَاوَاتٍ ۚ وَهُوَ بِكُلِّ شَيْءٍ عَلِيمٌ ﴿٢٩﴾
وَإِذْ قَالَ رَبُّكَ لِلْمَلَائِكَةِ إِنِّي
جَاعِلٌ فِي الْأَرْضِ خَلِيفَةً ۖ قَالُوا
أَتَجْعَلُ فِيهَا مَن يُفْسِدُ فِيهَا
وَيَسْفِكُ الدِّمَاءَ وَنَحْنُ نُسَبِّحُ
بِحَمْدِكَ وَنُقَدِّسُ لَكَ ۖ قَالَ
إِنِّي أَعْلَمُ مَا لَا تَعْلَمُونَ ﴿٣٠﴾
وَعَلَّمَ آدَمَ الْأَسْمَاءَ كُلَّهَا ثُمَّ
عَرَضَهُمْ عَلَى الْمَلَائِكَةِ فَقَالَ أَنبِئُونِي
بِأَسْمَاءِ هَٰؤُلَاءِ إِن كُنتُمْ صَادِقِينَ ﴿٣١﴾
قَالُوا سُبْحَانَكَ لَا عِلْمَ لَنَا إِلَّا مَا

what Thou hast taught us: in truth it is Thou Who art perfect in knowledge and wisdom."

33. He said: "O Adam ! tell them their names." When he had told them their names, Allah said: "Did I not tell you that I know the secrets of heaven and earth, and I know what ye reveal and what ye conceal?"

34. And behold, We said to the angels: "Bow down to Adam:" and they bowed down: not so Iblis: he refused and was haughty: he was of those who reject Faith.

35. And We said: "O Adam! dwell thou and thy wife in the Garden; and eat of the bountiful things therein as (where and when) ye will; but approach not this tree, or ye run into harm and transgression."

36. Then did Satan make them slip from the (Garden), and get them out of the state (of felicity) in which they had been. And We said: "Get ye down, all (ye people), with enmity between yourselves. On earth will be your dwelling place and your means of livelihood— for a time".

37. Then learnt Adam from his Lord certain words and his Lord turned towards him; for He is Oft-Returning, Most Merciful.

38. We said: "Get ye down all from here; and if, as is sure, there comes to you guidance from Me, whosoever follows My guidance, on them shall be no fear, nor shall they grieve.

39. "But those who reject Faith and belie Our Signs, they shall be Companions of the Fire; they shall abide therein."

40. O Children of Israel! call to mind the (special) favour which I bestowed upon you, and fulfil your

ہمیں کچھ معلوم نہیں بیشک تو دانا اور حکمت والا ہے (٣٢)
(تب) خدا نے (آدم کو) حکم دیا کہ آدم! تم ان کو ان (چیزوں)
کے نام بتاؤ جب اُنہوں نے اُن کو ان کے نام بتائے
تو (فرشتوں سے) فرمایا کیوں میں نے تم سے نہیں کہا تھا
کہ میں آسمانوں اور زمین کی (سب) پوشیدہ باتیں جانتا ہوں
اور جو تم ظاہر کرتے ہو اور جو پوشیدہ کرتے ہو (سب) مجھکو معلوم ہے (٣٣)
اور جب ہم نے فرشتوں کو حکم دیا کہ آدم کے آگے سجدہ
کرو تو وہ سب سجدے میں گر پڑے مگر شیطان نے
انکار کیا اور غرور میں آکر کافر بن گیا (٣٤)
اور ہم نے کہا کہ اے آدم تم اور تمہاری بیوی بہشت
میں رہو اور جہاں سے چاہو بے روک ٹوک کھاؤ (پیو)
لیکن اِس درخت کے پاس نہ جانا نہیں تو ظالموں
میں (داخل) ہو جاؤ گے (٣٥)
پھر شیطان نے دونوں کو وہاں سے پھسلا دیا اور جس (عیش و نشاط) میں
تھے اُس سے اُنکو نکلوا دیا۔ تب ہمنے حکم دیا کہ (بہشت بریں سے) چلے
جاؤ تم ایک دوسرے کے دشمن ہو اور تمہارے لئے زمین میں
ایک وقت تک ٹھکانا اور معاش (مقرر کر دیا گیا) ہے (٣٦)
پھر آدم نے اپنے پروردگار سے کچھ کلمات سیکھے (اور معافی مانگی) تو اس
نے اُنکا قصور معاف کر دیا بیشک وہ معاف کرنیوالا (اور) صاحبِ رحم ہے (٣٧)
ہم نے فرمایا کہ تم سب یہاں سے اُتر جاؤ جب تمہارے پاس
میری طرف سے ہدایت پہنچے تو (اُسکی پیروی کرنا کہ) جنھوں
نے میری ہدایت کی پیروی کی اُن کو نہ کچھ خوف ہوگا اور
نہ وہ غمناک ہوں گے (٣٨)
اور جنہوں نے (اسکو) قبول نہ کیا اور ہماری آیتوں کو جھٹلایا
وہ دوزخ میں جانیوالے ہیں (اور) وہ ہمیشہ اسمیں رہیں گے (٣٩)
اے آلِ یعقوب! میرے وہ احسان یاد کرو جو میں نے تم پر
کئے تھے اور اُس اقرار کو پورا کرو جو تم نے مجھ سے کیا تھا

عَلَّمْتَنَا ۖ إِنَّكَ أَنتَ الْعَلِيمُ الْحَكِيمُ (٣٢)
قَالَ يَا آدَمُ أَنبِئْهُم بِأَسْمَائِهِمْ ۖ فَلَمَّا
أَنبَأَهُم بِأَسْمَائِهِمْ قَالَ أَلَمْ أَقُل
لَّكُمْ إِنِّي أَعْلَمُ غَيْبَ السَّمَاوَاتِ
وَالْأَرْضِ وَأَعْلَمُ مَا تُبْدُونَ وَمَا
كُنتُمْ تَكْتُمُونَ (٣٣)
وَإِذْ قُلْنَا لِلْمَلَائِكَةِ اسْجُدُوا لِآدَمَ
فَسَجَدُوا إِلَّا إِبْلِيسَ أَبَىٰ وَاسْتَكْبَرَ
وَكَانَ مِنَ الْكَافِرِينَ (٣٤)
وَقُلْنَا يَا آدَمُ اسْكُنْ أَنتَ وَزَوْجُكَ
الْجَنَّةَ وَكُلَا مِنْهَا رَغَدًا حَيْثُ شِئْتُمَا
وَلَا تَقْرَبَا هَٰذِهِ الشَّجَرَةَ فَتَكُونَا
مِنَ الظَّالِمِينَ (٣٥)
فَأَزَلَّهُمَا الشَّيْطَانُ عَنْهَا فَأَخْرَجَهُمَا
مِمَّا كَانَا فِيهِ ۖ وَقُلْنَا اهْبِطُوا بَعْضُكُمْ
لِبَعْضٍ عَدُوٌّ ۖ وَلَكُمْ فِي الْأَرْضِ
مُسْتَقَرٌّ وَمَتَاعٌ إِلَىٰ حِينٍ (٣٦)
فَتَلَقَّىٰ آدَمُ مِن رَّبِّهِ كَلِمَاتٍ فَتَابَ
عَلَيْهِ ۚ إِنَّهُ هُوَ التَّوَّابُ الرَّحِيمُ (٣٧)
قُلْنَا اهْبِطُوا مِنْهَا جَمِيعًا ۖ فَإِمَّا
يَأْتِيَنَّكُم مِّنِّي هُدًى فَمَن تَبِعَ
هُدَايَ فَلَا خَوْفٌ عَلَيْهِمْ وَلَا هُمْ
يَحْزَنُونَ (٣٨)
وَالَّذِينَ كَفَرُوا وَكَذَّبُوا بِآيَاتِنَا أُولَٰئِكَ
أَصْحَابُ النَّارِ ۖ هُمْ فِيهَا خَالِدُونَ (٣٩)
يَا بَنِي إِسْرَائِيلَ اذْكُرُوا نِعْمَتِيَ
الَّتِي أَنْعَمْتُ عَلَيْكُمْ وَأَوْفُوا

Covenant with Me and I shall fulfil My Covenant with you, and fear none but Me.

ہیں اس اقرار کو پورا کروں گا جو میں نے تم سے کیا تھا
اور مجھی سے ڈرتے رہو ﴿۴۰﴾

بِعَهْدِيْٓ اُوْفِ بِعَهْدِكُمْ ۚ وَاِيَّايَ
فَارْهَبُوْنِ ﴿۴۰﴾

41. And believe in what I reveal, confirming the revelation which is with you, and be not the first to reject Faith therein, nor sell My Signs for a small price; and fear Me, and Me alone.

اور جو کتاب میں نے (اپنے رسول محمدؐ پر) نازل کی ہے جو تمہاری
کتاب (تورات) کو سچا کہتی ہے اس پر ایمان لاؤ اور اس سے
منکرِ اول نہ بنو اور میری آیتوں میں (تحریف کر کے ان کے) بدلے تھوڑی سی
قیمت (یعنی دنیاوی منفعت) نہ حاصل کرو اور مجھی سے خوف رکھو ﴿۴۱﴾

وَاٰمِنُوْا بِمَآ اَنْزَلْتُ مُصَدِّقًا لِّمَا
مَعَكُمْ وَلَا تَكُوْنُوْٓا اَوَّلَ كَافِرٍ
بِهٖ ۠ وَلَا تَشْتَرُوْا بِاٰيٰتِيْ ثَمَنًا قَلِيْلًا ۡ
وَّاِيَّايَ فَاتَّقُوْنِ ﴿۴۱﴾

42. And cover not Truth with falsehood, nor conceal the Truth when ye know (what it is).

اور حق کو باطل کے ساتھ نہ ملاؤ اور سچی بات کو جان بوجھ
کر نہ چھپاؤ ﴿۴۲﴾

وَلَا تَلْبِسُوا الْحَقَّ بِالْبَاطِلِ وَتَكْتُمُوا
الْحَقَّ وَاَنْتُمْ تَعْلَمُوْنَ ﴿۴۲﴾

43. And be steadfast in prayer: give Zakat, and bow down your heads with those who bow down (in worship).

اور نماز پڑھا کرو اور زکوٰۃ دیا کرو اور (خدا کے آگے)
جھکنے والوں کے ساتھ جھکا کرو ﴿۴۳﴾

وَاَقِيْمُوا الصَّلٰوةَ وَاٰتُوا الزَّكٰوةَ
وَارْكَعُوْا مَعَ الرّٰكِعِيْنَ ﴿۴۳﴾

44. Do ye enjoin right conduct on the people, and forget (to practise it) yourselves, and yet ye study the Scripture? Will ye not understand?

(یہ) کیا (عقل کی بات ہے کہ) تم لوگوں کو نیکی کرنے کو
کہتے ہو اور اپنے تئیں فراموش کئے دیتے ہو حالانکہ
تم کتاب (خدا) بھی پڑھتے ہو کیا تم سمجھتے نہیں؟ ﴿۴۴﴾

اَتَاْمُرُوْنَ النَّاسَ بِالْبِرِّ وَتَنْسَوْنَ
اَنْفُسَكُمْ وَاَنْتُمْ تَتْلُوْنَ الْكِتٰبَ ۭ
اَفَلَا تَعْقِلُوْنَ ﴿۴۴﴾

45. Nay, seek (Allah's) help with patient perseverance and prayer: it is indeed hard, except to those who are humble.

اور (رنج و تکلیف میں) صبر اور نماز سے مدد لیا کرو اور بےشک
نماز گراں ہے مگر ان لوگوں پر (گراں) نہیں جو عجز کرنے والے ہیں ﴿۴۵﴾

وَاسْتَعِيْنُوْا بِالصَّبْرِ وَالصَّلٰوةِ ۭ
وَاِنَّهَا لَكَبِيْرَةٌ اِلَّا عَلَي الْخٰشِعِيْنَ ﴿۴۵﴾

46. Who bear in mind the certainty that they are to meet their Lord, and that they are to return to Him.

جو یقین کئے ہوئے ہیں کہ وہ اپنے پروردگار سے ملنے والے ہیں
اور اس کی طرف لوٹ کر جانے والے ہیں ﴿۴۶﴾

الَّذِيْنَ يَظُنُّوْنَ اَنَّهُمْ مُّلٰقُوْا
رَبِّهِمْ وَاَنَّهُمْ اِلَيْهِ رٰجِعُوْنَ ﴿۴۶﴾

47. O Children of Israel! call to mind the (special) favour which I bestowed upon you, and that I preferred you to all others.

اے یعقوب کی اولاد! میرے وہ احسان یاد کرو جو میں نے
تم پر کئے تھے اور یہ کہ میں نے تم کو جہان کے لوگوں
پر فضیلت بخشی تھی ﴿۴۷﴾

يٰبَنِيْٓ اِسْرَاۗءِيْلَ اذْكُرُوْا نِعْمَتِيَ الَّتِيْٓ
اَنْعَمْتُ عَلَيْكُمْ وَاَنِّىْ فَضَّلْتُكُمْ
عَلَي الْعٰلَمِيْنَ ﴿۴۷﴾

48. Then guard yourselves against a day when one soul shall not avail another nor shall intercession be accepted for her, nor shall compensation be taken from her, nor shall anyone be helped (from outside).

اور اس دن سے ڈرو جب کوئی کسی کے کچھ بھی کام
نہ آئے اور نہ کسی کی سفارش منظور کی جائے اور نہ کسی سے
کسی طرح کا بدلہ قبول کیا جائے اور نہ لوگ (کسی اور طرح)
مدد حاصل کر سکیں ﴿۴۸﴾

وَاتَّقُوْا يَوْمًا لَّا تَجْزِيْ نَفْسٌ عَنْ
نَّفْسٍ شَيْـًٔا وَّلَا يُقْبَلُ مِنْهَا شَفَاعَةٌ
وَّلَا يُؤْخَذُ مِنْهَا عَدْلٌ وَّلَا هُمْ
يُنْصَرُوْنَ ﴿۴۸﴾

49. And remember, We delivered you from the people of Pharaoh: they set you hard tasks and chastisement, slaughtered your sons and let your women-folk live;

اور (ہمارے ان احسانات کو یاد کرو) جب ہم نے تم کو قوم فرعون
سے مخلصی بخشی وہ (لوگ) تم کو بڑا دکھ دیتے تھے تمہارے بیٹوں
کو تو قتل کر ڈالتے تھے اور بیٹیوں کو زندہ رہنے دیتے تھے

وَاِذْ نَجَّيْنٰكُمْ مِّنْ اٰلِ فِرْعَوْنَ
يَسُوْمُوْنَكُمْ سُوْۗءَ الْعَذَابِ يُذَبِّحُوْنَ
اَبْنَاۗءَكُمْ وَيَسْتَحْيُوْنَ نِسَاۗءَكُمْ ۭ

therein was a tremendous trial from your Lord.

اور اس میں تمہارے پروردگار کی طرف سے بڑی
(سخت) آزمائش تھی ﴿۴۹﴾

وفی ذلکم بلاء من ربکم
عظیم ﴿۴۹﴾

50. And remember We divided the Sea for you and saved you and drowned Pharaoh's people within your very sight.

اور جب ہم نے تمہارے لئے دریا کو پھاڑ دیا تو تم کو
تو نجات دی اور فرعون کی قوم کو غرق کر دیا اور تم
دیکھ ہی تو رہے تھے ﴿۵۰﴾

واذ فرقنا بکم البحر فانجینکم
واغرقنا ال فرعون وانتم
تنظرون ﴿۵۰﴾

51. And remember We appointed forty nights for Moses, and in his absence ye took the calf (for worship), and ye did grievous wrong.

اور جب ہم نے موسیٰ سے چالیس رات کا وعدہ کیا تو تم نے اُن کے
پیچھے بچھڑے کو (معبود) مقرر کر لیا اور تم ظلم کر رہے تھے ﴿۵۱﴾

واذ وعدنا موسی اربعین لیلة ثم
اتخذتم العجل من بعده وانتم ظلمون ﴿۵۱﴾

52. Even then We did forgive you, there was a chance for you to be grateful.

پھر اُس کے بعد ہم نے تم کو معاف کر دیا تاکہ تم
شکر کرو ﴿۵۲﴾

ثم عفونا عنکم من بعد ذلک
لعلکم تشکرون ﴿۵۲﴾

53. And remember We gave Moses the Scripture and the Criterion (between right and wrong), there was a chance for you to be guided aright.

اور جب ہم نے موسیٰ کو کتاب اور معجزے عنایت
کئے تاکہ تم ہدایت حاصل کرو ﴿۵۳﴾

واذ اتینا موسی الکتب والفرقان
لعلکم تهتدون ﴿۵۳﴾

54. And remember Moses said to his people: "O my people! ye have indeed wronged yourselves by your worship of the calf: so turn (in repentance) to your Maker, and slay yourselves (the wrong-doers); that will be better for you in the sight of your Maker." Then He turned towards you (in forgiveness): for He is Oft-Returning, Most Merciful.

اور جب موسیٰ نے اپنی قوم کے لوگوں سے کہا کہ بھائیو
تم نے بچھڑے کو (معبود) ٹھیرانے میں (بڑا) ظلم
کیا ہے تو اپنے پیدا کرنے والے کے آگے توبہ کرو
اور اپنے تئیں ہلاک کر ڈالو۔ تمہارے خالق کے نزدیک
تمہارے حق میں یہی بہتر ہے پھر اُس نے تمہارا قصور
معاف کر دیا وہ بیشک معاف کرنے والا (اور) صاحبِ رحم ہے ﴿۵۴﴾

واذ قال موسی لقومه یقوم
انکم ظلمتم انفسکم باتخاذکم
العجل فتوبوا الی بارئکم
فاقتلوا انفسکم ذلکم خیر
لکم عند بارئکم فتاب علیکم
انه هو التواب الرحیم ﴿۵۴﴾

55. And remember ye said: "O Moses ! we shall never believe in thee until we see Allah manifestly," thereupon thunderbolt seized you.

اور جب تم نے (موسیٰ سے) کہا کہ موسیٰ جب تک ہم خدا
کو سامنے نہ دیکھ لیں گے تم پر ایمان نہیں لائیں گے تو تم
کو بجلی نے آ گھیرا اور تم دیکھ رہے تھے ﴿۵۵﴾

واذ قلتم یموسی لن نؤمن
لک حتی نری الله جهرة فاخذتکم
الصعقة وانتم تنظرون ﴿۵۵﴾

56. Then We raised you up after your death; ye had the chance to be grateful.

پھر موت آ جانے کے بعد ہم نے تم کو از سرِ نو زندہ
کر دیا تاکہ احسان مانو ﴿۵۶﴾

ثم بعثنکم من بعد موتکم
لعلکم تشکرون ﴿۵۶﴾

57. And We gave you the shade of clouds and sent down to you Manna and quails, saying: "Eat of the good things We have provided for you:" (but they rebelled); to Us they did no harm, but they harmed their own selves.

اور بادل کا تم پر سایہ کئے رکھا اور (تمہارے لئے) من و سلویٰ
اُتارتے رہے کہ جو پاکیزہ چیزیں ہم نے تم کو عطا فرمائی ہیں اُن کو کھاؤ
(پیو) مگر تمہارے بزرگوں نے اِن نعمتوں کی کچھ قدر نہ جانی (اور)
وہ ہمارا کچھ نہیں بگاڑتے تھے بلکہ اپنا ہی نقصان کرتے تھے ﴿۵۷﴾

وظللنا علیکم الغمام وانزلنا علیکم
المن والسلوی کلوا من طیبت
ما رزقنکم وما ظلمونا ولکن
کانوا انفسهم یظلمون ﴿۵۷﴾

58. And remember We said: "Enter this town, and eat of the

اور جب ہم نے (اُن سے) کہا کہ اس گاؤں میں داخل ہو جاؤ

واذ قلنا ادخلوا هذه القریة

plenty therein as ye wish; and enter the gate prostrating, and say: Forgive (us) We shall forgive you your faults and increase (the portion of) those who do good."

اوراس میں جہاں سے چاہو خوب کھاؤ (پیو) اور (دیکھنا)
دروازے میں داخل ہونا تو سجدہ کرنا اور حطۃ کہنا ہم
تمہارے گناہ معاف کردیں گے اور نیکی کرنے والوں
کو اور زیادہ دیں گے ﴿۵۸﴾

فَكُلُوا مِنْهَا حَيْثُ شِئْتُمْ رَغَدًا
وَّادْخُلُوا الْبَابَ سُجَّدًا وَّقُولُوا
حِطَّةٌ نَّغْفِرْ لَكُمْ خَطٰيٰكُمْ ؕ
وَسَنَزِيدُ الْمُحْسِنِينَ ﴿۵۸﴾

59. But the transgressors changed the word from that which had been given them; so We sent on the transgressors a plague from heaven, for that they infringed (Our command) repeatedly.

توجو ظالم تھے اُنہوں نے اس لفظ کو جس کا ان کو
حکم دیا تھا بدل کر اسکی جگہ اور لفظ کہنا شروع کیا
پس ہم نے (اُن) ظالموں پر آسمان سے عذاب نازل کیا
کیونکہ نافرمانیاں کئے جاتے تھے ﴿۵۹﴾

فَبَدَّلَ الَّذِينَ ظَلَمُوا قَوْلًا
غَيْرَ الَّذِي قِيلَ لَهُمْ فَأَنْزَلْنَا عَلَى
الَّذِينَ ظَلَمُوا رِجْزًا مِّنَ السَّمَاءِ
بِمَا كَانُوا يَفْسُقُونَ ﴿۵۹﴾ ع ٦ ١٣

60. And remember Moses prayed for water for his people; We said: "Strike the rock with thy staff." Then gushed forth therefrom twelve springs. Each group knew its own place for water. So eat and drink of the sustenance provided by Allah, and do no evil nor mischief on the (face of the) earth.

اور جب موسیٰ نے اپنی قوم کے لئے (خدا سے) پانی مانگا
تو ہم نے کہا کہ اپنی لاٹھی پتھر پر مارو (اُنہوں نے لاٹھی ماری)
تو پھر اُس میں سے بارہ چشمے پھوٹ نکلے
اور تمام لوگوں نے اپنا اپنا گھاٹ معلوم کر (کے پانی پی لیا)
(ہم نے حکم دیا کہ) خدا کی (عطا فرمائی ہوئی) روزی کھاؤ اور
پیو مگر زمین میں فساد نہ کرتے پھرنا ﴿۶۰﴾

وَإِذِ اسْتَسْقَىٰ مُوسَىٰ لِقَوْمِهِ
فَقُلْنَا اضْرِبْ بِّعَصَاكَ الْحَجَرَ ؕ
فَانْفَجَرَتْ مِنْهُ اثْنَتَا عَشْرَةَ عَيْنًا ؕ
قَدْ عَلِمَ كُلُّ أُنَاسٍ مَّشْرَبَهُمْ ؕ
كُلُوا وَاشْرَبُوا مِنْ رِّزْقِ اللَّهِ وَلَا
تَعْثَوْا فِي الْأَرْضِ مُفْسِدِينَ ﴿۶۰﴾

61. And remember ye said: "O Moses ! we cannot endure one kind of food (always); so beseech thy Lord for us to produce for us of what the earth groweth,—its pot-herbs, and cucumbers, its garlic, lentils, and onions." He said: "Will ye exchange the better for the worse ? Go ye down to any town, and ye shall find what ye want!" They were covered with humiliation and misery: they drew on themselves the wrath of Allah. This because they went on rejecting the Signs of Allah and slaying His Messengers without just cause. This because they rebelled and went on transgressing.

اور جب تم نے کہا کہ موسیٰ! ہم سے ایک (ہی) کھانے پر
صبر نہیں ہوسکتا تو اپنے پروردگار سے دُعا کیجیے کہ
ترکاری اور ککڑی اور گیہوں اور مسور اور پیاز (وغیرہ)
جو نباتات زمین سے اُگتی ہیں ہمارے لئے پیدا
کردے۔ اُنہوں نے کہا کہ بھلا عمدہ چیزیں چھوڑ کر
اُن کے بدلے ناقص چیزیں کیوں چاہتے ہو (اگر یہی
چیزیں مطلوب ہیں) تو کسی شہر میں جا اُترو وہاں جو مانگتے ہو
مل جائیگا اور (آخر کار) ذلّت (ورسوائی) اور محتاجی (وبے نوائی)
اُن سے چمٹا دی گئی اور وہ خدا کے غضب میں گرفتار
ہوگئے۔ یہ اسلئے کہ وہ خدا کی آیتوں سے انکار کرتے تھے
اور (اُسکے) نبیوں کو ناحق قتل کردیتے تھے (یعنی) یہ اسلئے
کہ نافرمانی کئے جاتے اور حد سے بڑھے جاتے تھے ﴿۶۱﴾

وَإِذْ قُلْتُمْ يٰمُوسَىٰ لَنْ نَّصْبِرَ عَلَىٰ
طَعَامٍ وَّاحِدٍ فَادْعُ لَنَا رَبَّكَ
يُخْرِجْ لَنَا مِمَّا تُنْبِتُ الْأَرْضُ مِنْ
بَقْلِهَا وَقِثَّائِهَا وَفُومِهَا وَعَدَسِهَا
وَبَصَلِهَا ؕ قَالَ أَتَسْتَبْدِلُونَ الَّذِي
هُوَ أَدْنَىٰ بِالَّذِي هُوَ خَيْرٌ ؕ اهْبِطُوا
مِصْرًا فَإِنَّ لَكُمْ مَّا سَأَلْتُمْ ؕ وَضُرِبَتْ
عَلَيْهِمُ الذِّلَّةُ وَالْمَسْكَنَةُ
وَبَاءُوا بِغَضَبٍ مِّنَ اللَّهِ ؕ ذٰلِكَ
بِأَنَّهُمْ كَانُوا يَكْفُرُونَ بِآيٰتِ اللَّهِ
وَيَقْتُلُونَ النَّبِيِّينَ بِغَيْرِ الْحَقِّ ؕ ذٰلِكَ
بِمَا عَصَوْا وَّكَانُوا يَعْتَدُونَ ﴿۶۱﴾ ع ٧ ١٠

62. Those who believe (in the Qur'an), and those who follow the

جو لوگ مسلمان ہیں یا یہودی یا عیسائی یا ستارہ پرست

إِنَّ الَّذِينَ آمَنُوا وَالَّذِينَ هَادُوا

Jewish (scriptures), and the Christians and the Sabians,— any who believe in Allah and the Last Day, and work righteousness, shall have their reward with their Lord on them shall be no fear, nor shall they grieve.

63. And remember We took your Covenant and We raised above you the Mount (Sinai) (saying): "Hold firmly to what We have given you and bring (ever) to remembrance what is therein: perchance ye may fear Allah."

64. But ye turned back thereafter: had it not been for the Grace and Mercy of Allah to you, ye had surely been among the lost.

65. And well ye knew those amongst you who transgressed in the matter of the Sabbath: We said to them: "Be ye apes, despised and rejected."

66. So We made it an example to their own time and to their posterity, and a lesson to those who fear Allah.

67. And remember Moses said to his people: "Allah commands that ye sacrifice a heifer." They said: "Makest thou a laughing-stock of us?" He said: "Allah save me from being an ignorant (fool)!"

68. They said: "Beseech on our behalf thy Lord to make plain to us What (heifer) it is!" He said: "He says: the heifer should be neither too old nor too young, but of middling age: now do what ye are commanded !"

69. They said: "Beseech on our behalf thy Lord to make plain to us her colour." He said: "He says: a fawn-coloured heifer, pure and rich in tone, the admiration of

(یعنی کوئی شخص کسی قوم و مذہب کا ہو) جو خدا اور روزِ قیامت
پر ایمان لائیگا اور عمل نیک کریگا تو ایسے لوگوں کو اُن
(کے اعمال) کا صلہ خدا کے ہاں ملیگا اور (قیامت کے دن)
اُنکو نہ کسی طرح کا خوف ہوگا اور نہ وہ غمناک ہونگے ﴿۶۲﴾
اور جب ہم نے تم سے عہد (کر) لیا اور کوہ طور کو تم پر
اُٹھا کھڑا کیا (اور حکم دیا) کہ جو کتاب ہم نے تمکو دی ہے اُسکو
زور سے پکڑے رہو اور جو اس میں (لکھا) ہے اُسے یاد رکھو
تاکہ (عذاب سے) محفوظ رہو ﴿۶۳﴾
تو تم اس کے بعد (عہد سے) پھر گئے اور اگر تم پر خدا کا
فضل اور اُس کی مہربانی نہ ہوتی تو تم خسارے میں
پڑ گئے ہوتے ﴿۶۴﴾
اور تم اُن لوگوں کو خوب جانتے ہو جو تم میں سے ہفتے
کے دن (مچھلی کا شکار کرنے) میں حد سے تجاوز کر گئے تھے
تو ہم نے اُن سے کہا کہ ذلیل و خوار بندر ہو جاؤ ﴿۶۵﴾
اور اس قصے کو اُس وقت کے لوگوں کیلئے اور جو اُنکے بعد آنیوالے
تھے عبرت اور پرہیزگاروں کیلئے نصیحت بنا دیا ﴿۶۶﴾
اور جب موسیٰ نے اپنی قوم کے لوگوں سے کہا کہ خدا تم
کو حکم دیتا ہے کہ ایک بیل ذبح کرو۔ وہ بولے کیا
تم ہم سے ہنسی کرتے ہو؟ (موسیٰ نے) کہا کہ میں خدا
کی پناہ مانگتا ہوں کہ نادان بنوں ﴿۶۷﴾
اُنہوں نے کہا اپنے پروردگار سے التجا کیجیے کہ وہ ہمیں
یہ بتائے کہ وہ بیل کس طرح کا ہو۔ (موسیٰ نے) کہا پروردگار
فرماتا ہے کہ وہ بیل نہ تو بوڑھا ہو اور نہ بچھڑا بلکہ اُنکے درمیان (یعنی
جوان) ہو سو جیسا تمکو حکم دیا گیا ہے ویسا کرو ﴿۶۸﴾
اُنہوں نے کہا اپنے پروردگار سے درخواست کیجیے کہ ہم کو
یہ بھی بتائے کہ اُس کا رنگ کیسا ہو موسیٰ نے کہا
پروردگار فرماتا ہے کہ اُس کا رنگ گہرا زرد ہو کہ دیکھنے والوں

وَالنَّصٰرٰى وَالصّٰبِـِٕيْنَ مَنْ اٰمَنَ
بِاللّٰهِ وَالْيَوْمِ الْاٰخِرِ وَعَمِلَ صَالِحًا
فَلَهُمْ اَجْرُهُمْ عِنْدَ رَبِّهِمْ ۚ وَلَا
خَوْفٌ عَلَيْهِمْ وَلَا هُمْ يَحْزَنُوْنَ ﴿٦٢﴾
وَاِذْ اَخَذْنَا مِيْثَاقَكُمْ وَرَفَعْنَا
فَوْقَكُمُ الطُّوْرَ ؕ خُذُوْا مَآ اٰتَيْنٰكُمْ
بِقُوَّةٍ وَّاذْكُرُوْا مَا فِيْهِ
لَعَلَّكُمْ تَتَّقُوْنَ ﴿٦٣﴾
ثُمَّ تَوَلَّيْتُمْ مِّنْۢ بَعْدِ ذٰلِكَ ۚ فَلَوْلَا
فَضْلُ اللّٰهِ عَلَيْكُمْ وَرَحْمَتُهٗ لَكُنْتُمْ
مِّنَ الْخٰسِرِيْنَ ﴿٦٤﴾
وَلَقَدْ عَلِمْتُمُ الَّذِيْنَ اعْتَدَوْا مِنْكُمْ
فِى السَّبْتِ فَقُلْنَا لَهُمْ كُوْنُوْا قِرَدَةً
خٰسِـِٕيْنَ ﴿٦٥﴾
فَجَعَلْنٰهَا نَكَالًا لِّمَا بَيْنَ يَدَيْهَا
وَمَا خَلْفَهَا وَمَوْعِظَةً لِّلْمُتَّقِيْنَ ﴿٦٦﴾
وَاِذْ قَالَ مُوْسٰى لِقَوْمِهٖٓ اِنَّ اللّٰهَ
يَاْمُرُكُمْ اَنْ تَذْبَحُوْا بَقَرَةً ؕ
قَالُوْٓا اَتَتَّخِذُنَا هُزُوًا ؕ قَالَ اَعُوْذُ
بِاللّٰهِ اَنْ اَكُوْنَ مِنَ الْجٰهِلِيْنَ ﴿٦٧﴾
قَالُوا ادْعُ لَنَا رَبَّكَ يُبَيِّنْ لَّنَا مَا هِىَ ؕ
قَالَ اِنَّهٗ يَقُوْلُ اِنَّهَا بَقَرَةٌ لَّا
فَارِضٌ وَّلَا بِكْرٌ ؕ عَوَانٌۢ بَيْنَ
ذٰلِكَ ؕ فَافْعَلُوْا مَا تُؤْمَرُوْنَ ﴿٦٨﴾
قَالُوا ادْعُ لَنَا رَبَّكَ يُبَيِّنْ لَّنَا
مَا لَوْنُهَا ؕ قَالَ اِنَّهٗ يَقُوْلُ اِنَّهَا
بَقَرَةٌ صَفْرَآءُ ۙ فَاقِعٌ لَّوْنُهَا

beholders!"

رکے دل) کو خوش کر دیتا ہو ﴿۶۹﴾

تَسُرُّ النّٰظِرِيْنَ ﴿٦٩﴾

70. They said: "Beseech on our behalf thy Lord to make plain to us what she is: to us are all heifers alike: we wish indeed for guidance, if Allah wills."

اُنہوں نے کہا کہ (اب کے) پروردگار سے پھر درخواست کیجیے کہ ہم کو یہ بتا دے
کہ وہ اور کس کس طرح کا ہو کیونکہ بہت سے بیل ہمیں ایک دوسرے کے
مشابہ معلوم ہوتے ہیں (پھر) خدا نے چاہا تو ہمیں ٹھیک بات معلوم ہو جائیگی ﴿۷۰﴾

قَالُوا ادْعُ لَنَا رَبَّكَ يُبَيِّنْ لَّنَا
مَا هِيَ ۙ اِنَّ الْبَقَرَ تَشٰبَهَ عَلَيْنَا ؕ
وَاِنَّآ اِنْ شَآءَ اللّٰهُ لَمُهْتَدُوْنَ ﴿٧٠﴾

71. He said: "He says: a heifer not trained to till the soil or water the fields; sound and without blemish." They said: "Now hast thou brought the truth." Then they offered her in sacrifice, and they scarcely did it.

موسیٰ نے کہا کہ خدا فرماتا ہے کہ وہ بیل کام میں لگا ہوا نہ ہو نہ تو زمین
جوتتا ہو اور نہ کھیتی کو پانی دیتا ہو اس میں کسی طرح کا داغ نہ ہو۔
کہنے لگے اب تم نے سب باتیں درست بتا دیں غرض (بڑی
مشکل سے) اُنہوں نے اس بیل کو ذبح کیا اور وہ ایسا کرنے والے تھے نہیں ﴿۷۱﴾

قَالَ اِنَّهٗ يَقُوْلُ اِنَّهَا بَقَرَةٌ لَّا
ذَلُوْلٌ تُثِيْرُ الْاَرْضَ وَلَا تَسْقِي الْحَرْثَ ۚ
مُسَلَّمَةٌ لَّا شِيَةَ فِيْهَا ؕ قَالُوا الْـٰٔنَ جِئْتَ
بِالْحَقِّ ؕ فَذَبَحُوْهَا وَمَا كَادُوْا يَفْعَلُوْنَ ﴿٧١﴾ ع

72. Remember ye slew a man and fell into a dispute among yourselves as to the crime: but Allah was to bring forth what ye did hide.

اور جب تم نے ایک شخص کو قتل کیا تو اس میں باہم جھگڑنے
لگے لیکن جو بات تم چھپا رہے تھے خدا اسکو ظاہر کرنیوالا تھا ﴿۷۲﴾

وَاِذْ قَتَلْتُمْ نَفْسًا فَادّٰرَءْتُمْ فِيْهَا ؕ
وَاللّٰهُ مُخْرِجٌ مَّا كُنْتُمْ تَكْتُمُوْنَ ﴿٧٢﴾ ۚ

73. So We said: "Strike the (body) with a piece of the (heifer)." Thus Allah bringeth the dead to life and showeth you His Signs: perchance ye may understand.

تو ہم نے کہا کہ اس بیل کا کوئی سا ٹکڑا مقتول کو مارو۔ اس
طرح خدا مُردوں کو زندہ کرتا ہے اور تم کو اپنی قدرت
کی نشانیاں دکھاتا ہے تاکہ تم سمجھو ﴿۷۳﴾

فَقُلْنَا اضْرِبُوْهُ بِبَعْضِهَا ؕ كَذٰلِكَ
يُحْيِ اللّٰهُ الْمَوْتٰى ۙ وَيُرِيْكُمْ اٰيٰتِهٖ
لَعَلَّكُمْ تَعْقِلُوْنَ ﴿٧٣﴾

74. Thenceforth were your hearts hardened: they became like a rock and even worse in hardness. For among rocks there are some from which rivers gush forth; others there are which when split asunder send forth water; and others which sink for fear of Allah, and Allah is not unmindful of what ye do.

پھر اس کے بعد تمہارے دل سخت ہو گئے گویا وہ پتھر ہیں
یا اُن سے بھی زیادہ سخت۔ اور پتھر تو بعضے ایسے ہوتے
ہیں کہ اُن میں سے چشمے پھوٹ نکلتے ہیں اور بعضے
ایسے ہوتے ہیں کہ پھٹ جاتے ہیں اور اُن میں سے
پانی نکلنے لگتا ہے اور بعضے ایسے ہوتے ہیں کہ خدا کے
خوف سے گر پڑتے ہیں۔ اور خدا تمہارے عملوں
سے بے خبر نہیں ﴿۷۴﴾

ثُمَّ قَسَتْ قُلُوْبُكُمْ مِّنْۢ بَعْدِ ذٰلِكَ
فَهِيَ كَالْحِجَارَةِ اَوْ اَشَدُّ قَسْوَةً ؕ
وَاِنَّ مِنَ الْحِجَارَةِ لَمَا يَتَفَجَّرُ
مِنْهُ الْاَنْهٰرُ ؕ وَاِنَّ مِنْهَا لَمَا
يَشَّقَّقُ فَيَخْرُجُ مِنْهُ الْمَآءُ ؕ وَاِنَّ
مِنْهَا لَمَا يَهْبِطُ مِنْ خَشْيَةِ اللّٰهِ ؕ
وَمَا اللّٰهُ بِغَافِلٍ عَمَّا تَعْمَلُوْنَ ﴿٧٤﴾

75. Can ye (O ye men of Faith) entertain the hope that they will believe in you ?—seeing that a party of them heard the Word of Allah, and perverted it knowingly after they understood it.

(مومنو) کیا تم اُمید رکھتے ہو کہ یہ لوگ تمہارے (دین کے)
قائل ہو جائینگے (حالانکہ) اُن میں سے کچھ لوگ کلامِ خدا
(یعنی تورات) کو سنتے پھر اُس کے سمجھ لینے کے بعد
اُسکو جان بوجھ کر بدل دیتے رہے ہیں ﴿۷۵﴾

اَفَتَطْمَعُوْنَ اَنْ يُّؤْمِنُوْا لَكُمْ وَقَدْ
كَانَ فَرِيْقٌ مِّنْهُمْ يَسْمَعُوْنَ كَلٰمَ
اللّٰهِ ثُمَّ يُحَرِّفُوْنَهٗ مِنْۢ بَعْدِ مَا
عَقَلُوْهُ وَهُمْ يَعْلَمُوْنَ ﴿٧٥﴾

76. Behold! when they meet the men of Faith, they say: "We believe": but when they meet each other in private, they say: "Shall you tell them what Allah hath

اور یہ لوگ جب مومنوں سے ملتے ہیں تو کہتے ہیں ہم
ایمان لے آئے ہیں۔ اور جس وقت آپس میں ایک دوسرے سے
ملتے ہیں تو کہتے ہیں جو بات خدا نے تم پر ظاہر فرمائی ہے وہ تم ان کو

وَاِذَا لَقُوا الَّذِيْنَ اٰمَنُوْا قَالُوْٓا اٰمَنَّا ۚ
وَاِذَا خَلَا بَعْضُهُمْ اِلٰى بَعْضٍ قَالُوْٓا
اَتُحَدِّثُوْنَهُمْ بِمَا فَتَحَ اللّٰهُ عَلَيْكُمْ

revealed to you, that they may engage you in argument about it before your Lord?"—Do ye not understand (their aim)?

اسلئے بتائے دیتے ہو کہ (قیامت کے دن) اسی کے حوالے سے تمہارے
پروردگار کے سامنے تمکو الزام دیں۔ کیا تم سمجھتے نہیں؟ (۷۶)

لِيُحَاجُّوكُم بِهِ عِندَ رَبِّكُمْ ط
أَفَلَا تَعْقِلُونَ ﴿٧٦﴾

77. Know they not that Allah knoweth what they conceal and what they reveal ?

کیا یہ لوگ یہ نہیں جانتے کہ جو کچھ یہ چھپاتے اور جو کچھ ظاہر
کرتے ہیں خدا کو (سب) معلوم ہے (۷۷)

أَوَلَا يَعْلَمُونَ أَنَّ اللَّهَ يَعْلَمُ مَا
يُسِرُّونَ وَمَا يُعْلِنُونَ ﴿٧٧﴾

78. And there are among them illiterates, who know not the Book, but (see therein their own) desires, and they do nothing but conjecture.

اور بعض اُن میں اَن پڑھ ہیں کہ اپنے خیالات باطل کے
سوا (خدا کی) کتاب سے واقف ہی نہیں اور وہ صرف ظن
سے کام لیتے ہیں (۷۸)

وَمِنْهُمْ أُمِّيُّونَ لَا يَعْلَمُونَ
الْكِتَابَ إِلَّا أَمَانِيَّ وَإِنْ هُمْ
إِلَّا يَظُنُّونَ ﴿٧٨﴾ النصف

79. Then woe to those who write the Book with their own hands, and then say: "This is from Allah," to traffic with it for a miserable price !— Woe to them for what their hands do write, and for the gain they make thereby.

تو اُن لوگوں پر افسوس ہے جو اپنے ہاتھ سے تو کتاب لکھتے ہیں
اور کہتے یہ ہیں کہ یہ خدا کے پاس سے آئی ہے تاکہ اسکے عوض
تھوڑی سی قیمت (یعنی دُنیوی منفعت) حاصل کریں۔ اُنپر
افسوس ہے اسلئے کہ (بے اصل باتیں) اپنے ہاتھ سے لکھتے ہیں
اور (پھر) اُن پر افسوس ہے اسلئے کہ ایسے کام کرتے ہیں (۷۹)

فَوَيْلٌ لِّلَّذِينَ يَكْتُبُونَ الْكِتَابَ
بِأَيْدِيهِمْ ثُمَّ يَقُولُونَ هَٰذَا مِنْ
عِندِ اللَّهِ لِيَشْتَرُوا بِهِ ثَمَنًا قَلِيلًا ط
فَوَيْلٌ لَّهُم مِّمَّا كَتَبَتْ أَيْدِيهِمْ
وَوَيْلٌ لَّهُم مِّمَّا يَكْسِبُونَ ﴿٧٩﴾

80. And they say: "The Fire shall not touch us but for a few numbered days:" say: "Have ye taken a promise from Allah, for He never breaks His promise? Or is it that ye say of Allah what ye do not know?"

اور کہتے ہیں کہ (دوزخ کی) آگ ہمیں چند روز کے سوا چھو
ہی نہیں سکیگی۔ اُن سے پوچھو کیا تم نے خدا سے اقرار لے رکھا
ہے کہ خدا اپنے اقرار کے خلاف نہیں کریگا (نہیں) بلکہ تم خدا کے
بارے میں ایسی باتیں کہتے ہو جنکا تمہیں مطلق علم نہیں (۸۰)

وَقَالُوا لَن تَمَسَّنَا النَّارُ إِلَّا أَيَّامًا
مَّعْدُودَةً ط قُلْ أَتَّخَذْتُمْ عِندَ اللَّهِ
عَهْدًا فَلَن يُخْلِفَ اللَّهُ عَهْدَهُ
أَمْ تَقُولُونَ عَلَى اللَّهِ مَا لَا تَعْلَمُونَ ﴿٨٠﴾

81. Nay, those who seek gain in Evil, and are girt round by their sins,—they are Companions of the Fire: therein shall they abide (for ever).

ہاں جو بُرے کام کرے اور اُسکے گناہ (ہر طرف سے) اُسکو
گھیر لیں تو ایسے لوگ دوزخ (میں جانے) والے ہیں (اور)
وہ ہمیشہ اسمیں (جلتے) رہیں گے (۸۱)

بَلَىٰ مَن كَسَبَ سَيِّئَةً وَأَحَاطَتْ
بِهِ خَطِيئَتُهُ فَأُولَٰئِكَ أَصْحَابُ
النَّارِ هُمْ فِيهَا خَالِدُونَ ﴿٨١﴾

82. But those who have faith and work righteousness, they are Companions of the Garden: therein shall they abide (for ever).

اور جو ایمان لائیں اور نیک کام کریں وہ جنت کے مالک ہونگے
(اور) ہمیشہ اُس میں (عیش کرتے) رہیں گے (۸۲)

وَالَّذِينَ آمَنُوا وَعَمِلُوا الصَّالِحَاتِ أُولَٰئِكَ
أَصْحَابُ الْجَنَّةِ هُمْ فِيهَا خَالِدُونَ ﴿٨٢﴾ ع ٩

83. And remember We took a Covenant from the Children of Israel (to this effect): worship none but Allah; treat with kindness your parents and kindred, and orphans and those in need; speak fair to the people; be steadfast in prayer; and give Zakat, then did ye turn back, except a few among you, and ye backslide (even now).

اور جب ہم نے بنی اسرائیل سے عہد لیا کہ خدا کے سوا کسی
کی عبادت نہ کرنا اور ماں باپ اور رشتہ داروں
اور یتیموں اور محتاجوں کے ساتھ بھلائی کرتے
رہنا اور لوگوں سے اچھی باتیں کہنا اور نماز
پڑھتے اور زکوٰۃ دیتے رہنا۔ تو چند شخصوں کے سوا
تم سب (اس عہد سے) منہ پھیر کر پھر بیٹھے (۸۳)

وَإِذْ أَخَذْنَا مِيثَاقَ بَنِي إِسْرَائِيلَ لَا
تَعْبُدُونَ إِلَّا اللَّهَ وَبِالْوَالِدَيْنِ
إِحْسَانًا وَذِي الْقُرْبَىٰ وَالْيَتَامَىٰ وَ
الْمَسَاكِينِ وَقُولُوا لِلنَّاسِ حُسْنًا وَ
أَقِيمُوا الصَّلَاةَ وَآتُوا الزَّكَاةَ ط ثُمَّ
تَوَلَّيْتُمْ إِلَّا قَلِيلًا مِّنكُمْ وَأَنتُم مُّعْرِضُونَ ﴿٨٣﴾

84. And remember We took your Covenant (to this effect): Shed no blood amongst you, nor turn out your own people from your homes: and this ye solemnly ratified. And to this ye were witness.

اور جب ہم نے تم سے عہد لیا کہ آپس میں کشت وخون
نہ کرنا اور اپنے کو اُنکے وطن سے نہ نکالنا تو تم نے
اقرار کر لیا اور تم (اس بات کے) گواہ ہو (۸۴)

وَاِذْ اَخَذْنَا مِيْثَاقَكُمْ لَا تَسْفِكُوْنَ
دِمَآءَكُمْ وَلَا تُخْرِجُوْنَ اَنْفُسَكُمْ مِّنْ
دِيَارِكُمْ ثُمَّ اَقْرَرْتُمْ وَاَنْتُمْ تَشْهَدُوْنَ (۸۴)

85. After this it is ye, the same people, who slay among yourselves, and banish a party of you from their homes; assist (their enemies) against them, in guilt and transgression; and if they come to you as captives, ye ransom them, though it was not lawful for you to banish them. Then is it only a part of the Book that ye believe in, and do ye reject the rest ? But what is the reward for those among you who behave like this but disgrace in this life?—And on the Day of Judgment they shall be consigned to the most grievous chastisement for Allah is not unmindful of what ye do.

پھر تم وہی ہو کہ اپنوں کو قتل بھی کر دیتے ہو اور اپنے
میں سے بعض لوگوں پر گناہ اور ظلم سے چڑھائی
کر کے اُنہیں وطن سے نکال بھی دیتے ہو اور اگر وہ تمہارے
پاس قید ہو کر آئیں تو بدلہ دے کر اُن کو چھڑا بھی لیتے ہو
حالانکہ اُن کا نکال دینا ہی تم کو حرام تھا (یہ) کیا
(بات ہے کہ) تم کتاب (خدا) کے بعض احکام کو تو مانتے ہو اور
بعض سے انکار کئے دیتے ہو تو جو تم میں سے ایسی حرکت کریں اُنکی
سزا اسکے سوا اور کیا ہو سکتی ہے کہ دنیا کی زندگی میں تو
رسوائی ہو اور قیامت کے دن سخت سے سخت عذاب میں ڈالدیئے
جائیں اور جو کام تم کرتے ہو خدا اُن سے غافل نہیں (۸۵)

ثُمَّ اَنْتُمْ هٰٓؤُلَآءِ تَقْتُلُوْنَ اَنْفُسَكُمْ
وَتُخْرِجُوْنَ فَرِيْقًا مِّنْكُمْ مِّنْ دِيَارِهِمْ ز
تَظٰهَرُوْنَ عَلَيْهِمْ بِالْاِثْمِ وَالْعُدْوَانِ ط
وَاِنْ يَّاْتُوْكُمْ اُسٰرٰى تُفٰدُوْهُمْ وَهُوَ
مُحَرَّمٌ عَلَيْكُمْ اِخْرَاجُهُمْ ط اَفَتُؤْمِنُوْنَ
بِبَعْضِ الْكِتٰبِ وَتَكْفُرُوْنَ بِبَعْضٍ ج
فَمَا جَزَآءُ مَنْ يَّفْعَلُ ذٰلِكَ مِنْكُمْ
اِلَّا خِزْيٌ فِى الْحَيٰوةِ الدُّنْيَا ج وَيَوْمَ
الْقِيٰمَةِ يُرَدُّوْنَ اِلٰٓى اَشَدِّ الْعَذَابِ ط
وَمَا اللّٰهُ بِغَافِلٍ عَمَّا تَعْمَلُوْنَ (۸۵)

86. These are the people who buy the life of this world at the price of the Hereafter: their chastisement shall not be lightened, nor shall they be helped.

یہ وہ لوگ ہیں جنہوں نے آخرت کے بدلے دُنیا کی
زندگی خریدی سو نہ تو اُن سے عذاب ہی ہلکا کیا جائیگا
اور نہ اُن کو (اور طرح کی) مدد ملے گی (۸۶)

اُولٰٓئِكَ الَّذِيْنَ اشْتَرَوُا الْحَيٰوةَ
الدُّنْيَا بِالْاٰخِرَةِ ز فَلَا يُخَفَّفُ عَنْهُمُ
الْعَذَابُ وَلَا هُمْ يُنْصَرُوْنَ (۸۶) ع

87. We gave Moses the Book and followed him up with a succession of Messengers; We gave Jesus the son of Mary clear (Signs) and strengthened him with the holy spirit. Is it that whenever there comes to you a Messenger with what ye yourselves desire not, ye are puffed up with pride ? —Some ye called impostors, and others ye slay !

اور ہم نے موسیٰ کو کتاب عنایت کی اور اُن کے پیچھے
یکے بعد دیگرے پیغمبر بھیجتے رہے اور عیسیٰ ابن مریم کو کھلے
نشانات بخشے اور روح القدس (یعنی جبرئیل) سے
اُن کو مدد دی۔ تو جب کوئی پیغمبر تمہارے پاس ایسی باتیں
لے کر آئے جن کو تمہارا جی نہیں چاہتا تھا تو تم سرکش
ہو جاتے رہے اور ایک گروہ (انبیاء) کو تو جھٹلاتے رہے
اور ایک گروہ کو قتل کرتے رہے (۸۷)

وَلَقَدْ اٰتَيْنَا مُوْسَى الْكِتٰبَ وَقَفَّيْنَا
مِنْ بَعْدِهٖ بِالرُّسُلِ ز وَاٰتَيْنَا عِيْسَى
ابْنَ مَرْيَمَ الْبَيِّنٰتِ وَاَيَّدْنٰهُ
بِرُوْحِ الْقُدُسِ ط اَفَكُلَّمَا جَآءَكُمْ
رَسُوْلٌ بِمَا لَا تَهْوٰٓى اَنْفُسُكُمُ
اسْتَكْبَرْتُمْ ج فَفَرِيْقًا كَذَّبْتُمْ ز
وَفَرِيْقًا تَقْتُلُوْنَ (۸۷)

88. They say, “Our hearts are the wrappings (which preserve Allah's Word: we need no more)” nay, Allah's curse is on them for their blasphemy: little is it they believe.

اور کہتے ہیں ہمارے دل پردے میں ہیں (نہیں) بلکہ
خدا نے اُن کے کفر کے سبب اُن پر لعنت کر رکھی ہے پس
یہ تھوڑے ہی پر ایمان لاتے ہیں (۸۸)

وَقَالُوْا قُلُوْبُنَا غُلْفٌ ط بَلْ لَّعَنَهُمُ
اللّٰهُ بِكُفْرِهِمْ فَقَلِيْلًا مَّا
يُؤْمِنُوْنَ (۸۸)

89. And when there comes; to them a Book from Allah, confirming

اور جب خدا کے ہاں سے اُنکے پاس کتاب آئی جو اُن کی

وَلَمَّا جَآءَهُمْ كِتٰبٌ مِّنْ عِنْدِ اللّٰهِ

what is with them,—although from of old they had prayed for victory against those without Faith,— when there comes to them that which they (should) have recognized, they refuse to believe in it, but the curse of Allah is on those without Faith.

90. Miserable is the price for which they have sold their souls, in that they deny (the revelation) which Allah has sent down, in insolent envy that Allah of His Grace should send it to any of His servants He pleases: thus have they drawn on themselves Wrath upon Wrath. And humiliating is the Chastisement of those who reject Faith.

91. When it is said to them, "Believe in what Allah hath sent down," they say, "We believe in what was sent down to us": yet they reject all besides, even if it be Truth confirming what is with them. Say: "Why then have ye slain the prophets of Allah in times gone by, if ye did indeed believe?"

92. There came to you Moses with clear (Signs); yet ye worshipped the Calf (even) after that, and ye did behave wrongfully.

93. And remember We took your Covenant and We raised above you the mount (Sinai): (saying): "Hold firmly to what We have given you, and hearken (to the Law)" they said: "We hear, and we disobey": and their hearts were filled (with the love) of the Calf because of their Faithlessness. Say: "Vile indeed are the behests of your Faith if ye have any faith!"

94. Say: "If the last Home, with Allah, be for you specially, and not for anyone else, then seek ye for

(آسمانی) کتاب کی بھی تصدیق کرتی ہے۔ اور وہ پہلے
(ہمیشہ) کافروں پر فتح مانگا کرتے تھے۔ تو جس چیز کو وہ
خوب پہچانتے تھے جب اُنکے پاس آپہنچی تو اُس سے کافر
ہوگئے پس کافروں پر خدا کی لعنت ﴿۸۹﴾

جس چیز کے بدلے اُنہوں نے اپنے تئیں بیچ ڈالا وہ بہت
بُری ہے یعنی اس جلن سے کہ خدا اپنے بندوں میں سے جس پر
چاہتا ہے اپنی مہربانی سے نازل فرماتا ہے خدا کی نازل کی
ہوئی کتاب سے کفر کرنے لگے تو وہ (اُس کے) غضب
بالائے غضب میں مبتلا ہوگئے۔ اور کافروں کیلئے ذلیل
کرنے والا عذاب ہے ﴿۹۰﴾

اور جب اُن سے کہا جاتا ہے کہ جو (کتاب) خدا نے (اب)
نازل فرمائی ہے اُسکو مانو تو کہتے ہیں کہ جو کتاب ہم پر (پہلے)
نازل ہو چکی ہے ہم تو اُسی کو مانتے ہیں (یعنی) یہ اسکے سوا اور (کتاب)
کو نہیں مانتے حالانکہ وہ (سراسر) سچی ہے اور جو اُن کی (آسمانی)
کتاب ہے اُسکی بھی تصدیق کرتی ہے (اُن سے) کہدو کہ اگر تم صاحبِ ایمان
ہوتے تو خدا کے پیغمبروں کو پہلے ہی کیوں قتل کیا کرتے ﴿۹۱﴾

اور موسیٰ تمہارے پاس کُھلے ہوئے معجزات لیکر آئے تو تم اُنکے
(کوہ طور پر جانیکے) بعد بچھڑے کو معبود بنا بیٹھے اور تم (اپنے
ہی حق میں) ظلم کرتے تھے ﴿۹۲﴾

اور جب ہم نے تم (لوگوں) سے عہد واثق لیا اور کوہ طور کو تم
پر اُٹھا کھڑا کیا (اور حکم دیا کہ) جو (کتاب) ہم نے تمکو دی ہے اسکو زور
سے پکڑو اور (جو تمہیں حکم ہوتا ہے اُسکو) سنو تو وہ (جو تمہارے بڑے تھے)
کہنے لگے کہ ہم نے سُن تو لیا لیکن مانتے نہیں۔ اور اُنکے کفر کے سبب
بچھڑا (گویا) اُنکے دلوں میں رچ گیا تھا (اے پیغمبر اُن سے) کہدو کہ اگر
تم مومن ہو تو تمہارا ایمان تم کو بُری بات بتاتا ہے ﴿۹۳﴾

کہہ دو کہ اگر آخرت کا گھر اور لوگوں (یعنی مسلمانوں) کیلئے
نہیں اور خدا کے نزدیک تمہارے ہی لئے مخصوص ہے تو اگر

مُصَدِّقٌ لِّمَا مَعَهُمْ وَكَانُوا مِن
قَبْلُ يَسْتَفْتِحُونَ عَلَى الَّذِينَ
كَفَرُوا فَلَمَّا جَاءَهُم مَّا عَرَفُوا
كَفَرُوا بِهِ فَلَعْنَةُ اللَّهِ عَلَى الْكَافِرِينَ ﴿٨٩﴾
بِئْسَمَا اشْتَرَوْا بِهِ أَنفُسَهُمْ أَن
يَكْفُرُوا بِمَا أَنزَلَ اللَّهُ بَغْيًا أَن
يُنَزِّلَ اللَّهُ مِن فَضْلِهِ عَلَىٰ مَن يَشَاءُ
مِنْ عِبَادِهِ فَبَاءُوا بِغَضَبٍ عَلَىٰ
غَضَبٍ ط وَلِلْكَافِرِينَ عَذَابٌ
مُّهِينٌ ﴿٩٠﴾
وَإِذَا قِيلَ لَهُمْ آمِنُوا بِمَا أَنزَلَ
اللَّهُ قَالُوا نُؤْمِنُ بِمَا أُنزِلَ عَلَيْنَا
وَيَكْفُرُونَ بِمَا وَرَاءَهُ وَهُوَ الْحَقُّ
مُصَدِّقًا لِّمَا مَعَهُمْ ط قُلْ فَلِمَ
تَقْتُلُونَ أَنبِيَاءَ اللَّهِ مِن قَبْلُ
إِن كُنتُم مُّؤْمِنِينَ ﴿٩١﴾
وَلَقَدْ جَاءَكُم مُّوسَىٰ بِالْبَيِّنَاتِ
ثُمَّ اتَّخَذْتُمُ الْعِجْلَ مِن بَعْدِهِ
وَأَنتُمْ ظَالِمُونَ ﴿٩٢﴾
وَإِذْ أَخَذْنَا مِيثَاقَكُمْ وَرَفَعْنَا
فَوْقَكُمُ الطُّورَ ط خُذُوا مَا آتَيْنَاكُم
بِقُوَّةٍ وَاسْمَعُوا ط قَالُوا سَمِعْنَا
وَعَصَيْنَا وَأُشْرِبُوا فِي قُلُوبِهِمُ
الْعِجْلَ بِكُفْرِهِمْ ط قُلْ بِئْسَمَا يَأْمُرُكُم
بِهِ إِيمَانُكُمْ إِن كُنتُم مُّؤْمِنِينَ ﴿٩٣﴾
قُلْ إِن كَانَتْ لَكُمُ الدَّارُ الْآخِرَةُ
عِندَ اللَّهِ خَالِصَةً مِّن دُونِ النَّاسِ

death, if ye are sincere."

95. But they shall never seek for death, on account of the (sins) which their hands have sent on before them. And Allah is well-acquainted with the wrong-doers.
96. Thou wilt indeed find them, of all people, most greedy of life,—even more than the idolaters: each one of them wishes he could be given a life of a thousand years: but the grant of such life will not save him from (due) chastisement, for Allah sees well all that they do.

97. Say: Whoever is an enemy to Gabriel—for he brings down the (revelation) to thy heart by Allah's will, a confirmation of what went before, and guidance and glad tidings for those who believe,—

98. Whoever is an enemy to Allah and His angels and prophets, to Gabriel and Michael,— lo ! Allah is an enemy to those who reject Faith.

99. We have sent down to thee manifest Signs (*āyāt*); and none reject them but those who are perverse.
100. Is it not (the case) that every time they make a Covenant, some party among them throw it aside?—Nay, most of them are faithless.

101. And when there came to them a Messenger from Allah, confirming what was with them, a party of the People of the Book threw away the Book of Allah behind their backs, as if (it had been something) they did not know !

102. They followed what the Satans recited over Solomon's Kingdom. Solomon did not disbelieve but Satans disbelieved, teaching men, magic, and such things as came down at Babylon to the angels Hārût and Mārût. But

فَتَمَنَّوُا الْمَوْتَ إِنْ كُنْتُمْ صٰدِقِينَ ﴿٩٤﴾
وَلَنْ يَتَمَنَّوْهُ أَبَدًا بِمَا قَدَّمَتْ
أَيْدِيهِمْ ۗ وَاللّٰهُ عَلِيمٌ بِالظّٰلِمِينَ ﴿٩٥﴾
وَلَتَجِدَنَّهُمْ أَحْرَصَ النَّاسِ عَلٰى
حَيٰوةٍ ۚ وَمِنَ الَّذِينَ أَشْرَكُوا ۚ
يَوَدُّ أَحَدُهُمْ لَوْ يُعَمَّرُ أَلْفَ سَنَةٍ ۚ
وَمَا هُوَ بِمُزَحْزِحِهِ مِنَ الْعَذَابِ أَنْ
يُعَمَّرَ ۗ وَاللّٰهُ بَصِيرٌ بِمَا يَعْمَلُونَ ﴿٩٦﴾
قُلْ مَنْ كَانَ عَدُوًّا لِجِبْرِيلَ فَإِنَّهُ
نَزَّلَهُ عَلٰى قَلْبِكَ بِإِذْنِ اللّٰهِ مُصَدِّقًا
لِمَا بَيْنَ يَدَيْهِ وَهُدًى وَبُشْرٰى
لِلْمُؤْمِنِينَ ﴿٩٧﴾
مَنْ كَانَ عَدُوًّا لِلّٰهِ وَمَلٰٓئِكَتِهِ
وَرُسُلِهِ وَجِبْرِيلَ وَمِيكٰلَ فَإِنَّ
اللّٰهَ عَدُوٌّ لِلْكٰفِرِينَ ﴿٩٨﴾
وَلَقَدْ أَنْزَلْنَا إِلَيْكَ آيٰتٍ بَيِّنٰتٍ ۚ
وَمَا يَكْفُرُ بِهَا إِلَّا الْفٰسِقُونَ ﴿٩٩﴾
أَوَكُلَّمَا عٰهَدُوا عَهْدًا نَبَذَهُ فَرِيقٌ
مِنْهُمْ ۚ بَلْ أَكْثَرُهُمْ لَا يُؤْمِنُونَ ﴿١٠٠﴾
وَلَمَّا جَاءَهُمْ رَسُولٌ مِنْ عِنْدِ اللّٰهِ
مُصَدِّقٌ لِمَا مَعَهُمْ نَبَذَ فَرِيقٌ
مِنَ الَّذِينَ أُوتُوا الْكِتٰبَ ۙ كِتٰبَ اللّٰهِ
وَرَاءَ ظُهُورِهِمْ كَأَنَّهُمْ لَا يَعْلَمُونَ ﴿١٠١﴾
وَاتَّبَعُوا مَا تَتْلُوا الشَّيٰطِينُ عَلٰى
مُلْكِ سُلَيْمٰنَ ۚ وَمَا كَفَرَ سُلَيْمٰنُ
وَلٰكِنَّ الشَّيٰطِينَ كَفَرُوا يُعَلِّمُونَ
النَّاسَ السِّحْرَ وَمَا أُنْزِلَ عَلَى

سچے ہو تو موت کی آرزو تو کرو ﴿۹۴﴾
لیکن ان اعمال کی وجہ سے جو ان کے ہاتھ آگے بھیج چکے ہیں یہ کبھی اس کی
آرزو نہیں کرینگے اور خدا ظالموں سے (خوب) واقف ہے ﴿۹۵﴾
بلکہ اُن کو تم اور لوگوں سے زندگی کے کہیں حریص دیکھو گے
یہاں تک کہ مشرکوں سے بھی۔ اُن میں سے ہر ایک یہی خواہش
کرتا ہے کہ کاش وہ ہزار برس جیتا رہے مگر اتنی لمبی عمر
اُس کو مل بھی جائے تو اُسے عذاب سے تو نہیں چھڑا سکتی
اور جو کام یہ کرتے ہیں خدا اُنکو دیکھ رہا ہے ﴿۹۶﴾
کہہ دو کہ جو شخص جبرئیل کا دشمن ہو (اُس کو غصے میں
مرجانا چاہیئے) اُس نے تو (یہ کتاب) خدا کے حکم سے
تمہارے دل پر نازل کی ہے جو پہلی کتابوں کی تصدیق کرتی
ہے اور ایمان والوں کیلئے ہدایت اور بشارت ہے ﴿۹۷﴾
جو شخص خدا کا اور اُس کے فرشتوں کا اور اُسکے پیغمبروں کا
اور جبرئیل اور میکائیل کا دشمن ہو تو ایسے کافروں کا
خدا دشمن ہے ﴿۹۸﴾
اور ہم نے تمہارے پاس سُلجھی ہوئی آیتیں ارسال فرمائی ہیں اور
اُن سے انکار وہی کرتے ہیں جو بدکردار ہیں ﴿۹۹﴾
اُن لوگوں نے جب جب (خدا سے) عہد واثق کیا تو اُنمیں سے ایک فریق نے
اُسکو (کسی چیز کی طرح) پھینک دیا۔ حقیقت یہ ہے کہ اُن میں اکثر بے ایمان ہیں ﴿۱۰۰﴾
اور جب اُنکے پاس خدا کی طرف سے پیغمبر (آخرالزماں) آئے
اور وہ اُن کی (آسمانی) کتاب کی تصدیق بھی کرتے ہیں
تو جن لوگوں کو کتاب دی گئی تھی اُنمیں سے ایک جماعت نے
خدا کی کتاب کو پیٹھ پیچھے پھینک دیا گویا وہ جانتے ہی نہیں ﴿۱۰۱﴾
اور اُن (ہزلیات) کے پیچھے لگ گئے جو سلیمان کے عہد سلطنت
میں شیاطین پڑھا کرتے تھے اور سلیمان نے مطلق کفر
کی بات نہیں کی بلکہ شیطان ہی کفر کرتے تھے کہ لوگوں
کو جادو سکھاتے تھے اور اُن باتوں کے بھی (پیچھے لگ گئے)

neither of these taught anyone (such things) without saying: "We are only for trial; so do not blaspheme." They learned from them the means to sow discord between man and wife. But they could not thus harm anyone except by Allah's permission. And they learned what harmed them, not what profited them. And they knew that the buyers of (magic) would have no share in the happiness of the Hereafter. And vile was the price for which they did sell their souls, if they but knew !

103. If they had kept their Faith and guarded themselves from evil, far better had been the reward from Allah, if they but knew!

104. O ye of Faith ! say not (to the Prophet) Ra'ina, but say, 'Unzurna and hearken (to him): to those without Faith is a grievous punishment.

105. It is never the wish of those without Faith among the People of the Book nor of the polytheists. That anything good should come down to you from your Lord. But Allah will choose for His special Mercy whom He will—for Allah is Lord of grace abounding.

106. None of Our revelations do We abrogate or cause to be forgotten, but We substitute something better or similar: knowest thou not that Allah hath power over all things ?

107. Knowest thou not that to Allah belongeth the dominion of the heavens and the earth ? And besides Him ye have neither patron nor helper.

108. Would ye question your Messenger as Moses was

جو شہر بابل میں دو فرشتوں (یعنی) ہاروت اور ماروت پر اتری
تھیں۔ اور وہ دونوں کسی کو کچھ نہیں سکھاتے تھے جب تک یہ نہ
کہہ دیتے کہ ہم تو (ذریعۂ) آزمائش ہیں۔ تم کفر میں نہ پڑو۔ غرض
لوگ اُن سے ایسا (جادو) سیکھتے جس سے میاں بیوی میں جُدائی
ڈال دیں۔ اور خدا کے حکم کے سوا وہ اس (جادو) سے
کسی کا کچھ بھی بگاڑ نہیں سکتے تھے۔ اور کچھ ایسے (منتر)
سیکھتے جو اُنکو نقصان ہی پہنچاتے اور فائدہ کچھ نہ دیتے۔
اور وہ جانتے تھے کہ جو شخص ایسی چیزوں (یعنی سحر اور منتر
وغیرہ) کا خریدار ہوگا اُس کا آخرت میں کچھ حصّہ نہیں
اور جس چیز کے عوض اُنہوں نے اپنی جانوں کو بیچ ڈالا
وہ بُری تھی۔ کاش وہ (اس بات کو) جانتے ﴿۱۰۲﴾
اور اگر وہ ایمان لاتے اور پرہیزگاری کرتے تو خدا کے ہاں سے
بہت اچھا صلہ ملتا۔ اے کاش وہ اس سے واقف ہوتے ﴿۱۰۳﴾
اے اہل ایمان (گفتگو کے وقت پیغمبر خدا سے) راعنا نہ کہا
کرو۔ اُنظرنا کہا کرو اور خوب سُن رکھو [29] اور کافروں
کے لئے دُکھ دینے والا عذاب ہے ﴿۱۰۴﴾
جو لوگ کافر ہیں اہل کتاب یا مشرک وہ اس بات کو
پسند نہیں کرتے کہ تم پر تمہارے پروردگار کی طرف سے
خیر (و برکت) نازل ہو اور خدا تو جس کو چاہتا ہے اپنی رحمت
کیساتھ خاص کر لیتا ہے اور خدا بڑے فضل کا مالک ہے ﴿۱۰۵﴾
ہم جس آیت کو منسوخ کر دیتے یا اُسے فراموش کرا دیتے
ہیں تو اُس سے بہتر یا ویسی ہی اور آیت بھیج دیتے ہیں
کیا تم نہیں جانتے کہ خدا ہر بات پر قادر ہے ﴿۱۰۶﴾
تمہیں معلوم نہیں کہ آسمانوں اور زمین کی بادشاہت
خدا ہی کی ہے۔ اور خدا کے سوا تمہارا کوئی دوست
اور مددگار نہیں ﴿۱۰۷﴾
کیا تم یہ چاہتے ہو کہ اپنے پیغمبر سے اُسی طرح کے

الْمَلَكَيْنِ بِبَابِلَ هَارُوتَ وَمَارُوتَ ۚ
وَمَا يُعَلِّمَانِ مِنْ أَحَدٍ حَتَّىٰ يَقُولَا
إِنَّمَا نَحْنُ فِتْنَةٌ فَلَا تَكْفُرْ ۖ
فَيَتَعَلَّمُونَ مِنْهُمَا مَا يُفَرِّقُونَ
بِهِ بَيْنَ الْمَرْءِ وَزَوْجِهِ ۚ وَمَا هُمْ
بِضَارِّينَ بِهِ مِنْ أَحَدٍ إِلَّا بِإِذْنِ
اللَّهِ ۚ وَيَتَعَلَّمُونَ مَا يَضُرُّهُمْ وَلَا
يَنْفَعُهُمْ ۚ وَلَقَدْ عَلِمُوا لَمَنِ اشْتَرَاهُ
مَا لَهُ فِي الْآخِرَةِ مِنْ خَلَاقٍ ۚ
وَلَبِئْسَ مَا شَرَوْا بِهِ أَنْفُسَهُمْ ۚ لَوْ كَانُوا
يَعْلَمُونَ ﴿١٠٢﴾
وَلَوْ أَنَّهُمْ آمَنُوا وَاتَّقَوْا لَمَثُوبَةٌ مِنْ
عِنْدِ اللَّهِ خَيْرٌ ۖ لَوْ كَانُوا يَعْلَمُونَ ﴿١٠٣﴾ ع ١٢
يَا أَيُّهَا الَّذِينَ آمَنُوا لَا تَقُولُوا رَاعِنَا
وَقُولُوا انْظُرْنَا وَاسْمَعُوا ۗ وَلِلْكَافِرِينَ
عَذَابٌ أَلِيمٌ ﴿١٠٤﴾
مَا يَوَدُّ الَّذِينَ كَفَرُوا مِنْ أَهْلِ الْكِتَابِ
وَلَا الْمُشْرِكِينَ أَنْ يُنَزَّلَ عَلَيْكُمْ مِنْ
خَيْرٍ مِنْ رَبِّكُمْ ۗ وَاللَّهُ يَخْتَصُّ بِرَحْمَتِهِ
مَنْ يَشَاءُ ۚ وَاللَّهُ ذُو الْفَضْلِ الْعَظِيمِ ﴿١٠٥﴾
مَا نَنْسَخْ مِنْ آيَةٍ أَوْ نُنْسِهَا نَأْتِ بِخَيْرٍ
مِنْهَا أَوْ مِثْلِهَا ۗ أَلَمْ تَعْلَمْ أَنَّ اللَّهَ
عَلَىٰ كُلِّ شَيْءٍ قَدِيرٌ ﴿١٠٦﴾
أَلَمْ تَعْلَمْ أَنَّ اللَّهَ لَهُ مُلْكُ
السَّمَاوَاتِ وَالْأَرْضِ ۗ وَمَا لَكُمْ مِنْ
دُونِ اللَّهِ مِنْ وَلِيٍّ وَلَا نَصِيرٍ ﴿١٠٧﴾
أَمْ تُرِيدُونَ أَنْ تَسْأَلُوا رَسُولَكُمْ

questioned of old ? But whoever changeth from Faith to Unbelief, hath strayed without doubt from the even way.

سوال کرو جس طرح کے سوال پہلے موسیٰ سے کئے
گئے تھے۔ اور جس شخص نے ایمان (چھوڑ کر اس) کے
بدلے کفر لیا وہ سیدھے رستے سے بھٹک گیا (۱۰۸)

كَمَا سُئِلَ مُوسَىٰ مِن قَبْلُ ۗ وَمَن
يَتَبَدَّلِ الْكُفْرَ بِالْإِيمَانِ فَقَدْ
ضَلَّ سَوَاءَ السَّبِيلِ ﴿١٠٨﴾

109. Quite a number of the People of the Book wish they could turn you (people) back to infidelity after ye have believed, from selfish envy, after the Truth hath become manifest unto them: but forgive and overlook, till Allah brings about His command; for Allah hath power over all things.

بہت سے اہل کتاب اپنے دل کی جلن سے یہ چاہتے
ہیں کہ ایمان لا چکنے کے بعد تم کو پھر کافر
بنا دیں۔ حالانکہ اُن پر حق ظاہر ہو چکا ہے۔
تو تم معاف کر دو اور درگذر کرو۔ یہاں تک
کہ خدا اپنا (دوسرا) حکم بھیجے۔ بیشک
خدا ہر بات پر قادر ہے (۱۰۹)

وَدَّ كَثِيرٌ مِّنْ أَهْلِ الْكِتَابِ لَوْ
يَرُدُّونَكُم مِّن بَعْدِ إِيمَانِكُمْ
كُفَّارًا ۚ حَسَدًا مِّنْ عِندِ أَنفُسِهِم
مِّن بَعْدِ مَا تَبَيَّنَ لَهُمُ الْحَقُّ ۖ
فَاعْفُوا وَاصْفَحُوا حَتَّىٰ يَأْتِيَ اللَّهُ
بِأَمْرِهِ ۗ إِنَّ اللَّهَ عَلَىٰ كُلِّ شَيْءٍ قَدِيرٌ ﴿١٠٩﴾

110. And be steadfast in prayer and give Zakat: and whatever good ye send forth for your souls before you, ye shall find it with Allah: for Allah sees well all that ye do.

اور نماز ادا کرتے رہو اور زکوٰۃ دیتے رہو۔
اور جو بھلائی اپنے لئے آگے بھیج رکھو گے
اُس کو خدا کے ہاں پا لوگے۔ کچھ شک نہیں
کہ خدا تمہارے سب کاموں کو دیکھ رہا ہے (۱۱۰)

وَأَقِيمُوا الصَّلَاةَ وَآتُوا الزَّكَاةَ ۚ
وَمَا تُقَدِّمُوا لِأَنفُسِكُم مِّنْ
خَيْرٍ تَجِدُوهُ عِندَ اللَّهِ ۗ إِنَّ
اللَّهَ بِمَا تَعْمَلُونَ بَصِيرٌ ﴿١١٠﴾

111. And they say: "None shall enter Paradise unless he be a Jew or a Christian" those are their (vain) desires. Say: "Produce your proof if ye are truthful."

اور (یہودی اور عیسائی) کہتے ہیں کہ یہودیوں اور
عیسائیوں کے سوا کوئی بہشت میں نہیں جانے کا
یہ اُن لوگوں کے خیالات باطل ہیں (اے پیغمبر اُن سے) کہہ دو
کہ اگر سچے ہو تو دلیل پیش کرو (۱۱۱)

وَقَالُوا لَن يَدْخُلَ الْجَنَّةَ إِلَّا
مَن كَانَ هُودًا أَوْ نَصَارَىٰ ۗ تِلْكَ
أَمَانِيُّهُمْ ۗ قُلْ هَاتُوا بُرْهَانَكُمْ
إِن كُنتُمْ صَادِقِينَ ﴿١١١﴾

112. Nay,—whoever submits his whole self to Allah and is a doer of good,—he will get his reward with his Lord; on such shall be no fear, nor shall they grieve.

ہاں جو شخص خدا کے آگے گردن جھکا دے (یعنی ایمان
لے آئے) اور وہ نیکوکار بھی ہو تو اُس کا صلہ اُس کے
پروردگار کے پاس ہے اور ایسے لوگوں کو (قیامت کے
دن) نہ کسی طرح کا خوف ہوگا اور نہ وہ غمناک ہونگے (۱۱۲)

بَلَىٰ مَنْ أَسْلَمَ وَجْهَهُ لِلَّهِ وَهُوَ
مُحْسِنٌ فَلَهُ أَجْرُهُ عِندَ رَبِّهِ
وَلَا خَوْفٌ عَلَيْهِمْ وَلَا هُمْ
يَحْزَنُونَ ﴿١١٢﴾

113. The Jews say: "The Christians have naught (to stand) upon; and the Christians say: "The Jews have naught (to stand) upon." Yet they (profess to) study the (same) Book. Like unto their word is what those say who know not; but Allah will judge between them in their quarrel

اور یہودی کہتے ہیں کہ عیسائی رستے پر نہیں اور عیسائی
کہتے ہیں کہ یہودی رستے پر نہیں۔ حالانکہ وہ کتاب (الٰہی)
پڑھتے ہیں۔ اسی طرح بالکل انہیں کی سی بات وہ
لوگ کہتے ہیں جو (کچھ) نہیں جانتے (یعنی مشرک)
تو جس بات میں یہ لوگ اختلاف کر رہے
ہیں خدا قیامت کے دن اُس کا اُن میں فیصلہ

وَقَالَتِ الْيَهُودُ لَيْسَتِ النَّصَارَىٰ
عَلَىٰ شَيْءٍ وَقَالَتِ النَّصَارَىٰ لَيْسَتِ
الْيَهُودُ عَلَىٰ شَيْءٍ وَهُمْ يَتْلُونَ
الْكِتَابَ ۗ كَذَٰلِكَ قَالَ الَّذِينَ لَا
يَعْلَمُونَ مِثْلَ قَوْلِهِمْ ۚ فَاللَّهُ
يَحْكُمُ بَيْنَهُمْ يَوْمَ الْقِيَامَةِ فِيمَا

كانوا فيه يختلفون (۱۱۳)

کردے گا (۱۱۳)

on the Day of Judgment.

ومن اظلم ممن منع مسجد
الله ان يذكر فيها اسمه وسعى
في خرابها اولئك ما كان لهم
ان يدخلوها الا خائفين لهم
في الدنيا خزي ولهم في الاخرة
عذاب عظيم (۱۱۴)

اور اس سے بڑھ کر ظالم کون جو خدا کی مسجدوں
میں خدا کے نام کا ذکر کئے جانے کو منع کرے اور اُن
کی ویرانی میں ساعی ہو۔ اُن لوگوں کو کچھ حق
نہیں کہ اُن میں داخل ہوں مگر ڈرتے ہوئے
اُن کے لئے دُنیا میں رسوائی ہے اور آخرت میں
بڑا عذاب (۱۱۴)

114. And who is more unjust than he who forbids that in places for the worship of Allah, His name should be celebrated ?—whose zeal is (in fact) to ruin them ? It was not fitting that such should themselves enter them except in fear. For them there is nothing but disgrace in this world, and in the world to come, an exceeding torment.

ولله المشرق والمغرب فاينما
تولوا فثم وجه الله ان الله
واسع عليم (۱۱۵)

اور مشرق اور مغرب سب خدا ہی کا ہے۔ تو جدھر
تم رُخ کرو اُدھر خدا کی ذات ہے۔ بیشک خدا
صاحبِ وسعت اور باخبر ہے (۱۱۵)

115. To Allah belong the East and the West: whithersoever ye turn, there is Allah's Face. For Allah is All-Embracing, All-Knowing.

وقالوا اتخذ الله ولدا سبحنه
بل له ما في السموت والارض
كل له قنتون (۱۱۶)

اور یہ لوگ اس بات کے قائل ہیں کہ خدا اولاد رکھتا ہے
(نہیں) وہ پاک ہے۔ بلکہ جو کچھ آسمانوں اور زمین میں ہے
سب اُسی کا ہے اور سب اُس کے فرمانبردار ہیں (۱۱۶)

116. They say: "Allah hath begotten a son": Glory be to Him.—Nay, to Him belongs all that is in the heavens and on earth: everything renders worship to Him.

بديع السموت والارض واذا
قضى امرا فانما يقول له كن
فيكون (۱۱۷)

(وہی) آسمانوں اور زمین کا پیدا کرنے والا ہے جب
کوئی کام کرنا چاہتا ہے تو اُس کو ارشاد فرما دیتا ہے کہ ہو جا
تو وہ ہو جاتا ہے (۱۱۷)

117. The Originator of the heavens and the earth: when He decreeth a matter, He saith to it: "Be," and it is.

وقال الذين لا يعلمون لولا
يكلمنا الله او تاتينا اية كذلك
قال الذين من قبلهم مثل
قولهم تشابهت قلوبهم قد
بينا الايت لقوم يوقنون (۱۱۸)

اور جو لوگ (کچھ) نہیں جانتے (یعنی مشرک) وہ کہتے ہیں
کہ خدا ہم سے کلام کیوں نہیں کرتا یا ہمارے پاس کوئی
نشانی کیوں نہیں آتی۔ اسی طرح جو لوگ اُن سے پہلے تھے وہ بھی
اُنہی کی سی باتیں کیا کرتے تھے اِن لوگوں کے دل آپس میں ملتے جلتے ہیں جو
لوگ صاحبِ یقین ہیں اُن کے (سمجھانے کے) لئے ہم نے نشانیاں بیان کر دی ہیں (۱۱۸)

118. Say those without knowledge: "Why speaketh not Allah unto us ? Or why cometh not unto us a Sign ? So said the people before them words of similar import. Their hearts are alike. We have indeed made clear the Signs unto any people who hold firmly to Faith (in their hearts).

انا ارسلنك بالحق بشيرا و
نذيرا ولا تسئل عن اصحب
الجحيم (۱۱۹)

(اے محمدؐ) ہم نے تم کو سچائی کے ساتھ خوشخبری سنانے والا
اور ڈرانے والا بنا کر بھیجا ہے اور اہلِ دوزخ کے بارے
میں تم سے کچھ پرسش نہیں ہوگی (۱۱۹)

119. Verily We have sent thee in truth as a bearer of glad tidings and a warner: but of thee no question shall be asked of the Companions of the Blazing Fire.

ولن ترضى عنك اليهود ولا
النصرى حتى تتبع ملتهم قل
ان هدى الله هو الهدى ولئن

اور تم سے نہ تو یہودی کبھی خوش ہوں گے اور نہ عیسائی
یہاں تک کہ اُن کے مذہب کی پیروی اختیار کر لو (اُن سے)
کہہ دو کہ خدا کی ہدایت (یعنی دینِ اسلام) ہی ہدایت ہے اور

120. Never will the Jews or the Christians be satisfied with thee unless thou follow their form of religion. Say: "The Guidance of Allah,–that is the (only) Guidance."

Wert thou to follow their desires after the knowledge which hath reached thee, then wouldst thou find neither Protector nor Helper against Allah.

(اے پیغمبر) اگر تم اپنے پاس علم (یعنی وحی خدا) کے آجانے پر بھی
اُن کی خواہشوں پر چلوگے تو تم کو (عذاب) خدا سے
(بچانے والا) نہ کوئی دوست ہوگا نہ کوئی مددگار ﴿۱۲۰﴾

اتبعت أهواءهم بعد الذي
جاءك من العلم ما لك من
الله من ولي ولا نصير ﴿١٢٠﴾

121. Those to whom We have given the Book study it as it should be studied: they are the ones that believe therein: those who reject faith therein,—the loss is their own.

جن لوگوں کو ہم نے کتاب عنایت کی ہے وہ اُس کو
(ایسا) پڑھتے ہیں جیسا اُس کے پڑھنے کا حق ہے۔
یہی لوگ اس پر ایمان رکھنے والے ہیں۔ اور جو اس کو
نہیں مانتے وہ خسارہ پانے والے ہیں ﴿۱۲۱﴾

الذين آتيناهم الكتاب يتلونه
حق تلاوته أولئك يؤمنون
به ومن يكفر به فأولئك
هم الخاسرون ﴿١٢١﴾

122. O Children of Israel ! call to mind the special favour which I bestowed upon you, and that I preferred you to all others.

اے بنی اسرائیل میرے وہ احسان یاد کرو جو میں
نے تم پر کئے اور یہ کہ میں نے تم کو اہلِ عالم پر
فضیلت بخشی ﴿۱۲۲﴾

يا بني إسرائيل اذكروا نعمتي
التي أنعمت عليكم وأني
فضلتكم على العالمين ﴿١٢٢﴾

123. Then guard yourselves against a Day when one soul shall not avail another, nor shall compensation be accepted from her nor shall intercession profit her nor shall anyone be helped (from outside).

اور اُس دن سے ڈرو جب کوئی شخص کسی شخص کے
کچھ کام نہ آئے اور نہ اُس سے بدلہ قبول کیا جائے
اور نہ اُس کو کسی کی سفارش کچھ فائدہ دے اور نہ لوگوں
کو (کسی اور طرح کی) مدد مل سکے ﴿۱۲۳﴾

واتقوا يوما لا تجزي نفس
عن نفس شيئا ولا يقبل منها
عدل ولا تنفعها شفاعة ولا
هم ينصرون ﴿١٢٣﴾

124. And remember that Abraham was tried by his Lord with certain Commands, which he fulfilled: He said: "I will make thee an Imām to the people. He pleaded: "And also (Imāms) from my offspring!" He answered: "But My Promise is not within the reach of evil-doers."

اور جب پروردگار نے چند باتوں میں ابراہیم کی
آزمائش کی تو وہ اُن میں پورے اُترے۔ خدا نے کہا
کہ میں تم کو لوگوں کا پیشوا بناؤں گا۔ انہوں نے کہا کہ (پروردگار)
میری اولاد میں سے بھی (پیشوا بنائیو) خدا نے فرمایا کہ
ہمارا اقرار ظالموں کیلئے نہیں ہوا کرتا ﴿۱۲۴﴾

وإذ ابتلى إبراهيم ربه بكلمات
فأتمهن قال إني جاعلك
للناس إماما قال ومن
ذريتي قال لا ينال عهدي
الظالمين ﴿١٢٤﴾

125. Remember We made the House a place of assembly for men and a place of safety; and take ye the Station of Abraham as a place of prayer; and We covenanted with Abraham and Ismā'il, that they should sanctify My House for those who compass it round, or use it as a retreat, or bow, or prostrate themselves (therein in prayer).

اور جب ہم نے خانہ کعبہ کو لوگوں کے لئے جمع ہونے
اور امن پانے کی جگہ مقرر کیا اور (حکم دیا کہ) جس مقام
پر ابراہیم کھڑے ہوئے تھے اُس کو نماز کی جگہ بنالو۔ اور
ابراہیم اور اسمٰعیل کو کہا کہ طواف کرنے والوں اور
اعتکاف کرنے والوں اور رکوع کرنے والوں اور سجدہ
کرنے والوں کیلئے میرے گھر کو پاک صاف رکھا کرو ﴿۱۲۵﴾

وإذ جعلنا البيت مثابة للناس
وأمنا واتخذوا من مقام
إبراهيم مصلى وعهدنا إلى
إبراهيم وإسماعيل أن طهرا
بيتي للطائفين والعاكفين
والركع السجود ﴿١٢٥﴾

126. And remember Abraham said: "My Lord, make this a City of Peace, and feed its People with fruits,–

اور جب ابراہیم نے دعا کی کہ اے پروردگار اس جگہ کو امن
کا شہر بنا اور اسکے رہنے والوں میں سے جو خدا پر اور

وإذ قال إبراهيم رب اجعل
هذا بلدا آمنا وارزق أهله

such of them as believe in Allah and the Last Day." He said: "(Yea), and such as reject Faith,–for a while will I grant them their pleasure, but will soon drive them to the torment of Fire,– an evil destination (indeed) !"

روزِ آخرت پر ایمان لائیں اُنکے کھانے کو میوے عطا
فرما۔ تو خدا نے فرمایا کہ جو کافر ہوگا میں اُسکو بھی کسی قدر
متمتع کرونگا مگر، پھر اسکو (عذاب) دوزخ کے (بھگتنے) کے
لئے ناچار کر دوں گا اور وہ بُری جگہ ہے ﴿١٢٦﴾

مِنَ الثَّمَرٰتِ مَنْ اٰمَنَ مِنْهُمْ
بِاللّٰهِ وَالْيَوْمِ الْاٰخِرِ ؕ قَالَ وَمَنْ
كَفَرَ فَاُمَتِّعُهٗ قَلِيْلًا ثُمَّ اَضْطَرُّهٗۤ
اِلٰى عَذَابِ النَّارِ ؕ وَبِئْسَ الْمَصِيْرُ ﴿١٢٦﴾

127. And remember Abraham and Ismā'il raised the foundations of the House (with this prayer): "Our Lord ! accept (this service) from us: for Thou art the All-Hearing, the All-Knowing.

128. "Our Lord! make of us Muslims, bowing to Thy (Will), and of our progeny a people Muslim, bowing to Thy (Will); and show us our places for the celebration of (due) rites; and turn unto us (in Mercy); for Thou art the Oft-Relenting Most Merciful.

اور جب ابراہیم اور اسمٰعیل بیت اللہ کی بنیادیں اونچی
کر رہے تھے (تو دُعا کئے جاتے تھے کہ) اے ہمارے پروردگار ہم سے
یہ خدمت قبول فرما۔ بیشک تُو سننے والا (اور) جاننے والا ہے ﴿١٢٧﴾
اے پروردگار ہم کو اپنا فرمانبردار بنائے رکھیو۔ اور
ہماری اولاد میں سے بھی ایک گروہ کو اپنا مطیع بنائے رہیو
اور (پروردگار) ہمیں ہمارے طریق عبادت بتا اور ہمارے حال پر (رحم
کے ساتھ) توجہ فرما۔ بیشک تُو توجہ فرمانے والا مہربان ہے ﴿١٢٨﴾

وَاِذْ يَرْفَعُ اِبْرٰهٖمُ الْقَوَاعِدَ مِنَ
الْبَيْتِ وَاِسْمٰعِيْلُ ؕ رَبَّنَا تَقَبَّلْ
مِنَّا ؕ اِنَّكَ اَنْتَ السَّمِيْعُ الْعَلِيْمُ ﴿١٢٧﴾
رَبَّنَا وَاجْعَلْنَا مُسْلِمَيْنِ لَكَ
وَمِنْ ذُرِّيَّتِنَآ اُمَّةً مُّسْلِمَةً لَّكَ ۪
وَاَرِنَا مَنَاسِكَنَا وَتُبْ عَلَيْنَا ۚ
اِنَّكَ اَنْتَ التَّوَّابُ الرَّحِيْمُ ﴿١٢٨﴾

129. "Our Lord ! send amongst them a Messenger of their own, who shall rehearse Thy Signs to them and instruct them in Scripture and Wisdom, and purify them: for Thou art the Exalted in Might, the Wise."

اے پروردگار ان (لوگوں) میں انہیں میں سے
ایک پیغمبر مبعوث کیجیو جو اُن کو تیری آیتیں پڑھ
پڑھ کر سُنایا کرے۔ اور کتاب اور دانائی سکھایا کرے
اور اُن (کے دلوں) کو پاک صاف کیا کرے۔ بیشک تُو
غالب (اور) صاحب حکمت ہے ﴿١٢٩﴾

رَبَّنَا وَابْعَثْ فِيْهِمْ رَسُوْلًا
مِّنْهُمْ يَتْلُوْا عَلَيْهِمْ اٰيٰتِكَ
وَيُعَلِّمُهُمُ الْكِتٰبَ وَالْحِكْمَةَ
وَيُزَكِّيْهِمْ ؕ اِنَّكَ اَنْتَ
الْعَزِيْزُ الْحَكِيْمُ ﴿١٢٩﴾ ع ١٥

130. And who turns away from the religion of Abraham but such as debase their souls with folly? Him We chose and rendered pure in this world: and he will be in the Hereafter in the ranks of the Righteous.

اور ابراہیم کے دین سے کون رُوگردانی کر سکتا ہے
بجز اس کے جو نہایت نادان ہو۔ ہم نے اُن کو
دنیا میں بھی منتخب کیا تھا اور آخرت میں بھی وہ
(زمرۂ) صلحاء میں ہوں گے ﴿١٣٠﴾

وَمَنْ يَّرْغَبُ عَنْ مِّلَّةِ اِبْرٰهٖمَ
اِلَّا مَنْ سَفِهَ نَفْسَهٗ ؕ وَلَقَدِ
اصْطَفَيْنٰهُ فِى الدُّنْيَا ۚ وَاِنَّهٗ
فِى الْاٰخِرَةِ لَمِنَ الصّٰلِحِيْنَ ﴿١٣٠﴾

131. Behold! his Lord said to him: Submit (thy will to Me):" He said: "I submit (my will) to the Lord and Cherisher of the Universe."

جب اُن سے اُنکے پروردگار نے فرمایا کہ اسلام لے آؤ تو انہوں
نے عرض کی کہ میں ربّ العالمین کے آگے سرِ اطاعت خم کرتا ہوں ﴿١٣١﴾

اِذْ قَالَ لَهٗ رَبُّهٗۤ اَسْلِمْ ۙ قَالَ
اَسْلَمْتُ لِرَبِّ الْعٰلَمِيْنَ ﴿١٣١﴾

132. And Abraham enjoined upon his sons and so did Jacob; "Oh my sons! Allah hath chosen the Faith for you; then die not except in the state of submission (to Me).

اور ابراہیم نے اپنے بیٹوں کو اسی بات کی وصیت
کی اور یعقوب نے بھی (اپنے فرزندوں سے یہی کہا)
کہ بیٹا خدا نے تمہارے لئے یہی دین پسند فرمایا ہے تو
مرنا تو مسلمان ہی مرنا ﴿١٣٢﴾

وَوَصّٰى بِهَآ اِبْرٰهٖمُ بَنِيْهِ
وَيَعْقُوْبُ ؕ يٰبَنِىَّ اِنَّ اللّٰهَ اصْطَفٰى
لَكُمُ الدِّيْنَ فَلَا تَمُوْتُنَّ
اِلَّا وَاَنْتُمْ مُّسْلِمُوْنَ ﴿١٣٢﴾ ؕ

133. Were ye witnesses when Death appeared before Jacob?

بھلا جس وقت یعقوب وفات پانے لگے تو

اَمْ كُنْتُمْ شُهَدَآءَ اِذْ حَضَرَ

Behold, he said to his sons: "What will ye worship after me?" They said: "We shall worship thy God and the God of thy fathers,—of Abraham, Ismā'il, and Isaac,—the One (True) God; to Him do we submit."

تم اُس وقت موجود تھے جب اُنہوں نے
اپنے بیٹوں سے پوچھا کہ میرے بعد تم کس کی عبادت
کرو گے۔ تو اُنہوں نے کہا کہ آپ کے معبود اور آپ
کے باپ دادا ابراہیم اور اسمٰعیل اور اسحٰق کے
معبود کی عبادت کریں گے جو معبود یکتا ہے اور
ہم اُسی کے حکم بردار ہیں ﴿۱۳۳﴾

يَعْقُوبَ الْمَوْتُ إِذْ قَالَ
لِبَنِيهِ مَا تَعْبُدُونَ مِنْ
بَعْدِي قَالُوا نَعْبُدُ إِلَٰهَكَ
وَإِلَٰهَ آبَائِكَ إِبْرَاهِيمَ وَإِسْمَاعِيلَ
وَإِسْحَاقَ إِلَٰهًا وَاحِدًا وَنَحْنُ
لَهُ مُسْلِمُونَ ﴿١٣٣﴾

134. That was a People that hath passed away. They shall reap the fruit of what they did, and ye of what ye do! Ye shall not be asked about what they did.

یہ جماعت گزر چکی ان کو ان کے اعمال (کا بدلہ
ملے گا) اور تم کو تمہارے اعمال (کا) اور
جو عمل وہ کرتے تھے اُن کی پرسش تم سے
نہیں ہوگی ﴿۱۳۴﴾

تِلْكَ أُمَّةٌ قَدْ خَلَتْ لَهَا
مَا كَسَبَتْ وَلَكُمْ مَا
كَسَبْتُمْ وَلَا تُسْأَلُونَ عَمَّا
كَانُوا يَعْمَلُونَ ﴿١٣٤﴾

135. They say: "Become Jews or Christians if ye would be guided (to salvation)." Say thou: "Nay! (I would rather) the Religion of Abraham the True, and he joined not gods with Allah."

اور (یہودی اور عیسائی) کہتے ہیں کہ یہودی یا
عیسائی ہو جاؤ تو سیدھے رستے پر لگ جاؤ (اے
پیغمبر ان سے) کہدو نہیں بلکہ (ہم) دین ابراہیم (اختیار کئے ہوئے
ہیں) جو ایک خدا کے ہو رہے تھے اور مشرکوں میں سے نہ تھے ﴿۱۳۵﴾

وَقَالُوا كُونُوا هُودًا أَوْ نَصَارَىٰ
تَهْتَدُوا قُلْ بَلْ مِلَّةَ إِبْرَاهِيمَ
حَنِيفًا وَمَا كَانَ مِنَ
الْمُشْرِكِينَ ﴿١٣٥﴾

136. Say ye: "We believe in Allah, and the revelation given to us, and to Abraham, Ismā'il, Isaac, Jacob, and the Tribes, and that given to Moses and Jesus, and that given to (all) Prophets from their Lord: we make no difference between one and another of them: and we submit to Allah.

(مسلمانو) کہو کہ ہم خدا پر ایمان لائے اور جو (کتاب) ہم پر
اُتری اُس پر اور جو (صحیفے) ابراہیم اور اسمٰعیل اور اسحٰق
اور یعقوب اور اُنکی اولاد پر نازل ہوئے اُن پر اور جو
(کتابیں) موسیٰ اور عیسیٰ کو عطا ہوئیں اُن پر اور جو
اور پیغمبروں کو اُنکے پروردگار کی طرف سے ملیں اُن پر
(سب پر) ایمان لائے ہم اُن پیغمبروں میں سے کسی میں کچھ فرق
نہیں کرتے اور ہم اُسی (خدائے واحد) کے فرمانبردار ہیں ﴿۱۳۶﴾

قُولُوا آمَنَّا بِاللَّهِ وَمَا أُنْزِلَ إِلَيْنَا
وَمَا أُنْزِلَ إِلَىٰ إِبْرَاهِيمَ وَإِسْمَاعِيلَ
وَإِسْحَاقَ وَيَعْقُوبَ وَالْأَسْبَاطِ وَمَا
أُوتِيَ مُوسَىٰ وَعِيسَىٰ وَمَا أُوتِيَ
النَّبِيُّونَ مِنْ رَبِّهِمْ لَا نُفَرِّقُ
بَيْنَ أَحَدٍ مِنْهُمْ وَنَحْنُ لَهُ
مُسْلِمُونَ ﴿١٣٦﴾

137. So if they believe as ye believe, they are indeed on the right path; but if they turn back, it is they who are in schism; but Allah will suffice thee as against them, and He is the All-Hearing, the All-Knowing.

تو اگر یہ لوگ بھی اُسی طرح ایمان لے آئیں جس
طرح تم ایمان لے آئے ہو تو ہدایت یاب ہو جائیں۔ اور
اگر مُنہ پھیر لیں (اور نہ مانیں) تو وہ (تمہارے)
مخالف ہیں۔ اور اُن کے مقابلے میں تمہیں خدا کافی ہے اور
وہ سننے والا (اور) جاننے والا ہے ﴿۱۳۷﴾

فَإِنْ آمَنُوا بِمِثْلِ مَا آمَنْتُمْ
بِهِ فَقَدِ اهْتَدَوْا وَإِنْ
تَوَلَّوْا فَإِنَّمَا هُمْ فِي شِقَاقٍ
فَسَيَكْفِيكَهُمُ اللَّهُ وَهُوَ
السَّمِيعُ الْعَلِيمُ ﴿١٣٧﴾

138. (Our religion) takes its hue from Allah and who can give a

(کہہ دو کہ ہم نے) خدا کا رنگ (اختیار کر لیا ہے) اور خدا

صِبْغَةَ اللَّهِ وَمَنْ أَحْسَنُ

hue than Allah. It is He Whom we worship.

139. Say: Will ye dispute with us about Allah, seeing that He is our Lord and your Lord; that we are responsible for our doings and ye for yours; and that we are sincere (in our faith) in Him ?

140. Or do ye say that Abraham, Ismā'il, Isaac, Jacob and the Tribes were Jews or Christians ? Say: Do ye know better than Allah ? Ah ! who is more unjust than those who conceal the testimony they have from Allah ? But Allah is not unmindful of what ye do !

141. That was a people that hath passed away. They shall reap the fruit of what they did, and ye of what ye do ! Ye shall not be asked !—about what they did.

142. The Fools among the people will say: "What hath turned them from the *Qibla* to which they were used ?" Say: to Allah belong both East and West: He guideth whom He will to a Way that is straight.

143. Thus have We made of you an *Ummat* justly balanced. That ye might be witnesses over the nations, and the Messenger a witness over yourselves; and We appointed the *Qibla* to which thou wast used, only to test those who followed the Messenger from those who would turn on their heels (from the Faith). Indeed it was (a change) momentous, except to those guided by Allah. And never would Allah

سے بہتر رنگ کس کا ہو سکتا ہے۔ اور ہم اُسی کی
عبادت کرنے والے ہیں ﴿۱۳۸﴾
(ان سے) کہو کیا تم خدا کے بارے میں ہم سے جھگڑتے
ہو حالانکہ وہی ہمارا اور تمہارا پروردگار ہے اور ہم کو
ہمارے اعمال (کا بدلہ ملیگا) اور تم کو تمہارے اعمال
(کا)، اور ہم خاص اُسی کی عبادت کرنیوالے ہیں ﴿۱۳۹﴾
(اے یہود و نصاریٰ) کیا تم اس بات کے قائل ہو
کہ ابراہیم اور اسمٰعیل اور اسحٰق اور یعقوب اور اُنکی
اولاد یہودی یا عیسائی تھے (اے محمد ان سے) کہو کہ بھلا تم
زیادہ جانتے ہو یا خدا؟ اور اس سے بڑھکر ظالم کون جو
خدا کی شہادت کو جو اسکے پاس (کتاب میں موجود) ہے چھپائے
اور جو کچھ تم لوگ کر رہے ہو خدا اس سے غافل نہیں ﴿۱۴۰﴾
یہ جماعت گزر چکی۔ اُنکو وہ (ملیگا) جو اُنہوں نے کیا
اور تم کو وہ جو تم نے کیا اور جو عمل وہ کرتے تھے
اُن کی پرسش تم سے نہیں ہوگی ﴿۱۴۱﴾
احمق لوگ کہیں گے کہ مسلمان جس قبلے پر (پہلے سے
چلے آتے) تھے (اب) اُس سے کیوں منہ پھیر بیٹھے
تم کہہ دو کہ مشرق اور مغرب سب خدا ہی کا ہے
وہ جس کو چاہتا ہے سیدھے رستے پر چلاتا ہے ﴿۱۴۲﴾
اور اسی طرح ہم نے تم کو اُمتِ معتدل بنایا ہے
تاکہ تم لوگوں پر گواہ بنو اور پیغمبر (آخر الزماں) تم
پر گواہ بنیں۔ اور جس قبلے پر تم (پہلے) تھے
اس کو ہم نے اس لئے مقرر کیا تھا کہ معلوم
کریں کہ کون (ہمارے) پیغمبر کا تابع رہتا ہے
اور کون اُلٹے پاؤں پھر جاتا ہے۔ اور یہ
بات (یعنی تحویل قبلہ لوگوں کو) گراں معلوم
ہوئی مگر جن کو خدا نے ہدایت بخشی ہے (وہ اسے

مِنَ اللّٰهِ صِبْغَةً ز وَّنَحْنُ
لَهٗ عٰبِدُوْنَ ﴿۱۳۸﴾
قُلْ اَتُحَآجُّوْنَنَا فِى اللّٰهِ وَهُوَ رَبُّنَا
وَرَبُّكُمْ ج وَلَنَآ اَعْمَالُنَا
وَلَكُمْ اَعْمَالُكُمْ ج وَنَحْنُ لَهٗ
مُخْلِصُوْنَ ﴿۱۳۹﴾
اَمْ تَقُوْلُوْنَ اِنَّ اِبْرٰهٖمَ وَاِسْمٰعِيْلَ
وَاِسْحٰقَ وَيَعْقُوْبَ وَالْاَسْبَاطَ
كَانُوْا هُوْدًا اَوْ نَصٰرٰى ط قُلْ ءَاَنْتُمْ
اَعْلَمُ اَمِ اللّٰهُ ط وَمَنْ اَظْلَمُ مِمَّنْ
كَتَمَ شَهَادَةً عِنْدَهٗ مِنَ اللّٰهِ ط
وَمَا اللّٰهُ بِغَافِلٍ عَمَّا تَعْمَلُوْنَ ﴿۱۴۰﴾
تِلْكَ اُمَّةٌ قَدْ خَلَتْ ج لَهَا مَا
كَسَبَتْ وَلَكُمْ مَّا كَسَبْتُمْ ج وَلَا
تُسْـَٔلُوْنَ عَمَّا كَانُوْا يَعْمَلُوْنَ ﴿۱۴۱﴾ ع
سَيَقُوْلُ السُّفَهَآءُ مِنَ النَّاسِ
مَا وَلّٰىهُمْ عَنْ قِبْلَتِهِمُ الَّتِىْ كَانُوْا
عَلَيْهَا ط قُلْ لِّلّٰهِ الْمَشْرِقُ وَالْمَغْرِبُ ط
يَهْدِىْ مَنْ يَّشَآءُ اِلٰى صِرَاطٍ مُّسْتَقِيْمٍ ﴿۱۴۲﴾
وَكَذٰلِكَ جَعَلْنٰكُمْ اُمَّةً وَّسَطًا
لِّتَكُوْنُوْا شُهَدَآءَ عَلَى النَّاسِ
وَيَكُوْنَ الرَّسُوْلُ عَلَيْكُمْ شَهِيْدًا ط
وَمَا جَعَلْنَا الْقِبْلَةَ الَّتِىْ كُنْتَ
عَلَيْهَآ اِلَّا لِنَعْلَمَ مَنْ يَّتَّبِعُ
الرَّسُوْلَ مِمَّنْ يَّنْقَلِبُ عَلٰى
عَقِبَيْهِ ط وَاِنْ كَانَتْ لَكَبِيْرَةً
اِلَّا عَلَى الَّذِيْنَ هَدَى اللّٰهُ ط

الجزء الثاني ۲

make your faith of no effect. For Allah is to all people most surely full of Kindness, Most Merciful.

گراں نہیں سمجھتے) اور خدا ایسا نہیں کہ تمہارے ایمان کو یونہی
کھو دے۔ خدا تو لوگوں پر بڑا مہربان (اور) صاحبِ رحمت ہے ﴿۱۴۳﴾

وَمَا كَانَ اللّٰهُ لِيُضِيْعَ اِيْمَانَكُمْ ؕ
اِنَّ اللّٰهَ بِالنَّاسِ لَرَءُوْفٌ رَّحِيْمٌ ﴿۱۴۳﴾

144. We see the turning of thy face (for guidance) to the heavens: now shall We turn thee to a *Qibla* that shall please thee. Turn then thy face in the direction of the Sacred Mosque: wherever ye are, turn your faces in that direction. The people of the Book know well that that is the truth from their Lord, nor is Allah unmindful of what they do.

(اے محمدؐ) ہم تمہارا آسمان کی طرف منہ پھیر پھیر کر
دیکھنا دیکھ رہے ہیں سو ہم تم کو اسی قبلے کی طرف جس کو
تم پسند کرتے ہو منہ کرنے کا حکم دینگے تو اپنا منہ
مسجد حرام (یعنی خانہ کعبہ) کی طرف پھیر لو۔ اور تم لوگ
جہاں ہوا کرو (نماز پڑھنے کے وقت) اسی مسجد کی طرف
منہ کر لیا کرو اور جن لوگوں کو کتاب دی گئی ہے وہ خوب
جانتے ہیں کہ (نیا قبلہ) ان کے پروردگار کی طرف سے
حق ہے۔ اور جو کام یہ لوگ کرتے ہیں خدا ان سے بیخبر نہیں ﴿۱۴۴﴾

قَدْ نَرٰى تَقَلُّبَ وَجْهِكَ فِى
السَّمَآءِ ۚ فَلَنُوَلِّيَنَّكَ قِبْلَةً
تَرْضٰىهَا ۠ فَوَلِّ وَجْهَكَ شَطْرَ
الْمَسْجِدِ الْحَرَامِ ؕ وَحَيْثُ مَا كُنْتُمْ
فَوَلُّوْا وُجُوْهَكُمْ شَطْرَهٗ ؕ وَاِنَّ
الَّذِيْنَ اُوْتُوا الْكِتٰبَ لَيَعْلَمُوْنَ
اَنَّهُ الْحَقُّ مِنْ رَّبِّهِمْ ؕ وَمَا اللّٰهُ
بِغَافِلٍ عَمَّا يَعْمَلُوْنَ ﴿۱۴۴﴾

145. Even if thou wert to bring to the people of the Book all the Signs (together), they would not follow thy *Qibla*; nor art thou going to follow their *Qibla*; nor indeed will they follow each other's *Qibla*. If thou after the knowledge hath reached thee, wert to follow their (vain) desires,—then wert thou indeed (clearly) in the wrong.

اور اگر تم ان اہل کتاب کے پاس تمام نشانیاں بھی
لے کر آؤ تو بھی یہ تمہارے قبلے کی پیروی نہ کریں۔ اور
تم بھی ان کے قبلے کی پیروی کرنیوالے نہیں ہو۔ اور ان
میں سے بھی بعض بعض کے قبلے کے پیرو نہیں۔ اور اگر
تم باوجود اس کے کہ تمہارے پاس دانش (یعنی وحی خدا)
آچکی ہے ان کی خواہشوں کے پیچھے چلو گے تو ظالموں
میں (داخل) ہو جاؤ گے ﴿۱۴۵﴾

وَلَئِنْ اَتَيْتَ الَّذِيْنَ اُوْتُوا الْكِتٰبَ
بِكُلِّ اٰيَةٍ مَّا تَبِعُوْا قِبْلَتَكَ ۚ وَمَآ
اَنْتَ بِتَابِعٍ قِبْلَتَهُمْ ۚ وَمَا بَعْضُهُمْ
بِتَابِعٍ قِبْلَةَ بَعْضٍ ؕ وَلَئِنِ اتَّبَعْتَ
اَهْوَآءَهُمْ مِّنْ بَعْدِ مَا جَآءَكَ
مِنَ الْعِلْمِ ۙ اِنَّكَ اِذًا لَّمِنَ
الظّٰلِمِيْنَ ﴿۱۴۵﴾ وقف لازم

146. The people of the Book know this as they know their own sons; but some of them conceal the truth which they themselves know.

جن لوگوں کو ہم نے کتاب دی ہے وہ ان (پیغمبر آخر الزماں)
کو اس طرح پہچانتے ہیں جس طرح اپنے بیٹوں کو پہچانا
کرتے ہیں مگر ایک فریق ان میں سے سچی بات کو جان
بوجھ کر چھپا رہا ہے ﴿۱۴۶﴾

الَّذِيْنَ اٰتَيْنٰهُمُ الْكِتٰبَ يَعْرِفُوْنَهٗ
كَمَا يَعْرِفُوْنَ اَبْنَآءَهُمْ ؕ وَاِنَّ
فَرِيْقًا مِّنْهُمْ لَيَكْتُمُوْنَ الْحَقَّ
وَهُمْ يَعْلَمُوْنَ ﴿۱۴۶﴾ وقف منزل

147. The Truth is from thy Lord; so be not at all in doubt.

(اے پیغمبر یہ نیا قبلہ) تمہارے پروردگار کی طرف سے حق ہے
تو تم ہرگز شک کرنے والوں میں نہ ہونا ﴿۱۴۷﴾

اَلْحَقُّ مِنْ رَّبِّكَ فَلَا تَكُوْنَنَّ
مِنَ الْمُمْتَرِيْنَ ﴿۱۴۷﴾ ع

148. To each is a goal to which Allah turns him; then strive together (as in a race) towards all that is good. Wheresoever ye are, Allah will bring you together. For Allah hath power over all things.

اور ہر ایک (فرقے) کیلئے ایک سمت (مقرر) ہے جدھر وہ
(عبادت کے وقت) منہ کیا کرتے ہیں تو تم نیکیوں میں سبقت
حاصل کرو۔ تم جہاں ہو گے خدا تم سب کو جمع کر لے گا
بیشک خدا ہر چیز پر قادر ہے ﴿۱۴۸﴾

وَلِكُلٍّ وِّجْهَةٌ هُوَ مُوَلِّيْهَا
فَاسْتَبِقُوا الْخَيْرٰتِ ؕ اَيْنَ مَا
تَكُوْنُوْا يَاْتِ بِكُمُ اللّٰهُ جَمِيْعًا ؕ
اِنَّ اللّٰهَ عَلٰى كُلِّ شَىْءٍ قَدِيْرٌ ﴿۱۴۸﴾ وقف النبی صلی اللہ علیہ وسلم

149. From whencesoever thou startest forth, turn thy face in the direction of the Sacred Mosque; that is indeed the truth from thy Lord. And Allah is not unmindful of what ye do.

اور تم جہاں سے نکلو (نماز میں) اپنا منہ مسجد محترم کی
طرف کر لیا کرو۔ بے شبہ وہ تمہارے پروردگار کی طرف
سے حق ہے۔ اور تم لوگ جو کچھ کرتے ہو خدا اُس
سے بے خبر نہیں ﴿۱۴۹﴾

وَمِنْ حَيْثُ خَرَجْتَ فَوَلِّ وَجْهَكَ
شَطْرَ الْمَسْجِدِ الْحَرَامِ ۖ وَإِنَّهُ
لَلْحَقُّ مِن رَّبِّكَ ۗ وَمَا اللَّهُ بِغَافِلٍ
عَمَّا تَعْمَلُونَ ﴿١٤٩﴾

150. So from whencesoever thou startest forth, turn thy face in the direction of the Sacred Mosque; and wheresoever ye are, turn your face thither: that there be no ground of dispute against you among the people. Except those of them that are bent on wickedness; so fear them not, but fear Me; and that I may complete My favours on you, and ye may (consent to) be guided;

اور تم جہاں سے نکلو مسجد محترم کی طرف مُنہ (کر کے
نماز پڑھا) کرو۔ اور مسلمانو تم جہاں ہوا کرو (اُسی
مسجد) کی طرف رُخ کیا کرو (یہ تاکید) اس لئے (کی
گئی ہے) کہ لوگ تم کو کسی طرح کا الزام نہ دے سکیں۔
مگر اُن میں سے جو ظالم ہیں (وہ الزام دیں تو دیں)
سو اُن سے مت ڈرنا اور مجھی سے ڈرتے رہنا۔ اور
یہ بھی مقصود ہے کہ میں تم کو اپنی تمام نعمتیں بخشوں
اور یہ بھی کہ تم راہِ راست پر چلو ﴿۱۵۰﴾

وَمِنْ حَيْثُ خَرَجْتَ فَوَلِّ وَجْهَكَ
شَطْرَ الْمَسْجِدِ الْحَرَامِ ۚ وَحَيْثُ مَا
كُنتُمْ فَوَلُّوا وُجُوهَكُمْ شَطْرَهُ لِئَلَّا
يَكُونَ لِلنَّاسِ عَلَيْكُمْ حُجَّةٌ
إِلَّا الَّذِينَ ظَلَمُوا مِنْهُمْ فَلَا
تَخْشَوْهُمْ وَاخْشَوْنِي وَلِأُتِمَّ
نِعْمَتِي عَلَيْكُمْ وَلَعَلَّكُمْ
تَهْتَدُونَ ﴿١٥٠﴾

151. A similar (favour have ye already received) in that We have sent among you a Messenger of your own, rehearsing to you Our Signs, and purifying you, and instructing you in Scripture and Wisdom, and in new Knowledge.

جس طرح (منجملہ اور نعمتوں کے) ہم نے تم میں تمہیں میں سے
ایک رسول بھیجے ہیں جو تم کو ہماری آیتیں پڑھ پڑھ کے
سُناتے اور تمہیں پاک بناتے اور کتاب (یعنی قرآن) اور
دانائی سکھاتے ہیں اور ایسی باتیں بتاتے ہیں جو تم پہلے نہیں جانتے تھے ﴿۱۵۱﴾

كَمَا أَرْسَلْنَا فِيكُمْ رَسُولًا مِّنكُمْ
يَتْلُو عَلَيْكُمْ آيَاتِنَا وَيُزَكِّيكُمْ
وَيُعَلِّمُكُمُ الْكِتَابَ وَالْحِكْمَةَ
وَيُعَلِّمُكُم مَّا لَمْ تَكُونُوا تَعْلَمُونَ ﴿١٥١﴾

152. Then do ye remember Me; I will remember you. Be grateful to Me, and reject not Faith.

سو تم مجھے یاد کیا کرو میں تمہیں یاد کیا کرونگا اور میرا
احسان مانتے رہنا اور ناشکری نہ کرنا ﴿۱۵۲﴾

فَاذْكُرُونِي أَذْكُرْكُمْ وَاشْكُرُوا لِي
وَلَا تَكْفُرُونِ ﴿١٥٢﴾

153. O ye who believe! seek help with patient Perseverance and Prayer: for God is with those who patiently persevere.

اے ایمان والو صبر اور نماز سے مدد لیا کرو بیشک
خدا صبر کرنے والوں کے ساتھ ہے ﴿۱۵۳﴾

يَا أَيُّهَا الَّذِينَ آمَنُوا اسْتَعِينُوا بِالصَّبْرِ
وَالصَّلَاةِ ۚ إِنَّ اللَّهَ مَعَ الصَّابِرِينَ ﴿١٥٣﴾

154. And say not of those who are slain in the way of Allah: "They are dead." Nay, they are living, though ye perceive (it) not.

اور جو لوگ خدا کی راہ میں مارے جائیں اُن کی
نسبت یہ نہ کہنا کہ وہ مرے ہوئے ہیں (وہ مُردہ نہیں)
بلکہ زندہ ہیں لیکن تم نہیں جانتے ﴿۱۵۴﴾

وَلَا تَقُولُوا لِمَن يُقْتَلُ فِي
سَبِيلِ اللَّهِ أَمْوَاتٌ ۚ بَلْ
أَحْيَاءٌ وَلَٰكِن لَّا تَشْعُرُونَ ﴿١٥٤﴾

155. Be sure We shall test you with something of fear and hunger, some loss in goods, lives and the fruits (of your toil), but give glad tidings to those who patiently persevere,—

اور ہم کسی قدر خوف اور بھوک اور مال اور جانوں
اور میووں کے نقصان سے تمہاری آزمائش کریں گے
تو صبر کرنیوالوں کو (خدا کی خوشنودی کی) بشارت سُنا دو ﴿۱۵۵﴾

وَلَنَبْلُوَنَّكُم بِشَيْءٍ مِّنَ الْخَوْفِ
وَالْجُوعِ وَنَقْصٍ مِّنَ الْأَمْوَالِ
وَالْأَنفُسِ وَالثَّمَرَاتِ ۗ وَبَشِّرِ الصَّابِرِينَ ﴿١٥٥﴾

156. Who say, when afflicted with calamity: "To Allah we belong, and

ان لوگوں پر جب کوئی مصیبت واقع ہوتی ہے تو کہتے

الَّذِينَ إِذَا أَصَابَتْهُم مُّصِيبَةٌ

to Him is our return":–

ہیں کہ ہم خدا ہی کا مال ہیں اور اُسی کیطرف لوٹ کر جانیوالے ہیں ﴿۱۵۶﴾

قَالُوْٓا اِنَّا لِلّٰهِ وَاِنَّآ اِلَيْهِ رٰجِعُوْنَ ﴿۱۵۶﴾

157. They are those on whom (Descend) blessings from their Lord, and Mercy. And they are the ones that receive guidance.

یہی لوگ ہیں جن پر اُن کے پروردگار
کی مہربانی اور رحمت ہے، اور یہی سیدھے
رستے پر ہیں ﴿۱۵۷﴾

اُولٰٓئِكَ عَلَيْهِمْ صَلَوٰتٌ مِّنْ
رَّبِّهِمْ وَرَحْمَةٌ قف وَاُولٰٓئِكَ
هُمُ الْمُهْتَدُوْنَ ﴿۱۵۷﴾

158. Behold! Safa and Marwa are among the Symbols of Allah. So if those who visit the House in the Season or at other times, should compass them round, it is no sin in them. And if anyone obeyeth his own impulse to Good,— be sure that Allah is He Who recogniseth and knoweth.

بیشک (کوہ) صفا اور مروہ خدا کی نشانیوں میں سے
ہیں۔ تو جو شخص خانہ کعبہ کا حج یا عمرہ کرے اُس پر کچھ گناہ
نہیں کہ دونوں کا طواف کرے (بلکہ طواف ایک قسم کا نیک کام ہے)
اور جو کوئی نیک کام کرے تو خدا قدر شناس اور
دانا ہے ﴿۱۵۸﴾

اِنَّ الصَّفَا وَالْمَرْوَةَ مِنْ شَعَآئِرِ
اللّٰهِ ج فَمَنْ حَجَّ الْبَيْتَ اَوِ اعْتَمَرَ
فَلَا جُنَاحَ عَلَيْهِ اَنْ يَّطَّوَّفَ بِهِمَا ط
وَمَنْ تَطَوَّعَ خَيْرًا لا فَاِنَّ اللّٰهَ
شَاكِرٌ عَلِيْمٌ ﴿۱۵۸﴾

159. Those who conceal the clear (Signs) We have sent down, and the Guidance, after We have made it clear for the People in the Book,— on them shall be Allah's curse, and the curse of those entitled to curse.—

جو لوگ ہمارے حکموں اور ہدایتوں کو جو ہم نے نازل
کی ہیں (کسی غرض فاسد سے) چھپاتے ہیں باوجودیکہ
ہم نے اُن لوگوں کے (سمجھانے کے) لئے اپنی کتاب
میں کھول کھول کر بیان کر دیا ہے ایسوں پر خدا اور
تمام لعنت کرنے والے لعنت کرتے ہیں ﴿۱۵۹﴾

اِنَّ الَّذِيْنَ يَكْتُمُوْنَ مَآ اَنْزَلْنَا
مِنَ الْبَيِّنٰتِ وَالْهُدٰى مِنْۢ بَعْدِ
مَا بَيَّنّٰهُ لِلنَّاسِ فِى الْكِتٰبِ لا
اُولٰٓئِكَ يَلْعَنُهُمُ اللّٰهُ وَيَلْعَنُهُمُ
اللّٰعِنُوْنَ لا ﴿۱۵۹﴾

160. Except those who repent and make amends and openly declare (the Truth): to them I turn; for I am Oft-Returning, Most Merciful.

ہاں جو توبہ کرتے ہیں اور اپنی حالت درست کر لیتے اور
(احکامِ الٰہی کو) صاف صاف بیان کر دیتے ہیں تو میں اُنکے قصور معاف
کر دیتا ہوں اور میں بڑا معاف کرنیوالا (اور) رحم والا ہوں ﴿۱۶۰﴾

اِلَّا الَّذِيْنَ تَابُوْا وَاَصْلَحُوْا وَبَيَّنُوْا
فَاُولٰٓئِكَ اَتُوْبُ عَلَيْهِمْ ج وَاَنَا
التَّوَّابُ الرَّحِيْمُ ﴿۱۶۰﴾

161. Those who reject Faith. And die rejecting,—on them is Allah's curse, and the curse of angels, and of all mankind;

جو لوگ کافر ہوئے اور کافر ہی مرے ایسوں پر
خدا کی اور فرشتوں کی اور لوگوں کی سب
کی لعنت ﴿۱۶۱﴾

اِنَّ الَّذِيْنَ كَفَرُوْا وَمَاتُوْا وَهُمْ
كُفَّارٌ اُولٰٓئِكَ عَلَيْهِمْ لَعْنَةُ اللّٰهِ
وَالْمَلٰٓئِكَةِ وَالنَّاسِ اَجْمَعِيْنَ لا ﴿۱۶۱﴾

162. They will abide therein: their penalty will not be lightened, nor will respite be their (lot).

وہ ہمیشہ اسی (لعنت) میں (گرفتار) رہیں گے اُن سے
نہ تو عذاب ہلکا ہی کیا جائیگا اور نہ اُنہیں (کچھ) مہلت ملیگی ﴿۱۶۲﴾

خٰلِدِيْنَ فِيْهَا ج لَا يُخَفَّفُ عَنْهُمُ
الْعَذَابُ وَلَا هُمْ يُنْظَرُوْنَ ﴿۱۶۲﴾

163. And your God is One God: there is no god but He, Most Gracious, Most Merciful.

اور (لوگو) تمہارا معبود خدائے واحد ہے۔ اُس بڑے مہربان
(اور) رحم والے کے سوا کوئی عبادت کے لائق نہیں ﴿۱۶۳﴾

وَاِلٰهُكُمْ اِلٰهٌ وَّاحِدٌ ج لَآ اِلٰهَ اِلَّا
هُوَ الرَّحْمٰنُ الرَّحِيْمُ ﴿۱۶۳﴾ ع

164. Behold! In the creation of the heavens and the earth; in the alternation of the Night and the Day; in the sailing of the ships through the Ocean for the profit of mankind;

بیشک آسمانوں اور زمین کے پیدا کرنے میں اور رات
اور دن کے ایک دوسرے کے پیچھے آنے جانے میں
اور کشتیوں (اور جہازوں) میں جو دریا میں لوگوں کے

اِنَّ فِىْ خَلْقِ السَّمٰوٰتِ وَالْاَرْضِ
وَاخْتِلَافِ الَّيْلِ وَالنَّهَارِ وَالْفُلْكِ
الَّتِىْ تَجْرِىْ فِى الْبَحْرِ بِمَا يَنْفَعُ

in the rain which Allah sends down from the skies, and the life which He gives therewith to an earth that is dead; in the beasts of all kinds that He scatters through the earth; in the change of the winds, and the clouds which they trail like their slaves between the sky and the earth;—(here) indeed are Signs for a people that are wise.

165. Yet there are men who take (for worship) others besides Allah, as equal (with Allah): they love them as they should love Allah. But those of Faith are overflowing in their love for Allah. If only the unrighteous could see, behold, they would see the Punishment: that to Allah belongs all power, and Allah will strongly enforce the Punishment.

166. Then would those who are followed clear themselves of those who follow (them): they would see the Chastisement and all relations between them would be cut off.

167. And those who followed would say: "If only we had one more chance, we would clear ourselves of them, as they have cleared themselves of us." Thus will Allah show them (the fruits of) their deeds as (nothing but) regrets. Nor will there be a way for them out of the Fire.

168. O ye people ! eat of what is on earth, lawful and good; and do not follow the footsteps of Satan for he is to you an avowed enemy.

169. For he commands you what is evil and shameful, and that ye should say of Allah that of which ye have no knowledge.

170. When it is said to them: "Follow what Allah hath revealed:" they say: "Nay ! we shall follow the ways of our fathers." What ! even though their fathers were void of

فائدے کیلئے رواں ہیں اور مینہ میں جس کو خدا آسمان سے
برساتا اور اُس سے زمین کو مرنے کے بعد زندہ (یعنی
خشک ہوئے پیچھے سرسبز) کر دیتا ہے اور زمین پر ہر قسم کے
جانور پھیلانے میں اور ہواؤں کے چلانے میں اور بادلوں میں
جو آسمان اور زمین کے درمیان گھرے رہتے ہیں عقلمندوں کیلئے
(خدا کی قدرت کی) نشانیاں ہیں (۱۶۴)
اور بعض لوگ ایسے ہیں جو غیر خدا کو شریک (خدا) بناتے
اور اُن سے خدا کی سی محبت کرتے ہیں لیکن جو ایمان
والے ہیں وہ تو خدا ہی کے سب سے زیادہ دوست دار ہیں
اور اے کاش ظالم لوگ جو بات عذاب کے وقت دیکھیں گے
اب دیکھ لیتے کہ سب طرح کی طاقت خدا ہی کو ہے اور یہ کہ
خدا سخت عذاب کرنے والا ہے (۱۶۵)
اُس دن (کفر کے) پیشوا اپنے پیرووں سے بیزاری ظاہر
کرینگے اور (دونوں) عذاب (الٰہی) دیکھ لیں گے اور اُنکے
آپس کے تعلقات منقطع ہو جائیں گے (۱۶۶)
(یہ حال دیکھکر) پیروی کرنیوالے (حسرت سے) کہینگے کہ اے کاش
ہمیں پھر دُنیا میں جانا نصیب ہوتا تاکہ جسطرح یہ ہم سے بیزار ہو رہے
ہیں اسی طرح ہم بھی اُنسے بیزار ہوں۔ اِسطرح خدا اُنکے اعمال
حسرت بنا کر دکھائیگا اور وہ دوزخ سے نکل نہیں سکینگے (۱۶۷)
لوگو جو چیزیں زمین میں حلال طیّب
ہیں وہ کھاؤ۔ اور شیطان کے قدموں پر
نہ چلو وہ تمہارا کھلا دشمن ہے (۱۶۸)
وہ تو تم کو بُرائی اور بے حیائی ہی کے کام کرنے کو کہتا ہے اور یہ بھی کہ خدا کی
نسبت ایسی باتیں کہو جن کا تمہیں (کچھ بھی) علم نہیں (۱۶۹)
اور جب اُن لوگوں سے کہا جاتا ہے کہ جو (کتاب) خدا نے
نازل فرمائی ہے اُس کی پیروی کرو تو کہتے ہیں (نہیں) بلکہ
ہم تو اُسی چیز کی پیروی کرینگے جس پر ہم نے اپنے باپ دادا کو

النَّاسَ وَمَآ اَنْزَلَ اللّٰهُ مِنَ السَّمَآءِ
مِنْ مَّآءٍ فَاَحْيَا بِهِ الْاَرْضَ بَعْدَ
مَوْتِهَا وَبَثَّ فِيْهَا مِنْ كُلِّ دَآبَّةٍ
وَّتَصْرِيْفِ الرِّيٰحِ وَالسَّحَابِ الْمُسَخَّرِ
بَيْنَ السَّمَآءِ وَالْاَرْضِ لَاٰيٰتٍ
لِّقَوْمٍ يَّعْقِلُوْنَ (١٦٤)
وَمِنَ النَّاسِ مَنْ يَّتَّخِذُ مِنْ
دُوْنِ اللّٰهِ اَنْدَادًا يُّحِبُّوْنَهُمْ
كَحُبِّ اللّٰهِ ۭ وَالَّذِيْنَ اٰمَنُوْٓا اَشَدُّ
حُبًّا لِّلّٰهِ ۭ وَلَوْ يَرَى الَّذِيْنَ ظَلَمُوْٓا
اِذْ يَرَوْنَ الْعَذَابَ ۙ اَنَّ الْقُوَّةَ لِلّٰهِ
جَمِيْعًا ۙ وَّاَنَّ اللّٰهَ شَدِيْدُ الْعَذَابِ (١٦٥)
اِذْ تَبَرَّاَ الَّذِيْنَ اتُّبِعُوْا مِنَ
الَّذِيْنَ اتَّبَعُوْا وَرَاَوُا الْعَذَابَ
وَتَقَطَّعَتْ بِهِمُ الْاَسْبَابُ (١٦٦)
وَقَالَ الَّذِيْنَ اتَّبَعُوْا لَوْ اَنَّ لَنَا كَرَّةً
فَنَتَبَرَّاَ مِنْهُمْ كَمَا تَبَرَّءُوْا مِنَّا ۭ
كَذٰلِكَ يُرِيْهِمُ اللّٰهُ اَعْمَالَهُمْ حَسَرٰتٍ عَلَيْهِمْ ۭ
وَمَا هُمْ بِخٰرِجِيْنَ مِنَ النَّارِ (١٦٧)
يٰٓاَيُّهَا النَّاسُ كُلُوْا مِمَّا فِي الْاَرْضِ
حَلٰلًا طَيِّبًا ۡ وَّلَا تَتَّبِعُوْا خُطُوٰتِ
الشَّيْطٰنِ ۭ اِنَّهٗ لَكُمْ عَدُوٌّ مُّبِيْنٌ (١٦٨)
اِنَّمَا يَاْمُرُكُمْ بِالسُّوْۗءِ وَالْفَحْشَاۗءِ
وَاَنْ تَقُوْلُوْا عَلَى اللّٰهِ مَا لَا تَعْلَمُوْنَ (١٦٩)
وَاِذَا قِيْلَ لَهُمُ اتَّبِعُوْا مَآ اَنْزَلَ
اللّٰهُ قَالُوْا بَلْ نَتَّبِعُ مَآ اَلْفَيْنَا عَلَيْهِ
اٰبَاۗءَنَا ۭ اَوَلَوْ كَانَ اٰبَاۗؤُهُمْ

لَا يَعْقِلُوْنَ شَيْـًٔا وَّ لَا يَهْتَدُوْنَ ﴿۱۷۰﴾

پایا۔ بھلا اگرچہ اُن کے باپ دادا نہ کچھ سمجھتے ہوں اور نہ سیدھے رستے پر ہوں (تب بھی وہ انہیں کی تقلید کئے جائینگے) ﴿۱۷۰﴾

wisdom and guidance?

وَمَثَلُ الَّذِيْنَ كَفَرُوْا كَمَثَلِ الَّذِيْ يَنْعِقُ بِمَا لَا يَسْمَعُ اِلَّا دُعَآءً وَّنِدَآءً ؕ صُمٌّۢ بُكْمٌ عُمْيٌ فَهُمْ لَا يَعْقِلُوْنَ ﴿۱۷۱﴾

جو لوگ کافر ہیں اُن کی مثال اُس شخص کی سی ہے جو کسی ایسی چیز کو آواز دے جو پکار اور آواز کے سوا کچھ سُن نہ سکے (یہ) بہرے ہیں گونگے ہیں اندھے ہیں کہ (کچھ) سمجھ ہی نہیں سکتے ﴿۱۷۱﴾

171. The parable of those who reject Faith is as if one were to shout like a goat-herd, to things that listen to nothing but calls and cries: deaf, dumb, and blind. They are void of wisdom.

يٰۤاَيُّهَا الَّذِيْنَ اٰمَنُوْا كُلُوْا مِنْ طَيِّبٰتِ مَا رَزَقْنٰكُمْ وَاشْكُرُوْا لِلّٰهِ اِنْ كُنْتُمْ اِيَّاهُ تَعْبُدُوْنَ ﴿۱۷۲﴾

اے اہلِ ایمان جو پاکیزہ چیزیں ہم نے تم کو عطا فرمائی ہیں اُن کو کھاؤ اور اگر خدا ہی کے بندے ہو تو (اس کی نعمتوں کا) شکر بھی ادا کرو ﴿۱۷۲﴾

172. O ye who believe ! eat of the good things that We have provided for you. And be grateful to Allah, if it is Him ye worship.

اِنَّمَا حَرَّمَ عَلَيْكُمُ الْمَيْتَةَ وَالدَّمَ وَلَحْمَ الْخِنْزِيْرِ وَمَآ اُهِلَّ بِهٖ لِغَيْرِ اللّٰهِ ۚ فَمَنِ اضْطُرَّ غَيْرَ بَاغٍ وَّلَا عَادٍ فَلَاۤ اِثْمَ عَلَيْهِ ؕ اِنَّ اللّٰهَ غَفُوْرٌ رَّحِيْمٌ ﴿۱۷۳﴾

اُس نے تم پر مرا ہوا جانور اور لہو اور سُور کا گوشت اور جس چیز پر خدا کے سوا کسی اور کا نام پکارا جائے حرام کر دیا ہے۔ ہاں جو ناچار ہو جائے (بشرطیکہ) خدا کی نافرمانی نہ کرے اور حد (ضرورت) سے باہر نہ نکل جائے اُس پر کچھ گناہ نہیں بیشک خدا بخشنے والا (اور) رحم کرنیوالا ہے ﴿۱۷۳﴾

173. He hath only forbidden you dead meat, and blood, and the flesh of swine, and that on which any other name hath been invoked besides that of Allah. But if one is forced by necessity, without wilful disobedience, nor transgressing due limits,—then is he guiltless. For Allah is Oft-Forgiving Most Merciful.

اِنَّ الَّذِيْنَ يَكْتُمُوْنَ مَآ اَنْزَلَ اللّٰهُ مِنَ الْكِتٰبِ وَيَشْتَرُوْنَ بِهٖ ثَمَنًا قَلِيْلًا ۙ اُولٰٓئِكَ مَا يَاْكُلُوْنَ فِيْ بُطُوْنِهِمْ اِلَّا النَّارَ وَلَا يُكَلِّمُهُمُ اللّٰهُ يَوْمَ الْقِيٰمَةِ وَلَا يُزَكِّيْهِمْ ۖۚ وَلَهُمْ عَذَابٌ اَلِيْمٌ ﴿۱۷۴﴾

جو لوگ (خدا کی) کتاب سے اُن (آیتوں اور ہدایتوں) کو جو اُس نے نازل فرمائی ہیں چھپاتے اور اُن کے بدلے تھوڑی سی قیمت (یعنی دُنیاوی منفعت) حاصل کرتے ہیں وہ اپنے پیٹوں میں محض آگ بھرتے ہیں ایسے لوگوں سے خدا قیامت کے دن نہ کلام کریگا اور نہ اُنکو (گناہوں سے) پاک کریگا اور اُن کیلئے دُکھ دینے والا عذاب ہے ﴿۱۷۴﴾

174. Those who conceal Allah's revelations in the Book, and purchase for them a miserable profit,—They swallow into themselves naught but Fire; Allah will not address them on the Day of Resurrection, nor purify them: grievous will be their Chastisement.

اُولٰٓئِكَ الَّذِيْنَ اشْتَرَوُا الضَّلٰلَةَ بِالْهُدٰى وَالْعَذَابَ بِالْمَغْفِرَةِ ۚ فَمَآ اَصْبَرَهُمْ عَلَى النَّارِ ﴿۱۷۵﴾

یہ وہ لوگ ہیں جنہوں نے ہدایت چھوڑ کر گمراہی اور بخشش چھوڑ کر عذاب خریدا۔ یہ آتش (جہنم) کی کیسی برداشت کرنے والے ہیں! ﴿۱۷۵﴾

175. They are the ones who buy Error in place of Guidance and Torment in place of Forgiveness. Ah ! what boldness (they show) for the Fire!

ذٰلِكَ بِاَنَّ اللّٰهَ نَزَّلَ الْكِتٰبَ بِالْحَقِّ ؕ وَاِنَّ الَّذِيْنَ اخْتَلَفُوْا فِى الْكِتٰبِ لَفِيْ شِقَاقٍۢ بَعِيْدٍ ﴿۱۷۶﴾ ع

یہ اس لئے کہ خدا نے کتاب سچائی کے ساتھ نازل فرمائی۔ اور جن لوگوں نے اس کتاب میں اختلاف کیا وہ ضد میں (آ کر نیکی سے) دُور (ہو گئے) ہیں ﴿۱۷۶﴾

176. (Their doom is) because Allah sent down the Book in truth but those who seek causes of dispute in the Book are in a schism far (from the purpose).

لَيْسَ الْبِرَّ اَنْ تُوَلُّوْا وُجُوْهَكُمْ

نیکی یہی نہیں کہ تم مشرق و مغرب (کو قبلہ سمجھ کر اُن)

177. It is not righteousness that ye turn your faces towards East or

West; but it is righteousness—to believe in Allah and the Last Day, and the Angels, and the Book, and the Messengers; to spend of your substance, out of love for Him, for your kin, for orphans, for the needy, for the wayfarer, for those who ask, and for the ransom of slaves; to be steadfast in prayer, and give Zakat, to fulfil the contracts which ye have made; and to be firm and patient, in pain (or suffering) and adversity, and throughout all periods of panic. Such are the people of truth, the God-fearing.

کی طرف مُنہ کرلو بلکہ نیکی یہ ہے کہ لوگ خدا پر
اور فرشتوں پر اور (خدا کی) کتاب پر اور پیغمبروں
پر ایمان لائیں۔ اور مال باوجود عزیز رکھنے کے
رشتہ داروں اور یتیموں اور مُحتاجوں اور مُسافروں
اور مانگنے والوں کو دیں اور گردنوں (کے چھڑانے)[43]
میں (خرچ کریں) اور نماز پڑھیں اور زکوٰۃ دیں
اور جب عہد کرلیں تو اُس کو پُورا کریں اور سختی اور
تکلیف میں اور (معرکۂ) کارزار کے وقت
ثابت قدم رہیں۔ یہی لوگ ہیں جو (ایمان میں)
سچے ہیں اور یہی ہیں جو (خدا سے) ڈرنے
والے ہیں (۱۷۷)

قِبَلَ الْمَشْرِقِ وَالْمَغْرِبِ وَلٰكِنَّ
الْبِرَّ مَنْ اٰمَنَ بِاللّٰهِ وَالْيَوْمِ الْاٰخِرِ
وَالْمَلٰٓئِكَةِ وَالْكِتٰبِ وَالنَّبِيّٖنَ ۚ وَاٰتَى
الْمَالَ عَلٰى حُبِّهٖ ذَوِى الْقُرْبٰى وَ
الْيَتٰمٰى وَالْمَسٰكِيْنَ وَابْنَ
السَّبِيْلِ ۙ وَالسَّآئِلِيْنَ وَفِى الرِّقَابِ ۚ
وَاَقَامَ الصَّلٰوةَ وَاٰتَى الزَّكٰوةَ ۚ
وَالْمُوْفُوْنَ بِعَهْدِهِمْ اِذَا عٰهَدُوْا ۚ
وَالصّٰبِرِيْنَ فِى الْبَاْسَآءِ وَالضَّرَّآءِ
وَحِيْنَ الْبَاْسِ ؕ اُولٰٓئِكَ الَّذِيْنَ صَدَقُوْا ؕ
وَاُولٰٓئِكَ هُمُ الْمُتَّقُوْنَ (١٧٧)

178. O ye who believe ! the law of equality is prescribed to you in cases of murder: the free for the free, the slave for the slave, the woman for the woman. But if any remission is made by the brother of the slain, then grant any reasonable demand, and compensate him with handsome gratitude. This is a concession and a Mercy from your Lord. After this whoever exceeds the limits shall be in grave chastisement.

مومنو! تم کو مقتولوں کے بارے میں قصاص
(یعنی خون کے بدلے خون) کا حکم دیا جاتا ہے
(اس طرح پر کہ) آزاد کے بدلے آزاد (مارا جائے) اور
غلام کے بدلے غلام اور عورت کے بدلے عورت[44]۔ اور اگر
قاتل کو اُسکے (مقتول) بھائی (کے قصاص میں) سے کچھ معاف
کر دیا جائے[45] تو (وارث مقتول کو) پسندیدہ طریق سے (قرارداد کی)
پیروی (یعنی مطالبۂ خونبہا) کرنا اور (قاتل کو) خوش خوئی کیساتھ
ادا کرنا چاہیے۔ یہ پروردگار کی طرف سے تمہارے لئے آسانی اور مہربانی ہے
جو اسکے بعد زیادتی کرے اُسکے لئے دُکھ کا عذاب ہے (۱۷۸)

يٰٓاَيُّهَا الَّذِيْنَ اٰمَنُوْا كُتِبَ عَلَيْكُمُ
الْقِصَاصُ فِى الْقَتْلٰى ؕ اَلْحُرُّ بِالْحُرِّ
وَالْعَبْدُ بِالْعَبْدِ وَالْاُنْثٰى بِالْاُنْثٰى ؕ
فَمَنْ عُفِىَ لَهٗ مِنْ اَخِيْهِ شَىْءٌ
فَاتِّبَاعٌ ۢ بِالْمَعْرُوْفِ وَاَدَآءٌ اِلَيْهِ
بِاِحْسَانٍ ؕ ذٰلِكَ تَخْفِيْفٌ مِّنْ
رَّبِّكُمْ وَرَحْمَةٌ ؕ فَمَنِ
اعْتَدٰى بَعْدَ ذٰلِكَ فَلَهٗ
عَذَابٌ اَلِيْمٌ (١٧٨)

179. In the Law of Equality there is (saving of) Life to you. O ye men of understanding; that ye may restrain yourselves.

اور اے اہلِ عقل (حکمِ) قصاص میں (تمہاری) زندگانی ہے
کہ تم (قتل و خونریزی سے) بچو (۱۷۹)

وَلَكُمْ فِى الْقِصَاصِ حَيٰوةٌ
يّٰٓاُولِى الْاَلْبَابِ لَعَلَّكُمْ تَتَّقُوْنَ (١٧٩)

180. It is prescribed, when death approaches any of you, if he leave any goods, that he make a bequest to parents and next of kin. According to reasonable usage; this is due from the God-fearing.

تم پر فرض کیا جاتا ہے کہ جب تم میں سے کسی کو
موت کا وقت آجائے تو اگر وہ کچھ مال چھوڑ جانیوالا
ہو تو ماں باپ اور رشتہ داروں کیلئے دستور کے مطابق وصیت
کر جائے (خدا سے) ڈرنے والوں پر یہ ایک حق ہے (۱۸۰)

كُتِبَ عَلَيْكُمْ اِذَا حَضَرَ اَحَدَكُمُ
الْمَوْتُ اِنْ تَرَكَ خَيْرًا ۖۚ الْوَصِيَّةُ
لِلْوَالِدَيْنِ وَالْاَقْرَبِيْنَ بِالْمَعْرُوْفِ ۚ
حَقًّا عَلَى الْمُتَّقِيْنَ ؕ (١٨٠)

181. If anyone changes the bequest after hearing it, the guilt

جو شخص وصیت کو سُننے کے بعد بدل ڈالے تو اُس (کے

فَمَنْ بَدَّلَهٗ بَعْدَ مَا سَمِعَهٗ فَاِنَّمَا

shall be on those who make the change. For Allah hears and knows (all things)..

بدلنے) کا گناہ اُنہیں لوگوں پر ہے جو اُس کو بدلیں
اور بیشک خدا سنتا جانتا ہے ﴿١٨١﴾

إِثْمُهُ عَلَى الَّذِينَ يُبَدِّلُونَهُ ط
إِنَّ اللَّهَ سَمِيعٌ عَلِيمٌ ﴿١٨١﴾

182. But if anyone fears partiality or wrong-doing on the part of the testator. And brings about a settlement among (the parties concerned), there is no wrong in him: for Allah is Oft-Forgiving, Most Merciful.

اگر کسی کو وصیت کرنیوالے کیطرف سے (کسی وارث کی) طرفداری یا
حق تلفی کا اندیشہ ہو تو اگر وہ (وصیت کو بدل کر) وارثوں میں صلح
کرادے تو اُس پر کچھ گناہ نہیں بیشک خدا بخشنے والا (اور) رحم والا ہے ﴿١٨٢﴾

فَمَنْ خَافَ مِن مُّوصٍ جَنَفًا
أَوْ إِثْمًا فَأَصْلَحَ بَيْنَهُمْ فَلَا إِثْمَ
عَلَيْهِ ط إِنَّ اللَّهَ غَفُورٌ رَّحِيمٌ ﴿١٨٢﴾ ع ٢٢

183. O ye who believe ! fasting is prescribed to you as it was prescribed to those before you, that ye may (learn) self-restraint.—

مومنو! تم پر روزے فرض کئے گئے ہیں۔
جس طرح تم سے پہلے لوگوں پر فرض کئے
گئے تھے تاکہ تم پرہیزگار بنو ﴿١٨٣﴾

يَا أَيُّهَا الَّذِينَ آمَنُوا كُتِبَ عَلَيْكُمُ
الصِّيَامُ كَمَا كُتِبَ عَلَى الَّذِينَ
مِن قَبْلِكُمْ لَعَلَّكُمْ تَتَّقُونَ ﴿١٨٣﴾

184. (Fasting) for a fixed number of days; but if any of you is ill, or on a journey, the prescribed number (should be made up) from days later. For those who can do it (with hardship), is a ransom, the feeding of one that is indigent. But he that will give more, of his own free-will,—it is better for him. And it is better for you that ye fast, if ye only knew.

(روزوں کے دن) گنتی کے چند روز ہیں تو جو
شخص تم میں سے بیمار ہو یا سفر میں ہو تو دوسرے
دنوں میں روزوں کا شمار پورا کرلے اور جو لوگ روزہ
رکھنے کی طاقت رکھیں (لیکن رکھیں نہیں) وہ روزے کے
بدلے محتاج کو کھانا کھلادیں۔ اور جو کوئی شوق سے
نیکی کرے تو اُسکے حق میں زیادہ اچھا ہے اور اگر سمجھو تو
روزہ رکھنا ہی تمہارے حق میں بہتر ہے ﴿١٨٤﴾

أَيَّامًا مَّعْدُودَاتٍ ط فَمَن كَانَ مِنكُم
مَّرِيضًا أَوْ عَلَىٰ سَفَرٍ فَعِدَّةٌ مِّنْ
أَيَّامٍ أُخَرَ ط وَعَلَى الَّذِينَ يُطِيقُونَهُ
فِدْيَةٌ طَعَامُ مِسْكِينٍ ط فَمَن
تَطَوَّعَ خَيْرًا فَهُوَ خَيْرٌ لَّهُ ط وَأَن
تَصُومُوا خَيْرٌ لَّكُمْ إِن كُنتُمْ
تَعْلَمُونَ ﴿١٨٤﴾

185. Ramadhān is the (month) in which was sent down the Qur'an, as a guide to mankind, also clear (Signs) for guidance and judgment (between right and wrong). So everyone of you who is present (at his home) during that month should spent it in fasting, but if anyone is ill, or on a journey, the prescribed period (should be made up) by days later. Allah intends every facility for you; He does not want to put you to difficulties. (He wants you) to complete the prescribed period, and to glorify Him in that He has guided you; and perchance ye shall be grateful.

(روزوں کا مہینہ) رمضان کا مہینہ (ہے) جس میں قرآن (اوّل
اوّل) نازل ہوا جو لوگوں کا رہنما ہے اور (جسمیں) ہدایت
کی کھلی نشانیاں ہیں اور (جو) حق و باطل کو) الگ الگ کرنیوالا ہے
تو جو کوئی تم میں سے اس مہینے میں موجود ہو چاہیئے کہ پورے
مہینے کے روزے رکھے اور جو بیمار ہو یا سفر میں ہو تو دوسرے
دنوں میں (رکھ کر) اُن کا شمار پورا کرلے خدا تمہارے حق
میں آسانی چاہتا ہے اور سختی نہیں چاہتا۔ اور (یہ
آسانی کا حکم) اسلئے (دیا گیا ہے) کہ تم روزوں کا شمار پورا
کرلو اور اس احسان کے بدلے کہ خدا نے تم کو ہدایت بخشی ہے
تم اُس کو بزرگی سے یاد کرو اور اُس کا شکر کرو ﴿١٨٥﴾

شَهْرُ رَمَضَانَ الَّذِي أُنزِلَ فِيهِ
الْقُرْآنُ هُدًى لِّلنَّاسِ وَبَيِّنَاتٍ
مِّنَ الْهُدَىٰ وَالْفُرْقَانِ ج فَمَن
شَهِدَ مِنكُمُ الشَّهْرَ فَلْيَصُمْهُ ط
وَمَن كَانَ مَرِيضًا أَوْ عَلَىٰ سَفَرٍ
فَعِدَّةٌ مِّنْ أَيَّامٍ أُخَرَ ط يُرِيدُ اللَّهُ
بِكُمُ الْيُسْرَ وَلَا يُرِيدُ بِكُمُ الْعُسْرَ ز
وَلِتُكْمِلُوا الْعِدَّةَ وَلِتُكَبِّرُوا اللَّهَ
عَلَىٰ مَا هَدَاكُمْ وَلَعَلَّكُمْ
تَشْكُرُونَ ﴿١٨٥﴾

186. When My servants ask thee concerning Me, I am indeed close (to them): I respond to the prayer

اور (اے پیغمبر) جب تم سے میرے بندے میرے بارے میں
دریافت کریں تو (کہہ دو کہ) میں تو (تمہارے) پاس ہوں۔

وَإِذَا سَأَلَكَ عِبَادِي عَنِّي فَإِنِّي
قَرِيبٌ ط أُجِيبُ دَعْوَةَ الدَّاعِ إِذَا

دَعَانِ فَلْيَسْتَجِيبُوا لِي
وَلْيُؤْمِنُوا بِي لَعَلَّهُمْ
يَرْشُدُونَ ﴿١٨٦﴾

جب کوئی پکارنے والا مجھے پکارتا ہے تو میں اس کی دعا قبول کرتا ہوں
تو ان کو چاہیئے کہ میرے حکموں کو مانیں اور مجھ پر ایمان
لائیں تاکہ نیک رستہ پائیں ﴿۱۸۶﴾

of every suppliant when he calleth on Me: let them also, with a will, listen to My call, and believe in Me: that they may walk in the right way.

أُحِلَّ لَكُمْ لَيْلَةَ الصِّيَامِ الرَّفَثُ
إِلَىٰ نِسَائِكُمْ ۚ هُنَّ لِبَاسٌ لَكُمْ
وَأَنْتُمْ لِبَاسٌ لَهُنَّ ۗ عَلِمَ اللَّهُ أَنَّكُمْ
كُنْتُمْ تَخْتَانُونَ أَنْفُسَكُمْ فَتَابَ
عَلَيْكُمْ وَعَفَا عَنْكُمْ ۖ فَالْآنَ
بَاشِرُوهُنَّ وَابْتَغُوا مَا كَتَبَ اللَّهُ
لَكُمْ ۚ وَكُلُوا وَاشْرَبُوا حَتَّىٰ يَتَبَيَّنَ
لَكُمُ الْخَيْطُ الْأَبْيَضُ مِنَ الْخَيْطِ
الْأَسْوَدِ مِنَ الْفَجْرِ ۖ ثُمَّ أَتِمُّوا
الصِّيَامَ إِلَى اللَّيْلِ ۚ وَلَا تُبَاشِرُوهُنَّ
وَأَنْتُمْ عَاكِفُونَ فِي الْمَسَاجِدِ ۗ
تِلْكَ حُدُودُ اللَّهِ فَلَا تَقْرَبُوهَا ۗ
كَذَٰلِكَ يُبَيِّنُ اللَّهُ آيَاتِهِ لِلنَّاسِ
لَعَلَّهُمْ يَتَّقُونَ ﴿١٨٧﴾

روزوں کی راتوں میں تمہارے لئے اپنی عورتوں کے
پاس جانا جائز کر دیا گیا ہے وہ تمہاری پوشاک ہیں
اور تم ان کی پوشاک ہو۔ خدا کو معلوم ہے کہ تم (ان کے پاس
جانے سے) اپنے حق میں خیانت کرتے تھے سو اس نے تم پر مہربانی
کی اور تمہاری حرکات سے درگذر فرمائی۔ اب (تم کو اختیار ہے کہ)
ان سے مباشرت کرو۔ اور خدا نے جو چیز تمہارے لئے لکھ رکھی ہے
(یعنی اولاد) اس کو (خدا سے) طلب کرو اور کھاؤ اور پیو یہاں تک
کہ صبح کی سفید دھاری (رات کی) سیاہ دھاری سے الگ
نظر آنے لگے پھر روزہ (رکھ کر) رات تک پورا کرو۔ اور
جب تم مسجدوں میں اعتکاف بیٹھے ہو تو ان سے
مباشرت نہ کرو۔ یہ خدا کی حدیں ہیں ان کے
پاس نہ جانا۔ اسی طرح خدا اپنی آیتیں لوگوں کے
(سمجھانے کے) لئے کھول کھول کر بیان فرماتا ہے
تاکہ وہ پرہیزگار بنیں ﴿۱۸۷﴾

187. Permitted to you on the night of the fasts, is the approach to your wives. They are your garments and ye are their garments. Allah knoweth what ye used to do secretly among yourselves: but He turned to you and forgave you; so now associate with them, and seek what Allah hath ordained for you, and eat and drink, until the white thread of dawn appear to you distinct from its black thread; then complete your fast till the night appears; but do not associate with your wives while ye are in retreat in the mosques. Those are limits (set by) Allah: approach not night thereto. Thus doth Allah make clear His Signs to men: that they may learn self-restraint.

وَلَا تَأْكُلُوا أَمْوَالَكُمْ بَيْنَكُمْ
بِالْبَاطِلِ وَتُدْلُوا بِهَا إِلَى الْحُكَّامِ
لِتَأْكُلُوا فَرِيقًا مِنْ أَمْوَالِ
النَّاسِ بِالْإِثْمِ وَأَنْتُمْ تَعْلَمُونَ ﴿١٨٨﴾

اور ایک دوسرے کا مال ناحق نہ کھاؤ اور نہ اس کو
(رشوۃً) حاکموں کے پاس پہنچاؤ تاکہ لوگوں کے مال کا
کچھ حصہ ناجائز طور پر نہ کھا جاؤ اور (اسے) تم
جانتے بھی ہو ﴿۱۸۸﴾

188. And do not eat up your property among yourselves for vanities, nor use it as bait for the judges, with intent that ye may eat up wrongfully and knowingly a little of (other) people's property.

يَسْأَلُونَكَ عَنِ الْأَهِلَّةِ ۖ قُلْ هِيَ
مَوَاقِيتُ لِلنَّاسِ وَالْحَجِّ ۗ وَلَيْسَ
الْبِرُّ بِأَنْ تَأْتُوا الْبُيُوتَ مِنْ
ظُهُورِهَا وَلَٰكِنَّ الْبِرَّ مَنِ
اتَّقَىٰ ۗ وَأْتُوا الْبُيُوتَ مِنْ
أَبْوَابِهَا ۚ وَاتَّقُوا اللَّهَ لَعَلَّكُمْ

(اے محمد) لوگ تم سے نئے چاند کے بارے میں
دریافت کرتے ہیں (کہ گھٹتا بڑھتا کیوں ہے) کہہ دو کہ
وہ لوگوں کے (کاموں کی میعادیں) اور حج کے وقت
معلوم ہونے کا ذریعہ ہے۔ اور نیکی اس بات میں نہیں کہ
(احرام کی حالت میں) گھروں میں ان کے پچھواڑے کی طرف سے آؤ
بلکہ نیکوکار وہ ہے جو پرہیزگار ہو اور گھروں میں ان کے دروازوں

189. They ask thee concerning the New Moons. Say: They are but signs to mark fixed periods of time in (the affairs of) men, and for Pilgrimage. It is no virtue if ye enter your houses from the back: it is virtue if ye fear Allah. Enter houses through the proper doors: and fear

Allah: that ye may prosper.

190. Fight in the cause of Allah those who fight you, but do not transgress limits; for Allah loveth not transgressors.

191. And slay them wherever ye catch them, and turn them out from where they have turned you out; for Persecution is worse than slaughter; but fight them not at the Sacred Mosque, unless they (first) fight you there; but if they fight you, slay them. Such is the reward of those who reject Faith.

192. But if they cease, Allah is Oft-Forgiving, Most Merciful.

193. And fight them on until there is no more Persecution and the religion becomes Allah's. But if they cease, let there be no hostility except to those who practise oppression.

194. The prohibited month for the prohibited month, —and so for all things prohibited,—there is the law of equality. If then anyone transgresses the prohibition against you, transgress ye likewise against him. But fear Allah, and know that Allah is with those who restrain themselves.

195. And spend of your substance in the cause of Allah, and make not your own hands contribute to (your) destruction; but do good; for Allah loveth those who do good.

196. And complete the *Hajj* or *'Umra* in the service of Allah, but if ye are prevented (from completing it), send an offering for sacrifice, such as ye may find, and do not shave your heads until the offering reaches the place of sacrifice. And

سے آیا کرو اور خدا سے ڈرتے رہو تاکہ نجات پاؤ ﴿۱۸۹﴾
اور جو لوگ تم سے لڑتے ہیں تم بھی خدا کی راہ میں اُن سے
لڑو مگر زیادتی نہ کرنا۔ کہ خدا زیادتی کرنے والوں کو
دوست نہیں رکھتا ﴿۱۹۰﴾
اور اُن کو جہاں پاؤ قتل کر دو۔ اور جہاں سے اُنہوں نے
تم کو نکالا ہے (یعنی مکے سے) وہاں سے تم بھی اُن کو
نکال دو۔ اور (دین سے گمراہ کرنے کا) فساد قتل خونریزی
سے کہیں بڑھ کر ہے۔ اور جب تک وہ تم سے مسجد محترم
(یعنی خانہ کعبہ) کے پاس نہ لڑیں تم بھی وہاں اُن سے نہ لڑنا۔ ہاں اگر
وہ تم سے لڑیں تو تم اُن کو قتل کر ڈالو۔ کافروں کی یہی سزا ہے ﴿۱۹۱﴾
اور اگر وہ باز آجائیں تو خدا بخشنے والا (اور) رحم کرنے والا ہے ﴿۱۹۲﴾
اور اُن سے اُس وقت تک لڑتے رہنا کہ فساد نابود ہو جائے
اور (ملک میں) خدا ہی کا دین ہو جائے۔ اور اگر وہ (فساد سے)
باز آجائیں تو ظالموں کے سوا کسی پر زیادتی نہیں
(کرنی چاہیئے) ﴿۱۹۳﴾
ادب کا مہینہ ادب کے مہینے کے مقابل ہے اور
ادب کی چیزیں ایک دوسرے کا بدلہ ہیں۔ پس اگر کوئی
تم پر زیادتی کرے تو جیسی زیادتی وہ تم پر کرے
ویسی ہی تم اُس پر کرو۔ اور خدا سے ڈرتے رہو اور
جان رکھو کہ خدا ڈرنے والوں کے ساتھ ہے ﴿۱۹۴﴾
اور خدا کی راہ میں (مال) خرچ کرو اور اپنے آپ کو
ہلاکت میں نہ ڈالو اور نیکی کرو بیشک خدا نیکی
کرنے والوں کو دوست رکھتا ہے ﴿۱۹۵﴾
اور خدا (کی خوشنودی) کے لئے حج اور عُمرے کو پورا
کرو۔ اور اگر (رستے میں) روک لئے جاؤ تو جیسی قربانی
میسر ہو (کر دو) اور جب تک قربانی اپنے مقام پر
نہ پہنچ جائے سر نہ منڈاؤ۔ اور اگر کوئی تم میں بیمار ہو

تُفْلِحُونَ ﴿١٨٩﴾
وَقَاتِلُوا فِي سَبِيلِ اللَّهِ الَّذِينَ
يُقَاتِلُونَكُمْ وَلَا تَعْتَدُوا ۚ إِنَّ
اللَّهَ لَا يُحِبُّ الْمُعْتَدِينَ ﴿١٩٠﴾
وَاقْتُلُوهُمْ حَيْثُ ثَقِفْتُمُوهُمْ
وَأَخْرِجُوهُمْ مِنْ حَيْثُ أَخْرَجُوكُمْ
وَالْفِتْنَةُ أَشَدُّ مِنَ الْقَتْلِ ۚ وَلَا
تُقَاتِلُوهُمْ عِنْدَ الْمَسْجِدِ الْحَرَامِ
حَتَّىٰ يُقَاتِلُوكُمْ فِيهِ ۖ فَإِنْ قَاتَلُوكُمْ
فَاقْتُلُوهُمْ ۗ كَذَٰلِكَ جَزَاءُ الْكَافِرِينَ ﴿١٩١﴾
فَإِنِ انْتَهَوْا فَإِنَّ اللَّهَ غَفُورٌ رَحِيمٌ ﴿١٩٢﴾
وَقَاتِلُوهُمْ حَتَّىٰ لَا تَكُونَ
فِتْنَةٌ وَيَكُونَ الدِّينُ لِلَّهِ ۖ
فَإِنِ انْتَهَوْا فَلَا عُدْوَانَ إِلَّا
عَلَى الظَّالِمِينَ ﴿١٩٣﴾
الشَّهْرُ الْحَرَامُ بِالشَّهْرِ الْحَرَامِ
وَالْحُرُمَاتُ قِصَاصٌ ۚ فَمَنِ اعْتَدَىٰ
عَلَيْكُمْ فَاعْتَدُوا عَلَيْهِ بِمِثْلِ
مَا اعْتَدَىٰ عَلَيْكُمْ ۚ وَاتَّقُوا اللَّهَ
وَاعْلَمُوا أَنَّ اللَّهَ مَعَ الْمُتَّقِينَ ﴿١٩٤﴾
وَأَنْفِقُوا فِي سَبِيلِ اللَّهِ وَلَا تُلْقُوا
بِأَيْدِيكُمْ إِلَى التَّهْلُكَةِ ۛ وَأَحْسِنُوا ۛ مع
إِنَّ اللَّهَ يُحِبُّ الْمُحْسِنِينَ ﴿١٩٥﴾ عند المتقدمين ١٠
وَأَتِمُّوا الْحَجَّ وَالْعُمْرَةَ لِلَّهِ ۚ فَإِنْ
أُحْصِرْتُمْ فَمَا اسْتَيْسَرَ مِنَ الْهَدْيِ ۖ
وَلَا تَحْلِقُوا رُءُوسَكُمْ حَتَّىٰ يَبْلُغَ
الْهَدْيُ مَحِلَّهُ ۚ فَمَنْ كَانَ مِنْكُمْ

if any of you is ill, or has an ailment in his scalp, (necessitating shaving), (he should) in compensation either fast, or feed the poor, or offer sacrifice; and when ye are in peaceful conditions (again), if anyone wishes to continue the *'Umra* on to the *Hajj*, he must make an offering such as he can afford, but if he cannot afford it, he should fast three days during the *Hajj*. And seven days on his return, making ten days in all. This is for those whose household is not in (the precincts of) the Sacred Mosque. And fear Allah, and know that Allah is strict in punishment.

یا اُس کے سر میں کسی طرح کی تکلیف ہو۔ تو اگر وہ سر
مُنڈا لے تو اُس کے بدلے روزے رکھے یا صدقہ دے
یا قربانی کرے۔ پھر جب (تکلیف دُور ہو کر) تم مطمئن ہو
جاؤ۔ تو جو (تم میں) حج کے وقت تک عُمرے سے فائدہ
اُٹھانا چاہے وہ جیسی قربانی میسّر ہو کرے۔ اور جس
کو (قربانی) نہ ملے وہ تین روزے ایّامِ حج میں رکھے
اور سات جب واپس ہو۔ یہ پُورے دس ہوئے۔
یہ حکم اُس شخص کیلئے ہے جس کے اہل و عیال مکّے
میں نہ رہتے ہوں اور خدا سے ڈرتے رہو اور جان رکھو
کہ خُدا سخت عذاب دینے والا ہے ﴿۱۹۶﴾

مريضا او به اذى من راسه
ففدية من صيام او صدقة
او نسك ۚ فاذا امنتم فمن تمتع
بالعمرة الى الحج فما استيسر
من الهدي ۚ فمن لم يجد فصيام
ثلثة ايام في الحج وسبعة اذا
رجعتم ۗ تلك عشرة كاملة ۗ
ذلك لمن لم يكن اهله حاضري
المسجد الحرام ۚ واتقوا الله واعلموا
ان الله شديد العقاب ﴿١٩٦﴾ ع

197. For *Hajj* are the months well known. If any one undertakes that duty therein, let there be no obscenity, nor wickedness, nor wrangling in the *Hajj*. And whatever good ye do, (be sure) Allah knoweth it. And take a provision (with you) for the journey, but the best of provisions is right conduct. So fear Me, O ye that are wise.

حج کے مہینے (معیّن ہیں جو) معلوم ہیں [۵۲]۔ تو جو شخص
ان مہینوں میں حج کی نیت کرلے تو حج (کے دنوں)
میں نہ عورتوں سے اختلاط کرے نہ کوئی بُرا کام کرے
اور نہ کسی سے جھگڑے۔ اور جو نیک کام تم کرو گے وہ خدا
کو معلوم ہوجائے گا۔ اور زادِ راہ (یعنی رستے کا خرچ)
ساتھ لے جاؤ کیونکہ بہتر (فائدہ) زادِ راہ (کا) پرہیزگاری
ہے۔ اور اے اہلِ عقل مجھ سے ڈرتے رہو ﴿۱۹۷﴾

الحج اشهر معلومت ۚ فمن
فرض فيهن الحج فلا رفث ولا
فسوق ولا جدال في الحج ۗ وما
تفعلوا من خير يعلمه
الله ۗ وتزودوا فان خير
الزاد التقوى واتقون يا اولي
الالباب ﴿١٩٧﴾

وقف النبی صلی اللہ علیہ وسلم

198. It is no crime in you if ye seek of the bounty of your Lord (during pilgrimage). Then when ye pour down from (Mount) 'Arafat, celebrate the praises of Allah at the Sacred Monument, and celebrate His praises as He has directed you, even though, before this, ye went astray.

اِس کا تمہیں کچھ گناہ نہیں کہ (حج کے دنوں میں بذریعۂ
تجارت) اپنے پروردگار سے روزی طلب کرو اور جب
عرفات سے واپس ہونے لگو تو مشعرِ حرام (یعنی مُزدلفے)
میں خدا کا ذکر کرو اور اسطرح ذکر کرو جس طرح اسنے تمکو سکھایا اور
اس سے پیشتر تم لوگ (ان طریقوں سے محض) ناواقف تھے ﴿۱۹۸﴾

ليس عليكم جناح ان تبتغوا
فضلا من ربكم ۗ فاذا افضتم
من عرفت فاذكروا الله عند
المشعر الحرام ۠ واذكروه كما هدىكم ۚ
وان كنتم من قبله لمن الضالين ﴿١٩٨﴾

199. Then return from the place whence it is usual for the multitude so to do, and ask for Allah's forgiveness. For Allah is Oft-Forgiving, Most Merciful.

پھر جہاں سے اور لوگ واپس ہوں وہیں سے تم بھی واپس ہو اور خدا سے
بخشش مانگو بیشک خدا بخشنے والا (اور) رحمت کرنیوالا ہے ﴿۱۹۹﴾

ثم افيضوا من حيث افاض الناس
واستغفروا الله ۗ ان الله غفور رحيم ﴿١٩٩﴾

200. So when ye have accomplished your rites, celebrate the praises of Allah, as ye used to celebrate the praises of your fathers,—yea, with far more heart

پھر جب حج کے تمام ارکان پُورے کرچکو تو (منیٰ میں) خدا
کو یاد کرو جس طرح اپنے باپ دادا کو یاد کیا کرتے تھے بلکہ
اس سے بھی زیادہ۔ اور بعض لوگ ایسے ہیں جو (خدا سے)

فاذا قضيتم مناسككم فاذكروا
الله كذكركم اباءكم او اشد
ذكرا ۗ فمن الناس من يقول

and soul. There are men who say: "Our Lord! Give us (Thy bounties) in this world!" But they will have no portion in the Hereafter.

التجا کرتے ہیں کہ اے پروردگار ہمکو (جو دینا ہے) دنیا ہی میں
عنایت کر ایسے لوگوں کا آخرت میں کچھ حصہ نہیں (۲۰۰)

رَبَّنَآ اٰتِنَا فِي الدُّنْيَا وَمَا لَهٗ فِي
الْاٰخِرَةِ مِنْ خَلَاقٍ ﴿۲۰۰﴾

201. And there are men who say: "Our Lord! Give us good in this world and good in the Hereafter. And save us from the torment of the Fire !"

اور بعضے ایسے ہیں کہ دعا کرتے ہیں کہ پروردگار ہم کو
دنیا میں بھی نعمت عطا فرما اور آخرت میں بھی نعمت بخشیو
اور دوزخ کے عذاب سے محفوظ رکھیو (۲۰۱)

وَمِنْهُمْ مَّنْ يَّقُوْلُ رَبَّنَآ اٰتِنَا فِي
الدُّنْيَا حَسَنَةً وَّفِي الْاٰخِرَةِ
حَسَنَةً وَّقِنَا عَذَابَ النَّارِ ﴿۲۰۱﴾

202. To these will be allotted what they have earned; and Allah is quick in account.

یہی لوگ ہیں جن کیلئے انکے کاموں کا حصہ (یعنی اجر نیک تیار) ہے
اور خدا جلد حساب لینے والا (اور جلد اجر دینے والا) ہے (۲۰۲)

اُولٰٓئِكَ لَهُمْ نَصِيْبٌ مِّمَّا كَسَبُوْا ۭ
وَاللّٰهُ سَرِيْعُ الْحِسَابِ ﴿۲۰۲﴾ النصف

203. Remember Allah during the Appointed Days, but if anyone hastens to leave in two days, there is no blame on him, and if anyone stays on, there is no blame on him, if his aim is to do right. Then fear Allah, and know that ye will surely be gathered unto Him.

اور (قیام منیٰ کے) دنوں میں (جو گنتی کے دن ہیں) خدا
کو یاد کرو۔ اگر کوئی جلدی کرے (اور) دو ہی دن میں
(چل دے) تو اس پر بھی کچھ گناہ نہیں۔ ۵۳ ق اور جو بعد تک
ٹھہرا رہے اس پر بھی کچھ گناہ نہیں۔ یہ باتیں اس شخص کیلئے
ہیں جو (خدا سے) ڈرے اور تم لوگ خدا سے ڈرتے رہو
اور جان رکھو کہ تم سب اسکے پاس جمع کئے جاؤ گے (۲۰۳)

وَاذْكُرُوا اللّٰهَ فِيْٓ اَيَّامٍ مَّعْدُوْدٰتٍ ۭ
فَمَنْ تَعَجَّلَ فِيْ يَوْمَيْنِ فَلَآ
اِثْمَ عَلَيْهِ ۚ وَمَنْ تَاَخَّرَ فَلَآ اِثْمَ
عَلَيْهِ ۙ لِمَنِ اتَّقٰى ۭ وَاتَّقُوا اللّٰهَ
وَاعْلَمُوْٓا اَنَّكُمْ اِلَيْهِ
تُحْشَرُوْنَ ﴿۲۰۳﴾

204. There is the type of man whose speech about this world's life may dazzle thee, and he calls Allah to witness about what is in his heart; yet is he the most contentious of enemies.

اور کوئی شخص تو ایسا ہے جس کی گفتگو دنیا کی زندگی میں
تم کو دلکش معلوم ہوتی ہے اور وہ اپنے مافی الضمیر
پر خدا کو گواہ بناتا ہے حالانکہ وہ سخت جھگڑالو ہے (۲۰۴)

وَمِنَ النَّاسِ مَنْ يُّعْجِبُكَ قَوْلُهٗ
فِي الْحَيٰوةِ الدُّنْيَا وَيُشْهِدُ اللّٰهَ
عَلٰي مَا فِيْ قَلْبِهٖ ۙ وَهُوَ اَلَدُّ الْخِصَامِ ﴿۲۰۴﴾

205. When he turns his back, his aim everywhere is to spread mischief through the earth and destroy crops and progeny but Allah loveth not mischief.

اور جب پیٹھ پھیر کر چلا جاتا ہے تو زمین میں دوڑتا پھرتا
ہے تاکہ اس میں فتنہ انگیزی کرے اور کھیتی کو (برباد)
اور (انسانوں اور حیوانوں کی) نسل کو نابود کر دے
اور خدا فتنہ انگیزی کو پسند نہیں کرتا (۲۰۵)

وَاِذَا تَوَلّٰى سَعٰى فِي الْاَرْضِ
لِيُفْسِدَ فِيْهَا وَيُهْلِكَ
الْحَرْثَ وَالنَّسْلَ ۭ وَاللّٰهُ لَا
يُحِبُّ الْفَسَادَ ﴿۲۰۵﴾

206. When it is said to him, "Fear Allah," he is led by arrogance to (more) crime. Enough for him is Hell;—an evil bed indeed (to lie on)!

اور جب اس سے کہا جاتا ہے کہ خدا سے خوف کر تو غرور
اس کو گناہ میں پھنسا دیتا ہے سو ایسے کو جہنم سزاوار ہے
اور وہ بہت برا ٹھکانا ہے (۲۰۶)

وَاِذَا قِيْلَ لَهُ اتَّقِ اللّٰهَ اَخَذَتْهُ
الْعِزَّةُ بِالْاِثْمِ فَحَسْبُهٗ جَهَنَّمُ ۭ
وَلَبِئْسَ الْمِهَادُ ﴿۲۰۶﴾

207. And there is the type of man who gives his life to earn the pleasure of Allah; and Allah is full of kindness to (His) devotees.

اور کوئی شخص ایسا ہے کہ خدا کی خوشنودی حاصل
کرنے کے لئے اپنی جان بیچ ڈالتا ہے۔ اور خدا
بندوں پر بہت مہربان ہے (۲۰۷)

وَمِنَ النَّاسِ مَنْ يَّشْرِيْ نَفْسَهُ
ابْتِغَاۗءَ مَرْضَاتِ اللّٰهِ ۭ وَاللّٰهُ
رَءُوْفٌۢ بِالْعِبَادِ ﴿۲۰۷﴾

208. O ye who believe ! enter into Islam whole-heartedly; and follow

مومنو! اسلام میں پورے پورے داخل ہو جاؤ

يٰٓاَيُّهَا الَّذِيْنَ اٰمَنُوا ادْخُلُوْا فِي

not the footsteps of the Satan for he is to you an avowed enemy.

اور شیطان کے پیچھے نہ چلو۔ وہ تو تمہارا صریح دشمن ہے ﴿۲۰۸﴾

السِّلْمِ كَافَّةً ۖ وَلَا تَتَّبِعُوا خُطُوٰتِ
الشَّيْطٰنِ ۚ إِنَّهُ لَكُمْ عَدُوٌّ مُّبِينٌ ﴿٢٠٨﴾

209. If ye backslide after the clear (Signs) have come to you, then know that Allah is Exalted in Power, Wise.

پھر اگر تم احکام روشن پہنچ جانے کے بعد لڑکھڑا جاؤ تو جان رکھو کہ خدا غالب (اور) حکمت والا ہے ﴿۲۰۹﴾

فَإِن زَلَلْتُم مِّن بَعْدِ مَا جَآءَتْكُمُ الْبَيِّنٰتُ
فَاعْلَمُوٓا أَنَّ اللّٰهَ عَزِيزٌ حَكِيمٌ ﴿٢٠٩﴾

210. Will they wait until Allah comes to them in canopies of clouds, with angels (in His train) and the question is (thus) settled? But to Allah do all questions go back (for decision).

کیا یہ لوگ اسی بات کے منتظر ہیں کہ ان پر خدا (کا عذاب) بادل کے سائبانوں میں آنازل ہو اور فرشتے بھی (اتر آئیں) اور کام تمام کر دیا جائے۔ اور سب کاموں کا رجوع خدا ہی کی طرف ہے ﴿۲۱۰﴾

هَلْ يَنظُرُونَ إِلَّآ أَن يَأْتِيَهُمُ اللّٰهُ
فِي ظُلَلٍ مِّنَ الْغَمَامِ وَالْمَلٰٓئِكَةُ
وَقُضِيَ الْأَمْرُ ۚ وَإِلَى اللّٰهِ تُرْجَعُ
الْأُمُورُ ﴿٢١٠﴾ ع ۲۵

211. Ask the Children of Israel how many clear (Signs) We have sent them. But if anyone, after Allah's favour has come to him, substitutes (something else), Allah is strict in punishment.

(اے محمد) بنی اسرائیل سے پوچھو کہ ہم نے ان کو کتنی کھلی نشانیاں دیں اور جو شخص خدا کی نعمت کو اپنے پاس آنے کے بعد بدل دے تو خدا سخت عذاب کرنے والا ہے ﴿۲۱۱﴾

سَلْ بَنِيٓ إِسْرَآءِيلَ كَمْ ءَاتَيْنٰهُم
مِّنْ ءَايَةٍۭ بَيِّنَةٍ ۗ وَمَن يُبَدِّلْ
نِعْمَةَ اللّٰهِ مِنۢ بَعْدِ مَا جَآءَتْهُ
فَإِنَّ اللّٰهَ شَدِيدُ الْعِقَابِ ﴿٢١١﴾

212. The life of this world is alluring to those who reject faith, and they scoff at those who believe. But the righteous will be above them on the Day of Resurrection; for Allah bestows His abundance without measure on whom He will.

اور جو کافر ہیں ان کے لئے دنیا کی زندگی خوشنما کر دی گئی ہے اور وہ مومنوں سے تمسخر کرتے ہیں لیکن جو پرہیزگار ہیں وہ قیامت کے دن ان پر غالب ہوں گے اور خدا جس کو چاہتا ہے بے شمار رزق دیتا ہے ﴿۲۱۲﴾

زُيِّنَ لِلَّذِينَ كَفَرُوا الْحَيٰوةُ
الدُّنْيَا وَيَسْخَرُونَ مِنَ الَّذِينَ
ءَامَنُوا ۘ وَالَّذِينَ اتَّقَوْا فَوْقَهُمْ
يَوْمَ الْقِيٰمَةِ ۗ وَاللّٰهُ يَرْزُقُ مَن
يَشَآءُ بِغَيْرِ حِسَابٍ ﴿٢١٢﴾

213. Mankind was one single nation. And Allah sent Messengers with glad tidings and warnings; and with them He sent the Book in truth, to judge between people in matters wherein they differed; but the People of the Book, after the clear Signs came to them, did not differ among themselves, except through selfish contumacy. Allah by His Grace guided the Believers to the Truth, concerning that wherein they differed. For Allah guides whom He will to a path that is straight.

(پہلے تو سب) لوگوں کا ایک ہی مذہب تھا (لیکن وہ آپس میں اختلاف کرنے لگے) تو خدا نے (ان کی طرف) بشارت دینے والے اور ڈر سنانے والے پیغمبر بھیجے اور ان پر سچائی کے ساتھ کتابیں نازل کیں تاکہ جن امور میں لوگ اختلاف کرتے تھے ان کا ان میں فیصلہ کر دے۔ اور اس میں اختلاف بھی انہیں لوگوں نے کیا جن کو کتاب دی گئی تھی باوجودیکہ ان کے پاس کھلے ہوئے احکام آ چکے تھے (اور یہ اختلاف انہوں نے صرف) آپس کی ضد سے کیا تو جس امر حق میں وہ اختلاف کرتے تھے خدا نے اپنی مہربانی سے مومنوں کو اس کی راہ دکھا دی اور خدا جس کو چاہتا ہے سیدھا رستہ دکھا دیتا ہے ﴿۲۱۳﴾

كَانَ النَّاسُ أُمَّةً وٰحِدَةً فَبَعَثَ
اللّٰهُ النَّبِيّٖنَ مُبَشِّرِينَ وَمُنذِرِينَ
وَأَنزَلَ مَعَهُمُ الْكِتٰبَ بِالْحَقِّ لِيَحْكُمَ
بَيْنَ النَّاسِ فِيمَا اخْتَلَفُوا فِيهِ ۚ
وَمَا اخْتَلَفَ فِيهِ إِلَّا الَّذِينَ
أُوتُوهُ مِنۢ بَعْدِ مَا جَآءَتْهُمُ الْبَيِّنٰتُ
بَغْيًۢا بَيْنَهُمْ ۖ فَهَدَى اللّٰهُ الَّذِينَ
ءَامَنُوا لِمَا اخْتَلَفُوا فِيهِ مِنَ الْحَقِّ
بِإِذْنِهِۦ ۗ وَاللّٰهُ يَهْدِي مَن
يَشَآءُ إِلَىٰ صِرٰطٍ مُّسْتَقِيمٍ ﴿٢١٣﴾

214. Or do ye think that ye shall enter the Garden (of Bliss) without such (trials) as came to those who passed away before you ? They encountered suffering and adversity, and were so shaken in spirit that even the Messenger and those of faith who were with him cried: "When (will come) the help of Allah ?" Ah ! verily, the help of Allah is (always) near !

کیاتم یہ خیال کرتے ہو کہ (یوں ہی) بہشت میں داخل ہو
جاؤ گے اور ابھی تم کو پہلے لوگوں کی سی (مشکلیں) تو پیش
آئی ہی نہیں۔ اُن کو (بڑی بڑی) سختیاں اور تکلیفیں پہنچیں
اور وہ (صعوبتوں میں) ہلا ہلا دیئے گئے یہاں تک کہ پیغمبر اور
مومن لوگ جو اُنکے ساتھ تھے سب پُکار اُٹھے کہ کب خدا کی
مدد آئے گی۔ دیکھو خدا کی مدد (عن) قریب
(آیا چاہتی) ہے ٢١٤

اَمْ حَسِبْتُمْ اَنْ تَدْخُلُوا الْجَنَّةَ
وَلَمَّا يَاْتِكُمْ مَّثَلُ الَّذِيْنَ خَلَوْا
مِنْ قَبْلِكُمْ ؕ مَسَّتْهُمُ الْبَاْسَآءُ
وَالضَّرَّآءُ وَزُلْزِلُوْا حَتّٰى يَقُوْلَ
الرَّسُوْلُ وَالَّذِيْنَ اٰمَنُوْا مَعَهٗ
مَتٰى نَصْرُ اللّٰهِ ؕ اَلَآ اِنَّ نَصْرَ اللّٰهِ
قَرِيْبٌ ٢١٤

215. They ask thee what they should spend (in charity). Say: Whatever wealth ye spend that is good, is for parents and kindred and orphans and those in want and for wayfarers. And whatever ye do that is good,—Allah knoweth it well.

(اے محمد) لوگ تم سے پُوچھتے ہیں کہ (خدا کی راہ میں)
کس طرح کا مال خرچ کریں۔ کہہ دو کہ (جو چاہو خرچ
کرو لیکن) جو مال خرچ کرنا چاہو وہ (درجہ بدرجہ اہلِ
استحقاق یعنی) ماں باپ کو اور قریب کے رشتہ داروں کو اور یتیموں
کو اور محتاجوں کو اور مسافروں کو (سب کو دو) اور جو
بھلائی تم کرو گے خدا اُس کو جانتا ہے ٢١٥

يَسْـَٔلُوْنَكَ مَاذَا يُنْفِقُوْنَ ؕ قُلْ
مَآ اَنْفَقْتُمْ مِّنْ خَيْرٍ
فَلِلْوَالِدَيْنِ وَالْاَقْرَبِيْنَ
وَالْيَتٰمٰى وَالْمَسٰكِيْنِ وَابْنِ
السَّبِيْلِ ؕ وَمَا تَفْعَلُوْا مِنْ خَيْرٍ
فَاِنَّ اللّٰهَ بِهٖ عَلِيْمٌ ٢١٥

216. Fighting is prescribed upon you, and ye dislike it. But it is possible that ye dislike a thing which is good for you, and that ye love a thing which is bad for you. But Allah knoweth, and ye know not.

(مُسلمانو) تم پر (خدا کے رستے میں) لڑنا فرض کر دیا
گیا ہے وہ تمہیں ناگوار تو ہوگا مگر عجب نہیں کہ
ایک چیز تم کو بُری لگے اور وہ تمہارے حق میں
بھلی ہو۔ اور عجب نہیں کہ ایک چیز تم کو بھلی لگے
اور وہ تمہارے لئے مضر ہو اور (ان باتوں کو) خدا ہی
بہتر جانتا ہے اور تم نہیں جانتے ٢١٦

كُتِبَ عَلَيْكُمُ الْقِتَالُ وَهُوَ
كُرْهٌ لَّكُمْ ۚ وَعَسٰٓى اَنْ تَكْرَهُوْا
شَيْـًٔا وَّهُوَ خَيْرٌ لَّكُمْ ۚ وَعَسٰٓى
اَنْ تُحِبُّوْا شَيْـًٔا وَّهُوَ شَرٌّ
لَّكُمْ ؕ وَاللّٰهُ يَعْلَمُ وَاَنْتُمْ
لَا تَعْلَمُوْنَ ٢١٦ ع ٢٦ ١٠

217. They ask thee concerning fighting in the Prohibited Month. Say: "Fighting therein is a grave (offence); but graver is it in the sight of Allah to prevent access to the path of Allah, to deny Him, to prevent access to the Sacred Mosque, and drive out its members." Tumult and oppression are worse than slaughter. Nor will they cease fighting you until they turn you back from your faith if they

(اے محمد) لوگ تم سے عزت والے مہینوں میں لڑائی
کرنیکے بارے میں دریافت کرتے ہیں۔ کہدو کہ ان میں
لڑنا بڑا (گناہ) ہے۔ اور خدا کی راہ سے روکنا اور اس سے کفر
کرنا اور مسجد حرام (یعنی خانہ کعبہ میں جانے) سے (بند کرنا)
اور اہلِ مسجد کو اس میں سے نکال دینا (جو یہ کفار کرتے
ہیں) خدا کے نزدیک اس سے بھی زیادہ (گناہ) ہے۔ اور
فتنہ انگیزی خونریزی سے بھی بڑھ کر ہے۔ اور یہ لوگ ہمیشہ
تم سے لڑتے رہیں گے یہاں تک کہ اگر مقدور

يَسْـَٔلُوْنَكَ عَنِ الشَّهْرِ الْحَرَامِ قِتَالٍ
فِيْهِ ؕ قُلْ قِتَالٌ فِيْهِ كَبِيْرٌ ؕ وَصَدٌّ
عَنْ سَبِيْلِ اللّٰهِ وَكُفْرٌ بِهٖ
وَالْمَسْجِدِ الْحَرَامِ ۗ وَاِخْرَاجُ
اَهْلِهٖ مِنْهُ اَكْبَرُ عِنْدَ اللّٰهِ ۚ
وَالْفِتْنَةُ اَكْبَرُ مِنَ الْقَتْلِ ؕ
وَلَا يَزَالُوْنَ يُقَاتِلُوْنَكُمْ حَتّٰى
يَرُدُّوْكُمْ عَنْ دِيْنِكُمْ اِنِ

can. And if any of you turn back from their faith and die in unbelief, their works will bear no fruit in this life and in the Hereafter: they will be companions of the Fire and will abide therein.

رکھیں تو تم کو تمہارے دین سے پھیر دیں۔
اور جو کوئی تم میں سے اپنے دین سے پھر کر (کافر ہو)
جائے گا اور کافر ہی مرے گا تو ایسے لوگوں کے
اعمال دنیا اور آخرت دونوں میں برباد ہو جائینگے اور
یہی لوگ دوزخ (میں جانے) والے ہیں جسمیں ہمیشہ رہیں گے ﴿٢١٧﴾

اسْتَطَاعُوا ۚ وَمَنْ يَرْتَدِدْ
مِنْكُمْ عَنْ دِينِهِ فَيَمُتْ وَهُوَ
كَافِرٌ فَأُولَٰئِكَ حَبِطَتْ أَعْمَالُهُمْ
فِي الدُّنْيَا وَالْآخِرَةِ ۖ وَأُولَٰئِكَ
أَصْحَابُ النَّارِ ۖ هُمْ فِيهَا خَالِدُونَ ﴿٢١٧﴾

218. Those who believed and those who suffered exile and fought (and strove and struggled) in the path of Allah,—they have the hope of the Mercy of Allah: and Allah is Oft-Forgiving, Most Merciful.

جو لوگ ایمان لائے اور خدا کیلئے وطن چھوڑ گئے اور
(کفار سے) جنگ کرتے رہے وہی خدا کی رحمت کے
اُمیدوار ہیں اور خدا بخشنے والا (اور) رحمت کرنیوالا ہے ﴿٢١٨﴾

إِنَّ الَّذِينَ آمَنُوا وَالَّذِينَ هَاجَرُوا
وَجَاهَدُوا فِي سَبِيلِ اللَّهِ أُولَٰئِكَ
يَرْجُونَ رَحْمَتَ اللَّهِ ۚ وَاللَّهُ غَفُورٌ رَحِيمٌ ﴿٢١٨﴾

219. They ask thee concerning wine and gambling. Say: "In them is great sin, and some profit, for men; but the sin is greater than the profit." They ask thee how much they are to spend; say: "What is beyond your needs." Thus doth Allah make clear to you His Signs: in order that ye may consider—

اے پیغمبر لوگ تم سے شراب اور جُوئے کا حکم
دریافت کرتے ہیں کہدو کہ ان میں نقصان بڑے ہیں
اور لوگوں کیلئے کچھ فائدے بھی ہیں مگر انکے نقصان
فائدوں سے کہیں زیادہ ہیں۔ اور یہ بھی تم سے پوچھتے ہیں
کہ (خدا کی راہ میں) کونسا مال خرچ کریں کہدو کہ جو
ضرورت سے زیادہ ہو۔ اس طرح خدا تمہارے لئے اپنے
احکام کھول کھول کر بیان فرماتا ہے تاکہ تم سوچو ﴿٢١٩﴾

يَسْأَلُونَكَ عَنِ الْخَمْرِ وَالْمَيْسِرِ ۖ
قُلْ فِيهِمَا إِثْمٌ كَبِيرٌ وَمَنَافِعُ
لِلنَّاسِ وَإِثْمُهُمَا أَكْبَرُ مِنْ
نَفْعِهِمَا ۗ وَيَسْأَلُونَكَ مَاذَا
يُنْفِقُونَ قُلِ الْعَفْوَ ۗ كَذَٰلِكَ
يُبَيِّنُ اللَّهُ لَكُمُ الْآيَاتِ
لَعَلَّكُمْ تَتَفَكَّرُونَ ﴿٢١٩﴾

220. (Their bearings) on this life and the Hereafter. They ask thee concerning orphans. Say: "The best thing to do is what is for their good; if ye mix their affairs with yours, they are your brethren; but Allah knows the man who means mischief from the man who means good. And if Allah had wished, He could have put you into difficulties: He is indeed exalted in Power, Wise."

(یعنی) دنیا اور آخرت (کی باتوں) میں غور کرو۔ اور تم سے
یتیموں کے بارے میں بھی دریافت کرتے ہیں کہدو کہ انکی (حالت کی)
اصلاح بہت اچھا کام ہے اور اگر تم انسے مل جلکر رہنا (یعنی خرچ
اکٹھا رکھنا) چاہو تو وہ تمہارے بھائی ہیں اور خدا خوب جانتا
ہے کہ خرابی کرنیوالا کون ہے اور اصلاح کرنیوالا کون۔ اور اگر خدا چاہتا
تو تمکو تکلیف میں ڈالدیتا۔ بیشک خدا غالب (اور) حکمت والا ہے ﴿٢٢٠﴾

فِي الدُّنْيَا وَالْآخِرَةِ ۗ وَيَسْأَلُونَكَ
عَنِ الْيَتَامَىٰ ۖ قُلْ إِصْلَاحٌ لَهُمْ
خَيْرٌ ۖ وَإِنْ تُخَالِطُوهُمْ
فَإِخْوَانُكُمْ ۚ وَاللَّهُ يَعْلَمُ الْمُفْسِدَ
مِنَ الْمُصْلِحِ ۚ وَلَوْ شَاءَ اللَّهُ
لَأَعْنَتَكُمْ ۚ إِنَّ اللَّهَ عَزِيزٌ حَكِيمٌ ﴿٢٢٠﴾

221. Do not marry unbelieving woman until they believe: a slave woman who believes is better than an unbelieving woman, even though she allure you. Nor marry (your girls) to unbelievers until they believe: a man slave who believes is better than an unbeliever, even though he allure you. Unbelievers do (but) beckon you to the Fire. But Allah

اور (مومنو) مشرک عورتوں سے جب تک کہ ایمان نہ لائیں نکاح
نہ کرنا کیونکہ مشرک عورت خواہ تم کو کیسی ہی بھلی لگے اُس
سے مومن لونڈی بہتر ہے۔ اور (اسی طرح) مشرک مرد جب تک
ایمان نہ لائیں مومن عورتوں کو اُن کی زوجیت میں
نہ دینا۔ کیونکہ مشرک (مرد) سے خواہ وہ تمکو کیسا ہی
بھلا لگے مومن غلام بہتر ہے یہ (مشرک لوگوں کو) دوزخ

وَلَا تَنْكِحُوا الْمُشْرِكَاتِ حَتَّىٰ يُؤْمِنَّ ۚ
وَلَأَمَةٌ مُؤْمِنَةٌ خَيْرٌ مِنْ
مُشْرِكَةٍ وَلَوْ أَعْجَبَتْكُمْ ۗ وَلَا
تُنْكِحُوا الْمُشْرِكِينَ حَتَّىٰ يُؤْمِنُوا ۚ
وَلَعَبْدٌ مُؤْمِنٌ خَيْرٌ مِنْ مُشْرِكٍ
وَلَوْ أَعْجَبَكُمْ ۗ أُولَٰئِكَ يَدْعُونَ إِلَى

النَّارِ ۖ وَاللّٰهُ يَدْعُوٓا اِلَى الْجَنَّةِ وَ
الْمَغْفِرَةِ بِاِذْنِهٖ ۚ وَيُبَيِّنُ اٰيٰتِهٖ
لِلنَّاسِ لَعَلَّهُمْ يَتَذَكَّرُوْنَ ﴿٢٢١﴾ ع ٢٧ ٥

کی طرف بُلاتے ہیں۔ اور خدا اپنی مہربانی سے بہشت
اور بخشش کی طرف بُلاتا ہے۔ اور اپنے حکم لوگوں سے کھول
کھولکر بیان کرتا ہے تاکہ نصیحت حاصل کریں ﴿٢٢١﴾

beckons by His Grace to the Garden (of Bliss) and forgiveness. And makes His Signs clear to mankind: that they may receive admonition.

وَيَسْـَٔلُوْنَكَ عَنِ الْمَحِيْضِ ۭ قُلْ
هُوَ اَذًى ۙ فَاعْتَزِلُوا النِّسَاۗءَ فِي
الْمَحِيْضِ ۙ وَلَا تَقْرَبُوْهُنَّ حَتّٰى
يَطْهُرْنَ ۚ فَاِذَا تَطَهَّرْنَ
فَاْتُوْهُنَّ مِنْ حَيْثُ اَمَرَكُمُ
اللّٰهُ ۭ اِنَّ اللّٰهَ يُحِبُّ التَّوَّابِيْنَ
وَيُحِبُّ الْمُتَطَهِّرِيْنَ ﴿٢٢٢﴾

اور تم سے حیض کے بارے میں دریافت کرتے ہیں کہدو
وہ تو نجاست ہے سو ایّامِ حیض میں عورتوں سے
کنارہ کش رہو۔ اور جب تک پاک نہ ہو جائیں اُن
سے مقاربت نہ کرو۔ ہاں جب پاک ہو جائیں تو جس
طریق سے خدا نے تمہیں ارشاد فرمایا ہے اُن کے پاس جاؤ
کچھ شک نہیں کہ خدا توبہ کرنے والوں اور پاک صاف
رہنے والوں کو دوست رکھتا ہے ﴿٢٢٢﴾

222. They ask thee concerning women's courses. Say: They are a hurt and a pollution: so keep away from women in their courses, and do not approach them until they are clean. But when they have purified themselves, ye may approach them as ordained for you by Allah for Allah loves those who turn to Him constantly and He loves those who keep themselves pure and clean.

نِسَاۗؤُكُمْ حَرْثٌ لَّكُمْ ۠ فَاْتُوْا
حَرْثَكُمْ اَنّٰى شِئْتُمْ ۡ وَقَدِّمُوْا
لِاَنْفُسِكُمْ ۭ وَاتَّقُوا اللّٰهَ وَاعْلَمُوْٓا
اَنَّكُمْ مُّلٰقُوْهُ ۭ وَبَشِّرِ
الْمُؤْمِنِيْنَ ﴿٢٢٣﴾

تمہاری عورتیں تمہاری کھیتی ہیں تو اپنی کھیتی میں
جس طرح چاہو جاؤ۔ اور اپنے لئے (نیک عمل) آگے
بھیجو۔ اور خدا سے ڈرتے رہو اور جان رکھو کہ (ایک
دن) تمہیں اسکے رُوبرو حاضر ہونا ہے ف٥٥ اور (اے پیغمبر)
ایمان والوں کو بشارت سُنادو ﴿٢٢٣﴾

223. Your wives are as a tilth unto you, so approach your tilth when or how ye will; but do some good act for your souls beforehand; and fear Allah, and know that ye are to meet Him (in the Hereafter), and give (these) good tidings to those who believe.

وَلَا تَجْعَلُوا اللّٰهَ عُرْضَةً لِّاَيْمَانِكُمْ
اَنْ تَبَرُّوْا وَتَتَّقُوْا وَتُصْلِحُوْا
بَيْنَ النَّاسِ ۭ وَاللّٰهُ سَمِيْعٌ عَلِيْمٌ ﴿٢٢٤﴾

اور خدا (کے نام) کو اس بات کا حیلہ نہ بنانا کہ (اُسکی)
قسمیں کھا کھا کر سلوک کرنے اور پرہیزگاری کرنے اور
لوگوں میں صلح و سازگاری کرانے سے رک جاؤ۔ اور خدا سب کچھ سنتا اور جانتا ہے ف٥٦ ﴿٢٢٤﴾

224. And make not Allah's (name) an excuse in your oaths against doing good, or acting rightly, or making peace between persons; for Allah is one Who heareth and knoweth all things.

لَا يُؤَاخِذُكُمُ اللّٰهُ بِاللَّغْوِ فِيْٓ اَيْمَانِكُمْ
وَلٰكِنْ يُّؤَاخِذُكُمْ بِمَا كَسَبَتْ
قُلُوْبُكُمْ ۭ وَاللّٰهُ غَفُوْرٌ حَلِيْمٌ ﴿٢٢٥﴾

خدا تمہاری لغو قسموں پر تم سے مواخذہ نہیں کرے گا۔
لیکن جو قسمیں تم قصدِ دلی سے کھاؤ گے اُن پر مواخذہ
کریگا اور خدا بخشنے والا بُردبار ہے ف٥٧ ﴿٢٢٥﴾

225. Allah will not call you to account for thoughtlessness in your oaths, but for the intention in your hearts, and He is Oft-Forgiving Most Forbearing.

لِلَّذِيْنَ يُؤْلُوْنَ مِنْ نِّسَاۗىِٕهِمْ
تَرَبُّصُ اَرْبَعَةِ اَشْهُرٍ ۚ فَاِنْ فَاۗءُوْ
فَاِنَّ اللّٰهَ غَفُوْرٌ رَّحِيْمٌ ﴿٢٢٦﴾

جو لوگ اپنی عورتوں کے پاس جانے کی قسم کھالیں اُن
کو چار مہینے انتظار کرنا چاہیئے اگر (اس عرصے میں قسم سے)
رجوع کرلیں تو خدا بخشنے والا مہربان ہے ﴿٢٢٦﴾

226. For those who take an oath for abstention from their wives, a waiting for four months is ordained; if then they return, Allah is Oft-Forgiving, Most Merciful.

وَاِنْ عَزَمُوا الطَّلَاقَ فَاِنَّ اللّٰهَ
سَمِيْعٌ عَلِيْمٌ ﴿٢٢٧﴾

اور اگر طلاق کا ارادہ کرلیں تو بھی خدا سُنتا (اور)
جانتا ہے ﴿٢٢٧﴾

227. But if their intention is firm for divorce, Allah heareth and knoweth all things.

وَالْمُطَلَّقٰتُ يَتَرَبَّصْنَ بِاَنْفُسِهِنَّ

اور طلاق والی عورتیں تین حیض تک ف٥٨ اپنے تئیں روکے

228. Divorced women shall wait concerning themselves for three

monthly periods. And it is not lawful for them to hide what Allah hath created in their wombs, if they have faith in Allah and the Last Day. And their husbands have the better right to take them back in that period, if they wish for reconciliation. And women shall have rights similar to the rights against them, according to what is equitable; but men have a degree over them and Allah is Exalted in Power, Wise.

229. A divorce is only permissible twice; after that, the parties should either hold together on equitable terms, or separate with kindness. It is not lawful for you, (men), to take back any of your gifts (from your wives), except when both parties fear that they would be unable to keep the limits ordained by Allah if ye (judges) do indeed fear that they would be unable to keep the limits ordained by Allah, there is no blame on either of them if she give something for her freedom, these are the limits ordained by Allah; so do not transgress them if any do transgress the limits ordained by Allah, such persons wrong (themselves as well as others).

230. So if a husband divorces his wife (irrevocably), he cannot, after that, re-marry her until after she has married another husband and he has divorced her. In that case there is no blame on either of them if they re-unite, provided they feel that they can keep the limits ordained by Allah. Such are the limits ordained by Allah, which He makes plain to those who know.

231. When ye divorce women, and they (are about to) fulfil the term of their *('Iddat)*, either take them back on equitable terms or set them free on equitable terms: but do not take

رہیں اور اگر وہ خدا اور روزِ قیامت پر
ایمان رکھتی ہیں تو اُن کو جائز نہیں کہ خدا نے
جو کچھ اُن کے شکم میں پیدا کیا ہے اُس کو چھپائیں
اور اُن کے خاوند اگر پھر موافقت چاہیں تو اس (مدت)
میں وہ اُن کو اپنی زوجیت میں لے لینے کے زیادہ حقدار
ہیں اور عورتوں کا حق (مردوں پر) ویسا ہی ہے جیسے دستور
کے مطابق (مردوں کا حق) عورتوں پر ہے البتہ مردوں کو
عورتوں پر فضیلت ہے اور خدا غالب (اور) صاحبِ حکمت ہے ﴿۲۲۸﴾
طلاق (صرف) دو بار ہے (یعنی جب دو دفعہ طلاق دیدی جائے تو) پھر
(عورتوں کو) یا تو بطریق شائستہ (نکاح میں) رہنے دینا ہے یا بھلائی
کے ساتھ چھوڑ دینا۔ اور یہ جائز نہیں کہ جو مہر تم انکو دے چکے ہو
اس میں سے کچھ واپس لے لو۔ ہاں اگر زن و شوہر کو خوف ہو کہ وہ خدا کی
حدوں کو قائم نہیں رکھ سکیں گے تو اگر عورت (خاوند کے ہاتھ سے)
رہائی پانے کے بدلے میں کچھ دے ڈالے تو دونوں پر کچھ
گناہ نہیں یہ خدا کی (مقرر کی ہوئی) حدیں ہیں اُن سے
باہر نہ نکلنا۔ اور جو لوگ خدا کی حدوں سے باہر نکل جائینگے
وہ گنہگار ہوں گے ﴿۲۲۹﴾
پھر اگر شوہر (دو طلاقوں کے بعد تیسری) طلاق عورت کو دیدے
تو اسکے بعد جب تک عورت کسی دوسرے شخص سے نکاح نہ کر لے اس (پہلے
شوہر) پر حلال نہ ہوگی۔ ہاں اگر دوسرا خاوند بھی طلاق دیدے اور عورت
اور پہلا خاوند پھر ایک دوسرے کیطرف رجوع کر لیں تو ان پر کچھ گناہ
نہیں بشرطیکہ دونوں یقین کریں کہ خدا کی حدوں کو قائم رکھ سکینگے
اور یہ خدا کی حدیں ہیں انکو وہ ان لوگوں کیلئے بیان فرماتا ہے
جو دانش رکھتے ہیں ﴿۲۳۰﴾
اور جب تم عورتوں کو (دو دفعہ) طلاق دے چکو اور انکی
عدت پوری ہو جائے تو اُنہیں یا تو حسنِ سلوک سے
نکاح میں رہنے دو یا بطریق شائستہ رخصت کر دو۔ اور

ثَلٰثَةَ قُرُوْٓءٍ ؕ وَلَا يَحِلُّ لَهُنَّ اَنْ
يَّكْتُمْنَ مَا خَلَقَ اللّٰهُ فِيْٓ اَرْحَامِهِنَّ
اِنْ كُنَّ يُؤْمِنَّ بِاللّٰهِ وَالْيَوْمِ الْاٰخِرِ ؕ
وَبُعُوْلَتُهُنَّ اَحَقُّ بِرَدِّهِنَّ فِيْ ذٰلِكَ
اِنْ اَرَادُوْٓا اِصْلَاحًا ؕ وَلَهُنَّ مِثْلُ
الَّذِيْ عَلَيْهِنَّ بِالْمَعْرُوْفِ ۪ وَلِلرِّجَالِ
عَلَيْهِنَّ دَرَجَةٌ ؕ وَاللّٰهُ عَزِيْزٌ
حَكِيْمٌ ﴿٢٢٨﴾ ع ٧ ١٤
اَلطَّلَاقُ مَرَّتٰنِ ۪ فَاِمْسَاكٌۢ بِمَعْرُوْفٍ
اَوْ تَسْرِيْحٌۢ بِاِحْسَانٍ ؕ وَلَا يَحِلُّ لَكُمْ
اَنْ تَاْخُذُوْا مِمَّآ اٰتَيْتُمُوْهُنَّ شَيْـًٔا
اِلَّآ اَنْ يَّخَافَآ اَلَّا يُقِيْمَا حُدُوْدَ اللّٰهِ ؕ
فَاِنْ خِفْتُمْ اَلَّا يُقِيْمَا حُدُوْدَ اللّٰهِ ۙ
فَلَا جُنَاحَ عَلَيْهِمَا فِيْمَا افْتَدَتْ
بِهٖ ؕ تِلْكَ حُدُوْدُ اللّٰهِ فَلَا تَعْتَدُوْهَا ۚ
وَمَنْ يَّتَعَدَّ حُدُوْدَ اللّٰهِ فَاُولٰٓئِكَ
هُمُ الظّٰلِمُوْنَ ﴿٢٢٩﴾
فَاِنْ طَلَّقَهَا فَلَا تَحِلُّ لَهٗ مِنْۢ بَعْدُ
حَتّٰى تَنْكِحَ زَوْجًا غَيْرَهٗ ؕ فَاِنْ
طَلَّقَهَا فَلَا جُنَاحَ عَلَيْهِمَآ اَنْ
يَّتَرَاجَعَآ اِنْ ظَنَّآ اَنْ يُّقِيْمَا
حُدُوْدَ اللّٰهِ ؕ وَتِلْكَ حُدُوْدُ
اللّٰهِ يُبَيِّنُهَا لِقَوْمٍ
يَّعْلَمُوْنَ ﴿٢٣٠﴾
وَاِذَا طَلَّقْتُمُ النِّسَآءَ فَبَلَغْنَ
اَجَلَهُنَّ فَاَمْسِكُوْهُنَّ بِمَعْرُوْفٍ
اَوْ سَرِّحُوْهُنَّ بِمَعْرُوْفٍ ۪ وَلَا

تُمْسِكُوهُنَّ ضِرَارًا لِّتَعْتَدُوا ۚ وَمَن
يَفْعَلْ ذَٰلِكَ فَقَدْ ظَلَمَ نَفْسَهُ ۚ
وَلَا تَتَّخِذُوا آيَاتِ اللَّهِ هُزُوًا ۚ وَّ
اذْكُرُوا نِعْمَتَ اللَّهِ عَلَيْكُمْ وَمَا
أَنزَلَ عَلَيْكُم مِّنَ الْكِتَابِ وَالْحِكْمَةِ
يَعِظُكُم بِهِ ۚ وَاتَّقُوا اللَّهَ وَاعْلَمُوا
أَنَّ اللَّهَ بِكُلِّ شَيْءٍ عَلِيمٌ ﴿٢٣١﴾

اس نیت سے اُنکو نکاح میں نہ رہنے دینا چاہیئے کہ اُنہیں
تکلیف دو اور اُن پر زیادتی کرو۔ اور جو ایسا کریگا وہ اپنا
ہی نقصان کریگا اور خدا کے احکام کو ہنسی (اور کھیل)
نہ بناؤ اور خدا نے تم کو جو نعمتیں بخشی ہیں اور تم پر جو کتاب
اور دانائی کی باتیں نازل کی ہیں جن سے وہ تمہیں نصیحت
فرماتا ہے اُن کو یاد کرو۔ اور خدا سے ڈرتے رہو اور جان رکھو
کہ خدا ہر چیز سے واقف ہے ﴿۲۳۱﴾

them back to injure them, (or) to take undue advantage; if anyone does that, he wrongs his own soul. Do not treat Allah's Signs as a jest, but solemnly rehearse Allah's favours on you, and the fact that He sent down to you the Book and Wisdom, for your instruction. And fear Allah, and know that Allah is well acquainted with all things.

وَإِذَا طَلَّقْتُمُ النِّسَاءَ فَبَلَغْنَ
أَجَلَهُنَّ فَلَا تَعْضُلُوهُنَّ أَن
يَنكِحْنَ أَزْوَاجَهُنَّ إِذَا تَرَاضَوْا
بَيْنَهُم بِالْمَعْرُوفِ ۗ ذَٰلِكَ يُوعَظُ
بِهِ مَن كَانَ مِنكُمْ يُؤْمِنُ بِاللَّهِ
وَالْيَوْمِ الْآخِرِ ۗ ذَٰلِكُمْ أَزْكَىٰ لَكُمْ
وَأَطْهَرُ ۗ وَاللَّهُ يَعْلَمُ وَأَنتُمْ لَا تَعْلَمُونَ ﴿٢٣٢﴾

اور جب تم عورتوں کو طلاق دے چکو اور اُن کی عدّت
پوری ہو جائے تو اُن کو دوسرے شوہروں کے ساتھ جب وہ
آپس میں جائز طور پر راضی ہو جائیں نکاح کرنے سے مت
روکو۔ اس (حکم) سے اُس شخص کو نصیحت کی جاتی ہے
جو تم میں خدا اور روزِ آخرت پر یقین رکھتا ہے۔ یہ
تمہارے لئے نہایت خوب اور بہت پاکیزگی کی بات
ہے۔ اور خدا جانتا ہے اور تم نہیں جانتے ﴿۲۳۲﴾

232. When ye divorce women, and they fulfil the term of their *('Iddat),* do not prevent them from marrying their (former) husbands, if they mutually agree on equitable terms. This instruction is for all amongst you, who believe in Allah and the Last Day. That is (the course making for) most virtue and purity amongst you. And Allah knows, and ye know not.

وَالْوَالِدَاتُ يُرْضِعْنَ أَوْلَادَهُنَّ
حَوْلَيْنِ كَامِلَيْنِ ۖ لِمَنْ أَرَادَ أَن
يُتِمَّ الرَّضَاعَةَ ۚ وَعَلَى الْمَوْلُودِ لَهُ
رِزْقُهُنَّ وَكِسْوَتُهُنَّ بِالْمَعْرُوفِ ۚ
لَا تُكَلَّفُ نَفْسٌ إِلَّا وُسْعَهَا ۚ لَا تُضَارَّ
وَالِدَةٌ بِوَلَدِهَا وَلَا مَوْلُودٌ لَّهُ
بِوَلَدِهِ ۚ وَعَلَى الْوَارِثِ مِثْلُ ذَٰلِكَ ۗ
فَإِنْ أَرَادَا فِصَالًا عَن تَرَاضٍ مِّنْهُمَا
وَتَشَاوُرٍ فَلَا جُنَاحَ عَلَيْهِمَا ۗ وَإِنْ
أَرَدتُّمْ أَن تَسْتَرْضِعُوا أَوْلَادَكُمْ
فَلَا جُنَاحَ عَلَيْكُمْ إِذَا سَلَّمْتُم
مَّا آتَيْتُم بِالْمَعْرُوفِ ۗ وَاتَّقُوا
اللَّهَ وَاعْلَمُوا أَنَّ اللَّهَ بِمَا

اور مائیں اپنے بچّوں کو پورے دو سال دُودھ پلائیں
یہ (حکم) اُس شخص کے لئے ہے جو پوری مدّت تک
دُودھ پلوانا چاہے اور دُودھ پلانے والی ماؤں کا کھانا اور
کپڑا دستور کے مطابق باپ کے ذمّے ہوگا۔ کسی شخص
کو اُس کی طاقت سے زیادہ تکلیف نہیں دی جاتی (تو
یاد رکھو کہ) نہ تو ماں کو اُس کے بچے کے سبب نقصان
پہنچایا جائے اور نہ باپ کو اُس کی اولاد کی وجہ سے
نقصان پہنچایا جائے اور اسی طرح (نان نفقہ) بچے
کے وارث کے ذمّے ہے۔ اور اگر دونوں (یعنی ماں باپ)
آپس کی رضامندی اور صلاح سے بچے کا دُودھ چھڑانا چاہیں
تو اُن پر کچھ گناہ نہیں۔ اور اگر تم اپنی اولاد کو دُودھ پلوانا
چاہو تو تم پر کچھ گناہ نہیں بشرطیکہ تم دُودھ پلانے والیوں کو
دستور کے مطابق اُنکا حق جو تم نے دینا کیا تھا دیدو۔ اور خدا سے

233. The mothers shall give suck to their offspring for two whole years, for him who desires to complete the term. But he shall bear the cost of their food and clothing on equitable terms. No soul shall have a burden laid on it greater than it can bear. No mother shall be treated unfairly on account of her child. Nor father on account of his child, an heir shall be chargeable in the same way, if they both decide on weaning, by mutual consent, and after due consultation, there is no blame on them. If ye decide on a foster-mother for your offspring there is no blame on you, provided ye pay (the foster mother) what ye offered, on equitable terms. But fear Allah and know that Allah

sees well what ye do.

ڈرتے رہو اور جان رکھو کہ جو کچھ تم کرتے ہو خدا اُس کو دیکھ رہا ہے (۲۳۳)

تَعْمَلُونَ بَصِيرٌ ﴿٢٣٣﴾

234. If any of you die and leave widows behind; they shall wait concerning themselves four months and ten days when they have fulfilled their term, there is no blame on you if they dispose of themselves in a just and reasonable manner. And Allah is well acquainted with what ye do.

اور جو لوگ تم میں سے مر جائیں اور عورتیں چھوڑ جائیں تو
عورتیں چار مہینے اور دس دن اپنے آپ کو روکے رہیں
اور جب (یہ) عدت پوری کر چکیں اور اپنے حق میں
پسندیدہ کام (یعنی نکاح) کر لیں تو تم پر کچھ
گناہ نہیں۔ اور خدا تمہارے سب کاموں سے
واقف ہے (۲۳۴)

وَالَّذِينَ يُتَوَفَّوْنَ مِنكُمْ وَ
يَذَرُونَ أَزْوَاجًا يَتَرَبَّصْنَ
بِأَنفُسِهِنَّ أَرْبَعَةَ أَشْهُرٍ وَعَشْرًا
فَإِذَا بَلَغْنَ أَجَلَهُنَّ فَلَا جُنَاحَ
عَلَيْكُمْ فِيمَا فَعَلْنَ فِي أَنفُسِهِنَّ
بِالْمَعْرُوفِ وَاللَّهُ بِمَا تَعْمَلُونَ خَبِيرٌ ﴿٢٣٤﴾

235. There is no blame on you if ye make an indirect offer of betrothal or hold it in your hearts. Allah knows that ye cherish them in your hearts: but do not make a secret contract with them except that you speak to them in terms honourable, nor resolve on the tie of marriage till the term prescribed is fulfilled. And know that Allah knoweth what is in your hearts, and take heed of Him; and know that Allah is Oft-Forgiving. Most Forbearing.

اگر تم کنائے کی باتوں میں عورتوں کو نکاح کا پیغام
بھیجو یا (نکاح کی خواہش کو) اپنے دلوں میں مخفی رکھو
تو تم پر کچھ گناہ نہیں۔ خدا کو معلوم ہے کہ تم اُن سے
(نکاح کا) ذکر کرو گے۔ مگر (ایام عدت میں) اسکے سوا
کہ دستور کے مطابق کوئی بات کہہ دو پوشیدہ طور پر
اُن سے قول و قرار نہ کرنا اور جب تک عدت پوری
نہ ہو لے نکاح کا پختہ ارادہ نہ کرنا اور جان رکھو کہ
جو کچھ تمہارے دلوں میں ہے خدا کو سب معلوم ہے
تو اس سے ڈرتے رہو اور جان رکھو کہ خدا بخشنے
والا (اور) حلم والا ہے (۲۳۵)

وَلَا جُنَاحَ عَلَيْكُمْ فِيمَا عَرَّضْتُم
بِهِ مِنْ خِطْبَةِ النِّسَاءِ أَوْ أَكْنَنتُمْ
فِي أَنفُسِكُمْ عَلِمَ اللَّهُ أَنَّكُمْ
سَتَذْكُرُونَهُنَّ وَلَٰكِن لَّا
تُوَاعِدُوهُنَّ سِرًّا إِلَّا أَن تَقُولُوا
قَوْلًا مَّعْرُوفًا وَلَا تَعْزِمُوا
عُقْدَةَ النِّكَاحِ حَتَّىٰ يَبْلُغَ الْكِتَابُ
أَجَلَهُ وَاعْلَمُوا أَنَّ اللَّهَ يَعْلَمُ
مَا فِي أَنفُسِكُمْ فَاحْذَرُوهُ وَ
اعْلَمُوا أَنَّ اللَّهَ غَفُورٌ حَلِيمٌ ﴿٢٣٥﴾ ع

236. There is no blame on you if ye divorce women before consummation or the fixation of their dower; but bestow on them (a suitable gift), the wealthy according to his means, and the poor according to his means;—a gift of a reasonable amount is due from those who wish to do the right thing.

اور اگر تم عورتوں کو اُن کے پاس جانے یا اُن کا مہر
مقرر کرنے سے پہلے طلاق دے دو تو تم پر کچھ گناہ
نہیں۔ ہاں اُن کو دستور کے مطابق کچھ خرچ ضرور دو
(یعنی) مقدور والا اپنے مقدور کے مطابق
دے اور تنگدست اپنی حیثیت کے مطابق۔ نیک
لوگوں پر یہ ایک طرح کا حق ہے (۲۳۶)

لَا جُنَاحَ عَلَيْكُمْ إِن طَلَّقْتُمُ
النِّسَاءَ مَا لَمْ تَمَسُّوهُنَّ أَوْ
تَفْرِضُوا لَهُنَّ فَرِيضَةً وَ
مَتِّعُوهُنَّ عَلَى الْمُوسِعِ قَدَرُهُ
وَعَلَى الْمُقْتِرِ قَدَرُهُ مَتَاعًا
بِالْمَعْرُوفِ حَقًّا عَلَى الْمُحْسِنِينَ ﴿٢٣٦﴾

237. And if ye divorce them before consummation, but after the fixation of a dower for them, then the half of the dower (is due to them), unless they remit it or (the man's half) is remitted by him in whose

اور اگر تم عورتوں کو اُن کے پاس جانے سے پہلے
طلاق دے دو لیکن مہر مقرر کر چکے ہو تو آدھا
مہر دینا ہوگا۔ ہاں اگر عورتیں مہر بخش دیں۔ یا مرد
جن کے ہاتھ میں عقد نکاح ہے (اپنا حق) چھوڑ دیں

وَإِن طَلَّقْتُمُوهُنَّ مِن قَبْلِ
أَن تَمَسُّوهُنَّ وَقَدْ فَرَضْتُمْ
لَهُنَّ فَرِيضَةً فَنِصْفُ مَا فَرَضْتُمْ
إِلَّا أَن يَعْفُونَ أَوْ يَعْفُوَ الَّذِي

بِيَدِهٖ عُقْدَةُ النِّكَاحِ ؕ وَاَنْ
تَعْفُوْٓا اَقْرَبُ لِلتَّقْوٰى ؕ وَلَا تَنْسَوُا
الْفَضْلَ بَيْنَكُمْ ؕ اِنَّ اللّٰهَ بِمَا
تَعْمَلُوْنَ بَصِيْرٌ ﴿٢٣٧﴾

(اور پورا مہر دے دیں تو ان کو اختیار ہے) اور اگر
تم مرد لوگ ہی اپنا حق چھوڑ دو تو یہ پرہیزگاری کی بات
ہے اور آپس میں بھلائی کرنے کو فراموش نہ کرنا کچھ شک
نہیں کہ خدا تمہارے سب کاموں کو دیکھ رہا ہے (۲۳۷)

hands is the marriage tie; and the remission (of the man's half) if the nearest to righteousness. And do not forget liberality between yourselves. For Allah sees well all that ye do.

حٰفِظُوْا عَلَى الصَّلَوٰتِ وَالصَّلٰوةِ
الْوُسْطٰى ۗ وَقُوْمُوْا لِلّٰهِ قٰنِتِيْنَ ﴿٢٣٨﴾

(مسلمانو) سب نمازیں خصوصاً بیچ کی نماز (یعنی نماز عصر) پورے التزام
کیساتھ ادا کرتے رہو اور خدا کے آگے ادب سے کھڑے رہا کرو (۲۳۸)

238. Guard strictly your (habit of) prayers. Especially the Middle Prayer; and stand before Allah in a devout (frame of mind).

فَاِنْ خِفْتُمْ فَرِجَالًا اَوْ رُكْبَانًا ۚ
فَاِذَآ اَمِنْتُمْ فَاذْكُرُوا اللّٰهَ
كَمَا عَلَّمَكُمْ مَّا لَمْ تَكُوْنُوْا
تَعْلَمُوْنَ ﴿٢٣٩﴾

اگر تم خوف کی حالت میں ہو تو پیادے یا سوار (جس
حال میں ہو نماز پڑھ لو) پھر جب امن (و اطمینان)
ہو جائے تو جس طریق سے خدا نے تم کو سکھایا ہے جو تم
پہلے نہیں جانتے تھے خدا کو یاد کرو (۲۳۹)

239. If ye fear (an enemy), pray on foot, or riding, (as may be most convenient), but when ye are in security, celebrate Allah's praises in the manner He has taught you, which ye knew not (before).

وَالَّذِيْنَ يُتَوَفَّوْنَ مِنْكُمْ وَ
يَذَرُوْنَ اَزْوَاجًا ۖۚ وَّصِيَّةً
لِّاَزْوَاجِهِمْ مَّتَاعًا اِلَى الْحَوْلِ
غَيْرَ اِخْرَاجٍ ۚ فَاِنْ خَرَجْنَ فَلَا
جُنَاحَ عَلَيْكُمْ فِيْ مَا فَعَلْنَ فِيْٓ
اَنْفُسِهِنَّ مِنْ مَّعْرُوْفٍ ؕ وَاللّٰهُ
عَزِيْزٌ حَكِيْمٌ ﴿٢٤٠﴾

اور جو لوگ تم میں سے مر جائیں اور عورتیں چھوڑ جائیں
وہ اپنی عورتوں کے حق میں وصیت کر جائیں کہ
ان کو ایک سال تک خرچ دیا جائے اور گھر
سے نہ نکالی جائیں۔ ہاں اگر وہ خود گھر سے
چلی جائیں اور اپنے حق میں پسندیدہ کام (یعنی
نکاح) کر لیں تو تم پر کچھ گناہ نہیں اور خدا زبردست
حکمت والا ہے (۲۴۰)

240. Those of you who die and leave widows should bequeath for their widows a year's maintenance without expulsion; but if they leave (the residence), there is no blame on you for what they do with themselves, provided it is reasonable. And Allah is Exalted in Power, Wise.

وَلِلْمُطَلَّقٰتِ مَتَاعٌۢ بِالْمَعْرُوْفِ ؕ
حَقًّا عَلَى الْمُتَّقِيْنَ ﴿٢٤١﴾

اور مطلقہ عورتوں کو بھی دستور کے مطابق نان و
نفقہ دینا چاہیئے پرہیزگاروں پر (یہ بھی) حق ہے (۲۴۱)

241. For divorced women is a suitable Gift this is a duty on the righteous.

كَذٰلِكَ يُبَيِّنُ اللّٰهُ لَكُمْ اٰيٰتِهٖ
لَعَلَّكُمْ تَعْقِلُوْنَ ﴿٢٤٢﴾ ع ٣١ ١٥

اسی طرح خدا اپنے احکام تمہارے لئے بیان فرماتا ہے
تاکہ تم سمجھو (۲۴۲)

242. Thus doth Allah make clear His Signs to you: in order that ye may understand.

اَلَمْ تَرَ اِلَى الَّذِيْنَ خَرَجُوْا مِنْ
دِيَارِهِمْ وَهُمْ اُلُوْفٌ حَذَرَ الْمَوْتِ ۪
فَقَالَ لَهُمُ اللّٰهُ مُوْتُوْا ثُمَّ اَحْيَاهُمْ ؕ
اِنَّ اللّٰهَ لَذُوْ فَضْلٍ عَلَى النَّاسِ
وَلٰكِنَّ اَكْثَرَ النَّاسِ لَا يَشْكُرُوْنَ ﴿٢٤٣﴾

بھلا تم نے ان لوگوں کو نہیں دیکھا جو (شمار میں)
ہزاروں ہی تھے اور موت کے ڈر سے اپنے گھروں
سے نکل بھاگے تھے تو خدا نے ان کو حکم دیا کہ مر جاؤ
پھر ان کو زندہ بھی کر دیا۔ کچھ شک نہیں کہ خدا لوگوں
پر مہربانی رکھتا ہے لیکن اکثر لوگ شکر نہیں کرتے (۲۴۳)

243. Didst thou not turn thy vision to those who abandoned their homes, though they were thousands (in number), for fear of death ? Allah said to them: "Die". Then He restored them to life. For Allah is full of bounty to mankind, but most of them are ungrateful.

وَقَاتِلُوْا فِيْ سَبِيْلِ اللّٰهِ وَاعْلَمُوْٓا

اور (مسلمانو) خدا کی راہ میں جہاد کرو اور جان رکھو کہ خدا

244. Then fight in the cause of Allah, and know that Allah heareth

and knoweth all things.

245. Who is he that will loan to Allah a beautiful loan, which Allah will double unto his credit and multiply many times ? It is Allah that giveth (you) Want or Plenty. And to Him shall be your return.

246. Has thou not turned thy vision to the Chiefs of the Children of Israel after (the time of) Moses? They said to a Prophet (that was) among them: "Appoint for us a King, that we may fight in the cause of Allah." He said; "Is it not possible, if ye were commanded to fight, that ye will not fight ?" They said: "How could we refuse to fight in the cause of Allah, seeing that we were turned out of our homes and our families?" But when they were commanded to fight, they turned back, except a small band among them. But Allah has full knowledge of those who do wrong.

247. Their Prophet said to them; "Allah hath appointed Tālût as king over you." They said: "How can he exercise authority over us when we are better fitted than he to exercise authority, and he is not even gifted, with wealth in abundance?" He said: "Allah hath chosen him above you, and hath gifted him abundantly with knowledge and bodily prowess: Allah granteth His authority to whom he pleaseth; Allah is All-Embracing, and He knoweth all things."

248. And (further) their Prophet said to them: "A Sign of his authority is that there shall come to you the Ark of the Covenant, with (an assurance) therein of security from

(سب کچھ) سنتا (اور سب کچھ) جانتا ہے ﴿۲۴۴﴾
کوئی ہے کہ خدا کو قرض حسنہ دے کہ وہ اس کے بدلے
اس کو کئی حصے زیادہ دے گا۔ اور خدا ہی روزی کو
تنگ کرتا اور (وہی اسے) کشادہ کرتا ہے اور تم اسی
کی طرف لوٹ کر جاؤ گے ﴿۲۴۵﴾
بھلا تم نے بنی اسرائیل کی ایک جماعت کو نہیں دیکھا
جس نے موسیٰ کے بعد اپنے پیغمبر سے کہا کہ آپ ہمارے
لئے ایک بادشاہ مقرر کر دیں تاکہ ہم خدا کی راہ میں
جہاد کریں۔ پیغمبر نے کہا کہ اگر تم کو جہاد کا حکم دیا جائے
تو عجب نہیں کہ لڑنے سے پہلو تہی کرو۔ وہ کہنے
لگے کہ ہم راہِ خدا میں کیوں نہ لڑیں گے۔ جب کہ ہم
وطن سے (خارج) اور بال بچوں سے جدا کر دیئے
گئے۔ لیکن جب ان کو جہاد کا حکم دیا گیا تو
چند اشخاص کے سوا سب پھر گئے۔ اور خدا ظالموں
سے خوب واقف ہے ﴿۲۴۶﴾
اور پیغمبر نے ان سے (یہ بھی) کہا کہ خدا نے تم پر طالوت
کو بادشاہ مقرر فرمایا ہے۔ وہ بولے کہ اسے ہم پر بادشاہی
کا حق کیونکر ہو سکتا ہے۔ بادشاہی کے مستحق تو ہم ہیں
اور اس کے پاس تو بہت سی دولت بھی نہیں۔ پیغمبر نے
کہا کہ خدا نے اس کو تم پر فضیلت دی ہے اور بادشاہی کیلئے
منتخب فرمایا ہے اس نے اسے علم بھی بہت سا بخشا
ہے اور تن و توش بھی (بڑا عطا کیا ہے) اور خدا (کو اختیار
ہے) جسے چاہے بادشاہی بخشے۔ وہ بڑا کشائش والا
(اور) دانا ہے ﴿۲۴۷﴾
اور پیغمبر نے ان سے کہا کہ ان کی بادشاہی کی نشانی یہ ہے
کہ تمہارے پاس ایک صندوق آئے گا جس کو فرشتے
اٹھائے ہوئے ہوں گے اس میں تمہارے پروردگار

أَنَّ اللَّهَ سَمِيعٌ عَلِيمٌ ﴿٢٤٤﴾
مَنْ ذَا الَّذِي يُقْرِضُ اللَّهَ قَرْضًا
حَسَنًا فَيُضَاعِفَهُ لَهُ أَضْعَافًا كَثِيرَةً
وَاللَّهُ يَقْبِضُ وَيَبْسُطُ وَإِلَيْهِ
تُرْجَعُونَ ﴿٢٤٥﴾
أَلَمْ تَرَ إِلَى الْمَلَإِ مِنْ بَنِي إِسْرَائِيلَ
مِنْ بَعْدِ مُوسَىٰ إِذْ قَالُوا لِنَبِيٍّ
لَهُمُ ابْعَثْ لَنَا مَلِكًا نُقَاتِلْ فِي (وقف لازم)
سَبِيلِ اللَّهِ قَالَ هَلْ عَسَيْتُمْ
إِنْ كُتِبَ عَلَيْكُمُ الْقِتَالُ أَلَّا
تُقَاتِلُوا قَالُوا وَمَا لَنَا أَلَّا نُقَاتِلَ
فِي سَبِيلِ اللَّهِ وَقَدْ أُخْرِجْنَا مِنْ
دِيَارِنَا وَأَبْنَائِنَا فَلَمَّا كُتِبَ
عَلَيْهِمُ الْقِتَالُ تَوَلَّوْا إِلَّا قَلِيلًا
مِنْهُمْ وَاللَّهُ عَلِيمٌ بِالظَّالِمِينَ ﴿٢٤٦﴾
وَقَالَ لَهُمْ نَبِيُّهُمْ إِنَّ اللَّهَ قَدْ
بَعَثَ لَكُمْ طَالُوتَ مَلِكًا قَالُوا
أَنَّىٰ يَكُونُ لَهُ الْمُلْكُ عَلَيْنَا وَ
نَحْنُ أَحَقُّ بِالْمُلْكِ مِنْهُ وَلَمْ
يُؤْتَ سَعَةً مِنَ الْمَالِ قَالَ
إِنَّ اللَّهَ اصْطَفَاهُ عَلَيْكُمْ وَ
زَادَهُ بَسْطَةً فِي الْعِلْمِ وَالْجِسْمِ
وَاللَّهُ يُؤْتِي مُلْكَهُ مَنْ يَشَاءُ
وَاللَّهُ وَاسِعٌ عَلِيمٌ ﴿٢٤٧﴾
وَقَالَ لَهُمْ نَبِيُّهُمْ إِنَّ آيَةَ مُلْكِهِ
أَنْ يَأْتِيَكُمُ التَّابُوتُ فِيهِ سَكِينَةٌ
مِنْ رَبِّكُمْ وَبَقِيَّةٌ مِمَّا تَرَكَ آلُ

مُوسٰى وَاٰلُ هٰرُوْنَ تَحْمِلُهُ الْمَلٰٓئِكَةُ ؕ
اِنَّ فِیْ ذٰلِكَ لَاٰيَةً لَّكُمْ اِنْ كُنْتُمْ
مُّؤْمِنِيْنَ ﴿۲۴۸﴾ ع

کی طرف سے تسلّی (بخشنے والی چیز) ہوگی اور کچھ اور چیزیں
بھی ہوں گی جو موسٰی اور ہارون چھوڑ گئے تھے۔ اگر تم
ایمان رکھتے ہو تو یہ تمہارے لئے ایک بڑی نشانی ہے ﴿۲۴۸﴾

your Lord, and the relics left by the family of Moses and the family of Aaron, carried by angels. In this is a Symbol for you if ye indeed have faith."

فَلَمَّا فَصَلَ طَالُوْتُ بِالْجُنُوْدِ ۙ قَالَ
اِنَّ اللّٰهَ مُبْتَلِيْكُمْ بِنَهَرٍ ۚ فَمَنْ
شَرِبَ مِنْهُ فَلَيْسَ مِنِّیْ ۚ وَمَنْ
لَّمْ يَطْعَمْهُ فَاِنَّهٗ مِنِّیْٓ اِلَّا مَنِ
اغْتَرَفَ غُرْفَةًۢ بِيَدِهٖ ۚ فَشَرِبُوْا
مِنْهُ اِلَّا قَلِيْلًا مِّنْهُمْ ؕ فَلَمَّا
جَاوَزَهٗ هُوَ وَالَّذِيْنَ اٰمَنُوْا مَعَهٗ ۙ
قَالُوْا لَا طَاقَةَ لَنَا الْيَوْمَ بِجَالُوْتَ
وَجُنُوْدِهٖ ؕ قَالَ الَّذِيْنَ يَظُنُّوْنَ
اَنَّهُمْ مُّلٰقُوا اللّٰهِ ۙ كَمْ مِّنْ
فِئَةٍ قَلِيْلَةٍ غَلَبَتْ فِئَةً كَثِيْرَةًۢ
بِاِذْنِ اللّٰهِ ؕ وَاللّٰهُ مَعَ الصّٰبِرِيْنَ ﴿۲۴۹﴾

غرض جب طالوت فوجیں لے کر روانہ ہوا تو اُس نے
(اُن سے) کہا کہ خدا ایک نہر سے تمہاری آزمائش
کرنے والا ہے۔ جو شخص اس میں سے پانی پی لیگا (اسکی
نسبت تصور کیا جائیگا کہ) وہ میرا نہیں۔ اور جو نہ پئے گا
وہ (سمجھا جائیگا کہ) میرا ہے۔ ہاں اگر کوئی ہاتھ سے چلّو بھر
پانی لے لے (تو خیر جب وہ لوگ نہر پر پہنچے) تو چند شخصوں
کے سوا سب نے پانی پی لیا۔ پھر جب طالوت اور
مومن لوگ جو اُسکے ساتھ تھے نہر کے پار ہو گئے تو کہنے لگے
کہ آج ہم میں جالوت اور اُسکے لشکر سے مقابلہ کرنیکی طاقت
نہیں۔ جو لوگ یقین رکھتے تھے کہ اُنکو خدا کے روبرو حاضر ہونا
ہے وہ کہنے لگے کہ بسا اوقات تھوڑی سی جماعت نے خدا کے حکم سے بڑی جماعت
پر فتح حاصل کی ہے اور خدا استقلال رکھنے والوں کے ساتھ ہے ﴿۲۴۹﴾

249. When Tālût set forth with the armies, he said: "Allah will test you at the stream; if any drinks of its water, he goes not with my army: only those who taste not of it go with me: a mere sip out of the hand is excused." But they drank of it, except a few. When they crossed the river,—he and the faithful ones with him,—they said: "This day we cannot cope with Goliath and his forces." But those who were convinced that they must meet Allah, said: "How oft, by Allah's will, hath a small force vanquished a big one ? Allah is with those who steadfastly persevere."

وَلَمَّا بَرَزُوْا لِجَالُوْتَ وَجُنُوْدِهٖ قَالُوْا
رَبَّنَآ اَفْرِغْ عَلَيْنَا صَبْرًا وَّثَبِّتْ
اَقْدَامَنَا وَانْصُرْنَا عَلَى الْقَوْمِ الْكٰفِرِيْنَ ﴿۲۵۰﴾ ؕ

اور جب وہ لوگ جالوت اور اُسکے لشکر کے مقابل میں آئے
تو (خدا سے) دُعا کی کہ اے پروردگار ہم پر صبر کے دہانے کھول دے اور
ہمیں (لڑائی میں) ثابت قدم رکھ اور (لشکر) کفار پر فتحیاب کر ﴿۲۵۰﴾

250. When they advanced to meet Goliath and his forces, they prayed: "Our Lord ! pour out constancy on us and make our steps firm: help us against those that reject faith."

فَهَزَمُوْهُمْ بِاِذْنِ اللّٰهِ ۙ۫ وَقَتَلَ
دَاوٗدُ جَالُوْتَ وَاٰتٰىهُ اللّٰهُ الْمُلْكَ
وَالْحِكْمَةَ وَعَلَّمَهٗ مِمَّا يَشَآءُ ؕ
وَلَوْلَا دَفْعُ اللّٰهِ النَّاسَ بَعْضَهُمْ
بِبَعْضٍ لَّفَسَدَتِ الْاَرْضُ وَلٰكِنَّ
اللّٰهَ ذُوْ فَضْلٍ عَلَى الْعٰلَمِيْنَ ﴿۲۵۱﴾

تو طالوت کی فوج نے خدا کے حکم سے اُن کو ہزیمت
دی اور داؤد نے جالوت کو قتل کر ڈالا۔ اور خدا نے
اُن کو بادشاہی اور دانائی بخشی اور جو کچھ چاہا سکھایا۔ اور
اگر خدا لوگوں کو ایک دوسرے (پر چڑھائی اور حملہ کرنے)
سے نہ ہٹاتا رہتا تو مُلک تباہ ہو جاتا لیکن خدا
اہلِ عالم پر بڑا مہربان ہے ﴿۲۵۱﴾

251. By Allah's will, they routed them; and David slew Goliath; and Allah gave him power and wisdom and taught him whatever (else) He willed. And did not Allah check one set of people by means of another, the earth would indeed be full of mischief: but Allah is full of bounty to all the worlds.

تِلْكَ اٰيٰتُ اللّٰهِ نَتْلُوْهَا عَلَيْكَ
بِالْحَقِّ ؕ وَاِنَّكَ لَمِنَ الْمُرْسَلِيْنَ ﴿۲۵۲﴾

یہ خدا کی آیتیں ہیں جو ہم تم کو سچائی کے ساتھ پڑھ کر
سُناتے ہیں اور (اے محمد) تم بلاشبہ پیغمبروں میں سے ہو ﴿۲۵۲﴾

252. These are the Signs of Allah: we rehearse them to thee in truth: verily thou art one of the Messengers.

253. Those Messengers We endowed with gifts, some above others: to some of them Allah spoke; others He raised to degrees (of honour); to Jesus the son of Mary We gave Clear (Signs), and strengthened him with the Holy Spirit. If Allah had so willed, succeeding generations would not have fought among each other, after Clear (Signs) had come to them, but they (chose) to wrangle, some believing and others rejecting. If Allah had so willed, they would not have fought each other; but Allah does what He wills.

یہ پیغمبر (جو ہم وقتاً فوقتاً بھیجتے رہے ہیں) ان میں سے
ہم نے بعض کو بعض پر فضیلت دی ہے بعض ایسے
ہیں جن سے خدا نے گفتگو کی اور بعض کے (دوسرے
امور میں) مرتبے بلند کئے۔ اور عیسیٰ ابن مریم کو ہم
نے کھلی ہوئی نشانیاں عطا کیں۔ اور روح القدس
سے ان کو مدد دی۔ اور اگر خدا چاہتا تو ان سے پچھلے
لوگ اپنے پاس کھلی نشانیاں آنے کے بعد آپس
میں نہ لڑتے لیکن انہوں نے اختلاف کیا تو ان
میں سے بعض تو ایمان لے آئے اور بعض کافر
ہی رہے اور اگر خدا چاہتا تو یہ لوگ باہم جنگ و
قتال نہ کرتے لیکن خدا جو چاہتا ہے کرتا ہے ﴿۲۵۳﴾

تِلْكَ الرُّسُلُ فَضَّلْنَا بَعْضَهُمْ
عَلٰى بَعْضٍ مِنْهُمْ مَّنْ كَلَّمَ اللّٰهُ
وَرَفَعَ بَعْضَهُمْ دَرَجٰتٍ ؕ وَاٰتَيْنَا
عِيْسَى ابْنَ مَرْيَمَ الْبَيِّنٰتِ
وَاَيَّدْنٰهُ بِرُوْحِ الْقُدُسِ ؕ وَلَوْ
شَآءَ اللّٰهُ مَا اقْتَتَلَ الَّذِيْنَ مِنْ
بَعْدِهِمْ مِّنْ بَعْدِ مَا جَآءَتْهُمُ
الْبَيِّنٰتُ وَلٰكِنِ اخْتَلَفُوْا فَمِنْهُمْ
مَّنْ اٰمَنَ وَمِنْهُمْ مَّنْ كَفَرَ ؕ
وَلَوْ شَآءَ اللّٰهُ مَا اقْتَتَلُوْا ۟ وَلٰكِنَّ
اللّٰهَ يَفْعَلُ مَا يُرِيْدُ ﴿٢٥٣﴾

254. O ye who believe ! spend out of (the bounties) We have provided for you, before the Day comes when no bargaining (will avail), nor friendship nor intercession. Those who reject Faith—they are the wrong-doers.

اے ایمان والو جو (مال) ہم نے تم کو دیا ہے اس
میں سے اس دن کے آنے سے پہلے پہلے خرچ کرلو
جس میں نہ (اعمال کا) سودا ہو۔ اور نہ دوستی اور
سفارش ہو سکے۔ اور کفر کرنے والے لوگ
ظالم ہیں ﴿۲۵۴﴾

يٰۤاَيُّهَا الَّذِيْنَ اٰمَنُوْۤا اَنْفِقُوْا
مِمَّا رَزَقْنٰكُمْ مِّنْ قَبْلِ اَنْ
يَّاْتِيَ يَوْمٌ لَّا بَيْعٌ فِيْهِ وَلَا خُلَّةٌ
وَّلَا شَفَاعَةٌ ؕ وَالْكٰفِرُوْنَ
هُمُ الظّٰلِمُوْنَ ﴿٢٥٤﴾

255. Allah ! There is no god but He,—the Living, the Self-subsisting, Supporter of all, no slumber can seize Him nor sleep. His are all things in the heavens and on earth. Who is thee can intercede in His presence except as He permitteth? He knoweth what (appeareth to His creatures as) Before or After or Behind them. Nor shall they compass aught of His knowledge except as He willeth. His Throne doth extend over the heavens and the earth, and He feeleth no fatigue in guarding and preserving them: for He is the Most High, the Supreme (in glory).

خدا (وہ معبود برحق ہے کہ) اسکے سوا کوئی عبادت کے لائق
نہیں۔ زندہ ہمیشہ رہنے والا۔ اسے نہ اونگھ آتی ہے نہ نیند
جو کچھ آسمانوں میں اور جو کچھ زمین میں ہے سب اسی
کا ہے۔ کون ہے کہ اس کی اجازت کے بغیر اس سے
(کسی کی) سفارش کر سکے۔ جو کچھ لوگوں کے روبرو ہو رہا ہے
اور جو کچھ ان کے پیچھے ہو چکا ہے اسے سب معلوم ہے اور وہ
اس کی معلومات میں سے کسی چیز پر دسترس حاصل نہیں
کر سکتے ہاں جس قدر وہ چاہتا ہے اسی قدر معلوم کرا دیتا ہے
اسکی بادشاہی (اور علم) آسمان اور زمین سب پر حاوی ہے اور
اسے انکی حفاظت کچھ بھی دشوار نہیں وہ بڑا عالی رتبہ اور جلیل القدر ہے ﴿۲۵۵﴾

اَللّٰهُ لَاۤ اِلٰهَ اِلَّا هُوَ ۚ اَلْحَيُّ الْقَيُّوْمُ ۚ
لَا تَاْخُذُهٗ سِنَةٌ وَّلَا نَوْمٌ ؕ
لَهٗ مَا فِي السَّمٰوٰتِ وَمَا فِي الْاَرْضِ ؕ
مَنْ ذَا الَّذِيْ يَشْفَعُ عِنْدَهٗۤ اِلَّا
بِاِذْنِهٖ ؕ يَعْلَمُ مَا بَيْنَ اَيْدِيْهِمْ
وَمَا خَلْفَهُمْ ۚ وَلَا يُحِيْطُوْنَ بِشَيْءٍ
مِّنْ عِلْمِهٖۤ اِلَّا بِمَا شَآءَ ۚ وَسِعَ
كُرْسِيُّهُ السَّمٰوٰتِ وَالْاَرْضَ ۚ وَلَا
يَـُٔوْدُهٗ حِفْظُهُمَا ۚ وَهُوَ الْعَلِيُّ
الْعَظِيْمُ ﴿٢٥٥﴾

256. Let there be no compulsion in religion: Truth stands out clear

دین (اسلام) میں زبردستی نہیں ہے۔ ہدایت (صاف طور پر

لَاۤ اِكْرَاهَ فِي الدِّيْنِ ۙ قَدْ تَّبَيَّنَ

from Error: whoever rejects Tagut and believes in Allah hath grasped the most trustworthy hand-hold, that never breaks. And Allah heareth and knoweth all things.

257. Allah is the Protector of those who have faith: from the depths of darkness He leads them forth into light. Of those who reject faith the patrons are the Tagut from light they will lead them forth into the depths of darkness. They will be Companions of the Fire, to dwell therein (for ever).

258. Hast thou not turned thy thought to one who disputed with Abraham about his Lord, because Allah had granted him power ? Abraham said: "My Lord is He Who giveth life and death." He said: "I give life and death." Said Abraham: "But it is Allah that causeth the sun to rise from the East: do thou then cause it to rise from the West." Thus was he confounded who (in arrogance) rejected Faith. Nor doth Allah give guidance to a people unjust.

259. Or (take) the similitude of one who passed by a hamlet, all in ruins to its roots. He said: "Oh! how shall Allah bring it (ever) to life, after (this) its death ?" But Allah caused him to die for a hundred years, then raised him up (again). He said: "How long didst thou tarry (thus) ?" He said: "(Perhaps) a day or part of a day." He said: "Nay, thou hast tarried thus a hundred years: but look at thy food and thy drink; they show no signs of age: and look at thy donkey: and that We may make of thee a Sign unto the people.

ظاہر اور) گمراہی سے الگ ہو چکی ہے۔ تو جو شخص
بُتوں سے اعتقاد نہ رکھے اور خدا پر ایمان لائے
اُس نے ایسی مضبوط رسّی ہاتھ میں پکڑ لی ہے جو کبھی ٹوٹنے
والی نہیں اور خدا (سب کچھ) سُنتا (اور سب کچھ) جانتا ہے (٢٥٦)
جو لوگ ایمان لائے ہیں اُن کا دوست خدا ہے کہ
اندھیرے سے نکال کر روشنی میں لے جاتا ہے
اور جو کافر ہیں اُن کے دوست شیطان ہیں
کہ اُن کو روشنی سے نکال کر اندھیرے میں لیجاتے ہیں
یہی لوگ اہل دوزخ ہیں کہ اُس میں ہمیشہ رہیں گے (٢٥٧)
بھلا تم نے اُس شخص کو نہیں دیکھا جو اس (غرور) کے
سبب سے کہ خدا نے اُس کو سلطنت بخشی تھی ابراہیم سے
پروردگار کے بارے میں جھگڑنے لگا۔ جب ابراہیم نے
کہا میرا پروردگار تو وہ ہے جو جلاتا ہے اور مارتا ہے۔
وہ بولا کہ جلا اور مار تو میں بھی سکتا ہوں۔ ابراہیم
نے کہا کہ خدا تو سورج کو مشرق سے نکالتا ہے
آپ اسے مغرب سے نکال دیجئے (یہ سُنکر) کافر حیران
رہ گیا۔ اور خدا بے انصافوں کو ہدایت نہیں دیا کرتا (٢٥٨)
یا اُسی طرح اس شخص کو (نہیں دیکھا) جسے ایک گاؤں
میں جو اپنی چھتوں پر گرا پڑا تھا اتفاق گذر ہوا
تو اُس نے کہا کہ خدا اس (کے باشندوں) کو مرنے کے
بعد کیونکر زندہ کرے گا۔ تو خدا نے اس کی روح قبض
کر لی (اور) سو برس تک (اُس کو مُردہ رکھا) پھر اُس کو
جلا اُٹھایا اور پوچھا تم کتنا عرصہ (مرے) رہے ہو اُس
نے جواب دیا کہ ایک دن یا اس سے بھی کم۔ خدا نے فرمایا
(نہیں) بلکہ سو برس (مرے) رہے ہو اور اپنے کھانے پینے
کی چیزوں کو دیکھو کہ (اتنی مدت میں مطلق) سڑی بُسی نہیں
اور اپنے گدھے کو بھی دیکھو (جو مرا پڑا ہے) غرض (ان باتوں سے) یہ ہے کہ ہم

الرُّشْدُ مِنَ الْغَيِّ ۚ فَمَنْ يَكْفُرْ
بِالطَّاغُوتِ وَيُؤْمِنْ بِاللَّهِ فَقَدِ
اسْتَمْسَكَ بِالْعُرْوَةِ الْوُثْقَىٰ لَا انْفِصَامَ
لَهَا ۗ وَاللَّهُ سَمِيعٌ عَلِيمٌ (٢٥٦)
اللَّهُ وَلِيُّ الَّذِينَ آمَنُوا يُخْرِجُهُمْ
مِنَ الظُّلُمَاتِ إِلَى النُّورِ ۖ وَالَّذِينَ
كَفَرُوا أَوْلِيَاؤُهُمُ الطَّاغُوتُ
يُخْرِجُونَهُمْ مِنَ النُّورِ إِلَى الظُّلُمَاتِ ۗ
أُولَٰئِكَ أَصْحَابُ النَّارِ ۖ هُمْ فِيهَا خَالِدُونَ (٢٥٧)
أَلَمْ تَرَ إِلَى الَّذِي حَاجَّ إِبْرَاهِيمَ
فِي رَبِّهِ أَنْ آتَاهُ اللَّهُ الْمُلْكَ إِذْ
قَالَ إِبْرَاهِيمُ رَبِّيَ الَّذِي يُحْيِي
وَيُمِيتُ قَالَ أَنَا أُحْيِي وَأُمِيتُ ۖ
قَالَ إِبْرَاهِيمُ فَإِنَّ اللَّهَ يَأْتِي
بِالشَّمْسِ مِنَ الْمَشْرِقِ فَأْتِ بِهَا
مِنَ الْمَغْرِبِ فَبُهِتَ الَّذِي كَفَرَ ۗ
وَاللَّهُ لَا يَهْدِي الْقَوْمَ الظَّالِمِينَ (٢٥٨)
أَوْ كَالَّذِي مَرَّ عَلَىٰ قَرْيَةٍ وَهِيَ
خَاوِيَةٌ عَلَىٰ عُرُوشِهَا ج قَالَ
أَنَّىٰ يُحْيِي هَٰذِهِ اللَّهُ بَعْدَ مَوْتِهَا
فَأَمَاتَهُ اللَّهُ مِائَةَ عَامٍ ثُمَّ
بَعَثَهُ ط قَالَ كَمْ لَبِثْتَ ط قَالَ
لَبِثْتُ يَوْمًا أَوْ بَعْضَ يَوْمٍ ط
قَالَ بَلْ لَبِثْتَ مِائَةَ عَامٍ فَانْظُرْ
إِلَىٰ طَعَامِكَ وَشَرَابِكَ لَمْ يَتَسَنَّهْ
وَانْظُرْ إِلَىٰ حِمَارِكَ وَلِنَجْعَلَكَ
آيَةً لِلنَّاسِ وَانْظُرْ إِلَى الْعِظَامِ

Look further at the bones, how We bring them together and clothe them with flesh." When this was shown clearly to him, he said: "I know that Allah hath power over all things."

تمکو لوگوں کیلئے (اپنی قدرت کی) نشانی بنائیں اور (ہاں گدھے
کی) ہڈیوں کو دیکھو کہ ہم انکو کیونکر جوڑے دیتے اور اُن پر (کس طرح)
گوشت پوست چڑھا دیتے ہیں جب یہ واقعات اُسکے مشاہدے میں
آئے تو بول اُٹھا کہ میں یقین کرتا ہوں کہ خدا ہر چیز پر قادر ہے (۲۵۹)

كَيْفَ نُنْشِزُهَا ثُمَّ نَكْسُوهَا
لَحْمًا ۚ فَلَمَّا تَبَيَّنَ لَهُ ۙ قَالَ
أَعْلَمُ أَنَّ اللَّهَ عَلَىٰ كُلِّ شَيْءٍ
قَدِيرٌ ﴿٢٥٩﴾

260. Behold! Abraham said: "My Lord ! show me how Thou givest life to the dead." He said: "Dost thou not then believe ?" He said: "Yea! but to satisfy my own heart." He said: "Take four birds; tie them (cut them into pieces), then put a portion of them: on every hill, and call to them: they will come to thee (flying) with speed. Then know that Allah is Exalted in Power, Wise."

اور جب ابراہیم نے (خدا سے) کہا کہ اے پروردگار
مجھے دکھا کہ تو مُردوں کو کیونکر زندہ کرے گا. خدا
نے فرمایا کیا تم نے (اس بات کو) باور نہیں کیا. انہوں نے
کہا کیوں نہیں لیکن (میں دیکھنا) اسلئے (چاہتا ہوں) کہ
میرا دل اطمینان کامل حاصل کرلے. خدا نے فرمایا کہ چار
جانور پکڑ کر اپنے پاس منگا لو (اور ٹکڑے ٹکڑے کرادو) پھر ان کا
ایک ایک ٹکڑا ہر ایک پہاڑ پر رکھدو پھر اُنکو بلاؤ تو وہ تمہارے پاس
دوڑتے چلے آئینگے اور جان رکھو کہ خدا غالب (اور) صاحب حکمت ہے (۲۶۰)

وَإِذْ قَالَ إِبْرَاهِيمُ رَبِّ أَرِنِي كَيْفَ
تُحْيِي الْمَوْتَىٰ ۖ قَالَ أَوَلَمْ تُؤْمِنْ ۖ
قَالَ بَلَىٰ وَلَٰكِنْ لِيَطْمَئِنَّ قَلْبِي ۖ
قَالَ فَخُذْ أَرْبَعَةً مِنَ الطَّيْرِ
فَصُرْهُنَّ إِلَيْكَ ثُمَّ اجْعَلْ عَلَىٰ
كُلِّ جَبَلٍ مِنْهُنَّ جُزْءًا ثُمَّ
ادْعُهُنَّ يَأْتِينَكَ سَعْيًا ۚ وَاعْلَمْ
أَنَّ اللَّهَ عَزِيزٌ حَكِيمٌ ﴿٢٦٠﴾ ع ٣٥ ٤

261. The parable of those who spend their wealth in the way of Allah is that of a grain of corn: it groweth seven ears, and each ear hath a hundred grains. Allah giveth manifold increase to whom He pleaseth: and Allah careth for all and He knoweth all things.

جو لوگ اپنا مال خدا کی راہ میں خرچ کرتے ہیں اُن
(کے مال) کی مثال اُس دانے کی سی ہے جس سے سات
بالیں اُگیں اور ہر ایک بال میں سو سو دانے ہوں اور
خدا جس (کے مال) کو چاہتا ہے زیادہ کرتا ہے وہ بڑی
کشائش والا (اور) سب کچھ جاننے والا ہے (۲۶۱)

مَثَلُ الَّذِينَ يُنْفِقُونَ أَمْوَالَهُمْ
فِي سَبِيلِ اللَّهِ كَمَثَلِ حَبَّةٍ أَنْبَتَتْ
سَبْعَ سَنَابِلَ فِي كُلِّ سُنْبُلَةٍ
مِائَةُ حَبَّةٍ ۗ وَاللَّهُ يُضَاعِفُ لِمَنْ
يَشَاءُ ۗ وَاللَّهُ وَاسِعٌ عَلِيمٌ ﴿٢٦١﴾

262. Those who spend their wealth in the cause of Allah, and follow not up their gifts with reminders of their generosity or with injury,—for them their reward is with their Lord: on them shall be no fear, nor shall they grieve.

جو لوگ اپنا مال خدا کے رستے میں صرف کرتے ہیں
پھر اس کے بعد نہ اس خرچ کا (کسی پر) احسان رکھتے
ہیں اور نہ (کسی کو) تکلیف دیتے ہیں. اُنکا صلہ اُن کے
پروردگار کے پاس (تیار) ہے اور (قیامت کے روز)
نہ اُن کو کچھ خوف ہوگا اور نہ وہ غمگین ہوں گے (۲۶۲)

الَّذِينَ يُنْفِقُونَ أَمْوَالَهُمْ فِي
سَبِيلِ اللَّهِ ثُمَّ لَا يُتْبِعُونَ مَا
أَنْفَقُوا مَنًّا وَلَا أَذًى ۙ لَهُمْ
أَجْرُهُمْ عِنْدَ رَبِّهِمْ وَلَا
خَوْفٌ عَلَيْهِمْ وَلَا هُمْ يَحْزَنُونَ ﴿٢٦٢﴾

263. Kind words and covering of faults are better than charity followed by injury. Allah is Free of all wants, and He is Most Forbearing.

جس خیرات دینے کے بعد (لینے والے کو) ایذا دی جائے
اُس سے تو نرم بات کہہ دینی اور (اسکی بے ادبی سے) درگزر
کرنا بہتر ہے اور خدا بے پروا (اور) بُردبار ہے (۲۶۳)

قَوْلٌ مَعْرُوفٌ وَمَغْفِرَةٌ خَيْرٌ
مِنْ صَدَقَةٍ يَتْبَعُهَا أَذًى ۗ وَ
اللَّهُ غَنِيٌّ حَلِيمٌ ﴿٢٦٣﴾

264. O ye who believe ! cancel not your charity by reminders of your generosity or by injury—like those

مومنو! اپنے صدقات (و خیرات) احسان رکھنے اور ایذا
دینے سے اُس شخص کی طرح برباد نہ کر دینا جو لوگوں کو

يَا أَيُّهَا الَّذِينَ آمَنُوا لَا تُبْطِلُوا
صَدَقَاتِكُمْ بِالْمَنِّ وَالْأَذَىٰ كَالَّذِي

يُنْفِقُ مَالَهُ رِئَآءَ النَّاسِ وَلَا
يُؤْمِنُ بِاللّٰهِ وَالْيَوْمِ الْاٰخِرِ ۭ
فَمَثَلُهٗ كَمَثَلِ صَفْوَانٍ عَلَيْهِ
تُرَابٌ فَاَصَابَهٗ وَابِلٌ فَتَرَكَهٗ
صَلْدًا ۭ لَا يَقْدِرُوْنَ عَلٰي شَيْءٍ
مِّمَّا كَسَبُوْا ۭ وَاللّٰهُ لَا يَهْدِي
الْقَوْمَ الْكٰفِرِيْنَ ﴿۲۶۴﴾

دکھاوے کیلئے مال خرچ کرتا ہے اور خدا اور روز
آخرت پر ایمان نہیں رکھتا تو اس (کے مال) کی
مثال اُس چٹان کی سی ہے جس پر تھوڑی سی مٹی
پڑی ہو اور اس پر زور کا مینہ برس کر اسے صاف
کر ڈالے۔ (اسی طرح) یہ (ریاکار) لوگ اپنے اعمال
کا کچھ بھی صلہ حاصل نہیں کر سکیں گے۔ اور خدا
ایسے ناشکروں کو ہدایت نہیں دیا کرتا ﴿۲۶۴﴾

who spend their wealth to be seen of men, but believe neither in Allah nor in the Last Day. They are in Parable like a hard, barren rock, on which is a little soil: on it falls heavy rain, which leaves it (just) a bare stone. They will be able to do nothing with aught they have earned. And Allah guideth not those who reject faith.

وَمَثَلُ الَّذِيْنَ يُنْفِقُوْنَ اَمْوَالَهُمُ
ابْتِغَآءَ مَرْضَاتِ اللّٰهِ وَتَثْبِيْتًا
مِّنْ اَنْفُسِهِمْ كَمَثَلِ جَنَّةٍۢ
بِرَبْوَةٍ اَصَابَهَا وَابِلٌ فَاٰتَتْ
اُكُلَهَا ضِعْفَيْنِ ۚ فَاِنْ لَّمْ يُصِبْهَا وَابِلٌ
فَطَلٌّ ۭ وَاللّٰهُ بِمَا تَعْمَلُوْنَ بَصِيْرٌ ﴿۲۶۵﴾

اور جو لوگ خدا کی خوشنودی حاصل کرنے کیلئے
اور خلوص نیّت سے اپنا مال خرچ کرتے ہیں
اُن کی مثال ایک باغ کی سی ہے جو اونچی جگہ
پر واقع ہو (جب) اس پر مینہ پڑے تو دُگنا
پھل لائے اور اگر مینہ نہ بھی پڑے تو خیر پھوار ہی سہی
اور خُدا تمہارے کاموں کو دیکھ رہا ہے ﴿۲۶۵﴾

265. And the likeness of those who spend their wealth seeking to please Allah and to strengthen their souls, is as a garden, high and fertile: heavy rain falls on it but makes it yield a double increase of harvest, and if it receives not heavy rain, light moisture Sufficeth it. Allah seeth well whatever ye do.

اَيَوَدُّ اَحَدُكُمْ اَنْ تَكُوْنَ لَهٗ
جَنَّةٌ مِّنْ نَّخِيْلٍ وَّاَعْنَابٍ
تَجْرِيْ مِنْ تَحْتِهَا الْاَنْهٰرُ ۙ لَهٗ
فِيْهَا مِنْ كُلِّ الثَّمَرٰتِ ۙ وَاَصَابَهُ
الْكِبَرُ وَلَهٗ ذُرِّيَّةٌ ضُعَفَاۗءُ
فَاَصَابَهَآ اِعْصَارٌ فِيْهِ نَارٌ
فَاحْتَرَقَتْ ۭ كَذٰلِكَ يُبَيِّنُ اللّٰهُ
لَكُمُ الْاٰيٰتِ لَعَلَّكُمْ تَتَفَكَّرُوْنَ ﴿۲۶۶﴾ ع

بھلا تم میں کوئی یہ چاہتا ہے کہ اس کا کھجوروں
اور انگوروں کا باغ ہو جس میں نہریں بہ رہی ہوں
اور اس میں اُس کے لئے ہر قسم کے میوے موجود ہوں
اور اسے بڑھاپا آ پکڑے اور اُس کے ننھے ننھے بچے
بھی ہوں تو (ناگہاں) اُس باغ پر آگ کا بھرا ہوا
بگولا چلے اور وہ جل (کر راکھ کا ڈھیر ہو) جائے
اس طرح خدا تم سے اپنی آیتیں کھول کھول کر
بیان فرماتا ہے تاکہ تم سوچو (اور سمجھو) ﴿۲۶۶﴾

266. Does any of you wish that he should have a garden with date-palms and vines and streams flowing underneath, and all kinds of fruit, while he is stricken with old age, and his children are not strong (enough to look after themselves)—that it should be caught in a whirlwind, with fire therein, and be burnt up ? Thus doth Allah make clear to you (His) Signs; that ye may consider.

يٰٓاَيُّهَا الَّذِيْنَ اٰمَنُوْٓا اَنْفِقُوْا
مِنْ طَيِّبٰتِ مَا كَسَبْتُمْ وَمِمَّآ
اَخْرَجْنَا لَكُمْ مِّنَ الْاَرْضِ ۠ وَلَا
تَيَمَّمُوا الْخَبِيْثَ مِنْهُ تُنْفِقُوْنَ
وَلَسْتُمْ بِاٰخِذِيْهِ اِلَّآ اَنْ تُغْمِضُوْا
فِيْهِ ۭ وَاعْلَمُوْٓا اَنَّ اللّٰهَ غَنِيٌّ

مومنو! جو پاکیزہ اور عمدہ مال تم کماتے ہو اور جو
چیزیں ہم تمہارے لئے زمین سے نکالتے
ہیں ان میں سے (راہِ خدا میں) خرچ کرو۔
اور بُری اور ناپاک چیزیں دینے کا قصد نہ کرنا کہ
(اگر وہ چیزیں تمہیں دی جائیں تو) بجز اس کے کہ (لیتے
وقت) آنکھیں بند کر لو اُن کو کبھی نہ لو۔ اور جان رکھو

267. O ye who believe ! give of the good things which ye have (honourably) earned, and of the fruits of the earth which We have produced for you, and do not aim at anything which is bad, out of it ye may give away something, when ye yourselves would not receive it except with closed eyes. And know that Allah is Free of all wants, and

Worthy of all praise.

کہ خدا بے پروا (اور) قابلِ ستائش ہے ﴿۲۶۷﴾

حَمِيدٌ ﴿٢٦٧﴾

268. Satan threatens you with poverty and bids you to conduct unseemly. Allah promiseth you His forgiveness and bounties. And Allah careth for all and He knoweth all things.

(اور دیکھنا) شیطان (کا کہا نہ ماننا وہ) تمہیں تنگدستی
کا خوف دلاتا اور بے حیائی کے کام کرنے کو کہتا ہے اور
خدا تم سے اپنی بخشش اور رحمت کا وعدہ کرتا ہے۔ اور خدا بڑی
کشائش والا (اور) سب کچھ جاننے والا ہے ﴿۲۶۸﴾

ٱلشَّيْطَٰنُ يَعِدُكُمُ ٱلْفَقْرَ وَيَأْمُرُكُم
بِٱلْفَحْشَآءِ ۖ وَٱللَّهُ يَعِدُكُم مَّغْفِرَةً
مِّنْهُ وَفَضْلًا ۗ وَٱللَّهُ وَٰسِعٌ
عَلِيمٌ ﴿٢٦٨﴾

269. He granteth wisdom to whom He pleaseth; and he to whom wisdom is granted receiveth indeed a benefit overflowing; but none will receive admonition but men of understanding.

وہ جس کو چاہتا ہے دانائی بخشتا ہے اور جس کو
دانائی ملی بےشک اس کو بڑی نعمت ملی۔
اور نصیحت تو وہی لوگ قبول کرتے ہیں جو عقلمند ہیں ﴿۲۶۹﴾

يُؤْتِى ٱلْحِكْمَةَ مَن يَشَآءُ ۚ وَمَن
يُؤْتَ ٱلْحِكْمَةَ فَقَدْ أُوتِىَ خَيْرًا
كَثِيرًا ۗ وَمَا يَذَّكَّرُ إِلَّآ أُو۟لُوا۟ ٱلْأَلْبَٰبِ ﴿٢٦٩﴾

270. And whatever ye spend in charity or whatever vow you make, be sure Allah knows it all. But the wrong-doers have no helpers.

اور تم (خدا کی راہ میں) جس طرح کا خرچ کرو یا کوئی
نذر مانو ف۶۷ خدا اس کو جانتا ہے اور ظالموں ف۶۸ کا کوئی
مددگار نہیں ﴿۲۷۰﴾

وَمَآ أَنفَقْتُم مِّن نَّفَقَةٍ أَوْ
نَذَرْتُم مِّن نَّذْرٍ فَإِنَّ ٱللَّهَ يَعْلَمُهُۥ ۗ
وَمَا لِلظَّٰلِمِينَ مِنْ أَنصَارٍ ﴿٢٧٠﴾

271. If ye disclose (acts of) charity, even so it is well, but if ye conceal them, and make them reach those (really) in need, that is best for you: it will remove from you some of your (stains of) evil. And Allah is well acquainted with what ye do.

اگر تم خیرات ظاہر دو تو وہ بھی خوب ہے اور اگر
پوشیدہ دو اور دو بھی اہلِ حاجت کو تو وہ خوب تر ہے
اور (اس طرح کا دینا) تمہارے گناہوں کو بھی دور
کر دیگا۔ اور خدا کو تمہارے سب کاموں کی خبر ہے ﴿۲۷۱﴾

إِن تُبْدُوا۟ ٱلصَّدَقَٰتِ فَنِعِمَّا هِىَ ۖ
وَإِن تُخْفُوهَا وَتُؤْتُوهَا ٱلْفُقَرَآءَ
فَهُوَ خَيْرٌ لَّكُمْ ۚ وَيُكَفِّرُ عَنكُم
مِّن سَيِّـَٔاتِكُمْ ۗ وَٱللَّهُ بِمَا تَعْمَلُونَ خَبِيرٌ ﴿٢٧١﴾

272. It is not for you to guide them to the right path. But Allah guides to the right path whom He pleaseth. Whatever of good ye give benefits your own souls, and ye shall only do so seeking the "Face" of Allah. Whatever good ye give, shall be rendered back to you, and ye shall not be dealt with unjustly.

(اے محمد) تم ان لوگوں کی ہدایت کے ذمہ دار نہیں ہو
بلکہ خدا ہی جس کو چاہتا ہے ہدایت بخشتا ہے۔ اور
(مومنو!) تم جو مال خرچ کرو گے تو اس کا فائدہ تمہیں کو ہے۔
اور تم تو جو خرچ کرو گے خدا کی خوشنودی کے لئے
کرو گے۔ اور جو مال تم خرچ کرو گے وہ تمہیں پورا پورا دیدیا
جائے گا۔ اور تمہارا کچھ نقصان نہیں کیا جائے گا ﴿۲۷۲﴾

لَّيْسَ عَلَيْكَ هُدَىٰهُمْ وَلَٰكِنَّ ٱللَّهَ
يَهْدِى مَن يَشَآءُ ۗ وَمَا تُنفِقُوا۟
مِنْ خَيْرٍ فَلِأَنفُسِكُمْ ۚ وَمَا تُنفِقُونَ
إِلَّا ٱبْتِغَآءَ وَجْهِ ٱللَّهِ ۚ وَمَا تُنفِقُوا۟
مِنْ خَيْرٍ يُوَفَّ إِلَيْكُمْ وَأَنتُمْ
لَا تُظْلَمُونَ ﴿٢٧٢﴾

273. (Charity is) for those in need, who, in Allah's cause, are restricted (from travel). And cannot move about in the land, seeking (for trade or work): the ignorant man thinks, because of their modesty, that they are free from want. Thou shalt know them by their (unfailing) mark: they beg not importunately from all and sundry. And whatever of good ye

(اور ہاں تم جو خرچ کرو گے تو) ان حاجتمندوں کیلئے جو خدا
کی راہ میں رکے بیٹھے ہیں اور ملک میں کسی طرف جانے کی طاقت
نہیں رکھتے (اور مانگنے سے عار رکھتے ہیں) یہاں تک کہ نہ مانگنے
کی وجہ سے ناواقف شخص ان کو غنی خیال کرتا ہے اور تم قیافے
سے ان کو صاف پہچان لو (کہ حاجتمند ہیں اور شرم کے سبب
لوگوں سے منہ پھوڑ کر (اور) لپٹ کر نہیں مانگ سکتے اور تم جو

لِلْفُقَرَآءِ ٱلَّذِينَ أُحْصِرُوا۟ فِى سَبِيلِ
ٱللَّهِ لَا يَسْتَطِيعُونَ ضَرْبًا فِى
ٱلْأَرْضِ يَحْسَبُهُمُ ٱلْجَاهِلُ
أَغْنِيَآءَ مِنَ ٱلتَّعَفُّفِ تَعْرِفُهُم
بِسِيمَٰهُمْ لَا يَسْـَٔلُونَ ٱلنَّاسَ
إِلْحَافًا ۗ وَمَا تُنفِقُوا۟ مِنْ خَيْرٍ

فَإِنَّ اللّٰهَ بِهٖ عَلِيْمٌ ﴿٢٧٣﴾
الَّذِيْنَ يُنْفِقُوْنَ اَمْوَالَهُمْ بِالَّيْلِ
وَالنَّهَارِ سِرًّا وَّعَلَانِيَةً فَلَهُمْ
اَجْرُهُمْ عِنْدَ رَبِّهِمْ ۚ وَلَا خَوْفٌ
عَلَيْهِمْ وَلَا هُمْ يَحْزَنُوْنَ ﴿٢٧٤﴾
الَّذِيْنَ يَاْكُلُوْنَ الرِّبٰوا لَا يَقُوْمُوْنَ
اِلَّا كَمَا يَقُوْمُ الَّذِيْ يَتَخَبَّطُهُ
الشَّيْطٰنُ مِنَ الْمَسِّ ۭ ذٰلِكَ
بِاَنَّهُمْ قَالُوْٓا اِنَّمَا الْبَيْعُ مِثْلُ
الرِّبٰوا ۘ وَاَحَلَّ اللّٰهُ الْبَيْعَ وَحَرَّمَ
الرِّبٰوا ۭ فَمَنْ جَاۗءَهٗ مَوْعِظَةٌ مِّنْ
رَّبِّهٖ فَانْتَهٰى فَلَهٗ مَا سَلَفَ ۭ وَاَمْرُهٗٓ
اِلَى اللّٰهِ ۭ وَمَنْ عَادَ فَاُولٰۗىِٕكَ اَصْحٰبُ
النَّارِ ۚ هُمْ فِيْهَا خٰلِدُوْنَ ﴿٢٧٥﴾
يَمْحَقُ اللّٰهُ الرِّبٰوا وَيُرْبِي الصَّدَقٰتِ ۭ
وَاللّٰهُ لَا يُحِبُّ كُلَّ كَفَّارٍ اَثِيْمٍ ﴿٢٧٦﴾
اِنَّ الَّذِيْنَ اٰمَنُوْا وَعَمِلُوا الصّٰلِحٰتِ
وَاَقَامُوا الصَّلٰوةَ وَاٰتَوُا الزَّكٰوةَ لَهُمْ
اَجْرُهُمْ عِنْدَ رَبِّهِمْ ۚ وَلَا خَوْفٌ
عَلَيْهِمْ وَلَا هُمْ يَحْزَنُوْنَ ﴿٢٧٧﴾
يٰٓاَيُّهَا الَّذِيْنَ اٰمَنُوا اتَّقُوا اللّٰهَ وَذَرُوْا
مَا بَقِيَ مِنَ الرِّبٰوٓا اِنْ كُنْتُمْ مُّؤْمِنِيْنَ ﴿٢٧٨﴾
فَاِنْ لَّمْ تَفْعَلُوْا فَاْذَنُوْا بِحَرْبٍ
مِّنَ اللّٰهِ وَرَسُوْلِهٖ ۚ وَاِنْ تُبْتُمْ
فَلَكُمْ رُءُوْسُ اَمْوَالِكُمْ ۚ لَا
تَظْلِمُوْنَ وَلَا تُظْلَمُوْنَ ﴿٢٧٩﴾
وَاِنْ كَانَ ذُوْ عُسْرَةٍ فَنَظِرَةٌ

مال خرچ کرو گے کچھ شک نہیں کہ خدا اُس کو جانتا ہے ﴿۲۷۳﴾
جو لوگ اپنا مال رات اور دن اور پوشیدہ اور ظاہر (راہِ خدا
میں) خرچ کرتے رہتے ہیں اُن کا صلہ پروردگار کے پاس
ہے۔ اور اُن کو (قیامت کے دن) نہ کسی طرح کا خوف
ہوگا اور نہ غم ﴿۲۷۴﴾
جو لوگ سُود کھاتے ہیں وہ (قبروں سے) اس طرح
(حواس باختہ) اُٹھیں گے جیسے کسی کو جن نے لپٹ کر
دیوانہ بنا دیا ہو۔ یہ اس لئے کہ وہ کہتے ہیں کہ سودا بیچنا
بھی تو (نفع کے لحاظ سے) ویسا ہی ہے جیسے سُود (لینا)
حالانکہ سودے کو خدا نے حلال کیا ہے اور سُود کو حرام
تو جس شخص کے پاس خدا کی نصیحت پہنچی اور وہ (سُود لینے سے)
باز آگیا تو جو پہلے ہو چکا وہ اس کا۔ اور (قیامت میں) اُس کا
معاملہ خدا کے سپرد۔ اور جو پھر لینے لگا تو ایسے لوگ دوزخی
ہیں کہ ہمیشہ دوزخ میں (جلتے) رہیں گے ف۶۹ ﴿۲۷۵﴾
خدا سُود کو نابود (یعنی بے برکت) کرتا اور خیرات (کی برکت)
کو بڑھاتا ہے اور خدا کسی ناشکرے گنہگار کو دوست نہیں رکھتا ﴿۲۷۶﴾
جو لوگ ایمان لائے اور نیک عمل کرتے اور نماز پڑھتے
اور زکوٰۃ دیتے رہے اُن کو اُن کے کاموں کا صلہ
خدا کے ہاں ملے گا اور (قیامت کے دن)
اُن کو نہ کچھ خوف ہوگا اور نہ وہ غمناک ہوں گے ﴿۲۷۷﴾
مومنو! خدا سے ڈرو اور اگر ایمان رکھتے ہو تو جتنا
سُود باقی رہ گیا ہے اُس کو چھوڑ دو ﴿۲۷۸﴾
اگر ایسا نہ کرو گے تو خبردار ہو جاؤ (کہ تم) خدا اور رسول
سے جنگ کرنے کیلئے (تیار ہوتے ہو) اور اگر توبہ کر لو گے
(اور سُود چھوڑ دو گے) تو تم کو اپنی اصلی رقم لینے کا حق ہے
جس میں نہ اوروں کا نقصان اور نہ تمہارا نقصان ﴿۲۷۹﴾
اور اگر قرض لینے والا تنگ دست ہو تو (اُسے) کشائش (کے

give, be assured Allah knoweth it well.

274. Those who (in charity) spend of their goods by night and by day, in secret and in public, have their reward with their Lord: on them shall be no fear, nor shall they grieve.

275. Those who devour usury will not stand except as stands one whom the Satan by his touch hath driven to madness. That is because they say: "Trade is like usury," but Allah hath permitted trade and forbidden usury. Those who after receiving admonition from their Lord, desist, shall be pardoned for the past; their case is for Allah (to judge); but those who repeat (the offence) are Companions of the Fire: they will abide therein (for ever).

276. Allah will deprive usury of all blessing, but will give increase for deeds of charity: for He loveth not any ungrateful sinner.

277. Those who believe, and do deeds of righteousness, and establish regular prayers and give Zakat, will have their reward with their Lord: on them shall be no fear, nor shall they grieve.

278. O ye who believe ! fear Allah, and give up What remains of your demand for usury, if ye are indeed believers.

279. If ye do it not, take notice of war from Allah and His Messenger: but if ye repent ye shall have your capital sums: deal not unjustly, and ye shall not be dealt with unjustly.

280. If the debtor is in a difficulty, grant him time till it is easy for him

to repay. But if ye remit it by way of charity, that is best for you if ye only knew.

281. And fear the Day when ye shall be brought back to Allah. Then shall every soul be paid what it earned, and none shall be dealt with unjustly.

282. O ye who believe ! when ye deal with each other, in transactions involving future obligations in a fixed period of time, reduce them to writing. Let a scribe write down faithfully as between the parties: let not the scribe refuse to write: as Allah has taught him, so let him write. Let him who incurs the liability dictate, but let him fear Allah, his Lord and not diminish aught of what he owes. If the party liable is mentally deficient, or weak, or unable himself to dictate, let his guardian dictate faithfully. And get two witnesses, out of your own men. And if there are not two men, then a man and two women, such as ye choose, for witnesses, so that if one of them errs, the other can remind her. The witnesses should not refuse when they are called on (for evidence). Disdain not to reduce to writing (your contract) for a future period, whether it be small or big; it is juster in the sight of Allah, more suitable as evidence, and more convenient to prevent doubts among yourselves, but if it be a transaction which ye carry out on the spot among yourselves, there is no blame on you if ye reduce it not to writing. But take witnesses whenever ye make a commercial

حاصل ہونے تک مُہلت (دو) اور اگر (زرِ قرض) بخش دو
تو وہ تمہارے لئے زیادہ اچھا ہے بشرطیکہ سمجھو (۲۸۰)
اور اُس دن سے ڈرو جبکہ تم خدا کے حضور میں لوٹ کر
جاؤ گے اور ہر شخص اپنے اعمال کا پُورا پُورا بدلہ پائے گا اور
کسی کو کچھ نقصان نہ ہو گا (۲۸۱)
مومنو! جب تم آپس میں کسی میعاد معین کے لئے قرض
کا معاملہ کرنے لگو تو اُس کو لکھ لیا کرو اور لکھنے والا
تم میں کسی کا نقصان نہ کرے بلکہ انصاف سے لکھے
نیز لکھنے والا جیسا خدا نے اُسے سکھایا ہے لکھنے سے انکار
بھی نہ کرے اور دستاویز لکھ دے۔ اور جو شخص قرض لے
وہی (دستاویز کا) مضمون بول کر لکھوائے اور خدا سے کہ
اُس کا مالک ہے خوف کرے اور زرِ قرض میں سے کچھ کم
نہ لکھوائے اور اگر قرض لینے والا بے عقل یا ضعیف ہو یا
مضمون لکھوانے کی قابلیت نہ رکھتا ہو تو جو اُس کا
ولی ہو وہ انصاف کے ساتھ مضمون لکھوائے اور
اپنے میں سے دو مردوں کو (ایسے معاملے کے)
گواہ کر لیا کرو۔ اور اگر دو مرد نہ ہوں تو ایک مرد
اور دو عورتیں جن کو تم گواہ پسند کرو (کافی ہیں)
کہ اگر ان میں سے ایک بھول جائے گی تو دوسری
اُسے یاد دلا دے گی۔ اور جب گواہ (گواہی کے لئے)
طلب کئے جائیں تو انکار نہ کریں۔ اور قرض تھوڑا ہو یا
بہت اس (کی دستاویز) کے لکھنے لکھانے میں کاہلی نہ کرنا
یہ بات خدا کے نزدیک نہایت قرینِ انصاف ہے
اور شہادت کے لئے بھی یہ بہت درست طریقہ ہے
اس سے تم کو کسی طرح کا شک و شبہ بھی نہیں پڑے گا
ہاں اگر سودا دست بدست ہو جو تم آپس میں لیتے
دیتے ہو تو اگر (ایسے معاملے کی) دستاویز نہ لکھو تو تم پر

إِلَىٰ مَيْسَرَةٍ ۚ وَأَن تَصَدَّقُوا
خَيْرٌ لَّكُمْ ۖ إِن كُنتُمْ تَعْلَمُونَ (۲۸۰)
وَاتَّقُوا يَوْمًا تُرْجَعُونَ فِيهِ
إِلَى اللَّهِ ۖ ثُمَّ تُوَفَّىٰ كُلُّ نَفْسٍ
مَّا كَسَبَتْ وَهُمْ لَا يُظْلَمُونَ (۲۸۱)
يَا أَيُّهَا الَّذِينَ آمَنُوا إِذَا تَدَايَنتُم
بِدَيْنٍ إِلَىٰ أَجَلٍ مُّسَمًّى فَاكْتُبُوهُ ۚ
وَلْيَكْتُب بَّيْنَكُمْ كَاتِبٌ بِالْعَدْلِ ۚ
وَلَا يَأْبَ كَاتِبٌ أَن يَكْتُبَ كَمَا
عَلَّمَهُ اللَّهُ ۚ فَلْيَكْتُبْ وَلْيُمْلِلِ
الَّذِي عَلَيْهِ الْحَقُّ وَلْيَتَّقِ اللَّهَ
رَبَّهُ وَلَا يَبْخَسْ مِنْهُ شَيْئًا ۚ
فَإِن كَانَ الَّذِي عَلَيْهِ الْحَقُّ
سَفِيهًا أَوْ ضَعِيفًا أَوْ لَا يَسْتَطِيعُ
أَن يُمِلَّ هُوَ فَلْيُمْلِلْ وَلِيُّهُ
بِالْعَدْلِ ۚ وَاسْتَشْهِدُوا شَهِيدَيْنِ
مِن رِّجَالِكُمْ ۖ فَإِن لَّمْ يَكُونَا
رَجُلَيْنِ فَرَجُلٌ وَامْرَأَتَانِ مِمَّن
تَرْضَوْنَ مِنَ الشُّهَدَاءِ أَن تَضِلَّ
إِحْدَاهُمَا فَتُذَكِّرَ إِحْدَاهُمَا
الْأُخْرَىٰ ۚ وَلَا يَأْبَ الشُّهَدَاءُ إِذَا
مَا دُعُوا ۚ وَلَا تَسْأَمُوا أَن تَكْتُبُوهُ
صَغِيرًا أَوْ كَبِيرًا إِلَىٰ أَجَلِهِ ۚ
ذَٰلِكُمْ أَقْسَطُ عِندَ اللَّهِ وَأَقْوَمُ
لِلشَّهَادَةِ وَأَدْنَىٰ أَلَّا تَرْتَابُوا ۖ
إِلَّا أَن تَكُونَ تِجَارَةً حَاضِرَةً
تُدِيرُونَهَا بَيْنَكُمْ فَلَيْسَ

contract; and let neither scribe nor witness suffer harm. If ye do (such harm), it would be wickedness in you. So fear Allah; for it is Allah that teaches you. And Allah is well acquainted with all things.

کچھ گناہ نہیں۔ اور جب خرید و فروخت کیا کرو
تو بھی گواہ کر لیا کرو۔ اور کاتب دستاویز اور گواہ
(معاملہ کرنے والوں کا) کسی طرح کا نقصان نہ کریں۔ اگر تم
(لوگ) ایسا کرو تو یہ تمہارے لئے گناہ کی بات ہے اور
خدا سے ڈرو اور دیکھو کہ وہ تم کو (کیسی مفید باتیں) سکھاتا
ہے اور خدا ہر چیز سے واقف ہے ﴿۲۸۲﴾

عَلَيْكُمْ جُنَاحٌ أَلَّا تَكْتُبُوهَا ۗ
وَأَشْهِدُوا إِذَا تَبَايَعْتُمْ ۚ وَلَا
يُضَارَّ كَاتِبٌ وَلَا شَهِيدٌ ۚ وَإِنْ
تَفْعَلُوا فَإِنَّهُ فُسُوقٌ بِكُمْ ۗ
وَاتَّقُوا اللَّهَ ۖ وَيُعَلِّمُكُمُ اللَّهُ ۗ
وَاللَّهُ بِكُلِّ شَيْءٍ عَلِيمٌ ﴿٢٨٢﴾

283. If ye are on a journey, and cannot find a scribe, a pledge with possession (may serve the purpose). And if one of you deposits a thing on trust with another, let the trustee (faithfully) discharge his trust, and let him fear Allah his Lord. Conceal not evidence; for whoever conceals it,—his heart is tainted with sin. And Allah knoweth all that ye do.

اور اگر تم سفر پر ہو اور (دستاویز لکھنے والا) نہ مل سکے
تو (کوئی چیز) رہن باقبضہ رکھ کر (قرض لے لو) اور اگر
کوئی کسی کو امین سمجھے (یعنی رہن کے بغیر قرض دیدے)
تو امانتدار کو چاہیئے کہ صاحب امانت کی امانت ادا کردے
اور خدا سے جو اس کا پروردگار ہے ڈرے۔ اور (دیکھنا)
شہادت کو مت چھپانا جو اس کو چھپائے گا وہ دل کا گنہگار
ہوگا۔ اور خدا تمہارے سب کاموں سے واقف ہے ﴿۲۸۳﴾

وَإِنْ كُنْتُمْ عَلَىٰ سَفَرٍ وَلَمْ تَجِدُوا
كَاتِبًا فَرِهَانٌ مَقْبُوضَةٌ ۖ فَإِنْ
أَمِنَ بَعْضُكُمْ بَعْضًا فَلْيُؤَدِّ
الَّذِي اؤْتُمِنَ أَمَانَتَهُ وَلْيَتَّقِ
اللَّهَ رَبَّهُ ۗ وَلَا تَكْتُمُوا الشَّهَادَةَ ۚ
وَمَنْ يَكْتُمْهَا فَإِنَّهُ آثِمٌ قَلْبُهُ ۗ
وَاللَّهُ بِمَا تَعْمَلُونَ عَلِيمٌ ﴿٢٨٣﴾

284. To Allah belongeth all that is in the heavens and on earth. Whether ye show what is in your minds or conceal it, Allah calleth you to account for it. He forgiveth whom He pleaseth, and punisheth whom He pleaseth. For Allah hath power over all things.

جو کچھ آسمانوں میں اور جو کچھ زمین میں ہے سب خدا ہی کا ہے
تم اپنے دلوں کی بات کو ظاہر کرو گے تو اور چھپاؤ گے تو
خدا تم سے اسکا حساب لے گا۔ پھر وہ جسے چاہے مغفرت
کرے اور جسے چاہے عذاب دے۔ اور خدا ہر چیز پر
قادر ہے ﴿۲۸۴﴾

لِلَّهِ مَا فِي السَّمَاوَاتِ وَمَا فِي الْأَرْضِ ۗ
وَإِنْ تُبْدُوا مَا فِي أَنْفُسِكُمْ أَوْ
تُخْفُوهُ يُحَاسِبْكُمْ بِهِ اللَّهُ ۖ فَيَغْفِرُ
لِمَنْ يَشَاءُ وَيُعَذِّبُ مَنْ يَشَاءُ ۗ
وَاللَّهُ عَلَىٰ كُلِّ شَيْءٍ قَدِيرٌ ﴿٢٨٤﴾

285. The Messenger believeth in what hath been revealed to him from his Lord, as do the men of faith, each one (of them) believeth in Allah, His angels, His books, and His Messengers. "We make no distinction (they say) between one and another of his Messengers." And they say: "We hear, and we obey: (we seek) Thy forgiveness, our Lord, and to Thee is the end of all journeys."

رسول اس کتاب پر جو ان کے پروردگار کی طرف سے ان پر
نازل ہوئی ایمان رکھتے ہیں اور مومن بھی۔ سب خدا پر اور
اسکے فرشتوں پر اور اسکی کتابوں پر اور اسکے پیغمبروں پر
ایمان رکھتے ہیں (اور کہتے ہیں کہ) ہم اسکے پیغمبروں سے
کسی میں کچھ فرق نہیں کرتے اور وہ (خدا سے) عرض کرتے
ہیں کہ ہم نے (تیرا حکم) سنا اور قبول کیا اے پروردگار ہم
تیری بخشش مانگتے ہیں اور تیری ہی طرف لوٹ کر جانا ہے ﴿۲۸۵﴾

آمَنَ الرَّسُولُ بِمَا أُنْزِلَ إِلَيْهِ
مِنْ رَبِّهِ وَالْمُؤْمِنُونَ ۚ كُلٌّ
آمَنَ بِاللَّهِ وَمَلَائِكَتِهِ وَكُتُبِهِ
وَرُسُلِهِ لَا نُفَرِّقُ بَيْنَ أَحَدٍ
مِنْ رُسُلِهِ ۚ وَقَالُوا سَمِعْنَا
وَأَطَعْنَا ۖ غُفْرَانَكَ رَبَّنَا وَإِلَيْكَ
الْمَصِيرُ ﴿٢٨٥﴾

286. On no soul doth Allah place a burden greater than it can bear. It gets every good that it earns, and it suffers every ill that it earns. (Pray:)

خدا کسی شخص کو اسکی طاقت سے زیادہ تکلیف نہیں دیتا
اچھے کام کریگا تو اس کو ان کا فائدہ ملے گا برے کریگا

لَا يُكَلِّفُ اللَّهُ نَفْسًا إِلَّا وُسْعَهَا ۚ
لَهَا مَا كَسَبَتْ وَعَلَيْهَا مَا اكْتَسَبَتْ ۗ

SÛRA–3
ÃL-I-'IMRÃN
(INTRODUCTION)

This Sûra is cognate to Sûra 2, but the matter is here treated from a different point of view. The references to Badr (Ramadhãn, H. 2) and Uḥud (Shawwãl, H. 3) give a clue to the dates of those passages.

Like Sûra 2, it takes a general view of the religious history of mankind, with special reference to the People of the Book, proceeds to explain the birth of the new People of Islam and their ordinances, insists on the need of struggle and fighting in the cause of Truth, and exhorts those who have been blessed with Islam to remain constant in Faith, pray for guidance, and maintain their spiritual hope for the Future.

The new points of view developed are: (1) The emphasis is here laid on the duty of the Christians to accept the new light; the Christians are here specially appealed to as the jews were specially appealed to in the last Sûra; (2) the lessons of the battles of Badr and Uḥud are set out for the Muslim community; and (3) the responsibilities of that community are insisted on both internally and in their relations to those outside.

"Our Lord ! condemn us not if we forget or fall into error; our Lord ! lay not on us a burden like that which Thou didst lay on those before us; our Lord ! lay not on us a burden greater than we have strength to bear. Blot out our sins, and grant us forgiveness. Have mercy on us. Thou art our Protector; grant us victory over the unbelievers.

تو اُسے اُن کا نقصان پہنچے گا۔ اے پروردگار اگر ہم سے
بھول یا چوک ہوگئی ہو تو ہم سے مواخذہ نہ کیجیو۔ اے
پروردگار ہم پر ایسا بوجھ نہ ڈالیو جیسا تو نے ہم سے پہلے
لوگوں پر ڈالا تھا۔ اے پروردگار جتنا بوجھ اُٹھانے
کی ہم میں طاقت نہیں اُتنا ہمارے سر پر نہ رکھیو۔ اور
(اے پروردگار) ہمارے گناہوں سے درگزر کر۔ اور ہمیں بخش دے
اور ہم پر رحم فرما۔ تو ہی ہمارا مالک ہے۔ اور ہم کو کافروں پر
غالب کر ﴿۲۸۶﴾

رَبَّنَا لَا تُؤَاخِذْنَآ اِنْ نَّسِيْنَآ اَوْ
اَخْطَاْنَا ۚ رَبَّنَا وَلَا تَحْمِلْ عَلَيْنَآ
اِصْرًا كَمَا حَمَلْتَهٗ عَلَى الَّذِيْنَ
مِنْ قَبْلِنَا ۚ رَبَّنَا وَلَا تُحَمِّلْنَا مَا
لَا طَاقَةَ لَنَا بِهٖ ۚ وَاعْفُ عَنَّا ۥ وقفة
وَاغْفِرْ لَنَا ۥ وقفة وَارْحَمْنَا ۥ وقفة اَنْتَ
مَوْلٰىنَا فَانْصُرْنَا عَلَى الْقَوْمِ
ع الْكٰفِرِيْنَ ﴿۲۸۶﴾

Āl-'Imrān, or the Family of 'Imrān

سورۂ آل عمران مدنی ہے اور اس میں دو سو آیتیں اور بیس رکوع ہیں

سُوْرَةُ اٰلِ عِمْرٰنَ مَدَنِيَّةٌ وَّهِيَ مِائَتَا اٰيَةٍ وَّعِشْرُوْنَ رُكُوْعًا

In the name of Allah, Most Gracious, Most Merciful.

شروع خدا کا نام لے کر جو بڑا مہربان نہایت رحم والا ہے

بِسْمِ اللّٰهِ الرَّحْمٰنِ الرَّحِيْمِ

1. A. L. M.
2. Allah ! There is no god but He,—the Living, the Self-Subsisting, the Supporter of all.

الم ﴿۱﴾ خدا (جو معبود برحق ہے) اُس کے سوا کوئی عبادت
کے لائق نہیں زندہ ہمیشہ رہنے والا ﴿۲﴾

الٓمّٓ ﴿۱﴾ اللّٰهُ لَآ اِلٰهَ اِلَّا هُوَ الْحَيُّ
الْقَيُّوْمُ ﴿۲﴾

3. It is He Who sent down to thee (step by step), in truth, the Book, confirming what went before it; and He sent down the Torah (of Moses) and the Gospel (of Jesus).

اُس نے (اے محمدؐ) تم پر سچی کتاب نازل کی جو پہلی (آسمانی)
کتابوں کی تصدیق کرتی ہے اور اُسی نے تورات اور
انجیل نازل کی ﴿۳﴾

نَزَّلَ عَلَيْكَ الْكِتٰبَ بِالْحَقِّ
مُصَدِّقًا لِّمَا بَيْنَ يَدَيْهِ وَ
اَنْزَلَ التَّوْرٰىةَ وَالْاِنْجِيْلَ ﴿۳﴾

4. Before this, as a guide to mankind, and He sent down the Criterion (of judgment between right and wrong). Then those who reject Faith in the Signs of Allah will suffer the severest chastisement and Allah is Exalted in Might, Lord of Retribution.

(یعنی) لوگوں کی ہدایت کیلئے (تورات اور انجیل اتاری)
اور (پھر قرآن جو حق اور باطل کو) الگ الگ کرنے والا ہے
نازل کیا۔ جو لوگ خدا کی آیتوں کا انکار کرتے ہیں اُن
کو سخت عذاب ہوگا۔ اور خدا زبردست (اور) بدلہ
لینے والا ہے ﴿۴﴾

مِنْ قَبْلُ هُدًى لِّلنَّاسِ وَ
اَنْزَلَ الْفُرْقَانَ ۥ اِنَّ الَّذِيْنَ
كَفَرُوْا بِاٰيٰتِ اللّٰهِ لَهُمْ
عَذَابٌ شَدِيْدٌ ؕ وَاللّٰهُ عَزِيْزٌ
ذُو انْتِقَامٍ ﴿۴﴾

5. From Allah, verily nothing is hidden on earth or in the heavens.

خدا (ایسا خبیر و بصیر ہے کہ) کوئی چیز اُس سے پوشیدہ نہیں
نہ زمین میں اور نہ آسمان میں ﴿۵﴾

اِنَّ اللّٰهَ لَا يَخْفٰى عَلَيْهِ شَيْءٌ فِي
الْاَرْضِ وَلَا فِي السَّمَآءِ ﴿۵﴾

6. He it is Who shapes you in the wombs as He pleases. There is no god but He, the Exalted in Might, the Wise.

وہی تو ہے جو (ماں کے) پیٹ میں جیسی چاہتا ہے
تمہاری صورتیں بناتا ہے۔ اُس غالب حکمت والے
کے سوا کوئی عبادت کے لائق نہیں ﴿۶﴾

هُوَ الَّذِيْ يُصَوِّرُكُمْ فِي الْاَرْحَامِ
كَيْفَ يَشَآءُ ؕ لَآ اِلٰهَ اِلَّا هُوَ
الْعَزِيْزُ الْحَكِيْمُ ﴿۶﴾

7. He it is Who has sent down to thee the Book: in it are verses basic or fundamental clear (in meaning);

وہی تو ہے جس نے تم پر کتاب نازل کی جس کی
بعض آیتیں محکم ہیں (اور) وہی اصل کتاب ہیں

هُوَ الَّذِيْٓ اَنْزَلَ عَلَيْكَ الْكِتٰبَ
مِنْهُ اٰيٰتٌ مُّحْكَمٰتٌ هُنَّ اُمُّ

they are the foundation of the Book: others are not entirely clear. But those in whose hearts is perversity follow the part thereof that is not entirely clear. Seeking discord, and searching for its interpretation, but no one knows its true meanings except Allah. And those who are firmly grounded in knowledge say: "We believe in it, the whole of it is from our Lord:" and none will grasp the Message except men of understanding.

اور بعض متشابہ ہیں، تو جن لوگوں کے دلوں
میں کجی ہے وہ متشابہات کا اتباع کرتے ہیں
تاکہ فتنہ برپا کریں اور مُراد اصلی کا پتہ لگائیں
حالانکہ مُراد اصلی خدا کے سوا کوئی نہیں جانتا
اور جو لوگ علم میں دستگاہ کامل رکھتے ہیں وہ
یہ کہتے ہیں کہ ہم ان پر ایمان لائے۔ یہ سب
ہمارے پروردگار کی طرف سے ہیں۔ اور نصیحت تو عقلمند
ہی قبول کرتے ہیں ⑦

الْكِتٰبِ وَأُخَرُ مُتَشٰبِهٰتٌ ۖ فَأَمَّا
الَّذِيْنَ فِيْ قُلُوْبِهِمْ زَيْغٌ
فَيَتَّبِعُوْنَ مَا تَشٰبَهَ مِنْهُ ابْتِغَآءَ
الْفِتْنَةِ وَابْتِغَآءَ تَأْوِيْلِهٖ ۚ وَمَا
يَعْلَمُ تَأْوِيْلَهٗٓ إِلَّا اللّٰهُ ۘ وَالرّٰسِخُوْنَ
فِي الْعِلْمِ يَقُوْلُوْنَ اٰمَنَّا بِهٖ ۙ كُلٌّ
مِّنْ عِنْدِ رَبِّنَا ۚ وَمَا يَذَّكَّرُ
إِلَّآ أُولُوا الْأَلْبَابِ ﴿٧﴾

8. "O Lord !" (they say), "Let not our hearts deviate now after Thou hast guided us, but grant us mercy from Thee: for Thou art the Grantor of bounties without measure.

اے پروردگار جب تُو نے ہمیں ہدایت بخشی ہے تو اس کے
بعد ہمارے دلوں میں کجی نہ پیدا کر دیجیو اور ہمیں اپنے ہاں
سے نعمت عطا فرما تُو تو بڑا عطا فرمانے والا ہے ⑧

رَبَّنَا لَا تُزِغْ قُلُوْبَنَا بَعْدَ إِذْ
هَدَيْتَنَا وَهَبْ لَنَا مِنْ لَّدُنْكَ
رَحْمَةً ۚ إِنَّكَ أَنْتَ الْوَهَّابُ ﴿٨﴾

9. "Our Lord ! Thou art He that will gather mankind together against a Day about which there is no doubt; for Allah never fails in His promise."

اے پروردگار تُو اُس روز جس (کے آنے) میں کچھ بھی
شک نہیں سب لوگوں کو (اپنے حضور میں) جمع کر لے گا
بیشک خدا خلاف وعدہ نہیں کرتا ⑨

رَبَّنَآ إِنَّكَ جَامِعُ النَّاسِ لِيَوْمٍ
لَّا رَيْبَ فِيْهِ ۚ إِنَّ اللّٰهَ لَا يُخْلِفُ
الْمِيْعَادَ ﴿٩﴾

10. Those who reject Faith,—neither their possessions nor their (numerous) progeny will avail them aught against Allah: they are themselves but fuel for the Fire.

جو لوگ کافر ہوئے (اس دن) نہ تو اُن کا مال ہی خدا
(کے عذاب) سے اُن کو بچا سکے گا اور نہ اُن کی اولاد ہی
(کچھ کام آئیگی) اور یہ لوگ آتش (جہنم) کا ایندھن ہوں گے ⑩

إِنَّ الَّذِيْنَ كَفَرُوْا لَنْ تُغْنِيَ عَنْهُمْ
أَمْوَالُهُمْ وَلَآ أَوْلَادُهُمْ مِّنَ
اللّٰهِ شَيْـًٔا ۖ وَأُولٰٓئِكَ هُمْ وَقُوْدُ النَّارِ ﴿١٠﴾

11. (Their plight will be) no better than that of the people of Pharaoh, and their predecessors: they denied our Signs, and Allah called them to account for their sins. For Allah is strict in punishment.

اُن کا حال بھی فرعونیوں اور اُن سے پہلے لوگوں کا سا
ہوگا جنہوں نے ہماری آیتوں کی تکذیب کی تھی تو خدا
نے اُن کو اُن کے گناہوں کے سبب (عذاب میں) پکڑ لیا
تھا اور خدا سخت عذاب کرنے والا ہے ⑪

كَدَأْبِ اٰلِ فِرْعَوْنَ ۙ وَالَّذِيْنَ
مِنْ قَبْلِهِمْ ۚ كَذَّبُوْا بِاٰيٰتِنَا ۚ
فَأَخَذَهُمُ اللّٰهُ بِذُنُوْبِهِمْ ۗ
وَاللّٰهُ شَدِيْدُ الْعِقَابِ ﴿١١﴾

12. Say to those who reject Faith: "Soon will ye be vanquished and gathered together to Hell,—an evil bed indeed (to lie on) !

(اے پیغمبر) کافروں سے کہہ دو کہ تم (دنیا میں بھی) عنقریب
مغلوب ہو جاؤ گے اور (آخرت میں) جہنم کی طرف ہانکے
جاؤ گے اور وہ بُری جگہ ہے ⑫

قُلْ لِّلَّذِيْنَ كَفَرُوْا سَتُغْلَبُوْنَ
وَتُحْشَرُوْنَ إِلٰى جَهَنَّمَ ۗ وَبِئْسَ
الْمِهَادُ ﴿١٢﴾

13. "There has already been for you a Sign in the two armies that met (in combat): one was fighting in the Cause of Allah, the other resisting Allah; these saw with their

تمہارے لئے دو گروہوں میں جو (جنگ بدر کے دن) آپس
میں بھڑ گئے (قدرت خدا کی عظیم الشان) نشانی تھی
ایک گروہ (مسلمانوں کا تھا وہ) خدا کی راہ میں لڑ رہا تھا اور دوسرا

قَدْ كَانَ لَكُمْ اٰيَةٌ فِيْ فِئَتَيْنِ
الْتَقَتَا ۖ فِئَةٌ تُقَاتِلُ فِيْ سَبِيْلِ اللّٰهِ
وَأُخْرٰى كَافِرَةٌ يَّرَوْنَهُمْ مِّثْلَيْهِمْ

own eyes twice their number. But Allah doth support with His aid whom He pleaseth. In this is a lesson for such as have eyes to see."

گروہ (کافروں کا تھا وہ) ان کو اپنی آنکھوں سے اپنے سے
دوگنا مشاہدہ کر رہا تھا اور خدا اپنی نصرت سے جسکو چاہتا ہے مدد
دیتا ہے جو اہلِ بصارت ہیں اُن کیلئے اِس (واقعے) میں بڑی عبرت ہے (۱۳)

رَأْيَ الْعَيْنِ ۚ وَاللَّهُ يُؤَيِّدُ بِنَصْرِهِ
مَنْ يَشَاءُ ۗ إِنَّ فِي ذَٰلِكَ لَعِبْرَةً
لِأُولِي الْأَبْصَارِ (۱۳)

14. Fair in the eyes of men is the love of things they covet: women and sons; heaped-up hoards of gold and silver; horses branded (for blood and excellence); and (wealth of) cattle and well-tilled land. Such are the possessions of this world's life; but with Allah is the best of the goals (to return to).

لوگوں کو ان کی خواہشوں کی چیزیں یعنی عورتیں
اور بیٹے اور سونے اور چاندی کے بڑے بڑے
ڈھیر اور نشان لگے ہوئے گھوڑے اور مویشی
اور کھیتی بڑی زینت دار معلوم ہوتی ہیں
(مگر) یہ سب دنیا ہی کی زندگی کے سامان ہیں۔ اور
خدا کے پاس بہت اچھا ٹھکانا ہے (۱۴)

زُيِّنَ لِلنَّاسِ حُبُّ الشَّهَوَاتِ
مِنَ النِّسَاءِ وَالْبَنِينَ وَالْقَنَاطِيرِ
الْمُقَنْطَرَةِ مِنَ الذَّهَبِ وَالْفِضَّةِ
وَالْخَيْلِ الْمُسَوَّمَةِ وَالْأَنْعَامِ
وَالْحَرْثِ ۗ ذَٰلِكَ مَتَاعُ الْحَيَاةِ الدُّنْيَا ۖ
وَاللَّهُ عِنْدَهُ حُسْنُ الْمَآبِ (۱۴)

15. Say: Shall I give you glad tidings of things far better than those ? For the righteous are Gardens in nearness to their Lord with rivers flowing beneath; therein is their eternal home; with spouses purified and the good pleasure of Allah. For in Allah's sight are (all) His servants,—

(اے پیغمبر ان سے) کہو کہ بھلا میں تم کو ایسی چیز بتاؤں جو اِن
چیزوں سے کہیں اچھی ہو (سنو) جو لوگ پرہیزگار ہیں ان
کیلئے خدا کے ہاں باغات (بہشت) ہیں جن کے نیچے
نہریں بہ رہی ہیں ان میں وہ ہمیشہ رہیں گے۔ اور پاکیزہ عورتیں ہیں
اور (سب سے بڑھ کر) خدا کی خوشنودی۔ اور خدا (اپنے نیک)
بندوں کو دیکھ رہا ہے (۱۵)

قُلْ أَؤُنَبِّئُكُمْ بِخَيْرٍ مِنْ ذَٰلِكُمْ ۚ
لِلَّذِينَ اتَّقَوْا عِنْدَ رَبِّهِمْ
جَنَّاتٌ تَجْرِي مِنْ تَحْتِهَا الْأَنْهَارُ
خَالِدِينَ فِيهَا وَأَزْوَاجٌ مُطَهَّرَةٌ
وَرِضْوَانٌ مِنَ اللَّهِ ۗ وَاللَّهُ بَصِيرٌ
بِالْعِبَادِ (۱۵)

16. (Namely), those who say: "Our Lord ! we have indeed believed: forgive us, then, our sins, and save us from the agony of the Fire;"—

جو خدا سے التجا کرتے ہیں کہ اے پروردگار ہم ایمان لے آئے
سو ہم کو ہمارے گناہ معاف فرما اور دوزخ کے عذاب سے محفوظ رکھ (۱۶)

الَّذِينَ يَقُولُونَ رَبَّنَا إِنَّنَا آمَنَّا
فَاغْفِرْ لَنَا ذُنُوبَنَا وَقِنَا عَذَابَ النَّارِ (۱۶)

17. Those who show patience, (firmness and self-control;) who are true (in word and deed); who worship devoutly; who spend (in the way of Allah); and who pray for forgiveness in the early hours of the morning.

یہ وہ لوگ ہیں جو (مشکلات میں) صبر کرتے اور سچ
بولتے اور عبادت میں لگے رہتے اور (راہِ خدا میں) خرچ
کرتے اور اوقاتِ سحر میں گناہوں کی معافی مانگا کرتے ہیں (۱۷)

الصَّابِرِينَ وَالصَّادِقِينَ وَ
الْقَانِتِينَ وَالْمُنْفِقِينَ وَالْمُسْتَغْفِرِينَ
بِالْأَسْحَارِ (۱۷)

18. There is no god but He: that is the witness of Allah, His angels, and those endued with knowledge, standing firm on justice. There is no god but He, the Exalted in Power, the Wise.

خدا تو اِس بات کی گواہی دیتا ہے کہ اُسکے سوا کوئی معبود
نہیں اور فرشتے اور علم والے لوگ جو انصاف پر قائم
ہیں وہ بھی (گواہی دیتے ہیں کہ) اُس غالب حکمت والے
کے سوا کوئی لائق عبادت نہیں (۱۸)

شَهِدَ اللَّهُ أَنَّهُ لَا إِلَٰهَ إِلَّا هُوَ
وَالْمَلَائِكَةُ وَأُولُو الْعِلْمِ قَائِمًا
بِالْقِسْطِ ۚ لَا إِلَٰهَ إِلَّا هُوَ الْعَزِيزُ
الْحَكِيمُ (۱۸) النصف

19. The Religion before Allah is Islam (submission to His Will): nor did the People of the Book dissent therefrom except through envy of each other, after knowledge had

دین تو خدا کے نزدیک اسلام ہے۔ اور اہلِ کتاب
نے جو (اس دین سے) اختلاف کیا تو علم حاصل ہونے
کے بعد آپس کی ضد سے کیا۔ اور جو شخص خدا کی آیتوں

إِنَّ الدِّينَ عِنْدَ اللَّهِ الْإِسْلَامُ ۗ
وَمَا اخْتَلَفَ الَّذِينَ أُوتُوا الْكِتَابَ
إِلَّا مِنْ بَعْدِ مَا جَاءَهُمُ الْعِلْمُ

come to them. But if any deny the Signs of Allah, Allah is swift in calling to account.

20. So if they dispute with thee, say: "I have submitted my whole self to Allah and so have those who follow me." And say to the People of the Book and to those who are unlearned: "Do ye (also) submit yourselves ?" If they do, they are in right guidance, but if they turn back, thy duty is to convey the Message; and in Allah's sight are (all) His servants.

21. As to those who deny the Signs of Allah, and in defiance of right, slay the prophets, and slay those who teach just dealing with mankind, announce to them a grievous chastisement.

22. They are those whose works will bear no fruit in this world and in the Hereafter, nor will they have anyone to help.

23. Hast thou not turned thy thought to those who have been given a portion of the Book? They are invited to the Book of Allah, to settle their dispute, but a party of them turn back and decline (the arbitration).

24. This because they say: "The Fire shall not touch us but for a few numbered days": for their forgeries deceive them as to their own religion.

25. But how (will they fare) when We gather them together against a Day about which there is no doubt, and each soul will be paid out just what it has earned, without (favour or) injustice?

26. Say: "O Allah! Lord of Power (and Rule), Thou givest Power to

کو نہ مانے تو خدا جلد حساب لینے والا (اور سزا
دینے والا) ہے (۱۹)
(اے پیغمبر) اگر یہ لوگ تم سے جھگڑنے لگیں تو کہنا کہ
میں اور میرے پیرو تو خدا کے فرمانبردار ہو چکے۔ اور
اہلِ کتاب اور اَن پڑھ لوگوں سے کہو کہ کیا تم بھی (خدا
کے فرمانبردار بنتے اور) اسلام لاتے ہو؟ اگر یہ لوگ اسلام
لے آئیں تو بیشک ہدایت پالیں اور اگر (تمہارا کہا) نہ مانیں تو تمہارا
کام صرف خدا کا پیغام پہنچا دینا ہے۔ اور خدا (اپنے) بندوں کو دیکھ رہا ہے (۲۰)
جو لوگ خدا کی آیتوں کو نہیں مانتے اور انبیاء کو
ناحق قتل کرتے رہے ہیں اور جو انصاف کا
حکم دیتے ہیں اُنہیں بھی مار ڈالتے ہیں اُن
کو دُکھ دینے والے عذاب کی خوشخبری سُنا دو (۲۱)
یہ ایسے لوگ ہیں جن کے اعمال دُنیا اور آخرت
دونوں میں برباد ہیں اور ان کا کوئی مددگار
نہیں (ہوگا) (۲۲)
بھلا تم نے اُن لوگوں کو نہیں دیکھا جن کو کتابِ خدا (یعنی
تورات) سے بہرہ دیا گیا اور وہ (اس) کتاب اللہ کی طرف
بُلائے جاتے ہیں تاکہ وہ (اُنکے تنازعات کا) اُن میں فیصلہ کردے
تو ایک فریق اُن میں سے کج ادائی کے ساتھ مُنہ پھیر لیتا ہے (۲۳)
یہ اِس لئے کہ یہ اس بات کے قائل ہیں کہ (دوزخ
کی) آگ ہمیں چند روز کے سوا چھو ہی نہیں سکے گی۔
اور جو کچھ یہ دین کے بارے میں بُہتان باندھتے رہے ہیں
اُس نے ان کو دھوکے میں ڈال رکھا ہے (۲۴)
تو اُس وقت کیا حال ہوگا جب ہم اُنکو جمع کرینگے (یعنی) اُس
روز جس (کے آنے) میں کچھ بھی شک نہیں اور ہر نفس اپنے
اعمال کا پُورا پُورا بدلہ پائیگا اور اُن پر ظلم نہیں کیا جائیگا (۲۵)
کہو کہ اے خُدا (اے) بادشاہی کے مالک تو جس کو چاہے

بَغْيًا بَيْنَهُمْ ۗ وَمَن يَكْفُرْ بِآيَاتِ
اللَّهِ فَإِنَّ اللَّهَ سَرِيعُ الْحِسَابِ (١٩)
فَإِنْ حَاجُّوكَ فَقُلْ أَسْلَمْتُ وَجْهِيَ
لِلَّهِ وَمَنِ اتَّبَعَنِ ۗ وَقُل لِّلَّذِينَ
أُوتُوا الْكِتَابَ وَالْأُمِّيِّينَ أَأَسْلَمْتُمْ ۚ
فَإِنْ أَسْلَمُوا فَقَدِ اهْتَدَوا ۖ وَّإِن
تَوَلَّوْا فَإِنَّمَا عَلَيْكَ الْبَلَاغُ ۗ وَاللَّهُ
ع بَصِيرٌ بِالْعِبَادِ (٢٠)
إِنَّ الَّذِينَ يَكْفُرُونَ بِآيَاتِ اللَّهِ
وَيَقْتُلُونَ النَّبِيِّينَ بِغَيْرِ حَقٍّ
وَيَقْتُلُونَ الَّذِينَ يَأْمُرُونَ بِالْقِسْطِ
مِنَ النَّاسِ فَبَشِّرْهُم بِعَذَابٍ أَلِيمٍ (٢١)
أُولَٰئِكَ الَّذِينَ حَبِطَتْ أَعْمَالُهُمْ
فِي الدُّنْيَا وَالْآخِرَةِ وَمَا لَهُم
مِّن نَّاصِرِينَ (٢٢)
أَلَمْ تَرَ إِلَى الَّذِينَ أُوتُوا نَصِيبًا
مِّنَ الْكِتَابِ يُدْعَوْنَ إِلَىٰ كِتَابِ
اللَّهِ لِيَحْكُمَ بَيْنَهُمْ ثُمَّ يَتَوَلَّىٰ
فَرِيقٌ مِّنْهُمْ وَهُم مُّعْرِضُونَ (٢٣)
ذَٰلِكَ بِأَنَّهُمْ قَالُوا لَن تَمَسَّنَا
النَّارُ إِلَّا أَيَّامًا مَّعْدُودَاتٍ ۖ
وَغَرَّهُمْ فِي دِينِهِم مَّا كَانُوا
يَفْتَرُونَ (٢٤)
فَكَيْفَ إِذَا جَمَعْنَاهُمْ لِيَوْمٍ لَّا رَيْبَ
فِيهِ وَوُفِّيَتْ كُلُّ نَفْسٍ مَّا كَسَبَتْ
وَهُمْ لَا يُظْلَمُونَ (٢٥)
قُلِ اللَّهُمَّ مَالِكَ الْمُلْكِ تُؤْتِي

whom Thou pleasest, and Thou strippest off Power from whom Thou pleasest: Thou enduest with honour whom Thou pleasest, and Thou bringest low whom Thou pleasest: in Thy hand is all Good. Verily, over all things thou hast power.

27. "Thou causest the Night to gain on the Day, and Thou causest the Day to gain on the Night; Thou bringest the Living out of the Dead, and Thou bringest the Dead out of the Living; and Thou givest sustenance to whom Thou pleasest without measure."

28. Let not the Believers take for friends or helpers Unbelievers rather than Believers: if any do that, shall have no relation left with Allah except by way of precaution, that ye may guard yourselves from them. But Allah cautions you (to fear) Himself; for the final goal is to Allah.

29. Say: "Whether ye hide what is in your hearts or reveal it, Allah knows it all: He knows what is in the heavens, and what is on earth. And Allah has power over all things.

30. "On the Day when every soul will be confronted with all the good it has done, and all the evil it has done, it will wish there were a great distance between it and its evil. But Allah cautions you (to fear) Him and Allah is full of kindness to those that serve Him."

31. Say: "If ye do love Allah, follow me: Allah will love you and forgive you your sins: for Allah is Oft-Forgiving, Most Merciful."

32. Say: "Obey Allah and His Messenger": but if they turn back,

بادشاہی بخشے اور جس سے چاہے بادشاہی چھین
لے اور جس کو چاہے عزت دے اور جسے چاہے
ذلیل کرے۔ ہر طرح کی بھلائی تیرے ہی ہاتھ ہے
اور بے شک تو ہر چیز پر قادر ہے ﴿٢٦﴾
تو ہی رات کو دن میں داخل کرتا اور تو ہی دن کو
رات میں داخل کرتا ہے تو ہی بے جان سے جاندار
پیدا کرتا ہے اور تو ہی جاندار سے بے جان پیدا کرتا ہے
اور تو ہی جس کو چاہتا ہے بےشمار رزق بخشتا ہے ﴿٢٧﴾
مومنوں کو چاہیئے کہ مومنوں کے سوا کافروں کو
دوست نہ بنائیں۔ اور جو ایسا کرے گا اُس سے
خدا کا کچھ (عہد) نہیں۔ ہاں اگر اس طریق سے تم ان
(کے شر) سے بچاؤ کی صورت پیدا کرو (تو مضائقہ نہیں)
اور خدا تم کو اپنے (غضب) سے ڈراتا ہے۔ اور خدا ہی
کی طرف (تم کو) لوٹ کر جانا ہے ﴿٢٨﴾
(اے پیغمبر لوگوں سے) کہہ دو کہ کوئی بات تم اپنے دلوں
میں مخفی رکھو یا اُسے ظاہر کرو خدا اُس کو جانتا ہے
اور جو کچھ آسمانوں میں اور جو کچھ زمین میں ہے اُسکو
سب کی خبر ہے اور وہ ہر چیز پر قادر ہے ﴿٢٩﴾
جس دن ہر شخص اپنے اعمال کی نیکی
کو موجود پالے گا اور اُن کی بُرائی کو بھی
دیکھ لیگا، تو آرزو کرے گا کہ اے کاش اس میں اور
اس بُرائی میں دُور کی مسافت ہو جاتی۔ اور خدا تم کو اپنے
(غضب) سے ڈراتا ہے۔ اور خدا اپنے بندوں پر نہایت مہربان ہے ﴿٣٠﴾
(اے پیغمبر لوگوں سے) کہہ دو کہ اگر تم خدا کو دوست رکھتے ہو
تو میری پیروی کرو خدا بھی تمہیں دوست رکھے گا اور تمہارے
گناہ معاف کر دے گا اور خدا بخشنے والا مہربان ہے ﴿٣١﴾
کہہ دو کہ خدا اور اُس کے رسول کا حکم مانو۔ اگر نہ مانیں

الْمُلْكَ مَنْ تَشَاءُ وَتَنْزِعُ الْمُلْكَ
مِمَّنْ تَشَاءُ وَتُعِزُّ مَنْ تَشَاءُ وَ
تُذِلُّ مَنْ تَشَاءُ ۖ بِيَدِكَ الْخَيْرُ ۖ
إِنَّكَ عَلَىٰ كُلِّ شَيْءٍ قَدِيرٌ ﴿٢٦﴾
تُولِجُ اللَّيْلَ فِي النَّهَارِ وَتُولِجُ
النَّهَارَ فِي اللَّيْلِ ۖ وَتُخْرِجُ الْحَيَّ مِنَ
الْمَيِّتِ وَتُخْرِجُ الْمَيِّتَ مِنَ الْحَيِّ ۖ
وَتَرْزُقُ مَنْ تَشَاءُ بِغَيْرِ حِسَابٍ ﴿٢٧﴾
لَا يَتَّخِذِ الْمُؤْمِنُونَ الْكَافِرِينَ
أَوْلِيَاءَ مِنْ دُونِ الْمُؤْمِنِينَ ۖ
وَمَنْ يَفْعَلْ ذَٰلِكَ فَلَيْسَ مِنَ
اللَّهِ فِي شَيْءٍ إِلَّا أَنْ تَتَّقُوا مِنْهُمْ
تُقَاةً ۗ وَيُحَذِّرُكُمُ اللَّهُ نَفْسَهُ ۗ
وَإِلَى اللَّهِ الْمَصِيرُ ﴿٢٨﴾
قُلْ إِنْ تُخْفُوا مَا فِي صُدُورِكُمْ
أَوْ تُبْدُوهُ يَعْلَمْهُ اللَّهُ ۗ وَيَعْلَمُ
مَا فِي السَّمَاوَاتِ وَمَا فِي الْأَرْضِ ۗ
وَاللَّهُ عَلَىٰ كُلِّ شَيْءٍ قَدِيرٌ ﴿٢٩﴾
يَوْمَ تَجِدُ كُلُّ نَفْسٍ مَا عَمِلَتْ
مِنْ خَيْرٍ مُحْضَرًا وَمَا عَمِلَتْ
مِنْ سُوءٍ تَوَدُّ لَوْ أَنَّ بَيْنَهَا
وَبَيْنَهُ أَمَدًا بَعِيدًا ۗ وَيُحَذِّرُكُمُ
اللَّهُ نَفْسَهُ ۗ وَاللَّهُ رَءُوفٌ بِالْعِبَادِ ﴿٣٠﴾
قُلْ إِنْ كُنْتُمْ تُحِبُّونَ اللَّهَ فَاتَّبِعُونِي
يُحْبِبْكُمُ اللَّهُ وَيَغْفِرْ لَكُمْ ذُنُوبَكُمْ ۗ
وَاللَّهُ غَفُورٌ رَحِيمٌ ﴿٣١﴾
قُلْ أَطِيعُوا اللَّهَ وَالرَّسُولَ ۖ فَإِنْ

Allah loveth not those who reject Faith.

33. Allah did choose Adam and Noah, the family of Abraham, and the family of 'Imrān above all people,–

34. Offspring, one of the other: and Allah heareth and knoweth all things.

35. Behold ! wife of 'Imrān said: "O my Lord ! I do dedicate into Thee what is in my womb for Thy special service: so accept this of me: for Thou hearest and knowest all things."

36. When she was delivered, she said: "O my Lord !' behold ! I am delivered of a female child !"—And Allah knew best what she brought forth—"And is not the male like the female. I have named her Mary, and I commend her and her offspring to Thy. protection from Satan, the Rejected."

37. Right graciously did her Lord accept her: He made her grow in purity and beauty: to the care of Zakariya was she assigned. Every time that he entered (her) chamber to see her, he found her supplied with sustenance. He said: "O Mary! Whence (comes) this to you ?" She said: "From Allah: for Allah provides sustenance to whom He pleases, without measure.

38. There did Zakariya pray to his Lord, saying: 'O my Lord ! Grant unto me from Thee a progeny that is pure: for Thou art He that heareth prayer !

39. While he was standing in prayer in the chamber, the angels called unto him: "Allah doth give thee glad tidings of Yahyā, confirming the truth of a Word from

تو خدا بھی کافروں کو دوست نہیں رکھتا ﴿۳۲﴾
خدا نے آدم اور نوح اور خاندان ابراہیم اور خاندان
عمران کو تمام جہان کے لوگوں میں منتخب فرمایا تھا ﴿۳۳﴾
اُن میں سے بعض بعض کی اولاد تھے ۔ اور خدا
سُننے والا (اور) جاننے والا ہے ﴿۳۴﴾
(وہ وقت یاد کرنے کے لائق ہے) جب عمران کی بیوی نے کہا کہ اے پروردگار
جو (بچہ) میرے پیٹ میں ہے میں اُس کو تیری نذر کرتی ہوں اُسے دنیا کے کاموں
سے آزاد رکھوں گی تو (اُسے) میری طرف سے قبول فرما تو تو سننے والا (اور) جاننے والا ہے ﴿۳۵﴾
جب اُن کے ہاں بچہ پیدا ہوا اور جو کچھ ان کے ہاں پیدا
ہوا تھا خدا کو خوب معلوم تھا ۔ تو کہنے لگیں کہ پروردگار!
میرے تو لڑکی ہوئی ہے اور (نذر کے لئے) لڑکا (موزوں تھا کہ وہ)
لڑکی کی طرح (ناتواں) نہیں ہوتا اور میں نے اس کا نام
مریم رکھا ہے اور میں اس کو اور اس کی اولاد کو شیطان مردود
سے تیری پناہ میں دیتی ہوں ﴿۳۶﴾
تو پروردگار نے اُس کو پسندیدگی کے ساتھ قبول
فرمایا اور اُسے اچھی طرح پرورش کیا اور زکریا کو
اس کا متکفل بنایا ۔ زکریا جب کبھی عبادت گاہ
میں اس کے پاس جاتے تو اس کے پاس کھانا
پاتے (یہ کیفیت دیکھ کر ایک دن مریم سے) پوچھنے لگے کہ مریم
یہ کھانا تمہارے پاس کہاں سے آتا ہے ۔ وہ بولیں خدا کے ہاں سے
(آتا ہے) بیشک خدا جسے چاہتا ہے بے شمار رزق دیتا ہے ﴿۳۷﴾
اُس وقت زکریا نے اپنے پروردگار سے دُعا کی (اور)
کہا کہ پروردگار مجھے اپنی جناب سے اولاد صالح عطا فرما ۔
تو بیشک دعا سننے (اور قبول کرنے) والا ہے ﴿۳۸﴾
وہ ابھی عبادت گاہ میں کھڑے نماز ہی پڑھ رہے تھے
کہ فرشتوں نے آواز دی کہ (زکریا) خدا تمہیں یحییٰ کی
بشارت دیتا ہے جو خدا کے فیض (یعنی عیسیٰ) کی تصدیق

تَوَلَّوْا فَإِنَّ اللّٰهَ لَا يُحِبُّ الْكٰفِرِيْنَ ﴿٣٢﴾
إِنَّ اللّٰهَ اصْطَفٰٓى اٰدَمَ وَنُوْحًا وَّاٰلَ
إِبْرٰهِيْمَ وَاٰلَ عِمْرٰنَ عَلَى الْعٰلَمِيْنَ ﴿٣٣﴾
ذُرِّيَّةً بَعْضُهَا مِنْ بَعْضٍ ۗ وَاللّٰهُ
سَمِيْعٌ عَلِيْمٌ ﴿٣٤﴾ ۚ
إِذْ قَالَتِ امْرَاَتُ عِمْرٰنَ رَبِّ إِنِّىْ
نَذَرْتُ لَكَ مَا فِىْ بَطْنِىْ مُحَرَّرًا فَتَقَبَّلْ
مِنِّىْ ۚ إِنَّكَ أَنْتَ السَّمِيْعُ الْعَلِيْمُ ﴿٣٥﴾
فَلَمَّا وَضَعَتْهَا قَالَتْ رَبِّ إِنِّىْ
وَضَعْتُهَآ أُنْثٰى ۗ وَاللّٰهُ أَعْلَمُ بِمَا
وَضَعَتْ ۗ وَلَيْسَ الذَّكَرُ
كَالْأُنْثٰى ۚ وَإِنِّىْ سَمَّيْتُهَا مَرْيَمَ
وَإِنِّىْٓ أُعِيْذُهَا بِكَ وَذُرِّيَّتَهَا
مِنَ الشَّيْطٰنِ الرَّجِيْمِ ﴿٣٦﴾
فَتَقَبَّلَهَا رَبُّهَا بِقَبُوْلٍ حَسَنٍ وَّ
أَنْبَتَهَا نَبَاتًا حَسَنًا ۙ وَّكَفَّلَهَا
زَكَرِيَّا ۗ كُلَّمَا دَخَلَ عَلَيْهَا زَكَرِيَّا
الْمِحْرَابَ ۙ وَجَدَ عِنْدَهَا رِزْقًا ۚ
قَالَ يٰمَرْيَمُ أَنّٰى لَكِ هٰذَا ۗ قَالَتْ
هُوَ مِنْ عِنْدِ اللّٰهِ ۗ إِنَّ اللّٰهَ يَرْزُقُ
مَنْ يَّشَآءُ بِغَيْرِ حِسَابٍ ﴿٣٧﴾
هُنَالِكَ دَعَا زَكَرِيَّا رَبَّهٗ ۚ قَالَ
رَبِّ هَبْ لِىْ مِنْ لَّدُنْكَ ذُرِّيَّةً
طَيِّبَةً ۚ إِنَّكَ سَمِيْعُ الدُّعَآءِ ﴿٣٨﴾
فَنَادَتْهُ الْمَلٰٓئِكَةُ وَهُوَ قَآئِمٌ
يُّصَلِّىْ فِى الْمِحْرَابِ ۙ أَنَّ اللّٰهَ
يُبَشِّرُكَ بِيَحْيٰى مُصَدِّقًا بِكَلِمَةٍ

Allah, and (be besides) noble, chaste, and a Prophet,—of the (goodly) company of the righteous."

مِّنَ اللّٰهِ وَسَيِّدًا وَّحَصُوْرًا وَّ
نَبِيًّا مِّنَ الصّٰلِحِيْنَ ﴿٣٩﴾

کرینگے اور سردار ہونگے اور عورتوں سے رغبت نہ رکھنے والے اور
(خدا کے) پیغمبر (یعنی) نیکوکاروں میں ہوں گے ﴿٣٩﴾

40. He said: "O my Lord ! how shall I have a son, seeing I am very old, and my wife is barren?" "Thus," was the answer, "doth Allah accomplish what He willeth."

قَالَ رَبِّ اَنّٰى يَكُوْنُ لِيْ غُلٰمٌ وَّقَدْ
بَلَغَنِيَ الْكِبَرُ وَامْرَاَتِيْ عَاقِرٌ ط
قَالَ كَذٰلِكَ اللّٰهُ يَفْعَلُ مَا يَشَآءُ ﴿٤٠﴾

زکریا نے کہا اے پروردگار میرے ہاں لڑکا کیونکر پیدا
ہوگا کہ میں تو بڈھا ہوگیا ہوں اور میری بیوی بانجھ ہے
خدا نے فرمایا اسی طرح خدا جو چاہتا ہے کرتا ہے ﴿٤٠﴾

41. He said: "O my Lord ! give me a Sign !" "Thy Sign," was the answer, "shall be that thou shalt speak to no man for three days but with signals. Then celebrate the praises of thy Lord again and again, and glorify Him in the evening and in the morning."

قَالَ رَبِّ اجْعَلْ لِّيْٓ اٰيَةً ط قَالَ
اٰيَتُكَ اَلَّا تُكَلِّمَ النَّاسَ ثَلٰثَةَ
اَيَّامٍ اِلَّا رَمْزًا ط وَاذْكُرْ رَّبَّكَ
ع ١١ ١٢ كَثِيْرًا وَّسَبِّحْ بِالْعَشِيِّ وَالْاِبْكَارِ ﴿٤١﴾ ع

زکریا نے کہا کہ پروردگار میرے لئے کوئی نشانی مقرر فرما
خدا نے فرمایا نشانی یہ ہے کہ تم لوگوں سے تین دن اشارے
کے سوا بات نہ کرسکو گے تو (ان دنوں میں) اپنے پروردگار
کی کثرت سے یاد اور صبح و شام اس کی تسبیح کرنا ﴿٤١﴾

42. Behold ! the angels said: "O Mary ! Allah hath chosen thee and purified thee—chosen thee above the women of all nations.

وَاِذْ قَالَتِ الْمَلٰٓئِكَةُ يٰمَرْيَمُ اِنَّ
اللّٰهَ اصْطَفٰكِ وَطَهَّرَكِ وَ
اصْطَفٰكِ عَلٰى نِسَآءِ الْعٰلَمِيْنَ ﴿٤٢﴾

اور جب فرشتوں نے (مریم سے) کہا کہ مریم! خدا نے تم
کو برگزیدہ کیا ہے اور پاک بنایا ہے اور جہان کی عورتوں
میں منتخب کیا ہے ﴿٤٢﴾

43. "O Mary ! worship the Lord devoutly: prostrate thyself, and bow down (in prayer) with those who bow down."

يٰمَرْيَمُ اقْنُتِيْ لِرَبِّكِ وَاسْجُدِيْ
وَارْكَعِيْ مَعَ الرّٰكِعِيْنَ ﴿٤٣﴾

مریم اپنے پروردگار کی فرمانبرداری کرنا اور سجدہ کرنا اور
رکوع کرنے والوں کے ساتھ رکوع کرنا ﴿٤٣﴾

44. This is part of the tidings of the things unseen, which We reveal unto thee (O Prophet !) by inspiration: thou wast not with them when they cast lots with pens, as to which of them should be charged with the care of Mary: nor wast thou with them when they disputed (the point).

ذٰلِكَ مِنْ اَنْۢبَآءِ الْغَيْبِ نُوْحِيْهِ
اِلَيْكَ ط وَمَا كُنْتَ لَدَيْهِمْ اِذْ
يُلْقُوْنَ اَقْلَامَهُمْ اَيُّهُمْ يَكْفُلُ
مَرْيَمَ ص وَمَا كُنْتَ لَدَيْهِمْ اِذْ
يَخْتَصِمُوْنَ ﴿٤٤﴾

(اے محمدؐ) یہ باتیں اخبار غیب میں سے ہیں جو ہم تمہارے
پاس بھیجتے ہیں۔ اور جب وہ لوگ اپنے قلم (بطور قرعہ)
ڈال رہے تھے کہ مریم کا متکفل کون بنے تو تم اُن کے
پاس نہیں تھے۔ اور نہ اس وقت ہی اُن کے پاس تھے
جب وہ آپس میں جھگڑ رہے تھے ﴿٤٤﴾

45. Behold ! the angels said: "O Mary ! Allah giveth thee glad tidings of a Word from Him: his name will be Christ Jesus, the son of Mary, held in honour in this world and the Hereafter and of (the company of) those nearest to Allah;

اِذْ قَالَتِ الْمَلٰٓئِكَةُ يٰمَرْيَمُ اِنَّ
اللّٰهَ يُبَشِّرُكِ بِكَلِمَةٍ مِّنْهُ ق اسْمُهُ
الْمَسِيْحُ عِيْسَى ابْنُ مَرْيَمَ وَجِيْهًا
فِي الدُّنْيَا وَالْاٰخِرَةِ وَمِنَ
الْمُقَرَّبِيْنَ ﴿٤٥﴾

(وہ وقت بھی یاد کرنے کے لائق ہے) جب فرشتوں نے
(مریم سے کہا) کہ مریم خدا تم کو اپنی طرف سے ایک فیض کی بشارت
دیتا ہے جس کا نام مسیح (اور مشہور) عیسیٰ ابن مریم ہوگا (اور جو)
دُنیا اور آخرت میں باآبرو اور (خدا کے) خاصوں
میں سے ہوگا ﴿٤٥﴾

46. "He shall speak to the people in childhood and in maturity. And he shall be (of the company of the righteous."

وَيُكَلِّمُ النَّاسَ فِي الْمَهْدِ وَكَهْلًا
وَّمِنَ الصّٰلِحِيْنَ ﴿٤٦﴾

اور ماں کی گود میں اور بڑی عمر کا ہو کر (دونوں حالتوں میں)
لوگوں سے (یکساں) گفتگو کریگا اور نیکوکاروں میں ہوگا ﴿٤٦﴾

47. She said: "O my Lord ! how shall I have a son when no man

قَالَتْ رَبِّ اَنّٰى يَكُوْنُ لِيْ وَلَدٌ

مریم نے کہا۔ پروردگار میرے ہاں بچہ کیونکر ہوگا کہ کسی

hath touched me ? He said: "Even so; Allah createth what He willeth: when He hath decreed a matter, He but saith to it, 'Be,' and it is !

انسان نے مجھے ہاتھ تک تو لگایا نہیں فرمایا کہ خدا
اسی طرح جو چاہتا ہے پیدا کرتا ہے جب وہ کوئی کام
کرنا چاہتا ہے تو ارشاد فرما دیتا ہے کہ ہو جا تو وہ ہو جاتا ہے (٤٧)

وَلَمْ يَمْسَسْنِي بَشَرٌ ؕ قَالَ كَذٰلِكِ
اللّٰهُ يَخْلُقُ مَا يَشَآءُ ؕ اِذَا قَضٰٓى
اَمْرًا فَاِنَّمَا يَقُوْلُ لَهٗ كُنْ فَيَكُوْنُ (٤٧)

48. "And Allah will teach him the Book and Wisdom, the Torah and the Gospel,

اور وہ انہیں لکھنا (پڑھنا) اور دانائی اور تورات
اور انجیل سکھائے گا (٤٨)

وَيُعَلِّمُهُ الْكِتٰبَ وَالْحِكْمَةَ وَالتَّوْرٰىةَ
وَالْاِنْجِيْلَ (٤٨)

49. "And (appoint him) a messenger to the Children of Israel, (with this message): "I have come to you, with a Sign from your Lord, in that I make for you out of clay, as it were, the figure of a bird, and breathe into it, and it becomes a bird by Allah's leave: and I heal those born blind, and the lepers, and I bring the dead into life, by Allah's leave; and I declare to you what ye eat, and what ye store in your houses. Surely therein is a Sign for you if ye did believe;

اور (عیسیٰ) بنی اسرائیل کی طرف پیغمبر (ہو کر جائیں گے
اور کہیں گے) کہ میں تمہارے پاس تمہارے پروردگار کی
طرف سے نشانی لیکر آیا ہوں وہ یہ کہ تمہارے سامنے مٹی کی مورت
بشکل پرند بناتا ہوں پھر اسمیں پھونک مارتا ہوں تو وہ
خدا کے حکم سے (سچ مچ) جانور ہو جاتا ہے۔ اور اندھے اور ابرص
کو تندرست کر دیتا ہوں۔ اور خدا کے حکم سے مُردے میں
جان ڈال دیتا ہوں۔ اور جو کچھ تم کھا کر آتے ہو اور جو
اپنے گھروں میں جمع کر رکھتے ہو سب تم کو بتا دیتا ہوں
اگر تم صاحب ایمان ہو تو ان باتوں میں تمہارے لئے
(قدرت خدا کی) نشانی ہے (٤٩)

وَرَسُوْلًا اِلٰى بَنِىٓ اِسْرَآءِيْلَ ۙ اَنِّىْ
قَدْ جِئْتُكُمْ بِاٰيَةٍ مِّنْ رَّبِّكُمْ ۙ
اَنِّىْٓ اَخْلُقُ لَكُمْ مِّنَ الطِّيْنِ
كَهَيْـَٔةِ الطَّيْرِ فَاَنْفُخُ فِيْهِ فَيَكُوْنُ
طَيْرًا بِاِذْنِ اللّٰهِ ۚ وَاُبْرِئُ الْاَكْمَهَ
وَالْاَبْرَصَ وَاُحْيِ الْمَوْتٰى بِاِذْنِ
اللّٰهِ ۚ وَاُنَبِّئُكُمْ بِمَا تَاْكُلُوْنَ وَمَا
تَدَّخِرُوْنَ ۙ فِىْ بُيُوْتِكُمْ ؕ اِنَّ
فِىْ ذٰلِكَ لَاٰيَةً لَّكُمْ اِنْ كُنْتُمْ
مُّؤْمِنِيْنَ (٤٩)

50. " '(I have come to you), to attest the Torah which was before me. And to make lawful to you part of what was (before) forbidden to you; I have come to you with a Sign from your Lord. So fear Allah, and obey me.

اور مجھ سے پہلے جو تورات (نازل ہوئی) تھی اسکی تصدیق بھی
کرتا ہوں اور (میں) اسلئے بھی (آیا ہوں) کہ بعض چیزیں
جو تم پر حرام تھیں انکو تمہارے لئے حلال کردوں اور میں تو تمہارے
پروردگار کیطرف سے نشانی لیکر آیا ہوں تو خدا سے ڈرو اور میرا کہا مانو (٥٠)

وَمُصَدِّقًا لِّمَا بَيْنَ يَدَىَّ مِنَ
التَّوْرٰىةِ وَلِاُحِلَّ لَكُمْ بَعْضَ الَّذِىْ
حُرِّمَ عَلَيْكُمْ وَجِئْتُكُمْ بِاٰيَةٍ مِّنْ
رَّبِّكُمْ فَاتَّقُوا اللّٰهَ وَاَطِيْعُوْنِ (٥٠)

51. " 'It is Allah who is my Lord and your Lord; then worship Him. This is a Way that is straight.' "

کچھ شک نہیں کہ خدا ہی میرا اور تمہارا پروردگار ہے تو اُسی
کی عبادت کرو یہی سیدھا رستہ ہے (٥١)

اِنَّ اللّٰهَ رَبِّىْ وَرَبُّكُمْ فَاعْبُدُوْهُ ؕ
هٰذَا صِرَاطٌ مُّسْتَقِيْمٌ (٥١)

52. When Jesus found unbelief on their part, he said: "Who will be my helpers to (the work of) Allah ? Said the Disciples:" We are Allah's helpers: we believe in Allah, and do thou bear witness that we are Muslims.

جب عیسیٰ نے اُن کی طرف سے نافرمانی (اور نیت قتل)
دیکھی تو کہنے لگے کہ کوئی ہے جو خدا کا طرفدار اور میرا مددگار
ہو۔ حواری بولے کہ ہم خدا کے (طرفدار اور آپکے) مددگار ہیں
ہم خدا پر ایمان لائے اور آپ گواہ رہیں کہ ہم فرمانبردار ہیں (٥٢)

فَلَمَّآ اَحَسَّ عِيْسٰى مِنْهُمُ الْكُفْرَ
قَالَ مَنْ اَنْصَارِىْٓ اِلَى اللّٰهِ ؕ قَالَ
الْحَوَارِيُّوْنَ نَحْنُ اَنْصَارُ اللّٰهِ ۚ
اٰمَنَّا بِاللّٰهِ ۚ وَاشْهَدْ بِاَنَّا مُسْلِمُوْنَ (٥٢)

53. "Our Lord ! we believe in what Thou hast revealed, and we follow the Messenger: then write us down among those who bear witness."

اے پروردگار جو (کتاب) تُو نے نازل فرمائی ہے ہم اُس پر ایمان
لے آئے اور (تیرے) پیغمبر کے متبع ہو چکے تو ہمکو ماننے والوں میں لکھ رکھ (٥٣)

رَبَّنَآ اٰمَنَّا بِمَآ اَنْزَلْتَ وَاتَّبَعْنَا
الرَّسُوْلَ فَاكْتُبْنَا مَعَ الشّٰهِدِيْنَ (٥٣)

54. And (the unbelievers) plotted and planned, and Allah too planned, and the best of planners is Allah.

اور وہ (یعنی یہود قتل عیسیٰ کے بارے میں ایک) چال چلے اور خدا
بھی (عیسیٰ کو بچانے کیلئے) چال چلا اور خدا خوب چال چلنے والا ہے (۵۴)

وَمَكَرُوْا وَمَكَرَ اللّٰهُ ۭ وَاللّٰهُ خَيْرُ
الْمٰكِرِيْنَ ۵۴ ع

55. Behold! Allah said: "O Jesus! I will take thee and raise thee to Myself and clear thee (of the falsehoods) of those who blaspheme; I will make those who follow thee superior to those who reject Faith, to the Day of Resurrection: then shall ye all return unto Me, and I will judge between you of the matters wherein ye dispute.

اس وقت خدا نے فرمایا کہ عیسیٰ! میں تمہاری دنیا میں رہنے کی
مدت پوری کر کے تم کو اپنی طرف اُٹھا لوں گا اور تمہیں کافروں
(کی صحبت) سے پاک کر دوں گا۔ اور جو لوگ تمہاری پیروی
کرینگے اُن کو کافروں پر قیامت تک فائق (و غالب)
رکھوں گا پھر تم سب میرے پاس لوٹ کر آؤ گے تو جن
باتوں میں تم اختلاف کرتے تھے اس دن تم میں ان کا
فیصلہ کر دوں گا (۵۵)

اِذْ قَالَ اللّٰهُ يٰعِيْسٰٓى اِنِّىْ مُتَوَفِّيْكَ
وَرَافِعُكَ اِلَىَّ وَمُطَهِّرُكَ مِنَ
الَّذِيْنَ كَفَرُوْا وَجَاعِلُ الَّذِيْنَ
اتَّبَعُوْكَ فَوْقَ الَّذِيْنَ كَفَرُوْٓا
اِلٰى يَوْمِ الْقِيٰمَةِ ۚ ثُمَّ اِلَيَّ مَرْجِعُكُمْ
فَاَحْكُمُ بَيْنَكُمْ فِيْمَا كُنْتُمْ فِيْهِ
تَخْتَلِفُوْنَ ۵۵

56. "As to those who reject Faith, I will punish them with severe chastisement in this world and in the Hereafter nor will they have anyone to help.

یعنی جو کافر ہوئے اُن کو دُنیا اور آخرت (دونوں)
میں سخت عذاب دُوں گا اور اُن کا کوئی مددگار
نہ ہوگا (۵۶)

فَاَمَّا الَّذِيْنَ كَفَرُوْا فَاُعَذِّبُهُمْ
عَذَابًا شَدِيْدًا فِى الدُّنْيَا وَ
الْاٰخِرَةِ ۡ وَمَا لَهُمْ مِّنْ نّٰصِرِيْنَ ۵۶

57. "As to those who believe and work righteousness, Allah will pay them (in full) their reward; but Allah loveth not those who do wrong.

اور جو ایمان لائے اور عمل نیک کرتے رہے اُن کو
خدا پورا پورا صلہ دے گا۔ اور خدا ظالموں کو دوست
نہیں رکھتا (۵۷)

وَاَمَّا الَّذِيْنَ اٰمَنُوْا وَعَمِلُوا
الصّٰلِحٰتِ فَيُوَفِّيْهِمْ اُجُوْرَهُمْ ۭ
وَاللّٰهُ لَا يُحِبُّ الظّٰلِمِيْنَ ۵۷

58. "This is what We rehearse unto thee of the Signs and the Message of Wisdom."

(اے محمد) یہ ہم تم کو (خدا کی) آیتیں اور حکمت بھری
نصیحتیں پڑھ پڑھ کر سُناتے ہیں (۵۸)

ذٰلِكَ نَتْلُوْهُ عَلَيْكَ مِنَ الْاٰيٰتِ
وَالذِّكْرِ الْحَكِيْمِ ۵۸

59. The similitude of Jesus before Allah is as that of Adam; He created him from dust, then said to him: "Be": and he was.

عیسیٰ کا حال خدا کے نزدیک آدم کا سا ہے کہ اُس
نے (پہلے) مٹی سے ان کا قالب بنایا پھر فرمایا کہ
(انسان) ہو جا تو وہ (انسان) ہو گئے (۵۹)

اِنَّ مَثَلَ عِيْسٰى عِنْدَ اللّٰهِ كَمَثَلِ
اٰدَمَ ۭ خَلَقَهٗ مِنْ تُرَابٍ ثُمَّ
قَالَ لَهٗ كُنْ فَيَكُوْنُ ۵۹

60. The Truth (comes) from thy Lord alone; so be not of those who doubt.

(یہ بات) تمہارے پروردگار کی طرف سے حق ہے تو تم
ہرگز شک کرنے والوں میں نہ ہونا (۶۰)

اَلْحَقُّ مِنْ رَّبِّكَ فَلَا تَكُنْ مِّنَ
الْمُمْتَرِيْنَ ۶۰

61. If anyone disputes in this matter with thee, now after (full) knowledge hath come to thee, say: "Come ! let us gather together,—our sons and your sons, our women and your women, ourselves and yourselves: then let us earnestly pray, and invoke the curse of Allah

پھر اگر یہ لوگ عیسیٰ کے بارے میں تم سے جھگڑا کریں
اور تم کو حقیقت الحال تو معلوم ہو ہی چلی ہے۔ تو ان
سے کہنا کہ آؤ ہم اپنے بیٹوں اور عورتوں کو بُلائیں
تم اپنے بیٹوں اور عورتوں کو بُلاؤ اور ہم خود بھی آئیں اور
تم خود بھی آؤ۔ پھر دونوں فریق (خدا سے) دُعا و التجا

فَمَنْ حَاۗجَّكَ فِيْهِ مِنْۢ بَعْدِ مَا
جَاۗءَكَ مِنَ الْعِلْمِ فَقُلْ تَعَالَوْا
نَدْعُ اَبْنَاۗءَنَا وَاَبْنَاۗءَكُمْ وَ
نِسَاۗءَنَا وَنِسَاۗءَكُمْ وَاَنْفُسَنَا وَ
اَنْفُسَكُمْ ۣ ثُمَّ نَبْتَهِلْ فَنَجْعَلْ

on those who lie!"

کریں اور جھوٹوں پر خدا کی لعنت بھیجیں (۶۱)

لَّعْنَتَ اللّٰهِ عَلَى الْكٰذِبِيْنَ ﴿٦١﴾

62. This is the true account: there is no god except Allah; and Allah—He is indeed the Exalted in Power, the Wise.

یہ تمام بیانات صحیح ہیں۔ اور خدا کے
سوا کوئی معبود نہیں۔ اور بیشک خدا
غالب (اور) صاحب حکمت ہے (۶۲)

اِنَّ هٰذَا لَهُوَ الْقَصَصُ الْحَقُّ ۚ
وَمَا مِنْ اِلٰهٍ اِلَّا اللّٰهُ ۭ وَاِنَّ اللّٰهَ
لَهُوَ الْعَزِيْزُ الْحَكِيْمُ ﴿٦٢﴾

63. But if they turn back, Allah hath full knowledge of those who do mischief.

تو اگر یہ لوگ پھر جائیں تو خدا مفسدوں کو خوب جانتا ہے (۶۳)

فَاِنْ تَوَلَّوْا فَاِنَّ اللّٰهَ عَلِيْمٌۢ بِالْمُفْسِدِيْنَ ﴿٦٣﴾ ع

64. Say: "O People of the Book ! come to common terms as between us and you: that we worship none but Allah; that we associate no partners with Him; that we erect not, from among ourselves, lords and patrons other than Allah." If then they turn back, say ye: "Bear witness that we (at least) are Muslims (bowing to Allah's Will)."

کہہ دو کہ اے اہل کتاب جو بات ہمارے اور تمہارے
دونوں کے درمیان یکساں (تسلیم کی گئی) ہے اس کی طرف
آؤ وہ یہ کہ خدا کے سوا ہم کسی کی عبادت نہ کریں۔ اور اُس
کے ساتھ کسی چیز کو شریک نہ بنائیں۔ اور ہم میں کوئی
کسی کو خدا کے سوا اپنا کارساز نہ سمجھے۔ اگر یہ لوگ (اس بات
کو) نہ مانیں تو (اُن سے) کہہ دو کہ تم گواہ رہو کہ ہم (خدا کے) فرمانبردار ہیں (۶۴)

قُلْ يٰٓاَهْلَ الْكِتٰبِ تَعَالَوْا اِلٰى
كَلِمَةٍ سَوَاۗءٍۢ بَيْنَنَا وَبَيْنَكُمْ اَلَّا
نَعْبُدَ اِلَّا اللّٰهَ وَلَا نُشْرِكَ بِهٖ
شَيْـــًٔـا وَّلَا يَتَّخِذَ بَعْضُنَا بَعْضًا
اَرْبَابًا مِّنْ دُوْنِ اللّٰهِ ۭ فَاِنْ تَوَلَّوْا
فَقُوْلُوا اشْهَدُوْا بِاَنَّا مُسْلِمُوْنَ ﴿٦٤﴾

65. Ye People of the Book ! why dispute ye about Abraham, when the Torah and the Gospel were not revealed till after him ? Have ye no understanding ?

اے اہل کتاب تم ابراہیم کے بارے میں کیوں جھگڑتے ہو
حالانکہ تورات اور انجیل اُن کے بعد اُتری ہیں
(اور وہ پہلے ہو چکے) تو کیا تم عقل نہیں رکھتے (۶۵)

يٰٓاَهْلَ الْكِتٰبِ لِمَ تُحَاۗجُّوْنَ فِيْٓ
اِبْرٰهِيْمَ وَمَآ اُنْزِلَتِ التَّوْرٰىةُ وَالْاِنْجِيْلُ
اِلَّا مِنْۢ بَعْدِهٖ ۭ اَفَلَا تَعْقِلُوْنَ ﴿٦٥﴾

66. Ah ! Ye are those who fell to disputing (even) in matters of which ye had some Knowledge! But why dispute ye in matters of which ye have no knowledge? It is Allah Who knows, and ye who know not !

دیکھو ایسی بات میں تو تم نے جھگڑا کیا ہی تھا جس کا
تمہیں کچھ علم تھا بھی۔ مگر ایسی بات میں کیوں
جھگڑتے ہو جس کا تم کو کچھ بھی علم نہیں۔ اور خدا
جانتا ہے اور تم نہیں جانتے (۶۶)

هٰٓاَنْتُمْ هٰٓؤُلَاۗءِ حَاجَجْتُمْ فِيْمَا
لَكُمْ بِهٖ عِلْمٌ فَلِمَ تُحَاۗجُّوْنَ فِيْمَا
لَيْسَ لَكُمْ بِهٖ عِلْمٌ ۭ وَاللّٰهُ يَعْلَمُ
وَاَنْتُمْ لَا تَعْلَمُوْنَ ﴿٦٦﴾

67. Abraham was not a Jew nor yet a Christian; but he was Upright, and bowed his will to Allah's, (which is Islam), and he joined not gods with Allah.

ابراہیم نہ تو یہودی تھے اور نہ عیسائی بلکہ سب سے
بے تعلق ہو کر ایک (خدا) کے ہو رہے تھے اور اسی
کے فرمانبردار تھے اور مشرکوں میں نہ تھے (۶۷)

مَا كَانَ اِبْرٰهِيْمُ يَهُوْدِيًّا وَّلَا
نَصْرَانِيًّا وَّلٰكِنْ كَانَ حَنِيْفًا مُّسْلِمًا ۭ
وَمَا كَانَ مِنَ الْمُشْرِكِيْنَ ﴿٦٧﴾

68. Without doubt, among men, the nearest of kin to Abraham, are those who follow him, as are also this Prophet and those who believe: and Allah is the Protector of those who have Faith.

ابراہیم سے قرب رکھنے والے تو وہ لوگ ہیں جو اُن کی
پیروی کرتے ہیں اور یہ پیغمبر آخر الزماں اور وہ لوگ جو
ایمان لائے ہیں۔ اور خدا مومنوں کا کارساز ہے (۶۸)

اِنَّ اَوْلَى النَّاسِ بِاِبْرٰهِيْمَ لَلَّذِيْنَ
اتَّبَعُوْهُ وَھٰذَا النَّبِيُّ وَالَّذِيْنَ
اٰمَنُوْا ۭ وَاللّٰهُ وَلِيُّ الْمُؤْمِنِيْنَ ﴿٦٨﴾

69. It is the wish of a section of the People of the Book to lead you astray. But they shall lead astray (not you), but themselves, and they do not perceive !

(اے اہل اسلام) بعضے اہل کتاب اس بات کی خواہش
رکھتے ہیں کہ تم کو گمراہ کر دیں۔ مگر یہ (تم کو کیا گمراہ کریں گے
اپنے آپ کو ہی گمراہ کر رہے ہیں اور نہیں جانتے (۶۹)

وَدَّتْ طَّاۗىِٕفَةٌ مِّنْ اَھْلِ الْكِتٰبِ
لَوْ يُضِلُّوْنَكُمْ ۭ وَمَا يُضِلُّوْنَ اِلَّآ
اَنْفُسَھُمْ وَمَا يَشْعُرُوْنَ ﴿٦٩﴾

70. Ye People of the Book ! why reject ye the Signs of Allah, of which ye are (yourselves) witnesses ?

71. Ye People of the Book! why do ye clothe truth with falsehood, and conceal the Truth, while ye have knowledge ?

72. A section of the People of the Book say: "Believe in the morning what is revealed to the Believers, but reject it at the end of the day: perchance they may (themselves) turn back;

73. "And believe no one unless he follows your religion." Say: "True guidance is the guidance of Allah: (fear ye) lest a revelation be sent to someone (else) like unto that which was sent unto you. Or that those (receiving such revelation) should engage you in argument before your Lord ? Say: "All bounties are in the hand of Allah: He granteth them to whom He pleaseth: and Allah careth for all, and He knoweth all things."

74. For His Mercy He specially chooseth whom He pleaseth: for Allah is the Lord of bounties unbounded.

75. Among the People of the Book are some who, if entrusted with a hoard of gold, will (readily) pay it back; others, who, if entrusted with a single silver coin, will not repay it unless thou constantly stoodest demanding, because, they say: "There is no way over us as to the unlettered people," but they tell a lie against Allah, and (well) they know it.

76. Nay,—Those that keep their plighted faith and act aright,—verily Allah loves those who act aright.

77. As for those who sell the faith they owe to Allah and their own

اے اہلِ کتاب تم خدا کی آیتوں سے کیوں انکار کرتے ہو
اور تم (تورات کو) مانتے تو ہو ﴿۷۰﴾
اے اہلِ کتاب تم سچ کو جھوٹ کے ساتھ خلط ملط
کیوں کرتے ہو اور حق کو کیوں چھپاتے ہو اور تم
جانتے بھی ہو ﴿۷۱﴾
اور اہلِ کتاب ایک دوسرے سے کہتے ہیں کہ جو
(کتاب) مومنوں پر نازل ہوئی ہے اُس پر دن کے
شروع میں تو ایمان لے آیا کرو اور اس کے آخر میں انکار
کر دیا کرو تاکہ وہ (اسلام سے) برگشتہ ہو جائیں ﴿۷۲﴾
اور اپنے دین کے پیرو کے سوا کسی اور کے قائل نہ ہونا
(اے پیغمبر) کہہ دو کہ ہدایت تو خدا ہی کی ہدایت ہے (وہ یہ بھی
کہتے ہیں) یہ بھی (نہ ماننا) کہ جو چیز تم کو ملی ہے ویسی کسی
اور کو ملے گی یا وہ تمہیں خدا کے روبرو قائل معقول کر سکیں گے
یہ بھی کہہ دو کہ بزرگی خدا ہی کے ہاتھ میں ہے وہ جسے چاہتا
ہے دیتا ہے اور خدا کشائش والا (اور) علم والا ہے ﴿۷۳﴾
وہ اپنی رحمت سے جس کو چاہتا ہے خاص کر لیتا ہے اور خدا
بڑے فضل کا مالک ہے ﴿۷۴﴾
اور اہلِ کتاب میں سے کوئی تو ایسا ہے کہ اگر تم اس کے
پاس (روپوں کا) ڈھیر امانت رکھ دو تو تم کو (فوراً) واپس
دیدے اور کوئی اس طرح کا ہے کہ اگر اسکے پاس ایک دینار بھی
امانت رکھو تو جب تک اسکے سر پر ہر وقت کھڑے نہ رہو
تمہیں دے ہی نہیں یہ اسلئے کہ وہ کہتے ہیں کہ امیوں کے بارے
میں ہم سے مواخذہ نہیں ہوگا یہ خدا پر محض جھوٹ بولتے
ہیں اور (اس بات کو) جانتے بھی ہیں ﴿۷۵﴾
ہاں جو شخص اپنے اقرار کو پورا کرے اور (خدا سے) ڈرے
تو خدا ڈرنے والوں کو دوست رکھتا ہے ﴿۷۶﴾
جو لوگ خدا کے اقراروں اور اپنی قسموں (کو بیچ ڈالتے

يٰۤاَهۡلَ الۡكِتٰبِ لِمَ تَكۡفُرُوۡنَ بِاٰيٰتِ
اللّٰهِ وَاَنۡتُمۡ تَشۡهَدُوۡنَ ﴿۷۰﴾
يٰۤاَهۡلَ الۡكِتٰبِ لِمَ تَلۡبِسُوۡنَ الۡحَقَّ
بِالۡبَاطِلِ وَتَكۡتُمُوۡنَ الۡحَقَّ وَاَنۡتُمۡ
تَعۡلَمُوۡنَ ﴿۷۱﴾ ع ۷ ۵
وَقَالَتۡ طَّآئِفَةٌ مِّنۡ اَهۡلِ الۡكِتٰبِ
اٰمِنُوۡا بِالَّذِىۡۤ اُنۡزِلَ عَلَى الَّذِيۡنَ
اٰمَنُوۡا وَجۡهَ النَّهَارِ وَاكۡفُرُوۡۤا
اٰخِرَهٗ لَعَلَّهُمۡ يَرۡجِعُوۡنَ ﴿۷۲﴾
وَلَا تُؤۡمِنُوۡۤا اِلَّا لِمَنۡ تَبِعَ دِيۡنَكُمۡ
قُلۡ اِنَّ الۡهُدٰى هُدَى اللّٰهِ اَنۡ
يُّؤۡتٰٓى اَحَدٌ مِّثۡلَ مَاۤ اُوۡتِيۡتُمۡ اَوۡ
يُحَآجُّوۡكُمۡ عِنۡدَ رَبِّكُمۡ قُلۡ اِنَّ
الۡفَضۡلَ بِيَدِ اللّٰهِ يُؤۡتِيۡهِ مَنۡ
يَّشَآءُ وَاللّٰهُ وَاسِعٌ عَلِيۡمٌ ﴿۷۳﴾
يَّخۡتَصُّ بِرَحۡمَتِهٖ مَنۡ يَّشَآءُ وَاللّٰهُ
ذُو الۡفَضۡلِ الۡعَظِيۡمِ ﴿۷۴﴾
وَمِنۡ اَهۡلِ الۡكِتٰبِ مَنۡ اِنۡ تَاۡمَنۡهُ
بِقِنۡطَارٍ يُّؤَدِّهٖۤ اِلَيۡكَ وَمِنۡهُمۡ مَّنۡ
اِنۡ تَاۡمَنۡهُ بِدِيۡنَارٍ لَّا يُؤَدِّهٖۤ اِلَيۡكَ
اِلَّا مَا دُمۡتَ عَلَيۡهِ قَآئِمًا ذٰلِكَ
بِاَنَّهُمۡ قَالُوۡا لَيۡسَ عَلَيۡنَا فِى
الۡاُمِّيّٖنَ سَبِيۡلٌ وَيَقُوۡلُوۡنَ
عَلَى اللّٰهِ الۡكَذِبَ وَهُمۡ يَعۡلَمُوۡنَ ﴿۷۵﴾
بَلٰى مَنۡ اَوۡفٰى بِعَهۡدِهٖ وَاتَّقٰى
فَاِنَّ اللّٰهَ يُحِبُّ الۡمُتَّقِيۡنَ ﴿۷۶﴾
اِنَّ الَّذِيۡنَ يَشۡتَرُوۡنَ بِعَهۡدِ

solemn plighted word for a small price, they shall have no portion in the Hereafter: nor will Allah (deign to) speak to them or look at them on the Day of Judgment, nor will He cleanse them (of sin): they shall have a grievous Chastisement.

78. There is among them a section who distort the Book with their tongues; (as they read) so that you would think it is a part of the Book, but it is no part of the Book; and they say, "That is from Allah," but it is not from Allah: it is they who tell a lie against Allah, and (well) they know it !

79. It is not (possible) that a man, to whom is given the Book, and Wisdom, and the Prophetic Office, should say to people: "Be ye my worshippers rather than Allah's": on the contrary (he would say): "Be ye worshippers of Him (Who is truly the Cherisher of all): for ye have taught the Book and ye have studied it earnestly."

80. Nor would he instruct you to take angels and prophets for Lords and Patrons. What ! would he bid you to unbelief after ye have bowed your will (to Allah in Islam) ?

81. Behold ! Allah took the Covenant of the Prophets, saying: "I give you a Book and Wisdom: then comes to you a Messenger, confirming what is with you; do ye believe in him and render him help." Allah said: "Do ye agree, and take this My Covenant as binding on you ?" They said: "We agree." He said: "Then bear witness, and I am with you among the witnesses."

ہیں اور اُن کے عوض تھوڑی سی قیمت حاصل کرتے
ہیں اُن کا آخرت میں کچھ حصہ نہیں۔ اُن سے خدا
نہ تو کلام کرے گا اور نہ قیامت کے روز اُن کی طرف
دیکھے گا اور نہ اُن کو پاک کرے گا اور اُن کو دُکھ
دینے والا عذاب ہوگا ۝٧٧
اور ان (اہلِ کتاب) میں بعض ایسے ہیں کہ کتاب (تورات)
کو زبان مروڑ مروڑ کر پڑھتے ہیں تاکہ تم سمجھو کہ جو کچھ وہ
پڑھتے ہیں کتاب میں سے ہے حالانکہ وہ کتاب میں
سے نہیں ہوتا اور کہتے ہیں کہ وہ خدا کی طرف سے
(نازل ہوا) ہے حالانکہ وہ خدا کی طرف سے نہیں ہوتا اور خدا
پر جھوٹ بولتے ہیں اور (یہ بات) جانتے بھی ہیں ۝٧٨
کسی آدمی کو شایاں نہیں کہ خدا تو اُسے کتاب اور
حکومت اور نبوت عطا فرمائے اور وہ لوگوں سے کہے
کہ خدا کو چھوڑ کر میرے بندے ہو جاؤ۔ بلکہ (اسکو یہ کہنا
سزاوار ہے کہ اے اہلِ کتاب تم (علمائے) ربانی ہو جاؤ
کیونکہ تم کتاب (خدا) پڑھتے پڑھاتے رہتے ہو ۝٧٩
اور اس کو یہ بھی نہیں کہنا چاہئیے کہ تم فرشتوں اور
پیغمبروں کو خدا بنا لو۔ بھلا جب تم مسلمان ہو چکے تو
کیا اُسے زیبا ہے کہ تمہیں کافر ہونے کو کہے ۝٨٠
اور جب خدا نے پیغمبروں سے عہد لیا کہ جب میں تم کو کتاب
اور دانائی عطا کروں پھر تمہارے پاس کوئی پیغمبر آئے جو
تمہاری کتاب کی تصدیق کرے تو تمہیں ضرور اُس پر
ایمان لانا ہوگا اور ضرور اُسکی مدد کرنی ہوگی۔ اور (عہد لینے
کے بعد) پوچھا کہ بھلا تم نے اقرار کیا اور اس اقرار پر میرا
ذمہ لیا (یعنی مجھے ضامن ٹھہرایا) اُنہوں نے کہا
(ہاں) ہم نے اقرار کیا۔ (خدا نے) فرمایا کہ تم (اس عہد و
پیمان کے) گواہ رہو اور میں بھی تمہارے ساتھ گواہ ہوں ۝٨١

اللّٰهِ وَاَيْمَانِهِمْ ثَمَنًا قَلِيْلًا
اُولٰٓئِكَ لَا خَلَاقَ لَهُمْ فِي
الْاٰخِرَةِ وَلَا يُكَلِّمُهُمُ اللّٰهُ
وَلَا يَنْظُرُ اِلَيْهِمْ يَوْمَ الْقِيٰمَةِ
وَلَا يُزَكِّيْهِمْ وَلَهُمْ عَذَابٌ اَلِيْمٌ ۝٧٧
وَاِنَّ مِنْهُمْ لَفَرِيْقًا يَّلْوٗنَ
اَلْسِنَتَهُمْ بِالْكِتٰبِ لِتَحْسَبُوْهُ مِنَ
الْكِتٰبِ وَمَا هُوَ مِنَ الْكِتٰبِ ۚ وَ
يَقُوْلُوْنَ هُوَ مِنْ عِنْدِ اللّٰهِ وَمَا هُوَ
مِنْ عِنْدِ اللّٰهِ ۚ وَيَقُوْلُوْنَ عَلَى اللّٰهِ
الْكَذِبَ وَهُمْ يَعْلَمُوْنَ ۝٧٨
مَا كَانَ لِبَشَرٍ اَنْ يُّؤْتِيَهُ اللّٰهُ الْكِتٰبَ
وَالْحُكْمَ وَالنُّبُوَّةَ ثُمَّ يَقُوْلَ
لِلنَّاسِ كُوْنُوْا عِبَادًا لِّيْ مِنْ دُوْنِ
اللّٰهِ وَلٰكِنْ كُوْنُوْا رَبّٰنِيّٖنَ بِمَا كُنْتُمْ
تُعَلِّمُوْنَ الْكِتٰبَ وَبِمَا كُنْتُمْ تَدْرُسُوْنَ ۝٧٩
وَلَا يَاْمُرَكُمْ اَنْ تَتَّخِذُوا الْمَلٰٓئِكَةَ
وَالنَّبِيّٖنَ اَرْبَابًا ۭ اَيَاْمُرُكُمْ
بِالْكُفْرِ بَعْدَ اِذْ اَنْتُمْ مُّسْلِمُوْنَ ۝٨٠
وَاِذْ اَخَذَ اللّٰهُ مِيْثَاقَ النَّبِيّٖنَ
لَمَآ اٰتَيْتُكُمْ مِّنْ كِتٰبٍ وَّحِكْمَةٍ
ثُمَّ جَاۗءَكُمْ رَسُوْلٌ مُّصَدِّقٌ
لِّمَا مَعَكُمْ لَتُؤْمِنُنَّ بِهٖ وَ
لَتَنْصُرُنَّهٗ ۭ قَالَ ءَاَقْرَرْتُمْ وَ
اَخَذْتُمْ عَلٰي ذٰلِكُمْ اِصْرِيْ ۭ قَالُوْٓا
اَقْرَرْنَا ۭ قَالَ فَاشْهَدُوْا وَاَنَا مَعَكُمْ
مِّنَ الشّٰهِدِيْنَ ۝٨١

82. If any turn back after this, they are perverted transgressors.

تو جو اس کے بعد پھر جائیں وہ بدکردار
ہیں ﴿۸۲﴾

فَمَنْ تَوَلّٰى بَعْدَ ذٰلِكَ فَاُولٰٓئِكَ
هُمُ الْفٰسِقُوْنَ ﴿٨٢﴾

83. Do they seek for other than the Religion of Allah?—while all creatures in the heavens and on earth have, willing or unwilling, bowed to His Will (accepted Islam), and to Him shall they all be brought back.

کیا یہ (کافر) خدا کے دین کے سوا کسی اور دین کے
طالب ہیں حالانکہ سب اہلِ آسمان و زمین خوشی یا زبردستی
سے خدا کے فرمانبردار ہیں اور اُسی کی طرف لَوٹ کر جانے والے ہیں ﴿۸۳﴾

اَفَغَيْرَ دِيْنِ اللّٰهِ يَبْغُوْنَ وَلَهٗٓ اَسْلَمَ
مَنْ فِي السَّمٰوٰتِ وَالْاَرْضِ طَوْعًا
وَّكَرْهًا وَّاِلَيْهِ يُرْجَعُوْنَ ﴿٨٣﴾

84. Say: "We believe in Allah, and in what has been revealed to us and what was revealed to Abraham, Isma'īl; Isaac, Jacob, and the Tribes, and in (the Books) given to Moses, Jesus, and the Prophets, from their Lord: we make no distinction between one and another among them, and to Allah do we bow our will (in Islam)."

کہو کہ ہم خدا پر ایمان لائے اور جو کتاب ہم پر
نازل ہوئی اور جو صحیفے ابراہیم اور اسمٰعیل
اور اسحاق اور یعقوب اور اُن کی اولاد پر
اُترے اور جو کتابیں موسیٰ اور عیسیٰ اور دوسرے انبیاء کو
پروردگار کی طرف سے ملیں سب پر ایمان لائے ہم ان
پیغمبروں میں سے کسی میں کچھ فرق نہیں کرتے اور ہم
اُسی (خدائے واحد) کے فرمانبردار ہیں ﴿۸۴﴾

قُلْ اٰمَنَّا بِاللّٰهِ وَمَآ اُنْزِلَ
عَلَيْنَا وَمَآ اُنْزِلَ عَلٰٓى اِبْرٰهِيْمَ
وَاِسْمٰعِيْلَ وَاِسْحٰقَ وَيَعْقُوْبَ
وَالْاَسْبَاطِ وَمَآ اُوْتِيَ مُوْسٰى وَ
عِيْسٰى وَالنَّبِيُّوْنَ مِنْ رَّبِّهِمْ
لَا نُفَرِّقُ بَيْنَ اَحَدٍ مِّنْهُمْ ز
وَنَحْنُ لَهٗ مُسْلِمُوْنَ ﴿٨٤﴾

85. If anyone desires a religion other than Islam (submission to Allah), never will it be accepted of him; and in the Hereafter he will be in the ranks of those who have lost.

اور جو شخص اسلام کے سوا کسی اور دین کا طالب ہوگا
وہ اس سے ہرگز قبول نہیں کیا جائے گا اور ایسا شخص
آخرت میں نقصان اُٹھانے والوں میں ہوگا ﴿۸۵﴾

وَمَنْ يَّبْتَغِ غَيْرَ الْاِسْلَامِ دِيْنًا
فَلَنْ يُّقْبَلَ مِنْهُ ج وَهُوَ فِي
الْاٰخِرَةِ مِنَ الْخٰسِرِيْنَ ﴿٨٥﴾

86. How shall Allah guide those who reject Faith after they accepted it and bore witness that the Messenger was true and that Clear Signs had come unto them ? But Allah guides not a people unjust.

خدا ایسے لوگوں کو کیونکر ہدایت دے جو ایمان لانے کے
بعد کافر ہو گئے اور (پہلے) اس بات کی گواہی دے
چکے کہ یہ پیغمبر برحق ہے اور اُن کے پاس دلائل بھی
آ گئے اور خدا بے انصافوں کو ہدایت نہیں دیتا ﴿۸۶﴾

كَيْفَ يَهْدِي اللّٰهُ قَوْمًا كَفَرُوْا
بَعْدَ اِيْمَانِهِمْ وَشَهِدُوْٓا اَنَّ
الرَّسُوْلَ حَقٌّ وَّجَآءَهُمُ الْبَيِّنٰتُ ط
وَاللّٰهُ لَا يَهْدِي الْقَوْمَ الظّٰلِمِيْنَ ﴿٨٦﴾

87. Of such the reward is that on them (rests) the curse of Allah, of His angels, and of all mankind;—

ان لوگوں کی سزا یہ ہے کہ اُن پر خدا کی اور فرشتوں
کی اور انسانوں کی سب کی لعنت ہو ﴿۸۷﴾

اُولٰٓئِكَ جَزَآؤُهُمْ اَنَّ عَلَيْهِمْ لَعْنَةَ
اللّٰهِ وَالْمَلٰٓئِكَةِ وَالنَّاسِ اَجْمَعِيْنَ ﴿٨٧﴾

88. In that will they dwell; nor will their punishment be lightened, nor respite be their (lot);—

ہمیشہ اس لعنت میں (گرفتار) رہیں گے اُن سے نہ تو
عذاب ہلکا کیا جائے گا اور نہ اُنہیں مہلت دی جائیگی ﴿۸۸﴾

خٰلِدِيْنَ فِيْهَا ج لَا يُخَفَّفُ عَنْهُمُ
الْعَذَابُ وَلَا هُمْ يُنْظَرُوْنَ ﴿٨٨﴾

89. Except for those that repent (even) after that, and make amends; for verily Allah is Oft-Forgiving, Most Merciful.

ہاں جنہوں نے اسکے بعد توبہ کی اور اپنی حالت درست
کر لی تو خدا بخشنے والا مہربان ہے ﴿۸۹﴾

اِلَّا الَّذِيْنَ تَابُوْا مِنْ بَعْدِ ذٰلِكَ
وَاَصْلَحُوْا قف فَاِنَّ اللّٰهَ غَفُوْرٌ رَّحِيْمٌ ﴿٨٩﴾

90. But those who reject Faith after they accepted it, and then go on adding to their defiance of Faith,— never will their repentance be

جو لوگ ایمان لانے کے بعد کافر ہو گئے پھر کفر
میں بڑھتے گئے۔ ایسوں کی توبہ ہرگز قبول نہیں ہوگی

اِنَّ الَّذِيْنَ كَفَرُوْا بَعْدَ اِيْمَانِهِمْ
ثُمَّ ازْدَادُوْا كُفْرًا لَّنْ تُقْبَلَ

accepted: for they are those who have gone astray.

91. As to those who reject Faith, and die rejecting,—never would be accepted from any such as much gold as the earth contains, though they should offer it for ransom. For such is (in store) a chastisement grievous and they will find no helpers.

92. By no means shall ye attain righteousness unless ye give (freely) of that which ye love: and whatever ye give, Allah knoweth it well.

93. All food was lawful to the Children of Israel, except what Israel made unlawful for himself before the Torah was revealed. Say: "Bring ye the Torah and study it, if ye be men of truth."

94. If any, after this, invent a lie and attribute it to Allah, they are indeed unjust wrong-doers.

95. Say: "Allah speaketh the Truth: follow the religion of Abraham, the sane in faith: he was not of the Pagans."

96. The first House (of worship) appointed for men was that at Bakka: full of blessing and of guidance for all the worlds.

97. In it are Signs Manifest; the Station of Abraham; whoever enters it attains security; pilgrimage thereto is a duty men owe to Allah,—those who can afford the journey; but if any deny faith, Allah stands not in need of any of His creatures.

98. Say: "O People of the Book ! why reject ye the Signs of Allah,

اور یہ لوگ گمراہ ہیں ﴿۹۰﴾
جو لوگ کافر ہوئے اور کفر ہی کی حالت میں مر گئے
وہ اگر (نجات حاصل کرنی چاہیں اور) بدلے میں
زمین بھر کر سونا دیں تو ہرگز قبول نہیں کیا جائے گا۔
ان لوگوں کو دکھ دینے والا عذاب ہوگا۔ اور ان کی
کوئی مدد نہیں کرے گا ﴿۹۱﴾
(مومنو!) جب تک تم اُن چیزوں میں سے جو تمہیں عزیز
ہیں (راہِ خدا میں) صرف نہ کرو گے کبھی نیکی حاصل نہ کر سکو گے
اور جو چیز تم صرف کرو گے خدا اُس کو جانتا ہے ﴿۹۲﴾
بنی اسرائیل کے لئے (تورات کے نازل ہونے سے)
پہلے کھانے کی تمام چیزیں حلال تھیں بجز اُن کے
جو یعقوب نے خود اپنے اُوپر حرام کر لی تھیں
کہہ دو کہ اگر سچے ہو تو تورات لاؤ اور اُسے پڑھو
(یعنی دلیل پیش کرو) ﴿۹۳﴾
جو اس کے بعد بھی خدا پر جھوٹے افترا کریں تو ایسے
لوگ ہی بے انصاف ہیں ﴿۹۴﴾
کہہ دو کہ خدا نے سچ فرما دیا پس دین ابراہیم کی پیروی کرو
جو سب سے بے تعلق ہو کر ایک (خدا) کے ہو رہے تھے اور مشرکوں سے نہ تھے ﴿۹۵﴾
پہلا گھر جو لوگوں (کے عبادت کرنے) کیلئے مقرر کیا گیا تھا
وہی ہے جو مکے میں ہے۔ بابرکت اور جہان کیلئے موجب ہدایت ﴿۹۶﴾
اس میں کھلی ہوئی نشانیاں ہیں جن میں سے ایک ابراہیم
کے کھڑے ہونے کی جگہ ہے۔ جو شخص اس (مبارک گھر) میں
داخل ہوا اس نے امن پا لیا۔ اور لوگوں پر خدا کا حق (یعنی
فرض) ہے کہ جو اس گھر تک جانے کا مقدور رکھے وہ اس کا حج
کرے۔ اور جو اس حکم کی تعمیل نہ کریگا تو خدا بھی اہلِ عالم
سے بے نیاز ہے ﴿۹۷﴾
کہو کہ اے اہلِ کتاب! تم خدا کی آیتوں سے کیوں کر

تَوْبَتُهُمْ ۚ وَاُولٰٓئِكَ هُمُ الضَّآلُّوْنَ ۝٩٠
اِنَّ الَّذِيْنَ كَفَرُوْا وَمَاتُوْا وَهُمْ
كُفَّارٌ فَلَنْ يُّقْبَلَ مِنْ اَحَدِهِمْ
مِّلْءُ الْاَرْضِ ذَهَبًا وَّلَوِ افْتَدٰى
بِهٖ ۭ اُولٰٓئِكَ لَهُمْ عَذَابٌ اَلِيْمٌ
وَّمَا لَهُمْ مِّنْ نّٰصِرِيْنَ ۝٩١
لَنْ تَنَالُوا الْبِرَّ حَتّٰى تُنْفِقُوْا مِمَّا
تُحِبُّوْنَ ڛ وَمَا تُنْفِقُوْا مِنْ شَيْءٍ
فَاِنَّ اللّٰهَ بِهٖ عَلِيْمٌ ۝٩٢
كُلُّ الطَّعَامِ كَانَ حِلًّا لِّبَنِيْٓ
اِسْرَاۗءِيْلَ اِلَّا مَا حَرَّمَ اِسْرَاۗءِيْلُ
عَلٰي نَفْسِهٖ مِنْ قَبْلِ اَنْ تُنَزَّلَ
التَّوْرٰىةُ ۭ قُلْ فَاْتُوْا بِالتَّوْرٰىةِ
فَاتْلُوْهَآ اِنْ كُنْتُمْ صٰدِقِيْنَ ۝٩٣
فَمَنِ افْتَرٰى عَلَي اللّٰهِ الْكَذِبَ مِنْۢ
بَعْدِ ذٰلِكَ فَاُولٰٓئِكَ هُمُ الظّٰلِمُوْنَ ۝٩٤
قُلْ صَدَقَ اللّٰهُ ۣ فَاتَّبِعُوْا مِلَّةَ اِبْرٰهِيْمَ
حَنِيْفًا ۭ وَمَا كَانَ مِنَ الْمُشْرِكِيْنَ ۝٩٥
اِنَّ اَوَّلَ بَيْتٍ وُّضِعَ لِلنَّاسِ لَلَّذِيْ
بِبَكَّةَ مُبٰرَكًا وَّھُدًى لِّلْعٰلَمِيْنَ ۝٩٦
فِيْهِ اٰيٰتٌۢ بَيِّنٰتٌ مَّقَامُ اِبْرٰهِيْمَ ڬ
وَمَنْ دَخَلَهٗ كَانَ اٰمِنًا ۭ وَلِلّٰهِ
عَلَي النَّاسِ حِجُّ الْبَيْتِ مَنِ
اسْتَطَاعَ اِلَيْهِ سَبِيْلًا ۭ وَمَنْ
كَفَرَ فَاِنَّ اللّٰهَ غَنِيٌّ عَنِ
الْعٰلَمِيْنَ ۝٩٧
قُلْ يٰٓاَهْلَ الْكِتٰبِ لِمَ تَكْفُرُوْنَ بِاٰيٰتِ

ع ۹ الجزء الرابع

وقف جبریل علیہ السلام

when Allah is Himself witness to all ye do ?"

کرتے ہو اور خدا تمہارے سب اعمال سے باخبر ہے ﴿۹۸﴾

اللّٰهِ ۖ وَاللّٰهُ شَهِيْدٌ عَلٰى مَا تَعْمَلُوْنَ ﴿٩٨﴾

99. Say: "O ye People of the Book! why obstruct ye those who believe, from the Path of Allah, seeking to make it crooked, while ye were yourselves witnesses (to Allah's Covenant)? But Allah is not unmindful of all that ye do."

کہو کہ اے اہلِ کتاب تم مومنوں کو خدا کے رستے سے
کیوں روکتے ہو اور باوجودیکہ تم اس سے واقف ہو
اُس میں کجی نکالتے ہو اور خدا تمہارے کاموں سے
بے خبر نہیں ﴿۹۹﴾

قُلْ يٰٓاَهْلَ الْكِتٰبِ لِمَ تَصُدُّوْنَ
عَنْ سَبِيْلِ اللّٰهِ مَنْ اٰمَنَ
تَبْغُوْنَهَا عِوَجًا وَّاَنْتُمْ شُهَدَآءُ ۭ
وَمَا اللّٰهُ بِغَافِلٍ عَمَّا تَعْمَلُوْنَ ﴿٩٩﴾

100. O ye who believe ! if ye listen to a faction among the People of the Book, they would (indeed) render you apostates after ye have believed!

مومنو! اگر تم اہلِ کتاب کے کسی فریق کا کہا مان لوگے
تو وہ تمہیں ایمان لانے کے بعد کافر
بنا دیں گے ﴿۱۰۰﴾

يٰٓاَيُّهَا الَّذِيْنَ اٰمَنُوْٓا اِنْ تُطِيْعُوْا
فَرِيْقًا مِّنَ الَّذِيْنَ اُوْتُوا الْكِتٰبَ
يَرُدُّوْكُمْ بَعْدَ اِيْمَانِكُمْ كٰفِرِيْنَ ﴿١٠٠﴾

101. And how would ye deny Faith while unto you are rehearsed the Signs of Allah, and among you lives the Messenger ? Whoever holds firmly to Allah will be shown a Way that is straight.

اور تم کیونکر کفر کرو گے جبکہ تم کو خدا کی آیتیں پڑھ پڑھ کر
سُنائی جاتی ہیں اور تم میں اُسکے پیغمبر موجود ہیں۔ اور جس نے
خدا (کی ہدایت کی رسّی) کو مضبوط پکڑ لیا وہ سیدھے رستے لگ گیا ﴿۱۰۱﴾

وَكَيْفَ تَكْفُرُوْنَ وَاَنْتُمْ تُتْلٰى عَلَيْكُمْ
اٰيٰتُ اللّٰهِ وَفِيْكُمْ رَسُوْلُهٗ ۭ وَمَنْ يَّعْتَصِمْ
بِاللّٰهِ فَقَدْ هُدِيَ اِلٰى صِرَاطٍ مُّسْتَقِيْمٍ ﴿١٠١﴾ ع

102. O ye who believe ! fear Allah as He should be feared, and die not except in a state of Islam.

مومنو! خدا سے ڈرو جیسا کہ اُس سے ڈرنے کا حق ہے
اور مرنا تو مسلمان ہی مرنا ﴿۱۰۲﴾

يٰٓاَيُّهَا الَّذِيْنَ اٰمَنُوا اتَّقُوا اللّٰهَ حَقَّ
تُقٰتِهٖ وَلَا تَمُوْتُنَّ اِلَّا وَاَنْتُمْ مُّسْلِمُوْنَ ﴿١٠٢﴾

103. And hold fast, all together, by the Rope which Allah (stretches out for you), and be not divided among yourselves; and remember with gratitude Allah's favour on you; for ye were enemies and He joined your hearts in love, so that by His Grace, ye became brethren; and ye were on the brink of the Pit of Fire, and He saved you from it. Thus doth Allah make His Signs clear to you: that ye may be guided.

اور سب مل کر خدا کی (ہدایت کی) رسّی کو مضبوط
پکڑے رہنا اور متفرق نہ ہونا۔ اور خدا کی اُس مہربانی
کو یاد کرو جب تم ایک دوسرے کے دشمن تھے تو
اُس نے تمہارے دلوں میں اُلفت ڈال دی اور تم اُسکی
مہربانی سے بھائی بھائی ہوگئے اور تم آگ کے گڑھے
کے کنارے تک پہنچ چکے تھے تو خدا نے تمکو اُس سے بچا لیا اسطرح
خدا تمکو اپنی آیتیں کھول کھول کر سناتا ہے تاکہ تم ہدایت پاؤ ﴿۱۰۳﴾

وَاعْتَصِمُوْا بِحَبْلِ اللّٰهِ جَمِيْعًا وَّلَا
تَفَرَّقُوْا ۠ وَاذْكُرُوْا نِعْمَتَ اللّٰهِ عَلَيْكُمْ
اِذْ كُنْتُمْ اَعْدَآءً فَاَلَّفَ بَيْنَ
قُلُوْبِكُمْ فَاَصْبَحْتُمْ بِنِعْمَتِهٖٓ اِخْوَانًا ۚ
وَكُنْتُمْ عَلٰى شَفَا حُفْرَةٍ مِّنَ
النَّارِ فَاَنْقَذَكُمْ مِّنْهَا ۭ كَذٰلِكَ يُبَيِّنُ
اللّٰهُ لَكُمْ اٰيٰتِهٖ لَعَلَّكُمْ تَهْتَدُوْنَ ﴿١٠٣﴾

104. Let there arise out of you a band of people inviting to all that is good, enjoining what is right, and forbidding what is wrong: they are the ones to attain felicity.

اور تم میں ایک جماعت ایسی ہونی چاہیے جو لوگوں کو نیکی
کی طرف بُلائے اور اچھے کام کرنے کا حکم دے
اور بُرے کاموں سے منع کرے یہی لوگ ہیں جو
نجات پانے والے ہیں ﴿۱۰۴﴾

وَلْتَكُنْ مِّنْكُمْ اُمَّةٌ يَّدْعُوْنَ
اِلَى الْخَيْرِ وَيَاْمُرُوْنَ بِالْمَعْرُوْفِ
وَيَنْهَوْنَ عَنِ الْمُنْكَرِ ۭ وَاُولٰۗىِٕكَ
هُمُ الْمُفْلِحُوْنَ ﴿١٠٤﴾

105. Be not like those who are divided amongst themselves and fall into disputations after receiving Clear Signs: for them is a dreadful Chastisement,—

اور اُن لوگوں کی طرح نہ ہونا جو متفرق ہوگئے اور احکام
بیّن آنےکے بعد ایک دوسرے سے (خلاف و) اختلاف کرنے لگے
یہ وہ لوگ ہیں جنکو قیامت کے دن بڑا عذاب ہوگا ﴿۱۰۵﴾

وَلَا تَكُوْنُوْا كَالَّذِيْنَ تَفَرَّقُوْا وَاخْتَلَفُوْا
مِنْ بَعْدِ مَا جَاۗءَهُمُ الْبَيِّنٰتُ ۭ
وَاُولٰۗىِٕكَ لَهُمْ عَذَابٌ عَظِيْمٌ ﴿١٠٥﴾

106. On the Day when some faces will be (lit up with) white, and some faces will be (in the gloom of) black: to those whose faces will be black, (will be said): "Did ye reject Faith after accepting it ? Taste then the Chastisement for rejecting Faith."

جس دن بہت سے مُنہ سفید ہونگے اور بہت سے سیاہ۔ تو جن
لوگوں کے مُنہ سیاہ ہونگے (اُن سے خدا فرمائے گا) کیا
تم ایمان لاکر کافر ہو گئے تھے؟ سو (اب) اُس کفر کے
بدلے عذاب (کے مزے) چکھو ﴿۱۰۶﴾

يَّوۡمَ تَبۡيَضُّ وُجُوۡهٌ وَّتَسۡوَدُّ وُجُوۡهٌ ۚ
فَاَمَّا الَّذِيۡنَ اسۡوَدَّتۡ وُجُوۡهُهُمۡ ۚ
اَكَفَرۡتُمۡ بَعۡدَ اِيۡمَانِكُمۡ فَذُوۡقُوا
الۡعَذَابَ بِمَا كُنۡتُمۡ تَكۡفُرُوۡنَ ﴿۱۰۶﴾

107. But those whose faces will be (lit with) white,—they will be in (the light of) Allah's mercy: therein to dwell (for ever).

اور جن لوگوں کے مُنہ سفید ہونگے وہ خدا کی رحمت
(کے باغوں) میں ہونگے اور اُن میں ہمیشہ رہیں گے ﴿۱۰۷﴾

وَاَمَّا الَّذِيۡنَ ابۡيَضَّتۡ وُجُوۡهُهُمۡ فَفِىۡ
رَحۡمَةِ اللّٰهِ ؕ هُمۡ فِيۡهَا خٰلِدُوۡنَ ﴿۱۰۷﴾

108. These are the Signs of Allah: We rehearse them to thee in Truth: and Allah means no injustice to any of His creatures.

یہ خدا کی آیتیں ہیں جو ہم تمکو صحت کیساتھ پڑھ کر
سُناتے ہیں۔ اور خدا اہلِ عالم پر ظلم نہیں کرنا چاہتا ﴿۱۰۸﴾

تِلۡكَ اٰيٰتُ اللّٰهِ نَتۡلُوۡهَا عَلَيۡكَ بِالۡحَقِّ ؕ
وَمَا اللّٰهُ يُرِيۡدُ ظُلۡمًا لِّلۡعٰلَمِيۡنَ ﴿۱۰۸﴾

109. To Allah belongs all that is in the heavens and earth: to Allah do all matters return.

اور جو کچھ آسمانوں میں اور جو کچھ زمین میں ہے سب خدا ہی کا ہے
اور سب کاموں کا رجوع (اور انجام) خدا ہی کی طرف ہے ﴿۱۰۹﴾

وَلِلّٰهِ مَا فِى السَّمٰوٰتِ وَمَا فِى الۡاَرۡضِ ؕ
وَاِلَى اللّٰهِ تُرۡجَعُ الۡاُمُوۡرُ ﴿۱۰۹﴾ ع

110. Ye are the best of Peoples, evolved for mankind, enjoining what is right, forbidding what is wrong, and believing in Allah. If only the People of the Book had Faith, it were best for them: among them are some who have Faith, but most of them are perverted transgressors.

(مومنو!) جتنی اُمتیں (یعنی قومیں) لوگوں میں
پیدا ہوئیں تم ان سب سے بہتر ہو کہ نیک کام کرنے کو کہتے ہو
اور بُرے کاموں سے منع کرتے ہو اور خدا پر ایمان رکھتے ہو
اور اگر اہلِ کتاب بھی ایمان لے آتے تو اُن کے لئے
بہت اچھا ہوتا۔ ان میں ایمان لانے والے بھی ہیں
(لیکن تھوڑے) اور اکثر نافرمان ہیں ﴿۱۱۰﴾

كُنۡتُمۡ خَيۡرَ اُمَّةٍ اُخۡرِجَتۡ لِلنَّاسِ
تَاۡمُرُوۡنَ بِالۡمَعۡرُوۡفِ وَتَنۡهَوۡنَ
عَنِ الۡمُنۡكَرِ وَتُؤۡمِنُوۡنَ بِاللّٰهِ ؕ وَلَوۡ
اٰمَنَ اَهۡلُ الۡكِتٰبِ لَكَانَ خَيۡرًا
لَّهُمۡ ؕ مِنۡهُمُ الۡمُؤۡمِنُوۡنَ وَاَكۡثَرُهُمُ
الۡفٰسِقُوۡنَ ﴿۱۱۰﴾

111. They will do you no harm, barring a trifling annoyance: if they come out to fight you, they will show you their backs, and no help shall they get.

اور یہ تمہیں خفیف سی تکلیف کے سوا کچھ نقصان
نہیں پہنچا سکیں گے اور اگر تم سے لڑینگے تو پیٹھ پھیر کر
بھاگ جائینگے۔ پھر اُن کو مدد بھی (کہیں سے) نہیں ملے گی ﴿۱۱۱﴾

لَنۡ يَّضُرُّوۡكُمۡ اِلَّاۤ اَذًى ؕ وَاِنۡ
يُّقَاتِلُوۡكُمۡ يُوَلُّوۡكُمُ الۡاَدۡبَارَ ۚ
ثُمَّ لَا يُنۡصَرُوۡنَ ﴿۱۱۱﴾

112. Shame is pitched over them (like a tent) wherever they are found, except when under a covenant (of protection) from Allah and from men; they draw on themselves wrath from Allah, and pitched over them is (the tent of) destitution. This because they rejected the Signs of Allah, and slew the Prophets in defiance of right: this because they rebelled and transgressed beyond bounds.

یہ جہاں نظر آئیں گے ذلّت (کو دیکھو گے کہ) ان سے
چمٹ رہی ہے۔ بجز اس کے کہ یہ خدا اور (مسلمان)
لوگوں کی پناہ میں آجائیں اور یہ لوگ خدا کے غضب
میں گرفتار ہیں اور ناداری ان سے لپٹ رہی ہے۔
یہ اِس لئے کہ خدا کی آیتوں سے انکار کرتے تھے
اور (اُس کے) پیغمبروں کو ناحق قتل کر دیتے تھے۔ یہ
اسلئے کہ یہ نافرمانی کئے جاتے اور حد سے بڑھے جاتے تھے ﴿۱۱۲﴾

ضُرِبَتۡ عَلَيۡهِمُ الذِّلَّةُ اَيۡنَ مَا
ثُقِفُوۡۤا اِلَّا بِحَبۡلٍ مِّنَ اللّٰهِ وَحَبۡلٍ
مِّنَ النَّاسِ وَبَآءُوۡ بِغَضَبٍ مِّنَ
اللّٰهِ وَضُرِبَتۡ عَلَيۡهِمُ الۡمَسۡكَنَةُ ؕ
ذٰلِكَ بِاَنَّهُمۡ كَانُوۡا يَكۡفُرُوۡنَ بِاٰيٰتِ
اللّٰهِ وَيَقۡتُلُوۡنَ الۡاَنۡۢبِيَآءَ بِغَيۡرِ حَقٍّ ؕ
ذٰلِكَ بِمَا عَصَوۡا وَّكَانُوۡا يَعۡتَدُوۡنَ ﴿۱۱۲﴾

113. Not all of them are alike: of the People of the Book are a portion

یہ بھی سب ایک جیسے نہیں ہیں ان اہلِ کتاب

لَيۡسُوۡا سَوَآءً ؕ مِنۡ اَهۡلِ الۡكِتٰبِ

that stand (for the right); they rehearse the Signs of Allah all night long, and they prostrate themselves in adoration.

میں کچھ لوگ (حکمِ خدا پر) قائم بھی ہیں۔ جو رات کے وقت خدا کی
آیتیں پڑھتے اور (اُسکے آگے) سجدے کرتے ہیں ﴿١١٣﴾

أُمَّةٌ قَآئِمَةٌ يَّتْلُوْنَ اٰيٰتِ اللّٰهِ
اٰنَآءَ الَّيْلِ وَهُمْ يَسْجُدُوْنَ ﴿١١٣﴾

114. They believe in Allah and the Last Day; they enjoin what is right, and forbid what is wrong; and they hasten (in emulation) in (all) good works: they are in the ranks of the righteous.

(اور) خدا پر اور روزِ آخرت پر ایمان رکھتے اور اچھے
کام کرنے کو کہتے اور بُری باتوں سے منع کرتے
اور نیکیوں پر لپکتے ہیں اور یہی لوگ
نیکوکار ہیں ﴿١١٤﴾

يُؤْمِنُوْنَ بِاللّٰهِ وَالْيَوْمِ الْاٰخِرِ وَ
يَاْمُرُوْنَ بِالْمَعْرُوْفِ وَيَنْهَوْنَ
عَنِ الْمُنْكَرِ وَيُسَارِعُوْنَ فِى الْخَيْرٰتِ ط
وَاُولٰٓئِكَ مِنَ الصّٰلِحِيْنَ ﴿١١٤﴾

115. Of the good that they do, nothing will be rejected of them; for Allah knoweth well those that do right.

اور یہ جس طرح کی نیکی کرینگے اسکی ناقدری نہیں کی جائیگی
اور خدا پرہیزگاروں کو خوب جانتا ہے ﴿١١٥﴾

وَمَا يَفْعَلُوْا مِنْ خَيْرٍ فَلَنْ يُّكْفَرُوْهُ ط
وَاللّٰهُ عَلِيْمٌ بِالْمُتَّقِيْنَ ﴿١١٥﴾

116. Those who reject Faith,— neither their possessions nor their (numerous) progeny will avail them aught against Allah: they will be Companions of the Fire,— dwelling therein (for ever).

جو لوگ کافر ہیں اُن کے مال اور اولاد خدا کے عذاب
کو ہرگز نہیں ٹال سکیں گے۔ اور یہ لوگ اہلِ دوزخ
ہیں کہ ہمیشہ اسی میں رہیں گے ﴿١١٦﴾

اِنَّ الَّذِيْنَ كَفَرُوْا لَنْ تُغْنِىَ عَنْهُمْ
اَمْوَالُهُمْ وَلَآ اَوْلَادُهُمْ مِّنَ اللّٰهِ شَيْئًا ط
وَاُولٰٓئِكَ اَصْحٰبُ النَّارِ هُمْ فِيْهَا خٰلِدُوْنَ ﴿١١٦﴾

117. What they spend in the life of this (material) world may be likened to a Wind which brings a nipping frost: it strikes and destroys the harvest of men who have wronged their own souls: it is not Allah that hath wronged them, but they wrong themselves.

یہ جو مال دُنیا کی زندگی میں خرچ کرتے ہیں
اُسکی مثال ہَوا کی سی ہے جس میں سخت سردی ہو اور
وہ ایسے لوگوں کی کھیتی پر جو اپنے آپ پر ظلم کرتے
تھے چلے اور اُسے تباہ کردے اور خدا نے اُن پر کچھ ظلم
نہیں کیا بلکہ یہ خود اپنے اوپر ظلم کر رہے ہیں ﴿١١٧﴾

مَثَلُ مَا يُنْفِقُوْنَ فِىْ هٰذِهِ الْحَيٰوةِ
الدُّنْيَا كَمَثَلِ رِيْحٍ فِيْهَا صِرٌّ
اَصَابَتْ حَرْثَ قَوْمٍ ظَلَمُوْٓا اَنْفُسَهُمْ
فَاَهْلَكَتْهُ ط وَمَا ظَلَمَهُمُ اللّٰهُ
وَلٰكِنْ اَنْفُسَهُمْ يَظْلِمُوْنَ ﴿١١٧﴾

118. O ye who believe ! take not into your intimacy those outside your ranks: they will not fail to corrupt you. They only desire for you to suffer: rank hatred has already appeared from their mouths: what their hearts conceal is far worse. We have made plain to you the Signs, if ye have wisdom.

مومنو! کسی غیر (مذہب کے آدمی) کو اپنا رازدار نہ بنانا
یہ لوگ تمہاری خرابی (اور فتنہ انگیزی کرنے) میں کسی طرح
کی کوتاہی نہیں کرتے اور چاہتے ہیں کہ (جس طرح ہو) تمہیں تکلیف
پہنچے۔ اُن کی زبانوں سے تو دشمنی ظاہر ہو ہی چکی ہے۔ اور
جو (کینے) اُن کے سینوں میں مخفی ہیں وہ کہیں زیادہ ہیں۔
اگر تم عقل رکھتے ہو تو ہم نے تم کو اپنی آیتیں کھول
کھول کر سُنا دی ہیں ﴿١١٨﴾

يٰٓاَيُّهَا الَّذِيْنَ اٰمَنُوْا لَا تَتَّخِذُوْا
بِطَانَةً مِّنْ دُوْنِكُمْ لَا يَاْلُوْنَكُمْ
خَبَالًا ط وَدُّوْا مَا عَنِتُّمْ ج قَدْ
بَدَتِ الْبَغْضَآءُ مِنْ اَفْوَاهِهِمْ صلے
وَمَا تُخْفِىْ صُدُوْرُهُمْ اَكْبَرُ ط
قَدْ بَيَّنَّا لَكُمُ الْاٰيٰتِ اِنْ كُنْتُمْ
تَعْقِلُوْنَ ﴿١١٨﴾

119. Ah ! ye are those who love them, but they love you not,— though ye believe in the whole of the Book, when they meet you, they say, "We believe": but when they are alone, they bite off the very tips of their fingers at you in their rage.

دیکھو تم ایسے (صاف دل) لوگ ہو کہ اُن لوگوں سے دوستی رکھتے ہو
حالانکہ وہ تم سے دوستی نہیں رکھتے اور تم سب کتابوں پر
ایمان رکھتے ہو اور وہ تمہاری کتاب کو نہیں مانتے) اور جب تم
سے ملتے ہیں تو کہتے ہیں ہم ایمان لے آئے ہیں اور جب الگ ہوتے

هٰٓاَنْتُمْ اُولَآءِ تُحِبُّوْنَهُمْ وَلَا
يُحِبُّوْنَكُمْ وَتُؤْمِنُوْنَ بِالْكِتٰبِ
كُلِّهٖ وَاِذَا لَقُوْكُمْ قَالُوْٓا اٰمَنَّا صلے
وَاِذَا خَلَوْا عَضُّوْا عَلَيْكُمُ الْاَنَامِلَ

Say: "Perish in your rage; Allah knoweth well all the secrets of the heart."

ہیں تو تم پر غصے کے سبب انگلیاں کاٹ کاٹ کھاتے ہیں (اُنسے) کہدو
کہ (بدبختو) غصے میں مر جاؤ۔ خدا تمہارے دلوں کی باتوں سے خوب واقف ہی (۱۱۹)

مِنَ الْغَيْظِ ۭ قُلْ مُوْتُوْا بِغَيْظِكُمْ ۭ
اِنَّ اللّٰهَ عَلِيْمٌۢ بِذَاتِ الصُّدُوْرِ (۱۱۹)

120. If aught that is good befalls you, it grieves them; but if some misfortune overtakes you, they rejoice at it. But if ye are patient and do right, not the least harm will their cunning do to you; for Allah compasseth round about all that they do.

اگر تمہیں آسودگی حاصل ہو تو اُن کو بُری لگتی ہو اور اگر
رنج پہنچے تو خوش ہوتے ہیں اور اگر تم تکلیفوں کی
برداشت اور (ان سی) کنارہ کشی کرتے رہو گے تو اُن کا
فریب تمہیں کچھ بھی نقصان نہ پہنچا سکے گا۔ یہ جو کچھ
کرتے ہیں خدا اُس پر احاطہ کئے ہوئے ہے (۱۲۰)

اِنْ تَمْسَسْكُمْ حَسَنَةٌ تَسُؤْھُمْ ۡ
وَاِنْ تُصِبْكُمْ سَيِّئَةٌ يَّفْرَحُوْا
بِهَا ۭ وَاِنْ تَصْبِرُوْا وَتَتَّقُوْا
لَا يَضُرُّكُمْ كَيْدُھُمْ شَـيْـــًٔـا ۭ
اِنَّ اللّٰهَ بِمَا يَعْمَلُوْنَ مُحِيْطٌ (۱۲۰) ع

121. (Remember that morning) thou didst leave thy household (early) to post the Faithful at their stations for battle: and Allah heareth and knoweth all things:

اور (اُس وقت کو یاد کرو) جب تم صبح کو اپنے گھر سے روانہ
ہو کر ایمان والوں کو لڑائی کیلئے مورچوں پر (موقع بموقع)
متعیّن کرنے لگے اور خدا سب کچھ سُنتا (اور) جانتا ہی (۱۲۱)

وَاِذْ غَدَوْتَ مِنْ اَھْلِكَ تُبَوِّئُ
الْمُؤْمِنِيْنَ مَقَاعِدَ لِلْقِتَالِ ۭ
وَاللّٰهُ سَمِيْعٌ عَلِيْمٌ (۱۲۱)

122. Remember two of your parties meditated cowardice; but Allah was their protector, and in Allah should the Faithful (ever) put their trust.

اُس وقت تم میں سے دو جماعتوں نے جی چھوڑ دینا
چاہا۔ مگر خدا اُن کا مددگار تھا۔ اور مومنوں کو خدا ہی
پر بھروسہ کرنا چاہیئے (۱۲۲)

اِذْ ھَمَّتْ طَّاۗىِٕفَتٰنِ مِنْكُمْ
اَنْ تَفْشَلَا ۙ وَاللّٰهُ وَلِيُّهُمَا ۭ وَعَلَي
اللّٰهِ فَلْيَتَوَكَّلِ الْمُؤْمِنُوْنَ (۱۲۲)

123. Allah had helped you at Badr, when ye were helpless: then fear Allah: thus may ye show your gratitude.

اور خدا نے جنگ بدر میں بھی تمہاری مدد کی تھی اور
اُس وقت بھی تم بے سروسامان تھے پس خدا سے
ڈرو (اور ان احسانوں کو یاد کرو) تاکہ شکر کرو (۱۲۳)

وَلَقَدْ نَصَرَكُمُ اللّٰهُ بِبَدْرٍ وَّاَنْتُمْ
اَذِلَّةٌ ۚ فَاتَّقُوا اللّٰهَ لَعَلَّكُمْ
تَشْكُرُوْنَ (۱۲۳)

124. Remember thou saidst to the Faithful: "Is it not enough for you that Allah should help you with three thousand angels (specially) sent down?

جب تم مومنوں سی یہ کہہ (کر اُنکے دل بڑھا) رہے تھے کہ کیا
یہ کافی نہیں کہ پروردگار تین ہزار فرشتے نازل کر کے
تمہیں مدد دے (۱۲۴)

اِذْ تَقُوْلُ لِلْمُؤْمِنِيْنَ اَلَنْ يَّكْفِيَكُمْ
اَنْ يُّمِدَّكُمْ رَبُّكُمْ بِثَلٰثَةِ اٰلٰفٍ
مِّنَ الْمَلٰۗىِٕكَةِ مُنْزَلِيْنَ (۱۲۴)

125. "Yea,—if ye remain firm, and act aright, even if the enemy should rush here on you in hot haste, your Lord would help you with five thousand angels clearly marked.

ہاں اگر تم دل کو مضبوط رکھو۔ اور (خدا سے)
ڈرتے رہو اور کافر تم پر جوش کے ساتھ
دفعۃً حملہ کر دیں تو پروردگار پانچ ہزار فرشتے
جن پر نشان ہوں گے تمہاری مدد کو بھیجے گا (۱۲۵)

بَلٰٓى ۙ اِنْ تَصْبِرُوْا وَتَتَّقُوْا وَ
يَاْتُوْكُمْ مِّنْ فَوْرِھِمْ ھٰذَا يُمْدِدْكُمْ
رَبُّكُمْ بِخَمْسَةِ اٰلٰفٍ مِّنَ الْمَلٰۗىِٕكَةِ
مُسَوِّمِيْنَ (۱۲۵)

126. Allah made it but a message of hope for you, and an assurance to your hearts: (in any case) there is no victory except from Allah, the Exalted, the Wise:

اور اس مدد کو تو خدا نے تمہارے لئے (ذریعۂ) بشارت بنایا
یعنی اس لئے کہ تمہارے دلوں کو اس سے تسلی حاصل ہو
ورنہ مدد تو خدا ہی کی ہی۔ جو غالب (اور) حکمت والا ہی (۱۲۶)

وَمَا جَعَلَهُ اللّٰهُ اِلَّا بُشْرٰى لَكُمْ
وَلِتَطْمَىِٕنَّ قُلُوْبُكُمْ بِهٖ ۭ وَمَا النَّصْرُ
اِلَّا مِنْ عِنْدِ اللّٰهِ الْعَزِيْزِ الْحَكِيْمِ (۱۲۶)

127. That He might cut off a fringe of the Unbelievers or expose them

(یہ خدا نے) اس لئے (کیا) کہ کافروں کی ایک جماعت

لِيَقْطَعَ طَرَفًا مِّنَ الَّذِيْنَ

to infamy, and they should then be turned back, frustrated of their purpose.

کو ہلاک یا اُنہیں ذلیل و مغلوب کردے کہ (جیسے آئے
تھے ویسے ہی) ناکام واپس جائیں (۱۲۷)

كَفَرُوا أَوْ يَكْبِتَهُمْ فَيَنْقَلِبُوا
خَائِبِينَ (١٢٧)

128. Not for thee, (but for Allah), is the decision: whether He turn in mercy to them, or punish them; for they are indeed wrong-doers.

(اے پیغمبر) اس کام میں تمہارا کچھ اختیار نہیں (اب دو صورتیں ہیں)
یا خدا اُنکے حال پر مہربانی کرے یا اُنہیں عذاب دے کہ یہ ظالم لوگ ہیں (۱۲۸)

لَيْسَ لَكَ مِنَ الْأَمْرِ شَيْءٌ أَوْ يَتُوبَ
عَلَيْهِمْ أَوْ يُعَذِّبَهُمْ فَإِنَّهُمْ ظَٰلِمُونَ (١٢٨)

129. To Allah belongeth all that is in the heavens and on earth. He forgiveth whom He pleaseth and punisheth whom He pleaseth; but Allah is Oft-Forgiving, Most Merciful.

اور جو کچھ آسمانوں میں ہے اور جو کچھ زمین میں ہے سب
خدا ہی کا ہے۔ وہ جسے چاہے بخش دے اور جسے چاہے عذاب
کرے۔ اور خدا بخشنے والا مہربان ہے (۱۲۹)

وَلِلَّهِ مَا فِي السَّمَٰوَٰتِ وَمَا فِي الْأَرْضِ
يَغْفِرُ لِمَنْ يَشَاءُ وَيُعَذِّبُ مَنْ
يَشَاءُ وَاللَّهُ غَفُورٌ رَحِيمٌ (١٢٩)

130. O ye who believe ! devour not Usury, doubled and multiplied; but fear Allah; that ye may (really) prosper.

اے ایمان والو! دُگنا چوگنا سُود
نہ کھاؤ اور خدا سے ڈرو تاکہ نجات
حاصل کرو (۱۳۰)

يَٰأَيُّهَا الَّذِينَ ءَامَنُوا لَا تَأْكُلُوا
الرِّبَوٰا أَضْعَٰفًا مُضَٰعَفَةً وَاتَّقُوا
اللَّهَ لَعَلَّكُمْ تُفْلِحُونَ (١٣٠)

131. And fear the Fire, which is prepared for those who reject Faith:

اور (دوزخ کی) آگ سے بچو جو کافروں کیلئے تیار کی گئی ہے (۱۳۱)

وَاتَّقُوا النَّارَ الَّتِي أُعِدَّتْ لِلْكَٰفِرِينَ (١٣١)

132. And obey Allah and the Messenger; that ye may obtain mercy.

اور خدا اور اُس کے رسول کی اطاعت کرو تاکہ تم پر
رحمت کی جائے (۱۳۲)

وَأَطِيعُوا اللَّهَ وَالرَّسُولَ لَعَلَّكُمْ
تُرْحَمُونَ (١٣٢)

133. Be quick in the race for forgiveness from your Lord and for a Garden whose width is that (of the whole) of the heavens and of the earth, prepared for the righteous,—

اور اپنے پروردگار کی بخشش اور بہشت کی طرف
لپکو جس کا عرض آسمان اور زمین کے برابر ہے اور جو
(خدا سے) ڈرنے والوں کے لئے تیار کی گئی ہے (۱۳۳)

وَسَارِعُوا إِلَىٰ مَغْفِرَةٍ مِنْ رَبِّكُمْ
وَجَنَّةٍ عَرْضُهَا السَّمَٰوَٰتُ وَالْأَرْضُ
أُعِدَّتْ لِلْمُتَّقِينَ (١٣٣)

134. Those who spend (freely), whether in prosperity, or in adversity; who restrain anger, and pardon (all) men;— for Allah loves those who do good:

جو آسودگی اور تنگی میں (اپنا مال خدا کی راہ میں)
خرچ کرتے ہیں اور غصے کو روکتے اور لوگوں
کے قصور معاف کرتے ہیں اور خدا نیکوکاروں کو
دوست رکھتا ہے (۱۳۴)

الَّذِينَ يُنْفِقُونَ فِي السَّرَّاءِ وَ
الضَّرَّاءِ وَالْكَٰظِمِينَ الْغَيْظَ
وَالْعَافِينَ عَنِ النَّاسِ وَاللَّهُ
يُحِبُّ الْمُحْسِنِينَ (١٣٤)

135. And those who, having done an act of indecency or wronged their own souls. Remember Allah and ask for forgiveness for their sins,—and who can forgive sins except Allah ?— and are never obstinate in persisting knowingly in (the wrong) they have done.

اور وہ کہ جب کوئی کھلا گناہ یا اپنے حق میں
کوئی اور برائی کر بیٹھتے ہیں تو خدا کو یاد کرتے
اور اپنے گناہوں کی بخشش مانگتے ہیں اور خدا کے
سوا گناہ بخش بھی کون سکتا ہے؟ اور جان بوجھ کر
اپنے افعال پر اڑے نہیں رہتے (۱۳۵)

وَالَّذِينَ إِذَا فَعَلُوا فَٰحِشَةً أَوْ
ظَلَمُوا أَنْفُسَهُمْ ذَكَرُوا اللَّهَ
فَاسْتَغْفَرُوا لِذُنُوبِهِمْ وَمَنْ يَغْفِرُ
الذُّنُوبَ إِلَّا اللَّهُ وَلَمْ يُصِرُّوا
عَلَىٰ مَا فَعَلُوا وَهُمْ يَعْلَمُونَ (١٣٥)

136. For such the reward is forgiveness from their Lord, and Gardens with rivers flowing

ایسے ہی لوگوں کا صلہ پروردگار کی طرف سے
بخشش اور باغ ہیں جن کے نیچے نہریں بہ رہی

أُولَٰئِكَ جَزَاؤُهُمْ مَغْفِرَةٌ مِنْ
رَبِّهِمْ وَجَنَّٰتٌ تَجْرِي مِنْ تَحْتِهَا

underneath,— an eternal dwelling: how excellent a recompense for those who work (and strive) !

ہیں (اور) وہ اُن میں ہمیشہ بستے رہیں گے۔ اور
(اچھے) کام کرنے والوں کا بدلہ بہت اچھا ہے (۱۳۶)

الْأَنْهٰرُ خٰلِدِيْنَ فِيْهَا ۭ وَنِعْمَ
اَجْرُ الْعٰمِلِيْنَ (١٣٦)

137. There have been examples that have passed away before you: travel through the earth, and see what was the end of those who rejected Truth.

تم لوگوں سے پہلے بھی بہت سے واقعات گذر چکے
ہیں۔ تو تم زمین میں سیر کر کے دیکھ لو کہ جھٹلانے
والوں کا کیسا انجام ہوا (۱۳۷)

قَدْ خَلَتْ مِنْ قَبْلِكُمْ سُنَنٌ ۙ
فَسِيْرُوْا فِي الْاَرْضِ فَانْظُرُوْا
كَيْفَ كَانَ عَاقِبَةُ الْمُكَذِّبِيْنَ (١٣٧)

138. Here is a plain statement to men, a guidance and instruction to those who fear Allah !

یہ (قرآن) لوگوں کے لئے بیان صریح اور اہلِ تقویٰ
کے لئے ہدایت اور نصیحت ہے (۱۳۸)

هٰذَا بَيَانٌ لِّلنَّاسِ وَهُدًى وَّ
مَوْعِظَةٌ لِّلْمُتَّقِيْنَ (١٣٨)

139. So lose not heart, nor fall into despair: for ye must gain mastery if ye are true in Faith.

اور (دیکھو) بیدل نہ ہونا اور نہ کسی طرح کا غم کرنا اگر تم
مومن (صادق) ہو تو تم ہی غالب رہو گے (۱۳۹)

وَلَا تَهِنُوْا وَلَا تَحْزَنُوْا وَاَنْتُمُ
الْاَعْلَوْنَ اِنْ كُنْتُمْ مُّؤْمِنِيْنَ (١٣٩)

140. If a wound hath touched you, be sure a similar wound hath touched the others. Such days (of varying fortunes) We give to men and men by turns: that Allah may know those that believe, and that He may take to Himself from your ranks martyr-witnesses (to Truth). And Allah loveth not those that do wrong.

اگر تمہیں زخم (شکست) لگا ہے تو اُن لوگوں کو بھی
ایسا زخم لگ چکا ہے۔ اور یہ دن ہیں کہ ہم ان کو
لوگوں میں بدلتے رہتے ہیں۔ اور اس سے یہ بھی
مقصود تھا کہ خدا ایمان والوں کو متمیز کر دے اور تم
میں سے گواہ بنائے اور خدا بے انصافوں کو پسند نہیں کرتا (۱۴۰)

اِنْ يَّمْسَسْكُمْ قَرْحٌ فَقَدْ مَسَّ
الْقَوْمَ قَرْحٌ مِّثْلُهٗ ۭ وَتِلْكَ
الْاَيَّامُ نُدَاوِلُهَا بَيْنَ النَّاسِ ۚ
وَلِيَعْلَمَ اللّٰهُ الَّذِيْنَ اٰمَنُوْا وَيَتَّخِذَ
مِنْكُمْ شُهَدَاۗءَ ۭ وَاللّٰهُ لَا يُحِبُّ الظّٰلِمِيْنَ (١٤٠)

141. Allah's object also is to purge those that are true in Faith and to deprive of blessing those that resist Faith.

اور یہ بھی مقصود تھا کہ خدا ایمان والوں کو خالص
(مومن) بنادے اور کافروں کو نابود کر دے (۱۴۱)

وَلِيُمَحِّصَ اللّٰهُ الَّذِيْنَ اٰمَنُوْا
وَيَمْحَقَ الْكٰفِرِيْنَ (١٤١)

142. Did ye think that ye would enter Heaven without Allah testing those of you who fought hard (in His Cause) and remained steadfast ?

کیا تم یہ سمجھتے ہو کہ (بے آزمائش) بہشت میں جا داخل ہو گے (حالانکہ
ابھی خدا نے تم میں سے جہاد کرنیوالوں کو تو اچھی طرح معلوم کیا ہی نہیں اور
(یہ بھی مقصود ہے کہ) وہ ثابت قدم رہنے والوں کو معلوم کرے (۱۴۲)

اَمْ حَسِبْتُمْ اَنْ تَدْخُلُوا الْجَنَّةَ
وَلَمَّا يَعْلَمِ اللّٰهُ الَّذِيْنَ جٰهَدُوْا
مِنْكُمْ وَيَعْلَمَ الصّٰبِرِيْنَ (١٤٢)

143. Ye did indeed wish for Death before ye encountered it: now ye have seen it with your own eyes, (and ye flinch !)

اور تم موت (شہادت) کے آنے سے پہلے اس کی تمنا
کیا کرتے تھے سو تم نے اُس کو آنکھوں سے
دیکھ لیا (۱۴۳)

وَلَقَدْ كُنْتُمْ تَمَنَّوْنَ الْمَوْتَ
مِنْ قَبْلِ اَنْ تَلْقَوْهُ ۠ فَقَدْ
رَاَيْتُمُوْهُ وَاَنْتُمْ تَنْظُرُوْنَ (١٤٣) ع

144. Muhammad is no more than a Messenger: many were the Messengers that passed away before Him. If he died or were slain, will ye then turn back on your heels? If any did turn back on his heels, not the least harm will he do to Allah; but Allah (on the other hand) will swiftly reward those who (serve him) with gratitude.

اور محمد (صلی اللہ علیہ وسلم) تو صرف (خدا کے) پیغمبر ہیں انسے
پہلے بھی بہت سے پیغمبر ہو گذرے ہیں۔ بھلا اگر یہ مر جائیں
یا مارے جائیں تو تم اُلٹے پاؤں پھر جاؤ؟ (یعنی مُرتد ہو جاؤ؟)
اور جو اُلٹے پاؤں پھر جائیگا تو خدا کا کچھ نقصان نہیں کر سکے گا
اور خدا شکر گذاروں کو (بڑا) ثواب دے گا (۱۴۴)

وَمَا مُحَمَّدٌ اِلَّا رَسُوْلٌ ۚ قَدْ خَلَتْ
مِنْ قَبْلِهِ الرُّسُلُ ۭ اَفَا۟ىِٕنْ مَّاتَ
اَوْ قُتِلَ انْقَلَبْتُمْ عَلٰٓى اَعْقَابِكُمْ ۭ
وَمَنْ يَّنْقَلِبْ عَلٰي عَقِبَيْهِ فَلَنْ يَّضُرَّ
اللّٰهَ شَـيْـــًٔـا ۭ وَسَيَجْزِي اللّٰهُ الشّٰكِرِيْنَ (١٤٤)

145. Nor can a soul die except by Allah's leave, the term being fixed as by writing. If any do desire a reward in this life, We shall give it to him; and if any do desire a reward in the Hereafter, We shall give it to him. And swiftly shall We reward those that (serve Us with) gratitude.

اور کسی شخص میں طاقت نہیں کہ خدا کے حکم کے بغیر
مر جائے (اس نے موت کا) وقت مقرر کر کے لکھ رکھا ہے
اور جو شخص دنیا میں (اپنے اعمال کا) بدلہ چاہے اسکو ہم یہیں بدلہ دیدینگے
اور جو آخرت میں طالب ثواب ہو اسکو وہاں اجر عطا کرینگے
اور ہم شکر گزاروں کو عنقریب (بہت اچھا) صلہ دینگے (۱۴۵)

وَمَا كَانَ لِنَفْسٍ اَنْ تَمُوْتَ اِلَّا
بِاِذْنِ اللّٰهِ كِتٰبًا مُّؤَجَّلًا ؕ وَمَنْ
يُّرِدْ ثَوَابَ الدُّنْيَا نُؤْتِهٖ مِنْهَا ۚ
وَمَنْ يُّرِدْ ثَوَابَ الْاٰخِرَةِ نُؤْتِهٖ
مِنْهَا ؕ وَسَنَجْزِى الشّٰكِرِيْنَ ﴿۱۴۵﴾

146. How many of the Prophets fought (in Allah's way), and with them (fought) large bands of godly men ? But they never lost heart if they met with disaster in Allah's way, nor did they weaken (in will) nor give in. And Allah loves those who are firm and steadfast.

اور بہت سے نبی ہوئے ہیں جنکے ساتھ ہو کر اکثر اہل اللہ (خدا کے
دشمنوں سے) لڑے ہیں۔ تو جو مصیبتیں اُن پر راہ خدا میں
واقع ہوئیں اُنکے سبب انہوں نے نہ تو ہمت ہاری اور نہ بزدلی کی نہ
(کافروں سے) دبے اور خدا استقلال رکھنے والوں کو دوست رکھتا ہے (۱۴۶)

وَكَاَيِّنْ مِّنْ نَّبِيٍّ قٰتَلَ ۙ مَعَهٗ
رِبِّيُّوْنَ كَثِيْرٌ ۚ فَمَا وَهَنُوْا لِمَآ
اَصَابَهُمْ فِىْ سَبِيْلِ اللّٰهِ وَمَا ضَعُفُوْا
وَمَا اسْتَكَانُوْا ؕ وَاللّٰهُ يُحِبُّ الصّٰبِرِيْنَ ﴿۱۴۶﴾

147. All that they said was: "Our Lord ! forgive us our sins and anything we may have done that transgressed our duty: establish our feet firmly, and help us against those that resist Faith."

اور (اس حالت میں) اُن کے مُنہ سے کوئی بات نکلتی
تو یہی کہ اے پروردگار ہمارے گناہ اور زیادتیاں
جو ہم اپنے کاموں میں کرتے رہے ہیں معاف فرما۔
اور ہمکو ثابت قدم رکھ اور کافروں پر فتح عنایت کر (۱۴۷)

وَمَا كَانَ قَوْلَهُمْ اِلَّاۤ اَنْ قَالُوْا
رَبَّنَا اغْفِرْ لَنَا ذُنُوْبَنَا وَاِسْرَافَنَا
فِىْۤ اَمْرِنَا وَثَبِّتْ اَقْدَامَنَا وَانْصُرْنَا
عَلَى الْقَوْمِ الْكٰفِرِيْنَ ﴿۱۴۷﴾

148. And Allah gave them a reward in this world, and the excellent reward of the Hereafter. For Allah loveth those who do good.

تو خدا نے اُن کو دنیا میں بھی بدلہ دیا اور آخرت
میں بھی بہت اچھا بدلہ (دے گا) اور خدا نیکوکاروں
کو دوست رکھتا ہے (۱۴۸)

فَاٰتٰىهُمُ اللّٰهُ ثَوَابَ الدُّنْيَا وَ
حُسْنَ ثَوَابِ الْاٰخِرَةِ ؕ وَاللّٰهُ
يُحِبُّ الْمُحْسِنِيْنَ ﴿۱۴۸﴾ ع

149. O ye who believe ! If ye obey the Unbelievers, they will drive you back on your heels, and ye will turn back (from Faith) to your own loss.

مومنو! اگر تم کافروں کا کہا مان لوگے تو
وہ تم کو اُلٹے پاؤں پھیر (کر مرتد کر) دیں گے
پھر تم بڑے خسارے میں پڑ جاؤ گے (۱۴۹)

يٰۤاَيُّهَا الَّذِيْنَ اٰمَنُوْۤا اِنْ تُطِيْعُوا
الَّذِيْنَ كَفَرُوْا يَرُدُّوْكُمْ عَلٰٓى
اَعْقَابِكُمْ فَتَنْقَلِبُوْا خٰسِرِيْنَ ﴿۱۴۹﴾

150. Nay, Allah is your Protector, and He is the best of helpers.

(یہ تمہارے مددگار نہیں ہیں) بلکہ خدا تمہارا مددگار ہے
اور وہ سب سے بہتر مددگار ہے (۱۵۰)

بَلِ اللّٰهُ مَوْلٰٮكُمْ ۚ وَهُوَ
خَيْرُ النّٰصِرِيْنَ ﴿۱۵۰﴾

151. Soon shall We cast terror into the hearts of the Unbelievers, for that they joined partners with Allah, for which He had sent no authority: their abode will be the Fire: and evil is the home of the wrong-doers !

ہم عنقریب کافروں کے دلوں میں تمہارا رُعب بٹھا
دینگے کیونکہ یہ خدا کے ساتھ شرک کرتے ہیں جس کی
اُس نے کوئی بھی دلیل نازل نہیں کی۔ اور اُن کا
ٹھکانا دوزخ ہے وہ ظالموں کا بہت بُرا ٹھکانا ہے (۱۵۱)

سَنُلْقِىْ فِىْ قُلُوْبِ الَّذِيْنَ كَفَرُوا
الرُّعْبَ بِمَاۤ اَشْرَكُوْا بِاللّٰهِ مَا لَمْ
يُنَزِّلْ بِهٖ سُلْطٰنًا ۚ وَمَاْوٰٮهُمُ
النَّارُ ؕ وَبِئْسَ مَثْوَى الظّٰلِمِيْنَ ﴿۱۵۱﴾

152. Allah did indeed fulfil His promise to you when ye with His permission were about to annihilate your enemy,— until ye flinched and

اور خدا نے اپنا وعدہ سچا کر دیا (یعنی) اُس وقت جبکہ
تم کافروں کو اس کے حکم سے قتل کر رہے تھے یہاں

وَلَقَدْ صَدَقَكُمُ اللّٰهُ وَعْدَهٗۤ اِذْ
تَحُسُّوْنَهُمْ بِاِذْنِهٖ ۚ حَتّٰۤى اِذَا فَشِلْتُمْ

fell to disputing about the order, and disobeyed it after He brought you in sight (of the Victory) which ye covet. Among you are some that hanker after this world and some that desire the Hereafter. Then did He divert you from your foes in order to test you. But He forgave you: for Allah is full of grace to those who believe.

153. Behold ! ye were climbing up the high ground, without even casting a side glance at anyone, and the Messenger in your rear was calling you back. There did Allah give you one distress after another by way of requital, to teach you not to grieve for (the booty) that had escaped you and for (the ill) that had befallen you. For Allah is well aware of all that ye do.

154. After (the excitement) of the distress, He sent down calm on a band of you overcome with slumber, while another band was stirred to anxiety by their own feelings, moved by wrong suspicions of Allah—suspicions due to Ignorance. They said: "Have we any hand in the affair?" Say thou: "Indeed, this affair is wholly Allah's." They hide in their minds what they dare not reveal to thee. They say (to themselves); "If we had had anything to do with this affair, we should not have been in the slaughter here." Say: "Even if you had remained in your homes, those for whom death was decreed would certainly have gone forth to the place of their death": but (all this was) that Allah might test what is in your breasts and purge what

تک کہ جو تم چاہتے تھے خدا نے تم کو دکھا دیا۔ اس کے
بعد تم نے ہمت ہار دی اور حکم (پیغمبر) میں جھگڑا کرنے
لگے اور اُس کی نافرمانی کی۔ بعض تو تم میں سے دنیا کے
خواستگار تھے اور بعض آخرت کے طالب۔ اُس وقت خدا
نے تم کو اُن (کے مقابلے) سے پھیر (کر بھگا) دیا تاکہ
تمہاری آزمائش کرے اور اُس نے تمہارا قصور معاف
کر دیا۔ اور خدا مومنوں پر بڑا فضل کرنے والا ہے ﴿۱۵۲﴾
(وہ وقت بھی یاد کرنے کے لائق ہے) جب تم لوگ دُور
بھاگے جاتے تھے اور کسی کو پیچھے پھر کر نہیں دیکھتے تھے اور
رسول اللہ تم کو تمہارے پیچھے کھڑے بلا رہے تھے تو خدا نے
تم کو غم پر غم پہنچایا تاکہ جو چیز تمہارے ہاتھ سے جاتی رہی
یا جو مصیبت تم پر واقع ہوئی ہے اس سے تم اندوہناک نہ ہو
اور خدا تمہارے سب اعمال سے خبردار ہے ﴿۱۵۳﴾
پھر خدا نے غم و رنج کے بعد تم پر تسلی نازل فرمائی۔
(یعنی) نیند کہ تم میں سے ایک جماعت پر طاری ہو گئی
اور کچھ لوگ جن کو جان کے لالے پڑ رہے تھے خدا کے
بارے میں ناحق (ایام) کفر کے سے گمان کرتے تھے۔
اور کہتے تھے بھلا ہمارے اختیار کی کچھ بات ہے؟ تم کہہ دو
کہ بے شک سب باتیں خدا ہی کے اختیار میں ہیں۔ یہ لوگ
(بہت سی باتیں) دلوں میں مخفی رکھتے ہیں جو تم پر
ظاہر نہیں کرتے تھے۔ کہتے تھے کہ ہمارے بس کی بات
ہوتی تو ہم یہاں قتل ہی نہ کیے جاتے۔ کہہ دو کہ اگر
تم اپنے گھروں میں بھی ہوتے تو جن کی تقدیر میں
مارا جانا لکھا تھا وہ اپنی اپنی قتل گاہوں کی
طرف ضرور نکل آتے۔ اس سے غرض یہ تھی کہ
خدا تمہارے سینوں کی باتوں کو آزمائے اور جو کچھ
تمہارے دلوں میں ہے اس کو خالص اور صاف کرے۔

وَتَنَازَعْتُمْ فِي الْأَمْرِ وَعَصَيْتُمْ
مِّنْ بَعْدِ مَا أَرَاكُمْ مَّا تُحِبُّونَ ۚ
مِنكُم مَّن يُرِيدُ الدُّنْيَا وَ
مِنكُم مَّن يُرِيدُ الْآخِرَةَ ۚ
ثُمَّ صَرَفَكُمْ عَنْهُمْ لِيَبْتَلِيَكُمْ ۖ
وَلَقَدْ عَفَا عَنكُمْ ۗ وَاللَّهُ ذُو
فَضْلٍ عَلَى الْمُؤْمِنِينَ ﴿١٥٢﴾
إِذْ تُصْعِدُونَ وَلَا تَلْوُونَ عَلَىٰ
أَحَدٍ وَالرَّسُولُ يَدْعُوكُمْ
فِي أُخْرَاكُمْ فَأَثَابَكُمْ غَمًّا
بِغَمٍّ لِّكَيْلَا تَحْزَنُوا عَلَىٰ مَا
فَاتَكُمْ وَلَا مَا أَصَابَكُمْ ۗ وَاللَّهُ
خَبِيرٌ بِمَا تَعْمَلُونَ ﴿١٥٣﴾
ثُمَّ أَنزَلَ عَلَيْكُم مِّن بَعْدِ
الْغَمِّ أَمَنَةً نُّعَاسًا يَغْشَىٰ
طَائِفَةً مِّنكُمْ ۖ وَطَائِفَةٌ قَدْ
أَهَمَّتْهُمْ أَنفُسُهُمْ يَظُنُّونَ
بِاللَّهِ غَيْرَ الْحَقِّ ظَنَّ الْجَاهِلِيَّةِ ۖ
يَقُولُونَ هَل لَّنَا مِنَ الْأَمْرِ
مِن شَيْءٍ ۗ قُلْ إِنَّ الْأَمْرَ كُلَّهُ
لِلَّهِ ۗ يُخْفُونَ فِي أَنفُسِهِم مَّا
لَا يُبْدُونَ لَكَ ۖ يَقُولُونَ لَوْ
كَانَ لَنَا مِنَ الْأَمْرِ شَيْءٌ مَّا قُتِلْنَا
هَاهُنَا ۗ قُل لَّوْ كُنتُمْ فِي بُيُوتِكُمْ
لَبَرَزَ الَّذِينَ كُتِبَ عَلَيْهِمُ الْقَتْلُ
إِلَىٰ مَضَاجِعِهِمْ ۖ وَلِيَبْتَلِيَ اللَّهُ
مَا فِي صُدُورِكُمْ وَلِيُمَحِّصَ مَا فِي

is in your hearts. For Allah knoweth well the secrets of your hearts.

اور خدا دلوں کی باتوں سے خوب واقف ہے (۱۵۴)

قُلُوبِكُمْ ۗ وَاللَّهُ عَلِيمٌ بِذَاتِ الصُّدُورِ ﴿١٥٤﴾

155. Those of you who turned back on the day the two hosts met,—it was Satan who caused them to fail, because of some (evil) they had done. But Allah has blotted out (their fault): for Allah is Oft-Forgiving, Most Forbearing.

جو لوگ تم میں سے (اُحد کے دن) جبکہ (مومنوں اور کافروں
کی) دو جماعتیں ایک دوسرے سے گتھ گئیں (جنگ سے) بھاگ گئے
تو اُن کے بعض افعال کے سبب شیطان نے اُن کو پھسلا دیا مگر خدا نے
اُن کا قصور معاف کر دیا۔ بیشک خدا بخشنے والا (اور) بُردبار ہے (۱۵۵)

إِنَّ الَّذِينَ تَوَلَّوْا مِنْكُمْ يَوْمَ الْتَقَى
الْجَمْعَانِ إِنَّمَا اسْتَزَلَّهُمُ الشَّيْطَانُ
بِبَعْضِ مَا كَسَبُوا ۖ وَلَقَدْ عَفَا اللَّهُ
عَنْهُمْ ۗ إِنَّ اللَّهَ غَفُورٌ حَلِيمٌ ﴿١٥٥﴾

156. O ye who believe ! be not like the Unbelievers, who say of their brethren, when they are travelling through the earth or engaged in fighting: "If they had stayed with us, they would not have died, or been slain." This that Allah may make it a cause of sighs and regrets in their hearts. It is Allah that gives Life and Death, and Allah sees well all that ye do.

مومنو! اُن لوگوں جیسے نہ ہونا جو کفر کرتے ہیں اور
اُن کے (مسلمان) بھائی جب (خدا کی راہ میں) سفر کریں
(اور مر جائیں) یا جہاد کو نکلیں (اور مارے جائیں) تو اُن کی
نسبت کہتے ہیں کہ اگر وہ ہمارے پاس رہتے تو نہ مرتے اور نہ
مارے جاتے۔ ان باتوں سے مقصود یہ ہے کہ خدا اُن لوگوں کے دلوں
میں افسوس پیدا کر دے۔ اور زندگی اور موت تو خدا ہی دیتا ہے
اور خدا تمہارے سب کاموں کو دیکھ رہا ہے (۱۵۶)

يَا أَيُّهَا الَّذِينَ آمَنُوا لَا تَكُونُوا
كَالَّذِينَ كَفَرُوا وَقَالُوا لِإِخْوَانِهِمْ
إِذَا ضَرَبُوا فِي الْأَرْضِ أَوْ كَانُوا
غُزًّى لَوْ كَانُوا عِنْدَنَا مَا مَاتُوا وَمَا قُتِلُوا
لِيَجْعَلَ اللَّهُ ذَٰلِكَ حَسْرَةً فِي
قُلُوبِهِمْ ۗ وَاللَّهُ يُحْيِي وَيُمِيتُ ۗ
وَاللَّهُ بِمَا تَعْمَلُونَ بَصِيرٌ ﴿١٥٦﴾

157. And if ye are slain, or die, in the way of Allah, forgiveness and mercy from Allah are far better than all they could amass:

اور اگر تم خدا کے رستے میں مارے جاؤ یا مر جاؤ تو جو (مال
ومتاع) لوگ جمع کرتے ہیں اس سے خدا کی بخشش
اور رحمت کہیں بہتر ہے (۱۵۷)

وَلَئِنْ قُتِلْتُمْ فِي سَبِيلِ اللَّهِ
أَوْ مُتُّمْ لَمَغْفِرَةٌ مِنَ اللَّهِ وَ
رَحْمَةٌ خَيْرٌ مِمَّا يَجْمَعُونَ ﴿١٥٧﴾

158. And if ye die, or are slain, lo ! it is unto Allah that ye are brought together.

اور اگر تم مر جاؤ یا مارے جاؤ خدا کے حضور میں
ضرور اکٹھے کئے جاؤ گے (۱۵۸)

وَلَئِنْ مُتُّمْ أَوْ قُتِلْتُمْ لَإِلَى
اللَّهِ تُحْشَرُونَ ﴿١٥٨﴾

159. It is part of the Mercy of Allah that thou dost deal gently with them. Wert thou severe or harsh-hearted, they would have broken away from about thee: so pass over (their faults), and ask for (Allah's) forgiveness for them; and consult them in affairs (of moment). Then, when thou hast taken a decision, put thy trust in Allah. For Allah loves those who put their trust (in Him).

(اے محمدؐ) خدا کی مہربانی سے تمہاری اُفتادِ مزاج اُن
لوگوں کے لئے نرم واقع ہوئی ہے اور اگر تم بدخو اور
سخت دل ہوتے تو یہ تمہارے پاس سے بھاگ کھڑے
ہوتے۔ تو اُن کو معاف کر دو اور اُن کے لئے (خدا سے) مغفرت
مانگو اور اپنے کاموں میں اُن سے مشورت لیا کرو۔ اور جب (کسی کام کا) عزم مصمم
کر لو تو خدا پر بھروسہ رکھو۔ بیشک خدا بھروسہ رکھنے والوں کو دوست رکھتا ہے (۱۵۹)

فَبِمَا رَحْمَةٍ مِنَ اللَّهِ لِنْتَ لَهُمْ ۖ
وَلَوْ كُنْتَ فَظًّا غَلِيظَ الْقَلْبِ
لَانْفَضُّوا مِنْ حَوْلِكَ ۖ فَاعْفُ
عَنْهُمْ وَاسْتَغْفِرْ لَهُمْ وَشَاوِرْهُمْ
فِي الْأَمْرِ ۖ فَإِذَا عَزَمْتَ فَتَوَكَّلْ عَلَى
اللَّهِ ۚ إِنَّ اللَّهَ يُحِبُّ الْمُتَوَكِّلِينَ ﴿١٥٩﴾

160. If Allah helps you, none can overcome you: if He forsakes you, who is there, after that, that can help you ? In Allah, then, let Believers put their trust.

اگر خدا تمہارا مددگار ہے تو تم پر کوئی غالب نہیں آ سکتا
اور اگر وہ تمہیں چھوڑ دے تو پھر کون ہے کہ تمہاری مدد کرے
اور مومنوں کو چاہیئے کہ خدا ہی پر بھروسہ رکھیں (۱۶۰)

إِنْ يَنْصُرْكُمُ اللَّهُ فَلَا غَالِبَ لَكُمْ ۖ
وَإِنْ يَخْذُلْكُمْ فَمَنْ ذَا الَّذِي يَنْصُرُكُمْ
مِنْ بَعْدِهِ ۗ وَعَلَى اللَّهِ فَلْيَتَوَكَّلِ الْمُؤْمِنُونَ ﴿١٦٠﴾

161. No prophet could (ever) act dishonestly if any person acts

اور کبھی نہیں ہو سکتا کہ پیغمبر (خدا) خیانت کریں۔ اور

وَمَا كَانَ لِنَبِيٍّ أَنْ يَغُلَّ ۚ وَمَنْ

dishonestly he shall, on the Day of Judgment, restore what he misappropriated; then shall every soul receive its due whatever it earned,—and none shall be dealt with unjustly.

162. Is the man who follows the good pleasure of Allah like the man who draws on himself the wrath of Allah, and whose abode is in Hell?—a woeful refuge !

163. They are in varying grades in the sight of Allah, and Allah sees well all that they do.

164. Allah did confer a great favour on the Believers when He sent among them a Messenger from among themselves, rehearsing unto them the Signs of Allah, purifying them, and instructing them in Scripture and Wisdom, while, before that, they had been in manifest error.

165. What ! When a single disaster smites you, although ye smote (your enemies) with one twice as great, do ye say ?— "Whence is this?" Say (to them): "It is from yourselves: for Allah hath power over all things."

166. What ye suffered on the day the two armies met, was with the leave of Allah, in order that He might test the Believers,—

167. And the Hypocrites also. These were told: "Come, fight in the way of Allah, or (at least) drive (the foe from your city)." They said: "Had we known there would be a fight, we should certainly have followed you." They were that day nearer to Unbelief than to Faith, saying with their lips what was not in their hearts. But Allah hath full knowledge of all they conceal.

خیانت کرنیوالوں کو قیامت کے دن خیانت کی ہوئی چیز
خدا کے رُوبرو لا حاضر کرنی ہوگی۔ پھر ہر شخص کو اسکے اعمال کا
پورا پورا بدلہ دیا جائے گا اور بے انصافی نہیں کی جائیگی (١٦١)
بھلا جو شخص خدا کی خوشنودی کا تابع ہو وہ اس شخص کی
طرح (مرتکب خیانت) ہو سکتا ہے جو خدا کی ناخوشی میں
گرفتار ہو اور جس کا ٹھکانا دوزخ ہے اور وہ بُرا ٹھکانا ہے (١٦٢)
ان لوگوں کے خدا کے ہاں (مختلف اور متفاوت) درجے ہیں
اور خدا اُن کے سب اعمال کو دیکھ رہا ہے (١٦٣)
خدا نے مومنوں پر بڑا احسان کیا ہے کہ ان میں
انہیں میں سے ایک پیغمبر بھیجے جو اُن کو
خدا کی آیتیں پڑھ پڑھ کر سناتے اور اُن کو
پاک کرتے اور (خدا کی) کتاب اور دانائی سکھاتے
ہیں۔ اور پہلے تو یہ لوگ صریح گمراہی میں تھے (١٦٤)
(بھلا یہ) کیا بات ہے کہ جب (اُحد کے دن کفار کے
ہاتھ سے) تم پر مصیبت واقع ہوئی حالانکہ (جنگ بدر میں)
اس سے دو چند مصیبت تمہارے ہاتھ سے اُن پر پڑ چکی ہے تو تم چلا اٹھے
کہ (ہائے) آفت (ہم پر) کہاں سے آ پڑی کہدو کہ یہ تمہاری شامت اعمال ہے
(کہ تم نے پیغمبر کے حکم کے خلاف کیا) بیشک خدا ہر چیز پر قادر ہے (١٦٥)
اور جو مصیبت تم پر دونوں جماعتوں کے مقابلے کے
دن واقع ہوئی سو خدا کے حکم سے (واقع ہوئی) اور (اس
سے) یہ مقصود تھا کہ خدا مومنوں کو اچھی طرح معلوم کرلے (١٦٦)
اور منافقوں کو بھی معلوم کرلے اور (جب) اُن سے کہا گیا
کہ آؤ خدا کے رستے میں جنگ کرو یا (کافروں کے) حملوں کو
روکو۔ تو کہنے لگے کہ اگر ہم کو لڑائی کی خبر ہوتی تو ہم ضرور
تمہارے ساتھ رہتے۔ یہ اُس دن ایمان کی نسبت کفر سے
زیادہ قریب تھے مُنہ سے وہ باتیں کہتے ہیں جو اُنکے دلمیں
نہیں ہیں۔ اور جو کچھ یہ چھپاتے ہیں خدا اُس سے خوب واقف ہے (١٦٧)

يَغْلُلْ يَأْتِ بِمَا غَلَّ يَوْمَ الْقِيٰمَةِ ۚ
ثُمَّ تُوَفّٰى كُلُّ نَفْسٍ مَّا كَسَبَتْ
وَهُمْ لَا يُظْلَمُوْنَ (١٦١)
اَفَمَنِ اتَّبَعَ رِضْوَانَ اللّٰهِ كَمَنْۢ
بَآءَ بِسَخَطٍ مِّنَ اللّٰهِ وَمَاْوٰىهُ
جَهَنَّمُ ۗ وَبِئْسَ الْمَصِيْرُ (١٦٢)
هُمْ دَرَجٰتٌ عِنْدَ اللّٰهِ ۗ وَاللّٰهُ
بَصِيْرٌۢ بِمَا يَعْمَلُوْنَ (١٦٣)
لَقَدْ مَنَّ اللّٰهُ عَلَى الْمُؤْمِنِيْنَ
اِذْ بَعَثَ فِيْهِمْ رَسُوْلًا مِّنْ
اَنْفُسِهِمْ يَتْلُوْا عَلَيْهِمْ اٰيٰتِهٖ
وَيُزَكِّيْهِمْ وَيُعَلِّمُهُمُ الْكِتٰبَ وَالْحِكْمَةَ ۚ
وَاِنْ كَانُوْا مِنْ قَبْلُ لَفِيْ ضَلٰلٍ مُّبِيْنٍ (١٦٤) النصف
اَوَلَمَّآ اَصَابَتْكُمْ مُّصِيْبَةٌ
قَدْ اَصَبْتُمْ مِّثْلَيْهَا ۙ قُلْتُمْ
اَنّٰى هٰذَا ۗ قُلْ هُوَ مِنْ عِنْدِ
اَنْفُسِكُمْ ۗ اِنَّ اللّٰهَ عَلٰى كُلِّ
شَيْءٍ قَدِيْرٌ (١٦٥)
وَمَآ اَصَابَكُمْ يَوْمَ الْتَقَى
الْجَمْعٰنِ فَبِاِذْنِ اللّٰهِ وَلِيَعْلَمَ
الْمُؤْمِنِيْنَ (١٦٦)
وَلِيَعْلَمَ الَّذِيْنَ نَافَقُوْا ۖ وَقِيْلَ لَهُمْ
تَعَالَوْا قَاتِلُوْا فِيْ سَبِيْلِ اللّٰهِ اَوِ ادْفَعُوْا ۗ
قَالُوْا لَوْ نَعْلَمُ قِتَالًا لَّا اتَّبَعْنٰكُمْ ۗ هُمْ
لِلْكُفْرِ يَوْمَئِذٍ اَقْرَبُ مِنْهُمْ لِلْاِيْمَانِ ۚ
يَقُوْلُوْنَ بِاَفْوَاهِهِمْ مَّا لَيْسَ فِيْ قُلُوْبِهِمْ ۗ
وَاللّٰهُ اَعْلَمُ بِمَا يَكْتُمُوْنَ (١٦٧)

168. (They are) the ones that say, (of their brethren slain), while they themselves sit (at ease): "If only they had listened to us, they would not have been slain." Say: "Avert death from your own selves, if ye speak the truth."

یہ خود تو (جنگ سے بچ کر) بیٹھ ہی رہے تھے مگر (جنہوں نے
راہ خدا میں جانیں قربان کر دیں) اپنے (اُن) بھائیوں کے
بارے میں بھی کہتے ہیں کہ اگر ہمارا کہا مانتے تو قتل نہ ہوتے
کہہ دو کہ اگر سچے ہو تو اپنے اوپر سے موت کو ٹال دینا ﴿۱۶۸﴾

اَلَّذِيْنَ قَالُوْا لِاِخْوَانِهِمْ
وَقَعَدُوْا لَوْ اَطَاعُوْنَا مَا قُتِلُوْا ؕ
قُلْ فَادْرَءُوْا عَنْ اَنْفُسِكُمُ
الْمَوْتَ اِنْ كُنْتُمْ صٰدِقِيْنَ ﴿۱۶۸﴾

169. Think not of those who are slain in Allah's way as dead. Nay, they live, finding their sustenance from their Lord.

جو لوگ خدا کی راہ میں مارے گئے اُن کو مرے ہوئے
نہ سمجھنا (وہ مرے ہوئے نہیں ہیں) بلکہ خدا کے نزدیک
زندہ ہیں اور اُن کو رزق مل رہا ہے ﴿۱۶۹﴾

وَلَا تَحْسَبَنَّ الَّذِيْنَ قُتِلُوْا
فِيْ سَبِيْلِ اللّٰهِ اَمْوَاتًا ؕ بَلْ
اَحْيَآءٌ عِنْدَ رَبِّهِمْ يُرْزَقُوْنَ ﴿۱۶۹﴾

170. They rejoice in the Bounty provided by Allah: and with regard to those left behind, who have not yet joined them (in their bliss), the (martyrs) glory in the fact that on them is no fear, nor have they (cause to) grieve.

جو کچھ خدا نے اُن کو اپنے فضل سے بخش رکھا ہے اُس
میں خوش ہیں اور جو لوگ اُن کے پیچھے رہ گئے اور (شہید
ہو کر) ان میں شامل نہیں ہو سکے اُن کی نسبت خوشیاں
منا رہے ہیں کہ (قیامت کے دن) اُن کو بھی نہ کچھ خوف
ہوگا اور نہ وہ غمناک ہوں گے ﴿۱۷۰﴾

فَرِحِيْنَ بِمَآ اٰتٰهُمُ اللّٰهُ مِنْ
فَضْلِهٖ ۙ وَيَسْتَبْشِرُوْنَ بِالَّذِيْنَ
لَمْ يَلْحَقُوْا بِهِمْ مِّنْ خَلْفِهِمْ ۙ
اَلَّا خَوْفٌ عَلَيْهِمْ وَلَا هُمْ
يَحْزَنُوْنَ ﴿۱۷۰﴾ وقف لازم

171. They rejoice in the Grace and the Bounty from Allah, and in the fact that Allah suffereth not the reward of the Faithful to be lost (in the least).

اور خدا کے انعامات اور فضل سے خوش ہو رہے ہیں
اور اس سے کہ خدا مومنوں کا اجر ضائع
نہیں کرتا ﴿۱۷۱﴾

يَسْتَبْشِرُوْنَ بِنِعْمَةٍ مِّنَ اللّٰهِ
وَفَضْلٍ ۙ وَّاَنَّ اللّٰهَ لَا يُضِيْعُ اَجْرَ
الْمُؤْمِنِيْنَ ﴿۱۷۱﴾ ع

172. Of those who answered the call of Allah and the Messenger, even after being wounded, those who do right and refrain from wrong have a great reward;—

جنہوں نے باوجود زخم کھانے کے خدا اور رسُول
(کے حکم) کو قبول کیا۔ جو لوگ ان میں نیکوکار
اور پرہیزگار ہیں اُن کے لئے بڑا
ثواب ہے ﴿۱۷۲﴾

اَلَّذِيْنَ اسْتَجَابُوْا لِلّٰهِ وَالرَّسُوْلِ
مِنْ بَعْدِ مَآ اَصَابَهُمُ الْقَرْحُ ۛ
لِلَّذِيْنَ اَحْسَنُوْا مِنْهُمْ وَاتَّقَوْا
اَجْرٌ عَظِيْمٌ ﴿۱۷۲﴾ ج

173. Those to whom men said: "A great army is gathering against you, so fear them": but it (only) increased their Faith: they said: "For us Allah sufficeth, and He is the best Guardian."

(جب) اُن سے لوگوں نے آکر بیان کیا کہ کفّار
نے تمہارے (مقابلے کے) لئے (لشکر کثیر) جمع کیا ہے
تو اُن سے ڈرو۔ تو اُن کا ایمان اور زیادہ ہو گیا۔
اور کہنے لگے ہم کو خدا کافی ہے اور وہ بہت اچھا کارساز ہے ﴿۱۷۳﴾

اَلَّذِيْنَ قَالَ لَهُمُ النَّاسُ اِنَّ
النَّاسَ قَدْ جَمَعُوْا لَكُمْ فَاخْشَوْهُمْ
فَزَادَهُمْ اِيْمَانًا ۖۗ وَّقَالُوْا حَسْبُنَا
اللّٰهُ وَنِعْمَ الْوَكِيْلُ ﴿۱۷۳﴾

174. And they returned with Grace and Bounty from Allah: no harm ever touched them: for they followed the good pleasure of Allah: and Allah is the Lord of bounties unbounded.

پھر وہ خدا کی نعمتوں اور اُس کے فضل کے ساتھ (خوش و
خرم) واپس آئے اُن کو کسی طرح کا ضرر نہ پہنچا اور
وہ خدا کی خوشنودی کے تابع رہے اور خدا بڑے فضل کا مالک ہے ﴿۱۷۴﴾

فَانْقَلَبُوْا بِنِعْمَةٍ مِّنَ اللّٰهِ وَفَضْلٍ
لَّمْ يَمْسَسْهُمْ سُوْٓءٌ ۙ لا وَّاتَّبَعُوْا
رِضْوَانَ اللّٰهِ ۭ وَاللّٰهُ ذُوْ فَضْلٍ عَظِيْمٍ ﴿۱۷۴﴾

175. It is only the Satan that suggests to you the fear of his

یہ (خوف دلانے والا) تو شیطان ہے جو اپنے دوستوں

اِنَّمَا ذٰلِكُمُ الشَّيْطٰنُ يُخَوِّفُ

votaries: be ye not afraid of them, but fear Me, if ye have Faith.

سے ڈراتا ہے۔ تو اگر تم مومن ہو تو اُن سے مت
ڈرنا اور مجھی سے ڈرتے رہنا ﴿۱۷۵﴾

أَوْلِيَاءَهُ فَلَا تَخَافُوهُمْ وَخَافُونِ
إِن كُنتُم مُّؤْمِنِينَ ﴿١٧٥﴾

176. Let not those grieve thee who rush headlong into Unbelief: not the least harm will they do to Allah: Allah's Plan is that He will give them no portion in the Hereafter, but a severe punishment.

اور جو لوگ کفر میں جلدی کرتے ہیں اُن (کی وجہ)
سے غمگین نہ ہونا۔ یہ خدا کا کچھ نقصان نہیں
کر سکتے خدا چاہتا ہے کہ آخرت میں اُن کو کچھ حصہ
نہ دے اور اُن کیلئے بڑا عذاب (تیار) ہے ﴿۱۷۶﴾

وَلَا يَحْزُنكَ الَّذِينَ يُسَارِعُونَ
فِي الْكُفْرِ ۚ إِنَّهُمْ لَن يَضُرُّوا اللَّهَ
شَيْئًا ۗ يُرِيدُ اللَّهُ أَلَّا يَجْعَلَ لَهُمْ حَظًّا
فِي الْآخِرَةِ ۖ وَلَهُمْ عَذَابٌ عَظِيمٌ ﴿١٧٦﴾

177. Those who purchase unbelief at the price of faith,— not the least harm will they do to Allah, but they will have a grievous punishment.

جن لوگوں نے ایمان کے بدلے کفر خریدا وہ
خدا کا کچھ نہیں بگاڑ سکتے اور اُن کو دُکھ دینے
والا عذاب ہوگا ﴿۱۷۷﴾

إِنَّ الَّذِينَ اشْتَرَوُا الْكُفْرَ
بِالْإِيمَانِ لَن يَضُرُّوا اللَّهَ شَيْئًا ۚ
وَلَهُمْ عَذَابٌ أَلِيمٌ ﴿١٧٧﴾

178. Let not the Unbelievers think that Our respite to them is good for themselves: We grant them respite that they may grow in their iniquity: but they will have a shameful punishment.

اور کافر لوگ یہ نہ خیال کریں کہ ہم جو اُن کو مہلت
دیئے جاتے ہیں تو یہ اُن کے حق میں اچھا ہے (نہیں
بلکہ) ہم ان کو اسلئے مہلت دیتے ہیں کہ اور گناہ کرلیں
آخر کار اُن کو ذلیل کرنے والا عذاب ہوگا ﴿۱۷۸﴾

وَلَا يَحْسَبَنَّ الَّذِينَ كَفَرُوا
أَنَّمَا نُمْلِي لَهُمْ خَيْرٌ لِّأَنفُسِهِمْ ۚ
إِنَّمَا نُمْلِي لَهُمْ لِيَزْدَادُوا إِثْمًا ۚ
وَلَهُمْ عَذَابٌ مُّهِينٌ ﴿١٧٨﴾

179. Allah will not leave the Believers in the state in which ye are now, until He separates what is evil from what is good nor will Allah disclose to you the secrets of the Unseen, but He chooses of His Messengers whom He pleases. So believe in Allah and His Messengers: and if ye believe and do right, ye have a great reward without measure.

(لوگو) جب تک خدا ناپاک کو پاک سے الگ
نہ کردے گا مومنوں کو اس حال میں جس میں
تم ہو ہرگز نہیں رہنے دے گا۔ اور اللہ تم کو غیب
کی باتوں سے بھی مطلع نہیں کرے گا۔ البتہ خدا اپنے
پیغمبروں میں سے جسے چاہتا ہے انتخاب کرلیتا ہے
تو تم خدا پر اور اسکے رسولوں پر ایمان لاؤ۔ اور اگر ایمان
لاؤ گے اور پرہیزگاری کروگے تو تمکو اجر عظیم ملے گا ﴿۱۷۹﴾

مَا كَانَ اللَّهُ لِيَذَرَ الْمُؤْمِنِينَ
عَلَىٰ مَا أَنتُمْ عَلَيْهِ حَتَّىٰ يَمِيزَ
الْخَبِيثَ مِنَ الطَّيِّبِ ۗ وَمَا
كَانَ اللَّهُ لِيُطْلِعَكُمْ عَلَى الْغَيْبِ وَلَٰكِنَّ
اللَّهَ يَجْتَبِي مِن رُّسُلِهِ مَن يَشَاءُ ۖ
فَآمِنُوا بِاللَّهِ وَرُسُلِهِ ۚ وَإِن تُؤْمِنُوا
وَتَتَّقُوا فَلَكُمْ أَجْرٌ عَظِيمٌ ﴿١٧٩﴾

180. And let not those who covetously withhold of the gifts which Allah hath given them of His Grace, think that it is good for them: nay, it will be the worse for them: soon it will be tied to their necks like a twisted collar, on the Day of Judgment. To Allah belongs the heritage of the heavens and the earth; and Allah is well-acquainted with all that ye do.

جو لوگ مال میں جو خدا نے اپنے فضل سے
اُن کو عطا فرمایا ہے بخل کرتے ہیں وہ اس بخل
کو اپنے حق میں اچھا نہ سمجھیں (وہ اچھا نہیں)
بلکہ اُن کے لئے بُرا ہے وہ جس مال میں بخل کرتے
ہیں قیامت کے دن اس کا طوق بنا کر اُن کی گردنوں
میں ڈالا جائیگا اور آسمانوں اور زمین کا وارث خدا ہی ہے
اور جو عمل تم کرتے ہو خدا کو معلوم ہے ﴿۱۸۰﴾

وَلَا يَحْسَبَنَّ الَّذِينَ يَبْخَلُونَ
بِمَا آتَاهُمُ اللَّهُ مِن فَضْلِهِ هُوَ
خَيْرًا لَّهُم ۖ بَلْ هُوَ شَرٌّ لَّهُمْ ۖ
سَيُطَوَّقُونَ مَا بَخِلُوا بِهِ يَوْمَ
الْقِيَامَةِ ۗ وَلِلَّهِ مِيرَاثُ السَّمَاوَاتِ
وَالْأَرْضِ ۗ وَاللَّهُ بِمَا تَعْمَلُونَ
خَبِيرٌ ﴿١٨٠﴾

181. Allah hath heard the taunt of those who say: "Truly, Allah is indigent and we are rich !"— We shall certainly record their word and (their act) of slaying the Prophets in defiance of right, and We shall say: "Taste ye the Chastisement of the scorching Fire !

خدا نے اُن لوگوں کا قول سُن لیا ہے جو کہتے ہیں
کہ خدا فقیر ہے اور ہم امیر ہیں۔ یہ جو کچھ کہتے ہیں ہم
اسکو لکھ لیں گے اور پیغمبروں کو جو یہ ناحق قتل کرتے
رہے ہیں اسکو بھی (قلمبند کر رکھیں گے) اور (قیامت کے روز)
کہیں گے کہ عذاب (آتش) سوزاں کے مزے چکھتے رہو ﴿١٨١﴾

لَقَدْ سَمِعَ اللّٰهُ قَوْلَ الَّذِيْنَ قَالُوْآ
اِنَّ اللّٰهَ فَقِيْرٌ وَّنَحْنُ اَغْنِيَآءُ م
سَنَكْتُبُ مَا قَالُوْا وَقَتْلَهُمُ الْاَنْبِيَآءَ
بِغَيْرِ حَقٍّ لا وَّنَقُوْلُ ذُوْقُوْا عَذَابَ
الْحَرِيْقِ ﴿١٨١﴾

وقف لازم

182. "This is because of the (unrighteous deeds) which your hands sent on before ye: for Allah never do injustice to those who serve Him."

یہ اُن کاموں کی سزا ہے جو تمہارے ہاتھ آگے بھیجتے رہے ہیں
اور خدا تو بندوں پر مطلق ظلم نہیں کرتا ﴿١٨٢﴾

ذٰلِكَ بِمَا قَدَّمَتْ اَيْدِيْكُمْ وَ
اَنَّ اللّٰهَ لَيْسَ بِظَلَّامٍ لِّلْعَبِيْدِ ﴿١٨٢﴾

183. They (also) said: "Allah took our promise not to believe in a messenger unless he showed us a sacrifice consumed by fire (from heaven)." Say: "There came to you Messengers before me, with clear Signs and even with what ye ask for: why then did ye slay them, if ye speak the truth?"

جو لوگ کہتے ہیں کہ خدا نے ہمیں حکم بھیجا کہ جب تک
کوئی پیغمبر ہمارے پاس ایسی نیاز لے کر نہ آئے
جسکو آگ (آکر) کھا جائے تب تک ہم اُس پر ایمان نہ لائینگے
(اے پیغمبر ان سے) کہہ دو کہ مجھ سے پہلے کئی پیغمبر تمہارے
پاس کھلی ہوئی نشانیاں لیکر آئے اور وہ (معجزہ) بھی لائے جو تم
کہتے ہو تو اگر سچے ہو تو تم نے اُن کو قتل کیوں کیا؟ ﴿١٨٣﴾

اَلَّذِيْنَ قَالُوْآ اِنَّ اللّٰهَ عَهِدَ
اِلَيْنَآ اَلَّا نُؤْمِنَ لِرَسُوْلٍ حَتّٰى
يَاْتِيَنَا بِقُرْبَانٍ تَاْكُلُهُ النَّارُ ط
قُلْ قَدْ جَآءَكُمْ رُسُلٌ مِّنْ قَبْلِىْ
بِالْبَيِّنٰتِ وَبِالَّذِىْ قُلْتُمْ فَلِمَ
قَتَلْتُمُوْهُمْ اِنْ كُنْتُمْ صٰدِقِيْنَ ﴿١٨٣﴾

184. Then if they reject thee, so were rejected messengers before thee, who came with clear Signs, and the Scriptures, and the Book of Enlightenment.

پھر اگر یہ لوگ تم کو سچا نہ سمجھیں تو تم سے پہلے بہت سے پیغمبر
کھلی ہوئی نشانیاں اور صحیفے اور روشن کتابیں لیکر
آچکے ہیں اور لوگوں نے اُن کو بھی سچا نہیں سمجھا ﴿١٨٤﴾

فَاِنْ كَذَّبُوْكَ فَقَدْ كُذِّبَ رُسُلٌ
مِّنْ قَبْلِكَ جَآءُوْ بِالْبَيِّنٰتِ وَالزُّبُرِ
وَالْكِتٰبِ الْمُنِيْرِ ﴿١٨٤﴾

185. Every soul shall have a taste of death: and only on the Day of Judgment shall you be paid your full recompense. Only he who is saved far from the Fire and admitted to the Garden will have succeeded: for the life of this world is but goods and chattels of deception.

ہر متنفس کو موت کا مزا چکھنا ہے۔ اور تم کو قیامت کے دن
تمہارے اعمال کا پورا پورا بدلہ دیا جائے گا تو جو شخص آتش جہنم
سے دُور رکھا گیا اور بہشت میں داخل کیا گیا وہ مُراد کو پہنچ
گیا۔ اور دُنیا کی زندگی تو دھوکے کا سامان ہے ﴿١٨٥﴾

كُلُّ نَفْسٍ ذَآئِقَةُ الْمَوْتِ ط وَاِنَّمَا
تُوَفَّوْنَ اُجُوْرَكُمْ يَوْمَ الْقِيٰمَةِ ط فَمَنْ
زُحْزِحَ عَنِ النَّارِ وَاُدْخِلَ الْجَنَّةَ فَقَدْ
فَازَ ط وَمَا الْحَيٰوةُ الدُّنْيَآ اِلَّا مَتَاعُ الْغُرُوْرِ ﴿١٨٥﴾

186. Ye shall certainly be tried and tested in your possessions and in yourselves; and ye shall certainly hear much that will grieve you, from those who received the Book before you and from those who worship partners besides Allah. But if ye persevere patiently, and guard against evil,—then that indeed is a matter of great resolution.

(اے اہلِ ایمان) تمہارے مال و جان میں تمہاری آزمائش
کی جائے گی اور تم اہلِ کتاب سے اور اُن لوگوں سے جو مشرک
ہیں بہت سی ایذا کی باتیں سُنو گے۔ تو اگر صبر اور
پرہیزگاری کرتے رہو گے تو یہ بڑی ہمت کے
کام ہیں ﴿١٨٦﴾

لَتُبْلَوُنَّ فِىْٓ اَمْوَالِكُمْ وَاَنْفُسِكُمْ
وَلَتَسْمَعُنَّ مِنَ الَّذِيْنَ اُوْتُوا الْكِتٰبَ
مِنْ قَبْلِكُمْ وَمِنَ الَّذِيْنَ اَشْرَكُوْآ
اَذًى كَثِيْرًا ط وَاِنْ تَصْبِرُوْا وَتَتَّقُوْا
فَاِنَّ ذٰلِكَ مِنْ عَزْمِ الْاُمُوْرِ ﴿١٨٦﴾

187. And remember Allah took a Covenant from the People of the Book, to make it known and clear

اور جب خدا نے اُن لوگوں سے جن کو کتاب
عنایت کی گئی تھی اقرار لیا کہ (اس میں جو کچھ لکھا ہے) اُسے

وَاِذْ اَخَذَ اللّٰهُ مِيْثَاقَ الَّذِيْنَ
اُوْتُوا الْكِتٰبَ لَتُبَيِّنُنَّهٗ لِلنَّاسِ

to mankind, and not to hide it; but they threw it away behind their backs, and purchased with it some miserable gain ! And vile was the bargain they made !

188. Think not that those who exult in what they have brought about, and love to be praised for what they have not done,— think not that they can escape the Chastisement. For them is a Chastisement grievous indeed.

189. To Allah belongeth the dominion of the heavens and the earth; and Allah hath power over all things.

190. Behold ! In the creation of the heavens and the earth, and the alternation of Night and Day,— there are indeed Signs for men of understanding,—

191. Men who remember Allah standing, sitting, and lying down on their sides, and contemplate the (wonders of) creation in the heavens and the earth, (with the saying): "Our Lord not for naught hast Thou created (all) this ! Glory to Thee! Give us salvation from the Chastisement of the Fire.

192. "Our Lord ! any whom Thou dost admit to the Fire, truly Thou coverest with shame, and never will wrong-doers find any helpers !

193. "Our Lord ! we have heard the call of one calling (us) to Faith, 'Believe ye in the Lord,' and we have believed. Our Lord ! forgive us our sins, blot out from us our iniquities, and take to Thyself our souls in the company of the righteous.

194. "Our Lord ! Grant us what Thou didst promise unto us through Thy Messengers, and save us from shame on the Day of Judgment: for Thou never breakest Thy promise."

صاف صاف بیان کرتے رہنا اور اس (کی کسی بات) کو
نہ چھپانا تو انہوں نے اسکو پس پشت پھینک دیا. اور اُسکے
بدلے تھوڑی سی قیمت حاصل کی یہ جو کچھ حاصل کرتے ہیں بُرا ہے (۱۸۷)
جو لوگ اپنے (ناپسند) کاموں سے خوش ہوتے ہیں
اور (پسندیدہ کام) جو کرتے نہیں اُن کیلئے چاہتے ہیں
کہ اُنکی تعریف کی جائے اُنکی نسبت خیال نہ کرنا کہ وہ عذاب سے
رستگار ہو جائینگے۔ اور انہیں درد دینے والا عذاب ہوگا (۱۸۸)
اور آسمانوں اور زمین کی بادشاہی خدا ہی کو ہے
اور خدا ہر چیز پر قادر ہے (۱۸۹)
بیشک آسمانوں اور زمین کی پیدائش اور رات
اور دن کے بدل بدل کر آنے جانے میں عقل
والوں کے لئے نشانیاں ہیں (۱۹۰)
جو کھڑے اور بیٹھے اور لیٹے (ہر حال میں) خدا کو
یاد کرتے اور آسمان اور زمین کی پیدائش میں غور کرتے
(اور کہتے) ہیں کہ اے پروردگار تو نے اس (مخلوق) کو
بے فائدہ نہیں پیدا کیا. تو پاک ہے. تو (قیامت کے
دن) ہمیں دوزخ کے عذاب سے بچائیو (۱۹۱)
اے پروردگار جس کو تو نے دوزخ میں ڈالا اُسے
رُسوا کیا اور ظالموں کا کوئی مددگار نہیں (۱۹۲)
اے پروردگار ہم نے ایک ندا کرنے والے کو سُنا کہ
ایمان کے لئے پکار رہا تھا (یعنی) اپنے پروردگار
پر ایمان لاؤ تو ہم ایمان لے آئے. اے پروردگار ہمارے
گناہ معاف فرما. اور ہماری بُرائیوں کو ہم سے محو کر
اور ہم کو دنیا سے نیک بندوں کے ساتھ اُٹھا (۱۹۳)
اے پروردگار تو نے جن جن چیزوں کے ہم سے اپنے
پیغمبروں کے ذریعے سے وعدے کئے ہیں وہ ہمیں عطا فرما اور
قیامت کے دن ہمیں رسوا نہ کیجیو کچھ شک نہیں کہ تو خلاف وعدہ نہیں کرتا (۱۹۴)

وَلَا تَكْتُمُوْنَهٗ ز فَنَبَذُوْهُ
وَرَآءَ ظُهُوْرِهِمْ وَاشْتَرَوْا بِهٖ
ثَمَنًا قَلِيْلًا ط فَبِئْسَ مَا يَشْتَرُوْنَ ﴿۱۸۷﴾
لَا تَحْسَبَنَّ الَّذِيْنَ يَفْرَحُوْنَ
بِمَآ اَتَوْا وَّيُحِبُّوْنَ اَنْ يُّحْمَدُوْا
بِمَا لَمْ يَفْعَلُوْا فَلَا تَحْسَبَنَّهُمْ بِمَفَازَةٍ
مِّنَ الْعَذَابِ ج وَلَهُمْ عَذَابٌ اَلِيْمٌ ﴿۱۸۸﴾
وَلِلّٰهِ مُلْكُ السَّمٰوٰتِ وَالْاَرْضِ ط
ع وَاللّٰهُ عَلٰى كُلِّ شَيْءٍ قَدِيْرٌ ع ﴿۱۸۹﴾
اِنَّ فِيْ خَلْقِ السَّمٰوٰتِ وَالْاَرْضِ
وَاخْتِلَافِ الَّيْلِ وَالنَّهَارِ لَاٰيٰتٍ
لِّاُولِي الْاَلْبَابِ ﴿۱۹۰﴾
الَّذِيْنَ يَذْكُرُوْنَ اللّٰهَ قِيٰمًا
وَّقُعُوْدًا وَّعَلٰى جُنُوْبِهِمْ وَيَتَفَكَّرُوْنَ
فِيْ خَلْقِ السَّمٰوٰتِ وَالْاَرْضِ ج رَبَّنَا
مَا خَلَقْتَ هٰذَا بَاطِلًا ج سُبْحٰنَكَ فَقِنَا
عَذَابَ النَّارِ ﴿۱۹۱﴾
رَبَّنَآ اِنَّكَ مَنْ تُدْخِلِ النَّارَ فَقَدْ
اَخْزَيْتَهٗ ط وَمَا لِلظّٰلِمِيْنَ مِنْ اَنْصَارٍ ﴿۱۹۲﴾
رَبَّنَآ اِنَّنَا سَمِعْنَا مُنَادِيًا يُّنَادِيْ
لِلْاِيْمَانِ اَنْ اٰمِنُوْا بِرَبِّكُمْ
فَاٰمَنَّا ق رَبَّنَا فَاغْفِرْ لَنَا ذُنُوْبَنَا
وَكَفِّرْ عَنَّا سَيِّاٰتِنَا وَتَوَفَّنَا مَعَ
الْاَبْرَارِ ج ﴿۱۹۳﴾
رَبَّنَا وَاٰتِنَا مَا وَعَدْتَّنَا عَلٰى
رُسُلِكَ وَلَا تُخْزِنَا يَوْمَ الْقِيٰمَةِ ط
اِنَّكَ لَا تُخْلِفُ الْمِيْعَادَ ﴿۱۹۴﴾

195. And their Lord hath accepted of them, and answered them: "Never will I suffer to be lost the work of any of you, be he male or female: ye are members, one of another: those who have left their homes, and were driven out therefrom, and suffered harm in My Cause, and fought and were slain,— verily, I will blot out from them their iniquites, and admit them into Gardens with rivers flowing beneath;—a reward from Allah and from Allah is the best of rewards."

تو اُن کے پروردگار نے اُن کی دعا قبول کرلی (اور
فرمایا) کہ میں کسی عمل کرنے والے کے عمل کو مرد ہو
یا عورت ضائع نہیں کرتا تم ایک دوسرے کی جنس ہو۔
تو جو لوگ میرے لئے وطن چھوڑ گئے اور اپنے
گھروں سے نکالے گئے اور ستائے گئے اور لڑے
اور قتل کئے گئے میں اُن کے گناہ دُور کردوں گا
اور اُن کو بہشتوں میں داخل کروں گا جن کے نیچے
نہریں بہ رہی ہیں۔ (یہ) خدا کے ہاں سے بدلہ ہے
اور خدا کے ہاں اچھا بدلہ ہے (١٩٥)

فَاسْتَجَابَ لَهُمْ رَبُّهُمْ أَنِّي لَا
أُضِيعُ عَمَلَ عَامِلٍ مِّنكُم مِّن
ذَكَرٍ أَوْ أُنثَىٰ ۖ بَعْضُكُم مِّن بَعْضٍ ۖ
فَالَّذِينَ هَاجَرُوا وَأُخْرِجُوا مِن
دِيَارِهِمْ وَأُوذُوا فِي سَبِيلِي
وَقَاتَلُوا وَقُتِلُوا لَأُكَفِّرَنَّ عَنْهُمْ
سَيِّئَاتِهِمْ وَلَأُدْخِلَنَّهُمْ جَنَّاتٍ
تَجْرِي مِن تَحْتِهَا الْأَنْهَارُ ثَوَابًا مِّنْ
عِندِ اللَّهِ ۗ وَاللَّهُ عِندَهُ حُسْنُ الثَّوَابِ (١٩٥)

196. Let not the strutting about of the Unbelievers through the land deceive thee:

(اے پیغمبر) کافروں کا شہروں میں چلنا پھرنا تمہیں دھوکا
نہ دے (١٩٦)

لَا يَغُرَّنَّكَ تَقَلُّبُ الَّذِينَ كَفَرُوا
فِي الْبِلَادِ (١٩٦)

197. Little is it for enjoyment: their Ultimate abode is Hell: what an evil bed (to lie on) !

(یہ دنیا کا) تھوڑا سا فائدہ ہے۔ پھر (آخرت میں) تو اُن
کا ٹھکانا دوزخ ہے۔ اور وہ بُری جگہ ہے ٨١ (١٩٧)

مَتَاعٌ قَلِيلٌ ثُمَّ مَأْوَاهُمْ جَهَنَّمُ ۚ
وَبِئْسَ الْمِهَادُ (١٩٧)

198. On the other hand, for those who fear their Lord, are Gardens, with rivers flowing beneath; therein are they to dwell (for ever),— an entertainment from Allah; and that which is from Allah is the best (bliss) for the righteous.

لیکن جو لوگ اپنے پروردگار سے ڈرتے رہے اُن
کے لئے باغ ہیں جن کے نیچے نہریں بہ رہی ہیں
(اور) اُن میں ہمیشہ رہیں گے (یہ) خدا کے ہاں سے (اُنکی) مہمانی ہے
اور جو کچھ خدا کے ہاں ہے وہ نیکو کاروں کیلئے بہت اچھا ہے (١٩٨)

لَٰكِنِ الَّذِينَ اتَّقَوْا رَبَّهُمْ لَهُمْ
جَنَّاتٌ تَجْرِي مِن تَحْتِهَا الْأَنْهَارُ
خَالِدِينَ فِيهَا نُزُلًا مِّنْ عِندِ اللَّهِ ۗ
النصف وَمَا عِندَ اللَّهِ خَيْرٌ لِّلْأَبْرَارِ (١٩٨)

199. And there are, certainly, among the People of the Book, those who believe in Allah, in the revelation to you, and in the revelation to them, bowing in humility to Allah: they will not sell the Signs of Allah for a miserable gain ! For them is a reward with their Lord, and Allah is swift in account.

اور بعض اہلِ کتاب ایسے بھی ہیں جو خدا پر اور
اُس (کتاب) پر جو تم پر نازل ہوئی اور اُس پر جو
اُن پر نازل ہوئی ایمان رکھتے ہیں اور خدا کے آگے
عاجزی کرتے ہیں اور خدا کی آیتوں کے بدلے تھوڑی سی
قیمت نہیں لیتے۔ یہی لوگ ہیں جن کا صلہ اُن کے پروردگار
کے ہاں (تیار) ہے اور خدا جلد حساب لینے والا ہے (١٩٩)

وَإِنَّ مِنْ أَهْلِ الْكِتَابِ لَمَن
يُؤْمِنُ بِاللَّهِ وَمَا أُنزِلَ إِلَيْكُمْ
وَمَا أُنزِلَ إِلَيْهِمْ خَاشِعِينَ لِلَّهِ
لَا يَشْتَرُونَ بِآيَاتِ اللَّهِ ثَمَنًا قَلِيلًا ۗ
أُولَٰئِكَ لَهُمْ أَجْرُهُمْ عِندَ رَبِّهِمْ ۗ
إِنَّ اللَّهَ سَرِيعُ الْحِسَابِ (١٩٩)

200. O ye who believe ! persevere in patience and constancy; vie in such perseverance; strengthen each other; and fear Allah; that ye may prosper.

اے اہلِ ایمان (کفار کے مقابلے میں) ثابت قدم رہو
اور استقامت رکھو اور (مورچوں پر) جمے رہو۔ اور
خدا سے ڈرو۔ تاکہ مراد حاصل کرو (٢٠٠)

يَا أَيُّهَا الَّذِينَ آمَنُوا اصْبِرُوا
وَصَابِرُوا وَرَابِطُوا وَاتَّقُوا اللَّهَ
ع لَعَلَّكُمْ تُفْلِحُونَ (٢٠٠)

SÛRA–4
AN-NISÃA
(INTRODUCTION)

This Sûra is closely connected chronologically with Sûra 3. Its subject-matter deals with the social problems which the Muslim community had to face immediately after Uḥud. While the particular occasion made the necessity urgent, the principles laid down have permanently governed Muslim Law and social practice.

Broadly speaking, the Sûra consists of two parts: (1) that dealing with women, orphans, inheritance, marriage and family rights generally, and (2) that dealing with the recalcitrants in the larger family, the community at Medina, viz. the Hypocrites and their accomplices.

An-Nisãa, or The Women

In the name of Allah, Most Gracious Most Merciful.

1. O mankind ! fear your Guardian Lord, Who created you from a single Person, created, out of it, His mate, and from them twain scattered (like seeds) countless men and women;— fear Allah, through Whom ye demand your mutual (rights), and be heedful of the wombs (that bore you): for Allah ever watches over you.

2. To orphans restore their property (when they reach their age), nor substitute (your) worthless things for (their) good ones; and devour not their substance (by mixing it up) with your own. For this is indeed a great sin.

3. If ye fear that ye shall not be able to deal justly with the orphans, marry women of your choice, two, or three, or four; but if ye fear that ye shall not be able to deal justly (with them), then only one, or that which your right hands possess. That will be more suitable, to prevent you from doing injustice.

4. And give the women (on marriage) their dower as an obligation; but if they, of their own good pleasure, remit any part of it to you, take it and enjoy it with right good cheer.

5. To those weak of understanding give not your property which Allah has assigned to you to manage, but feed and clothe them therewith, and speak to them words of kindness and justice.

6. Make trial of orphans until they reach the age of marriage; if then ye find sound judgment in

سورۂ نساء مدنی ہے اور اس میں ایک سو چھہتر آیتیں اور چوبیس رکوع ہیں

شروع خدا کا نام لے کر جو بڑا مہربان نہایت رحم والا ہے ○
لوگو اپنے پروردگار سے ڈرو جس نے تم کو ایک شخص
سے پیدا کیا (یعنی اوّل) اُس سے اُس کا جوڑا بنایا۔
پھر ان دونوں سے کثرت سے مرد و عورت (پیدا
کرکے رُوئے زمین پر) پھیلا دیئے۔ اور خدا سے جس کے
نام کو تم اپنی حاجت براری کا ذریعہ بناتے ہو ڈرو اور
(قطع مودّت) ارحام سے (بچو) کچھ شک نہیں کہ خدا تمہیں دیکھ رہا ہے ①
اور یتیموں کا مال (جو تمہاری تحویل میں ہو) اُن کے
حوالے کر دو اور اُن کے پاکیزہ (اور عمدہ) مال کو (اپنے
ناقص اور) بُرے مال سے نہ بدلو۔ اور نہ اُن کا مال
اپنے مال میں ملا کر کھاؤ۔ کہ یہ بڑا سخت گناہ ہے ②
اور اگر تم کو اس بات کا خوف ہو کہ یتیم لڑکیوں کے
بارے میں انصاف نہ کرسکو گے تو اُن کے سوا جو عورتیں
تم کو پسند ہوں دو دو یا تین تین یا چار چار اُن سے
نکاح کر لو۔ اور اگر اس بات کا اندیشہ ہو کہ (سب عورتوں
سے) یکساں سلوک نہ کرسکو گے تو ایک عورت (کافی ہے) یا
لونڈی جسکے تم مالک ہو۔ اس سے تم بے انصافی سے بچ جاؤ گے ③
اور عورتوں کو اُن کے مہر خوشی سے دے دیا کرو ہاں اگر
وہ اپنی خوشی سے اس میں سے کچھ تم کو چھوڑ دیں۔
تو اسے ذوق شوق سے کھا لو ④
اور بے عقلوں کو اُن کا مال جسے خدا نے تم لوگوں
کے لئے سبب معیشت بنایا ہے مت دو (ہاں)
اس میں سے اُن کو کھلاتے اور پہناتے رہو اور اُن
سے معقول باتیں کہتے رہو ⑤
اور یتیموں کو بالغ ہونے تک کام کاج میں مصروف
رکھو پھر (بالغ ہونے پر) اگر اُن میں عقل کی

سُورَةُ النِّسَاءِ مَدَنِيَّةٌ وَّهِيَ مِائَةٌ وَّسِتٌّ وَّسَبْعُونَ اٰيَةً وَّاَرْبَعٌ وَّعِشْرُونَ رُكُوعًا

بِسْمِ اللّٰهِ الرَّحْمٰنِ الرَّحِيْمِ ○
يٰۤاَيُّهَا النَّاسُ اتَّقُوْا رَبَّكُمُ الَّذِيْ
خَلَقَكُمْ مِّنْ نَّفْسٍ وَّاحِدَةٍ وَّ
خَلَقَ مِنْهَا زَوْجَهَا وَبَثَّ مِنْهُمَا
رِجَالًا كَثِيْرًا وَّنِسَآءً ۚ وَاتَّقُوا
اللّٰهَ الَّذِيْ تَسَآءَلُوْنَ بِهٖ وَالْاَرْحَامَ ؕ
اِنَّ اللّٰهَ كَانَ عَلَيْكُمْ رَقِيْبًا ①
وَاٰتُوا الْيَتٰمٰۤى اَمْوَالَهُمْ وَلَا تَتَبَدَّلُوا
الْخَبِيْثَ بِالطَّيِّبِ ۠ وَلَا تَاْكُلُوْۤا
اَمْوَالَهُمْ اِلٰۤى اَمْوَالِكُمْ ؕ اِنَّهٗ
كَانَ حُوْبًا كَبِيْرًا ②
وَاِنْ خِفْتُمْ اَلَّا تُقْسِطُوْا فِي الْيَتٰمٰى
فَانْكِحُوْا مَا طَابَ لَكُمْ مِّنَ
النِّسَآءِ مَثْنٰى وَثُلٰثَ وَرُبٰعَ ۚ
فَاِنْ خِفْتُمْ اَلَّا تَعْدِلُوْا فَوَاحِدَةً
اَوْ مَا مَلَكَتْ اَيْمَانُكُمْ ؕ ذٰلِكَ
اَدْنٰۤى اَلَّا تَعُوْلُوْا ③
وَاٰتُوا النِّسَآءَ صَدُقٰتِهِنَّ نِحْلَةً ؕ
فَاِنْ طِبْنَ لَكُمْ عَنْ شَيْءٍ مِّنْهُ
نَفْسًا فَكُلُوْهُ هَنِيْٓـًٔا مَّرِيْٓـًٔا ④
وَلَا تُؤْتُوا السُّفَهَآءَ اَمْوَالَكُمُ الَّتِيْ
جَعَلَ اللّٰهُ لَكُمْ قِيٰمًا وَّارْزُقُوْهُمْ
فِيْهَا وَاكْسُوْهُمْ وَقُوْلُوْا لَهُمْ
قَوْلًا مَّعْرُوْفًا ⑤
وَابْتَلُوا الْيَتٰمٰى حَتّٰۤى اِذَا بَلَغُوا
النِّكَاحَ ۚ فَاِنْ اٰنَسْتُمْ مِّنْهُمْ رُشْدًا

فَادْفَعُوٓا اِلَيْهِمْ اَمْوَالَهُمْ ۚ وَلَا
تَاْكُلُوْهَآ اِسْرَافًا وَّبِدَارًا اَنْ
يَّكْبَرُوْا ؕ وَمَنْ كَانَ غَنِيًّا
فَلْيَسْتَعْفِفْ ۚ وَمَنْ كَانَ فَقِيْرًا
فَلْيَاْكُلْ بِالْمَعْرُوْفِ ؕ فَاِذَا دَفَعْتُمْ
اِلَيْهِمْ اَمْوَالَهُمْ فَاَشْهِدُوْا عَلَيْهِمْ ؕ
وَكَفٰى بِاللّٰهِ حَسِيْبًا ﴿٦﴾

پختگی دیکھو تو اُن کا مال اُنکے حوالے کردو۔ اور اس خوف
سے کہ وہ بڑے ہو جائینگے (یعنی بڑے ہو کر تم سے اپنا مال
واپس لے لینگے) اسکو فضول خرچی اور جلدی میں نہ اُڑا دینا۔
جو شخص آسودہ حال ہو اُسکو ایسے مال سے قطعی طور پر پرہیز رکھنا
چاہیئے اور جو بے مقدور ہو وہ مناسب طور پر (یعنی بقدر خدمت)
کچھ لے لے۔ اور جب اُنکا مال اُنکے حوالے کرنے لگو تو گواہ کر لیا کرو
اور حقیقت میں تو خدا ہی (گواہ اور) حساب لینے والا کافی ہے ﴿٦﴾

them, release their property to them; but consume it not wastefully, nor in haste against their growing up. If the guardian is well-off, let him claim no remuneration, but if he is poor, let him have for himself what is just and reasonable. When ye release their property to them, take witnesses in their presence: but all-sufficient is Allah in taking account.

لِلرِّجَالِ نَصِيْبٌ مِّمَّا تَرَكَ الْوَالِدٰنِ
وَالْاَقْرَبُوْنَ ۪ وَلِلنِّسَآءِ نَصِيْبٌ مِّمَّا تَرَكَ
الْوَالِدٰنِ وَالْاَقْرَبُوْنَ مِمَّا قَلَّ مِنْهُ
اَوْ كَثُرَ ؕ نَصِيْبًا مَّفْرُوْضًا ﴿٧﴾

جو مال ماں باپ اور رشتہ دار چھوڑ مریں
تھوڑا ہو یا بہت اُس میں مردوں کا بھی حصہ
ہے اور عورتوں کا بھی۔ یہ حصّے (خدا کے)
مقرر کئے ہوئے ہیں ﴿٧﴾

7. From what is left by parents and those nearest related there is a share for men and a share for women, whether the property be small or large,—a determinate share.

وَاِذَا حَضَرَ الْقِسْمَةَ اُولُوا الْقُرْبٰى
وَالْيَتٰمٰى وَالْمَسٰكِيْنُ فَارْزُقُوْهُمْ
مِّنْهُ وَقُوْلُوْا لَهُمْ قَوْلًا
مَّعْرُوْفًا ﴿٨﴾

اور جب میراث کی تقسیم کے وقت (غیر وارث)
رشتہ دار اور یتیم اور محتاج آجائیں تو اُن کو بھی
اس میں سے کچھ دے دیا کرو۔ اور شیریں کلامی
سے پیش آیا کرو ﴿٨﴾

8. But if at the time of division other relatives, or orphans, or poor, are present, give them out of the (property), and speak to them words of kindness and justice.

وَلْيَخْشَ الَّذِيْنَ لَوْ تَرَكُوْا مِنْ
خَلْفِهِمْ ذُرِّيَّةً ضِعٰفًا خَافُوْا
عَلَيْهِمْ ۖ فَلْيَتَّقُوا اللّٰهَ وَلْيَقُوْلُوْا
قَوْلًا سَدِيْدًا ﴿٩﴾

اور ایسے لوگوں کو ڈرنا چاہیئے جو ایسی حالت میں ہوں کہ
اپنے بعد ننھے ننھے بچے چھوڑ جائیں اور اُن کو اُنکی نسبت
خوف ہو (کہ اُنکے مرنے کے بعد ان بیچاروں کا کیا حال ہوگا)
پس چاہیئے کہ یہ لوگ خدا سے ڈریں اور معقول بات کہیں ﴿٩﴾

9. Let those (disposing of an estate) have the same fear in their minds as they would have for their own if they had left a helpless family behind: let them fear Allah, and speak appropriate words.

اِنَّ الَّذِيْنَ يَاْكُلُوْنَ اَمْوَالَ الْيَتٰمٰى
ظُلْمًا اِنَّمَا يَاْكُلُوْنَ فِيْ بُطُوْنِهِمْ
نَارًا ؕ وَسَيَصْلَوْنَ سَعِيْرًا ﴿١٠﴾ ع

جو لوگ یتیموں کا مال ناجائز طور پر کھاتے ہیں وہ
اپنے پیٹ میں آگ بھرتے ہیں۔ اور دوزخ
میں ڈالے جائیں گے ﴿١٠﴾

10. Those who unjustly eat up the property of orphans, eat up a Fire into their own bodies: they will soon be enduring a blazing Fire !

يُوْصِيْكُمُ اللّٰهُ فِيْٓ اَوْلَادِكُمْ ۗ
لِلذَّكَرِ مِثْلُ حَظِّ الْاُنْثَيَيْنِ ۚ
فَاِنْ كُنَّ نِسَآءً فَوْقَ اثْنَتَيْنِ
فَلَهُنَّ ثُلُثَا مَا تَرَكَ ۚ وَاِنْ كَانَتْ
وَاحِدَةً فَلَهَا النِّصْفُ ؕ وَلِاَبَوَيْهِ

خدا تمہاری اولاد کے بارے میں تم کو ارشاد
فرماتا ہے کہ ایک لڑکے کا حصہ دو لڑکیوں کے
حصے کے برابر ہے اور اگر اولادِ میت صرف لڑکیاں
ہی ہوں (یعنی دو یا) دو سے زیادہ تو کُل ترکے میں
اُن کا دو تہائی۔ اور اگر صرف ایک لڑکی ہو تو اُس کا حصہ

11. Allah (thus) directs you as regards your children's (inheritance): to the male, a portion equal to that of two females: if only daughters, two or more, their share is two-thirds of the inheritance; if only one, her share is a half.

For parents, a sixth share of the inheritance to each, if the deceased left children; if no children, and the parents are the (only) heirs, the mother has a third: if the deceased left brothers (or sisters), the mother has a sixth. (The distribution in all cases is) after the payment of legacies and debts. Ye know not whether your parents or your children are nearest to you in benefit. These are settled portions ordained by Allah: and Allah is All-knowing, All-wise.

12. In what your wives leave, your share is a half, if they leave no child, but if they leave a child, ye get a fourth; after payment of legacies and debts. In what ye leave; their share is a fourth, if ye leave no child; but if ye leave a child, they get an eighth; after payment of legacies and debts.

If the man or woman whose inheritance is in question, has left neither ascendants nor descendants, but has left a brother or a sister, each one of the two gets a sixth; but if more than two, they share in a third; after payment of legacies and debts; so that no loss is caused (to anyone). Thus is it ordained by Allah; and Allah is All-knowing, Most Forbearing.

13. Those are limits set by Allah: those who obey Allah and His

نصف۔ اور میت کے ماں باپ کا یعنی دونوں میں سے
ہر ایک کا ترکے میں چھٹا حصہ بشرطیکہ میت کے اولاد ہو
اور اگر اولاد نہ ہو اور صرف ماں باپ ہی اسکے وارث ہوں تو ایک تہائی
ماں کا حصہ۔ اور اگر میت کے بھائی بھی ہوں تو ماں کا چھٹا حصہ۔ اور
تقسیم ترکہ میت کی وصیت (کی تعمیل) کے بعد جو اُس نے کی ہو یا قرض
کے (ادا ہونیکے بعد جو اُسکے ذمے ہو) عمل میں آئیگی۔ تمکو معلوم نہیں
کہ تمہارے باپ دادوں اور بیٹوں پوتوں میں سے فائدے کے لحاظ سے
کون تم سے زیادہ قریب ہے یہ حصے خدا کے مقرر کئے ہوئے ہیں
اور خدا سب کچھ جاننے والا اور حکمت والا ہے ﴿١١﴾
اور جو مال تمہاری عورتیں چھوڑ مریں۔ اگر اُن کے اولاد
نہ ہو تو اس میں نصف حصہ تمہارا۔ اور اگر اولاد ہو
تو ترکے میں تمہارا حصہ چوتھائی۔ (لیکن یہ تقسیم
وصیت (کی تعمیل) کے بعد جو انہوں نے کی ہو یا
قرض کے (ادا ہونے کے بعد جو اُنکے ذمے ہو۔ کی جائیگی)
اور جو مال تم (مرد) چھوڑ مرو۔ اگر تمہارے اولاد نہ ہو
تو تمہاری عورتوں کا اس میں چوتھا حصہ۔ اور اگر اولاد ہو تو
اُنکا آٹھواں حصہ (یہ حصے) تمہاری وصیت (کی تعمیل)
کے بعد جو تم نے کی ہو۔ اور (ادائے) قرض کے (بعد
تقسیم کئے جائیں گے) اور اگر ایسے مرد یا عورت
کی میراث ہو جس کے نہ باپ ہو نہ بیٹا مگر اسکے
بھائی یا بہن ہو تو اُن میں سے ہر ایک کا چھٹا حصہ
اور اگر ایک سے زیادہ ہوں تو سب ایک تہائی میں
شریک ہونگے (یہ حصے بھی) بعد ادائے وصیت و قرض
بشرطیکہ ان سے میت نے کسی کا نقصان نہ کیا ہو (تقسیم
کئے جائینگے) یہ خدا کا فرمان ہے۔ اور خدا نہایت علم والا
(اور) نہایت حلم والا ہے ﴿١٢﴾
(تمام احکام) خدا کی حدیں ہیں۔ اور جو شخص خدا اور

لِكُلِّ وَاحِدٍ مِّنْهُمَا السُّدُسُ مِمَّا
تَرَكَ إِنْ كَانَ لَهُ وَلَدٌ فَإِنْ لَّمْ
يَكُنْ لَّهُ وَلَدٌ وَّوَرِثَهُ أَبَوَاهُ
فَلِأُمِّهِ الثُّلُثُ فَإِنْ كَانَ لَهُ
إِخْوَةٌ فَلِأُمِّهِ السُّدُسُ مِنْ
بَعْدِ وَصِيَّةٍ يُّوصِي بِهَا أَوْ دَيْنٍ
آبَاؤُكُمْ وَأَبْنَاؤُكُمْ لَا تَدْرُونَ
أَيُّهُمْ أَقْرَبُ لَكُمْ نَفْعًا فَرِيضَةً مِّنَ
اللَّهِ إِنَّ اللَّهَ كَانَ عَلِيمًا حَكِيمًا ﴿١١﴾
وَلَكُمْ نِصْفُ مَا تَرَكَ أَزْوَاجُكُمْ
إِنْ لَّمْ يَكُنْ لَّهُنَّ وَلَدٌ فَإِنْ كَانَ
لَهُنَّ وَلَدٌ فَلَكُمُ الرُّبُعُ مِمَّا
تَرَكْنَ مِنْ بَعْدِ وَصِيَّةٍ يُّوصِينَ
بِهَا أَوْ دَيْنٍ وَلَهُنَّ الرُّبُعُ مِمَّا
تَرَكْتُمْ إِنْ لَّمْ يَكُنْ لَّكُمْ وَلَدٌ
فَإِنْ كَانَ لَكُمْ وَلَدٌ فَلَهُنَّ
الثُّمُنُ مِمَّا تَرَكْتُمْ مِّنْ بَعْدِ
وَصِيَّةٍ تُوصُونَ بِهَا أَوْ دَيْنٍ
وَإِنْ كَانَ رَجُلٌ يُّورَثُ كَلَالَةً
أَوِ امْرَأَةٌ وَّلَهُ أَخٌ أَوْ أُخْتٌ
فَلِكُلِّ وَاحِدٍ مِّنْهُمَا السُّدُسُ
فَإِنْ كَانُوا أَكْثَرَ مِنْ ذَٰلِكَ
فَهُمْ شُرَكَاءُ فِي الثُّلُثِ مِنْ بَعْدِ
وَصِيَّةٍ يُّوصَىٰ بِهَا أَوْ دَيْنٍ غَيْرَ
مُضَارٍّ وَصِيَّةً مِّنَ اللَّهِ وَاللَّهُ
عَلِيمٌ حَلِيمٌ ﴿١٢﴾
تِلْكَ حُدُودُ اللَّهِ وَمَنْ يُّطِعِ

Messenger will be admitted to Gardens with rivers flowing beneath, to abide therein (for ever) and that will be the Supreme achievement.

اُس کے پیغمبر کی فرمانبرداری کرے گا۔ خدا اس کو
بہشتوں میں داخل کرے گا جن میں نہریں بہ رہی
ہیں۔ وہ اُن میں ہمیشہ رہیں گے اور یہ بڑی کامیابی ہے ﴿۱۳﴾

اللّٰهَ وَرَسُوْلَهٗ يُدْخِلْهُ جَنّٰتٍ
تَجْرِيْ مِنْ تَحْتِهَا الْاَنْهٰرُ خٰلِدِيْنَ
فِيْهَا ؕ وَذٰلِكَ الْفَوْزُ الْعَظِيْمُ ﴿۱۳﴾

14. But those who disobey Allah and His Messenger and transgress His limits will be admitted to a Fire, to abide therein: and they shall have a humiliating punishment.

اور جو خدا اور اُس کے رسُول کی نافرمانی کرے گا
اور اُس کی حدوں سے نکل جائے گا اُس کو خدا
دوزخ میں ڈالے گا جہاں وہ ہمیشہ رہے گا اور اسکو
ذلت کا عذاب ہوگا ﴿۱۴﴾

وَمَنْ يَّعْصِ اللّٰهَ وَرَسُوْلَهٗ وَ
يَتَعَدَّ حُدُوْدَهٗ يُدْخِلْهُ نَارًا
خَالِدًا فِيْهَا ۪ وَلَهٗ عَذَابٌ
مُّهِيْنٌ ﴿۱۴﴾

15. If any of your women are guilty of lewdness, take the evidence of four (reliable) witnesses from amongst you against them; and if they testify, confine them to houses until death do claim them, or Allah ordain for them some (other) way.

مسلمانو! تمہاری عورتوں میں جو بدکاری کا ارتکاب
کر بیٹھیں اُن پر اپنے لوگوں میں سے چار شخصوں کی
شہادت لو اگر وہ (اُنکی بدکاری کی) گواہی دیں تو اُن
عورتوں کو گھروں میں بند رکھو یہاں تک کہ موت اُنکا کام
تمام کردے یا خدا اُن کیلئے کوئی اور سبیل (پیدا) کرے ﴿۱۵﴾

وَالّٰتِيْ يَاْتِيْنَ الْفَاحِشَةَ مِنْ
نِّسَآئِكُمْ فَاسْتَشْهِدُوْا عَلَيْهِنَّ
اَرْبَعَةً مِّنْكُمْ ۚ فَاِنْ شَهِدُوْا
فَاَمْسِكُوْهُنَّ فِي الْبُيُوْتِ حَتّٰى يَتَوَفّٰهُنَّ
الْمَوْتُ اَوْ يَجْعَلَ اللّٰهُ لَهُنَّ سَبِيْلًا ﴿۱۵﴾

16. If two persons among you are guilty of lewdness, punish them both. If they repent and amend, leave them alone; for Allah is Oft-Returning, Most Merciful.

اور جو دو مرد تم میں سے بدکاری کریں تو اُن کو ایذا دو
پھر اگر وہ توبہ کرلیں اور نیکوکار ہوجائیں تو اُنکا پیچھا
چھوڑ دو۔ بیشک خدا توبہ قبول کرنیوالا (اور) مہربان ہے ﴿۱۶﴾

وَالَّذٰنِ يَاْتِيٰنِهَا مِنْكُمْ فَاٰذُوْهُمَا ۚ فَاِنْ
تَابَا وَاَصْلَحَا فَاَعْرِضُوْا عَنْهُمَا ؕ
اِنَّ اللّٰهَ كَانَ تَوَّابًا رَّحِيْمًا ﴿۱۶﴾

17. Allah accepts the repentance of those who do evil in ignorance and repent soon afterwards; to them will Allah turn in mercy: for Allah is full of knowledge and wisdom.

خدا اُنہیں لوگوں کی توبہ قبول فرماتا ہے جو نادانی سے
بُری حرکت کر بیٹھتے ہیں پھر جلد توبہ کرلیتے ہیں پس
ایسے لوگوں پر خدا مہربانی کرتا ہے۔ اور وہ سب کچھ
جانتا (اور) حکمت والا ہے ﴿۱۷﴾

اِنَّمَا التَّوْبَةُ عَلَى اللّٰهِ لِلَّذِيْنَ يَعْمَلُوْنَ
السُّوْٓءَ بِجَهَالَةٍ ثُمَّ يَتُوْبُوْنَ مِنْ
قَرِيْبٍ فَاُولٰٓئِكَ يَتُوْبُ اللّٰهُ عَلَيْهِمْ ؕ
وَكَانَ اللّٰهُ عَلِيْمًا حَكِيْمًا ﴿۱۷﴾

18. Of no effect is the repentance of those who continue to do evil, until death faces one of them, and he says, "Now have I repented indeed;" nor of those who die rejecting Faith: for them have We prepared a chastisement most grievous.

اور ایسے لوگوں کی توبہ قبول نہیں ہوتی جو
(ساری عمر) بُرے کام کرتے رہیں یہاں تک کہ
جب اُن میں سے کسی کی موت آموجود ہو تو اُس وقت
کہنے لگے کہ اب میں توبہ کرتا ہوں اور نہ اُنکی (توبہ قبول ہوتی ہے)
جو کفر کی حالت میں مریں ایسے لوگوں کیلئے ہم نے عذاب الیم تیار کر رکھا ہے ﴿۱۸﴾

وَلَيْسَتِ التَّوْبَةُ لِلَّذِيْنَ يَعْمَلُوْنَ
السَّيِّاٰتِ ۚ حَتّٰٓى اِذَا حَضَرَ اَحَدَهُمُ
الْمَوْتُ قَالَ اِنِّيْ تُبْتُ الْـٰٔنَ
وَلَا الَّذِيْنَ يَمُوْتُوْنَ وَهُمْ كُفَّارٌ ؕ
اُولٰٓئِكَ اَعْتَدْنَا لَهُمْ عَذَابًا اَلِيْمًا ﴿۱۸﴾

19. O ye who believe! ye are forbidden to inherit women against their will. Nor should ye treat them with harshness, that ye may take away part of the dower ye have

مومنو! تم کو جائز نہیں کہ زبردستی عورتوں کے
وارث بن جاؤ۔ اور (دیکھنا) اِس نیت سے کہ
جو کچھ تم نے اُن کو دیا ہے اُس میں سے کچھ لے لو

يٰٓاَيُّهَا الَّذِيْنَ اٰمَنُوْا لَا يَحِلُّ
لَكُمْ اَنْ تَرِثُوا النِّسَآءَ كَرْهًا ؕ
وَلَا تَعْضُلُوْهُنَّ لِتَذْهَبُوْا بِبَعْضِ

given them,—except where they have been guilty of open lewdness; on the contrary live with them on a footing of kindness and equity. If ye take a dislike to them it may be that ye dislike a thing, and Allah brings about through it a great deal of good.

انہیں (گھروں میں) مت روک رکھنا۔ ہاں اگر وہ کھلے طور پر بدکاری کی مرتکب ہوں (تو روکنا نامناسب نہیں) اور اُن کے ساتھ اچھی طرح سے رہو سہو۔ اگر وہ تم کو ناپسند ہوں تو عجب نہیں کہ تم کسی چیز کو ناپسند کرو اور خدا اس میں بہت سی بھلائی پیدا کر دے ﴿۱۹﴾

مَآ اٰتَیْتُمُوْھُنَّ اِلَّآ اَنْ یَّاْتِیْنَ
بِفَاحِشَةٍ مُّبَیِّنَةٍ ۚ وَعَاشِرُوْھُنَّ
بِالْمَعْرُوْفِ ۚ فَاِنْ كَرِھْتُمُوْھُنَّ فَعَسٰٓى
اَنْ تَكْرَھُوْا شَیْـًٔا وَّیَجْعَلَ اللّٰهُ فِیْهِ
خَیْرًا كَثِیْرًا ﴿۱۹﴾

20. But if ye decide to take one wife in place of another, even if ye had given the latter a whole treasure for dower, take not the least bit of it back: would ye take it by slander and a manifest sin?

اور اگر تم ایک عورت کو چھوڑ کر دوسری عورت کرنی چاہو اور پہلی عورت کو بہت سا مال دے چکے ہو تو اس میں سے کچھ مت لینا۔ بھلا تم ناجائز طور پر اور صریح ظلم سے اپنا مال اس سے واپس لو گے؟ ﴿۲۰﴾

وَاِنْ اَرَدْتُّمُ اسْتِبْدَالَ زَوْجٍ مَّكَانَ
زَوْجٍ ۙ وَّاٰتَیْتُمْ اِحْدٰىھُنَّ قِنْطَارًا فَلَا
تَاْخُذُوْا مِنْهُ شَیْـًٔا ؕ اَتَاْخُذُوْنَهٗ بُھْتَانًا
وَّاِثْمًا مُّبِیْنًا ﴿۲۰﴾

21. And how could ye take it when ye have gone in unto each other, and they have taken from you a solemn covenant?

اور تم دیا ہوا مال کیونکر واپس لے سکتے ہو جبکہ تم ایک دوسرے کے ساتھ صحبت کر چکے ہو اور وہ تم سے عہد واثق بھی لے چکی ہیں ﴿۲۱﴾

وَكَیْفَ تَاْخُذُوْنَهٗ وَقَدْ اَفْضٰى بَعْضُكُمْ
اِلٰى بَعْضٍ وَّاَخَذْنَ مِنْكُمْ مِّیْثَاقًا غَلِیْظًا ﴿۲۱﴾

22. And marry not women whom your fathers married,—except what is past: it was shameful and odious,—an abominable custom indeed.

اور جن عورتوں سے تمہارے باپ نے نکاح کیا ہو اُن سے نکاح نہ کرنا مگر (جاہلیت میں) جو ہو چکا (سو ہو چکا) یہ نہایت بےحیائی اور (خدا کی) ناخوشی کی بات تھی۔ اور بہت بُرا دستور تھا ﴿۲۲﴾

وَلَا تَنْكِحُوْا مَا نَكَحَ اٰبَآؤُكُمْ مِّنَ النِّسَآءِ
اِلَّا مَا قَدْ سَلَفَ ؕ اِنَّهٗ كَانَ فَاحِشَةً
وَّمَقْتًا ؕ وَسَآءَ سَبِیْلًا ﴿۲۲﴾ ع ۱۴

23. Prohibited to you (for marriage) are:—your mothers, daughters, sisters; father's sisters, mother's sisters; brother's daughters, sister's daughters; foster-mothers (who gave you suck), foster-sisters; your wives' mothers; your step-daughters under your guardianship, born of your wives to whom ye have gone in,—no prohibition if ye have not gone in,— (those who have been) wives of your sons proceeding from your loins; and two sisters in wedlock at one and the same time, except for what is past; for Allah is Oft-Forgiving, Most Merciful;—

تم پر تمہاری مائیں اور بیٹیاں اور بہنیں اور پھوپھیاں اور خالائیں اور بھتیجیاں اور بھانجیاں اور وہ مائیں جنہوں نے تم کو دودھ پلایا ہو [ف ۸۲] اور رضاعی بہنیں اور ساسیں حرام کر دی گئی ہیں اور جن عورتوں سے تم مباشرت کر چکے ہو اُن کی لڑکیاں جنہیں تم پرورش کرتے ہو (وہ بھی تم پر حرام ہیں) ہاں اگر اُن کے ساتھ تم نے مباشرت نہ کی ہو تو (اُن کی لڑکیوں کے ساتھ نکاح کر لینے میں) تم پر کچھ گناہ نہیں۔ اور تمہارے صُلبی بیٹوں کی عورتیں بھی۔ اور دو بہنوں کا اکٹھا کرنا بھی (حرام ہے) مگر جو ہو چکا (سو ہو چکا) [ف ۸۳] بے شک خدا بخشنے والا (اور) رحم والا ہے ﴿۲۳﴾

حُرِّمَتْ عَلَیْكُمْ اُمَّھٰتُكُمْ وَبَنٰتُكُمْ وَاَخَوٰتُكُمْ
وَعَمّٰتُكُمْ وَخٰلٰتُكُمْ وَبَنٰتُ الْاَخِ وَبَنٰتُ
الْاُخْتِ وَاُمَّھٰتُكُمُ الّٰتِیْٓ اَرْضَعْنَكُمْ وَ
اَخَوٰتُكُمْ مِّنَ الرَّضَاعَةِ وَاُمَّھٰتُ نِسَآئِكُمْ
وَرَبَآئِبُكُمُ الّٰتِیْ فِیْ حُجُوْرِكُمْ مِّنْ نِّسَآئِكُمُ
الّٰتِیْ دَخَلْتُمْ بِھِنَّ ۫ فَاِنْ لَّمْ تَكُوْنُوْا
دَخَلْتُمْ بِھِنَّ فَلَا جُنَاحَ عَلَیْكُمْ ۫
وَحَلَآئِلُ اَبْنَآئِكُمُ الَّذِیْنَ مِنْ
اَصْلَابِكُمْ ۙ وَاَنْ تَجْمَعُوْا بَیْنَ
الْاُخْتَیْنِ اِلَّا مَا قَدْ سَلَفَ ؕ اِنَّ
اللّٰهَ كَانَ غَفُوْرًا رَّحِیْمًا ﴿۲۳﴾

24. Also (prohibited are) women already married, except those whom your right hands possess: thus hath Allah ordained (prohibitions) against you: except for these, all others are lawful, provided ye seek (them in marriage) with gifts from your property,—desiring chastity, not fornication. Give them their dowery for the enjoyment you have of them as a duty; but if, after a dower is prescribed, ye agree mutually (to vary it), there is no blame on you, and Allah is All-Knowing All-Wise.

اور شوہر والی عورتیں بھی (تم پر حرام ہیں) مگر وہ جو اسیر
ہو کر لونڈیوں کے طور پر) تمہارے قبضے میں آجائیں (یہ حکم)
خدا نے تم کو لکھ دیا ہے۔ اور ان (محرمات) کے سوا اور عورتیں
تم کو حلال ہیں اس طرح سے کہ مال خرچ کر کے اُن سے
نکاح کر لو بشرطیکہ (نکاح سے) مقصود عفت قائم رکھنا ہو
نہ شہوت رانی۔ تو جن عورتوں سے تم فائدہ حاصل کرو اُن کا
مہر جو مقرر کیا ہو ادا کر دو اور اگر مقرر کرنے کے بعد آپس کی
رضامندی سے مہر میں کمی بیشی کر لو تو تم پر کچھ گناہ نہیں۔
بیشک خدا سب کچھ جاننے والا (اور) حکمت والا ہے ۲۴

الجزء الخامس ٥

وَّالْمُحْصَنٰتُ مِنَ النِّسَآءِ اِلَّا مَا
مَلَكَتْ اَيْمَانُكُمْ ۚ كِتٰبَ اللّٰهِ عَلَيْكُمْ ۚ
وَاُحِلَّ لَكُمْ مَّا وَرَآءَ ذٰلِكُمْ اَنْ
تَبْتَغُوْا بِاَمْوَالِكُمْ مُّحْصِنِيْنَ غَيْرَ
مُسٰفِحِيْنَ ؕ فَمَا اسْتَمْتَعْتُمْ بِهٖ
مِنْهُنَّ فَاٰتُوْهُنَّ اُجُوْرَهُنَّ فَرِيْضَةً ؕ
وَلَا جُنَاحَ عَلَيْكُمْ فِيْمَا تَرٰضَيْتُمْ
بِهٖ مِنْۢ بَعْدِ الْفَرِيْضَةِ ؕ اِنَّ اللّٰهَ
كَانَ عَلِيْمًا حَكِيْمًا ۲۴

25. If any of you have not the means wherewith to wed free believing women, they may wed believing girls from among those whom your right hands possess: and Allah hath full knowledge about your Faith. Ye are one from another: wed them with the leave of their owners, and give them their dowers, according to what is reasonable: they should be chaste, not fornicators, nor taking adulterous: when they are taken in wedlock, if they commit indecency their punishment is half that for free women. This (permission) is for those among you who fear sin; but it is better for you that ye practise self-restraint. And Allah is Oft-Forgiving, Most Merciful.

اور جو شخص تم میں سے مومن آزاد عورتوں (یعنی بیبیوں)
سے نکاح کرنے کا مقدور نہ رکھے تو مومن لونڈیوں ہی سے جو تمہارے
قبضے میں آگئی ہوں (نکاح کرلے) اور خدا تمہارے ایمان کو
اچھی طرح جانتا ہے۔ تم آپس میں ایک دوسرے کے ہم جنس ہو۔ تو ان
لونڈیوں کے ساتھ اُنکے مالکوں سے اجازت حاصل کر کے نکاح کر لو اور دستور کے
مطابق انکا مہر بھی ادا کر دو بشرطیکہ عفیفہ ہوں نہ ایسی کہ کھلم کھلا
بدکاری کریں اور نہ درپردہ دوستی کرنا چاہیں۔ پھر اگر نکاح میں آکر
بدکاری کا ارتکاب کر بیٹھیں تو جو سزا آزاد عورتوں (یعنی بیبیوں)
کیلئے ہے اسکی آدھی اُنکو (دی جائے) یہ (لونڈی کے ساتھ
نکاح کرنے کی) اجازت اس شخص کو ہے جسے گناہ کر بیٹھنے
کا اندیشہ ہو۔ اور اگر صبر کرو تو یہ تمہارے لئے بہت اچھا ہے
اور خدا بخشنے والا مہربان ہے ۲۵

وَمَنْ لَّمْ يَسْتَطِعْ مِنْكُمْ طَوْلًا اَنْ
يَّنْكِحَ الْمُحْصَنٰتِ الْمُؤْمِنٰتِ فَمِنْ
مَّا مَلَكَتْ اَيْمَانُكُمْ مِّنْ فَتَيٰتِكُمُ
الْمُؤْمِنٰتِ ؕ وَاللّٰهُ اَعْلَمُ بِاِيْمَانِكُمْ ؕ
بَعْضُكُمْ مِّنْۢ بَعْضٍ ۚ فَانْكِحُوْهُنَّ
بِاِذْنِ اَهْلِهِنَّ وَاٰتُوْهُنَّ اُجُوْرَهُنَّ
بِالْمَعْرُوْفِ مُحْصَنٰتٍ غَيْرَ مُسٰفِحٰتٍ
وَّلَا مُتَّخِذٰتِ اَخْدَانٍ ۚ فَاِذَآ اُحْصِنَّ
فَاِنْ اَتَيْنَ بِفَاحِشَةٍ فَعَلَيْهِنَّ نِصْفُ
مَا عَلَى الْمُحْصَنٰتِ مِنَ الْعَذَابِ ؕ
ذٰلِكَ لِمَنْ خَشِيَ الْعَنَتَ مِنْكُمْ ؕ وَاَنْ
تَصْبِرُوْا خَيْرٌ لَّكُمْ ؕ وَاللّٰهُ غَفُوْرٌ رَّحِيْمٌ ۲۵ ع

26. Allah doth wish to make clear to you and to guide you into the ways of those before you; and (He doth wish to) turn to you (in Mercy): and Allah is All-Knowing, All-Wise.

خدا چاہتا ہے کہ (اپنی آیتیں) تم سے کھول کھول کر بیان
فرمائے اور تم کو اگلے لوگوں کے طریقے بتائے۔ اور تم پر
مہربانی کرے۔ اور خدا جاننے والا (اور) حکمت والا ہے ۲۶

يُرِيْدُ اللّٰهُ لِيُبَيِّنَ لَكُمْ وَيَهْدِيَكُمْ
سُنَنَ الَّذِيْنَ مِنْ قَبْلِكُمْ وَيَتُوْبَ
عَلَيْكُمْ ؕ وَاللّٰهُ عَلِيْمٌ حَكِيْمٌ ۲۶

27. Allah doth wish to turn to you, but the wish of those who follow their lusts is that ye should turn away (from Him),— far, far away.

اور خدا تو چاہتا ہے کہ تم پر مہربانی کرے۔ اور جو لوگ اپنی
خواہشوں کے پیچھے چلتے ہیں وہ چاہتے ہیں کہ تم سیدھے
رستے سے بھٹک کر دُور جا پڑو ۲۷

وَاللّٰهُ يُرِيْدُ اَنْ يَّتُوْبَ عَلَيْكُمْ ۫ وَ
يُرِيْدُ الَّذِيْنَ يَتَّبِعُوْنَ الشَّهَوٰتِ
اَنْ تَمِيْلُوْا مَيْلًا عَظِيْمًا ۲۷

28. Allah doth wish to lighten your (burdens): for man was created weak (in resolution).

خدا چاہتا ہے کہ تم پر سے بوجھ ہلکا کرے اور انسان
(طبعاً) کمزور پیدا ہوا ہے ﴿۲۸﴾

يُرِيْدُ اللّٰهُ اَنْ يُّخَفِّفَ عَنْكُمْ ۚ وَ
خُلِقَ الْاِنْسَانُ ضَعِيْفًا ﴿۲۸﴾

29. O ye who believe ! eat not up your property among yourselves in vanities: but let there be amongst you traffic and trade by mutual good-will: nor kill (or destroy) yourselves: for verily Allah hath been to you Most Merciful !

مومنو! ایک دوسرے کا مال ناحق نہ کھاؤ ہاں اگر
آپس کی رضامندی سے تجارت کا لین دین ہو (اور
اس سے مالی فائدہ حاصل ہو جائے تو وہ جائز ہے)
اور اپنے آپ کو ہلاک نہ کرو۔ کچھ شک نہیں کہ خدا تم پر
مہربان ہے ﴿۲۹﴾

يٰۤاَيُّهَا الَّذِيْنَ اٰمَنُوْا لَا تَاْكُلُوْۤا اَمْوَالَكُمْ
بَيْنَكُمْ بِالْبَاطِلِ اِلَّاۤ اَنْ تَكُوْنَ
تِجَارَةً عَنْ تَرَاضٍ مِّنْكُمْ ۟ وَ لَا
تَقْتُلُوْۤا اَنْفُسَكُمْ ؕ اِنَّ اللّٰهَ كَانَ
بِكُمْ رَحِيْمًا ﴿۲۹﴾

30. If any do that in rancour and injustice,— soon shall We cast him into the Fire: and easy it is for Allah.

اور جو تعدی اور ظلم سے ایسا کرے گا ہم اُس کو
عنقریب جہنّم میں داخل کریں گے۔ اور یہ خدا کو
آسان ہے ﴿۳۰﴾

وَمَنْ يَّفْعَلْ ذٰلِكَ عُدْوَانًا وَّظُلْمًا
فَسَوْفَ نُصْلِيْهِ نَارًا ؕ وَكَانَ ذٰلِكَ
عَلَى اللّٰهِ يَسِيْرًا ﴿۳۰﴾

31. If ye (but) eschew the most heinous of the things which ye are forbidden to do, We shall remit your evil deeds, and admit you to a Gate of great honour.

اگر تم بڑے بڑے گناہوں سے جن سے تم کو منع کیا
جاتا ہے اجتناب رکھو گے تو ہم تمہارے (چھوٹے چھوٹے) گناہ
معاف کر دیں گے اور تمہیں عزت کے مکانوں میں داخل کریں گے ﴿۳۱﴾

اِنْ تَجْتَنِبُوْا كَبٰۤىِٕرَ مَا تُنْهَوْنَ عَنْهُ
نُكَفِّرْ عَنْكُمْ سَيِّاٰتِكُمْ وَنُدْخِلْكُمْ
مُّدْخَلًا كَرِيْمًا ﴿۳۱﴾

32. And in no wise covet those things in which Allah hath bestowed His gifts more freely on some of you than on others: to men is allotted what they earn, and to women what they earn: but ask Allah of His bounty. For Allah hath full knowledge of all things.

اور جس چیز میں خدا نے تم میں سے بعض کو بعض پر
فضیلت دی ہے اس کی ہوس مت کرو۔ مردوں کو ان کاموں کا
ثواب ہے جو انہوں نے کئے۔ اور عورتوں کو ان کاموں کا ثواب ہے
جو انہوں نے کئے۔ اور خدا سے اس کا فضل (و کرم) مانگتے رہو
کچھ شک نہیں کہ خدا ہر چیز سے واقف ہے ﴿۳۲﴾

وَلَا تَتَمَنَّوْا مَا فَضَّلَ اللّٰهُ بِهٖ بَعْضَكُمْ
عَلٰى بَعْضٍ ؕ لِلرِّجَالِ نَصِيْبٌ مِّمَّا
اكْتَسَبُوْا ؕ وَلِلنِّسَآءِ نَصِيْبٌ مِّمَّا
اكْتَسَبْنَ ؕ وَسْـَٔلُوا اللّٰهَ مِنْ فَضْلِهٖ ؕ
اِنَّ اللّٰهَ كَانَ بِكُلِّ شَيْءٍ عَلِيْمًا ﴿۳۲﴾

33. To (benefit) everyone, We have appointed sharers and heirs to property left by parents and relatives. To those, also, to whom your right hand was pledged, give their due portion. For truly Allah is witness to all things.

اور جو مال ماں باپ اور رشتہ دار چھوڑ مریں تو (حقداروں
میں تقسیم کر دو کہ) ہم نے ہر ایک کے حقدار مقرر کر دیئے ہیں۔ اور
جن لوگوں سے تم عہد کر چکے ہو ان کو بھی ان کا حصّہ دو۔
بے شک خدا ہر چیز کے سامنے ہے ﴿۳۳﴾

وَلِكُلٍّ جَعَلْنَا مَوَالِيَ مِمَّا تَرَكَ
الْوَالِدٰنِ وَالْاَقْرَبُوْنَ ؕ وَالَّذِيْنَ
عَقَدَتْ اَيْمَانُكُمْ فَاٰتُوْهُمْ نَصِيْبَهُمْ ؕ
اِنَّ اللّٰهَ كَانَ عَلٰى كُلِّ شَيْءٍ شَهِيْدًا ﴿۳۳﴾ ع ٥

34. Men are the protectors and maintainers of women, because Allah has given the one more (strength) than the other, and because they support them from their means. Therefore the righteous women are devoutly obedient, and guard in (the husband's) absence

مرد عورتوں پر مسلط و حاکم ہیں اس لئے کہ خدا نے بعض کو
بعض سے افضل بنایا ہے اور اس لئے بھی کہ مرد اپنا مال
خرچ کرتے ہیں۔ تو جو نیک بیبیاں ہیں وہ مردوں کے
حکم پر چلتی ہیں اور ان کے پیٹھ پیچھے خدا کی حفاظت میں
(مال و آبرو کی) خبرداری کرتی ہیں اور جن عورتوں کی نسبت

اَلرِّجَالُ قَوّٰمُوْنَ عَلَى النِّسَآءِ بِمَا
فَضَّلَ اللّٰهُ بَعْضَهُمْ عَلٰى بَعْضٍ وَّ
بِمَاۤ اَنْفَقُوْا مِنْ اَمْوَالِهِمْ ؕ فَالصّٰلِحٰتُ
قٰنِتٰتٌ حٰفِظٰتٌ لِّلْغَيْبِ بِمَا حَفِظَ
اللّٰهُ ؕ وَالّٰتِيْ تَخَافُوْنَ نُشُوْزَهُنَّ

what Allah would have them guard. As to those women on whose part ye fear disloyalty and ill-conduct, admonish them (first), (next), refuse to share their beds, (and last) beat them (lightly); but if they return to obedience, seek not against them means (of annoyance): for Allah is Most High, Great (above you all).

تمہیں معلوم ہو کہ سرکشی (اور بدخوئی) کرنے لگی ہیں تو (پہلے)
اُن کو (زبانی) سمجھاؤ (اگر نہ سمجھیں تو) پھر اُنکے ساتھ سونا ترک کر دو
اگر اس پر بھی باز نہ آئیں تو زدوکوب کرو۔ اور اگر فرمانبردار ہو جائیں
تو پھر اُن کو ایذا دینے کا کوئی بہانہ مت ڈھونڈو۔ بیشک خدا
سب سے اعلےٰ (اور) جلیل القدر ہے ﴿٣٤﴾

فَعِظُوهُنَّ وَاهْجُرُوهُنَّ فِي
الْمَضَاجِعِ وَاضْرِبُوهُنَّ ۚ فَإِنْ
أَطَعْنَكُمْ فَلَا تَبْغُوا عَلَيْهِنَّ
سَبِيلًا ۗ إِنَّ اللَّهَ كَانَ عَلِيًّا
كَبِيرًا ﴿٣٤﴾

35. If ye fear a breach between them twain, appoint (two) arbiters, one from his family, and the other from hers; if they seek to set things aright, Allah will cause their reconciliation: for Allah hath full knowledge, and is acquainted with all things.

اور اگر تم کو معلوم ہو کہ میاں بیوی میں اَن بن ہے تو
ایک مُنصف مرد کے خاندان میں سے اور ایک مُنصف عورت
کے خاندان میں سے مقرر کرو۔ وہ اگر صُلح کرا دینی چاہیں گے تو
خُدا اُن میں موافقت پیدا کر دیگا۔ کچھ شک نہیں کہ خدا
سب کچھ جانتا اور سب باتوں سے خبردار ہے ﴿٣٥﴾

وَإِنْ خِفْتُمْ شِقَاقَ بَيْنِهِمَا فَابْعَثُوا
حَكَمًا مِّنْ أَهْلِهِ وَحَكَمًا مِّنْ
أَهْلِهَا ۚ إِن يُرِيدَا إِصْلَاحًا
يُوَفِّقِ اللَّهُ بَيْنَهُمَا ۗ إِنَّ اللَّهَ كَانَ
عَلِيمًا خَبِيرًا ﴿٣٥﴾

36. Serve Allah, and join not any partners with Him; and do good— to parents, kinsfolk, orphans, those in need, neighbours who are of kin neighbours who are strangers, the Companion by your side, the way-farer (ye meet), and what your right hands possess: for Allah loveth not the arrogant, the vainglorious;—

اور خُدا ہی کی عبادت کرو اور اس کے ساتھ کسی چیز کو
شریک نہ بناؤ اور ماں باپ اور قرابت والوں اور یتیموں
اور محتاجوں اور رشتہ دار ہمسایوں اور اجنبی ہمسایوں
اور رفقائے پہلو (یعنی پاس بیٹھنے والوں) اور مُسافروں
اور جو لوگ تمہارے قبضے میں ہوں سب کے ساتھ احسان کرو
کہ خُدا احسان کرنیوالوں کو دوست رکھتا ہے اور تکبر کرنے
والے بڑائی مارنے والے کو دوست نہیں رکھتا ﴿٣٦﴾

وَاعْبُدُوا اللَّهَ وَلَا تُشْرِكُوا بِهِ
شَيْئًا ۖ وَبِالْوَالِدَيْنِ إِحْسَانًا وَبِذِي
الْقُرْبَىٰ وَالْيَتَامَىٰ وَالْمَسَاكِينِ وَ
الْجَارِ ذِي الْقُرْبَىٰ وَالْجَارِ الْجُنُبِ
وَالصَّاحِبِ بِالْجَنبِ وَابْنِ السَّبِيلِ
وَمَا مَلَكَتْ أَيْمَانُكُمْ ۗ إِنَّ اللَّهَ
لَا يُحِبُّ مَن كَانَ مُخْتَالًا فَخُورًا ﴿٣٦﴾

37. (Nor) those who are niggardly, enjoin niggardliness on others, hide the bounties which Allah hath bestowed on them; for We have prepared, for those who resist Faith, a Punishment that steeps them in contempt;—

جو خود بھی بُخل کریں اور لوگوں کو بھی بُخل سکھائیں اور
جو (مال) خدا نے اُن کو اپنے فضل سے عطا فرمایا ہے اُسے
چھپا چھپا کے رکھیں اور ہم نے ناشکروں کے لئے ذلّت
کا عذاب تیار کر رکھا ہے ﴿٣٧﴾

الَّذِينَ يَبْخَلُونَ وَيَأْمُرُونَ النَّاسَ
بِالْبُخْلِ وَيَكْتُمُونَ مَا آتَاهُمُ اللَّهُ
مِن فَضْلِهِ ۗ وَأَعْتَدْنَا لِلْكَافِرِينَ
عَذَابًا مُّهِينًا ﴿٣٧﴾

38. Nor those who spend of their substance, to be seen of men, and have no faith in Allah and the Last Day: if any take the Satan for their intimate, what a dreadful intimate he is!

اور خرچ بھی کریں تو (خُدا کے لئے نہیں بلکہ) لوگوں کے
دکھانے کو۔ اور ایمان نہ خدا پر لائیں نہ روزِ آخرت
پر (ایسے لوگوں کا ساتھی شیطان ہے) اور جس کا ساتھی
شیطان ہوا تو (کچھ شک نہیں کہ) وہ بُرا ساتھی ہے ﴿٣٨﴾

وَالَّذِينَ يُنفِقُونَ أَمْوَالَهُمْ
رِئَاءَ النَّاسِ وَلَا يُؤْمِنُونَ
بِاللَّهِ وَلَا بِالْيَوْمِ الْآخِرِ ۗ وَمَن يَكُنِ
الشَّيْطَانُ لَهُ قَرِينًا فَسَاءَ قَرِينًا ﴿٣٨﴾

39. And what burden were it on them if they had faith in Allah and in the Last Day, and they spent out of what Allah hath given them for

اور اگر یہ لوگ خدا پر اور روزِ قیامت پر ایمان لاتے اور جو کچھ
خدا نے اُن کو دیا تھا اُس میں سے خرچ کرتے۔ تو اُن کا کیا

وَمَاذَا عَلَيْهِمْ لَوْ آمَنُوا بِاللَّهِ وَالْيَوْمِ
الْآخِرِ وَأَنفَقُوا مِمَّا رَزَقَهُمُ اللَّهُ ۚ

sustenance ? For Allah hath full knowledge of them.

40. Allah is never unjust in the least degree: if there is any good (done), He doubleth it, and giveth from His Own self a great reward.

41. How then if We brought from each People a witness, and We brought thee as a witness against these People !

42. On that day those who reject Faith and disobey the Messenger will wish that the earth were made one with them: but never will they hide a single fact from Allah !

43. O ye who believe ! approach not prayers in a state of intoxication, until ye can understand all that ye say,— nor in a state of ceremonial impurity except when you are passing by (through the mosque). Until after washing your whole body. If ye are ill, or on a journey, or one of you cometh from the privy, or ye have been in contact with women, and ye find no water, then take for yourselves clean sand (or earth), and rub therewith your faces and hands. For Allah doth blot out sins and forgive again and again.

44. Hast thou not turned thy thought to those who were given a portion of the Book ? They traffic in error, and wish that ye should lose the right path.

45. But Allah hath full knowledge of your enemies: Allah is enough for a Protector, and Allah is enough for a Helper.

46. Of the Jews there are those who displace words from their (right) places, and say: "We hear and we disobey"; and "Here, may you not hear;" and *"Rā'ina"* with a twist of their tongues and a slander to Faith. If only they had said: "We

نقصان ہوتا اور خدا اُن کو خوب جانتا ہے ﴿۳۹﴾
خدا کسی کی ذرا بھی حق تلفی نہیں کرتا اور اگر نیکی (کی)
ہوگی تو اُس کو دوچند کردے گا۔ اور اپنے ہاں سے
اجرِ عظیم بخشے گا ﴿۴۰﴾
بھلا اُس دن کیا حال ہوگا جب ہم ہر اُمت میں سے احوال بتانے والے
کو بلائینگے اور تم کو اُن لوگوں کا (حال بتانے کو) گواہ طلب کرینگے ﴿۴۱﴾
اُس روز کافر اور پیغمبر کے نافرمان آرزو کریں گے کہ کاش
اُن کو زمین میں مدفون کرکے مٹی برابر کردی جاتی۔ اور
خدا سے کوئی بات چھپا نہیں سکیں گے ﴿۴۲﴾
مومنو! جب تم نشے کی حالت میں ہو تو جب تک (اُن
الفاظ کو) جو مُنہ سے کہو سمجھنے (نہ) لگو۔ نماز کے پاس نہ جاؤ
اور جنابت کی حالت میں بھی (نماز کے پاس نہ جاؤ) جب
تک کہ غسل (نہ) کرلو۔ ہاں اگر بحالتِ سفر رستے چلے جا رہے
ہو (اور پانی نہ ملنے کے سبب غسل نہ کرسکو تو تیمم کرکے نماز پڑھ لو)
اور اگر تم بیمار ہو یا سفر میں ہو یا تم میں سے کوئی بیت الخلاء سے
ہو کر آیا ہو یا تم عورتوں سے ہمبستر ہوئے ہو اور تمہیں
پانی نہ ملے تو پاک مٹی لو اور مُنہ اور ہاتھوں کا مسح (کرکے تیمم)
کرلو۔ بیشک خدا معاف کرنے والا (اور) بخشنے والا ہے ﴿۴۳﴾
بھلا تم نے اُن لوگوں کو نہیں دیکھا جن کو کتاب سے حصہ
دیا گیا تھا کہ وہ گمراہی کو خریدتے ہیں اور چاہتے ہیں کہ
تم بھی رستے سے بھٹک جاؤ ﴿۴۴﴾
اور خدا تمہارے دشمنوں سے خوب واقف ہے۔ اور خدا ہی
کافی کارساز اور کافی مددگار ہے ﴿۴۵﴾
اور یہ جو یہودی ہیں ان میں کچھ لوگ ایسے بھی ہیں کہ
کلمات کو اُن کے مقامات سے بدل دیتے ہیں اور
کہتے ہیں کہ ہم نے سُن لیا اور نہیں مانا اور سُنیئے نہ سنوائے جاؤ
اور زبان کو مروڑ کر اور دین میں طعن کی راہ سے (تم سے گفتگو

وَكَانَ اللّٰهُ بِهِمْ عَلِيْمًا ﴿٣٩﴾
إِنَّ اللّٰهَ لَا يَظْلِمُ مِثْقَالَ ذَرَّةٍ ۚ وَ
إِنْ تَكُ حَسَنَةً يُّضٰعِفْهَا وَيُؤْتِ
مِنْ لَّدُنْهُ أَجْرًا عَظِيْمًا ﴿٤٠﴾
فَكَيْفَ إِذَا جِئْنَا مِنْ كُلِّ أُمَّةٍ بِشَهِيْدٍ
وَّجِئْنَا بِكَ عَلٰى هٰٓؤُلَآءِ شَهِيْدًا ﴿٤١﴾ ط
يَوْمَئِذٍ يَّوَدُّ الَّذِيْنَ كَفَرُوْا وَ
عَصَوُا الرَّسُوْلَ لَوْ تُسَوّٰى بِهِمُ
الْأَرْضُ ۖ وَلَا يَكْتُمُوْنَ اللّٰهَ حَدِيْثًا ﴿٤٢﴾ ع
يٰٓأَيُّهَا الَّذِيْنَ اٰمَنُوْا لَا تَقْرَبُوا الصَّلٰوةَ
وَأَنْتُمْ سُكٰرٰى حَتّٰى تَعْلَمُوْا مَا
تَقُوْلُوْنَ وَلَا جُنُبًا إِلَّا عَابِرِيْ
سَبِيْلٍ حَتّٰى تَغْتَسِلُوْا ۭ وَإِنْ كُنْتُمْ
مَّرْضٰٓى أَوْ عَلٰى سَفَرٍ أَوْ جَآءَ أَحَدٌ
مِّنْكُمْ مِّنَ الْغَآئِطِ أَوْ لٰمَسْتُمُ النِّسَآءَ
فَلَمْ تَجِدُوْا مَآءً فَتَيَمَّمُوْا صَعِيْدًا
طَيِّبًا فَامْسَحُوْا بِوُجُوْهِكُمْ وَأَيْدِيْكُمْ ۭ
إِنَّ اللّٰهَ كَانَ عَفُوًّا غَفُوْرًا ﴿٤٣﴾
أَلَمْ تَرَ إِلَى الَّذِيْنَ أُوْتُوْا نَصِيْبًا مِّنَ
الْكِتٰبِ يَشْتَرُوْنَ الضَّلٰلَةَ وَيُرِيْدُوْنَ
أَنْ تَضِلُّوا السَّبِيْلَ ﴿٤٤﴾ ط
وَاللّٰهُ أَعْلَمُ بِأَعْدَآئِكُمْ ۭ وَكَفٰى بِاللّٰهِ
وَلِيًّا ۙ وَّكَفٰى بِاللّٰهِ نَصِيْرًا ﴿٤٥﴾
مِنَ الَّذِيْنَ هَادُوْا يُحَرِّفُوْنَ الْكَلِمَ
عَنْ مَّوَاضِعِهٖ وَيَقُوْلُوْنَ سَمِعْنَا
وَعَصَيْنَا وَاسْمَعْ غَيْرَ مُسْمَعٍ وَّرَاعِنَا
لَيًّا بِأَلْسِنَتِهِمْ وَطَعْنًا فِي الدِّيْنِ ۭ وَلَوْ

وقف النبي عليه السلام

hear and we obey"; and "Do hear"; and "Do look at us": it would have been better for them, and more proper; but Allah hath cursed them for their Unbelief; and but few of them will believe.

47. O ye People of the Book ! believe in what We have (now) revealed, confirming what was (already) with you, before We change the face and fame of some (of you) beyond all recognition, and turn them hindwards, or curse them as We cursed the Sabbath-breakers, for the decision of Allah must be carried out.

48. Allah forgiveth not that partners should be set up with Him; but He forgiveth anything else, to whom he pleaseth; to set up partners with Allah is to devise a sin most heinous indeed.

49. Hast thou not turned thy thought to those who claim purity for themselves ? Nay—but Allah doth purify whom He pleaseth. And they will not be wronged a whit.

50. Behold ! how they invent a lie against Allah! But that by itself is a manifest sin !

51. Hast thou not turned thy thought to those who were given a portion of the Book ? They believe in Sorcery and Tagut and say to the Unbelievers that they are better guided in the (right) way than the Believers !

52. They are (men) whom Allah hath cursed: and those whom Allah hath cursed, thou wilt find, have no one to help.

53. Have they a share in dominion or power ? Behold, they give not a farthing to their fellow-men ?

54. Or do they envy mankind for what Allah hath given them of His bounty ? But We had already given

کے وقت) راعنا کہتے ہیں اور اگر (یوں) کہتے کہ ہم نے سن لیا اور
مان لیا اور (صرف) اسمع اور (راعنا کی جگہ) انظرنا (کہتے) تو انکے
حق میں بہتر ہوتا اور بات بھی بہت درست ہوتی لیکن خدا نے انکے کفر
کے سبب اُن پر لعنت کر رکھی ہے تو یہ کچھ تھوڑے ہی ایمان لاتے ہیں (۴۶)
اے کتاب والو! قبل اسکے کہ ہم لوگوں کے مونہوں کو بگاڑ کر
اُن کی پیٹھ کی طرف پھیر دیں یا اُن پر اس طرح لعنت
کریں جس طرح ہفتے والوں پر کی تھی۔ ہماری نازل فرمائی
ہوئی کتاب پر جو تمہاری کتاب کی بھی تصدیق کرتی ہے ایمان
لے آؤ۔ اور خدا نے جو حکم فرمایا سو (سمجھ لو کہ) ہو چکا (۴۷)
خدا اس گناہ کو نہیں بخشے گا کہ کسی کو اس کا شریک بنایا
جائے اور اس کے سوا اور گناہ جس کو چاہے معاف کر دے۔
اور جس نے خدا کا شریک مقرر کیا اس نے بڑا بہتان باندھا (۴۸)
کیا تم نے اُن لوگوں کو نہیں دیکھا جو اپنے تئیں پاکیزہ کہتے
ہیں (نہیں) بلکہ خدا ہی جس کو چاہتا ہے پاکیزہ کرتا ہے۔ اور
اُن پر دھاگے برابر بھی ظلم نہیں ہوگا (۴۹)
دیکھو یہ خدا پر کیسا جھوٹ (طوفان) باندھتے ہیں۔
اور یہی گناہ صریح کافی ہے (۵۰)
بھلا تم نے اُن لوگوں کو نہیں دیکھا جن کو کتاب
سے حصہ دیا گیا ہے کہ بتوں اور شیطان کو مانتے ہیں
اور کفار کے بارے میں کہتے ہیں کہ یہ لوگ مومنوں
کی نسبت سیدھے رستے پر ہیں (۵۱)
یہی لوگ ہیں جن پر خدا نے لعنت کی ہے۔ اور جس پر خدا
لعنت کرے تو تم اس کا کسی کو مددگار نہ پاؤ گے (۵۲)
کیا ان کے پاس بادشاہی کا کچھ حصہ ہے (تو) لوگوں
کو تل برابر بھی نہ دیں گے (۵۳)
یا جو خدا نے لوگوں کو اپنے فضل سے دے رکھا ہے
اس کا حسد کرتے ہیں۔ تو ہم نے خاندان ابراہیم کو

أَنَّهُمْ قَالُوا سَمِعْنَا وَأَطَعْنَا وَاسْمَعْ
وَانْظُرْنَا لَكَانَ خَيْرًا لَّهُمْ وَأَقْوَمَ
وَلٰكِن لَّعَنَهُمُ اللّٰهُ بِكُفْرِهِمْ فَلَا
يُؤْمِنُونَ إِلَّا قَلِيلًا ﴿٤٦﴾
يٰٓأَيُّهَا الَّذِينَ أُوتُوا الْكِتٰبَ اٰمِنُوا بِمَا
نَزَّلْنَا مُصَدِّقًا لِّمَا مَعَكُم مِّن قَبْلِ
أَن نَّطْمِسَ وُجُوهًا فَنَرُدَّهَا عَلٰى
أَدْبَارِهَا أَوْ نَلْعَنَهُمْ كَمَا لَعَنَّا أَصْحٰبَ
السَّبْتِ وَكَانَ أَمْرُ اللّٰهِ مَفْعُولًا ﴿٤٧﴾
إِنَّ اللّٰهَ لَا يَغْفِرُ أَن يُشْرَكَ بِهِ وَيَغْفِرُ
مَا دُونَ ذٰلِكَ لِمَن يَشَاءُ ج وَمَن
يُشْرِكْ بِاللّٰهِ فَقَدِ افْتَرٰى إِثْمًا عَظِيمًا ﴿٤٨﴾
أَلَمْ تَرَ إِلَى الَّذِينَ يُزَكُّونَ أَنفُسَهُمْ
بَلِ اللّٰهُ يُزَكِّي مَن يَشَاءُ وَلَا
يُظْلَمُونَ فَتِيلًا ﴿٤٩﴾
اُنظُرْ كَيْفَ يَفْتَرُونَ عَلَى اللّٰهِ الْكَذِبَ
وَكَفٰى بِهِ إِثْمًا مُّبِينًا ﴿٥٠﴾ ع
أَلَمْ تَرَ إِلَى الَّذِينَ أُوتُوا نَصِيبًا
مِّنَ الْكِتٰبِ يُؤْمِنُونَ بِالْجِبْتِ وَالطَّاغُوتِ
وَيَقُولُونَ لِلَّذِينَ كَفَرُوا هٰٓؤُلَاءِ
أَهْدٰى مِنَ الَّذِينَ اٰمَنُوا سَبِيلًا ﴿٥١﴾
أُولٰٓئِكَ الَّذِينَ لَعَنَهُمُ اللّٰهُ وَمَن
يَلْعَنِ اللّٰهُ فَلَن تَجِدَ لَهُ نَصِيرًا ﴿٥٢﴾
أَمْ لَهُمْ نَصِيبٌ مِّنَ الْمُلْكِ فَإِذًا لَّا
يُؤْتُونَ النَّاسَ نَقِيرًا ﴿٥٣﴾
أَمْ يَحْسُدُونَ النَّاسَ عَلٰى مَا اٰتٰهُمُ
اللّٰهُ مِن فَضْلِهِ فَقَدْ اٰتَيْنَا اٰلَ

the people of Abraham the Book and Wisdom, and conferred upon them a great kingdom.

55. Some of them believed, and some of them averted their faces from him: and enough is Hell for a burning fire.

56. Those who reject our Signs, We shall soon cast into the Fire: as often as their skins are roasted through, We shall change them for fresh skins, that they may taste the Chastisement: for Allah is Exalted in Power, Wise.

57. But those who believe and do deeds of righteousness, We shall soon admit to Gardens, with rivers flowing beneath,— their eternal home: therein shall they have spouses purified We shall admit them to shades, cool and ever deepening.

58. Allah doth command you to render back your Trusts to those to whom they are due; and when ye judge between people that ye judge with justice: verily how excellent is the teaching which He giveth you ! For Allah is He Who heareth and seeth all things.

59. O ye who believe ! obey Allah, and obey the Messenger, and those charged with authority among you. If ye differ in anything among yourselves, refer it to Allah and His Messenger, if ye do believe in Allah and the Last Day: that is best, and most suitable for final determination.

60. Hast thou not turned thy thought to those who declare that they believe in the revelations that have come to thee and to those before thee? Their (real) wish is to resort together for judgment (in their disputes) to the Evil (Tagut) though they were ordered to reject him.

کتاب اور دانائی عنایت فرمائی تھی اور سلطنت عظیم
بھی بخشی تھی ﴿۵۴﴾
پھر لوگوں میں سے کسی نے تو اس کتاب کو مانا اور کوئی اس سے رکا (اور ہٹا)
رہا تو ان نہ ماننے والوں (کے جلانے) کو دوزخ کی جلتی ہوئی آگ کافی ہے ﴿۵۵﴾
جن لوگوں نے ہماری آیتوں سے کفر کیا ان کو ہم عنقریب
آگ میں داخل کریں گے۔ جب ان کی کھالیں گل (اور جل)
جائیں گی تو ہم اور کھالیں بدل دیں گے تاکہ (ہمیشہ) عذاب
(کا مزہ) چکھتے رہیں۔ بیشک خدا غالب حکمت والا ہے ﴿۵۶﴾
اور جو ایمان لائے اور عمل نیک کرتے رہے ان کو
ہم بہشتوں میں داخل کریں گے جن کے نیچے نہریں
بہ رہی ہیں وہ ان میں ہمیشہ ہمیشہ رہیں گے۔ وہاں
ان کے لئے پاک بیبیاں ہیں۔ اور ان کو ہم گھنے سائے
میں داخل کریں گے ﴿۵۷﴾
خدا تم کو حکم دیتا ہے کہ امانت والوں کی امانتیں انکے
حوالے کر دیا کرو۔ اور جب لوگوں میں فیصلہ کرنے لگو
تو انصاف سے فیصلہ کیا کرو۔ خدا تمہیں بہت خوب
نصیحت کرتا ہے۔ بیشک خدا سنتا (اور) دیکھتا ہے ﴿۵۸﴾
مومنو! خدا اور اسکے رسول کی فرمانبرداری کرو اور جو تم میں
سے صاحب حکومت ہیں ان کی بھی۔ اور اگر کسی بات میں
تم میں اختلاف واقع ہو تو اگر خدا اور روز آخرت پر ایمان
رکھتے ہو تو اس میں خدا اور اسکے رسول (کے حکم) کی طرف
رجوع کرو۔ یہ بہت اچھی بات ہے اور اسکا مآل بھی اچھا ہے ﴿۵۹﴾
کیا تم نے ان لوگوں کو نہیں دیکھا جو دعویٰ تو یہ کرتے ہیں کہ جو
(کتاب) تم پر نازل ہوئی اور جو (کتابیں) تم سے پہلے نازل ہوئیں
ان سب پر ایمان رکھتے ہیں۔ اور چاہتے یہ ہیں کہ اپنا مقدمہ ایک
سرکش کے پاس لیجا کر فیصلہ کرائیں حالانکہ ان کو حکم دیا گیا تھا
کہ اس سے اعتقاد نہ رکھیں اور شیطان (تو یہ) چاہتا ہے کہ

إِبْرٰهِيمَ الْكِتٰبَ وَالْحِكْمَةَ وَاٰتَيْنٰهُمْ
مُّلْكًا عَظِيمًا ﴿٥٤﴾
فَمِنْهُمْ مَّنْ اٰمَنَ بِهٖ وَمِنْهُمْ مَّنْ
صَدَّ عَنْهُ ۚ وَكَفٰى بِجَهَنَّمَ سَعِيرًا ﴿٥٥﴾
إِنَّ الَّذِينَ كَفَرُوا بِاٰيٰتِنَا سَوْفَ
نُصْلِيهِمْ نَارًا ۗ كُلَّمَا نَضِجَتْ جُلُودُهُمْ
بَدَّلْنٰهُمْ جُلُودًا غَيْرَهَا لِيَذُوقُوا
الْعَذَابَ ۗ إِنَّ اللّٰهَ كَانَ عَزِيزًا حَكِيمًا ﴿٥٦﴾ ربع
وَالَّذِينَ اٰمَنُوا وَعَمِلُوا الصّٰلِحٰتِ
سَنُدْخِلُهُمْ جَنّٰتٍ تَجْرِي مِنْ
تَحْتِهَا الْأَنْهٰرُ خٰلِدِينَ فِيهَا أَبَدًا ۖ
لَهُمْ فِيهَا أَزْوٰجٌ مُّطَهَّرَةٌ ۖ وَّنُدْخِلُهُمْ
ظِلًّا ظَلِيلًا ﴿٥٧﴾
إِنَّ اللّٰهَ يَأْمُرُكُمْ أَنْ تُؤَدُّوا الْأَمٰنٰتِ
إِلٰى أَهْلِهَا ۙ وَإِذَا حَكَمْتُمْ بَيْنَ النَّاسِ
أَنْ تَحْكُمُوا بِالْعَدْلِ ۚ إِنَّ اللّٰهَ نِعِمَّا
يَعِظُكُمْ بِهٖ ۗ إِنَّ اللّٰهَ كَانَ سَمِيعًا بَصِيرًا ﴿٥٨﴾
يٰأَيُّهَا الَّذِينَ اٰمَنُوا أَطِيعُوا اللّٰهَ وَأَطِيعُوا
الرَّسُولَ وَأُولِي الْأَمْرِ مِنْكُمْ ۚ فَإِنْ
تَنٰزَعْتُمْ فِي شَيْءٍ فَرُدُّوهُ إِلَى اللّٰهِ وَ
الرَّسُولِ إِنْ كُنْتُمْ تُؤْمِنُونَ بِاللّٰهِ وَالْيَوْمِ
الْاٰخِرِ ۚ ذٰلِكَ خَيْرٌ وَّأَحْسَنُ تَأْوِيلًا ﴿٥٩﴾ ع ٨
أَلَمْ تَرَ إِلَى الَّذِينَ يَزْعُمُونَ أَنَّهُمْ
اٰمَنُوا بِمَا أُنْزِلَ إِلَيْكَ وَمَا أُنْزِلَ
مِنْ قَبْلِكَ يُرِيدُونَ أَنْ يَتَحَاكَمُوا
إِلَى الطَّاغُوتِ وَقَدْ أُمِرُوا أَنْ
يَكْفُرُوا بِهٖ ۗ وَيُرِيدُ الشَّيْطٰنُ أَنْ

يُضِلَّهُمْ ضَلٰلًا بَعِيدًا ﴿٦٠﴾
وَإِذَا قِيلَ لَهُمْ تَعَالَوْا إِلٰى مَآ أَنْزَلَ
اللّٰهُ وَإِلَى الرَّسُولِ رَأَيْتَ الْمُنٰفِقِينَ
يَصُدُّونَ عَنْكَ صُدُودًا ﴿٦١﴾
فَكَيْفَ إِذَآ أَصَابَتْهُمْ مُّصِيبَةٌ بِمَا
قَدَّمَتْ أَيْدِيهِمْ ثُمَّ جَآءُوكَ
يَحْلِفُونَ بِاللّٰهِ إِنْ أَرَدْنَآ إِلَّآ إِحْسَانًا
وَّتَوْفِيقًا ﴿٦٢﴾
أُولٰٓئِكَ الَّذِينَ يَعْلَمُ اللّٰهُ مَا فِي قُلُوبِهِمْ
فَأَعْرِضْ عَنْهُمْ وَعِظْهُمْ وَقُلْ
لَّهُمْ فِيٓ أَنْفُسِهِمْ قَوْلًا بَلِيغًا ﴿٦٣﴾
وَمَآ أَرْسَلْنَا مِنْ رَّسُولٍ إِلَّا لِيُطَاعَ
بِإِذْنِ اللّٰهِ وَلَوْ أَنَّهُمْ إِذْ ظَّلَمُوٓا
أَنْفُسَهُمْ جَآءُوكَ فَاسْتَغْفَرُوا اللّٰهَ
وَاسْتَغْفَرَ لَهُمُ الرَّسُولُ لَوَجَدُوا
اللّٰهَ تَوَّابًا رَّحِيمًا ﴿٦٤﴾
فَلَا وَرَبِّكَ لَا يُؤْمِنُونَ حَتّٰى يُحَكِّمُوكَ
فِيمَا شَجَرَ بَيْنَهُمْ ثُمَّ لَا يَجِدُوا فِيٓ
أَنْفُسِهِمْ حَرَجًا مِّمَّا قَضَيْتَ وَ
يُسَلِّمُوا تَسْلِيمًا ﴿٦٥﴾
وَلَوْ أَنَّا كَتَبْنَا عَلَيْهِمْ أَنِ اقْتُلُوٓا
أَنْفُسَكُمْ أَوِ اخْرُجُوا مِنْ دِيَارِكُمْ
مَّا فَعَلُوهُ إِلَّا قَلِيلٌ مِّنْهُمْ وَلَوْ
أَنَّهُمْ فَعَلُوا مَا يُوعَظُونَ بِهٖ لَكَانَ
خَيْرًا لَّهُمْ وَأَشَدَّ تَثْبِيتًا ﴿٦٦﴾
وَّإِذًا لَّاٰتَيْنٰهُمْ مِّنْ لَّدُنَّآ أَجْرًا عَظِيمًا ﴿٦٧﴾
وَّلَهَدَيْنٰهُمْ صِرَاطًا مُّسْتَقِيمًا ﴿٦٨﴾

اُن کو بہکا کر رستے سے دور ڈال دے ﴿۶۰﴾
اور جب اُن سے کہا جاتا ہے کہ جو حکم خدا نے نازل فرمایا ہے
اُس کی طرف (رجوع کرو) اور پیغمبر کی طرف آؤ تو تم منافقوں
کو دیکھتے ہو کہ تم سے اعراض کرتے اور رُکے جاتے ہیں ﴿۶۱﴾
تو کیسی (ندامت کی) بات ہے کہ جب اُنکے اعمال (کی شامت)
سے اُن پر کوئی مصیبت واقع ہوتی ہے تو تمہارے پاس
بھاگے آتے ہیں اور قسمیں کھاتے ہیں کہ واللہ ہمارا مقصود
تو بھلائی اور موافقت تھا ﴿۶۲﴾
ان لوگوں کے دلوں میں جو جو کچھ ہے خدا اُس کو (خوب)
جانتا ہے تم ان (کی باتوں) کا کچھ خیال نہ کرو۔ اور انہیں نصیحت کرو
اور اُن سے ایسی باتیں کہو جو اُن کے دلوں میں اثر کر جائیں ﴿۶۳﴾
اور ہم نے جو پیغمبر بھیجا ہے اس لئے بھیجا ہے کہ خدا کے
فرمان کے مطابق اُس کا حکم مانا جائے۔ اور یہ لوگ
جب اپنے حق میں ظلم کر بیٹھے تھے اگر تمہارے پاس آتے اور
خدا سے بخشش مانگتے اور رسولِ خدا بھی اُن کیلئے بخشش
طلب کرتے تو خدا کو معاف کرنے والا اور مہربان پاتے ﴿۶۴﴾
تمہارے پروردگار کی قسم یہ لوگ جب تک اپنے تنازعات
میں تمہیں منصف نہ بنائیں۔ اور جو فیصلہ تم کر دو اُس سے
اپنے دل میں تنگ نہ ہوں بلکہ اُس کو خوشی سے مان لیں
تب تک مومن نہیں ہوں گے ﴿۶۵﴾
اور اگر ہم اُنہیں حکم دیتے کہ اپنے آپ کو قتل کر ڈالو یا اپنے
گھر چھوڑ کر نکل جاؤ تو اُن میں سے تھوڑے ہی ایسا
کرتے۔ اور اگر یہ اس نصیحت پر کاربند ہوتے جو اُن کو
کی جاتی ہے تو اُن کے حق میں بہتر اور (دین میں)
زیادہ ثابت قدمی کا موجب ہوتا ﴿۶۶﴾
اور ہم اُن کو اپنے ہاں سے اجرِ عظیم بھی عطا فرماتے ﴿۶۷﴾
اور سیدھا رستہ بھی دکھاتے ﴿۶۸﴾

But Satan's wish is to lead them astray far away (from the Right).

61. When it is said to them: "Come to what Allah hath revealed, and to the Messenger": thou seest the Hypocrites avert their faces from thee in disgust.

62. How then, when they are seized by misfortune, because of the deeds which their hands have sent forth? Then they come to thee, swearing by Allah: "We meant no more than good-will and conciliation!"

63. Those men,—Allah knows what is in their heart; so keep clear of them but admonish them, and speak to them a word to reach their very souls.

64. We sent not a Messenger, but to be obeyed, in accordance with the leave of Allah. If they had only, when they were unjust to themselves, come unto thee and asked Allah's forgiveness. And the Messenger had asked forgiveness for them, they would have found Allah indeed Oft-Returning, Most Merciful.

65. But no, by thy Lord, they can have no (real) Faith, until they make thee judge in all disputes between them, and find in their souls no resistance against thy decisions, but accept them with the fullest conviction.

66. If We had ordered them to sacrifice their lives or to leave their homes, very few of them would have done it: but if they had done what they were (actually) told, it would have been best for them, and would have gone farthest to strengthen their (faith);

67. And We should then have given them from Ourselves a great reward;

68. And We should have shown them the Straight Way.

69. All who obey Allah and the Messenger are in the Company of those on whom is the Grace of Allah,—of the Prophets (who teach), the Sincere (lovers of Truth), the martyres, and the Righteous (who do good): Ah ! How beautiful is their Company.

70. Such is the Bounty from Allah: and sufficient is it that Allah knoweth all.

71. O ye who believe ! take your precautions, and either go forth in parties or go forth all together.

72. There are certainly among you men who would tarry behind: if a misfortune befalls you, they say: "Allah did favour us in that we were not present among them."

73. But if good fortune comes to you from Allah, they would be sure to say—as if there had never been ties of affection between you and them—"Oh ! I wish I had been with them: a fine thing should I then have made of it !"

74. Let those fight In the cause of Allah who sell the life of this world for the Hereafter. To him who fighteth in the cause of Allah,—whether he is slain or gets victory—soon shall We give him a reward of great (value).

75. And why should ye not fight in the cause of Allah and of those who, being weak, are ill-treated (and oppressed) ?— men, women, and children, whose cry is: "Our Lord ! rescue us from this town, whose people are oppressors; and raise for us from Thee one who will protect; and raise for us from Thee one who will help !"

76. Those who believe fight in the cause of Allah, and those who reject Faith fight in the cause of Evil (Tagut): so fight ye against the friends, of Satan: feeble indeed is the cunning of Satan.

اور جو لوگ خدا اور اُس کے رسول کی اطاعت کرتے ہیں وہ
(قیامت کے روز) اُن لوگوں کے ساتھ ہونگے جن پر خدا نے
بڑا فضل کیا یعنی انبیاء اور صدیق اور شہید اور نیک لوگ
اور اُن لوگوں کی رفاقت بہت ہی خوب ہے ﴿٦٩﴾
یہ خدا کا فضل ہے۔ اور خدا جاننے والا کافی ہے ﴿٧٠﴾
مومنو! جہاد کے لئے ہتھیار لے لیا کرو پھر یا تو جماعت
جماعت ہو کر نکلا کرو یا سب اکٹھے کُوچ کیا کرو ﴿٧١﴾
اور تم میں کوئی ایسا بھی ہے کہ (عمداً) دیر لگاتا ہے۔ پھر
اگر تم پر کوئی مصیبت پڑ جائے تو کہتا ہے کہ خدا نے مجھ پر
بڑی مہربانی کی کہ میں اُن میں موجود نہ تھا ﴿٧٢﴾
اور اگر خدا تم پر فضل کرے تو اس طرح سے کہ گویا تم میں
اس میں دوستی تھی ہی نہیں (افسوس کرتا اور) کہتا ہے کہ
کاش میں بھی اُن کے ساتھ ہوتا تو مقصدِ عظیم حاصل ہوتا ﴿٧٣﴾
تو جو لوگ آخرت (کو خریدتے اور اس) کے بدلے دُنیا کی
زندگی کو بیچنا چاہتے ہیں اُن کو چاہیئے کہ خدا کی راہ میں
جنگ کریں۔ اور جو شخص خدا کی راہ میں جنگ کرے پھر
شہید ہو جائے یا غلبہ پائے ہم عنقریب اُسکو بڑا ثواب دینگے ﴿٧٤﴾
اور تم کو کیا ہوا ہے کہ خدا کی راہ میں اور اُن بےبس مردوں
اور عورتوں اور بچوں کی خاطر نہیں لڑتے جو دُعائیں کیا
کرتے ہیں کہ اے پروردگار ہم کو اس شہر سے جس کے
رہنے والے ظالم ہیں نکال کر کہیں اور لے جا۔ اور اپنی
طرف سے کسی کو ہمارا حامی بنا۔ اور اپنی ہی طرف
سے کسی کو ہمارا مددگار مقرر فرما ﴿٧٥﴾
جو مومن ہیں وہ تو خدا کے لئے لڑتے ہیں اور جو کافر
ہیں وہ بتوں کے لئے لڑتے ہیں سو تم شیطان کے
مددگاروں سے لڑو (اور ڈرو مت) کیونکہ شیطان کا
داؤ بودا ہوتا ہے ﴿٧٦﴾

وَمَنْ يُّطِعِ اللّٰهَ وَالرَّسُوْلَ فَاُولٰٓئِكَ
مَعَ الَّذِيْنَ اَنْعَمَ اللّٰهُ عَلَيْهِمْ مِّنَ
النَّبِيّٖنَ وَالصِّدِّيْقِيْنَ وَالشُّهَدَآءِ وَ
الصّٰلِحِيْنَ ۚ وَحَسُنَ اُولٰٓئِكَ رَفِيْقًا ﴿٦٩﴾
ع ذٰلِكَ الْفَضْلُ مِنَ اللّٰهِ ۭ وَكَفٰى بِاللّٰهِ عَلِيْمًا ﴿٧٠﴾
يٰٓاَيُّهَا الَّذِيْنَ اٰمَنُوْا خُذُوْا حِذْرَكُمْ
فَانْفِرُوْا ثُبَاتٍ اَوِ انْفِرُوْا جَمِيْعًا ﴿٧١﴾
وَاِنَّ مِنْكُمْ لَمَنْ لَّيُبَطِّئَنَّ ۚ فَاِنْ
اَصَابَتْكُمْ مُّصِيْبَةٌ قَالَ قَدْ اَنْعَمَ اللّٰهُ
عَلَيَّ اِذْ لَمْ اَكُنْ مَّعَهُمْ شَهِيْدًا ﴿٧٢﴾
وَلَئِنْ اَصَابَكُمْ فَضْلٌ مِّنَ اللّٰهِ لَيَقُوْلَنَّ
كَاَنْ لَّمْ تَكُنْ بَيْنَكُمْ وَبَيْنَهٗ مَوَدَّةٌ
يّٰلَيْتَنِيْ كُنْتُ مَعَهُمْ فَاَفُوْزَ فَوْزًا عَظِيْمًا ﴿٧٣﴾
فَلْيُقَاتِلْ فِيْ سَبِيْلِ اللّٰهِ الَّذِيْنَ
يَشْرُوْنَ الْحَيٰوةَ الدُّنْيَا بِالْاٰخِرَةِ ۭ وَ
مَنْ يُّقَاتِلْ فِيْ سَبِيْلِ اللّٰهِ فَيُقْتَلْ اَوْ
يَغْلِبْ فَسَوْفَ نُؤْتِيْهِ اَجْرًا عَظِيْمًا ﴿٧٤﴾
وَمَا لَكُمْ لَا تُقَاتِلُوْنَ فِيْ سَبِيْلِ اللّٰهِ
وَالْمُسْتَضْعَفِيْنَ مِنَ الرِّجَالِ وَ
النِّسَآءِ وَالْوِلْدَانِ الَّذِيْنَ يَقُوْلُوْنَ
رَبَّنَآ اَخْرِجْنَا مِنْ هٰذِهِ الْقَرْيَةِ الظَّالِمِ
اَهْلُهَا ۚ وَاجْعَلْ لَّنَا مِنْ لَّدُنْكَ وَلِيًّا ۚ
وَّاجْعَلْ لَّنَا مِنْ لَّدُنْكَ نَصِيْرًا ﴿٧٥﴾
اَلَّذِيْنَ اٰمَنُوْا يُقَاتِلُوْنَ فِيْ سَبِيْلِ اللّٰهِ ۚ
وَالَّذِيْنَ كَفَرُوْا يُقَاتِلُوْنَ فِيْ سَبِيْلِ
الطَّاغُوْتِ فَقَاتِلُوْٓا اَوْلِيَآءَ الشَّيْطٰنِ ۚ
ع اِنَّ كَيْدَ الشَّيْطٰنِ كَانَ ضَعِيْفًا ﴿٧٦﴾

77. Hast thou not turned thy thought to those who were told to hold back their hands (from fight) but establish regular prayers and spend in regular Zakat ? When (at length) the order for fighting was issued to them, behold ! a section of them feared men as—or even more than—they should have feared Allah: they said: "Our Lord! why hast Thou ordered us to fight? Wouldst Thou not grant us respite to our (natural) term, near (enough)? Say: "Short is the enjoyment of this world: the Hereafter is the best for those who do right: never will ye be dealt with unjustly in the very least!

78. "Wherever ye are, death will find you out, even if ye are in towers built up strong and high!"

If some good befalls them they say, "This is from Allah"; but if evil, they say, "This is from thee" (O Prophet). Say: "All things are from Allah." But what hath come to these people, that they fail to understand a single fact?

79. Whatever good, (O man !) happens to thee, is from Allah; but whatever evil happens to thee, is from thyself and We have sent thee as a Messenger to (instruct) mankind. And enough is Allah for a witness.

80. He who obeys the Messenger, obeys Allah: but if any turn away, We have not sent thee to watch over them.

81. They have "Obedience" on their lips; but when they leave thee, a section of them meditate all night on things very different from what thou tellest them. But Allah records their nightly (plots): so keep clear of them, and put thy trust in Allah, and enough is Allah as a disposer of affairs.

82. Do they not ponder on the Qur'an ? Had it been from other than Allah, they would surely have found therein much discrepancy.

بھلا تم نے ان لوگوں کو نہیں دیکھا جن کو (پہلے یہ) حکم دیا
گیا تھا کہ اپنے ہاتھوں کو (جنگ سے) روکے رہو اور نماز پڑھتے اور زکوٰة
دیتے رہو۔ پھر جب ان پر جہاد فرض کر دیا گیا تو بعض لوگ ان میں سے لوگوں
سے یوں ڈرنے لگے جیسے خدا سے ڈرا کرتے ہیں بلکہ اس سے بھی زیادہ۔
اور بڑبڑانے لگے کہ اے خدا تو نے ہم پر جہاد (جلد) کیوں
فرض کر دیا۔ تھوڑی مدت اور ہمیں کیوں مہلت نہ دی (اے پیغمبر
ان سے) کہہ دو کہ دنیا کا فائدہ بہت تھوڑا ہے اور بہت اچھی
چیز تو پرہیزگار کیلئے (نجات) آخرت ہے اور تم پر دھاگے برابر
بھی ظلم نہیں کیا جائے گا ﴿۷۷﴾
(اے جہاد سے ڈرنے والو) تم کہیں رہو موت تو تمہیں
آ کر رہے گی خواہ بڑے بڑے محلوں میں رہو۔ اور ان
لوگوں کو اگر کوئی فائدہ پہنچتا ہے تو کہتے ہیں یہ خدا کی طرف سے ہے
اور اگر کوئی گزند پہنچتا ہے تو (اے محمد تم سے) کہتے ہیں کہ یہ (گزند)
آپ کی وجہ سے (ہمیں پہنچا) ہے۔ کہہ دو کہ (رنج و راحت) سب اللہ ہی
کی طرف سے ہے ان لوگوں کو کیا ہو گیا ہے کہ بات بھی نہیں سمجھ سکتے ﴿۷۸﴾
(اے آدم زاد) تجھ کو جو فائدہ پہنچے وہ خدا کی طرف سے ہے اور جو نقصان
پہنچے وہ تیری ہی (شامت اعمال کی) وجہ سے ہے اور (اے محمد) ہم نے تم کو
لوگوں (کی ہدایت) کیلئے پیغمبر بنا کر بھیجا ہے اور (اس بات کا) خدا ہی گواہ کافی ہے ﴿۷۹﴾
جو شخص رسول کی فرمانبرداری کریگا تو بیشک اس نے خدا کی فرمانبرداری کی
اور جو نافرمانی کرے تو اے پیغمبر تمہیں ہم نے ان کا نگہبان بنا کر نہیں بھیجا ﴿۸۰﴾
اور یہ لوگ منہ سے تو کہتے ہیں کہ (آپ کی) فرمانبرداری (دل سے منظور) ہے
لیکن جب تمہارے پاس سے چلے جاتے ہیں تو ان میں سے بعض لوگ رات کو
تمہاری باتوں کے خلاف مشورے کرتے ہیں اور جو مشورے یہ کرتے ہیں خدا ان کو
لکھ لیتا ہے۔ تو ان کا کچھ خیال نہ کرو اور خدا پر بھروسہ رکھو اور خدا ہی کافی کارساز ہے ﴿۸۱﴾
بھلا یہ قرآن میں غور کیوں نہیں کرتے۔ اگر یہ خدا کے سوا
کسی اور کا (کلام) ہوتا تو اس میں (بہت سا)
اختلاف پاتے ﴿۸۲﴾

أَلَمْ تَرَ إِلَى الَّذِينَ قِيلَ لَهُمْ كُفُّوٓا
أَيْدِيَكُمْ وَأَقِيمُوا الصَّلٰوةَ وَاٰتُوا الزَّكٰوةَ
فَلَمَّا كُتِبَ عَلَيْهِمُ الْقِتَالُ إِذَا فَرِيقٌ
مِّنْهُمْ يَخْشَوْنَ النَّاسَ كَخَشْيَةِ اللّٰهِ
أَوْ أَشَدَّ خَشْيَةً ۚ وَقَالُوا رَبَّنَا لِمَ
كَتَبْتَ عَلَيْنَا الْقِتَالَ ۚ لَوْلَآ أَخَّرْتَنَآ
إِلٰٓى أَجَلٍ قَرِيبٍ ۗ قُلْ مَتَاعُ الدُّنْيَا
قَلِيلٌ ۚ وَالْاٰخِرَةُ خَيْرٌ لِّمَنِ اتَّقٰى ۚ
وَلَا تُظْلَمُونَ فَتِيلًا ﴿٧٧﴾
أَيْنَ مَا تَكُونُوا يُدْرِكْكُّمُ الْمَوْتُ وَلَوْ كُنْتُمْ
فِي بُرُوجٍ مُّشَيَّدَةٍ ۗ وَإِنْ تُصِبْهُمْ حَسَنَةٌ
يَّقُولُوا هٰذِهٖ مِنْ عِنْدِ اللّٰهِ ۚ وَإِنْ
تُصِبْهُمْ سَيِّئَةٌ يَّقُولُوا هٰذِهٖ مِنْ عِنْدِكَ ۚ
قُلْ كُلٌّ مِّنْ عِنْدِ اللّٰهِ ۖ فَمَالِ هٰٓؤُلَآءِ
الْقَوْمِ لَا يَكَادُونَ يَفْقَهُونَ حَدِيثًا ﴿٧٨﴾
مَآ أَصَابَكَ مِنْ حَسَنَةٍ فَمِنَ اللّٰهِ ۖ وَمَآ
أَصَابَكَ مِنْ سَيِّئَةٍ فَمِنْ نَّفْسِكَ ۚ وَ
أَرْسَلْنٰكَ لِلنَّاسِ رَسُولًا ۚ وَكَفٰى بِاللّٰهِ شَهِيدًا ﴿٧٩﴾
مَنْ يُّطِعِ الرَّسُولَ فَقَدْ أَطَاعَ اللّٰهَ ۚ
وَمَنْ تَوَلّٰى فَمَآ أَرْسَلْنٰكَ عَلَيْهِمْ حَفِيظًا ﴿٨٠﴾
وَيَقُولُونَ طَاعَةٌ ۡ فَإِذَا بَرَزُوا مِنْ
عِنْدِكَ بَيَّتَ طَآئِفَةٌ مِّنْهُمْ غَيْرَ الَّذِي
تَقُولُ ۚ وَاللّٰهُ يَكْتُبُ مَا يُبَيِّتُونَ ۚ فَأَعْرِضْ
عَنْهُمْ وَتَوَكَّلْ عَلَى اللّٰهِ ۚ وَكَفٰى بِاللّٰهِ وَكِيلًا ﴿٨١﴾
أَفَلَا يَتَدَبَّرُونَ الْقُرْاٰنَ ۚ وَلَوْ كَانَ
مِنْ عِنْدِ غَيْرِ اللّٰهِ لَوَجَدُوا فِيهِ
اخْتِلَافًا كَثِيرًا ﴿٨٢﴾

83. When there comes to them some matter touching (public) safety or fear, they divulge it. If they had only referred it to the Messenger or to those charged with authority among them, the proper investigators would have known it from them (direct). Were it not for the Grace and Mercy of Allah unto you, all but a few of you would have followed Satan.

84. Then fight in Allah's cause—thou art held responsible only for thyself—and rouse the Believers. It may be that Allah will restrain the fury of the Unbelievers; for Allah is the strongest in might and in punishment.

اور جب اُن کے پاس امن یا خوف کی کوئی خبر پہنچتی ہے
تو اُسے مشہور کر دیتے ہیں۔ اور اگر اس کو پیغمبر اور اپنے
سرداروں کے پاس پہنچاتے تو تحقیق کرنے والے اُس کی تحقیق
کر لیتے۔ اور اگر تم پر خدا کا فضل اور اُس کی مہربانی نہ ہوتی تو چند
اشخاص کے سوا سب شیطان کے پیرو ہو جاتے (۸۳)
تو (اے محمدؐ) تم خدا کی راہ میں لڑو۔ تم اپنے سوا کسی کے
ذمہ دار نہیں ہو۔ اور مومنوں کو بھی ترغیب دو۔
قریب ہے کہ خدا کافروں کی لڑائی کو بند کر دے۔ اور
خدا لڑائی کے اعتبار سے بہت سخت ہے اور سزا
کے لحاظ سے بہت سخت ہے (۸۴)

وَإِذَا جَآءَهُمْ أَمْرٌ مِّنَ الْأَمْنِ أَوِ الْخَوْفِ
أَذَاعُوا بِهِۦ ۖ وَلَوْ رَدُّوهُ إِلَى الرَّسُولِ وَإِلَىٰٓ
أُولِى الْأَمْرِ مِنْهُمْ لَعَلِمَهُ الَّذِينَ
يَسْتَنۢبِطُونَهُۥ مِنْهُمْ ۗ وَلَوْلَا فَضْلُ اللَّهِ عَلَيْكُمْ
وَرَحْمَتُهُۥ لَاتَّبَعْتُمُ الشَّيْطَٰنَ إِلَّا قَلِيلًا ﴿٨٣﴾
فَقَٰتِلْ فِى سَبِيلِ اللَّهِ لَا تُكَلَّفُ
إِلَّا نَفْسَكَ ۚ وَحَرِّضِ الْمُؤْمِنِينَ ۖ
عَسَى اللَّهُ أَن يَكُفَّ بَأْسَ الَّذِينَ
كَفَرُوا ۚ وَاللَّهُ أَشَدُّ بَأْسًا وَأَشَدُّ
تَنكِيلًا ﴿٨٤﴾

85. Whoever intercedes in a good cause becomes a partner therein: and whoever recommends and helps an evil cause, shares in its burden: and Allah hath power over all things.

جو شخص نیک بات کی سفارش کرے تو اُس کو اُس
(کے ثواب) میں سے حصہ ملے گا۔ اور جو بُری بات کی
سفارش کرے اُس کو اُس (کے عذاب) میں سے حصہ ملیگا۔
اور خدا ہر چیز پر قدرت رکھتا ہے (۸۵)

مَّن يَشْفَعْ شَفَٰعَةً حَسَنَةً يَكُن
لَّهُۥ نَصِيبٌ مِّنْهَا ۖ وَمَن يَشْفَعْ
شَفَٰعَةً سَيِّئَةً يَكُن لَّهُۥ كِفْلٌ مِّنْهَا ۗ
وَكَانَ اللَّهُ عَلَىٰ كُلِّ شَىْءٍ مُّقِيتًا ﴿٨٥﴾

86. When a (courteous) greeting is offered you, meet it with a greeting still more courteous, or (at least) of equal courtesy. Allah takes careful account of all things.

اور جب تم کو کوئی دُعا دے تو (جواب میں) تم اُس سے بہتر
(کلمے) سے (اُسے) دُعا دو یا انہیں لفظوں سے دُعا دو۔
بیشک خدا ہر چیز کا حساب لینے والا ہے (۸۶)

وَإِذَا حُيِّيتُم بِتَحِيَّةٍ فَحَيُّوا بِأَحْسَنَ
مِنْهَآ أَوْ رُدُّوهَآ ۗ إِنَّ اللَّهَ كَانَ عَلَىٰ
كُلِّ شَىْءٍ حَسِيبًا ﴿٨٦﴾ النصف

87. Allah ! There is no god but He: of a surety he will gather you together on the Day of Judgment, about which there is no doubt. And whose word can be truer than Allah's?

خدا (وہ معبود برحق ہے کہ) اُس کے سوا کوئی عبادت کے
لائق نہیں۔ وہ قیامت کے دن تم سب کو ضرور جمع کریگا
اور خدا سے بڑھ کر بات کا سچا کون ہے؟ (۸۷)

اللَّهُ لَآ إِلَٰهَ إِلَّا هُوَ ۚ لَيَجْمَعَنَّكُمْ إِلَىٰ
يَوْمِ الْقِيَٰمَةِ لَا رَيْبَ فِيهِ ۗ وَمَنْ
أَصْدَقُ مِنَ اللَّهِ حَدِيثًا ﴿٨٧﴾

88. Why should ye be divided into two parties about the Hypocrites ? Allah hath cast them off for their (evil) deeds. Would ye guide those whom Allah hath thrown out of the Way ? For those whom Allah hath thrown out of the Way, never shalt thou find the Way.

تو کیا سبب ہے کہ تم منافقوں کے بارے میں دو گروہ ہو رہے ہو
حالانکہ خدا نے اُن کو اُنکے کرتوتوں کے سبب اوندھا کر دیا ہے۔ کیا تم چاہتے
ہو کہ جس شخص کو خدا نے گمراہ کر دیا ہے اُس کو رستے پر لے آؤ۔
اور جس شخص کو خدا گمراہ کر دے تم اُس کے لئے کبھی بھی
رستہ نہیں پاؤ گے (۸۸)

فَمَا لَكُمْ فِى الْمُنَٰفِقِينَ فِئَتَيْنِ وَاللَّهُ
أَرْكَسَهُم بِمَا كَسَبُوٓا ۚ أَتُرِيدُونَ
أَن تَهْدُوا مَنْ أَضَلَّ اللَّهُ ۖ
وَمَن يُضْلِلِ اللَّهُ فَلَن تَجِدَ
لَهُۥ سَبِيلًا ﴿٨٨﴾

89. They but wish that ye should reject Faith, as they do, and thus be on the same footing (as they): so take not friends from their ranks

وہ تو یہی چاہتے ہیں کہ جس طرح وہ خود کافر ہیں (اسی طرح)
تم بھی کافر ہو کر (سب) برابر ہو جاؤ تو جب تک وہ خدا کی

وَدُّوا لَوْ تَكْفُرُونَ كَمَا كَفَرُوا فَتَكُونُونَ
سَوَآءً ۖ فَلَا تَتَّخِذُوا مِنْهُمْ أَوْلِيَآءَ حَتَّىٰ

until they flee in the way of Allah (from what is forbidden). But if they turn renegades, seize them and slay them wherever ye find them; and (in any case) take no friends or helpers from their ranks:—

90. Except those who join a group between whom and you there is a treaty (of peace), or those who approach you with hearts restraining them from fighting you or fighting their own People. If Allah had pleased, He could have given them power over you, and they would have fought you: therefore if they withdraw from you but fight you not, and (instead) send you (guarantees of) peace, then Allah hath opened no way for you (to war against them).

91. Others you will find that wish to be secure from you as well as that of their people: every time they are sent back to temptation, they succumb thereto: if they withdraw not from you nor give you (guarantees of peace besides restraining their hands, seize them and slay them wherever ye get them: in their case We have provided you with a clear argument against them.

92. Never should a Believer kill a Believer; except by mistake, and whoever kills a Believer by mistake it is ordained that he should free a believing slave. And pay blood-money to the deceased's family, unless they remit it freely. If the deceased belonged to a people at war with you, and he was a Believer, the freeing of a believing slave (is enough). If he belonged to a people with whom ye have a treaty of mutual alliance, blood-money should be paid to his family, and a believing slave be freed. For those who find this beyond their means, (is prescribed) a fast for two months running: by way of repentance to Allah: for Allah hath

راہ میں وطن نہ چھوڑ جائیں اُن میں سے کسی کو دوست
نہ بنانا۔ اگر (ترکِ وطن کو) قبول نہ کریں تو اُنکو پکڑ لو اور جہاں
پاؤ قتل کر دو۔ اور ان میں سے کسی کو اپنا رفیق اور مددگار نہ بناؤ ﴿٨٩﴾
مگر جو لوگ ایسے لوگوں سے جا ملے ہوں جن میں اور تم میں (صلح کا)
عہد ہو یا اس حال میں کہ اُنکے دل تمہارے ساتھ یا اپنی قوم کیساتھ
لڑنے سے رُک گئے ہوں تمہارے پاس آجائیں (تو احتراز
ضرور نہیں) اور اگر خدا چاہتا تو اُنکو تم پر غالب کر دیتا تو وہ تم
سے ضرور لڑتے پھر اگر وہ تم سے (جنگ کرنے سے) کنارہ کشی کریں اور
لڑیں نہیں اور تمہاری طرف صلح (کا پیغام) بھیجیں تو خدا نے تمہارے
لئے اُن پر (زبردستی کرنیکی) کوئی سبیل مقرر نہیں کی ﴿٩٠﴾
تم کچھ اور لوگ ایسے بھی پاؤ گے جو یہ چاہتے ہیں کہ تم سے
بھی امن میں رہیں اور اپنی قوم سے بھی امن میں رہیں۔
لیکن جب فتنہ انگیزی کو بلائے جائیں تو اُس میں اوندھے مُنہ
گر پڑیں تو ایسے لوگ اگر تم سے (لڑنے سے) کنارہ کشی نہ کریں اور
نہ تمہاری طرف (پیغام) صلح بھیجیں اور نہ اپنے ہاتھوں کو روکیں
تو اُنکو پکڑ لو اور جہاں پاؤ قتل کر دو۔ ان لوگوں کے مقابلے
میں ہم نے تمہارے لئے سندِ صریح مقرر کر دی ہے ﴿٩١﴾
اور کسی مومن کو شایاں نہیں کہ مومن کو مار ڈالے مگر
بھول کر۔ اور جو بھول کر بھی مومن کو مار ڈالے
تو (ایک تو) ایک مسلمان غلام آزاد کر دے اور (دوسرے) مقتول کے
وارثوں کو خُون بہا دے ہاں اگر وہ معاف کر دیں (تو اُنکو اختیار ہے)
اگر مقتول تمہارے دشمنوں کی جماعت میں سے ہو اور وہ خود مومن ہو
تو صرف ایک مسلمان غلام آزاد کرنا چاہیئے اور اگر مقتول ایسے
لوگوں میں سے ہو جن میں اور تم میں صلح کا عہد ہو تو وارثانِ
مقتول کو خون بہا دینا اور ایک مسلمان غلام آزاد کرنا چاہیئے
اور جس کو یہ میسر نہ ہو وہ متواتر دو مہینے کے روزے رکھے یہ
(کفارہ) خدا کی طرف سے (قبول) توبہ (کے لئے) ہے

يُهَاجِرُوا فِي سَبِيلِ اللَّهِ ۚ فَإِن تَوَلَّوْا
فَخُذُوهُمْ وَاقْتُلُوهُمْ حَيْثُ وَجَدتُّمُوهُمْ ۖ
وَلَا تَتَّخِذُوا مِنْهُمْ وَلِيًّا وَلَا نَصِيرًا ﴿٨٩﴾
إِلَّا الَّذِينَ يَصِلُونَ إِلَىٰ قَوْمٍ بَيْنَكُمْ
وَبَيْنَهُم مِّيثَاقٌ أَوْ جَاءُوكُمْ حَصِرَتْ
صُدُورُهُمْ أَن يُقَاتِلُوكُمْ أَوْ يُقَاتِلُوا
قَوْمَهُمْ ۚ وَلَوْ شَاءَ اللَّهُ لَسَلَّطَهُمْ
عَلَيْكُمْ فَلَقَاتَلُوكُمْ ۚ فَإِنِ اعْتَزَلُوكُمْ
فَلَمْ يُقَاتِلُوكُمْ وَأَلْقَوْا إِلَيْكُمُ السَّلَمَ
فَمَا جَعَلَ اللَّهُ لَكُمْ عَلَيْهِمْ سَبِيلًا ﴿٩٠﴾
سَتَجِدُونَ آخَرِينَ يُرِيدُونَ أَن
يَأْمَنُوكُمْ وَيَأْمَنُوا قَوْمَهُمْ كُلَّمَا
رُدُّوا إِلَى الْفِتْنَةِ أُرْكِسُوا فِيهَا ۚ
فَإِن لَّمْ يَعْتَزِلُوكُمْ وَيُلْقُوا إِلَيْكُمُ
السَّلَمَ وَيَكُفُّوا أَيْدِيَهُمْ فَخُذُوهُمْ
وَاقْتُلُوهُمْ حَيْثُ ثَقِفْتُمُوهُمْ ۚ وَأُولَٰئِكُمْ
جَعَلْنَا لَكُمْ عَلَيْهِمْ سُلْطَانًا مُّبِينًا ﴿٩١﴾ ع
وَمَا كَانَ لِمُؤْمِنٍ أَن يَقْتُلَ مُؤْمِنًا
إِلَّا خَطَأً ۚ وَمَن قَتَلَ مُؤْمِنًا خَطَأً
فَتَحْرِيرُ رَقَبَةٍ مُّؤْمِنَةٍ وَدِيَةٌ مُّسَلَّمَةٌ
إِلَىٰ أَهْلِهِ إِلَّا أَن يَصَّدَّقُوا ۚ فَإِن
كَانَ مِن قَوْمٍ عَدُوٍّ لَّكُمْ وَهُوَ مُؤْمِنٌ
فَتَحْرِيرُ رَقَبَةٍ مُّؤْمِنَةٍ ۖ وَإِن كَانَ
مِن قَوْمٍ بَيْنَكُمْ وَبَيْنَهُم مِّيثَاقٌ
فَدِيَةٌ مُّسَلَّمَةٌ إِلَىٰ أَهْلِهِ وَتَحْرِيرُ
رَقَبَةٍ مُّؤْمِنَةٍ ۖ فَمَن لَّمْ يَجِدْ فَصِيَامُ
شَهْرَيْنِ مُتَتَابِعَيْنِ تَوْبَةً مِّنَ اللَّهِ

وَكَانَ اللّٰهُ عَلِيْمًا حَكِيْمًا ﴿٩٢﴾

اور خدا سب کچھ جانتا (اور) بڑی حکمت والا ہے ﴿۹۲﴾

all knowledge and all wisdom.

وَمَنْ يَّقْتُلْ مُؤْمِنًا مُّتَعَمِّدًا فَجَزَآؤُهٗ
جَهَنَّمُ خَالِدًا فِيْهَا وَغَضِبَ اللّٰهُ
عَلَيْهِ وَلَعَنَهٗ وَاَعَدَّ لَهٗ عَذَابًا
عَظِيْمًا ﴿٩٣﴾

اور جو شخص مسلمان کو قصداً مار ڈالے گا تو اُس کی سزا
دوزخ ہے جس میں وہ ہمیشہ (جلتا) رہے گا اور خدا اس
پر غضبناک ہوگا اور اُس پر لعنت کریگا اور ایسے شخص کیلئے
اُس نے بڑا (سخت) عذاب تیار کر رکھا ہے ﴿۹۳﴾

93. If a man kills a Believer intentionally, his recompense is Hell, to abide therein (for ever): and the wrath and the curse of Allah are upon him, and a dreadful chastisement is prepared for him.

يٰۤاَيُّهَا الَّذِيْنَ اٰمَنُوْۤا اِذَا ضَرَبْتُمْ فِيْ
سَبِيْلِ اللّٰهِ فَتَبَيَّنُوْا وَلَا تَقُوْلُوْا
لِمَنْ اَلْقٰۤى اِلَيْكُمُ السَّلٰمَ لَسْتَ مُؤْمِنًا ۚ
تَبْتَغُوْنَ عَرَضَ الْحَيٰوةِ الدُّنْيَا ؗ
فَعِنْدَ اللّٰهِ مَغَانِمُ كَثِيْرَةٌ ؕ كَذٰلِكَ
كُنْتُمْ مِّنْ قَبْلُ فَمَنَّ اللّٰهُ
عَلَيْكُمْ فَتَبَيَّنُوْا ؕ اِنَّ اللّٰهَ كَانَ بِمَا
تَعْمَلُوْنَ خَبِيْرًا ﴿٩٤﴾

مومنو! جب تم خدا کی راہ میں باہر نکلا کرو تو تحقیق
سے کام لیا کرو اور جو شخص تم سے سلام علیک
کرے اُس سے یہ نہ کہو کہ تم مومن نہیں ہو۔ اور اس
سے تمہاری غرض یہ ہو کہ دنیا کی زندگی کا فائدہ حاصل
کرو۔ سو خدا کے نزدیک بہت سی غنیمتیں ہیں تم بھی
تو پہلے ایسے ہی تھے۔ پھر خدا نے تم پر احسان کیا تو
(آئندہ) تحقیق کر لیا کرو۔ اور جو عمل تم کرتے ہو خدا کو
سب کی خبر ہے ﴿۹۴﴾

94. O ye who believe ! when ye go out in the cause of Allah, investigate carefully, and say not to anyone who offers you a salutation: "Thou art none of a Believer !" Coveting the perishable goods of this life: with Allah are profits and spoils abundant. Even thus were ye yourselves before, till Allah conferred on you His favours: therefore carefully investigate. For Allah is well aware of all that ye do.

لَا يَسْتَوِي الْقٰعِدُوْنَ مِنَ الْمُؤْمِنِيْنَ
غَيْرُ اُولِي الضَّرَرِ وَالْمُجٰهِدُوْنَ فِيْ
سَبِيْلِ اللّٰهِ بِاَمْوَالِهِمْ وَاَنْفُسِهِمْ ؕ
فَضَّلَ اللّٰهُ الْمُجٰهِدِيْنَ بِاَمْوَالِهِمْ
وَاَنْفُسِهِمْ عَلَى الْقٰعِدِيْنَ دَرَجَةً ؕ
وَكُلًّا وَّعَدَ اللّٰهُ الْحُسْنٰى ؕ وَفَضَّلَ اللّٰهُ
الْمُجٰهِدِيْنَ عَلَى الْقٰعِدِيْنَ اَجْرًا عَظِيْمًا ﴿٩٥﴾
دَرَجٰتٍ مِّنْهُ وَمَغْفِرَةً وَّرَحْمَةً ؕ
وَكَانَ اللّٰهُ غَفُوْرًا رَّحِيْمًا ﴿٩٦﴾ ع ١٣

جو مسلمان (گھروں میں) بیٹھ رہتے (اور لڑنے سے جی چراتے)
ہیں اور کوئی عذر نہیں رکھتے وہ اور جو خدا کی راہ میں
اپنے مال اور جان سے لڑتے ہیں وہ دونوں برابر نہیں
ہو سکتے۔ مال اور جان سے جہاد کرنیوالوں کو بیٹھ رہنے والوں
پر اللہ نے درجے میں فضیلت بخشی ہے۔ اور (گو) نیک
وعدہ سب سے ہے لیکن اجر عظیم کے لحاظ سے خدا نے
جہاد کرنیوالوں کو بیٹھ رہنے والوں پر کہیں فضیلت بخشی ہے ﴿۹۵﴾
(یعنی) خدا کی طرف سے درجات میں اور بخشش میں اور
رحمت میں۔ اور خدا بڑا بخشنے والا (اور) مہربان ہے ﴿۹۶﴾

95. Not equal are those Believers who sit (at home), except those who are disabled. And those who strive and fight in the cause of Allah with their goods and their persons. Allah hath granted a grade higher to those who strive and fight with their goods and persons than to those who sit (at home). Unto all (in Faith) hath Allah promised good: but those who strive and fight hath He distinguished above those who sit (at home) by a great reward.,—

96. Ranks specially bestowed by Him and Forgiveness and Mercy. For Allah is Oft-Forgiving, Most Merciful.

اِنَّ الَّذِيْنَ تَوَفّٰهُمُ الْمَلٰٓئِكَةُ ظَالِمِيْۤ
اَنْفُسِهِمْ قَالُوْا فِيْمَ كُنْتُمْ ؕ قَالُوْا كُنَّا
مُسْتَضْعَفِيْنَ فِي الْاَرْضِ ؕ قَالُوْۤا اَلَمْ
تَكُنْ اَرْضُ اللّٰهِ وَاسِعَةً فَتُهَاجِرُوْا
فِيْهَا ؕ فَاُولٰٓئِكَ مَاْوٰىهُمْ جَهَنَّمُ ؕ وَسَآءَتْ

جو لوگ اپنی جانوں پر ظلم کرتے ہیں جب فرشتے اُن کی
جان قبض کرنے لگتے ہیں تو اُن سے پوچھتے ہیں کہ تم کس
حال میں تھے۔ وہ کہتے ہیں کہ ہم مُلک میں عاجز و ناتوان
تھے۔ فرشتے کہتے ہیں کیا خدا کا ملک فراخ نہیں تھا
کہ تم اُس میں ہجرت کر جاتے۔ ایسے لوگوں کا ٹھکانا دوزخ ہے

97. When angels take the souls of those who die in sin against their souls, they say: "In what (plight) were ye ?" They reply: "Weak and oppressed were we in the earth". They say: "Was not the earth of Allah spacious enough for you to move yourselves away (from evil)?"

Such men will find their abode in Hell.—What an evil Refuge!—

98. Except those who are (really) weak and oppressed—men, women, and children who have no means in their power, nor can they find a way (to escape)

99. For these, there is hope that Allah will forgive: for Allah doth blot out (sins) and forgive again and again.

100. He who forsakes his home in the cause of Allah, finds in the earth many a refuge. And abundance should he die as a refugee from home for Allah and His Messenger, His reward becomes due and sure with Allah: and Allah is Oft-Forgiving Most Merciful.

101. When ye travel through the earth, there is no blame on you if ye shorten your prayers, for fear the Unbelievers may attack you: for the Unbelievers are unto you open enemies.

102. When thou (O Messenger) art with them, and standest to lead them in prayer, let one party of them stand up (in prayer) with thee. Taking their arms with them: when they finish their prostrations, let them take their position in the rear, and let the other party come up which hath not yet prayed—and let them pray with thee, taking all precautions, and bearing arms: the Unbelievers wish, if ye were negligent of your arms and your baggage, to assault you in a single rush. But there is no blame on you if ye put away your arms because of the inconvenience of rain or because ye are ill; but take (every) precaution for yourselves. For the Unbelievers Allah hath prepared a humiliating punishment.

اور وہ بری جگہ ہے ﴿٩٧﴾
ہاں جو مرد اور عورتیں اور بچے بے بس ہیں کہ نہ تو
کوئی چارہ کر سکتے ہیں اور نہ رستہ جانتے
ہیں ﴿٩٨﴾
قریب ہے کہ خدا ایسوں کو معاف کر دے۔
اور خدا معاف کرنے والا (اور) بخشنے والا ہے ﴿٩٩﴾
اور جو شخص خدا کی راہ میں گھر بار چھوڑ جائے
وہ زمین میں بہت سی جگہ اور کشائش پائیگا۔ اور جو شخص
خدا اور اُس کے رسول کی طرف ہجرت کر کے گھر سے
نکل جائے پھر اُس کو موت آ پکڑے۔ تو اس کا ثواب
خدا کے ذمے ہو چکا۔ اور خدا بخشنے والا مہربان ہے ﴿١٠٠﴾
اور جب تم سفر کو جاؤ تو تم پر کچھ گناہ نہیں کہ نماز کو
کم کر کے پڑھو بشرطیکہ تم کو خوف ہو کہ کافر لوگ تم کو
ایذا دیں گے۔ بے شک کافر تمہارے کھلے دشمن
ہیں ف۹ ﴿١٠١﴾
اور (اے پیغمبر) جب تم اُن (مجاہدین کے لشکر)
میں ہو اور اُن کو نماز پڑھانے لگو تو چاہیئے
کہ اُن کی ایک جماعت تمہارے ساتھ مسلح ہو کر
کھڑی رہے۔ جب وہ سجدہ کر چکیں تو پرے
ہو جائیں پھر دوسری جماعت جس نے نماز نہیں پڑھی
(اُنکی جگہ) آئے اور ہوشیار اور مسلح ہو کر تمہارے ساتھ نماز
ادا کرے۔ کافر اس گھات میں ہیں کہ تم ذرا اپنے
ہتھیاروں اور سامان سے غافل ہو جاؤ کہ تم پر
یکبارگی حملہ کر دیں۔ اگر تم بارش کے سبب
تکلیف میں ہو یا بیمار ہو تو تم پر کچھ گناہ نہیں کہ ہتھیار
اُتار رکھو مگر ہوشیار ضرور رہنا خدا نے کافروں کے لئے
ذلت کا عذاب تیار کر رکھا ہے ﴿١٠٢﴾

مَصِيرًا ﴿٩٧﴾
إِلَّا الْمُسْتَضْعَفِينَ مِنَ الرِّجَالِ
وَالنِّسَاءِ وَالْوِلْدَانِ لَا يَسْتَطِيعُونَ
حِيلَةً وَلَا يَهْتَدُونَ سَبِيلًا ﴿٩٨﴾
فَأُولَٰئِكَ عَسَى اللَّهُ أَنْ يَعْفُوَ عَنْهُمْ
وَكَانَ اللَّهُ عَفُوًّا غَفُورًا ﴿٩٩﴾
وَمَنْ يُهَاجِرْ فِي سَبِيلِ اللَّهِ يَجِدْ
فِي الْأَرْضِ مُرَاغَمًا كَثِيرًا وَسَعَةً وَمَنْ
يَخْرُجْ مِنْ بَيْتِهِ مُهَاجِرًا إِلَى اللَّهِ وَ
رَسُولِهِ ثُمَّ يُدْرِكْهُ الْمَوْتُ فَقَدْ وَقَعَ
ع أَجْرُهُ عَلَى اللَّهِ وَكَانَ اللَّهُ غَفُورًا رَحِيمًا ﴿١٠٠﴾
وَإِذَا ضَرَبْتُمْ فِي الْأَرْضِ فَلَيْسَ عَلَيْكُمْ
جُنَاحٌ أَنْ تَقْصُرُوا مِنَ الصَّلَاةِ
إِنْ خِفْتُمْ أَنْ يَفْتِنَكُمُ الَّذِينَ كَفَرُوا
إِنَّ الْكَافِرِينَ كَانُوا لَكُمْ عَدُوًّا مُبِينًا ﴿١٠١﴾
وَإِذَا كُنْتَ فِيهِمْ فَأَقَمْتَ لَهُمُ الصَّلَاةَ
فَلْتَقُمْ طَائِفَةٌ مِنْهُمْ مَعَكَ وَ
لْيَأْخُذُوا أَسْلِحَتَهُمْ فَإِذَا سَجَدُوا
فَلْيَكُونُوا مِنْ وَرَائِكُمْ وَلْتَأْتِ
طَائِفَةٌ أُخْرَىٰ لَمْ يُصَلُّوا فَلْيُصَلُّوا
مَعَكَ وَلْيَأْخُذُوا حِذْرَهُمْ وَأَسْلِحَتَهُمْ
وَدَّ الَّذِينَ كَفَرُوا لَوْ تَغْفُلُونَ عَنْ
أَسْلِحَتِكُمْ وَأَمْتِعَتِكُمْ فَيَمِيلُونَ
عَلَيْكُمْ مَيْلَةً وَاحِدَةً وَلَا جُنَاحَ
عَلَيْكُمْ إِنْ كَانَ بِكُمْ أَذًى مِنْ مَطَرٍ أَوْ
كُنْتُمْ مَرْضَىٰ أَنْ تَضَعُوا أَسْلِحَتَكُمْ وَخُذُوا
حِذْرَكُمْ إِنَّ اللَّهَ أَعَدَّ لِلْكَافِرِينَ عَذَابًا مُهِينًا ﴿١٠٢﴾

103. When ye have performed the prayers, remember Allah, standing, sitting down, or lying down on your sides; but when ye are free from danger, set up regular Prayers: for such prayers are enjoined on Believers at stated times.

104. And slacken not in following up the enemy: if ye are suffering hardships, they are suffering similar hardships: but you hope from Allah, what they have not. And Allah is full of knowledge and wisdom.

105. We have sent down to thee the Book in truth, that thou mightest judge between people by that which Allah has shown thee; so be not an advocate for those who betray their trust;

106. But seek the forgiveness of Allah; for Allah is Oft-Forgiving, Most Merciful.

107. Contend not on behalf of such as betray their own souls; for Allah loveth not one given to perfidy and sin:—

108. They seek to hide themselves from the people but they cannot hide from Allah, while he is with them when they plot by night. In words that He cannot approve: and Allah doth ompass round all that they do.

109. Ah ! these are the sort of men on whose behalf ye may contend in this world; but who will contend with Allah on their behalf on the Day of Judgment, or who will carry their affairs through?

110. If anyone does evil or wrongs his own soul but afterwards seeks Allah's Forgiveness, he will find Allah Oft-Forgiving, Most Merciful.

111. And if anyone earns sin, he earns it against his own soul: for Allah is full of knowledge and wisdom.

112. But if anyone earns a fault or a sin and throws it on to one that is

پھر جب تم نماز تمام کر چکو تو کھڑے اور بیٹھے اور لیٹے (ہر
حالت میں) خدا کو یاد کرو۔ پھر جب خوف جاتا رہے تو (اس طرح
سے) نماز پڑھو (جس طرح امن کی حالت میں پڑھتے ہو)
بیشک نماز کا مومنوں پر اوقات (مقررہ) میں ادا کرنا فرض ہے ﴿۱۰۳﴾
اور کفار کے پیچھا کرنے میں سستی نہ کرنا۔ اگر تم بے آرام
ہوتے ہو تو جس طرح تم بے آرام ہوتے ہو اسی طرح
وہ بھی بے آرام ہوتے ہیں اور تم خدا سے ایسی ایسی امیدیں رکھتے ہو جو
وہ نہیں رکھ سکتے اور خدا سب کچھ جانتا اور بڑی حکمت والا ہے ﴿۱۰۴﴾
(اے پیغمبر) ہم نے تم پر سچی کتاب نازل کی ہے تاکہ
خدا کی ہدایات کے مطابق لوگوں کے مقدمات فیصل کرو
اور (دیکھو) دغابازوں کی حمایت میں کبھی بحث نہ کرنا ﴿۱۰۵﴾
اور خدا سے بخشش مانگنا۔ بے شک خدا بخشنے والا
مہربان ہے ﴿۱۰۶﴾
اور جو لوگ اپنے ہم جنسوں کی خیانت کرتے ہیں ان کی طرف سے
بحث نہ کرنا کیونکہ خدا خائن اور مرتکب جرائم کو دوست نہیں رکھتا ﴿۱۰۷﴾
یہ لوگوں سے تو چھپتے ہیں اور خدا سے نہیں چھپتے
حالانکہ جب وہ راتوں کو ایسی باتوں کے مشورے کیا کرتے
ہیں جن کو وہ پسند نہیں کرتا تو ان کے ساتھ ہوا کرتا ہے اور
خدا ان کے (تمام) کاموں پر احاطہ کئے ہوئے ہے ﴿۱۰۸﴾
بھلا تم لوگ دنیا کی زندگی میں تو ان کی طرف سے
بحث کر لیتے ہو قیامت کو ان کی طرف سے خدا کے ساتھ
کون جھگڑے گا اور کون ان کا وکیل بنے گا ﴿۱۰۹﴾
اور جو شخص کوئی برا کام کر بیٹھے یا اپنے حق میں ظلم کرلے
پھر خدا سے بخشش مانگے تو خدا کو بخشنے والا اور مہربان پائے گا ﴿۱۱۰﴾
اور جو کوئی گناہ کرتا ہے تو اس کا وبال اسی پر ہے
اور خدا جاننے والا (اور) حکمت والا ہے ﴿۱۱۱﴾
اور جو شخص کوئی قصور یا گناہ تو خود کرے لیکن اس سے کسی بے گناہ

فَاِذَا قَضَيْتُمُ الصَّلٰوةَ فَاذْكُرُوا اللّٰهَ
قِيَامًا وَّقُعُوْدًا وَّعَلٰى جُنُوْبِكُمْ ۚ فَاِذَا
اطْمَاْنَنْتُمْ فَاَقِيْمُوا الصَّلٰوةَ ۚ اِنَّ الصَّلٰوةَ
كَانَتْ عَلَى الْمُؤْمِنِيْنَ كِتٰبًا مَّوْقُوْتًا ﴿۱۰۳﴾
وَلَا تَهِنُوْا فِي ابْتِغَآءِ الْقَوْمِ ؕ اِنْ تَكُوْنُوْا
تَاْلَمُوْنَ فَاِنَّهُمْ يَاْلَمُوْنَ كَمَا تَاْلَمُوْنَ ۚ
وَتَرْجُوْنَ مِنَ اللّٰهِ مَا لَا يَرْجُوْنَ ؕ وَ
كَانَ اللّٰهُ عَلِيْمًا حَكِيْمًا ﴿۱۰۴﴾ ع
اِنَّآ اَنْزَلْنَآ اِلَيْكَ الْكِتٰبَ بِالْحَقِّ لِتَحْكُمَ
بَيْنَ النَّاسِ بِمَآ اَرٰىكَ اللّٰهُ ؕ وَلَا تَكُنْ
لِّلْخَآئِنِيْنَ خَصِيْمًا ﴿۱۰۵﴾
وَّاسْتَغْفِرِ اللّٰهَ ؕ اِنَّ اللّٰهَ كَانَ غَفُوْرًا
رَّحِيْمًا ﴿۱۰۶﴾
وَلَا تُجَادِلْ عَنِ الَّذِيْنَ يَخْتَانُوْنَ اَنْفُسَهُمْ ؕ
اِنَّ اللّٰهَ لَا يُحِبُّ مَنْ كَانَ خَوَّانًا اَثِيْمًا ﴿۱۰۷﴾
يَّسْتَخْفُوْنَ مِنَ النَّاسِ وَلَا يَسْتَخْفُوْنَ
مِنَ اللّٰهِ وَهُوَ مَعَهُمْ اِذْ يُبَيِّتُوْنَ
مَا لَا يَرْضٰى مِنَ الْقَوْلِ ؕ وَكَانَ اللّٰهُ
بِمَا يَعْمَلُوْنَ مُحِيْطًا ﴿۱۰۸﴾
هٰۤاَنْتُمْ هٰۤؤُلَآءِ جٰدَلْتُمْ عَنْهُمْ فِي
الْحَيٰوةِ الدُّنْيَا ۫ فَمَنْ يُّجَادِلُ اللّٰهَ عَنْهُمْ
يَوْمَ الْقِيٰمَةِ اَمْ مَّنْ يَّكُوْنُ عَلَيْهِمْ وَكِيْلًا ﴿۱۰۹﴾
وَمَنْ يَّعْمَلْ سُوْٓءًا اَوْ يَظْلِمْ نَفْسَهٗ ثُمَّ
يَسْتَغْفِرِ اللّٰهَ يَجِدِ اللّٰهَ غَفُوْرًا رَّحِيْمًا ﴿۱۱۰﴾
وَمَنْ يَّكْسِبْ اِثْمًا فَاِنَّمَا يَكْسِبُهٗ
عَلٰى نَفْسِهٖ ؕ وَكَانَ اللّٰهُ عَلِيْمًا حَكِيْمًا ﴿۱۱۱﴾
وَمَنْ يَّكْسِبْ خَطِيْٓئَةً اَوْ اِثْمًا ثُمَّ يَرْمِ

innocent, He carries (on himself) (both) a false charge and a flagrant sin.

113. But for the Grace of Allah to thee and His Mercy, a party of them would certainly have plotted to lead thee astray. But (in fact) they will only lead their own souls astray, and to thee they can do no harm in the least. For Allah hath sent down to thee the Book and Wisdom and taught thee what thou knewest not (before): and great is the Grace of Allah unto thee.

114. In most of their secret talks there is no good: but if one exhorts to a deed of charity or goodness or conciliation between people (secrecy is permissible): to him who does this, seeking the good pleasure of Allah, We shall soon give a reward of the highest (value).

115. If anyone contends with the Messenger even after guidance has been plainly conveyed to him, and follows a path other than that becoming to men to Faith, We shall leave him in the path he has chosen, and land him in Hell,—what an evil refuge !

116. Allah forgiveth not (the sin of) joining other gods with Him; but He forgiveth whom He pleaseth other sins than this: one who joins other gods with Allah, hath strayed far, far away (from the Right).

117. (The Pagans), leaving Him, call but upon female deities: they call but upon Satan the persistent rebel !

118. Allah did curse him, but he said: "I will take of Thy servants a portion marked off:

119. "I will mislead them, and I will create in them false desires; I will order them to slit the ears of cattle, and to deface the (fair) nature created by Allah," Whoever, forsaking Allah, takes Satan for a friend, hath of a surety suffered a

کو متہم کردے تو اُس نے بہتان اور صریح گناہ کا بوجھ اپنے سر رکھا ﴿١١٢﴾
اور اگر تم پر خدا کا فضل اور مہربانی نہ ہوتی تو ان میں
سے ایک جماعت تم کو بہکانے کا قصد کر ہی چکی تھی۔ اور
یہ اپنے سوا (کسی کو) بہکا نہیں سکتے اور نہ تمہارا کچھ بگاڑ
سکتے ہیں۔ اور خدا نے تم پر کتاب اور دانائی نازل فرمائی
ہے اور تمہیں وہ باتیں سکھائی ہیں جو تم جانتے نہیں تھے
اور تم پر خدا کا بڑا فضل ہے ﴿١١٣﴾
ان لوگوں کی بہت سی مشورتیں اچھی نہیں ہاں
(اُس شخص کی مشورت اچھی ہو سکتی ہے) جو خیرات یا
نیک بات یا لوگوں میں صلح کرنے کو کہے۔ اور جو ایسے
کام خدا کی خوشنودی حاصل کرنے کے لئے کرے گا تو
ہم اُس کو بڑا ثواب دیں گے ﴿١١٤﴾
اور جو شخص سیدھا رستہ معلوم ہونے کے بعد پیغمبر کی
مخالفت کرے اور مومنوں کے رستے کے سوا اور
رستے پر چلے تو جدھر وہ چلتا ہے ہم اُسے اُدھر ہی چلنے دینگے
اور (قیامت کے دن) جہنم میں داخل کرینگے۔ اور وہ بُری جگہ ہے ﴿١١٥﴾
خدا اس گناہ کو نہیں بخشے گا کہ کسی کو اُس کا شریک بنایا جائے
اور اس کے سوا اور گناہ جس کو چاہے گا بخش دے گا۔
اور جس نے خدا کے ساتھ شریک بنایا وہ رستے سے دور جا پڑا ﴿١١٦﴾
یہ جو خدا کے سوا پرستش کرتے ہیں تو عورتوں ہی کی۔
اور پکارتے ہیں تو شیطان سرکش ہی کو ﴿١١٧﴾
جس پر خدا نے لعنت کی ہے (جو خدا سے) کہنے لگا میں تیرے
بندوں سے (غیر خدا کی نذر دلوا کر مال کا) ایک مقرر حصہ لے لیا کروں گا ﴿١١٨﴾
اور ان کو گمراہ کرتا اور اُمیدیں دلاتا رہوں گا اور یہ
سکھاتا رہوں گا کہ جانوروں کے کان چیرتے رہیں
اور (یہ بھی) کہتا رہوں گا کہ وہ خدا کی بنی ہوئی صورتوں
کو بدلتے رہیں۔ اور جس شخص نے خدا کو چھوڑ کر شیطان کو

ع ١٦ ١٤ بِهٖ بَرِيْٓـًٔا فَقَدِ احْتَمَلَ بُهْتَانًا وَّاِثْمًا مُّبِيْنًا ع ﴿١١٢﴾
وَلَوْلَا فَضْلُ اللّٰهِ عَلَيْكَ وَرَحْمَتُهٗ
لَهَمَّتْ طَّآئِفَةٌ مِّنْهُمْ اَنْ يُّضِلُّوْكَ ؕ وَمَا
يُضِلُّوْنَ اِلَّآ اَنْفُسَهُمْ وَمَا يَضُرُّوْنَكَ
مِنْ شَيْءٍ ؕ وَاَنْزَلَ اللّٰهُ عَلَيْكَ الْكِتٰبَ
وَالْحِكْمَةَ وَعَلَّمَكَ مَا لَمْ تَكُنْ تَعْلَمُ ؕ
وَكَانَ فَضْلُ اللّٰهِ عَلَيْكَ عَظِيْمًا ﴿١١٣﴾ النصف
لَا خَيْرَ فِيْ كَثِيْرٍ مِّنْ نَّجْوٰىهُمْ اِلَّا
مَنْ اَمَرَ بِصَدَقَةٍ اَوْ مَعْرُوْفٍ اَوْ
اِصْلَاحٍۢ بَيْنَ النَّاسِ ؕ وَمَنْ يَّفْعَلْ
ذٰلِكَ ابْتِغَآءَ مَرْضَاتِ اللّٰهِ فَسَوْفَ
نُؤْتِيْهِ اَجْرًا عَظِيْمًا ﴿١١٤﴾
وَمَنْ يُّشَاقِقِ الرَّسُوْلَ مِنْۢ بَعْدِ مَا
تَبَيَّنَ لَهُ الْهُدٰى وَيَتَّبِعْ غَيْرَ سَبِيْلِ
الْمُؤْمِنِيْنَ نُوَلِّهٖ مَا تَوَلّٰى وَنُصْلِهٖ
ع ١٧ ١٥ جَهَنَّمَ ؕ وَسَآءَتْ مَصِيْرًا ع ﴿١١٥﴾
اِنَّ اللّٰهَ لَا يَغْفِرُ اَنْ يُّشْرَكَ بِهٖ وَيَغْفِرُ
مَا دُوْنَ ذٰلِكَ لِمَنْ يَّشَآءُ ؕ وَمَنْ
يُّشْرِكْ بِاللّٰهِ فَقَدْ ضَلَّ ضَلٰلًۢا بَعِيْدًا ﴿١١٦﴾
اِنْ يَّدْعُوْنَ مِنْ دُوْنِهٖٓ اِلَّآ اِنٰثًا ۚ
وَاِنْ يَّدْعُوْنَ اِلَّا شَيْطٰنًا مَّرِيْدًا ﴿١١٧﴾
وقف لازم لَّعَنَهُ اللّٰهُ ۘ وَقَالَ لَاَتَّخِذَنَّ مِنْ
عِبَادِكَ نَصِيْبًا مَّفْرُوْضًا ﴿١١٨﴾
وَّلَاُضِلَّنَّهُمْ وَلَاُمَنِّيَنَّهُمْ وَلَاٰمُرَنَّهُمْ
فَلَيُبَتِّكُنَّ اٰذَانَ الْاَنْعَامِ وَلَاٰمُرَنَّهُمْ
فَلَيُغَيِّرُنَّ خَلْقَ اللّٰهِ ؕ وَمَنْ يَّتَّخِذِ
الشَّيْطٰنَ وَلِيًّا مِّنْ دُوْنِ اللّٰهِ فَقَدْ

loss that is manifest.

120. Satan makes them promises, and creates in them false hopes, but Satan's promises are nothing but deception.
121. They (his dupes) will have their dwelling in Hell, and from it they will find no way of escape.

122. But those who believe and do deeds of righteousness,—We shall soon admit them to Gardens, with rivers flowing beneath,—to dwell therein for ever. Allah's promise is the truth, and whose word can be truer than Allah's ?

123. Not your desires, nor those of the People of the Book (can prevail): whoever works evil, will be requited accordingly. Nor will he find, besides Allah, any protector or helper.
124. If any do deeds of righteousness,—be they male or female—and have faith, they will enter Heaven, and not the least injustice will be done to them.

125. Who can be better in religion than one who submits his whole self to Allah, does good, and follows the way of Abraham the true in faith? For Allah did take Abraham for a friend.

126. But to Allah belong all things in the heavens and on earth: and He it is that encompasseth all things.
127. They ask thy instruction concerning the Women. Say: Allah doth instruct you about them: and (remember) what hath been rehearsed unto you in the Book, concerning the orphaned women to whom ye give not the portions prescribed, and yet whom ye desire

دوست بنایا وہ صریح نقصان میں پڑ گیا (۱۱۹)
وہ ان کو وعدے دیتا ہے اور اُمیدیں دلاتا ہے اور جو کچھ
شیطان اُنہیں وعدے دیتا ہے وہ دھوکا ہی دھوکا ہے (۱۲۰)
ایسے لوگوں کا ٹھکانا جہنم ہے اور وہ وہاں سے مخلصی
نہیں پا سکیں گے (۱۲۱)
اور جو لوگ ایمان لائے اور نیک کام کرتے رہے اُن
کو ہم بہشتوں میں داخل کریں گے جن کے نیچے نہریں
جاری ہیں۔ ابدالآباد اُن میں رہیں گے۔
یہ خدا کا سچا وعدہ ہے اور خدا سے زیادہ بات کا سچا
کون ہو سکتا ہے (۱۲۲)
(نجات) نہ تو تمہاری آرزوؤں پر ہے اور نہ اہلِ کتاب کی
آرزوؤں پر۔ جو شخص بُرے عمل کرے گا اُسے اُسی طرح کا بدلہ
دیا جائے گا اور وہ خدا کے سوا نہ کسی کو حمایتی پائے گا اور نہ مددگار (۱۲۳)
اور جو نیک کام کرے گا مرد ہو یا عورت اور وہ صاحب
ایمان بھی ہوگا تو ایسے لوگ بہشت میں داخل ہوں گے
اور اُن کی تل برابر بھی حق تلفی نہ کی جائے گی (۱۲۴)
اور اس شخص سے کس کا دین اچھا ہو سکتا ہے
جس نے حکمِ خدا کو قبول کیا اور وہ نیکوکار بھی ہے
اور ابراہیم کے دین کا پیرو ہے جو یکسو (مسلمان) تھے۔ اور خدا نے
ابراہیم کو اپنا دوست بنایا تھا (۱۲۵)
اور آسمان اور زمین میں جو کچھ ہے سب خدا ہی کا ہے
اور خدا ہر چیز پر احاطہ کئے ہوئے ہے (۱۲۶)
(اے پیغمبر) لوگ تم سے (یتیم) عورتوں کے بارے میں فتویٰ
طلب کرتے ہیں۔ کہہ دو کہ خدا تم کو اُنکے (ساتھ نکاح کرنے کے)
معاملے میں اجازت دیتا ہے اور جو حکم اس کتاب میں پہلے
دیا گیا ہے وہ ان یتیم عورتوں کے بارے میں ہے جن کو تم اُن کا
حق تو دیتے نہیں اور خواہش رکھتے ہو کہ اُن کے

خَسِرَ خُسْرَانًا مُّبِيْنًا ﴿١١٩﴾
يَعِدُهُمْ وَيُمَنِّيْهِمْ ۭ وَمَا يَعِدُهُمُ
الشَّيْطٰنُ اِلَّا غُرُوْرًا ﴿١٢٠﴾
اُولٰۗىِٕكَ مَاْوٰىهُمْ جَهَنَّمُ ۡ وَلَا يَجِدُوْنَ
عَنْهَا مَحِيْصًا ﴿١٢١﴾
وَالَّذِيْنَ اٰمَنُوْا وَعَمِلُوا الصّٰلِحٰتِ
سَنُدْخِلُهُمْ جَنّٰتٍ تَجْرِيْ مِنْ
تَحْتِهَا الْاَنْهٰرُ خٰلِدِيْنَ فِيْهَآ اَبَدًا ۭ
وَعْدَ اللّٰهِ حَقًّا ۭ وَمَنْ اَصْدَقُ مِنَ
اللّٰهِ قِيْلًا ﴿١٢٢﴾
لَيْسَ بِاَمَانِيِّكُمْ وَلَآ اَمَانِيِّ اَهْلِ
الْكِتٰبِ ۭ مَنْ يَّعْمَلْ سُوْۗءًا يُّجْزَ بِهٖ ۙ وَلَا
يَجِدْ لَهٗ مِنْ دُوْنِ اللّٰهِ وَلِيًّا وَّلَا نَصِيْرًا ﴿١٢٣﴾
وَمَنْ يَّعْمَلْ مِنَ الصّٰلِحٰتِ مِنْ ذَكَرٍ اَوْ
اُنْثٰى وَهُوَ مُؤْمِنٌ فَاُولٰۗىِٕكَ يَدْخُلُوْنَ
الْجَنَّةَ وَلَا يُظْلَمُوْنَ نَقِيْرًا ﴿١٢٤﴾
وَمَنْ اَحْسَنُ دِيْنًا مِّمَّنْ اَسْلَمَ
وَجْهَهٗ لِلّٰهِ وَهُوَ مُحْسِنٌ وَّاتَّبَعَ مِلَّةَ
اِبْرٰهِيْمَ حَنِيْفًا ۭ وَاتَّخَذَ اللّٰهُ
اِبْرٰهِيْمَ خَلِيْلًا ﴿١٢٥﴾
وَلِلّٰهِ مَا فِي السَّمٰوٰتِ وَمَا فِي الْاَرْضِ ۭ
وَكَانَ اللّٰهُ بِكُلِّ شَيْءٍ مُّحِيْطًا ﴿١٢٦﴾ ع
وَيَسْتَفْتُوْنَكَ فِي النِّسَاۗءِ ۭ قُلِ اللّٰهُ
يُفْتِيْكُمْ فِيْهِنَّ ۙ وَمَا يُتْلٰى عَلَيْكُمْ
فِي الْكِتٰبِ فِيْ يَتٰمَى النِّسَاۗءِ الّٰتِيْ لَا
تُؤْتُوْنَهُنَّ مَا كُتِبَ لَهُنَّ وَتَرْغَبُوْنَ
اَنْ تَنْكِحُوْهُنَّ وَالْمُسْتَضْعَفِيْنَ

مِنَ الْوِلْدَانِ ۙ وَأَنْ تَقُومُوا لِلْيَتَامَىٰ
بِالْقِسْطِ ۚ وَمَا تَفْعَلُوا مِنْ خَيْرٍ
فَإِنَّ اللَّهَ كَانَ بِهِ عَلِيمًا ﴿١٢٧﴾
وَإِنِ امْرَأَةٌ خَافَتْ مِنْ بَعْلِهَا
نُشُوزًا أَوْ إِعْرَاضًا فَلَا جُنَاحَ
عَلَيْهِمَا أَنْ يُصْلِحَا بَيْنَهُمَا صُلْحًا ۚ
وَالصُّلْحُ خَيْرٌ ۗ وَأُحْضِرَتِ الْأَنْفُسُ
الشُّحَّ ۚ وَإِنْ تُحْسِنُوا وَتَتَّقُوا فَإِنَّ
اللَّهَ كَانَ بِمَا تَعْمَلُونَ خَبِيرًا ﴿١٢٨﴾
وَلَنْ تَسْتَطِيعُوا أَنْ تَعْدِلُوا بَيْنَ النِّسَاءِ
وَلَوْ حَرَصْتُمْ ۖ فَلَا تَمِيلُوا كُلَّ الْمَيْلِ
فَتَذَرُوهَا كَالْمُعَلَّقَةِ ۚ وَإِنْ تُصْلِحُوا
وَتَتَّقُوا فَإِنَّ اللَّهَ كَانَ غَفُورًا رَحِيمًا ﴿١٢٩﴾
وَإِنْ يَتَفَرَّقَا يُغْنِ اللَّهُ كُلًّا
مِنْ سَعَتِهِ ۚ وَكَانَ اللَّهُ وَاسِعًا
حَكِيمًا ﴿١٣٠﴾
وَلِلَّهِ مَا فِي السَّمَاوَاتِ وَمَا فِي الْأَرْضِ ۗ
وَلَقَدْ وَصَّيْنَا الَّذِينَ أُوتُوا الْكِتَابَ
مِنْ قَبْلِكُمْ وَإِيَّاكُمْ أَنِ اتَّقُوا اللَّهَ ۚ
وَإِنْ تَكْفُرُوا فَإِنَّ لِلَّهِ مَا فِي السَّمَاوَاتِ
وَمَا فِي الْأَرْضِ ۚ وَكَانَ اللَّهُ غَنِيًّا
حَمِيدًا ﴿١٣١﴾
وَلِلَّهِ مَا فِي السَّمَاوَاتِ وَمَا فِي الْأَرْضِ ۚ
وَكَفَىٰ بِاللَّهِ وَكِيلًا ﴿١٣٢﴾
إِنْ يَشَأْ يُذْهِبْكُمْ أَيُّهَا النَّاسُ وَيَأْتِ
بِآخَرِينَ ۚ وَكَانَ اللَّهُ عَلَىٰ ذَٰلِكَ قَدِيرًا ﴿١٣٣﴾
مَنْ كَانَ يُرِيدُ ثَوَابَ الدُّنْيَا

ساتھ نکاح کر لو اور (نیز) بیچارے بے کس بچوں کے
بارے میں۔ اور یہ (بھی حکم دیتا ہے) کہ یتیموں کے بارے میں انصاف پر
قائم رہو۔ اور جو بھلائی تم کرو گے خدا اُس کو جانتا ہے ﴿١٢٧﴾
اور اگر کسی عورت کو اپنے خاوند کی طرف سے زیادتی
یا بے رغبتی کا اندیشہ ہو تو میاں بیوی پر کچھ گناہ
نہیں کہ آپس میں کسی قرارداد پر صُلح کر لیں
اور صُلح خوب (چیز) ہے اور طبیعتیں تو بُخل کی طرف
مائل ہوتی ہیں ف۹۲ اور اگر تم نیکوکاری اور پرہیزگاری
کرو گے تو خدا تمہارے سب کاموں سے واقف ہے ﴿١٢٨﴾
اور تم خواہ کتنا ہی چاہو عورتوں میں ہرگز برابری نہیں کر سکو گے
تو ایسا بھی نہ کرنا کہ ایک ہی کی طرف ڈھل جاؤ۔ اور دوسری کو
(ایسی حالت میں) چھوڑ دو کہ گویا ادھر میں لٹک رہی ہے ف۹۳ اور اگر آپس میں
موافقت کر لو اور پرہیزگاری کرو تو خدا بخشنے والا مہربان ہے ﴿١٢٩﴾
اور اگر میاں بیوی (میں موافقت نہ ہو سکے) اور ایک دوسرے
سے جُدا ہو جائیں تو خدا ہر ایک کو اپنی دولت سے غنی کر دے گا
اور خدا بڑی کشائش والا اور حکمت والا ہے ﴿١٣٠﴾
اور جو کچھ آسمانوں میں اور جو کچھ زمین میں ہے سب خدا
ہی کا ہے اور جن لوگوں کو تم سے پہلے کتاب دی گئی تھی
اُن کو بھی اور (اے محمد) تم کو بھی ہم نے حکم تاکیدی کیا ہے
کہ خدا سے ڈرتے رہو۔ اور اگر کفر کرو گے تو (سمجھ رکھو کہ)
جو کچھ آسمانوں میں اور جو کچھ زمین میں ہے سب خدا ہی کا ہے
اور خدا بے پروا اور سزاوار حمد و ثنا ہے ﴿١٣١﴾
اور (پھر سُن رکھو کہ) جو کچھ آسمانوں میں اور جو کچھ زمین میں ہے
سب خدا ہی کا ہے۔ اور خدا ہی کارساز کافی ہے ﴿١٣٢﴾
لوگو اگر وہ چاہے تو تم کو فنا کر دے اور (تمہاری جگہ) اور
لوگوں کو پیدا کر دے۔ اور خدا اس بات پر قادر ہے ﴿١٣٣﴾
جو شخص دُنیا (میں عملوں) کی جزا کا طالب ہو تو

to marry, as also concerning the children who are weak and oppressed: that ye stand firm for justice to orphans. There is not a good deed which ye do, but Allah is well-acquainted therewith.

128. If a wife fears cruelty or desertion on her husband's part, there is no blame on them if they arrange an amicable settlement between themselves; and such settlement is best; even though men's souls are swayed by greed. But if ye do good and practise self-restraint, Allah is well-acquainted with all that ye do.

129. Ye are never able to do justice between wives even if it is your ardent desire: but turn not away (from a woman) altogether, so as to leave her (as it were) hanging (in the air). If ye come to a friendly understanding, and practise self-restraint, Allah is Oft-Forgiving, Most Merciful.

130. But if they separate Allah will provide abundance for each of them from His all-reaching bounty: for Allah is He that careth for all and is Wise.

131. To Allah belong all things in the heavens and on earth. Verily We have directed the People of the Book before you, and you (O Muslims) to fear Allah. But if ye deny Him, lo ! unto Allah belong all things in the heavens and on earth, and Allah is free of all wants, worthy of all praise.

132. Yea, unto Allah belong all things in the heavens and on earth, and enough is Allah to carry through all affairs.

133. If it were His Will, He could destroy you, O mankind, and create another race; for He hath power this to do.

134. If any one desires a reward in this life, in Allah's (gift) is the reward

فَعِنْدَ اللّٰهِ ثَوَابُ الدُّنْيَا وَالْاٰخِرَةِ ؕ
وَكَانَ اللّٰهُ سَمِيْعًۢا بَصِيْرًا ﴿۱۳۴﴾ ع ١٩ ١٦

خدا کے پاس دُنیا اور آخرت (دونوں) کیلئے اجر (موجود)
ہیں۔اور خدا سُنتا دیکھتا ہے (۱۳۴)

(both) of this life and of the Hereafter: for Allah is He that heareth and seeth (all things).

يٰۤاَيُّهَا الَّذِيْنَ اٰمَنُوْا كُوْنُوْا قَوّٰمِيْنَ
بِالْقِسْطِ شُهَدَآءَ لِلّٰهِ وَلَوْ عَلٰۤى
اَنْفُسِكُمْ اَوِ الْوَالِدَيْنِ وَالْاَقْرَبِيْنَ ۚ
اِنْ يَّكُنْ غَنِيًّا اَوْ فَقِيْرًا فَاللّٰهُ اَوْلٰى
بِهِمَا ۫ فَلَا تَتَّبِعُوا الْهَوٰۤى اَنْ
تَعْدِلُوْا ۚ وَاِنْ تَلْوٗۤا اَوْ تُعْرِضُوْا
فَاِنَّ اللّٰهَ كَانَ بِمَا تَعْمَلُوْنَ خَبِيْرًا ﴿۱۳۵﴾

اے ایمان والو! انصاف پر قائم رہو اور خدا کیلئے
سچی گواہی دو خواہ (اس میں) تمہارا یا تمہارے ماں باپ
اور رشتہ داروں کا نقصان ہی ہو۔ اگر کوئی امیر ہے یا
فقیر تو خدا اُن کا خیر خواہ ہے۔ تو تم خواہش نفس کے
پیچھے چل کر عدل کو نہ چھوڑ دینا۔ اگر تم پیچدار شہادت دو گے
یا (شہادت سے) بچنا چاہو گے تو (جان رکھو) خدا تمہارے
سب کاموں سے واقف ہے (۱۳۵)

135. O ye who believe ! stand out firmly for justice, as witnesses to Allah, even as against yourselves, or your parents, or your kin, and whether it be (against) rich or poor: for Allah can best protect both. Follow not the lusts (of your hearts), lest ye swerve, and if ye distort (justice) or decline to do justice, verily Allah is well-acquainted with all that ye do.

يٰۤاَيُّهَا الَّذِيْنَ اٰمَنُوْۤا اٰمِنُوْا بِاللّٰهِ وَ
رَسُوْلِهٖ وَالْكِتٰبِ الَّذِىْ نَزَّلَ عَلٰى
رَسُوْلِهٖ وَالْكِتٰبِ الَّذِىْۤ اَنْزَلَ مِنْ
قَبْلُ ؕ وَمَنْ يَّكْفُرْ بِاللّٰهِ وَمَلٰٓئِكَتِهٖ
وَكُتُبِهٖ وَرُسُلِهٖ وَالْيَوْمِ الْاٰخِرِ فَقَدْ
ضَلَّ ضَلٰلًاۢ بَعِيْدًا ﴿۱۳۶﴾

مومنو! خدا پر اور اُس کے رسول پر اور جو کتاب اُس
نے اپنے پیغمبر (آخر الزماں) پر نازل کی ہے اور جو
کتابیں اس سے پہلے نازل کی تھیں سب پر ایمان لاؤ۔
اور جو شخص خدا اور اُس کے فرشتوں اور اُسکی کتابوں
اور اُس کے پیغمبروں اور روز قیامت سے انکار کرے وہ
رستے سے بھٹک کر دور جا پڑا (۱۳۶)

136. O ye who believe ! believe in Allah and His Messenger, and the scripture which He hath sent to His Messenger and the scripture which He sent to those before (him). Any who denieth Allah, His angels, His Books, His Messengers, and the Day of Judgment, hath gone far, far astray.

اِنَّ الَّذِيْنَ اٰمَنُوْا ثُمَّ كَفَرُوْا ثُمَّ اٰمَنُوْا
ثُمَّ كَفَرُوْا ثُمَّ ازْدَادُوْا كُفْرًا لَّمْ يَكُنِ اللّٰهُ
لِيَغْفِرَ لَهُمْ وَلَا لِيَهْدِيَهُمْ سَبِيْلًا ؕ ﴿۱۳۷﴾
بَشِّرِ الْمُنٰفِقِيْنَ بِاَنَّ لَهُمْ عَذَابًا
اَلِيْمًا ۙ ﴿۱۳۸﴾
اۨلَّذِيْنَ يَتَّخِذُوْنَ الْكٰفِرِيْنَ اَوْلِيَآءَ مِنْ
دُوْنِ الْمُؤْمِنِيْنَ ؕ اَيَبْتَغُوْنَ عِنْدَهُمُ
الْعِزَّةَ فَاِنَّ الْعِزَّةَ لِلّٰهِ جَمِيْعًا ؕ ﴿۱۳۹﴾

جو لوگ ایمان لائے پھر کافر ہو گئے۔ پھر ایمان لائے
پھر کافر ہو گئے پھر کفر میں بڑھتے گئے اُن کو خدا نہ
تو بخشے گا اور نہ سیدھا رستہ دکھائے گا (۱۳۷)
(اے پیغمبر) منافقوں (یعنی دو رُخے لوگوں) کو بشارت
سُنا دو کہ اُن کیلئے دکھ دینے والا عذاب (تیار) ہے (۱۳۸)
جو مومنوں کو چھوڑ کر کافروں کو دوست بناتے ہیں۔ کیا
یہ اُن کے ہاں عزت حاصل کرنی چاہتے ہیں تو عزت تو
سب خدا ہی کی ہے (۱۳۹)

137. Those who believe, then reject Faith, then believe (again) and (again) reject Faith, and go on increasing in Unbelief,—Allah will not forgive them, nor guide them on the Way.

138. To the Hypocrites give the good tidings that there is for them a grievous Chastisement;—

139. Those who take for friends Unbelievers rather than Believers: is it honour they seek among them? Nay,— all honour is with Allah.

وَقَدْ نَزَّلَ عَلَيْكُمْ فِى الْكِتٰبِ اَنْ اِذَا
سَمِعْتُمْ اٰيٰتِ اللّٰهِ يُكْفَرُ بِهَا وَيُسْتَهْزَاُ بِهَا
فَلَا تَقْعُدُوْا مَعَهُمْ حَتّٰى يَخُوْضُوْا فِىْ حَدِيْثٍ
غَيْرِهٖۤ ۖ اِنَّكُمْ اِذًا مِّثْلُهُمْ ؕ اِنَّ اللّٰهَ جَامِعُ

اور خدا نے تم (مومنوں) پر اپنی کتاب میں (یہ حکم) نازل
فرمایا ہے کہ جب تم (کہیں) سُنو کہ خدا کی آیتوں سے انکار ہو رہا ہے
اور اُنکی ہنسی اُڑائی جاتی ہے تو جب تک وہ لوگ اور باتیں (نہ) کرنے
لگیں اُنکے پاس مت بیٹھو ورنہ تم بھی اُنہیں جیسے ہو جاؤ گے۔ کچھ

140. Already has He sent you in the Book, that when ye hear the Message of Allah held in defiance and ridicule, ye are not to sit with them unless they turn to a different theme: if ye did, ye would be like them. For Allah will collect the

الْمُنٰفِقِيْنَ وَالْكٰفِرِيْنَ فِيْ جَهَنَّمَ جَمِيْعًا ﴿۱۴۰﴾

شک نہیں کہ خدا منافقوں اور کافروں سب کو دوزخ میں اکٹھا کرنے والا ہے (۱۴۰)

Hypocrites and those who defy Faith—all in Hell;—

الَّذِيْنَ يَتَرَبَّصُوْنَ بِكُمْ ۚ فَاِنْ
كَانَ لَكُمْ فَتْحٌ مِّنَ اللّٰهِ قَالُوْٓا اَلَمْ
نَكُنْ مَّعَكُمْ ۖ وَاِنْ كَانَ لِلْكٰفِرِيْنَ
نَصِيْبٌ ۙ قَالُوْٓا اَلَمْ نَسْتَحْوِذْ عَلَيْكُمْ
وَنَمْنَعْكُمْ مِّنَ الْمُؤْمِنِيْنَ ۚ فَاللّٰهُ يَحْكُمُ
بَيْنَكُمْ يَوْمَ الْقِيٰمَةِ ۗ وَلَنْ يَّجْعَلَ اللّٰهُ
لِلْكٰفِرِيْنَ عَلَى الْمُؤْمِنِيْنَ سَبِيْلًا ﴿۱۴۱﴾ ع

جو تم کو دیکھتے رہتے ہیں۔ اگر خدا کی طرف سے
تم کو فتح ملے تو کہتے ہیں کیا ہم تمہارے ساتھ
نہ تھے۔ اور اگر کافروں کو (فتح) نصیب ہو تو
(ان سے) کہتے ہیں کہ کیا ہم تم پر غالب نہیں تھے
اور تم کو مسلمانوں (کے ہاتھ) سے بچایا نہیں تو خدا تم
میں قیامت کے دن فیصلہ کر دے گا اور خدا کافروں
کو مومنوں پر ہرگز غلبہ نہیں دے گا (۱۴۱)

141. (These are) the ones who wait and watch about you: if ye do gain a victory from Allah, they say: "Were we not with you ?"—but if the Unbelievers gain a success, they say (to them): "Did we not gain an advantage over you, and did we not guard you from the Believers?" But Allah will judge Betwixt you on the Day of Judgment. And never will Allah grant to the Unbelievers a way (to triumph) over the Believers.

اِنَّ الْمُنٰفِقِيْنَ يُخٰدِعُوْنَ اللّٰهَ وَهُوَ
خَادِعُهُمْ ۚ وَاِذَا قَامُوْٓا اِلَى الصَّلٰوةِ
قَامُوْا كُسَالٰى ۙ يُرَآءُوْنَ النَّاسَ وَلَا
يَذْكُرُوْنَ اللّٰهَ اِلَّا قَلِيْلًا ﴿۱۴۲﴾

منافق (ان چالوں سے اپنے نزدیک) خدا کو دھوکا دیتے ہیں۔
(یہ اسکو کیا دھوکا دینگے) وہ انہیں کو دھوکے میں ڈالنے والا ہے اور
جب یہ نماز کو کھڑے ہوتے ہیں تو سست اور کاہل ہو کر (صرف) لوگوں کے
دکھانے کو اور خدا کی یاد ہی نہیں کرتے مگر بہت کم (۱۴۲)

142. The Hypocrites— they seek to deceive Allah but it is Allah Who deceive them. When they stand up to prayer, they stand without earnestness, to be seen of men, but little do they hold Allah in remembrance;

مُّذَبْذَبِيْنَ بَيْنَ ذٰلِكَ ۖ لَآ اِلٰى
هٰٓؤُلَآءِ وَلَآ اِلٰى هٰٓؤُلَآءِ ۗ وَمَنْ يُّضْلِلِ
اللّٰهُ فَلَنْ تَجِدَ لَهٗ سَبِيْلًا ﴿۱۴۳﴾

بیچ میں پڑے لٹک رہے ہیں نہ ان کی طرف (ہوتے
ہیں) نہ ان کی طرف۔ اور جس کو خدا بھٹکائے تو تم اس
کے لئے کبھی بھی رستہ نہ پاؤ گے (۱۴۳)

143. (They are) wavering between this and that belonging neither to these nor those whom Allah leaves straying,— never wilt thou find for him the Way.

يٰٓاَيُّهَا الَّذِيْنَ اٰمَنُوْا لَا تَتَّخِذُوا الْكٰفِرِيْنَ
اَوْلِيَآءَ مِنْ دُوْنِ الْمُؤْمِنِيْنَ ۚ اَتُرِيْدُوْنَ
اَنْ تَجْعَلُوْا لِلّٰهِ عَلَيْكُمْ سُلْطٰنًا مُّبِيْنًا ﴿۱۴۴﴾

اے اہل ایمان مومنوں کے سوا کافروں کو دوست
نہ بناؤ۔ کیا تم چاہتے ہو کہ اپنے اوپر خدا کا
صریح الزام لو۔ (۱۴۴)

144. O ye who believe ! take not for friends Unbelievers rather than Believers: do ye wish to offer Allah an open proof against yourselves?

اِنَّ الْمُنٰفِقِيْنَ فِي الدَّرْكِ الْاَسْفَلِ
مِنَ النَّارِ ۚ وَلَنْ تَجِدَ لَهُمْ نَصِيْرًا ﴿۱۴۵﴾

کچھ شک نہیں کہ منافق لوگ دوزخ کے سب سے
نچلے درجے میں ہوں گے اور تم ان کا کسی کو مددگار نہ پاؤ گے (۱۴۵)

145. The Hypocrites will be in the lowest depths of the Fire: no helper wilt thou find for them;—

اِلَّا الَّذِيْنَ تَابُوْا وَاَصْلَحُوْا وَاعْتَصَمُوْا
بِاللّٰهِ وَاَخْلَصُوْا دِيْنَهُمْ لِلّٰهِ فَاُولٰٓئِكَ
مَعَ الْمُؤْمِنِيْنَ ۭ وَسَوْفَ يُؤْتِ اللّٰهُ
الْمُؤْمِنِيْنَ اَجْرًا عَظِيْمًا ﴿۱۴۶﴾

ہاں جنہوں نے توبہ کی اور اپنی حالت کو درست کیا اور
خدا (کی رسی) کو مضبوط پکڑا اور خاص خدا کے حکم بردار
ہو گئے تو ایسے لوگ مومنوں کے زمرے میں ہوں گے
اور خدا عنقریب مومنوں کو بڑا ثواب دے گا (۱۴۶)

146. Except for those who repent, mend (their life), hold fast to Allah, and make their religious devotion sincere to Allah: if so they will be (numbered) with the Believers. And soon will Allah grant to the Believers a reward of immense value.

مَا يَفْعَلُ اللّٰهُ بِعَذَابِكُمْ اِنْ شَكَرْتُمْ
وَاٰمَنْتُمْ ۭ وَكَانَ اللّٰهُ شَاكِرًا عَلِيْمًا ﴿۱۴۷﴾

اگر تم (خدا کے) شکر گزار رہو اور (اس پر) ایمان لے آؤ تو
خدا تم کو عذاب دے کر کیا کرے گا۔ اور خدا تو قدر شناس (اور) دانا ہے (۱۴۷)

147. What can Allah gain by your punishment, if ye are grateful and ye believe ? Nay, it is Allah That recogniseth (all good), and knoweth all things.

148. Allah loveth not the shouting of evil words in public speech, except by one who has been wronged, for Allah is He Who heareth and knoweth all things.

خدا اس بات کو پسند نہیں کرتا کہ کوئی کسی کو علانیہ بُرا
کہے مگر وہ جو مظلوم ہو۔ اور خدا (سب کچھ)
سُنتا (اور) جانتا ہے ﴿١٤٨﴾

لَا يُحِبُّ اللّٰهُ الْجَهْرَ بِالسُّوْٓءِ مِنَ
الْقَوْلِ اِلَّا مَنْ ظُلِمَ ؕ وَكَانَ اللّٰهُ
سَمِيْعًا عَلِيْمًا ﴿١٤٨﴾

149. Whether you do openly a good deed or conceal it or cover evil with pardon, surely Allah is ever pardoning Powerful.

اگر تم لوگ بھلائی کھلم کھلا کرو گے یا چھپا کر۔ یا بُرائی سے درگزر
کرو گے تو خدا بھی معاف کرنے والا (اور) صاحب قدرت ہے ﴿١٤٩﴾

اِنْ تُبْدُوْا خَيْرًا اَوْ تُخْفُوْهُ اَوْ تَعْفُوْا عَنْ
سُوْٓءٍ فَاِنَّ اللّٰهَ كَانَ عَفُوًّا قَدِيْرًا ﴿١٤٩﴾

150. Those who deny Allah and His Messengers, and wish to separate between Allah and His Messengers, saying: "We believe in some but reject others": and wish to take a course midway,—

جو لوگ خدا سے اور اُس کے پیغمبروں سے کفر کرتے
ہیں اور خدا اور اُس کے پیغمبروں میں فرق کرنا چاہتے
ہیں اور کہتے ہیں کہ ہم بعض کو مانتے ہیں اور بعض کو نہیں
مانتے۔ اور ایمان اور کفر کے بیچ میں ایک راہ
نکالنی چاہتے ہیں ﴿١٥٠﴾

اِنَّ الَّذِيْنَ يَكْفُرُوْنَ بِاللّٰهِ وَرُسُلِهٖ
وَيُرِيْدُوْنَ اَنْ يُّفَرِّقُوْا بَيْنَ اللّٰهِ
وَرُسُلِهٖ وَيَقُوْلُوْنَ نُؤْمِنُ بِبَعْضٍ
وَّنَكْفُرُ بِبَعْضٍ ۙ وَّيُرِيْدُوْنَ اَنْ
يَّتَّخِذُوْا بَيْنَ ذٰلِكَ سَبِيْلًا ۙ ﴿١٥٠﴾

151. They are in truth Unbelievers; and We have prepared for Unbelievers a humiliating punishement.

وہ بلا اشتباہ کافر ہیں۔ اور کافروں کے لئے ہم
نے ذلت کا عذاب تیار کر رکھا ہے ﴿١٥١﴾

اُولٰٓئِكَ هُمُ الْكٰفِرُوْنَ حَقًّا ۚ وَاَعْتَدْنَا
لِلْكٰفِرِيْنَ عَذَابًا مُّهِيْنًا ﴿١٥١﴾

152. To those who believe in Allah and His messengers and make no distinction between any of the messengers, We shall soon give their (due) rewards: for Allah is Oft-Forgiving, Most Merciful.

اور جو لوگ خدا اور اُس کے پیغمبروں پر ایمان لائے
اور اُن میں سے کسی میں فرق نہ کیا (یعنی سب کو مانا)
ایسے لوگوں کو وہ عنقریب اُن (کی نیکیوں) کے صلے عطا
فرمائے گا۔ اور خدا بخشنے والا مہربان ہے ﴿١٥٢﴾

وَالَّذِيْنَ اٰمَنُوْا بِاللّٰهِ وَرُسُلِهٖ وَلَمْ
يُفَرِّقُوْا بَيْنَ اَحَدٍ مِّنْهُمْ اُولٰٓئِكَ
سَوْفَ يُؤْتِيْهِمْ اُجُوْرَهُمْ ؕ وَكَانَ
اللّٰهُ غَفُوْرًا رَّحِيْمًا ﴿١٥٢﴾ ع ٢١

153. The People of the Book ask thee to cause a book to descend to them from heaven: indeed they asked Moses for an even greater (miracle), for they said: "Show us Allah in public," but they were seized for their presumption, by thunder and lightning. Yet they worshipped the calf even after clear Signs had come to them; even so We forgave them; and gave Moses manifest proofs of authority.

(اے محمدؐ) اہل کتاب تم سے درخواست کرتے ہیں کہ تم اُن پر
ایک (لکھی ہوئی) کتاب آسمان سے اُتار لاؤ تو یہ موسیٰ سے
اس سے بھی بڑی بڑی درخواستیں کر چکے ہیں (اُن سے)
کہتے تھے ہمیں خدا کو ظاہر (یعنی آنکھوں سے) دکھا دو
سو اُن کے گناہ کی وجہ سے اُن کو بجلی نے آ پکڑا۔
پھر کھلی نشانیاں آئے پیچھے بچھڑے کو (معبود) بنا بیٹھے تو
اس سے بھی ہم نے درگزر کی۔ اور موسیٰ کو صریح غلبہ دیا ﴿١٥٣﴾

يَسْـَٔلُكَ اَهْلُ الْكِتٰبِ اَنْ تُنَزِّلَ
عَلَيْهِمْ كِتٰبًا مِّنَ السَّمَآءِ فَقَدْ سَاَلُوْا
مُوْسٰٓى اَكْبَرَ مِنْ ذٰلِكَ فَقَالُوْٓا
اَرِنَا اللّٰهَ جَهْرَةً فَاَخَذَتْهُمُ الصّٰعِقَةُ
بِظُلْمِهِمْ ۚ ثُمَّ اتَّخَذُوا الْعِجْلَ مِنْ
بَعْدِ مَا جَآءَتْهُمُ الْبَيِّنٰتُ فَعَفَوْنَا عَنْ
ذٰلِكَ ۚ وَاٰتَيْنَا مُوْسٰى سُلْطٰنًا مُّبِيْنًا ﴿١٥٣﴾

154. And for their Covenant We raised over them the Mount (Sinai); and (on another occasion) We said: "Enter the gate with humility"; and (once again) We commanded them: "Transgress not in the matter of the Sabbath." And We took from them a solemn Covenant.

اور اُن سے عہد لینے کو ہم نے اُن پر کوہ طور اُٹھا کھڑا کیا
اور اُنہیں حکم دیا کہ (شہر کے) دروازے میں (داخل ہونا تو) سجدہ
کرتے ہوئے داخل ہونا اور یہ بھی حکم دیا کہ ہفتے کے دن (مچھلیاں)
پکڑنے میں تجاوز (یعنی حکم کے خلاف) نہ کرنا غرض ہم نے اُن سے مضبوط عہد لیا ﴿١٥٤﴾

وَرَفَعْنَا فَوْقَهُمُ الطُّوْرَ بِمِيْثَاقِهِمْ
وَقُلْنَا لَهُمُ ادْخُلُوا الْبَابَ سُجَّدًا وَّ
قُلْنَا لَهُمْ لَا تَعْدُوْا فِي السَّبْتِ وَ
اَخَذْنَا مِنْهُمْ مِّيْثَاقًا غَلِيْظًا ﴿١٥٤﴾

فَبِمَا نَقْضِهِمْ مِّيْثَاقَهُمْ وَكُفْرِهِمْ
بِاٰيٰتِ اللّٰهِ وَقَتْلِهِمُ الْاَنْۢبِيَآءَ بِغَيْرِ
حَقٍّ وَّقَوْلِهِمْ قُلُوْبُنَا غُلْفٌ ؕ بَلْ
طَبَعَ اللّٰهُ عَلَيْهَا بِكُفْرِهِمْ فَلَا
يُؤْمِنُوْنَ اِلَّا قَلِيْلًا ﴿١٥٥﴾
وَّبِكُفْرِهِمْ وَقَوْلِهِمْ عَلٰى مَرْيَمَ
بُهْتَانًا عَظِيْمًا ﴿١٥٦﴾
وَّقَوْلِهِمْ اِنَّا قَتَلْنَا الْمَسِيْحَ عِيْسَى
ابْنَ مَرْيَمَ رَسُوْلَ اللّٰهِ ۚ وَمَا قَتَلُوْهُ
وَمَا صَلَبُوْهُ وَلٰكِنْ شُبِّهَ لَهُمْ ؕ
وَاِنَّ الَّذِيْنَ اخْتَلَفُوْا فِيْهِ لَفِيْ
شَكٍّ مِّنْهُ ؕ مَا لَهُمْ بِهٖ مِنْ
عِلْمٍ اِلَّا اتِّبَاعَ الظَّنِّ ۚ وَمَا قَتَلُوْهُ
يَقِيْنًا ﴿١٥٧﴾
بَلْ رَّفَعَهُ اللّٰهُ اِلَيْهِ ؕ وَكَانَ اللّٰهُ
عَزِيْزًا حَكِيْمًا ﴿١٥٨﴾
وَاِنْ مِّنْ اَهْلِ الْكِتٰبِ اِلَّا لَيُؤْمِنَنَّ بِهٖ
قَبْلَ مَوْتِهٖ ۚ وَيَوْمَ الْقِيٰمَةِ يَكُوْنُ عَلَيْهِمْ شَهِيْدًا ﴿١٥٩﴾
فَبِظُلْمٍ مِّنَ الَّذِيْنَ هَادُوْا حَرَّمْنَا
عَلَيْهِمْ طَيِّبٰتٍ اُحِلَّتْ لَهُمْ وَ
بِصَدِّهِمْ عَنْ سَبِيْلِ اللّٰهِ كَثِيْرًا ﴿١٦٠﴾
وَّاَخْذِهِمُ الرِّبٰوا وَقَدْ نُهُوْا عَنْهُ وَ
اَكْلِهِمْ اَمْوَالَ النَّاسِ بِالْبَاطِلِ ؕ وَ
اَعْتَدْنَا لِلْكٰفِرِيْنَ مِنْهُمْ عَذَابًا اَلِيْمًا ﴿١٦١﴾
لٰكِنِ الرّٰسِخُوْنَ فِي الْعِلْمِ مِنْهُمْ وَ
الْمُؤْمِنُوْنَ يُؤْمِنُوْنَ بِمَآ اُنْزِلَ
اِلَيْكَ وَمَآ اُنْزِلَ مِنْ قَبْلِكَ وَ

(لیکن اُنہوں نے عہد کو توڑ ڈالا) تو اُنکے عہد توڑ دینے اور خدا
کی آیتوں سے کفر کرنے اور انبیاء کو ناحق مار ڈالنے اور یہ کہنے کے
سبب کہ ہمارے دلوں پر پردے (پڑے ہوئے) ہیں (خدا نے انکو مردود
کر دیا۔ اور اُنکے دلوں پر پردے نہیں ہیں) بلکہ انکے کفر کے سبب
خدا نے اُن پر مُہر کر دی ہے تو یہ کم ہی ایمان لاتے ہیں ﴿١٥٥﴾
اور اُن کے کفر کے سبب اور مریم پر ایک بہتان عظیم
باندھنے کے سبب ﴿١٥٦﴾
اور یہ کہنے کے سبب کہ ہم نے مریم کے بیٹے عیسیٰ مسیح کو
جو خدا کے پیغمبر (کہلاتے) تھے قتل کر دیا ہے (خدا نے انکو ملعون کر دیا)
اور انہوں نے عیسیٰ کو قتل نہیں کیا اور نہ اُنہیں سُولی پر
چڑھایا بلکہ اُن کو اُن کی سی صورت معلوم ہوئی۔ اور جو لوگ
اُن کے بارے میں اختلاف کرتے ہیں وہ اُنکے حال سے
شک میں پڑے ہوئے ہیں۔ اور پیروی ظن کے سوا اُنکو اسکا
مطلق علم نہیں۔ اور اُنہوں نے عیسیٰ کو یقیناً قتل نہیں کیا ﴿١٥٧﴾
بلکہ خدا نے اُن کو اپنی طرف اُٹھا لیا۔ اور خدا غالب (اور)
حکمت والا ہے ﴿١٥٨﴾
اور کوئی اہل کتاب نہیں ہوگا مگر اُنکی موت سے پہلے اُن پر
ایمان لے آئیگا اور وہ قیامت کے دن اُن پر گواہ ہونگے ﴿١٥٩﴾
تو ہم نے یہودیوں کے ظلموں کے سبب (بہت سی)
پاکیزہ چیزیں جو اُن کو حلال تھیں حرام کر دیں۔ اور اس
سبب سے بھی کہ وہ اکثر خدا کے رستے سے (لوگوں کو) روکتے تھے ﴿١٦٠﴾
اور اس سبب سے بھی کہ باوجود منع کئے جانیکے سُود لیتے تھے اور
اس سبب سے بھی کہ لوگوں کا مال ناحق کھاتے تھے۔ اور ان میں سے جو کافر
ہیں اُنکے لئے ہم نے درد دینے والا عذاب تیار کر رکھا ہے ﴿١٦١﴾
مگر جو لوگ اُن میں سے علم میں پکے ہیں اور جو مومن
ہیں وہ اس (کتاب) پر جو تم پر نازل ہوئی اور جو
(کتابیں) تم سے پہلے نازل ہوئیں (سب پر) ایمان

155. (They have incurred divine displeasure): in that they broke their Covenant; that they rejected the Signs of Allah; that they slew the Messengers in defiance of right; that they said, "Our hearts are the Wrappings";—nay, Allah hath set the seal on their hearts for their blasphemy, and little is it they believe;—

156. That they rejected Faith; that they uttered against Mary a grave false charge;

157. That they said (in boast), "We killed Christ Jesus the son of Mary, the Messenger of Allah";— but they killed him not, nor crucified him. Only a likeness of that was shown to them. And those who differ therein are full of doubts, with no (certain) knowledge. But only conjecture to follow, for of a surety they killed him not:—

158. Nay, Allah raised him up unto Himself; and Allah is Exalted in Power, Wise;—

159. And there is none of the People of the Book but must believe in him before his death; and on the Day of Judgment He will be a witness against them;—

160. For the iniquity of the Jews We made unlawful for them certain (foods) good and wholesome which had been lawful for them;—and that they hindered many from Allah's Way;—

161. That they took usury, though they were forbidden; and that they devoured men's wealth wrongfully;— We have prepared for those among them who reject Faith a grievous chastisement.

162. But those among them who are well-grounded in knowledge, and the Believers, believe in what hath been revealed to thee and what was revealed before thee: and

(especially) those who establish regular prayer and pay Zakat and believe in Allah and in the Last Day: to them shall We soon give a great reward.

رکھتے ہیں اور نماز پڑھتے ہیں اور زکوٰۃ دیتے ہیں
اور خدا اور روزِ آخرت کو مانتے ہیں. اُن کو ہم
عنقریب اجرِ عظیم دیں گے ١٦٢

الْمُقِيْمِيْنَ الصَّلٰوةَ وَالْمُؤْتُوْنَ الزَّكٰوةَ
وَالْمُؤْمِنُوْنَ بِاللّٰهِ وَالْيَوْمِ الْاٰخِرِ ط
اُولٰٓئِكَ سَنُؤْتِيْهِمْ اَجْرًا عَظِيْمًا ١٦٢ ع

163. We have sent thee inspiration, as We sent it to Noah and the Messengers after him: We sent inspiration to Abraham. Ismā'īl, Isaac, Jacob and the Tribes, to Jesus, Job, Jonah, Aaron, and Solomon, and to David We gave the Psalms.

(اے محمدؐ) ہم نے تمہاری طرف اسی طرح وحی بھیجی
ہے جس طرح نوحؑ اور اُن سے پچھلے پیغمبروں کی
طرف بھیجی تھی. اور ابراہیم اور اسمٰعیل اور اسحٰق اور
یعقوب اور اولادِ یعقوب اور عیسیٰ اور ایوب اور
یُونس اور ہارُون اور سلیمان کی طرف بھی ہم نے وحی
بھیجی تھی اور داؤد کو ہم نے زبور بھی عنایت کی تھی ١٦٣

اِنَّآ اَوْحَيْنَآ اِلَيْكَ كَمَآ اَوْحَيْنَآ اِلٰى
نُوْحٍ وَّالنَّبِيّٖنَ مِنْۢ بَعْدِهٖ ۚ وَاَوْحَيْنَآ
اِلٰٓى اِبْرٰهِيْمَ وَاِسْمٰعِيْلَ وَاِسْحٰقَ وَ
يَعْقُوْبَ وَالْاَسْبَاطِ وَعِيْسٰى وَاَيُّوْبَ
وَيُوْنُسَ وَهٰرُوْنَ وَسُلَيْمٰنَ ۚ وَاٰتَيْنَا
دَاوٗدَ زَبُوْرًا ١٦٣

164. Of some messengers We have already told thee the story; of others We have not;— and to Moses Allah spoke direct;—

اور بہت سے پیغمبر ہیں کہ جن کے حالات ہم تم سے
پیشتر بیان کر چکے ہیں اور بہت سے پیغمبر ہیں جنکے حالات
تم سے بیان نہیں کیے. اور موسیٰ سے تو خدا نے باتیں بھی کیں ١٦٤

وَرُسُلًا قَدْ قَصَصْنٰهُمْ عَلَيْكَ مِنْ
قَبْلُ وَرُسُلًا لَّمْ نَقْصُصْهُمْ عَلَيْكَ ط
وَكَلَّمَ اللّٰهُ مُوْسٰى تَكْلِيْمًا ١٦٤

165. Messengers who gave good news as well as warning, that mankind, after (the coming) of the messengers, should have no plea against Allah: for Allah is Exalted in Power, Wise.

(سب) پیغمبروں کو (خدا نے) خوشخبری سنانے والے اور ڈرانے والے
(بنا کر بھیجا تھا) تاکہ پیغمبروں کے آنے کے بعد لوگوں کو خدا پر
الزام کا موقع نہ رہے. اور خدا غالب حکمت والا ہے ١٦٥

رُسُلًا مُّبَشِّرِيْنَ وَمُنْذِرِيْنَ لِئَلَّا
يَكُوْنَ لِلنَّاسِ عَلَى اللّٰهِ حُجَّةٌ ۢ بَعْدَ
الرُّسُلِ ط وَكَانَ اللّٰهُ عَزِيْزًا حَكِيْمًا ١٦٥

166. But Allah beareth witness that what He hath sent unto thee He hath sent with His (own) knowledge, and the angels bear witness: but enough is Allah for a witness.

لیکن خدا نے جو (کتاب) تم پر نازل کی ہے اُس کی
نسبت خدا گواہی دیتا ہے کہ اُس نے اپنے علم سے نازل کی ہے
اور فرشتے بھی گواہی دیتے ہیں. اور گواہ تو خدا ہی کافی ہے ١٦٦

لٰكِنِ اللّٰهُ يَشْهَدُ بِمَآ اَنْزَلَ اِلَيْكَ
اَنْزَلَهٗ بِعِلْمِهٖ ۚ وَالْمَلٰٓئِكَةُ يَشْهَدُوْنَ ط
وَكَفٰى بِاللّٰهِ شَهِيْدًا ١٦٦

167. Those who reject Faith and keep off (men) from the Way of Allah, have verily strayed far, far away from the Path.

جن لوگوں نے کفر کیا اور (لوگوں کو) خدا کے رستے سے
روکا وہ رستے سے بھٹک کر دُور جا پڑے ١٦٧

اِنَّ الَّذِيْنَ كَفَرُوْا وَصَدُّوْا عَنْ
سَبِيْلِ اللّٰهِ قَدْ ضَلُّوْا ضَلٰلًا ۢ بَعِيْدًا ١٦٧

168. Those who reject Faith and do wrong,— Allah will not forgive them, nor guide them to any way—

جو لوگ کافر ہوئے اور ظلم کرتے رہے خدا اُن کو بخشنے والا
نہیں اور نہ اُنہیں رستہ ہی دکھائے گا ١٦٨

اِنَّ الَّذِيْنَ كَفَرُوْا وَظَلَمُوْا لَمْ يَكُنِ
اللّٰهُ لِيَغْفِرَ لَهُمْ وَلَا لِيَهْدِيَهُمْ طَرِيْقًا ١٦٨

169. Except the way of Hell, to dwell therein for ever. And this to Allah is easy.

ہاں دوزخ کا رستہ جس میں وہ ہمیشہ (جلتے) رہیں گے
اور یہ (بات) خدا کو آسان ہے ١٦٩

اِلَّا طَرِيْقَ جَهَنَّمَ خٰلِدِيْنَ فِيْهَآ اَبَدًا ط
وَكَانَ ذٰلِكَ عَلَى اللّٰهِ يَسِيْرًا ١٦٩

170. O mankind ! the Messenger hath come to you in truth from Allah: believe in him: it is best for you. But if ye reject Faith, to Allah belong all things in the heavens and on earth:

لوگو! خدا کے پیغمبر تمہارے پاس تمہارے پروردگار کی طرف سے
حق بات لیکر آئے ہیں تو (اُن پر) ایمان لاؤ (یہی) تمہارے حق
میں بہتر ہے. اور اگر کفر کرو گے تو (جان رکھو کہ) جو کچھ آسمانوں اور

يٰٓاَيُّهَا النَّاسُ قَدْ جَآءَكُمُ الرَّسُوْلُ
بِالْحَقِّ مِنْ رَّبِّكُمْ فَاٰمِنُوْا خَيْرًا لَّكُمْ ط
وَاِنْ تَكْفُرُوْا فَاِنَّ لِلّٰهِ مَا فِي السَّمٰوٰتِ

and Allah is All-Knowing, All-Wise.

171. O People of the Book! commit no excesses in your religion: nor say of Allah aught but the truth. Christ Jesus the son of Mary was (no more than) a Messenger of Allah, and His Word, which He bestowed on Mary, and a Spirit proceeding from Him: so believe in Allah and His Messengers. Say not "Three": desist: it will be better for you: for Allah is One God: glory be to Him: (far Exalted is He) above having a son. To Him belong all things in the heavens and on earth. And enough is Allah as a Disposer of affairs.

172. Christ disdaineth not to serve and worship Allah, nor do the angels, those nearest (to Allah): those who disdain His worship and are arrogant, He will gather them all together unto Himself to (answer).

173. But to those who believe and do deeds of righteousness, He will give their (due) rewards,—and more, out of His bounty: but those who are disdainful and arrogant, He will punish with a grievous chastisement: nor will they find, besides Allah, any to protect or help them.

174. O mankind! Verily there hath come to you a convincing proof from your Lord for We have sent unto you a light (that is) manifest.

175. Then those who believe in Allah, and hold fast to Him,—soon will He admit them to Mercy and Grace from Himself, and guide them to Himself by a straight Way.

176. They ask thee for a legal decision, say: Allah directs (thus)

زمین میں ہے سب خدا ہی کا ہے اور خدا سب کچھ جاننے والا اور حکمت والا ہے ﴿۱۷۰﴾
اے اہلِ کتاب اپنے دین (کی بات) میں حد سے نہ بڑھو
اور خدا کے بارے میں حق کے سوا کچھ نہ کہو۔ مسیح (یعنی) مریم
کے بیٹے عیسیٰ (نہ خدا تھے نہ خدا کے بیٹے بلکہ) خدا کے رسُول
اور اُسکا کلمہ (بشارت) تھے جو اُس نے مریم کی طرف بھیجا تھا اور
اُسکی طرف سے ایک رُوح تھے۔ تو خدا اور اُسکے رسُولوں پر ایمان لاؤ۔
اور (یہ) نہ کہو کہ (خدا) تین (ہیں۔ اس اعتقاد سے) باز آؤ کہ یہ تمہارے
حق میں بہتر ہے۔ خدا ہی معبود واحد ہے۔ اور اس سے پاک ہے
کہ اُس کے اولاد ہو۔ جو کچھ آسمانوں میں اور جو کچھ زمین
میں ہے سب اُسی کا ہے۔ اور خدا ہی کارساز کافی ہے ﴿۱۷۱﴾
مسیح اس بات سے عار نہیں رکھتے کہ خدا کے بندے
ہوں اور نہ مُقرب فرشتے (عار رکھتے ہیں)
اور جو شخص خدا کا بندہ ہونے کو موجبِ عار سمجھے اور
سرکشی کرے تو خدا سب کو اپنے پاس جمع کر لے گا ﴿۱۷۲﴾
تو جو لوگ ایمان لائے اور نیک کام کرتے رہے وہ اُن کو
اُن کا پُورا بدلہ دے گا اور اپنے فضل سے (کچھ) زیادہ
بھی عنایت کرے گا۔ اور جنہوں نے (بندہ ہونے سے)
عار و انکار اور تکبر کیا اُن کو وہ تکلیف دینے والا عذاب دیگا ﴿۱۷۳﴾
اور وہ خدا کے سوا اپنا حامی اور مددگار نہ
پائیں گے ﴿۱۷۳﴾
لوگو! تمہارے پروردگار کی طرف سے تمہارے پاس دلیل
(روشن) آ چکی ہے اور ہم نے (کفر و ضلالت کا اندھیرا دُور
کرنے کو) تمہاری طرف چمکتا ہوا نُور بھیج دیا ہے ﴿۱۷۴﴾
پس جو لوگ خدا پر ایمان لائے اور اُس (کے دین کی رسّی) کو
مضبوط پکڑے رہے اُنکو وہ اپنی رحمت اور فضل (کی بہشتوں) میں
داخل کریگا اور اپنی طرف (پہنچنے کا) سیدھا رستہ دکھائیگا ﴿۱۷۵﴾
(اے پیغمبر) لوگ تم سے (کلالہ کے بارے میں) حکم (خدا) دریافت

وَالْاَرْضِ ؕ وَكَانَ اللّٰهُ عَلِيْمًا حَكِيْمًا ﴿۱۷۰﴾
يٰۤاَهْلَ الْكِتٰبِ لَا تَغْلُوْا فِيْ دِيْنِكُمْ
وَلَا تَقُوْلُوْا عَلَى اللّٰهِ اِلَّا الْحَقَّ ؕ اِنَّمَا
الْمَسِيْحُ عِيْسَى ابْنُ مَرْيَمَ رَسُوْلُ اللّٰهِ
وَكَلِمَتُهٗ ۚ اَلْقٰهَاۤ اِلٰى مَرْيَمَ وَرُوْحٌ
مِّنْهُ ۫ فَاٰمِنُوْا بِاللّٰهِ وَرُسُلِهٖ ۚ وَلَا
تَقُوْلُوْا ثَلٰثَةٌ ؕ اِنْتَهُوْا خَيْرًا لَّكُمْ ؕ
اِنَّمَا اللّٰهُ اِلٰهٌ وَّاحِدٌ ؕ سُبْحٰنَهٗۤ اَنْ
يَّكُوْنَ لَهٗ وَلَدٌ ۘ لَهٗ مَا فِي السَّمٰوٰتِ
وَمَا فِي الْاَرْضِ ؕ وَكَفٰى بِاللّٰهِ وَكِيْلًا ﴿۱۷۱﴾ ع
لَنْ يَّسْتَنْكِفَ الْمَسِيْحُ اَنْ يَّكُوْنَ
عَبْدًا لِّلّٰهِ وَلَا الْمَلٰٓئِكَةُ الْمُقَرَّبُوْنَ ؕ
وَمَنْ يَّسْتَنْكِفْ عَنْ عِبَادَتِهٖ وَ
يَسْتَكْبِرْ فَسَيَحْشُرُهُمْ اِلَيْهِ جَمِيْعًا ﴿۱۷۲﴾
فَاَمَّا الَّذِيْنَ اٰمَنُوْا وَعَمِلُوا الصّٰلِحٰتِ
فَيُوَفِّيْهِمْ اُجُوْرَهُمْ وَيَزِيْدُهُمْ
مِّنْ فَضْلِهٖ ۚ وَاَمَّا الَّذِيْنَ اسْتَنْكَفُوْا
وَاسْتَكْبَرُوْا فَيُعَذِّبُهُمْ عَذَابًا اَلِيْمًا ۙ
وَّلَا يَجِدُوْنَ لَهُمْ مِّنْ دُوْنِ اللّٰهِ
وَلِيًّا وَّلَا نَصِيْرًا ﴿۱۷۳﴾
يٰۤاَيُّهَا النَّاسُ قَدْ جَآءَكُمْ بُرْهَانٌ
مِّنْ رَّبِّكُمْ وَاَنْزَلْنَاۤ اِلَيْكُمْ
نُوْرًا مُّبِيْنًا ﴿۱۷۴﴾
فَاَمَّا الَّذِيْنَ اٰمَنُوْا بِاللّٰهِ وَاعْتَصَمُوْا بِهٖ
فَسَيُدْخِلُهُمْ فِيْ رَحْمَةٍ مِّنْهُ وَفَضْلٍ ۙ
وَّيَهْدِيْهِمْ اِلَيْهِ صِرَاطًا مُّسْتَقِيْمًا ﴿۱۷۵﴾
يَسْتَفْتُوْنَكَ ؕ قُلِ اللّٰهُ يُفْتِيْكُمْ فِي

SÛRA–5

AL-MÃÎDAH

(INTRODUCTION)

This Sûra deals, by way of recapitulation, with the backsliding of the Jews and Christians from their pure religions, to which the coping stone was placed by Islam. It refers particularly to the Christians, and to their solemn Sacrament of the Last Supper, to whose mystic meaning they are declared to have been false.

As a logical corollary to the corruption of the earlier religions of Allah, the practical precepts of Islam, about food, cleanliness, justice, and fidelity are recapitulated.

The third verse contains the memorable declaration : "This day have I perfected your religion for you"; which was promulgated in 10 H., during the Apostle's last Pilgrimage to Makkah. Chronologically it was the last verse to be revealed.

about those who leave no descendants or ascendants as heirs. If it is a man, that dies, leaving a sister but no child, she shall have half the inheritance: if (such a deceased was) a woman, who left no child, her brother takes her inheritance: if there are two sisters, they shall have two-thirds of the inheritance (between them): if there are brothers and sisters, (they share), the male having twice the share of the female. Thus doth Allah make clear to you (His law), lest ye err. And Allah Hath knowledge of all things.

Al-Mã'ida or The Table Spread

In the name of Allah, Most Gracious, Most Merciful.

1. O ye who believe ! fulfil (all) obligations.

Lawful unto you (for food) are all beasts of cattle with the exceptions named: but animals of the chase are forbidden while ye are in the Sacred Precincts or in the state of pilgrimage: for Allah doth command according to His Will and Plan.

2. O ye who believe ! violate not the sanctity of the rites of Allah, nor of the Sacred Month, nor of the animals brought for sacrifice, nor the garlands that mark out such animals, nor the people resorting to the Sacred House, seeking of the bounty and good pleasure of their Lord. But when ye are clear of the Sacred Precincts and of the state of pilgrimage, ye may hunt and let not the hatred of some people in (once) shutting you out of the Sacred Mosque lead you to transgression (and hostility on your part). Help ye one another in righteousness and piety, but help ye not one another in sin and rancour: fear Allah: for Allah is strict in punishment.

کرتے ہیں۔ کہہ دو کہ خدا کلالہ کے بارے میں یہ حکم دیتا ہے کہ اگر کوئی ایسا مرد مر جائے جسکے اولاد نہ ہو (اور نہ ماں باپ) اور اسکے بہن ہو تو اسکو بھائی کے ترکے میں سے آدھا حصہ ملیگا اور اگر بہن مر جائے اور اسکے اولاد نہ ہو تو اسکے تمام مال کا وارث بھائی ہوگا۔ اور اگر (مرنیوالے بھائی کی) دو بہنیں ہوں تو دونوں کو بھائی کے ترکے میں سے دو تہائی۔ اور اگر بھائی اور بہن یعنی مرد اور عورتیں ملے جلے وارث ہوں تو مرد کا حصہ دو عورتوں کے حصے کے برابر ہے (یہ احکام) خدا تم سے اس لئے بیان فرماتا ہے کہ بھٹکتے نہ پھرو اور خدا ہر چیز سے واقف ہے ﴿۱۷۶﴾

سورۂ مائدہ مدنی ہے اور اس میں ایک سو بیس آیتیں اور سولہ رکوع ہیں

شروع خدا کا نام لیکر جو بڑا مہربان نہایت رحم والا ہے ○
اے ایمان والو اپنے اقراروں کو پورا کرو۔ تمہارے لئے چارپائے جانور (جو چرنے والے ہیں) حلال کر دیئے گئے ہیں بجز اُن کے جو تمہیں پڑھ کر سنائے جاتے ہیں۔ مگر احرام (حج) میں شکار کو حلال نہ جاننا۔ خدا جیسا چاہتا ہے حکم دیتا ہے ﴿۱﴾
مومنو! خدا کے نام کی چیزوں کی بے حرمتی نہ کرنا اور نہ ادب کے مہینے کی اور نہ قربانی کے جانوروں کی اور نہ اُن جانوروں کی (جو خدا کی نذر کر دیئے گئے ہوں اور) جنکے گلوں میں پٹے بندھے ہوں اور نہ اُن لوگوں کی جو عزت کے گھر (یعنی بیت اللہ) کو جا رہے ہوں (اور) اپنے پروردگار کے فضل اور اسکی خوشنودی کے طلبگار ہوں۔ اور جب احرام اُتار دو تو (پھر اختیار ہے کہ) شکار کرو۔ اور لوگوں کی دشمنی اس وجہ سے کہ انہوں نے تمکو عزت والی مسجد سے روکا تھا تمہیں اس بات پر آمادہ نہ کرے کہ تم اُن پر زیادتی کرنے لگو۔ اور (دیکھو) نیکی اور پرہیزگاری کے کاموں میں ایک دوسرے کی مدد کیا کرو۔ اور گناہ اور ظلم کی باتوں میں مدد نہ کیا کرو اور خدا سے ڈرتے رہو۔ کچھ شک نہیں کہ خدا کا عذاب سخت ہے ﴿۲﴾

الْكَلٰلَةِ ۭ اِنِ امْرُؤٌا هَلَكَ لَيْسَ لَهٗ
وَلَدٌ وَّلَهٗٓ اُخْتٌ فَلَهَا نِصْفُ مَا
تَرَكَ ۚ وَهُوَ يَرِثُهَآ اِنْ لَّمْ يَكُنْ
لَّهَا وَلَدٌ ۚ فَاِنْ كَانَتَا اثْنَتَيْنِ
فَلَهُمَا الثُّلُثٰنِ مِمَّا تَرَكَ ۭ وَاِنْ
كَانُوْٓا اِخْوَةً رِّجَالًا وَّنِسَاۗءً
فَلِلذَّكَرِ مِثْلُ حَظِّ الْاُنْثَيَيْنِ ۭ
يُبَيِّنُ اللّٰهُ لَكُمْ اَنْ تَضِلُّوْا ۭ وَاللّٰهُ
بِكُلِّ شَيْءٍ عَلِيْمٌ ﴿۱۷۶﴾ ع ٢٤

سُوْرَةُ الْمَاۗىِٕدَةِ مَدَنِيَّةٌ وَّهِيَ مِائَةٌ وَّعِشْرُوْنَ اٰيَةً وَّسِتَّةَ عَشَرَ رُكُوْعًا

بِسْمِ اللّٰهِ الرَّحْمٰنِ الرَّحِيْمِ ○
يٰٓاَيُّهَا الَّذِيْنَ اٰمَنُوْٓا اَوْفُوْا بِالْعُقُوْدِ ۭ
اُحِلَّتْ لَكُمْ بَهِيْمَةُ الْاَنْعَامِ اِلَّا
مَا يُتْلٰى عَلَيْكُمْ غَيْرَ مُحِلِّي الصَّيْدِ
وَاَنْتُمْ حُرُمٌ ۭ اِنَّ اللّٰهَ يَحْكُمُ مَا
يُرِيْدُ ﴿۱﴾
يٰٓاَيُّهَا الَّذِيْنَ اٰمَنُوْا لَا تُحِلُّوْا شَعَاۗىِٕرَ
اللّٰهِ وَلَا الشَّهْرَ الْحَرَامَ وَلَا الْهَدْيَ وَلَا
الْقَلَاۗىِٕدَ وَلَآ اٰۗمِّيْنَ الْبَيْتَ الْحَرَامَ
يَبْتَغُوْنَ فَضْلًا مِّنْ رَّبِّهِمْ وَرِضْوَانًا ۭ
وَاِذَا حَلَلْتُمْ فَاصْطَادُوْا ۭ وَلَا
يَجْرِمَنَّكُمْ شَنَاٰنُ قَوْمٍ اَنْ صَدُّوْكُمْ
عَنِ الْمَسْجِدِ الْحَرَامِ اَنْ تَعْتَدُوْا ۘ وَ
تَعَاوَنُوْا عَلَى الْبِرِّ وَالتَّقْوٰى ۠
وَلَا تَعَاوَنُوْا عَلَى الْاِثْمِ وَ
الْعُدْوَانِ ۠ وَاتَّقُوا اللّٰهَ ۭ اِنَّ
اللّٰهَ شَدِيْدُ الْعِقَابِ ﴿۲﴾ الربع

3. Forbidden to you (for food) are: dead meat, blood, the flesh of swine, and that on which hath been invoked the name of other than Allah; that which hath been killed by strangling, or by a violent blow, or by a headlong fall, or by being gored to death; that which hath been (partly) eaten by a wild animal; unless ye are able to slaughter it (in due form); that which is sacrificed on stone (altars); (forbidden) also is the division (of meat) by raffling with arrows: that is impiety.

This day have those who reject Faith given up all hope of your religion: yet fear them not but fear Me. This day have I perfected your religion for you, completed My favour upon you, and have chosen for you Islam as your religion.

But if any is forced by hunger, with no inclination to transgression, Allah is indeed Oft-Forgiving, Most Merciful.

تم پر مرا ہوا جانور اور (بہتا) لہو اور سور کا
گوشت اور جس چیز پر خدا کے سوا کسی اور کا نام پکارا
جائے اور جو جانور گلا گھٹ کر مر جائے اور جو چوٹ لگ کر مر جائے
اور جو گر کر مر جائے اور جو سینگ لگ کر مر جائے یہ سب حرام ہیں
اور وہ جانور بھی جسکو درندے پھاڑ کھائیں مگر جسکو تم (مرنے
سے پہلے) ذبح کر لو اور وہ جانور بھی جو تھان پر ذبح کیا جائے اور
یہ بھی کہ پانسوں سے قسمت معلوم کرو [٩٩] یہ سب گناہ (کے کام) ہیں
آج کافر تمہارے دین سے ناامید ہو گئے ہیں تو اُن
سے مت ڈرو اور مجھی سے ڈرتے رہو۔ (اور) آج ہم
نے تمہارے لئے تمہارا دین کامل کر دیا اور اپنی نعمتیں تم
پر پوری کر دیں اور تمہارے لئے اسلام کو دین پسند کیا
ہاں جو شخص بھوک میں ناچار ہو جائے (بشرطیکہ) گناہ کی
طرف مائل نہ ہو تو خدا بخشنے والا مہربان ہے ③

حُرِّمَتْ عَلَيْكُمُ الْمَيْتَةُ وَالدَّمُ وَ
لَحْمُ الْخِنْزِيرِ وَمَا أُهِلَّ لِغَيْرِ اللَّهِ
بِهِ وَالْمُنْخَنِقَةُ وَالْمَوْقُوذَةُ وَالْمُتَرَدِّيَةُ
وَالنَّطِيحَةُ وَمَا أَكَلَ السَّبُعُ إِلَّا مَا
ذَكَّيْتُمْ وَمَا ذُبِحَ عَلَى النُّصُبِ
وَأَنْ تَسْتَقْسِمُوا بِالْأَزْلَامِ ذَٰلِكُمْ
فِسْقٌ الْيَوْمَ يَئِسَ الَّذِينَ كَفَرُوا
مِنْ دِينِكُمْ فَلَا تَخْشَوْهُمْ وَاخْشَوْنِ
الْيَوْمَ أَكْمَلْتُ لَكُمْ دِينَكُمْ وَ
أَتْمَمْتُ عَلَيْكُمْ نِعْمَتِي وَرَضِيتُ
لَكُمُ الْإِسْلَامَ دِينًا فَمَنِ اضْطُرَّ
فِي مَخْمَصَةٍ غَيْرَ مُتَجَانِفٍ لِإِثْمٍ
فَإِنَّ اللَّهَ غَفُورٌ رَحِيمٌ ③

4. They ask thee what is lawful to them (as food). Say: Lawful unto you are (all) things good and pure: and what ye have taught the beasts and birds of prey, training them to hunt in the manner directed to you by Allah: eat what they catch for you, but pronounce the name of Allah over it: and fear Allah; for Allah is swift in taking account.

تم سے پوچھتے ہیں کہ کون کونسی چیزیں اُن کیلئے حلال
ہیں (اُنسے) کہہ دو کہ سب پاکیزہ چیزیں تمکو حلال ہیں اور
وہ (شکار) بھی حلال ہے جو تمہارے لئے اُن شکاری جانوروں
نے پکڑا ہو جنکو تم نے سدھا رکھا ہو اور جس (طریق) سے خدا نے تمہیں (شکار
کرنا) سکھایا ہے (اس طریق سے) تم نے انکو سکھایا ہو تو جو شکار وہ تمہارے
لئے پکڑ رکھیں اُسکو کھا لیا کرو (اور شکاری جانوروں کے چھوڑتے وقت)
خدا کا نام لے لیا کرو اور خدا سے ڈرتے رہو بیشک خدا جلد حساب لینے والا ہے ④

يَسْأَلُونَكَ مَاذَا أُحِلَّ لَهُمْ قُلْ
أُحِلَّ لَكُمُ الطَّيِّبَاتُ وَمَا عَلَّمْتُمْ
مِنَ الْجَوَارِحِ مُكَلِّبِينَ تُعَلِّمُونَهُنَّ
مِمَّا عَلَّمَكُمُ اللَّهُ فَكُلُوا مِمَّا
أَمْسَكْنَ عَلَيْكُمْ وَاذْكُرُوا
اسْمَ اللَّهِ عَلَيْهِ وَاتَّقُوا اللَّهَ إِنَّ
اللَّهَ سَرِيعُ الْحِسَابِ ④

5. This day are (all) things good and pure made lawful unto you. The food of the People of the Book is lawful unto you and yours is lawful unto them. (Lawful unto you in marriage) are (not only) chaste women who are believers, but chaste women among the People of the Book, revealed before your time,— when ye give them their due dowers, and desire chastity, not lewdness, taking them as lovers. If any one rejects faith,

آج تمہارے لئے سب پاکیزہ چیزیں حلال کر دی گئیں اور
اہل کتاب کا کھانا بھی تم کو حلال ہے اور تمہارا کھانا
اُن کو حلال ہے۔ اور پاک دامن مومن عورتیں اور
پاک دامن اہل کتاب عورتیں بھی (حلال ہیں)
جبکہ اُن کا مہر دے دو۔ اور اُن سے عفت قائم
رکھنی مقصود ہو نہ کھلی بدکاری کرنی اور نہ چھپی
دوستی کرنی۔ اور جو شخص ایمان کا منکر ہوا

الْيَوْمَ أُحِلَّ لَكُمُ الطَّيِّبَاتُ وَطَعَامُ
الَّذِينَ أُوتُوا الْكِتَابَ حِلٌّ لَكُمْ
وَطَعَامُكُمْ حِلٌّ لَهُمْ وَالْمُحْصَنَاتُ
مِنَ الْمُؤْمِنَاتِ وَالْمُحْصَنَاتُ مِنَ
الَّذِينَ أُوتُوا الْكِتَابَ مِنْ قَبْلِكُمْ
إِذَا آتَيْتُمُوهُنَّ أُجُورَهُنَّ مُحْصِنِينَ
غَيْرَ مُسَافِحِينَ وَلَا مُتَّخِذِي أَخْدَانٍ

fruitless is his work, and in the Hereafter he will be in the ranks of those who have lost (all spiritual good).

6. O ye who believe ! when ye prepare for prayer, wash your faces, and your hands (and arms) to the elbows; rub your heads (with water); and (wash) your feet to the ankles. If ye are in a state of ceremonial impurity, bathe your whole body. But if ye are ill, or on a journey, or one of you cometh from the privy, or ye have been in contact with women, and ye find no water, then take for yourselves clean sand or earth, and rub therewith your faces and hands. Allah doth not wish to place you in a difficulty, but to make you clean, and to complete His favour to you, that ye may be grateful.

7. And call in remembrance the favour of Allah unto you, and His Covenant, which He ratified with you, when ye said: "We hear and we obey": and fear Allah, for Allah knoweth well the secrets of your hearts.

8. O ye who believe ! stand out firmly for Allah, as witnesses to fair dealing, and let not the hatred of others to you make you swerve to wrong and depart from justice. Be just: that is next to Piety: and fear Allah. For Allah is well-acquainted with all that ye do.

9. To those who believe and do deeds of righteousness hath Allah promised forgiveness and a great reward.

10. Those who reject Faith and deny Our Signs will be Companions of Hell- fire.

11. O ye who believe ! call in remembrance the favour of Allah

وَمَنْ يَّكْفُرْ بِالْاِيْمَانِ فَقَدْ حَبِطَ عَمَلُهٗ	اُس کے عمل ضائع ہو گئے. اور وہ آخرت میں
وَهُوَ فِي الْاٰخِرَةِ مِنَ الْخٰسِرِيْنَ ۝٥ ع	نقصان پانے والوں میں ہو گا ۝٥
يٰۤاَيُّهَا الَّذِيْنَ اٰمَنُوْۤا اِذَا قُمْتُمْ اِلَى الصَّلٰوةِ	مومنو! جب تم نماز پڑھنے کا قصد کیا کرو تو منہ
فَاغْسِلُوْا وُجُوْهَكُمْ وَاَيْدِيَكُمْ اِلَى الْمَرَافِقِ	اور کہنیوں تک ہاتھ دھو لیا کرو اور سر کا مسح کر لیا
وَامْسَحُوْا بِرُءُوْسِكُمْ وَاَرْجُلَكُمْ اِلَى الْكَعْبَيْنِ	کرو. اور ٹخنوں تک پاؤں (دھو لیا کرو) اور اگر نہانے کی
وَاِنْ كُنْتُمْ جُنُبًا فَاطَّهَّرُوْا وَاِنْ كُنْتُمْ مَّرْضٰۤى	حاجت ہو تو (نہا کر) پاک ہو جایا کرو. اور اگر بیمار ہو
اَوْ عَلٰى سَفَرٍ اَوْ جَآءَ اَحَدٌ مِّنْكُمْ مِّنَ	یا سفر میں ہو یا کوئی تم میں سے بیت الخلا
الْغَآئِطِ اَوْ لٰمَسْتُمُ النِّسَآءَ فَلَمْ	سے ہو کر آیا ہو یا تم عورتوں سے ہمبستر ہوئے
تَجِدُوْا مَآءً فَتَيَمَّمُوْا صَعِيْدًا طَيِّبًا	ہو اور تمہیں پانی نہ مل سکے تو پاک مٹی لو اور اُس
فَامْسَحُوْا بِوُجُوْهِكُمْ وَاَيْدِيْكُمْ مِّنْهُ	سے منہ اور ہاتھوں کا مسح (یعنی تیمم) کر لو.
مَا يُرِيْدُ اللّٰهُ لِيَجْعَلَ عَلَيْكُمْ مِّنْ حَرَجٍ	خدا تم پر کسی طرح کی تنگی نہیں کرنا چاہتا بلکہ
وَّلٰكِنْ يُّرِيْدُ لِيُطَهِّرَكُمْ وَلِيُتِمَّ	یہ چاہتا ہے کہ تمہیں پاک کرے اور اپنی نعمتیں
نِعْمَتَهٗ عَلَيْكُمْ لَعَلَّكُمْ تَشْكُرُوْنَ ۝٦	تم پر پوری کرے تاکہ تم شکر کرو ۝٦
وَاذْكُرُوْا نِعْمَةَ اللّٰهِ عَلَيْكُمْ وَمِيْثَاقَهُ	اور خدا نے جو تم پر احسان کئے ہیں اُن کو یاد کرو اور
الَّذِيْ وَاثَقَكُمْ بِهٖۤ اِذْ قُلْتُمْ سَمِعْنَا	اُس عہد کو بھی جس کا تم سے قول لیا تھا (یعنی) جب تم
وَاَطَعْنَا وَاتَّقُوا اللّٰهَ اِنَّ اللّٰهَ عَلِيْمٌ	نے کہا تھا کہ ہم نے (خدا کا حکم) سن لیا اور قبول کیا. اور اللہ
بِذَاتِ الصُّدُوْرِ ۝٧	ڈرو کچھ شک نہیں کہ خدا دلوں کی باتوں (تک) سے واقف ہے ۝٧
يٰۤاَيُّهَا الَّذِيْنَ اٰمَنُوْا كُوْنُوْا قَوّٰمِيْنَ	اے ایمان والو! خدا کیلئے انصاف کی گواہی دینے کے لئے
لِلّٰهِ شُهَدَآءَ بِالْقِسْطِ وَلَا يَجْرِمَنَّكُمْ	کھڑے ہو جایا کرو. اور لوگوں کی دشمنی تم کو اس بات پر
شَنَاٰنُ قَوْمٍ عَلٰۤى اَلَّا تَعْدِلُوْا اِعْدِلُوْا	آمادہ نہ کرے کہ انصاف چھوڑ دو. انصاف کیا کرو
هُوَ اَقْرَبُ لِلتَّقْوٰى وَاتَّقُوا اللّٰهَ اِنَّ	کہ یہی پرہیزگاری کی بات ہے اور خدا سے ڈرتے رہو.
اللّٰهَ خَبِيْرٌ بِمَا تَعْمَلُوْنَ ۝٨	کچھ شک نہیں کہ خدا تمہارے سب اعمال سے خبردار ہے ۝٨
وَعَدَ اللّٰهُ الَّذِيْنَ اٰمَنُوْا وَعَمِلُوا الصّٰلِحٰتِ	جو لوگ ایمان لائے اور نیک کام کرتے رہے اُن سے خدا نے
لَهُمْ مَّغْفِرَةٌ وَّاَجْرٌ عَظِيْمٌ ۝٩	وعدہ فرمایا ہے کہ اُن کیلئے بخشش اور اجر عظیم ہے ۝٩
وَالَّذِيْنَ كَفَرُوْا وَكَذَّبُوْا بِاٰيٰتِنَاۤ	اور جنہوں نے کفر کیا اور ہماری آیتوں کو جھٹلایا
اُولٰۤئِكَ اَصْحٰبُ الْجَحِيْمِ ۝١٠	وہ جہنمی ہیں ۝١٠
يٰۤاَيُّهَا الَّذِيْنَ اٰمَنُوا اذْكُرُوْا نِعْمَتَ اللّٰهِ	اے ایمان والو! خدا نے جو تم پر احسان کیا ہے اُس کو

unto you when certain men formed the design to stretch out their hands against you, but (Allah) held back their hands from you: so fear Allah. And on Allah let Believers put (all) their trust.

یاد کرو جب ایک جماعت نے ارادہ کیا کہ تم پر دست درازی
کریں تو اُس نے اُن کے ہاتھ روک دیئے اور خدا
سے ڈرتے رہو۔ اور مومنوں کو خدا ہی پر بھروسہ رکھنا چاہیے ﴿۱۱﴾

عَلَيْكُمْ إِذْ هَمَّ قَوْمٌ أَنْ يَّبْسُطُوْٓا إِلَيْكُمْ
أَيْدِيَهُمْ فَكَفَّ أَيْدِيَهُمْ عَنْكُمْ ۚ وَ
اتَّقُوا اللّٰهَ ۗ وَعَلَى اللّٰهِ فَلْيَتَوَكَّلِ الْمُؤْمِنُوْنَ ﴿١١﴾ ع ٢

12. Allah did aforetime take a Covenant from the Children of Israel, and We appointed twelve chieftains among them. And Allah said: "I am with you: if ye (but) establish regular Prayers, pay Zakat believe in My Messengers, honour and assist them, and loan to Allah a beautiful loan, verily I will wipe out from you your evils, and admit you to Gardens with rivers flowing beneath; but if any of you, after this, resisteth faith, he hath truly wandered from the path of rectitude."

اور خدا نے بنی اسرائیل سے اقرار لیا اور اُن میں
ہم نے بارہ سردار مقرر کئے۔ پھر خدا نے فرمایا
کہ میں تمہارے ساتھ ہوں۔ اگر تم نماز پڑھتے
اور زکوٰۃ دیتے رہو گے اور میرے پیغمبروں پر
ایمان لاؤ گے اور اُن کی مدد کرو گے اور خدا کو
قرض حسنہ دو گے تو میں تم سے تمہارے
گناہ دُور کر دوں گا اور تم کو بہشتوں میں داخل
کروں گا جن کے نیچے نہریں بہ رہی ہیں پھر جس نے
اسکے بعد تم میں سے کفر کیا وہ سیدھے رستے سے بھٹک گیا ﴿۱۲﴾

وَلَقَدْ أَخَذَ اللّٰهُ مِيْثَاقَ بَنِيْٓ إِسْرَآءِيْلَ ۚ
وَبَعَثْنَا مِنْهُمُ اثْنَيْ عَشَرَ نَقِيْبًا ۗ وَقَالَ
اللّٰهُ إِنِّيْ مَعَكُمْ ۗ لَئِنْ أَقَمْتُمُ الصَّلٰوةَ
وَاٰتَيْتُمُ الزَّكٰوةَ وَاٰمَنْتُمْ بِرُسُلِيْ وَ
عَزَّرْتُمُوْهُمْ وَأَقْرَضْتُمُ اللّٰهَ قَرْضًا
حَسَنًا لَّأُكَفِّرَنَّ عَنْكُمْ سَيِّاٰتِكُمْ وَ
لَأُدْخِلَنَّكُمْ جَنّٰتٍ تَجْرِيْ مِنْ تَحْتِهَا
الْأَنْهٰرُ ۚ فَمَنْ كَفَرَ بَعْدَ ذٰلِكَ مِنْكُمْ
فَقَدْ ضَلَّ سَوَآءَ السَّبِيْلِ ﴿١٢﴾

13. But because of their breach of their Covenant, We cursed them, and made their hearts grow hard: they change the words from their (right) places and forget a good part of the Message that was sent them, nor wilt thou cease to find them— barring a few—ever bent on (new) deceits: but forgive them, and overlook (their misdeeds): for Allah loveth those who are kind.

تو ان لوگوں کے عہد توڑ دینے کے سبب ہم نے اُن پر
لعنت کی اور اُنکے دلوں کو سخت کر دیا یہ لوگ کلمات کتاب
کو اپنے مقامات سے بدل دیتے ہیں۔ اور جن باتوں کی اُن کو
نصیحت کی گئی تھی اُنکا بھی ایک حصہ فراموش کر بیٹھے اور
تھوڑے آدمیوں کے سوا ہمیشہ تم اُنکی (ایک نہ ایک) خیانت کی
خبر پاتے رہتے ہو تو اُنکی خطائیں معاف کر دو اور (اُنسے) درگذر
کرو کہ خدا احسان کرنے والوں کو دوست رکھتا ہے ﴿۱۳﴾

فَبِمَا نَقْضِهِمْ مِّيْثَاقَهُمْ لَعَنّٰهُمْ وَجَعَلْنَا
قُلُوْبَهُمْ قٰسِيَةً ۚ يُحَرِّفُوْنَ الْكَلِمَ عَنْ
مَّوَاضِعِهٖ ۙ وَنَسُوْا حَظًّا مِّمَّا ذُكِّرُوْا
بِهٖ ۚ وَلَا تَزَالُ تَطَّلِعُ عَلٰى خَآئِنَةٍ
مِّنْهُمْ إِلَّا قَلِيْلًا مِّنْهُمْ فَاعْفُ
عَنْهُمْ وَاصْفَحْ ۗ إِنَّ اللّٰهَ يُحِبُّ
الْمُحْسِنِيْنَ ﴿١٣﴾

14. From those, too, who call themselves Christians, We did take a Covenant, but they forgot a good part of the Message that was sent them: so We stirred up enmity and hatred between the one and the other, to the Day of Judgment. And soon will Allah show them what it is they have done.

اور جو لوگ (اپنے تئیں) کہتے ہیں کہ ہم نصاریٰ ہیں ہم
نے اُن سے بھی عہد لیا تھا مگر انہوں نے بھی اُس نصیحت کا
جو اُن کو کی گئی تھی ایک حصہ فراموش کر دیا تو ہم نے اُنکے
باہم قیامت تک کیلئے دشمنی اور کینہ ڈالدیا۔ اور جو کچھ وہ کرتے
رہے خدا عنقریب اُن کو اس سے آگاہ کرے گا ﴿۱۴﴾

وَمِنَ الَّذِيْنَ قَالُوْٓا إِنَّا نَصٰرٰٓى أَخَذْنَا
مِيْثَاقَهُمْ فَنَسُوْا حَظًّا مِّمَّا ذُكِّرُوْا
بِهٖ فَأَغْرَيْنَا بَيْنَهُمُ الْعَدَاوَةَ وَالْبَغْضَآءَ
إِلٰى يَوْمِ الْقِيٰمَةِ ۗ وَسَوْفَ يُنَبِّئُهُمُ اللّٰهُ
بِمَا كَانُوْا يَصْنَعُوْنَ ﴿١٤﴾

15. O people of the Book ! there hath come to you Our Messenger, revealing to you much that ye used to hide in the Book, and passing over much (that is now unnecessary): there hath come to

اے اہل کتاب تمہارے پاس ہمارے پیغمبر (آخر الزماں) آ گئے
ہیں کہ جو کچھ تم کتاب (الٰہی) میں سے چھپاتے تھے وہ اُس میں سے بہت
کچھ تمہیں کھول کھول کر بتا دیتے ہیں۔ اور تمہارے بہت سے قصور معاف

يٰٓأَهْلَ الْكِتٰبِ قَدْ جَآءَكُمْ رَسُوْلُنَا
يُبَيِّنُ لَكُمْ كَثِيْرًا مِّمَّا كُنْتُمْ تُخْفُوْنَ
مِنَ الْكِتٰبِ وَيَعْفُوْا عَنْ كَثِيْرٍ ۚ قَدْ

جَآءَكُم مِّنَ اللّٰهِ نُورٌ وَّكِتٰبٌ مُّبِينٌ ﴿١٥﴾
يَّهْدِي بِهِ اللّٰهُ مَنِ اتَّبَعَ رِضْوَانَهٗ
سُبُلَ السَّلٰمِ وَيُخْرِجُهُم مِّنَ الظُّلُمٰتِ إِلَى
النُّورِ بِإِذْنِهٖ وَيَهْدِيهِمْ إِلٰى صِرَاطٍ مُّسْتَقِيمٍ ﴿١٦﴾
لَقَدْ كَفَرَ الَّذِينَ قَالُوٓا إِنَّ اللّٰهَ هُوَ
الْمَسِيحُ ابْنُ مَرْيَمَ ۚ قُلْ فَمَن يَّمْلِكُ
مِنَ اللّٰهِ شَيْئًا إِنْ أَرَادَ أَن يُّهْلِكَ
الْمَسِيحَ ابْنَ مَرْيَمَ وَأُمَّهٗ وَمَن
فِي الْأَرْضِ جَمِيعًا ۗ وَلِلّٰهِ مُلْكُ السَّمٰوٰتِ
وَالْأَرْضِ وَمَا بَيْنَهُمَا ۚ يَخْلُقُ مَا يَشَآءُ ۚ
وَاللّٰهُ عَلٰى كُلِّ شَيْءٍ قَدِيرٌ ﴿١٧﴾
وَقَالَتِ الْيَهُودُ وَالنَّصٰرٰى نَحْنُ أَبْنٰٓؤُا
اللّٰهِ وَأَحِبَّٰٓؤُهٗ ۚ قُلْ فَلِمَ يُعَذِّبُكُم
بِذُنُوبِكُم ۖ بَلْ أَنتُم بَشَرٌ مِّمَّنْ
خَلَقَ ۚ يَغْفِرُ لِمَن يَشَآءُ وَيُعَذِّبُ
مَن يَشَآءُ ۚ وَلِلّٰهِ مُلْكُ السَّمٰوٰتِ وَ
الْأَرْضِ وَمَا بَيْنَهُمَا ۖ وَإِلَيْهِ الْمَصِيرُ ﴿١٨﴾
يٰٓأَهْلَ الْكِتٰبِ قَدْ جَآءَكُمْ رَسُولُنَا
يُبَيِّنُ لَكُمْ عَلٰى فَتْرَةٍ مِّنَ الرُّسُلِ
أَن تَقُولُوا مَا جَآءَنَا مِن بَشِيرٍ وَّلَا
نَذِيرٍ ۫ فَقَدْ جَآءَكُم بَشِيرٌ وَّنَذِيرٌ ۗ
ع وَاللّٰهُ عَلٰى كُلِّ شَيْءٍ قَدِيرٌ ﴿١٩﴾
وَإِذْ قَالَ مُوسٰى لِقَوْمِهٖ يٰقَوْمِ اذْكُرُوا
نِعْمَةَ اللّٰهِ عَلَيْكُمْ إِذْ جَعَلَ فِيكُمْ
أَنۢبِيَآءَ وَجَعَلَكُم مُّلُوكًا ۖ وَّاٰتٰىكُم
مَّا لَمْ يُؤْتِ أَحَدًا مِّنَ الْعٰلَمِينَ ﴿٢٠﴾
يٰقَوْمِ ادْخُلُوا الْأَرْضَ الْمُقَدَّسَةَ

کر دیتے ہیں بیشک تمہارے پاس خدا کی طرف سے نُور اور روشن کتاب آچکی ہے ﴿۱۵﴾
جس سے خدا اپنی رضا پر چلنے والوں کو نجات کے رستے
دکھاتا ہے اور اپنے حکم سے اندھیرے میں سے نکال کر روشنی کی
طرف لے جاتا اور ان کو سیدھے رستے پر چلاتا ہے ﴿۱۶﴾
جو لوگ اس بات کے قائل ہیں کہ عیسیٰ ابن مریم خدا
ہیں وہ بیشک کافر ہیں۔ (اُن سے) کہہ دو کہ اگر خدا عیسیٰ ابن
مریم کو اور انکی والدہ کو اور جتنے لوگ زمین میں ہیں سب کو
ہلاک کرنا چاہے تو اُسکے آگے کس کی پیش چل سکتی ہے؟
اور آسمان اور زمین اور جو کچھ ان دونوں میں ہے سب پر
خدا ہی کی بادشاہی ہے وہ جو چاہتا ہے پیدا کرتا ہے
اور خدا ہر چیز پر قادر ہے ﴿۱۷﴾
اور یہود اور نصاریٰ کہتے ہیں کہ ہم خدا کے بیٹے اور اُسکے
پیارے ہیں۔ کہو کہ پھر وہ تمہاری بداعمالیوں کے سبب
تمہیں عذاب کیوں دیتا ہے (نہیں) بلکہ تم اسکی مخلوقات
میں (دوسروں کی طرح کے) انسان ہو۔ وہ جسے چاہے بخشے اور
جسے چاہے عذاب دے۔ اور آسمان اور زمین اور جو کچھ ان دونوں
میں ہے سب پر خدا ہی کی حکومت ہے اور (سب کو) اسی کی طرف لوٹ کر جانا ہے ﴿۱۸﴾
اے اہلِ کتاب پیغمبروں کے آنے کا سلسلہ جو (ایک عرصے تک)
منقطع رہا تو (اب) تمہارے پاس ہمارے پیغمبر آگئے ہیں جو تم سے
(ہمارے احکام) بیان کرتے ہیں تاکہ تم یہ نہ کہو کہ ہمارے پاس کوئی
خوشخبری یا ڈر سنانے والا نہیں آیا سو (اب) تمہارے پاس خوشخبری
اور ڈر سنانے والے آگئے ہیں۔ اور خدا ہر چیز پر قادر ہے ﴿۱۹﴾
اور جب موسیٰ نے اپنی قوم سے کہا کہ بھائیو تم پر خدا نے
جو احسان کیے ہیں ان کو یاد کرو کہ اُس نے تم میں پیغمبر
پیدا کیے اور تمہیں بادشاہ بنایا اور تم کو اتنا کچھ عنایت کیا
کہ اہلِ عالم میں سے کسی کو نہیں دیا ﴿۲۰﴾
تو بھائیو تم ارضِ مقدس (یعنی ملکِ شام) میں جسے خدا

you from Allah a (new) light and a perspicuous Book,—

16. Wherewith Allah guideth all who seek His good pleasure to ways of peace and safety, and leadeth them out of darkness, by His Will, unto the light,—guideth them to a Path that is Straight.

17. They disbelieved indeed those that say that Allah is Christ the son of Mary say: "Who then hath the least power against Allah, if His Will were to destroy Christ the son of Mary, his mother, and all—everyone that is on the earth? For to Allah belongeth the dominion of the heavens and the earth, and all that is between. He createth what He pleaseth. For Allah hath power over all things."

18. (Both) the Jews and the Christians say: "We are sons of Allah, and His beloved." Say: "Why then doth He punish you for your sins ? Nay, ye are but men,— of the men He hath created: He forgiveth whom He pleaseth. And He punisheth whom He pleaseth: and to Allah belongeth the dominion of the heavens and the earth, and all that is between: and unto Him is the final goal (of all)."

19. O People of the Book ! now hath come unto you, making (things) clear unto you. Our Messenger, after the break in (the series of) our messengers, lest ye should say: "There came unto us no bringer of glad tidings and no warner": but now hath come unto you a bringer of glad tidings and a warner. And Allah hath power over all things.

20. Remember Moses said to his people: "O my People ! call in remembrance the favour of Allah unto you, when He produced prophets among you, made you kings, and gave you what He had not given to any other among the peoples.

21. "O my people ! enter the holy land which Allah hath assigned unto

you, and turn not back ignominiously, for then will ye be overthrown, to your own ruin."

22. They said: "O Moses ! in this land are a people of exceeding strength: never shall we enter it until they leave it: If (once) they leave, then shall we enter."

23. (But) among (their) God-fearing men were two on whom Allah had bestowed His grace: they said: "Assault them at the (proper) Gate: when once ye are in, victory will be yours; but on Allah put your trust if ye have faith."

24. They said: "O Moses ! We shall never enter it as long as they are in it. Go thou, and thy Lord, and fight ye two, while we sit here."

25. He said: "O my Lord ! I have power only over myself and my brother: so separate us from this rebellious people !"

26. Allah said: "Therefore will the land be out of their reach for forty years: in distraction will they wander through the land: but sorrow thou not over these rebellious people."

27. Recite to them the truth of the story of the two sons of Adam. Behold ! they each presented a sacrifice (to Allah): it was accepted from one, but not from the other. Said the latter: "Be sure I will slay thee." "Surely," said the former, "Allah doth accept of the sacrifice of those who are righteous.

28. "If thou dost stretch thy hand against me, to slay me, it is not for me to stretch my hand against thee to slay thee: for I do fear Allah, the Cherisher of the Worlds.

نے تمہارے لئے لکھ رکھا ہے چل داخل ہو اور (دیکھنا مقابلے
کے وقت) پیٹھ نہ پھیر دینا ورنہ نقصان میں پڑ جاؤ گے ﴿٢١﴾
وہ کہنے لگے کہ موسیٰ وہاں تو بڑے زبردست لوگ (رہتے)
ہیں۔ اور جب تک وہ اس سرزمین سے نکل نہ جائیں ہم وہاں جا نہیں سکتے
ہاں اگر وہ وہاں سے نکل جائیں تو ہم جا داخل ہونگے ﴿٢٢﴾
جو لوگ (خدا سے) ڈرتے تھے اُن میں سے دو شخص جن پر
خدا کی عنایت تھی کہنے لگے کہ اُن لوگوں پر دروازے کے
رستے سے حملہ کر دو جب تم دروازے میں داخل ہو گئے
تو فتح تمہاری ہے۔ اور خدا ہی پر بھروسہ رکھو بشرطیکہ
صاحب ایمان ہو ﴿٢٣﴾
وہ بولے کہ موسیٰ جب تک وہ لوگ وہاں ہیں ہم کبھی وہاں
نہیں جا سکتے (اگر لڑنا ہی ضرور ہے) تو تم اور تمہارا خدا
جاؤ اور لڑو۔ ہم یہیں بیٹھے رہیں گے ﴿٢٤﴾
موسیٰ نے (خدا سے) التجا کی کہ پروردگار میں اپنے اور اپنے
بھائی کے سوا اور کسی پر اختیار نہیں رکھتا تو ہم میں
اور اُن نافرمان لوگوں میں جدائی کر دے ﴿٢٥﴾
خدا نے فرمایا کہ وہ ملک اُن پر چالیس برس تک کے لئے
حرام کر دیا گیا (کہ وہاں جانے نہ پائینگے اور جنگل کی) زمین میں
سرگرداں پھرتے رہیں گے تو ان نافرمان لوگوں کے حال پر افسوس نہ کرو ﴿٢٦﴾
اور (اے محمدؐ) اُن کو آدم کے دو بیٹوں (ہابیل اور قابیل) کے
حالات (جو بالکل) سچے (ہیں) پڑھ کر سنا دو کہ جب اُن دونوں نے
(خدا کی جناب میں) کچھ نیازیں چڑھائیں تو ایک کی نیاز تو قبول ہو گئی
اور دوسرے کی قبول نہ ہوئی (تب قابیل ہابیل سے) کہنے لگا کہ میں تجھے
قتل کر دونگا اُس نے کہا کہ خدا پرہیزگاروں ہی کی نیاز قبول فرمایا کرتا ہے ﴿٢٧﴾
اور اگر تو مجھے قتل کرنے کیلئے مجھ پر ہاتھ چلائے گا تو میں
تجھ کو قتل کرنے کیلئے تجھ پر ہاتھ نہیں چلاؤں گا۔ مجھے
تو خدائے رب العالمین سے ڈر لگتا ہے ﴿٢٨﴾

الَّتِيْ كَتَبَ اللّٰهُ لَكُمْ وَلَا تَرْتَدُّوْا عَلٰٓى
اَدْبَارِكُمْ فَتَنْقَلِبُوْا خٰسِرِيْنَ ﴿٢١﴾
قَالُوْا يٰمُوْسٰٓى اِنَّ فِيْهَا قَوْمًا جَبَّارِيْنَ ۖ
وَاِنَّا لَنْ نَّدْخُلَهَا حَتّٰى يَخْرُجُوْا مِنْهَا ۚ
فَاِنْ يَّخْرُجُوْا مِنْهَا فَاِنَّا دٰخِلُوْنَ ﴿٢٢﴾
قَالَ رَجُلٰنِ مِنَ الَّذِيْنَ يَخَافُوْنَ اَنْعَمَ
اللّٰهُ عَلَيْهِمَا ادْخُلُوْا عَلَيْهِمُ الْبَابَ ۚ
فَاِذَا دَخَلْتُمُوْهُ فَاِنَّكُمْ غٰلِبُوْنَ ۚ
وَعَلَى اللّٰهِ فَتَوَكَّلُوْٓا اِنْ كُنْتُمْ
مُّؤْمِنِيْنَ ﴿٢٣﴾
قَالُوْا يٰمُوْسٰٓى اِنَّا لَنْ نَّدْخُلَهَآ اَبَدًا
مَّا دَامُوْا فِيْهَا فَاذْهَبْ اَنْتَ وَرَبُّكَ
فَقَاتِلَآ اِنَّا هٰهُنَا قٰعِدُوْنَ ﴿٢٤﴾
قَالَ رَبِّ اِنِّيْ لَآ اَمْلِكُ اِلَّا نَفْسِيْ وَ
اَخِيْ فَافْرُقْ بَيْنَنَا وَبَيْنَ الْقَوْمِ
الْفٰسِقِيْنَ ﴿٢٥﴾
قَالَ فَاِنَّهَا مُحَرَّمَةٌ عَلَيْهِمْ اَرْبَعِيْنَ
سَنَةً ۚ يَتِيْهُوْنَ فِي الْاَرْضِ ۭ فَلَا تَاْسَ
عَلَى الْقَوْمِ الْفٰسِقِيْنَ ﴿٢٦﴾
وَاتْلُ عَلَيْهِمْ نَبَاَ ابْنَيْ اٰدَمَ بِالْحَقِّ ۘ
اِذْ قَرَّبَا قُرْبَانًا فَتُقُبِّلَ مِنْ اَحَدِهِمَا
وَلَمْ يُتَقَبَّلْ مِنَ الْاٰخَرِ ۭ قَالَ
لَاَقْتُلَنَّكَ ۭ قَالَ اِنَّمَا يَتَقَبَّلُ اللّٰهُ
مِنَ الْمُتَّقِيْنَ ﴿٢٧﴾
لَىِٕنْ بَسَطْتَّ اِلَيَّ يَدَكَ لِتَقْتُلَنِيْ مَآ
اَنَا بِبَاسِطٍ يَّدِيَ اِلَيْكَ لِاَقْتُلَكَ ۚ اِنِّيْٓ
اَخَافُ اللّٰهَ رَبَّ الْعٰلَمِيْنَ ﴿٢٨﴾

29. "For me, I intend to let thee draw on thyself my sin as well as thine, for thou wilt be among the Companions of the Fire, and that is the reward of those who do wrong."

إِنِّي أُرِيدُ أَنْ تَبُوءَ بِإِثْمِي وَإِثْمِكَ
فَتَكُونَ مِنْ أَصْحَابِ النَّارِ ۚ وَذَٰلِكَ
جَزَاءُ الظَّالِمِينَ ﴿٢٩﴾

میں چاہتا ہوں کہ تو میرے گناہ میں بھی ماخوذ ہو اور اپنے
گناہ میں بھی پھر (زمرۂ) اہلِ دوزخ میں ہو۔ اور
ظالموں کی یہی سزا ہے (۲۹)

30. The (selfish) soul of the other led him to the murder of his brother: he murdered him, and became (himself) one of the lost ones.

فَطَوَّعَتْ لَهُ نَفْسُهُ قَتْلَ أَخِيهِ فَقَتَلَهُ
فَأَصْبَحَ مِنَ الْخَاسِرِينَ ﴿٣٠﴾

مگر اُس کے نفس نے اُس کو بھائی کے قتل ہی کی ترغیب
دی تو اُس نے اُسے قتل کر دیا اور خسارہ اٹھانے والوں میں ہو گیا (۳۰)

31. Then Allah sent a raven, who scratched the ground, to show him how to hide the naked body of his brother. "Woe is me !" said he; "Was I not even able to be as this raven, and to hide the naked body of my brother ?" Then he became full of regrets—

فَبَعَثَ اللَّهُ غُرَابًا يَبْحَثُ فِي الْأَرْضِ
لِيُرِيَهُ كَيْفَ يُوَارِي سَوْءَةَ أَخِيهِ ۚ
قَالَ يَا وَيْلَتَا أَعَجَزْتُ أَنْ أَكُونَ مِثْلَ
هَٰذَا الْغُرَابِ فَأُوَارِيَ سَوْءَةَ أَخِي ۖ
فَأَصْبَحَ مِنَ النَّادِمِينَ ﴿٣١﴾

اب خدا نے ایک کوا بھیجا جو زمین کریدنے لگا تاکہ اُسے
دکھائے کہ اپنے بھائی کی لاش کو کیونکر چھپائے۔ کہنے
لگا اے ہے مجھ سے اتنا بھی نہ ہو سکا کہ اس کوّے
کے برابر ہوتا کہ اپنے بھائی کی لاش چھپا دیتا۔ پھر
وہ پشیمان ہوا (۳۱)

32. On that account: We ordained for the Children of Israel that if any one slew a person—unless it be for murder or for speading mischief in the land— it would be as if he slew the whole people: and if any one saved a life. It would be as if he saved the life of the whole people. Then although there came to them Our Messengers with Clear Signs, yet, even after that, many of them continued to commit excesses in the land.

مِنْ أَجْلِ ذَٰلِكَ كَتَبْنَا عَلَىٰ بَنِي
إِسْرَائِيلَ أَنَّهُ مَنْ قَتَلَ نَفْسًا بِغَيْرِ
نَفْسٍ أَوْ فَسَادٍ فِي الْأَرْضِ فَكَأَنَّمَا
قَتَلَ النَّاسَ جَمِيعًا وَمَنْ أَحْيَاهَا
فَكَأَنَّمَا أَحْيَا النَّاسَ جَمِيعًا ۚ وَلَقَدْ
جَاءَتْهُمْ رُسُلُنَا بِالْبَيِّنَاتِ ثُمَّ إِنَّ
كَثِيرًا مِنْهُمْ بَعْدَ ذَٰلِكَ فِي الْأَرْضِ
لَمُسْرِفُونَ ﴿٣٢﴾

اس (قتل) کی وجہ سے ہم نے بنی اسرائیل پر یہ حکم نازل
کیا کہ جو شخص کسی کو (ناحق) قتل کرے گا (یعنی) بغیر اسکے
کہ جان کا بدلہ لیا جائے یا ملک میں خرابی کرنے کی سزا دی جائے
اُس نے گویا تمام لوگوں کو قتل کیا۔ اور جو اسکی زندگانی
کا موجب ہوا تو گویا تمام لوگوں کی زندگانی کا موجب
ہوا اور ان لوگوں کے پاس ہمارے پیغمبر روشن دلیلیں
لا چکے ہیں پھر اس کے بعد بھی اُن میں بہت سے لوگ
ملک میں حدِ اعتدال سے نکل جاتے ہیں (۳۲)

33. The punishment of those who wage war against Allah and His Messenger, and strive with might and main for mischief through the land is: execution, or crucifixion, or the cutting off of hands and feet from opposite sides, or exile from the land: that is their disgrace in this world, and a heavy punishment is theirs in the Hereafter;

إِنَّمَا جَزَاءُ الَّذِينَ يُحَارِبُونَ اللَّهَ وَ
رَسُولَهُ وَيَسْعَوْنَ فِي الْأَرْضِ فَسَادًا
أَنْ يُقَتَّلُوا أَوْ يُصَلَّبُوا أَوْ تُقَطَّعَ أَيْدِيهِمْ
وَأَرْجُلُهُمْ مِنْ خِلَافٍ أَوْ يُنْفَوْا
مِنَ الْأَرْضِ ۚ ذَٰلِكَ لَهُمْ خِزْيٌ فِي الدُّنْيَا ۖ
وَلَهُمْ فِي الْآخِرَةِ عَذَابٌ عَظِيمٌ ﴿٣٣﴾

جو لوگ خدا اور اُس کے رسول سے لڑائی کریں اور ملک
میں فساد کرنے کو دوڑتے پھریں اُن کی یہی سزا ہے
کہ قتل کر دیے جائیں یا سولی چڑھا دیے جائیں یا اُن
کے ایک ایک طرف کے ہاتھ اور ایک ایک طرف کے پاؤں
کاٹ دیے جائیں یا ملک سے نکال دیے جائیں یہ تو دنیا میں
انکی رسوائی ہے اور آخرت میں اُنکے لئے بڑا (بھاری) عذاب (تیار) ہے (۳۳)

34. Except for those who repent before they fall into your Power: in that case, know that Allah is Oft-Forgiving, Most Merciful.

إِلَّا الَّذِينَ تَابُوا مِنْ قَبْلِ أَنْ تَقْدِرُوا
عَلَيْهِمْ ۖ فَاعْلَمُوا أَنَّ اللَّهَ غَفُورٌ رَحِيمٌ ﴿٣٤﴾

ہاں جن لوگوں نے اس سے پیشتر کہ تمہارے قابو آ جائیں
توبہ کر لی تو جان رکھو کہ خدا بخشنے والا مہربان ہے (۳۴)

35. O ye who believe ! do your duty to Allah, seek the means of

يَا أَيُّهَا الَّذِينَ آمَنُوا اتَّقُوا اللَّهَ وَابْتَغُوا

اے ایمان والو! خدا سے ڈرتے رہو اور اس کا قرب

approach unto Him, and strive (with might and main) in His cause: that ye may prosper.

36. As to those who reject Faith,—if they had everything on earth, and twice repeated, to give as ransom for the Chastisement of the Day of Judgment, it would never be accepted of them. Theirs would be a grievous Chastisement.

37. Their wish will be to get out of the Fire. But never will they get out therefrom: their Chastisement will be one that endures.

38. As to the thief, Male or female, cut off his or her hands: a retribution for their deed and exemplary punishment from Allah, and Allah is Exalted in Power, full of Wisdom.

39. But if the thief repent after his crime, and amend his conduct, Allah turneth to him in forgiveness; for Allah is Oft-Forgiving, Most Merciful.

40. Knowest thou not that to Allah (alone) belongeth the dominion of the heavens and the earth ? He punisheth whom He pleaseth, and He forgiveth whom He pleaseth: and Allah hath power over all things.

41. O Messenger ! let not those grieve thee, who race each other into Unbelief: (whether it be) among those who say "We believe" with their lips but whose hearts have no faith; or it be among the Jews—men who will listen to any lie,—will listen even to others who have never so much as come to thee. They change the words from their (right) places they say, "If ye are given this, take it, but if not, beware!" If any one's trial is intended by Allah, thou hast no authority in the least for him against Allah. For such—it is not Allah's

حاصل کرنے کا ذریعہ تلاش کرتے رہو اور اُسکے رستے
میں جہاد کرو تاکہ رُستگاری پاؤ ﴿۳۵﴾
جو لوگ کافر ہیں اگر اُن کے پاس رُوئے زمین (کے
تمام خزانے اور اس) کا سب مال ومتاع ہو اور اسکے ساتھ اسی قدر
اور بھی ہو تاکہ قیامت کے روز عذاب (سے رُستگاری) حاصل
کرنے) کا بدلہ دیں تو اُن سے قبول نہیں کیا جائے گا۔ اور
اُن کو درد دینے والا عذاب ہوگا ﴿۳۶﴾
(ہر چند) چاہیں گے کہ آگ سے نکل جائیں مگر اس سے
نہیں نکل سکیں گے اور اُنکے لئے ہمیشہ کا عذاب ہے ﴿۳۷﴾
اور جو چوری کرے مرد ہو یا عورت اُن کے ہاتھ کاٹ
ڈالو۔ یہ اُن کے فعلوں کی سزا اور خدا کی طرف سے عبرت
ہے۔ اور خدا زبردست (اور) صاحب حکمت ہے ﴿۳۸﴾
اور جو شخص گناہ کے بعد توبہ کرلے اور نیکوکار ہو جائے
تو خدا اُس کو معاف کر دے گا۔ کچھ شک نہیں کہ خُدا
بخشنے والا مہربان ہے ﴿۳۹﴾
کیا تم کو معلوم نہیں کہ آسمانوں اور زمین میں خُدا ہی
کی سلطنت ہے جس کو چاہے عذاب کرے اور جسے چاہے
بخش دے۔ اور خُدا ہر چیز پر قادر ہے ﴿۴۰﴾
اے پیغمبر جو لوگ کفر میں جلدی کرتے ہیں (کچھ تو) اُن
میں سے (ہیں) جو مُنہ سے کہتے ہیں کہ ہم مومن ہیں
لیکن اُن کے دل مومن نہیں ہیں اور (کچھ) اُن میں سے جو
یہودی ہیں اُنکی وجہ سے غمناک نہ ہونا یہ غلط باتیں بنانے
کیلئے جاسوسی کرتے پھرتے ہیں اور ایسے لوگوں (کے بہکانے
کیلئے جاسوس بنے ہیں جو ابھی تمہارے پاس نہیں آئے (صحیح)
باتوں کو اُنکے مقامات (میں ثابت ہونے) کے بعد بدل دیتے
ہیں اور (لوگوں سے) کہتے ہیں کہ اگر تم کو یہی (حکم) ملے تو اسے
قبول کرلینا اور اگر نہ ملے تو (اس سے) احتراز کرنا اور اگر کسی کو

إِلَيْهِ الْوَسِيلَةَ وَجَاهِدُوا فِي سَبِيلِهِ
لَعَلَّكُمْ تُفْلِحُونَ ﴿٣٥﴾
إِنَّ الَّذِينَ كَفَرُوا لَوْ أَنَّ لَهُم مَّا
فِي الْأَرْضِ جَمِيعًا وَمِثْلَهُ مَعَهُ
لِيَفْتَدُوا بِهِ مِنْ عَذَابِ يَوْمِ
الْقِيَامَةِ مَا تُقُبِّلَ مِنْهُمْ ۖ وَلَهُمْ
عَذَابٌ أَلِيمٌ ﴿٣٦﴾
يُرِيدُونَ أَن يَخْرُجُوا مِنَ النَّارِ وَمَا هُم
بِخَارِجِينَ مِنْهَا ۖ وَلَهُمْ عَذَابٌ مُّقِيمٌ ﴿٣٧﴾
وَالسَّارِقُ وَالسَّارِقَةُ فَاقْطَعُوا
أَيْدِيَهُمَا جَزَاءً بِمَا كَسَبَا نَكَالًا مِّنَ
اللَّهِ ۗ وَاللَّهُ عَزِيزٌ حَكِيمٌ ﴿٣٨﴾
فَمَن تَابَ مِن بَعْدِ ظُلْمِهِ وَأَصْلَحَ
فَإِنَّ اللَّهَ يَتُوبُ عَلَيْهِ ۗ إِنَّ اللَّهَ
غَفُورٌ رَّحِيمٌ ﴿٣٩﴾
أَلَمْ تَعْلَمْ أَنَّ اللَّهَ لَهُ مُلْكُ السَّمَاوَاتِ
وَالْأَرْضِ يُعَذِّبُ مَن يَشَاءُ وَيَغْفِرُ
لِمَن يَشَاءُ ۗ وَاللَّهُ عَلَىٰ كُلِّ شَيْءٍ قَدِيرٌ ﴿٤٠﴾
يَا أَيُّهَا الرَّسُولُ لَا يَحْزُنكَ الَّذِينَ
يُسَارِعُونَ فِي الْكُفْرِ مِنَ الَّذِينَ
قَالُوا آمَنَّا بِأَفْوَاهِهِمْ وَلَمْ تُؤْمِن
قُلُوبُهُمْ ۛ وَمِنَ الَّذِينَ هَادُوا ۛ مع
سَمَّاعُونَ لِلْكَذِبِ سَمَّاعُونَ لِقَوْمٍ عند المتقدمين ۱۲
آخَرِينَ لَمْ يَأْتُوكَ ۖ يُحَرِّفُونَ الْكَلِمَ
مِن بَعْدِ مَوَاضِعِهِ ۖ يَقُولُونَ إِنْ
أُوتِيتُمْ هَٰذَا فَخُذُوهُ وَإِن لَّمْ
تُؤْتَوْهُ فَاحْذَرُوا ۚ وَمَن يُرِدِ اللَّهُ

will to purify their hearts. For them there is disgrace in this world, and in the Hereafter a heavy punishment.

خدا گمراہ کرنا چاہے تو اس کیلئے تم کچھ بھی خدا سے (ہدایت کا)
اختیار نہیں رکھتے۔ یہ وہ لوگ ہیں جن کے دلوں کو خدا نے
پاک کرنا نہیں چاہا۔ اُن کیلئے دنیا میں بھی ذلت ہے اور
آخرت میں بھی بڑا عذاب ہے[99] ﴿۴۱﴾

فِتْنَتَهٗ فَلَنْ تَمْلِكَ لَهٗ مِنَ اللّٰهِ شَيْـًٔا ؕ
اُولٰٓئِكَ الَّذِيْنَ لَمْ يُرِدِ اللّٰهُ اَنْ يُّطَهِّرَ
قُلُوْبَهُمْ ؕ لَهُمْ فِى الدُّنْيَا خِزْىٌ ۚۖ وَّ
لَهُمْ فِى الْاٰخِرَةِ عَذَابٌ عَظِيْمٌ ﴿۴۱﴾

42. (They are fond of) listening to falsehood, of devouring anything forbidden. If they do come to thee, either judge between them, or decline to interfere. If thou decline, they cannot hurt thee in the least. If thou judge, judge in equity between them. For Allah loveth those who judge in equity.

(یہ) جھوٹی باتیں بنانے کیلئے جاسوسی کرنیوالے اور رشوت کا
حرام مال کھانیوالے ہیں۔ اگر یہ تمہارے پاس (کوئی مقدمہ فیصل کرانے کو)
آئیں تو تم ان میں فیصلہ کردینا یا اعراض کرنا۔ اور اگر ان سے
اعراض کرو گے تو وہ تمہارا کچھ بھی نہیں بگاڑ سکیں گے۔
اور اگر فیصلہ کرنا چاہو تو انصاف کا فیصلہ کرنا کہ خدا
انصاف کرنے والوں کو دوست رکھتا ہے ﴿۴۲﴾

سَمّٰعُوْنَ لِلْكَذِبِ اَكّٰلُوْنَ لِلسُّحْتِ ؕ
فَاِنْ جَآءُوْكَ فَاحْكُمْ بَيْنَهُمْ اَوْ اَعْرِضْ
عَنْهُمْ ۚ وَاِنْ تُعْرِضْ عَنْهُمْ فَلَنْ
يَّضُرُّوْكَ شَيْـًٔا ؕ وَاِنْ حَكَمْتَ فَاحْكُمْ
بَيْنَهُمْ بِالْقِسْطِ ؕ اِنَّ اللّٰهَ يُحِبُّ
الْمُقْسِطِيْنَ ﴿۴۲﴾

43. But why do they come to thee for decision, when they have (their own) Torah before them?—Therein is the (plain) Command of Allah; yet even after that, they would turn away. For they are not (really) People of Faith.

اور یہ تم سے (اپنے مقدمات) کیونکر فیصلہ کرائینگے جبکہ خود انکے پاس
تورات (موجود) ہے جس میں خدا کا حکم (لکھا ہوا) ہے (یہ اسے جانتے ہیں)
پھر اسکے بعد اس سے پھر جاتے ہیں اور یہ لوگ ایمان ہی نہیں رکھتے ﴿۴۳﴾

وَكَيْفَ يُحَكِّمُوْنَكَ وَعِنْدَهُمُ التَّوْرٰىةُ
فِيْهَا حُكْمُ اللّٰهِ ثُمَّ يَتَوَلَّوْنَ مِنْۢ بَعْدِ
ذٰلِكَ ؕ وَمَآ اُولٰٓئِكَ بِالْمُؤْمِنِيْنَ ﴿۴۳﴾ ع

44. It was We who revealed the Torah (to Moses): therein was guidance and light. By its standard have been judged the Jews, by the Prophets who bowed (as in Islam) to Allah's Will, by the Rabbis and the Doctors of Law: for to them was entrusted the protection of Allah's Book, and they were witnesses thereto: therefore fear not men, but fear Me, and sell not My Signs for a miserable price. If any do fail to judge by what Allah hath revealed, they are Unbelievers.

بیشک ہم نے تورات نازل فرمائی جس میں ہدایت اور
روشنی ہے۔ اسی کے مطابق انبیاء جو (خدا کے) فرمانبردار تھے
یہودیوں کو حکم دیتے رہے ہیں اور مشائخ اور علماء بھی کیونکہ وہ
کتاب خدا کے نگہبان مقرر کئے گئے تھے اور اس پر گواہ تھے
(یعنی حکم الٰہی کا یقین رکھتے تھے) تو تم لوگوں سے
مت ڈرنا اور مجھی سے ڈرتے رہنا اور میری آیتوں کے
بدلے تھوڑی سی قیمت نہ لینا۔ اور جو خدا کے نازل فرمائے ہوئے
احکام کے مطابق حکم نہ دے تو ایسے ہی لوگ کافر ہیں ﴿۴۴﴾

اِنَّآ اَنْزَلْنَا التَّوْرٰىةَ فِيْهَا هُدًى وَّنُوْرٌ ۚ
يَحْكُمُ بِهَا النَّبِيُّوْنَ الَّذِيْنَ اَسْلَمُوْا
لِلَّذِيْنَ هَادُوْا وَالرَّبّٰنِيُّوْنَ وَالْاَحْبَارُ
بِمَا اسْتُحْفِظُوْا مِنْ كِتٰبِ اللّٰهِ وَكَانُوْا
عَلَيْهِ شُهَدَآءَ ۚ فَلَا تَخْشَوُا النَّاسَ
وَاخْشَوْنِ وَلَا تَشْتَرُوْا بِاٰيٰتِىْ ثَمَنًا
قَلِيْلًا ؕ وَمَنْ لَّمْ يَحْكُمْ بِمَآ اَنْزَلَ اللّٰهُ
فَاُولٰٓئِكَ هُمُ الْكٰفِرُوْنَ ﴿۴۴﴾

45. We ordained therein for them: "Life for life, eye for eye, nose for nose, ear for ear, tooth for tooth, and wounds equal for equal." But if anyone remits the retaliation by way of charity, it is an act of atonement for himself. And if any fail to judge by what Allah hath revealed, they are wrong-doers.

اور ہم نے ان لوگوں کے لئے تورات میں یہ حکم لکھ دیا تھا
کہ جان کے بدلے جان اور آنکھ کے بدلے آنکھ اور ناک
کے بدلے ناک اور کان کے بدلے کان اور دانت کے بدلے
دانت اور سب زخموں کا اسی طرح بدلہ ہے۔ لیکن جو شخص
بدلہ معاف کردے وہ اس کے لئے کفارہ ہوگا۔ اور جو خدا کے نازل
فرمائے ہوئے احکام کے مطابق حکم نہ دے تو ایسے ہی لوگ بے انصاف ہیں ﴿۴۵﴾

وَكَتَبْنَا عَلَيْهِمْ فِيْهَآ اَنَّ النَّفْسَ
بِالنَّفْسِ ۙ وَالْعَيْنَ بِالْعَيْنِ وَالْاَنْفَ
بِالْاَنْفِ وَالْاُذُنَ بِالْاُذُنِ وَالسِّنَّ
بِالسِّنِّ ۙ وَالْجُرُوْحَ قِصَاصٌ ؕ فَمَنْ
تَصَدَّقَ بِهٖ فَهُوَ كَفَّارَةٌ لَّهٗ ؕ وَمَنْ لَّمْ
يَحْكُمْ بِمَآ اَنْزَلَ اللّٰهُ فَاُولٰٓئِكَ هُمُ الظّٰلِمُوْنَ ﴿۴۵﴾

46. And in their footsteps We sent Jesus the son of Mary, confirming the Torah that had come before him: We sent him the Gospel: therein was guidance and light. And confirmation of the Torah that had come before him: a guidance and an admonition to those who fear Allah.

اور ان پیغمبروں کے بعد انہیں کے قدموں پر ہم نے
عیسیٰ ابن مریم کو بھیجا جو اپنے سے پہلے کی کتاب تورات
کی تصدیق کرتے تھے اور اُن کو انجیل عنایت کی
جس میں ہدایت اور نُور ہے اور تورات کی جو اُس سے
پہلی (کتاب) ہے تصدیق کرتی ہے اور پرہیزگاروں کو راہ
بتاتی اور نصیحت کرتی ہے ﴿۴۶﴾

وَقَفَّيْنَا عَلَىٰٓ اٰثَارِهِمْ بِعِيْسَى ابْنِ
مَرْيَمَ مُصَدِّقًا لِّمَا بَيْنَ يَدَيْهِ
مِنَ التَّوْرٰىةِ ۪ وَاٰتَيْنٰهُ الْاِنْجِيْلَ
فِيْهِ هُدًى وَّنُوْرٌ ۙ وَّمُصَدِّقًا لِّمَا
بَيْنَ يَدَيْهِ مِنَ التَّوْرٰىةِ وَهُدًى
وَّمَوْعِظَةً لِّلْمُتَّقِيْنَ ۭ﴿٤٦﴾

47. Let the People of the Gospel judge by what Allah hath revealed therein. If any do fail to judge by what Allah hath revealed, they are those who rebel.

اور اہلِ انجیل کو چاہیئے کہ جو احکام خدا نے اسمیں نازل فرمائے ہیں
اُس کے مطابق حکم دیا کریں۔ اور جو خدا کے نازل کئے ہوئے
احکام کے مطابق حکم نہ دیگا تو ایسے لوگ نافرمان ہیں ﴿۴۷﴾

وَلْيَحْكُمْ اَهْلُ الْاِنْجِيْلِ بِمَآ اَنْزَلَ اللّٰهُ
فِيْهِ ۭ وَمَنْ لَّمْ يَحْكُمْ بِمَآ اَنْزَلَ اللّٰهُ
فَاُولٰۗىِٕكَ هُمُ الْفٰسِقُوْنَ ﴿٤٧﴾

48. To thee We sent the Scripture in truth, confirming the scripture that came before it, and guarding it in safety: so judge between them by what Allah hath revealed, and follow not their vain desires, diverging from the Truth that hath come to thee. To each among you have We prescribed a Law and an Open Way. If Allah had so willed, He would have made you a single People, but (His Plan is) to test you in what He hath given you: so strive as in a race in all virtues. The goal of you all is to Allah; it is He that will show you the truth of the matters in which ye dispute;

اور (اے پیغمبر) ہم نے تم پر سچی کتاب نازل کی ہے جو اپنے
سے پہلی کتابوں کی تصدیق کرتی ہے اور اُن (سب)
پر شامل ہے تو جو حکم خدا نے نازل فرمایا ہے اُسکے مطابق اُنکا
فیصلہ کرنا اور حق جو تمہارے پاس آچکا ہے اُسکو چھوڑ کر اُنکی
خواہشوں کی پیروی نہ کرنا۔ ہم نے تم میں سے ہر ایک (فرقے)
کیلئے ایک دستور اور طریقہ مقرر کیا ہے۔ اور اگر خدا چاہتا تو تم سب کو
ایک ہی شریعت پر کر دیتا مگر جو حکم اُسنے تمکو دیئے ہیں اُنمیں وہ
تمہاری آزمائش کرنی چاہتا ہے سو نیک کاموں میں جلدی کرو
تم سب کو خدا کی طرف لوٹ کر جانا ہے پھر جن باتوں میں
تم کو اختلاف تھا وہ تم کو بتا دے گا ﴿۴۸﴾

وَاَنْزَلْنَآ اِلَيْكَ الْكِتٰبَ بِالْحَقِّ مُصَدِّقًا
لِّمَا بَيْنَ يَدَيْهِ مِنَ الْكِتٰبِ وَمُهَيْمِنًا
عَلَيْهِ فَاحْكُمْ بَيْنَهُمْ بِمَآ اَنْزَلَ اللّٰهُ
وَلَا تَتَّبِعْ اَهْوَاۗءَهُمْ عَمَّا جَاۗءَكَ
مِنَ الْحَقِّ ۭ لِكُلٍّ جَعَلْنَا مِنْكُمْ شِرْعَةً
وَّمِنْهَاجًا ۭ وَلَوْ شَاۗءَ اللّٰهُ لَجَعَلَكُمْ
اُمَّةً وَّاحِدَةً وَّلٰكِنْ لِّيَبْلُوَكُمْ فِيْ
مَآ اٰتٰىكُمْ فَاسْتَبِقُوا الْخَيْرٰتِ ۭ اِلَى
اللّٰهِ مَرْجِعُكُمْ جَمِيْعًا فَيُنَبِّئُكُمْ بِمَا
كُنْتُمْ فِيْهِ تَخْتَلِفُوْنَ ﴿٤٨﴾ۙ

49. And this (He commands): Judge thou between them by what Allah hath revealed, and follow not their vain desires, but beware of them lest they beguile thee from any of that (teaching) which Allah hath sent down to thee. And if they turn away, be assured that for some of their crimes it is Allah's purpose to punish them. And truly most men are rebellious.

اور (ہم پھر تاکید کرتے ہیں کہ) جو (حکم) خدا نے نازل فرمایا ہے
اُسی کے مطابق اُنمیں فیصلہ کرنا اور اُنکی خواہشوں کی پیروی نہ
کرنا اور اُن سے بچتے رہنا کہ کسی حکم سے جو خدا نے تم پر نازل فرمایا ہے
یہ کہیں تمکو بہکا نہ دیں۔ اگر یہ نہ مانیں تو جان لو کہ خدا چاہتا ہے
کہ اُنکے بعض گناہوں کے سبب اُن پر مصیبت نازل کرے
اور اکثر لوگ تو نافرمان ہیں ﴿۴۹﴾

وَاَنِ احْكُمْ بَيْنَهُمْ بِمَآ اَنْزَلَ اللّٰهُ وَلَا
تَتَّبِعْ اَهْوَاۗءَهُمْ وَاحْذَرْهُمْ اَنْ
يَّفْتِنُوْكَ عَنْۢ بَعْضِ مَآ اَنْزَلَ اللّٰهُ
اِلَيْكَ ۭ فَاِنْ تَوَلَّوْا فَاعْلَمْ اَنَّمَا يُرِيْدُ
اللّٰهُ اَنْ يُّصِيْبَهُمْ بِبَعْضِ ذُنُوْبِهِمْ ۭ
وَاِنَّ كَثِيْرًا مِّنَ النَّاسِ لَفٰسِقُوْنَ ﴿٤٩﴾

50. Do they then seek after a judgment of (the Days of) Ignorance? But who, for a people whose faith is assured, can give better judgment than Allah ?

کیا یہ زمانہ جاہلیت کے حکم کے خواہشمند ہیں۔ اور جو یقین
رکھتے ہیں اُن کیلئے خدا سے اچھا حکم کس کا ہے ﴿۵۰﴾

اَفَحُكْمَ الْجَاهِلِيَّةِ يَبْغُوْنَ ۭ وَمَنْ
اَحْسَنُ مِنَ اللّٰهِ حُكْمًا لِّقَوْمٍ يُّوْقِنُوْنَ ﴿٥٠﴾ ع ٧

51. O ye who believe ! take not the Jews and the Christians for your friends and protectors: they are but friends and protectors to each other. And he amongst you that turns to them (for friendship) is of them. Verily Allah guideth not a people unjust.

52. Those in whose hearts is a disease—thou seest how eagerly they run about amongst them, saying: "We do fear lest a change of fortune bring us disaster." Ah ! perhaps Allah will give (thee) victory, or a decision from Him then will they regret of the thoughts which they secretly harboured in their hearts.

53. And those who believe will say: "Are these the men who swore their strongest oaths by Allah, that they were with you ? All that they do will be in vain, and they will fall into (nothing but) ruin.

اے ایمان والو! یہود اور نصاریٰ کو دوست نہ بناؤ
یہ ایک دوسرے کے دوست ہیں اور جو شخص تم
میں سے اُن کو دوست بنائے گا وہ بھی اُنہیں
میں سے ہوگا۔ بیشک خدا ظالم لوگوں کو ہدایت نہیں دیتا ﴿۵۱﴾
تو جن لوگوں کے دلوں میں (نفاق کا) مرض ہے تم
اُن کو دیکھو گے کہ اُن میں دوڑ دوڑ کے ملے جاتے ہیں۔
کہتے ہیں کہ ہمیں خوف ہے کہ کہیں ہم پر زمانے کی گردش نہ آجائے
سو قریب ہے کہ خدا فتح بھیجے یا اپنے ہاں سے کوئی اور امر (نازل فرمائے)
پھر یہ اپنے دل کی باتوں پر جو چھپایا کرتے تھے پشیمان ہو کر رہ جائینگے ﴿۵۲﴾
اور (اُس وقت) مسلمان (تعجب سے) کہیں گے کہ کیا یہ وہی
ہیں جو خدا کی سخت سخت قسمیں کھایا کرتے تھے۔ کہ ہم تمہارے
ساتھ ہیں۔ اُن کے عمل اکارت گئے اور وہ خسارے
میں پڑ گئے ﴿۵۳﴾

يٰۤاَيُّهَا الَّذِيْنَ اٰمَنُوْا لَا تَتَّخِذُوا الْيَهُوْدَ
وَالنَّصٰرٰۤى اَوْلِيَآءَ ۘ بَعْضُهُمْ اَوْلِيَآءُ
بَعْضٍ ؕ وَمَنْ يَّتَوَلَّهُمْ مِّنْكُمْ فَاِنَّهٗ
مِنْهُمْ ؕ اِنَّ اللّٰهَ لَا يَهْدِى الْقَوْمَ الظّٰلِمِيْنَ ﴿۵۱﴾
فَتَرَى الَّذِيْنَ فِىْ قُلُوْبِهِمْ مَّرَضٌ
يُّسَارِعُوْنَ فِيْهِمْ يَقُوْلُوْنَ نَخْشٰٓى
اَنْ تُصِيْبَنَا دَآئِرَةٌ ؕ فَعَسَى اللّٰهُ اَنْ
يَّاْتِىَ بِالْفَتْحِ اَوْ اَمْرٍ مِّنْ عِنْدِهٖ فَيُصْبِحُوْا
عَلٰى مَاۤ اَسَرُّوْا فِىْۤ اَنْفُسِهِمْ نٰدِمِيْنَ ﴿۵۲﴾
وَيَقُوْلُ الَّذِيْنَ اٰمَنُوْۤا اَهٰٓؤُلَآءِ
الَّذِيْنَ اَقْسَمُوْا بِاللّٰهِ جَهْدَ اَيْمَانِهِمْ
اِنَّهُمْ لَمَعَكُمْ ؕ حَبِطَتْ اَعْمَالُهُمْ
فَاَصْبَحُوْا خٰسِرِيْنَ ﴿۵۳﴾

54. O ye who believe ! if any from among you turn back from his Faith, soon will Allah produce a people whom He will love as they will love Him,—lowly with the Believers, mighty against the Rejecters, fighting in the Way of Allah, and never afraid of the reproaches of such as find fault. That is the Grace of Allah, which He will bestow on whom He pleaseth. And Allah encompasseth all, and He knoweth all things.

اے ایمان والو اگر کوئی تم میں سے اپنے دین سے پھر جائیگا
تو خدا ایسے لوگ پیدا کر دیگا جن کو وہ دوست رکھے اور
جسے وہ دوست رکھیں اور جو مومنوں کے حق میں نرمی
کریں اور کافروں سے سختی سے پیش آئیں۔ خدا کی راہ میں جہاد
کریں اور کسی ملامت کرنیوالے کی ملامت سے نہ ڈریں۔ یہ خدا
کا فضل ہے۔ وہ جسے چاہتا ہے دیتا ہے۔
اور خدا بڑی کشایش والا (اور) جاننے والا ہے ﴿۵۴﴾

يٰۤاَيُّهَا الَّذِيْنَ اٰمَنُوْا مَنْ يَّرْتَدَّ مِنْكُمْ
عَنْ دِيْنِهٖ فَسَوْفَ يَاْتِى اللّٰهُ بِقَوْمٍ
يُّحِبُّهُمْ وَيُحِبُّوْنَهٗۤ ۙ اَذِلَّةٍ عَلَى الْمُؤْمِنِيْنَ
اَعِزَّةٍ عَلَى الْكٰفِرِيْنَ يُجَاهِدُوْنَ فِىْ
سَبِيْلِ اللّٰهِ وَلَا يَخَافُوْنَ لَوْمَةَ لَآئِمٍ ؕ
ذٰلِكَ فَضْلُ اللّٰهِ يُؤْتِيْهِ مَنْ يَّشَآءُ ؕ
وَاللّٰهُ وَاسِعٌ عَلِيْمٌ ﴿۵۴﴾

55. Your (real) friends are (no less than) Allah, His Messenger, and the Believers,—those who establish regular prayers and pay Zakat and they bow down humbly (in worship).

56. As to those who turn (for friendship) to Allah, His Messenger, and the Believers,—it is the party of Allah that must certainly triumph.

تمہارے دوست تو خدا اور اُس کے پیغمبر اور مومن لوگ
ہی ہیں جو نماز پڑھتے اور زکوٰۃ دیتے اور (خدا کے
آگے) جھکتے ہیں ﴿۵۵﴾
اور جو شخص خدا اور اُسکے پیغمبر اور مومنوں سے دوستی کریگا تو (وہ خدا
کی جماعت میں داخل ہوگا اور) خدا کی جماعت ہی غلبہ پانیوالی ہے ﴿۵۶﴾

اِنَّمَا وَلِيُّكُمُ اللّٰهُ وَرَسُوْلُهٗ وَالَّذِيْنَ
اٰمَنُوا الَّذِيْنَ يُقِيْمُوْنَ الصَّلٰوةَ وَ
يُؤْتُوْنَ الزَّكٰوةَ وَهُمْ رٰكِعُوْنَ ﴿۵۵﴾
وَمَنْ يَّتَوَلَّ اللّٰهَ وَرَسُوْلَهٗ وَالَّذِيْنَ
اٰمَنُوْا فَاِنَّ حِزْبَ اللّٰهِ هُمُ الْغٰلِبُوْنَ ﴿۵۶﴾

57. O ye who believe ! take not for friends and protectors those who take your religion for a mockery or sport,—whether among those who

اے ایمان والو جن لوگوں کو تم سے پہلے کتابیں
دی گئی تھیں اُن کو اور کافروں کو جنہوں نے تمہارے

يٰۤاَيُّهَا الَّذِيْنَ اٰمَنُوْا لَا تَتَّخِذُوا الَّذِيْنَ
اتَّخَذُوْا دِيْنَكُمْ هُزُوًا وَّلَعِبًا مِّنَ

received the Scripture before you, or among those who reject Faith: but fear ye Allah, if ye have Faith (indeed).

58. When ye proclaim your call to prayer, they take it (but) as mockery and sport; that is because they are a people without understanding.

59. Say: "O people of the Book ! Do ye disapprove of us for no other reason than that we believe in Allah, and the revelation that hath come to us and that which came before (us), and (perhaps) that most of you are rebellious and disobedient?"

60. Say: "Shall I point out to you something much worse than this, (as judged) by the treatment it received from Allah ? Those who incurred the curse of Allah and His wrath, those of whom some He transformed into apes and swine, those who worshipped Evil (Tagut)— these are (many times) worse in rank, and far more astray from the even Path !"

61. When they come to thee, they say: "We believe": but in fact they enter with a disbelief, and they go out with the same. But Allah knoweth fully all that they hide.

62. Many of them dost thou see, racing each other in sin and transgression and their eating of things forbidden. Evil indeed are the things that they do.

63. Why do not the Rabbis and the doctors of law forbid them from their (habit of) uttering sinful words and eating things forbidden ? Evil indeed are their works.

64. The Jews say: "Allah's hand is tied up," Be *their* hands tied up and be they accursed for the (blasphemy) they utter. Nay, both His hands are widely outstretched: He giveth and spendeth (of His bounty) as He pleaseth. But the revelation that cometh to thee from Allah increaseth in most of them their obstinate rebellion and blasphemy. Amongst them We

دین کو ہنسی اور کھیل بنا رکھا ہو دوست نہ بناؤ اور
مومن ہو تو خدا سے ڈرتے رہو ﴿۵۷﴾
اور جب تم لوگ نماز کے لئے اذان دیتے ہو تو یہ اُسے
بھی ہنسی اور کھیل بناتے ہیں یہ اسلئے کہ سمجھ نہیں رکھتے ﴿۵۸﴾
کہو کہ اے اہلِ کتاب تم ہم میں بُرائی ہی کیا دیکھتے ہو سوا اسکے
کہ ہم خدا پر اور جو کتاب ہم پر نازل ہوئی اس پر اور جو کتابیں
پہلے نازل ہوئیں اُن پر ایمان لائے ہیں اور تم میں اکثر بدکردار ہیں ﴿۵۹﴾
کہو کہ میں تمہیں بتاؤں کہ خدا کے ہاں اس سے بھی
بدتر جزا پانے والے کون ہیں؟ وہ لوگ ہیں جن پر
خدا نے لعنت کی اور جن پر وہ غضبناک ہوا اور (جنکو)
اُن میں سے بندر اور سُور بنا دیا اور جنہوں نے شیطان کی پرستش کی
ایسے لوگوں کا بُرا ٹھکانا ہے اور وہ سیدھے رستے سے بہت دور ہیں ﴿۶۰﴾
اور جب یہ لوگ تمہارے پاس آتے ہیں تو کہتے ہیں کہ ہم
ایمان لے آئے حالانکہ کفر لے کر آتے ہیں اور اُسی کو لیکر جاتے
ہیں۔ اور جن باتوں کو یہ مخفی رکھتے ہیں خدا اُنکو خوب جانتا ہے ﴿۶۱﴾
اور تم دیکھو گے کہ ان میں اکثر گناہ اور زیادتی اور حرام
کھانے میں جلدی کر رہے ہیں۔ بیشک یہ جو کچھ کرتے
ہیں بُرا کرتے ہیں ﴿۶۲﴾
بھلا ان کے مشائخ اور علماء انہیں گناہ کی باتوں
اور حرام کھانے سے منع کیوں نہیں کرتے؟
بلاشبہ وہ بھی بُرا کرتے ہیں ﴿۶۳﴾
اور یہود کہتے ہیں کہ خدا کا ہاتھ (گردن سے) بندھا ہوا ہے
(یعنی اللہ بخیل ہے) انہیں کے ہاتھ باندھے جائیں اور ایسا کہنے
کے سبب اُن پر لعنت ہو بلکہ اسکے دونوں ہاتھ کھلے ہیں۔ وہ
جسطرح (اور جتنا) چاہتا ہے خرچ کرتا ہے اور (اے محمدؐ) یہ (کتاب)
جو تمہارے پروردگار کی طرف سے تم پر نازل ہوئی اس سے اُن میں سے
اکثر کی شرارت اور انکار اور بڑھیگا۔ اور ہم نے انکی باہم عداوت

الَّذِينَ أُوتُوا الْكِتَابَ مِنْ قَبْلِكُمْ وَالْكُفَّارَ
أَوْلِيَاءَ ۚ وَاتَّقُوا اللَّهَ إِنْ كُنْتُمْ مُؤْمِنِينَ ﴿٥٧﴾
وَإِذَا نَادَيْتُمْ إِلَى الصَّلَاةِ اتَّخَذُوهَا هُزُوًا
وَلَعِبًا ۚ ذَٰلِكَ بِأَنَّهُمْ قَوْمٌ لَا يَعْقِلُونَ ﴿٥٨﴾
قُلْ يَا أَهْلَ الْكِتَابِ هَلْ تَنْقِمُونَ مِنَّا إِلَّا
أَنْ آمَنَّا بِاللَّهِ وَمَا أُنْزِلَ إِلَيْنَا وَمَا
أُنْزِلَ مِنْ قَبْلُ وَأَنَّ أَكْثَرَكُمْ فَاسِقُونَ ﴿٥٩﴾
قُلْ هَلْ أُنَبِّئُكُمْ بِشَرٍّ مِنْ ذَٰلِكَ
مَثُوبَةً عِنْدَ اللَّهِ ۚ مَنْ لَعَنَهُ اللَّهُ وَ
غَضِبَ عَلَيْهِ وَجَعَلَ مِنْهُمُ الْقِرَدَةَ
وَالْخَنَازِيرَ وَعَبَدَ الطَّاغُوتَ ۚ أُولَٰئِكَ
شَرٌّ مَكَانًا وَأَضَلُّ عَنْ سَوَاءِ السَّبِيلِ ﴿٦٠﴾
وَإِذَا جَاءُوكُمْ قَالُوا آمَنَّا وَقَدْ دَخَلُوا
بِالْكُفْرِ وَهُمْ قَدْ خَرَجُوا بِهِ ۚ وَاللَّهُ
أَعْلَمُ بِمَا كَانُوا يَكْتُمُونَ ﴿٦١﴾
وَتَرَىٰ كَثِيرًا مِنْهُمْ يُسَارِعُونَ فِي
الْإِثْمِ وَالْعُدْوَانِ وَأَكْلِهِمُ السُّحْتَ ۚ
لَبِئْسَ مَا كَانُوا يَعْمَلُونَ ﴿٦٢﴾
لَوْلَا يَنْهَاهُمُ الرَّبَّانِيُّونَ وَالْأَحْبَارُ
عَنْ قَوْلِهِمُ الْإِثْمَ وَأَكْلِهِمُ السُّحْتَ ۚ
لَبِئْسَ مَا كَانُوا يَصْنَعُونَ ﴿٦٣﴾
وَقَالَتِ الْيَهُودُ يَدُ اللَّهِ مَغْلُولَةٌ ۚ
غُلَّتْ أَيْدِيهِمْ وَلُعِنُوا بِمَا قَالُوا ۘ وقف لازم
بَلْ يَدَاهُ مَبْسُوطَتَانِ يُنْفِقُ كَيْفَ
يَشَاءُ ۚ وَلَيَزِيدَنَّ كَثِيرًا مِنْهُمْ مَا
أُنْزِلَ إِلَيْكَ مِنْ رَبِّكَ طُغْيَانًا وَ
كُفْرًا ۚ وَأَلْقَيْنَا بَيْنَهُمُ الْعَدَاوَةَ وَ

have placed enmity and hatred till the Day of Judgment. Every time they kindle the fire of war, Allah doth extinguish it; but they (ever) strive to do mischief on earth. And Allah loveth not those who do mischief.

65. If only the People of the Book had believed and been righteous. We should indeed have blotted out their iniquities and admitted them to Gardens of Bliss.

66. If only they had stood fast by the Torah, the Gospel, and all the revelation that was sent to them from their Lord, they would have eaten both from above them and from below their feet. There is from among them a party of the right course: but many of them follow a course that is evil.

67. O Messenger ! proclaim the (Message) which hath been sent to thee from thy Lord. If thou didst not, thou wouldst not have fulfilled and proclaimed His Mission. And Allah will defend thee from men (who mean mischief). For Allah guideth not those who reject Faith.

68. Say: "O People of the Book ! ye have no ground to stand upon unless ye stand fast by the Torah. The Gospel, and all the revelation that has come to you from your Lord." It is the revelation that cometh to thee from thy Lord, that increaseth in most of them their obstinate rebellion and blasphemy. But sorrow thou not over (these) people without Faith.

69 . Those who believe (in the Qur'an). Those who follow the Jewish (scriptures), and the Sabians and the Christians,— any who believe in Allah and the Last Day, and work righteousness,— on them shall be no fear, nor shall they grieve.

70. We took the Covenant of the Children of Israel and sent them

اور بغض قیامت تک کیلئے ڈال دیا ہے۔ یہ جب لڑائی کیلئے
آگ جلاتے ہیں تو خدا اُس کو بجھا دیتا ہے۔ اور یہ ملک میں
فساد کیلئے دوڑتے پھرتے ہیں۔ اور خدا فساد کرنیوالوں
کو دوست نہیں رکھتا ﴿۶۴﴾
اور اگر اہل کتاب ایمان لاتے اور پرہیزگاری کرتے
تو ہم ان سے اُن کے گناہ محو کر دیتے اور اُن کو نعمت
کے باغوں میں داخل کرتے ﴿۶۵﴾
اور اگر وہ تورات اور انجیل کو اور جو (اور کتابیں) اُن کے
پروردگار کی طرف سے اُن پر نازل ہوئیں اُن کو قائم رکھتے
تو (اُن پر رزق مینہ کی طرح برستا کہ) اپنے اوپر سے اور پاؤں
کے نیچے سے کھاتے۔ ان میں کچھ لوگ میانہ رو ہیں اور
بہت سے ایسے ہیں جن کے اعمال بُرے ہیں ﴿۶۶﴾
اے پیغمبر جو ارشادات خدا کی طرف سے تم پر نازل ہوئے
ہیں سب لوگوں کو پہنچا دو۔ اور اگر ایسا نہ کیا تو تم خدا کے
پیغام پہنچانے میں قاصر رہے (یعنی پیغمبری کا فرض ادا نہ کیا)
اور خدا تم کو لوگوں سے بچائے رکھیگا بیشک خدا منکروں کو ہدایت نہیں کرتا ﴿۶۷﴾
کہو کہ اے اہل کتاب جب تک تم تورات اور انجیل کو اور
جو (اور کتابیں) تمہارے پروردگار کی طرف سے تم لوگوں پر
نازل ہوئیں اُن کو قائم نہ رکھو گے کچھ بھی راہ پر نہیں ہو سکتے
اور (یہ قرآن) جو تمہارے پروردگار کی طرف سے تم پر نازل ہوا ہے
اس سے اُن میں سے اکثر کی سرکشی اور کفر اور بڑھیگا۔
تو تم قوم کفار پر افسوس نہ کرو ﴿۶۸﴾
جو لوگ خدا پر اور روز آخرت پر ایمان لائیں گے
اور عمل نیک کریں گے خواہ وہ مسلمان ہوں یا
یہودی یا ستارہ پرست یا عیسائی اُن کو قیامت
کے دن) نہ کچھ خوف ہوگا اور نہ وہ غمناک ہونگے ﴿۶۹﴾
ہم نے بنی اسرائیل سے عہد بھی لیا اور اُنکی طرف پیغمبر بھی

ٱلْبَغْضَآءَ إِلَىٰ يَوْمِ ٱلْقِيَٰمَةِ ۚ كُلَّمَآ
أَوْقَدُوا۟ نَارًا لِّلْحَرْبِ أَطْفَأَهَا ٱللَّهُ ۚ
وَيَسْعَوْنَ فِى ٱلْأَرْضِ فَسَادًا ۚ وَٱللَّهُ
لَا يُحِبُّ ٱلْمُفْسِدِينَ ﴿٦٤﴾
وَلَوْ أَنَّ أَهْلَ ٱلْكِتَٰبِ ءَامَنُوا۟ وَٱتَّقَوْا۟
لَكَفَّرْنَا عَنْهُمْ سَيِّـَٔاتِهِمْ وَلَأَدْخَلْنَٰهُمْ
جَنَّٰتِ ٱلنَّعِيمِ ﴿٦٥﴾
وَلَوْ أَنَّهُمْ أَقَامُوا۟ ٱلتَّوْرَىٰةَ وَٱلْإِنجِيلَ
وَمَآ أُنزِلَ إِلَيْهِم مِّن رَّبِّهِمْ لَأَكَلُوا۟
مِن فَوْقِهِمْ وَمِن تَحْتِ أَرْجُلِهِم ۚ
مِّنْهُمْ أُمَّةٌ مُّقْتَصِدَةٌ ۖ وَكَثِيرٌ
مِّنْهُمْ سَآءَ مَا يَعْمَلُونَ ﴿٦٦﴾ ع ۹ ۱۰ ۱۴
يَٰٓأَيُّهَا ٱلرَّسُولُ بَلِّغْ مَآ أُنزِلَ إِلَيْكَ
مِن رَّبِّكَ ۖ وَإِن لَّمْ تَفْعَلْ فَمَا بَلَّغْتَ
رِسَالَتَهُۥ ۚ وَٱللَّهُ يَعْصِمُكَ مِنَ ٱلنَّاسِ ۗ
إِنَّ ٱللَّهَ لَا يَهْدِى ٱلْقَوْمَ ٱلْكَٰفِرِينَ ﴿٦٧﴾
قُلْ يَٰٓأَهْلَ ٱلْكِتَٰبِ لَسْتُمْ عَلَىٰ شَىْءٍ
حَتَّىٰ تُقِيمُوا۟ ٱلتَّوْرَىٰةَ وَٱلْإِنجِيلَ
وَمَآ أُنزِلَ إِلَيْكُم مِّن رَّبِّكُمْ ۗ
وَلَيَزِيدَنَّ كَثِيرًا مِّنْهُم مَّآ أُنزِلَ
إِلَيْكَ مِن رَّبِّكَ طُغْيَٰنًا وَكُفْرًا ۖ
فَلَا تَأْسَ عَلَى ٱلْقَوْمِ ٱلْكَٰفِرِينَ ﴿٦٨﴾
إِنَّ ٱلَّذِينَ ءَامَنُوا۟ وَٱلَّذِينَ هَادُوا۟ وَ
ٱلصَّٰبِـُٔونَ وَٱلنَّصَٰرَىٰ مَنْ ءَامَنَ بِٱللَّهِ
وَٱلْيَوْمِ ٱلْءَاخِرِ وَعَمِلَ صَٰلِحًا فَلَا
خَوْفٌ عَلَيْهِمْ وَلَا هُمْ يَحْزَنُونَ ﴿٦٩﴾
لَقَدْ أَخَذْنَا مِيثَٰقَ بَنِىٓ إِسْرَٰٓءِيلَ

Messengers. Every time there came to them a Messenger with what they themselves desired not—some (of these) they called impostors, and some they slay.

71. They thought there would be no trial (or punishment); so they became blind and deaf; yet Allah (in mercy) turned to them; yet again many of them became blind and deaf. But Allah sees well all that they do.

72. Certainly they disbelieve who say: "Allah is Christ the son of Mary." But said Christ: "O Children of Israel ! worship Allah, my Lord and your Lord." Whoever joins other gods with Allah,—Allah will forbid him the Garden, and the Fire will be his abode. There will for the wrong-doers be no one to help.

73. They disbelieve who say: Allah is one of three (in a Trinity:) for there is no god except one God. If they desist not from their word (of blasphemy), verily a grievous chastisement will befall the disbelievers among them.

74. Why turn they not to Allah and seek His forgiveness ? For Allah is Oft-Forgiving, Most Merciful.

75. Christ the son of Mary was no more than a Messenger; many were the Messengers that passed away before him. His mother was a woman of truth. They had both to eat their (daily) food. See how Allah doth make His Signs clear to them; yet see in what ways they are deluded away from the truth !

76. Say: "Will ye worship, besides Allah, something which hath no power either to harm or benefit you? But Allah,—He it is that heareth and knoweth all things."

بھیجے (لیکن) جب کوئی پیغمبر انکے پاس ایسی باتیں لیکر
آتا جن کو اُنکے دل نہیں چاہتے تھے تو وہ (انبیاء کی) ایک
جماعت کو تو جھٹلا دیتے اور ایک جماعت کو قتل کر دیتے تھے (٧٠)
اور یہ خیال کرتے تھے کہ (اس سے) اُن پر کوئی آفت نہیں آنیکی تو
وہ اندھے اور بہرے ہو گئے پھر خدا نے اُن پر مہربانی
فرمائی (لیکن) پھر اُن میں سے بہت سے اندھے اور بہرے ہو گئے
اور خدا اُن کے سب کاموں کو دیکھ رہا ہے (٧١)
وہ لوگ بےشبہ کافر ہیں جو کہتے ہیں کہ مریم کے
بیٹے (عیسیٰ) مسیح خدا ہیں۔ حالانکہ مسیح یہود سے
یہ کہا کرتے تھے کہ اے بنی اسرائیل خدا ہی کی عبادت
کرو جو میرا بھی پروردگار ہے اور تمہارا بھی (اور جان رکھو کہ)
جو شخص خدا کیساتھ شرک کریگا خدا اُس پر بہشت کو حرام کر دیگا۔
اور اُسکا ٹھکانا دوزخ ہے اور ظالموں کا کوئی مددگار نہیں (٧٢)
وہ لوگ (بھی) کافر ہیں جو اس بات کے قائل ہیں کہ
خدا تین میں کا تیسرا ہے۔ حالانکہ اُس معبود یکتا کے سوا
کوئی عبادت کے لائق نہیں۔ اگر یہ لوگ ایسے اقوال
(وعقائد) سے باز نہیں آئیں گے تو اُن میں جو کافر
ہوئے ہیں وہ تکلیف دینے والا عذاب پائیں گے (٧٣)
تو یہ کیوں خدا کے آگے توبہ نہیں کرتے اور اس سے گناہوں
کی معافی نہیں مانگتے اور خدا تو بخشنے والا مہربان ہے (٧٤)
مسیح ابن مریم تو صرف (خدا کے) پیغمبر تھے ان سے پہلے بھی بہت سے رسول گزر
چکے تھے اور اُنکی والدہ (مریم خدا کی) ولی (اور سچی فرمانبردار) تھیں۔
دونوں (انسان تھے اور) کھانا کھاتے تھے دیکھو ہم ان لوگوں کیلئے اپنی
آیتیں کسطرح کھول کھول کر بیان کرتے ہیں پھر (یہ) دیکھو کہ یہ کدھر الٹے جا رہے ہیں (٧٥)
کہو کہ تم خدا کے سوا ایسی چیز کی کیوں پرستش کرتے ہو جسکو
تمہارے نفع اور نقصان کا کچھ بھی اختیار نہیں اور خدا
ہی سب کچھ سنتا جانتا ہے (٧٦)

وَأَرْسَلْنَا إِلَيْهِمْ رُسُلًا ۖ كُلَّمَا جَاءَهُمْ
رَسُولٌ بِمَا لَا تَهْوَىٰ أَنفُسُهُمْ فَرِيقًا
كَذَّبُوا وَفَرِيقًا يَقْتُلُونَ (٧٠)
وَحَسِبُوا أَلَّا تَكُونَ فِتْنَةٌ فَعَمُوا وَ
صَمُّوا ثُمَّ تَابَ اللَّهُ عَلَيْهِمْ ثُمَّ
عَمُوا وَصَمُّوا كَثِيرٌ مِّنْهُمْ ۚ وَاللَّهُ
بَصِيرٌ بِمَا يَعْمَلُونَ (٧١)
لَقَدْ كَفَرَ الَّذِينَ قَالُوا إِنَّ اللَّهَ هُوَ
الْمَسِيحُ ابْنُ مَرْيَمَ ۖ وَقَالَ الْمَسِيحُ
يَا بَنِي إِسْرَائِيلَ اعْبُدُوا اللَّهَ رَبِّي
وَرَبَّكُمْ ۖ إِنَّهُ مَن يُشْرِكْ بِاللَّهِ فَقَدْ
حَرَّمَ اللَّهُ عَلَيْهِ الْجَنَّةَ وَمَأْوَاهُ النَّارُ ۖ
وَمَا لِلظَّالِمِينَ مِنْ أَنصَارٍ (٧٢)
لَقَدْ كَفَرَ الَّذِينَ قَالُوا إِنَّ اللَّهَ ثَالِثُ
ثَلَاثَةٍ ۘ وَمَا مِنْ إِلَٰهٍ إِلَّا إِلَٰهٌ وَاحِدٌ ۚ
وَإِن لَّمْ يَنتَهُوا عَمَّا يَقُولُونَ
لَيَمَسَّنَّ الَّذِينَ كَفَرُوا مِنْهُمْ عَذَابٌ
أَلِيمٌ (٧٣)
أَفَلَا يَتُوبُونَ إِلَى اللَّهِ وَيَسْتَغْفِرُونَهُ ۚ
وَاللَّهُ غَفُورٌ رَّحِيمٌ (٧٤)
مَّا الْمَسِيحُ ابْنُ مَرْيَمَ إِلَّا رَسُولٌ قَدْ
خَلَتْ مِن قَبْلِهِ الرُّسُلُ وَأُمُّهُ صِدِّيقَةٌ ۖ
كَانَا يَأْكُلَانِ الطَّعَامَ ۗ انظُرْ كَيْفَ نُبَيِّنُ
لَهُمُ الْآيَاتِ ثُمَّ انظُرْ أَنَّىٰ يُؤْفَكُونَ (٧٥)
قُلْ أَتَعْبُدُونَ مِن دُونِ اللَّهِ مَا لَا
يَمْلِكُ لَكُمْ ضَرًّا وَلَا نَفْعًا ۚ وَاللَّهُ هُوَ
السَّمِيعُ الْعَلِيمُ (٧٦)

77. Say: "O People of the Book! Exceed not in your religion the bounds (of what is proper), trespassing beyond the truth, nor follow the vain desires of people who went wrong in times gone by,—who misled many, and strayed (themselves) from the even Way.

78. Curses were pronounced on those among the Children of Israel who rejected Faith, by the tongue of David and of Jesus the son of Mary: because they disobeyed and persisted in Excesses.

79. Nor did they forbid one another the iniquities which they committed: evil indeed were the deeds which they did.

80. Thou seest many of them turning in friendship to the Unbelievers. Evil indeed are (the works) which their souls have sent forward before them (with the result), that Allah's wrath is on them, and in torment will they abide.

81. If only they had believed in Allah, in the Prophet, and in what hath been revealed to him, never would they have taken them for friends and protectors, but most of them are rebellious wrong-doers.

82. Strongest among men in enmity to the Believers wilt thou find the Jews and Pagans; and nearest among them in love to the Believers wilt thou find those who say, "We are Christians": because amongst these are men devoted to learning. And men who have renounced the world, and they are not arrogant.

83. And when they listen to the revelation received by the Messenger, thou wilt see their eyes overflowing with tears, for they recognise the truth: they pray: "Our Lord! we believe, write us down among the witnesses.

84. "What cause can we have not to believe in Allah and the truth which has come to us, seeing that we long for our Lord to admit us to

کہو کہ اے اہل کتاب اپنے دین (کی بات) میں ناحق
مبالغہ نہ کرو اور ایسے لوگوں کی خواہشوں کے پیچھے نہ چلو
جو (خود بھی) پہلے گمراہ ہوئے اور اور بھی اکثروں کو گمراہ
کر گئے اور سیدھے رستے سے بھٹک گئے ﴿۷۷﴾
جو لوگ بنی اسرائیل میں کافر ہوئے ان پر داؤد اور عیسیٰ
ابن مریم کی زبان سے لعنت کی گئی۔ یہ اس لئے کہ نافرمانی کرتے
تھے اور حد سے تجاوز کئے جاتے تھے ﴿۷۸﴾
(اور) برے کاموں سے جو وہ کرتے تھے ایک دوسرے کو
روکتے نہیں تھے۔ بلاشبہ وہ برا کرتے تھے ﴿۷۹﴾
تم ان میں سے بہتوں کو دیکھو گے کہ کافروں سے دوستی
رکھتے ہیں۔ انہوں نے جو کچھ آگے بھیجا ہے برا ہے۔
(وہ یہ) کہ خدا ان سے ناخوش ہوا اور وہ ہمیشہ عذاب
میں (مبتلا) رہیں گے ﴿۸۰﴾
اور اگر وہ خدا پر اور پیغمبر پر اور جو کتاب ان پر نازل
ہوئی تھی اس پر یقین رکھتے تو ان لوگوں کو دوست
نہ بناتے لیکن ان میں اکثر بدکردار ہیں ﴿۸۱﴾
(اے پیغمبر) تم دیکھو گے کہ مومنوں کے ساتھ سب سے زیادہ دشمنی کرنے والے
یہودی اور مشرک ہیں۔ اور دوستی کے لحاظ سے مومنوں سے قریب تر
ان لوگوں کو پاؤ گے جو کہتے ہیں کہ ہم نصاریٰ ہیں۔ یہ اس لئے
کہ ان میں عالم بھی ہیں اور مشائخ بھی اور وہ تکبر
نہیں کرتے ﴿۸۲﴾
اور جب اس (کتاب) کو سنتے ہیں جو (سب سے پچھلے پیغمبر (محمدؐ) پر نازل ہوئی تو
تم دیکھتے ہو کہ ان کی آنکھوں سے آنسو جاری ہو جاتے ہیں اس لئے کہ انہوں نے حق بات
پہچان لی۔ اور وہ (خدا کی جناب میں) عرض کرتے ہیں کہ اے
پروردگار ہم ایمان لے آئے تو ہم کو ماننے والوں میں لکھ لے ﴿۸۳﴾
اور ہمیں کیا ہوا ہے کہ خدا پر اور حق بات پر جو ہمارے پاس
آئی ہے ایمان نہ لائیں۔ اور ہم امید رکھتے ہیں کہ پروردگار ہم کو

قُلْ يَٰٓأَهْلَ ٱلْكِتَٰبِ لَا تَغْلُوا۟ فِى دِينِكُمْ
غَيْرَ ٱلْحَقِّ وَلَا تَتَّبِعُوٓا۟ أَهْوَآءَ قَوْمٍ
قَدْ ضَلُّوا۟ مِن قَبْلُ وَأَضَلُّوا۟ كَثِيرًا
وَضَلُّوا۟ عَن سَوَآءِ ٱلسَّبِيلِ ﴿٧٧﴾
لُعِنَ ٱلَّذِينَ كَفَرُوا۟ مِنۢ بَنِىٓ إِسْرَٰٓءِيلَ
عَلَىٰ لِسَانِ دَاوُۥدَ وَعِيسَى ٱبْنِ مَرْيَمَ
ذَٰلِكَ بِمَا عَصَوا۟ وَّكَانُوا۟ يَعْتَدُونَ ﴿٧٨﴾
كَانُوا۟ لَا يَتَنَاهَوْنَ عَن مُّنكَرٍ فَعَلُوهُ
لَبِئْسَ مَا كَانُوا۟ يَفْعَلُونَ ﴿٧٩﴾
تَرَىٰ كَثِيرًا مِّنْهُمْ يَتَوَلَّوْنَ ٱلَّذِينَ
كَفَرُوا۟ لَبِئْسَ مَا قَدَّمَتْ لَهُمْ أَنفُسُهُمْ
أَن سَخِطَ ٱللَّهُ عَلَيْهِمْ وَفِى ٱلْعَذَابِ
هُمْ خَٰلِدُونَ ﴿٨٠﴾
وَلَوْ كَانُوا۟ يُؤْمِنُونَ بِٱللَّهِ وَٱلنَّبِىِّ وَمَآ
أُنزِلَ إِلَيْهِ مَا ٱتَّخَذُوهُمْ أَوْلِيَآءَ وَ
لَٰكِنَّ كَثِيرًا مِّنْهُمْ فَٰسِقُونَ ﴿٨١﴾
لَتَجِدَنَّ أَشَدَّ ٱلنَّاسِ عَدَٰوَةً لِّلَّذِينَ
ءَامَنُوا۟ ٱلْيَهُودَ وَٱلَّذِينَ أَشْرَكُوا۟ ۖ وَلَتَجِدَنَّ
أَقْرَبَهُم مَّوَدَّةً لِّلَّذِينَ ءَامَنُوا۟ ٱلَّذِينَ
قَالُوٓا۟ إِنَّا نَصَٰرَىٰ ۚ ذَٰلِكَ بِأَنَّ مِنْهُمْ
قِسِّيسِينَ وَرُهْبَانًا وَأَنَّهُمْ لَا يَسْتَكْبِرُونَ ﴿٨٢﴾
وَإِذَا سَمِعُوا۟ مَآ أُنزِلَ إِلَى ٱلرَّسُولِ
تَرَىٰٓ أَعْيُنَهُمْ تَفِيضُ مِنَ ٱلدَّمْعِ
مِمَّا عَرَفُوا۟ مِنَ ٱلْحَقِّ ۖ يَقُولُونَ رَبَّنَآ
ءَامَنَّا فَٱكْتُبْنَا مَعَ ٱلشَّٰهِدِينَ ﴿٨٣﴾
وَمَا لَنَا لَا نُؤْمِنُ بِٱللَّهِ وَمَا جَآءَنَا
مِنَ ٱلْحَقِّ وَنَطْمَعُ أَن يُدْخِلَنَا رَبُّنَا

the company of the righteous ?"

85. And for this their prayer hath Allah rewarded them with Gardens, with rivers flowing underneath,—their eternal Home. Such is the recompense of those who do good.

86. But those who reject Faith and belie Our Signs,—they shall be Companions of Hell-fire.

87. O ye who believe ! make not unlawful the good things which Allah hath made lawful for you, but commit no excess: for Allah loveth not those given to excess.

88. Eat to the things which Allah hath provided for you, lawful and good; but fear Allah, in Whom ye believe.

89. Allah will not call you to account for what is void in your oaths, but He will call you to account for your deliberate oaths: for expiation, feed ten indigent persons, on a scale of the average for the food of your families; or clothe them; or give a slave his freedom. If that is beyond your means, fast for three days. That is the expiation for the oaths ye have sworn. But keep to your oaths. Thus doth Allah make clear to you His Signs, that ye May be grateful.

90. O ye who believe ! intoxicants and gambling, sacrificing to stones, and (divination by) arrows, are an abomination,— of Satan's handiwork: eschew such (abomination), that ye may prosper.

91. Satan's plan is (but) to excite enmity and hatred between you, with intoxicants and gambling, and hinder you from the remembrance of Allah, and from prayer: will ye

نیک بندوں کیساتھ (بہشت میں) داخل کرے گا ﴿٨٤﴾
تو خدا نے اُن کو اس کہنے کے عوض (بہشت کے) باغ عطا
فرمائے جن کے نیچے نہریں بہ رہی ہیں وہ ہمیشہ اُن میں
رہیں گے۔ اور نیکوکاروں کا یہی صلہ ہے ﴿٨٥﴾
اور جن لوگوں نے کفر کیا اور ہماری آیتوں کو جھٹلایا وہ
جہنمی ہیں ﴿٨٦﴾
مومنو! جو پاکیزہ چیزیں خدا نے تمہارے لئے حلال کی
ہیں اُن کو حرام نہ کرو اور حد سے نہ بڑھو کہ خدا حد سے
بڑھنے والوں کو دوست نہیں رکھتا ﴿٨٧﴾
اور جو حلال طیب روزی خدا نے تم کو دی ہے اُسے کھاؤ
اور خدا سے جس پر ایمان رکھتے ہو ڈرتے رہو ﴿٨٨﴾
خدا تمہاری بے ارادہ قسموں پر تم سے مواخذہ نہیں کریگا
لیکن پختہ قسموں پر (جن کے خلاف کروگے) مواخذہ
کرے گا تو اس کا کفارہ دس محتاجوں کو اوسط درجے
کا کھانا کھلانا ہے جو تم اپنے اہل وعیال کو کھلاتے ہو
یا اُن کو کپڑے دینا یا ایک غلام آزاد کرنا۔ اور جسکو یہ میسر نہ ہو
وہ تین روزے رکھے۔ یہ تمہاری قسموں کا کفارہ ہے جب
تم قسم کھالو (اور اسے توڑ دو) اور (تم کو) چاہیئے کہ اپنی قسموں
کی حفاظت کرو۔ اس طرح خدا تمہارے (سمجھانے کے) لئے اپنی آیتیں
کھول کھول کر بیان فرماتا ہے تاکہ تم شکر کرو ﴿٨٩﴾
اے ایمان والو! شراب اور جوا اور بت اور
پانسے (یہ سب) ناپاک کام اعمالِ شیطان
سے ہیں سو ان سے بچتے رہنا تاکہ
نجات پاؤ ﴿٩٠﴾
شیطان تو یہ چاہتا ہے کہ شراب اور جوئے کے
سبب تمہارے آپس میں دشمنی اور رنجش ڈلوا دے
اور تمہیں خدا کی یاد سے اور نماز سے روک دے تو تم کو

مَعَ الْقَوْمِ الصّٰلِحِيْنَ ﴿٨٤﴾
فَاَثَابَهُمُ اللّٰهُ بِمَا قَالُوْا جَنّٰتٍ تَجْرِيْ
مِنْ تَحْتِهَا الْاَنْهٰرُ خٰلِدِيْنَ فِيْهَا ؕ
وَذٰلِكَ جَزَآءُ الْمُحْسِنِيْنَ ﴿٨٥﴾
وَالَّذِيْنَ كَفَرُوْا وَكَذَّبُوْا بِاٰيٰتِنَآ اُولٰٓئِكَ
ع اَصْحٰبُ الْجَحِيْمِ ﴿٨٦﴾
يٰٓاَيُّهَا الَّذِيْنَ اٰمَنُوْا لَا تُحَرِّمُوْا طَيِّبٰتِ
مَآ اَحَلَّ اللّٰهُ لَكُمْ وَلَا تَعْتَدُوْا ؕ
اِنَّ اللّٰهَ لَا يُحِبُّ الْمُعْتَدِيْنَ ﴿٨٧﴾
وَكُلُوْا مِمَّا رَزَقَكُمُ اللّٰهُ حَلٰلًا طَيِّبًا
وَّاتَّقُوا اللّٰهَ الَّذِيْٓ اَنْتُمْ بِهٖ مُؤْمِنُوْنَ ﴿٨٨﴾
لَا يُؤَاخِذُكُمُ اللّٰهُ بِاللَّغْوِ فِيْٓ اَيْمَانِكُمْ
وَلٰكِنْ يُّؤَاخِذُكُمْ بِمَا عَقَّدْتُّمُ
الْاَيْمَانَ ۚ فَكَفَّارَتُهٗٓ اِطْعَامُ عَشَرَةِ
مَسٰكِيْنَ مِنْ اَوْسَطِ مَا تُطْعِمُوْنَ
اَهْلِيْكُمْ اَوْ كِسْوَتُهُمْ اَوْ تَحْرِيْرُ رَقَبَةٍ ؕ
فَمَنْ لَّمْ يَجِدْ فَصِيَامُ ثَلٰثَةِ اَيَّامٍ ؕ
ذٰلِكَ كَفَّارَةُ اَيْمَانِكُمْ اِذَا حَلَفْتُمْ ؕ
وَاحْفَظُوْٓا اَيْمَانَكُمْ ؕ كَذٰلِكَ يُبَيِّنُ
اللّٰهُ لَكُمْ اٰيٰتِهٖ لَعَلَّكُمْ تَشْكُرُوْنَ ﴿٨٩﴾
يٰٓاَيُّهَا الَّذِيْنَ اٰمَنُوْٓا اِنَّمَا الْخَمْرُ وَالْمَيْسِرُ
وَالْاَنْصَابُ وَالْاَزْلَامُ رِجْسٌ مِّنْ
عَمَلِ الشَّيْطٰنِ فَاجْتَنِبُوْهُ لَعَلَّكُمْ
تُفْلِحُوْنَ ﴿٩٠﴾
اِنَّمَا يُرِيْدُ الشَّيْطٰنُ اَنْ يُّوْقِعَ بَيْنَكُمُ
الْعَدَاوَةَ وَالْبَغْضَآءَ فِي الْخَمْرِ وَ
الْمَيْسِرِ وَيَصُدَّكُمْ عَنْ ذِكْرِ اللّٰهِ وَعَنِ

not then abstain ?

92. Obey Allah, and obey the Messenger. And beware (of evil): if ye do turn back, know ye that it is Our Messenger's duty to proclaim (the Message) in the clearest manner.

93. On those who believe and do deeds of righteousness there is no blame for what they ate (in the past), when they guard themselves from evil, and believe, and do deeds of righteousness,— then again, guard themselves from evil and believe,— then again, guard themselves from evil and do good. For Allah loveth those who do good.

94. O ye who believe ! Allah doth but make a trial of you in a little matter of game well within reach of your hands and your lances, that He may test who feareth Him unseen: any who transgress thereafter, will have a grievous chastisement.

95. O ye who believe ! kill not game while in the Sacred precincts or in the state of pilgrimage if any of you doth so intentionally, the compensation is an offering, brought to the Ka'ba, of a domestic animal equivalent to the one he killed. As adjudged by two just men among you; or by way of atonement, the feeding of the indigent; or its equivalent in fasts: that he may taste of the penalty of his deed. Allah Forgives what is past: for repetition Allah will punish him for Allah is Exalted, and Lord of Retribution.

96. Lawful to you is the pursuit of water-game and its use for food,— for the benefit of yourselves and those who travel; but forbidden is the pursuit of land-game:—as long as ye are in the Sacred Precincts or in the state of pilgrimage and fear Allah, to Whom ye shall be gathered back.

97. Allah made the Ka'ba, the Sacred House, a means of support for men, as also the Sacred Months, the animals for offerings, and the

(ان کاموں سے) باز رہنا چاہیئے ﴿٩١﴾
اور خدا کی فرمانبرداری اور رسُول (خدا) کی اطاعت
کرتے رہو اور ڈرتے رہو. اگر مُنہ پھیر لوگے تو جان رکھو کہ ہمارے
پیغمبر کے ذمّے تو صرف پیغام کا کھول کر پہنچا دینا ہے ﴿٩٢﴾
جو لوگ ایمان لائے اور نیک عمل کرتے رہے اُن پر
اُن چیزوں کا کچھ گناہ نہیں جو وہ کھا چکے. جب کہ اُنہوں
نے پرہیز کیا اور ایمان لائے اور نیک کام کئے پھر پرہیز
کیا اور ایمان لائے پھر پرہیز کیا اور نیکو کاری کی. اور خدا
نیکو کاروں کو دوست رکھتا ہے ﴿٩٣﴾
مومنو! کسی قدر شکار سے جن کو تم ہاتھوں اور نیزوں
سے پکڑ سکو خدا تمہاری آزمائش کریگا (یعنی حالتِ احرام میں
شکار کی ممانعت سے) تاکہ معلوم کرے کہ اُس سے غائبانہ کون ڈرتا ہے
تو جو اسکے بعد زیادتی کرے اُسکے لیئے دُکھ دینے والا عذاب (تیار) ہے ﴿٩٤﴾
مومنو! جب تم احرام کی حالت میں ہو تو شکار نہ مارنا.
اور جو تم میں سے جان بُوجھ کر اُسے مارے تو (یا تو اس کا)
بدلہ (دے اور وہ یہ ہے کہ) اسی طرح کا چارپایہ جسے
تم میں سے دو معتبر شخص مقرر کر دیں قربانی (کرکے) اور یہ قربانی
کعبے پہنچائی جائے یا کفارہ (دے اور وہ) مسکینوں کو کھانا
کھلانا (ہے) یا اسکے برابر روزے رکھے تاکہ اپنے کام کی سزا (کا مزہ) چکھے
(اور) جو پہلے ہو چکا وہ خدا نے معاف کر دیا اور جو پھر (ایسا کام) کریگا
تو خدا اُس سے انتقام لیگا. اور خدا غالب (اور) انتقام لینے والا ہے ﴿٩٥﴾
تمہارے لئے دریا (کی چیزوں) کا شکار اور اُن کا کھانا حلال کر دیا
گیا ہے (یعنی) تمہارے اور مسافروں کے فائدے کیلئے اور جنگل (کی
چیزوں) کا شکار جب تک تم احرام کی حالت میں ہو تم پر حرام ہے
اور خدا سے جس کے پاس تم (سب) جمع کئے جاؤ گے ڈرتے رہو ﴿٩٦﴾
خدا نے عزت کے گھر (یعنی) کعبے کو لوگوں کیلئے موجبِ امن
مقرر فرمایا ہے اور عزت کے مہینوں کو اور قربانی کو اور اُن

الصَّلٰوةِ ۚ فَهَلْ اَنْتُمْ مُّنْتَهُوْنَ ﴿٩١﴾
وَاَطِيْعُوا اللّٰهَ وَاَطِيْعُوا الرَّسُوْلَ
وَاحْذَرُوْا ۚ فَاِنْ تَوَلَّيْتُمْ فَاعْلَمُوْٓا
اَنَّمَا عَلٰى رَسُوْلِنَا الْبَلٰغُ الْمُبِيْنُ ﴿٩٢﴾
لَيْسَ عَلَى الَّذِيْنَ اٰمَنُوْا وَعَمِلُوا الصّٰلِحٰتِ
جُنَاحٌ فِيْمَا طَعِمُوْٓا اِذَا مَا اتَّقَوْا وَّ
اٰمَنُوْا وَعَمِلُوا الصّٰلِحٰتِ ثُمَّ اتَّقَوْا وَّ
اٰمَنُوْا ثُمَّ اتَّقَوْا وَّاَحْسَنُوْا ؕ وَاللّٰهُ
يُحِبُّ الْمُحْسِنِيْنَ ﴿٩٣﴾ ع ١٢
يٰٓاَيُّهَا الَّذِيْنَ اٰمَنُوْا لَيَبْلُوَنَّكُمُ اللّٰهُ بِشَيْءٍ
مِّنَ الصَّيْدِ تَنَالُهٗٓ اَيْدِيْكُمْ وَرِمَاحُكُمْ
لِيَعْلَمَ اللّٰهُ مَنْ يَّخَافُهٗ بِالْغَيْبِ ۚ فَمَنِ
اعْتَدٰى بَعْدَ ذٰلِكَ فَلَهٗ عَذَابٌ اَلِيْمٌ ﴿٩٤﴾
يٰٓاَيُّهَا الَّذِيْنَ اٰمَنُوْا لَا تَقْتُلُوا الصَّيْدَ وَ
اَنْتُمْ حُرُمٌ ؕ وَمَنْ قَتَلَهٗ مِنْكُمْ مُّتَعَمِّدًا
فَجَزَآءٌ مِّثْلُ مَا قَتَلَ مِنَ النَّعَمِ
يَحْكُمُ بِهٖ ذَوَا عَدْلٍ مِّنْكُمْ هَدْيًا
بٰلِغَ الْكَعْبَةِ اَوْ كَفَّارَةٌ طَعَامُ مَسٰكِيْنَ
اَوْ عَدْلُ ذٰلِكَ صِيَامًا لِّيَذُوْقَ وَبَالَ
اَمْرِهٖ ؕ عَفَا اللّٰهُ عَمَّا سَلَفَ ؕ وَمَنْ عَادَ
فَيَنْتَقِمُ اللّٰهُ مِنْهُ ؕ وَاللّٰهُ عَزِيْزٌ ذُو انْتِقَامٍ ﴿٩٥﴾
اُحِلَّ لَكُمْ صَيْدُ الْبَحْرِ وَطَعَامُهٗ مَتَاعًا
لَّكُمْ وَلِلسَّيَّارَةِ ۚ وَحُرِّمَ عَلَيْكُمْ صَيْدُ
الْبَرِّ مَا دُمْتُمْ حُرُمًا ؕ وَاتَّقُوا اللّٰهَ الَّذِيْٓ
اِلَيْهِ تُحْشَرُوْنَ ﴿٩٦﴾
جَعَلَ اللّٰهُ الْكَعْبَةَ الْبَيْتَ الْحَرَامَ
قِيٰمًا لِّلنَّاسِ وَالشَّهْرَ الْحَرَامَ وَالْهَدْيَ

garlands that mark them: that ye may know that Allah hath knowledge of what is in the heavens and on earth and that Allah is well acquainted with all things.

98. Know ye that Allah is strict in punishment and that Allah is Oft-Forgiving, Most Merciful.

99. The Messenger's duty is but to proclaim (the Message). But Allah knoweth all that ye reveal and ye conceal.

100. Say: "Not equal are things that are bad and things that are good, even though the abundance of the bad may dazzle thee; so fear Allah, O ye that understand; that (so) ye may prosper."

101. O ye who believe ! ask not questions about things which, if made plain to you, may cause you trouble. But if ye ask about things when the Qur'an is being Revealed, they will be made plain to you, Allah will forgive those: for Allah is Oft-Forgiving, Most Forbearing.

102. Some people before you did ask such questions, and on that account lost their faith.

103. It was not Allah Who instituted (superstitions like those of) a slit-ear she-camel, or a she-camel let loose for free pasture, or idol sacrifices for twin-births in animals, or stallion-camels freed from work: it is the disbelievers who invent a lie against Allah; but most of them lack wisdom.

104. When it is said to them: "Come to what Allah hath revealed; come to the Messenger": they say: "Enough for us are the ways we found our fathers following." What! even though their fathers were void of knowledge and guidance ?

105. O ye who believe ! guard your own souls: if ye follow (right) guidance. No hurt can come to you from those who stray. The return of

جانوروں کو جنکے گلے میں پٹے بندھے ہوں۔ یہ اسلئے کہ تم
جان لو کہ جو کچھ آسمانوں میں ہے اور جو کچھ زمین میں ہے خدا سب
کو جانتا ہے اور یہ کہ خدا کو ہر چیز کا علم ہے ﴿٩٧﴾
جان رکھو کہ خدا سخت عذاب دینے والا ہے اور یہ کہ
خدا بخشنے والا مہربان بھی ہے ﴿٩٨﴾
پیغمبر کے ذمے تو صرف (پیغام خدا کا) پہنچا دینا ہے اور جو کچھ
تم ظاہر کرتے ہو اور جو کچھ مخفی کرتے ہو خدا کو سب معلوم ہے ﴿٩٩﴾
کہہ دو کہ ناپاک چیزیں اور پاک چیزیں برابر نہیں ہوتیں گو
ناپاک چیزوں کی کثرت تمہیں خوش ہی لگے۔ تو عقل والو
خدا سے ڈرتے رہو تاکہ رستگاری حاصل کرو ﴿١٠٠﴾
مومنو! ایسی چیزوں کے بارے میں مت سوال کرو کہ اگر ان کی
حقیقتیں تم پر ظاہر کر دی جائیں تو تمہیں بری لگیں۔ اور اگر قرآن
کے نازل ہونے کے ایام میں ایسی باتیں پوچھو گے تو تم پر ظاہر بھی
کر دی جائیں گی (اب تو) خدا نے ایسی باتوں (کے پوچھنے) سے
درگزر فرمایا ہے اور خدا بخشنے والا بردبار ہے ﴿١٠١﴾
اس طرح کی باتیں تم سے پہلے لوگوں نے بھی پوچھی تھیں
(مگر جب بتائی گئیں تو) پھر ان سے منکر ہو گئے ﴿١٠٢﴾
خدا نے نہ تو بحیرہ کچھ چیز بنایا ہے اور نہ سائبہ
اور نہ وصیلہ اور نہ حام بلکہ کافر خدا پر جھوٹ
افترا کرتے ہیں۔ اور یہ اکثر عقل نہیں
رکھتے ﴿١٠٣﴾
اور جب ان لوگوں سے کہا جاتا ہے کہ جو کتاب خدا نے نازل فرمائی ہے
اس کی اور رسول اللہ کی طرف رجوع کرو تو کہتے ہیں کہ جس طریق پر ہم نے اپنے
باپ دادا کو پایا ہے وہی ہمیں کافی ہے۔ بھلا اگر انکے باپ دادا نہ تو کچھ
جانتے ہوں اور نہ سیدھے رستے پر ہوں (تب بھی)؟ ﴿١٠٤﴾
اے ایمان والو! اپنی جانوں کی حفاظت کرو جب تم ہدایت
پر ہو تو کوئی گمراہ تمہارا کچھ بھی بگاڑ نہیں سکتا تم سب کو خدا کی

وَالْقَلَآئِدَ ذٰلِكَ لِتَعْلَمُوْٓا اَنَّ اللّٰهَ يَعْلَمُ
مَا فِي السَّمٰوٰتِ وَمَا فِي الْاَرْضِ وَاَنَّ
اللّٰهَ بِكُلِّ شَيْءٍ عَلِيْمٌ ﴿٩٧﴾
اِعْلَمُوْٓا اَنَّ اللّٰهَ شَدِيْدُ الْعِقَابِ وَ
اَنَّ اللّٰهَ غَفُوْرٌ رَّحِيْمٌ ﴿٩٨﴾
مَا عَلَى الرَّسُوْلِ اِلَّا الْبَلٰغُ ۭ وَاللّٰهُ يَعْلَمُ
مَا تُبْدُوْنَ وَمَا تَكْتُمُوْنَ ﴿٩٩﴾
قُلْ لَّا يَسْتَوِي الْخَبِيْثُ وَالطَّيِّبُ وَلَوْ
اَعْجَبَكَ كَثْرَةُ الْخَبِيْثِ ۚ فَاتَّقُوا اللّٰهَ
يٰٓاُولِي الْاَلْبَابِ لَعَلَّكُمْ تُفْلِحُوْنَ ﴿١٠٠﴾ ع
يٰٓاَيُّهَا الَّذِيْنَ اٰمَنُوْا لَا تَسْـَٔلُوْا عَنْ اَشْيَاۗءَ
اِنْ تُبْدَ لَكُمْ تَسُؤْكُمْ ۚ وَاِنْ
تَسْـَٔلُوْا عَنْهَا حِيْنَ يُنَزَّلُ الْقُرْاٰنُ
تُبْدَ لَكُمْ ۭ عَفَا اللّٰهُ عَنْهَا ۭ وَاللّٰهُ
غَفُوْرٌ حَلِيْمٌ ﴿١٠١﴾
قَدْ سَاَلَهَا قَوْمٌ مِّنْ قَبْلِكُمْ ثُمَّ اَصْبَحُوْا
بِهَا كٰفِرِيْنَ ﴿١٠٢﴾
مَا جَعَلَ اللّٰهُ مِنْۢ بَحِيْرَةٍ وَّلَا سَاۗىِٕبَةٍ
وَّلَا وَصِيْلَةٍ وَّلَا حَامٍ ۙ وَّلٰكِنَّ الَّذِيْنَ
كَفَرُوْا يَفْتَرُوْنَ عَلَى اللّٰهِ الْكَذِبَ ۭ
وَاَكْثَرُهُمْ لَا يَعْقِلُوْنَ ﴿١٠٣﴾
وَاِذَا قِيْلَ لَهُمْ تَعَالَوْا اِلٰى مَآ اَنْزَلَ
اللّٰهُ وَاِلَى الرَّسُوْلِ قَالُوْا حَسْبُنَا مَا
وَجَدْنَا عَلَيْهِ اٰبَاۗءَنَا ۭ اَوَلَوْ كَانَ
اٰبَاۗؤُهُمْ لَا يَعْلَمُوْنَ شَيْـــًٔا وَّلَا يَهْتَدُوْنَ ﴿١٠٤﴾
يٰٓاَيُّهَا الَّذِيْنَ اٰمَنُوْا عَلَيْكُمْ اَنْفُسَكُمْ ۚ لَا
يَضُرُّكُمْ مَّنْ ضَلَّ اِذَا اهْتَدَيْتُمْ ۭ

you all is to Allah: it is He That will inform you of all that ye do.

106. O ye who believe ! when death approaches any of you, (take) witnesses among yourselves when making bequest,—two just men of your own (brotherhood) or others from outside if ye are journeying through the earth, and the chance of death befalls you (thus). If ye doubt (their truth), detain them both after prayer, and let them both swear by Allah: "We will not take for it a price even though the (beneficiary) be our near relation: we shall hide not the evidence we owe to Allah if we do, then behold ! we shall be sinners.

107. But if it gets known that these two were guilty of the sin (of perjury), let two others stand forth in their places,—nearest in kin from among those who claim a lawful right: let them swear by Allah: "We affirm that our witness is truer than that of those two, and that we have not trespassed (beyond the truth): if we did, behold ! we will be wrong-doers."

108. That is most suitable: that they may give the evidence in its true nature and shape, or else they would fear that other oaths would be taken after their oaths. But fear Allah, and listen (to His counsel): for Allah guideth not a rebellious people.

109. On the day when Allah will gather the Messengers together, and ask: "What was the response ye received (from men to your teaching)?" They will say: "We have no knowledge: it is Thou Who knowest in full all that is hidden."

110. Then will Allah say: "O Jesus the son of Mary ! recount My favour to thee and to thy mother. Behold ! I strengthened thee with the Holy Spirit. So that thou didst speak to the people in childhood and in old

طرف لوٹ کر جانا ہے اُس وقت وہ تم کو تمہارے سب کاموں سے جو
(دنیا میں) کیے تھے آگاہ کریگا (اور اُنکا بدلہ دیگا) ﴿١٠٥﴾
مومنو! جب تم میں سے کسی کی موت آموجود ہو تو شہادت
(کا نصاب) یہ ہے کہ وصیت کے وقت تم (مسلمانوں) میں سے
دو مرد عادل (یعنی صاحب اعتبار) گواہ ہوں۔ یا اگر (مسلمان نہ
ملیں اور) تم سفر کر رہے ہو اور (اُس وقت) تم پر موت کی مصیبت
واقع ہو تو کسی دوسرے مذہب کے دو (شخصوں کو) گواہ کر لو۔ اگر تم کو
ان گواہوں کی نسبت کچھ شک ہو تو اُنکو (عصر کی) نماز کے بعد کھڑا
کرو اور دونوں خدا کی قسمیں کھائیں کہ ہم شہادت کا کچھ عوض نہیں لینگے
گو ہمارا رشتہ دار ہی ہو۔ اور نہ ہم اللہ کی شہادت کو چھپائینگے
اگر ایسا کریں گے تو گنہگار ہوں گے ﴿١٠٦﴾
پھر اگر معلوم ہو جائے کہ ان دونوں نے (جھوٹ بول کر) گناہ حاصل کیا ہے
تو جن (لوگوں) کا اُنہوں نے حق مارنا چاہا تھا اُنمیں سے اُنکی جگہ اور دو گواہ
کھڑے ہوں جو (میت سے) قرابت قریبہ رکھتے ہوں۔ پھر وہ خدا کی
قسمیں کھائیں کہ ہماری شہادت اُنکی شہادت سے بہت سچی ہے اور ہم نے
کوئی زیادتی نہیں کی۔ ایسا کیا ہو تو ہم بے انصاف ہیں ﴿١٠٧﴾
اس طریق سے بہت قریب ہے کہ یہ لوگ صحیح صحیح شہادت دیں یا
اس بات سے خوف کریں کہ (ہماری) قسمیں اُنکی قسموں کے بعد رد کر دی
جائیں گی۔ اور خدا سے ڈرو اور اُسکے حکموں کو گوش ہوش سے سنو
اور خدا نافرمان لوگوں کو ہدایت نہیں دیتا ﴿١٠٨﴾
(وہ دن یاد رکھنے کے لائق ہے) جس دن خدا پیغمبروں کو جمع
کریگا پھر اُن سے پوچھے گا کہ تمہیں کیا جواب ملا تھا وہ عرض کرینگے
کہ ہمیں کچھ معلوم نہیں۔ تو ہی غیب کی باتوں سے واقف ہے ﴿١٠٩﴾
جب خدا (عیسیٰ سے) فرمائے گا کہ اے عیسیٰ ابن مریم! میرے
اُن احسانوں کو یاد کرو جو میں نے تم پر اور تمہاری والدہ پر کیے
جب میں نے روح القدس (یعنی جبرئیل) سے تمہاری مدد کی۔
تم جھولے میں اور جوان ہو کر (ایک ہی نسق پر) لوگوں سے

إلى الله مرجعكم جميعا فينبئكم
بما كنتم تعملون ﴿١٠٥﴾
يا أيها الذين آمنوا شهادة بينكم
إذا حضر أحدكم الموت حين
الوصية اثنان ذوا عدل منكم أو
آخران من غيركم إن أنتم ضربتم
في الأرض فأصابتكم مصيبة الموت
تحبسونهما من بعد الصلاة فيقسمان
بالله إن ارتبتم لا نشتري به ثمنا
ولو كان ذا قربى ولا نكتم شهادة
الله إنا إذا لمن الآثمين ﴿١٠٦﴾
فإن عثر على أنهما استحقا إثما
فآخران يقومان مقامهما من الذين
استحق عليهم الأوليان فيقسمان بالله
لشهادتنا أحق من شهادتهما وما
اعتدينا إنا إذا لمن الظالمين ﴿١٠٧﴾
ذلك أدنى أن يأتوا بالشهادة على
وجهها أو يخافوا أن ترد أيمان بعد
أيمانهم واتقوا الله واسمعوا والله
لا يهدي القوم الفاسقين ﴿١٠٨﴾
يوم يجمع الله الرسل فيقول ماذا
أجبتم قالوا لا علم لنا إنك أنت
علام الغيوب ﴿١٠٩﴾
إذ قال الله يا عيسى ابن مريم اذكر
نعمتي عليك وعلى والدتك إذ
أيدتك بروح القدس تكلم
الناس في المهد وكهلا وإذ علمتك

age. Behold ! I taught thee the Book and Wisdom, the Torah and the Gospel. And behold! thou makest out of clay, as it were, the figure of a bird, by My leave. And thou breathest into it, and it becometh a bird by My leave, and thou healest those born blind, and the lepers, by My leave. And behold ! thou bringest forth the dead by My leave. And behold ! I did restrain the Children of Israel from (violence to) thee when thou didst show them the Clear Signs, and the unbelievers among them said: 'This is nothing but evident magic.'

111. "And behold ! I inspired the Disciples to have faith in Me and Mine Messenger: they said. 'We have faith, and do thou bear witness that we bow to Allah as Muslims'."

112. Behold ! the Disciples said: "O Jesus the son of Mary ! can thy Lord send down to us a Table set (with viands) from heaven ?" Said Jesus: "Fear Allah, if ye have faith".

113. They said: "We only wish to eat thereof and satisfy our hearts, and to know that thou has indeed told us the truth; and that we ourselves may be witnesses to the miracle."

114. Said Jesus the son of Mary: "O Allah our Lord ! send us from heaven a Table set (with viands), that there may be for us—for the first and the last of us—a solemn festival and a Sign from Thee; and provide for our sustenance, for Thou art the best sustainer (of our needs)."

115. Allah said: "I will send it down unto you: but if any of you after that resisteth faith, I will punish him with a chastisement such as I have not inflicted on any one among all the peoples.

116. And behold ! Allah will say: "O Jesus the son of Mary ! didst thou say unto men, 'Take me and

گفتگو کرتے تھے۔ اور جب میں نے تم کو کتاب اور دانائی اور
تورات اور انجیل سکھائی اور جب تم میرے حکم سے مٹی کا جانور بنا کر
اُس میں پھونک مار دیتے تھے تو وہ میرے حکم سے اڑنے لگتا تھا
اور مادر زاد اندھے اور سفید داغ والے کو میرے حکم سے چنگا کر دیتے
تھے اور مُردے کو (زندہ کرکے قبر سے) نکال کھڑا کرتے تھے۔ اور جب
میں نے بنی اسرائیل (کے ہاتھوں) کو تم سے روک دیا جب
تم اُن کے پاس کھلے ہوئے نشان لیکر آئے تو جو اُن میں سے کافر تھے
کہنے لگے کہ یہ تو صریح جادو ہے ﴿۱۱۰﴾
اور جب میں نے حواریوں کی طرف حکم بھیجا کہ مجھ پر اور میرے
پیغمبر پر ایمان لاؤ۔ وہ کہنے لگے کہ (پروردگار) ہم ایمان لائے
تو شاہد رہیو کہ ہم فرمانبردار ہیں ﴿۱۱۱﴾
(وہ قصہ بھی یاد کرو) جب حواریوں نے کہا کہ اے عیسیٰ ابن
مریم! کیا تمہارا پروردگار ایسا کر سکتا ہے کہ ہم پر آسمان سے
(طعام کا) خوان نازل کرے؟ اُنہوں نے کہا کہ اگر ایمان رکھتے
ہو تو خدا سے ڈرو ﴿۱۱۲﴾
وہ بولے کہ ہماری یہ خواہش ہے کہ ہم اس میں سے کھائیں
اور ہمارے دل تسلی پائیں اور ہم جان لیں کہ تم نے ہم سے
سچ کہا ہے اور ہم اس (خوان کے نزول) پر گواہ رہیں ﴿۱۱۳﴾
(تب) عیسیٰ ابن مریم نے دعا کی کہ اے ہمارے پروردگار ہم پر
آسمان سے خوان نازل فرما کہ ہمارے لئے (وہ دن) عید قرار
پائے یعنی ہمارے اگلوں اور پچھلوں (سب) کیلئے اور وہ تیری طرف
سے نشانی ہو اور ہمیں رزق دے تو بہتر رزق دینے والا ہے ﴿۱۱۴﴾
خدا نے فرمایا میں تم پر ضرور خوان نازل فرماؤں گا لیکن جو
اس کے بعد تم میں سے کفر کرے گا اُسے ایسا عذاب دونگا
کہ اہل عالم میں کسی کو ایسا عذاب نہ دوں گا ﴿۱۱۵﴾
اور (اُس وقت کو بھی یاد رکھو) جب خدا فرمائیگا کہ اے عیسیٰ
ابن مریم! کیا تم نے لوگوں سے کہا تھا کہ خدا کے سوا مجھے اور

الْكِتٰبَ وَالْحِكْمَةَ وَالتَّوْرٰىةَ وَالْاِنْجِيْلَ ۚ
وَاِذْ تَخْلُقُ مِنَ الطِّيْنِ كَهَيْـَٔةِ الطَّيْرِ
بِاِذْنِيْ فَتَنْفُخُ فِيْهَا فَتَكُوْنُ طَيْرًا بِاِذْنِيْ
وَتُبْرِئُ الْاَكْمَهَ وَالْاَبْرَصَ بِاِذْنِيْ ۚ
وَاِذْ تُخْرِجُ الْمَوْتٰى بِاِذْنِيْ ۚ وَاِذْ كَفَفْتُ
بَنِيْٓ اِسْرَآءِيْلَ عَنْكَ اِذْ جِئْتَهُمْ
بِالْبَيِّنٰتِ فَقَالَ الَّذِيْنَ كَفَرُوْا مِنْهُمْ
اِنْ هٰذَآ اِلَّا سِحْرٌ مُّبِيْنٌ ﴿١١٠﴾
وَاِذْ اَوْحَيْتُ اِلَى الْحَوَارِيّٖنَ اَنْ اٰمِنُوْا
بِيْ وَبِرَسُوْلِيْ ۚ قَالُوْٓا اٰمَنَّا وَاشْهَدْ
بِاَنَّنَا مُسْلِمُوْنَ ﴿١١١﴾
اِذْ قَالَ الْحَوَارِيُّوْنَ يٰعِيْسَى ابْنَ
مَرْيَمَ هَلْ يَسْتَطِيْعُ رَبُّكَ اَنْ يُّنَزِّلَ
عَلَيْنَا مَآئِدَةً مِّنَ السَّمَآءِ ۗ قَالَ اتَّقُوا
اللّٰهَ اِنْ كُنْتُمْ مُّؤْمِنِيْنَ ﴿١١٢﴾
قَالُوْا نُرِيْدُ اَنْ نَّاْكُلَ مِنْهَا وَتَطْمَئِنَّ
قُلُوْبُنَا وَنَعْلَمَ اَنْ قَدْ صَدَقْتَنَا وَ
ربع نَكُوْنَ عَلَيْهَا مِنَ الشّٰهِدِيْنَ ﴿١١٣﴾
قَالَ عِيْسَى ابْنُ مَرْيَمَ اللّٰهُمَّ رَبَّنَآ
اَنْزِلْ عَلَيْنَا مَآئِدَةً مِّنَ السَّمَآءِ تَكُوْنُ
لَنَا عِيْدًا لِّاَوَّلِنَا وَاٰخِرِنَا وَاٰيَةً مِّنْكَ ۚ
وَارْزُقْنَا وَاَنْتَ خَيْرُ الرّٰزِقِيْنَ ﴿١١٤﴾
قَالَ اللّٰهُ اِنِّيْ مُنَزِّلُهَا عَلَيْكُمْ ۚ فَمَنْ
يَّكْفُرْ بَعْدُ مِنْكُمْ فَاِنِّيْٓ اُعَذِّبُهٗ عَذَابًا
ع ١٥ لَّآ اُعَذِّبُهٗٓ اَحَدًا مِّنَ الْعٰلَمِيْنَ ﴿١١٥﴾ ع
وَاِذْ قَالَ اللّٰهُ يٰعِيْسَى ابْنَ مَرْيَمَ
ءَاَنْتَ قُلْتَ لِلنَّاسِ اتَّخِذُوْنِيْ وَاُمِّيَ

SÛRA–6
AL-AN'ÃM
(INTRODUCTION)

This is a Sûra of the late Makkan period. The greater part of it was revealed entire. Its place in the traditional order of arrangement is justified by logical considerations. We have alreay had the spiritual history of mankind, a discussion of the earlier revelations and how they were lost or corrupted, the regulations for the outer life of the new Community and the points in which the Jews and Christians failed to maintain the central doctrine of Islam—the unity of Allah. The next step now taken is to expound this doctrine in relation to Pagan Arabia.

my mother for two gods beside Allah'?" He will say: "Glory to Thee! never could I say what I had no right (to say). Had I said such a thing. Thou wouldst indeed have known it. Thou knowest what is in my heart, though I know not what is in Thine. For Thou knowest in full all that is hidden.

میری والدہ کو معبود مقرر کرو؟ وہ کہیں گے کہ تو پاک ہے مجھے کب
شایاں تھا کہ میں ایسی بات کہتا جس کا مجھے کچھ حق نہیں۔
اگر میں نے ایسا کہا ہوگا تو تجھ کو معلوم ہوگا (کیونکہ) جو بات
میرے دل میں ہے تو اسے جانتا ہے اور جو تیرے ضمیر میں ہے اُسے
میں نہیں جانتا۔ بے شک تو علام الغیوب ہے ﴿۱۱۶﴾

اِلٰهَيْنِ مِنْ دُوْنِ اللّٰهِ ۭ قَالَ سُبْحٰنَكَ
مَا يَكُوْنُ لِيْٓ اَنْ اَقُوْلَ مَا لَيْسَ لِيْ ۤ
بِحَقٍّ ۭ اِنْ كُنْتُ قُلْتُهٗ فَقَدْ عَلِمْتَهٗ ۭ
تَعْلَمُ مَا فِيْ نَفْسِيْ وَلَآ اَعْلَمُ مَا فِيْ
نَفْسِكَ ۭ اِنَّكَ اَنْتَ عَلَّامُ الْغُيُوْبِ ﴿١١٦﴾

وقف النبي صلى الله عليه وسلم

117. "Never said I to them aught except what Thou didst command me to say, to wit, 'Worship Allah, my Lord and your Lord': and I was a witness over them whilst I dwelt amongst them; when thou didst take me up Thou wast the Watcher over them, and Thou art a witness to all things.

میں نے اُن سے کچھ نہیں کہا بجز اسکے جس کا تو نے مجھے
حکم دیا ہے وہ یہ کہ تم خدا کی عبادت کرو جو میرا اور تمہارا سب کا
پروردگار ہے۔ اور جب تک میں اُن میں رہا اُن (کے حالات)
کی خبر رکھتا رہا جب تو نے مجھے دنیا سے اُٹھا لیا تو تو اُن کا
نگراں تھا اور تو ہر چیز سے خبردار ہے ﴿۱۱۷﴾

مَا قُلْتُ لَهُمْ اِلَّا مَآ اَمَرْتَنِيْ بِهٖٓ اَنِ
اعْبُدُوا اللّٰهَ رَبِّيْ وَرَبَّكُمْ ۚ وَكُنْتُ
عَلَيْهِمْ شَهِيْدًا مَّا دُمْتُ فِيْهِمْ ۚ
فَلَمَّا تَوَفَّيْتَنِيْ كُنْتَ اَنْتَ الرَّقِيْبَ
عَلَيْهِمْ ۭ وَاَنْتَ عَلٰي كُلِّ شَيْءٍ شَهِيْدٌ ﴿١١٧﴾

118. "If Thou dost punish them, they are Thy servants: if Thou dost forgive them, Thou art the Exalted in power, the Wise."

اگر تو اُن کو عذاب دے تو یہ تیرے بندے ہیں۔ اور اگر بخش
دے تو (تیری مہربانی ہے) بے شک تو غالب (اور) حکمت
والا ہے ﴿۱۱۸﴾

اِنْ تُعَذِّبْهُمْ فَاِنَّهُمْ عِبَادُكَ ۚ وَ
اِنْ تَغْفِرْ لَهُمْ فَاِنَّكَ اَنْتَ الْعَزِيْزُ
الْحَكِيْمُ ﴿١١٨﴾

119. Allah will say; "This is a day on which the truthful will profit from their truth: theirs are Gardens, with rivers flowing beneath,—their eternal home: Allah well-pleased with them, and they with Allah: that is the mighty Triumph (the fulfillment of all desires).

خدا فرمائے گا کہ آج وہ دن ہے کہ راستبازوں کو اُنکی سچائی
ہی فائدہ دے گی۔ اُن کے لئے باغ ہیں جن کے
نیچے نہریں بہ رہی ہیں۔ ابدالآباد اُن میں بستے
رہیں گے۔ خدا اُن سے خوش ہے اور وہ خدا سے
خوش ہیں۔ یہ بڑی کامیابی ہے ﴿۱۱۹﴾

قَالَ اللّٰهُ هٰذَا يَوْمُ يَنْفَعُ الصّٰدِقِيْنَ
صِدْقُهُمْ ۭ لَهُمْ جَنّٰتٌ تَجْرِيْ مِنْ
تَحْتِهَا الْاَنْهٰرُ خٰلِدِيْنَ فِيْهَآ اَبَدًا ۭ
رَضِيَ اللّٰهُ عَنْهُمْ وَرَضُوْا عَنْهُ ۭ ذٰلِكَ
الْفَوْزُ الْعَظِيْمُ ﴿١١٩﴾

120. To Allah doth belong the dominion of the heavens and the earth, and all that is therein, and it is He who hath power over all things.

آسمان اور زمین اور جو کچھ ان (دونوں) میں ہے سب پر
خدا ہی کی بادشاہی ہے۔ اور وہ ہر چیز پر قادر ہے ﴿۱۲۰﴾

لِلّٰهِ مُلْكُ السَّمٰوٰتِ وَالْاَرْضِ وَمَا
فِيْهِنَّ ۭ وَهُوَ عَلٰي كُلِّ شَيْءٍ قَدِيْرٌ ﴿١٢٠﴾ ع ١٥

Al-An'ām, or Cattle.

سورہ انعام مکی ہے اور اسمیں ایک سو پینسٹھ یا چھیاسٹھ آیتیں اور بیس رکوع ہیں

سُوْرَةُ الْاَنْعَامِ مَكِّيَّةٌ وَّهِيَ مِائَةٌ وَّخَمْسٌ وَّسِتُّوْنَ اٰيَةً وَّعِشْرُوْنَ رُكُوْعًا

In the name of Allah, Most Gracious, Most Merciful.

شروع خدا کا نام لے کر جو بڑا مہربان نہایت رحم والا ہے

بِسْمِ اللّٰهِ الرَّحْمٰنِ الرَّحِيْمِ

1. Praise be to Allah, Who created the heavens and the earth, and made the Darkness and the Light. Yet those who reject Faith hold (others) as equal with their Guardian Lord.

ہر طرح کی تعریف خدا ہی کو سزاوار ہے جس نے آسمانوں
اور زمین کو پیدا کیا اور اندھیرا اور روشنی بنائی پھر بھی کافر
(اور چیزوں کو) خدا کے برابر ٹھیراتے ہیں ﴿۱﴾

اَلْحَمْدُ لِلّٰهِ الَّذِيْ خَلَقَ السَّمٰوٰتِ وَ
الْاَرْضَ وَجَعَلَ الظُّلُمٰتِ وَالنُّوْرَ ۥ
ثُمَّ الَّذِيْنَ كَفَرُوْا بِرَبِّهِمْ يَعْدِلُوْنَ ﴿١﴾

2. He it is Who created you from clay, and then decreed a stated term (for you). And there is with Him another determined term; yet

وہی تو ہے جس نے تم کو مٹی سے پیدا کیا پھر (مرنے کا) ایک
وقت مقرر کر دیا۔ اور ایک مدت اسکے ہاں اور مقرر ہے پھر بھی

هُوَ الَّذِيْ خَلَقَكُمْ مِّنْ طِيْنٍ ثُمَّ قَضٰٓى
اَجَلًا ۭ وَاَجَلٌ مُّسَمًّى عِنْدَهٗ ثُمَّ

Ye doubt within yourselves !

3. And He is Allah in the heavens and in earth. He knoweth what ye hide, and what ye reveal, and He knoweth the (recompense) which ye earn (by your deeds).

4. But never did a single one of the Signs of their Lord reach them, but they turned away therefrom.

5. And now they reject the truth when it reaches them: but soon shall come to them the news of what they used to mock at.

6. See they not how many of those before them We did destroy?— Generations We had established on the earth, in strength such as We have not given to you— for whom We poured out rain from the skies in abundance, and gave streams flowing beneath their (feet): yet for their sins We destroyed them, and raised in their wake fresh generations (to succeed them).

7. If We had sent unto thee a written (Message) on parchment, so that they could touch it with their hands, the Unbelievers would have been sure to say: "This is nothing but obvious magic !"

8. They say: "Why is not an angel sent down to him ?" If We did send down an angel, the matter would be settled at once, and no respite would be granted them.

9. If We had made it an angel, We should have sent him as a man. And We should certainly have caused them confusion in a matter which they have already covered with confusion.

10. Mocked were (many) Messengers before thee; but their scoffers were hemmed in by the thing that they mocked.

11. Say: "Travel through the earth and see what was the end of those who rejected Truth."

تم (اے کافرو خدا کے بارے میں) شک کرتے ہو (٢)
اور آسمان اور زمین میں وہی (ایک) خدا ہے۔ تمہاری
پوشیدہ اور ظاہر سب باتیں جانتا ہے۔ اور تم جو عمل
کرتے ہو سب سے واقف ہے (٣)
اور خدا کی نشانیوں میں سے کوئی نشانی ان لوگوں کے
پاس نہیں آتی مگر یہ اس سے منہ پھیر لیتے ہیں (٤)
جب ان کے پاس حق آیا تو اس کو بھی جھٹلا دیا سو ان کو
ان چیزوں کا جن سے یہ استہزاء کرتے ہیں عنقریب انجام
معلوم ہو جائے گا (٥)
کیا انہوں نے نہیں دیکھا کہ ہم نے ان سے پہلے کتنی امتوں
کو ہلاک کر دیا جن کے پاؤں ملک میں ایسے جما دیئے تھے
کہ تمہارے پاؤں بھی ایسے نہیں جمائے اور ان پر آسمان
سے لگاتار مینہ برسایا اور نہریں بنا دیں جو ان کے (مکانوں کے)
نیچے بہہ رہی تھیں پھر ان کو ان کے گناہوں کے سبب ہلاک کر دیا
اور ان کے بعد اور امتیں پیدا کر دیں (٦)
اور اگر ہم تم پر کاغذوں پر لکھی ہوئی کتاب نازل کرتے
اور یہ اسے اپنے ہاتھوں سے ٹٹول بھی لیتے۔ تو جو کافر ہیں
وہ یہی کہہ دیتے کہ یہ تو (صاف اور) صریح جادو ہے (٧)
اور کہتے ہیں کہ ان (پیغمبر) پر فرشتہ کیوں نازل نہ ہوا۔ (جو
ان کی تصدیق کرتا) اگر ہم فرشتہ نازل کرتے تو کام ہی فیصل
ہو جاتا پھر انہیں (مطلق) مہلت نہ دی جاتی (٨)
نیز اگر ہم کسی فرشتے کو بھیجتے تو اسے مرد کی صورت میں بھیجتے
اور جو شبہ (اب) کرتے ہیں اسی شبے میں پھر انہیں ڈال دیتے (٩)
اور تم سے پہلے بھی پیغمبروں کے ساتھ تمسخر ہوتے رہے ہیں سو جو لوگ
ان میں سے تمسخر کیا کرتے تھے ان کو تمسخر کی سزا نے آ گھیرا (١٠)
کہو کہ (اے منکرین رسالت) ملک میں چلو پھرو۔ پھر دیکھو
کہ جھٹلانے والوں کا کیا انجام ہوا (١١)

أَنْتُمْ تَمْتَرُونَ (٢)
وَهُوَ اللّٰهُ فِي السَّمٰوٰتِ وَفِي الْأَرْضِ ۖ
يَعْلَمُ سِرَّكُمْ وَجَهْرَكُمْ وَيَعْلَمُ مَا
تَكْسِبُونَ (٣)
وَمَا تَأْتِيهِمْ مِنْ آيَةٍ مِنْ آيَاتِ رَبِّهِمْ
إِلَّا كَانُوا عَنْهَا مُعْرِضِينَ (٤)
فَقَدْ كَذَّبُوا بِالْحَقِّ لَمَّا جَاءَهُمْ ۖ
فَسَوْفَ يَأْتِيهِمْ أَنْبَاءُ مَا كَانُوا بِهِ
يَسْتَهْزِئُونَ (٥)
أَلَمْ يَرَوْا كَمْ أَهْلَكْنَا مِنْ قَبْلِهِمْ مِنْ
قَرْنٍ مَكَّنَّاهُمْ فِي الْأَرْضِ مَا لَمْ نُمَكِّنْ
لَكُمْ وَأَرْسَلْنَا السَّمَاءَ عَلَيْهِمْ مِدْرَارًا
وَجَعَلْنَا الْأَنْهَارَ تَجْرِي مِنْ تَحْتِهِمْ
فَأَهْلَكْنَاهُمْ بِذُنُوبِهِمْ وَأَنْشَأْنَا مِنْ
بَعْدِهِمْ قَرْنًا آخَرِينَ (٦)
وَلَوْ نَزَّلْنَا عَلَيْكَ كِتَابًا فِي قِرْطَاسٍ
فَلَمَسُوهُ بِأَيْدِيهِمْ لَقَالَ الَّذِينَ
كَفَرُوا إِنْ هٰذَا إِلَّا سِحْرٌ مُبِينٌ (٧)
وَقَالُوا لَوْلَا أُنْزِلَ عَلَيْهِ مَلَكٌ ۖ وَلَوْ
أَنْزَلْنَا مَلَكًا لَقُضِيَ الْأَمْرُ ثُمَّ لَا
يُنْظَرُونَ (٨)
وَلَوْ جَعَلْنَاهُ مَلَكًا لَجَعَلْنَاهُ رَجُلًا وَ
لَلَبَسْنَا عَلَيْهِمْ مَا يَلْبِسُونَ (٩)
وَلَقَدِ اسْتُهْزِئَ بِرُسُلٍ مِنْ قَبْلِكَ فَحَاقَ
بِالَّذِينَ سَخِرُوا مِنْهُمْ مَا كَانُوا بِهِ يَسْتَهْزِئُونَ (١٠)
قُلْ سِيرُوا فِي الْأَرْضِ ثُمَّ انْظُرُوا
كَيْفَ كَانَ عَاقِبَةُ الْمُكَذِّبِينَ (١١)

12. Say: "To whom belongeth all that is in the heavens and on earth?" Say: "To Allah. He hath inscribed for Himself (the rule of) Mercy. That He will gather you together for the Day of Judgment, there is no doubt whatever, it is they who have lost their own souls, that will not believe.

(اُن سے) پوچھو کہ آسمان اور زمین میں جو کچھ ہے کس کا ہے
کہدو خدا کا۔ اُس نے اپنی ذات (پاک) پر رحمت کو لازم کر لیا ہے وہ
تم سب کو قیامت کے دن جس میں کچھ بھی شک نہیں ضرور جمع کرے گا
جن لوگوں نے اپنے تئیں نقصان میں ڈال رکھا ہے وہ ایمان نہیں لاتے (١٢)

قُلْ لِّمَنْ مَّا فِي السَّمٰوٰتِ وَالْاَرْضِ ۭ قُلْ
لِّلّٰهِ ۭ كَتَبَ عَلٰي نَفْسِهِ الرَّحْمَةَ ۭ لَيَجْمَعَنَّكُمْ
اِلٰى يَوْمِ الْقِيٰمَةِ لَا رَيْبَ فِيْهِ ۭ اَلَّذِيْنَ
خَسِرُوْٓا اَنْفُسَهُمْ فَهُمْ لَا يُؤْمِنُوْنَ (١٢)

13. To him belongeth all that dwelleth (or lurketh) in the Night and the Day, for He is the one Who heareth and knoweth all things.

اور جو مخلوق رات اور دن میں بستی ہے سب اسی کی ہے۔
اور وہ سنتا جانتا ہے (١٣)

وَلَهٗ مَا سَكَنَ فِي الَّيْلِ وَالنَّهَارِ ۭ وَهُوَ
السَّمِيْعُ الْعَلِيْمُ (١٣)

14. Say: "Shall I take for my protector any other than Allah, the Maker of the heavens and the earth? And He it is that feedeth but is not fed." Say: "Nay ! but I am commanded to be the first of those who bow to Allah (in Islam), and be not thou of the company of those who join gods with Allah."

کہو کیا میں خدا کو چھوڑ کر کسی اور کو مددگار بناؤں۔ کہ (وہی تو) آسمانوں
اور زمین کا پیدا کرنیوالا ہے اور وہی (سب کو) کھانا دیتا ہے اور خود
کسی سے کھانا نہیں لیتا (یہ بھی) کہدو کہ مجھے یہ حکم ہوا ہے کہ میں سب سے
پہلے اسلام لانیوالا ہوں اور یہ کہ تم (اے پیغمبر) مشرکوں میں نہ ہونا (١٤)

قُلْ اَغَيْرَ اللّٰهِ اَتَّخِذُ وَلِيًّا فَاطِرِ السَّمٰوٰتِ
وَالْاَرْضِ وَهُوَ يُطْعِمُ وَلَا يُطْعَمُ ۭ قُلْ
اِنِّىْٓ اُمِرْتُ اَنْ اَكُوْنَ اَوَّلَ مَنْ اَسْلَمَ
وَلَا تَكُوْنَنَّ مِنَ الْمُشْرِكِيْنَ (١٤)

15. Say: "I would, if I disobeyed my Lord, indeed have fear of the Chastisement of a Mighty Day.

(یہ بھی) کہہ دو کہ اگر میں اپنے پروردگار کی نافرمانی کروں۔
تو مجھے بڑے دن کے عذاب کا خوف ہے (١٥)

قُلْ اِنِّىْٓ اَخَافُ اِنْ عَصَيْتُ رَبِّيْ
عَذَابَ يَوْمٍ عَظِيْمٍ (١٥)

16. "On that day, if the Penalty is averted from any, it is due to Allah's Mercy; and that would be a Mighty Triumph.

جس شخص سے اُس روز عذاب ٹال دیا گیا اُس پر خدا نے (بڑی)
مہربانی فرمائی۔ اور یہ کھلی کامیابی ہے (١٦)

مَنْ يُّصْرَفْ عَنْهُ يَوْمَىِٕذٍ فَقَدْ
رَحِمَهٗ ۭ وَذٰلِكَ الْفَوْزُ الْمُبِيْنُ (١٦)

17. "If Allah touch thee with affliction, none can remove it but He; if He touch thee with happiness, He hath power over all things.

اور اگر خدا تم کو کوئی سختی پہنچائے تو اُسکے سوا اس کو کوئی
دُور کرنے والا نہیں اور اگر نعمت (وراحت) عطا کرے تو
(کوئی اُس کو روکنے والا نہیں) وہ ہر چیز پر قادر ہے (١٧)

وَاِنْ يَّمْسَسْكَ اللّٰهُ بِضُرٍّ فَلَا كَاشِفَ
لَهٗٓ اِلَّا هُوَ ۭ وَاِنْ يَّمْسَسْكَ بِخَيْرٍ
فَهُوَ عَلٰي كُلِّ شَيْءٍ قَدِيْرٌ (١٧)

18. "He is irresistibly Supreme over His servants. And He is the Wise, acquainted with all things."

اور وہ اپنے بندوں پر غالب ہے۔ اور وہ دانا
(اور) خبردار ہے (١٨)

وَهُوَ الْقَاهِرُ فَوْقَ عِبَادِهٖ ۭ وَهُوَ
الْحَكِيْمُ الْخَبِيْرُ (١٨)

19. Say: "What thing is most weighty in evidence ?" Say: "Allah is witness between me and you; this Qur'an hath been revealed to me by inspiration. That I may warn you and all whom it reaches. Can ye possibly bear witness that besides Allah there are other gods?" Say: "Nay! I cannot bear witness!" Say: "But in truth He is the One God. And I truly am innocent of (your blasphemy of) joining others with Him."

ان سے پوچھو کہ سب سے بڑھ کر (قرین انصاف) کس کی شہادت ہے
کہہ دو کہ خدا ہی مجھ میں اور تم میں گواہ ہے۔ اور یہ قرآن مجھ پر
اسلئے اتارا گیا ہے کہ اسکے ذریعے سے تم کو اور جس شخص تک وہ
پہنچ سکے آگاہ کردوں۔ کیا تم لوگ اس بات کی شہادت دیتے ہو
کہ خدا کیساتھ اور بھی معبود ہیں (اے محمد) کہہ دو کہ میں تو (ایسی)
شہادت نہیں دیتا۔ کہہ دو کہ صرف وہی ایک معبود ہے اور
جن کو تم لوگ شریک بناتے ہو میں اُن سے بیزار ہوں (١٩)

قُلْ اَيُّ شَيْءٍ اَكْبَرُ شَهَادَةً ۭ قُلِ اللّٰهُ ڐ
شَهِيْدٌۢ بَيْنِيْ وَبَيْنَكُمْ ۣ وَاُوْحِيَ اِلَيَّ
هٰذَا الْقُرْاٰنُ لِاُنْذِرَكُمْ بِهٖ وَمَنْۢ
بَلَغَ ۭ اَىِٕنَّكُمْ لَتَشْهَدُوْنَ اَنَّ مَعَ
اللّٰهِ اٰلِهَةً اُخْرٰى ۭ قُلْ لَّآ اَشْهَدُ ۚ
قُلْ اِنَّمَا هُوَ اِلٰهٌ وَّاحِدٌ وَّاِنَّنِيْ
بَرِيْۗءٌ مِّمَّا تُشْرِكُوْنَ (١٩)

20. Those to whom We have given the Book know this as they

جن لوگوں کو ہم نے کتاب دی ہے وہ ان (ہمارے پیغمبر) کو اس

اَلَّذِيْنَ اٰتَيْنٰهُمُ الْكِتٰبَ يَعْرِفُوْنَهٗ

know their own sons. Those who have lost their own souls refuse therefore to believe.

طرح پہچانتے ہیں جس طرح اپنے بیٹوں کو پہچانا کرتے ہیں جنہوں
نے اپنے تئیں نقصان میں ڈال رکھا ہے وہ ایمان نہیں لاتے ﴿۲۰﴾

كَمَا يَعْرِفُونَ أَبْنَاءَهُمْ الَّذِينَ خَسِرُوا
أَنفُسَهُمْ فَهُمْ لَا يُؤْمِنُونَ ﴿٢٠﴾

21. Who doth more wrong than he who inventeth a lie against Allah or rejecteth His Signs ? But verily the wrong-doers never shall prosper.

اور اُس شخص سے زیادہ کون ظالم ہے جس نے خدا پر
جھوٹ افترا کیا یا اُس کی آیتوں کو جھٹلایا کچھ شک نہیں کہ
ظالم لوگ نجات نہیں پائیں گے ﴿۲۱﴾

وَمَنْ أَظْلَمُ مِمَّنِ افْتَرَىٰ عَلَى اللَّهِ
كَذِبًا أَوْ كَذَّبَ بِآيَاتِهِ إِنَّهُ لَا يُفْلِحُ
الظَّالِمُونَ ﴿٢١﴾

22. On the day shall We gather them all together: We shall say to those who ascribed partners (to Us): "Where are the partners whom ye (invented and) talked about !

اور جس دن ہم سب لوگوں کو جمع کریں گے پھر مشرکوں
سے پوچھیں گے کہ (آج) وہ تمہارے شریک کہاں ہیں
جن کا تمہیں دعویٰ تھا؟ ﴿۲۲﴾

وَيَوْمَ نَحْشُرُهُمْ جَمِيعًا ثُمَّ نَقُولُ
لِلَّذِينَ أَشْرَكُوا أَيْنَ شُرَكَاؤُكُمُ
الَّذِينَ كُنتُمْ تَزْعُمُونَ ﴿٢٢﴾

23. There will then be (left) no excuse for them but to say: "By Allah our Lord we were not those who joined gods with Allah."

تو اُن سے کچھ عذر نہ بن پڑیگا اور بجز اسکے (کچھ چارہ نہ ہوگا)
کہ کہیں خدا کی قسم جو ہمارا پروردگار ہے ہم شریک نہیں بناتے تھے ﴿۲۳﴾

ثُمَّ لَمْ تَكُن فِتْنَتُهُمْ إِلَّا أَن قَالُوا وَ
اللَّهِ رَبِّنَا مَا كُنَّا مُشْرِكِينَ ﴿٢٣﴾

24. Behold ! how they lie against themselves but the (lie) which they invented will leave them in the lurch.

دیکھو انہوں نے اپنے اُوپر کیسا جھوٹ بولا اور
جو کچھ یہ افترا کیا کرتے تھے سب اُن سے
جاتا رہا ﴿۲۴﴾

انظُرْ كَيْفَ كَذَبُوا عَلَىٰ أَنفُسِهِمْ
وَضَلَّ عَنْهُم مَّا كَانُوا
يَفْتَرُونَ ﴿٢٤﴾

25. Of them there are some who (pretend to) listen to thee; but We have thrown veils on their hearts, so they understand it not, and deafness in their ears; if they saw everyone of the Signs, they will not believe in them; in so much that when they come to thee, they (but) dispute with thee; the Unbelievers say: "These are nothing but tales of the ancients."

اور اُن میں بعض ایسے ہیں کہ تمہاری (باتوں کی) طرف کان
رکھتے ہیں اور ہم نے اُنکے دلوں پر تو پردے ڈالدیے ہیں کہ
اُنکو سمجھ نہ سکیں اور کانوں میں ثقل پیدا کر دیا ہے (کہ سُن نہ سکیں) اور
اگر یہ تمام نشانیاں بھی دیکھ لیں تب بھی تو ان پر ایمان نہ لائیں یہاں تک
کہ جب تمہارے پاس تم سے بحث کرنےکو آتے ہیں تو جو کافر ہیں کہتے ہیں
یہ (قرآن) اور کچھ بھی نہیں صرف پہلے لوگوں کی کہانیاں ہیں ﴿۲۵﴾

وَمِنْهُم مَّن يَسْتَمِعُ إِلَيْكَ وَجَعَلْنَا
عَلَىٰ قُلُوبِهِمْ أَكِنَّةً أَن يَفْقَهُوهُ وَفِي
آذَانِهِمْ وَقْرًا وَإِن يَرَوْا كُلَّ آيَةٍ
لَّا يُؤْمِنُوا بِهَا حَتَّىٰ إِذَا جَاءُوكَ
يُجَادِلُونَكَ يَقُولُ الَّذِينَ كَفَرُوا إِنْ
هَٰذَا إِلَّا أَسَاطِيرُ الْأَوَّلِينَ ﴿٢٥﴾

26. Others they forbid it and themselves they keep away; but they only destroy themselves and they perceive it not.

وہ اس سے (اوروں کو بھی) روکتے ہیں اور خود بھی پرے
رہتے ہیں۔ مگر (ان باتوں سے) اپنے آپ ہی کو ہلاک کرتے
ہیں اور (اس سے) بے خبر ہیں ﴿۲۶﴾

وَهُمْ يَنْهَوْنَ عَنْهُ وَيَنْأَوْنَ عَنْهُ
وَإِن يُهْلِكُونَ إِلَّا أَنفُسَهُمْ وَمَا
يَشْعُرُونَ ﴿٢٦﴾

27. If thou couldst but see when they shall be made to stand by the Fire they will say: "Would that we were but sent back ! Then would we not reject the Signs of our Lord, but would be amongst those who believe!"

کاش تم (اُن کو اُس وقت) دیکھو جب یہ دوزخ کے کنارے
کھڑے کیے جائینگے اور کہیں گے کہ اے کاش ہم پھر (دنیا میں) لوٹا
دیے جائیں تاکہ اپنے پروردگار کی آیتوں کی تکذیب نہ کریں اور مومن ہو جائیں ﴿۲۷﴾

وَلَوْ تَرَىٰ إِذْ وُقِفُوا عَلَى النَّارِ فَقَالُوا
يَا لَيْتَنَا نُرَدُّ وَلَا نُكَذِّبَ بِآيَاتِ رَبِّنَا
وَنَكُونَ مِنَ الْمُؤْمِنِينَ ﴿٢٧﴾

28. Yea, in their own (eyes) will become manifest what before they concealed. But if they were returned, they would certainly relapse to the

ہاں یہ جو کچھ پہلے چھپایا کرتے تھے (آج) اُن پر ظاہر ہو گیا ہے
اور اگر یہ (دنیا میں) لوٹائے بھی جائیں تو جن (کاموں) سے اُن کو منع

بَلْ بَدَا لَهُم مَّا كَانُوا يُخْفُونَ مِن
قَبْلُ وَلَوْ رُدُّوا لَعَادُوا لِمَا نُهُوا

عَنْهُ وَاِنَّهُمْ لَكٰذِبُوْنَ ﴿٢٨﴾
وَقَالُوْٓا اِنْ هِيَ اِلَّا حَيَاتُنَا الدُّنْيَا
وَمَا نَحْنُ بِمَبْعُوْثِيْنَ ﴿٢٩﴾
وَلَوْ تَرٰٓى اِذْ وُقِفُوْا عَلٰى رَبِّهِمْ ۭ قَالَ
اَلَيْسَ هٰذَا بِالْحَقِّ ۭ قَالُوْا بَلٰى وَرَبِّنَا ۭ
قَالَ فَذُوْقُوا الْعَذَابَ بِمَا كُنْتُمْ
تَكْفُرُوْنَ ﴿٣٠﴾

کیا گیا تھا وہی پھر کرنے لگیں کچھ شک نہیں کہ یہ جھوٹے ہیں ﴿۲۸﴾
اور کہتے ہیں کہ ہماری جو دنیا کی زندگی ہے بس یہی (زندگی) ہے اور
ہم (مرنے کے بعد) پھر زندہ نہیں کیے جائیں گے ﴿۲۹﴾
اور کاش تم (ان کو اس وقت) دیکھو جب یہ اپنے پروردگار کے
سامنے کھڑے کیے جائیں گے اور وہ فرمائے گا کیا یہ (دوبارہ زندہ ہونا)
برحق نہیں تو کہیں گے کیوں نہیں پروردگار کی قسم (بالکل برحق ہے)
خدا فرمائے گا اب کفر کے بدلے (جو دنیا میں کرتے تھے) عذاب کے مزے چکھو ﴿۳۰﴾

things they were forbidden, for they are indeed liars.

29. And they (sometimes) say: "There is nothing except our life on this earth, and never shall we be raised up again."

30. If thou couldst but see when they shall be made to stand before their Lord he will say: "Is not this the truth ?" They will say: "Yea, by our Lord" he will say: "Taste ye then the Chastisement because ye rejected Faith."

قَدْ خَسِرَ الَّذِيْنَ كَذَّبُوْا بِلِقَاۗءِ اللّٰهِ ۭ
حَتّٰٓي اِذَا جَاۗءَتْهُمُ السَّاعَةُ بَغْتَةً قَالُوْا
يٰحَسْرَتَنَا عَلٰي مَا فَرَّطْنَا فِيْهَا ۙ وَهُمْ
يَحْمِلُوْنَ اَوْزَارَهُمْ عَلٰي ظُهُوْرِهِمْ ۭ
اَلَا سَاۗءَ مَا يَزِرُوْنَ ﴿٣١﴾

جن لوگوں نے خدا کے روبرو کھڑے ہونے کو جھوٹ سمجھا وہ گھاٹے
میں آ گئے۔ یہاں تک کہ جب ان پر قیامت ناگہاں آ موجود ہوگی
تو بول اٹھیں گے کہ (ہائے) اس تقصیر پر افسوس ہے جو ہم نے قیامت کے
بارے میں کی۔ اور وہ اپنے (اعمال کے) بوجھ اپنی پیٹھوں پر اٹھائے
ہوئے ہوں گے۔ دیکھو جو بوجھ یہ اٹھا رہے ہیں بہت برا ہے ﴿۳۱﴾

31. Lost indeed are they who treat it as a falsehood that they must meet Allah,—until on a sudden the hour is on them, and they say: "Ah! woe unto us that we neglected; for they bear their burdens on their backs, and evil indeed are the burdens that they bear ?

وَمَا الْحَيٰوةُ الدُّنْيَآ اِلَّا لَعِبٌ وَّلَهْوٌ ۭ
وَلَلدَّارُ الْاٰخِرَةُ خَيْرٌ لِّلَّذِيْنَ يَتَّقُوْنَ ۭ
اَفَلَا تَعْقِلُوْنَ ﴿٣٢﴾

اور دنیا کی زندگی تو ایک کھیل اور مشغلہ ہے۔ اور بہت اچھا گھر
تو آخرت کا گھر ہے (یعنی) ان کے لیے جو (خدا سے) ڈرتے ہیں۔
کیا تم سمجھتے نہیں ﴿۳۲﴾

32. Nothing is the life of this world but play and amusement. But best is the Home in the Hereafter, for those who are righteous. Will ye not then understand ?

قَدْ نَعْلَمُ اِنَّهٗ لَيَحْزُنُكَ الَّذِيْ يَقُوْلُوْنَ
فَاِنَّهُمْ لَا يُكَذِّبُوْنَكَ وَلٰكِنَّ الظّٰلِمِيْنَ
بِاٰيٰتِ اللّٰهِ يَجْحَدُوْنَ ﴿٣٣﴾

ہم کو معلوم ہے کہ ان (کافروں) کی باتیں تمہیں رنج پہنچاتی
ہیں (مگر) یہ تمہاری تکذیب نہیں کرتے بلکہ ظالم خدا کی آیتوں
سے انکار کرتے ہیں ﴿۳۳﴾

33. We know indeed the grief which their words do cause thee: it is not thee they reject: it is the Signs of Allah, which the wicked deny.

وَلَقَدْ كُذِّبَتْ رُسُلٌ مِّنْ قَبْلِكَ فَصَبَرُوْا
عَلٰي مَا كُذِّبُوْا وَاُوْذُوْا حَتّٰٓي اَتٰىهُمْ
نَصْرُنَا ۚ وَلَا مُبَدِّلَ لِكَلِمٰتِ اللّٰهِ ۚ وَلَقَدْ
جَاۗءَكَ مِنْ نَّبَاِى الْمُرْسَلِيْنَ ﴿٣٤﴾

اور تم سے پہلے بھی پیغمبر جھٹلائے جاتے رہے۔ تو وہ تکذیب
اور ایذا پر صبر کرتے رہے یہاں تک کہ ان کے پاس ہماری مدد
پہنچتی رہی۔ اور خدا کی باتوں کو کوئی بھی بدلنے والا نہیں۔ اور تم کو
پیغمبروں (کے احوال) کی خبریں پہنچ چکی ہیں (تو تم بھی صبر سے کام لو) ﴿۳۴﴾

34. Rejected were the Messengers before thee: with patience and constancy they bore their rejection and their persecution until Our aid did reach them: there is none that can alter the Words (and Decrees) of Allah already hast thou received some account of those Messengers.

وَاِنْ كَانَ كَبُرَ عَلَيْكَ اِعْرَاضُهُمْ
فَاِنِ اسْتَطَعْتَ اَنْ تَبْتَغِيَ نَفَقًا فِي
الْاَرْضِ اَوْ سُلَّمًا فِي السَّمَاۗءِ فَتَاْتِيَهُمْ
بِاٰيَةٍ ۭ وَلَوْ شَاۗءَ اللّٰهُ لَجَمَعَهُمْ عَلَي
الْهُدٰي فَلَا تَكُوْنَنَّ مِنَ

اور اگر ان کی روگردانی تم پر شاق گزرتی ہے
تو اگر طاقت ہو تو زمین میں کوئی سرنگ ڈھونڈھ
نکالو یا آسمان میں سیڑھی (تلاش کرو) پھر ان کے
پاس کوئی معجزہ لاؤ۔ اور اگر خدا چاہتا تو سب کو ہدایت
پر جمع کر دیتا۔ پس تم ہرگز نادانوں میں

35. If their spurning is hard on thee, yet if thou wert able to seek a tunnel in the ground or a ladder to the skies and bring them a Sign,—(what good ?). If it were Allah's Will, He could gather them together unto true guidance: so be not thou amongst those who are swayed by

ignorance (and impatience) !

نہ ہونا ﴿٣٥﴾

الجهلين ﴿٣٥﴾

النصف

36. Those who listen (in truth), be sure, will accept: as to the dead, Allah will raise them up; then will they be returned unto Him.

بات یہ ہے کہ حق کو قبول وہی کرتے ہیں جو سنتے بھی ہیں اور مُردوں کو
تو خدا قیامت ہی کو اُٹھائیگا پھر اُسی کیطرف لوٹکر جائینگے ﴿٣٦﴾

انما يستجيب الذين يسمعون ط و
الموتى يبعثهم الله ثم اليه يرجعون ﴿٣٦﴾

37. They say: "Why is not a Sign sent down to him from his Lord !" Say: "Allah hath certainly power to send down a Sign: But most of them understand not."

اور کہتے ہیں کہ اُن پر اُنکے پروردگار کے پاس سے کوئی نشانی
کیوں نازل نہیں ہوئی۔ کہہ دو کہ خدا نشانی اُتارنے پر
قادر ہے لیکن اکثر لوگ نہیں جانتے ﴿٣٧﴾

وقالوا لولا نزل عليه اية من
ربه قل ان الله قادر على ان
ينزل اية ولكن اكثرهم لا يعلمون ﴿٣٧﴾

38. There is not an animal (that lives) on the earth, nor a being that flies on its wings, but (forms part of) communities like you. Nothing have We omitted from the Book, and they (all) shall be gathered to their Lord in the end.

اور زمین میں جو چلنے پھرنے والا (حیوان) یا دو پروں سے
اُڑنے والا جانور ہے اُنکی بھی تم لوگوں کی طرح جماعتیں
ہیں۔ ہم نے کتاب (یعنی لوح محفوظ) میں کسی چیز (کے لکھنے)
میں کوتاہی نہیں کی پھر سب اپنے پروردگار کیطرف جمع کئے جائینگے ﴿٣٨﴾

وما من دابة في الارض ولا طير
يطير بجناحيه الا امم امثالكم
ما فرطنا في الكتب من شيء ثم
الى ربهم يحشرون ﴿٣٨﴾

39. Those who reject our Signs are deaf and dumb,— in the midst of darkness profound: whom Allah willeth. He leaveth to wander: whom He willeth. He placeth on the Way that is Straight.

اور جن لوگوں نے ہماری آیتوں کو جھٹلایا وہ بہرے اور
گونگے ہیں (اسکے علاوہ) اندھیرے میں (پڑے ہوئے)
جسکو خدا چاہے گمراہ کردے اور جسے چاہے سیدھے رستے پر چلادے ﴿٣٩﴾

والذين كذبوا باياتنا صم وبكم
في الظلمت من يشا الله يضلله
ومن يشا يجعله على صراط مستقيم ﴿٣٩﴾

40. Say: "Think ye to yourselves, if there come upon you the Punishment of Allah, or the Hour (that ye dread). Would ye then call upon other than Allah ?— (reply) if ye are truthful !

کہو (کافرو) بھلا دیکھو تو اگر تم پر خدا کا عذاب آجائے یا
قیامت آموجود ہو۔ تو کیا تم (ایسی حالت میں) خدا کے سوا
کسی اور کو پکارو گے؟ اگر سچے ہو (تو بتاؤ) ﴿٤٠﴾

قل ارءيتكم ان اتكم عذاب الله
او اتتكم الساعة اغير الله تدعون
ان كنتم صدقين ﴿٤٠﴾

41. "Nay,—on Him would ye call, and if it be his Will, He would remove (the distress) which occasioned your call upon Him, and ye would forget (the false gods) which ye join with Him !"

(نہیں) بلکہ (مصیبت کے وقت تم) اُسی کو پکارتے ہو تو جس
دکھ کیلئے اُسے پکارتے ہو وہ اگر چاہتا ہے تو اسکو دور کر دیتا ہے
اور جن کو تم شریک بناتے ہو (اُس وقت) انہیں بھول جاتے ہو ﴿٤١﴾

بل اياه تدعون فيكشف ما
تدعون اليه ان شاء وتنسون
ما تشركون ﴿٤١﴾ ع

42. Before thee We sent (messengers) to many nations, and We afflicted the nations with suffering and adversity, that they call (Allah) in humility.

اور ہم نے تم سے پہلے بہت سی اُمتوں کی طرف پیغمبر بھیجے۔
پھر (اُن کی نافرمانیوں کے سبب) ہم انہیں سختیوں اور
تکلیفوں میں پکڑتے رہے تاکہ عاجزی کریں ﴿٤٢﴾

ولقد ارسلنا الى امم من قبلك
فاخذنهم بالباساء والضراء لعلهم
يتضرعون ﴿٤٢﴾

43. When the suffering reached them from Us, why then did they not call (Allah) in humility? On the contrary their hearts became hardened, and Satan made their (sinful) acts seem alluring to them.

تو جب اُن پر ہمارا عذاب آتا رہا کیوں نہیں عاجزی کرتے
رہے۔ مگر اُن کے تو دل ہی سخت ہو گئے تھے اور جو کام وہ کرتے
تھے شیطان اُن کو (اُن کی نظروں میں) آراستہ کر دکھاتا تھا ﴿٤٣﴾

فلولا اذ جاءهم باسنا تضرعوا
ولكن قست قلوبهم وزين لهم
الشيطن ما كانوا يعملون ﴿٤٣﴾

44. But when they forgot the warning they had received, We opened to them the gates of all

پھر جب اُنہوں نے اُس نصیحت کو جو اُن کو کی گئی تھی فراموش
کر دیا تو ہم نے اُن پر ہر چیز کے دروازے کھول دیئے۔

فلما نسوا ما ذكروا به فتحنا
عليهم ابواب كل شيء حتى اذا

فَرِحُوا بِمَا أُوتُوا أَخَذْنَاهُمْ بَغْتَةً
فَإِذَا هُمْ مُبْلِسُونَ ﴿٤٤﴾
فَقُطِعَ دَابِرُ الْقَوْمِ الَّذِينَ ظَلَمُوا ۚ
وَالْحَمْدُ لِلَّهِ رَبِّ الْعَالَمِينَ ﴿٤٥﴾
قُلْ أَرَأَيْتُمْ إِنْ أَخَذَ اللَّهُ سَمْعَكُمْ
وَأَبْصَارَكُمْ وَخَتَمَ عَلَىٰ قُلُوبِكُمْ
مَنْ إِلَٰهٌ غَيْرُ اللَّهِ يَأْتِيكُمْ بِهِ ۗ انْظُرْ
كَيْفَ نُصَرِّفُ الْآيَاتِ ثُمَّ هُمْ يَصْدِفُونَ ﴿٤٦﴾
قُلْ أَرَأَيْتَكُمْ إِنْ أَتَاكُمْ عَذَابُ اللَّهِ
بَغْتَةً أَوْ جَهْرَةً هَلْ يُهْلَكُ إِلَّا الْقَوْمُ الظَّالِمُونَ ﴿٤٧﴾
وَمَا نُرْسِلُ الْمُرْسَلِينَ إِلَّا مُبَشِّرِينَ
وَمُنْذِرِينَ ۖ فَمَنْ آمَنَ وَأَصْلَحَ فَلَا
خَوْفٌ عَلَيْهِمْ وَلَا هُمْ يَحْزَنُونَ ﴿٤٨﴾
وَالَّذِينَ كَذَّبُوا بِآيَاتِنَا يَمَسُّهُمُ الْعَذَابُ
بِمَا كَانُوا يَفْسُقُونَ ﴿٤٩﴾
قُلْ لَا أَقُولُ لَكُمْ عِنْدِي خَزَائِنُ اللَّهِ
وَلَا أَعْلَمُ الْغَيْبَ وَلَا أَقُولُ لَكُمْ إِنِّي
مَلَكٌ ۖ إِنْ أَتَّبِعُ إِلَّا مَا يُوحَىٰ إِلَيَّ ۚ
قُلْ هَلْ يَسْتَوِي الْأَعْمَىٰ وَالْبَصِيرُ ۚ
أَفَلَا تَتَفَكَّرُونَ ﴿٥٠﴾ ع ٥
وَأَنْذِرْ بِهِ الَّذِينَ يَخَافُونَ أَنْ يُحْشَرُوا
إِلَىٰ رَبِّهِمْ ۙ لَيْسَ لَهُمْ مِنْ دُونِهِ وَلِيٌّ
وَلَا شَفِيعٌ لَعَلَّهُمْ يَتَّقُونَ ﴿٥١﴾
وَلَا تَطْرُدِ الَّذِينَ يَدْعُونَ رَبَّهُمْ
بِالْغَدَاةِ وَالْعَشِيِّ يُرِيدُونَ وَجْهَهُ ۖ
مَا عَلَيْكَ مِنْ حِسَابِهِمْ مِنْ شَيْءٍ وَمَا
مِنْ حِسَابِكَ عَلَيْهِمْ مِنْ شَيْءٍ

یہاں تک کہ جب ان چیزوں سے جو اُنکو دی گئی تھیں خوب خوش
ہو گئے تو ہم نے اُنکو ناگہاں پکڑ لیا اور وہ اُس وقت مایوس ہو کر رہ گئے ﴿۴۴﴾
غرض ظالم لوگوں کی جڑ کاٹ دی گئی اور سب تعریف
خدائے رب العالمین ہی کو (سزاوار) ہے ﴿۴۵﴾
(ان کافروں سے) کہو کہ بھلا دیکھو تو اگر خدا تمہارے کان اور آنکھیں
چھین لے اور تمہارے دلوں پر مُہر لگادے تو خدا کے سوا کونسا معبود
ہے جو تمہیں یہ نعمتیں پھر بخشے؟ دیکھو ہم کس کس طرح اپنی آیتیں
بیان کرتے ہیں۔ پھر بھی یہ لوگ رُوگردانی کئے جاتے ہیں ﴿۴۶﴾
کہو کہ بھلا بتاؤ تو اگر تم پر خدا کا عذاب بیخبری میں یا خبر
آنے کے بعد آئے تو کیا ظالم لوگوں کے سوا کوئی اور بھی ہلاک ہوگا؟ ﴿۴۷﴾
اور ہم جو پیغمبروں کو بھیجتے رہے ہیں تو خوشخبری سنانے اور ڈرانے کو
پھر جو شخص ایمان لائے اور نیکوکار ہو جائے تو ایسے لوگوں کو نہ کچھ
خوف ہوگا اور نہ وہ اندوہناک ہوں گے ﴿۴۸﴾
اور جنہوں نے ہماری آیتوں کو جھٹلایا اُن کی نافرمانیوں
کے سبب اُنہیں عذاب ہوگا ﴿۴۹﴾
کہہ دو کہ میں تم سے یہ نہیں کہتا کہ میرے پاس اللہ تعالےٰ
کے خزانے ہیں اور نہ (یہ کہ) میں غیب جانتا ہوں اور نہ
تم سے یہ کہتا ہوں کہ میں فرشتہ ہوں۔ میں تو صرف اُس حکم پر
چلتا ہوں جو مجھے (خدا کی طرف سے) آتا ہے۔ کہہ دو کہ بھلا اندھا
اور آنکھ والا برابر ہوتے ہیں؟ تو پھر تم غور (کیوں) نہیں کرتے؟ ﴿۵۰﴾
اور جو لوگ خوف رکھتے ہیں کہ اپنے پروردگار کے رُوبرو حاضر کئے جائینگے
(اور جانتے ہیں کہ) اُسکے سوا نہ تو اُنکا کوئی دوست ہوگا اور نہ سفارش کرنیوالا
اُن کو اس (قرآن) کے ذریعے سے نصیحت کر دو تاکہ پرہیزگار بنیں ﴿۵۱﴾
اور جو لوگ صبح و شام اپنے پروردگار سے دُعا کرتے ہیں (اور) اُسکی
ذات کے طالب ہیں اُن کو (اپنے پاس سے) مت نکالو۔ اُنکے حساب
(اعمال) کی جوابدہی تم پر کچھ نہیں اور تمہارے حساب کی جوابدہی
اُن پر کچھ نہیں۔ (پس ایسا نہ کرنا) اگر اُن کو نکالو گے

(good) things, until, in the midst of their enjoyment of Our gifts, on a sudden, We called them to account, when lo! they were plunged in despair!

45. Of the wrong-doers the last remnant was cut off Praise be to Allah, the Cherisher of the Worlds.

46. Say: "Think ye, if Allah took away your hearing and your sight, and sealed up your hearts, who—a god other than Allah—could restore them to you ?" See how We explain the Signs by various (symbols); yet they turn aside.

47. Say: "Think ye, if the Punishment of Allah comes to you, whether suddenly or openly, will any be destroyed except those who do wrong?

48. We send the Messengers only to give good news and to warn: so those who believe and mend (their lives),—upon them shall be no fear, nor shall they grieve.

49. But those who reject our Signs,—them shall punishment touch, for that they ceased not from transgressing.

50. Say: "I tell you not that with me are the Treasures of Allah, nor do I know what is hidden. Nor do I tell you I am an angel. I but follow what is revealed to me." Say: "Can the blind be held equal to the seeing?" Will ye then consider not?

51. Give this warning to those in whose (hearts) is the fear that they will be brought (to Judgment) before their Lord: except for Him they will have no protector nor intercessor: that they may guard (against evil).

52. Send not away those who call on their Lord morning and evening, seeking His Face. In naught art thou accountable for them, and in naught are they accountable for thee, that thou shouldst turn them away, and thus be (one)

فَتَطْرُدَهُمْ فَتَكُونَ مِنَ الظّٰلِمِينَ ﴿٥٢﴾

تو ظالموں میں ہو جاؤ گے ﴿۵۲﴾

of the unjust.

وَكَذٰلِكَ فَتَنَّا بَعْضَهُمْ بِبَعْضٍ لِّيَقُولُوٓا
أَهٰٓؤُلَآءِ مَنَّ اللّٰهُ عَلَيْهِمْ مِّنْۢ بَيْنِنَا ؕ
أَلَيْسَ اللّٰهُ بِأَعْلَمَ بِالشّٰكِرِينَ ﴿٥٣﴾

اور اسی طرح ہم نے بعض لوگوں کو بعض سے آزمائش کی ہے کہ (جو دولتمند
ہیں وہ غریبوں کی نسبت) کہتے ہیں کیا یہی لوگ ہیں جن پر خدا نے
ہم میں سے فضل کیا ہے (خدا نے فرمایا) بھلا خدا شکر کرنیوالوں سے واقف نہیں؟ ﴿۵۳﴾

53. Thus did We test some of them by others, that they should say: "Is it these then that Allah hath favoured from amongst us?" Doth not Allah know best those who are grateful?

وَإِذَا جَآءَكَ الَّذِينَ يُؤْمِنُونَ بِـَٔايٰتِنَا
فَقُلْ سَلٰمٌ عَلَيْكُمْ كَتَبَ رَبُّكُمْ عَلٰى
نَفْسِهِ الرَّحْمَةَ ۙ أَنَّهُۥ مَنْ عَمِلَ مِنْكُمْ
سُوٓءًۢا بِجَهٰلَةٍ ثُمَّ تَابَ مِنْۢ بَعْدِهِۦ وَ
أَصْلَحَ فَأَنَّهُۥ غَفُورٌ رَّحِيمٌ ﴿٥٤﴾

اور جب تمہارے پاس ایسے لوگ آیا کریں جو ہماری آیتوں پر
ایمان لاتے ہیں تو (ان سے) سلام علیکم کہا کرو خدا نے
اپنی ذات (پاک) پر رحمت کو لازم کر لیا ہے کہ جو کوئی تم میں
سے نادانی سے کوئی بُری حرکت کر بیٹھے پھر اسکے بعد توبہ
کرلے اور نیکوکار ہو جائے تو وہ بخشنے والا مہربان ہے ﴿۵۴﴾

54. When those come to thee who believe in Our Signs, say: "Peace be on you: your Lord hath inscribed for Himself (the rule of) Mercy: verily, if any of you did evil in ingnorance, and thereafter repented, and amended (his conduct), lo! He is Oft-Forgiving, Most Merciful.

وَكَذٰلِكَ نُفَصِّلُ الْأٰيٰتِ وَلِتَسْتَبِينَ
سَبِيلُ الْمُجْرِمِينَ ﴿٥٥﴾ ع

اور اسی طرح ہم اپنی آیتیں کھول کھول کر بیان کرتے ہیں (تاکہ
تم لوگ ان پر عمل کرو) اور اسلئے کہ گنہگاروں کا رستہ ظاہر ہو جائے ﴿۵۵﴾

55. Thus do We explain the Signs in detail: that the way of the sinners may be shown up.

قُلْ إِنِّى نُهِيتُ أَنْ أَعْبُدَ الَّذِينَ
تَدْعُونَ مِنْ دُونِ اللّٰهِ ؕ قُلْ لَّآ أَتَّبِعُ
أَهْوَآءَكُمْ ۙ قَدْ ضَلَلْتُ إِذًا وَّمَآ أَنَا
مِنَ الْمُهْتَدِينَ ﴿٥٦﴾

(اے پیغمبر کفار سے) کہہ دو کہ جن کو تم خدا کے سوا پکارتے ہو
مجھے ان کی عبادت سے منع کیا گیا ہے۔ (یہ بھی) کہہ دو
کہ میں تمہاری خواہشوں کی پیروی نہیں کروں گا ایسا
کروں تو گمراہ ہو جاؤں اور ہدایت یافتہ لوگوں میں نہ رہوں ﴿۵۶﴾

56. Say: "I am forbidden" to worship those—others than Allah—whom ye call upon," say: "I will not follow your vain desires: if I did, I would stray from the path, and be not of the company of those who receive guidance."

قُلْ إِنِّى عَلٰى بَيِّنَةٍ مِّنْ رَّبِّى وَكَذَّبْتُمْ
بِهِۦ ؕ مَا عِنْدِى مَا تَسْتَعْجِلُونَ بِهِۦٓ ؕ إِنِ
الْحُكْمُ إِلَّا لِلّٰهِ ؕ يَقُصُّ الْحَقَّ وَهُوَ
خَيْرُ الْفٰصِلِينَ ﴿٥٧﴾

کہہ دو کہ میں تو اپنے پروردگار کی دلیل روشن پر ہوں اور تم
اس کی تکذیب کرتے ہو جس چیز (یعنی عذاب) کے لئے تم جلدی
کر رہے ہو وہ میرے پاس نہیں ہے (ایسا) حکم اللہ ہی کے اختیار
میں ہے وہ سچی بات بیان فرماتا ہے اور وہ سب سے بہتر فیصلہ کرنیوالا ہے ﴿۵۷﴾

57. Say: "For me, I am on a clear Sign from my Lord, but ye reject Him. What ye would see hastened, is not in my power. The Command rests with none but Allah: He declares the Truth, and He is the best of judges."

قُلْ لَّوْ أَنَّ عِنْدِى مَا تَسْتَعْجِلُونَ بِهِۦ
لَقُضِىَ الْأَمْرُ بَيْنِى وَبَيْنَكُمْ ؕ وَاللّٰهُ
أَعْلَمُ بِالظّٰلِمِينَ ﴿٥٨﴾

کہہ دو کہ جس چیز کیلئے تم جلدی کر رہے ہو اگر وہ میرے اختیار
میں ہوتی تو مجھ میں اور تم میں فیصلہ ہو چکا ہوتا اور خدا
ظالموں سے خوب واقف ہے ﴿۵۸﴾

58. Say: "If what ye would see hastened were in my power, the matter would be settled at once between you and me. But Allah knoweth best those who do wrong."

وَعِنْدَهُۥ مَفَاتِحُ الْغَيْبِ لَا يَعْلَمُهَآ
إِلَّا هُوَ ؕ وَيَعْلَمُ مَا فِى الْبَرِّ وَالْبَحْرِ ؕ
وَمَا تَسْقُطُ مِنْ وَّرَقَةٍ إِلَّا يَعْلَمُهَا
وَلَا حَبَّةٍ فِى ظُلُمٰتِ الْأَرْضِ وَلَا رَطْبٍ
وَّلَا يَابِسٍ إِلَّا فِى كِتٰبٍ مُّبِينٍ ﴿٥٩﴾

اور اسی کے پاس غیب کی کنجیاں ہیں جن کو اس کے سوا
کوئی نہیں جانتا اور اسے جنگلوں اور دریاؤں کی سب
چیزوں کا علم ہے اور کوئی پتا نہیں جھڑتا مگر وہ اس کو جانتا
ہے اور زمین کے اندھیروں میں کوئی دانہ اور کوئی ہری یا سوکھی
چیز نہیں ہے مگر کتاب روشن میں (لکھی ہوئی) ہے ﴿۵۹﴾

59. With Him are the keys of the Unseen, the treasures that none knoweth but He. He knoweth whatever there is on the earth and in the sea. Not a leaf doth fall but with His knowledge: there is not a grain in the darkness (or depths) of the earth, nor anything fresh or dry (green or withered), but is (inscribed) in a Record clear (to those who can read).

60. It is He Who doth take your souls by night, and hath knowledge of all that ye have done by day: by day doth He raise you up again; that a term appointed be fulfilled; in the end unto Him will be your return; then will He show you the truth of all that ye did.

61. He is Irresistibly, supreme over His servants and He sets guardians over you. At length, when death approaches one of you, Our angels take his soul, and they never fail in their duty.

62. Then are they returned unto Allah, their True Protector, surely His is the Command, and He is the Swiftest in taking account.

63. Say: "Who is it that delivereth you from the dark recesses of land and sea, when ye call upon Him in humility and in secret: 'If He only delivers us from these (dangers), (we vow) we shall truly show our gratitude'.?"

64. Say: "It is Allah That delivereth you from these and all (other) distresses: and yet ye worship false gods!"

65. Say: "He hath power to send calamities on you, from above and below, or to cover you with confusion in party strife, giving you a taste of mutual vengeance—each from the other". See how We explain the Signs in diverse ways; that they may understand.

66. But thy people reject this, though it is the Truth. Say: "Not mine is the responsibility for arranging your affairs;

67. For every Prophecy is a limit of time, and soon shall ye know it."

68. When thou seest men engaged in vain discourse about Our Sings, turn away from them unless they turn to a different theme. If Satan ever makes thee forget, then after recollection, sit

اور وہی تو ہے جو رات کو (سونے کی حالت میں) تمہاری روح قبض کر لیتا ہے
اور جو کچھ تم دن میں کرتے ہو اس سے خبر رکھتا ہے پھر تمہیں دن کو اٹھا دیتا ہے
تاکہ (یہی سلسلہ جاری رکھ کر زندگی کی) مدت معین پوری کر دی جائے
پھر تم (سب) کو اسی کی طرف لوٹ کر جانا ہے (اس روز) وہ تم کو تمہارے
عمل جو تم کرتے ہو (ایک ایک کر کے) بتائے گا (۶۰)
اور وہ اپنے بندوں پر غالب ہے اور تم پر نگہبان مقرر کیے رکھتا ہے
یہاں تک کہ جب تم میں سے کسی کی موت آتی ہے تو ہمارے فرشتے اس کی
روح قبض کر لیتے ہیں اور کسی طرح کی کوتاہی نہیں کرتے (۶۱)
پھر (قیامت کے دن تمام) لوگ اپنے مالک برحق خدائے تعالیٰ کے پاس
واپس بلائے جائیں گے سن لو کہ حکم اسی کا ہے اور وہ نہایت جلد حساب لینے والا ہے (۶۲)
کہو بھلا تم کو جنگلوں اور دریاؤں کے اندھیروں سے کون مخلصی
دیتا ہے (جب) کہ تم اسے عاجزی اور نیاز پنہانی سے پکارتے ہو
(اور کہتے ہو) اگر خدا ہم کو اس (تنگی) سے نجات بخشے تو ہم اس کے
بہت شکر گزار ہوں (۶۳)
کہو کہ خدا ہی تم کو اس (تنگی) سے اور ہر سختی سے نجات بخشتا ہے
پھر (تم) اس کے ساتھ شرک کرتے ہو (۶۴)
کہہ دو کہ وہ (اس پر بھی) قدرت رکھتا ہے کہ تم پر
اوپر کی طرف سے یا تمہارے پاؤں کے نیچے سے عذاب
بھیجے یا تمہیں فرقہ فرقہ کر دے اور ایک کو دوسرے سے لڑا کر
آپس کی لڑائی کا مزا چکھا دے۔ دیکھو ہم اپنی آیتوں کو کس
کس طرح بیان کرتے ہیں تاکہ یہ لوگ سمجھیں (۶۵)
اور اس (قرآن) کو تمہاری قوم نے جھٹلایا حالانکہ وہ سراسر
حق ہے کہہ دو کہ میں تمہارا داروغہ نہیں ہوں (۶۶)
ہر خبر کے لیے ایک وقت مقرر ہے اور تم کو عنقریب معلوم ہو جائے گا (۶۷)
اور جب تم ایسے لوگوں کو دیکھو جو ہماری آیتوں کے بارے میں
بیہودہ بکواس کر رہے ہیں تو ان سے الگ ہو جاؤ یہاں
تک کہ اور باتوں میں مصروف ہو جائیں اور اگر (یہ بات)

وهو الذي يتوفىكم باليل ويعلم
ما جرحتم بالنهار ثم يبعثكم فيه
ليقضى اجل مسمى ثم اليه
مرجعكم ثم ينبئكم بما كنتم
تعملون ﴿٦٠﴾
وهو القاهر فوق عباده ويرسل عليكم
حفظة حتى اذا جاء احدكم الموت
توفته رسلنا وهم لا يفرطون ﴿٦١﴾
ثم ردوا الى الله مولىهم الحق الا
له الحكم وهو اسرع الحاسبين ﴿٦٢﴾
قل من ينجيكم من ظلمت البر
والبحر تدعونه تضرعا وخفية
لئن انجىنا من هذه لنكونن من
الشكرين ﴿٦٣﴾
قل الله ينجيكم منها ومن كل كرب
ثم انتم تشركون ﴿٦٤﴾
قل هو القادر على ان يبعث عليكم عذابا
من فوقكم او من تحت ارجلكم او
يلبسكم شيعا ويذيق بعضكم باس
بعض انظر كيف نصرف الايت لعلهم
يفقهون ﴿٦٥﴾
وكذب به قومك وهو الحق قل
لست عليكم بوكيل ﴿٦٦﴾
لكل نبا مستقر وسوف تعلمون ﴿٦٧﴾
واذا رايت الذين يخوضون في ايتنا
فاعرض عنهم حتى يخوضوا في حديث
غيره واما ينسينك الشيطن فلا

not thou in the company of those who do wrong.

69. On their account no responsibility falls on the righteous, but (their duty) is to remind them, that they may (learn to) fear Allah.

70. Leave alone those who take their religion to be mere play and amusement, and are deceived by the life of this world. But continue to admonish them with it (Al-Qur'an) lest a soul is caught in its own ruin by its own action: it will find for itself no protector or intercessor except Allah: if it offered every ransom, (or reparation), none will be accepted: such is (the end of) those who deliver themselves to ruin by their own acts: they will have for drink (only) boiling water, and for punishment one most grievous: for they persisted in rejecting Allah.

71. Say. "Shall we call on others besides Allah,—things that can do us neither good nor harm,—and turn on our heels after receiving guidance from Allah?—like one whom the Satans have made into a fool, wandering bewildered through the earth, his friends calling 'Come to us', (vainly) guiding him to the Path." Say: "Allah's guidance is the (only) guidance, and we have been directed to submit ourselves to the Lord of the worlds;—

72. "To establish regular prayers and to fear Allah: for it is to Him that we shall be gathered together."

73. It is He Who created the heavens and the earth with truth: the day He saith, "Be," behold! it is. His Word is the Truth. His will be the dominion the day the trumpet will be blown. He knoweth the Unseen as well as that which is Open. For He is the Wise, well acquainted (with all things).

74. Lo! Abraham said to his father Āzar: "Takest thou idols for gods? For I see thee and thy people in manifest error."

شیطان تمہیں بھلا دے تو یاد آنے پر ظالم لوگوں کے ساتھ نہ بیٹھو ﴿۶۸﴾
اور پرہیزگاروں پر اُن لوگوں کے حساب کی کچھ بھی جوابدہی
نہیں. ہاں نصیحت تاکہ وہ بھی پرہیزگار ہوں ﴿۶۹﴾
اور جن لوگوں نے اپنے دین کو کھیل اور تماشا بنا رکھا ہے اور دنیا کی زندگی
نے اُنکو دھوکے میں ڈال رکھا ہے اُنسے کچھ کام نہ رکھو ہاں اس (قرآن) کے
ذریعے سے نصیحت کرتے رہو تاکہ (قیامت کے دن) کوئی اپنے اعمال کی سزا
میں ہلاکت میں نہ ڈالا جائے. (اُس روز) خدا کے سوا نہ تو کوئی اُسکا دوست ہوگا
اور نہ سفارش کرنیوالا اور اگر وہ ہر چیز (جو روئے زمین پر ہے بطور) معاوضہ دینا
چاہے تو وہ اُس سے قبول نہ ہو. یہی لوگ ہیں کہ اپنے اعمال کے وبال میں ہلاکت
میں ڈالے گئے اُنکے لئے پینے کو کھولتا ہوا پانی اور دکھ دینے والا عذاب ہے اسلئے کہ کفر کرتے تھے ﴿۷۰﴾
کہو. کیا ہم خدا کے سوا ایسی چیز کو پکاریں جو نہ ہمارا بھلا
کر سکے نہ بُرا. اور جب ہم کو خدا نے سیدھا رستہ دکھا دیا تو (کیا)
ہم اُلٹے پاؤں پھر جائیں؟ (پھر ہماری ایسی مثال ہو) جیسے کسی کو
جنات نے جنگل میں بھلا دیا ہو اور وہ حیران (ہو رہا ہو) اور
اُسکے کچھ رفیق ہوں جو اُسکو رستے کی طرف بلائیں کہ ہمارے پاس
چلا آ. کہدو کہ رستہ تو وہی ہے جو خدا نے بتایا ہے اور ہمیں تو یہ حکم
ملا ہے کہ ہم خدائے رب العالمین کے فرمانبردار ہوں ﴿۷۱﴾
اور یہ (بھی) کہ نماز پڑھتے رہو اور اُس سے ڈرتے رہو. اور
وہی تو ہے جس کے پاس تم جمع کئے جاؤ گے ﴿۷۲﴾
اور وہی تو ہے جس نے آسمانوں اور زمین کو تدبیر سے پیدا کیا ہے
اور جس دن وہ فرمائیگا کہ ہو جا تو (حشر برپا) ہو جائیگا ﴿۷۳﴾
اُس کا ارشاد برحق ہے اور جس دن صُور پھونکا جائیگا (اُس دن)
اسی کی بادشاہت ہوگی. وہی پوشیدہ اور ظاہر (سب) کا جاننے
والا ہے اور وہی دانا اور خبردار ہے ﴿۷۳﴾
اور (وہ وقت بھی یاد کرنے کے لائق ہے) جب ابراہیم نے
اپنے باپ آزر سے کہا کہ تم کیا بتوں کو معبود بناتے ہو. میں
دیکھتا ہوں کہ تم اور تمہاری قوم صریح گمراہی میں ہو ﴿۷۴﴾

تَقْعُدْ بَعْدَ الذِّكْرٰى مَعَ الْقَوْمِ الظّٰلِمِيْنَ ﴿٦٨﴾
وَمَا عَلَى الَّذِيْنَ يَتَّقُوْنَ مِنْ حِسَابِهِمْ
مِّنْ شَيْءٍ وَّلٰكِنْ ذِكْرٰى لَعَلَّهُمْ يَتَّقُوْنَ ﴿٦٩﴾
وَذَرِ الَّذِيْنَ اتَّخَذُوْا دِيْنَهُمْ لَعِبًا وَّ
لَهْوًا وَّغَرَّتْهُمُ الْحَيٰوةُ الدُّنْيَا وَذَكِّرْ
بِهٖٓ اَنْ تُبْسَلَ نَفْسٌۢ بِمَا كَسَبَتْ ۖ لَيْسَ لَهَا
مِنْ دُوْنِ اللّٰهِ وَلِيٌّ وَّلَا شَفِيْعٌ ۚ وَاِنْ
تَعْدِلْ كُلَّ عَدْلٍ لَّا يُؤْخَذْ مِنْهَا ۗ اُولٰٓئِكَ
الَّذِيْنَ اُبْسِلُوْا بِمَا كَسَبُوْا ۚ لَهُمْ شَرَابٌ
مِّنْ حَمِيْمٍ وَّعَذَابٌ اَلِيْمٌۢ بِمَا كَانُوْا يَكْفُرُوْنَ ﴿٧٠﴾ ع ۱۴
قُلْ اَنَدْعُوْا مِنْ دُوْنِ اللّٰهِ مَا لَا
يَنْفَعُنَا وَلَا يَضُرُّنَا وَنُرَدُّ عَلٰٓى اَعْقَابِنَا
بَعْدَ اِذْ هَدٰىنَا اللّٰهُ كَالَّذِي اسْتَهْوَتْهُ
الشَّيٰطِيْنُ فِي الْاَرْضِ حَيْرَانَ ۠ لَهٗٓ
اَصْحٰبٌ يَّدْعُوْنَهٗٓ اِلَى الْهُدَى ائْتِنَا ۭ
قُلْ اِنَّ هُدَى اللّٰهِ هُوَ الْهُدٰى ۭ وَ
اُمِرْنَا لِنُسْلِمَ لِرَبِّ الْعٰلَمِيْنَ ﴿٧١﴾
وَاَنْ اَقِيْمُوا الصَّلٰوةَ وَاتَّقُوْهُ ۭ وَهُوَ
الَّذِيْٓ اِلَيْهِ تُحْشَرُوْنَ ﴿٧٢﴾
وَهُوَ الَّذِيْ خَلَقَ السَّمٰوٰتِ وَالْاَرْضَ
بِالْحَقِّ ۭ وَيَوْمَ يَقُوْلُ كُنْ فَيَكُوْنُ ۭ النصف
قَوْلُهُ الْحَقُّ ۭ وَلَهُ الْمُلْكُ يَوْمَ يُنْفَخُ
فِي الصُّوْرِ ۭ عٰلِمُ الْغَيْبِ وَالشَّهَادَةِ ۭ
وَهُوَ الْحَكِيْمُ الْخَبِيْرُ ﴿٧٣﴾
وَاِذْ قَالَ اِبْرٰهِيْمُ لِاَبِيْهِ اٰزَرَ اَتَتَّخِذُ
اَصْنَامًا اٰلِهَةً ۚ اِنِّيْٓ اَرٰىكَ وَقَوْمَكَ
فِيْ ضَلٰلٍ مُّبِيْنٍ ﴿٧٤﴾

75. So also did We show Abraham the kingdom of the heavens and the earth, that he might have certitude.

76. When the night covered him over, he saw a star: he said: "This is my Lord." But when it set, he said. "I love not those that set."

77. When he saw the moon rising in splendour, He said: "This is my Lord." But when the moon set, he said: "Unless my Lord guide me, I shall surely be among those who go astray."

78. When he saw the sun rising (in splendour,) he said: "This is my Lord; this is the greatest (of all)." But when the sun set, he said: "O my people! I am indeed free from your (guilt) of giving partners to Allah.

79. "For me, I have set my face, firmly and truly, towards Him Who created the heavens and the earth, and never shall I give partners to Allah."

80. His people disputed with him. He said: "(Come) ye to dispute with me, about Allah, when He (Himself) hath guided me? I fear not (the beings) ye associate with Allah: unless my Lord willeth, (nothing can happen), my Lord comprehendeth in His knowledge all things. Will ye not (yourselves) be admonished?

81. "How should I fear (the beings) ye associate with Allah, when ye fear not to give partners to Allah without any warrant having been given to you? Which of (us) two parties hath more right to security? (tell me) if ye know.

82. "It is those who believe and mix not their beliefs with wrong—that are (truly) in security, for they are on (right) guidance."

83. That was Our argument which We gave to Abraham (to use) against his people: We raise whom We will, degree after degree: for thy Lord is full of wisdom and knowledge.

84. We gave him Isaac and Jacob: all (three) We guided: and

اور ہم اس طرح ابراہیم کو آسمانوں اور زمین کے عجائبات
دکھانے لگے تاکہ وہ خوب یقین کرنیوالوں میں ہو جائیں ﴿۷۵﴾
(یعنی) جب رات نے اُن کو (پردۂ تاریکی سے) ڈھانپ لیا تو
(آسمان میں) ایک ستارا نظر پڑا کہنے لگے یہ میرا پروردگار ہے. جب
وہ غائب ہو گیا تو کہنے لگے کہ مجھے غائب ہو جانیوالے تو پسند نہیں ﴿۷۶﴾
پھر جب چاند کو دیکھا کہ چمک رہا ہے تو کہنے لگے یہ میرا پروردگار ہے.
لیکن جب وہ بھی چھپ گیا تو بول اُٹھے کہ اگر میرا پروردگار مجھے
سیدھا رستہ نہیں دکھائیگا تو میں اُن لوگوں میں ہو جاؤنگا جو بھٹک رہے ہیں ﴿۷۷﴾
پھر جب سُورج کو دیکھا کہ جگمگا رہا ہے تو کہنے لگے میرا پروردگار
یہ ہے یہ سب سے بڑا ہے. مگر جب وہ بھی غروب ہو گیا تو کہنے لگے لوگو
جن چیزوں کو تم (خدا کا) شریک بناتے ہو میں اُنسے بیزار ہوں ﴿۷۸﴾
میں نے سب سے یکسو ہو کر اپنے تئیں اُسی ذات کیطرف متوجہ کیا جس نے
آسمانوں اور زمین کو پیدا کیا ہے اور میں مشرکوں میں سے نہیں ہوں ﴿۷۹﴾
اور اُنکی قوم اُنسے بحث کرنے لگی تو انہوں نے کہا کہ تم مجھ سے خدا کے بارے
میں (کیا) بحث کرتے ہو. اُسنے تو مجھے سیدھا رستہ دکھا دیا ہے. اور جن چیزوں کو
تم اُسکا شریک بناتے ہو میں اُنسے نہیں ڈرتا ہاں جو میرا پروردگار کچھ چاہے.
میرا پروردگار اپنے علم سے ہر چیز پر احاطہ کئے ہوئے ہے. کیا تم خیال نہیں کرتے؟ ﴿۸۰﴾
بھلا میں اُن چیزوں سے جنکو تم (خدا کا) شریک بناتے ہو کیونکر
ڈروں جبکہ تم اِس سے نہیں ڈرتے کہ خدا کیساتھ شریک بناتے ہو جسکی
اُس نے کوئی سند نازل نہیں کی. اب دونوں فریق میں سے کونسا
فریق امن (اور جمعیت خاطر) کا مستحق ہے اگر سمجھ رکھتے ہو (تو بتاؤ) ﴿۸۱﴾
جو لوگ ایمان لائے اور اپنے ایمان کو (شرک کے) ظلم سے مخلوط نہیں
کیا اُن کیلئے امن (اور جمعیت خاطر) ہے اور وہی ہدایت پانیوالے ہیں ﴿۸۲﴾
اور یہ ہماری دلیل تھی جو ہم نے ابراہیم کو اُنکی قوم کے مقابلے
میں عطا کی تھی. ہم جسکے چاہتے ہیں درجے بلند کر دیتے ہیں.
بیشک تمہارا پروردگار دانا (اور) خبردار ہے ﴿۸۳﴾
اور ہم نے اُن کو اسحٰق اور یعقوب بخشے (اور) سب کو ہدایت

وَكَذٰلِكَ نُرِيْٓ اِبْرٰهِيْمَ مَلَكُوْتَ السَّمٰوٰتِ
وَالْاَرْضِ وَلِيَكُوْنَ مِنَ الْمُوْقِنِيْنَ ﴿٧٥﴾
فَلَمَّا جَنَّ عَلَيْهِ الَّيْلُ رَاٰ كَوْكَبًا ۚ قَالَ
هٰذَا رَبِّيْ ۚ فَلَمَّآ اَفَلَ قَالَ لَآ اُحِبُّ
الْاٰفِلِيْنَ ﴿٧٦﴾
فَلَمَّا رَاَ الْقَمَرَ بَازِغًا قَالَ هٰذَا رَبِّيْ ۚ
فَلَمَّآ اَفَلَ قَالَ لَئِنْ لَّمْ يَهْدِنِيْ رَبِّيْ
لَاَكُوْنَنَّ مِنَ الْقَوْمِ الضَّآلِّيْنَ ﴿٧٧﴾
فَلَمَّا رَاَ الشَّمْسَ بَازِغَةً قَالَ هٰذَا
رَبِّيْ هٰذَآ اَكْبَرُ ۚ فَلَمَّآ اَفَلَتْ قَالَ
يٰقَوْمِ اِنِّيْ بَرِيْٓءٌ مِّمَّا تُشْرِكُوْنَ ﴿٧٨﴾
اِنِّيْ وَجَّهْتُ وَجْهِيَ لِلَّذِيْ فَطَرَ السَّمٰوٰتِ
وَالْاَرْضَ حَنِيْفًا وَّمَآ اَنَا مِنَ الْمُشْرِكِيْنَ ﴿٧٩﴾
وَحَآجَّهٗ قَوْمُهٗ ۚ قَالَ اَتُحَآجُّوْٓنِّيْ فِي
اللّٰهِ وَقَدْ هَدٰىنِ ۚ وَلَآ اَخَافُ مَا تُشْرِكُوْنَ
بِهٖٓ اِلَّآ اَنْ يَّشَآءَ رَبِّيْ شَيْئًا ۚ وَسِعَ رَبِّيْ
كُلَّ شَيْءٍ عِلْمًا ۚ اَفَلَا تَتَذَكَّرُوْنَ ﴿٨٠﴾
وَكَيْفَ اَخَافُ مَآ اَشْرَكْتُمْ وَلَا تَخَافُوْنَ
اَنَّكُمْ اَشْرَكْتُمْ بِاللّٰهِ مَا لَمْ يُنَزِّلْ بِهٖ
عَلَيْكُمْ سُلْطٰنًا ۚ فَاَيُّ الْفَرِيْقَيْنِ اَحَقُّ
بِالْاَمْنِ ۚ اِنْ كُنْتُمْ تَعْلَمُوْنَ ﴿٨١﴾
اَلَّذِيْنَ اٰمَنُوْا وَلَمْ يَلْبِسُوْٓا اِيْمَانَهُمْ بِظُلْمٍ
اُولٰٓئِكَ لَهُمُ الْاَمْنُ وَهُمْ مُّهْتَدُوْنَ ﴿٨٢﴾
وَتِلْكَ حُجَّتُنَآ اٰتَيْنٰهَآ اِبْرٰهِيْمَ عَلٰى قَوْمِهٖ ۚ
نَرْفَعُ دَرَجٰتٍ مَّنْ نَّشَآءُ ۚ اِنَّ رَبَّكَ
حَكِيْمٌ عَلِيْمٌ ﴿٨٣﴾
وَوَهَبْنَا لَهٗٓ اِسْحٰقَ وَيَعْقُوْبَ ۚ كُلًّا هَدَيْنَا ۚ

before him, We guided Noah, and among his progeny, David, Solomon, Job, Joseph, Moses, and Aaron: thus do We reward those who do good:

85. And Zakarîya and John, and Jesus and Elias: all in the ranks of the Righteous:

86. And Isma'îl and Elisha, and Jonas, and Lot: and to all We gave favour above the nations:

87. (To them) and to their fathers, and progeny and brethren: We chose them, and We guided them to a straight Way.

88. This is the Guidance of Allah: He giveth that guidance to whom He pleaseth, of His servants if they were to join other gods with Him, all that they did would be vain for them.

89. These were the men to whom We gave the Book, and Judgement, and Prophethood: if these (their descendants) reject them, behold! We shall entrust their charge to a new People who reject them not.

90. Those were the (prophets) who received Allah's guidance. Follow the guidance they received; say: "No reward for this do I ask of you: this is but a Reminder to the nations.

91. No just estimate of Allah do they make when they say: "Nothing doth Allah send down to man (by way of revelation)": say: "Who then sent down the Book which Moses brought?—a light and guidance to man: but ye make it into (separate) sheets for show, while ye conceal much (of its contents): therein were ye taught that which ye knew not—neither ye nor your fathers." Say: "Allah (sent it down)": then leave them to plunge in vain discourse and trifling.

92. And this is a Book which We have sent down, bringing blessings, and confirming (the revelations) which came before it: that thou

دی اور پہلے نوح کو بھی ہدایت دی تھی اور اُن کی اولاد
میں سے داؤد اور سلیمان اور ایّوب اور یوسف اور موسٰی
اور ہارون کو بھی۔ اور ہم نیک لوگوں کو ایسا ہی بدلہ دیا کرتے ہیں ﴿۸۵﴾
اور زکریا اور یحیٰی اور عیسٰی اور الیاس کو بھی۔ یہ سب
نیکو کار تھے ﴿۸۶﴾
اور اسمٰعیل اور الیسع اور یونس اور لُوط کو بھی۔ اور ان
سب کو جہان کے لوگوں پر فضیلت بخشی تھی ﴿۸۷﴾
اور بعض بعض کو اُنکے باپ دادا اور اولاد اور بھائیوں میں
سے بھی۔ اور اُنکو برگزیدہ بھی کیا تھا اور سیدھا رستہ بھی دکھایا تھا ﴿۸۸﴾
یہ خدا کی ہدایت ہے اس پر اپنے بندوں میں سے جسے چاہے
چلائے اور اگر وہ لوگ شرک کرتے تو جو عمل وہ کرتے تھے
سب ضائع ہو جاتے ﴿۸۹﴾
یہ وہ لوگ تھے جن کو ہم نے کتاب اور حکم (شریعت) اور نبوت
عطا فرمائی تھی۔ اگر یہ (کفار) ان باتوں سے انکار کریں تو ہم نے اُن پر (ایمان
لانے کیلئے) ایسے لوگ مقرر کر دیئے ہیں کہ وہ اُن سے کبھی انکار کرنے والے نہیں ﴿۹۰﴾
یہ وہ لوگ ہیں جن کو خدا نے ہدایت دی تھی تو تم اُنہیں کی ہدایت
کی پیروی کرو۔ کہہ دو کہ میں تم سے اِس (قرآن) کا صلہ نہیں مانگتا۔
یہ تو جہان کے لوگوں کے لئے محض نصیحت ہے ﴿۹۱﴾
اور ان لوگوں نے خدا کی قدر جیسے جاننی چاہیے تھی نہ جانی جب
اُنہوں نے کہا کہ خدا نے انسان پر (وحی اور کتاب وغیرہ) کچھ بھی نازل
نہیں کیا۔ کہو کہ جو کتاب موسٰی لیکر آئے تھے اسے کس نے نازل کیا تھا؟ جو
لوگوں کیلئے نور اور ہدایت تھی اور جسے تم نے علیحدہ علیحدہ اوراق (پر نقل)
کر رکھا ہے اُن (کے کچھ حصے) کو تو ظاہر کرتے ہو اور اکثر کو چھپاتے ہو اور تم کو
وہ باتیں سکھائی گئیں جنکو نہ تم جانتے تھے اور نہ تمہارے باپ دادا۔ کہہ دو (اس کتاب کو)
خدا ہی نے نازل کیا تھا پھر اُنکو چھوڑ دو کہ اپنی بیہودہ بکواس میں کھیلتے رہیں ﴿۹۲﴾
اور (ویسی ہی) یہ کتاب ہے جسے ہم نے نازل کیا ہے بابرکت جو اپنے سے
پہلی (کتابوں) کی تصدیق کرتی ہے اور (جو) اسلئے (نازل کی گئی ہے)

وَنُوحًا هَدَيْنَا مِنْ قَبْلُ وَمِنْ ذُرِّيَّتِهِ
دَاوُدَ وَسُلَيْمٰنَ وَأَيُّوبَ وَيُوسُفَ وَمُوسٰى
وَهٰرُونَ ۚ وَكَذٰلِكَ نَجْزِي الْمُحْسِنِينَ ﴿٨٤﴾
وَزَكَرِيَّا وَيَحْيٰى وَعِيسٰى وَإِلْيَاسَ ۖ
كُلٌّ مِّنَ الصّٰلِحِينَ ﴿٨٥﴾
وَإِسْمٰعِيلَ وَالْيَسَعَ وَيُونُسَ وَلُوطًا ۚ
وَكُلًّا فَضَّلْنَا عَلَى الْعٰلَمِينَ ﴿٨٦﴾
وَمِنْ آبَائِهِمْ وَذُرِّيّٰتِهِمْ وَإِخْوَانِهِمْ ۖ وَ
اجْتَبَيْنٰهُمْ وَهَدَيْنٰهُمْ إِلٰى صِرٰطٍ مُّسْتَقِيمٍ ﴿٨٧﴾
ذٰلِكَ هُدَى اللّٰهِ يَهْدِي بِهِ مَنْ يَّشَاءُ
مِنْ عِبَادِهِ ۚ وَلَوْ أَشْرَكُوا لَحَبِطَ عَنْهُمْ
مَّا كَانُوا يَعْمَلُونَ ﴿٨٨﴾
أُولٰٓئِكَ الَّذِينَ آتَيْنٰهُمُ الْكِتٰبَ وَالْحُكْمَ
وَالنُّبُوَّةَ ۚ فَإِنْ يَّكْفُرْ بِهَا هٰٓؤُلَآءِ فَقَدْ
وَكَّلْنَا بِهَا قَوْمًا لَّيْسُوا بِهَا بِكٰفِرِينَ ﴿٨٩﴾
أُولٰٓئِكَ الَّذِينَ هَدَى اللّٰهُ فَبِهُدٰىهُمُ
اقْتَدِهْ ۗ قُلْ لَّآ أَسْأَلُكُمْ عَلَيْهِ أَجْرًا ۖ
إِنْ هُوَ إِلَّا ذِكْرٰى لِلْعٰلَمِينَ ﴿٩٠﴾ ع
وَمَا قَدَرُوا اللّٰهَ حَقَّ قَدْرِهِ إِذْ قَالُوا
مَآ أَنْزَلَ اللّٰهُ عَلٰى بَشَرٍ مِّنْ شَيْءٍ ۗ قُلْ
مَنْ أَنْزَلَ الْكِتٰبَ الَّذِي جَآءَ بِهِ
مُوسٰى نُورًا وَّهُدًى لِّلنَّاسِ تَجْعَلُونَهُ
قَرَاطِيسَ تُبْدُونَهَا وَتُخْفُونَ كَثِيرًا ۚ
وَعُلِّمْتُمْ مَّا لَمْ تَعْلَمُوٓا أَنْتُمْ وَلَآ آبَاؤُكُمْ ۖ
قُلِ اللّٰهُ ۙ ثُمَّ ذَرْهُمْ فِي خَوْضِهِمْ يَلْعَبُونَ ﴿٩١﴾
وَهٰذَا كِتٰبٌ أَنْزَلْنٰهُ مُبٰرَكٌ مُّصَدِّقُ
الَّذِي بَيْنَ يَدَيْهِ وَلِتُنْذِرَ أُمَّ الْقُرٰى

وَمَنْ حَوْلَهَا ۚ وَالَّذِينَ يُؤْمِنُونَ بِالْآخِرَةِ
يُؤْمِنُونَ بِهِ ۖ وَهُمْ عَلَىٰ صَلَاتِهِمْ يُحَافِظُونَ ﴿٩٢﴾
وَمَنْ أَظْلَمُ مِمَّنِ افْتَرَىٰ عَلَى اللَّهِ كَذِبًا
أَوْ قَالَ أُوحِيَ إِلَيَّ وَلَمْ يُوحَ إِلَيْهِ شَيْءٌ وَمَنْ
قَالَ سَأُنْزِلُ مِثْلَ مَا أَنْزَلَ اللَّهُ ۗ وَلَوْ تَرَىٰ
إِذِ الظَّالِمُونَ فِي غَمَرَاتِ الْمَوْتِ وَالْمَلَائِكَةُ
بَاسِطُو أَيْدِيهِمْ أَخْرِجُوا أَنْفُسَكُمُ ۖ الْيَوْمَ
تُجْزَوْنَ عَذَابَ الْهُونِ بِمَا كُنْتُمْ تَقُولُونَ
عَلَى اللَّهِ غَيْرَ الْحَقِّ وَكُنْتُمْ عَنْ آيَاتِهِ تَسْتَكْبِرُونَ ﴿٩٣﴾
وَلَقَدْ جِئْتُمُونَا فُرَادَىٰ كَمَا خَلَقْنَاكُمْ
أَوَّلَ مَرَّةٍ وَتَرَكْتُمْ مَا خَوَّلْنَاكُمْ
وَرَاءَ ظُهُورِكُمْ ۖ وَمَا نَرَىٰ مَعَكُمْ
شُفَعَاءَكُمُ الَّذِينَ زَعَمْتُمْ أَنَّهُمْ
فِيكُمْ شُرَكَاءُ ۚ لَقَدْ تَقَطَّعَ بَيْنَكُمْ وَ
ع ضَلَّ عَنْكُمْ مَا كُنْتُمْ تَزْعُمُونَ ﴿٩٤﴾
إِنَّ اللَّهَ فَالِقُ الْحَبِّ وَالنَّوَىٰ ۖ يُخْرِجُ
الْحَيَّ مِنَ الْمَيِّتِ وَمُخْرِجُ الْمَيِّتِ
مِنَ الْحَيِّ ۚ ذَٰلِكُمُ اللَّهُ ۖ فَأَنَّىٰ تُؤْفَكُونَ ﴿٩٥﴾
فَالِقُ الْإِصْبَاحِ وَجَعَلَ اللَّيْلَ سَكَنًا
وَالشَّمْسَ وَالْقَمَرَ حُسْبَانًا ۚ ذَٰلِكَ
تَقْدِيرُ الْعَزِيزِ الْعَلِيمِ ﴿٩٦﴾
وَهُوَ الَّذِي جَعَلَ لَكُمُ النُّجُومَ لِتَهْتَدُوا
بِهَا فِي ظُلُمَاتِ الْبَرِّ وَالْبَحْرِ ۗ قَدْ
فَصَّلْنَا الْآيَاتِ لِقَوْمٍ يَعْلَمُونَ ﴿٩٧﴾
وَهُوَ الَّذِي أَنْشَأَكُمْ مِنْ نَفْسٍ
وَاحِدَةٍ فَمُسْتَقَرٌّ وَمُسْتَوْدَعٌ ۗ
قَدْ فَصَّلْنَا الْآيَاتِ لِقَوْمٍ يَفْقَهُونَ ﴿٩٨﴾

کہ تم مکے اور اُس کے آس پاس کے لوگوں کو آگاہ کردو۔ اور جو لوگ آخرت پر ایمان
رکھتے ہیں وہ اس کتاب پر بھی ایمان رکھتے ہیں اور وہ اپنی نمازوں کی (پوری) خبر رکھتے ہیں ﴿٩٣﴾
اور اس سے بڑھ کر ظالم کون ہوگا جو خدا پر جھوٹ افترا کرے یا یہ کہے کہ
مجھ پر وحی آئی ہے حالانکہ اس پر کچھ بھی وحی نہ آئی ہو۔ اور جو یہ کہے کہ
جس طرح کی کتاب خدا نے نازل کی ہے اس طرح کی میں بھی بنا لیتا ہوں
اور کاش تم ان ظالم (یعنی مشرک) لوگوں کو اس وقت دیکھو جب موت کی
سختیوں میں (مبتلا) ہوں اور فرشتے (ان کی طرف عذاب کیلئے) ہاتھ بڑھا
رہے ہوں کہ نکالو اپنی جانیں۔ آج تم کو ذلت کے عذاب کی سزا دی جائیگی
اس لئے کہ تم خدا پر جھوٹ بولا کرتے تھے اور اس کی آیتوں سے سرکشی کرتے تھے ﴿٩٤﴾
اور جیسا ہم نے تم کو پہلی دفعہ پیدا کیا تھا ایسا ہی آج اکیلے
اکیلے ہمارے پاس آئے۔ اور جو (مال و) متاع ہم نے تمہیں عطا
فرمایا تھا وہ سب اپنی پیٹھ پیچھے چھوڑ آئے اور ہم تمہارے ساتھ تمہارے
سفارشیوں کو بھی نہیں دیکھتے جن کی نسبت تم خیال کرتے تھے کہ
وہ تمہارے (شفیع اور ہمارے) شریک ہیں (آج) تمہارے آپس کے
سب تعلقات منقطع ہو گئے اور جو دعوے تم کیا کرتے تھے سب جاتے رہے ﴿٩٥﴾
بیشک خدا ہی دانے اور گٹھلی کو پھاڑ کر (ان سے درخت وغیرہ) اگاتا ہے
وہی جاندار کو بے جان سے نکالتا ہے اور وہی بے جان کا جاندار
سے نکالنے والا ہے۔ یہی تو خدا ہے۔ پھر تم کہاں بہکے پھرتے ہو؟ ﴿٩٦﴾
وہی (رات کے اندھیرے سے) صبح کی روشنی پھاڑ نکالتا ہے اور اسی نے
رات کو (موجب) آرام (ٹھہرایا) اور سورج اور چاند کو (ذرائع) شمار بنایا ہے
یہ خدا کے (مقرر کئے ہوئے) اندازے ہیں جو غالب (اور) علم والا ہے ﴿٩٧﴾
اور وہی تو ہے جس نے تمہارے لئے ستارے بنائے تاکہ جنگلوں اور
دریاؤں کے اندھیروں میں ان سے رستے معلوم کرو۔ عقل والوں کے
لئے ہم نے اپنی آیتیں کھول کھول کر بیان کر دی ہیں ﴿٩٨﴾
اور وہی تو ہے جس نے تم کو ایک شخص سے پیدا کیا پھر (تمہارے لئے)
ایک ٹھہرنے کی جگہ ہے اور ایک سپرد ہونے کی۔ سمجھنے والوں کے
لئے ہم نے (اپنی) آیتیں کھول کھول کر بیان کر دی ہیں ﴿٩٩﴾

mayest warn the Mother of Cities and all around her. Those who believe in the Hereafter believe in this (Book), and they are constant in guarding their Prayers.

93. Who can be more wicked than one who inventeth a lie against Allah, or saith, "I have received inspiration," when he hath received none, or (again) who saith, "I can reveal the like of what Allah hath revealed"? If thou couldst but see how the wicked (do fare) in the agonies of death!—the angels stretch forth their hands, (saying), "Yield up your souls: this day shall ye receive your reward,—a chastisement of disgrace, for that ye used to tell lies against Allah, and scornfully to reject of His Signs!"

94. "And behold! ye come to Us bare and alone as We created you for the first time: ye have left behind you all (the favours) which We bestowed on you: We see not with you your intercessors whom ye thought to be partners in your affairs: so now all relations between you have been cut off, and your (pet) fancies have left you in the lurch!

95. It is Allah Who causeth the seed-grain and the date-stone to split and sprout. He causeth the living to issue from the dead. And He is the One to cause the dead to issue from the living. That is Allah: then how are ye deluded away from the truth?

96. He it is that cleaveth the day-break (from the dark): He makes the night for rest and tranquillity, and the sun and moon for the reckoning (of time): such is the judgment and ordering of (Him), the Exalted in Power, the Omniscient.

97. It is He Who maketh the stars (as beacons) for you, that ye may guide yourselves, with their help, through the dark spaces of land and sea: We detail Our Signs for people who know.

98. It is He Who hath produced you from a single soul: then there is a resting place and a repository: We detail Our signs for people who understand.

99. It is He Who sendeth down rain from the skies: with it We produce vegetation of all kinds: from some We produce green (crops), out of which we produce, close-compounded grain out of the date-palm and its sheaths (or spathes) (come) clusters of dates hanging low and near: and (then there are) gardens of grapes, and olives, and pomegranates, each similar (in kind) yet different (in variety): when they begin to bear fruit, feast your eyes with the fruit and the ripeness thereof. Behold! in these things there are Signs for people who believe.

100. Yet they make the Jinns equals with Allah, though Allah did create the Jinns; and they falsely, having no knowledge, attribute to Him sons and daughters, praise and glory be to Him! (for He is) above what they attribute to Him!

101. Wonderful Originator of the heavens and the earth: how can He have a son when He hath no consort? He created all things, and He hath full knowledge of all things.

102. That is Allah, your Lord! there is no god but He, the Creator of all things: then worship ye Him: and He hath power to dispose of all affairs.

103. No vision can grasp Him, but His grasp is over all vision; He is subtle well-aware.

104. "Now have come to you, from your Lord proofs (to open your eyes): if any will see, it will be for (the good of) his own soul: if any will be blind, it will be to his own (Harm): I am not (here) to watch over your doings."

105. Thus do We explain the Signs by various (ways) that they may say, "Thou hast learnt this (from somebody), and that We may make the matter clear to those who know.

106. Follow what thou art taught by inspiration from thy Lord: there is no

اور وہی تو ہے جو آسمان سے مینہ برساتا ہے۔ پھر ہم ہی (جو مینہ
برساتے ہیں) اُس سے ہر طرح کی روئیدگی اُگاتے ہیں۔ پھر
اُس میں سے سبز سبز کونپلیں نکالتے ہیں اور ان کونپلوں میں سے
ایک دوسرے کیساتھ جُڑے ہوئے دانے نکالتے ہیں۔ اور کھجور کے گابھے
میں سے لٹکتے ہوئے گُچھے اور انگوروں کے باغ اور زیتون اور
انار جو ایک دُوسرے سے ملتے جُلتے بھی ہیں اور نہیں بھی ملتے۔
یہ چیزیں جب پھلتی ہیں تو ان کے پھلوں پر اور (جب پکتی ہیں تو)
اِن کے پکنے پر نظر کرو۔ ان میں اُن لوگوں کیلئے جو ایمان
لاتے ہیں (قدرت خدا کی بہت سی) نشانیاں ہیں ﴿۱۰۰﴾
اور اُن لوگوں نے جنوں کو خدا کا شریک ٹھیرایا حالانکہ انکو اُسی نے پیدا کیا۔
اور بے سمجھے (جھوٹ بہتان) اُسکے لئے بیٹے اور بیٹیاں بنا کھڑی کیں۔
وہ اِن باتوں سے جو اُسکی نسبت بیان کرتے ہیں پاک ہے اور (اُسکی شان) ان سے بلند ہے ﴿۱۰۱﴾
(وہی) آسمانوں اور زمین کا پیدا کرنے والا (ہے)۔ اُس کے اولاد
کہاں سے ہو جب کہ اُس کی بیوی ہی نہیں۔ اور اُس نے
ہر چیز کو پیدا کیا ہے اور وہ ہر چیز سے باخبر ہے ﴿۱۰۲﴾
یہی (اوصاف رکھنے والا) خدا تمہارا پروردگار ہے۔ اُسکے سوا
کوئی معبود نہیں (وہی) ہر چیز کا پیدا کرنیوالا (ہے) تو اُسی کی عبادت
کرو اور وہ ہر چیز کا نگراں ہے ﴿۱۰۳﴾
(وہ ایسا ہے کہ) نگاہیں اُس کا ادراک نہیں کر سکتیں اور وہ نگاہوں
کا ادراک کر سکتا ہے۔ اور وہ بھید جاننے والا خبردار ہے ﴿۱۰۴﴾
(اے محمدؐ ان سے کہہ دو کہ) تمہارے (پاس) پروردگار کیطرف سے (روشن)
دلیلیں پہنچ چکی ہیں تو جس نے (انکو آنکھ کھولکر) دیکھا اُسنے اپنا بھلا کیا اور
جو اندھا بنا رہا اُس نے اپنے حق میں بُرا کیا اور میں تمہارا نگہبان نہیں ہوں ﴿۱۰۵﴾
اور ہم اسی طرح اپنی آیتیں پھیر پھیر کر بیان کرتے ہیں تاکہ کافر یہ
نہ کہیں کہ تم (یہ باتیں اہلِ کتاب سے) سیکھے ہوئے ہو اور تاکہ سمجھنے
والے لوگوں کے لئے تشریح کر دیں ﴿۱۰۶﴾
اور جو حکم تمہارے پروردگار کیطرف سے تمہارے پاس آتا ہے اسی کی پیروی کرو

وَهُوَ الَّذِيْٓ اَنْزَلَ مِنَ السَّمَآءِ مَآءً ج
فَاَخْرَجْنَا بِهٖ نَبَاتَ كُلِّ شَيْءٍ فَاَخْرَجْنَا
مِنْهُ خَضِرًا نُّخْرِجُ مِنْهُ حَبًّا مُّتَرَاكِبًا ج
وَمِنَ النَّخْلِ مِنْ طَلْعِهَا قِنْوَانٌ دَانِيَةٌ
وَّجَنّٰتٍ مِّنْ اَعْنَابٍ وَّالزَّيْتُوْنَ وَ
الرُّمَّانَ مُشْتَبِهًا وَّغَيْرَ مُتَشَابِهٍ ط
اُنْظُرُوْٓا اِلٰى ثَمَرِهٖٓ اِذَآ اَثْمَرَ وَيَنْعِهٖ ط
اِنَّ فِيْ ذٰلِكُمْ لَاٰيٰتٍ لِّقَوْمٍ
يُّؤْمِنُوْنَ ﴿٩٩﴾
وَجَعَلُوْا لِلّٰهِ شُرَكَآءَ الْجِنَّ وَخَلَقَهُمْ
وَخَرَقُوْا لَهٗ بَنِيْنَ وَبَنٰتٍ بِغَيْرِ عِلْمٍ ط
سُبْحٰنَهٗ وَتَعٰلٰى عَمَّا يَصِفُوْنَ ﴿١٠٠﴾ ع ١٢ ١٨
بَدِيْعُ السَّمٰوٰتِ وَالْاَرْضِ ط اَنّٰى يَكُوْنُ
لَهٗ وَلَدٌ وَّلَمْ تَكُنْ لَّهٗ صَاحِبَةٌ ط وَخَلَقَ
كُلَّ شَيْءٍ ج وَهُوَ بِكُلِّ شَيْءٍ عَلِيْمٌ ﴿١٠١﴾
ذٰلِكُمُ اللّٰهُ رَبُّكُمْ ج لَآ اِلٰهَ اِلَّا هُوَ ج
خَالِقُ كُلِّ شَيْءٍ فَاعْبُدُوْهُ ج وَهُوَ
عَلٰى كُلِّ شَيْءٍ وَّكِيْلٌ ﴿١٠٢﴾
لَا تُدْرِكُهُ الْاَبْصَارُ ز وَهُوَ يُدْرِكُ
الْاَبْصَارَ ج وَهُوَ اللَّطِيْفُ الْخَبِيْرُ ﴿١٠٣﴾
قَدْ جَآءَكُمْ بَصَآئِرُ مِنْ رَّبِّكُمْ ج فَمَنْ
اَبْصَرَ فَلِنَفْسِهٖ ج وَمَنْ عَمِيَ فَعَلَيْهَا ط وَ
مَآ اَنَا عَلَيْكُمْ بِحَفِيْظٍ ﴿١٠٤﴾
وَكَذٰلِكَ نُصَرِّفُ الْاٰيٰتِ وَ
لِيَقُوْلُوْا دَرَسْتَ وَلِنُبَيِّنَهٗ لِقَوْمٍ
يَّعْلَمُوْنَ ﴿١٠٥﴾
اِتَّبِعْ مَآ اُوْحِيَ اِلَيْكَ مِنْ رَّبِّكَ ج لَآ

إِلٰهَ إِلَّا هُوَ ۚ وَأَعْرِضْ عَنِ الْمُشْرِكِينَ ﴿١٠٦﴾
وَلَوْ شَاءَ اللّٰهُ مَا أَشْرَكُوا ۗ وَمَا جَعَلْنَاكَ
عَلَيْهِمْ حَفِيظًا ۚ وَمَا أَنْتَ عَلَيْهِمْ بِوَكِيلٍ ﴿١٠٧﴾
وَلَا تَسُبُّوا الَّذِينَ يَدْعُونَ مِنْ دُونِ
اللّٰهِ فَيَسُبُّوا اللّٰهَ عَدْوًا بِغَيْرِ عِلْمٍ ۗ
كَذٰلِكَ زَيَّنَّا لِكُلِّ أُمَّةٍ عَمَلَهُمْ
ثُمَّ إِلٰى رَبِّهِمْ مَرْجِعُهُمْ فَيُنَبِّئُهُمْ
بِمَا كَانُوا يَعْمَلُونَ ﴿١٠٨﴾

اُس (پروردگار) کے سوا کوئی معبود نہیں۔ اور مشرکوں سے کنارہ کرلو ﴿۱۰۷﴾
اور اگر خدا چاہتا تو یہ لوگ شرک نہ کرتے۔ اور (اے پیغمبر) ہم نے تم کو
اُن پر نگہبان مقرر نہیں کیا۔ اور نہ تم اُن کے داروغہ ہو ﴿۱۰۸﴾
اور جن لوگوں کو یہ مشرک خدا کے سوا پکارتے ہیں اُن کو بُرا نہ کہنا
کہ یہ بھی کہیں خدا کو بے ادبی سے بے سمجھے بُرا (نہ) کہہ بیٹھیں۔
اس طرح ہم نے ہر ایک فرقے کے اعمال (اُنکی نظروں میں) اچھے
کر دکھائے ہیں۔ پھر اُن کو اپنے پروردگار کی طرف لوٹ کر جانا ہے
تب وہ اُن کو بتائے گا کہ وہ کیا کیا کرتے تھے ﴿۱۰۹﴾

god but He: and turn aside from those Who join gods with Allah.

107. If it had been Allah's Will, they would not have taken false gods: but We made thee not one to watch over their doings, nor art thou set over them to dispose of their affairs.

108. Revile not ye those whom they call upon besides Allah, lest they out of spite revile Allah in their ignorance. Thus have We made alluring to each people its own doings. In the end will they return to their Lord and He shall then tell them the truth of all that they did.

وَأَقْسَمُوا بِاللّٰهِ جَهْدَ أَيْمَانِهِمْ لَئِنْ
جَاءَتْهُمْ آيَةٌ لَيُؤْمِنُنَّ بِهَا ۚ
قُلْ إِنَّمَا الْآيَاتُ عِنْدَ اللّٰهِ ۖ وَمَا
يُشْعِرُكُمْ أَنَّهَا إِذَا جَاءَتْ لَا
يُؤْمِنُونَ ﴿١٠٩﴾

اور یہ لوگ خدا کی سخت سخت قسمیں کھاتے ہیں کہ اگر اُن کے پاس
کوئی نشانی آئے تو وہ اس پر ضرور ایمان لے آئیں۔ کہہ دو کہ
نشانیاں تو سب خدا ہی کے پاس ہیں۔ اور (مومنو!) تمہیں کیا
معلوم ہے (یہ تو ایسے بدبخت ہیں) کہ اُن کے پاس نشانیاں
آ بھی جائیں تب بھی ایمان نہ لائیں ﴿۱۱۰﴾

109. They swear their strongest oaths by Allah, that if a (special) Sign came to them, by it they would believe. Say: "Certainly (all) Signs are in the power of Allah: but what will make you (Muslims) realise that (even) if (special) Signs came, they will not believe."?

وَنُقَلِّبُ أَفْئِدَتَهُمْ وَأَبْصَارَهُمْ كَمَا
لَمْ يُؤْمِنُوا بِهِ أَوَّلَ مَرَّةٍ وَنَذَرُهُمْ
فِي طُغْيَانِهِمْ يَعْمَهُونَ ﴿١١٠﴾
وَلَوْ أَنَّنَا نَزَّلْنَا إِلَيْهِمُ الْمَلٰئِكَةَ
وَكَلَّمَهُمُ الْمَوْتٰى وَحَشَرْنَا عَلَيْهِمْ
كُلَّ شَيْءٍ قُبُلًا مَا كَانُوا لِيُؤْمِنُوا إِلَّا
أَنْ يَشَاءَ اللّٰهُ وَلٰكِنَّ أَكْثَرَهُمْ
يَجْهَلُونَ ﴿١١١﴾

اور ہم اُن کے دلوں اور آنکھوں کو اُلٹ دینگے (تو) جیسے یہ
اس (قرآن) پر پہلی دفعہ ایمان نہیں لائے (ویسے پھر نہ لائینگے)
اور اُن کو چھوڑ دینگے کہ اپنی سرکشی میں بہکتے رہیں ﴿۱۱۱﴾
اور اگر ہم اُن پر فرشتے بھی اُتار دیتے اور مُردے
بھی اُن سے گفتگو کرنے لگتے اور ہم سب چیزوں
کو اُن کے سامنے لا موجود بھی کر دیتے تو بھی یہ
ایمان لانے والے نہ تھے۔ اِلّا ماشاء اللہ۔ بات یہ ہے
کہ یہ اکثر نادان ہیں ﴿۱۱۲﴾

110. We (too) shall turn to (confusion) their hearts and their eyes, even as they refused to believe in this in the first instance: We shall leave them in their trespasses, to (stumble blindly).

111. Even if We did send unto them angels, and the dead did speak unto them, and We gathered together all things before their very eyes, they are not the ones to believe, unless it is in Allah's Plan. But most of them ignore (the truth).

وَكَذٰلِكَ جَعَلْنَا لِكُلِّ نَبِيٍّ عَدُوًّا
شَيٰطِينَ الْإِنْسِ وَالْجِنِّ يُوحِي بَعْضُهُمْ
إِلٰى بَعْضٍ زُخْرُفَ الْقَوْلِ غُرُورًا ۚ
وَلَوْ شَاءَ رَبُّكَ مَا فَعَلُوهُ فَذَرْهُمْ
وَمَا يَفْتَرُونَ ﴿١١٢﴾
وَلِتَصْغٰى إِلَيْهِ أَفْئِدَةُ الَّذِينَ لَا

اور اسی طرح ہم نے شیطان (سیرت) انسانوں اور جنوں
کو ہر پیغمبر کا دشمن بنا دیا تھا۔ وہ دھوکا دینے کے
لئے ایک دوسرے کے دل میں ملمع کی باتیں ڈالتے رہتے
تھے اور اگر تمہارا پروردگار چاہتا تو وہ ایسا نہ کرتے تو اُن
کو اور جو کچھ یہ افترا کرتے ہیں اُسے چھوڑ دو ﴿۱۱۳﴾
اور (وہ ایسے کام) اسلئے بھی (کرتے تھے) کہ جو لوگ آخرت پر

112. Likewise did We make for every Messenger an enemy,— satans among men and Jinns, inspiring each other with flowery discourses by way of deception. If thy Lord had so willed, they would not have done it: so leave them and what they forge.

113. To such (deceit) let the hearts of those incline, who have no faith

in the Hereafter: and let them delight in it, and let them earn from it what they may.

ایمان نہیں رکھتے اُنکے دل اُن کی باتوں پر مائل ہوں اور
وہ انہیں پسند کریں اور جو کام وہ کرتے تھے وہی کرنے لگیں ﴿١١٣﴾

يؤمنون بالآخرة وليرضوه و
ليقترفوا ما هم مقترفون ﴿١١٣﴾

114. Say: "Shall I seek for judge other than Allah?— When He it is Who hath sent unto you the Book, explained in detail." They know full well, to whom We have given the Book, that it hath been sent down from thy Lord in truth. Never be then of those who doubt.

کہو، کیا میں خدا کے سوا اور منصف تلاش کروں حالانکہ
اُس نے تمہاری طرف واضح المطالب کتاب بھیجی ہے۔ اور
جن لوگوں کو ہم نے کتاب (تورات) دی ہے وہ جانتے ہیں
کہ وہ تمہارے پروردگار کی طرف سے برحق نازل ہوئی ہے تو تم
ہرگز شک کرنے والوں میں نہ ہونا ﴿١١٤﴾

أفغير الله أبتغي حكما وهو الذي
أنزل إليكم الكتاب مفصلا و
الذين آتيناهم الكتاب يعلمون أنه
منزل من ربك بالحق فلا تكونن
من الممترين ﴿١١٤﴾

115. The Word of thy Lord doth find its fulfilment in truth and in justice: none can change His Words: for He is the one Who heareth and knoweth all.

اور تمہارے پروردگار کی باتیں سچائی اور انصاف میں پوری
ہیں اُسکی باتوں کو کوئی بدلنے والا نہیں اور وہ سنتا جانتا ہے ﴿١١٥﴾

وتمت كلمت ربك صدقا وعدلا
لا مبدل لكلماته وهو السميع العليم ﴿١١٥﴾

116. Wert thou to follow the common run of those on earth, they will lead thee away from the Way of Allah. They follow nothing but conjecture: they do nothing but lie.

اور اکثر لوگ جو زمین پر آباد ہیں (گمراہ ہیں) اگر تم اُن کا کہا
مان لوگے تو وہ تمہیں خدا کا رستہ بھلا دینگے۔ یہ محض خیال
کے پیچھے چلتے اور نرے اٹکل کے تیر چلاتے ہیں ﴿١١٦﴾

وإن تطع أكثر من في الأرض يضلوك
عن سبيل الله إن يتبعون إلا
الظن وإن هم إلا يخرصون ﴿١١٦﴾

117. Thy Lord knoweth best who strayeth from His Way: He knoweth best those who are rightly guided.

تمہارا پروردگار اُن لوگوں کو خوب جانتا ہے جو اُسکے رستے سے
بھٹکے ہوئے ہیں اور اُن سے بھی خوب واقف ہے جو رستے پر چل رہے ہیں ﴿١١٧﴾

إن ربك هو أعلم من يضل عن
سبيله وهو أعلم بالمهتدين ﴿١١٧﴾

118. So eat of (meats) on which Allah's name hath been pronounced, if ye have faith in His Signs.

تو جس چیز پر (ذبح کے وقت) خدا کا نام لیا جائے اگر تم اسکی
آیتوں پر ایمان رکھتے ہو تو اُسے کھا لیا کرو ﴿١١٨﴾

فكلوا مما ذكر اسم الله عليه
إن كنتم بآياته مؤمنين ﴿١١٨﴾

119. Why should ye not eat of (meats) on which Allah's name hath been pronounced, when He hath explained to you in detail what is forbidden to you—except under compulsion of necessity? But many do mislead (men) by low desires without knowledge. Thy Lord knoweth best those who transgress.

اور سبب کیا ہے کہ جس چیز پر خدا کا نام لیا جائے تم اُسے نہ کھاؤ حالانکہ
جو چیزیں اُس نے تمہارے لئے حرام ٹھہرا دی ہیں وہ ایک ایک کر کے بیان
کر دی ہیں (بیشک اُن کو نہیں کھانا چاہیے) مگر اس صورت میں کہ اُنکے
کھانے کے لئے ناچار ہو جاؤ۔ اور بہت سے لوگ بے سمجھے بوجھے
اپنے نفس کی خواہشوں سے لوگوں کو بہکا رہے ہیں کچھ شک نہیں کہ ایسے لوگوں
کو جو (خدا کی مقرر کی ہوئی) حد سے باہر نکل جاتے ہیں تمہارا پروردگار خوب جانتا ہے ﴿١١٩﴾

وما لكم ألا تأكلوا مما ذكر اسم الله
عليه وقد فصل لكم ما حرم عليكم
إلا ما اضطررتم إليه وإن
كثيرا ليضلون بأهوائهم
بغير علم إن ربك هو أعلم
بالمعتدين ﴿١١٩﴾

120. Eschew all sin, open or secret: those who earn sin will get due recompense for their "earnings."

اور ظاہری اور پوشیدہ (ہر طرح کا) گناہ ترک کر دو۔
جو لوگ گناہ کرتے ہیں وہ عنقریب اپنے کئے کی
سزا پائیں گے ﴿١٢٠﴾

وذروا ظاهر الإثم وباطنه
إن الذين يكسبون الإثم سيجزون
بما كانوا يقترفون ﴿١٢٠﴾

121. Eat not of (meats) on which Allah's name hath not been pronounced: that would be impiety. But the satans ever inspire their

اور جس چیز پر خدا کا نام نہ لیا جائے اسے مت کھاؤ کہ اسکا کھانا گناہ ہے
اور شیطان (لوگ) اپنے رفیقوں کے دلوں میں یہ بات ڈالتے

ولا تأكلوا مما لم يذكر اسم الله
عليه وإنه لفسق وإن الشياطين

ليوحون الى اوليئهم ليجادلوكم ج
ع ١٤ وان اطعتموهم انكم لمشركون ﴿١٢١﴾
او من كان ميتا فاحيينه وجعلنا
له نورا يمشي به في الناس كمن
مثله في الظلمت ليس بخارج
منها ط كذلك زين للكفرين ما
كانوا يعملون ﴿١٢٢﴾
وكذلك جعلنا في كل قرية اكبر
مجرميها ليمكروا فيها ط وما يمكرون
الا بانفسهم وما يشعرون ﴿١٢٣﴾
واذا جاءتهم اية قالوا لن نؤمن
حتى نؤتى مثل ما اوتي رسل
الله م الله اعلم حيث يجعل
رسلته ط سيصيب الذين اجرموا
صغار عند الله وعذاب شديد
بما كانوا يمكرون ﴿١٢٤﴾
فمن يرد الله ان يهديه يشرح
صدره للاسلام ج ومن يرد ان
يضله يجعل صدره ضيقا حرجا
كانما يصعد في السماء ط كذلك يجعل
الله الرجس على الذين لا يؤمنون ﴿١٢٥﴾
وهذا صراط ربك مستقيما ط قد
فصلنا الايت لقوم يذكرون ﴿١٢٦﴾
لهم دار السلم عند ربهم وهو
وليهم بما كانوا يعملون ﴿١٢٧﴾
ويوم يحشرهم جميعا ج يمعشر الجن
قد استكثرتم من الانس ج وقال

وقف لازم
وقف منزل

ہیں کہ تم سے جھگڑا کریں اور اگر تم لوگ اُن کے کہے پر
چلے تو بیشک تم بھی مشرک ہوئے ﴿١٢٢﴾
بھلا جو پہلے مُردہ تھا پھر ہم نے اُس کو زندہ کیا اور اُسکے
لئے روشنی کر دی جس کے ذریعے سے وہ لوگوں میں چلتا
پھرتا ہے کہیں اُس شخص جیسا ہو سکتا ہے جو اندھیرے
میں پڑا ہوا ہو اور اُس سے نکل ہی نہ سکے۔ اسی طرح کافر جو عمل
کر رہے ہیں وہ اُنہیں اچھے معلوم ہوتے ہیں ﴿١٢٣﴾
اور اسی طرح ہم نے ہر بستی میں بڑے بڑے مجرم پیدا کئے کہ
اُن میں مکّاریاں کرتے رہیں۔ اور جو مکّاریاں یہ کرتے
ہیں اُن کا نقصان انہیں کو ہے اور (اس سے) بے خبر ہیں ﴿١٢٤﴾
اور جب اُن کے پاس کوئی آیت آتی ہے تو کہتے ہیں کہ جس طرح
کی رسالت خدا کے پیغمبروں کو ملی ہے جبتک اُسی طرح کی رسالت
ہم کو نہ ملے ہم ہرگز ایمان نہیں لائیں گے اس کو خدا ہی
خوب جانتا ہے کہ (رسالت کا کونسا محل ہے اور) وہ اپنی پیغمبری
کسے عنایت فرمائے۔ جو لوگ جرم کرتے ہیں اُن کو خدا کے
ہاں ذلت اور عذاب شدید ہوگا اسلئے کہ مکّاریاں کرتے تھے ﴿١٢٥﴾
تو جس شخص کو خدا چاہتا ہے کہ ہدایت بخشے اُس کا سینہ
اسلام کے لئے کھول دیتا ہے اور جسے چاہتا ہے کہ
گمراہ کرے اُس کا سینہ تنگ اور گھٹا ہوا کر دیتا ہے۔ گویا
وہ آسمان پر چڑھ رہا ہے۔ اس طرح خدا اُن لوگوں پر جو ایمان
نہیں لاتے عذاب بھیجتا ہے ﴿١٢٦﴾
اور یہی تمہارے پروردگار کا سیدھا رستہ ہے جو لوگ غور کرنیوالے
ہیں اُن کیلئے ہم نے اپنی آیتیں کھول کھولکر بیان کر دی ہیں ﴿١٢٧﴾
اُن کیلئے اُن کے اعمال کے صلے میں پروردگار کے ہاں
سلامتی کا گھر ہے۔ اور وہی اُن کا دوستدار ہے ﴿١٢٨﴾
اور جس دن وہ سب (جن و انس) کو جمع کریگا (اور فرمائیگا کہ)
اے گروہِ جنّات تم نے انسانوں سے بہت (فائدے) حاصل کیے۔ تو جو انسانوں

friends to contend with you if ye were to obey them, ye would indeed be Pagans.

122. Can he who was dead, to whom We gave life, and a Light whereby he can walk amongst men, be like him who is in the depths of darkness, from which he can never come out? Thus to those without Faith their own deeds seem pleasing.

123. Thus have We placed leaders in every town, its wicked men, to plot (and burrow) therein: but they only plot against their own souls, and they perceive it not.

124. When there comes to them a Sign (from Allah), they say: "We shall not believe until we receive one (exactly) like those received by Allah's messengers." Allah knoweth best where to Place His mission. Soon will the wicked be overtaken by humiliation before Allah, and a severe chastisement, for all their plots.

125. Those whom Allah willeth to guide,— He openeth their breast to Islam; those whom He willeth to leave straying,— He maketh their breast close and constricted, as if they had to climb up to the skies: thus doth Allah lay abomination on those who refuse to believe.

126. This is the Way of thy Lord, leading straight: We have detailed the Signs for those who receive admonition.

127. For them will be a Home of Peace with their Lord: He will be their Friend, because they practised (righteousness).

128. On the day when He will gather them all together, (and say): "O ye assembly of Jinns much (toll) did ye take of men." Their friends

amongst men will say: "Our Lord! we made profit from each other: but (alas!) we reached our term—which Thou didst appoint for us." He will say: "The Fire be your dwelling-place: you will dwell therein for ever, except as Allah willeth. For thy Lord is full of wisdom and knowledge.

129. Thus do We make the wrong-doers turn to each other, because of what they earn.

130. "O ye assembly of Jinns and men! came there not unto you messengers from amongst you, setting forth unto you My Signs, and warning you of the meeting of this Day of yours?" They will say: "We bear witness against ourselves." It was the life of this world that deceived them. So against themselves will they bear witness that they rejected Faith.

131. (The messengers were sent) thus, for thy Lord would not destroy the towns unjustly whilst their occupants were unwarned.

132. To all are degrees (or ranks) according to their deeds: for thy Lord is not unmindful of anything that they do.

133. Thy Lord is Self-sufficient, full of Mercy: if it were His Will, He could destroy you, and in your place appoint whom He will as your successors, even as He raised you up from the posterity of other people.

134. All that hath been promised unto you will come to pass: nor can ye frustrate it (in the least bit).

135. Say: "O my people! do whatever ye can: I will do (my part): soon will ye know who it is whose end will be (best) in the Hereafter: certain it is that the wrong-doers will not prosper."

136. Out of what Allah hath produced in abundance in tilth and in cattle, they assigned Him a share: they say, according to their

میں اُن کے دوستدار ہونگے وہ کہیں گے کہ پروردگار ہم ایک
دوسرے سے فائدہ حاصل کرتے رہے اور (آخر) اُس وقت
کو پہنچ گئے جو تو نے ہمارے لئے مقرر کیا تھا. خدا فرمائے گا
(اب) تمہارا ٹھکانا دوزخ ہے ہمیشہ اس میں (جلتے) رہو گے
مگر جو خدا چاہے. بیشک تمہارا پروردگار دانا اور خبردار ہے ﴿۱۲۹﴾
اور اسی طرح ہم ظالموں کو اُن کے اعمال کے سبب جو وہ
کرتے تھے ایک دوسرے پر مسلّط کر دیتے ہیں ﴿۱۳۰﴾
اے جنوں اور انسانوں کی جماعت کیا تمہارے پاس تم ہی
میں سے پیغمبر نہیں آتے رہے جو میری آیتیں تم کو پڑھ پڑھ کر
سناتے اور اس دن کے سامنے آموجود ہونے سے ڈراتے تھے.
وہ کہیں گے کہ (پروردگار) ہمیں اپنے گناہوں کا اقرار ہے.
ان لوگوں کو دنیا کی زندگی نے دھوکے میں ڈال رکھا تھا.
اور (اب) خود اپنے اوپر گواہی دی کہ کفر کرتے تھے ﴿۱۳۱﴾
(اے محمدؐ) یہ (جو پیغمبر آتے رہے اور کتابیں نازل ہوتی رہیں تو) اسلئے کہ تمہارا پروردگار
ایسا نہیں کہ بستیوں کو ظلم سے ہلاک کر دے اور وہاں کے رہنے والوں کو کچھ بھی خبر نہ ہو ﴿۱۳۲﴾
اور سب لوگوں کے بلحاظ اعمال درجے (مقرر) ہیں اور جو کام یہ
لوگ کرتے ہیں خدا اُن سے بے خبر نہیں ﴿۱۳۳﴾
اور تمہارا پروردگار بے پروا (اور) صاحب رحمت ہے. اگر چاہے
(تو اے بندو) تمہیں نابود کر دے اور تمہارے بعد جن لوگوں کو چاہے
تمہارا جانشین بنا دے جیسا تم کو بھی دوسرے لوگوں کی نسل سے پیدا کیا ہے ﴿۱۳۴﴾
کچھ شک نہیں کہ جو وعدہ تم سے کیا جاتا ہے وہ (وقوع میں)
آنے والا ہے. اور تم (خدا کو) مغلوب نہیں کر سکتے ﴿۱۳۵﴾
کہہ دو کہ لوگو تم اپنی جگہ عمل کئے جاؤ میں (اپنی جگہ) عمل کئے
جاتا ہوں. عنقریب تم کو معلوم ہو جائیگا کہ آخرت میں (بہشت)
کس کا گھر ہوگا. کچھ شک نہیں کہ مشرک نجات نہیں پانے کے ﴿۱۳۶﴾
اور (یہ لوگ) خدا ہی کی پیدا کی ہوئی چیزوں یعنی کھیتی اور
چوپایوں میں خدا کا بھی ایک حصہ مقرر کرتے ہیں اور اپنے

أَوْلِيَآؤُهُم مِّنَ الْإِنسِ رَبَّنَا اسْتَمْتَعَ
بَعْضُنَا بِبَعْضٍ وَبَلَغْنَا أَجَلَنَا الَّذِيٓ
أَجَّلْتَ لَنَا ۚ قَالَ النَّارُ مَثْوَاكُمْ
خَالِدِينَ فِيهَا إِلَّا مَا شَآءَ اللَّهُ ۗ إِنَّ
رَبَّكَ حَكِيمٌ عَلِيمٌ ﴿١٢٨﴾
وَكَذَٰلِكَ نُوَلِّي بَعْضَ الظَّالِمِينَ بَعْضًا
بِمَا كَانُوا يَكْسِبُونَ ﴿١٢٩﴾ ع ١٥ ع ٢
يَا مَعْشَرَ الْجِنِّ وَالْإِنسِ أَلَمْ يَأْتِكُمْ
رُسُلٌ مِّنكُمْ يَقُصُّونَ عَلَيْكُمْ آيَاتِي
وَيُنذِرُونَكُمْ لِقَآءَ يَوْمِكُمْ هَٰذَا ۚ
قَالُوا شَهِدْنَا عَلَىٰ أَنفُسِنَا ۖ وَغَرَّتْهُمُ
الْحَيَاةُ الدُّنْيَا وَشَهِدُوا عَلَىٰ أَنفُسِهِمْ
أَنَّهُمْ كَانُوا كَافِرِينَ ﴿١٣٠﴾
ذَٰلِكَ أَن لَّمْ يَكُن رَّبُّكَ مُهْلِكَ
الْقُرَىٰ بِظُلْمٍ وَأَهْلُهَا غَافِلُونَ ﴿١٣١﴾
وَلِكُلٍّ دَرَجَاتٌ مِّمَّا عَمِلُوا ۚ وَمَا رَبُّكَ
بِغَافِلٍ عَمَّا يَعْمَلُونَ ﴿١٣٢﴾
وَرَبُّكَ الْغَنِيُّ ذُو الرَّحْمَةِ ۚ إِن يَشَأْ
يُذْهِبْكُمْ وَيَسْتَخْلِفْ مِن بَعْدِكُم مَّا
يَشَآءُ كَمَا أَنشَأَكُم مِّن ذُرِّيَّةِ قَوْمٍ آخَرِينَ ﴿١٣٣﴾
إِنَّ مَا تُوعَدُونَ لَآتٍ ۖ وَمَا أَنتُم
بِمُعْجِزِينَ ﴿١٣٤﴾
قُلْ يَا قَوْمِ اعْمَلُوا عَلَىٰ مَكَانَتِكُمْ إِنِّي
عَامِلٌ ۖ فَسَوْفَ تَعْلَمُونَ مَن تَكُونُ
لَهُ عَاقِبَةُ الدَّارِ ۗ إِنَّهُ لَا يُفْلِحُ الظَّالِمُونَ ﴿١٣٥﴾
وَجَعَلُوا لِلَّهِ مِمَّا ذَرَأَ مِنَ الْحَرْثِ وَ
الْأَنْعَامِ نَصِيبًا فَقَالُوا هَٰذَا لِلَّهِ بِزَعْمِهِمْ

fancies: "This is for Allah, and this"—for Our "partners"! But the share of their "partners" reacheth not Allah, whilst the share of Allah reacheth their "partners"! Evil (and unjust) is their judgment.

137. Even so, in the eyes of most of the Pagans, their "partners" made alluring the slaughter of their children, in order to lead them to their own destruction, and cause confusion in their religion if Allah had willed, they would not have done so: but leave alone them and what they forged.

138. And they say that such and such cattle and crops are forbidden, and none should eat of them except those whom—so they say—We wish; further, there are cattle forbidden to yoke or burden, and cattle on which, (at slaughter) the name of Allah is not pronounced:—forging a lie against Allah's name: soon will He requite them for what they forged.

139. They say: "What is in the wombs of such and such cattle is specially reserved (for food) for our men, and forbidden to our women; but if it is still-born, then all have shares therein. For their (false) attribution (of superstitions to Allah), He will soon punish them: for He is full of wisdom and knowledge.

140. Lost are those who slay their children, from folly, without knowledge, and forbid food which Allah hath provided for them, forging (lies) against Allah, they have indeed gone astray and heeded no guidance.

141. It is He who produceth gardens, with trellises and without, and dates, and tilth with produce of all kinds, 'and olives and pomegranates, similar (in kind) and different (in variety): eat of their fruit in their season, but render the dues that are proper on the day that the harvest is gathered. But waste not by excess: for Allah

خیال (باطل) سے کہتے ہیں کہ یہ (حصہ) تو خدا کا اور یہ ہمارے شریکوں
(یعنی بتوں) کا۔ تو جو حصہ اُنکے شریکوں کا ہوتا ہے وہ تو خدا کی طرف نہیں
جاسکتا۔ اور جو حصہ خدا کا ہوتا ہے وہ اُن کے شریکوں کی
طرف جاسکتا ہے۔ یہ کیسا بُرا انصاف ہے ﴿۱۳۶﴾

اسی طرح بہت سے مشرکوں کو اُن کے شریکوں نے اُن کے بچّوں کو
جان سے مار ڈالنا اچھا کر دکھایا ہے تاکہ اُنہیں ہلاکت
میں ڈال دیں اور اُنکے دین کو اُن پر خلط ملط کر دیں۔ اور اگر
خدا چاہتا تو وہ ایسا نہ کرتے تو انکو چھوڑ دو کہ وہ جانیں اور انکا جھوٹ ﴿۱۳۷﴾
اور اپنے خیال سے یہ بھی کہتے ہیں کہ یہ چارپائے اور کھیتی منع ہے۔
اُسے اُس شخص کے سوا جسے ہم چاہیں کوئی نہ کھائے اور (بعض) چارپائے
ایسے ہیں کہ اُنکی پیٹھ پر چڑھنا منع کر دیا گیا ہے۔ اور بعض مویشی ایسے
ہیں جن پر (ذبح کرتے وقت) خدا کا نام نہیں لیتے سب خدا پر
جھوٹ ہے۔ وہ عنقریب اُن کو اُن کے جھوٹ کا بدلہ دیگا ﴿۱۳۸﴾
اور یہ بھی کہتے ہیں کہ جو بچّہ ان چارپایوں کے پیٹ میں ہے
وہ خاص ہمارے مردوں کیلئے ہے۔ اور ہماری عورتوں کو (اُس کا
کھانا) حرام ہے۔ اور اگر وہ بچّہ مرا ہوا ہو تو سب اس میں شریک
ہیں (یعنی اسے مرد اور عورتیں سب کھائیں) عنقریب خدا اُن کو انکے
ڈھکوسلوں کی سزا دیگا۔ بیشک وہ حکمت والا خبردار ہے ﴿۱۳۹﴾
جن لوگوں نے اپنی اولاد کو بیوقوفی سے بے سمجھی سے قتل کیا اور
خدا پر افترا کر کے اسکی عطا فرمائی ہوئی روزی کو حرام ٹھیرایا وہ
گھاٹے میں پڑ گئے۔ وہ بے شُبہ گمراہ ہیں اور ہدایت یافتہ نہیں ہیں ﴿۱۴۰﴾
اور خدا ہی تو ہے جس نے باغ پیدا کئے چھتریوں پر چڑھائے ہوئے بھی اور
جو چھتریوں پر نہیں چڑھائے ہوئے وہ بھی۔ اور کھجور اور کھیتی جنکے
طرح طرح کے پھل ہوتے ہیں اور زیتون اور انار جو (بعض باتوں میں)
ایک دوسرے سے ملتے جلتے ہیں اور (بعض باتوں میں) نہیں ملتے۔
جب یہ چیزیں پھلیں تو انکے پھل کھاؤ اور جس دن (پھل توڑو اور کھیتی)
کاٹو تو خدا کا حق بھی اس میں سے ادا کرو اور بیجا نہ اڑانا کہ

وَهٰذَا لِشُرَكَآئِنَا ۚ فَمَا كَانَ لِشُرَكَآئِهِمْ
فَلَا يَصِلُ إِلَى اللّٰهِ ۚ وَمَا كَانَ لِلّٰهِ فَهُوَ
يَصِلُ إِلٰى شُرَكَآئِهِمْ ۗ سَآءَ
مَا يَحْكُمُوْنَ ﴿۱۳۶﴾
وَكَذٰلِكَ زَيَّنَ لِكَثِيْرٍ مِّنَ الْمُشْرِكِيْنَ
قَتْلَ أَوْلَادِهِمْ شُرَكَآؤُهُمْ لِيُرْدُوْهُمْ
وَلِيَلْبِسُوْا عَلَيْهِمْ دِيْنَهُمْ ۗ وَلَوْ شَآءَ
اللّٰهُ مَا فَعَلُوْهُ فَذَرْهُمْ وَمَا يَفْتَرُوْنَ ﴿۱۳۷﴾
وَقَالُوْا هٰذِهٖٓ أَنْعَامٌ وَّحَرْثٌ حِجْرٌ ۖ لَّا
يَطْعَمُهَآ إِلَّا مَنْ نَّشَآءُ بِزَعْمِهِمْ وَ
أَنْعَامٌ حُرِّمَتْ ظُهُوْرُهَا وَأَنْعَامٌ لَّا
يَذْكُرُوْنَ اسْمَ اللّٰهِ عَلَيْهَا افْتِرَآءً
عَلَيْهِ ۗ سَيَجْزِيْهِمْ بِمَا كَانُوْا يَفْتَرُوْنَ ﴿۱۳۸﴾
وَقَالُوْا مَا فِيْ بُطُوْنِ هٰذِهِ الْأَنْعَامِ
خَالِصَةٌ لِّذُكُوْرِنَا وَمُحَرَّمٌ عَلٰٓى
أَزْوَاجِنَا ۚ وَإِنْ يَّكُنْ مَّيْتَةً فَهُمْ
فِيْهِ شُرَكَآءُ ۗ سَيَجْزِيْهِمْ وَصْفَهُمْ ۗ
إِنَّهٗ حَكِيْمٌ عَلِيْمٌ ﴿۱۳۹﴾
قَدْ خَسِرَ الَّذِيْنَ قَتَلُوْٓا أَوْلَادَهُمْ سَفَهًا
بِغَيْرِ عِلْمٍ وَّحَرَّمُوْا مَا رَزَقَهُمُ اللّٰهُ افْتِرَآءً
عَلَى اللّٰهِ ۚ قَدْ ضَلُّوْا وَمَا كَانُوْا مُهْتَدِيْنَ ﴿۱۴۰﴾ ع
وَهُوَ الَّذِيْٓ أَنْشَاَ جَنّٰتٍ مَّعْرُوْشٰتٍ
وَّغَيْرَ مَعْرُوْشٰتٍ وَّالنَّخْلَ وَالزَّرْعَ
مُخْتَلِفًا أُكُلُهٗ وَالزَّيْتُوْنَ وَالرُّمَّانَ
مُتَشَابِهًا وَّغَيْرَ مُتَشَابِهٍ ۚ كُلُوْا مِنْ ثَمَرِهٖٓ
إِذَآ أَثْمَرَ وَاٰتُوْا حَقَّهٗ يَوْمَ حَصَادِهٖ ۖ
وَلَا تُسْرِفُوْا ۚ إِنَّهٗ لَا يُحِبُّ

loveth not the wasters.

142. Of the cattle are some for burden and some for meat: eat what Allah hath provided for you, and follow not the footsteps of Satan: for he is to you an avowed enemy.

143. (Take) eight (head of cattle) in (four) pairs: of sheep a pair; and of goats a pair, say, hath He forbidden the two males, or the two females, or (the young) which the wombs of the two females enclose? Tell me with knowledge if ye are truthful:

144. Of camels a pair, and of oxen a pair; say, hath He forbidden the two males, or the two females, or (the young) which the wombs of the two females enclose?—Were ye present when Allah ordered you such a thing? But who doth more wrong than one who invents a lie against Allah, to lead astray men without knowledge? For Allah guideth not people who do wrong.

145. Say: "I find not in the Message received by me by inspiration any (meat) forbidden to be eaten by one who wishes to eat it, unless it be dead meat, or blood poured forth, or the flesh of swine,—for it is an abomination—or what is impious, (meat) on which a name has been invoked, other than Allah's." But (even so), if a person is forced by necessity, without wilful disobedience, nor transgressing due limits,—thy Lord is Oft-Forgiving, Most Merciful.

146. For those who followed the Jewish Law, We forbade every (animal) with undivided hoof, and We forbade them the fat of the ox and the sheep, except what adheres to their backs or their entrails, or is mixed up with a bone: this in recompense for their wilful disobedience: for We are True (in Our ordinances).

خدا بیجا اُڑانے والوں کو دوست نہیں رکھتا ﴿۱۴۱﴾
اور چارپایوں میں بوجھ اُٹھانے والے (یعنی بڑے بڑے) بھی پیدا کیے اور
زمین سے لگے ہوئے (یعنی چھوٹے چھوٹے) بھی (پس) خدا کا دیا ہوا رزق
کھاؤ اور شیطان کے قدموں پر نہ چلو۔ وہ تمہارا صریح دشمن ہے ﴿۱۴۲﴾
(یہ بڑے چھوٹے چارپائے) آٹھ قسم کے (ہیں) دو (دو) بھیڑوں
میں سے اور دو (دو) بکریوں میں سے (یعنی ایک ایک نر اور ایک
ایک مادہ) (اے پیغمبر ان سے) پوچھو کہ (خدا نے) دونوں (کے) نروں کو
حرام کیا ہے یا دونوں (کی) مادینوں کو یا جو بچہ مادینوں کے پیٹ میں
لپٹ رہا ہو اُسے اگر سچے ہو تو مجھے سند سے بتاؤ ﴿۱۴۳﴾
اور دو (دو) اُونٹوں میں سے اور دو (دو) گایوں میں سے (ان کے بارے
میں بھی ان سے) پوچھو کہ (خدا نے) دونوں (کے) نروں کو حرام کیا ہے یا
دونوں (کی) مادینوں کو یا جو بچہ مادینوں کے پیٹ میں لپٹا ہو اُسکو۔
بھلا جس وقت خدا نے تم کو اس کا حکم دیا تھا تم اُس وقت
موجود تھے؟ تو اس شخص سے زیادہ کون ظالم ہے جو خدا پر
جھوٹ افترا کرے تاکہ ازراہِ بیدانشی لوگوں کو گمراہ کرے۔
کچھ شک نہیں کہ خدا ظالم لوگوں کو ہدایت نہیں دیتا ﴿۱۴۴﴾
کہو کہ جو احکام مجھ پر نازل ہوئے ہیں مَیں اُن میں کوئی
چیز جسے کھانے والا کھائے حرام نہیں پاتا بجز اسکے کہ وہ
مرا ہوا جانور ہو یا بہتا لہو یا سُور کا گوشت کہ یہ سب ناپاک ہیں
یا کوئی گناہ کی چیز ہو کہ اس پر خدا کے سوا کسی اور کا نام لیا گیا
ہو۔ اور اگر کوئی مجبور ہو جائے لیکن نہ تو نافرمانی کرے اور نہ حد سے
باہر نکل جائے تو تمہارا پروردگار بخشنے والا مہربان ہے ﴿۱۴۵﴾
اور یہودیوں پر ہم نے سب ناخن والے جانور حرام کر دیئے تھے۔
اور گایوں اور بکریوں سے اُنکی چربی حرام کر دی تھی سوا اسکے
جو اُنکی پیٹھ پر لگی ہو یا اوجھڑی میں ہو یا ہڈی میں ملی ہو۔
یہ سزا ہم نے اُن کو اُن کی شرارت کے سبب دی تھی اور
ہم تو سچ کہنے والے ہیں ﴿۱۴۶﴾ ع ۱۳

الْمُسْرِفِينَ ﴿١٤١﴾
وَمِنَ الْأَنْعَامِ حَمُولَةً وَفَرْشًا كُلُوا
مِمَّا رَزَقَكُمُ اللَّهُ وَلَا تَتَّبِعُوا خُطُوَاتِ
الشَّيْطَانِ إِنَّهُ لَكُمْ عَدُوٌّ مُبِينٌ ﴿١٤٢﴾
ثَمَانِيَةَ أَزْوَاجٍ مِنَ الضَّأْنِ اثْنَيْنِ
وَمِنَ الْمَعْزِ اثْنَيْنِ قُلْ آلذَّكَرَيْنِ
حَرَّمَ أَمِ الْأُنْثَيَيْنِ أَمَّا اشْتَمَلَتْ
عَلَيْهِ أَرْحَامُ الْأُنْثَيَيْنِ نَبِّئُونِي بِعِلْمٍ
إِنْ كُنْتُمْ صَادِقِينَ ﴿١٤٣﴾
وَمِنَ الْإِبِلِ اثْنَيْنِ وَمِنَ الْبَقَرِ اثْنَيْنِ
قُلْ آلذَّكَرَيْنِ حَرَّمَ أَمِ الْأُنْثَيَيْنِ
أَمَّا اشْتَمَلَتْ عَلَيْهِ أَرْحَامُ الْأُنْثَيَيْنِ
أَمْ كُنْتُمْ شُهَدَاءَ إِذْ وَصَّاكُمُ اللَّهُ
بِهَٰذَا فَمَنْ أَظْلَمُ مِمَّنِ افْتَرَىٰ عَلَى
اللَّهِ كَذِبًا لِيُضِلَّ النَّاسَ بِغَيْرِ عِلْمٍ
إِنَّ اللَّهَ لَا يَهْدِي الْقَوْمَ الظَّالِمِينَ ﴿١٤٤﴾ ع ١٧
قُلْ لَا أَجِدُ فِي مَا أُوحِيَ إِلَيَّ مُحَرَّمًا
عَلَىٰ طَاعِمٍ يَطْعَمُهُ إِلَّا أَنْ يَكُونَ
مَيْتَةً أَوْ دَمًا مَسْفُوحًا أَوْ لَحْمَ خِنْزِيرٍ
فَإِنَّهُ رِجْسٌ أَوْ فِسْقًا أُهِلَّ لِغَيْرِ اللَّهِ
بِهِ فَمَنِ اضْطُرَّ غَيْرَ بَاغٍ وَلَا عَادٍ
فَإِنَّ رَبَّكَ غَفُورٌ رَحِيمٌ ﴿١٤٥﴾
وَعَلَى الَّذِينَ هَادُوا حَرَّمْنَا كُلَّ ذِي
ظُفُرٍ وَمِنَ الْبَقَرِ وَالْغَنَمِ حَرَّمْنَا عَلَيْهِمْ
شُحُومَهُمَا إِلَّا مَا حَمَلَتْ ظُهُورُهُمَا
أَوِ الْحَوَايَا أَوْ مَا اخْتَلَطَ بِعَظْمٍ ذَٰلِكَ
جَزَيْنَاهُمْ بِبَغْيِهِمْ وَإِنَّا لَصَادِقُونَ ﴿١٤٦﴾

147. If they accuse thee of falsehood, say: "Your Lord is full of mercy all-embracing; but from people in guilt never will His wrath be turned back.

148. Those who give partners (to Allah) will say: "If Allah had wished, we should not have given partners to Him, nor would our fathers; nor should we have had any forbidden thing." So did their ancestors argue falsely, until they tasted of Our wrath. Say: "Have ye any (certain) knowledge? If so, produce it before us. Ye follow nothing but conjecture: ye do nothing but lie."

149. Say: "With Allah is the argument that reaches home: if it had been His Will. He could indeed have guided you all."

150. Say: "Bring forward your witnesses to prove that Allah did forbid so and so." If they bring such witnesses, be not thou amongst them: nor follow thou the vain desires of such as treat Our Signs as falsehoods, and such as believe not in the Hereafter: for they hold others as equal with their Guardian Lord.

151. Say: "Come, I will rehearse what Allah hath (really) prohibited you from": join not anything with Him: Be good to your parents; kill not your children on a plea of want;—We provide sustenance for you and for them;—come not nigh to indecent deeds, whether open or secret; take not life, which Allah hath made sacred, except by way of justice and law: thus doth He command you, that ye may learn wisdom.

152. And come not nigh to the orphan's property, except to improve it, until he attain the age of full strength; give measure and weight with (full) justice;—no burden do We place on any soul,

اور اگر یہ لوگ تمہاری تکذیب کریں تو کہہ دو کہ تمہارا پروردگار
صاحب رحمت وسیع ہے مگر اس کا عذاب گنہگار لوگوں
سے نہیں ٹلے گا ﴿۱۴۷﴾
جو لوگ شرک کرتے ہیں وہ کہیں گے کہ اگر خدا چاہتا تو ہم
شرک نہ کرتے اور نہ ہمارے باپ دادا (شرک کرتے) اور نہ ہم
کسی چیز کو حرام ٹھہراتے۔ اسی طرح ان لوگوں نے تکذیب کی تھی
جو اُن سے پہلے تھے یہاں تک کہ ہمارے عذاب کا مزہ چکھ کر رہے کہہ دو
کیا تمہارے پاس کوئی سند ہے؟ اگر ہے تو اسے ہمارے سامنے نکالو۔ تم
محض خیال کے پیچھے چلتے اور اٹکل کے تیر چلاتے ہو ﴿۱۴۸﴾
کہہ دو کہ خدا ہی کی حجت غالب ہے اگر وہ چاہتا تو تم سب کو
ہدایت دے دیتا ﴿۱۴۹﴾
کہو کہ اپنے گواہوں کو لاؤ جو بتائیں کہ خدا نے یہ چیزیں حرام
کی ہیں۔ پھر اگر وہ (آکر) گواہی دیں تو تم اُن کے ساتھ گواہی
نہ دینا۔ اور نہ اُن کی خواہشوں کی پیروی کرنا جو ہماری آیتوں کو
جھٹلاتے ہیں اور جو آخرت پر ایمان نہیں لاتے اور (بتوں کو)
اپنے پروردگار کے برابر ٹھہراتے ہیں ﴿۱۵۰﴾
کہو کہ (لوگو) آؤ میں تمہیں وہ چیزیں پڑھ کر سناؤں جو تمہارے پروردگار نے
تم پر حرام کر دی ہیں (ان کی نسبت اس نے اس طرح ارشاد فرمایا ہے) کہ کسی چیز کو خدا
کا شریک نہ بنانا اور ماں باپ (سے بد سلوکی نہ کرنا بلکہ) سلوک کرتے رہنا
اور ناداری (کے اندیشے) سے اپنی اولاد کو قتل نہ کرنا کیونکہ تم کو اور
اُن کو ہم ہی رزق دیتے ہیں۔ اور بےحیائی کے کام ظاہر ہوں یا
پوشیدہ اُن کے پاس نہ پھٹکنا۔ اور کسی جان (والے) کو جس کے قتل کو خدا
نے حرام کر دیا ہے قتل نہ کرنا مگر جائز طور پر (یعنی جس کا شریعت حکم
دے) ان باتوں کی وہ تمہیں تاکید کرتا ہے تاکہ تم سمجھو ﴿۱۵۱﴾
اور یتیم کے مال کے پاس بھی نہ جانا مگر ایسے طریق سے کہ بہت ہی پسندیدہ
ہو۔ یہاں تک کہ وہ جوانی کو پہنچ جائے۔ اور ناپ اور تول انصاف کے
ساتھ پوری پوری کیا کرو۔ ہم کسی کو تکلیف نہیں دیتے مگر اس کی

فَإِنْ كَذَّبُوكَ فَقُلْ رَّبُّكُمْ ذُوْ رَحْمَةٍ
وَّاسِعَةٍ ۚ وَلَا يُرَدُّ بَأْسُهٗ عَنِ الْقَوْمِ
الْمُجْرِمِيْنَ ﴿۱۴۷﴾
سَيَقُوْلُ الَّذِيْنَ اَشْرَكُوْا لَوْ شَآءَ اللّٰهُ مَآ
اَشْرَكْنَا وَلَآ اٰبَآؤُنَا وَلَا حَرَّمْنَا مِنْ
شَيْءٍ ۚ كَذٰلِكَ كَذَّبَ الَّذِيْنَ مِنْ قَبْلِهِمْ
حَتّٰى ذَاقُوْا بَاْسَنَا ۭ قُلْ هَلْ عِنْدَكُمْ
مِّنْ عِلْمٍ فَتُخْرِجُوْهُ لَنَا ۭ اِنْ تَتَّبِعُوْنَ
اِلَّا الظَّنَّ وَاِنْ اَنْتُمْ اِلَّا تَخْرُصُوْنَ ﴿۱۴۸﴾
قُلْ فَلِلّٰهِ الْحُجَّةُ الْبَالِغَةُ ۚ فَلَوْ شَآءَ
لَهَدٰىكُمْ اَجْمَعِيْنَ ﴿۱۴۹﴾
قُلْ هَلُمَّ شُهَدَآءَكُمُ الَّذِيْنَ يَشْهَدُوْنَ
اَنَّ اللّٰهَ حَرَّمَ هٰذَا ۚ فَاِنْ شَهِدُوْا فَلَا
تَشْهَدْ مَعَهُمْ ۚ وَلَا تَتَّبِعْ اَهْوَآءَ الَّذِيْنَ
كَذَّبُوْا بِاٰيٰتِنَا وَالَّذِيْنَ لَا يُؤْمِنُوْنَ
بِالْاٰخِرَةِ وَهُمْ بِرَبِّهِمْ يَعْدِلُوْنَ ﴿۱۵۰﴾ ع
قُلْ تَعَالَوْا اَتْلُ مَا حَرَّمَ رَبُّكُمْ
عَلَيْكُمْ اَلَّا تُشْرِكُوْا بِهٖ شَيْـًٔا وَّ
بِالْوَالِدَيْنِ اِحْسَانًا ۚ وَلَا تَقْتُلُوْٓا اَوْلَادَكُمْ
مِّنْ اِمْلَاقٍ ۭ نَحْنُ نَرْزُقُكُمْ وَاِيَّاهُمْ ۚ
وَلَا تَقْرَبُوا الْفَوَاحِشَ مَا ظَهَرَ مِنْهَا
وَمَا بَطَنَ ۚ وَلَا تَقْتُلُوا النَّفْسَ الَّتِيْ
حَرَّمَ اللّٰهُ اِلَّا بِالْحَقِّ ۭ ذٰلِكُمْ وَصّٰىكُمْ
بِهٖ لَعَلَّكُمْ تَعْقِلُوْنَ ﴿۱۵۱﴾
وَلَا تَقْرَبُوْا مَالَ الْيَتِيْمِ اِلَّا بِالَّتِيْ
هِيَ اَحْسَنُ حَتّٰى يَبْلُغَ اَشُدَّهٗ ۚ وَاَوْفُوا
الْكَيْلَ وَالْمِيْزَانَ بِالْقِسْطِ ۚ لَا نُكَلِّفُ

نَفْسًا اِلَّا وُسْعَهَا ۚ وَاِذَا قُلْتُمْ فَاعْدِلُوْا
وَلَوْ كَانَ ذَا قُرْبٰى ۚ وَبِعَهْدِ اللّٰهِ اَوْفُوْا ۭ
ذٰلِكُمْ وَصّٰىكُمْ بِهٖ لَعَلَّكُمْ تَذَكَّرُوْنَ ﴿١٥٢﴾
وَاَنَّ هٰذَا صِرَاطِيْ مُسْتَقِيْمًا فَاتَّبِعُوْهُ ۚ
وَلَا تَتَّبِعُوا السُّبُلَ فَتَفَرَّقَ بِكُمْ عَنْ
سَبِيْلِهٖ ۭ ذٰلِكُمْ وَصّٰىكُمْ بِهٖ لَعَلَّكُمْ تَتَّقُوْنَ ﴿١٥٣﴾
ثُمَّ اٰتَيْنَا مُوْسَى الْكِتٰبَ تَمَامًا عَلَى
الَّذِيْٓ اَحْسَنَ وَتَفْصِيْلًا لِّكُلِّ شَيْءٍ
وَّهُدًى وَّرَحْمَةً لَّعَلَّهُمْ بِلِقَاۗءِ
ع ١٩ رَبِّهِمْ يُؤْمِنُوْنَ ﴿١٥٤﴾
وَهٰذَا كِتٰبٌ اَنْزَلْنٰهُ مُبٰرَكٌ فَاتَّبِعُوْهُ
وَاتَّقُوْا لَعَلَّكُمْ تُرْحَمُوْنَ ﴿١٥٥﴾
اَنْ تَقُوْلُوْٓا اِنَّمَآ اُنْزِلَ الْكِتٰبُ عَلٰي
طَاۗىِٕفَتَيْنِ مِنْ قَبْلِنَا ۠ وَاِنْ كُنَّا
عَنْ دِرَاسَتِهِمْ لَغٰفِلِيْنَ ﴿١٥٦﴾
اَوْ تَقُوْلُوْا لَوْ اَنَّآ اُنْزِلَ عَلَيْنَا الْكِتٰبُ
لَكُنَّآ اَهْدٰى مِنْهُمْ ۚ فَقَدْ جَاۗءَكُمْ
بَيِّنَةٌ مِّنْ رَّبِّكُمْ وَهُدًى وَّرَحْمَةٌ ۚ
فَمَنْ اَظْلَمُ مِمَّنْ كَذَّبَ بِاٰيٰتِ اللّٰهِ
وَصَدَفَ عَنْهَا ۭ سَنَجْزِي الَّذِيْنَ
يَصْدِفُوْنَ عَنْ اٰيٰتِنَا سُوْۗءَ الْعَذَابِ
بِمَا كَانُوْا يَصْدِفُوْنَ ﴿١٥٧﴾
هَلْ يَنْظُرُوْنَ اِلَّآ اَنْ تَاْتِيَهُمُ الْمَلٰۗىِٕكَةُ
اَوْ يَاْتِيَ رَبُّكَ اَوْ يَاْتِيَ بَعْضُ اٰيٰتِ رَبِّكَ ۭ
يَوْمَ يَاْتِيْ بَعْضُ اٰيٰتِ رَبِّكَ لَا يَنْفَعُ
نَفْسًا اِيْمَانُهَا لَمْ تَكُنْ اٰمَنَتْ مِنْ
قَبْلُ اَوْ كَسَبَتْ فِيْٓ اِيْمَانِهَا خَيْرًا ۭ

طاقت کے مطابق۔ اور جب (کسی کی نسبت) کوئی بات کہو تو انصاف سے
کہو گو وہ (تمہارا) رشتہ دار ہی ہو اور خدا کے عہد کو پورا کرو۔ ان
باتوں کا خدا تمہیں حکم دیتا ہے تاکہ تم نصیحت قبول کرو ﴿۱۵۲﴾
اور یہ کہ میرا سیدھا رستہ یہی ہے تو تم اسی پر چلنا اور اور
رستوں پر نہ چلنا کہ (ان پر چل کر) خدا کے رستے سے الگ ہو جاؤ گے
ان باتوں کا خدا تمہیں حکم دیتا ہے تاکہ تم پرہیزگار بنو ﴿۱۵۳﴾
(ہاں) پھر (سن لو کہ) ہم نے موسیٰ کو کتاب عنایت کی تھی تاکہ
ان لوگوں پر جو نیکوکار ہیں نعمت پوری کر دیں اور (اس میں) ہر
چیز کا بیان (ہے) اور ہدایت (ہے) اور رحمت ہے تاکہ (ان کی امت کے
لوگ) اپنے پروردگار کے روبرو حاضر ہونے کا یقین کریں ﴿۱۵۴﴾
اور (اے کفر کرنے والو) یہ کتاب بھی ہمیں نے اتاری ہے برکت والی۔
تو اس کی پیروی کرو اور (خدا سے) ڈرو تاکہ تم پر مہربانی کی جائے ﴿۱۵۵﴾
(اور اس لئے اتاری ہے) کہ (تم یوں نہ) کہو کہ ہم سے پہلے دو ہی
گروہوں پر کتابیں اتری ہیں اور ہم ان کے پڑھنے سے
(معذور اور) بے خبر تھے ﴿۱۵۶﴾
یا (یہ نہ) کہو کہ اگر ہم پر بھی کتاب نازل ہوتی تو ہم ان لوگوں
کی نسبت کہیں سیدھے رستے پر ہوتے سو تمہارے پاس تمہارے
پروردگار کی طرف سے دلیل اور ہدایت اور رحمت آ گئی ہے۔
تو اس سے بڑھ کر ظالم کون ہوگا جو خدا کی آیتوں کی تکذیب
کرے اور ان سے (لوگوں کو) پھیرے۔ جو لوگ ہماری آیتوں سے
پھیرتے ہیں اس پھیرنے کے سبب ہم ان کو برے عذاب
کی سزا دیں گے ﴿۱۵۷﴾
یہ اس کے سوا اور کس بات کے منتظر ہیں کہ ان کے پاس فرشتے آئیں یا
خود تمہارا پروردگار آئے یا تمہارے پروردگار کی کچھ نشانیاں آئیں
مگر جس روز تمہارے پروردگار کی نشانیاں آ جائیں گی تو جو شخص
پہلے ایمان نہیں لایا ہوگا اس وقت اسے ایمان لانا کچھ فائدہ نہیں
دے گا یا اپنے ایمان (کی حالت) میں نیک عمل نہیں کئے ہوں گے (تو گناہوں سے توبہ کرنا مفید

but that which it can bear;—whenever ye speak, speak justly, even if a near relative is concerned; and fulfil the Covenant of Allah: thus doth He command you, that ye may remember.

153. Verily, this is My Way leading straight: follow it: follow not (other) paths: they will scatter you about from His Path: thus doth He command you, that ye may be righteous.

154. Moreover, We gave Moses the Book, completing (our favour) to those who would do right, and explaining all things in detail,—and a guide and a mercy, that they might believe in the meeting with their Lord.

155. And this is a Book which We have revealed as a blessing: so follow it and be righteous, that ye may receive mercy:

156. Lest ye should say: "The Book was sent down to two Peoples before us, and for our part, we remained unacquainted with all that they learned by assiduous study;"

157. Or lest ye should say: "If the Book had only been sent down to us, we should have followed its guidance better than they." Now then hath come unto you a Clear (Sign) from your Lord,—and a guide and a mercy: then who could do more wrong than one who rejecteth Allah's Signs, and turneth away therefrom? In good time shall We requite those who turn away from Our Signs, with a dreadful chastisement for their turning away.

158. Are they waiting to see if the angels come to them, or thy Lord (Himself), or certain of the Signs of thy Lord! the day that certain of the Signs of the Lord do come, no good will it do to a soul to believe then, if it believed not before nor earned righteousness through its Faith.

SÛRA–7
AL-A'RÃF
(INTRODUCTION)

This Sûra is closely connected, both chronologically and in respect of the argument, with the previous Sûra. But it expounds the doctrine of revelation and man's spiritual history by illustrations from Adam onwards, through various Prophets, and the details of Moses's struggles, to the time of the Apostle Muḥammad, in whom Allah's revelation is completed.

Say: "Wait ye: we too are waiting"

159. As for those who divide their religion and break up into sects, thou hast no part in them in the least: their affair is with Allah: He will in the end tell them the truth of all that they did.

160. He that doeth good shall have ten times as much to his credit: he that doeth evil shall only be recompensed according to his evil: no wrong shall be done unto them.

161. Say: "Verily, my Lord hath guided me to a Way that is straight,—a religion of right,— the Path (trod) by Abraham the true in faith, and he (certainly) joined not gods with Allah."

162. Say: "Truly, my prayer and my service of sacrifice, my life and my death, are (all) for Allah, the Cherisher of the Worlds:

163. No partner hath He: this am I commanded, and I am the first of those who submit to His Will.

164. Say: "Shall I seek for (my) Lord other than Allah. When He is the Cherisher of all things (that exist)? Every soul draws the meed of its acts on none but itself: no bearer of burdens can bear the burden of another. Your return in the end is towards Allah: He will tell you the truth of the things wherein ye disputed."

165. It is He Who hath made you the inheritors of the earth: He hath raised you in ranks, some above others: that He may try you in the gifts He hath given you: for thy Lord is quick in punishment: yet He is indeed Oft-Forgiving Most Merciful.

Al-A'râf. or The Heights.

In the name of Allah, Most Gracious, Most Merciful.

1. Alif, Lam, Mim, Sad.
2. A Book revealed unto thee,— so let thy heart be oppressed no more by any difficulty on that

ہو گا اے پیغمبر ان سے کہہ دو کہ تم بھی انتظار کرو ہم بھی انتظار کرتے ہیں (۱۵۸)
جن لوگوں نے اپنے دین میں (بہت سے) رستے نکالے اور
کئی کئی فرقے ہو گئے اُن سے تم کو کچھ کام نہیں ان کا کام خدا
کے حوالے پھر جو کچھ وہ کرتے رہے ہیں وہ اُنکو (سب) بتائے گا (۱۵۹)
جو کوئی (خدا کے حضور) نیکی لیکر آئیگا اُسکو ویسی دس نیکیاں
ملیں گی۔ اور جو بُرائی لائے گا اُسے سزا ویسی ہی ملے گی
اور اُن پر ظلم نہیں کیا جائے گا (۱۶۰)
کہہ دو کہ مجھے میرے پروردگار نے سیدھا رستہ دکھا دیا ہے
(یعنی دین صحیح) مذہب ابراہیم کا جو ایک (خدا) ہی کی طرف
کے تھے۔ اور مشرکوں میں سے نہ تھے (۱۶۱)
(یہ بھی) کہہ دو کہ میری نماز اور میری عبادت اور میرا جینا اور
میرا مرنا سب خدائے رب العالمین ہی کیلئے ہے (۱۶۲)
جس کا کوئی شریک نہیں اور مجھ کو اسی بات کا حکم ملا ہے
اور میں سب سے اوّل فرمانبردار ہوں (۱۶۳)
کہو کیا میں خدا کے سوا اور پروردگار تلاش کروں۔ اور
وہی تو ہر چیز کا مالک ہے اور جو کوئی (بُرا) کام کرتا ہے تو
اُس کا ضرر اُسی کو ہوتا ہے اور کوئی شخص کسی (کے گناہ) کا بوجھ
نہیں اُٹھائیگا پھر تم (سب) کو اپنے پروردگار کیطرف لوٹ کر جانا ہے
تو جن جن باتوں میں تم اختلاف کیا کرتے تھے وہ تم کو بتائیگا (۱۶۴)
اور وہی تو ہے جس نے زمین میں تم کو اپنا نائب بنایا اور
ایک کے دوسرے پر درجے بلند کئے تاکہ جو کچھ اُس نے تمہیں
بخشا ہے اس میں تمہاری آزمائش کرے بیشک تمہارا پروردگار
جلد عذاب دینے والا ہے اور بیشک وہ بخشنے والا مہربان بھی ہے (۱۶۵)

سورۂ اعراف مکی ہے اور اس میں دو سو چھ آیتیں اور چوبیس رکوع ہیں

شروع خدا کا نام لے کر جو بڑا مہربان نہایت رحم والا ہے
المص (۱) (اے محمدؐ یہ) کتاب (جو) تم پر نازل ہوئی ہے اس سے
تمہیں تنگدل نہیں ہونا چاہیئے (یہ نازل) اسلئے (ہوئی ہے) کہ تم اسکے

قُلِ انْتَظِرُوْٓا اِنَّا مُنْتَظِرُوْنَ ﴿۱۵۸﴾
اِنَّ الَّذِيْنَ فَرَّقُوْا دِيْنَهُمْ وَكَانُوْا شِيَعًا
لَّسْتَ مِنْهُمْ فِيْ شَيْءٍ ۭ اِنَّمَآ اَمْرُهُمْ اِلَى
اللّٰهِ ثُمَّ يُنَبِّئُهُمْ بِمَا كَانُوْا يَفْعَلُوْنَ ﴿۱۵۹﴾
مَنْ جَآءَ بِالْحَسَنَةِ فَلَهٗ عَشْرُ اَمْثَالِهَا ۚ
وَمَنْ جَآءَ بِالسَّيِّئَةِ فَلَا يُجْزٰٓى اِلَّا
مِثْلَهَا وَهُمْ لَا يُظْلَمُوْنَ ﴿۱۶۰﴾
قُلْ اِنَّنِيْ هَدٰىنِيْ رَبِّيْٓ اِلٰى صِرَاطٍ
مُّسْتَقِيْمٍ ڬ دِيْنًا قِيَمًا مِّلَّةَ اِبْرٰهِيْمَ
حَنِيْفًا ۚ وَمَا كَانَ مِنَ الْمُشْرِكِيْنَ ﴿۱۶۱﴾
قُلْ اِنَّ صَلَاتِيْ وَنُسُكِيْ وَمَحْيَايَ وَ
مَمَاتِيْ لِلّٰهِ رَبِّ الْعٰلَمِيْنَ ﴿۱۶۲﴾
لَا شَرِيْكَ لَهٗ ۚ وَبِذٰلِكَ اُمِرْتُ وَاَنَا
اَوَّلُ الْمُسْلِمِيْنَ ﴿۱۶۳﴾
قُلْ اَغَيْرَ اللّٰهِ اَبْغِيْ رَبًّا وَّهُوَ رَبُّ
كُلِّ شَيْءٍ ۭ وَلَا تَكْسِبُ كُلُّ نَفْسٍ اِلَّا
عَلَيْهَا ۚ وَلَا تَزِرُ وَازِرَةٌ وِّزْرَ اُخْرٰى ۚ
ثُمَّ اِلٰى رَبِّكُمْ مَّرْجِعُكُمْ فَيُنَبِّئُكُمْ
بِمَا كُنْتُمْ فِيْهِ تَخْتَلِفُوْنَ ﴿۱۶۴﴾
وَهُوَ الَّذِيْ جَعَلَكُمْ خَلٰٓئِفَ الْاَرْضِ
وَرَفَعَ بَعْضَكُمْ فَوْقَ بَعْضٍ دَرَجٰتٍ
لِّيَبْلُوَكُمْ فِيْ مَآ اٰتٰىكُمْ ۭ اِنَّ رَبَّكَ سَرِيْعُ
الْعِقَابِ ڮ وَاِنَّهٗ لَغَفُوْرٌ رَّحِيْمٌ ﴿۱۶۵﴾

سُوْرَةُ الْاَعْرَافِ مَكِّيَّةٌ وَّهِيَ مِائَتَانِ وَسِتُّ اٰيَاتٍ وَّاَرْبَعٌ وَّعِشْرُوْنَ رُكُوْعًا

بِسْمِ اللّٰهِ الرَّحْمٰنِ الرَّحِيْمِ
الٓمّٓصٓ ﴿۱﴾ كِتٰبٌ اُنْزِلَ اِلَيْكَ فَلَا
يَكُنْ فِيْ صَدْرِكَ حَرَجٌ مِّنْهُ لِتُنْذِرَ

account,—that with it thou mightest warn (the erring) and a reminder to the Believers.

3. Follow (O men!) the revelation given unto you from your Lord, and follow not, as friends or protectors, other than Him. Little it is ye remember of admonition.

4. How many towns have We destroyed (for their sins)? Our punishment took them on a sudden by night or while they slept for their afternoon rest.

5. When (thus) Our punishment took them, no cry did they utter but this: "Indeed we did wrong."

6. Then shall we question those to whom Our Message was sent and those by whom we sent it.

7. And verily, We shall recount their whole story with knowledge, for We were never absent (at any time or place).

8. The balance that day will be true (to a nicety): those whose scale (of good) will be heavy, will prosper:

9. Those whose scale will be light, will find their souls in perdition, for that they wrongfully treated Our Signs.

10. It is We Who have placed you with authority on earth, and provided you therein with means for the fulfilment of your life: small are the thanks that ye give!

11. It is We Who created you and gave you shape: then We bade the angels prostrate to Adam, and they prostrated, not so Iblis; he refused to be of those who prostrate.

12. (Allah) said: "What prevented thee from prostrating when I commanded thee?" He said: "I am better than he: Thou didst create me from fire, and him from clay".

13. (Allah) said: "Get thee down from it: it is not for thee to be arrogant here: get out, for thou art of the meanest (of creatures)."

ذریعے سے (لوگوں کو) ڈر سناؤ اور (یہ) ایمان والوں کے لیے نصیحت ہے ﴿۲﴾
(لوگو) جو کتاب تم پر تمہارے پروردگار کے ہاں سے نازل ہوئی
ہے اس کی پیروی کرو اور اس کے سوا اور رفیقوں کی پیروی
نہ کرو (اور) تم کم ہی نصیحت قبول کرتے ہو ﴿۳﴾
اور کتنی ہی بستیاں ہیں کہ ہم نے تباہ کر ڈالیں جن پر ہمارا عذاب (یا تو رات کو)
آتا تھا جبکہ وہ سوتے تھے یا (دن کو) جب وہ قیلولہ (یعنی دوپہر کو آرام) کرتے تھے ﴿۴﴾
تو جس وقت ان پر عذاب آتا تھا ان کے منہ سے یہی نکلتا تھا کہ
(ہائے) ہم (اپنے اوپر) ظلم کرتے رہے ﴿۵﴾
تو جن لوگوں کی طرف پیغمبر بھیجے گئے ہم ان سے بھی پرسش
کریں گے اور پیغمبروں سے بھی پوچھیں گے ﴿۶﴾
پھر اپنے علم سے ان کے حالات بیان کریں گے اور ہم
کہیں غائب تو نہیں تھے ﴿۷﴾
اور اس روز (اعمال کا) تلنا برحق ہے۔ تو جن لوگوں کے
(عملوں کے) وزن بھاری ہوں گے وہ تو نجات پانے والے ہیں ﴿۸﴾
اور جن کے وزن ہلکے ہوں گے تو یہی لوگ ہیں جنہوں نے
اپنے تئیں خسارے میں ڈالا اس لیے کہ ہماری آیتوں کے
بارے میں بے انصافی کرتے تھے ﴿۹﴾
اور ہم ہی نے زمین میں تمہارا ٹھکانا بنایا اور اس میں تمہارے
لیے سامان معیشت پیدا کیے (مگر) تم کم ہی شکر کرتے ہو ﴿۱۰﴾
اور ہم ہی نے تم کو (ابتدا میں مٹی سے) پیدا کیا پھر تمہاری شکل
صورت بنائی پھر فرشتوں کو حکم دیا کہ آدم کے آگے سجدہ کرو تو (سب نے) سجدہ
کیا لیکن ابلیس۔ کہ وہ سجدہ کرنے میں (شامل) نہ ہوا ﴿۱۱﴾
(خدا نے) فرمایا جب میں نے تجھ کو حکم دیا تو کس چیز نے تجھے سجدہ
کرنے سے باز رکھا۔ اس نے کہا کہ میں اس سے افضل ہوں مجھے
تو نے آگ سے پیدا کیا ہے اور اسے مٹی سے بنایا ہے ﴿۱۲﴾
فرمایا تو (بہشت سے) اتر جا تجھے شایاں نہیں کہ یہاں غرور کرے
پس نکل جا۔ تو ذلیل ہے ﴿۱۳﴾

بِهٖ وَذِكْرٰى لِلْمُؤْمِنِيْنَ ﴿٢﴾
اِتَّبِعُوْا مَآ اُنْزِلَ اِلَيْكُمْ مِّنْ رَّبِّكُمْ
وَلَا تَتَّبِعُوْا مِنْ دُوْنِهٖٓ اَوْلِيَآءَ ط
قَلِيْلًا مَّا تَذَكَّرُوْنَ ﴿٣﴾
وَكَمْ مِّنْ قَرْيَةٍ اَهْلَكْنٰهَا فَجَآءَهَا
بَاْسُنَا بَيَاتًا اَوْ هُمْ قَآئِلُوْنَ ﴿٤﴾
فَمَا كَانَ دَعْوٰىهُمْ اِذْ جَآءَهُمْ بَاْسُنَآ
اِلَّآ اَنْ قَالُوْٓا اِنَّا كُنَّا ظٰلِمِيْنَ ﴿٥﴾
فَلَنَسْئَلَنَّ الَّذِيْنَ اُرْسِلَ اِلَيْهِمْ وَ
لَنَسْئَلَنَّ الْمُرْسَلِيْنَ ﴿٦﴾
فَلَنَقُصَّنَّ عَلَيْهِمْ بِعِلْمٍ وَّمَا كُنَّا
غَآئِبِيْنَ ﴿٧﴾
وَالْوَزْنُ يَوْمَئِذِ نِ الْحَقُّ ج فَمَنْ ثَقُلَتْ
مَوَازِيْنُهٗ فَاُولٰٓئِكَ هُمُ الْمُفْلِحُوْنَ ﴿٨﴾
وَمَنْ خَفَّتْ مَوَازِيْنُهٗ فَاُولٰٓئِكَ
الَّذِيْنَ خَسِرُوْٓا اَنْفُسَهُمْ بِمَا كَانُوْا
بِاٰيٰتِنَا يَظْلِمُوْنَ ﴿٩﴾
وَلَقَدْ مَكَّنّٰكُمْ فِي الْاَرْضِ وَجَعَلْنَا
لَكُمْ فِيْهَا مَعَايِشَ ط قَلِيْلًا مَّا تَشْكُرُوْنَ ﴿١٠﴾ ع
وَلَقَدْ خَلَقْنٰكُمْ ثُمَّ صَوَّرْنٰكُمْ ثُمَّ
قُلْنَا لِلْمَلٰٓئِكَةِ اسْجُدُوْا لِاٰدَمَ ق فَسَجَدُوْٓا
اِلَّآ اِبْلِيْسَ ط لَمْ يَكُنْ مِّنَ السّٰجِدِيْنَ ﴿١١﴾
قَالَ مَا مَنَعَكَ اَلَّا تَسْجُدَ اِذْ اَمَرْتُكَ ط
قَالَ اَنَا خَيْرٌ مِّنْهُ ج خَلَقْتَنِيْ مِنْ نَّارٍ
وَّخَلَقْتَهٗ مِنْ طِيْنٍ ﴿١٢﴾
قَالَ فَاهْبِطْ مِنْهَا فَمَا يَكُوْنُ لَكَ اَنْ
تَتَكَبَّرَ فِيْهَا فَاخْرُجْ اِنَّكَ مِنَ الصّٰغِرِيْنَ ﴿١٣﴾

14. He said: "Give me respite till the day they are raised up."

15. (Allah) said: "Be thou among those who have respite."

16. He said: "Because thou hast thrown me out (of the Way), lo! I will lie in wait for them on Thy Straight Way:

17. "Then will I assault them from before them and behind them, from their right and their left: nor wilt Thou find, in most of them, gratitude (for Thy mercies)."

18. (Allah) said: "Get out from this, despised and expelled. If any of them follow thee,—hell will I fill with you all.

19. "O Adam! dwell thou and thy wife in the Garden, and enjoy (its good things) as ye wish: but approach not this tree, lest you become of the unjust."

20. Then began Satan to whisper suggestions to them, in order to reveal to them their shame that was hidden from them (before): he said: "Your Lord only forbade you this tree, lest ye should become angels or such beings as live for ever."

21. And he swore to them both, that he was their sincere adviser.

22. So by deceit he brought about their fall: when they tasted of the tree, their shameful parts became manifest to them, and they began to sew together the leaves of the Garden over their bodies. And their Lord called unto them: "Did I not forbid you that tree, and tell you that Satan was an avowed enemy unto you?"

23. They said: "Our Lord we have wronged our own souls: if Thou forgive us not and bestow not upon us Thy Mercy, we shall certainly be lost.

24. (Allah) said: "Get ye down, with enmity between yourselves. On earth will be your dwelling-place and your means of livelihood,—for a time."

اُس نے کہا کہ مجھے اُس دن تک مہلت عطا فرما جس دن لوگ قبروں سے اُٹھائے جائینگے (١٤)
فرمایا (اچھا) تجھ کو مہلت دی جاتی ہے (١٥)
(پھر) شیطان نے کہا کہ مجھے تو تُو نے ملعون کیا ہی ہے میں بھی تیرے
سیدھے رستے پر اُن (کو گمراہ کرنے) کے لئے بیٹھوں گا (١٦)
پھر اُن کے آگے سے اور پیچھے سے اور دائیں سے اور بائیں سے
(غرض ہر طرف سے) آؤنگا (اور اُن کی راہ ماروں گا) اور تو ان
میں اکثر کو شکر گزار نہیں پائے گا (١٧)
(خدا نے) فرمایا نکل جا یہاں سے پاجی مردود جو لوگ اُنمیں سے تیری
پیروی کرینگے میں (اُنکو اور تجھکو جہنم میں ڈالکر) تم سب سے جہنم کو بھر دونگا (١٨)
اور (ہم نے) آدم (سے کہا کہ) تم اور تمہاری بیوی بہشت میں
رہو سہو اور جہاں سے چاہو (اور جو چاہو) نوش جان کرو مگر
اس درخت کے پاس نہ جانا۔ ورنہ گنہگار ہو جاؤ گے (١٩)
تو شیطان دونوں کو بہکانے لگا تاکہ اُن کے ستر کی چیزیں جو
اُن سے پوشیدہ تھیں کھول دے اور کہنے لگا کہ تم کو تمہارے
پروردگار نے اس درخت سے صرف اس لئے منع کیا ہے کہ تم
فرشتے نہ بن جاؤ یا ہمیشہ جیتے نہ رہو (٢٠)
اور اُن سے قسم کھا کر کہا کہ میں تو تمہارا خیر خواہ ہوں (٢١)
غرض (مردود نے) دھوکا دیکر انکو معصیت کیطرف کھینچ ہی لیا جب انہوں نے
اس درخت (کے پھل) کو کھا لیا تو انکے ستر کی چیزیں کھل گئیں اور وہ
بہشت کے (درختوں کے) پتے (توڑ توڑ کر) اپنے اوپر چپکانے (اور ستر چھپانے) لگے
تب اُنکے پروردگار نے اُنکو پکارا کہ کیا میں نے تمکو اس درخت (کے پاس جانے)
سے منع نہیں کیا تھا اور جتا نہیں دیا تھا کہ شیطان تمہارا کھلم کھلا دشمن ہے؟ (٢٢)
دونوں عرض کرنے لگے کہ پروردگار ہم نے اپنی جانوں پر ظلم کیا اور اگر
تو ہمیں نہیں بخشیگا اور ہم پر رحم نہیں کریگا تو ہم تباہ ہو جائینگے (٢٣)
(خدا نے) فرمایا (تم سب بہشت سے) اُتر جاؤ (اب سے) تم ایک دوسرے
کے دشمن ہو اور تمہارے لئے ایک وقت (خاص) تک زمین پر
ٹھکانا اور (زندگی کا) سامان (کر دیا گیا) ہے (٢٤)

قَالَ أَنظِرْنِي إِلَىٰ يَوْمِ يُبْعَثُونَ (١٤)
قَالَ إِنَّكَ مِنَ الْمُنظَرِينَ (١٥)
قَالَ فَبِمَا أَغْوَيْتَنِي لَأَقْعُدَنَّ لَهُمْ
صِرَاطَكَ الْمُسْتَقِيمَ (١٦)
ثُمَّ لَآتِيَنَّهُم مِّن بَيْنِ أَيْدِيهِمْ وَمِنْ
خَلْفِهِمْ وَعَنْ أَيْمَانِهِمْ وَعَن شَمَائِلِهِمْ
وَلَا تَجِدُ أَكْثَرَهُمْ شَاكِرِينَ (١٧)
قَالَ اخْرُجْ مِنْهَا مَذْءُومًا مَّدْحُورًا لَّمَن
تَبِعَكَ مِنْهُمْ لَأَمْلَأَنَّ جَهَنَّمَ مِنكُمْ أَجْمَعِينَ (١٨)
وَيَا آدَمُ اسْكُنْ أَنتَ وَزَوْجُكَ الْجَنَّةَ
فَكُلَا مِنْ حَيْثُ شِئْتُمَا وَلَا تَقْرَبَا
هَٰذِهِ الشَّجَرَةَ فَتَكُونَا مِنَ الظَّالِمِينَ (١٩)
فَوَسْوَسَ لَهُمَا الشَّيْطَانُ لِيُبْدِيَ لَهُمَا
مَا وُورِيَ عَنْهُمَا مِن سَوْآتِهِمَا وَقَالَ
مَا نَهَاكُمَا رَبُّكُمَا عَنْ هَٰذِهِ الشَّجَرَةِ إِلَّا
أَن تَكُونَا مَلَكَيْنِ أَوْ تَكُونَا مِنَ الْخَالِدِينَ (٢٠)
وَقَاسَمَهُمَا إِنِّي لَكُمَا لَمِنَ النَّاصِحِينَ (٢١)
فَدَلَّاهُمَا بِغُرُورٍ فَلَمَّا ذَاقَا الشَّجَرَةَ
بَدَتْ لَهُمَا سَوْآتُهُمَا وَطَفِقَا يَخْصِفَانِ
عَلَيْهِمَا مِن وَرَقِ الْجَنَّةِ وَنَادَاهُمَا
رَبُّهُمَا أَلَمْ أَنْهَكُمَا عَن تِلْكُمَا الشَّجَرَةِ
وَأَقُل لَّكُمَا إِنَّ الشَّيْطَانَ لَكُمَا عَدُوٌّ مُّبِينٌ (٢٢)
قَالَا رَبَّنَا ظَلَمْنَا أَنفُسَنَا وَإِن لَّمْ
تَغْفِرْ لَنَا وَتَرْحَمْنَا لَنَكُونَنَّ مِنَ الْخَاسِرِينَ (٢٣)
قَالَ اهْبِطُوا بَعْضُكُمْ لِبَعْضٍ عَدُوٌّ
وَلَكُمْ فِي الْأَرْضِ مُسْتَقَرٌّ وَمَتَاعٌ
إِلَىٰ حِينٍ (٢٤)

25. He said: "Therein shall ye live, and therein shall ye die: but from it shall ye be taken out (at last)."

(یعنی) کہا کہ اُسی میں تمہارا جینا ہوگا اور اسی میں مرنا اور
اُسی میں سے (قیامت کو زندہ کر کے) نکالے جاؤ گے ﴿۲۵﴾

قَالَ فِيهَا تَحْيَوْنَ وَفِيهَا تَمُوتُونَ وَ
مِنْهَا تُخْرَجُونَ ﴿٢٥﴾

26. O ye Children of Adam! We have bestowed raiment upon you to cover your shame, as well as to be an adornment to you, but the raiment of righteousness— that is the best. Such are among the Signs of Allah, that they may receive admonition!

اے بنی آدم ہم نے تم پر پوشاک اُتاری کہ تمہارا ستر ڈھانکے اور
(تمہارے بدن کو) زینت (دے) اور (جو) پرہیزگاری کا لباس
ہے، وہ سب سے اچھا ہے یہ خدا کی نشانیاں ہیں تاکہ لوگ نصیحت پکڑیں ﴿۲۶﴾

يَٰبَنِيٓ ءَادَمَ قَدْ أَنزَلْنَا عَلَيْكُمْ لِبَاسًا يُوَٰرِي
سَوْءَٰتِكُمْ وَرِيشًا ۖ وَلِبَاسُ ٱلتَّقْوَىٰ ذَٰلِكَ
خَيْرٌ ۚ ذَٰلِكَ مِنْ ءَايَٰتِ ٱللَّهِ لَعَلَّهُمْ يَذَّكَّرُونَ ﴿٢٦﴾

27. O ye Children of Adam! let not Satan seduce you, in the same manner as he got your parents out of the Garden, stripping them of their raiment, to expose their shame: for he and his tribe see you from a position where ye cannot see them: We made the Satans friends (only) to those without Faith.

اے بنی آدم (دیکھنا کہیں) شیطان تمہیں بہکا نہ دے جس طرح تمہارے
ماں باپ کو (بہکا کر) بہشت سے نکلوا دیا اور اُن سے اُنکے کپڑے اُتروا
دیئے تاکہ اُنکے ستر اُنکو کھول کر دکھا دے۔ وہ اور اُسکے بھائی تم کو
ایسی جگہ سے دیکھتے رہتے ہیں جہاں سے تم اُنکو نہیں دیکھ سکتے ہم نے
شیطانوں کو اُنہی لوگوں کا رفیق بنایا ہے جو ایمان نہیں رکھتے ہیں ﴿۲۷﴾

يَٰبَنِيٓ ءَادَمَ لَا يَفْتِنَنَّكُمُ ٱلشَّيْطَٰنُ كَمَآ
أَخْرَجَ أَبَوَيْكُم مِّنَ ٱلْجَنَّةِ يَنزِعُ
عَنْهُمَا لِبَاسَهُمَا لِيُرِيَهُمَا سَوْءَٰتِهِمَآ ۗ إِنَّهُۥ
يَرَىٰكُمْ هُوَ وَقَبِيلُهُۥ مِنْ حَيْثُ لَا تَرَوْنَهُمْ ۗ إِنَّا
جَعَلْنَا ٱلشَّيَٰطِينَ أَوْلِيَآءَ لِلَّذِينَ لَا يُؤْمِنُونَ ﴿٢٧﴾

28. When they commit an indecency, they say: "We found our fathers doing so"; and "Allah commanded us thus": Say: "Nay, Allah never command what is Indecent: do ye say of Allah what ye know not?

اور جب کوئی بے حیائی کا کام کرتے ہیں تو کہتے ہیں کہ ہم نے
اپنے بزرگوں کو اسی طرح کرتے دیکھا ہے اور خدا نے بھی ہم کو یہی حکم دیا ہے
کہہ دو کہ خدا بے حیائی کے کام کرنیکا ہرگز حکم نہیں دیتا۔ بھلا تم
خدا کی نسبت ایسی بات کیوں کہتے ہو جس کا تمہیں علم نہیں ﴿۲۸﴾

وَإِذَا فَعَلُوا۟ فَٰحِشَةً قَالُوا۟ وَجَدْنَا
عَلَيْهَآ ءَابَآءَنَا وَٱللَّهُ أَمَرَنَا بِهَا ۗ قُلْ
إِنَّ ٱللَّهَ لَا يَأْمُرُ بِٱلْفَحْشَآءِ ۖ أَتَقُولُونَ
عَلَى ٱللَّهِ مَا لَا تَعْلَمُونَ ﴿٢٨﴾

29. Say: "My Lord hath commanded justice; and that ye set your whole selves (to Him) at every time and place of prayer, and call upon Him, making your devotion sincere such as He created you in the beginning, so shall ye return."

کہہ دو کہ میرے پروردگار نے تو انصاف کرنیکا حکم دیا ہے اور یہ کہ
ہر نماز کے وقت سیدھا (قبلے کی طرف) رُخ کیا کرو۔ اور خاص
اُسی کی عبادت کرو اور اُسی کو پکارو۔ اُس نے جس طرح تمکو
ابتدا میں پیدا کیا تھا اسی طرح تم پھر پیدا ہو گے ﴿۲۹﴾

قُلْ أَمَرَ رَبِّى بِٱلْقِسْطِ ۖ وَأَقِيمُوا۟ وُجُوهَكُمْ
عِندَ كُلِّ مَسْجِدٍ وَٱدْعُوهُ مُخْلِصِينَ
لَهُ ٱلدِّينَ ۚ كَمَا بَدَأَكُمْ
تَعُودُونَ ﴿٢٩﴾

30. Some He hath guided: others have deserved the loss of their way; in that they took the Satans in preference to Allah, for their friends and protectors, and think that they receive guidance.

ایک فریق کو تو اُس نے ہدایت دی اور ایک فریق پر گمراہی ثابت
ہو چکی۔ اُن لوگوں نے خدا کو چھوڑ کر شیطانوں کو رفیق بنا لیا
اور سمجھتے (یہ) ہیں کہ ہدایت یاب ہیں ﴿۳۰﴾

فَرِيقًا هَدَىٰ وَفَرِيقًا حَقَّ عَلَيْهِمُ ٱلضَّلَٰلَةُ ۗ
إِنَّهُمُ ٱتَّخَذُوا۟ ٱلشَّيَٰطِينَ أَوْلِيَآءَ مِن
دُونِ ٱللَّهِ وَيَحْسَبُونَ أَنَّهُم مُّهْتَدُونَ ﴿٣٠﴾

31. O Children of Adam! wear your beautiful apparel at every time and place of prayer: eat and drink: but waste not by excess, for Allah loveth not the wasters.

اے بنی آدم! ہر نماز کے وقت اپنے تئیں مزین کیا کرو اور
کھاؤ اور پیو اور بے جا نہ اُڑاؤ کہ خدا بے جا اُڑانے والوں
کو دوست نہیں رکھتا ﴿۳۱﴾

يَٰبَنِيٓ ءَادَمَ خُذُوا۟ زِينَتَكُمْ عِندَ كُلِّ
مَسْجِدٍ وَكُلُوا۟ وَٱشْرَبُوا۟ وَلَا تُسْرِفُوٓا۟ ۚ
إِنَّهُۥ لَا يُحِبُّ ٱلْمُسْرِفِينَ ﴿٣١﴾

32. Say: Who hath forbidden the beautiful (gifts) of Allah, which He hath produced for His servants, and the things, clean and pure, (which He hath provided) for sustenance?

پوچھو تو کہ جو زینت (و آرائش) اور کھانے (پینے) کی پاکیزہ چیزیں
خدا نے اپنے بندوں کیلئے پیدا کی ہیں اُن کو حرام کس نے کیا ہے؟
کہہ دو کہ یہ چیزیں دُنیا کی زندگی میں ایمان والوں کیلئے ہیں۔

قُلْ مَنْ حَرَّمَ زِينَةَ ٱللَّهِ ٱلَّتِىٓ أَخْرَجَ
لِعِبَادِهِۦ وَٱلطَّيِّبَٰتِ مِنَ ٱلرِّزْقِ ۚ قُلْ
هِىَ لِلَّذِينَ ءَامَنُوا۟ فِى ٱلْحَيَوٰةِ ٱلدُّنْيَا

say: They are, in the life of this world, for those who believe, (and) purely for them on the Day of Judgment. Thus do We explain the Signs in detail for those who know.
33. Say: The things that my Lord hath indeed forbidden are: indecent deeds, whether open or secret; sins and trespasses against truth or reason; assigning of partners to Allah, for which He hath given no authority; and saying things about Allah of which ye have no knowledge.
34. To every People is a term appointed: when their term is reached, not an hour can they cause delay, nor (an hour) can they advance (it in anticipation).
35. O ye Children of Adam! whenever there come to you Messengers from amongst you, rehearsing My Signs unto you,—those who are righteous and mend (their lives),— on them shall be no fear nor shall they grieve.

36. But those who reject Our Signs and treat them with arrogance,—they are Companions of the Fire, to dwell therein (for ever).
37. Who is more unjust than one who forges a lie against Allah or rejects His Signs? For such, their portion appointed must reach them from the Book (of Decrees): until, when Our messengers (of death) arrive and take their souls, they say: "Where are the things that ye used to invoke besides Allah?" They will reply, "They have left us in the lurch," and they will bear witness against themselves, that they had rejected Allah.
38. He will say: "Enter ye in the company of the Peoples who passed away before you—men and Jinns,—into the Fire. Every time a new People enters, it curses its sister-People (that went before), until they follow each other, all into the Fire. Saith the last about the first: "Our Lord! it is these that misled us: so give them a double punishment in the Fire." He will say:

اور قیامت کے دن خاص انہی کا حصہ ہوں گی۔ اسی طرح
خدا اپنی آیتیں سمجھنے والوں کیلئے کھول کھول کر بیان فرماتا ہے (۳۲)
کہہ دو کہ میرے پروردگار نے تو بے حیائی کی باتوں کو ظاہر ہوں
یا پوشیدہ اور گناہ کو اور ناحق زیادتی کرنے کو حرام کیا ہے۔
اور اس کو بھی کہ تم کسی کو خدا کا شریک بناؤ جس کی اُس نے
کوئی سند نازل نہیں کی اور اس کو بھی کہ خدا کے بارے میں
ایسی باتیں کہو جن کا تمہیں کچھ علم نہیں (۳۳)
اور ہر ایک فرقے کے لئے (موت کا) ایک وقت مقرر ہے جب
وہ آجاتا ہے تو نہ تو ایک گھڑی دیر کر سکتے ہیں نہ جلدی (۳۴)
اے بنی آدم (ہم تم کو یہ نصیحت ہمیشہ کرتے رہے ہیں کہ) جب ہمارے
پیغمبر تمہارے پاس آیا کریں اور ہماری آیتیں تم کو سنایا کریں (تو اُن پر
ایمان لایا کرو کہ) جو شخص (اُن پر ایمان لاکر خدا سے) ڈرتا رہیگا اور
اپنی حالت درست رکھیگا تو ایسے لوگوں کو نہ کچھ خوف ہوگا اور نہ وہ غمناک ہونگے (۳۵)
اور جنہوں نے ہماری آیتوں کو جھٹلایا اور اُن سے سرتابی کی وہی
دوزخی ہیں کہ ہمیشہ اس میں (جلتے) رہیں گے (۳۶)
تو اس سے زیادہ ظالم کون ہے جو خدا پر جھوٹ باندھے
یا اُس کی آیتوں کو جھٹلائے۔ اُن کو اُن کے نصیب کا لکھا ملتا
ہی رہیگا۔ یہاں تک کہ جب اُنکے پاس ہمارے بھیجے ہوئے
(فرشتے) جان نکالنے آئیں گے۔ تو کہیں گے کہ جن کو تم خدا کے
سوا پکارا کرتے تھے۔ وہ (اب) کہاں ہیں؟ وہ کہیں گے (معلوم نہیں)
کہ وہ ہم سے (کہاں) غائب ہوگئے اور اقرار کرینگے کہ بیشک وہ کافر تھے (۳۷)
تو خدا فرمائے گا کہ جنوں اور انسانوں کی جو جماعتیں تم سے پہلے
ہو گزری ہیں اُن ہی کیساتھ تم بھی داخل جہنم ہو جاؤ۔ جب ایک
جماعت (وہاں) جا داخل ہوگی تو اپنی (مذہبی) بہن (یعنی اپنے جیسی
دوسری جماعت) پر لعنت کریگی۔ یہانتک کہ جب سب اسمیں داخل
ہو جائینگے تو پچھلی جماعت پہلی کی نسبت کہے گی کہ اے پروردگار
ان ہی لوگوں نے ہمکو گمراہ کیا تھا تو انکو آتش جہنم کا دگنا عذاب دے

خَالِصَةً يَّوْمَ الْقِيٰمَةِ ۗ كَذٰلِكَ نُفَصِّلُ
الْاٰيٰتِ لِقَوْمٍ يَّعْلَمُوْنَ ﴿۳۲﴾
قُلْ اِنَّمَا حَرَّمَ رَبِّيَ الْفَوَاحِشَ مَا
ظَهَرَ مِنْهَا وَمَا بَطَنَ وَالْاِثْمَ وَالْبَغْيَ
بِغَيْرِ الْحَقِّ وَاَنْ تُشْرِكُوْا بِاللّٰهِ مَا لَمْ
يُنَزِّلْ بِهٖ سُلْطٰنًا وَّاَنْ تَقُوْلُوْا عَلَى
اللّٰهِ مَا لَا تَعْلَمُوْنَ ﴿۳۳﴾
وَلِكُلِّ اُمَّةٍ اَجَلٌ ۚ فَاِذَا جَآءَ اَجَلُهُمْ
لَا يَسْتَاْخِرُوْنَ سَاعَةً وَّلَا يَسْتَقْدِمُوْنَ ﴿۳۴﴾
يٰبَنِيْٓ اٰدَمَ اِمَّا يَاْتِيَنَّكُمْ رُسُلٌ مِّنْكُمْ
يَقُصُّوْنَ عَلَيْكُمْ اٰيٰتِيْ ۙ فَمَنِ اتَّقٰى وَ
اَصْلَحَ فَلَا خَوْفٌ عَلَيْهِمْ وَلَا هُمْ
يَحْزَنُوْنَ ﴿۳۵﴾
وَالَّذِيْنَ كَذَّبُوْا بِاٰيٰتِنَا وَاسْتَكْبَرُوْا عَنْهَآ
اُولٰٓئِكَ اَصْحٰبُ النَّارِ ۚ هُمْ فِيْهَا خٰلِدُوْنَ ﴿۳۶﴾
فَمَنْ اَظْلَمُ مِمَّنِ افْتَرٰى عَلَى اللّٰهِ كَذِبًا
اَوْ كَذَّبَ بِاٰيٰتِهٖ ۗ اُولٰٓئِكَ يَنَالُهُمْ نَصِيْبُهُمْ
مِّنَ الْكِتٰبِ ۗ حَتّٰٓى اِذَا جَآءَتْهُمْ رُسُلُنَا
يَتَوَفَّوْنَهُمْ ۙ قَالُوْٓا اَيْنَ مَا كُنْتُمْ تَدْعُوْنَ
مِنْ دُوْنِ اللّٰهِ ۗ قَالُوْا ضَلُّوْا عَنَّا وَشَهِدُوْا
عَلٰٓى اَنْفُسِهِمْ اَنَّهُمْ كَانُوْا كٰفِرِيْنَ ﴿۳۷﴾
قَالَ ادْخُلُوْا فِيْٓ اُمَمٍ قَدْ خَلَتْ مِنْ
قَبْلِكُمْ مِّنَ الْجِنِّ وَالْاِنْسِ فِي النَّارِ ۗ كُلَّمَا
دَخَلَتْ اُمَّةٌ لَّعَنَتْ اُخْتَهَا ۗ حَتّٰٓى اِذَا
ادَّارَكُوْا فِيْهَا جَمِيْعًا ۙ قَالَتْ اُخْرٰىهُمْ
لِاُوْلٰىهُمْ رَبَّنَا هٰٓؤُلَآءِ اَضَلُّوْنَا فَاٰتِهِمْ
عَذَابًا ضِعْفًا مِّنَ النَّارِ ۗ قَالَ لِكُلٍّ

"Doubled for all": but this ye do not know.

39. Then the first will say to the last: "See then! no advantage have ye over us; so taste ye of the Chastisement for all that ye did!"

40. To those who reject Our Signs and treat them with arrogance, no opening will there be of the gates of heaven, nor will they enter the Garden, until the camel can pass through the eye of the needle: such is Our reward for those in sin.

41. For them there is hell, as a couch (below) and folds and folds of covering above: such is Our requital of those who do wrong.

42. But those who believe and work righteousness,—no burden do We place on any soul, but that which it can bear,— they will be Companions of the Garden, therein to dwell (for ever).

43. And We shall remove from their hearts any rancour; beneath them will be rivers flowing;—and they shall say: "Praise be to Allah, Who hath guided us to this (felicity): never could we have found guidance, had it not been for the guidance of Allah: indeed it was the truth that the Messengers of our Lord brought unto us." And they shall hear the cry: "Behold! the Garden before you! Ye have been made its inheritors, for your deeds (of righteousness)."

44. The Companions of the Garden will call out to the Companions of the Fire: "We have indeed found the promises of our Lord to us true have you also found your Lord's promises true?" They shall say, "Yes": but a Crier shall proclaim between them: "The curse of Allah is on the wrong-doers;—

45. "Those who would hinder (men) from the path of Allah desiring to make something crooked: they were those who denied the Hereafter."

46. Between them shall be a veil, and on the Heights will be men who would know everyone by his marks: they will call out to the

خدا فرمائیگا کہ (تم) سب کو دُگنا (عذاب دیا جائیگا) مگر تم نہیں جانتے ﴿۳۸﴾
اور پہلی جماعت پچھلی سے کہیگی کہ تم کو ہم پر کچھ بھی فضیلت نہ ہوئی۔
تو جو (عمل) تم کیا کرتے تھے اسکے بدلے میں عذاب کے مزے چکھو ﴿۳۹﴾
جن لوگوں نے ہماری آیتوں کو جھٹلایا اور اُن سے سرتابی کی
اُن کے لئے نہ آسمان کے دروازے کھولے جائینگے اور نہ وہ بہشت
میں داخل ہونگے یہانتک کہ اونٹ سوئی کے ناکے میں سے نہ نکل جائے
اور گنہگاروں کو ہم ایسی ہی سزا دیا کرتے ہیں ﴿۴۰﴾
ایسے لوگوں کیلئے (نیچے) بچھونا بھی (آتش) جہنم کا ہوگا اور اوپر
سے اوڑھنا بھی (اسی کا)، اور ظالموں کو ہم ایسی ہی سزا دیتے ہیں ﴿۴۱﴾
اور جو لوگ ایمان لائے اور عمل نیک کرتے رہے (اور ہم عملوں کیلئے)
کسی شخص کو اُسکی طاقت سے زیادہ تکلیف دیتے ہی نہیں۔ ایسے ہی
لوگ اہل بہشت ہیں (کہ) اس میں ہمیشہ رہیں گے ﴿۴۲﴾
اور جو کینے اُنکے سینوں میں ہونگے ہم سب نکال ڈالینگے اُن کے
(محلوں کے) نیچے نہریں بہ رہی ہونگی۔ اور کہیں گے کہ خدا کا شکر ہے
جس نے ہمکو یہاں کا رستہ دکھایا اور اگر خدا ہم کو رستہ نہ دکھاتا
تو ہم رستہ نہ پا سکتے۔ بیشک ہمارے پروردگار کے رسُول حق بات
لیکر آئے تھے۔ اور (اُس روز) منادی کردیجائیگی کہ تم اُن اعمال کے صلے
میں جو (دنیا میں) کرتے تھے اس بہشت کے مالک بنا دیئے گئے ہو ﴿۴۳﴾
اور اہل بہشت دوزخیوں سے پکار کر کہینگے کہ جو وعدہ ہمارے پروردگار
نے ہم سے کیا تھا ہم نے تو اُسے سچا پالیا۔ بھلا جو وعدہ تمہارے
پروردگار نے تم سے کیا تھا تم نے بھی اُسے سچا پایا؟ وہ کہیں گے
ہاں۔ تو (اُس وقت) اُن میں ایک پکارنے والا پکار دے گا
کہ بے انصافوں پر خدا کی لعنت ﴿۴۴﴾
جو خدا کی راہ سے روکتے اور اس میں کجی ڈھونڈتے اور
آخرت سے انکار کرتے تھے ﴿۴۵﴾
ان دونوں (یعنی بہشت اور دوزخ) کے درمیان (اعراف نام) ایک دیوار ہوگی اور اعراف پر کچھ
آدمی ہونگے جو سب کو انکی صورتوں سے پہچان لینگے تو وہ اہل بہشت کو پکار کر کہینگے کہ

ضِعْفٌ وَّلٰكِنْ لَّا تَعْلَمُوْنَ ﴿٣٨﴾
وَقَالَتْ اُوْلٰىهُمْ لِاُخْرٰىهُمْ فَمَا كَانَ لَكُمْ عَلَيْنَا
مِنْ فَضْلٍ فَذُوْقُوا الْعَذَابَ بِمَا كُنْتُمْ تَكْسِبُوْنَ ﴿٣٩﴾
اِنَّ الَّذِيْنَ كَذَّبُوْا بِاٰيٰتِنَا وَاسْتَكْبَرُوْا
عَنْهَا لَا تُفَتَّحُ لَهُمْ اَبْوَابُ السَّمَآءِ وَلَا
يَدْخُلُوْنَ الْجَنَّةَ حَتّٰى يَلِجَ الْجَمَلُ
فِيْ سَمِّ الْخِيَاطِ ۭ وَكَذٰلِكَ نَجْزِي الْمُجْرِمِيْنَ ﴿٤٠﴾
لَهُمْ مِّنْ جَهَنَّمَ مِهَادٌ وَّمِنْ فَوْقِهِمْ
غَوَاشٍ ۭ وَكَذٰلِكَ نَجْزِي الظّٰلِمِيْنَ ﴿٤١﴾
وَالَّذِيْنَ اٰمَنُوْا وَعَمِلُوا الصّٰلِحٰتِ لَا
نُكَلِّفُ نَفْسًا اِلَّا وُسْعَهَآ اُولٰۗىِٕكَ
اَصْحٰبُ الْجَنَّةِ ۚ هُمْ فِيْهَا خٰلِدُوْنَ ﴿٤٢﴾
وَنَزَعْنَا مَا فِيْ صُدُوْرِهِمْ مِّنْ غِلٍّ
تَجْرِيْ مِنْ تَحْتِهِمُ الْاَنْهٰرُ ۚ وَقَالُوا الْحَمْدُ
لِلّٰهِ الَّذِيْ هَدٰىنَا لِهٰذَا ۣ وَمَا كُنَّا لِنَهْتَدِيَ
لَوْلَآ اَنْ هَدٰىنَا اللّٰهُ ۚ لَقَدْ جَاۗءَتْ
رُسُلُ رَبِّنَا بِالْحَقِّ ۭ وَنُوْدُوْٓا اَنْ تِلْكُمُ
الْجَنَّةُ اُوْرِثْتُمُوْهَا بِمَا كُنْتُمْ تَعْمَلُوْنَ ﴿٤٣﴾
وَنَادٰٓى اَصْحٰبُ الْجَنَّةِ اَصْحٰبَ النَّارِ اَنْ
قَدْ وَجَدْنَا مَا وَعَدَنَا رَبُّنَا حَقًّا فَهَلْ
وَجَدْتُّمْ مَّا وَعَدَ رَبُّكُمْ حَقًّا ۭ قَالُوْا نَعَمْ ۚ
فَاَذَّنَ مُؤَذِّنٌۢ بَيْنَهُمْ اَنْ لَّعْنَةُ اللّٰهِ
عَلَى الظّٰلِمِيْنَ ﴿٤٤﴾
الَّذِيْنَ يَصُدُّوْنَ عَنْ سَبِيْلِ اللّٰهِ وَ
يَبْغُوْنَهَا عِوَجًا ۚ وَهُمْ بِالْاٰخِرَةِ كٰفِرُوْنَ ﴿٤٥﴾
وَبَيْنَهُمَا حِجَابٌ ۚ وَعَلَى الْاَعْرَافِ رِجَالٌ
يَّعْرِفُوْنَ كُلًّا بِسِيْمٰىهُمْ ۚ وَنَادَوْا اَصْحٰبَ الْجَنَّةِ

Companions of the Garden, "Peace be upon you" they have not entered it, but they still hoped to (enter it).

47. When their eyes shall be turned towards the Companions of the Fire, they will say: "Our Lord! send us not to the company of the wrong-doers".

48. The men on the Heights will call to certain men whom they will know from their marks, saying "Of what profit to you were your hoards and your arrogant ways?

49. "Behold! are these not the men whom you swore that Allah with His Mercy would never bless? Enter ye the Garden: no fear shall be on you, nor shall ye grieve."

50. The Companions of the Fire will call to the Companions of the Garden: "Pour down to us water or anything that Allah doth provide for your sustenance." They will say: "Both these things hath Allah forbidden to those who rejected Him;—

51. "Such as took their religion to be mere amusement and play, and were deceived by the life of the world." That day shall We forget them as they forgot the meeting of this day of theirs, and as they were wont to reject Our Signs.

52. For We had certainly sent unto them a Book, based on knowledge, which We explained in detail,—a guide and a mercy to all who believe.

53. Are they waiting for its fulfilment? On the day when it is fulfilled those who have forgotten it before will say: "The Messengers of our Lord did indeed bring true (tidings). Have we no intercessors now to intercede on our behalf? Or could we be sent back? Then should we behave differently from our behaviour in the past." In fact they will have lost their souls, and

تم پر سلامتی ہو۔ یہ لوگ (ابھی) بہشت میں داخل تو نہیں ہوئے ہونگے مگر امید رکھتے ہونگے (۴۶)
اور جب اُن کی نگاہیں پلٹ کر اہلِ دوزخ کی طرف جائیں گی
تو عرض کریں گے کہ اے ہمارے پروردگار ہم کو ظالم لوگوں کے
ساتھ (شامل) نہ کیجیو (۴۷)
اور اہلِ اعراف (کافر) لوگوں کو جنہیں اُنکی صورتوں سے شناخت
کرتے ہونگے پکاریں گے اور کہیں گے (کہ آج) نہ تو تمہاری جماعت
ہی تمہارے کچھ کام آئی اور نہ تمہارا تکبر (ہی سُود مند ہوا) (۴۸)
(پھر مومنوں کی طرف اشارہ کر کے کہینگے) کیا یہ وہی لوگ ہیں جنکے بارے
میں تم قسمیں کھایا کرتے تھے کہ خدا اپنی رحمت سے انکی دستگیری نہیں کریگا (تو مومنو تم
بہشت میں داخل ہو جاؤ تمہیں کچھ خوف نہیں اور نہ تمکو کچھ رنج و اندوہ ہوگا (۴۹)
اور دوزخی بہشتیوں سے (گڑگڑا کر) کہیں گے کہ کسی قدر ہم پر
پانی بہاؤ یا جو رزق خدا نے تمہیں عنایت فرمایا ہے ان میں سے
(کچھ ہمیں بھی دو) وہ جواب دینگے کہ خدا نے بہشت کا پانی
اور رزق کافروں پر حرام کر دیا ہے (۵۰)
جنہوں نے اپنے دین کو تماشا اور کھیل بنا رکھا تھا اور دُنیا
کی زندگی نے اُن کو دھوکے میں ڈال رکھا تھا۔ تو جس طرح
یہ لوگ اس دن کے آنے کو بھولے ہوئے اور ہماری آیتوں
سے منکر ہو رہے تھے اسی طرح آج ہم بھی انہیں بھلا دینگے (۵۱)
اور ہم نے اُن کے پاس کتاب پہنچا دی ہے جس کو علم و دانش
کے ساتھ کھول کھول کر بیان کر دیا ہے (اور) وہ مومن لوگوں
کے لئے ہدایت اور رحمت ہے (۵۲)
کیا یہ لوگ اسکے وقوع کے منتظر ہیں جس دن وہ واقع
ہو جائیگا۔ تو جو لوگ اسکو پہلے سے بھولے ہوئے ہونگے وہ بول
اُٹھیں گے کہ بیشک ہمارے پروردگار کے رسُول حق لیکر آئے تھے بھلا
(آج) ہمارے کوئی سفارشی ہیں کہ ہماری سفارش کریں یا ہم (دنیا میں) پھر
لوٹا دیئے جائیں کہ جو عمل (بد) ہم (پہلے) کرتے تھے (وہ نہ کریں بلکہ) اُنکے
سوا اور (نیک) عمل کریں۔ بیشک ان لوگوں نے اپنا نقصان

أَن سَلَٰمٌ عَلَيْكُمْ لَمْ يَدْخُلُوهَا وَهُمْ يَطْمَعُونَ (٤٦)
وَإِذَا صُرِفَتْ أَبْصَٰرُهُمْ تِلْقَآءَ أَصْحَٰبِ
ٱلنَّارِ قَالُوا رَبَّنَا لَا تَجْعَلْنَا مَعَ ٱلْقَوْمِ
ٱلظَّٰلِمِينَ (٤٧)
وَنَادَىٰٓ أَصْحَٰبُ ٱلْأَعْرَافِ رِجَالًا يَعْرِفُونَهُم
بِسِيمَىٰهُمْ قَالُوا مَآ أَغْنَىٰ عَنكُمْ جَمْعُكُمْ
وَمَا كُنتُمْ تَسْتَكْبِرُونَ (٤٨)
أَهَٰٓؤُلَآءِ ٱلَّذِينَ أَقْسَمْتُمْ لَا يَنَالُهُمُ ٱللَّهُ
بِرَحْمَةٍ ٱدْخُلُوا ٱلْجَنَّةَ لَا خَوْفٌ عَلَيْكُمْ
وَلَآ أَنتُمْ تَحْزَنُونَ (٤٩)
وَنَادَىٰٓ أَصْحَٰبُ ٱلنَّارِ أَصْحَٰبَ ٱلْجَنَّةِ
أَنْ أَفِيضُوا عَلَيْنَا مِنَ ٱلْمَآءِ أَوْ مِمَّا
رَزَقَكُمُ ٱللَّهُ قَالُوٓا إِنَّ ٱللَّهَ حَرَّمَهُمَا
عَلَى ٱلْكَٰفِرِينَ (٥٠)
ٱلَّذِينَ ٱتَّخَذُوا دِينَهُمْ لَهْوًا وَلَعِبًا وَ
غَرَّتْهُمُ ٱلْحَيَوٰةُ ٱلدُّنْيَا فَٱلْيَوْمَ
نَنسَىٰهُمْ كَمَا نَسُوا لِقَآءَ يَوْمِهِمْ هَٰذَا
وَمَا كَانُوا بِـَٔايَٰتِنَا يَجْحَدُونَ (٥١)
وَلَقَدْ جِئْنَٰهُم بِكِتَٰبٍ فَصَّلْنَٰهُ عَلَىٰ
عِلْمٍ هُدًى وَرَحْمَةً لِّقَوْمٍ
يُؤْمِنُونَ (٥٢)
هَلْ يَنظُرُونَ إِلَّا تَأْوِيلَهُ يَوْمَ يَأْتِى
تَأْوِيلُهُ يَقُولُ ٱلَّذِينَ نَسُوهُ مِن قَبْلُ
قَدْ جَآءَتْ رُسُلُ رَبِّنَا بِٱلْحَقِّ فَهَل
لَّنَا مِن شُفَعَآءَ فَيَشْفَعُوا لَنَآ أَوْ نُرَدُّ
فَنَعْمَلَ غَيْرَ ٱلَّذِى كُنَّا نَعْمَلُ قَدْ
خَسِرُوٓا أَنفُسَهُمْ وَضَلَّ عَنْهُم مَّا

the things they forged will leave them in the lurch.

54. Your Guardian Lord is Allah, Who created the heavens and the earth in six Days, then He settled Himself on the Throne: He draweth the night as a veil o'er the day, each seeking the other in rapid succession: and the sun, the moon, and the stars, (all) are subserviant by His Command. Verily, His are the creation and the Command blessed be Allah, the Cherisher and Sustainer of the Worlds!

55. Call on your Lord with humility and in private: for Allah loveth not those who trespass beyond bounds.

56. Do not mischief on the earth, after it hath been set in order, but call on Him with fear and longing (in your hearts): for the Mercy of Allah is (always) near to those who do good.

57. It is He Who sendeth the Winds like heralds of glad tidings, going before His Mercy: when they have carried the heavy-laden clouds. We drive them to a land that is dead, make rain to descend thereon, and produce every kind of harvest therewith: thus shall We raise up the dead: perchance ye may remember.

58. From the land that is clean and good, by the Will of its Cherisher, springs up produce, (rich) after its kind: but from the land that is bad, springs up nothing but that which is scanty thus do we explain the Signs by various (symbols) to those who are grateful.

59. We sent Noah to his people. He said: "O my people ! worship Allah! ye have no other god but Him. I fear for you the Punishment of a dreadful Day!"

60. The leaders of his people Said: "Ah! we see thee in evident error."

كَانُوا يَفْتَرُونَ ۝٥٣
کیا اور جو کچھ یہ افترا کیا کرتے تھے اُن سے سب جاتا رہا (۵۳)

إِنَّ رَبَّكُمُ اللّٰهُ الَّذِي خَلَقَ السَّمٰوٰتِ
کچھ شک نہیں کہ تمہارا پروردگار خدا ہی ہے جس نے آسمانوں

وَالْأَرْضَ فِي سِتَّةِ أَيَّامٍ ثُمَّ اسْتَوٰى
اور زمین کو چھ دن میں پیدا کیا پھر عرش پر جا ٹھیرا۔ وہی رات

عَلَى الْعَرْشِ يُغْشِي الَّيْلَ النَّهَارَ
کو دن کا لباس پہناتا ہے کہ وہ اسکے پیچھے دوڑتا چلا آتا ہے

يَطْلُبُهُ حَثِيثًا وَّالشَّمْسَ وَالْقَمَرَ وَ
اور اسی نے سورج اور چاند اور ستاروں کو پیدا کیا سب اسکے حکم کے مطابق

النُّجُومَ مُسَخَّرٰتٍ بِأَمْرِهِ أَلَا لَهُ الْخَلْقُ
کام میں لگے ہوئے ہیں۔ دیکھو سب مخلوق بھی اسی کی ہے اور حکم بھی اُسی کا

وَالْأَمْرُ تَبٰرَكَ اللّٰهُ رَبُّ الْعٰلَمِينَ ۝٥٤
ہے۔ یہ خدائے رب العالمین بڑی برکت والا ہے (۵۴)

اُدْعُوا رَبَّكُمْ تَضَرُّعًا وَّخُفْيَةً إِنَّهُ
(لوگو) اپنے پروردگار سے عاجزی سے اور چپکے چپکے دعائیں مانگا کرو۔

لَا يُحِبُّ الْمُعْتَدِينَ ۝٥٥
وہ حد سے بڑھنے والوں کو دوست نہیں رکھتا (۵۵)

وَلَا تُفْسِدُوا فِي الْأَرْضِ بَعْدَ إِصْلَاحِهَا
اور ملک میں اصلاح کے بعد خرابی نہ کرنا اور خدا سے خوف

وَادْعُوهُ خَوْفًا وَّطَمَعًا إِنَّ رَحْمَتَ اللّٰهِ
کرتے ہوئے اور اُمید رکھکر دعائیں مانگتے رہنا۔ کچھ شک نہیں کہ

قَرِيبٌ مِّنَ الْمُحْسِنِينَ ۝٥٦
خدا کی رحمت نیکی کرنے والوں سے قریب ہے (۵۶)

وَهُوَ الَّذِي يُرْسِلُ الرِّيٰحَ بُشْرًا بَيْنَ
اور وہی تو ہے جو اپنی رحمت (یعنی مینہ) سے پہلے ہواؤں کو خوشخبری (بنا کر)

يَدَيْ رَحْمَتِهِ حَتّٰى إِذَا أَقَلَّتْ سَحَابًا
بھیجتا ہے۔ یہاں تک کہ جب وہ بھاری بھاری بادلوں کو اٹھا لاتی ہے تو ہم

ثِقَالًا سُقْنٰهُ لِبَلَدٍ مَّيِّتٍ فَأَنْزَلْنَا
اسکو ایک مری ہوئی بستی کیطرف ہانک دیتے ہیں پھر بادل سے مینہ برساتے ہیں پھر

بِهِ الْمَاءَ فَأَخْرَجْنَا بِهِ مِنْ كُلِّ الثَّمَرٰتِ
مینہ سے ہر طرح کے پھل پیدا کرتے ہیں۔ اسی طرح ہم مردوں کو (زمین سے) زندہ کرکے

كَذٰلِكَ نُخْرِجُ الْمَوْتٰى لَعَلَّكُمْ تَذَكَّرُونَ ۝٥٧
باہر نکالینگے۔ یہ آیات اسلئے بیان کی جاتی ہیں تاکہ تم نصیحت پکڑو (۵۷)

وَالْبَلَدُ الطَّيِّبُ يَخْرُجُ نَبَاتُهُ بِإِذْنِ
(جو) زمین پاکیزہ (ہے) اس میں سے سبزہ بھی پروردگار کے حکم سے (نفیس ہی)

رَبِّهِ وَالَّذِي خَبُثَ لَا يَخْرُجُ إِلَّا
نکلتا ہے اور جو خراب ہے اُس میں جو کچھ نکلتا ہے ناقص ہوتا

نَكِدًا كَذٰلِكَ نُصَرِّفُ الْاٰيٰتِ لِقَوْمٍ
ہے۔ اسی طرح ہم آیتوں کو شکرگزار لوگوں کے لئے پھیر پھیر کر

يَّشْكُرُونَ ۝٥٨
بیان کرتے ہیں (۵۸)

لَقَدْ أَرْسَلْنَا نُوحًا إِلٰى قَوْمِهِ فَقَالَ
ہم نے نوح کو اُن کی قوم کی طرف بھیجا تو انہوں نے (اُن سے)

يٰقَوْمِ اعْبُدُوا اللّٰهَ مَا لَكُمْ مِّنْ إِلٰهٍ
کہا اے میری برادری کے لوگو خدا کی عبادت کرو اس کے سوا

غَيْرُهُ إِنِّي أَخَافُ عَلَيْكُمْ عَذَابَ
تمہارا کوئی معبود نہیں مجھے تمہارے بارے میں بڑے دن

يَوْمٍ عَظِيمٍ ۝٥٩
کے عذاب کا (بہت ہی) ڈر ہے (۵۹)

قَالَ الْمَلَأُ مِنْ قَوْمِهِ إِنَّا لَنَرٰىكَ فِي
تو جو اُن کی قوم میں سردار تھے وہ کہنے لگے کہ ہم تمہیں صریح

ضَلٰلٍ مُّبِينٍ ۝٦٠
گمراہی میں (مبتلا) دیکھتے ہیں (۶۰)

61. He said: "O my people! there is no error in me: on the contrary I am a messenger from the Lord and Cherisher of the Worlds!"

62. "I but convey to you" the Message of my Lord. Sincere is my advice to you, and I know from Allah something that ye know not.

63. "Do ye wonder that there hath come to you a reminder from your Lord, through a man of your own people, to warn you,—so that ye may fear Allah and haply receive His Mercy?"

64. But they rejected him, and We delivered him, and those with him, in the Ark: but We overwhelmed in the Flood those who rejected Our Signs, they were indeed a blind people!

65. To the 'Ād people, (We sent) Hûd, one of their (own) brethren: he said: "O my people! worship Allah! ye have no other god but Him. Will ye not fear (Allah)?"

66. The leaders of the unbelievers among his people said: "Ah! we see thou art in folly!" and "We think thou art a liar!"

67. He said: "O my people! there is no folly in me" but (I am) a messenger from the Lord and Cherisher of the Worlds!

68. "I but convey to you the messages of my Lord: I am to you a sincere and trustworthy adviser".

69. "Do ye wonder that there hath come to you a message from your Lord through a man of your own people, to warn you? Call in remembrance that He made you inheritors after the people of Noah, and gave you a stature tall among the nations. Call in remembrance the benefits (ye have received) from Allah: that so ye may prosper."

70. They said: "Comest thou to us, that we may worship Allah alone, and give up that which our fathers used to worship bring us what thou threatenest us with, if so be that thou tellest the truth!"

قَالَ يٰقَوْمِ لَيْسَ بِيْ ضَلٰلَةٌ وَّلٰكِنِّيْ
رَسُوْلٌ مِّنْ رَّبِّ الْعٰلَمِيْنَ ﴿٦١﴾
اُبَلِّغُكُمْ رِسٰلٰتِ رَبِّيْ وَاَنْصَحُ لَكُمْ وَاَعْلَمُ
مِنَ اللّٰهِ مَا لَا تَعْلَمُوْنَ ﴿٦٢﴾
اَوَعَجِبْتُمْ اَنْ جَآءَكُمْ ذِكْرٌ مِّنْ رَّبِّكُمْ
عَلٰى رَجُلٍ مِّنْكُمْ لِيُنْذِرَكُمْ وَلِتَتَّقُوْا
وَلَعَلَّكُمْ تُرْحَمُوْنَ ﴿٦٣﴾
فَكَذَّبُوْهُ فَاَنْجَيْنٰهُ وَالَّذِيْنَ مَعَهٗ فِي
الْفُلْكِ وَاَغْرَقْنَا الَّذِيْنَ كَذَّبُوْا بِاٰيٰتِنَا ؕ
ع ١٥ اِنَّهُمْ كَانُوْا قَوْمًا عَمِيْنَ ﴿٦٤﴾
وَاِلٰى عَادٍ اَخَاهُمْ هُوْدًا ؕ قَالَ يٰقَوْمِ
اعْبُدُوا اللّٰهَ مَا لَكُمْ مِّنْ اِلٰهٍ غَيْرُهٗ ؕ
اَفَلَا تَتَّقُوْنَ ﴿٦٥﴾
قَالَ الْمَلَاُ الَّذِيْنَ كَفَرُوْا مِنْ قَوْمِهٖۤ اِنَّا لَنَرٰىكَ
فِيْ سَفَاهَةٍ وَّاِنَّا لَنَظُنُّكَ مِنَ الْكٰذِبِيْنَ ﴿٦٦﴾
قَالَ يٰقَوْمِ لَيْسَ بِيْ سَفَاهَةٌ وَّلٰكِنِّيْ
رَسُوْلٌ مِّنْ رَّبِّ الْعٰلَمِيْنَ ﴿٦٧﴾
اُبَلِّغُكُمْ رِسٰلٰتِ رَبِّيْ وَاَنَا لَكُمْ نَاصِحٌ
اَمِيْنٌ ﴿٦٨﴾
اَوَعَجِبْتُمْ اَنْ جَآءَكُمْ ذِكْرٌ مِّنْ رَّبِّكُمْ
عَلٰى رَجُلٍ مِّنْكُمْ لِيُنْذِرَكُمْ ؕ وَاذْكُرُوْۤا
اِذْ جَعَلَكُمْ خُلَفَآءَ مِنْۢ بَعْدِ قَوْمِ
نُوْحٍ وَّزَادَكُمْ فِي الْخَلْقِ بَصْطَةً ۚ
فَاذْكُرُوْۤا اٰلَآءَ اللّٰهِ لَعَلَّكُمْ تُفْلِحُوْنَ ﴿٦٩﴾
قَالُوْۤا اَجِئْتَنَا لِنَعْبُدَ اللّٰهَ وَحْدَهٗ وَ
نَذَرَ مَا كَانَ يَعْبُدُ اٰبَآؤُنَا ۚ فَاْتِنَا بِمَا
تَعِدُنَآ اِنْ كُنْتَ مِنَ الصّٰدِقِيْنَ ﴿٧٠﴾

اُنہوں نے کہا اے قوم مجھ میں کسی طرح کی گمراہی نہیں ہے بلکہ
میں پروردگار عالم کا پیغمبر ہوں ﴿٦١﴾
تمہیں اپنے پروردگار کے پیغام پہنچاتا ہوں اور تمہاری خیرخواہی کرتا
ہوں اور مجھ کو خدا کی طرف سے ایسی باتیں معلوم ہیں جن سے تم بےخبر ہو ﴿٦٢﴾
کیا تم کو اس بات سے تعجب ہوا ہے کہ تم میں سے ایک شخص کے ہاتھ
تمہارے پروردگار کی طرف سے تمہارے پاس نصیحت آئی تاکہ وہ
تم کو ڈرائے اور تاکہ تم پرہیزگار بنو اور تاکہ تم پر رحم کیا جائے ﴿٦٣﴾
مگر ان لوگوں نے ان کی تکذیب کی۔ تو ہم نے نوح کو اور جو ان کے ساتھ کشتی
میں سوار تھے ان کو تو بچا لیا اور جن لوگوں نے ہماری آیتوں کو جھٹلایا تھا
انہیں غرق کر دیا کچھ شک نہیں کہ وہ اندھے لوگ تھے ﴿٦٤﴾
اور اسی طرح قوم عاد کی طرف ان کے بھائی ہود کو بھیجا۔ انہوں
نے کہا کہ بھائیو خدا ہی کی عبادت کرو۔ اس کے سوا تمہارا کوئی
معبود نہیں کیا تم ڈرتے نہیں؟ ﴿٦٥﴾
تو ان کی قوم کے سردار جو کافر تھے کہنے لگے کہ تم ہمیں احمق نظر
آتے ہو اور ہم تمہیں جھوٹا خیال کرتے ہیں ﴿٦٦﴾
انہوں نے کہا کہ میری قوم! مجھ میں حماقت کی کوئی بات نہیں ہے
بلکہ میں رب العالمین کا پیغمبر ہوں ﴿٦٧﴾
میں تمہیں خدا کے پیغام پہنچاتا ہوں اور تمہارا امانتدار
خیرخواہ ہوں ﴿٦٨﴾
کیا تم کو اس بات سے تعجب ہوا ہے کہ تم میں سے ایک شخص
کے ہاتھ تمہارے پروردگار کی طرف سے تمہارے پاس نصیحت آئی
تاکہ وہ تمہیں ڈرائے۔ اور یاد تو کرو جب اس نے تم کو قوم نوح
کے بعد سردار بنایا اور تم کو پھیلاؤ زیادہ دیا پس خدا کی
نعمتوں کو یاد کرو تاکہ نجات حاصل کرو ﴿٦٩﴾
وہ کہنے لگے کیا تم ہمارے پاس اس لئے آئے ہو کہ ہم اکیلے خدا ہی
کی عبادت کریں اور جن کو ہمارے باپ دادا پوجتے چلے آئے ہیں
ان کو چھوڑ دیں؟ تو اگر سچے ہو تو جس چیز سے ہمیں ڈراتے ہو اسے لے آؤ ﴿٧٠﴾

71. He said: "Punishment and wrath have already come upon you from your Lord: dispute ye with me over names which ye have devised—ye and your fathers,—without authority from Allah? Then wait: I am amongst you, also waiting."

ھود نے کہا کہ تمہارے پروردگار کی طرف سے تم پر عذاب اور غضب
رکا نازل ہونا مقرر ہو چکا ہے کیا تم مجھ سے ایسے ناموں کے
بارے میں جھگڑتے ہو جو تم نے اور تمہارے باپ دادا نے (اپنی
طرف سے) رکھ لئے ہیں جن کی خدا نے کوئی سند نازل نہیں کی۔
تو تم بھی انتظار کرو میں بھی تمہارے ساتھ انتظار کرتا ہوں (٧١)

قَالَ قَدْ وَقَعَ عَلَيْكُمْ مِّنْ رَّبِّكُمْ رِجْسٌ
وَّغَضَبٌ أَتُجَادِلُوْنَنِيْ فِيْ أَسْمَاءٍ
سَمَّيْتُمُوْهَا أَنْتُمْ وَآبَاؤُكُمْ مَّا نَزَّلَ اللّٰهُ
بِهَا مِنْ سُلْطٰنٍ فَانْتَظِرُوْا إِنِّيْ مَعَكُمْ
مِّنَ الْمُنْتَظِرِيْنَ (٧١)

72. We saved him and those who adhered to him, by Our Mercy and We cut off the roots of those who rejected Our Signs and did not believe.

پھر ہم نے ہود کو اور جو لوگ اُن کے ساتھ تھے اُن کو نجات
بخشی اور جنہوں نے ہماری آیتوں کو جھٹلایا تھا اُن کی جڑ
کاٹ دی۔ اور وہ ایمان لانے والے تھے ہی نہیں (٧٢)

فَأَنْجَيْنٰهُ وَالَّذِيْنَ مَعَهٗ بِرَحْمَةٍ مِّنَّا
وَقَطَعْنَا دَابِرَ الَّذِيْنَ كَذَّبُوْا بِاٰيٰتِنَا
وَمَا كَانُوْا مُؤْمِنِيْنَ (٧٢)

73. To the Thamûd people (We sent) Ṣâlih, one of their own brethren: he said: "O my people! worship Allah; ye have no other god but Him. Now hath come unto you a clear (Sign) from your Lord! This she-camel of Allah is a Sign unto you: so leave her to graze in Allah's earth, and let her come to no harm, or ye shall be seized with a grievous punishment."

اور قوم ثمود کی طرف اُن کے بھائی صالح کو بھیجا۔ (تو) صالح نے کہا
اے قوم! خدا ہی کی عبادت کرو اس کے سوا تمہارا کوئی معبود
نہیں۔ تمہارے پاس تمہارے پروردگار کی طرف سے ایک معجزہ آ چکا ہے (یعنی)
یہی خدا کی اونٹنی تمہارے لئے معجزہ ہے۔ تو اسے (آزاد) چھوڑ دو کہ
خدا کی زمین میں چرتی پھرے اور تم اُسے بُری نیت سے ہاتھ بھی
نہ لگانا۔ ورنہ عذاب الیم تمہیں پکڑ لے گا (٧٣)

وَإِلٰى ثَمُوْدَ أَخَاهُمْ صٰلِحًا قَالَ
يٰقَوْمِ اعْبُدُوا اللّٰهَ مَا لَكُمْ مِّنْ إِلٰهٍ
غَيْرُهٗ قَدْ جَاءَتْكُمْ بَيِّنَةٌ مِّنْ رَّبِّكُمْ
هٰذِهٖ نَاقَةُ اللّٰهِ لَكُمْ اٰيَةً فَذَرُوْهَا
تَأْكُلْ فِيْ أَرْضِ اللّٰهِ وَلَا تَمَسُّوْهَا
بِسُوْءٍ فَيَأْخُذَكُمْ عَذَابٌ أَلِيْمٌ (٧٣)

74. "And remember how He made you inheritors After the 'Âd people and gave you habitations in the land: ye build for yourselves palaces and castles in (open) plains, and carve out homes in the mountains; so bring to remembrance the benefits (ye have received) from Allah, and refrain from evil and mischief on the earth."

اور یاد تو کرو جب اُس نے تم کو قوم عاد کے بعد سردار
بنایا اور زمین پر آباد کیا۔ کہ نرم زمین سے (مٹی لے لے کر)
محل تعمیر کرتے ہو اور پہاڑوں کو تراش تراش کر
گھر بناتے ہو۔ پس خدا کی نعمتوں کو یاد کرو اور زمین
میں فساد نہ کرتے پھرو (٧٤)

وَاذْكُرُوْا إِذْ جَعَلَكُمْ خُلَفَاءَ مِنْ بَعْدِ
عَادٍ وَّبَوَّأَكُمْ فِي الْأَرْضِ تَتَّخِذُوْنَ مِنْ
سُهُوْلِهَا قُصُوْرًا وَّتَنْحِتُوْنَ الْجِبَالَ
بُيُوْتًا فَاذْكُرُوْا اٰلَاءَ اللّٰهِ وَلَا تَعْثَوْا
فِي الْأَرْضِ مُفْسِدِيْنَ (٧٤)

75. The leaders of the arrogant party among his people said to those who were reckoned powerless—those among them who believed: "Know ye indeed that Sâlih is a messenger from his Lord?" They said: "We do indeed believe in the revelation which hath been sent through him."

تو اُن کی قوم میں سردار لوگ جو غرور رکھتے تھے غریب لوگوں
سے جو اُن میں سے ایمان لے آئے تھے کہنے لگے بھلا تم یقین کرتے ہو
کہ صالح اپنے پروردگار کی طرف سے بھیجے گئے ہیں؟ انہوں نے کہا
ہاں جو چیز دیکر وہ بھیجے گئے ہیں ہم اُس پر بلاشبہ ایمان رکھتے ہیں (٧٥)

قَالَ الْمَلَأُ الَّذِيْنَ اسْتَكْبَرُوْا مِنْ قَوْمِهٖ
لِلَّذِيْنَ اسْتُضْعِفُوْا لِمَنْ اٰمَنَ مِنْهُمْ
أَتَعْلَمُوْنَ أَنَّ صٰلِحًا مُّرْسَلٌ مِّنْ رَّبِّهٖ
قَالُوْا إِنَّا بِمَا أُرْسِلَ بِهٖ مُؤْمِنُوْنَ (٧٥)

76. The arrogant party said: "For our part, we reject what ye believe in."

تو سرداران مغرور کہنے لگے کہ جس چیز پر تم ایمان لائے ہو ہم
تو اس کو نہیں مانتے (٧٦)

قَالَ الَّذِيْنَ اسْتَكْبَرُوْا إِنَّا بِالَّذِيْ اٰمَنْتُمْ
بِهٖ كٰفِرُوْنَ (٧٦)

77. Then they ham-strung the she-camel, and insolently defied the order of their Lord, saying: "O Sâlih! bring about thy threats, if

آخر انہوں نے اونٹنی (کی کونچوں) کو کاٹ ڈالا اور اپنے پروردگار
کے حکم سے سرکشی کی اور کہنے لگے کہ صالح جس چیز سے تم ہمیں

فَعَقَرُوا النَّاقَةَ وَعَتَوْا عَنْ أَمْرِ رَبِّهِمْ
وَقَالُوْا يٰصٰلِحُ ائْتِنَا بِمَا تَعِدُنَا إِنْ كُنْتَ

thou art a messenger (of Allah)!"

78. So the earthquake took them unawares, and they lay prostrate in their homes in the morning!

79. So Sālih left them, saying: "O my people! I did indeed convey to you the message for which I was sent by my Lord: I gave you good counsel, but ye love not good counsellors!"

80. We also (sent) Lût: he said to his people: "Do ye commit lewdness such as no people in creation (ever) committed before you?

81. "For ye practise your lusts on men in preference to women: ye are indeed a people transgressing beyond bounds".

82. And his people gave no answer but this: they said, "Drive them out of your city: these are indeed men who want to be clean and pure!"

83. But We saved him and his family, except his wife: she was of those who lagged behind

84. And we rained down on them a shower (of brimstone): then see what was the end of those who indulged in sin and crime!

85. To the Madyan people we sent Shu'aib, one of their own brethren: he said: "O my people! worship Allah; ye have no other god but Him. Now hath come unto you a clear (Sign) from your Lord! Give just measure and weight, nor withhold from the people the things that are their due; and do no mischief on the earth after it has been set in order: that will be best for you, if ye have Faith."

86. "And squat not on every road, breathing threats, hindering from the path of Allah those who believe in Him, and seek to make it crooked; but remember how ye

ڈراتے تھے اگر تم (خدا کے) پیغمبر ہو تو اُسے ہم پر لے آؤ ﴿٧٧﴾
تو اُن کو بھونچال نے آ پکڑا اور وہ اپنے گھروں میں اوندھے
پڑے رہ گئے ﴿٧٨﴾
پھر صالح اُن سے (ناامید ہو کر) پھرے اور کہا کہ میری قوم!
میں نے تم کو خدا کا پیغام پہنچا دیا اور تمہاری خیرخواہی کی مگر تم
ایسے ہو کہ خیرخواہوں کو دوست ہی نہیں رکھتے ﴿٧٩﴾
اور اسی طرح جب ہم نے لوط کو (پیغمبر بنا کر بھیجا تو) اُس
وقت اُنہوں نے اپنی قوم سے کہا کہ تم ایسی بےحیائی کا کام کیوں
کرتے ہو کہ تم سے پہلے اہل عالم میں سے کسی نے اس طرح کا کام نہیں کیا ﴿٨٠﴾
یعنی خواہش نفسانی پورا کرنے کے لئے عورتوں کو چھوڑ کر لونڈوں
پر گرتے ہو حقیقت یہ ہے کہ تم لوگ حد سے نکل جانے والے ہو ﴿٨١﴾
تو اُن سے اس کا جواب کچھ نہ بن پڑا اور بولے تو یہ بولے کہ ان
لوگوں (یعنی لوط اور اس کے گھر والوں کو) اپنے گاؤں سے نکال دو
(کہ) یہ لوگ پاک بننا چاہتے ہیں ﴿٨٢﴾
تو ہم نے اُن کو اور اُن کے گھر والوں کو بچا لیا مگر اُن کی بی بی
(نہ بچی) کہ وہ پیچھے رہنے والوں میں تھی ﴿٨٣﴾
اور ہم نے اُن پر (پتھروں کا) مینہ برسایا سو دیکھ لو کہ
گنہگاروں کا کیسا انجام ہوا ﴿٨٤﴾
اور مدین کی طرف اُن کے بھائی شعیب کو بھیجا تو اُنہوں نے
کہا کہ قوم! خدا ہی کی عبادت کرو اُس کے سوا تمہارا کوئی معبود نہیں۔
تمہارے پاس تمہارے پروردگار کی طرف سے نشانی آ چکی ہے تو تم ناپ
اور تول پوری کیا کرو اور لوگوں کو چیزیں کم نہ دیا کرو۔ اور زمین
میں اصلاح کے بعد خرابی نہ کرو۔ اگر تم صاحبِ ایمان ہو تو سمجھ لو کہ
یہ بات تمہارے حق میں بہتر ہے ﴿٨٥﴾
اور ہر رستے پر مت بیٹھا کرو کہ جو شخص خدا پر ایمان لاتا ہے
اُسے تم ڈراتے اور راہِ خدا سے روکتے اور اُس میں کجی
ڈھونڈتے ہو اور (اُس وقت کو) یاد کرو جب تم تھوڑے سے

مِنَ الْمُرْسَلِيْنَ ﴿٧٧﴾
فَاَخَذَتْهُمُ الرَّجْفَةُ فَاَصْبَحُوْا فِيْ
دَارِهِمْ جٰثِمِيْنَ ﴿٧٨﴾
فَتَوَلّٰى عَنْهُمْ وَقَالَ يٰقَوْمِ لَقَدْ اَبْلَغْتُكُمْ
رِسَالَةَ رَبِّيْ وَنَصَحْتُ لَكُمْ وَلٰكِنْ لَّا
تُحِبُّوْنَ النّٰصِحِيْنَ ﴿٧٩﴾
وَلُوْطًا اِذْ قَالَ لِقَوْمِهٖٓ اَتَاْتُوْنَ
الْفَاحِشَةَ مَا سَبَقَكُمْ بِهَا مِنْ اَحَدٍ
مِّنَ الْعٰلَمِيْنَ ﴿٨٠﴾
اِنَّكُمْ لَتَاْتُوْنَ الرِّجَالَ شَهْوَةً مِّنْ
دُوْنِ النِّسَآءِ ؕ بَلْ اَنْتُمْ قَوْمٌ مُّسْرِفُوْنَ ﴿٨١﴾
وَمَا كَانَ جَوَابَ قَوْمِهٖٓ اِلَّآ اَنْ قَالُوْٓا
اَخْرِجُوْهُمْ مِّنْ قَرْيَتِكُمْ ۚ اِنَّهُمْ اُنَاسٌ
يَّتَطَهَّرُوْنَ ﴿٨٢﴾
فَاَنْجَيْنٰهُ وَاَهْلَهٗٓ اِلَّا امْرَاَتَهٗ ۖ كَانَتْ
مِنَ الْغٰبِرِيْنَ ﴿٨٣﴾
وَاَمْطَرْنَا عَلَيْهِمْ مَّطَرًا ؕ فَانْظُرْ كَيْفَ
كَانَ عَاقِبَةُ الْمُجْرِمِيْنَ ﴿٨٤﴾ ع
وَاِلٰى مَدْيَنَ اَخَاهُمْ شُعَيْبًا ؕ قَالَ يٰقَوْمِ
اعْبُدُوا اللّٰهَ مَا لَكُمْ مِّنْ اِلٰهٍ غَيْرُهٗ ؕ قَدْ
جَآءَتْكُمْ بَيِّنَةٌ مِّنْ رَّبِّكُمْ فَاَوْفُوا الْكَيْلَ
وَالْمِيْزَانَ وَلَا تَبْخَسُوا النَّاسَ اَشْيَآءَهُمْ
وَلَا تُفْسِدُوْا فِى الْاَرْضِ بَعْدَ اِصْلَاحِهَا ؕ
ذٰلِكُمْ خَيْرٌ لَّكُمْ اِنْ كُنْتُمْ مُّؤْمِنِيْنَ ﴿٨٥﴾
وَلَا تَقْعُدُوْا بِكُلِّ صِرَاطٍ تُوْعِدُوْنَ
وَتَصُدُّوْنَ عَنْ سَبِيْلِ اللّٰهِ مَنْ اٰمَنَ
بِهٖ وَتَبْغُوْنَهَا عِوَجًا ۚ وَاذْكُرُوْٓا اِذْ

were little, and He gave you increase. And see what was the end of those who did mischief.

87. "And if there is a party among you who believes in the Message with which I have been sent, and a party which does not believe, hold yourselves in patience until Allah doth decide between us: for He is the best to decide."

88. The leaders, the arrogant party among his people, said: "O Shu'aib! we shall certainly drive thee out of our city—(thee) and those who believe with thee; or else ye (thou and they) shall have to return to our religion." He said: "What! even though we do detest (them)?

89. "We should indeed forge a lie against Allah, if we returned to your religion after Allah hath rescued us therefrom; nor could we by any manner of means return thereto unless it be as in the will of Allah, our Lord. Our Lord comprehends all things in His knowledge in Allah is our trust. Our Lord ! Decide thou between us and our people in truth, for thou art the best to decide."

90. The leaders, the Unbelievers among his people, said: "If ye follow Shu'aib, be sure then ye are ruined!"

91. But the earthquake took them unawares, and they lay prostrate in their homes before the morning!

92. The men who rejected Shu'aib became as if they had never been in the homes where they had flourished: the men who rejected Shu'aib—it was they who were ruined !

93. So Shu'aib left them, saying: "O my people! I did indeed convey to you the Messages for which I was sent by my Lord: I gave you good counsel, but how shall I lament over a people who refuse to believe!"

تھے تو خدا نے تم کو جماعت کثیر کر دیا اور دیکھ لو کہ خرابی
کرنے والوں کا انجام کیسا ہوا[ف۱۲۹] ﴿۸۶﴾
اور اگر تم میں سے ایک جماعت میری رسالت پر ایمان
لے آئی ہے اور ایک جماعت ایمان نہیں لائی تو صبر کئے
رہو یہاں تک کہ خدا ہمارے تمہارے درمیان فیصلہ کردے۔
اور وہ سب سے بہتر فیصلہ کرنے والا ہے ﴿۸۷﴾
(تو) اُن کی قوم میں جو لوگ سردار اور بڑے آدمی تھے وہ
کہنے لگے۔ کہ شعیب (یا تو) ہم تم کو اور جو لوگ تمہارے ساتھ ایمان
لائے ہیں اُن کو اپنے شہر سے نکال دینگے۔ یا تم ہمارے مذہب
میں آجاؤ۔ اُنہوں نے کہا خواہ ہم (تمہارے دین سے) بیزار ہی ہوں (تو بھی)؟ ﴿۸۸﴾
اگر ہم اسکے بعد کہ خدا ہمیں اس سے نجات بخش چکا ہو تمہارے
مذہب میں لوٹ جائیں تو بیشک ہم نے خدا پر جھوٹ (افترا) باندھا
اور ہمیں شایاں نہیں کہ ہم اس میں لوٹ جائیں ہاں خدا
جو ہمارا پروردگار ہے وہ چاہے تو (ہم مجبور ہیں) ہمارے
پروردگار کا علم ہر چیز پر احاطہ کئے ہوئے ہے۔ ہمارا خدا ہی
پر بھروسا ہے۔ اے پروردگار ہم میں اور ہماری قوم میں انصاف
کے ساتھ فیصلہ کردے اور تُو سب سے بہتر فیصلہ کرنے والا ہے ﴿۸۹﴾
اور اُنکی قوم میں سے سردار لوگ جو کافر تھے کہنے لگے کہ (بھائیو) اگر تم
نے شعیب کی پیروی کی تو بیشک تم خسارے میں پڑ گئے ﴿۹۰﴾
تو اُن کو بھونچال نے آپکڑا اور وہ اپنے گھروں میں اوندھے
پڑے رہ گئے ﴿۹۱﴾
(یہ لوگ) جنہوں نے شعیب کی تکذیب کی تھی ایسے برباد ہوئے
تھے کہ گویا وہ اُن میں کبھی آباد ہی نہیں ہوئے تھے (غرض) جنہوں
نے شعیب کو جھٹلایا وہ خسارے میں پڑ گئے ﴿۹۲﴾
تو شعیب اُن میں سے نکل آئے اور کہا کہ بھائیو میں نے تم کو
اپنے پروردگار کے پیغام پہنچا دیئے ہیں اور تمہاری خیرخواہی کی
تھی تو میں کافروں پر (عذاب نازل ہونے سے) رنج و غم کیوں کروں ﴿۹۳﴾

كُنْتُمْ قَلِيلًا فَكَثَّرَكُمْ ۖ وَانْظُرُوا كَيْفَ
كَانَ عَاقِبَةُ الْمُفْسِدِينَ ﴿٨٦﴾
وَإِنْ كَانَ طَائِفَةٌ مِنْكُمْ آمَنُوا بِالَّذِي
أُرْسِلْتُ بِهِ وَطَائِفَةٌ لَمْ يُؤْمِنُوا
فَاصْبِرُوا حَتَّىٰ يَحْكُمَ اللَّهُ بَيْنَنَا ۚ
وَهُوَ خَيْرُ الْحَاكِمِينَ ﴿٨٧﴾
قَالَ الْمَلَأُ الَّذِينَ اسْتَكْبَرُوا مِنْ
قَوْمِهِ لَنُخْرِجَنَّكَ يَا شُعَيْبُ وَالَّذِينَ
آمَنُوا مَعَكَ مِنْ قَرْيَتِنَا أَوْ لَتَعُودُنَّ
فِي مِلَّتِنَا ۚ قَالَ أَوَلَوْ كُنَّا كَارِهِينَ ﴿٨٨﴾
قَدِ افْتَرَيْنَا عَلَى اللَّهِ كَذِبًا إِنْ عُدْنَا
فِي مِلَّتِكُمْ بَعْدَ إِذْ نَجَّانَا اللَّهُ مِنْهَا ۚ
وَمَا يَكُونُ لَنَا أَنْ نَعُودَ فِيهَا إِلَّا
أَنْ يَشَاءَ اللَّهُ رَبُّنَا ۚ وَسِعَ رَبُّنَا كُلَّ
شَيْءٍ عِلْمًا ۚ عَلَى اللَّهِ تَوَكَّلْنَا ۚ رَبَّنَا
افْتَحْ بَيْنَنَا وَبَيْنَ قَوْمِنَا بِالْحَقِّ وَأَنْتَ
خَيْرُ الْفَاتِحِينَ ﴿٨٩﴾
وَقَالَ الْمَلَأُ الَّذِينَ كَفَرُوا مِنْ قَوْمِهِ
لَئِنِ اتَّبَعْتُمْ شُعَيْبًا إِنَّكُمْ إِذًا لَخَاسِرُونَ ﴿٩٠﴾
فَأَخَذَتْهُمُ الرَّجْفَةُ فَأَصْبَحُوا فِي
دَارِهِمْ جَاثِمِينَ ﴿٩١﴾
الَّذِينَ كَذَّبُوا شُعَيْبًا كَأَنْ لَمْ يَغْنَوْا
فِيهَا ۚ الَّذِينَ كَذَّبُوا شُعَيْبًا كَانُوا
هُمُ الْخَاسِرِينَ ﴿٩٢﴾
فَتَوَلَّىٰ عَنْهُمْ وَقَالَ يَا قَوْمِ لَقَدْ أَبْلَغْتُكُمْ
رِسَالَاتِ رَبِّي وَنَصَحْتُ لَكُمْ ۖ فَكَيْفَ
آسَىٰ عَلَىٰ قَوْمٍ كَافِرِينَ ﴿٩٣﴾

94. Whenever We sent a prophet to a town, We took up its people in suffering and adversity, in order that they might call in humility.

اور ہم نے کسی شہر میں کوئی پیغمبر نہیں بھیجا مگر وہاں کے رہنے والوں
کو (جو ایمان نہ لائے) دکھوں اور مصیبتوں میں مبتلا کیا تاکہ
وہ عاجزی اور زاری کریں ﴿۹۴﴾

وَمَآ اَرْسَلْنَا فِیْ قَرْیَةٍ مِّنْ نَّبِیٍّ اِلَّآ
اَخَذْنَآ اَهْلَهَا بِالْبَاْسَآءِ وَالضَّرَّآءِ
لَعَلَّهُمْ یَضَّرَّعُوْنَ ﴿۹۴﴾

95. Then We changed their suffering into prosperity, until they grew and multiplied, and began to say: "Our fathers (too) were touched by suffering and affluence". Behold! We took them to account of a sudden, while they realised not (their peril).

پھر ہم نے تکلیف کو آسودگی سے بدل دیا یہاں تک کہ
(مال واولاد میں) زیادہ ہو گئے تو کہنے لگے کہ اسی طرح کا
رنج و راحت ہمارے بڑوں کو بھی پہنچتا رہا ہے تو ہم نے اُن کو
ناگہاں پکڑ لیا اور وہ (اپنے حال میں) بے خبر تھے ﴿۹۵﴾

ثُمَّ بَدَّلْنَا مَكَانَ السَّیِّئَةِ الْحَسَنَةَ
حَتّٰی عَفَوْا وَّقَالُوْا قَدْ مَسَّ اٰبَآءَنَا
الضَّرَّآءُ وَالسَّرَّآءُ فَاَخَذْنٰهُمْ بَغْتَةً
وَّهُمْ لَا یَشْعُرُوْنَ ﴿۹۵﴾

96. If the people of the towns had but believed and feared Allah, We should indeed have opened out to them (all kinds of) blessings from heaven and earth; but they rejected (the truth), and We brought them to book for their misdeeds.

اگر ان بستیوں کے لوگ ایمان لے آتے اور پرہیزگار ہو جاتے تو
ہم اُن پر آسمان اور زمین کی برکات (کے دروازے)
کھول دیتے مگر اُنہوں نے تو تکذیب کی۔ سو اُن کے
اعمال کی سزا میں ہم نے اُن کو پکڑ لیا ﴿۹۶﴾

وَلَوْ اَنَّ اَهْلَ الْقُرٰۤی اٰمَنُوْا وَاتَّقَوْا
لَفَتَحْنَا عَلَیْهِمْ بَرَكٰتٍ مِّنَ السَّمَآءِ وَ
الْاَرْضِ وَلٰكِنْ كَذَّبُوْا فَاَخَذْنٰهُمْ بِمَا
كَانُوْا یَكْسِبُوْنَ ﴿۹۶﴾

97. Did the people of the towns feel secure against the coming of Our wrath by night while they were asleep?

کیا بستیوں کے رہنے والے اس سے بےخوف ہیں۔ کہ اُن پر ہمارا
عذاب رات کو واقع ہو اور وہ (بے خبر) سو رہے ہوں ﴿۹۷﴾

اَفَاَمِنَ اَهْلُ الْقُرٰۤی اَنْ یَّاْتِیَهُمْ بَاْسُنَا
بَیَاتًا وَّهُمْ نَآىِٕمُوْنَ ﴿۹۷﴾

98. Or else did they feel secure against its coming in broad daylight while they played about (care-free)?

اور کیا اہلِ شہر اس سے نڈر ہیں کہ ان پر ہمارا عذاب دن چڑھے
آنازل ہو اور وہ کھیل رہے ہوں ﴿۹۸﴾

اَوَاَمِنَ اَهْلُ الْقُرٰۤی اَنْ یَّاْتِیَهُمْ بَاْسُنَا
ضُحًی وَّهُمْ یَلْعَبُوْنَ ﴿۹۸﴾

99. Did they then feel secure against Allah's devising but no one can feel secure from the Plan of Allah, except those (doomed) to ruin!

کیا یہ لوگ خدا کے داؤں کا ڈر نہیں رکھتے (سُن لو کہ) خدا کے
داؤں سے وہی لوگ نڈر ہوتے ہیں جو خسارہ پانے والے ہیں ﴿۹۹﴾

اَفَاَمِنُوْا مَكْرَ اللّٰهِ ۚ فَلَا یَاْمَنُ مَكْرَ اللّٰهِ
اِلَّا الْقَوْمُ الْخٰسِرُوْنَ ﴿۹۹﴾ ع

100. To those who inherit the earth in succession to its (previous) possessors, is it not a guiding (lesson) that, if We so willed, we could punish them (too) for their sins, and seal up their hearts so that they could not hear?

کیا ان لوگوں کو جو اہلِ زمین کے (مر جانے کے) بعد زمین کے مالک
ہوتے ہیں یہ امر موجبِ ہدایت نہیں ہوا کہ اگر ہم چاہیں تو اُنکے
گناہوں کے سبب اُن پر مصیبت ڈال دیں اور اُنکے دلوں پر
مُہر لگا دیں کہ کچھ سُن ہی نہ سکیں ﴿۱۰۰﴾

اَوَلَمْ یَهْدِ لِلَّذِیْنَ یَرِثُوْنَ الْاَرْضَ
مِنْۢ بَعْدِ اَهْلِهَاۤ اَنْ لَّوْ نَشَآءُ اَصَبْنٰهُمْ
بِذُنُوْبِهِمْ ۚ وَنَطْبَعُ عَلٰی قُلُوْبِهِمْ
فَهُمْ لَا یَسْمَعُوْنَ ﴿۱۰۰﴾

101. Such were the towns whose story We (thus) relate unto thee: there came indeed to them their Messengers with clear (Signs); but they would not believe what they had rejected before. Thus doth Allah seal up the hearts of those who reject Faith.

یہ بستیاں ہیں جن کے کچھ حالات ہم تم کو سُناتے ہیں اور
اُن کے پاس اُن کے پیغمبر نشانیاں لے کر آئے مگر وہ ایسے
نہیں تھے کہ جس چیز کو پہلے جُھٹلا چکے ہوں اُسے
مان لیں اسی طرح خدا کافروں کے دلوں پر مُہر
لگا دیتا ہے ﴿۱۰۱﴾

تِلْكَ الْقُرٰی نَقُصُّ عَلَیْكَ مِنْ اَنْۢبَآىِٕهَا ۚ
وَلَقَدْ جَآءَتْهُمْ رُسُلُهُمْ بِالْبَیِّنٰتِ ۚ
فَمَا كَانُوْا لِیُؤْمِنُوْا بِمَا كَذَّبُوْا مِنْ
قَبْلُ ۚ كَذٰلِكَ یَطْبَعُ اللّٰهُ عَلٰی قُلُوْبِ
الْكٰفِرِیْنَ ﴿۱۰۱﴾

102. Most of them We found not men (true) to their covenant: but

اور ہم نے اُن میں سے اکثروں میں عہد (کا نباہ) نہیں دیکھا۔

وَمَا وَجَدْنَا لِاَكْثَرِهِمْ مِّنْ عَهْدٍ ۚ

most of them We found rebellious and disobedient.

103. Then after them We sent Moses with Our Signs to Pharaoh and his chiefs. But they wrongfully rejected them: so see what was the end of those who made mischief.

104. Moses said: "O Pharaoh!" I am a messenger from the Lord of the Worlds,–

105. One for whom it is right to say nothing but truth about Allah. Now have I come unto you (people), from your Lord with a clear (Sign): so let the Children of Israel depart along with me."

106. (Pharaoh) said: "If indeed thou hast come with a Sign, show it forth,—if thou tellest the truth."

107. Then (Moses) threw his rod, and behold! it was a serpent, plain (for all to see)!

108. And he drew out his hand, and behold! it was white to all beholders!

109. Said the Chiefs of the people of Pharaoh: "This is indeed a sorcerer well-versed.

110. "His plan is to get you out of your land: then what is it ye counsel?"

111. They said: "Keep him and his brother in suspense (for a while); and send to the cities men to collect—

112. And bring up to thee all (our) sorcerers well-versed."

113. So there came the sorcerers to Pharaoh: they said, "Of course we shall have a (suitable) reward if we win!"

114. He said: "Yea, (and more),—for ye shall in that case be (raised to posts) nearest (to my person)."

115. They said: "O Moses! wilt thou throw (first), or shall we have the (first) throw?"

116. Said Moses: "Throw ye (first)." So when they threw, they bewitched the eyes of the people, and struck terror into them: and

اور ان میں اکثروں کو (دیکھا تو) بدکار ہی دیکھا (١٠٢)
پھر ان (پیغمبروں) کے بعد ہم نے موسیٰ کو نشانیاں دے کر فرعون اور
اُس کے اعیانِ سلطنت کے پاس بھیجا۔ تو انہوں نے اُن کے ساتھ کفر
کیا سو دیکھ لو کہ خرابی کرنے والوں کا انجام کیا ہوا (١٠٣)
اور موسیٰ نے کہا کہ اے فرعون میں رب العالمین کا
پیغمبر ہوں (١٠٤)
مجھ پر واجب ہے کہ خدا کی طرف سے جو کچھ کہوں سچ ہی
کہوں میں تمہارے پاس تمہارے پروردگار کی طرف سے نشانی لے کر
آیا ہوں سو بنی اسرائیل کو میرے ساتھ جانے کی رخصت دیجیئے (١٠٥)
فرعون نے کہا اگر تم نشانی لے کر آئے ہو تو اگر سچے ہو تو
لاؤ (دکھاؤ) (١٠٦)
موسیٰ نے اپنی لاٹھی (زمین پر) ڈال دی تو وہ اسی وقت صریح اژدہا (ہو گیا) (١٠٧)
اور اپنا ہاتھ باہر نکالا تو اسی دم دیکھنے والوں کی نگاہوں میں سفید براق (تھا) (١٠٨)
تو قوم فرعون میں جو سردار تھے وہ کہنے لگے کہ یہ بڑا علامہ
جادوگر ہے (١٠٩)
اس کا ارادہ یہ ہے کہ تم کو تمہارے ملک سے نکال دے۔ بھلا
تمہاری کیا صلاح ہے؟ (١١٠)
انہوں نے (فرعون سے) کہا کہ فی الحال موسیٰ اور اس کے بھائی
کے معاملے کو موقوف رکھیے اور شہروں میں نقیب روانہ کر دیجیے (١١١)
کہ تمام ماہر جادوگروں کو آپ کے پاس لے آئیں (١١٢)
(چنانچہ ایسا ہی کیا گیا) اور جادوگر فرعون کے پاس آ پہنچے (اور)
کہنے لگے کہ اگر ہم جیت گئے تو ہمیں صلہ عطا کیا جائے (١١٣)
(فرعون نے) کہا ہاں (ضرور) اور اس کے علاوہ تم مقربوں میں داخل کر لیے جاؤ گے (١١٤)
(جب فریقین روز مقررہ پر جمع ہوئے تو) جادوگروں نے کہا کہ موسیٰ یا
تو تم (جادو کی چیز) ڈالو یا ہم ڈالتے ہیں (١١٥)
(موسیٰ نے) کہا تم ہی ڈالو۔ جب انہوں نے (جادو کی چیزیں) ڈالیں
تو لوگوں کی آنکھوں پر جادو کر دیا (یعنی نظربندی کر دی) اور (لاٹھیوں

وَإِنْ وَجَدْنَا أَكْثَرَهُمْ لَفٰسِقِينَ (١٠٢)
ثُمَّ بَعَثْنَا مِنْ بَعْدِهِمْ مُوسٰى بِاٰيٰتِنَا
إِلٰى فِرْعَوْنَ وَمَلَا۠ئِهٖ فَظَلَمُوا بِهَا ۚ
فَانْظُرْ كَيْفَ كَانَ عَاقِبَةُ الْمُفْسِدِينَ (١٠٣)
وَقَالَ مُوسٰى يٰفِرْعَوْنُ إِنِّي رَسُولٌ مِّنْ
رَّبِّ الْعٰلَمِينَ (١٠٤)
حَقِيقٌ عَلٰى أَنْ لَّا أَقُولَ عَلَى اللّٰهِ إِلَّا
الْحَقَّ ۚ قَدْ جِئْتُكُمْ بِبَيِّنَةٍ مِّنْ رَّبِّكُمْ
فَأَرْسِلْ مَعِيَ بَنِي إِسْرَآءِيلَ (١٠٥)
قَالَ إِنْ كُنْتَ جِئْتَ بِاٰيَةٍ فَأْتِ بِهَا
إِنْ كُنْتَ مِنَ الصّٰدِقِينَ (١٠٦)
فَأَلْقٰى عَصَاهُ فَإِذَا هِيَ ثُعْبَانٌ مُّبِينٌ (١٠٧)
وَنَزَعَ يَدَهٗ فَإِذَا هِيَ بَيْضَآءُ لِلنّٰظِرِينَ (١٠٨)
قَالَ الْمَلَأُ مِنْ قَوْمِ فِرْعَوْنَ إِنَّ هٰذَا
لَسٰحِرٌ عَلِيمٌ (١٠٩)
يُرِيدُ أَنْ يُخْرِجَكُمْ مِّنْ أَرْضِكُمْ ۚ فَمَاذَا
تَأْمُرُونَ (١١٠)
قَالُوٓا أَرْجِهْ وَأَخَاهُ وَأَرْسِلْ فِي الْمَدَآئِنِ
حٰشِرِينَ (١١١)
يَأْتُوكَ بِكُلِّ سٰحِرٍ عَلِيمٍ (١١٢)
وَجَآءَ السَّحَرَةُ فِرْعَوْنَ قَالُوٓا إِنَّ لَنَا
لَأَجْرًا إِنْ كُنَّا نَحْنُ الْغٰلِبِينَ (١١٣)
قَالَ نَعَمْ وَإِنَّكُمْ لَمِنَ الْمُقَرَّبِينَ (١١٤)
قَالُوا يٰمُوسٰى إِمَّآ أَنْ تُلْقِيَ وَإِمَّآ أَنْ
نَّكُونَ نَحْنُ الْمُلْقِينَ (١١٥)
قَالَ أَلْقُوا ۚ فَلَمَّآ أَلْقَوْا سَحَرُوٓا أَعْيُنَ
النَّاسِ وَاسْتَرْهَبُوهُمْ وَجَآءُو

they showed a great (feat of) magic.

117. We revealed to Moses "Throw thy rod": and behold! it swallows up all the falsehoods which they fake!

118. Thus truth was confirmed. And all that they did was made of no effect.

119. So they were vanquished there and then, and turned about humble.

120. But the sorcerers fell down prostrate in adoration.

121. Saying: "We believe in the Lord of the Worlds.

122. "The Lord of Moses and Aaron."

123. Said Pharaoh: "Believe ye in Him before I give you permission? Surely this is a trick which ye have planned in the City to drive out its people: but soon shall ye know (the consequences)."

124. "Be sure I will cut off your hands and your feet on opposite sides, and I will crucify you all."

125. They said: "For us, we are but sent back unto our Lord."

126. "But thou dost wreak thy vengeance on us simply because we believed in the Signs of our Lord when they reached us! Our Lord! pour out on us patience and constancy, and take our souls unto Thee as Muslims (who bow to Thy Will)!"

127. Said the chiefs of Pharaoh's people: "Wilt thou leave Moses and his people, to spread mischief in the land, and to abandon thee and thy gods?" He said "Their male children will we slay; (only) their females will we save alive; and we have over them (power) irresistible."

128. Said Moses to his people: "Pray for help from Allah," and (wait) in patience and constancy: for the earth is Allah's, to give as a heritage to such of His servants as He pleaseth; and the end is (best) for the righteous.

اور رسیوں کے سانپ بنا بنا کر) انہیں ڈرا دیا اور بہت بڑا جادو دکھایا ﴿۱۱۶﴾
(اور اُس وقت) ہم نے موسیٰ کی طرف وحی بھیجی کہ تم بھی اپنی لاٹھی ڈال دو وہ فوراً
(سانپ بن کر) جادوگروں کے بنائے ہوئے سانپوں کو (ایک ایک کر کے) نگل جائے گی ﴿۱۱۷﴾
(پھر) تو حق ثابت ہو گیا اور جو کچھ فرعونی کرتے تھے
باطل ہو گیا ﴿۱۱۸﴾
اور وہ مغلوب ہو گئے اور ذلیل ہو کر رہ گئے ﴿۱۱۹﴾
(اور یہ کیفیت دیکھ کر) جادوگر سجدے میں گر پڑے ﴿۱۲۰﴾
(اور) کہنے لگے کہ ہم جہان کے پروردگار پر ایمان لائے ﴿۱۲۱﴾
(یعنی) موسیٰ اور ہارون کے پروردگار پر ﴿۱۲۲﴾
فرعون نے کہا کہ بیشتر اس کے کہ میں تمہیں اجازت دوں
تم اس پر ایمان لے آئے؟ بے شک یہ فریب ہے جو تم نے
مل کر شہر میں کیا ہے تاکہ اہل شہر کو یہاں سے نکال دو۔
سو عنقریب (اس کا نتیجہ) معلوم کر لو گے ﴿۱۲۳﴾
میں (پہلے تو) تمہارے ایک طرف کے ہاتھ اور دوسری طرف کے
پاؤں کاٹ دوں گا پھر تم سب کو سولی چڑھا دوں گا ﴿۱۲۴﴾
وہ بولے کہ ہم تو اپنے پروردگار کی طرف لوٹ کر جانے والے ہیں ﴿۱۲۵﴾
اور اس کے سوا تجھ کو ہماری کونسی بات بری لگی ہے کہ جب ہمارے
پروردگار کی نشانیاں ہمارے پاس آ گئیں تو ہم ان پر ایمان لے آئے۔ اے
پروردگار ہم پر صبر و استقامت کے دہانے کھول دے اور ہمیں (ماریو تو) مسلمان ہی ماریو ﴿۱۲۶﴾
اور قوم فرعون میں جو سردار تھے کہنے لگے کہ کیا آپ موسیٰ اور
اس کی قوم کو چھوڑ دیجیے گا کہ ملک میں خرابی کریں اور
آپ سے اور آپ کے معبودوں سے دست کش ہو جائیں۔ وہ
بولے کہ ہم ان کے لڑکوں کو تو قتل کر ڈالیں گے اور لڑکیوں کو
زندہ رہنے دیں گے اور بے شبہ ہم ان پر غالب ہیں ﴿۱۲۷﴾
موسیٰ نے اپنی قوم سے کہا کہ خدا سے مدد مانگو اور ثابت قدم رہو
زمین تو خدا کی ہے۔ وہ اپنے بندوں میں سے جسے چاہتا ہے
اس کا مالک بناتا ہے۔ اور آخر بھلا تو ڈرنے والوں کا ہے ﴿۱۲۸﴾

بِسِحۡرٍ عَظِيۡمٍ ﴿۱۱۶﴾
وَاَوۡحَيۡنَاۤ اِلٰى مُوۡسٰٓى اَنۡ اَلۡقِ عَصَاكَۚ
فَاِذَا هِىَ تَلۡقَفُ مَا يَاۡفِكُوۡنَۚ ﴿۱۱۷﴾
فَوَقَعَ الۡحَـقُّ وَبَطَلَ مَا كَانُوۡا
يَعۡمَلُوۡنَۚ ﴿۱۱۸﴾
فَغُلِبُوۡا هُنَالِكَ وَانۡقَلَبُوۡا صٰغِرِيۡنَۚ ﴿۱۱۹﴾
وَاُلۡقِىَ السَّحَرَةُ سٰجِدِيۡنَ ﴿۱۲۰﴾
قَالُوۡۤا اٰمَنَّا بِرَبِّ الۡعٰلَمِيۡنَ ﴿۱۲۱﴾
رَبِّ مُوۡسٰى وَهٰرُوۡنَ ﴿۱۲۲﴾
قَالَ فِرۡعَوۡنُ اٰمَنۡتُمۡ بِهٖ قَبۡلَ اَنۡ اٰذَنَ
لَـكُمۡ ۚ اِنَّ هٰذَا لَمَكۡرٌ مَّكَرۡتُمُوۡهُ فِى
الۡمَدِيۡنَةِ لِتُخۡرِجُوۡا مِنۡهَاۤ اَهۡلَهَا ۚ فَسَوۡفَ
تَعۡلَمُوۡنَ ﴿۱۲۳﴾
لَاُقَطِّعَنَّ اَيۡدِيَكُمۡ وَاَرۡجُلَكُمۡ مِّنۡ خِلَافٍ
ثُمَّ لَاُصَلِّبَنَّكُمۡ اَجۡمَعِيۡنَ ﴿۱۲۴﴾
قَالُوۡۤا اِنَّاۤ اِلٰى رَبِّنَا مُنۡقَلِبُوۡنَۚ ﴿۱۲۵﴾
وَمَا تَنۡقِمُ مِنَّاۤ اِلَّاۤ اَنۡ اٰمَنَّا بِاٰيٰتِ
رَبِّنَا لَمَّا جَآءَتۡنَا ؕ رَبَّنَاۤ اَفۡرِغۡ عَلَيۡنَا
صَبۡرًا وَّتَوَفَّنَا مُسۡلِمِيۡنَ ﴿۱۲۶﴾ ع ۱۴
وَقَالَ الۡمَلَاُ مِنۡ قَوۡمِ فِرۡعَوۡنَ اَتَذَرُ
مُوۡسٰى وَقَوۡمَهٗ لِيُفۡسِدُوۡا فِى الۡاَرۡضِ
وَيَذَرَكَ وَاٰلِهَتَكَ ؕ قَالَ سَنُقَتِّلُ اَبۡنَآءَهُمۡ
وَنَسۡتَحۡىٖ نِسَآءَهُمۡ ۚ وَاِنَّا فَوۡقَهُمۡ
قٰهِرُوۡنَ ﴿۱۲۷﴾
قَالَ مُوۡسٰى لِقَوۡمِهِ اسۡتَعِيۡنُوۡا بِاللّٰهِ
وَاصۡبِرُوۡا ۚ اِنَّ الۡاَرۡضَ لِلّٰهِ ۙ يُوۡرِثُهَا
مَنۡ يَّشَآءُ مِنۡ عِبَادِهٖ ؕ وَالۡعَاقِبَةُ لِلۡمُتَّقِيۡنَ ﴿۱۲۸﴾

129. They said: "We have had (nothing but) trouble, both before and after thou camest to us." He said: "It may be that your Lord will destroy your enemy and make you inheritors in the earth; that so He may see how ye act."

130. We punished the people of Pharaoh with years (of drought) and shortness of crops; that they might receive admonition.

131. But when good (times) came, they said, "This is due to us;" when gripped by calamity, they ascribed it to evil omens connected with Moses and those with him! Behold! in truth the omens of evil are theirs in Allah's sight, but most of them do not understand!

132. They said (to Moses): "Whatever be the Signs Thou bringest, to work therewith thy sorcery on us, we shall never believe in thee."

133. So We sent on them: wholesale Death, Locusts, Lice, frogs, and Blood: Signs openly Self-explained: but they were steeped in arrogance, a people given to sin.

134. And when the Plague fell on them, they said: "O Moses! on our behalf call on thy Lord in virtue of his promise to thee: if thou wilt remove the Plague from us, we shall truly believe in thee, and we shall send away the Children of Israel with thee."

135. But when We removed the Plague from them according to a fixed term which they had to fulfil,—behold! they broke their word!

136. So We exacted retribution from them: We drowned them in the sea, because they rejected Our Signs, and failed to take warning from them.

137. And We made a people, considered weak (and of no account), inheritors of lands in both East and West,—lands whereon We sent down Our blessings. The fair promise of thy Lord was fulfilled for the Children of Israel, because

قَالُوْٓا اُوْذِيْنَا مِنْ قَبْلِ اَنْ تَاْتِيَنَا وَمِنْۢ
بَعْدِ مَا جِئْتَنَا ۭ قَالَ عَسٰى رَبُّكُمْ اَنْ
يُّهْلِكَ عَدُوَّكُمْ وَيَسْتَخْلِفَكُمْ فِي الْاَرْضِ
فَيَنْظُرَ كَيْفَ تَعْمَلُوْنَ ١٢٩
وَلَقَدْ اَخَذْنَآ اٰلَ فِرْعَوْنَ بِالسِّنِيْنَ وَ
نَقْصٍ مِّنَ الثَّمَرٰتِ لَعَلَّهُمْ يَذَّكَّرُوْنَ ١٣٠
فَاِذَا جَاۗءَتْهُمُ الْحَسَنَةُ قَالُوْا لَنَا هٰذِهٖ ۚ
وَاِنْ تُصِبْهُمْ سَيِّئَةٌ يَّطَّيَّرُوْا بِمُوْسٰى
وَمَنْ مَّعَهٗ ۭ اَلَآ اِنَّمَا طٰۗىِٕرُهُمْ عِنْدَ
اللّٰهِ وَلٰكِنَّ اَكْثَرَهُمْ لَا يَعْلَمُوْنَ ١٣١
وَقَالُوْا مَهْمَا تَاْتِنَا بِهٖ مِنْ اٰيَةٍ لِّتَسْحَرَنَا
بِهَا ۙ فَمَا نَحْنُ لَكَ بِمُؤْمِنِيْنَ ١٣٢
فَاَرْسَلْنَا عَلَيْهِمُ الطُّوْفَانَ وَالْجَرَادَ وَ
الْقُمَّلَ وَالضَّفَادِعَ وَالدَّمَ اٰيٰتٍ مُّفَصَّلٰتٍ ۣ
فَاسْتَكْبَرُوْا وَكَانُوْا قَوْمًا مُّجْرِمِيْنَ ١٣٣
وَلَمَّا وَقَعَ عَلَيْهِمُ الرِّجْزُ قَالُوْا يٰمُوْسَى
ادْعُ لَنَا رَبَّكَ بِمَا عَهِدَ عِنْدَكَ ۚ لَىِٕنْ
كَشَفْتَ عَنَّا الرِّجْزَ لَنُؤْمِنَنَّ لَكَ وَ
لَنُرْسِلَنَّ مَعَكَ بَنِيْٓ اِسْرَاۗءِيْلَ ١٣٤
فَلَمَّا كَشَفْنَا عَنْهُمُ الرِّجْزَ اِلٰٓى اَجَلٍ هُمْ
بٰلِغُوْهُ اِذَا هُمْ يَنْكُثُوْنَ ١٣٥
فَانْتَقَمْنَا مِنْهُمْ فَاَغْرَقْنٰهُمْ فِي الْيَمِّ
بِاَنَّهُمْ كَذَّبُوْا بِاٰيٰتِنَا وَكَانُوْا عَنْهَا غٰفِلِيْنَ ١٣٦
وَاَوْرَثْنَا الْقَوْمَ الَّذِيْنَ كَانُوْا يُسْتَضْعَفُوْنَ
مَشَارِقَ الْاَرْضِ وَمَغَارِبَهَا الَّتِيْ بٰرَكْنَا
فِيْهَا ۭ وَتَمَّتْ كَلِمَتُ رَبِّكَ الْحُسْنٰى عَلٰي
بَنِيْٓ اِسْرَاۗءِيْلَ ڏ بِمَا صَبَرُوْا ۭ وَدَمَّرْنَا

وہ بولے کہ تمہارے آنے سے پہلے بھی ہم کو اذیتیں پہنچتی
رہیں اور آنے کے بعد بھی۔ موسیٰ نے کہا کہ قریب ہے کہ
تمہارا پروردگار تمہارے دشمن کو ہلاک کر دے اور اسکی جگہ
تمہیں زمین میں خلیفہ بنائے پھر دیکھے کہ تم کیسے عمل کرتے ہو ۱۲۹
اور ہم نے فرعونیوں کو قحطوں اور میووں کے نقصان میں
پکڑا تاکہ نصیحت حاصل کریں ۱۳۰
تو جب اُن کو آسائش حاصل ہوتی تو کہتے کہ ہم اسکے
مستحق ہیں اور اگر سختی پہنچتی تو موسیٰ اور اُن کے
رفیقوں کی بدشگونی بتاتے دیکھو اُن کی بدشگونی خدا کے
ہاں (مقدر) ہے لیکن ان میں اکثر نہیں جانتے ۱۳۱
اور کہنے لگے کہ تم ہمارے پاس (خواہ) کوئی ہی نشانی لاؤ تاکہ
اس سے ہم پر جادو کرو مگر ہم تم پر ایمان لانے والے نہیں ہیں ۱۳۲
تو ہم نے اُن پر طوفان اور ٹڈیاں اور جوئیں اور مینڈک اور
خون کتنی کھلی ہوئی نشانیاں بھیجیں۔ مگر وہ تکبر ہی کرتے رہے
اور وہ لوگ تھے ہی گنہگار ۱۳۳
اور جب اُن پر عذاب واقع ہوتا تو کہتے کہ موسیٰ ہمارے
لئے اپنے پروردگار سے دُعا کرو جیسا اُس نے تم سے عہد
کر رکھا ہے اگر تم ہم سے عذاب کو ٹال دوگے تو ہم تم پر ایمان بھی لے
آئینگے اور بنی اسرائیل کو بھی تمہارے ساتھ جانے (کی اجازت) دینگے ۱۳۴
پھر جب ہم ایک مدت کیلئے جس تک اُنکو پہنچنا تھا اُن سے
عذاب دُور کر دیتے تو وہ عہد کو توڑ ڈالتے ۱۳۵
تو ہم نے اُن سے بدلہ لے کر ہی چھوڑا کہ اُن کو دریا میں ڈبو دیا
اسلئے کہ وہ ہماری آیتوں کو جھٹلاتے اور اُن سے بے پروائی کرتے تھے ۱۳۶
اور جو لوگ کمزور سمجھے جاتے تھے اُن کو زمین (شام) کے
مشرق و مغرب کا جس میں ہم نے برکت دی تھی وارث
کر دیا اور بنی اسرائیل کے بارے میں اُنکے صبر کی وجہ سے تمہارے
پروردگار کا وعدۂ نیک پورا ہوا اور فرعون اور قوم فرعون جو

they had patience and constancy, and We levelled to the ground the great Works and fine Buildings which Pharaoh and his people erected (with such pride).

138. We took the Children of Israel (with safety) across the sea. They came upon a people devoted entirely to some idols they had. They said: "O Moses! fashion for us a god like unto the gods they have." He said: "Surely ye are a people without knowledge".

139. "As to these folk,—the cult they are in is bound to destruction, and vain is the (worship) which they practise."

140. He said: "Shall I seek for you a god other than Allah, when it is He who hath endowed you with gifts above the nations?"

141. And remember We rescued you from Pharaoh's people, who afflicted you with the worst of punishment who slew your male children and saved alive your females: in that was a momentous trial from your Lord.

142. We appointed for Moses thirty nights, and completed (the period) with ten (more): thus was completed the term with his Lord, forty nights. And Moses had charged his brother Aaron (before he went up): "Act for me amongst my people: do right, and follow not the way of those who do mischief."

143. When Moses came to the place appointed by Us, and his Lord addressed him, he said: "O my Lord! show (Thyself) to me, that I may look upon Thee." Allah said: "By no means canst thou see Me (direct); but look upon the mount; if it abide in its place, then shalt thou see Me." When his Lord manifested Himself to the Mount, He made it as dust, and Moses fell down in a swoon. When he recovered his senses he said: "Glory be to Thee! To Thee I turn in repentance, and I am the first to believe."

محل) بناتے اور (انگور کے باغ) جو چھتریوں پر چڑھاتے
تھے سب کو ہم نے تباہ کر دیا ﴿۱۳۷﴾
اور ہم نے بنی اسرائیل کو دریا کے پار اتارا تو وہ ایسے لوگوں کے
پاس جا پہنچے جو اپنے بتوں (کی عبادت) کے لئے بیٹھے رہتے تھے۔
(بنی اسرائیل) کہنے لگے کہ موسیٰ جیسے ان لوگوں کے معبود ہیں ہمارے
لئے بھی ایک معبود بنا دو۔ موسیٰ نے کہا کہ تم بڑے ہی جاہل لوگ ہو ﴿۱۳۸﴾
یہ لوگ جس شغل میں (پھنسے ہوئے) ہیں وہ برباد ہونے والا ہے
اور جو کام یہ کرتے ہیں سب بیہودہ ہیں ﴿۱۳۹﴾
(اور یہ بھی) کہا کہ بھلا میں خدا کے سوا تمہارے لئے کوئی اور
معبود تلاش کروں حالانکہ اس نے تم کو تمام اہل عالم پر فضیلت بخشی ہے ﴿۱۴۰﴾
اور (ہمارے ان احسانوں کو یاد کرو) جب ہم نے تم کو فرعونیوں
(کے ہاتھ) سے نجات بخشی وہ لوگ تم کو بڑا دکھ دیتے تھے تمہارے
بیٹوں کو قتل کر ڈالتے تھے اور بیٹیوں کو زندہ رہنے دیتے تھے اور
اس میں تمہارے پروردگار کی طرف سے سخت آزمائش تھی ﴿۱۴۱﴾
اور ہم نے موسیٰ سے تیس رات کی میعاد مقرر کی اور دس (راتیں)
اور ملا کر اسے پورا (چلہ) کر دیا تو اس کے پروردگار کی چالیس
رات کی میعاد پوری ہو گئی۔ اور موسیٰ نے اپنے بھائی ہارون
سے کہا کہ میرے (کوہ طور پر جانے کے) بعد تم میری قوم میں میرے
جانشین ہو (ان کی) اصلاح کرتے رہنا اور شریروں کے رستے نہ چلنا ﴿۱۴۲﴾
اور جب موسیٰ ہمارے مقرر کئے ہوئے وقت پر (کوہ طور پر) پہنچے اور
ان کے پروردگار نے ان سے کلام کیا تو کہنے لگے کہ اے پروردگار
مجھے (جلوہ) دکھا کہ میں تیرا دیدار (بھی) دیکھوں۔ پروردگار نے کہا کہ تم
مجھے ہرگز نہ دیکھ سکو گے۔ ہاں پہاڑ کی طرف دیکھتے رہو اگر یہ اپنی جگہ
قائم رہا تو تم مجھ کو دیکھ سکو گے۔ جب ان کا پروردگار پہاڑ پر نمودار
ہوا تو (تجلی انوار ربانی) نے اس کو ریزہ ریزہ کر دیا۔ اور موسیٰ بےہوش
ہو کر گر پڑے۔ جب ہوش میں آئے تو کہنے لگے کہ تیری ذات پاک ہے
اور میں تیرے حضور میں توبہ کرتا ہوں اور جو ایمان لانے والے ہیں ان میں سب سے اول ہوں ﴿۱۴۳﴾

مَا كَانَ يَصْنَعُ فِرْعَوْنُ وَقَوْمُهُ وَمَا
كَانُوا يَعْرِشُونَ ﴿١٣٧﴾
وَجَاوَزْنَا بِبَنِي إِسْرَاءِيلَ الْبَحْرَ فَأَتَوْا
عَلَى قَوْمٍ يَعْكُفُونَ عَلَى أَصْنَامٍ لَهُمْ
قَالُوا يَا مُوسَى اجْعَلْ لَنَا إِلَٰهًا كَمَا لَهُمْ
آلِهَةٌ قَالَ إِنَّكُمْ قَوْمٌ تَجْهَلُونَ ﴿١٣٨﴾
إِنَّ هَٰؤُلَاءِ مُتَبَّرٌ مَا هُمْ فِيهِ وَبَاطِلٌ
مَا كَانُوا يَعْمَلُونَ ﴿١٣٩﴾
قَالَ أَغَيْرَ اللَّهِ أَبْغِيكُمْ إِلَٰهًا وَهُوَ
فَضَّلَكُمْ عَلَى الْعَالَمِينَ ﴿١٤٠﴾
وَإِذْ أَنْجَيْنَاكُمْ مِنْ آلِ فِرْعَوْنَ يَسُومُونَكُمْ
سُوءَ الْعَذَابِ يُقَتِّلُونَ أَبْنَاءَكُمْ وَ
يَسْتَحْيُونَ نِسَاءَكُمْ وَفِي ذَٰلِكُمْ بَلَاءٌ
مِنْ رَبِّكُمْ عَظِيمٌ ﴿١٤١﴾
وَوَاعَدْنَا مُوسَى ثَلَاثِينَ لَيْلَةً وَأَتْمَمْنَاهَا
بِعَشْرٍ فَتَمَّ مِيقَاتُ رَبِّهِ أَرْبَعِينَ لَيْلَةً
وَقَالَ مُوسَى لِأَخِيهِ هَارُونَ اخْلُفْنِي
فِي قَوْمِي وَأَصْلِحْ وَلَا تَتَّبِعْ سَبِيلَ
الْمُفْسِدِينَ ﴿١٤٢﴾
وَلَمَّا جَاءَ مُوسَى لِمِيقَاتِنَا وَكَلَّمَهُ
رَبُّهُ قَالَ رَبِّ أَرِنِي أَنْظُرْ إِلَيْكَ
قَالَ لَنْ تَرَانِي وَلَٰكِنِ انْظُرْ إِلَى الْجَبَلِ
فَإِنِ اسْتَقَرَّ مَكَانَهُ فَسَوْفَ
تَرَانِي فَلَمَّا تَجَلَّى رَبُّهُ لِلْجَبَلِ جَعَلَهُ
دَكًّا وَخَرَّ مُوسَى صَعِقًا فَلَمَّا أَفَاقَ
قَالَ سُبْحَانَكَ تُبْتُ إِلَيْكَ وَأَنَا أَوَّلُ
الْمُؤْمِنِينَ ﴿١٤٣﴾

144. (Allah) said: "O Moses! I have chosen thee above (other) men, by the messages I (have given thee) and the words I (have spoken to thee); take then the (revelation) which I give thee, and be of those who give thanks."

145. And We ordained for him in the Tablets in all matters, Admonition and explanation of all things, (and said): "Take and hold these with firmness, and enjoin thy people to hold fast by the best in the precepts: soon shall I show you the homes of the wicked,—(how they lie desolate)."

146. Those who behave arrogantly on the earth in defiance of right—them will I turn away from My Signs: even if they see all the Signs, they will not believe in them; and if they see the way of right conduct, they will not adopt it as the Way; but if they see the way of error, that is the Way they will adopt. For they have rejected our Signs, and failed to take warning from them.

147. Those who reject Our Signs and the Meeting in the Hereafter,—vain are their deeds: can they expect to be rewarded except as they have wrought?

148. The people of Moses made, in his absence, out of their ornaments, the body of a calf, (for worship): having lowing sound did they not see that it could neither speak to them, nor show them the Way? They took it for worship and they did wrong.

149. When they repented, and saw that they had erred, they said: "If our Lord have not mercy upon us and forgive us, we shall indeed be among the Losers.

150. When Moses came back to his people, angry and grieved, he said: "Evil it is that ye Have done in my place in my absence: did ye make haste to bring on the judgment of your Lord?" He put down the Tablets, seized his brother by (the hair of) his head,

(خدا نے) فرمایا موسیٰ میں نے تم کو اپنے پیغام اور اپنے کلام سے
لوگوں سے ممتاز کیا ہے۔ تو جو میں نے تم کو عطا کیا ہے اُسے پکڑ رکھو
اور (میرا) شکر بجا لاؤ ﴿١٤٤﴾
اور ہم نے (تورات کی) تختیوں میں اُن کے لئے ہر قسم کی نصیحت اور ہر چیز
کی تفصیل لکھ دی پھر (ارشاد فرمایا کہ) اسے زور سے پکڑے رہو اور
اپنی قوم سے بھی کہہ دو کہ ان باتوں کو جو اس میں (مندرج ہیں اور)
بہت بہتر ہیں پکڑے رہیں۔ میں عنقریب تم کو نافرمان لوگوں کا گھر دکھاؤں گا ﴿١٤٥﴾
جو لوگ زمین میں ناحق غرور کرتے ہیں اُن کو اپنی آیتوں سے
پھیر دوں گا۔ اگر یہ سب نشانیاں بھی دیکھ لیں تب بھی ان پر
ایمان نہ لائیں اور اگر راستی کا رستہ دیکھیں تو اُسے (اپنا)
رستہ نہ بنائیں۔ اور اگر گمراہی کی راہ دیکھیں تو اُسے
رستہ بنالیں۔ یہ اس لئے کہ اُنہوں نے ہماری آیات کو
جھٹلایا اور اُن سے غفلت کرتے رہے ﴿١٤٦﴾
اور جن لوگوں نے ہماری آیتوں اور آخرت کے آنے کو جھٹلایا
اُن کے اعمال ضائع ہو جائیں گے۔ یہ جیسے عمل کرتے ہیں ویسا
ہی اُن کو بدلہ ملے گا ﴿١٤٧﴾
اور قوم موسیٰ نے موسیٰ کے بعد اپنے زیور کا ایک بچھڑا بنا لیا (وہ)
ایک جسم (تھا) جس میں سے بیل کی آواز نکلتی تھی۔ ان لوگوں نے
یہ نہ دیکھا کہ وہ نہ ان سے بات کر سکتا ہے اور نہ ان کو رستہ دکھا سکتا ہے۔
اُس کو انہوں نے (معبود) بنا لیا اور (اپنے حق میں) ظلم کیا ﴿١٤٨﴾
اور جب وہ نادم ہوئے اور دیکھا کہ گمراہ ہو گئے ہیں تو کہنے لگے
کہ اگر ہمارا پروردگار ہم پر رحم نہیں کرے گا اور ہم کو معاف
نہیں فرمائے گا تو ہم برباد ہو جائیں گے ﴿١٤٩﴾
اور جب موسیٰ اپنی قوم میں نہایت غصے اور افسوس کی حالت
میں واپس آئے تو کہنے لگے کہ تم نے میرے بعد بہت ہی بداطواری
کی۔ کیا تم نے اپنے پروردگار کا حکم (یعنی میرا اپنے پاس آنا) جلد
چاہا (یہ کہا) اور (شدت غضب سے تورات کی) تختیاں ڈال دیں اور

قَالَ يٰمُوْسٰٓى اِنِّى اصْطَفَيْتُكَ عَلَى
النَّاسِ بِرِسٰلٰتِىْ وَبِكَلَامِىْ ۖ فَخُذْ مَآ
اٰتَيْتُكَ وَكُنْ مِّنَ الشّٰكِرِيْنَ ﴿١٤٤﴾
وَكَتَبْنَا لَهٗ فِى الْاَلْوَاحِ مِنْ كُلِّ شَىْءٍ
مَّوْعِظَةً وَّتَفْصِيْلًا لِّكُلِّ شَىْءٍ ۚ
فَخُذْهَا بِقُوَّةٍ وَّاْمُرْ قَوْمَكَ يَاْخُذُوْا
بِاَحْسَنِهَا ؕ سَاُورِيْكُمْ دَارَ الْفٰسِقِيْنَ ﴿١٤٥﴾
سَاَصْرِفُ عَنْ اٰيٰتِىَ الَّذِيْنَ يَتَكَبَّرُوْنَ
فِى الْاَرْضِ بِغَيْرِ الْحَقِّ ؕ وَاِنْ يَّرَوْا
كُلَّ اٰيَةٍ لَّا يُؤْمِنُوْا بِهَا ۚ وَاِنْ يَّرَوْا
سَبِيْلَ الرُّشْدِ لَا يَتَّخِذُوْهُ سَبِيْلًا ۚ وَاِنْ
يَّرَوْا سَبِيْلَ الْغَىِّ يَتَّخِذُوْهُ سَبِيْلًا ؕ ذٰلِكَ
بِاَنَّهُمْ كَذَّبُوْا بِاٰيٰتِنَا وَكَانُوْا عَنْهَا غٰفِلِيْنَ ﴿١٤٦﴾
وَالَّذِيْنَ كَذَّبُوْا بِاٰيٰتِنَا وَلِقَآءِ الْاٰخِرَةِ
حَبِطَتْ اَعْمَالُهُمْ ؕ هَلْ يُجْزَوْنَ اِلَّا
مَا كَانُوْا يَعْمَلُوْنَ ﴿١٤٧﴾ ع ركوع ١٧
وَاتَّخَذَ قَوْمُ مُوْسٰى مِنْ بَعْدِهٖ مِنْ
حُلِيِّهِمْ عِجْلًا جَسَدًا لَّهٗ خُوَارٌ ؕ اَلَمْ
يَرَوْا اَنَّهٗ لَا يُكَلِّمُهُمْ وَلَا يَهْدِيْهِمْ
سَبِيْلًا ۘ اِتَّخَذُوْهُ وَكَانُوْا ظٰلِمِيْنَ ﴿١٤٨﴾ وقف لازم
وَلَمَّا سُقِطَ فِىْٓ اَيْدِيْهِمْ وَرَاَوْا اَنَّهُمْ
قَدْ ضَلُّوْا ۙ قَالُوْا لَئِنْ لَّمْ يَرْحَمْنَا رَبُّنَا
وَيَغْفِرْ لَنَا لَنَكُوْنَنَّ مِنَ الْخٰسِرِيْنَ ﴿١٤٩﴾
وَلَمَّا رَجَعَ مُوْسٰٓى اِلٰى قَوْمِهٖ غَضْبَانَ
اَسِفًا ۙ قَالَ بِئْسَمَا خَلَفْتُمُوْنِىْ مِنْ بَعْدِىْ ۚ
اَعَجِلْتُمْ اَمْرَ رَبِّكُمْ ۚ وَاَلْقَى الْاَلْوَاحَ وَ
اَخَذَ بِرَاْسِ اَخِيْهِ يَجُرُّهٗ اِلَيْهِ ؕ قَالَ

and dragged him. To him Aaron said: "Son of my mother! The people did indeed reckon me as naught, and went near to slaying me! Make not the enemies rejoice over my misfortune, nor count thou me amongst the people of sin."

151. Moses prayed: "O my Lord! forgive me and my brother! Admit us to thy mercy! for Thou art the Most Merciful of those who show mercy!"

152. Those who took the calf (for worship) will indeed be overwhelmed with wrath from their Lord and with shame in this life: thus do We recompense those who invent (falsehoods).

153. But those who do wrong but repent thereafter and (truly) believe,—verily Thy Lord is thereafter Oft-Forgiving, Most Merciful.

154. When the anger of Moses was appeased, he took up the Tablets: in the writing thereon was Guidance and Mercy for such as fear their Lord.

155. And Moses chose seventy of his people for Our place of meeting: when they were seized with violent quaking, he prayed: "O my Lord! if it had been Thy Will thou couldst have destroyed, long before, both them and me: wouldst Thou destroy us for the deeds of the foolish ones among us? This is no more than thy trial: by it Thou causest whom Thou wilt stray, and Thou leadest whom Thou wilt into the right path. Thou art our Protector: so forgive us and give us Thy mercy; for Thou art the Best of those who forgive.

156. "And ordain for us that which is good, in this life and in the Hereafter: for we have turned unto Thee." He said: "I afflict My Punishment on whom I will; but My Mercy extendeth to all things. That (Mercy) I shall ordain for those who do right, and pay Zakat and

اپنے بھائی کے سر کے بالوں کو پکڑ کر اپنی طرف کھینچنے لگے انہوں
نے کہا کہ بھائی جان لوگ تو مجھے کمزور سمجھتے تھے اور قریب تھا
کہ قتل کر دیں۔ تو ایسا کام نہ کیجئے کہ دشمن مجھ پر ہنسیں اور مجھے ظالم لوگوں میں مت ملایئے ﴿۱۵۰﴾
تب انہوں نے دعا کی کہ اے میرے پروردگار مجھے اور میرے بھائی کو معاف کر
اور ہمیں اپنی رحمت میں داخل کر تو سب سے بڑھ کر رحم کرنے والا ہے ﴿۱۵۱﴾
(خدا نے فرمایا کہ) جن لوگوں نے بچھڑے کو (معبود) بنا لیا تھا ان پر پروردگار
کا غضب واقع ہوگا اور دنیا کی زندگی میں ذلت (نصیب ہوگی)
اور ہم افترا پردازوں کو ایسا ہی بدلہ دیا کرتے ہیں ﴿۱۵۲﴾
اور جنہوں نے برے کام کئے پھر اس کے بعد توبہ کر لی اور
ایمان لے آئے۔ تو کچھ شک نہیں کہ تمہارا پروردگار اس کے
بعد (بخش دے گا کہ وہ) بخشنے والا مہربان ہے ﴿۱۵۳﴾
اور جب موسیٰ کا غصہ فرو ہوا تو (تورات کی) تختیاں اٹھا لیں۔
اور جو کچھ ان میں لکھا تھا وہ ان لوگوں کے لئے جو اپنے
پروردگار سے ڈرتے ہیں ہدایت اور رحمت تھی ﴿۱۵۴﴾
اور موسیٰ نے اس میعاد پر جو ہم نے مقرر کی تھی اپنی قوم کے
ستر آدمی منتخب (کر کے کوہ طور پر حاضر) کئے۔ جب ان کو زلزلے نے
پکڑا تو موسیٰ نے کہا کہ اے پروردگار اگر تو چاہتا تو ان کو اور مجھ کو پہلے
ہی سے ہلاک کر دیتا کیا تو اس فعل کی سزا میں جو ہم میں سے بے عقل
لوگوں نے کیا ہے ہمیں ہلاک کر دیگا؟ یہ تو تیری آزمائش ہے اس سے تو جس کو
چاہے گمراہ کرے اور جسے چاہے ہدایت بخشے۔ تو ہی ہمارا کارساز
ہے تو ہمیں (ہمارے گناہ) بخش دے اور ہم پر رحم کر اور تو
سب سے بہتر بخشنے والا ہے ﴿۱۵۵﴾
اور ہمارے لئے اس دنیا میں بھی بھلائی لکھ دے اور آخرت میں
بھی۔ ہم تیری طرف رجوع ہو چکے۔ فرمایا کہ جو میرا
عذاب ہے اسے تو جس پر چاہتا ہوں نازل کرتا ہوں اور
جو میری رحمت ہے وہ ہر چیز کو شامل ہے۔ میں اس کو
ان لوگوں کے لئے لکھ دوں گا جو پرہیزگاری کرتے اور زکوٰۃ

ابن أم إن القوم استضعفوني وكادوا
يقتلونني فلا تشمت بي الأعداء ولا
تجعلني مع القوم الظالمين ﴿١٥٠﴾
قال رب اغفر لي ولأخي وأدخلنا
في رحمتك وأنت أرحم الراحمين ﴿١٥١﴾ ع
إن الذين اتخذوا العجل سينالهم
غضب من ربهم وذلة في الحياة
الدنيا وكذلك نجزي المفترين ﴿١٥٢﴾
والذين عملوا السيئات ثم تابوا من
بعدها وآمنوا إن ربك من بعدها
لغفور رحيم ﴿١٥٣﴾
ولما سكت عن موسى الغضب أخذ
الألواح وفي نسختها هدى ورحمة
للذين هم لربهم يرهبون ﴿١٥٤﴾
واختار موسى قومه سبعين رجلا
لميقاتنا فلما أخذتهم الرجفة قال
رب لو شئت أهلكتهم من قبل
وإياي أتهلكنا بما فعل السفهاء
منا إن هي إلا فتنتك تضل بها
من تشاء وتهدي من تشاء أنت
ولينا فاغفر لنا وارحمنا وأنت
خير الغافرين ﴿١٥٥﴾
واكتب لنا في هذه الدنيا حسنة
وفي الآخرة إنا هدنا إليك قال
عذابي أصيب به من أشاء ورحمتي
وسعت كل شيء فسأكتبها للذين
يتقون ويؤتون الزكاة والذين

هُمْ بِآيَاتِنَا يُؤْمِنُونَ ﴿١٥٦﴾
الَّذِينَ يَتَّبِعُونَ الرَّسُولَ النَّبِيَّ الْأُمِّيَّ
الَّذِي يَجِدُونَهُ مَكْتُوبًا عِنْدَهُمْ فِي
التَّوْرَاةِ وَالْإِنْجِيلِ يَأْمُرُهُمْ بِالْمَعْرُوفِ
وَيَنْهَاهُمْ عَنِ الْمُنْكَرِ وَيُحِلُّ لَهُمُ الطَّيِّبَاتِ
وَيُحَرِّمُ عَلَيْهِمُ الْخَبَائِثَ وَيَضَعُ عَنْهُمْ
إِصْرَهُمْ وَالْأَغْلَالَ الَّتِي كَانَتْ عَلَيْهِمْ ۚ
فَالَّذِينَ آمَنُوا بِهِ وَعَزَّرُوهُ وَنَصَرُوهُ
وَاتَّبَعُوا النُّورَ الَّذِي أُنْزِلَ مَعَهُ ۙ
أُولَٰئِكَ هُمُ الْمُفْلِحُونَ ﴿١٥٧﴾ ع ١٩ ٩
قُلْ يَا أَيُّهَا النَّاسُ إِنِّي رَسُولُ اللَّهِ إِلَيْكُمْ
جَمِيعًا الَّذِي لَهُ مُلْكُ السَّمَاوَاتِ وَ
الْأَرْضِ ۖ لَا إِلَٰهَ إِلَّا هُوَ يُحْيِي وَيُمِيتُ ۖ
فَآمِنُوا بِاللَّهِ وَرَسُولِهِ النَّبِيِّ الْأُمِّيِّ
الَّذِي يُؤْمِنُ بِاللَّهِ وَكَلِمَاتِهِ وَاتَّبِعُوهُ
لَعَلَّكُمْ تَهْتَدُونَ ﴿١٥٨﴾
وَمِنْ قَوْمِ مُوسَىٰ أُمَّةٌ يَهْدُونَ بِالْحَقِّ
وَبِهِ يَعْدِلُونَ ﴿١٥٩﴾
وَقَطَّعْنَاهُمُ اثْنَتَيْ عَشْرَةَ أَسْبَاطًا أُمَمًا ۚ
وَأَوْحَيْنَا إِلَىٰ مُوسَىٰ إِذِ اسْتَسْقَاهُ قَوْمُهُ
أَنِ اضْرِبْ بِعَصَاكَ الْحَجَرَ ۖ فَانْبَجَسَتْ
مِنْهُ اثْنَتَا عَشْرَةَ عَيْنًا ۖ قَدْ عَلِمَ كُلُّ
أُنَاسٍ مَشْرَبَهُمْ ۚ وَظَلَّلْنَا عَلَيْهِمُ الْغَمَامَ
وَأَنْزَلْنَا عَلَيْهِمُ الْمَنَّ وَالسَّلْوَىٰ ۖ كُلُوا
مِنْ طَيِّبَاتِ مَا رَزَقْنَاكُمْ ۚ وَمَا ظَلَمُونَا
وَلَٰكِنْ كَانُوا أَنْفُسَهُمْ يَظْلِمُونَ ﴿١٦٠﴾
وَإِذْ قِيلَ لَهُمُ اسْكُنُوا هَٰذِهِ الْقَرْيَةَ

دیتے اور ہماری آیتوں پر ایمان رکھتے ہیں ﴿١٥٦﴾
وہ جو (محمدؐ) رسول (اللہ) کی جو نبی اُمّی ہیں پیروی کرتے ہیں
جن (کے اوصاف) کو وہ اپنے ہاں تورات اور انجیل میں لکھا ہوا پاتے
ہیں۔ وہ اُنہیں نیک کام کا حکم دیتے ہیں اور بُرے کام سے روکتے ہیں۔
اور پاک چیزوں کو اُن کیلئے حلال کرتے ہیں اور ناپاک چیزوں
کو اُن پر حرام ٹھیراتے ہیں اور اُن پر سے بوجھ اور طوق جو اُن
(کے سر) پر (اور گلے میں) تھے اُتارتے ہیں۔ تو جو لوگ اُن پر ایمان
لائے اور اُنکی رفاقت کی اور اُنہیں مدد دی۔ اور جو نُور اُنکے
ساتھ نازل ہوا ہے اُس کی پیروی کی وہی مُراد پانے
والے ہیں ﴿١٥٧﴾
(اے محمدؐ) کہہ دو کہ لوگو میں تم سب کی طرف خدا کا بھیجا ہوا
ہوں (یعنی اُس کا رسول ہوں) (وہ) جو آسمانوں اور زمین کا
بادشاہ ہے۔ اسکے سوا کوئی معبود نہیں وہی زندگانی بخشتا ہے اور
وہی موت دیتا ہے۔ تو خدا پر اور اسکے رسول پیغمبر اُمّی پر جو خدا پر اور
اُس کے تمام کلام پر ایمان رکھتے ہیں ایمان لاؤ اور اُن کی
پیروی کرو تاکہ ہدایت پاؤ ﴿١٥٨﴾
اور قوم موسیٰ میں کچھ لوگ ایسے بھی ہیں جو حق کا رستہ بتاتے
اور اسی کے ساتھ انصاف کرتے ہیں ﴿١٥٩﴾
اور ہم نے اُنکو (یعنی بنی اسرائیل کو) الگ الگ کر کے بارہ قبیلے (اور)
بڑی بڑی جماعتیں بنا دیا اور جب موسیٰ سے اُنکی قوم نے پانی
طلب کیا تو ہم نے اُنکی طرف وحی بھیجی کہ اپنی لاٹھی پتھر پر مار دو۔ تو
اسمیں سے بارہ چشمے پھوٹ نکلے اور سب لوگوں نے اپنا اپنا گھاٹ معلوم
کر لیا۔ اور ہم نے اُن (کے سروں) پر بادل کو سائبان بنائے رکھا اور
اُن پر منّ و سلویٰ اُتارتے رہے۔ (اور اُن سے کہا کہ) جو پاکیزہ چیزیں ہم
تمہیں دیتے ہیں اُنہیں کھاؤ۔ اور ان لوگوں نے ہمارا کچھ نقصان
نہیں کیا۔ بلکہ (جو نقصان کیا) اپنا ہی کیا ﴿١٦٠﴾
اور (یاد کرو) جب اُن سے کہا گیا کہ اس شہر میں سکونت اختیار کرلو

those who believe in Our Signs;—

157. "Those who follow the Messenger, the unlettered Prophet, whom they find mentioned in their own (Scriptures),— in the Taurat and the Gospel;—for he commands them what is just and forbids them what is evil; he allows them as lawful what is good (and pure) and prohibits them from what is bad (and impure): He releases them from their heavy burdens and from the yokes that are upon them. So it is those who believe in him, honour him, help him, and follow the Light which is sent down with him,—it is they who will prosper."

158. Say: "O men! I am sent unto you all, as the Messenger of Allah, to Whom belongeth the dominion of the heavens and the earth: there is no god but He: it is He that giveth both life and death. So believe in Allah and His Messenger. The unlettered Prophet, who believeth in Allah and His Words: follow him that (so) ye may be guided."

159. Of the people of Moses there is a section who guide and do justice in the light of truth.

160. We divided them into twelve Tribes or nations. We directed Moses by inspiration, when his (thirsty) people asked him for Water: "Strike the rock with thy staff": out of it there gushed forth twelve springs: each group knew its own place for water. We gave them the shade of clouds, and sent down to them manna and quails, (saying): "Eat of the good things We have provided for you": (but they rebelled); to Us they did no harm, but they harmed their own souls.

161. And remember it was said to them: "Dwell in this town and eat

therein as ye wish, but say forgive (us) and enter the gate in a posture of humility: We shall forgive you your faults; We shall increase (the portion of) those who do good."

اور اسمیں جہاں سے جی چاہے کھانا پینا، اور (ہاں شہر میں جانا تو)
حِطّۃٌ کہنا اور دروازے میں داخل ہونا تو سجدہ کرنا۔ ہم تمہارے
گناہ معاف کر دینگے (اور) نیکی کرنیوالوں کو اور زیادہ دینگے (۱۶۱)

وَكُلُوا مِنْهَا حَيْثُ شِئْتُمْ وَقُولُوا حِطَّةٌ
وَّادْخُلُوا الْبَابَ سُجَّدًا نَّغْفِرْ لَكُمْ
خَطِيٓـٰٔتِكُمْ سَنَزِيدُ الْمُحْسِنِينَ ﴿١٦١﴾

162. But the transgressors among them changed the word from that which had been given them so we sent on them a plague from heaven. For that they repeatedly transgressed.

مگر جو اُن میں ظالم تھے اُنہوں نے اُس لفظ کو جس کا اُن کو
حکم دیا گیا تھا بدل کر اُس کی جگہ اور لفظ کہنا شروع
کیا تو ہم نے اُن پر آسمان سے عذاب بھیجا اس لئے
کہ ظلم کرتے تھے (۱۶۲)

فَبَدَّلَ الَّذِينَ ظَلَمُوا مِنْهُمْ قَوْلًا
غَيْرَ الَّذِي قِيلَ لَهُمْ فَأَرْسَلْنَا
عَلَيْهِمْ رِجْزًا مِّنَ السَّمَآءِ بِمَا كَانُوا
يَظْلِمُونَ ﴿١٦٢﴾ ع

163. Ask them concerning the town standing close by the sea. Behold! they transgressed in the matter of the Sabbath, for on the day of their Sabbath their fish did come to them, openly (holding up their heads,) but on the day they had no Sabbath, they came not: thus did We make a trial of them, for they were given to transgression.

اور ان سے اس گاؤں کا حال تو پوچھو جو لبِ دریا واقع
تھا جب یہ لوگ ہفتے کے دن کے بارے میں حد سے تجاوز کرنے
لگے (یعنی) اُس وقت کہ اُنکے ہفتے کے دن مچھلیاں اُنکے سامنے
پانی کے اُوپر آتیں اور جب ہفتے کا دن نہ ہوتا تو نہ آتیں اسی طرح ہم
اُن لوگوں کو اُنکی نافرمانیوں کے سبب آزمائش میں ڈالنے لگے (۱۶۳)

وَسْـَٔلْهُمْ عَنِ الْقَرْيَةِ الَّتِي كَانَتْ
حَاضِرَةَ الْبَحْرِ إِذْ يَعْدُونَ فِي السَّبْتِ
إِذْ تَأْتِيهِمْ حِيتَانُهُمْ يَوْمَ سَبْتِهِمْ شُرَّعًا
وَّيَوْمَ لَا يَسْبِتُونَ لَا تَأْتِيهِمْ كَذَٰلِكَ
نَبْلُوهُمْ بِمَا كَانُوا يَفْسُقُونَ ﴿١٦٣﴾

164. When some of them said: "Why do ye preach to a people whom Allah will destroy or visit with a terrible punishment?"— said the preachers: "To discharge our duty to your Lord and perchance they may fear Him."

اور جب اُن میں سے ایک جماعت نے کہا کہ تم ایسے لوگوں کو کیوں
نصیحت کرتے ہو جن کو خدا ہلاک کرنیوالا یا سخت عذاب دینے والا ہے
تو اُنہوں نے کہا اس لئے کہ تمہارے پروردگار کے سامنے معذرت
کر سکیں اور عجب نہیں کہ وہ پرہیزگاری اختیار کریں (۱۶۴)

وَإِذْ قَالَتْ أُمَّةٌ مِّنْهُمْ لِمَ تَعِظُونَ
قَوْمًا اللَّهُ مُهْلِكُهُمْ أَوْ مُعَذِّبُهُمْ عَذَابًا
شَدِيدًا قَالُوا مَعْذِرَةً إِلَىٰ رَبِّكُمْ
وَلَعَلَّهُمْ يَتَّقُونَ ﴿١٦٤﴾

165. When they disregarded the warnings that had been given them, we rescued those who forbade evil; but We visited the wrong-doers with a grievous punishment, because they were given to transgression.

جب اُنہوں نے ان باتوں کو فراموش کر دیا جن کی اُنکو نصیحت
کی گئی تھی تو جو لوگ بُرائی سے منع کرتے تھے اُنکو ہم نے نجات دی اور جو
ظلم کرتے تھے اُنکو بُرے عذاب میں پکڑ لیا کہ نافرمانی کیے جاتے تھے (۱۶۵)

فَلَمَّا نَسُوا مَا ذُكِّرُوا بِهِ أَنجَيْنَا الَّذِينَ
يَنْهَوْنَ عَنِ السُّوٓءِ وَأَخَذْنَا الَّذِينَ
ظَلَمُوا بِعَذَابٍ بَـِٔيسٍ بِمَا كَانُوا يَفْسُقُونَ ﴿١٦٥﴾

166. When in their insolence they transgressed (all) prohibitions, We said to them: "Be ye apes, despised and rejected."

غرض جن اعمال (بد) سے اُنکو منع کیا گیا تھا جب وہ اُن (پر اصرار اور
ہمارے حکم) سے گردن کشی کرنے لگے تو ہم نے اُنکو حکم دیا کہ ذلیل بندر ہو جاؤ (۱۶۶)

فَلَمَّا عَتَوْا عَن مَّا نُهُوا عَنْهُ قُلْنَا لَهُمْ
كُونُوا قِرَدَةً خَاسِـِٔينَ ﴿١٦٦﴾

167. Behold! thy Lord did declare that He would send against them, to the Day of Judgment, those who would afflict them with grievous Chastisement. Thy Lord is quick in retribution, but He is also Oft-Forgiving, Most Merciful.

اور (اُس وقت کو یاد کرو) جب تمہارے پروردگار نے (یہود کو) آگاہ
کر دیا تھا کہ وہ اُن پر قیامت تک ایسے شخص کو مسلط رکھے گا جو
اُن کو بُری بُری تکلیفیں دیتا رہے بیشک تمہارا پروردگار جلد عذاب
کرنے والا ہے اور وہ بخشنے والا مہربان بھی ہے (۱۶۷)

وَإِذْ تَأَذَّنَ رَبُّكَ لَيَبْعَثَنَّ عَلَيْهِمْ إِلَىٰ
يَوْمِ الْقِيَٰمَةِ مَن يَسُومُهُمْ سُوٓءَ الْعَذَابِ
إِنَّ رَبَّكَ لَسَرِيعُ الْعِقَابِ وَإِنَّهُ
لَغَفُورٌ رَّحِيمٌ ﴿١٦٧﴾

168. We broke them up into sections on this earth. There are among them some that are the

اور ہم نے اُن کو جماعت جماعت کر کے مُلک میں منتشر کر دیا۔
بعض اُن میں سے نیکوکار ہیں اور بعض اور طرح کے (یعنی بدکار)

وَقَطَّعْنَٰهُمْ فِي الْأَرْضِ أُمَمًا مِّنْهُمُ
الصَّٰلِحُونَ وَمِنْهُمْ دُونَ ذَٰلِكَ

righteous, and some that are the opposite. We have tried them with both prosperity and adversity: in order that they might turn (to Us).

169. After them succeeded an (evil) generation: they inherited the Book, but they chose (for themselves) the vanities of this world, saying (for excuse): "(Everything) will be forgiven us." (Even so), if similar vanities came their way, they would (again) seize them. Was not the Covenant of the Book taken from them, that they would not ascribe to Allah anything but the truth? And they study what is in the Book. But best for the righteous is the Home in the Hereafter. Will ye not understand?

170. As to those who hold fast by the Book and establish regular Prayer,—never shall we suffer the reward of the righteous to perish.

171. When We raised the Mount over them, as if it had been a canopy, and they thought it was going to fall on them (We said): "Hold firmly to what We have given you, and bring (ever) to remembrance what is therein; perchance ye may fear Allah".

172. When thy Lord drew forth from the Children of Adam—from their loins—their descendants, and made them testify concerning themselves, (saying): "Am I not your Lord (Who cherishes and sustains you)?"—They said: "Yea! we do testify!" (This), lest ye should say on the Day of Judgment: "Of this we were never mindful":

173. Or lest ye should say: "Our fathers before us took false gods, but we are (their) descendants after them: wilt Thou then destroy us because of the deeds of men who followed falsehood?"

174. Thus do We explain the Signs in detail; and perchance they may turn (unto Us).

175. Relate to them the story of the man to whom We sent Our Signs, but he passed them by: so Satan followed him up, and he went astray.

اور ہم آسائشوں اور تکلیفوں (دونوں) سے اُن کی آزمائش
کرتے رہے تاکہ (ہماری طرف) رجوع کریں ﴿۱۶۸﴾
پھر انکے بعد ناخلف انکے قائم مقام ہوئے جو کتاب کے وارث بنے
یہ (بے تأمل) اس دُنیائے دنی کا مال و متاع لے لیتے ہیں اور کہتے
ہیں کہ ہم بخش دیئے جائینگے (اور لوگ ایسوں پر طعن کرتے ہیں) اگر
انکے سامنے بھی ویسا ہی مال آجاتا ہے تو وہ بھی اسے لے لیتے ہیں۔
کیا انسے کتاب کی نسبت عہد نہیں لیا گیا کہ خدا پر سچ کے سوا اور کچھ
نہیں کہینگے! اور جو کچھ اس (کتاب) میں ہے اسکو انہوں نے پڑھ بھی لیا ہے۔
اور آخرت کا گھر پرہیزگاروں کیلئے بہتر ہے کیا تم سمجھتے نہیں ﴿۱۶۹﴾
اور جو لوگ کتاب کو مضبوط پکڑے ہوئے ہیں اور نماز کا التزام رکھتے ہیں
(انکو ہم اجر دینگے کہ) ہم نیکوکاروں کا اجر ضائع نہیں کرتے ﴿۱۷۰﴾
اور جب ہم نے اُن (کے سروں) پر پہاڑ اُٹھا کھڑا کیا گویا وہ سائبان تھا
اور اُنہوں نے خیال کیا کہ وہ اُن پر گرتا ہے تو (ہم نے کہا کہ) جو
ہم نے تمہیں دیا ہے اُسے زور سے پکڑے رہو اور جو اس میں لکھا ہے
اس پر عمل کرو تاکہ بچ جاؤ ﴿۱۷۱﴾
اور جب تمہارے پروردگار نے بنی آدم سے یعنی اُن کی پیٹھوں سے
اُن کی اولاد نکالی تو اُن سے خود اُن کے مقابلے میں اقرار کرا لیا
(یعنی اُن سے پوچھا کہ) کیا میں تمہارا پروردگار نہیں ہوں۔ وہ
کہنے لگے کیوں نہیں ہم گواہ ہیں (کہ تو ہمارا پروردگار ہے) (یہ اقرار اسلئے
کرایا تھا) کہ قیامت کے دن (کہیں یوں نہ) کہنے لگو کہ ہم کو تو اسکی خبر ہی نہ تھی ﴿۱۷۲﴾
یا یہ (نہ) کہو کہ شرک تو پہلے ہمارے بڑوں نے کیا تھا۔ اور ہم تو انکی
اولاد تھے (جو) اُنکے بعد (پیدا ہوئے) تو کیا جو کام اہل باطل
کرتے رہے اس کے بدلے تو ہمیں ہلاک کرتا ہے؟ ﴿۱۷۳﴾
اور اسی طرح ہم (اپنی) آیتیں کھول کھول کر بیان کرتے ہیں تاکہ یہ رجوع کریں ﴿۱۷۴﴾
اور ان کو اس شخص کا حال پڑھ کر سنا دو جس کو ہم نے اپنی آیتیں
عطا فرمائیں (اور ہفت پارچہ علم شرائع سے مزین کیا) تو اسنے انکو
اُتار دیا پھر شیطان اُسکے پیچھے لگا تو وہ گمراہوں میں ہو گیا ﴿۱۷۵﴾

وَبَلَوْنٰهُمْ بِالْحَسَنٰتِ وَالسَّيِّاٰتِ لَعَلَّهُمْ
يَرْجِعُوْنَ ﴿۱۶۸﴾
فَخَلَفَ مِنْ بَعْدِهِمْ خَلْفٌ وَّرِثُوا الْكِتٰبَ
يَاْخُذُوْنَ عَرَضَ هٰذَا الْاَدْنٰى وَيَقُوْلُوْنَ
سَيُغْفَرُ لَنَا ۚ وَاِنْ يَّاْتِهِمْ عَرَضٌ مِّثْلُهٗ
يَاْخُذُوْهُ ؕ اَلَمْ يُؤْخَذْ عَلَيْهِمْ مِّيْثَاقُ الْكِتٰبِ
اَنْ لَّا يَقُوْلُوْا عَلَى اللّٰهِ اِلَّا الْحَقَّ وَدَرَسُوْا
مَا فِيْهِ ؕ وَالدَّارُ الْاٰخِرَةُ خَيْرٌ لِّلَّذِيْنَ
يَتَّقُوْنَ ؕ اَفَلَا تَعْقِلُوْنَ ﴿۱۶۹﴾
وَالَّذِيْنَ يُمَسِّكُوْنَ بِالْكِتٰبِ وَاَقَامُوا
الصَّلٰوةَ ؕ اِنَّا لَا نُضِيْعُ اَجْرَ الْمُصْلِحِيْنَ ﴿۱۷۰﴾
وَاِذْ نَتَقْنَا الْجَبَلَ فَوْقَهُمْ كَاَنَّهٗ ظُلَّةٌ
وَّظَنُّوْۤا اَنَّهٗ وَاقِعٌۢ بِهِمْ ۚ خُذُوْا مَاۤ
اٰتَيْنٰكُمْ بِقُوَّةٍ وَّاذْكُرُوْا مَا فِيْهِ
لَعَلَّكُمْ تَتَّقُوْنَ ﴿۱۷۱﴾ ع ۲۱/۹
وَاِذْ اَخَذَ رَبُّكَ مِنْۢ بَنِیْۤ اٰدَمَ مِنْ
ظُهُوْرِهِمْ ذُرِّيَّتَهُمْ وَاَشْهَدَهُمْ عَلٰۤى
اَنْفُسِهِمْ ۚ اَلَسْتُ بِرَبِّكُمْ ؕ قَالُوْا بَلٰى ۛۚ مع
شَهِدْنَا ۛۚ اَنْ تَقُوْلُوْا يَوْمَ الْقِيٰمَةِ اِنَّا كُنَّا
عَنْ هٰذَا غٰفِلِيْنَ ﴿۱۷۲﴾ عند المتأخرين ۱۲
اَوْ تَقُوْلُوْۤا اِنَّمَاۤ اَشْرَكَ اٰبَآؤُنَا مِنْ قَبْلُ
وَكُنَّا ذُرِّيَّةً مِّنْۢ بَعْدِهِمْ ۚ اَفَتُهْلِكُنَا
بِمَا فَعَلَ الْمُبْطِلُوْنَ ﴿۱۷۳﴾
وَكَذٰلِكَ نُفَصِّلُ الْاٰيٰتِ وَلَعَلَّهُمْ يَرْجِعُوْنَ ﴿۱۷۴﴾
وَاتْلُ عَلَيْهِمْ نَبَاَ الَّذِیْۤ اٰتَيْنٰهُ اٰيٰتِنَا
فَانْسَلَخَ مِنْهَا فَاَتْبَعَهُ الشَّيْطٰنُ فَكَانَ
مِنَ الْغٰوِيْنَ ﴿۱۷۵﴾

176. If it had been Our Will, We should have elevated him with Our Signs: but he inclined to the earth, and followed his own vain desires. His similitude is that of a dog: if you attack him, he lolls out his tongue, or if you leave him alone, he (still) lolls out his tongue. That is the similitude of those who reject Our Signs; so relate the story; perchance they may reflect.

177. Evil as the example are people who reject Our Signs and wrong their own souls.

178. Whom Allah doth guide,—he is on the right path: whom He rejects from His guidance,— such are the persons who lose.

179. Many are the Jinns and men We have made for Hell: they have hearts wherewith they understand not, eyes wherewith they see not, and ears wherewith they hear not. They are like cattle,—nay more misguided: for they are heedless (of warning).

180. The most beautiful names belong to Allah: so call on Him by them; but shun such men as distort His names: for what they do, they will soon be requited.

181. Of those We have created are people who direct (others) with truth, and dispense justice therewith.

182. Those who reject Our Signs, We will lead them step by step to ruin while they know not:

183. Respite will I grant unto them: for My scheme is strong (and unfailing).

184. Do they not reflect? Their Companion is not seized with madness: he is but a perspicuous warner.

185. Do they see nothing in the kingdom of the heavens and the earth and all that Allah hath created? (Do they not see) that it may well be that their term is nigh

اور اگر ہم چاہتے تو ان آیتوں سے اس (کے درجے) کو بلند
کر دیتے۔ مگر وہ تو پستی کی طرف مائل ہوگیا اور اپنی خواہش کے
پیچھے چل پڑا۔ تو اس کی مثال کُتّے کی سی ہوگئی کہ اگر سختی
کرو تو زبان نکالے رہے اور یُوں ہی چھوڑ دو تو بھی زبان
نکالے رہے۔ یہی مثال اُن لوگوں کی ہے جنہوں نے ہماری آیتوں
کو جُھٹلایا تو (اُن سے) یہ قصہ بیان کر دو تاکہ وہ فکر کریں (١٧٦)
جن لوگوں نے ہماری آیتوں کی تکذیب کی اُن کی مثال بُری
ہے اور انہوں نے نقصان (کیا تو) اپنا ہی کیا (١٧٧)
جس کو خدا ہدایت دے وہی راہ یاب ہے۔ اور جس کو گمراہ کرے
تو ایسے ہی لوگ نقصان اُٹھانے والے ہیں (١٧٨)
اور ہم نے بہت سے جن اور انسان دوزخ کیلئے پیدا کئے ہیں اُنکے
دل ہیں لیکن اُنسے سمجھتے نہیں اور اُنکی آنکھیں ہیں مگر اُن سے
دیکھتے نہیں۔ اور اُنکے کان ہیں پر اُنسے سنتے نہیں۔ یہ لوگ (بالکل)
چار پایوں کی طرح ہیں بلکہ اُنسے بھی بھٹکے ہوئے۔ یہی وہ
ہیں جو غفلت میں پڑے ہوئے ہیں (١٧٩)
اور خدا کے سب نام اچھے ہی اچھے ہیں تو اُس کو اُسکے ناموں سے
پکارا کرو۔ اور جو لوگ اسکے ناموں میں کجی (اختیار) کرتے
ہیں اُنکو چھوڑ دو۔ وہ جو کچھ کر رہے ہیں عنقریب اُسکی سزا پائینگے (١٨٠)
اور ہماری مخلوقات میں سے ایک وہ لوگ ہیں جو حق کا رستہ بتاتے ہیں اور اسی کے ساتھ انصاف کرتے ہیں (١٨١)
اور جن لوگوں نے ہماری آیتوں کو جھٹلایا اُن کو بتدریج اس طریق
سے پکڑیں گے کہ اُن کو معلوم ہی نہ ہوگا (١٨٢)
اور میں اُنکو مہلت دیئے جاتا ہوں میری تدبیر (بڑی) مضبوط ہے (١٨٣)
کیا اُنہوں نے غور نہیں کیا کہ انکے رفیق (محمد) کو (کسی طرح کا بھی) جنون
نہیں ہے۔ وہ تو ظاہر ظہور ڈر سنانے والے ہیں (١٨٤)
کیا اُنہوں نے آسمان اور زمین کی بادشاہت میں اور جو چیزیں
خدا نے پیدا کی ہیں اُن پر نظر نہیں کی۔ اور اس بات پر (خیال
نہیں کیا) کہ عجب نہیں (اُن کی موت) کا وقت نزدیک پہنچ

وَلَوْ شِئْنَا لَرَفَعْنٰهُ بِهَا وَلٰكِنَّهٗۤ اَخْلَدَ
اِلَى الْاَرْضِ وَاتَّبَعَ هَوٰىهُ ۚ فَمَثَلُهٗ كَمَثَلِ
الْكَلْبِ ۚ اِنْ تَحْمِلْ عَلَيْهِ يَلْهَثْ اَوْ
تَتْرُكْهُ يَلْهَثْ ؕ ذٰلِكَ مَثَلُ الْقَوْمِ
الَّذِيْنَ كَذَّبُوْا بِاٰيٰتِنَا ۚ فَاقْصُصِ
الْقَصَصَ لَعَلَّهُمْ يَتَفَكَّرُوْنَ (١٧٦)
سَآءَ مَثَلَا ۨالْقَوْمُ الَّذِيْنَ كَذَّبُوْا بِاٰيٰتِنَا
وَاَنْفُسَهُمْ كَانُوْا يَظْلِمُوْنَ (١٧٧)
مَنْ يَّهْدِ اللّٰهُ فَهُوَ الْمُهْتَدِيْ ۚ وَمَنْ
يُّضْلِلْ فَاُولٰٓئِكَ هُمُ الْخٰسِرُوْنَ (١٧٨)
وَلَقَدْ ذَرَاْنَا لِجَهَنَّمَ كَثِيْرًا مِّنَ الْجِنِّ وَ
الْاِنْسِ ۖ لَهُمْ قُلُوْبٌ لَّا يَفْقَهُوْنَ بِهَا ۟
وَلَهُمْ اَعْيُنٌ لَّا يُبْصِرُوْنَ بِهَا ۟ وَلَهُمْ
اٰذَانٌ لَّا يَسْمَعُوْنَ بِهَا ؕ اُولٰٓئِكَ كَالْاَنْعَامِ
بَلْ هُمْ اَضَلُّ ؕ اُولٰٓئِكَ هُمُ الْغٰفِلُوْنَ (١٧٩)
وَلِلّٰهِ الْاَسْمَآءُ الْحُسْنٰى فَادْعُوْهُ بِهَا ۠ وَذَرُوا
الَّذِيْنَ يُلْحِدُوْنَ فِيْۤ اَسْمَآئِهٖ ؕ سَيُجْزَوْنَ
مَا كَانُوْا يَعْمَلُوْنَ (١٨٠)
ع ٢٢ ١٠ ١٢ وَمِمَّنْ خَلَقْنَاۤ اُمَّةٌ يَّهْدُوْنَ بِالْحَقِّ وَبِهٖ يَعْدِلُوْنَ (١٨١)
وَالَّذِيْنَ كَذَّبُوْا بِاٰيٰتِنَا سَنَسْتَدْرِجُهُمْ
مِّنْ حَيْثُ لَا يَعْلَمُوْنَ ۚ (١٨٢)
وَاُمْلِيْ لَهُمْ ؕ اِنَّ كَيْدِيْ مَتِيْنٌ (١٨٣)
اَوَلَمْ يَتَفَكَّرُوْا ٚ مَا بِصَاحِبِهِمْ مِّنْ جِنَّةٍ ؕ
اِنْ هُوَ اِلَّا نَذِيْرٌ مُّبِيْنٌ (١٨٤)
اَوَلَمْ يَنْظُرُوْا فِيْ مَلَكُوْتِ السَّمٰوٰتِ وَ
الْاَرْضِ وَمَا خَلَقَ اللّٰهُ مِنْ شَيْءٍ ۙ وَّ
اَنْ عَسٰۤى اَنْ يَّكُوْنَ قَدِ اقْتَرَبَ

drawing to an end? In what Message after this will they then believe?

186. To such as Allah rejects from His guidance, there can be no guide: He will Leave them in their trespasses, wandering in distraction.
187. They ask thee about the (final) Hour—when will be its appointed time? Say: "The knowledge thereof is with my Lord (alone): none but He can reveal as to when it will occur. Heavy were its burden through the heavens and the earth. Only, all of a sudden will it come to you." They ask thee as if thou wert eager in search thereof: say: "The knowledge thereof is with Allah (alone), but most men know not."
188. Say: "I have no power over any good or harm to myself except as Allah willeth. If I had knowledge of the unseen, I should have multiplied all good, and no evil should have touched me: I am but a warner, and a bringer of glad tidings to those who have faith."

189. It is He Who created you from a single person, and made his mate of like nature, in order that he might dwell with her (in love). When they are united, she bears a light burden and carries it about (unnoticed). When she grows heavy, they both pray to Allah their Lord (saying): "if Thou givest us a goodly child, we vow we shall (ever) be grateful."
190. But when He giveth them a goodly child, they ascribe to others a share in the gift they have received: but Allah is exalted high above the partners they ascribe to Him.
191. Do they indeed ascribe to Him as partners things that can create nothing, but are themselves created?
192. No aid can they give them, nor can they aid themselves!
193. If ye call them to guidance, they will not obey: for you it is the same whether ye call them or ye keep silent.

گیا ہو۔ تو اس کے بعد وہ اور کس بات پر ایمان
لائیں گے؟ ﴿۱۸۵﴾
جس شخص کو خدا گمراہ کرے اُسکو کوئی ہدایت دینے والا نہیں۔
اور وہ ان گمراہوں کو چھوڑے رکھتا ہے کہ اپنی سرکشی میں پڑے بہکتے رہیں ﴿۱۸۶﴾
(یہ لوگ) تم سے قیامت کے بارے میں پوچھتے ہیں کہ اسکے واقع
ہونے کا وقت کب ہے کہہ دو کہ اسکا علم تو میرے پروردگار ہی
کو ہے وہی اُسے اُسکے وقت پر ظاہر کر دیگا۔ وہ آسمان اور زمین میں ایک
بھاری بات ہوگی۔ اور ناگہاں تم پر آجائیگی۔ یہ تم سے اس طرح دریافت
کرتے ہیں کہ گویا تم اس سے بخوبی واقف ہو۔ کہو کہ اس کا علم تو
خدا ہی کو ہے لیکن اکثر لوگ یہ نہیں جانتے ﴿۱۸۷﴾
کہہ دو کہ میں اپنے فائدے اور نقصان کا کچھ بھی اختیار
نہیں رکھتا مگر جو خدا چاہے۔ اور اگر میں غیب کی باتیں
جانتا ہوتا تو بہت سے فائدے جمع کر لیتا اور مجھ کو کوئی
تکلیف نہ پہنچتی۔ میں تو مومنوں کو ڈر اور خوشخبری
سُنانے والا ہوں ﴿۱۸۸﴾
وہ خدا ہی تو ہے جس نے تم کو ایک شخص سے پیدا کیا اور اُس سے اسکا جوڑا بنایا
تاکہ اُس سے راحت حاصل کرے سو جب وہ اسکے پاس جاتا ہے تو اُسے ہلکا سا
حمل رہ جاتا ہے اور وہ اسکے ساتھ چلتی پھرتی ہے۔ پھر جب کچھ بوجھ معلوم کرتی
(یعنی بچہ پیٹ میں بڑا ہوتا) ہے تو دونوں میاں بیوی اپنے پروردگار خدائے عزوجل سے
التجا کرتے ہیں کہ اگر تو ہمیں صحیح و سالم (بچہ) دیگا تو ہم تیرے شکرگزار ہونگے ﴿۱۸۹﴾
جب وہ انکو صحیح و سالم بچہ دیتا ہے تو اُس (بچے) میں جو وہ انکو دیتا ہے اُسکا شریک مقرر
کرتے ہیں۔ جو وہ شرک کرتے ہیں خدا کا رتبہ اس سے بلند ہے ﴿۱۹۰﴾
کیا وہ ایسوں کو شریک بناتے ہیں جو کچھ بھی پیدا نہیں کر سکتے اور خود پیدا کئے جاتے ہیں ﴿۱۹۱﴾
اور نہ اُن کی مدد کی طاقت رکھتے ہیں اور نہ اپنی ہی مدد
کر سکتے ہیں ﴿۱۹۲﴾
اگر تم اُن کو سیدھے رستے کی طرف بلاؤ تو تمہارا کہا نہ مانیں۔
تمہارے لئے برابر ہے کہ تم اُن کو بلاؤ یا چپکے ہو رہو ﴿۱۹۳﴾

أَجَلُهُمْ ۖ فَبِأَيِّ حَدِيثٍ بَعْدَهُ
يُؤْمِنُونَ ﴿١٨٥﴾
مَن يُضْلِلِ اللَّهُ فَلَا هَادِيَ لَهُ ۚ وَيَذَرُهُمْ
فِي طُغْيَانِهِمْ يَعْمَهُونَ ﴿١٨٦﴾
يَسْأَلُونَكَ عَنِ السَّاعَةِ أَيَّانَ مُرْسَاهَا ۖ
قُلْ إِنَّمَا عِلْمُهَا عِندَ رَبِّي ۖ لَا يُجَلِّيهَا
لِوَقْتِهَا إِلَّا هُوَ ۚ ثَقُلَتْ فِي السَّمَاوَاتِ وَ
الْأَرْضِ ۚ لَا تَأْتِيكُمْ إِلَّا بَغْتَةً ۗ يَسْأَلُونَكَ
كَأَنَّكَ حَفِيٌّ عَنْهَا ۖ قُلْ إِنَّمَا عِلْمُهَا
عِندَ اللَّهِ وَلَٰكِنَّ أَكْثَرَ النَّاسِ لَا يَعْلَمُونَ ﴿١٨٧﴾
قُل لَّا أَمْلِكُ لِنَفْسِي نَفْعًا وَلَا ضَرًّا إِلَّا
مَا شَاءَ اللَّهُ ۚ وَلَوْ كُنتُ أَعْلَمُ الْغَيْبَ
لَاسْتَكْثَرْتُ مِنَ الْخَيْرِ ۚ وَمَا مَسَّنِيَ
السُّوءُ ۚ إِنْ أَنَا إِلَّا نَذِيرٌ وَبَشِيرٌ
لِّقَوْمٍ يُؤْمِنُونَ ﴿١٨٨﴾
هُوَ الَّذِي خَلَقَكُم مِّن نَّفْسٍ وَاحِدَةٍ
وَجَعَلَ مِنْهَا زَوْجَهَا لِيَسْكُنَ إِلَيْهَا ۖ
فَلَمَّا تَغَشَّاهَا حَمَلَتْ حَمْلًا خَفِيفًا فَمَرَّتْ
بِهِ ۖ فَلَمَّا أَثْقَلَت دَّعَوَا اللَّهَ رَبَّهُمَا لَئِنْ
آتَيْتَنَا صَالِحًا لَّنَكُونَنَّ مِنَ الشَّاكِرِينَ ﴿١٨٩﴾
فَلَمَّا آتَاهُمَا صَالِحًا جَعَلَا لَهُ شُرَكَاءَ
فِيمَا آتَاهُمَا ۚ فَتَعَالَى اللَّهُ عَمَّا يُشْرِكُونَ ﴿١٩٠﴾
أَيُشْرِكُونَ مَا لَا يَخْلُقُ شَيْئًا وَهُمْ يُخْلَقُونَ ﴿١٩١﴾
وَلَا يَسْتَطِيعُونَ لَهُمْ نَصْرًا وَلَا أَنفُسَهُمْ
يَنصُرُونَ ﴿١٩٢﴾
وَإِن تَدْعُوهُمْ إِلَى الْهُدَىٰ لَا يَتَّبِعُوكُمْ ۚ
سَوَاءٌ عَلَيْكُمْ أَدَعَوْتُمُوهُمْ أَمْ أَنتُمْ صَامِتُونَ ﴿١٩٣﴾

194. Verily those whom ye call upon besides Allah are servants like unto you: call upon them, and let them listen to your prayer, if ye are (indeed) truthful!

(مشرکو) جن کو تم خدا کے سوا پکارتے ہو تمہاری طرح کے بندے
ہی ہیں (اچھا) تم اُن کو پکارو اگر سچے ہو تو چاہیئے کہ وہ تم
کو جواب بھی دیں ﴿۱۹۴﴾

إِنَّ الَّذِينَ تَدْعُونَ مِنْ دُونِ اللَّهِ
عِبَادٌ أَمْثَالُكُمْ فَادْعُوهُمْ فَلْيَسْتَجِيبُوا
لَكُمْ إِنْ كُنْتُمْ صَادِقِينَ ﴿١٩٤﴾

195. Have they feet to walk with? Or hands to lay hold with? Or eyes to see with? Or ears to hear with? Say: "Call your 'god-partners', scheme (your worst) against me, and give me no respite!

بھلا اُن کے پاؤں ہیں جن سے چلیں یا ہاتھ ہیں جن سے پکڑیں
یا آنکھیں ہیں جن سے دیکھیں یا کان ہیں جن سے سُنیں؟
کہہ دو کہ اپنے شریکوں کو بلا لو اور میرے بارے میں (جو تدبیر
(کرنی ہو) کر لو اور مجھے کچھ مہلت بھی نہ دو (پھر دیکھو کہ وہ
میرا کیا کر سکتے ہیں) ﴿۱۹۵﴾

أَلَهُمْ أَرْجُلٌ يَمْشُونَ بِهَا أَمْ لَهُمْ
أَيْدٍ يَبْطِشُونَ بِهَا أَمْ لَهُمْ أَعْيُنٌ
يُبْصِرُونَ بِهَا أَمْ لَهُمْ آذَانٌ يَسْمَعُونَ
بِهَا قُلِ ادْعُوا شُرَكَاءَكُمْ ثُمَّ
كِيدُونِ فَلَا تُنْظِرُونِ ﴿١٩٥﴾

196. "For my Protector is Allah, Who revealed the Book, (from time to time), and He will befriend the righteous.

197. "But those ye call upon besides Him, are unable to help you, and indeed to help themselves."

198. If thou callest them to guidance, they hear not. Thou wilt see them looking at thee, but they see not.

میرا مددگار تو خدا ہی ہے جس نے کتاب (برحق) نازل کی اور
نیک لوگوں کا وہی دوستدار ہے ﴿۱۹۶﴾
اور جن کو تم خدا کے سوا پکارتے ہو وہ نہ تمہاری ہی مدد کی
طاقت رکھتے ہیں اور نہ خود اپنی ہی مدد کر سکتے ہیں ﴿۱۹۷﴾
اور اگر تم اُن کو سیدھے رستے کی طرف بلاؤ تو سُن نہ سکیں.
اور تم انہیں دیکھتے ہو کہ (بظاہر) آنکھیں کھولے تمہاری
طرف دیکھ رہے ہیں مگر (فی الواقع) کچھ نہیں دیکھتے ﴿۱۹۸﴾

إِنَّ وَلِيِّيَ اللَّهُ الَّذِي نَزَّلَ الْكِتَابَ
وَهُوَ يَتَوَلَّى الصَّالِحِينَ ﴿١٩٦﴾
وَالَّذِينَ تَدْعُونَ مِنْ دُونِهِ لَا يَسْتَطِيعُونَ
نَصْرَكُمْ وَلَا أَنْفُسَهُمْ يَنْصُرُونَ ﴿١٩٧﴾
وَإِنْ تَدْعُوهُمْ إِلَى الْهُدَىٰ لَا يَسْمَعُوا
وَتَرَاهُمْ يَنْظُرُونَ إِلَيْكَ وَهُمْ
لَا يُبْصِرُونَ ﴿١٩٨﴾

199. Hold to forgiveness; command what is right; but turn away from the ignorant.

(اے محمدؐ) عفو اختیار کرو اور نیک کام کرنے کا حکم دو اور جاہلوں
سے کنارہ کر لو ﴿۱۹۹﴾

خُذِ الْعَفْوَ وَأْمُرْ بِالْعُرْفِ وَأَعْرِضْ
عَنِ الْجَاهِلِينَ ﴿١٩٩﴾

200. If a suggestion from Satan assail thy (mind), seek refuge with Allah; for He heareth and knoweth (all things).

201. Those who fear Allah, when a thought of evil from Satan assaults them, bring Allah to remembrance, when lo! they see (aright)!

اور اگر شیطان کی طرف سے تمہارے دل میں کسی طرح کا وسوسہ پیدا ہو
تو خدا سے پناہ مانگو. بیشک وہ سننے والا (اور) سب کچھ جاننے والا ہے ﴿۲۰۰﴾
جو لوگ پرہیزگار ہیں جب اُن کو شیطان کی طرف سے کوئی وسوسہ
پیدا ہوتا ہے تو چونک پڑتے ہیں اور (دل کی آنکھیں
کھول کر) دیکھنے لگتے ہیں ﴿۲۰۱﴾

وَإِمَّا يَنْزَغَنَّكَ مِنَ الشَّيْطَانِ نَزْغٌ
فَاسْتَعِذْ بِاللَّهِ إِنَّهُ سَمِيعٌ عَلِيمٌ ﴿٢٠٠﴾
إِنَّ الَّذِينَ اتَّقَوْا إِذَا مَسَّهُمْ طَائِفٌ
مِنَ الشَّيْطَانِ تَذَكَّرُوا فَإِذَا هُمْ
مُبْصِرُونَ ﴿٢٠١﴾

202. But their brethren (the evil ones) plunge them deeper into error, and never relax (their efforts).

اور ان (کفار) کے بھائی انہیں گمراہی میں کھینچے جاتے ہیں
پھر (اس میں کسی طرح کی) کوتاہی نہیں کرتے ﴿۲۰۲﴾

وَإِخْوَانُهُمْ يَمُدُّونَهُمْ فِي الْغَيِّ ثُمَّ
لَا يُقْصِرُونَ ﴿٢٠٢﴾

203. If thou bring them not a revelation, they say: "Why hast thou not got it together?" Say: "I but follow what is revealed to me from my Lord: this is (nothing but) Lights

اور جب تم اُن کے پاس (کچھ دنوں تک) کوئی آیت نہیں لاتے تو کہتے ہیں
کہ تم نے (اپنی طرف سے) کیوں نہیں بنا لی. کہہ دو کہ میں تو اسی حکم کی پیروی کرتا ہوں
جو میرے پروردگار کی طرف سے میرے پاس آتا ہے. یہ قرآن تمہارے پروردگار کی جانب سے

وَإِذَا لَمْ تَأْتِهِمْ بِآيَةٍ قَالُوا لَوْلَا اجْتَبَيْتَهَا
قُلْ إِنَّمَا أَتَّبِعُ مَا يُوحَىٰ إِلَيَّ مِنْ رَبِّي
هَٰذَا بَصَائِرُ مِنْ رَبِّكُمْ وَهُدًى وَ

SÛRA–8
AL-ANFÃL
(INTRODUCTION)

In the previous Introductions to the Sûras we have shown how each Sûra is a step or gradation in the teaching of the Qur-ãn. The first seven Sûras, comprising a little less than one-third of the Qur-ãn, form a gradation, sketching the early spiritual history of man and leading up to the formation of the new Ummat or Community of the Holy Apostle. Now we begin another gradation, consolidating that Ummat and directing us as to various phases in our new collective life.

In this chapter we have the lessons of the Battle of Badr enforced in their larger aspects: (1) the question of war booty; (2) the true virtues necessary for fighting the good fight; (3) victory against odds; (4) clemency and consideration for one's own and for others in the hour of victory.

As regards booty taken in battle, the first point to note, is that that should never be our aim in war. It is only an advertitious circumstance, a sort of windfall. Secondly, no soldier or troop has any inherent right to it. A righteous war is a community affair, and any accessions resulting from it belong to Allah, or the community or Cause. Thirdly, certain equitable principles of division should be laid down to check human greed and selfishness. A fifth share goes to the Commander, and he can use it at his discretion; for his own expenses, and for the relief of the poor and suffering, and the orphans and widows (8: 41). The remainder was divided, according to the Prophet's practice, not only among those who were actually in the fight physically, but all who were in the enterprise, young and old, provided they loyally did some duty assigned to them. Fourthly, there should be no disputes, as they interfere with internal discipline and harmony.

These principles are followed in the best modern practice of civilised nations. All acquisition of war belong absolutely to the Sovereign as representing the commonwealth. In the distribution of booty not only the actual captors but also the "joint captors" and the "constructive captors" share. See Sir R. Phillimore's *International Law* (1885), vol. 3, pp. 209-10, 221-4.

As regards the military virtues, which are the types of virtues throughtout life, we are shown by an analysis of the incidents of Badr how, against the greatest odds, Allah's help will give the victory if men are fighting not for themselves but for the sacred Cause of Allah. And directions are given for the treatment of prisoners and for maintaining the solidarity of the Muslim community.

The date of this Sûra is shortly after the battle of Badr, which was fought on Friday, the 17th of Ramadhãn in the second year of the Hijra.

from your Lord, and Guidance, and Mercy, for any who have Faith."

204. When the Qur'an is read, listen to it with attention, and hold your peace: that ye may receive Mercy.

205. And do thou (O reader!) bring thy Lord to remembrance in thy (very) soul, with humility and remember without loudness in words, in the mornings and evenings; and be not thou of those who are unheedful.

206. Those who are near to thy Lord, disdain not to worship Him: they glorify Him and prostrate before Him.

Al-Anfãl, or the Spoils of War

In the name of Allah, Most Gracious, Most Merciful.

1. They ask thee concerning (things taken as) spoils, of war. Say: "(Such) spoils are at the disposal of Allah and the Messenger: so fear Allah, and keep straight the relations between yourselves: obey Allah and His Messenger, if ye do believe."

2. For, believers are those who, when Allah is mentioned, fell a tremor in their hearts, and when they hear His revelations rehearsed, find their faith strengthened, and put (all) their trust in their Lord;

3. Who establish regular prayers and spend (freely) out of the gifts We have given them for sustenance:

4. Such in truth are the Believers: they have grades of dignity with their Lord, and forgiveness, and generous sustenance:

5. Just as thy Lord ordered thee out of thy house in truth, even though a party among the Believers disliked it,

6. Disputing with thee concerning the truth after it was made manifest, as if they were being driven to death while they see it.

7. Behold! Allah promised you one of the two parties, that it should be yours: ye wished that the one unarmed should be yours, but Allah

دانش و بصیرت اور مومنوں کے لئے ہدایت اور رحمت ہے ﴿۲۰۳﴾
اور جب قرآن پڑھا جائے تو توجہ سے سُنا کرو اور خاموش رہا کرو
تاکہ تم پر رحم کیا جائے ﴿۲۰۴﴾
اور اپنے پروردگار کو دل ہی دل میں عاجزی اور خوف سے
اور پست آواز سے صبح و شام یاد کرتے رہو اور (دیکھنا)
غافل نہ ہونا ﴿۲۰۵﴾
جو لوگ تمہارے پروردگار کے پاس ہیں وہ اس کی عبادت سے گردن کشی نہیں
کرتے اور اُس پاک ذات کو یاد کرتے اور اس کے آگے سجدے کرتے رہتے ہیں ﴿۲۰۶﴾

سورۃ انفال مدنی ہے اور اس میں پچھتر آیتیں اور دس رُکوع ہیں

شروع خدا کا نام لے کر جو بڑا مہربان نہایت رحم والا ہے
(اے محمد مجاہد لوگ) تم سے غنیمت کے مال کے بارے میں دریافت
کرتے ہیں (کہ کیا حکم ہے) کہہ دو کہ غنیمت خدا اور اس کے رسول کا مال ہے
تو خدا سے ڈرو اور آپس میں صلح رکھو اور اگر ایمان رکھتے ہو تو
خدا اور اس کے رسول کے حکم پر چلو ﴿۱﴾
مومن تو وہ ہیں کہ جب خدا کا ذکر کیا جاتا ہے تو ان کے دل ڈر جاتے
ہیں اور جب انہیں اس کی آیتیں پڑھ کر سنائی جاتی ہیں تو ان کا ایمان
اور بڑھ جاتا ہے۔ اور وہ اپنے پروردگار پر بھروسا رکھتے ہیں ﴿۲﴾
(اور) وہ جو نماز پڑھتے ہیں اور جو مال ہم نے ان کو دیا ہے اس میں سے (نیک کاموں میں) خرچ کرتے ہیں ﴿۳﴾
یہی سچے مومن ہیں اور ان کے لئے پروردگار کے ہاں
(بڑے بڑے) درجے اور بخشش اور عزت کی
روزی ہے ﴿۴﴾
(ان لوگوں کو اپنے گھروں سے اسی طرح نکلنا چاہیے تھا) جس طرح تمہارے پروردگار
نے تم کو تدبیر کے ساتھ اپنے گھر سے نکالا اور (اس وقت) مومنوں کی ایک جماعت ناخوش تھی ﴿۵﴾
وہ لوگ حق بات میں اس کے ظاہر ہوئے پیچھے تم سے جھگڑنے لگے
گویا موت کی طرف دھکیلے جاتے ہیں اور اسے دیکھ رہے ہیں ﴿۶﴾
اور (اس وقت کو یاد کرو) جب خدا تم سے وعدہ کرتا تھا کہ
(ابو سفیان اور ابو جہل کے) دو گروہوں میں سے ایک گروہ تمہارا

رَحْمَةٌ لِّقَوْمٍ يُّؤْمِنُوْنَ ﴿٢٠٣﴾
وَاِذَا قُرِئَ الْقُرْاٰنُ فَاسْتَمِعُوْا لَهٗ وَ
اَنْصِتُوْا لَعَلَّكُمْ تُرْحَمُوْنَ ﴿٢٠٤﴾
وَاذْكُرْ رَّبَّكَ فِیْ نَفْسِكَ تَضَرُّعًا وَّ
خِيْفَةً وَّدُوْنَ الْجَهْرِ مِنَ الْقَوْلِ
بِالْغُدُوِّ وَالْاٰصَالِ وَلَا تَكُنْ مِّنَ الْغٰفِلِيْنَ ﴿٢٠٥﴾
اِنَّ الَّذِيْنَ عِنْدَ رَبِّكَ لَا يَسْتَكْبِرُوْنَ
عَنْ عِبَادَتِهٖ وَيُسَبِّحُوْنَهٗ وَلَهٗ يَسْجُدُوْنَ ﴿٢٠٦﴾

سُوْرَةُ الْاَنْفَالِ مَدَنِيَّةٌ وَّهِيَ خَمْسٌ وَّسَبْعُوْنَ اٰيَةً وَّعَشْرُ رُكُوْعَاتٍ

بِسْمِ اللّٰهِ الرَّحْمٰنِ الرَّحِيْمِ
يَسْـَٔلُوْنَكَ عَنِ الْاَنْفَالِ ؕ قُلِ الْاَنْفَالُ
لِلّٰهِ وَالرَّسُوْلِ ۚ فَاتَّقُوا اللّٰهَ وَاَصْلِحُوْا ذَاتَ
بَيْنِكُمْ ۪ وَاَطِيْعُوا اللّٰهَ وَرَسُوْلَهٗۤ اِنْ كُنْتُمْ
مُّؤْمِنِيْنَ ﴿١﴾
اِنَّمَا الْمُؤْمِنُوْنَ الَّذِيْنَ اِذَا ذُكِرَ اللّٰهُ وَجِلَتْ
قُلُوْبُهُمْ وَاِذَا تُلِيَتْ عَلَيْهِمْ اٰيٰتُهٗ زَادَتْهُمْ
اِيْمَانًا وَّعَلٰى رَبِّهِمْ يَتَوَكَّلُوْنَ ﴿٢﴾
الَّذِيْنَ يُقِيْمُوْنَ الصَّلٰوةَ وَمِمَّا رَزَقْنٰهُمْ يُنْفِقُوْنَ ﴿٣﴾
اُولٰٓئِكَ هُمُ الْمُؤْمِنُوْنَ حَقًّا ؕ لَهُمْ
دَرَجٰتٌ عِنْدَ رَبِّهِمْ وَمَغْفِرَةٌ وَّرِزْقٌ
كَرِيْمٌ ﴿٤﴾
كَمَاۤ اَخْرَجَكَ رَبُّكَ مِنْ بَيْتِكَ بِالْحَقِّ ۪
وَاِنَّ فَرِيْقًا مِّنَ الْمُؤْمِنِيْنَ لَكٰرِهُوْنَ ﴿٥﴾
يُجَادِلُوْنَكَ فِی الْحَقِّ بَعْدَ مَا تَبَيَّنَ كَاَنَّمَا
يُسَاقُوْنَ اِلَى الْمَوْتِ وَهُمْ يَنْظُرُوْنَ ﴿٦﴾
وَاِذْ يَعِدُكُمُ اللّٰهُ اِحْدَى الطَّآئِفَتَيْنِ
اَنَّهَا لَكُمْ وَتَوَدُّوْنَ اَنَّ غَيْرَ ذَاتِ

willed to establish the Truth according to His words, and to cut off the roots of the Unbelievers;–

مسخر ہو جائے گا۔ اور تم چاہتے تھے کہ جو قافلہ بے (شان و) شوکت
(یعنی بے ہتھیار) ہے وہ تمہارے ہاتھ آ جائے اور خدا چاہتا تھا کہ
اپنے فرمان سے حق کو قائم رکھے اور کافروں کی جڑ کاٹ (کر پھینک) دے[١٣٣] (٧)

الشَّوْكَةِ تَكُونُ لَكُمْ وَيُرِيدُ اللَّهُ أَنْ
يُحِقَّ الْحَقَّ بِكَلِمَاتِهِ وَيَقْطَعَ دَابِرَ
الْكَافِرِينَ (٧)

8. That He might establish Truth and prove Falsehood false, distasteful though it be to those in guilt.

تاکہ سچ کو سچ اور جھوٹ کو جھوٹ کر دے۔ گو مشرک
ناخوش ہی ہوں (٨)

لِيُحِقَّ الْحَقَّ وَيُبْطِلَ الْبَاطِلَ وَلَوْ
كَرِهَ الْمُجْرِمُونَ (٨)

9. Remember ye implored the assistance of your Lord. And He answered you: "I will assist you with a thousand of the angels, ranks on ranks."

جب تم اپنے پروردگار سے فریاد کرتے تھے تو اس نے تمہاری
دعا قبول کر لی (اور فرمایا) کہ (تسلی رکھو) ہم ہزار فرشتوں سے جو
ایک دوسرے کے پیچھے آتے جائیں گے تمہاری مدد کریں گے (٩)

إِذْ تَسْتَغِيثُونَ رَبَّكُمْ فَاسْتَجَابَ لَكُمْ
أَنِّي مُمِدُّكُمْ بِأَلْفٍ مِنَ الْمَلَائِكَةِ
مُرْدِفِينَ (٩)

10. Allah made it but a message of hope, and an assurance to your hearts: (in any case) there is no help except from Allah: and Allah is Exalted in Power, Wise.

اور اس مدد کو خدا نے محض بشارت بنایا تھا کہ تمہارے دل
اس سے اطمینان حاصل کریں۔ اور مدد تو اللہ ہی کی طرف سے ہے۔
بے شک خدا غالب حکمت والا ہے (١٠)

وَمَا جَعَلَهُ اللَّهُ إِلَّا بُشْرَىٰ وَلِتَطْمَئِنَّ
بِهِ قُلُوبُكُمْ وَمَا النَّصْرُ إِلَّا مِنْ عِنْدِ اللَّهِ
ع ١٥ إِنَّ اللَّهَ عَزِيزٌ حَكِيمٌ (١٠)

11. Remember He covered you with drowsiness, to give you calm as from himself, and he caused rain to descend on you from heaven, to clean you therewith, to remove from you the stain of Satan, to strengthen your hearts, and to plant your feet firmly therewith.

جب اس نے (تمہاری) تسکین کیلئے اپنی طرف سے تمہیں نیند
کی چادر (اڑھا دی اور تم پر آسمان سے پانی برسا دیا تاکہ تم
کو اس سے (نہلا کر) پاک کر دے اور شیطانی نجاست کو تم سے
دور کر دے اور اس لئے بھی کہ تمہارے دلوں کو مضبوط کر دے
اور اس سے تمہارے پاؤں جمائے رکھے (١١)

إِذْ يُغَشِّيكُمُ النُّعَاسَ أَمَنَةً مِنْهُ وَ
يُنَزِّلُ عَلَيْكُمْ مِنَ السَّمَاءِ مَاءً لِيُطَهِّرَكُمْ
بِهِ وَيُذْهِبَ عَنْكُمْ رِجْزَ الشَّيْطَانِ وَ
لِيَرْبِطَ عَلَىٰ قُلُوبِكُمْ وَيُثَبِّتَ بِهِ
الْأَقْدَامَ (١١)

12. Remember thy Lord inspired the angels (with the message): "I am with you: give firmness to the Believers: I will instil terror into the hearts of the Unbelievers: smite ye above their necks and smite all their finger-tips off them."

جب تمہارا پروردگار فرشتوں کو ارشاد فرماتا تھا کہ میں تمہارے
ساتھ ہوں تم مومنوں کو تسلی دو کہ ثابت قدم رہیں میں ابھی
ابھی کافروں کے دلوں میں رعب و ہیبت ڈالے دیتا ہوں تو
ان کے سر مار (کر) اڑا دو۔ اور ان کا پور پور مار (کر) توڑ دو[١٣٤] (١٢)

إِذْ يُوحِي رَبُّكَ إِلَى الْمَلَائِكَةِ أَنِّي مَعَكُمْ
فَثَبِّتُوا الَّذِينَ آمَنُوا سَأُلْقِي فِي قُلُوبِ
الَّذِينَ كَفَرُوا الرُّعْبَ فَاضْرِبُوا فَوْقَ
الْأَعْنَاقِ وَاضْرِبُوا مِنْهُمْ كُلَّ بَنَانٍ (١٢)

13. This because they contended against Allah and His Messenger: if any contend against Allah and His Messenger. Allah is strict in punishment.

یہ (سزا) اس لئے دی گئی کہ انہوں نے خدا اور اس کے رسول کی
مخالفت کی اور جو شخص خدا اور اس کے رسول کی مخالفت کرتا ہے
تو خدا بھی سخت عذاب دینے والا ہے (١٣)

ذَٰلِكَ بِأَنَّهُمْ شَاقُّوا اللَّهَ وَرَسُولَهُ وَ
مَنْ يُشَاقِقِ اللَّهَ وَرَسُولَهُ فَإِنَّ اللَّهَ
شَدِيدُ الْعِقَابِ (١٣)

14. Thus (will it be said): "Taste ye then of the (punishment): for those who reject is the chastisement of the Fire."

یہ (مزہ) تو یہاں چکھو اور یہ (جانے رہو) کہ کافروں کیلئے
(آخرت میں) دوزخ کا عذاب (بھی تیار) ہے (١٤)

ذَٰلِكُمْ فَذُوقُوهُ وَأَنَّ لِلْكَافِرِينَ
عَذَابَ النَّارِ (١٤)

15. O ye who believe! when ye meet the Unbelievers in hostile array, never turn your backs to them.

اے اہل ایمان جب میدان جنگ میں کفار سے تمہارا مقابلہ
ہو تو ان سے پیٹھ نہ پھیرنا (١٥)

يَا أَيُّهَا الَّذِينَ آمَنُوا إِذَا لَقِيتُمُ الَّذِينَ
كَفَرُوا زَحْفًا فَلَا تُوَلُّوهُمُ الْأَدْبَارَ (١٥)

16. If any do turn his back to them on such a day— unless it be in a stratagem of war, or to retreat to a troop (of his own)— he draws on himself the wrath of Allah, and his abode is Hell,— an evil refuge (indeed)!

17. It is not ye who slew them; it was Allah: when thou threwest (a handful of dust), it was not thy act, but Allah's: in order that He might confer on the Believers a gracious benefit from Himself: for Allah is He Who heareth and knoweth (all things).

18. That, and also because Allah is He Who makes feeble the Plans and strategems of the Unbelievers.

19. (O Unbelievers!) if ye prayed for victory and judgment, now hath the judgment come to you: if ye desist (from wrong), it will be best for you: if ye return (to the attack), so shall We. Not the least good will your forces be to you even if they were multiplied: for verily Allah is with those who believe!

20. O ye who believe! obey Allah and His Messenger, and turn not away from him when ye hear (him speak).

21. Nor be like those who say, "We hear," but listen not:

22. For the worst of beasts in the sight of Allah are the deaf and the dumb,—those who understand not.

23. If Allah had found in them any good, He would indeed have made them listen: (as it is), if He had made them listen, they would but have turned back and declined (faith).

24. O ye who believe! give your response to Allah and His Messenger, when He calleth you to that which will give you life; and know that Allah cometh in between a man and his heart, and that it is He to Whom ye shall (all) be gathered.

25. And fear the trial which affecteth not in particular (only) those of you who do wrong: and know that Allah is strict in

اور جو شخص جنگ کے روز اس صورت کے سوا کہ لڑائی کے لئے
کنارے کنارے چلے (یعنی حکمت عملی سے دشمن کو مارے) یا اپنی فوج
میں جا ملنا چاہے اُن سے پیٹھ پھیرے گا (تو سمجھو کہ) وہ خدا کے غضب میں
گرفتار ہو گیا اور اسکا ٹھکانا دوزخ ہے اور وہ بہت ہی بُری جگہ ہے (۱۶)
تم لوگوں نے ان (کفار) کو قتل نہیں کیا بلکہ خدا نے انہیں قتل کیا۔
اور (اے محمدؐ) جس وقت تم نے کنکریاں پھینکی تھیں تو وہ تم نے نہیں
پھینکی تھیں بلکہ اللہ نے پھینکی تھیں اس سے یہ غرض تھی کہ مومنوں
کو اپنے (احسانوں) سے اچھی طرح آزما لے بیشک خدا سنتا جانتا ہے (۱۷)
(بات) یہ (ہے) کچھ شک نہیں کہ خدا کافروں کی تدبیر کو کمزور کر دینے والا ہے (۱۸)
(کافرو) اگر تم (محمد صلی اللہ علیہ وسلم پر) فتح چاہتے ہو تو تمہارے پاس فتح آ چکی
(دیکھو) اگر تم (اپنے افعال سے) باز آجاؤ تو تمہارے حق میں بہتر ہے اور
اگر پھر (نافرمانی) کرو گے تو ہم بھی پھر تمہیں عذاب کرینگے اور تمہاری جماعت
خواہ کتنی ہی کثیر ہو تمہارے کچھ بھی کام نہ آئیگی اور خدا تو مومنوں کے ساتھ ہے (۱۹)
اے ایمان والو خدا اور اسکے رسُول کے حکم پر چلو اور اس سے روگردانی
نہ کرو اور تم سُنتے ہو (۲۰)
اور ان لوگوں جیسے نہ ہونا جو کہتے ہیں کہ ہم نے (حکم خدا)
سُن لیا مگر (حقیقت میں) نہیں سُنتے (۲۱)
کچھ شک نہیں کہ خدا کے نزدیک تمام جانداروں سے بدتر
بہرے گُونگے ہیں جو کچھ نہیں سمجھتے (۲۲)
اور اگر خدا ان میں نیکی (کا مادہ) دیکھتا تو انکو سننے کی توفیق بخشتا
اور اگر (بغیر صلاحیت ہدایت کے) سماعت دیتا تو وہ منہ پھیر کر بھاگ جاتے (۲۳)
مومنو! خدا اور اسکے رسول کا حکم قبول کرو جبکہ رسول خدا تمہیں
ایسے کام کیلئے بلاتے ہیں جو تم کو زندگی (جاوداں) بخشتا ہے اور جان
رکھو کہ خدا آدمی اور اسکے دل کے درمیان حائل ہو جاتا ہے
اور یہ بھی کہ تم سب اسکے روبرو جمع کئے جاؤ گے (۲۴)
اور اس فتنے سے ڈرو جو خصوصیت کے ساتھ اُنہی لوگوں
پر واقع نہ ہوگا جو تم میں گنہگار ہیں اور جان رکھو کہ خدا سخت

وَمَنْ يُّوَلِّهِمْ يَوْمَئِذٍ دُبُرَهٗۤ اِلَّا مُتَحَرِّفًا
لِّقِتَالٍ اَوْ مُتَحَيِّزًا اِلٰى فِئَةٍ فَقَدْ بَآءَ
بِغَضَبٍ مِّنَ اللّٰهِ وَمَاْوٰىهُ جَهَنَّمُ ؕ
وَبِئْسَ الْمَصِيْرُ ﴿١٦﴾
فَلَمْ تَقْتُلُوْهُمْ وَلٰكِنَّ اللّٰهَ قَتَلَهُمْ ۪
وَمَا رَمَيْتَ اِذْ رَمَيْتَ وَلٰكِنَّ اللّٰهَ رَمٰى ۚ
وَلِيُبْلِيَ الْمُؤْمِنِيْنَ مِنْهُ بَلَآءً حَسَنًا ؕ
اِنَّ اللّٰهَ سَمِيْعٌ عَلِيْمٌ ﴿١٧﴾
ذٰلِكُمْ وَاَنَّ اللّٰهَ مُوْهِنُ كَيْدِ الْكٰفِرِيْنَ ﴿١٨﴾
اِنْ تَسْتَفْتِحُوْا فَقَدْ جَآءَكُمُ الْفَتْحُ ۚ
وَاِنْ تَنْتَهُوْا فَهُوَ خَيْرٌ لَّكُمْ ۚ وَاِنْ
تَعُوْدُوْا نَعُدْ ۚ وَلَنْ تُغْنِيَ عَنْكُمْ فِئَتُكُمْ
شَيْئًا وَّلَوْ كَثُرَتْ ۙ وَاَنَّ اللّٰهَ مَعَ الْمُؤْمِنِيْنَ ﴿١٩﴾ ع
يٰۤاَيُّهَا الَّذِيْنَ اٰمَنُوْۤا اَطِيْعُوا اللّٰهَ وَ
رَسُوْلَهٗ وَلَا تَوَلَّوْا عَنْهُ وَاَنْتُمْ تَسْمَعُوْنَ ﴿٢٠﴾
وَلَا تَكُوْنُوْا كَالَّذِيْنَ قَالُوْا سَمِعْنَا وَهُمْ
لَا يَسْمَعُوْنَ ﴿٢١﴾
اِنَّ شَرَّ الدَّوَآبِّ عِنْدَ اللّٰهِ الصُّمُّ
الْبُكْمُ الَّذِيْنَ لَا يَعْقِلُوْنَ ﴿٢٢﴾
وَلَوْ عَلِمَ اللّٰهُ فِيْهِمْ خَيْرًا لَّاَسْمَعَهُمْ ؕ
وَلَوْ اَسْمَعَهُمْ لَتَوَلَّوْا وَّهُمْ مُّعْرِضُوْنَ ﴿٢٣﴾
يٰۤاَيُّهَا الَّذِيْنَ اٰمَنُوا اسْتَجِيْبُوْا لِلّٰهِ وَ
لِلرَّسُوْلِ اِذَا دَعَاكُمْ لِمَا يُحْيِيْكُمْ ۚ وَ
اعْلَمُوْۤا اَنَّ اللّٰهَ يَحُوْلُ بَيْنَ الْمَرْءِ وَ
قَلْبِهٖ وَاَنَّهٗۤ اِلَيْهِ تُحْشَرُوْنَ ﴿٢٤﴾
وَاتَّقُوْا فِتْنَةً لَّا تُصِيْبَنَّ الَّذِيْنَ ظَلَمُوْا
مِنْكُمْ خَآصَّةً ۚ وَاعْلَمُوْۤا اَنَّ اللّٰهَ شَدِيْدُ

punishment.

26. Call to mind when ye were a small (band), deemed weak through the land, and afraid that men might despoil and kidnap you; but He provided a safe asylum for you, strengthened you with His aid, and gave you good things for sustenance: that ye might be grateful.

27. O ye that believe! betray not the trust of Allah and the Messenger, nor misappropriate knowingly things entrusted to you.

28. And know ye that your possessions and your progeny are but a trial: and that it is Allah with whom lies your highest reward.

29. O ye who believe! if ye fear Allah, He will grant you a Criterion (to judge between right and wrong), remove from you (all) evil deeds and forgive you: for Allah is the Lord of grace unbounded.

30. Remember how the Unbelievers plotted against thee, to keep thee in bonds, or slay thee, or get thee out (of thy home). They plot and plan, and Allah too plans, but the best of planners is Allah.

31. When Our Signs are rehearsed to them, they say: "We have heard this (before): if we wished, we could say (words) like these: these are nothing but tales of the ancients."

32. Remember how they said: "O Allah! if this is indeed the Truth from Thee, rain down on us a shower of stones from the sky, or send us a grievous chastisement."

33. But Allah was not going to send them a Chastisement: whilst thou wast amongst them; nor was He going to send it whilst they could ask for pardon.

34. But what plea have they that Allah should not punish them, when they keep out (men) from the Sacred Mosque—and they are not its guardians? No men can be its guardians except the righteous; but most of them do not understand.

عذاب دینے والا ہے ﴿٢٥﴾
اور (اس وقت کو) یاد کرو جب تم زمین (مکہ) میں قلیل اور ضعیف سمجھے
جاتے تھے اور ڈرتے رہتے تھے کہ لوگ تمہیں اُڑا (نہ) لے جائیں
(یعنی بے خانماں نہ کردیں) تو اس نے تم کو جگہ دی اور اپنی مدد
سے تم کو تقویت بخشی اور پاکیزہ چیزیں کھانے کو دیں تاکہ (اُس کا) شکر کرو ﴿٢٦﴾
اے ایمان والو! نہ تو خدا اور رسول کی امانت میں خیانت کرو اور نہ
اپنی امانتوں میں خیانت کرو اور تم (ان باتوں کو) جانتے ہو ﴿٢٧﴾
اور جان رکھو کہ تمہارا مال اور اولاد بڑی آزمائش ہے اور یہ کہ
خدا کے پاس (نیکیوں کا) بڑا ثواب ہے ﴿٢٨﴾
مومنو! اگر تم خدا سے ڈرو گے تو وہ تمہارے لئے امر فارق
پیدا کر دیگا (یعنی تم کو ممتاز کر دیگا) اور تمہارے گناہ مٹا دیگا
اور تمہیں بخش دے گا اور خدا بڑے فضل والا ہے ﴿٢٩﴾
اور (اے محمد اس وقت کو یاد کرو) جب کافر لوگ تمہارے بارے میں چال چل
رہے تھے کہ تم کو قید کر دیں یا جان سے مار دیں یا (وطن سے) نکال دیں تو (ادھر تو)
وہ چال چل رہے تھے اور (ادھر) خدا چال چل رہا تھا اور خدا سب سے بہتر چال چلنے والا ہے ﴿٣٠﴾
اور جب اُنکو ہماری آیتیں پڑھ کر سنائی جاتی ہیں۔ تو کہتے ہیں (یہ
کلام) ہم نے سن لیا ہے اگر ہم چاہیں تو اسی طرح کا (کلام) ہم بھی کہدیں
اور یہ ہے ہی کیا صرف اگلے لوگوں کی حکایتیں ہیں ﴿٣١﴾
اور جب اُنہوں نے کہا کہ اے خدا اگر یہ (قرآن) تیری طرف سے برحق
ہے تو ہم پر آسمان سے پتھر برسا یا کوئی اور تکلیف دینے والا
عذاب بھیج ﴿٣٢﴾
اور خدا ایسا نہ تھا کہ جب تک تم ان میں تھے انہیں عذاب دیتا۔
اور نہ ایسا تھا کہ وہ بخشش مانگیں اور انہیں عذاب دے ﴿٣٣﴾
اور (اب) اُن کیلئے کونسی وجہ ہے کہ وہ انہیں عذاب نہ دے
جب کہ وہ مسجد محترم (میں نماز پڑھنے) سے روکتے ہیں اور وہ
اس مسجد کے متولی بھی نہیں ہیں۔ اسکے متولی تو صرف پرہیزگار
ہیں لیکن اُن میں کے اکثر نہیں جانتے ﴿٣٤﴾

العقاب ﴿٢٥﴾
واذكروا اذ انتم قليل مستضعفون
في الارض تخافون ان يتخطفكم
الناس فاوىكم وايدكم بنصره ورزقكم
من الطيبت لعلكم تشكرون ﴿٢٦﴾
يايها الذين امنوا لا تخونوا الله و
الرسول وتخونوا امنتكم وانتم تعلمون ﴿٢٧﴾
واعلموا انما اموالكم واولادكم فتنة
وان الله عنده اجر عظيم ﴿٢٨﴾ ع ٣/١٧
يايها الذين امنوا ان تتقوا الله يجعل
لكم فرقانا ويكفر عنكم سياتكم و
يغفر لكم والله ذو الفضل العظيم ﴿٢٩﴾
واذ يمكر بك الذين كفروا ليثبتوك او
يقتلوك او يخرجوك ويمكرون ويمكر
الله والله خير الماكرين ﴿٣٠﴾
واذا تتلى عليهم ايتنا قالوا قد سمعنا
لو نشاء لقلنا مثل هذا ان هذا
الا اساطير الاولين ﴿٣١﴾
واذ قالوا اللهم ان كان هذا هو
الحق من عندك فامطر علينا حجارة
من السماء او ائتنا بعذاب اليم ﴿٣٢﴾
وما كان الله ليعذبهم وانت فيهم وما
كان الله معذبهم وهم يستغفرون ﴿٣٣﴾
وما لهم الا يعذبهم الله وهم يصدون
عن المسجد الحرام وما كانوا اولياءه ان
اولياؤه الا المتقون ولكن اكثرهم
لا يعلمون ﴿٣٤﴾

35. Their prayer at the House (of Allah) is nothing but whistling and clapping of hands: (its only answer can be), "Taste ye the Chastisement because ye blasphemed."

36. The Unbelievers spend their wealth to hinder (men) from the path of Allah, and so will they continue to spend; but in the end they will have (only) regrets and sighs; at length they will be overcome: and the Unbelievers will be gathered together to Hell;—

37. In order that Allah may separate the impure from the pure. Put the impure, one on another, heap them together, and cast them into Hell. They will be the ones to have lost.

38. Say to the Unbelievers, if (now) they desist (from Unbelief), their past would be forgiven them; but if they persist, the punishment of those before them is already (a matter of warning for them).

39. And fight them on until there is no more persecution, and religion becomes Allah's in its entirety but if they cease, verily Allah doth see all that they do.

40. If they refuse, be sure that Allah is your Protector—the Best to protect and the Best to help.

41. And know that out of all the booty that ye may acquire (in war), a fifth share is assigned to Allah,—and to the Messenger, and to near relatives, orphans, the needy, and the wayfarer,— if ye do believe in Allah and in the revelation We sent down to Our Servant on the Day of Discrimination—the Day of the meeting of the two forces. For Allah hath power over all things.

42. Remember ye were on the hither side of the valley, and they on the farther side, and the caravan on lower ground than ye. Even if ye had made a mutual appointment to meet, ye would certainly have failed in the appointment: But (thus ye met), that Allah might

اور ان لوگوں کی نماز خانۂ کعبہ کے پاس سیٹیاں اور تالیاں بجانے
کے سوا کچھ نہ تھی۔ تو تم جو کفر کرتے تھے اب اس کے بدلے عذاب (کا مزہ) چکھو ﴿۳۵﴾
جو لوگ کافر ہیں اپنا مال خرچ کرتے ہیں کہ (لوگوں کو) خدا کے
رستے سے روکیں سو ابھی اور خرچ کریں گے مگر آخر وہ (خرچ کرنا) ان کے
لئے (موجب) افسوس ہوگا اور وہ مغلوب ہو جائیں گے۔
اور کافر لوگ دوزخ کی طرف ہانکے جائیں گے ﴿۳۶﴾
تاکہ خدا پاک سے ناپاک کو الگ کر دے اور ناپاک کو ایک
دوسرے پر رکھ کر ایک ڈھیر بنا دے۔ پھر اس کو دوزخ میں ڈال دے
یہی لوگ خسارہ پانے والے ہیں ﴿۳۷﴾
(اے پیغمبر) کفار سے کہہ دو کہ اگر وہ اپنے افعال سے باز آ جائیں تو جو ہو چکا وہ
انہیں معاف کر دیا جائے گا اور اگر پھر (وہی حرکات) کرنے لگیں گے تو اگلے لوگوں کا
(جو) طریق جاری ہو چکا ہے (وہی ان کے حق میں برتا جائے گا) ﴿۳۸﴾
اور ان لوگوں سے لڑتے رہو یہاں تک کہ فتنہ (یعنی کفر کا فساد)
باقی نہ رہے اور دین سب خدا ہی کا ہو جائے اور اگر باز آ جائیں
تو خدا ان کے کاموں کو دیکھ رہا ہے ﴿۳۹﴾
اور اگر روگردانی کریں تو جان رکھو کہ خدا تمہارا حمایتی ہے
(اور) وہ خوب حمایتی اور خوب مددگار ہے ﴿۴۰﴾
اور جان رکھو کہ جو چیز تم (کفار سے) لوٹ کر لاؤ اس میں سے
پانچواں حصہ خدا کا اور اس کے رسول کا اور اہل قرابت کا اور
یتیموں کا اور محتاجوں کا اور مسافروں کا ہے۔ اگر تم خدا پر
اور اس (نصرت) پر ایمان رکھتے ہو جو (حق و باطل میں) فرق کرنے کے
دن (یعنی جنگ بدر میں) جس دن دونوں فوجوں میں مڈبھیڑ ہو گئی۔ اپنے
بندے (محمدؐ) پر نازل فرمائی۔ اور خدا ہر چیز پر قادر ہے ﴿۴۱﴾
جس وقت تم (مدینے سے) قریب کے ناکے پر تھے اور کافر بعید کے
ناکے پر اور قافلہ تم سے نیچے (اتر گیا) تھا۔ اور اگر تم (جنگ کے لئے)
آپس میں قرار داد کر لیتے تو وقت معین (پر جمع ہونے) میں تقدیم و تاخیر
ہو جاتی لیکن خدا کو منظور تھا کہ جو کام ہو کر رہنے والا تھا اسے

وَمَا كَانَ صَلَاتُهُمْ عِندَ الْبَيْتِ إِلَّا مُكَاءً وَتَصْدِيَةً
فَذُوقُوا الْعَذَابَ بِمَا كُنتُمْ تَكْفُرُونَ ﴿٣٥﴾
إِنَّ الَّذِينَ كَفَرُوا يُنفِقُونَ أَمْوَالَهُمْ
لِيَصُدُّوا عَن سَبِيلِ اللَّهِ فَسَيُنفِقُونَهَا
ثُمَّ تَكُونُ عَلَيْهِمْ حَسْرَةً ثُمَّ يُغْلَبُونَ ۗ
وَالَّذِينَ كَفَرُوا إِلَىٰ جَهَنَّمَ يُحْشَرُونَ ﴿٣٦﴾
لِيَمِيزَ اللَّهُ الْخَبِيثَ مِنَ الطَّيِّبِ وَيَجْعَلَ
الْخَبِيثَ بَعْضَهُ عَلَىٰ بَعْضٍ فَيَرْكُمَهُ جَمِيعًا
فَيَجْعَلَهُ فِي جَهَنَّمَ ۚ أُولَٰئِكَ هُمُ الْخَاسِرُونَ ﴿٣٧﴾
قُل لِّلَّذِينَ كَفَرُوا إِن يَنتَهُوا يُغْفَرْ لَهُم
مَّا قَدْ سَلَفَ وَإِن يَعُودُوا فَقَدْ مَضَتْ
سُنَّتُ الْأَوَّلِينَ ﴿٣٨﴾
وَقَاتِلُوهُمْ حَتَّىٰ لَا تَكُونَ فِتْنَةٌ وَيَكُونَ
الدِّينُ كُلُّهُ لِلَّهِ ۚ فَإِنِ انتَهَوْا فَإِنَّ اللَّهَ
بِمَا يَعْمَلُونَ بَصِيرٌ ﴿٣٩﴾
وَإِن تَوَلَّوْا فَاعْلَمُوا أَنَّ اللَّهَ مَوْلَاكُمْ ۚ
نِعْمَ الْمَوْلَىٰ وَنِعْمَ النَّصِيرُ ﴿٤٠﴾
وَاعْلَمُوا أَنَّمَا غَنِمْتُم مِّن شَيْءٍ فَأَنَّ
لِلَّهِ خُمُسَهُ وَلِلرَّسُولِ وَلِذِي الْقُرْبَىٰ
وَالْيَتَامَىٰ وَالْمَسَاكِينِ وَابْنِ السَّبِيلِ
إِن كُنتُمْ آمَنتُم بِاللَّهِ وَمَا أَنزَلْنَا عَلَىٰ
عَبْدِنَا يَوْمَ الْفُرْقَانِ يَوْمَ الْتَقَى الْجَمْعَانِ ۗ
وَاللَّهُ عَلَىٰ كُلِّ شَيْءٍ قَدِيرٌ ﴿٤١﴾
إِذْ أَنتُم بِالْعُدْوَةِ الدُّنْيَا وَهُم بِالْعُدْوَةِ
الْقُصْوَىٰ وَالرَّكْبُ أَسْفَلَ مِنكُمْ ۚ وَلَوْ
تَوَاعَدتُّمْ لَاخْتَلَفْتُمْ فِي الْمِيعَادِ ۙ وَلَٰكِن
لِّيَقْضِيَ اللَّهُ أَمْرًا كَانَ مَفْعُولًا

accomplish a matter already decided; that those who died might die after a clear Sign (had been given), and those who lived might live after a clear Sign (had been given). And verily Allah is He Who heareth and knoweth (all things).

43. Remember in thy dream Allah showed them to thee as few: if He had shown them to thee as many, ye would surely have been discouraged, and ye would surely have disputed in (your) decision: but Allah saved (you): for He knoweth well the (secrets) of (all) hearts.

44. And remember when ye met, He showed them to you as few in your eyes, and He made you appear as contemptible in their eyes: that Allah might accomplish a matter already decided and unto Allah are all matters returned.

45. O ye who believe! when ye meet a force, be firm, and call Allah in remembrance much (and often); that ye may prosper:

46. And obey Allah and His Messenger; and fall into no disputes, lest ye lose heart and your power depart; and be patient and persevering: for Allah is with those who patiently persevere:

47. And be not like those who started from their homes insolently and to be seen of men, and to hinder (men) from the path of Allah: for Allah compasseth all that they do.

48. Remember Satan made their (sinful) acts seem alluring to them, and said: "No one among men can overcome you this day, while I am near to you": but when the two forces came in sight of each other, he turned on his heels, and said: "Lo! I am clear of you; lo! I see what ye see not; lo! I fear Allah; for Allah is strict in punishment"

49. Lo! the Hypocrites and those in whose hearts is a disease: say: "these people,—their religion has misled them." But if any trust in Allah, behold! Allah is Exalted in might, Wise.

کرہی ڈالے تاکہ جو مرے بصیرت پر (یعنی یقین جان کر) مرے اور جو
جیتا رہے وہ بھی بصیرت پر (یعنی حق پہچان کر) جیتا رہے۔
اور کچھ شک نہیں کہ خدا سنتا جانتا ہے ﴿۴۲﴾

اُس وقت خدا نے تمہیں خواب میں کافروں کو تھوڑی تعداد میں
دکھایا اور اگر بہت کر کے دکھاتا تو تم لوگ جی چھوڑ دیتے اور
(جو) کام (درپیش تھا اُس) میں جھگڑنے لگتے لیکن خدا نے
(تمہیں اس سے) بچا لیا بیشک وہ سینوں کی باتوں تک سے واقف ہے ﴿۴۳﴾

اور اُس وقت جب تم ایک دوسرے کے مقابل ہوئے تو کافروں کو تمہاری نظروں
میں تھوڑا کر کے دکھاتا تھا اور تم کو اُن کی نگاہوں میں تھوڑا کر کے دکھاتا تھا
تاکہ خدا کو جو کام کرنا منظور تھا اُسے کر ڈالے اور سب کاموں کا رجوع خدا ہی کی طرف ہے ﴿۴۴﴾

مومنو! جب (کفار کی) کسی جماعت سے تمہارا مقابلہ ہو تو ثابت قدم رہو
اور خدا کو بہت یاد کرو تاکہ مراد حاصل کرو ﴿۴۵﴾

اور خدا اور اس کے رسُول کے حکم پر چلو اور آپس میں جھگڑا نہ
کرنا کہ (ایسا کرو گے تو) تم بزدل ہو جاؤ گے اور تمہارا اقبال جاتا
رہیگا اور صبر سے کام لو کہ خدا صبر کرنے والوں کا مددگار ہے ﴿۴۶﴾

اور اُن لوگوں جیسے نہ ہونا جو اتراتے ہوئے (یعنی حق کا مقابلہ کرنے
کیلئے) اور لوگوں کو دکھانے کیلئے گھروں سے نکل آئے اور لوگوں کو خدا کی
راہ سے روکتے ہیں۔ اور جو اعمال یہ کرتے ہیں خدا اُن پر احاطہ کئے ہوئے ہے ﴿۴۷﴾

اور جب شیطانوں نے اُنکے اعمال اُنکو آراستہ کر دکھائے اور کہا کہ آج کے دن
لوگوں میں کوئی تم پر غالب نہ ہوگا۔ اور میں تمہارا رفیق ہوں (لیکن) جب
دونوں فوجیں ایک دوسرے کے مقابل (صف آرا) ہوئیں تو پسپا ہو کر
چل دیا۔ اور کہنے لگا کہ مجھے تم سے کوئی واسطہ نہیں میں تو ایسی
چیزیں دیکھ رہا ہوں جو تم نہیں دیکھ سکتے، مجھے تو خدا سے ڈر لگتا ہے۔
اور خدا سخت عذاب کرنے والا ہے ﴿۴۸﴾

اُس وقت منافق اور (کافر) جن کے دلوں میں مرض تھا کہتے تھے
کہ اِن لوگوں کو ان کے دین نے مغرور کر رکھا ہے۔ اور جو شخص
خدا پر بھروسا رکھتا ہے تو خدا غالب حکمت والا ہے ﴿۴۹﴾

لِّيَهْلِكَ مَنْ هَلَكَ عَنْۢ بَيِّنَةٍ وَّيَحْيٰى
مَنْ حَيَّ عَنْۢ بَيِّنَةٍ ؕ وَاِنَّ اللّٰهَ لَسَمِيْعٌ
عَلِيْمٌ ۙ ﴿۴۲﴾
اِذْ يُرِيْكَهُمُ اللّٰهُ فِيْ مَنَامِكَ قَلِيْلًا ؕ وَلَوْ
اَرٰىكَهُمْ كَثِيْرًا لَّفَشِلْتُمْ وَلَتَنَازَعْتُمْ
فِي الْاَمْرِ وَلٰكِنَّ اللّٰهَ سَلَّمَ ؕ اِنَّهٗ عَلِيْمٌۢ
بِذَاتِ الصُّدُوْرِ ﴿۴۳﴾
وَاِذْ يُرِيْكُمُوْهُمْ اِذِ الْتَقَيْتُمْ فِيْۤ اَعْيُنِكُمْ
قَلِيْلًا وَّيُقَلِّلُكُمْ فِيْۤ اَعْيُنِهِمْ لِيَقْضِيَ اللّٰهُ
اَمْرًا كَانَ مَفْعُوْلًا ؕ وَاِلَى اللّٰهِ تُرْجَعُ الْاُمُوْرُ ﴿۴۴﴾ ع
يٰۤاَيُّهَا الَّذِيْنَ اٰمَنُوْۤا اِذَا لَقِيْتُمْ فِئَةً فَاثْبُتُوْا
وَاذْكُرُوا اللّٰهَ كَثِيْرًا لَّعَلَّكُمْ تُفْلِحُوْنَ ﴿۴۵﴾
وَاَطِيْعُوا اللّٰهَ وَرَسُوْلَهٗ وَلَا تَنَازَعُوْا
فَتَفْشَلُوْا وَتَذْهَبَ رِيْحُكُمْ وَاصْبِرُوْا ؕ
اِنَّ اللّٰهَ مَعَ الصّٰبِرِيْنَ ﴿۴۶﴾
وَلَا تَكُوْنُوْا كَالَّذِيْنَ خَرَجُوْا مِنْ دِيَارِهِمْ
بَطَرًا وَّرِئَآءَ النَّاسِ وَيَصُدُّوْنَ عَنْ
سَبِيْلِ اللّٰهِ ؕ وَاللّٰهُ بِمَا يَعْمَلُوْنَ مُحِيْطٌ ﴿۴۷﴾
وَاِذْ زَيَّنَ لَهُمُ الشَّيْطٰنُ اَعْمَالَهُمْ وَ
قَالَ لَا غَالِبَ لَكُمُ الْيَوْمَ مِنَ النَّاسِ وَ
اِنِّيْ جَارٌ لَّكُمْ ۚ فَلَمَّا تَرَآءَتِ الْفِئَتٰنِ
نَكَصَ عَلٰى عَقِبَيْهِ وَقَالَ اِنِّيْ بَرِيْٓءٌ
مِّنْكُمْ اِنِّيْۤ اَرٰى مَا لَا تَرَوْنَ اِنِّيْۤ اَخَافُ
اللّٰهَ ؕ وَاللّٰهُ شَدِيْدُ الْعِقَابِ ﴿۴۸﴾ ع
اِذْ يَقُوْلُ الْمُنٰفِقُوْنَ وَالَّذِيْنَ فِيْ قُلُوْبِهِمْ
مَّرَضٌ غَرَّ هٰۤؤُلَآءِ دِيْنُهُمْ ؕ وَمَنْ يَّتَوَكَّلْ
عَلَى اللّٰهِ فَاِنَّ اللّٰهَ عَزِيْزٌ حَكِيْمٌ ﴿۴۹﴾

50. If thou couldst see, when the angels take the souls of the Unbelievers (at death), (how) they smite their faces and their backs, (saying): "Taste the chastisement of the blazing Fire—

51. This is "because of (the deeds) which your (own) hands sent forth. For Allah is never unjust to His servants."

52. "(Deeds) after the manner of the People of Pharaoh and of those before them: they rejected the Signs of Allah, and Allah punished them for their crimes: for Allah is Strong, and Strict in punishment:

53. "Because Allah will never change the Grace which He hath bestowed on a people until they change what is in their (own) souls: and verily Allah is He who heareth and knoweth (all things)."

54. "(Deeds) after the manner of the People of Pharaoh and those before them": they treated as false the Signs of their Lord so We destroyed them for their crimes, and We drowned the People of Pharaoh: for they were all oppressors and wrong-doers.

55. For the worst of beasts in the sight of Allah are those who reject Him: they will not believe.

56. They are those with whom thou didst make a covenant, but they break their covenant every time, and they have not the fear (of Allah).

57. If ye gain the mastery over them in war, disperse, with them, those who follow them, that they may remember.

58. If thou fearest treachery from any group, throw back (their Covenant) to them, (so as to be) on equal terms: for Allah loveth not the treacherous.

59. Let not the Unbelievers think that they have escaped, they will never frustrate (them).

60. Against them make ready your strength to the utmost of your power, including steeds of war, to

اور کاش تم اُس وقت (کی کیفیت) دیکھو جب فرشتے کافروں
کی جانیں نکالتے ہیں اُن کے مونہوں اور پیٹھوں پر (کوڑے
اور ہتھوڑے وغیرہ) مارتے (رہیں اور کہتے ہیں کہ اب) عذابِ آتش (کا مزہ) چکھو ﴿۵۰﴾
یہ اُن (اعمال) کی سزا ہے جو تمہارے ہاتھوں نے آگے بھیجے ہیں۔ اور یہ
(جان رکھو) کہ خدا بندوں پر ظلم نہیں کرتا ﴿۵۱﴾
جیسا حال فرعونیوں اور اُن سے پہلے لوگوں کا (ہوا تھا ویسا ہی
ان کا ہوا کہ) انہوں نے خدا کی آیتوں سے کفر کیا تو خدا نے اُن کے
گناہوں کی سزا میں اُنکو پکڑ لیا۔ بیشک خدا زبردست (اور) سخت عذاب دینے والا ہے ﴿۵۲﴾
یہ اس لئے کہ جو نعمت خدا کسی قوم کو دیا کرتا ہے جب تک وہ
خود اپنے دلوں کی حالت نہ بدل ڈالیں خدا اُسے نہیں بدلا کرتا
اور اس لئے کہ خدا سنتا جانتا ہے ﴿۵۳﴾
جیسا حال فرعونیوں اور اُن سے پہلے لوگوں کا (ہوا تھا ویسا ہی اُن کا ہوا)
انہوں نے اپنے پروردگار کی آیتوں کو جھٹلایا تو ہم نے اُنکو اُنکے گناہوں کے
سبب ہلاک کر ڈالا اور فرعونیوں کو ڈبو دیا۔ اور وہ سب ظالم تھے ﴿۵۴﴾
جانداروں میں سب سے بدتر خدا کے نزدیک وہ لوگ ہیں جو کافر ہیں
سو وہ ایمان نہیں لاتے ﴿۵۵﴾
جن لوگوں سے تم نے (صلح کا) عہد کیا ہے پھر وہ ہر بار اپنے عہد کو
توڑ ڈالتے ہیں اور (خدا سے) نہیں ڈرتے ﴿۵۶﴾
اگر تم اُنکو لڑائی میں پاؤ تو انہیں ایسی سزا دو کہ جو لوگ اُنکے پس پشت ہوں
وہ اُنکو دیکھ کر بھاگ جائیں عجب نہیں کہ اُن کو (اس سے) عبرت ہو ﴿۵۷﴾
اور اگر تم کو کسی قوم سے دغابازی کا خوف ہو تو (اُن کا عہد)
اُنہیں کی طرف پھینک دو (اور) برابر (کا جواب دو) کچھ
شک نہیں کہ خدا دغابازوں کو دوست نہیں رکھتا ﴿۵۸﴾
اور کافر یہ نہ خیال کریں کہ وہ بھاگ نکلے ہیں وہ (اپنی چالوں
سے ہم کو) ہرگز عاجز نہیں کرسکتے ﴿۵۹﴾
اور جہاں تک ہو سکے (فوج کی جمعیت کے) زور سے اور
گھوڑوں کے تیار رکھنے سے اُن کے (مقابلے کے) لئے

وَلَوْ تَرٰٓی اِذْ یَتَوَفَّی الَّذِیْنَ کَفَرُوا الْمَلٰٓئِکَةُ
یَضْرِبُوْنَ وُجُوْهَهُمْ وَاَدْبَارَهُمْ وَذُوْقُوْا
عَذَابَ الْحَرِیْقِ ﴿۵۰﴾
ذٰلِکَ بِمَا قَدَّمَتْ اَیْدِیْکُمْ وَاَنَّ اللّٰهَ
لَیْسَ بِظَلَّامٍ لِّلْعَبِیْدِ ﴿۵۱﴾
کَدَاْبِ اٰلِ فِرْعَوْنَ وَالَّذِیْنَ مِنْ قَبْلِهِمْ
کَفَرُوْا بِاٰیٰتِ اللّٰهِ فَاَخَذَهُمُ اللّٰهُ بِذُنُوْبِهِمْ
اِنَّ اللّٰهَ قَوِیٌّ شَدِیْدُ الْعِقَابِ ﴿۵۲﴾
ذٰلِکَ بِاَنَّ اللّٰهَ لَمْ یَکُ مُغَیِّرًا نِّعْمَةً
اَنْعَمَهَا عَلٰی قَوْمٍ حَتّٰی یُغَیِّرُوْا مَا بِاَنْفُسِهِمْ
وَاَنَّ اللّٰهَ سَمِیْعٌ عَلِیْمٌ ﴿۵۳﴾
کَدَاْبِ اٰلِ فِرْعَوْنَ وَالَّذِیْنَ مِنْ قَبْلِهِمْ
کَذَّبُوْا بِاٰیٰتِ رَبِّهِمْ فَاَهْلَکْنٰهُمْ بِذُنُوْبِهِمْ وَ
اَغْرَقْنَآ اٰلَ فِرْعَوْنَ وَکُلٌّ کَانُوْا ظٰلِمِیْنَ ﴿۵۴﴾
اِنَّ شَرَّ الدَّوَآبِّ عِنْدَ اللّٰهِ الَّذِیْنَ کَفَرُوْا
فَهُمْ لَا یُؤْمِنُوْنَ ﴿۵۵﴾
اَلَّذِیْنَ عٰهَدْتَّ مِنْهُمْ ثُمَّ یَنْقُضُوْنَ عَهْدَهُمْ
فِیْ کُلِّ مَرَّةٍ وَّهُمْ لَا یَتَّقُوْنَ ﴿۵۶﴾
فَاِمَّا تَثْقَفَنَّهُمْ فِی الْحَرْبِ فَشَرِّدْ بِهِمْ مَّنْ
خَلْفَهُمْ لَعَلَّهُمْ یَذَّکَّرُوْنَ ﴿۵۷﴾
وَاِمَّا تَخَافَنَّ مِنْ قَوْمٍ خِیَانَةً فَانْۢبِذْ
اِلَیْهِمْ عَلٰی سَوَآءٍ ۭ اِنَّ اللّٰهَ لَا یُحِبُّ
الْخَآئِنِیْنَ ﴿۵۸﴾ ع
وَلَا یَحْسَبَنَّ الَّذِیْنَ کَفَرُوْا سَبَقُوْا ۭ
اِنَّهُمْ لَا یُعْجِزُوْنَ ﴿۵۹﴾
وَاَعِدُّوْا لَهُمْ مَّا اسْتَطَعْتُمْ مِّنْ قُوَّةٍ
وَّمِنْ رِّبَاطِ الْخَیْلِ تُرْهِبُوْنَ بِهٖ عَدُوَّ

اللّٰهِ وَعَدُوَّكُمْ وَاٰخَرِيْنَ مِنْ دُوْنِهِمْ ۚ لَا
تَعْلَمُوْنَهُمْ ۚ اَللّٰهُ يَعْلَمُهُمْ ۭ وَمَا تُنْفِقُوْا
مِنْ شَيْءٍ فِيْ سَبِيْلِ اللّٰهِ يُوَفَّ اِلَيْكُمْ وَ
اَنْتُمْ لَا تُظْلَمُوْنَ ﴿۶۰﴾
وَاِنْ جَنَحُوْا لِلسَّلْمِ فَاجْنَحْ لَهَا وَتَوَكَّلْ
عَلَى اللّٰهِ ۭ اِنَّهٗ هُوَ السَّمِيْعُ الْعَلِيْمُ ﴿۶۱﴾
وَاِنْ يُّرِيْدُوْٓا اَنْ يَّخْدَعُوْكَ فَاِنَّ حَسْبَكَ
اللّٰهُ ۭ هُوَ الَّذِيْٓ اَيَّدَكَ بِنَصْرِهٖ وَبِالْمُؤْمِنِيْنَ ﴿۶۲﴾
وَاَلَّفَ بَيْنَ قُلُوْبِهِمْ ۭ لَوْ اَنْفَقْتَ مَا فِي
الْاَرْضِ جَمِيْعًا مَّآ اَلَّفْتَ بَيْنَ قُلُوْبِهِمْ
وَلٰكِنَّ اللّٰهَ اَلَّفَ بَيْنَهُمْ ۭ اِنَّهٗ عَزِيْزٌ
حَكِيْمٌ ﴿۶۳﴾
يٰٓاَيُّهَا النَّبِيُّ حَسْبُكَ اللّٰهُ وَمَنِ اتَّبَعَكَ
مِنَ الْمُؤْمِنِيْنَ ﴿۶۴﴾ ع
يٰٓاَيُّهَا النَّبِيُّ حَرِّضِ الْمُؤْمِنِيْنَ عَلَى
الْقِتَالِ ۭ اِنْ يَّكُنْ مِّنْكُمْ عِشْرُوْنَ صٰبِرُوْنَ
يَغْلِبُوْا مِائَتَيْنِ ۚ وَاِنْ يَّكُنْ مِّنْكُمْ مِّائَةٌ
يَّغْلِبُوْٓا اَلْفًا مِّنَ الَّذِيْنَ كَفَرُوْا بِاَنَّهُمْ
قَوْمٌ لَّا يَفْقَهُوْنَ ﴿۶۵﴾
اَلْئٰنَ خَفَّفَ اللّٰهُ عَنْكُمْ وَعَلِمَ اَنَّ فِيْكُمْ
ضَعْفًا ۭ فَاِنْ يَّكُنْ مِّنْكُمْ مِّائَةٌ صَابِرَةٌ
يَّغْلِبُوْا مِائَتَيْنِ ۚ وَاِنْ يَّكُنْ مِّنْكُمْ
اَلْفٌ يَّغْلِبُوْٓا اَلْفَيْنِ بِاِذْنِ اللّٰهِ ۭ وَاللّٰهُ
مَعَ الصّٰبِرِيْنَ ﴿۶۶﴾
مَا كَانَ لِنَبِيٍّ اَنْ يَّكُوْنَ لَهٗٓ اَسْرٰى
حَتّٰى يُثْخِنَ فِي الْاَرْضِ ۭ تُرِيْدُوْنَ عَرَضَ
الدُّنْيَا ۖ وَاللّٰهُ يُرِيْدُ الْاٰخِرَةَ ۭ وَاللّٰهُ

مستعد رہو کہ اس سے خدا کے دشمنوں اور تمہارے دشمنوں اور
ان کے سوا اور لوگوں پر جن کو تم نہیں جانتے اور خدا جانتا ہے
ہیبت بیٹھی رہے گی۔ اور تم جو کچھ راہ خدا میں خرچ کرو گے
اُس کا ثواب تم کو پورا پورا دیا جائیگا اور تمہارا ذرا نقصان نہ کیا جائیگا (۶۰)
اور اگر یہ لوگ صلح کیطرف مائل ہوں تو تم بھی اسکی طرف مائل ہو جاؤ اور خدا
پر بھروسا رکھو۔ کچھ شک نہیں کہ وہ سب کچھ سنتا اور جانتا ہے (۶۱)
اور اگر یہ چاہیں کہ تم کو فریب دیں تو خدا تمہیں کفایت کریگا۔ وہی تو
ہے جس نے تم کو اپنی مدد سے اور مسلمانوں (کی جمعیت) سے تقویت بخشی (۶۲)
اور ان کے دلوں میں اُلفت پیدا کر دی۔ اور اگر تم دُنیا بھر کی
دولت خرچ کرتے تب بھی اُن کے دلوں میں اُلفت پیدا نہ
کر سکتے۔ مگر خدا ہی نے ان میں اُلفت ڈال دی۔ بیشک وہ
زبردست (اور) حکمت والا ہے (۶۳)
اے نبی! خدا تم کو اور مومنوں کو جو تمہارے پیرو ہیں
کافی ہے (۶۴)
اے نبی! مسلمانوں کو جہاد کی ترغیب دو۔ اگر تم میں بیس آدمی
ثابت قدم رہنے والے ہوں گے تو دو سو کافروں پر غالب
رہیں گے۔ اور اگر سو (ایسے) ہوں گے تو ہزار پر
غالب رہیں گے۔ اس لئے کہ کافر ایسے لوگ ہیں کہ کچھ
بھی سمجھ نہیں رکھتے (۶۵)
اب خدا نے تم پر سے بوجھ ہلکا کر دیا اور معلوم کر لیا کہ (ابھی)
تم میں کسی قدر کمزوری ہے۔ پس اگر تم میں ایک سو ثابت قدم
رہنے والے ہوں گے تو دو سو پر غالب رہیں گے اور
اگر ایک ہزار ہوں گے تو خدا کے حکم سے دو ہزار پر غالب رہیں گے
اور خدا ثابت قدم رہنے والوں کا مددگار ہے (۶۶)
پیغمبر کو شایاں نہیں کہ اس کے قبضے میں قیدی رہیں جب تک
(کافروں کو قتل کر کے) زمین میں کثرت سے خون (نہ) بہا دے
تم لوگ دنیا کے مال کے طالب ہو اور خدا آخرت (کی بھلائی)

strike terror into (the hearts of) the enemies, of Allah and your enemies, and others besides, whom ye may not know, but whom Allah doth know. Whatever ye shall spend in the Cause of Allah, shall be repaid unto you, and ye shall not be treated unjustly.

61. But if the enemy incline towards peace, do thou (also) incline towards peace, and trust in Allah: for He is the One that heareth and knoweth (all things).

62. Should they intend to deceive thee,—verily Allah sufficeth thee: He it is that hath strengthened thee with His aid and with (the company of) the Believers,

63. And (moreover) He hath put affection between their hearts: not if thou hadst spent all that is in the earth, couldst thou have produced that affection, but Allah Hath done it: for He is Exalted in might, Wise.

64. O Prophet ! Sufficient unto thee is Allah,—and unto those Who follow thee among the Believers.

65. O Prophet! rouse the Believers to the fight. If there are twenty amongst you, patient and persevering, they will vanquish two hundred: if a hundred. They will vanquish a thousand of the Unbelievers: for these are a people without understanding.

66. For the present, Allah hath lightened your (burden), for He knoweth that there is a weak spot in you: but (even so), if there are a hundred of you, patient and persevering, they will vanquish two hundred, and if a thousand, they will vanquish two thousand, with the leave of Allah: for Allah is with those who patiently persevere.

67. It is not fitting for a Prophet that he should have prisoners of war until He hath thoroughly subdued the land. Ye look for the temporal goods of this world; but Allah looketh to the Hereafter: and

Allah is Exalted in might, Wise.

68. Had it not been for a previous ordainment from Allah, a severe punishment would have reached you for the (ransom) that ye took.

69. But (now) enjoy what ye took in war, lawful and good: but fear Allah: for Allah is Oft-Forgiving, Most Merciful.

70. O Prophet! say to those who are captives in your hands: "If Allah findeth any good in your hearts, He will give you something better than what has been taken from you, and He will forgive you: for Allah is Oft-Forgiving, Most Merciful."

71. But if they have treacherous designs against thee, (O Messenger!), they have already been in treason against Allah, and so hath He given (thee) power over them. And Allah is He Who hath (full) knowledge and wisdom.

72. Those who believed, and emigrated and fought for the Faith, with their property and their persons, in the Cause of Allah, as well as those who gave (them) asylum and aid,—these are (all) Friends and protectors, one of another. As to those who believed but did not emigrate ye owe no duty of protection to them until they emigrate; but if they seek your aid in religion, it is your duty to help them, except against a people with whom ye have a treaty of mutual alliance. And (remember) Allah seeth all that ye do.

73. The Unbelievers are protectors, one of another: unless ye do this. (Protect each other), there would be tumult and oppression on earth, and great mischief.

74. Those who believe, and emigrate, and fight for the Faith, in the Cause of Allah, as well as those who give (them) asylum and aid,—these are (all) in very truth the Believers: for them is the forgiveness of sins and a provision most generous.

75. And those who accept Faith subsequently, and emigrate, and

چاہتا ہے اور خدا غالب حکمت والا ہے ﴿۶۷﴾
اگر خدا کا حکم پہلے نہ ہو چکا ہوتا تو جو (فدیہ) تم نے لیا ہے اُس کے
بدلے تم پر بڑا عذاب (نازل) ہوتا ﴿۶۸﴾
تو جو مال غنیمت تمہیں ملا ہے اُسے کھاؤ کہ وہ تمہارے لئے حلال طیب
(ہے) اور خدا سے ڈرتے رہو بیشک خدا بخشنے والا مہربان ہے ﴿۶۹﴾
اے پیغمبر جو قیدی تمہارے ہاتھ میں (گرفتار) ہیں ان سے کہہ دو
کہ اگر خدا تمہارے دلوں میں نیکی معلوم کریگا تو جو مال تم سے
چھن گیا ہے اس سے بہتر تمہیں عنایت فرمائے گا اور تمہارے
گناہ بھی معاف کردیگا۔ اور خدا بخشنے والا مہربان ہے ﴿۷۰﴾
اور اگر یہ لوگ تم سے دغا کرنا چاہیں گے تو یہ پہلے ہی خدا سے دغا
کرچکے ہیں تو اس نے ان کو (تمہارے) قبضے میں کردیا۔ اور
خدا دانا حکمت والا ہے ﴿۷۱﴾
جو لوگ ایمان لائے اور وطن سے ہجرت کر گئے اور خدا کی
راہ میں اپنے مال اور جان سے لڑے۔ وہ اور جنہوں نے (ہجرت
کرنے والوں کو) جگہ دی اور (اُن کی) مدد کی وہ آپس میں ایک
دوسرے کے رفیق ہیں اور جو لوگ ایمان تو لے آئے لیکن ہجرت
نہیں کی تو جب تک وہ ہجرت نہ کریں تم کو اُن کی رفاقت سے
کچھ سروکار نہیں۔ اور اگر وہ تم سے دین (کے معاملات) میں مدد طلب کریں تو
تم کو مدد کرنی لازم ہے۔ مگر ان لوگوں کے مقابلے میں کہ تم میں اور اُن میں (صلح کا)
عہد ہو (مدد نہیں کرنی چاہیے) اور خدا تمہارے سب کاموں کو دیکھ رہا ہے ﴿۷۲﴾
اور جو لوگ کافر ہیں (وہ بھی) ایک دوسرے کے رفیق ہیں۔ تو (مومنو) اگر
تم یہ (کام) نہ کرو گے تو ملک میں فتنہ برپا ہو جائے گا اور بڑا فساد مچے گا ﴿۷۳﴾
اور جو لوگ ایمان لائے اور وطن سے ہجرت کر گئے اور
خدا کی راہ میں لڑائیاں کرتے رہے۔ اور جنہوں نے (ہجرت
کرنے والوں کو) جگہ دی اور ان کی مدد کی۔ یہی لوگ سچے مسلمان
ہیں ان کیلئے (خدا کے ہاں) بخشش اور عزت کی روزی ہے ﴿۷۴﴾
اور جو لوگ بعد میں ایمان لائے اور وطن سے ہجرت کر گئے اور

عَزِيزٌ حَكِيمٌ ﴿٦٧﴾
لَوْلَا كِتٰبٌ مِّنَ اللّٰهِ سَبَقَ لَمَسَّكُمْ
فِيمَآ أَخَذْتُمْ عَذَابٌ عَظِيمٌ ﴿٦٨﴾
فَكُلُوا مِمَّا غَنِمْتُمْ حَلٰلًا طَيِّبًا ۖ وَّ
اتَّقُوا اللّٰهَ ۚ إِنَّ اللّٰهَ غَفُورٌ رَّحِيمٌ ﴿٦٩﴾ ع ۹ ۵
يٰٓأَيُّهَا النَّبِيُّ قُلْ لِّمَنْ فِيٓ أَيْدِيكُمْ
مِّنَ الْأَسْرٰٓى إِنْ يَّعْلَمِ اللّٰهُ فِي قُلُوبِكُمْ
خَيْرًا يُّؤْتِكُمْ خَيْرًا مِّمَّآ أُخِذَ مِنْكُمْ
وَيَغْفِرْ لَكُمْ ۗ وَاللّٰهُ غَفُورٌ رَّحِيمٌ ﴿٧٠﴾
وَإِنْ يُّرِيدُوا خِيَانَتَكَ فَقَدْ خَانُوا
اللّٰهَ مِنْ قَبْلُ فَأَمْكَنَ مِنْهُمْ ۗ وَاللّٰهُ
عَلِيمٌ حَكِيمٌ ﴿٧١﴾
إِنَّ الَّذِينَ اٰمَنُوا وَهَاجَرُوا وَجٰهَدُوا
بِأَمْوَالِهِمْ وَأَنْفُسِهِمْ فِي سَبِيلِ اللّٰهِ
وَالَّذِينَ اٰوَوْا وَّنَصَرُوٓا أُولٰٓئِكَ بَعْضُهُمْ
أَوْلِيَآءُ بَعْضٍ ۚ وَالَّذِينَ اٰمَنُوا وَلَمْ
يُهَاجِرُوا مَا لَكُمْ مِّنْ وَّلَايَتِهِمْ مِّنْ شَيْءٍ
حَتّٰى يُهَاجِرُوا ۚ وَإِنِ اسْتَنْصَرُوكُمْ فِي
الدِّينِ فَعَلَيْكُمُ النَّصْرُ إِلَّا عَلٰى قَوْمٍ بَيْنَكُمْ
وَبَيْنَهُمْ مِّيثَاقٌ ۗ وَاللّٰهُ بِمَا تَعْمَلُونَ بَصِيرٌ ﴿٧٢﴾
وَالَّذِينَ كَفَرُوا بَعْضُهُمْ أَوْلِيَآءُ بَعْضٍ ۚ إِلَّا
تَفْعَلُوهُ تَكُنْ فِتْنَةٌ فِي الْأَرْضِ وَفَسَادٌ كَبِيرٌ ﴿٧٣﴾
وَالَّذِينَ اٰمَنُوا وَهَاجَرُوا وَجٰهَدُوا
فِي سَبِيلِ اللّٰهِ وَالَّذِينَ اٰوَوْا وَّنَصَرُوٓا
أُولٰٓئِكَ هُمُ الْمُؤْمِنُونَ حَقًّا ۚ لَهُمْ
مَّغْفِرَةٌ وَّرِزْقٌ كَرِيمٌ ﴿٧٤﴾
وَالَّذِينَ اٰمَنُوا مِنْ بَعْدُ وَهَاجَرُوا

SÛRA–9
AT-TAUBA
(INTRODUCTION)

Logically this Sûra follows up the argument of the last Sûra (8), and indeed may be considered a part of it, although chronologically the two are separated by an interval of seven years.

We saw that Sûra 8 dealt with the large questions arising at the outset of the life of a new Ummat or organised nation: questions of defence under attack, distribution of war acquisitions after victory, the virtues needed for concerted action, and clemency and consideration for one's own and for enemies in the hour of victory. We pass on in this Sûra to deal with the question : What is to be done if the enemy breaks faith and is guilty of treachery? No nation can go on with a treaty if the other party violates it at will; but it is laid down that a period of four months should be allowed by way of notice after denunciation of the treaty; that due protection should be accorded in the intervening period; that there should always be open the door to repentance and reunion with the people of Allah; and that if all these fail, and war must be undertaken, it must be pushed with utmost vigour.

These are the general principles deducible from the Sûra. The immediate occasion for their promulgation may be considered in connection with the chronological place of the Sûra.

Chronologically, verses 1-29 were a notable declaration of State policy promulgated about the month of Shwwãl, A.H. 9, and read out by Ḥadhrat 'Alî at the Pilgrimage two months later in order to give the policy the widest publicity possible. The remainder of the Sûra, verses 30-129, was revealed a little earlier, say, about the month of Ramadhãn, A.H. 9, and sums up the lessons of the Apostle's Tabûk expedition in the summer of A.H. 9 (say October 630).

Tabûk is a place near the frontier of Arabia, quite close to what was then Byzantine territory in the Province of Syria (which includes Palestine). It is about 350 miles northwest of Madinah, and 150 miles south of Ma'ãn. It had a fort and a spring of sweet water. In consequence of strong and persistent rumours that the Byzantines (Romans) were preparing to invade Arabia and that the Byzantine Emperor himself had arrived near the frontier for the purpose, the Apostle collected as large a force as he could, and marched to Tubûk. The Byzantine invasion did not come off. But the Apostle took the opportunity of consolidating the Muslim position in that direction and making treaties of alliance with certain Christain and Jewish tribes near the Gulf of 'Aqaba. On his return to Madinah he considered the situation. During his absence the Hypocrites had played, as always, a double game, and the policy hitherto followed, of free access to the sacred centre of Islam, to Muslims and Pagans alike, was now altered, as it had been abused by the enemies of Islam.

This is the only Sûra to which the usual formula of *Bismillãh* is not prefixed. It was among the last of the Sûras revealed, and though the Apostle had directed that it should follow Sûra 8, it was not clear whether it was to form a separate Sûra or only a part of Sûra 8. It is now treated as a separate Sûra, but the *Bismillãh* is not prefixed to it, as there is no warrant for supposing that the Apostle used the *Bismillãh* before it in his recittion of the Qur-ãn. The Sûra is known under many names: the two most commonly used are (1) *Tauba* (Repentance), with reference to 9: 104 and (2) *Barãat* (Immunity), the opening word of the Sûra.

fight for the Faith in your company,—they are of you. But kindred by blood have prior rights against each other in the Book of Allah. Verily Allah is well—acquainted with all things.

At-Tauba (Repentance) or Barāat (Immunity)

1. A (declaration) of immunity from Allah and His Messenger, to those of the Pagans with whom ye have contracted mutual alliances:—

2. Go ye, then for four months, (as ye will), throughout the land, but know yet that ye cannot frustrate Allah (by your falsehood but that Allah will cover with shame those who reject Him.

3. And an announcement from Allah and His Messenger, to the people (assembled) on the day of the Great Pilgrimage,—that Allah and His Messenger dissolve (treaty) obligations with the Pagans. If, then, ye repent, it were best for you; but if ye turn away, know ye that ye cannot frustrate Allah, and proclaim a grievous chastisement to those who reject Faith.

4. (But the treaties are) not dissolved with those Pagans with whom ye have entered into alliance and who have not subsequently failed you in aught, nor aided anyone against you. So fulfil your engagements with them to the end of their term: for Allah loveth the righteous.

5. But when the forbidden months are past, then fight and slay the Pagans wherever ye find them, and seize them, beleaguer them, and lie in wait for them in every stratagem (of war); but if they repent, and establish regular prayers and pay Zakat then open the way for them: for Allah is Oft-Forgiving, Most Merciful.

6. If one amongst the Pagans ask thee for asylum, grant it to him,

وَجَاهَدُوا مَعَكُمْ فَأُولَٰئِكَ مِنْكُمْ ۚ
وَأُولُوا الْأَرْحَامِ بَعْضُهُمْ أَوْلَىٰ بِبَعْضٍ
فِي كِتَابِ اللَّهِ ۗ إِنَّ اللَّهَ بِكُلِّ شَيْءٍ عَلِيمٌ ﴿٧٥﴾

سُورَةُ التَّوْبَةِ مَدَنِيَّةٌ وَهِيَ مِائَةٌ وَتِسْعٌ وَعِشْرُونَ آيَةً وَسِتَّةَ عَشَرَ رُكُوعًا

بَرَاءَةٌ مِنَ اللَّهِ وَرَسُولِهِ إِلَى الَّذِينَ
عَاهَدْتُمْ مِنَ الْمُشْرِكِينَ ﴿١﴾
فَسِيحُوا فِي الْأَرْضِ أَرْبَعَةَ أَشْهُرٍ وَ
اعْلَمُوا أَنَّكُمْ غَيْرُ مُعْجِزِي اللَّهِ ۙ وَأَنَّ
اللَّهَ مُخْزِي الْكَافِرِينَ ﴿٢﴾
وَأَذَانٌ مِنَ اللَّهِ وَرَسُولِهِ إِلَى النَّاسِ
يَوْمَ الْحَجِّ الْأَكْبَرِ أَنَّ اللَّهَ بَرِيءٌ مِنَ
الْمُشْرِكِينَ ۙ وَرَسُولُهُ ۚ فَإِنْ تُبْتُمْ
فَهُوَ خَيْرٌ لَكُمْ ۖ وَإِنْ تَوَلَّيْتُمْ فَاعْلَمُوا
أَنَّكُمْ غَيْرُ مُعْجِزِي اللَّهِ ۗ وَبَشِّرِ الَّذِينَ
كَفَرُوا بِعَذَابٍ أَلِيمٍ ﴿٣﴾
إِلَّا الَّذِينَ عَاهَدْتُمْ مِنَ الْمُشْرِكِينَ
ثُمَّ لَمْ يَنْقُصُوكُمْ شَيْئًا وَلَمْ يُظَاهِرُوا
عَلَيْكُمْ أَحَدًا فَأَتِمُّوا إِلَيْهِمْ عَهْدَهُمْ
إِلَىٰ مُدَّتِهِمْ ۚ إِنَّ اللَّهَ يُحِبُّ
الْمُتَّقِينَ ﴿٤﴾
فَإِذَا انْسَلَخَ الْأَشْهُرُ الْحُرُمُ فَاقْتُلُوا
الْمُشْرِكِينَ حَيْثُ وَجَدْتُمُوهُمْ
وَخُذُوهُمْ وَاحْصُرُوهُمْ وَاقْعُدُوا
لَهُمْ كُلَّ مَرْصَدٍ ۚ فَإِنْ تَابُوا وَأَقَامُوا
الصَّلَاةَ وَآتَوُا الزَّكَاةَ فَخَلُّوا
سَبِيلَهُمْ ۚ إِنَّ اللَّهَ غَفُورٌ رَحِيمٌ ﴿٥﴾
وَإِنْ أَحَدٌ مِنَ الْمُشْرِكِينَ اسْتَجَارَكَ

تمہارے ساتھ ہو کر جہاد کرتے رہے وہ بھی تم ہی میں سے
ہیں اور رشتہ دار خدا کے حکم کی رُو سے ایک دوسرے کے زیادہ
حق دار ہیں کچھ شک نہیں کہ خدا ہر چیز سے واقف ہے ﴿٧٥﴾

سُورۂ توبہ مدنی ہے اور اس میں ایک سو اُنتیس آیتیں اور سولہ رکوع ہیں

(اے اہلِ اسلام اب) خدا اور اسکے رسول کیطرف سے مشرکوں سے
جن سے تم نے عہد کر رکھا تھا بیزاری (اور جنگ کی تیاری) ہے ﴿١﴾
تو (مشرکو تم) زمین میں چار مہینے چل پھر لو اور جان رکھو کہ تم
خدا کو عاجز نہ کر سکو گے۔ اور یہ بھی کہ خدا کافروں کو رسوا
کرنے والا ہے ﴿٢﴾
اور حج اکبر کے دن خدا اور اس کے رسول کی طرف
سے لوگوں کو آگاہ کیا جاتا ہے کہ خدا مشرکوں سے
بیزار ہے اور اس کا رسول بھی (ان سے دست بردار ہے)
پس اگر تم توبہ کر لو تو تمہارے حق میں بہتر ہے اور اگر نہ مانو
(اور خدا سے مقابلہ کرو) تو جان رکھو کہ تم خدا کو ہرا نہیں سکو گے۔
اور (اے پیغمبر) کافروں کو دُکھ دینے والے عذاب کی خبر سُنا دو ﴿٣﴾
البتہ جن مشرکوں کے ساتھ تم نے عہد کیا ہو
اور اُنہوں نے تمہارا کسی طرح کا قصور نہ کیا
ہو اور نہ تمہارے مقابلے میں کسی کی مدد کی ہو تو جس مدت
تک اُن کے ساتھ عہد کیا ہو اُسے پورا کرو (کہ) خدا
پرہیزگاروں کو دوست رکھتا ہے ﴿٤﴾
جب عزت کے مہینے گزر جائیں تو مشرکوں کو جہاں
پاؤ قتل کر دو۔ اور پکڑ لو۔ اور گھیر لو۔ اور ہر گھات
کی جگہ اُن کی تاک میں بیٹھے رہو۔ پھر اگر
وہ توبہ کر لیں اور نماز پڑھنے اور زکوٰۃ
دینے لگیں تو اُن کی راہ چھوڑ دو۔ بے شک
خدا بخشنے والا مہربان ہے ﴿٥﴾
اور اگر کوئی مشرک تم سے پناہ کا خواستگار ہو تو

so that he may hear the Word of Allah; and then escort him to where he can be secure, that is because they are men without knowledge.

7. How can there be a covenant before Allah and His Messenger, with the Pagans, except those with whom ye made a treaty near the Sacred Mosque? As long as these stand true to you, stand ye true to them: for Allah doth love the righteous.

8. How (can there be such a covenant) seeing that if they get an advantage over you, they respect not in you the ties either of kinship or of covenant? With (fair words from) their mouths they please you, but their hearts are averse from you; and most of them are rebellious and wicked.

9. The Words of Allah have they sold for a miserable price, and (many) have they hindered from His Way: evil indeed are the deeds thy have done.

10. In a Believer they respect not the ties either of kinship or of covenant! It is they who have transgressed all bounds.

11. But (even so), if they repent, establish regular prayers, and pay Zakat they are your brethren in Faith: (thus) do We explain the Signs in detail, for those who understand.

12. But if they violate their oaths after their covenant, and attack your Faith,—fight ye the chiefs of Unfaith: for their oaths are nothing to them: that thus they may be restrained.

13. Will ye not fight people who violated their oaths, plotted to expel the Messenger, and attacked you first? Do ye fear them? Nay, it is Allah Whom ye should more justly fear, if ye believe!

اس کو پناہ دو یہاں تک کہ کلامِ خدا
سُننے لگے۔ پھر اُس کو امن کی جگہ واپس پہنچا دو۔
اس لئے کہ یہ بے خبر لوگ ہیں ﴿٦﴾
بھلا مشرکوں کے لئے (جنہوں نے عہد توڑ ڈالا) خدا اور
اُس کے رسُول کے نزدیک عہد کیونکر (قائم) رہ سکتا ہے
ہاں جن لوگوں کے ساتھ تم نے مسجد محترم (یعنی خانہ کعبہ)
کے نزدیک عہد کیا ہے اگر وہ (اپنے عہد پر) قائم رہیں تو تم
بھی (اپنے قول وقرار پر) قائم رہو بیشک خدا پرہیزگاروں کو دوست رکھتا ہے ﴿٧﴾
(بھلا اُن سے عہد کیونکر پورا کیا جائے جب ان کا یہ حال ہے)
کہ اگر تم پر غلبہ پالیں تو نہ قرابت کا لحاظ کریں نہ عہد کا۔ یہ منہ
سے تو تمہیں خوش کر دیتے ہیں لیکن انکے دل (ان باتوں کو)
قبول نہیں کرتے اور ان میں اکثر نافرمان ہیں ﴿٨﴾
یہ خدا کی آیتوں کے عوض تھوڑا سا فائدہ حاصل کرتے اور لوگوں
کو خدا کے رستے سے روکتے ہیں کچھ شک نہیں کہ جو کام یہ کرتے ہیں بُرے ہیں ﴿٩﴾
یہ لوگ کسی مومن کے حق میں نہ تو رشتہ داری کا پاس کرتے ہیں
نہ عہد کا اور یہ حد سے تجاوز کرنے والے ہیں ﴿١٠﴾
اگر یہ توبہ کر لیں اور نماز پڑھنے اور زکٰوۃ دینے لگیں تو دین
میں تمہارے بھائی ہیں اور سمجھنے والے لوگوں کے لئے ہم
اپنی آیتیں کھول کھول کر بیان کرتے ہیں ﴿١١﴾
اور اگر عہد کرنے کے بعد اپنی قسموں کو توڑ ڈالیں اور تمہارے
دین میں طعنے کرنے لگیں تو ان کفر کے پیشواؤں سے جنگ کرو (یہ بے ایمان
لوگ ہیں اور) انکی قسموں کا کچھ اعتبار نہیں۔ عجب نہیں کہ (اپنی حرکات سے) باز آجائیں ﴿١٢﴾
بھلا تم ایسے لوگوں سے کیوں نہ لڑو جنہوں نے اپنی قسموں کو توڑ
ڈالا اور پیغمبر (خدا) کے جلاوطن کرنے کا عزمِ مصمم کر لیا اور اُنہوں
نے تم سے (عہد شکنی کی) ابتدا کی۔ کیا تم ایسے لوگوں
سے ڈرتے ہو حالانکہ ڈرنے کے لائق خدا ہے بشرطیکہ
ایمان رکھتے ہو ﴿١٣﴾

فَأَجِرْهُ حَتّٰى يَسْمَعَ كَلٰمَ اللّٰهِ
ثُمَّ أَبْلِغْهُ مَأْمَنَهٗ ۚ ذٰلِكَ بِأَنَّهُمْ
قَوْمٌ لَّا يَعْلَمُونَ ﴿٦﴾ ع
كَيْفَ يَكُونُ لِلْمُشْرِكِينَ عَهْدٌ عِنْدَ
اللّٰهِ وَعِنْدَ رَسُولِهٖٓ إِلَّا الَّذِينَ عٰهَدْتُّمْ
عِنْدَ الْمَسْجِدِ الْحَرَامِ ۚ فَمَا اسْتَقَامُوا
لَكُمْ فَاسْتَقِيمُوا لَهُمْ ۚ إِنَّ اللّٰهَ يُحِبُّ
الْمُتَّقِينَ ﴿٧﴾
كَيْفَ وَإِنْ يَّظْهَرُوا عَلَيْكُمْ لَا يَرْقُبُوا
فِيكُمْ إِلًّا وَّلَا ذِمَّةً ۚ يُرْضُونَكُمْ
بِأَفْوَاهِهِمْ وَتَأْبٰى قُلُوبُهُمْ ۚ وَأَكْثَرُهُمْ
فٰسِقُونَ ﴿٨﴾
اِشْتَرَوْا بِاٰيٰتِ اللّٰهِ ثَمَنًا قَلِيلًا فَصَدُّوا
عَنْ سَبِيلِهٖ ۚ إِنَّهُمْ سَآءَ مَا كَانُوا يَعْمَلُونَ ﴿٩﴾
لَا يَرْقُبُونَ فِي مُؤْمِنٍ إِلًّا وَّلَا ذِمَّةً ۚ
وَأُولٰٓئِكَ هُمُ الْمُعْتَدُونَ ﴿١٠﴾
فَإِنْ تَابُوا وَأَقَامُوا الصَّلٰوةَ وَاٰتَوُا
الزَّكٰوةَ فَإِخْوَانُكُمْ فِي الدِّينِ ۗ وَنُفَصِّلُ
الْاٰيٰتِ لِقَوْمٍ يَّعْلَمُونَ ﴿١١﴾
وَإِنْ نَّكَثُوٓا أَيْمَانَهُمْ مِّنْ بَعْدِ عَهْدِهِمْ
وَطَعَنُوا فِي دِينِكُمْ فَقَاتِلُوٓا أَئِمَّةَ الْكُفْرِ ۙ
إِنَّهُمْ لَآ أَيْمَانَ لَهُمْ لَعَلَّهُمْ يَنْتَهُونَ ﴿١٢﴾
أَلَا تُقَاتِلُونَ قَوْمًا نَّكَثُوٓا أَيْمَانَهُمْ
وَهَمُّوا بِإِخْرَاجِ الرَّسُولِ وَهُمْ
بَدَءُوكُمْ أَوَّلَ مَرَّةٍ ۚ أَتَخْشَوْنَهُمْ ۚ
فَاللّٰهُ أَحَقُّ أَنْ تَخْشَوْهُ إِنْ كُنْتُمْ
مُّؤْمِنِينَ ﴿١٣﴾

14. Fight them, and Allah will punish them by your hands, and disgrace them help you (to victory) over them, heal the breasts of Believers.

15. And still the indignation of their hearts. For Allah will turn (in mercy) to whom He will: and Allah is All-Knowing, All-Wise.

16. Do you think that you would be left alone while Allah has not yet known those among you who strive with might and main, and take none for friends and protectors except Allah, His Messenger, and the (community of) Believers? And Allah is well-acquainted with (all) that ye do.

17. It is not for such as join gods with Allah, to maintain the mosques of Allah while they witness against their own souls to infidelity. The works of such bear no fruit: in Fire shall they dwell.

18. The mosques of Allah shall be visited and maintained by such as believe in Allah and the Last Day, establish regular prayers, and pay Zakat, and fear none (at all) except Allah it is they who are expected to be on true guidance.

19. Do ye consider the giving of drink to pilgrims, or the maintenance of the Sacred Mosque, equal to (the pious service of) those who believe in Allah and the Last Day, and strive with might and main in the cause of Allah? They are not equal in the sight of Allah: and Allah guides not those who do wrong.

20. Those who believe, and emigrate and strive with might and main, in Allah's cause, with their goods and their persons have the highest rank in the sight of Allah: they are the people who will achieve (salvation).

21. Their Lord doth give them glad tidings of a Mercy from Himself, of His good pleasure. And of Gardens for them, wherein are delights that endure:

22. They will dwell therein for ever. Verily with Allah is a reward,

ان سے (خوب) لڑو۔ خدا ان کو تمہارے ہاتھوں سے عذاب
میں ڈالے گا اور رسوا کرے گا اور تم کو ان پر غلبہ دے گا اور
مومن لوگوں کے سینوں کو شفا بخشے گا (١٤)
اور ان کے دلوں سے غصہ دور کرے گا اور جس پر چاہے گا رحمت
کرے گا۔ اور خدا سب کچھ جانتا (اور) حکمت والا ہے (١٥)
کیا تم لوگ یہ خیال کرتے ہو کہ (بے آزمائش) چھوڑ دیئے جاؤ گے
اور ابھی تو خدا نے ایسے لوگوں کو متمیز کیا ہی نہیں جنہوں نے
تم میں سے جہاد کئے اور خدا اور اسکے رسول اور مومنوں کے سوا کسی کو
دلی دوست نہیں بنایا۔ اور خدا تمہارے سب کاموں سے واقف ہے (١٦)
مشرکوں کو زیبا نہیں کہ خدا کی مسجدوں کو آباد کریں جب کہ
وہ اپنے آپ پر کفر کی گواہی دے رہے ہوں۔ ان
لوگوں کے سب اعمال بے کار ہیں۔ اور یہ ہمیشہ دوزخ
میں رہیں گے (١٧)
خدا کی مسجدوں کو تو وہ لوگ آباد کرتے ہیں جو خدا پر اور
روز قیامت پر ایمان لاتے اور نماز پڑھتے اور زکوٰة
دیتے ہیں اور خدا کے سوا کسی سے نہیں ڈرتے یہی لوگ
اُمید ہے کہ ہدایت یافتہ لوگوں میں (داخل) ہوں (١٨)
کیا تم نے حاجیوں کو پانی پلانا اور مسجد محترم (یعنی خانہ کعبہ)
کو آباد کرنا اس شخص کے اعمال جیسا خیال کیا ہے جو خدا اور روز آخر
پر ایمان رکھتا ہے اور خدا کی راہ میں جہاد کرتا ہے؟ یہ لوگ خدا کے نزدیک
برابر نہیں ہیں۔ اور خدا ظالم لوگوں کو ہدایت نہیں دیا کرتا (١٩)
جو لوگ ایمان لائے اور وطن چھوڑ گئے اور خدا کی راہ میں مال
اور جان سے جہاد کرتے رہے خدا کے ہاں ان کے درجے
بہت بڑے ہیں۔ اور وہی مراد کو پہنچنے والے ہیں (٢٠)
اُن کا پروردگار اُن کو اپنی رحمت کی اور خوشنودی کی اور
بہشتوں کی خوشخبری دیتا ہے جن میں انکے لئے نعمت ہائے جاودانی ہے (٢١)
(اور وہ) اُن میں ابد الآباد رہیں گے۔ کچھ شک نہیں کہ خدا

قَاتِلُوهُمْ يُعَذِّبْهُمُ اللَّهُ بِأَيْدِيكُمْ
وَيُخْزِهِمْ وَيَنصُرْكُمْ عَلَيْهِمْ وَيَشْفِ
صُدُورَ قَوْمٍ مُّؤْمِنِينَ ﴿١٤﴾
وَيُذْهِبْ غَيْظَ قُلُوبِهِمْ ۗ وَيَتُوبُ اللَّهُ
عَلَىٰ مَن يَشَاءُ ۗ وَاللَّهُ عَلِيمٌ حَكِيمٌ ﴿١٥﴾
أَمْ حَسِبْتُمْ أَن تُتْرَكُوا وَلَمَّا يَعْلَمِ اللَّهُ
الَّذِينَ جَاهَدُوا مِنكُمْ وَلَمْ يَتَّخِذُوا
مِن دُونِ اللَّهِ وَلَا رَسُولِهِ وَلَا الْمُؤْمِنِينَ
وَلِيجَةً ۚ وَاللَّهُ خَبِيرٌ بِمَا تَعْمَلُونَ ﴿١٦﴾ ع ١٠
مَا كَانَ لِلْمُشْرِكِينَ أَن يَعْمُرُوا مَسَاجِدَ
اللَّهِ شَاهِدِينَ عَلَىٰ أَنفُسِهِم بِالْكُفْرِ ۚ
أُولَٰئِكَ حَبِطَتْ أَعْمَالُهُمْ وَفِي النَّارِ
هُمْ خَالِدُونَ ﴿١٧﴾
إِنَّمَا يَعْمُرُ مَسَاجِدَ اللَّهِ مَنْ آمَنَ بِاللَّهِ
وَالْيَوْمِ الْآخِرِ وَأَقَامَ الصَّلَاةَ وَآتَى
الزَّكَاةَ وَلَمْ يَخْشَ إِلَّا اللَّهَ ۖ فَعَسَىٰ أُولَٰئِكَ
أَن يَكُونُوا مِنَ الْمُهْتَدِينَ ﴿١٨﴾
أَجَعَلْتُمْ سِقَايَةَ الْحَاجِّ وَعِمَارَةَ
الْمَسْجِدِ الْحَرَامِ كَمَنْ آمَنَ بِاللَّهِ وَالْيَوْمِ
الْآخِرِ وَجَاهَدَ فِي سَبِيلِ اللَّهِ ۚ لَا يَسْتَوُونَ
عِندَ اللَّهِ ۗ وَاللَّهُ لَا يَهْدِي الْقَوْمَ الظَّالِمِينَ ﴿١٩﴾ وقف لازم
الَّذِينَ آمَنُوا وَهَاجَرُوا وَجَاهَدُوا فِي
سَبِيلِ اللَّهِ بِأَمْوَالِهِمْ وَأَنفُسِهِمْ أَعْظَمُ
دَرَجَةً عِندَ اللَّهِ ۚ وَأُولَٰئِكَ هُمُ الْفَائِزُونَ ﴿٢٠﴾
يُبَشِّرُهُمْ رَبُّهُم بِرَحْمَةٍ مِّنْهُ وَرِضْوَانٍ
وَجَنَّاتٍ لَّهُمْ فِيهَا نَعِيمٌ مُّقِيمٌ ﴿٢١﴾
خَالِدِينَ فِيهَا أَبَدًا ۚ إِنَّ اللَّهَ عِندَهُ

the greatest (of all).

کے ہاں بڑا صلہ (تیار) ہے (۲۲)

أَجْرٌ عَظِيمٌ ﴿٢٢﴾

23. O ye who believe! Take not for protectors your fathers and your brothers if they love infidelity above Faith: if any of you do so, they do wrong.

اے اہلِ ایمان! اگر تمہارے (ماں) باپ اور (بہن) بھائی
ایمان کے مقابل کفر کو پسند کریں تو اُن سے دوستی
نہ رکھو۔ اور جو اُن سے دوستی رکھیں گے وہ
ظالم ہیں (۲۳)

يَا أَيُّهَا الَّذِينَ آمَنُوا لَا تَتَّخِذُوا آبَاءَكُمْ
وَإِخْوَانَكُمْ أَوْلِيَاءَ إِنِ اسْتَحَبُّوا الْكُفْرَ
عَلَى الْإِيمَانِ ۚ وَمَنْ يَتَوَلَّهُمْ مِنْكُمْ
فَأُولَٰئِكَ هُمُ الظَّالِمُونَ ﴿٢٣﴾

24. Say: If it be that your fathers, your sons, your brothers, your mates, or your kindred: the wealth that ye have gained; the commerce in which ye fear a decline: or the dwellings in which ye delight— are dearer to you than Allah or His Messenger, or the striving in His cause;—then wait until Allah brings about His Decision: and Allah guides not the rebellious.

کہہ دو کہ اگر تمہارے باپ اور بیٹے اور بھائی اور
عورتیں اور خاندان کے آدمی اور مال جو تم کماتے ہو
اور تجارت جس کے بند ہونے سے ڈرتے ہو اور مکانات
جن کو پسند کرتے ہو خدا اور اُسکے رسول سے اور خدا کی راہ میں
جہاد کرنے سے تمہیں زیادہ عزیز ہوں تو ٹھیرے رہو یہاں تک کہ خدا
اپنا حکم (یعنی عذاب) بھیجے۔ اور خدا نافرمان لوگوں کو ہدایت نہیں دیا کرتا (۲۴)

قُلْ إِنْ كَانَ آبَاؤُكُمْ وَأَبْنَاؤُكُمْ وَإِخْوَانُكُمْ
وَأَزْوَاجُكُمْ وَعَشِيرَتُكُمْ وَأَمْوَالٌ اقْتَرَفْتُمُوهَا
وَتِجَارَةٌ تَخْشَوْنَ كَسَادَهَا وَمَسَاكِنُ تَرْضَوْنَهَا
أَحَبَّ إِلَيْكُمْ مِنَ اللَّهِ وَرَسُولِهِ وَجِهَادٍ
فِي سَبِيلِهِ فَتَرَبَّصُوا حَتَّىٰ يَأْتِيَ اللَّهُ بِأَمْرِهِ ۗ
وَاللَّهُ لَا يَهْدِي الْقَوْمَ الْفَاسِقِينَ ﴿٢٤﴾

25. Assuredly Allah did help you in many battle-fields and on the day of Hunain: behold! your great numbers elated you, but they availed you naught; the land. For all that it is wide, did constrain you, and ye turned back in retreat.

خدا نے بہت سے موقعوں پر تم کو مدد دی ہے اور (جنگ) حُنین کے
دن جب کہ تم کو اپنی (جماعت کی) کثرت پر غرّہ تھا تو وہ تمہارے
کچھ بھی کام نہ آئی اور زمین باوجود (اتنی بڑی) فراخی کے تم پر
تنگ ہوگئی۔ پھر تم پیٹھ پھیر کر پھر گئے (۲۵)

لَقَدْ نَصَرَكُمُ اللَّهُ فِي مَوَاطِنَ كَثِيرَةٍ ۙ
وَيَوْمَ حُنَيْنٍ ۙ إِذْ أَعْجَبَتْكُمْ كَثْرَتُكُمْ فَلَمْ
تُغْنِ عَنْكُمْ شَيْئًا وَضَاقَتْ عَلَيْكُمُ الْأَرْضُ
بِمَا رَحُبَتْ ثُمَّ وَلَّيْتُمْ مُدْبِرِينَ ﴿٢٥﴾

26. But Allah did pour His calm on the Messenger and on the Believers and sent down forces which ye saw not: He punished the Unbelievers: thus doth He reward those without Faith.

پھر خدا نے اپنے پیغمبر پر اور مومنوں پر اپنی طرف سے تسکین نازل
فرمائی اور (تمہاری مدد کو فرشتوں کے) لشکر جو تمہیں نظر نہیں آتے تھے
(آسمان سے) اُتارے اور کافروں کو عذاب دیا۔ اور کفر کرنے والوں کی یہی سزا ہے (۲۶)

ثُمَّ أَنْزَلَ اللَّهُ سَكِينَتَهُ عَلَىٰ رَسُولِهِ وَ
عَلَى الْمُؤْمِنِينَ وَأَنْزَلَ جُنُودًا لَمْ تَرَوْهَا
وَعَذَّبَ الَّذِينَ كَفَرُوا ۚ وَذَٰلِكَ جَزَاءُ الْكَافِرِينَ ﴿٢٦﴾

27. Again will Allah, after this, turn (in mercy) to whom He will: for Allah is Oft-Forgiving, Most Merciful.

پھر خدا اس کے بعد جس پر چاہے مہربانی سے توجہ فرمائے
اور خدا بخشنے والا مہربان ہے (۲۷)

ثُمَّ يَتُوبُ اللَّهُ مِنْ بَعْدِ ذَٰلِكَ عَلَىٰ مَنْ
يَشَاءُ ۗ وَاللَّهُ غَفُورٌ رَحِيمٌ ﴿٢٧﴾

28. O ye who believe! Truly the Pagans are unclean; so let them not, after this year of theirs, approach the Sacred Mosque. And if ye fear poverty, soon will Allah enrich you, if He wills, out of His bounty, for Allah is All-Knowing, All-Wise.

مومنو! مشرک تو پلید ہیں تو اس برس کے
بعد وہ خانہ کعبہ کے پاس نہ جانے پائیں اور اگر
تم کو مفلسی کا خوف ہو تو خدا چاہے گا تو
تم کو اپنے فضل سے غنی کر دے گا۔ بے شک
خدا سب کچھ جانتا اور حکمت والا ہے (۲۸)

يَا أَيُّهَا الَّذِينَ آمَنُوا إِنَّمَا الْمُشْرِكُونَ
نَجَسٌ فَلَا يَقْرَبُوا الْمَسْجِدَ الْحَرَامَ بَعْدَ
عَامِهِمْ هَٰذَا ۚ وَإِنْ خِفْتُمْ عَيْلَةً فَسَوْفَ
يُغْنِيكُمُ اللَّهُ مِنْ فَضْلِهِ إِنْ شَاءَ ۚ إِنَّ
اللَّهَ عَلِيمٌ حَكِيمٌ ﴿٢٨﴾

29. Fight those who believe not in Allah nor the Last Day, nor hold that forbidden which hath been forbidden by Allah and His

جو لوگ اہلِ کتاب میں سے خدا پر ایمان نہیں لاتے اور
نہ روزِ آخرت پر (یقین رکھتے ہیں) اور نہ ان چیزوں

قَاتِلُوا الَّذِينَ لَا يُؤْمِنُونَ بِاللَّهِ وَلَا بِالْيَوْمِ
الْآخِرِ وَلَا يُحَرِّمُونَ مَا حَرَّمَ اللَّهُ وَرَسُولُهُ

وَلَا يَدِينُونَ دِينَ الْحَقِّ مِنَ الَّذِينَ
أُوتُوا الْكِتَابَ حَتَّىٰ يُعْطُوا الْجِزْيَةَ عَنْ
يَدٍ وَهُمْ صَاغِرُونَ ﴿٢٩﴾ ع
وَقَالَتِ الْيَهُودُ عُزَيْرٌ ابْنُ اللَّهِ وَقَالَتِ
النَّصَارَى الْمَسِيحُ ابْنُ اللَّهِ ۖ ذَٰلِكَ قَوْلُهُمْ
بِأَفْوَاهِهِمْ ۖ يُضَاهِئُونَ قَوْلَ الَّذِينَ
كَفَرُوا مِنْ قَبْلُ ۚ قَاتَلَهُمُ اللَّهُ ۚ أَنَّىٰ
يُؤْفَكُونَ ﴿٣٠﴾
اتَّخَذُوا أَحْبَارَهُمْ وَرُهْبَانَهُمْ أَرْبَابًا
مِنْ دُونِ اللَّهِ وَالْمَسِيحَ ابْنَ مَرْيَمَ
وَمَا أُمِرُوا إِلَّا لِيَعْبُدُوا إِلَٰهًا وَاحِدًا ۖ
لَا إِلَٰهَ إِلَّا هُوَ ۚ سُبْحَانَهُ عَمَّا يُشْرِكُونَ ﴿٣١﴾
يُرِيدُونَ أَنْ يُطْفِئُوا نُورَ اللَّهِ بِأَفْوَاهِهِمْ
وَيَأْبَى اللَّهُ إِلَّا أَنْ يُتِمَّ نُورَهُ وَلَوْ كَرِهَ
الْكَافِرُونَ ﴿٣٢﴾
هُوَ الَّذِي أَرْسَلَ رَسُولَهُ بِالْهُدَىٰ وَ
دِينِ الْحَقِّ لِيُظْهِرَهُ عَلَى الدِّينِ كُلِّهِ
وَلَوْ كَرِهَ الْمُشْرِكُونَ ﴿٣٣﴾ النصف
يَا أَيُّهَا الَّذِينَ آمَنُوا إِنَّ كَثِيرًا مِنَ الْأَحْبَارِ
وَالرُّهْبَانِ لَيَأْكُلُونَ أَمْوَالَ النَّاسِ
بِالْبَاطِلِ وَيَصُدُّونَ عَنْ سَبِيلِ اللَّهِ ۗ
وَالَّذِينَ يَكْنِزُونَ الذَّهَبَ وَالْفِضَّةَ وَلَا
يُنْفِقُونَهَا فِي سَبِيلِ اللَّهِ فَبَشِّرْهُمْ بِعَذَابٍ أَلِيمٍ ﴿٣٤﴾
يَوْمَ يُحْمَىٰ عَلَيْهَا فِي نَارِ جَهَنَّمَ فَتُكْوَىٰ بِهَا
جِبَاهُهُمْ وَجُنُوبُهُمْ وَظُهُورُهُمْ ۖ هَٰذَا
مَا كَنَزْتُمْ لِأَنْفُسِكُمْ فَذُوقُوا مَا كُنْتُمْ
تَكْنِزُونَ ﴿٣٥﴾

کو حرام سمجھتے ہیں جو خدا اور اُس کے رسُول نے حرام کی
ہیں اور نہ دینِ حق کو قبول کرتے ہیں ان سے جنگ کرو
یہاں تک کہ ذلیل ہوکر اپنے ہاتھ سے جزیہ دیں ﴿۲۹﴾
اور یہود کہتے ہیں کہ عُزیر خدا کے بیٹے ہیں اور عیسائی
کہتے ہیں کہ مسیح خدا کے بیٹے ہیں۔ یہ اُن کے منہ کی باتیں
ہیں۔ پہلے کافر بھی اسی طرح کی باتیں کہا کرتے تھے یہ بھی
انہیں کی ریس کرنے لگے ہیں خدا انکو ہلاک کرے۔ یہ
کہاں بہکے پھرتے ہیں ﴿۳۰﴾
انہوں نے اپنے علماء اور مشائخ اور مسیح ابن مریم کو اللہ
کے سوا خدا بنالیا حالانکہ اُن کو یہ حکم دیا گیا تھا کہ خدائے
واحد کے سوا کسی کی عبادت نہ کریں اس کے سوا کوئی
معبود نہیں۔ اور وہ ان لوگوں کے شریک مقرر کرنے سے پاک ہے ﴿۳۱﴾
یہ چاہتے ہیں کہ خدا کے نور کو اپنے منہ سے (پھونک مار کر)
بجھا دیں۔ اور خدا اپنے نور کو پورا کئے بغیر رہنے کا نہیں۔
اگرچہ کافروں کو بُرا ہی لگے ﴿۳۲﴾
وہی تو ہے جس نے اپنے پیغمبر کو ہدایت اور دینِ حق دیکر
بھیجا تاکہ اس (دین) کو (دُنیا کے) تمام دینوں پر غالب
کرے اگرچہ کافر ناخوش ہی ہوں ﴿۳۳﴾
مومنو! (اہلِ کتاب کے) بہت سے عالم اور مشائخ لوگوں کا
مال ناحق کھاتے اور (اُن کو) راہ خدا سے روکتے ہیں اور
جو لوگ سونا اور چاندی جمع کرتے ہیں اور اس کو خدا کے
رستے میں خرچ نہیں کرتے اُن کو اُس دن کے عذاب الیم
کی خبر سُنا دو ﴿۳۴﴾
جس دن وہ (مال) دوزخ کی آگ میں (خوب) گرم کیا
جائے گا۔ پھر اس سے ان (بخیلوں) کی پیشانیاں اور پہلو
اور پیٹھیں داغی جائیں گی (اور کہا جائے گا کہ) یہ وہی ہے
جو تم نے اپنے لئے جمع کیا تھا سو جو تم جمع کرتے تھے (اب) اسکا مزہ چکھو ﴿۳۵﴾

Messenger, nor acknowledge the Religion of Truth, from among the People of the Book, until they pay the *Jizya* with willing submission, and feel themselves subdued.

30. The Jews call 'Uzair a son of Allah, and the Christians call Christ the Son of Allah. That is a saying from their mouth; (in this) they but imitate what the Unbelievers of old used to say. Allah's curse be on them: how they are deluded away from the Truth!

31. They take their priests and their anchorites to be their lords beside Allah. And (they take as their Lord) Christ the son of Mary; yet they were commanded to worship but One God: there is no god but He. Praise and glory to Him: (far is He) from having the partners they associate (with Him).

32. Fain would they extinguish Allah's Light with their mouths, but Allah will not allow but that His Light should be perfected, even though the Unbelievers May detest (it).

33. It is He Who hath sent His Messenger with Guidance and the Religion of Truth, to cause it to prevail over all religion, even though the Pagans may detest (it).

34. O ye who believe! There are Indeed many among the priests and anchorites, who in falsehood devour the wealth of men and hinder (them) from the Way of Allah. And there are those who hoard gold and silver and spend it not in the Way of Allah: announce unto them a most grievous chastisment—

35. On the Day when it will be heated in the fire of Hell, and with it will be branded their foreheads, their flanks, and their backs,—"This is the (treasure) which ye Hoarded for yourselves: taste ye, then, the (treasures) ye hoarded"

36. The number of months in the sight of Allah is twelve (in a year)—so ordained by Him the day He created the heavens and the earth; of them four are sacred: that is the right religion so wrong not yourselves therein, and fight the Pagans all together as they fight you all together. But know that Allah is with those who restrain themselves.

37. Verily the transposing (of a prohibited month) is an addition to Unbelief: the Unbelievers are led to wrong thereby: for they make it lawful one year, and forbidden another year, in order to agree with the number of months forbidden by Allah and make such forbidden ones Lawful. The evil of their course seems pleasing to them. But Allah guideth not those who reject Faith.

38. O ye who believe! what is the matter with you, that, when ye are asked to go forth in the Cause of Allah, ye cling heavily to the earth? Do ye prefer the life of this world to the Hereafter? But little is the comfort of this life, as compared with the Hereafter.

39. Unless ye go forth, He will punish you with a grievous penalty, and put others in your place; but Him ye would not harm in the least, for Allah Hath power over all things.

40. If ye help not (the Prophet), (it is no matter): for Allah did indeed help him, when the Unbelievers drove him out: being the second of the two they two were in the Cave, and he said to his companion, "Have no fear, for Allah is with us": then Allah sent down His peace upon him, and strengthened him with forces which ye saw not, and humbled to the depths the word of the Unbelievers. But the word of Allah is exalted to the heights: for Allah is Exalted in might, Wise.

خدا کے نزدیک مہینے گنتی میں (بارہ ہیں یعنی) اس روز (سے)
کہ اُس نے آسمانوں اور زمین کو پیدا کیا۔ کتاب خدا میں (برس کے)
بارہ مہینے (لکھے ہوئے) ہیں ان میں سے چار مہینے ادب کے ہیں یہی [ف ۱۲۹]
دین (کا) سیدھا رستہ ہے تو ان (مہینوں) میں (قتال ناحق سے)
اپنے آپ پر ظلم نہ کرنا۔ اور تم سب کے سب مشرکوں سے لڑو جیسے وہ سب کے
سب تم سے لڑتے ہیں۔ اور جان رکھو کہ خدا پرہیزگاروں کے ساتھ ہے ﴿۳۶﴾

امن کے کسی مہینے کو ہٹا کر آگے پیچھے کر دینا کفر میں اضافہ کرتا ہے
اس سے کافر گمراہی میں پڑے رہتے ہیں۔ ایک سال تو اسکو حلال سمجھ لیتے
ہیں اور دوسرے سال حرام تاکہ ادب کے مہینوں کی جو خدا نے مقرر کئے
ہیں گنتی پوری کر لیں۔ اور جو خدا نے منع کیا ہے اسکو جائز کر لیں۔ اُنکے
بُرے اعمال انکو بھلے دکھائی دیتے ہیں اور خدا کافر لوگوں کو ہدایت نہیں دیا کرتا ﴿۳۷﴾

مومنو! تمہیں کیا ہوا ہے کہ جب تم سے کہا جاتا ہے کہ خدا کی راہ میں
(جہاد کیلئے) نکلو تو تم (کاہلی کے سبب سے) زمین پر گرے جاتے ہو (یعنی
گھروں سے نکلنا نہیں چاہتے) کیا تم آخرت (کی نعمتوں) کو چھوڑ کر دنیا کی
زندگی پر خوش ہو بیٹھے ہو۔ دُنیا کی زندگی کے فائدے تو آخرت
کے مقابل بہت ہی کم ہیں ﴿۳۸﴾

اگر تم نہ نکلو گے تو خدا تم کو بڑی تکلیف کا عذاب دے گا۔ اور
تمہاری جگہ اور لوگ پیدا کر دیگا (جو خدا کے پورے فرمانبردار ہونگے)
اور تم اس کو کچھ نقصان نہ پہنچا سکو گے اور خدا ہر چیز پر قدرت رکھتا ہے ﴿۳۹﴾

اگر تم پیغمبر کی مدد نہ کرو گے تو خدا اُن کا مددگار ہے۔ (وہ وقت تم
کو یاد ہوگا) جب ان کو کافروں نے گھر سے نکال دیا (اُس
وقت) دو ہی شخص تھے جن (میں (ایک ابوبکر تھے) دوسرے
(خود رسول اللہ) جب وہ دونوں غار (ثور) میں تھے اُس وقت
پیغمبر اپنے رفیق کو تسلی دیتے تھے کہ غم نہ کرو خدا ہمارے ساتھ ہے۔
تو خدا نے اُن پر تسکین نازل فرمائی اور اُن کو ایسے لشکروں سے
مدد دی جو تم کو نظر نہیں آتے تھے اور کافروں کی بات کو پست کر دیا
اور بات تو خدا ہی کی بلند ہے۔ اور خدا زبردست (اور) حکمت والا ہے ﴿۴۰﴾

إِنَّ عِدَّةَ الشُّهُورِ عِنْدَ اللَّهِ اثْنَا عَشَرَ شَهْرًا
فِي كِتَابِ اللَّهِ يَوْمَ خَلَقَ السَّمَاوَاتِ وَالْأَرْضَ
مِنْهَا أَرْبَعَةٌ حُرُمٌ ذَٰلِكَ الدِّينُ الْقَيِّمُ
فَلَا تَظْلِمُوا فِيهِنَّ أَنْفُسَكُمْ وَقَاتِلُوا
الْمُشْرِكِينَ كَافَّةً كَمَا يُقَاتِلُونَكُمْ كَافَّةً
وَاعْلَمُوا أَنَّ اللَّهَ مَعَ الْمُتَّقِينَ ﴿٣٦﴾
إِنَّمَا النَّسِيءُ زِيَادَةٌ فِي الْكُفْرِ يُضَلُّ بِهِ
الَّذِينَ كَفَرُوا يُحِلُّونَهُ عَامًا وَيُحَرِّمُونَهُ
عَامًا لِيُوَاطِئُوا عِدَّةَ مَا حَرَّمَ اللَّهُ فَيُحِلُّوا
مَا حَرَّمَ اللَّهُ زُيِّنَ لَهُمْ سُوءُ أَعْمَالِهِمْ
وَاللَّهُ لَا يَهْدِي الْقَوْمَ الْكَافِرِينَ ﴿٣٧﴾ ع ٥
يَا أَيُّهَا الَّذِينَ آمَنُوا مَا لَكُمْ إِذَا قِيلَ
لَكُمُ انْفِرُوا فِي سَبِيلِ اللَّهِ اثَّاقَلْتُمْ
إِلَى الْأَرْضِ أَرَضِيتُمْ بِالْحَيَاةِ الدُّنْيَا
مِنَ الْآخِرَةِ فَمَا مَتَاعُ الْحَيَاةِ الدُّنْيَا
فِي الْآخِرَةِ إِلَّا قَلِيلٌ ﴿٣٨﴾
إِلَّا تَنْفِرُوا يُعَذِّبْكُمْ عَذَابًا أَلِيمًا
وَيَسْتَبْدِلْ قَوْمًا غَيْرَكُمْ وَلَا تَضُرُّوهُ
شَيْئًا وَاللَّهُ عَلَىٰ كُلِّ شَيْءٍ قَدِيرٌ ﴿٣٩﴾
إِلَّا تَنْصُرُوهُ فَقَدْ نَصَرَهُ اللَّهُ إِذْ أَخْرَجَهُ
الَّذِينَ كَفَرُوا ثَانِيَ اثْنَيْنِ إِذْ هُمَا
فِي الْغَارِ إِذْ يَقُولُ لِصَاحِبِهِ لَا تَحْزَنْ
إِنَّ اللَّهَ مَعَنَا فَأَنْزَلَ اللَّهُ سَكِينَتَهُ
عَلَيْهِ وَأَيَّدَهُ بِجُنُودٍ لَمْ تَرَوْهَا وَجَعَلَ
كَلِمَةَ الَّذِينَ كَفَرُوا السُّفْلَىٰ وَ
كَلِمَةُ اللَّهِ هِيَ الْعُلْيَا وَاللَّهُ عَزِيزٌ
حَكِيمٌ ﴿٤٠﴾

41. Go ye forth, (whether equipped) lightly or heavily, and strive and struggle, with your goods and your persons, in the Cause of Allah. That is best for you, if ye (but knew).

تم سبکبار ہو یا گراں بار (یعنی مال و اسباب تھوڑا رکھتے ہو یا بہت۔ گھروں سے) نکل آؤ اور خدا کے رستے میں مال اور جان سے لڑو۔ یہی تمہارے حق میں بہتر ہے بشرطیکہ سمجھو ﴿۴۱﴾

انْفِرُوْا خِفَافًا وَّثِقَالًا وَّجَاهِدُوْا بِاَمْوَالِكُمْ
وَاَنْفُسِكُمْ فِيْ سَبِيْلِ اللّٰهِ ذٰلِكُمْ خَيْرٌ
لَّكُمْ اِنْ كُنْتُمْ تَعْلَمُوْنَ ﴿٤١﴾

42. If there had been immediate gain (in sight), and the journey easy, they would (all) without doubt have followed thee, but the distance was long, (and weighed) on them. They would indeed swear by Allah, "If we only could, We should certainly have come out with you:" They would destroy their own souls; for Allah doth know that they are certainly lying.

اگر مال غنیمت سہل الحصول اور سفر بھی ہلکا ہوتا تو تمہارے ساتھ (شوق سے) چل دیتے لیکن مسافت ان کو دور (دراز) نظر آئی (تو عذر کریں گے) اور خدا کی قسمیں کھائیں گے کہ اگر ہم طاقت رکھتے تو آپ کے ساتھ ضرور نکل پڑتے یہ ایسے عذر سے اپنے تئیں ہلاک کر رہے ہیں اور خدا جانتا ہے کہ یہ جھوٹے ہیں ﴿۴۲﴾

لَوْ كَانَ عَرَضًا قَرِيْبًا وَّسَفَرًا قَاصِدًا
لَّاتَّبَعُوْكَ وَلٰكِنْ بَعُدَتْ عَلَيْهِمُ
الشُّقَّةُ وَسَيَحْلِفُوْنَ بِاللّٰهِ لَوِ اسْتَطَعْنَا
لَخَرَجْنَا مَعَكُمْ يُهْلِكُوْنَ اَنْفُسَهُمْ
وَاللّٰهُ يَعْلَمُ اِنَّهُمْ لَكٰذِبُوْنَ ﴿٤٢﴾ ع

43. God give thee grace! Why didst thou grant them exemption until those who told the truth were seen by thee in a clear light, and thou hadst proved the liars?

خدا تمہیں معاف کرے۔ تم نے پیشتر اس کے کہ تم پر وہ لوگ بھی ظاہر ہو جاتے جو سچے ہیں اور وہ بھی تمہیں معلوم ہو جاتے جو جھوٹے ہیں ان کو اجازت کیوں دی؟ ﴿۴۳﴾

عَفَا اللّٰهُ عَنْكَ لِمَ اَذِنْتَ لَهُمْ حَتّٰى
يَتَبَيَّنَ لَكَ الَّذِيْنَ صَدَقُوْا وَتَعْلَمَ
الْكٰذِبِيْنَ ﴿٤٣﴾

44. Those who believe in Allah and the Last Day ask thee for no exemption from fighting with their goods and persons. And Allah knoweth well those who do their duty.

جو لوگ خدا پر اور روز آخرت پر ایمان رکھتے ہیں وہ تم سے اجازت نہیں مانگتے کہ (پیچھے رہ جائیں بلکہ چاہتے ہیں کہ) اپنے مال اور جان سے جہاد کریں اور خدا پرہیزگاروں سے واقف ہے ﴿۴۴﴾

لَا يَسْتَاْذِنُكَ الَّذِيْنَ يُؤْمِنُوْنَ بِاللّٰهِ وَ
الْيَوْمِ الْاٰخِرِ اَنْ يُّجَاهِدُوْا بِاَمْوَالِهِمْ
وَاَنْفُسِهِمْ وَاللّٰهُ عَلِيْمٌۢ بِالْمُتَّقِيْنَ ﴿٤٤﴾

45. Only those ask thee for exemption who believe not in Allah and the Last Day, and whose hearts are in doubt, so that they are tossed in their doubts to and fro.

اجازت وہی لوگ مانگتے ہیں جو خدا پر اور پچھلے دن پر ایمان نہیں رکھتے اور ان کے دل شک میں پڑے ہوئے ہیں۔ سو وہ اپنے شک میں ڈانواں ڈول ہو رہے ہیں ﴿۴۵﴾

اِنَّمَا يَسْتَاْذِنُكَ الَّذِيْنَ لَا يُؤْمِنُوْنَ
بِاللّٰهِ وَالْيَوْمِ الْاٰخِرِ وَارْتَابَتْ قُلُوْبُهُمْ
فَهُمْ فِيْ رَيْبِهِمْ يَتَرَدَّدُوْنَ ﴿٤٥﴾

46. If they had intended to come out, they would certainly have made some preparation therefor: but Allah was averse to their being sent forth; so He made them lag behind, and they were told, "Sit ye among those who sit (inactive)."

اور اگر وہ نکلنے کا ارادہ کرتے تو اس کیلئے سامان تیار کرتے لیکن خدا نے ان کا اٹھنا (اور نکلنا) پسند ہی نہ کیا تو ان کو ہلنے جلنے ہی نہ دیا اور (ان سے) کہہ دیا گیا کہ جہاں (معذور) بیٹھے ہیں تم بھی ان کے ساتھ بیٹھے رہو ﴿۴۶﴾

وَلَوْ اَرَادُوا الْخُرُوْجَ لَاَعَدُّوْا لَهٗ عُدَّةً
وَّلٰكِنْ كَرِهَ اللّٰهُ انْۢبِعَاثَهُمْ
فَثَبَّطَهُمْ وَقِيْلَ اقْعُدُوْا مَعَ
الْقٰعِدِيْنَ ﴿٤٦﴾

47. If they had come out with you, they would not have added to your (strength) but only (made for) disorder, hurrying to and fro in your midst and sowing sedition among you, and there would have been some among you who would have listened to them. But Allah knoweth well those who do wrong.

اگر وہ تم میں (شامل ہو کر) نکل بھی کھڑے ہوتے تو تمہارے حق میں شرارت کرتے اور تم میں فساد ڈلوانے کی غرض سے دوڑے دوڑے پھرتے اور تم میں ان کے جاسوس بھی ہیں اور خدا ظالموں کو خوب جانتا ہے ﴿۴۷﴾

لَوْ خَرَجُوْا فِيْكُمْ مَّا زَادُوْكُمْ اِلَّا خَبَالًا
وَّلَاۡاَوْضَعُوْا خِلٰلَكُمْ يَبْغُوْنَكُمُ الْفِتْنَةَ
وَفِيْكُمْ سَمّٰعُوْنَ لَهُمْ وَاللّٰهُ عَلِيْمٌۢ بِالظّٰلِمِيْنَ ﴿٤٧﴾

48. Indeed they had plotted sedition before, and upset matters for thee,—until the Truth arrived, and the Decree of Allah became manifest, much to their disgust.

یہ پہلے بھی طالب فساد رہے ہیں اور بہت سی باتوں میں تمہارے لئے الٹ پھیر کرتے رہے ہیں یہاں تک کہ حق آپہنچا اور خدا کا حکم غالب ہوا اور وہ برا مانتے ہی رہ گئے ﴿۴۸﴾

لَقَدِ ابْتَغَوُا الْفِتْنَةَ مِنْ قَبْلُ وَقَلَّبُوْا لَكَ
الْاُمُوْرَ حَتّٰى جَآءَ الْحَقُّ وَظَهَرَ اَمْرُ اللّٰهِ
وَهُمْ كٰرِهُوْنَ ﴿٤٨﴾

وَمِنْهُمْ مَّنْ يَّقُوْلُ ائْذَنْ لِّيْ وَلَا تَفْتِنِّيْ ؕ
اَلَا فِي الْفِتْنَةِ سَقَطُوْا ؕ وَاِنَّ جَهَنَّمَ لَمُحِيْطَةٌ ۢ
بِالْكٰفِرِيْنَ ﴿۴۹﴾

اور ان میں کوئی ایسا بھی ہے جو کہتا ہے کہ مجھے تو اجازت
ہی دیجئے۔ اور آفت میں نہ ڈالئے۔ دیکھو یہ آفت میں پڑ گئے ہیں۔
اور دوزخ سب کافروں کو گھیرے ہوئے ہے ﴿۴۹﴾

49. Among them is (many) a man who says: "Grant me exemption and draw me not into trial." Have they not fallen into trial already? And indeed Hell surrounds the Unbelievers (on all sides).

اِنْ تُصِبْكَ حَسَنَةٌ تَسُؤْهُمْ ۚ وَاِنْ
تُصِبْكَ مُصِيْبَةٌ يَّقُوْلُوْا قَدْ اَخَذْنَآ
اَمْرَنَا مِنْ قَبْلُ وَيَتَوَلَّوْا وَّهُمْ فَرِحُوْنَ ﴿۵۰﴾

(اے پیغمبر) اگر تم کو آسائش حاصل ہوتی ہے تو ان کو بری
لگتی ہے۔ اور اگر کوئی مشکل پڑتی ہے تو کہتے ہیں کہ ہم نے
اپنا کام پہلے ہی (درست) کر لیا تھا اور خوشیاں مناتے لوٹ جاتے ہیں ﴿۵۰﴾

50. If good befalls thee, it grieves them; but if a misfortune befalls thee, they say, "We took indeed our precautions beforehand," and they turn away rejoicing.

قُلْ لَّنْ يُّصِيْبَنَآ اِلَّا مَا كَتَبَ اللّٰهُ لَنَا ۚ هُوَ
مَوْلٰىنَا ۚ وَعَلَى اللّٰهِ فَلْيَتَوَكَّلِ الْمُؤْمِنُوْنَ ﴿۵۱﴾

کہہ دو کہ ہم کو کوئی مصیبت نہیں پہنچ سکتی بجز اس کے جو خدا نے ہمارے
لئے لکھ دی ہو وہی ہمارا کارساز ہے اور مومنوں کو خدا ہی کا بھروسا رکھنا چاہئے ﴿۵۱﴾

51. Say: "Nothing will happen to us except what Allah has decreed for us: He is our Protector": and on Allah let the Believers put their trust.

قُلْ هَلْ تَرَبَّصُوْنَ بِنَآ اِلَّآ اِحْدَى
الْحُسْنَيَيْنِ ۭ وَنَحْنُ نَتَرَبَّصُ بِكُمْ اَنْ
يُّصِيْبَكُمُ اللّٰهُ بِعَذَابٍ مِّنْ عِنْدِهٖٓ اَوْ
بِاَيْدِيْنَا ڮ فَتَرَبَّصُوْٓا اِنَّا مَعَكُمْ
مُّتَرَبِّصُوْنَ ﴿۵۲﴾

کہہ دو کہ تم ہمارے حق میں دو بھلائیوں میں سے ایک کے منتظر ہو
اور ہم تمہارے حق میں اس بات کے منتظر ہیں کہ خدا (یا تو)
اپنے پاس سے تم پر کوئی عذاب نازل کرے یا ہمارے ہاتھوں
سے (عذاب دلوائے) تو تم بھی انتظار کرو ہم بھی تمہارے
ساتھ انتظار کرتے ہیں ﴿۵۲﴾

52. Say: "Can you expect for us (any fate) other than one of two glorious things—(martyrdom or victory)? But we can expect for you either that Allah will send His punishment from Him or by our hands. So wait (Expectant); we too will wait with you."

قُلْ اَنْفِقُوْا طَوْعًا اَوْ كَرْهًا لَّنْ يُّتَقَبَّلَ
مِنْكُمْ ۭ اِنَّكُمْ كُنْتُمْ قَوْمًا فٰسِقِيْنَ ﴿۵۳﴾

کہہ دو کہ تم (مال) خوشی سے خرچ کرو یا ناخوشی سے تم سے
ہرگز قبول نہیں کیا جائے گا۔ تم نافرمان لوگ ہو ﴿۵۳﴾

53. Say: "Spend (for the Cause) willingly or unwillingly: not from you will it be accepted: for ye are indeed a people rebellious and wicked."

وَمَا مَنَعَهُمْ اَنْ تُقْبَلَ مِنْهُمْ نَفَقٰتُهُمْ اِلَّآ
اَنَّهُمْ كَفَرُوْا بِاللّٰهِ وَبِرَسُوْلِهٖ وَلَا يَاْتُوْنَ
الصَّلٰوةَ اِلَّا وَهُمْ كُسَالٰى وَلَا يُنْفِقُوْنَ
اِلَّا وَهُمْ كٰرِهُوْنَ ﴿۵۴﴾

اور ان کے خرچ (اموال) کے قبول ہونے سے کوئی چیز مانع
نہیں ہوئی سوا اس کے کہ انہوں نے خدا سے اور اس کے رسول سے
کفر کیا اور نماز کو آتے ہیں تو سست و کاہل ہو کر اور خرچ
کرتے ہیں تو ناخوشی سے ﴿۵۴﴾

54. The only reasons why their contributions are not accepted are: that they reject Allah and His Messenger; that they come not to prayer save lazily and that they offer contributions unwillingly.

فَلَا تُعْجِبْكَ اَمْوَالُهُمْ وَلَآ اَوْلَادُهُمْ ۭ اِنَّمَا
يُرِيْدُ اللّٰهُ لِيُعَذِّبَهُمْ بِهَا فِي الْحَيٰوةِ
الدُّنْيَا وَتَزْهَقَ اَنْفُسُهُمْ وَهُمْ كٰفِرُوْنَ ﴿۵۵﴾

تم ان کے مال اور اولاد سے تعجب نہ کرنا خدا چاہتا ہے کہ ان
چیزوں سے دنیا کی زندگی میں ان کو عذاب دے اور (جب) ان
کی جان نکلے تو (اس وقت بھی) وہ کافر ہی ہوں ﴿۵۵﴾

55. Let not their wealth nor their children dazzle thee: in reality Allah's Wish is to punish them with these things in this life, and that their souls may perish in their (very) denial of Allah.

وَيَحْلِفُوْنَ بِاللّٰهِ اِنَّهُمْ لَمِنْكُمْ ۭ وَمَا هُمْ
مِّنْكُمْ وَلٰكِنَّهُمْ قَوْمٌ يَّفْرَقُوْنَ ﴿۵۶﴾

اور خدا کی قسمیں کھاتے ہیں کہ وہ تم ہی میں سے ہیں حالانکہ وہ
تم میں سے نہیں ہیں۔ اصل یہ ہے کہ یہ ڈرپوک لوگ ہیں ﴿۵۶﴾

56. They swear by Allah that they are indeed of you: but they are not of you: yet they are afraid (of you).

لَوْ يَجِدُوْنَ مَلْجَاً اَوْ مَغٰرٰتٍ اَوْ مُدَّخَلًا
لَّوَلَّوْا اِلَيْهِ وَهُمْ يَجْمَحُوْنَ ﴿۵۷﴾

اگر ان کو کوئی بچاؤ کی جگہ (جیسے قلعہ) یا غار و مغاک یا زمین کے اندر
گھسنے کی جگہ مل جائے تو اسی طرف رسیاں تڑاتے ہوئے بھاگ جائیں ﴿۵۷﴾

57. If they could find a place to flee to, or caves, or a place of concealment, they would Turn straightway thereto with an obstinate rush.

وَمِنْهُمْ مَّنْ يَّلْمِزُكَ فِي الصَّدَقٰتِ ۚ فَاِنْ

اور ان میں بعض ایسے بھی ہیں کہ (تقسیم) صدقات میں تم پر طعنہ زنی

58. And among them are men who slander thee in the matter of

(the distribution of) the alms. If they are given part thereof, they are pleased, but if not, behold! they are indignant!

59. If only they had been content with what Allah and His Messenger gave them, and had said, "Sufficient unto us is Allah! Allah and His mesenger will soon give us of His bounty: to Allah do we turn our hopes!" (That would have been the right Course).

60. Alms are for the poor and the needy, and those employed to administer the (funds): for those whose hearts have been (recently) reconciled (to Truth); for those in bondage and in debt; in the cause of Allah; and for the wayfarer: (thus is it) ordained by Allah. And Allah is full of knowledge and wisdom.

61. Among them are men who molest the Prophet and say, "He is (all) ear." Say, "He listens to what is best for you: he believes in Allah, has faith in the Believers, and is a Mercy to those of you who believe." But those who molest the Prophet will have a grievous chastisement

62. To you they swear by Allah. In order to please you: but it is more fitting that they should please Allah and His Messenger, if they are Believers.

63. Know they not that for those who oppose Allah and His Messenger, is the Fire of Hell?—wherein they shall dwell. That is the supreme disgrace.

64. The Hypocrites are afraid lest a Sûra should be sent down about them, showing them what is (really passing) in their hearts. Say: "Mock ye! But verily Allah will bring to light all that ye fear (should be revealed).

65. If thou dost question them, they declare (with emphasis): "We were only talking idly and in play.": Say: "Was it at Allah, and His Signs, and His Messenger, that ye were mocking?"

66. Make ye no excuses: ye have rejected Faith after ye had accepted

کرتے ہیں. اگر ان کو اس میں سے (خاطر خواہ) مل جائے تو خوش
رہیں اور اگر (اس قدر) نہ ملے تو جھٹ خفا ہو جائیں ﴿۵۸﴾
اور اگر وہ اس پر خوش رہتے جو خدا اور اسکے رسول نے انکو دیا تھا اور کہتے
کہ ہمیں خدا کافی ہے اور خدا اپنے فضل سے اور اسکے پیغمبر (اپنی مہربانی سے) ہمیں
(پھر) دینگے اور ہمیں تو خدا ہی کی خواہش ہے تو انکے حق میں بہتر ہوتا ﴿۵۹﴾
صدقات (یعنی زکوٰۃ و خیرات) تو مفلسوں اور محتاجوں اور کارکنان صدقات کا حق ہے
اور ان لوگوں کا جنکی تالیف قلوب منظور ہے اور غلاموں کے آزاد کرانے میں اور
قرضداروں (کے قرض ادا کرنے) میں اور خدا کی راہ میں اور مسافروں (کی مدد) میں (بھی یہ مال
خرچ کرنا چاہئے یہ حقوق) خدا کی طرف سے مقرر کر دیئے گئے ہیں اور خدا جاننے والا (اور) حکمت والا ہے ﴿۶۰﴾
اور ان میں بعض ایسے ہیں جو پیغمبر کو ایذا دیتے ہیں اور کہتے ہیں کہ یہ شخص
نرا کان ہے (ان سے) کہدو کہ (وہ) کان (ہے تو) تمہاری بھلائی کیلئے
وہ خدا کا اور مومنوں (کی بات) کا یقین رکھتا ہے. اور جو لوگ تم میں
ایمان لائے ہیں ان کیلئے رحمت ہے[140] اور جو لوگ رسول خدا کو رنج
پہنچاتے ہیں اُن کے لئے عذاب الیم (تیار) ہے ﴿۶۱﴾
مومنو! یہ لوگ تمہارے سامنے خدا کی قسمیں کھاتے ہیں تاکہ تم کو خوش
کر دیں. حالانکہ اگر یہ (دل سے) مومن ہوتے تو خدا اور اسکے پیغمبر
خوش کرنے کے زیادہ مستحق ہیں ﴿۶۲﴾
کیا ان لوگوں کو معلوم نہیں کہ جو شخص خدا اور اسکے رسول
سے مقابلہ کرتا ہے تو اسکے لئے جہنم کی آگ (تیار) ہے جس میں وہ ہمیشہ
(جلتا) رہے گا. یہ بڑی رسوائی ہے ﴿۶۳﴾
منافق ڈرتے رہتے ہیں کہ ان (کے پیغمبر) پر کہیں کوئی ایسی سورت (نہ)
اُتر آئے کہ انکے دل کی باتوں کو ان (مسلمانوں) پر ظاہر کر دے. کہہ دو کہ
ہنسی کئے جاؤ. جس بات سے تم ڈرتے ہو خدا اسکو ضرور ظاہر کر دیگا ﴿۶۴﴾
اور اگر تم ان سے (اس بارے میں) دریافت کرو تو کہیں گے کہ ہم تو یوں
ہی بات چیت اور دل لگی کرتے تھے. کہو کیا تم خدا اور اسکی آیتوں
اور اس کے رسول سے ہنسی کرتے تھے؟ ﴿۶۵﴾
بہانے مت بناؤ تم ایمان لانے کے بعد کافر ہو چکے ہو.

أُعْطُوا مِنْهَا رَضُوا وَإِن لَّمْ يُعْطَوْا مِنْهَا
إِذَا هُمْ يَسْخَطُونَ ﴿٥٨﴾
وَلَوْ أَنَّهُمْ رَضُوا مَا آتَاهُمُ اللَّهُ وَرَسُولُهُ
وَقَالُوا حَسْبُنَا اللَّهُ سَيُؤْتِينَا اللَّهُ مِن
فَضْلِهِ وَرَسُولُهُ إِنَّا إِلَى اللَّهِ رَاغِبُونَ ﴿٥٩﴾
إِنَّمَا الصَّدَقَاتُ لِلْفُقَرَاءِ وَالْمَسَاكِينِ وَ
الْعَامِلِينَ عَلَيْهَا وَالْمُؤَلَّفَةِ قُلُوبُهُمْ وَفِي
الرِّقَابِ وَالْغَارِمِينَ وَفِي سَبِيلِ اللَّهِ وَابْنِ
السَّبِيلِ فَرِيضَةً مِّنَ اللَّهِ وَاللَّهُ عَلِيمٌ حَكِيمٌ ﴿٦٠﴾
وَمِنْهُمُ الَّذِينَ يُؤْذُونَ النَّبِيَّ وَيَقُولُونَ
هُوَ أُذُنٌ قُلْ أُذُنُ خَيْرٍ لَّكُمْ يُؤْمِنُ بِاللَّهِ
وَيُؤْمِنُ لِلْمُؤْمِنِينَ وَرَحْمَةٌ لِّلَّذِينَ
آمَنُوا مِنكُمْ وَالَّذِينَ يُؤْذُونَ رَسُولَ
اللَّهِ لَهُمْ عَذَابٌ أَلِيمٌ ﴿٦١﴾
يَحْلِفُونَ بِاللَّهِ لَكُمْ لِيُرْضُوكُمْ وَاللَّهُ
وَرَسُولُهُ أَحَقُّ أَن يُرْضُوهُ إِن كَانُوا
مُؤْمِنِينَ ﴿٦٢﴾
أَلَمْ يَعْلَمُوا أَنَّهُ مَن يُحَادِدِ اللَّهَ وَ
رَسُولَهُ فَأَنَّ لَهُ نَارَ جَهَنَّمَ خَالِدًا فِيهَا
ذَٰلِكَ الْخِزْيُ الْعَظِيمُ ﴿٦٣﴾
يَحْذَرُ الْمُنَافِقُونَ أَن تُنَزَّلَ عَلَيْهِمْ
سُورَةٌ تُنَبِّئُهُم بِمَا فِي قُلُوبِهِمْ قُلِ
اسْتَهْزِئُوا إِنَّ اللَّهَ مُخْرِجٌ مَّا تَحْذَرُونَ ﴿٦٤﴾
وَلَئِن سَأَلْتَهُمْ لَيَقُولُنَّ إِنَّمَا كُنَّا نَخُوضُ
وَنَلْعَبُ قُلْ أَبِاللَّهِ وَآيَاتِهِ وَرَسُولِهِ
كُنتُمْ تَسْتَهْزِئُونَ ﴿٦٥﴾
لَا تَعْتَذِرُوا قَدْ كَفَرْتُم بَعْدَ إِيمَانِكُمْ

it. If We pardon some of you, We will punish others amongst you, for that they are sinners.

67. The Hypocrites, men and women, are alike: they enjoin evil, and forbid what is just, and tighten their purse's strings. They have forgotten Allah: so He Hath forgotten them. Verily the Hypocrites are rebellious and perverse.

68. Allah hath promised the Hypocrites men and women, and the rejecters, of Faith, the fire of Hell: therein shall they dwell: sufficient is it for them: for them is the curse of Allah. And an enduring punishment,—

69. As in the case of those before you: they were mightier than you in power, and more flourishing in wealth and children. They had their enjoyment of their portion: and ye have of yours, as did those before you; and ye indulge in idle talk as they did. They!—their works are fruitless in this world and in the Hereafter, and they are the Losers.

70. Hath not the story reached them of those before them?—The people of Noah, and 'Ād, and Thamud; the people of Abraham, the men of Midian, and the Cities overthrown. To them came their messengers with Clear Signs. It is not Allah Who wrongs them, but they wrong their own souls.

71. The Believers, men and women, are protectors, one of another: they enjoin what is just, and forbid what is evil: they observe regular prayers, pay Zakat and obey Allah and His Messenger. On them will Allah pour His mercy: for Allah is Exalted in power, Wise.

72. Allah hath promised to Believers, men and women, Gardens under which rivers flow, to dwell therein, and beautiful

اگر ہم تم میں سے ایک جماعت کو معاف کر دیں تو دوسری
جماعت کو سزا بھی دینگے کیونکہ وہ گناہ کرتے رہے ہیں (۶۶)
منافق مرد اور منافق عورتیں ایکدوسرے کے ہمجنس (یعنی ایک ہی طرح
کے) ہیں کہ بُرے کام کرنے کو کہتے اور نیک کاموں سے منع کرتے
اور (خرچ کرنے سے) ہاتھ بند کئے رہتے ہیں انہوں نے خدا کو بھلا
دیا تو خدا نے اُن کو بھلا دیا بیشک منافق نافرمان ہیں (۶۷)
اللہ نے منافق مردوں اور منافق عورتوں اور کافروں سے
آتش جہنم کا وعدہ کیا ہے جس میں ہمیشہ (جلتے) رہیں گے وہی ان کے
لائق ہے اور خدا نے ان پر لعنت کر دی ہے اور اُنکے لئے ہمیشہ کا عذاب (تیار) ہے (۶۸)
(تم منافق لوگ) ان لوگوں کی طرح ہو جو تم سے پہلے ہو چکے
ہیں۔ وہ تم سے بہت طاقتور اور مال و اولاد میں کہیں زیادہ
تھے تو وہ اپنے حصے سے بہرہ یاب ہو چکے سو جس طرح تم سے
پہلے لوگ اپنے حصے سے فائدہ اٹھا چکے ہیں اسی طرح تم نے اپنے حصے سے
فائدہ اٹھا لیا۔ اور جس طرح وہ باطل میں ڈوبے رہے اسی طرح تم باطل میں ڈوبے رہے
یہ وہ لوگ ہیں جن کے اعمال دنیا اور آخرت میں ضائع ہو گئے اور یہی نقصان اٹھانے والے ہیں (۶۹)
کیا ان کو اُن لوگوں (کے حالات) کی خبر نہیں پہنچی جو اُن سے
پہلے تھے (یعنی) نوح اور عاد اور ثمود کی قوم اور ابراہیم کی
قوم اور مدین والے اور اُلٹی ہوئی بستیوں والے۔ اُن کے
پاس پیغمبر نشانیاں لے لیکر آئے۔ اور خدا تو ایسا نہ تھا کہ اُن پر
ظلم کرتا لیکن وہی اپنے آپ پر ظلم کرتے تھے (۷۰)
اور مومن مرد اور مومن عورتیں ایک دوسرے کے دوست
ہیں کہ اچھے کام کرنے کو کہتے اور بُری باتوں سے منع
کرتے اور نماز پڑھتے اور زکوٰۃ دیتے اور خدا اور اُسکے
پیغمبر کی اطاعت کرتے ہیں۔ یہی لوگ ہیں جن پر خدا
رحم کرے گا بیشک خدا غالب حکمت والا ہے (۷۱)
خدا نے مومن مردوں اور مومن عورتوں سے بہشتوں کا
وعدہ کیا ہے جن کے نیچے نہریں بہ رہی ہیں (وہ) ان میں

إِن نَّعْفُ عَن طَآئِفَةٍ مِّنكُمْ نُعَذِّبْ
طَآئِفَةً بِأَنَّهُمْ كَانُوا مُجْرِمِينَ ﴿٦٦﴾
الْمُنَافِقُونَ وَالْمُنَافِقَاتُ بَعْضُهُم مِّن بَعْضٍ
يَأْمُرُونَ بِالْمُنكَرِ وَيَنْهَوْنَ عَنِ الْمَعْرُوفِ
وَيَقْبِضُونَ أَيْدِيَهُمْ نَسُوا اللَّهَ فَنَسِيَهُمْ
إِنَّ الْمُنَافِقِينَ هُمُ الْفَاسِقُونَ ﴿٦٧﴾
وَعَدَ اللَّهُ الْمُنَافِقِينَ وَالْمُنَافِقَاتِ وَالْكُفَّارَ
نَارَ جَهَنَّمَ خَالِدِينَ فِيهَا هِيَ حَسْبُهُمْ
وَلَعَنَهُمُ اللَّهُ وَلَهُمْ عَذَابٌ مُّقِيمٌ ﴿٦٨﴾
كَالَّذِينَ مِن قَبْلِكُمْ كَانُوا أَشَدَّ مِنكُمْ
قُوَّةً وَأَكْثَرَ أَمْوَالًا وَأَوْلَادًا فَاسْتَمْتَعُوا
بِخَلَاقِهِمْ فَاسْتَمْتَعْتُم بِخَلَاقِكُمْ كَمَا اسْتَمْتَعَ
الَّذِينَ مِن قَبْلِكُم بِخَلَاقِهِمْ وَخُضْتُمْ
كَالَّذِي خَاضُوا أُولَٰئِكَ حَبِطَتْ أَعْمَالُهُمْ
فِي الدُّنْيَا وَالْآخِرَةِ وَأُولَٰئِكَ هُمُ الْخَاسِرُونَ ﴿٦٩﴾
أَلَمْ يَأْتِهِمْ نَبَأُ الَّذِينَ مِن قَبْلِهِمْ قَوْمِ
نُوحٍ وَعَادٍ وَثَمُودَ وَقَوْمِ إِبْرَاهِيمَ
وَأَصْحَابِ مَدْيَنَ وَالْمُؤْتَفِكَاتِ أَتَتْهُمْ
رُسُلُهُم بِالْبَيِّنَاتِ فَمَا كَانَ اللَّهُ لِيَظْلِمَهُمْ
وَلَٰكِن كَانُوا أَنفُسَهُمْ يَظْلِمُونَ ﴿٧٠﴾
وَالْمُؤْمِنُونَ وَالْمُؤْمِنَاتُ بَعْضُهُمْ أَوْلِيَاءُ
بَعْضٍ يَأْمُرُونَ بِالْمَعْرُوفِ وَيَنْهَوْنَ
عَنِ الْمُنكَرِ وَيُقِيمُونَ الصَّلَاةَ وَيُؤْتُونَ
الزَّكَاةَ وَيُطِيعُونَ اللَّهَ وَرَسُولَهُ أُولَٰئِكَ
سَيَرْحَمُهُمُ اللَّهُ إِنَّ اللَّهَ عَزِيزٌ حَكِيمٌ ﴿٧١﴾
وَعَدَ اللَّهُ الْمُؤْمِنِينَ وَالْمُؤْمِنَاتِ جَنَّاتٍ
تَجْرِي مِن تَحْتِهَا الْأَنْهَارُ خَالِدِينَ فِيهَا وَ

مَسٰكِنَ طَيِّبَةً فِيْ جَنّٰتِ عَدْنٍ ۭ وَرِضْوَانٌ
مِّنَ اللّٰهِ اَكْبَرُ ۭ ذٰلِكَ هُوَ الْفَوْزُ الْعَظِيْمُ ﴿٧٢﴾
يٰٓاَيُّهَا النَّبِيُّ جَاهِدِ الْكُفَّارَ وَالْمُنٰفِقِيْنَ
وَاغْلُظْ عَلَيْهِمْ ۭ وَمَاْوٰىهُمْ جَهَنَّمُ ۭ وَ
بِئْسَ الْمَصِيْرُ ﴿٧٣﴾
يَحْلِفُوْنَ بِاللّٰهِ مَا قَالُوْا ۭ وَلَقَدْ قَالُوْا كَلِمَةَ
الْكُفْرِ وَكَفَرُوْا بَعْدَ اِسْلَامِهِمْ وَهَمُّوْا
بِمَا لَمْ يَنَالُوْا ۚ وَمَا نَقَمُوْٓا اِلَّآ اَنْ اَغْنٰىهُمُ
اللّٰهُ وَرَسُوْلُهٗ مِنْ فَضْلِهٖ ۚ فَاِنْ يَّتُوْبُوْا
يَكُ خَيْرًا لَّهُمْ ۚ وَاِنْ يَّتَوَلَّوْا يُعَذِّبْهُمُ
اللّٰهُ عَذَابًا اَلِيْمًا ۙ فِي الدُّنْيَا وَالْاٰخِرَةِ ۚ وَمَا
لَهُمْ فِي الْاَرْضِ مِنْ وَّلِيٍّ وَّلَا نَصِيْرٍ ﴿٧٤﴾
وَمِنْهُمْ مَّنْ عٰهَدَ اللّٰهَ لَىِٕنْ اٰتٰىنَا مِنْ فَضْلِهٖ
لَنَصَّدَّقَنَّ وَلَنَكُوْنَنَّ مِنَ الصّٰلِحِيْنَ ﴿٧٥﴾
فَلَمَّآ اٰتٰىهُمْ مِّنْ فَضْلِهٖ بَخِلُوْا بِهٖ وَتَوَلَّوْا
وَّهُمْ مُّعْرِضُوْنَ ﴿٧٦﴾
فَاَعْقَبَهُمْ نِفَاقًا فِيْ قُلُوْبِهِمْ اِلٰى يَوْمِ
يَلْقَوْنَهٗ بِمَآ اَخْلَفُوا اللّٰهَ مَا وَعَدُوْهُ وَبِمَا
كَانُوْا يَكْذِبُوْنَ ﴿٧٧﴾
اَلَمْ يَعْلَمُوْٓا اَنَّ اللّٰهَ يَعْلَمُ سِرَّهُمْ وَ
نَجْوٰىهُمْ وَاَنَّ اللّٰهَ عَلَّامُ الْغُيُوْبِ ﴿٧٨﴾
اَلَّذِيْنَ يَلْمِزُوْنَ الْمُطَّوِّعِيْنَ مِنَ
الْمُؤْمِنِيْنَ فِي الصَّدَقٰتِ وَالَّذِيْنَ لَا
يَجِدُوْنَ اِلَّا جُهْدَهُمْ فَيَسْخَرُوْنَ مِنْهُمْ ۭ
سَخِرَ اللّٰهُ مِنْهُمْ ۡ وَلَهُمْ عَذَابٌ اَلِيْمٌ ﴿٧٩﴾
اِسْتَغْفِرْ لَهُمْ اَوْ لَا تَسْتَغْفِرْ لَهُمْ ۭ اِنْ
تَسْتَغْفِرْ لَهُمْ سَبْعِيْنَ مَرَّةً فَلَنْ يَّغْفِرَ

ہمیشہ رہیں گے اور بہشت ہائے جاودانی میں نفیس مکانات کا
(وعدہ کیا ہے) اور خدا کی رضامندی تو سب سے بڑھکر نعمت ہے یہی بڑی کامیابی ہے ﴿٧٢﴾
اے پیغمبر کافروں اور منافقوں سے لڑو۔ اور اُن پر سختی
کرو۔ اور اُن کا ٹھکانا دوزخ ہے۔ اور وہ بُری
جگہ ہے ﴿٧٣﴾
یہ خدا کی قسمیں کھاتے ہیں کہ انہوں نے (تو کچھ) نہیں کہا
حالانکہ اُنہوں نے کفر کا کلمہ کہا ہے اور یہ اسلام لانے کے بعد
کافر ہو گئے ہیں اور ایسی بات کا قصد کر چکے ہیں جس پر قدرت
نہیں پا سکے۔ اور انہوں نے (مسلمانوں میں) عیب ہی کونسا دیکھا ہے سوا
اسکے کہ خدا نے اپنے فضل سے اور اسکے پیغمبر نے (اپنی مہربانی سے) انکو دولت مند
کر دیا ہے۔ تو اگر یہ لوگ توبہ کر لیں تو انکے حق میں بہتر ہوگا اور اگر منہ پھیر لیں تو خدا انکو دنیا
اور آخرت میں دُکھ دینے والا عذاب دیگا۔ اور زمین میں انکا کوئی دوست اور مددگار نہ ہوگا ﴿٧٤﴾
اور ان میں بعض ایسے ہیں جنہوں نے خدا سے عہد کیا تھا کہ اگر وہ ہمکو اپنی
مہربانی سے (مال) عطا فرمائیگا تو ہم ضرور خیرات کیا کرینگے اور نیکوکاروں میں ہو جائینگے ﴿٧٥﴾
لیکن جب خدا نے ان کو اپنے فضل سے (مال) دیا تو اس میں بخل
کرنے لگے اور (اپنے عہد سے) روگردانی کر کے پھر بیٹھے ﴿٧٦﴾
تو خدا نے اسکا انجام یہ کیا کہ اُس روز تک کیلئے جسمیں وہ خدا کے روبرو
حاضر ہونگے اُنکے دلوں میں نفاق ڈالدیا اسلئے کہ انہوں نے خدا سے جو
وعدہ کیا تھا اسکے خلاف کیا اور اسلئے کہ وہ جھوٹ بولتے تھے ﴿٧٧﴾
کیا اُنکو معلوم نہیں کہ خدا انکے بھیدوں اور مشوروں تک سے واقف ہے
اور یہ کہ وہ غیب کی باتیں جاننے والا ہے ﴿٧٨﴾
جو (ذی استطاعت) مسلمان دل کھول کر خیرات کرتے ہیں اور جو (بیچارے
غریب صرف) اتنا ہی کما سکتے ہیں جتنی مزدوری کرتے (اور تھوڑی سی
کمائی میں سے بھی خرچ کرتے) ہیں اُن پر جو (منافق) طعن کرتے اور
ہنستے ہیں خدا اُن پر ہنستا ہے اور اُن کیلئے تکلیف دینے والا عذاب (تیار) ہے ﴿٧٩﴾
تم اُن کے لئے بخشش مانگو یا نہ مانگو (بات ایک ہی ہے) اگر انکے
لئے ستر دفعہ بھی بخشش مانگو گے تو بھی خدا اُن کو نہیں بخشے گا

mansions in Gardens of everlasting stay but the greatest bliss is the Good Pleasure of Allah: that is the supreme triumph.

73. O Prophet! strive hard against the Unbelievers and the Hypocrites, and be firm against them. Their abode is Hell,—an evil refuge indeed.

74. They swear by Allah that they said nothing (evil), but indeed they uttered blasphemy, and they uttered it after accepting Islam: and they meditated a plot which they were unable to carry out: this revenge of theirs was (their) only return for the bounty with which Allah and His Messenger had enriched them! If they repent, it will be best for them: but if they turn back (to their evil ways), Allah will punish them with a grievous chastisement in this life and in the Hereafter: they shall have none on earth to protect or help them.

75. Amongst them are men who made a Covenant with Allah, that if He bestowed on them of His bounty; they would give (largely) in charity, and be truly amongst those who are righteous.

76. But when He did bestow of His bounty, they became misers, and turned back (from their Covenant), averse (from its fulfilment).

77. So He hath put as a consequence hypocrisy into their hearts, (to last) till the Day whereon they shall meet Him: because they broke their Covenant with Allah, and because they lied (again and again).

78. Know they not that Allah doth know their secret (thoughts) and their secret counsels, and that Allah knoweth well all things unseen?

79. Those who slander such of the Believers as give themselve freely to (deeds of) charity, as well as those who give according to their means,—and throw ridicule on them,—Allah will throw back their ridicule on them: and they shall have a grievous chastisement.

80. Whether thou ask for their forgiveness, or not, (their sin is unforgivable): if thou ask seventy times for their forgiveness, Allah

will not forgive them: because they have rejected Allah and His Messenger: and Allah guideth not those who are perversely rebellious.

81. Those who were left behind (in the Tabûk expedition) rejoiced in their sitting back behind the Messenger of Allah: they hated to strive and fight, with their goods and their persons, in the Cause of Allah: they said, "Go not forth in the heat." Say, "The fire of Hell is fiercer in heat," if only they could understand!

82. Let them laugh a little: much will they weep: a recompense for the (evil) that they do.

83. If, then, Allah bring thee back to any of them, and they ask Thy permission to come out (with thee), say: "Never shall ye come out with me, nor fight an enemy with me: for ye preferred to sit inactive on the first occasion: then sit ye (now) with those who stay behind."

84. Nor do thou ever pray for any of them that dies, nor stand at his grave; for they rejected Allah and His Messenger, and died in a state of perverse rebellion.

85. Nor let their wealth nor their children dazzle thee: Allah's Wish is to punish them with these things in this world, and that their souls may depart while they are unbelievers.

86. When a Sûra comes down, enjoining them to believe in Allah and to strive and fight along with His Messenger, those with wealth and influence among them ask thee for exemption, and say: "Leave us (behind): we would be with those who sit (at home)."

87. They prefer to be with (the women), who remain behind (at home): their hearts are sealed and so they understand not.

88. But the Messenger, and those who believe with him, strive and fight with their wealth and their persons: for them are (all) good

یہ اس لئے کہ انہوں نے خدا اور اس کے رسول سے کفر
کیا۔ اور خدا نافرمان لوگوں کو ہدایت نہیں دیتا ﴿۸۰﴾
جو لوگ (غزوۂ تبوک میں) پیچھے رہ گئے وہ پیغمبر خدا کی (مرضی)
کے خلاف بیٹھ رہنے سے خوش ہوئے اور اس بات کو ناپسند
کیا کہ خدا کی راہ میں اپنے مال اور جان سے جہاد کریں۔ اور
(اوروں سے بھی) کہنے لگے کہ گرمی میں مت نکلنا (ان سے) کہہ دو کہ دوزخ
کی آگ اس سے کہیں زیادہ گرم ہے کاش یہ (اس بات کو) سمجھتے ﴿۸۱﴾
یہ (دنیا میں) تھوڑا سا ہنس لیں اور (آخرت میں) ان کو ان اعمال
کے بدلے جو کرتے رہے ہیں بہت سا رونا ہوگا ﴿۸۲﴾
پھر اگر خدا تم کو ان میں سے کسی گروہ کی طرف لے جائے اور وہ
تم سے نکلنے کی اجازت طلب کریں تو کہہ دینا کہ تم میرے
ساتھ ہرگز نہیں نکلو گے اور نہ میرے ساتھ (مددگار ہو کر)
دشمن سے لڑائی کرو گے۔ تم پہلی دفعہ بیٹھ رہنے سے خوش
ہوئے تو اب بھی پیچھے رہنے والوں کے ساتھ بیٹھے رہو ﴿۸۳﴾
اور (اے پیغمبر) ان میں سے کوئی مر جائے تو کبھی اس (کے جنازے)
پر نماز نہ پڑھنا اور نہ اس کی قبر پر (جا کر) کھڑے ہونا۔ یہ خدا اور
اس کے رسول کے ساتھ کفر کرتے رہے اور مرے بھی نافرمان (ہی مرے) ﴿۸۴﴾
اور ان کے مال اور اولاد سے تعجب نہ کرنا۔ ان چیزوں سے خدا
یہ چاہتا ہے کہ ان کو دنیا میں عذاب کرے۔ اور (جب) ان
کی جان نکلے تو (اس وقت بھی) یہ کافر ہی ہوں ﴿۸۵﴾
اور جب کوئی سورت نازل ہوتی ہے کہ خدا پر ایمان لاؤ اور اس کے رسول کے ساتھ
ہو کر لڑائی کرو تو جو ان میں دولتمند ہیں وہ تم سے اجازت طلب کرتے ہیں اور
کہتے ہیں کہ ہمیں تو رہنے ہی دیجئے کہ جو لوگ گھروں میں رہیں گے ہم بھی ان کے ساتھ رہیں ﴿۸۶﴾
یہ اس بات سے خوش ہیں کہ عورتوں کے ساتھ جو پیچھے رہ جاتی ہیں (گھروں میں)
بیٹھ (رہیں) ان کے دلوں پر مہر لگا دی گئی ہے تو یہ سمجھتے ہی نہیں ﴿۸۷﴾
لیکن پیغمبر اور جو لوگ ان کے ساتھ ایمان لائے سب اپنے مال اور
جان سے لڑے۔ انہی لوگوں کے لئے بھلائیاں ہیں اور یہی

اللهُ لَهُمْ ذٰلِكَ بِاَنَّهُمْ كَفَرُوْا بِاللّٰهِ
وَرَسُوْلِهٖ وَاللّٰهُ لَا يَهْدِي الْقَوْمَ الْفٰسِقِيْنَ ﴿٨٠﴾
فَرِحَ الْمُخَلَّفُوْنَ بِمَقْعَدِهِمْ خِلٰفَ
رَسُوْلِ اللّٰهِ وَكَرِهُوْٓا اَنْ يُّجَاهِدُوْا
بِاَمْوَالِهِمْ وَاَنْفُسِهِمْ فِيْ سَبِيْلِ اللّٰهِ
وَقَالُوْا لَا تَنْفِرُوْا فِي الْحَرِّ قُلْ نَارُ
جَهَنَّمَ اَشَدُّ حَرًّا لَوْ كَانُوْا يَفْقَهُوْنَ ﴿٨١﴾
فَلْيَضْحَكُوْا قَلِيْلًا وَّلْيَبْكُوْا كَثِيْرًا ج
جَزَآءً بِمَا كَانُوْا يَكْسِبُوْنَ ﴿٨٢﴾
فَاِنْ رَّجَعَكَ اللّٰهُ اِلٰى طَآئِفَةٍ مِّنْهُمْ
فَاسْتَاْذَنُوْكَ لِلْخُرُوْجِ فَقُلْ لَّنْ تَخْرُجُوْا
مَعِيَ اَبَدًا وَّلَنْ تُقَاتِلُوْا مَعِيَ عَدُوًّا اِنَّكُمْ
رَضِيْتُمْ بِالْقُعُوْدِ اَوَّلَ مَرَّةٍ فَاقْعُدُوْا
مَعَ الْخَالِفِيْنَ ﴿٨٣﴾
وَلَا تُصَلِّ عَلٰٓى اَحَدٍ مِّنْهُمْ مَّاتَ اَبَدًا
وَّلَا تَقُمْ عَلٰى قَبْرِهٖ اِنَّهُمْ كَفَرُوْا بِاللّٰهِ
وَرَسُوْلِهٖ وَمَاتُوْا وَهُمْ فٰسِقُوْنَ ﴿٨٤﴾
وَلَا تُعْجِبْكَ اَمْوَالُهُمْ وَاَوْلَادُهُمْ
اِنَّمَا يُرِيْدُ اللّٰهُ اَنْ يُّعَذِّبَهُمْ بِهَا فِي
الدُّنْيَا وَتَزْهَقَ اَنْفُسُهُمْ وَهُمْ كٰفِرُوْنَ ﴿٨٥﴾
وَاِذَآ اُنْزِلَتْ سُوْرَةٌ اَنْ اٰمِنُوْا بِاللّٰهِ وَ
جَاهِدُوْا مَعَ رَسُوْلِهِ اسْتَاْذَنَكَ اُولُوا
الطَّوْلِ مِنْهُمْ وَقَالُوْا ذَرْنَا نَكُنْ مَّعَ الْقٰعِدِيْنَ ﴿٨٦﴾
رَضُوْا بِاَنْ يَّكُوْنُوْا مَعَ الْخَوَالِفِ وَطُبِعَ
عَلٰى قُلُوْبِهِمْ فَهُمْ لَا يَفْقَهُوْنَ ﴿٨٧﴾
لٰكِنِ الرَّسُوْلُ وَالَّذِيْنَ اٰمَنُوْا مَعَهٗ
جَاهَدُوْا بِاَمْوَالِهِمْ وَاَنْفُسِهِمْ وَاُولٰٓئِكَ

things: and it is they who will prosper.

مراد پانے والے ہیں (۸۸)

لهم الخيرات وأولئك هم المفلحون ٨٨

89. Allah hath prepared for them Gardens under which rivers flow, to dwell therein: that is the supreme triumph.

خدا نے اُن کے لئے باغات تیار کر رکھے ہیں
جن کے نیچے نہریں بہ رہی ہیں ہمیشہ ان میں رہیں گے
یہ بڑی کامیابی ہے (۸۹)

أعد الله لهم جنات تجري من تحتها
الأنهار خالدين فيها ذلك الفوز
العظيم ٨٩

90. And there were, among the desert Arabs (also), men who made excuses and came to claim exemption: and those who were false to Allah and His Messenger (merely) sat behind: soon will a grievous chastisement seize the Unbelievers among them.

اور صحرانشینوں میں سے بھی کچھ لوگ عذر کرتے ہوئے (تمہارے
پاس) آئے کہ ان کو بھی اجازت دی جائے اور جنہوں نے خدا اور
اس کے رسول سے جھوٹ بولا وہ (گھر میں) بیٹھ رہے سو جو لوگ
ان میں سے کافر ہوئے ہیں ان کو دکھ دینے والا عذاب پہنچے گا (۹۰)

وجاء المعذرون من الأعراب ليؤذن
لهم وقعد الذين كذبوا الله ورسوله
سيصيب الذين كفروا منهم
عذاب أليم ٩٠

91. There is no blame on those who are infirm, or ill, or who find no resources to spend (on the Cause), if they are sincere (in duty) to Allah and His Messenger: no ground (of complaint) can there be against such as do right: and Allah is Oft-Forgiving, Most Merciful.

نہ تو ضعیفوں پر کچھ گناہ ہے اور نہ بیماروں پر اور نہ اُن پر
جن کے پاس خرچ موجود نہیں (کہ شریک جہاد ہوں یعنی)
جبکہ خدا اور اسکے رسول کے خیر اندیش (اور دل سے انکے
ساتھ) ہوں۔ نیکوکاروں پر کسی طرح کا الزام نہیں ہے۔ اور
خدا بخشنے والا مہربان ہے (۹۱)

ليس على الضعفاء ولا على المرضى
ولا على الذين لا يجدون ما ينفقون
حرج إذا نصحوا لله ورسوله ما على
المحسنين من سبيل والله غفور
رحيم ٩١

92. Nor (is there blame) on those who came to thee to be provided with mounts. And when thou saidst, "I can find no mounts for you," they turned back, their eyes streaming with tears of grief that they had no resources wherewith to provide the expenses.

اور نہ ان (بے سروسامان) لوگوں پر (الزام) ہے کہ تمہارے پاس
آئے کہ اُن کو سواری دو اور تم نے کہا کہ میرے پاس کوئی ایسی
چیز نہیں جس پر تم کو سوار کروں تو وہ لوٹ گئے اور اس غم سے کہ
انکے پاس خرچ موجود نہ تھا انکی آنکھوں سے آنسو بہ رہے تھے (۹۲)

ولا على الذين إذا ما أتوك لتحملهم
قلت لا أجد ما أحملكم عليه
تولوا وأعينهم تفيض من الدمع
حزنا ألا يجدوا ما ينفقون ٩٢

93. The ground (of complaint) is only against such as claim exemption while they are rich. They prefer to stay with the (women) who remain behind: Allah hath sealed their hearts: so they know not.

الزام تو اُن لوگوں پر ہے جو دولتمند ہیں اور (پھر) تم
سے اجازت طلب کرتے ہیں (یعنی) اس بات سے خوش
ہیں کہ عورتوں کے ساتھ جو پیچھے رہ جاتی ہیں (گھروں میں بیٹھ)
رہیں۔ خدا نے اُن کے دلوں پر مُہر کر دی ہے پس وہ سمجھتے ہی نہیں (۹۳)

إنما السبيل على الذين يستأذنونك
وهم أغنياء رضوا بأن يكونوا مع
الخوالف وطبع الله على قلوبهم فهم
لا يعلمون ٩٣

94. They will present their excuses to you when ye return to them. Say thou: "Present no excuses: we shall not believe you: Allah hath already informed us of the true state of matters concerning you: it is your actions that Allah and His Messenger will observe: in the end will ye be brought back to Him who knoweth what is hidden and what is open: then will He show you the truth of all that ye did."

جب تم اُن کے پاس واپس جاؤ گے تو تم سے عذر کریں گے
تم کہنا کہ عذر مت کرو ہم ہرگز تمہاری بات نہیں مانیں گے
خدا نے ہم کو تمہارے سب حالات بتا دیئے ہیں۔ اور ابھی
خدا اور اُس کا رسول تمہارے عملوں کو (اور) دیکھیں گے پھر
تم غائب و حاضر کے جاننے والے (خدائے واحد) کی طرف
لوٹائے جاؤ گے اور جو عمل تم کرتے رہے ہو وہ سب تمہیں بتائے گا (۹۴)

يعتذرون إليكم إذا رجعتم إليهم
قل لا تعتذروا لن نؤمن لكم قد
نبأنا الله من أخباركم وسيرى
الله عملكم ورسوله ثم تردون إلى
عالم الغيب والشهادة فينبئكم بما
كنتم تعملون ٩٤

سَيَحْلِفُونَ بِاللّٰهِ لَكُمْ إِذَا انْقَلَبْتُمْ إِلَيْهِمْ
لِتُعْرِضُوا عَنْهُمْ ۖ فَأَعْرِضُوا عَنْهُمْ ۖ إِنَّهُمْ
رِجْسٌ ۖ وَّمَأْوٰىهُمْ جَهَنَّمُ ۚ جَزَآءًۢ بِمَا
كَانُوا يَكْسِبُونَ ﴿٩٥﴾

جب تم اُن کے پاس لوٹ کر جاؤ گے تو تمہارے روبرو
خدا کی قسمیں کھائیں گے تاکہ تم اُن سے درگزر کرو سو اُن کی
طرف التفات نہ کرنا یہ ناپاک ہیں اور جو کام یہ کرتے رہے ہیں
اُن کے بدلے اُن کا ٹھکانا دوزخ ہے ﴿۹۵﴾

95. They will swear to you by Allah, when ye return to them, that ye may leave them alone. So leave them alone: for they are an abomination, and Hell is their dwelling-place,—a fitting recompense for the (evil) that they did.

يَحْلِفُونَ لَكُمْ لِتَرْضَوْا عَنْهُمْ ۚ فَإِنْ
تَرْضَوْا عَنْهُمْ فَإِنَّ اللّٰهَ لَا يَرْضٰى عَنِ
الْقَوْمِ الْفٰسِقِينَ ﴿٩٦﴾

یہ تمہارے آگے قسمیں کھائیں گے تاکہ تم اُن سے خوش ہو جاؤ
لیکن اگر تم ان سے خوش ہو جاؤ گے تو خدا تو نافرمان لوگوں
سے خوش نہیں ہوتا ﴿۹۶﴾

96. They will swear unto you, that ye may be pleased with them. But if ye are pleased with them. Allah is not pleased with those who disobey.

اَلْأَعْرَابُ أَشَدُّ كُفْرًا وَّنِفَاقًا وَّ
أَجْدَرُ أَلَّا يَعْلَمُوا حُدُودَ مَآ
أَنْزَلَ اللّٰهُ عَلٰى رَسُولِهٖ ۗ وَاللّٰهُ عَلِيمٌ
حَكِيمٌ ﴿٩٧﴾

دیہاتی لوگ سخت کافر اور سخت منافق ہیں اور اس قابل
ہیں کہ جو احکام (شریعت) خدا نے اپنے رسول پر نازل
فرمائے ہیں ان سے واقف (ہی) نہ ہوں۔ اور خدا جاننے
والا (اور) حکمت والا ہے ﴿۹۷﴾

97. The Bedouin Arabs are the worst in unbelief and hypocrisy, and most fitted to be in ignorance of the command which Allah hath sent down to His Messenger: but Allah is All-Knowing, All-Wise.

وَمِنَ الْأَعْرَابِ مَنْ يَّتَّخِذُ مَا يُنْفِقُ
مَغْرَمًا وَّيَتَرَبَّصُ بِكُمُ الدَّوَآئِرَ ۚ عَلَيْهِمْ
دَآئِرَةُ السَّوْءِ ۗ وَاللّٰهُ سَمِيعٌ عَلِيمٌ ﴿٩٨﴾

اور بعض دیہاتی ایسے ہیں کہ جو کچھ خرچ کرتے ہیں اُسے تاوان
سمجھتے ہیں اور تمہارے حق میں مصیبتوں کے منتظر ہیں۔ انہی پر
بری مصیبت (واقع) ہو۔ اور خدا سننے والا (اور) جاننے والا ہے ﴿۹۸﴾

98. Some of the Bedouin Arabs look upon their payments as a fine, and watch for disasters for you: on them be the disaster of Evil: for Allah is He that heareth and knoweth (all things).

وَمِنَ الْأَعْرَابِ مَنْ يُّؤْمِنُ بِاللّٰهِ وَالْيَوْمِ
الْاٰخِرِ وَيَتَّخِذُ مَا يُنْفِقُ قُرُبٰتٍ عِنْدَ اللّٰهِ
وَصَلَوٰتِ الرَّسُولِ ۗ أَلَآ إِنَّهَا قُرْبَةٌ
لَّهُمْ ۗ سَيُدْخِلُهُمُ اللّٰهُ فِي رَحْمَتِهٖ ۗ
إِنَّ اللّٰهَ غَفُورٌ رَّحِيمٌ ﴿٩٩﴾

اور بعض دیہاتی ایسے ہیں کہ خدا پر اور روز آخرت پر ایمان
رکھتے ہیں اور جو کچھ خرچ کرتے ہیں اُس کو خدا کی قربت اور
پیغمبر کی دعاؤں کا ذریعہ سمجھتے ہیں۔ دیکھو وہ بے شبہ
اُن کے لئے (موجب) قربت ہے۔ خدا ان کو عنقریب اپنی
رحمت میں داخل کرے گا۔ بے شک خدا بخشنے والا مہربان ہے ﴿۹۹﴾

99. But some of the Bedouin Arabs believe in Allah and the Last Day, and look on their payments as pious gifts bringing them nearer to Allah and obtaining the prayers of the Messenger. Aye, indeed they bring them nearer (to Him): soon will Allah Admit them to His Mercy: for Allah is Oft-Forgiving, Most Merciful.

وَالسّٰبِقُونَ الْأَوَّلُونَ مِنَ الْمُهٰجِرِينَ وَ
الْأَنْصَارِ وَالَّذِينَ اتَّبَعُوهُمْ بِإِحْسَانٍ ۙ
رَّضِيَ اللّٰهُ عَنْهُمْ وَرَضُوا عَنْهُ وَأَعَدَّ لَهُمْ
جَنّٰتٍ تَجْرِي تَحْتَهَا الْأَنْهٰرُ خٰلِدِينَ فِيهَآ
أَبَدًا ۚ ذٰلِكَ الْفَوْزُ الْعَظِيمُ ﴿١٠٠﴾

جن لوگوں نے سبقت کی (یعنی سب سے) پہلے (ایمان لائے) مہاجرین
میں سے بھی اور انصار میں سے بھی اور جنہوں نے نیکوکاری کے ساتھ اُن کی
پیروی کی خدا اُن سے خوش ہے اور وہ خدا سے خوش ہیں اور اس نے
اُن کیلئے باغات تیار کئے ہیں جن کے نیچے نہریں بہ رہی ہیں (اور)
ہمیشہ ان میں رہیں گے۔ یہ بڑی کامیابی ہے ﴿۱۰۰﴾

100. The vanguard (of Islam)—the first of those who forsook (their homes) and of those who gave them aid, and (also) those who follow them in (all) good deeds,—Well-pleased is Allah with them, as are they with Him: for them hath He prepared Gardens under which rivers flow, to dwell therein for ever: that is the supreme Triumph.

وَمِمَّنْ حَوْلَكُمْ مِّنَ الْأَعْرَابِ مُنٰفِقُونَ ۛ
وَمِنْ أَهْلِ الْمَدِينَةِ ۛ مَرَدُوا عَلَى النِّفَاقِ
لَا تَعْلَمُهُمْ ۖ نَحْنُ نَعْلَمُهُمْ ۚ سَنُعَذِّبُهُمْ

اور تمہارے گردونواح کے بعض دیہاتی منافق ہیں اور بعض
مدینے والے بھی نفاق پر اڑے ہوئے ہیں تم انہیں نہیں جانتے
ہم جانتے ہیں۔ ہم اُن کو دوہرا عذاب دیں گے۔ پھر وہ بڑے

101. Certain of the desert Arabs round about you are Hypocrites, as well as among the Madinah folk: they are obstinate in hypocrisy: thou knowest them not: We know them: twice shall We punish them: and in

addition shall they be sent to a grievous Chastisement..

102. Others (there are who) have acknowledged their wrong-doings: they have mixed an act that was good with another that was evil. Perhaps Allah will turn unto them (in mercy): for Allah is Oft-Forgiving, Most Merciful.

103. Of their wealth take alms, that so thou mightest purify and sanctify them; and pray on their behalf. Verily thy prayers are a source of security for them: And Allah is One Who heareth and knoweth.

104. Know they not that Allah doth accept repentance from His votaries and receives their gifts of charity, and that Allah is verily He, the Oft-Returning, Most Merciful?

105. And say: "Work (righteousness): soon will Allah observe your work, and His Messenger, and the Believers: soon will ye be brought back to the Knower of what is hidden and what is open: then will He show you the truth of all that ye did."

106. There are (yet) others, held in suspense for the command of Allah, whether He will punish them, or turn in mercy to them: and Allah is All-Knowing, Wise.

107. And there are those who put up a mosque by way of mischief and infidelity—to disunite the Believers—and in preparation for one who warred against Allah and His Messenger aforetime. They will indeed swear that their intention is nothing but good; but Allah doth declare that they are certainly liars.

108. Never stand thou forth therein. There is a mosque whose foundation was laid from the first day on piety; it is more worthy of thy standing forth (for prayer) therein. In it are men who love to be purified; and Allah loveth those who make themselves pure.

109. Which then is best?—he that layeth his foundation on piety to

عذاب کی طرف لوٹائے جائیں گے (۱۰۱)
اور کچھ اور لوگ ہیں کہ اپنے گناہوں کا (صاف) اقرار
کرتے ہیں۔ انہوں نے اچھے اور بُرے عملوں کو ملا جلا
دیا تھا۔ قریب ہے کہ خدا اُن پر مہربانی سے توجہ فرمائے۔
بے شک خدا بخشنے والا مہربان ہے (۱۰۲)
اُن کے مال میں سے زکوٰة قبول کرلو کہ اس سے تم ان کو (ظاہر میں
بھی) پاک اور (باطن میں بھی) پاکیزہ کرتے ہو اور اُنکے حق میں دعائے خیر
کرو کہ تمہاری دُعا اُنکے لئے موجب تسکین ہے اور خدا سننے والا (اور) جاننے والا ہے (۱۰۳)
کیا یہ لوگ نہیں جانتے کہ خدا ہی اپنے بندوں سے توبہ قبول فرماتا
اور صدقات (وخیرات) لیتا ہے اور بے شک خدا ہی توبہ
قبول کرنے والا مہربان ہے (۱۰۴)
اور ان سے کہہ دو کہ عمل کئے جاؤ۔ خدا اور اسکا رسول اور
مومن (سب) تمہارے عملوں کو دیکھ لیں گے۔ اور تم غائب و
حاضر کے جاننے والے (خدائے واحد) کی طرف لوٹائے جاؤ گے۔
پھر جو کچھ تم کرتے رہے ہو وہ سب تم کو بتا دے گا (۱۰۵)
اور کچھ اور لوگ ہیں جن کا کام خدا کے حکم پر موقوف ہے چاہے اُن کو
عذاب دے اور چاہے معاف کر دے۔ اور خدا جاننے والا (اور) حکمت والا ہے (۱۰۶)
اور (ان میں ایسے بھی ہیں) جنہوں نے اس غرض سے مسجد بنائی
ہے کہ ضرر پہنچائیں اور کفر کریں اور مومنوں میں تفرقہ ڈالیں
اور جو لوگ خدا اور اسکے رسول سے پہلے جنگ کر چکے ہیں
اُن کیلئے گھات کی جگہ بنائیں اور قسمیں کھائیں گے کہ ہمارا مقصود
تو صرف بھلائی تھی مگر خدا گواہی دیتا ہے کہ یہ جھوٹے ہیں (۱۰۷)
تم اس (مسجد) میں کبھی (جاکر) کھڑے بھی نہ ہونا۔ البتہ وہ مسجد جس کی
بنیاد پہلے دن سے تقویٰ پر رکھی گئی ہے اس قابل ہے کہ
اس میں جایا (اور نماز پڑھایا) کرو اس میں ایسے لوگ ہیں
جو پاک رہنے کو پسند کرتے ہیں اور خدا پاک رہنے والوں ہی کو پسند کرتا ہے (۱۰۸)
بھلا جس شخص نے اپنی عمارت کی بنیاد خدا کے خوف اور اسکی

مرتين ثم يردون إلى عذاب عظيم ١٠١
وآخرون اعترفوا بذنوبهم خلطوا
عملا صالحا وآخر سيئا عسى الله
أن يتوب عليهم ۚ إن الله غفور
رحيم ١٠٢
خذ من أموالهم صدقة تطهرهم
وتزكيهم بها وصل عليهم ۖ إن صلوتك
سكن لهم ۗ والله سميع عليم ١٠٣
ألم يعلموا أن الله هو يقبل التوبة
عن عباده ويأخذ الصدقت وأن
الله هو التواب الرحيم ١٠٤
وقل اعملوا فسيرى الله عملكم
ورسوله والمؤمنون ۖ وستردون إلى
علم الغيب والشهدة فينبئكم بما
كنتم تعملون ١٠٥
وآخرون مرجون لأمر الله إما يعذبهم
وإما يتوب عليهم ۗ والله عليم حكيم ١٠٦
والذين اتخذوا مسجدا ضرارا وكفرا
وتفريقا بين المؤمنين وإرصادا
لمن حارب الله ورسوله من قبل ۚ
وليحلفن إن أردنا إلا الحسنى ۖ والله
يشهد إنهم لكذبون ١٠٧
لا تقم فيه أبدا ۚ لمسجد أسس على
التقوى من أول يوم أحق أن تقوم
فيه ۚ فيه رجال يحبون أن يتطهروا ۚ
والله يحب المطهرين ١٠٨
أفمن أسس بنينه على تقوى من الله

Allah and His Good Pleasure?—or he that layeth his foundation on an undermined sand-cliff ready to crumble to pieces? And it doth crumble to pieces with him, into the fire of Hell. And Allah guideth not People that do wrong.

110. The foundation of those who so build is never free from suspicion and shakiness in their hearts, until their hearts are cut to pieces. And Allah is All-Knowing, Wise.

111. Allah hath purchased of the Believers their persons and their goods; for theirs (in return) is the Garden (of Paradise): they fight in His Cause, and slay and are slain: a promise binding on Him in Truth, through the Torah, the Gospel, and the Qur'an: and who is more faithful to his Covenant than Allah? Then rejoice in the bargain which ye have concluded: that is the achievement supreme.

112. Those that turn (to Allah) in repentance; that serve Him, and praise Him; that wander in devotion to Cause of Allah; that bow down and prostrate themselves in prayer; that enjoin good and forbid evil; and observe the limits set by Allah,—(these do rejoice). So proclaim the glad tidings to the Believers.

113. It is not fitting, for the Prophet and those who believe, that they should pray for forgiveness for Pagans, even though they be of kin, after it is clear to them that they are companions of the Fire.

114. And Abraham prayed for his father's forgiveness only because of a promise he had made to him. But when it became clear to him that he was an enemy to Allah, he dissociated himself from him: for Abraham was most tender hearted, forbearing.

115. And Allah will not mislead a people after He hath guided them until he makes clear to them as to what they should avoid, for Allah hath knowledge of all things.

رضامندی پر رکھی وہ اچھا ہے یا وہ جس نے اپنی عمارت
کی بنیاد گر جانیوالی کھائی کے کنارے پر رکھی کہ وہ اسکو دوزخ
کی آگ میں لے گری[142] اور خدا ظالم لوگوں کو ہدایت نہیں دیتا ﴿۱۰۹﴾
یہ عمارت جو انہوں نے بنائی ہے ہمیشہ اُنکے دلوں میں (موجب) خلجان
رہے گی (اور اُن کو متردد رکھے گی) مگر یہ کہ اُنکے دل پاش پاش
ہو جائیں۔ اور خدا جاننے والا اور حکمت والا ہے ﴿۱۱۰﴾
خدا نے مومنوں سے اُن کی جانیں اور اُن کے مال خرید لئے
ہیں (اور اسکے) عوض میں اُنکے لئے بہشت (تیار کی) ہے یہ
لوگ خدا کی راہ میں لڑتے ہیں تو مارتے بھی ہیں اور مارے
جاتے بھی ہیں۔ یہ تورات اور انجیل اور قرآن میں سچا وعدہ ہے
جس کا پورا کرنا اُسے ضرور ہے۔ اور خدا سے زیادہ وعدہ پورا
کرنے والا کون ہے؟ تو جو سودا تم نے اُس سے کیا ہے اُس
سے خوش رہو۔ اور یہی بڑی کامیابی ہے ﴿۱۱۱﴾
توبہ کرنیوالے۔ عبادت کرنیوالے۔ حمد کرنیوالے۔ روزہ رکھنےوالے۔
رکوع کرنیوالے۔ سجدہ کرنیوالے۔ نیک کاموں کا امر کرنیوالے۔
بُری باتوں سے منع کرنیوالے۔ خدا کی حدوں کی حفاظت کرنیوالے
(یہی مومن لوگ ہیں) اور اے پیغمبر مومنوں کو (بہشت کی) خوشخبری سنا دو ﴿۱۱۲﴾
پیغمبر اور مسلمانوں کو شایاں نہیں کہ جب اُن پر ظاہر ہو گیا
کہ مشرک اہل دوزخ ہیں تو اُن کے لئے بخشش مانگیں۔
گو وہ اُن کے قرابت دار ہی ہوں ﴿۱۱۳﴾
اور ابراہیم کا اپنے باپ کے لئے بخشش مانگنا تو ایک وعدے
کے سبب تھا جو وہ اُس سے کر چکے تھے لیکن جب ان کو
معلوم ہو گیا کہ وہ خدا کا دشمن ہے تو اُس سے بیزار ہو گئے۔
کچھ شک نہیں کہ ابراہیم بڑے نرم دل اور متحمل تھے ﴿۱۱۴﴾
اور خدا ایسا نہیں کہ کسی قوم کو ہدایت دینے کے بعد
گمراہ کر دے جب تک ان کو وہ چیز نہ بتا دے جس سے وہ
پرہیز کریں۔ بے شک خدا ہر چیز سے واقف ہے ﴿۱۱۵﴾

وَرِضْوَانٍ خَيْرٌ أَمْ مَّنْ أَسَّسَ بُنْيَانَهُ
عَلَىٰ شَفَا جُرُفٍ هَارٍ فَانْهَارَ بِهِ فِي نَارِ
جَهَنَّمَ ۗ وَاللَّهُ لَا يَهْدِي الْقَوْمَ الظَّالِمِينَ ﴿١٠٩﴾
لَا يَزَالُ بُنْيَانُهُمُ الَّذِي بَنَوْا رِيبَةً فِي
قُلُوبِهِمْ إِلَّا أَنْ تَقَطَّعَ قُلُوبُهُمْ ۗ وَاللَّهُ
عَلِيمٌ حَكِيمٌ ﴿١١٠﴾
إِنَّ اللَّهَ اشْتَرَىٰ مِنَ الْمُؤْمِنِينَ أَنْفُسَهُمْ
وَأَمْوَالَهُمْ بِأَنَّ لَهُمُ الْجَنَّةَ ۚ يُقَاتِلُونَ
فِي سَبِيلِ اللَّهِ فَيَقْتُلُونَ وَيُقْتَلُونَ ۖ وَعْدًا
عَلَيْهِ حَقًّا فِي التَّوْرَاةِ وَالْإِنْجِيلِ وَالْقُرْآنِ ۚ
وَمَنْ أَوْفَىٰ بِعَهْدِهِ مِنَ اللَّهِ ۚ فَاسْتَبْشِرُوا
بِبَيْعِكُمُ الَّذِي بَايَعْتُمْ بِهِ ۚ وَذَٰلِكَ هُوَ
الْفَوْزُ الْعَظِيمُ ﴿١١١﴾
التَّائِبُونَ الْعَابِدُونَ الْحَامِدُونَ السَّائِحُونَ
الرَّاكِعُونَ السَّاجِدُونَ الْآمِرُونَ بِالْمَعْرُوفِ
وَالنَّاهُونَ عَنِ الْمُنْكَرِ وَالْحَافِظُونَ لِحُدُودِ
اللَّهِ ۗ وَبَشِّرِ الْمُؤْمِنِينَ ﴿١١٢﴾
مَا كَانَ لِلنَّبِيِّ وَالَّذِينَ آمَنُوا أَنْ يَسْتَغْفِرُوا
لِلْمُشْرِكِينَ وَلَوْ كَانُوا أُولِي قُرْبَىٰ مِنْ
بَعْدِ مَا تَبَيَّنَ لَهُمْ أَنَّهُمْ أَصْحَابُ الْجَحِيمِ ﴿١١٣﴾
وَمَا كَانَ اسْتِغْفَارُ إِبْرَاهِيمَ لِأَبِيهِ إِلَّا
عَنْ مَوْعِدَةٍ وَعَدَهَا إِيَّاهُ فَلَمَّا تَبَيَّنَ
لَهُ أَنَّهُ عَدُوٌّ لِلَّهِ تَبَرَّأَ مِنْهُ ۚ إِنَّ
إِبْرَاهِيمَ لَأَوَّاهٌ حَلِيمٌ ﴿١١٤﴾
وَمَا كَانَ اللَّهُ لِيُضِلَّ قَوْمًا بَعْدَ إِذْ
هَدَاهُمْ حَتَّىٰ يُبَيِّنَ لَهُمْ مَا يَتَّقُونَ ۚ إِنَّ
اللَّهَ بِكُلِّ شَيْءٍ عَلِيمٌ ﴿١١٥﴾

116. Unto Allah belongeth the dominion of the heavens and the earth. He giveth life and He taketh it. Except for Him ye have no protector nor helper.

117. Allah turned with favour to the Prophet, the Muhajirs. And the Ansār,—who followed Him in a time of distress, after that the hearts of a part of them had nearly swerved (from duty); but He turned to them (also): for He is unto them Most Kind, Most Merciful.

118. (He turned in mercy also) to the three who were left behind; (they felt guilty) to such a degree that the earth seemed constrained to them, for all its speciousness, and their (very) souls seemed straitened to them,—and they perceived that there is no fleeing from Allah (and no refuge) but to Himself. Then He turned to them, that they might repent: for Allah is Oft-Returning, Most Merciful.

119. O ye who believe! Fear Allah and be with those who are truthful.

120. It was not fitting for the people of Madinah and the Bedouin Arabs of the neighbourhood, to stay behind Allah's Messenger, nor to prefer their own lives to his: because nothing could they suffer or do, but was reckoned to their credit as a deed of righteousness,—whether they suffered thirst, or fatigue, or hunger, in the Cause of Allah, or trod paths to raise the ire of the Unbelievers, or gain any gain from an enemy: for Allah suffereth not the reward to be lost of those who do good;—

121. Nor could they spend anything (for the Cause)—small or great—nor cut across a valley, but the deed is inscribed to their credit; that Allah may requite them with the best (possible reward).

122. It is not for the Believers to go forth together: if a contingent from

خدا ہی ہے جس کے لئے آسمانوں اور زمین کی بادشاہت
ہے۔ وہی زندگانی بخشتا اور (وہی) موت دیتا ہے اور
خدا کے سوا تمہارا کوئی دوست اور مددگار نہیں ﴿۱۱۶﴾
بے شک خدا نے پیغمبر پر مہربانی کی اور مہاجرین اور انصار
پر جو باوجود اس کے کہ ان میں سے بعضوں کے دل جلد
پھر جانے کو تھے مشکل کی گھڑی میں پیغمبر کے ساتھ رہے۔
پھر خدا نے اُن پر مہربانی فرمائی۔ بیشک وہ اُن پر نہایت
شفقت کرنے والا (اور) مہربان ہے ﴿۱۱۷﴾
اور اُن تینوں پر بھی جن کا معاملہ ملتوی کیا گیا تھا۔ یہاں
تک کہ جب زمین باوجود فراخی کے اُن پر تنگ ہوگئی اور
اُن کی جانیں بھی اُن پر دُوبھر ہوگئیں اور اُنہوں نے جان لیا
کہ خدا (کے ہاتھ) سے خود اُسکے سوا کوئی پناہ نہیں پھر خدا نے اُن پر
مہربانی کی تاکہ توبہ کریں۔ بیشک خدا توبہ قبول کرنیوالا مہربان ہے ﴿۱۱۸﴾
اے اہلِ ایمان! خدا سے ڈرتے رہو اور راستبازوں کے
ساتھ رہو ﴿۱۱۹﴾
اہل مدینہ کو اور جو اُن کے آس پاس دیہاتی رہتے ہیں اُنکو
شایاں نہ تھا کہ پیغمبر خدا سے پیچھے رہ جائیں اور نہ
یہ کہ اپنی جانوں کو اُن کی جان سے زیادہ عزیز رکھیں۔
یہ اس لئے کہ انہیں خدا کی راہ میں جو تکلیف پہنچتی ہے
پیاس کی یا محنت کی یا بھوک کی یا وہ ایسی جگہ چلتے ہیں کہ
کافروں کو غصہ آئے یا دشمنوں سے کوئی چیز لیتے ہیں تو ہر
بات پر اُن کے لئے عمل نیک لکھا جاتا ہے۔ کچھ شک نہیں
کہ خدا نیکوکاروں کا اجر ضائع نہیں کرتا ﴿۱۲۰﴾
اور (اسی طرح) وہ جو خرچ کرتے ہیں تھوڑا یا بہت یا کوئی
میدان طے کرتے ہیں تو یہ سب کچھ اُنکے لئے (اعمالِ صالحہ میں)
لکھ لیا جاتا ہے تاکہ خدا اُن کو اُنکے اعمال کا بہت اچھا بدلہ دے ﴿۱۲۱﴾
اور یہ تو ہو نہیں سکتا کہ مومن سب کے سب نکل آئیں تو یوں کیوں نہ کیا

إِنَّ اللَّهَ لَهُ مُلْكُ السَّمٰوٰتِ وَالْأَرْضِ
يُحْيِي وَيُمِيتُ وَمَا لَكُمْ مِّنْ دُونِ اللَّهِ
مِنْ وَّلِيٍّ وَّلَا نَصِيرٍ ﴿١١٦﴾
لَقَدْ تَّابَ اللَّهُ عَلَى النَّبِيِّ وَالْمُهٰجِرِينَ
وَالْأَنْصَارِ الَّذِينَ اتَّبَعُوهُ فِي سَاعَةِ
الْعُسْرَةِ مِنْ بَعْدِ مَا كَادَ يَزِيغُ قُلُوبُ
فَرِيقٍ مِّنْهُمْ ثُمَّ تَابَ عَلَيْهِمْ إِنَّهُ
بِهِمْ رَءُوفٌ رَّحِيمٌ ﴿١١٧﴾
وَّعَلَى الثَّلٰثَةِ الَّذِينَ خُلِّفُوا حَتّٰى إِذَا
ضَاقَتْ عَلَيْهِمُ الْأَرْضُ بِمَا رَحُبَتْ وَ
ضَاقَتْ عَلَيْهِمْ أَنْفُسُهُمْ وَظَنُّوا أَنْ لَّا
مَلْجَأَ مِنَ اللَّهِ إِلَّا إِلَيْهِ ثُمَّ تَابَ عَلَيْهِمْ
لِيَتُوبُوا إِنَّ اللَّهَ هُوَ التَّوَّابُ الرَّحِيمُ ﴿١١٨﴾
يٰأَيُّهَا الَّذِينَ اٰمَنُوا اتَّقُوا اللَّهَ وَكُونُوا
مَعَ الصّٰدِقِينَ ﴿١١٩﴾
مَا كَانَ لِأَهْلِ الْمَدِينَةِ وَمَنْ حَوْلَهُمْ
مِّنَ الْأَعْرَابِ أَنْ يَّتَخَلَّفُوا عَنْ رَّسُولِ
اللَّهِ وَلَا يَرْغَبُوا بِأَنْفُسِهِمْ عَنْ نَّفْسِهِ
ذٰلِكَ بِأَنَّهُمْ لَا يُصِيبُهُمْ ظَمَأٌ وَّلَا نَصَبٌ
وَّلَا مَخْمَصَةٌ فِي سَبِيلِ اللَّهِ وَلَا يَطَـُٔونَ
مَوْطِئًا يَّغِيظُ الْكُفَّارَ وَلَا يَنَالُونَ مِنْ
عَدُوٍّ نَّيْلًا إِلَّا كُتِبَ لَهُمْ بِهِ عَمَلٌ
صَالِحٌ إِنَّ اللَّهَ لَا يُضِيعُ أَجْرَ الْمُحْسِنِينَ ﴿١٢٠﴾
وَلَا يُنْفِقُونَ نَفَقَةً صَغِيرَةً وَّلَا كَبِيرَةً
وَّلَا يَقْطَعُونَ وَادِيًا إِلَّا كُتِبَ لَهُمْ
لِيَجْزِيَهُمُ اللَّهُ أَحْسَنَ مَا كَانُوا يَعْمَلُونَ ﴿١٢١﴾
وَمَا كَانَ الْمُؤْمِنُونَ لِيَنْفِرُوا كَافَّةً

every expedition go forth to devote themselves to studies in religion, and admonish the people when they return to them,—that thus they (may learn) to guard themselves (against evil).

کہ ہر ایک جماعت میں سے چند اشخاص نکل جاتے
تاکہ دین (کا علم سیکھتے اور اُس) میں سمجھ پیدا
کرتے۔ اور جب اپنی قوم کی طرف واپس آتے تو اُن کو
ڈر سناتے تاکہ وہ حذر کرتے ﴿١٢٢﴾

فَلَوْلَا نَفَرَ مِنْ كُلِّ فِرْقَةٍ مِّنْهُمْ
طَآئِفَةٌ لِّيَتَفَقَّهُوا فِي الدِّينِ وَلِيُنذِرُوا
قَوْمَهُمْ إِذَا رَجَعُوٓا إِلَيْهِمْ لَعَلَّهُمْ
يَحْذَرُونَ ﴿١٢٢﴾ ع ١٥

123. O ye who believe! Fight the Unbelievers who are near to you and let them find harshness in you: and know that Allah is with those who fear Him.

اے اہل ایمان! اپنے نزدیک کے (رہنے والے) کافروں سے
جنگ کرو۔ اور چاہیئے کہ وہ تم میں سختی (یعنی محنت و قوتِ جنگ) معلوم
کریں۔ اور جان رکھو کہ خدا پرہیزگاروں کے ساتھ ہے ﴿١٢٣﴾

يَٰٓأَيُّهَا الَّذِينَ ءَامَنُوا قَٰتِلُوا الَّذِينَ يَلُونَكُم
مِّنَ الْكُفَّارِ وَلْيَجِدُوا فِيكُمْ غِلْظَةً ۚ
وَاعْلَمُوٓا أَنَّ اللَّهَ مَعَ الْمُتَّقِينَ ﴿١٢٣﴾ الربع

124. Whenever there cometh down a Sûra, some of them say: "Which of you has had His faith increased by it?" Yea, those who believe,—their faith is increased, and they do rejoice.

اور جب کوئی سورت نازل ہوتی ہے تو بعض منافق (استہزا کرتے اور)
پوچھتے ہیں کہ اس سورت نے تم میں سے کس کا ایمان زیادہ کیا ہے۔
سو جو ایمان والے ہیں اُنکا تو ایمان زیادہ کیا اور وہ خوش ہوتے ہیں ﴿١٢٤﴾

وَإِذَا مَآ أُنزِلَتْ سُورَةٌ فَمِنْهُم مَّن يَقُولُ
أَيُّكُمْ زَادَتْهُ هَٰذِهِۦٓ إِيمَٰنًا ۚ فَأَمَّا الَّذِينَ
ءَامَنُوا فَزَادَتْهُمْ إِيمَٰنًا وَهُمْ يَسْتَبْشِرُونَ ﴿١٢٤﴾

125. But those in whose hearts is a disease,—it will add doubt to their doubt, and they will die in a state of Unbelief.

اور جن کے دلوں میں مرض ہے اُنکے حق میں خبث پر خبث زیادہ
کیا۔ اور وہ مرے بھی تو کافر کے کافر ﴿١٢٥﴾

وَأَمَّا الَّذِينَ فِي قُلُوبِهِم مَّرَضٌ فَزَادَتْهُمْ
رِجْسًا إِلَىٰ رِجْسِهِمْ وَمَاتُوا وَهُمْ كَٰفِرُونَ ﴿١٢٥﴾

126. See they not that they are tried every year once or twice? Yet they turn not in repentance, and they take no heed.

کیا یہ دیکھتے نہیں کہ یہ ہر سال ایک یا دو بار بلا میں پھنسا
دیئے جاتے ہیں پھر بھی توبہ نہیں کرتے اور نہ
نصیحت پکڑتے ہیں ﴿١٢٦﴾

أَوَلَا يَرَوْنَ أَنَّهُمْ يُفْتَنُونَ فِي كُلِّ
عَامٍ مَّرَّةً أَوْ مَرَّتَيْنِ ثُمَّ لَا يَتُوبُونَ
وَلَا هُمْ يَذَّكَّرُونَ ﴿١٢٦﴾

127. Whenever there cometh down a Sûra, they look at each other, (saying), "Doth anyone see you?" Then they turn away: Allah hath turned their hearts (from the light); for they are a people that understand not.

اور جب کوئی سورت نازل ہوتی ہے تو ایک دوسرے کی طرف
دیکھنے لگتے ہیں (اور پوچھتے ہیں کہ) بھلا تمہیں کوئی دیکھتا
ہے؟ پھر پھر جاتے ہیں۔ خدا نے اُن کے دلوں کو پھیر
رکھا ہے کیونکہ یہ ایسے لوگ ہیں کہ سمجھ سے کام نہیں لیتے ﴿١٢٧﴾

وَإِذَا مَآ أُنزِلَتْ سُورَةٌ نَّظَرَ بَعْضُهُمْ
إِلَىٰ بَعْضٍ هَلْ يَرَىٰكُم مِّنْ أَحَدٍ ثُمَّ
انصَرَفُوا ۚ صَرَفَ اللَّهُ قُلُوبَهُم بِأَنَّهُمْ
قَوْمٌ لَّا يَفْقَهُونَ ﴿١٢٧﴾

128. Now hath come unto you a Messenger from amongst yourselves: it grieves him that ye should suffer, ardently anxious is he over you: to the Believers is he most kind and merciful.

(لوگو) تمہارے پاس تم ہی میں سے ایک پیغمبر آئے ہیں تمہاری
تکلیف اُن کو گراں معلوم ہوتی ہے اور تمہاری بھلائی کے بہت
خواہشمند ہیں۔ اور مومنوں پر نہایت شفقت کرنیوالے (اور) مہربان ہیں ﴿١٢٨﴾

لَقَدْ جَآءَكُمْ رَسُولٌ مِّنْ أَنفُسِكُمْ عَزِيزٌ
عَلَيْهِ مَا عَنِتُّمْ حَرِيصٌ عَلَيْكُم بِالْمُؤْمِنِينَ
رَءُوفٌ رَّحِيمٌ ﴿١٢٨﴾

129. But if they turn away, say: "Allah sufficeth me: there is no god but He on Him is my trust,— He the Lord of the Throne Supreme!"

پھر اگر یہ لوگ پھر جائیں (اور نہ مانیں) تو کہہ دو کہ خدا مجھے
کفایت کرتا ہے اُس کے سوا کوئی معبود نہیں۔ اُسی پر میرا
بھروسا ہے اور وہی عرش عظیم کا مالک ہے ﴿١٢٩﴾

فَإِن تَوَلَّوْا فَقُلْ حَسْبِيَ اللَّهُ لَآ إِلَٰهَ
إِلَّا هُوَ ۖ عَلَيْهِ تَوَكَّلْتُ ۖ وَهُوَ رَبُّ
الْعَرْشِ الْعَظِيمِ ﴿١٢٩﴾ ع ١٦

SÛRA–10
YÛNUS
(INTRODUCTION)

Chronologically this Sûra and the five that follow (Sûras 9, 12, 13, 14, and 15) are closely connected, and were revealed in the late Makkan period, as the great event of the Hijrat was gradually approaching down the stream of Time. But their chronology has no particular significance.

On the other hand their arrangement in the gradation of Quranic teaching fits in with the subject-matter. S. 8 and S. 9 were mainly concerned with the first questions that arose on the formation of the new and organised Community of Islam in its conflict with those who wished to suppress or destroy it or use force to prevent its growth and the consolidation of its ideals. See Introductions to those Sûras. The present group leads us to the questions that face us when external hostility has been met, and our relations to Allah have to be considered from a higher standpoint than that of sale-preservation. How does revelation work? What is the meaning of divine grace and its withdrawal? How do the Messengers of Allah deliver their Message? How should we receive it?

All these question revolve round the revelation of the Qur-ãn and each Sûra of this group except the 13 has the Abbreviated Letters A.L.R. attached to it. S. 13 has the letters A.L.M.R., and we shall discuss this variation when we come to S. 13.

The Abbreviated Letters are mystic symbols, about whose meaning there is no authoritative explanation. If the present group A.L.R. is cognate to the group A.L.M., we have to consider and form some idea in our minds as to the probable meaning of the variation. We think A.L.M. to be a symbol of those Sûras that deal with the beginning, the middle, and the end of man's spiritual history,—the origin, the present position, and the things to come in the Last Days (eschatology, to use a theological term). A.L. stand as symbols of the first two, and M. of the last. In the present group of Sûras we find hardly any eschatological matter, and therefore we can understand the absence of M., the symbol standing for such matter. In its place comes R., which is phonetically allied to L.L. is produced by the impact of the tongue to the front of the palate, and R. to the middle of the palate. In many languages the letters L. and R. are interchangeable; e.g. in Arabic, al-Raḥmãn becomes ar-Raḥmãn, and R. in imperfect enunciation becomes L., as in Chinese lallations. If L. is a symbol of present-day things looking to the future, we may take R. as a symbol of present-day things looking within, i.e. into the interior of the organisation of the Ummat. And this symbolism fits in with the subject-matter of the Sûras in question. But no one should be dogmatic in speculation about mystic Symbols.

Let us now consider Sûra 10 alone. The central theme is that Allah's wonderful Creation must not be viewed by us as a creation of material things only, once made and finished with. Most wonderful of all is how He reveals Himself to men through Apostles and Scriptures; how apostles are rejected by men, and the Message disbelieved until it is too late for repentance; and how, as in the case of Yûnus (Jonah) and his people, even the rejection (when repentance supervenes) does not prevent Allah's grace and mercy from working, and how far that working is beyond man's comprehension.

Yûnus, or Jonah

In the name of Allah, Most Gracious, Most Merciful

1. **A. L. R.** These are the Ayats of the Book of Wisdom.

2. Is it a matter of wonderment to men that We have sent our inspiration to a man from among themselves?—that he should warn mankind (of their danger), and give the good news to the Believers that they have before their Lord the good actions they have advanced (but) say the Unbelievers: "This is indeed an evident sorcerer!"

3. Verily your Lord is Allah, who created the heavens and the earth in six Days, then He established Himself on the Throne, regulating and governing all things. No intercessor (can plead with Him) except after His leave (hath been obtained). This is Allah your Lord; Him therefore serve ye; will ye not receive admonition?

4. To Him will be your return—of all of you. The promise of Allah is true and sure. It is He who beginneth the process of creation, and repeateth it, that He may reward with justice those who believe and work righteousness; but those who reject Him will have draughts of boiling fluids, and a Chastisement grievous, because they did reject Him.

5. It is He Who made the sun to be a shining glory and the moon to be a light (of beauty), and measured out stages for it, that ye might know the number of years and the count (of time). Nowise did Allah create this but in truth and righteousness. (Thus) doth He explain His Signs in detail, for those who know!

6. Verily, in the alternation of the Night and the Day, and in all that Allah hath created, in the heavens and the earth, are Signs for those who fear Him.

7. Those who rest not their hope on their meeting with Us, but are pleased and satisfied with the life of the Present, and those who heed

سورۂ یونس مکی ہے اور اسمیں ایک سو نو آیتیں اور گیارہ رکوع ہیں

شروع خدا کا نام لے کر جو بڑا مہربان نہایت رحم والا ہے
آلرا یہ بڑی دانائی کی کتاب کی آیتیں ہیں (۱)
کیا لوگوں کو تعجب ہوا کہ ہم نے اُنہی میں سے ایک
مرد کو حکم بھیجا کہ لوگوں کو ڈر سنا دو اور ایمان
لانے والوں کو خوشخبری دے دو کہ ان کے پروردگار
کے ہاں ان کا سچا درجہ ہے (ایسے شخص کی نسبت) کافر کہتے
ہیں کہ یہ تو صریح جادوگر ہے (۲)
تمہارا پروردگار تو خدا ہی ہے جس نے آسمان اور زمین چھ
دن میں بنائے پھر عرش (تخت شاہی) پر قائم ہوا وہی
ہر ایک کام کا انتظام کرتا ہے۔ کوئی (اسکے پاس) اس کا اذن
حاصل کئے بغیر کسی کی سفارش نہیں کر سکتا یہی خدا تمہارا
پروردگار ہے تو اُسی کی عبادت کرو۔ بھلا تم غور کیوں نہیں کرتے (۳)
اسی کے پاس تم سب کو لوٹ کر جانا ہے۔ خدا کا وعدہ سچا ہے۔
وہی خلقت کو پہلی بار پیدا کرتا ہے۔ پھر وہی اس کو دوبارہ
پیدا کرے گا تاکہ ایمان والوں اور نیک کام کرنے والوں کو
انصاف کیساتھ بدلہ دے۔ اور جو کافر ہیں اُنکے لئے پینے کو نہایت
گرم پانی اور درد دینے والا عذاب ہوگا کیونکہ (خدا سے) انکار کرتے تھے (۴)
وہی تو ہے جس نے سورج کو روشن اور چاند کو منور بنایا
اور چاند کی منزلیں مقرر کیں تاکہ تم برسوں کا شمار اور (کاموں کا)
حساب معلوم کرو۔ یہ (سب کچھ) خدا نے تدبیر سے پیدا کیا ہے
سمجھنے والوں کیلئے وہ اپنی آیتیں کھول کھول کر بیان فرماتا ہے (۵)
رات اور دن کے (ایک دوسرے کے پیچھے) آنے جانے میں
اور جو چیزیں خدا نے آسمان اور زمین میں پیدا کی ہیں (سب)
میں ڈرنے والوں کے لئے نشانیاں ہیں (۶)
جن لوگوں کو ہم سے ملنے کی توقع نہیں اور دنیا کی زندگی
سے خوش اور اسی پر مطمئن ہو بیٹھے اور ہماری نشانیوں سے

سورة يونس مكية وهي مائة وتسع ايات واحد عشر ركوعا

المنزل الثالث ۳

بِسْمِ اللّٰهِ الرَّحْمٰنِ الرَّحِيْمِ
الٓرٰ تِلْكَ اٰيٰتُ الْكِتٰبِ الْحَكِيْمِ (۱)
اَكَانَ لِلنَّاسِ عَجَبًا اَنْ اَوْحَيْنَآ اِلٰى
رَجُلٍ مِّنْهُمْ اَنْ اَنْذِرِ النَّاسَ وَبَشِّرِ
الَّذِيْنَ اٰمَنُوْٓا اَنَّ لَهُمْ قَدَمَ صِدْقٍ
عِنْدَ رَبِّهِمْ ؕ قَالَ الْكٰفِرُوْنَ اِنَّ
هٰذَا لَسٰحِرٌ مُّبِيْنٌ (۲)
اِنَّ رَبَّكُمُ اللّٰهُ الَّذِيْ خَلَقَ السَّمٰوٰتِ
وَالْاَرْضَ فِيْ سِتَّةِ اَيَّامٍ ثُمَّ اسْتَوٰى
عَلَى الْعَرْشِ يُدَبِّرُ الْاَمْرَ ؕ مَا مِنْ
شَفِيْعٍ اِلَّا مِنْۢ بَعْدِ اِذْنِهٖ ؕ ذٰلِكُمُ اللّٰهُ
رَبُّكُمْ فَاعْبُدُوْهُ ؕ اَفَلَا تَذَكَّرُوْنَ (۳)
اِلَيْهِ مَرْجِعُكُمْ جَمِيْعًا ؕ وَعْدَ اللّٰهِ حَقًّا ؕ
اِنَّهٗ يَبْدَؤُا الْخَلْقَ ثُمَّ يُعِيْدُهٗ لِيَجْزِيَ
الَّذِيْنَ اٰمَنُوْا وَعَمِلُوا الصّٰلِحٰتِ بِالْقِسْطِ ؕ
وَالَّذِيْنَ كَفَرُوْا لَهُمْ شَرَابٌ مِّنْ حَمِيْمٍ
وَّعَذَابٌ اَلِيْمٌۢ بِمَا كَانُوْا يَكْفُرُوْنَ (۴)
هُوَ الَّذِيْ جَعَلَ الشَّمْسَ ضِيَآءً وَّالْقَمَرَ
نُوْرًا وَّقَدَّرَهٗ مَنَازِلَ لِتَعْلَمُوْا عَدَدَ
السِّنِيْنَ وَالْحِسَابَ ؕ مَا خَلَقَ اللّٰهُ ذٰلِكَ
اِلَّا بِالْحَقِّ ۚ يُفَصِّلُ الْاٰيٰتِ لِقَوْمٍ يَّعْلَمُوْنَ (۵)
اِنَّ فِي اخْتِلَافِ الَّيْلِ وَالنَّهَارِ وَمَا خَلَقَ
اللّٰهُ فِي السَّمٰوٰتِ وَالْاَرْضِ لَاٰيٰتٍ
لِّقَوْمٍ يَّتَّقُوْنَ (۶)
اِنَّ الَّذِيْنَ لَا يَرْجُوْنَ لِقَآءَنَا وَرَضُوْا
بِالْحَيٰوةِ الدُّنْيَا وَاطْمَاَنُّوْا بِهَا وَالَّذِيْنَ

وقف النبي صلى الله عليه وسلم

not Our Signs,—

8. Their abode is the Fire, because of the (evil) they earned.

9. Those who believe, and work righteousness,— their Lord will guide them because of their Faith: beneath them will flow rivers in Gardens of Bliss.

10. (This will be) their prayer therein: "Glory to Thee, O Allah!" and "Peace" will be their greeting therein and the end of their prayer will be: "Praise be to Allah, the Cherisher and Sustainer of the Worlds!"

11. If Allah were to hasten for men the ill (they have earned) as they would fain hasten on the good,— then would their respite be settled at once. But We leave those who rest not their hope on their meeting with Us, in their trespasses, wandering in distraction blindly.

12. When trouble toucheth a man, he crieth unto Us (in all postures)— lying down on his side, or sitting, or standing. But when We have removed his affliction, he passeth on his way as if he had never cried to Us for the affliction that touched him! Thus do the deeds of transgressors seem fair in their eyes!

13. Generations before you We destroyed when they did wrong: their Messengers came to them with clear Signs, but they would not believe! Thus do We requite those who sin!

14. Then We made you heirs in the land after them, to see how ye would behave!

15. But when Our clear Signs are rehearsed unto them, those who rest not their hope on their meeting with Us, say: "Bring us a Qur'an other than this, or change this," Say: "It is not for me, of my own accord, to change it: I follow naught

غافل ہو رہے ہیں ﴿٧﴾
اُن کا ٹھکانا اُن (اعمال) کے سبب جو وہ کرتے ہیں دوزخ ہے ﴿٨﴾
اور جو لوگ ایمان لائے اور نیک کام کرتے رہے اُن کو
پروردگار اُنکے ایمان کی وجہ سے (ایسے محلوں کی) راہ دکھائیگا
(کہ) ان کے نیچے نعمت کے باغوں میں نہریں بہ رہی ہونگی ﴿٩﴾
(جب وہ) اُن میں (اُن کی نعمتوں کو دیکھیں گے تو بیساختہ
کہینگے سُبحان اللہ۔ اور آپس میں اُنکی دعا سلامٌ علیکم ہوگی۔ اور اُنکا
آخری قول یہ (ہوگا) کہ خدائے ربّ العالمین کی حمد (اور اُسکا شکر) ہے ﴿١٠﴾
اور اگر خدا لوگوں کی بُرائی میں جلدی کرتا جس طرح وہ طلبِ خیر
میں جلدی کرتے ہیں تو ان کی (عمر کی) میعاد پوری ہو چکی
ہوتی۔ سو جن لوگوں کو ہم سے ملنے کی توقع نہیں انہیں ہم
چھوڑے رکھتے ہیں کہ اپنی سرکشی میں بہکتے رہیں ﴿١١﴾
اور جب انسان کو تکلیف پہنچتی ہے تو لیٹا اور بیٹھا اور کھڑا
(ہر حال میں) ہمیں پکارتا ہے۔ پھر جب ہم اس تکلیف کو اُس
سے دُور کر دیتے ہیں تو (بے لحاظ ہو جاتا اور) اس طرح گزر جاتا ہے
کہ گویا کسی تکلیف پہنچنے پر ہمیں کبھی پکارا ہی نہ تھا اسی طرح حد سے
نکل جانے والوں کو اُنکے اعمال آراستہ کر کے دکھائے گئے ہیں ﴿١٢﴾
اور تم سے پہلے ہم کئی اُمتوں کو جب اُنہوں نے ظلم اختیار کیا
ہلاک کر چکے ہیں۔ اور اُن کے پاس پیغمبر کھلی نشانیاں لیکر
آئے مگر وہ ایسے نہ تھے کہ ایمان لاتے۔ ہم گنہگاروں کو
اسی طرح بدلہ دیا کرتے ہیں ﴿١٣﴾
پھر ہم نے ان کے بعد تم لوگوں کو مُلک میں خلیفہ بنایا
تاکہ دیکھیں کہ تم کیسے کام کرتے ہو ﴿١٤﴾
اور جب ان کو ہماری آیتیں پڑھ کر سُنائی جاتی ہیں تو جن
لوگوں کو ہم سے ملنے کی اُمید نہیں وہ کہتے ہیں کہ (یا تو)
اس کے سوا کوئی اور قرآن (بنا) لاؤ یا اس کو بدل دو۔
کہہ دو کہ مجھ کو اختیار نہیں ہے کہ اسے اپنی طرف سے بدل

هُمْ عَنْ آيَاتِنَا غَافِلُونَ ﴿٧﴾
أُولَٰئِكَ مَأْوَاهُمُ النَّارُ بِمَا كَانُوا يَكْسِبُونَ ﴿٨﴾
إِنَّ الَّذِينَ آمَنُوا وَعَمِلُوا الصَّالِحَاتِ يَهْدِيهِمْ
رَبُّهُم بِإِيمَانِهِمْ ۖ تَجْرِي مِن تَحْتِهِمُ
الْأَنْهَارُ فِي جَنَّاتِ النَّعِيمِ ﴿٩﴾
دَعْوَاهُمْ فِيهَا سُبْحَانَكَ اللَّهُمَّ وَتَحِيَّتُهُمْ
فِيهَا سَلَامٌ ۚ وَآخِرُ دَعْوَاهُمْ أَنِ الْحَمْدُ
لِلَّهِ رَبِّ الْعَالَمِينَ ﴿١٠﴾ ع
وَلَوْ يُعَجِّلُ اللَّهُ لِلنَّاسِ الشَّرَّ اسْتِعْجَالَهُم
بِالْخَيْرِ لَقُضِيَ إِلَيْهِمْ أَجَلُهُمْ ۖ فَنَذَرُ
الَّذِينَ لَا يَرْجُونَ لِقَاءَنَا فِي طُغْيَانِهِمْ
يَعْمَهُونَ ﴿١١﴾
وَإِذَا مَسَّ الْإِنسَانَ الضُّرُّ دَعَانَا لِجَنبِهِ
أَوْ قَاعِدًا أَوْ قَائِمًا فَلَمَّا كَشَفْنَا عَنْهُ
ضُرَّهُ مَرَّ كَأَن لَّمْ يَدْعُنَا إِلَىٰ ضُرٍّ
مَّسَّهُ ۚ كَذَٰلِكَ زُيِّنَ لِلْمُسْرِفِينَ مَا
كَانُوا يَعْمَلُونَ ﴿١٢﴾
وَلَقَدْ أَهْلَكْنَا الْقُرُونَ مِن قَبْلِكُمْ
لَمَّا ظَلَمُوا ۙ وَجَاءَتْهُمْ رُسُلُهُم بِالْبَيِّنَاتِ
وَمَا كَانُوا لِيُؤْمِنُوا ۚ كَذَٰلِكَ نَجْزِي
الْقَوْمَ الْمُجْرِمِينَ ﴿١٣﴾
ثُمَّ جَعَلْنَاكُمْ خَلَائِفَ فِي الْأَرْضِ مِن
بَعْدِهِمْ لِنَنظُرَ كَيْفَ تَعْمَلُونَ ﴿١٤﴾
وَإِذَا تُتْلَىٰ عَلَيْهِمْ آيَاتُنَا بَيِّنَاتٍ ۙ قَالَ
الَّذِينَ لَا يَرْجُونَ لِقَاءَنَا ائْتِ بِقُرْآنٍ
غَيْرِ هَٰذَا أَوْ بَدِّلْهُ ۚ قُلْ مَا يَكُونُ لِي
أَنْ أُبَدِّلَهُ مِن تِلْقَاءِ نَفْسِي ۖ إِنْ

but what is revealed unto me: if I were to disobey my Lord, I should myself fear the Chastisement of a Great Day (to come)."

دوں۔ میں تو اسی حکم کا تابع ہوں جو میری طرف آتا ہے۔ اگر میں اپنے
پروردگار کی نافرمانی کروں تو مجھے بڑے (سخت) دن کے عذاب سے خوف آتا ہے ﴿۱۵﴾

اَتَّبِعُ اِلَّا مَا يُوْحٰٓى اِلَيَّ ۚ اِنِّيْٓ اَخَافُ اِنْ
عَصَيْتُ رَبِّيْ عَذَابَ يَوْمٍ عَظِيْمٍ ﴿۱۵﴾

16. Say: "If Allah had so willed, I should not have rehearsed it to you, nor should He have made it known to you. A whole life-time before this have I tarried amongst you: will ye not then understand?"

(یہ بھی) کہہ دو کہ اگر خدا چاہتا تو (نہ تو) میں ہی یہ کتاب تم کو پڑھ کر سناتا
اور نہ وہی تمہیں اس سے واقف کرتا۔ میں اس سے پہلے تم میں ایک عمر رہا
ہوں (اور کبھی ایک کلمہ بھی اس طرح کا نہیں کہا) بھلا تم سمجھتے نہیں ﴿۱۶﴾

قُلْ لَّوْ شَآءَ اللّٰهُ مَا تَلَوْتُهٗ عَلَيْكُمْ وَلَآ
اَدْرٰىكُمْ بِهٖ ۖ فَقَدْ لَبِثْتُ فِيْكُمْ عُمُرًا
مِّنْ قَبْلِهٖ ۭ اَفَلَا تَعْقِلُوْنَ ﴿۱۶﴾

17. Who doth more wrong than such as forge a lie against Allah, or deny His Signs? But never will prosper those who sin.

تو اس سے بڑھ کر ظالم کون ہوگا جو خدا پر جھوٹ افترا کرے
اور اس کی آیتوں کو جھٹلائے؟ بے شک گنہگار فلاح
نہیں پائیں گے ﴿۱۷﴾

فَمَنْ اَظْلَمُ مِمَّنِ افْتَرٰى عَلَى اللّٰهِ
كَذِبًا اَوْ كَذَّبَ بِاٰيٰتِهٖ ۭ اِنَّهٗ لَا يُفْلِحُ
الْمُجْرِمُوْنَ ﴿۱۷﴾

18. They serve, besides Allah, what can hurt them not nor profit them, and they say: "These are our intercessors with Allah." Say: "Do ye indeed inform Allah of something He knows not, in the heavens or on earth?—Glory to Him! And far is He above the partners they ascribe (to Him)!"

اور یہ (لوگ) خدا کے سوا ایسی چیزوں کی پرستش کرتے ہیں
جو نہ ان کا کچھ بگاڑ ہی سکتی ہیں اور نہ کچھ بھلا ہی کرسکتی ہیں۔ اور کہتے
ہیں کہ یہ خدا کے پاس ہماری سفارش کرنے والے ہیں۔ کہہ دو کیا تم
خدا کو ایسی چیز بتاتے ہو جس کا وجود اسے نہ آسمانوں میں معلوم ہے
اور نہ زمین میں؟ وہ پاک ہے اور (اس کی شان) ان کے شرک کرنے سے بہت بلند ہے ﴿۱۸﴾

وَيَعْبُدُوْنَ مِنْ دُوْنِ اللّٰهِ مَا لَا يَضُرُّهُمْ
وَلَا يَنْفَعُهُمْ وَيَقُوْلُوْنَ هٰٓؤُلَاۗءِ شُفَعَاۗؤُنَا
عِنْدَ اللّٰهِ ۭ قُلْ اَتُنَبِّـــُٔوْنَ اللّٰهَ بِمَا لَا يَعْلَمُ
فِي السَّمٰوٰتِ وَلَا فِي الْاَرْضِ ۭ سُبْحٰنَهٗ
وَتَعٰلٰى عَمَّا يُشْرِكُوْنَ ﴿۱۸﴾

19. Mankind was but one nation, but differed (later). Had it not been for a Word that went forth before from thy Lord, their differences would have been settled between them.

اور (سب) لوگ (پہلے) ایک ہی امت (یعنی ایک ہی ملت پر) تھے پھر
جدا جدا ہوگئے۔ اور اگر ایک بات جو تمہارے پروردگار کی طرف سے پہلے
ہوچکی ہے نہ ہوتی تو جن باتوں میں وہ اختلاف کرتے ہیں ان میں فیصلہ کردیا جاتا ﴿۱۹﴾

وَمَا كَانَ النَّاسُ اِلَّآ اُمَّةً وَّاحِدَةً
فَاخْتَلَفُوْا ۭ وَلَوْلَا كَلِمَةٌ سَبَقَتْ مِنْ
رَّبِّكَ لَقُضِيَ بَيْنَهُمْ فِيْمَا فِيْهِ يَخْتَلِفُوْنَ ﴿۱۹﴾

20. They say: "Why is not a Sign sent down to him from his Lord?" Say: "The Unseen is only for Allah (to know). Then wait ye: I too will wait with you".

اور کہتے ہیں کہ اس پر اس کے پروردگار کی طرف سے کوئی نشانی کیوں نازل
نہیں ہوئی؟ کہہ دو کہ غیب (کا علم) تو خدا ہی کو ہے سو تم انتظار
کرو میں بھی تمہارے ساتھ انتظار کرتا ہوں ﴿۲۰﴾

وَيَقُوْلُوْنَ لَوْلَآ اُنْزِلَ عَلَيْهِ اٰيَةٌ مِّنْ
رَّبِّهٖ ۚ فَقُلْ اِنَّمَا الْغَيْبُ لِلّٰهِ فَانْتَظِرُوْا ۚ
اِنِّيْ مَعَكُمْ مِّنَ الْمُنْتَظِرِيْنَ ﴿۲۰﴾ ع

21. When We make mankind taste of some mercy after adversity hath touched them, behold! they take to plotting against Our Signs! Say: "Swifter to plan is Allah!" Verily, Our messengers record all the plots that ye make!"

اور جب ہم لوگوں کو تکلیف پہنچنے کے بعد (اپنی) رحمت (سے
آسائش) کا مزہ چکھاتے ہیں تو وہ ہماری آیتوں میں حیلے کرنے
لگتے ہیں۔ کہہ دو کہ خدا بہت جلد حیلہ کرنے والا ہے اور جو حیلے
تم کرتے ہو ہمارے فرشتے ان کو لکھتے جاتے ہیں ﴿۲۱﴾

وَاِذَآ اَذَقْنَا النَّاسَ رَحْمَةً مِّنْۢ بَعْدِ
ضَرَّاۗءَ مَسَّتْهُمْ اِذَا لَهُمْ مَّكْرٌ فِيْٓ اٰيَاتِنَا ۭ
قُلِ اللّٰهُ اَسْرَعُ مَكْرًا ۭ اِنَّ رُسُلَنَا يَكْتُبُوْنَ
مَا تَمْكُرُوْنَ ﴿۲۱﴾

22. He it is who enableth you to traverse through land and sea; till when ye even board ships;—they sail with them with a favourable wind, and they rejoice thereat; then comes a stormy wind and the waves come to them from all sides,

وہی تو ہے جو تم کو جنگل اور دریا میں چلنے پھرنے اور سیر کرنے کی
توفیق دیتا ہے۔ یہاں تک کہ جب تم کشتیوں میں (سوار) ہوتے ہو اور کشتیاں
پاکیزہ ہوا کے نرم نرم جھونکوں سے سواروں کو لے کر چلنے لگتی ہیں اور وہ ان سے
خوش ہوتے ہیں تو ناگہاں زناٹے کی ہوا چل پڑتی ہے اور لہریں ہر طرف سے

هُوَ الَّذِيْ يُسَيِّرُكُمْ فِي الْبَرِّ وَالْبَحْرِ ۭ حَتّٰى
اِذَا كُنْتُمْ فِي الْفُلْكِ ۚ وَجَرَيْنَ بِهِمْ بِرِيْحٍ
طَيِّبَةٍ وَّفَرِحُوْا بِهَا جَاۗءَتْهَا رِيْحٌ عَاصِفٌ
وَّجَاۗءَهُمُ الْمَوْجُ مِنْ كُلِّ مَكَانٍ وَّظَنُّوْٓا

and they think they are being
overwhelmed: they pray unto Allah,
sincerely offering (their) duty unto
Him, saying, "If Thou dost deliver
us from this, we shall truly show
our gratitude!"
23. But when he delivereth them,
behold! they transgress insolently
through the earth in defiance of right!
O mankind! your insolence is against
your own souls,—an enjoyment of
the life of the Present: in the end, to
Us is your return, and We shall show
you the truth of all that ye did.
24. The likeness of the life of the
Present is as the rain which We
send down from the skies: by its
mingling arises the produce of the
earth—which provides food for men
and animals: (it grows) till the earth
is clad with its golden ornaments
and is decked out (in beauty): the
people to whom it belongs think they
have all powers of disposal over it:
there reaches it Our command by
night or by day, and We make it like
a harvest clean-mown, as if it had
not flourished only the day before!
Thus do We explain the Signs in
detail for those who reflect.
25. But Allah doth call to the
Home of Peace: He doth guide
whom He pleaseth to a Way that is
straight.
26. To those who do right is a
goodly (reward)—Yea, more (than
in measure)! No darkness nor
abasement shall cover their faces!
They will Companions of the Garden;
they will abide therein (for aye)!
27. But those who have earned
evil will have a reward of like evil:
ignominy will cover their (faces): no
defender will they have from (the
wrath of) Allah: their faces will be
covered, as it were, with pieces from
the depth of the darkness of Night:
they are Inhabitants of the Fire: they
will abide therein (for aye)!
28. One Day shall We gather
them all together. Then shall We
say to those who joined gods (with
Us): "To your place! ye and those
ye joined as 'partners'." We shall

اُن پر جوش مارتی ہوئی آنے لگتی ہیں اور وہ خیال کرتے ہیں کہ (اب تو) لہروں
میں گھر گئے۔ تو اُس وقت خالص خدا ہی کی عبادت کر کے اُس سے دعا مانگنے لگتے ہیں
(کہ اے خدا) اگر تو ہم کو اس سے نجات بخشے تو ہم (تیرے) بہت ہی شکر گزار ہوں ﴿۲۲﴾
لیکن جب وہ انکو نجات دے دیتا ہے تو ملک میں ناحق شرارت کرنے
لگتے ہیں۔ لوگو! تمہاری شرارت کا وبال تمہاری ہی جانوں پر ہو گا
تم دنیا کی زندگی کے فائدے اٹھا لو پھر تم کو ہمارے ہی پاس لوٹ کر
آنا ہے۔ اُس وقت ہم تم کو بتائیں گے جو کچھ تم کیا کرتے تھے ﴿۲۳﴾
دنیا کی زندگی کی مثال مینہ کی سی ہے کہ ہم نے اُسکو آسمان سے برسایا۔
پھر اسکے ساتھ سبزہ جسے آدمی اور جانور کھاتے ہیں مل کر نکلا یہانتک
کہ زمین سبزے سے خوشنما اور آراستہ ہو گئی۔ اور زمین والوں نے خیال کیا
کہ وہ اس پر پوری دسترس رکھتے ہیں ناگہاں رات کو یا دن کو ہمارا حکم
(عذاب) آپہنچا تو ہم نے اس کو کاٹ (کر ایسا کر) ڈالا کہ
گویا کل وہاں کچھ تھا ہی نہیں۔ جو لوگ غور کرنے والے
ہیں اُن کے لئے ہم (اپنی قدرت کی) نشانیاں اسی
طرح کھول کھول کر بیان کرتے ہیں ﴿۲۴﴾
اور خدا سلامتی کے گھر کی طرف بلاتا ہے اور جس کو چاہتا
ہے سیدھا رستہ دکھاتا ہے ﴿۲۵﴾
جن لوگوں نے نیکوکاری کی اُن کے لئے بھلائی ہے اور
(مزید برآں) اور بھی۔ اور ان کے مونہوں پر نہ تو سیاہی چھائے گی
اور نہ رسوائی۔ یہی جنتی ہیں کہ اس میں ہمیشہ رہیں گے ﴿۲۶﴾
اور جنہوں نے بُرے کام کئے تو بُرائی کا بدلہ ویسا ہی ہو گا
اور انکے مونہوں پر ذلت چھا جائے گی۔ اور کوئی ان کو خدا
سے بچانے والا نہ ہو گا۔ انکے مونہوں (کی سیاہی کا یہ عالم
ہو گا کہ ان) پر گویا اندھیری رات کے ٹکڑے اُڑھا دیئے
گئے ہیں۔ یہی دوزخی ہیں کہ ہمیشہ اس میں رہیں گے ﴿۲۷﴾
اور جس دن ہم ان سب کو جمع کریں گے پھر مشرکوں سے کہیں گے کہ تم اور
تمہارے شریک اپنی اپنی جگہ ٹھہرے رہو۔ تو ہم انمیں تفرقہ ڈال

أَنَّهُمْ أُحِيطَ بِهِمْ دَعَوُا اللَّهَ مُخْلِصِينَ
لَهُ الدِّينَ لَئِنْ أَنْجَيْتَنَا مِنْ هَٰذِهِ
لَنَكُونَنَّ مِنَ الشَّاكِرِينَ ﴿٢٢﴾
فَلَمَّا أَنْجَاهُمْ إِذَا هُمْ يَبْغُونَ فِي الْأَرْضِ
بِغَيْرِ الْحَقِّ يَا أَيُّهَا النَّاسُ إِنَّمَا بَغْيُكُمْ
عَلَىٰ أَنْفُسِكُمْ مَتَاعَ الْحَيَاةِ الدُّنْيَا ثُمَّ
إِلَيْنَا مَرْجِعُكُمْ فَنُنَبِّئُكُمْ بِمَا كُنْتُمْ تَعْمَلُونَ ﴿٢٣﴾
إِنَّمَا مَثَلُ الْحَيَاةِ الدُّنْيَا كَمَاءٍ أَنْزَلْنَاهُ
مِنَ السَّمَاءِ فَاخْتَلَطَ بِهِ نَبَاتُ الْأَرْضِ
مِمَّا يَأْكُلُ النَّاسُ وَالْأَنْعَامُ حَتَّىٰ
إِذَا أَخَذَتِ الْأَرْضُ زُخْرُفَهَا وَازَّيَّنَتْ
وَظَنَّ أَهْلُهَا أَنَّهُمْ قَادِرُونَ عَلَيْهَا
أَتَاهَا أَمْرُنَا لَيْلًا أَوْ نَهَارًا فَجَعَلْنَاهَا
حَصِيدًا كَأَنْ لَمْ تَغْنَ بِالْأَمْسِ كَذَٰلِكَ
نُفَصِّلُ الْآيَاتِ لِقَوْمٍ يَتَفَكَّرُونَ ﴿٢٤﴾
وَاللَّهُ يَدْعُو إِلَىٰ دَارِ السَّلَامِ وَيَهْدِي
مَنْ يَشَاءُ إِلَىٰ صِرَاطٍ مُسْتَقِيمٍ ﴿٢٥﴾
لِلَّذِينَ أَحْسَنُوا الْحُسْنَىٰ وَزِيَادَةٌ وَلَا
يَرْهَقُ وُجُوهَهُمْ قَتَرٌ وَلَا ذِلَّةٌ أُولَٰئِكَ
أَصْحَابُ الْجَنَّةِ هُمْ فِيهَا خَالِدُونَ ﴿٢٦﴾
وَالَّذِينَ كَسَبُوا السَّيِّئَاتِ جَزَاءُ سَيِّئَةٍ
بِمِثْلِهَا وَتَرْهَقُهُمْ ذِلَّةٌ مَا لَهُمْ مِنَ
اللَّهِ مِنْ عَاصِمٍ كَأَنَّمَا أُغْشِيَتْ وُجُوهُهُمْ
قِطَعًا مِنَ اللَّيْلِ مُظْلِمًا أُولَٰئِكَ أَصْحَابُ
النَّارِ هُمْ فِيهَا خَالِدُونَ ﴿٢٧﴾
وَيَوْمَ نَحْشُرُهُمْ جَمِيعًا ثُمَّ نَقُولُ لِلَّذِينَ
أَشْرَكُوا مَكَانَكُمْ أَنْتُمْ وَشُرَكَاؤُكُمْ فَزَيَّلْنَا بَيْنَهُمْ

separate them, and their "partners" shall say: "It was not us that ye worshipped!
29. "Enough is Allah for a witness between us and you: we certainly knew nothing of your worship of us!"
30. There will every soul see (the fruits of) the deeds it sent before: they will be brought back to Allah their rightful Lord, and their invented falsehoods will leave them in the lurch.
31. Say: "Who is it that sustains you (in life) from the sky and from the earth? Or who is it that has power over hearing and sight? And who is it that brings out the living from the dead and the dead from the living? And who is it that rules and regulates all affairs?" They will soon say, "Allah". Say, "Will ye not then show piety (to Him)?"
32. Such is Allah, your true Lord: apart from the Truth, what (remains) but error? How then are ye turned away?
33. Thus is the Word of thy Lord proved true against those who rebel: verily they will not believe.
34. Say: "Of your 'partners', can any originate creation and repeat it?" Say: "It is Allah Who originates creation and repeats it: then how are ye deluded away (from the truth)?"
35. Say: "Of your 'partners' is there any that can give any guidance towards Truth?" Say: "It is Allah Who gives guidance towards Truth. Is then He Who gives guidance to Truth more worthy to be followed, or he who finds not guidance (Himself) unless he is guided? What then is the matter with you? How judge ye?
36. But most of them follow nothing but conjecture: truly conjecture can be of no avail against Truth. Verily Allah is well aware of all that they do.
37. This Qur'an is not such as can be produced by other than Allah; on the contrary it is a confirmation of (revelations) that

دینگے اور اُنکے شریک (اُنسے) کہینگے کہ تم ہمکو تو نہیں پوجا کرتے تھے ﴿۲۸﴾
ہمارے اور تمہارے درمیان خدا ہی گواہ کافی ہے۔ ہم تمہاری
پرستش سے بالکل بے خبر تھے ﴿۲۹﴾
وہاں ہر شخص (اپنے اعمال کی) جو اُس نے آگے بھیجے ہونگے
آزمائش کرلے گا ۱۲۵ اور وہ اپنے سچے مالک کی طرف لوٹائے
جائینگے اور جو کچھ وہ بہتان باندھا کرتے تھے سب اُنسے جاتا رہیگا ﴿۳۰﴾
(اُن سے) پوچھو کہ تم کو آسمان اور زمین میں رزق کون دیتا
ہے یا (تمہارے) کانوں اور آنکھوں کا مالک کون ہے اور بے جان
سے جاندار کون پیدا کرتا ہے اور جاندار سے بے جان کون
پیدا کرتا ہے اور دُنیا کے کاموں کا انتظام کون کرتا ہے؟ جھٹ
کہہ دینگے کہ خدا۔ تو کہو کہ پھر تم (خدا سے) ڈرتے کیوں نہیں ﴿۳۱﴾
یہی خدا تو تمہارا پروردگار برحق ہے اور حق بات کے ظاہر ہونیکے بعد
گمراہی کے سوا ہے ہی کیا؟ تو تم کہاں پھرے جاتے ہو؟ ﴿۳۲﴾
اسی طرح خدا کا ارشاد ان نافرمانوں کے حق میں ثابت ہو کر رہا
کہ یہ ایمان نہیں لائیں گے ﴿۳۳﴾
(ان سے) پوچھو کہ بھلا تمہارے شریکوں میں کوئی ایسا ہے کہ مخلوقات
کو ابتداءً پیدا کرے (اور) پھر اسکو دوبارہ بنائے کہدو کہ خدا ہی پہلی
بار پیدا کرتا ہے پھر وہی اسکو دوبارہ پیدا کریگا تو تم کہاں اُلٹے جارہے ہو ﴿۳۴﴾
پوچھو کہ بھلا تمہارے شریکوں میں کون ایسا ہے کہ حق کا رستہ دکھائے کہدو کہ
خدا ہی حق کا رستہ دکھاتا ہے بھلا جو حق کا رستہ دکھائے وہ اس قابل ہے
کہ اسکی پیروی کیجائے۔ یا وہ کہ جب تک کوئی اسے رستہ نہ بتائے
رستہ نہ پائے۔ تو تم کو کیا ہوا ہے کیسا انصاف کرتے ہو؟ ﴿۳۵﴾
اور اُن میں کے اکثر صرف ظن کی پیروی کرتے ہیں۔ اور کچھ
شک نہیں کہ ظن حق کے مقابلے میں کچھ بھی کارآمد نہیں
ہوسکتا۔ بیشک خدا تمہارے (سب) اعمال سے واقف ہے ﴿۳۶﴾
اور یہ قرآن ایسا نہیں کہ خدا کے سوا کوئی اس کو اپنی طرف
سے بنالائے۔ ہاں (ہاں یہ خدا کا کلام ہے) جو (کتابیں) اس

وَقَالَ شُرَكَاۤؤُهُمۡ مَّا كُنۡتُمۡ اِيَّانَا تَعۡبُدُوۡنَ ﴿۲۸﴾
فَكَفٰى بِاللّٰهِ شَهِيۡدًاۢ بَيۡنَنَا وَبَيۡنَكُمۡ اِنۡ كُنَّا
عَنۡ عِبَادَتِكُمۡ لَغٰفِلِيۡنَ ﴿۲۹﴾
هُنَالِكَ تَبۡلُوۡا كُلُّ نَفۡسٍ مَّاۤ اَسۡلَفَتۡ وَ
رُدُّوۡۤا اِلَى اللّٰهِ مَوۡلٰٮهُمُ الۡحَـقِّ وَضَلَّ عَنۡهُمۡ
مَّا كَانُوۡا يَفۡتَرُوۡنَ ﴿۳۰﴾
قُلۡ مَنۡ يَّرۡزُقُكُمۡ مِّنَ السَّمَاۤءِ وَالۡاَرۡضِ
اَمَّنۡ يَّمۡلِكُ السَّمۡعَ وَالۡاَبۡصَارَ وَمَنۡ يُّخۡرِجُ
الۡحَـىَّ مِنَ الۡمَيِّتِ وَيُخۡرِجُ الۡمَيِّتَ مِنَ
الۡحَـىِّ وَمَنۡ يُّدَبِّرُ الۡاَمۡرَ ؕ فَسَيَـقُوۡلُوۡنَ اللّٰهُ ۚ
فَقُلۡ اَفَلَا تَتَّقُوۡنَ ﴿۳۱﴾
فَذٰلِكُمُ اللّٰهُ رَبُّكُمُ الۡحَـقُّ ۚ فَمَاذَا بَعۡدَ
الۡحَـقِّ اِلَّا الضَّلٰلُ ۖ ۚ فَاَنّٰى تُصۡرَفُوۡنَ ﴿۳۲﴾
كَذٰلِكَ حَقَّتۡ كَلِمَتُ رَبِّكَ عَلَى الَّذِيۡنَ
فَسَقُوۡۤا اَنَّهُمۡ لَا يُؤۡمِنُوۡنَ ﴿۳۳﴾
قُلۡ هَلۡ مِنۡ شُرَكَاۤٮِٕكُمۡ مَّنۡ يَّبۡدَؤُا
الۡخَـلۡقَ ثُمَّ يُعِيۡدُهٗ ؕ قُلِ اللّٰهُ يَبۡدَؤُا
الۡخَـلۡقَ ثُمَّ يُعِيۡدُهٗ فَاَنّٰى تُؤۡفَكُوۡنَ ﴿۳۴﴾
قُلۡ هَلۡ مِنۡ شُرَكَاۤٮِٕكُمۡ مَّنۡ يَّهۡدِىۡۤ
اِلَى الۡحَـقِّ ؕ قُلِ اللّٰهُ يَهۡدِىۡ لِلۡحَـقِّ ؕ اَفَمَنۡ
يَّهۡدِىۡۤ اِلَى الۡحَـقِّ اَحَقُّ اَنۡ يُّتَّبَعَ اَمَّنۡ لَّا
يَهِدِّىۡۤ اِلَّاۤ اَنۡ يُّهۡدٰى ۚ فَمَا لَـكُمۡ كَيۡفَ تَحۡكُمُوۡنَ ﴿۳۵﴾
وَمَا يَتَّبِعُ اَكۡثَرُهُمۡ اِلَّا ظَنًّا ؕ اِنَّ الظَّنَّ
لَا يُغۡنِىۡ مِنَ الۡحَـقِّ شَيۡـًٔا ؕ اِنَّ اللّٰهَ عَلِيۡمٌۢ
بِمَا يَفۡعَلُوۡنَ ﴿۳۶﴾
وَمَا كَانَ هٰذَا الۡقُرۡاٰنُ اَنۡ يُّفۡتَرٰى مِنۡ
دُوۡنِ اللّٰهِ وَلٰـكِنۡ تَصۡدِيۡقَ الَّذِىۡ

went before it, and a fuller explanation of the Book—wherein there is no doubt— from the Lord of the Worlds.

سے پہلے (کی) ہیں۔ اُن کی تصدیق کرتا ہے اور اُنہی کتابوں کی (اس میں) تفصیل ہے اس میں کچھ شک نہیں (کہ یہ) رب العالمین کی طرف سے (نازل ہوا) ہے ﴿٣٧﴾

بَيْنَ يَدَيْهِ وَتَفْصِيلَ الْكِتَٰبِ لَا رَيْبَ فِيهِ مِن رَّبِّ الْعَٰلَمِينَ ﴿٣٧﴾

38. Or do they say, "He forged it"? Say: "Bring then a Sûra like unto it, and call (to your aid) anyone you can, besides Allah, if it be ye speak the truth!"

کیا یہ لوگ کہتے ہیں کہ پیغمبر نے اس کو اپنی طرف سے بنا لیا ہے کہہ دو کہ اگر سچے ہو تو تم بھی اس طرح کی ایک سورت بنا لاؤ اور خدا کے سوا جن کو تم بلا سکو بلا بھی لو ﴿٣٨﴾

أَمْ يَقُولُونَ افْتَرَىٰهُ ۖ قُلْ فَأْتُوا بِسُورَةٍ مِّثْلِهِ وَادْعُوا مَنِ اسْتَطَعْتُم مِّن دُونِ اللَّهِ إِن كُنتُمْ صَٰدِقِينَ ﴿٣٨﴾

39. Nay, they charge with falsehood that whose knowledge they cannot compass, even before the interpretation thereof hath reached them: thus did those before them make charges of falsehood: but see what was the end of those who did wrong!

حقیقت یہ ہے کہ جس چیز کے علم پر یہ قابو نہیں پا سکے اس کو (نادانی سے) جھٹلا دیا اور ابھی اس کی حقیقت ان پر کھلی ہی نہیں۔ اسی طرح جو لوگ ان سے پہلے تھے اُنہوں نے تکذیب کی تھی سو دیکھ لو کہ ظالموں کا کیسا انجام ہوا؟ ﴿٣٩﴾

بَلْ كَذَّبُوا بِمَا لَمْ يُحِيطُوا بِعِلْمِهِ وَلَمَّا يَأْتِهِمْ تَأْوِيلُهُ ۚ كَذَٰلِكَ كَذَّبَ الَّذِينَ مِن قَبْلِهِمْ ۖ فَانظُرْ كَيْفَ كَانَ عَٰقِبَةُ الظَّٰلِمِينَ ﴿٣٩﴾

40. Of them there are some who believe therein, and some who do not: and thy Lord knoweth best those who are out for mischief.

اور ان میں سے کچھ تو ایسے ہیں کہ اس پر ایمان لے آتے ہیں اور کچھ ایسے ہیں کہ ایمان نہیں لاتے۔ اور تمہارا پروردگار شریروں سے خوب واقف ہے ﴿٤٠﴾

وَمِنْهُم مَّن يُؤْمِنُ بِهِ وَمِنْهُم مَّن لَّا يُؤْمِنُ بِهِ ۚ وَرَبُّكَ أَعْلَمُ بِالْمُفْسِدِينَ ﴿٤٠﴾

41. If they charge thee with falsehood, say: "My work to me, and yours to you! Ye are free from responsibility for what I do, and I for what ye do!"

اور اگر یہ تمہاری تکذیب کریں تو کہہ دو کہ مجھ کو میرے اعمال کا بدلہ ملے گا۔ اور تم کو تمہارے اعمال (کا)۔ تم میرے عملوں کے جوابدہ نہیں ہو اور میں تمہارے عملوں کا جوابدہ نہیں ہوں ﴿٤١﴾

وَإِن كَذَّبُوكَ فَقُل لِّي عَمَلِي وَلَكُمْ عَمَلُكُمْ ۖ أَنتُم بَرِيٓـُٔونَ مِمَّآ أَعْمَلُ وَأَنَا۠ بَرِيٓءٌ مِّمَّا تَعْمَلُونَ ﴿٤١﴾

42. Among them are some who (pretend to) listen to thee: but canst thou make the deaf to hear,—even though they are without understanding

اور ان میں بعض ایسے ہیں کہ تمہاری طرف کان لگاتے ہیں تو کیا تم بہروں کو سناؤ گے اگرچہ کچھ بھی (سنتے) سمجھتے نہ ہوں ﴿٤٢﴾

وَمِنْهُم مَّن يَسْتَمِعُونَ إِلَيْكَ ۚ أَفَأَنتَ تُسْمِعُ الصُّمَّ وَلَوْ كَانُوا لَا يَعْقِلُونَ ﴿٤٢﴾

43. And among them are some who look at thee: but canst thou guide the blind,—even though they will not see?

اور بعض ایسے ہیں کہ تمہاری طرف دیکھتے ہیں تو کیا تم اندھوں کو رستہ دکھاؤ گے اگرچہ کچھ بھی دیکھتے (بھالتے) نہ ہوں[146] ﴿٤٣﴾

وَمِنْهُم مَّن يَنظُرُ إِلَيْكَ ۚ أَفَأَنتَ تَهْدِي الْعُمْيَ وَلَوْ كَانُوا لَا يُبْصِرُونَ ﴿٤٣﴾

44. Verily Allah will not deal unjustly with man in aught: it is man that wrongs his own soul.

خدا تو لوگوں پر کچھ ظلم نہیں کرتا لیکن لوگ ہی اپنے آپ پر ظلم کرتے ہیں ﴿٤٤﴾

إِنَّ اللَّهَ لَا يَظْلِمُ النَّاسَ شَيْـًٔا وَلَٰكِنَّ النَّاسَ أَنفُسَهُمْ يَظْلِمُونَ ﴿٤٤﴾

45. And on the day when He will gather them together: (it will be) as if they had tarried but an hour of a day: they will recognise each other: assuredly those will be lost who denied the meeting with Allah and refused to receive true guidance.

اور جس دن خدا اُن کو جمع کرے گا (تو وہ دنیا کی نسبت ایسا خیال کریں گے کہ) گویا (وہاں) گھڑی بھر دن سے زیادہ رہے ہی نہیں تھے (اور) آپس میں ایک دوسرے کو شناخت بھی کریں گے جن لوگوں نے خدا کے روبرو حاضر ہونے کو جھٹلایا وہ خسارے میں پڑ گئے اور راہ یاب نہ ہوئے ﴿٤٥﴾

وَيَوْمَ يَحْشُرُهُمْ كَأَن لَّمْ يَلْبَثُوٓا إِلَّا سَاعَةً مِّنَ النَّهَارِ يَتَعَارَفُونَ بَيْنَهُمْ ۚ قَدْ خَسِرَ الَّذِينَ كَذَّبُوا بِلِقَآءِ اللَّهِ وَمَا كَانُوا مُهْتَدِينَ ﴿٤٥﴾

46. Whether We show thee (realised in thy life-time) some part

اور اگر ہم کوئی عذاب جس کا ان لوگوں سے وعدہ کرتے ہیں تمہاری آنکھوں

وَإِمَّا نُرِيَنَّكَ بَعْضَ الَّذِي نَعِدُهُمْ

of what We promise them,—or We take thy soul (before that),—in any case, to Us is their return: ultimately Allah is witness to all that they do.
47. To every people (was sent) a Messenger: when their Messenger comes (before them), the matter will be judged between them with justice, and they will not be wronged.
48. They say: "When will this promise come to pass,—if ye speak the truth?"
49. Say: "I have no power over any harm or profit to myself except as Allah willeth. To every People is a term appointed: when their term is reached, not an hour can they cause delay, not (an hour) can they advance (it in anticipation)."
50. Say: Do ye see,—if His punishment should come to you by night or by day,—what portion of it would the Sinners wish to hasten?
51. "Would ye then believe in it at last, when it actually cometh to pass? (It will then be said:) 'Ah! now? and ye wanted (aforetime) to hasten it on!'
52. "At length will be said to the wrong-doers: 'Taste ye the enduring punishment! Ye get but the recompense of what ye earned!'"
53. They seek to be informed by thee: "Is that true?" Say: "Aye! by my Lord! It is the very truth! And ye cannot frustrate it!"
54. Every soul that hath sinned, if it possessed all that is on earth, would fain give it in ransom: they would declare (their) repentance when they see the Chastisement: but the judgment between them will be with justice, and no wrong will be done unto them.
55. Is it not (the case) that to Allah belongeth whatever is in the heavens and on earth? Is it not (the case) that Allah's promise is assuredly true? Yet most of them do not know.
56. It is He who giveth life and who taketh it, and to Him shall ye all be brought back.

کے سامنے (نازل) کریں یا اس وقت جب تمہاری مدت حیات پوری کریں
تو انکو ہمارے ہی پاس لوٹ کر آنا ہی پھر جو کچھ یہ کر رہے ہیں خدا اسکو دیکھ رہا ہے (۴۶)
اور ہر ایک امت کی طرف پیغمبر بھیجا گیا جب ان کا پیغمبر آتا ہے تو
ان میں انصاف کے ساتھ فیصلہ کر دیا جاتا ہے اور انپر کچھ ظلم نہیں کیا جاتا (۴۷)
اور یہ کہتے ہیں کہ اگر تم سچے ہو تو (جس عذاب کا) یہ وعدہ ہے
وہ آئے گا، کب (۴۸)
کہہ دو کہ میں تو اپنے نقصان اور فائدے کا بھی کچھ اختیار نہیں
رکھتا، مگر جو خدا چاہے ہر ایک امت کے لئے (موت کا) ایک
وقت مقرر ہے جب وہ وقت آجاتا ہے تو ایک گھڑی بھی
دیر نہیں کر سکتے اور نہ جلدی کر سکتے ہیں (۴۹)
کہہ دو کہ بھلا دیکھو تو اگر اس کا عذاب تم پر (ناگہاں) آجائے
رات کو یا دن کو تو پھر گنہگار کس بات کی جلدی کرینگے (۵۰)
کیا جب وہ آ واقع ہو گا تب اس پر ایمان لاؤ گے (اُس وقت کہا جائیگا
کہ) اور اب (ایمان لائے؟) اسی کیلئے تو تم جلدی مچایا کرتے تھے (۵۱)
پھر ظالم لوگوں سے کہا جائے گا کہ عذاب دائمی کا مزہ
چکھو (اب)، تم انہی (اعمال) کا بدلہ پاؤ گے جو (دنیا میں)
کرتے رہے (۵۲)
اور تم سے دریافت کرتے ہیں کہ آیا یہ سچ ہے کہہ دو ہاں
خدا کی قسم سچ ہے اور تم (بھاگ کر خدا کو) عاجز نہیں کر سکو گے (۵۳)
اور اگر ہر ایک نافرمان شخص کے پاس روئے زمین کی تمام چیزیں ہوں
تو (عذاب سے بچنے کے) بدلے میں (سب) دے ڈالے اور جب وہ عذاب
کو دیکھیں گے تو پچھتائیں گے (اور) ندامت کو چھپائیں گے اور انمیں انصاف کے
ساتھ فیصلہ کر دیا جائیگا اور (کسی طرح کا) ان پر ظلم نہیں ہوگا (۵۴)
سن رکھو کہ جو کچھ آسمانوں اور زمین میں ہے سب خدا ہی
کا ہے۔ اور یہ بھی سن رکھو کہ خدا کا وعدہ سچا ہے لیکن اکثر
لوگ نہیں جانتے (۵۵)
وہی جان بخشتا اور (وہی) موت دیتا ہے اور تم لوگ اسی کی طرف لوٹ کر جاؤ گے (۵۶)

أَوْ نَتَوَفَّيَنَّكَ فَإِلَيْنَا مَرْجِعُهُمْ ثُمَّ اللَّهُ
شَهِيدٌ عَلَىٰ مَا يَفْعَلُونَ ﴿٤٦﴾
وَلِكُلِّ أُمَّةٍ رَّسُولٌ ۖ فَإِذَا جَاءَ رَسُولُهُمْ
قُضِيَ بَيْنَهُم بِالْقِسْطِ وَهُمْ لَا يُظْلَمُونَ ﴿٤٧﴾
وَيَقُولُونَ مَتَىٰ هَٰذَا الْوَعْدُ إِن كُنتُمْ
صَادِقِينَ ﴿٤٨﴾
قُل لَّا أَمْلِكُ لِنَفْسِي ضَرًّا وَلَا نَفْعًا
إِلَّا مَا شَاءَ اللَّهُ ۗ لِكُلِّ أُمَّةٍ أَجَلٌ ۚ
إِذَا جَاءَ أَجَلُهُمْ فَلَا يَسْتَأْخِرُونَ
سَاعَةً ۖ وَلَا يَسْتَقْدِمُونَ ﴿٤٩﴾
قُلْ أَرَأَيْتُمْ إِنْ أَتَاكُمْ عَذَابُهُ بَيَاتًا
أَوْ نَهَارًا مَّاذَا يَسْتَعْجِلُ مِنْهُ الْمُجْرِمُونَ ﴿٥٠﴾
أَثُمَّ إِذَا مَا وَقَعَ آمَنتُم بِهِ ۚ آلْآنَ
وَقَدْ كُنتُم بِهِ تَسْتَعْجِلُونَ ﴿٥١﴾
ثُمَّ قِيلَ لِلَّذِينَ ظَلَمُوا ذُوقُوا عَذَابَ
الْخُلْدِ هَلْ تُجْزَوْنَ إِلَّا بِمَا كُنتُمْ
تَكْسِبُونَ ﴿٥٢﴾
وَيَسْتَنبِئُونَكَ أَحَقٌّ هُوَ ۖ قُلْ إِي وَرَبِّي
إِنَّهُ لَحَقٌّ ۖ وَمَا أَنتُم بِمُعْجِزِينَ ﴿٥٣﴾
وَلَوْ أَنَّ لِكُلِّ نَفْسٍ ظَلَمَتْ مَا فِي الْأَرْضِ
لَافْتَدَتْ بِهِ ۗ وَأَسَرُّوا النَّدَامَةَ لَمَّا
رَأَوُا الْعَذَابَ ۖ وَقُضِيَ بَيْنَهُم بِالْقِسْطِ ۚ
وَهُمْ لَا يُظْلَمُونَ ﴿٥٤﴾
أَلَا إِنَّ لِلَّهِ مَا فِي السَّمَاوَاتِ وَالْأَرْضِ ۗ
أَلَا إِنَّ وَعْدَ اللَّهِ حَقٌّ وَلَٰكِنَّ أَكْثَرَهُمْ
لَا يَعْلَمُونَ ﴿٥٥﴾
هُوَ يُحْيِي وَيُمِيتُ وَإِلَيْهِ تُرْجَعُونَ ﴿٥٦﴾

وقف النبی علیہ السلام

يَٰٓأَيُّهَا ٱلنَّاسُ قَدْ جَآءَتْكُم مَّوْعِظَةٌ مِّن رَّبِّكُمْ وَشِفَآءٌ لِّمَا فِى ٱلصُّدُورِ وَهُدًى وَرَحْمَةٌ لِّلْمُؤْمِنِينَ ﴿٥٧﴾

لوگو تمہارے پاس تمہارے پروردگار کی طرف سے نصیحت اور دلوں کی بیماریوں کی شفا اور مومنوں کے لئے ہدایت اور رحمت آ پہنچی ہے ﴿۵۷﴾

57. O mankind! there hath come to you an admonition from your Lord and a healing for the (diseases) in your hearts,—and for those who believe, a Guidance and a Mercy.

قُلْ بِفَضْلِ ٱللَّهِ وَبِرَحْمَتِهِۦ فَبِذَٰلِكَ فَلْيَفْرَحُوا۟ هُوَ خَيْرٌ مِّمَّا يَجْمَعُونَ ﴿٥٨﴾

کہہ دو کہ (یہ کتاب) خدا کے فضل اور اس کی مہربانی سے (نازل ہوئی ہے) تو چاہیئے کہ لوگ اس سے خوش ہوں یہ اس سے کہیں بہتر ہے جو وہ جمع کرتے ہیں ﴿۵۸﴾

58. Say: "In the Bounty of Allah. And in His Mercy,—in that let them rejoice": that is better than the (wealth) they hoard.

قُلْ أَرَءَيْتُم مَّآ أَنزَلَ ٱللَّهُ لَكُم مِّن رِّزْقٍ فَجَعَلْتُم مِّنْهُ حَرَامًا وَحَلَٰلًا قُلْ ءَآللَّهُ أَذِنَ لَكُمْ أَمْ عَلَى ٱللَّهِ تَفْتَرُونَ ﴿٥٩﴾

کہو کہ بھلا دیکھو تو خدا نے تمہارے لئے جو رزق نازل فرمایا تو تم نے اس میں سے (بعض کو) حرام ٹھہرایا اور (بعض کو) حلال (ان سے) پوچھو کیا خدا نے اس کا تمہیں حکم دیا ہے یا تم خدا پر افترا کرتے ہو؟ ﴿۵۹﴾

59. Say: "See ye what things Allah hath sent down to you for sustenance? Yet ye hold forbidden some things thereof and (some things) lawful." Say: "Hath Allah indeed permitted you, or do ye forge (things) to attribute to Allah?"

وَمَا ظَنُّ ٱلَّذِينَ يَفْتَرُونَ عَلَى ٱللَّهِ ٱلْكَذِبَ يَوْمَ ٱلْقِيَٰمَةِ إِنَّ ٱللَّهَ لَذُو فَضْلٍ عَلَى ٱلنَّاسِ وَلَٰكِنَّ أَكْثَرَهُمْ لَا يَشْكُرُونَ ﴿٦٠﴾

اور جو لوگ خدا پر افترا کرتے ہیں وہ قیامت کے دن کی نسبت کیا خیال رکھتے ہیں؟ بےشک خدا لوگوں پر مہربان ہے لیکن اکثر لوگ شکر نہیں کرتے ﴿۶۰﴾

60. And what think those who forge lies against Allah, on the Day of Judgment? Verily Allah is full of Bounty to mankind, but most of them are ungrateful.

وَمَا تَكُونُ فِى شَأْنٍ وَمَا تَتْلُوا۟ مِنْهُ مِن قُرْءَانٍ وَلَا تَعْمَلُونَ مِنْ عَمَلٍ إِلَّا كُنَّا عَلَيْكُمْ شُهُودًا إِذْ تُفِيضُونَ فِيهِ وَمَا يَعْزُبُ عَن رَّبِّكَ مِن مِّثْقَالِ ذَرَّةٍ فِى ٱلْأَرْضِ وَلَا فِى ٱلسَّمَآءِ وَلَآ أَصْغَرَ مِن ذَٰلِكَ وَلَآ أَكْبَرَ إِلَّا فِى كِتَٰبٍ مُّبِينٍ ﴿٦١﴾

اور تم جس حال میں ہوتے ہو یا قرآن میں سے کچھ پڑھتے ہو یا تم لوگ کوئی (اور) کام کرتے ہو جب اس میں مصروف ہوتے ہو ہم تمہارے سامنے ہوتے ہیں اور تمہارے پروردگار سے ذرہ برابر بھی کوئی چیز پوشیدہ نہیں ہے نہ زمین میں اور نہ آسمان میں اور نہ کوئی چیز اس سے چھوٹی ہے یا بڑی مگر کتاب روشن میں (لکھی ہوئی) ہے ﴿۶۱﴾

61. In whatever business thou mayest be, and whatever portion thou mayest be reciting from the Qur'an,—and whatever deed ye (mankind) may be doing,—We are Witnesses thereof when ye are deeply engrossed therein. Nor is hidden from the Lord (so much as) the weight of an atom on the earth or in heaven. And not the smallest and not the greatest of these things but are recorded in a clear Record.

أَلَآ إِنَّ أَوْلِيَآءَ ٱللَّهِ لَا خَوْفٌ عَلَيْهِمْ وَلَا هُمْ يَحْزَنُونَ ﴿٦٢﴾

سن رکھو کہ جو خدا کے دوست ہیں ان کو نہ کچھ خوف ہوگا اور نہ وہ غمناک ہوں گے ﴿۶۲﴾

62. Behold! verily on the friends of Allah there is no fear, nor shall they grieve;

ٱلَّذِينَ ءَامَنُوا۟ وَكَانُوا۟ يَتَّقُونَ ﴿٦٣﴾

(یعنی) وہ جو ایمان لائے اور پرہیزگار رہے ﴿۶۳﴾

63. Those who believe and (constantly) guard against evil;—

لَهُمُ ٱلْبُشْرَىٰ فِى ٱلْحَيَوٰةِ ٱلدُّنْيَا وَفِى ٱلْءَاخِرَةِ لَا تَبْدِيلَ لِكَلِمَٰتِ ٱللَّهِ ذَٰلِكَ هُوَ ٱلْفَوْزُ ٱلْعَظِيمُ ﴿٦٤﴾

ان کے لئے دنیا کی زندگی میں بھی بشارت ہے اور آخرت میں بھی۔ خدا کی باتیں بدلتی نہیں۔ یہی تو بڑی کامیابی ہے ﴿۶۴﴾

64. For them are Glad Tidings, in the life of the Present and in the Hereafter: no change can there be in the Words of Allah. This is indeed the supreme Triumph.

وَلَا يَحْزُنكَ قَوْلُهُمْ إِنَّ ٱلْعِزَّةَ لِلَّهِ جَمِيعًا هُوَ ٱلسَّمِيعُ ٱلْعَلِيمُ ﴿٦٥﴾

اور (اے پیغمبر) ان لوگوں کی باتوں سے آزردہ نہ ہونا (کیونکہ) عزت سب خدا ہی کی ہے وہ (سب کچھ) سنتا (اور) جانتا ہے ﴿۶۵﴾

65. Let not their speech grieve thee: for all power and honour belong to Allah: It is He Who heareth and knoweth (all things).

أَلَآ إِنَّ لِلَّهِ مَن فِى ٱلسَّمَٰوَٰتِ وَمَن فِى

سن رکھو کہ جو مخلوق آسمانوں میں ہے اور جو زمین میں ہے سب

66. Behold! verily to Allah belong

الْأَرْضِ ۗ وَمَا يَتَّبِعُ الَّذِينَ يَدْعُونَ
مِن دُونِ اللَّهِ شُرَكَاءَ ۚ إِن يَتَّبِعُونَ
إِلَّا الظَّنَّ وَإِنْ هُمْ إِلَّا يَخْرُصُونَ ﴿٦٦﴾

خدا ہی کے (بندے اور اسکے مملوک) ہیں اور یہ جو خدا کے سوا
(اپنے بنائے ہوئے) شریکوں کو پکارتے ہیں وہ (کسی اور چیز کے) پیچھے نہیں
چلتے۔ صرف ظن کے پیچھے چلتے ہیں اور محض اٹکلیں دوڑا رہے ہیں (۶۶)

all creatures, in the heavens and on earth. What do they follow who worship as His "partners" other than Allah? They follow nothing but conjecture, and they do nothing but lie.

هُوَ الَّذِي جَعَلَ لَكُمُ اللَّيْلَ لِتَسْكُنُوا
فِيهِ وَالنَّهَارَ مُبْصِرًا ۚ إِنَّ فِي ذَٰلِكَ لَآيَاتٍ
لِّقَوْمٍ يَسْمَعُونَ ﴿٦٧﴾

وہی تو ہے جس نے تمہارے لئے رات بنائی تاکہ اس میں
آرام کرو۔ اور روز روشن بنایا (تاکہ اس میں کام کرو) جو لوگ
مادہ سماعت رکھتے ہیں اُن کیلئے ان میں نشانیاں ہیں (۶۷)

67. He it is that hath made you the Night that ye may rest therein, and the Day to make things visible (to you). Verily in this are Signs for those who listen (to His Message).

قَالُوا اتَّخَذَ اللَّهُ وَلَدًا ۗ سُبْحَانَهُ ۖ هُوَ الْغَنِيُّ
لَهُ مَا فِي السَّمَاوَاتِ وَمَا فِي الْأَرْضِ ۚ إِنْ
عِندَكُم مِّن سُلْطَانٍ بِهَٰذَا ۚ أَتَقُولُونَ
عَلَى اللَّهِ مَا لَا تَعْلَمُونَ ﴿٦٨﴾

(بعض لوگ) کہتے ہیں کہ خدا نے بیٹا بنا لیا ہے (اسکی ذات اولاد سے)
پاک ہے (اور) وہ بے نیاز ہے جو کچھ آسمانوں میں اور جو کچھ زمین میں ہے
سب اسی کا ہے (اے افترا پردازو) تمہارے پاس اس (قول باطل) کی
کوئی دلیل نہیں ہے۔ تم خدا کی نسبت ایسی بات کیوں کہتے ہو جو جانتے نہیں (۶۸)

68. They say, "Allah hath begotten a son!"—Glory be to Him! He is Self-Sufficient! His are all things in the heavens and on earth! No warrant have ye for this! Say ye about Allah what ye know not?

قُلْ إِنَّ الَّذِينَ يَفْتَرُونَ عَلَى اللَّهِ الْكَذِبَ
لَا يُفْلِحُونَ ﴿٦٩﴾

کہہ دو کہ جو لوگ خدا پر جھوٹ باندھتے ہیں فلاح
نہیں پائیں گے (۶۹)

69. Say: "Those who forge a lie against Allah will never prosper."

مَتَاعٌ فِي الدُّنْيَا ثُمَّ إِلَيْنَا مَرْجِعُهُمْ ثُمَّ
نُذِيقُهُمُ الْعَذَابَ الشَّدِيدَ بِمَا كَانُوا
يَكْفُرُونَ ﴿٧٠﴾ ع

(اُن کیلئے جو فائدے ہیں) دُنیا میں (ہیں) پھر ان کو ہماری
ہی طرف لوٹ کر آنا ہے اُس وقت ہم انکو عذاب شدید (کے
مزے) چکھائیں گے کیونکہ کفر (کی باتیں) کیا کرتے تھے (۷۰)

70. A little enjoyment in this world!—and then, to Us will be their return. Then shall We make them taste the severest Chastisement for their disbelief.

النصف

وقف لازم

وَاتْلُ عَلَيْهِمْ نَبَأَ نُوحٍ إِذْ قَالَ لِقَوْمِهِ يَا قَوْمِ
إِن كَانَ كَبُرَ عَلَيْكُم مَّقَامِي وَتَذْكِيرِي
بِآيَاتِ اللَّهِ فَعَلَى اللَّهِ تَوَكَّلْتُ فَأَجْمِعُوا
أَمْرَكُمْ وَشُرَكَاءَكُمْ ثُمَّ لَا يَكُنْ أَمْرُكُمْ عَلَيْكُمْ
غُمَّةً ثُمَّ اقْضُوا إِلَيَّ وَلَا تُنظِرُونِ ﴿٧١﴾

اور انکو نوح کا قصہ پڑھکر سنا دو جب اُنہوں نے اپنی قوم سے کہا کہ اے
قوم! اگر تم کو میرا تم میں رہنا اور خدا کی آیتوں سے نصیحت کرنا ناگوار ہو
تو میں تو خدا پر بھروسہ رکھتا ہوں تم اپنے شریکوں کے ساتھ ملکر ایک کام
(جو میرے بارے میں کرنا چاہو) مقرر کر لو اور وہ تمہاری تمام جماعت (کو معلوم ہو جائے اور
کسی) سے پوشیدہ نہ رہے پھر وہ کام میرے حق میں کر گزرو اور مجھے مہلت نہ دو (۷۱)

71. Relate to them the story of Noah. Behold! he said to his People: "O my People, if it be hard on your (mind) that I should stay (with you) and remind (you) the Signs of Allah,—yet I put my trust in Allah get ye then an agreement about your plan and among your Partners, so your plan be not to you dark and dubious. Then pass your sentence on me, and give me no respite.

فَإِن تَوَلَّيْتُمْ فَمَا سَأَلْتُكُم مِّنْ أَجْرٍ ۖ
إِنْ أَجْرِيَ إِلَّا عَلَى اللَّهِ ۖ وَأُمِرْتُ أَنْ
أَكُونَ مِنَ الْمُسْلِمِينَ ﴿٧٢﴾

اور اگر تم نے منہ پھیر لیا تو (تم جانتے ہو کہ) میں نے تم سے کچھ معاوضہ
نہیں مانگا میرا معاوضہ تو خدا کے ذمے ہے اور مجھے حکم ہوا
ہے کہ میں فرمانبرداروں میں رہوں (۷۲)

72. But if ye turn back, (consider): no reward have I asked of you: my reward is only due from Allah, and I have been commanded to be of those who submit to Allah's Will (in Islām)."

فَكَذَّبُوهُ فَنَجَّيْنَاهُ وَمَن مَّعَهُ فِي الْفُلْكِ
وَجَعَلْنَاهُمْ خَلَائِفَ وَأَغْرَقْنَا الَّذِينَ
كَذَّبُوا بِآيَاتِنَا ۖ فَانظُرْ كَيْفَ كَانَ عَاقِبَةُ
الْمُنذَرِينَ ﴿٧٣﴾

لیکن ان لوگوں نے ان کی تکذیب کی تو ہم نے ان کو اور
جو لوگ اُنکے ساتھ کشتی میں سوار تھے سب کو (طوفان سے) بچا لیا
اور انہیں (زمین میں) خلیفہ بنا دیا اور جن لوگوں نے ہماری آیتوں کو
جھٹلایا اُنکو غرق کر دیا تو دیکھ لو کہ جو لوگ ڈرائے گئے تھے انکا کیسا انجام ہوا (۷۳)

73. They rejected him, but We delivered him, and those with him, in the Ark, and We made them inherit (the earth), while We drowned in the Flood those who rejected Our Signs. Then see what was the end of those who were warned (but heeded not)!

74. Then after him We sent (many) messengers to their Peoples: they brought them Clear Signs, but they would not believe what they had already rejected beforehand. Thus do We seal the hearts of the transgressors.

پھر نوح کے بعد ہم نے اور پیغمبر اپنی اپنی قوم کی طرف بھیجے۔ تو وہ اُنکے پاس کھلی نشانیاں لیکر آئے مگر وہ لوگ ایسے نہ تھے کہ جس چیز کی پہلے تکذیب کر چکے تھے اس پر ایمان لے آتے۔ اسی طرح ہم زیادتی کرنیوالوں کے دلوں پر مُہر لگا دیتے ہیں ﴿۷۴﴾

ثُمَّ بَعَثْنَا مِنْ بَعْدِهٖ رُسُلًا اِلٰى قَوْمِهِمْ فَجَآءُوْهُمْ بِالْبَيِّنٰتِ فَمَا كَانُوْا لِيُؤْمِنُوْا بِمَا كَذَّبُوْا بِهٖ مِنْ قَبْلُ ۚ كَذٰلِكَ نَطْبَعُ عَلٰى قُلُوْبِ الْمُعْتَدِيْنَ ﴿٧٤﴾

75. Then after them sent We Moses and Aaron to Pharaoh and his chiefs with Our Signs. But they were arrogant: they were a wicked people.

پھر اُن کے بعد ہم نے موسیٰ اور ہارون کو اپنی نشانیاں دیکر فرعون اور اس کے سرداروں کے پاس بھیجا تو اُنہوں نے تکبر کیا اور وہ گنہگار لوگ تھے ﴿۷۵﴾

ثُمَّ بَعَثْنَا مِنْ بَعْدِهِمْ مُّوْسٰى وَهٰرُوْنَ اِلٰى فِرْعَوْنَ وَمَلَا۟ئِهٖ بِاٰيٰتِنَا فَاسْتَكْبَرُوْا وَكَانُوْا قَوْمًا مُّجْرِمِيْنَ ﴿٧٥﴾

76. When the Truth did come to them from Us, they said: "This is indeed evident sorcery!"

تو جب اُن کے پاس ہمارے ہاں سے حق آیا تو کہنے لگے کہ یہ تو صریح جادو ہے ﴿۷۶﴾

فَلَمَّا جَآءَهُمُ الْحَقُّ مِنْ عِنْدِنَا قَالُوْٓا اِنَّ هٰذَا لَسِحْرٌ مُّبِيْنٌ ﴿٧٦﴾

77. Said Moses: "Say ye (this) about the Truth when it hath (actually) reached you? Is it sorcery (like) this? But sorcerers will not prosper."

موسیٰ نے کہا کیا تم حق کے بارے میں جب وہ تمہارے پاس آیا یہ کہتے ہو کہ یہ جادو ہے حالانکہ جادوگر فلاح نہیں پانے کے ﴿۷۷﴾

قَالَ مُوْسٰٓى اَتَقُوْلُوْنَ لِلْحَقِّ لَمَّا جَآءَكُمْ ۚ اَسِحْرٌ هٰذَا ۚ وَلَا يُفْلِحُ السّٰحِرُوْنَ ﴿٧٧﴾

78. They said: "Hast thou come to us to turn us away from the ways we found our fathers following,—in order that thou and thy brother may have greatness in the land? But not we shall believe in you!"

وہ بولے کیا تم ہمارے پاس اسلئے آئے ہو کہ جس (راہ) پر ہم اپنے باپ دادا کو پاتے رہے ہیں اس سے ہمکو پھیر دو۔ اور (اس) ملک میں تم دونوں ہی کی سرداری ہو جائے؟ اور ہم تم پر ایمان لانیوالے نہیں ہیں ﴿۷۸﴾

قَالُوْٓا اَجِئْتَنَا لِتَلْفِتَنَا عَمَّا وَجَدْنَا عَلَيْهِ اٰبَآءَنَا وَتَكُوْنَ لَكُمَا الْكِبْرِيَآءُ فِى الْاَرْضِ ۗ وَمَا نَحْنُ لَكُمَا بِمُؤْمِنِيْنَ ﴿٧٨﴾

79. Said Pharaoh: "Bring me every sorcerer well versed."

اور فرعون نے حکم دیا کہ سب کامل فن جادوگروں کو ہمارے پاس لے آؤ ﴿۷۹﴾

وَقَالَ فِرْعَوْنُ ائْتُوْنِيْ بِكُلِّ سٰحِرٍ عَلِيْمٍ ﴿٧٩﴾

80. When the sorcerers came, Moses said to them: "Throw ye what ye (wish) to throw!"

جب جادوگر آئے تو موسیٰ نے اُن سے کہا کہ جو تم کو ڈالنا ہو ڈالو ﴿۸۰﴾

فَلَمَّا جَآءَ السَّحَرَةُ قَالَ لَهُمْ مُّوْسٰٓى اَلْقُوْا مَآ اَنْتُمْ مُّلْقُوْنَ ﴿٨٠﴾

81. When they had had their throw, Moses said: "What ye have brought is sorcery: Allah will surely make it of no effect: for Allah Prospereth not the work of those who make mischief.

جب اُنہوں نے (اپنی رسیوں اور لاٹھیوں کو) ڈالا تو موسیٰ نے کہا کہ جو چیزیں تم (بنا کر) لائے ہو جادو ہے خدا اس کو ابھی نیست و نابود کر دیگا خدا شریروں کے کام سنوارا نہیں کرتا ﴿۸۱﴾

فَلَمَّآ اَلْقَوْا قَالَ مُوْسٰى مَا جِئْتُمْ بِهِ السِّحْرُ ۗ اِنَّ اللّٰهَ سَيُبْطِلُهٗ ۗ اِنَّ اللّٰهَ لَا يُصْلِحُ عَمَلَ الْمُفْسِدِيْنَ ﴿٨١﴾

82. "And Allah by His Words doth prove and establish the Truth, however much the Sinners may hate it!"

اور خدا اپنے حکم سے سچ کو سچ ہی کر دے گا اگرچہ گنہگار بُرا ہی مانیں ﴿۸۲﴾

وَيُحِقُّ اللّٰهُ الْحَقَّ بِكَلِمٰتِهٖ وَلَوْ كَرِهَ الْمُجْرِمُوْنَ ﴿٨٢﴾ ع

83. But none believed in Moses except some children of his People, because of the fear of Pharaoh and his chiefs, lest they should persecute them; and certainly Pharaoh was mighty on the earth and one who transgressed all bounds.

تو موسیٰ پر کوئی ایمان نہ لایا۔ مگر اس کی قوم میں سے چند لڑکے (اور وہ بھی) فرعون اور اُس کے اہل دربار سے ڈرتے ڈرتے کہ کہیں وہ اُن کو آفت میں نہ پھنسا دے۔ اور فرعون مُلک میں متکبر و متغلب اور (کبر و کفر میں) حد سے بڑھا ہوا تھا ﴿۸۳﴾

فَمَآ اٰمَنَ لِمُوْسٰٓى اِلَّا ذُرِّيَّةٌ مِّنْ قَوْمِهٖ عَلٰى خَوْفٍ مِّنْ فِرْعَوْنَ وَمَلَا۟ئِهِمْ اَنْ يَّفْتِنَهُمْ ۗ وَاِنَّ فِرْعَوْنَ لَعَالٍ فِى الْاَرْضِ ۚ وَاِنَّهٗ لَمِنَ الْمُسْرِفِيْنَ ﴿٨٣﴾

84. Moses said: "O my People! If ye do (really) believe in Allah, then

اور موسیٰ نے کہا کہ قوم! اگر تم خدا پر ایمان لائے ہو تو اگر دل سے

وَقَالَ مُوْسٰى يٰقَوْمِ اِنْ كُنْتُمْ اٰمَنْتُمْ

in Him put your trust if ye submit (your will to His)."

85. They said: "In Allah do we put our trust. Our Lord make us not a trial for those who practise oppression;

86. "And deliver us by Thy Mercy from those who reject (Thee)."

87. We inspired Moses and his brother with this Message: "Provide dwellings for your People in Egypt, make your dwellings into places of worship, and establish regular prayers: and give Glad Tidings to those who believe!"

88. Moses prayed: "Our Lord! Thou hast indeed bestowed on Pharaoh and his Chiefs splendour and wealth in the life of the Present, and so, our Lord they mislead (men) from Thy Path. Deface our Lord the features of their wealth, and send hardness to their hearts, so they will not believe until they see the grievous Chastisement."

89. Allah said: "Accepted is your prayer (O Moses and Aaron)! So stand ye straight, and follow not the path of those who know not."

90. We took the Children of Israel across the sea: Pharaoh and his hosts followed them in insolence and spite. At length, when overwhelmed with the flood, he said: "I believe that there is no god except Him Whom the Children of Israel believe in: I am of those who submit (to Allah in Islãm)."

91. (It was said to him:) "Ah now!—but a little while before, wast thou in rebellion!—and thou didst mischief (and violence)!

92. "This day shall We save thee in thy body, that thou mayest be a Sign to those who come after thee! But verily, many among mankind are heedless of Our Signs!"

93. We settled the Children of Israel in an honourable dwelling-place, and provided for them sustenance of the best: it was after knowledge had been granted to them, that they fell into schisms.

فرمانبردار رہو تو اُسی پر بھروسا رکھو ﴿۸۴﴾
تو وہ بولے کہ ہم خدا ہی پر بھروسا رکھتے ہیں اے ہمارے پروردگار
ہم کو ظالم لوگوں کے ہاتھ سے آزمائش میں نہ ڈال ﴿۸۵﴾
اور اپنی رحمت سے قوم کفار سے نجات بخش ﴿۸۶﴾
اور ہم نے موسیٰ اور اسکے بھائی کی طرف وحی بھیجی کہ اپنے لوگوں
کے لئے مصر میں گھر بناؤ اور اپنے گھروں کو قبلہ (یعنی مسجدیں)
ٹھیراؤ۔ اور نماز پڑھو۔ اور مومنوں کو خوشخبری سنا دو ﴿۸۷﴾
اور موسیٰ نے کہا اے ہمارے پروردگار تو نے فرعون اور اس کے
سرداروں کو دنیا کی زندگی میں (بہت سا) ساز و برگ اور مال و
زر دے رکھا ہے۔ اے پروردگار۔ ان کا مآل یہ ہے کہ تیرے
رستے سے گمراہ کر دیں اے پروردگار انکے مال کو برباد کر دے اور
انکے دلوں کو سخت کر دے کہ ایمان نہ لائیں جبتک عذاب الیم نہ دیکھ لیں ﴿۸۸﴾
(خدا نے) فرمایا کہ تمہاری دعا قبول کر لی گئی تو تم ثابت قدم رہنا
اور بے عقلوں کے رستے نہ چلنا ﴿۸۹﴾
اور ہم نے بنی اسرائیل کو دریا سے پار کر دیا تو فرعون اور اس
کے لشکر نے سرکشی اور تعدی سے ان کا تعاقب کیا۔ یہاں تک
کہ جب اس کو غرق (کے عذاب) نے آپکڑا تو کہنے لگا میں
ایمان لایا کہ جس (خدا) پر بنی اسرائیل ایمان لائے ہیں اسکے سوا
کوئی معبود نہیں اور میں فرمانبرداروں میں ہوں ﴿۹۰﴾
(جواب ملا کہ) اب (ایمان لاتا ہے) حالانکہ تو پہلے نافرمانی
کرتا رہا اور مفسد بنا رہا؟ ﴿۹۱﴾
تو آج ہم تیرے بدن کو (دریا سے) نکال لیں گے تاکہ تو
پچھلوں کے لئے عبرت ہو اور بہت سے لوگ ہماری
نشانیوں سے بےخبر ہیں ﴿۹۲﴾
اور ہم نے بنی اسرائیل کو رہنے کو عمدہ جگہ دی اور کھانے کو
پاکیزہ چیزیں عطا کیں۔ لیکن وہ باوجود علم ہونے کے اختلاف
کرتے رہے۔ بیشک جن باتوں میں وہ اختلاف کرتے رہے ہیں

بِاللّٰهِ فَعَلَيْهِ تَوَكَّلُوْٓا اِنْ كُنْتُمْ مُّسْلِمِيْنَ ﴿۸۴﴾
فَقَالُوْا عَلَى اللّٰهِ تَوَكَّلْنَا ۚ رَبَّنَا لَا تَجْعَلْنَا
فِتْنَةً لِّلْقَوْمِ الظّٰلِمِيْنَ ﴿۸۵﴾
وَنَجِّنَا بِرَحْمَتِكَ مِنَ الْقَوْمِ الْكٰفِرِيْنَ ﴿۸۶﴾
وَاَوْحَيْنَآ اِلٰى مُوْسٰى وَاَخِيْهِ اَنْ تَبَوَّاٰ
لِقَوْمِكُمَا بِمِصْرَ بُيُوْتًا وَّاجْعَلُوْا بُيُوْتَكُمْ
قِبْلَةً وَّاَقِيْمُوا الصَّلٰوةَ ۗ وَبَشِّرِ الْمُؤْمِنِيْنَ ﴿۸۷﴾
وَقَالَ مُوْسٰى رَبَّنَآ اِنَّكَ اٰتَيْتَ فِرْعَوْنَ
وَمَلَاَهٗ زِيْنَةً وَّاَمْوَالًا فِي الْحَيٰوةِ الدُّنْيَا ۙ
رَبَّنَا لِيُضِلُّوْا عَنْ سَبِيْلِكَ ۚ رَبَّنَا اطْمِسْ
عَلٰٓى اَمْوَالِهِمْ وَاشْدُدْ عَلٰى قُلُوْبِهِمْ
فَلَا يُؤْمِنُوْا حَتّٰى يَرَوُا الْعَذَابَ الْاَلِيْمَ ﴿۸۸﴾
قَالَ قَدْ اُجِيْبَتْ دَّعْوَتُكُمَا فَاسْتَقِيْمَا
وَلَا تَتَّبِعٰٓنِّ سَبِيْلَ الَّذِيْنَ لَا يَعْلَمُوْنَ ﴿۸۹﴾
وَجٰوَزْنَا بِبَنِيْٓ اِسْرَآءِيْلَ الْبَحْرَ فَاَتْبَعَهُمْ
فِرْعَوْنُ وَجُنُوْدُهٗ بَغْيًا وَّعَدْوًا ۭ حَتّٰٓى
اِذَآ اَدْرَكَهُ الْغَرَقُ ۙ قَالَ اٰمَنْتُ اَنَّهٗ
لَآ اِلٰهَ اِلَّا الَّذِيْٓ اٰمَنَتْ بِهٖ بَنُوْٓا
اِسْرَآءِيْلَ وَاَنَا مِنَ الْمُسْلِمِيْنَ ﴿۹۰﴾
آٰلْئٰنَ وَقَدْ عَصَيْتَ قَبْلُ وَكُنْتَ
مِنَ الْمُفْسِدِيْنَ ﴿۹۱﴾
فَالْيَوْمَ نُنَجِّيْكَ بِبَدَنِكَ لِتَكُوْنَ لِمَنْ
خَلْفَكَ اٰيَةً ۭ وَاِنَّ كَثِيْرًا مِّنَ النَّاسِ
عَنْ اٰيٰتِنَا لَغٰفِلُوْنَ ﴿۹۲﴾ ع
وَلَقَدْ بَوَّاْنَا بَنِيْٓ اِسْرَآءِيْلَ مُبَوَّاَ صِدْقٍ
وَّرَزَقْنٰهُمْ مِّنَ الطَّيِّبٰتِ ۚ فَمَا اخْتَلَفُوْا
حَتّٰى جَاۗءَهُمُ الْعِلْمُ ۭ اِنَّ رَبَّكَ يَقْضِيْ

Verily Allah will judge between them as to the schisms amongst them, on the Day of Judgment.

94. If thou wert in doubt as to what We have revealed unto thee, then ask those who have been reading the Book from before thee: the Truth hath indeed come to thee from thy Lord: so be in no wise of those in doubt.

95. Nor be of those who reject the Signs of Allah, or thou shalt be of those who perish

96. Those against whom the Word of thy Lord hath been verified would not believe—

97. Even if every Sign was brought unto them,—until they see (for themselves) the Chastisement Grievous.

98. If only there had been a single township (among those We warned), which believed,—so its Faith should have profited it,—except the People of Jonah? When they believed, We removed from them the Chastisement of Ignominy in the life of the Present, and permitted them to enjoy (their life) for a while.

99. If it had been thy Lord's Will, they would all have believed,— all who are on earth! Wilt thou then compel mankind, against their will, to believe!

100. No soul can believe, except by the Will of Allah, and He will place abomination on those who will not understand.

101. Say: "Behold all that is in the heavens and on earth"; but neither Signs nor Warners profit those who believe not.

102. Do they then expect (any thing) but the like of (what happened in) the days of the men who passed away before them? Say: "Wait ye then: for I, too, will wait with you."

103. In the end We deliver Our messengers and those who believe: thus is it fitting on Our part that We should deliver those who believe!

تمہارا پروردگار قیامت کے دن ان میں ان باتوں کا فیصلہ کر دیگا ﴿٩٣﴾
اگر تم کو اس (کتاب کے) بارے میں جو ہم نے تم پر نازل کی ہے کچھ
شک ہو تو جو لوگ تم سے پہلے کی (اُتری ہوئی) کتابیں پڑھتے ہیں
ان سے پوچھ لو۔ تمہارے پروردگار کی طرف سے تمہارے پاس حق آچکا ہے
تو تم ہرگز شک کرنے والوں میں نہ ہونا ﴿٩٤﴾
اور نہ اُن لوگوں میں ہونا جو خدا کی آیتوں کی تکذیب کرتے
ہیں نہیں تو نقصان اُٹھاؤ گے ﴿٩٥﴾
جن لوگوں کے بارے میں خدا کا حکم (عذاب) قرار پا چکا ہے
وہ ایمان نہیں لانے کے ﴿٩٦﴾
جب تک کہ عذاب الیم نہ دیکھ لیں خواہ ان کے پاس ہر طرح
کی نشانی آجائے ﴿٩٧﴾
تو کوئی بستی ایسی کیوں نہ ہوئی کہ ایمان لاتی تو اسکا ایمان
اُسے نفع دیتا۔ ہاں یونس کی قوم کہ جب ایمان لائی تو ہم نے
دنیا کی زندگی میں اُن سے ذلت کا عذاب دُور کر دیا اور
ایک مدت تک (فوائد دنیاوی سے) اُن کو بہرہ مند رکھا ﴿٩٨﴾
اور اگر تمہارا پروردگار چاہتا تو جتنے لوگ زمین میں ہیں
سب کے سب ایمان لے آتے۔ تو کیا تم لوگوں پر زبردستی
کرنا چاہتے ہو کہ وہ مومن ہو جائیں؟ ﴿٩٩﴾
حالانکہ کسی شخص کو قدرت نہیں ہے کہ خدا کے حکم کے بغیر ایمان لائے
اور جو لوگ بے عقل ہیں اُن پر وہ (کفر و ذلت کی) نجاست ڈالتا ہے ﴿١٠٠﴾
(ان کفار سے) کہو کہ دیکھو تو آسمانوں اور زمین میں کیا کیا کچھ ہے؟
مگر جو لوگ ایمان نہیں رکھتے اُنکے نشانیاں اور ڈراوے کچھ کام نہیں آتے ﴿١٠١﴾
سو جیسے (بُرے) دن اُن سے پہلے لوگوں پر گزر چکے ہیں اسی
طرح کے دنوں کے، یہ منتظر ہیں۔ کہہ دو کہ تم بھی انتظار کرو
میں بھی تمہارے ساتھ انتظار کرتا ہوں ﴿١٠٢﴾
اور ہم اپنے پیغمبروں کو اور مومنوں کو نجات دیتے رہے ہیں
اسی طرح ہمارا ذمہ ہے کہ مسلمانوں کو نجات دیں ﴿١٠٣﴾

بَيْنَهُمْ يَوْمَ الْقِيٰمَةِ فِيْمَا كَانُوْا فِيْهِ يَخْتَلِفُوْنَ ﴿٩٣﴾
فَاِنْ كُنْتَ فِيْ شَكٍّ مِّمَّآ اَنْزَلْنَآ اِلَيْكَ
فَسْئَلِ الَّذِيْنَ يَقْرَءُوْنَ الْكِتٰبَ مِنْ
قَبْلِكَ ۚ لَقَدْ جَآءَكَ الْحَقُّ مِنْ رَّبِّكَ فَلَا
تَكُوْنَنَّ مِنَ الْمُمْتَرِيْنَ ﴿٩٤﴾
وَلَا تَكُوْنَنَّ مِنَ الَّذِيْنَ كَذَّبُوْا بِاٰيٰتِ
اللّٰهِ فَتَكُوْنَ مِنَ الْخٰسِرِيْنَ ﴿٩٥﴾
اِنَّ الَّذِيْنَ حَقَّتْ عَلَيْهِمْ كَلِمَتُ رَبِّكَ
لَا يُؤْمِنُوْنَ ﴿٩٦﴾
وَلَوْ جَآءَتْهُمْ كُلُّ اٰيَةٍ حَتّٰى يَرَوُا
الْعَذَابَ الْاَلِيْمَ ﴿٩٧﴾
فَلَوْلَا كَانَتْ قَرْيَةٌ اٰمَنَتْ فَنَفَعَهَآ
اِيْمَانُهَآ اِلَّا قَوْمَ يُوْنُسَ ۚ لَمَّآ اٰمَنُوْا
كَشَفْنَا عَنْهُمْ عَذَابَ الْخِزْيِ فِي الْحَيٰوةِ
الدُّنْيَا وَمَتَّعْنٰهُمْ اِلٰى حِيْنٍ ﴿٩٨﴾
وَلَوْ شَآءَ رَبُّكَ لَاٰمَنَ مَنْ فِي الْاَرْضِ
كُلُّهُمْ جَمِيْعًا ۚ اَفَاَنْتَ تُكْرِهُ النَّاسَ
حَتّٰى يَكُوْنُوْا مُؤْمِنِيْنَ ﴿٩٩﴾
وَمَا كَانَ لِنَفْسٍ اَنْ تُؤْمِنَ اِلَّا بِاِذْنِ اللّٰهِ ۚ
وَيَجْعَلُ الرِّجْسَ عَلَى الَّذِيْنَ لَا يَعْقِلُوْنَ ﴿١٠٠﴾
قُلِ انْظُرُوْا مَاذَا فِي السَّمٰوٰتِ وَالْاَرْضِ ۚ وَمَا
تُغْنِي الْاٰيٰتُ وَالنُّذُرُ عَنْ قَوْمٍ لَّا يُؤْمِنُوْنَ ﴿١٠١﴾
فَهَلْ يَنْتَظِرُوْنَ اِلَّا مِثْلَ اَيَّامِ الَّذِيْنَ
خَلَوْا مِنْ قَبْلِهِمْ ۚ قُلْ فَانْتَظِرُوْٓا اِنِّيْ
مَعَكُمْ مِّنَ الْمُنْتَظِرِيْنَ ﴿١٠٢﴾
ثُمَّ نُنَجِّيْ رُسُلَنَا وَالَّذِيْنَ اٰمَنُوْا كَذٰلِكَ ۚ
حَقًّا عَلَيْنَا نُنْجِ الْمُؤْمِنِيْنَ ﴿١٠٣﴾ ع ١١ / ١٥

SÛRA–11
HÛD
(INTRODUCTION)

For the chronological place of this Sûra and the general arguments of Sûras 10 to 15, see Introduction to S.10.

In subject-matter this Sûra supplements the preceding one. In the last Sûra stress was laid on that side of Allah's dealings with man which leads to Mercy: here stress is laid on the side which deals with justice and the punishment of Sin when all Grace is resisted.

104. Say: "O ye men! If ye are in doubt as to my religion, (behold!) I worship not what ye worship other than Allah! But I worship Allah—Who will take your souls (at death): I am commanded to be (in the ranks) of the Believers,

105. "And further (thus): set thy face towards Religion with true piety, and never in any wise be of the Unbelievers;

106. "Nor call on any, other than Allah;—such can neither profit thee nor hurt thee: if thou dost, behold! thou shalt certainly be of those who do wrong."

107. If Allah do touch thee with hurt, there is none can remove it but He: if He do design some benefit for thee, there is none can keep back His favour: He causeth it to reach whomsoever of His servants He pleaseth. And He is the Oft-Forgiving, Most Merciful.

108. Say: "O ye men! Now Truth hath reached you from your Lord! Those, who receive guidance, do so for the good of their own souls; those who stray, do so to their own loss: and I am not (set) over you to arrange your affairs."

109. Follow thou the inspiration sent unto thee, and be patient and constant, till Allah, do decide: for He is the Best to decide.

(اے پیغمبر) کہہ دو کہ لوگو اگر تم کو میرے دین میں کسی طرح کا شک ہو تو (سن رکھو کہ)
جن لوگوں کی تم خدا کے سوا عبادت کرتے ہو میں اُنکی عبادت نہیں کرتا۔
بلکہ میں خدا کی عبادت کرتا ہوں جو تمہاری روحیں قبض کر لیتا ہے۔
اور مجھکو یہی حکم ہوا ہے کہ ایمان لانے والوں میں ہُوں (۱۰۴)
اور یہ کہ (اے محمدؐ سب سے) یکسو ہو کر دین (اسلام) کی پیروی کئے
جاؤ اور مُشرکوں میں ہرگز نہ ہونا (۱۰۵)
اور خدا کو چھوڑ کر ایسی چیز کو نہ پکارنا جو نہ تمہارا کچھ بھلا کر سکے
اور نہ کچھ بگاڑ سکے اگر ایسا کرو گے تو ظالموں میں ہو جاؤ گے (۱۰۶)
اور اگر خدا تم کو کوئی تکلیف پہنچائے۔ تو اسکے سوا اس کا کوئی
دُور کرنیوالا نہیں۔ اور اگر تم سے بھلائی کرنی چاہے تو اسکے فضل
کو کوئی روکنے والا نہیں۔ وہ اپنے بندوں میں سے جسے چاہتا ہے
فائدہ پہنچاتا ہے۔ اور وہ بخشنے والا مہربان ہے (۱۰۷)
کہہ دو کہ لوگو تمہارے پروردگار کے ہاں سے تمہارے پاس حق
آچکا ہے تو جو کوئی ہدایت حاصل کرتا ہے تو ہدایت سے اپنے ہی
حق میں بھلائی کرتا ہے اور جو گمراہی اختیار کرتا ہے تو گمراہی سے
اپنا ہی نقصان کرتا ہے۔ اور میں تمہارا وکیل نہیں ہُوں (۱۰۸)
اور (اے پیغمبر) تم کو جو حکم بھیجا جاتا ہے اس کی پیروی کئے جاؤ
اور (تکلیفوں پر) صبر کرو۔ یہاں تک کہ خدا فیصلہ کر دے
اور وہ سب سے بہتر فیصلہ کرنے والا ہے (۱۰۹)

قُلْ يٰۤاَيُّهَا النَّاسُ اِنْ كُنْتُمْ فِيْ شَكٍّ
مِّنْ دِيْنِيْ فَلَاۤ اَعْبُدُ الَّذِيْنَ تَعْبُدُوْنَ
مِنْ دُوْنِ اللّٰهِ وَلٰكِنْ اَعْبُدُ اللّٰهَ الَّذِيْ
يَتَوَفّٰىكُمْ ۖۚ وَاُمِرْتُ اَنْ اَكُوْنَ مِنَ الْمُؤْمِنِيْنَ ﴿۱۰۴﴾
وَاَنْ اَقِمْ وَجْهَكَ لِلدِّيْنِ حَنِيْفًا ۚ وَلَا
تَكُوْنَنَّ مِنَ الْمُشْرِكِيْنَ ﴿۱۰۵﴾
وَلَا تَدْعُ مِنْ دُوْنِ اللّٰهِ مَا لَا يَنْفَعُكَ وَلَا
يَضُرُّكَ ۚ فَاِنْ فَعَلْتَ فَاِنَّكَ اِذًا مِّنَ الظّٰلِمِيْنَ ﴿۱۰۶﴾
وَاِنْ يَّمْسَسْكَ اللّٰهُ بِضُرٍّ فَلَا كَاشِفَ لَهٗۤ
اِلَّا هُوَ ۚ وَاِنْ يُّرِدْكَ بِخَيْرٍ فَلَا رَآدَّ
لِفَضْلِهٖ ؕ يُصِيْبُ بِهٖ مَنْ يَّشَآءُ مِنْ
عِبَادِهٖ ؕ وَهُوَ الْغَفُوْرُ الرَّحِيْمُ ﴿۱۰۷﴾
قُلْ يٰۤاَيُّهَا النَّاسُ قَدْ جَآءَكُمُ الْحَقُّ مِنْ
رَّبِّكُمْ ۚ فَمَنِ اهْتَدٰى فَاِنَّمَا يَهْتَدِيْ
لِنَفْسِهٖ ۚ وَمَنْ ضَلَّ فَاِنَّمَا يَضِلُّ عَلَيْهَا ۚ
وَمَاۤ اَنَا عَلَيْكُمْ بِوَكِيْلٍ ؕ ﴿۱۰۸﴾
وَاتَّبِعْ مَا يُوْحٰۤى اِلَيْكَ وَاصْبِرْ
حَتّٰى يَحْكُمَ اللّٰهُ ۚ وَهُوَ خَيْرُ
الْحٰكِمِيْنَ ع ﴿۱۰۹﴾

Hûd (The Prophet Hûd)

In the name of Allah, Most Gracious, Most Merciful.

1. **A. L. R.** (This is) a Book, with verses fundamental (of established meaning), further explained in detail,— from One Who is Wise and Well-Acquainted (with all things):

2. (It teacheth) that ye should worship none but Allah. (Say:) "Verily I am (sent) unto you from Him to warn and to bring Glad tidings:

3. "(And to preach thus), 'Seek ye the forgiveness of your Lord,

سُورہ ہُود مکّی ہے اور اسمیں ایک سو تئیس آیتیں اور دس رکوع ہیں

شروع خدا کا نام لے کر جو بڑا مہربان نہایت رحم والا ہے
الرا۔ یہ وہ کتاب ہے جس کی آیتیں مستحکم ہیں اور خدائے
حکیم و خبیر کی طرف سے بہ تفصیل بیان کر دی
گئی ہے (۱)
(وہ یہ) کہ خدا کے سوا کسی کی عبادت نہ کرو اور میں اُس کی
طرف سے تم کو ڈر سُنانے والا اور خوشخبری دینے والا ہوں (۲)
اور یہ کہ اپنے پروردگار سے بخشش مانگو اور اسکے آگے توبہ

سُوْرَةُ هُوْدٍ مَّكِّيَّةٌ وَّهِيَ مِائَةٌ وَّثَلٰثٌ وَّعِشْرُوْنَ اٰيَةً وَّعَشْرُ رُكُوْعَاتٍ

بِسْمِ اللّٰهِ الرَّحْمٰنِ الرَّحِيْمِ
الٓرٰ ۟ كِتٰبٌ اُحْكِمَتْ اٰيٰتُهٗ ثُمَّ
فُصِّلَتْ مِنْ لَّدُنْ حَكِيْمٍ
خَبِيْرٍ ۙ ﴿۱﴾
اَلَّا تَعْبُدُوْۤا اِلَّا اللّٰهَ ؕ اِنَّنِيْ لَكُمْ مِّنْهُ
نَذِيْرٌ وَّبَشِيْرٌ ۙ ﴿۲﴾
وَّاَنِ اسْتَغْفِرُوْا رَبَّكُمْ ثُمَّ تُوْبُوْۤا اِلَيْهِ

and turn to Him in repentance; that He may grant you enjoyment, good (and true), for a term appointed, and bestow His abounding grace on all who abound in merit! But if ye turn away, then I fear for you the Chastisement of a Great Day:

کرو وہ تم کو ایک وقت مقرر تک متاعِ نیک سے بہرہ مند
کرے گا اور ہر صاحب بزرگی کو اس کی بزرگی (کی داد) دیگا۔
اور اگر رُوگردانی کرو گے تو مجھے تمہارے بارے میں (قیامت کے)
بڑے دن کے عذاب کا ڈر ہے (٣)

يُمَتِّعْكُمْ مَّتَاعًا حَسَنًا إِلَىٰ أَجَلٍ مُّسَمًّى
وَيُؤْتِ كُلَّ ذِي فَضْلٍ فَضْلَهُ ۖ وَإِن
تَوَلَّوْا فَإِنِّي أَخَافُ عَلَيْكُمْ عَذَابَ
يَوْمٍ كَبِيرٍ (٣)

4. "To Allah is your return, and He hath power over all things."

تم (سب) کو خدا کی طرف لوٹ کر جانا ہے۔ اور وہ ہر چیز
پر قادر ہے (٤)

إِلَى اللَّهِ مَرْجِعُكُمْ ۖ وَهُوَ عَلَىٰ كُلِّ شَيْءٍ
قَدِيرٌ (٤)

5. Behold! they fold up their hearts, that they may lie hid from Him! Ah! even when they cover themselves with their garments, He knoweth what they conceal, and what they reveal: for He knoweth well the (inmost secrets) of the hearts.

دیکھو یہ اپنے سینوں کو دوہرا کرتے ہیں تاکہ خدا سے پردہ کریں۔
سُن رکھو جس وقت یہ کپڑوں میں لپٹ کر پڑتے ہیں (تب بھی)
وہ اُن کی چھپی اور کھلی باتوں کو جانتا ہے۔ وہ تو دلوں تک
کی باتوں سے آگاہ ہے (٥)

أَلَا إِنَّهُمْ يَثْنُونَ صُدُورَهُمْ لِيَسْتَخْفُوا
مِنْهُ ۚ أَلَا حِينَ يَسْتَغْشُونَ ثِيَابَهُمْ
يَعْلَمُ مَا يُسِرُّونَ وَمَا يُعْلِنُونَ ۚ
إِنَّهُ عَلِيمٌ بِذَاتِ الصُّدُورِ (٥)

6. There is no moving creature on earth but its sustenance dependeth on Allah: He knoweth its resting place and its temporary deposit: all is in a clear Record.

اور زمین پر کوئی چلنے پھرنے والا نہیں مگر اس کا رزق خدا
کے ذمے ہے وہ جہاں رہتا ہے اُسے بھی جانتا ہے اور جہاں سونپا
جاتا ہے اُسے بھی۔ یہ سب کچھ کتاب روشن میں (لکھا ہوا) ہے (٦)

وَمَا مِن دَابَّةٍ فِي الْأَرْضِ إِلَّا
عَلَى اللَّهِ رِزْقُهَا وَيَعْلَمُ مُسْتَقَرَّهَا
وَمُسْتَوْدَعَهَا ۚ كُلٌّ فِي كِتَابٍ مُّبِينٍ (٦)

7. He it is Who created the heavens and the earth in six Days—and His Throne was over the Waters—that He might try you, which of you is best in conduct. But if thou wert to say to them, "Ye shall indeed be raised up after death", the Unbelievers would be sure to say, "This is nothing but obvious sorcery!"

اور وہی تو ہے جس نے آسمانوں اور زمین کو چھ دن میں
بنایا اور (اس وقت) اُس کا عرش پانی پر تھا (تمہارے پیدا
کرنے سے) مقصود یہ ہے کہ وہ تم کو آزمائے کہ تم میں عمل کے
لحاظ سے کون بہتر ہے۔ اور اگر تم کہو کہ تم لوگ مرنے کے بعد
(زندہ کر کے) اُٹھائے جاؤ گے تو کافر کہہ دینگے کہ یہ تو کھلا جادو ہے (٧)

وَهُوَ الَّذِي خَلَقَ السَّمَاوَاتِ وَالْأَرْضَ
فِي سِتَّةِ أَيَّامٍ وَكَانَ عَرْشُهُ عَلَى الْمَاءِ
لِيَبْلُوَكُمْ أَيُّكُمْ أَحْسَنُ عَمَلًا ۗ وَلَئِن قُلْتَ
إِنَّكُم مَّبْعُوثُونَ مِن بَعْدِ الْمَوْتِ لَيَقُولَنَّ
الَّذِينَ كَفَرُوا إِنْ هَٰذَا إِلَّا سِحْرٌ مُّبِينٌ (٧)

8. If We delay the chastisement for them for a definite term, they are sure to say, "What keeps it back?" Ah! On the day it (actually) reaches them, nothing will turn it away from them, and they will be completely encircled by that which they used to mock at!

اور اگر ایک مدت معیّن تک ہم اُن سے عذاب روک دیں تو
کہیں گے کہ کونسی چیز عذاب کو روکے ہوئے ہے؟ دیکھو جس روز وہ
اُن پر واقع ہوگا (پھر) ٹلنے کا نہیں۔ اور جس چیز کے ساتھ
یہ استہزاء کیا کرتے ہیں وہ اُن کو گھیر لے گی (٨)

وَلَئِنْ أَخَّرْنَا عَنْهُمُ الْعَذَابَ إِلَىٰ أُمَّةٍ
مَّعْدُودَةٍ لَّيَقُولُنَّ مَا يَحْبِسُهُ ۗ أَلَا يَوْمَ
يَأْتِيهِمْ لَيْسَ مَصْرُوفًا عَنْهُمْ وَحَاقَ بِهِم
مَّا كَانُوا بِهِ يَسْتَهْزِئُونَ (٨) ع

9. If We give man a taste of mercy from Ourselves, and then withdraw it from him, behold! he is in despair and (falls into) ingratitude,

اور اگر ہم انسان کو اپنے پاس سے نعمت بخشیں پھر اس سے اس کو
چھین لیں تو ناامید (اور) ناشکرا (ہو جاتا) ہے (٩)

وَلَئِنْ أَذَقْنَا الْإِنسَانَ مِنَّا رَحْمَةً ثُمَّ
نَزَعْنَاهَا مِنْهُ إِنَّهُ لَيَئُوسٌ كَفُورٌ (٩)

10. But if We give him a taste of (Our) favours after adversity hath touched him, he is sure to say, "All evil has departed from me:" behold! he falls into exultation and pride.

اور اگر تکلیف پہنچنے کے بعد آسائش کا مزہ چکھائیں تو (خوش
ہو کر) کہتا ہے کہ (آہا) سب سختیاں مجھ سے دور ہوگئیں بیشک
وہ خوشیاں منانے والا (اور) فخر کرنے والا ہے (١٠)

وَلَئِنْ أَذَقْنَاهُ نَعْمَاءَ بَعْدَ ضَرَّاءَ مَسَّتْهُ
لَيَقُولَنَّ ذَهَبَ السَّيِّئَاتُ عَنِّي ۚ إِنَّهُ
لَفَرِحٌ فَخُورٌ (١٠)

11. Not so do those who show patience and constancy, and work righteousness; for them is forgiveness (of sins) and a great reward.

ہاں جنہوں نے صبر کیا اور عمل نیک کئے یہی ہیں جن کے لئے
بخشش اور اجر عظیم ہے (۱۱)

إِلَّا الَّذِينَ صَبَرُوا وَعَمِلُوا الصَّٰلِحَٰتِ
أُولَٰٓئِكَ لَهُم مَّغْفِرَةٌ وَأَجْرٌ كَبِيرٌ ﴿١١﴾

12. Perchance thou mayest (feel the inclination) to give up a part of what is revealed unto thee, and thy heart feeleth straitened because they say, "Why is not a treasure sent down unto him, or why does not an angel come down with him?" But thou art there only to warn! It is Allah that arrangeth all affairs!

شاید تم کچھ چیز وحی میں سے جو تمہارے پاس آتی ہے
چھوڑ دو اور اس (خیال) سے تمہارا دل تنگ ہو کہ (کافر)
یہ کہنے لگیں کہ اس پر کوئی خزانہ کیوں نہیں نازل ہوا یا اسکے
ساتھ کوئی فرشتہ کیوں نہیں آیا۔ اے محمد تم تو صرف نصیحت
کرنے والے ہو۔ اور خدا ہر چیز کا نگہبان ہے (۱۲)

فَلَعَلَّكَ تَارِكٌۢ بَعْضَ مَا يُوحَىٰٓ إِلَيْكَ
وَضَآئِقٌۢ بِهِۦ صَدْرُكَ أَن يَقُولُوا لَوْلَآ
أُنزِلَ عَلَيْهِ كَنزٌ أَوْ جَآءَ مَعَهُۥ مَلَكٌ
إِنَّمَآ أَنتَ نَذِيرٌ وَاللَّهُ عَلَىٰ كُلِّ
شَيْءٍ وَكِيلٌ ﴿١٢﴾

13. Or they may say, "He forged it." Say. "Bring ye then ten Suras forged, like unto it, and call (to your aid) whomsoever ye can, other than Allah!—If ye speak the truth!

یہ کیا کہتے ہیں کہ اس نے قرآن از خود بنا لیا ہے کہہ دو کہ اگر
سچے ہو تو تم بھی ایسی دس سورتیں بنا لاؤ اور خدا کے سوا جس
جس کو بلا سکتے ہو بلا بھی لو (۱۳)

أَمْ يَقُولُونَ افْتَرَىٰهُ قُلْ فَأْتُوا بِعَشْرِ
سُوَرٍ مِّثْلِهِۦ مُفْتَرَيَٰتٍ وَادْعُوا مَنِ
اسْتَطَعْتُم مِّن دُونِ اللَّهِ إِن كُنتُمْ صَٰدِقِينَ ﴿١٣﴾

14. "If then they (your false gods) answer not your (call), know ye that this Revelation is sent down (replete) with the knowledge of Allah, and that there is no god but He! Will ye even then submit (to Islam)?"

اگر وہ تمہاری بات قبول نہ کریں تو جان لو کہ وہ خدا کے
علم سے اترا ہے اور یہ کہ اس کے سوا کوئی معبود نہیں تو
تمہیں بھی اسلام لے آنا چاہیئے (۱۴)

فَإِلَّمْ يَسْتَجِيبُوا لَكُمْ فَاعْلَمُوٓا أَنَّمَآ
أُنزِلَ بِعِلْمِ اللَّهِ وَأَن لَّآ إِلَٰهَ إِلَّا هُوَ
فَهَلْ أَنتُم مُّسْلِمُونَ ﴿١٤﴾

15. Those who desire the life of the Present and its glitter,—to them We shall pay (the price of) their deeds therein,—without diminution.

جو لوگ دنیا کی زندگی اور اس کی زیب و زینت کے
طالب ہوں ہم ان کے اعمال کا بدلہ انہیں دنیا ہی میں
دے دیتے ہیں اور اس میں ان کی حق تلفی نہیں کی جاتی (۱۵)

مَن كَانَ يُرِيدُ الْحَيَوٰةَ الدُّنْيَا وَ
زِينَتَهَا نُوَفِّ إِلَيْهِمْ أَعْمَٰلَهُمْ فِيهَا
وَهُمْ فِيهَا لَا يُبْخَسُونَ ﴿١٥﴾

16. They are those for whom there is nothing in the Hereafter but the Fire: vain are the designs they frame therein, and of no effect are the deeds that they do!

یہ وہ لوگ ہیں جن کیلئے آخرت میں آتش (جہنم) کے سوا اور کچھ
نہیں اور جو عمل انہوں نے دنیا میں کئے سب برباد اور
جو کچھ وہ کرتے رہے سب ضائع ہوا (۱۶)

أُولَٰٓئِكَ الَّذِينَ لَيْسَ لَهُمْ فِي الْءَاخِرَةِ
إِلَّا النَّارُ وَحَبِطَ مَا صَنَعُوا فِيهَا
وَبَٰطِلٌ مَّا كَانُوا يَعْمَلُونَ ﴿١٦﴾

17. Can they be (like) those who accept a Clear (Sign) from their Lord and followed by a witness from Him and before him is the Book of Moses—a guide and a mercy? They believe therein; but those of the Sects that reject it,—the Fire will be their promised meeting-place. Be not then in doubt thereon: for it is the Truth from thy Lord: yet many among men do not believe!

بھلا جو لوگ اپنے پروردگار کی طرف سے دلیل (روشن)
رکھتے ہوں اور ان کے ساتھ ایک (آسمانی) گواہ بھی اسکی جانب سے
ہو اور اس سے پہلے موسیٰ کی کتاب ہو جو پیشوا اور رحمت ہو
(تو کیا وہ قرآن پر ایمان نہیں لائینگے) یہی لوگ تو اس پر ایمان لاتے
ہیں اور جو کوئی اور فرقوں میں سے اس سے منکر ہو تو اس کا ٹھکانا آگ
ہے تو تم اس (قرآن) سے شک میں نہ ہونا۔ یہ تمہارے پروردگار
کی طرف سے حق ہے لیکن اکثر لوگ ایمان نہیں لاتے (۱۷)

أَفَمَن كَانَ عَلَىٰ بَيِّنَةٍ مِّن رَّبِّهِۦ وَ
يَتْلُوهُ شَاهِدٌ مِّنْهُ وَمِن قَبْلِهِۦ كِتَٰبُ
مُوسَىٰٓ إِمَامًا وَرَحْمَةً أُولَٰٓئِكَ يُؤْمِنُونَ
بِهِۦ وَمَن يَكْفُرْ بِهِۦ مِنَ الْأَحْزَابِ فَالنَّارُ
مَوْعِدُهُۥ فَلَا تَكُ فِي مِرْيَةٍ مِّنْهُ
إِنَّهُ الْحَقُّ مِن رَّبِّكَ وَلَٰكِنَّ أَكْثَرَ
النَّاسِ لَا يُؤْمِنُونَ ﴿١٧﴾

18. Who doth more wrong than those who forge a lie against Allah?

اور اس سے بڑھ کر ظالم کون ہوگا جو خدا پر جھوٹ افترا

وَمَنْ أَظْلَمُ مِمَّنِ افْتَرَىٰ عَلَى اللَّهِ

They will be brought before their Lord, and the witnesses will say, "These are the ones who lied against their Lord! Behold! the Curse of Allah is on those who do wrong!—

19. "Those who hinder (men) from the path of Allah and wish it, to be crooked: these were they who denied the Hereafter!"

20. They will not escape in earth, nor have they protectors besides Allah! Their chastisement will be doubled! They could not hear, nor they could see!

21. They are the ones who have lost their own souls: and the (fancies) they forged have left them in the lurch!

22. Without a doubt, these are the very ones who will lose most in the Hereafter!

23. But those who believe and work righteousness, and humble themselves before their Lord—they will be Companions of the Garden, to dwell therein for aye!

24. These two kinds (of men) may be compared to the blind and deaf, and those who can see and hear well. Are they equal when compared? Will ye not then take heed?

25. We sent Noah to his People (with a mission); "I have come to you as a clear warner.

26. "That ye serve none but Allah: verily I do fear for you the punishment of a Grievous Day.

27. But the Chiefs of the Unbelievers among his People said: "We see (in) thee nothing but a man like ourselves: nor do we see that any follow thee but the meanest among us, apparently nor do we see in you (all) any merit above us: in fact we think ye are liars!"

کرے ہ ایسے لوگ خدا کے سامنے پیش کئے جائیں گے اور
گواہ کہیں گے کہ یہی لوگ ہیں جنہوں نے اپنے پروردگار پر جھوٹ
بولا تھا۔ سُن رکھو کہ ظالموں پر خدا کی لعنت ہے (١٨)
جو خدا کے رستے سے روکتے اور اس میں کجی چاہتے ہیں۔ اور
وہ آخرت سے بھی انکار کرتے ہیں (١٩)
یہ لوگ زمین میں (کہیں بھاگ کر خدا کو) ہرا نہیں سکتے۔
اور نہ خدا کے سوا کوئی ان کا حمایتی ہے۔ (اے
پیغمبر) ان کو دُگنا عذاب دیا جائے گا۔ کیونکہ یہ
(شدّتِ کفر سے تمہاری بات) نہیں سُن سکتے تھے
اور نہ (تم کو) دیکھ سکتے تھے (٢٠)
یہی ہیں جنہوں نے اپنے تئیں خسارے میں ڈالا۔ اور جو
کچھ وہ افترا کیا کرتے تھے اُن سے جاتا رہا (٢١)
بلاشُبہ یہ لوگ آخرت میں سب سے زیادہ نقصان پانے والے ہیں (٢٢)
جو لوگ ایمان لائے اور عمل نیک کئے۔ اور اپنے پروردگار
کے آگے عاجزی کی۔ یہی صاحبِ جنّت ہیں۔ ہمیشہ اس
میں رہیں گے (٢٣)
دونوں فرقوں (یعنی کافر و مومن) کی مثال ایسی ہے جیسے ایک اندھا بہرا (٢٤)
ہو اور ایک دیکھتا سنتا۔ بھلا دونوں کا حال یکساں ہو سکتا ہے؟ پھر تم سوچتے کیوں نہیں۔
اور ہم نے نوح کو اُن کی قوم کی طرف بھیجا (تو اُنہوں نے اُن سے کہا) کہ
میں تم کو کھول کھول کر ڈر سُنانے (اور یہ پیغام پہنچانے) آیا ہوں (٢٥)
کہ خدا کے سوا کسی کی عبادت نہ کرو۔ مجھے تمہاری نسبت
عذاب الیم کا خوف ہے (٢٦)
تو اُن کی قوم کے سردار جو کافر تھے کہنے لگے کہ ہم تم کو اپنے
ہی جیسا ایک آدمی دیکھتے ہیں اور یہ بھی دیکھتے ہیں کہ تمہارے
پیرو وہی لوگ ہوئے ہیں جو ہم میں ادنیٰ درجے کے ہیں۔ اور
وہ بھی رائے ظاہر سے (نہ غور و تعمق سے) اور ہم تم میں اپنے اوپر
کسی طرح کی فضیلت نہیں دیکھتے بلکہ تمہیں جھوٹا خیال کرتے ہیں (٢٧)

كَذَبَا ۚ أُولٰٓئِكَ يُعْرَضُونَ عَلٰى رَبِّهِمْ
وَيَقُولُ الْاَشْهَادُ هٰٓؤُلَآءِ الَّذِيْنَ كَذَبُوْا
عَلٰى رَبِّهِمْ ۚ اَلَا لَعْنَةُ اللّٰهِ عَلَى الظّٰلِمِيْنَ (١٨)
الَّذِيْنَ يَصُدُّوْنَ عَنْ سَبِيْلِ اللّٰهِ وَ
يَبْغُوْنَهَا عِوَجًا ۖ وَهُمْ بِالْاٰخِرَةِ هُمْ كٰفِرُوْنَ (١٩)
اُولٰٓئِكَ لَمْ يَكُوْنُوْا مُعْجِزِيْنَ فِى الْاَرْضِ
وَمَا كَانَ لَهُمْ مِّنْ دُوْنِ اللّٰهِ مِنْ
اَوْلِيَآءَ ۘ يُضٰعَفُ لَهُمُ الْعَذَابُ ۚ مَا
كَانُوْا يَسْتَطِيْعُوْنَ السَّمْعَ وَمَا كَانُوْا
يُبْصِرُوْنَ (٢٠)
اُولٰٓئِكَ الَّذِيْنَ خَسِرُوْٓا اَنْفُسَهُمْ وَضَلَّ
عَنْهُمْ مَّا كَانُوْا يَفْتَرُوْنَ (٢١)
لَا جَرَمَ اَنَّهُمْ فِى الْاٰخِرَةِ هُمُ الْاَخْسَرُوْنَ (٢٢)
اِنَّ الَّذِيْنَ اٰمَنُوْا وَعَمِلُوا الصّٰلِحٰتِ وَ
اَخْبَتُوْٓا اِلٰى رَبِّهِمْ ۙ اُولٰٓئِكَ اَصْحٰبُ
الْجَنَّةِ ۚ هُمْ فِيْهَا خٰلِدُوْنَ (٢٣)
مَثَلُ الْفَرِيْقَيْنِ كَالْاَعْمٰى وَالْاَصَمِّ وَالْبَصِيْرِ
وَالسَّمِيْعِ ۭ هَلْ يَسْتَوِيٰنِ مَثَلًا ۭ اَفَلَا تَذَكَّرُوْنَ (٢٤)
وَلَقَدْ اَرْسَلْنَا نُوْحًا اِلٰى قَوْمِهٖٓ ۡ اِنِّىْ لَكُمْ
نَذِيْرٌ مُّبِيْنٌ (٢٥)
اَنْ لَّا تَعْبُدُوْٓا اِلَّا اللّٰهَ ۭ اِنِّىْٓ اَخَافُ
عَلَيْكُمْ عَذَابَ يَوْمٍ اَلِيْمٍ (٢٦)
فَقَالَ الْمَلَاُ الَّذِيْنَ كَفَرُوْا مِنْ قَوْمِهٖ
مَا نَرٰىكَ اِلَّا بَشَرًا مِّثْلَنَا وَمَا نَرٰىكَ
اتَّبَعَكَ اِلَّا الَّذِيْنَ هُمْ اَرَاذِلُنَا
بَادِىَ الرَّاْىِ ۚ وَمَا نَرٰى لَكُمْ عَلَيْنَا مِنْ
فَضْلٍ بَلْ نَظُنُّكُمْ كٰذِبِيْنَ (٢٧)

28. He said: "O my People! see ye if (it be that) I have a Clear Sign from my Lord and that He hath sent Mercy unto me from Him, but that the Mercy hath been obscured from your sight? Shall we compel you to accept it when ye are averse to it?

29. "And O my People! I ask you for no wealth I return: my reward is from none but Allah: but I will not drive away (in contempt) those who believe: for verily they are to meet their Lord, and ye I see are the ignorant ones!

30. "And O my People! who would help me against Allah if I drove them away? Will ye not then take heed?

31. "I tell you not that with me are the Treasures of Allah, nor do I know what is hidden, nor claim I to be an angel. Nor yet do I say, of those whom your eyes do despise that Allah will not grant them (all) that is good: Allah knoweth best what is in their souls: I should, if I did, indeed be a wrong-doer."

32. They said: "O Noah! thou hast disputed with us, and (much) hast thou prolonged the dispute with us: now bring upon us what thou threatenest us with, if thou speakest the truth!?"

33. He said: "Truly, Allah will bring it on you if He wills,—and then, ye will not be able to frustrate it!

34. "Of no profit will be my counsel to you, much as I desire to give you (good) counsel, if it be that Allah willeth to leave you astray: He is your Lord! and to Him will ye return!"

35. Or do they say, "He has forged it"? Say: "If I had forged it, on me were my sin! And I am free of the sins of which ye are guilty!

36. It was revealed to Noah: "None of thy People will believe except those who have believed already! So grieve no longer over

قَالَ يٰقَوْمِ اَرَءَيْتُمْ اِنْ كُنْتُ عَلٰى بَيِّنَةٍ
مِّنْ رَّبِّيْ وَاٰتٰىنِيْ رَحْمَةً مِّنْ عِنْدِهٖ فَعُمِّيَتْ
عَلَيْكُمْ ؕ اَنُلْزِمُكُمُوْهَا وَاَنْتُمْ لَهَا كٰرِهُوْنَ ﴿٢٨﴾
وَيٰقَوْمِ لَاۤ اَسْـَٔلُكُمْ عَلَيْهِ مَالًا ؕ اِنْ
اَجْرِيَ اِلَّا عَلَى اللّٰهِ وَمَاۤ اَنَا بِطَارِدِ
الَّذِيْنَ اٰمَنُوْا ؕ اِنَّهُمْ مُّلٰقُوْا رَبِّهِمْ وَ
لٰكِنِّيْۤ اَرٰىكُمْ قَوْمًا تَجْهَلُوْنَ ﴿٢٩﴾
وَيٰقَوْمِ مَنْ يَّنْصُرُنِيْ مِنَ اللّٰهِ اِنْ
طَرَدْتُّهُمْ ؕ اَفَلَا تَذَكَّرُوْنَ ﴿٣٠﴾
وَلَاۤ اَقُوْلُ لَكُمْ عِنْدِيْ خَزَآئِنُ اللّٰهِ
وَلَاۤ اَعْلَمُ الْغَيْبَ وَلَاۤ اَقُوْلُ اِنِّيْ
مَلَكٌ وَّلَاۤ اَقُوْلُ لِلَّذِيْنَ تَزْدَرِيْۤ
اَعْيُنُكُمْ لَنْ يُّؤْتِيَهُمُ اللّٰهُ خَيْرًا ؕ اَللّٰهُ
اَعْلَمُ بِمَا فِيْۤ اَنْفُسِهِمْ ۖۚ اِنِّيْۤ اِذًا
لَّمِنَ الظّٰلِمِيْنَ ﴿٣١﴾
قَالُوْا يٰنُوْحُ قَدْ جٰدَلْتَنَا فَاَكْثَرْتَ
جِدَالَنَا فَاْتِنَا بِمَا تَعِدُنَاۤ اِنْ كُنْتَ
مِنَ الصّٰدِقِيْنَ ﴿٣٢﴾
قَالَ اِنَّمَا يَاْتِيْكُمْ بِهِ اللّٰهُ اِنْ شَآءَ
وَمَاۤ اَنْتُمْ بِمُعْجِزِيْنَ ﴿٣٣﴾
وَلَا يَنْفَعُكُمْ نُصْحِيْۤ اِنْ اَرَدْتُّ اَنْ
اَنْصَحَ لَكُمْ اِنْ كَانَ اللّٰهُ يُرِيْدُ اَنْ
يُّغْوِيَكُمْ ؕ هُوَ رَبُّكُمْ ۫ وَاِلَيْهِ تُرْجَعُوْنَ ﴿٣٤﴾
اَمْ يَقُوْلُوْنَ افْتَرٰىهُ ؕ قُلْ اِنِ افْتَرَيْتُهٗ
فَعَلَيَّ اِجْرَامِيْ وَاَنَا بَرِيْٓءٌ مِّمَّا تُجْرِمُوْنَ ﴿٣٥﴾
وَاُوْحِيَ اِلٰى نُوْحٍ اَنَّهٗ لَنْ يُّؤْمِنَ مِنْ
قَوْمِكَ اِلَّا مَنْ قَدْ اٰمَنَ فَلَا تَبْتَئِسْ

انہوں نے کہا کہ اے قوم! دیکھو تو اگر میں اپنے پروردگار کی طرف سے دلیلِ روشن
رکھتا ہوں اور اُس نے مجھے اپنے ہاں سے رحمت بخشی ہو جس کی حقیقت تم سے
پوشیدہ رکھی گئی ہے تو کیا ہم اسکے لئے تمہیں مجبور کر سکتے ہیں اور تم ہو کہ اس سے ناخوش ہو رہے ہو ﴿٢٨﴾
اور اے قوم! میں اس (نصیحت) کے بدلے تم سے مال و زر کا
خواہاں نہیں ہوں میرا صلہ تو خدا کے ذمے ہے اور جو لوگ ایمان
لائے ہیں میں اُن کو نکالنے والا بھی نہیں ہوں۔ وہ تو اپنے پروردگار
سے ملنے والے ہیں لیکن میں دیکھتا ہوں کہ تم لوگ نادانی کر رہے ہو ﴿٢٩﴾
اور برادرانِ ملت اگر میں ان کو نکال دوں تو (عذاب) خدا سے
بچانے کیلئے کون میری مدد کر سکتا ہے؟ بھلا تم غور کیوں نہیں کرتے؟ ﴿٣٠﴾
میں نہ تم سے یہ کہتا ہوں کہ میرے پاس خدا کے خزانے ہیں اور نہ
یہ کہ میں غیب جانتا ہوں اور نہ یہ کہتا ہوں کہ میں فرشتہ ہوں
اور نہ ان لوگوں کی نسبت جن کو تم حقارت کی نظر سے دیکھتے ہو
یہ کہتا ہوں کہ خدا ان کو بھلائی (یعنی اعمال کی جزائے نیک)
نہیں دے گا۔ جو ان کے دلوں میں ہے اُسے خدا خوب جانتا ہے۔
اگر میں ایسا کہوں تو بے انصافوں میں ہوں ﴿٣١﴾
اُنہوں نے کہا کہ نوح تم نے ہم سے جھگڑا تو کیا اور جھگڑا
بھی بہت کیا لیکن اگر سچے ہو تو جس چیز سے ہمیں ڈراتے ہو
وہ ہم پر لا نازل کرو ﴿٣٢﴾
نوح نے کہا کہ اس کو تو خدا ہی چاہے گا تو نازل کرے گا۔
اور تم (اس کو کسی طرح) ہرا نہیں سکتے ﴿٣٣﴾
اور اگر میں یہ چاہوں کہ تمہاری خیر خواہی کروں اور خدا یہ
چاہے کہ تمہیں گمراہ کرے تو میری خیر خواہی تم کو کچھ فائدہ نہیں
دے سکتی۔ وہی تمہارا پروردگار ہے اور تمہیں اسی کی طرف لوٹ کر جانا ہے ﴿٣٤﴾
کیا یہ کہتے ہیں کہ اس پیغمبر نے قرآن اپنے دل سے بنا لیا ہے کہہ دو کہ اگر میں نے دل سے
بنا لیا ہے تو میرے گناہ کا وبال مجھ پر اور جو گناہ تم کرتے ہو اس سے میں بری الذمہ ہوں ﴿٣٥﴾
اور نوح کی طرف وحی کی گئی کہ تمہاری قوم میں جو لوگ
ایمان لا چکے (لا چکے) ان کے سوا اور کوئی ایمان نہیں لائے گا

their (evil) deeds.

37. "But construct an Ark under Our eyes and Our inspiration, and address Me no (further) on behalf of those who are in sin: for they are about to be overwhelmed (in the Flood)."

38. Forthwith he (starts) constructing the Ark: every time that the Chiefs of his People passed by him, they threw ridicule on him. He said: "If ye ridicule us now, we (in our turn) can look down on you with ridicule likewise!

39. "But soon will ye know who it is on whom will descend a Chastisement that will cover them with shame,—on whom will be unloosed a Chastisement lasting.:"

40. At length, behold! there came Our Command, and the fountains of the earth gushed forth! We said: "Embark therein, of each kind two, male and female, and your family—except those against whom the Word has already gone forth,— and the believers." But only a few believed with him.

41. So he said: "Embark ye on the Ark in the name of Allah, whether it move or be at rest! For my Lord is, be sure, Oft-Forgiving, Most Merciful!"

42. So the Ark sailed with them on the waves (towering) like mountains, and Noah called out to his son, who had separated himself (from the rest): "O my son! embark with us, and be not with the Unbelievers!"

43. The son replied: "I will betake myself to some mountain: it will save me from the water." Noah said: "This day nothing can save, from the Command of Allah, any but those on whom He hath mercy!"— and the waves came between them, and the son was among those who were drowned.

44. Then the word went forth: "O earth! swallow up thy water, and O sky! withhold (thy rain)!" And the water abated, and the matter was ended. The Ark rested on Mount Jûdî, and the word went forth: "Away with those who do wrong!"

45. And Noah called upon His Lord and said: "O my Lord! surely

توجو کام یہ کر رہے ہیں اُن کی وجہ سے غم نہ کھاؤ (۳۶)
اور ایک کشتی ہمارے حکم سے ہمارے روبرو بناؤ۔ اور جو لوگ ظالم ہیں انکے
بارے میں ہم سے کچھ نہ کہنا کیونکہ وہ ضرور غرق کر دیئے جائینگے (۳۷)
تو نوح نے کشتی بنانی شروع کر دی۔ اور جب انکی قوم کے سردار انکے
پاس سے گزرتے تو اُن سے تمسخر کرتے۔ وہ کہتے کہ اگر تم ہم سے تمسخر کرتے
ہو تو جس طرح تم ہم سے تمسخر کرتے ہو اسی طرح (ایک وقت) ہم بھی تم سے تمسخر کرینگے (۳۸)
اور تم کو جلد معلوم ہو جائے گا کہ کس پر عذاب آتا ہے جو اُسے رسوا
کرے گا اور کس پر ہمیشہ کا عذاب نازل ہوتا ہے؟ (۳۹)
یہاں تک کہ جب ہمارا حکم آپہنچا اور تنور جوش مارنے لگا۔ تو ہم نے (نوح کو)
حکم دیا کہ ہر قسم (کے جانداروں) میں سے جوڑا جوڑا (یعنی) دو (دو) جانور
ایک ایک نر اور ایک ایک مادہ لے لو اور جس شخص کی نسبت حکم ہو چکا ہے
(کہ ہلاک ہو جائیگا) اس کو چھوڑ کر اپنے گھر والوں کو اور جو ایمان
لایا ہو اسکو کشتی میں سوار کر لو اور انکے ساتھ ایمان بہت ہی کم لوگ لائے تھے (۴۰)
(نوح نے) کہا کہ خدا کا نام لیکر (کہ اسی کے ہاتھ میں) اسکا چلنا اور ٹھہرنا
(ہے) اس میں سوار ہو جاؤ بیشک میرا پروردگار بخشنے والا مہربان ہے (۴۱)
اور وہ اُن کو لیکر (طوفان کی) لہروں میں چلنے لگی (لہریں کیا
تھیں) گویا پہاڑ (تھے) اس وقت نوح نے اپنے بیٹے کو کہ (کشتی
سے) الگ تھا پکارا کہ بیٹا ہمارے ساتھ سوار ہو جا اور کافروں میں شامل نہ ہو (۴۲)
اس نے کہا کہ میں (ابھی) پہاڑ سے جا لگوں گا وہ مجھے پانی سے
بچالے گا۔ انہوں نے کہا کہ آج خدا کے عذاب سے کوئی بچانے والا نہیں
(اور نہ کوئی بچ سکتا ہے) مگر جس پر خدا رحم کرے۔ اتنے میں دونوں
کے درمیان لہر آحائل ہوئی اور وہ ڈوب کر رہ گیا (۴۳)
اور حکم دیا گیا کہ اے زمین اپنا پانی نگل جا اور اے
آسمان تھم جا۔ تو پانی خشک ہو گیا اور کام تمام
کر دیا گیا اور کشتی کوہ جودی پر جا ٹھہری۔ اور کہہ دیا
گیا کہ بے انصاف لوگوں پر لعنت (۴۴)
اور نوح نے اپنے پروردگار کو پکارا اور کہا کہ پروردگار

بِمَا كَانُوا يَفْعَلُونَ (٣٦)
وَاصْنَعِ الْفُلْكَ بِأَعْيُنِنَا وَوَحْيِنَا وَلَا
تُخَاطِبْنِي فِي الَّذِينَ ظَلَمُوا إِنَّهُم مُّغْرَقُونَ (٣٧)
وَيَصْنَعُ الْفُلْكَ وَكُلَّمَا مَرَّ عَلَيْهِ مَلَأٌ
مِّن قَوْمِهِ سَخِرُوا مِنْهُ قَالَ إِن تَسْخَرُوا
مِنَّا فَإِنَّا نَسْخَرُ مِنكُمْ كَمَا تَسْخَرُونَ (٣٨)
فَسَوْفَ تَعْلَمُونَ مَن يَأْتِيهِ عَذَابٌ
يُخْزِيهِ وَيَحِلُّ عَلَيْهِ عَذَابٌ مُّقِيمٌ (٣٩)
حَتَّىٰ إِذَا جَاءَ أَمْرُنَا وَفَارَ التَّنُّورُ قُلْنَا
احْمِلْ فِيهَا مِن كُلٍّ زَوْجَيْنِ اثْنَيْنِ
وَأَهْلَكَ إِلَّا مَن سَبَقَ عَلَيْهِ الْقَوْلُ
وَمَنْ آمَنَ وَمَا آمَنَ مَعَهُ إِلَّا
قَلِيلٌ (٤٠)
وَقَالَ ارْكَبُوا فِيهَا بِسْمِ اللَّهِ مَجْرٖىهَا
وَمُرْسَاهَا إِنَّ رَبِّي لَغَفُورٌ رَّحِيمٌ (٤١)
وَهِيَ تَجْرِي بِهِمْ فِي مَوْجٍ كَالْجِبَالِ
وَنَادَىٰ نُوحٌ ابْنَهُ وَكَانَ فِي مَعْزِلٍ
يَا بُنَيَّ ارْكَب مَّعَنَا وَلَا تَكُن مَّعَ الْكَافِرِينَ (٤٢)
قَالَ سَآوِي إِلَىٰ جَبَلٍ يَعْصِمُنِي مِنَ
الْمَاءِ قَالَ لَا عَاصِمَ الْيَوْمَ مِنْ أَمْرِ اللَّهِ
إِلَّا مَن رَّحِمَ وَحَالَ بَيْنَهُمَا الْمَوْجُ
فَكَانَ مِنَ الْمُغْرَقِينَ (٤٣)
وَقِيلَ يَا أَرْضُ ابْلَعِي مَاءَكِ وَيَا سَمَاءُ
أَقْلِعِي وَغِيضَ الْمَاءُ وَقُضِيَ الْأَمْرُ وَ
اسْتَوَتْ عَلَى الْجُودِيِّ وَقِيلَ بُعْدًا
لِّلْقَوْمِ الظَّالِمِينَ (٤٤) الربع
وَنَادَىٰ نُوحٌ رَّبَّهُ فَقَالَ رَبِّ إِنَّ ابْنِي

مِنْ اَهْلِىْ وَاِنَّ وَعْدَكَ الْحَقُّ وَاَنْتَ
اَحْكَمُ الْحٰكِمِيْنَ ﴿٤٥﴾
قَالَ يٰنُوْحُ اِنَّهٗ لَيْسَ مِنْ اَهْلِكَ ۚ اِنَّهٗ
عَمَلٌ غَيْرُ صَالِحٍ ۖ فَلَا تَسْـَٔلْنِ مَا لَيْسَ
لَكَ بِهٖ عِلْمٌ ۗ اِنِّىْٓ اَعِظُكَ اَنْ تَكُوْنَ
مِنَ الْجٰهِلِيْنَ ﴿٤٦﴾
قَالَ رَبِّ اِنِّىْٓ اَعُوْذُ بِكَ اَنْ اَسْـَٔلَكَ
مَا لَيْسَ لِىْ بِهٖ عِلْمٌ ۗ وَاِلَّا تَغْفِرْ لِىْ
وَتَرْحَمْنِىْٓ اَكُنْ مِّنَ الْخٰسِرِيْنَ ﴿٤٧﴾
قِيْلَ يٰنُوْحُ اهْبِطْ بِسَلٰمٍ مِّنَّا وَبَرَكٰتٍ
عَلَيْكَ وَعَلٰٓى اُمَمٍ مِّمَّنْ مَّعَكَ ۗ وَ
اُمَمٌ سَنُمَتِّعُهُمْ ثُمَّ يَمَسُّهُمْ مِّنَّا
عَذَابٌ اَلِيْمٌ ﴿٤٨﴾
تِلْكَ مِنْ اَنْۢبَآءِ الْغَيْبِ نُوْحِيْهَآ اِلَيْكَ ۚ
مَا كُنْتَ تَعْلَمُهَآ اَنْتَ وَلَا قَوْمُكَ مِنْ
قَبْلِ هٰذَا ۛ فَاصْبِرْ ۛ اِنَّ الْعَاقِبَةَ لِلْمُتَّقِيْنَ ﴿٤٩﴾
وَاِلٰى عَادٍ اَخَاهُمْ هُوْدًا ۗ قَالَ يٰقَوْمِ
اعْبُدُوا اللّٰهَ مَا لَكُمْ مِّنْ اِلٰهٍ غَيْرُهٗ ۗ
اِنْ اَنْتُمْ اِلَّا مُفْتَرُوْنَ ﴿٥٠﴾
يٰقَوْمِ لَآ اَسْـَٔلُكُمْ عَلَيْهِ اَجْرًا ۗ اِنْ
اَجْرِىَ اِلَّا عَلَى الَّذِىْ فَطَرَنِىْ ۗ اَفَلَا
تَعْقِلُوْنَ ﴿٥١﴾
وَيٰقَوْمِ اسْتَغْفِرُوْا رَبَّكُمْ ثُمَّ تُوْبُوْٓا
اِلَيْهِ يُرْسِلِ السَّمَآءَ عَلَيْكُمْ مِّدْرَارًا وَّ
يَزِدْكُمْ قُوَّةً اِلٰى قُوَّتِكُمْ وَلَا تَتَوَلَّوْا
مُجْرِمِيْنَ ﴿٥٢﴾
قَالُوْا يٰهُوْدُ مَا جِئْتَنَا بِبَيِّنَةٍ وَّمَا نَحْنُ

میرا بیٹا بھی میرے گھر والوں میں ہے (تو اس کو بھی نجات
دے) تیرا وعدہ سچا ہے اور تو سب سے بہتر حاکم ہے ﴿٤٥﴾
خدا نے فرمایا کہ نوح وہ تیرے گھر والوں میں نہیں ہے۔
وہ تو ناشائستہ افعال ہے تو جس چیز کی تم کو حقیقت
معلوم نہیں اس کے بارے میں مجھ سے سوال ہی نہ کرو۔ اور
میں تم کو نصیحت کرتا ہوں کہ نادان نہ بنو ﴿٤٦﴾
نوح نے کہا پروردگار میں تجھ سے پناہ مانگتا ہوں کہ ایسی
چیز کا تجھ سے سوال کروں جس کی حقیقت مجھے معلوم نہیں اور
اگر تو مجھے نہیں بخشیگا اور مجھ پر رحم نہیں کریگا تو میں تباہ ہو جاؤنگا ﴿٤٧﴾
حکم ہوا کہ نوح ہماری طرف سے سلامتی اور برکتوں کے ساتھ (جو
تم پر اور تمہارے ساتھ کی جماعتوں پر نازل کی گئی ہیں)
اُتر آؤ۔ اور کچھ اور جماعتیں ہونگی جن کو ہم (دنیا کے فوائد سے)
محظوظ کرینگے پھر ان کو ہماری طرف سے عذاب الیم پہنچیگا ﴿٤٨﴾
یہ (حالات) منجملہ غیب کی خبروں کے ہیں جو ہم تمہاری طرف بھیجتے ہیں۔ اور
اس سے پہلے نہ تم ہی ان کو جانتے تھے اور نہ تمہاری قوم (ہی ان سے واقف
تھی) تو صبر کرو کہ انجام پرہیزگاروں ہی کا (بھلا) ہے ﴿٤٩﴾
اور ہم نے عاد کی طرف ان کے بھائی ہود کو بھیجا۔ انہوں نے
کہا کہ میری قوم! خدا ہی کی عبادت کرو اس کے سوا تمہارا
کوئی معبود نہیں۔ تم (شرک کر کے خدا پر) محض بہتان باندھتے ہو ﴿٥٠﴾
میری قوم! میں اس (وعظ و نصیحت) کا تم سے کچھ صلہ نہیں مانگتا۔
میرا صلہ تو اس کے ذمے ہے جس نے مجھے پیدا کیا۔ بھلا
تم سمجھتے کیوں نہیں؟ ﴿٥١﴾
اور اے قوم! اپنے پروردگار سے بخشش مانگو پھر اس کے
آگے توبہ کرو۔ وہ تم پر آسمان سے موسلا دھار مینہ برسائے گا
اور تمہاری طاقت پر طاقت بڑھائیگا۔ اور (دیکھو) گنہگار
بن کر روگردانی نہ کرو ﴿٥٢﴾
وہ بولے ہود تم ہمارے پاس کوئی دلیل ظاہر نہیں لائے۔ اور

my son is of my family and Thy promise is true, and Thou art the Justest of Judges!"

46. He said: "O Noah! he is not of thy family: for his conduct is unrighteous. So ask not of Me that of which thou hast no knowledge! I give thee counsel, lest thou become one of the ignorants!"

47. Noah said: "O my Lord! I do seek refuge with Thee, from asking Thee for that of which I have no knowledge and unless Thou forgive me and have Mercy on me, I should indeed be among the losers!

48. The word came: "O Noah! come down (from the Ark) with Peace from Us, and Blessing on thee and on some of the Peoples (who will spring) from those with thee: but (there will be other) Peoples to whom We shall grant their pleasures (for a time), but in the end will a grievous Chastisement reach them from Us."

49. Such are some of the stories of the Unseen, which We have revealed unto thee: before this, neither thou nor thy People knew them. So persevere patiently: for the End is for those who are righteous.

50. To the 'Ād People (We sent) Hûd, one of their own brethren. He said: "O my people! worship Allah! ye have no other god but Him. You are only forgers.

51. "O my people! I ask of you no reward for this (Message). My reward is from none but Him who created me: will ye not then understand?

52. "And O my people! Ask forgiveness of your Lord, and turn to Him (in repentance): He will send you the skies pouring abundant rain, and add strength to your strength: so turn ye not back in sin!"

53. They said: "O Hûd! no Clear (Sign) hast thou brought us, and

we are not the ones to desert our gods on thy word! Nor shall we believe in thee!

54. "We say nothing but that (perhaps) some of our gods may have seized thee with evil." He said: "I call Allah to witness, and do ye bear witness, that I am free from the sin of ascribing, to Him,

55. "Other gods as partners! so scheme (your worst) against me, all of you, and give me no respite.

56. "I put my trust in Allah, my Lord and your Lord! There is not a moving creature, but He hath grasp of its fore-lock. Verily, it is my Lord that is on a straight Path.

57. "If ye turn away,—I (at least) have conveyed the Message with which i was sent to you. My Lord will make another People to succeed you, and you will not harm Him in the least. For my Lord hath care and watch over all things."

58. So when Our decree issued, We saved Hûd and those who believed with him, by (special) Grace from Us: We saved them from a severe Chastisement.

59. Such were the 'Ãd People: they rejected the Signs of their Lord and Cherisher; disobeyed His Messengers; and followed the command of every powerful, obstinate Transgressor.

60. And they were pursued by a Curse in this Life,—and on the Day of Judgment. Ah! Behold! For the 'Ãd rejected their Lord and Cherisher! Away with 'Ãd the People of Hûd!

61. To the Thamud People (We sent) Sãlih, one of their own brethren he said: "O my People! worship Allah: ye have no other God but Him. It is He Who hath produced you from the earth and settled you therein: then ask forgiveness of Him, and turn to Him (in repentance): for my Lord is (always) near, ready to answer."

ہم (صرف) تمہارے کہنے سے نہ اپنے معبودوں کو چھوڑنے
والے ہیں اور نہ تم پر ایمان لانے والے ہیں ﴿۵۳﴾
ہم تو یہ سمجھتے ہیں کہ ہمارے کسی معبود نے تمہیں آسیب پہنچا (کر دیوانہ کر)
دیا ہے۔ انہوں نے کہا کہ میں خدا کو گواہ کرتا ہوں اور تم بھی گواہ
رہو کہ جن کو تم (خدا کا) شریک بناتے ہو میں اس سے بیزار ہوں ﴿۵۴﴾
(یعنی جن کی) خدا کے سوا عبادت کرتے ہو (تو تم سب مل کر میرے
بارے میں (جو تدبیر کرنی چاہو) کر لو اور مجھے مہلت نہ دو ﴿۵۵﴾
میں خدا پر جو میرا اور تمہارا (سب کا) پروردگار ہے بھروسہ رکھتا ہوں
(زمین پر) جو چلنے پھرنے والا ہے وہ اس کو چوٹی سے پکڑے ہوئے ہے
بیشک میرا پروردگار سیدھے رستے پر ہے ﴿۵۶﴾
اگر تم روگردانی کرو گے تو جو پیغام میرے ہاتھ تمہاری طرف
بھیجا گیا ہے وہ میں نے تمہیں پہنچا دیا ہے اور میرا پروردگار
تمہاری جگہ اور لوگوں کو لا بسائے گا۔ اور تم خدا کا کچھ بھی
نقصان نہیں کر سکتے میرا پروردگار تو ہر چیز پر نگہبان ہے ﴿۵۷﴾
اور جب ہمارا حکم (عذاب) آ پہنچا تو ہم نے ہود کو اور جو لوگ
ان کے ساتھ ایمان لائے تھے ان کو اپنی مہربانی سے بچا لیا۔
اور انہیں عذاب شدید سے نجات دی ﴿۵۸﴾
یہ (وہی) عاد ہیں جنہوں نے خدا کی نشانیوں سے انکار کیا اور اس کے
پیغمبروں کی نافرمانی کی اور ہر سرکش و متکبر کا کہا مانا ﴿۵۹﴾
تو اس دنیا میں بھی لعنت ان کے پیچھے لگی رہی اور قیامت کے
دن بھی (لگی رہے گی)۔ دیکھو عاد نے اپنے پروردگار سے
کفر کیا (اور) سن رکھو ہود کی قوم عاد پر پھٹکار ہے ﴿۶۰﴾
اور ثمود کی طرف ان کے بھائی صالح کو (بھیجا) تو انہوں نے
کہا کہ قوم! خدا ہی کی عبادت کرو۔ اس کے سوا تمہارا کوئی
معبود نہیں۔ اسی نے تم کو زمین سے پیدا کیا۔ اور اس میں آباد کیا۔
تو اس سے مغفرت مانگو۔ اور اس کے آگے توبہ کرو۔ بیشک میرا پروردگار
نزدیک (بھی ہے اور دعا کا) قبول کرنے والا (بھی) ہے ﴿۶۱﴾

بِتَارِكِيٓ اٰلِهَتِنَا عَنْ قَوْلِكَ وَمَا نَحْنُ
لَكَ بِمُؤْمِنِيْنَ ﴿٥٣﴾
اِنْ نَّقُوْلُ اِلَّا اعْتَرٰىكَ بَعْضُ اٰلِهَتِنَا
بِسُوْٓءٍ ۗ قَالَ اِنِّيْٓ اُشْهِدُ اللّٰهَ وَاشْهَدُوْٓا
اَنِّيْ بَرِيْٓءٌ مِّمَّا تُشْرِكُوْنَ ﴿٥٤﴾
مِنْ دُوْنِهٖ فَكِيْدُوْنِيْ جَمِيْعًا ثُمَّ
لَا تُنْظِرُوْنِ ﴿٥٥﴾
اِنِّيْ تَوَكَّلْتُ عَلَى اللّٰهِ رَبِّيْ وَرَبِّكُمْ ۭ
مَا مِنْ دَاۗبَّةٍ اِلَّا هُوَ اٰخِذٌۢ بِنَاصِيَتِهَا ۭ
اِنَّ رَبِّيْ عَلٰي صِرَاطٍ مُّسْتَقِيْمٍ ﴿٥٦﴾
فَاِنْ تَوَلَّوْا فَقَدْ اَبْلَغْتُكُمْ مَّآ اُرْسِلْتُ
بِهٖٓ اِلَيْكُمْ ۭ وَيَسْتَخْلِفُ رَبِّيْ قَوْمًا غَيْرَكُمْ ۚ
وَلَا تَضُرُّوْنَهٗ شَيْـًٔا ۭ اِنَّ رَبِّيْ عَلٰي كُلِّ
شَيْءٍ حَفِيْظٌ ﴿٥٧﴾
وَلَمَّا جَاۗءَ اَمْرُنَا نَجَّيْنَا هُوْدًا وَّالَّذِيْنَ
اٰمَنُوْا مَعَهٗ بِرَحْمَةٍ مِّنَّا ۚ وَنَجَّيْنٰهُمْ مِّنْ
عَذَابٍ غَلِيْظٍ ﴿٥٨﴾
وَتِلْكَ عَادٌ جَحَدُوْا بِاٰيٰتِ رَبِّهِمْ وَعَصَوْا
رُسُلَهٗ وَاتَّبَعُوْٓا اَمْرَ كُلِّ جَبَّارٍ عَنِيْدٍ ﴿٥٩﴾
وَاُتْبِعُوْا فِيْ هٰذِهِ الدُّنْيَا لَعْنَةً وَّيَوْمَ
الْقِيٰمَةِ ۭ اَلَآ اِنَّ عَادًا كَفَرُوْا رَبَّهُمْ ۭ اَلَا
بُعْدًا لِّعَادٍ قَوْمِ هُوْدٍ ﴿٦٠﴾ ع ۵ وقف لازم
وَاِلٰى ثَمُوْدَ اَخَاهُمْ صٰلِحًا ۘ قَالَ يٰقَوْمِ
اعْبُدُوا اللّٰهَ مَا لَكُمْ مِّنْ اِلٰهٍ غَيْرُهٗ ۭ هُوَ
اَنْشَاَكُمْ مِّنَ الْاَرْضِ وَاسْتَعْمَرَكُمْ فِيْهَا
فَاسْتَغْفِرُوْهُ ثُمَّ تُوْبُوْٓا اِلَيْهِ ۭ اِنَّ رَبِّيْ
قَرِيْبٌ مُّجِيْبٌ ﴿٦١﴾

62. They Said: "O Ṣâlih! Thou hast been of us!—A centre of our hopes hitherto! Dost thou (now) forbid us the worship of what our fathers worshipped? But we are really in suspicious (disquieting) doubt as to that to which thou invitest us."

63. He said: "O my people! Do ye see?—If I have a Clear (Sign) from my Lord and He hath sent Mercy unto me from Himself,—who then can help me against Allah if I were to disobey Him? What then would ye add to my (portion) but perdition?

64. "And O my people! This she-camel of Allah is a sign to you: leave her to feed on Allah's (free) earth, and inflict no harm on her, or a swift Punishment will seize you!"

65. But they did ham-string her. So he said: "Enjoy yourselves in your homes for three days: (then will be your ruin): (behold) there a promise not to be belied!"

66. When Our Decree issued, We saved Ṣâlih and those who believed with him, by (special) Grace from Us—and from the Ignominy of that Day. For thy Lord—He is they Strong One, and the Mighty.

67. The (mighty) Blast overtook the wrong-doers, and they lay prostrate in their homes before the morning,—

68. As if they had never dwelt and flourished there. Ah! Behold! For the Thamûd rejected their Lord and Cherisher! So away with the Thamûd

69. There came Our Messengers to Abraham with glad tidings. They said, "Peace!" He answered, "Peace!" and hastened to entertain them with a roasted calf.

70. But when he saw their hands not reaching towards the (meal), he felt some mistrust of them, and conceived a fear of them. They said: "Fear not: we have been sent against the people of Lût."

71. And his wife was standing (there), and she laughed: but We gave her glad tidings of Isaac, and after him, of Jacob.

اُنہوں نے کہا کہ صالح اس سے پہلے ہم تم سے (کئی طرح
کی) اُمیدیں رکھتے تھے (اب وہ منقطع ہو گئیں) کیا تم ہم کو
ان چیزوں سے منع کرتے ہو جن کو ہمارے بزرگ پوجتے آئے ہیں۔
اور جس بات کی طرف تم ہمیں بلاتے ہو اس میں ہمیں قوی شبہ ہے ﴿٦٢﴾
(صالح نے) کہا قوم! بھلا دیکھو تو اگر میں اپنے پروردگار کی
طرف سے کھلی دلیل پر ہوں اور اس نے مجھے اپنے ہاں سے
(نبوّت کی) نعمت بخشی ہو تو اگر میں خدا کی نافرمانی کروں تو اسکے سامنے
میری کون مدد کریگا؟ تم تو (کفر کی باتوں سے) میرا نقصان کرتے ہو ﴿٦٣﴾
اور یہ بھی کہا کہ اے قوم! یہ خدا کی اونٹنی تمہارے لئے ایک نشانی (یعنی معجزہ)
ہے۔ تو اس کو چھوڑ دو کہ خدا کی زمین میں (جہاں چاہے) چرے
اور اس کو کسی طرح کی تکلیف نہ دینا ورنہ تمہیں جلد عذاب آ پکڑیگا ﴿٦٤﴾
مگر انہوں نے اسکی کونچیں کاٹ ڈالیں۔ تو (صالح نے) کہا کہ اپنے گھروں
میں تین دن (اور) فائدے اٹھا لو۔ یہ وعدہ ہے کہ جھوٹا نہ ہوگا ﴿٦٥﴾
جب ہمارا حکم آگیا تو ہم نے صالح کو اور جو لوگ ان کے ساتھ
ایمان لائے تھے اُن کو اپنی مہربانی سے بچا لیا اور اس دن کی
رسوائی سے (محفوظ رکھا) بیشک تمہارا پروردگار طاقتور (اور) زبردست ہے ﴿٦٦﴾
اور جن لوگوں نے ظلم کیا تھا ان کو چنگھاڑ (کی صورت میں عذاب)
نے آ پکڑا تو وہ اپنے گھروں میں اوندھے پڑے رہ گئے ﴿٦٧﴾
گویا کبھی ان میں بسے ہی نہ تھے۔ سُن رکھو کہ ثمود نے اپنے پروردگار
سے کفر کیا۔ اور سُن رکھو ثمود پر پھٹکار ہے ﴿٦٨﴾
اور ہمارے فرشتے ابراہیم کے پاس بشارت لیکر آئے تو سلام کہا۔ انہوں نے بھی (جواب
میں) سلام کہا۔ ابھی کچھ وقفہ نہیں ہوا تھا کہ (ابراہیم) ایک بُھنا ہوا بچھڑا لے آئے ﴿٦٩﴾
جب دیکھا کہ ان کے ہاتھ کھانے کی طرف نہیں جاتے (یعنی وہ
کھانا نہیں کھاتے) تو ان کو اجنبی سمجھ کر دل میں خوف کیا۔ (فرشتوں نے) کہا کہ
خوف نہ کیجئے ہم قوم لوط کی طرف (انکے ہلاک کرنے کو) بھیجے گئے ہیں ﴿٧٠﴾
اور ابراہیم کی بیوی (جو پاس) کھڑی تھی ہنس پڑی تو ہم نے
اس کو اسحٰق کی اور اسحٰق کے بعد یعقوب کی خوشخبری دی ﴿٧١﴾

قَالُوْا يٰصٰلِحُ قَدْ كُنْتَ فِيْنَا مَرْجُوًّا
قَبْلَ هٰذَآ اَتَنْهٰىنَآ اَنْ نَّعْبُدَ مَا يَعْبُدُ
اٰبَآؤُنَا وَاِنَّنَا لَفِيْ شَكٍّ مِّمَّا تَدْعُوْنَآ
اِلَيْهِ مُرِيْبٍ ﴿٦٢﴾
قَالَ يٰقَوْمِ اَرَءَيْتُمْ اِنْ كُنْتُ عَلٰى
بَيِّنَةٍ مِّنْ رَّبِّيْ وَاٰتٰىنِيْ مِنْهُ رَحْمَةً
فَمَنْ يَّنْصُرُنِيْ مِنَ اللّٰهِ اِنْ عَصَيْتُهٗ
فَمَا تَزِيْدُوْنَنِيْ غَيْرَ تَخْسِيْرٍ ﴿٦٣﴾
وَيٰقَوْمِ هٰذِهٖ نَاقَةُ اللّٰهِ لَكُمْ اٰيَةً
فَذَرُوْهَا تَاْكُلْ فِيْٓ اَرْضِ اللّٰهِ وَلَا
تَمَسُّوْهَا بِسُوْٓءٍ فَيَاْخُذَكُمْ عَذَابٌ قَرِيْبٌ ﴿٦٤﴾
فَعَقَرُوْهَا فَقَالَ تَمَتَّعُوْا فِيْ دَارِكُمْ
ثَلٰثَةَ اَيَّامٍ ذٰلِكَ وَعْدٌ غَيْرُ مَكْذُوْبٍ ﴿٦٥﴾
فَلَمَّا جَآءَ اَمْرُنَا نَجَّيْنَا صٰلِحًا وَّالَّذِيْنَ
اٰمَنُوْا مَعَهٗ بِرَحْمَةٍ مِّنَّا وَمِنْ خِزْيِ
يَوْمِئِذٍ اِنَّ رَبَّكَ هُوَ الْقَوِيُّ الْعَزِيْزُ ﴿٦٦﴾
وَاَخَذَ الَّذِيْنَ ظَلَمُوا الصَّيْحَةُ فَاَصْبَحُوْا
فِيْ دِيَارِهِمْ جٰثِمِيْنَ ﴿٦٧﴾
كَاَنْ لَّمْ يَغْنَوْا فِيْهَا اَلَآ اِنَّ ثَمُوْدَا۟ كَفَرُوْا
رَبَّهُمْ اَلَا بُعْدًا لِّثَمُوْدَ ﴿٦٨﴾
وَلَقَدْ جَآءَتْ رُسُلُنَآ اِبْرٰهِيْمَ بِالْبُشْرٰى قَالُوْا
سَلٰمًا قَالَ سَلٰمٌ فَمَا لَبِثَ اَنْ جَآءَ بِعِجْلٍ حَنِيْذٍ ﴿٦٩﴾
فَلَمَّا رَآ اَيْدِيَهُمْ لَا تَصِلُ اِلَيْهِ نَكِرَهُمْ
وَاَوْجَسَ مِنْهُمْ خِيْفَةً قَالُوْا لَا تَخَفْ
اِنَّآ اُرْسِلْنَآ اِلٰى قَوْمِ لُوْطٍ ﴿٧٠﴾
وَامْرَاَتُهٗ قَآئِمَةٌ فَضَحِكَتْ فَبَشَّرْنٰهَا
بِاِسْحٰقَ وَمِنْ وَّرَآءِ اِسْحٰقَ يَعْقُوْبَ ﴿٧١﴾

72. She said: "Alas for me! Shall I bear a child, seeing I am an old woman, and my husband here is an old man? That would indeed be a wonderful thing!"

اُس نے کہا اے ہے میرے بچہ ہوگا؟ میں تو بڑھیا ہوں اور
یہ میرے میاں بھی بوڑھے ہیں یہ تو بڑی عجیب بات ہے ﴿۷۲﴾

قَالَتْ يٰوَيْلَتٰىٓ ءَاَلِدُ وَاَنَا عَجُوْزٌ وَّهٰذَا
بَعْلِيْ شَيْخًا ۭ اِنَّ هٰذَا لَشَيْءٌ عَجِيْبٌ ﴿۷۲﴾

73. They said: "Dost thou wonder at Allah's decree? The grace of Allah and His blessings on you, O ye people of the house! for He is indeed worthy of all praise, full of all glory!"

انہوں نے کہا کیا تم خدا کی قدرت سے تعجب کرتی ہو؟ اے
اہل بیت تم پر خدا کی رحمت اور اُس کی برکتیں ہیں۔ وہ سزاوار تعریف
اور بزرگوار ہے ﴿۷۳﴾

قَالُوْٓا اَتَعْجَبِيْنَ مِنْ اَمْرِ اللّٰهِ رَحْمَتُ اللّٰهِ
وَبَرَكٰتُهٗ عَلَيْكُمْ اَهْلَ الْبَيْتِ ۭ اِنَّهٗ
حَمِيْدٌ مَّجِيْدٌ ﴿۷۳﴾

74. When fear had passed from (the mind of) Abraham and the glad tidings had reached him, he began to plead with Us for Lût's people.

جب ابراہیم سے خوف جاتا رہا اور اُن کو خوشخبری بھی مل گئی
تو قوم لوط کے بارے میں لگے ہم سے بحث کرنے ﴿۷۴﴾

فَلَمَّا ذَهَبَ عَنْ اِبْرٰهِيْمَ الرَّوْعُ وَجَاۗءَتْهُ
الْبُشْرٰى يُجَادِلُنَا فِيْ قَوْمِ لُوْطٍ ﴿۷۴﴾

75. For Abraham was, without doubt, forbearing (of faults), compassionate, and given to penitence.

بے شک ابراہیم بڑے تحمل والے نرم دل اور رجوع کرنے والے تھے ﴿۷۵﴾

اِنَّ اِبْرٰهِيْمَ لَحَلِيْمٌ اَوَّاهٌ مُّنِيْبٌ ﴿۷۵﴾

76. O Abraham! seek not this. The decree of thy Lord hath gone forth: for them there cometh a Chastisement that cannot be turned back!

اے ابراہیم اس بات کو جانے دو۔ تمہارے پروردگار کا حکم
آپہنچا ہے۔ اور ان لوگوں پر عذاب آنے والا ہے جو کبھی
نہیں ٹلنے کا ﴿۷۶﴾

يٰٓاِبْرٰهِيْمُ اَعْرِضْ عَنْ هٰذَا ۚ اِنَّهٗ قَدْ
جَاۗءَ اَمْرُ رَبِّكَ ۚ وَاِنَّهُمْ اٰتِيْهِمْ عَذَابٌ
غَيْرُ مَرْدُوْدٍ ﴿۷۶﴾

77. When Our Messengers came to Lût, he was grieved on their account and felt himself powerless (to protect) them. He said: "This is a distressful day."

اور جب ہمارے فرشتے لوط کے پاس آئے تو وہ اُن (کے آنے)
سے غمناک اور تنگ دل ہوئے اور کہنے لگے کہ آج کا دن
بڑی مشکل کا دن ہے ﴿۷۷﴾

وَلَمَّا جَاۗءَتْ رُسُلُنَا لُوْطًا سِيْۗءَ بِهِمْ وَ
ضَاقَ بِهِمْ ذَرْعًا وَّقَالَ هٰذَا يَوْمٌ
عَصِيْبٌ ﴿۷۷﴾

78. And his people came rushing towards him, and they had been long in the habit of practising abominations. He said: "O my people! here are my daughters: they are purer for you (if ye marry)! Now fear Allah, and cover me not with disgrace about my guests! Is there not among you a single right-minded man?"

اور لوط کی قوم کے لوگ اُن کے پاس بے تحاشا دوڑتے ہوئے
آئے اور یہ لوگ پہلے ہی سے فعل شنیع کیا کرتے تھے۔ (لوط نے)
کہا کہ اے قوم! یہ (جو) میری (قوم کی) لڑکیاں ہیں یہ تمہارے لئے
(جائز اور) پاک ہیں۔ تو خدا سے ڈرو اور میرے مہمانوں (کے بارے) میں
میری آبرو نہ کھوؤ۔ کیا تم میں کوئی بھی شائستہ آدمی نہیں؟ ﴿۷۸﴾

وَجَاۗءَهٗ قَوْمُهٗ يُهْرَعُوْنَ اِلَيْهِ ۭ وَمِنْ
قَبْلُ كَانُوْا يَعْمَلُوْنَ السَّـيِّاٰتِ ۭ قَالَ
يٰقَوْمِ هٰٓؤُلَاۗءِ بَنَاتِيْ هُنَّ اَطْهَرُ لَكُمْ
فَاتَّقُوا اللّٰهَ وَلَا تُخْزُوْنِ فِيْ ضَيْفِيْ ۭ اَلَيْسَ
مِنْكُمْ رَجُلٌ رَّشِيْدٌ ﴿۷۸﴾

79. They said: "Well dost thou know we have no need of thy daughters: indeed thou knowest quite well what we want!"

وہ بولے تم کو معلوم ہے کہ تمہاری (قوم کی) بیٹیوں کی ہمیں کچھ
حاجت نہیں۔ اور جو ہماری غرض ہے اُسے تم (خوب) جانتے ہو ﴿۷۹﴾

قَالُوْا لَقَدْ عَلِمْتَ مَا لَنَا فِيْ بَنٰتِكَ مِنْ
حَقٍّ ۚ وَاِنَّكَ لَتَعْلَمُ مَا نُرِيْدُ ﴿۷۹﴾

80. He said: "Would that I had power to suppress you or that I could betake myself to some powerful support".

(لوط نے) کہا اے کاش مجھ میں تمہارے مقابلے کی طاقت ہوتی
یا کسی مضبوط قلعے میں پناہ پکڑ سکتا ﴿۸۰﴾

قَالَ لَوْ اَنَّ لِيْ بِكُمْ قُوَّةً اَوْ اٰوِيْٓ اِلٰى
رُكْنٍ شَدِيْدٍ ﴿۸۰﴾

81. (The Messengers) said: "O Lût! we are Messengers from thy Lord! By no means shall they reach thee! Now travel with thy family while yet a part of the night remains, and let not any of you look back: but thy wife (will remain behind): to

فرشتوں نے کہا کہ لوط ہم تمہارے پروردگار کے فرشتے ہیں یہ لوگ
ہرگز تم تک نہیں پہنچ سکیں گے تو کچھ رات رہے سے اپنے
گھر والوں کو لے کر چل دو اور تم میں سے کوئی شخص پیچھے پھر کر نہ
دیکھے۔ مگر تمہاری بیوی کہ جو آفت اُن پر پڑنے والی ہے وہی اُس پر

قَالُوْا يٰلُوْطُ اِنَّا رُسُلُ رَبِّكَ لَنْ يَّصِلُوْٓا
اِلَيْكَ فَاَسْرِ بِاَهْلِكَ بِقِطْعٍ مِّنَ الَّيْلِ
وَلَا يَلْتَفِتْ مِنْكُمْ اَحَدٌ اِلَّا امْرَاَتَكَ ۭ
اِنَّهٗ مُصِيْبُهَا مَآ اَصَابَهُمْ ۭ اِنَّ مَوْعِدَهُمُ

الصُّبْحُ ۚ أَلَيْسَ الصُّبْحُ بِقَرِيبٍ ﴿٨١﴾
فَلَمَّا جَاءَ أَمْرُنَا جَعَلْنَا عَالِيَهَا سَافِلَهَا
وَأَمْطَرْنَا عَلَيْهَا حِجَارَةً مِّن سِجِّيلٍ
مَّنضُودٍ ﴿٨٢﴾
مُّسَوَّمَةً عِندَ رَبِّكَ ۖ وَمَا هِيَ مِنَ
الظَّالِمِينَ بِبَعِيدٍ ﴿٨٣﴾
وَإِلَىٰ مَدْيَنَ أَخَاهُمْ شُعَيْبًا ۚ قَالَ
يَا قَوْمِ اعْبُدُوا اللَّهَ مَا لَكُم مِّنْ إِلَٰهٍ
غَيْرُهُ ۖ وَلَا تَنقُصُوا الْمِكْيَالَ وَالْمِيزَانَ
إِنِّي أَرَاكُم بِخَيْرٍ وَإِنِّي أَخَافُ عَلَيْكُمْ
عَذَابَ يَوْمٍ مُّحِيطٍ ﴿٨٤﴾
وَيَا قَوْمِ أَوْفُوا الْمِكْيَالَ وَالْمِيزَانَ بِالْقِسْطِ
وَلَا تَبْخَسُوا النَّاسَ أَشْيَاءَهُمْ وَلَا تَعْثَوْا
فِي الْأَرْضِ مُفْسِدِينَ ﴿٨٥﴾
بَقِيَّتُ اللَّهِ خَيْرٌ لَّكُمْ إِن كُنتُم
مُّؤْمِنِينَ ۚ وَمَا أَنَا عَلَيْكُم بِحَفِيظٍ ﴿٨٦﴾
قَالُوا يَا شُعَيْبُ أَصَلَاتُكَ تَأْمُرُكَ أَن
نَّتْرُكَ مَا يَعْبُدُ آبَاؤُنَا أَوْ أَن نَّفْعَلَ
فِي أَمْوَالِنَا مَا نَشَاءُ ۖ إِنَّكَ لَأَنتَ
الْحَلِيمُ الرَّشِيدُ ﴿٨٧﴾
قَالَ يَا قَوْمِ أَرَأَيْتُمْ إِن كُنتُ عَلَىٰ بَيِّنَةٍ
مِّن رَّبِّي وَرَزَقَنِي مِنْهُ رِزْقًا حَسَنًا ۚ
وَمَا أُرِيدُ أَنْ أُخَالِفَكُمْ إِلَىٰ مَا
أَنْهَاكُمْ عَنْهُ ۚ إِنْ أُرِيدُ إِلَّا
الْإِصْلَاحَ مَا اسْتَطَعْتُ ۚ وَمَا تَوْفِيقِي
إِلَّا بِاللَّهِ ۚ عَلَيْهِ تَوَكَّلْتُ وَإِلَيْهِ
أُنِيبُ ﴿٨٨﴾

پڑے گی) اُن کے (عذاب کے) وعدے کا وقت صبح ہے اور کیا صبح کچھ دور ہے؟ ﴿٨١﴾
تو جب ہمارا حکم آیا ہم نے اُس بستی کو (اُلٹ کر) نیچے اُوپر کر دیا۔
اور اُن پر پتھر کی تہ بہ تہ (یعنی پے در پے) کنکریاں
برسائیں ﴿٨٢﴾
جن پر تمہارے پروردگار کے ہاں سے نشان کئے ہوئے تھے۔
اور وہ (بستی ان) ظالموں سے کچھ دور نہیں ﴿٨٣﴾
اور مدین کی طرف اُن کے بھائی شعیب کو (بھیجا) تو انہوں نے
کہا کہ اے قوم! خدا ہی کی عبادت کرو کہ اس کے سوا تمہارا کوئی
معبود نہیں۔ اور ماپ اور تول میں کمی نہ کیا کرو میں تو تم کو
آسودہ حال دیکھتا ہوں اور (اگر تم ایمان نہ لاؤ گے تو) مجھے
تمہارے بارے میں ایک ایسے دن کے عذاب کا خوف ہے جو تم کو گھیر کر رہے گا ﴿٨٤﴾
اور قوم! ماپ اور تول انصاف کے ساتھ پوری پوری کیا
کرو اور لوگوں کو اُن کی چیزیں کم نہ دیا کرو۔ اور زمین میں
خرابی کرتے نہ پھرو ﴿٨٥﴾
اگر تم کو (میرے کہنے کا) یقین ہو تو خدا کا دیا ہوا نفع ہی تمہارے
لئے بہتر ہے اور میں تمہارا نگہبان نہیں ہوں ﴿٨٦﴾
اُنہوں نے کہا شعیب کیا تمہاری نماز تمہیں یہ سکھاتی ہے
کہ جن کو ہمارے باپ دادا پوجتے آئے ہیں ہم اُن کو ترک کر دیں
یا اپنے مال میں تصرف کرنا چاہیں تو نہ کریں تم تو بڑے
نرم دل اور راست باز ہو ﴿٨٧﴾
اُنہوں نے کہا کہ اے قوم! دیکھو تو اگر میں اپنے پروردگار کی طرف
سے دلیل روشن پر ہوں اور اُس نے اپنے ہاں سے مجھے نیک
روزی دی ہو (تو کیا میں ان کے خلاف کروں گا؟) اور میں نہیں چاہتا کہ جس امر سے
میں تمہیں منع کروں خود اُس کو کرنے لگوں۔ میں تو جہاں تک مجھ سے
ہو سکے (تمہارے معاملات کی) اصلاح چاہتا ہوں اور (اس بارے
میں) مجھے توفیق کا ملنا خدا ہی (کے فضل) سے ہے۔ میں اُسی پر
بھروسہ رکھتا ہوں اور اسی کی طرف رجوع کرتا ہوں ﴿٨٨﴾

her will happen what happens to the people. Morning is their time appointed: is not the morning nigh?"

82. When Our decree issued, We turned (the cities) upside down, and rained down on them brimstones hard as baked clay, spread, layer on layer,—

83. Marked from thy Lord; nor are they ever far from those who do wrong!

84. To the Madyan people (We sent) Shu'aib, one of their own brethren: he said: "O my people! worship Allah: ye have no other god but Him. And give not short measure or weight: I see you in prosperity, but I fear for you the Chastisement of a Day that will compass (you) all round.

85. "And O my people! give just measure and weight, nor withhold from the people the things that are their due: commit not evil in the land with intent to do mischief.

86. 'That which is left you by Allah is best for you, if ye (but) believed! But I am not set over you to keep watch!"

87. They said: "O Shu'aib! does thy prayer command thee that we leave off the worship which our fathers practised, or that we leave off doing what we like with our property? Truly, thou art the one that forbeareth with faults and is right-minded!"

88. He said: "O my people! see ye whether I have a Clear (Sign) from my Lord, and He hath given me sustenance (pure and) good as from Himself? I wish not, in opposition to you, to do that which I forbid you to do. I only desire (your) betterment to the best of my power; and my success (in my task) can only come from Allah. In Him I trust, and unto Him I turn.

89. "And O my people! let not my dissent (from you) cause you to sin, lest ye suffer a fate similar to that of the people of Noah or of Hûd or of Ṣâlih, nor are the people of Lût far off from you!
90. "But ask forgiveness of your Lord, and turn unto Him (in repentance): for my Lord is indeed full of mercy and loving-kindness."
91. They said: "O Shu'aib! much of what thou sayest we do not understand! In fact among us we see that thou hast no strength! Were it not for thy family, we should certainly have stoned thee! For thou hast among us no great position!"
92. He said: "O my people! is then my family of more consideration with you than Allah? For ye cast Him away behind your backs (with contempt). But verily my Lord encompasseth all that ye do!
93. "And O my people! do whatever ye can: I will do (my part): soon will ye know who it is on whom descends the Chastisement of ignominy, and who is a liar! And watch ye! For I too am watching with you!"
94. When Our decree issued, We saved Shu'aib and those who believed with him, by (special) Mercy from Us: but the (mighty) Blast did seize the wrong-doers, and they lay prostrate in their homes by the morning,—

95. As if they had never dwelt and flourished there! So away with Madyan as were Thamûd gone away.
96. And We sent Moses, with Our Clear (Signs) and an authority manifest,
97. Unto Pharaoh and his Chiefs: but they followed the command of Pharaoh, and the command of Pharaoh was not rightly guided.
98. He will go before his people on the Day of Judgment, and lead them into the Fire but woeful indeed will be the place to which they are led!
99. And they are followed by a curse in this (life) and on the Day of Judgment: and woeful is the gift which shall be given (unto them)!

اور اے قوم! میری مخالفت تم سے کوئی ایسا کام نہ کرا دے کہ جیسی مصیبت
نوح کی قوم یا ہود کی قوم یا صالح کی قوم پر واقع ہوئی تھی ویسی ہی مصیبت
تم پر واقع ہو اور لوط کی قوم (کا زمانہ تو) تم سے کچھ دور نہیں ﴿٨٩﴾
اور اپنے پروردگار سے بخشش مانگو اور اُسکے آگے توبہ کرو۔
بیشک میرا پروردگار رحم والا (اور) محبت والا ہے ﴿٩٠﴾
انہوں نے کہا کہ شعیب تمہاری بہت سی باتیں ہماری سمجھ میں نہیں
آتیں اور ہم دیکھتے ہیں کہ تم ہم میں کمزور بھی ہو اور اگر تمہارے بھائی نہ
ہوتے تو ہم تم کو سنگسار کر دیتے اور تم ہم پر کسی طرح بھی غالب نہیں ہو ﴿٩١﴾
اُنہوں نے کہا کہ قوم! کیا میرے بھائی بندوں کا دباؤ تم پر خدا سے
زیادہ ہے؟ اور اس کو تم نے پیٹھ پیچھے ڈال رکھا ہے۔ میرا
پروردگار تو تمہارے سب اعمال پر احاطہ کئے ہوئے ہے ﴿٩٢﴾
اور برادران ملت تم اپنی جگہ کام کئے جاؤ میں (اپنی جگہ) کام کئے
جاتا ہوں تم کو عنقریب معلوم ہو جائیگا کہ رسوا کرنیوالا عذاب کس پر آتا ہے
اور جھوٹا کون ہے؟ اور تم بھی انتظار کرو میں بھی تمہارے ساتھ انتظار کرتا ہوں ﴿٩٣﴾
اور جب ہمارا حکم آ پہنچا تو ہم نے شعیب کو اور جو لوگ اُن کے
ساتھ ایمان لائے تھے اُن کو تو اپنی رحمت سے بچا لیا اور جو
ظالم تھے اُن کو چنگھاڑ نے آ دبوچا تو وہ اپنے گھروں
میں اوندھے پڑے رہ گئے ﴿٩٤﴾
گویا اُن میں کبھی بسے ہی نہ تھے سُن رکھو کہ مدین پر
(ویسی ہی) پھٹکار ہے جیسی ثمود پر پھٹکار تھی ﴿٩٥﴾
اور ہم نے موسیٰ کو اپنی نشانیاں اور دلیل روشن دیکر بھیجا ﴿٩٦﴾
(یعنی) فرعون اور اسکے سرداروں کی طرف تو وہ فرعون ہی کے
حکم پر چلے۔ اور فرعون کا حکم درست نہیں تھا ﴿٩٧﴾
وہ قیامت کے دن اپنی قوم کے آگے آگے چلیگا اور انکو دوزخ
میں جا اُتاریگا۔ اور جس مقام پر وہ اُتارے جائینگے وہ بُرا ہے ﴿٩٨﴾
اور اس جہان میں بھی لعنت اُنکے پیچھے لگا دی گئی اور قیامت
کے دن بھی (پیچھے لگی رہے گی)، جو انعام ان کو ملا ہے بُرا ہے ﴿٩٩﴾

وَيٰقَوْمِ لَا يَجْرِمَنَّكُمْ شِقَاقِيْٓ اَنْ يُّصِيْبَكُمْ
مِّثْلُ مَآ اَصَابَ قَوْمَ نُوْحٍ اَوْ قَوْمَ هُوْدٍ
اَوْ قَوْمَ صٰلِحٍ ؕ وَمَا قَوْمُ لُوْطٍ مِّنْكُمْ بِبَعِيْدٍ ﴿٨٩﴾
وَاسْتَغْفِرُوْا رَبَّكُمْ ثُمَّ تُوْبُوْٓا اِلَيْهِ ؕ اِنَّ
رَبِّيْ رَحِيْمٌ وَّدُوْدٌ ﴿٩٠﴾
قَالُوْا يٰشُعَيْبُ مَا نَفْقَهُ كَثِيْرًا مِّمَّا تَقُوْلُ
وَاِنَّا لَنَرٰىكَ فِيْنَا ضَعِيْفًا ۚ وَلَوْلَا رَهْطُكَ
لَرَجَمْنٰكَ ؗ وَمَآ اَنْتَ عَلَيْنَا بِعَزِيْزٍ ﴿٩١﴾
قَالَ يٰقَوْمِ اَرَهْطِيْٓ اَعَزُّ عَلَيْكُمْ مِّنَ اللّٰهِ ؕ
وَاتَّخَذْتُمُوْهُ وَرَآءَكُمْ ظِهْرِيًّا ؕ اِنَّ رَبِّيْ
بِمَا تَعْمَلُوْنَ مُحِيْطٌ ﴿٩٢﴾
وَيٰقَوْمِ اعْمَلُوْا عَلٰى مَكَانَتِكُمْ اِنِّيْ عَامِلٌ ؕ
سَوْفَ تَعْلَمُوْنَ ۙ مَنْ يَّاْتِيْهِ عَذَابٌ يُّخْزِيْهِ
وَمَنْ هُوَ كَاذِبٌ ؕ وَارْتَقِبُوْٓا اِنِّيْ مَعَكُمْ رَقِيْبٌ ﴿٩٣﴾
وَلَمَّا جَآءَ اَمْرُنَا نَجَّيْنَا شُعَيْبًا وَّالَّذِيْنَ
اٰمَنُوْا مَعَهٗ بِرَحْمَةٍ مِّنَّا ۚ وَاَخَذَتِ
الَّذِيْنَ ظَلَمُوا الصَّيْحَةُ فَاَصْبَحُوْا فِيْ
دِيَارِهِمْ جٰثِمِيْنَ ﴿٩٤﴾
كَاَنْ لَّمْ يَغْنَوْا فِيْهَا ؕ اَلَا بُعْدًا لِّمَدْيَنَ
كَمَا بَعِدَتْ ثَمُوْدُ ﴿٩٥﴾ ع
وَلَقَدْ اَرْسَلْنَا مُوْسٰى بِاٰيٰتِنَا وَسُلْطٰنٍ مُّبِيْنٍ ﴿٩٦﴾
اِلٰى فِرْعَوْنَ وَمَلَا۟ئِهٖ فَاتَّبَعُوْٓا اَمْرَ فِرْعَوْنَ ۚ
وَمَآ اَمْرُ فِرْعَوْنَ بِرَشِيْدٍ ﴿٩٧﴾
يَقْدُمُ قَوْمَهٗ يَوْمَ الْقِيٰمَةِ فَاَوْرَدَهُمُ
النَّارَ ؕ وَبِئْسَ الْوِرْدُ الْمَوْرُوْدُ ﴿٩٨﴾
وَاُتْبِعُوْا فِيْ هٰذِهٖ لَعْنَةً وَّيَوْمَ الْقِيٰمَةِ ؕ
بِئْسَ الرِّفْدُ الْمَرْفُوْدُ ﴿٩٩﴾

ذٰلِكَ مِنْ اَنْۢبَآءِ الْقُرٰى نَقُصُّهٗ عَلَيْكَ
مِنْهَا قَآئِمٌ وَّحَصِيْدٌ ﴿١٠٠﴾

یہ (پرانی) بستیوں کے تھوڑے سے حالات ہیں جو ہم تم سے بیان کرتے
ہیں۔ ان میں سے بعض تو باقی ہیں اور بعض کا تہس نہس ہو گیا (۱۰۰)

100. These are some of the stories of communities which We relate unto thee: of them some are standing, and some have been mown down (by the sickle of time).

وَمَا ظَلَمْنٰهُمْ وَلٰكِنْ ظَلَمُوْٓا اَنْفُسَهُمْ فَمَآ
اَغْنَتْ عَنْهُمْ اٰلِهَتُهُمُ الَّتِيْ يَدْعُوْنَ مِنْ
دُوْنِ اللّٰهِ مِنْ شَيْءٍ لَّمَّا جَآءَ اَمْرُ رَبِّكَ ؕ وَمَا
زَادُوْهُمْ غَيْرَ تَتْبِيْبٍ ﴿١٠١﴾

اور ہم نے ان لوگوں پر ظلم نہیں کیا بلکہ انہوں نے خود اپنے اوپر
ظلم کیا غرض جب تمہارے پروردگار کا حکم آپہنچا تو جن معبودوں
کو وہ خدا کے سوا پکارا کرتے تھے وہ اُن کے کچھ بھی کام نہ
آئے۔ اور تباہ کرنے کے سوا اُنکے حق میں اور کچھ نہ کر سکے (۱۰۱)

101. It was not We that wronged them: they wronged their own souls: the deities, other than Allah, whom they invoked, profited them no whit when there issued the decree of thy Lord: nor did they add aught (to their lot) but perdition!

وَكَذٰلِكَ اَخْذُ رَبِّكَ اِذَآ اَخَذَ الْقُرٰى
وَهِيَ ظَالِمَةٌ ؕ اِنَّ اَخْذَهٗٓ اَلِيْمٌ شَدِيْدٌ ﴿١٠٢﴾

اور تمہارا پروردگار جب نافرمان بستیوں کو پکڑا کرتا ہے تو اسکی پکڑ
اسی طرح کی ہوتی ہے۔ بیشک اسکی پکڑ دُکھ دینے والی (اور سخت) ہے (۱۰۲)

102. Such is the chastisement of thy Lord when He chastises communities in the midst of their wrong: grievous, indeed, and severe is His chastisement.

اِنَّ فِيْ ذٰلِكَ لَاٰيَةً لِّمَنْ خَافَ عَذَابَ
الْاٰخِرَةِ ؕ ذٰلِكَ يَوْمٌ مَّجْمُوْعٌ ۙ لَّهُ النَّاسُ
وَذٰلِكَ يَوْمٌ مَّشْهُوْدٌ ﴿١٠٣﴾

اِن (قصوں) میں اس شخص کے لئے جو عذابِ آخرت سے
ڈرے عبرت ہے۔ یہ وہ دن ہوگا جس میں سب لوگ اکٹھے کئے جائینگے
اور یہی وہ دن ہوگا جسمیں سب (خدا کے رُوبرو) حاضر کئے جائینگے (۱۰۳)

103. In that is a Sign for those who fear the Chastisement of the Hereafter; that is a Day for which mankind will be gathered together: that will be a Day of Testimony.

وَمَا نُؤَخِّرُهٗٓ اِلَّا لِاَجَلٍ مَّعْدُوْدٍ ؕ ﴿١٠٤﴾

اور ہم اسکے لانے میں ایک وقتِ معین تک تاخیر کر رہے ہیں (۱۰۴)

104. Nor shall We delay it but for a term appointed.

يَوْمَ يَاْتِ لَا تَكَلَّمُ نَفْسٌ اِلَّا بِاِذْنِهٖ ۚ
فَمِنْهُمْ شَقِيٌّ وَّسَعِيْدٌ ﴿١٠٥﴾

جس روز وہ آجائے گا تو کوئی متنفس خدا کے حکم کے بغیر بول بھی
نہیں سکیگا۔ پھر ان میں سے کچھ بدبخت ہونگے اور کچھ نیک بخت (۱۰۵)

105. The day it arrives, no soul shall speak except by His leave: of those (gathered) some will be wretched and some will be blessed.

فَاَمَّا الَّذِيْنَ شَقُوْا فَفِي النَّارِ لَهُمْ فِيْهَا
زَفِيْرٌ وَّشَهِيْقٌ ۙ ﴿١٠٦﴾

توجو بدبخت ہوں گے وہ دوزخ میں (ڈال دیئے جائینگے)
اُس میں اُن کو چلّانا اور دھاڑنا ہوگا (۱۰۶)

106. Those who are wretched shall be in the Fire: there will be for them therein (nothing but) the heaving of sighs and sobs:

خٰلِدِيْنَ فِيْهَا مَا دَامَتِ السَّمٰوٰتُ وَالْاَرْضُ
اِلَّا مَا شَآءَ رَبُّكَ ؕ اِنَّ رَبَّكَ فَعَّالٌ لِّمَا
يُرِيْدُ ﴿١٠٧﴾

(اور) جب تک آسمان اور زمین ہیں اُسی میں رہیں گے۔
مگر جتنا تمہارا پروردگار چاہے۔ بیشک تمہارا پروردگار
جو چاہتا ہے کر دیتا ہے (۱۰۷)

107. They will dwell therein so long as the heavens and the earth endure, except as thy Lord willeth: for thy Lord is the (sure) Accomplisher of what He planneth.

وَاَمَّا الَّذِيْنَ سُعِدُوْا فَفِي الْجَنَّةِ خٰلِدِيْنَ
فِيْهَا مَا دَامَتِ السَّمٰوٰتُ وَالْاَرْضُ اِلَّا
مَا شَآءَ رَبُّكَ ؕ عَطَآءً غَيْرَ مَجْذُوْذٍ ﴿١٠٨﴾

اور جو نیک بخت ہونگے وہ بہشت میں (داخل کئے جائینگے اور) جب تک
آسمان اور زمین ہیں ہمیشہ اسی میں رہیں گے مگر جتنا تمہارا پروردگار
چاہے۔ یہ (خدا کی) بخشش ہے جو کبھی منقطع نہیں ہوگی (۱۰۸)

108. And those who are blessed shall be in the Garden: they will dwell therein so long as the heavens and the earth endure, except as thy Lord willeth: a gift without break.

فَلَا تَكُ فِيْ مِرْيَةٍ مِّمَّا يَعْبُدُ هٰٓؤُلَآءِ ؕ
مَا يَعْبُدُوْنَ اِلَّا كَمَا يَعْبُدُ اٰبَآؤُهُمْ
مِّنْ قَبْلُ ؕ وَاِنَّا لَمُوَفُّوْهُمْ نَصِيْبَهُمْ
غَيْرَ مَنْقُوْصٍ ﴿١٠٩﴾ ع

تو یہ لوگ جو (غیر خدا کی) پرستش کرتے ہیں۔ اس سے تم خلجان
میں نہ پڑنا۔ یہ (اسی طرح) پرستش کرتے ہیں جس طرح پہلے سے انکے
باپ دادا پرستش کرتے آئے ہیں۔ اور ہم ان کو ان کا حصہ
پورا پورا بلا کم و کاست دینے والے ہیں (۱۰۹)

109. Be not then in doubt as to what these men worship. They worship nothing but what their fathers worshipped before (them): but verily We shall pay them back (in full) their portion without (the least) abatement.

وَلَقَدْ اٰتَيْنَا مُوْسَى الْكِتٰبَ فَاخْتُلِفَ فِيْهِ ؕ

اور ہم نے موسیٰ کو کتاب دی تو اس میں اختلاف کیا گیا۔ اور اگر

110. We certainly gave the Book to Moses, but differences arose

وَلَوْلَا كَلِمَةٌ سَبَقَتْ مِن رَّبِّكَ لَقُضِيَ بَيْنَهُمْ
وَإِنَّهُمْ لَفِي شَكٍّ مِّنْهُ مُرِيبٍ ﴿١١٠﴾
وَإِنَّ كُلًّا لَّمَّا لَيُوَفِّيَنَّهُمْ رَبُّكَ أَعْمَالَهُمْ
إِنَّهُ بِمَا يَعْمَلُونَ خَبِيرٌ ﴿١١١﴾
فَاسْتَقِمْ كَمَا أُمِرْتَ وَمَن تَابَ مَعَكَ
وَلَا تَطْغَوْا إِنَّهُ بِمَا تَعْمَلُونَ بَصِيرٌ ﴿١١٢﴾
وَلَا تَرْكَنُوا إِلَى الَّذِينَ ظَلَمُوا فَتَمَسَّكُمُ
النَّارُ وَمَا لَكُم مِّن دُونِ اللَّهِ مِنْ
أَوْلِيَاءَ ثُمَّ لَا تُنصَرُونَ ﴿١١٣﴾
وَأَقِمِ الصَّلَاةَ طَرَفَيِ النَّهَارِ وَزُلَفًا
مِّنَ اللَّيْلِ إِنَّ الْحَسَنَاتِ يُذْهِبْنَ السَّيِّئَاتِ
ذَٰلِكَ ذِكْرَىٰ لِلذَّاكِرِينَ ﴿١١٤﴾
وَاصْبِرْ فَإِنَّ اللَّهَ لَا يُضِيعُ أَجْرَ
الْمُحْسِنِينَ ﴿١١٥﴾
فَلَوْلَا كَانَ مِنَ الْقُرُونِ مِن قَبْلِكُمْ
أُولُو بَقِيَّةٍ يَنْهَوْنَ عَنِ الْفَسَادِ فِي
الْأَرْضِ إِلَّا قَلِيلًا مِّمَّنْ أَنجَيْنَا مِنْهُمْ
وَاتَّبَعَ الَّذِينَ ظَلَمُوا مَا أُتْرِفُوا
فِيهِ وَكَانُوا مُجْرِمِينَ ﴿١١٦﴾
وَمَا كَانَ رَبُّكَ لِيُهْلِكَ الْقُرَىٰ بِظُلْمٍ
وَأَهْلُهَا مُصْلِحُونَ ﴿١١٧﴾
وَلَوْ شَاءَ رَبُّكَ لَجَعَلَ النَّاسَ أُمَّةً
وَاحِدَةً وَلَا يَزَالُونَ مُخْتَلِفِينَ ﴿١١٨﴾
إِلَّا مَن رَّحِمَ رَبُّكَ وَلِذَٰلِكَ خَلَقَهُمْ
وَتَمَّتْ كَلِمَةُ رَبِّكَ لَأَمْلَأَنَّ جَهَنَّمَ
مِنَ الْجِنَّةِ وَالنَّاسِ أَجْمَعِينَ ﴿١١٩﴾
وَكُلًّا نَّقُصُّ عَلَيْكَ مِنْ أَنبَاءِ الرُّسُلِ

تمہارے پروردگار کی طرف سے ایک بات پہلے نہ ہو چکی ہوتی تو ان میں
فیصلہ کر دیا جاتا۔ اور وہ تو اس سے قوی شبہے میں (پڑے ہوئے) ہیں ﴿١١٠﴾
اور تمہارا پروردگار ان سب کو (قیامت کے دن) ان کے اعمال کا پورا
پورا بدلہ دے گا۔ بیشک جو عمل یہ کرتے ہیں وہ اس سے واقف ہے ﴿١١١﴾
سو (اے پیغمبر) جیسا تم کو حکم ہوتا ہے (اس پر) تم اور جو لوگ تمہارے ساتھ
تائب ہوئے ہیں قائم رہو۔ اور حد سے تجاوز نہ کرنا۔ وہ تمہارے سب اعمال کو دیکھ رہا ہے ﴿١١٢﴾
اور جو لوگ ظالم ہیں اُن کی طرف مائل نہ ہونا نہیں تو تمہیں (دوزخ
کی) آگ آ لپٹے گی اور خدا کے سوا تمہارے اور دوست نہیں ہیں اگر تم
ظالموں کی طرف مائل ہو گئے تو پھر تم کو (کہیں سے) مدد نہ مل سکے گی ﴿١١٣﴾
اور دن کے دونوں سروں (یعنی صبح اور شام کے اوقات میں) اور رات
کی چند (پہلی) ساعات میں نماز پڑھا کرو۔ کچھ شک نہیں کہ نیکیاں گناہوں
کو دور کر دیتی ہیں۔ یہ اُن کے لئے نصیحت ہے جو نصیحت قبول کرنے والے ہیں ﴿١١٤﴾
اور صبر کئے رہو کہ خدا نیکوکاروں کا اجر ضائع
نہیں کرتا ﴿١١٥﴾
تو جو اُمتیں تم سے پہلے گزر چکی ہیں ان میں ایسے ہوشمند
کیوں نہ ہوئے جو ملک میں خرابی کرنے سے روکتے ہاں
(ایسے) تھوڑے سے (تھے) جن کو ہم نے ان میں سے
مخلصی بخشی۔ اور جو ظالم تھے وہ اُنہی باتوں کے پیچھے لگے رہے
جن میں عیش و آرام تھا اور وہ گناہوں میں ڈوبے ہوئے تھے ﴿١١٦﴾
اور تمہارا پروردگار ایسا نہیں ہے کہ بستیوں کو جبکہ وہاں کے
باشندے نیکوکار ہوں ازراہِ ظلم تباہ کر دے ﴿١١٧﴾
اور اگر تمہارا پروردگار چاہتا تو تمام لوگوں کو ایک ہی جماعت
کر دیتا لیکن وہ ہمیشہ اختلاف کرتے رہیں گے ﴿١١٨﴾
مگر جن پر تمہارا پروردگار رحم کرے اور اسی لئے اس نے ان
کو پیدا کیا ہے اور تمہارے پروردگار کا قول پورا ہو گیا کہ میں
دوزخ کو جنوں اور انسانوں سب سے بھر دوں گا ﴿١١٩﴾
(اے محمدؐ) اور پیغمبروں کے وہ سب حالات جو ہم تم سے بیان

therein: had it not been that a Word had gone forth before from thy Lord the matter would have been decided between them: but they are in suspicious doubt concerning it.

111. And, of a surety, to all will your Lord pay back (in full the recompense) of their deeds: for He knoweth well all that they do.

112. Therefore stand firm (in the straight Path) as thou art commanded,— thou and those who with thee turn (unto Allah); and transgress not (from the Path): for He seeth well all that ye do.

113. And incline not to those who do wrong, or the Fire will touch you; and ye have no protectors other than Allah, nor shall ye be helped.

114. And establish regular prayers at the two ends of the day and at the approaches of the night: for those things that are good remove those that are evil: that is a reminder for the mindful

115. And be steadfast in patience; for verily Allah will not suffer the reward of the righteous to perish.

116. If only there had been of the generations before you, men of righteousness who prohibited men from mischief in the earth (but there were none) except a few among them whom We saved (from harm)? But the wrong-doers pursued the enjoyment of the good things of life which were given them, and persisted in sin.

117. Nor would thy Lord be the One to destroy the towns unjustly while their people are Righteous.

118. If thy Lord had so willed, He could have made mankind one People: but they will not cease to differ,

119. Except those on whom thy Lord hath bestowed His Mercy: and for this did He create them: and the Word of thy Lord shall be fulfilled: "I will fill Hell with jinns and men all together."

120. All that we relate to thee of the stories of the messengers,—

SÛRA–12
YÛSUF
(INTRODUCTION)

For the chronological place of this Sûra and the general argument of Sûras 10 to 15 see Introduction to Sura 10.

In subject-matter this Sûra is entirely taken up with the story (recapitulated rather than told) of Joseph, the youngest (but one) of the twelve sons of the patriarch Jacob.The story is called the most beautiful of stories (12:3) for many reasons: (1) it is the most detailed of any in the Qur-ãn; (2) it is full of human vicissitudes, and has therefore deservedly appealed to men and women of all classes; (3) it paints in vivid colours, with their spiritual implications, the most varied aspects of life—the patriarch's old age and the confidence between him and his litle best-beloved son, the elder brother's jealousy of this little son, their plot and their father's grief, the sale of the father's darling into slavery for a miserable little price, carnal love contrasted with purity and chastity, false charges, prison, the interpretation of dreams, low life and high life, Innocence raised to honour; the sweet "revenge" of Forgiveness and Benevolence, high matters of State and administration, humility in exaltation, filial love, and the beauty of Piety and Truth.

The story is similar to but not identical with the Biblical story; but the atmosphere is wholly diferent. The Biblical story is like a folk-tale in which morality has no place. Its tendency is to exalt the clever and financially-minded Jew against the Egyptian, and to explain certain ethnic and tribal peculiarities in later Jewish history. Joseph is shown as buying up all the cattle and the land of the poor Egyptians for the State under the stress of famine conditions, and making the Israelites "rulers" over Pharaoh's cattle.The Quranic story, on the other hand, is less a narrative than a highly spiritual sermon of allegory explaining the seeming contradictions in life, the enduring nature of virtue in a world full of flux and change, and the marvellous working of Allah's eternal purpose in His Plan as unfolded to us on the wide canvas of history. This aspect of the matter has been a favourite with Muslim poets and Ṣufi exegetists.

with it We make firm thy heart: in them there cometh to thee the Truth, as well as an exhortation and a message of remembrance to those who believe.

121. Say to those who do not believe: "Do whatever ye can: we shall do our part;

122. "And wait ye! We too shall wait."

123. To Allah do belong the unseen (secrets) of the heavens and the earth, and to Him goeth back every affair (for decision): so worship Him, and put thy trust in Him: and thy Lord is not Unmindful of aught that ye do.

کرتے ہیں ان سے ہم تمہارے دل کو قائم رکھتے ہیں اور ان (قصص)
میں تمہارے پاس حق پہنچ گیا اور (یہ) مومنوں کیلئے نصیحت اور عبرت ہے (۱۲۰)
اور جو لوگ ایمان نہیں لائے اُن سے کہہ دو کہ تم اپنی جگہ عمل کئے
جاؤ ہم (اپنی جگہ) عمل کئے جاتے ہیں (۱۲۱)
اور (نتیجہ اعمال کا) تم بھی انتظار کرو ہم بھی انتظار کرتے ہیں (۱۲۲)
اور آسمانوں اور زمین کی چھپی چیزوں کا علم خدا ہی کو ہے
اور تمام امور کا رجوع اسی کی طرف ہے۔ تو اسی کی عبادت
کرو اور اسی پر بھروسا رکھو۔ اور جو کچھ تم کر رہے ہو تمہارا
پروردگار اس سے بے خبر نہیں (۱۲۳)

مَا نُثَبِّتُ بِهٖ فُؤَادَكَ ۚ وَجَآءَكَ فِيْ هٰذِهِ
الْحَقُّ وَمَوْعِظَةٌ وَّذِكْرٰى لِلْمُؤْمِنِيْنَ ﴿۱۲۰﴾
وَقُلْ لِّلَّذِيْنَ لَا يُؤْمِنُوْنَ اعْمَلُوْا عَلٰى
مَكَانَتِكُمْ ۭ اِنَّا عٰمِلُوْنَ ﴿۱۲۱﴾
وَانْتَظِرُوْا ۚ اِنَّا مُنْتَظِرُوْنَ ﴿۱۲۲﴾
وَلِلّٰهِ غَيْبُ السَّمٰوٰتِ وَالْاَرْضِ وَاِلَيْهِ
يُرْجَعُ الْاَمْرُ كُلُّهٗ فَاعْبُدْهُ وَ
تَوَكَّلْ عَلَيْهِ ۭ وَمَا رَبُّكَ بِغَافِلٍ
عَمَّا تَعْمَلُوْنَ ﴿۱۲۳﴾

Yûsuf, or Joseph

سورۂ یوسف مکی ہے اور اسمیں ایک سو گیارہ آیتیں اور بارہ رکوع ہیں

سُوْرَةُ يُوْسُفَ مَكِّيَّةٌ وَّهِيَ مِائَةٌ وَّاِحْدٰى عَشْرَةَ اٰيَةً وَّاثْنَا عَشَرَ رُكُوْعًا

In the name of Allah, Most Gracious, Most Merciful.

1. **A. L. R.** These are the Verses of the Perspicuous Book.

2. We have sent it down as an Arabic Qur'an, in order that ye may learn wisdom.

3. We do relate unto thee the most beautiful of stories, in that We reveal to thee this (portion of the) Qur'an: before this, thou too was among those who knew it not.

4. Behold, Joseph said to his father: "O my father! I did see eleven stars and the sun and the moon: I saw them prostrate themselves to me!"

5. Said (the father): "My (dear) little son! relate not thy vision to thy brothers, lest they concoct a plot against thee: for Satan is to man an avowed enemy!

6. "Thus will thy Lord choose thee and teach thee the interpretation of stories (and events) an perfect His favour to thee and to the posterity of Jacob— even as He perfected it to thy fathers Abraham and Isaac

شروع خدا کا نام لے کر جو بڑا مہربان نہایت رحم والا ہے
آلرا۔ یہ کتاب روشن کی آیتیں ہیں (۱)
ہم نے اس قرآن کو عربی میں نازل کیا ہے تاکہ تم
سمجھ سکو (۲)
(اے پیغمبر) ہم اس قرآن کے ذریعے سے جو ہم نے تمہاری
طرف بھیجا ہے تمہیں ایک نہایت اچھا قصہ سناتے ہیں اور
تم اس سے پہلے بے خبر تھے (۳)
جب یوسف نے اپنے والد سے کہا کہ ابا میں نے (خواب میں)
گیارہ ستاروں اور سورج اور چاند کو دیکھا ہے۔ دیکھتا
(کیا) ہوں کہ وہ مجھے سجدہ کر رہے ہیں (۴)
اُنہوں نے کہا کہ بیٹا! اپنے خواب کا ذکر اپنے بھائیوں سے نہ کرنا
نہیں تو وہ تمہارے حق میں کوئی فریب کی چال چلیں گے کچھ
شک نہیں کہ شیطان انسان کا کھلا دشمن ہے (۵)
اور اسی طرح خدا تمہیں برگزیدہ (و ممتاز) کرے گا اور (خواب کی)
باتوں کی تعبیر کا علم سکھائے گا۔ اور جس طرح اس نے اپنی
نعمت پہلے تمہارے دادا پردادا ابراہیم اور اسحاق پر پوری کی
تھی اسی طرح تم پر اور اولاد یعقوب پر پوری کریگا بیشک

بِسْمِ اللّٰهِ الرَّحْمٰنِ الرَّحِيْمِ
الٓرٰ ۟ تِلْكَ اٰيٰتُ الْكِتٰبِ الْمُبِيْنِ ﴿۱﴾
اِنَّآ اَنْزَلْنٰهُ قُرْءٰنًا عَرَبِيًّا لَّعَلَّكُمْ
تَعْقِلُوْنَ ﴿۲﴾
نَحْنُ نَقُصُّ عَلَيْكَ اَحْسَنَ الْقَصَصِ
بِمَآ اَوْحَيْنَآ اِلَيْكَ هٰذَا الْقُرْاٰنَ ۖ وَ
اِنْ كُنْتَ مِنْ قَبْلِهٖ لَمِنَ الْغٰفِلِيْنَ ﴿۳﴾
اِذْ قَالَ يُوْسُفُ لِاَبِيْهِ يٰٓاَبَتِ اِنِّيْ رَاَيْتُ
اَحَدَ عَشَرَ كَوْكَبًا وَّالشَّمْسَ وَالْقَمَرَ
رَاَيْتُهُمْ لِيْ سٰجِدِيْنَ ﴿۴﴾
قَالَ يٰبُنَيَّ لَا تَقْصُصْ رُءْيَاكَ عَلٰٓى
اِخْوَتِكَ فَيَكِيْدُوْا لَكَ كَيْدًا ۭ اِنَّ
الشَّيْطٰنَ لِلْاِنْسَانِ عَدُوٌّ مُّبِيْنٌ ﴿۵﴾
وَكَذٰلِكَ يَجْتَبِيْكَ رَبُّكَ وَيُعَلِّمُكَ مِنْ
تَاْوِيْلِ الْاَحَادِيْثِ وَيُتِمُّ نِعْمَتَهٗ عَلَيْكَ
وَعَلٰٓى اٰلِ يَعْقُوْبَ كَمَآ اَتَمَّهَا عَلٰٓى اَبَوَيْكَ
مِنْ قَبْلُ اِبْرٰهِيْمَ وَاِسْحٰقَ ۭ اِنَّ رَبَّكَ

aforetime! For thy Lord is full of knowledge and wisdom.

تمہارا پروردگار (سب کچھ) جاننے والا (اور) حکمت والا ہے ﴿۶﴾

عَلِيۡمٌ حَكِيۡمٌ ﴿٦﴾ ع

7. Verily in Joseph and his brethren are Signs for Seekers (after Truth)

ہاں یوسف اور ان کے بھائیوں (کے قصے) میں پوچھنے والوں
کیلئے (بہت سی) نشانیاں ہیں ﴿۷﴾ ۱۴۹

لَقَدۡ كَانَ فِيۡ يُوۡسُفَ وَاِخۡوَتِهٖۤ اٰيٰتٌ
لِّلسَّآئِلِيۡنَ ﴿٧﴾

8. They said: "Truly Joseph and his brother are loved more by our father than we: but we are a goodly body! Really our father is obviously in error!

جب انہوں نے (آپس میں) تذکرہ کیا کہ یوسف اور اس کا
بھائی ابّا کو ہم سے زیادہ پیارے ہیں حالانکہ ہم جماعت (کی جماعت)
ہیں۔ کچھ شک نہیں کہ ابّا صریح غلطی پر ہیں ﴿۸﴾ ۱۵۰

اِذۡ قَالُوۡا لَيُوۡسُفُ وَاَخُوۡهُ اَحَبُّ اِلٰٓى
اَبِيۡنَا مِنَّا وَنَحۡنُ عُصۡبَةٌ ؕ اِنَّ اَبَانَا
لَفِيۡ ضَلٰلٍ مُّبِيۡنِ ۖ ﴿٨﴾

9. "Slay ye Joseph or cast him out to some (unknown) land, that so the favour of your father may be given to you alone: (there will be time enough) for you to be righteous after that!

تو یوسف کو (یا تو جان سے) مار ڈالو یا کسی ملک میں پھینک آؤ۔
پھر ابّا کی توجہ صرف تمہاری طرف ہو جائے گی۔ اور اس کے
بعد تم اچھی حالت میں ہو جاؤ گے ﴿۹﴾

اۨقۡتُلُوۡا يُوۡسُفَ اَوِ اطۡرَحُوۡهُ اَرۡضًا يَّخۡلُ
لَكُمۡ وَجۡهُ اَبِيۡكُمۡ وَتَكُوۡنُوۡا مِنۡۢ بَعۡدِهٖ
قَوۡمًا صٰلِحِيۡنَ ﴿٩﴾

10. Said one of them: "Slay not Joseph, but if ye must do something, throw him down to the bottom of the well: he will be picked up by some caravan of travellers."

ان میں سے ایک کہنے والے نے کہا کہ یوسف کو جان سے
نہ مارو کسی گہرے کنوئیں میں ڈال دو کہ کوئی راہگیر نکال (کر
اور ملک میں) لے جائیگا۔ اگر تم کو کرنا ہی (ہے تو یوں کرو) ﴿۱۰﴾

قَالَ قَآئِلٌ مِّنۡهُمۡ لَا تَقۡتُلُوۡا يُوۡسُفَ وَ
اَلۡقُوۡهُ فِيۡ غَيٰبَتِ الۡجُبِّ يَلۡتَقِطۡهُ بَعۡضُ
السَّيَّارَةِ اِنۡ كُنۡتُمۡ فٰعِلِيۡنَ ﴿١٠﴾

11. They said: "O our father! why dost thou not Trust us with Joseph,—seeing we are indeed his sincere well-wishers?

(یہ مشورہ کر کے وہ یعقوب سے) کہنے لگے کہ ابّا جان کیا سبب ہے کہ آپ
یوسف کے بارے میں ہمارا اعتبار نہیں کرتے حالانکہ ہم اسکے خیرخواہ ہیں ﴿۱۱﴾

قَالُوۡا يٰۤاَبَانَا مَا لَكَ لَا تَاۡمَنَّا عَلٰى يُوۡسُفَ
وَاِنَّا لَهٗ لَنٰصِحُوۡنَ ﴿١١﴾

12. "Send him with us tomorrow to enjoy himself and play, and we shall take every care of him."

کل اُسے ہمارے ساتھ بھیج دیجئے کہ خوب میوے کھائے اور کھیلے
کودے ہم اُس کے نگہبان ہیں ﴿۱۲﴾

اَرۡسِلۡهُ مَعَنَا غَدًا يَّرۡتَعۡ وَيَلۡعَبۡ وَاِنَّا
لَهٗ لَحٰفِظُوۡنَ ﴿١٢﴾

13. (Jacob) said: "Really it saddens me that ye should take him away: I fear lest the wolf should devour him while ye attend not to him."

اُنہوں نے کہا کہ یہ امر مجھے غمناک کئے دیتا ہے کہ تم اُسے
لے جاؤ (یعنی وہ مجھ سے جدا ہو جائے) اور مجھے یہ بھی خوف ہے
کہ تم (کھیل میں) اُس سے غافل ہو جاؤ اور اُسے بھیڑیا کھا جائے ﴿۱۳﴾

قَالَ اِنِّىۡ لَيَحۡزُنُنِىۡۤ اَنۡ تَذۡهَبُوۡا بِهٖ وَ
اَخَافُ اَنۡ يَّاۡكُلَهُ الذِّئۡبُ وَاَنۡتُمۡ
عَنۡهُ غٰفِلُوۡنَ ﴿١٣﴾

14. They said: "If the wolf were to devour him while we are (so large) a party, then should we be the losers!"

وہ کہنے لگے کہ اگر ہماری موجودگی میں کہ ہم ایک طاقتور جماعت
ہیں اُسے بھیڑیا کھا گیا تو ہم بڑے نقصان میں پڑ گئے ﴿۱۴﴾

قَالُوۡا لَئِنۡ اَكَلَهُ الذِّئۡبُ وَنَحۡنُ عُصۡبَةٌ
اِنَّاۤ اِذًا لَّخٰسِرُوۡنَ ﴿١٤﴾

15. So they did take him away, and they all agreed to throw him down to the bottom of the well: and We put into his heart (this Message): 'Of a surety thou shall (one day) tell them the truth of this their affair while they perceive not.'

غرض جب وہ اس کو لے گئے اور اس بات پر اتفاق کر لیا کہ
اسکو گہرے کنوئیں میں ڈالدیں تو ہم نے یوسف کی طرف وحی بھیجی کہ (ایک وقت ایسا آئیگا
کہ) تم انکے اس سلوک سے آگاہ کرو گے اور انکو (اس وحی کی) کچھ خبر نہ ہوگی ﴿۱۵﴾ ۱۵۱

فَلَمَّا ذَهَبُوۡا بِهٖ وَاَجۡمَعُوۡۤا اَنۡ يَّجۡعَلُوۡهُ
فِيۡ غَيٰبَتِ الۡجُبِّ ۚ وَاَوۡحَيۡنَاۤ اِلَيۡهِ لَـتُنَـبِّئَنَّهُمۡ
بِاَمۡرِهِمۡ هٰذَا وَهُمۡ لَا يَشۡعُرُوۡنَ ﴿١٥﴾

16. Then they came to their father in the early part of the night, weeping.

(یہ حرکت کر کے) وہ رات کے وقت باپ کے پاس روتے ہوئے آئے ﴿۱۶﴾

وَجَآءُوۡۤ اَبَاهُمۡ عِشَآءً يَّبۡكُوۡنَ ﴿١٦﴾

17. They said: "O our father! we went racing with one another, and left Joseph with our things; and the wolf devoured him. But thou wilt

(اور) کہنے لگے کہ ابّا جان ہم تو دوڑنے اور ایک دوسرے سے آگے نکلنے میں
مصروف ہو گئے اور یوسف کو اپنے اسباب کے پاس چھوڑ گئے تو اسے بھیڑیا

قَالُوۡا يٰۤاَبَانَاۤ اِنَّا ذَهَبۡنَا نَسۡتَبِقُ وَتَرَكۡنَا
يُوۡسُفَ عِنۡدَ مَتَاعِنَا فَاَكَلَهُ الذِّئۡبُ ۚ

never believe us even though we tell the truth."

18. They stained his shirt with false blood. He said: "Nay, but your minds have made up a tale (that may pass) with you, (for me) patience is most fitting: against that which ye assert, it is Allah (alone) Whose help can be sought"...

19. Then there came a caravan of travellers: they sent their water-carrier (for water), and he let down his bucket (into the well)... He said: "Ah there! Good news! Here is a (fine) young man!" So they concealed him as a treasure! But Allah knoweth well all that they do!

20. The (Brethren) sold him for a miserable price,— for a few dirhams counted out: in such low estimation did they hold him!

21. The man in Egypt who bought him, said to his wife: "Make his stay (among us) honourable: may be he will bring us much good, or we shall adopt him as a son." Thus did We establish Joseph in the land, that We might teach him the interpretation of stories (and events). And Allah Hath full power and control over His affairs; but most among mankind know it not.

22. When Joseph attained His full manhood, We gave him power and knowledge: thus do We reward those who do right.

23. But she in whose house he was, sought to seduce him and she fastened the doors, and said: "Now come," He said: "Allah forbid! truly (thy husband) is my lord ! he made my sojourn agreeable! truly to no good come those who do wrong

24. And (with passion) did she desire him, and he would have desired her, but that he saw the evidence of his Lord: thus (did We order) that We might turn away from him (all) evil and indecent deeds: for he was one of Our servants chosen.

25. So they both raced each other to the door, and she tore his shirt

کھا گیا۔ اور آپ ہماری بات کو گو ہم سچ ہی کہتے ہوں باور نہیں کرینگے (17)
اور انکے کرتے پر جھوٹ موٹ کا لہو بھی لگا لائے یعقوب نے کہا (کہ حقیقۃ الحال
یوں نہیں ہے) بلکہ تم اپنے دل سے (یہ) بات بنا لائے ہو [152] اچھا صبر (کہ وہی
خوب ہے) اور جو تم بیان کرتے ہو اسکے بارے میں خدا ہی سے مدد مطلوب ہے (18)
(اب خدا کی شان دیکھو کہ اس کنوئیں کے قریب) ایک قافلہ آوارد ہوا اور
انہوں نے (پانی کیلئے) اپنا سقا بھیجا اس نے کنوئیں میں ڈول لٹکایا
(تو یوسف اس سے لٹک گئے) وہ بولا زہے قسمت یہ تو (نہایت حسین) لڑکا ہے
اور اسکو قیمتی سرمایہ سمجھکر چھپا لیا اور جو کچھ وہ کرتے تھے خدا کو سب معلوم تھا (19)
اور اس کو تھوڑی سی قیمت (یعنی) معدودے چند درہموں پر بیچ
ڈالا اور انہیں ان (کے بارے) میں کچھ لالچ بھی نہ تھا (20)
اور مصر میں جس شخص نے اس کو خریدا [153] اس نے اپنی بیوی سے
(جس کا نام زلیخا تھا) کہا کہ اس کو عزت واکرام سے رکھو۔
عجب نہیں کہ یہ ہمیں فائدہ دے یا ہم اسے بیٹا بنا لیں اس طرح
ہم نے یوسف کو سرزمین (مصر) میں جگہ دی اور غرض یہ تھی کہ ہم ان
کو (خواب کی) باتوں کی تعبیر سکھائیں۔ اور خدا اپنے کام پر غالب ہے
لیکن اکثر لوگ نہیں جانتے (21)
اور جب وہ اپنی جوانی کو پہنچے تو ہم نے ان کو دانائی اور علم بخشا
اور نیکو کاروں کو ہم اسی طرح بدلہ دیا کرتے ہیں (22)
تو جس عورت کے گھر میں وہ رہتے تھے اس نے انکو اپنی طرف مائل کرنا چاہا
اور دروازے بند کرکے کہنے لگی (یوسف) جلدی آؤ انہوں نے کہا کہ خدا
پناہ میں رکھے وہ (یعنی تمہارے میاں) تو میرے آقا ہیں انہوں نے مجھے اچھی
طرح سے رکھا ہے (میں ایسا ظلم نہیں کر سکتا) بیشک ظالم لوگ فلاح نہیں پائیں گے (23)
اور اس عورت نے ان کا قصد کیا اور انہوں نے اس کا قصد کیا
اگر وہ اپنے پروردگار کی نشانی نہ دیکھتے (تو جو ہوتا سو ہوتا)۔ یوں
اس لئے (کیا گیا) کہ ہم ان سے برائی اور بے حیائی کو روک
دیں [154] بیشک وہ ہمارے خالص بندوں میں سے تھے (24)
اور دونوں دروازے کی طرف بھاگے (آگے یوسف پیچھے زلیخا) اور

وَمَآ اَنْتَ بِمُؤْمِنٍ لَّنَا وَلَوْ كُنَّا صٰدِقِيْنَ (17)
وَجَآءُوْ عَلٰى قَمِيْصِهٖ بِدَمٍ كَذِبٍ ۭ قَالَ
بَلْ سَوَّلَتْ لَكُمْ اَنْفُسُكُمْ اَمْرًا ۭ فَصَبْرٌ
جَمِيْلٌ ۭ وَاللّٰهُ الْمُسْتَعَانُ عَلٰى مَا تَصِفُوْنَ (18)
وَجَآءَتْ سَيَّارَةٌ فَاَرْسَلُوْا وَارِدَهُمْ
فَاَدْلٰى دَلْوَهٗ ۭ قَالَ يٰبُشْرٰى هٰذَا غُلٰمٌ ۭ
وَاَسَرُّوْهُ بِضَاعَةً ۭ وَاللّٰهُ عَلِيْمٌۢ بِمَا
يَعْمَلُوْنَ (19)
وَشَرَوْهُ بِثَمَنٍۢ بَخْسٍ دَرَاهِمَ مَعْدُوْدَةٍ ۚ
وَكَانُوْا فِيْهِ مِنَ الزّٰهِدِيْنَ (20)
وَقَالَ الَّذِي اشْتَرٰىهُ مِنْ مِّصْرَ لِامْرَاَتِهٖٓ
اَكْرِمِيْ مَثْوٰىهُ عَسٰٓى اَنْ يَّنْفَعَنَآ اَوْ نَتَّخِذَهٗ
وَلَدًا ۭ وَكَذٰلِكَ مَكَّنَّا لِيُوْسُفَ فِي الْاَرْضِ
وَلِنُعَلِّمَهٗ مِنْ تَاْوِيْلِ الْاَحَادِيْثِ ۭ وَاللّٰهُ
غَالِبٌ عَلٰٓى اَمْرِهٖ وَلٰكِنَّ اَكْثَرَ النَّاسِ
لَا يَعْلَمُوْنَ (21)
وَلَمَّا بَلَغَ اَشُدَّهٗٓ اٰتَيْنٰهُ حُكْمًا وَّعِلْمًا ۭ
وَكَذٰلِكَ نَجْزِي الْمُحْسِنِيْنَ (22)
وَرَاوَدَتْهُ الَّتِيْ هُوَ فِيْ بَيْتِهَا عَنْ نَّفْسِهٖ
وَغَلَّقَتِ الْاَبْوَابَ وَقَالَتْ هَيْتَ لَكَ ۭ
قَالَ مَعَاذَ اللّٰهِ اِنَّهٗ رَبِّيْٓ اَحْسَنَ مَثْوَايَ ۭ
اِنَّهٗ لَا يُفْلِحُ الظّٰلِمُوْنَ (23)
وَلَقَدْ هَمَّتْ بِهٖ ۚ وَهَمَّ بِهَا ۚ لَوْلَآ اَنْ
رَّاٰ بُرْهَانَ رَبِّهٖ ۭ كَذٰلِكَ لِنَصْرِفَ عَنْهُ
السُّوْۗءَ وَالْفَحْشَاۗءَ ۭ اِنَّهٗ مِنْ عِبَادِنَا
الْمُخْلَصِيْنَ (24)
وَاسْتَبَقَا الْبَابَ وَقَدَّتْ قَمِيْصَهٗ مِنْ

دُبُرٍ وَّاَلْفَيَا سَيِّدَهَا لَدَا الْبَابِ ؕ قَالَتْ
مَا جَزَآءُ مَنْ اَرَادَ بِاَهْلِكَ سُوْٓءًا اِلَّآ
اَنْ يُّسْجَنَ اَوْ عَذَابٌ اَلِيْمٌ ﴿۲۵﴾

عورت نے اُنکا کرتا پیچھے سے (پکڑ کر جو کھینچا تو) پھاڑ ڈالا اور دونوں
کو دروازے کے پاس عورت کا خاوند مل گیا تو عورت بولی کہ جو شخص تمہاری بیوی
کیساتھ برا ارادہ کرے اُس کی اسکے سوا کیا سزا ہے کہ یا تو قید کیا جائے یا دکھ کا عذاب دیا جائے ﴿۲۵﴾

from the back: they both found her lord near the door. She said: "What is the (fitting) punishment for one who formed an evil design against thy wife, but prison or a grievous chastisement?"

قَالَ هِيَ رَاوَدَتْنِيْ عَنْ نَّفْسِيْ وَشَهِدَ
شَاهِدٌ مِّنْ اَهْلِهَا ۚ اِنْ كَانَ قَمِيْصُهٗ
قُدَّ مِنْ قُبُلٍ فَصَدَقَتْ وَهُوَ مِنَ
الْكٰذِبِيْنَ ﴿۲۶﴾

(یوسف نے) کہا اسی نے مجھ کو اپنی طرف مائل کرنا چاہا تھا۔
اس کے قبیلے میں سے ایک فیصلہ کرنے والے نے یہ فیصلہ کیا کہ
اگر اس کا کُرتا آگے سے پھٹا ہو تو یہ سچّی اور یوسف
جھوٹا ہے ﴿۲۶﴾

26. He said: "It was she that sought to seduce me— from my (true) self." And one of her household saw (this) and bore witness, (thus):— "If it be that his shirt is rent from the front, then is her tale true, and he is a liar!

وَاِنْ كَانَ قَمِيْصُهٗ قُدَّ مِنْ دُبُرٍ فَكَذَبَتْ
وَهُوَ مِنَ الصّٰدِقِيْنَ ﴿۲۷﴾

اور اگر کُرتا پیچھے سے پھٹا ہو تو یہ جھوٹی اور
وہ سچا ہے ﴿۲۷﴾

27. "But if it be that his shirt is torn from the back, then is she the liar, and he is telling the truth!"

فَلَمَّا رَاٰ قَمِيْصَهٗ قُدَّ مِنْ دُبُرٍ قَالَ اِنَّهٗ
مِنْ كَيْدِكُنَّ ؕ اِنَّ كَيْدَكُنَّ
عَظِيْمٌ ﴿۲۸﴾

جب اُس کا کرتا دیکھا (تو) پیچھے سے پھٹا تھا (تب اُس
نے زلیخا سے کہا) کہ یہ تمہارا ہی فریب ہے۔ اور کچھ شک نہیں کہ تم
عورتوں کے فریب بڑے (بھاری) ہوتے ہیں ﴿۲۸﴾

28. So when he saw his shirt,—that it was torn at the back,—(her husband) said: "Behold! it is a snare of you women! Truly, mighty is your snare!

يُوْسُفُ اَعْرِضْ عَنْ هٰذَا ٚ وَاسْتَغْفِرِيْ
لِذَنْۢبِكِ ۚۖ اِنَّكِ كُنْتِ مِنَ الْخٰطِـِٕيْنَ ﴿۲۹﴾ ع

یوسف! اس بات کا خیال نہ کر۔ اور (زلیخا) تو اپنے گناہ کی
بخشش مانگ۔ بیشک خطا تیری ہی ہے ﴿۲۹﴾

29. "O Joseph, pass this over! (O wife), ask forgiveness for thy sin, for truly thou hast been at fault!"

وَقَالَ نِسْوَةٌ فِي الْمَدِيْنَةِ امْرَاَتُ الْعَزِيْزِ
تُرَاوِدُ فَتٰىهَا عَنْ نَّفْسِهٖ ۚ قَدْ شَغَفَهَا حُبًّا ؕ
اِنَّا لَنَرٰىهَا فِيْ ضَلٰلٍ مُّبِيْنٍ ﴿۳۰﴾

اور شہر میں عورتیں گفتگوئیں کرنے لگیں کہ عزیز کی بیوی اپنے
غلام کو اپنی طرف مائل کرنا چاہتی ہے اور اسکی محبت اسکے دل میں
گھر کر گئی ہے۔ ہم دیکھتی ہیں کہ وہ صریح گمراہی میں ہے ﴿۳۰﴾

30. Ladies said in the City: "The wife of the (great) 'Aziz is seeking to seduce her slave truly hath he inspired her with violent love: we see she is evidently going astray."

فَلَمَّا سَمِعَتْ بِمَكْرِهِنَّ اَرْسَلَتْ اِلَيْهِنَّ
وَاَعْتَدَتْ لَهُنَّ مُتَّكَاً وَّاٰتَتْ كُلَّ
وَاحِدَةٍ مِّنْهُنَّ سِكِّيْنًا وَّقَالَتِ
اخْرُجْ عَلَيْهِنَّ ۚ فَلَمَّا رَاَيْنَهٗٓ اَكْبَرْنَهٗ
وَقَطَّعْنَ اَيْدِيَهُنَّ ز وَقُلْنَ حَاشَ لِلّٰهِ
مَا هٰذَا بَشَرًا ؕ اِنْ هٰذَآ اِلَّا مَلَكٌ
كَرِيْمٌ ﴿۳۱﴾

جب زلیخا نے ان عورتوں کی (گفتگو جو حقیقت میں دیدار یوسف
کے لئے ایک) چال (تھی) سُنی تو اُنکے پاس (دعوت کا) پیغام بھیجا
اور اُنکے لئے ایک محفل مرتب کی۔ اور (پھل تراشنے کیلئے) ہر ایک کو ایک ایک چھری
دی اور (یوسف سے) کہا کہ ان کے سامنے باہر آؤ۔ جب عورتوں نے انکو
دیکھا تو اُن کا رعب (حسن) اُن پر (ایسا) چھا گیا کہ (پھل تراشتے
تراشتے) اپنے ہاتھ کاٹ لئے اور بیساختہ بول اُٹھیں کہ سبحان اللہ
(یہ حسن) یہ آدمی نہیں کوئی بزرگ فرشتہ ہے ﴿۳۱﴾

31. When she heard of their malicious talk, she sent for them and prepared a banquet for them: she gave each of them a knife: and she said (to Joseph), "Come out before them." When they saw him, they did extol him, and (in their amazement) cut their hands: they said, "Allah preserve us! no mortal is this! This is none other than a noble angel!"

قَالَتْ فَذٰلِكُنَّ الَّذِيْ لُمْتُنَّنِيْ فِيْهِ ؕ وَ
لَقَدْ رَاوَدْتُّهٗ عَنْ نَّفْسِهٖ فَاسْتَعْصَمَ ؕ
وَلَئِنْ لَّمْ يَفْعَلْ مَآ اٰمُرُهٗ لَيُسْجَنَنَّ

تب (زلیخا نے) کہا یہ وہی ہے جسکے بارے میں تم مجھے طعنے دیتی
تھیں اور بیشک میں نے اس کو اپنی طرف مائل کرنا چاہا مگر یہ بچا
رہا اور اگر یہ وہ کام نہ کرے گا جو میں اسے کہتی ہوں تو قید

32. She said: "There before you is the man about whom ye did blame me! I did seek to seduce him from his (true) self but he did firmly save himself guiltless!... And now, if he doth not my bidding, he

shall certainly be cast into prison, and (what is more) be of the company of the vilest!"

33. He said: "O my Lord! The prison is dearer to my liking than that to which they invite me: unless Thou turn away their snare from me, I should feel inclined towards them and join the ranks of the ignorant."

34. So his Lord hearkened to him (in his prayer) and turned away from him their snare: verily He heareth and knoweth (all things).

35. Then it occurred to them after they had seen the Signs, (that it was best) to imprison him for a time.

36. Now with him there came into the prison two young men. Said one of them; "I see myself (in a dream) pressing wine." Said the other: "I see myself (in a dream) carrying bread on my head, and birds are eating thereof." "Tell us" (they said) "the truth and meaning thereof: for we see thou art one that doth good (to all).

37. He said: "Before any food comes (in due course) to feed either of you I will surely reveal to you the truth and meaning of this ere it befall you. That is part of the (Duty) which my Lord hath taught me I have (I assure you) abandoned the ways of a people that believe not in Allah and that (even) deny the Hereafter.

38. "And I follow the ways of my fathers,—Abraham, Isaac and Jacob; and never could we attribute any partners whatever to Allah: that (comes) of the grace of Allah to us and to mankind: yet Most men are not grateful.

39. "O my two companions. Of the prison! (I ask you): are many lords differing among themselves better, or Allah the One, Supreme and Irresistible?

40. Whatever ye worship apart from Him is nothing but names which ye have named, ye and your

کر دیا جائے گا اور ذلیل ہوگا ﴿۳۲﴾
یوسف نے دعا کی کہ پروردگار جس کام کی طرف یہ مجھے بلاتی ہیں اس کی
نسبت مجھے قید پسند ہے اور اگر تو مجھ سے ان کے فریب کو نہ ہٹائیگا تو میں ان کی
طرف مائل ہو جاؤں گا اور نادانوں میں داخل ہو جاؤنگا ﴿۳۳﴾
تو خدا نے اُن کی دعا قبول کر لی اور ان سے عورتوں کا مکر دفع
کر دیا۔ بیشک وہ سننے (اور) جاننے والا ہے ﴿۳۴﴾
پھر باوجود اس کے کہ وہ لوگ نشان دیکھ چکے تھے اُن کی
رائے یہی ٹھہری کہ کچھ عرصے کیلئے اُن کو قید ہی کر دیں ﴿۳۵﴾
اور ان کے ساتھ دو اور جوان بھی داخل زنداں ہوئے ایک نے
اُن میں سے کہا کہ (میں نے خواب دیکھا ہے) دیکھتا (کیا) ہوں کہ شراب (کیلئے
انگور) نچوڑ رہا ہوں دوسرے نے کہا کہ (میں نے بھی خواب دیکھا ہے) یہ
دیکھتا ہوں کہ اپنے سر پر روٹیاں اٹھائے ہوئے ہوں اور جانور اُن میں سے
کھا رہے ہیں (تو ہمیں) ان کی تعبیر بتا دیجئے کہ ہم تمہیں نیکوکار دیکھتے ہیں ﴿۳۶﴾
یوسف نے کہا کہ جو کھانا تم کو ملنے والا ہے وہ آنے نہیں پائیگا
کہ میں اس سے پہلے تم کو اس کی تعبیر بتا دوں گا۔ یہ اُن
(باتوں) میں سے ہے جو میرے پروردگار نے مجھے سکھائی ہیں
جو لوگ خدا پر ایمان نہیں لاتے اور روز آخرت سے انکار کرتے
ہیں میں اُن کا مذہب چھوڑے ہوئے ہوں ﴿۳۷﴾
اور اپنے باپ دادا ابراہیم اور اسحاق اور یعقوب کے مذہب
پر چلتا ہوں۔ ہمیں شایاں نہیں ہے کہ کسی چیز کو خدا
کے ساتھ شریک بنائیں یہ خدا کا فضل ہے ہم پر بھی
اور لوگوں پر بھی ہے۔ لیکن اکثر لوگ شکر
نہیں کرتے ﴿۳۸﴾
میرے جیل خانے کے رفیقو! بھلا کئی جدا جدا آقا اچھے
یا (ایک) خدائے یکتا و غالب؟ ﴿۳۹﴾
جن چیزوں کی تم خدا کے سوا پرستش کرتے ہو وہ صرف نام ہی
نام ہیں جو تم نے اور تمہارے باپ دادا نے رکھ لئے ہیں

وَلَيَكُونًا مِّنَ الصّٰغِرِينَ ﴿۳۲﴾
قَالَ رَبِّ السِّجْنُ أَحَبُّ إِلَيَّ مِمَّا يَدْعُونَنِيٓ
إِلَيْهِ ۚ وَإِلَّا تَصْرِفْ عَنِّي كَيْدَهُنَّ
أَصْبُ إِلَيْهِنَّ وَأَكُن مِّنَ الْجٰهِلِينَ ﴿۳۳﴾
فَاسْتَجَابَ لَهُ رَبُّهُ فَصَرَفَ عَنْهُ
كَيْدَهُنَّ ۚ إِنَّهُ هُوَ السَّمِيعُ الْعَلِيمُ ﴿۳۴﴾
ثُمَّ بَدَا لَهُم مِّنۢ بَعْدِ مَا رَأَوُا الْاٰيٰتِ
لَيَسْجُنُنَّهُ حَتّٰى حِينٍ ﴿۳۵﴾
وَدَخَلَ مَعَهُ السِّجْنَ فَتَيَانِ ۚ قَالَ
أَحَدُهُمَآ إِنِّيٓ أَرٰىنِيٓ أَعْصِرُ خَمْرًا ۖ وَقَالَ
الْاٰخَرُ إِنِّيٓ أَرٰىنِيٓ أَحْمِلُ فَوْقَ رَأْسِي
خُبْزًا تَأْكُلُ الطَّيْرُ مِنْهُ ۖ نَبِّئْنَا
بِتَأْوِيلِهِ ۖ إِنَّا نَرٰىكَ مِنَ الْمُحْسِنِينَ ﴿۳۶﴾
قَالَ لَا يَأْتِيكُمَا طَعَامٌ تُرْزَقٰنِهِ إِلَّا
نَبَّأْتُكُمَا بِتَأْوِيلِهِ قَبْلَ أَن يَأْتِيَكُمَا ۚ
ذٰلِكُمَا مِمَّا عَلَّمَنِي رَبِّي ۚ إِنِّي
تَرَكْتُ مِلَّةَ قَوْمٍ لَّا يُؤْمِنُونَ بِاللّٰهِ وَهُم
بِالْاٰخِرَةِ هُمْ كٰفِرُونَ ﴿۳۷﴾
وَاتَّبَعْتُ مِلَّةَ اٰبَآءِيٓ إِبْرٰهِيمَ وَإِسْحٰقَ
وَيَعْقُوبَ ۚ مَا كَانَ لَنَآ أَن نُّشْرِكَ بِاللّٰهِ
مِن شَيْءٍ ۚ ذٰلِكَ مِن فَضْلِ اللّٰهِ عَلَيْنَا
وَعَلَى النَّاسِ وَلٰكِنَّ أَكْثَرَ النَّاسِ لَا
يَشْكُرُونَ ﴿۳۸﴾
يٰصٰحِبَيِ السِّجْنِ ءَأَرْبَابٌ مُّتَفَرِّقُونَ
خَيْرٌ أَمِ اللّٰهُ الْوٰحِدُ الْقَهَّارُ ﴿۳۹﴾
مَا تَعْبُدُونَ مِن دُونِهِۦٓ إِلَّآ أَسْمَآءً
سَمَّيْتُمُوهَآ أَنتُمْ وَاٰبَآؤُكُم مَّآ أَنزَلَ

fathers,— for which Allah hath sent down no authority: the Command is for none but Allah: He hath commanded that ye worship none but Him: that is the right religion, but most men understand not...

خدا نے اُن کی کوئی سند نازل نہیں کی (سُن رکھو کہ) خدا
کے سوا کسی کی حکومت نہیں ہے اُس نے ارشاد فرمایا ہے
کہ اس کے سوا کسی کی عبادت نہ کرو یہی سیدھا دین ہے
لیکن اکثر لوگ نہیں جانتے (۴۰)

اللّٰهُ بِهَا مِنْ سُلْطٰنٍ ۭ اِنِ الْحُكْمُ اِلَّا
لِلّٰهِ ۭ اَمَرَ اَلَّا تَعْبُدُوْٓا اِلَّآ اِيَّاهُ ۭ ذٰلِكَ
الدِّيْنُ الْقَيِّمُ وَلٰكِنَّ اَكْثَرَ النَّاسِ
لَا يَعْلَمُوْنَ (۴۰)

41. "O my two companions of the prison! As to one of you, he will pour out the wine for his lord to drink; as for the other, he will hang from the cross, and the birds will eat from off his head. (So) hath been decreed that matter whereof ye twain do enquire"...

42. And of the two, to that one whom he considered about to be saved, he said: "Mention me to thy lord," but Satan made him forget to mention him to his lord: and (Joseph) lingered in prison a few (more) years.

میرے جیل خانے کے رفیقو تم میں سے ایک (جو پہلا خواب
بیان کرنے والا ہے وہ) تو اپنے آقا کو شراب پلایا کرے گا۔
اور جو دوسرا ہے وہ سُولی دیا جائے گا اور جانور اُس کا سر کھا
جائیں گے۔ جو امر تم مجھ سے پوچھتے تھے وہ فیصل ہو چکا ہے (۴۱)
اور دونوں شخصوں میں سے جس کی نسبت (یوسف نے) خیال
کیا کہ وہ رہائی پا جائے گا اس سے کہا کہ اپنے آقا سے میرا
ذکر بھی کرنا لیکن شیطان نے اُن کا اپنے آقا سے ذکر کرنا بھلا
دیا اور (یوسف) کئی برس جیل خانے ہی میں رہے (۴۲)

يٰصَاحِبَيِ السِّجْنِ اَمَّآ اَحَدُكُمَا
فَيَسْقِيْ رَبَّهٗ خَمْرًا ۚ وَاَمَّا الْاٰخَرُ فَيُصْلَبُ
فَتَاْكُلُ الطَّيْرُ مِنْ رَّاْسِهٖ ۭ قُضِيَ الْاَمْرُ
الَّذِيْ فِيْهِ تَسْتَفْتِيٰنِ (۴۱)
وَقَالَ لِلَّذِيْ ظَنَّ اَنَّهٗ نَاجٍ مِّنْهُمَا
اذْكُرْنِيْ عِنْدَ رَبِّكَ ۡ فَاَنْسٰىهُ
الشَّيْطٰنُ ذِكْرَ رَبِّهٖ فَلَبِثَ فِي السِّجْنِ
بِضْعَ سِنِيْنَ (۴۲) ع ۵

43. The king (of Egypt) said: "I do see (in a vision) seven fat kine, whom seven lean ones devour,— and seven green ears of corn, and seven (others) withered. O ye chiefs! expound to me my vision if it be that ye can interpret visions."

اور بادشاہ نے کہا کہ میں (نے خواب دیکھا ہے) دیکھتا
(کیا) ہوں کہ سات موٹی گائیں ہیں جن کو سات دُبلی گائیں
کھا رہی ہیں۔ اور سات خوشے سبز ہیں اور (سات) خشک
اے سردارو اگر تم خوابوں کی تعبیر دے سکتے ہو تو مجھے میرے
خواب کی تعبیر بتاؤ (۴۳)

وَقَالَ الْمَلِكُ اِنِّىْٓ اَرٰى سَبْعَ بَقَرٰتٍ
سِمَانٍ يَّاْكُلُهُنَّ سَبْعٌ عِجَافٌ وَّسَبْعَ
سُنْۢبُلٰتٍ خُضْرٍ وَّاُخَرَ يٰبِسٰتٍ ۭ يٰٓاَيُّهَا
الْمَلَاُ اَفْتُوْنِيْ فِيْ رُءْيَايَ اِنْ كُنْتُمْ لِلرُّءْيَا
تَعْبُرُوْنَ (۴۳)

44. They said: "A confused medley of dreams: and we are not skilled in the interpretation of dreams."

45. But the man who had been released, one of the two (who had been in prison) and who now remembered him after (so long) a space of time, said: "I will tell you the truth of its interpretation: send ye me (therefore)."

46. "O Joseph!" (he said) "O man of truth! expound to us (the dream) of seven fat kine whom seven lean ones devour, and of seven green ears of corn and (seven) others withered: that I may return to the people, and that they may know."

47. (Joseph) said: "For seven years shall ye diligently sow as is your wont: and the harvests that ye

انہوں نے کہا یہ تو پریشان سے خواب ہیں اور ہمیں ایسے
خوابوں کی تعبیر نہیں آتی (۴۴)
اب وہ شخص جو دونوں قیدیوں میں سے رہائی پا گیا تھا اور جسے مدت کے بعد وہ
بات یاد آگئی بول اُٹھا کہ میں آپ کو اس کی تعبیر (لا) بتاتا ہوں مجھے (جیلخانے) جانے کی اجازت دیجیے (۴۵)
(غرض وہ یوسف کے پاس آیا اور کہنے لگا) یوسف اے بڑے سچے
(یوسف) ہمیں (اس خواب) کی تعبیر بتائیے کہ سات موٹی گایوں کو سات دُبلی
گائیں کھا رہی ہیں۔ اور سات خوشے سبز ہیں اور سات سوکھے تاکہ میں لوگوں کے پاس
واپس جا کر (تعبیر) بتاؤں عجب نہیں کہ وہ (تمہاری قدر) جانیں (۴۶)
اُنہوں نے کہا کہ تم لوگ سات سال متواتر کھیتی کرتے رہو گے
تو جو (غلہ) کاٹو تو تھوڑے سے غلے کے سوا جو کھانے میں آئے

قَالُوْٓا اَضْغَاثُ اَحْلَامٍ ۚ وَمَا نَحْنُ بِتَاْوِيْلِ
الْاَحْلَامِ بِعٰلِمِيْنَ (۴۴)
وَقَالَ الَّذِيْ نَجَا مِنْهُمَا وَادَّكَرَ بَعْدَ
اُمَّةٍ اَنَا اُنَبِّئُكُمْ بِتَاْوِيْلِهٖ فَاَرْسِلُوْنِ (۴۵)
يُوْسُفُ اَيُّهَا الصِّدِّيْقُ اَفْتِنَا فِيْ سَبْعِ
بَقَرٰتٍ سِمَانٍ يَّاْكُلُهُنَّ سَبْعٌ عِجَافٌ
وَّسَبْعِ سُنْۢبُلٰتٍ خُضْرٍ وَّاُخَرَ يٰبِسٰتٍ ۙ
لَّعَلِّيْٓ اَرْجِعُ اِلَى النَّاسِ لَعَلَّهُمْ يَعْلَمُوْنَ (۴۶)
قَالَ تَزْرَعُوْنَ سَبْعَ سِنِيْنَ دَاَبًا ۚ
فَمَا حَصَدْتُّمْ فَذَرُوْهُ فِيْ سُنْۢبُلِهٖٓ

reap, ye shall leave them in the ear,—except a little, of which ye shall eat.

48. "Then will come after that (period) seven dreadful (years), which will devour what ye shall have laid by in advance for them,—(all) except a little which ye shall have (specially) guarded.

49. "Then will come after that (period) a year in which the people will have abundant water, and in which they will press (wine and oil.)"

50. So the king said: "Bring ye him unto me." But when the messenger came to him, (Joseph) said: "Go thou back to thy lord, and ask him, 'What was the matter with the ladies who cut their hands'? For my Lord is certainly well aware of their snare."

51. (The king) said (to the ladies): "What was your affair when ye did seek to seduce Joseph?" The ladies said: "Allah preserve us! no evil know we against him!" Said the 'Aziz's wife: "Now is the truth manifest (to all): it was I who sought to seduce him he is indeed of those who are (ever) true (and virtuous).

52. 'This (say I), in order that he may know that I have never been false to him in his absence, and that Allah will never guide the snare of the false ones

53. "Yet I do not absolve myself (of blame): the (human) soul certainly incites evil, unless my Lord do bestow His Mercy: but surely my Lord is Oft-Forgiving, Most Merciful."

54. So the king said: "Bring him unto me; I will take him specially to serve about my own person." Therefore when he had spoken to him, he said: "Be assured this day, thou art of high standing with us, invested with all trust."

55. (Joseph) said: "Set me over the store-houses of the land: I am a good keeper, knowledgeable."

اُسے خوشوں میں ہی رہنے دینا ﴿۴۷﴾
پھر اس کے بعد (خشک سالی کے) سات سخت (سال) آئینگے
کہ جو (غلہ) تم نے جمع کر رکھا ہوگا وہ اس سب کو کھا جائیں گے۔
صرف وہی تھوڑا سا رہ جائے گا جو تم احتیاط سے رکھ چھوڑو گے ﴿۴۸﴾
پھر اس کے بعد ایک ایسا سال آئے گا کہ خوب مینہ برسے گا
اور لوگ اس میں رس نچوڑیں گے ﴿۴۹﴾
(یہ تعبیر سُن کر) بادشاہ نے حکم دیا کہ یوسف کو میرے پاس
لے آؤ۔ جب قاصد اُن کے پاس گیا۔ تو اُنہوں نے کہا
کہ اپنے آقا کے پاس واپس جاؤ اور ان سے پوچھو کہ اُن
عورتوں کا کیا حال ہے جنہوں نے اپنے ہاتھ کاٹ لئے تھے۔
بیشک میرا پروردگار ان کے مکروں سے خوب واقف ہے ﴿۵۰﴾
(بادشاہ نے عورتوں سے) پوچھا کہ بھلا اُس وقت کیا ہُوا تھا
جب تم نے یوسف کو اپنی طرف مائل کرنا چاہا؟ (سب) بول
اٹھیں کہ حاشاللہ ہم نے اس میں کوئی بُرائی معلوم نہیں کی۔
عزیز کی عورت نے کہا اب سچی بات تو ظاہر ہو ہی گئی ہے (اصل یہ ہے کہ)
میں نے اسکو اپنی طرف مائل کرنا چاہا تھا اور وہ بیشک سچا ہے ﴿۵۱﴾
(یوسف نے کہا کہ میں نے) یہ بات اس لئے (پوچھی ہے) کہ عزیز
کو یقین ہو جائے کہ میں نے اسکی پیٹھ پیچھے اسکی (امانت میں) خیانت
نہیں کی اور خدا خیانت کرنیوالوں کے مکروں کو روبراہ نہیں کرتا ﴿۵۲﴾
اور میں اپنے تئیں پاک صاف نہیں کہتا کیونکہ نفس (امارہ)
انسان کو بُرائی ہی سکھاتا رہتا ہے مگر یہ کہ میرا پروردگار
رحم کرے۔ بیشک میرا پروردگار بخشنے والا مہربان ہے ﴿۵۳﴾
بادشاہ نے حکم دیا کہ اسے میرے پاس لاؤ میں اُسے اپنا
مصاحب خاص بناؤں گا۔ پھر جب اُن سے گفتگو کی تو کہا کہ
آج سے تم ہمارے ہاں صاحب منزلت (اور) صاحب اعتبار ہو ﴿۵۴﴾
(یوسف نے) کہا مجھے اس ملک کے خزانوں پر مقرر کر دیجئے
کیونکہ میں حفاظت بھی کر سکتا ہوں اور اس کام سے واقف بھی ہوں ﴿۵۵﴾

إِلَّا قَلِيلًا مِّمَّا تَأْكُلُونَ ﴿٤٧﴾
ثُمَّ يَأْتِي مِن بَعْدِ ذَٰلِكَ سَبْعٌ شِدَادٌ
يَأْكُلْنَ مَا قَدَّمْتُمْ لَهُنَّ إِلَّا قَلِيلًا
مِّمَّا تُحْصِنُونَ ﴿٤٨﴾
ثُمَّ يَأْتِي مِن بَعْدِ ذَٰلِكَ عَامٌ فِيهِ
ع ٧ يُغَاثُ النَّاسُ وَفِيهِ يَعْصِرُونَ ﴿٤٩﴾
وَقَالَ الْمَلِكُ ائْتُونِي بِهِ ۖ فَلَمَّا
جَاءَهُ الرَّسُولُ قَالَ ارْجِعْ إِلَىٰ
رَبِّكَ فَاسْأَلْهُ مَا بَالُ النِّسْوَةِ اللَّاتِي
قَطَّعْنَ أَيْدِيَهُنَّ ۚ إِنَّ رَبِّي بِكَيْدِهِنَّ
عَلِيمٌ ﴿٥٠﴾
قَالَ مَا خَطْبُكُنَّ إِذْ رَاوَدتُّنَّ يُوسُفَ
عَن نَّفْسِهِ ۚ قُلْنَ حَاشَ لِلَّهِ مَا عَلِمْنَا عَلَيْهِ
مِن سُوءٍ ۚ قَالَتِ امْرَأَتُ الْعَزِيزِ الْآنَ
حَصْحَصَ الْحَقُّ أَنَا رَاوَدتُّهُ عَن
نَّفْسِهِ وَإِنَّهُ لَمِنَ الصَّادِقِينَ ﴿٥١﴾
ذَٰلِكَ لِيَعْلَمَ أَنِّي لَمْ أَخُنْهُ بِالْغَيْبِ
وَأَنَّ اللَّهَ لَا يَهْدِي كَيْدَ
الْخَائِنِينَ ﴿٥٢﴾
الجزء الثالث عشر ١٣ وَمَا أُبَرِّئُ نَفْسِي ۚ إِنَّ النَّفْسَ
لَأَمَّارَةٌ بِالسُّوءِ إِلَّا مَا رَحِمَ رَبِّي ۚ
إِنَّ رَبِّي غَفُورٌ رَّحِيمٌ ﴿٥٣﴾
وَقَالَ الْمَلِكُ ائْتُونِي بِهِ أَسْتَخْلِصْهُ
لِنَفْسِي ۖ فَلَمَّا كَلَّمَهُ قَالَ إِنَّكَ الْيَوْمَ
لَدَيْنَا مَكِينٌ أَمِينٌ ﴿٥٤﴾
قَالَ اجْعَلْنِي عَلَىٰ خَزَائِنِ الْأَرْضِ ۖ
إِنِّي حَفِيظٌ عَلِيمٌ ﴿٥٥﴾

56. Thus did we give established power to Joseph in the land, to take possession therein as, when, or where he pleased. We bestow of Our mercy on whom We please, and We suffer not, to be lost, the reward of those who do good.

57. But verily the reward of the Hereafter is the best, for those who believe, and are constant in righteousness.

58. Then came Joseph's brethren: They entered his presence, and he knew them, but they knew him not.

59. And when he had furnished them forth with provisions (suitable) for them, he said: "Bring unto me a brother ye have, of the same father as yourselves, (but a different mother): see ye not that I pay out full measure, and that I do provide the best hospitality?

60. "Now if ye bring him not to me, ye shall have no measure (of corn) from me, nor shall ye (even) come near me."

61. They said: "We shall try to win him from his father: indeed we shall do it."

62. And (Joseph) told his servants to put their stock-in-trade (with which they had bartered) into their saddle-bags, so they should know it only when they returned to their people, in order that they might come back

63. Now when they returned to their father, they said: "O our father! No more measure of grain shall we get (unless we take our brother): so send our brother with us, that we may get our measure; and we will indeed take every care of him."

64. He said: "Shall I trust you with him with any result other than when I trusted you with his brother aforetime? But Allah is the best to take care (of him), and He is the Most Merciful of those who show mercy!"

65. Then when they opened their baggage, they found their stock-in-trade had been returned to them. They said: "O our father! What (more) can we desire? This our Stock-in-trade has been returned to us: so we

اس طرح ہم نے یوسف کو ملک (مصر) میں جگہ دی۔ اور وہ اس
ملک میں جہاں چاہتے تھے رہتے تھے ہم اپنی رحمت جس پر چاہتے ہیں
کرتے ہیں اور نیکوکاروں کے اجر کو ضائع نہیں کرتے ﴿٥٦﴾
اور جو لوگ ایمان لائے اور ڈرتے رہے اُن کیلئے آخرت
کا اجر بہت بہتر ہے ﴿٥٧﴾
اور یوسف کے بھائی (کنعان سے مصر میں غلہ خریدنے کیلئے) آئے تو
یوسف کے پاس گئے تو یوسف نے اُنکو پہچان لیا اور وہ اُنکو نہ پہچان سکے ﴿٥٨﴾
جب یوسف نے اُنکے لئے اُنکا سامان تیار کر دیا تو کہا کہ (پھر آنا تو) جو باپ کی
طرف سے تمہارا ایک اور بھائی ہے اُسے بھی میرے پاس لیتے آنا کیا تم نہیں دیکھتے
کہ میں ماپ بھی پوری پوری دیتا ہوں اور مہمانداری بھی خوب کرتا ہوں ﴿٥٩﴾
اور اگر تم اُسے میرے پاس نہ لاؤ گے تو نہ تمہیں میرے ہاں
سے غلہ ملے گا اور نہ تم میرے پاس ہی آسکو گے ﴿٦٠﴾
انہوں نے کہا کہ ہم اُس کے بارے میں اسکے والد سے تذکرہ
کرینگے۔ اور ہم (یہ کام) کر کے رہیں گے ﴿٦١﴾
اور (یوسف نے) اپنے خدام سے کہا کہ ان کا سرمایہ (یعنی
غلے کی قیمت) ان کے شلیتوں میں رکھ دو عجب نہیں کہ جب
یہ اپنے اہل و عیال میں جائیں تو اسے پہچان لیں (اور)
عجب نہیں کہ یہ پھر یہاں آئیں ﴿٦٢﴾
جب وہ اپنے باپ کے پاس واپس گئے تو کہنے لگے کہ ابا (جب تک ہم
بنیامین کو ساتھ نہ لیجائیں) ہمارے لئے غلے کی بندش کر دی گئی ہے تو ہمارے ساتھ
ہمارے بھائی کو بھیج دیجئے تاکہ ہم پھر غلہ لائیں اور ہم اسکے نگہبان ہیں ﴿٦٣﴾
(یعقوب نے) کہا کہ میں اسکے بارے میں تمہارا اعتبار نہیں کرتا مگر ویسا ہی
جیسا پہلے اس کے بھائی کے بارے میں کیا تھا سو خدا ہی بہتر
نگہبان ہے اور وہ سب سے زیادہ رحم کرنے والا ہے ﴿٦٤﴾
اور جب انہوں نے اپنا اسباب کھولا تو دیکھا کہ اُن کا سرمایہ
واپس کر دیا گیا ہے۔ کہنے لگے ابا ہمیں (اور) کیا چاہیے (دیکھئے)
یہ ہماری پونجی بھی ہمیں واپس کر دی گئی ہے۔ اب ہم اپنے اہل و

وَكَذٰلِكَ مَكَّنَّا لِيُوسُفَ فِي الْأَرْضِ
يَتَبَوَّأُ مِنْهَا حَيْثُ يَشَاءُ ۚ نُصِيبُ بِرَحْمَتِنَا
مَنْ نَشَاءُ ۖ وَلَا نُضِيعُ أَجْرَ الْمُحْسِنِينَ ﴿٥٦﴾
وَلَأَجْرُ الْآخِرَةِ خَيْرٌ لِلَّذِينَ آمَنُوا وَ
كَانُوا يَتَّقُونَ ﴿٥٧﴾ ع
وَجَاءَ إِخْوَةُ يُوسُفَ فَدَخَلُوا عَلَيْهِ
فَعَرَفَهُمْ وَهُمْ لَهُ مُنْكِرُونَ ﴿٥٨﴾
وَلَمَّا جَهَّزَهُمْ بِجَهَازِهِمْ قَالَ ائْتُونِي
بِأَخٍ لَكُمْ مِنْ أَبِيكُمْ ۚ أَلَا تَرَوْنَ أَنِّي
أُوفِي الْكَيْلَ وَأَنَا خَيْرُ الْمُنْزِلِينَ ﴿٥٩﴾
فَإِنْ لَمْ تَأْتُونِي بِهِ فَلَا كَيْلَ لَكُمْ
عِنْدِي وَلَا تَقْرَبُونِ ﴿٦٠﴾
قَالُوا سَنُرَاوِدُ عَنْهُ أَبَاهُ وَإِنَّا
لَفَاعِلُونَ ﴿٦١﴾
وَقَالَ لِفِتْيَانِهِ اجْعَلُوا بِضَاعَتَهُمْ
فِي رِحَالِهِمْ لَعَلَّهُمْ يَعْرِفُونَهَا
إِذَا انْقَلَبُوا إِلَىٰ أَهْلِهِمْ لَعَلَّهُمْ
يَرْجِعُونَ ﴿٦٢﴾
فَلَمَّا رَجَعُوا إِلَىٰ أَبِيهِمْ قَالُوا يَا أَبَانَا مُنِعَ
مِنَّا الْكَيْلُ فَأَرْسِلْ مَعَنَا أَخَانَا نَكْتَلْ
وَإِنَّا لَهُ لَحَافِظُونَ ﴿٦٣﴾
قَالَ هَلْ آمَنُكُمْ عَلَيْهِ إِلَّا كَمَا
أَمِنْتُكُمْ عَلَىٰ أَخِيهِ مِنْ قَبْلُ ۖ فَاللَّهُ
خَيْرٌ حَافِظًا ۖ وَهُوَ أَرْحَمُ الرَّاحِمِينَ ﴿٦٤﴾
وَلَمَّا فَتَحُوا مَتَاعَهُمْ وَجَدُوا بِضَاعَتَهُمْ
رُدَّتْ إِلَيْهِمْ ۖ قَالُوا يَا أَبَانَا مَا نَبْغِي ۖ هَٰذِهِ
بِضَاعَتُنَا رُدَّتْ إِلَيْنَا ۖ وَنَمِيرُ أَهْلَنَا وَ

shall get (more) food for our family; we shall take care of our brother; and add (at the same time) a full camel's load (of grain to our provisions). This is but a small quantity.

66. (Jacob) said: "Never will I send him with you until ye swear a solemn oath to me, in Allah's name, that ye will be sure to bring him back to me unless ye are yourselves Hemmed in (and made powerless). And when they had sworn their solemn oath, He said: "Over all that we say, be Allah the Witness and Guardian!"

67. Further he said: "O my sons! enter not all by one gate: enter ye by different gates. Not that I can profit you aught against Allah (with my advice): none can command except Allah: on Him do I put my trust: and let all that trust put their trust on Him."

68. And when they entered in the manner their father had enjoined, it did not profit them in the least against (the Plan of) Allah: it served only to satisfy Jacob's heartfelt desire. For he was, by Our instruction, full of knowledge (and experience): but most men know not.

69. Now when they came into Joseph's presence, he received his (full) brother to stay with him. He said (to him): "Behold! I am thy (own) brother; so grieve not at aught of their doings."

70. At length when he had furnished them forth with provisions (suitable) for them, he put the drinking cup into his brother's saddle-bag. Then shouted out a Crier: "O ye (in) the Caravan! behold! ye are thieves, without doubt!"

71. They said, turning towards them: "What is it that ye miss?"

72. They said: "We miss the great beaker of the king; for him who produces it. Is (the reward of) a camel load; I will be bound by it."

73. (The brothers) said: "By Allah! well ye know that we came not to make mischief in the land, and we are no thieves!"

74. (The Egyptians) said: "What then shall be the penalty of this, if ye are (proved) to have lied?"

نحفظ اخانا ونزداد كيل بعير ذلك
كيل يسير ﴿٦٥﴾
قال لن ارسله معكم حتى تؤتون
موثقا من الله لتأتنني به الا ان
يحاط بكم فلما اتوه موثقهم قال
الله على ما نقول وكيل ﴿٦٦﴾
وقال يبني لا تدخلوا من باب واحد
وادخلوا من ابواب متفرقة وما اغني
عنكم من الله من شيء ان الحكم الا لله
عليه توكلت وعليه فليتوكل المتوكلون ﴿٦٧﴾
ولما دخلوا من حيث امرهم ابوهم
ما كان يغني عنهم من الله من شيء
الا حاجة في نفس يعقوب قضها
وانه لذو علم لما علمنه ولكن
اكثر الناس لا يعلمون ﴿٦٨﴾
ولما دخلوا على يوسف اوى اليه
اخاه قال اني انا اخوك فلا تبتئس
بما كانوا يعملون ﴿٦٩﴾
فلما جهزهم بجهازهم جعل السقاية
في رحل اخيه ثم اذن مؤذن ايتها
العير انكم لسارقون ﴿٧٠﴾
قالوا واقبلوا عليهم ماذا تفقدون ﴿٧١﴾
قالوا نفقد صواع الملك ولمن جاء
به حمل بعير وانا به زعيم ﴿٧٢﴾
قالوا تالله لقد علمتم ما جئنا لنفسد
في الارض وما كنا سارقين ﴿٧٣﴾
قالوا فما جزاؤه ان كنتم كذبين ﴿٧٤﴾

عیال کیلئے پھر غلہ لائیں گے اور اپنے بھائی کی نگہبانی کرینگے اور
ایک بار شتر زیادہ لائیں گے کہ یہ غلہ (جو ہم لائے ہیں) تھوڑا ہے ﴿۶۵﴾
(یعقوب نے) کہا کہ جبتک تم خدا کا عہد نہ دو کہ اسکو میرے پاس (صحیح سالم)
لے آؤ گے میں اسے ہرگز تمہارے ساتھ نہیں بھیجنے کا۔ مگر یہ کہ تم
گھیر لئے جاؤ (یعنی بے بس ہو جاؤ تو مجبوری ہے) جب اُنہوں نے
اُنسے عہد کر لیا تو (یعقوب نے) کہا کہ جو قول و قرار ہم کر رہے ہیں اسکا خدا ضامن ہے ﴿۶۶﴾
اور ہدایت کی کہ بیٹا ایک ہی دروازے سے داخل نہ ہونا بلکہ
جُدا جُدا دروازوں سے داخل ہونا۔ اور میں خدا کی تقدیر تو
تم سے نہیں روک سکتا۔ (بیشک) حکم اسی کا ہے۔ میں اسی پر بھروسا
رکھتا ہوں اور اہل توکل کو اسی پر بھروسا رکھنا چاہیئے ﴿۶۷﴾
اور جب وہ اُن اُن مقامات سے داخل ہوئے جہاں جہاں
سے (داخل ہونے کیلئے) باپ نے اُن سے کہا تھا تو وہ تدبیر خدا
کے حکم کو ذرا بھی ٹال نہیں سکتی تھی۔ ہاں وہ یعقوب کے دل کی
خواہش تھی جو اُنہوں نے پوری کی تھی اور بیشک وہ صاحب علم تھے
کیونکہ ہم نے اُن کو علم سکھایا تھا لیکن اکثر لوگ نہیں جانتے ﴿۶۸﴾
اور جب وہ لوگ یوسف کے پاس پہنچے تو یوسف نے اپنے حقیقی بھائی
کو اپنے پاس جگہ دی اور کہا کہ میں تمہارا بھائی ہوں تو جو سلوک
یہ (ہمارے ساتھ) کرتے رہے ہیں اس پر افسوس نہ کرنا ﴿۶۹﴾
جب اُن کا اسباب تیار کر دیا تو اپنے بھائی کے شلیتے میں گلاس
رکھ دیا پھر (جب وہ آبادی سے باہر نکل گئے تو) ایک پکارنے والے
نے آواز دی کہ قافلے والو! تم تو چور ہو[155] ﴿۷۰﴾
وہ اُن کی طرف متوجہ ہو کر کہنے لگے کہ تمہاری کیا چیز کھوئی گئی ہے ﴿۷۱﴾
وہ بولے کہ بادشاہ (کے پانی پینے) کا گلاس کھو گیا ہے اور جو شخص
اسکو لے آئے اسکے لئے ایک بار شتر (انعام) اور میں اسکا ضامن ہوں ﴿۷۲﴾
وہ کہنے لگے کہ خدا کی قسم تم کو معلوم ہے کہ ہم (اس) ملک میں
اسلئے نہیں آئے کہ خرابی کریں اور نہ ہم چوری کیا کرتے ہیں ﴿۷۳﴾
بولے کہ اگر تم جھوٹے نکلے (یعنی چوری ثابت ہوئی) تو اسکی سزا کیا ﴿۷۴﴾

75. They said: "The penalty should be that he in whose saddle-bag it is found, should be held (as bondman) to atone for the (crime). Thus it is we punish the wrong-doers!"

76. So he began (the search) with their baggage, before (he came to) the baggage of his brother: at length he brought it out of his brother's baggage. Thus did We plan for Joseph. He could not take his brother by the law of the king except that Allah willed it (so). We raise to degrees (of wisdom) whom We please: but over all endued with knowledge is One, the All-Knowing.

77. They said: "If he steals, there was a brother of his who did steal before (him)." But these things did Joseph keep locked in his heart, revealing not the secrets to them he (simply) said (to himself): "Ye are the worse situated; and Allah knoweth best the truth of what ye assert!"

78. They said: "O exalted one! Behold! he has a father, aged and venerable, (who will grieve for him); so take one of us in his place; for we see that thou art (gracious) in doing good."

79. He said: "Allah forbid that we take other than him with whom we found our property: indeed (if we did so), we should be acting wrongfully.

80. Now when they saw no hope of his (yielding), they held a conference in private. The leader among them said: "Know ye not that your father did take an oath from you in Allah's name, and how before this, ye did fail in your duty with Joseph? Therefore will I not leave this land until my father permits me, or Allah judges for me; and He is the best to judge.

81. "Turn ye back to your father, and say, 'O our father! behold! thy son committed theft! We bear witness only to what we know, and we could not well guard against the unseen!

82. "Ask at the town where we have been and the caravan in which we returned, and (you will find) we are indeed telling the truth."

اُنہوں نے کہا کہ اس کی سزا یہ کہ جس کے شلیتے میں وہ دستیاب ہو وہی اس کا
بدل قرار دیا جائے ف۱۵۶ ہم ظالموں کو یہی سزا دیا کرتے ہیں ﴿۷۵﴾
پھر (یوسف نے) اپنے بھائی کے شلیتے سے پہلے اُنکے شلیتوں کو دیکھنا
شروع کیا۔ پھر اپنے بھائی کے شلیتے میں سے اُسکو نکال لیا۔ اس طرح
ہم نے یوسف کیلئے تدبیر کی (ورنہ) بادشاہ کے قانون کے مطابق
وہ مشیت خدا کے سوا اپنے بھائی کو لے نہیں سکتے تھے ف۱۵۷ ہم جسکو چاہتے ہیں
درجے بلند کرتے ہیں اور ہر علم والے سے دوسرا علم والا بڑھ کر ہے ﴿۷۶﴾
(برادرانِ یوسف نے) کہا کہ اگر اس نے چوری کی ہو تو (کچھ عجب
نہیں کہ) اسکے ایک بھائی نے بھی پہلے چوری کی تھی ف۱۵۸ یوسف نے
اس بات کو اپنے دل میں مخفی رکھا اور اُن پر ظاہر نہ ہونے دیا
(اور) کہا کہ تم بڑے بدقماش ہو۔ اور جو تم بیان کرتے ہو خدا اُسے خوب جانتا ہے ﴿۷۷﴾
وہ کہنے لگے کہ اے عزیز اسکے والد بہت بوڑھے ہیں (اور اس سے
بہت محبت رکھتے ہیں) تو (اس کو چھوڑ دیجئے اور) اسکی جگہ ہم میں سے
کسی کو رکھ لیجئے ہم دیکھتے ہیں کہ آپ احسان کرنے والے ہیں ﴿۷۸﴾
(یوسف نے) کہا کہ خدا پناہ میں رکھے کہ جس شخص کے پاس ہم نے اپنی چیز
پائی ہے اسکے سوا کسی اور کو پکڑ لیں ایسا کریں تو ہم (بڑے) بے انصاف ہیں ﴿۷۹﴾ ف
جب وہ اس سے نا اُمید ہو گئے تو الگ ہو کر صلاح کرنے
لگے۔ سب سے بڑے نے کہا کیا تم نہیں جانتے کہ تمہارے والد نے تم
سے خدا کا عہد لیا ہے اور اس سے پہلے بھی تم یوسف کے بارے
میں قصور کر چکے ہو تو جب تک والد صاحب مجھے حکم نہ دیں۔
میں تو اس جگہ سے ہلنے کا نہیں یا خدا میرے لئے کوئی اور تدبیر
کرے۔ اور وہ سب سے بہتر فیصلہ کرنے والا ہے ﴿۸۰﴾
تم سب والد صاحب کے پاس واپس جاؤ اور کہو کہ ابا آپکے صاحبزادے نے
(وہاں جا کر) چوری کی۔ اور ہم نے تو اپنی دانست کے مطابق آپ سے اسکے لے
آنیکا عہد کیا تھا مگر ہم غیب (کی باتوں) کے (جاننے اور) یاد رکھنے والے تو نہیں تھے ﴿۸۱﴾
اور جس بستی میں ہم (ٹھیرے) تھے وہاں سے (یعنی اہل مصر سے) اور جس قافلے میں
آئے ہیں اس سے دریافت کر لیجئے اور ہم (اس بیان میں) بالکل سچے ہیں ﴿۸۲﴾

قَالُوْا جَزَآؤُهٗ مَنْ وُّجِدَ فِیْ رَحْلِهٖ فَهُوَ
جَزَآؤُهٗ ؕ كَذٰلِكَ نَجْزِی الظّٰلِمِیْنَ ﴿۷۵﴾
فَبَدَاَ بِاَوْعِیَتِهِمْ قَبْلَ وِعَآءِ اَخِیْهِ ثُمَّ
اسْتَخْرَجَهَا مِنْ وِّعَآءِ اَخِیْهِ ؕ كَذٰلِكَ كِدْنَا
لِیُوْسُفَ ؕ مَا كَانَ لِیَاْخُذَ اَخَاهُ فِیْ دِیْنِ
الْمَلِكِ اِلَّاۤ اَنْ یَّشَآءَ اللّٰهُ ؕ نَرْفَعُ دَرَجٰتٍ
مَّنْ نَّشَآءُ ؕ وَ فَوْقَ كُلِّ ذِیْ عِلْمٍ عَلِیْمٌ ﴿۷۶﴾
قَالُوْۤا اِنْ یَّسْرِقْ فَقَدْ سَرَقَ اَخٌ لَّهٗ
مِنْ قَبْلُ ۚ فَاَسَرَّهَا یُوْسُفُ فِیْ نَفْسِهٖ
وَ لَمْ یُبْدِهَا لَهُمْ ۚ قَالَ اَنْتُمْ شَرٌّ
مَّكَانًا ۚ وَ اللّٰهُ اَعْلَمُ بِمَا تَصِفُوْنَ ﴿۷۷﴾
قَالُوْا یٰۤاَیُّهَا الْعَزِیْزُ اِنَّ لَهٗۤ اَبًا شَیْخًا
كَبِیْرًا فَخُذْ اَحَدَنَا مَكَانَهٗ ۚ اِنَّا نَرٰىكَ
مِنَ الْمُحْسِنِیْنَ ﴿۷۸﴾
قَالَ مَعَاذَ اللّٰهِ اَنْ نَّاْخُذَ اِلَّا مَنْ وَّجَدْنَا
مَتَاعَنَا عِنْدَهٗۤ ۙ اِنَّاۤ اِذًا لَّظٰلِمُوْنَ ﴿۷۹﴾ ع
فَلَمَّا اسْتَایْــَٔسُوْا مِنْهُ خَلَصُوْا نَجِیًّا ؕ قَالَ
كَبِیْرُهُمْ اَلَمْ تَعْلَمُوْۤا اَنَّ اَبَاكُمْ قَدْ
اَخَذَ عَلَیْكُمْ مَّوْثِقًا مِّنَ اللّٰهِ وَ مِنْ
قَبْلُ مَا فَرَّطْتُّمْ فِیْ یُوْسُفَ ۚ فَلَنْ
اَبْرَحَ الْاَرْضَ حَتّٰی یَاْذَنَ لِیْۤ اَبِیْۤ اَوْ
یَحْكُمَ اللّٰهُ لِیْ ۚ وَ هُوَ خَیْرُ الْحٰكِمِیْنَ ﴿۸۰﴾
اِرْجِعُوْۤا اِلٰۤی اَبِیْكُمْ فَقُوْلُوْا یٰۤاَبَانَاۤ اِنَّ
ابْنَكَ سَرَقَ ۚ وَ مَا شَهِدْنَاۤ اِلَّا بِمَا
عَلِمْنَا وَ مَا كُنَّا لِلْغَیْبِ حٰفِظِیْنَ ﴿۸۱﴾
وَ سْـَٔلِ الْقَرْیَةَ الَّتِیْ كُنَّا فِیْهَا وَ الْعِیْرَ
الَّتِیْۤ اَقْبَلْنَا فِیْهَا ؕ وَ اِنَّا لَصٰدِقُوْنَ ﴿۸۲﴾

83. Jacob said: "Nay, but ye have yourselves contrived a story (good enough) for you. So patience is most fitting (for me). May be Allah will bring them (back) all to me (in the end). For He is indeed full of knowledge and wisdom."

(جب انہوں نے یہ بات یعقوب سے آکر کہی تو) انہوں نے کہا کہ (حقیقت یوں نہیں ہے) بلکہ یہ بات تم نے اپنے دل سے بنالی ہے تو صبر ہی بہتر ہے۔ عجب نہیں کہ خدا ان سب کو میرے پاس لے آئے۔ بیشک وہ دانا (اور) حکمت والا ہے ﴿۸۳﴾

قَالَ بَلْ سَوَّلَتْ لَكُمْ أَنْفُسُكُمْ
أَمْرًا فَصَبْرٌ جَمِيلٌ عَسَى اللَّهُ أَنْ
يَأْتِيَنِي بِهِمْ جَمِيعًا إِنَّهُ هُوَ الْعَلِيمُ
الْحَكِيمُ ﴿٨٣﴾

84. And he turned away from them, and said: "How great is my grief for Joseph! And his eyes became white with sorrow, and he was suppressed with silent sorrow.

پھر ان کے پاس سے چلے گئے اور کہنے لگے کہ ہائے افسوس یوسف (ہائے افسوس) اور رنج والم میں (اس قدر روئے کہ) ان کی آنکھیں سفید ہوگئیں اور ان کا دل غم سے بھر رہا تھا ﴿۸۴﴾

وَتَوَلَّىٰ عَنْهُمْ وَقَالَ يَا أَسَفَىٰ عَلَىٰ يُوسُفَ
وَابْيَضَّتْ عَيْنَاهُ مِنَ الْحُزْنِ فَهُوَ كَظِيمٌ ﴿٨٤﴾

85. They said: "By Allah! (never) wilt thou cease to remember Joseph until thou reach the last extremity of illness, or until thou die!"

بیٹے کہنے لگے کہ واللہ اگر آپ یوسف کو اسی طرح یاد ہی کرتے رہیں گے تو یا تو بیمار ہوجائیں گے یا جان ہی دے دیں گے ﴿۸۵﴾

قَالُوا تَاللَّهِ تَفْتَأُ تَذْكُرُ يُوسُفَ حَتَّىٰ
تَكُونَ حَرَضًا أَوْ تَكُونَ مِنَ الْهَالِكِينَ ﴿٨٥﴾

86. He said: "I only complain of my distraction and anguish to Allah, and I know from Allah that which ye know not...

انہوں نے کہا کہ میں تو اپنے غم واندوہ کا اظہار خدا سے کرتا ہوں۔ اور خدا کی طرف سے وہ باتیں جانتا ہوں جو تم نہیں جانتے ﴿۸۶﴾

قَالَ إِنَّمَا أَشْكُو بَثِّي وَحُزْنِي إِلَى
اللَّهِ وَأَعْلَمُ مِنَ اللَّهِ مَا لَا تَعْلَمُونَ ﴿٨٦﴾

87. "O my sons! go ye and enquire about Joseph and his brother, and never give up hope of Allah's soothing Mercy: truly no one despairs of Allah's soothing Mercy, except those who have no faith."

بیٹا یوں کرو کہ ایک دفعہ پھر جاؤ اور یوسف اور اُس کے بھائی کو تلاش کرو اور خدا کی رحمت سے نااُمید نہ ہو کہ خدا کی رحمت سے بےایمان لوگ نااُمید ہوا کرتے ہیں ﴿۸۷﴾

يَا بَنِيَّ اذْهَبُوا فَتَحَسَّسُوا مِنْ يُوسُفَ
وَأَخِيهِ وَلَا تَيْأَسُوا مِنْ رَوْحِ اللَّهِ
إِنَّهُ لَا يَيْأَسُ مِنْ رَوْحِ اللَّهِ إِلَّا الْقَوْمُ
الْكَافِرُونَ ﴿٨٧﴾

88. Then, when they came (back) into (Joseph's) presence they said: "O exalted one! distress has seized us and our family: we have (now) brought but scanty capital: so pay us full measure, (we pray thee), and treat it as charity to us; for Allah doth reward the charitable."

جب وہ یوسف کے پاس گئے تو کہنے لگے کہ عزیز ہمیں اور ہمارے اہل وعیال کو بڑی تکلیف ہو رہی ہے اور ہم تھوڑا سا سرمایہ لائے ہیں آپ ہمیں (اس کے عوض) پورا غلّہ دیجیے اور خیرات کیجیے کہ خدا خیرات کرنے والوں کو ثواب دیتا ہے ﴿۸۸﴾

فَلَمَّا دَخَلُوا عَلَيْهِ قَالُوا يَا أَيُّهَا الْعَزِيزُ
مَسَّنَا وَأَهْلَنَا الضُّرُّ وَجِئْنَا بِبِضَاعَةٍ
مُزْجَاةٍ فَأَوْفِ لَنَا الْكَيْلَ وَتَصَدَّقْ
عَلَيْنَا إِنَّ اللَّهَ يَجْزِي الْمُتَصَدِّقِينَ ﴿٨٨﴾

89. He said: "Know ye how ye dealt with Joseph and his brother, not knowing (what ye were doing)?"

(یوسف نے) کہا تمہیں معلوم ہے جب تم نادانی میں پھنسے ہوئے تھے تو تم نے یوسف اور اُس کے بھائی کے ساتھ کیا کیا تھا؟ ﴿۸۹﴾

قَالَ هَلْ عَلِمْتُمْ مَا فَعَلْتُمْ بِيُوسُفَ
وَأَخِيهِ إِذْ أَنْتُمْ جَاهِلُونَ ﴿٨٩﴾

90. They said: "Art thou indeed Joseph?" He said, "I am Joseph, and this is my brother: Allah has indeed been gracious to us (all): behold, he that is righteous and patient,—never will Allah suffer the reward to be lost, of those who do right."

وہ بولے کیا تم ہی یوسف ہو؟ انہوں نے کہا ہاں میں ہی یوسف ہوں۔ اور (بنیامین کی طرف اشارہ کرکے کہنے لگے) یہ میرا بھائی ہے خدا نے ہم پر بڑا احسان کیا ہے۔ جو شخص خدا سے ڈرتا اور صبر کرتا ہے تو خدا نیکوکاروں کا اجر ضائع نہیں کرتا ﴿۹۰﴾

قَالُوا أَإِنَّكَ لَأَنْتَ يُوسُفُ قَالَ
أَنَا يُوسُفُ وَهَٰذَا أَخِي قَدْ مَنَّ
اللَّهُ عَلَيْنَا إِنَّهُ مَنْ يَتَّقِ وَيَصْبِرْ
فَإِنَّ اللَّهَ لَا يُضِيعُ أَجْرَ الْمُحْسِنِينَ ﴿٩٠﴾

91. They said: "By Allah! Indeed has Allah preferred thee above us, and we certainly have been guilty of sin!"

وہ بولے خدا کی قسم خدا نے تم کو ہم پر فضیلت بخشی ہے اور بےشک ہم خطاکار تھے ﴿۹۱﴾

قَالُوا تَاللَّهِ لَقَدْ آثَرَكَ اللَّهُ عَلَيْنَا
وَإِنْ كُنَّا لَخَاطِئِينَ ﴿٩١﴾

92. He said: "This day let no reproach be (cast) on you: Allah

(یوسف نے) کہا کہ آج کے دن (سے) تم پر کچھ عتاب (وملامت)

قَالَ لَا تَثْرِيبَ عَلَيْكُمُ الْيَوْمَ

يَغْفِرُ اللّٰهُ لَكُمْ وَهُوَ اَرْحَمُ
الرّٰحِمِيْنَ ﴿۹۲﴾

نہیں ہے۔ خدا تم کو معاف کرے۔ اور وہ بہت
رحم کرنے والا ہے ﴿۹۲﴾

will forgive you, and He is the Most Merciful of those who show mercy!

اِذْهَبُوْا بِقَمِيْصِيْ هٰذَا فَاَلْقُوْهُ عَلٰى
وَجْهِ اَبِيْ يَاْتِ بَصِيْرًا ۚ وَاْتُوْنِيْ بِاَهْلِكُمْ
اَجْمَعِيْنَ ﴿۹۳﴾

یہ میرا کرتہ لے جاؤ اور اسے والد صاحب کے منہ پر ڈال دو۔
وہ بینا ہو جائیں گے۔ اور اپنے تمام اہل وعیال کو
میرے پاس لے آؤ ﴿۹۳﴾

93. "Go with this my shirt, and cast it over the face of my father: he will come to see (clearly). Then come ye (here) to me together with all your family."

وَلَمَّا فَصَلَتِ الْعِيْرُ قَالَ اَبُوْهُمْ اِنِّيْ
لَاَجِدُ رِيْحَ يُوْسُفَ لَوْلَآ اَنْ تُفَنِّدُوْنِ ﴿۹۴﴾
قَالُوْا تَاللّٰهِ اِنَّكَ لَفِيْ ضَلٰلِكَ الْقَدِيْمِ ﴿۹۵﴾

اور جب قافلہ (مصر سے) روانہ ہوا۔ تو انکے والد کہنے لگے کہ اگر مجھ کو
یہ نہ کہو کہ (بوڑھا) بہک گیا ہے تو مجھے تو یوسف کی بو آرہی ہے ﴿۹۴﴾
وہ بولے کہ واللہ آپ اسی قدیم غلطی میں (مبتلا) ہیں ﴿۹۵﴾

94. When the Caravan left (Egypt), their father said: "I do indeed scent the presence of Joseph: nay, think me not a dotard."
95. They said: "By Allah! truly thou art in thine old wandering illusion."

فَلَمَّآ اَنْ جَآءَ الْبَشِيْرُ اَلْقٰىهُ عَلٰى
وَجْهِهٖ فَارْتَدَّ بَصِيْرًا ۚ قَالَ اَلَمْ اَقُلْ
لَّكُمْ ۚ اِنِّيْٓ اَعْلَمُ مِنَ اللّٰهِ مَا لَا تَعْلَمُوْنَ ﴿۹۶﴾
قَالُوْا يٰٓاَبَانَا اسْتَغْفِرْ لَنَا ذُنُوْبَنَآ اِنَّا
كُنَّا خٰطِـِٕيْنَ ﴿۹۷﴾

جب خوشخبری دینے والا آپہنچا تو کرتہ یعقوب کے منہ پر ڈال دیا۔
اور وہ بینا ہو گئے۔ (اور بیٹوں سے) کہنے لگے۔ کیا میں نے تم سے نہیں
کہا تھا کہ میں خدا کی طرف سے وہ باتیں جانتا ہوں جو تم نہیں جانتے ﴿۹۶﴾
بیٹوں نے کہا کہ ابا ہمارے لئے ہمارے گناہ کی مغفرت مانگئے۔
بیشک ہم خطا کار تھے ﴿۹۷﴾

96. Then when the bearer of the good news came, he cast (the shirt) over his face, and he forthwith regained clear sight. He said: "Did I not say to you, 'I know from Allah that which ye know not?' "
97. They said: "O our father! ask for us forgiveness for our sins, for we were truly at fault.

قَالَ سَوْفَ اَسْتَغْفِرُ لَكُمْ رَبِّيْ ۭ اِنَّهٗ
هُوَ الْغَفُوْرُ الرَّحِيْمُ ﴿۹۸﴾
فَلَمَّا دَخَلُوْا عَلٰى يُوْسُفَ اٰوٰٓى اِلَيْهِ
اَبَوَيْهِ وَقَالَ ادْخُلُوْا مِصْرَ اِنْ شَآءَ
اللّٰهُ اٰمِنِيْنَ ﴿۹۹﴾

انہوں نے کہا کہ میں اپنے پروردگار سے تمہارے لئے بخشش
مانگوں گا۔ بیشک وہ بخشنے والا مہربان ہے ﴿۹۸﴾
جب (یہ سب لوگ) یوسف کے پاس پہنچے تو (یوسف نے)
اپنے والدین کو اپنے پاس بٹھایا اور کہا مصر میں داخل
ہو جائیے خدا نے چاہا تو خاطر جمع سے رہیے گا ﴿۹۹﴾

98. He said: "Soon will I ask my Lord for forgiveness for you: for He is indeed Oft-Forgiving, Most Merciful."
99. Then when they entered the presence of Joseph, he provided a home for his parents with himself, and said: "Enter ye Egypt (all) in safety if it please Allah.

وَرَفَعَ اَبَوَيْهِ عَلَى الْعَرْشِ وَخَرُّوْا لَهٗ
سُجَّدًا ۚ وَقَالَ يٰٓاَبَتِ هٰذَا تَاْوِيْلُ
رُءْيَايَ مِنْ قَبْلُ ۡ قَدْ جَعَلَهَا رَبِّيْ حَقًّا ۭ
وَقَدْ اَحْسَنَ بِيْٓ اِذْ اَخْرَجَنِيْ مِنَ السِّجْنِ
وَجَآءَ بِكُمْ مِّنَ الْبَدْوِ مِنْۢ بَعْدِ اَنْ
نَّزَغَ الشَّيْطٰنُ بَيْنِيْ وَبَيْنَ اِخْوَتِيْ ۭ
اِنَّ رَبِّيْ لَطِيْفٌ لِّمَا يَشَآءُ ۭ اِنَّهٗ هُوَ
الْعَلِيْمُ الْحَكِيْمُ ﴿۱۰۰﴾

اور اپنے والدین کو تخت پر بٹھایا اور سب یوسف کے آگے سجدے
میں گر پڑے اور (اس وقت) یوسف نے کہا ابا جان یہ میرے اس خواب
کی تعبیر ہے جو میں نے پہلے (بچپن میں) دیکھا تھا میرے پروردگار نے
اسے سچ کر دیا [۱۵۹] اور اس نے مجھ پر (بہت سے) احسان کئے ہیں کہ مجھ کو جیلخانے سے نکالا۔
اور اس کے بعد کہ شیطان نے مجھ میں اور میرے بھائیوں
میں فساد ڈال دیا تھا آپ کو گاؤں سے یہاں لایا۔
بیشک میرا پروردگار جو چاہتا ہے تدبیر سے کرتا ہے۔ وہ
دانا اور حکمت والا ہے ﴿۱۰۰﴾

100. And he raised his parents high on the throne and they fell down in prostration, (all) before him. He said: "O my father! this is the fulfilment of my vision of old! Allah hath made it come true! He was indeed good to me when he took me out of prison and brought you (all here) out of the desert, (even) after Satan had sown enmity between me and my brothers. Verily my Lord is Gracious to whom He wills for verily He is full of knowledge and wisdom.

رَبِّ قَدْ اٰتَيْتَنِيْ مِنَ الْمُلْكِ وَعَلَّمْتَنِيْ

(جب یہ سب باتیں ہولیں تو یوسف نے خدا سے دعا کی کہ)

101. "O my Lord! Thou hast indeed bestowed on me some power, and

taught me something of the interpretation of dreams,—O thou Creator of the heavens and the earth! Thou art my Protector in this world and in the Hereafter. Take Thou my soul (at death) as one submitting to Thy Will (as a Muslim), and unite me with the righteous."
102. Such is one of the stories of what happened unseen, which We reveal by inspiration unto thee: nor wast thou (present) with them when they concerted their plans together in the process of weaving their plots.
103. Yet no faith will the greater part of mankind have, however ardently thou dost desire it.
104. And no reward dost thou ask of them for this: it is no less than a Message for all creatures.
105. And how many Signs in the heavens and the earth do they pass by? Yet they turn (their faces) away from them!
106. And most of them believe not in Allah without associating (others as partners) with Him!

107. Do they then feel secure from the coming against them of the covering veil of the wrath of Allah.—Or of the coming against them of the (final) Hour all of a sudden while they perceive not?
108. Say thou. "This is my Way; I do invite unto Allah,—with a certain knowledge I and whoever follows me. Glory to Allah! and never will I join gods with Allah!"
109. Nor did We send before thee (as Messengers) any but men, whom We did inspire, –(men) from the peoples of the towns. Do they not travel through the earth, and see what was the end of those before them? But the home of the Hereafter is best, for those who do right. Will ye not then understand?

110. (Respite will be granted) until, when the messengers give up hope (of their people) and (come to) think that they were treated as liars, there

اے میرے پروردگار تو نے مجھ کو حکومت سے بہرہ دیا اور خوابوں کی
تعبیر کا علم بخشا۔ اے آسمانوں اور زمین کے پیدا کرنیوالے توہی دنیا اور آخرت
میں میرا کارساز ہے۔ تو مجھے (دنیا سے) اپنی اطاعت (کی حالت)
میں اُٹھائیو اور (آخرت میں) اپنے نیک بندوں میں داخل کیجیو ﴿۱۰۱﴾
(اے پیغمبر) یہ اخبار غیب میں سے ہیں۔ جو ہم تمہاری طرف بھیجتے
ہیں۔ اور جب برادران یوسف نے اپنی بات پر اتفاق کیا تھا اور وہ
فریب کر رہے تھے تو تم اُن کے پاس تو نہ تھے ﴿۱۰۲﴾
اور بہت سے آدمی گو تم (کتنی ہی) خواہش کرو ایمان لانیوالے نہیں ہیں ﴿۱۰۳﴾
اور تم ان سے اس (خیر خواہی) کا کچھ صلہ بھی تو نہیں مانگتے یہ
(قرآن) اور کچھ نہیں تمام عالم کے لئے نصیحت ہے ﴿۱۰۴﴾
اور آسمان و زمین میں بہت سی نشانیاں ہیں جن پر یہ گزرتے
ہیں اور ان سے اعراض کرتے ہیں ﴿۱۰۵﴾
اور یہ اکثر خدا پر ایمان نہیں رکھتے مگر (اس کے ساتھ)
شرک کرتے ہیں ف۱۶۱ ﴿۱۰۶﴾

کیا یہ اس (بات) سے بے خوف ہیں کہ ان پر خدا کا عذاب نازل
ہو کر ان کو ڈھانپ لے یا اُن پر ناگہاں قیامت آجائے
اور انہیں خبر بھی نہ ہو ﴿۱۰۷﴾
کہدو میرا رستہ تو یہ ہے میں خدا کی طرف بُلاتا ہوں (از رُوئے یقین و برہان)
سمجھ بُوجھ کر میں بھی (لوگوں کو خدا کی طرف بلاتا ہوں) اور میرے پیرو بھی۔
اور خدا پاک ہے اور میں شرک کرنے والوں میں سے نہیں ہوں ﴿۱۰۸﴾
اور ہم نے تم سے پہلے بستیوں کے رہنے والوں میں سے مرد ہی
بھیجے تھے جن کی طرف ہم وحی بھیجتے تھے کیا ان لوگوں نے
ملک میں سیر (و سیاحت) نہیں کی کہ دیکھ لیتے کہ جو لوگ ان سے
پہلے تھے اُن کا انجام کیا ہوا۔ اور متقیوں کے لئے آخرت
کا گھر بہت اچھا ہے کیا تم سمجھتے نہیں؟ ﴿۱۰۹﴾
یہاں تک کہ جب پیغمبر نااُمید ہو گئے اور انہوں نے خیال کیا کہ
(اپنی نصرت کے بارے میں جو بات اُنہوں نے کہی تھی اس

مِنْ تَأْوِيلِ الْأَحَادِيثِ ۚ فَاطِرَ السَّمٰوٰتِ
وَالْأَرْضِ ۚ أَنْتَ وَلِيِّي فِي الدُّنْيَا وَ
الْآخِرَةِ ۖ تَوَفَّنِي مُسْلِمًا وَأَلْحِقْنِي
بِالصّٰلِحِينَ ﴿١٠١﴾
ذٰلِكَ مِنْ أَنْبَاءِ الْغَيْبِ نُوحِيهِ إِلَيْكَ ۚ
وَمَا كُنْتَ لَدَيْهِمْ إِذْ أَجْمَعُوا أَمْرَهُمْ
وَهُمْ يَمْكُرُونَ ﴿١٠٢﴾
وَمَا أَكْثَرُ النَّاسِ وَلَوْ حَرَصْتَ بِمُؤْمِنِينَ ﴿١٠٣﴾
وَمَا تَسْأَلُهُمْ عَلَيْهِ مِنْ أَجْرٍ ۚ إِنْ هُوَ
ع ١١ / ٥ إِلَّا ذِكْرٌ لِلْعٰلَمِينَ ﴿١٠٤﴾
وَكَأَيِّنْ مِنْ آيَةٍ فِي السَّمٰوٰتِ وَالْأَرْضِ
يَمُرُّونَ عَلَيْهَا وَهُمْ عَنْهَا مُعْرِضُونَ ﴿١٠٥﴾
وَمَا يُؤْمِنُ أَكْثَرُهُمْ بِاللّٰهِ إِلَّا وَهُمْ
مُشْرِكُونَ ﴿١٠٦﴾
أَفَأَمِنُوا أَنْ تَأْتِيَهُمْ غَاشِيَةٌ مِنْ عَذَابِ
اللّٰهِ أَوْ تَأْتِيَهُمُ السَّاعَةُ بَغْتَةً وَهُمْ
لَا يَشْعُرُونَ ﴿١٠٧﴾
قُلْ هٰذِهِ سَبِيلِي أَدْعُو إِلَى اللّٰهِ ۚ
عَلٰى بَصِيرَةٍ أَنَا وَمَنِ اتَّبَعَنِي ۖ وَسُبْحٰنَ
اللّٰهِ وَمَا أَنَا مِنَ الْمُشْرِكِينَ ﴿١٠٨﴾
وَمَا أَرْسَلْنَا مِنْ قَبْلِكَ إِلَّا رِجَالًا
نُوحِي إِلَيْهِمْ مِنْ أَهْلِ الْقُرٰى ۗ أَفَلَمْ
يَسِيرُوا فِي الْأَرْضِ فَيَنْظُرُوا كَيْفَ
كَانَ عَاقِبَةُ الَّذِينَ مِنْ قَبْلِهِمْ ۗ وَلَدَارُ
الْآخِرَةِ خَيْرٌ لِلَّذِينَ اتَّقَوْا ۗ أَفَلَا تَعْقِلُونَ ﴿١٠٩﴾
حَتّٰى إِذَا اسْتَيْأَسَ الرُّسُلُ وَظَنُّوا
أَنَّهُمْ قَدْ كُذِبُوا جَاءَهُمْ نَصْرُنَا ۙ

وقف النبي عليه الصلوٰة والسلام

SÛRA–13
AR-RA'D
(INTRODUCTION)

The chronological place of this Sûra and the general argument of Sûras 10 to 15 has been described in the Introduction to S. 10.

The special argument of this Sûra deals with that aspect of Allah's revelation of Himself to man and His dealings with him, which is concerned with certain contrasts which are here pointd out. There is the revelation to the Prophets, which comes in spoken words adapted to the language of the various men and groups of men to whom it comes; and there is the parallel revelation or Signs in the constant laws of external nature, on this earth and in the visible heavens. There is the contrast between recurring life and death already in the external world: why should men disbelieve in the life after death? They mock at the idea of punishment because it is deferred: but can they not see Allah's power and glory in thunder and the forces of nature? All creation praises Him: it is the good that endures and the evil that is swept away like froth or scum. Not only in miracles but in the normal working of the world, are shown Allah's power and mercy. What is Punishment in this world, compared to that in the life to come? Even here there are Signs of the working of His law: plot or plan as men will, it is Allah's Will that must prevail. This is illustrated in Joseph's story in the preceding Sûra.

reaches them Our help, and those whom We will are delivered into safety. But never will be warded off Our punishment from those who are in sin.

111. There is, in their stories, instruction for men endued with understanding. It is not a tale invented, but a confirmation of what went before it,— a detailed exposition of all things, and a Guide and a Mercy to any such as believe.

Al-Ra'd, or Thunder

In the name of Allah, Most Gracious, Most Merciful.

1. **A.L.M.R.** These are the verses of the Book: that which hath been revealed unto thee from thy Lord is the Truth; but most men believe not.

2. Allah is He Who raised the heavens without any pillars that ye can see; then He established Himself on the Throne. He has subjected the sun and the moon! Each one runs (its course) for a term appointed. He doth regulate all affairs, explaining the Signs in detail, that ye may believe with certainty in the meeting with your Lord.

3. And it is He Who spread out the earth, and set thereon Mountains standing firm, and (flowing) rivers: and fruit of every kind He made in pairs, two and two: He draweth the Night as a veil O'er the Day. Behold, verily in these things there are Signs for those who consider!

4. And in the earth are tracts (diverse though) neighbouring, and gardens of vines and fields sown with corn, and palm trees—growing out of single roots or otherwise: watered with the same water, yet some of them We make more excellent than others to eat. Behold,

ہیں) وہ سچے نہ نکلے تو اُن کے پاس ہماری مدد آپہنچی۔ پھر جسے ہم نے
چاہا بچا دیا اور ہمارا عذاب (اُتر کر) گنہگار لوگوں سے پھرا نہیں کرتا (۱۱۰)
ان کے قصے میں عقلمندوں کے لئے عبرت ہے۔ یہ (قرآن)
ایسی بات نہیں ہے جو (اپنے دل سے) بنائی گئی ہو
بلکہ جو (کتابیں) اس سے پہلے (نازل ہوئی) ہیں اُن
کی تصدیق (کرنے والا) ہے اور ہر چیز کی تفصیل (کرنے
والا) اور مومنوں کے لئے ہدایت اور رحمت ہے (۱۱۱)

سورہ رعد مکی ہے اور اسمیں تینتالیس آیتیں اور چھ رکوع ہیں

شروع خدا کا نام لے کر جو بڑا مہربان نہایت رحم والا ہے
المرا (اے محمد) یہ کتاب (الٰہی) کی آیتیں ہیں۔ اور جو تمہارے
پروردگار کی طرف سے تم پر نازل ہوا ہے حق ہے لیکن اکثر لوگ
ایمان نہیں لاتے (۱)
خدا وہی تو ہے جس نے ستونوں کے بغیر آسمان جیسا کہ تم دیکھتے
ہو (اتنے) اونچے بنائے۔ پھر عرش پر جا ٹھہرا اور سورج اور چاند
کو کام میں لگا دیا۔ ہر ایک ایک میعاد معین تک گردش کر رہا ہے
وہی (دنیا کے) کاموں کا انتظام کرتا ہے (اس طرح) وہ اپنی
آیتیں کھول کھول کر بیان کرتا ہے کہ تم اپنے پروردگار کے
روبرو جانے کا یقین کرو (۲)
اور وہ وہی ہے جس نے زمین کو پھیلایا اور
اس میں پہاڑ اور دریا پیدا کئے۔ اور ہر طرح
کے میووں کی دو دو قسمیں بنائیں۔ وہی رات
کو دن کا لباس پہناتا ہے۔ غور کرنے والوں کے لئے
اس میں بہت سی نشانیاں ہیں (۳)
اور زمین میں کئی طرح کے قطعات ہیں۔ ایک دوسرے
سے ملے ہوئے اور انگور کے باغ اور کھیتی اور کھجور کے درخت۔ بعض
کی بہت سی شاخیں ہیں اور بعض کی اتنی نہیں ہوتیں (باوجودیکہ)
پانی سب کو ایک ہی ملتا ہے۔ اور ہم بعض میووں کو بعض پر لذت

فَنُجِّيَ مَنْ نَّشَآءُ ۭ وَلَا يُرَدُّ بَاْسُنَا عَنِ
الْقَوْمِ الْمُجْرِمِيْنَ ﴿۱۱۰﴾
لَقَدْ كَانَ فِيْ قَصَصِهِمْ عِبْرَةٌ لِّاُولِي
الْاَلْبَابِ ۭ مَا كَانَ حَدِيْثًا يُّفْتَرٰى وَ
لٰكِنْ تَصْدِيْقَ الَّذِيْ بَيْنَ يَدَيْهِ وَ
تَفْصِيْلَ كُلِّ شَيْءٍ وَّهُدًى وَّرَحْمَةً
لِّقَوْمٍ يُّؤْمِنُوْنَ ﴿۱۱۱﴾

سُوْرَةُ الرَّعْدِ مَدَنِيَّةٌ وَهِيَ ثَلٰثٌ وَّاَرْبَعُوْنَ اٰيَةً وَّسِتُّ رُكُوْعَاتٍ

بِسْمِ اللّٰهِ الرَّحْمٰنِ الرَّحِيْمِ
الٓمّٓرٰ ۣ تِلْكَ اٰيٰتُ الْكِتٰبِ ۭ وَالَّذِيْٓ
اُنْزِلَ اِلَيْكَ مِنْ رَّبِّكَ الْحَقُّ وَلٰكِنَّ
اَكْثَرَ النَّاسِ لَا يُؤْمِنُوْنَ ﴿۱﴾
اَللّٰهُ الَّذِيْ رَفَعَ السَّمٰوٰتِ بِغَيْرِ عَمَدٍ
تَرَوْنَهَا ثُمَّ اسْتَوٰى عَلَى الْعَرْشِ وَ
سَخَّرَ الشَّمْسَ وَالْقَمَرَ ۭ كُلٌّ يَّجْرِيْ
لِاَجَلٍ مُّسَمًّى ۭ يُدَبِّرُ الْاَمْرَ يُفَصِّلُ
الْاٰيٰتِ لَعَلَّكُمْ بِلِقَاۗءِ رَبِّكُمْ
تُوْقِنُوْنَ ﴿۲﴾
وَهُوَ الَّذِيْ مَدَّ الْاَرْضَ وَجَعَلَ فِيْهَا
رَوَاسِيَ وَاَنْهٰرًا ۭ وَمِنْ كُلِّ الثَّمَرٰتِ
جَعَلَ فِيْهَا زَوْجَيْنِ اثْنَيْنِ يُغْشِي
الَّيْلَ النَّهَارَ ۭ اِنَّ فِيْ ذٰلِكَ لَاٰيٰتٍ
لِّقَوْمٍ يَّتَفَكَّرُوْنَ ﴿۳﴾
وَفِي الْاَرْضِ قِطَعٌ مُّتَجٰوِرٰتٌ وَّجَنّٰتٌ
مِّنْ اَعْنَابٍ وَّزَرْعٌ وَّنَخِيْلٌ صِنْوَانٌ
وَّغَيْرُ صِنْوَانٍ يُّسْقٰى بِمَاۗءٍ وَّاحِدٍ ۣ وَ
نُفَضِّلُ بَعْضَهَا عَلٰي بَعْضٍ فِي الْاُكُلِ ۭ

verily in these things there are Signs for those who understand!

5. If thou dost marvel (at their want of faith), strange is their saying: "When we are (actually) dust, shall we indeed then be in a creation renewed?" They are those who deny their Lord! They are those round whose necks will be yokes (of servitude): they will be Companions of the Fire, to dwell therein (for aye)!

6. They ask thee to hasten on the evil in preference to the good yet have come to pass, before them, (many) exemplary punishments! But verily thy Lord is full of forgiveness for mankind for their wrong-doing. And verily thy Lord is (also) strict in punishment.

7. And the Unbelievers say: "Why is not a Sign sent down to him from his Lord?" But thou art truly a warner, and to every people a guide.

8. Allah doth know what every female (womb) doth bear, by how much the wombs fall short (of their time or number) or do exceed. Every single thing is with Him in (due) proportion.

9. He knoweth the Unseen and that which is open: He is the Great, the most High.

10. It is the same (to Him) whether any of you conceal his speech or declare it openly; whether he lie hid by night or walk forth freely by day.

11. For each (such person) there are (angels) in succession, before and behind him; they guard him by command of Allah. Verily never will Allah change the condition of a people until they change what is in themselves but when (once) Allah willeth a people's punishment, there can be no turning it back, nor will they find, besides Him, any to protect

12. It is He Who doth show you the lightning, by way both of fear

میں فضیلت دیتے ہیں اور اس میں سمجھنے والوں کیلئے بہت سی نشانیاں ہیں (۴)
اگر تم عجیب بات سننی چاہو تو کافروں کا یہ کہنا عجیب
ہے کہ جب ہم (مرکر) مٹی ہو جائیں گے تو کیا از سرِ نو
پیدا ہوں گے؟ یہی لوگ ہیں جو اپنے پروردگار سے منکر
ہوئے ہیں۔ اور یہی ہیں جن کی گردنوں میں طوق ہوں گے۔
اور یہی اہلِ دوزخ ہیں کہ ہمیشہ اس میں (جلتے) رہیں گے (۵)
اور یہ لوگ بھلائی سے پہلے تم سے بُرائی کے جلد خواستگار
(یعنی طالب عذاب) ہیں حالانکہ اُن سے پہلے عذاب (واقع)
ہو چکے ہیں۔ اور تمہارا پروردگار لوگوں کو باوجود اُنکی بے انصافیوں کے
معاف کرنیوالا ہے۔ اور بیشک تمہارا پروردگار سخت عذاب دینے والا ہے (۶)
اور کافر لوگ کہتے ہیں کہ اس (پیغمبر) پر اسکے پروردگار کی طرف سے
کوئی نشانی نازل نہیں ہوئی۔ سو (اے محمد) تم تو صرف
ہدایت کرنے والے ہو اور ہر ایک قوم کیلئے رہنما ہوا کرتا ہے (۷)
خدا ہی اُس بچے سے واقف ہے جو عورت کے پیٹ میں ہوتا
ہے اور پیٹ کے سکڑنے اور بڑھنے سے بھی (واقف ہے)
اور ہر چیز کا اس کے ہاں ایک اندازہ مقرر ہے (۸)
وہ دانائے نہاں و آشکار ہے سب سے بزرگ (اور) عالی رتبہ ہے (۹)
کوئی تم میں سے چپکے سے بات کہے یا پکار کر۔ یا رات کو
کہیں چھپ جائے یا دن (کی روشنی) میں کھلم کھلا چلے
پھرے (اس کے نزدیک) برابر ہے (۱۰)
اُس کے آگے اور پیچھے خدا کے چوکیدار ہیں جو خدا کے حکم
سے اُس کی حفاظت کرتے ہیں۔ خدا اس (نعمت) کو جو
کسی قوم کو (حاصل) ہے نہیں بدلتا جب تک کہ وہ اپنی
حالت کو نہ بدلے۔ اور جب خدا کسی قوم کے ساتھ بُرائی کا
ارادہ کرتا ہے تو پھر وہ پھر نہیں سکتی۔ اور خدا کے سوا اُن
کا کوئی مددگار نہیں ہوتا (۱۱)
اور وہی تو ہے جو تم کو ڈرانے اور امید دلانے کیلئے بجلی دکھاتا

إِنَّ فِي ذَٰلِكَ لَآيَاتٍ لِّقَوْمٍ يَعْقِلُونَ ﴿٤﴾
وَإِن تَعْجَبْ فَعَجَبٌ قَوْلُهُمْ أَإِذَا كُنَّا
تُرَابًا أَإِنَّا لَفِي خَلْقٍ جَدِيدٍ ۗ أُولَٰئِكَ
الَّذِينَ كَفَرُوا بِرَبِّهِمْ ۖ وَأُولَٰئِكَ
الْأَغْلَالُ فِي أَعْنَاقِهِمْ ۖ وَأُولَٰئِكَ أَصْحَابُ
النَّارِ ۖ هُمْ فِيهَا خَالِدُونَ ﴿٥﴾
وَيَسْتَعْجِلُونَكَ بِالسَّيِّئَةِ قَبْلَ الْحَسَنَةِ
وَقَدْ خَلَتْ مِن قَبْلِهِمُ الْمَثُلَاتُ ۗ وَإِنَّ
رَبَّكَ لَذُو مَغْفِرَةٍ لِّلنَّاسِ عَلَىٰ ظُلْمِهِمْ ۖ
وَإِنَّ رَبَّكَ لَشَدِيدُ الْعِقَابِ ﴿٦﴾
وَيَقُولُ الَّذِينَ كَفَرُوا لَوْلَا أُنزِلَ
عَلَيْهِ آيَةٌ مِّن رَّبِّهِ ۗ إِنَّمَا أَنتَ مُنذِرٌ ۖ
ع وَلِكُلِّ قَوْمٍ هَادٍ ﴿٧﴾
اللَّهُ يَعْلَمُ مَا تَحْمِلُ كُلُّ أُنثَىٰ وَمَا
تَغِيضُ الْأَرْحَامُ وَمَا تَزْدَادُ ۖ وَكُلُّ
شَيْءٍ عِندَهُ بِمِقْدَارٍ ﴿٨﴾
عَالِمُ الْغَيْبِ وَالشَّهَادَةِ الْكَبِيرُ الْمُتَعَالِ ﴿٩﴾
سَوَاءٌ مِّنكُم مَّنْ أَسَرَّ الْقَوْلَ وَمَن
جَهَرَ بِهِ وَمَنْ هُوَ مُسْتَخْفٍ بِاللَّيْلِ
وَسَارِبٌ بِالنَّهَارِ ﴿١٠﴾
لَهُ مُعَقِّبَاتٌ مِّن بَيْنِ يَدَيْهِ وَمِنْ
خَلْفِهِ يَحْفَظُونَهُ مِنْ أَمْرِ اللَّهِ ۗ إِنَّ
اللَّهَ لَا يُغَيِّرُ مَا بِقَوْمٍ حَتَّىٰ يُغَيِّرُوا
مَا بِأَنفُسِهِمْ ۗ وَإِذَا أَرَادَ اللَّهُ بِقَوْمٍ
سُوءًا فَلَا مَرَدَّ لَهُ ۚ وَمَا لَهُم مِّن دُونِهِ
مِن وَالٍ ﴿١١﴾
هُوَ الَّذِي يُرِيكُمُ الْبَرْقَ خَوْفًا وَ

and of hope: it is He Who doth raise up the clouds, heavy with (fertilising) rain!

13. Nay, thunder repeateth His praises, and so do the angels, with awe: He flingeth the loud-voiced Thunder-bolts, and therewith He striketh whomsoever He will... yet these (are the men) the while they are disputing about Allah He is Mighty in Power.

14. To Him is due the true prayer any others that they call upon besides Him hear them no more than if they were to stretch forth their hands for water to reach their mouths but it reaches them not: for the prayer of those without Faith is nothing but vain prayer.

15. Whatever beings there are in the heavens and the earth do prostrate themselves to Allah — with good-will or in spite of themselves: so do their shadows in the mornings and evenings.

16. Say: "Who is the Lord and Sustainer of the heavens and the earth?" Say:"(It is) Allah." Say: "Do ye then take (for worship) protectors other than Him, such as have no power either for good or for harm to themselves?" Say: "Are the blind equal with those who see? Or the depths of darkness equal with Light?" Or do they assign to Allah partners who have created (anything) as He has created, so that the creation seemed to them similar? Say: "Allah is the Creator of all things: He is the One, the Supreme and Irresistible."

17. He sends down water from the skies, and the channels flow, each according to its measure: But the torrent bears away the foam that mounts up to the surface. Even so, from that (ore) which they heat in the fire, to make ornaments or utensils therewith, there is a scum likewise. Thus doth Allah (by parables) show forth Truth and falsehood. For the scum disappears like froth cast out; while that which is for the good of mankind remains on the earth. Thus doth Allah set forth parables.

اور بھاری بھاری بادل پیدا کرتا ہے ﴿۱۲﴾
اور رعد اور فرشتے سب اُس کے خوف سے اُس کی تسبیح
وتحمید کرتے رہتے ہیں۔ اور وہی بجلیاں بھیجتا ہے پھر جس
پر چاہتا ہے گرا بھی دیتا ہے۔ اور وہ خدا کے بارے میں
جھگڑتے ہیں اور وہ بڑی قوت والا ہے ﴿۱۳﴾
سُود مند پکارنا تو اسی کا ہے اور جنکو یہ لوگ اُسکے سوا پکارتے ہیں
وہ اُنکی پکار کو کسی طرح قبول نہیں کرتے مگر اس شخص کی طرح جو
اپنے دونوں ہاتھ پانی کیطرف پھیلادے تاکہ (دور ہی سے) اُسکے منہ تک آپہنچے
حالانکہ وہ (اس تک کبھی بھی نہیں آسکتا اور اسی طرح کافروں کی پکار بیکار ہے ﴿۱۴﴾
اور جتنی مخلوقات آسمانوں اور زمین میں ہے خوشی سے یا زبردستی سے
خدا کے آگے سجدہ کرتی ہے اور اُنکے سائے بھی صبح و شام سجدے کرتے ہیں ﴿۱۵﴾
ان سے پوچھو کہ آسمانوں اور زمین کا پروردگار کون ہے؟
(انہیں ان کی طرف سے) کہہ دو کہ خدا۔ پھر (ان سے) کہو کہ
تم نے خدا کو چھوڑ کر ایسے لوگوں کو کیوں کارساز بنایا ہے جو خود اپنے
نفع ونقصان کا بھی اختیار نہیں رکھتے۔ (یہ بھی) پوچھو کیا اندھا
اور آنکھوں والا برابر ہیں؟ یا اندھیرا اور اُجالا برابر ہو سکتا ہے؟
بھلا ان لوگوں نے جنکو خدا کا شریک مقرر کیا ہے کیا انہوں نے خدا کی سی
مخلوقات پیدا کی ہے جسکے سبب انکو مخلوقات مشتبہ ہوگئی ہے کہہ دو کہ خدا
ہی ہر چیز کا پیدا کرنے والا ہے اور وہ یکتا (اور) زبردست ہے ﴿۱۶﴾
اسی نے آسمان سے مینہ برسایا پھر اس سے اپنے اپنے
اندازے کے مطابق نالے بہ نکلے پھر نالے پر پھولا ہوا
جھاگ آگیا۔ اور جس چیز کو زیور یا کوئی اور سامان بنانے
کے لئے آگ میں تپاتے ہیں اس میں بھی ایسا ہی جھاگ
ہوتا ہے۔ اس طرح خدا حق اور باطل کی مثال بیان فرماتا
ہے۔ سو جھاگ تو سوکھ کر زائل ہو جاتا ہے اور (پانی) جو
لوگوں کو فائدہ پہنچاتا ہے وہ زمین میں ٹھہرا رہتا ہے اس
طرح خدا (صحیح اور غلط کی) مثالیں بیان فرماتا ہے تاکہ تم سمجھو ﴿۱۷﴾

طَمَعًا وَّيُنْشِئُ السَّحَابَ الثِّقَالَ ﴿١٢﴾
وَيُسَبِّحُ الرَّعْدُ بِحَمْدِهٖ وَالْمَلٰٓئِكَةُ مِنْ
خِيْفَتِهٖ ۚ وَيُرْسِلُ الصَّوَاعِقَ فَيُصِيْبُ
بِهَا مَنْ يَّشَآءُ وَهُمْ يُجَادِلُوْنَ فِى
اللّٰهِ ۚ وَهُوَ شَدِيْدُ الْمِحَالِ ﴿١٣﴾
لَهٗ دَعْوَةُ الْحَقِّ ۗ وَالَّذِيْنَ يَدْعُوْنَ مِنْ
دُوْنِهٖ لَا يَسْتَجِيْبُوْنَ لَهُمْ بِشَيْءٍ اِلَّا كَبَاسِطِ
كَفَّيْهِ اِلَى الْمَآءِ لِيَبْلُغَ فَاهُ وَمَا هُوَ
بِبَالِغِهٖ ۚ وَمَا دُعَآءُ الْكٰفِرِيْنَ اِلَّا فِىْ ضَلٰلٍ ﴿١٤﴾
وَلِلّٰهِ يَسْجُدُ مَنْ فِى السَّمٰوٰتِ وَالْاَرْضِ
طَوْعًا وَّكَرْهًا وَّظِلٰلُهُمْ بِالْغُدُوِّ وَالْاٰصَالِ ﴿١٥﴾ السجدة ۲
قُلْ مَنْ رَّبُّ السَّمٰوٰتِ وَالْاَرْضِ ۚ
قُلِ اللّٰهُ ۚ قُلْ اَفَاتَّخَذْتُمْ مِّنْ دُوْنِهٖٓ
اَوْلِيَآءَ لَا يَمْلِكُوْنَ لِاَنْفُسِهِمْ نَفْعًا وَّ
لَا ضَرًّا ۚ قُلْ هَلْ يَسْتَوِى الْاَعْمٰى
وَالْبَصِيْرُ ۙ اَمْ هَلْ تَسْتَوِى الظُّلُمٰتُ
وَالنُّوْرُ ۚ اَمْ جَعَلُوْا لِلّٰهِ شُرَكَآءَ خَلَقُوْا
كَخَلْقِهٖ فَتَشَابَهَ الْخَلْقُ عَلَيْهِمْ ۚ قُلِ اللّٰهُ
خَالِقُ كُلِّ شَيْءٍ وَّهُوَ الْوَاحِدُ الْقَهَّارُ ﴿١٦﴾
اَنْزَلَ مِنَ السَّمَآءِ مَآءً فَسَالَتْ اَوْدِيَةٌ
بِقَدَرِهَا فَاحْتَمَلَ السَّيْلُ زَبَدًا
رَّابِيًا ۚ وَمِمَّا يُوْقِدُوْنَ عَلَيْهِ
فِى النَّارِ ابْتِغَآءَ حِلْيَةٍ اَوْ مَتَاعٍ
زَبَدٌ مِّثْلُهٗ ۚ كَذٰلِكَ يَضْرِبُ اللّٰهُ
الْحَقَّ وَالْبَاطِلَ ۚ فَاَمَّا الزَّبَدُ فَيَذْهَبُ
جُفَآءً ۚ وَاَمَّا مَا يَنْفَعُ النَّاسَ فَيَمْكُثُ
فِى الْاَرْضِ ۚ كَذٰلِكَ يَضْرِبُ اللّٰهُ الْاَمْثَالَ ﴿١٧﴾

18. For those who respond to their Lord, are (all) good things. But those who respond not to Him,—even if they had all that is in the heavens and on earth, and as much more, (in vain) would they offer it for ransom. For them will the reckoning be terrible: their abode will be Hell,—what a bed of misery!

19. Is then one who doth know that that which hath been revealed unto thee from thy Lord is the Truth, like one who is blind? It is those who are endued with understanding that receive admonition;—

20. Those who fulfil the Covenant of Allah and fail not in their plighted word;

21. Those who join together those things which Allah hath commanded to be joined, hold their Lord in awe, and fear the terrible reckoning;

22. Those who patiently persevere, seeking the countenance of their Lord; establish regular prayers; spend, out of (the gifts) We have bestowed for their sustenance, secretly and openly; and turn off Evil with good: for such there is the final attainment of the (Eternal) Home,—

23. Gardens of perpetual bliss: they shall enter there, as well as the righteous among their fathers, their spouses and their offspring and angels shall enter unto them from every gate (with the salutation)

24. "Peace unto you for that ye persevered in patience! Now how excellent is the final Home!"

25. But those who break the Covenant of Allah, after having plighted their word thereto, and cut asunder those things which Allah has commanded to be joined, and work mischief in the land; — on them is the Curse; for them is the terrible Home!

26. Allah doth enlarge, or grant by (strict) measure, the Sustenance

جن لوگوں نے خدا کے حکم کو قبول کیا انکی حالت بہت بہتر
ہوگی۔ اور جنہوں نے اُس کو قبول نہ کیا اگر روئے زمین
کے سب خزانے اُنکے اختیار میں ہوں تو وہ سب کے سب اور اُنکے
ساتھ اتنے ہی اور اُنکے (بدلے میں صرف کرڈالیں (مگر نجات کہاں؟)
ایسے لوگوں کا حساب بھی بُرا ہوگا اور اُنکا ٹھکانا بھی دوزخ ہے اور وہ بُری جگہ ہے (۱۸)
بھلا جو شخص یہ جانتا ہے کہ جو کچھ تمہارے پروردگار کی طرف
سے تم پر نازل ہوا ہے حق ہے وہ اُس شخص کی طرح ہے
جو اندھا ہے؟ اور سمجھتے تو وہی ہیں جو عقلمند ہیں (۱۹)
جو خدا کے عہد کو پورا کرتے ہیں اور اقرار کو نہیں
توڑتے (۲۰)
اور جن (رشتہ ہائے قرابت) کے جوڑے رکھنے کا خدا نے
حکم دیا ہے اُن کو جوڑے رکھتے اور اپنے پروردگار سے ڈرتے
رہتے اور بُرے حساب سے خوف رکھتے ہیں (۲۱)
اور جو پروردگار کی خوشنودی حاصل کرنے کیلئے (مصائب
پر) صبر کرتے ہیں۔ اور نماز پڑھتے ہیں اور جو (مال) ہم نے
اُن کو دیا ہے اُس میں سے پوشیدہ اور ظاہر خرچ کرتے ہیں اور نیکی
سے بُرائی کو دور کرتے ہیں یہی لوگ ہیں جنکے لئے عاقبت کا گھر ہے (۲۲)
(یعنی) ہمیشہ رہنے کے باغات جن میں وہ داخل ہونگے اور انکے باپ دادا
اور بیبیوں اور اولاد میں سے جو نیکوکار ہونگے وہ بھی (بہشت میں جائینگے)
اور فرشتے (بہشت کے) ہر ایک دروازے سے انکے پاس آئینگے (۲۳)
(اور کہیں گے) تم پر رحمت ہو (یہ) تمہاری ثابت قدمی کا
بدلہ ہے۔ اور عاقبت کا گھر خوب (گھر) ہے (۲۴)
اور جو لوگ خدا سے عہد واثق کر کے اُس کو توڑ ڈالتے اور
جن (رشتہ ہائے قرابت) کے جوڑے رکھنے کا خدا نے حکم دیا ہے
اُن کو قطع کر دیتے اور ملک میں فساد کرتے ہیں ایسوں
پر لعنت ہے اور اُن کے لئے گھر بھی بُرا ہے (۲۵)
خدا جس کا چاہتا ہے رزق فراخ کر دیتا ہے اور (جس کا) چاہتا

لِلَّذِينَ اسْتَجَابُوا لِرَبِّهِمُ الْحُسْنَىٰ ۚ
وَالَّذِينَ لَمْ يَسْتَجِيبُوا لَهُ لَوْ أَنَّ لَهُمْ
مَا فِي الْأَرْضِ جَمِيعًا وَمِثْلَهُ مَعَهُ
لَافْتَدَوْا بِهِ ۚ أُولَٰئِكَ لَهُمْ سُوءُ الْحِسَابِ
وَمَأْوَاهُمْ جَهَنَّمُ ۖ وَبِئْسَ الْمِهَادُ (۱۸)
أَفَمَنْ يَعْلَمُ أَنَّمَا أُنْزِلَ إِلَيْكَ مِنْ
رَبِّكَ الْحَقُّ كَمَنْ هُوَ أَعْمَىٰ ۚ إِنَّمَا
يَتَذَكَّرُ أُولُو الْأَلْبَابِ (۱۹)
الَّذِينَ يُوفُونَ بِعَهْدِ اللَّهِ وَلَا
يَنْقُضُونَ الْمِيثَاقَ (۲۰)
وَالَّذِينَ يَصِلُونَ مَا أَمَرَ اللَّهُ بِهِ أَنْ
يُوصَلَ وَيَخْشَوْنَ رَبَّهُمْ وَيَخَافُونَ
سُوءَ الْحِسَابِ (۲۱)
وَالَّذِينَ صَبَرُوا ابْتِغَاءَ وَجْهِ رَبِّهِمْ
وَأَقَامُوا الصَّلَاةَ وَأَنْفَقُوا مِمَّا رَزَقْنَاهُمْ
سِرًّا وَعَلَانِيَةً وَيَدْرَءُونَ بِالْحَسَنَةِ
السَّيِّئَةَ أُولَٰئِكَ لَهُمْ عُقْبَى الدَّارِ (۲۲)
جَنَّاتُ عَدْنٍ يَدْخُلُونَهَا وَمَنْ صَلَحَ
مِنْ آبَائِهِمْ وَأَزْوَاجِهِمْ وَذُرِّيَّاتِهِمْ
وَالْمَلَائِكَةُ يَدْخُلُونَ عَلَيْهِمْ مِنْ كُلِّ بَابٍ (۲۳)
سَلَامٌ عَلَيْكُمْ بِمَا صَبَرْتُمْ ۚ فَنِعْمَ
عُقْبَى الدَّارِ (۲۴)
وَالَّذِينَ يَنْقُضُونَ عَهْدَ اللَّهِ مِنْ بَعْدِ
مِيثَاقِهِ وَيَقْطَعُونَ مَا أَمَرَ اللَّهُ بِهِ
أَنْ يُوصَلَ وَيُفْسِدُونَ فِي الْأَرْضِ ۙ
أُولَٰئِكَ لَهُمُ اللَّعْنَةُ وَلَهُمْ سُوءُ الدَّارِ (۲۵)
اللَّهُ يَبْسُطُ الرِّزْقَ لِمَنْ يَشَاءُ وَيَقْدِرُ ۚ

وقف النبي عليه الصلوٰة والسلام
النصف

(which He giveth) to whomso He pleaseth. (The worldly) rejoice in the life of this world: but the life of this world is but little comfort compared to the Hereafter.

27. The Unbelievers say: "Why is not a Sign sent down to him from his Lord?" Say: "Truly Allah leaveth, to stray, whom He will; but He guideth to Himself those who turn to Him in penitence,—

28. "Those who believe, and whose hearts find satisfaction in the remembrance of Allah: for without doubt in the remembrance of Allah do hearts find satisfaction.

29. "For those who believe and work righteousness, is (every) blessedness, and a beautiful place of (final) return."

30. Thus have We sent thee amongst a People before whom (long since) have (other) Peoples (gone and) passed away; in order that thou mightest rehearse unto them what We send down unto thee by inspiration; yet do they reject (Him), the Most Gracious! Say: "He is my Lord! There is no god but He! On Him is my trust, and to Him do I turn!"

31. If there were a Qur'an with which mountains were moved, or the earth were cloven asunder, or the dead were made to speak, (this would be the one!) but, truly, the Command is with Allah in all things! Do not the Believers know, that, had Allah (so) willed, He could have guided all mankind (to the Right)? But the Unbelievers,—never will disaster cease to seize them for their (ill) deeds, or to settle close to their homes, until the promise of Allah come to pass, for, verily, Allah will not fail in His promise.

32. Mocked were (many) messengers before thee: but I granted respite to the Unbelievers, and finally I punished them: then how (terrible) was My requital!

ہے تنگ کر دیتا ہے۔ اور کافر لوگ دنیا کی زندگی پر خوش ہو رہے
ہیں۔ اور دنیا کی زندگی آخرت (کے مقابلے) میں (بہت) تھوڑا فائدہ ہے ﴿٢٦﴾
اور کافر کہتے ہیں کہ اس (پیغمبر) پر اس کے پروردگار کی طرف
سے کوئی نشانی کیوں نازل نہیں ہوئی؟ کہہ دو کہ خدا جسے
چاہتا ہے گمراہ کرتا ہے اور جو (اس کی طرف) رجوع ہوتا ہے
اس کو اپنی طرف کا رستہ دکھاتا ہے ﴿٢٧﴾
(یعنی) جو لوگ ایمان لاتے اور جن کے دل یاد خدا سے
آرام پاتے ہیں (ان کو) اور سن رکھو کہ خدا کی یاد سے
دل آرام پاتے ہیں ﴿٢٨﴾
جو لوگ ایمان لائے اور عمل نیک کئے ان کے لئے
خوش حالی اور عمدہ ٹھکانا ہے ﴿٢٩﴾
(جس طرح ہم اور پیغمبر بھیجتے رہے ہیں) اسی طرح (اے محمدؐ) ہم نے
تم کو اس امت میں جس سے پہلے بہت سی امتیں گزر چکی ہیں
بھیجا ہے تاکہ تم ان کو وہ (کتاب) جو ہم نے تمہاری طرف بھیجی ہے پڑھ کر سنا دو۔
اور یہ لوگ رحمٰن کو نہیں مانتے کہہ دو۔ وہی تو میرا پروردگار ہے اس کے سوا
کوئی معبود نہیں میں اسی پر بھروسہ رکھتا ہوں اور اسی کی طرف رجوع کرتا ہوں ﴿٣٠﴾
اور اگر کوئی قرآن ایسا ہوتا کہ اس (کی تاثیر) سے پہاڑ
چل پڑتے یا زمین پھٹ جاتی یا مردوں سے کلام کر سکتے
(تو یہی قرآن ان اوصاف سے متصف ہوتا مگر) بات یہ
ہے کہ سب باتیں خدا کے اختیار میں ہیں۔ تو کیا مومنوں کو
اس سے اطمینان نہیں ہوا کہ اگر خدا چاہتا تو سب لوگوں کو ہدایت کے
رستے پر چلا دیتا۔ اور کافروں پر ہمیشہ ان کے اعمال کے بدلے بلا آتی رہے گی۔
یا ان کے مکانات کے قریب نازل ہوتی رہے گی۔ یہاں تک کہ خدا کا وعدہ
آپہنچے۔ بے شک خدا وعدہ خلاف نہیں کرتا ﴿٣١﴾
اور تم سے پہلے بھی رسولوں کے ساتھ تمسخر ہوتے رہے
ہیں تو ہم نے کافروں کو مہلت دی پھر پکڑ لیا سو (دیکھ لو کہ)
ہمارا عذاب کیسا تھا ﴿٣٢﴾

وَفَرِحُوْا بِالْحَيٰوةِ الدُّنْيَا ۗ وَمَا الْحَيٰوةُ
الدُّنْيَا فِي الْاٰخِرَةِ اِلَّا مَتَاعٌ ﴿٢٦﴾
وَيَقُوْلُ الَّذِيْنَ كَفَرُوْا لَوْلَآ اُنْزِلَ
عَلَيْهِ اٰيَةٌ مِّنْ رَّبِّهٖ ۗ قُلْ اِنَّ اللّٰهَ
يُضِلُّ مَنْ يَّشَآءُ وَيَهْدِيْٓ اِلَيْهِ
مَنْ اَنَابَ ﴿٢٧﴾
اَلَّذِيْنَ اٰمَنُوْا وَتَطْمَئِنُّ قُلُوْبُهُمْ
بِذِكْرِ اللّٰهِ ۗ اَلَا بِذِكْرِ اللّٰهِ تَطْمَئِنُّ
الْقُلُوْبُ ﴿٢٨﴾
اَلَّذِيْنَ اٰمَنُوْا وَعَمِلُوا الصّٰلِحٰتِ طُوْبٰى
لَهُمْ وَحُسْنُ مَاٰبٍ ﴿٢٩﴾
كَذٰلِكَ اَرْسَلْنٰكَ فِيْٓ اُمَّةٍ قَدْ خَلَتْ
مِنْ قَبْلِهَآ اُمَمٌ لِّتَتْلُوَا۟ عَلَيْهِمُ الَّذِيْٓ
اَوْحَيْنَآ اِلَيْكَ وَهُمْ يَكْفُرُوْنَ بِالرَّحْمٰنِ ۗ
قُلْ هُوَ رَبِّيْ لَآ اِلٰهَ اِلَّا هُوَ ۚ عَلَيْهِ
تَوَكَّلْتُ وَاِلَيْهِ مَتَابِ ﴿٣٠﴾
وَلَوْ اَنَّ قُرْاٰنًا سُيِّرَتْ بِهِ الْجِبَالُ اَوْ
قُطِّعَتْ بِهِ الْاَرْضُ اَوْ كُلِّمَ بِهِ الْمَوْتٰى ۗ
بَلْ لِّلّٰهِ الْاَمْرُ جَمِيْعًا ۗ اَفَلَمْ يَايْــَٔسِ الَّذِيْنَ
اٰمَنُوْٓا اَنْ لَّوْ يَشَآءُ اللّٰهُ لَهَدَى النَّاسَ جَمِيْعًا ۗ
وَلَا يَزَالُ الَّذِيْنَ كَفَرُوْا تُصِيْبُهُمْ
بِمَا صَنَعُوْا قَارِعَةٌ اَوْ تَحُلُّ قَرِيْبًا مِّنْ
دَارِهِمْ حَتّٰى يَاْتِيَ وَعْدُ اللّٰهِ ۗ اِنَّ اللّٰهَ
لَا يُخْلِفُ الْمِيْعَادَ ﴿٣١﴾
وَلَقَدِ اسْتُهْزِئَ بِرُسُلٍ مِّنْ قَبْلِكَ
فَاَمْلَيْتُ لِلَّذِيْنَ كَفَرُوْا ثُمَّ اَخَذْتُهُمْ ۫
فَكَيْفَ كَانَ عِقَابِ ﴿٣٢﴾

33. Is then He Who standeth over every soul (and knoweth) all that it doth, (like any others)? And yet they ascribe partners to Allah. Say: "But name them! Is it that ye will inform Him of something He knoweth not on earth, or is it (just) a show of words?" Nay! to those who believe not, their devising seems pleasing, but they are kept back (thereby) from the Path. And those whom Allah leads astray, no one can guide

34. For them is a Penalty in the life of this world, but harder, truly, is the Chastisement of the Hereafter: and defender have they none against Allah.

35. The parable of the Garden which the righteous are promised!—beneath it flow rivers: perpetual is the fruits thereof and the shade therein: such is the End of the Righteous; and the End of Unbelievers is the Fire.

36. Those to whom We have given the Book rejoice at what hath been revealed unto thee: but there are among the clans those who reject a part thereof. Say: "I am commanded to worship Allah, and not to join partners with Him. Unto Him do I call, and unto Him is my return."

37. Thus have We revealed it to be a judgment of authority in Arabic. Wert thou to follow their (vain) desires after the knowledge which hath reached thee, then wouldst thou find neither protector nor defender against Allah.

38. We did send messengers before thee, and appointed for them wives and children: and it was never the part of a messenger to bring a Sign except as Allah permitted (or commanded). For each period is an appointment).

39. Allah doth blot out or confirm what He pleaseth: with Him is the Mother of the Book.

تو کیا جو (خدا) ہر متنفس کے اعمال کا نگراں (ونگہبان) ہے (وہ
بتوں کی طرح بےعلم وبےخبر ہوسکتا ہے؟) اور ان لوگوں نے خدا کے شریک
مقرر کر رکھے ہیں۔ ان سے کہو کہ (ذرا) ان کے نام تو لو کیا تم اسے
ایسی چیزیں بتاتے ہو جسکو وہ زمین میں (کہیں بھی) معلوم نہیں کرتا یا
(محض) ظاہری (باطل اور جھوٹی) بات کی (تقلید کرتے ہو) اصل یہ ہے کہ
کافروں کو انکے فریب خوبصورت معلوم ہوتے ہیں اور وہ (ہدایت کے) رستے سے
روک لئے گئے ہیں۔ اور جسے خدا گمراہ کرے اُسے کوئی ہدایت کرنیوالا نہیں ٣٣
ان کو دنیا کی زندگی میں بھی عذاب ہے۔ اور آخرت کا
عذاب تو بہت ہی سخت ہے اور اُن کو خدا (کے عذاب)
سے کوئی بھی بچانے والا نہیں ٣٤
جس باغ کا متقیوں سے وعدہ کیا گیا ہے۔ اُس کے
اوصاف یہ ہیں کہ اُس کے نیچے نہریں بہ رہی ہیں اُسکے
پھل ہمیشہ (قائم رہنے والے) ہیں اور اسکے سائے بھی۔ یہ
اُن لوگوں کا انجام ہے جو متقی ہیں۔ اور کافروں کا انجام دوزخ ہے ٣٥
اور جن لوگوں کو ہم نے کتاب دی ہے وہ اُس (کتاب) سے جو تم پر نازل
ہوئی ہے خوش ہوتے ہیں اور بعض فرقے اسکی بعض باتیں نہیں بھی مانتے
کہہ دو کہ مجھکو یہی حکم ہوا ہے کہ خدا ہی کی عبادت کروں اور اسکے ساتھ کسی کو
شریک نہ بناؤں۔ میں اُسی کی طرف بلاتا ہوں اور اُسی کی طرف مجھے لوٹنا ہے ٣٦
اور اسی طرح ہم نے اس قرآن کو عربی زبان کا فرمان نازل
کیا ہے۔ اور اگر تم علم (ودانش) آنے کے بعد اُن لوگوں کی خواہشوں کے
پیچھے چلو گے تو خدا کے سامنے کوئی نہ تمہارا مددگار ہوگا اور نہ کوئی بچانیوالا ٣٧
اور (اے محمدؐ) ہم نے تم سے پہلے بھی پیغمبر بھیجے تھے اور اُن کو
بیبیاں اور اولاد بھی دی تھی۔ اور کسی پیغمبر کے اختیار کی
بات نہ تھی کہ خدا کے حکم کے بغیر کوئی نشانی لائے۔ ہر
حکم (قضا) (کتاب میں) مرقوم ہے ٣٨
خدا جس کو چاہتا ہے مٹا دیتا ہے اور جس کو چاہتا ہے
قائم رکھتا ہے اور اُسی کے پاس اصل کتاب ہے ٣٩

أَفَمَنْ هُوَ قَآئِمٌ عَلَىٰ كُلِّ نَفْسٍ بِمَا
كَسَبَتْ ۗ وَجَعَلُوا لِلَّهِ شُرَكَآءَ ؕ قُلْ
سَمُّوهُمْ ؕ أَمْ تُنَبِّئُونَهُ بِمَا لَا يَعْلَمُ
فِى الْأَرْضِ أَمْ بِظَاهِرٍ مِّنَ الْقَوْلِ ؕ
بَلْ زُيِّنَ لِلَّذِينَ كَفَرُوا مَكْرُهُمْ
وَصُدُّوا عَنِ السَّبِيلِ ؕ وَمَنْ يُّضْلِلِ
اللّٰهُ فَمَا لَهُ مِنْ هَادٍ ٣٣
لَهُمْ عَذَابٌ فِى الْحَيٰوةِ الدُّنْيَا وَلَعَذَابُ
الْاٰخِرَةِ اَشَقُّ ۚ وَمَا لَهُمْ مِّنَ اللّٰهِ مِنْ
وَّاقٍ ٣٤
مَثَلُ الْجَنَّةِ الَّتِىْ وُعِدَ الْمُتَّقُوْنَ ؕ
تَجْرِىْ مِنْ تَحْتِهَا الْاَنْهٰرُ ؕ اُكُلُهَا
دَآئِمٌ وَّظِلُّهَا ؕ تِلْكَ عُقْبَى الَّذِيْنَ
اتَّقَوْا ۖ وَّعُقْبَى الْكٰفِرِيْنَ النَّارُ ٣٥
وَالَّذِيْنَ اٰتَيْنٰهُمُ الْكِتٰبَ يَفْرَحُوْنَ بِمَآ
اُنْزِلَ اِلَيْكَ وَمِنَ الْاَحْزَابِ مَنْ يُّنْكِرُ
بَعْضَهٗ ؕ قُلْ اِنَّمَآ اُمِرْتُ اَنْ اَعْبُدَ اللّٰهَ
وَلَآ اُشْرِكَ بِهٖ ؕ اِلَيْهِ اَدْعُوْا وَاِلَيْهِ مَاٰبِ ٣٦
وَكَذٰلِكَ اَنْزَلْنٰهُ حُكْمًا عَرَبِيًّا ؕ وَلَئِنِ
اتَّبَعْتَ اَهْوَآءَهُمْ بَعْدَ مَا جَآءَكَ مِنَ الْعِلْمِ ۙ
مَا لَكَ مِنَ اللّٰهِ مِنْ وَّلِىٍّ وَّلَا وَاقٍ ٣٧ ع
وَلَقَدْ اَرْسَلْنَا رُسُلًا مِّنْ قَبْلِكَ وَ
جَعَلْنَا لَهُمْ اَزْوَاجًا وَّذُرِّيَّةً ؕ وَمَا
كَانَ لِرَسُوْلٍ اَنْ يَّاْتِىَ بِاٰيَةٍ اِلَّا بِاِذْنِ
اللّٰهِ ؕ لِكُلِّ اَجَلٍ كِتَابٌ ٣٨
يَمْحُوا اللّٰهُ مَا يَشَآءُ وَيُثْبِتُ ۚ وَعِنْدَهٗ
اُمُّ الْكِتٰبِ ٣٩

SÛRA–14
IBRÃHÎM
(INTRODUCTION)

For the chronology and the general argument of this Sûra in the series Sûras 10 to 15, see Introduction to S. 10.

The special subject-matter of this Sûra is a continuation of the conculding portion of the last Sûra, which explained how Allah's revelation gains ground in spite of selfish men's opposition. Here illustrations are given from the story of Moses and Abraham, and Abraham's Prayer for Makkah forms the core of the Sûra.

40. Whether We shall show thee (within thy life-time) part of what We promised them or take to Us thy soul (before it is all accomplished). Thy duty is to make (the Message) reach them: It is Our part to call them to account.

اور اگر ہم کوئی عذاب جس کا ان لوگوں سے وعدہ کرتے ہیں تمہیں دکھائیں (یعنی تمہارے روبرو
ان پر نازل کریں) یا تمہاری مدت حیات پوری کر دیں (یعنی تمہارے انتقال کے بعد عذاب
بھیجیں) تو تمہارا کام (ہمارے احکام کا) پہنچا دینا ہے اور ہمارا کام حساب لینا ہے (۴۰)

وَإِن مَّا نُرِيَنَّكَ بَعْضَ الَّذِي نَعِدُهُمْ
أَوْ نَتَوَفَّيَنَّكَ فَإِنَّمَا عَلَيْكَ الْبَلٰغُ
وَعَلَيْنَا الْحِسَابُ ﴿٤٠﴾

41. See they not that We gradually reduce the land from its outlying borders?. (Where) Allah commands, there is none to put back His command: and He is Swift in calling to account.

کیا انہوں نے نہیں دیکھا کہ ہم زمین کو اس کے کناروں سے گھٹاتے
چلے آتے ہیں[١٦١] اور خدا (جیسا چاہتا ہے) حکم کرتا ہے کوئی اس کے حکم
کا رد کرنے والا نہیں۔ اور وہ جلد حساب لینے والا ہے (۴۱)

أَوَلَمْ يَرَوْا أَنَّا نَأْتِي الْأَرْضَ نَنقُصُهَا
مِنْ أَطْرَافِهَا ۚ وَاللّٰهُ يَحْكُمُ لَا مُعَقِّبَ
لِحُكْمِهِ ۚ وَهُوَ سَرِيعُ الْحِسَابِ ﴿٤١﴾

42. Those before them did (also) devise plots; but in all things Allah is the devising altogether. He knoweth the doings of every soul: and soon will the Unbelievers know who gets home in the End.

جو لوگ ان سے پہلے تھے وہ بھی (بہتیری) چالیں چلتے رہے
ہیں سو چال تو سب اللہ ہی کی ہے ہر متنفس جو کچھ کر رہا ہے وہ اسے
جانتا ہے اور کافر جلد معلوم کریں گے کہ عاقبت کا گھر (یعنی انجام محمود) کس کے لئے ہے (۴۲)

وَقَدْ مَكَرَ الَّذِينَ مِن قَبْلِهِمْ فَلِلّٰهِ الْمَكْرُ
جَمِيعًا ۖ يَعْلَمُ مَا تَكْسِبُ كُلُّ نَفْسٍ ۗ وَ
سَيَعْلَمُ الْكُفّٰرُ لِمَنْ عُقْبَى الدَّارِ ﴿٤٢﴾

43. The Unbelievers say: "No messenger art thou." Say: "Enough for a witness between me and you is Allah, and such as have knowledge of the Book."

اور کافر لوگ کہتے ہیں کہ تم (خدا کے) رسول نہیں ہو۔ کہہ دو کہ
میرے اور تمہارے درمیان خدا اور وہ شخص جس کے پاس
کتاب (آسمانی) کا علم ہے گواہ کافی ہیں[١٦٢] (۴۳)

وَيَقُولُ الَّذِينَ كَفَرُوا لَسْتَ مُرْسَلًا ۚ
قُلْ كَفٰى بِاللّٰهِ شَهِيدًا بَيْنِي وَبَيْنَكُمْ
وَمَنْ عِندَهُ عِلْمُ الْكِتٰبِ ﴿٤٣﴾ ع

Ibrāhîm, or Abraham

سورۂ ابراہیم مکی ہے اور اس میں باون آیتیں اور سات رکوع ہیں

سُورَةُ إِبْرٰهِيمَ مَكِّيَّةٌ وَهِيَ اثْنَتَانِ وَخَمْسُونَ آيَةً وَسَبْعُ رُكُوعَاتٍ

In the name of Allah, Most Gracious, Most Merciful.

شروع خدا کا نام لے کر جو بڑا مہربان نہایت رحم والا ہے

بِسْمِ اللّٰهِ الرَّحْمٰنِ الرَّحِيمِ

1. **A. L. R.** A Book which We have revealed unto thee, in order that thou mightest lead mankind out of the depths of darkness into light—by the leave of their Lord—to the Way of (Him) the Exalted in Power, Worthy of all Praise!—

الٓرا (یہ) ایک (پرنور) کتاب (ہے) اس کو ہم نے تم پر اس لئے نازل کیا ہے کہ
لوگوں کو اندھیرے سے نکال کر روشنی کی طرف لے جاؤ (یعنی) ان کے
پروردگار کے حکم سے غالب اور قابل تعریف (خدا) کے رستے کی طرف (۱)

الٓرٰ ۚ كِتٰبٌ أَنزَلْنٰهُ إِلَيْكَ لِتُخْرِجَ النَّاسَ
مِنَ الظُّلُمٰتِ إِلَى النُّورِ بِإِذْنِ رَبِّهِمْ
إِلٰى صِرَاطِ الْعَزِيزِ الْحَمِيدِ ﴿١﴾

2. Of Allah, to Whom do belong all things in the heavens and on earth! But alas for the Unbelievers for a terrible Chastisement (their Unfaith will bring them)!—

وہ خدا کہ جو کچھ آسمانوں اور زمین میں ہے
سب اسی کا ہے۔ اور کافروں کے لئے عذاب سخت
(کی وجہ) سے خرابی ہے (۲)

اللّٰهِ الَّذِي لَهُ مَا فِي السَّمٰوٰتِ وَمَا فِي
الْأَرْضِ ۗ وَوَيْلٌ لِّلْكٰفِرِينَ مِنْ
عَذَابٍ شَدِيدٍ ﴿٢﴾

3. Those who prefer the life of this world to the Hereafter, who hinder (men) from the Path of Allah and seek to make it crooked: they are astray by a long distance.

جو آخرت کی نسبت دنیا کو پسند کرتے اور (لوگوں کو)
خدا کے رستے سے روکتے اور اس میں کجی
چاہتے ہیں۔ یہ لوگ پرلے سرے کی گمراہی
میں ہیں (۳)

الَّذِينَ يَسْتَحِبُّونَ الْحَيٰوةَ الدُّنْيَا
عَلَى الْآخِرَةِ وَيَصُدُّونَ عَن سَبِيلِ
اللّٰهِ وَيَبْغُونَهَا عِوَجًا ۚ أُولٰئِكَ فِي
ضَلٰلٍ بَعِيدٍ ﴿٣﴾

4. We sent not a messenger except (to teach) in the language of his (own) people, in order to make (things) clear to them. So Allah leads astray those whom He pleases and guides whom He

اور ہم نے کوئی پیغمبر نہیں بھیجا مگر اپنی قوم کی زبان بولتا
تھا تاکہ انہیں (احکام خدا) کھول کھول کر بتا دے
پھر خدا جسے چاہتا ہے گمراہ کرتا ہے۔ اور جسے چاہتا ہے ہدایت

وَمَا أَرْسَلْنَا مِن رَّسُولٍ إِلَّا بِلِسَانِ
قَوْمِهِ لِيُبَيِّنَ لَهُمْ ۖ فَيُضِلُّ اللّٰهُ مَن
يَشَاءُ وَيَهْدِي مَن يَشَاءُ ۚ وَهُوَ

pleases and He is Exalted in power, Full of Wisdom.

5. We sent Moses with Our Signs (and the command). "Bring out thy people from the depths of darkness into light, and remind them of the Days of Allah." Verily in this there are Signs for such as are firmly patient and constant,—grateful and appreciative.

6. Remember! Moses said to his people: "Call to mind the favour of Allah to you when He delivered you from the people of Pharaoh: they set you hard tasks and punishments, slaughtered your sons, and let your women-folk live: therein was a tremendous trial from your Lord."

7. And remember! your Lord caused to be declared (publicly): "If ye are grateful, I will add more (favours) unto you; but if ye show ingratitude, truly My punishment is terrible indeed."

8. And Moses said: "If ye show ingratitude, ye and all on earth together,—yet is Allah free of all wants, Worthy of all praise.

9. Has not the story reached you, (O people!), of those who (went) before you?— of the People of Noah, and 'Ād, and Thamud?—And of those who (came) after them? None knows them but Allah. To them came Messengers with Clear (Signs); but they put their hands up to their mouths, and said: "We do deny (the mission) on which ye have been sent, and we are really in suspicious (disquieting) doubt as to that to which ye invite us."

10. Their messengers said: "Is there a doubt about Allah, the Creator of the heavens and the earth? It is He Who invites you, in order that He may forgive you your sins and give you respite for a term appointed!" They said: "Ah! ye are no more than human, like

دیتا ہے اور وہ غالب (اور) حکمت والا ہے ④
اور ہم نے موسیٰ کو اپنی نشانیاں دیکر بھیجا کہ اپنی قوم کو
تاریکی سے نکال کر روشنی میں لے جاؤ۔ اور اُن کو خدا کے
دن یاد دلاؤ۔ اور اس میں ان لوگوں کے لئے جو صابر و
شاکر ہیں (قدرتِ خدا کی) نشانیاں ہیں ⑤
اور جب موسیٰ نے اپنی قوم سے کہا۔ کہ خدا نے جو تم پر مہربانیاں
کی ہیں اُنکو یاد کرو جبکہ تم کو فرعون کی قوم (کے ہاتھ) سے مخلصی
دی۔ وہ لوگ تمہیں بڑے عذاب دیتے تھے اور تمہارے بیٹوں کو
مار ڈالتے تھے اور عورت ذات (یعنی) تمہاری (لڑکیوں) کو زندہ رہنے
دیتے تھے۔ اور اسمیں تمہارے پروردگار کی طرف سے بڑی سخت آزمائش تھی ⑥
اور جب تمہارے پروردگار نے (تم کو) آگاہ کیا کہ اگر شکر کرو گے
تو میں تمہیں زیادہ دوں گا اور اگر ناشکری کرو گے تو
(یاد رکھو کہ) میرا عذاب (بھی) سخت ہے ⑦
اور موسیٰ نے (صاف صاف) کہہ دیا کہ اگر تم اور جتنے اور
لوگ زمین میں ہیں سب کے سب ناشکری کرو تو خدا بھی
بے نیاز (اور) قابلِ تعریف ہے ⑧
بھلا تم کو اُن لوگوں (کے حالات) کی خبر نہیں پہنچی جو تم
سے پہلے تھے۔ (یعنی) نوح اور عاد اور ثمود کی قوم اور جو اُنکے
بعد تھے جن کا علم خدا کے سوا کسی کو نہیں۔ (جب) انکے پاس
پیغمبر نشانیاں لے کر آئے تو اُنہوں نے اپنے ہاتھ اُن کے
مُونہوں پر رکھ دیئے (کہ خاموش رہو) اور کہنے لگے کہ ہم
تو تمہاری رسالت کو تسلیم نہیں کرتے اور جس چیز کی طرف
تم ہمیں بلاتے ہو ہم اس سے قوی شک میں ہیں ⑨
اُن کے پیغمبروں نے کہا کیا (تم کو) خدا (کے بارے) میں
شک ہے جو آسمانوں اور زمین کا پیدا کرنے والا ہے۔ وہ تمہیں
اسلئے بلاتا ہے کہ تمہارے گناہ بخشے اور (فائدہ پہنچانے کیلئے) ایک
مدت مقرر تک تمکو مہلت دے۔ وہ بولے کہ تم تو ہمارے ہی جیسے آدمی ہو۔

الْعَزِيزُ الْحَكِيمُ ④
وَلَقَدْ أَرْسَلْنَا مُوسَىٰ بِآيَاتِنَا أَنْ أَخْرِجْ
قَوْمَكَ مِنَ الظُّلُمَاتِ إِلَى النُّورِ وَذَكِّرْهُمْ
بِأَيَّامِ اللَّهِ ۚ إِنَّ فِي ذَٰلِكَ لَآيَاتٍ لِكُلِّ
صَبَّارٍ شَكُورٍ ⑤
وَإِذْ قَالَ مُوسَىٰ لِقَوْمِهِ اذْكُرُوا نِعْمَةَ
اللَّهِ عَلَيْكُمْ إِذْ أَنْجَاكُمْ مِنْ آلِ فِرْعَوْنَ
يَسُومُونَكُمْ سُوءَ الْعَذَابِ وَيُذَبِّحُونَ
أَبْنَاءَكُمْ وَيَسْتَحْيُونَ نِسَاءَكُمْ ۚ وَفِي
ذَٰلِكُمْ بَلَاءٌ مِنْ رَبِّكُمْ عَظِيمٌ ⑥ ع ۱۳ ۲
وَإِذْ تَأَذَّنَ رَبُّكُمْ لَئِنْ شَكَرْتُمْ
لَأَزِيدَنَّكُمْ ۖ وَلَئِنْ كَفَرْتُمْ إِنَّ عَذَابِي
لَشَدِيدٌ ⑦
وَقَالَ مُوسَىٰ إِنْ تَكْفُرُوا أَنْتُمْ وَمَنْ
فِي الْأَرْضِ جَمِيعًا فَإِنَّ اللَّهَ لَغَنِيٌّ
حَمِيدٌ ⑧
أَلَمْ يَأْتِكُمْ نَبَأُ الَّذِينَ مِنْ قَبْلِكُمْ
قَوْمِ نُوحٍ وَعَادٍ وَثَمُودَ ۛ وَالَّذِينَ
مِنْ بَعْدِهِمْ ۛ لَا يَعْلَمُهُمْ إِلَّا اللَّهُ ۚ مع
جَاءَتْهُمْ رُسُلُهُمْ بِالْبَيِّنَاتِ فَرَدُّوا عند المتقدمين ۱۲
أَيْدِيَهُمْ فِي أَفْوَاهِهِمْ وَقَالُوا إِنَّا كَفَرْنَا
بِمَا أُرْسِلْتُمْ بِهِ وَإِنَّا لَفِي شَكٍّ مِمَّا
تَدْعُونَنَا إِلَيْهِ مُرِيبٍ ⑨ الثلاثة
قَالَتْ رُسُلُهُمْ أَفِي اللَّهِ شَكٌّ فَاطِرِ
السَّمَاوَاتِ وَالْأَرْضِ ۖ يَدْعُوكُمْ لِيَغْفِرَ لَكُمْ
مِنْ ذُنُوبِكُمْ وَيُؤَخِّرَكُمْ إِلَىٰ أَجَلٍ
مُسَمًّى ۚ قَالُوا إِنْ أَنْتُمْ إِلَّا بَشَرٌ مِثْلُنَا

ourselves! Ye wish to turn us away from what our fathers used to worship; then bring us some clear authority.

11. Their messengers said to them: "True, we are human like yourselves, but Allah doth grant His grace to such of His servants as He pleases. It is not for us to bring you an authority except as Allah permits. And on Allah let all men of faith put their trust.

12. Why we should not put our trust on Allah. Indeed He has guided us to the Ways we (follow). We shall certainly bear with patience all the hurt you caused us. For those who put their trust should put their trust on Allah."

13. And the Unbelievers said to their messengers: "Be sure we shall drive you out of our land, or ye shall return to our religion." But their Lord inspired (this Message) to them: "Verily We shall cause the wrong-doers to perish!

14. "And verily, We shall cause you to abide in the land, and succeed them. This for such as fear the time when they shall stand before My tribunal,—such as fear My Punishment."

15. But they sought victory and decision (there and then), and frustration was the lot of every powerful obstinate transgressor.

16. In front of such a one is Hell, and he is given, for drink, boiling fetid water.

17. In gulps will he sip it, but never will he be near swallowing it down his throat; death will come to him from every quarter, yet will he not die; and in front of him will be a chastisement unrelenting.

18. The parable of those who reject their Lord is that their works are as ashes, on which the wind blows furiously on a tempestuous day: no power have they over aught that they have earned: that is the straying far, far (from the goal).

تمہارا یہ منشا ہے کہ جن چیزوں کو ہمارے بڑے پوجتے رہے ہیں ان کے
پوجنے سے ہم کو بند کر دو تو (اچھا) کوئی کھلی دلیل لاؤ (یعنی معجزہ دکھاؤ) (10)
پیغمبروں نے اُن سے کہا کہ ہاں ہم تمہارے ہی جیسے آدمی ہیں لیکن
خدا اپنے بندوں میں سے جس پر چاہتا ہے (نبوت کا) احسان
کرتا ہے۔ اور ہمارے اختیار کی بات نہیں کہ ہم خدا کے حکم
کے بغیر تم کو (تمہاری فرمائش کے مطابق) معجزہ دکھائیں۔
اور خدا ہی پر مومنوں کو بھروسا رکھنا چاہیے (11)
اور ہم کیونکر خدا پر بھروسا نہ رکھیں حالانکہ اُس نے ہم کو ہمارے (دین کے)
سیدھے رستے بتائے ہیں اور جو تکلیفیں تم ہم کو دیتے ہو اس پر
صبر کریں گے۔ اور اہل توکل کو خدا ہی پر بھروسا رکھنا چاہیے (12)
اور جو کافر تھے انہوں نے اپنے پیغمبروں سے کہا کہ (یا تو) ہم
تم کو اپنے ملک سے باہر نکال دینگے یا ہمارے مذہب میں
داخل ہو جاؤ۔ تو پروردگار نے اُن کی طرف وحی بھیجی کہ
ہم ظالموں کو ہلاک کر دیں گے (13)
اور اُن کے بعد تم کو اس زمین میں آباد کر دیں گے۔ یہ اُس
شخص کیلئے ہے جو (قیامت کے روز) میرے سامنے کھڑے ہونے سے
ڈرے اور میرے عذاب سے خوف کرے (14)
اور پیغمبروں نے (خدا سے اپنی) فتح چاہی تو ہر سرکش ضدی نامراد رہ گیا (15)
اس کے پیچھے دوزخ ہے اور اُسے پیپ کا پانی پلایا
جائے گا (16)
وہ اُس کو گھونٹ گھونٹ پیے گا اور گلے سے نہیں اُتار
سکے گا اور ہر طرف سے اُسے موت آ رہی ہو گی مگر وہ مرنے
میں نہیں آئے گا اور اسکے پیچھے سخت عذاب ہو گا (17)
جن لوگوں نے اپنے پروردگار سے کفر کیا اُنکے اعمال کی مثال
راکھ کی سی ہے کہ آندھی کے دن اس پر زور کی ہوا چلے
(اور) اُسے اڑا لے جائے۔ (اسی طرح) جو کام وہ کرتے رہے اُن پر
اُن کو کچھ دسترس نہ ہو گی۔ یہی تو پرلے سرے کی گمراہی ہے (18)

تُرِيدُونَ أَن تَصُدُّونَا عَمَّا كَانَ يَعْبُدُ
آبَاؤُنَا فَأْتُونَا بِسُلْطَانٍ مُّبِينٍ (10)
قَالَتْ لَهُمْ رُسُلُهُمْ إِن نَّحْنُ إِلَّا بَشَرٌ
مِّثْلُكُمْ وَلَٰكِنَّ اللَّهَ يَمُنُّ عَلَىٰ مَن
يَشَاءُ مِنْ عِبَادِهِ ۖ وَمَا كَانَ لَنَا أَن
نَّأْتِيَكُم بِسُلْطَانٍ إِلَّا بِإِذْنِ اللَّهِ ۚ وَ
عَلَى اللَّهِ فَلْيَتَوَكَّلِ الْمُؤْمِنُونَ (11)
وَمَا لَنَا أَلَّا نَتَوَكَّلَ عَلَى اللَّهِ وَقَدْ هَدَانَا
سُبُلَنَا ۚ وَلَنَصْبِرَنَّ عَلَىٰ مَا آذَيْتُمُونَا ۚ
وَعَلَى اللَّهِ فَلْيَتَوَكَّلِ الْمُتَوَكِّلُونَ (12)
وَقَالَ الَّذِينَ كَفَرُوا لِرُسُلِهِمْ
لَنُخْرِجَنَّكُم مِّنْ أَرْضِنَا أَوْ لَتَعُودُنَّ
فِي مِلَّتِنَا ۖ فَأَوْحَىٰ إِلَيْهِمْ رَبُّهُمْ
لَنُهْلِكَنَّ الظَّالِمِينَ (13)
وَلَنُسْكِنَنَّكُمُ الْأَرْضَ مِن بَعْدِهِمْ ۚ
ذَٰلِكَ لِمَنْ خَافَ مَقَامِي وَخَافَ
وَعِيدِ (14)
وَاسْتَفْتَحُوا وَخَابَ كُلُّ جَبَّارٍ عَنِيدٍ (15)
مِّن وَرَائِهِ جَهَنَّمُ وَيُسْقَىٰ مِن مَّاءٍ
صَدِيدٍ (16)
يَتَجَرَّعُهُ وَلَا يَكَادُ يُسِيغُهُ وَيَأْتِيهِ
الْمَوْتُ مِن كُلِّ مَكَانٍ وَمَا هُوَ بِمَيِّتٍ ۖ
وَمِن وَرَائِهِ عَذَابٌ غَلِيظٌ (17)
مَّثَلُ الَّذِينَ كَفَرُوا بِرَبِّهِمْ ۖ أَعْمَالُهُمْ
كَرَمَادٍ اشْتَدَّتْ بِهِ الرِّيحُ فِي يَوْمٍ
عَاصِفٍ ۖ لَّا يَقْدِرُونَ مِمَّا كَسَبُوا عَلَىٰ
شَيْءٍ ۚ ذَٰلِكَ هُوَ الضَّلَالُ الْبَعِيدُ (18)

19. Seest thou not that Allah created the heavens and the earth in Truth? If He so will, He can remove you and put (in your place) a new Creation?

کیا تم نے نہیں دیکھا کہ خدا نے آسمانوں اور زمین کو تدبیر
سے پیدا کیا ہے؟ اگر وہ چاہے تو تم کو نابود کر دے اور
(تمہاری جگہ) نئی مخلوق پیدا کر دے ﴿١٩﴾

أَلَمْ تَرَ أَنَّ اللّٰهَ خَلَقَ السَّمٰوٰتِ وَ
الْأَرْضَ بِالْحَقِّ ۚ إِنْ يَّشَأْ يُذْهِبْكُمْ
وَيَأْتِ بِخَلْقٍ جَدِيْدٍ ﴿١٩﴾

20. Nor is that for Allah any great matter.

اور یہ خدا کو کچھ بھی مشکل نہیں ﴿٢٠﴾

وَّمَا ذٰلِكَ عَلَى اللّٰهِ بِعَزِيْزٍ ﴿٢٠﴾

21. They will all be marshalled before Allah together: then will the weak say to those who were arrogant, "For us, we but followed you; can ye then avail us at all against the Wrath of Allah?" They will reply, "If we had received the guidance of Allah, we should have given it to you; to us it makes no difference (now) whether we rage, or bear (these torments) with patience: for ourselves there is no way of escape."

اور (قیامت کے دن) سب لوگ خدا کے سامنے کھڑے ہوں گے
تو ضعیف (العقل متبع اپنے رؤسائے) متکبرین سے کہیں گے
کہ ہم تو تمہارے پیرو تھے۔ کیا تم خدا کا کچھ عذاب ہم پر سے دفع
کر سکتے ہو؟ وہ کہیں گے کہ اگر خدا ہم کو ہدایت کرتا تو ہم
تم کو ہدایت کرتے۔ اب ہم گھبرائیں یا صبر کریں ہمارے حق میں
برابر ہے۔ کوئی جگہ (گریز اور) رہائی کی ہمارے لئے نہیں ہے ﴿٢١﴾

وَبَرَزُوْا لِلّٰهِ جَمِيْعًا فَقَالَ الضُّعَفٰٓؤُا
لِلَّذِيْنَ اسْتَكْبَرُوْٓا إِنَّا كُنَّا لَكُمْ تَبَعًا
فَهَلْ أَنْتُمْ مُّغْنُوْنَ عَنَّا مِنْ عَذَابِ
اللّٰهِ مِنْ شَيْءٍ ۚ قَالُوْا لَوْ هَدٰىنَا اللّٰهُ
لَهَدَيْنٰكُمْ ۚ سَوَآءٌ عَلَيْنَآ أَجَزِعْنَآ أَمْ
صَبَرْنَا مَا لَنَا مِنْ مَّحِيْصٍ ﴿٢١﴾ ع ٩ ١٥

22. And Satan will say when the matter is decided: "It was Allah Who gave you a promise of Truth: I too promised, but I failed in my promise to you. I had no authority over you except to call you, but ye listened to me; then reproach not me, but reproach your own souls. I cannot listen to your cries, nor can ye listen to mine. I reject your former act in associating me with Allah. For wrong-doers there must be a grievous Chastisement."

جب (حساب کتاب کا) کام فیصلہ ہو چکے گا تو شیطان کہے گا
(جو) وعدہ خدا نے تم سے کیا تھا وہ تو سچا (تھا) اور (جو) وعدہ
میں نے تم سے کیا تھا وہ جھوٹا تھا۔ اور میرا تم پر کسی طرح کا
زور نہیں تھا۔ ہاں میں نے تم کو (گمراہی اور باطل کی طرف) بلایا
تو تم نے (جلدی سے اور بے دلیل) میرا کہنا مان لیا۔ تو آج مجھے ملامت نہ کرو
اپنے آپ ہی کو ملامت کرو۔ نہ میں تمہاری فریاد رسی کر سکتا ہوں اور نہ تم میری
فریاد رسی کر سکتے ہو۔ میں اس بات سے انکار کرتا ہوں کہ تم پہلے مجھے شریک
بناتے تھے۔ بیشک جو ظالم ہیں ان کے لئے درد دینے والا عذاب ہے ﴿٢٢﴾

وَقَالَ الشَّيْطٰنُ لَمَّا قُضِيَ الْأَمْرُ إِنَّ
اللّٰهَ وَعَدَكُمْ وَعْدَ الْحَقِّ وَوَعَدْتُّكُمْ
فَأَخْلَفْتُكُمْ ۚ وَمَا كَانَ لِيَ عَلَيْكُمْ مِّنْ
سُلْطٰنٍ إِلَّآ أَنْ دَعَوْتُكُمْ فَاسْتَجَبْتُمْ
لِيْ ۚ فَلَا تَلُوْمُوْنِيْ وَلُوْمُوْٓا أَنْفُسَكُمْ ۚ
مَآ أَنَا بِمُصْرِخِكُمْ وَمَآ أَنْتُمْ بِمُصْرِخِيَّ ۚ
إِنِّيْ كَفَرْتُ بِمَآ أَشْرَكْتُمُوْنِ مِنْ قَبْلُ ۗ
إِنَّ الظّٰلِمِيْنَ لَهُمْ عَذَابٌ أَلِيْمٌ ﴿٢٢﴾

23. But those who believe and work righteousness will be admitted to Gardens beneath which rivers flow,—to dwell therein for aye with the leave of their Lord. Their greeting therein will be: "Peace!"

اور جو ایمان لائے اور عمل نیک کئے وہ بہشتوں میں داخل کئے
جائیں گے جن کے نیچے نہریں بہ رہی ہیں اپنے پروردگار کے
حکم سے ہمیشہ ان میں رہیں گے۔ وہاں ان کی صاحب سلامت سلام ہوگا ﴿٢٣﴾

وَأُدْخِلَ الَّذِيْنَ اٰمَنُوْا وَعَمِلُوا الصّٰلِحٰتِ
جَنّٰتٍ تَجْرِيْ مِنْ تَحْتِهَا الْأَنْهٰرُ خٰلِدِيْنَ
فِيْهَا بِإِذْنِ رَبِّهِمْ ۚ تَحِيَّتُهُمْ فِيْهَا سَلٰمٌ ﴿٢٣﴾

24. Seest thou not how Allah sets forth a parable?—A goodly Word like a goodly tree, whose root is firmly fixed, and its branches (reach) to the heavens,—

کیا تم نے نہیں دیکھا کہ خدا نے پاک بات کی کیسی مثال
بیان فرمائی ہے (وہ ایسی ہے) جیسے پاکیزہ درخت جس کی جڑ مضبوط
(یعنی زمین کو پکڑے ہوئے) ہو اور شاخیں آسمان میں[١٦٤٣] ﴿٢٤﴾

أَلَمْ تَرَ كَيْفَ ضَرَبَ اللّٰهُ مَثَلًا كَلِمَةً
طَيِّبَةً كَشَجَرَةٍ طَيِّبَةٍ أَصْلُهَا ثَابِتٌ
وَّفَرْعُهَا فِي السَّمَآءِ ﴿٢٤﴾

25. It brings forth its fruit at all times, by the leave of its Lord so Allah sets forth parables for men, in order that they may receive admonition.

اپنے پروردگار کے حکم سے ہر وقت پھل لاتا (اور میوے دیتا)
ہو۔ اور خدا لوگوں کیلئے مثالیں بیان فرماتا ہے تاکہ وہ
نصیحت پکڑیں ﴿٢٥﴾

تُؤْتِيْٓ أُكُلَهَا كُلَّ حِيْنٍ بِإِذْنِ رَبِّهَا ۗ
وَيَضْرِبُ اللّٰهُ الْأَمْثَالَ لِلنَّاسِ لَعَلَّهُمْ
يَتَذَكَّرُوْنَ ﴿٢٥﴾

26. And the parable of an evil Word is that of an evil tree: it is torn up by the root from the surface of the earth: it has no stability.

27. Allah will establish in strength those who believe, with the Word that stands firm, in this world and in the Hereafter; but Allah will leave, to stray, those who do wrong: Allah doeth what He willeth.

28. Hast thou not turned thy thought to those who exchanged the favour of Allah. With ingratitude and caused their people to descend to the House of Perdition?—

29. Into Hell? They will burn therein,—an evil place to stay in!

30. And they set up (idols) as equal to Allah, to mislead (men) from His Path! Say: "Enjoy (your brief power)! But verily ye are making straightway for Hell!"

31. Speak to my servants who have believed, that they may establish regular prayers, and spend (in charity) out of the Sustenance We have given them, secretly and openly, before the coming of a Day in which there will be neither mutual bargaining nor befriending.

32. It is Allah Who hath created the heavens and the earth and sendeth down rain from the skies, and with it bringeth our fruits wherewith to feed you; it is He Who hath made the ships subject to you, that they may sail through the sea by His Command; and the rivers (also) hath He made subject to you.

33. And He hath made subject to you the sun and the moon, both diligently pursuing their courses; and the Night and the Day hath He (also) made subject to you.

34. And He giveth you of all that ye ask for but if ye count the favours of Allah, never will ye be able to number them. Verily, man is given up to injustice and ingratitude.

اور ناپاک بات کی مثال ناپاک درخت کی سی ہے (نہ جڑ مستحکم
نہ شاخیں بلند) زمین کے اوپر ہی سے اکھیڑ کر پھینک دیا جائے۔
اس کو ذرا بھی قرار (وثبات) نہیں ۱۶۴ ف ﴿۲۶﴾
خدا مومنوں (کے دلوں) کو (صحیح اور) پکی بات سے دنیا کی
زندگی میں بھی مضبوط رکھتا ہے اور آخرت میں بھی (رکھے گا)
اور خدا بے انصافوں کو گمراہ کر دیتا ہے اور خدا جو چاہتا ہے کرتا ہے ﴿۲۷﴾
کیا تم نے ان لوگوں کو نہیں دیکھا جنہوں نے خدا کے احسان
کو ناشکری سے بدل دیا۔ اور اپنی قوم کو تباہی کے
گھر میں اتارا ﴿۲۸﴾
(وہ گھر) دوزخ (ہے سب ناشکرے) اس میں داخل ہوں گے اور وہ برا ٹھکانا ہے ﴿۲۹﴾
اور ان لوگوں نے خدا کے شریک مقرر کئے کہ (لوگوں کو) اس کے
رستے سے گمراہ کریں۔ کہہ دو کہ (چند روز) فائدے اٹھا لو
آخر کار تم کو دوزخ کی طرف لوٹ کر جانا ہے ﴿۳۰﴾
(اے پیغمبر) میرے مومن بندوں سے کہہ دو کہ نماز پڑھا کریں
اور اس دن کے آنے سے پیشتر جس میں نہ (اعمال کا) سودا
ہوگا اور نہ دوستی (کام آئے گی) ہمارے دیئے ہوئے مال
میں سے درپردہ اور ظاہر خرچ کرتے رہیں ﴿۳۱﴾
خدا ہی تو ہے جس نے آسمانوں اور زمین کو پیدا کیا اور
آسمان سے مینہ برسایا۔ پھر اس سے تمہارے کھانے
کے لئے پھل پیدا کئے۔ اور کشتیوں (اور جہازوں) کو تمہارے
زیر فرمان کیا تاکہ دریا (اور سمندر) میں اس کے حکم سے چلیں
اور نہروں کو بھی تمہارے زیر فرمان کیا ﴿۳۲﴾
اور سورج اور چاند کو تمہارے لئے کام میں لگا دیا کہ دونوں (دن رات)
ایک دستور پر چل رہے ہیں۔ اور رات اور دن کو بھی تمہاری خاطر کام میں لگا دیا ﴿۳۳﴾
اور جو کچھ تم نے مانگا سب میں سے تم کو عنایت کیا اور اگر خدا
کے احسان گننے لگو تو شمار نہ کر سکو (مگر لوگ نعمتوں کا شکر نہیں کرتے)
کچھ شک نہیں کہ انسان بڑا بے انصاف اور ناشکرا ہے ﴿۳۴﴾

وَمَثَلُ كَلِمَةٍ خَبِيثَةٍ كَشَجَرَةٍ خَبِيثَةٍ
اِجْتُثَّتْ مِنْ فَوْقِ الْاَرْضِ مَا لَهَا
مِنْ قَرَارٍ ﴿٢٦﴾
يُثَبِّتُ اللّٰهُ الَّذِيْنَ اٰمَنُوْا بِالْقَوْلِ الثَّابِتِ
فِى الْحَيٰوةِ الدُّنْيَا وَفِى الْاٰخِرَةِ ۚ وَيُضِلُّ
اللّٰهُ الظّٰلِمِيْنَ ۚ وَيَفْعَلُ اللّٰهُ مَا يَشَآءُ ﴿٢٧﴾ ع ۲ ۱۶
اَلَمْ تَرَ اِلَى الَّذِيْنَ بَدَّلُوْا نِعْمَتَ
اللّٰهِ كُفْرًا وَّاَحَلُّوْا قَوْمَهُمْ
دَارَ الْبَوَارِ ﴿٢٨﴾
جَهَنَّمَ ۚ يَصْلَوْنَهَا ۗ وَبِئْسَ الْقَرَارُ ﴿٢٩﴾
وَجَعَلُوْا لِلّٰهِ اَنْدَادًا لِّيُضِلُّوْا عَنْ
سَبِيْلِهٖ ۗ قُلْ تَمَتَّعُوْا فَاِنَّ مَصِيْرَكُمْ
اِلَى النَّارِ ﴿٣٠﴾
قُلْ لِّعِبَادِىَ الَّذِيْنَ اٰمَنُوْا يُقِيْمُوا
الصَّلٰوةَ وَيُنْفِقُوْا مِمَّا رَزَقْنٰهُمْ سِرًّا
وَّعَلَانِيَةً مِّنْ قَبْلِ اَنْ يَّاْتِىَ يَوْمٌ
لَّا بَيْعٌ فِيْهِ وَلَا خِلٰلٌ ﴿٣١﴾
اَللّٰهُ الَّذِىْ خَلَقَ السَّمٰوٰتِ وَالْاَرْضَ
وَاَنْزَلَ مِنَ السَّمَآءِ مَآءً فَاَخْرَجَ بِهٖ
مِنَ الثَّمَرٰتِ رِزْقًا لَّكُمْ ۚ وَسَخَّرَ لَكُمُ
الْفُلْكَ لِتَجْرِىَ فِى الْبَحْرِ بِاَمْرِهٖ ۚ وَسَخَّرَ
لَكُمُ الْاَنْهٰرَ ﴿٣٢﴾
وَسَخَّرَ لَكُمُ الشَّمْسَ وَالْقَمَرَ دَآئِبَيْنِ ۚ
وَسَخَّرَ لَكُمُ الَّيْلَ وَالنَّهَارَ ﴿٣٣﴾
وَاٰتٰكُمْ مِّنْ كُلِّ مَا سَاَلْتُمُوْهُ ۗ وَاِنْ
تَعُدُّوْا نِعْمَتَ اللّٰهِ لَا تُحْصُوْهَا ۗ اِنَّ
الْاِنْسَانَ لَظَلُوْمٌ كَفَّارٌ ﴿٣٤﴾ ع ۵ ۱۷

35. Remember Abraham said: "O my Lord! make this city one of peace and security; and preserve me and my sons from worshipping idols.

اور جب ابراہیم نے دُعا کی کہ میرے پروردگار اس شہر کو
(لوگوں کے لئے) امن کی جگہ بنادے اور مجھے اور میری اولاد
کو اس بات سے کہ بُتوں کی پرستش کرنے لگیں بچائے رکھ ﴿٣٥﴾

وَإِذْ قَالَ إِبْرٰهِيمُ رَبِّ اجْعَلْ هٰذَا
الْبَلَدَ اٰمِنًا وَّاجْنُبْنِىْ وَبَنِىَّ اَنْ نَّعْبُدَ
الْاَصْنَامَ ﴿٣٥﴾

36. "O my Lord! they have indeed led astray many among mankind; he then who follows my (ways) is of me, and he that disobeys me,— but Thou art indeed Oft-Forgiving, Most Merciful.

اے پروردگار انہوں نے بہت سے لوگوں کو
گمراہ کیا ہے۔ سو جس شخص نے میرا کہا مانا وہ میرا
ہے اور جس نے میری نافرمانی کی تو تُو بخشنے والا
مہربان ہے ﴿٣٦﴾

رَبِّ اِنَّهُنَّ اَضْلَلْنَ كَثِيْرًا مِّنَ
النَّاسِ ۚ فَمَنْ تَبِعَنِىْ فَاِنَّهٗ مِنِّىْ ۚ
وَمَنْ عَصَانِىْ فَاِنَّكَ غَفُوْرٌ
رَّحِيْمٌ ﴿٣٦﴾

37. "O our Lord! I have made some of my offspring to dwell in a valley without cultivation, by Thy Sacred House; in order, O our Lord! that they may establish regular Prayer: so fill the hearts of some among men with love towards them, and feed them with Fruits: so that they may give thanks.

اے پروردگار میں نے اپنی اولاد میدان (مکہ) میں جہاں
کھیتی نہیں تیرے عزت (وادب) والے گھر کے پاس۔
لا بسائی ہے۔ اے پروردگار تاکہ یہ نماز پڑھیں تو
لوگوں کے دلوں کو ایسا کردے کہ ان کی طرف جھکے رہیں
اور اُن کو میووں سے روزی دے تاکہ (تیرا) شکر کریں ﴿٣٧﴾

رَبَّنَآ اِنِّىْٓ اَسْكَنْتُ مِنْ ذُرِّيَّتِىْ بِوَادٍ
غَيْرِ ذِىْ زَرْعٍ عِنْدَ بَيْتِكَ الْمُحَرَّمِ ۙ
رَبَّنَا لِيُقِيْمُوا الصَّلٰوةَ فَاجْعَلْ اَفْئِدَةً
مِّنَ النَّاسِ تَهْوِىْٓ اِلَيْهِمْ وَارْزُقْهُمْ
مِّنَ الثَّمَرٰتِ لَعَلَّهُمْ يَشْكُرُوْنَ ﴿٣٧﴾

38. "O our Lord! truly Thou dost know what we conceal and what we reveal: for nothing whatever is hidden from Allah, whether on earth or in heaven.

اے پروردگار جو بات ہم چھپاتے اور جو ظاہر کرتے ہیں۔
تو سب جانتا ہے اور خدا سے کوئی چیز مخفی نہیں (نہ)
زمین میں نہ آسمان میں ﴿٣٨﴾

رَبَّنَآ اِنَّكَ تَعْلَمُ مَا نُخْفِىْ وَمَا نُعْلِنُ ۗ
وَمَا يَخْفٰى عَلَى اللّٰهِ مِنْ شَىْءٍ فِى الْاَرْضِ
وَلَا فِى السَّمَآءِ ﴿٣٨﴾

39. "Praise be to Allah, Who hath granted unto me in old age Ismā'īl and Isaac: for truly my Lord is He, the Hearer of Prayer!

خدا کا شکر ہے جس نے مجھ کو بڑی عمر میں
اسمٰعیل اور اسحاق بخشے۔ بیشک میرا پروردگار
دُعا سننے والا ہے ﴿٣٩﴾

اَلْحَمْدُ لِلّٰهِ الَّذِىْ وَهَبَ لِىْ عَلَى الْكِبَرِ
اِسْمٰعِيْلَ وَاِسْحٰقَ ۚ اِنَّ رَبِّىْ
لَسَمِيْعُ الدُّعَآءِ ﴿٣٩﴾

40. "O my Lord! make me one who establishes regular Prayer, and also (raise such) among my offspring O our Lord! and accept Thou my Prayer.

اے پروردگار مجھ کو (ایسی توفیق عنایت) کر کہ نماز پڑھتا رہوں اور
میری اولاد کو بھی (یہ توفیق بخش) اے پروردگار میری دُعا قبول فرما ﴿٤٠﴾

رَبِّ اجْعَلْنِىْ مُقِيْمَ الصَّلٰوةِ وَمِنْ
ذُرِّيَّتِىْ ۖ رَبَّنَا وَتَقَبَّلْ دُعَآءِ ﴿٤٠﴾

41. "O our Lord ! cover (us) with Thy Forgiveness— me, my parents, and (all) Believers, on the Day that the Reckoning will be established!

اے پروردگار حساب (کتاب) کے دن مجھ کو اور میرے ماں
باپ کو اور مومنوں کو مغفرت کیجو ﴿٤١﴾

رَبَّنَا اغْفِرْ لِىْ وَلِوَالِدَىَّ وَلِلْمُؤْمِنِيْنَ
يَوْمَ يَقُوْمُ الْحِسَابُ ﴿٤١﴾ ع

42. Think not that Allah doth not heed the deeds of those who do wrong. He but giveth them respite against a Day when the eyes will fixedly stare in horror,—

اور (مومنو) مت خیال کرنا کہ یہ ظالم جو عمل کر رہے ہیں خدا اُن
سے بے خبر ہے۔ وہ اُن کو اُس دن تک مہلت دے رہا ہے
جبکہ (دہشت کے سبب) آنکھیں کھلی کی کھلی رہ جائیں گی ﴿٤٢﴾

وَلَا تَحْسَبَنَّ اللّٰهَ غَافِلًا عَمَّا يَعْمَلُ
الظّٰلِمُوْنَ ۚ اِنَّمَا يُؤَخِّرُهُمْ لِيَوْمٍ
تَشْخَصُ فِيْهِ الْاَبْصَارُ ﴿٤٢﴾

43. They running forward with necks outstretched, their heads uplifted, their gaze returning not

(اور لوگ) سر اُٹھائے ہوئے (میدان قیامت کی طرف) دوڑ
رہے ہونگے اُن کی نگاہیں اُن کی طرف لوٹ نہ سکیں گی۔

مُهْطِعِيْنَ مُقْنِعِىْ رُءُوْسِهِمْ لَا
يَرْتَدُّ اِلَيْهِمْ طَرْفُهُمْ ۚ وَاَفْئِدَتُهُمْ

towards them, and their hearts a (gaping) void!

اور انکے دل (مارے خوف کے) ہوا ہو رہے ہونگے ﴿۴۳﴾

هَوَآءٌ ﴿٤٣﴾

44. So warn mankind of the Day when the Wrath will reach them: then will the wrong-doers say: "Our Lord respite us (if only) for a short Term: we will answer Thy Call, and follow the messengers!" "What! were ye not wont to swear aforetime that ye should suffer no decline?

اور لوگوں کو اُس دن سے آگاہ کر دو جب اُن پر عذاب آ جائیگا
تب ظالم لوگ کہیں گے کہ اے ہمارے پروردگار ہمیں تھوڑی سی
مدت مہلت عطا کر تاکہ ہم تیری دعوت (توحید) قبول کریں اور (تیرے)
پیغمبروں کے پیچھے چلیں (تو جواب ملیگا) کیا تم پہلے قسمیں نہیں کھایا کرتے تھے کہ
تمکو (اس حال سے جس میں تم ہو) زوال (اور قیامت کو حساب اعمال) نہیں ہوگا ﴿۴۴﴾

وَاَنْذِرِ النَّاسَ يَوْمَ يَاْتِيْهِمُ الْعَذَابُ
فَيَقُوْلُ الَّذِيْنَ ظَلَمُوْا رَبَّنَآ اَخِّرْنَآ
اِلٰٓى اَجَلٍ قَرِيْبٍ ۙ نُّجِبْ دَعْوَتَكَ وَ
نَتَّبِعِ الرُّسُلَ ؕ اَوَلَمْ تَكُوْنُوْٓا اَقْسَمْتُمْ
مِّنْ قَبْلُ مَا لَكُمْ مِّنْ زَوَالٍ ﴿٤٤﴾

45. "And ye dwelt in the dwellings of men who wronged themselves ye were clearly shown how We dealt with them; and We put forth (many) Parables in your behoof!"

اور جو لوگ اپنے آپ پر ظلم کرتے تھے تم اُنکے مکانوں میں رہتے تھے اور
تم پر ظاہر ہو چکا تھا کہ ہم نے ان لوگوں کے ساتھ کس طرح
(کا معاملہ) کیا تھا۔ اور تمہارے (سمجھانے کیلئے) مثالیں بیان کر دی تھیں ﴿۴۵﴾

وَّسَكَنْتُمْ فِيْ مَسٰكِنِ الَّذِيْنَ ظَلَمُوْٓا
اَنْفُسَهُمْ وَتَبَيَّنَ لَكُمْ كَيْفَ فَعَلْنَا بِهِمْ
وَضَرَبْنَا لَكُمُ الْاَمْثَالَ ﴿٤٥﴾

46. Mighty indeed were the plots which they made, but their plots were (well) within the sight of Allah, even though they were such as to shake the hills!

اور اُنہوں نے (بڑی بڑی) تدبیریں کیں اور انکی (سب) تدبیریں خدا کے ہاں
لکھی ہوئی ہیں گو وہ تدبیریں ایسی (غضب کی) تھیں کہ اُن سے پہاڑ بھی ٹل جائیں ﴿۴۶﴾

وَقَدْ مَكَرُوْا مَكْرَهُمْ وَعِنْدَ اللّٰهِ مَكْرُهُمْ ؕ
وَاِنْ كَانَ مَكْرُهُمْ لِتَزُوْلَ مِنْهُ الْجِبَالُ ﴿٤٦﴾

47. Never think that Allah would fail His messengers in His promise: for Allah is Exalted in Power,—the Lord of Retribution.

تو ایسا خیال نہ کرنا کہ خدا نے جو اپنے پیغمبروں سے وعدہ کیا ہے اسکے
خلاف کرے گا۔ بیشک خدا زبردست (اور) بدلہ لینے والا ہے ﴿۴۷﴾

فَلَا تَحْسَبَنَّ اللّٰهَ مُخْلِفَ وَعْدِهٖ رُسُلَهٗ ؕ
اِنَّ اللّٰهَ عَزِيْزٌ ذُو انْتِقَامٍ ﴿٤٧﴾

48. One day the Earth will be changed to a different Earth, and so will be the Heavens, and (men) will be marshalled forth, before Allah, the One, the Irresistible;

جس دن یہ زمین دوسری زمین سے بدل دی جائیگی اور آسمان بھی (بدل
دیئے جائینگے) اور سب لوگ خدائے یگانہ و زبردست کے سامنے نکل کھڑے ہونگے ﴿۴۸﴾

يَوْمَ تُبَدَّلُ الْاَرْضُ غَيْرَ الْاَرْضِ وَ
السَّمٰوٰتُ وَبَرَزُوْا لِلّٰهِ الْوَاحِدِ الْقَهَّارِ ﴿٤٨﴾

49. And thou wilt see the Sinners that day bound together in fetters:—

اور اُس دن تم گنہگاروں کو دیکھو گے کہ زنجیروں میں
جکڑے ہوئے ہیں ﴿۴۹﴾

وَتَرَى الْمُجْرِمِيْنَ يَوْمَئِذٍ مُّقَرَّنِيْنَ
فِى الْاَصْفَادِ ﴿٤٩﴾

50. Their garments of liquid pitch, and their faces covered with Fire;

اُنکے کرتے گندھک کے ہونگے اور اُنکے مونہوں کو آگ لپٹ رہی ہو گی ﴿۵۰﴾

سَرَابِيْلُهُمْ مِّنْ قَطِرَانٍ وَّتَغْشٰى وُجُوْهَهُمُ النَّارُ ﴿٥٠﴾

51. That Allah may requite each soul according to its deserts; and verily Allah is Swift in calling to account.

یہ اس لئے کہ خدا ہر شخص کو اُس کے اعمال کا بدلہ دے۔
بیشک خدا جلد حساب لینے والا ہے ﴿۵۱﴾

لِيَجْزِيَ اللّٰهُ كُلَّ نَفْسٍ مَّا كَسَبَتْ ؕ اِنَّ
اللّٰهَ سَرِيْعُ الْحِسَابِ ﴿٥١﴾

52. Here is a Message for mankind: that they may take warning therefrom, and may know that He is One Allah: let men of understanding take heed.

یہ (قرآن) لوگوں کے نام (خدا کا پیغام) ہے تاکہ اُن کو اس سے
ڈرایا جائے اور تاکہ وہ جان لیں کہ وہی اکیلا معبود ہے اور تاکہ اہل عقل نصیحت پکڑیں ﴿۵۲﴾

هٰذَا بَلٰغٌ لِّلنَّاسِ وَلِيُنْذَرُوْا بِهٖ وَلِيَعْلَمُوْٓا اَنَّمَا
هُوَ اِلٰهٌ وَّاحِدٌ وَّلِيَذَّكَّرَ اُولُوا الْاَلْبَابِ ﴿٥٢﴾ ع ۱۹

SÛRA–15
AL-ḤIJR
(INTRODUCTION)

This is the last of the six Sûras of the A.L.M. series (10 to 15). Its place in chronology is the late Makkan period, probably somewhere near the middle of that period. See Introduction to S. 10 where will be found also an indication of the general subject-matter of the whole series in the gradation of Quranic teaching.

The special subject-matter of this, Sûra is the protection of Allah's Revelation and Allah's Truth. Evil arose from Pride and the warping of man's will, but Allah's Mercy is the antidote, as was proved in the case of Abraham and Lot, and might have been proved by the people of the Aika and the Ḥijr if they had only attended to Allah's "Signs". The Qur-ãn, beginning with the Seven Oft-repeated Verses, is the precious vehicle for the praises of Allah.

Al-Ḥijr, or The Rocky Tract

In the name of Allah, Most Gracious, Most Merciful.

1. **A.L.R.** These are the Ayats of Revelation,— of a Qur-ān that makes things clear.

2. Often will those who disbelieve, wish that they had been Muslims.

3. Leave them alone, to eat and enjoy and let (false) hope distract them: soon for they will soon know.

4. Never did We destroy a population that had not a term decreed and assigned beforehand.

5. Neither can a people anticipate its Term, nor delay it.

6. They say: "O thou to whom the Message is being revealed! Truly thou art mad (or possessed)!

7. "Why bringest thou not angels to us if it be that thou hast the Truth?"

8. We send not the angels down except for just cause: if they came (to the ungodly), behold! no respite would they have!

9. We have, without doubt, sent down the Message; and We will assuredly guard it (from corruption).

10. We did send messengers before thee amongst the sects of old:

11. But never came a messenger to them but they mocked him.

12. Even so do We let it creep into the hearts of the sinners—

13. They do not believe in the Message, such has been the way of those who went before them.

14. Even if We opened out to them a gate from heaven, and they

سورۂ حجر مکی ہے اور اس میں ننانوے آیتیں اور چھ رکوع ہیں

شروع خدا کا نام لے کر جو بڑا مہربان نہایت رحم والا ہے
الرٰ۔ یہ (خدا کی) کتاب اور قرآن روشن کی آیتیں ہیں (۱)
کسی وقت کافر لوگ آرزو کریں گے کہ اے کاش وہ
مسلمان ہوتے (۲)
(اے محمدؐ) انکو انکے حال پر رہنے دو کہ کھالیں اور فائدے اٹھالیں اور
(طول) امل انکو دنیا میں مشغول کئے رہے عنقریب انکو اسکا انجام معلوم ہو جائیگا (۳)
اور ہم نے کوئی بستی ہلاک نہیں کی مگر اس کا وقت
مقرر و معین تھا (۴)
کوئی جماعت اپنی مدت (وفات) سے نہ آگے نکل سکتی ہے
نہ پیچھے رہ سکتی ہے (۵)
اور (کفار) کہتے ہیں کہ اے شخص جس پر نصیحت (کی کتاب)
نازل ہوئی ہے تو تو دیوانہ ہے (۶)
اگر تو سچا ہے تو ہمارے پاس فرشتوں کو کیوں نہیں
لے آتا (۷)
(کہہ دو) ہم فرشتوں کو نازل نہیں کیا کرتے مگر حق کے ساتھ
اور اس وقت ان کو مہلت نہیں ملتی (۸)
بیشک یہ (کتاب) نصیحت ہمیں نے اتاری ہے اور
ہم ہی اس کے نگہبان ہیں (۹)
اور ہم نے تم سے پہلے لوگوں میں بھی پیغمبر
بھیجے تھے (۱۰)
اور ان کے پاس کوئی پیغمبر نہیں آتا تھا مگر وہ اسکے
ساتھ استہزا کرتے تھے (۱۱)
اسی طرح ہم اس (تکذیب و ضلال) کو گنہگاروں کے دلوں میں داخل کر دیتے ہیں (۱۲)
سو وہ اس پر ایمان نہیں لاتے اور پہلوں کی روش بھی
یہی رہی ہے (۱۳)
اور اگر ہم آسمان کا کوئی دروازہ ان پر کھول دیں اور

سُورَةُ الْحِجْرِ مَكِّيَّةٌ وَهِيَ تِسْعٌ وَتِسْعُونَ آيَةً وَسِتُّ رُكُوعَاتٍ

الجزء الرابع عشر ١٤

بِسْمِ اللَّهِ الرَّحْمَٰنِ الرَّحِيمِ
الٓر ۚ تِلْكَ آيَاتُ الْكِتَابِ وَقُرْآنٍ مُبِينٍ (١)
رُبَمَا يَوَدُّ الَّذِينَ كَفَرُوا لَوْ
كَانُوا مُسْلِمِينَ (٢)
ذَرْهُمْ يَأْكُلُوا وَيَتَمَتَّعُوا وَيُلْهِهِمُ
الْأَمَلُ ۖ فَسَوْفَ يَعْلَمُونَ (٣)
وَمَا أَهْلَكْنَا مِنْ قَرْيَةٍ إِلَّا وَلَهَا
كِتَابٌ مَعْلُومٌ (٤)
مَا تَسْبِقُ مِنْ أُمَّةٍ أَجَلَهَا وَمَا
يَسْتَأْخِرُونَ (٥)
وَقَالُوا يَا أَيُّهَا الَّذِي نُزِّلَ عَلَيْهِ الذِّكْرُ
إِنَّكَ لَمَجْنُونٌ (٦)
لَوْ مَا تَأْتِينَا بِالْمَلَائِكَةِ إِنْ كُنْتَ
مِنَ الصَّادِقِينَ (٧)
مَا نُنَزِّلُ الْمَلَائِكَةَ إِلَّا بِالْحَقِّ وَمَا
كَانُوا إِذًا مُنْظَرِينَ (٨)
إِنَّا نَحْنُ نَزَّلْنَا الذِّكْرَ وَإِنَّا لَهُ
لَحَافِظُونَ (٩)
وَلَقَدْ أَرْسَلْنَا مِنْ قَبْلِكَ فِي شِيَعِ
الْأَوَّلِينَ (١٠)
وَمَا يَأْتِيهِمْ مِنْ رَسُولٍ إِلَّا كَانُوا
بِهِ يَسْتَهْزِئُونَ (١١)
كَذَٰلِكَ نَسْلُكُهُ فِي قُلُوبِ الْمُجْرِمِينَ (١٢)
لَا يُؤْمِنُونَ بِهِ ۖ وَقَدْ خَلَتْ سُنَّةُ
الْأَوَّلِينَ (١٣)
وَلَوْ فَتَحْنَا عَلَيْهِمْ بَابًا مِنَ السَّمَاءِ

were to continue (all day) ascending therein,

15. They would only say: "Our eyes have been intoxicated: nay, we have been bewitched by sorcery."

16. It is We Who have set out constellations in the heavens and made them fair-seeming to (all) beholders;

17. And (moreover) We haveguarded them from every accursed Satan.

18. But any that gains a hearing by stealth, is pursued by a fiery comet, bright (to see).

19. And the earth We have spread out (like a carpet); set thereon mountains firm and immovable; and produced therein all kinds of things in due balance.

20. And We have provided therein means of subsistence,—for you and for those for whose sustenance ye are not responsible.

21. And there is not a thing but its (sources and) treasures (inexhaustible) are with Us; but We only send down thereof in due and ascertainable measures.

22. And We send the fecundating winds, then cause the rain to descend from the sky, therewith providing you with water (in abundance), though ye are not the guardians of its stores.

23. And verily, it is We Who give life, and Who give death: it is We Who remain inheritors (after all else passes away).

24. To Us are known those of you who hasten forward, and those who lag behind.

25. Assuredly it is thy Lord who will gather them together: for He is Perfect in Wisdom and Knowledge

26. We created man from sounding clay, from mud moulded into shape;

27. And the Jinn race, We had created before, from the fire of a scorching wind.

وہ اس میں چڑھنے بھی لگیں (۱۴)
تو بھی یہی کہیں کہ ہماری آنکھیں مخمور ہوگئی ہیں بلکہ
ہم پر جادو کر دیا گیا ہے (۱۵)
اور ہم ہی نے آسمان میں بُرج بنائے اور دیکھنے والوں
کے لئے اس کو سجا دیا (۱۶)
اور ہر شیطان راندہ درگاہ سے اسے محفوظ کر دیا (۱۷)
ہاں اگر کوئی چوری سے سننا چاہے تو چمکتا ہوا
انگارا اس کے پیچھے لپکتا ہے (۱۸)
اور زمین کو بھی ہم ہی نے پھیلایا اور اس پر
پہاڑ (بنا کر) رکھ دیئے اور اس میں ہر ایک
سنجیدہ چیز اگائی (۱۹)
اور ہم ہی نے تمہارے لئے اور اُن لوگوں کیلئے جن کو
تم روزی نہیں دیتے اس میں معاش کے سامان پیدا کئے (۲۰)
اور ہمارے ہاں ہر چیز کے خزانے ہیں اور ہم ان
کو بمقدار مناسب اُتارتے رہتے ہیں (۲۱)
اور ہم ہی ہوائیں چلاتے ہیں (جو بادلوں کے پانی سے) بھری ہوئی
(ہوتی ہیں) اور ہم ہی آسمان سے مینہ برساتے ہیں اور ہم ہی تم کو
اس کا پانی پلاتے ہیں اور تم تو اس کا خزانہ نہیں رکھتے (۲۲)
اور ہم ہی حیات بخشتے اور ہم ہی موت دیتے ہیں اور ہم ہی سب کے وارث (مالک) ہیں (۲۳)
اور جو لوگ تم میں پہلے گزر چکے ہیں ہم کو معلوم ہیں اور جو
پیچھے آنے والے ہیں وہ بھی ہم کو معلوم ہیں (۲۴)
اور تمہارا پروردگار (قیامت کے دن) ان سب کو جمع
کریگا۔ وہ بڑا دانا (اور) خبردار ہے (۲۵)
اور ہم نے انسان کو کھنکھناتے سڑے ہوئے گارے
سے پیدا کیا ہے (۲۶)
اور جنوں کو اس سے بھی پہلے بے دھوئیں کی آگ
سے پیدا کیا تھا (۲۷)

فَظَلُّوا فِيهِ يَعْرُجُونَ (۱۴)
لَقَالُوٓا إِنَّمَا سُكِّرَتْ أَبْصَارُنَا بَلْ
نَحْنُ قَوْمٌ مَّسْحُورُونَ (۱۵)
وَلَقَدْ جَعَلْنَا فِي السَّمَآءِ بُرُوجًا وَّزَيَّنّٰهَا
لِلنّٰظِرِينَ (۱۶)
وَحَفِظْنٰهَا مِنْ كُلِّ شَيْطٰنٍ رَّجِيمٍ (۱۷)
إِلَّا مَنِ اسْتَرَقَ السَّمْعَ فَأَتْبَعَهُ
شِهَابٌ مُّبِينٌ (۱۸)
وَالْأَرْضَ مَدَدْنٰهَا وَأَلْقَيْنَا فِيهَا
رَوَاسِيَ وَأَنْۢبَتْنَا فِيهَا مِنْ كُلِّ شَيْءٍ
مَّوْزُونٍ (۱۹)
وَجَعَلْنَا لَكُمْ فِيهَا مَعَايِشَ وَمَنْ لَّسْتُمْ
لَهُ بِرٰزِقِينَ (۲۰)
وَإِنْ مِّنْ شَيْءٍ إِلَّا عِنْدَنَا خَزَآئِنُهُ
وَمَا نُنَزِّلُهُ إِلَّا بِقَدَرٍ مَّعْلُومٍ (۲۱)
وَأَرْسَلْنَا الرِّيٰحَ لَوَاقِحَ فَأَنْزَلْنَا مِنَ
السَّمَآءِ مَآءً فَأَسْقَيْنٰكُمُوهُ وَمَا أَنْتُمْ
لَهُ بِخٰزِنِينَ (۲۲)
وَإِنَّا لَنَحْنُ نُحْيِۦ وَنُمِيتُ وَنَحْنُ الْوٰرِثُونَ (۲۳)
وَلَقَدْ عَلِمْنَا الْمُسْتَقْدِمِينَ مِنْكُمْ
وَلَقَدْ عَلِمْنَا الْمُسْتَأْخِرِينَ (۲۴)
وَإِنَّ رَبَّكَ هُوَ يَحْشُرُهُمْ إِنَّهُ حَكِيمٌ
عَلِيمٌ (۲۵)
وَلَقَدْ خَلَقْنَا الْإِنْسٰنَ مِنْ صَلْصٰلٍ
مِّنْ حَمَإٍ مَّسْنُونٍ (۲۶)
وَالْجَآنَّ خَلَقْنٰهُ مِنْ قَبْلُ مِنْ نَّارِ
السَّمُومِ (۲۷)

28. Behold! thy Lord said to the angels: "I am about to creat man, from sounding clay from mud moulded into shape;

29. "When I have fashioned him (in due proportion) and breathed into him of My spirit, fall ye down in obeisance unto him."

30. So the angels prostrated themselves, all of them together:

31. Not so Iblîs: he refused to be among those who prostrated themselves.

32. (Allah) said: "O Iblîs! What is your reason for not being among those who prostrated themselves?"

33. (Iblîs) said: "I am not one to prostrate myself to man, whom Thou didst create from sounding clay, from mud moulded into shape."

34. (Allah) said: "Then get thee out from here; for thou art rejected, accursed.

35. "And the Curse shall be on thee till the Day of Judgment."

36. (Iblîs) said: "O my Lord! give me then respite till the Day the (dead) are raised."

37. (Allah) said: "Respite is granted thee—

38. "Till the Day of the Time Appointed."

39. (Iblîs) said: "O my Lord! because Thou hast put me in the wrong, I will make (wrong) fair-seeming to them on the earth, and I will put them all in the wrong,—

40. "Except Thy chosen servants among them,

41. (Allah) said: "This is for me a straight path.

42. "For over My servants no authority shalt thou have, except such as put themselves in the wrong and follow thee."

43. And verily, Hell is the promised abode for them all!

44. To it are seven Gates: for each of those Gates is a (special) class (of sinners) assigned.

45. The righteous (will be) amid Gardens and fountains (of clear-flowing water).

اور جب تمہارے پروردگار نے فرشتوں سے فرمایا کہ
میں کھنکھناتے سڑے ہوئے گارے سے ایک بشر بنانے والا ہوں ﴿۲۸﴾
جب اسکو (صورت انسانیہ میں) درست کرلوں اور اسمیں اپنی (بے بہا
چیز یعنی) روح پھونک دوں تو اسکے آگے سجدے میں گر پڑنا ﴿۲۹﴾
تو فرشتے تو سب کے سب سجدے میں گر پڑے ﴿۳۰﴾
مگر شیطان کہ اُس نے سجدہ کرنے والوں کے ساتھ
ہونے سے انکار کیا ﴿۳۱﴾
(خدا نے) فرمایا کہ ابلیس! تجھے کیا ہُوا کہ تو سجدہ کرنے
والوں میں شامل نہ ہُوا ﴿۳۲﴾
(اُس نے) کہا میں ایسا نہیں ہوں کہ انسان کو جس کو تُو نے
کھنکھناتے سڑے ہوئے گارے سے بنایا ہو سجدہ کروں ﴿۳۳﴾
(خدا نے) فرمایا یہاں سے نکل جا تُو مردود ہے ﴿۳۴﴾
اور تجھ پر قیامت کے دن تک لعنت (برسے گی) ﴿۳۵﴾
(اس نے) کہا کہ پروردگار مجھے اس دن تک مہلت
دے جب لوگ (مرنے کے بعد) زندہ کئے جائینگے ﴿۳۶﴾
فرمایا کہ تجھے مہلت دی جاتی ہے ﴿۳۷﴾
وقت مقرر (یعنی قیامت) کے دن تک ﴿۳۸﴾
(اس نے) کہا کہ پروردگار جیسا تو نے مجھے رستے سے الگ کیا ہے میں بھی
زمین میں لوگوں کیلئے (گناہوں کو) آراستہ کر دکھاؤنگا اور سب کو بہکاؤنگا ﴿۳۹﴾
ہاں ان میں جو تیرے مخلص بندے ہیں (اُن پر قابو چلنا مشکل ہے) ﴿۴۰﴾
(خدا نے) فرمایا کہ مجھ تک (پہنچنے کا) یہی سیدھا رستہ ہے ﴿۴۱﴾
جو میرے (مخلص) بندے ہیں اُن پر تجھے کچھ قدرت نہیں (کہ
اُنکو گناہ میں ڈال سکے) ہاں بداہوں میں سے جو تیرے پیچھے چل پڑے ﴿۴۲﴾
اور اُن سب کے وعدے کی جگہ جہنم ہے ﴿۴۳﴾
اس کے سات دروازے ہیں ہر ایک دروازے کیلئے
اُن میں سے جماعتیں تقسیم کر دی گئی ہیں ﴿۴۴﴾
جو متقی ہیں وہ باغوں اور چشموں میں ہوں گے ﴿۴۵﴾

وَإِذْ قَالَ رَبُّكَ لِلْمَلَٰٓئِكَةِ إِنِّي خَالِقٌۢ
بَشَرًا مِّن صَلْصَٰلٍ مِّنْ حَمَإٍ مَّسْنُونٍ ﴿۲۸﴾
فَإِذَا سَوَّيْتُهُۥ وَنَفَخْتُ فِيهِ مِن رُّوحِي
فَقَعُوا لَهُۥ سَٰجِدِينَ ﴿۲۹﴾
فَسَجَدَ الْمَلَٰٓئِكَةُ كُلُّهُمْ أَجْمَعُونَ ﴿۳۰﴾
إِلَّآ إِبْلِيسَ أَبَىٰٓ أَن يَكُونَ مَعَ
السَّٰجِدِينَ ﴿۳۱﴾
قَالَ يَٰٓإِبْلِيسُ مَا لَكَ أَلَّا تَكُونَ مَعَ
السَّٰجِدِينَ ﴿۳۲﴾
قَالَ لَمْ أَكُن لِّأَسْجُدَ لِبَشَرٍ خَلَقْتَهُۥ مِن
صَلْصَٰلٍ مِّنْ حَمَإٍ مَّسْنُونٍ ﴿۳۳﴾
قَالَ فَاخْرُجْ مِنْهَا فَإِنَّكَ رَجِيمٌ ﴿۳۴﴾
وَإِنَّ عَلَيْكَ اللَّعْنَةَ إِلَىٰ يَوْمِ الدِّينِ ﴿۳۵﴾
قَالَ رَبِّ فَأَنظِرْنِيٓ إِلَىٰ يَوْمِ
يُبْعَثُونَ ﴿۳۶﴾
قَالَ فَإِنَّكَ مِنَ الْمُنظَرِينَ ﴿۳۷﴾
إِلَىٰ يَوْمِ الْوَقْتِ الْمَعْلُومِ ﴿۳۸﴾
قَالَ رَبِّ بِمَآ أَغْوَيْتَنِي لَأُزَيِّنَنَّ لَهُمْ
فِي الْأَرْضِ وَلَأُغْوِيَنَّهُمْ أَجْمَعِينَ ﴿۳۹﴾
إِلَّا عِبَادَكَ مِنْهُمُ الْمُخْلَصِينَ ﴿۴۰﴾
قَالَ هَٰذَا صِرَٰطٌ عَلَيَّ مُسْتَقِيمٌ ﴿۴۱﴾
إِنَّ عِبَادِي لَيْسَ لَكَ عَلَيْهِمْ سُلْطَٰنٌ
إِلَّا مَنِ اتَّبَعَكَ مِنَ الْغَاوِينَ ﴿۴۲﴾
وَإِنَّ جَهَنَّمَ لَمَوْعِدُهُمْ أَجْمَعِينَ ﴿۴۳﴾
لَهَا سَبْعَةُ أَبْوَٰبٍ لِّكُلِّ بَابٍ مِّنْهُمْ
جُزْءٌ مَّقْسُومٌ ﴿۴۴﴾ ع ۳ ۴
إِنَّ الْمُتَّقِينَ فِي جَنَّٰتٍ وَعُيُونٍ ﴿۴۵﴾

46. (Their greeting will be); "Enter ye here in Peace and Security."
47. And We shall remove from their hearts any lurking sense of injury; (they will be) brothers (Joyfully) facing each other on raised couches.
48. There no sense of fatigue shall touch them, nor shall they (ever) be asked to leave.
49. Tell My servants that I am indeed the Oft-Forgiving, Most Merciful;
50. And that My Chastisement will be indeed the most grievous Chastisement
51. Tell them about the guests of Abraham.
52. When they entered his presence and said, "Peace!" He said, "We feel afraid of you!"
53. They said: "Fear not! We give thee glad tidings of a son endowed with knowledge''
54. He said: "Do ye give me such glad tidings even though old age has seized me? Of what, then, is your good news?"
55. They said: "We give thee glad tidings in truth; be not then in despair!"
56. He said: "And who despairs of the mercy of his Lord, but such as go astray?"
57. Abraham said: "What then is the business on which ye (have come), O ye Messengers (of Allah)?"
58. They said: "We have been sent to a people (deep) in sin,
59. "Excepting the adherents of Lût: them we are certainly (charged) to save (from harm),—all—
60. "Except his wife, who, We bave ascertained, will be among those who will lag behind."
61. At length when the messengers arrived among the adherents of Lût.
62. He said; "Ye appear to be uncommon folk."
63. They said: "Yea, We have come to thee to accomplish that of which they doubt.
64. "We have come to thee with the Truth and assuredly We tell the truth.
65. "Then travel by night with thy household, when a portion of the

(اُن سے کہا جائیگا کہ) ان میں سلامتی (اور) خاطر جمع سے داخل ہوجاؤ ﴿٤٦﴾
اور انکے دلوں میں جو کدورت ہوگی اُنکو ہم نکال کر (صاف کر) دینگے
(گویا) بھائی بھائی تختوں پر ایک دوسرے کے سامنے بیٹھے ہوئے ہیں ﴿٤٧﴾
نہ اُن کو وہاں کوئی تکلیف پہنچے گی اور نہ وہ وہاں سے
نکالے جائیں گے ﴿٤٨﴾
(اے پیغمبر) میرے بندوں کو بتادو کہ میں بڑا بخشنے والا (اور) مہربان ہوں ﴿٤٩﴾
اور یہ کہ میرا عذاب بھی درد دینے والا عذاب ہے ﴿٥٠﴾
اور ان کو ابراہیم کے مہمانوں کا احوال سُنادو ﴿٥١﴾
جب وہ ابراہیم کے پاس آئے تو سلام کہا۔ (اُنہوں نے)
کہا کہ ہمیں تو تم سے ڈر لگتا ہے ﴿٥٢﴾
(مہمانوں نے) کہا کہ ڈریئے نہیں ہم آپکو ایک دانشمند لڑکے کی خوشخبری دیتے ہیں ﴿٥٣﴾
(وہ) بولے کہ جب مجھے بڑھاپے نے آپکڑا تو تم خوشخبری
دینے لگے۔ اب کاہے کی خوشخبری دیتے ہو ﴿٥٤﴾
(اُنھوں نے) کہا کہ ہم آپ کو سچّی خوشخبری دیتے ہیں
آپ مایوس نہ ہوجیے ﴿٥٥﴾
(ابراہیم نے) کہا کہ خدا کی رحمت سے (میں) مایوس کیوں
ہونے لگا اس سے) مایوس ہونا گمراہوں کا کام ہے ﴿٥٦﴾
پھر کہنے لگے کہ فرشتو! تمہیں (اور) کیا کام ہے ﴿٥٧﴾
(انہوں نے) کہا کہ ہم ایک گنہگار قوم کیطرف بھیجے گئے ہیں (کہ اسکو عذاب کریں) ﴿٥٨﴾
مگر لُوط کے گھر والے کہ ان سب کو ہم بچالیں گے ﴿٥٩﴾
البتہ اُنکی عورت (کہ) اُسکے لئے ہم نے ٹھہرا دیا ہے کہ وہ پیچھے رہ جائیگی ﴿٦٠﴾
پھر جب فرشتے لُوط کے گھر گئے ﴿٦١﴾
(تو لُوط نے) کہا تم تو نا آشنا سے لوگ ہو ﴿٦٢﴾
وہ بولے کہ (نہیں) بلکہ ہم آپ کے پاس وہ چیز لےکر آئے
ہیں جس میں لوگ شک کرتے تھے ﴿٦٣﴾
اور ہم آپکے پاس یقینی بات لیکر آئے ہیں اور ہم سچ کہتے ہیں ﴿٦٤﴾
تو آپ کچھ رات رہے سے اپنے گھر والوں کو لے نکلیں

ادخلوها بسلام آمنين ﴿٤٦﴾
ونزعنا ما في صدورهم من غل
إخوانا على سرر متقابلين ﴿٤٧﴾
لا يمسهم فيها نصب وما هم منها
بمخرجين ﴿٤٨﴾
نبئ عبادي أني أنا الغفور الرحيم ﴿٤٩﴾
وأن عذابي هو العذاب الأليم ﴿٥٠﴾
ونبئهم عن ضيف إبراهيم ﴿٥١﴾
إذ دخلوا عليه فقالوا سلاما قال
إنا منكم وجلون ﴿٥٢﴾
قالوا لا توجل إنا نبشرك بغلام عليم ﴿٥٣﴾
قال أبشرتموني على أن مسني الكبر
فبم تبشرون ﴿٥٤﴾
قالوا بشرناك بالحق فلا تكن من
القانطين ﴿٥٥﴾
قال ومن يقنط من رحمة ربه
إلا الضالون ﴿٥٦﴾
قال فما خطبكم أيها المرسلون ﴿٥٧﴾
قالوا إنا أرسلنا إلى قوم مجرمين ﴿٥٨﴾
إلا آل لوط إنا لمنجوهم أجمعين ﴿٥٩﴾
إلا امرأته قدرنا إنها لمن الغابرين ﴿٦٠﴾
فلما جاء آل لوط المرسلون ﴿٦١﴾
قال إنكم قوم منكرون ﴿٦٢﴾
قالوا بل جئناك بما كانوا فيه
يمترون ﴿٦٣﴾
وأتيناك بالحق وإنا لصادقون ﴿٦٤﴾
فأسر بأهلك بقطع من الليل واتبع

night (yet remains), and do thou go behind them: let no one amongst you look back, but pass on whither ye are ordered."
66. And We made known this decree to him, that the last remnants of those (sinners) should be cut off by the morning.
67. The inhabitants of the City came in (mad) joy (at news of the young men).
68. Lût said: "These are my guests: disgrace me not:
69. "But fear Allah, and shame me not."
70. They said: "Did we not forbid thee (to speak) for all and sundry?"
71. He said: "There are my daughters (to marry), if ye must act (so)."
72. Verily, by thy life (O Prophet), in their wild intoxication, they wander in distraction, to and fro.
73. But the (mighty) Blast overtook them at sunrise,
74. And We turned (the cities) upside down, and rained down on them brimstones hard as baked clay.
75. Behold! in this are Signs for those who by tokens do understand.
76. And the (Cities were) right on the high-road.
77. Behold! in this is a Sign for those who believe!
78. And the Companions of the Wood were also wrong-doers;
79. So We exacted retribution from them. They were both on an open highway, plain to see.
80. The Companions of the Rocky Tract also rejected the messengers:
81. We sent them Our Signs, but they persisted in turning away from them.
82. Out of the mountains did they hew (their) edifices, (feeling themselves) secure.
83. But the (mighty) Blast seized them of a morning,
84. And of no avail to them was all that they did (with such art and care)!
85. We created not the heavens, the earth, and all between them, but for just ends. And the Hour is surely coming (when this will be manifest). So overlook (any human faults) with gracious forgiveness.
86. For verily it is thy Lord Who is the All-Creator, Knowing all things.

اور خود اُن کے پیچھے چلیں اور آپ میں سے کوئی شخص
پیچھے مڑ کر نہ دیکھے۔ اور جہاں آپکو حکم ہو وہاں چلے جائیے ﴿۶۵﴾
اور ہم نے لوط کی طرف وحی بھیجی کہ ان لوگوں کی جڑ صبح
ہوتے ہوتے کاٹ دی جائے گی ﴿۶۶﴾
اور اہل شہر (لوط کے پاس) خوش خوش (دوڑے) آئے ﴿۶۷﴾
(لوط نے) کہا کہ یہ میرے مہمان ہیں (کہیں انکے بارے میں) مجھے رسوا نہ کرنا ﴿۶۸﴾
اور خدا سے ڈرو۔ اور میری بے آبروئی نہ کیجیو ﴿۶۹﴾
وہ بولے کیا ہم نے تم کو سارے جہان (کی حمایت وطرفداری) سے منع نہیں کیا ﴿۷۰﴾
(انہوں نے) کہا کہ اگر تمہیں کرنا ہی ہے تو یہ میری (قوم کی) لڑکیاں ہیں (ان سے شادی کرلو) ﴿۷۱﴾
(اے محمد) تمہاری جان کی قسم وہ اپنی مستی میں مدہوش (ہو رہے) تھے ﴿۷۲﴾
سو اُن کو سورج نکلتے نکلتے چنگھاڑ نے آپکڑا ﴿۷۳﴾
اور ہم نے اس (شہر) کو (الٹ کر) نیچے اوپر کر دیا۔ اور
ان پر کھنگر کی پتھریاں برسائیں ﴿۷۴﴾
بیشک اس (قصے) میں اہل فراست کے لئے نشانیاں ہیں ﴿۷۵﴾
اور وہ (شہر) اب تک سیدھے رستے پر (موجود) ہے ﴿۷۶﴾
بیشک اس میں ایمان لانے والوں کیلئے نشانی ہے ﴿۷۷﴾
اور بَن کے رہنے والے (یعنی قوم شعیب کے لوگ) بھی گنہگار تھے ﴿۷۸﴾
تو ہم نے اُن سے بھی بدلہ لیا اور یہ دونوں شہر کھلے رستے پر (موجود) ہیں ﴿۷۹﴾
اور (وادئ) حجر کے رہنے والوں نے بھی پیغمبروں کی تکذیب کی ﴿۸۰﴾
ہم نے انکو اپنی نشانیاں دیں اور وہ اُنسے منہ پھیرتے رہے ﴿۸۱﴾
اور وہ پہاڑوں کو تراش تراش کر گھر بناتے تھے (کہ) امن (واطمینان) سے رہیں گے ﴿۸۲﴾
تو چیخ نے ان کو صبح ہوتے ہوتے آپکڑا ﴿۸۳﴾
اور جو کام وہ کرتے تھے وہ اُن کے کچھ بھی کام نہ آئے ﴿۸۴﴾
اور ہم نے آسمانوں اور زمین کو اور جو (مخلوقات) اُن میں
ہے اُس کو تدبیر کے ساتھ پیدا کیا ہے۔ اور قیامت تو ضرور
آکر رہے گی تو تم (ان لوگوں سے) اچھی طرح سے درگزر کرو ﴿۸۵﴾
کچھ شک نہیں کہ تمہارا پروردگار ہی (سب کچھ) پیدا کرنیوالا (اور) جاننے والا ہے ﴿۸۶﴾

أَدْبَارَهُمْ وَلَا يَلْتَفِتْ مِنكُمْ أَحَدٌ
وَامْضُوا حَيْثُ تُؤْمَرُونَ ﴿٦٥﴾
وَقَضَيْنَا إِلَيْهِ ذَٰلِكَ الْأَمْرَ أَنَّ دَابِرَ
هَٰؤُلَاءِ مَقْطُوعٌ مُّصْبِحِينَ ﴿٦٦﴾
وَجَاءَ أَهْلُ الْمَدِينَةِ يَسْتَبْشِرُونَ ﴿٦٧﴾
قَالَ إِنَّ هَٰؤُلَاءِ ضَيْفِي فَلَا تَفْضَحُونِ ﴿٦٨﴾
وَاتَّقُوا اللَّهَ وَلَا تُخْزُونِ ﴿٦٩﴾
قَالُوا أَوَلَمْ نَنْهَكَ عَنِ الْعَالَمِينَ ﴿٧٠﴾
قَالَ هَٰؤُلَاءِ بَنَاتِي إِن كُنتُمْ فَاعِلِينَ ﴿٧١﴾
لَعَمْرُكَ إِنَّهُمْ لَفِي سَكْرَتِهِمْ يَعْمَهُونَ ﴿٧٢﴾
فَأَخَذَتْهُمُ الصَّيْحَةُ مُشْرِقِينَ ﴿٧٣﴾
فَجَعَلْنَا عَالِيَهَا سَافِلَهَا وَأَمْطَرْنَا عَلَيْهِمْ
حِجَارَةً مِّن سِجِّيلٍ ﴿٧٤﴾
إِنَّ فِي ذَٰلِكَ لَآيَاتٍ لِّلْمُتَوَسِّمِينَ ﴿٧٥﴾
وَإِنَّهَا لَبِسَبِيلٍ مُّقِيمٍ ﴿٧٦﴾
إِنَّ فِي ذَٰلِكَ لَآيَةً لِّلْمُؤْمِنِينَ ﴿٧٧﴾
وَإِن كَانَ أَصْحَابُ الْأَيْكَةِ لَظَالِمِينَ ﴿٧٨﴾
فَانتَقَمْنَا مِنْهُمْ وَإِنَّهُمَا لَبِإِمَامٍ مُّبِينٍ ﴿٧٩﴾
وَلَقَدْ كَذَّبَ أَصْحَابُ الْحِجْرِ الْمُرْسَلِينَ ﴿٨٠﴾
وَآتَيْنَاهُمْ آيَاتِنَا فَكَانُوا عَنْهَا مُعْرِضِينَ ﴿٨١﴾
وَكَانُوا يَنْحِتُونَ مِنَ الْجِبَالِ بُيُوتًا آمِنِينَ ﴿٨٢﴾
فَأَخَذَتْهُمُ الصَّيْحَةُ مُصْبِحِينَ ﴿٨٣﴾
فَمَا أَغْنَىٰ عَنْهُم مَّا كَانُوا يَكْسِبُونَ ﴿٨٤﴾
وَمَا خَلَقْنَا السَّمَاوَاتِ وَالْأَرْضَ وَمَا
بَيْنَهُمَا إِلَّا بِالْحَقِّ ۗ وَإِنَّ السَّاعَةَ لَآتِيَةٌ ۖ
فَاصْفَحِ الصَّفْحَ الْجَمِيلَ ﴿٨٥﴾
إِنَّ رَبَّكَ هُوَ الْخَلَّاقُ الْعَلِيمُ ﴿٨٦﴾

SÛRA–16

AN-NAḤL

(INTRODUCTION)

Chronologically this Sûra, like the six which preceded it, belongs to the late Makkan period, except perhaps verse 110 and some of the verses that follow, but the chronology has no significance. In subject-matter it sums up, from a new point of view, the arguments on the great questions of Allah's dealings with man, His Self-revelation to man and how the Messengers and the Message are writ large in every phase of Allah's Creation and the life of Man. The new point of view is that Nature points to Nature's Allah.

87. And We have bestowed upon thee the Seven Oft-repeated (Verses) and the Grand Qur'an.

88. Strain not thine eyes (wistfully) at what We have bestowed on certain classes of them, nor grieve over them: but lower thy wing (in gentleness) to the Believers.

89. And say: "I am indeed he that warneth openly and without ambiguity,"—

90. (Of just such wrath) as We sent down on those who divided (Scripture into arbitrary parts),—

91. (So also on such) who have made Qur'an into shreds (as they please).

92. Therefore, by thy Lord, we will, of a surety, call them to account,

93. For all their deeds.

94. Therefore expound openly what thou art commanded, and turn away from those who join false gods with Allah.

95. For sufficient are We unto thee against those who scoff.—

96. Those who adopt, with Allah, another god: but soon will they come to know.

97. We do indeed know how thy heart is distressed at what they say.

98. But celebrate the praises of thy Lord and be of those who prostrate themselves in adoration.

99. And serve thy Lord until there come unto thee the Hour that is Certain.

اور ہم نے تم کو سات (آیتیں) جو (نماز میں) دُہرا کر پڑھی جاتی
ہیں (یعنی سورۂ الحمد) اور عظمت والا قرآن عطا فرمایا ہے ﴿٨٧﴾
اور ہم نے کفار کی کئی جماعتوں کو جو (فوائد دنیاوی سے)
متمتع کیا ہے تم اُن کی طرف (رغبت سے) آنکھ اُٹھا کر نہ دیکھنا
اور نہ اُنکے حال پر تأسف کرنا اور مومنوں سے خاطر اور تواضع سے پیش آنا ﴿٨٨﴾
اور کہہ دو کہ میں تو علانیہ ڈر سنانے والا ہوں ﴿٨٩﴾
(اور ہم ان کفار پر اسی طرح عذاب نازل کرینگے) جسطرح اُن لوگوں پر نازل کیا جنہوں نے تقسیم کر دیا ﴿٩٠﴾
یعنی قرآن کو (کچھ ماننے اور کچھ نہ ماننے سے) ٹکڑے ٹکڑے کر ڈالا ﴿٩١﴾
تمہارے پروردگار کی قسم ہم اُن سے ضرور پرسش کرینگے ﴿٩٢﴾
اُن کاموں کی جو وہ کرتے رہے ﴿٩٣﴾
پس جو حکم تم کو (خدا کی طرف سے) ملا ہے وہ (لوگوں کو) سُنا دو
اور مشرکوں کا (ذرا) خیال نہ کرو ﴿٩٤﴾
ہم تمہیں ان لوگوں (کے شر) سے بچانے کیلئے جو تم سے استہزاء کرتے ہیں کافی ہیں ﴿٩٥﴾
جو خدا کے ساتھ اور معبود قرار دیتے ہیں سو عنقریب ان کو
(ان باتوں کا انجام) معلوم ہو جائے گا ﴿٩٦﴾
اور ہم جانتے ہیں کہ ان کی باتوں سے تمہارا دل تنگ
ہوتا ہے ﴿٩٧﴾
تو تم اپنے پروردگار کی تسبیح کہتے اور (اسکی) خوبیاں
بیان کرتے رہو اور سجدہ کرنے والوں میں داخل رہو ﴿٩٨﴾
اور اپنے پروردگار کی عبادت کئے جاؤ یہاں تک کہ تمہاری موت (کا وقت) آجائے ﴿٩٩﴾

وَلَقَدْ اٰتَيْنٰكَ سَبْعًا مِّنَ الْمَثَانِيْ وَ
الْقُرْاٰنَ الْعَظِيْمَ ﴿٨٧﴾
لَا تَمُدَّنَّ عَيْنَيْكَ اِلٰى مَا مَتَّعْنَا بِهٖٓ
اَزْوَاجًا مِّنْهُمْ وَلَا تَحْزَنْ عَلَيْهِمْ وَ
اخْفِضْ جَنَاحَكَ لِلْمُؤْمِنِيْنَ ﴿٨٨﴾
وَقُلْ اِنِّيْٓ اَنَا النَّذِيْرُ الْمُبِيْنُ ﴿٨٩﴾
كَمَآ اَنْزَلْنَا عَلَى الْمُقْتَسِمِيْنَ ﴿٩٠﴾
الَّذِيْنَ جَعَلُوا الْقُرْاٰنَ عِضِيْنَ ﴿٩١﴾
فَوَرَبِّكَ لَنَسْـَٔلَنَّهُمْ اَجْمَعِيْنَ ﴿٩٢﴾
عَمَّا كَانُوْا يَعْمَلُوْنَ ﴿٩٣﴾
فَاصْدَعْ بِمَا تُؤْمَرُ وَاَعْرِضْ عَنِ
الْمُشْرِكِيْنَ ﴿٩٤﴾
اِنَّا كَفَيْنٰكَ الْمُسْتَهْزِءِيْنَ ﴿٩٥﴾
الَّذِيْنَ يَجْعَلُوْنَ مَعَ اللّٰهِ اِلٰهًا اٰخَرَ
فَسَوْفَ يَعْلَمُوْنَ ﴿٩٦﴾
وَلَقَدْ نَعْلَمُ اَنَّكَ يَضِيْقُ صَدْرُكَ
بِمَا يَقُوْلُوْنَ ﴿٩٧﴾
فَسَبِّحْ بِحَمْدِ رَبِّكَ وَكُنْ مِّنَ
السّٰجِدِيْنَ ﴿٩٨﴾
وَاعْبُدْ رَبَّكَ حَتّٰى يَاْتِيَكَ الْيَقِيْنُ ﴿٩٩﴾

An-Nahl, or The Bee

سورۂ نحل مکی ہے اور اس میں ایک سو اٹھائیس آیتیں اور سولہ رکوع ہیں

سُوْرَةُ النَّحْلِ مَكِّيَّةٌ وَّهِيَ مِائَةٌ وَّثَمَانٌ وَّعِشْرُوْنَ اٰيَةً وَّسِتَّةَ عَشَرَ رُكُوْعًا

In the name of Allah, Most Gracious, Most Merciful.

1. (Inevitable) cometh (to pass) the Command of Allah: seek ye not then to hasten it: glory to Him, and far is He above having the partners they ascribe unto Him!

2. He doth send down His angels with inspiration of His Command, to such of His servants as He pleaseth, (saying): "Warn (Man) that there is no god but I: so do your duty unto Me."

شروع خدا کا نام لے کر جو بڑا مہربان نہایت رحم والا ہے
خدا کا حکم (یعنی عذاب گویا) آ ہی پہنچا تو (کافرو) اسکے لئے جلدی
مت کرو۔ یہ لوگ جو (خدا کا) شریک بناتے ہیں وہ اس سے پاک اور بالاتر ہے ﴿١﴾
وہی فرشتوں کو پیغام دے کر اپنے حکم سے اپنے بندوں میں
سے جس کے پاس چاہتا ہے بھیجتا ہے کہ (لوگوں کو) بتا دو
کہ میرے سوا کوئی معبود نہیں تو مجھی سے ڈرو ﴿٢﴾

بِسْمِ اللّٰهِ الرَّحْمٰنِ الرَّحِيْمِ
اَتٰٓى اَمْرُ اللّٰهِ فَلَا تَسْتَعْجِلُوْهُ ؕ سُبْحٰنَهٗ
وَتَعٰلٰى عَمَّا يُشْرِكُوْنَ ﴿١﴾
يُنَزِّلُ الْمَلٰٓئِكَةَ بِالرُّوْحِ مِنْ اَمْرِهٖ
عَلٰى مَنْ يَّشَآءُ مِنْ عِبَادِهٖٓ اَنْ
اَنْذِرُوْٓا اَنَّهٗ لَآ اِلٰهَ اِلَّآ اَنَا فَاتَّقُوْنِ ﴿٢﴾

خَلَقَ السَّمٰوٰتِ وَالْاَرْضَ بِالْحَقِّ ؕ
تَعٰلٰى عَمَّا يُشْرِكُوْنَ ﴿۳﴾
خَلَقَ الْاِنْسَانَ مِنْ نُّطْفَةٍ فَاِذَا هُوَ
خَصِيْمٌ مُّبِيْنٌ ﴿۴﴾
وَالْاَنْعَامَ خَلَقَهَا ۚ لَكُمْ فِيْهَا دِفْءٌ وَّ
مَنَافِعُ وَمِنْهَا تَاْكُلُوْنَ ﴿۵﴾
وَلَكُمْ فِيْهَا جَمَالٌ حِيْنَ تُرِيْحُوْنَ
وَحِيْنَ تَسْرَحُوْنَ ﴿۶﴾
وَتَحْمِلُ اَثْقَالَكُمْ اِلٰى بَلَدٍ لَّمْ تَكُوْنُوْا
بٰلِغِيْهِ اِلَّا بِشِقِّ الْاَنْفُسِ ؕ اِنَّ رَبَّكُمْ
لَرَءُوْفٌ رَّحِيْمٌ ﴿۷﴾
وَّالْخَيْلَ وَالْبِغَالَ وَالْحَمِيْرَ لِتَرْكَبُوْهَا
وَزِيْنَةً ؕ وَيَخْلُقُ مَا لَا تَعْلَمُوْنَ ﴿۸﴾
وَعَلَى اللّٰهِ قَصْدُ السَّبِيْلِ وَمِنْهَا جَآئِرٌ ؕ
وَلَوْ شَآءَ لَهَدٰىكُمْ اَجْمَعِيْنَ ﴿۹﴾ ع
هُوَ الَّذِيْٓ اَنْزَلَ مِنَ السَّمَآءِ مَآءً لَّكُمْ
مِّنْهُ شَرَابٌ وَّمِنْهُ شَجَرٌ فِيْهِ تُسِيْمُوْنَ ﴿۱۰﴾
يُنْۢبِتُ لَكُمْ بِهِ الزَّرْعَ وَالزَّيْتُوْنَ وَ
النَّخِيْلَ وَالْاَعْنَابَ وَمِنْ كُلِّ الثَّمَرٰتِ ؕ
اِنَّ فِيْ ذٰلِكَ لَاٰيَةً لِّقَوْمٍ يَّتَفَكَّرُوْنَ ﴿۱۱﴾
وَسَخَّرَ لَكُمُ الَّيْلَ وَالنَّهَارَ ۙ وَالشَّمْسَ
وَالْقَمَرَ ؕ وَالنُّجُوْمُ مُسَخَّرٰتٌۢ بِاَمْرِهٖ ؕ
اِنَّ فِيْ ذٰلِكَ لَاٰيٰتٍ لِّقَوْمٍ يَّعْقِلُوْنَ ﴿۱۲﴾
وَمَا ذَرَاَ لَكُمْ فِي الْاَرْضِ مُخْتَلِفًا اَلْوَانُهٗ ؕ
اِنَّ فِيْ ذٰلِكَ لَاٰيَةً لِّقَوْمٍ يَّذَّكَّرُوْنَ ﴿۱۳﴾
وَهُوَ الَّذِيْ سَخَّرَ الْبَحْرَ لِتَاْكُلُوْا مِنْهُ
لَحْمًا طَرِيًّا وَّتَسْتَخْرِجُوْا مِنْهُ حِلْيَةً

اُسی نے آسمانوں اور زمین کو مبنی برحکمت پیدا کیا۔ اس
کی ذات ان (کافروں) کے شرک سے اونچی ہے ﴿۳﴾
اسی نے انسان کو نطفے سے بنایا مگر وہ اُس (خالق)
کے بارے میں علانیہ جھگڑنے لگا ﴿۴﴾
اور چارپایوں کو بھی اُسی نے پیدا کیا۔ انمیں تمہارے لئے
جڑاول اور بہت سے فائدے ہیں۔ اور انمیں سے بعض کو تم کھاتے بھی ہو ﴿۵﴾
اور جب شام کو انہیں (جنگل سے) لاتے ہو اور جب صبح کو (جنگل)
چرانے لیجاتے ہو تو اُن سے تمہاری عزت و شان ہے ﴿۶﴾
اور (دور دراز) شہروں میں جہاں تم زحمت شاقہ کے
بغیر پہنچ نہیں سکتے وہ تمہارے بوجھ اُٹھا کر لیجاتے ہیں کچھ شک
نہیں کہ تمہارا پروردگار نہایت شفقت والا اور مہربان ہے ﴿۷﴾
اور اسی نے گھوڑے اور خچر اور گدھے پیدا کئے تاکہ تم ان پر سوار ہو اور (وہ تمہارے
لئے) رونق و زینت (بھی ہیں) اور وہ (اور چیزیں بھی) پیدا کرتا ہے جنکی تمکو خبر نہیں ﴿۸﴾
اور سیدھا رستہ تو خدا تک جا پہنچتا ہے۔ اور بعض رستے ٹیڑھے ہیں (وہ
اُس تک نہیں پہنچتے) اور اگر وہ چاہتا تو تم سب کو سیدھے رستے پر چلا دیتا ﴿۹﴾
وہی تو ہے جس نے آسمان سے پانی برسایا جسے تم پیتے ہو اور اس سے
درخت بھی (شاداب ہوتے) ہیں جنمیں تم اپنے چارپایوں کو چراتے ہو ﴿۱۰﴾
اسی پانی سے وہ تمہارے لئے کھیتی اور زیتون اور کھجور اور انگور
(اور اور بیشمار درخت) اُگاتا ہے اور ہر طرح کے پھل (پیدا کرتا ہے)
غور کرنیوالوں کیلئے اسمیں (قدرت خدا کی بڑی) نشانی ہے ﴿۱۱﴾
اور اسی نے تمہارے لئے رات اور دن اور سورج اور چاند کو کام
میں لگایا اور اُسی کے حکم سے ستارے بھی کام میں لگے ہوئے
ہیں۔ سمجھنے والوں کیلئے اسمیں (قدرت خدا کی بہت سی) نشانیاں ہیں ﴿۱۲﴾
اور جو طرح طرح کے رنگوں کی چیزیں اُس نے زمین میں پیدا کیں
(سب تمہارے زیر فرمان کردیں) نصیحت پکڑنے والوں کیلئے اسمیں نشانی ہے ﴿۱۳﴾
اور وہی تو ہے جس نے دریا کو تمہارے اختیار میں کیا تاکہ اس میں سے تازہ گوشت
کھاؤ۔ اور اس سے زیور (موتی وغیرہ) نکالو جسے تم پہنتے ہو۔ اور تم دیکھتے

3. He has created the heavens and the earth with truth far is He above having the partners they ascribe to Him!

4. He has created man from a sperm-drop and behold this same (man) becomes an open disputer!

5. And cattle He has created for you (men): from them ye derive warmth, and numerous benefits, and of their (meat) ye eat.

6. And ye have a sense of pride and beauty in them as ye drive them home in the evening, and as ye lead them forth to pasture in the morning.

7. And they carry your heavy loads to lands that ye could not (otherwise) reach except with souls distressed: for your Lord is indeed Most Kind, Most Merciful.

8. And (He has created) horses, mules, and donkeys, for you to ride and as an adornment; and He has created (other) things of which ye have no knowledge.

9. Allah alone can show the right path but there are ways that turn aside; if Allah had willed, He could have guided all of you.

10. It is He Who sends down rain from the sky from it ye drink, and out of it (grows) the vegetation on which ye feed your cattle.

11. With it He produces for you corn, olives, date-palms, grapes, and every kind of fruit: verily in this is a Sign for those who give thought.

12. He has made subject to you the Night and the Day; the Sun and the Moon; and the Stars are in subjection by His Command: verily in this are Signs for men who are wise.

13. And the things on this earth which He has multiplied in varying colours (and qualities); verily in this is a Sign for men who are mindful.

14. It is He Who has made the sea subject, that ye may eat thereof flesh that is fresh and tender, and that ye may extract therefrom ornaments to

wear; and thou seest the ships therein that plough the waves, that ye may seek (thus) of the bounty of Allah and that ye may be grateful.

15. And He has set up on the earth mountains standing firm, lest it should shake with you; and rivers and ways: that ye may guide yourselves;

16. And marks and sign-posts; and by the stars (men) guide themselves.

17. Is then He Who creates like one that creates not? Will ye not receive admonition?

18. If ye would count up the favours of Allah, never would ye be able to number them: for Allah is Oft-Forgiving, Most Merciful.

19. And Allah doth know what ye conceal, and what ye reveal.

20. Those whom they invoke besides Allah create nothing and are themselves created.

21. (They are things) dead, lifeless: nor do they know when they will be raised up.

22. Your God is One God: as to those who believe not in the Hereafter, their hearts refuse to know, and they are arrogant.

23. Undoubtedly Allah doth know What they conceal, and what they reveal: verily He loveth not the arrogant.

24. When it is said to them, "What is it that your Lord has revealed?" they say, "Tales of the ancients!"

25. That they may bear, on the Day of Judgment, their own burdens in full, and also (something) of the burdens of those without knowledge, whom they misled. Alas, how grievous the burdens they will bear!

26. Those before them did also plot (against Allah's Way): but Allah took their structures from their foundations, and the roof fell down on them from above; and the Wrath

تَلْبَسُونَهَا ۚ وَتَرَى الْفُلْكَ مَوَاخِرَ فِيهِ
وَلِتَبْتَغُوا مِنْ فَضْلِهِ وَلَعَلَّكُمْ تَشْكُرُونَ ﴿١٤﴾
وَأَلْقَىٰ فِي الْأَرْضِ رَوَاسِيَ أَنْ تَمِيدَ بِكُمْ
وَأَنْهَارًا وَسُبُلًا لَعَلَّكُمْ تَهْتَدُونَ ﴿١٥﴾
وَعَلَامَاتٍ ۚ وَبِالنَّجْمِ هُمْ يَهْتَدُونَ ﴿١٦﴾
أَفَمَنْ يَخْلُقُ كَمَنْ لَا يَخْلُقُ ۗ أَفَلَا
تَذَكَّرُونَ ﴿١٧﴾
وَإِنْ تَعُدُّوا نِعْمَةَ اللَّهِ لَا تُحْصُوهَا ۗ
إِنَّ اللَّهَ لَغَفُورٌ رَحِيمٌ ﴿١٨﴾
وَاللَّهُ يَعْلَمُ مَا تُسِرُّونَ وَمَا تُعْلِنُونَ ﴿١٩﴾
وَالَّذِينَ يَدْعُونَ مِنْ دُونِ اللَّهِ لَا
يَخْلُقُونَ شَيْئًا وَهُمْ يُخْلَقُونَ ﴿٢٠﴾
أَمْوَاتٌ غَيْرُ أَحْيَاءٍ ۖ وَمَا يَشْعُرُونَ
أَيَّانَ يُبْعَثُونَ ﴿٢١﴾
إِلَٰهُكُمْ إِلَٰهٌ وَاحِدٌ ۚ فَالَّذِينَ لَا
يُؤْمِنُونَ بِالْآخِرَةِ قُلُوبُهُمْ مُنْكِرَةٌ
وَهُمْ مُسْتَكْبِرُونَ ﴿٢٢﴾
لَا جَرَمَ أَنَّ اللَّهَ يَعْلَمُ مَا يُسِرُّونَ
وَمَا يُعْلِنُونَ ۚ إِنَّهُ لَا يُحِبُّ الْمُسْتَكْبِرِينَ ﴿٢٣﴾
وَإِذَا قِيلَ لَهُمْ مَاذَا أَنْزَلَ رَبُّكُمْ ۙ
قَالُوا أَسَاطِيرُ الْأَوَّلِينَ ﴿٢٤﴾
لِيَحْمِلُوا أَوْزَارَهُمْ كَامِلَةً يَوْمَ
الْقِيَامَةِ ۙ وَمِنْ أَوْزَارِ الَّذِينَ يُضِلُّونَهُمْ
بِغَيْرِ عِلْمٍ ۗ أَلَا سَاءَ مَا يَزِرُونَ ﴿٢٥﴾
قَدْ مَكَرَ الَّذِينَ مِنْ قَبْلِهِمْ فَأَتَى اللَّهُ
بُنْيَانَهُمْ مِنَ الْقَوَاعِدِ فَخَرَّ عَلَيْهِمُ
السَّقْفُ مِنْ فَوْقِهِمْ وَأَتَاهُمُ الْعَذَابُ

ہو کہ کشتیاں دریا میں پانی کو پھاڑتی چلی جاتی ہیں۔ اور اسلئے بھی (دریا
کو تمہارے اختیار میں کیا) کہ تم خدا کے فضل سے (معاش) تلاش کرو اور تاکہ (اسکا) شکر کرو ﴿۱۴﴾
اور اُسی نے زمین پر پہاڑ (بناکر) رکھدیئے کہ تمکو لیکر کہیں جھک نہ جائے
اور نہریں اور رستے بنادیئے تاکہ ایک مقام سے دوسرے مقام تک (آسانی سے) جاسکو ﴿۱۵﴾
اور (رستوں میں) نشانات بنادیئے اور لوگ ستاروں سے بھی رستے معلوم کرتے ہیں ﴿۱۶﴾
تو جو (اتنی مخلوقات) پیدا کرے۔ کیا وہ ویسا ہے جو کچھ بھی پیدا
نہ کرسکے تو پھر تم غور کیوں نہیں کرتے؟ ﴿۱۷﴾
اور اگر تم خدا کی نعمتوں کو شمار کرنا چاہو تو گن نہ سکو۔ بیشک
خدا بخشنے والا مہربان ہے ﴿۱۸﴾
اور جو کچھ تم چھپاتے اور جو کچھ ظاہر کرتے ہو سب سے خدا واقف ہے ﴿۱۹﴾
اور جن لوگوں کو یہ خدا کے سوا پکارتے ہیں وہ کوئی چیز بھی
تو نہیں بنا سکتے بلکہ خود اُن کو اور بناتے ہیں ﴿۲۰﴾
(وہ) لاشیں ہیں بے جان۔ ان کو یہ بھی تو معلوم نہیں کہ
اُٹھائے کب جائیں گے ﴿۲۱﴾
تمہارا معبود تو اکیلا خدا ہے۔ تو جو آخرت پر ایمان نہیں
رکھتے اُن کے دل انکار کر رہے ہیں اور وہ سرکش ہو
رہے ہیں ﴿۲۲﴾
یہ جو کچھ چھپاتے ہیں اور جو ظاہر کرتے ہیں خدا ضرور اس
کو جانتا ہے۔ وہ (خدا) سرکشوں کو ہرگز پسند نہیں کرتا ﴿۲۳﴾
اور جب ان (کافروں) سے کہا جاتا ہے کہ تمہارے پروردگار
نے کیا اُتارا ہے تو کہتے ہیں کہ (وہ تو) پہلے لوگوں کی حکایتیں ہیں ﴿۲۴﴾
(اے پیغمبر ان کو بکنے دو) یہ قیامت کے دن اپنے (اعمال کے)
پورے بوجھ بھی اٹھائینگے اور جن کو یہ بےتحقیق گمراہ کرتے
ہیں اُنکے بوجھ بھی (اٹھائینگے) سُن رکھو کہ جو بوجھ یہ اٹھا رہے ہیں بُرے ہیں ﴿۲۵﴾
ان سے پہلے لوگوں نے بھی (ایسی ہی) مکاریاں کی تھیں
تو خدا (کا حکم) اُنکی عمارت کے ستونوں پر آپہنچا اور چھت اُن پر
اُن کے اوپر سے گر پڑی۔ اور (ایسی) طرف سے اُن پر عذاب

seized them from directions they did not perceive.

27. Then, on the Day of Judgment, He will cover them with shame, and say: "Where are My 'partners' concerning whom ye used to dispute (with the godly)?" Those endued with knowledge will say: "This Day, indeed, are the Unbelievers covered with Shame and Misery,—

28. "(Namely) those whose lives the angels take in a state of wrong-doing to their own souls." Then would they offer submission (with the pretence), We did no evil (knowingly)." (The angels will reply), "Nay, but verily Allah knoweth all that ye did;

29. "So enter the gates of Hell, to dwell therein. Thus evil indeed is the abode of the arrogant."

30. To the righteous (when) it is said, "What is it that your Lord has revealed?" they say, "All that is good." To those who do good, there is good in this world, and the Home of the Hereafter is even better and excellent indeed is the Home of the righteous,—

31. Gardens of Eternity which they will enter: beneath them flow (pleasant) rivers: they will have therein all that they wish: thus doth Allah reward the righteous,—

32. (Namely) those whose lives the angels take in a state of purity, saying (to them), "Peace be on you; enter ye the Garden, because of (the good) which ye did (in the world)."

33. Do the (ungodly) wait but for the angels to come to them, or there comes the Command of thy Lord (for their doom)? So did those who went before them. But Allah wronged them not: nay, they wronged their own souls.

34. But the evil results of their deeds overtook them, and that every (Wrath) at which they had scoffed hemmed them in.

آ واقع ہوا جہاں سے اُن کو خیال بھی نہ تھا ﴿٢٦﴾
پھر وہ ان کو قیامت کے دن بھی ذلیل کرے گا اور کہیگا
کہ میرے وہ شریک کہاں ہیں جن کے بارے میں تم جھگڑا
کرتے تھے؟ جن لوگوں کو علم دیا گیا تھا وہ کہیں گے کہ
آج کافروں کی رسوائی اور بُرائی ہے ﴿٢٧﴾
(ان کا حال یہ ہے کہ) جب فرشتے ان کی روحیں قبض
کرنے لگتے ہیں (اور یہ) اپنے ہی حق میں ظلم کرنیوالے ہوتے
ہیں، تو مطیع و منقاد ہو جاتے ہیں (اور کہتے ہیں) کہ ہم کوئی بُرا کام
نہیں کرتے تھے۔ ہاں جو کچھ تم کیا کرتے تھے خدا اُسے خوب جانتا ہے ﴿٢٨﴾
سو دوزخ کے دروازوں میں داخل ہو جاؤ۔ ہمیشہ اس میں
رہو گے۔ اب تکبر کرنے والوں کا بُرا ٹھکانا ہے ﴿٢٩﴾
اور (جب) پرہیزگاروں سے پوچھا جاتا ہے کہ تمہارے پروردگار
نے کیا نازل کیا ہے۔ تو کہتے ہیں کہ بہترین (کلام)۔ جو لوگ
نیکوکار ہیں ان کے لئے اس دنیا میں بھی بھلائی ہے اور
آخرت کا گھر تو بہت ہی اچھا ہے اور پرہیزگاروں کا گھر بہت خوب ہے ﴿٣٠﴾
(وہ) بہشت جاودانی (ہیں) جن میں وہ داخل ہوں گے
اُن کے نیچے نہریں بہ رہی ہیں وہاں جو چاہیں گے اُنکے
لئے میسر ہو گا۔ خدا پرہیزگاروں کو ایسا ہی بدلہ دیتا ہے ﴿٣١﴾
(ان کی کیفیت یہ ہے کہ) جب فرشتے اُن کی جانیں نکالنے
لگتے ہیں! اور یہ (کفر و شرک سے) پاک ہوتے ہیں تو سلام علیکم کہتے ہیں اور
کہتے ہیں کہ جو عمل تم کیا کرتے تھے اُنکے بدلے میں بہشت میں داخل ہو جاؤ ﴿٣٢﴾
کیا یہ (کافر) اس بات کے منتظر ہیں کہ فرشتے اُنکے پاس (جان
نکالنے) آئیں یا تمہارے پروردگار کا حکم (عذاب) آ پہنچے۔ اسی
طرح اُن لوگوں نے کیا تھا جو اُن سے پہلے تھے اور خدا نے
اُن پر ظلم نہیں کیا بلکہ وہ خود اپنے آپ پر ظلم کرتے تھے ﴿٣٣﴾
تو اُن کو اُن کے اعمال کے بُرے بدلے ملے اور جس چیز کے
ساتھ وہ ٹھٹھے کیا کرتے تھے اُس نے اُنکو (ہر طرف سے) گھیر لیا ﴿٣٤﴾

مِنْ حَيْثُ لَا يَشْعُرُوْنَ ﴿٢٦﴾
ثُمَّ يَوْمَ الْقِيٰمَةِ يُخْزِيْهِمْ وَيَقُوْلُ
اَيْنَ شُرَكَآءِيَ الَّذِيْنَ كُنْتُمْ تُشَآقُّوْنَ
فِيْهِمْ ۭ قَالَ الَّذِيْنَ اُوْتُوا الْعِلْمَ اِنَّ
الْخِزْيَ الْيَوْمَ وَالسُّوْٓءَ عَلَى الْكٰفِرِيْنَ ﴿٢٧﴾
الَّذِيْنَ تَتَوَفّٰىهُمُ الْمَلٰٓئِكَةُ ظَالِمِيْٓ
اَنْفُسِهِمْ ۠ فَاَلْقَوُا السَّلَمَ مَا كُنَّا
نَعْمَلُ مِنْ سُوْٓءٍ ۭ بَلٰٓى اِنَّ اللّٰهَ عَلِيْمٌۢ
بِمَا كُنْتُمْ تَعْمَلُوْنَ ﴿٢٨﴾
فَادْخُلُوْٓا اَبْوَابَ جَهَنَّمَ خٰلِدِيْنَ فِيْهَا ۭ
فَلَبِئْسَ مَثْوَى الْمُتَكَبِّرِيْنَ ﴿٢٩﴾
وَقِيْلَ لِلَّذِيْنَ اتَّقَوْا مَاذَآ اَنْزَلَ
رَبُّكُمْ ۭ قَالُوْا خَيْرًا ۭ لِلَّذِيْنَ اَحْسَنُوْا
فِيْ هٰذِهِ الدُّنْيَا حَسَنَةٌ ۭ وَلَدَارُ الْاٰخِرَةِ
خَيْرٌ ۭ وَلَنِعْمَ دَارُ الْمُتَّقِيْنَ ﴿٣٠﴾
جَنّٰتُ عَدْنٍ يَّدْخُلُوْنَهَا تَجْرِيْ مِنْ
تَحْتِهَا الْاَنْهٰرُ لَهُمْ فِيْهَا مَا يَشَآءُوْنَ ۭ
كَذٰلِكَ يَجْزِي اللّٰهُ الْمُتَّقِيْنَ ﴿٣١﴾
الَّذِيْنَ تَتَوَفّٰىهُمُ الْمَلٰٓئِكَةُ طَيِّبِيْنَ ۙ
يَقُوْلُوْنَ سَلٰمٌ عَلَيْكُمُ ادْخُلُوا الْجَنَّةَ
بِمَا كُنْتُمْ تَعْمَلُوْنَ ﴿٣٢﴾
هَلْ يَنْظُرُوْنَ اِلَّآ اَنْ تَاْتِيَهُمُ الْمَلٰٓئِكَةُ
اَوْ يَاْتِيَ اَمْرُ رَبِّكَ ۭ كَذٰلِكَ فَعَلَ الَّذِيْنَ
مِنْ قَبْلِهِمْ ۭ وَمَا ظَلَمَهُمُ اللّٰهُ وَلٰكِنْ
كَانُوْٓا اَنْفُسَهُمْ يَظْلِمُوْنَ ﴿٣٣﴾
فَاَصَابَهُمْ سَيِّاٰتُ مَا عَمِلُوْا وَحَاقَ
بِهِمْ مَّا كَانُوْا بِهٖ يَسْتَهْزِءُوْنَ ﴿٣٤﴾

35. The worshippers of false gods say: "If Allah had so willed, we should not have worshipped aught but Him—neither we nor our fathers,—nor should we have prescribed prohibitions other than His." So did those who went before them. But what is the mission of messengers but to preach the Clear Message?

36. For We assuredly sent amongst every People a Messenger, (with the Command), "Serve Allah, and eschew Evil": of the people were some whom Allah guided, and some on whom Error became inevitably (established). So travel through the earth, and see what was the end of those who denied (the Truth).

37. If thou art anxious for their guidance, yet Allah guideth not such as he leaves to stray, and there is none to help them.

38. They swear their strongest oath by Allah, that Allah will not raise up those who die: nay, but it is a promise (binding) on Him in truth: but most among mankind know it not.

39. (They must be raised up), in order that He may manifest to them the truth of that wherein they differ, and that the rejecters of Truth may realise that they were liars.

40. For to anything which We have willed, We but say "Be," and it is.

41. To those who leave their homes in the cause of Allah, after suffering oppression,— We will assuredly give a goodly home in this world; but truly the reward of the Hereafter will be greater. If they only realised (this)!

42. (They are) those who persevere in patience, and put their trust on their Lord.

43. And before thee We sent none but men, to whom We granted inspiration: if ye realise this not, ask of those who possess the Message.

44. (We sent them) with Clear Signs and Scriptures and We have

اور مشرک کہتے ہیں کہ اگر خدا چاہتا تو نہ ہم ہی اُس کے
سوا کسی چیز کو پُوجتے اور نہ ہمارے بڑے ہی (پُوجتے)
اور نہ اُسکے (فرمان کے) بغیر ہم کسی چیز کو حرام ٹھہراتے۔
(اے پیغمبر) اسی طرح اُن سے اگلے لوگوں نے کیا تھا۔ تو پیغمبروں کے
ذمے (خدا کے احکام کو) کھولکر سنا دینے کے سوا اور کچھ نہیں ﴿۳۵﴾
اور ہم نے ہر جماعت میں پیغمبر بھیجا کہ خدا ہی کی عبادت
کرو اور بتوں (کی پرستش) سے اجتناب کرو۔ تو ان میں
بعض ایسے ہیں جنکو خدا نے ہدایت دی اور بعض ایسے
ہیں جن پر گمراہی ثابت ہوئی سو زمین میں چل پھر کر دیکھ لو
کہ جھٹلانے والوں کا انجام کیسا ہوا ﴿۳۶﴾
اگر تم ان (کفار) کی ہدایت کیلئے للچاؤ تو جس کو خدا گمراہ کرتا
ہے اسکو وہ ہدایت نہیں دیا کرتا اور ایسے لوگوں کا کوئی مددگار بھی نہیں ہوتا ﴿۳۷﴾
اور یہ خدا کی سخت سخت قسمیں کھاتے ہیں کہ جو مر جاتا ہے خدا اُسے
(قیامت کے دن قبر سے) نہیں اُٹھائیگا۔ ہرگز نہیں۔ یہ (خدا کا)
وعدہ سچا ہے اور اُسکا پورا کرنا اُسے ضرور ہے لیکن اکثر لوگ نہیں جانتے ﴿۳۸﴾
تاکہ جن باتوں میں یہ اختلاف کرتے ہیں وہ اُن پر ظاہر کر دے
اور اسلئے کہ کافر جان لیں کہ وہ جھوٹے تھے ﴿۳۹﴾
جب ہم کسی چیز کا ارادہ کرتے ہیں تو ہماری بات یہی ہے
کہ اسکو کہہ دیتے ہیں کہ ہو جا تو وہ ہو جاتی ہے ﴿۴۰﴾
اور جن لوگوں نے ظلم سہنے کے بعد خدا کے لئے وطن چھوڑا
ہم اُنکو دنیا میں اچھا ٹھکانا دینگے اور آخرت کا اجر تو
بہت بڑا ہے۔ کاش وہ (اُسے) جانتے ﴿۴۱﴾
یعنی وہ لوگ جو صبر کرتے ہیں اور اپنے پروردگار پر بھروسا رکھتے ہیں ﴿۴۲﴾
اور ہم نے تم سے پہلے مردوں ہی کو پیغمبر بنا کر بھیجا تھا
جن کی طرف ہم وحی بھیجا کرتے تھے اگر تم لوگ نہیں جانتے
تو اہل کتاب سے پوچھ لو ﴿۴۳﴾
(اور ان پیغمبروں کو) دلیلیں اور کتابیں دے کر (بھیجا تھا)

وَقَالَ الَّذِينَ أَشْرَكُوا لَوْ شَاءَ اللَّهُ
مَا عَبَدْنَا مِنْ دُونِهِ مِنْ شَيْءٍ نَحْنُ
وَلَا آبَاؤُنَا وَلَا حَرَّمْنَا مِنْ دُونِهِ مِنْ
شَيْءٍ ۚ كَذَٰلِكَ فَعَلَ الَّذِينَ مِنْ قَبْلِهِمْ ۚ
فَهَلْ عَلَى الرُّسُلِ إِلَّا الْبَلَاغُ الْمُبِينُ ﴿٣٥﴾
وَلَقَدْ بَعَثْنَا فِي كُلِّ أُمَّةٍ رَسُولًا
أَنِ اعْبُدُوا اللَّهَ وَاجْتَنِبُوا الطَّاغُوتَ ۖ
فَمِنْهُمْ مَنْ هَدَى اللَّهُ وَمِنْهُمْ مَنْ حَقَّتْ
عَلَيْهِ الضَّلَالَةُ ۚ فَسِيرُوا فِي الْأَرْضِ
فَانْظُرُوا كَيْفَ كَانَ عَاقِبَةُ الْمُكَذِّبِينَ ﴿٣٦﴾
إِنْ تَحْرِصْ عَلَىٰ هُدَاهُمْ فَإِنَّ اللَّهَ لَا
يَهْدِي مَنْ يُضِلُّ ۖ وَمَا لَهُمْ مِنْ نَاصِرِينَ ﴿٣٧﴾
وَأَقْسَمُوا بِاللَّهِ جَهْدَ أَيْمَانِهِمْ ۙ لَا يَبْعَثُ
اللَّهُ مَنْ يَمُوتُ ۚ بَلَىٰ وَعْدًا عَلَيْهِ حَقًّا
وَلَٰكِنَّ أَكْثَرَ النَّاسِ لَا يَعْلَمُونَ ﴿٣٨﴾
لِيُبَيِّنَ لَهُمُ الَّذِي يَخْتَلِفُونَ فِيهِ وَ
لِيَعْلَمَ الَّذِينَ كَفَرُوا أَنَّهُمْ كَانُوا كَاذِبِينَ ﴿٣٩﴾
إِنَّمَا قَوْلُنَا لِشَيْءٍ إِذَا أَرَدْنَاهُ أَنْ نَقُولَ
لَهُ كُنْ فَيَكُونُ ﴿٤٠﴾ ع ۵
وَالَّذِينَ هَاجَرُوا فِي اللَّهِ مِنْ بَعْدِ
مَا ظُلِمُوا لَنُبَوِّئَنَّهُمْ فِي الدُّنْيَا حَسَنَةً ۖ
وَلَأَجْرُ الْآخِرَةِ أَكْبَرُ ۚ لَوْ كَانُوا يَعْلَمُونَ ﴿٤١﴾ وقف لازم
الَّذِينَ صَبَرُوا وَعَلَىٰ رَبِّهِمْ يَتَوَكَّلُونَ ﴿٤٢﴾
وَمَا أَرْسَلْنَا مِنْ قَبْلِكَ إِلَّا رِجَالًا
نُوحِي إِلَيْهِمْ ۚ فَاسْأَلُوا أَهْلَ الذِّكْرِ إِنْ
كُنْتُمْ لَا تَعْلَمُونَ ﴿٤٣﴾
بِالْبَيِّنَاتِ وَالزُّبُرِ ۗ وَأَنْزَلْنَا إِلَيْكَ الذِّكْرَ

لِتُبَيِّنَ لِلنَّاسِ مَا نُزِّلَ إِلَيْهِمْ وَلَعَلَّهُمْ
يَتَفَكَّرُونَ ﴿٤٤﴾

اور ہم نے تم پر بھی یہ کتاب نازل کی ہے تاکہ جو (ارشادات)
لوگوں پر نازل ہوئے ہیں وہ اُن پر ظاہر کر دو۔ اور تاکہ وہ غور کریں ﴿۴۴﴾

sent down unto thee (also) the Message; that thou mayest explain clearly to men what is sent for them, and that they may give thought.

النصف

أَفَأَمِنَ الَّذِينَ مَكَرُوا السَّيِّئَاتِ أَنْ
يَخْسِفَ اللَّهُ بِهِمُ الْأَرْضَ أَوْ يَأْتِيَهُمُ
الْعَذَابُ مِنْ حَيْثُ لَا يَشْعُرُونَ ﴿٤٥﴾

کیا جو لوگ بُری بُری چالیں چلتے ہیں اس بات سے بےخوف
ہیں کہ خدا اُنکو زمین میں دھنسا دے یا (ایسی طرف سے)
اُن پر عذاب آجائے جہاں سے اُن کو خبر ہی نہ ہو ﴿۴۵﴾

45. Do then those who devise evil (plots) feel secure that Allah will not cause the earth to swallow them up, or that the Wrath will not seize them from directions they little perceive?—

أَوْ يَأْخُذَهُمْ فِي تَقَلُّبِهِمْ فَمَا هُمْ بِمُعْجِزِينَ ﴿٤٦﴾

یا اُنکو چلتے پھرتے پکڑ لے وہ (خدا کو) عاجز نہیں کر سکتے ﴿۴۶﴾

46. Or that He may not call them to account in the midst of their goings to and fro, without a chance of their frustrating Him?—

أَوْ يَأْخُذَهُمْ عَلَىٰ تَخَوُّفٍ فَإِنَّ رَبَّكُمْ
لَرَءُوفٌ رَحِيمٌ ﴿٤٧﴾

یا جب اُن کو عذاب کا ڈر پیدا ہو گیا ہو تو اُنکو پکڑ لے بیشک
تمہارا پروردگار بہت شفقت کرنے والا اور مہربان ہے ﴿۴۷﴾

47. Or that He may not call them to account by a process of slow wastage—for thy Lord is indeed full of kindness and mercy.

أَوَلَمْ يَرَوْا إِلَىٰ مَا خَلَقَ اللَّهُ مِنْ شَيْءٍ
يَتَفَيَّأُ ظِلَالُهُ عَنِ الْيَمِينِ وَالشَّمَائِلِ
سُجَّدًا لِلَّهِ وَهُمْ دَاخِرُونَ ﴿٤٨﴾

کیا ان لوگوں نے خدا کی مخلوقات میں سے ایسی چیزیں نہیں دیکھیں
جنکے سائے دائیں سے (بائیں کو) اور بائیں سے (دائیں کو) لَوٹتے رہتے
ہیں (یعنی) خدا کے آگے عاجز ہو کر سجدے میں پڑے رہتے ہیں ﴿۴۸﴾

48. Do they not look at Allah's creation. Among things,—how their shadows turn round, from the right and the left, prostrating themselves to Allah, and that in the humblest manner?

وَلِلَّهِ يَسْجُدُ مَا فِي السَّمَاوَاتِ وَمَا فِي
الْأَرْضِ مِنْ دَابَّةٍ وَالْمَلَائِكَةُ وَهُمْ
لَا يَسْتَكْبِرُونَ ﴿٤٩﴾

اور تمام جاندار جو آسمانوں میں ہیں اور جو زمین میں ہیں
سب خدا کے آگے سجدہ کرتے ہیں اور فرشتے بھی۔
اور وہ ذرا غرور نہیں کرتے ﴿۴۹﴾

49. And to Allah doth prostrate all that is in the heavens and on earth, whether moving creatures or the angels: for none are arrogant (before their Lord).

يَخَافُونَ رَبَّهُمْ مِنْ فَوْقِهِمْ وَيَفْعَلُونَ
مَا يُؤْمَرُونَ ﴿٥٠﴾ ۩

اور اپنے پروردگار سے جو اُن کے اُوپر ہے ڈرتے ہیں۔
اور جو اُن کو ارشاد ہوتا ہے اس پر عمل کرتے ہیں ﴿۵۰﴾

السجدة ع ٦

50. They all fear their Lord, high above them, and they do all that they are commanded.

وَقَالَ اللَّهُ لَا تَتَّخِذُوا إِلَٰهَيْنِ اثْنَيْنِ
إِنَّمَا هُوَ إِلَٰهٌ وَاحِدٌ فَإِيَّايَ فَارْهَبُونِ ﴿٥١﴾

اور خدا نے فرمایا ہے کہ دو دو معبود نہ بناؤ معبود وہی
ایک ہے تو مجھی سے ڈرتے رہو ﴿۵۱﴾

51. Allah has said: "Take not (for worship two gods: for He is just One God: then fear Me (and Me alone)."

وَلَهُ مَا فِي السَّمَاوَاتِ وَالْأَرْضِ وَلَهُ
الدِّينُ وَاصِبًا أَفَغَيْرَ اللَّهِ تَتَّقُونَ ﴿٥٢﴾

اور جو کچھ آسمانوں میں اور جو کچھ زمین میں ہے سب اُسی کا ہے
اور اُسی کی عبادت لازم ہے تو تم خدا کے سوا اوروں سے کیوں ڈرتے ہو؟ ﴿۵۲﴾

52. To Him belongs whatever is in the heavens and on earth and to Him is the religion always: then will ye fear other— than Allah?

وَمَا بِكُمْ مِنْ نِعْمَةٍ فَمِنَ اللَّهِ ثُمَّ
إِذَا مَسَّكُمُ الضُّرُّ فَإِلَيْهِ
تَجْأَرُونَ ﴿٥٣﴾

اور جو نعمتیں تم کو میسر ہیں سب خدا کی طرف سے ہیں۔ پھر
جب تم کو کوئی تکلیف پہنچتی ہے تو اُسی کے آگے
چلاتے ہو ﴿۵۳﴾

53. And ye have no good thing but is from Allah: and moreover, when ye are touched by distress, unto Him ye cry with groans,

ثُمَّ إِذَا كَشَفَ الضُّرَّ عَنْكُمْ إِذَا
فَرِيقٌ مِنْكُمْ بِرَبِّهِمْ يُشْرِكُونَ ﴿٥٤﴾

پھر جب وہ تم سے تکلیف کو دور کر دیتا ہے تو کچھ لوگ
تم میں سے خدا کے ساتھ شریک کرنے لگتے ہیں ﴿۵۴﴾

54. Yet, when He removes the distress from you, behold! Some of you turn to other gods to join with their Lord—

لِيَكْفُرُوا بِمَا آتَيْنَاهُمْ فَتَمَتَّعُوا فَسَوْفَ
تَعْلَمُونَ ﴿٥٥﴾

تاکہ جو (نعمتیں) ہمنے اُنکو عطا فرمائی ہیں اُنکی ناشکری کریں تو (مشرکو) دنیا
میں فائدے اٹھا لو عنقریب تمکو (اسکا انجام) معلوم ہو جائیگا ﴿۵۵﴾

55. To show their ingratitude for the favours We have bestowed on them! Then enjoy (your brief day); but soon will ye know (your folly)!

56. And they (even) assign, to things they do not know, a portion out of that which We have bestowed for their sustenance! By Allah, ye shall certainly be called to account for your false inventions.
57. And they assign daughters for Allah!— Glory be to Him!— and for themselves what they desire!

اور ہمارے دیئے ہوئے مال میں سے ایسی چیزوں کا حصہ مقرر
کرتے ہیں جن کو جانتے ہی نہیں (کافرو) خدا کی قسم کہ جو تم
افترا کرتے ہو اس کی تم سے ضرور پرسش ہوگی ﴿۵۶﴾
اور یہ لوگ خدا کے لئے تو بیٹیاں تجویز کرتے ہیں (اور) وہ اُن
سے پاک ہے اور اپنے لئے (بیٹے) جو مرغوب (و دلپسند) ہیں ﴿۵۷﴾

وَيَجْعَلُوْنَ لِمَا لَا يَعْلَمُوْنَ نَصِيْبًا
مِّمَّا رَزَقْنٰهُمْ ؕ تَاللّٰهِ لَتُسْـَٔلُنَّ عَمَّا
كُنْتُمْ تَفْتَرُوْنَ ﴿٥٦﴾
وَيَجْعَلُوْنَ لِلّٰهِ الْبَنٰتِ سُبْحٰنَهٗ ۙ
وَلَهُمْ مَّا يَشْتَهُوْنَ ﴿٥٧﴾

58. When news is brought to one of them, of (the birth of) a female (child), his face darkens, and he is filled with inward grief!
59. With shame does he hide himself from his people, because of the bad news he has had! Shall he retain it on (sufferance and) Contempt, or bury it in the dust? Ah! what an evil (choice) they decide on?
60. To those who believe not in the Hereafter, applies the similitude of evil: to Allah applies the highest similitude: for He is the Exalted in Power, full of Wisdom.

حالانکہ جب اُنہیں سے کسی کو بیٹی (کے پیدا ہونے) کی خبر ملتی ہے تو اسکا
منہ (غم کے سبب) کالا پڑ جاتا ہے اور (اسکے دل کو دیکھو تو) وہ اندوہناک ہو جاتا ہے ﴿۵۸﴾
اور اس خبر بد سے (جو وہ سنتا ہے) لوگوں سے چھپتا
پھرتا ہے (اور) سوچتا ہے۔ کہ آیا ذلت برداشت
کرکے لڑکی کو زندہ رہنے دے یا زمین میں گاڑ دے
دیکھو یہ جو تجویز کرتے ہیں بہت بری ہے ﴿۵۹﴾
جو لوگ آخرت پر ایمان نہیں رکھتے انہی کے لئے
بری باتیں (شایاں) ہیں اور خدا کو صفت اعلیٰ (زیب
دیتی ہے) اور وہ غالب حکمت والا ہے ﴿۶۰﴾

وَاِذَا بُشِّرَ اَحَدُهُمْ بِالْاُنْثٰى ظَلَّ
وَجْهُهٗ مُسْوَدًّا وَّهُوَ كَظِيْمٌ ﴿٥٨﴾ ۚ
يَتَوَارٰى مِنَ الْقَوْمِ مِنْ سُوْٓءِ مَا
بُشِّرَ بِهٖ ؕ اَيُمْسِكُهٗ عَلٰى هُوْنٍ اَمْ
يَدُسُّهٗ فِى التُّرَابِ ؕ اَلَا سَآءَ مَا
يَحْكُمُوْنَ ﴿٥٩﴾
لِلَّذِيْنَ لَا يُؤْمِنُوْنَ بِالْاٰخِرَةِ مَثَلُ
السَّوْءِ ۚ وَلِلّٰهِ الْمَثَلُ الْاَعْلٰى ؕ وَهُوَ
الْعَزِيْزُ الْحَكِيْمُ ﴿٦٠﴾ ع

61. If Allah were to punish men for their wrong-doing, he would not leave, on the (earth), a single living creature: but He gives them respite for a stated Term: when their Term expires, they would not be able to delay (the punishment) for a single hour, just as they would not be able to anticipate it (for a single hour).
62. They attribute to Allah what they hate (for themselves), and their tongues assert the falsehood that the reward most fair is for themselves: without doubt for them is the Fire, and they will be the first to be hastened on into it!

اور اگر خدا لوگوں کو ان کے ظلم کے سبب پکڑنے لگے
تو ایک جاندار کو زمین پر نہ چھوڑے۔ لیکن اُن کو ایک
وقت مقرر تک مہلت دیئے جاتا ہے۔ جب وہ وقت
آجاتا ہے تو ایک گھڑی نہ پیچھے رہ سکتے ہیں نہ آگے
بڑھ سکتے ہیں ﴿۶۱﴾
اور یہ خدا کے لئے ایسی چیزیں تجویز کرتے ہیں جن کو
خود ناپسند کرتے ہیں اور زبان سے جھوٹ بکے جاتے ہیں کہ ان کو
(قیامت کے دن) بھلائی (یعنی نجات) ہوگی۔ کچھ شک نہیں کہ انکے لئے
(دوزخ کی) آگ (تیار) ہے اور یہ (دوزخ میں) سب سے آگے بھیجے جائینگے ﴿۶۲﴾

وَلَوْ يُؤَاخِذُ اللّٰهُ النَّاسَ بِظُلْمِهِمْ
مَّا تَرَكَ عَلَيْهَا مِنْ دَآبَّةٍ وَّلٰكِنْ
يُّؤَخِّرُهُمْ اِلٰٓى اَجَلٍ مُّسَمًّى ۚ فَاِذَا
جَآءَ اَجَلُهُمْ لَا يَسْتَاْخِرُوْنَ سَاعَةً
وَّلَا يَسْتَقْدِمُوْنَ ﴿٦١﴾
وَيَجْعَلُوْنَ لِلّٰهِ مَا يَكْرَهُوْنَ وَتَصِفُ
اَلْسِنَتُهُمُ الْكَذِبَ اَنَّ لَهُمُ الْحُسْنٰى ؕ
لَا جَرَمَ اَنَّ لَهُمُ النَّارَ وَاَنَّهُمْ
مُّفْرَطُوْنَ ﴿٦٢﴾

63. By Allah, We (also) sent (our prophets) to Peoples before thee; but Satan Madm, (to the wicked), their own acts seem alluring: he is their patron today, so but they shall have a most grievous chastisement.
64. And We sent down the Book to thee so that that thou shouldst

خدا کی قسم ہم نے تم سے پہلی امتوں کی طرف بھی پیغمبر بھیجے
تو شیطان نے اُن کے کردار (ناشائستہ) اُن کو آراستہ کر دکھائے
تو آج بھی وہی اُن کا دوست ہے اور اُنکے لئے عذاب الیم ہے ﴿۶۳﴾
اور ہم نے جو تم پر کتاب نازل کی ہے تو اسکے لئے کہ جس

تَاللّٰهِ لَقَدْ اَرْسَلْنَآ اِلٰٓى اُمَمٍ مِّنْ
قَبْلِكَ فَزَيَّنَ لَهُمُ الشَّيْطٰنُ اَعْمَالَهُمْ
فَهُوَ وَلِيُّهُمُ الْيَوْمَ وَلَهُمْ عَذَابٌ اَلِيْمٌ ﴿٦٣﴾
وَمَآ اَنْزَلْنَا عَلَيْكَ الْكِتٰبَ اِلَّا لِتُبَيِّنَ

make clear to them those things in which they differ, and that it should be a guide and a mercy to those who believe.

65. And Allah sends down rain from the skies, and gives therewith life to the earth after its death: verily in this is a sign for those who listen.

66. And verily in cattle (too) will ye find an instructive Sign. From what is within their bodies, between excretions and blood, we produce, for your drink, milk, pure and agreeable to those who drink it.

67. And from the fruit of the date-palm and the vine, ye get out strong drink, and wholesome food: behold, in this also is a sign for those who are wise.

68. And thy Lord taught the Bee to build its cells in hills, on trees, and in (men's) habitations;

69. Then to eat of all the produce (of the earth), and follow the ways of Thy Lord made smooth: there issues from within their bodies a drink of varying colours, wherein is healing for men: verily in this is a Sign for those who give thought.

70. It is Allah Who creates you and takes your souls at death; and of you there are some who are sent back to a feeble age, so that they know nothing after having known (much): for Allah is All-Knowing, All-Powerful.

71. Allah has bestowed His gifts of sustenance more freely on some of you than on others: those more favoured are not going to throw back their gifts to those whom their right hands possess, so as to be equal in that respect. Will they then deny the favours of Allah?

امر میں ان لوگوں کو اختلاف ہے تم اس کا فیصلہ کر دو۔
اور (یہ) مومنوں کے لئے ہدایت اور رحمت ہے ﴿۶۴﴾
اور خدا ہی نے آسمان سے پانی برسایا پھر اُس سے زمین
کو اسکے مرنے کے بعد زندہ کیا بے شک اس میں
سننے والوں کے لئے نشانی ہے ﴿۶۵﴾
اور تمہارے لئے چارپایوں میں بھی (مقام) عبرت (و غور) ہے
کہ اُن کے پیٹوں میں جو گوبر اور لہو ہے اس سے ہم تم کو
خالص دودھ پلاتے ہیں جو پینے والوں کیلئے خوشگوار ہے ﴿۶۶﴾
اور کھجور اور انگور کے میووں سے بھی (تم پینے کی چیزیں
تیار کرتے ہو) کہ ان سے شراب بناتے ہو[167] اور عمدہ رزق (کھاتے
ہو) جو لوگ سمجھ رکھتے ہیں انکے لئے ان (چیزوں) میں (قدرت خدا کی) نشانی ہے ﴿۶۷﴾
اور تمہارے پروردگار نے شہد کی مکھیوں کو ارشاد فرمایا
کہ پہاڑوں میں اور درختوں میں اور (اُونچی اُونچی)[168]
چھتریوں میں جو لوگ بناتے ہیں گھر بنا ﴿۶۸﴾
اور ہر قسم کے میوے کھا۔ اور اپنے پروردگار کے صاف
رستوں پر چلی جا۔ اس کے پیٹ سے پینے کی چیز نکلتی ہے
جس کے مختلف رنگ ہوتے ہیں اس میں لوگوں (کے کئی
امراض) کی شفا ہے بیشک سوچنے والوں کے لئے اس
میں بھی نشانی ہے ﴿۶۹﴾
اور خدا ہی نے تم کو پیدا کیا۔ پھر وہی تم کو موت دیتا ہے
اور تم میں بعض ایسے ہوتے ہیں کہ نہایت خراب عمر کو پہنچ
جاتے ہیں اور (بہت کچھ) جاننے کے بعد ہر چیز سے بے علم ہو جاتے
ہیں بیشک خدا (سب کچھ) جاننے والا (اور) قدرت والا ہے ﴿۷۰﴾
اور خدا نے رزق (و دولت) میں بعض کو بعض پر فضیلت
دی ہے تو جن لوگوں کو فضیلت دی ہے وہ اپنا رزق اپنے
مملوکوں کو تو دے ڈالنے والے ہیں نہیں کہ سب اسمیں برابر
ہو جائیں تو کیا یہ لوگ نعمت الٰہی کے منکر ہیں؟ ﴿۷۱﴾

لَهُمُ الَّذِي اخْتَلَفُوا فِيهِ ۙ وَهُدًى
وَّرَحْمَةً لِّقَوْمٍ يُّؤْمِنُونَ ﴿٦٤﴾
وَاللّٰهُ أَنْزَلَ مِنَ السَّمَآءِ مَآءً فَأَحْيَا
بِهِ الْأَرْضَ بَعْدَ مَوْتِهَا ۗ إِنَّ فِي ذٰلِكَ
لَاٰيَةً لِّقَوْمٍ يَّسْمَعُونَ ﴿٦٥﴾
وَإِنَّ لَكُمْ فِي الْأَنْعَامِ لَعِبْرَةً ۗ نُسْقِيكُمْ
مِّمَّا فِي بُطُونِهِ مِنْ بَيْنِ فَرْثٍ وَّدَمٍ
لَّبَنًا خَالِصًا سَآئِغًا لِّلشّٰرِبِينَ ﴿٦٦﴾
وَمِنْ ثَمَرٰتِ النَّخِيلِ وَالْأَعْنَابِ
تَتَّخِذُونَ مِنْهُ سَكَرًا وَّرِزْقًا حَسَنًا ۗ
إِنَّ فِي ذٰلِكَ لَاٰيَةً لِّقَوْمٍ يَّعْقِلُونَ ﴿٦٧﴾
وَأَوْحٰى رَبُّكَ إِلَى النَّحْلِ أَنِ اتَّخِذِي
مِنَ الْجِبَالِ بُيُوتًا وَّمِنَ الشَّجَرِ
وَمِمَّا يَعْرِشُونَ ﴿٦٨﴾
ثُمَّ كُلِي مِنْ كُلِّ الثَّمَرٰتِ فَاسْلُكِي
سُبُلَ رَبِّكِ ذُلُلًا ۗ يَخْرُجُ مِنْ بُطُونِهَا
شَرَابٌ مُّخْتَلِفٌ أَلْوَانُهُ فِيهِ شِفَآءٌ
لِّلنَّاسِ ۗ إِنَّ فِي ذٰلِكَ لَاٰيَةً لِّقَوْمٍ
يَّتَفَكَّرُونَ ﴿٦٩﴾
وَاللّٰهُ خَلَقَكُمْ ثُمَّ يَتَوَفّٰىكُمْ ۚ وَمِنْكُمْ
مَّنْ يُّرَدُّ إِلٰى أَرْذَلِ الْعُمُرِ لِكَيْ لَا
يَعْلَمَ بَعْدَ عِلْمٍ شَيْـًٔا ۗ إِنَّ اللّٰهَ عَلِيمٌ
قَدِيرٌ ﴿٧٠﴾
وَاللّٰهُ فَضَّلَ بَعْضَكُمْ عَلٰى بَعْضٍ فِي
الرِّزْقِ ۚ فَمَا الَّذِينَ فُضِّلُوا بِرَآدِّي
رِزْقِهِمْ عَلٰى مَا مَلَكَتْ أَيْمَانُهُمْ فَهُمْ
فِيهِ سَوَآءٌ ۗ أَفَبِنِعْمَةِ اللّٰهِ يَجْحَدُونَ ﴿٧١﴾

72. And Allah has made for you mates of your own nature, and made for you, out of them, sons and daughters and grandchildren, and provided for you sustenance of the best: will they then believe in vain things, and be ungrateful for Allah's favours?—

اور خدا ہی نے تم میں سے تمہارے لئے عورتیں پیدا کیں
اور عورتوں سے تمہارے بیٹے اور پوتے پیدا کئے اور کھانے
کو تمہیں پاکیزہ چیزیں دیں تو کیا بے اصل چیزوں پر
اعتقاد رکھتے اور خدا کی نعمتوں سے انکار کرتے
ہیں؟ ﴿۷۲﴾

وَاللّٰهُ جَعَلَ لَكُمْ مِّنْ اَنْفُسِكُمْ
اَزْوَاجًا وَّجَعَلَ لَكُمْ مِّنْ اَزْوَاجِكُمْ
بَنِيْنَ وَحَفَدَةً وَّرَزَقَكُمْ مِّنَ
الطَّيِّبٰتِ ؕ اَفَبِالْبَاطِلِ يُؤْمِنُوْنَ وَ
بِنِعْمَتِ اللّٰهِ هُمْ يَكْفُرُوْنَ ﴿۷۲﴾

73. And worship others than Allah,— such as have no power of providing them, for sustenance, with anything in heavens or earth, and cannot possibly have such power?

اور خدا کے سوا ایسوں کو پوجتے ہیں جو اُن کو آسمانوں
اور زمین میں روزی دینے کا ذرا بھی اختیار نہیں رکھتے
اور نہ (کسی اور طرح کا) مقدور رکھتے ہیں ﴿۷۳﴾

وَيَعْبُدُوْنَ مِنْ دُوْنِ اللّٰهِ مَا لَا
يَمْلِكُ لَهُمْ رِزْقًا مِّنَ السَّمٰوٰتِ
وَالْاَرْضِ شَيْـًٔا وَّلَا يَسْتَطِيْعُوْنَ ﴿۷۳﴾

74. Invent not similitudes for Allah: for Allah knoweth, and ye know not.

تو (لوگو) خدا کے بارے میں (غلط) مثالیں نہ بناؤ (صحیح
مثالوں کا طریقہ) خدا ہی جانتا ہے اور تم نہیں جانتے ﴿۷۴﴾

فَلَا تَضْرِبُوْا لِلّٰهِ الْاَمْثَالَ ؕ اِنَّ اللّٰهَ
يَعْلَمُ وَاَنْتُمْ لَا تَعْلَمُوْنَ ﴿۷۴﴾

75. Allah sets forth the Parable (of two men: one) a slave under the dominion of another; he has no power of any sort; and (the other) a man on whom We have bestowed goodly favours from Ourselves, and he spends thereof (freely), privately and publicly: are the two equal? (By no means;) praise be to Allah. But most of them know not.

خدا ایک اور مثال بیان فرماتا ہے کہ ایک غلام ہے جو (بالکل) دوسرے
کے اختیار میں ہے اور کسی چیز پر قدرت نہیں رکھتا اور ایک ایسا شخص ہے
جس کو ہم نے اپنے ہاں سے (بہت سا) مال طیب عطا فرمایا ہے اور وہ اس میں
سے (رات دن) پوشیدہ اور ظاہر خرچ کرتا رہتا ہے تو کیا یہ دونوں شخص
برابر ہیں؟ (ہرگز نہیں) الحمد للہ لیکن ان میں سے اکثر لوگ نہیں سمجھ رکھتے ﴿۷۵﴾

ضَرَبَ اللّٰهُ مَثَلًا عَبْدًا مَّمْلُوْكًا لَّا
يَقْدِرُ عَلٰى شَيْءٍ وَّمَنْ رَّزَقْنٰهُ مِنَّا
رِزْقًا حَسَنًا فَهُوَ يُنْفِقُ مِنْهُ سِرًّا
وَّجَهْرًا ؕ هَلْ يَسْتَوٗنَ ؕ اَلْحَمْدُ لِلّٰهِ ؕ
بَلْ اَكْثَرُهُمْ لَا يَعْلَمُوْنَ ﴿۷۵﴾

76. Allah sets forth (another) parable of two men: one of them dumb, with no power of any sort; a wearisome burden is he to his master; whichever way he directs him, he brings no good: is such a man equal with one who commands justice, and is on a Straight Way?

اور خدا ایک اور مثال بیان فرماتا ہے کہ دو آدمی ہیں ایک
اُن میں سے گونگا اور دوسرے کی ملک ہے (اور بے اختیار و ناتواں)
کہ کسی چیز پر قدرت نہیں رکھتا۔ اور اپنے مالک کو دو بھر ہو رہا ہے
وہ جہاں اُسے بھیجتا ہے (خیر سے کبھی) بھلائی نہیں لاتا کیا ایسا
(گونگا بہرا) اور وہ شخص جو (سنتا بولتا اور) لوگوں کو انصاف
کرنے کا حکم دیتا ہے اور خود سیدھے رستے پر چل رہا ہے دونوں برابر ہیں؟ ﴿۷۶﴾

وَضَرَبَ اللّٰهُ مَثَلًا رَّجُلَيْنِ اَحَدُهُمَاۤ
اَبْكَمُ لَا يَقْدِرُ عَلٰى شَيْءٍ وَّهُوَ
كَلٌّ عَلٰى مَوْلٰىهُ ۙ اَيْنَمَا يُوَجِّهْهُّ
لَا يَاْتِ بِخَيْرٍ ؕ هَلْ يَسْتَوِيْ هُوَ ۙ
وَمَنْ يَّاْمُرُ بِالْعَدْلِ ۙ وَهُوَ عَلٰى
صِرَاطٍ مُّسْتَقِيْمٍ ﴿۷۶﴾ ع

77. To Allah belongeth the Unseen of the heavens and the earth. And the matter of the Hour (of Judgement) is as the twinkling of an eye, or even quicker: for Allah hath power over all things.

اور آسمانوں اور زمین کا علم خدا ہی کو ہے اور (خدا کے نزدیک)
قیامت کا آنا یوں ہے جیسے آنکھ کا جھپکنا بلکہ اس سے بھی جلد تر
کچھ شک نہیں کہ خدا ہر چیز پر قادر ہے ﴿۷۷﴾

وَلِلّٰهِ غَيْبُ السَّمٰوٰتِ وَالْاَرْضِ ؕ وَمَاۤ
اَمْرُ السَّاعَةِ اِلَّا كَلَمْحِ الْبَصَرِ اَوْ هُوَ
اَقْرَبُ ؕ اِنَّ اللّٰهَ عَلٰى كُلِّ شَيْءٍ قَدِيْرٌ ﴿۷۷﴾

78. It is He Who brought you forth from the wombs of your mothers when ye knew nothing; and He gave you hearing and sight and intelligence and affections: that ye

اور خدا ہی نے تم کو تمہاری ماؤں کے شکم سے پیدا کیا
کہ تم کچھ نہیں جانتے تھے۔ اور اس نے تم کو کان اور
آنکھیں اور دل (اور ان کے علاوہ اور اعضا) بخشے تاکہ

وَاللّٰهُ اَخْرَجَكُمْ مِّنْ بُطُوْنِ اُمَّهٰتِكُمْ
لَا تَعْلَمُوْنَ شَيْـًٔا ۙ وَّجَعَلَ لَكُمُ
السَّمْعَ وَالْاَبْصَارَ وَالْاَفْـِٕدَةَ ۙ لَعَلَّكُمْ

may give thanks (to Allah).

79. Do they not look at the birds, held poised in the midst of (the air and) the sky? Nothing holds them up but (the power of) Allah. Verily in this are Signs for those who believe.

80. It is Allah Who made your habitations homes of rest and quiet for you; and made for you, out of the skins of animals, (tents for) dwellings, which ye find so light (and handy) when ye travel and when ye stop (in your travels), and out of their wool, and their soft fibres (between wool and hair), and their, rich stuff and articles of convenience (to serve you) for a time

81. It is Allah Who made out of the things He created, some things to give you shade; of the hills He made some for your shelter; He made you garments to protect you from heat, and coats of mail to protect you from your (mutual) violence. Thus does He complete his favours on you, that ye may surrender to His Will (in Islām).

82. But if they turn away, thy duty is only to preach the Clear Message.

83. They recognise the favours of Allah; then they deny them; and most of them are (creatures) ungrateful.

84. On the Day We shall raise from all Peoples a Witness; then will no excuse be accepted from Unbelievers, nor will they be allowed to make amends.

85. When the wrong-doers (actually) see the Chastisement then will it in no way be mitigated, nor will they then receive respite.

86. When those who gave partners to Allah will see their "partners", they will say: "Our Lord! These are our 'partners', those whom we used to invoke besides Thee," But they will throw their word at them (and say): "Indeed ye are liars!'

87. That day shall they (openly) show (their) submission to Allah;

تم شکر کرو ﴿۷۸﴾
کیا ان لوگوں نے پرندوں کو نہیں دیکھا کہ آسمان کی ہوا میں
گھرے ہوئے (اُڑتے رہتے) ہیں۔ ان کو خدا ہی تھامے رکھتا ہے
ایمان والوں کیلئے اس میں (بہت سی) نشانیاں ہیں ﴿۷۹﴾
اور خدا ہی نے تمہارے لئے گھروں کو رہنے کی جگہ بنایا اور
اُسی نے چوپایوں کی کھالوں سے تمہارے لئے ڈیرے بنائے
جنکو تم سبک دیکھ کر سفر اور حضر میں کام میں لاتے ہو اور اُن کی
اُون اور پشم اور بالوں سے تم اسباب اور برتنے کی چیزیں (بناتے
ہو جو) مدت تک (کام دیتی ہیں) ﴿۸۰﴾
اور خدا ہی نے تمہارے (آرام کے) لئے اپنی پیدا کی ہوئی
چیزوں کے سائے بنائے اور پہاڑوں میں غاریں بنائیں اور
کُرتے بنائے جو تم کو گرمی سے بچائیں۔ اور (ایسے) کُرتے (بھی)
جو تم کو (اسلحہ) جنگ (کے ضرر) سے محفوظ رکھیں۔ اسی طرح خدا
اپنا احسان تم پر پورا کرتا ہے تاکہ تم فرمانبردار بنو ﴿۸۱﴾
اور اگر یہ لوگ اعراض کریں تو (اے پیغمبر) تمہارا کام فقط کھول کر سنا دینا ہے ﴿۸۲﴾
یہ خدا کی نعمتوں سے واقف ہیں مگر (واقف ہو کر) اُن سے
انکار کرتے ہیں۔ اور یہ اکثر ناشکرے ہیں ﴿۸۳﴾
اور جس دن ہم ہر اُمت میں سے گواہ (یعنی پیغمبر) کھڑا
کریں گے تو نہ تو کفار کو (بولنے کی) اجازت ملے گی اور نہ
اُن کے عذر قبول کئے جائیں گے ﴿۸۴﴾
اور جب ظالم لوگ عذاب دیکھ لینگے تو پھر نہ تو اُن کے عذاب ہی
میں تخفیف کی جائے گی اور نہ اُن کو مہلت ہی دی جائیگی ﴿۸۵﴾
اور جب مشرک اپنے (بنائے ہوئے) شریکوں کو دیکھیں گے تو
کہیں گے کہ پروردگار یہ وہی ہمارے شریک ہیں جنکو ہم تیرے سوا
پکارا کرتے تھے۔ تو وہ (اُن کے کلام کو مسترد کر دیں گے اور
اُن سے کہیں گے کہ تم تو جھوٹے ہو ﴿۸۶﴾
اور اُس دن خدا کے سامنے سرنگوں ہو جائیں گے اور جو طوفان

تَشْكُرُونَ ﴿٧٨﴾
أَلَمْ يَرَوْا إِلَى الطَّيْرِ مُسَخَّرَاتٍ فِي جَوِّ
السَّمَاءِ مَا يُمْسِكُهُنَّ إِلَّا اللَّهُ ۗ إِنَّ فِي
ذَٰلِكَ لَآيَاتٍ لِقَوْمٍ يُؤْمِنُونَ ﴿٧٩﴾
وَاللَّهُ جَعَلَ لَكُمْ مِنْ بُيُوتِكُمْ سَكَنًا
وَجَعَلَ لَكُمْ مِنْ جُلُودِ الْأَنْعَامِ
بُيُوتًا تَسْتَخِفُّونَهَا يَوْمَ ظَعْنِكُمْ وَيَوْمَ
إِقَامَتِكُمْ ۙ وَمِنْ أَصْوَافِهَا وَأَوْبَارِهَا
وَأَشْعَارِهَا أَثَاثًا وَمَتَاعًا إِلَىٰ حِينٍ ﴿٨٠﴾
وَاللَّهُ جَعَلَ لَكُمْ مِمَّا خَلَقَ ظِلَالًا
وَجَعَلَ لَكُمْ مِنَ الْجِبَالِ أَكْنَانًا وَ
جَعَلَ لَكُمْ سَرَابِيلَ تَقِيكُمُ الْحَرَّ وَ
سَرَابِيلَ تَقِيكُمْ بَأْسَكُمْ ۚ كَذَٰلِكَ يُتِمُّ
نِعْمَتَهُ عَلَيْكُمْ لَعَلَّكُمْ تُسْلِمُونَ ﴿٨١﴾
فَإِنْ تَوَلَّوْا فَإِنَّمَا عَلَيْكَ الْبَلَاغُ الْمُبِينُ ﴿٨٢﴾
يَعْرِفُونَ نِعْمَتَ اللَّهِ ثُمَّ يُنْكِرُونَهَا
وَأَكْثَرُهُمُ الْكَافِرُونَ ﴿٨٣﴾
وَيَوْمَ نَبْعَثُ مِنْ كُلِّ أُمَّةٍ شَهِيدًا
ثُمَّ لَا يُؤْذَنُ لِلَّذِينَ كَفَرُوا وَلَا هُمْ
يُسْتَعْتَبُونَ ﴿٨٤﴾
وَإِذَا رَأَى الَّذِينَ ظَلَمُوا الْعَذَابَ فَلَا
يُخَفَّفُ عَنْهُمْ وَلَا هُمْ يُنْظَرُونَ ﴿٨٥﴾
وَإِذَا رَأَى الَّذِينَ أَشْرَكُوا شُرَكَاءَهُمْ
قَالُوا رَبَّنَا هَٰؤُلَاءِ شُرَكَاؤُنَا الَّذِينَ
كُنَّا نَدْعُو مِنْ دُونِكَ ۖ فَأَلْقَوْا إِلَيْهِمُ
الْقَوْلَ إِنَّكُمْ لَكَاذِبُونَ ﴿٨٦﴾
وَأَلْقَوْا إِلَى اللَّهِ يَوْمَئِذٍ السَّلَمَ ۖ وَضَلَّ

and all their inventions shall leave them in the lurch.

وہ باندھا کرتے تھے سب اُن سے جاتا رہے گا (۸۷)

عَنْهُمْ مَّا كَانُوْا يَفْتَرُوْنَ (۸۷)

88. Those who reject Allah and hinder (men) from the Path of Allah—for them will We add Chastisement to Chastisement; for that they used to spread mischief.

جن لوگوں نے کفر کیا اور (لوگوں کو) خدا کے رستے سے روکا
ہم اُن کو عذاب پر عذاب دیں گے۔ اس لئے کہ شرارت
کیا کرتے تھے (۸۸)

اَلَّذِيْنَ كَفَرُوْا وَصَدُّوْا عَنْ سَبِيْلِ
اللّٰهِ زِدْنٰهُمْ عَذَابًا فَوْقَ الْعَذَابِ
بِمَا كَانُوْا يُفْسِدُوْنَ (۸۸)

89. On the day We shall raise from all Peoples a witness against them, from amongst themselves: and We shall bring thee as a witness against these (thy people): and We have sent down to thee the Book explaining all things, a Guide, a Mercy and Glad Tidings to Muslims.

اور (اُس دن کو یاد کرو) جس دن ہم ہر اُمت میں
سے خود اُن پر گواہ کھڑے کریں گے۔ اور (اے پیغمبر)
تم کو ان لوگوں پر گواہ لائیں گے۔ اور ہم نے تم پر
(ایسی) کتاب نازل کی ہے کہ (اسمیں) ہر چیز کا بیان (مفصل)
ہے اور مسلمانوں کیلئے ہدایت اور رحمت اور بشارت ہے (۸۹)

وَيَوْمَ نَبْعَثُ فِيْ كُلِّ اُمَّةٍ شَهِيْدًا عَلَيْهِمْ
مِّنْ اَنْفُسِهِمْ وَجِئْنَا بِكَ شَهِيْدًا عَلٰى
هٰٓؤُلَآءِ ۚ وَنَزَّلْنَا عَلَيْكَ الْكِتٰبَ تِبْيَانًا
لِّكُلِّ شَيْءٍ وَّهُدًى وَّرَحْمَةً وَّبُشْرٰى
ع ١٢ ١٨ لِلْمُسْلِمِيْنَ (۸۹)

90. Allah commands justice, the doing of good, and giving to kith and kin, and He forbids all indecent deeds, and evil and rebellion: He instructs you, that ye may receive admonition.

خدا تم کو انصاف اور احسان کرنے اور رشتہ داروں کو
(خرچ سے مدد) دینے کا حکم دیتا ہے۔ اور بے حیائی اور
نامعقول کاموں سے اور سرکشی سے منع کرتا ہے (اور)
تمہیں نصیحت کرتا ہے تاکہ تم یاد رکھو (۹۰)

اِنَّ اللّٰهَ يَاْمُرُ بِالْعَدْلِ وَالْاِحْسَانِ
وَاِيْتَآئِ ذِي الْقُرْبٰى وَيَنْهٰى عَنِ
الْفَحْشَآءِ وَالْمُنْكَرِ وَالْبَغْيِ ۚ يَعِظُكُمْ
لَعَلَّكُمْ تَذَكَّرُوْنَ (۹۰)

91. Fulfil the Covenant of Allah when ye have entered into it, and break not your oaths after ye have confirmed them; indeed ye have made Allah your surety; for Allah knoweth all that ye do.

اور جب خدا سے عہد (واثق) کرو تو اُس کو پورا کرو اور جب
پکی قسمیں کھاؤ تو اُن کو مت توڑو کہ تم خدا کو اپنا ضامن
مقرر کر چکے ہو اور جو کچھ تم کرتے ہو خدا اس
کو جانتا ہے (۹۱)

وَاَوْفُوْا بِعَهْدِ اللّٰهِ اِذَا عٰهَدْتُّمْ
وَلَا تَنْقُضُوا الْاَيْمَانَ بَعْدَ تَوْكِيْدِهَا
وَقَدْ جَعَلْتُمُ اللّٰهَ عَلَيْكُمْ كَفِيْلًا ۚ
اِنَّ اللّٰهَ يَعْلَمُ مَا تَفْعَلُوْنَ (۹۱)

92. And be not like a woman who breaks into untwisted strands the yarn which she has spun, after it has become strong. Using your oaths to deceive one another, lest one party should be more numerous than another: for Allah will test you by this; and on the Day of Judgment He will certainly make clear to you (the truth of) that wherein ye disagree.

اور اُس عورت کی طرح نہ ہونا جس نے محنت سے تو سُوت
کاتا پھر اس کو توڑ کر ٹکڑے ٹکڑے کر ڈالا کہ تم اپنی قسموں
کو آپس میں اس بات کا ذریعہ بنانے لگو کہ ایک گروہ
دوسرے گروہ سے زیادہ غالب رہے۔ بات یہ ہے
کہ خدا تمہیں اس سے آزماتا ہے اور جن باتوں میں تم
اختلاف کرتے ہو قیامت کو اُس کی حقیقت تم پر ظاہر کر دیگا (۹۲)

وَلَا تَكُوْنُوْا كَالَّتِيْ نَقَضَتْ غَزْلَهَا
مِنْ بَعْدِ قُوَّةٍ اَنْكَاثًا ۭ تَتَّخِذُوْنَ
اَيْمَانَكُمْ دَخَلًا بَيْنَكُمْ اَنْ تَكُوْنَ
اُمَّةٌ هِيَ اَرْبٰى مِنْ اُمَّةٍ ۭ اِنَّمَا يَبْلُوْكُمُ
اللّٰهُ بِهٖ ۭ وَلَيُبَيِّنَنَّ لَكُمْ يَوْمَ الْقِيٰمَةِ
مَا كُنْتُمْ فِيْهِ تَخْتَلِفُوْنَ (۹۲)

93. If Allah so willed, He could make you all one People: but He leaves straying whom He pleases, and He guides whom He pleases: but ye shall certainly be called to account for all your actions.

اور اگر خدا چاہتا تو تم (سب) کو ایک ہی جماعت بنا دیتا
لیکن وہ جسے چاہتا ہے گمراہ کرتا ہے اور جسے چاہتا ہے ہدایت دیتا ہے اور
جو عمل تم کرتے ہو (اُس دن) اُن کے بارے میں تم سے ضرور پوچھا جائیگا (۹۳)

وَلَوْ شَآءَ اللّٰهُ لَجَعَلَكُمْ اُمَّةً وَّاحِدَةً
وَّلٰكِنْ يُّضِلُّ مَنْ يَّشَآءُ وَيَهْدِيْ مَنْ
يَّشَآءُ ۭ وَلَتُسْـَٔلُنَّ عَمَّا كُنْتُمْ تَعْمَلُوْنَ (۹۳)

94. And take not your oaths, to practise deception between

اور اپنی قسموں کو آپس میں اس بات کا ذریعہ نہ بناؤ کہ (لوگوں

وَلَا تَتَّخِذُوْٓا اَيْمَانَكُمْ دَخَلًا بَيْنَكُمْ

yourselves. With the result that someone's foot may slip after it was firmly planted, and ye may have to taste the evil (consequences) of having hindered (men) from the Path of Allah and a mighty Wrath descend on you.

95. Nor sell the Covenant of Allah for a miserable price: for with Allah is (a prize) far better for you, if ye only knew.

96. What is with you must vanish: what is with Allah will endure. And We will certainly bestow, on those who patiently persevere, their reward according to the best of their actions.

97. Whoever works righteousness, man or woman, and has Faith, verily, to him will We give a life that is good and pure, and We will bestow on such their reward according to the best of their actions.

98. When thou dost read the Qur'an, seek Allah's protection from Satan the Rejected One.

99. No authority has he over those who believe and put their trust in their Lord.

100. His authority is over those only, who take him as patron and who join partners with Allah.

101. When We substitute one revelation for another,—and, Allah knows best what He reveals (in stages),— they say, "Thou art but a forger" but most of them know not.

102. Say, the Holy Spirit has brought the revelation from the Lord in truth, in other to strengthen those who believe, and as a Guide and Glad Tidings to Muslims.

103. We know indeed that they say, "It is a man that teaches him." The tongue of him they wickedly point to is notably foreign, while this is Arabic, pure and clear.

کے) قدم جم چکنے کے بعد لڑکھڑا جائیں اور اس وجہ سے
کہ تم نے لوگوں کو خدا کے رستے سے روکا۔ تم کو عقوبت کا مزا
چکھنا پڑے۔ اور بڑا سخت عذاب ملے ﴿۹۴﴾
اور خدا سے جو تم نے عہد کیا ہے (اس کو مت بیچو اور) اسکے
بدلے تھوڑی سی قیمت نہ لو۔ (کیونکہ ایفائے عہد کا) جو (صلہ)
خدا کے ہاں مقرر ہے وہ اگر سمجھو تو تمہارے لئے بہتر ہے ﴿۹۵﴾
جو کچھ تمہارے پاس ہے وہ ختم ہو جاتا ہے اور جو خدا کے
پاس ہے وہ باقی ہے (کہ کبھی ختم نہیں ہوگا) اور جن لوگوں نے
صبر کیا ہم اُن کو اُن کے اعمال کا بہت اچھا بدلہ دیں گے ﴿۹۶﴾
جو شخص نیک اعمال کریگا مرد ہو یا عورت اور وہ مومن بھی
ہوگا تو ہم اسکو (دنیا میں) پاک (اور آرام کی) زندگی سے زندہ
رکھیں گے اور (آخرت میں) اُنکے اعمال کا نہایت اچھا صلہ دینگے ﴿۹۷﴾
اور جب تم قرآن پڑھنے لگو تو شیطان مردود سے پناہ
مانگ لیا کرو ﴿۹۸﴾
کہ جو مومن ہیں اور اپنے پروردگار پر بھروسا رکھتے ہیں
اُن پر اُس کا کچھ زور نہیں چلتا ﴿۹۹﴾
اُس کا زور انہی لوگوں پر چلتا ہے جو اسکو رفیق بناتے ہیں اور
اُسکے (وسوسے کے) سبب (خدا کیساتھ) شریک مقرر کرتے ہیں ﴿۱۰۰﴾
اور جب ہم کوئی آیت کسی آیت کی جگہ بدل دیتے ہیں۔ اور خدا جو
کچھ نازل فرماتا ہے اُسے خوب جانتا ہے تو (کافر) کہتے ہیں کہ تم تو (یونہی)
اپنی طرف سے بنا لاتے ہو حقیقت یہ ہے کہ اُن میں اکثر نادان ہیں ﴿۱۰۱﴾
کہہ دو کہ اسکو روح القدس تمہارے پروردگار کی طرف سے سچائی کے
ساتھ لیکر نازل ہوئے ہیں تاکہ یہ (قرآن) مومنوں کو ثابت قدم رکھے
اور حکم ماننے والوں کیلئے تو (یہ) ہدایت اور بشارت ہے ﴿۱۰۲﴾
اور ہمیں معلوم ہے کہ یہ کہتے ہیں کہ اس (پیغمبر) کو ایک شخص
سکھا جاتا ہے مگر جس کی طرف (تعلیم کی) نسبت کرتے ہیں اسکی
زبان تو عجمی ہے اور یہ صاف عربی زبان ہے ﴿۱۰۳﴾

فَتَزِلَّ قَدَمٌۢ بَعْدَ ثُبُوتِهَا وَتَذُوقُوا
السُّوٓءَ بِمَا صَدَدْتُّمْ عَنْ سَبِيلِ اللّٰهِ ۚ
وَلَكُمْ عَذَابٌ عَظِيمٌ ﴿٩٤﴾
وَلَا تَشْتَرُوا بِعَهْدِ اللّٰهِ ثَمَنًا قَلِيلًا ۚ
إِنَّمَا عِنْدَ اللّٰهِ هُوَ خَيْرٌ لَّكُمْ إِنْ
كُنْتُمْ تَعْلَمُونَ ﴿٩٥﴾
مَا عِنْدَكُمْ يَنْفَدُ ۖ وَمَا عِنْدَ اللّٰهِ بَاقٍ ۗ
وَلَنَجْزِيَنَّ الَّذِينَ صَبَرُوٓا أَجْرَهُمْ
بِأَحْسَنِ مَا كَانُوا يَعْمَلُونَ ﴿٩٦﴾
مَنْ عَمِلَ صَالِحًا مِّنْ ذَكَرٍ أَوْ أُنْثٰى وَهُوَ
مُؤْمِنٌ فَلَنُحْيِيَنَّهُ حَيٰوةً طَيِّبَةً ۖ وَلَنَجْزِيَنَّهُمْ
أَجْرَهُمْ بِأَحْسَنِ مَا كَانُوا يَعْمَلُونَ ﴿٩٧﴾
فَإِذَا قَرَأْتَ الْقُرْاٰنَ فَاسْتَعِذْ بِاللّٰهِ
مِنَ الشَّيْطٰنِ الرَّجِيمِ ﴿٩٨﴾
إِنَّهُ لَيْسَ لَهُ سُلْطٰنٌ عَلَى الَّذِينَ
اٰمَنُوا وَعَلٰى رَبِّهِمْ يَتَوَكَّلُونَ ﴿٩٩﴾
إِنَّمَا سُلْطٰنُهُ عَلَى الَّذِينَ يَتَوَلَّوْنَهُ
وَالَّذِينَ هُمْ بِهِ مُشْرِكُونَ ﴿١٠٠﴾ ع ١٣ ١١ ١٩
وَإِذَا بَدَّلْنَا اٰيَةً مَّكَانَ اٰيَةٍ ۙ وَّاللّٰهُ
أَعْلَمُ بِمَا يُنَزِّلُ قَالُوٓا إِنَّمَا أَنْتَ
مُفْتَرٍ ۚ بَلْ أَكْثَرُهُمْ لَا يَعْلَمُونَ ﴿١٠١﴾
قُلْ نَزَّلَهُ رُوحُ الْقُدُسِ مِنْ رَّبِّكَ
بِالْحَقِّ لِيُثَبِّتَ الَّذِينَ اٰمَنُوا وَهُدًى
وَّبُشْرٰى لِلْمُسْلِمِينَ ﴿١٠٢﴾
وَلَقَدْ نَعْلَمُ أَنَّهُمْ يَقُولُونَ إِنَّمَا يُعَلِّمُهُ
بَشَرٌ ۗ لِسَانُ الَّذِي يُلْحِدُونَ إِلَيْهِ
أَعْجَمِيٌّ وَّهٰذَا لِسَانٌ عَرَبِيٌّ مُّبِينٌ ﴿١٠٣﴾

104. Those who believe not in the Signs of Allah,— Allah will not guide them, and their will be a grievous Chastisement.

یہ لوگ خدا کی آیتوں پر ایمان نہیں لاتے ان کو خدا ہدایت
نہیں دیتا اور اُن کے لئے عذاب الیم ہے ﴿١٠٤﴾

إِنَّ الَّذِينَ لَا يُؤْمِنُونَ بِآيَاتِ اللَّهِ لَا
يَهْدِيهِمُ اللَّهُ وَلَهُمْ عَذَابٌ أَلِيمٌ ﴿١٠٤﴾

105. It is those who believe not in the Signs of Allah, that forge falsehood: it is they who lie!

جھوٹ افترا تو وہی لوگ کیا کرتے ہیں
جو خدا کی آیتوں پر ایمان نہیں لاتے۔ اور
وہی جھوٹے ہیں ﴿١٠٥﴾

إِنَّمَا يَفْتَرِي الْكَذِبَ الَّذِينَ لَا
يُؤْمِنُونَ بِآيَاتِ اللَّهِ ۖ وَأُولَٰئِكَ هُمُ
الْكَاذِبُونَ ﴿١٠٥﴾

106. Anyone who, after accepting faith in Allah, utters Unbelief,— except under compulsion, his heart remaining firm in Faith—but such as open their breast to Unbelief,— on them is Wrath from Allah, and theirs will be a dreadful Chastisement.

جو شخص ایمان لانے کے بعد خدا کے ساتھ کفر کرے
وہ نہیں جو (کفر پر زبردستی) مجبور کیا جائے اور اس کا
دل ایمان کے ساتھ مطمئن ہو۔ بلکہ وہ جو (دل سے اور)
دل کھول کر کفر کرے۔ تو ایسوں پر اللہ کا غضب ہے
اور اُن کو بڑا سخت عذاب ہوگا ﴿١٠٦﴾

مَنْ كَفَرَ بِاللَّهِ مِنْ بَعْدِ إِيمَانِهِ إِلَّا
مَنْ أُكْرِهَ وَقَلْبُهُ مُطْمَئِنٌّ بِالْإِيمَانِ
وَلَٰكِنْ مَنْ شَرَحَ بِالْكُفْرِ صَدْرًا
فَعَلَيْهِمْ غَضَبٌ مِنَ اللَّهِ وَلَهُمْ
عَذَابٌ عَظِيمٌ ﴿١٠٦﴾

107. This because they love the life of this world better than the Hereafter: and Allah will not guide those who reject Faith.

یہ اس لئے کہ انہوں نے دنیا کی زندگی کو آخرت کے
مقابلے میں عزیز رکھا۔ اور اس لئے کہ خدا کافر
لوگوں کو ہدایت نہیں دیتا ﴿١٠٧﴾

ذَٰلِكَ بِأَنَّهُمُ اسْتَحَبُّوا الْحَيَاةَ الدُّنْيَا
عَلَى الْآخِرَةِ وَأَنَّ اللَّهَ لَا يَهْدِي
الْقَوْمَ الْكَافِرِينَ ﴿١٠٧﴾

108. Those are they whose hearts, ears, and eyes Allah has sealed up and they take no heed.

یہی لوگ ہیں جن کے دلوں پر اور کانوں پر اور
آنکھوں پر خدا نے مُہر لگا رکھی ہے اور یہی غفلت
میں پڑے ہوئے ہیں ﴿١٠٨﴾

أُولَٰئِكَ الَّذِينَ طَبَعَ اللَّهُ عَلَىٰ قُلُوبِهِمْ
وَسَمْعِهِمْ وَأَبْصَارِهِمْ ۖ وَأُولَٰئِكَ
هُمُ الْغَافِلُونَ ﴿١٠٨﴾

109. Without doubt, in the Hereafter they will be the losers.

کچھ شک نہیں کہ یہ آخرت میں خسارہ اُٹھانے والے
ہوں گے ﴿١٠٩﴾

لَا جَرَمَ أَنَّهُمْ فِي الْآخِرَةِ هُمُ
الْخَاسِرُونَ ﴿١٠٩﴾

110. But verily thy Lord,—to those who leave their homes after trials and persecutions,—and who thereafter strive and fight for the Faith and patiently persevere,—thy Lord after all this is Oft-Foregiving, Most Merciful.

پھر جن لوگوں نے ایذائیں اٹھانے کے بعد ترکِ وطن کیا پھر
جہاد کئے اور ثابت قدم رہے تمہارا پروردگار اُنکو بیشک
ان آزمائشوں کے بعد بخشنے والا اور اُنپر رحمت کرنیوالا ہے ﴿١١٠﴾

ثُمَّ إِنَّ رَبَّكَ لِلَّذِينَ هَاجَرُوا مِنْ
بَعْدِ مَا فُتِنُوا ثُمَّ جَاهَدُوا وَصَبَرُوا
إِنَّ رَبَّكَ مِنْ بَعْدِهَا لَغَفُورٌ رَحِيمٌ ﴿١١٠﴾ ع

111. On the Day every soul will come up pleading for itself, and every soul will be recompensed (fully) for all its actions, and none will be unjustly dealt with.

جس دن ہر متنفس اپنی طرف سے جھگڑا کرنے آئیگا۔ اور ہر شخص
کو اسکے اعمال کا پورا پورا بدلہ دیا جائیگا اور کسی کا نقصان
نہیں کیا جائے گا ﴿١١١﴾

يَوْمَ تَأْتِي كُلُّ نَفْسٍ تُجَادِلُ عَنْ
نَفْسِهَا وَتُوَفَّىٰ كُلُّ نَفْسٍ مَا عَمِلَتْ
وَهُمْ لَا يُظْلَمُونَ ﴿١١١﴾

112. Allah sets forth a Parable: a city enjoying security and quiet, abundantly supplied with sustenance from every place: yet was it ungrateful for the favours of Allah: so Allah made it taste of

اور خدا ایک بستی کی مثال بیان فرماتا ہے کہ (ہر طرح) امن
چین سے بستی تھی۔ ہر طرف سے رزق بافراغت چلا آتا
تھا مگر اُن لوگوں نے خدا کی نعمتوں کی ناشکری کی تو

وَضَرَبَ اللَّهُ مَثَلًا قَرْيَةً كَانَتْ آمِنَةً
مُطْمَئِنَّةً يَأْتِيهَا رِزْقُهَا رَغَدًا مِنْ
كُلِّ مَكَانٍ فَكَفَرَتْ بِأَنْعُمِ اللَّهِ

hunger and terror (in extremes) (closing in on it) like a garment (from every side), because of the (evil) which (its people) wrought.

خدا نے اُن کے اعمال کے سبب اُن کو بھوک اور خوف
کا لباس پہنا کر (ناشکری کا) مزہ چکھا دیا ﴿۱۱۲﴾

فَاَذَاقَهَا اللّٰهُ لِبَاسَ الْجُوْعِ وَالْخَوْفِ
بِمَا كَانُوْا يَصْنَعُوْنَ ﴿١١٢﴾

113. And there came to them a Messenger from among themselves, but they falsely rejected him; so the Wrath seized them even in the midst of their iniquities.

اور اُن کے پاس انہی میں سے ایک پیغمبر آیا تو اُنہوں
نے اس کو جھٹلایا سو اُن کو عذاب نے آپکڑا اور وہ
ظالم تھے ﴿۱۱۳﴾

وَلَقَدْ جَآءَهُمْ رَسُوْلٌ مِّنْهُمْ
فَكَذَّبُوْهُ فَاَخَذَهُمُ الْعَذَابُ وَهُمْ
ظٰلِمُوْنَ ﴿١١٣﴾

114. So eat of the sustenance which Allah has provided for you, lawful and good; and be grateful for the favours of Allah, if it is He Whom ye serve.

پس خدا نے جو تم کو حلال طیب رزق دیا ہے اُسے
کھاؤ اور اللہ کی نعمتوں کا شکر کرو۔ اگر اسی کی
عبادت کرتے ہو ﴿۱۱۴﴾

فَكُلُوْا مِمَّا رَزَقَكُمُ اللّٰهُ حَلٰلًا
طَيِّبًا ۪ وَّاشْكُرُوْا نِعْمَتَ اللّٰهِ اِنْ
كُنْتُمْ اِيَّاهُ تَعْبُدُوْنَ ﴿١١٤﴾

115. He has only forbidden you dead meat, and blood, and the flesh or swine, and any (food) over which the name of other than Allah has been invoked. But if one is forced by necessity, without wilful disobedience, nor transgressing due limits,— then Allah is Oft-Forgiving, Most Merciful.

اُس نے تم پر مُردار اور لہو اور سؤر کا گوشت حرام کر دیا
ہے اور جس چیز پر خدا کے سوا کسی اور کا نام پکارا جائے
(اس کو بھی) ہاں اگر کوئی ناچار ہو جائے تو بشرطیکہ گناہ
کرنیوالا نہ ہو اور نہ حد سے نکلنے والا تو خدا بخشنے والا مہربان ہے ﴿۱۱۵﴾

اِنَّمَا حَرَّمَ عَلَيْكُمُ الْمَيْتَةَ وَالدَّمَ
وَلَحْمَ الْخِنْزِيْرِ وَمَآ اُهِلَّ لِغَيْرِ اللّٰهِ
بِهٖ ۚ فَمَنِ اضْطُرَّ غَيْرَ بَاغٍ وَّلَا عَادٍ
فَاِنَّ اللّٰهَ غَفُوْرٌ رَّحِيْمٌ ﴿١١٥﴾

116. But say not—for any false thing that your tongues may put forth,— "This is lawful, and this is forbidden," so as to ascribe false things to Allah. For those who ascribe false things to Allah, will never prosper.

اور یونہی جھوٹ جو تمہاری زبان پر آجائے مت کہہ دیا
کرو کہ یہ حلال ہے اور یہ حرام ہے۔ کہ خدا پر جھوٹ
بہتان باندھنے لگو جو لوگ خدا پر جھوٹ بہتان باندھتے
ہیں اُن کا بھلا نہیں ہوگا ﴿۱۱۶﴾

وَلَا تَقُوْلُوْا لِمَا تَصِفُ اَلْسِنَتُكُمُ
الْكَذِبَ هٰذَا حَلٰلٌ وَّهٰذَا حَرَامٌ
لِّتَفْتَرُوْا عَلَى اللّٰهِ الْكَذِبَ ؕ اِنَّ الَّذِيْنَ
يَفْتَرُوْنَ عَلَى اللّٰهِ الْكَذِبَ لَا يُفْلِحُوْنَ ﴿١١٦﴾

117. In such falsehood is but a paltry profit; but they will have a most grievous Chastisement.

(جھوٹ کا) فائدہ تو تھوڑا سا ہوگا مگر (اسکے بدلے) اُنکو عذاب الیم (بہت) ہوگا ﴿۱۱۷﴾

مَتَاعٌ قَلِيْلٌ ۪ وَّلَهُمْ عَذَابٌ اَلِيْمٌ ﴿١١٧﴾

118. To the Jews We prohibited such things as We have mentioned to thee before: We did them no wrong, but they were used to doing wrong to themselves.

اور جو چیزیں ہم تم سے پہلے بیان کر چکے ہیں وہ ہم نے
یہودیوں پر حرام کر دی تھیں۔ اور ہم نے اُن پر کچھ ظلم نہیں
کیا بلکہ وہی اپنے آپ پر ظلم کرتے تھے ﴿۱۱۸﴾

وَعَلَى الَّذِيْنَ هَادُوْا حَرَّمْنَا مَا قَصَصْنَا
عَلَيْكَ مِنْ قَبْلُ ۚ وَمَا ظَلَمْنٰهُمْ وَلٰكِنْ
كَانُوْٓا اَنْفُسَهُمْ يَظْلِمُوْنَ ﴿١١٨﴾

119. But verily the Lord, to those who do wrong in ignorance, but who thereafter repent and make amends, thy Lord after all this, is Oft-Forgiving, Most Merciful.

پھر جن لوگوں نے نادانی سے بُرا کام کیا۔ پھر اس کے بعد
توبہ کی اور نیکوکار ہو گئے تو تمہارا پروردگار (اُن کو)
توبہ کرنے اور نیکوکار ہو جانے کے بعد بخشنے والا (اور
اُن پر) رحمت کرنے والا ہے ﴿۱۱۹﴾

ثُمَّ اِنَّ رَبَّكَ لِلَّذِيْنَ عَمِلُوا السُّوْٓءَ
بِجَهَالَةٍ ثُمَّ تَابُوْا مِنْۢ بَعْدِ ذٰلِكَ وَ
اَصْلَحُوْٓا ۙ اِنَّ رَبَّكَ مِنْۢ بَعْدِهَا لَغَفُوْرٌ
رَّحِيْمٌ ﴿١١٩﴾ ع

120. Abraham was indeed a model, devoutly obedient to Allah, (and) true in faith, and he joined not gods with Allah.

بیشک ابراہیم (لوگوں کے) امام (اور) خدا کے فرمانبردار
تھے۔ جو ایک طرف کے ہو رہے تھے اور مشرکوں میں سے نہ تھے ﴿۱۲۰﴾

اِنَّ اِبْرٰهِيْمَ كَانَ اُمَّةً قَانِتًا لِّلّٰهِ
حَنِيْفًا ۭ وَلَمْ يَكُ مِنَ الْمُشْرِكِيْنَ ﴿١٢٠﴾

121. He showed his gratitude for the favours of Allah, who chose

اُس کی نعمتوں کے شکرگزار تھے۔ خدا نے اُن کو برگزیدہ کیا

شَاكِرًا لِّاَنْعُمِهٖ ۭ اِجْتَبٰىهُ وَهَدٰىهُ اِلٰى

SÛRA–17
AL-ISRÃA
(INTRODUCTION)

In the gradation of spiritual teaching (see Introduction to Sûra 7), we saw that the first seven Sûras sketched the early spiritual history of man, and led up to the formation of the new Ummat of Islam. Sûras 8 to 16 formed another series dealing with the formation of the new Ummat and its consolidation, and Allah's dealing with man taken as an Ummat and considered in his social relation in organised communities (see Introduction to Sûras 8, 10, and 16). We now come to a fresh series, (Sûras 17-29), which may be considered in three parts. Sûras 17-21 begin with an allusion to the *Mi'rãj* (of which more later), and proceed to spiritual history as touching individuals rather than nations. The old prophets and stories of the past are now referred to from this point of view. Sûras 22-25 refer to Ḥajj (pilgrimage), worship and prayer, chastity, privacy, etc., as related to a man's individual spiritual growth. Sûras 26-29 go back to the old prophets and stories of the past, as illustrating the growth of the individual soul in the reactions against the lives of the communities, and the reactions of the communities to the lives of its great individual souls.

Let us now consider S. 17 itself. It opens with the mystic Vision of the Ascension of the Holy Prophet: he was transported from the Sacred Mosque (of Makkah) to the Farthest Mosque (of Jerusalem) in a night and shown some of the Signs of Allah. The majority of Commentators take this Night Journey literally, but allow that there were other occasions on which a spiritual Journey or Vision occurred. Even on the supposition of a miraculous bodily Journey, it is conceded that the body was almost transformed into a spiritual fineness. The Ḥadîth literature gives details of this Journey and its study helps to elucidate its mystic meaning. The Holy Prophet was first transported to the seat of the earlier revelations in Jerusalem, and then taken throutgh the seven heavens, even to the Sublime Throne, and initiated into the spiritual mysteries of the human soul struggling in Space and Time. The Spaniard, Miguel Asin, Arabic Professor in the University of Madrid, has shown that this *Mi'rãj* literature had a great influence on the Mediaeval literature of Europe, and especially on the great Italian poem, the *Divine Comedy* (or Drama) of Dante, which towers like a landmark in mediaeval European literature.

The reference to this great mystic story of the *Mi'rãj* is a fitting prelude to the journey of the human soul in its spiritual growth in life. The first steps in such growth must be through moral conduct—the reciprocal rights of parents and childern, kindness to our fellow-men, courage and firmness in the hour of danger, a sense of personal responsibility, and a sense of Allah's Presence through prayer and praise.

The *Mi'rāj* is usually dated to the 27th night of the month of Rajab (though other dates, e.g. 17th of Rabi' I, are also given) in the year before the Hijra. This fixes the date of the opening verse of the Sûra, though portions of the Sûra may have been a little earlier.

him, and guided him to a Straight Way.

122. And We gave him Good in this world, and he will be, in the Hereafter, in the ranks of the Righteous.

123. Then We revealed to thee "Follow the ways of Abraham the True in Faith, and he joined not gods with Allah."

124. The Sabbath was only made (strict) for those who disagreed (as to its observance); but Allah will judge between them on the Day of Judgement, as to their differences.

125. Invite (all) to the Way of the Lord with wisdom and beautiful preaching; and argue with them in ways that are best and most gracious: for thy Lord knoweth best, who have strayed from His path, and who receive guidance.

126. And if ye punish, let your punishment be proportionate to the wrong that has been done to you: but if ye show patience, that is indeed the best (course) for those who are patient.

127. And do thou be patient, for thy patience is but with the help from Allah; nor grieve over them: and distress not thyself because of their plots.

128. For Allah is with those who restrain themselves, and those who do good.

Bani Isrã-îl, or the Children of Israel or Al-Isrã

In the name of Allah, Most Gracious Most Merciful.

1. Glory to (Allah) Who did take His Servant for a Journey by night from the Sacred Mosque to the Farthest Mosque whose precincts We did bless,—in order that We might show him some of Our Signs: for He is the One Who heareth and seeth (all things).

2. We gave Moses the Book, and made it a Guide to the Children of Israel, (commanding): "Take not other than Me as Disposer of (your)

تھا۔ اور (اپنی) سیدھی راہ پر چلایا تھا ﴿١٢١﴾
اور ہم نے اُن کو دنیا میں بھی خوبی دی تھی۔ اور وہ آخرت
میں بھی نیک لوگوں میں ہوں گے ﴿١٢٢﴾
پھر ہم نے تمہاری طرف وحی بھیجی کہ دین ابراہیم
کی پیروی اختیار کرو جو ایک طرف کے ہو رہے تھے۔
اور مشرکوں میں سے نہ تھے ﴿١٢٣﴾
ہفتے کا دن تو انہی لوگوں کیلئے مقرر کیا گیا تھا جنہوں نے
اس میں اختلاف کیا۔ اور تمہارا پروردگار قیامت کے دن انمیں
ان باتوں کا فیصلہ کر دیگا جن میں وہ اختلاف کرتے تھے ﴿١٢٤﴾
(اے پیغمبر) لوگوں کو دانش اور نیک نصیحت سے اپنے پروردگار کے رستے
کی طرف بلاؤ۔ اور بہت ہی اچھے طریق سے اُنسے مناظرہ کرو۔ جو
اسکے رستے سے بھٹک گیا تمہارا پروردگار اسے بھی خوب جانتا ہے
اور جو رستے پر چلنے والے ہیں اُن سے بھی خوب واقف ہے ﴿١٢٥﴾
اور اگر تم اُنکو تکلیف دینی چاہو تو اتنی ہی دو جتنی تکلیف تمکو
اُنسے پہنچی۔ اور اگر صبر کرو تو وہ صبر کرنیوالوں کیلئے بہت اچھا ہے ﴿١٢٦﴾
اور صبر ہی کرو اور تمہارا صبر بھی خدا ہی کی مدد سے ہے۔ اور انکے
بارے میں غم نہ کرو اور جو یہ بداندیشی کرتے ہیں اس سے تنگدل نہ ہو ﴿١٢٧﴾
کچھ شک نہیں کہ جو پرہیزگار ہیں اور جو نیکوکار ہیں خدا
اُن کا مددگار ہے ﴿١٢٨﴾

سورۃ الاسراء مکی ہے اور اسمیں ایک سو گیارہ آیتیں اور بارہ رکوع ہیں

شروع خدا کا نام لے کر جو بڑا مہربان نہایت رحم والا ہے
وہ (ذات) پاک ہے جو ایک رات اپنے بندے[١٦٩] کو مسجد الحرام
(یعنی خانہ کعبہ) سے مسجد اقصیٰ (یعنی بیت المقدس) تک
جسکے گرداگرد ہم نے برکتیں رکھی ہیں لے گیا تاکہ ہم اسے اپنی (قدرت کی)
نشانیاں دکھائیں۔ بیشک وہ سننے والا (اور) دیکھنے والا ہے ﴿١﴾
اور ہم نے موسیٰ کو کتاب عنایت کی تھی اور اسکو بنی اسرائیل
کے لئے رہنما مقرر کیا تھا کہ میرے سوا کسی کو کارساز

صِرَاطٍ مُّسْتَقِيمٍ ﴿١٢١﴾
وَآتَيْنَاهُ فِي الدُّنْيَا حَسَنَةً ۖ وَإِنَّهُ فِي
الْآخِرَةِ لَمِنَ الصَّالِحِينَ ﴿١٢٢﴾
ثُمَّ أَوْحَيْنَا إِلَيْكَ أَنِ اتَّبِعْ مِلَّةَ
إِبْرَاهِيمَ حَنِيفًا ۖ وَمَا كَانَ مِنَ
الْمُشْرِكِينَ ﴿١٢٣﴾
إِنَّمَا جُعِلَ السَّبْتُ عَلَى الَّذِينَ اخْتَلَفُوا
فِيهِ ۚ وَإِنَّ رَبَّكَ لَيَحْكُمُ بَيْنَهُمْ يَوْمَ
الْقِيَامَةِ فِيمَا كَانُوا فِيهِ يَخْتَلِفُونَ ﴿١٢٤﴾
ادْعُ إِلَىٰ سَبِيلِ رَبِّكَ بِالْحِكْمَةِ وَ
الْمَوْعِظَةِ الْحَسَنَةِ ۖ وَجَادِلْهُمْ بِالَّتِي
هِيَ أَحْسَنُ ۚ إِنَّ رَبَّكَ هُوَ أَعْلَمُ بِمَنْ
ضَلَّ عَنْ سَبِيلِهِ ۖ وَهُوَ أَعْلَمُ بِالْمُهْتَدِينَ ﴿١٢٥﴾
وَإِنْ عَاقَبْتُمْ فَعَاقِبُوا بِمِثْلِ مَا عُوقِبْتُمْ
بِهِ ۖ وَلَئِنْ صَبَرْتُمْ لَهُوَ خَيْرٌ لِلصَّابِرِينَ ﴿١٢٦﴾
وَاصْبِرْ وَمَا صَبْرُكَ إِلَّا بِاللَّهِ ۚ وَلَا تَحْزَنْ
عَلَيْهِمْ وَلَا تَكُ فِي ضَيْقٍ مِمَّا يَمْكُرُونَ ﴿١٢٧﴾
إِنَّ اللَّهَ مَعَ الَّذِينَ اتَّقَوْا وَالَّذِينَ
هُمْ مُحْسِنُونَ ﴿١٢٨﴾ ع ١٦ ٢٢

سُورَةُ الْإِسْرَاءِ مَكِّيَّةٌ وَهِيَ مِائَةٌ وَإِحْدَىٰ عَشْرَةَ آيَةً وَاثْنَا عَشَرَ رُكُوعًا

بِسْمِ اللَّهِ الرَّحْمَٰنِ الرَّحِيمِ
سُبْحَانَ الَّذِي أَسْرَىٰ بِعَبْدِهِ لَيْلًا
مِنَ الْمَسْجِدِ الْحَرَامِ إِلَى الْمَسْجِدِ
الْأَقْصَى الَّذِي بَارَكْنَا حَوْلَهُ لِنُرِيَهُ
مِنْ آيَاتِنَا ۚ إِنَّهُ هُوَ السَّمِيعُ الْبَصِيرُ ﴿١﴾
وَآتَيْنَا مُوسَى الْكِتَابَ وَجَعَلْنَاهُ هُدًى
لِبَنِي إِسْرَائِيلَ أَلَّا تَتَّخِذُوا مِنْ

الجزء الخامس عشر ١٥ . المنزل الرابع ٤

دُونِي وَكِيلًا ﴿٢﴾

نہ ٹھہرانا ﴿٢﴾

affairs."

ذُرِّيَّةَ مَنْ حَمَلْنَا مَعَ نُوحٍ ۚ إِنَّهُ
كَانَ عَبْدًا شَكُورًا ﴿٣﴾

اے اُن لوگوں کی اولاد جن کو ہم نے نوح کے ساتھ (کشتی
میں) سوار کیا تھا بیشک نوح (ہمارے) شکر گزار بندے تھے ﴿٣﴾

3. O ye that are sprung from those whom We carried (in the Ark) with Noah! verily he was a devotee most grateful.

وَقَضَيْنَا إِلَىٰ بَنِي إِسْرَائِيلَ فِي الْكِتَابِ
لَتُفْسِدُنَّ فِي الْأَرْضِ مَرَّتَيْنِ وَ
لَتَعْلُنَّ عُلُوًّا كَبِيرًا ﴿٤﴾

اور ہم نے کتاب میں بنی اسرائیل سے کہہ دیا تھا
کہ تم زمین میں دو دفعہ فساد مچاؤ گے اور بڑی سرکشی
کرو گے ﴿٤﴾

4. And we decreed for the Children of Israel in the Book, that twice would they do mischief on the earth and be elated with mighty arrogance (and twice would they be punished)!

فَإِذَا جَاءَ وَعْدُ أُولَاهُمَا بَعَثْنَا عَلَيْكُمْ
عِبَادًا لَّنَا أُولِي بَأْسٍ شَدِيدٍ فَجَاسُوا
خِلَالَ الدِّيَارِ ۚ وَكَانَ وَعْدًا مَّفْعُولًا ﴿٥﴾

پس جب پہلے (وعدے) کا وقت آیا تو ہم نے اپنے
سخت لڑائی لڑنے والے بندے تم پر مُسلط کر دیے اور
وہ شہروں کے اندر پھیل گئے۔ اور وہ وعدہ پورا ہو کر رہا ﴿٥﴾

5. When the first of the warnings came to pass, We sent against you Our servants given to terrible warfare: they entered the very inmost parts of your homes; and it was a warning (completely) fulfilled.

ثُمَّ رَدَدْنَا لَكُمُ الْكَرَّةَ عَلَيْهِمْ وَ
أَمْدَدْنَاكُم بِأَمْوَالٍ وَبَنِينَ وَجَعَلْنَاكُمْ
أَكْثَرَ نَفِيرًا ﴿٦﴾

پھر ہم نے دوسری بار تم کو اُن پر غلبہ دیا اور مال اور
بیٹوں سے تمہاری مدد کی۔ اور تم کو جماعت کثیر
بنا دیا ﴿٦﴾

6. Then did We grant you victory over them: We gave you increase in resources and sons, and made you the more numerous in man-power.

إِنْ أَحْسَنتُمْ أَحْسَنتُمْ لِأَنفُسِكُمْ ۖ
وَإِنْ أَسَأْتُمْ فَلَهَا ۚ فَإِذَا جَاءَ وَعْدُ
الْآخِرَةِ لِيَسُوءُوا وُجُوهَكُمْ وَلِيَدْخُلُوا
الْمَسْجِدَ كَمَا دَخَلُوهُ أَوَّلَ مَرَّةٍ وَ
لِيُتَبِّرُوا مَا عَلَوْا تَتْبِيرًا ﴿٧﴾

اگر تم نیکو کاری کرو گے تو اپنی جانوں کیلئے کرو گے اور اگر اعمال بد کرو گے
تو اُنکا (وبال بھی) تمہاری ہی جانوں پر ہوگا پھر جب دوسرے (وعدے) کا
وقت آیا تو ہم نے پھر اپنے بندے بھیجے تاکہ تمہارے چہروں کو بگاڑ دیں۔
اور جسطرح پہلی دفعہ مسجد (بیت المقدس) میں داخل ہوگئے تھے اُسی
طرح پھر اسمیں داخل ہو جائیں اور جس چیز پر غلبہ پائیں اُسے تباہ کر دیں ﴿٧﴾

7. If ye did well, ye did well for yourselves; if ye did evil, (ye did it) against yourselves. So when the second of the warnings came to pass, (We permitted your enemies) to disfigure your faces, and to enter your Temple as they had entered it before, and to visit with destruction all that fell into their power.

عَسَىٰ رَبُّكُمْ أَن يَرْحَمَكُمْ ۚ وَإِنْ عُدتُّمْ
عُدْنَا ۘ وَجَعَلْنَا جَهَنَّمَ لِلْكَافِرِينَ
حَصِيرًا ﴿٨﴾

اُمید ہے کہ تمہارا پروردگار تم پر رحم کرے۔ اور اگر تم پھر وہی
(حرکتیں) کرو گے تو ہم بھی وہی (پہلا سلوک) کریں گے
اور ہم نے جہنم کو کافروں کیلئے قید خانہ بنا رکھا ہے ﴿٨﴾

8. It may be that your Lord may (yet) show mercy unto you; but if ye revert (to your sins), We shall revert (to Our punishments): and We have made Hell a prison for those who reject (all Faith).

إِنَّ هَٰذَا الْقُرْآنَ يَهْدِي لِلَّتِي هِيَ
أَقْوَمُ وَيُبَشِّرُ الْمُؤْمِنِينَ الَّذِينَ
يَعْمَلُونَ الصَّالِحَاتِ أَنَّ لَهُمْ أَجْرًا كَبِيرًا ﴿٩﴾

یہ قرآن وہ رستہ دکھاتا ہے جو سب سے سیدھا ہے
اور مومنوں کو جو نیک عمل کرتے ہیں بشارت دیتا ہے کہ
اُن کے لئے اجرِ عظیم ہے ﴿٩﴾

9. Verily this Qur'an doth guide to that which is most right (or stable), and giveth the glad tidings to the Believers who work deeds of righteousness, that they shall have a magnificent reward;

وَأَنَّ الَّذِينَ لَا يُؤْمِنُونَ بِالْآخِرَةِ
أَعْتَدْنَا لَهُمْ عَذَابًا أَلِيمًا ﴿١٠﴾

اور یہ بھی (بتاتا ہے) کہ جو آخرت پر ایمان نہیں رکھتے اُن
کیلئے ہم نے دُکھ دینے والا عذاب تیار کر رکھا ہے ﴿١٠﴾

10. And to those who believe not in the Hereafter, (it announceth) that We have prepared for them a Chastisement grievous (indeed).

وَيَدْعُ الْإِنسَانُ بِالشَّرِّ دُعَاءَهُ
بِالْخَيْرِ ۖ وَكَانَ الْإِنسَانُ عَجُولًا ﴿١١﴾

اور انسان جس طرح (جلدی سے) بھلائی مانگتا ہے اسی طرح بُرائی
مانگتا ہے۔ اور انسان جلد باز (پیدا ہوا) ہے ﴿١١﴾

11. Man prays for evil as fervently as he prays for good for man is given to haste.

وَجَعَلْنَا الَّيْلَ وَالنَّهَارَ اٰيَتَيْنِ
فَمَحَوْنَآ اٰيَةَ الَّيْلِ وَجَعَلْنَآ اٰيَةَ
النَّهَارِ مُبْصِرَةً لِّتَبْتَغُوْا فَضْلًا مِّنْ
رَّبِّكُمْ وَلِتَعْلَمُوْا عَدَدَ السِّنِيْنَ
وَالْحِسَابَ ؕ وَكُلَّ شَيْءٍ فَصَّلْنٰهُ
تَفْصِيْلًا ﴿۱۲﴾

اور ہم نے دن اور رات کو دو نشانیاں بنایا ہے
رات کی نشانی کو تاریک بنایا۔ اور دن کی نشانی کو
روشن۔ تاکہ تم اپنے پروردگار کا فضل (یعنی روزی) تلاش
کرو اور برسوں کا شمار اور حساب جانو۔ اور
ہم نے ہر چیز کی (بخوبی) تفصیل
کر دی ہے ﴿۱۲﴾

12. We have made the Night and the Day as two (of Our) Signs: the Sign of the Night have We made dark while the Sign of the Day We have made bright that ye may seek bounty from your Lord and that ye may know the number and count of the years: all things have We explained in detail.

وَكُلَّ اِنْسَانٍ اَلْزَمْنٰهُ طٰٓئِرَهٗ فِيْ
عُنُقِهٖ ؕ وَنُخْرِجُ لَهٗ يَوْمَ الْقِيٰمَةِ كِتٰبًا
يَّلْقٰىهُ مَنْشُوْرًا ﴿۱۳﴾

اور ہم نے ہر انسان کے اعمال کو (بصورتِ کتاب)
اس کے گلے میں لٹکا دیا ہے۔ اور قیامت کے روز (وہ)
کتاب اُسے نکال دکھائینگے جسے وہ کھلا ہوا دیکھے گا ﴿۱۳﴾

13. Every man's fate We have fastened on his own neck: on the Day of Judgment We shall bring out for him a scroll, which he will see spread open.

اِقْرَاْ كِتٰبَكَ ؕ كَفٰى بِنَفْسِكَ الْيَوْمَ
عَلَيْكَ حَسِيْبًا ؕ ﴿۱۴﴾

(کہا جائے گا کہ) اپنی کتاب پڑھ لے۔ تو آج اپنا آپ ہی
محاسب کافی ہے ﴿۱۴﴾

14. (It will be said to him:) "Read thine (own) record: sufficient is thy soul this day to make out an account against thee."

مَنِ اهْتَدٰى فَاِنَّمَا يَهْتَدِيْ لِنَفْسِهٖ ۚ
وَمَنْ ضَلَّ فَاِنَّمَا يَضِلُّ عَلَيْهَا ؕ وَلَا
تَزِرُ وَازِرَةٌ وِّزْرَ اُخْرٰى ؕ وَمَا كُنَّا
مُعَذِّبِيْنَ حَتّٰى نَبْعَثَ رَسُوْلًا ﴿۱۵﴾

جو شخص ہدایت اختیار کرتا ہے تو اپنے لئے اختیار
کرتا ہے اور جو گمراہ ہوتا ہے تو گمراہی کا ضرر بھی اُسی کو
ہوگا اور کوئی شخص کسی دوسرے کا بوجھ نہیں اُٹھائیگا۔
اور جبتک ہم پیغمبر نہ بھیج لیں عذاب نہیں دیا کرتے ﴿۱۵﴾

15. Who receiveth guidance, receiveth it for his own benefit: who goeth astray doth so to his own loss: no bearer of burdens can bear the burden of another: nor would We punish until We had sent a messenger (to give warning).

وَاِذَآ اَرَدْنَآ اَنْ نُّهْلِكَ قَرْيَةً اَمَرْنَا
مُتْرَفِيْهَا فَفَسَقُوْا فِيْهَا فَحَقَّ عَلَيْهَا
الْقَوْلُ فَدَمَّرْنٰهَا تَدْمِيْرًا ﴿۱۶﴾

اور جب ہمارا ارادہ کسی بستی کے ہلاک کرنیکا ہوا تو وہاں کے آسودہ
لوگوں کو (فواحش پر) مامور کر دیا تو وہ نافرمانیاں کرتے رہے پھر اُس پر
(عذاب کا) حکم ثابت ہوگیا۔ اور ہم نے اُسے ہلاک کر ڈالا ﴿۱۶﴾

16. When We decide to destroy a town, We command those among them who are given the good things of this life (to be obedient) but they continued to transgress; so that the word is proved true against them: then We destroy them utterly.

وَكَمْ اَهْلَكْنَا مِنَ الْقُرُوْنِ مِنْۢ بَعْدِ
نُوْحٍ ؕ وَكَفٰى بِرَبِّكَ بِذُنُوْبِ عِبَادِهٖ
خَبِيْرًاۢ بَصِيْرًا ﴿۱۷﴾

اور ہم نے نوح کے بعد بہت سی اُمتوں کو ہلاک کر ڈالا۔
اور تمہارا پروردگار اپنے بندوں کے گناہوں کو جاننے
اور دیکھنے والا کافی ہے ﴿۱۷﴾

17. How many generations have We destroyed after Noah? And enough is thy Lord to note and see the sins of His servants.

مَنْ كَانَ يُرِيْدُ الْعَاجِلَةَ عَجَّلْنَا لَهٗ
فِيْهَا مَا نَشَآءُ لِمَنْ نُّرِيْدُ ثُمَّ جَعَلْنَا
لَهٗ جَهَنَّمَ ۚ يَصْلٰىهَا مَذْمُوْمًا مَّدْحُوْرًا ﴿۱۸﴾

جو شخص دنیا (کی آسودگی) کا خواہشمند ہو تو ہم اسمیں سے جسے چاہتے ہیں اور
جتنا چاہتے ہیں جلد دے دیتے ہیں پھر اسکے لئے جہنم کو (ٹھکانا) مقرر کر رکھا ہے
جسمیں وہ نفرین سُن کر اور درگاہ خدا سے راندہ ہو کر داخل ہوگا ﴿۱۸﴾

18. If any do wish for the transitory things (of this life), We readily grant them—such things as We will, to such persons as We will: in the end have We provided Hell for them: they will burn therein, disgraced and rejected.

وَمَنْ اَرَادَ الْاٰخِرَةَ وَسَعٰى لَهَا سَعْيَهَا وَهُوَ
مُؤْمِنٌ فَاُولٰٓئِكَ كَانَ سَعْيُهُمْ مَّشْكُوْرًا ﴿۱۹﴾

اور جو شخص آخرت کا خواستگار ہو اور اسمیں اتنی کوشش کرے جتنی
اُسے لائق ہے اور وہ مومن بھی ہو تو ایسے ہی لوگوں کی کوشش ٹھکانے لگتی ہے ﴿۱۹﴾

19. Those who do wish for the (things of) the Hereafter, and strive therefor with all due striving, and have Faith,—they are the ones whose striving will be thanked (by Allah).

كُلًّا نُّمِدُّ هٰٓؤُلَآءِ وَهٰٓؤُلَآءِ مِنْ عَطَآءِ

ہم انکو اور ان کو سب کو تمہارے پروردگار کی بخشش سے مدد دیتے

20. Of the bounties of thy Lord We bestow freely on all—these as

well as those: the bounties of thy Lord are not closed (to anyone).

ہیں اور تمہارے پروردگار کی بخشش (کسی سے) رُکی ہوئی نہیں ﴿۲۰﴾

رَبِّكَ ۚ وَمَا كَانَ عَطَآءُ رَبِّكَ مَحْظُوْرًا ﴿٢٠﴾

21. See how We have bestowed more on some than on others; but verily the Hereafter is more in rank and gradation and more in excellence.

دیکھو ہم نے کس طرح بعض کو بعض پر فضیلت بخشی ہے اور آخرت
درجوں میں (دُنیا سے) بہت برتر اور برتری میں کہیں بڑھکر ہے ﴿۲۱﴾

اُنْظُرْ كَيْفَ فَضَّلْنَا بَعْضَهُمْ عَلٰى بَعْضٍ ۚ
وَلَلْاٰخِرَةُ اَكْبَرُ دَرَجٰتٍ وَّاَكْبَرُ تَفْضِيْلًا ﴿٢١﴾

22. Take not with Allah another god; or thou (O man!) wilt sit in disgrace and destitution.

اور خدا کے ساتھ کوئی اور معبود نہ بنانا کہ ملامتیں سُن کر اور
بےکس ہو کر بیٹھے رہ جاؤ گے ﴿۲۲﴾

لَا تَجْعَلْ مَعَ اللّٰهِ اِلٰهًا اٰخَرَ فَتَقْعُدَ
مَذْمُوْمًا مَّخْذُوْلًا ﴿٢٢﴾

23. Thy Lord hath decreed that ye worship none but Him, and that ye be kind to parents. Whether one or both of them attain old age in thy life, say not to them a word of contempt, nor repel them but address them, in terms of honour.

اور تمہارے پروردگار نے ارشاد فرمایا ہے کہ اُسکے سوا کسی کی
عبادت نہ کرو اور ماں باپ کے ساتھ بھلائی کرتے رہو اگر
اُن میں سے ایک یا دونوں تمہارے سامنے بڑھاپے کو پہنچ
جائیں تو اُن کو اُف تک نہ کہنا اور نہ اُنہیں جھڑکنا اور
اُن سے بات ادب کے ساتھ کرنا ﴿۲۳﴾

وَقَضٰى رَبُّكَ اَلَّا تَعْبُدُوْٓا اِلَّآ اِيَّاهُ
وَبِالْوَالِدَيْنِ اِحْسَانًا ۚ اِمَّا يَبْلُغَنَّ
عِنْدَكَ الْكِبَرَ اَحَدُهُمَآ اَوْ كِلٰهُمَا
فَلَا تَقُلْ لَّهُمَآ اُفٍّ وَّلَا تَنْهَرْهُمَا وَ
قُلْ لَّهُمَا قَوْلًا كَرِيْمًا ﴿٢٣﴾

24. And, out of kindness, lower to them the wing of humility, and say: "My Lord! bestow on them Thy Mercy even as they cherished me in childhood."

اور عجز و نیاز سے اُن کے آگے جھکے رہو اور اُنکے حق میں دُعا
کرو کہ اے پروردگار جیسا اُنہوں نے مجھے بچپن میں (شفقت سے)
پرورش کیا ہے تو بھی اُن (کے حال) پر رحمت فرما ﴿۲۴﴾

وَاخْفِضْ لَهُمَا جَنَاحَ الذُّلِّ مِنَ
الرَّحْمَةِ وَقُلْ رَّبِّ ارْحَمْهُمَا كَمَا
رَبَّيٰنِيْ صَغِيْرًا ﴿٢٤﴾

25. Your Lord knoweth best what is in your hearts: if ye do deeds of righteousness, verily He is Most Forgiving to those who turn to Him again and again (in true penitence).

جو کچھ تمہارے دلوں میں ہے تمہارا پروردگار اس سے بخوبی
واقف ہے۔ اگر تم نیک ہو گے تو وہ رجوع لانے والوں
کو بخش دینے والا ہے ﴿۲۵﴾

رَبُّكُمْ اَعْلَمُ بِمَا فِيْ نُفُوْسِكُمْ ۚ اِنْ
تَكُوْنُوْا صٰلِحِيْنَ فَاِنَّهٗ كَانَ لِلْاَوَّابِيْنَ
غَفُوْرًا ﴿٢٥﴾

26. And render to the kindred their due rights, as (also) to those in want and to the wayfarer: but squander not (your wealth) in the manner of a spendthrift.

اور رشتہ داروں اور محتاجوں اور مسافروں کو اُن کا
حق ادا کرو اور فضول خرچی سے مال نہ اُڑاؤ ﴿۲۶﴾

وَاٰتِ ذَا الْقُرْبٰى حَقَّهٗ وَالْمِسْكِيْنَ
وَابْنَ السَّبِيْلِ وَلَا تُبَذِّرْ تَبْذِيْرًا ﴿٢٦﴾

27. Verily spendthrifts are brothers of the Satans; and the Satan is to his Lord (Himself) ungrateful.

کہ فضول خرچی کرنیوالے تو شیطان کے بھائی ہیں اور شیطان
اپنے پروردگار (کی نعمتوں) کا کفران کرنیوالا (یعنی ناشکرا) ہے ﴿۲۷﴾

اِنَّ الْمُبَذِّرِيْنَ كَانُوْٓا اِخْوَانَ الشَّيٰطِيْنِ ۚ
وَكَانَ الشَّيْطٰنُ لِرَبِّهٖ كَفُوْرًا ﴿٢٧﴾

28. And even if thou hast to turn away from them in pursuit of the Mercy from thy Lord which thou dost expect, yet speak to them a word of easy kindness.

اگر تم اپنے پروردگار کی رحمت (یعنی فراخ دستی) کے انتظار
میں جس کی تمہیں اُمید ہو (اُن مستحقین) کی طرف توجہ نہ کر سکو
تو اُن سے نرمی سے بات کہہ دیا کرو ﴿۲۸﴾

وَاِمَّا تُعْرِضَنَّ عَنْهُمُ ابْتِغَآءَ رَحْمَةٍ
مِّنْ رَّبِّكَ تَرْجُوْهَا فَقُلْ لَّهُمْ قَوْلًا
مَّيْسُوْرًا ﴿٢٨﴾

29. Make not thy hand tied (Like a niggard's) to thy neck, nor stretch it forth to its utmost reach, so that thou become blameworthy and destitute.

اور اپنے ہاتھ کو نہ تو گردن سے بندھا ہوا (یعنی بہت تنگ)
کر لو (کہ کسی کو کچھ دو ہی نہیں) اور نہ بالکل کھول ہی دو (کہ سبھی
کچھ دے ڈالو اور انجام یہ ہو) کہ ملامت زدہ اور درماندہ ہو کر بیٹھ جاؤ ﴿۲۹﴾

وَلَا تَجْعَلْ يَدَكَ مَغْلُوْلَةً اِلٰى عُنُقِكَ
وَلَا تَبْسُطْهَا كُلَّ الْبَسْطِ فَتَقْعُدَ
مَلُوْمًا مَّحْسُوْرًا ﴿٢٩﴾

30. Verily thy Lord doth provide sustenance in abundance for whom

بیشک تمہارا پروردگار جس کی روزی چاہتا ہے فراخ کر دیتا ہے

اِنَّ رَبَّكَ يَبْسُطُ الرِّزْقَ لِمَنْ يَّشَآءُ

He pleaseth, and He straiten it for He doth know and regard all His servants.

اور جس کی روزی چاہتا ہے تنگ کر دیتا ہے وہ اپنے بندوں
سے خبردار ہے اور (ان کو) دیکھ رہا ہے ﴿۳۰﴾

وَيَقْدِرُ ۚ إِنَّهُ كَانَ بِعِبَادِهِ خَبِيرًا
بَصِيرًا ﴿٣٠﴾

31. Kill not your children for fear of want: We shall provide, sustenance for them as well as for you. Verily the killing of them is a great sin.

اور اپنی اولاد کو مفلسی کے خوف سے قتل نہ کرنا (کیونکہ
اُن کو اور تم کو ہم ہی رزق دیتے ہیں۔ کچھ شک نہیں کہ
ان کا مار ڈالنا بڑا سخت گناہ ہے ﴿۳۱﴾

وَلَا تَقْتُلُوا أَوْلَادَكُمْ خَشْيَةَ إِمْلَاقٍ ۖ
نَحْنُ نَرْزُقُهُمْ وَإِيَّاكُمْ ۚ إِنَّ قَتْلَهُمْ
كَانَ خِطْئًا كَبِيرًا ﴿٣١﴾

32. Nor come nigh to adultery: for it is an indecent (deed) and an evil way

اور زنا کے بھی پاس نہ جانا کہ وہ بے حیائی اور بُری
راہ ہے ﴿۳۲﴾

وَلَا تَقْرَبُوا الزِّنَىٰ ۖ إِنَّهُ كَانَ فَاحِشَةً
وَسَاءَ سَبِيلًا ﴿٣٢﴾

33. Nor take life—which Allah has made sacred—except for just cause. And if anyone is slain wrongfully, We have given his heir authority (to demand Qiṣāṣ or to forgive): but let him not exceed bounds in the matter of taking life; for he is helped (by the Law).

اور جس جاندار کا مارنا خدا نے حرام کیا ہے اُسے قتل نہ کرنا مگر جائز
طور پر (یعنی بفتوائے شریعت) اور جو شخص ظلم سے قتل کیا جائے
ہم نے اسکے وارث کو اختیار دیا ہے (کہ ظالم قاتل سے بدلہ لے) تو
اسکو چاہیئے کہ قتل (کے قصاص) میں زیادتی نہ کرے کہ وہ منصور و فتحیاب ہے ﴿۳۳﴾

وَلَا تَقْتُلُوا النَّفْسَ الَّتِي حَرَّمَ اللَّهُ إِلَّا
بِالْحَقِّ ۗ وَمَنْ قُتِلَ مَظْلُومًا فَقَدْ
جَعَلْنَا لِوَلِيِّهِ سُلْطَانًا فَلَا يُسْرِفْ
فِي الْقَتْلِ ۖ إِنَّهُ كَانَ مَنْصُورًا ﴿٣٣﴾

34. Come not nigh to the orphan's property except to improve it, until he attains the age of full strength; and fulfil (every) engagement, for (every) engagement will be enquired into (on the Day of Reckoning).

اور یتیم کے مال کے پاس بھی نہ پھٹکنا۔ مگر ایسے
طریق سے کہ بہت بہتر ہو یہاں تک کہ وہ جوانی
کو پہنچ جائے۔ اور عہد کو پورا کرو کہ عہد کے بارے
میں ضرور پرسش ہوگی ﴿۳۴﴾

وَلَا تَقْرَبُوا مَالَ الْيَتِيمِ إِلَّا بِالَّتِي
هِيَ أَحْسَنُ حَتَّىٰ يَبْلُغَ أَشُدَّهُ ۚ وَ
أَوْفُوا بِالْعَهْدِ ۖ إِنَّ الْعَهْدَ كَانَ
مَسْئُولًا ﴿٣٤﴾

35. Give full measure when ye measure, and weigh with a balance that is straight: that is better and fairer in the final determination.

اور جب (کوئی چیز) ماپ کر دینے لگو تو پیمانہ پورا بھرا کرو اور
جب تول کر دو۔ تو ترازو سیدھی رکھ کر تولا کرو۔ یہ بہت اچھی
بات اور انجام کے لحاظ سے بھی بہت بہتر ہے ﴿۳۵﴾

وَأَوْفُوا الْكَيْلَ إِذَا كِلْتُمْ وَزِنُوا
بِالْقِسْطَاسِ الْمُسْتَقِيمِ ۚ ذَٰلِكَ خَيْرٌ
وَأَحْسَنُ تَأْوِيلًا ﴿٣٥﴾

36. And pursue not that of which thou hast no knowledge; for surely the hearing, the sight, the heart all of those shall be questioned of.

اور (اے بندے) جس چیز کا تجھے علم نہیں اس کے پیچھے
نہ پڑ۔ کہ کان اور آنکھ اور دل ان سب (جوارح) سے
ضرور باز پرس ہوگی ﴿۳۶﴾

وَلَا تَقْفُ مَا لَيْسَ لَكَ بِهِ عِلْمٌ ۚ إِنَّ
السَّمْعَ وَالْبَصَرَ وَالْفُؤَادَ كُلُّ أُولَٰئِكَ
كَانَ عَنْهُ مَسْئُولًا ﴿٣٦﴾

37. Nor walk on the earth with insolence: for thou canst not rend the earth asunder, nor reach the mountains in height.

اور زمین پر اکڑ کر (اور تن کر) مت چل کہ تو زمین کو
پھاڑ تو نہیں ڈالے گا اور نہ لمبا ہو کر پہاڑوں (کی
چوٹی) تک پہنچ جائے گا ﴿۳۷﴾

وَلَا تَمْشِ فِي الْأَرْضِ مَرَحًا ۖ إِنَّكَ
لَنْ تَخْرِقَ الْأَرْضَ وَلَنْ تَبْلُغَ الْجِبَالَ
طُولًا ﴿٣٧﴾

38. Of all such things the evil is hateful in the sight of thy Lord.

ان سب (عادتوں) کی بُرائی تیرے پروردگار کے
نزدیک بہت ناپسند ہے ﴿۳۸﴾

كُلُّ ذَٰلِكَ كَانَ سَيِّئُهُ عِنْدَ رَبِّكَ
مَكْرُوهًا ﴿٣٨﴾

39. These are among the (precepts of) wisdom, which thy

(اے پیغمبر) یہ اُن (ہدایتوں) میں سے ہیں جو خدا نے دانائی کی باتیں

ذَٰلِكَ مِمَّا أَوْحَىٰ إِلَيْكَ رَبُّكَ مِنَ

الْحِكْمَةِ ۗ وَلَا تَجْعَلْ مَعَ اللَّهِ إِلَٰهًا آخَرَ
فَتُلْقَىٰ فِي جَهَنَّمَ مَلُومًا مَدْحُورًا ﴿٣٩﴾
أَفَأَصْفَاكُمْ رَبُّكُمْ بِالْبَنِينَ وَاتَّخَذَ
مِنَ الْمَلَائِكَةِ إِنَاثًا ۚ إِنَّكُمْ لَتَقُولُونَ
قَوْلًا عَظِيمًا ﴿٤٠﴾
وَلَقَدْ صَرَّفْنَا فِي هَٰذَا الْقُرْآنِ
لِيَذَّكَّرُوا وَمَا يَزِيدُهُمْ إِلَّا نُفُورًا ﴿٤١﴾
قُلْ لَوْ كَانَ مَعَهُ آلِهَةٌ كَمَا يَقُولُونَ
إِذًا لَابْتَغَوْا إِلَىٰ ذِي الْعَرْشِ سَبِيلًا ﴿٤٢﴾
سُبْحَانَهُ وَتَعَالَىٰ عَمَّا يَقُولُونَ عُلُوًّا
كَبِيرًا ﴿٤٣﴾
تُسَبِّحُ لَهُ السَّمَاوَاتُ السَّبْعُ وَالْأَرْضُ
وَمَنْ فِيهِنَّ ۚ وَإِنْ مِنْ شَيْءٍ إِلَّا
يُسَبِّحُ بِحَمْدِهِ وَلَٰكِنْ لَا تَفْقَهُونَ
تَسْبِيحَهُمْ ۗ إِنَّهُ كَانَ حَلِيمًا غَفُورًا ﴿٤٤﴾
وَإِذَا قَرَأْتَ الْقُرْآنَ جَعَلْنَا بَيْنَكَ
وَبَيْنَ الَّذِينَ لَا يُؤْمِنُونَ بِالْآخِرَةِ
حِجَابًا مَسْتُورًا ﴿٤٥﴾
وَجَعَلْنَا عَلَىٰ قُلُوبِهِمْ أَكِنَّةً أَنْ
يَفْقَهُوهُ وَفِي آذَانِهِمْ وَقْرًا ۚ وَإِذَا
ذَكَرْتَ رَبَّكَ فِي الْقُرْآنِ وَحْدَهُ
وَلَّوْا عَلَىٰ أَدْبَارِهِمْ نُفُورًا ﴿٤٦﴾
نَحْنُ أَعْلَمُ بِمَا يَسْتَمِعُونَ بِهِ إِذْ
يَسْتَمِعُونَ إِلَيْكَ وَإِذْ هُمْ نَجْوَىٰ
إِذْ يَقُولُ الظَّالِمُونَ إِنْ تَتَّبِعُونَ
إِلَّا رَجُلًا مَسْحُورًا ﴿٤٧﴾
انْظُرْ كَيْفَ ضَرَبُوا لَكَ الْأَمْثَالَ فَضَلُّوا

تمہاری طرف وحی کی ہیں اور خدا کے ساتھ کوئی اور معبود نہ بنانا کہ (ایسا کرنے سے)
ملامت زدہ اور (درگاہ خدا سے) راندہ بنا کر جہنم میں ڈال دیے جاؤ گے ﴿۳۹﴾
(مشرکو!) کیا تمہارے پروردگار نے تم کو تو لڑکے دیے
اور خود فرشتوں کو بیٹیاں بنایا۔ کچھ شک نہیں کہ (یہ)
تم بڑی (نامعقول) بات کہتے ہو ﴿۴۰﴾
اور ہم نے اس قرآن میں طرح طرح کی باتیں بیان کی ہیں تاکہ
لوگ نصیحت پکڑیں مگر وہ اس سے اور بدک جاتے ہیں ﴿۴۱﴾
کہہ دو کہ اگر خدا کے ساتھ اور معبود ہوتے جیسا کہ یہ کہتے ہیں تو وہ ضرور
(خدائے) مالک عرش کی طرف (لڑنے بھڑنے کیلئے) رستہ نکالتے ﴿۴۲﴾
وہ پاک ہے اور جو کچھ یہ بکواس کرتے ہیں اس سے (اس کا
رتبہ) بہت عالی ہے ﴿۴۳﴾
ساتوں آسمان اور زمین اور جو لوگ ان میں ہیں سب
اسی کی تسبیح کرتے ہیں۔ اور (مخلوقات میں سے) کوئی چیز نہیں
مگر اس کی تعریف کے ساتھ تسبیح کرتی ہے لیکن تم ان کی
تسبیح کو نہیں سمجھتے۔ بے شک وہ بردبار (اور) غفار ہے ﴿۴۴﴾
اور جب تم قرآن پڑھا کرتے ہو تو ہم تم میں اور ان لوگوں
میں جو آخرت پر ایمان نہیں رکھتے حجاب پر
حجاب کر دیتے ہیں ﴿۴۵﴾
اور ان کے دلوں پر پردہ ڈال دیتے ہیں کہ اسے
سمجھ نہ سکیں اور ان کے کانوں میں ثقل پیدا کر دیتے
ہیں۔ اور جب تم قرآن میں اپنے پروردگار یکتا کا ذکر کرتے ہو
تو وہ بدک جاتے اور پیٹھ پھیر کر چل دیتے ہیں ﴿۴۶﴾
یہ لوگ جب تمہاری طرف کان لگاتے ہیں تو جس نیت
سے یہ سنتے ہیں ہم اسے خوب جانتے ہیں اور جب یہ
سرگوشیاں کرتے ہیں (یعنی) جب ظالم کہتے ہیں کہ تم ایک
ایسے شخص کی پیروی کرتے ہو جس پر جادو کیا گیا ہے ﴿۴۷﴾
دیکھو انہوں نے کس کس طرح کی تمہارے بارے میں باتیں

Lord has revealed to thee. Take not, with Allah, another object of worship, lest thou shouldst be thrown into Hell, blameworthy and rejected.

40. Has then your Lord, (O Pagans!) preferred for you sons, and taken for Himself daughters among the angels? Truly ye utter a most dreadful saying!

41. We have explained (things) in various (ways) in this Qur'an, in order that they may receive admonition, but it only increases their flight (from the Truth)!

42. Say: if there had been (other) gods with Him,—as they say,—behold, they would certainly have sought out a way in submitting to the Lord of the Throne!

43. Glory to Him! He is high above all that they say! Exalted and Great (beyond measure)!

44. The seven heavens and the earth, and all beings therein, declare His glory: there is not a thing but celebrates His praise; and yet ye understand not how they declare His glory! Verily He is Oft-Forbearing, Most Forgiving!

45. When thou dost recite the Qur'an, We put, between thee and those who believe not in the Hereafter, a veil invisible:

46. And We put coverings over their hearts (and minds) lest they should understand the Qur'an, and deafness into their ears: when thou dost mention thy Lord—and Him alone—in the Qur'an, they turn on their backs, fleeing (from the Truth).

47. We know best what it is they listen, when they listen to thee; and when they meet in private behold, the wicked say, "Ye follow none other than a man bewitched!"

48. See what similes they strike for thee: but they have gone astray,

and never can they find a way.

49. They say: "What! when we are reduced to bones and dust, should we really be raised up (to be) a new creation?

50. Say: (Nay!) be ye stones or iron,

51. "Or any created matter which, in your minds, is hardest (to be raised up,)— (yet shall ye be raised up)!" Then will they say: "Who will cause us to return?" Say: "He Who created you first!" Then will they wag their heads towards thee, and say, "When will that be?" Say, "May be it will be quite soon!

52. "It will be on the Day when He will call you, and ye will answer (His call) with (words of) His praise, and ye will think that ye tarried but a little while!"

53. Say to My servants that they should (only) say those things that are best: for Satan doth sow dissensions among them: for Satan is to man an avowed enemy.

54. It is your Lord That knoweth you best: if He please, He granteth you mercy, or if He please, punishment: We have not sent thee to be a disposer of their affairs for them.

55. And it is your Lord That knoweth best all beings that are in the heavens and on earth: and We made some of the Prophets to excel others and We gave to David the Psalms.

56. Say: "Call on those—besides Him—whom ye fancy: they have neither the power to remove your troubles from you nor to change them."

57. Those whom they call upon do seek (for themselves) means of access to their Lord,—as to who are nearest: they hope for His Mercy and fear His Wrath: for the

بنائی ہیں۔ سو یہ گمراہ ہو رہے ہیں اور رستہ نہیں پا سکتے ﴿۴۸﴾
اور کہتے ہیں کہ جب ہم (مر کر بوسیدہ) ہڈیاں اور چُور چُور
ہو جائینگے تو کیا از سرِ نو پیدا ہو کر اُٹھیں گے؟ ﴿۴۹﴾
کہہ دو کہ (خواہ تم) پتھر ہو جاؤ یا لوہا ﴿۵۰﴾
یا کوئی اور چیز جو تمہارے نزدیک (پتھر اور لوہے سے بھی)
بڑی (سخت) ہو (جھٹ) کہیں گے کہ (بھلا) ہمیں دوبارہ کون
جِلائے گا؟ کہہ دو کہ وہی جس نے تم کو پہلی بار پیدا کیا۔ تو
(تعجب سے) تمہارے آگے سر ہلائیں گے اور پوچھیں گے کہ ایسا
کب ہوگا؟ کہہ دو اُمید ہے کہ جلد ہوگا ﴿۵۱﴾
جس دن وہ تمہیں پکاریگا تو تم اسکی تعریف کیساتھ جواب
دو گے اور خیال کرو گے کہ تم (دنیا میں) بہت کم (مدت) رہے ﴿۵۲﴾
اور میرے بندوں سے کہہ دو کہ (لوگوں سے) ایسی باتیں
کہا کریں جو بہت پسندیدہ ہوں۔ کیونکہ شیطان (بُری
باتوں سے) اُن میں فساد ڈلوا دیتا ہے۔ کچھ شک نہیں
کہ شیطان انسان کا کھلا دشمن ہے ﴿۵۳﴾
تمہارا پروردگار تم سے خوب واقف ہے۔ اگر چاہے تو
تم پر رحم کرے یا اگر چاہے تو تمہیں عذاب دے۔ اور ہم
نے تم کو اُن پر داروغہ (بنا کر) نہیں بھیجا ﴿۵۴﴾
اور جو لوگ آسمانوں اور زمین میں ہیں تمہارا پروردگار
ان سے خوب واقف ہے۔ اور ہم نے بعض پیغمبروں کو بعض پر
فضیلت بخشی اور داؤد کو زبور عنایت کی ﴿۵۵﴾
کہو کہ (مشرکو) جن لوگوں کی نسبت تمہیں (معبود ہونیکا)
گمان ہے اُن کو بلا دیکھو۔ وہ تم سے تکلیف کے دُور کرنے
یا اسکے بدل دینے کا کچھ بھی اختیار نہیں رکھتے ﴿۵۶﴾
یہ لوگ جن کو (خدا کے سوا) پکارتے ہیں وہ خود اپنے پروردگار کے
ہاں ذریعۂ (تقرب) تلاش کرتے رہتے ہیں کہ کون ان میں (خدا کا)
زیادہ مقرب (ہوتا) ہے اور اسکی رحمت کے اُمیدوار رہتے ہیں اور اُسکے

فَلَا يَسْتَطِيعُونَ سَبِيلًا ﴿٤٨﴾
وَقَالُوٓا ءَاِذَا كُنَّا عِظَامًا وَّرُفَاتًا ءَاِنَّا
لَمَبْعُوثُونَ خَلْقًا جَدِيدًا ﴿٤٩﴾
قُلْ كُونُوا حِجَارَةً اَوْ حَدِيدًا ﴿٥٠﴾
اَوْ خَلْقًا مِّمَّا يَكْبُرُ فِي صُدُورِكُمْ
فَسَيَقُولُونَ مَنْ يُّعِيدُنَا قُلِ الَّذِي
فَطَرَكُمْ اَوَّلَ مَرَّةٍ فَسَيُنْغِضُونَ
اِلَيْكَ رُءُوسَهُمْ وَيَقُولُونَ مَتٰى هُوَ
قُلْ عَسٰٓى اَنْ يَّكُونَ قَرِيبًا ﴿٥١﴾
يَوْمَ يَدْعُوكُمْ فَتَسْتَجِيبُونَ بِحَمْدِهٖ
وَتَظُنُّونَ اِنْ لَّبِثْتُمْ اِلَّا قَلِيلًا ﴿٥٢﴾
وَقُلْ لِّعِبَادِي يَقُولُوا الَّتِي هِيَ
اَحْسَنُ اِنَّ الشَّيْطٰنَ يَنْزَغُ بَيْنَهُمْ
اِنَّ الشَّيْطٰنَ كَانَ لِلْاِنْسَانِ عَدُوًّا
مُّبِينًا ﴿٥٣﴾
رَبُّكُمْ اَعْلَمُ بِكُمْ اِنْ يَّشَاْ يَرْحَمْكُمْ
اَوْ اِنْ يَّشَاْ يُعَذِّبْكُمْ وَمَآ اَرْسَلْنٰكَ
عَلَيْهِمْ وَكِيلًا ﴿٥٤﴾
وَرَبُّكَ اَعْلَمُ بِمَنْ فِي السَّمٰوٰتِ وَ
الْاَرْضِ وَلَقَدْ فَضَّلْنَا بَعْضَ النَّبِيّٖنَ
عَلٰى بَعْضٍ وَّاٰتَيْنَا دَاوٗدَ زَبُورًا ﴿٥٥﴾
قُلِ ادْعُوا الَّذِينَ زَعَمْتُمْ مِّنْ دُونِهٖ
فَلَا يَمْلِكُونَ كَشْفَ الضُّرِّ عَنْكُمْ
وَلَا تَحْوِيلًا ﴿٥٦﴾
اُولٰٓئِكَ الَّذِينَ يَدْعُونَ يَبْتَغُونَ اِلٰى
رَبِّهِمُ الْوَسِيلَةَ اَيُّهُمْ اَقْرَبُ وَيَرْجُونَ
رَحْمَتَهٗ وَيَخَافُونَ عَذَابَهٗ اِنَّ عَذَابَ

Wrath of thy Lord is something to take heed of.

58. There is not a population but We shall destroy it before the Day of Judgment or punish it with a dreadful Chastisement. That is written in the (eternal) Record.

59. And We refrain from sending the Signs, only because the men of former generations treated them as false: We sent the She-camel to the Thamûd—a visible Sign— but they treated her wrongfully: We only sent the Signs by way of frightening (and warning from evil).

60. Behold! We told thee that thy Lord doth encompass mankind round about: We granted the vision which We showed thee, but as a trial for men,— as also the Cursed Tree (mentioned) in the Qur'an: We put fear (and warning) into them, but it only increases their inordinate transgression!

61. Behold! We said to the angels: "Prostrate unto Adam": they prostrated except Iblîs: he said, "Shall I prostrate to one whom Thou didst create from clay?"

62. He said, "Seest Thou? This is the one whom Thou hast honoured above me! If Thou wilt but respite me to the Day of Judgment, I will surely bring his descendants under my sway—all but a few!"

63. (Allah) said: "Go thy way; if any of them follow thee, verily Hell will be the recompense of you (all)— an ample recompense.

64. And Arouse those whom thou canst among them, with thy (seductive) voice; make assaults on them with thy cavalry and thy infantry; mutually share with them wealth and children; and make promises to them." But Satan promises them nothing but deceit.

65. "As for My servants, no authority shalt thou have over them:" Enough is thy Lord for a Disposer of affairs.

66. Your Lord is He That maketh the Ship go smoothly for you

عذاب سے خوف رکھتے ہیں بیشک تمہارے پروردگار کا عذاب ڈرنے کی چیز ہے ﴿٥٧﴾
اور (کفر کرنیوالوں کی) کوئی بستی نہیں مگر قیامت کے دن سے
پہلے ہم اُسے ہلاک کر دینگے یا سخت عذاب سے معذب کرینگے۔ یہ
کتاب (یعنی تقدیر) میں لکھا جا چکا ہے ﴿٥٨﴾
اور ہم نے نشانیاں بھیجنی اس لئے موقوف کر دیں کہ اگلے لوگوں
نے اس کی تکذیب کی تھی۔ اور ہم نے ثمود کو اُونٹنی (نبوت صالح
کی کھلی) نشانی دی تو انہوں نے اس پر ظلم کیا۔ اور ہم جو نشانیاں
بھیجا کرتے ہیں تو ڈرانے کو ﴿٥٩﴾
جب ہم نے تم سے کہا کہ تمہارا پروردگار لوگوں کو احاطہ کئے
ہوئے ہے۔ اور جو نمائش ہم نے تمہیں دکھائی اسکو لوگوں
کے لئے آزمائش کیا اور اسی طرح (تھوہر کے) درخت کو جس پر
قرآن میں لعنت کی گئی۔ اور ہم انہیں ڈراتے ہیں تو اُن کو اس سے
بڑی (سخت) سرکشی پیدا ہوتی ہے ﴿٦٠﴾
اور جب ہم نے فرشتوں سے کہا کہ آدم کو سجدہ کرو تو سب نے سجدہ کیا مگر ابلیس
نے نہ کیا۔ بولا کہ بھلا میں ایسے شخص کو سجدہ کروں جسکو تو نے مٹی سے پیدا کیا ہے ﴿٦١﴾
(اور ازراہِ طنز) کہنے لگا کہ دیکھ تو یہی وہ ہے جسے تو نے مجھ پر فضیلت
دی ہے۔ اگر تو مجھ کو قیامت کے دن تک کی مہلت دے تو میں تھوڑے
سے شخصوں کے سوا اس کی (تمام) اولاد کی جڑ کاٹتا رہوں گا ﴿٦٢﴾
خدا نے فرمایا (یہاں سے) چلا جا۔ جو شخص ان میں سے تیری
پیروی کریگا تو تم سب کی جزا جہنم ہے (اور وہ) پوری سزا ہے ﴿٦٣﴾
اور ان میں سے جس کو بہکا سکے اپنی آواز سے بہکاتا رہ۔ اور
اُن پر اپنے سواروں اور پیادوں کو چڑھا کر لاتا رہ اور
اُن کے مال اور اولاد میں شریک ہوتا رہ اور اُن سے
وعدے کرتا رہ۔ اور شیطان جو وعدے اُنسے کرتا ہے سب دھوکا ہے ﴿٦٤﴾
جو میرے مخلص بندے ہیں اُن پر تیرا کچھ زور نہیں۔ اور
(اے پیغمبر) تمہارا پروردگار کارساز کافی ہے ﴿٦٥﴾
تمہارا پروردگار وہ ہے جو تمہارے لئے دریا میں کشتیاں

رَبِّكَ كَانَ مَحْذُوْرًا ﴿٥٧﴾
وَاِنْ مِّنْ قَرْيَةٍ اِلَّا نَحْنُ مُهْلِكُوْهَا
قَبْلَ يَوْمِ الْقِيٰمَةِ اَوْ مُعَذِّبُوْهَا عَذَابًا
شَدِيْدًا ؕ كَانَ ذٰلِكَ فِي الْكِتٰبِ مَسْطُوْرًا ﴿٥٨﴾
وَمَا مَنَعَنَآ اَنْ نُّرْسِلَ بِالْاٰيٰتِ اِلَّآ اَنْ
كَذَّبَ بِهَا الْاَوَّلُوْنَ ؕ وَاٰتَيْنَا ثَمُوْدَ النَّاقَةَ
مُبْصِرَةً فَظَلَمُوْا بِهَا ؕ وَمَا نُرْسِلُ
بِالْاٰيٰتِ اِلَّا تَخْوِيْفًا ﴿٥٩﴾
وَاِذْ قُلْنَا لَكَ اِنَّ رَبَّكَ اَحَاطَ بِالنَّاسِ ؕ
وَمَا جَعَلْنَا الرُّءْيَا الَّتِيْٓ اَرَيْنٰكَ اِلَّا
فِتْنَةً لِّلنَّاسِ وَالشَّجَرَةَ الْمَلْعُوْنَةَ
فِي الْقُرْاٰنِ ؕ وَنُخَوِّفُهُمْ ۙ فَمَا يَزِيْدُهُمْ
اِلَّا طُغْيَانًا كَبِيْرًا ﴿٦٠﴾ ع ٦ ٨ ٦
وَاِذْ قُلْنَا لِلْمَلٰٓئِكَةِ اسْجُدُوْا لِاٰدَمَ فَسَجَدُوْٓا
اِلَّآ اِبْلِيْسَ ؕ قَالَ ءَاَسْجُدُ لِمَنْ خَلَقْتَ طِيْنًا ﴿٦١﴾
قَالَ اَرَءَيْتَكَ هٰذَا الَّذِيْ كَرَّمْتَ
عَلَيَّ ؗ لَئِنْ اَخَّرْتَنِ اِلٰى يَوْمِ الْقِيٰمَةِ
لَاَحْتَنِكَنَّ ذُرِّيَّتَهٗٓ اِلَّا قَلِيْلًا ﴿٦٢﴾
قَالَ اذْهَبْ فَمَنْ تَبِعَكَ مِنْهُمْ فَاِنَّ
جَهَنَّمَ جَزَآؤُكُمْ جَزَآءً مَّوْفُوْرًا ﴿٦٣﴾
وَاسْتَفْزِزْ مَنِ اسْتَطَعْتَ مِنْهُمْ بِصَوْتِكَ
وَاَجْلِبْ عَلَيْهِمْ بِخَيْلِكَ وَرَجِلِكَ وَشَارِكْهُمْ
فِي الْاَمْوَالِ وَالْاَوْلَادِ وَعِدْهُمْ ؕ وَمَا
يَعِدُهُمُ الشَّيْطٰنُ اِلَّا غُرُوْرًا ﴿٦٤﴾
اِنَّ عِبَادِيْ لَيْسَ لَكَ عَلَيْهِمْ سُلْطٰنٌ ؕ
وَكَفٰى بِرَبِّكَ وَكِيْلًا ﴿٦٥﴾
رَبُّكُمُ الَّذِيْ يُزْجِيْ لَكُمُ الْفُلْكَ فِي الْبَحْرِ

لِتَبْتَغُوْا مِنْ فَضْلِهٖ ۭ اِنَّهٗ كَانَ بِكُمْ
رَحِيْمًا ﴿۶۶﴾
وَاِذَا مَسَّكُمُ الضُّرُّ فِي الْبَحْرِ ضَلَّ مَنْ
تَدْعُوْنَ اِلَّآ اِيَّاهُ ۚ فَلَمَّا نَجّٰىكُمْ اِلَى
الْبَرِّ اَعْرَضْتُمْ ۭ وَكَانَ الْاِنْسَانُ كَفُوْرًا ﴿۶۷﴾
اَفَاَمِنْتُمْ اَنْ يَّخْسِفَ بِكُمْ جَانِبَ الْبَرِّ
اَوْ يُرْسِلَ عَلَيْكُمْ حَاصِبًا ثُمَّ لَا تَجِدُوْا
لَكُمْ وَكِيْلًا ۙ ﴿۶۸﴾
اَمْ اَمِنْتُمْ اَنْ يُّعِيْدَكُمْ فِيْهِ تَارَةً
اُخْرٰى فَيُرْسِلَ عَلَيْكُمْ قَاصِفًا مِّنَ
الرِّيْحِ فَيُغْرِقَكُمْ بِمَا كَفَرْتُمْ ۙ ثُمَّ
لَا تَجِدُوْا لَكُمْ عَلَيْنَا بِهٖ تَبِيْعًا ﴿۶۹﴾
وَلَقَدْ كَرَّمْنَا بَنِيْٓ اٰدَمَ وَحَمَلْنٰهُمْ
فِي الْبَرِّ وَالْبَحْرِ وَرَزَقْنٰهُمْ مِّنَ
الطَّيِّبٰتِ وَفَضَّلْنٰهُمْ عَلٰي كَثِيْرٍ
مِّمَّنْ خَلَقْنَا تَفْضِيْلًا ﴿۷۰﴾ ع
يَوْمَ نَدْعُوْا كُلَّ اُنَاسٍۢ بِاِمَامِهِمْ ۚ
فَمَنْ اُوْتِيَ كِتٰبَهٗ بِيَمِيْنِهٖ فَاُولٰۗىِٕكَ
يَقْرَءُوْنَ كِتٰبَهُمْ وَلَا يُظْلَمُوْنَ
فَتِيْلًا ﴿۷۱﴾
وَمَنْ كَانَ فِيْ هٰذِهٖٓ اَعْمٰى فَهُوَ فِي
الْاٰخِرَةِ اَعْمٰى وَاَضَلُّ سَبِيْلًا ﴿۷۲﴾
وَاِنْ كَادُوْا لَيَفْتِنُوْنَكَ عَنِ الَّذِيْٓ
اَوْحَيْنَآ اِلَيْكَ لِتَفْتَرِيَ عَلَيْنَا غَيْرَهٗ ڰ
وَاِذًا لَّاتَّخَذُوْكَ خَلِيْلًا ﴿۷۳﴾
وَلَوْلَآ اَنْ ثَبَّتْنٰكَ لَقَدْ كِدْتَّ تَرْكَنُ
اِلَيْهِمْ شَيْـًٔا قَلِيْلًا ﴿۷۴﴾

چلاتا ہے تاکہ تم اُس کے فضل سے (روزی) تلاش کرو۔
بے شک وہ تم پر مہربان ہے ﴿۶۶﴾
اور جب تم کو دریا میں تکلیف پہنچتی ہے (یعنی ڈوبنے کا خوف ہوتا ہے) تو
جنکو تم پکارا کرتے ہو سب اُس (پروردگار) کے سوا گم ہو جاتے ہیں پھر جب وہ
تمکو ڈوبنے سے بچا کر خشکی کیطرف لیجاتا ہے تو تم منہ پھیر لیتے ہو اور انسان ہے ہی ناشکرا ﴿۶۷﴾
کیا تم (اس سے) بے خوف ہو کہ خدا تمہیں خشکی کی طرف (لیجا کر
زمین میں) دھنسا دے یا تم پر سنگریزوں کی بھری ہوئی آندھی
چلا دے۔ پھر تم اپنا کوئی نگہبان نہ پاؤ ﴿۶۸﴾
یا (اس سے) بے خوف ہو کہ تم کو دوسری دفعہ دریا میں
لے جائے پھر تم پر تیز ہوا چلائے اور تمہارے
کفر کے سبب تمہیں ڈبو دے۔ پھر تم اُس غرق کے سبب
اپنے لئے کوئی پیچھا کرنے والا نہ پاؤ ﴿۶۹﴾
اور ہم نے بنی آدم کو عزّت بخشی اور اُن کو
جنگل اور دریا میں سواری دی اور پاکیزہ
روزی عطا کی اور اپنی بہت سی مخلوقات پر
فضیلت دی ﴿۷۰﴾
جس دن ہم سب لوگوں کو اُن کے پیشواؤں کے ساتھ
بُلائیں گے۔ تو جن (کے اعمال) کی کتاب اُن کے داہنے
ہاتھ میں دی جائے گی وہ اپنی کتاب کو (خوش ہو ہو کر) پڑھینگے
اور اُن پر دھاگے برابر بھی ظلم نہ ہوگا ﴿۷۱﴾
اور جو شخص اس (دنیا) میں اندھا ہو وہ آخرت میں بھی
اندھا ہوگا اور (نجات کے) رستے سے بہت دُور ﴿۷۲﴾
اور اے پیغمبر جو وحی ہم نے تمہاری طرف بھیجی ہے قریب تھا
کہ یہ (کافر) لوگ تم کو اس سے بچلا دیں تاکہ تم اسکے سوا اور
باتیں ہماری نسبت بنا لو۔ اور اسوقت وہ تمکو دوست بنا لیتے ﴿۷۳﴾
اور اگر ہم تم کو ثابت قدم نہ رہنے دیتے تو تم کسی قدر
اُن کی طرف مائل ہونے ہی لگے تھے ﴿۷۴﴾

through the sea, in order that ye may seek of His Bounty. For He is unto you Most Merciful.

67. When distress seizes you at sea, those that ye call upon— besides Himself—leave you in the lurch! but when He brings you back safe to land, ye turn away (from Him). Most ungrateful is man!

68. Do ye then feel secure that He will not cause you to be swallowed up beneath the earth when ye are on land, or that He will not send against you a violent tornado (with showers of stones) so that ye shall find no protector

69. Or do ye feel secure that He will not send you back a second time to sea and send against you a heavy gale to drown you because of your ingratitude, so that ye find no helper therein against Us?

70. We have honoured the sons of Adam; provided them with transport on land and sea; given them for sustenance things good and pure; and conferred on them special favours, above a great part of Our Creation.

71. On the day We shall call together all human beings with their (respective) Imāms: those who are given their record in their right hand will read it (with pleasure), and they will not be dealt with unjustly in the least.

72. But those who were blind in this world, will be blind in the Hereafter, and most astray from the Path.

73. And their purpose was to tempt thee away from that which We had revealed unto thee, to substitute in Our name something quite different: (in that case), behold! they would certainly have made thee (their) friend!

74. And had We not given thee strength, thou wouldst nearly have inclined to them a little.

75. In that case We should have made thee taste double portion (of punishment) in this life, and an equal portion in death: and moreover thou wouldst have found none to help thee against Us!

76. Their purpose was to scare thee off the land, in order to expel thee; but in that case they would not have stayed (therein) after thee, except for a little while.

77. (This was Our) way with the messengers We sent before thee: thou wilt find no change in Our ways.

78. Establish regular prayers—at the sun's decline till the darkness of the night, and the recital of the Qur'an in morning prayer for the recital of dawn is witnessed.

79. And as for the night keep awake a part of it as an additional prayer for thee: soon will thy Lord raise thee to a Station of Praise and Glory!

80. Say: "O my Lord! let my entry be by the Gate of Truth and Honour, and likewise my exit by the Gate of Truth and Honour; and grant me from Thee an authority to aid (me)

81. And say: "Truth has (now) arrived, and Falsehood perished: for Falsehood is (by its nature) bound to perish."

82. We send down (stage by stage) of the Qur'an that which is a healing and a mercy to those who believe: to the unjust it causes nothing but loss after loss.

83. Yet when We bestow Our favours on man, he turns away and becomes remote on his side (instead of coming to Us), and when evil seizes him he gives himself up to despair!

84. Say: "Everyone acts according to his own disposition: but your Lord knows best who it is that is best guided on the Way."

85. They ask thee concerning the Spirit say: "The Spirit is of the command of my Lord of knowledge it is only a little that is communicated to you, (O men!)"

اس وقت ہم تم کو زندگی میں بھی (عذاب کا) دُونا اور
مرنے پر بھی دُونا مزہ چکھاتے۔ پھر تم ہمارے مقابلے میں
کسی کو اپنا مددگار نہ پاتے ﴿٧٥﴾
اور قریب تھا کہ یہ لوگ تمہیں زمین (مکّہ) سے پھسلا
دیں تاکہ تمہیں وہاں سے جلاوطن کر دیں۔ اور اس
وقت تمہارے پیچھے یہ بھی نہ رہتے مگر کم ﴿٧٦﴾
جو پیغمبر ہمنے تم سے پہلے بھیجے تھے اُنکا اور اُنکے بارے میں ہمارا
یہی) طریق رہا ہی اور تم ہمارے طریق میں تغیر و تبدل نہ پاؤگے ﴿٧٧﴾
(اے محمد) سُورج کے ڈھلنے سے رات کے اندھیرے تک (ظہر۔ عصر۔
مغرب۔ عشا کی) نمازیں اور صبح کو قرآن پڑھا کرو۔ کیونکہ
صبح کے وقت قرآن کا پڑھنا موجب حضور (ملائکہ) ہی ﴿٧٨﴾
اور بعض حصۂ شب میں بیدار رہا کرو (اور تہجد کی نماز پڑھا کرو یہ شب خیزی) تمہارے لئے
(سبب) زیادت ہی قریب ہی کہ خدا تم کو مقام محمود میں داخل کرے ﴿٧٩﴾
اور کہو کہ اے پروردگار مجھے (مدینے میں) اچھی طرح داخل کیجیو
اور (مکّے سے) اچھی طرح نکالیو۔ اور اپنے ہاں سے
زور و قوت کو میرا مددگار بنائیو ﴿٨٠﴾
اور کہہ دو کہ حق آگیا اور باطل نابود ہوگیا بے شک
باطل نابود ہونے والا ہے ﴿٨١﴾
اور ہم قرآن (کے ذریعے) سے وہ چیز نازل کرتے ہیں
جو مومنوں کے لئے شفا اور رحمت ہے اور ظالموں
کے حق میں تو اس سے نقصان ہی بڑھتا ہے ﴿٨٢﴾
اور جب ہم انسان کو نعمت بخشتے ہیں تو روگرداں ہو جاتا
اور پہلو پھیر لیتا ہی۔ اور جب اُسے سختی پہنچتی ہی تو ناامید ہو جاتا ہی ﴿٨٣﴾
کہہ دو کہ ہر شخص اپنے طریق کے مطابق عمل کرتا ہی۔ سو تمہارا پروردگار
اس شخص سے خوب واقف ہی جو سب سے زیادہ سیدھے رستے پر ہی ﴿٨٤﴾
اور تم سے رُوح کے بارے میں سوال کرتے ہیں۔ کہدو کہ وہ میرے پروردگار
کی ایک شان ہی اور تم لوگوں کو (بہت ہی کم) علم دیا گیا ہے ﴿٨٥﴾

إِذًا لَّأَذَقْنٰكَ ضِعْفَ الْحَيٰوةِ وَضِعْفَ
الْمَمَاتِ ثُمَّ لَا تَجِدُ لَكَ عَلَيْنَا
نَصِيْرًا ﴿٧٥﴾
وَإِنْ كَادُوْا لَيَسْتَفِزُّوْنَكَ مِنَ
الْأَرْضِ لِيُخْرِجُوْكَ مِنْهَا وَإِذًا لَّا
يَلْبَثُوْنَ خِلٰفَكَ إِلَّا قَلِيْلًا ﴿٧٦﴾
سُنَّةَ مَنْ قَدْ أَرْسَلْنَا قَبْلَكَ مِنْ
رُّسُلِنَا وَلَا تَجِدُ لِسُنَّتِنَا تَحْوِيْلًا ﴿٧٧﴾
أَقِمِ الصَّلٰوةَ لِدُلُوْكِ الشَّمْسِ إِلٰى
غَسَقِ الَّيْلِ وَقُرْاٰنَ الْفَجْرِ إِنَّ قُرْاٰنَ
الْفَجْرِ كَانَ مَشْهُوْدًا ﴿٧٨﴾
وَمِنَ الَّيْلِ فَتَهَجَّدْ بِهٖ نَافِلَةً لَّكَ
عَسٰى أَنْ يَّبْعَثَكَ رَبُّكَ مَقَامًا مَّحْمُوْدًا ﴿٧٩﴾
وَقُلْ رَّبِّ أَدْخِلْنِيْ مُدْخَلَ صِدْقٍ
وَّأَخْرِجْنِيْ مُخْرَجَ صِدْقٍ وَّاجْعَلْ
لِّيْ مِنْ لَّدُنْكَ سُلْطٰنًا نَّصِيْرًا ﴿٨٠﴾
وَقُلْ جَآءَ الْحَقُّ وَزَهَقَ الْبَاطِلُ إِنَّ
الْبَاطِلَ كَانَ زَهُوْقًا ﴿٨١﴾
وَنُنَزِّلُ مِنَ الْقُرْاٰنِ مَا هُوَ شِفَآءٌ
وَّرَحْمَةٌ لِّلْمُؤْمِنِيْنَ وَلَا يَزِيْدُ
الظّٰلِمِيْنَ إِلَّا خَسَارًا ﴿٨٢﴾
وَإِذَآ أَنْعَمْنَا عَلَى الْإِنْسَانِ أَعْرَضَ وَ
نَاٰ بِجَانِبِهٖ وَإِذَا مَسَّهُ الشَّرُّ كَانَ يَئُوْسًا ﴿٨٣﴾
قُلْ كُلٌّ يَّعْمَلُ عَلٰى شَاكِلَتِهٖ فَرَبُّكُمْ
أَعْلَمُ بِمَنْ هُوَ أَهْدٰى سَبِيْلًا ﴿٨٤﴾
وَيَسْأَلُوْنَكَ عَنِ الرُّوْحِ قُلِ الرُّوْحُ مِنْ
أَمْرِ رَبِّيْ وَمَآ أُوْتِيْتُمْ مِّنَ الْعِلْمِ إِلَّا قَلِيْلًا ﴿٨٥﴾

86. If it were Our Will, We could take away that which We have sent thee by inspiration: then wouldst thou find none to plead thy affair in that matter as against Us,—

87. Except for Mercy from thy Lord; for His Bounty is to thee (indeed) great.

88. Say: "If the whole of mankind and Jinns were to gather together to produce the like of this Qur'an, they could not produce the like thereof, even if they backed up each other with help and support.

89. And We have explained to man, in this Qur'an, every kind of similitude: yet the greater part of men refuse (to receive it) except with ingratitude!

90. They say: "We shall not believe in thee, until thou cause a spring to gush forth for us from the earth,

91. "Or (until) thou have a garden of date trees and vines, and cause rivers to gush forth in their midst, carrying abundant water;

92. "Or thou cause the sky to fall in pieces, as thou sayest (will happen), against us; or thou bring Allah and the angels before (us) face to face;

93. "Or thou have a house adorned with gold, or thou mount a ladder right into the skies. No, we shall not even believe in thy mounting until thou send down to us a book that we could read." Say: "Glory to my Lord! Am I aught but a man,— a messenger?"

94. What kept men back from Belief when Guidance came to them, was nothing but this: they said, "Has Allah sent a man (like us) to be (His) Messenger?"

95. Say, "If there were settled, on earth, angels walking about in peace and quiet, We should certainly have sent them down from the heavens an angel for a messenger."

اور اگر ہم چاہیں تو جو کتاب ہم تمہاری طرف بھیجتے ہیں اُسے (دلوں سے)
محو کردیں۔ پھر تم اسکے لئے ہمارے مقابلے میں کسی کو مددگار نہ پاؤ ﴿۸۶﴾
مگر (اس کا قائم رہنا) تمہارے پروردگار کی رحمت ہے۔ کچھ
شک نہیں کہ تم پر اس کا بڑا فضل ہے ﴿۸۷﴾
کہہ دو کہ اگر انسان اور جن اس بات پر مجتمع ہوں
کہ اس قرآن جیسا بنا لائیں تو اس جیسا
نہ لاسکیں گے اگرچہ وہ ایک دوسرے کے
مددگار ہوں ﴿۸۸﴾
اور ہم نے قرآن میں سب باتیں طرح طرح سے بیان
کردی ہیں مگر اکثر لوگوں نے انکار کرنے کے سوا
قبول نہ کیا ﴿۸۹﴾
اور کہنے لگے کہ ہم تم پر ایمان نہیں لائینگے جبتک کہ (عجیب و
غریب باتیں نہ دکھاؤ یعنی یا تو) ہمارے لئے زمین سے چشمہ جاری کردو ﴿۹۰﴾
یا تمہارا کھجوروں اور انگوروں کا کوئی باغ ہو اور اسکے بیچ میں
نہریں بہا نکالو ﴿۹۱﴾
یا جیسا تم کہا کرتے ہو ہم پر آسمان کے ٹکڑے لا گراؤ یا خدا
اور فرشتوں کو (ہمارے) سامنے لے آؤ ﴿۹۲﴾
یا تو تمہارا سونے کا گھر ہو۔ یا تم آسمان پر چڑھ جاؤ اور ہم تمہارے
چڑھنے کو بھی نہیں مانیں گے جب تک کہ کوئی کتاب نہ لاؤ
جسے ہم پڑھ بھی لیں کہہ دو کہ میرا پروردگار پاک ہے میں تو
صرف ایک پیغام پہنچانے والا انسان ہوں ﴿۹۳﴾
اور جب لوگوں کے پاس ہدایت آگئی تو ان کو ایمان لانے
سے اس کے سوا کوئی چیز مانع نہ ہوئی کہ کہنے لگے کہ کیا خدا
نے آدمی کو پیغمبر کر کے بھیجا ہے ﴿۹۴﴾
کہہ دو کہ اگر زمین میں فرشتے ہوتے (کہ اس میں) چلتے
پھرتے (اور) آرام کرتے (یعنی بستے) تو ہم اُن کے پاس
فرشتے کو پیغمبر بنا کر بھیجتے ﴿۹۵﴾

وَلَئِنْ شِئْنَا لَنَذْهَبَنَّ بِالَّذِيٓ اَوْحَيْنَآ
اِلَيْكَ ثُمَّ لَا تَجِدُ لَكَ بِهٖ عَلَيْنَا وَكِيْلًا ﴿۸۶﴾
اِلَّا رَحْمَةً مِّنْ رَّبِّكَ ۭ اِنَّ فَضْلَهٗ كَانَ
عَلَيْكَ كَبِيْرًا ﴿۸۷﴾
قُلْ لَّئِنِ اجْتَمَعَتِ الْاِنْسُ وَالْجِنُّ
عَلٰٓي اَنْ يَّاْتُوْا بِمِثْلِ هٰذَا الْقُرْاٰنِ لَا
يَاْتُوْنَ بِمِثْلِهٖ وَلَوْ كَانَ بَعْضُهُمْ لِبَعْضٍ
ظَهِيْرًا ﴿۸۸﴾
وَلَقَدْ صَرَّفْنَا لِلنَّاسِ فِيْ هٰذَا الْقُرْاٰنِ
مِنْ كُلِّ مَثَلٍ ۡ فَاَبٰٓى اَكْثَرُ النَّاسِ
اِلَّا كُفُوْرًا ﴿۸۹﴾
وَقَالُوْا لَنْ نُّؤْمِنَ لَكَ حَتّٰى تَفْجُرَ لَنَا
مِنَ الْاَرْضِ يَنْۢبُوْعًا ﴿۹۰﴾
اَوْ تَكُوْنَ لَكَ جَنَّةٌ مِّنْ نَّخِيْلٍ وَّعِنَبٍ
فَتُفَجِّرَ الْاَنْهٰرَ خِلٰلَهَا تَفْجِيْرًا ﴿۹۱﴾
اَوْ تُسْقِطَ السَّمَاۗءَ كَمَا زَعَمْتَ عَلَيْنَا
كِسَفًا اَوْ تَاْتِيَ بِاللّٰهِ وَالْمَلٰۗىِٕكَةِ قَبِيْلًا ﴿۹۲﴾
اَوْ يَكُوْنَ لَكَ بَيْتٌ مِّنْ زُخْرُفٍ اَوْ
تَرْقٰى فِي السَّمَاۗءِ ۭ وَلَنْ نُّؤْمِنَ لِرُقِيِّكَ
حَتّٰى تُنَزِّلَ عَلَيْنَا كِتٰبًا نَّقْرَؤُهٗ ۭ قُلْ
سُبْحَانَ رَبِّيْ هَلْ كُنْتُ اِلَّا بَشَرًا رَّسُوْلًا ﴿۹۳﴾
وَمَا مَنَعَ النَّاسَ اَنْ يُّؤْمِنُوْٓا اِذْ جَاۗءَهُمُ
الْهُدٰٓى اِلَّآ اَنْ قَالُوْٓا اَبَعَثَ اللّٰهُ بَشَرًا
رَّسُوْلًا ﴿۹۴﴾
قُلْ لَّوْ كَانَ فِي الْاَرْضِ مَلٰۗىِٕكَةٌ
يَّمْشُوْنَ مُطْمَىِٕنِّيْنَ لَنَزَّلْنَا عَلَيْهِمْ
مِّنَ السَّمَاۗءِ مَلَكًا رَّسُوْلًا ﴿۹۵﴾

96. Say: "Enough is Allah for a witness between me and you: for He is well acquainted with His servants, and He sees (all things).

کہہ دو کہ میرے اور تمہارے درمیان خدا ہی گواہ کافی ہے وہی اپنے بندوں سے خبردار (اور اُن کو) دیکھنے والا ہے ﴿۹۶﴾

قُلْ كَفَىٰ بِاللَّهِ شَهِيدًا بَيْنِي وَبَيْنَكُمْ ۚ إِنَّهُ كَانَ بِعِبَادِهِ خَبِيرًا بَصِيرًا ﴿٩٦﴾

97. It is he whom Allah guides, that is on true guidance; but he whom He leaves astray—for such wilt thou find no protector besides Him. On the Day of Judgment We shall gather them together, prone on their faces, blind, dumb, and deaf: their abode will be Hell: every time it shows abatement, We shall increase for them the fierceness of the Fire.

اور جس شخص کو خدا ہدایت دے وہی ہدایت یاب ہے۔ اور جن کو گمراہ کرے تو تم خدا کے سوا اُن کے رفیق نہیں پاؤ گے۔ اور ہم اُن کو قیامت کے دن اوندھے مُنہ اندھے گونگے اور بہرے (بنا کر) اُٹھائینگے اور اُن کا ٹھکانا دوزخ ہے۔ جب (اس کی آگ) بجھنے کو ہوگی تو ہم اُن کو (عذاب دینے کیلئے) اور بھڑکا دینگے ﴿۹۷﴾

وَمَن يَهْدِ اللَّهُ فَهُوَ الْمُهْتَدِ ۖ وَمَن يُضْلِلْ فَلَن تَجِدَ لَهُمْ أَوْلِيَاءَ مِن دُونِهِ ۖ وَنَحْشُرُهُمْ يَوْمَ الْقِيَامَةِ عَلَىٰ وُجُوهِهِمْ عُمْيًا وَبُكْمًا وَصُمًّا ۖ مَّأْوَاهُمْ جَهَنَّمُ ۖ كُلَّمَا خَبَتْ زِدْنَاهُمْ سَعِيرًا ﴿٩٧﴾

98. That is their recompense, because they rejected Our Signs, and said, "When we are reduced to bones and broken dust, should we really be raised up (to be) a new Creation?"

یہ اُنکی سزا ہے اسلئے کہ وہ ہماری آیتوں سے کفر کرتے تھے اور کہتے تھے کہ جب ہم (مر کر بوسیدہ) ہڈیاں اور ریزہ ریزہ ہو جائینگے تو کیا از سرِ نو پیدا کئے جائیں گے؟ ﴿۹۸﴾

ذَٰلِكَ جَزَاؤُهُم بِأَنَّهُمْ كَفَرُوا بِآيَاتِنَا وَقَالُوا أَإِذَا كُنَّا عِظَامًا وَرُفَاتًا أَإِنَّا لَمَبْعُوثُونَ خَلْقًا جَدِيدًا ﴿٩٨﴾

99. See they not that Allah, Who created the heavens and the earth, has power to create the like of them (anew)? Only He has decreed a term appointed, of which there is no doubt. But the unjust refuse (to receive it) except with ingratitude.

کیا انہوں نے نہیں دیکھا کہ خدا جس نے آسمانوں اور زمین کو پیدا کیا ہے اس بات پر قادر ہے کہ اُن جیسے (لوگ) پیدا کردے۔ اور اس نے اُنکے لئے ایک وقت مقرر کر دیا ہے جسمیں کچھ بھی شک نہیں۔ تو ظالموں نے انکار کرنیکے سوا (اُسے) قبول نہ کیا ﴿۹۹﴾

أَوَلَمْ يَرَوْا أَنَّ اللَّهَ الَّذِي خَلَقَ السَّمَاوَاتِ وَالْأَرْضَ قَادِرٌ عَلَىٰ أَن يَخْلُقَ مِثْلَهُمْ وَجَعَلَ لَهُمْ أَجَلًا لَّا رَيْبَ فِيهِ فَأَبَى الظَّالِمُونَ إِلَّا كُفُورًا ﴿٩٩﴾

100. Say: "If ye had Control of the Treasures of the Mercy of my Lord, behold, ye would keep them back, for fear of spending them: for man is (ever) niggardly!"

کہہ دو کہ اگر میرے پروردگار کی رحمت کے خزانے تمہارے ہاتھ میں ہوتے تو تم خرچ ہو جانے کے خوف سے (اُن کو) بند کر رکھتے۔ اور انسان دل کا بہت تنگ ہے ﴿۱۰۰﴾

قُل لَّوْ أَنتُمْ تَمْلِكُونَ خَزَائِنَ رَحْمَةِ رَبِّي إِذًا لَّأَمْسَكْتُمْ خَشْيَةَ الْإِنفَاقِ ۚ وَكَانَ الْإِنسَانُ قَتُورًا ﴿١٠٠﴾

101. To Moses We did give nine Clear Signs: ask the Children of Israel: when he came to them, Pharaoh said to him: "O Moses! I consider thee, indeed, to have been worked upon by sorcery!

اور ہم نے موسیٰ کو نو کھلی نشانیاں دیں تو بنی اسرائیل سے دریافت کر لو کہ جب وہ اُنکے پاس آئے تو فرعون نے اُن سے کہا کہ موسیٰ! میں خیال کرتا ہوں کہ تم پر جادو کیا گیا ہے ﴿۱۰۱﴾

وَلَقَدْ آتَيْنَا مُوسَىٰ تِسْعَ آيَاتٍ بَيِّنَاتٍ ۖ فَاسْأَلْ بَنِي إِسْرَائِيلَ إِذْ جَاءَهُمْ فَقَالَ لَهُ فِرْعَوْنُ إِنِّي لَأَظُنُّكَ يَا مُوسَىٰ مَسْحُورًا ﴿١٠١﴾

102. Moses said, "Thou knowest well that these things have been sent down by none but the Lord of the heavens and the earth as eye-opening evidence: and I consider thee indeed, O Pharaoh, to be one doomed to destruction!"

انہوں نے کہا کہ تم یہ جانتے ہو کہ آسمانوں اور زمین کے پروردگار کے سوا اسکو کسی نے نازل نہیں کیا۔ (اور وہ بھی تم لوگوں کے) سمجھانے کو اور اے فرعون! میں خیال کرتا ہوں کہ تم ہلاک ہو جاؤ گے ﴿۱۰۲﴾

قَالَ لَقَدْ عَلِمْتَ مَا أَنزَلَ هَٰؤُلَاءِ إِلَّا رَبُّ السَّمَاوَاتِ وَالْأَرْضِ بَصَائِرَ وَإِنِّي لَأَظُنُّكَ يَا فِرْعَوْنُ مَثْبُورًا ﴿١٠٢﴾

103. So he resolved to remove them from the face of the earth: but We did drown him and all who were with him.

تو اُس نے چاہا کہ ان کو سرزمین (مصر) سے نکال دے تو ہم نے اُس کو اور جو اسکے ساتھ تھے سب کو ڈبو دیا ﴿۱۰۳﴾

فَأَرَادَ أَن يَسْتَفِزَّهُم مِّنَ الْأَرْضِ فَأَغْرَقْنَاهُ وَمَن مَّعَهُ جَمِيعًا ﴿١٠٣﴾

104. And We said thereafter to the Children of Israel, "Dwell securely

اور اس کے بعد بنی اسرائیل سے کہا کہ تم اس ملک میں

وَقُلْنَا مِن بَعْدِهِ لِبَنِي إِسْرَائِيلَ اسْكُنُوا

SÛRA–18
AL-KAHF
(INTRODUCTION)

It has been explained in the Introduction to S. 17 how the five Sûras 17 to 21 develop the theme of the individual soul's spiritual history, and how they fit into the general scheme of exposition.

This particular Makkan Sûra may be called a lesson on the brevity and mystery of Life. First there is the story of the Companions of the Cave who slept therein for a long period, and yet thought they had been there only a day or less. Then there is the story of the mysterious Teacher who shows Moses how Life itself is a parable. And further there is the story of Ẓul-qarnain, the two horned one, the powerful ruler of west and east, who made an iron wall to protect the weak against the strong. The parables refer to the brevity, uncertainty, and vanity of this life; to the many paradoxes in it, which can only be understood by patience and the fulness of knowledge; and to the need of guarding our spiritual gains against the incursions of evil.

الْأَرْضَ فَإِذَا جَاءَ وَعْدُ الْآخِرَةِ جِئْنَا
بِكُمْ لَفِيفًا ﴿١٠٤﴾
وَبِالْحَقِّ أَنْزَلْنَاهُ وَبِالْحَقِّ نَزَلَ ۗ وَمَا
أَرْسَلْنَاكَ إِلَّا مُبَشِّرًا وَنَذِيرًا ﴿١٠٥﴾
وَقُرْآنًا فَرَقْنَاهُ لِتَقْرَأَهُ عَلَى النَّاسِ
عَلَىٰ مُكْثٍ وَنَزَّلْنَاهُ تَنْزِيلًا ﴿١٠٦﴾
قُلْ آمِنُوا بِهِ أَوْ لَا تُؤْمِنُوا ۚ إِنَّ الَّذِينَ
أُوتُوا الْعِلْمَ مِنْ قَبْلِهِ إِذَا يُتْلَىٰ عَلَيْهِمْ
يَخِرُّونَ لِلْأَذْقَانِ سُجَّدًا ﴿١٠٧﴾
وَيَقُولُونَ سُبْحَانَ رَبِّنَا إِنْ كَانَ وَعْدُ
رَبِّنَا لَمَفْعُولًا ﴿١٠٨﴾
وَيَخِرُّونَ لِلْأَذْقَانِ يَبْكُونَ وَيَزِيدُهُمْ
خُشُوعًا ﴿١٠٩﴾
قُلِ ادْعُوا اللَّهَ أَوِ ادْعُوا الرَّحْمَٰنَ ۖ
أَيًّا مَا تَدْعُوا فَلَهُ الْأَسْمَاءُ الْحُسْنَىٰ ۚ
وَلَا تَجْهَرْ بِصَلَاتِكَ وَلَا تُخَافِتْ بِهَا
وَابْتَغِ بَيْنَ ذَٰلِكَ سَبِيلًا ﴿١١٠﴾
وَقُلِ الْحَمْدُ لِلَّهِ الَّذِي لَمْ يَتَّخِذْ وَلَدًا
وَلَمْ يَكُنْ لَهُ شَرِيكٌ فِي الْمُلْكِ وَلَمْ
يَكُنْ لَهُ وَلِيٌّ مِنَ الذُّلِّ ۖ وَكَبِّرْهُ
تَكْبِيرًا ﴿١١١﴾ ع ١٢

رہو سہو۔ پھر جب آخرت کا وعدہ آجائے گا تو ہم تم سب
کو جمع کر کے لے آئیں گے ﴿۱۰۴﴾
اور ہم نے اس قرآن کو سچائی کیساتھ نازل کیا ہے اور وہ سچائی کیساتھ نازل ہوا ﴿۱۰۵﴾
اور (اے محمد) ہم نے تمکو صرف خوشخبری دینے والا اور ڈر سنانے والا بناکر بھیجا ہے
اور ہم نے قرآن کو جزو جزو کر کے نازل کیا ہے تاکہ تم لوگوں کو
ٹھیر ٹھیر کر پڑھ کر سناؤ اور ہم نے اسکو آہستہ آہستہ اتارا ہے ﴿۱۰۶﴾
کہہ دو کہ تم اس پر ایمان لاؤ یا نہ لاؤ (یہ فی نفسہ حق ہے) جن
لوگوں کو اس سے پہلے علم (کتاب) دیا گیا ہے جب وہ انکو پڑھ کر
سنایا جاتا ہے تو وہ ٹھوڑیوں کے بل سجدے میں گر پڑتے ہیں ﴿۱۰۷﴾
اور کہتے ہیں کہ ہمارا پروردگار پاک ہے۔ بے شک ہمارے
پروردگار کا وعدہ پورا ہو کر رہا ﴿۱۰۸﴾
اور وہ ٹھوڑیوں کے بل گر پڑتے ہیں (اور) روتے جاتے ہیں
اور اس سے اُن کو اور زیادہ عاجزی پیدا ہوتی ہے ﴿۱۰۹﴾
کہہ دو کہ تم (خدا کو) اللہ (کے نام سے) پکارو یا رحمٰن (کے
نام سے) جس نام سے پکارو اُس کے سب نام اچھے ہیں۔
اور نماز نہ بلند آواز سے پڑھو اور نہ آہستہ بلکہ اس کے
بیچ کا طریقہ اختیار کرو ﴿۱۱۰﴾
اور کہو کہ سب تعریف خدا ہی کو ہے جس نے نہ تو کسی کو بیٹا
بنایا ہے اور نہ اس کی بادشاہی میں کوئی شریک ہے۔ اور
نہ اس وجہ سے کہ وہ عاجز و ناتوان ہے کوئی اس کا مددگار
ہے اور اس کو بڑا جان کر اس کی بڑائی کرتے رہو ﴿۱۱۱﴾

in the land (of promise)": but when the second of the warnings came to pass, We gathered you together in a mingled crowd.

105. We sent down the (Qur'an) in Truth, and in Truth has it descended: and We sent thee but to give Glad Tidings and to warn (sinners).

106. (It is) a Qur'an which We have divided (into parts from time to time), in order that thou mightest recite it to men at intervals: We have revealed it by stages.

107. Say "Whether ye believe in it or not, it is true that those who were given knowledge beforehand, when it is recited to them, fall down on their faces in humble prostration,

108. "And they say: 'Glory to our Lord! Truly has the promise of our Lord been fulfilled!'

109. They fall down on their faces in tears, and it increases their (earnest) humility.

110. Say: "Call upon Allah, or call upon Raḥmān: by whatever name ye call upon Him, (it is well): for to Him belong the Most Beautiful Names. Neither speak thy Prayer aloud, nor speak it in a low tone, but seek a middle course between."

111. Say: "Praise be to Allah, Who begets no son, and has no partner in (His) dominion: nor (needs) He any to protect Him from humiliation: yea, magnify Him for His greatness and glory!"

سُورَةُ الْكَهْفِ مَكِّيَّةٌ وَهِيَ مِائَةٌ وَعَشْرُ آيَاتٍ وَفِيهَا اثْنَا عَشَرَ رُكُوعًا

سورۂ کہف مکی ہے اور اسمیں ایک سو دس آیتیں اور بارہ رکوع ہیں

Al-Kahf, or the Cave

بِسْمِ اللَّهِ الرَّحْمَٰنِ الرَّحِيمِ
الْحَمْدُ لِلَّهِ الَّذِي أَنْزَلَ عَلَىٰ عَبْدِهِ
الْكِتَابَ وَلَمْ يَجْعَلْ لَهُ عِوَجًا ۜ ﴿١﴾
قَيِّمًا لِيُنْذِرَ بَأْسًا شَدِيدًا مِنْ لَدُنْهُ
وَيُبَشِّرَ الْمُؤْمِنِينَ الَّذِينَ يَعْمَلُونَ

شروع خدا کا نام لے کر جو بڑا مہربان نہایت رحم والا ہے
سب تعریف خدا ہی کو ہے جس نے اپنے بندے (محمد) پر (یہ) کتاب
نازل کی اور اس میں کسی طرح کی کجی (اور پیچیدگی) نہ رکھی ﴿۱﴾
(بلکہ) سیدھی (اور سلیس اتاری) تاکہ (لوگوں کو) عذاب سخت
سے جو اسکی طرف سے (آنیوالا) ہے ڈرائے اور مومنوں کو جو نیک عمل کرتے

In the name of Allah, Most Gracious, Most Merciful.

1. Praise be to Allah, Who hath sent to His Servant the Book, and hath allowed therein no Crookedness:

2. (He hath made it) Straight (and Clear) in order that He may warn (the godless) of a terrible Punishment from Him, and that He may

الصّٰلِحٰتِ اَنَّ لَهُمْ اَجْرًا حَسَنًا ﴿۲﴾
مّٰكِثِيْنَ فِيْهِ اَبَدًا ﴿۳﴾
وَّيُنْذِرَ الَّذِيْنَ قَالُوا اتَّخَذَ اللّٰهُ وَلَدًا ﴿۴﴾
مَا لَهُمْ بِهٖ مِنْ عِلْمٍ وَّلَا لِاٰبَآىِٕهِمْ ؕ
كَبُرَتْ كَلِمَةً تَخْرُجُ مِنْ اَفْوَاهِهِمْ ؕ
اِنْ يَّقُوْلُوْنَ اِلَّا كَذِبًا ﴿۵﴾
فَلَعَلَّكَ بَاخِعٌ نَّفْسَكَ عَلٰٓى اٰثَارِهِمْ
اِنْ لَّمْ يُؤْمِنُوْا بِهٰذَا الْحَدِيْثِ اَسَفًا ﴿۶﴾
اِنَّا جَعَلْنَا مَا عَلَى الْاَرْضِ زِيْنَةً لَّهَا
لِنَبْلُوَهُمْ اَيُّهُمْ اَحْسَنُ عَمَلًا ﴿۷﴾
وَاِنَّا لَجٰعِلُوْنَ مَا عَلَيْهَا صَعِيْدًا
جُرُزًا ﴿۸﴾
اَمْ حَسِبْتَ اَنَّ اَصْحٰبَ الْكَهْفِ
وَالرَّقِيْمِ كَانُوْا مِنْ اٰيٰتِنَا عَجَبًا ﴿۹﴾
اِذْ اَوَى الْفِتْيَةُ اِلَى الْكَهْفِ فَقَالُوْا
رَبَّنَآ اٰتِنَا مِنْ لَّدُنْكَ رَحْمَةً وَّهَيِّئْ لَنَا
مِنْ اَمْرِنَا رَشَدًا ﴿۱۰﴾
فَضَرَبْنَا عَلٰٓى اٰذَانِهِمْ فِى الْكَهْفِ
سِنِيْنَ عَدَدًا ﴿۱۱﴾
ثُمَّ بَعَثْنٰهُمْ لِنَعْلَمَ اَىُّ الْحِزْبَيْنِ
ع اَحْصٰى لِمَا لَبِثُوْٓا اَمَدًا ﴿۱۲﴾
نَحْنُ نَقُصُّ عَلَيْكَ نَبَاَهُمْ بِالْحَقِّ ؕ
اِنَّهُمْ فِتْيَةٌ اٰمَنُوْا بِرَبِّهِمْ وَزِدْنٰهُمْ
هُدًى ﴿۱۳﴾
وَّرَبَطْنَا عَلٰى قُلُوْبِهِمْ اِذْ قَامُوْا
فَقَالُوْا رَبُّنَا رَبُّ السَّمٰوٰتِ وَالْاَرْضِ
لَنْ نَّدْعُوَا مِنْ دُوْنِهٖٓ اِلٰهًا لَّقَدْ

ہیں خوشخبری سنائے کہ اُن کے لئے (اُن کے کاموں کا) نیک بدلہ (یعنی بہشت) ہے ﴿۲﴾
جس میں وہ ابدالآباد رہیں گے ﴿۳﴾
اور اُن لوگوں کو بھی ڈرائے جو کہتے ہیں کہ خدا نے (کسی کو) بیٹا بنالیا ہے ﴿۴﴾
اُن کو اس بات کا کچھ بھی علم نہیں اور نہ اُن کے باپ دادا
ہی کو تھا۔ (یہ) بڑی سخت بات ہے جو اُن کے منہ سے نکلتی ہے (اور
کچھ شک نہیں کہ) یہ جو کچھ کہتے ہیں محض جھوٹ ہے ﴿۵﴾
(اے پیغمبر) اگر یہ اس کلام پر ایمان نہ لائیں تو شاید تم ان کے
پیچھے رنج کر کر کے اپنے تئیں ہلاک کردو گے ﴿۶﴾
جو چیز زمین پر ہے ہم نے اس کو زمین کیلئے آرائش بنایا ہے
تاکہ لوگوں کی آزمائش کریں کہ اُن میں کون اچھے عمل کرنے والا ہے ﴿۷﴾
اور جو چیز زمین پر ہے ہم اس کو (نابود کر کے) بنجر
میدان کردیں گے ﴿۸﴾
کیا تم خیال کرتے ہو کہ غار اور لوح والے ہماری
نشانیوں میں سے عجیب تھے؟ ﴿۹﴾
جب وہ جوان غار میں جا رہے تو کہنے لگے کہ اے ہمارے
پروردگار ہم پر اپنے ہاں سے رحمت نازل فرما۔ اور ہمارے
کام میں درستی (کے سامان) مہیا کر ﴿۱۰﴾
تو ہم نے غار میں کئی سال تک ان کے کانوں پر (نیند کا)
پردہ ڈالے (یعنی ان کو سلائے) رکھا ﴿۱۱﴾
پھر اُن کو جگا اُٹھایا تاکہ معلوم کریں کہ جتنی مدت وہ
(غار میں) رہے دونوں جماعتوں میں سے اس کی مقدار کس کو خوب یاد ہے ﴿۱۲﴾
ہم ان کے حالات تم سے صحیح صحیح بیان کرتے ہیں۔ وہ
کئی جوان تھے جو اپنے پروردگار پر ایمان لائے تھے اور
ہم نے اُن کو اور زیادہ ہدایت دی تھی ﴿۱۳﴾
اور اُن کے دلوں کو مربوط (یعنی مضبوط) کر دیا جب
وہ (اُٹھ) کھڑے ہوئے تو کہنے لگے کہ ہمارا پروردگار
آسمانوں اور زمین کا مالک ہے ہم اُس کے سوا کسی کو معبود (سمجھ کر)

give Glad Tidings to the Believers who work Righteous deeds, that they shall have a goodly Reward,

3. Wherein they shall remain for ever:

4. Further, that He may warn those (also) who say, "Allah hath begotten a son":

5. No knowledge have they of such a thing, nor had their fathers. It is a grievous thing that issues from their mouths as a saying. What they say is nothing but falsehood!

6. Thou wouldst only, perchance, Fret thyself to death, following after them, in grief, if they believe not in this Message.

7. That which is on earth We have made but as a glittering show for it, in order that We may test them—as to which of them are best in conduct.

8. Verily what is on earth We shall make but as dust and dry soil (without growth or herbage).

9. Or dost thou think that the Companions of the Cave and of the Inscription were wonders among Our Signs?

10. Behold, the youths betook themselves to the Cave: they said, "Our Lord! bestow on us mercy from Thyself, and dispose of our affair for us in the right way!"

11. Then We drew (a veil) over their ears, for a number of years, in the Cave, (so that they heard not):

12. Then We roused them, in order to test which of the two parties was best at calculating the term of years they had tarried!

13. We relate to thee their story in truth: they were youths who believed in their Lord, and We increased them in guidance:

14. We gave strength to their hearts: behold, they stood up and said: "Our Lord is the Lord of the heavens and of the earth: never shall we call upon any god other

than Him: if we did, we should indeed have uttered an enormity!

15. "These our people have taken for worship gods other than Him: why do they not bring forward an authority clear (and convincing) for what they do? Who doth more wrong than such as invent a falsehood against Allah?

16. "When ye turn away from them and the things they worship other than Allah, betake yourselves to the Cave: your Lord will shower His mercies on you and dispose of your affair towards comfort and ease."

17. Thou wouldst have seen the sun, when it rose, declining to the right from their Cave, and when it set, turning away from them to the left, while they lay in the open space in the midst of the Cave. Such are among the Signs of Allah: he whom Allah guides is rightly guided; but he whom Allah leaves to stray,—for him wilt thou find no protector to lead him to the Right Way.

18. Thou wouldst have thought them awake, whilst they were asleep, and We turned them on their right and on their left sides: their dog stretching forth his two fore-legs on the threshold: if thou hadst looked at them, thou wouldst have certainly turned back from them in flight, and wouldst certainly have been filled with terror of them.

19. Such (being their state), We raised them up (from sleep), that they might question each other. Said one of them, "How long have ye stayed (here)?" They said, "We have stayed (perhaps) a day, or part of a day." (At length) they (all) said, "Allah (alone) knows best how long ye have stayed here... Now send ye then one of you with this money of yours to the town: let him find out which is the best food (to be had) and bring some to you, (that ye may satisfy your hunger therewith) and let him behave with care and courtesy, and let him not inform anyone about you.

نہ پکارینگے (اگر ایسا کیا) تو اس وقت ہم نے بعید از عقل بات کہی ﴿١٤﴾
ان ہماری قوم کے لوگوں نے اس کے سوا اور معبود
بنا رکھے ہیں۔ بھلا یہ اُن (کے خدا ہونے) پر کوئی کھلی
دلیل کیوں نہیں لاتے۔ تو اس سے زیادہ کون ظالم ہے
جو خدا پر جھوٹ افترا کرے ﴿١٥﴾
اور جب تم نے ان (مشرکوں) سے اور جن کو یہ خدا کے
سوا عبادت کرتے ہیں ان سے کنارہ کر لیا ہے تو غار میں
چل رہو۔ تمہارا پروردگار تمہارے لئے اپنی رحمت وسیع کر دیگا
اور تمہارے کاموں میں آسانی (کے سامان) مہیا کریگا[١٤٢] ﴿١٦﴾
اور جب سورج نکلے تو تم دیکھو کہ (دھوپ) ان کے غار
سے داہنی طرف سمٹ جائے اور جب غروب ہو تو ان
سے بائیں طرف کترا جائے اور وہ اُس کے میدان میں تھے۔
یہ خدا کی نشانیوں میں سے ہیں۔ جس کو خدا ہدایت دے وہ
ہدایت یاب ہے۔ اور جس کو گمراہ کرے تو تم اس کے لئے
کوئی دوست راہ بتانے والا نہ پاؤ گے[١٤٣] ﴿١٧﴾
اور تم اُن کو خیال کرو کہ جاگ رہے ہیں۔ حالانکہ وہ سوتے
ہیں۔ اور ہم اُن کو دائیں اور بائیں کروٹ بدلاتے تھے۔
اور اُن کا کتا چوکھٹ پر دونوں ہاتھ پھیلائے ہوئے تھا۔
اگر تم اُن کو جھانک کر دیکھتے تو پیٹھ پھیر کر بھاگ جاتے
اور اُن سے دہشت میں آجاتے ﴿١٨﴾
اور اسی طرح ہم نے اُن کو اٹھایا تاکہ آپس میں ایک دوسرے
سے دریافت کریں۔ ایک کہنے والے نے کہا کہ تم (یہاں) کتنی
مدت رہے؟ اُنہوں نے کہا کہ ایک دن یا اس سے بھی کم۔
اُنہوں نے کہا کہ جتنی مدت تم رہے ہو تمہارا پروردگار ہی
اس کو خوب جانتا ہے۔ تو اپنے میں سے کسی کو یہ روپیہ دیکر
شہر کو بھیجو وہ دیکھے کہ نفیس کھانا کونسا ہے تو اُس میں سے کھانا لے
آئے اور آہستہ آہستہ آئے جائے اور تمہارا حال کسی کو نہ بتائے ﴿١٩﴾

قُلْنَآ اِذًا شَطَطًا ﴿١٤﴾
هٰٓؤُلَآءِ قَوْمُنَا اتَّخَذُوْا مِنْ دُوْنِهٖٓ
اٰلِهَةً ؕ لَوْلَا يَاْتُوْنَ عَلَيْهِمْ بِسُلْطٰنٍۢ
بَيِّنٍ ؕ فَمَنْ اَظْلَمُ مِمَّنِ افْتَرٰى عَلَى
اللّٰهِ كَذِبًا ﴿١٥﴾
وَاِذِ اعْتَزَلْتُمُوْهُمْ وَمَا يَعْبُدُوْنَ
اِلَّا اللّٰهَ فَاْوٗٓا اِلَى الْكَهْفِ يَنْشُرْ لَكُمْ
رَبُّكُمْ مِّنْ رَّحْمَتِهٖ وَيُهَيِّئْ لَكُمْ
مِّنْ اَمْرِكُمْ مِّرْفَقًا ﴿١٦﴾
وَتَرَى الشَّمْسَ اِذَا طَلَعَتْ تَّزٰوَرُ
عَنْ كَهْفِهِمْ ذَاتَ الْيَمِيْنِ وَاِذَا غَرَبَتْ
تَّقْرِضُهُمْ ذَاتَ الشِّمَالِ وَهُمْ فِيْ فَجْوَةٍ
مِّنْهُ ؕ ذٰلِكَ مِنْ اٰيٰتِ اللّٰهِ ؕ مَنْ يَّهْدِ
اللّٰهُ فَهُوَ الْمُهْتَدِ ۚ وَمَنْ يُّضْلِلْ فَلَنْ
تَجِدَ لَهٗ وَلِيًّا مُّرْشِدًا ﴿١٧﴾ ع ١٤
وَتَحْسَبُهُمْ اَيْقَاظًا وَّهُمْ رُقُوْدٌ ۖ
وَّنُقَلِّبُهُمْ ذَاتَ الْيَمِيْنِ وَذَاتَ
الشِّمَالِ ۖ وَكَلْبُهُمْ بَاسِطٌ ذِرَاعَيْهِ
بِالْوَصِيْدِ ؕ لَوِ اطَّلَعْتَ عَلَيْهِمْ لَوَلَّيْتَ
مِنْهُمْ فِرَارًا وَّلَمُلِئْتَ مِنْهُمْ رُعْبًا ﴿١٨﴾
وَكَذٰلِكَ بَعَثْنٰهُمْ لِيَتَسَآءَلُوْا بَيْنَهُمْ ؕ
قَالَ قَآئِلٌ مِّنْهُمْ كَمْ لَبِثْتُمْ ؕ قَالُوْا
لَبِثْنَا يَوْمًا اَوْ بَعْضَ يَوْمٍ ؕ قَالُوْا رَبُّكُمْ
اَعْلَمُ بِمَا لَبِثْتُمْ ؕ فَابْعَثُوْٓا اَحَدَكُمْ
بِوَرِقِكُمْ هٰذِهٖٓ اِلَى الْمَدِيْنَةِ فَلْيَنْظُرْ
اَيُّهَآ اَزْكٰى طَعَامًا فَلْيَاْتِكُمْ بِرِزْقٍ
مِّنْهُ وَلْيَتَلَطَّفْ وَلَا يُشْعِرَنَّ بِكُمْ اَحَدًا ﴿١٩﴾

نصف القرآن بعدد الحروف الی حرف التاء من کلمۃ ولیتلطف

20. "For if they should come upon you, they would stone you or force you to return to their religion, and in that case ye would never attain prosperity."

21. Thus did We make their case know to the people, that they might know that the promise of Allah is true, and that there can be no doubt about the Hour of Judgment. Behold, they dispute among themselves as to their affair. (Some) said, "Construct a building over them": their Lord knows best about them: those who prevailed over their affair said, "Let us surely build a place of worship over them."

22. (Some) say they were three, the dog being the fourth among them; (others) say they were five, the dog being the sixth,—doubtfully guessing at the unknown; (yet others) say they were seven, the dog being the eighth. Say thou: "My Lord knoweth best their number; it is but few that know their (real case)." Enter not, therefore, into controversies concerning them, except on a matter that is clear, nor consult any of them about (the affair of) the Sleepers.

23. Nor say of anything, "I shall be sure to do so and so tomorrow"—

24. Except "If Allah so wills" and remember thy Lord when thou forgettest, and say, "I hope that my Lord will guide me ever closer (even) than this to the right course."

25. So they stayed in their Cave three hundred years, and nine (more).

26. Say: "Allah knows best how long they stayed: with Him is (the knowledge of) the secrets of the heavens and the earth: how clearly He sees, how finely He hears (everything)! They have no protector other than Him; nor does He share His Command with any person whatsoever.

27. And recite (and teach) what has been revealed to thee of the Book of thy Lord: none can change His Words, and none wilt thou find as a refuge other than Him.

28. And keep yourself content with those who call on their Lord

اگر وہ تم پر دسترس پالیں گے تو تمہیں سنگسار کر دیں گے۔ یا
پھر اپنے مذہب میں داخل کر لیں گے اور اُس وقت تم کبھی فلاح نہیں پاؤ گے ﴿۲۰﴾
اور اسی طرح ہم نے (لوگوں کو) ان (کے حال) سے خبردار کر دیا تاکہ وہ
جانیں کہ خدا کا وعدہ سچا ہے اور یہ کہ قیامت (جس کا وعدہ کیا جاتا ہے)
اس میں کچھ شک نہیں۔ اس وقت لوگ ان کے بارے میں
باہم جھگڑنے لگے اور کہنے لگے کہ ان (کے غار) پر عمارت بنا دو۔ ان کا پروردگار
اُن (کے حال) سے خوب واقف ہے۔ جو لوگ اُن کے معاملے میں غلبہ رکھتے تھے
وہ کہنے لگے کہ ہم ان (کے غار) پر مسجد بنائیں گے ﴿۲۱﴾
(بعض لوگ) اٹکل پچو کہیں گے کہ وہ تین تھے (اور) چوتھا
اُن کا کتّا تھا اور (بعض) کہیں گے کہ وہ پانچ تھے اور چھٹا
اُن کا کتّا تھا۔ اور (بعض) کہیں گے کہ وہ سات تھے اور آٹھواں
اُن کا کتّا تھا۔ کہہ دو کہ میرا پروردگار ہی اُن کے شمار سے خوب واقف ہے اُن کو
جانتے بھی ہیں تو تھوڑے ہی لوگ (جانتے ہیں) تو تم اُن (کے معاملے) میں گفتگو
نہ کرنا مگر سرسری سی گفتگو۔ اور نہ ان کے بارے میں اُن میں سے کسی سے کچھ دریافت ہی کرنا ﴿۲۲﴾
اور کسی کام کی نسبت نہ کہنا کہ میں اسے کل کر دوں گا ﴿۲۳﴾
مگر (ان شاء اللہ کہہ کر یعنی اگر) خدا چاہے تو (کر دوں گا) اور
جب خدا کا نام لینا بھول جاؤ تو یاد آنے پر لے لو۔ اور کہہ دو کہ امید ہے
کہ میرا پروردگار مجھے اس سے بھی زیادہ ہدایت کی باتیں بتائے ﴿۲۴﴾
اور اصحاب کہف اپنے غار میں نو اُوپر تین سو سال
رہے ﴿۲۵﴾
کہہ دو کہ جتنی مدت وہ رہے اُسے خدا ہی خوب جانتا ہے۔ اسی کو آسمانوں
اور زمین کی پوشیدہ باتیں (معلوم) ہیں۔ وہ کیا خوب دیکھنے والا اور کیا خوب
سننے والا ہے۔ اس کے سوا ان کا کوئی کارساز نہیں اور نہ وہ اپنے حکم میں کسی کو شریک کرتا ہے ﴿۲۶﴾
اور اپنے پروردگار کی کتاب کو جو تمہارے پاس بھیجی جاتی ہے
پڑھتے رہا کرو۔ اُس کی باتوں کو کوئی بدلنے والا نہیں۔ اور
اُس کے سوا تم کہیں پناہ بھی نہیں پاؤ گے ﴿۲۷﴾
اور جو لوگ صبح و شام اپنے پروردگار کو پکارتے اور اس

إِنَّهُمْ إِن يَظْهَرُوا عَلَيْكُمْ يَرْجُمُوكُمْ أَوْ
يُعِيدُوكُمْ فِي مِلَّتِهِمْ وَلَن تُفْلِحُوا إِذًا أَبَدًا ﴿٢٠﴾
وَكَذَٰلِكَ أَعْثَرْنَا عَلَيْهِمْ لِيَعْلَمُوا أَنَّ
وَعْدَ اللَّهِ حَقٌّ وَأَنَّ السَّاعَةَ لَا رَيْبَ
فِيهَا إِذْ يَتَنَازَعُونَ بَيْنَهُمْ أَمْرَهُمْ
فَقَالُوا ابْنُوا عَلَيْهِم بُنْيَانًا رَّبُّهُمْ
أَعْلَمُ بِهِمْ قَالَ الَّذِينَ غَلَبُوا عَلَىٰ
أَمْرِهِمْ لَنَتَّخِذَنَّ عَلَيْهِم مَّسْجِدًا ﴿٢١﴾
سَيَقُولُونَ ثَلَاثَةٌ رَّابِعُهُمْ كَلْبُهُمْ وَ
يَقُولُونَ خَمْسَةٌ سَادِسُهُمْ كَلْبُهُمْ رَجْمًا
بِالْغَيْبِ وَيَقُولُونَ سَبْعَةٌ وَثَامِنُهُمْ كَلْبُهُمْ
قُل رَّبِّي أَعْلَمُ بِعِدَّتِهِم مَّا يَعْلَمُهُمْ إِلَّا
قَلِيلٌ فَلَا تُمَارِ فِيهِمْ إِلَّا مِرَاءً ظَاهِرًا
وَلَا تَسْتَفْتِ فِيهِم مِّنْهُمْ أَحَدًا ﴿٢٢﴾
وَلَا تَقُولَنَّ لِشَيْءٍ إِنِّي فَاعِلٌ ذَٰلِكَ غَدًا ﴿٢٣﴾
إِلَّا أَن يَشَاءَ اللَّهُ وَاذْكُر رَّبَّكَ إِذَا
نَسِيتَ وَقُلْ عَسَىٰ أَن يَهْدِيَنِ رَبِّي
لِأَقْرَبَ مِنْ هَٰذَا رَشَدًا ﴿٢٤﴾
وَلَبِثُوا فِي كَهْفِهِمْ ثَلَاثَ مِائَةٍ سِنِينَ
وَازْدَادُوا تِسْعًا ﴿٢٥﴾
قُلِ اللَّهُ أَعْلَمُ بِمَا لَبِثُوا لَهُ غَيْبُ السَّمَاوَاتِ
وَالْأَرْضِ أَبْصِرْ بِهِ وَأَسْمِعْ مَا لَهُم مِّن
دُونِهِ مِن وَلِيٍّ وَلَا يُشْرِكُ فِي حُكْمِهِ أَحَدًا ﴿٢٦﴾
وَاتْلُ مَا أُوحِيَ إِلَيْكَ مِن كِتَابِ رَبِّكَ
لَا مُبَدِّلَ لِكَلِمَاتِهِ وَلَن تَجِدَ مِن
دُونِهِ مُلْتَحَدًا ﴿٢٧﴾
وَاصْبِرْ نَفْسَكَ مَعَ الَّذِينَ يَدْعُونَ

morning and evening, seeking His Face; and let not thine eyes pass beyond them, seeking the pomp and glitter of this Life; nor obey any whose heart We have permitted to neglect the remembrance of Us, one who follows his own desires, and his affair has become all excess.

رَبَّهُمْ بِالْغَدٰوةِ وَالْعَشِيِّ يُرِيْدُوْنَ
وَجْهَهٗ وَلَا تَعْدُ عَيْنٰكَ عَنْهُمْ ۚ تُرِيْدُ
زِيْنَةَ الْحَيٰوةِ الدُّنْيَا ۚ وَلَا تُطِعْ مَنْ
اَغْفَلْنَا قَلْبَهٗ عَنْ ذِكْرِنَا وَاتَّبَعَ هَوٰىهُ
وَكَانَ اَمْرُهٗ فُرُطًا ﴿٢٨﴾ النصف

کی خوشنودی کے طالب ہیں اُن کے ساتھ صبر کرتے
رہو۔ اور تمہاری نگاہیں ان میں سے (گزر کر اور طرف)
نہ دوڑیں۔ کہ تم آرائش زندگانی دنیا کے خواستگار ہو جاؤ۔ اور
جس شخص کے دل کو ہم نے اپنی یاد سے غافل کر دیا ہے اور وہ اپنی خواہش
کی پیروی کرتا ہے اور اسکا کام حد سے بڑھ گیا ہے اس کا کہنا نہ ماننا ﴿٢٨﴾

29. Say, "The Truth is from your Lord" let him who will, believe, and let him who will, reject (it): for the wrong-doers We have prepared a Fire whose (smoke and flames), like the walls and roof of a tent, will hem them in: if they implore relief they will be granted water like melted brass, that will scald their faces, how dreadful the drink! How uncomfortable a couch to recline on!

وَقُلِ الْحَقُّ مِنْ رَّبِّكُمْ ۫ فَمَنْ شَآءَ
فَلْيُؤْمِنْ وَّمَنْ شَآءَ فَلْيَكْفُرْ ۚ اِنَّآ اَعْتَدْنَا
لِلظّٰلِمِيْنَ نَارًا ۙ اَحَاطَ بِهِمْ سُرَادِقُهَا ؕ وَاِنْ
يَّسْتَغِيْثُوْا يُغَاثُوْا بِمَآءٍ كَالْمُهْلِ يَشْوِي
الْوُجُوْهَ ؕ بِئْسَ الشَّرَابُ ؕ وَسَآءَتْ مُرْتَفَقًا ﴿٢٩﴾

اور کہہ دو کہ (لوگو) یہ قرآن تمہارے پروردگار کی طرف سے برحق ہے تو جو
چاہے ایمان لائے اور جو چاہے کافر رہے۔ ہم نے ظالموں کیلئے (دوزخ کی)
آگ تیار کر رکھی ہے جسکی قناتیں اُنکو گھیر رہی ہونگی۔ اور اگر فریاد کرینگے
تو ایسے کھولتے ہوئے پانی سے انکی دادرسی کیجائیگی جو پگھلے ہوئے تانبے کی طرح
(گرم ہوگا اور جو) مونہوں کو بھون ڈالیگا (انکے پینے کا) پانی بھی بُرا اور آرامگاہ بھی بُری ﴿٢٩﴾

30. As to those who believe and work righteousness, verily We shall not suffer to perish the reward of any who do a (single) righteous deed.

اِنَّ الَّذِيْنَ اٰمَنُوْا وَعَمِلُوا الصّٰلِحٰتِ
اِنَّا لَا نُضِيْعُ اَجْرَ مَنْ اَحْسَنَ عَمَلًا ۚ ﴿٣٠﴾

(اور) جو ایمان لائے اور کام بھی نیک کرتے رہے تو ہم نیک
کام کرنے والوں کا اجر ضائع نہیں کرتے ﴿٣٠﴾

31. For them will be Gardens of Eternity; beneath them rivers will flow: they will be adorned therein with bracelets of gold, and they will wear green garments of fine silk and heavy brocade; they will recline therein on raised thrones. How good the recompense! How beautiful a couch to recline on!

اُولٰٓئِكَ لَهُمْ جَنّٰتُ عَدْنٍ تَجْرِيْ مِنْ
تَحْتِهِمُ الْاَنْهٰرُ يُحَلَّوْنَ فِيْهَا مِنْ اَسَاوِرَ
مِنْ ذَهَبٍ وَّيَلْبَسُوْنَ ثِيَابًا خُضْرًا مِّنْ
سُنْدُسٍ وَّاِسْتَبْرَقٍ مُّتَّكِـِٕيْنَ فِيْهَا عَلَى
الْاَرَآئِكِ ؕ نِعْمَ الثَّوَابُ ؕ وَحَسُنَتْ مُرْتَفَقًا ﴿٣١﴾ ع ٤/١٦

ایسے لوگوں کے لئے ہمیشہ رہنے کے باغ ہیں جن میں اُنکے
(محلوں کے) نیچے نہریں بہ رہی ہیں۔ اُن کو وہاں سونے
کے کنگن پہنائے جائیں گے اور وہ باریک دیبا اور اطلس
کے سبز کپڑے پہنا کرینگے۔ (اور) تختوں پر تکیے لگا کر بیٹھا کرینگے
(کیا) خوب بدلہ اور (کیا) خوب آرامگاہ ہے ﴿٣١﴾

32. Set forth to them the parable of two men: For one of them We provided two gardens of grapevines and surrounded them with date palms; in between the two We placed tillage.

وَاضْرِبْ لَهُمْ مَّثَلًا رَّجُلَيْنِ جَعَلْنَا
لِاَحَدِهِمَا جَنَّتَيْنِ مِنْ اَعْنَابٍ وَّ
حَفَفْنٰهُمَا بِنَخْلٍ وَّجَعَلْنَا بَيْنَهُمَا زَرْعًا ؕ ﴿٣٢﴾

اور ان سے دو شخصوں کا حال بیان کرو جن میں سے ایک کو
ہم نے انگور کے دو باغ (عنایت) کئے تھے اور اُنکے گرداگرد
کھجوروں کے درخت لگا دیئے تھے اور اُنکے درمیان کھیتی پیدا کر دی تھی ﴿٣٢﴾

33. Each of those gardens brought forth its produce, and failed not in the least therein: in the midst of them We caused a river to flow.

كِلْتَا الْجَنَّتَيْنِ اٰتَتْ اُكُلَهَا وَلَمْ تَظْلِمْ
مِّنْهُ شَيْـًٔا ۙ وَّفَجَّرْنَا خِلٰلَهُمَا نَهَرًا ۙ ﴿٣٣﴾

دونوں باغ (کثرت سے) پھل لاتے۔ اور اس (کی پیداوار) میں
کسی طرح کی کمی نہ ہوتی اور دونوں میں ہم نے ایک نہر بھی جاری کر رکھی تھی ﴿٣٣﴾

34. (Abundant) was the produce this man had: he said to his companion, in the course of a mutual argument: "More wealth have I than you, and more honour and power in (my following of) men."

وَّكَانَ لَهٗ ثَمَرٌ ۚ فَقَالَ لِصَاحِبِهٖ وَهُوَ
يُحَاوِرُهٗٓ اَنَا اَكْثَرُ مِنْكَ مَالًا وَّاَعَزُّ
نَفَرًا ﴿٣٤﴾

اور (اسطرح) اُس (شخص) کو (اُنکی) پیداوار (ملتی رہتی) تھی تو (ایک دن) جبکہ
وہ اپنے دوست سے باتیں کر رہا تھا کہنے لگا کہ میں تم سے مال (و دولت)
میں بھی زیادہ ہوں اور جتھے (اور جماعت) کے لحاظ سے بھی زیادہ عزت والا ہوں ﴿٣٤﴾

35. He went into his garden while he wronged himself: he said, "I deem not that this will ever perish,"

وَدَخَلَ جَنَّتَهٗ وَهُوَ ظَالِمٌ لِّنَفْسِهٖ ۚ
قَالَ مَآ اَظُنُّ اَنْ تَبِيْدَ هٰذِهٖٓ اَبَدًا ۙ ﴿٣٥﴾

اور (ایسی شیخیوں سے) اپنے حق میں ظلم کرتا ہوا اپنے باغ میں داخل
ہوا کہنے لگا کہ میں نہیں خیال کرتا کہ یہ باغ کبھی تباہ ہو ﴿٣٥﴾

36. "Nor do I deem that the Hour (of Judgment) will (ever) come: even if I am brought back to my Lord. I shall surely find (there) something better in exchange."

اور نہ خیال کرتا ہوں کہ قیامت برپا ہو۔ اور اگر میں اپنے
پروردگار کی طرف لوٹایا بھی جاؤں۔ تو (وہاں) ضرور اس
سے اچھی جگہ پاؤں گا (۳۶)

وَّمَآ اَظُنُّ السَّاعَةَ قَآئِمَةً ۙ وَّلَئِنۡ
رُّدِدۡتُّ اِلٰى رَبِّىۡ لَاَجِدَنَّ خَيۡرًا مِّنۡهَا
مُنۡقَلَبًا ۚ (۳۶)

37. His companion said to him, in the course of the argument with him: "Dost thou deny Him Who created thee out of dust, then out of a sperm-drop, then fashioned thee into a man?

تو اس کا دوست جو اس سے گفتگو کر رہا تھا کہنے لگا کہ کیا
تم اس (خدا) سے کفر کرتے ہو جس نے تم کو مٹی سے پیدا کیا پھر
نطفے سے پھر تمہیں پورا مرد بنایا (۳۷)

قَالَ لَهٗ صَاحِبُهٗ وَهُوَ يُحَاوِرُهٗۤ اَكَفَرۡتَ
بِالَّذِىۡ خَلَقَكَ مِنۡ تُرَابٍ ثُمَّ مِنۡ
نُّطۡفَةٍ ثُمَّ سَوّٰٮكَ رَجُلًا ؕ (۳۷)

38. "But as for my part Allah is my Lord, and none shall I associate with my Lord.

مگر میں تو یہ کہتا ہوں کہ خدا ہی میرا پروردگار ہے اور میں
اپنے پروردگار کے ساتھ کسی کو شریک نہیں کرتا (۳۸)

لٰـكِنَّا۟ هُوَ اللّٰهُ رَبِّىۡ وَلَاۤ اُشۡرِكُ بِرَبِّىۡۤ
اَحَدًا (۳۸)

39. "Why didst thou not, as thou wentest into Thy garden, say: 'Allah's Will (be done)! There is no power but from Allah!' If thou dost see me less than thee in wealth and sons,

اور (بھلا) جب تم اپنے باغ میں داخل ہوئے تو تم نے
ماشاءاللہ لاقوۃ الا باللہ کیوں نہ کہا؟ اگر تم مجھے مال و
اولاد میں اپنے سے کمتر دیکھتے ہو (۳۹)

وَلَوۡلَاۤ اِذۡ دَخَلۡتَ جَنَّتَكَ قُلۡتَ مَا شَآءَ
اللّٰهُ ۙ لَا قُوَّةَ اِلَّا بِاللّٰهِ ۚ اِنۡ تَرَنِ اَنَا
اَقَلَّ مِنۡكَ مَالًا وَّوَلَدًا ۚ (۳۹)

40. "It may be that my Lord will give me something better than thy garden, and that He will send on thy garden thunderbolts (by way of reckoning) from heaven, making it (but) slippery sand!—

تو عجب نہیں کہ میرا پروردگار مجھے تمہارے باغ سے بہتر عطا
فرمائے۔ اور اس (تمہارے باغ) پر آسمان سے آفت بھیج دے
تو وہ صاف میدان ہو جائے (۴۰)

فَعَسٰى رَبِّىۡۤ اَنۡ يُّؤۡتِيَنِ خَيۡرًا مِّنۡ
جَنَّتِكَ وَيُرۡسِلَ عَلَيۡهَا حُسۡبَانًا مِّنَ
السَّمَآءِ فَتُصۡبِحَ صَعِيۡدًا زَلَقًا ۙ (۴۰)

41. "Or the water of the garden will run off underground so that thou wilt never be able to find it."

یا اس (کی نہر) کا پانی گہرا ہو جائے تو پھر تم اسے
نہ لا سکو (۴۱)

اَوۡ يُصۡبِحَ مَآؤُهَا غَوۡرًا فَلَنۡ تَسۡتَطِيۡعَ
لَهٗ طَلَبًا (۴۱)

42. So his fruits were encompassed (with ruin), and he remained twisting and turning his hands over what he had spent on his property, which had (now) tumbled to pieces to its very foundations, and he could only say, "Woe is me! Would I had never ascribed partners to my Lord and Cherisher!"

اور اس کے میووں کو عذاب نے آ گھیرا اور وہ اپنی
چھتریوں پر گر کر رہ گیا۔ تو جو مال اس نے اس پر خرچ
کیا تھا اس پر (حسرت سے) ہاتھ ملنے لگا۔ اور کہنے لگا کاش
میں اپنے پروردگار کے ساتھ کسی کو شریک نہ بناتا (۴۲)

وَاُحِيۡطَ بِثَمَرِهٖ فَاَصۡبَحَ يُقَلِّبُ كَفَّيۡهِ
عَلٰى مَاۤ اَنۡفَقَ فِيۡهَا وَهِىَ خَاوِيَةٌ عَلٰى
عُرُوۡشِهَا وَيَقُوۡلُ يٰلَيۡتَنِىۡ لَمۡ اُشۡرِكۡ
بِرَبِّىۡۤ اَحَدًا (۴۲)

43. Nor had he numbers to help him against Allah, nor was he able to deliver himself.

(اس وقت) خدا کے سوا کوئی جماعت اس کی مددگار نہ
ہوئی اور نہ وہ بدلہ لے سکا (۴۳)

وَلَمۡ تَكُنۡ لَّهٗ فِئَةٌ يَّنۡصُرُوۡنَهٗ مِنۡ
دُوۡنِ اللّٰهِ وَمَا كَانَ مُنۡتَصِرًا ؕ (۴۳)

44. There, the (only) protection comes from Allah, the True One. He is the Best to reward, and the Best to give success.

یہاں (سے ثابت ہوا کہ) حکومت سب خدائے برحق کی ہے
اسی کا صلہ بہتر اور (اسی کا) بدلہ اچھا ہے (۴۴)

هُنَالِكَ الۡوَلَايَةُ لِلّٰهِ الۡحَقِّ ؕ هُوَ خَيۡرٌ ۵
ثَوَابًا وَّخَيۡرٌ عُقۡبًا ۚ (۴۴) ع ۱۳ ۱۷

45. Set forth to them the similitude of the life of this world: it is like the rain which We send down from the skies: the earth's vegetation absorbs it, but soon it becomes dry

اور ان سے دنیا کی زندگی کی مثال بھی بیان کر دو (وہ)
ایسی ہے جیسے پانی جسے ہم نے آسمان سے برسایا۔ تو
اس کے ساتھ زمین کی روئیدگی مل گئی پھر وہ چورا چورا

وَاضۡرِبۡ لَهُمۡ مَّثَلَ الۡحَيٰوةِ الدُّنۡيَا
كَمَآءٍ اَنۡزَلۡنٰهُ مِنَ السَّمَآءِ فَاخۡتَلَطَ
بِهٖ نَبَاتُ الۡاَرۡضِ فَاَصۡبَحَ هَشِيۡمًا

stubble, which the winds do scatter: it is (only) Allah Who prevails over all things.

ہوگئی کہ ہوائیں اُسے اُڑاتی پھرتی ہیں۔ اور خدا تو ہر چیز
پر قدرت رکھتا ہے ﴿٤٥﴾

تَذْرُوْهُ الرِّيٰحُ ۗ وَكَانَ اللّٰهُ عَلٰى كُلِّ
شَيْءٍ مُّقْتَدِرًا ﴿٤٥﴾

46. Wealth and sons are allurements of the life of this world: but the things that endure, Good Deeds, are best in the sight of thy Lord, as rewards, and best as (the foundation for) hopes.

مال اور بیٹے تو دنیا کی زندگی کی (رونق و) زینت ہیں۔
اور نیکیاں جو باقی رہنے والی ہیں وہ ثواب کے لحاظ سے تمہارے
پروردگار کے ہاں بہت اچھی اور اُمید کے لحاظ سے بہت بہتر ہیں ﴿٤٦﴾

اَلْمَالُ وَالْبَنُوْنَ زِيْنَةُ الْحَيٰوةِ الدُّنْيَا ۚ
وَالْبٰقِيٰتُ الصّٰلِحٰتُ خَيْرٌ عِنْدَ رَبِّكَ
ثَوَابًا وَّخَيْرٌ اَمَلًا ﴿٤٦﴾

47. On the Day We shall remove the mountains, and thou wilt see the earth as a level stretch, and We shall gather them, all together, nor shall We leave out anyone of them.

اور جس دن ہم پہاڑوں کو چلائیں گے اور تم زمین کو صاف
میدان دیکھو گے اور ان (لوگوں) کو ہم جمع کرلیں گے تو
ان میں سے کسی کو بھی نہیں چھوڑیں گے ﴿٤٧﴾

وَيَوْمَ نُسَيِّرُ الْجِبَالَ وَتَرَى الْاَرْضَ
بَارِزَةً ۙ وَّحَشَرْنٰهُمْ فَلَمْ نُغَادِرْ مِنْهُمْ
اَحَدًا ﴿٤٧﴾

48. And they will be marshalled before thy Lord in ranks (with the announcement) , "Now have ye come to Us (bare) as We created you first: aye, ye thought We shall not fulfil the appointment made to you to meet (Us)!":

اور سب تمہارے پروردگار کے سامنے صف باندھ کر لائے جائینگے
(تو ہم اُن سے کہیں گے کہ) جس طرح ہم نے تم کو پہلی بار پیدا کیا تھا
(اسی طرح آج) تم ہمارے سامنے آئے لیکن تم نے تو یہ خیال کر رکھا
تھا کہ ہم نے تمہارے لئے (قیامت کا) کوئی وقت مقرر ہی نہیں کیا ﴿٤٨﴾

وَعُرِضُوْا عَلٰى رَبِّكَ صَفًّا ۗ لَقَدْ
جِئْتُمُوْنَا كَمَا خَلَقْنٰكُمْ اَوَّلَ مَرَّةٍ ۭ
بَلْ زَعَمْتُمْ اَلَّنْ نَّجْعَلَ لَكُمْ
مَّوْعِدًا ﴿٤٨﴾

49. And the Book (of Deeds) will be placed (before you); and thou wilt see the sinful in great terror because of what is (recorded) therein; they will say, "Ah! woe to us! What a book is this! It leaves out nothing small or great, but takes account thereof!" They will find all that they did, placed before them: and not one will thy Lord treat with injustice.

اور (عملوں کی) کتاب (کھول کر) رکھی جائے گی تو تم گنہگاروں کو
دیکھو گے کہ جو کچھ اسمیں (لکھا) ہوگا اس سے ڈر رہے ہونگے۔
اور کہیں گے۔ ہائے شامت یہ کیسی کتاب ہے کہ نہ چھوٹی بات کو
چھوڑتی ہے نہ بڑی کو (کوئی بات بھی نہیں) مگر اسے لکھ رکھا ہے اور جو
عمل کئے ہونگے سب کو حاضر پائینگے اور تمہارا پروردگار کسی پر ظلم نہیں کریگا ﴿٤٩﴾

وَوُضِعَ الْكِتٰبُ فَتَرَى الْمُجْرِمِيْنَ
مُشْفِقِيْنَ مِمَّا فِيْهِ وَيَقُوْلُوْنَ يٰوَيْلَتَنَا
مَالِ هٰذَا الْكِتٰبِ لَا يُغَادِرُ صَغِيْرَةً
وَّلَا كَبِيْرَةً اِلَّآ اَحْصٰىهَا ۚ وَوَجَدُوْا مَا
عَمِلُوْا حَاضِرًا ۭ وَلَا يَظْلِمُ رَبُّكَ اَحَدًا ﴿٤٩﴾

50. Behold! We said to the angels, "Prostrate to Adam": they prostrated except Iblîs. He was one of the Jinns, and he broke the Command of his Lord will ye then take him and his progeny as protectors rather thàn Me? And they are enemies to you! Evil would be the exchange for the wrong-doers!

اور جب ہم نے فرشتوں کو حکم دیا کہ آدم کو سجدہ کرو تو سب نے
سجدہ کیا مگر ابلیس (نے نہ کیا) وہ جنات میں سے تھا تو اپنے
پروردگار کے حکم سے باہر ہوگیا۔ کیا تم اس کو اور اُسکی اولاد
کو میرے سوا دوست بناتے ہو حالانکہ وہ تمہارے دشمن ہیں۔
اور (شیطان کی دوستی) ظالموں کے لئے (خدا کی دوستی کا)
بُرا بدل ہے ﴿٥٠﴾

وَاِذْ قُلْنَا لِلْمَلٰٓئِكَةِ اسْجُدُوْا لِاٰدَمَ
فَسَجَدُوْٓا اِلَّآ اِبْلِيْسَ ۭ كَانَ مِنَ الْجِنِّ
فَفَسَقَ عَنْ اَمْرِ رَبِّهٖ ۭ اَفَتَتَّخِذُوْنَهٗ
وَذُرِّيَّتَهٗٓ اَوْلِيَاۗءَ مِنْ دُوْنِيْ وَهُمْ
لَكُمْ عَدُوٌّ ۭ بِئْسَ لِلظّٰلِمِيْنَ
بَدَلًا ﴿٥٠﴾

51. I called them not to witness the creation of the heavens and the earth, not (even) their own creation: nor is it for Me to take as helpers such as Lead (men) astray!

میں نے اُن کو نہ تو آسمانوں اور زمین کے پیدا کرنے کے
وقت بُلایا تھا اور نہ خود اُن کے پیدا کرنے کے وقت۔ اور
میں ایسا نہ تھا کہ گمراہ کرنے والوں کو مددگار بناتا ﴿٥١﴾

مَآ اَشْهَدْتُّهُمْ خَلْقَ السَّمٰوٰتِ وَ
الْاَرْضِ وَلَا خَلْقَ اَنْفُسِهِمْ ۠ وَمَا كُنْتُ
مُتَّخِذَ الْمُضِلِّيْنَ عَضُدًا ﴿٥١﴾

52. On the Day He will say, "Call on those whom ye thought to be

اور جس دن خدا فرمائیگا کہ (اب) میرے شریکوں کو جن کی

وَيَوْمَ يَقُوْلُ نَادُوْا شُرَكَاۗءِيَ الَّذِيْنَ

My partners." And they will call on them, but they will not listen to them; and We shall make for them a place of common perdition.

53. And the Sinful shall see the Fire and apprehend that they have to fall therein: no means will they find to turn away therefrom.

54. We have explained in detail in this Qur'an, for the benefit of mankind, every kind of similitude: but man is, in most things, contentious.

55. And what is there to keep back men from believing, now that guidance has come to them, nor from praying for forgiveness from their Lord but that (they wait for) the ways of the ancients to overtake them, or the Wrath be brought to them face to face?

56. We only send the Messengers to give glad tidings and to give warnings: but the Unbelievers dispute with vain argument, in order therewith to weaken the truth, and they treat My Signs and warnings as a jest.

57. And who doth more wrong than one who is reminded of the Signs of his Lord but turns away from them, forgetting the (deeds) which his hands have sent forth? Verily We have set veils over their hearts so that they understand this not, and over their ears, deafness. If thou callest them to guidance, even then will they never accept guidance.

58. But your Lord is Most Forgiving, full of Mercy. If He were yo call them (at once) to account for what they have earned, then surely He would have hastened their Punishment: but they have their appointed time, beyond which they will find no refuge.

59. Such were the towns We destroyed when they committed iniquities; but We fixed an appointed time for their destruction.

60. Behold, Moses said to his attendant, "I will not give up until Ireach

نسبت تم گمان (الوہیت) رکھتے تھے بلاؤ تو وہ انکو بلائینگے مگر وہ
انکو کچھ جواب دینگے۔ اور ہم انکے بیچ میں ایک ہلاکت کی جگہ بنا دینگے ﴿۵۲﴾
اور گنہگار لوگ دوزخ کو دیکھیں گے تو یقین کرلینگے کہ وہ اسمیں
پڑنے والے ہیں۔ اور اس سے بچنے کا کوئی رستہ نہ پائینگے ﴿۵۳﴾
اور ہم نے اس قرآن میں لوگوں (کے سمجھانے) کیلئے طرح طرح
کی مثالیں بیان فرمائی ہیں لیکن انسان سب چیزوں سے
بڑھ کر جھگڑالو ہے ﴿۵۴﴾
اور لوگوں کے پاس جب ہدایت آگئی تو اُن کو کس چیز نے
منع کیا کہ ایمان لائیں اور اپنے پروردگار سے بخشش مانگیں بجز
اسکے کہ (اس بات کے منتظر ہوں کہ) انہیں بھی پہلوں کا سا
معاملہ پیش آئے۔ یا اُن پر عذاب سامنے موجود ہو ﴿۵۵﴾
اور ہم جو پیغمبروں کو بھیجا کرتے ہیں تو صرف اسلئے کہ (لوگوں کو
خدا کی نعمتوں کی) خوشخبریاں سنائیں اور (عذاب سے) ڈرائیں۔ اور جو کافر
ہیں وہ باطل (کی سند) سے جھگڑا کرتے ہیں تاکہ اس سے حق کو پھسلا دیں
اور اُنہوں نے ہماری آیتوں کو اور جس چیز سے انکو ڈرایا جاتا ہے ہنسی بنا لیا ﴿۵۶﴾
اور اُس سے ظالم کون جس کو اُسکے پروردگار کے کلام سے سمجھایا
گیا تو اُس نے اُس سے منہ پھیر لیا۔ اور جو اعمال وہ آگے کر چکا
اُس کو بھول گیا۔ ہم نے انکے دلوں پر پردے ڈال دیئے کہ اسے
سمجھ نہ سکیں۔ اور کانوں میں ثقل (پیدا کر دیا ہے کہ سن نہ سکیں)
اور اگر تم انکو رستے کی طرف بلاؤ تو کبھی رستے پر نہ آئینگے ﴿۵۷﴾
اور تمہارا پروردگار بخشنے والا صاحب رحمت ہے۔ اگر وہ اُن
کے کرتوتوں پر اُن کو پکڑنے لگے تو اُن پر جھٹ عذاب بھیج دے
مگر اُن کے لئے ایک وقت (مقرر کر رکھا) ہے کہ اسکے عذاب
سے کوئی پناہ کی جگہ نہ پائیں گے ﴿۵۸﴾
اور یہ بستیاں (جو ویران پڑی ہیں) جب اُنہوں نے (کفر سے)
ظلم کیا تو ہم نے انکو تباہ کر دیا۔ اور انکی تباہی کیلئے ایک وقت مقرر کر دیا تھا ﴿۵۹﴾
اور جب موسیٰ نے اپنے شاگرد سے کہا کہ جب تک میں دو دریاؤں کے

زَعَمْتُمْ فَدَعَوْهُمْ فَلَمْ يَسْتَجِيبُوا لَهُمْ
وَجَعَلْنَا بَيْنَهُمْ مَّوْبِقًا ﴿٥٢﴾
وَرَاَ الْمُجْرِمُونَ النَّارَ فَظَنُّوا أَنَّهُمْ
مُّوَاقِعُوهَا وَلَمْ يَجِدُوا عَنْهَا مَصْرِفًا ﴿٥٣﴾ ع ٧ ١٩
وَلَقَدْ صَرَّفْنَا فِي هٰذَا الْقُرْاٰنِ لِلنَّاسِ
مِنْ كُلِّ مَثَلٍ ۚ وَكَانَ الْإِنْسَانُ أَكْثَرَ
شَيْءٍ جَدَلًا ﴿٥٤﴾
وَمَا مَنَعَ النَّاسَ أَنْ يُؤْمِنُوا إِذْ جَاءَهُمُ
الْهُدٰى وَيَسْتَغْفِرُوا رَبَّهُمْ إِلَّا أَنْ
تَأْتِيَهُمْ سُنَّةُ الْأَوَّلِينَ أَوْ يَأْتِيَهُمُ
الْعَذَابُ قُبُلًا ﴿٥٥﴾
وَمَا نُرْسِلُ الْمُرْسَلِينَ إِلَّا مُبَشِّرِينَ
وَمُنْذِرِينَ ۚ وَيُجَادِلُ الَّذِينَ كَفَرُوا
بِالْبَاطِلِ لِيُدْحِضُوا بِهِ الْحَقَّ وَاتَّخَذُوا
اٰيٰتِي وَمَا أُنْذِرُوا هُزُوًا ﴿٥٦﴾
وَمَنْ أَظْلَمُ مِمَّنْ ذُكِّرَ بِاٰيٰتِ رَبِّهِ
فَأَعْرَضَ عَنْهَا وَنَسِيَ مَا قَدَّمَتْ يَدَاهُ ط
إِنَّا جَعَلْنَا عَلٰى قُلُوبِهِمْ أَكِنَّةً أَنْ
يَفْقَهُوهُ وَفِي اٰذَانِهِمْ وَقْرًا ۖ وَإِنْ تَدْعُهُمْ
إِلَى الْهُدٰى فَلَنْ يَهْتَدُوا إِذًا أَبَدًا ﴿٥٧﴾
وَرَبُّكَ الْغَفُورُ ذُو الرَّحْمَةِ ۖ لَوْ يُؤَاخِذُهُمْ
بِمَا كَسَبُوا لَعَجَّلَ لَهُمُ الْعَذَابَ ۚ بَلْ
لَهُمْ مَوْعِدٌ لَنْ يَجِدُوا مِنْ دُونِهِ
مَوْئِلًا ﴿٥٨﴾
وَتِلْكَ الْقُرٰى أَهْلَكْنٰهُمْ لَمَّا ظَلَمُوا وَ
جَعَلْنَا لِمَهْلِكِهِمْ مَوْعِدًا ﴿٥٩﴾ ع ٨ ٢٠
وَإِذْ قَالَ مُوسٰى لِفَتٰىهُ لَا أَبْرَحُ حَتّٰى

the junction of the two seas or (until) I spend years and years in travel."
61. But when they reached the Junction, they forgot (about) their Fish, which took its course through the sea (straight) as in a tunnel.
62. When they had passed on (some distance), Moses said to his attendant: "Bring us our early meal; truly we have suffered much fatigue at this (stage of) our journey."
63. He replied: "Sawest thou (what happened) when we betook ourselves to the rock? I did indeed forget (about) the Fish: none but Satan made me forget to tell (you) about It: it took its course through the sea in a marvellous way!"
64. Moses said: "That was what we were seeking after: so they went back on their footsteps, following (the path they had come).
65. So they found one of Our servants. On whom We had bestowed Mercy from Ourselves and whom We had taught knowledge from Our own presence.
66. Moses said to him: "May I follow thee, on the footing that Thou teach me something of the (Higher) Truth which thou hast been taught?"
67. (The other) said: "Verily Thou wilt not be able to have patience with me!
68. "For how canst thou have patience about things which are beyond your knowledge?"
69. Moses said: "Thou wilt find me, if Allah so will, (truly) patient: nor shall I disobey thee in aught."
70. The other said: "If then thou wouldst follow me, ask me no questions about anything until I Myself speak to thee concerning it."
71. So they both proceeded: until, when they were in the boat, he scuttled it. Said Moses: "Hast thou scuttled it in order to drown those in it? Truly a strange thing hast thou done!"
72. He answered: "Did I not tell thee that thou canst have no patience with me?"
73. Moses said: Rebuke me not for forgetting, nor grieve me by

ملنے کی جگہ تک پہنچ جاؤں ہٹنے کا نہیں خواہ برسوں چلتا رہوں ﴿٦٠﴾
جب اُن کے ملنے کے مقام پر پہنچے تو اپنی مچھلی بھول گئے۔
تو اُس نے دریا میں سُرنگ کی طرح اپنا رستہ بنا لیا ﴿٦١﴾
جب آگے چلے تو (موسیٰ نے) اپنے شاگرد سے کہا کہ ہمارے
لئے کھانا لاؤ اس سفر سے ہم کو بہت تکان ہو گئی ہے ﴿٦٢﴾
(اس نے) کہا کہ بھلا آپ نے دیکھا کہ جب ہم نے پتھر کے
پاس آرام کیا تھا تو میں مچھلی (وہیں) بھول گیا۔ اور مجھے
(آپ سے) اُس کا ذکر کرنا شیطان نے بھلا دیا۔ اور اُس نے
عجب طرح سے دریا میں اپنا رستہ لیا ﴿٦٣﴾
(موسیٰ نے) کہا یہی تو (وہ مقام) ہے جسے ہم تلاش کرتے
تھے تو وہ اپنے پاؤں کے نشان دیکھتے دیکھتے لوٹ گئے ﴿٦٤﴾
(وہاں) انہوں نے ہمارے بندوں میں سے ایک بندہ دیکھا جس کو ہم نے اپنے
ہاں سے رحمت (یعنی نبوت یا نعمت ولایت) دی تھی اور اپنے پاس سے علم بخشا تھا ﴿٦٥﴾
موسیٰ نے اُن سے (جن کا نام خضر تھا) کہا کہ جو علم (خدا کی طرف سے) آپ کو سکھایا
گیا ہے اگر آپ اس میں سے مجھے کچھ بھلائی (کی باتیں) سکھائیں تو میں آپ کے ساتھ رہوں ﴿٦٦﴾
(خضر نے) کہا کہ تم میرے ساتھ رہ کر صبر نہیں کر سکو گے ﴿٦٧﴾
اور جس بات کی تمہیں خبر ہی نہیں اس پر صبر بھی کیونکر کر سکتے ہو ﴿٦٨﴾
(موسیٰ نے) کہا خدا نے چاہا تو آپ مجھے صابر پایئے گا۔ اور میں
آپ کے ارشاد کے خلاف نہیں کروں گا ﴿٦٩﴾
(خضر نے) کہا اگر تم میرے ساتھ رہنا چاہو تو (شرط یہ ہے کہ) مجھ
سے کوئی بات نہ پوچھنا جب تک میں خود اس کا ذکر تم سے نہ کروں ﴿٧٠﴾
تو دونوں چل پڑے یہاں تک کہ جب کشتی میں سوار ہوئے تو (خضر نے)
کشتی کو پھاڑ ڈالا۔ (موسیٰ نے) کہا کیا آپ نے اس کو اس لئے پھاڑا ہے
کہ سواروں کو غرق کر دیں۔ یہ تو آپ نے بڑی (عجیب) بات کی ﴿٧١﴾
(خضر نے) کہا۔ کیا میں نے نہیں کہا تھا کہ تم میرے ساتھ
صبر نہ کر سکو گے ﴿٧٢﴾
(موسیٰ نے) کہا کہ جو بھول مجھ سے ہوئی اس پر مواخذہ نہ

أَبْلُغَ مَجْمَعَ الْبَحْرَيْنِ أَوْ أَمْضِيَ حُقُبًا ﴿٦٠﴾
فَلَمَّا بَلَغَا مَجْمَعَ بَيْنِهِمَا نَسِيَا حُوتَهُمَا
فَاتَّخَذَ سَبِيلَهُ فِي الْبَحْرِ سَرَبًا ﴿٦١﴾
فَلَمَّا جَاوَزَا قَالَ لِفَتَاهُ آتِنَا غَدَاءَنَا
لَقَدْ لَقِينَا مِنْ سَفَرِنَا هَٰذَا نَصَبًا ﴿٦٢﴾
قَالَ أَرَأَيْتَ إِذْ أَوَيْنَا إِلَى الصَّخْرَةِ
فَإِنِّي نَسِيتُ الْحُوتَ وَمَا أَنْسَانِيهُ إِلَّا
الشَّيْطَانُ أَنْ أَذْكُرَهُ ۚ وَاتَّخَذَ سَبِيلَهُ
فِي الْبَحْرِ ۖ عَجَبًا ﴿٦٣﴾
قَالَ ذَٰلِكَ مَا كُنَّا نَبْغِ ۚ فَارْتَدَّا عَلَىٰ
آثَارِهِمَا قَصَصًا ﴿٦٤﴾
فَوَجَدَا عَبْدًا مِنْ عِبَادِنَا آتَيْنَاهُ رَحْمَةً
مِنْ عِنْدِنَا وَعَلَّمْنَاهُ مِنْ لَدُنَّا عِلْمًا ﴿٦٥﴾
قَالَ لَهُ مُوسَىٰ هَلْ أَتَّبِعُكَ عَلَىٰ أَنْ
تُعَلِّمَنِ مِمَّا عُلِّمْتَ رُشْدًا ﴿٦٦﴾
قَالَ إِنَّكَ لَنْ تَسْتَطِيعَ مَعِيَ صَبْرًا ﴿٦٧﴾
وَكَيْفَ تَصْبِرُ عَلَىٰ مَا لَمْ تُحِطْ بِهِ خُبْرًا ﴿٦٨﴾
قَالَ سَتَجِدُنِي إِنْ شَاءَ اللَّهُ صَابِرًا وَلَا
أَعْصِي لَكَ أَمْرًا ﴿٦٩﴾
قَالَ فَإِنِ اتَّبَعْتَنِي فَلَا تَسْأَلْنِي عَنْ
شَيْءٍ حَتَّىٰ أُحْدِثَ لَكَ مِنْهُ ذِكْرًا ﴿٧٠﴾ ع
فَانْطَلَقَا حَتَّىٰ إِذَا رَكِبَا فِي السَّفِينَةِ
خَرَقَهَا ۖ قَالَ أَخَرَقْتَهَا لِتُغْرِقَ أَهْلَهَا
لَقَدْ جِئْتَ شَيْئًا إِمْرًا ﴿٧١﴾
قَالَ أَلَمْ أَقُلْ إِنَّكَ لَنْ تَسْتَطِيعَ مَعِيَ
صَبْرًا ﴿٧٢﴾
قَالَ لَا تُؤَاخِذْنِي بِمَا نَسِيتُ وَلَا

raising difficulties in my case."

74. Then they proceeded: until, when they met a young boy, he slew him. Moses said: "Hast thou slain an innocent person who had slain none? Truly a foul (unheard-of) thing hast thou done!"

75. He answered: "Did I not tell thee that thou canst have no patience with me?"

76. (Moses) said: "If ever I ask thee about anything after this, keep me not in thy company: then wouldst thou have received (full) excuse from my side.

77. Then they proceeded: until, when they came to the inhabitants of a town, they asked them for food, but they refused them hospitality. They found there a wall on the point of falling down, but he set it up straight. (Moses) said: "If thou hadst wished, surely thou couldst have exacted some recompense for it!

78. He answered: "This is the parting between me and thee: now will I tell thee the interpretation of (those things) over which thou wast unable to hold patience.

79. "As for the boat, it belonged to certain men in dire want: they plied on the water: I but wished to render it unserviceable, for there was after them a certain king who seized on every boat by force.

80. "As for the youth, his parents were people of Faith, and we feared that he would grieve them by obstinate rebellion and ingratitude (to Allah)

81. "So we desired that their Lord would give them in exchange (a son) better in purity (of conduct) and closer in affection.

82. "As for the wall, it belonged to two youths, orphans, in the Town; there was, beneath it; a buried treasure, to which they were entitled; their father had been a

کیجئے۔ اور میرے معاملے میں مجھ پر مشکل نہ ڈالیے ﴿٧٣﴾

پھر دونوں چلے۔ یہاں تک کہ (رستے میں) ایک لڑکا ملا تو (خضر
نے) اُسے مار ڈالا۔ (موسیٰ نے) کہا کہ آپ نے ایک بے گناہ شخص کو
(ناحق) بغیر قصاص کے مار ڈالا۔ (یہ تو) آپ نے بُری بات کی ﴿٧٤﴾

(خضر نے) کہا کیا میں نے نہیں کہا تھا کہ تم سے میرے
ساتھ صبر نہیں ہو سکے گا؟ ﴿٧٥﴾

اُنہوں نے کہا کہ اگر میں اس کے بعد (پھر) کوئی بات
پوچھوں (یعنی اعتراض کروں) تو مجھے اپنے ساتھ نہ رکھیے گا
کہ آپ میری طرف سے عذر کے قبول کرنے میں غایت کو پہنچ گئے ﴿٧٦﴾

پھر دونوں چلے۔ یہاں تک کہ ایک گاؤں والوں کے پاس پہنچے
اور اُن سے کھانا طلب کیا۔ اُنہوں نے اُنکی ضیافت کرنے سے انکار
کیا۔ پھر اُنہوں نے وہاں ایک دیوار دیکھی جو (جھک کر) گرا چاہتی تھی تو
(خضر نے) اُس کو سیدھا کر دیا۔ (موسیٰ نے) کہا کہ اگر آپ چاہتے
تو اُن سے (اس کا) معاوضہ لیتے (تاکہ کھانے کا کام چلتا) ﴿٧٧﴾

(خضر نے) کہا کہ اب مجھ میں اور تم میں علیحدگی۔ (مگر) جن باتوں پر
تم صبر نہ کر سکے میں اُن کا تمہیں بھید بتلائے دیتا ہوں ﴿٧٨﴾

(کہ وہ) جو کشتی (تھی) غریب لوگوں کی تھی جو دریا میں محنت
(کر کے یعنی کشتیاں چلا کر گذارہ) کرتے تھے۔ اور اُن کے سامنے
(کی طرف) ایک بادشاہ تھا جو ہر ایک کشتی کو زبردستی چھین لیتا تھا تو
میں نے چاہا کہ اُسے عیب دار کر دوں (تاکہ وہ اُسے غصب نہ کر سکے) ﴿٧٩﴾

اور وہ جو لڑکا تھا اسکے ماں باپ دونوں مومن تھے ہمیں اندیشہ ہوا
کہ وہ (بڑا ہو کر بدکردار ہو گا کہیں) اُنکو سرکشی اور کفر میں نہ پھنسا دے ﴿٨٠﴾

تو ہم نے چاہا کہ اُن کا پروردگار اسکی جگہ اُنکو اور (بچہ) عطا
فرمائے جو پاک طینتی میں بہتر اور محبت میں زیادہ قریب ہو ﴿٨١﴾

اور وہ جو دیوار تھی سو دو یتیم لڑکوں کی تھی (جو) شہر میں
(رہتے تھے) اور اُسکے نیچے اُن کا خزانہ (مدفون) تھا اور اُن کا
باپ ایک نیک آدمی تھا۔ تو تمہارے پروردگار نے چاہا کہ

تُرْهِقْنِي مِنْ أَمْرِي عُسْرًا ﴿٧٣﴾
فَانْطَلَقَا حَتَّىٰ إِذَا لَقِيَا غُلَامًا فَقَتَلَهُ
قَالَ أَقَتَلْتَ نَفْسًا زَكِيَّةً بِغَيْرِ نَفْسٍ
لَقَدْ جِئْتَ شَيْئًا نُكْرًا ﴿٧٤﴾
قَالَ أَلَمْ أَقُلْ لَكَ إِنَّكَ لَنْ تَسْتَطِيعَ
مَعِيَ صَبْرًا ﴿٧٥﴾
قَالَ إِنْ سَأَلْتُكَ عَنْ شَيْءٍ بَعْدَهَا
فَلَا تُصَاحِبْنِي قَدْ بَلَغْتَ مِنْ لَدُنِّي
عُذْرًا ﴿٧٦﴾
فَانْطَلَقَا حَتَّىٰ إِذَا أَتَيَا أَهْلَ قَرْيَةٍ
اسْتَطْعَمَا أَهْلَهَا فَأَبَوْا أَنْ يُضَيِّفُوهُمَا
فَوَجَدَا فِيهَا جِدَارًا يُرِيدُ أَنْ يَنْقَضَّ
فَأَقَامَهُ قَالَ لَوْ شِئْتَ لَاتَّخَذْتَ عَلَيْهِ
أَجْرًا ﴿٧٧﴾
قَالَ هَٰذَا فِرَاقُ بَيْنِي وَبَيْنِكَ سَأُنَبِّئُكَ
بِتَأْوِيلِ مَا لَمْ تَسْتَطِعْ عَلَيْهِ صَبْرًا ﴿٧٨﴾
أَمَّا السَّفِينَةُ فَكَانَتْ لِمَسَاكِينَ يَعْمَلُونَ
فِي الْبَحْرِ فَأَرَدْتُ أَنْ أَعِيبَهَا وَكَانَ
وَرَاءَهُمْ مَلِكٌ يَأْخُذُ كُلَّ سَفِينَةٍ
غَصْبًا ﴿٧٩﴾
وَأَمَّا الْغُلَامُ فَكَانَ أَبَوَاهُ مُؤْمِنَيْنِ
فَخَشِينَا أَنْ يُرْهِقَهُمَا طُغْيَانًا وَكُفْرًا ﴿٨٠﴾
فَأَرَدْنَا أَنْ يُبْدِلَهُمَا رَبُّهُمَا خَيْرًا مِنْهُ
زَكَاةً وَأَقْرَبَ رُحْمًا ﴿٨١﴾
وَأَمَّا الْجِدَارُ فَكَانَ لِغُلَامَيْنِ يَتِيمَيْنِ
فِي الْمَدِينَةِ وَكَانَ تَحْتَهُ كَنْزٌ لَهُمَا
وَكَانَ أَبُوهُمَا صَالِحًا فَأَرَادَ رَبُّكَ

righteous man: so thy Lord desired that they should attain their age of full strength and get out their treasure—a mercy (and favour) from thy Lord. I did it not of my own accord. Such is the interpretation of (those things) over which thou wast unable to hold patience."

83. They ask thee concerning *Zul-qarnain*. Say, "I will rehearse to you something of his story."

84. Verily We established his power on earth, and We gave him the ways and the means to all ends.

85. One (such) way he followed,

86. Until, when he reached the setting of the sun, he found it set in a spring of murky water: near it he found a People: We said: "O Zul-qarnain! (thou hast authority,) either to punish them, or to treat them with kindness."

87. He said: "Whoever doth wrong, him shall we punish; then shall he be sent back to his Lord; and He will punish him with a punishment unheard-of (before).

88. "But whoever believes, and works righteousness,—he shall have a goodly reward, and easy will be his task as we order it by our command."

89. Then followed he (another) way,

90. Until, when he came to the rising of the sun, he found it rising on a people for whom We had provided no covering protection against the sun.

91. (He left them) as they were: We completely understood what was before him.

92. Then followed he (another) way,

93. Until, when he reached (a tract) between two mountains, he found, beneath them, a people who scarcely understood a word.

94. They said: "O Zul-qarnain! the Gog and Magog (people) do great mischief on earth: shall we then render thee tribute in order that thou mightest erect a barrier

وہ اپنی جوانی کو پہنچ جائیں اور (پھر) اپنا خزانہ نکالیں۔
یہ تمہارے پروردگار کی مہربانی ہے۔ اور یہ کام میں نے اپنی طرف سے
نہیں کئے۔ یہ ان باتوں کی حقیقت ہے جن پر تم صبر نہ کرسکے ﴿۸۲﴾
اور تم سے ذوالقرنین کے بارے میں دریافت کرتے ہیں کہہ دو
کہ میں اس کا کسی قدر حال تمہیں پڑھ کر سناتا ہوں ﴿۸۳﴾
ہم نے اُس کو زمین میں بڑی دست رس دی تھی اور ہر طرح
کا سامان عطا کیا تھا ﴿۸۴﴾
تو اُس نے (سفر کا) ایک سامان کیا ﴿۸۵﴾
یہاں تک کہ جب سورج کے غروب ہونے کی جگہ پہنچا تو اُسے
ایسا پایا کہ ایک کیچڑ کی ندی میں ڈوب رہا ہے اور اُس (ندی) کے
پاس ایک قوم دیکھی۔ ہم نے کہا ذوالقرنین! تم انکو خواہ تکلیف دو
خواہ اُن (کے بارے) میں بھلائی اختیار کرو (دونوں باتوں کی تمکو قدرت ہے) ﴿۸۶﴾
(ذوالقرنین نے) کہا کہ جو (کفر و بدکرداری سے) ظلم کریگا اُسے ہم عذاب دینگے
پھر (جب) وہ اپنے پروردگار کی طرف لوٹایا جائیگا تو وہ بھی اُسے بُرا عذاب دیگا ﴿۸۷﴾
اور جو ایمان لائیگا اور عمل نیک کریگا اسکے لئے بہت اچھا بدلہ ہے اور ہم
اپنے معاملے میں (اس پر کسی طرح کی سختی نہیں کرینگے بلکہ) اس سے نرم بات کہینگے ﴿۸۸﴾
پھر اُس نے ایک اور سامان (سفر کا) کیا ﴿۸۹﴾
یہاں تک کہ سورج کے طلوع ہونیکے مقام پر پہنچا تو دیکھا
کہ وہ ایسے لوگوں پر طلوع کرتا ہے جن کیلئے ہم نے سورج
کے اس طرف کوئی اوٹ نہیں بنائی تھی ﴿۹۰﴾
(حقیقت الحال) یوں (تھی) اور جو کچھ اُسکے پاس تھا ہمکو سب کی خبر تھی ﴿۹۱﴾
پھر اُس نے ایک اور سامان کیا ﴿۹۲﴾
یہاں تک کہ دو دیواروں کے درمیان پہنچا تو دیکھا کہ اُنکے
اس طرف کچھ لوگ ہیں کہ بات کو سمجھ نہیں سکتے ﴿۹۳﴾
اُن لوگوں نے کہا کہ ذوالقرنین! یاجوج اور ماجوج
زمین میں فساد کرتے رہتے ہیں۔ بھلا ہم آپ کے
لئے خرچ (کا انتظام) کر دیں کہ آپ ہمارے اور اُن کے

أَنْ يَّبْلُغَآ أَشُدَّهُمَا وَيَسْتَخْرِجَا كَنْزَهُمَا
رَحْمَةً مِّنْ رَّبِّكَ ۚ وَمَا فَعَلْتُهُ عَنْ أَمْرِي ۚ
ذٰلِكَ تَأْوِيلُ مَا لَمْ تَسْطِعْ عَّلَيْهِ صَبْرًا ﴿٨٢﴾
وَيَسْأَلُونَكَ عَنْ ذِي الْقَرْنَيْنِ ۖ قُلْ
سَأَتْلُوا عَلَيْكُمْ مِّنْهُ ذِكْرًا ﴿٨٣﴾
إِنَّا مَكَّنَّا لَهُ فِي الْأَرْضِ وَآتَيْنٰهُ مِنْ
كُلِّ شَيْءٍ سَبَبًا ﴿٨٤﴾
فَأَتْبَعَ سَبَبًا ﴿٨٥﴾
حَتّٰى إِذَا بَلَغَ مَغْرِبَ الشَّمْسِ وَجَدَهَا
تَغْرُبُ فِي عَيْنٍ حَمِئَةٍ وَّوَجَدَ عِنْدَهَا
قَوْمًا ۗ قُلْنَا يٰذَا الْقَرْنَيْنِ إِمَّآ أَنْ تُعَذِّبَ
وَإِمَّآ أَنْ تَتَّخِذَ فِيهِمْ حُسْنًا ﴿٨٦﴾
قَالَ أَمَّا مَنْ ظَلَمَ فَسَوْفَ نُعَذِّبُهُ
ثُمَّ يُرَدُّ إِلٰى رَبِّهِ فَيُعَذِّبُهُ عَذَابًا نُّكْرًا ﴿٨٧﴾
وَأَمَّا مَنْ آمَنَ وَعَمِلَ صَالِحًا فَلَهُ جَزَآءً
الْحُسْنٰى ۚ وَسَنَقُولُ لَهُ مِنْ أَمْرِنَا يُسْرًا ﴿٨٨﴾
ثُمَّ أَتْبَعَ سَبَبًا ﴿٨٩﴾
حَتّٰى إِذَا بَلَغَ مَطْلِعَ الشَّمْسِ وَجَدَهَا
تَطْلُعُ عَلٰى قَوْمٍ لَّمْ نَجْعَلْ لَّهُمْ مِّنْ
دُونِهَا سِتْرًا ﴿٩٠﴾
كَذٰلِكَ وَقَدْ أَحَطْنَا بِمَا لَدَيْهِ خُبْرًا ﴿٩١﴾
ثُمَّ أَتْبَعَ سَبَبًا ﴿٩٢﴾
حَتّٰى إِذَا بَلَغَ بَيْنَ السَّدَّيْنِ وَجَدَ مِنْ
دُونِهِمَا قَوْمًا لَّا يَكَادُونَ يَفْقَهُونَ قَوْلًا ﴿٩٣﴾
قَالُوا يٰذَا الْقَرْنَيْنِ إِنَّ يَأْجُوجَ وَ
مَأْجُوجَ مُفْسِدُونَ فِي الْأَرْضِ فَهَلْ
نَجْعَلُ لَكَ خَرْجًا عَلٰى أَنْ تَجْعَلَ

between us and them?

درمیان ایک دیوار کھینچ دیں ﴿٩٤﴾

بَيْنَنَا وَبَيْنَهُمْ سَدًّا ﴿٩٤﴾

95. He said: "(The power) in which my Lord has established me is better (than tribute): help me therefore with strength (and labour): I will erect a strong barrier between you and them:

ذوالقرنین نے کہا کہ خرچ کا جو مقدور خدا نے مجھے بخشا ہے وہ بہت اچھا ہے تم مجھے قوت (بازو) سے مدد دو۔ میں تمہارے اور اُنکے درمیان ایک مضبوط اوٹ بنا دونگا ﴿٩٥﴾

قَالَ مَا مَكَّنِّيْ فِيْهِ رَبِّيْ خَيْرٌ فَاَعِيْنُوْنِيْ بِقُوَّةٍ اَجْعَلْ بَيْنَكُمْ وَبَيْنَهُمْ رَدْمًا ﴿٩٥﴾

96. "Bring me blocks of iron." At length, when he had filled up the space between the two steep mountain-sides, he said, "Blow (with your bellows)" then, when he had made it (red) as fire, he said: "Bring me, that I may pour over it, molten lead."

تو تم لوہے کے (بڑے بڑے) تختے لاؤ (چنانچہ کام جاری کر دیا گیا) یہانتک کہ جب اُس نے دونوں پہاڑوں کے درمیان (کا حصہ) برابر کر دیا (اور) کہا کہ (اب اسے) دھونکو۔ یہانتک کہ جب اسکو (دھونک دھونک کر) آگ کر دیا تو کہا کہ (اب) میرے پاس تانبہ لاؤ کہ اس پر پگھلا کر ڈالدوں ﴿٩٦﴾

اٰتُوْنِيْ زُبَرَ الْحَدِيْدِ ۭ حَتّٰٓى اِذَا سَاوٰى بَيْنَ الصَّدَفَيْنِ قَالَ انْفُخُوْا ۭ حَتّٰٓى اِذَا جَعَلَهٗ نَارًا ۙ قَالَ اٰتُوْنِيْٓ اُفْرِغْ عَلَيْهِ قِطْرًا ﴿٩٦﴾

97. Thus were they made powerless to scale it or to dig through it.

پھر اُن میں یہ قدرت نہ رہی کہ اس پر چڑھ سکیں اور نہ یہ طاقت رہی کہ اس میں نقب لگا سکیں ﴿٩٧﴾

فَمَا اسْطَاعُوْٓا اَنْ يَّظْهَرُوْهُ وَمَا اسْتَطَاعُوْا لَهٗ نَقْبًا ﴿٩٧﴾

98. He said: "This is a mercy from my Lord: but when the promise of my Lord comes to pass, He will make it into dust; and the promise of my Lord is true."

بولا کہ یہ میرے پروردگار کی مہربانی ہے جب میرے پروردگار کا وعدہ آپہنچے گا تو اس کو (ڈھا کر) ہموار کر دیگا۔ اور میرے پروردگار کا وعدہ سچا ہے ﴿٩٨﴾

قَالَ هٰذَا رَحْمَةٌ مِّنْ رَّبِّيْ ۚ فَاِذَا جَاۗءَ وَعْدُ رَبِّيْ جَعَلَهٗ دَكَّاۗءَ ۚ وَكَانَ وَعْدُ رَبِّيْ حَقًّا ﴿٩٨﴾

99. On that day We shall leave them to surge like waves on one another: the trumpet will be blown, and We shall collect them all together.

(اس روز) ہم اُن کو چھوڑ دینگے کہ (روئے زمین پر پھیل کر) ایک دوسرے میں گھس جائیں گے اور صور پھونکا جائیگا تو ہم سب کو جمع کر لیں گے ﴿٩٩﴾

وَتَرَكْنَا بَعْضَهُمْ يَوْمَىِٕذٍ يَّمُوْجُ فِيْ بَعْضٍ وَّنُفِخَ فِي الصُّوْرِ فَجَمَعْنٰهُمْ جَمْعًا ﴿٩٩﴾

100. And We shall present Hell that day for Unbelievers to see, all spread out,—

اور اس روز جہنم کو کافروں کے سامنے لائیں گے ﴿١٠٠﴾

وَّعَرَضْنَا جَهَنَّمَ يَوْمَىِٕذٍ لِّلْكٰفِرِيْنَ عَرْضَا ﴿١٠٠﴾

101. (Unbelievers) whose eyes had been under a veil from Remembrance of Me, and who had been unable even to hear.

جن کی آنکھیں میری یاد سے پردے میں تھیں اور وہ سُننے کی طاقت نہیں رکھتے تھے ﴿١٠١﴾

الَّذِيْنَ كَانَتْ اَعْيُنُهُمْ فِيْ غِطَاۗءٍ عَنْ ذِكْرِيْ وَكَانُوْا لَا يَسْتَطِيْعُوْنَ سَمْعًا ﴿١٠١﴾ ع ١٩

102. Do the Unbelievers think that they can take My servants as protectors besides Me? Verily We have prepared Hell for the Unbelievers for (their) entertainment.

کیا کافر یہ خیال کرتے ہیں کہ وہ ہمارے بندوں کو ہمارے سوا (اپنا) کارساز بنائیں گے (تو ہم خفا نہیں ہونگے) ہم نے (ایسے) کافروں کیلئے جہنم کی مہمانی تیار کر رکھی ہے ﴿١٠٢﴾

اَفَحَسِبَ الَّذِيْنَ كَفَرُوْٓا اَنْ يَّتَّخِذُوْا عِبَادِيْ مِنْ دُوْنِيْٓ اَوْلِيَاۗءَ ۭ اِنَّآ اَعْتَدْنَا جَهَنَّمَ لِلْكٰفِرِيْنَ نُزُلًا ﴿١٠٢﴾

103. Say: "Shall we tell you of those who lose most in respect of their deeds?—

کہہ دو کہ ہم تمہیں بتائیں جو عملوں کے لحاظ سے بڑے نقصان میں ہیں ﴿١٠٣﴾

قُلْ هَلْ نُنَبِّئُكُمْ بِالْاَخْسَرِيْنَ اَعْمَالًا ﴿١٠٣﴾

104. "Those whose efforts have been wasted in this life, while they thought that they were acquiring

وہ لوگ جن کی سعی دُنیا کی زندگی میں برباد ہو گئی۔ اور وہ یہ سمجھے ہوئے ہیں کہ اچھے کام کر رہے

اَلَّذِيْنَ ضَلَّ سَعْيُهُمْ فِي الْحَيٰوةِ الدُّنْيَا وَهُمْ يَحْسَبُوْنَ اَنَّهُمْ يُحْسِنُوْنَ

SÛRA–19
MARYAM
(INTRODUCTION)

The spiritual growth of man as an individual soul having been explained in S. 17 as beginning with the first principles of moral conduct and in S. 18 as being dependent upon our realisation of the brevity and mystery of this life and the true use of power as in the story of Ẓul-qarnain, we now pass on to the story of individual Messengers of Allah in their personal relations with their environment,—Yaḥyã with his father Zakarîya, Jesus with his mother Mary, Abraham with his unbelieving father, Moses with his brother Aaron, Ismã'îl with his family, and Idrîs in the high station to which he was called. Seeing how these great ones fited into the scheme of life, man is condemned for his want of faith, or for degrading his faith to superstition, and warned of the Hereafter.

In chronology, it was revealed before the first resort of the batch of Muslims to Abyssinia, say seven years before the Hijrat.

good by their works?"

105. They are those who deny the Signs of their Lord and the fact of their having to meet Him (in the Hereafter): vain will be their works, nor shall We, on the Day of Judgment, give them any Weight.
106. That is their reward, Hell; because they rejected Faith, and took My Signs and My Messengers by way of jest.
107. As to those who believe and work righteous deeds, they have, for their entertainment, the Gardens of Paradise,
108. Wherein they shall dwell (for aye): no change will they wish for from them.
109. Say: "If the ocean were ink (wherewith to write out) the words of my Lord, sooner would the ocean be exhausted than would the words of my Lord, even if we added another ocean like it, for its aid."
110. Say: "I am but a man like yourselves, (but) the inspiration has come to me, that your God is One God: whoever expects to meet his Lord, let him work righteousness, and, in the worship of his Lord, admit no one as partner.

Maryam, or Mary

In the name of Allah, Most Gracious, Most Merciful.

1. Kãf. Hã. Yã. 'Ain. Ṣãd.

2. (This is) a mention of the Mercy of thy Lord to His servant Zakarîya.
3. Behold! he cried to his Lord in secret.
4. Praying: "O my Lord! infirm indeed are my bones, and the hair of my head doth glisten with grey: but never am I unblest, O my Lord, in my prayer to Thee!

5. "Now I fear (what) my relatives (and colleagues) (will do) after me: but my wife is barren: so give me an heir as from Thyself,—

ہیں ﴿۱۰۴﴾
یہ وہ لوگ ہیں جنہوں نے اپنے پروردگار کی آیتوں اور
اسکے سامنے جانے سے انکار کیا تو اُن کے اعمال ضائع ہوگئے
اور ہم قیامت کے دن اُن کیلئے کچھ بھی وزن قائم نہیں کرینگے ﴿۱۰۵﴾
یہ اُنکی سزا ہے (یعنی) جہنم۔ اسلئے کہ انہوں نے کفر کیا اور
ہماری آیتوں اور ہمارے پیغمبروں کی ہنسی اُڑائی ﴿۱۰۶﴾
جو لوگ ایمان لائے اور عمل نیک کئے اُن کے لئے
بہشت کے باغ مہمانی ہوں گے ﴿۱۰۷﴾
ہمیشہ اُن میں رہیں گے اور وہاں سے مکان بدلنا نہ چاہیں گے ﴿۱۰۸﴾
کہہ دو کہ اگر سمندر میرے پروردگار کی باتوں کے (لکھنے کے) لئے
سیاہی ہو تو قبل اسکے کہ میرے پروردگار کی باتیں تمام ہوں
سمندر ختم ہو جائے اگرچہ ہم ویسا ہی اور اسکی مدد کو لائیں ﴿۱۰۹﴾
کہہ دو کہ میں تمہاری طرح کا ایک بشر ہوں۔ (البتہ) میری طرف
وحی آتی ہے کہ تمہارا معبود (وہی) ایک معبود ہے۔ تو جو شخص اپنے پروردگار
سے ملنے کی اُمید رکھے چاہیے کہ عمل نیک کرے اور اپنے
پروردگار کی عبادت میں کسی کو شریک نہ بنائے ﴿۱۱۰﴾

سورۂ مریم مکی ہے اور اس میں اٹھانوے آیتیں اور چھ رکوع ہیں

شروع خدا کا نام لیکر جو بڑا مہربان نہایت رحم والا ہے
کہیعص ﴿۱﴾ (یہ) تمہارے پروردگار کی مہربانی کا بیان
(ہے جو اس نے) اپنے بندے زکریا پر (کی تھی) ﴿۲﴾
جب اُنہوں نے اپنے پروردگار کو دبی آواز سے پکارا ﴿۳﴾
(اور) کہا کہ اے میرے پروردگار میری ہڈیاں بڑھاپے
کے سبب کمزور ہوگئی ہیں اور سر شعلہ مارنے لگا ہے اور اے میرے
پروردگار میں تجھ سے مانگ کر کبھی محروم نہیں رہا ﴿۴﴾
اور میں اپنے بعد اپنے بھائی بندوں سے ڈرتا ہوں
اور میری بیوی بانجھ ہے تو مجھے اپنے پاس سے
ایک وارث عطا فرما ﴿۵﴾

صُنْعًا ﴿١٠٤﴾
أُولَٰئِكَ الَّذِينَ كَفَرُوا بِآيَاتِ رَبِّهِمْ
وَلِقَائِهِ فَحَبِطَتْ أَعْمَالُهُمْ فَلَا نُقِيمُ
لَهُمْ يَوْمَ الْقِيَامَةِ وَزْنًا ﴿١٠٥﴾
ذَٰلِكَ جَزَاؤُهُمْ جَهَنَّمُ بِمَا كَفَرُوا
وَاتَّخَذُوا آيَاتِي وَرُسُلِي هُزُوًا ﴿١٠٦﴾
إِنَّ الَّذِينَ آمَنُوا وَعَمِلُوا الصَّالِحَاتِ
كَانَتْ لَهُمْ جَنَّاتُ الْفِرْدَوْسِ نُزُلًا ﴿١٠٧﴾
خَالِدِينَ فِيهَا لَا يَبْغُونَ عَنْهَا حِوَلًا ﴿١٠٨﴾
قُلْ لَوْ كَانَ الْبَحْرُ مِدَادًا لِكَلِمَاتِ
رَبِّي لَنَفِدَ الْبَحْرُ قَبْلَ أَنْ تَنْفَدَ
كَلِمَاتُ رَبِّي وَلَوْ جِئْنَا بِمِثْلِهِ مَدَدًا ﴿١٠٩﴾
قُلْ إِنَّمَا أَنَا بَشَرٌ مِثْلُكُمْ يُوحَىٰ إِلَيَّ
أَنَّمَا إِلَٰهُكُمْ إِلَٰهٌ وَاحِدٌ فَمَنْ
كَانَ يَرْجُو لِقَاءَ رَبِّهِ فَلْيَعْمَلْ عَمَلًا
صَالِحًا وَلَا يُشْرِكْ بِعِبَادَةِ رَبِّهِ أَحَدًا ﴿١١٠﴾

سُورَةُ مَرْيَمَ مَكِّيَّةٌ وَهِيَ ثَمَانٍ وَتِسْعُونَ آيَةً وَسِتُّ رُكُوعَاتٍ

بِسْمِ اللَّهِ الرَّحْمَٰنِ الرَّحِيمِ
كهيعص ﴿١﴾ ذِكْرُ رَحْمَتِ رَبِّكَ
عَبْدَهُ زَكَرِيَّا ﴿٢﴾
إِذْ نَادَىٰ رَبَّهُ نِدَاءً خَفِيًّا ﴿٣﴾
قَالَ رَبِّ إِنِّي وَهَنَ الْعَظْمُ مِنِّي
وَاشْتَعَلَ الرَّأْسُ شَيْبًا وَلَمْ أَكُنْ
بِدُعَائِكَ رَبِّ شَقِيًّا ﴿٤﴾
وَإِنِّي خِفْتُ الْمَوَالِيَ مِنْ وَرَائِي
وَكَانَتِ امْرَأَتِي عَاقِرًا فَهَبْ لِي مِنْ
لَدُنْكَ وَلِيًّا ﴿٥﴾

6. "(One that) will (truly) inherit me, and inherit the posterity of Jacob; and make him, O my Lord! One with whom Thou art well-pleased!"
7. (His prayer was answered): "O Zakarîya! We give thee good news of a son: his name shall be Yahya: on none by that name have We conferred distinction before."
8. He said: "O my Lord! how shall I have a son, when my wife is barren and I have grown quite decrepit from old age?"

9. He said: "So (it will be): thy Lord saith, 'That is easy for Me: I did indeed create thee before, when thou hadst been nothing!"

10. (Zakarîya) said: "O my Lord! give me a Sign," "Thy Sign," was the answer, "Shall be that thou shalt speak to no man for three nights, although thou art not dumb."
11. So Zakarîya came out to his people from his chamber: he told them by signs to celebrate Allah's praises in the morning and in the evening.
12. (To his son came the command): "O Yaḥyā! take hold of the Book with might": and We gave him Wisdom even as a youth,
13. And pity (for all creatures) as from Us, and purity: he was devout,

14. And kind to his parents, and he was not overbearing or rebellious.
15. So Peace on him the day he was born, the day that he dies, and the day that he will be raised up to life (again)!
16. Relate in the Book (the story of) Mary, when she withdrew from her family to a place in the East.

17. She placed a screen (to screen herself) from them: then We sent to her Our angel, and he appeared before her as a man in all respects.
18. She said: "I seek refuge from thee to (Allah) Most Gracious: (come not near) if thou dost fear Allah."

جو میری اور اولادِ یعقوب کی میراث کا مالک ہو۔ اور
(اے) میرے پروردگار اُس کو خوش اطوار بنائیو ۱۷۹ف ﴿۶﴾
اے زکریا ہم تم کو ایک لڑکے کی بشارت دیتے ہیں جس کا نام
یحییٰ ہے۔ اس سے پہلے ہم نے اس نام کا کوئی شخص پیدا نہیں کیا ﴿۷﴾
اُنہوں نے کہا پروردگار میرے ہاں کس طرح لڑکا ہوگا۔
جس حال میں میری بیوی بانجھ ہے اور میں بڑھاپے کی
انتہا کو پہنچ گیا ہوں ﴿۸﴾
حکم ہوا کہ اسی طرح (ہوگا) تمہارے پروردگار نے فرمایا ہے
کہ مجھے یہ آسان ہے اور میں پہلے تم کو بھی تو پیدا کر چکا
ہوں اور تم کچھ چیز نہ تھے ﴿۹﴾
کہا کہ پروردگار میرے لئے کوئی نشانی مقرر فرما۔ فرمایا نشانی یہ ہے کہ تم
صحیح سالم ہو کر تین رات (دن) لوگوں سے بات نہ کر سکو گے ﴿۱۰﴾
پھر وہ (عبادت کے) حجرے سے نکل کر اپنی قوم کے پاس آئے
تو اُن سے اشارے سے کہا کہ صبح و شام (خدا کو) یاد کرتے رہو ﴿۱۱﴾
اے یحییٰ (ہماری) کتاب کو زور سے پکڑے رہو۔ اور ہم نے انکو
لڑکپن ہی میں دانائی عطا فرمائی تھی ﴿۱۲﴾
اور اپنے پاس سے شفقت اور پاکیزگی (دی تھی) اور
وہ پرہیزگار تھے ﴿۱۳﴾
اور ماں باپ کے ساتھ نیکی کرنیوالے تھے اور سرکش (اور) نافرمان نہیں تھے ﴿۱۴﴾
اور جس دن وہ پیدا ہوئے اور جس دن وفات پائینگے اور جس
دن زندہ کر کے اٹھائے جائینگے اُن پر سلام (اور رحمت) ہے ﴿۱۵﴾
اور کتاب (قرآن) میں مریم کا بھی مذکور کرو جب وہ اپنے
لوگوں سے الگ ہو کر مشرق کی طرف چلی گئیں ﴿۱۶﴾
تو اُنہوں نے انکی طرف سے پردہ کر لیا (اُس وقت) ہم نے انکی طرف اپنا
فرشتہ بھیجا تو وہ اُن کے سامنے ٹھیک آدمی (کی شکل) بن گیا ﴿۱۷﴾
(مریم) بولیں کہ اگر تم پرہیزگار ہو تو میں تم سے خدا کی
پناہ مانگتی ہوں ﴿۱۸﴾

يَّرِثُنِيْ وَيَرِثُ مِنْ اٰلِ يَعْقُوْبَ ۖ
وَاجْعَلْهُ رَبِّ رَضِيًّا ﴿۶﴾
يٰزَكَرِيَّآ اِنَّا نُبَشِّرُكَ بِغُلٰمِ ِۨ اسْمُهٗ
يَحْيٰى ۙ لَمْ نَجْعَلْ لَّهٗ مِنْ قَبْلُ سَمِيًّا ﴿۷﴾
قَالَ رَبِّ اَنّٰى يَكُوْنُ لِيْ غُلٰمٌ وَّكَانَتِ
امْرَاَتِيْ عَاقِرًا وَّقَدْ بَلَغْتُ مِنَ الْكِبَرِ
عِتِيًّا ﴿۸﴾
قَالَ كَذٰلِكَ ۚ قَالَ رَبُّكَ هُوَ عَلَيَّ هَيِّنٌ
وَّقَدْ خَلَقْتُكَ مِنْ قَبْلُ وَلَمْ تَكُ
شَيْـًٔا ﴿۹﴾
قَالَ رَبِّ اجْعَلْ لِّيْٓ اٰيَةً ۚ قَالَ اٰيَتُكَ
اَلَّا تُكَلِّمَ النَّاسَ ثَلٰثَ لَيَالٍ سَوِيًّا ﴿۱۰﴾
فَخَرَجَ عَلٰى قَوْمِهٖ مِنَ الْمِحْرَابِ فَاَوْحٰٓى
اِلَيْهِمْ اَنْ سَبِّحُوْا بُكْرَةً وَّعَشِيًّا ﴿۱۱﴾
يٰيَحْيٰى خُذِ الْكِتٰبَ بِقُوَّةٍ ۚ وَاٰتَيْنٰهُ
الْحُكْمَ صَبِيًّا ﴿۱۲﴾
وَّحَنَانًا مِّنْ لَّدُنَّا وَزَكٰوةً ۚ وَكَانَ
تَقِيًّا ﴿۱۳﴾
وَّبَرًّا بِوَالِدَيْهِ وَلَمْ يَكُنْ جَبَّارًا عَصِيًّا ﴿۱۴﴾
وَسَلٰمٌ عَلَيْهِ يَوْمَ وُلِدَ وَيَوْمَ يَمُوْتُ
وَيَوْمَ يُبْعَثُ حَيًّا ﴿۱۵﴾ ع
وَاذْكُرْ فِي الْكِتٰبِ مَرْيَمَ ۘ اِذِ انْتَبَذَتْ
مِنْ اَهْلِهَا مَكَانًا شَرْقِيًّا ﴿۱۶﴾
فَاتَّخَذَتْ مِنْ دُوْنِهِمْ حِجَابًا ۪ فَاَرْسَلْنَآ
اِلَيْهَا رُوْحَنَا فَتَمَثَّلَ لَهَا بَشَرًا سَوِيًّا ﴿۱۷﴾
قَالَتْ اِنِّيْٓ اَعُوْذُ بِالرَّحْمٰنِ مِنْكَ
اِنْ كُنْتَ تَقِيًّا ﴿۱۸﴾

19. He said: "Nay, I am only a messenger from thy Lord (to announce) to thee the gift of a pure son."

انہوں نے کہا کہ میں تو تمہارے پروردگار کا بھیجا ہوا (یعنی فرشتہ) ہوں (اور اسلئے آیا ہوں) کہ تمہیں پاکیزہ لڑکا بخشوں ﴿١٩﴾

قَالَ اِنَّمَآ اَنَا رَسُوۡلُ رَبِّكِ ۖ لِاَهَبَ
لَكِ غُلٰمًا زَكِيًّا ﴿١٩﴾

20. She said: "How shall I have a son, seeing that no man has touched me, and I am not unchaste?"

(مریم نے) کہا کہ میرے ہاں لڑکا کیونکر ہوگا مجھے کسی بشر نے چھوا تک نہیں۔ اور میں بدکار بھی نہیں ہوں ﴿٢٠﴾

قَالَتۡ اَنّٰى يَكُوۡنُ لِىۡ غُلٰمٌ وَّلَمۡ يَمۡسَسۡنِىۡ
بَشَرٌ وَّلَمۡ اَكُ بَغِيًّا ﴿٢٠﴾

21. He said: "So (it will be): thy Lord saith, 'That is easy for Me: and (We wish) to appoint him as a Sign unto men and a Mercy from Us': it is a matter (so) decreed."

(فرشتے نے) کہا کہ یونہی (ہوگا) تمہارے پروردگار نے فرمایا کہ یہ مجھے آسان ہے اور (میں اُسے اسی طریق پر پیدا کرونگا) تاکہ اسکو لوگوں کیلئے اپنی طرف سے نشانی اور (ذریعہ) رحمت (و مہربانی) بناؤں اور یہ کام مقرر ہو چکا ہے ﴿٢١﴾

قَالَ كَذٰلِكِ ۚ قَالَ رَبُّكِ هُوَ عَلَىَّ
هَيِّنٌ ۚ وَلِنَجۡعَلَهٗۤ اٰيَةً لِّلنَّاسِ وَرَحۡمَةً
مِّنَّا ۚ وَكَانَ اَمۡرًا مَّقۡضِيًّا ﴿٢١﴾

22. So she conceived him, and she retired with him to a remote place.

تو وہ اس (بچے) کے ساتھ حاملہ ہو گئیں اور اُسے لیکر ایک دور جگہ چلی گئیں ﴿٢٢﴾

فَحَمَلَتۡهُ فَانْتَبَذَتۡ بِهٖ مَكَانًا قَصِيًّا ﴿٢٢﴾

23. And the pains of childbirth drove her to the trunk of a palm-tree: she cried (in her anguish): "Ah! would that I had died before this! would that I had been a thing forgotten.

پھر درد زہ اُن کو کھجور کے تنے کی طرف لے آیا۔ کہنے لگیں کہ کاش میں اس سے پہلے مر چکتی اور بھولی بسری ہو گئی ہوتی ﴿٢٣﴾

فَاَجَآءَهَا الۡمَخَاضُ اِلٰى جِذۡعِ النَّخۡلَةِ ۚ
قَالَتۡ يٰلَيۡتَنِىۡ مِتُّ قَبۡلَ هٰذَا وَكُنۡتُ
نَسۡيًا مَّنۡسِيًّا ﴿٢٣﴾

24. But (a voice) cried to her from beneath the (palm-tree): "Grieve not! for thy Lord hath provided a rivulet beneath thee;

اس وقت اُنکے نیچے کی جانب سے فرشتے نے اُنکو آواز دی کہ غمناک نہ ہو۔ تمہارے پروردگار نے تمہارے نیچے ایک چشمہ پیدا کر دیا ہے ﴿٢٤﴾

فَنَادٰٮهَا مِنۡ تَحۡتِهَاۤ اَلَّا تَحۡزَنِىۡ قَدۡ
جَعَلَ رَبُّكِ تَحۡتَكِ سَرِيًّا ﴿٢٤﴾

25. "And shake towards thyself the trunk of the palm-tree: it will let fall fresh ripe dates upon thee.

اور کھجور کے تنے کو پکڑ کر اپنی طرف ہلاؤ تم پر تازہ تازہ کھجوریں جھڑ پڑیں گی ﴿٢٥﴾

وَهُزِّىۡۤ اِلَيۡكِ بِجِذۡعِ النَّخۡلَةِ تُسٰقِطۡ
عَلَيۡكِ رُطَبًا جَنِيًّا ﴿٢٥﴾

26. "So eat and drink and cool (thine) eye. And if thou dost see any man, say, 'I have vowed a fast to (Allah) Most Gracious, and this day will I enter into no talk with any human being".'

تو کھاؤ اور پیو اور آنکھیں ٹھنڈی کرو۔ اگر تم کسی آدمی کو دیکھو تو کہنا کہ میں نے خدا کے لئے روزے کی منّت مانی تو آج میں کسی آدمی سے ہرگز کلام نہیں کروں گی ﴿٢٦﴾

فَكُلِىۡ وَاشۡرَبِىۡ وَقَرِّىۡ عَيۡنًا ۚ فَاِمَّا
تَرَيِنَّ مِنَ الۡبَشَرِ اَحَدًا ۙ فَقُوۡلِىۡۤ اِنِّىۡ
نَذَرۡتُ لِلرَّحۡمٰنِ صَوۡمًا فَلَنۡ اُكَلِّمَ
الۡيَوۡمَ اِنۡسِيًّا ۚ ﴿٢٦﴾

27. At length she brought the (babe) to her people, carrying him (in her arms), they said: "O Mary! truly a strange thing has thou brought!

پھر وہ اس (بچے) کو اٹھا کر اپنی قوم کے لوگوں کے پاس لے آئیں۔ وہ کہنے لگے کہ مریم یہ تو تُو نے بُرا کام کیا ﴿٢٧﴾

فَاَتَتۡ بِهٖ قَوۡمَهَا تَحۡمِلُهٗ ؕ قَالُوۡا يٰمَرۡيَمُ
لَقَدۡ جِئۡتِ شَيۡـًٔـا فَرِيًّا ﴿٢٧﴾

28. "O sister of Aaron! thy father was not a man of evil, nor thy mother a woman unchaste!"

اے ہارون کی بہن (ف ١٨٠) نہ تو تیرا باپ ہی بداطوار آدمی تھا اور نہ تیری ماں ہی بدکار تھی ﴿٢٨﴾

يٰۤاُخۡتَ هٰرُوۡنَ مَا كَانَ اَبُوۡكِ امۡرَاَ سَوۡءٍ
وَّمَا كَانَتۡ اُمُّكِ بَغِيًّا ۖ ﴿٢٨﴾

29. But she pointed to the babe. They said: "How can we talk to one who is a child in the cradle?"

تو مریم نے اس لڑکے کی طرف اشارہ کیا۔ وہ بولے کہ ہم اس سے کہ گود کا بچہ ہے کیونکر بات کریں ﴿٢٩﴾

فَاَشَارَتۡ اِلَيۡهِ ؕ قَالُوۡا كَيۡفَ نُكَلِّمُ مَنۡ
كَانَ فِى الۡمَهۡدِ صَبِيًّا ﴿٢٩﴾

30. He said: "I am indeed a servant of Allah: He hath given me revelation and made me a prophet:

(بچے نے) کہا کہ میں خدا کا بندہ ہوں اُس نے مجھے کتاب دی ہے اور نبی بنایا ہے ﴿٣٠﴾

قَالَ اِنِّىۡ عَبۡدُ اللّٰهِ ؕ اٰتٰٮنِىَ الۡكِتٰبَ
وَجَعَلَنِىۡ نَبِيًّا ۙ ﴿٣٠﴾

31. "And He hath made me blessed wheresoever I be, and hath enjoined on me prayer and zakat as long as I live;

اور میں جہاں ہوں (اور جس حال میں ہوں) مجھے صاحبِ برکت کیا ہے
اور جب تک زندہ ہوں مجھ کو نماز اور زکوٰۃ کا ارشاد فرمایا ہے (۳۱)

وَّجَعَلَنِیْ مُبٰرَكًا اَیْنَ مَا كُنْتُ ۪ وَاَوْصٰنِیْ
بِالصَّلٰوةِ وَالزَّكٰوةِ مَا دُمْتُ حَیًّا ﴿۳۱﴾

32. "(He hath made me) kind to my mother, and not overbearing or unblest;

اور (مجھے) اپنی ماں کے ساتھ نیک سلوک کرنے والا (بنایا ہے)
اور سرکش و بدبخت نہیں بنایا (۳۲)

وَّبَرًّۢا بِوَالِدَتِیْ ۫ وَلَمْ یَجْعَلْنِیْ جَبَّارًا
شَقِیًّا ﴿۳۲﴾

33. "So Peace is on me the day I was born, the day that I die, and the day that I shall be raised up to life (again)"!

اور جس دن میں پیدا ہوا اور جس دن مروں گا اور جس دن
زندہ کر کے اٹھایا جاؤں گا مجھ پر سلام (ورحمت) ہے (۳۳)

وَالسَّلٰمُ عَلَیَّ یَوْمَ وُلِدْتُّ وَیَوْمَ
اَمُوْتُ وَیَوْمَ اُبْعَثُ حَیًّا ﴿۳۳﴾

34. Such (was) Jesus the son of Mary: (it is) a statement of truth, about which they (vainly) dispute.

یہ مریم کے بیٹے عیسیٰ ہیں (اور یہ) سچی بات ہے جس میں
لوگ شک کرتے ہیں (۳۴)

ذٰلِكَ عِیْسَی ابْنُ مَرْیَمَ ۚ قَوْلَ الْحَقِّ
الَّذِیْ فِیْهِ یَمْتَرُوْنَ ﴿۳۴﴾

35. It is not befitting to (the majesty of) Allah that He should beget a son. Glory be to Him! when He determines a matter, He only says to it, "Be", and it is.

خدا کو سزاوار نہیں کہ کسی کو بیٹا بنائے وہ پاک ہے
جب کسی چیز کا ارادہ کرتا ہے تو اس کو یہی کہتا ہے
کہ ہو جا تو وہ ہو جاتی ہے (۳۵)

مَا كَانَ لِلّٰهِ اَنْ یَّتَّخِذَ مِنْ وَّلَدٍ ۙ
سُبْحٰنَهٗ ؕ اِذَا قَضٰۤی اَمْرًا فَاِنَّمَا یَقُوْلُ
لَهٗ كُنْ فَیَكُوْنُ ﴿۳۵﴾ ؕ

36. Verily Allah is my Lord and your Lord: Him therefore serve ye: this is a Way that is straight.

اور بیشک خدا ہی میرا اور تمہارا پروردگار ہے تو اسی
کی عبادت کرو یہی سیدھا رستہ ہے (۳۶)

وَاِنَّ اللّٰهَ رَبِّیْ وَرَبُّكُمْ فَاعْبُدُوْهُ ؕ
هٰذَا صِرَاطٌ مُّسْتَقِیْمٌ ﴿۳۶﴾

37. But the sects differ among themselves: and woe to the Unbelievers because of the (coming) Judgment of an awful Day!

پھر (اہل کتاب کے) فرقوں نے باہم اختلاف کیا سو جو لوگ کافر
ہوئے ہیں ان کو بڑے دن (یعنی قیامت کے روز) حاضر ہونے سے خرابی ہے (۳۷)

فَاخْتَلَفَ الْاَحْزَابُ مِنْ بَیْنِهِمْ ۚ فَوَیْلٌ
لِّلَّذِیْنَ كَفَرُوْا مِنْ مَّشْهَدِ یَوْمٍ عَظِیْمٍ ﴿۳۷﴾

38. How plainly will they see and hear, the Day that they will appear before Us! but the unjust today are in error manifest!

وہ جس دن ہمارے سامنے آئینگے کیسے سننے والے اور کیسے دیکھنے والے
ہوں گے مگر ظالم آج صریح گمراہی میں ہیں (۳۸)

اَسْمِعْ بِهِمْ وَاَبْصِرْ ۙ یَوْمَ یَاْتُوْنَنَا لٰكِنِ
الظّٰلِمُوْنَ الْیَوْمَ فِیْ ضَلٰلٍ مُّبِیْنٍ ﴿۳۸﴾

39. But warn them of the Day of Distress, when the matter will be determined: for (behold,) they are negligent and they do not believe!

اور ان کو حسرت (و افسوس) کے دن سے ڈراؤ جب بات فیصل کر دی جائیگی
اور (ابھی) وہ غفلت میں (پڑے ہوئے) ہیں اور ایمان نہیں لاتے (۳۹)

وَاَنْذِرْهُمْ یَوْمَ الْحَسْرَةِ اِذْ قُضِیَ الْاَمْرُ ۘ (وقف لازم)
وَهُمْ فِیْ غَفْلَةٍ وَّهُمْ لَا یُؤْمِنُوْنَ ﴿۳۹﴾

40. It is We Who will inherit the earth, and all beings thereon: to Us will they all be returned.

ہم ہی زمین کے اور جو لوگ اس پر (بستے) ہیں ان کے وارث
ہیں۔ اور ہماری ہی طرف ان کو لوٹنا ہوگا (۴۰)

اِنَّا نَحْنُ نَرِثُ الْاَرْضَ وَمَنْ عَلَیْهَا
وَاِلَیْنَا یُرْجَعُوْنَ ﴿۴۰﴾ ع ۵

41. (Also) mention in the Book (the story of) Abraham: he was a man of Truth, a prophet.

اور کتاب میں ابراہیم کو یاد کرو۔ بیشک وہ نہایت
سچے پیغمبر تھے (۴۱)

وَاذْكُرْ فِی الْكِتٰبِ اِبْرٰهِیْمَ ۬ؕ اِنَّهٗ كَانَ
صِدِّیْقًا نَّبِیًّا ﴿۴۱﴾

42. Behold, he said to his father: "O my father! why worship that which heareth not and seeth not, and can profit thee nothing?

جب انہوں نے اپنے باپ سے کہا کہ ابا آپ ایسی چیزوں کو کیوں پوجتے
ہیں جو نہ سنیں اور نہ دیکھیں اور نہ آپ کے کچھ کام آسکیں (۴۲)

اِذْ قَالَ لِاَبِیْهِ یٰۤاَبَتِ لِمَ تَعْبُدُ مَا لَا
یَسْمَعُ وَلَا یُبْصِرُ وَلَا یُغْنِیْ عَنْكَ شَیْـًٔا ﴿۴۲﴾

43. "O my father! to me hath come knowledge which hath not reached thee: so follow me: I will guide thee to a Way that is even and straight.

ابا مجھے ایسا علم ملا ہے جو آپ کو نہیں ملا تو میرے ساتھ ہو جیے
میں آپ کو سیدھی راہ پر چلا دوں گا (۴۳)

یٰۤاَبَتِ اِنِّیْ قَدْ جَآءَنِیْ مِنَ الْعِلْمِ مَا لَمْ
یَاْتِكَ فَاتَّبِعْنِیْۤ اَهْدِكَ صِرَاطًا سَوِیًّا ﴿۴۳﴾

44. "O my father! serve not Satan: for Satan is a rebel against (Allah) Most Gracious.

ابا شیطان کی پوجا نہ کیجئے بےشک شیطان خدا کا نافرمان ہے (۴۴)

يَا أَبَتِ لَا تَعْبُدِ الشَّيْطَانَ إِنَّ الشَّيْطَانَ كَانَ لِلرَّحْمَٰنِ عَصِيًّا (۴۴)

45. "O my father! I fear lest a Chastisement afflict thee from (Allah) Most Gracious, so that thou become to Satan a friend."

ابا مجھے ڈر لگتا ہے کہ آپ کو خدا کا عذاب آپکڑے تو آپ شیطان کے ساتھی ہو جائیں (۴۵)

يَا أَبَتِ إِنِّي أَخَافُ أَن يَمَسَّكَ عَذَابٌ مِّنَ الرَّحْمَٰنِ فَتَكُونَ لِلشَّيْطَانِ وَلِيًّا (۴۵)

46. (The father) replied: art thou shrinking from my gods, O Abraham? If thou forbear not, I will indeed stone thee: now get away from me for a good long while!"

اُس نے کہا کہ ابراہیم کیا تو میرے معبودوں سے برگشتہ ہے؟ اگر تو باز نہ آئیگا تو میں تجھے سنگسار کردونگا۔ اور تو ہمیشہ کیلئے مجھ سے دور ہو جا (۴۶)

قَالَ أَرَاغِبٌ أَنتَ عَنْ آلِهَتِي يَا إِبْرَاهِيمُ لَئِن لَّمْ تَنتَهِ لَأَرْجُمَنَّكَ وَاهْجُرْنِي مَلِيًّا (۴۶)

47. Abraham said: "Peace be on thee: I will pray to my Lord for thy forgiveness: for He is to me Most Gracious.

(ابراہیم نے) سلام علیکم کہا (اور کہا کہ) میں آپکے لئے اپنے پروردگار سے بخشش مانگوں گا۔ بیشک وہ مجھ پر نہایت مہربان ہے (۴۷)

قَالَ سَلَامٌ عَلَيْكَ سَأَسْتَغْفِرُ لَكَ رَبِّي إِنَّهُ كَانَ بِي حَفِيًّا (۴۷)

48. "And I will turn away from you (all) and from those whom ye invoke besides Allah: I will call on my Lord perhaps, by my prayer to my Lord, I shall be not unblest."!

اور میں آپ لوگوں سے اور جن کو آپ خدا کے سوا پکارا کرتے ہیں اُن سے کنارہ کرتا ہوں اور اپنے پروردگار ہی کو پکارونگا امید ہے کہ میں اپنے پروردگار کو پکار کر محروم نہیں رہونگا (۴۸)

وَأَعْتَزِلُكُمْ وَمَا تَدْعُونَ مِن دُونِ اللَّهِ وَأَدْعُو رَبِّي عَسَىٰ أَلَّا أَكُونَ بِدُعَاءِ رَبِّي شَقِيًّا (۴۸)

49. When he had turned away from them and from those whom they worshipped besides Allah, We bestowed on him Isaac and Jacob, and each one of them We made a prophet.

اور جب ابراہیم اُن لوگوں سے اور جن کی وہ خدا کے سوا پرستش کرتے تھے الگ ہو گئے تو ہم نے اُن کو اسحاق اور (اسحاق کو) یعقوب بخشے۔ اور سب کو پیغمبر بنایا (۴۹)

فَلَمَّا اعْتَزَلَهُمْ وَمَا يَعْبُدُونَ مِن دُونِ اللَّهِ وَهَبْنَا لَهُ إِسْحَاقَ وَيَعْقُوبَ وَكُلًّا جَعَلْنَا نَبِيًّا (۴۹)

50. And We bestowed of Our Mercy on them, and We granted them lofty honour on the tongue of truth.

اور اُن کو اپنی رحمت سے (بہت سی چیزیں) عنایت کیں۔ اور اُن کا ذکر جمیل بلند کیا (۵۰)

وَوَهَبْنَا لَهُم مِّن رَّحْمَتِنَا وَجَعَلْنَا لَهُمْ لِسَانَ صِدْقٍ عَلِيًّا (۵۰) ع ۳ ۶

51. Also mention in the Book (the story of) Moses: for he was specially chosen. And he was a messenger and a prophet.

اور کتاب میں موسیٰ کا بھی ذکر کرو بیشک وہ (ہمارے) برگزیدہ اور پیغمبر مرسل تھے (۵۱)

وَاذْكُرْ فِي الْكِتَابِ مُوسَىٰ إِنَّهُ كَانَ مُخْلَصًا وَكَانَ رَسُولًا نَّبِيًّا (۵۱)

52. And We called him from the right side of Mount (Sinai), and made him draw near to Us, for converse in secret

اور ہم نے اُن کو طور کی داہنی طرف پکارا اور باتیں کرنے کے لئے نزدیک بلایا (۵۲)

وَنَادَيْنَاهُ مِن جَانِبِ الطُّورِ الْأَيْمَنِ وَقَرَّبْنَاهُ نَجِيًّا (۵۲)

53. And, out of Our Mercy, We gave him his brother Aaron, (also) a prophet.

اور اپنی مہربانی سے اُن کو اُن کا بھائی ہارون پیغمبر عطا کیا (۵۳)

وَوَهَبْنَا لَهُ مِن رَّحْمَتِنَا أَخَاهُ هَارُونَ نَبِيًّا (۵۳)

54. Also mention in the Book (the story of) Ismā'īl: he was (strictly) true to what he promised, and he was a messenger (and) a prophet.

اور کتاب میں اسمٰعیل کا بھی ذکر کرو وہ وعدے کے سچے اور (ہمارے) بھیجے ہوئے نبی تھے (۵۴)

وَاذْكُرْ فِي الْكِتَابِ إِسْمَاعِيلَ إِنَّهُ كَانَ صَادِقَ الْوَعْدِ وَكَانَ رَسُولًا نَّبِيًّا (۵۴)

55. He used to enjoin on his people Prayer and zakat and he was most acceptable in the sight of his Lord.

اور اپنے گھر والوں کو نماز اور زکوٰۃ کا حکم کرتے تھے اور اپنے پروردگار کے ہاں پسندیدہ (وبرگزیدہ) تھے (۵۵)

وَكَانَ يَأْمُرُ أَهْلَهُ بِالصَّلَاةِ وَالزَّكَاةِ وَكَانَ عِندَ رَبِّهِ مَرْضِيًّا (۵۵)

56. Also mention in the Book Idrîs: he was a man of truth (and sincerity), (and) a prophet:

اور کتاب میں ادریس کا بھی ذکر کرو۔ وہ بھی نہایت سچے نبی تھے (۵۶)

وَاذْكُرْ فِي الْكِتٰبِ إِدْرِيْسَ إِنَّهُ كَانَ
صِدِّيْقًا نَّبِيًّا ﴿٥٦﴾

57. And We raised him to a lofty station.

اور ہم نے اُن کو اونچی جگہ اُٹھا لیا تھا (۵۷)

وَّرَفَعْنٰهُ مَكَانًا عَلِيًّا ﴿٥٧﴾

58. Those were some of the prophets on whom Allah did bestow His Grace,—of the posterity of Adam, and of those whom We carried (in the Ark) with Noah, and of the posterity of Abraham and Israel—of those whom We guided and chose. Whenever the Signs of (Allah) Most Gracious were rehearsed to them, they would fall down in prostrate adoration and in tears.

یہ وہ لوگ ہیں جن پر خدا نے اپنے پیغمبروں میں سے فضل کیا (یعنی) اولاد آدم میں سے اور اُن لوگوں میں سے جن کو ہم نے نوح کے ساتھ (کشتی میں) سوار کیا اور ابراہیم اور یعقوب کی اولاد میں سے اور اُن لوگوں میں سے جنکو ہم نے ہدایت دی اور برگزیدہ کیا جب اُنکے سامنے ہماری آیتیں پڑھی جاتی تھیں تو سجدے میں گر پڑتے اور روتے رہتے تھے (۵۸)

أُولٰٓئِكَ الَّذِيْنَ أَنْعَمَ اللّٰهُ عَلَيْهِمْ مِّنَ
النَّبِيّٖنَ مِنْ ذُرِّيَّةِ اٰدَمَ وَمِمَّنْ
حَمَلْنَا مَعَ نُوْحٍ وَّمِنْ ذُرِّيَّةِ إِبْرٰهِيْمَ
وَإِسْرَآءِيْلَ وَمِمَّنْ هَدَيْنَا وَاجْتَبَيْنَا
إِذَا تُتْلٰى عَلَيْهِمْ اٰيٰتُ الرَّحْمٰنِ
خَرُّوْا سُجَّدًا وَّبُكِيًّا ﴿٥٨﴾ السجدة ٥

59. But after them there followed a posterity who missed prayers and followed after lusts soon, then, will they face Destruction,—

پھر اُن کے بعد چند ناخلف اُن کے جانشین ہوئے جنہوں نے نماز کو (چھوڑ دیا گویا اُسے) کھو دیا۔ اور خواہشاتِ نفسانی کے پیچھے لگ گئے۔ سو عنقریب انکو گمراہی (کی سزا) ملیگی (۵۹)

فَخَلَفَ مِنْ بَعْدِهِمْ خَلْفٌ أَضَاعُوا
الصَّلٰوةَ وَاتَّبَعُوا الشَّهَوٰتِ فَسَوْفَ
يَلْقَوْنَ غَيًّا ﴿٥٩﴾

60. Except those who repent and believe, and work Righteousness: for these will enter the Garden and will not be wronged in the least,—

ہاں جس نے توبہ کی اور ایمان لایا اور عمل نیک کئے تو ایسے لوگ بہشت میں داخل ہوں گے اور اُن کا ذرا نقصان نہ کیا جائے گا (۶۰)

إِلَّا مَنْ تَابَ وَاٰمَنَ وَعَمِلَ صَالِحًا
فَأُولٰٓئِكَ يَدْخُلُوْنَ الْجَنَّةَ وَلَا يُظْلَمُوْنَ
شَيْـًٔا ﴿٦٠﴾

61. Gardens of Eternity, those which (Allah) Most Gracious has promised to His servants in the Unseen: for His promise must (necessarily) come to pass.

(یعنی) بہشت جاودانی (میں) جسکا خدا نے اپنے بندوں سے وعدہ کیا ہوا اور جو انکی آنکھوں سے پوشیدہ (ہے) بیشک اسکا وعدہ (نیکوکاروں کے) سامنے آنے والا ہے (۶۱)

جَنّٰتِ عَدْنِ الَّتِيْ وَعَدَ الرَّحْمٰنُ عِبَادَهُ
بِالْغَيْبِ إِنَّهُ كَانَ وَعْدُهُ مَأْتِيًّا ﴿٦١﴾

62. They will not there hear any vain discourse, but only salutations of Peace: and they will have therein their sustenance, morning and evening.

وہ اس میں سلام کے سوا کوئی بیہودہ کلام نہ سُنیں گے اور اُن کے لئے صبح و شام کھانا تیار ہوگا (۶۲)

لَا يَسْمَعُوْنَ فِيْهَا لَغْوًا إِلَّا سَلٰمًا وَلَهُمْ
رِزْقُهُمْ فِيْهَا بُكْرَةً وَّعَشِيًّا ﴿٦٢﴾

63. Such is the Garden which We give as an inheritance to those of Our Servants who guard against evil.

یہی وہ جنت ہے جس کا ہم اپنے بندوں میں سے ایسے شخص کو مالک بنائیں گے جو پرہیزگار ہوگا (۶۳)

تِلْكَ الْجَنَّةُ الَّتِيْ نُوْرِثُ مِنْ عِبَادِنَا
مَنْ كَانَ تَقِيًّا ﴿٦٣﴾

64. (The angels say:) "We descend not but by command of thy Lord: to Him belongeth what is before us and what is behind us, and what is between: and thy Lord never doth forget,—

اور (فرشتوں نے پیغمبر کو جواب دیا کہ) ہم تمہارے پروردگار کے حکم کے سوا اُتر نہیں سکتے۔ جو کچھ ہمارے آگے ہے اور جو پیچھے ہے اور جو انکے درمیان ہے سب اسی کا ہے اور تمہارا پروردگار بھولنے والا نہیں (۶۴)

وَمَا نَتَنَزَّلُ إِلَّا بِأَمْرِ رَبِّكَ لَهُ مَا بَيْنَ
أَيْدِيْنَا وَمَا خَلْفَنَا وَمَا بَيْنَ ذٰلِكَ
وَمَا كَانَ رَبُّكَ نَسِيًّا ﴿٦٤﴾

65. Lord of the heavens and of the earth, and of all that is between them: so worship Him, and be constant and patient in His worship: knowest thou of any who is worthy of the same Name as He?

(یعنی) آسمان اور زمین کا اور جو اُن دونوں کے درمیان ہے سب کا پروردگار ہے تو اسی کی عبادت کرو اور اسکی عبادت پر ثابت قدم رہو۔ بھلا تم کوئی اسکا ہم نام جانتے ہو (۶۵)

رَبُّ السَّمٰوٰتِ وَالْأَرْضِ وَمَا بَيْنَهُمَا فَاعْبُدْهُ
وَاصْطَبِرْ لِعِبَادَتِهِ هَلْ تَعْلَمُ لَهُ سَمِيًّا ﴿٦٥﴾ ع ٤

66. Man says: "What! when I am

اور (کافر) انسان کہتا ہے کہ جب میں مرجاؤں گا تو کیا زندہ

وَيَقُوْلُ الْإِنْسَانُ ءَإِذَا مَا مِتُّ لَسَوْفَ

dead, shall I then be raised up alive?"

67. But does not man call to mind that We created him before out of nothing?

68. So, by thy Lord, without doubt, We shall gather them together, and (also) Satans (with them); then shall We bring them forth on their knees round about Hell;

69. Then shall We certainly drag out from every sect all those who were worst in obstinate rebellion against (Allah) Most Gracious.

70. And certainly We know best those who are most worthy of being burned therein.

71. Not one of you but will pass over it: this is, with thy Lord, a Decree which must be accomplished.

72. But We shall save those who guarded against evil, and We shall leave the wrong-doers therein, (humbled) to their knees.

73. When Our Clear Signs are rehearsed to them, the Unbelievers say to those who believe, "Which of the two sides is best in point of position and fairer in assembly,"

74. But how many (countless) generations before them have We destroyed, who were even better in equipment and in glitter to the eye?

75. Say: "Whoever goes astray, (Allah) Most Gracious extends (the rope) to them, until, when they see the warning of Allah (being fulfilled)—either in punishment or in (the approach of) the Hour,—they will at length realise who is worst in position, and (who) weakest in forces!

76. "And Allah doth increase in guidance those who seek guidance: and the things that endure, Good Deeds, are best in the sight of thy Lord, as rewards, and best in respect of (their) eventual returns."

77. Has thou then seen the (sort of) man who rejects Our Signs, yet says: "I shall certainly be given wealth and children?"

کر کے نکالا جاؤں گا؟ (۶۶)
کیا (ایسا) انسان یاد نہیں کرتا کہ ہم نے اس کو پہلے بھی
تو پیدا کیا تھا اور وہ کچھ بھی چیز نہ تھا (۶۷)
تمہارے پروردگار کی قسم ہم ان کو جمع کریں گے اور شیطانوں کو بھی پھر ان سب کو
جہنم کے گرد حاضر کریں گے (اور وہ) گھٹنوں پر گرے ہوئے (ہوں گے) (۶۸)
پھر ہر جماعت میں سے ہم ایسے لوگوں کو کھینچ نکالیں گے جو
خدا سے سخت سرکشی کرتے تھے (۶۹)
اور ہم اُن لوگوں سے خوب واقف ہیں جو اُن میں داخل
ہونے کے زیادہ لائق ہیں (۷۰)
اور تم میں کوئی (شخص) نہیں مگر اُسے اس پر گزرنا ہوگا۔ یہ
تمہارے پروردگار پر لازم اور مقرر ہے (۷۱)
پھر ہم پرہیزگاروں کو نجات دیں گے۔ اور ظالموں کو
اس میں گھٹنوں کے بل پڑا ہوا چھوڑ دیں گے (۷۲)
اور جب اُن لوگوں کے سامنے ہماری آیتیں پڑھی جاتی ہیں
تو جو کافر ہیں وہ مومنوں سے کہتے ہیں کہ دونوں فریق میں سے
مکان کس کے اچھے اور مجلسیں کس کی بہتر ہیں؟ (۷۳)
اور ہم نے ان سے پہلے بہت سی اُمتیں ہلاک کر دیں وہ لوگ
(ان سے) ٹھاٹھ اور نمود میں کہیں اچھے تھے (۷۴)
کہہ دو کہ جو شخص گمراہی میں پڑا ہوا ہے۔ خدا اس کو آہستہ آہستہ
مہلت دیئے جاتا ہے یہاں تک کہ جب اس چیز کو
دیکھ لیں گے جس کا ان سے وعدہ کیا جاتا ہے خواہ عذاب اور خواہ قیامت
تو اس وقت جان لیں گے کہ مکان کس کا بُرا ہے اور لشکر کس کا کمزور ہے (۷۵)
اور جو لوگ ہدایت یاب ہیں خدا اُن کو زیادہ ہدایت دیتا ہے
اور نیکیاں جو باقی رہنے والی ہیں وہ تمہارے پروردگار کے
صلے کے لحاظ سے خوب اور انجام کے اعتبار سے بہتر ہیں (۷۶)
بھلا تم نے اُس شخص کو دیکھا جس نے ہماری آیتوں سے کفر کیا اور کہنے
لگا کہ (اگر میں ازسرِنو زندہ ہوا بھی تو یہی) مال اور اولاد مجھے (وہاں) ملے گا (۷۷)

أُخْرَجُ حَيًّا ﴿٦٦﴾
أَوَلَا يَذْكُرُ الْإِنْسَانُ أَنَّا خَلَقْنٰهُ مِنْ
قَبْلُ وَلَمْ يَكُ شَيْئًا ﴿٦٧﴾
فَوَرَبِّكَ لَنَحْشُرَنَّهُمْ وَالشَّيٰطِينَ ثُمَّ
لَنُحْضِرَنَّهُمْ حَوْلَ جَهَنَّمَ جِثِيًّا ﴿٦٨﴾
ثُمَّ لَنَنْزِعَنَّ مِنْ كُلِّ شِيعَةٍ أَيُّهُمْ
أَشَدُّ عَلَى الرَّحْمٰنِ عِتِيًّا ﴿٦٩﴾
ثُمَّ لَنَحْنُ أَعْلَمُ بِالَّذِينَ هُمْ أَوْلٰى بِهَا
صِلِيًّا ﴿٧٠﴾
وَإِنْ مِنْكُمْ إِلَّا وَارِدُهَا ۚ كَانَ عَلٰى
رَبِّكَ حَتْمًا مَقْضِيًّا ﴿٧١﴾
ثُمَّ نُنَجِّي الَّذِينَ اتَّقَوْا وَنَذَرُ الظّٰلِمِينَ
فِيهَا جِثِيًّا ﴿٧٢﴾
وَإِذَا تُتْلٰى عَلَيْهِمْ اٰيٰتُنَا بَيِّنٰتٍ قَالَ
الَّذِينَ كَفَرُوا لِلَّذِينَ اٰمَنُوا ۙ أَيُّ
الْفَرِيقَيْنِ خَيْرٌ مَقَامًا وَأَحْسَنُ نَدِيًّا ﴿٧٣﴾
وَكَمْ أَهْلَكْنَا قَبْلَهُمْ مِنْ قَرْنٍ هُمْ
أَحْسَنُ أَثَاثًا وَرِئْيًا ﴿٧٤﴾
قُلْ مَنْ كَانَ فِي الضَّلٰلَةِ فَلْيَمْدُدْ لَهُ
الرَّحْمٰنُ مَدًّا ۚ حَتّٰى إِذَا رَأَوْا مَا يُوعَدُونَ
إِمَّا الْعَذَابَ وَإِمَّا السَّاعَةَ ۖ فَسَيَعْلَمُونَ
مَنْ هُوَ شَرٌّ مَكَانًا وَأَضْعَفُ جُنْدًا ﴿٧٥﴾
وَيَزِيدُ اللّٰهُ الَّذِينَ اهْتَدَوْا هُدًى ۗ
وَالْبٰقِيٰتُ الصّٰلِحٰتُ خَيْرٌ عِنْدَ رَبِّكَ
ثَوَابًا وَخَيْرٌ مَرَدًّا ﴿٧٦﴾
أَفَرَأَيْتَ الَّذِي كَفَرَ بِاٰيٰتِنَا وَقَالَ
لَأُوتَيَنَّ مَالًا وَوَلَدًا ﴿٧٧﴾

78. Has he penetrated to the Unseen, or has he taken a promise with the Most Gracious?

79. Nay! We shall record what he says, and We shall add and add to his punishment.

80. To Us shall return all that he talks of, and he shall appear before Us bare and alone.

81. And they have taken (for worship) gods other than Allah, to give them power and glory!

82. Instead, they shall reject their worship, and become adversaries against them.

83. Seest thou not that We have set Satans on against the Unbelievers, to incite them with fury?

84. So make no haste against them, for We but count out to them a (limited) number (of days).

85. The day We shall gather the righteous to (Allah) Most Gracious, like a band (presented before a king for honours.)

86. And We shall drive the sinners to hell, (like thirsty cattle driven down to water,—)

87. None shall have the power of intercession, but such a one as has received permission (or promise) from (Allah) Most Gracious.

88. They say: "The Most Gracious has betaken a son!"

89. Indeed ye have put forth a thing most monstrous!

90. At it the skies are about to burst, the earth to split asunder, and the mountains to fall down in utter ruin,

91. That they attributed a son to the Most Gracious.

92. For it is not consonant with the majesty of the Most Gracious that He should beget a son.

93. Not one of the beings in the heavens and the earth but must come to the Most Gracious as a servant.

94. He does take an account of them (all), and hath numbered them (all) exactly.

95. And everyone of them will come to Him singly on the Day of Judgment.

96. On those who believe and work deeds of righteousness, will

کیا اس نے غیب کی خبر پالی ہے یا خدا کے یہاں (سے)
عہد لے لیا ہے؟ ﴿۷۸﴾
ہرگز نہیں۔ یہ جو کچھ کہتا ہے ہم اس کو لکھتے جاتے اور
آہستہ آہستہ عذاب بڑھاتے جاتے ہیں ﴿۷۹﴾
اور جو چیزیں یہ بتاتا ہے اسکے ہم وارث ہونگے اور یہ اکیلا ہمارے سامنے آئیگا ﴿۸۰﴾
اور ان لوگوں نے خدا کے سوا اور معبود بنا لئے ہیں تاکہ وہ انکے
لئے (موجب عزت و) مدد ہوں ﴿۸۱﴾
ہرگز نہیں۔ وہ (معبودانِ باطل) اُن کی پرستش سے انکار
کریں گے اور اُن کے دشمن (و مخالف) ہوں گے ﴿۸۲﴾
کیا تم نے نہیں دیکھا کہ ہم نے شیطانوں کو کافروں پر چھوڑ
رکھا ہے کہ وہ اُن کو برانگیختہ کرتے رہتے ہیں ﴿۸۳﴾
تو تم اُن پر (عذاب کے لئے) جلدی نہ کرو۔ ہم تو اُن کیلئے (دن) شمار کر رہے ہیں ﴿۸۴﴾
جس روز ہم پرہیزگاروں کو خدا کے سامنے (بطور) مہمان جمع کریں گے ﴿۸۵﴾
اور گنہگاروں کو دوزخ کی طرف پیاسے ہانک لے جائیں گے ﴿۸۶﴾
(تو لوگ) کسی کی سفارش کا اختیار نہ رکھیں گے مگر جس نے
خدا سے اقرار لیا ہو ﴿۸۷﴾
اور کہتے ہیں خدا بیٹا رکھتا ہے ﴿۸۸﴾
(ایسا کہنے والو یہ تو تم) بُری بات (زبان پر) لاتے ہو ﴿۸۹﴾
قریب ہے کہ اس (افترا) سے آسمان پھٹ پڑیں اور زمین
شق ہو جائے اور پہاڑ پارہ پارہ ہو کر گر پڑیں ﴿۹۰﴾
کہ اُنہوں نے خدا کے لئے بیٹا تجویز کیا ﴿۹۱﴾
اور خدا کو شایاں نہیں کہ کسی کو بیٹا بنائے ﴿۹۲﴾
تمام شخص جو آسمانوں اور زمین میں ہیں سب خدا کے
روبرو بندے ہو کر آئیں گے ﴿۹۳﴾
اُس نے اُن (سب) کو (اپنے علم سے) گھیر رکھا اور (ایک ایک کو) شمار کر رکھا ہے ﴿۹۴﴾
اور سب قیامت کے دن اسکے سامنے اکیلے اکیلے حاضر ہوں گے ﴿۹۵﴾
اور جو لوگ ایمان لائے اور عمل نیک کئے خدا اُن کی محبت

أَطَّلَعَ الْغَيْبَ أَمِ اتَّخَذَ عِنْدَ الرَّحْمٰنِ
عَهْدًا ﴿٧٨﴾
كَلَّا سَنَكْتُبُ مَا يَقُولُ وَنَمُدُّ لَهُ مِنَ
الْعَذَابِ مَدًّا ﴿٧٩﴾
وَنَرِثُهُ مَا يَقُولُ وَيَأْتِينَا فَرْدًا ﴿٨٠﴾
وَاتَّخَذُوا مِنْ دُونِ اللّٰهِ آلِهَةً لِيَكُونُوا
لَهُمْ عِزًّا ﴿٨١﴾
كَلَّا سَيَكْفُرُونَ بِعِبَادَتِهِمْ وَيَكُونُونَ
عَلَيْهِمْ ضِدًّا ﴿٨٢﴾
أَلَمْ تَرَ أَنَّا أَرْسَلْنَا الشَّيٰطِينَ عَلَى
الْكٰفِرِينَ تَؤُزُّهُمْ أَزًّا ﴿٨٣﴾
فَلَا تَعْجَلْ عَلَيْهِمْ إِنَّمَا نَعُدُّ لَهُمْ عَدًّا ﴿٨٤﴾
يَوْمَ نَحْشُرُ الْمُتَّقِينَ إِلَى الرَّحْمٰنِ وَفْدًا ﴿٨٥﴾
وَنَسُوقُ الْمُجْرِمِينَ إِلَىٰ جَهَنَّمَ وِرْدًا ﴿٨٦﴾
لَا يَمْلِكُونَ الشَّفَاعَةَ إِلَّا مَنِ اتَّخَذَ
عِنْدَ الرَّحْمٰنِ عَهْدًا ﴿٨٧﴾
وَقَالُوا اتَّخَذَ الرَّحْمٰنُ وَلَدًا ﴿٨٨﴾
لَقَدْ جِئْتُمْ شَيْئًا إِدًّا ﴿٨٩﴾
تَكَادُ السَّمٰوٰتُ يَتَفَطَّرْنَ مِنْهُ وَتَنْشَقُّ
الْأَرْضُ وَتَخِرُّ الْجِبَالُ هَدًّا ﴿٩٠﴾
أَنْ دَعَوْا لِلرَّحْمٰنِ وَلَدًا ﴿٩١﴾
وَمَا يَنْبَغِي لِلرَّحْمٰنِ أَنْ يَتَّخِذَ وَلَدًا ﴿٩٢﴾
إِنْ كُلُّ مَنْ فِي السَّمٰوٰتِ وَالْأَرْضِ إِلَّا
آتِي الرَّحْمٰنِ عَبْدًا ﴿٩٣﴾
لَقَدْ أَحْصٰىهُمْ وَعَدَّهُمْ عَدًّا ﴿٩٤﴾
وَكُلُّهُمْ آتِيهِ يَوْمَ الْقِيٰمَةِ فَرْدًا ﴿٩٥﴾
إِنَّ الَّذِينَ آمَنُوا وَعَمِلُوا الصّٰلِحٰتِ

SÛRA–20

ṬÃ-HÃ

(INTRODUCTION)

The chronology of this Sûra has some significance: it has some relation to the spiritual lessons which it teaches.

It was used with great effect in that remarkable scene which resulted in Ḥadhrat 'Umar's conversion, and which took place about the seventh year before the Hijrat.

The scene is described with dramatic details by Ibn Hishãm. 'Umar had previously been one of the greatest enemies and persecutors of Islam. Like his blood-thirsty kinsmen the Quraish, he meditated slaying the Prophet, when it was suggested to him that there were near relations of his that had embraced Islam. His sister Fã îma and her husband Sa'îd were Muslims, but in those days of persecution they had kept their faith secret. When 'Umar went to their house, he heard them reciting this Sûra from a written copy they had. For a while they concealed the copy. 'Umar attacked his sister and her husband, but they bore the attack with exemplary patience, and declared their faith. 'Umar was so struck with their sincerity and fortitude that he asked to see the leaf from which they had been reading. It was given to him: his soul was touched, and he not only came into the Faith but became one of its strongest supporters and champions.

The leaf contained some portion of this Sûra, perhaps the introductory portion. The mystic leters *Ṭã-Hã* are prefixed to this Sûra. What do they mean? The earliest tradition is that they denote a dialectical interjection meaning "O man!" If so, the title is particularly appropriate in two ways: (1) It was a direct and personal address to a man in a high state of excitement tempted by his temper to do grievous wrong, but called by Allah's Grace, as by a personal appeal, to face the realities, for Allah knew his inmost secret thoughts (20: 7) : the revelation was sent by Allah Most Gracious, out of His Grace and Mercy (20: 5). (2) It takes up the story from the last Sûra, of man as a spiritual being and illustrates it in further details. It tells the story of Moses in the crisis of his life when he received Allah's Commission and in his personal relations with his mother, and how he came to be brought up in the Pharaoh's house, to learn all the wisdom of the Egyptians, for use in Allah's service, and in his personal relations with Pharaoh, whom we take to be his adoptive father (28: 9). If further tells the story of a fallen soul who misled the Israelites into idolatry, and recalls how man's Arch-enemy Satan caused his fall. Prayer and praise are necessary to man to cure his spiritual blindness and enable him to appreciate Allah's revelation.

the Most Gracious bestow Love.

97. So have We made the (Qur'ān) easy in thine own tongue, that with it thou mayest give glad tidings to the righteous, and warnings to people given to contention.

98. But how many (countless) generations before them have We destroyed? Canst thou find a single one of them (now) or hear (so much as) a whisper of them?

Ṭā-Hā

In the name of Allah, Most Gracious, Most Merciful.

1. Tā-Hā.

2. We have not sent down the Qur-ān to thee to be (an occasion) for thy distress,

3. But only as an admonition to those who fear (Allah),—

4. A revelation from Him Who created the earth and the heavens on high.

5. The Most Gracious is firmly established on the throne.

6. To Him belongs what is in the heavens and on earth, and all between them, and all beneath the soil.

7. If thou pronounce the word aloud, (it is no matter): for verily He knoweth what is secret and what is yet more hidden.

8. Allah! there is no god but He! To Him belong the Most Beautiful Names.

9. Was the story of Moses reached thee?

10. Behold, he saw a fire: so he said to his family, "Tarry ye; I perceive a fire; perhaps I can bring you some burning brand therefrom, or find some guidance at the fire."

11. But when he came to the fire, He was called "O Moses!

12. "Verily I am thy Lord! Therefore put off thy shoes: thou art in the sacred valley Tuwā.

13. "I have chosen thee: listen, then to the inspiration (given to thee).

14. "Verily, I am Allah: there is no god but I: so serve thou Me (only),

(مخلوقات کے دل میں) پیدا کر دے گا ۹۶

(اے پیغمبر) ہم نے یہ (قرآن) تمہاری زبان میں آسان (نازل) کیا ہے تاکہ تم اس سے پرہیزگاروں کو خوشخبری پہنچا دو اور جھگڑالوؤں کو ڈر سنا دو ۹۷

اور ہم نے ان سے پہلے بہت سے گروہوں کو ہلاک کر دیا ہے بھلا تم ان میں سے کسی کو دیکھتے ہو یا کہیں ان کی بھنک سنتے ہو ۹۸

سورہ طٰہٰ مکی ہے اور اس میں ایک سو پینتیس آیتیں اور آٹھ رکوع ہیں

شروع خدا کا نام لے کر جو بڑا مہربان نہایت رحم والا ہے

طٰہٰ ۱ (اے محمدؐ) ہم نے تم پر قرآن اس لئے نازل نہیں کیا کہ تم مشقت میں پڑ جاؤ ۲

بلکہ اس شخص کو نصیحت دینے کے لئے (نازل کیا ہے) جو خوف رکھتا ہے ۳

یہ اس ذات کا اتارا ہوا ہے جس نے زمین اور اونچے اونچے آسمان بنائے ۴

(یعنی خدائے) رحمٰن جس نے عرش پر قرار پکڑا ۵

جو کچھ آسمانوں میں ہے اور جو کچھ زمین میں ہے اور جو کچھ ان دونوں کے بیچ میں ہے اور جو کچھ (زمین کی) مٹی کے نیچے ہے سب اسی کا ہے ۶

اور اگر تم پکار کر بات کہو تو وہ تو چھپے بھید اور نہایت پوشیدہ بات تک کو جانتا ہے ۷

(وہ معبود برحق ہے کہ) اس کے سوا کوئی معبود نہیں اس کے (سب) نام اچھے ہیں ۸

اور کیا تمہیں موسیٰ کے حال کی خبر ملی ہے ۹

جب انہوں نے آگ دیکھی تو اپنے گھر کے لوگوں سے کہا کہ تم (یہاں) ٹھہرو میں نے آگ دیکھی ہے (میں وہاں جاتا ہوں) شاید اس میں سے میں تمہارے پاس انگاری لاؤں یا آگ (کے مقام) کا رستہ معلوم کر سکوں ۱۰

جب وہاں پہنچے تو آواز آئی کہ موسیٰ ۱۱

میں تو تمہارا پروردگار ہوں تو اپنی جوتیاں اتار دو تم (یہاں) پاک میدان (یعنی) طویٰ میں ہو ۱۲

اور میں نے تم کو انتخاب کر لیا ہے تو جو حکم دیا جائے اسے سنو ۱۳

بیشک میں ہی خدا ہوں میرے سوا کوئی معبود نہیں تو میری

سَيَجْعَلُ لَهُمُ الرَّحْمٰنُ وُدًّا ۹۶

فَاِنَّمَا يَسَّرْنٰهُ بِلِسَانِكَ لِتُبَشِّرَ بِهِ الْمُتَّقِيْنَ وَتُنْذِرَ بِهٖ قَوْمًا لُّدًّا ۹۷

وَكَمْ اَهْلَكْنَا قَبْلَهُمْ مِّنْ قَرْنٍ ۭ هَلْ تُحِسُّ مِنْهُمْ مِّنْ اَحَدٍ اَوْ تَسْمَعُ لَهُمْ رِكْزًا ۹۸

سُوْرَةُ طٰهٰ مَكِّيَّةٌ وَّهِيَ مِائَةٌ وَّخَمْسٌ وَّثَلٰثُوْنَ اٰيَةً وَّثَمَانُ رُكُوْعَاتٍ

بِسْمِ اللّٰهِ الرَّحْمٰنِ الرَّحِيْمِ

طٰهٰ ۱ مَآ اَنْزَلْنَا عَلَيْكَ الْقُرْاٰنَ لِتَشْقٰٓى ۲

اِلَّا تَذْكِرَةً لِّمَنْ يَّخْشٰى ۳

تَنْزِيْلًا مِّمَّنْ خَلَقَ الْاَرْضَ وَالسَّمٰوٰتِ الْعُلٰى ۴

اَلرَّحْمٰنُ عَلَى الْعَرْشِ اسْتَوٰى ۵

لَهٗ مَا فِي السَّمٰوٰتِ وَمَا فِي الْاَرْضِ وَمَا بَيْنَهُمَا وَمَا تَحْتَ الثَّرٰى ۶

وَاِنْ تَجْهَرْ بِالْقَوْلِ فَاِنَّهٗ يَعْلَمُ السِّرَّ وَاَخْفٰى ۷

اَللّٰهُ لَآ اِلٰهَ اِلَّا هُوَ ۭ لَهُ الْاَسْمَاۗءُ الْحُسْنٰى ۸

وَهَلْ اَتٰىكَ حَدِيْثُ مُوْسٰى ۹

اِذْ رَاٰ نَارًا فَقَالَ لِاَهْلِهِ امْكُثُوْٓا اِنِّىْٓ اٰنَسْتُ نَارًا لَّعَلِّيْٓ اٰتِيْكُمْ مِّنْهَا بِقَبَسٍ اَوْ اَجِدُ عَلَى النَّارِ هُدًى ۱۰

فَلَمَّآ اَتٰىهَا نُوْدِيَ يٰمُوْسٰى ۱۱

اِنِّىْٓ اَنَا رَبُّكَ فَاخْلَعْ نَعْلَيْكَ ۚ اِنَّكَ بِالْوَادِ الْمُقَدَّسِ طُوًى ۱۲

وَاَنَا اخْتَرْتُكَ فَاسْتَمِعْ لِمَا يُوْحٰى ۱۳

اِنَّنِيْٓ اَنَا اللّٰهُ لَآ اِلٰهَ اِلَّآ اَنَا فَاعْبُدْنِيْ

and establish regular prayer for My remembrance.

عبادت کیا کرو۔ اور میری یاد کے لئے نماز پڑھا کرو ﴿١٤﴾

وَأَقِمِ الصَّلٰوةَ لِذِكْرِي ﴿١٤﴾

15. "Verily the Hour is coming— I have almost kept it hidden—for every soul to receive its reward by the measure of its Endeavour.

قیامت یقیناً آنیوالی ہے میں چاہتا ہوں کہ اُس (کے وقت) کو
پوشیدہ رکھوں تاکہ ہر شخص جو کوشش کرے اسکا بدلہ پائے ﴿١٥﴾

إِنَّ السَّاعَةَ اٰتِيَةٌ أَكَادُ أُخْفِيهَا لِتُجْزٰى
كُلُّ نَفْسٍ بِمَا تَسْعٰى ﴿١٥﴾

16. "Therefore let not such as believe not therein but follow their own lusts, divert thee therefrom, lest thou perish!"...

تو جو شخص اس پر ایمان نہیں رکھتا اور اپنی خواہش کے پیچھے چلتا ہے (کہیں)
تمکو اس (کے یقین) سے روک نہ دے تو (اس صورت میں) تم ہلاک ہو جاؤ ﴿١٦﴾

فَلَا يَصُدَّنَّكَ عَنْهَا مَنْ لَّا يُؤْمِنُ بِهَا
وَاتَّبَعَ هَوٰىهُ فَتَرْدٰى ﴿١٦﴾

17. "And what is that in thy right hand, O Moses?"

اور موسیٰ یہ تمہارے داہنے ہاتھ میں کیا ہے؟ ﴿١٧﴾

وَمَا تِلْكَ بِيَمِينِكَ يٰمُوسٰى ﴿١٧﴾

18. He said, "It is my rod: on it I lean; with it I beat down fodder for my flocks; and in it I find other uses."

اُنہوں نے کہا یہ میری لاٹھی ہے اس پر میں سہارا لگاتا ہوں
اور اس سے اپنی بکریوں کے لئے پتے جھاڑتا ہوں اور
اس میں میرے اور بھی کئی فائدے ہیں ﴿١٨﴾

قَالَ هِيَ عَصَايَ أَتَوَكَّؤُا عَلَيْهَا وَ
أَهُشُّ بِهَا عَلٰى غَنَمِي وَلِيَ فِيهَا مَاٰرِبُ
أُخْرٰى ﴿١٨﴾

19. (Allah) said, "Throw it, O Moses!"

فرمایا کہ موسیٰ اسے ڈال دو ﴿١٩﴾

قَالَ أَلْقِهَا يٰمُوسٰى ﴿١٩﴾

20. He threw it, and behold! it was a snake, active in motion.

تو اُنہوں نے اسکو ڈال دیا اور وہ ناگہاں سانپ بنکر دوڑنے لگا ﴿٢٠﴾

فَأَلْقٰىهَا فَإِذَا هِيَ حَيَّةٌ تَسْعٰى ﴿٢٠﴾

21. (Allah) said, "Seize it, and fear not: We shall return it at once to its former condition"...

خدا نے فرمایا کہ اسے پکڑ لو اور ڈرنا مت۔ ہم اس کو ابھی اسکی
پہلی حالت پر لوٹا دیں گے ﴿٢١﴾

قَالَ خُذْهَا وَلَا تَخَفْ سَنُعِيدُهَا
سِيرَتَهَا الْأُولٰى ﴿٢١﴾

22. "Now draw thy hand close to thy side: it shall come forth white (and shining), without harm (or stain),—as another Sign,—

اور اپنا ہاتھ اپنی بغل سے لگا لو وہ کسی عیب (و بیماری) کے
بغیر سفید (چمکتا دمکتا) نکلے گا۔ (یہ) دوسری نشانی (ہے) ﴿٢٢﴾

وَاضْمُمْ يَدَكَ إِلٰى جَنَاحِكَ تَخْرُجْ
بَيْضَاءَ مِنْ غَيْرِ سُوْٓءٍ اٰيَةً أُخْرٰى ﴿٢٢﴾

23. "In order that We may show thee of our Greater Signs.

تاکہ ہم تمہیں اپنے نشانات عظیم دکھائیں ﴿٢٣﴾

لِنُرِيَكَ مِنْ اٰيٰتِنَا الْكُبْرٰى ﴿٢٣﴾

24. "Go thou to Pharaoh, for he has indeed transgressed all bounds."

تم فرعون کے پاس جاؤ (کہ) وہ سرکش ہو رہا ہے ﴿٢٤﴾

اِذْهَبْ إِلٰى فِرْعَوْنَ إِنَّهُ طَغٰى ﴿٢٤﴾ ع

25. (Moses) said: "O my Lord! expand me my breast;

کہا میرے پروردگار (اس کام کے لئے) میرا سینہ کھول دے ﴿٢٥﴾

قَالَ رَبِّ اشْرَحْ لِي صَدْرِي ﴿٢٥﴾

26. "Ease my task for me;

اور میرا کام آسان کر دے ﴿٢٦﴾

وَيَسِّرْ لِي أَمْرِي ﴿٢٦﴾

27. "And remove the impediment from my speech,

اور میری زبان کی گرہ کھول دے ﴿٢٧﴾

وَاحْلُلْ عُقْدَةً مِّنْ لِّسَانِي ﴿٢٧﴾

28. "So they may understand what I say:

تاکہ وہ میری بات سمجھ لیں ﴿٢٨﴾

يَفْقَهُوا قَوْلِي ﴿٢٨﴾

29. "And give me a Minister from my family,

اور میرے گھر والوں میں سے (ایک کو) میرا وزیر (یعنی مددگار) مقرر فرما ﴿٢٩﴾

وَاجْعَلْ لِّي وَزِيرًا مِّنْ أَهْلِي ﴿٢٩﴾

30. "Aaron, my brother;

(یعنی) میرے بھائی ہارون کو ﴿٣٠﴾

هٰرُونَ أَخِي ﴿٣٠﴾

31. "Add to my strength through him.

اس سے میری قوت کو مضبوط کر ﴿٣١﴾

اشْدُدْ بِهٖٓ أَزْرِي ﴿٣١﴾

32. "And make him share My task:

اور اسے میرے کام میں شریک کر ﴿٣٢﴾

وَأَشْرِكْهُ فِي أَمْرِي ﴿٣٢﴾

33. "That we may celebrate Thy praise without stint,

تاکہ ہم تیری بہت سی تسبیح کریں ﴿٣٣﴾

كَيْ نُسَبِّحَكَ كَثِيرًا ﴿٣٣﴾

34. "And remember Thee without stint:

اور تجھے کثرت سے یاد کریں ﴿٣٤﴾

وَّنَذْكُرَكَ كَثِيرًا ﴿٣٤﴾

35. "For Thou art ever seeing

36. (Allah) said: "Granted is thy prayer, O Moses!"

37. "And indeed We conferred a favour on thee another time (before).

38. "Behold! We sent to thy mother, by inspiration, the message:

39. " 'Throw (the child) into the chest, and throw (the chest) into the river: the river will cast him up on the bank, and he will be taken up by one who is an enemy to Me and an enemy to him': but I endued thee with love from Me: and (this) in order that thou mayest be reared under Mine eye.

40. "Behold! thy sister goeth forth and saith, 'Shall I show you one who will nurse and rear the (child)?' So We brought thee back to thy mother, that her eye might be cooled and she should not grieve. Then thou didst slay a man, but We saved thee from trouble, and We tried thee in various ways. Then didst thou tarry a number of years with the people of Midian. Then didst thou come hither as ordained, O Moses!

41. "And I have prepared thee for Myself (for service)"...

42. Go, thou and thy brother, with My signs, and slacken not, either of you, in keeping Me in remembrance.

43. "Go, both of you, to Pharaoh, for he has indeed transgressed all bounds;

44. "But speak to him mildly; perchance he may take warning or fear (Allah)."

45. They (Moses and Aaron) said: "Our Lord! we fear lest he hasten with insolence against us, or lest he transgress all bounds."

46. He said: "Fear not: for I am with you: I hear and see (everything).

47. "So go ye both to him, and say, 'Verily we are messengers sent by thy Lord: send forth, therefore, the Children of Israel with us, and

تُو ہم کو (ہر حال میں) دیکھ رہا ہے ﴿٣٥﴾
فرمایا۔ موسیٰ تمہاری دُعا قبول کی گئی ﴿٣٦﴾
اور ہم نے تم پر ایک بار اور بھی احسان کیا تھا ﴿٣٧﴾
جب ہم نے تمہاری والدہ کو الہام کیا تھا جو تمہیں بتایا جاتا ہے ﴿٣٨﴾
(وہ یہ تھا) کہ اسے (یعنی موسیٰ کو) صندوق میں رکھو پھر اس (صندوق)
کو دریا میں ڈال دو تو دریا اسکو کنارے پر ڈال دیگا (اور) میرا اور اسکا دشمن اُسے
اٹھا لیگا۔ اور (موسیٰ) میں نے تم پر اپنی طرف سے محبت ڈال دی (اسلئے کہ تم پر
مہربانی کیجائے) اور اسلئے کہ تم میرے سامنے پرورش پاؤ ﴿٣٩﴾
جب تمہاری بہن (فرعون کے ہاں) گئی اور کہنے لگی کہ میں تمہیں ایسا
شخص بتاؤں جو اسکو پالے تو (اس طریق سے) ہم نے تمکو تمہاری ماں کے پاس
پہنچا دیا تاکہ انکی آنکھیں ٹھنڈی ہوں اور وہ رنج نہ کریں
اور تم نے ایک شخص کو مار ڈالا تو ہم نے تم کو غم سے
مخلصی دی اور ہم نے تمہاری (کئی بار) آزمائش کی۔ پھر
تم کئی سال اہل مدین میں ٹھیرے رہے۔ پھر اے موسیٰ تم
(قابلیت رسالت کے) اندازے پر آ پہنچے ﴿٤٠﴾
اور میں نے تم کو اپنے (کام کے) لئے بنایا ہے ﴿٤١﴾
تو تم اور تمہارا بھائی دونوں ہماری نشانیاں لے کر جاؤ
اور میری یاد میں سُستی نہ کرنا ﴿٤٢﴾
دونوں فرعون کے پاس جاؤ وہ سرکش ہو رہا ہے ﴿٤٣﴾
اور اس سے نرمی سے بات کرنا شاید وہ غور کرے یا
ڈر جائے ﴿٤٤﴾
دونوں کہنے لگے کہ ہمارے پروردگار ہمیں خوف ہے کہ وہ ہم پر
تعدّی کرنے لگے یا زیادہ سرکش ہو جائے ﴿٤٥﴾
(خدا نے) فرمایا کہ ڈرو مت میں تمہارے ساتھ ہوں (اور)
سنتا اور دیکھتا ہوں ﴿٤٦﴾
(اچھا) تو اسکے پاس جاؤ اور کہو کہ ہم آپکے پروردگار کے
بھیجے ہوئے ہیں۔ تو بنی اسرائیل کو ہمارے ساتھ جانے کی اجازت

إِنَّكَ كُنتَ بِنَا بَصِيرًا ﴿٣٥﴾
قَالَ قَدْ أُوتِيتَ سُؤْلَكَ يٰمُوسٰى ﴿٣٦﴾
وَلَقَدْ مَنَنَّا عَلَيْكَ مَرَّةً أُخْرٰى ﴿٣٧﴾
إِذْ أَوْحَيْنَا إِلٰى أُمِّكَ مَا يُوحٰى ﴿٣٨﴾
أَنِ اقْذِفِيهِ فِي التَّابُوتِ فَاقْذِفِيهِ فِي
الْيَمِّ فَلْيُلْقِهِ الْيَمُّ بِالسَّاحِلِ يَأْخُذْهُ
عَدُوٌّ لِّي وَعَدُوٌّ لَّهُ ۚ وَأَلْقَيْتُ عَلَيْكَ
مَحَبَّةً مِّنِّي ۚ وَلِتُصْنَعَ عَلٰى عَيْنِي ﴿٣٩﴾ م
إِذْ تَمْشِي أُخْتُكَ فَتَقُولُ هَلْ أَدُلُّكُمْ
عَلٰى مَن يَكْفُلُهُ ۖ فَرَجَعْنٰكَ إِلٰى أُمِّكَ
كَيْ تَقَرَّ عَيْنُهَا وَلَا تَحْزَنَ ۚ
وَقَتَلْتَ نَفْسًا فَنَجَّيْنٰكَ مِنَ الْغَمِّ وَ
فَتَنّٰكَ فُتُونًا ۚ فَلَبِثْتَ سِنِينَ فِي
أَهْلِ مَدْيَنَ ۚ ثُمَّ جِئْتَ عَلٰى قَدَرٍ
يٰمُوسٰى ﴿٤٠﴾
وَاصْطَنَعْتُكَ لِنَفْسِي ﴿٤١﴾ ج
اِذْهَبْ أَنتَ وَأَخُوكَ بِاٰيٰتِي وَلَا تَنِيَا
فِي ذِكْرِي ﴿٤٢﴾ ج
اِذْهَبَا إِلٰى فِرْعَوْنَ إِنَّهُ طَغٰى ﴿٤٣﴾ ج
فَقُولَا لَهُ قَوْلًا لَّيِّنًا لَّعَلَّهُ يَتَذَكَّرُ أَوْ
يَخْشٰى ﴿٤٤﴾
قَالَا رَبَّنَا إِنَّنَا نَخَافُ أَن يَفْرُطَ عَلَيْنَا
أَوْ أَن يَطْغٰى ﴿٤٥﴾
قَالَ لَا تَخَافَا إِنَّنِي مَعَكُمَا أَسْمَعُ وَ
أَرٰى ﴿٤٦﴾
فَأْتِيٰهُ فَقُولَا إِنَّا رَسُولَا رَبِّكَ فَأَرْسِلْ
مَعَنَا بَنِي إِسْرَاءِيلَ ۙ وَلَا تُعَذِّبْهُمْ

وقف لازم

قَدْ جِئْنٰكَ بِاٰيَةٍ مِّنْ رَّبِّكَ ؕ وَالسَّلٰمُ
عَلٰى مَنِ اتَّبَعَ الْهُدٰى ﴿۴۷﴾
اِنَّا قَدْ اُوْحِيَ اِلَيْنَآ اَنَّ الْعَذَابَ عَلٰى
مَنْ كَذَّبَ وَتَوَلّٰى ﴿۴۸﴾
قَالَ فَمَنْ رَّبُّكُمَا يٰمُوْسٰى ﴿۴۹﴾
قَالَ رَبُّنَا الَّذِيْٓ اَعْطٰى كُلَّ شَيْءٍ خَلْقَهٗ
ثُمَّ هَدٰى ﴿۵۰﴾
قَالَ فَمَا بَالُ الْقُرُوْنِ الْاُوْلٰى ﴿۵۱﴾
قَالَ عِلْمُهَا عِنْدَ رَبِّيْ فِيْ كِتٰبٍ ۚ لَا يَضِلُّ
رَبِّيْ وَلَا يَنْسَى ﴿۵۲﴾
الَّذِيْ جَعَلَ لَكُمُ الْاَرْضَ مَهْدًا وَّ
سَلَكَ لَكُمْ فِيْهَا سُبُلًا وَّاَنْزَلَ مِنَ السَّمَآءِ
مَآءً ؕ فَاَخْرَجْنَا بِهٖٓ اَزْوَاجًا مِّنْ نَّبَاتٍ شَتّٰى ﴿۵۳﴾
كُلُوْا وَارْعَوْا اَنْعَامَكُمْ ؕ اِنَّ فِيْ ذٰلِكَ
لَاٰيٰتٍ لِّاُولِي النُّهٰى ﴿۵۴﴾ ع
مِنْهَا خَلَقْنٰكُمْ وَفِيْهَا نُعِيْدُكُمْ وَمِنْهَا
نُخْرِجُكُمْ تَارَةً اُخْرٰى ﴿۵۵﴾
وَلَقَدْ اَرَيْنٰهُ اٰيٰتِنَا كُلَّهَا فَكَذَّبَ وَاَبٰى ﴿۵۶﴾
قَالَ اَجِئْتَنَا لِتُخْرِجَنَا مِنْ اَرْضِنَا
بِسِحْرِكَ يٰمُوْسٰى ﴿۵۷﴾
فَلَنَاْتِيَنَّكَ بِسِحْرٍ مِّثْلِهٖ فَاجْعَلْ بَيْنَنَا
وَبَيْنَكَ مَوْعِدًا لَّا نُخْلِفُهٗ نَحْنُ وَلَآ
اَنْتَ مَكَانًا سُوًى ﴿۵۸﴾
قَالَ مَوْعِدُكُمْ يَوْمُ الزِّيْنَةِ وَاَنْ يُّحْشَرَ
النَّاسُ ضُحًى ﴿۵۹﴾
فَتَوَلّٰى فِرْعَوْنُ فَجَمَعَ كَيْدَهٗ ثُمَّ اَتٰى ﴿۶۰﴾
قَالَ لَهُمْ مُّوْسٰى وَيْلَكُمْ لَا تَفْتَرُوْا عَلَى

دیجئے اور انہیں عذاب نہ کیجئے ہم آپکے پاس آپکے پروردگار کیطرف سے نشانی
لیکر آئے ہیں۔ اور جو ہدایت کی بات مانے اسکو سلامتی ہو ﴿۴۷﴾
ہماری طرف یہ وحی آئی ہے کہ جو جھٹلائے اور منہ پھیرے
اس کے لئے عذاب (تیار) ہے ﴿۴۸﴾
(غرض موسیٰ اور ہارون فرعون کے پاس گئے) اسنے کہا کہ موسیٰ تمہارا پروردگار کون ہے؟ ﴿۴۹﴾
کہا کہ ہمارا پروردگار وہ ہے جس نے ہر چیز کو اس کی شکل و
صورت بخشی پھر راہ دکھائی ﴿۵۰﴾
کہا تو پہلی جماعتوں کا کیا حال؟ ﴿۵۱﴾
کہا کہ اُن کا علم میرے پروردگار کو ہے (جو) کتاب میں
(لکھا ہوا ہے) میرا پروردگار نہ چوکتا ہے نہ بھولتا ہے ﴿۵۲﴾
وہ (وہی تو ہے) جس نے تم لوگوں کے لئے زمین کو فرش بنایا
اور اس میں تمہارے لئے رستے جاری کئے اور آسمان سے
پانی برسایا پھر اس سے انواع واقسام کی مختلف روئیدگیاں پیدا کیں ﴿۵۳﴾
(کہ خود بھی) کھاؤ اور اپنے چارپایوں کو بھی چراؤ۔ بیشک ان
(باتوں) میں عقل والوں کے لئے (بہت سی) نشانیاں ہیں ﴿۵۴﴾
اسی (زمین) سے ہم نے تم کو پیدا کیا اور اسی میں تمہیں لوٹائینگے
اور اسی سے دوسری دفعہ نکالیں گے ﴿۵۵﴾
اور ہم نے فرعون کو اپنی سب نشانیاں دکھائیں مگر وہ تکذیب اور انکار ہی کرتا رہا ﴿۵۶﴾
کہنے لگا کہ موسیٰ کیا تم ہمارے پاس اس لئے آئے ہو کہ اپنے
جادو (کے زور) سے ہمیں ہمارے ملک سے نکال دو ﴿۵۷﴾
تو ہم بھی تمہارے مقابل ایسا ہی جادو لائیں گے تو ہمارے
اور اپنے درمیان ایک وقت مقرر کرلو کہ نہ تو ہم اسکے خلاف
کریں اور نہ تم (اور یہ مقابلہ) ایک ہموار میدان میں (ہوگا) ﴿۵۸﴾
(موسیٰ نے) کہا کہ آپ کے لئے یوم زینت کا وعدہ ہے
اور یہ کہ لوگ اُس دن چاشت کے وقت اکٹھے ہو جائیں ﴿۵۹﴾
تو فرعون لوٹ گیا اور اپنے سامان جمع کر کے پھر آیا ﴿۶۰﴾
موسیٰ نے اُن (جادوگروں) سے کہا کہ ہائے تمہاری کمبختی

afflict them not: with a Sign, indeed, have we come from thy Lord! And Peace to all who follow guidance!

48. " 'Verily it has been revealed to us that the Chastisement (awaits) those who reject and turn away.' "

49. (When this message was delivered), (Pharaoh) said: "Who then, O Moses, is the Lord of you two?"
50. He said: "Our Lord He Who gave to each (created) thing its form then, gave (it) guidance."

51. (Pharaoh) said: "What then is the condition of previous generations?"
52. He replied: "The knowledge of that is with my Lord, duly recorded: my Lord never errs, nor forgets,—
53. "He Who has made for you the earth like a carpet spread out; has enabled you to go about therein by roads (and channels); and has sent down water from the sky." With it have We produced diverse pairs of plants each separate from the others.
54. Eat (for yourselves) and pasture your cattle: verily, in this are Signs for men endued with understanding.
55. From the (earth) did We create you, and into it shall We return you, and from it shall We bring you out once again.
56. And We showed Pharaoh all Our Signs, but he did reject and refuse.
57. He said: "Hast thou come to drive us out of our land with thy magic, O Moses?
58. "But we can surely produce magic to match thine! So make a tryst between us and thee, which we shall not fail to keep—neither we nor thou— in a place where both shall have even chances."
59. Moses said: "Your tryst is the Day of the Festival, and let the people be assembled when the sun is well up,"
60. So Pharaoh withdrew: He concerted his plan, and then came (back).
61. Moses said to them "Woe to you! Forge not ye a lie against

Allah, lest He destroy you (at once) utterly by chastisement: the forger must suffer failure."

62. So they disputed, one with another, over their affair, but they kept their talk secret.

63. They said: "These two are certainly (expert) magicians: their object is to drive you out from your land with their magic, and to do away with your most cherished way.

64. "Therefore concert your plan, and then assemble in (serried) ranks: he wins (all along) today who gains the upper hand."

65. They said: "O Moses! whether wilt thou that thou throw (first) or that we be the first to throw?"

66. He said, "Nay, throw ye first!" Then behold their ropes and their rods—so it seemed to him on account of their magic—began to be in lively motion!

67. So Moses conceived in his mind a (sort of) fear.

68. We said: "Fear not! for thou hast indeed the upper hand:

69. "Throw that which is in thy right hand: quickly will it swallow up that which they have faked: what they have faked is but a magician's trick: and the magician succeeds not.

70. So the magicians were thrown down to prostration: they said, "We believe in the Lord of Aaron and Moses".

71. (Pharaoh) said: "Believe ye in Him before I give you permission? Surely this must be your leader, who has taught you magic! Be sure I will cut off your hands and feet on opposite sides, and I will have you crucified on trunks of palm-trees: so shall ye know for certain, which of us can give the more severe and the more lasting Punishment!"

72. They said: "Never shall we prefer thee to what has come to us of the Clear Signs Him Who created

خدا پر جھوٹ افترا نہ کرو کہ وہ تمہیں عذاب سے فنا
کردے گا۔ اور جس نے افترا کیا وہ نامراد رہا ﴿٦١﴾
تو وہ باہم اپنے معاملے میں جھگڑنے اور چپکے چپکے سرگوشی کرنے لگے ﴿٦٢﴾
کہنے لگے یہ دونوں جادوگر ہیں چاہتے ہیں کہ اپنے جادو
(کے زور) سے تم کو تمہارے ملک سے نکال دیں۔ اور
تمہارے شائستہ مذہب کو نابود کردیں ﴿٦٣﴾
تو تم (جادو کا) سامان اکٹھا کرلو اور پھر قطار باندھ کر آؤ۔
آج جو غالب رہا وہی کامیاب ہوا ﴿٦٤﴾
بولے کہ موسیٰ یا تو تم (اپنی چیز) ڈالو یا ہم (اپنی چیزیں)
پہلے ڈالتے ہیں ﴿٦٥﴾
موسیٰ نے کہا نہیں تم ہی ڈالو (جب انہوں نے چیزیں ڈالیں)
تو ناگہاں اُن کی رسیاں اور لاٹھیاں موسیٰ کے خیال میں
ایسی آنے لگیں کہ وہ (میدان میں ادھر اُدھر) دوڑ رہی ہیں ﴿٦٦﴾
(اُس وقت) موسیٰ نے اپنے دل میں خوف معلوم کیا ﴿٦٧﴾
ہم نے کہا خوف نہ کرو بلاشبہ تم ہی غالب ہو ﴿٦٨﴾
اور جو چیز (یعنی لاٹھی) تمہارے داہنے ہاتھ میں ہے اسے ڈال دو کہ جو کچھ انہوں نے
بنایا ہے اُس کو نگل جائیگی جو کچھ انہوں نے بنایا ہے (یہ تو) جادوگروں کے ہتھکنڈے
ہیں اور جادوگر جہاں جائے فلاح نہیں پائے گا ﴿٦٩﴾
(القصہ یوں ہی ہوا) تو جادوگر سجدے میں گر پڑے (اور) کہنے
لگے کہ ہم موسیٰ اور ہارون کے پروردگار پر ایمان لائے ﴿٧٠﴾
(فرعون) بولا کہ پیشتر اسکے کہ میں تمہیں اجازت دوں تم اس
پر ایمان لے آئے۔ بیشک وہ تمہارا بڑا (یعنی اُستاد) ہے جس نے
تم کو جادو سکھایا ہے سو میں تمہارے ہاتھ اور پاؤں (جانب) خلاف
سے کٹوا دونگا اور کھجور کے تنوں پر سولی چڑھوا دونگا (اُس وقت) تم کو
معلوم ہوگا کہ ہم میں سے کس کا عذاب زیادہ سخت اور دیر تک رہنے والا ہے ﴿٧١﴾
اُنہوں نے کہا کہ جو دلائل ہمارے پاس آگئے ہیں اُن پر اور جس نے
ہم کو پیدا کیا ہے اُس پر ہم آپ کو ہرگز ترجیح نہیں دینگے۔ تو آپ

اللّٰهِ كَذِبًا فَيُسْحِتَكُمْ بِعَذَابٍ ۚ وَقَدْ
خَابَ مَنِ افْتَرٰى ﴿٦١﴾
فَتَنَازَعُوْٓا اَمْرَهُمْ بَيْنَهُمْ وَاَسَرُّوا النَّجْوٰى ﴿٦٢﴾
قَالُوْٓا اِنْ هٰذٰنِ لَسٰحِرٰنِ يُرِيْدٰنِ اَنْ
يُّخْرِجٰكُمْ مِّنْ اَرْضِكُمْ بِسِحْرِهِمَا وَ
يَذْهَبَا بِطَرِيْقَتِكُمُ الْمُثْلٰى ﴿٦٣﴾
فَاَجْمِعُوْا كَيْدَكُمْ ثُمَّ ائْتُوْا صَفًّا ۚ وَقَدْ
اَفْلَحَ الْيَوْمَ مَنِ اسْتَعْلٰى ﴿٦٤﴾
قَالُوْا يٰمُوْسٰٓى اِمَّآ اَنْ تُلْقِيَ وَاِمَّآ اَنْ
نَّكُوْنَ اَوَّلَ مَنْ اَلْقٰى ﴿٦٥﴾
قَالَ بَلْ اَلْقُوْا ۚ فَاِذَا حِبَالُهُمْ وَ
عِصِيُّهُمْ يُخَيَّلُ اِلَيْهِ مِنْ سِحْرِهِمْ
اَنَّهَا تَسْعٰى ﴿٦٦﴾
فَاَوْجَسَ فِيْ نَفْسِهٖ خِيْفَةً مُّوْسٰى ﴿٦٧﴾
قُلْنَا لَا تَخَفْ اِنَّكَ اَنْتَ الْاَعْلٰى ﴿٦٨﴾
وَاَلْقِ مَا فِيْ يَمِيْنِكَ تَلْقَفْ مَا صَنَعُوْا ۭ
اِنَّمَا صَنَعُوْا كَيْدُ سٰحِرٍ ۭ وَلَا يُفْلِحُ
السّٰحِرُ حَيْثُ اَتٰى ﴿٦٩﴾
فَاُلْقِيَ السَّحَرَةُ سُجَّدًا قَالُوْٓا اٰمَنَّا
بِرَبِّ هٰرُوْنَ وَمُوْسٰى ﴿٧٠﴾
قَالَ اٰمَنْتُمْ لَهٗ قَبْلَ اَنْ اٰذَنَ لَكُمْ ۭ
اِنَّهٗ لَكَبِيْرُكُمُ الَّذِيْ عَلَّمَكُمُ السِّحْرَ ۚ
فَلَاُقَطِّعَنَّ اَيْدِيَكُمْ وَاَرْجُلَكُمْ مِّنْ
خِلَافٍ وَّلَاُصَلِّبَنَّكُمْ فِيْ جُذُوْعِ
النَّخْلِ ۡ وَلَتَعْلَمُنَّ اَيُّنَآ اَشَدُّ عَذَابًا وَّاَبْقٰى ﴿٧١﴾
قَالُوْا لَنْ نُّؤْثِرَكَ عَلٰى مَا جَاۗءَنَا مِنَ
الْبَيِّنٰتِ وَالَّذِيْ فَطَرَنَا فَاقْضِ مَآ اَنْتَ

us! So decree whatever thou desirest to decree: for thou canst only decree (touching) the life of this world.

73. "For us, we have believed in our Lord: may He forgive us our faults, and the magic to which thou didst compel us: for Allah is Best and Most Abiding."

74. Verily he who comes to his Lord as a sinner (at Judgment),—for him is Hell: therein shall he neither die nor live.

75. But such as come to Him as Believers who have worked righteous deeds,—for them are ranks exalted,—

76. Gardens of Eternity, beneath which flow rivers: they will dwell therein for aye: such is the reward of those who purify themselves (from evil).

77. We sent an inspiration to Moses: "Travel by night with My servants, and strike a dry path for them through the sea, without fear of being overtaken (by Pharaoh) and without (any other) fear."

78. Then Pharaoh pursued them with his forces, but the waters completely overwhelmed them and covered them up.

79. Pharaoh led his people astray instead of leading them aright.

80. O ye Children of Israel! We delivered you from your enemy, and We made a Convenant with you on the right side of Mount (Sinai), and We sent down to you Manna and quails:

81. "Eat of the good things We have provided for your sustenance, but commit no excess therein, lest My Wrath should descend on you: and those on whom descends My Wrath do perish indeed!

82. "But, without doubt, I am (also) He that forgives again and again, to those who repent, believe, and do right,—who, in fine, are on true guidance."

83. (When Moses was up on the Mount, Allah said:) "What made thee hasten in advance of thy people, O Moses?"

84. He replied: "Behold, they are

کو جو حکم دینا ہو دے دیجئے اور آپ (جو حکم دے سکتے ہیں) وہ صرف
اسی دنیا کی زندگی میں (دے سکتے ہیں) ﴿۷۲﴾
ہم اپنے پروردگار پر ایمان لے آئے تاکہ وہ ہمارے گناہوں کو
معاف کرے اور (اسے بھی) جو آپ نے ہم سے زبردستی جادو کرایا
اور خدا بہتر اور باقی رہنے والا ہے ﴿۷۳﴾
جو شخص اپنے پروردگار کے پاس گنہگار ہو کر آئے گا تو اس کے
لئے جہنم ہے جس میں نہ مرے گا نہ جئے گا ﴿۷۴﴾
اور جو اس کے روبرو ایماندار ہو کر آئے گا اور عمل بھی نیک کئے
ہونگے تو ایسے لوگوں کے لئے اونچے اونچے درجے ہیں ﴿۷۵﴾
(یعنی) ہمیشہ رہنے کے باغ جن کے نیچے نہریں بہ رہی ہیں۔
ہمیشہ ان میں رہیں گے اور یہ اس شخص کا بدلہ ہے جو پاک ہوا ﴿۷۶﴾
اور ہم نے موسیٰ کی طرف وحی بھیجی کہ ہمارے بندوں کو راتوں رات نکال لیجاؤ
پھر اُن کیلئے دریا میں (لاٹھی مار کر) خشک رستہ بنا دو پھر تمکو نہ تو
(فرعون کے) آپکڑنے کا خوف ہو گا اور نہ (غرق ہونے کا) ڈر ﴿۷۷﴾
پھر فرعون نے اپنے لشکر کے ساتھ انکا تعاقب کیا۔ تو دریا (کی
موجوں) نے اُن پر چڑھ کر اُنہیں ڈھانک لیا (یعنی ڈبو دیا) ﴿۷۸﴾
اور فرعون نے اپنی قوم کو گمراہ کر دیا اور سیدھے رستے پر نہ ڈالا ﴿۷۹﴾
اے آل یعقوب ہم نے تم کو تمہارے دشمن سے نجات دی اور
تورات دینے کے لئے تم سے کوہ طور کی داہنی طرف مقرر کی اور
تم پر من اور سلویٰ نازل کیا ﴿۸۰﴾
اور حکم دیا کہ جو پاکیزہ چیزیں ہم نے تم کو دی ہیں اُنکو کھاؤ اور
اس میں حد سے نہ نکلنا۔ ورنہ تم پر میرا غضب نازل ہو گا۔
اور جس پر میرا عذاب نازل ہوا وہ ہلاک ہو گیا ﴿۸۱﴾
اور جو توبہ کرے اور ایمان لائے اور عمل نیک کرے پھر سیدھے
رستے چلے اس کو میں بخش دینے والا ہوں ﴿۸۲﴾
اور اے موسیٰ تم نے اپنی قوم سے آگے چلے آنے میں کیوں جلدی کی؟ ﴿۸۳﴾
کہا وہ میرے پیچھے (آ رہے) ہیں اور اے میرے پروردگار میں نے

قَاضٍ ۖ إِنَّمَا تَقْضِي هٰذِهِ الْحَيٰوةَ
الدُّنْيَا ﴿۷۲﴾
إِنَّا آمَنَّا بِرَبِّنَا لِيَغْفِرَ لَنَا خَطٰيٰنَا وَمَا
أَكْرَهْتَنَا عَلَيْهِ مِنَ السِّحْرِ ۗ وَاللّٰهُ
خَيْرٌ وَّأَبْقٰى ﴿۷۳﴾
إِنَّهُ مَنْ يَّأْتِ رَبَّهُ مُجْرِمًا فَإِنَّ لَهُ
جَهَنَّمَ ۖ لَا يَمُوتُ فِيهَا وَلَا يَحْيٰى ﴿۷۴﴾
وَمَنْ يَّأْتِهِ مُؤْمِنًا قَدْ عَمِلَ الصّٰلِحٰتِ
فَأُولٰٓئِكَ لَهُمُ الدَّرَجٰتُ الْعُلٰى ﴿۷۵﴾
جَنّٰتُ عَدْنٍ تَجْرِي مِنْ تَحْتِهَا الْأَنْهٰرُ
خٰلِدِينَ فِيهَا ۚ وَذٰلِكَ جَزٰٓؤُا مَنْ تَزَكّٰى ﴿۷۶﴾
وَلَقَدْ أَوْحَيْنَآ إِلٰى مُوسٰىٓ أَنْ أَسْرِ
بِعِبَادِي فَاضْرِبْ لَهُمْ طَرِيقًا فِي الْبَحْرِ
يَبَسًا ۙ لَّا تَخٰفُ دَرَكًا وَّلَا تَخْشٰى ﴿۷۷﴾
فَأَتْبَعَهُمْ فِرْعَوْنُ بِجُنُودِهِ فَغَشِيَهُمْ
مِّنَ الْيَمِّ مَا غَشِيَهُمْ ﴿۷۸﴾
وَأَضَلَّ فِرْعَوْنُ قَوْمَهُ وَمَا هَدٰى ﴿۷۹﴾
يٰبَنِيٓ إِسْرَآءِيلَ قَدْ أَنْجَيْنٰكُمْ مِّنْ
عَدُوِّكُمْ وَوٰعَدْنٰكُمْ جَانِبَ الطُّورِ
الْأَيْمَنَ وَنَزَّلْنَا عَلَيْكُمُ الْمَنَّ وَالسَّلْوٰى ﴿۸۰﴾
كُلُوا مِنْ طَيِّبٰتِ مَا رَزَقْنٰكُمْ وَلَا
تَطْغَوْا فِيهِ فَيَحِلَّ عَلَيْكُمْ غَضَبِي ۚ
وَمَنْ يَّحْلِلْ عَلَيْهِ غَضَبِي فَقَدْ هَوٰى ﴿۸۱﴾
وَإِنِّي لَغَفَّارٌ لِّمَنْ تَابَ وَآمَنَ وَعَمِلَ
صَالِحًا ثُمَّ اهْتَدٰى ﴿۸۲﴾
وَمَآ أَعْجَلَكَ عَنْ قَوْمِكَ يٰمُوسٰى ﴿۸۳﴾
قَالَ هُمْ أُولَآءِ عَلٰىٓ أَثَرِي وَعَجِلْتُ

close on my footsteps: I hastened to Thee, O my Lord, to please Thee."

85. (Allah) said: "We have tested thy people in thy absence: the Sãmiri has led them Astray."

86. So Moses returned to his people in a state of anger and sorrow. He said: "O my people! did not your Lord make a handsome promise to you? Did then the promise seem to you long (in coming)? Or did ye desire that Wrath should descend from your Lord on you, and so ye broke your promise to me?"

87. They said: "We broke not the promise to thee, as far as lay in our power: but we were made to carry the weight of the ornaments of the (whole) people, and we threw them (into the fire), and that was what the Sãmiri suggested.

88. "Then he brought out (of the fire) before the (people) the image of a calf: it seemed to low: so they said: 'This is your god, and the god of Moses, but (Moses) has forgotten!"

89. Could they not see that itcould not return them a word (for answer), and that it had no power either to harm them or to do them good?

90. Aaron had already, before this said to them: "O my people! ye are being tested in this: for verily your Lord is (Allah) Most Gracious: so follow me and obey my command."

91. They had said: "We will not cease to worship it, will devote ourselves to it until Moses returns to us."

92. (Moses) said: "O Aaron! what kept thee back, when thou sawest them going wrong.

93. "From following me? Didst thou then disobey my order?"

94. (Aaron) replied: "O son of my mother! Seize (me) not by my beard nor by (the hair of) my head! Truly I feared lest thou shouldst say, 'Thou hast caused a division among the Children of Israel, and thou didst

تیری طرف (آنے کی) جلدی اس لئے کی کہ تو خوش ہو ۸۴
فرمایا کہ ہم نے تمہاری قوم کو تمہارے بعد آزمائش میں ڈال دیا ہے
اور سامری نے اُن کو بہکا دیا ہے ۸۵
اور موسیٰ غصے اور غم کی حالت میں اپنی قوم کے پاس واپس آئے
(اور) کہنے لگے کہ اے قوم کیا تمہارے پروردگار نے تم سے اچھا وعدہ
نہیں کیا تھا؟ کیا (میری جدائی کی) مدت تمہیں دراز (معلوم) ہوئی
یا تم نے چاہا کہ تم پر تمہارے پروردگار کی طرف سے غضب نازل ہو۔ اور (اس لئے)
تم نے مجھ سے جو وعدہ کیا تھا (اس کے) خلاف کیا ۸۶
وہ کہنے لگے کہ ہم نے اپنے اختیار سے تم سے وعدہ خلاف نہیں کیا۔ بلکہ ہم
لوگوں کے زیوروں کا بوجھ اٹھائے ہوئے تھے پھر ہم نے اُس کو (آگ
میں) ڈال دیا اور اسی طرح سامری نے ڈال دیا ۸۷
تو اس نے اُن کیلئے ایک بچھڑا بنا دیا (یعنی اس کا) قالب جس
کی آواز گائے کی سی تھی۔ تو لوگ کہنے لگے کہ یہی تمہارا معبود ہے اور
یہی موسیٰ کا معبود ہے مگر وہ بھول گئے ہیں ۸۸
کیا یہ لوگ نہیں دیکھتے کہ وہ اُن کی کسی بات کا جواب نہیں دیتا۔
اور نہ اُن کے نقصان اور نفع کا کچھ اختیار رکھتا ہے ۸۹
اور ہارون نے ان سے پہلے ہی کہہ دیا تھا کہ لوگو اس سے
صرف تمہاری آزمائش کی گئی ہے۔ اور تمہارا پروردگار تو
خدا ہے تو میری پیروی کرو اور میرا کہا مانو ۹۰
وہ کہنے لگے کہ جب تک موسیٰ ہمارے پاس واپس نہ آئیں
ہم تو اس (کی پوجا) پر قائم رہیں گے ۹۱
(پھر موسیٰ نے ہارون سے) کہا کہ ہارون جب تم نے ان کو
دیکھا تھا کہ گمراہ ہو گئے ہیں تو تم کو کس چیز نے روکا ۹۲
(یعنی) اس بات سے کہ تم میرے پیچھے چلے آؤ۔ بھلا تم نے میرے حکم کے خلاف کیوں کیا؟ ۹۳
کہنے لگے کہ بھائی میری ڈاڑھی اور سر (کے بالوں)
کو نہ پکڑیئے میں تو اس سے ڈرا کہ آپ یہ نہ کہیں کہ تم
نے بنی اسرائیل میں تفرقہ ڈال دیا اور میری بات کو

إِلَيْكَ رَبِّ لِتَرْضَىٰ ٨٤
قَالَ فَإِنَّا قَدْ فَتَنَّا قَوْمَكَ مِنْ بَعْدِكَ
وَأَضَلَّهُمُ السَّامِرِيُّ ٨٥
فَرَجَعَ مُوسَىٰ إِلَىٰ قَوْمِهِ غَضْبَانَ أَسِفًا
قَالَ يَٰقَوْمِ أَلَمْ يَعِدْكُمْ رَبُّكُمْ وَعْدًا
حَسَنًا أَفَطَالَ عَلَيْكُمُ الْعَهْدُ أَمْ
أَرَدْتُمْ أَنْ يَحِلَّ عَلَيْكُمْ غَضَبٌ مِنْ
رَبِّكُمْ فَأَخْلَفْتُمْ مَوْعِدِي ٨٦
قَالُوا مَا أَخْلَفْنَا مَوْعِدَكَ بِمَلْكِنَا
وَلَٰكِنَّا حُمِّلْنَا أَوْزَارًا مِنْ زِينَةِ الْقَوْمِ
فَقَذَفْنَاهَا فَكَذَٰلِكَ أَلْقَى السَّامِرِيُّ ٨٧
فَأَخْرَجَ لَهُمْ عِجْلًا جَسَدًا لَهُ خُوَارٌ
فَقَالُوا هَٰذَا إِلَٰهُكُمْ وَإِلَٰهُ مُوسَىٰ
فَنَسِيَ ٨٨
أَفَلَا يَرَوْنَ أَلَّا يَرْجِعُ إِلَيْهِمْ قَوْلًا وَلَا
يَمْلِكُ لَهُمْ ضَرًّا وَلَا نَفْعًا ٨٩
وَلَقَدْ قَالَ لَهُمْ هَٰرُونُ مِنْ قَبْلُ
يَٰقَوْمِ إِنَّمَا فُتِنْتُمْ بِهِ وَإِنَّ رَبَّكُمُ
الرَّحْمَٰنُ فَاتَّبِعُونِي وَأَطِيعُوا أَمْرِي ٩٠
قَالُوا لَنْ نَبْرَحَ عَلَيْهِ عَٰكِفِينَ حَتَّىٰ
يَرْجِعَ إِلَيْنَا مُوسَىٰ ٩١
قَالَ يَٰهَٰرُونُ مَا مَنَعَكَ إِذْ رَأَيْتَهُمْ
ضَلُّوا ٩٢
أَلَّا تَتَّبِعَنِ أَفَعَصَيْتَ أَمْرِي ٩٣
قَالَ يَبْنَؤُمَّ لَا تَأْخُذْ بِلِحْيَتِي
وَلَا بِرَأْسِي إِنِّي خَشِيتُ أَنْ تَقُولَ
فَرَّقْتَ بَيْنَ بَنِي إِسْرَٰءِيلَ وَلَمْ

not observe my word!' "

95. (Moses) said: "What then is thy case, O Sãmĩri?"

96. He replied: "I saw what they saw not: so I took a handful (of dust) from the footprint of the Messenger, and threw it (into the calf): thus did my soul suggest to me."

97. (Moses) said: "Get thee gone! But thy (punishment) in this life will be that thou wilt say, 'Touch me not'; and moreover (for a future penalty) thou hast a promise that will not fail: now look at thy god, of whom thou hast become a devoted worshipper: we will certainly burn it in a blazing fire and scatter it broadcast in the sea!"

98. But the God of you all is Allah: there is no god but He: all things He comprehends in His knowledge.

99. Thus do We relate to thee some stories of what happened before: for We have sent thee a reminder from Us.

100. If any do turn away therefrom, verily they will bear a burden on the Day of Judgment;

101. They will abide in this (state): and grievous will the burden be to them on that Day,—

102. The Day when the Trumpet will be sounded: that Day, We shall gather the sinful, blear-eyed (with terror).

103. In whispers will they consult each other: "Ye tarried not longer than ten (Days)";

104. We know best what they will say, when the best of them in judgment will say: "Ye tarried not longer than a day!"

105. They ask thee concerning the Mountains: say, "My Lord will uproot them and scatter them as dust;

106. "He will leave them as plains smooth and level;

107. "Nothing crooked or curved wilt thou see in their place."

ملحوظ نہ رکھا ﴿۹۴﴾
(پھر سامری سے) کہنے لگے کہ سامری تیرا کیا حال ہے؟ ﴿۹۵﴾
اُس نے کہا کہ میں نے ایسی چیز دیکھی جو اَوروں نے نہیں دیکھی تو میں نے
فرشتے کے نقش پا سے مٹی کی ایک مٹھی بھر لی پھر اسکو (بچھڑے کے
قالب میں) ڈال دیا اور مجھے میرے جی نے (اس کام کو) اچھا بتایا ﴿۹۶﴾
(موسیٰ نے) کہا جا تجھ کو (دنیا کی) زندگی میں یہ (سزا) ہے کہ
کہتا رہے کہ مجھ کو ہاتھ نہ لگانا[۱۸۴] اور تیرے لئے ایک اور وعدہ ہے
(یعنی عذاب کا) جو تجھ سے ٹل نہ سکے گا اور جس معبود کی پوجا (پر تو
قائم و) معتکف تھا اسکو دیکھ ہم اسے جلا دینگے پھر اس (کی
راکھ) کو اڑا کر دریا میں بکھیر دیں گے ﴿۹۷﴾
تمہارا معبود خدا ہی ہے جس کے سوا کوئی معبود نہیں اس کا
علم ہر چیز پر محیط ہے ﴿۹۸﴾
اس طرح پر ہم تم سے وہ حالات بیان کرتے ہیں جو گزر چکے
ہیں اور ہم نے تمہیں اپنے پاس سے نصیحت (کی کتاب) عطا فرمائی ہے ﴿۹۹﴾
جو شخص اس سے منہ پھیرے گا وہ قیامت کے دن (گناہ کا)
بوجھ اٹھائے گا ﴿۱۰۰﴾
(ایسے لوگ) ہمیشہ اس (عذاب) میں (مبتلا) رہیں گے اور یہ بوجھ
قیامت کے روز ان کے لئے بُرا ہوگا ﴿۱۰۱﴾
جس روز صور پھونکا جائے گا اور ہم گنہگاروں کو اکٹھا
کرینگے اور اُن کی آنکھیں نیلی نیلی ہوں گی ﴿۱۰۲﴾
(تو) وہ آپس میں آہستہ آہستہ کہیں گے کہ تم (دنیا میں) صرف دس ہی دن رہے ہو ﴿۱۰۳﴾
جو باتیں یہ کرینگے ہم خوب جانتے ہیں اسوقت انمیں سب سے اچھی راہ والا
(یعنی عاقل و ہوشمند) کہے گا کہ (نہیں بلکہ) صرف ایک ہی روز ٹھیرے ہو ﴿۱۰۴﴾
اور تم سے پہاڑوں کے بارے میں دریافت کرتے ہیں کہہ دو کہ
خدا ان کو اڑا کر بکھیر دے گا ﴿۱۰۵﴾
اور زمین کو ہموار میدان کر چھوڑے گا ﴿۱۰۶﴾
جس میں نہ تم کجی (اور پستی) دیکھو گے نہ ٹیلا (اور بلندی) ﴿۱۰۷﴾

تَرْقُبْ قَوْلِي ﴿٩٤﴾
قَالَ فَمَا خَطْبُكَ يَٰسَٰمِرِيُّ ﴿٩٥﴾
قَالَ بَصُرْتُ بِمَا لَمْ يَبْصُرُوا بِهِ فَقَبَضْتُ
قَبْضَةً مِّنْ أَثَرِ الرَّسُولِ فَنَبَذْتُهَا وَ
كَذَٰلِكَ سَوَّلَتْ لِي نَفْسِي ﴿٩٦﴾
قَالَ فَاذْهَبْ فَإِنَّ لَكَ فِي الْحَيَوٰةِ أَن
تَقُولَ لَا مِسَاسَ وَإِنَّ لَكَ مَوْعِدًا
لَّن تُخْلَفَهُ وَانظُرْ إِلَىٰ إِلَٰهِكَ الَّذِي
ظَلْتَ عَلَيْهِ عَاكِفًا لَّنُحَرِّقَنَّهُ ثُمَّ
لَنَنسِفَنَّهُ فِي الْيَمِّ نَسْفًا ﴿٩٧﴾
إِنَّمَا إِلَٰهُكُمُ اللَّهُ الَّذِي لَا إِلَٰهَ إِلَّا هُوَ
وَسِعَ كُلَّ شَيْءٍ عِلْمًا ﴿٩٨﴾
كَذَٰلِكَ نَقُصُّ عَلَيْكَ مِنْ أَنبَاءِ مَا
قَدْ سَبَقَ وَقَدْ آتَيْنَاكَ مِن لَّدُنَّا ذِكْرًا ﴿٩٩﴾
مَّنْ أَعْرَضَ عَنْهُ فَإِنَّهُ يَحْمِلُ يَوْمَ
الْقِيَامَةِ وِزْرًا ﴿١٠٠﴾
خَالِدِينَ فِيهِ وَسَاءَ لَهُمْ يَوْمَ الْقِيَامَةِ
حِمْلًا ﴿١٠١﴾
يَوْمَ يُنفَخُ فِي الصُّورِ وَنَحْشُرُ الْمُجْرِمِينَ
يَوْمَئِذٍ زُرْقًا ﴿١٠٢﴾
يَتَخَافَتُونَ بَيْنَهُمْ إِن لَّبِثْتُمْ إِلَّا عَشْرًا ﴿١٠٣﴾
نَّحْنُ أَعْلَمُ بِمَا يَقُولُونَ إِذْ يَقُولُ
أَمْثَلُهُمْ طَرِيقَةً إِن لَّبِثْتُمْ إِلَّا يَوْمًا ﴿١٠٤﴾
وَيَسْأَلُونَكَ عَنِ الْجِبَالِ فَقُلْ يَنسِفُهَا
رَبِّي نَسْفًا ﴿١٠٥﴾
فَيَذَرُهَا قَاعًا صَفْصَفًا ﴿١٠٦﴾
لَّا تَرَىٰ فِيهَا عِوَجًا وَلَا أَمْتًا ﴿١٠٧﴾

108. On that Day will they follow the caller (straight): no crookedness in him: and the voices will be hushed to The Most Gracious: so that thou hearest not but murmuring.

109. On that Day shall no intercession avail except for those for whom permission has been granted by The Most Gracious and whose word is acceptable to Him.

110. He knows what is before or after or behind them: but they shall comprehend Him not.

111. (All) faces shall be humbled before—the Living, the Self-Subsisting, The Sustainer: hopeless indeed will be the man that carries iniquity (on his back).

112. But he who works deeds of righteousness, and has faith, will have no fear of harm nor of any curtailment (of what is his due).

113. Thus have We sent this down—an Arabic Qur'an—and explained therein in detail some of the warnings, in order that they may fear Allah, or that it may cause their remembrance (of Him).

114. High above all is Allah, the King, the Truth! Be not in haste with the Qur'an before its revelation to thee is completed, but say, "O my Lord! increase me in knowledge."

115. We had already, beforehand, taken the covenant of Adam, but he forgot: and We found on his part no firm resolve.

116. When We said to the angels, "Prostrate yourselves to Adam", they prostrated themselves, but not Iblīs: he refused.

117. Then We said: "O Adam! verily, this is an enemy to thee and thy wife: so let him not get you both out of the Garden, so that thou art landed in misery.

118. "There is therein (enough provision) for thee not to go hungry nor to go naked,

119. "Nor to suffer from thirst, nor from the sun's heat."

120. But Satan whispered evil to him: he said, "O Adam! shall I lead

اس روز لوگ ایک پکارنے والے کے پیچھے چلیں گے اور اسکی پیروی سے
انحراف نہ کر سکیں گے۔ اور خدا کے سامنے آوازیں پست ہو جائینگی
تو تم آواز خفی کے سوا کوئی آواز نہ سنو گے ﴿۱۰۸﴾
اس روز کسی کی سفارش کچھ فائدہ نہ دے گی مگر اس شخص
کی جسے خدا اجازت دے اور اسکی بات کو پسند فرمائے ﴿۱۰۹﴾
جو کچھ ان کے آگے ہے اور جو کچھ ان کے پیچھے ہے وہ اس کو
جانتا ہے اور وہ (اپنے) علم سے خدا کے (علم) پر احاطہ نہیں کر سکتے ﴿۱۱۰﴾
اور اس زندہ و قائم کے روبرو منہ نیچے ہو جائیں گے۔ اور
جس نے ظلم کا بوجھ اٹھایا وہ نامراد رہا ﴿۱۱۱﴾
اور جو نیک کام کرے گا اور مومن بھی ہوگا تو اس کو نہ ظلم کا
خوف ہوگا اور نہ نقصان کا ﴿۱۱۲﴾
اور ہم نے اس کو اسی طرح کا قرآن عربی نازل کیا ہے اور اس
میں طرح طرح کے ڈراوے بیان کر دیئے ہیں تاکہ لوگ پرہیزگار
بنیں۔ یا خدا ان کے لئے نصیحت پیدا کر دے ﴿۱۱۳﴾
تو خدا جو سچا بادشاہ ہے عالی قدر ہے۔ اور قرآن کی وحی جو تمہاری
طرف بھیجی جاتی ہے اسکے پورا ہونے سے پہلے قرآن کے (پڑھنے کے)
لئے جلدی نہ کیا کرو اور دعا کرو کہ میرے پروردگار مجھے اور زیادہ علم دے ﴿۱۱۴﴾
اور ہم نے پہلے آدم سے عہد لیا تھا مگر وہ (اسے) بھول گئے اور
ہم نے ان میں صبر و ثبات نہ دیکھا ﴿۱۱۵﴾
اور جب ہم نے فرشتوں سے کہا کہ آدم کے آگے سجدہ کرو تو
سب سجدے میں گر پڑے مگر ابلیس نے انکار کیا ﴿۱۱۶﴾
ہم نے فرمایا کہ آدم یہ تمہارا اور تمہاری بیوی کا دشمن ہے
تو یہ کہیں تم دونوں کو بہشت سے نکلوا نہ دے پھر تم
تکلیف میں پڑ جاؤ ﴿۱۱۷﴾
یہاں تم کو یہ (آسائش) ہے کہ نہ بھوکے رہو نہ ننگے ﴿۱۱۸﴾
اور یہ کہ نہ پیاسے رہو اور نہ دھوپ کھاؤ ﴿۱۱۹﴾
تو شیطان نے ان کے دل میں وسوسہ ڈالا۔ اور کہا کہ

يَوْمَئِذٍ يَّتَّبِعُوْنَ الدَّاعِيَ لَا عِوَجَ
لَهٗ ۚ وَخَشَعَتِ الْاَصْوَاتُ لِلرَّحْمٰنِ
فَلَا تَسْمَعُ اِلَّا هَمْسًا ﴿۱۰۸﴾
يَوْمَئِذٍ لَّا تَنْفَعُ الشَّفَاعَةُ اِلَّا مَنْ
اَذِنَ لَهُ الرَّحْمٰنُ وَرَضِيَ لَهٗ قَوْلًا ﴿۱۰۹﴾
يَعْلَمُ مَا بَيْنَ اَيْدِيْهِمْ وَمَا خَلْفَهُمْ
وَلَا يُحِيْطُوْنَ بِهٖ عِلْمًا ﴿۱۱۰﴾
وَعَنَتِ الْوُجُوْهُ لِلْحَيِّ الْقَيُّوْمِ ۭ وَقَدْ
خَابَ مَنْ حَمَلَ ظُلْمًا ﴿۱۱۱﴾
وَمَنْ يَّعْمَلْ مِنَ الصّٰلِحٰتِ وَهُوَ
مُؤْمِنٌ فَلَا يَخٰفُ ظُلْمًا وَّلَا هَضْمًا ﴿۱۱۲﴾
وَكَذٰلِكَ اَنْزَلْنٰهُ قُرْاٰنًا عَرَبِيًّا وَّصَرَّفْنَا
فِيْهِ مِنَ الْوَعِيْدِ لَعَلَّهُمْ يَتَّقُوْنَ اَوْ
يُحْدِثُ لَهُمْ ذِكْرًا ﴿۱۱۳﴾
فَتَعٰلَى اللّٰهُ الْمَلِكُ الْحَقُّ ۚ وَلَا تَعْجَلْ
بِالْقُرْاٰنِ مِنْ قَبْلِ اَنْ يُّقْضٰٓى اِلَيْكَ
وَحْيُهٗ ۡ وَقُلْ رَّبِّ زِدْنِيْ عِلْمًا ﴿۱۱۴﴾
وَلَقَدْ عَهِدْنَآ اِلٰٓى اٰدَمَ مِنْ قَبْلُ
فَنَسِيَ وَلَمْ نَجِدْ لَهٗ عَزْمًا ﴿۱۱۵﴾ ع
وَاِذْ قُلْنَا لِلْمَلٰٓئِكَةِ اسْجُدُوْا لِاٰدَمَ
فَسَجَدُوْٓا اِلَّآ اِبْلِيْسَ ۭ اَبٰى ﴿۱۱۶﴾
فَقُلْنَا يٰٓاٰدَمُ اِنَّ هٰذَا عَدُوٌّ لَّكَ
وَلِزَوْجِكَ فَلَا يُخْرِجَنَّكُمَا مِنَ الْجَنَّةِ
فَتَشْقٰى ﴿۱۱۷﴾
اِنَّ لَكَ اَلَّا تَجُوْعَ فِيْهَا وَلَا تَعْرٰى ﴿۱۱۸﴾
وَاَنَّكَ لَا تَظْمَؤُا فِيْهَا وَلَا تَضْحٰى ﴿۱۱۹﴾
فَوَسْوَسَ اِلَيْهِ الشَّيْطٰنُ قَالَ يٰٓاٰدَمُ

هَلْ اَدُلُّكَ عَلٰى شَجَرَةِ الْخُلْدِ وَمُلْكٍ
لَّا يَبْلٰى ﴿١٢٠﴾

آدم بھلا میں تم کو (ایسا) درخت بتاؤں (جو) ہمیشہ کی
زندگی کا (ثمرہ دے) اور (ایسی) بادشاہت کہ کبھی زائل نہ ہو ﴿١٢٠﴾

thee to the Tree of Eternity and to a kingdom that never decays?"

فَاَكَلَا مِنْهَا فَبَدَتْ لَهُمَا سَوْاٰتُهُمَا
وَطَفِقَا يَخْصِفٰنِ عَلَيْهِمَا مِنْ وَّرَقِ
الْجَنَّةِ ۫ وَعَصٰٓى اٰدَمُ رَبَّهٗ
فَغَوٰى ﴿١٢١﴾

تو دونوں نے اس درخت کا پھل کھا لیا تو ان پر ان کی شرمگاہیں
ظاہر ہو گئیں اور وہ اپنے (بدنوں) پر بہشت کے پتے چپکانے لگے اور
آدم نے اپنے پروردگار کے (حکم کے) خلاف کیا تو (وہ
اپنے مطلوب سے) بے راہ ہو گئے ﴿١٢١﴾

121. In the result, they both ate of the tree, and so their nakedness appeared to them: they began to sew together, for their covering, leaves from the Garden: thus did Adam disobey his Lord, and fell into error.

ثُمَّ اجْتَبٰهُ رَبُّهٗ فَتَابَ عَلَيْهِ
وَهَدٰى ﴿١٢٢﴾

پھر ان کے پروردگار نے ان کو نوازا تو ان پر مہربانی سے
توجہ فرمائی اور سیدھی راہ بتائی ﴿١٢٢﴾

122. But his Lord chose him (for His Grace): He turned to him, and gave him guidance.

قَالَ اهْبِطَا مِنْهَا جَمِيْعًا ۢ بَعْضُكُمْ لِبَعْضٍ
عَدُوٌّ ۚ فَاِمَّا يَاْتِيَنَّكُمْ مِّنِّىْ هُدًى ۙ فَمَنِ
اتَّبَعَ هُدَاىَ فَلَا يَضِلُّ وَلَا يَشْقٰى ﴿١٢٣﴾

فرمایا کہ تم دونوں یہاں سے نیچے اتر جاؤ تم میں بعض بعض کے دشمن (ہونگے)
پھر اگر میری طرف سے تمہارے پاس ہدایت آئے تو جو شخص میری
ہدایت کی پیروی کریگا وہ نہ گمراہ ہوگا اور نہ تکلیف میں پڑیگا ﴿١٢٣﴾

123. He said: "Get ye down, both of you,—all together, from the Garden, with enmity one to another: but if, as is sure, there comes to you guidance from Me, whosoever follows My guidance, will not Lose his way, nor fall into misery.

وَمَنْ اَعْرَضَ عَنْ ذِكْرِىْ فَاِنَّ لَهٗ مَعِيْشَةً
ضَنْكًا وَّنَحْشُرُهٗ يَوْمَ الْقِيٰمَةِ اَعْمٰى ﴿١٢٤﴾

اور جو میری نصیحت سے منہ پھیریگا اس کی زندگی تنگ
ہو جائیگی اور قیامت کو ہم اسے اندھا کر کے اٹھائینگے ﴿١٢٤﴾

124. "But whosoever turns away from My Message, verily for him is a life narrowed down, and We shall raise him up blind on the Day of Judgment."

قَالَ رَبِّ لِمَ حَشَرْتَنِىْٓ اَعْمٰى وَقَدْ
كُنْتُ بَصِيْرًا ﴿١٢٥﴾

وہ کہے گا کہ میرے پروردگار تو نے مجھے اندھا کر کے کیوں
اٹھایا میں تو دیکھتا بھالتا تھا ﴿١٢٥﴾

125. He will say: "O my Lord! why hast thou raised me up blind, while I had sight (before)?"

قَالَ كَذٰلِكَ اَتَتْكَ اٰيٰتُنَا فَنَسِيْتَهَا ۚ وَ
كَذٰلِكَ الْيَوْمَ تُنْسٰى ﴿١٢٦﴾

خدا فرمائے گا کہ ایسا ہی (چاہئے تھا) تیرے پاس ہماری آیتیں
آئیں تو تو نے انکو بھلا دیا۔ اسی طرح آج ہم تجھ کو بھلا دینگے ﴿١٢٦﴾

126. (Allah) will say: "Thus didst thou, when Our Signs came unto thee, forgot them: so wilt thou, this day, be forgotten."

وَكَذٰلِكَ نَجْزِىْ مَنْ اَسْرَفَ وَلَمْ يُؤْمِنْۢ
بِاٰيٰتِ رَبِّهٖ ۭ وَلَعَذَابُ الْاٰخِرَةِ اَشَدُّ
وَاَبْقٰى ﴿١٢٧﴾

اور جو شخص حد سے نکل جائے اور اپنے پروردگار کی آیتوں پر ایمان
نہ لائے ہم اس کو ایسا ہی بدلہ دیتے ہیں۔ اور آخرت کا عذاب
بہت سخت اور بہت دیر رہنے والا ہے ﴿١٢٧﴾

127. And thus do We recompense him who transgresses beyond bounds and believes not in the Signs of his Lord: and the Chastisement of the Hereafter is far more grievous and more enduring.

اَفَلَمْ يَهْدِ لَهُمْ كَمْ اَهْلَكْنَا قَبْلَهُمْ
مِّنَ الْقُرُوْنِ يَمْشُوْنَ فِىْ مَسٰكِنِهِمْ ۭ
اِنَّ فِىْ ذٰلِكَ لَاٰيٰتٍ لِّاُولِى النُّهٰى ﴿١٢٨﴾

کیا یہ بات ان لوگوں کیلئے موجب ہدایت نہ ہوئی کہ ہم ان
سے پہلے بہت سے قرنوں کو ہلاک کر چکے ہیں جنکے رہنے کے مقامات
میں یہ چلتے پھرتے ہیں عقل والوں کیلئے اسمیں (بہت سی) نشانیاں ہیں ﴿١٢٨﴾

128. Is it not a guidance to such men (to call to mind) how many generations before them We destroyed, in whose haunts they (now) move? Verily, in this are Signs for men endued with understanding.

وَلَوْلَا كَلِمَةٌ سَبَقَتْ مِنْ رَّبِّكَ لَكَانَ
لِزَامًا وَّاَجَلٌ مُّسَمًّى ﴿١٢٩﴾

اور اگر ایک بات تمہارے پروردگار کی طرف سے پہلے صادر اور (جزائے اعمال کیلئے)
ایک میعاد مقرر نہ ہو چکی ہوتی تو (نزول) عذاب لازم ہو جاتا ﴿١٢٩﴾

129. Had it not been for a Word that went forth before from thy Lord, (their punishment) must necessarily have come; but there is a term appointed (for respite).

فَاصْبِرْ عَلٰى مَا يَقُوْلُوْنَ وَسَبِّحْ بِحَمْدِ
رَبِّكَ قَبْلَ طُلُوْعِ الشَّمْسِ وَقَبْلَ

پس جو کچھ یہ بکواس کرتے ہیں اس پر صبر کرو۔ اور سورج کے نکلنے سے پہلے اور
اسکے غروب ہونے سے پہلے اپنے پروردگار کی تسبیح و تحمید کیا کرو اور رات کی

130. Therefore be patient with what they say, and celebrate (constantly) the praises of thy Lord, before the

SÛRA–21
AL-ANBIYÃA
(INTRODUCTION)

The last Sûra dealt with the individual story (spiritual) of Moses and Aaron, and contrasted it with the growth of evil in individuals like Pharaoh and the Samirî, and ended with a warning against Evil, and an exhortation to the purification of the soul with prayer and praise. This Sûra begins with the external obstacles placed by Evil against such purification, and gives the assurance of Allah's power to defend men, illustrating this with reference to Abraham's fight against idolatry, Lot's fight against unnatural wickedness, Noah's against unbelief, that of David and Solomon against injustice and failure to proclaim Allah's glory by making full use of man's Allah-given faculties and powers, that of Job against impatience and want of self-confidence, that of Isma'îl Idrîs and Ẓul-kifl against want of steady perseverance, that of Ẓun-nun against hasty anger, that of Zakariyã against spiritual isolation, and that of Mary against the lusts of this world. In each illusion there is a special point about the soul's purification. The common point is that the Prophets were not, as the vulgar suppose, just irresistible men. They had to win their ground inch by inch against all kinds of resistance from evil.

The chronology of this Sûra has no significance. It probably dates from the middle of the Makkan period of inspiration.

rising of the sun, and before its setting; yea, celebrate them for part of the hours of the night, and at the sides of the day: that thou may be pleased.

131. Nor strain thine eyes in longing for the things We have given for enjoyment to parties of them, the splendour of the life of this world, through which We test them: but the provision of thy Lord is better and more enduring.

132. Enjoin prayer on thy people, And be constant therein. We ask thee not to provide sustenance: We provide it for thee. But the (fruit of) the Hereafter is for Righteousness.

133. They say: "Why does he not bring us a Sign from his Lord?" Has not a Clear Sign come to them of all that was in the former Books of revelation?

134. Had We destroyed them with a punishment before this. They would have said: "Our Lord! If only thou Hadst sent us a messenger, we should certainly have followed Thy Signs before we were humbled and put to shame."

135. Say: "Each one (of us) is waiting: wait ye, therefore, and soon shall ye know who it is that is on the straight and even way, and who it is that has received guidance."

Al-Anbiyãa, or The Prophets

In the name of Allah, Most Gracious, Most Merciful.

1. Closer and closer to mankind comes their Reckoning: yet they heed not and they turn away.

2. Never comes (aught) to them of a renewed Message from their Lord, but they listen to it as in jest,—

3. Their hearts toying as with trifles. The wrong-doers conceal their private counsels, (saying, "Is this (one) more than a man like yourselves? Will ye go to witchcraft with your eyes open?"

ساعات (اولین) میں بھی اسکی تسبیح کیا کرو اور دن کی اطراف (یعنی
دوپہر کے قریب ظہر کے وقت بھی) تاکہ تم خوش ہو جاؤ ﴿١٣٠﴾
اور کئی طرح کے لوگوں کو جو ہم نے دنیا کی (زندگی میں) آرائش کی چیزوں سے
بہرہ مند کیا ہے تاکہ اُنکی آزمائش کریں اُن پر نگاہ نہ کرنا اور تمہارے
پروردگار کی (عطا فرمائی ہوئی) روزی بہت بہتر اور باقی رہنے والی ہے ﴿١٣١﴾
اور اپنے گھر والوں کو نماز کا حکم کرو اور اس پر قائم رہو ہم تم سے
روزی کے خواستگار نہیں بلکہ تمہیں ہم روزی دیتے ہیں.
اور (نیک) انجام (اہل) تقوٰی کا ہے ﴿١٣٢﴾
اور کہتے ہیں کہ یہ (پیغمبر) اپنے پروردگار کیطرف سے ہمارے پاس کوئی نشانی
کیوں نہیں لاتے کیا انکے پاس پہلی کتابوں کی نشانی نہیں آئی ﴿١٣٣﴾
اور اگر ہم اُن کو پیغمبر (کے بھیجنے) سے پیشتر کسی عذاب سے
ہلاک کر دیتے تو وہ کہتے کہ اے ہمارے پروردگار تو نے ہماری
طرف کوئی پیغمبر کیوں نہ بھیجا کہ ہم ذلیل اور رسوا ہونے
سے پہلے تیرے کلام (واحکام) کی پیروی کرتے ﴿١٣٤﴾
کہہ دو کہ سب (نتائج اعمال کے) منتظر ہیں سو تم بھی منتظر رہو۔
عنقریب تمکو معلوم ہو جائیگا کہ (دین کے) سیدھے رستے پر چلنے والے
کون ہیں اور (جنت کیطرف) راہ پانے والے کون ہیں (ہم یا تم) ﴿١٣٥﴾

سورۂ انبیاء مکی ہے اور اس میں ایک سو بارہ آیتیں اور سات رکوع ہیں

شروع خدا کا نام لے کر جو بڑا مہربان نہایت رحم والا ہے
لوگوں کا حساب (اعمال کا وقت) نزدیک آپہنچا ہے اور
وہ غفلت میں (پڑے اس سے) منہ پھیر رہے ہیں ﴿١﴾
ان کے پاس کوئی نئی نصیحت اُن کے پروردگار کی طرف سے
نہیں آتی مگر وہ اُسے کھیلتے ہوئے سنتے ہیں ﴿٢﴾
اُن کے دل غفلت میں پڑے ہوئے ہیں۔ اور ظالم
لوگ (آپس میں) چپکے چپکے باتیں کرتے ہیں کہ یہ
(شخص کچھ بھی) نہیں مگر تمہارے جیسا آدمی ہے تو تم آنکھوں
دیکھتے جادو (کی لپیٹ) میں کیوں آتے ہو ﴿٣﴾ ١٨٥

غُرُوبِهَا ۚ وَمِنْ آنَاءِ اللَّيْلِ فَسَبِّحْ وَ
أَطْرَافَ النَّهَارِ لَعَلَّكَ تَرْضَىٰ ﴿١٣٠﴾
وَلَا تَمُدَّنَّ عَيْنَيْكَ إِلَىٰ مَا مَتَّعْنَا بِهِ
أَزْوَاجًا مِّنْهُمْ زَهْرَةَ الْحَيَاةِ الدُّنْيَا ۙ
لِنَفْتِنَهُمْ فِيهِ ۚ وَرِزْقُ رَبِّكَ خَيْرٌ وَأَبْقَىٰ ﴿١٣١﴾
وَأْمُرْ أَهْلَكَ بِالصَّلَاةِ وَاصْطَبِرْ عَلَيْهَا ۖ
لَا نَسْأَلُكَ رِزْقًا ۖ نَّحْنُ نَرْزُقُكَ ۗ وَ
الْعَاقِبَةُ لِلتَّقْوَىٰ ﴿١٣٢﴾
وَقَالُوا لَوْلَا يَأْتِينَا بِآيَةٍ مِّن رَّبِّهِ ۚ
أَوَلَمْ تَأْتِهِم بَيِّنَةُ مَا فِي الصُّحُفِ الْأُولَىٰ ﴿١٣٣﴾
وَلَوْ أَنَّا أَهْلَكْنَاهُم بِعَذَابٍ مِّن قَبْلِهِ
لَقَالُوا رَبَّنَا لَوْلَا أَرْسَلْتَ إِلَيْنَا رَسُولًا
فَنَتَّبِعَ آيَاتِكَ مِن قَبْلِ أَن نَّذِلَّ
وَنَخْزَىٰ ﴿١٣٤﴾
قُلْ كُلٌّ مُّتَرَبِّصٌ فَتَرَبَّصُوا ۖ
فَسَتَعْلَمُونَ مَنْ أَصْحَابُ الصِّرَاطِ
ع ٧ السَّوِيِّ وَمَنِ اهْتَدَىٰ ﴿١٣٥﴾

سُورَةُ الْأَنْبِيَاءِ مَكِّيَّةٌ وَهِيَ مِائَةٌ وَاثْنَتَا عَشْرَةَ آيَةً وَسَبْعُ رُكُوعَاتٍ

بِسْمِ اللَّهِ الرَّحْمَٰنِ الرَّحِيمِ
اقْتَرَبَ لِلنَّاسِ حِسَابُهُمْ وَهُمْ الجزء السابع عشر ١٧
فِي غَفْلَةٍ مُّعْرِضُونَ ﴿١﴾
مَا يَأْتِيهِم مِّن ذِكْرٍ مِّن رَّبِّهِم مُّحْدَثٍ
إِلَّا اسْتَمَعُوهُ وَهُمْ يَلْعَبُونَ ﴿٢﴾
لَاهِيَةً قُلُوبُهُمْ ۗ وَأَسَرُّوا النَّجْوَى ۖ
الَّذِينَ ظَلَمُوا هَلْ هَٰذَا إِلَّا بَشَرٌ
مِّثْلُكُمْ ۖ أَفَتَأْتُونَ السِّحْرَ وَأَنتُمْ
تُبْصِرُونَ ﴿٣﴾

4. Say: "My Lord knoweth (every) word (spoken) in the heavens and on earth: He is the One that heareth and knoweth (all things)."

5. "Nay," they say, "(these are) medleys of dreams!—Nay, he forged it!—Nay, he is (but) a poet! Let him then bring us a Sign like the ones that were sent to (Prophets) of old!"

6. (As to those) before them, not one of the towns which We destroyed believed: will these believe?

7. Before thee, also, the messengers We sent were but men, to whom We granted inspiration: if ye know this not, ask of those who possess the Message.

8. Nor did We give them bodies that ate no food, nor were they immortals.

9. Then We fulfilled to them Our promise, and We saved them and those whom We willed but We destroyed those who transgressed beyond bounds.

10. We have revealed for you (O men!) a book which will give you eminence. Will ye not then understand?

11. How many were the towns. We utterly destroyed because of their iniquities, setting up in their places other peoples?

12. Yet, when they felt Our Punishment (coming), behold, they (tried to) flee from it.

13. Flee not, but return to the good things of this life which were given you, and to your homes, in order that ye may be called to account.

14. They said: "Ah! woe to us! We were indeed wrong-doers!"

15. And that cry of theirs ceased not, till We made them as a field that is mown, as ashes silent and quenched.

16. Not for (idle) sport did We create the heavens and the earth

(پیغمبر نے) کہا کہ جو بات آسمان اور زمین میں (کہی جاتی) ہے میرا
پروردگار اُسے جانتا ہے۔ اور وہ سننے والا (اور) جاننے والا ہے (٤)
بلکہ (ظالم) کہنے لگے کہ (یہ قرآن) پریشان (باتیں ہیں جو) خواب (میں دیکھ لی) ہیں (نہیں)
بلکہ اس نے اسکو اپنی طرف سے بنا لیا ہے (نہیں) بلکہ یہ (شعر ہے جو اس) شاعر (کا نتیجہ طبع) ہے ف١٨٦
تو جیسے پہلے (پیغمبر نشانیاں دیکر) بھیجے گئے تھے (اسی طرح) یہ بھی ہمارے پاس کوئی نشانی لائے (٥)
ان سے پہلے جن بستیوں کو ہم نے ہلاک کیا وہ ایمان نہیں
لاتی تھیں. تو کیا یہ ایمان لے آئیں گے (٦)
اور ہم نے تم سے پہلے مرد ہی (پیغمبر بناکر) بھیجے جن کی طرف
ہم وحی بھیجتے تھے۔ اگر تم نہیں جانتے تو جو یاد رکھتے ہیں
اُن سے پوچھ لو (٧)
اور ہم نے اُن کے ایسے جسم نہیں بنائے تھے کہ کھانا نہ کھائیں
اور نہ وہ ہمیشہ رہنے والے تھے (٨)
پھر ہم نے اُن کے بارے میں (اپنا) وعدہ سچا کر دیا تو اُن کو
اور جس کو چاہا نجات دی اور حد سے نکل جانیوالوں کو ہلاک کر دیا (٩)
ہم نے تمہاری طرف ایسی کتاب نازل کی ہے جس میں
تمہارا تذکرہ ہے کیا تم نہیں سمجھتے؟ (١٠)
اور ہم نے بہت سی بستیوں کو جو ستمگار تھیں ہلاک کر مارا
اور اُن کے بعد اور لوگ پیدا کر دیئے (١١)
جب انہوں نے ہمارے (مقدمۂ) عذاب کو دیکھا تو لگے
اس سے بھاگنے (١٢)
مت بھاگو اور جن (نعمتوں) میں تم عیش و آسائش
کرتے تھے ان کی اور اپنے گھروں کی طرف لوٹ جاؤ۔
شاید تم سے (اس بارے میں) دریافت کیا جائے (١٣)
کہنے لگے ہائے شامت بے شک ہم ظالم تھے (١٤)
تو وہ ہمیشہ اسی طرح پکارتے رہے یہاں تک کہ ہم نے اُن کو
(کھیتی کی طرح) کاٹ کر (اور آگ کی طرح) بجھا کر ڈھیر کر دیا (١٥)
اور ہم نے آسمان اور زمین کو اور جو (مخلوقات) ان دونوں کے

قٰلَ رَبِّيْ يَعْلَمُ الْقَوْلَ فِي السَّمَآءِ وَ
الْاَرْضِ وَهُوَ السَّمِيْعُ الْعَلِيْمُ (٤)
بَلْ قَالُوْٓا اَضْغَاثُ اَحْلَامٍۢ بَلِ
افْتَرٰىهُ بَلْ هُوَ شَاعِرٌ ۚۖ فَلْيَاْتِنَا
بِاٰيَةٍ كَمَآ اُرْسِلَ الْاَوَّلُوْنَ (٥)
مَآ اٰمَنَتْ قَبْلَهُمْ مِّنْ قَرْيَةٍ اَهْلَكْنٰهَا ۚ
اَفَهُمْ يُؤْمِنُوْنَ (٦)
وَمَآ اَرْسَلْنَا قَبْلَكَ اِلَّا رِجَالًا نُّوْحِيْٓ
اِلَيْهِمْ فَسْئَلُوْٓا اَهْلَ الذِّكْرِ اِنْ
كُنْتُمْ لَا تَعْلَمُوْنَ (٧)
وَمَا جَعَلْنٰهُمْ جَسَدًا لَّا يَاْكُلُوْنَ
الطَّعَامَ وَمَا كَانُوْا خٰلِدِيْنَ (٨)
ثُمَّ صَدَقْنٰهُمُ الْوَعْدَ فَاَنْجَيْنٰهُمْ وَمَنْ
نَّشَآءُ وَاَهْلَكْنَا الْمُسْرِفِيْنَ (٩)
لَقَدْ اَنْزَلْنَآ اِلَيْكُمْ كِتٰبًا فِيْهِ ذِكْرُكُمْ ۭ
ع اَفَلَا تَعْقِلُوْنَ (١٠)
وَكَمْ قَصَمْنَا مِنْ قَرْيَةٍ كَانَتْ ظَالِمَةً
وَّاَنْشَاْنَا بَعْدَهَا قَوْمًا اٰخَرِيْنَ (١١)
فَلَمَّآ اَحَسُّوْا بَاْسَنَآ اِذَا هُمْ مِّنْهَا
يَرْكُضُوْنَ (١٢)
لَا تَرْكُضُوْا وَارْجِعُوْٓا اِلٰى مَآ
اُتْرِفْتُمْ فِيْهِ وَمَسٰكِنِكُمْ لَعَلَّكُمْ
تُسْئَلُوْنَ (١٣)
قَالُوْا يٰوَيْلَنَآ اِنَّا كُنَّا ظٰلِمِيْنَ (١٤)
فَمَا زَالَتْ تِّلْكَ دَعْوٰىهُمْ حَتّٰى جَعَلْنٰهُمْ
حَصِيْدًا خٰمِدِيْنَ (١٥)
وَمَا خَلَقْنَا السَّمَآءَ وَالْاَرْضَ وَمَا بَيْنَهُمَا

لٰعِبِيْنَ ﴿۱۶﴾

درمیان ہے اس کو لہو و لعب کے لئے پیدا نہیں کیا (۱۶)

and all that is between!

لَوْ اَرَدْنَآ اَنْ نَّتَّخِذَ لَهْوًا لَّاتَّخَذْنٰهُ مِنْ
لَّدُنَّآ ۖ اِنْ كُنَّا فٰعِلِيْنَ ﴿۱۷﴾

اگر ہم چاہتے کہ کھیل (کی چیزیں یعنی زن و فرزند) بنائیں
تو اگر ہم کو کرنا ہی ہوتا تو ہم اپنے پاس سے بنا لیتے (۱۷)

17. If it had been Our wish to take (just) a pastime, We should surely have taken it from the things nearest to Us, if We would do (such a thing)!

بَلْ نَقْذِفُ بِالْحَقِّ عَلَى الْبَاطِلِ
فَيَدْمَغُهٗ فَاِذَا هُوَ زَاهِقٌ ۚ وَلَكُمُ
الْوَيْلُ مِمَّا تَصِفُوْنَ ﴿۱۸﴾

(نہیں) بلکہ ہم سچ کو جھوٹ پر کھینچ مارتے ہیں تو وہ اس کا
سر توڑ دیتا ہے اور جھوٹ اسی وقت نابود ہو جاتا ہے۔ اور جو
باتیں تم بناتے ہو اُن سے تمہاری ہی خرابی ہے (۱۸)

18. Nay, We hurl the Truth against falsehood, and it knocks out its brain, and behold, falsehood doth perish! Ah! woe be to you for the (false) things ye ascribe (to Us).

وَلَهٗ مَنْ فِى السَّمٰوٰتِ وَالْاَرْضِ ۭ وَمَنْ
عِنْدَهٗ لَا يَسْتَكْبِرُوْنَ عَنْ عِبَادَتِهٖ
وَلَا يَسْتَحْسِرُوْنَ ﴿۱۹﴾

اور جو لوگ آسمانوں میں اور جو زمین میں ہیں سب اسی کے
(مملوک اور اسی کا مال) ہیں۔ اور جو (فرشتے) اسکے پاس ہیں
وہ اُسکی عبادت سے نہ کنیاتے ہیں اور نہ اُکتاتے ہیں (۱۹)

19. To Him belong all (creatures) in the heavens and on earth: even those who are with Him are not too proud to serve Him, nor are they (ever) weary (of His service):

يُسَبِّحُوْنَ الَّيْلَ وَالنَّهَارَ لَا يَفْتُرُوْنَ ﴿۲۰﴾

رات دن (اسکی) تسبیح کرتے رہتے ہیں (نہ تھکتے ہیں نہ) تھمتے ہیں (۲۰)

20. They celebrate His praises night and day, nor do they ever flag or intermit.

اَمِ اتَّخَذُوْٓا اٰلِهَةً مِّنَ الْاَرْضِ هُمْ
يُنْشِرُوْنَ ﴿۲۱﴾

بھلا لوگوں نے جو زمین کی چیزوں سے (بعض کو) معبود بنا لیا ہے
(تو کیا) وہ ان کو (مرنے کے بعد) اٹھا کھڑا کرینگے؟ (۲۱)

21. Or have they taken (for worship) gods from the earth who can raise (the dead)?

لَوْ كَانَ فِيْهِمَآ اٰلِهَةٌ اِلَّا اللّٰهُ لَفَسَدَتَا ۚ
فَسُبْحٰنَ اللّٰهِ رَبِّ الْعَرْشِ عَمَّا
يَصِفُوْنَ ﴿۲۲﴾

اگر آسمان اور زمین میں خدا کے سوا اور معبود ہوتے تو زمین
و آسمان درہم برہم ہو جاتے۔ جو باتیں یہ لوگ بتاتے ہیں
خدائے مالک عرش اُن سے پاک ہے (۲۲)

22. If there were, in the heavens and the earth, other gods besides Allah, there would have been ruin in both! But glory to Allah, the Lord of the Throne: (High is He) above what they attribute to Him!

لَا يُسْـَٔلُ عَمَّا يَفْعَلُ وَهُمْ يُسْـَٔلُوْنَ ﴿۲۳﴾

وہ جو کام کرتا ہے اسکی پرسش نہیں ہوگی اور (جو کام یہ لوگ کرتے ہیں) اسکی (ان سے) پرسش ہوگی (۲۳)

23. He cannot be questioned for His acts, but they will be questioned (for theirs).

اَمِ اتَّخَذُوْا مِنْ دُوْنِهٖٓ اٰلِهَةً ۭ قُلْ
هَاتُوْا بُرْهَانَكُمْ ۚ هٰذَا ذِكْرُ مَنْ
مَّعِىَ وَذِكْرُ مَنْ قَبْلِىْ ۭ بَلْ اَكْثَرُهُمْ
لَا يَعْلَمُوْنَ ۙ الْحَقَّ فَهُمْ مُّعْرِضُوْنَ ﴿۲۴﴾

کیا لوگوں نے خدا کو چھوڑ کر اور معبود بنا لئے ہیں کہدو کہ (اس بات پر) اپنی
دلیل پیش کرو۔ یہ (میری اور) میرے ساتھ والوں کی کتاب بھی ہے اور جو مجھ سے
پہلے (پیغمبر) ہوئے ہیں۔ اُنکی کتابیں بھی ہیں۔ بلکہ (بات یہ ہے کہ) اُن میں اکثر حق
بات کو نہیں جانتے اور اس لئے اس سے منہ پھیر لیتے ہیں (۲۴)

24. Or have they taken for worship (other) gods besides Him? Say, "Bring your convincing proof: this is the Message of those with me and the Message of those before me." But most of them know not the Truth, and so turn away.

وَمَآ اَرْسَلْنَا مِنْ قَبْلِكَ مِنْ رَّسُوْلٍ
اِلَّا نُوْحِىْٓ اِلَيْهِ اَنَّهٗ لَآ اِلٰهَ اِلَّآ اَنَا
فَاعْبُدُوْنِ ﴿۲۵﴾

اور جو پیغمبر ہم نے تم سے پہلے بھیجے اُن کی طرف یہی
وحی بھیجی کہ میرے سوا کوئی معبود نہیں تو میری ہی
عبادت کرو (۲۵)

25. Not a messenger did We send before thee without this inspiration sent by Us to him: that there is no god but I; therefore worship and serve Me.

وَقَالُوا اتَّخَذَ الرَّحْمٰنُ وَلَدًا سُبْحٰنَهٗ ۭ
بَلْ عِبَادٌ مُّكْرَمُوْنَ ﴿۲۶﴾

اور کہتے ہیں کہ خدا بیٹا رکھتا ہے وہ پاک ہے (اسکے نہ بیٹا ہے نہ بیٹی) بلکہ
(جنکو یہ لوگ اسکے بیٹے بیٹیاں سمجھتے ہیں) وہ اسکے عزت والے بندے ہیں (۲۶)

26. And they say: "The Most Gracious has taken a son." Glory to Him! They are (but) servants raised to honour.

لَا يَسْبِقُوْنَهٗ بِالْقَوْلِ وَهُمْ بِاَمْرِهٖ
يَعْمَلُوْنَ ﴿۲۷﴾

اس کے آگے بڑھ کر بول نہیں سکتے۔ اور اس کے حکم پر
عمل کرتے ہیں (۲۷)

27. They speak not before He speaks, and they act (in all things) by His command.

28. He knows what is before them, and what is behind them, and they offer no intercession except for those with whom He is well-pleased and they stand in awe and reverence of His (glory).

جو کچھ اُن کے آگے ہو چکا ہے اور جو پیچھے ہوگا وہ سب سے واقف ہے
اور وہ (اس کے پاس کسی کی) سفارش نہیں کر سکتے مگر اس
شخص کی جس سے خدا خوش ہو اور وہ اس کی ہیبت سے ڈرتے رہتے ہیں ﴿۲۸﴾

يَعْلَمُ مَا بَيْنَ أَيْدِيهِمْ وَمَا خَلْفَهُمْ
وَلَا يَشْفَعُونَ إِلَّا لِمَنِ ارْتَضَىٰ وَهُم
مِّنْ خَشْيَتِهِ مُشْفِقُونَ ﴿٢٨﴾

29. If any of them should say, "I am a god besides Him", such a one We should reward with Hell: thus do We reward those who do wrong.

اور جو شخص اُن میں سے یہ کہے کہ خدا کے سوا میں معبود
ہوں تو اُسے ہم دوزخ کی سزا دیں گے اور ظالموں
کو ہم ایسی ہی سزا دیا کرتے ہیں ﴿۲۹﴾

وَمَن يَقُلْ مِنْهُمْ إِنِّي إِلَٰهٌ مِّن دُونِهِ
فَذَٰلِكَ نَجْزِيهِ جَهَنَّمَ كَذَٰلِكَ نَجْزِي
الظَّالِمِينَ ﴿٢٩﴾

30. Do not the Unbelievers see that the heavens and the earth were joined together (as one unit of Creation), before We clove them asunder? We made from water every living thing. Will they not then believe?

کیا کافروں نے نہیں دیکھا کہ آسمان اور زمین دونوں
ملے ہوئے تھے تو ہم نے جُدا جُدا کر دیا۔ اور تمام
جاندار چیزیں ہم نے پانی سے بنائیں پھر یہ لوگ ایمان
کیوں نہیں لاتے ﴿۳۰﴾

أَوَلَمْ يَرَ الَّذِينَ كَفَرُوا أَنَّ السَّمَاوَاتِ
وَالْأَرْضَ كَانَتَا رَتْقًا فَفَتَقْنَاهُمَا وَ
جَعَلْنَا مِنَ الْمَاءِ كُلَّ شَيْءٍ حَيٍّ أَفَلَا
يُؤْمِنُونَ ﴿٣٠﴾

31. And We have set on the earth mountains standing firm, lest it should shake with them, and We have made therein broad highways (between mountains) for them to pass through: that they may find their way.

اور ہم نے زمین میں پہاڑ بنائے تاکہ لوگوں (کے بوجھ) سے
ہلنے (اور جھکنے) نہ لگے اور اس میں کشادہ رستے بنائے تاکہ لوگ اُن پر چلیں ﴿۳۱﴾

وَجَعَلْنَا فِي الْأَرْضِ رَوَاسِيَ أَن تَمِيدَ بِهِمْ
وَجَعَلْنَا فِيهَا فِجَاجًا سُبُلًا لَّعَلَّهُمْ يَهْتَدُونَ ﴿٣١﴾

32. And We have made the heavens as a canopy well guarded: yet do they turn away from the Signs which these things (point to)!

اور آسمان کو محفوظ چھت بنایا۔ اس پر بھی وہ ہماری
نشانیوں سے منہ پھیر رہے ہیں ﴿۳۲﴾

وَجَعَلْنَا السَّمَاءَ سَقْفًا مَّحْفُوظًا وَهُمْ
عَنْ آيَاتِهَا مُعْرِضُونَ ﴿٣٢﴾

33. It is He Who created the Night and the Day, and the sun and the moon: all (the celestial bodies) swim along, each in its rounded course.

اور وہی تو ہے جس نے رات اور دن اور سورج اور چاند کو بنایا (یہ سب
(یعنی سورج اور چاند اور ستارے) آسمان میں (اس طرح چلتے ہیں گویا) تیر رہے ہیں ﴿۳۳﴾

وَهُوَ الَّذِي خَلَقَ اللَّيْلَ وَالنَّهَارَ وَالشَّمْسَ
وَالْقَمَرَ كُلٌّ فِي فَلَكٍ يَسْبَحُونَ ﴿٣٣﴾

34. We granted not to any man before thee permanent life (here): if then thou shouldst die, would they live permanently?

اور (اے پیغمبر) ہم نے تم سے پہلے کسی آدمی کو بقائے دوام
نہیں بخشا۔ بھلا اگر تم مرجاؤ تو کیا یہ لوگ ہمیشہ رہیں گے ﴿۳۴﴾

وَمَا جَعَلْنَا لِبَشَرٍ مِّن قَبْلِكَ الْخُلْدَ أَفَإِن
مِّتَّ فَهُمُ الْخَالِدُونَ ﴿٣٤﴾

35. Every soul shall have a taste of death: and We test you by evil and by good by way of trial. To Us must ye return.

ہر متنفس کو موت کا مزہ چکھنا ہے۔ اور ہم تم لوگوں کو سختی اور آسودگی
میں آزمائش کے طور پر مبتلا کرتے ہیں۔ اور تم ہماری طرف ہی لوٹ کر آؤ گے ﴿۳۵﴾

كُلُّ نَفْسٍ ذَائِقَةُ الْمَوْتِ وَنَبْلُوكُم
بِالشَّرِّ وَالْخَيْرِ فِتْنَةً وَإِلَيْنَا تُرْجَعُونَ ﴿٣٥﴾

36. When the Unbelievers see thee, they treat thee not except with ridicule. "Is this," (they say), "The one who talks of your gods?" And they blaspheme at the mention of The Most Gracious!

اور جب کافر تم کو دیکھتے ہیں تو تم سے استہزا
کرتے ہیں۔ کہ کیا یہی شخص ہے جو تمہارے معبودوں
کا ذکر (برائی سے) کیا کرتا ہے حالانکہ وہ خود رحمٰن کے
نام سے منکر ہیں ﴿۳۶﴾

وَإِذَا رَآكَ الَّذِينَ كَفَرُوا إِن
يَتَّخِذُونَكَ إِلَّا هُزُوًا أَهَٰذَا الَّذِي
يَذْكُرُ آلِهَتَكُمْ وَهُم بِذِكْرِ الرَّحْمَٰنِ
هُمْ كَافِرُونَ ﴿٣٦﴾

37. Man is a creature of haste: soon (enough) will I show you My Signs; so ask Me not to hasten them!

انسان (کچھ ایسا) جلد باز ہے کہ گویا جلد بازی ہی سے بنایا گیا ہے۔ میں
تم لوگوں کو عنقریب اپنی نشانیاں دکھاؤں گا تو تم جلدی نہ کرو ﴿۳۷﴾

خُلِقَ الْإِنسَانُ مِنْ عَجَلٍ سَأُرِيكُمْ
آيَاتِي فَلَا تَسْتَعْجِلُونِ ﴿٣٧﴾

38. They say: "When will this promise come to pass, if ye are

اور کہتے ہیں کہ اگر تم سچے ہو تو (جس عذاب کی) یہ وعید

وَيَقُولُونَ مَتَىٰ هَٰذَا الْوَعْدُ إِن كُنتُمْ

telling the truth?"

39. If only the Unbelievers knew (the time) when they will not be able to ward off the Fire from their faces, nor yet from their backs, and (when) no help can reach them!

40. Nay, it may come to them all of a sudden and confound them: no power will they have then to avert it, nor will they (then) get respite.

41. Mocked were (many) messengers before thee; but their scoffers were hemmed in by the thing that they mocked.

42. Say, "Who can keep you safe by night and by day from (the Wrath of) The Most Gracious?" Yet they turn away from the remembrance of their Lord.

43. Or have they gods that can guard them from Us? They have no power to aid themselves, nor can they be defended from Us.

44. Nay, We gave the good things of this life to these men and their fathers until the period grew long for them; see they not that We gradually reduce the land (in their control) from its outlying borders? Is it then they who will win?

45. Say, "I do but warn you according to revelation": but the deaf will not hear the call, (even) when they are warned!

46. If but a breath of the Wrath of thy Lord do touch them they will then say, "Woe to us! we did wrong indeed!"

47. We shall set up scales of justice for the day of Judgment, so that not a soul will be dealt with unjustly in the least. And if there be (no more than) the weight of a mustard seed, We will bring it (to account): and enough are We to take account.

رہے وہ) کب آئے گا (۳۸)
اے کاش کافر اس وقت کو جانیں جب وہ اپنے مونہوں
پر سے (دوزخ کی) آگ کو روک نہ سکیں گے اور نہ اپنی
پیٹھوں پر سے اور نہ اُن کا کوئی مددگار ہوگا (۳۹)
بلکہ قیامت اُن پر ناگہاں آ واقع ہوگی اور اُنکے ہوش کھو دیگی پھر
نہ تو وہ اسکو ہٹا سکیں گے اور نہ اُنکو مہلت دی جائے گی (۴۰)
اور تم سے پہلے بھی پیغمبروں کے ساتھ استہزا ہوتا رہا ہے تو جو
لوگ ان میں سے تمسخر کیا کرتے تھے اُن کو اسی (عذاب)
نے جس کی ہنسی اُڑاتے تھے آ گھیرا (۴۱)
کہو کہ رات اور دن میں خدا سے تمہاری کون حفاظت
کر سکتا ہے؟ بات یہ ہے کہ یہ اپنے پروردگار کی یاد
سے منہ پھیرے ہوئے ہیں (۴۲)
کیا ہمارے سوا ان کے اور معبود ہیں کہ ان کو (مصائب)
بچا سکیں۔ وہ آپ اپنی مدد تو کر ہی نہیں سکیں گے اور
نہ ہم سے پناہ ہی دیئے جائیں گے (۴۳)
بلکہ ہم ان لوگوں کو اور ان کے باپ دادا کو متمتع کرتے رہے
یہاں تک کہ (اسی حالت میں) اُنکی عمریں بسر ہوگئیں۔ کیا یہ
نہیں دیکھتے کہ ہم زمین کو اسکے کناروں سے گھٹاتے چلے
آتے ہیں۔ تو کیا یہ لوگ غلبہ پانے والے ہیں؟ (۴۴)
کہہ دو کہ میں تم کو حکمِ خدا کے مطابق نصیحت کرتا ہوں اور
بہروں کو جب نصیحت کی جائے تو وہ پکار کو سنتے ہی نہیں (۴۵)
اور اگر اُن کو تمہارے پروردگار کا تھوڑا سا عذاب بھی پہنچے تو
کہنے لگیں کہ ہائے کم بختی ہم بے شک گنہگار تھے (۴۶)
اور ہم قیامت کے دن انصاف کی ترازو کھڑی کریں گے
تو کسی شخص کی ذرا بھی حق تلفی نہ کی جائے گی۔ اور اگر رائی کے
دانے کے برابر بھی (کسی کا عمل) ہوگا تو ہم اُسکو لا موجود کرینگے
اور ہم حساب کرنے کو کافی ہیں (۴۷)

صٰدِقِينَ (۳۸)
لَوْ يَعْلَمُ الَّذِينَ كَفَرُوا حِينَ لَا
يَكُفُّونَ عَن وُّجُوهِهِمُ النَّارَ وَلَا
عَن ظُهُورِهِمْ وَلَا هُمْ يُنصَرُونَ (۳۹)
بَلْ تَأْتِيهِم بَغْتَةً فَتَبْهَتُهُمْ فَلَا
يَسْتَطِيعُونَ رَدَّهَا وَلَا هُمْ يُنظَرُونَ (۴۰)
وَلَقَدِ اسْتُهْزِئَ بِرُسُلٍ مِّن قَبْلِكَ
فَحَاقَ بِالَّذِينَ سَخِرُوا مِنْهُم مَّا كَانُوا
بِهِ يَسْتَهْزِءُونَ (۴۱) ع
قُلْ مَن يَكْلَؤُكُم بِاللَّيْلِ وَ
النَّهَارِ مِنَ الرَّحْمٰنِ بَلْ هُمْ عَن
ذِكْرِ رَبِّهِم مُّعْرِضُونَ (۴۲)
أَمْ لَهُمْ آلِهَةٌ تَمْنَعُهُم مِّن دُونِنَا
لَا يَسْتَطِيعُونَ نَصْرَ أَنفُسِهِمْ وَلَا هُم
مِّنَّا يُصْحَبُونَ (۴۳)
بَلْ مَتَّعْنَا هٰؤُلَاءِ وَآبَاءَهُمْ حَتّٰى
طَالَ عَلَيْهِمُ الْعُمُرُ أَفَلَا يَرَوْنَ أَنَّا
نَأْتِي الْأَرْضَ نَنقُصُهَا مِنْ أَطْرَافِهَا
أَفَهُمُ الْغٰلِبُونَ (۴۴)
قُلْ إِنَّمَا أُنذِرُكُم بِالْوَحْيِ وَلَا يَسْمَعُ
الصُّمُّ الدُّعَاءَ إِذَا مَا يُنذَرُونَ (۴۵)
وَلَئِن مَّسَّتْهُمْ نَفْحَةٌ مِّنْ عَذَابِ
رَبِّكَ لَيَقُولُنَّ يٰوَيْلَنَا إِنَّا كُنَّا ظٰلِمِينَ (۴۶)
وَنَضَعُ الْمَوَازِينَ الْقِسْطَ لِيَوْمِ الْقِيٰمَةِ
فَلَا تُظْلَمُ نَفْسٌ شَيْئًا وَإِن كَانَ
مِثْقَالَ حَبَّةٍ مِّنْ خَرْدَلٍ أَتَيْنَا بِهَا
وَكَفٰى بِنَا حٰسِبِينَ (۴۷)

48. In the past We granted to Moses and Aaron the Criterion (for judgment). And a Light and a Message for those who would do right,—

اور ہمنے موسیٰ اور ہارون کو (ہدایت اور گمراہی میں) فرق کردینے والی
اور (سرتاپا) روشنی اور نصیحت (کی کتاب) عطا کی (یعنی) پرہیزگاروں کیلئے ﴿۴۸﴾

وَلَقَدْ اٰتَيْنَا مُوْسٰى وَهٰرُوْنَ الْفُرْقَانَ
وَضِيَآءً وَّذِكْرًا لِّلْمُتَّقِيْنَ ﴿٤٨﴾

49. Those who fear their Lord in their most secret thoughts, and who hold the Hour (of Judgment) in awe.

جو بِن دیکھے اپنے پروردگار سے ڈرتے ہیں اور قیامت
کا بھی خوف رکھتے ہیں ﴿۴۹﴾

الَّذِيْنَ يَخْشَوْنَ رَبَّهُمْ بِالْغَيْبِ وَهُمْ
مِّنَ السَّاعَةِ مُشْفِقُوْنَ ﴿٤٩﴾

50. And this is a blessed Message which We have sent down: will ye then reject it?

اور یہ مبارک نصیحت ہے جسے ہم نے نازل فرمایا ہے تو کیا
تم اس سے انکار کرتے ہو؟ ﴿۵۰﴾

وَهٰذَا ذِكْرٌ مُّبٰرَكٌ اَنْزَلْنٰهُ ۭ اَفَاَنْتُمْ
لَهٗ مُنْكِرُوْنَ ﴿٥٠﴾

51. We bestowed aforetime on Abraham his rectitude of conduct, and well were We acquainted with him.

اور ہم نے ابراہیم کو پہلے ہی سے ہدایت دی تھی اور ہم اُن
(کے حال) سے واقف تھے ﴿۵۱﴾

وَلَقَدْ اٰتَيْنَآ اِبْرٰهِيْمَ رُشْدَهٗ مِنْ
قَبْلُ وَكُنَّا بِهٖ عٰلِمِيْنَ ﴿٥١﴾

52. Behold! he said to his father and his people, "What are these images, to which ye are (so assiduously) devoted?"

جب انہوں نے اپنے باپ اور اپنی قوم کے لوگوں سے کہا کہ یہ
کیا مُورتیں ہیں جن (کی پرستش) پر تم معتکف (و قائم) ہو ﴿۵۲﴾

اِذْ قَالَ لِاَبِيْهِ وَقَوْمِهٖ مَا هٰذِهِ التَّمَاثِيْلُ
الَّتِيْٓ اَنْتُمْ لَهَا عٰكِفُوْنَ ﴿٥٢﴾

53. They said, "We found our fathers worshipping them."

وہ کہنے لگے کہ ہم نے اپنے باپ دادا کو انکی پرستش کرتے دیکھا ہے ﴿۵۳﴾

قَالُوْا وَجَدْنَآ اٰبَآءَنَا لَهَا عٰبِدِيْنَ ﴿٥٣﴾

54. He said, "Indeed ye have been in manifest error—ye and your fathers."

(ابراہیم نے) کہا کہ تم بھی (گمراہ ہو) اور تمہارے باپ دادا بھی
صریح گمراہی میں پڑے رہے ﴿۵۴﴾

قَالَ لَقَدْ كُنْتُمْ اَنْتُمْ وَاٰبَآؤُكُمْ
فِيْ ضَلٰلٍ مُّبِيْنٍ ﴿٥٤﴾

55. They said, "Have you brought us the Truth, or are you one of those who jest?"

وہ بولے کیا تم ہمارے پاس (واقعی) حق لائے ہو یا (ہم سے) کھیل (کی باتیں) کرتے ہو ﴿۵۵﴾

قَالُوْٓا اَجِئْتَنَا بِالْحَقِّ اَمْ اَنْتَ مِنَ اللّٰعِبِيْنَ ﴿٥٥﴾

56. He said, "Nay, your Lord is the Lord of the heavens and the earth, He Who created them (from nothing): and I am a witness to this (truth).

(ابراہیم نے) کہا (نہیں) بلکہ تمہارا پروردگار آسمانوں اور زمین کا
پروردگار ہے جس نے ان کو پیدا کیا ہے اور میں اس (بات)
کا گواہ (اور اسی کا قائل) ہوں ﴿۵۶﴾

قَالَ بَلْ رَّبُّكُمْ رَبُّ السَّمٰوٰتِ وَالْاَرْضِ
الَّذِيْ فَطَرَهُنَّ ڮ وَاَنَا عَلٰى ذٰلِكُمْ مِّنَ
الشّٰهِدِيْنَ ﴿٥٦﴾

57. "And by Allah, I will certainly plan against your idols—after ye go away and turn your backs"...

اور خدا کی قسم جب تم پیٹھ پھیر کر چلے جاؤ گے تو میں تمہارے
بتوں سے ایک چال چلوں گا ﴿۵۷﴾

وَتَاللّٰهِ لَاَكِيْدَنَّ اَصْنَامَكُمْ بَعْدَ اَنْ
تُوَلُّوْا مُدْبِرِيْنَ ﴿٥٧﴾

58. So he broke them to pieces, (all) but the biggest of them, that they might turn (and address themselves) to it.

پھر ان کو توڑ کر ریزہ ریزہ کر دیا مگر ایک بڑے (بت) کو
(نہ توڑا) تاکہ وہ اس کی طرف رجوع کریں ﴿۵۸﴾

فَجَعَلَهُمْ جُذٰذًا اِلَّا كَبِيْرًا لَّهُمْ لَعَلَّهُمْ
اِلَيْهِ يَرْجِعُوْنَ ﴿٥٨﴾

59. They said, "Who has done this to our gods? He must indeed be one of the unjust one.

کہنے لگے کہ ہمارے معبودوں کے ساتھ یہ معاملہ کس نے کیا؟
وہ تو کوئی ظالم ہے ﴿۵۹﴾

قَالُوْا مَنْ فَعَلَ هٰذَا بِاٰلِهَتِنَآ اِنَّهٗ لَمِنَ
الظّٰلِمِيْنَ ﴿٥٩﴾

60. They said, "We heard a youth talk of them: he is called Abraham."

لوگوں نے کہا کہ ہم نے ایک جوان کو اُن کا ذکر کرتے ہوئے
سُنا ہے اُسے ابراہیم کہتے ہیں ﴿۶۰﴾

قَالُوْا سَمِعْنَا فَتًى يَّذْكُرُهُمْ يُقَالُ
لَهٗٓ اِبْرٰهِيْمُ ۭ ﴿٦٠﴾

61. They said, "Then bring him before the eyes of the people, that they may bear witness:"

وہ بولے کہ اُسے لوگوں کے سامنے لاؤ تاکہ وہ
گواہ رہیں ﴿۶۱﴾

قَالُوْا فَاْتُوْا بِهٖ عَلٰٓى اَعْيُنِ النَّاسِ
لَعَلَّهُمْ يَشْهَدُوْنَ ﴿٦١﴾

62. They said, "Art thou the one that did this with our gods, O Abraham?"

(جب ابراہیم آئے تو بت پرستوں نے) کہا کہ ابراہیم بھلا یہ کام
ہمارے معبودوں کے ساتھ تو نے کیا ہے؟ ﴿۶۲﴾

قَالُوْٓا ءَاَنْتَ فَعَلْتَ هٰذَا بِاٰلِهَتِنَا
يٰٓاِبْرٰهِيْمُ ﴿٦٢﴾

63. He said: "Nay, this was done by this the biggest one! Ask them, if they can talk."

(ابراہیم نے) کہا بلکہ یہ اُن کے ان بڑے (بت) نے کیا
(ہوگا)۔ اگر یہ بولتے ہوں تو ان سے پوچھ لو ﴿۶۳﴾

قَالَ بَلْ فَعَلَهٗ ۖ كَبِيْرُهُمْ هٰذَا فَسْـَٔلُوْهُمْ
اِنْ كَانُوْا يَنْطِقُوْنَ ﴿٦٣﴾

64. So they turned to themselves and said, "Surely ye are the ones in the wrong!"

انہوں نے اپنے دل میں غور کیا تو آپس میں کہنے لگے
بیشک تم ہی بے انصاف ہو ﴿۶۴﴾

فَرَجَعُوْٓا اِلٰٓى اَنْفُسِهِمْ فَقَالُوْٓا اِنَّكُمْ
اَنْتُمُ الظّٰلِمُوْنَ ﴿٦٤﴾

65. Then were they confounded with shame: (they said), "Thou knowest full well that these (idols) do not speak!"

پھر (شرمندہ ہو کر) سر نیچا کر لیا (اس پر بھی ابراہیم سے
کہنے لگے کہ) تم جانتے ہو یہ بولتے نہیں ﴿۶۵﴾

ثُمَّ نُكِسُوْا عَلٰى رُءُوْسِهِمْ ۚ لَقَدْ عَلِمْتَ
مَا هٰٓؤُلَآءِ يَنْطِقُوْنَ ﴿٦٥﴾

66. (Abraham) said, "Do ye then worship, besides Allah, things that can neither be of any good to you nor do you harm?

ابراہیم نے کہا کہ پھر تم خدا کو چھوڑ کر کیوں ایسی چیزوں کو پوجتے ہو جو
نہ تمہیں کچھ فائدہ دے سکیں اور نہ نقصان پہنچا سکیں؟ ﴿۶۶﴾

قَالَ اَفَتَعْبُدُوْنَ مِنْ دُوْنِ اللّٰهِ مَا لَا
يَنْفَعُكُمْ شَيْـًٔا وَّلَا يَضُرُّكُمْ ﴿٦٦﴾

67. "Fie upon you, and upon the things that ye worship besides Allah! Have ye no sense?"...

تف ہے تم پر اور جن کو تم خدا کے سوا پوجتے ہو اُن پر۔ کیا تم
عقل نہیں رکھتے؟ ﴿۶۷﴾

اُفٍّ لَّكُمْ وَلِمَا تَعْبُدُوْنَ مِنْ دُوْنِ
اللّٰهِ ۭ اَفَلَا تَعْقِلُوْنَ ﴿٦٧﴾

68. They said, "Burn him and protect your gods, if ye do (anything at all)!"

(تب وہ) کہنے لگے کہ اگر تمہیں (اس سے اپنے معبود کا انتقام لینا
اور) کچھ کرنا ہے تو اس کو جلا ڈالو اور اپنے معبودوں کی مدد کرو ﴿۶۸﴾

قَالُوْا حَرِّقُوْهُ وَانْصُرُوْٓا اٰلِهَتَكُمْ اِنْ
كُنْتُمْ فٰعِلِيْنَ ﴿٦٨﴾

69. We said, "O Fire! be thou cool, and (a means of) safety for Abraham!"

ہم نے حکم دیا اے آگ سرد ہو جا اور ابراہیم پر
(موجب) سلامتی (بن جا) ﴿۶۹﴾

قُلْنَا يٰنَارُ كُوْنِيْ بَرْدًا وَّسَلٰمًا عَلٰٓى
اِبْرٰهِيْمَ ﴿٦٩﴾

70. Then they planned against him: but We made them the Greater losers.

اُن لوگوں نے برا تو اُن کا چاہا تھا مگر ہم نے انہی کو نقصان میں ڈال دیا ﴿۷۰﴾

وَاَرَادُوْا بِهٖ كَيْدًا فَجَعَلْنٰهُمُ الْاَخْسَرِيْنَ ﴿٧٠﴾

71. But We delivered him and (his nephew) Lût (and directed them) to the land which We have blessed for the nations.

اور ابراہیم اور لوط کو اس سرزمین کی طرف بچا نکالا جس میں
ہم نے اہل عالم کے لئے برکت رکھی تھی ﴿۷۱﴾

وَنَجَّيْنٰهُ وَلُوْطًا اِلَى الْاَرْضِ الَّتِيْ
بٰرَكْنَا فِيْهَا لِلْعٰلَمِيْنَ ﴿٧١﴾

72. And We bestowed on him Isaac and, as an additional gift, (a grandson), Jacob, and We made righteous men of every one (of them).

اور ہم نے ابراہیم کو اسحٰق عطا کئے۔ اور مستزاد برآں یعقوب۔
اور سب کو نیک کیا ﴿۷۲﴾

وَوَهَبْنَا لَهٗٓ اِسْحٰقَ ۭ وَيَعْقُوْبَ نَافِلَةً ۭ
وَكُلًّا جَعَلْنَا صٰلِحِيْنَ ﴿٧٢﴾

73. And We made them leaders, guiding (men) by Our Command, and We inspired them to do good deeds, to establish regular prayers, and to Give zakat and they constantly served Us (and Us only).

اور اُن کو پیشوا بنایا کہ ہمارے حکم سے ہدایت کرتے
تھے اور اُن کو نیک کام کرنے اور نماز پڑھنے اور
زکوٰۃ دینے کا حکم بھیجا اور وہ ہماری عبادت کیا
کرتے تھے ﴿۷۳﴾

وَجَعَلْنٰهُمْ اَىِٕمَّةً يَّهْدُوْنَ بِاَمْرِنَا وَ
اَوْحَيْنَآ اِلَيْهِمْ فِعْلَ الْخَيْرٰتِ وَاِقَامَ
الصَّلٰوةِ وَاِيْتَاۗءَ الزَّكٰوةِ ۚ وَكَانُوْا
لَنَا عٰبِدِيْنَ ﴿٧٣﴾

74. And to Lût, too, We gave Judgment and Knowledge, and We saved him from the town which practised abominations: truly they

اور لوط (کا قصہ یاد کرو) جب اُن کو ہم نے حکم (یعنی حکمت و
نبوت) اور علم بخشا اور اس بستی سے جہاں کے لوگ گندے کام کیا کرتے

وَلُوْطًا اٰتَيْنٰهُ حُكْمًا وَّعِلْمًا وَّنَجَّيْنٰهُ
مِنَ الْقَرْيَةِ الَّتِيْ كَانَتْ تَّعْمَلُ الْخَبٰۗىِٕثَ ۭ

were a people given to Evil, a rebellious people.

تھے بچا نکالا بیشک وہ بُرے اور بدکردار لوگ تھے ﴿۷۴﴾

إِنَّهُمْ كَانُوا قَوْمَ سَوْءٍ فَاسِقِينَ ﴿٧٤﴾

75. And We admitted him to Our Mercy: for he was one of the Righteous.

اور انہیں اپنی رحمت (کے محل) میں داخل کیا۔ کچھ شک
نہیں کہ وہ نیک کرداروں میں تھے ﴿۷۵﴾

وَأَدْخَلْنَاهُ فِي رَحْمَتِنَا ۖ إِنَّهُ مِنَ
الصَّالِحِينَ ﴿٧٥﴾

76. (Remember) Noah, when he cried (to Us) aforetime: We listened to his (prayer) and delivered him and his family from great distress.

اور نوح (کا قصہ بھی یاد کرو) جب (اس سے) پیشتر انہوں
نے ہمیں پکارا تو ہم نے ان کی دعا قبول فرمائی اور انکو اور
انکے ساتھیوں کو بڑی گھبراہٹ سے نجات دی ﴿۷۶﴾

وَنُوحًا إِذْ نَادَىٰ مِنْ قَبْلُ فَاسْتَجَبْنَا
لَهُ فَنَجَّيْنَاهُ وَأَهْلَهُ مِنَ الْكَرْبِ
الْعَظِيمِ ﴿٧٦﴾

77. We helped him against people who rejected Our Signs: truly they were a people given to Evil: so We drowned them (in the Flood) all together.

اور جو لوگ ہماری آیتوں کی تکذیب کرتے تھے اُن پر
نصرت بخشی۔ وہ بیشک بُرے لوگ تھے سو ہم نے اُن
سب کو غرق کر دیا ﴿۷۷﴾

وَنَصَرْنَاهُ مِنَ الْقَوْمِ الَّذِينَ كَذَّبُوا بِآيَاتِنَا ۚ
إِنَّهُمْ كَانُوا قَوْمَ سَوْءٍ فَأَغْرَقْنَاهُمْ
أَجْمَعِينَ ﴿٧٧﴾

78. And remember David and Solomon, when they gave judgment in the matter of the field into which the sheep of certain people had strayed by night: We did witness their judgment.

اور داؤد اور سلیمان (کا حال بھی سُن لو کہ) جب وہ ایک کھیتی کا
مقدمہ فیصل کرنے لگے جس میں کچھ لوگوں کی بکریاں رات کو چر گئی
(اور اسے روند گئی) تھیں اور ہم انکے فیصلے کے وقت موجود تھے ﴿۷۸﴾

وَدَاوُودَ وَسُلَيْمَانَ إِذْ يَحْكُمَانِ فِي
الْحَرْثِ إِذْ نَفَشَتْ فِيهِ غَنَمُ الْقَوْمِ ۚ
وَكُنَّا لِحُكْمِهِمْ شَاهِدِينَ ﴿٧٨﴾

79. To Solomon We inspired the (right) understanding of the matter: to each (of them) We gave Judgment and Knowledge; it was Our power that made the hills and the birds celebrate Our praises, with David: it was We Who did (all these things).

تو ہم نے فیصلہ (کرنے کا طریق) سلیمان کو سمجھا دیا۔ اور ہم نے دونوں کو حکم
(یعنی حکمت و نبوت) اور علم بخشا تھا اور ہم نے پہاڑوں کو داؤد کا مسخر کر دیا تھا کہ انکے
ساتھ تسبیح کرتے تھے اور جانوروں کو بھی (مسخر کر دیا تھا) اور ہم ہی (ایسا) کرنے والے تھے ﴿۷۹﴾

فَفَهَّمْنَاهَا سُلَيْمَانَ ۚ وَكُلًّا آتَيْنَا حُكْمًا
وَعِلْمًا ۚ وَسَخَّرْنَا مَعَ دَاوُودَ الْجِبَالَ
يُسَبِّحْنَ وَالطَّيْرَ ۚ وَكُنَّا فَاعِلِينَ ﴿٧٩﴾

80. It was We Who taught him the making of coats of mail for your benefit, to guard you from each other's violence: will ye then be grateful?

اور ہم نے تمہارے لئے اُن کو ایک (طرح کا) لباس بنانا بھی سکھا دیا
تاکہ تم کو لڑائی (کے ضرر) سے بچائے پس تم کو شکرگزار ہونا چاہیے ﴿۸۰﴾

وَعَلَّمْنَاهُ صَنْعَةَ لَبُوسٍ لَكُمْ لِتُحْصِنَكُمْ
مِنْ بَأْسِكُمْ ۖ فَهَلْ أَنْتُمْ شَاكِرُونَ ﴿٨٠﴾

81. (It was Our power that made) the violent (unruly) wind flow (tamely) for Solomon, to his order, to the land which We had blessed: for We do know all things.

اور ہم نے تیز ہوا سلیمان کے تابع (فرمان) کر دی تھی جو اُن کے
حکم سے اس ملک میں چلتی تھی جس میں ہم نے برکت دی تھی
(یعنی شام) اور ہم ہر چیز سے خبردار ہیں ﴿۸۱﴾

وَلِسُلَيْمَانَ الرِّيحَ عَاصِفَةً تَجْرِي بِأَمْرِهِ
إِلَى الْأَرْضِ الَّتِي بَارَكْنَا فِيهَا ۚ وَكُنَّا
بِكُلِّ شَيْءٍ عَالِمِينَ ﴿٨١﴾

82. And of Satans were some who dived for him, and did other work besides; and it was We Who guarded them.

اور دیووں (کی جماعت کو بھی اُن کے تابع کر دیا تھا کہ اُن)
میں سے بعض اُن کے لئے غوطے مارتے تھے اور اسکے سوا اور
کام بھی کرتے تھے۔ اور ہم اُن کے نگہبان تھے ﴿۸۲﴾

وَمِنَ الشَّيَاطِينِ مَنْ يَغُوصُونَ لَهُ
وَيَعْمَلُونَ عَمَلًا دُونَ ذَٰلِكَ ۖ وَكُنَّا
لَهُمْ حَافِظِينَ ﴿٨٢﴾

83. And (remember) Job, when he cried to his Lord "Truly distress has seized me, but Thou art the Most Merciful of those that are Merciful."

اور ایوب (کو یاد کرو) جب انہوں نے اپنے پروردگار سے دعا کی کہ
مجھے ایذا ہو رہی ہے اور تو سب سے بڑھ کر رحم کرنے والا ہے ﴿۸۳﴾

وَأَيُّوبَ إِذْ نَادَىٰ رَبَّهُ أَنِّي مَسَّنِيَ
الضُّرُّ وَأَنْتَ أَرْحَمُ الرَّاحِمِينَ ﴿٨٣﴾

84. So We listened to him: We removed the distress that was on him, and We restored his people to him, and doubled their number,—

تو ہم نے اُن کی دعا قبول کر لی اور جو اُن کو تکلیف تھی
وہ دُور کر دی اور اُن کو بال بچے بھی عطا فرمائے اور

فَاسْتَجَبْنَا لَهُ فَكَشَفْنَا مَا بِهِ مِنْ
ضُرٍّ ۖ وَآتَيْنَاهُ أَهْلَهُ وَمِثْلَهُمْ مَعَهُمْ

as a Grace from Ourselves, and a thing for commemoration, for all who serve Us.

اپنی مہربانی سے اُن کے ساتھ اتنے ہی اور (بخشے) اور
عبادت کرنے والوں کے لئے (یہ) نصیحت ہے ﴿۸۴﴾

رَحْمَةً مِّنْ عِنْدِنَا وَذِكْرٰى
لِلْعٰبِدِيْنَ ﴿۸۴﴾

85. And (remember) Ismã'îl Idrîs, and Zul-kifl, all (men) of constancy and patience;

اور اسمٰعیل اور ادریس اور ذوالکفل (کو بھی یاد کرو)
یہ سب صبر کرنے والے تھے ﴿۸۵﴾

وَاِسْمٰعِيْلَ وَاِدْرِيْسَ وَذَا الْكِفْلِ ؕ
كُلٌّ مِّنَ الصّٰبِرِيْنَ ﴿۸۵﴾ ۚۖ

86. We admitted them to Our Mercy: for they were of the Righteous ones.

اور ہم نے اُن کو اپنی رحمت میں داخل کیا۔ بلاشبہ وہ
نیکوکار تھے ﴿۸۶﴾

وَاَدْخَلْنٰهُمْ فِيْ رَحْمَتِنَا ؕ اِنَّهُمْ
مِّنَ الصّٰلِحِيْنَ ﴿۸۶﴾

87. And remember Zun-nûn, when he departed in wrath: he imagined that We had no power over him! but he cried through the depths of darkness, "There is no god but Thou: glory to Thee: I was indeed wrong!"

اور ذوالنون (کو یاد کرو) جب وہ (اپنی قوم سے ناراض ہو کر)
غصے کی حالت میں چل دیئے اور خیال کیا کہ ہم اُن پر قابو
نہیں پاسکیں گے آخر اندھیرے میں (خدا کو) پکارنے لگے کہ تیرے
سوا کوئی معبود نہیں۔ تو پاک ہے (اور) بیشک میں قصوروار ہوں ﴿۸۷﴾

وَذَا النُّوْنِ اِذْ ذَّهَبَ مُغَاضِبًا فَظَنَّ
اَنْ لَّنْ نَّقْدِرَ عَلَيْهِ فَنَادٰى فِي الظُّلُمٰتِ
اَنْ لَّآ اِلٰهَ اِلَّآ اَنْتَ سُبْحٰنَكَ ۖ اِنِّيْ
كُنْتُ مِنَ الظّٰلِمِيْنَ ﴿۸۷﴾ ۚۖ

88. So We listened to him: and delivered him from distress: and thus do We deliver those who have faith.

تو ہم نے انکی دعا قبول کرلی اور ان کو غم سے نجات بخشی۔ اور
ایمان والوں کو ہم اسی طرح نجات دیا کرتے ہیں ﴿۸۸﴾

فَاسْتَجَبْنَا لَهٗ ۙ وَنَجَّيْنٰهُ مِنَ الْغَمِّ ؕ
وَكَذٰلِكَ نُـْۨجِي الْمُؤْمِنِيْنَ ﴿۸۸﴾

89. And (remember) Zakarîyã, when he cried to his Lord: "O my Lord! leave me not without offspring, though Thou art the best of inheritors."

اور زکریا (کو یاد کرو) جب اُنہوں نے اپنے پروردگار کو پکارا کہ
پروردگار! مجھے اکیلا نہ چھوڑ اور تو سب سے بہتر وارث ہے ﴿۸۹﴾

وَزَكَرِيَّآ اِذْ نَادٰى رَبَّهٗ رَبِّ لَا تَذَرْنِيْ
فَرْدًا وَّاَنْتَ خَيْرُ الْوٰرِثِيْنَ ﴿۸۹﴾ ۚۖ

90. So We listened to him: and We granted him Yahyã: We cured his wife's (barrenness) for him. These (three) were ever quick in doing in good works: they used to call on Us in yearning and awe and humble themselves before Us.

تو ہم نے اُن کی پکار سن لی اور اُن کو یحیٰی بخشے اور انکی
بیوی کو اولاد کے قابل بنا دیا۔ یہ لوگ لپک لپک کر
نیکیاں کرتے اور ہمیں اُمید اور خوف سے پکارتے اور
ہمارے آگے عاجزی کیا کرتے تھے ﴿۹۰﴾

فَاسْتَجَبْنَا لَهٗ ۫ وَوَهَبْنَا لَهٗ يَحْيٰى وَ
اَصْلَحْنَا لَهٗ زَوْجَهٗ ؕ اِنَّهُمْ كَانُوْا
يُسٰرِعُوْنَ فِي الْخَيْرٰتِ وَيَدْعُوْنَنَا
رَغَبًا وَّرَهَبًا ؕ وَكَانُوْا لَنَا خٰشِعِيْنَ ﴿۹۰﴾

91. And (remember) her who guarded her chastity: We breathed into her from Our spirit, and We made her and her son a Sign for all peoples.

اور اُن (مریم) کو (بھی یاد کرو) جنہوں نے اپنی عفت کو
محفوظ رکھا۔ تو ہم نے اُن میں اپنی رُوح پھونک دی اور اُنکو
اور اُن کے بیٹے کو اہل عالم کے لئے نشانی بنا دیا ﴿۹۱﴾

وَالَّتِيْٓ اَحْصَنَتْ فَرْجَهَا فَنَفَخْنَا فِيْهَا
مِنْ رُّوْحِنَا وَجَعَلْنٰهَا وَابْنَهَآ اٰيَةً
لِّلْعٰلَمِيْنَ ﴿۹۱﴾

92. Verily, this Ummah of yours is a single Ummah and I am your Lord and Cherisher: therefore serve Me (and no other).

یہ تمہاری جماعت ایک ہی جماعت ہے اور میں تمہارا
پروردگار ہوں تو میری ہی عبادت کیا کرو ﴿۹۲﴾

اِنَّ هٰذِهٖٓ اُمَّتُكُمْ اُمَّةً وَّاحِدَةً ۖ وَّاَنَا
رَبُّكُمْ فَاعْبُدُوْنِ ﴿۹۲﴾

93. But (later generations) cut off their affair (of unity), one from another: (yet) will they all return to Us.

اور یہ لوگ اپنے معاملے میں باہم متفرق ہو گئے۔ (مگر) سب
ہماری طرف رجوع کرنے والے ہیں ﴿۹۳﴾

وَتَقَطَّعُوْٓا اَمْرَهُمْ بَيْنَهُمْ ؕ كُلٌّ اِلَيْنَا
رٰجِعُوْنَ ﴿۹۳﴾ ع ع

94. Whoever works any act of Righteousness and has Faith,— his endeavour will not be rejected: We shall record it in his favour.

جو نیک کام کریگا اور مومن بھی ہوگا تو اسکی کوشش رائیگاں
نہ جائیگی۔ اور ہم اُس کے لئے (ثواب اعمال) لکھ رہے ہیں ﴿۹۴﴾

فَمَنْ يَّعْمَلْ مِنَ الصّٰلِحٰتِ وَهُوَ مُؤْمِنٌ
فَلَا كُفْرَانَ لِسَعْيِهٖ ۚ وَاِنَّا لَهٗ كٰتِبُوْنَ ﴿۹۴﴾

95. But there is a ban on any population which We have destroyed: that they shall not return,

اور جس بستی (والوں) کو ہم نے ہلاک کر دیا محال ہے کہ (رجوع کریں) وہ رجوع نہیں کریں گے ﴿٩٥﴾ ف ١٨٩

وَحَرَامٌ عَلَىٰ قَرْيَةٍ أَهْلَكْنَاهَا أَنَّهُمْ لَا يَرْجِعُونَ ﴿٩٥﴾

96. Until the Gog and Magog (people) are let through (their barrier), and they swiftly swarm from every hill.

یہاں تک کہ یاجوج اور ماجوج کھول دیئے جائیں اور وہ ہر بلندی سے دوڑ رہے ہوں ﴿٩٦﴾

حَتَّىٰ إِذَا فُتِحَتْ يَأْجُوجُ وَمَأْجُوجُ وَهُم مِّن كُلِّ حَدَبٍ يَنسِلُونَ ﴿٩٦﴾

97. Then will the True Promise draw nigh (of fulfilment): then behold! the eyes of the Unbelievers will fixedly stare in horror: "Ah! woe to us! we were indeed heedless of this; nay; we truly did wrong!

اور (قیامت کا) سچا وعدہ قریب آجائے. تو ناگاہ کافروں کی آنکھیں کھلی کی کھلی رہ جائیں (اور کہنے لگیں کہ) ہائے شامت ہم اس (حال) سے غفلت میں رہے بلکہ ہم (اپنے حق میں) ظالم تھے ﴿٩٧﴾

وَاقْتَرَبَ الْوَعْدُ الْحَقُّ فَإِذَا هِيَ شَاخِصَةٌ أَبْصَارُ الَّذِينَ كَفَرُوا يَا وَيْلَنَا قَدْ كُنَّا فِي غَفْلَةٍ مِّنْ هَٰذَا بَلْ كُنَّا ظَالِمِينَ ﴿٩٧﴾

98. Verily ye, (Unbelievers), and the (false) gods that ye worship besides Allah, are (but) fuel for Hell! To it will ye (surely) come!

(کافرو اس روز) تم اور جن کی تم خدا کے سوا عبادت کرتے ہو دوزخ کا ایندھن ہونگے (اور تم (سب) اسمیں داخل ہو کر رہو گے ﴿٩٨﴾

إِنَّكُمْ وَمَا تَعْبُدُونَ مِن دُونِ اللَّهِ حَصَبُ جَهَنَّمَ أَنتُمْ لَهَا وَارِدُونَ ﴿٩٨﴾

99. If these had been gods, they would not have got there! But each one will abide therein.

اگر یہ لوگ (درحقیقت) معبود ہوتے تو اسمیں داخل نہ ہوتے سب اس میں ہمیشہ (جلتے) رہیں گے ﴿٩٩﴾

لَوْ كَانَ هَٰؤُلَاءِ آلِهَةً مَّا وَرَدُوهَا وَكُلٌّ فِيهَا خَالِدُونَ ﴿٩٩﴾

100. There, sobbing will be their lot, nor will they there hear (aught else).

وہاں اُن کو چلّانا ہوگا اور اس میں (کچھ) نہ سُن سکیں گے ﴿١٠٠﴾

لَهُمْ فِيهَا زَفِيرٌ وَهُمْ فِيهَا لَا يَسْمَعُونَ ﴿١٠٠﴾

101. Those for whom the Good from Us has gone before, will be removed far therefrom.

جن لوگوں کے لئے ہماری طرف سے پہلے بھلائی مقرر ہو چکی ہے وہ اس سے دور رکھے جائیں گے ﴿١٠١﴾

إِنَّ الَّذِينَ سَبَقَتْ لَهُم مِّنَّا الْحُسْنَىٰ أُولَٰئِكَ عَنْهَا مُبْعَدُونَ ﴿١٠١﴾

102. Not the slightest sound will they hear of Hell: what their souls desired, in that will they dwell.

(یہانتک کہ) اسکی آواز بھی تو نہیں سنیں گے اور جو کچھ انکا جی چاہیگا اسمیں (یعنی ہر طرح کے عیش اور لطف میں) ہمیشہ رہیں گے ﴿١٠٢﴾

لَا يَسْمَعُونَ حَسِيسَهَا وَهُمْ فِي مَا اشْتَهَتْ أَنفُسُهُمْ خَالِدُونَ ﴿١٠٢﴾

103. The Great Terror will bring them no grief: but the angels will meet them (with mutual greetings): "This is your Day,—(the Day) that ye were promised."

اُن کو (اس دن کا) بڑا بھاری خوف غمگین نہیں کرے گا. اور فرشتے اُن کو لینے آئیں گے (اور کہیں گے کہ) یہی وہ دن ہے جس کا تم سے وعدہ کیا جاتا تھا ﴿١٠٣﴾

لَا يَحْزُنُهُمُ الْفَزَعُ الْأَكْبَرُ وَتَتَلَقَّاهُمُ الْمَلَائِكَةُ هَٰذَا يَوْمُكُمُ الَّذِي كُنتُمْ تُوعَدُونَ ﴿١٠٣﴾

104. The Day that We roll up the heavens like a scroll rolled up for books (completed),—even as We produced the first Creation, so shall We produce a new one: a promise We have undertaken: truly shall We fulfil it.

جس دن ہم آسمان کو اس طرح لپیٹ لینگے جیسے خطوں کا طومار لپیٹ لیتے ہیں جس طرح ہم نے (کائنات کو) پہلے پیدا کیا تھا اسی طرح دوبارہ پیدا کر دینگے (یہ) وعدہ (ہے جسکا پورا کرنا) لازم ہے ہم (ایسا) ضرور کرنیوالے ہیں ﴿١٠٤﴾

يَوْمَ نَطْوِي السَّمَاءَ كَطَيِّ السِّجِلِّ لِلْكُتُبِ كَمَا بَدَأْنَا أَوَّلَ خَلْقٍ نُّعِيدُهُ وَعْدًا عَلَيْنَا إِنَّا كُنَّا فَاعِلِينَ ﴿١٠٤﴾

105. Before this We wrote in the Psalms, after the Message (given to Moses): "My servants, the righteous, shall inherit the earth."

اور ہم نے نصیحت (کی کتاب یعنی تورات) کے بعد زبور میں لکھ دیا تھا کہ میرے نیکوکار بندے ملک کے وارث ہوں گے ﴿١٠٥﴾

وَلَقَدْ كَتَبْنَا فِي الزَّبُورِ مِن بَعْدِ الذِّكْرِ أَنَّ الْأَرْضَ يَرِثُهَا عِبَادِيَ الصَّالِحُونَ ﴿١٠٥﴾

106. Verily in this (Qur'an) is a Message for people who would (truly) worship Allah.

عبادت کرنیوالے لوگوں کیلیئے اس میں (خدا کے حکموں کی) تبلیغ ہے ﴿١٠٦﴾

إِنَّ فِي هَٰذَا لَبَلَاغًا لِّقَوْمٍ عَابِدِينَ ﴿١٠٦﴾

SÛRA–22
AL-ḤAJJ
(INTRODUCTION)

We now come to a new series of four Sûras, dealing with the environments and methods contributing to our spiritual progress, as the last five Sûras dealt with the Messengers who came in various ways to proclaim the Truth and conquer evil. See Introduction to S. 17.

The subject-matter of this particular Sûra is concerned mainly with the spiritual implications of the Sacred House, the Pilgrimage, the Sacrifices, Striving and Fighting in defence of Truth when attacked, and other acts that make for Unselfishness and uproot Falsehood.

On the chronology of this Sûra, opinion is divided. Some parts were probably revealed in the later Makkan period, and some in Madinah. But the chronological question has no significance here.

107. We sent thee not, but as a Mercy for all creatures.
108. Say: "What has come to me by inspiration is that your God is One God: will ye therefore bow to His Will (in Islãm)?"
109. But if they turn back, say: "I have proclaimed the Message to you all alike and in truth; but I know not whether that which ye are promised is near or far.

110. "It is He Who knows what is open in speech and what ye hide (in your hearts).

111. "I know not but that it may be a trial for you, and a grant of (worldly) livelihood (to you) for a time."
112. Say: "O my Lord! judge Thou in truth!" "Our Lord Most Gracious is the One Whose assistance should be sought against the blasphemies ye utter!"

Al-Ḥajj, or The Pilgrimage

In the name of Allah, Most Gracious, Most Merciful.

1. O mankind! Fear your Lord! for the convulsion of the Hour (of Judgment) will be a thing terrible!

2. The Day ye shall see it, every mother giving suck shall forget her suckling-babe, and every pregnant female shall drop her load (unformed): thou shalt see mankind as in a drunken riot, yet not drunk: but dreadful will be the Chastisement of Allah.
3. And yet among men there are such as dispute about Allah, without knowledge, and follow every Satan obstinate in rebellion!
4. About whom (Satan) it is decreed that whoever turns to him for friendship, him will he lead astray, and he will guide him to the Chastisement of the Fire.
5. O mankind! if ye have a doubt about the Resurrection, (consider) that We created you out of dust, then out of sperm, then out of a leech-like clot, then out of a morsel

اور (اے محمدؐ) ہم نے تم کو تمام جہان کیلئے رحمت (بنا کر) بھیجا ہے ﴿١٠٧﴾
کہہ دو کہ مجھ پر (خدا کی طرف سے) یہ وحی آتی ہے کہ تم سب کا معبود
خدائے واحد ہے۔ تو تم کو چاہیئے کہ فرمانبردار ہو جاؤ ﴿١٠٨﴾
اگر یہ لوگ منہ پھیریں تو کہہ دو کہ میں نے تم سب کو یکساں (احکام
الہٰی سے) آگاہ کر دیا ہے۔ اور مجھ کو معلوم نہیں کہ جس چیز کا تم سے
وعدہ کیا جاتا ہے وہ (عنقریب آنیوالی) ہے یا (اسکا وقت) دور ہے ﴿١٠٩﴾
جو بات پکار کر کی جائے وہ اسے بھی جانتا ہے اور جو تم پوشیدہ
کرتے ہو اس سے بھی واقف ہے ﴿١١٠﴾
اور میں نہیں جانتا شاید وہ تمہارے لئے آزمائش ہو اور ایک
مدت تک (تم اس سے) فائدہ (اٹھاتے رہو) ﴿١١١﴾
(پیغمبر نے) کہا کہ اے میرے پروردگار حق کیساتھ فیصلہ کر دے اور ہمارا
پروردگار بڑا مہربان ہے اسی سے ان باتوں میں جو تم بیان کرتے ہو مدد مانگی جاتی ہے ﴿١١٢﴾

وَمَآ اَرْسَلْنٰكَ اِلَّا رَحْمَةً لِّلْعٰلَمِيْنَ ﴿١٠٧﴾
قُلْ اِنَّمَا يُوْحٰٓى اِلَيَّ اَنَّمَآ اِلٰهُكُمْ اِلٰهٌ
وَّاحِدٌ فَهَلْ اَنْتُمْ مُّسْلِمُوْنَ ﴿١٠٨﴾
فَاِنْ تَوَلَّوْا فَقُلْ اٰذَنْتُكُمْ عَلٰى سَوَآءٍ
وَاِنْ اَدْرِيْٓ اَقَرِيْبٌ اَمْ بَعِيْدٌ مَّا
تُوْعَدُوْنَ ﴿١٠٩﴾
اِنَّهٗ يَعْلَمُ الْجَهْرَ مِنَ الْقَوْلِ وَيَعْلَمُ
مَا تَكْتُمُوْنَ ﴿١١٠﴾
وَاِنْ اَدْرِيْ لَعَلَّهٗ فِتْنَةٌ لَّكُمْ وَمَتَاعٌ
اِلٰى حِيْنٍ ﴿١١١﴾
قٰلَ رَبِّ احْكُمْ بِالْحَقِّ وَرَبُّنَا الرَّحْمٰنُ
الْمُسْتَعَانُ عَلٰى مَا تَصِفُوْنَ ﴿١١٢﴾ ع

سورۂ حج مدنی ہے اور اس میں اٹھتر آیتیں اور دس رکوع ہیں

سُوْرَةُ الْحَجِّ مَدَنِيَّةٌ وَّهِيَ ثَمَانٌ وَّسَبْعُوْنَ اٰيَةً وَّعَشْرُ رُكُوْعَاتٍ

شروع خدا کا نام لے کر جو بڑا مہربان نہایت رحم والا ہے
لوگو اپنے پروردگار سے ڈرو کہ قیامت کا زلزلہ ایک
حادثہ عظیم ہے ﴿١﴾
(اے مخاطب) جس دن تو اسکو دیکھے گا (اس دن یہ حال ہو گا کہ) تمام دودھ پلانے
والی عورتیں اپنے بچوں کو بھول جائینگی۔ اور تمام حمل والیوں کے حمل گر پڑینگے
اور لوگ تجھکو متوالے نظر آئینگے مگر وہ متوالے نہیں ہونگے بلکہ (عذاب
دیکھ کر) مدہوش ہو رہے ہونگے بیشک خدا کا عذاب بڑا سخت ہے ﴿٢﴾
اور بعض لوگ ایسے ہیں جو خدا (کی شان) میں علم (و دانش) کے
بغیر جھگڑتے اور ہر شیطان سرکش کی پیروی کرتے ہیں ﴿٣﴾
جس کے بارے میں لکھ دیا گیا ہے کہ جو اسے دوست رکھے گا تو
وہ اسکو گمراہ کر دیگا اور دوزخ کے عذاب کا رستہ دکھائیگا ﴿٤﴾
لوگو اگر تم کو (مرنے کے بعد) جی اٹھنے میں کچھ شک ہو تو
ہم نے تم کو (پہلی بار بھی تو) پیدا کیا تھا (یعنی ابتدا میں)
مٹی سے پھر اس سے نطفہ بنا کر۔ پھر اس سے خون کا لوتھڑا بنا کر۔ پھر اس سے

بِسْمِ اللّٰهِ الرَّحْمٰنِ الرَّحِيْمِ
يٰٓاَيُّهَا النَّاسُ اتَّقُوْا رَبَّكُمْ اِنَّ زَلْزَلَةَ
السَّاعَةِ شَيْءٌ عَظِيْمٌ ﴿١﴾
يَوْمَ تَرَوْنَهَا تَذْهَلُ كُلُّ مُرْضِعَةٍ
عَمَّآ اَرْضَعَتْ وَتَضَعُ كُلُّ ذَاتِ حَمْلٍ
حَمْلَهَا وَتَرَى النَّاسَ سُكٰرٰى وَمَا هُمْ
بِسُكٰرٰى وَلٰكِنَّ عَذَابَ اللّٰهِ شَدِيْدٌ ﴿٢﴾
وَمِنَ النَّاسِ مَنْ يُّجَادِلُ فِي اللّٰهِ بِغَيْرِ
عِلْمٍ وَّيَتَّبِعُ كُلَّ شَيْطٰنٍ مَّرِيْدٍ ﴿٣﴾
كُتِبَ عَلَيْهِ اَنَّهٗ مَنْ تَوَلَّاهُ فَاَنَّهٗ
يُضِلُّهٗ وَيَهْدِيْهِ اِلٰى عَذَابِ السَّعِيْرِ ﴿٤﴾
يٰٓاَيُّهَا النَّاسُ اِنْ كُنْتُمْ فِيْ رَيْبٍ مِّنَ
الْبَعْثِ فَاِنَّا خَلَقْنٰكُمْ مِّنْ تُرَابٍ ثُمَّ
مِنْ نُّطْفَةٍ ثُمَّ مِنْ عَلَقَةٍ ثُمَّ مِنْ مُّضْغَةٍ

مُّخَلَّقَةٍ وَّغَيْرِ مُخَلَّقَةٍ لِّنُبَيِّنَ لَكُمْ ۚ وَنُقِرُّ
فِي الْأَرْحَامِ مَا نَشَاءُ إِلَىٰ أَجَلٍ مُّسَمًّى
ثُمَّ نُخْرِجُكُمْ طِفْلًا ثُمَّ لِتَبْلُغُوا أَشُدَّكُمْ ۖ
وَمِنكُم مَّن يُتَوَفَّىٰ وَمِنكُم مَّن يُرَدُّ
إِلَىٰ أَرْذَلِ الْعُمُرِ لِكَيْلَا يَعْلَمَ مِن بَعْدِ
عِلْمٍ شَيْئًا ۚ وَتَرَى الْأَرْضَ هَامِدَةً
فَإِذَا أَنزَلْنَا عَلَيْهَا الْمَاءَ اهْتَزَّتْ وَ
رَبَتْ وَأَنبَتَتْ مِن كُلِّ زَوْجٍ بَهِيجٍ ٥
ذَٰلِكَ بِأَنَّ اللَّهَ هُوَ الْحَقُّ وَأَنَّهُ يُحْيِي
الْمَوْتَىٰ وَأَنَّهُ عَلَىٰ كُلِّ شَيْءٍ قَدِيرٌ ٦
وَأَنَّ السَّاعَةَ آتِيَةٌ لَّا رَيْبَ فِيهَا
وَأَنَّ اللَّهَ يَبْعَثُ مَن فِي الْقُبُورِ ٧
وَمِنَ النَّاسِ مَن يُجَادِلُ فِي اللَّهِ بِغَيْرِ
عِلْمٍ وَلَا هُدًى وَلَا كِتَابٍ مُّنِيرٍ ٨
ثَانِيَ عِطْفِهِ لِيُضِلَّ عَن سَبِيلِ اللَّهِ ۖ لَهُ
فِي الدُّنْيَا خِزْيٌ ۖ وَنُذِيقُهُ يَوْمَ الْقِيَامَةِ
عَذَابَ الْحَرِيقِ ٩
ذَٰلِكَ بِمَا قَدَّمَتْ يَدَاكَ وَأَنَّ اللَّهَ لَيْسَ
بِظَلَّامٍ لِّلْعَبِيدِ ١٠ ع
وَمِنَ النَّاسِ مَن يَعْبُدُ اللَّهَ عَلَىٰ
حَرْفٍ ۖ فَإِنْ أَصَابَهُ خَيْرٌ اطْمَأَنَّ
بِهِ ۖ وَإِنْ أَصَابَتْهُ فِتْنَةٌ انقَلَبَ عَلَىٰ
وَجْهِهِ خَسِرَ الدُّنْيَا وَالْآخِرَةَ ۚ ذَٰلِكَ
هُوَ الْخُسْرَانُ الْمُبِينُ ١١
يَدْعُو مِن دُونِ اللَّهِ مَا لَا يَضُرُّهُ وَمَا
لَا يَنفَعُهُ ۚ ذَٰلِكَ هُوَ الضَّلَالُ الْبَعِيدُ ١٢
يَدْعُو لَمَن ضَرُّهُ أَقْرَبُ مِن نَّفْعِهِ ۚ

بوٹی بناکر جسکی بناوٹ کامل بھی ہوتی ہے اور ناقص بھی تاکہ تم پر (اپنی خالقیت)
ظاہر کردیں۔ اور ہم جسکو چاہتے ہیں ایک میعاد مقرر تک پیٹ میں ٹھہرائے
رکھتے ہیں۔ پھر تمکو بچہ بناکر نکالتے ہیں۔ پھر تم جوانی کو پہنچتے ہو۔ ف ۱۹۰
اور بعض (قبل از پیری) مرجاتے ہیں۔ اور بعض (شیخ فانی ہوجاتے
اور بڑھاپے کی) نہایت خراب عمر کی طرف لوٹائے جاتے ہیں کہ
(بہت کچھ) جاننے کے بعد بالکل بے علم ہوجاتے ہیں۔ اور (اے دیکھنے والے)
تو دیکھتا ہے (کہ ایک وقت میں) زمین خشک (پڑی ہوتی ہے) پھر جب ہم اس پر مینہ
برساتے ہیں تو وہ شاداب ہوجاتی اور اُبھرنے لگتی ہے اور طرح طرح کی بارونق چیزیں اُگاتی ہے ۵
اِن قدرتوں سے ظاہر ہے کہ خدا ہی (قادر مطلق ہے جو) برحق ہے۔ اور یہ کہ
وہ مُردوں کو زندہ کردیتا ہے اور یہ کہ وہ ہر چیز پر قدرت رکھتا ہے ۶
اور یہ کہ قیامت آنے والی ہے۔ اس میں کچھ شک نہیں اور یہ کہ خدا
سب لوگوں کو جو قبروں میں ہیں جلا اُٹھائے گا ۷
اور لوگوں میں کوئی ایسا بھی ہے جو خدا (کی شان) میں بغیر
علم (ودانش) کے اور بغیر ہدایت کے اور بغیر کتاب روشن کے جھگڑتا ہے ۸
(اور تکبر سے) گردن موڑ لیتا ہے تاکہ (لوگوں کو) خدا کے رستے سے
گمراہ کردے۔ اس کیلئے دنیا میں ذلت ہے۔ اور قیامت کے دن
ہم اسے عذاب (آتش) سوزاں کا مزا چکھائیں گے ۹
(اے سرکش) یہ اُس (کفر) کی سزا ہے جو تیرے ہاتھوں نے آگے
بھیجا ہے اور خدا اپنے بندوں پر ظلم کرنے والا نہیں ۱۰
اور لوگوں میں بعض ایسا بھی ہے جو کنارے پر (کھڑا ہوکر) خدا کی
عبادت کرتا ہے۔ اگر اس کو کوئی (دنیاوی) فائدہ پہنچے تو
اسکے سبب مطمئن ہوجائے اور اگر کوئی آفت پڑے تو منہ کے بل
لَوٹ جائے (یعنی پھر کافر ہوجائے) اُس نے دنیا میں بھی
نقصان اٹھایا اور آخرت میں بھی یہی تو نقصان صریح ہے ۱۱
یہ خدا کے سوا ایسی چیز کو پکارتا ہے جو نہ اُسے نقصان پہنچائے
اور نہ فائدہ دے سکے یہی تو پرلے درجے کی گمراہی ہے ۱۲
(بلکہ) ایسے شخص کو پکارتا ہے جس کا نقصان فائدہ سے زیادہ

of flesh, partly formed and partly unformed, in order that We may manifest (Our power) to you; and We cause whom We will to rest in the wombs for an appointed term, then do We bring you out as babes, then (foster you) that ye may reach your age of full strength; and some of you are called to die, and some are sent back to the feeblest old age, so that they know nothing after having known (much). And (further), thou seest the earth barren and lifeless, but when We pour down rain on it, it is stirred (to life), it swells, and it puts forth every kind of beautiful growth (in pairs).

6. This is so, because Allah is the Reality: it is He Who gives life to the dead, and it is He Who has power over all things.

7. And verily the Hour will come: there can be no doubt about it, or about (the fact) that Allah will raise up all who are in the graves.

8. Yet there is among men such a one as disputes about Allah, without knowledge, without guidance, and without a Book of Enlightenment,—

9. (Disdainfully) bending his side, in order to lead (men) astray from the Path of Allah: for him there is disgrace in this life, and on the Day of Judgment We shall make him taste the chastisement of burning (Fire).

10. (It will be said): "This is because of the deeds which thy hands sent forth, for verily Allah is not unjust to His servants."

11. There are among men some who serve Allah, as it were, on the verge: if good befalls them, they are, therewith, well content; but if a trial comes to them, they turn on their faces: they lose both this world and the Hereafter: that is indeed the manifest loss.

12. They call on such deities, besides Allah, as can neither hurt nor profit them: that is straying far indeed (from the Way)!

13. (Perhaps) they call on one whose hurt is nearer than his profit:

evil, indeed, is the patron, and evil the companion (for help)!

14. Verily Allah will admit those who believe and work righteous deeds, to Gardens, beneath which rivers flow: for Allah carries out all that He desires.

15. If any think that Allah will not help him (His Messenger) in this world and the Hereafter, let him stretch out a rope to the ceiling and cut (himself) off: then let him see whether his plan will remove that which enrages (him)!

16. Thus have We sent down Clear Signs; and verily Allah doth guide whom He will!

17. Those who believe (in the Qur'an), those who follow the Jewish (scriptures), and the Sabians, Christians, Magians, and Polytheists,— Allah will judge between them on the Day of Judgment: for Allah is witness of all things.

18. Seest thou not that to Allah prostrate all things that are in the heavens and on earth,— the sun, the moon, the stars; the hills, the trees, the animals; and a great number among mankind? But a great number are (also) such as unto whom the Chastisement is justly due. And such as Allah shall disgrace,— none can raise to honour: for Allah carries out all that He wills.

19. These two antagonists dispute with each other about their Lord: but those who deny (their Lord),—for them will be cut out a garment of Fire: over their heads will be poured out boiling water.

20. With it will be melted what is within their bodies, as well as (their) skins.

21. In addition there will be maces of iron (to punish) them.

22. Every time they wish to get away therefrom, from anguish, they

قریب ہے۔ ایسا دوست بھی بُرا اور ایسا ہم صحبت بھی بُرا (۱۳)
جو لوگ ایمان لائے اور عمل نیک کرتے رہے خدا ان کو بہشتوں
میں داخل کریگا جن کے نیچے نہریں چل رہی ہیں۔ کچھ
شک نہیں کہ خدا جو چاہتا ہے کرتا ہے (۱۴)
جو شخص یہ گمان کرتا ہو کہ خدا اس کو دنیا اور آخرت میں
مدد نہیں دیگا تو اُس کو چاہیئے کہ اُوپر کی طرف (یعنی اپنے گھر
کی چھت میں) ایک رسی باندھے پھر (اس سے اپنا) گلا گھونٹ لے
پھر دیکھے کہ آیا یہ تدبیر اسکے غصے کو دُور کر دیتی ہے (۱۵)
اور اسی طرح ہم نے اس قرآن کو اتارا ہے (جس کی تمام) باتیں کھلی
ہوئی (ہیں) اور یہ (یاد رکھو) کہ خدا جسکو چاہتا ہے ہدایت دیتا ہے (۱۶)
جو لوگ مومن (یعنی مسلمان) ہیں اور جو یہودی ہیں اور
ستارہ پرست اور عیسائی اور مجوسی اور مشرک خدا ان
(سب) میں قیامت کے دن فیصلہ کر دے گا بیشک
خدا ہر چیز سے باخبر ہے (۱۷)
کیا تم نے نہیں دیکھا کہ جو (مخلوق) آسمانوں میں ہے
اور جو زمین میں ہے اور سورج اور چاند اور ستارے
اور پہاڑ اور درخت اور چارپائے اور بہت
سے انسان خدا کو سجدہ کرتے ہیں۔
اور بہت سے ایسے ہیں جن پر عذاب ثابت ہو چکا ہے۔ اور
جس شخص کو خدا ذلیل کرے اسکو کوئی عزت دینے والا نہیں
بے شک خدا جو چاہتا ہے کرتا ہے (۱۸)
یہ دو (فریق) ایک دوسرے کے دشمن اپنے پروردگار (کے بارے)
میں جھگڑتے ہیں۔ تو جو کافر ہیں اُن کیلئے آگ کے کپڑے قطع
کئے جائینگے۔ (اور) انکے سروں پر جلتا ہوا پانی ڈالا جائے گا (۱۹)
اس سے اُنکے پیٹ کے اندر کی چیزیں اور کھالیں گل جائینگی (۲۰)
اور اُن (کے مارنے ٹھوکنے) کیلئے لوہے کے ہتھوڑے ہونگے (۲۱)
جب وہ چاہیں گے کہ اس رنج (و تکلیف) کی وجہ سے دوزخ سے نکل جائیں

لَبِئْسَ الْمَوْلٰى وَلَبِئْسَ الْعَشِيْرُ ﴿١٣﴾
اِنَّ اللّٰهَ يُدْخِلُ الَّذِيْنَ اٰمَنُوْا وَعَمِلُوا
الصّٰلِحٰتِ جَنّٰتٍ تَجْرِيْ مِنْ تَحْتِهَا
الْاَنْهٰرُ ؕ اِنَّ اللّٰهَ يَفْعَلُ مَا يُرِيْدُ ﴿١٤﴾
مَنْ كَانَ يَظُنُّ اَنْ لَّنْ يَّنْصُرَهُ اللّٰهُ
فِي الدُّنْيَا وَالْاٰخِرَةِ فَلْيَمْدُدْ بِسَبَبٍ
اِلَى السَّمَآءِ ثُمَّ لْيَقْطَعْ فَلْيَنْظُرْ هَلْ
يُذْهِبَنَّ كَيْدُهٗ مَا يَغِيْظُ ﴿١٥﴾
وَكَذٰلِكَ اَنْزَلْنٰهُ اٰيٰتٍۭ بَيِّنٰتٍ ۙ وَّاَنَّ
اللّٰهَ يَهْدِيْ مَنْ يُّرِيْدُ ﴿١٦﴾
اِنَّ الَّذِيْنَ اٰمَنُوْا وَالَّذِيْنَ هَادُوْا وَ
الصّٰبِـِٔيْنَ وَالنَّصٰرٰى وَالْمَجُوْسَ وَ
الَّذِيْنَ اَشْرَكُوْٓا ۖ اِنَّ اللّٰهَ يَفْصِلُ بَيْنَهُمْ
يَوْمَ الْقِيٰمَةِ ؕ اِنَّ اللّٰهَ عَلٰى كُلِّ شَيْءٍ شَهِيْدٌ ﴿١٧﴾
اَلَمْ تَرَ اَنَّ اللّٰهَ يَسْجُدُ لَهٗ مَنْ فِي
السَّمٰوٰتِ وَمَنْ فِي الْاَرْضِ وَالشَّمْسُ
وَالْقَمَرُ وَالنُّجُوْمُ وَالْجِبَالُ وَالشَّجَرُ
وَالدَّوَآبُّ وَكَثِيْرٌ مِّنَ النَّاسِ ؕ
وَكَثِيْرٌ حَقَّ عَلَيْهِ الْعَذَابُ ؕ وَمَنْ
يُّهِنِ اللّٰهُ فَمَا لَهٗ مِنْ مُّكْرِمٍ ؕ اِنَّ اللّٰهَ
يَفْعَلُ مَا يَشَآءُ ۩ ﴿١٨﴾ السجدة
هٰذٰنِ خَصْمٰنِ اخْتَصَمُوْا فِيْ رَبِّهِمْ ۫
فَالَّذِيْنَ كَفَرُوْا قُطِّعَتْ لَهُمْ ثِيَابٌ مِّنْ
نَّارٍ ؕ يُصَبُّ مِنْ فَوْقِ رُءُوْسِهِمُ الْحَمِيْمُ ﴿١٩﴾
يُصْهَرُ بِهٖ مَا فِيْ بُطُوْنِهِمْ وَالْجُلُوْدُ ﴿٢٠﴾
وَلَهُمْ مَّقَامِعُ مِنْ حَدِيْدٍ ﴿٢١﴾
كُلَّمَآ اَرَادُوْٓا اَنْ يَّخْرُجُوْا مِنْهَا مِنْ غَمٍّ

will be forced back therein, and (it will be said). "Taste ye the Chastisement of Burning!"

23. Allah will admit those who believe and work righteous deeds, to Gardens beneath which rivers flow: they shall be adorned therein with bracelets of gold and pearls; and their garments there will be of silk.

24. For they have been guided (in this life) to the purest of speeches; they have been guided to the Path of Him Who is Worthy of (all) Praise.

25. As to those who have rejected (Allah), and would keep back (men) from the Way of Allah, and from the Sacred Mosque, which We have made (open) to (all) men— equal is the dweller there and the visitor from the country— and any whose purpose therein is profanity wrongfully them will We cause to taste of a most grievous Chastisement.

26. Behold! We pointed the site, to Abraham, of the (Sacred) House, (saying): "Associate not anything (in worship) with Me; and sanctify My House for those who compass it round, or stand up, or bow, or prostrate themselves (therein in prayer).

27. "And proclaim the Pilgrimage among men: they will come to thee on foot and (mounted) on every camel, lean (on account of journeys) through deep and distant mountain highways;

28. "That they may witness the benefits (provided) for them, and celebrate the name of Allah, through the Days appointed, over the cattle which He has provided for them (for sacrifice): then eat ye thereof and feed the distressed ones in want.

29. "Then let them complete the rites prescribed for them, fulfil their vows, and (again) circumambulate the Ancient House."

30. Such (is the Pilgrimage): whoever honours the sacred rites of Allah, for him it is good in the sight of his Lord. Lawful to you (forfood

تو پھر اسی میں لوٹا دیئے جائینگے اور کہا جائیگا کہ جلنے کے عذاب کا مزا چکھتے رہو (۲۲)
جو لوگ ایمان لائے اور عمل نیک کرتے رہے خدا اُن کو بہشتوں میں
داخل کریگا جن کے تلے نہریں بہ رہی ہیں۔ وہاں اُن کو
سونے کے کنگن پہنائے جائینگے اور موتی۔ اور وہاں اُن کا
لباس ریشمی ہوگا (۲۳)
اور اُن کو پاکیزہ کلام کی ہدایت کی گئی اور (خدائے) حمید
کی راہ بتائی گئی (۲۴)
جو لوگ کافر ہیں اور (لوگوں کو) خدا کے رستے سے اور
مسجد محترم سے جسے ہم نے لوگوں کیلئے یکساں (عبادت گاہ)
بنایا ہے روکتے ہیں خواہ وہ وہاں کے رہنے والے ہوں یا باہر سے
آنے والے۔ اور جو اس میں شرارت سے کجروی (و کفر) کرنا چاہے
اُس کو ہم درد دینے والے عذاب کا مزہ چکھائینگے (۲۵)
اور (ایک وقت تھا) جب ہم نے ابراہیم کے لئے خانہ کعبہ کو مقام
مقرر کیا (اور ارشاد فرمایا) کہ میرے ساتھ کسی چیز کو شریک
نہ کیجو اور طواف کرنے والوں اور قیام کرنیوالوں اور رکوع کرنے
والوں (اور) سجدہ کرنیوالوں کیلئے میرے گھر کو صاف رکھا کرو (۲۶)
اور لوگوں میں حج کے لئے ندا کر دو کہ تمہاری طرف پیدل اور
دُبلے دُبلے اونٹوں پر جو دور (دراز) رستوں سے چلے
آتے ہوں (سوار ہوکر) چلے آئیں (۲۷)
تاکہ اپنے فائدے کے کاموں کے لئے حاضر ہوں۔ اور (قربانی
کے) ایام معلوم میں چہار پایاں مویشی (کے ذبح کے وقت)
جو خدا نے اُن کو دیئے ہیں اُن پر خدا کا نام لیں۔ اس میں سے
تم خود بھی کھاؤ اور فقیر درماندہ کو بھی کھلاؤ (۲۸)
پھر چاہیے کہ لوگ اپنا میل کچیل دور کریں اور نذریں پوری
کریں اور خانہ قدیم (یعنی بیت اللہ) کا طواف کریں (۲۹)
یہ (ہمارا حکم ہے) اور جو شخص ادب کی چیزوں کی جو خدا نے مقرر کی
ہیں عظمت رکھے تو یہ پروردگار کے نزدیک اسکے حق میں بہتر ہے

أُعِيدُوا فِيهَا وَذُوقُوا عَذَابَ الْحَرِيقِ ﴿٢٢﴾
إِنَّ اللَّهَ يُدْخِلُ الَّذِينَ آمَنُوا وَعَمِلُوا
الصَّالِحَاتِ جَنَّاتٍ تَجْرِي مِنْ تَحْتِهَا
الْأَنْهَارُ يُحَلَّوْنَ فِيهَا مِنْ أَسَاوِرَ مِنْ
ذَهَبٍ وَلُؤْلُؤًا وَلِبَاسُهُمْ فِيهَا حَرِيرٌ ﴿٢٣﴾
وَهُدُوا إِلَى الطَّيِّبِ مِنَ الْقَوْلِ
وَهُدُوا إِلَىٰ صِرَاطِ الْحَمِيدِ ﴿٢٤﴾
إِنَّ الَّذِينَ كَفَرُوا وَيَصُدُّونَ عَنْ
سَبِيلِ اللَّهِ وَالْمَسْجِدِ الْحَرَامِ الَّذِي
جَعَلْنَاهُ لِلنَّاسِ سَوَاءً الْعَاكِفُ فِيهِ
وَالْبَادِ وَمَنْ يُرِدْ فِيهِ بِإِلْحَادٍ بِظُلْمٍ
نُذِقْهُ مِنْ عَذَابٍ أَلِيمٍ ﴿٢٥﴾
وَإِذْ بَوَّأْنَا لِإِبْرَاهِيمَ مَكَانَ الْبَيْتِ
أَنْ لَا تُشْرِكْ بِي شَيْئًا وَطَهِّرْ بَيْتِيَ
لِلطَّائِفِينَ وَالْقَائِمِينَ وَالرُّكَّعِ
السُّجُودِ ﴿٢٦﴾
وَأَذِّنْ فِي النَّاسِ بِالْحَجِّ يَأْتُوكَ رِجَالًا
وَعَلَىٰ كُلِّ ضَامِرٍ يَأْتِينَ مِنْ كُلِّ
فَجٍّ عَمِيقٍ ﴿٢٧﴾
لِيَشْهَدُوا مَنَافِعَ لَهُمْ وَيَذْكُرُوا اسْمَ
اللَّهِ فِي أَيَّامٍ مَعْلُومَاتٍ عَلَىٰ مَا رَزَقَهُمْ
مِنْ بَهِيمَةِ الْأَنْعَامِ فَكُلُوا مِنْهَا وَ
أَطْعِمُوا الْبَائِسَ الْفَقِيرَ ﴿٢٨﴾
ثُمَّ لْيَقْضُوا تَفَثَهُمْ وَلْيُوفُوا نُذُورَهُمْ
وَلْيَطَّوَّفُوا بِالْبَيْتِ الْعَتِيقِ ﴿٢٩﴾
ذَٰلِكَ وَمَنْ يُعَظِّمْ حُرُمَاتِ اللَّهِ فَهُوَ
خَيْرٌ لَهُ عِنْدَ رَبِّهِ وَأُحِلَّتْ لَكُمُ الْأَنْعَامُ

in Pilgrimage) are cattle, except those mentioned to you (as exceptions): so shun the abomination of idols, and shun the word that is false,—
31. Being true in faith to Allah, and never assigning partners to Him: if anyone assigns partners to Allah, he is as if he had fallen from heaven and been snatched up by birds, or the wind had swooped (like a bird on its prey) and thrown him into a far-distant place.
32. Such (is his state): and whoever holds in honour the Rites of Allah, (in the sacrifice of animals), such (honour) should come truly from piety of heart.
33. In them ye have benefits for a term appointed: in the end their place of sacrifice is near the Ancient House.
34. To every people did We appoint rites (of sacrifice), that they might celebrate the name of Allah over the sustenance He gave them from animals (fit for food). But your God is One God: submit then your wills to Him (in Islam): and give thou the good news to those who humble themselves,—
35. To those whose hearts, when Allah is mentioned, are filled with fear, who show patient perseverance over their afflictions, keep up regular prayer, and spend (in charity) out of what We have bestowed upon them.
36. The sacrificial camels We have made for you as among the Signs from Allah: in them is (much) good for you: then pronounce the name of Allah over them as they line up (for sacrifice): when they are down on their sides (after slaughter), eat ye thereof, and feed such as (beg not but) live in contentment, and such as beg with due humility: thus have We made animals subject to you, that ye may be grateful.
37. It is not their meat nor their blood, that reaches Allah: it is your piety that reaches Him: He has thus made them subject to you, that ye may glorify Allah for His guidance to you: and proclaim the Good News to all who do good.
38. Verily Allah will defend (from ill) those who believe: verily, Allah

اور تمہارے لئے مویشی حلال کر دیئے گئے ہیں سوائے انکے جو تمہیں پڑھ کر
سنائے جاتے ہیں. تو بتوں کی پلیدی سے بچو اور جھوٹی بات سے اجتناب کرو (۳۰)
صرف ایک خدا کے ہوکر اور اس کے ساتھ شریک نہ ٹھیرا کر
اور جو شخص (کسی کو) خدا کے ساتھ شریک مقرر کرے تو وہ گویا
ایسا ہے جیسے آسمان سے گر پڑے پھر اسکو پرندے اُچک
لے جائیں یا ہوا کسی دُور جگہ اُڑا کر پھینک دے (۳۱)
یہ (ہمارا حکم ہے) اور جو شخص ادب کی چیزوں کی جو خدا نے مقرر
کی ہیں عظمت رکھے تو یہ (فعل) دلوں کی پرہیزگاری میں سے ہے (۳۲)
ان میں ایک وقت مقرر تک تمہارے لئے فائدے ہیں پھر ان کو
خانۂ قدیم (یعنی بیت اللہ) تک پہنچانا (اور ذبح ہونا) ہے (۳۳)
اور ہم نے ہر ایک اُمت کے لئے قربانی کا طریق مقرر کر دیا ہے
تاکہ جو مویشی چارپائے خدا نے اُن کو دیئے ہیں (اُن کے ذبح
کرنے کے وقت) اُن پر خدا کا نام لیں سو تمہارا معبود ایک ہی ہے
تو اسی کے فرمانبردار ہو جاؤ. اور عاجزی کرنیوالوں کو خوشخبری سنا دو (۳۴)
یہ وہ لوگ ہیں کہ جب خدا کا نام لیا جاتا ہے تو انکے دل ڈر جاتے ہیں
اور (جب) اُن پر مصیبت پڑتی ہے تو صبر کرتے ہیں اور نماز آداب سے پڑھتے
ہیں اور جو (مال) ہمنے انکو عطا فرمایا ہے اس میں سے (نیک کاموں میں) خرچ کرتے ہیں (۳۵)
اور قربانی کے اونٹوں کو بھی ہم نے تمہارے لئے شعائر خدا (والے) مقرر
کیا ہے. ان میں تمہارے لئے فائدے ہیں تو (قربانی کرنیکے وقت)
قطار باندھ کر اُن پر خدا کا نام لو. جب پہلو کے بل گر پڑیں تو ان
میں سے کھاؤ اور قناعت سے بیٹھ رہنے والوں اور سوال کرنیوالوں کو بھی کھلاؤ
اس طرح ہمنے انکو تمہارے زیر فرمان کر دیا ہے تاکہ تم شکر کرو (۳۶)
خدا تک نہ اُن کا گوشت پہنچتا ہے اور نہ خون. بلکہ اس تک
تمہاری پرہیزگاری پہنچتی ہے. اسی طرح خدا نے اُن کو تمہارا
مسخر کر دیا ہے تاکہ اس بات کے بدلے کہ اس نے تمکو ہدایت بخشی ہے
اُسے بزرگی سے یاد کرو. اور (اے پیغمبر) نیکوکاروں کو خوشخبری سنا دو (۳۷)
خدا تو مومنوں سے اُنکے دشمنوں کو ہٹاتا رہتا ہے. بیشک خدا

إِلَّا مَا يُتْلَىٰ عَلَيْكُمْ فَاجْتَنِبُوا الرِّجْسَ مِنَ
الْأَوْثَانِ وَاجْتَنِبُوا قَوْلَ الزُّورِ ﴿٣٠﴾
حُنَفَاءَ لِلَّهِ غَيْرَ مُشْرِكِينَ بِهِ ۚ وَمَنْ
يُشْرِكْ بِاللَّهِ فَكَأَنَّمَا خَرَّ مِنَ السَّمَاءِ
فَتَخْطَفُهُ الطَّيْرُ أَوْ تَهْوِي بِهِ الرِّيحُ
فِي مَكَانٍ سَحِيقٍ ﴿٣١﴾
ذَٰلِكَ ۖ وَمَنْ يُعَظِّمْ شَعَائِرَ اللَّهِ فَإِنَّهَا
مِنْ تَقْوَى الْقُلُوبِ ﴿٣٢﴾
لَكُمْ فِيهَا مَنَافِعُ إِلَىٰ أَجَلٍ مُسَمًّى ثُمَّ
مَحِلُّهَا إِلَى الْبَيْتِ الْعَتِيقِ ﴿٣٣﴾
وَلِكُلِّ أُمَّةٍ جَعَلْنَا مَنْسَكًا لِيَذْكُرُوا
اسْمَ اللَّهِ عَلَىٰ مَا رَزَقَهُمْ مِنْ بَهِيمَةِ
الْأَنْعَامِ ۗ فَإِلَٰهُكُمْ إِلَٰهٌ وَاحِدٌ فَلَهُ أَسْلِمُوا ۗ
وَبَشِّرِ الْمُخْبِتِينَ ﴿٣٤﴾
الَّذِينَ إِذَا ذُكِرَ اللَّهُ وَجِلَتْ قُلُوبُهُمْ
وَالصَّابِرِينَ عَلَىٰ مَا أَصَابَهُمْ وَالْمُقِيمِي
الصَّلَاةِ وَمِمَّا رَزَقْنَاهُمْ يُنْفِقُونَ ﴿٣٥﴾
وَالْبُدْنَ جَعَلْنَاهَا لَكُمْ مِنْ شَعَائِرِ اللَّهِ
لَكُمْ فِيهَا خَيْرٌ ۖ فَاذْكُرُوا اسْمَ اللَّهِ
عَلَيْهَا صَوَافَّ ۖ فَإِذَا وَجَبَتْ جُنُوبُهَا
فَكُلُوا مِنْهَا وَأَطْعِمُوا الْقَانِعَ وَالْمُعْتَرَّ ۚ
كَذَٰلِكَ سَخَّرْنَاهَا لَكُمْ لَعَلَّكُمْ تَشْكُرُونَ ﴿٣٦﴾
لَنْ يَنَالَ اللَّهَ لُحُومُهَا وَلَا دِمَاؤُهَا
وَلَٰكِنْ يَنَالُهُ التَّقْوَىٰ مِنْكُمْ ۚ كَذَٰلِكَ
سَخَّرَهَا لَكُمْ لِتُكَبِّرُوا اللَّهَ عَلَىٰ مَا هَدَاكُمْ ۗ
وَبَشِّرِ الْمُحْسِنِينَ ﴿٣٧﴾
إِنَّ اللَّهَ يُدَافِعُ عَنِ الَّذِينَ آمَنُوا ۗ إِنَّ

loveth not any that is unfaithful, ungrateful.

39. To those against whom war is made, permission is given to (fight), because they are wronged;— and verily, Allah is Most Powerful for their aid;—

40. (They are those who have been expelled from their homes in defiance of right,— (for no cause) except that they say, "Our Lord is Allah". Did not Allah check one set of people by means of another, there would surely have been pulled down monasteries, churches, synagogues, and mosques, in which the name of Allah is commemorated in abundant measure. Allah will certainly aid those who aid His (cause);— for verily Allah is Full of strength, Exalted in Might, (Able to enforce His Will).

41. (They are) those who, if We establish them in the land, establish regular prayer and give zakat, enjoin the right and forbid wrong: with Allah rests the end (and decision) of (all) affairs.

42. If they disbelieve you so did the Peoples before them (with their Prophets),— the People of Noah, and 'Ad and Thamûd;

43. And those of Abraham and Lût;

44. And the Companions of the Madyan people; and Moses was rejected (in the same way). But I granted respite to the Unbelievers, and (only) after that did I punish them: but how (terrible) was My punishment (of them)!

45. How many populations have We destroyed, which were given to wrong-doing? They tumbled down on their roofs. And how many wells are lying idle and neglected, and castles lofty and well-built?

46. Do they not travel through the land, so that their hearts (and minds) may thus learn wisdom and their ears may thus learn to hear? Truly it is not the eyes that are blind, but the hearts which are in their breasts.

کسی خیانت کرنیوالے اور کفرانِ نعمت کرنیوالے کو دوست نہیں رکھتا ﴿۳۸﴾
جن مسلمانوں سے (خواہ مخواہ) لڑائی کی جاتی ہے اُنکو اجازت ہے (کہ وہ بھی لڑیں)
کیونکہ اُن پر ظلم ہو رہا ہے۔ اور خدا (اُنکی مدد کریگا وہ) یقیناً اُنکی مدد پر قادر ہے ﴿۳۹﴾
یہ وہ لوگ ہیں کہ اپنے گھروں سے ناحق نکال دیئے گئے (انہوں
نے کچھ قصور نہیں کیا)، ہاں یہ کہتے ہیں کہ ہمارا پروردگار خدا ہے
اور اگر خدا لوگوں کو ایک دوسرے سے نہ ہٹاتا رہتا تو (راہبوں
کے) صومعے اور (عیسائیوں کے) گرجے اور (یہودیوں کے)
عبادت خانے اور (مسلمانوں کی) مسجدیں جن میں خدا کا بہت سا
ذکر کیا جاتا ہے گرائی جا چکی ہوتیں۔ اور جو شخص خدا کی مدد کرتا ہے
خدا اُسکی ضرور مدد کرتا ہے۔ بیشک خدا توانا اور غالب ہے ﴿۴۰﴾
یہ وہ لوگ ہیں کہ اگر ہم اُن کو ملک میں دسترس دیں تو
نماز پڑھیں اور زکوٰۃ ادا کریں اور نیک کام کرنیکا حکم دیں
اور بُرے کاموں سے منع کریں اور سب کاموں کا انجام
خدا ہی کے اختیار میں ہے ﴿۴۱﴾
اور اگر یہ لوگ تم کو جھٹلاتے ہیں تو اُن سے پہلے نوح کی قوم
اور عاد اور ثمود بھی (اپنے پیغمبروں کو) جھٹلا چکے ہیں ﴿۴۲﴾
اور قوم ابراہیم اور قوم لوط بھی ﴿۴۳﴾
اور مدین کے رہنے والے بھی۔ اور موسیٰ بھی تو جھٹلائے جا چکے
ہیں لیکن میں کافروں کو مہلت دیتا رہا پھر اُن کو پکڑ لیا۔
تو (دیکھ لو کہ) میرا عذاب کیسا (سخت) تھا ﴿۴۴﴾
اور بہت سی بستیاں ہیں کہ ہم نے اُن کو تباہ کر ڈالا کہ وہ
نافرمان تھیں سو وہ اپنی چھتوں پر گری پڑی ہیں۔ اور
(بہت سے) کنوئیں بیکار اور (بہت سے) محل ویران (پڑے ہیں) ﴿۴۵﴾
کیا ان لوگوں نے ملک میں سیر نہیں کی تاکہ اُنکے دل (ایسے)
ہوتے کہ اُن سے سمجھ سکتے اور کان (ایسے) ہوتے کہ اُن
سے سن سکتے۔ بات یہ ہے کہ آنکھیں اندھی نہیں ہوتیں بلکہ دل
جو سینوں میں ہیں (وہ) اندھے ہوتے ہیں ﴿۴۶﴾

اللّٰهَ لَا يُحِبُّ كُلَّ خَوَّانٍ كَفُوْرٍ ﴿۳۸﴾
اُذِنَ لِلَّذِيْنَ يُقٰتَلُوْنَ بِاَنَّهُمْ ظُلِمُوْا ؕ
وَاِنَّ اللّٰهَ عَلٰى نَصْرِهِمْ لَقَدِيْرُ ﴿۳۹﴾
الَّذِيْنَ اُخْرِجُوْا مِنْ دِيَارِهِمْ بِغَيْرِ
حَقٍّ اِلَّاۤ اَنْ يَّقُوْلُوْا رَبُّنَا اللّٰهُ ؕ وَلَوْلَا
دَفْعُ اللّٰهِ النَّاسَ بَعْضَهُمْ بِبَعْضٍ
لَّهُدِّمَتْ صَوَامِعُ وَبِيَعٌ وَّصَلَوٰتٌ
وَّمَسٰجِدُ يُذْكَرُ فِيْهَا اسْمُ اللّٰهِ كَثِيْرًا ؕ
وَلَيَنْصُرَنَّ اللّٰهُ مَنْ يَّنْصُرُهٗ ؕ اِنَّ اللّٰهَ
لَقَوِيٌّ عَزِيْزٌ ﴿۴۰﴾
اَلَّذِيْنَ اِنْ مَّكَّنّٰهُمْ فِى الْاَرْضِ اَقَامُوا
الصَّلٰوةَ وَاٰتَوُا الزَّكٰوةَ وَاَمَرُوْا
بِالْمَعْرُوْفِ وَنَهَوْا عَنِ الْمُنْكَرِ ؕ وَلِلّٰهِ
عَاقِبَةُ الْاُمُوْرِ ﴿۴۱﴾
وَاِنْ يُّكَذِّبُوْكَ فَقَدْ كَذَّبَتْ قَبْلَهُمْ
قَوْمُ نُوْحٍ وَّعَادٌ وَّثَمُوْدُ ﴿۴۲﴾
وَقَوْمُ اِبْرٰهِيْمَ وَقَوْمُ لُوْطٍ ﴿۴۳﴾
وَّاَصْحٰبُ مَدْيَنَ ۚ وَكُذِّبَ مُوْسٰى
فَاَمْلَيْتُ لِلْكٰفِرِيْنَ ثُمَّ اَخَذْتُهُمْ ۚ فَكَيْفَ
كَانَ نَكِيْرِ ﴿۴۴﴾
فَكَاَيِّنْ مِّنْ قَرْيَةٍ اَهْلَكْنٰهَا وَهِىَ
ظَالِمَةٌ فَهِىَ خَاوِيَةٌ عَلٰى عُرُوْشِهَا
وَبِئْرٍ مُّعَطَّلَةٍ وَّقَصْرٍ مَّشِيْدٍ ﴿۴۵﴾
اَفَلَمْ يَسِيْرُوْا فِى الْاَرْضِ فَتَكُوْنَ لَهُمْ
قُلُوْبٌ يَّعْقِلُوْنَ بِهَاۤ اَوْ اٰذَانٌ يَّسْمَعُوْنَ
بِهَا ۚ فَاِنَّهَا لَا تَعْمَى الْاَبْصَارُ وَلٰكِنْ
تَعْمَى الْقُلُوْبُ الَّتِىْ فِى الصُّدُوْرِ ﴿۴۶﴾

وقف منزل

47. Yet they ask thee to hasten on the Punishment! But Allah will not fail in His promise. Verily a Day in the sight of thy Lord is like a thousand years of your reckoning.

48. And to how many populations did I give respite, which were given to wrong-doing? In the end I punished them. To Me is the destination (of all).

49. Say: O men! I am (sent) to you only to give a clear warning:

50. "Those who believe and work righteousness, for them is forgiveness and a sustenance most generous.

51. "But those who strive against Our Signs, to frustrate them,—they will be companions of the Fire."

52. Never did We send a messenger or a prophet before thee, but, when he framed a desire, Satan threw some (vanity) into his desire: but Allah will cancel anything (vain) that Satan throws in, and Allah will confirm (and establish) His Signs: for Allah is full of knowledge and wisdom:

53. That He may make the suggestions thrown in by Satan, but a trial for those in whose hearts is a disease and who are hardened of heart: verily the wrong-doers are in a schism far (from the Truth):

54. And that those on whom knowledge has been bestowed may learn that the (Qur'an) is the Truth from thy Lord, and that they may believe therein, and their hearts may be made humbly (open) to it: for verily Allah is the Guide of those who believe, to the Straight Way.

55. Those who reject Faith will not cease to be in doubt concerning (Revelation) until the Hour (of Judgment) comes suddenly upon them, or there comes to them the Chastisement of a barren day.

اور (یہ) لوگ تم سے عذاب کیلئے جلدی کر رہے ہیں اور خدا اپنا
وعدہ ہرگز خلاف نہیں کریگا۔ اور بیشک تمہارے پروردگار کے
نزدیک ایک روز تمہارے حساب کے رو سے ہزار برس کے برابر ہے ﴿۴۷﴾
اور بہت سی بستیاں ہیں کہ میں اُن کو مہلت دیتا رہا اور وہ نافرمان
تھیں پھر میں نے اُن کو پکڑ لیا۔ اور میری ہی طرف لوٹ کر آنا ہے ﴿۴۸﴾
(اے پیغمبر) کہہ دو کہ لوگو! میں تم کو کھلم کھلا نصیحت کرنے
والا ہوں ﴿۴۹﴾
تو جو لوگ ایمان لائے اور کام نیک کئے اُن کیلئے بخشش
اور آبرو کی روزی ہے ﴿۵۰﴾
اور جن لوگوں نے ہماری آیتوں میں (اپنے زعم باطل میں)
ہمیں عاجز کرنے کیلئے سعی کی وہ اہل دوزخ ہیں ﴿۵۱﴾
اور ہم نے تم سے پہلے کوئی رسول اور نبی نہیں بھیجا مگر
(اس کا یہ حال تھا کہ) جب وہ کوئی آرزو کرتا تھا تو
شیطان اُس کی آرزو میں (وسوسہ) ڈال دیتا تھا
تو جو (وسوسہ) شیطان ڈالتا ہے خدا اُسکو دور کر دیتا ہے پھر خدا اپنی
آیتوں کو مضبوط کر دیتا ہے۔ اور خدا علم والا اور حکمت والا ہے ﴿۵۲﴾
غرض (اس سے) یہ ہے کہ جو (وسوسہ) شیطان ڈالتا ہے اُسکو اُن
لوگوں کے لئے جن کے دلوں میں بیماری ہے اور جن کے دل
سخت ہیں ذریعۂ آزمائش ٹھہرائے۔ بے شک ظالم
پرلے درجے کی مخالفت میں ہیں ﴿۵۳﴾
اور یہ بھی غرض ہے کہ جن لوگوں کو علم عطا ہوا ہے وہ جان
لیں کہ وہ (یعنی وحی) تمہارے پروردگار کی طرف سے حق ہے تو وہ
اس پر ایمان لائیں اور اُن کے دل خدا کے آگے عاجزی کریں اور جو
لوگ ایمان لائے ہیں خدا اُنکو سیدھے رستے کی طرف ہدایت کرتا ہے ﴿۵۴﴾
اور کافر لوگ ہمیشہ اس سے شک میں رہیں گے یہاں تک کہ قیامت
اُن پر ناگہاں آ جائے یا ایک نامبارک دن کا عذاب اُن
پر آ واقع ہو ﴿۵۵﴾

وَيَسْتَعْجِلُونَكَ بِالْعَذَابِ وَلَنْ يُخْلِفَ
اللَّهُ وَعْدَهُ وَإِنَّ يَوْمًا عِنْدَ رَبِّكَ
كَأَلْفِ سَنَةٍ مِمَّا تَعُدُّونَ ﴿۴۷﴾
وَكَأَيِّنْ مِنْ قَرْيَةٍ أَمْلَيْتُ لَهَا وَهِيَ
ظَالِمَةٌ ثُمَّ أَخَذْتُهَا وَإِلَيَّ الْمَصِيرُ ﴿۴۸﴾
قُلْ يَا أَيُّهَا النَّاسُ إِنَّمَا أَنَا لَكُمْ
نَذِيرٌ مُبِينٌ ﴿۴۹﴾
فَالَّذِينَ آمَنُوا وَعَمِلُوا الصَّالِحَاتِ لَهُمْ
مَغْفِرَةٌ وَرِزْقٌ كَرِيمٌ ﴿۵۰﴾
وَالَّذِينَ سَعَوْا فِي آيَاتِنَا مُعَاجِزِينَ
أُولَٰئِكَ أَصْحَابُ الْجَحِيمِ ﴿۵۱﴾
وَمَا أَرْسَلْنَا مِنْ قَبْلِكَ مِنْ
رَسُولٍ وَلَا نَبِيٍّ إِلَّا إِذَا تَمَنَّىٰ
أَلْقَى الشَّيْطَانُ فِي أُمْنِيَّتِهِ
فَيَنْسَخُ اللَّهُ مَا يُلْقِي الشَّيْطَانُ ثُمَّ
يُحْكِمُ اللَّهُ آيَاتِهِ وَاللَّهُ عَلِيمٌ حَكِيمٌ ﴿۵۲﴾
لِيَجْعَلَ مَا يُلْقِي الشَّيْطَانُ فِتْنَةً
لِلَّذِينَ فِي قُلُوبِهِمْ مَرَضٌ وَالْقَاسِيَةِ
قُلُوبُهُمْ وَإِنَّ الظَّالِمِينَ لَفِي شِقَاقٍ
بَعِيدٍ ﴿۵۳﴾
وَلِيَعْلَمَ الَّذِينَ أُوتُوا الْعِلْمَ أَنَّهُ الْحَقُّ
مِنْ رَبِّكَ فَيُؤْمِنُوا بِهِ فَتُخْبِتَ لَهُ
قُلُوبُهُمْ وَإِنَّ اللَّهَ لَهَادِ الَّذِينَ
آمَنُوا إِلَىٰ صِرَاطٍ مُسْتَقِيمٍ ﴿۵۴﴾
وَلَا يَزَالُ الَّذِينَ كَفَرُوا فِي مِرْيَةٍ
مِنْهُ حَتَّىٰ تَأْتِيَهُمُ السَّاعَةُ بَغْتَةً
أَوْ يَأْتِيَهُمْ عَذَابُ يَوْمٍ عَقِيمٍ ﴿۵۵﴾

56. On that Day the Dominion will be that of Allah: He will judge between them: so those who believe and work righteous deeds will be in Gardens of Delight.

اس روز بادشاہی خدا ہی کی ہوگی۔ (اور) وہ ان میں فیصلہ کردے گا۔ تو جو لوگ ایمان لائے اور عمل نیک کرتے رہے وہ نعمت کے باغوں میں ہوں گے (۵۶)

اَلْمُلْكُ يَوْمَئِذٍ لِّلّٰهِ ؕ يَحْكُمُ بَيْنَهُمْ ؕ
فَالَّذِيْنَ اٰمَنُوْا وَعَمِلُوا الصّٰلِحٰتِ فِيْ
جَنّٰتِ النَّعِيْمِ (۵۶)

57. And for those who reject Faith and deny Our Signs, there will be a humiliating punishment.

اور جو کافر ہوئے اور ہماری آیتوں کو جھٹلاتے رہے اُن کے لئے ذلیل کرنے والا عذاب ہوگا (۵۷)

وَالَّذِيْنَ كَفَرُوْا وَكَذَّبُوْا بِاٰيٰتِنَا فَاُولٰٓئِكَ
لَهُمْ عَذَابٌ مُّهِيْنٌ (۵۷) ع ۹ ۱۴

58. Those who leave their homes in the cause of Allah, and are then slain or die,— on them will Allah bestow verily a goodly Provision: truly Allah is He Who bestows the best Provision.

اور جن لوگوں نے خدا کی راہ میں ہجرت کی پھر مارے گئے یا مر گئے۔ اُن کو خدا اچھی روزی دیگا۔ اور بیشک خدا سب سے بہتر رزق دینے والا ہے (۵۸)

وَالَّذِيْنَ هَاجَرُوْا فِيْ سَبِيْلِ اللّٰهِ ثُمَّ
قُتِلُوْٓا اَوْ مَاتُوْا لَيَرْزُقَنَّهُمُ اللّٰهُ رِزْقًا حَسَنًا ؕ
وَاِنَّ اللّٰهَ لَهُوَ خَيْرُ الرّٰزِقِيْنَ (۵۸)

59. Verily He will admit them to a place with which they shall be well pleased: for Allah is All-Knowing, Most Forbearing.

وہ اُن کو ایسے مقام میں داخل کریگا جسے وہ پسند کرینگے اور خدا تو جاننے والا (اور) بُردبار ہے (۵۹)

لَيُدْخِلَنَّهُمْ مُّدْخَلًا يَّرْضَوْنَهٗ ؕ وَاِنَّ
اللّٰهَ لَعَلِيْمٌ حَلِيْمٌ (۵۹)

60. That (is so). And if one has retaliated to no greater extent than the injury he received, and is again set upon inordinately, Allah will help Him: for Allah is One That blots out (sins) and forgives (again and again).

یہ (بات خدا کے ہاں ٹھہر چکی ہے) اور جو شخص (کسی کو) اتنی ہی ایذا دے جتنی ایذا اُسکو دی گئی پھر اُس شخص پر زیادتی کیجائے تو خدا اسکی مدد کریگا۔ بیشک خدا معاف کرنیوالا (اور) بخشنے والا ہے (۶۰)

ذٰلِكَ ۚ وَمَنْ عَاقَبَ بِمِثْلِ مَا عُوْقِبَ
بِهٖ ثُمَّ بُغِيَ عَلَيْهِ لَيَنْصُرَنَّهُ اللّٰهُ ؕ اِنَّ
اللّٰهَ لَعَفُوٌّ غَفُوْرٌ (۶۰)

61. That is because Allah merges Night into Day, and He merges Day into Night, and verily it is Allah Who hears and sees (all things).

یہ اس لئے کہ خدا رات کو دن میں داخل کرتا ہے اور دن کو رات میں داخل کرتا ہے اور خدا تو سننے والا دیکھنے والا ہے (۶۱)

ذٰلِكَ بِاَنَّ اللّٰهَ يُوْلِجُ الَّيْلَ فِي النَّهَارِ
وَيُوْلِجُ النَّهَارَ فِي الَّيْلِ وَاَنَّ اللّٰهَ سَمِيْعٌ
بَصِيْرٌ (۶۱)

62. That is because Allah—He is the Reality; and those besides Him whom they invoke,— they are but vain Falsehood: verily Allah is He, Most High, Most Great.

یہ اس لئے کہ خدا ہی برحق ہے اور جس چیز کو (کافر) خدا کے سوا پکارتے ہیں وہ باطل ہے اور اس لئے کہ خدا رفیع الشان اور بڑا ہے (۶۲)

ذٰلِكَ بِاَنَّ اللّٰهَ هُوَ الْحَقُّ وَاَنَّ مَا
يَدْعُوْنَ مِنْ دُوْنِهٖ هُوَ الْبَاطِلُ وَ
اَنَّ اللّٰهَ هُوَ الْعَلِيُّ الْكَبِيْرُ (۶۲)

63. Seest thou not that Allah sends down rain from the sky, and forthwith the earth becomes clothed with green? For Allah is All-subtle, All-Aware.

کیا تم نہیں دیکھتے کہ خدا آسمان سے مینہ برساتا ہے تو زمین سرسبز ہوجاتی ہے۔ بے شک خدا مہربان اور خبردار ہے (۶۳)

اَلَمْ تَرَ اَنَّ اللّٰهَ اَنْزَلَ مِنَ السَّمَآءِ مَآءً ز
فَتُصْبِحُ الْاَرْضُ مُخْضَرَّةً ؕ اِنَّ اللّٰهَ
لَطِيْفٌ خَبِيْرٌ (۶۳)

64. To Him belongs all that is in the heavens and on earth: for verily Allah,—He is free of all wants, worthy of all praise.

جو کچھ آسمانوں میں ہے اور جو کچھ زمین میں ہے اُسی کا ہے۔ اور بیشک خدا بے نیاز (اور) قابل ستائش ہے (۶۴)

لَهٗ مَا فِي السَّمٰوٰتِ وَمَا فِي الْاَرْضِ ؕ وَ
اِنَّ اللّٰهَ لَهُوَ الْغَنِيُّ الْحَمِيْدُ (۶۴) ع ۱۰ ۱۵

65. Seest thou not that Allah has made subject to you (men) all that is on the earth, and the ships that sail through the sea by His command? He withholds the sky

کیا تم نہیں دیکھتے کہ جتنی چیزیں زمین میں ہیں (سب) خدا نے تمہارے زیر فرمان کر رکھی ہیں۔ اور کشتیاں (بھی) جو اُسی کے حکم سے دریا میں چلتی ہیں۔ اور وہ آسمان کو تھامے رہتا ہے

اَلَمْ تَرَ اَنَّ اللّٰهَ سَخَّرَ لَكُمْ مَّا فِي
الْاَرْضِ وَالْفُلْكَ تَجْرِيْ فِي الْبَحْرِ
بِاَمْرِهٖ ؕ وَيُمْسِكُ السَّمَآءَ اَنْ تَقَعَ

عَلَى الْأَرْضِ إِلَّا بِإِذْنِهِ ۗ إِنَّ اللَّهَ
بِالنَّاسِ لَرَءُوفٌ رَّحِيمٌ ﴿٦٥﴾

کہ زمین پر نہ گر پڑے مگر اُس کے حکم سے۔ بیشک خدا
لوگوں پر نہایت شفقت کرنے والا مہربان ہے ﴿۶۵﴾

from falling on the earth except by His leave: for Allah is Most Kind and Most Merciful to man.

وَهُوَ الَّذِي أَحْيَاكُمْ ثُمَّ يُمِيتُكُمْ ثُمَّ
يُحْيِيكُمْ ۗ إِنَّ الْإِنسَانَ لَكَفُورٌ ﴿٦٦﴾

اور وہی تو ہے جس نے تمکو حیات بخشی۔ پھر تم کو مارتا ہی پھر
تمہیں زندہ بھی کریگا۔ اور انسان تو بڑا ناشکر ہے ﴿۶۶﴾

66. It is He Who gave you life, will cause you to die, and will again give you Life: truly man is a most ungrateful creature!

لِّكُلِّ أُمَّةٍ جَعَلْنَا مَنسَكًا هُمْ نَاسِكُوهُ ۖ
فَلَا يُنَازِعُنَّكَ فِي الْأَمْرِ ۚ وَادْعُ إِلَىٰ
رَبِّكَ ۖ إِنَّكَ لَعَلَىٰ هُدًى مُّسْتَقِيمٍ ﴿٦٧﴾

ہم نے ہر ایک اُمت کے لئے ایک شریعت مقرر کر دی ہی جس
پر وہ چلتے ہیں۔ تو یہ لوگ تمسے اس امر میں جھگڑا نہ کریں اور تم (لوگوں) کو
اپنے پروردگار کیطرف بلاتے رہو۔ بیشک تم سیدھے رستے پر ہو ﴿۶۷﴾

67. To every People have We appointed rites which they must follow: let them not then dispute with thee on the matter, but do thou invite (them) to thy Lord: for thou art assuredly on the Right Way.

وَإِن جَادَلُوكَ فَقُلِ اللَّهُ أَعْلَمُ بِمَا
تَعْمَلُونَ ﴿٦٨﴾

اور اگر یہ تم سے جھگڑا کریں تو کہہ دو کہ جو عمل تم کرتے ہو خدا
اُن سے خوب واقف ہے ﴿۶۸﴾

68. If they do wrangle with thee, say, "Allah knows best what it is ye are doing."

اللَّهُ يَحْكُمُ بَيْنَكُمْ يَوْمَ الْقِيَامَةِ فِيمَا
كُنتُمْ فِيهِ تَخْتَلِفُونَ ﴿٦٩﴾

جن باتوں میں تم اختلاف کرتے ہو خدا تم میں قیامت
کے روز اُن کا فیصلہ کر دے گا ﴿۶۹﴾

69. "Allah will judge between you on the Day of Judgment concerning the matters in which ye differ."

أَلَمْ تَعْلَمْ أَنَّ اللَّهَ يَعْلَمُ مَا فِي السَّمَاءِ
وَالْأَرْضِ ۗ إِنَّ ذَٰلِكَ فِي كِتَابٍ ۚ إِنَّ
ذَٰلِكَ عَلَى اللَّهِ يَسِيرٌ ﴿٧٠﴾

کیا تم نہیں جانتے کہ جو کچھ آسمان اور زمین میں ہے خدا
اس کو جانتا ہے۔ یہ (سب کچھ) کتاب میں (لکھا ہوا) ہے۔
بیشک یہ سب خدا کو آسان ہے ﴿۷۰﴾

70. Knowest thou not that Allah knows all that is in heaven and on earth? Indeed it is all in a record, and that is easy for Allah.

وَيَعْبُدُونَ مِن دُونِ اللَّهِ مَا لَمْ يُنَزِّلْ
بِهِ سُلْطَانًا وَمَا لَيْسَ لَهُم بِهِ عِلْمٌ ۗ
وَمَا لِلظَّالِمِينَ مِن نَّصِيرٍ ﴿٧١﴾

اور (یہ لوگ) خدا کے سوا ایسی چیزوں کی عبادت کرتے ہیں جنکی اُس
نے کوئی سند نازل نہیں فرمائی اور نہ اُنکے پاس اسکی کوئی دلیل ہی
اور ظالموں کا کوئی بھی مددگار نہیں ہوگا ﴿۷۱﴾

71. Yet they worship, besides Allah, things for which no authority has been sent down to them, and of which they have (really) no knowledge: for those that do wrong there is no helper.

وَإِذَا تُتْلَىٰ عَلَيْهِمْ آيَاتُنَا بَيِّنَاتٍ
تَعْرِفُ فِي وُجُوهِ الَّذِينَ كَفَرُوا
الْمُنكَرَ ۖ يَكَادُونَ يَسْطُونَ بِالَّذِينَ
يَتْلُونَ عَلَيْهِمْ آيَاتِنَا ۗ قُلْ أَفَأُنَبِّئُكُم
بِشَرٍّ مِّن ذَٰلِكُمُ ۗ النَّارُ وَعَدَهَا اللَّهُ
الَّذِينَ كَفَرُوا ۖ وَبِئْسَ الْمَصِيرُ ﴿٧٢﴾ ع ٩

اور جب اُن کو ہماری آیتیں پڑھ کر سنائی جاتی ہیں تو (اُن
کی شکل بگڑ جاتی ہے اور) تم اُنکے چہروں میں صاف طور پر ناخوشی
(کے آثار) دیکھتے ہو۔ قریب ہوتے ہیں کہ جو لوگ اُنکو ہماری
آیتیں پڑھ کر سناتے ہیں اُن پر حملہ کر دیں۔ کہہ دو کہ میں تمکو اس
سے بھی بُری چیز بتاؤں؟ وہ (دوزخ کی) آگ ہے جسکا خدا نے
کافروں سے وعدہ کیا ہے اور وہ بُرا ٹھکانا ہے ﴿۷۲﴾

72. When Our Clear Signs are rehearsed to them, thou wilt notice a denial on the faces of the Unbelievers! They nearly attack with violence those who rehearse Our Signs to them. Say, "Shall I tell you of something (far) worse than that? It is the Fire (of Hell)! Allah has promised it to the Unbelievers! And evil is that destination!"

يَا أَيُّهَا النَّاسُ ضُرِبَ مَثَلٌ فَاسْتَمِعُوا لَهُ ۚ
إِنَّ الَّذِينَ تَدْعُونَ مِن دُونِ اللَّهِ
لَن يَخْلُقُوا ذُبَابًا وَلَوِ اجْتَمَعُوا لَهُ ۖ وَإِن
يَسْلُبْهُمُ الذُّبَابُ شَيْئًا لَّا يَسْتَنقِذُوهُ

لوگو! ایک مثال بیان کی جاتی ہے اسے غور سے سنو کہ جن
لوگوں کو تم خدا کے سوا پکارتے ہو وہ ایک مکھی بھی نہیں
بنا سکتے۔ اگرچہ اس کے لئے سب مجتمع ہو جائیں اور اگر اُن
سے مکھی کوئی چیز چھین لے جائے تو اُسے اُس سے چھڑا نہیں سکتے

73. O men! Here is a parable set forth! Listen to it! Those on whom, besides Allah, ye call, cannot create (even) a fly, if they all met together for the purpose! And if the fly should snatch away anything from them, they would have no power to release

SÛRA–23
AL-MÛMINÛN
(INTRODUCTION)

This Sûra deals with the virtues which are the seed-bed of Faith, especially in an environment in which Truth is denied and its votaries insulted and persecuted. But Truth is One and must prevail. Those who do wrong will be filled with vain regrets when it is too late for repentance.

It belongs to the late Makkan period.

it from the fly. Feeble are those who petition and those whom they petition!

74. They do not have right estimate of Allah, for Allah is Powerful and Mighty.

75. Allah chooses Messengers from angels and from men for Allah is He Who hears and sees (all things).

76. He knows what is before them and what is behind them: and to Allah go back all affairs (for decision).

77. O ye who believe! bow down, prostrate yourselves, and adore your Lord; and do good; that ye may prosper.

78. And strive in His cause as ye ought to strive, (with sincerity and under discipline). He has chosen you, and has imposed no difficulties on you in religion; it is the religion of your father Abraham. It is He Who has named you Muslims, both before and in this (Revelation); that the Messenger may be a witness for you, and ye be witnesses for mankind! So establish regular Prayer, give zakat and hold fast to Allah! He is your Protector—the Best to protect and the Best to help!

Al-Mûminûn, or The Believers

In the name of Allah, Most Gracious, Most Merciful.

1. Successful indeed are the Believers,—
2. Those who humble themselves in their prayers;
3. Who avoid vain talk;
4. Who are active in giving zakat;
5. Who guard their modesty,
6. Except with those joined to them in the marriage bond, or (the captives) whom their right hands possess,— for (in their case) they are free from blame,
7. But those whose desires

طالب (یعنی عابد) اور مطلوب (یعنی معبود دونوں) گئے گزرے ہیں ﴿۷۳﴾
ان لوگوں نے خدا کی قدر جیسی کرنی چاہیے تھی نہیں کی کچھ
شک نہیں کہ خدا زبردست (اور) غالب ہے ﴿۷۴﴾
خدا فرشتوں میں سے پیغام پہنچانے والے منتخب کرلیتا ہے
اور انسانوں میں سے بھی۔ بیشک خدا سننے والا (اور) دیکھنے والا ہے ﴿۷۵﴾
جو اُن کے آگے ہے اور جو اُن کے پیچھے ہے وہ اس سے واقف ہے۔
اور سب کاموں کا رجوع خدا ہی کی طرف ہے ﴿۷۶﴾
مومنو! رکوع کرتے اور سجدے کرتے اور اپنے پروردگار
کی عبادت کرتے رہو اور نیک کام کرو تاکہ
فلاح پاؤ ﴿۷۷﴾
اور خدا (کی راہ) میں جہاد کرو۔ جیسا جہاد کرنے کا حق ہے اُس
نے تمکو برگزیدہ کیا ہے اور تم پر دین (کی کسی بات) میں تنگی نہیں کی۔
(اور تمہارے لئے) تمہارے باپ ابراہیم کا دین (پسند کیا) اُسی نے پہلے (یعنی پہلی
کتابوں میں) تمہارا نام مسلمان رکھا تھا اور اس کتاب میں بھی (وہی نام رکھا ہے
تو جہاد کرو) تاکہ پیغمبر تمہارے بارے میں شاہد ہوں۔ اور تم لوگوں کے مقابلے
میں شاہد ہو۔ اور نماز پڑھو اور زکوٰۃ دو اور خدا (کے دین کی رسی) کو پکڑے
رہو۔ وہی تمہارا دوست ہے۔ اور خوب دوست اور خوب مددگار ہے ﴿۷۸﴾

سورۂ مومنون مکی ہے اور اس میں ایک سو اٹھارہ آیتیں اور چھ رکوع ہیں

شروع خدا کا نام لے کر جو بڑا مہربان نہایت رحم والا ہے
بیشک ایمان والے رستگار ہوگئے ﴿۱﴾
جو نماز میں عجز و نیاز کرتے ہیں ﴿۲﴾
اور جو بیہودہ باتوں سے منہ موڑے رہتے ہیں ﴿۳﴾
اور جو زکوٰۃ ادا کرتے ہیں ﴿۴﴾
اور جو اپنی شرمگاہوں کی حفاظت کرتے ہیں ﴿۵﴾
مگر اپنی بیویوں سے یا (کنیزوں سے) جو اُن کی ملک
ہوتی ہیں کہ (اُن سے) مباشرت کرنے سے) انہیں ملامت نہیں ﴿۶﴾
اور جو ان کے سوا اوروں کے طالب ہوں وہ (خدا کی مقرر

مِنْهُ ضَعُفَ الطَّالِبُ وَالْمَطْلُوبُ ﴿٧٣﴾
مَا قَدَرُوا اللّٰهَ حَقَّ قَدْرِهٖ اِنَّ اللّٰهَ
لَقَوِيٌّ عَزِيزٌ ﴿٧٤﴾
اَللّٰهُ يَصْطَفِيْ مِنَ الْمَلٰٓئِكَةِ رُسُلًا وَّ
مِنَ النَّاسِ اِنَّ اللّٰهَ سَمِيْعٌ بَصِيْرٌ ﴿٧٥﴾
يَعْلَمُ مَا بَيْنَ اَيْدِيْهِمْ وَمَا خَلْفَهُمْ
وَاِلَى اللّٰهِ تُرْجَعُ الْاُمُوْرُ ﴿٧٦﴾
يٰۤاَيُّهَا الَّذِيْنَ اٰمَنُوا ارْكَعُوْا وَاسْجُدُوْا وَ
اعْبُدُوْا رَبَّكُمْ وَافْعَلُوا الْخَيْرَ لَعَلَّكُمْ
تُفْلِحُوْنَ ﴿٧٧﴾
وَجَاهِدُوْا فِي اللّٰهِ حَقَّ جِهَادِهٖ هُوَ اجْتَبٰىكُمْ
وَمَا جَعَلَ عَلَيْكُمْ فِي الدِّيْنِ مِنْ حَرَجٍ
مِلَّةَ اَبِيْكُمْ اِبْرٰهِيْمَ هُوَ سَمّٰىكُمُ الْمُسْلِمِيْنَ
مِنْ قَبْلُ وَفِيْ هٰذَا لِيَكُوْنَ الرَّسُوْلُ
شَهِيْدًا عَلَيْكُمْ وَتَكُوْنُوْا شُهَدَآءَ عَلَى النَّاسِ
فَاَقِيْمُوا الصَّلٰوةَ وَاٰتُوا الزَّكٰوةَ وَاعْتَصِمُوْا
بِاللّٰهِ هُوَ مَوْلٰىكُمْ فَنِعْمَ الْمَوْلٰى وَنِعْمَ النَّصِيْرُ ﴿٧٨﴾

سُوْرَةُ الْمُؤْمِنُوْنَ مَكِّيَّةٌ وَهِيَ مِائَةٌ وَثَمَانَ عَشْرَةَ اٰيَةً وَسِتُّ رُكُوْعَاتٍ

بِسْمِ اللّٰهِ الرَّحْمٰنِ الرَّحِيْمِ
قَدْ اَفْلَحَ الْمُؤْمِنُوْنَ ﴿١﴾
الَّذِيْنَ هُمْ فِيْ صَلَاتِهِمْ خٰشِعُوْنَ ﴿٢﴾
وَالَّذِيْنَ هُمْ عَنِ اللَّغْوِ مُعْرِضُوْنَ ﴿٣﴾
وَالَّذِيْنَ هُمْ لِلزَّكٰوةِ فٰعِلُوْنَ ﴿٤﴾
وَالَّذِيْنَ هُمْ لِفُرُوْجِهِمْ حٰفِظُوْنَ ﴿٥﴾
اِلَّا عَلٰۤى اَزْوَاجِهِمْ اَوْ مَا مَلَكَتْ اَيْمَانُهُمْ
فَاِنَّهُمْ غَيْرُ مَلُوْمِيْنَ ﴿٦﴾
فَمَنِ ابْتَغٰى وَرَآءَ ذٰلِكَ فَاُولٰٓئِكَ هُمُ

السجدة عند الامام الشافعي ۲۰

ع ۱۰

الجزء الثامن عشر ۱۸

الْعٰدُوْنَ ﴿۷﴾

کی ہوئی) حد سے نکل جانے والے ہیں ﴿۷﴾

exceed those limits are transgressors;—

وَالَّذِيْنَ هُمْ لِاَمٰنٰتِهِمْ وَعَهْدِهِمْ رٰعُوْنَ ﴿۸﴾

اور جو امانتوں اور اقراروں کو ملحوظ رکھتے ہیں ﴿۸﴾

8. Those who faithfully observe their trusts and their covenants;

وَالَّذِيْنَ هُمْ عَلٰى صَلَوٰتِهِمْ يُحَافِظُوْنَ ﴿۹﴾

اور جو نمازوں کی پابندی کرتے ہیں ﴿۹﴾

9. And who (strictly) guard their prayers;—

اُولٰٓئِكَ هُمُ الْوٰرِثُوْنَ ﴿۱۰﴾

یہی لوگ میراث حاصل کرنے والے ہیں ﴿۱۰﴾

10. These will be the heirs,

الَّذِيْنَ يَرِثُوْنَ الْفِرْدَوْسَ ؕ هُمْ فِيْهَا خٰلِدُوْنَ ﴿۱۱﴾

(یعنی) جو بہشت کی میراث حاصل کریں گے۔ (اور) اُس میں ہمیشہ رہیں گے ﴿۱۱﴾

11. Who will inherit Paradise: they will dwell therein (for ever).

وَلَقَدْ خَلَقْنَا الْاِنْسَانَ مِنْ سُلٰلَةٍ مِّنْ طِيْنٍ ﴿۱۲﴾

اور ہم نے انسان کو مٹی کے خلاصے[۱۹۲] سے پیدا کیا ہے ﴿۱۲﴾

12. Man We did create from a quintessence (of clay);

ثُمَّ جَعَلْنٰهُ نُطْفَةً فِيْ قَرَارٍ مَّكِيْنٍ ﴿۱۳﴾

پھر اس کو ایک مضبوط (اور محفوظ) جگہ میں نطفہ بنا کر رکھا ﴿۱۳﴾

13. Then We placed him as (a drop of) sperm in a place of rest, firmly fixed;

ثُمَّ خَلَقْنَا النُّطْفَةَ عَلَقَةً فَخَلَقْنَا الْعَلَقَةَ مُضْغَةً فَخَلَقْنَا الْمُضْغَةَ عِظٰمًا فَكَسَوْنَا الْعِظٰمَ لَحْمًا ۗ ثُمَّ اَنْشَاْنٰهُ خَلْقًا اٰخَرَ ؕ فَتَبٰرَكَ اللّٰهُ اَحْسَنُ الْخٰلِقِيْنَ ﴿۱۴﴾

پھر نطفے کا لوتھڑا بنایا۔ پھر لوتھڑے کی بوٹی بنائی پھر بوٹی کی ہڈیاں بنائیں پھر ہڈیوں پر گوشت (پوست) چڑھایا۔ پھر اُس کو نئی صورت میں بنا دیا۔ تو خدا جو سب سے بہتر بنانے والا بڑا بابرکت ہے ﴿۱۴﴾

14. Then We made the sperm into a clot of congealed blood; then of that clot We made a (foetus) lump; then We made out of that lump bones and clothed the bones with flesh; then We developed out of it another creature. So blessed be Allah, the Best to create!

ثُمَّ اِنَّكُمْ بَعْدَ ذٰلِكَ لَمَيِّتُوْنَ ﴿۱۵﴾

پھر اس کے بعد تم مر جاتے ہو ﴿۱۵﴾

15. After that, at length ye will die.

ثُمَّ اِنَّكُمْ يَوْمَ الْقِيٰمَةِ تُبْعَثُوْنَ ﴿۱۶﴾

پھر قیامت کے روز اُٹھا کھڑے کئے جاؤ گے ﴿۱۶﴾

16. Again, on the Day of Judgment, will ye be raised up.

وَلَقَدْ خَلَقْنَا فَوْقَكُمْ سَبْعَ طَرَآئِقَ ۖ وَمَا كُنَّا عَنِ الْخَلْقِ غٰفِلِيْنَ ﴿۱۷﴾

اور ہم نے تمہارے اُوپر (کی جانب) سات آسمان پیدا کئے اور ہم خلقت سے غافل نہیں ہیں ﴿۱۷﴾

17. And We have made, above you, seven tracts; and We are never unmindful of (Our) Creation.

وَاَنْزَلْنَا مِنَ السَّمَآءِ مَآءً بِقَدَرٍ فَاَسْكَنّٰهُ فِى الْاَرْضِ ۖ وَاِنَّا عَلٰى ذَهَابٍ بِهٖ لَقٰدِرُوْنَ ﴿۱۸﴾

اور ہم ہی نے آسمان سے ایک انداز کے ساتھ پانی نازل کیا۔ پھر اُس کو زمین میں ٹھیرا دیا اور ہم اُس کے نابود کر دینے پر بھی قادر ہیں ﴿۱۸﴾

8. And We send down water from the sky according to (due) measure, and We cause it to soak in the soil; and We certainly are able to drain it off (with ease).

فَاَنْشَاْنَا لَكُمْ بِهٖ جَنّٰتٍ مِّنْ نَّخِيْلٍ وَّاَعْنَابٍ ۘ لَكُمْ فِيْهَا فَوَاكِهُ كَثِيْرَةٌ وَّمِنْهَا تَاْكُلُوْنَ ﴿۱۹﴾

پھر ہم نے اُس سے تمہارے لئے کھجوروں اور انگوروں کے باغ بنائے۔ ان میں تمہارے لئے بہت سے میوے پیدا ہوتے ہیں اور اُن میں سے تم کھاتے ہو ﴿۱۹﴾

19. With it We grow for you gardens of date-palms and vines: in them have ye abundant fruits: and of them ye eat (and have enjoyment),—

وَشَجَرَةً تَخْرُجُ مِنْ طُوْرِ سَيْنَآءَ تَنْۢبُتُ بِالدُّهْنِ وَصِبْغٍ لِّلْاٰكِلِيْنَ ﴿۲۰﴾

اور وہ درخت بھی (ہم ہی نے پیدا کیا) جو طور سینا میں پیدا ہوتا ہے (یعنی زیتون کا درخت کہ) کھانے کیلئے روغن اور سالن لئے ہوئے اُگتا ہے ﴿۲۰﴾

20. Also a tree springing out of Mount Sinai, which produces oil, and relish for those who use it for food.

وَاِنَّ لَكُمْ فِى الْاَنْعَامِ لَعِبْرَةً ۚ نُسْقِيْكُمْ

اور تمہارے لئے چارپایوں میں بھی عبرت (اور نشانی) ہے کہ جو اُن کے

21. And in cattle (too) ye have an instructive example: from within

their bodies We produce (milk) for you to drink; there are, in them, (besides), numerous (other) benefits for you; and of their (meat) ye eat;

22. And on them, as well as in ships, ye ride.

23. And certainly we sent Noah to his people: he said, "O my people! worship Allah! Ye have no other god but Him. Will ye not fear (Him)?"

24. The chiefs of the Unbelievers among his people said: "he is no more than a man like yourselves: his wish is to assert his superiority over you: if Allah had wished (to send messengers), He could have sent down angels: never did we hear such a thing (as he says), among our ancestors of old."

25. (And some said): "He is only a man possessed: wait (and have patience) with him for a time."

26. (Noah) said: "O my Lord! help me: for that they accuse me of falsehood!"

27. So We inspired him (with this message); "Construct the Ark within Our sight and under Our guidance: then when comes Our command, and the oven gushes forth, take thou on board pairs of every species, male and female, and thy family—except those of them against whom the Word has already gone forth: and address Me not in favour of the wrong-doers: for they shall be drowned (in the Flood).

28. And when thou hast embarked On the Ark—thou and those with thee,—say: "Praise be to Allah, Who has saved us from the people who do wrong."

29. And say: "O my Lord! enable me to disembark with Thy blessing: for Thou Art the Best to enable (us) to disembark."

30. Verily in this there are Signs (for men to understand); lo! We put (men) to test.

31. Then We raised after them another generation.

32. And We sent to them a messenger from among

پیٹوں میں ہے اس سے ہم تمہیں (دودھ) پلاتے ہیں۔ اور تمہارے لئے
اُنمیں (اور بھی) بہت سے فائدے ہیں اور بعض کو تم کھاتے بھی ہو (۲۱)
اور اُن پر اور کشتیوں پر تم سوار ہوتے ہو (۲۲)
اور ہم نے نوحؑ کو اُن کی قوم کی طرف بھیجا تو انہوں نے
اُن سے کہا کہ اے قوم خدا ہی کی عبادت کرو اس کے سوا
تمہارا کوئی معبود نہیں کیا تم ڈرتے نہیں؟ (۲۳)
تو اُن کی قوم کے سردار جو کافر تھے کہنے لگے کہ یہ تو تم ہی
جیسا آدمی ہے تم پر بڑائی حاصل کرنی چاہتا ہے۔ اور اگر
خدا چاہتا تو فرشتے اتار دیتا۔ ہم نے اپنے اگلے باپ دادا
میں تو یہ بات کبھی سُنی نہیں (۲۴)
اِس آدمی کو تو دیوانگی (کا عارضہ) ہے۔ تو اس کے بارے
میں کچھ مدت انتظار کرو (۲۵)
(نوحؑ نے) کہا کہ پروردگار اُنہوں نے مجھے جھٹلایا ہے تو میری مدد کر (۲۶)
پس ہم نے اُن کی طرف وحی بھیجی کہ ہمارے سامنے اور ہمارے
حکم سے ایک کشتی بناؤ۔ پھر جب ہمارا حکم آ پہنچے اور تنور (پانی سے
بھر کر) جوش مارنے لگے تو سب (قسم کے حیوانات) میں سے جوڑا جوڑا
(یعنی نر اور مادہ) دو دو کشتی میں بٹھالو اور اپنے گھر والوں کو بھی۔
سوا اُن کے جنکی نسبت اُن میں سے (ہلاک ہونیکا) حکم پہلے (صادر) ہو چکا ہے
اور ظالموں کے بارے میں ہم سے کچھ نہ کہنا۔ وہ ضرور ڈبو دیئے جائینگے (۲۷)
اور جب تم اور تمہارے ساتھی کشتی میں بیٹھ جاؤ تو (خدا کا شکر
کرنا اور) کہنا کہ سب تعریف خدا ہی کو (سزاوار) ہے جس نے
ہم کو ظالم لوگوں سے نجات بخشی (۲۸)
اور (یہ بھی) دعا کرنا کہ اے پروردگار ہم کو مبارک جگہ اتاریو
اور تو سب سے بہتر اتارنے والا ہے (۲۹)
بیشک اِس (قصے) میں نشانیاں ہیں اور ہمیں تو آزمائش کرنی تھی (۳۰)
پھر ان کے بعد ہم نے ایک اور جماعت پیدا کی (۳۱)
اور اُنہی میں سے اُن میں ایک پیغمبر بھیجا (جس نے اُن

مِّمَّا فِي بُطُونِهَا وَلَكُمْ فِيهَا مَنَافِعُ كَثِيرَةٌ
وَمِنْهَا تَأْكُلُونَ ﴿٢١﴾
وَعَلَيْهَا وَعَلَى الْفُلْكِ تُحْمَلُونَ ﴿٢٢﴾
وَلَقَدْ أَرْسَلْنَا نُوحًا إِلَىٰ قَوْمِهِ فَقَالَ
يَا قَوْمِ اعْبُدُوا اللَّهَ مَا لَكُم مِّنْ إِلَٰهٍ
غَيْرُهُ أَفَلَا تَتَّقُونَ ﴿٢٣﴾
فَقَالَ الْمَلَأُ الَّذِينَ كَفَرُوا مِن قَوْمِهِ
مَا هَٰذَا إِلَّا بَشَرٌ مِّثْلُكُمْ يُرِيدُ أَن
يَتَفَضَّلَ عَلَيْكُمْ وَلَوْ شَاءَ اللَّهُ لَأَنزَلَ
مَلَائِكَةً مَّا سَمِعْنَا بِهَٰذَا فِي آبَائِنَا الْأَوَّلِينَ ﴿٢٤﴾
إِنْ هُوَ إِلَّا رَجُلٌ بِهِ جِنَّةٌ فَتَرَبَّصُوا
بِهِ حَتَّىٰ حِينٍ ﴿٢٥﴾
قَالَ رَبِّ انصُرْنِي بِمَا كَذَّبُونِ ﴿٢٦﴾
فَأَوْحَيْنَا إِلَيْهِ أَنِ اصْنَعِ الْفُلْكَ بِأَعْيُنِنَا
وَوَحْيِنَا فَإِذَا جَاءَ أَمْرُنَا وَفَارَ التَّنُّورُ
فَاسْلُكْ فِيهَا مِن كُلٍّ زَوْجَيْنِ اثْنَيْنِ
وَأَهْلَكَ إِلَّا مَن سَبَقَ عَلَيْهِ الْقَوْلُ
مِنْهُمْ وَلَا تُخَاطِبْنِي فِي الَّذِينَ ظَلَمُوا
إِنَّهُم مُّغْرَقُونَ ﴿٢٧﴾
فَإِذَا اسْتَوَيْتَ أَنتَ وَمَن مَّعَكَ عَلَى
الْفُلْكِ فَقُلِ الْحَمْدُ لِلَّهِ الَّذِي نَجَّانَا
مِنَ الْقَوْمِ الظَّالِمِينَ ﴿٢٨﴾
وَقُل رَّبِّ أَنزِلْنِي مُنزَلًا مُّبَارَكًا وَأَنتَ
خَيْرُ الْمُنزِلِينَ ﴿٢٩﴾
إِنَّ فِي ذَٰلِكَ لَآيَاتٍ وَإِن كُنَّا لَمُبْتَلِينَ ﴿٣٠﴾
ثُمَّ أَنشَأْنَا مِن بَعْدِهِمْ قَرْنًا آخَرِينَ ﴿٣١﴾
فَأَرْسَلْنَا فِيهِمْ رَسُولًا مِّنْهُمْ أَنِ اعْبُدُوا

themselves, (saying), "Worship Allah! Ye have no other god but Him. Will ye not fear (Him)?"

33. And the chiefs of his people, who disbelieved and denied the Meeting in the Hereafter, and on whom We had bestowed the good things of this life, said: "He is no more than a man like yourselves: he eats and drinks of what ye drink.

34. "If ye obey a man like yourselves, behold, it is certain ye will be lost.

35. "Does he promise that when ye die and become dust and bones, ye shall be brought forth (again)?

36. "Far, very far is that which ye are promised!

37. "There is nothing but our life in this world! We shall die and we live! But we shall never be raised up again!

38. "He is only a man who invents a lie against Allah, but we are not the ones to believe in him!

39. (The prophet) said: "O my Lord help me: for that they accuse me of falsehood."

40. (Allah) said: "In but a little while, they are sure to be sorry!"

41. Then the Blast overtook them with justice, and We made them as rubbish of dead leaves so away with the people who do wrong!

42. Then We raised after them other generations.

43. No people can hasten their term, nor can they delay (it).

44. Then sent We Our messengers in succession: every time there came to a people their messenger, they accused him of falsehood: so We made them follow each other (in punishment): We made them as a tale (that is told): so away with a people that will not believe!

45. Then We sent Moses and his brother Aaron, with Our Signs and

سے کہا) کہ خدا ہی کی عبادت کرو (کہ) اسکے سوا تمہارا کوئی
معبود نہیں۔ تو کیا تم ڈرتے نہیں؟ ﴿٣٢﴾
تو اُن کی قوم کے سردار جو کافر تھے اور آخرت کے آنے کو
جھوٹ سمجھتے تھے اور دنیا کی زندگی میں ہم نے ان کو
آسودگی دے رکھی تھی کہنے لگے کہ یہ تو تم ہی جیسا آدمی ہے
جس قسم کا کھانا تم کھاتے ہو اسی طرح کا یہ بھی کھاتا ہے
اور جو (پانی) تم پیتے ہو اسی قسم کا یہ بھی پیتا ہے ﴿٣٣﴾
اور اگر تم نے اپنے ہی جیسے آدمی کا کہا مان لیا تو
گھاٹے میں پڑ گئے ﴿٣٤﴾
کیا یہ تم سے یہ کہتا ہے کہ جب تم مر جاؤ گے اور مٹی ہو جاؤ گے اور
استخوان (کے سوا کچھ نہ رہیگا) تو تم (زمین سے) نکالے جاؤ گے ﴿٣٥﴾
جس بات کا تم سے وعدہ کیا جاتا ہے (بہت) بعید اور (بہت) بعید ہے ﴿٣٦﴾
زندگی تو یہی ہماری دنیا کی زندگی ہے کہ (اسی میں) ہم مرتے
اور جیتے ہیں اور ہم پھر نہیں اٹھائے جائیں گے ﴿٣٧﴾
یہ تو ایک ایسا آدمی ہے جس نے خدا پر جھوٹ افترا کیا
ہے اور ہم اس کو ماننے والے نہیں ﴿٣٨﴾
پیغمبر نے کہا کہ اے پروردگار انہوں نے مجھے جھوٹا سمجھا ہے تو میری مدد کر ﴿٣٩﴾
فرمایا کہ یہ تھوڑے ہی عرصے میں پشیمان ہو کر رہ جائیں گے ﴿٤٠﴾
تو اُن کو (وعدہ) برحق (کے مطابق) زور کی آواز نے آپکڑا
تو ہم نے اُن کو کوڑا کر ڈالا پس ظالم لوگوں پر لعنت ہے ﴿٤١﴾
پھر اُن کے بعد ہم نے اور جماعتیں پیدا کیں ﴿٤٢﴾
کوئی جماعت اپنے وقت سے نہ آگے جا سکتی ہے نہ پیچھے رہ سکتی ہے ﴿٤٣﴾
پھر ہم پے در پے اپنے پیغمبر بھیجتے رہے جب کسی اُمت کے پاس
اُس کا پیغمبر آتا تھا تو وہ اُسے جھٹلا دیتے تھے۔ تو ہم بھی بعض کو
بعض کے پیچھے (ہلاک کرتے اور اُن پر عذاب) لاتے رہے اور اُنکے
افسانے بناتے رہے پس جو لوگ ایمان نہیں لاتے اُن پر لعنت ﴿٤٤﴾
پھر ہم نے موسیٰ اور اُن کے بھائی ہارون کو اپنی نشانیاں

اللّٰهَ مَا لَكُمۡ مِّنۡ اِلٰهٍ غَيۡرُهٗ ؕ اَفَلَا
ع تَتَّقُوۡنَ ﴿٣٢﴾
وَقَالَ الۡمَلَاُ مِنۡ قَوۡمِهِ الَّذِيۡنَ كَفَرُوۡا
وَكَذَّبُوۡا بِلِقَآءِ الۡاٰخِرَةِ وَاَتۡرَفۡنٰهُمۡ
فِى الۡحَيٰوةِ الدُّنۡيَا ۙ مَا هٰذَاۤ اِلَّا بَشَرٌ
مِّثۡلُكُمۡ ۙ يَاۡكُلُ مِمَّا تَاۡكُلُوۡنَ مِنۡهُ
وَيَشۡرَبُ مِمَّا تَشۡرَبُوۡنَ ۙ ﴿٣٣﴾
وَلَئِنۡ اَطَعۡتُمۡ بَشَرًا مِّثۡلَكُمۡ ۙ اِنَّكُمۡ
اِذًا لَّخٰسِرُوۡنَ ۙ ﴿٣٤﴾
اَيَعِدُكُمۡ اَنَّكُمۡ اِذَا مِتُّمۡ وَكُنۡتُمۡ تُرَابًا
وَّعِظَامًا اَنَّكُمۡ مُّخۡرَجُوۡنَ ۙ ﴿٣٥﴾
هَيۡهَاتَ هَيۡهَاتَ لِمَا تُوۡعَدُوۡنَ ۙ ﴿٣٦﴾
اِنۡ هِىَ اِلَّا حَيَاتُنَا الدُّنۡيَا نَمُوۡتُ وَ
نَحۡيَا وَمَا نَحۡنُ بِمَبۡعُوۡثِيۡنَ ۙ ﴿٣٧﴾
اِنۡ هُوَ اِلَّا رَجُلُ ۨافۡتَرٰى عَلَى اللّٰهِ
كَذِبًا وَّمَا نَحۡنُ لَهٗ بِمُؤۡمِنِيۡنَ ﴿٣٨﴾
قَالَ رَبِّ انۡصُرۡنِىۡ بِمَا كَذَّبُوۡنِ ﴿٣٩﴾
قَالَ عَمَّا قَلِيۡلٍ لَّيُصۡبِحُنَّ نٰدِمِيۡنَ ۚ ﴿٤٠﴾
فَاَخَذَتۡهُمُ الصَّيۡحَةُ بِالۡحَقِّ فَجَعَلۡنٰهُمۡ
غُثَآءً ۚ فَبُعۡدًا لِّلۡقَوۡمِ الظّٰلِمِيۡنَ ﴿٤١﴾
ثُمَّ اَنۡشَاۡنَا مِنۡۢ بَعۡدِهِمۡ قُرُوۡنًا اٰخَرِيۡنَ ﴿٤٢﴾
مَا تَسۡبِقُ مِنۡ اُمَّةٍ اَجَلَهَا وَمَا يَسۡتَاۡخِرُوۡنَ ﴿٤٣﴾
ثُمَّ اَرۡسَلۡنَا رُسُلَنَا تَتۡرَا ؕ كُلَّمَا جَآءَ
اُمَّةً رَّسُوۡلُهَا كَذَّبُوۡهُ فَاَتۡبَعۡنَا بَعۡضَهُمۡ
بَعۡضًا وَّجَعَلۡنٰهُمۡ اَحَادِيۡثَ ۚ فَبُعۡدًا
لِّقَوۡمٍ لَّا يُؤۡمِنُوۡنَ ﴿٤٤﴾
ثُمَّ اَرۡسَلۡنَا مُوۡسٰى وَاَخَاهُ هٰرُوۡنَ ۙ

authority manifest,

46. To Pharaoh and his Chiefs: but these behaved insolently: they were an arrogant people.

47. They said: "Shall we believe in two men like ourselves? And their people are subject to us!"

48. So they rejected them and they became of those who were destroyed.

49. And We gave Moses the Book, in order that they might receive guidance.

50. And We made the son of Mary and his mother as a Sign: We gave them both shelter on high ground, affording rest and security and furnished with springs.

51. O ye messengers! enjoy (all) things good and pure, and work righteousness: for I am well-acquainted with (all) that ye do.

52. And verily this Ummah of yours is a single Ummah and I am your Lord and Cherisher: therefore fear Me (and no other).

53. But people have cut off their affair (of unity), between them, into sects: each party rejoices in that which is with itself.

54. But leave them in their confused ignorance for a time.

55. Do they think that because We have granted them abundance of wealth and sons,

56. We would hasten them on in every good? Nay they do not perceive.

57. Verily those who live in awe for fear of their Lord;

58. Those who believe in the Signs of their Lord;

59. Those who join not (in worship) partners with their Lord;

60. And those who dispense their charity with their hearts full of fear, because they will return to their Lord;—

اور دلیل ظاہر دے کر بھیجا ﴿۴۵﴾
(یعنی) فرعون اور اُسکی جماعت کی طرف. تو انہوں نے تکبر کیا
اور وہ سرکش لوگ تھے ﴿۴۶﴾
کہنے لگے کہ کیا ہم اُن اپنے جیسے دو آدمیوں پر ایمان
لے آئیں اور اُن کی قوم کے لوگ ہمارے خدمتگار ہیں ﴿۴۷﴾
تو اُن لوگوں نے اُنکی تکذیب کی سو آخر ہلاک کر دیئے گئے ﴿۴۸﴾
اور ہم نے مُوسیٰ کو کتاب دی تھی تاکہ وہ لوگ ہدایت
پائیں ﴿۴۹﴾
اور مریم کے بیٹے (عیسیٰ) اور اُنکی ماں کو (اپنی) نشانی بنایا تھا اور اُنکو ایک اونچی جگہ پر
جو رہنے کے لائق تھی اور جہاں (نتھرا ہوا) پانی جاری تھا پناہ دی تھی ﴿۵۰﴾
اے پیغمبرو! پاکیزہ چیزیں کھاؤ اور عمل نیک کرو. جو عمل تم
کرتے ہو میں اُن سے واقف ہوں ﴿۵۱﴾
اور یہ تمہاری جماعت (حقیقت میں) ایک ہی جماعت ہے اور میں
تمہارا پروردگار ہوں تو مجھ سے ڈرو ﴿۵۲﴾
پھر اُنہوں نے آپس میں اپنے کام کو متفرق کر کے جُدا جُدا کر دیا
جو چیز جس فرقے کے پاس ہے وہ اس سے خوش ہو رہا ہے ﴿۵۳﴾
تو اُن کو ایک مدت تک ان کی غفلت ہی میں رہنے دو ﴿۵۴﴾
کیا یہ لوگ یہ خیال کرتے ہیں کہ ہم جو دنیا میں اُن کو مال
اور بیٹوں سے مدد دیتے ہیں ﴿۵۵﴾
(تو اس سے) اُنکی بھلائی میں جلدی کر رہے ہیں. (نہیں) بلکہ یہ
سمجھتے ہی نہیں ﴿۵۶﴾
جو لوگ اپنے پروردگار کے خوف سے ڈرتے
ہیں ﴿۵۷﴾
اور جو اپنے پروردگار کی آیتوں پر ایمان رکھتے ہیں ﴿۵۸﴾
اور جو اپنے پروردگار کے ساتھ شریک نہیں کرتے ﴿۵۹﴾
اور جو دے سکتے ہیں دیتے ہیں اور اُنکے دل اس بات سے ڈرتے
رہتے ہیں کہ اُن کو اپنے پروردگار کی طرف لوٹ کر جانا ہے ﴿۶۰﴾

بِاٰیٰتِنَا وَسُلْطٰنٍ مُّبِیْنٍ ﴿۴۵﴾
اِلٰی فِرْعَوْنَ وَمَلَا۠ئِهٖ فَاسْتَكْبَرُوْا وَكَانُوْا
قَوْمًا عَالِیْنَ ﴿۴۶﴾
فَقَالُوْٓا اَنُؤْمِنُ لِبَشَرَیْنِ مِثْلِنَا وَقَوْمُهُمَا
لَنَا عٰبِدُوْنَ ﴿۴۷﴾
فَكَذَّبُوْهُمَا فَكَانُوْا مِنَ الْمُهْلَكِیْنَ ﴿۴۸﴾
وَلَقَدْ اٰتَیْنَا مُوْسَی الْكِتٰبَ لَعَلَّهُمْ
یَهْتَدُوْنَ ﴿۴۹﴾
وَجَعَلْنَا ابْنَ مَرْیَمَ وَاُمَّهٗٓ اٰیَةً وَّ
اٰوَیْنٰهُمَآ اِلٰی رَبْوَةٍ ذَاتِ قَرَارٍ وَّمَعِیْنٍ ﴿۵۰﴾
یٰٓاَیُّهَا الرُّسُلُ كُلُوْا مِنَ الطَّیِّبٰتِ وَ
اعْمَلُوْا صَالِحًا ؕ اِنِّیْ بِمَا تَعْمَلُوْنَ عَلِیْمٌ ﴿۵۱﴾
وَاِنَّ هٰذِهٖٓ اُمَّتُكُمْ اُمَّةً وَّاحِدَةً وَّ
اَنَا رَبُّكُمْ فَاتَّقُوْنِ ﴿۵۲﴾
فَتَقَطَّعُوْٓا اَمْرَهُمْ بَیْنَهُمْ زُبُرًا ؕ كُلُّ
حِزْبٍۭ بِمَا لَدَیْهِمْ فَرِحُوْنَ ﴿۵۳﴾
فَذَرْهُمْ فِیْ غَمْرَتِهِمْ حَتّٰی حِیْنٍ ﴿۵۴﴾
اَیَحْسَبُوْنَ اَنَّمَا نُمِدُّهُمْ بِهٖ مِنْ مَّالٍ
وَّبَنِیْنَ ﴿۵۵﴾
نُسَارِعُ لَهُمْ فِی الْخَیْرٰتِ ؕ بَلْ لَّا
یَشْعُرُوْنَ ﴿۵۶﴾
اِنَّ الَّذِیْنَ هُمْ مِّنْ خَشْیَةِ رَبِّهِمْ
مُّشْفِقُوْنَ ﴿۵۷﴾
وَالَّذِیْنَ هُمْ بِاٰیٰتِ رَبِّهِمْ یُؤْمِنُوْنَ ﴿۵۸﴾
وَالَّذِیْنَ هُمْ بِرَبِّهِمْ لَا یُشْرِكُوْنَ ﴿۵۹﴾
وَالَّذِیْنَ یُؤْتُوْنَ مَآ اٰتَوْا وَّقُلُوْبُهُمْ
وَجِلَةٌ اَنَّهُمْ اِلٰی رَبِّهِمْ رٰجِعُوْنَ ﴿۶۰﴾

61. It is these who hasten in every good work, and these who are foremost in them.

یہی لوگ نیکیوں میں جلدی کرتے اور یہی اُن کیلئے آگے
نکل جاتے ہیں ﴿٦١﴾

أُولَٰٓئِكَ يُسَٰرِعُونَ فِي ٱلْخَيْرَٰتِ وَهُمْ
لَهَا سَٰبِقُونَ ﴿٦١﴾

62. On no soul do We place a burden greater than it can bear: before Us is a record which clearly speaks the truth. They will never be wronged.

اور ہم کسی شخص کو اسکی طاقت سے زیادہ تکلیف نہیں دیتے اور ہمارے پاس
کتاب ہے جو سچ سچ کہہ دیتی ہے اور ان (لوگوں) پر ظلم نہیں کیا جائیگا ﴿٦٢﴾

وَلَا نُكَلِّفُ نَفْسًا إِلَّا وُسْعَهَا وَلَدَيْنَا
كِتَٰبٌ يَنطِقُ بِٱلْحَقِّ وَهُمْ لَا يُظْلَمُونَ ﴿٦٢﴾

63. But their hearts are in confused ignorance of this; and there are, besides that, deeds of theirs, which they will (continue) to do,—

مگر اُنکے دل اِن (باتوں) کیطرف سے غفلت میں (پڑے ہوئے) ہیں
اور اُنکے سوا اور اعمال بھی ہیں جو یہ کرتے رہتے ہیں ﴿٦٣﴾

بَلْ قُلُوبُهُمْ فِي غَمْرَةٍ مِّنْ هَٰذَا وَلَهُمْ
أَعْمَٰلٌ مِّن دُونِ ذَٰلِكَ هُمْ لَهَا عَٰمِلُونَ ﴿٦٣﴾

64. Until, when We seize in Punishment those of them who received the good things of this world, behold, they will groan in supplication!

یہاں تک کہ جب ہم نے اُن میں سے آسودہ حال لوگوں کو
پکڑ لیا تو وہ اُس وقت تلملا اُٹھیں گے ﴿٦٤﴾

حَتَّىٰٓ إِذَآ أَخَذْنَا مُتْرَفِيهِم بِٱلْعَذَابِ
إِذَا هُمْ يَجْـَٔرُونَ ﴿٦٤﴾

65. (It will be said): "Groan not in supplication this day; for ye shall certainly not be helped by Us.

آج مت تلملاؤ تم کو ہم سے کچھ مدد نہیں ملے گی ﴿٦٥﴾

لَا تَجْـَٔرُوا ٱلْيَوْمَ إِنَّكُم مِّنَّا لَا تُنصَرُونَ ﴿٦٥﴾

66. "My Signs used to be rehearsed to you, but ye used to turn back on your heels—

میری آیتیں تم کو پڑھ پڑھ کر سنائی جاتی تھیں اور تم اُلٹے
پاؤں پھر پھر جاتے تھے ﴿٦٦﴾

قَدْ كَانَتْ ءَايَٰتِي تُتْلَىٰ عَلَيْكُمْ فَكُنتُمْ
عَلَىٰٓ أَعْقَٰبِكُمْ تَنكِصُونَ ﴿٦٦﴾

67. "In arrogance: talking nonsense about the (Qur'an), like one telling fables by night."

اُن سے سرکشی کرتے. کہانیوں میں مشغول ہوتے (اور) بیہودہ بکواس کرتے تھے ﴿٦٧﴾

مُسْتَكْبِرِينَ بِهِۦ سَٰمِرًا تَهْجُرُونَ ﴿٦٧﴾

68. Do they not ponder over the Word (of Allah), or has anything (new) come to them that did not come to their fathers of old?

کیا انہوں نے اس کلام میں غور نہیں کیا یا اُنکے پاس کوئی ایسی
چیز آئی ہے جو اُنکے اگلے باپ دادا کے پاس نہیں آئی تھی ﴿٦٨﴾

أَفَلَمْ يَدَّبَّرُوا ٱلْقَوْلَ أَمْ جَآءَهُم
مَّا لَمْ يَأْتِ ءَابَآءَهُمُ ٱلْأَوَّلِينَ ﴿٦٨﴾

69. Or do they not recognise their Messenger, that they deny him?

یا یہ اپنے پیغمبر کو جانتے پہچانتے نہیں اِس وجہ سے اُن کو
نہیں مانتے؟ ﴿٦٩﴾

أَمْ لَمْ يَعْرِفُوا رَسُولَهُمْ فَهُمْ لَهُۥ
مُنكِرُونَ ﴿٦٩﴾

70. Or do they say, "He is Possessed"? Nay, he has brought them the Truth, but most of them hate the Truth.

کیا یہ کہتے ہیں کہ اسے سودا ہے (نہیں) بلکہ وہ اُن کے
پاس حق کو لیکر آئے ہیں اور اُنمیں سے اکثر حق کو ناپسند کرتے ہیں ﴿٧٠﴾

أَمْ يَقُولُونَ بِهِۦ جِنَّةٌۢ بَلْ جَآءَهُم
بِٱلْحَقِّ وَأَكْثَرُهُمْ لِلْحَقِّ كَٰرِهُونَ ﴿٧٠﴾

71. If the Truth had been in accord with their desires, truly the heavens and the earth, and all beings therein would have been in ruin nay, We have sent them their admonition, but they turn away from their admonition.

اور اگر (خدائے بر) حق اُن کی خواہشوں پر چلے تو آسمان اور
زمین اور جو اُن میں ہیں سب درہم برہم ہو جائیں بلکہ
ہم نے اُن کے پاس اُن کی نصیحت (کی کتاب) پہنچا دی ہے
اور وہ اپنی (کتاب) نصیحت سے مُنہ پھیر رہے ہیں ﴿٧١﴾

وَلَوِ ٱتَّبَعَ ٱلْحَقُّ أَهْوَآءَهُمْ لَفَسَدَتِ
ٱلسَّمَٰوَٰتُ وَٱلْأَرْضُ وَمَن فِيهِنَّ
بَلْ أَتَيْنَٰهُم بِذِكْرِهِمْ فَهُمْ عَن ذِكْرِهِم
مُّعْرِضُونَ ﴿٧١﴾

72. Or is it that thou asked them for some recompense? But the recompense of thy Lord is best: He is the Best of those who give sustenance.

کیا تم اُن سے (تبلیغ کے صلے میں) کچھ مال مانگتے ہو. تو تمہارے پروردگار کا
مال بہت اچھا ہے اور وہ سب سے بہتر رزق دینے والا ہے ﴿٧٢﴾

أَمْ تَسْـَٔلُهُمْ خَرْجًا فَخَرَاجُ رَبِّكَ خَيْرٌ
وَهُوَ خَيْرُ ٱلرَّٰزِقِينَ ﴿٧٢﴾

73. But verily thou callest them to the Straight Way;

اور تم تو اُن کو سیدھے رستے کی طرف بلاتے ہو ﴿٧٣﴾

وَإِنَّكَ لَتَدْعُوهُمْ إِلَىٰ صِرَٰطٍ مُّسْتَقِيمٍ ﴿٧٣﴾

74. And verily those who believe not in the Hereafter are deviating from that Way.

اور جو لوگ آخرت پر ایمان نہیں لاتے وہ رستے سے
الگ ہو رہے ہیں ﴿٧٤﴾

وَإِنَّ ٱلَّذِينَ لَا يُؤْمِنُونَ بِٱلْـَٔاخِرَةِ عَنِ
ٱلصِّرَٰطِ لَنَٰكِبُونَ ﴿٧٤﴾

75. If We had mercy on them and removed the distress which is on them, they would obstinately persist in their transgression, wandering in distraction to and fro.
76. We inflicted Punishment on them, but they humbled not themselves to their Lord, nor do they submissively entreat (Him)!—
77. Until We open on them a gate leading to a severe Punishment: then lo! they will be plunged in despair therein!
78. It is He Who has created for you (the faculties of) hearing, sight, feeling and understanding: little thanks it is ye give!
79. And He Has multiplied you through the earth, and to Him shall ye be gathered back.
80. It is He Who gives life and death, and to Him (is due) the alternation of Night and Day: will ye not then understand?
81. On the contrary they say things similar to what the ancients said.
82. They say: "What! When we die and become dust and bones, could we really be raised up again?
83. "Such things have been promised to us and to our fathers before! They are nothing but tales of the ancients!"
84. Say: "To whom belong the earth and all beings therein? (Say) if ye know!"
85. They will say, "To Allah!" Say: "Yet will ye not receive admonition?"
86. Say: "Who is the Lord of the seven heavens, and the Lord of the Mighty Throne
87. They will say, "(They belong) to Allah." Say: "Will ye not then fear.
88. Say: "Who is it in whose hands is the sovereignty of all things,—Who protects (all), but is not protected (of any)? (Say) if ye know."
89. They will say, "(It belongs) to Allah." Say: "Then how are ye deluded?"

اور اگر ہم اُن پر رحم کریں اور جو تکلیفیں اُنکو پہنچ رہی ہیں وہ دُور
کر دیں تو اپنی سرکشی پر اڑے رہیں (اور) بھٹکتے (پھریں) ﴿٧٥﴾
اور ہم نے اُن کو عذاب میں بھی پکڑا تو بھی اُنہوں نے خدا کے آگے
عاجزی نہ کی اور وہ عاجزی کرتے ہی نہیں ﴿٧٦﴾
یہاں تک کہ جب ہم نے اُن پر عذاب شدید کا دروازہ
کھول دیا تو اُس وقت وہاں نا اُمید ہو گئے ﴿٧٧﴾
اور وہی تو ہے جس نے تمہارے کان اور آنکھیں اور
دل بنائے۔ (لیکن) تم کم شکر گزاری کرتے ہو ﴿٧٨﴾
اور وہی تو ہے جس نے تم کو زمین میں پیدا کیا اور اُسی
کی طرف تم جمع ہو کر جاؤ گے ﴿٧٩﴾
اور وہی ہے جو زندگی بخشتا اور موت دیتا ہے اور رات
اور دن کا بدلتے رہنا اسی کا تصرف ہے کیا تم سمجھتے نہیں؟ ﴿٨٠﴾
بات یہ ہے کہ جو بات اگلے (کافر) کہتے تھے اسیطرح کی (بات) یہ کہتے ہیں ﴿٨١﴾
کہتے ہیں کہ جب ہم مرجائینگے اور مٹی ہو جائینگے اور استخوان
(بوسیدہ) کے سوا کچھ نہ رہیگا، تو کیا ہم پھر اٹھائے جائینگے؟ ﴿٨٢﴾
یہ وعدہ ہم سے اور ہم سے پہلے ہمارے باپ دادا سے بھی
ہوتا چلا آیا ہے (اجی) یہ تو صرف اگلے لوگوں کی کہانیاں ہیں ﴿٨٣﴾
کہو کہ اگر تم جانتے ہو تو بتاؤ کہ زمین اور جو کچھ زمین
میں ہے (سب) کس کا مال ہے ﴿٨٤﴾
جھٹ بول اٹھیں گے کہ خدا کا۔ کہو کہ پھر تم سوچتے
کیوں نہیں ﴿٨٥﴾
(ان سے) پوچھو کہ سات آسمانوں کا کون مالک ہے اور
عرش عظیم کا (کون) مالک (ہے)؟ ﴿٨٦﴾
بیساختہ کہہ دینگے کہ (یہ چیزیں) خدا ہی کی ہیں کہو کہ پھر تم ڈرتے کیوں نہیں ﴿٨٧﴾
کہو کہ اگر تم جانتے ہو تو بتاؤ کہ وہ کون ہے جسکے ہاتھ میں ہر چیز کی بادشاہی ہے
اور وہ پناہ دیتا ہے اور اُسکے مقابل کوئی کسی کو پناہ نہیں دے سکتا ﴿٨٨﴾
فوراً کہہ دینگے کہ (ایسی بادشاہی تو) خدا ہی کی ہے کہو پھر تم کہاں سے جادو میں پڑجاتے ہو ﴿٨٩﴾

وَلَوْ رَحِمْنٰهُمْ وَكَشَفْنَا مَا بِهِمْ مِّنْ ضُرٍّ
لَّلَجُّوْا فِيْ طُغْيَانِهِمْ يَعْمَهُوْنَ ﴿٧٥﴾
وَلَقَدْ اَخَذْنٰهُمْ بِالْعَذَابِ فَمَا اسْتَكَانُوْا
لِرَبِّهِمْ وَمَا يَتَضَرَّعُوْنَ ﴿٧٦﴾
حَتّٰى اِذَا فَتَحْنَا عَلَيْهِمْ بَابًا ذَا عَذَابٍ
شَدِيْدٍ اِذَا هُمْ فِيْهِ مُبْلِسُوْنَ ﴿٧٧﴾
وَهُوَ الَّذِيْ اَنْشَاَ لَكُمُ السَّمْعَ وَالْاَبْصَارَ
وَالْاَفْئِدَةَ قَلِيْلًا مَّا تَشْكُرُوْنَ ﴿٧٨﴾
وَهُوَ الَّذِيْ ذَرَاَكُمْ فِي الْاَرْضِ
وَاِلَيْهِ تُحْشَرُوْنَ ﴿٧٩﴾
وَهُوَ الَّذِيْ يُحْيٖ وَيُمِيْتُ وَلَهُ اخْتِلَافُ
الَّيْلِ وَالنَّهَارِ اَفَلَا تَعْقِلُوْنَ ﴿٨٠﴾
بَلْ قَالُوْا مِثْلَ مَا قَالَ الْاَوَّلُوْنَ ﴿٨١﴾
قَالُوْٓا ءَاِذَا مِتْنَا وَكُنَّا تُرَابًا وَّعِظَامًا
ءَاِنَّا لَمَبْعُوْثُوْنَ ﴿٨٢﴾
لَقَدْ وُعِدْنَا نَحْنُ وَاٰبَاۗؤُنَا هٰذَا مِنْ
قَبْلُ اِنْ هٰذَآ اِلَّآ اَسَاطِيْرُ الْاَوَّلِيْنَ ﴿٨٣﴾
قُلْ لِّمَنِ الْاَرْضُ وَمَنْ فِيْهَآ اِنْ
كُنْتُمْ تَعْلَمُوْنَ ﴿٨٤﴾
سَيَقُوْلُوْنَ لِلّٰهِ قُلْ اَفَلَا
تَذَكَّرُوْنَ ﴿٨٥﴾
قُلْ مَنْ رَّبُّ السَّمٰوٰتِ السَّبْعِ وَرَبُّ
الْعَرْشِ الْعَظِيْمِ ﴿٨٦﴾
سَيَقُوْلُوْنَ لِلّٰهِ قُلْ اَفَلَا تَتَّقُوْنَ ﴿٨٧﴾
قُلْ مَنْ بِيَدِهٖ مَلَكُوْتُ كُلِّ شَيْءٍ وَّهُوَ
يُجِيْرُ وَلَا يُجَارُ عَلَيْهِ اِنْ كُنْتُمْ تَعْلَمُوْنَ ﴿٨٨﴾
سَيَقُوْلُوْنَ لِلّٰهِ قُلْ فَاَنّٰى تُسْحَرُوْنَ ﴿٨٩﴾

90. We have sent them the Truth: but they indeed are liars.

91. No son did Allah beget, nor is there any god along with Him: (if there were many gods), behold, each god would have taken away what he had created, and some would have lorded it over others! Glory to Allah! (He is free) from the (sort of) things they attribute to Him!

92. He knows what is hidden and what is open: too high is He for the partners they attribute to Him!

93. Say: "O my Lord! if Thou wilt show me (in my lifetime) that which they are warned against,—

94. "Then, O my Lord! put me not amongst the people who do wrong!"

95. And We are certainly able to show thee (in fulfilment) that against which they are warned.

96. Repel evil with that which is best: We are well acquainted with the things they say.

97. And say "O my Lord! I seek refuge with Thee from the suggestions of the Satans.

98. "And I seek refuge with Thee O my Lord! lest they should come near me."

99. Until, when death comes to one of them, he says: "O my Lord! send me back (to life),—

100. "In order that I may work righteousness in the things I neglected."— "By no means! it is but a word he says."—Before them is a Partition till the Day they are raised up.

101. Then when the Trumpet is blown, there will be no more relationships between them that day, nor will one ask after another!

102. Then those whose balance (of good deeds) is heavy,—they will be successful.

103. But those whose balance is light, will be those who have lost their souls; in Hell will they abide.

بات یہ ہے کہ ہم نے انکے پاس حق پہنچا دیا ہے اور جو بت پرستی کئے جاتے ہیں بیشک جھوٹے ہیں ﴿۹۰﴾
خدا نے نہ تو کسی کو (اپنا) بیٹا بنایا ہے اور نہ اُس کے ساتھ
کوئی اور معبود ہے ایسا ہوتا تو ہر معبود اپنی اپنی مخلوقات
کو لے کر چل دیتا اور ایک دوسرے پر غالب آجاتا یہ لوگ
جو کچھ (خدا کے بارے میں) بیان کرتے ہیں خدا اس سے پاک ہے ﴿۹۱﴾
وہ پوشیدہ اور ظاہر کو جانتا ہے اور (مشرک) جو اسکے ساتھ
شریک کرتے ہیں (اسکی شان) اس سے بلند ہے ﴿۹۲﴾
(اے محمد) کہو کہ اے پروردگار جس عذاب کا ان (کفار) سے وعدہ ہو رہا ہے اگر
تو میری زندگی میں اُن پر نازل کر کے مجھے بھی دکھائے ﴿۹۳﴾
تو اے پروردگار مجھے (اس سے محفوظ رکھیو اور) ان ظالموں میں شامل نہ کیجیو ﴿۹۴﴾
اور جو وعدہ ہم اُن سے کر رہے ہیں ہم تم کو دکھا کر اُن پر نازل
کرنے پر قادر ہیں ﴿۹۵﴾
اور بُری بات کے جواب میں ایسی بات کہو جو نہایت اچھی ہو
اور یہ جو کچھ بیان کرتے ہیں ہمیں خوب معلوم ہے ﴿۹۶﴾
اور کہو کہ اے پروردگار میں شیطانوں کے وسوسوں سے تیری پناہ مانگتا ہوں ﴿۹۷﴾
اور اے پروردگار اس سے بھی تیری پناہ مانگتا ہوں کہ وہ میرے پاس آموجود ہوں ﴿۹۸﴾
(یہ لوگ اسی طرح غفلت میں رہیں گے) یہاں تک کہ جب ان میں سے کسی کے پاس موت
آجائیگی تو کہیگا کہ اے پروردگار مجھے پھر دنیا میں واپس بھیج دے ﴿۹۹﴾
تاکہ میں اس میں جسے چھوڑ آیا ہوں نیک کام کیا کروں ہرگز نہیں یہ ایک ایسی بات
ہے کہ وہ اسے زبان سے کہہ رہا ہوگا (اور اسکے ساتھ عمل نہیں ہوگا) اور انکے پیچھے برزخ
(حائل) ہے (جہاں وہ) اس دن تک کہ (دوبارہ) اٹھائے جائینگے (رہیں گے) ﴿۱۰۰﴾
پھر جب صور پھونکا جائے گا تو نہ تو ان میں قرابتیں رہیں گی
اور نہ ایک دوسرے کو پوچھیں گے ﴿۱۰۱﴾
تو جن کے (عملوں کے) بوجھ بھاری ہوں گے وہ فلاح
پانے والے ہیں ﴿۱۰۲﴾
اور جن کے بوجھ ہلکے ہوں گے وہ وہ لوگ ہیں جنہوں نے
اپنے تئیں خسارے میں ڈالا ہمیشہ دوزخ میں رہیں گے ﴿۱۰۳﴾

بَلْ أَتَيْنٰهُمْ بِالْحَقِّ وَإِنَّهُمْ لَكٰذِبُوْنَ ﴿٩٠﴾
مَا اتَّخَذَ اللّٰهُ مِنْ وَّلَدٍ وَّمَا كَانَ مَعَهٗ
مِنْ إِلٰهٍ إِذًا لَّذَهَبَ كُلُّ إِلٰهٍ بِمَا خَلَقَ
وَلَعَلَا بَعْضُهُمْ عَلٰى بَعْضٍ سُبْحٰنَ
اللّٰهِ عَمَّا يَصِفُوْنَ ﴿٩١﴾
عٰلِمِ الْغَيْبِ وَالشَّهَادَةِ فَتَعٰلٰى عَمَّا
يُشْرِكُوْنَ ﴿٩٢﴾ ع ١٥ ٥
قُلْ رَّبِّ إِمَّا تُرِيَنِّيْ مَا
يُوْعَدُوْنَ ﴿٩٣﴾
رَبِّ فَلَا تَجْعَلْنِيْ فِي الْقَوْمِ الظّٰلِمِيْنَ ﴿٩٤﴾
وَإِنَّا عَلٰى أَنْ نُّرِيَكَ مَا نَعِدُهُمْ
لَقٰدِرُوْنَ ﴿٩٥﴾
اِدْفَعْ بِالَّتِيْ هِيَ أَحْسَنُ السَّيِّئَةَ نَحْنُ
أَعْلَمُ بِمَا يَصِفُوْنَ ﴿٩٦﴾
وَقُلْ رَّبِّ أَعُوْذُ بِكَ مِنْ هَمَزٰتِ الشَّيٰطِيْنِ ﴿٩٧﴾
وَأَعُوْذُ بِكَ رَبِّ أَنْ يَّحْضُرُوْنِ ﴿٩٨﴾
حَتّٰى إِذَا جَاءَ أَحَدَهُمُ الْمَوْتُ قَالَ
رَبِّ ارْجِعُوْنِ ﴿٩٩﴾
لَعَلِّيْ أَعْمَلُ صَالِحًا فِيْمَا تَرَكْتُ كَلَّا
إِنَّهَا كَلِمَةٌ هُوَ قَائِلُهَا وَمِنْ وَّرَائِهِمْ
بَرْزَخٌ إِلٰى يَوْمِ يُبْعَثُوْنَ ﴿١٠٠﴾
فَإِذَا نُفِخَ فِي الصُّوْرِ فَلَا أَنْسَابَ بَيْنَهُمْ
يَوْمَئِذٍ وَّلَا يَتَسَاءَلُوْنَ ﴿١٠١﴾
فَمَنْ ثَقُلَتْ مَوَازِيْنُهٗ فَأُولٰٓئِكَ هُمُ
الْمُفْلِحُوْنَ ﴿١٠٢﴾
وَمَنْ خَفَّتْ مَوَازِيْنُهٗ فَأُولٰٓئِكَ الَّذِيْنَ
خَسِرُوْا أَنْفُسَهُمْ فِيْ جَهَنَّمَ خٰلِدُوْنَ ﴿١٠٣﴾

104. The Fire will burn their faces, and they will therein grin, with their lips displaced.

105. "Were not My Signs rehearsed to you, and ye did but treat them as falsehoods?"

106. They will say: "Our Lord! our misfortune overwhelmed us, and we became a people astray!

107. "Our Lord! bring us out of this: if ever we return (to evil), then shall we be wrong-doers indeed!"

108. He will say: "Be ye driven into it (with ignominy)! and speak ye not to Me!

109. "A part of My servants there was, who used to pray, 'Our Lord! we believe; then do Thou forgive us, and have mercy upon us: for Thou art the Best of those who show mercy!'

110. "But ye treated them with ridicule, so much so that (ridicule of) them made you forget My Message while ye were laughing at them!

111. "I have rewarded them this day for their patience and constancy: they are indeed the ones that have achieved Bliss..."

112. He will say: "What number of years did ye stay on earth?"

113. They will say: "We stayed a day or part of a day: but ask those who keep account."

114. He will say: "Ye stayed not but a little,—if ye had only known!

115. "Did ye then think that We had created you in jest, and that ye Would not be brought back to Us (for account)?"

116. Therefore exalted be Allah, the King, the Reality: there is no god but He, the Lord of the Throne of Honour!

117. If anyone invokes, besides Allah, any other god, he has no authority thereof; and his reckoning will be only with his Lord! and verily

آگ اُن کے مُونہوں کو جھلس دے گی اور وہ اس میں
تیوری چڑھائے ہوں گے ﴿١٠٤﴾
کیا تم کو میری آیتیں پڑھ کر سنائی جاتی تھیں (نہیں) تم
اُن کو سُنتے تھے اور جُھٹلاتے تھے ﴿١٠٥﴾
اے ہمارے پروردگار ہم پر ہماری کمبختی غالب ہوگئی اور
ہم رستے سے بھٹک گئے ﴿١٠٦﴾
اے پروردگار ہم کو اس میں سے نکال دے. اگر ہم پھر
(ایسے کام) کریں تو ظالم ہوں گے ﴿١٠٧﴾
(خدا) فرمائیگا کہ اسی میں ذلت کیساتھ پڑے رہو اور مجھ سے بات نہ کرو ﴿١٠٨﴾
میرے بندوں میں ایک گروہ تھا جو دعا کیا کرتا تھا کہ اے
ہمارے پروردگار ہم ایمان لائے تو تُو ہم کو بخش دے اور ہم
پر رحم کر اور تو سب سے بہتر رحم کرنے والا ہے ﴿١٠٩﴾
تو تم اُن سے تمسخر کرتے رہے یہاں تک کہ انکے پیچھے میری یاد
بھی بھول گئے. اور تم (ہمیشہ) اُن سے ہنسی کیا کرتے تھے ﴿١١٠﴾
آج میں نے اُن کو اُن کے صبر کا بدلہ دیا کہ وہ کامیاب
ہو گئے ﴿١١١﴾
(خدا) پوچھے گا کہ تم زمین میں کتنے برس رہے؟ ﴿١١٢﴾
وہ کہیں گے کہ ہم ایک روز یا ایک روز سے بھی کم رہے
تھے شمار کرنے والوں سے پوچھ لیجئے ﴿١١٣﴾
(خدا) فرمائے گا کہ (وہاں) تم (بہت ہی) کم رہے. کاش تم
جانتے ہوتے ﴿١١٤﴾
کیا تم یہ خیال کرتے ہو کہ ہم نے تم کو بے فائدہ پیدا کیا ہے
اور یہ کہ تم ہماری طرف لوٹ کر نہیں آؤ گے؟ ﴿١١٥﴾
تو خدا جو سچا بادشاہ ہے (اسکی شان) اس سے اُونچی ہے. اُسکے
سوا کوئی معبود نہیں (وہی) عرش بزرگ کا مالک ہے ﴿١١٦﴾
اور جو شخص خدا کے ساتھ اور معبود کو پکارتا ہے جس کی اُسکے
پاس کچھ بھی سند نہیں تو اس کا حساب خدا ہی کے ہاں ہوگا.

تَلْفَحُ وُجُوهَهُمُ النَّارُ وَهُمْ فِيهَا
كَالِحُونَ ﴿١٠٤﴾
أَلَمْ تَكُنْ آيَاتِي تُتْلَىٰ عَلَيْكُمْ فَكُنتُم
بِهَا تُكَذِّبُونَ ﴿١٠٥﴾
قَالُوا رَبَّنَا غَلَبَتْ عَلَيْنَا شِقْوَتُنَا وَكُنَّا
قَوْمًا ضَالِّينَ ﴿١٠٦﴾
رَبَّنَا أَخْرِجْنَا مِنْهَا فَإِنْ عُدْنَا فَإِنَّا
ظَالِمُونَ ﴿١٠٧﴾
قَالَ اخْسَئُوا فِيهَا وَلَا تُكَلِّمُونِ ﴿١٠٨﴾
إِنَّهُ كَانَ فَرِيقٌ مِّنْ عِبَادِي يَقُولُونَ
رَبَّنَا آمَنَّا فَاغْفِرْ لَنَا وَارْحَمْنَا وَأَنتَ
خَيْرُ الرَّاحِمِينَ ﴿١٠٩﴾
فَاتَّخَذْتُمُوهُمْ سِخْرِيًّا حَتَّىٰ أَنسَوْكُمْ
ذِكْرِي وَكُنتُم مِّنْهُمْ تَضْحَكُونَ ﴿١١٠﴾
إِنِّي جَزَيْتُهُمُ الْيَوْمَ بِمَا صَبَرُوا أَنَّهُمْ
هُمُ الْفَائِزُونَ ﴿١١١﴾
قَالَ كَمْ لَبِثْتُمْ فِي الْأَرْضِ عَدَدَ سِنِينَ ﴿١١٢﴾
قَالُوا لَبِثْنَا يَوْمًا أَوْ بَعْضَ يَوْمٍ فَاسْأَلِ
الْعَادِّينَ ﴿١١٣﴾
قَالَ إِن لَّبِثْتُمْ إِلَّا قَلِيلًا لَّوْ أَنَّكُمْ
كُنتُمْ تَعْلَمُونَ ﴿١١٤﴾
أَفَحَسِبْتُمْ أَنَّمَا خَلَقْنَاكُمْ عَبَثًا وَأَنَّكُمْ
إِلَيْنَا لَا تُرْجَعُونَ ﴿١١٥﴾
فَتَعَالَى اللَّهُ الْمَلِكُ الْحَقُّ لَا إِلَٰهَ إِلَّا
هُوَ رَبُّ الْعَرْشِ الْكَرِيمِ ﴿١١٦﴾
وَمَن يَدْعُ مَعَ اللَّهِ إِلَٰهًا آخَرَ لَا بُرْهَانَ
لَهُ بِهِ فَإِنَّمَا حِسَابُهُ عِندَ رَبِّهِ إِنَّهُ

SÛRA–24
AN-NÛR
(INTRODUCTION)

The environmental and social influences which most frequently wreck our spiritual ideals have to do with sex, and especially with its misuse, whether in the form of unregulated behaviour, of false charges or scandals, or breach of the refined conventions of personal or domestic privacy. Our complete conquest of all pitfalls in such matters enables us to rise to the higher regions of Light and of Allah-created Nature, about which a mystic doctrine is suggested. This subject is continued in the next Sûra.

As the reprobation of false slanders about women (24: 11-20) is connected with an incident that happened to Ḥadhrat 'Ãi-sha in A.H. 5-6, that fixes the chronological place of this Madinah Sûra.

لَا يُفْلِحُ الْكٰفِرُوْنَ ﴿١١٧﴾
وَقُلْ رَّبِّ اغْفِرْ وَارْحَمْ وَاَنْتَ خَيْرُ
الرّٰحِمِيْنَ ﴿١١٨﴾ ع

سُوْرَةُ النُّوْرِ مَدَنِيَّةٌ وَّهِيَ اَرْبَعٌ وَّسِتُّوْنَ اٰيَةً وَّتِسْعُ رُكُوْعَاتٍ

بِسْمِ اللّٰهِ الرَّحْمٰنِ الرَّحِيْمِ
سُوْرَةٌ اَنْزَلْنٰهَا وَفَرَضْنٰهَا وَاَنْزَلْنَا فِيْهَآ
اٰيٰتٍۢ بَيِّنٰتٍ لَّعَلَّكُمْ تَذَكَّرُوْنَ ﴿١﴾
اَلزَّانِيَةُ وَالزَّانِيْ فَاجْلِدُوْا كُلَّ وَاحِدٍ
مِّنْهُمَا مِائَةَ جَلْدَةٍ ۖ وَّلَا تَاْخُذْكُمْ
بِهِمَا رَاْفَةٌ فِيْ دِيْنِ اللّٰهِ اِنْ كُنْتُمْ
تُؤْمِنُوْنَ بِاللّٰهِ وَالْيَوْمِ الْاٰخِرِ ۚ وَلْيَشْهَدْ
عَذَابَهُمَا طَآئِفَةٌ مِّنَ الْمُؤْمِنِيْنَ ﴿٢﴾
اَلزَّانِيْ لَا يَنْكِحُ اِلَّا زَانِيَةً اَوْ
مُشْرِكَةً ۫ وَّالزَّانِيَةُ لَا يَنْكِحُهَآ اِلَّا
زَانٍ اَوْ مُشْرِكٌ ۚ وَحُرِّمَ ذٰلِكَ عَلَى
الْمُؤْمِنِيْنَ ﴿٣﴾
وَالَّذِيْنَ يَرْمُوْنَ الْمُحْصَنٰتِ ثُمَّ لَمْ
يَاْتُوْا بِاَرْبَعَةِ شُهَدَآءَ فَاجْلِدُوْهُمْ
ثَمٰنِيْنَ جَلْدَةً وَّلَا تَقْبَلُوْا لَهُمْ شَهَادَةً
اَبَدًا ۚ وَاُولٰٓئِكَ هُمُ الْفٰسِقُوْنَ ﴿٤﴾
اِلَّا الَّذِيْنَ تَابُوْا مِنْۢ بَعْدِ ذٰلِكَ وَ
اَصْلَحُوْا ۚ فَاِنَّ اللّٰهَ غَفُوْرٌ رَّحِيْمٌ ﴿٥﴾
وَالَّذِيْنَ يَرْمُوْنَ اَزْوَاجَهُمْ وَلَمْ يَكُنْ
لَّهُمْ شُهَدَآءُ اِلَّآ اَنْفُسُهُمْ فَشَهَادَةُ
اَحَدِهِمْ اَرْبَعُ شَهٰدٰتٍۢ بِاللّٰهِ ۙ اِنَّهٗ لَمِنَ
الصّٰدِقِيْنَ ﴿٦﴾
وَالْخَامِسَةُ اَنَّ لَعْنَتَ اللّٰهِ عَلَيْهِ اِنْ

کچھ شک نہیں کہ کافر رستگاری نہیں پائیں گے ﴿١١٧﴾
اور خدا سے دعا کرو کہ میرے پروردگار مجھے بخش دے اور
(مجھ پر) رحم کر اور تو سب سے بہتر رحم کرنے والا ہے ﴿١١٨﴾

سورۂ نور مدنی ہے اور اس میں چونسٹھ آیتیں اور نو رکوع ہیں

شروع خدا کا نام لے کر جو بڑا مہربان نہایت رحم والا ہے
یہ (ایک) سورت ہے جس کو ہم نے نازل کیا اور اس (کے احکام)
کو فرض کر دیا اور اس میں واضح المطالب آیتیں نازل کیں تاکہ تم یاد رکھو ﴿١﴾
بدکاری کرنے والی عورت اور بدکاری کرنے والا مرد (جب
ان کی بدکاری ثابت ہو جائے تو) دونوں میں سے ہر ایک کو
سو درے مارو۔ اور اگر تم خدا اور روز آخرت پر ایمان رکھتے ہو
تو شرع خدا (کے حکم) میں تمہیں ان پر ہرگز ترس نہ آئے۔ اور چاہیئے
کہ ان کی سزا کے وقت مسلمانوں کی ایک جماعت بھی موجود ہو ﴿٢﴾
بدکار مرد تو بدکار یا مشرک عورت کے سوا نکاح نہیں کرتا اور
بدکار عورت کو بھی بدکار یا مشرک مرد کے سوا اور کوئی نکاح
میں نہیں لاتا [١٩٣] اور یہ (یعنی بدکار عورت سے نکاح کرنا)
مومنوں پر حرام ہے ﴿٣﴾
اور جو لوگ پرہیزگار عورتوں کو بدکاری کا عیب لگائیں
اور اس پر چار گواہ نہ لائیں تو ان کو اسی درے مارو
اور کبھی ان کی شہادت قبول نہ کرو اور یہی
بدکردار ہیں ﴿٤﴾
ہاں جو اس کے بعد توبہ کر لیں اور (اپنی حالت) سنوار
لیں تو خدا (بھی) بخشنے والا مہربان ہے ﴿٥﴾
اور جو لوگ اپنی عورتوں پر بدکاری کی تہمت لگائیں اور
خود ان کے سوا ان کے گواہ نہ ہوں تو ہر ایک کی شہادت
یہ ہے کہ پہلے تو چار بار خدا کی قسم کھائے کہ بے شک
وہ سچا ہے ﴿٦﴾
اور پانچویں (بار) یہ (کہے) کہ اگر وہ جھوٹا ہو تو اس پر

the Unbelievers shall not prosper.

118. So say; "O my lord! grant Thou forgiveness and mercy! for Thou art the Best of those who show mercy!"

An-Nûr, or Light

In the name of Allah, Most Gracious, Most Merciful.

1. A Sûra which We have sent down and which We have ordained: in it have We sent down Clear Signs, in order that ye may receive admonition.

2. The woman and the man guilty of fornication,— flog each of them with a hundred stripes: let not compassion move you in their case, in a matter prescribed by Allah, if ye believe in Allah and the Last Day: and let a party of the Believers witness their punishment.

3. The adulterer cannot have sexual relations with any but an adulteress or an idolatress, and the adulteress, none can have sexual relations with her but an adulterer or an idolater; to the believers such a thing is forbidden.

4. And those who launch a charge against chaste women, and produce not four witnesses (to support their allegations),— flog them with eighty stripes; and reject their evidence ever after: for such men are wicked transgressors;—

5. Except those who repent thereafter and mend (their conduct); for Allah is Oft-Forgiving, Most Merciful.

6. And for those who launch a charge against their wives, and have (in support) no evidence but their own,— let one of them testify four times by Allah that he is of those who speak the Truth.

7. And the fifth (oath) (should be) that he solemnly invokes the curse

of Allah on himself if he tells a lie.

8. But it would avert the punishment from the wife, if she bears witness four times (with an oath) by Allah, that (her husband) is telling a lie;

9. And the fifth (oath) should be that she solemnly invokes the wrath of Allah on herself if (her accuser) is telling the truth.

10. If it were not for Allah's grace and mercy on you, and that Allah is Oft-Returning, full of Wisdom,—(ye would be ruined indeed).

11. Those who brought forward the lie are a body among yourselves: think it not to be an evil to you; on the contrary it is good for you: to every man among them (will come the punishment) of the sin that he earned, and to him who took on himself the lead among them, will be a Chastisement grievous.

12. Why did not the Believers—men and women —when ye heard of the affair,—thought well of their people and say, "This (charge) is an obvious lie"?

13. Why did they not bring four witnesses to prove it? When they have not brought the witnesses, such men, in the sight of Allah, (stand forth) themselves as liars!

14. Were it not for the grace and mercy of Allah on you, in this world and the Hereafter, a grievous chastisement would have seized you in that ye rushed glibly into this affair.

15. Behold, ye received it on your tongues, and said out of your mouths things of which ye had no knowledge; and ye thought it to be a light matter, while it was most serious in the sight of Allah.

16. And why did ye not, when ye heard it, say?— "It is not right of us to speak of this: glory to Thee (our Lord) this is a most serious slander!"

17. Allah doth admonish you, that ye may never repeat such (conduct), if ye are (true) Believers.

خدا کی لعنت ⑦
اور عورت سے سزا کو یہ بات ٹال سکتی ہے کہ وہ پہلے چار بار
خدا کی قسم کھائے کہ بے شک یہ جھوٹا ہے ⑧
اور پانچویں (دفعہ) یوں (کہے) کہ اگر یہ سچا ہو تو مجھ پر
خدا کا غضب (نازل ہو) ⑨
اور اگر تم پر خدا کا فضل اور اسکی مہربانی نہ ہوتی تو بہت سی خرابیاں
پیدا ہو جاتیں مگر وہ صاحب کرم ہے اور یہ کہ خدا توبہ قبول کرنیوالا اور حکیم ہے ⑩
جن لوگوں نے بہتان باندھا ہے تم ہی میں سے ایک جماعت ہے
اسکو اپنے حق میں برا نہ سمجھنا۔ بلکہ وہ تمہارے لئے اچھا ہے۔ ان میں سے
جس شخص نے گناہ کا جتنا حصہ لیا اسکے لئے اتنا وبال ہے۔ اور جس نے
ان میں سے اس بہتان کا بڑا بوجھ اٹھایا ہے اسکو بڑا عذاب ہوگا ⑪
جب تم نے وہ بات سنی تھی تو مومن مردوں اور عورتوں نے
کیوں اپنے دلوں میں نیک گمان نہ کیا۔ اور (کیوں نہ)
کہا کہ یہ صریح طوفان ہے ⑫
یہ (افترا پرداز) اپنی بات (کی تصدیق) کے (لئے) چار گواہ کیوں نہ
لائے۔ تو جب یہ گواہ نہیں لا سکے تو خدا کے نزدیک یہی جھوٹے ہیں ⑬
اور اگر دنیا اور آخرت میں تم پر خدا کا فضل اور اسکی رحمت
نہ ہوتی تو جس شغل میں تم منہمک تھے اس کی وجہ سے
تم پر بڑا (سخت) عذاب نازل ہوتا ⑭
جب تم اپنی زبانوں سے اس کا ایک دوسرے سے ذکر
کرتے تھے اور اپنے منہ سے ایسی بات کہتے تھے جسکا تم کو کچھ بھی علم نہ تھا
اور تم اسے ایک ہلکی بات سمجھتے تھے اور خدا کے نزدیک وہ بڑی (بھاری) بات تھی ⑮
اور جب تم نے اسے سنا تھا تو کیوں نہ کہہ دیا کہ ہمیں شایاں
نہیں کہ ایسی بات زبان پر لائیں۔ (پروردگار) تو پاک ہے
یہ تو (بہت) بڑا بہتان ہے ⑯
خدا تمہیں نصیحت کرتا ہے کہ اگر مومن ہو تو پھر کبھی ایسا
(کام) نہ کرنا ⑰

كَانَ مِنَ الْكٰذِبِيْنَ ⑦
وَيَدْرَؤُا عَنْهَا الْعَذَابَ اَنْ تَشْهَدَ اَرْبَعَ
شَهٰدٰتٍۭ بِاللّٰهِ اِنَّهٗ لَمِنَ الْكٰذِبِيْنَ ⑧
وَالْخَامِسَةَ اَنَّ غَضَبَ اللّٰهِ عَلَيْهَآ اِنْ
كَانَ مِنَ الصّٰدِقِيْنَ ⑨
وَلَوْلَا فَضْلُ اللّٰهِ عَلَيْكُمْ وَرَحْمَتُهٗ وَ
ع اَنَّ اللّٰهَ تَوَّابٌ حَكِيْمٌ ⑩
اِنَّ الَّذِيْنَ جَآءُوْ بِالْاِفْكِ عُصْبَةٌ مِّنْكُمْ
لَا تَحْسَبُوْهُ شَرًّا لَّكُمْ بَلْ هُوَ خَيْرٌ لَّكُمْ
لِكُلِّ امْرِئٍ مِّنْهُمْ مَّا اكْتَسَبَ مِنَ الْاِثْمِ
وَالَّذِيْ تَوَلّٰى كِبْرَهٗ مِنْهُمْ لَهٗ عَذَابٌ عَظِيْمٌ ⑪
لَوْلَآ اِذْ سَمِعْتُمُوْهُ ظَنَّ الْمُؤْمِنُوْنَ وَ
الْمُؤْمِنٰتُ بِاَنْفُسِهِمْ خَيْرًا وَّقَالُوْا هٰذَآ
اِفْكٌ مُّبِيْنٌ ⑫
لَوْلَا جَآءُوْ عَلَيْهِ بِاَرْبَعَةِ شُهَدَآءَ فَاِذْ لَمْ
يَاْتُوْا بِالشُّهَدَآءِ فَاُولٰٓئِكَ عِنْدَ اللّٰهِ هُمُ الْكٰذِبُوْنَ ⑬
وَلَوْلَا فَضْلُ اللّٰهِ عَلَيْكُمْ وَرَحْمَتُهٗ فِي
الدُّنْيَا وَالْاٰخِرَةِ لَمَسَّكُمْ فِيْ مَآ اَفَضْتُمْ
فِيْهِ عَذَابٌ عَظِيْمٌ ⑭
اِذْ تَلَقَّوْنَهٗ بِاَلْسِنَتِكُمْ وَتَقُوْلُوْنَ بِاَفْوَاهِكُمْ
مَّا لَيْسَ لَكُمْ بِهٖ عِلْمٌ وَّتَحْسَبُوْنَهٗ هَيِّنًا
وَّهُوَ عِنْدَ اللّٰهِ عَظِيْمٌ ⑮
وَلَوْلَآ اِذْ سَمِعْتُمُوْهُ قُلْتُمْ مَّا يَكُوْنُ لَنَآ
اَنْ نَّتَكَلَّمَ بِهٰذَا سُبْحٰنَكَ هٰذَا بُهْتَانٌ
عَظِيْمٌ ⑯
يَعِظُكُمُ اللّٰهُ اَنْ تَعُوْدُوْا لِمِثْلِهٖٓ اَبَدًا
اِنْ كُنْتُمْ مُّؤْمِنِيْنَ ⑰

18. And Allah makes the Signs plain to you: for Allah is full of knowledge and wisdom.

19. Those who love (to see) scandal circulate among the Believers, will have a grievous Chastisement in this life and in the Hereafter: Allah knows, and ye know not.

20. Were it not for the grace and mercy of Allah on you, and that Allah is full of kindness and mercy, (ye would be ruined indeed).

21. O ye who believe! follow not Satan's footsteps: if any will follow the footsteps of Satan, he will (but) command what is indecent and wrong: and were it not for the grace and mercy of Allah on you, not one of you would ever have been pure: but Allah doth purify whom He pleases: and Allah is One Who hears and knows (all things).

22. Let not those among you who are endued with grace and amplitude of means resolve by oath against helping their kinsmen, those in want, and those who have left their homes in Allah's cause: let them forgive and overlook, do you not wish that Allah should forgive you? For Allah is Oft-Forgiving, Most Merciful.

23. Those who slander chaste, indiscreet and believing women are cursed in this life and in the Hereafter: for them is a grievous Chastisement—

24. On the Day when their tongues, their hands, and their feet will bear witness against them as to their actions.

25. On that Day Allah will pay them back (all) their just dues, and they will realise that Allah is the (very) Truth, that makes all things manifest.

26. Women impure are for men impure, and men impure for women

اور خدا تمہارے (سمجھانے کے) لئے اپنی آیتیں کھول کھول کر
بیان فرماتا ہے اور خدا جاننے والا (اور) حکمت والا ہے ﴿١٨﴾
جو لوگ اس بات کو پسند کرتے ہیں کہ مومنوں میں بیحیائی
(یعنی تہمت بدکاری کی خبر) پھیلے اُن کو دنیا اور آخرت
میں دُکھ دینے والا عذاب ہوگا اور خدا جانتا ہے اور
تم نہیں جانتے ﴿١٩﴾
اور اگر تم پر خدا کا فضل اور اسکی رحمت نہ ہوتی (تو کیا کچھ نہ ہوتا
مگر وہ کریم ہے) اور یہ کہ خدا نہایت مہربان (اور) رحیم ہے ﴿٢٠﴾
مومنو! شیطان کے قدموں پر نہ چلنا۔ اور جو شخص شیطان
کے قدموں پر چلے گا تو شیطان تو بے حیائی (کی باتیں) اور
بُرے کام ہی بتائے گا اور اگر تم پر خدا کا فضل اور اُسکی
مہربانی نہ ہوتی تو ایک شخص بھی تم میں پاک نہ ہو سکتا
مگر خدا جس کو چاہتا ہے پاک کر دیتا ہے اور خدا سننے
والا (اور) جاننے والا ہے ﴿٢١﴾
اور جو لوگ تم میں صاحبِ فضل اور صاحبِ وسعت ہیں
وہ اس بات کی قسم نہ کھائیں کہ رشتہ داروں اور محتاجوں اور
وطن چھوڑ جانے والوں کو کچھ خرچ پات نہیں دینگے۔ اُنکو چاہیے
کہ معاف کر دیں اور درگزر کریں کیا تم پسند نہیں کرتے کہ خدا
تم کو بخش دے؟ اور خدا تو بخشنے والا مہربان ہے ﴿٢٢﴾
جو لوگ پرہیزگار (اور) بُرے کاموں سے بے خبر اور ایماندار عورتوں
پر بدکاری کی تہمت لگاتے ہیں اُن پر دنیا اور آخرت (دونوں)
میں لعنت ہے اور اُن کو سخت عذاب ہوگا ﴿٢٣﴾
(یعنی قیامت کے روز) جس دن اُن کی زبانیں اور ہاتھ اور
پاؤں سب اُن کے کاموں کی گواہی دیں گے ﴿٢٤﴾
اُس دن خدا اُن کو (اُنکے اعمال کا) پورا پورا (اور) ٹھیک بدلہ
دیگا اور اُنکو معلوم ہو جائیگا کہ خدا برحق (اور حق کو) ظاہر کرنیوالا ہے ﴿٢٥﴾
ناپاک عورتیں ناپاک مردوں کیلئے ہیں اور ناپاک مرد ناپاک

وَيُبَيِّنُ اللّٰهُ لَكُمُ الْاٰيٰتِ ۭ وَاللّٰهُ عَلِيْمٌ
حَكِيْمٌ ﴿١٨﴾
اِنَّ الَّذِيْنَ يُحِبُّوْنَ اَنْ تَشِيْعَ الْفَاحِشَةُ
فِي الَّذِيْنَ اٰمَنُوْا لَهُمْ عَذَابٌ اَلِيْمٌ ۙ فِي
الدُّنْيَا وَالْاٰخِرَةِ ۭ وَاللّٰهُ يَعْلَمُ وَاَنْتُمْ
لَا تَعْلَمُوْنَ ﴿١٩﴾
وَلَوْلَا فَضْلُ اللّٰهِ عَلَيْكُمْ وَرَحْمَتُهٗ وَاَنَّ
اللّٰهَ رَءُوْفٌ رَّحِيْمٌ ﴿٢٠﴾
يٰٓاَيُّهَا الَّذِيْنَ اٰمَنُوْا لَا تَتَّبِعُوْا خُطُوٰتِ
الشَّيْطٰنِ ۭ وَمَنْ يَّتَّبِعْ خُطُوٰتِ الشَّيْطٰنِ
فَاِنَّهٗ يَاْمُرُ بِالْفَحْشَاۗءِ وَالْمُنْكَرِ ۭ وَلَوْلَا فَضْلُ
اللّٰهِ عَلَيْكُمْ وَرَحْمَتُهٗ مَا زَكٰى مِنْكُمْ مِّنْ
اَحَدٍ اَبَدًا ۙ وَّلٰكِنَّ اللّٰهَ يُزَكِّيْ مَنْ يَّشَاۗءُ ۭ
وَاللّٰهُ سَمِيْعٌ عَلِيْمٌ ﴿٢١﴾
وَلَا يَاْتَلِ اُولُوا الْفَضْلِ مِنْكُمْ وَالسَّعَةِ
اَنْ يُّؤْتُوْٓا اُولِي الْقُرْبٰى وَالْمَسٰكِيْنَ وَ
الْمُهٰجِرِيْنَ فِيْ سَبِيْلِ اللّٰهِ ۠ وَلْيَعْفُوْا
وَلْيَصْفَحُوْا ۭ اَلَا تُحِبُّوْنَ اَنْ يَّغْفِرَ اللّٰهُ
لَكُمْ ۭ وَاللّٰهُ غَفُوْرٌ رَّحِيْمٌ ﴿٢٢﴾
اِنَّ الَّذِيْنَ يَرْمُوْنَ الْمُحْصَنٰتِ الْغٰفِلٰتِ
الْمُؤْمِنٰتِ لُعِنُوْا فِي الدُّنْيَا وَالْاٰخِرَةِ ۠
وَلَهُمْ عَذَابٌ عَظِيْمٌ ﴿٢٣﴾
يَّوْمَ تَشْهَدُ عَلَيْهِمْ اَلْسِنَتُهُمْ وَاَيْدِيْهِمْ
وَاَرْجُلُهُمْ بِمَا كَانُوْا يَعْمَلُوْنَ ﴿٢٤﴾
يَوْمَىِٕذٍ يُّوَفِّيْهِمُ اللّٰهُ دِيْنَهُمُ الْحَقَّ وَ
يَعْلَمُوْنَ اَنَّ اللّٰهَ هُوَ الْحَقُّ الْمُبِيْنُ ﴿٢٥﴾
اَلْخَبِيْثٰتُ لِلْخَبِيْثِيْنَ وَالْخَبِيْثُوْنَ

لِلْخَبِيثَٰتِ ۚ وَالطَّيِّبَٰتُ لِلطَّيِّبِينَ وَ
الطَّيِّبُونَ لِلطَّيِّبَٰتِ ۚ أُولَٰٓئِكَ مُبَرَّءُونَ
مِمَّا يَقُولُونَ ۖ لَهُم مَّغْفِرَةٌ وَرِزْقٌ
كَرِيمٌ ﴿٢٦﴾

عورتوں کیلئے۔ اور پاک عورتیں پاک مردوں کیلئے ہیں۔
اور پاک مرد پاک عورتوں کیلئے۔ یہ (پاک لوگ) ان (بدگویوں)
کی باتوں سے بری ہیں (اور) اُن کیلئے بخشش اور
نیک روزی ہے ﴿٢٦﴾

impure, and women of purity are for men of purity, and men of purity are for women of purity: these are innocent of all what people say: for them there is forgiveness, and a provision honourable.

يَٰٓأَيُّهَا الَّذِينَ ءَامَنُوا لَا تَدْخُلُوا بُيُوتًا
غَيْرَ بُيُوتِكُمْ حَتَّىٰ تَسْتَأْنِسُوا وَتُسَلِّمُوا
عَلَىٰٓ أَهْلِهَا ۚ ذَٰلِكُمْ خَيْرٌ لَّكُمْ لَعَلَّكُمْ
تَذَكَّرُونَ ﴿٢٧﴾

مومنو! اپنے گھروں کے سوا دوسرے (لوگوں کے) گھروں میں
گھر والوں سے اجازت لئے اور اُن کو سلام کئے بغیر
داخل نہ ہوا کرو۔ یہ تمہارے حق میں بہتر ہے (اور ہم یہ نصیحت
اس لئے کرتے ہیں کہ) شاید تم یاد رکھو ﴿٢٧﴾

27. O ye who believe! enter not houses other than your own, until ye have asked permission and saluted those in them: that is best for you, in order that ye may heed (what is seemly).

فَإِن لَّمْ تَجِدُوا فِيهَآ أَحَدًا فَلَا تَدْخُلُوهَا
حَتَّىٰ يُؤْذَنَ لَكُمْ ۖ وَإِن قِيلَ لَكُمُ ارْجِعُوا
فَارْجِعُوا ۖ هُوَ أَزْكَىٰ لَكُمْ ۚ وَاللَّهُ بِمَا تَعْمَلُونَ
عَلِيمٌ ﴿٢٨﴾

اگر تم گھر میں کسی کو موجود نہ پاؤ تو جب تک تم کو اجازت
نہ دی جائے اسمیں مت داخل ہو۔ اور اگر یہ کہا جائے کہ (اس وقت)
لوٹ جاؤ تو لوٹ جایا کرو۔ یہ تمہارے لئے بڑی پاکیزگی کی بات ہے
اور جو کام تم کرتے ہو خدا سب جانتا ہے ﴿٢٨﴾

28. If ye find no one in the house, enter not until permission is given to you: if ye are asked to go back, go back: that makes for greater purity for yourselves: and Allah knows well all that ye do.

لَّيْسَ عَلَيْكُمْ جُنَاحٌ أَن تَدْخُلُوا بُيُوتًا
غَيْرَ مَسْكُونَةٍ فِيهَا مَتَٰعٌ لَّكُمْ ۚ وَاللَّهُ يَعْلَمُ
مَا تُبْدُونَ وَمَا تَكْتُمُونَ ﴿٢٩﴾

(ہاں) اگر تم کسی ایسے مکان میں جاؤ جس میں کوئی نہ بستا ہو
اور اسمیں تمہارا اسباب (رکھا) ہو تو تم پر کچھ گناہ نہیں۔ اور جو کچھ
تم ظاہر کرتے ہو اور جو پوشیدہ کرتے ہو خدا کو سب معلوم ہے ﴿٢٩﴾

29. It is no fault on your part to enter houses not used for living in, which serve some (other) use for you: and Allah has knowledge of what ye reveal and what ye conceal.

قُل لِّلْمُؤْمِنِينَ يَغُضُّوا مِنْ أَبْصَٰرِهِمْ
وَيَحْفَظُوا فُرُوجَهُمْ ۚ ذَٰلِكَ أَزْكَىٰ لَهُمْ ۗ
إِنَّ اللَّهَ خَبِيرٌۢ بِمَا يَصْنَعُونَ ﴿٣٠﴾

مومن مردوں سے کہہ دو کہ اپنی نظریں نیچی رکھا کریں اور
اپنی شرمگاہوں کی حفاظت کیا کریں۔ یہ اُن کیلئے بڑی پاکیزگی
کی بات ہے (اور) جو کام یہ کرتے ہیں خدا اُن سے خبردار ہے ﴿٣٠﴾

30. Say to the believing men that they should lower their gaze and guard their modesty: that will make for greater purity for them: and Allah is well acquainted with all that they do.

وَقُل لِّلْمُؤْمِنَٰتِ يَغْضُضْنَ مِنْ
أَبْصَٰرِهِنَّ وَيَحْفَظْنَ فُرُوجَهُنَّ وَلَا
يُبْدِينَ زِينَتَهُنَّ إِلَّا مَا ظَهَرَ مِنْهَا ۖ
وَلْيَضْرِبْنَ بِخُمُرِهِنَّ عَلَىٰ جُيُوبِهِنَّ ۖ
وَلَا يُبْدِينَ زِينَتَهُنَّ إِلَّا لِبُعُولَتِهِنَّ أَوْ
ءَابَآئِهِنَّ أَوْ ءَابَآءِ بُعُولَتِهِنَّ أَوْ أَبْنَآئِهِنَّ
أَوْ أَبْنَآءِ بُعُولَتِهِنَّ أَوْ إِخْوَٰنِهِنَّ أَوْ بَنِىٓ
إِخْوَٰنِهِنَّ أَوْ بَنِىٓ أَخَوَٰتِهِنَّ أَوْ نِسَآئِهِنَّ
أَوْ مَا مَلَكَتْ أَيْمَٰنُهُنَّ أَوِ التَّٰبِعِينَ غَيْرِ

اور مومن عورتوں سے بھی کہہ دو کہ وہ بھی اپنی نگاہیں نیچی
رکھا کریں اور اپنی شرمگاہوں کی حفاظت کیا کریں اور اپنی آرائش
(یعنی زیور کے مقامات) کو ظاہر نہ ہونے دیا کریں مگر جو اُس میں سے
کھلا رہتا ہو۔ اور اپنے سینوں پر اوڑھنیاں اوڑھے رہا کریں
اور اپنے خاوند اور باپ اور خسر اور بیٹوں اور خاوند
کے بیٹوں اور بھائیوں اور بھتیجوں اور بھانجوں اور
اپنی (ہی قسم کی) عورتوں اور لونڈی غلاموں کے سوا
نیز اُن خدام کے جو عورتوں کی خواہش نہ رکھیں یا
ایسے لڑکوں کے جو عورتوں کے پردے کی چیزوں سے واقف نہ

31. And say to the believing women that they should lower their gaze and guard their modesty; that they should not display their beauty and ornaments except what (ordinarily) appear thereof; that they should draw their veils over their bosoms and not display their beauty except to their husbands, their fathers, their husbands' fathers, their sons, their husbands' sons, their brothers or their brothers' sons, or their sisters' sons, or their women, or the slaves whom their right hands possess, or male attendants free of sexual desires. Or small children who have no

carnal knowledge of women; and that they should not strike their feet in order to draw attention to their hidden ornaments. And O ye Believers! turn ye all together towards Allah in repentance that ye may be successful.

ہوں (غرض ان لوگوں کے سوا کسی پر) اپنی زینت (اور سنگار
کے مقامات) کو ظاہر نہ ہونے دیں۔ اور اپنے پاؤں (ایسے
طور سے زمین پر) نہ ماریں کہ (جھنکار کانوں میں پہنچے
اور) اُن کا پوشیدہ زیور معلوم ہو جائے اور مومنو سب
خدا کے آگے توبہ کرو تاکہ فلاح پاؤ (۳۱)

أُولِي الْإِرْبَةِ مِنَ الرِّجَالِ أَوِ الطِّفْلِ
الَّذِينَ لَمْ يَظْهَرُوا عَلَىٰ عَوْرَاتِ النِّسَاءِ ۖ
وَلَا يَضْرِبْنَ بِأَرْجُلِهِنَّ لِيُعْلَمَ مَا يُخْفِينَ
مِن زِينَتِهِنَّ ۚ وَتُوبُوا إِلَى اللَّهِ جَمِيعًا
أَيُّهَ الْمُؤْمِنُونَ لَعَلَّكُمْ تُفْلِحُونَ (۳۱)

32. Marry those among you who are single, and the virtuous ones among your slaves, male or female: if they are in poverty, Allah will give them means out of His grace: for Allah is Ample-giving, and He knoweth all things.

33. Let those who find not the wherewithal for marriage keep themselves chaste, until Allah gives them means out of His grace. And if any of your slaves ask for a deed in writing (for emancipation) give them such a deed if ye know any good in them; yea, give them something yourselves out of the means which Allah has given to you. But force not your maids to prostitution when they desire chastity, in order that ye may make a gain in the goods of this life. But if anyone compels them, yet, after such compulsion, is Allah Oft-Forgiving, Most Merciful (to them).

34. We have already sent down to you verses making things clear, an illustration from (the story of) people who passed away before you, and an admonition for those who fear (Allah).

اور اپنی قوم کی بیوہ عورتوں کے نکاح کر دیا کرو۔ اور اپنے غلاموں
اور لونڈیوں کے بھی جو نیک ہوں (نکاح کر دیا کرو) اگر وہ مفلس ہونگے تو خدا
اُنکو اپنے فضل سے خوشحال کر دیگا اور خدا (بہت) وسعت والا (اور سب کچھ) جاننے والا ہے (۳۲)
اور جن کو بیاہ کا مقدور نہ ہو وہ پاکدامنی کو اختیار کئے
رہیں یہاں تک کہ خدا اُن کو اپنے فضل سے غنی کر دے۔ اور جو
غلام تم سے مکاتبت چاہیں اگر تم اُنمیں (صلاحیت اور) نیکی پاؤ
تو اُن سے مکاتبت کر لو اور خدا نے جو مال تم کو بخشا ہے اُس میں سے
اُن کو بھی دو۔ اور اپنی لونڈیوں کو اگر وہ پاک دامن رہنا چاہیں
تو (بے شرمی سے) دنیاوی زندگی کے فوائد حاصل کرنے کیلئے
بدکاری پر مجبور نہ کرنا اور جو اُن کو مجبور کریگا تو اُن (بیچاریوں) کے
مجبور کئے جانے کے بعد خدا بخشنے والا مہربان ہے (۳۳)
اور ہم نے تمہاری طرف روشن آیتیں نازل کی ہیں اور جو
لوگ تم سے پہلے گزر چکے ہیں اُن کی خبریں اور پرہیزگاروں
کے لئے نصیحت (۳۴)

وَأَنكِحُوا الْأَيَامَىٰ مِنكُمْ وَالصَّالِحِينَ مِنْ
عِبَادِكُمْ وَإِمَائِكُمْ ۚ إِن يَكُونُوا فُقَرَاءَ
يُغْنِهِمُ اللَّهُ مِن فَضْلِهِ ۗ وَاللَّهُ وَاسِعٌ عَلِيمٌ (۳۲)
وَلْيَسْتَعْفِفِ الَّذِينَ لَا يَجِدُونَ نِكَاحًا حَتَّىٰ
يُغْنِيَهُمُ اللَّهُ مِن فَضْلِهِ ۗ وَالَّذِينَ يَبْتَغُونَ
الْكِتَابَ مِمَّا مَلَكَتْ أَيْمَانُكُمْ فَكَاتِبُوهُمْ إِنْ
عَلِمْتُمْ فِيهِمْ خَيْرًا ۖ وَآتُوهُم مِّن مَّالِ
اللَّهِ الَّذِي آتَاكُمْ ۚ وَلَا تُكْرِهُوا فَتَيَاتِكُمْ
عَلَى الْبِغَاءِ إِنْ أَرَدْنَ تَحَصُّنًا لِّتَبْتَغُوا عَرَضَ
الْحَيَاةِ الدُّنْيَا ۚ وَمَن يُكْرِههُّنَّ فَإِنَّ اللَّهَ
مِن بَعْدِ إِكْرَاهِهِنَّ غَفُورٌ رَّحِيمٌ (۳۳)
وَلَقَدْ أَنزَلْنَا إِلَيْكُمْ آيَاتٍ مُّبَيِّنَاتٍ وَمَثَلًا
مِّنَ الَّذِينَ خَلَوْا مِن قَبْلِكُمْ وَمَوْعِظَةً
لِّلْمُتَّقِينَ (۳٤) ع

35. Allah is the Light of the heavens and the earth. The parable of His Light is as if there were a Niche and within it a Lamp: the Lamp enclosed in Glass: the glass as it were a brilliant star: lit from a blessed Tree, an Olive, neither of the East nor of the West, whose Oil is well-nigh luminous, though fire scarce touched it: Light upon Light! Allah doth guide whom He will to His Light: Allah doth set forth Parables for men: and Allah doth know all things.

خدا آسمانوں اور زمین کا نور ہے۔ اُس کے نور کی مثال
ایسی ہے کہ گویا ایک طاق ہے جس میں چراغ ہے۔ اور چراغ
ایک قندیل میں ہے اور قندیل (ایسی صاف شفاف ہے کہ) گویا موتی
کا سا چمکتا ہوا تارا ہے (اس میں) ایک مبارک درخت کا تیل جلایا جاتا ہے
(یعنی) زیتون کہ نہ مشرق کی طرف ہے نہ مغرب کی طرف (ایسا معلوم
ہوتا ہے کہ) اس کا تیل خواہ آگ اُسے نہ بھی چھوئے جلنے کو تیار ہے (بڑی)
روشنی پر روشنی (ہو رہی ہے) خدا اپنے نور سے جس کو چاہتا ہے سیدھی راہ دکھاتا ہے
اور خدا جو مثالیں بیان فرماتا ہے (تو) لوگوں کے (سمجھانے کے) لئے اور خدا ہر چیز سے واقف ہے (۳۵)

اللَّهُ نُورُ السَّمَاوَاتِ وَالْأَرْضِ ۚ مَثَلُ نُورِهِ
كَمِشْكَاةٍ فِيهَا مِصْبَاحٌ ۖ الْمِصْبَاحُ فِي
زُجَاجَةٍ ۖ الزُّجَاجَةُ كَأَنَّهَا كَوْكَبٌ دُرِّيٌّ
يُوقَدُ مِن شَجَرَةٍ مُّبَارَكَةٍ زَيْتُونَةٍ لَّا شَرْقِيَّةٍ
وَلَا غَرْبِيَّةٍ يَكَادُ زَيْتُهَا يُضِيءُ وَلَوْ لَمْ
تَمْسَسْهُ نَارٌ ۚ نُّورٌ عَلَىٰ نُورٍ ۗ يَهْدِي اللَّهُ
لِنُورِهِ مَن يَشَاءُ ۚ وَيَضْرِبُ اللَّهُ الْأَمْثَالَ
لِلنَّاسِ ۗ وَاللَّهُ بِكُلِّ شَيْءٍ عَلِيمٌ (۳۵)

فِي بُيُوتٍ أَذِنَ اللّٰهُ أَنْ تُرْفَعَ وَيُذْكَرَ
فِيهَا اسْمُهُ يُسَبِّحُ لَهُ فِيهَا بِالْغُدُوِّ وَ
الْآصَالِ ﴿٣٦﴾

(وہ قندیل) اُن گھروں میں (ہے) جنکے بارے میں خدا نے ارشاد فرمایا ہے
کہ بلند کیے جائیں۔ اور وہاں خدا کے نام کا ذکر کیا جائے (اور)
اُن میں صبح و شام اس کی تسبیح کرتے رہیں ﴿٣٦﴾

36. (Lit is such a Light) in houses, which Allah hath permitted to be raised to honour; for the celebration, in them, of His name: in them is He glorified in the mornings and in the evenings, (again and again),—

رِجَالٌ لَا تُلْهِيهِمْ تِجَارَةٌ وَلَا بَيْعٌ
عَنْ ذِكْرِ اللّٰهِ وَإِقَامِ الصَّلٰوةِ وَإِيتَاءِ
الزَّكٰوةِ يَخَافُونَ يَوْمًا تَتَقَلَّبُ فِيهِ
الْقُلُوبُ وَالْأَبْصَارُ ﴿٣٧﴾

(یعنی ایسے) لوگ جن کو خدا کے ذکر اور نماز پڑھنے اور زکوٰۃ دینے
سے نہ سوداگری غافل کرتی ہے نہ خرید و فروخت۔ وہ اُس
دن سے جب دل (خوف اور گھبراہٹ کے سبب) اُلٹ جائینگے
اور آنکھیں (اوپر چڑھ جائینگی) ڈرتے ہیں ﴿٣٧﴾

37. By men whom neither trade nor sale can divert from the Remembrance of Allah, nor from regular Prayer, nor from paying zakat their (only) fear is for the Day when hearts and eyes will be turned about,—

لِيَجْزِيَهُمُ اللّٰهُ أَحْسَنَ مَا عَمِلُوا وَيَزِيدَهُمْ
مِنْ فَضْلِهِ وَاللّٰهُ يَرْزُقُ مَنْ يَشَاءُ
بِغَيْرِ حِسَابٍ ﴿٣٨﴾

تاکہ خدا اُن کو اُن کے عملوں کا بہت اچھا بدلہ دے۔ اور
اپنے فضل سے زیادہ بھی عطا کرے۔ اور خدا جسکو چاہتا
ہے بے شمار رزق دیتا ہے ﴿٣٨﴾

38. That Allah may reward them according to the best of their deeds, and add even more for them out of His Grace: for Allah doth provide for those whom He will, without measure.

وَالَّذِينَ كَفَرُوا أَعْمَالُهُمْ كَسَرَابٍ بِقِيعَةٍ
يَحْسَبُهُ الظَّمْآنُ مَاءً حَتّٰى إِذَا جَاءَهُ
لَمْ يَجِدْهُ شَيْئًا وَوَجَدَ اللّٰهَ عِنْدَهُ فَوَفّٰهُ
حِسَابَهُ وَاللّٰهُ سَرِيعُ الْحِسَابِ ﴿٣٩﴾

اور جن لوگوں نے کفر کیا اُن کے اعمال (کی مثال ایسی ہے)
جیسے میدان میں ریت کہ پیاسا اُسے پانی سمجھے۔ یہاں تک
کہ جب اسکے پاس آئے تو اُسے کچھ بھی نہ پائے۔ اور خدا ہی کو اپنے
پاس دیکھے تو وہ اُسے اسکا حساب پورا پورا چکا دے اور خدا جلد حساب کرنیوالا ہے ﴿٣٩﴾

39. But the Unbelievers,— their deeds are like a mirage in sandy deserts, which the man parched with thirst mistakes for water; until when he comes up to it, he finds it to be nothing: but he finds Allah there, and Allah will pay him his account: and Allah is swift in taking account.

أَوْ كَظُلُمٰتٍ فِي بَحْرٍ لُجِّيٍّ يَغْشٰهُ مَوْجٌ
مِنْ فَوْقِهِ مَوْجٌ مِنْ فَوْقِهِ سَحَابٌ
ظُلُمٰتٌ بَعْضُهَا فَوْقَ بَعْضٍ إِذَا أَخْرَجَ
يَدَهُ لَمْ يَكَدْ يَرٰهَا وَمَنْ لَمْ يَجْعَلِ اللّٰهُ
لَهُ نُورًا فَمَا لَهُ مِنْ نُورٍ ﴿٤٠﴾ ع

یا (انکے اعمال کی مثال ایسی ہے) جیسے دریائے عمیق میں اندھیرے
جس پر لہر چڑھی چلی آتی ہو (اور) اُس کے اُوپر اور لہر (آرہی ہو) (اور)
اُسکے اُوپر بادل ہو غرض اندھیرے ہی اندھیرے ہوں۔ ایک
پر ایک (چھایا ہوا) جب اپنا ہاتھ نکالے تو کچھ نہ دیکھ سکے۔ اور جسکو
خدا روشنی نہ دے اُسکو (کہیں بھی) روشنی نہیں (مل سکتی) ﴿٤٠﴾

40. Or (the Unbelievers' state) is like the depths of darkness in a vast deep ocean, overwhelmed with billow topped by billow, topped by (dark) clouds: depths of darkness, one above another: if a man stretches out his hand, he can hardly see it! For any to whom Allah giveth not light, there is no light!

أَلَمْ تَرَ أَنَّ اللّٰهَ يُسَبِّحُ لَهُ مَنْ فِي السَّمٰوٰتِ
وَالْأَرْضِ وَالطَّيْرُ صٰٓفّٰتٍ كُلٌّ قَدْ عَلِمَ
صَلَاتَهُ وَتَسْبِيحَهُ وَاللّٰهُ عَلِيمٌ بِمَا
يَفْعَلُونَ ﴿٤١﴾

کیا تم نے نہیں دیکھا کہ جو لوگ آسمانوں اور زمین میں ہیں
خدا کی تسبیح کرتے رہتے ہیں۔ اور پر پھیلائے ہوئے جانور
بھی۔ اور سب اپنی نماز اور تسبیح (کے طریقے) سے واقف ہیں
اور جو کچھ وہ کرتے ہیں (سب) خدا کو معلوم ہے ﴿٤١﴾

41. Seest thou not that it is Allah Whose praises all being in the heavens and on earth do celebrate, and the birds (of the air) with wings outspread? Each one knows its own (mode of) prayer and praise. And Allah knows well all that they do.

وَلِلّٰهِ مُلْكُ السَّمٰوٰتِ وَالْأَرْضِ وَإِلَى
اللّٰهِ الْمَصِيرُ ﴿٤٢﴾

اور آسمان اور زمین کی بادشاہی خدا ہی کے لئے ہے اور
خدا ہی کی طرف لوٹ کر جانا ہے ﴿٤٢﴾

42. Yea, to Allah belongs the dominion of the heavens and the earth; and to Allah is the return.

أَلَمْ تَرَ أَنَّ اللّٰهَ يُزْجِي سَحَابًا ثُمَّ يُؤَلِّفُ
بَيْنَهُ ثُمَّ يَجْعَلُهُ رُكَامًا فَتَرَى الْوَدْقَ

کیا تم نے نہیں دیکھا کہ خدا ہی بادلوں کو چلاتا ہے پھر اُنکو آپس
میں ملا دیتا ہے پھر اُنکو تہ بتہ کر دیتا ہے پھر تم دیکھتے ہو کہ بادل

43. Seest thou not that Allah makes the clouds move gently, then joins them together, then makes them into a heap?—then wilt thou

see rain issue forth from their midst. And He sends down from the sky mountain masses (of clouds) wherein is hail: He strikes therewith whom He pleases and He turns it away from whom He pleases. The vivid flash of its lightning well-nigh blinds the sight.

44. It is Allah Who alternates the Night and the Day: verily in these things is an instructive example for those who have vision!

45. And Allah has created every animal from water: of them there are some that creep on their bellies; some that walk on two legs: and some that walk on four. Allah creates what He wills; for verily Allah has power over all things.

46. We have indeed sent down Signs that make things manifest: and Allah guides whom He wills to a Way that is straight.

47. They say, "We believe in Allah and in the Messenger, and we obey": but even after that, some of them turn away: they are not (really) Believers.

48. When they are summoned to Allah and His Messenger, in order that he may judge between them, behold, some of them decline (to come).

49. But if the right is on their side, they come to him with all submission.

50. Is it that there is a disease in their hearts? Or do they doubt, or are they in fear, that Allah and His Messenger will deal unjustly with them? Nay, it is they themselves who do wrong.

51. The answer of the Believers, when summoned to Allah and His Messenger, in order that he may judge between them, is no other than this: they say, "We hear and we obey": it is such as these that will prosper.

52. It is such as obey Allah and His Messenger, and fear Allah and do right, that will triumph.

میں سے مینہ نکل (کر برس) رہا ہے اور آسمان میں جو (اولوں کے) پہاڑ ہیں
اُن سے اولے نازل کرتا ہے تو جس پر چاہتا ہے اسکو برسا دیتا ہے اور
جس سے چاہتا ہے ہٹا رکھتا ہے۔ اور (بادل میں جو) بجلی ہوتی ہے اسکی
چمک آنکھوں کو (خیرہ کر کے بینائی کو) اُچکے لئے جاتی ہے (٤٣)
خدا ہی رات اور دن کو بدلتا رہتا ہے۔ اہلِ بصارت کے لئے
اس میں بڑی عبرت ہے (٤٤)
اور خدا ہی نے ہر چلنے پھرنے والے جاندار کو پانی سے پیدا
کیا۔ تو اُن میں سے بعضے ایسے ہیں کہ پیٹ کے بل چلتے ہیں
اور بعض ایسے ہیں جو دو پاؤں پر چلتے ہیں اور بعض ایسے ہیں
جو چار پاؤں پر چلتے ہیں۔ خدا جو چاہتا ہے پیدا کرتا ہے بیشک
خدا ہر چیز پر قادر ہے (٤٥)
ہم ہی نے روشن آیتیں نازل کی ہیں۔ اور خدا جس کو
چاہتا ہے سیدھے رستے کی طرف ہدایت کرتا ہے (٤٦)
اور (بعض لوگ) کہتے ہیں کہ ہم خدا پر اور رسول پر ایمان لائے
اور (اُن کا) حکم مان لیا۔ پھر اس کے بعد اُن میں سے ایک
فرقہ پھر جاتا ہے اور یہ لوگ صاحبِ ایمان ہی نہیں ہیں (٤٧)
اور جب اُنکو خدا اور اُسکے رسول کی طرف بلایا جاتا ہے تاکہ (رسولِ خدا)
اُنکا قضیہ چکا دیں تو اُنمیں سے ایک فرقہ مُنہ پھیر لیتا ہے (٤٨)
اور اگر (معاملہ) حق (ہو اور) اُنکو (پہنچتا) ہو تو اُنکی طرف مطیع ہو کر چلے آتے ہیں (٤٩)
کیا ان کے دلوں میں بیماری ہے یا (یہ) شک میں ہیں یا
اُن کو یہ خوف ہے کہ خدا اور اس کا رسول اُن کے حق میں
ظلم کریں گے؟ (نہیں) بلکہ یہ خود ظالم ہیں (٥٠)
مومنوں کی تو یہ بات ہے کہ جب خدا اور اسکے رسول کی طرف
بلائے جائیں تاکہ وہ اُن میں فیصلہ کریں تو کہیں کہ ہم نے (حکم) سُن لیا
اور مان لیا۔ اور یہی لوگ فلاح پانے والے ہیں (٥١)
اور جو شخص خدا اور اُسکے رسول کی فرمانبرداری کریگا اور اُس سے ڈریگا
تو ایسے ہی لوگ مُراد کو پہنچنے والے ہیں (٥٢)

يَخْرُجُ مِنْ خِلٰلِهٖ ۚ وَيُنَزِّلُ مِنَ السَّمَآءِ
مِنْ جِبَالٍ فِيْهَا مِنْ بَرَدٍ فَيُصِيْبُ بِهٖ
مَنْ يَّشَآءُ وَيَصْرِفُهٗ عَنْ مَّنْ يَّشَآءُ ۗ
يَكَادُ سَنَا بَرْقِهٖ يَذْهَبُ بِالْاَبْصَارِ ؕ (٤٣)
يُقَلِّبُ اللّٰهُ الَّيْلَ وَالنَّهَارَ ؕ اِنَّ فِيْ ذٰلِكَ
لَعِبْرَةً لِّاُولِي الْاَبْصَارِ (٤٤)
وَاللّٰهُ خَلَقَ كُلَّ دَآبَّةٍ مِّنْ مَّآءٍ ۚ فَمِنْهُمْ
مَّنْ يَّمْشِيْ عَلٰى بَطْنِهٖ ۚ وَمِنْهُمْ مَّنْ
يَّمْشِيْ عَلٰى رِجْلَيْنِ ۚ وَمِنْهُمْ مَّنْ يَّمْشِيْ
عَلٰٓى اَرْبَعٍ ؕ يَخْلُقُ اللّٰهُ مَا يَشَآءُ ؕ اِنَّ اللّٰهَ
عَلٰى كُلِّ شَيْءٍ قَدِيْرٌ (٤٥)
لَقَدْ اَنْزَلْنَآ اٰيٰتٍ مُّبَيِّنٰتٍ ؕ وَاللّٰهُ يَهْدِيْ
مَنْ يَّشَآءُ اِلٰى صِرَاطٍ مُّسْتَقِيْمٍ (٤٦)
وَيَقُوْلُوْنَ اٰمَنَّا بِاللّٰهِ وَبِالرَّسُوْلِ وَاَطَعْنَا
ثُمَّ يَتَوَلّٰى فَرِيْقٌ مِّنْهُمْ مِّنْ بَعْدِ ذٰلِكَ ؕ
وَمَآ اُولٰٓئِكَ بِالْمُؤْمِنِيْنَ (٤٧)
وَاِذَا دُعُوْٓا اِلَى اللّٰهِ وَرَسُوْلِهٖ لِيَحْكُمَ
بَيْنَهُمْ اِذَا فَرِيْقٌ مِّنْهُمْ مُّعْرِضُوْنَ (٤٨)
وَاِنْ يَّكُنْ لَّهُمُ الْحَقُّ يَاْتُوْٓا اِلَيْهِ مُذْعِنِيْنَ ؕ (٤٩)
اَفِيْ قُلُوْبِهِمْ مَّرَضٌ اَمِ ارْتَابُوْٓا اَمْ يَخَافُوْنَ
اَنْ يَّحِيْفَ اللّٰهُ عَلَيْهِمْ وَرَسُوْلُهٗ ؕ بَلْ
اُولٰٓئِكَ هُمُ الظّٰلِمُوْنَ ۧ (٥٠)
اِنَّمَا كَانَ قَوْلَ الْمُؤْمِنِيْنَ اِذَا دُعُوْٓا اِلَى
اللّٰهِ وَرَسُوْلِهٖ لِيَحْكُمَ بَيْنَهُمْ اَنْ يَّقُوْلُوْا
سَمِعْنَا وَاَطَعْنَا ؕ وَاُولٰٓئِكَ هُمُ الْمُفْلِحُوْنَ (٥١)
وَمَنْ يُّطِعِ اللّٰهَ وَرَسُوْلَهٗ وَيَخْشَ اللّٰهَ
وَيَتَّقْهِ فَاُولٰٓئِكَ هُمُ الْفَآئِزُوْنَ (٥٢)

وَاَقْسَمُوْا بِاللّٰهِ جَهْدَ اَيْمَانِهِمْ لَئِنْ اَمَرْتَهُمْ
لَيَخْرُجُنَّ ؕ قُلْ لَّا تُقْسِمُوْا ۚ طَاعَةٌ مَّعْرُوْفَةٌ ؕ
اِنَّ اللّٰهَ خَبِيْرٌۢ بِمَا تَعْمَلُوْنَ ﴿۵۳﴾
قُلْ اَطِيْعُوا اللّٰهَ وَاَطِيْعُوا الرَّسُوْلَ ۚ
فَاِنْ تَوَلَّوْا فَاِنَّمَا عَلَيْهِ مَا حُمِّلَ وَ
عَلَيْكُمْ مَّا حُمِّلْتُمْ ؕ وَاِنْ تُطِيْعُوْهُ
تَهْتَدُوْا ؕ وَمَا عَلَى الرَّسُوْلِ اِلَّا
الْبَلٰغُ الْمُبِيْنُ ﴿۵۴﴾

اور (یہ) خدا کی سخت سخت قسمیں کھاتے ہیں کہ اگر تم انکو حکم دو تو
(سب گھروں سے) نکل کھڑے ہوں۔ کہہ دو کہ قسمیں مت کھاؤ
پسندیدہ فرمانبرداری (درکار ہے) بیشک خدا تمہارے سب اعمال سے خبردار ہے (۵۳)
کہہ دو کہ خدا کی فرمانبرداری کرو اور رسولِ (خدا) کے حکم پر چلو اگر
منہ موڑو گے تو رسول پر (اس چیز کا) ادا کرنا ہے جو انکے ذمے ہے
اور تم پر (اس چیز کا) ادا کرنا ہے جو تمہارے ذمے ہے اور اگر تم انکے
فرمان پر چلو گے تو سیدھا رستہ پا لو گے اور رسول کے ذمے
تو صاف صاف (احکامِ خدا کا) پہنچا دینا ہے (۵۴)

53. They swear their strongest oaths by Allah that, if only thou wouldst command them, they would leave (their homes). Say: "Swear ye not; obedience is (more) reasonable; verily, Allah is well acquainted with all that ye do."
54. Say: "Obey Allah, and obey the Messenger: but if ye turn away, he is only responsible for the duty placed on him and ye for that placed on you. If ye obey him, ye shall be on right guidance. The Messenger's duty is only to preach the clear (Message)".

وَعَدَ اللّٰهُ الَّذِيْنَ اٰمَنُوْا مِنْكُمْ وَعَمِلُوا
الصّٰلِحٰتِ لَيَسْتَخْلِفَنَّهُمْ فِى الْاَرْضِ
كَمَا اسْتَخْلَفَ الَّذِيْنَ مِنْ قَبْلِهِمْ ۪ وَ
لَيُمَكِّنَنَّ لَهُمْ دِيْنَهُمُ الَّذِى ارْتَضٰى لَهُمْ
وَلَيُبَدِّلَنَّهُمْ مِّنْۢ بَعْدِ خَوْفِهِمْ اَمْنًا ؕ
يَعْبُدُوْنَنِىْ لَا يُشْرِكُوْنَ بِىْ شَيْــًٔا ؕ وَمَنْ
كَفَرَ بَعْدَ ذٰلِكَ فَاُولٰٓئِكَ هُمُ الْفٰسِقُوْنَ ﴿۵۵﴾
وَاَقِيْمُوا الصَّلٰوةَ وَاٰتُوا الزَّكٰوةَ وَاَطِيْعُوا
الرَّسُوْلَ لَعَلَّكُمْ تُرْحَمُوْنَ ﴿۵۶﴾
لَا تَحْسَبَنَّ الَّذِيْنَ كَفَرُوْا مُعْجِزِيْنَ فِى
الْاَرْضِ ۚ وَمَاْوٰىهُمُ النَّارُ ؕ وَلَبِئْسَ الْمَصِيْرُ ﴿۵۷﴾
يٰۤاَيُّهَا الَّذِيْنَ اٰمَنُوْا لِيَسْتَاْذِنْكُمُ الَّذِيْنَ
مَلَكَتْ اَيْمَانُكُمْ وَالَّذِيْنَ لَمْ يَبْلُغُوا الْحُلُمَ
مِنْكُمْ ثَلٰثَ مَرّٰتٍ ؕ مِنْ قَبْلِ صَلٰوةِ الْفَجْرِ وَ
حِيْنَ تَضَعُوْنَ ثِيَابَكُمْ مِّنَ الظَّهِيْرَةِ وَ
مِنْۢ بَعْدِ صَلٰوةِ الْعِشَآءِ ۫ ثَلٰثُ عَوْرٰتٍ
لَّكُمْ ؕ لَيْسَ عَلَيْكُمْ وَلَا عَلَيْهِمْ جُنَاحٌۢ بَعْدَهُنَّ ؕ
طَوّٰفُوْنَ عَلَيْكُمْ بَعْضُكُمْ عَلٰى بَعْضٍ ؕ كَذٰلِكَ
يُبَيِّنُ اللّٰهُ لَكُمُ الْاٰيٰتِ ؕ وَاللّٰهُ عَلِيْمٌ حَكِيْمٌ ﴿۵۸﴾

جو لوگ تم میں سے ایمان لائے اور نیک کام کرتے رہے۔
ان سے خدا کا وعدہ ہے کہ ان کو ملک کا حاکم بنا دیگا جیسا ان
سے پہلے لوگوں کو حاکم بنایا تھا اور انکے دین کو جسے اس نے
انکے لئے پسند کیا ہے مستحکم و پائیدار کریگا اور خوف کے بعد ان کو امن
بخشے گا۔ وہ میری عبادت کرینگے اور میرے ساتھ کسی چیز کو شریک
نہ بنائیں گے۔ اور جو اسکے بعد کفر کرے تو ایسے لوگ
بدکردار ہیں (۵۵)
اور نماز پڑھتے رہو اور زکوٰۃ دیتے رہو اور پیغمبر (خدا)
کے فرمان پر چلتے رہو تاکہ تم پر رحمت کی جائے (۵۶)
(اور) ایسا خیال نہ کرنا کہ کافر لوگ (ہمکو) زمین میں مغلوب کر دینگے (یہ)
جا ہی کہاں سکتے ہیں انکا ٹھکانا دوزخ ہے اور وہ بہت برا ٹھکانا ہے (۵۷)
مومنو تمہارے غلام لونڈیاں اور جو بچے تم میں سے بلوغ
کو نہیں پہنچے تین دفعہ (یعنی تین اوقات میں) تم سے
اجازت لیا کریں۔ (ایک تو) نماز صبح سے پہلے اور (دوسرے
گرمی کی) دوپہر کو جب تم کپڑے اتار دیتے ہو اور (تیسرے) عشاء کی
نماز کے بعد (یہ) تین (وقت) تمہارے پردے (کے) ہیں انکے (آگے)
پیچھے (یعنی دوسرے وقتوں میں) نہ تم پر کچھ گناہ ہے اور نہ ان پر کہ کام کاج
کیلئے ایک دوسرے کے پاس آتے رہتے ہو۔ اس طرح خدا اپنی آیتیں کھول کھول کر
بیان فرماتا ہے۔ اور خدا بڑا علم والا اور بڑا حکمت والا ہے (۵۸)

55. Allah has promised, to those among you who believe and work righteous deeds, that He will, of a surety, grant them in the land, inheritance (of power), as He granted it to those before them; that He will establish in authority their religion—the one which He has chosen for them; and that He will change (their state), after the fear in which they (lived), to one of security and peace: 'They will worship Me (alone) and not associate aught with Me. If any do reject Faith after this, they are rebellious and wicked.
56. So establish regular Prayer and give zakat and obey the Messenger; that ye may receive mercy.
57. Never think thou that the Unbelievers can escape in the earth their abode is the Fire,— and it is indeed an evil refuge!
58. O ye who believe! let those whom your right hands possess, and the (children) among you who have not come of age ask your permission (before they come to your presence), on three occasions: before morning prayer; the while ye doff your clothes for the noonday heat; and after the late-night prayer: these are your three times of undress: outside those times it is not wrong for you or for them to move about attending to each other: thus does Allah make clear the Signs to you: for Allah is full of knowledge and wisdom.

59. But when the children among you come of age, let them (also) ask for permission, as do those before them: thus does Allah make clear His Signs to you: for Allah is full of knowledge and wisdom.

اور جب تمہارے لڑکے بالغ ہو جائیں تو انکو بھی اسی طرح اجازت
لینی چاہیے جس طرح اُن سے اگلے (یعنی بڑے آدمی) اجازت حاصل کرتے
رہے ہیں۔ اسطرح خدا تم سے اپنی آیتیں کھول کھول کر بیان فرماتا ہے
اور خدا جاننے والا اور حکمت والا ہے ﴿۵۹﴾

وَاِذَا بَلَغَ الْاَطْفَالُ مِنْكُمُ الْحُلُمَ
فَلْيَسْتَاْذِنُوْا كَمَا اسْتَاْذَنَ الَّذِيْنَ مِنْ
قَبْلِهِمْ ۗ كَذٰلِكَ يُبَيِّنُ اللّٰهُ لَكُمْ اٰيٰتِهٖ ۗ
وَاللّٰهُ عَلِيْمٌ حَكِيْمٌ ﴿۵۹﴾

60. Such elderly women as are past the prospect of marriage,—there is no blame on them if they lay aside their (outer) garments, provided they make not a wanton display of their beauty: but it is best for them to be modest: and Allah is One Who sees and knows all things.

اور بڑی عمر کی عورتیں جن کو نکاح کی توقع نہیں رہی اور
وہ کپڑے اتار کر سر ننگا کر) لیا کریں تو اُن پر کچھ گناہ نہیں
بشرطیکہ اپنی زینت کی چیزیں نہ ظاہر کریں۔ اور اگر اس سے
بھی بچیں تو یہ) اُنکے حق میں بہتر ہے اور خدا سنتا جانتا ہے ﴿۶۰﴾

وَالْقَوَاعِدُ مِنَ النِّسَآءِ الّٰتِيْ لَا يَرْجُوْنَ
نِكَاحًا فَلَيْسَ عَلَيْهِنَّ جُنَاحٌ اَنْ يَّضَعْنَ
ثِيَابَهُنَّ غَيْرَ مُتَبَرِّجٰتٍ بِزِيْنَةٍ ۗ وَاَنْ
يَّسْتَعْفِفْنَ خَيْرٌ لَّهُنَّ ۗ وَاللّٰهُ سَمِيْعٌ عَلِيْمٌ ﴿۶۰﴾

61. It is no fault in the blind nor in one born lame, nor in one afflicted with illness, nor in yourselves, that ye should eat in your own houses, or those of your fathers, or your mothers, or your brothers, or your sisters, or your father's brothers or your father's sisters, or your mother's brothers, or your mother's sisters, or in houses of which the keys are in your possession, or in the house of a sincere friend of yours: there is no blame on you, whether ye eat in company or separately. But if ye enter houses, salute each other—a greeting of blessing and purity as from Allah. Thus does Allah make clear the Signs to you: that ye may understand.

نہ تو اندھے پر کچھ گناہ ہے اور نہ لنگڑے پر اور نہ بیمار پر اور
نہ خود تم پر کہ اپنے گھروں سے کھانا کھاؤ یا اپنے
باپوں کے گھروں سے یا اپنی ماؤں کے گھروں سے
یا بھائیوں کے گھروں سے یا اپنی بہنوں کے
گھروں سے یا اپنے چچاؤں کے گھروں سے
یا اپنی پھوپھیوں کے گھروں سے یا اپنے ماموؤں کے
گھروں سے یا اپنی خالاؤں کے گھروں سے یا اُس گھر
سے جس کی کنجیاں تمہارے ہاتھ میں ہوں یا اپنے دوستوں
کے گھروں سے (اور اس کا بھی) تم پر کچھ گناہ نہیں کہ
سب مل کر کھانا کھاؤ یا جُدا جُدا۔ اور جب گھروں میں
جایا کرو تو اپنے (گھر والوں) کو سلام کیا کرو (یہ) خدا
کی طرف سے مبارک اور پاکیزہ تحفہ ہے۔ اس طرح
خدا اپنی آیتیں کھول کھول کر بیان فرماتا ہے تاکہ تم سمجھو ﴿۶۱﴾

لَيْسَ عَلَى الْاَعْمٰى حَرَجٌ وَّلَا عَلَى الْاَعْرَجِ
حَرَجٌ وَّلَا عَلَى الْمَرِيْضِ حَرَجٌ وَّلَا عَلٰٓى
اَنْفُسِكُمْ اَنْ تَاْكُلُوْا مِنْ بُيُوْتِكُمْ اَوْ بُيُوْتِ
اٰبَآئِكُمْ اَوْ بُيُوْتِ اُمَّهٰتِكُمْ اَوْ بُيُوْتِ اِخْوَانِكُمْ
اَوْ بُيُوْتِ اَخَوٰتِكُمْ اَوْ بُيُوْتِ اَعْمَامِكُمْ
اَوْ بُيُوْتِ عَمّٰتِكُمْ اَوْ بُيُوْتِ اَخْوَالِكُمْ اَوْ
بُيُوْتِ خٰلٰتِكُمْ اَوْ مَا مَلَكْتُمْ مَّفَاتِحَهٗٓ اَوْ
صَدِيْقِكُمْ ۗ لَيْسَ عَلَيْكُمْ جُنَاحٌ اَنْ
تَاْكُلُوْا جَمِيْعًا اَوْ اَشْتَاتًا ۗ فَاِذَا دَخَلْتُمْ
بُيُوْتًا فَسَلِّمُوْا عَلٰٓى اَنْفُسِكُمْ تَحِيَّةً مِّنْ
عِنْدِ اللّٰهِ مُبٰرَكَةً طَيِّبَةً ۗ كَذٰلِكَ
يُبَيِّنُ اللّٰهُ لَكُمُ الْاٰيٰتِ لَعَلَّكُمْ
تَعْقِلُوْنَ ﴿۶۱﴾ ع

62. Only those are Believers, who believe in Allah and His Messenger: when they are with him on a matter requiring collective action, they do not depart until they have asked for his leave; those who ask for the leave are those who believe in Allah and His Messenger; so when they ask for thy leave, for some business of their, give leave to those of them whom thou wilt, and ask Allah for

مومن تو وہ ہیں جو خدا پر اور اُس کے رسول پر ایمان
لائے اور جب کبھی ایسے کام کے لئے جو جمع ہو کر کرنے کا ہو
پیغمبر خدا کے پاس جمع ہوں تو اُن سے اجازت لئے بغیر چلے نہیں جاتے۔
اے پیغمبر جو لوگ تم سے اجازت حاصل کرتے ہیں وہی خدا پر اور اسکے رسول پر
ایمان رکھتے ہیں سو جب یہ لوگ تم سے کسی کام کیلئے اجازت مانگا کریں
تو اُن میں سے جسے چاہا کرو اجازت دے دیا کرو اور اُنکے لئے خدا سے بخشش

اِنَّمَا الْمُؤْمِنُوْنَ الَّذِيْنَ اٰمَنُوْا بِاللّٰهِ وَرَسُوْلِهٖ وَ
اِذَا كَانُوْا مَعَهٗ عَلٰٓى اَمْرٍ جَامِعٍ لَّمْ يَذْهَبُوْا حَتّٰى
يَسْتَاْذِنُوْهُ ۗ اِنَّ الَّذِيْنَ يَسْتَاْذِنُوْنَكَ
اُولٰٓئِكَ الَّذِيْنَ يُؤْمِنُوْنَ بِاللّٰهِ وَرَسُوْلِهٖ ۚ
فَاِذَا اسْتَاْذَنُوْكَ لِبَعْضِ شَاْنِهِمْ فَاْذَنْ
لِّمَنْ شِئْتَ مِنْهُمْ وَاسْتَغْفِرْ لَهُمُ

SÛRA–25
AL-FURQÃN
(INTRODUCTION)

This Sûra further develops the contrast between Light and Darkness, as symbolical of knowledge and ignorance, righteousness and sin, spiritual progress and degradation. It closes with a definition of the deeds by which the righteous are known in the environement of this world.

It is mainly an early Makkan Sûra, but its date has no significance.

their forgiveness; for Allah is Oft-Forgiving, Most Merciful.

63. Deem not the summons of the Messenger among yourselves like the summons of one of you to another: Allah doth know those of you who slip away under shelter of some excuse: then let those beware who withstand the Messenger's order, lest some trial befall them, or a grievous Chastisement be inflicted on them.

64. Be quite sure that to Allah doth belong whatever is in the heavens and on earth. Well doth He know what ye are intent upon: and the day they will be brought back to Him, He will tell them the truth of what they did: for Allah doth know all things.

Al-Furqān, or The Criterion

In the name of Allah, Most Gracious Most Merciful.

1. Blessed is He Who sent down the Criterion to His servant, that it may be an admonition to all creatures;—

2. He to Whom belongs the dominion of the heavens and the earth: no son has He begotten, nor has He a partner in His dominion: it is He Who created all things, and ordered them in due proportions.

3. Yet have they taken, besides Him, gods that can create nothing but are themselves created; that have no control of hurt or good to themselves; nor can they control Death nor Life nor Resurrection.

4. But the Misbelievers say: "Naught is this but a lie which he has forged, and others have helped him at it." In truth it is they who have put forward an iniquity and a falsehood.

5. And they say: "Tales of the ancients, which he has caused to be written: and they are dictated before him morning and evening."

مانگاکرو کچھ شک نہیں کہ خدا بخشنے والا مہربان ہے (٦٢)
مومنو پیغمبر کے بلانے کو ایسا خیال نہ کرنا جیسا تم آپس
میں ایک دوسرے کو بلاتے ہو۔ بیشک خدا کو وہ لوگ معلوم
ہیں جو تم میں سے آنکھ بچا کر چل دیتے ہیں تو جو لوگ اُن
کے حکم کی مخالفت کرتے ہیں اُن کو ڈرنا چاہئے کہ (ایسا
نہ ہو کہ) اُن پر کوئی آفت پڑ جائے یا تکلیف دینے والا
عذاب نازل ہو (٦٣)

دیکھو جو کچھ آسمانوں اور زمین میں ہے سب خدا ہی کا ہے
جس (طریق) پر تم ہو وہ اُسے جانتا ہے۔ اور جس روز
لوگ اس کی طرف لوٹائے جائیں گے تو جو عمل وہ کرتے رہے
وہ اُن کو بتادے گا۔ اور خدا ہر چیز سے واقف ہے (٦٤)

سورۂ فرقان مکی ہے اور اس میں ستتر آیتیں اور چھ رکوع ہیں

شروع خدا کا نام لے کر جو بڑا مہربان نہایت رحم والا ہے
وہ (خدائے عزوجل) بہت ہی بابرکت ہے جس نے اپنے بندے پر قرآن
نازل فرمایا تاکہ اہلِ عالم کو ہدایت کرے (١)
وہی کہ آسمانوں اور زمین کی بادشاہی اسی کی ہے اور جس
نے (کسی کو) بیٹا نہیں بنایا اور جس کا بادشاہی میں کوئی شریک
نہیں اور جس نے ہر چیز کو پیدا کیا پھر اُس کا ایک اندازہ ٹھہرایا (٢)
اور (لوگوں نے) اُس کے سوا اور معبود بنا لئے ہیں جو کوئی
چیز بھی پیدا نہیں کر سکتے اور خود پیدا کئے گئے ہیں اور
نہ اپنے نقصان اور نفع کا کچھ اختیار رکھتے ہیں اور نہ مرنا اُنکے
اختیار میں ہے اور نہ جینا اور نہ (مر کر) اُٹھ کھڑے ہونا (٣)
اور کافر کہتے ہیں کہ یہ (قرآن) من گھڑت باتیں ہیں جو اس
(مدعیٔ رسالت) نے بنا لی ہیں۔ اور اور لوگوں نے اسمیں اُسکی
مدد کی ہے۔ یہ لوگ (ایسا کہنے سے) ظلم اور جھوٹ پر اُتر آئے ہیں (٤)
اور کہتے ہیں کہ یہ پہلے لوگوں کی کہانیاں ہیں جنکو اُس نے جمع کر رکھا
ہے اور وہ صبح و شام اُس کو پڑھ پڑھ کر سنائی جاتی ہیں (٥)

اللَّهَ ۚ إِنَّ اللَّهَ غَفُورٌ رَّحِيمٌ (٦٢)
لَّا تَجْعَلُوا دُعَاءَ الرَّسُولِ بَيْنَكُمْ
كَدُعَاءِ بَعْضِكُم بَعْضًا ۚ قَدْ يَعْلَمُ
اللَّهُ الَّذِينَ يَتَسَلَّلُونَ مِنكُمْ لِوَاذًا ۚ
فَلْيَحْذَرِ الَّذِينَ يُخَالِفُونَ عَنْ أَمْرِهِ
أَن تُصِيبَهُمْ فِتْنَةٌ أَوْ يُصِيبَهُمْ عَذَابٌ
أَلِيمٌ (٦٣)
أَلَا إِنَّ لِلَّهِ مَا فِي السَّمَاوَاتِ وَالْأَرْضِ ۖ
قَدْ يَعْلَمُ مَا أَنتُمْ عَلَيْهِ وَيَوْمَ يُرْجَعُونَ
إِلَيْهِ فَيُنَبِّئُهُم بِمَا عَمِلُوا ۗ وَاللَّهُ بِكُلِّ
شَيْءٍ عَلِيمٌ (٦٤)

سُورَةُ الْفُرْقَانِ مَكِّيَّةٌ وَهِيَ سَبْعٌ وَسَبْعُونَ آيَةً وَسِتُّ رُكُوعَاتٍ

بِسْمِ اللَّهِ الرَّحْمَٰنِ الرَّحِيمِ
تَبَارَكَ الَّذِي نَزَّلَ الْفُرْقَانَ عَلَىٰ عَبْدِهِ
لِيَكُونَ لِلْعَالَمِينَ نَذِيرًا (١)
الَّذِي لَهُ مُلْكُ السَّمَاوَاتِ وَالْأَرْضِ وَ
لَمْ يَتَّخِذْ وَلَدًا وَلَمْ يَكُن لَّهُ شَرِيكٌ فِي
الْمُلْكِ وَخَلَقَ كُلَّ شَيْءٍ فَقَدَّرَهُ تَقْدِيرًا (٢)
وَاتَّخَذُوا مِن دُونِهِ آلِهَةً لَّا يَخْلُقُونَ
شَيْئًا وَهُمْ يُخْلَقُونَ وَلَا يَمْلِكُونَ
لِأَنفُسِهِمْ ضَرًّا وَلَا نَفْعًا وَلَا يَمْلِكُونَ
مَوْتًا وَلَا حَيَاةً وَلَا نُشُورًا (٣)
وَقَالَ الَّذِينَ كَفَرُوا إِنْ هَٰذَا إِلَّا إِفْكٌ
افْتَرَاهُ وَأَعَانَهُ عَلَيْهِ قَوْمٌ آخَرُونَ ۖ
فَقَدْ جَاءُوا ظُلْمًا وَزُورًا (٤)
وَقَالُوا أَسَاطِيرُ الْأَوَّلِينَ اكْتَتَبَهَا
فَهِيَ تُمْلَىٰ عَلَيْهِ بُكْرَةً وَأَصِيلًا (٥)

6. Say: "The (Qur'an) was sent down by Him Who knows the secret (that is) in the heavens and the earth: verily He is Oft-Forgiving, Most Merciful."	کہہ دو کہ اُس کو اس نے اتارا ہے جو آسمانوں اور زمین کی پوشیدہ باتوں کو جانتا ہے۔ بیشک وہ بخشنے والا مہربان ہے ⑥	قُلْ أَنْزَلَهُ الَّذِي يَعْلَمُ السِّرَّ فِي السَّمٰوٰتِ وَالْأَرْضِ ۗ إِنَّهُ كَانَ غَفُورًا رَّحِيمًا ⑥
7. And they say: "What sort of a messenger is this, who eats food, and walks through the streets? Why has not an angel been sent down to him to give admonition with him?	اور کہتے ہیں یہ کیسا پیغمبر ہے کہ کھانا کھاتا ہے اور بازاروں میں چلتا پھرتا ہے۔ اس پر کوئی فرشتہ کیوں نازل نہیں کیا گیا کہ اس کے ساتھ ہدایت کرنے کو رہتا ⑦	وَقَالُوا مَالِ هٰذَا الرَّسُولِ يَأْكُلُ الطَّعَامَ وَيَمْشِي فِي الْأَسْوَاقِ ۗ لَوْلَا أُنْزِلَ إِلَيْهِ مَلَكٌ فَيَكُونَ مَعَهُ نَذِيرًا ⑦
8. "Or (why) has not a treasure been bestowed on him, or why has he (not) a garden for enjoyment?" The wicked say: "Ye follow none other than a man bewitched."	یا اُس کی طرف (آسمان سے) خزانہ اُتارا جاتا یا اُس کا کوئی باغ ہوتا کہ اس میں سے کھایا کرتا۔ اور ظالم کہتے ہیں کہ تم تو ایک جادو زدہ شخص کی پیروی کرتے ہو ⑧	أَوْ يُلْقٰى إِلَيْهِ كَنْزٌ أَوْ تَكُونُ لَهُ جَنَّةٌ يَأْكُلُ مِنْهَا ۗ وَقَالَ الظّٰلِمُونَ إِنْ تَتَّبِعُونَ إِلَّا رَجُلًا مَّسْحُورًا ⑧
9. See what kinds of comparisons they make for thee! But they have gone astray, and never a way will they be able to find!	(اے پیغمبر) دیکھو تو یہ تمہارے بارے میں کس کس طرح کی باتیں کرتے ہیں سو گمراہ ہو گئے اور رستہ نہیں پا سکتے ⑨	اُنْظُرْ كَيْفَ ضَرَبُوا لَكَ الْأَمْثَالَ فَضَلُّوا فَلَا يَسْتَطِيعُونَ سَبِيلًا ⑨ ع ٩ ١٦
10. Blessed is He Who, if that were His Will, could give thee better (things) than those,—Gardens beneath which rivers flow; and He could give thee Palaces (secure to dwell in).	وہ (خدا) بہت بابرکت ہے جو اگر چاہے تو تمہارے لئے اس سے بہتر (چیزیں) بنا دے (یعنی) باغات جن کے نیچے نہریں بہہ رہی ہوں نیز تمہارے لئے محل بنا دے ⑩	تَبٰرَكَ الَّذِي إِنْ شَاءَ جَعَلَ لَكَ خَيْرًا مِّنْ ذٰلِكَ جَنّٰتٍ تَجْرِي مِنْ تَحْتِهَا الْأَنْهٰرُ ۙ وَيَجْعَلْ لَّكَ قُصُورًا ⑩
11. Nay, they deny the Hour (of the Judgment to come): but We have prepared a Blazing Fire for such as deny the Hour:	بلکہ یہ تو قیامت ہی کو جھٹلاتے ہیں اور ہم نے قیامت کے جھٹلانے والوں کے لئے دوزخ تیار کر رکھی ہے ⑪	بَلْ كَذَّبُوا بِالسَّاعَةِ وَأَعْتَدْنَا لِمَنْ كَذَّبَ بِالسَّاعَةِ سَعِيرًا ⑪
12. When it sees them from a place far off, they will hear its fury and its raging sigh.	جس وقت وہ انکو دُور سے دیکھے گی تو (غضبناک ہو رہی ہوگی اور یہ) اُسکے جوش (غضب) اور چیخنے چلّانے کو سنیں گے ⑫	إِذَا رَأَتْهُمْ مِّنْ مَّكَانٍ بَعِيدٍ سَمِعُوا لَهَا تَغَيُّظًا وَّزَفِيرًا ⑫
13. And when they are cast, bound together, into a constricted place therein, they will plead for destruction there and then!	اور جب یہ دوزخ کی کسی تنگ جگہ میں (زنجیروں میں) جکڑ کر ڈالے جائیں گے تو وہاں موت کو پکاریں گے ⑬	وَإِذَا أُلْقُوا مِنْهَا مَكَانًا ضَيِّقًا مُّقَرَّنِينَ دَعَوْا هُنَالِكَ ثُبُورًا ⑬
14. "This day plead not for a single destruction: plead for destruction oft-repeated!"	آج ایک ہی موت کو نہ پکارو بہت سی موتوں کو پکارو ⑭	لَا تَدْعُوا الْيَوْمَ ثُبُورًا وَّاحِدًا وَّادْعُوا ثُبُورًا كَثِيرًا ⑭
15. Say: "Is that best, or the eternal Garden, promised to the righteous? For them, that is a reward as well as a final abode.	پوچھو کہ یہ بہتر ہے یا بہشتِ جاودانی جس کا پرہیزگاروں سے وعدہ ہے۔ یہ اُن (کے عملوں) کا بدلہ اور رہنے کا ٹھکانا ہوگا ⑮	قُلْ أَذٰلِكَ خَيْرٌ أَمْ جَنَّةُ الْخُلْدِ الَّتِي وُعِدَ الْمُتَّقُونَ ۗ كَانَتْ لَهُمْ جَزَاءً وَّ مَصِيرًا ⑮
16. "For them there will be therein all that they wish for: they will dwell (there) for aye: a promise binding upon thy Lord."	وہاں جو چاہیں گے اُن کیلئے (میسر ہوگا) ہمیشہ اُسمیں رہیں گے یہ وعدہ خدا کو (پورا کرنا) لازم ہے اور اس لائق ہے کہ مانگ لیا جائے ⑯	لَهُمْ فِيهَا مَا يَشَاءُونَ خٰلِدِينَ ۗ كَانَ عَلٰى رَبِّكَ وَعْدًا مَّسْئُولًا ⑯
17. The Day He will gather them together as well as those whom	اور جس دن (خدا) ان کو اور اُن کو جنہیں یہ خدا کے سوا پوجتے	وَيَوْمَ يَحْشُرُهُمْ وَمَا يَعْبُدُونَ مِنْ

they worship besides Allah, He will ask: "Was it ye who led these My servants astray, or did they stray from the Path themselves?"

18. They will say: "Glory to Thee! not meet was it for us that we should take for protectors others besides Thee: but Thou didst bestow, on them and their fathers, good things (in life), until they forgot the Message: for they were a people destroyed".

19. (Allah will say): "Now have they proved you liars in what ye say: so ye cannot avert (your penalty) nor (get) help." And whoever among you does wrong, him shall We cause to taste of a grievous Chastisement.

20. And the messengers whom We sent before thee were all (men) who ate food and walked through the markets. We have made some of you as a trial for others: will ye have patience? For Allah is One Who sees (all things).

21. Those who do not hope to meet Us (for Judgment) say: "Why are not the angels sent down to us, or (why) do we not see our Lord?" Indeed they have an arrogant conceit of themselves, and mighty is the insolence of their impiety!

22. The Day they see the angels,— no joy will there be to the sinners that Day: the (angels) will say: "There is a barrier forbidden (to you) altogether!"

23. And We shall turn to whatever deeds they did (in this life), and We shall make such deeds as floating dust scattered about.

24. The Companions of the Garden will be well, that Day, in their abode, and have the fairest of places for repose.

25. The Day the heaven shall be rent asunder with clouds, and angels shall be sent down, Descending (in ranks),—

26. That Day, the dominion right by shall be (wholly) for The Most Gracious: it will be a Day of dire difficulty for the Misbelievers.

ہیں جمع کرے گا تو فرمائے گا کیا تم نے میرے ان بندوں
کو گمراہ کیا تھا یا یہ خود گمراہ ہو گئے تھے ﴿١٧﴾
وہ کہیں گے تو پاک ہے ہمیں یہ بات شایاں نہ تھی کہ تیرے
سوا اوروں کو دوست بناتے لیکن تو نے ہی ان کو اور انکے
باپ دادا کو برتنے کو نعمتیں دیں۔ یہاں تک کہ وہ تیری یاد
کو بھول گئے اور یہ ہلاک ہونے والے لوگ تھے ﴿١٨﴾
تو (کافرو) انہوں نے تو تم کو تمہاری بات میں جھٹلا دیا پس
(اب) تم (عذاب کو) نہ پھیر سکتے ہو نہ (کسی سے) مدد لے سکتے ہو۔ اور جو شخص
تم میں سے ظلم کریگا ہم اسکو بڑے عذاب کا مزہ چکھائیں گے ﴿١٩﴾
اور ہم نے تم سے پہلے جتنے پیغمبر بھیجے ہیں سب کھانا کھاتے
تھے اور بازاروں میں چلتے پھرتے تھے۔ اور ہم نے تمہیں
ایک دوسرے کیلئے آزمائش بنایا۔ کیا تم صبر کرو گے اور
تمہارا پروردگار تو دیکھنے والا ہے ﴿٢٠﴾
اور جو لوگ ہم سے ملنے کی امید نہیں رکھتے۔ کہتے ہیں کہ ہم پر فرشتے
کیوں نہ نازل کئے گئے۔ یا ہم آنکھ سے اپنے پروردگار کو دیکھ لیں۔
یہ اپنے خیال میں بڑائی رکھتے ہیں اور (اسی بنا پر) بڑے
سرکش ہو رہے ہیں ﴿٢١﴾
جس دن یہ فرشتوں کو دیکھیں گے اس دن گنہگاروں کیلئے کوئی خوشی
کی بات نہیں ہوگی اور کہینگے (خدا کرے تم) روک لئے (اور) بند کر دیئے جاؤ[ف ١٩٦] ﴿٢٢﴾
اور جو انہوں نے عمل کئے ہوں گے ہم اُن کی طرف متوجہ
ہونگے تو اُن کو اُڑتی خاک کر دیں گے ﴿٢٣﴾
اُس دن اہلِ جنت کا ٹھکانا بھی بہتر ہوگا اور مقام آرام
بھی خوب ہوگا ﴿٢٤﴾
اور جس دن آسمان ابر کے ساتھ پھٹ جائے گا[ف ١٩٧] اور فرشتے
نازل کئے جائیں گے ﴿٢٥﴾
اُس دن سچی بادشاہی خدا ہی کی ہوگی۔ اور وہ دن
کافروں پر (سخت) مشکل ہوگا ﴿٢٦﴾

دُونِ اللَّهِ فَيَقُولُ ءَأَنتُمْ أَضْلَلْتُمْ
عِبَادِي هَٰؤُلَاءِ أَمْ هُمْ ضَلُّوا السَّبِيلَ ﴿١٧﴾
قَالُوا سُبْحَانَكَ مَا كَانَ يَنبَغِي لَنَا أَن
نَّتَّخِذَ مِن دُونِكَ مِنْ أَوْلِيَاءَ وَلَٰكِن
مَّتَّعْتَهُمْ وَآبَاءَهُمْ حَتَّىٰ نَسُوا الذِّكْرَ
وَكَانُوا قَوْمًا بُورًا ﴿١٨﴾
فَقَدْ كَذَّبُوكُم بِمَا تَقُولُونَ فَمَا تَسْتَطِيعُونَ
صَرْفًا وَلَا نَصْرًا ۚ وَمَن يَظْلِم مِّنكُمْ
نُذِقْهُ عَذَابًا كَبِيرًا ﴿١٩﴾
وَمَا أَرْسَلْنَا قَبْلَكَ مِنَ الْمُرْسَلِينَ إِلَّا
إِنَّهُمْ لَيَأْكُلُونَ الطَّعَامَ وَيَمْشُونَ فِي
الْأَسْوَاقِ ۗ وَجَعَلْنَا بَعْضَكُمْ لِبَعْضٍ فِتْنَةً
أَتَصْبِرُونَ ۗ وَكَانَ رَبُّكَ بَصِيرًا ﴿٢٠﴾
وَقَالَ الَّذِينَ لَا يَرْجُونَ لِقَاءَنَا لَوْلَا
أُنزِلَ عَلَيْنَا الْمَلَائِكَةُ أَوْ نَرَىٰ رَبَّنَا ۗ
لَقَدِ اسْتَكْبَرُوا فِي أَنفُسِهِمْ وَعَتَوْ
عُتُوًّا كَبِيرًا ﴿٢١﴾
يَوْمَ يَرَوْنَ الْمَلَائِكَةَ لَا بُشْرَىٰ يَوْمَئِذٍ
لِّلْمُجْرِمِينَ وَيَقُولُونَ حِجْرًا مَّحْجُورًا ﴿٢٢﴾
وَقَدِمْنَا إِلَىٰ مَا عَمِلُوا مِنْ عَمَلٍ
فَجَعَلْنَاهُ هَبَاءً مَّنثُورًا ﴿٢٣﴾
أَصْحَابُ الْجَنَّةِ يَوْمَئِذٍ خَيْرٌ مُّسْتَقَرًّا
وَأَحْسَنُ مَقِيلًا ﴿٢٤﴾
وَيَوْمَ تَشَقَّقُ السَّمَاءُ بِالْغَمَامِ وَنُزِّلَ
الْمَلَائِكَةُ تَنزِيلًا ﴿٢٥﴾
الْمُلْكُ يَوْمَئِذٍ الْحَقُّ لِلرَّحْمَٰنِ ۚ وَكَانَ
يَوْمًا عَلَى الْكَافِرِينَ عَسِيرًا ﴿٢٦﴾

وَيَوْمَ يَعَضُّ الظَّالِمُ عَلَىٰ يَدَيْهِ يَقُولُ
يَا لَيْتَنِي اتَّخَذْتُ مَعَ الرَّسُولِ سَبِيلًا ﴿٢٧﴾
يَا وَيْلَتَىٰ لَيْتَنِي لَمْ أَتَّخِذْ فُلَانًا
خَلِيلًا ﴿٢٨﴾
لَقَدْ أَضَلَّنِي عَنِ الذِّكْرِ بَعْدَ إِذْ جَاءَنِي ۗ
وَكَانَ الشَّيْطَانُ لِلْإِنْسَانِ خَذُولًا ﴿٢٩﴾
وَقَالَ الرَّسُولُ يَا رَبِّ إِنَّ قَوْمِي اتَّخَذُوا
هَٰذَا الْقُرْآنَ مَهْجُورًا ﴿٣٠﴾

اور جس دن (ناعاقبت اندیش) ظالم اپنے ہاتھ کاٹ کاٹ کھائیگا (اور کہیگا
کہ اے کاش میں نے پیغمبر کے ساتھ رستہ اختیار کیا ہوتا ﴿۲۷﴾
ہائے شامت کاش میں نے فلاں شخص کو دوست نہ بنایا
ہوتا ﴿۲۸﴾
اُس نے مجھ کو (کتاب) نصیحت کے میرے پاس آنیکے بعد بہکا
دیا۔ اور شیطان انسان کو وقت پر دغا دینے والا ہے ﴿۲۹﴾
اور پیغمبر کہیں گے کہ اے پروردگار میری قوم نے اس قرآن
کو چھوڑ رکھا تھا [۱۹۸] ﴿۳۰﴾

27. The Day that the wrong-doer will bite at his hands, he will say, "Oh! would that I had taken a (straight) path with the Messenger!

28. "Ah! woe is me! would that I had never taken such a one for a friend!

29. "He did lead me astray from the Message (of Allah) after it had come to me! Ah! the Satan is but a traitor to man!

30. Then the Messenger will say: "O my Lord, Truly my people treated this Qur'an with neglect."

وَكَذَٰلِكَ جَعَلْنَا لِكُلِّ نَبِيٍّ عَدُوًّا مِنَ
الْمُجْرِمِينَ ۗ وَكَفَىٰ بِرَبِّكَ هَادِيًا وَنَصِيرًا ﴿٣١﴾
وَقَالَ الَّذِينَ كَفَرُوا لَوْلَا نُزِّلَ عَلَيْهِ
الْقُرْآنُ جُمْلَةً وَاحِدَةً ۚ كَذَٰلِكَ ۚ
لِنُثَبِّتَ بِهِ فُؤَادَكَ ۖ وَرَتَّلْنَاهُ تَرْتِيلًا ﴿٣٢﴾
وَلَا يَأْتُونَكَ بِمَثَلٍ إِلَّا جِئْنَاكَ بِالْحَقِّ
وَأَحْسَنَ تَفْسِيرًا ﴿٣٣﴾
الَّذِينَ يُحْشَرُونَ عَلَىٰ وُجُوهِهِمْ إِلَىٰ جَهَنَّمَ
أُولَٰئِكَ شَرٌّ مَكَانًا وَأَضَلُّ سَبِيلًا ﴿٣٤﴾

اور اسی طرح ہم نے گنہگاروں میں سے ہر پیغمبر کا دشمن بنا دیا
اور تمہارا پروردگار ہدایت دینے اور مدد کرنے کو کافی ہے ﴿۳۱﴾
اور کافر کہتے ہیں کہ اس پر قرآن ایک ہی دفعہ کیوں نہیں
اُتارا گیا۔ اس طرح (آہستہ آہستہ) اسلئے اُتارا گیا کہ اس سے تمہارے دل کو
قائم رکھیں۔ اور اسی واسطے ہم اسکو ٹھہر ٹھہر کر پڑھتے رہے ہیں ﴿۳۲﴾
اور یہ لوگ تمہارے پاس جو (اعتراض کی) بات لاتے ہیں ہم تمہارے
پاس اسکا معقول اور خوب مشرح جواب بھیجدیتے ہیں ﴿۳۳﴾
جو لوگ اپنے مونہوں کے بل دوزخ کی طرف جمع کئے جائینگے
اُن کا ٹھکانا بھی بُرا ہے اور وہ رستے سے بھی بہکے ہوئے ہیں ﴿۳۴﴾

31. Thus have We made for every prophet an enemy among the sinners: but enough is thy Lord to guide and to help.

32. Those who reject Faith say: "Why is not the Qur'an revealed to him all at once? Thus (is it revealed), that We may strengthen thy heart thereby, and We have rehearsed it to thee in slow, well-arranged stages, gradually.

33. And no question do they bring to thee but We reveal to thee the truth and the best explanation (thereof).

34. Those who will be gathered to Hell (prone) on their faces,—they will be in an evil plight, and, as to Path, most astray.

وَلَقَدْ آتَيْنَا مُوسَى الْكِتَابَ وَجَعَلْنَا مَعَهُ
أَخَاهُ هَارُونَ وَزِيرًا ﴿٣٥﴾
فَقُلْنَا اذْهَبَا إِلَى الْقَوْمِ الَّذِينَ كَذَّبُوا
بِآيَاتِنَا فَدَمَّرْنَاهُمْ تَدْمِيرًا ﴿٣٦﴾
وَقَوْمَ نُوحٍ لَمَّا كَذَّبُوا الرُّسُلَ أَغْرَقْنَاهُمْ
وَجَعَلْنَاهُمْ لِلنَّاسِ آيَةً ۖ وَأَعْتَدْنَا
لِلظَّالِمِينَ عَذَابًا أَلِيمًا ﴿٣٧﴾
وَعَادًا وَثَمُودَ وَأَصْحَابَ الرَّسِّ وَقُرُونًا
بَيْنَ ذَٰلِكَ كَثِيرًا ﴿٣٨﴾
وَكُلًّا ضَرَبْنَا لَهُ الْأَمْثَالَ ۖ وَكُلًّا تَبَّرْنَا

اور ہم نے موسیٰ کو کتاب دی اور اُنکے بھائی ہارون کو مددگار
بنا کر اُن کے ساتھ ملا دیا ﴿۳۵﴾
اور کہا کہ دونوں اُن لوگوں کے پاس جاؤ جنہوں نے ہماری
آیتوں کی تکذیب کی (جب تکذیب پر اڑے رہے) تو ہمنے اُنکو ہلاک کر ڈالا ﴿۳۶﴾
اور نوح کی قوم نے بھی جب پیغمبروں کو جھٹلایا تو ہم نے
انہیں غرق کر دیا اور لوگوں کے لئے نشانی بنا دیا۔ اور ظالموں
کیلئے ہم نے دُکھ دینے والا عذاب تیار کر رکھا ہے ﴿۳۷﴾
اور عاد اور ثمود اور کنوئیں والوں اور اُن کے درمیان اور
بہت سی جماعتوں کو بھی (ہلاک کر دیا) ﴿۳۸﴾
اور سب کے (سمجھانے کے) لئے ہم نے مثالیں بیان کیں اور

35. (Before this), We sent Moses the Book, and appointed his brother Aaron with him as Minister;

36. And We commanded: "Go ye both, to the people who have rejected our Signs:" and those (people) We destroyed with utter destruction.

37. And the people of Noah,—when they rejected the messengers, We drowned them, and We made them as a Sign for mankind; and We have prepared for (all) wrong-doers a grievous Chastisement:

38. As also 'Ād and Thamûd, and the Companions of the Rass, and many a generation between them.

39. To each one We set forth Parables and examples; and each

one We broke to utter annihilation (for their sins).

40. And the (Unbelievers) must indeed have passed by the town on which was rained a shower of evil: did they not then see it (with their own eyes)? But they expect not to be raised again.

41. When they see thee, they treat thee no otherwise than in mockery: "Is this the one whom Allah has sent as a messenger?"

42. "He indeed would well-nigh have misled us from our gods, had it not been that we were constant to them!"—Soon will they know, when they see the Chastisement, who it is that is most misled in Path!

43. Seest thou such a one as taketh for his god his own passion (or impulse)? Couldst thou be a disposer of affairs for him?

44. Or thinkest thou that most of them listen or understand? They are only like cattle,—nay, they are farther astray from the way.

45. Hast thou not seen how thy Lord?— Doth prolong the Shadow! If He willed, He could make it stationary! Then do We make the sun its guide;

46. Then We draw it in towards Ourselves,— a contraction by easy stages.

47. And He it is Who makes the Night as a Robe for you, and Sleep as Repose and makes the Day (as it were) a Resurrection.

48. And He it is Who sends the Winds as heralds of glad tidings, going before His Mercy, and We send down pure water from the sky,—

49. That with it We may give life to a dead land, and slake the thirst of things We have created,— cattle and men in great numbers.

50. And We have distributed the (water) amongst them, in order that they may be mindful but most men are averse (to aught) but (rank) ingratitude.

(نہ ماننے پر) سب کا تہس نہس کر دیا ﴿٣٩﴾
اور یہ (کافر) اس بستی پر بھی گزر چکے ہیں جس پر بُری طرح کا
مینہ برسایا گیا تھا وہ اس کو دیکھتے نہ ہوں گے بلکہ اُن کو
تو (مرنے کے بعد) جی اُٹھنے کی امید ہی نہیں ﴿٤٠﴾
اور یہ لوگ جب تم کو دیکھتے ہیں تو تمہاری ہنسی اُڑاتے ہیں
کہ کیا یہی شخص ہے جس کو خدا نے پیغمبر بنا کر بھیجا ہے ﴿٤١﴾
اگر ہم اپنے معبودوں کے بارے میں ثابت قدم نہ رہتے
تو یہ ضرور ہم کو بہکا دیتا (اور) اُن سے (پھیر دیتا) اور یہ
عنقریب معلوم کر لیں گے جب عذاب دیکھیں گے کہ سیدھے
رستے سے کون بھٹکا ہوا ہے ﴿٤٢﴾
کیا تم نے اس شخص کو دیکھا جس نے خواہشِ نفس کو معبود
بنا رکھا ہے تو کیا تم اس پر نگہبان ہو سکتے ہو؟ ﴿٤٣﴾
یا تم یہ خیال کرتے ہو کہ ان میں اکثر سُنتے یا سمجھتے ہیں؟
(نہیں) یہ تو چوپایوں کی طرح کے ہیں بلکہ اُن سے بھی
زیادہ گمراہ ہیں ﴿٤٤﴾
بھلا تم نے اپنے پروردگار کی قدرت کو نہیں دیکھا کہ وہ
سائے کو کس طرح دراز کر (کے پھیلا) دیتا ہے اور اگر وہ چاہتا تو اس کو
بے حرکت (ٹھیرا) رکھتا پھر سورج کو اس کا رہنما بنا دیتا ہے ﴿٤٥﴾
پھر ہم اس کو آہستہ آہستہ اپنی طرف سمیٹ لیتے ہیں ﴿٤٦﴾
اور وہی تو ہے جس نے رات کو تمہارے لئے پردہ اور نیند کو
آرام بنایا اور دن کو اُٹھ کھڑے ہونے کا وقت ٹھیرایا ﴿٤٧﴾
اور وہی تو ہے جو اپنی رحمت کے مینہ کے آگے ہواؤں کو خوشخبری بنا کر
بھیجتا ہے اور ہم آسمان سے پاک (اور نتھرا ہوا) پانی برساتے ہیں ﴿٤٨﴾
تاکہ اس سے شہرِ مُردہ (یعنی زمینِ اُفتادہ) کو زندہ کر دیں اور پھر ہم
اُسے بہت سے چوپایوں اور آدمیوں کو جو ہم نے پیدا کئے ہیں پلاتے ہیں ﴿٤٩﴾
اور ہم نے اس (قرآن کی آیتوں) کو طرح طرح سے لوگوں میں بیان کیا تاکہ
نصیحت پکڑیں مگر بہت سے لوگوں نے انکار کے سوا قبول نہ کیا ﴿٥٠﴾

تَتْبِيرًا ﴿٣٩﴾
وَلَقَدْ أَتَوْا عَلَى الْقَرْيَةِ الَّتِي أُمْطِرَتْ
مَطَرَ السَّوْءِ ۚ أَفَلَمْ يَكُونُوا يَرَوْنَهَا ۚ بَلْ
كَانُوا لَا يَرْجُونَ نُشُورًا ﴿٤٠﴾
وَإِذَا رَأَوْكَ إِنْ يَتَّخِذُونَكَ إِلَّا هُزُوًا ط
أَهَٰذَا الَّذِي بَعَثَ اللَّهُ رَسُولًا ﴿٤١﴾
إِنْ كَادَ لَيُضِلُّنَا عَنْ آلِهَتِنَا لَوْلَا
أَنْ صَبَرْنَا عَلَيْهَا ۚ وَسَوْفَ يَعْلَمُونَ
حِينَ يَرَوْنَ الْعَذَابَ مَنْ أَضَلُّ
سَبِيلًا ﴿٤٢﴾
أَرَأَيْتَ مَنِ اتَّخَذَ إِلَٰهَهُ هَوَاهُ أَفَأَنْتَ
تَكُونُ عَلَيْهِ وَكِيلًا ﴿٤٣﴾
أَمْ تَحْسَبُ أَنَّ أَكْثَرَهُمْ يَسْمَعُونَ أَوْ
يَعْقِلُونَ ۚ إِنْ هُمْ إِلَّا كَالْأَنْعَامِ ۖ بَلْ
هُمْ أَضَلُّ سَبِيلًا ﴿٤٤﴾ ع
أَلَمْ تَرَ إِلَىٰ رَبِّكَ كَيْفَ مَدَّ الظِّلَّ ۚ وَلَوْ شَاءَ
لَجَعَلَهُ سَاكِنًا ثُمَّ جَعَلْنَا الشَّمْسَ
عَلَيْهِ دَلِيلًا ﴿٤٥﴾
ثُمَّ قَبَضْنَاهُ إِلَيْنَا قَبْضًا يَسِيرًا ﴿٤٦﴾
وَهُوَ الَّذِي جَعَلَ لَكُمُ اللَّيْلَ لِبَاسًا وَ
النَّوْمَ سُبَاتًا وَجَعَلَ النَّهَارَ نُشُورًا ﴿٤٧﴾
وَهُوَ الَّذِي أَرْسَلَ الرِّيَاحَ بُشْرًا بَيْنَ يَدَيْ
رَحْمَتِهِ ۚ وَأَنْزَلْنَا مِنَ السَّمَاءِ مَاءً طَهُورًا ﴿٤٨﴾
لِنُحْيِيَ بِهِ بَلْدَةً مَيْتًا وَنُسْقِيَهُ مِمَّا خَلَقْنَا
أَنْعَامًا وَأَنَاسِيَّ كَثِيرًا ﴿٤٩﴾
وَلَقَدْ صَرَّفْنَاهُ بَيْنَهُمْ لِيَذَّكَّرُوا فَأَبَىٰ
أَكْثَرُ النَّاسِ إِلَّا كُفُورًا ﴿٥٠﴾

51. Had it been Our Will, We could have sent a warner to every town.

52. Therefore listen not to the Unbelievers, but strive against them with the utmost strenuousness, with the (Qur'an).

53. It is He Who has let free the two bodies of flowing water: one palatable and sweet, and the other salt and bitter; yet has He made a barrier between them, a partition that is not to be passed.

54. It is He Who has created man from water: then has He established relationships of lineage and marriage: for thy Lord has power (over all things).

55. Yet do they worship, besides Allah, things that can neither profit them nor harm them: and the misbeliever is a helper (of Evil), against his own Lord!

56. But thee We only sent to give glad tidings and warnings.

57. Say: "No reward do I ask of you for it but this: that each one who will may take a (straight) Path to his Lord:"

58. And put thy trust in Him Who lives and dies not; and celebrate His praise; and enough is He to be acquainted with the faults of His servants;—

59. He Who created the heavens and the earth and all that is between, in six days, then He established Himself on the Throne: Allah Most Gracious: ask thou, then, about Him of any acquainted (with such things).

60. When it is said to them, "Adore ye the Most Gracious!", They say, "And what is (Allah) Most Gracious? Shall we adore that which thou commandest us?" And it increases them in aversion.

61. Blessed is He Who made constellations in the skies, and placed therein a Lamp and a Moon giving light;

62. And it is He Who made the Night and the Day to follow each other for such as desire to be

اور اگر ہم چاہتے تو ہر بستی میں ڈرانے والا بھیج دیتے ﴿۵۱﴾
تو تم کافروں کا کہا نہ مانو اور اُن سے اس قرآن کے حکم
کے مطابق بڑے شد و مد سے لڑو ﴿۵۲﴾
اور وہی تو ہے جس نے دو دریاؤں کو ملا دیا۔ ایک کا پانی شیریں
ہے پیاس بجھانے والا اور دوسرے کا کھاری چھاتی جلانے والا
اور دونوں کے درمیان ایک آڑ اور مضبوط اوٹ بنا دی ﴿۵۳﴾
اور وہی تو ہے جس نے پانی سے آدمی پیدا کیا پھر اسکو صاحب نسب اور صاحب
قرابت دامادی بنایا[199]۔ اور تمہارا پروردگار (ہر طرح کی) قدرت رکھتا ہے ﴿۵۴﴾
اور یہ لوگ خدا کو چھوڑ کر ایسی چیز کی پرستش کرتے ہیں کہ جو نہ
اُن کو فائدہ پہنچا سکے اور نہ نقصان۔ اور کافر اپنے پروردگار
کی مخالفت میں بڑا زور مارتا ہے ﴿۵۵﴾
اور ہم نے (اے محمد) تم کو صرف خوشی اور عذاب کی خبر سنانے کو بھیجا ہے ﴿۵۶﴾
کہہ دو کہ میں تم سے اس (کام) کی اُجرت نہیں مانگتا۔ ہاں
جو شخص چاہے اپنے پروردگار کی طرف (جانے کا) رستہ اختیار کرے ﴿۵۷﴾
اور اُس (خدائے) زندہ پر بھروسہ رکھو جو (کبھی) نہیں مریگا اور
اُس کی تعریف کیساتھ تسبیح کرتے رہو۔ اور وہ اپنے بندوں کے
گناہوں سے خبر رکھنے کو کافی ہے ﴿۵۸﴾
جس نے آسمانوں اور زمین کو اور جو کچھ ان دونوں کے درمیان ہے
چھ دن میں پیدا کیا پھر عرش پر جا ٹھہرا وہ (جسکا نام) رحمٰن (یعنی)
بڑا مہربان (ہے) تو اس کا حال کسی باخبر سے دریافت کر لو ﴿۵۹﴾
اور جب ان (کفار) سے کہا جاتا ہے کہ رحمٰن کو سجدہ کرو تو
کہتے ہیں کہ رحمٰن کیا ہے؟ کیا جس کے لئے تم ہم سے کہتے ہو ہم
اس کے آگے سجدہ کریں اور اس سے بدکتے ہیں ﴿۶۰﴾
(اور خدا) بڑی برکت والا ہے جس نے آسمانوں میں برج بنائے اور اُنمیں
(آفتاب کا نہایت روشن) چراغ اور چمکتا ہوا چاند بھی بنایا ﴿۶۱﴾
اور وہی تو ہے جس نے رات اور دن کو ایک دوسرے کے پیچھے آنے جانے
والا بنایا (یہ باتیں) اس شخص کیلئے جو غور کرنا چاہے یا شکرگزاری

وَلَوْ شِئْنَا لَبَعَثْنَا فِيْ كُلِّ قَرْيَةٍ نَّذِيْرًا ﴿٥١﴾
فَلَا تُطِعِ الْكٰفِرِيْنَ وَجَاهِدْهُمْ بِهٖ
جِهَادًا كَبِيْرًا ﴿٥٢﴾
وَهُوَ الَّذِيْ مَرَجَ الْبَحْرَيْنِ هٰذَا عَذْبٌ
فُرَاتٌ وَّهٰذَا مِلْحٌ اُجَاجٌ ۚ وَجَعَلَ
بَيْنَهُمَا بَرْزَخًا وَّحِجْرًا مَّحْجُوْرًا ﴿٥٣﴾
وَهُوَ الَّذِيْ خَلَقَ مِنَ الْمَآءِ بَشَرًا فَجَعَلَهٗ
نَسَبًا وَّصِهْرًا ۭ وَكَانَ رَبُّكَ قَدِيْرًا ﴿٥٤﴾
وَيَعْبُدُوْنَ مِنْ دُوْنِ اللّٰهِ مَا لَا يَنْفَعُهُمْ
وَلَا يَضُرُّهُمْ ۭ وَكَانَ الْكَافِرُ عَلٰى رَبِّهٖ
ظَهِيْرًا ﴿٥٥﴾
وَمَآ اَرْسَلْنٰكَ اِلَّا مُبَشِّرًا وَّنَذِيْرًا ﴿٥٦﴾
قُلْ مَآ اَسْـَٔلُكُمْ عَلَيْهِ مِنْ اَجْرٍ اِلَّا
مَنْ شَآءَ اَنْ يَّتَّخِذَ اِلٰى رَبِّهٖ سَبِيْلًا ﴿٥٧﴾
وَتَوَكَّلْ عَلَى الْحَيِّ الَّذِيْ لَا يَمُوْتُ وَ
سَبِّحْ بِحَمْدِهٖ ۭ وَكَفٰى بِهٖ بِذُنُوْبِ عِبَادِهٖ
خَبِيْرًا ﴿٥٨﴾ مع
اِۨلَّذِيْ خَلَقَ السَّمٰوٰتِ وَالْاَرْضَ وَمَا
بَيْنَهُمَا فِيْ سِتَّةِ اَيَّامٍ ثُمَّ اسْتَوٰى عَلَى
الْعَرْشِ ۚ اَلرَّحْمٰنُ فَسْـَٔلْ بِهٖ خَبِيْرًا ﴿٥٩﴾
وَاِذَا قِيْلَ لَهُمُ اسْجُدُوْا لِلرَّحْمٰنِ قَالُوْا
وَمَا الرَّحْمٰنُ ۤ اَنَسْجُدُ لِمَا تَاْمُرُنَا وَ
زَادَهُمْ نُفُوْرًا ﴿٦٠﴾
تَبٰرَكَ الَّذِيْ جَعَلَ فِي السَّمَآءِ بُرُوْجًا وَّ
جَعَلَ فِيْهَا سِرٰجًا وَّقَمَرًا مُّنِيْرًا ﴿٦١﴾
وَهُوَ الَّذِيْ جَعَلَ الَّيْلَ وَالنَّهَارَ خِلْفَةً
لِّمَنْ اَرَادَ اَنْ يَّذَّكَّرَ اَوْ اَرَادَ

mindful or to show their gratitude.

کا ارادہ کرے (سوچنے اور سمجھنے کی ہیں) ﴿۶۲﴾

شُكُوْرًا ﴿٦٢﴾

63. And the servants of (Allah) Most Gracious are those who walk on the earth in humility, and when the ignorant address them, they say, "Peace!";

اور خدا کے بندے تو وہ ہیں جو زمین پر آہستگی سے چلتے ہیں
اور جب جاہل لوگ اُن سے (جاہلانہ) گفتگو کرتے ہیں تو
سلام کہتے ہیں ﴿۶۳﴾

وَعِبَادُ الرَّحْمٰنِ الَّذِيْنَ يَمْشُوْنَ عَلَى
الْاَرْضِ هَوْنًا وَّاِذَا خَاطَبَهُمُ الْجٰهِلُوْنَ
قَالُوْا سَلٰمًا ﴿٦٣﴾

64. Those who spend the night in adoration of their Lord prostrate and standing;

اور وہ جو اپنے پروردگار کے آگے سجدے کرکے اور (عجز وادب سے)
کھڑے رہ کر راتیں بسر کرتے ہیں ﴿۶۴﴾

وَالَّذِيْنَ يَبِيْتُوْنَ لِرَبِّهِمْ سُجَّدًا وَّ
قِيَامًا ﴿٦٤﴾

65. Those who say, "Our Lord! avert from us the Wrath of Hell, for its Wrath is indeed an affliction grievous,—
66. "Evil indeed is it as an abode, and as a place to rest in";
67. Those who, when they spend, are not extravagant and not niggardly, but hold a just (balance) between those (extremes);
68. Those who invoke not, with Allah, any other god, nor slay such life as Allah has made sacred, except for just cause, nor commit fornication;—and any that does this (not only) meets punishment,

اور وہ جو دُعا مانگتے رہتے ہیں کہ اے پروردگار دوزخ کے
عذاب کو ہم سے دُور رکھیو کہ اُس کا عذاب بڑی تکلیف کی چیز ہے ﴿۶۵﴾
اور دوزخ ٹھیرنے اور رہنے کی بہت بُری جگہ ہے ﴿۶۶﴾
اور وہ کہ جب خرچ کرتے ہیں تو نہ بیجا اُڑاتے ہیں اور نہ تنگی کو کام
میں لاتے ہیں بلکہ اعتدال کے ساتھ نہ ضرورت سے زیادہ نہ کم ﴿۶۷﴾
اور وہ جو خدا کے ساتھ کسی اور معبود کو نہیں پکارتے اور جس
جاندار کو مار ڈالنا خدا نے حرام کیا ہے اس کو قتل نہیں کرتے
مگر جائز طریق پر (یعنی شریعت کے حکم سے) اور بدکاری نہیں
کرتے۔ اور جو یہ کام کرے گا سخت گناہ میں مبتلا ہوگا ﴿۶۸﴾

وَالَّذِيْنَ يَقُوْلُوْنَ رَبَّنَا اصْرِفْ عَنَّا
عَذَابَ جَهَنَّمَ ۖ اِنَّ عَذَابَهَا كَانَ غَرَامًا ﴿٦٥﴾
اِنَّهَا سَآءَتْ مُسْتَقَرًّا وَّمُقَامًا ﴿٦٦﴾
وَالَّذِيْنَ اِذَآ اَنْفَقُوْا لَمْ يُسْرِفُوْا وَلَمْ
يَقْتُرُوْا وَكَانَ بَيْنَ ذٰلِكَ قَوَامًا ﴿٦٧﴾
وَالَّذِيْنَ لَا يَدْعُوْنَ مَعَ اللّٰهِ اِلٰهًا
اٰخَرَ وَلَا يَقْتُلُوْنَ النَّفْسَ الَّتِيْ حَرَّمَ
اللّٰهُ اِلَّا بِالْحَقِّ وَلَا يَزْنُوْنَ ۚ وَمَنْ
يَّفْعَلْ ذٰلِكَ يَلْقَ اَثَامًا ﴿٦٨﴾

69. (But) the Chastisement on the Day of Judgment will be doubled to him, and he will dwell therein in ignominy,—
70. Unless he repents, believes, and works righteous deeds, for Allah will change the evil of such persons into good, and Allah is Oft-Forgiving, Most Merciful,

قیامت کے دن اس کو دُونا عذاب ہوگا اور ذلّت وخواری
سے ہمیشہ اس میں رہے گا ﴿۶۹﴾
مگر جس نے توبہ کی اور ایمان لایا اور اچھے کام کئے تو
ایسے لوگوں کے گناہوں کو خدا نیکیوں سے بدل دے گا
اور خدا تو بخشنے والا مہربان ہے ﴿۷۰﴾

يُّضٰعَفْ لَهُ الْعَذَابُ يَوْمَ الْقِيٰمَةِ وَ
يَخْلُدْ فِيْهِ مُهَانًا ﴿٦٩﴾
اِلَّا مَنْ تَابَ وَاٰمَنَ وَعَمِلَ عَمَلًا
صَالِحًا فَاُولٰٓئِكَ يُبَدِّلُ اللّٰهُ سَيِّاٰتِهِمْ
حَسَنٰتٍ ۗ وَكَانَ اللّٰهُ غَفُوْرًا رَّحِيْمًا ﴿٧٠﴾

71. And whoever repents and does good has truly turned to Allah in repentance:

اور جو توبہ کرتا اور عمل نیک کرتا ہے تو بیشک وہ خدا
کی طرف رجوع کرتا ہے ﴿۷۱﴾

وَمَنْ تَابَ وَعَمِلَ صَالِحًا فَاِنَّهٗ يَتُوْبُ
اِلَى اللّٰهِ مَتَابًا ﴿٧١﴾

72. Those who witness no falsehood and, if they pass by futility, they pass by it with honourable (avoidance);
73. Those who, when they are admonished with the Signs of their Lord, droop not down at them as if they were deaf or blind;
74. And those who pray, "Our Lord! Grant unto us wives and

اور وہ جو جھوٹی گواہی نہیں دیتے اور جب اُنکو بیہودہ چیزوں کے
پاس سے گزرنے کا اتفاق ہو تو بزرگانہ انداز سے گزرتے ہیں ﴿۷۲﴾
اور وہ کہ جب اُنکو پروردگار کی باتیں سمجھائی جاتی ہیں تو اُن پر
اندھے اور بہرے ہو کر نہیں گرتے (بلکہ غور و فکر سے سنتے ہیں) ﴿۷۳﴾
اور وہ جو (خدا سے) دُعا مانگتے ہیں کہ اے پروردگار ہمکو ہماری

وَالَّذِيْنَ لَا يَشْهَدُوْنَ الزُّوْرَ ۙ وَاِذَا
مَرُّوْا بِاللَّغْوِ مَرُّوْا كِرَامًا ﴿٧٢﴾
وَالَّذِيْنَ اِذَا ذُكِّرُوْا بِاٰيٰتِ رَبِّهِمْ لَمْ
يَخِرُّوْا عَلَيْهَا صُمًّا وَّعُمْيَانًا ﴿٧٣﴾
وَالَّذِيْنَ يَقُوْلُوْنَ رَبَّنَا هَبْ لَنَا مِنْ

SÛRA–26
ASH-SHU'ARÃA
(INTRODUCTION)

This Sûra begins a new series of four Sûras (26-29), which illustrate the contrast between the spirit of Prophecy and spiritual Light and the reaction to it in the communities among whom it appeared, by going back to old Prophets and the stories of the Past, as explained in the Introduction to S. 17.

In this particular Sûra we have the story of Moses in his fight with Pharaoh and of Pharaoh's discomfiture. Other Prophets mentioned are Abraham, Noah, Hûd, Ṣãliḥ, Lut and Shu'aib. The lesson is drawn that the Qur-ãn is a continuation and fulfilment of previous Revelations, and is pure Truth, unlike the poerty of vain poets.

Chronologically, the Sûra belongs to the middle Makkan period, when the contact of the Light of Prophecy with the milieu of Pagan Makkah was testing the Makkans in their most arrogant mood.

offspring who will be the comfort of our eyes, and give us (the grace) to lead the righteous."

75. Those are the ones who will be rewarded with the highest place in heaven, because of their patient constancy: therein shall they be met with salutations and peace,

76. Dwelling therein;—how beautiful an abode and place of rest!

77. Say (to the Rejecters): "My Lord would not concern Himself with you but for your call on Him: but ye have indeed rejected (Him), and soon will come the inevitable (punishment) !"

Ash-Shu'arāa, or The Poets

In the name of Allah, Most Gracious, Most Merciful.

1. Ṭā. Sīn. Mīm.
2. These are Verses of the Book that makes (things) clear.
3. It may be thou will kill thyself with grief, that they do not become Believers.
4. If (such) were Our Will, We could send down to them from the sky a Sign, to which they would bend their necks in humility.
5. But there comes not to them a newly-revealed Message from The Most Gracious, but they turn away therefrom.
6. They have indeed rejected (the Message): so they will know soon (enough) the truth of what they mocked at!
7. Do they not look at the earth, —how many noble things of all kinds We have produced therein?
8. Verily, in this is a Sign: but most of them do not believe.
9. And verily, thy Lord is He, the Exalted in Might, Most Merciful.
10. Behold, thy Lord called Moses: "Go to the people of iniquity,—
11. "The people of Pharaoh: will they not fear Allah?"
12. He said: "O my Lord! I do fear that they will charge me with falsehood:

بیویوں کی طرف سے (دل کا چین) اور اولاد کی طرف سے آنکھ کی
ٹھنڈک عطا فرما اور ہمیں پرہیزگاروں کا امام بنا ﴿٧٤﴾
ان (صفات) کے لوگوں کو ان کے صبر کے بدلے اونچے اونچے محل دیئے جائیں گے
اور وہاں فرشتے ان سے دعا و سلام کے ساتھ ملاقات کریں گے ﴿٧٥﴾
اس میں وہ ہمیشہ رہیں گے۔ اور وہ ٹھہرنے اور رہنے کی بہت ہی عمدہ جگہ ہے ﴿٧٦﴾
کہہ دو کہ اگر تم (خدا کو) نہیں پکارتے تو میرا پروردگار بھی تمہاری کچھ پروا
نہیں کرتا۔ تم نے تکذیب کی ہے سو اس کی سزا تمہارے لئے لازم ہوگی ﴿٧٧﴾

سورۂ شعراء مکی ہے اور اس میں دو سو ستائیس آیتیں اور گیارہ رکوع ہیں

شروع خدا کا نام لے کر جو بڑا مہربان نہایت رحم والا ہے
طسم ﴿١﴾ یہ کتاب روشن کی آیتیں ہیں ﴿٢﴾
(اے پیغمبر) شاید تم اس (رنج) سے کہ یہ لوگ ایمان نہیں
لاتے اپنے تئیں ہلاک کردو گے ﴿٣﴾
اگر ہم چاہیں تو ان پر آسمان سے نشانی اتار دیں پھر ان کی
گردنیں اس کے آگے جھک جائیں ﴿٤﴾
اور ان کے پاس (خدائے) رحمٰن کی طرف سے کوئی نئی نصیحت نہیں
آتی مگر اس سے منہ پھیر لیتے ہیں ﴿٥﴾
سو یہ تو جھٹلا چکے اب ان کو اس چیز کی حقیقت معلوم
ہوگی جس کی ہنسی اڑاتے تھے ﴿٦﴾
کیا انہوں نے زمین کی طرف نہیں دیکھا کہ ہم نے اس میں
ہر قسم کی کتنی نفیس چیزیں اگائی ہیں ﴿٧﴾
کچھ شک نہیں کہ اس میں (قدرت خدا کی) نشانی ہے
مگر یہ اکثر ایمان لانے والے نہیں ﴿٨﴾
اور تمہارا پروردگار غالب (اور) مہربان ہے ﴿٩﴾
اور جب تمہارے پروردگار نے موسیٰ کو پکارا کہ ظالم
لوگوں کے پاس جاؤ ﴿١٠﴾
(یعنی) قوم فرعون کے پاس۔ کیا یہ ڈرتے نہیں ﴿١١﴾
انہوں نے کہا کہ میرے پروردگار میں ڈرتا ہوں کہ یہ مجھے جھوٹا سمجھیں ﴿١٢﴾

أَزْوَاجِنَا وَذُرِّيّٰتِنَا قُرَّةَ أَعْيُنٍ وَّاجْعَلْنَا
لِلْمُتَّقِيْنَ إِمَامًا ﴿٧٤﴾
أُولٰٓئِكَ يُجْزَوْنَ الْغُرْفَةَ بِمَا صَبَرُوْا
وَيُلَقَّوْنَ فِيْهَا تَحِيَّةً وَّسَلٰمًا ﴿٧٥﴾
خٰلِدِيْنَ فِيْهَا حَسُنَتْ مُسْتَقَرًّا وَّمُقَامًا ﴿٧٦﴾
قُلْ مَا يَعْبَؤُا بِكُمْ رَبِّيْ لَوْلَا دُعَآؤُكُمْ
فَقَدْ كَذَّبْتُمْ فَسَوْفَ يَكُوْنُ لِزَامًا ﴿٧٧﴾

سُوْرَةُ الشُّعَرَآءِ مَكِّيَّةٌ وَّهِيَ مِائَتَانِ وَسَبْعٌ وَّعِشْرُوْنَ اٰيَةً وَّاِحْدٰى عَشَرَ رُكُوْعًا

بِسْمِ اللّٰهِ الرَّحْمٰنِ الرَّحِيْمِ
طٰسٓمٓ ﴿١﴾ تِلْكَ اٰيٰتُ الْكِتٰبِ الْمُبِيْنِ ﴿٢﴾
لَعَلَّكَ بَاخِعٌ نَّفْسَكَ أَلَّا يَكُوْنُوْا
مُؤْمِنِيْنَ ﴿٣﴾
إِنْ نَّشَأْ نُنَزِّلْ عَلَيْهِمْ مِّنَ السَّمَآءِ اٰيَةً
فَظَلَّتْ أَعْنَاقُهُمْ لَهَا خٰضِعِيْنَ ﴿٤﴾
وَمَا يَأْتِيْهِمْ مِّنْ ذِكْرٍ مِّنَ الرَّحْمٰنِ
مُحْدَثٍ إِلَّا كَانُوْا عَنْهُ مُعْرِضِيْنَ ﴿٥﴾
فَقَدْ كَذَّبُوْا فَسَيَأْتِيْهِمْ أَنْۢبٰٓؤُا مَا كَانُوْا
بِهٖ يَسْتَهْزِءُوْنَ ﴿٦﴾
أَوَلَمْ يَرَوْا إِلَى الْأَرْضِ كَمْ أَنْۢبَتْنَا فِيْهَا
مِنْ كُلِّ زَوْجٍ كَرِيْمٍ ﴿٧﴾
إِنَّ فِيْ ذٰلِكَ لَاٰيَةً وَمَا كَانَ أَكْثَرُهُمْ
مُّؤْمِنِيْنَ ﴿٨﴾
وَإِنَّ رَبَّكَ لَهُوَ الْعَزِيْزُ الرَّحِيْمُ ﴿٩﴾
وَإِذْ نَادٰى رَبُّكَ مُوْسٰٓى أَنِ ائْتِ الْقَوْمَ
الظّٰلِمِيْنَ ﴿١٠﴾
قَوْمَ فِرْعَوْنَ أَلَا يَتَّقُوْنَ ﴿١١﴾
قَالَ رَبِّ إِنِّيْ أَخَافُ أَنْ يُّكَذِّبُوْنِ ﴿١٢﴾

13. "My breast will be straitened, and my tongue will not speak (plainly): so send unto Aaron.

14. "And (further), they have a charge of crime against me; and I fear they may slay me."

15. Allah said: "By no means! proceed then, both of you, with Our Signs; We are with you, and will listen (to your call).

16. "So go forth, both of you, to Pharaoh, and say: 'We have been sent by the Lord and Cherisher of the Worlds;

17. " 'Send thou with us the Children of Israel.' "

18. (Pharaoh) said: "Did we not cherish thee as a child among us, and didst thou not stay in our midst many years of thy life?

19. "And thou didst a deed of thine which (thou knowest) thou didst, and thou art an ungrateful!"

20. Moses said: "I did it then, when I was in error.

21. "So I fled from you (all) when I feared you; but my Lord has (since) invested me with judgment (and wisdom) and appointed me as one of the messengers.

22. "And this is the favour with which thou dost reproach me,— that you hast enslaved the Children of Israel!"

23. Pharaoh said: "And what is the Lord and Cherisher of the Worlds?"

24. (Moses) said: "The Lord and Cherisher of the heavens and the earth, and all between,— if ye had but sure belief."

25. (Pharaoh) said to those around: "Do ye not listen (to what he says)?"

26. (Moses) said: "Your Lord and the Lord of your fathers from the beginning!"

27. (Pharaoh) said: "Truly your messenger who has been sent to you is a veritable madman!"

28. (Moses) said: "Lord of the East and the West, and all between! If ye only had sense!"

29. (Pharaoh) said: "If thou takest any god other than me, I will

اور میرا دل تنگ ہوتا ہے اور میری زبان رکتی ہے تو ہارون
کو حکم بھیج (کہ میرے ساتھ چلیں) ﴿۱۳﴾
اور اُن لوگوں کا مجھ پر ایک گناہ (یعنی قبطی کے خون کا دعویٰ)
بھی ہے سو مجھے یہ بھی ڈر ہے کہ مجھ کو مار ہی ڈالیں ﴿۱۴﴾
فرمایا ہرگز نہیں۔ تم دونوں ہماری نشانیاں لے کر جاؤ ہم تمہارے ساتھ سننے والے ہیں ﴿۱۵﴾
تو دونوں فرعون کے پاس جاؤ اور کہو کہ ہم تمام جہان کے
مالک کے بھیجے ہوئے ہیں ﴿۱۶﴾
(اور اس لئے آئے ہیں) کہ آپ بنی اسرائیل کو ہمارے ساتھ جانے کی اجازت دیں ﴿۱۷﴾
(فرعون نے موسیٰ سے) کہا کیا ہم نے تم کو کہ ابھی بچّے تھے
پرورش نہیں کیا اور تم نے برسوں ہمارے ہاں عمر بسر (نہیں) کی؟ ﴿۱۸﴾
اور تم نے ایک اور کام کیا تھا جو کیا تم ناشکرے معلوم
ہوتے ہو ﴿۱۹﴾
(موسیٰ نے) کہا کہ (ہاں) وہ حرکت مجھ سے ناگہاں سرزد ہوئی تھی اور میں خطا کاروں میں تھا ﴿۲۰﴾
تو جب مجھے تم سے ڈر لگا تو تم میں سے بھاگ گیا۔ پھر خدا نے
مجھ کو نبوت و علم بخشا اور مجھے پیغمبروں میں سے کیا ﴿۲۱﴾
اور (کیا) یہی احسان ہے جو آپ مجھ پر رکھتے ہیں کہ آپ نے
بنی اسرائیل کو غلام بنا رکھا ہے ﴿۲۲﴾
فرعون نے کہا کہ تمام جہان کا مالک کیا؟ ﴿۲۳﴾
کہا کہ آسمانوں اور زمین اور جو کچھ ان دونوں میں ہے
سب کا مالک۔ بشرطیکہ تم لوگوں کو یقین ہو ﴿۲۴﴾
فرعون نے اپنے اہالی موالی سے کہا کہ کیا تم سنتے نہیں؟ ﴿۲۵﴾
(موسیٰ نے) کہا کہ تمہارا اور تمہارے پہلے باپ دادا کا مالک ﴿۲۶﴾
(فرعون نے) کہا کہ (یہ) پیغمبر جو تمہاری طرف بھیجا گیا
ہے باؤلا ہے ﴿۲۷﴾
(موسیٰ نے) کہا کہ مشرق اور مغرب اور جو کچھ ان دونوں
میں ہے سب کا مالک بشرطیکہ تم کو سمجھ ہو ﴿۲۸﴾
(فرعون نے) کہا کہ اگر تم نے میرے سوا کسی اور کو معبود

وَيَضِيقُ صَدْرِي وَلَا يَنْطَلِقُ لِسَانِي
فَأَرْسِلْ إِلَىٰ هَارُونَ ﴿١٣﴾
وَلَهُمْ عَلَيَّ ذَنْبٌ فَأَخَافُ أَنْ
يَقْتُلُونِ ﴿١٤﴾
قَالَ كَلَّا ۖ فَاذْهَبَا بِآيَاتِنَا ۖ إِنَّا مَعَكُمْ مُسْتَمِعُونَ ﴿١٥﴾
فَأْتِيَا فِرْعَوْنَ فَقُولَا إِنَّا رَسُولُ رَبِّ
الْعَالَمِينَ ﴿١٦﴾
أَنْ أَرْسِلْ مَعَنَا بَنِي إِسْرَائِيلَ ﴿١٧﴾
قَالَ أَلَمْ نُرَبِّكَ فِينَا وَلِيدًا وَلَبِثْتَ
فِينَا مِنْ عُمُرِكَ سِنِينَ ﴿١٨﴾
وَفَعَلْتَ فَعْلَتَكَ الَّتِي فَعَلْتَ وَأَنْتَ
مِنَ الْكَافِرِينَ ﴿١٩﴾
قَالَ فَعَلْتُهَا إِذًا وَأَنَا مِنَ الضَّالِّينَ ﴿٢٠﴾
فَفَرَرْتُ مِنْكُمْ لَمَّا خِفْتُكُمْ فَوَهَبَ لِي
رَبِّي حُكْمًا وَجَعَلَنِي مِنَ الْمُرْسَلِينَ ﴿٢١﴾
وَتِلْكَ نِعْمَةٌ تَمُنُّهَا عَلَيَّ أَنْ عَبَّدْتَ
بَنِي إِسْرَائِيلَ ﴿٢٢﴾
قَالَ فِرْعَوْنُ وَمَا رَبُّ الْعَالَمِينَ ﴿٢٣﴾
قَالَ رَبُّ السَّمَاوَاتِ وَالْأَرْضِ وَمَا بَيْنَهُمَا ۖ
إِنْ كُنْتُمْ مُوقِنِينَ ﴿٢٤﴾
قَالَ لِمَنْ حَوْلَهُ أَلَا تَسْتَمِعُونَ ﴿٢٥﴾
قَالَ رَبُّكُمْ وَرَبُّ آبَائِكُمُ الْأَوَّلِينَ ﴿٢٦﴾
قَالَ إِنَّ رَسُولَكُمُ الَّذِي أُرْسِلَ إِلَيْكُمْ
لَمَجْنُونٌ ﴿٢٧﴾
قَالَ رَبُّ الْمَشْرِقِ وَالْمَغْرِبِ وَمَا بَيْنَهُمَا ۖ
إِنْ كُنْتُمْ تَعْقِلُونَ ﴿٢٨﴾
قَالَ لَئِنِ اتَّخَذْتَ إِلَٰهًا غَيْرِي لَأَجْعَلَنَّكَ

certainly put thee in prison!"

30. (Moses) said: "Even if I showed you something clear (and) convincing?"
31. (Pharaoh) said: "Show it then, if thou tellest the truth!"
32. So (Moses) threw his rod, and behold, it was a serpent, plain (for all to see)!
33. And he drew out his hand,and behold, it was white to all beholders!
34. (Pharaoh) said to the Chiefs around him: "This is indeed a sorcerer well-versed:
35. "His plan is to get you out of your land by his sorcery; then what is it ye counsel?"
36. They said: "Keep him and his brother in suspense (for a while), and dispatch to the Cities heralds to collect—
37. "And bring up to thee all (our) sorcerers well-versed."
38. So the sorcerers were got together for the appointment of a day well-known,
39. And the people were told: "Are ye (now) assembled?"—
40. "That we may follow the sorcerers if they win?"
41. So when the sorcerers arrived, they said to Pharaoh: "Of course—shall we have a (suitable) reward if we win?"
42. He said: "Yea, (and more),—for ye shall in that case be (raised to posts) nearest (to my person)."
43. Moses said to them: "Throw ye–that which ye are about to throw!"
44. So they threw their ropes and their rods, and said: "By the might of Pharaoh, it is we who will certainly win!"
45. Then Moses threw his rod, when, behold, it straightway swallows up all the falsehoods which they fake!
46. Then did the sorcerers fall down, prostrate in adoration,
47. Saying: "We believe in the Lord of the Worlds.
48. "The Lord of Moses and Aaron."
49. Said (Pharaoh): "Believe ye in Him before I give you permission? Surely he is your leader, who has taught you sorcery!

مِنَ الْمَسْجُونِينَ ﴿٢٩﴾
قَالَ أَوَلَوْ جِئْتُكَ بِشَيْءٍ مُبِينٍ ﴿٣٠﴾
قَالَ فَأْتِ بِهِ إِنْ كُنْتَ مِنَ الصَّادِقِينَ ﴿٣١﴾
فَأَلْقَىٰ عَصَاهُ فَإِذَا هِيَ ثُعْبَانٌ مُبِينٌ ﴿٣٢﴾
وَنَزَعَ يَدَهُ فَإِذَا هِيَ بَيْضَاءُ لِلنَّاظِرِينَ ﴿٣٣﴾
قَالَ لِلْمَلَإِ حَوْلَهُ إِنَّ هَٰذَا لَسَاحِرٌ عَلِيمٌ ﴿٣٤﴾
يُرِيدُ أَنْ يُخْرِجَكُمْ مِنْ أَرْضِكُمْ بِسِحْرِهِ
فَمَاذَا تَأْمُرُونَ ﴿٣٥﴾
قَالُوا أَرْجِهْ وَأَخَاهُ وَابْعَثْ فِي الْمَدَائِنِ
حَاشِرِينَ ﴿٣٦﴾
يَأْتُوكَ بِكُلِّ سَحَّارٍ عَلِيمٍ ﴿٣٧﴾
فَجُمِعَ السَّحَرَةُ لِمِيقَاتِ يَوْمٍ مَعْلُومٍ ﴿٣٨﴾
وَقِيلَ لِلنَّاسِ هَلْ أَنْتُمْ مُجْتَمِعُونَ ﴿٣٩﴾
لَعَلَّنَا نَتَّبِعُ السَّحَرَةَ إِنْ كَانُوا هُمُ الْغَالِبِينَ ﴿٤٠﴾
فَلَمَّا جَاءَ السَّحَرَةُ قَالُوا لِفِرْعَوْنَ أَئِنَّ
لَنَا لَأَجْرًا إِنْ كُنَّا نَحْنُ الْغَالِبِينَ ﴿٤١﴾
قَالَ نَعَمْ وَإِنَّكُمْ إِذًا لَمِنَ الْمُقَرَّبِينَ ﴿٤٢﴾
قَالَ لَهُمْ مُوسَىٰ أَلْقُوا مَا أَنْتُمْ مُلْقُونَ ﴿٤٣﴾
فَأَلْقَوْا حِبَالَهُمْ وَعِصِيَّهُمْ وَقَالُوا بِعِزَّةِ
فِرْعَوْنَ إِنَّا لَنَحْنُ الْغَالِبُونَ ﴿٤٤﴾
فَأَلْقَىٰ مُوسَىٰ عَصَاهُ فَإِذَا هِيَ تَلْقَفُ
مَا يَأْفِكُونَ ﴿٤٥﴾
فَأُلْقِيَ السَّحَرَةُ سَاجِدِينَ ﴿٤٦﴾
قَالُوا آمَنَّا بِرَبِّ الْعَالَمِينَ ﴿٤٧﴾
رَبِّ مُوسَىٰ وَهَارُونَ ﴿٤٨﴾
قَالَ آمَنْتُمْ لَهُ قَبْلَ أَنْ آذَنَ لَكُمْ
إِنَّهُ لَكَبِيرُكُمُ الَّذِي عَلَّمَكُمُ السِّحْرَ

بنایا تو میں تمہیں قید کر دوں گا ﴿٢٩﴾
(موسیٰ نے) کہا خواہ میں آپ کے پاس روشن چیز لاؤں (یعنی معجزہ) ﴿٣٠﴾
(فرعون نے) کہا اگر سچے ہو تو اسے لاؤ (دکھاؤ) ﴿٣١﴾
پس انہوں نے اپنی لاٹھی ڈالدی تو وہ اسی وقت صریح اژدہا بن گئی ﴿٣٢﴾
اور اپنا ہاتھ نکالا تو اسی دم دیکھنے والوں کیلئے سفید براق نظر آنے لگا ﴿٣٣﴾
فرعون نے اپنے گرد کے سرداروں سے کہا کہ یہ تو کامل فن جادوگر ہے ﴿٣٤﴾
چاہتا ہے کہ تم کو اپنے جادو (کے زور) سے تمہارے ملک سے
نکال دے تو تمہاری کیا رائے ہے؟ ﴿٣٥﴾
انہوں نے کہا کہ اسکے اور اسکے بھائی (کے بارے) میں کچھ توقف کیجئے
اور شہروں میں نقیب بھیج دیجئے ﴿٣٦﴾
کہ سب ماہر جادوگروں کو (جمع کر کے) آپکے پاس لے آئیں ﴿٣٧﴾
تو جادوگر ایک مقررہ دن کی میعاد پر جمع ہو گئے ﴿٣٨﴾
اور لوگوں سے کہہ دیا گیا کہ تم (سب) کو اکٹھے ہو جانا چاہیے ﴿٣٩﴾
تاکہ اگر جادوگر غالب رہیں تو ہم انکے پیرو ہو جائیں ﴿٤٠﴾
جب جادوگر آگئے تو فرعون سے کہنے لگے کہ اگر ہم غالب
رہے تو ہمیں صلہ بھی عطا ہو گا؟ ﴿٤١﴾
فرعون نے کہا ہاں اور تم مقربوں میں بھی داخل کر لئے جاؤ گے ﴿٤٢﴾
موسیٰ نے اُن سے کہا کہ جو چیز ڈالنی چاہتے ہو ڈالو ﴿٤٣﴾
تو انہوں نے اپنی رسیاں اور لاٹھیاں ڈالیں اور کہنے
لگے کہ فرعون کے اقبال کی قسم! ہم ضرور غالب رہیں گے ﴿٤٤﴾
پھر موسیٰ نے اپنی لاٹھی ڈالی تو وہ ان چیزوں کو جو جادوگروں
نے بنائی تھیں نگلنے لگی ﴿٤٥﴾
تب جادوگر سجدے میں گر پڑے ﴿٤٦﴾
(اور) کہنے لگے کہ ہم تمام جہان کے مالک پر ایمان لائے ﴿٤٧﴾
جو موسیٰ اور ہارون کا مالک ہے ﴿٤٨﴾
فرعون نے کہا کیا اس سے پہلے کہ میں تم کو اجازت دوں
تم اس پر ایمان لے آئے بیشک یہ تمہارا بڑا ہے جس نے تم کو

فَلَسَوْفَ تَعْلَمُونَ ۚ لَأُقَطِّعَنَّ أَيْدِيَكُمْ وَأَرْجُلَكُم مِّنْ خِلَافٍ وَلَأُصَلِّبَنَّكُمْ أَجْمَعِينَ ﴿٤٩﴾

جادو سکھایا ہے سو عنقریب تم (اس کا انجام) معلوم کر لوگے کہ میں تمہارے ہاتھ اور پاؤں اطراف مخالف سے کاٹ دوں گا اور تم سب کو سولی پر چڑھا دوں گا ﴿٤٩﴾

But soon shall ye know! "Be sure I will cut off your hands and your feet on opposite sides, and I will crucify you all"

قَالُوا لَا ضَيْرَ ۖ إِنَّا إِلَىٰ رَبِّنَا مُنقَلِبُونَ ﴿٥٠﴾

انہوں نے کہا کچھ نقصان (کی بات) نہیں ہم اپنے پروردگار کی طرف لوٹ جانے والے ہیں ﴿٥٠﴾

50. They said: "No matter! For us, we shall but return to our Lord!

إِنَّا نَطْمَعُ أَن يَغْفِرَ لَنَا رَبُّنَا خَطَايَانَا أَن كُنَّا أَوَّلَ الْمُؤْمِنِينَ ﴿٥١﴾

ہمیں اُمید ہے کہ ہمارا پروردگار ہمارے گناہ بخش دے گا اس لئے کہ ہم اوّل ایمان لانیوالوں میں ہیں ﴿٥١﴾

51. "Only, our desire is that our Lord will forgive us our faults since we are the first to believe."

وَأَوْحَيْنَا إِلَىٰ مُوسَىٰ أَنْ أَسْرِ بِعِبَادِي إِنَّكُم مُّتَّبَعُونَ ﴿٥٢﴾

اور ہم نے موسیٰ کی طرف وحی بھیجی کہ ہمارے بندوں کو رات کو لے نکلو کہ (فرعونیوں کی طرف سے) تمہارا تعاقب کیا جائیگا ﴿٥٢﴾

52. By inspiration We told Moses: "Travel by night with My servants; for surely ye shall be pursued."

فَأَرْسَلَ فِرْعَوْنُ فِي الْمَدَائِنِ حَاشِرِينَ ﴿٥٣﴾

تو فرعون نے شہروں میں نقیب روانہ کئے ﴿٥٣﴾

53. Then Pharaoh sent heralds to (all) the Cities,

إِنَّ هَٰؤُلَاءِ لَشِرْذِمَةٌ قَلِيلُونَ ﴿٥٤﴾

(اور کہا) کہ یہ لوگ تھوڑی سی جماعت ہے ﴿٥٤﴾

54. (Saying): "These (Israelites) are but a small band,

وَإِنَّهُمْ لَنَا لَغَائِظُونَ ﴿٥٥﴾

اور یہ ہمیں غصہ دلا رہے ہیں ﴿٥٥﴾

55. "And they have surely enraged us;

وَإِنَّا لَجَمِيعٌ حَاذِرُونَ ﴿٥٦﴾

اور ہم سب باساز و سامان ہیں ﴿٥٦﴾

56. "And we are a multitude amply fore-warned."

فَأَخْرَجْنَاهُم مِّن جَنَّاتٍ وَعُيُونٍ ﴿٥٧﴾

تو ہم نے اُن کو باغوں اور چشموں سے نکال دیا ﴿٥٧﴾

57. So We expelled them from gardens, springs,

وَكُنُوزٍ وَمَقَامٍ كَرِيمٍ ﴿٥٨﴾

اور خزانوں اور نفیس مکانات سے ﴿٥٨﴾

58. Treasures, and every kind of honourable position;

كَذَٰلِكَ وَأَوْرَثْنَاهَا بَنِي إِسْرَائِيلَ ﴿٥٩﴾

(انکے ساتھ ہم نے) اس طرح (کیا) اور ان چیزوں کا وارث بنی اسرائیل کو کر دیا ﴿٥٩﴾

59. Thus it was, but We made the Children of Israel inheritors of such things.

فَأَتْبَعُوهُم مُّشْرِقِينَ ﴿٦٠﴾

تو انہوں نے سورج نکلتے (یعنی صبح کو) اُنکا تعاقب کیا ﴿٦٠﴾

60. So they pursued them at sunrise.

فَلَمَّا تَرَاءَى الْجَمْعَانِ قَالَ أَصْحَابُ مُوسَىٰ إِنَّا لَمُدْرَكُونَ ﴿٦١﴾

جب دونوں جماعتیں آمنے سامنے ہوئیں تو موسیٰ کے ساتھی کہنے لگے کہ ہم تو پکڑ لئے گئے ﴿٦١﴾

61. And when the two bodies saw each other, the people of Moses said: "We are sure to be overtaken."

قَالَ كَلَّا ۖ إِنَّ مَعِيَ رَبِّي سَيَهْدِينِ ﴿٦٢﴾

موسیٰ نے کہا ہرگز نہیں میرا پروردگار میرے ساتھ ہے وہ مجھے رستہ بتائیگا ﴿٦٢﴾

62. (Moses) said: "By no means! My Lord is with me! Soon will He guide me!"

فَأَوْحَيْنَا إِلَىٰ مُوسَىٰ أَنِ اضْرِب بِّعَصَاكَ الْبَحْرَ ۖ فَانفَلَقَ فَكَانَ كُلُّ فِرْقٍ كَالطَّوْدِ الْعَظِيمِ ﴿٦٣﴾

اس وقت ہم نے موسیٰ کی طرف وحی بھیجی کہ اپنی لاٹھی دریا پر مارو۔ تو دریا پھٹ گیا اور ہر ایک ٹکڑا (یوں) ہو گیا (کہ) گویا بڑا پہاڑ (ہے) ﴿٦٣﴾

63. Then We told Moses by inspiration: "Strike the sea with thy rod." So it divided, and each separate part became like the huge, firm mass of a mountain.

وَأَزْلَفْنَا ثَمَّ الْآخَرِينَ ﴿٦٤﴾

اور دوسروں کو وہاں ہم نے قریب کر دیا ﴿٦٤﴾

64. And We made the other party approach thither.

وَأَنجَيْنَا مُوسَىٰ وَمَن مَّعَهُ أَجْمَعِينَ ﴿٦٥﴾

اور موسیٰ اور اُن کے ساتھ والوں کو (تو) بچا لیا ﴿٦٥﴾

65. We delivered Moses and all who were with him;

ثُمَّ أَغْرَقْنَا الْآخَرِينَ ﴿٦٦﴾

پھر دوسروں کو ڈبو دیا ﴿٦٦﴾

66. But We drowned the others.

إِنَّ فِي ذَٰلِكَ لَآيَةً ۖ وَمَا كَانَ أَكْثَرُهُم مُّؤْمِنِينَ ﴿٦٧﴾

بے شک اس (قصے) میں نشانی ہے۔ لیکن یہ اکثر ایمان لانے والے نہیں ﴿٦٧﴾

67. Verily in this is a Sign: but most of them do not believe.

68. And verily thy Lord is He, the Exalted in Might, Most Merciful.
اور تمہارا پروردگار تو غالب (اور) مہربان ہے (٦٨)
وان ربك لهو العزيز الرحيم (٦٨)

69. And rehearse to them (something of) Abraham's story.
اور اُن کو ابراہیم کا حال پڑھ کر سُنا دو (٦٩)
واتل عليهم نبا ابرهيم (٦٩)

70. Behold, he said to his father and his people: "What worship ye?"
جب انہوں نے اپنے باپ اور اپنی قوم کے لوگوں سے کہا کہ تم کس چیز کو پوجتے ہو؟ (٧٠)
اذ قال لابيه وقومه ما تعبدون (٧٠)

71. They said: "We worship Idols, and we remain constantly in attendance on them."
وہ کہنے لگے کہ ہم بتوں کو پوجتے ہیں اور ان کی پوجا پر قائم ہیں (٧١)
قالوا نعبد اصناما فنظل لها عكفين (٧١)

72. He said: "Do they listen to you when ye call (on them),
(ابراہیم نے) کہا کہ جب تم ان کو پکارتے ہو تو کیا وہ تمہاری آواز سنتے ہیں؟ (٧٢)
قال هل يسمعونكم اذ تدعون (٧٢)

73. Or do you good or harm?"
یا تمہیں کچھ فائدہ دے سکتے یا نقصان پہنچا سکتے ہیں؟ (٧٣)
او ينفعونكم او يضرون (٧٣)

74. They said: "Nay, but we found our fathers doing thus (what we do)."
انہوں نے کہا (نہیں) بلکہ ہم نے اپنے باپ دادا کو اسی طرح کرتے دیکھا ہے (٧٤)
قالوا بل وجدنا اباءنا كذلك يفعلون (٧٤)

75. He said: "Do ye then see whom ye have been worshipping,—
(ابراہیم نے) کہا کیا تم نے دیکھا کہ جن کو تم پوجتے رہے ہو (٧٥)
قال افرءيتم ما كنتم تعبدون (٧٥)

76. "Ye and your fathers before you?—
تم بھی اور تمہارے اگلے باپ دادا بھی (٧٦)
انتم واباؤكم الاقدمون (٧٦)

77. "For they are enemies to me; not so the Lord and Cherisher of the Worlds;
وہ میرے دشمن ہیں۔ مگر خدائے رب العالمین (میرا دوست ہے) (٧٧)
فانهم عدو لي الا رب العلمين (٧٧)

78. "Who created me, and it is He Who guides me;
جس نے مجھے پیدا کیا ہے اور وہی مجھے رستہ دکھاتا ہے (٧٨)
الذي خلقني فهو يهدين (٧٨)

79. "Who gives me food and drink,
اور وہ جو مجھے کھلاتا اور پلاتا ہے (٧٩)
والذي هو يطعمني ويسقين (٧٩)

80. "And when I am ill, it is He who cures me;
اور جب میں بیمار پڑتا ہوں تو مجھے شفا بخشتا ہے (٨٠)
واذا مرضت فهو يشفين (٨٠)

81. "Who will cause me to die, and then to live (again);
اور وہ جو مجھے مارے گا اور پھر زندہ کرے گا (٨١)
والذي يميتني ثم يحيين (٨١)

82. "And who, I hope, will forgive me my faults on the Day of Judgment.
اور وہ جس سے میں امید رکھتا ہوں کہ قیامت کے دن میرے
گناہ بخشے گا (٨٢)
والذي اطمع ان يغفر لي خطيئتي
يوم الدين (٨٢)

83. "O my Lord! bestow wisdom on me, and join me with the righteous;
اے پروردگار مجھے علم و دانش عطا فرما اور نیکوکاروں میں شامل کر (٨٣)
رب هب لي حكما والحقني بالصلحين (٨٣)

84. "Grant me honourable mention on the tongue of truth among the latest (generations);
اور پچھلے لوگوں میں میرا ذکر نیک (جاری) کر (٨٤)
واجعل لي لسان صدق في الاخرين (٨٤)

85. "Make me one of the inheritors of the Garden of Bliss;
اور مجھے نعمت کی بہشت کے وارثوں میں کر (٨٥)
واجعلني من ورثة جنة النعيم (٨٥)

86. "Forgive my father, for that He is among those astray;
اور میرے باپ کو بخش دے کہ وہ گمراہوں میں سے ہے (٨٦)
واغفر لابي انه كان من الضالين (٨٦)

87. "And let me not be in disgrace on the Day when (men) will be raised up;—
اور جس دن لوگ اُٹھا کھڑے کئے جائینگے مجھے رُسوا نہ کیجیو (٨٧)
ولا تخزني يوم يبعثون (٨٧)

88. "The Day whereon neither wealth nor sons will avail,
جس دن نہ مال ہی کچھ فائدہ دے سکیگا اور نہ بیٹے (٨٨)
يوم لا ينفع مال ولا بنون (٨٨)

89. "But only he (will prosper) that brings to Allah a sound heart;
ہاں جو شخص خدا کے پاس پاک دل لیکر آیا (وہ بچ جائیگا) (٨٩)
الا من اتى الله بقلب سليم (٨٩)

90. "To the righteous, the Garden will be brought near,
اور بہشت پرہیزگاروں کے قریب کر دی جائے گی (٩٠)
وازلفت الجنة للمتقين (٩٠)

91. "And to those straying in evil, the Fire will be placed in full view;
اور دوزخ گمراہوں کے سامنے لائی جائے گی (٩١)
وبرزت الجحيم للغوين (٩١)

92. "And it shall be said to them: 'Where are the (gods) ye worshipped—
اور اُن سے کہا جائیگا کہ جن کو تم پوجتے تھے وہ کہاں ہیں؟ (٩٢)
وقيل لهم اين ما كنتم تعبدون (٩٢)

93. " 'Besides Allah? Can they
(یعنی جن کو) خدا کے سوا (پوجتے تھے) کیا وہ تمہاری مدد
من دون الله هل ينصرونكم او

help you or help themselves?' "	کر سکتے ہیں یا خود بدلہ لے سکتے ہیں؟ ﴿٩٣﴾	يَنتَصِرُونَ ﴿٩٣﴾
94. "Then they will be thrown headlong into the (Fire),—they and those straying in evil,	تو وہ اور گمراہ (یعنی بت اور بت پرست) اوندھے منہ دوزخ میں ڈال دیئے جائیں گے ﴿٩٤﴾	فَكُبْكِبُوا فِيهَا هُمْ وَالْغَاوُونَ ﴿٩٤﴾
95. "And the whole hosts of Iblîs together.	اور شیطان کے لشکر سب کے سب (داخل جہنم ہوں گے) ﴿٩٥﴾	وَجُنُودُ إِبْلِيسَ أَجْمَعُونَ ﴿٩٥﴾
96. "They will say there in their mutual bickerings:	وہاں وہ آپس میں جھگڑیں گے اور کہیں گے ﴿٩٦﴾	قَالُوا وَهُمْ فِيهَا يَخْتَصِمُونَ ﴿٩٦﴾
97. " 'By Allah, we were truly in an error manifest,	کہ خدا کی قسم ہم تو صریح گمراہی میں تھے ﴿٩٧﴾	تَاللَّهِ إِن كُنَّا لَفِي ضَلَالٍ مُّبِينٍ ﴿٩٧﴾
98. " 'When we held you as equals with the Lord of the Worlds;	جب کہ تمہیں (خدائے) رب العالمین کے برابر ٹھیراتے تھے ﴿٩٨﴾	إِذْ نُسَوِّيكُم بِرَبِّ الْعَالَمِينَ ﴿٩٨﴾
99. " 'And our seducers were only those who were steeped in guilt.	اور ہم کو ان گنہگاروں ہی نے گمراہ کیا تھا ﴿٩٩﴾	وَمَا أَضَلَّنَا إِلَّا الْمُجْرِمُونَ ﴿٩٩﴾
100. " 'Now, then, we have none to intercede (for us),	تو (آج) نہ کوئی ہمارا سفارش کرنے والا ہے ﴿١٠٠﴾	فَمَا لَنَا مِن شَافِعِينَ ﴿١٠٠﴾
101. " 'Nor a single intimate friend	اور نہ گرم جوش دوست ﴿١٠١﴾	وَلَا صَدِيقٍ حَمِيمٍ ﴿١٠١﴾
102. " 'Now if we only had a chance of return, we shall truly be of those who believe!' "	کاش ہمیں (دنیا میں) پھر جانا ہو تو ہم مومنوں میں ہو جائیں ﴿١٠٢﴾	فَلَوْ أَنَّ لَنَا كَرَّةً فَنَكُونَ مِنَ الْمُؤْمِنِينَ ﴿١٠٢﴾
103. Verily in this is a Sign but most of them do not believe.	بےشک اس میں نشانی ہے اور ان میں اکثر ایمان لانے والے نہیں ﴿١٠٣﴾	إِنَّ فِي ذَٰلِكَ لَآيَةً ۖ وَمَا كَانَ أَكْثَرُهُم مُّؤْمِنِينَ ﴿١٠٣﴾
104. And verily thy Lord is He, the Exalted in Might, Most Merciful.	اور تمہارا پروردگار تو غالب (اور) مہربان ہے ﴿١٠٤﴾	وَإِنَّ رَبَّكَ لَهُوَ الْعَزِيزُ الرَّحِيمُ ﴿١٠٤﴾
105. The people of Noah rejected the messengers.	قوم نوح نے بھی پیغمبروں کو جھٹلایا ﴿١٠٥﴾	كَذَّبَتْ قَوْمُ نُوحٍ الْمُرْسَلِينَ ﴿١٠٥﴾
106. Behold, their brother Noah said to them: "Will ye not Fear (Allah)?	جب ان سے انکے بھائی نوح نے کہا کہ تم ڈرتے کیوں نہیں ﴿١٠٦﴾	إِذْ قَالَ لَهُمْ أَخُوهُمْ نُوحٌ أَلَا تَتَّقُونَ ﴿١٠٦﴾
107. "I am to you a trustworthy messenger	میں تو تمہارا امانتدار پیغمبر ہوں ﴿١٠٧﴾	إِنِّي لَكُمْ رَسُولٌ أَمِينٌ ﴿١٠٧﴾
108. "So fear Allah, and obey me.	تو خدا سے ڈرو اور میرا کہا مانو ﴿١٠٨﴾	فَاتَّقُوا اللَّهَ وَأَطِيعُونِ ﴿١٠٨﴾
109. "No reward do I ask of you for it: my reward is only from the Lord of the Worlds:	اور میں اس کام کا تم سے صلہ نہیں مانگتا میرا صلہ تو خدائے رب العالمین ہی پر ہے ﴿١٠٩﴾	وَمَا أَسْأَلُكُمْ عَلَيْهِ مِنْ أَجْرٍ ۖ إِنْ أَجْرِيَ إِلَّا عَلَىٰ رَبِّ الْعَالَمِينَ ﴿١٠٩﴾
110. "So fear Allah, and obey me."	تو خدا سے ڈرو اور میرے کہنے پر چلو ﴿١١٠﴾	فَاتَّقُوا اللَّهَ وَأَطِيعُونِ ﴿١١٠﴾
111. They said: "Shall we believe in thee when it is the meanest that follow thee?"	وہ بولے کہ کیا ہم تم کو مان لیں اور تمہارے پیرو تو ذلیل لوگ ہوئے ہیں ﴿١١١﴾	قَالُوا أَنُؤْمِنُ لَكَ وَاتَّبَعَكَ الْأَرْذَلُونَ ﴿١١١﴾
112. He said: "And what do I know as to what they do?	(نوح نے) کہا کہ مجھے کیا معلوم کہ وہ کیا کرتے ہیں ﴿١١٢﴾	قَالَ وَمَا عِلْمِي بِمَا كَانُوا يَعْمَلُونَ ﴿١١٢﴾
113. "Their account is only with my Lord, if ye could (but) understand.	ان کا حساب (اعمال) میرے پروردگار کے ذمے ہے کاش تم سمجھو ﴿١١٣﴾	إِنْ حِسَابُهُمْ إِلَّا عَلَىٰ رَبِّي ۖ لَوْ تَشْعُرُونَ ﴿١١٣﴾
114. "I am not one to drive away those who believe.	اور میں مومنوں کو نکال دینے والا نہیں ہوں ﴿١١٤﴾	وَمَا أَنَا بِطَارِدِ الْمُؤْمِنِينَ ﴿١١٤﴾
115. "I am sent only as a plain warner".	میں تو صرف کھول کھول کر نصیحت کرنے والا ہوں ﴿١١٥﴾	إِنْ أَنَا إِلَّا نَذِيرٌ مُّبِينٌ ﴿١١٥﴾
116. They said: "If thou desist not, O Noah! thou shalt be stoned (to death).	انہوں نے کہا کہ نوح اگر تم باز نہ آؤ گے تو سنگسار کر دیئے جاؤ گے ﴿١١٦﴾	قَالُوا لَئِن لَّمْ تَنتَهِ يَا نُوحُ لَتَكُونَنَّ مِنَ الْمَرْجُومِينَ ﴿١١٦﴾

117. He said: "O my Lord! truly my people have rejected me.	(نوح نے) کہا کہ پروردگار میری قوم نے تو مجھے جھٹلا دیا (۱۱۷)	قَالَ رَبِّ إِنَّ قَوْمِي كَذَّبُونِ (۱۱۷)
118. "Judge thou, then, between me and them openly, and deliver me and those of the Believers who are with me."	سو تو میرے اور ان کے درمیان ایک کھلا فیصلہ کر دے اور مجھے اور جو مومن میرے ساتھ ہیں اُن کو بچا لے (۱۱۸)	فَافْتَحْ بَيْنِي وَبَيْنَهُمْ فَتْحًا وَنَجِّنِي وَمَنْ مَّعِيَ مِنَ الْمُؤْمِنِينَ (۱۱۸)
119. So We delivered him and those with him. In the Ark filled (with all creatures).	پس ہم نے انکو اور جو ان کے ساتھ بھری ہوئی کشتی میں (سوار) تھے انکو بچا لیا (۱۱۹)	فَأَنْجَيْنٰهُ وَمَنْ مَّعَهُ فِي الْفُلْكِ الْمَشْحُونِ (۱۱۹)
120. Thereafter We drowned those who remained behind.	پھر اس کے بعد باقی لوگوں کو ڈبو دیا (۱۲۰)	ثُمَّ أَغْرَقْنَا بَعْدُ الْبٰقِينَ (۱۲۰)
121. Verily in this is a Sign: but most of them do not believe.	بے شک اس میں نشانی ہے اور ان میں اکثر ایمان لانے والے نہیں تھے (۱۲۱)	إِنَّ فِي ذٰلِكَ لَاٰيَةً ۖ وَمَا كَانَ أَكْثَرُهُمْ مُّؤْمِنِينَ (۱۲۱)
122. And verily thy Lord is He, the Exalted in Might, Most Merciful.	اور تمہارا پروردگار تو غالب (اور) مہربان ہے (۱۲۲)	وَإِنَّ رَبَّكَ لَهُوَ الْعَزِيزُ الرَّحِيمُ (۱۲۲)
123. The 'Ād (people) rejected the messengers.	عاد نے بھی پیغمبروں کو جھٹلایا (۱۲۳)	كَذَّبَتْ عَادٌ الْمُرْسَلِينَ (۱۲۳)
124. Behold, their brother Hûd said to them: "Will ye not fear (Allah)?	جب اُن سے اُنکے بھائی ہُود نے کہا کیا تم ڈرتے نہیں؟ (۱۲۴)	إِذْ قَالَ لَهُمْ أَخُوهُمْ هُودٌ أَلَا تَتَّقُونَ (۱۲۴)
125. "I am to you a messenger worthy of all trust:	میں تو تمہارا امانتدار پیغمبر ہوں (۱۲۵)	إِنِّي لَكُمْ رَسُولٌ أَمِينٌ (۱۲۵)
126. "So fear Allah and obey me.	تو خدا سے ڈرو اور میرا کہا مانو (۱۲۶)	فَاتَّقُوا اللّٰهَ وَأَطِيعُونِ (۱۲۶)
127. "No reward do I ask of you for it: my reward is only from the Lord of the Worlds.	اور میں اس کا تم سے کچھ بدلہ نہیں مانگتا میرا بدلہ (خدائے) رب العالمین کے ذمے ہے (۱۲۷)	وَمَا أَسْـَٔلُكُمْ عَلَيْهِ مِنْ أَجْرٍ ۖ إِنْ أَجْرِيَ إِلَّا عَلٰى رَبِّ الْعٰلَمِينَ (۱۲۷)
128. "Do ye build a landmark on every high place to amuse yourselves?	بھلا تم ہر اونچی جگہ پر عبث نشان تعمیر کرتے ہو (۱۲۸)	أَتَبْنُونَ بِكُلِّ رِيعٍ اٰيَةً تَعْبَثُونَ (۱۲۸)
129. "And do ye get for yourselves fine buildings in the hope of living therein (for ever)?	اور محل بناتے ہو شاید تم ہمیشہ رہو گے (۱۲۹)	وَتَتَّخِذُونَ مَصَانِعَ لَعَلَّكُمْ تَخْلُدُونَ (۱۲۹)
130. "And when ye strike you strike like tyrants.	اور جب (کسی کو) پکڑتے ہو تو ظالمانہ پکڑتے ہو (۱۳۰)	وَإِذَا بَطَشْتُمْ بَطَشْتُمْ جَبَّارِينَ (۱۳۰)
131. "Now fear Allah, and obey me.	تو خدا سے ڈرو اور میری اطاعت کرو (۱۳۱)	فَاتَّقُوا اللّٰهَ وَأَطِيعُونِ (۱۳۱)
132. "Yea, fear Him Who has bestowed on you freely all that ye know.	اور اس سے جس نے تم کو ان چیزوں سے مدد دی جنکو تم جانتے ہو ڈرو (۱۳۲)	وَاتَّقُوا الَّذِي أَمَدَّكُمْ بِمَا تَعْلَمُونَ (۱۳۲)
133. "Freely has He bestowed on you cattle and sons,—	اس نے تمہیں چارپایوں اور بیٹوں سے مدد دی (۱۳۳)	أَمَدَّكُمْ بِأَنْعٰمٍ وَّبَنِينَ (۱۳۳)
134. "And Gardens and Springs.	اور باغوں اور چشموں سے (۱۳۴)	وَجَنّٰتٍ وَّعُيُونٍ (۱۳۴)
135. "Truly I fear for you the Chastisement of a Great Day.	مجھ کو تمہارے بارے میں بڑے (سخت) دن کے عذاب کا خوف ہے (۱۳۵)	إِنِّي أَخَافُ عَلَيْكُمْ عَذَابَ يَوْمٍ عَظِيمٍ (۱۳۵)
136. They said: "It is the same to us whether thou admonish us or be not among (our) admonishers!	وہ کہنے لگے ہمیں خواہ نصیحت کرو یا نہ کرو ہمارے لئے یکساں ہے (۱۳۶)	قَالُوا سَوَاءٌ عَلَيْنَا أَوَعَظْتَ أَمْ لَمْ تَكُنْ مِّنَ الْوٰعِظِينَ (۱۳۶)
137. "This is no other than a customary device of the ancients,	یہ تو اگلوں ہی کے طریق ہیں (۱۳۷)	إِنْ هٰذَا إِلَّا خُلُقُ الْأَوَّلِينَ (۱۳۷)
138. "And we are not the ones to receive Pains and Chastisement!"	اور ہم پر کوئی عذاب نہیں آئے گا (۱۳۸)	وَمَا نَحْنُ بِمُعَذَّبِينَ (۱۳۸)
139. So they rejected him, and We destroyed them. Verily in this is a	تو انہوں نے ہود کو جھٹلایا سو ہم نے اُن کو ہلاک کر ڈالا بیشک اس	فَكَذَّبُوهُ فَأَهْلَكْنٰهُمْ ۗ إِنَّ فِي ذٰلِكَ لَاٰيَةً ۗ

Sign: but most of them do not believe.	میں نشانی ہے۔ اور ان میں اکثر ایمان لانیوالے نہیں تھے ﴿۱۳۹﴾	وَمَا كَانَ أَكْثَرُهُمْ مُؤْمِنِينَ ﴿١٣٩﴾
140. And verily thy Lord is He, the Exalted in Might, Most Merciful.	اور تمہارا پروردگار تو غالب (اور) مہربان ہے ﴿۱۴۰﴾	وَإِنَّ رَبَّكَ لَهُوَ الْعَزِيزُ الرَّحِيمُ ﴿١٤٠﴾
141. The Thamûd (people) rejected the messengers.	(اور قوم) ثمود نے بھی پیغمبروں کو جھٹلایا ﴿۱۴۱﴾	كَذَّبَتْ ثَمُودُ الْمُرْسَلِينَ ﴿١٤١﴾
142. Behold, their brother Ṣâliḥ said to them: "Will you not fear (Allah)?	جب اُن سے اُنکے بھائی صالح نے کہا کہ تم ڈرتے کیوں نہیں؟ ﴿۱۴۲﴾	إِذْ قَالَ لَهُمْ أَخُوهُمْ صَالِحٌ أَلَا تَتَّقُونَ ﴿١٤٢﴾
143. "I am to you a messenger worthy of all trust.	میں تو تمہارا امانت دار پیغمبر ہوں ﴿۱۴۳﴾	إِنِّي لَكُمْ رَسُولٌ أَمِينٌ ﴿١٤٣﴾
144. "So fear Allah, and obey me.	تو خدا سے ڈرو اور میرا کہا مانو ﴿۱۴۴﴾	فَاتَّقُوا اللَّهَ وَأَطِيعُونِ ﴿١٤٤﴾
145. "No reward do I ask of you for it: my reward is only from the Lord of the Worlds.	اور میں اس کام کا تم سے بدلہ نہیں مانگتا۔ میرا بدلہ (خدائے) رب العالمین کے ذمّے ہے ﴿۱۴۵﴾	وَمَا أَسْأَلُكُمْ عَلَيْهِ مِنْ أَجْرٍ إِنْ أَجْرِيَ إِلَّا عَلَىٰ رَبِّ الْعَالَمِينَ ﴿١٤٥﴾
146. "Will ye be left secure, in (the enjoyment of) all that ye have here?—	کیا جو چیزیں (تمہیں) یہاں (میسر) ہیں اُن میں تم بےخوف چھوڑ دیئے جاؤ گے؟ ﴿۱۴۶﴾	أَتُتْرَكُونَ فِي مَا هَاهُنَا آمِنِينَ ﴿١٤٦﴾
147. "Gardens and Springs,	(یعنی) باغ اور چشمے ﴿۱۴۷﴾	فِي جَنَّاتٍ وَعُيُونٍ ﴿١٤٧﴾
148. "And corn-fields and date palms with spathes near breaking (with the weight of fruit)?	اور کھیتیاں اور کھجوریں جنکے خوشے لطیف و نازک ہوتے ہیں ﴿۱۴۸﴾	وَزُرُوعٍ وَنَخْلٍ طَلْعُهَا هَضِيمٌ ﴿١٤٨﴾
149. "And ye carve houses out of (rocky) mountains with great skill.	اور تکلف سے پہاڑوں میں تراش تراش کر گھر بناتے ہو ﴿۱۴۹﴾	وَتَنْحِتُونَ مِنَ الْجِبَالِ بُيُوتًا فَارِهِينَ ﴿١٤٩﴾
150. "But fear Allah and obey me;	تو خدا سے ڈرو اور میرے کہے پر چلو ﴿۱۵۰﴾	فَاتَّقُوا اللَّهَ وَأَطِيعُونِ ﴿١٥٠﴾
151. "And follow not the bidding of those who are extravagant,—	اور حد سے تجاوز کرنے والوں کی بات نہ مانو ﴿۱۵۱﴾	وَلَا تُطِيعُوا أَمْرَ الْمُسْرِفِينَ ﴿١٥١﴾
152. "Who make mischief in the land, and mend not (their ways)."	جو ملک میں فساد کرتے ہیں اور اصلاح نہیں کرتے ﴿۱۵۲﴾	الَّذِينَ يُفْسِدُونَ فِي الْأَرْضِ وَلَا يُصْلِحُونَ ﴿١٥٢﴾
153. They said: "Thou art only one of those bewitched!	وہ کہنے لگے کہ تم تو جادو زدہ ہو ﴿۱۵۳﴾	قَالُوا إِنَّمَا أَنْتَ مِنَ الْمُسَحَّرِينَ ﴿١٥٣﴾
154. "Thou art no more than a mortal like us: then bring us a Sign, if thou tellest the truth!"	تم اور کچھ نہیں ہماری ہی طرح کے آدمی ہو۔ اگر سچے ہو تو کوئی نشانی پیش کرو ﴿۱۵۴﴾	مَا أَنْتَ إِلَّا بَشَرٌ مِثْلُنَا فَأْتِ بِآيَةٍ إِنْ كُنْتَ مِنَ الصَّادِقِينَ ﴿١٥٤﴾
155. He said: "Here is a she-camel: she has a right of watering, and ye have a right of watering, (severally) on a day appointed.	(صالح نے) کہا (دیکھو) یہ اُونٹنی ہے (ایک دن) اسکی پانی پینے کی باری ہے اور ایک معین روز تمہاری باری ﴿۱۵۵﴾	قَالَ هَٰذِهِ نَاقَةٌ لَهَا شِرْبٌ وَلَكُمْ شِرْبُ يَوْمٍ مَعْلُومٍ ﴿١٥٥﴾
156. "Touch her not with harm, lest the Chastisement of a Great Day seize you."	اور اس کو کوئی تکلیف نہ دینا (نہیں تو) تم کو سخت عذاب آپکڑے گا ﴿۱۵۶﴾	وَلَا تَمَسُّوهَا بِسُوءٍ فَيَأْخُذَكُمْ عَذَابُ يَوْمٍ عَظِيمٍ ﴿١٥٦﴾
157. But they ham-strung her: then did they become full of regrets.	تو انہوں نے اسکی کونچیں کاٹ ڈالیں پھر نادم ہوئے ﴿۱۵۷﴾	فَعَقَرُوهَا فَأَصْبَحُوا نَادِمِينَ ﴿١٥٧﴾
158. But the Chastisement seized them. Verily in this is a Sign: but most of them do not believe.	سو اُن کو عذاب نے آپکڑا۔ بیشک اس میں نشانی ہے اور ان میں اکثر ایمان لانے والے نہیں تھے ﴿۱۵۸﴾	فَأَخَذَهُمُ الْعَذَابُ إِنَّ فِي ذَٰلِكَ لَآيَةً وَمَا كَانَ أَكْثَرُهُمْ مُؤْمِنِينَ ﴿١٥٨﴾
159. And verily thy Lord is He, the Exalted in Might, Most Merciful.	اور تمہارا پروردگار تو غالب (اور) مہربان ہے ﴿۱۵۹﴾	وَإِنَّ رَبَّكَ لَهُوَ الْعَزِيزُ الرَّحِيمُ ﴿١٥٩﴾
160. The people of Lût rejected the messengers.	(اور) قوم لوط نے بھی پیغمبروں کو جھٹلایا ﴿۱۶۰﴾	كَذَّبَتْ قَوْمُ لُوطٍ الْمُرْسَلِينَ ﴿١٦٠﴾

161. Behold, their brother Lûṭ said to them: "Will ye not fear (Allah)?
جب اُن سے اُن کے بھائی لوط نے کہا کہ تم کیوں نہیں ڈرتے (۱۶۱)
إِذْ قَالَ لَهُمْ أَخُوهُمْ لُوطٌ أَلَا تَتَّقُونَ ﴿١٦١﴾

162. "I am to you a messenger worthy of all trust.
میں تو تمہارا امانت دار پیغمبر ہوں (۱۶۲)
إِنِّي لَكُمْ رَسُولٌ أَمِينٌ ﴿١٦٢﴾

163. "So fear Allah and obey me.
تو خدا سے ڈرو اور میرا کہا مانو (۱۶۳)
فَاتَّقُوا اللَّهَ وَأَطِيعُونِ ﴿١٦٣﴾

164. "No reward do I ask of you for it: my reward is only from the Lord of the Worlds.
اور میں تم سے اس (کام) کا بدلہ نہیں مانگتا میرا بدلہ (خدائے) رب العالمین کے ذمے ہے (۱۶۴)
وَمَا أَسْأَلُكُمْ عَلَيْهِ مِنْ أَجْرٍ إِنْ أَجْرِيَ إِلَّا عَلَىٰ رَبِّ الْعَالَمِينَ ﴿١٦٤﴾

165. "Of all the creatures in the world, will ye approach males,
کیا تم اہل عالم میں سے لڑکوں پر مائل ہوتے ہو (۱۶۵)
أَتَأْتُونَ الذُّكْرَانَ مِنَ الْعَالَمِينَ ﴿١٦٥﴾

166. "And leave those whom Allah has created for you to be your mates? Nay, ye are a people transgressing (all limits)!"
اور تمہارے پروردگار نے جو تمہارے لئے تمہاری بیویاں پیدا کی ہیں اُنکو چھوڑ دیتے ہو حقیقت یہ ہے کہ تم حد سے نکل جانے والے لوگ ہو (۱۶۶)
وَتَذَرُونَ مَا خَلَقَ لَكُمْ رَبُّكُمْ مِنْ أَزْوَاجِكُمْ بَلْ أَنْتُمْ قَوْمٌ عَادُونَ ﴿١٦٦﴾

167. They said: "If thou desist not, O Lûṭ ! thou wilt assuredly be cast out!"
وہ کہنے لگے کہ لوط اگر تم باز نہ آؤ گے تو شہر بدر کر دیئے جاؤ گے (۱۶۷)
قَالُوا لَئِنْ لَمْ تَنْتَهِ يَا لُوطُ لَتَكُونَنَّ مِنَ الْمُخْرَجِينَ ﴿١٦٧﴾

168. He said: "I do detest your doings."
لوط نے کہا کہ میں تمہارے کام سے سخت بیزار ہوں (۱۶۸)
قَالَ إِنِّي لِعَمَلِكُمْ مِنَ الْقَالِينَ ﴿١٦٨﴾

169. "O my Lord! deliver me and my family from such things as they do!"
اے میرے پروردگار مجھکو اور میرے گھر والوں کو انکے کاموں (کے وبال) سے نجات دے (۱۶۹)
رَبِّ نَجِّنِي وَأَهْلِي مِمَّا يَعْمَلُونَ ﴿١٦٩﴾

170. So We delivered him and his family,—all
سو ہم نے اُن کو اور اُنکے گھر والوں کو سب کو نجات دی (۱۷۰)
فَنَجَّيْنَاهُ وَأَهْلَهُ أَجْمَعِينَ ﴿١٧٠﴾

171. Except an old woman who lingered behind.
مگر ایک بڑھیا کہ پیچھے رہ گئی (۱۷۱)
إِلَّا عَجُوزًا فِي الْغَابِرِينَ ﴿١٧١﴾

172. Then the rest We destroyed utterly.
پھر ہم نے اوروں کو ہلاک کر دیا (۱۷۲)
ثُمَّ دَمَّرْنَا الْآخَرِينَ ﴿١٧٢﴾

173. We rained down on them a shower (of brimstone): and evil was the shower on those who were admonished (But heeded not)!
اور ان پر مینہ برسایا سو جو مینہ ان (لوگوں) پر برسا جو ڈرائے گئے تھے وہ بُرا تھا (۱۷۳)
وَأَمْطَرْنَا عَلَيْهِمْ مَطَرًا فَسَاءَ مَطَرُ الْمُنْذَرِينَ ﴿١٧٣﴾

174. Verily in this is a Sign: but most of them do not believe.
بیشک اس میں نشانی ہے۔ اور اُن میں اکثر ایمان لانے والے نہیں تھے (۱۷۴)
إِنَّ فِي ذَٰلِكَ لَآيَةً وَمَا كَانَ أَكْثَرُهُمْ مُؤْمِنِينَ ﴿١٧٤﴾

175. And verily thy Lord is He, the Exalted in Might Most Merciful.
اور تمہارا پروردگار تو غالب (اور) مہربان ہے (۱۷۵)
وَإِنَّ رَبَّكَ لَهُوَ الْعَزِيزُ الرَّحِيمُ ﴿١٧٥﴾ ع ١٠

176. The Companions of the Wood rejected the messengers.
اور بن کے رہنے والوں نے بھی پیغمبروں کو جھٹلایا (۱۷۶)
كَذَّبَ أَصْحَابُ الْأَيْكَةِ الْمُرْسَلِينَ ﴿١٧٦﴾

177. Behold, Shu'aib said to them: "Will ye not fear (Allah)?
جب اُن سے شعیب نے کہا کہ تم ڈرتے کیوں نہیں (۱۷۷)
إِذْ قَالَ لَهُمْ شُعَيْبٌ أَلَا تَتَّقُونَ ﴿١٧٧﴾

178. "I am to you a messenger worthy of all trust.
میں تو تمہارا امانت دار پیغمبر ہوں (۱۷۸)
إِنِّي لَكُمْ رَسُولٌ أَمِينٌ ﴿١٧٨﴾

179. "So fear Allah and obey me.
تو خدا سے ڈرو اور میرا کہا مانو (۱۷۹)
فَاتَّقُوا اللَّهَ وَأَطِيعُونِ ﴿١٧٩﴾

180. "No reward do I ask of you for it: my reward is only from the Lord of the Worlds.
اور میں اس (کام) کا تم سے کچھ بدلہ نہیں مانگتا میرا بدلہ تو (خدائے) رب العالمین کے ذمے ہے (۱۸۰)
وَمَا أَسْأَلُكُمْ عَلَيْهِ مِنْ أَجْرٍ إِنْ أَجْرِيَ إِلَّا عَلَىٰ رَبِّ الْعَالَمِينَ ﴿١٨٠﴾

181. "Give just measure, and cause no loss (to others by fraud).
(دیکھو) پیمانہ پورا بھر کر دو اور نقصان نہ کیا کرو (۱۸۱)
أَوْفُوا الْكَيْلَ وَلَا تَكُونُوا مِنَ الْمُخْسِرِينَ ﴿١٨١﴾

182. "And weigh with scales true and upright.

وَزِنُوا بِالْقِسْطَاسِ الْمُسْتَقِيمِ ﴿١٨٢﴾

اور ترازو سیدھی رکھ کر تولا کرو ﴿١٨٢﴾

183. "And withhold not things justly due to men, nor do evil in the land, working mischief.

وَلَا تَبْخَسُوا النَّاسَ أَشْيَاءَهُمْ وَلَا تَعْثَوْا فِي الْأَرْضِ مُفْسِدِينَ ﴿١٨٣﴾

اور لوگوں کو اُن کی چیزیں کم نہ دیا کرو اور ملک میں فساد نہ کرتے پھرو ﴿١٨٣﴾

184. "And fear Him Who created you and (Who created) the generations before (you)."

وَاتَّقُوا الَّذِي خَلَقَكُمْ وَالْجِبِلَّةَ الْأَوَّلِينَ ﴿١٨٤﴾

اور اس سے ڈرو جس نے تم کو اور پہلی خلقت کو پیدا کیا ﴿١٨٤﴾

185. They said: "Thou art only one of those bewitched!

قَالُوا إِنَّمَا أَنتَ مِنَ الْمُسَحَّرِينَ ﴿١٨٥﴾

وہ کہنے لگے کہ تم جادو زدہ ہو ﴿١٨٥﴾

186. "Thou art no more than a mortal like us, and indeed we think thou art a liar!

وَمَا أَنتَ إِلَّا بَشَرٌ مِّثْلُنَا وَإِن نَّظُنُّكَ لَمِنَ الْكَاذِبِينَ ﴿١٨٦﴾

اور تم اور کچھ نہیں ہم ہی جیسے آدمی ہو۔ اور ہمارا خیال ہے کہ تم جھوٹے ہو ﴿١٨٦﴾

187. "Now cause a piece of the sky to fall on us, if thou art truthful!"

فَأَسْقِطْ عَلَيْنَا كِسَفًا مِّنَ السَّمَاءِ إِن كُنتَ مِنَ الصَّادِقِينَ ﴿١٨٧﴾

اگر سچے ہو تو ہم پر آسمان سے ایک ٹکڑا لا گراؤ ﴿١٨٧﴾

188. He said: "My Lord knows best what ye do."

قَالَ رَبِّي أَعْلَمُ بِمَا تَعْمَلُونَ ﴿١٨٨﴾

(شعیبؑ نے) کہا کہ جو کام تم کرتے ہو میرا پروردگار اس سے خوب واقف ہے ﴿١٨٨﴾

189. But they rejected him. Then the punishment of a day of overshadowing gloom seized them, and that was the Chastisement of a Great Day.

فَكَذَّبُوهُ فَأَخَذَهُمْ عَذَابُ يَوْمِ الظُّلَّةِ ۚ إِنَّهُ كَانَ عَذَابَ يَوْمٍ عَظِيمٍ ﴿١٨٩﴾

تو اُن لوگوں نے اُن کو جھٹلایا پس سائبان کے عذاب نے اُنکو آپکڑا۔ بے شک وہ بڑے (سخت) دن کا عذاب تھا ﴿١٨٩﴾

190. Verily in that is a Sign: but most of them do not believe.

إِنَّ فِي ذَٰلِكَ لَآيَةً ۖ وَمَا كَانَ أَكْثَرُهُم مُّؤْمِنِينَ ﴿١٩٠﴾

اس میں یقیناً نشانی ہے۔ اور ان میں اکثر ایمان لانے والے نہیں تھے ﴿١٩٠﴾

191. And verily thy Lord is He, the Exalted in Might Most Merciful.

وَإِنَّ رَبَّكَ لَهُوَ الْعَزِيزُ الرَّحِيمُ ﴿١٩١﴾

اور تمہارا پروردگار تو غالب (اور) مہربان ہے ﴿١٩١﴾

192. Verily this is a Revelation from the Lord of the Worlds:

وَإِنَّهُ لَتَنزِيلُ رَبِّ الْعَالَمِينَ ﴿١٩٢﴾

اور یہ (قرآن خدائے) پروردگار عالم کا اُتارا ہوا ہے ﴿١٩٢﴾

193. With it came down the Truthful spirit

نَزَلَ بِهِ الرُّوحُ الْأَمِينُ ﴿١٩٣﴾

اس کو امانت دار فرشتہ لے کر اُترا ہے ﴿١٩٣﴾

194. To thy heart that thou mayest admonish

عَلَىٰ قَلْبِكَ لِتَكُونَ مِنَ الْمُنذِرِينَ ﴿١٩٤﴾

(یعنی اُس نے) تمہارے دل پر (القا کیا ہے) تاکہ (لوگوں کو) نصیحت کرتے رہو ﴿١٩٤﴾

195. In the perspicuous Arabic tongue.

بِلِسَانٍ عَرَبِيٍّ مُّبِينٍ ﴿١٩٥﴾

(اور القا بھی) فصیح عربی زبان میں (کیا ہے) ﴿١٩٥﴾

196. Without doubt it is (announced) in the revealed Books of former peoples.

وَإِنَّهُ لَفِي زُبُرِ الْأَوَّلِينَ ﴿١٩٦﴾

اور اسکی خبر پہلے پیغمبروں کی کتابوں میں (لکھی ہوئی) ہے ﴿١٩٦﴾

197. Is it not a Sign to them that the Learned of the Children of Israel knew it (as true)?

أَوَلَمْ يَكُن لَّهُمْ آيَةً أَن يَعْلَمَهُ عُلَمَاءُ بَنِي إِسْرَائِيلَ ﴿١٩٧﴾

کیا اُن کے لئے یہ سند نہیں ہے کہ علمائے بنی اسرائیل اس (بات) کو جانتے ہیں ﴿١٩٧﴾

198. Had We revealed it to any of the non-Arabs,

وَلَوْ نَزَّلْنَاهُ عَلَىٰ بَعْضِ الْأَعْجَمِينَ ﴿١٩٨﴾

اور اگر ہم اس کو کسی غیر اہل زبان پر اتارتے ﴿١٩٨﴾

199. And had he recited it to them, they would not have believed in it.

فَقَرَأَهُ عَلَيْهِم مَّا كَانُوا بِهِ مُؤْمِنِينَ ﴿١٩٩﴾

اور وہ اسے ان (لوگوں) کو پڑھ کر سناتا تو یہ اسے کبھی نہ مانتے ﴿١٩٩﴾

200. Thus have We caused it to enter the hearts of the Sinners.

كَذَٰلِكَ سَلَكْنَاهُ فِي قُلُوبِ الْمُجْرِمِينَ ﴿٢٠٠﴾

اسی طرح ہم نے انکار کو گنہگاروں کے دلوں میں داخل کر دیا ﴿٢٠٠﴾

201. They will not believe in it until they see the grievous Chastisement

لَا يُؤْمِنُونَ بِهِ حَتَّىٰ يَرَوُا الْعَذَابَ الْأَلِيمَ ﴿٢٠١﴾

وہ جبتک درد دینے والا عذاب نہ دیکھ لیں اسکو نہیں مانیں گے ﴿٢٠١﴾

202. But it will come to them of a sudden, while they perceive it not;

فَيَأْتِيَهُم بَغْتَةً وَهُمْ لَا يَشْعُرُونَ ﴿٢٠٢﴾

وہ ان پر ناگہاں آواقع ہوگا اور انہیں خبر بھی نہ ہوگی ﴿٢٠٢﴾

203. Then they will say: "Shall we be respited?"
اُس وقت کہیں گے کیا ہمیں مہلت ملے گی؟ (٢٠٣)
فيقولوا هل نحن منظرون (٢٠٣)

204. Do they then ask for Our Chastisement to be hastened on?
تو کیا یہ ہمارے عذاب کو جلدی طلب کر رہے ہیں (٢٠٤)
أفبعذابنا يستعجلون (٢٠٤)

205. Seest thou? If We do let them enjoy (this life) for a few years,
بھلا دیکھو تو اگر ہم اُن کو برسوں فائدے دیتے رہیں (٢٠٥)
أفرءيت إن متعنٰهم سنين (٢٠٥)

206. Yet there comes to them at length the (Punishment) which they were promised!
پھر اُن پر وہ (عذاب) آ واقع ہو جس کا ان سے وعدہ کیا جاتا ہے (٢٠٦)
ثم جآءهم ما كانوا يوعدون (٢٠٦)

207. It will profit them not the enjoyment they were given.
تو جو فائدے یہ اٹھاتے رہے اُن کے کس کام آئیں گے (٢٠٧)
ما أغنى عنهم ما كانوا يمتعون (٢٠٧)

208. Never did We destroy a town but had its warners—
اور ہم نے کوئی بستی ہلاک نہیں کی مگر اسکے لئے نصیحت کرنے والے پہلے بھیج دیتے تھے (٢٠٨)
وما أهلكنا من قرية إلا لها منذرون (٢٠٨)

209. By way of reminder; and We never are unjust.
(تاکہ نصیحت کر دیں) اور ہم ظالم نہیں ہیں (٢٠٩)
ذكرى وما كنا ظٰلمين (٢٠٩)

210. The Satans did not bring it down:
اور اس (قرآن) کو شیطان لے کر نازل نہیں ہوئے (٢١٠)
وما تنزلت به الشيٰطين (٢١٠)

211. It is not meet for them, nor is it in their power
یہ کام نہ تو اُن کو سزاوار ہے اور نہ وہ اسکی طاقت رکھتے ہیں (٢١١)
وما ينبغي لهم وما يستطيعون (٢١١)

212. Indeed they are banished from hearing it.
وہ (آسمانی باتوں کے) سننے (کے مقامات) سے الگ کر دیئے گئے ہیں (٢١٢)
إنهم عن السمع لمعزولون (٢١٢)

213. So call not on any other god with Allah, or thou wilt be among those who will be punished.
تو خدا کے سوا کسی اور معبود کو مت پکارنا ورنہ تم کو عذاب دیا جائے گا (٢١٣)
فلا تدع مع الله إلٰها ءاخر فتكون من المعذبين (٢١٣)

214. And admonish thy nearest kinsmen,
اور اپنے قریب کے رشتہ داروں کو ڈر سنا دو (٢١٤)
وأنذر عشيرتك الأقربين (٢١٤)

215. And lower thy wing to the Believers who follow thee.
اور جو مومن تمہارے پیرو ہو گئے ہیں اُن سے متواضع پیش آؤ (٢١٥)
واخفض جناحك لمن اتبعك من المؤمنين (٢١٥)

216. Then if they disobey thee, say: "I am free (of responsibility) from what ye do!"
پھر اگر لوگ تمہاری نافرمانی کریں تو کہہ دو کہ میں تمہارے اعمال سے بےتعلق ہوں (٢١٦)
فإن عصوك فقل إني بريء مما تعملون (٢١٦)

217. And put thy trust on the Exalted in Might, the Merciful,—
اور (خدائے) غالب (اور) مہربان پر بھروسا رکھو (٢١٧)
وتوكل على العزيز الرحيم (٢١٧)

218. Who seeth thee standing forth (in prayer),
جو تم کو جب تم (تہجد کے وقت) اٹھتے ہو دیکھتا ہے (٢١٨)
الذي يرٰىك حين تقوم (٢١٨)

219. And thy movements among those who prostrate themselves.
اور نمازیوں میں تمہارے پھرنے کو بھی (٢١٩)
وتقلبك في السٰجدين (٢١٩)

220. For it is He Who heareth and knoweth all things.
بیشک وہ سننے والا (اور) جاننے والا ہے (٢٢٠)
إنه هو السميع العليم (٢٢٠)

221. Shall I inform you, (O people), on whom it is that the Satans descend?
(اچھا) میں تمہیں بتاؤں کہ شیطان کس پر اُترتے ہیں (٢٢١)
هل أنبئكم على من تنزل الشيٰطين (٢٢١)

222. They descend on every lying, wicked person,
ہر جھوٹے گنہگار پر اُترتے ہیں (٢٢٢)
تنزل على كل أفاك أثيم (٢٢٢)

223. They listen eagerly and most of them are liars.
جو سنی ہوئی بات (اسکے کان میں) لا ڈالتے ہیں اور وہ اکثر جھوٹے ہیں (٢٢٣)
يلقون السمع وأكثرهم كٰذبون (٢٢٣)

224. And the Poets,— it is those straying in Evil, who follow them:
اور شاعروں کی پیروی گمراہ لوگ کیا کرتے ہیں (٢٢٤)
والشعرآء يتبعهم الغاون (٢٢٤)

225. Seest thou not that they wander distracted in every valley?—
کیا تم نے نہیں دیکھا کہ وہ ہر وادی میں سر مارتے پھرتے ہیں (٢٢٥)
ألم تر أنهم في كل واد يهيمون (٢٢٥)

226. And that they say what they practise not?—
اور کہتے وہ ہیں جو کرتے نہیں (٢٢٦)
وأنهم يقولون ما لا يفعلون (٢٢٦)

227. Except those who believe, work righteousness, engaged much
مگر جو لوگ ایمان لائے اور نیک کام کئے اور خدا کو بہت یاد
إلا الذين ءامنوا وعملوا الصٰلحٰت و

SÛRA–27

AN-NAML

(INTRODUCTION)

This Sûra is cognate in subject to the one preceding it and the two following it. Its chronological place is also in the same group of four.

Here there is much mystic symbolism. Wonders in the physical world are types of greater wonders in the spiritual world. The Fire, the White Hand and the Rod, in the story of Moses; the speech of birds, the crowds of Jinns and men pitted against a humble ant, and the Hoopoe and the Queen of Sheba, in Solomon's story; the defeat of the plot of the nine wicked men in the story of Ṣãliḥ; and the crime of sin with open eyes in the story of Lot;—lead up to the lessons of true and false worship and the miracles of Allah's grace and revelation.

in the remembrance of Allah, and defend themselves after they are unjustly attacked. And soon will the unjust know what vicissitudes their affairs will take!

An-Naml, or the Ants

In the name of Allah, Most Gracious, Most Merciful.

1. Ṭā. Sīn. These are verses of the Qur'an,— A Book that makes (things) clear;

2. A Guide; and Glad Tidings for the Believers,—

3. Those who establish regular prayers and give zakat, and also have sure faith in the Hereafter.

4. As to those who believe not in the Hereafter, We have made their deeds pleasing in their eyes; and so they wander blindly.

5. Such are they for whom a grievous Chastisement is (waiting): and in the Hereafter theirs will be the greatest loss.

6. As for thee, thou receivest the Qur'an from One All-Wise, All-Knowing.

7. Behold ! Moses said to his family: "I perceive a fire; soon will I bring you from there some information, or I will bring you a burning brand (to light our fuel,) that ye may warm yourselves.

8. But when he came to the (Fire), a voice was heard: "Blessed are those in the Fire and those around: and Glory to Allah, the Lord of the Worlds.

9. "O Moses! Verily, I am Allah, the Exalted in Might, the Wise!...

10. "Now do thou throw thy rod!" But when he saw it moving (of its own accord) as if it had been a snake, He turned back in retreat, and retraced not his steps: "O Moses!" (it was said), "Fear not: truly, in My presence, those called as messengers have no fear,—

11. "But if any have done wrong and have thereafter substituted good to take the place of evil, truly, I am Oft-Forgiving, Most Merciful.

12. "Now put thy hand into thy bosom, and it will come forth white

کرتے رہے اور اپنے اُوپر ظلم ہونے کے بعد انتقام لیا اور
ظالم عنقریب جان لیں گے کہ کون سی جگہ لَوٹ کر
جاتے ہیں ﴿۲۲۷﴾

سُورۂ نمل مکّی ہے اور اس میں ترانوے آیتیں اور سات رکوع ہیں

شروع خدا کا نام لے کر جو بڑا مہربان نہایت رحم والا ہے
طٰسٓ۔ یہ قرآن اور کتاب روشن کی آیتیں ہیں ﴿۱﴾
مومنوں کے لئے ہدایت اور بشارت ہے ﴿۲﴾
وہ جو نماز پڑھتے اور زکوٰۃ دیتے اور آخرت کا یقین
رکھتے ہیں ﴿۳﴾
جو لوگ آخرت پر ایمان نہیں رکھتے ہم نے اُنکے اعمال اُن کے
لئے آراستہ کردیئے ہیں تو وہ سرگرداں ہو رہے ہیں ﴿۴﴾
یہی لوگ ہیں جن کے لئے بڑا عذاب ہے اور وہ آخرت میں
بھی بہت نقصان اُٹھانے والے ہیں ﴿۵﴾
اور تم کو قرآن (خدائے) حکیم و علیم کی طرف سے عطا
کیا جاتا ہے ﴿۶﴾
جب موسیٰ نے اپنے گھر والوں سے کہا کہ میں نے آگ دیکھی ہے
میں وہاں سے (رستے کا) پتہ لاتا ہوں یا سلگتا ہوا انگارا
تمہارے پاس لاتا ہوں تاکہ تم تاپو ﴿۷﴾
جب موسیٰ اسکے پاس آئے تو ندا آئی کہ وہ جو آگ میں (تجلّی دکھاتا) ہے
بابرکت ہے اور وہ جو آگ کے اردگرد ہیں اور خدا جو تمام عالم کا پروردگار ہے پاک ہے ﴿۸﴾
اے موسیٰ میں ہی خدائے غالب و دانا ہوں ﴿۹﴾
اور اپنی لاٹھی ڈال دو۔ جب اُسے دیکھا تو اس طرح ہل رہی تھی گویا
سانپ ہے تو پیٹھ پھیر کر بھاگے اور پیچھے مُڑ کر نہ دیکھا (حکم ہوا کہ)
موسیٰ ڈرو مت۔ ہمارے پاس پیغمبر ڈرا نہیں کرتے ﴿۱۰﴾
ہاں جس نے ظلم کیا پھر بُرائی کے بعد اسے نیکی سے بدل دیا
تو میں بخشنے والا مہربان ہوں ﴿۱۱﴾
اور اپنا ہاتھ اپنے گریبان میں ڈالو بے عیب سفید نکلے گا

ذَكَرُوا اللَّهَ كَثِيرًا وَانتَصَرُوا مِن بَعْدِ
مَا ظُلِمُوا ۗ وَسَيَعْلَمُ الَّذِينَ ظَلَمُوا
أَيَّ مُنقَلَبٍ يَنقَلِبُونَ ﴿٢٢٧﴾ ع ١٥

سُورَةُ النَّمْلِ مَكِّيَّةٌ وَهِيَ ثَلَاثٌ وَتِسْعُونَ آيَةً وَسَبْعُ رُكُوعَاتٍ

بِسْمِ اللَّهِ الرَّحْمَٰنِ الرَّحِيمِ
طس ۚ تِلْكَ آيَاتُ الْقُرْآنِ وَكِتَابٍ مُّبِينٍ ﴿١﴾
هُدًى وَبُشْرَىٰ لِلْمُؤْمِنِينَ ﴿٢﴾
الَّذِينَ يُقِيمُونَ الصَّلَاةَ وَيُؤْتُونَ الزَّكَاةَ
وَهُم بِالْآخِرَةِ هُمْ يُوقِنُونَ ﴿٣﴾
إِنَّ الَّذِينَ لَا يُؤْمِنُونَ بِالْآخِرَةِ زَيَّنَّا
لَهُمْ أَعْمَالَهُمْ فَهُمْ يَعْمَهُونَ ﴿٤﴾
أُولَٰئِكَ الَّذِينَ لَهُمْ سُوءُ الْعَذَابِ وَهُمْ
فِي الْآخِرَةِ هُمُ الْأَخْسَرُونَ ﴿٥﴾
وَإِنَّكَ لَتُلَقَّى الْقُرْآنَ مِن لَّدُنْ حَكِيمٍ
عَلِيمٍ ﴿٦﴾ النصف
إِذْ قَالَ مُوسَىٰ لِأَهْلِهِ إِنِّي آنَسْتُ نَارًا
سَآتِيكُم مِّنْهَا بِخَبَرٍ أَوْ آتِيكُم بِشِهَابٍ
قَبَسٍ لَّعَلَّكُمْ تَصْطَلُونَ ﴿٧﴾
فَلَمَّا جَاءَهَا نُودِيَ أَن بُورِكَ مَن فِي
النَّارِ وَمَنْ حَوْلَهَا وَسُبْحَانَ اللَّهِ رَبِّ الْعَالَمِينَ ﴿٨﴾
يَا مُوسَىٰ إِنَّهُ أَنَا اللَّهُ الْعَزِيزُ الْحَكِيمُ ﴿٩﴾
وَأَلْقِ عَصَاكَ ۚ فَلَمَّا رَآهَا تَهْتَزُّ كَأَنَّهَا
جَانٌّ وَلَّىٰ مُدْبِرًا وَلَمْ يُعَقِّبْ ۚ يَا مُوسَىٰ
لَا تَخَفْ إِنِّي لَا يَخَافُ لَدَيَّ الْمُرْسَلُونَ ﴿١٠﴾
إِلَّا مَن ظَلَمَ ثُمَّ بَدَّلَ حُسْنًا بَعْدَ سُوءٍ
فَإِنِّي غَفُورٌ رَّحِيمٌ ﴿١١﴾
وَأَدْخِلْ يَدَكَ فِي جَيْبِكَ تَخْرُجْ بَيْضَاءَ

without stain (or harm): (these are) among the nine Signs (thou wilt take) to Pharaoh and his people: for they are a people rebellious in transgression."

13. But when Our Signs came to them, visibly they said: "This is sorcery manifest!"

14. And they denied them, though their souls acknowledged them wrongfully and out of pride: so see what was the end of those who acted corruptly!

15. We gave knowledge to David and Solomon: and they both said: "Praise be to Allah, Who has favoured us above many of His servants who believe!"

16. And Solomon was David's heir. He said: "O ye people! we have been taught the speech of Birds, and we have been given of everything this is indeed Grace manifest (from Allah.)"

17. And before Solomon were marshalled his hosts,—of Jinns and men and birds, and they were all kept in order and ranks.

18. At length, when they came to a valley of ants, one of the ants said: "O ye ants, get into your habitations, lest Solomon and his hosts crush you (under foot) without knowing it."

19. So he smiled, amused at her speech; and he said: "O my Lord! so order me that I may be grateful for Thy favours, which Thou has bestowed on me and on my parents, and that I may work the righteousness that will please Thee: and admit me, by Thy Grace, to the ranks of Thy righteous Servants."

20. And he took a muster of the Birds; and he said: "Why is it I see not the Hoopoe? Or is he among the absentees?

21. "I will certainly punish him with a severe punishment, or execute him, unless he bring me a clear reason (for absence)."

22. But the Hoopoe tarried not far: he (came up and) said: "I have

(ان دو معجزوں کے ساتھ جو) نو معجزوں میں (داخل ہیں) فرعون
اور اس کی قوم کے پاس (جاؤ) کہ وہ بدکردار لوگ ہیں ﴿١٢﴾
جب اُن کے پاس ہماری روشن نشانیاں پہنچیں کہنے لگے
یہ صریح جادو ہے ﴿١٣﴾
اور بے انصافی اور غرور سے اُن سے انکار کیا۔ لیکن اُن کے
دل اُن کو مان چکے تھے سو دیکھ لو کہ فساد کرنیوالوں کا انجام کیسا ہوا ﴿١٤﴾
اور ہم نے داؤد اور سلیمان کو علم بخشا۔ اور اُنہوں نے کہا
کہ خدا کا شکر ہے جس نے ہمیں اپنے بہت سے مومن بندوں
پر فضیلت دی ﴿١٥﴾
اور سلیمان داؤد کے قائم مقام ہوئے۔ اور کہنے لگے کہ لوگو
ہمیں (خدا کی طرف سے) جانوروں کی بولی سکھائی گئی ہے
اور ہر چیز عنایت فرمائی گئی ہے۔ بیشک یہ (اس کا) صریح فضل ہے ﴿١٦﴾
اور سلیمان کے لئے جنّوں اور انسانوں اور پرندوں کے
لشکر جمع کئے گئے اور وہ قسم وار کئے گئے تھے ﴿١٧﴾
یہاں تک کہ جب چیونٹیوں کے میدان میں پہنچے تو ایک
چیونٹی نے کہا کہ چیونٹیو اپنے بلوں میں داخل ہو
جاؤ ایسا نہ ہو کہ سلیمان اور اسکے لشکر تم کو کچل ڈالیں اور
اُن کو خبر بھی نہ ہو ﴿١٨﴾
تو وہ اس کی بات سے ہنس پڑے اور کہنے لگے کہ اے پروردگار
مجھے توفیق عنایت کر کہ جو احسان تو نے مجھ پر اور میرے ماں
باپ پر کئے ہیں اُن کا شکر کروں اور ایسے نیک کام کروں کہ تو
اُن سے خوش ہو جائے اور مجھے اپنی رحمت سے اپنے نیک بندوں میں داخل فرما ﴿١٩﴾
اور جب اُنہوں نے جانوروں کا جائزہ لیا تو کہنے لگے کیا سبب ہے
کہ ہُدہُد نظر نہیں آتا۔ کیا کہیں غائب ہو گیا ہے؟ ﴿٢٠﴾
میں اسے سخت سزا دوں گا یا ذبح کر ڈالوں گا یا میرے سامنے
(اپنی بے قصوری کی) دلیل صریح پیش کرے ﴿٢١﴾
ابھی تھوڑی ہی دیر ہوئی تھی کہ ہُدہُد آ موجود ہوا اور کہنے

مِنْ غَيْرِ سُوٓءٍ فِى تِسْعِ ءَايَٰتٍ إِلَىٰ فِرْعَوْنَ
وَقَوْمِهِۦٓ إِنَّهُمْ كَانُوا۟ قَوْمًا فَٰسِقِينَ ﴿١٢﴾
فَلَمَّا جَآءَتْهُمْ ءَايَٰتُنَا مُبْصِرَةً قَالُوا۟ هَٰذَا
سِحْرٌ مُّبِينٌ ﴿١٣﴾
وَجَحَدُوا۟ بِهَا وَٱسْتَيْقَنَتْهَآ أَنفُسُهُمْ ظُلْمًا
وَعُلُوًّا فَٱنظُرْ كَيْفَ كَانَ عَٰقِبَةُ ٱلْمُفْسِدِينَ ﴿١٤﴾
وَلَقَدْ ءَاتَيْنَا دَاوُۥدَ وَسُلَيْمَٰنَ عِلْمًا وَقَالَا
ٱلْحَمْدُ لِلَّهِ ٱلَّذِى فَضَّلَنَا عَلَىٰ كَثِيرٍ مِّنْ
عِبَادِهِ ٱلْمُؤْمِنِينَ ﴿١٥﴾
وَوَرِثَ سُلَيْمَٰنُ دَاوُۥدَ وَقَالَ يَٰٓأَيُّهَا
ٱلنَّاسُ عُلِّمْنَا مَنطِقَ ٱلطَّيْرِ وَأُوتِينَا مِن
كُلِّ شَىْءٍ إِنَّ هَٰذَا لَهُوَ ٱلْفَضْلُ ٱلْمُبِينُ ﴿١٦﴾
وَحُشِرَ لِسُلَيْمَٰنَ جُنُودُهُۥ مِنَ ٱلْجِنِّ وَ
ٱلْإِنسِ وَٱلطَّيْرِ فَهُمْ يُوزَعُونَ ﴿١٧﴾
حَتَّىٰٓ إِذَآ أَتَوْا۟ عَلَىٰ وَادِ ٱلنَّمْلِ قَالَتْ
نَمْلَةٌ يَٰٓأَيُّهَا ٱلنَّمْلُ ٱدْخُلُوا۟ مَسَٰكِنَكُمْ
لَا يَحْطِمَنَّكُمْ سُلَيْمَٰنُ وَجُنُودُهُۥ وَهُمْ
لَا يَشْعُرُونَ ﴿١٨﴾
فَتَبَسَّمَ ضَاحِكًا مِّن قَوْلِهَا وَقَالَ رَبِّ
أَوْزِعْنِىٓ أَنْ أَشْكُرَ نِعْمَتَكَ ٱلَّتِىٓ أَنْعَمْتَ
عَلَىَّ وَعَلَىٰ وَٰلِدَىَّ وَأَنْ أَعْمَلَ صَٰلِحًا تَرْضَىٰهُ
وَأَدْخِلْنِى بِرَحْمَتِكَ فِى عِبَادِكَ ٱلصَّٰلِحِينَ ﴿١٩﴾
وَتَفَقَّدَ ٱلطَّيْرَ فَقَالَ مَا لِىَ لَآ أَرَى
ٱلْهُدْهُدَ أَمْ كَانَ مِنَ ٱلْغَآئِبِينَ ﴿٢٠﴾
لَأُعَذِّبَنَّهُۥ عَذَابًا شَدِيدًا أَوْ لَأَا۟ذْبَحَنَّهُۥٓ
أَوْ لَيَأْتِيَنِّى بِسُلْطَٰنٍ مُّبِينٍ ﴿٢١﴾
فَمَكَثَ غَيْرَ بَعِيدٍ فَقَالَ أَحَطتُ بِمَا

compassed which thou hast not compassed, and I have come to thee from Sabã with tidings true.

23. "I found (there) a woman ruling over them and provided with every requisite; and she has a magnificent throne.

24. "I found her and her people worshipping the sun besides Allah: Satan has made their deeds seem pleasing in their eyes, and has kept them away from the Path,—so they receive no guidance,—

25. "So that they worship not Allah who brings forth what is hidden in the heavens and the earth, and knows what ye hide and what ye reveal.

26. "Allah!—there is no god but He!—Lord of the Throne Supreme!"

27. (Solomon) said: "Soon shall we see whether thou hast told the truth or lied!

28. "Go thou, with this letter of mine, and deliver it to them: then draw back from them, and (wait to) see what answer they return"...

29. (The Queen) said: "Ye chiefs! here is—delivered to me—a letter worthy of respect.

30. "It is from Solomon, and is (as follows): 'In the name of Allah, Most Gracious, Most Merciful:

31. " 'Be ye not arrogant against me, but come to me in submission (to the true Religion).' "

32. She said: "Ye chiefs! advise me in (this) my affair: no affair have I decided except in your presence."

33. They said: "We are endued with strength, and given to vehement war: but the command is with thee; so consider what thou wilt command."

34. She said: "Kings, when they enter a country, despoil it, and make the noblest of its people its meanest thus do they behave.

35. "But I am going to send him a present, and (wait) to see with what

لگا کہ مجھے ایک ایسی چیز معلوم ہوئی ہے جسکی آپ کو خبر نہیں
اور میں آپکے پاس (شہر) سبا سے ایک یقینی خبر لیکر آیا ہوں ۝۲۲
میں نے ایک عورت دیکھی کہ ان لوگوں پر بادشاہت کرتی ہے
اور ہر چیز اسے میسر ہے اور اس کا ایک بڑا تخت ہے ۝۲۳
میں نے دیکھا کہ وہ اور اس کی قوم خدا کو چھوڑ کر آفتاب کو سجدہ
کرتے ہیں اور شیطان نے اُنکے اعمال انہیں آراستہ کر دکھائے ہیں
اور اُن کو رستے سے روک رکھا ہے پس وہ رستے پر نہیں آتے ۝۲۴
(اور نہیں سمجھتے) کہ خدا کو جو آسمانوں اور زمین میں چھپی چیزوں
کو ظاہر کر دیتا اور تمہارے پوشیدہ اور ظاہر اعمال کو جانتا ہے
کیوں سجدہ نہ کریں ۝۲۵
خدا کے سوا کوئی عبادت کے لائق نہیں وہی عرش عظیم کا مالک ہے ۝۲۶
(سلیمانؑ نے) کہا (اچھا) ہم دیکھیں گے تو نے سچ کہا ہے یا تو جھوٹا ہے ۝۲۷
یہ میرا خط لے جا اور اسے اُن کی طرف ڈال دے پھر اُن کے
پاس سے پھر آ اور دیکھ کہ وہ کیا جواب دیتے ہیں ۝۲۸
ملکہ نے کہا کہ دربار والو میری طرف ایک نامۂ گرامی
ڈالا گیا ہے ۝۲۹
وہ سلیمانؑ کی طرف سے ہے اور (مضمون یہ ہے) کہ شروع خدا کا نام
لے کر جو بڑا مہربان نہایت رحم والا ہے ۝۳۰
(بعد اسکے یہ) کہ مجھ سے سرکشی نہ کرو اور مطیع و منقاد ہو کر میرے پاس چلے آؤ ۝۳۱
(خط سنا کر) کہنے لگی کہ اے اہلِ دربار میرے اس معاملے میں مجھے
مشورہ دو جبتک تم حاضر نہ ہو اور صلاح نہ دو میں کسی کام کو فیصل کرنے والی نہیں ہوں ۝۳۲
وہ بولے کہ ہم بڑے زور آور اور سخت جنگجو ہیں اور حکم آپکے اختیار
ہے۔ تو جو حکم دیجئے گا (اُس کے مآل پر) نظر کر لیجئے گا ۝۳۳
اس نے کہا کہ بادشاہ جب کسی شہر میں داخل ہوتے ہیں
تو اس کو تباہ کر دیتے ہیں اور وہاں کے عزت والوں کو
ذلیل کر دیا کرتے ہیں اور اسی طرح یہ بھی کریں گے ۝۳۴
اور میں اُن کی طرف کچھ تحفہ بھیجتی ہوں اور دیکھتی ہوں کہ

لَمْ تُحِطْ بِهٖ وَجِئْتُكَ مِنْ سَبَاٍۢ بِنَبَاٍ
يَّقِيْنٍ ۝۲۲
اِنِّيْ وَجَدْتُّ امْرَاَةً تَمْلِكُهُمْ وَاُوْتِيَتْ
مِنْ كُلِّ شَيْءٍ وَّلَهَا عَرْشٌ عَظِيْمٌ ۝۲۳
وَجَدْتُّهَا وَقَوْمَهَا يَسْجُدُوْنَ لِلشَّمْسِ مِنْ
دُوْنِ اللّٰهِ وَزَيَّنَ لَهُمُ الشَّيْطٰنُ اَعْمَالَهُمْ
فَصَدَّهُمْ عَنِ السَّبِيْلِ فَهُمْ لَا يَهْتَدُوْنَ ۝۲۴
اَلَّا يَسْجُدُوْا لِلّٰهِ الَّذِيْ يُخْرِجُ الْخَبْءَ فِي
السَّمٰوٰتِ وَالْاَرْضِ وَيَعْلَمُ مَا تُخْفُوْنَ
وَمَا تُعْلِنُوْنَ ۝۲۵
اَللّٰهُ لَآ اِلٰهَ اِلَّا هُوَ رَبُّ الْعَرْشِ الْعَظِيْمِ ۝۲۶
قَالَ سَنَنْظُرُ اَصَدَقْتَ اَمْ كُنْتَ مِنَ الْكٰذِبِيْنَ ۝۲۷
اِذْهَبْ بِّكِتٰبِيْ هٰذَا فَاَلْقِهْ اِلَيْهِمْ
ثُمَّ تَوَلَّ عَنْهُمْ فَانْظُرْ مَاذَا يَرْجِعُوْنَ ۝۲۸
قَالَتْ يٰٓاَيُّهَا الْمَلَؤُا اِنِّيْٓ اُلْقِيَ اِلَيَّ كِتٰبٌ
كَرِيْمٌ ۝۲۹
اِنَّهٗ مِنْ سُلَيْمٰنَ وَاِنَّهٗ بِسْمِ اللّٰهِ الرَّحْمٰنِ
الرَّحِيْمِ ۝۳۰
اَلَّا تَعْلُوْا عَلَيَّ وَاْتُوْنِيْ مُسْلِمِيْنَ ۝۳۱
قَالَتْ يٰٓاَيُّهَا الْمَلَؤُا اَفْتُوْنِيْ فِيْٓ اَمْرِيْ
مَا كُنْتُ قَاطِعَةً اَمْرًا حَتّٰى تَشْهَدُوْنِ ۝۳۲
قَالُوْا نَحْنُ اُولُوْا قُوَّةٍ وَّاُولُوْا بَاْسٍ شَدِيْدٍ
وَّالْاَمْرُ اِلَيْكِ فَانْظُرِيْ مَاذَا تَاْمُرِيْنَ ۝۳۳
قَالَتْ اِنَّ الْمُلُوْكَ اِذَا دَخَلُوْا قَرْيَةً
اَفْسَدُوْهَا وَجَعَلُوْٓا اَعِزَّةَ اَهْلِهَآ اَذِلَّةً
وَكَذٰلِكَ يَفْعَلُوْنَ ۝۳۴
وَاِنِّيْ مُرْسِلَةٌ اِلَيْهِمْ بِهَدِيَّةٍ فَنٰظِرَةٌۢ بِمَ

(answer) return (my) ambassadors."

36. Now when (the embassy) came to Solomon, he said: "Will ye give me abundance in wealth? But that which Allah has given me is better than that which He has given you! Nay it is ye who rejoice in your gift!

37. "Go back to them, and be sure we shall come to them with such hosts as they will never be able to meet: we shall expel them from there in disgrace, and they will feel humbled (indeed)."

38. He said (to his own men): "Ye Chiefs! which of you can bring me her throne before they come to me in submission?"

39. A stalwart of the Jinn said: "I will bring it to thee before thou rise from thy council: indeed I have full strength for the purpose, and may be trusted."

40. Said one who had knowledge of the Book: "I will bring it to thee before ever thy glance returns to thee. Then when (Solomon) saw it placed firmly before him, he said: "This is by the grace of my Lord!—to test me whether I am grateful or ungrateful! And if any is grateful, truly his gratitude is (a gain) for his own soul; but if any is ungrateful, truly my Lord is Free of all Needs, Supreme in Honour!"

41. He said: "Disguise her throne. Let us see whether she is guided (to the truth) or is one of those who are not rightly guided."

42. So when she arrived, she was asked, "Is this thy throne?" She said, "It seems the same. And knowledge was bestowed on us in advance of this, and we have submitted to Allah (in Islām)."

43. And he diverted her from the worship of others besides Allah: for she was (sprung) of a people that had no faith.

44. She was asked to enter the lofty Palace: but when she saw it, she thought it was a lake of water, and she (tucked up her skirts), uncovering her legs. He said: "This is but a palace paved smooth with

قاصد کیا جواب لاتے ہیں ﴿٣٥﴾
جب (قاصد) سلیمان کے پاس پہنچا تو (سلیمان نے) کہا کیا تم مجھے مال سے
مدد دینا چاہتے ہو جو کچھ خدا نے مجھے عطا فرمایا ہے وہ اس سے بہتر ہے
جو تمہیں دیا ہے حقیقت یہ ہے کہ اپنے تحفے سے تم ہی خوش ہوتے ہوگے ﴿٣٦﴾
انکے پاس واپس جاؤ ہم اُن پر ایسے لشکر لیکر حملہ کرینگے جنکے مقابلے کی
اُن میں طاقت نہ ہوگی اور انکو وہاں سے بےعزت کرکے نکال دینگے اور وہ ذلیل ہونگے ﴿٣٧﴾
سلیمان نے کہا کہ اے دربار والو کوئی تم میں ایسا ہے کہ قبل اسکے کہ وہ لوگ
فرمانبردار ہوکر ہمارے پاس آئیں ملکہ کا تخت میرے پاس لے آئے ﴿٣٨﴾
جنّات میں سے ایک قوی ہیکل جن نے کہا کہ قبل اسکے کہ آپ اپنی
جگہ سے اُٹھیں میں اسکو آپکے پاس لا حاضر کرتا ہوں اور مجھے اس پر
قدرت (بھی) حاصل ہے (اور) امانت دار (بھی) ہوں ﴿٣٩﴾
ایک شخص جس کو کتاب (الٰہی) کا علم تھا کہنے لگا کہ میں آپکی آنکھ
کے جھپکنے سے پہلے پہلے اُسے آپکے پاس حاضر کئے دیتا ہوں جب سلیمان
نے تخت کو اپنے پاس رکھا ہوا دیکھا تو کہا کہ یہ میرے پروردگار کا
فضل ہے تاکہ مجھے آزمائے کہ میں شکر کرتا ہوں یا کفرانِ نعمت کرتا ہوں
اور جو شکر کرتا ہے تو اپنے ہی فائدے کے لئے شکر کرتا ہے اور جو ناشکری کرتا
ہے تو میرا پروردگار بے پروا (اور) کرم کرنے والا ہے ﴿٤٠﴾
سلیمان نے کہا کہ ملکہ کے (امتحانِ عقل کے) لئے اسکے تخت کی صورت بدل دو
دیکھیں کہ وہ سوجھ رکھتی ہے یا اُن لوگوں میں سے ہے جو سوجھ نہیں رکھتے ﴿٤١﴾
جب وہ آپہنچی تو پوچھا گیا کہ کیا آپکا تخت بھی اسی طرح کا ہے اس نے
کہا کہ یہ تو گویا ہو بہو وہی ہے۔ اور ہم کو اس سے پہلے ہی
(سلیمان کی عظمت وشان کا) علم ہوگیا تھا اور ہم فرمانبردار ہیں ﴿٤٢﴾
اور وہ جو خدا کے سوا (اور کی) پرستش کرتی تھی سلیمان نے اسکو
اس سے منع کیا (اس سے پہلے تو) وہ کافروں میں سے تھی ﴿٤٣﴾
(پھر) اس سے کہا گیا کہ محل میں چلیے۔ جب اس نے اس (کے فرش) کو
دیکھا تو اُسے پانی کا حوض سمجھا اور (کپڑا اٹھا کر) اپنی پنڈلیاں کھول دیں
سلیمان نے کہا یہ ایسا محل ہے جسکے (نیچے بھی) شیشے جڑے ہوئے ہیں۔

يَرْجِعُ الْمُرْسَلُوْنَ ﴿٣٥﴾
فَلَمَّا جَآءَ سُلَيْمٰنَ قَالَ اَتُمِدُّوْنَنِ بِمَالٍ
فَمَآ اٰتٰىنِۦَ اللّٰهُ خَيْرٌ مِّمَّآ اٰتٰىكُمْ ۚ بَلْ اَنْتُمْ
بِهَدِيَّتِكُمْ تَفْرَحُوْنَ ﴿٣٦﴾
اِرْجِعْ اِلَيْهِمْ فَلَنَاْتِيَنَّهُمْ بِجُنُوْدٍ لَّا قِبَلَ لَهُمْ بِهَا
وَلَنُخْرِجَنَّهُمْ مِّنْهَآ اَذِلَّةً وَّهُمْ صٰغِرُوْنَ ﴿٣٧﴾
قَالَ يٰٓاَيُّهَا الْمَلَؤُا اَيُّكُمْ يَاْتِيْنِيْ بِعَرْشِهَا
قَبْلَ اَنْ يَّاْتُوْنِيْ مُسْلِمِيْنَ ﴿٣٨﴾
قَالَ عِفْرِيْتٌ مِّنَ الْجِنِّ اَنَا اٰتِيْكَ بِهٖ
قَبْلَ اَنْ تَقُوْمَ مِنْ مَّقَامِكَ ۚ وَاِنِّيْ عَلَيْهِ
لَقَوِيٌّ اَمِيْنٌ ﴿٣٩﴾
قَالَ الَّذِيْ عِنْدَهٗ عِلْمٌ مِّنَ الْكِتٰبِ اَنَا
اٰتِيْكَ بِهٖ قَبْلَ اَنْ يَّرْتَدَّ اِلَيْكَ طَرْفُكَ ؕ
فَلَمَّا رَاٰهُ مُسْتَقِرًّا عِنْدَهٗ قَالَ هٰذَا مِنْ
فَضْلِ رَبِّيْ ۖ لِيَبْلُوَنِيْٓ ءَاَشْكُرُ اَمْ اَكْفُرُ ؕ
وَمَنْ شَكَرَ فَاِنَّمَا يَشْكُرُ لِنَفْسِهٖ ۚ وَمَنْ
كَفَرَ فَاِنَّ رَبِّيْ غَنِيٌّ كَرِيْمٌ ﴿٤٠﴾
قَالَ نَكِّرُوْا لَهَا عَرْشَهَا نَنْظُرْ اَتَهْتَدِيْٓ اَمْ
تَكُوْنُ مِنَ الَّذِيْنَ لَا يَهْتَدُوْنَ ﴿٤١﴾
فَلَمَّا جَآءَتْ قِيْلَ اَهٰكَذَا عَرْشُكِ ؕ قَالَتْ
كَاَنَّهٗ هُوَ ۚ وَاُوْتِيْنَا الْعِلْمَ مِنْ قَبْلِهَا وَ
كُنَّا مُسْلِمِيْنَ ﴿٤٢﴾
وَصَدَّهَا مَا كَانَتْ تَّعْبُدُ مِنْ دُوْنِ اللّٰهِ ؕ
اِنَّهَا كَانَتْ مِنْ قَوْمٍ كٰفِرِيْنَ ﴿٤٣﴾
قِيْلَ لَهَا ادْخُلِي الصَّرْحَ ۚ فَلَمَّا رَاَتْهُ
حَسِبَتْهُ لُجَّةً وَّكَشَفَتْ عَنْ سَاقَيْهَا ؕ
قَالَ اِنَّهٗ صَرْحٌ مُّمَرَّدٌ مِّنْ قَوَارِيْرَ ؕ

slabs of glass." She said: "O my Lord! I have indeed wronged my soul: I do (now) submit (in Islãm), with Solomon, to the Lord of the Worlds."

وہ بول اٹھی کہ پروردگار میں اپنے آپ پر ظلم کرتی رہی تھی اور
(اب) میں سلیمان کے ہاتھ پر خدائے رب العالمین پر ایمان لاتی ہوں ﴿۴۴﴾ ف ۲۰۹

قَالَتْ رَبِّ إِنِّي ظَلَمْتُ نَفْسِي وَأَسْلَمْتُ
ع ۳ / ۱۸ مَعَ سُلَيْمٰنَ لِلّٰهِ رَبِّ الْعٰلَمِينَ ﴿۴۴﴾

45. We sent (aforetime), to the <u>Th</u>amûd, their brother Ṣãliḥ, saying, "Serve Allah": but behold, they became two factions quarrelling with each other.

اور ہم نے ثمود کی طرف اُن کے بھائی صالح کو بھیجا کہ خدا
کی عبادت کرو تو وہ دو فریق ہو کر آپس میں جھگڑنے
لگے ﴿۴۵﴾

وَلَقَدْ أَرْسَلْنَا إِلَىٰ ثَمُودَ أَخَاهُمْ صٰلِحًا
أَنِ اعْبُدُوا اللّٰهَ فَإِذَا هُمْ فَرِيقٰنِ
يَخْتَصِمُونَ ﴿۴۵﴾

46. He said: "O my people! why ask ye to hasten on the evil before the good? If only ye ask Allah for forgiveness, ye may hope to receive mercy."

(صالح نے) کہا کہ اے قوم! تم بھلائی سے پہلے بُرائی کے
لئے کیوں جلدی کرتے ہو (اور) خدا سے بخشش کیوں
نہیں مانگتے تاکہ تم پر رحم کیا جائے ﴿۴۶﴾ ف ۲۱۰

قَالَ يٰقَوْمِ لِمَ تَسْتَعْجِلُونَ بِالسَّيِّئَةِ قَبْلَ
الْحَسَنَةِ ۚ لَوْلَا تَسْتَغْفِرُونَ اللّٰهَ لَعَلَّكُمْ
تُرْحَمُونَ ﴿۴۶﴾

47. They said: "Ill omen do we augur from thee and those that are with thee". He said: "Your ill omen is with Allah; yea, ye are a people under trial."

وہ کہنے لگے کہ تم اور تمہارے ساتھی ہمارے لئے شگون بد ہیں (صالح نے) کہا کہ
تمہاری بدشگونی خدا کی طرف سے ہے بلکہ تم ایسے لوگ ہو جن کی آزمائش کی جاتی ہے ﴿۴۷﴾

قَالُوا اطَّيَّرْنَا بِكَ وَبِمَنْ مَّعَكَ ۚ قَالَ
طٰٓئِرُكُمْ عِنْدَ اللّٰهِ بَلْ أَنْتُمْ قَوْمٌ تُفْتَنُونَ ﴿۴۷﴾

48. There were in the City nine men, who made mischief in the land, and would not reform.

اور شہر میں نو شخص تھے جو ملک میں فساد کیا کرتے تھے
اور اصلاح سے کام نہیں لیتے تھے ﴿۴۸﴾

وَكَانَ فِي الْمَدِينَةِ تِسْعَةُ رَهْطٍ يُّفْسِدُونَ
فِي الْأَرْضِ وَلَا يُصْلِحُونَ ﴿۴۸﴾

49. They said: "Swear a mutual oath by Allah that we shall make a secret night attack on him and his people, and that we shall then say to his heir (when he seeks vengeance): 'We were not present at the slaughter of his people, and we are positively telling the truth'."

کہنے لگے کہ خدا کی قسم کھاؤ کہ ہم رات کو اس پر اور اسکے گھر والوں
پر شبخون ماریں گے پھر اسکے وارثوں سے کہہ دینگے کہ ہم تو اسکے
گھر والوں کے موقع ہلاکت پر گئے ہی نہیں اور ہم سچ کہتے ہیں ﴿۴۹﴾

قَالُوا تَقَاسَمُوا بِاللّٰهِ لَنُبَيِّتَنَّهُ وَأَهْلَهُ ثُمَّ
لَنَقُولَنَّ لِوَلِيِّهِ مَا شَهِدْنَا مَهْلِكَ أَهْلِهِ
وَإِنَّا لَصٰدِقُونَ ﴿۴۹﴾

50. They plotted and planned, but We too planned, even while they perceived it not.

اور وہ ایک چال چلے اور ہم بھی ایک چال چلے اور ان کو
کچھ خبر نہ ہوئی ﴿۵۰﴾

وَمَكَرُوا مَكْرًا وَّمَكَرْنَا مَكْرًا وَّهُمْ لَا
يَشْعُرُونَ ﴿۵۰﴾

51. Then see what was the end of their plot!—this, that We destroyed them and their people, all (of them).

تو دیکھ لو کہ ان کی چال کا انجام کیسا ہوا؟ ہم نے ان کو اور
ان کی قوم سب کو ہلاک کر ڈالا ﴿۵۱﴾

فَانْظُرْ كَيْفَ كَانَ عٰقِبَةُ مَكْرِهِمْ ۙ أَنَّا
دَمَّرْنٰهُمْ وَقَوْمَهُمْ أَجْمَعِينَ ﴿۵۱﴾

52. Now such were their houses,—in utter ruin,—because they practised wrong-doing. Verily in this is a Sign for people of knowledge.

اب یہ اُن کے گھر اُن کے ظلم کے سبب خالی پڑے ہیں۔
جو لوگ دانش رکھتے ہیں اُن کیلئے اس میں نشانی ہے ﴿۵۲﴾

فَتِلْكَ بُيُوتُهُمْ خَاوِيَةً بِمَا ظَلَمُوا ۗ إِنَّ
فِي ذٰلِكَ لَآيَةً لِّقَوْمٍ يَّعْلَمُونَ ﴿۵۲﴾

53. And We saved those who believed and practised righteousness.

اور جو لوگ ایمان لائے اور ڈرتے تھے اُن کو ہم نے نجات دی ﴿۵۳﴾

وَأَنْجَيْنَا الَّذِينَ آمَنُوا وَكَانُوا يَتَّقُونَ ﴿۵۳﴾

54. (We also sent) Lût (as a messenger): behold, he said to his people, "Do ye do what is indecent though ye see (its iniquity)?

اور لوط کو (یاد کرو) جب انہوں نے اپنی قوم سے کہا کہ تم
بے حیائی (کے کام) کیوں کرتے ہو اور تم دیکھتے ہو ﴿۵۴﴾

وَلُوطًا إِذْ قَالَ لِقَوْمِهِ أَتَأْتُونَ الْفٰحِشَةَ
وَأَنْتُمْ تُبْصِرُونَ ﴿۵۴﴾

55. Would ye really approach men in your lusts rather than women? Nay, ye are a people (grossly) ignorant!

کیا تم عورتوں کو چھوڑ کر لذت (حاصل کرنے) کیلئے مردوں کی طرف
مائل ہوتے ہو۔ حقیقت یہ ہے کہ تم احمق لوگ ہو ﴿۵۵﴾

أَئِنَّكُمْ لَتَأْتُونَ الرِّجَالَ شَهْوَةً مِّنْ دُونِ
النِّسَاءِ ۚ بَلْ أَنْتُمْ قَوْمٌ تَجْهَلُونَ ﴿۵۵﴾

56. But his people gave no other answer but this: They said, "Drive

تو ان کی قوم کے لوگ (بولے تو) یہ بولے اور اس کے سوا انکا

فَمَا كَانَ جَوَابَ قَوْمِهِ إِلَّا أَنْ قَالُوا أَخْرِجُوا

اٰلَ لُوْطٍ مِّنْ قَرْيَتِكُمْ ۚ اِنَّهُمْ اُنَاسٌ
يَّتَطَهَّرُوْنَ ﴿٥٦﴾
فَاَنْجَيْنٰهُ وَاَهْلَهٗۤ اِلَّا امْرَاَتَهٗ ۫ قَدَّرْنٰهَا
مِنَ الْغٰبِرِيْنَ ﴿٥٧﴾ ع
وَاَمْطَرْنَا عَلَيْهِمْ مَّطَرًا ۚ فَسَآءَ مَطَرُ الْمُنْذَرِيْنَ ﴿٥٨﴾
قُلِ الْحَمْدُ لِلّٰهِ وَسَلٰمٌ عَلٰى عِبَادِهِ الَّذِيْنَ
اصْطَفٰى ؕ آٰللّٰهُ خَيْرٌ اَمَّا يُشْرِكُوْنَ ﴿٥٩﴾
اَمَّنْ خَلَقَ السَّمٰوٰتِ وَالْاَرْضَ وَاَنْزَلَ
لَكُمْ مِّنَ السَّمَآءِ مَآءً ۚ فَاَنْۢبَتْنَا بِهٖ حَدَآئِقَ
ذَاتَ بَهْجَةٍ ۚ مَا كَانَ لَكُمْ اَنْ تُنْۢبِتُوْا شَجَرَهَا ؕ
ءَاِلٰهٌ مَّعَ اللّٰهِ ؕ بَلْ هُمْ قَوْمٌ يَّعْدِلُوْنَ ﴿٦٠﴾
اَمَّنْ جَعَلَ الْاَرْضَ قَرَارًا وَّجَعَلَ خِلٰلَهَاۤ
اَنْهٰرًا وَّجَعَلَ لَهَا رَوَاسِيَ وَجَعَلَ بَيْنَ
الْبَحْرَيْنِ حَاجِزًا ؕ ءَاِلٰهٌ مَّعَ اللّٰهِ ؕ بَلْ
اَكْثَرُهُمْ لَا يَعْلَمُوْنَ ؕ ﴿٦١﴾
اَمَّنْ يُّجِيْبُ الْمُضْطَرَّ اِذَا دَعَاهُ وَ
يَكْشِفُ السُّوْٓءَ وَيَجْعَلُكُمْ خُلَفَآءَ الْاَرْضِ ؕ
ءَاِلٰهٌ مَّعَ اللّٰهِ ؕ قَلِيْلًا مَّا تَذَكَّرُوْنَ ؕ ﴿٦٢﴾
اَمَّنْ يَّهْدِيْكُمْ فِيْ ظُلُمٰتِ الْبَرِّ وَالْبَحْرِ
وَمَنْ يُّرْسِلُ الرِّيٰحَ بُشْرًاۢ بَيْنَ يَدَيْ
رَحْمَتِهٖ ؕ ءَاِلٰهٌ مَّعَ اللّٰهِ ؕ تَعٰلَى اللّٰهُ عَمَّا
يُشْرِكُوْنَ ؕ ﴿٦٣﴾
اَمَّنْ يَّبْدَؤُا الْخَلْقَ ثُمَّ يُعِيْدُهٗ وَمَنْ
يَّرْزُقُكُمْ مِّنَ السَّمَآءِ وَالْاَرْضِ ؕ ءَاِلٰهٌ
مَّعَ اللّٰهِ ؕ قُلْ هَاتُوْا بُرْهَانَكُمْ اِنْ كُنْتُمْ
صٰدِقِيْنَ ﴿٦٤﴾
قُلْ لَّا يَعْلَمُ مَنْ فِي السَّمٰوٰتِ وَالْاَرْضِ

کچھ جواب نہ تھا کہ لوط کے گھر والوں کو اپنے شہر سے نکال دو
یہ لوگ پاک بننا چاہتے ہیں ﴿۵۶﴾
تو ہم نے اُن کو اور اُن کے گھر والوں کو نجات دی مگر اُنکی بیوی کی کہ
نسبت ہمنے مقرر کر رکھا تھا کہ (وہ) پیچھے رہنے والوں میں ہوگی ﴿۵۷﴾
اور ہمنے اُنپر مینہ برسایا سو جو مینہ اُن لوگوں پر برسا جنکو متنبہ کر دیا گیا تھا برا تھا ﴿۵۸﴾
کہہ دو کہ سب تعریف خدا ہی کو سزاوار ہے اور اسکے بندوں پر سلام ہے جنکو
اس نے منتخب فرمایا۔ بھلا خدا بہتر ہے یا وہ جنکو یہ اُسکا شریک بناتے ہیں ﴿۵۹﴾
بھلا کس نے آسمانوں اور زمین کو پیدا کیا اور (کس نے) تمہارے
لئے آسمان سے پانی برسایا۔ (ہم نے) پھر ہم نے اس سے سرسبز
باغ اُگائے تمہارا کام تو نہ تھا کہ تم اُنکے درختوں کو اُگاتے تو کیا خدا
کیساتھ کوئی اور بھی معبود ہے؟ (ہرگز نہیں) بلکہ یہ لوگ رستے سے الگ ہو رہے ہیں ﴿۶۰﴾
بھلا کس نے زمین کو قرارگاہ بنایا اور اسکے بیچ نہریں بنائیں اور
اس کیلئے پہاڑ بنائے اور (کس نے) دو دریاؤں کے بیچ اوٹ
بنائی (یہ سب کچھ خدا نے بنایا) تو کیا خدا کیساتھ کوئی اور معبود بھی ہے؟
(ہرگز نہیں) بلکہ ان میں اکثر دانش نہیں رکھتے ﴿۶۱﴾
بھلا کون بیقرار کی التجا قبول کرتا ہے جب وہ اُس سے دعا کرتا ہے اور (کون اُسکی)
تکلیف کو دور کرتا ہے اور کون تمکو زمین میں (اگلوں کا) جانشین بناتا ہے (یہ سب کچھ
خدا کرتا ہے) تو کیا خدا کیساتھ کوئی اور معبود بھی ہے (ہرگز نہیں مگر) تم بہت کم غور کرتے ہو ﴿۶۲﴾
بھلا کون تم کو جنگل اور دریا کے اندھیروں میں رستہ بتاتا اور
(کون) ہواؤں کو اپنی رحمت کے آگے خوشخبری بنا کر بھیجتا ہے
(یہ سب کچھ خدا کرتا ہے) تو کیا خدا کیساتھ کوئی اور معبود بھی ہے؟ (ہرگز نہیں)
یہ لوگ جو شرک کرتے ہیں خدا (کی شان) اس سے بلند ہے ﴿۶۳﴾
بھلا کون خلقت کو پہلی بار پیدا کرتا۔ پھر اس کو بار بار پیدا
کرتا رہتا ہے اور (کون) تم کو آسمان اور زمین سے رزق
دیتا ہے (یہ سب کچھ خدا کرتا ہے) تو کیا خدا کیساتھ کوئی اور معبود
بھی ہے؟ (ہرگز نہیں) کہہ دو کہ (مشرکو) اگر تم سچے ہو تو دلیل پیش کرو ﴿۶۴﴾
کہہ دو کہ جو لوگ آسمانوں اور زمین میں ہیں خدا کے سوا غیب

out the followers of Lûṭ from your city: these are indeed men who want to be clean and pure!"

57. But We saved him and his family, except his wife: her We destined to be of those who lagged behind.

58. And We rained down on them a shower (of brimstone): and evil was the shower on those who were admonished (but heeded not)!

59. Say: Praise be to Allah, and Peace on His servants whom He has chosen (for His Message). (Who) is better?—Allah or the false gods they associate (with Him)?

60. On who has created the heavens and the earth, and who sends you down rain from the sky? Yea, with it We cause to grow well-planted orchards full of beauty and delight: it is not in your power to cause the growth of the trees in them. (Can there be another) god besides Allah? Nay, they are a people who swerve from justice.

61. Or, who has made the earth firm to live in; made rivers in its midst; set thereon mountains immovable; and made a separating bar between the two seas (can there be another) god besides Allah? Nay, most of them know not.

62. Or, who listens to the distressed when he calls on Him, and Who relieves his suffering, and makes you (mankind) inheritors of the earth? (Can there be another) god besides Allah? Little it is that ye heed!

63. Or, who guides you through the depths of darkness on land and sea, and who sends the winds as heralds of glad tidings, going before His Mercy? (Can there be another) god besides Allah?—High is Allah above what they associate with Him!

64. Or, who originates Creation, then repeats it, and who gives you sustenance from heaven and earth? (Can there be another) god besides Allah? Say, "Bring forth your argument, if ye are telling the truth!"

65. Say: None in the heavens or on earth, except Allah, knows what

is hidden: nor can they perceive when they shall be raised up (for Judgment).	کی باتیں نہیں جانتے اور نہ یہ جانتے ہیں کہ کب (زندہ کرکے) اُٹھائے جائیں گے ﴿۶۵﴾	الْغَيْبَ إِلَّا اللَّهُ ۚ وَمَا يَشْعُرُونَ أَيَّانَ يُبْعَثُونَ ﴿٦٥﴾
66. Nay, but their knowledge fails as to the Hereafter, they are in doubt and uncertainty thereanent; nay, they are blind thereunto!	بلکہ آخرت (کے بارے) میں اُنکا علم منتہی ہوچکا ہے بلکہ وہ اس سے شک میں ہیں بلکہ اس سے اندھے ہو رہے ہیں ﴿۶۶﴾	بَلِ ادَّارَكَ عِلْمُهُمْ فِي الْآخِرَةِ ۚ بَلْ هُمْ فِي شَكٍّ مِّنْهَا ۖ بَلْ هُم مِّنْهَا عَمُونَ ﴿٦٦﴾
67. The Unbelievers say "What! when we become dust,— we and our fathers,—shall we really be raised (from the dead)?	اور جو لوگ کافر ہیں کہتے ہیں کہ جب ہم اور ہمارے باپ دادا مٹی ہو جائیں گے تو کیا ہم پھر (قبروں سے) نکالے جائیں گے ﴿۶۷﴾	وَقَالَ الَّذِينَ كَفَرُوا أَإِذَا كُنَّا تُرَابًا وَآبَاؤُنَا أَئِنَّا لَمُخْرَجُونَ ﴿٦٧﴾
68. "It is true we were promised this,—we and our fathers before (us): these are nothing but tales of the ancients."	یہ وعدہ ہم سے اور ہمارے باپ دادا سے پہلے سے ہوتا چلا آیا ہے (کہاں کا اٹھنا اور کیسی قیامت) یہ تو صرف پہلے لوگوں کی کہانیاں ہیں ﴿۶۸﴾	لَقَدْ وُعِدْنَا هَٰذَا نَحْنُ وَآبَاؤُنَا مِن قَبْلُ إِنْ هَٰذَا إِلَّا أَسَاطِيرُ الْأَوَّلِينَ ﴿٦٨﴾
69. Say: "Go ye through the earth and see what has been the end of those guilty (of sin)."	کہہ دو کہ ملک میں چلو پھرو پھر دیکھو کہ گنہگاروں کا انجام کیا ہوا ہے ﴿۶۹﴾	قُلْ سِيرُوا فِي الْأَرْضِ فَانظُرُوا كَيْفَ كَانَ عَاقِبَةُ الْمُجْرِمِينَ ﴿٦٩﴾
70. But grieve not over them, nor distress thyself because of their plots.	اور اُن (کے حال) پر غم نہ کرنا اور نہ ان چالوں سے جو یہ کر رہے ہیں تنگ دل ہونا ﴿۷۰﴾	وَلَا تَحْزَنْ عَلَيْهِمْ وَلَا تَكُن فِي ضَيْقٍ مِّمَّا يَمْكُرُونَ ﴿٧٠﴾
71. They also say: "When will this promise (come to pass)? If ye are truthful."	اور کہتے ہیں کہ اگر تم سچے ہو تو یہ وعدہ کب پورا ہوگا؟ ﴿۷۱﴾	وَيَقُولُونَ مَتَىٰ هَٰذَا الْوَعْدُ إِن كُنتُمْ صَادِقِينَ ﴿٧١﴾
72. Say: "It may be that some of the events which ye wish to hasten on may be (close) in your pursuit!"	کہہ دو کہ جس (عذاب) کے لئے تم جلدی کر رہے ہو شاید اس میں سے کچھ تمہارے نزدیک آپہنچا ہو ﴿۷۲﴾	قُلْ عَسَىٰ أَن يَكُونَ رَدِفَ لَكُم بَعْضُ الَّذِي تَسْتَعْجِلُونَ ﴿٧٢﴾
73. But verily thy Lord is full of grace to mankind: yet most of them are ungrateful.	اور تمہارا پروردگار تو لوگوں پر فضل کرنے والا ہے لیکن ان میں سے اکثر شکر نہیں کرتے ﴿۷۳﴾	وَإِنَّ رَبَّكَ لَذُو فَضْلٍ عَلَى النَّاسِ وَلَٰكِنَّ أَكْثَرَهُمْ لَا يَشْكُرُونَ ﴿٧٣﴾
74. And verily thy Lord knoweth all that their hearts do hide, as well as all that they reveal.	اور جو باتیں اُنکے سینوں میں پوشیدہ ہوتی ہیں اور جو کام وہ ظاہر کرتے ہیں تمہارا پروردگار ان (سب) کو جانتا ہے ﴿۷۴﴾	وَإِنَّ رَبَّكَ لَيَعْلَمُ مَا تُكِنُّ صُدُورُهُمْ وَمَا يُعْلِنُونَ ﴿٧٤﴾
75. And there is nothing hidden in heaven or earth, but is (recorded) in a clear record.	اور آسمانوں اور زمین میں کوئی پوشیدہ چیز نہیں ہے مگر (وہ) کتاب روشن میں (لکھی ہوئی) ہے ﴿۷۵﴾	وَمَا مِنْ غَائِبَةٍ فِي السَّمَاءِ وَالْأَرْضِ إِلَّا فِي كِتَابٍ مُّبِينٍ ﴿٧٥﴾
76. Verily this Qur'an doth explain to the Children of Israel most of the matters in which they disagree.	بے شک یہ قرآن بنی اسرائیل کے سامنے اکثر باتیں جن میں وہ اختلاف کرتے ہیں بیان کر دیتا ہے ﴿۷۶﴾	إِنَّ هَٰذَا الْقُرْآنَ يَقُصُّ عَلَىٰ بَنِي إِسْرَائِيلَ أَكْثَرَ الَّذِي هُمْ فِيهِ يَخْتَلِفُونَ ﴿٧٦﴾
77. And it certainly is a Guide and a Mercy to those who believe.	اور بے شک یہ مومنوں کیلئے ہدایت اور رحمت ہے ﴿۷۷﴾	وَإِنَّهُ لَهُدًى وَرَحْمَةٌ لِّلْمُؤْمِنِينَ ﴿٧٧﴾
78. Verily thy Lord will decide between them by His Decree: and He is Exalted in Might, All-Knowing.	تمہارا پروردگار (قیامت کے روز) اُن میں اپنے حکم سے فیصلہ کر دے گا اور وہ غالب (اور) علم والا ہے ﴿۷۸﴾	إِنَّ رَبَّكَ يَقْضِي بَيْنَهُم بِحُكْمِهِ ۚ وَهُوَ الْعَزِيزُ الْعَلِيمُ ﴿٧٨﴾

فَتَوَكَّلْ عَلَى اللّٰهِ ۖ اِنَّكَ عَلَى الْحَقِّ الْمُبِيْنِ ﴿٧٩﴾
اِنَّكَ لَا تُسْمِعُ الْمَوْتٰى وَلَا تُسْمِعُ الصُّمَّ
الدُّعَآءَ اِذَا وَلَّوْا مُدْبِرِيْنَ ﴿٨٠﴾
وَمَآ اَنْتَ بِهٰدِى الْعُمْىِ عَنْ ضَلٰلَتِهِمْ ۭ
اِنْ تُسْمِعُ اِلَّا مَنْ يُّؤْمِنُ بِاٰيٰتِنَا فَهُمْ
مُّسْلِمُوْنَ ﴿٨١﴾

تو خدا پر بھروسا رکھو تم تو حق صریح پر ہو ﴿٧٩﴾
کچھ شک نہیں کہ تم مُردوں کو (بات) نہیں سُنا سکتے اور نہ
بہروں کو جبکہ وہ پیٹھ پھیر کر پھر جائیں آواز سُنا سکتے ہو ﴿٨٠﴾
اور نہ اندھوں کو گمراہی سے (نکال کر) رستہ دکھا سکتے ہو
تم تو انہی کو سُنا سکتے ہو جو ہماری آیتوں پر ایمان لاتے ہیں
اور وہ فرمانبردار ہو جاتے ہیں ﴿٨١﴾

79. So put thy trust in Allah: for thou art on (the Path of) manifest Truth.
80. Truly thou canst not cause the Dead to listen, nor canst thou cause the Deaf to hear the call, (especially) when they turn back in retreat.
81. Nor canst thou be a guide to the Blind, (to prevent them) from straying: only those wilt thou get to listen who believe in Our Signs, so they submit.

وَاِذَا وَقَعَ الْقَوْلُ عَلَيْهِمْ اَخْرَجْنَا لَهُمْ
دَآبَّةً مِّنَ الْاَرْضِ تُكَلِّمُهُمْ ۙ اَنَّ النَّاسَ
كَانُوْا بِاٰيٰتِنَا لَا يُوْقِنُوْنَ ﴿٨٢﴾ ع

اور جب اُن کے بارے میں (عذاب کا) وعدہ پُورا ہوگا تو ہم
اُن کے لئے زمین میں سے ایک جانور نکالیں گے جو اُن سے
بیان کر دیگا۔ اس لئے کہ لوگ ہماری آیتوں پر ایمان نہیں لاتے تھے ﴿٨٢﴾

82. And when the Word is fulfilled against them (the unjust), We shall bring forth from the earth a Beast to speak unto them because mankind had no faith in Our Signs.

وَيَوْمَ نَحْشُرُ مِنْ كُلِّ اُمَّةٍ فَوْجًا مِّمَّنْ
يُّكَذِّبُ بِاٰيٰتِنَا فَهُمْ يُوْزَعُوْنَ ﴿٨٣﴾
حَتّٰٓى اِذَا جَآءُوْ قَالَ اَكَذَّبْتُمْ بِاٰيٰتِىْ
وَلَمْ تُحِيْطُوْا بِهَا عِلْمًا اَمَّاذَا كُنْتُمْ
تَعْمَلُوْنَ ﴿٨٤﴾
وَوَقَعَ الْقَوْلُ عَلَيْهِمْ بِمَا ظَلَمُوْا فَهُمْ
لَا يَنْطِقُوْنَ ﴿٨٥﴾
اَلَمْ يَرَوْا اَنَّا جَعَلْنَا الَّيْلَ لِيَسْكُنُوْا
فِيْهِ وَالنَّهَارَ مُبْصِرًا ۭ اِنَّ فِىْ ذٰلِكَ لَاٰيٰتٍ
لِّقَوْمٍ يُّؤْمِنُوْنَ ﴿٨٦﴾

اور جس روز ہم ہر اُمت میں سے اس گروہ کو جمع کرینگے جو ہماری آیتوں
کی تکذیب کرتے تھے تو اُن کی جماعت بندی کی جائے گی ﴿٨٣﴾
یہاں تک کہ جب (سب) آجائینگے تو (خدا) فرمائے گا کہ کیا تم
نے میری آیتوں کو جھٹلا دیا تھا اور تم نے (اپنے) علم سے اُن کا
احاطہ تو کیا ہی نہ تھا۔ بھلا تم کیا کرتے تھے؟ ﴿٨٤﴾
اور اُن کے ظلم کے سبب اُن کے حق میں وعدہ (عذاب)
پُورا ہو کر رہے گا تو وہ بول بھی نہ سکیں گے ﴿٨٥﴾
کیا انہوں نے نہیں دیکھا کہ ہم نے رات کو (اسلئے) بنایا ہے کہ اسمیں آرام
کریں اور دن کو روشن (بنایا ہے کہ اسمیں کام کریں) بےشک اسمیں
مومن لوگوں کے لئے نشانیاں ہیں ﴿٨٦﴾

83. The Day We shall gather together from every people a troop of those who reject Our Signs, and they shall be kept in ranks,—
84. Until, when they come (before the Judgment-seat), (Allah) will say: "Did ye reject My Signs, though ye comprehended them not in knowledge, or what was it ye did?"
85. And the Word will be fulfilled against them, because of their wrong-doing, and they will be unable to speak (in plea).
86. See they not that We have made the Night for them to rest in and the Day to give them light? Verily in this are Signs for any people that believe!

وَيَوْمَ يُنْفَخُ فِى الصُّوْرِ فَفَزِعَ مَنْ فِى
السَّمٰوٰتِ وَمَنْ فِى الْاَرْضِ اِلَّا مَنْ
شَآءَ اللّٰهُ ۭ وَكُلٌّ اَتَوْهُ دٰخِرِيْنَ ﴿٨٧﴾
وَتَرَى الْجِبَالَ تَحْسَبُهَا جَامِدَةً وَّهِىَ تَمُرُّ
مَرَّ السَّحَابِ ۭ صُنْعَ اللّٰهِ الَّذِىْٓ اَتْقَنَ كُلَّ
شَىْءٍ ۭ اِنَّهٗ خَبِيْرٌۢ بِمَا تَفْعَلُوْنَ ﴿٨٨﴾
مَنْ جَآءَ بِالْحَسَنَةِ فَلَهٗ خَيْرٌ مِّنْهَا ۚ وَ
هُمْ مِّنْ فَزَعٍ يَّوْمَئِذٍ اٰمِنُوْنَ ﴿٨٩﴾

اور جس روز صُور پھونکا جائے گا تو جو لوگ آسمانوں اور
جو زمین میں ہیں سب گھبرا اُٹھیں گے مگر وہ جسے خدا چاہے
اور سب اس کے پاس عاجز ہو کر چلے آئیں گے ﴿٨٧﴾
اور تم پہاڑوں کو دیکھتے ہو تو خیال کرتے ہو کہ (اپنی جگہ پر) کھڑے ہیں
مگر وہ (اُس روز) اِس طرح اُڑتے پھرینگے جیسے بادل (یہ) خدا کی کاریگری ہے
جس نے ہر چیز کو مضبوط بنایا۔ بیشک وہ تمہارے سب افعال سے باخبر ہے ﴿٨٨﴾
جو شخص نیکی لیکر آئیگا تو اسکے لئے اس سے بہتر (بدلہ تیار) ہے
اور ایسے لوگ (اس روز) گھبراہٹ سے بےخوف ہوں گے ﴿٨٩﴾

87. And the Day that the Trumpet will be sounded—then will be smitten with terror those who are in the heavens, and those who are on earth, except such as Allah will please (to exempt): and all shall come to Him in utter humility.
88. Thou seest the mountains and thinkest them firmly fixed: but they shall pass away as the clouds pass away: (such is) the artistry of Allah, who disposes of all things in perfect order: for He is well acquainted with all that ye do.
89. If any do good, he will have better than it. And they will be secure from terror that Day.

SÛRA–28
AL-QAṢAṢ
(INTRODUCTION)

This Sûra continues the subject of Revelation and its reception by those to whom it is sent. But it emphasises new points : how the recipient of inspiration is prepared for his high destiny, even in the growth of his ordinary life, and how the rejection of Allah's Message by groups of men or by individuals is caused by overweening arrogance or avarice. The plight of those who reject the Truth is contrasted with the reward of the righteous.

With the possible exception of a few verses, it belongs to the late Makkan period, just preceding the Hijrat.

90. And if any do evil, their faces will be thrown headlong into the Fire: "Do ye receive a reward other than that which ye have earned by your deeds?"
91. For me, I have been commanded to serve the Lord of this City, Him Who has sanctified it and to Whom (belong) all things: and I am commanded to be of those who bow in Islam to Allah's Will,—
92. And to rehearse the Qur'an: and if any accept guidance, they do it for the good of their own souls, and if any stray, say: "I am only a Warner".
93. And say: "Praise be to Allah, Who will soon show you His Signs, so that ye shall know them:" and thy Lord is not unmindful of all that ye do.

Al-Qaṣaṣ, or the Narration

In the name of Allah, Most Gracious, Most Merciful.
1. Tā. Sīn. Mīm.
2. These are Verses of the Book that makes (things) clear.
3. We rehearse to thee some of the story of Moses and Pharaoh in Truth, for people who believe.
4. Truly Pharaoh elated himself in the land and divided its people into sections, depressing a group among them: their sons he slew, but he kept alive their females: for he was indeed an evil-doer.
5. And We wished to be gracious to those who were being depressed in the land, to make them leaders (in faith) and make them heirs,
6. To establish a firm place for them in the land, and to show Pharaoh, Hāmān, and their hosts, what they were dreading from them.
7. So We sent this inspiration to the mother of Moses: "Suckle (thy child), but when thou hast fears about him, cast him into the river, but fear not nor grieve: for We shall

اور جو بُرائی لیکر آئیگا تو ایسے لوگ اوندھے مُنہ دوزخ میں ڈالدیئے
جائینگے۔ تم کو تو اُن ہی اعمال کا بدلہ ملے گا جو تم کرتے رہے ہو ۹۰
(کہہ دو) مجھ کو یہی ارشاد ہوا ہے کہ اس شہر مکہ کے مالک کی عبادت
کروں جس نے اس کو محترم (و مقام ادب) بنایا ہے اور سب چیز
اسی کی ہے اور یہ بھی حکم ہوا ہے کہ اُس کا حکم بردار رہوں ۹۱
اور یہ بھی کہ قرآن پڑھا کروں تو جو شخص راہ راست اختیار
کرتا ہے تو اپنے ہی فائدے کیلئے اختیار کرتا ہے۔ اور جو گمراہ رہتا ہے
تو کہہ دو کہ میں تو صرف نصیحت کرنے والا ہوں ۹۲
اور کہو کہ خدا کا شکر ہے۔ وہ تم کو عنقریب اپنی نشانیاں دکھائے گا تو تم
انکو پہچان لوگے۔ اور جو کام تم کرتے ہو تمہارا پروردگار اُنسے بیخبر نہیں ہے ۹۳

سُورۂ قصص مکّی ہے اور اس میں اٹھاسی آیتیں اور نو رکوع ہیں

شروع خدا کا نام لے کر جو بڑا مہربان نہایت رحم والا ہے
طٰسم ۱ یہ کتاب روشن کی آیتیں ہیں ۲
(اے محمد) ہم تمہیں موسیٰ اور فرعون کے کچھ حالات مومن لوگوں
(کے سنانے) کے لئے صحیح صحیح سناتے ہیں ۳
کہ فرعون نے ملک میں سر اٹھا رکھا تھا اور وہاں کے
باشندوں کو گروہ گروہ بنا رکھا تھا اُن میں سے ایک گروہ کو
(یہاں تک) کمزور کر دیا تھا کہ اُنکے بیٹوں کو ذبح کر ڈالتا اور اُنکی
لڑکیوں کو زندہ رہنے دیتا۔ بیشک وہ مُفسدوں میں تھا ۴
اور ہم چاہتے تھے کہ جو لوگ ملک میں کمزور کر دیئے گئے ہیں
اُن پر احسان کریں اور اُن کو پیشوا بنائیں اور انہیں (ملک کا)
وارث کریں ۵
اور ملک میں اُن کو قدرت دیں اور فرعون اور ہامان اور
اُنکے لشکر کو وہ چیز دکھا دیں جس سے وہ ڈرتے تھے ۶
اور ہم نے موسیٰ کی ماں کی طرف وحی بھیجی کہ اسکو دودھ پلاؤ
جب تمکو اسکے بارے میں کچھ خوف پیدا ہو تو اسے دریا میں ڈالدینا
اور نہ تو خوف کرنا اور نہ رنج کرنا۔ ہم اس کو تمہارے پاس

وَمَنْ جَآءَ بِالسَّيِّئَةِ فَكُبَّتْ وُجُوهُهُمْ فِي
النَّارِ ۖ هَلْ تُجْزَوْنَ إِلَّا مَا كُنتُمْ تَعْمَلُونَ ۝٩٠
إِنَّمَآ أُمِرْتُ أَنْ أَعْبُدَ رَبَّ هَٰذِهِ الْبَلْدَةِ
الَّذِي حَرَّمَهَا وَلَهُ كُلُّ شَيْءٍ ۖ وَأُمِرْتُ
أَنْ أَكُونَ مِنَ الْمُسْلِمِينَ ۝٩١
وَأَنْ أَتْلُوَا الْقُرْآنَ ۖ فَمَنِ اهْتَدَىٰ فَإِنَّمَا
يَهْتَدِي لِنَفْسِهِ ۖ وَمَن ضَلَّ فَقُلْ إِنَّمَآ
أَنَا مِنَ الْمُنذِرِينَ ۝٩٢
وَقُلِ الْحَمْدُ لِلَّهِ سَيُرِيكُمْ آيَاتِهِ فَتَعْرِفُونَهَا ۚ
ع ١١ وَمَا رَبُّكَ بِغَافِلٍ عَمَّا تَعْمَلُونَ ۝٩٣

سُورَةُ الْقَصَصِ مَكِّيَّةٌ وَهِيَ ثَمَانٌ وَثَمَانُونَ آيَةً وَتِسْعُ رُكُوعَاتٍ

بِسْمِ اللَّهِ الرَّحْمَٰنِ الرَّحِيمِ
طسٓمٓ ۝١ تِلْكَ آيَاتُ الْكِتَابِ الْمُبِينِ ۝٢
نَتْلُوا عَلَيْكَ مِن نَّبَإِ مُوسَىٰ وَفِرْعَوْنَ
بِالْحَقِّ لِقَوْمٍ يُؤْمِنُونَ ۝٣
إِنَّ فِرْعَوْنَ عَلَا فِي الْأَرْضِ وَجَعَلَ أَهْلَهَا
شِيَعًا يَسْتَضْعِفُ طَائِفَةً مِّنْهُمْ يُذَبِّحُ
أَبْنَاءَهُمْ وَيَسْتَحْيِي نِسَاءَهُمْ ۚ إِنَّهُ
كَانَ مِنَ الْمُفْسِدِينَ ۝٤
وَنُرِيدُ أَن نَّمُنَّ عَلَى الَّذِينَ اسْتُضْعِفُوا
فِي الْأَرْضِ وَنَجْعَلَهُمْ أَئِمَّةً وَنَجْعَلَهُمُ
الْوَارِثِينَ ۝٥
وَنُمَكِّنَ لَهُمْ فِي الْأَرْضِ وَنُرِيَ فِرْعَوْنَ
وَهَامَانَ وَجُنُودَهُمَا مِنْهُم مَّا كَانُوا يَحْذَرُونَ ۝٦
وَأَوْحَيْنَا إِلَىٰ أُمِّ مُوسَىٰ أَنْ أَرْضِعِيهِ ۖ
فَإِذَا خِفْتِ عَلَيْهِ فَأَلْقِيهِ فِي الْيَمِّ وَلَا
تَخَافِي وَلَا تَحْزَنِي ۖ إِنَّا رَادُّوهُ إِلَيْكِ وَ

جَاعِلُوهُ مِنَ الْمُرْسَلِينَ ﴿٧﴾
فَالْتَقَطَهُ آلُ فِرْعَوْنَ لِيَكُونَ لَهُمْ عَدُوًّا
وَحَزَنًا ۗ إِنَّ فِرْعَوْنَ وَهَامَانَ وَجُنُودَهُمَا
كَانُوا خَاطِئِينَ ﴿٨﴾
وَقَالَتِ امْرَأَتُ فِرْعَوْنَ قُرَّتُ عَيْنٍ لِّي
وَلَكَ ۖ لَا تَقْتُلُوهُ عَسَىٰ أَن يَنفَعَنَا أَوْ
نَتَّخِذَهُ وَلَدًا وَهُمْ لَا يَشْعُرُونَ ﴿٩﴾
وَأَصْبَحَ فُؤَادُ أُمِّ مُوسَىٰ فَارِغًا ۖ إِن كَادَتْ
لَتُبْدِي بِهِ لَوْلَا أَن رَّبَطْنَا عَلَىٰ قَلْبِهَا
لِتَكُونَ مِنَ الْمُؤْمِنِينَ ﴿١٠﴾
وَقَالَتْ لِأُخْتِهِ قُصِّيهِ ۖ فَبَصُرَتْ بِهِ عَن
جُنُبٍ وَهُمْ لَا يَشْعُرُونَ ﴿١١﴾
وَحَرَّمْنَا عَلَيْهِ الْمَرَاضِعَ مِن قَبْلُ فَقَالَتْ
هَلْ أَدُلُّكُمْ عَلَىٰ أَهْلِ بَيْتٍ يَكْفُلُونَهُ
لَكُمْ وَهُمْ لَهُ نَاصِحُونَ ﴿١٢﴾
فَرَدَدْنَاهُ إِلَىٰ أُمِّهِ كَيْ تَقَرَّ عَيْنُهَا وَلَا تَحْزَنَ
وَلِتَعْلَمَ أَنَّ وَعْدَ اللَّهِ حَقٌّ وَلَٰكِنَّ أَكْثَرَهُمْ
لَا يَعْلَمُونَ ﴿١٣﴾
وَلَمَّا بَلَغَ أَشُدَّهُ وَاسْتَوَىٰ آتَيْنَاهُ حُكْمًا
وَعِلْمًا ۚ وَكَذَٰلِكَ نَجْزِي الْمُحْسِنِينَ ﴿١٤﴾
وَدَخَلَ الْمَدِينَةَ عَلَىٰ حِينِ غَفْلَةٍ مِّنْ
أَهْلِهَا فَوَجَدَ فِيهَا رَجُلَيْنِ يَقْتَتِلَانِ هَٰذَا مِن
شِيعَتِهِ وَهَٰذَا مِنْ عَدُوِّهِ ۖ فَاسْتَغَاثَهُ
الَّذِي مِن شِيعَتِهِ عَلَى الَّذِي مِنْ عَدُوِّهِ
فَوَكَزَهُ مُوسَىٰ فَقَضَىٰ عَلَيْهِ ۖ قَالَ هَٰذَا مِنْ
عَمَلِ الشَّيْطَانِ ۖ إِنَّهُ عَدُوٌّ مُّضِلٌّ مُّبِينٌ ﴿١٥﴾
قَالَ رَبِّ إِنِّي ظَلَمْتُ نَفْسِي فَاغْفِرْ لِي

واپس پہنچا دیں گے اور (پھر) اسے پیغمبر بنا دیں گے ﴿٧﴾
تو فرعون کے لوگوں نے اسکو اُٹھا لیا اسلئے کہ (نتیجہ یہ) ہونا تھا
کہ) وہ انکا دشمن اور (ان کیلئے موجب) غم ہو۔ بیشک فرعون
اور ہامان اور اُن کے لشکر چوک گئے ﴿٨﴾
اور فرعون کی بیوی نے کہا کہ (یہ) میری اور تمہاری (دونوں
کی) آنکھوں کی ٹھنڈک ہے اُسکو قتل نہ کرنا شاید یہ ہمیں فائدہ پہنچائے
یا ہم اسے بیٹا بنا لیں اور وہ (انجام سے) بے خبر تھے ﴿٩﴾
اور موسیٰ کی ماں کا دل بے قرار ہو گیا۔ اگر ہم اُنکے دل کو مضبوط
نہ کر دیتے تو قریب تھا کہ وہ اس (قصے) کو ظاہر کر دیں۔ غرض
یہ تھی کہ وہ مومنوں میں رہیں ﴿١٠﴾
اور اُس کی بہن سے کہا کہ اسکے پیچھے پیچھے چلی جا تو وہ اُسے
دُور سے دیکھتی رہی۔ اور اُن (لوگوں) کو کچھ خبر نہ تھی ﴿١١﴾
اور ہم نے پہلے ہی سے اس پر (دائیوں کے) دودھ حرام
کر دیئے تھے۔ تو موسیٰ کی بہن نے کہا کہ میں تمہیں ایسے گھر والے بتاؤں
تمہارے لئے اس (بچے) کو پالیں اور اسکی خیر خواہی (سے پرورش) کریں ﴿١٢﴾
تو ہم نے (اس طریق سے) اُنکو اُنکی ماں کے پاس واپس پہنچا دیا
تاکہ اُنکی آنکھیں ٹھنڈی ہوں اور وہ غم نہ کھائیں اور معلوم
کریں کہ خدا کا وعدہ سچا ہے لیکن یہ اکثر نہیں جانتے ﴿١٣﴾
اور جب موسیٰ جوانی کو پہنچے اور بھر پور (جوان) ہو گئے تو ہم نے اُنکو
حکمت اور علم عنایت کیا۔ اور ہم نیکوکاروں کو ایسا ہی بدلا دیا کرتے ہیں ﴿١٤﴾
اور وہ ایسے وقت شہر میں داخل ہوئے کہ وہاں کے باشندے
بے خبر ہو رہے تھے تو دیکھا کہ وہاں دو شخص لڑ رہے تھے ایک تو
موسیٰ کی قوم کا ہے اور دوسرا اُنکے دشمنوں میں سے۔ تو جو شخص اُنکی قوم میں سے تھا
اس نے دوسرے شخص کے مقابلے میں جو موسیٰ کے دشمنوں میں سے تھا مدد طلب
کی تو انہوں نے اسکو مکا مارا اور اسکا کام تمام کر دیا۔ کہنے لگے کہ یہ کام تو
(اغوائے) شیطان سے ہوا بیشک وہ (انسان کا) دشمن اور صریح بہکانے والا ہے ﴿١٥﴾
بولے کہ اے پروردگار میں نے اپنے آپ پر ظلم کیا تو مجھے بخش دے

restore him to thee, and We shall make him one of Our messengers."

8. Then the people of Pharaoh picked him up (from the river): (it was intended) that (Moses) should be to them an adversary and a cause of sorrow: for Pharaoh and Hāmān and (all) their hosts were men of sin.

9. The wife of Pharaoh said: "(Here is) a joy of the eye for me and for thee: slay him not. It may be that he will be of use to us, or we may adopt him as a son." And they perceived not (what they were doing)!

10. And the heart of the mother of Moses became void: she was going almost to disclose his (case), had We not strengthened her heart (with faith), so that she might remain a (firm) believer.

11. And she said to the sister of (Moses), "Trace him". So she (the sister) watched him from a distance and they perceived not.

12. And We ordained that he refused suck at first, until (his sister came up and) said: "Shall I point out to you the people of a house that will nourish and bring him up for you and take care of him."

13. Thus did We restore him to his mother, that her eye might be comforted, that she might not grieve, and that she might know that the promise of Allah is true: but most of them do not know.

14. When he reached full age, and was firmly established (in life), We bestowed on him wisdom and knowledge: for thus do We reward those who do good.

15. And he entered the City at a time when its people were not watching: and he found there two men fighting,— one of his own people, and the other, of his foes. Now the man of his own people appealed to him against his foe, and Moses struck him with his fist and killed him. He said: "This is a work of Satan: for he is an enemy that manifestly misleads!"

16. He prayed: "O my Lord! I have indeed wronged my soul! Do Thou

then forgive me !" So (Allah) forgave him: for He is the Oft-Forgiving, Most Merciful.

17. He said: "O my Lord! for that Thou hast bestowed Thy Grace on me, never shall I be a help to those who sin!"

18. In the morning, he was in the city, fearful and vigilant when behold, the man who had, the day before, sought his help called aloud for his help (again). Moses said to him: "Thou art truly, one erring manifestly."

19. Then, when he was about to lay his hands on their enemy the man said: "O Moses! is it thy intention to slay me as thou slewest a man yesterday? Thou only desire to become a tyrant in the land, and not to be one who sets things right!"

20. And there came a man, running, from the furthest end of the City. He said: "O Moses! the Chiefs are taking counsel together about thee, to slay thee: so get thee away, for I do give thee sincere advice."

21. He therefore got away therefrom, looking about, in a state of fear. He prayed: "O my Lord! save me from people given to wrong-doing."

22. Then, when he turned his face towards (the land of) Madyan, he said: "I do hope that my Lord will show me the smooth and straight Path."

23. And when he arrived at the watering (place) in Madyan, he found there a group of men watering (their flocks), and besides them he found two women who were keeping back (their flocks). He said: "What is the matter with you?" They said: "We cannot water (our flocks) until the shepherds take back (their flocks): and our father is a very old man."

24. So he watered (their flocks) for them; then he turned back to the shade, and said: "O my lord! truly am I in (desperate) need of any good that Thou dost send me!"...

25. Afterwards one of the (damsels) came (back) to him,

تو خدا نے اُن کو بخش دیا۔ بیشک وہ بخشنے والا مہربان ہے ﴿۱۶﴾
کہنے لگے کہ اے پروردگار تُو نے جو مجھ پر مہربانی فرمائی ہے میں
(آئندہ) کبھی گنہگاروں کا مددگار نہ بنوں ﴿۱۷﴾
الغرض صبح کے وقت شہر میں ڈرتے ڈرتے داخل ہوئے کہ دیکھیں
(کیا ہوتا ہے) تو ناگہاں وہی شخص جس نے کل اُن سے مدد مانگی تھی پھر اُن کو
پکار رہا ہے۔ موسیٰ نے اس سے کہا کہ تُو تو صریح گمراہ ہے ﴿۱۸﴾
جب مُوسیٰ نے ارادہ کیا کہ اس شخص کو جو ان دونوں کا دشمن تھا
پکڑ لیں تو وہ (یعنی مُوسیٰ کی قوم کا آدمی) بول اُٹھا کہ جس طرح
تم نے کل ایک شخص کو مار ڈالا تھا (اسی طرح) چاہتے ہو کہ
مجھے بھی مار ڈالو۔ تم تو یہی چاہتے ہو کہ ملک میں ظلم و ستم کرتے
پھرو اور یہ نہیں چاہتے کہ نیکوکاروں میں ہو ﴿۱۹﴾
اور ایک شخص شہر کی پرلی طرف سے دوڑتا ہوا آیا (اور) بولا
کہ موسیٰ (شہر کے) رئیس تمہارے بارے میں صلاحیں کرتے ہیں کہ تم کو
مار ڈالیں سو تم یہاں سے نکل جاؤ۔ میں تمہارا خیرخواہ ہوں ﴿۲۰﴾
موسیٰ وہاں سے ڈرتے ڈرتے نکل کھڑے ہوئے کہ دیکھیں (کیا ہوتا ہے اور)
دُعا کرنے لگے کہ اے پروردگار مجھے ظالم لوگوں سے نجات دے ﴿۲۱﴾
اور جب مدین کی طرف رُخ کیا تو کہنے لگے اُمید ہے کہ میرا
پروردگار مجھے سیدھا رستہ بتائے ﴿۲۲﴾
اور جب مدین کے پانی (کے مقام) پر پہنچے تو دیکھا کہ وہاں لوگ
جمع ہو رہے (اور اپنے چارپایوں کو) پانی پلا رہے ہیں۔ اور اُن کے
ایک طرف دو عورتیں (اپنی بکریوں کو) روکے کھڑی ہیں۔ موسیٰ نے (اُن سے) کہا
تمہارا کیا کام ہے۔ وہ بولیں کہ جب تک چرواہے (اپنے چارپایوں کو) لے نہ
جائیں ہم پانی نہیں پلا سکتے اور ہمارے والد بڑی عمر کے بوڑھے ہیں ﴿۲۳﴾
تو موسیٰ نے اُن کیلئے (بکریوں کو) پانی پلا دیا پھر سائے کی طرف
چلے گئے۔ اور کہنے لگے کہ پروردگار میں اس کا محتاج ہوں
کہ تو مجھ پر اپنی نعمت نازل فرمائے ﴿۲۴﴾
(تھوڑی دیر کے بعد) اُن میں سے ایک عورت جو شرماتی اور

فَغَفَرَ لَهٗ ۭ اِنَّهٗ هُوَ الْغَفُوْرُ الرَّحِيْمُ ﴿۱۶﴾
قَالَ رَبِّ بِمَآ اَنْعَمْتَ عَلَيَّ فَلَنْ اَكُوْنَ
ظَهِيْرًا لِّلْمُجْرِمِيْنَ ﴿۱۷﴾
فَاَصْبَحَ فِي الْمَدِيْنَةِ خَآئِفًا يَّتَرَقَّبُ فَاِذَا
الَّذِي اسْتَنْصَرَهٗ بِالْاَمْسِ يَسْتَصْرِخُهٗ ۭ
قَالَ لَهٗ مُوْسٰٓى اِنَّكَ لَغَوِيٌّ مُّبِيْنٌ ﴿۱۸﴾
فَلَمَّآ اَنْ اَرَادَ اَنْ يَّبْطِشَ بِالَّذِيْ هُوَ
عَدُوٌّ لَّهُمَا ۙ قَالَ يٰمُوْسٰٓى اَتُرِيْدُ اَنْ
تَقْتُلَنِيْ كَمَا قَتَلْتَ نَفْسًۢا بِالْاَمْسِ ۖ اِنْ
تُرِيْدُ اِلَّآ اَنْ تَكُوْنَ جَبَّارًا فِي الْاَرْضِ
وَمَا تُرِيْدُ اَنْ تَكُوْنَ مِنَ الْمُصْلِحِيْنَ ﴿۱۹﴾
وَجَآءَ رَجُلٌ مِّنْ اَقْصَا الْمَدِيْنَةِ يَسْعٰى ۡ
قَالَ يٰمُوْسٰٓى اِنَّ الْمَلَاَ يَاْتَمِرُوْنَ بِكَ
لِيَقْتُلُوْكَ فَاخْرُجْ اِنِّيْ لَكَ مِنَ النّٰصِحِيْنَ ﴿۲۰﴾
فَخَرَجَ مِنْهَا خَآئِفًا يَّتَرَقَّبُ ۡ قَالَ رَبِّ
نَجِّنِيْ مِنَ الْقَوْمِ الظّٰلِمِيْنَ ﴿۲۱﴾ ع ۲/۵
وَلَمَّا تَوَجَّهَ تِلْقَآءَ مَدْيَنَ قَالَ عَسٰى رَبِّيْٓ
اَنْ يَّهْدِيَنِيْ سَوَآءَ السَّبِيْلِ ﴿۲۲﴾
وَلَمَّا وَرَدَ مَآءَ مَدْيَنَ وَجَدَ عَلَيْهِ اُمَّةً
مِّنَ النَّاسِ يَسْقُوْنَ ۫ وَوَجَدَ مِنْ دُوْنِهِمُ
امْرَاَتَيْنِ تَذُوْدٰنِ ۚ قَالَ مَا خَطْبُكُمَا ۭ
قَالَتَا لَا نَسْقِيْ حَتّٰى يُصْدِرَ الرِّعَآءُ ۫ وَاَبُوْنَا
شَيْخٌ كَبِيْرٌ ﴿۲۳﴾
فَسَقٰى لَهُمَا ثُمَّ تَوَلّٰٓى اِلَى الظِّلِّ فَقَالَ
رَبِّ اِنِّيْ لِمَآ اَنْزَلْتَ اِلَيَّ مِنْ خَيْرٍ
فَقِيْرٌ ﴿۲۴﴾
فَجَآءَتْهُ اِحْدٰىهُمَا تَمْشِيْ عَلَى اسْتِحْيَآءٍ ۡ

walking bashfully. She said: "My father invites thee that he may reward thee for having watered (our flocks) for us." So when he came to him and narrated the story, he said: "Fear thou not: (well) hast thou escaped from unjust people."

26. Said one of the (damsels): "O my (dear) father! engage him on wages: truly the best of men for thee to employ is the (man) who is strong and trusty"...

27. He said: "I intend to wed one of these my daughters to thee, on condition that thou serve me for eight years; but if thou complete ten years, it will be (grace) from thee. But I intend not to place thee under a difficulty: thou wilt find me, indeed, if Allah wills, one of the righteous."

28. He said: "Be that (the agreement between me and thee: whichever of the two terms I fulfil, let there be no injustice to me. Be Allah a witness to what we say."

29. Now when Moses had fulfilled the term, and was travelling with his family, he perceived a fire in the direction of Mount Ṭûr. He said to his family: "Tarry ye; I perceive a fire; I hope to bring you from there some information, or a burning firebrand, that ye may warm yourselves."

30. But when he came to the (Fire), he was called from the right bank of the valley, from a tree in hallowed ground: "O Moses! Verily I am Allah, the Lord of the Worlds...

31. "Now do thou throw thy rod!" But when he saw it moving (of its own accord) as if it had been a snake, he turned back in retreat, and retraced not his steps: "O Moses!" (it was said), "Draw near, and fear not: for thou art of those who are secure.

32. "Thrust thy hand into thy bosom, and it will come forth white

لجاتی چلی آتی تھی موسیٰ کے پاس آئی (اور) کہنے لگی کہ تم کو میرے
والد بلاتے ہیں کہ تم نے جو ہمارے لئے پانی پلایا تھا اسکی تم کو
اُجرت دیں جب وہ اُنکے پاس آئے اور اُنسے (اپنا) ماجرا بیان کیا تو
انہوں نے کہا کہ کچھ خوف نہ کرو تم ظالم لوگوں سے بچ آئے ہو ﴿۲۵﴾
ایک لڑکی بولی کہ ابّا ان کو نوکر رکھ لیجئے کیونکہ بہتر نوکر
جو آپ رکھیں وہ ہے (جو) توانا اور امانت دار
(ہو) ﴿۲۶﴾
اُنہوں نے (موسیٰ سے) کہا کہ میں چاہتا ہوں اپنی ان دو
بیٹیوں میں سے ایک کو تم سے بیاہ دوں اس (عہد) پر کہ تم
آٹھ برس میری خدمت کرو اور اگر دس سال پورے کر دو
تو وہ تمہاری طرف سے (احسان) ہے اور میں تم پر تکلیف ڈالنی نہیں
چاہتا تم مجھے انشاء اللہ نیک لوگوں میں پاؤ گے ﴿۲۷﴾
موسیٰ نے کہا کہ مجھ میں اور آپ میں یہ (عہد پختہ ہوا) میں جونسی
مدت (چاہوں) پوری کر دوں پھر مجھ پر کوئی زیادتی نہ ہو
اور ہم جو معاہدہ کرتے ہیں خدا اس کا گواہ ہے ﴿۲۸﴾
جب موسیٰ نے مدت پوری کر دی اور اپنے گھر کے لوگوں
کو لے کر چلے تو طور کی طرف سے آگ دکھائی دی تو اپنے گھر
والوں سے کہنے لگے کہ (تم یہاں) ٹھہرو۔ مجھے آگ نظر آئی
ہے شاید میں وہاں سے (رستے کا) کچھ پتہ لاؤں یا آگ
کا انگارہ لے آؤں تاکہ تم تاپو ﴿۲۹﴾
جب اسکے پاس پہنچے تو میدان کے دائیں کنارے سے ایک
مبارک جگہ میں ایک درخت میں سے آواز آئی کہ موسیٰ میں تو
خدائے رب العالمین ہوں ﴿۳۰﴾
اور یہ کہ اپنی لاٹھی ڈال دو۔ جب دیکھا کہ وہ حرکت کر رہی ہے
گویا سانپ ہے تو پیٹھ پھیر کر چل دیئے اور پیچھے مُڑ کر بھی نہ دیکھا ﴿۳۱﴾
(ہم نے کہا کہ) موسیٰ آگے آؤ اور ڈرو مت تم امن پانے والوں میں ہو
اپنا ہاتھ گریبان میں ڈالو تو بغیر کسی عیب کے سفید نکل آئیگا

قَالَتْ إِنَّ أَبِي يَدْعُوكَ لِيَجْزِيَكَ أَجْرَ مَا
سَقَيْتَ لَنَا ۚ فَلَمَّا جَاءَهُ وَقَصَّ عَلَيْهِ
الْقَصَصَ قَالَ لَا تَخَفْ ۖ نَجَوْتَ مِنَ
الْقَوْمِ الظَّالِمِينَ ﴿٢٥﴾
قَالَتْ إِحْدَاهُمَا يَا أَبَتِ اسْتَأْجِرْهُ ۖ
إِنَّ خَيْرَ مَنِ اسْتَأْجَرْتَ الْقَوِيُّ
الْأَمِينُ ﴿٢٦﴾
قَالَ إِنِّي أُرِيدُ أَنْ أُنْكِحَكَ إِحْدَى
ابْنَتَيَّ هَاتَيْنِ عَلَىٰ أَنْ تَأْجُرَنِي ثَمَانِيَ
حِجَجٍ ۖ فَإِنْ أَتْمَمْتَ عَشْرًا فَمِنْ
عِنْدِكَ ۖ وَمَا أُرِيدُ أَنْ أَشُقَّ عَلَيْكَ ۚ
سَتَجِدُنِي إِنْ شَاءَ اللَّهُ مِنَ الصَّالِحِينَ ﴿٢٧﴾
قَالَ ذَٰلِكَ بَيْنِي وَبَيْنَكَ ۖ أَيَّمَا الْأَجَلَيْنِ
قَضَيْتُ فَلَا عُدْوَانَ عَلَيَّ ۖ وَاللَّهُ عَلَىٰ
مَا نَقُولُ وَكِيلٌ ﴿٢٨﴾
فَلَمَّا قَضَىٰ مُوسَى الْأَجَلَ وَسَارَ بِأَهْلِهِ
آنَسَ مِنْ جَانِبِ الطُّورِ نَارًا قَالَ لِأَهْلِهِ
امْكُثُوا إِنِّي آنَسْتُ نَارًا لَعَلِّي آتِيكُمْ مِنْهَا
بِخَبَرٍ أَوْ جَذْوَةٍ مِنَ النَّارِ لَعَلَّكُمْ
تَصْطَلُونَ ﴿٢٩﴾
فَلَمَّا أَتَاهَا نُودِيَ مِنْ شَاطِئِ الْوَادِ الْأَيْمَنِ
فِي الْبُقْعَةِ الْمُبَارَكَةِ مِنَ الشَّجَرَةِ أَنْ
يَا مُوسَىٰ إِنِّي أَنَا اللَّهُ رَبُّ الْعَالَمِينَ ﴿٣٠﴾
وَأَنْ أَلْقِ عَصَاكَ ۖ فَلَمَّا رَآهَا تَهْتَزُّ كَأَنَّهَا
جَانٌّ وَلَّىٰ مُدْبِرًا وَلَمْ يُعَقِّبْ ۚ يَا مُوسَىٰ
أَقْبِلْ وَلَا تَخَفْ ۖ إِنَّكَ مِنَ الْآمِنِينَ ﴿٣١﴾
اسْلُكْ يَدَكَ فِي جَيْبِكَ تَخْرُجْ بَيْضَاءَ

مِنْ غَيْرِ سُوْٓءٍ وَّاضْمُمْ اِلَيْكَ
جَنَاحَكَ مِنَ الرَّهْبِ فَذٰنِكَ بُرْهَانٰنِ
مِنْ رَّبِّكَ اِلٰى فِرْعَوْنَ وَمَلَا۟ئِهٖ ؕ اِنَّهُمْ
كَانُوْا قَوْمًا فٰسِقِيْنَ ﴿۳۲﴾

اور خوف دُور ہونے (کی وجہ) سے اپنے بازو کو اپنی طرف
سکیڑ لو۔ یہ دو دلیلیں تمہارے پروردگار کی طرف سے ہیں
(اُنکے ساتھ) فرعون اور اُسکے درباریوں کے پاس (جاؤ)
کہ وہ نافرمان لوگ ہیں ﴿۳۲﴾

without stain (or harm), and draw thy hand close to thy side (to guard) against fear. Those are the two credentials From thy Lord to Pharaoh and his Chiefs: for truly they are a people rebellious and wicked."

قَالَ رَبِّ اِنِّيْ قَتَلْتُ مِنْهُمْ نَفْسًا فَاَخَافُ
اَنْ يَّقْتُلُوْنِ ﴿۳۳﴾

(موسیٰ نے) کہا اے پروردگار اُنمیں کا ایک شخص میرے ہاتھ سے قتل ہو چکا
ہے سو مجھے خوف ہے کہ وہ (کہیں) مجھ کو مار نہ ڈالیں ﴿۳۳﴾

33. He said: "O my Lord! I have slain a man among them, and I fear lest they slay me.

وَاَخِيْ هٰرُوْنُ هُوَ اَفْصَحُ مِنِّيْ لِسَانًا
فَاَرْسِلْهُ مَعِيَ رِدْاً يُّصَدِّقُنِيْٓ ۡ اِنِّيْٓ اَخَافُ
اَنْ يُّكَذِّبُوْنِ ﴿۳۴﴾

اور ہارون (جو) میرا بھائی (ہے) اُسکی زبان مجھ سے زیادہ فصیح ہے
تو اسکو میرے ساتھ مددگار بنا کر بھیج کہ میری تصدیق کرے مجھے
خوف ہے کہ وہ لوگ میری تکذیب کریں گے ﴿۳۴﴾

34. "And my brother Aaron—he is more eloquent in speech than I: so send him with me as a helper, to confirm (and strengthen) me: for I fear that they may accuse me of falsehood."

قَالَ سَنَشُدُّ عَضُدَكَ بِاَخِيْكَ وَنَجْعَلُ
لَكُمَا سُلْطٰنًا فَلَا يَصِلُوْنَ اِلَيْكُمَا ۚۛ بِاٰيٰتِنَآ ۚۛ
اَنْتُمَا وَمَنِ اتَّبَعَكُمَا الْغٰلِبُوْنَ ﴿۳۵﴾

(خدا نے) فرمایا ہم تمہارے بھائی سے تمہارے بازو کو مضبوط کرینگے
اور تم دونوں کو غلبہ دینگے تو ہماری نشانیوں کے سبب وہ تم تک پہنچ نہ
سکیں گے (اور) تم اور جنہوں نے تمہاری پیروی کی غالب رہوگے ﴿۳۵﴾

35. He said: "We will certainly strengthen thy arm through thy brother, and invest you both with authority, so they shall not be able to touch you: with Our Signs shall ye triumph,—you two as well as those who follow you."

فَلَمَّا جَآءَهُمْ مُّوْسٰى بِاٰيٰتِنَا بَيِّنٰتٍ قَالُوْا
مَا هٰذَآ اِلَّا سِحْرٌ مُّفْتَرًى وَّمَا سَمِعْنَا
بِهٰذَا فِيْٓ اٰبَآئِنَا الْاَوَّلِيْنَ ﴿۳۶﴾

اور جب موسیٰ اُنکے پاس ہماری کھلی نشانیاں لیکر آئے تو وہ کہنے
لگے کہ یہ تو جادو ہے جو اس نے بنا کھڑا کیا ہے اور یہ (باتیں)
ہم نے اپنے اگلے باپ دادا میں تو کبھی سُنی نہیں ﴿۳۶﴾

36. When Moses came to them with Our Clear Signs, they said: "This is nothing but sorcery faked up: never did we hear the like among our fathers of old!"

وَقَالَ مُوْسٰى رَبِّيْٓ اَعْلَمُ بِمَنْ جَآءَ
بِالْهُدٰى مِنْ عِنْدِهٖ وَمَنْ تَكُوْنُ لَهٗ
عَاقِبَةُ الدَّارِ ؕ اِنَّهٗ لَا يُفْلِحُ الظّٰلِمُوْنَ ﴿۳۷﴾

اور موسیٰ نے کہا کہ میرا پروردگار اس شخص کو خوب جانتا
ہے جو اس کی طرف سے حق لے کر آیا ہے اور جس کے لئے
عاقبت کا گھر (یعنی بہشت) ہے۔ بیشک ظالم نجات نہیں پائینگے ﴿۳۷﴾

37. Moses said: "My Lord knows best who it is that comes with guidance from Him and whose End will be best in the Hereafter: certain it is that the wrong-doers will not prosper."

وَقَالَ فِرْعَوْنُ يٰٓاَيُّهَا الْمَلَاُ مَا عَلِمْتُ
لَكُمْ مِّنْ اِلٰهٍ غَيْرِيْ ۚ فَاَوْقِدْ لِيْ يٰهَامٰنُ
عَلَى الطِّيْنِ فَاجْعَلْ لِّيْ صَرْحًا لَّعَلِّيْٓ
اَطَّلِعُ اِلٰٓى اِلٰهِ مُوْسٰى ۙ وَاِنِّيْ لَاَظُنُّهٗ
مِنَ الْكٰذِبِيْنَ ﴿۳۸﴾

اور فرعون نے کہا کہ اے اہلِ دربار میں تمہارا اپنے سوا
کسی کو خدا نہیں جانتا تو ہامان میرے لئے گارے کو
آگ لگا (کر اینٹیں پکا) دو پھر ایک (اُونچا) محل
بنا دو تاکہ میں موسیٰ کے خدا کی طرف چڑھ جاؤں اور
میں تو اسے جھوٹا سمجھتا ہوں ﴿۳۸﴾

38. Pharaoh said: "O Chiefs! no god do I know for you but myself: therefore, O Hāmān! light me a (kiln to bake bricks) out of clay, and build me a lofty palace, that I may mount up to the god of Moses: but as far as I am concerned, I think (Moses) is a liar!"

وَاسْتَكْبَرَ هُوَ وَجُنُوْدُهٗ فِي الْاَرْضِ بِغَيْرِ
الْحَقِّ وَظَنُّوْٓا اَنَّهُمْ اِلَيْنَا لَا يُرْجَعُوْنَ ﴿۳۹﴾

اور وہ اور اسکے لشکر ملک میں ناحق مغرور ہو رہے تھے
اور خیال کرتے تھے کہ وہ ہماری طرف لوٹ کر نہیں آئینگے ﴿۳۹﴾

39. And he was arrogant and insolent in the land, beyond reason,— he and his hosts: they thought that they would not have to return to Us!"

فَاَخَذْنٰهُ وَجُنُوْدَهٗ فَنَبَذْنٰهُمْ فِي الْيَمِّ ۚ
فَانْظُرْ كَيْفَ كَانَ عَاقِبَةُ الظّٰلِمِيْنَ ﴿۴۰﴾

تو ہم نے اُنکو اور اُنکے لشکروں کو پکڑ لیا اور دریا میں ڈال دیا۔
سو دیکھ لو کہ ظالموں کا کیسا انجام ہوا ﴿۴۰﴾

40. So We seized him and his hosts, and We flung them into the sea: now behold what was the End of those who did wrong!

وَجَعَلْنٰهُمْ اَئِمَّةً يَّدْعُوْنَ اِلَى النَّارِ ۚ
وَيَوْمَ الْقِيٰمَةِ لَا يُنْصَرُوْنَ ﴿٤١﴾
وَاَتْبَعْنٰهُمْ فِيْ هٰذِهِ الدُّنْيَا لَعْنَةً ۚ وَ
يَوْمَ الْقِيٰمَةِ هُمْ مِّنَ الْمَقْبُوْحِيْنَ ﴿٤٢﴾ ع

اور ہم نے اُن کو پیشوا بنایا تھا وہ (لوگوں کو) دوزخ کی طرف بلاتے
تھے اور قیامت کے دن اُن کی مدد نہیں کی جائے گی ﴿۴۱﴾
اور اس دنیا میں ہم نے اُنکے پیچھے لعنت لگا دی اور وہ قیامت
کے روز بھی بدحالوں میں ہوں گے ﴿۴۲﴾

41. And We made them (but) leaders inviting to the Fire; and on the Day of Judgment no help shall they find.

42. In this world We made a Curse to follow them: and on the Day of Judgment they will be among the loathed (and despised).

وَلَقَدْ اٰتَيْنَا مُوْسَى الْكِتٰبَ مِنْ بَعْدِ
مَآ اَهْلَكْنَا الْقُرُوْنَ الْاُوْلٰى بَصَآئِرَ
لِلنَّاسِ وَهُدًى وَّرَحْمَةً لَّعَلَّهُمْ
يَتَذَكَّرُوْنَ ﴿٤٣﴾

اور ہم نے پہلی اُمتوں کے ہلاک کرنے کے
بعد موسیٰ کو کتاب دی جو لوگوں کے لئے بصیرت
اور ہدایت اور رحمت ہے تاکہ وہ نصیحت
پکڑیں ﴿۴۳﴾

43. We did reveal to Moses the Book after We had destroyed the earlier generations, (to give) Insight to men, and Guidance and Mercy, that they might receive admonition.

وَمَا كُنْتَ بِجَانِبِ الْغَرْبِيِّ اِذْ قَضَيْنَآ
اِلٰى مُوْسَى الْاَمْرَ وَمَا كُنْتَ مِنَ
الشّٰهِدِيْنَ ﴿٤٤﴾

اور جب ہم نے موسیٰ کی طرف حکم بھیجا تو تم (طور کی)
غرب کی طرف نہیں تھے اور نہ اس واقعے کے دیکھنے
والوں میں تھے ﴿۴۴﴾

44. Thou wast not on the Western side when We decreed the Commission to Moses, nor wast thou a witness (of those events).

وَلٰكِنَّآ اَنْشَاْنَا قُرُوْنًا فَتَطَاوَلَ عَلَيْهِمُ
الْعُمُرُ ۚ وَمَا كُنْتَ ثَاوِيًا فِيْٓ اَهْلِ مَدْيَنَ
تَتْلُوْا عَلَيْهِمْ اٰيٰتِنَا ۙ وَلٰكِنَّا كُنَّا
مُرْسِلِيْنَ ﴿٤٥﴾

لیکن ہم نے (موسیٰ کے بعد) کئی اُمتوں کو پیدا کیا پھر
اُن پر مدت طویل گزر گئی۔ اور نہ تم مدین والوں میں
رہنے والے تھے کہ اُن کو ہماری آیتیں پڑھ پڑھ کر سناتے
تھے۔ ہاں ہم ہی تو پیغمبر بھیجنے والے تھے ﴿۴۵﴾

45. But We raised up (new) generations, and long were the ages that passed over them; but thou wast not a dweller among the people of Madyan, rehearsing Our Signs to them; but it is We Who send Messengers (with inspiration).

وَمَا كُنْتَ بِجَانِبِ الطُّوْرِ اِذْ نَادَيْنَا
وَلٰكِنْ رَّحْمَةً مِّنْ رَّبِّكَ لِتُنْذِرَ قَوْمًا
مَّآ اَتٰىهُمْ مِّنْ نَّذِيْرٍ مِّنْ قَبْلِكَ لَعَلَّهُمْ
يَتَذَكَّرُوْنَ ﴿٤٦﴾

اور نہ تم اس وقت جب کہ ہم نے (موسیٰ کو) آواز دی طُور کے
کنارے تھے بلکہ (تمہارا بھیجا جانا) تمہارے پروردگار کی رحمت ہے
تاکہ تم اُن لوگوں کو جن کے پاس تم سے پہلے کوئی ہدایت
کرنے والا نہیں آیا ہدایت کرو تاکہ وہ نصیحت پکڑیں ﴿۴۶﴾

46. Nor wast thou at the side of (the Mountain of) Ṭûr when We called (to Moses). Yet (art thou sent) as a Mercy from thy Lord, to give warning to a people to whom no warner had come before thee: in order that they may receive admonition.

وَلَوْلَآ اَنْ تُصِيْبَهُمْ مُّصِيْبَةٌۢ بِمَا قَدَّمَتْ
اَيْدِيْهِمْ فَيَقُوْلُوْا رَبَّنَا لَوْلَآ اَرْسَلْتَ اِلَيْنَا
رَسُوْلًا فَنَتَّبِعَ اٰيٰتِكَ وَنَكُوْنَ مِنَ
الْمُؤْمِنِيْنَ ﴿٤٧﴾

اور (اے پیغمبر ہم نے تم کو اسلئے بھیجا ہے کہ) ایسا نہ ہو کہ اگر ان
(اعمال) کے سبب جو انکے ہاتھ آگے بھیج چکے ہیں اُن پر کوئی
مصیبت واقع ہو تو یہ کہنے لگیں کہ اے پروردگار تو نے ہماری طرف کوئی پیغمبر
کیوں نہ بھیجا کہ ہم تیری آیتوں کی پیروی کرتے اور ایمان لانے والوں میں ہوتے ﴿۴۷﴾

47. If (We had) not (sent thee to the Quraish),—in case a calamity should seize them for (the deeds) that their hands have sent forth, they might say: "Our Lord! why didst Thou not send us a messenger? We should then have followed the Signs and been amongst those who believe!"

فَلَمَّا جَآءَهُمُ الْحَقُّ مِنْ عِنْدِنَا قَالُوْا لَوْلَآ
اُوْتِيَ مِثْلَ مَآ اُوْتِيَ مُوْسٰى ۭ اَوَلَمْ يَكْفُرُوْا
بِمَآ اُوْتِيَ مُوْسٰى مِنْ قَبْلُ ۚ قَالُوْا سِحْرٰنِ
تَظٰهَرَا ۣ وَقَالُوْٓا اِنَّا بِكُلٍّ كٰفِرُوْنَ ﴿٤٨﴾

پھر جب اُنکے پاس ہماری طرف سے حق آپہنچا تو کہنے لگے کہ
جیسی (نشانیاں) موسیٰ کو ملی تھیں ویسی اس کو کیوں نہیں
ملیں کیا جو (نشانیاں) پہلے موسیٰ کو دی گئی تھیں اُنہوں نے اُنسے کفر نہیں کیا؟
کہنے لگے کہ دونوں جادوگر ہیں ایک دوسرے کے موافق۔ اور بولے کہ ہم سب سے منکر ہیں ﴿۴۸﴾

48. But (now), when the Truth has come to them from Ourselves, they say, "Why are not (Signs) sent to him, like those which were sent to Moses?" Do they not then reject (the Signs) which were formerly sent to Moses? They say: "Two kinds of sorcery, each assisting the other!" And they say: "For us, we reject all (such things)!"

49. Say: "Then bring ye a Book from Allah, which is a better Guide than either of them, that I may follow it! (Do), if ye are truthful!"

کہہ دو کہ اگر سچے ہو تو تم خدا کے پاس سے کوئی اور کتاب لے آؤ جو ان دونوں
(کتابوں) سے بڑھ کر ہدایت کرنیوالی ہو تا کہ میں بھی اسی کی پیروی کروں (۴۹)

قُلْ فَأْتُوا بِكِتٰبٍ مِّنْ عِنْدِ اللّٰهِ هُوَ
أَهْدٰى مِنْهُمَآ أَتَّبِعْهُ إِنْ كُنْتُمْ صٰدِقِيْنَ ﴿۴۹﴾

50. But if they hearken not to thee, know that they only follow their own lusts: and who is more astray than one who follows his own lusts, devoid of guidance from Allah? For Allah guides not people given to wrong-doing.

پھر اگر یہ تمہاری بات قبول نہ کریں تو جان لو کہ یہ صرف
اپنی خواہشوں کی پیروی کرتے ہیں۔ اور اس سے زیادہ
کون گمراہ ہوگا جو خدا کی ہدایت کو چھوڑ کر اپنی خواہش کے
پیچھے چلے۔ بیشک خدا ظالم لوگوں کو ہدایت نہیں دیتا (۵۰)

فَإِنْ لَّمْ يَسْتَجِيْبُوْا لَكَ فَاعْلَمْ أَنَّمَا
يَتَّبِعُوْنَ أَهْوَآءَهُمْ ۚ وَمَنْ أَضَلُّ مِمَّنِ
اتَّبَعَ هَوٰىهُ بِغَيْرِ هُدًى مِّنَ اللّٰهِ ۚ إِنَّ
اللّٰهَ لَا يَهْدِي الْقَوْمَ الظّٰلِمِيْنَ ﴿۵۰﴾ ع ۸

51. Now have We brought them the Word in order that they may receive admonition.

اور ہم پے در پے اُن لوگوں کے پاس (ہدایت کی) باتیں
بھیجتے رہے ہیں تا کہ نصیحت پکڑیں (۵۱)

وَلَقَدْ وَصَّلْنَا لَهُمُ الْقَوْلَ لَعَلَّهُمْ
يَتَذَكَّرُوْنَ ﴿۵۱﴾

52. Those to whom We sent the Book before this,—they do believe in this (Revelation);

جن لوگوں کو ہم نے اس سے پہلے کتاب دی تھی وہ اس پر
ایمان لے آتے ہیں (۵۲)

اَلَّذِيْنَ اٰتَيْنٰهُمُ الْكِتٰبَ مِنْ قَبْلِهِ هُمْ
بِهِ يُؤْمِنُوْنَ ﴿۵۲﴾ النصف

53. And when it is recited to them, they say: "We believe therein, for it is the Truth from our Lord: indeed we have been Muslims (bowing to Allah's Will) from before this."

اور جب (قرآن) اُن کو پڑھ کر سنایا جاتا ہے تو کہتے ہیں کہ ہم
اس پر ایمان لے آئے۔ بیشک وہ ہمارے پروردگار کی طرف
سے برحق ہے (اور) ہم تو اس سے پہلے کے حکم بردار ہیں (۵۳)

وَإِذَا يُتْلٰى عَلَيْهِمْ قَالُوْٓا اٰمَنَّا بِهِ إِنَّهُ
الْحَقُّ مِنْ رَّبِّنَآ إِنَّا كُنَّا مِنْ قَبْلِهِ
مُسْلِمِيْنَ ﴿۵۳﴾

54. Twice will they be given their reward, for that they have persevered, that they avert Evil with Good, and that they spend (in charity) out of what We have given them.

ان لوگوں کو دُگنا بدلہ دیا جائے گا کیونکہ صبر کرتے رہے ہیں
اور بھلائی کے ساتھ بُرائی کو دُور کرتے ہیں اور جو (مال) ہم
نے اُن کو دیا ہے اس میں سے خرچ کرتے ہیں (۵۴)

أُولٰٓئِكَ يُؤْتَوْنَ أَجْرَهُمْ مَّرَّتَيْنِ بِمَا
صَبَرُوْا وَيَدْرَءُوْنَ بِالْحَسَنَةِ السَّيِّئَةَ
وَمِمَّا رَزَقْنٰهُمْ يُنْفِقُوْنَ ﴿۵۴﴾

55. And when they hear vain talk, they turn away therefrom and say: "To us our deeds, and to you yours; peace be to you: we seek not the ignorant."

اور جب بیہودہ بات سُنتے ہیں تو اس سے مُنہ پھیر لیتے
ہیں اور کہتے ہیں کہ ہم کو ہمارے اعمال اور تم کو
تمہارے اعمال۔ تم کو سلام۔ ہم جاہلوں کے خواستگار
نہیں ہیں (۵۵)

وَإِذَا سَمِعُوا اللَّغْوَ أَعْرَضُوْا عَنْهُ وَ
قَالُوْا لَنَآ أَعْمَالُنَا وَلَكُمْ أَعْمَالُكُمْ ز
سَلٰمٌ عَلَيْكُمْ ز لَا نَبْتَغِي
الْجٰهِلِيْنَ ﴿۵۵﴾

56. It is true thou wilt not be able to guide everyone whom thou lovest; but Allah guides those whom He will and He knows best those who receive guidance.

(اے محمدؐ) تم جس کو دوست رکھتے ہو اُسے ہدایت نہیں کر سکتے
بلکہ خدا ہی جس کو چاہتا ہے ہدایت کرتا ہے اور وہ ہدایت
پانے والوں کو خوب جانتا ہے (۵۶)

إِنَّكَ لَا تَهْدِيْ مَنْ أَحْبَبْتَ وَلٰكِنَّ
اللّٰهَ يَهْدِيْ مَنْ يَّشَآءُ ۚ وَهُوَ أَعْلَمُ
بِالْمُهْتَدِيْنَ ﴿۵۶﴾

57. They say: "If we were to follow the guidance with thee, we should be snatched away from our land." Have We not established for them a secure sanctuary, to which are brought as tribute fruits of all kinds,—a provision from Ourselves? But

اور کہتے ہیں کہ اگر ہم تمہارے ساتھ ہدایت کی پیروی کریں
تو اپنے ملک سے اُچک لئے جائیں۔ کیا ہم نے اُن کو حرم
میں جو امن کا مقام ہے جگہ نہیں دی۔ جہاں ہر قسم کے
میوے پہنچائے جاتے ہیں (اور یہ) رزق ہماری طرف سے ہے

وَقَالُوْٓا إِنْ نَّتَّبِعِ الْهُدٰى مَعَكَ
نُتَخَطَّفْ مِنْ أَرْضِنَا ۚ أَوَلَمْ نُمَكِّنْ لَّهُمْ
حَرَمًا اٰمِنًا يُّجْبٰٓى إِلَيْهِ ثَمَرٰتُ كُلِّ
شَيْءٍ رِّزْقًا مِّنْ لَّدُنَّا وَلٰكِنَّ أَكْثَرَهُمْ

most of them understand not.

58. And how many towns We destroyed, which exulted in their life (of ease and plenty)! Now those habitations of theirs, after them, are deserted,— all but a (miserable) few! And We are their heirs!

59. Nor was thy Lord the one to destroy a town until He had sent to its Centre a messenger, rehearsing to them Our Signs; nor are We going to destroy a population except when its members practise iniquity.

60. The (material) things which ye are given are but the conveniences of this life and the glitter thereof; but that which is with Allah is better and more enduring: will ye not then be wise?

61. Are (these two) alike?—One to whom We have made a goodly promise, and who is going to reach its (fulfilment), and one to whom We have given the good things of this life, but who, on the Day of judgment, is to be among those brought up (for punishment)?

62. That Day (Allah) will call to them, and say: "Where are My 'partners'?— whom ye imagined (to be such)?"

63. Those against whom the charge will be proved, will say: "Our Lord! these are the ones whom we led astray: we led them astray, as we were astray ourselves: we free ourselves (from them) to you. It was not us they worshipped."

64. It will be said (to them): "Call upon your 'partners' (for help)": they will call upon them, but they will not listen to them; and they will see the Chastisement (before them); (how they will wish) 'If only they had been open to guidance!'

65. That Day (Allah) will call to them, and say: "What was the answer ye gave to the messengers?"

66. Then the arguments that day will be obscure to them and they will not be able (even) to question each other.

لیکن اُن میں سے اکثر نہیں جانتے ﴿۵۷﴾
اور ہم نے بہت سی بستیوں کو ہلاک کر ڈالا جو اپنی (فراخی) معیشت
میں اترا رہے تھے سو یہ اُنکے مکانات ہیں جو اُنکے بعد آباد ہی
نہیں ہوئے مگر بہت کم۔ اور اُنکے پیچھے ہم ہی اُنکے وارث ہوئے ﴿۵۸﴾
اور تمہارا پروردگار بستیوں کو ہلاک نہیں کیا کرتا جب تک
اُنکے بڑے شہر میں پیغمبر نہ بھیج لے جو اُنکو ہماری آیتیں پڑھ پڑھ کر سنائے
اور ہم بستیوں کو ہلاک نہیں کیا کرتے مگر اس حالت میں
کہ وہاں کے باشندے ظالم ہوں ﴿۵۹﴾
اور جو چیز تم کو دی گئی ہے وہ دنیا کی زندگی کا فائدہ اور
اس کی زینت ہے۔ اور جو خدا کے پاس ہے وہ بہتر اور
باقی رہنے والی ہے کیا تم سمجھتے نہیں؟ ﴿۶۰﴾
بھلا جس شخص سے ہم نے نیک وعدہ کیا اور اُس نے اُسے حاصل کر لیا تو کیا
وہ اس شخص کا سا ہے جسکو ہم نے دنیا کی زندگی کے فائدے سے بہرہ مند کیا
پھر وہ قیامت کے روز اُن لوگوں میں ہو جو (ہمارے روبرو) حاضر کئے جائینگے ﴿۶۱﴾
اور جس روز (خدا) اُنکو پکاریگا اور کہیگا کہ میرے وہ شریک
کہاں ہیں جن کا تمہیں دعویٰ تھا ﴿۶۲﴾
(تو) جن لوگوں پر (عذاب کا) حکم ثابت ہو چکا ہو گا وہ کہینگے
کہ ہمارے پروردگار یہ وہ لوگ ہیں جنکو ہم نے گمراہ کیا تھا اور جس طرح
ہم خود گمراہ ہوئے تھے اسی طرح اُنکو گمراہ کیا تھا (اب) ہم تیری طرف
(متوجہ ہو کر) اُن سے بیزار ہوتے ہیں یہ ہمیں نہیں پوجتے تھے ﴿۶۳﴾
اور کہا جائیگا کہ اپنے شریکوں کو بلاؤ۔ تو وہ اُن کو پکارینگے
اور وہ اُن کو جواب نہ دے سکیں گے اور (جب) عذاب کو دیکھ لینگے
(تو تمنا کریں گے کہ) کاش وہ ہدایت یاب ہوتے ﴿۶۴﴾
اور جس روز (خدا) اُن کو پکارے گا اور کہے گا کہ تم نے
پیغمبروں کو کیا جواب دیا ﴿۶۵﴾
تو وہ اس روز خبروں سے اندھے ہو جائیں گے، اور
آپس میں کچھ بھی پوچھ نہ سکیں گے ﴿۶۶﴾

لَا يَعْلَمُونَ ﴿٥٧﴾
وَكَمْ أَهْلَكْنَا مِنْ قَرْيَةٍ بَطِرَتْ مَعِيشَتَهَا
فَتِلْكَ مَسٰكِنُهُمْ لَمْ تُسْكَنْ مِّنْ بَعْدِهِمْ
إِلَّا قَلِيلًا وَكُنَّا نَحْنُ الْوٰرِثِينَ ﴿٥٨﴾
وَمَا كَانَ رَبُّكَ مُهْلِكَ الْقُرٰى حَتّٰى
يَبْعَثَ فِيْ أُمِّهَا رَسُولًا يَتْلُوا عَلَيْهِمْ
اٰيٰتِنَا وَمَا كُنَّا مُهْلِكِي الْقُرٰى إِلَّا
وَأَهْلُهَا ظٰلِمُونَ ﴿٥٩﴾
وَمَا أُوتِيتُمْ مِّنْ شَيْءٍ فَمَتَاعُ الْحَيٰوةِ
الدُّنْيَا وَزِينَتُهَا وَمَا عِنْدَ اللّٰهِ خَيْرٌ
وَّأَبْقٰى أَفَلَا تَعْقِلُونَ ﴿٦٠﴾ ع
أَفَمَنْ وَّعَدْنٰهُ وَعْدًا حَسَنًا فَهُوَ
لَاقِيهِ كَمَنْ مَّتَّعْنٰهُ مَتَاعَ الْحَيٰوةِ الدُّنْيَا
ثُمَّ هُوَ يَوْمَ الْقِيٰمَةِ مِنَ الْمُحْضَرِينَ ﴿٦١﴾
وَيَوْمَ يُنَادِيهِمْ فَيَقُولُ أَيْنَ شُرَكَاءِيَ
الَّذِينَ كُنْتُمْ تَزْعُمُونَ ﴿٦٢﴾
قَالَ الَّذِينَ حَقَّ عَلَيْهِمُ الْقَوْلُ رَبَّنَا
هٰؤُلَاءِ الَّذِينَ أَغْوَيْنَا أَغْوَيْنٰهُمْ
كَمَا غَوَيْنَا تَبَرَّأْنَا إِلَيْكَ مَا كَانُوا
إِيَّانَا يَعْبُدُونَ ﴿٦٣﴾
وَقِيلَ ادْعُوا شُرَكَاءَكُمْ فَدَعَوْهُمْ
فَلَمْ يَسْتَجِيبُوا لَهُمْ وَرَأَوُا الْعَذَابَ
لَوْ أَنَّهُمْ كَانُوا يَهْتَدُونَ ﴿٦٤﴾
وَيَوْمَ يُنَادِيهِمْ فَيَقُولُ مَاذَا أَجَبْتُمُ
الْمُرْسَلِينَ ﴿٦٥﴾
فَعَمِيَتْ عَلَيْهِمُ الْأَنْبَاءُ يَوْمَئِذٍ فَهُمْ
لَا يَتَسَاءَلُونَ ﴿٦٦﴾

67. But any that (in this life) had repented, believed, and worked righteousness, haply he shall be one of the successful.

لیکن جس نے توبہ کی اور ایمان لایا اور عمل نیک
کئے تو اُمید ہے کہ وہ نجات پانے والوں
میں ہو (۶۷)

فَأَمَّا مَنْ تَابَ وَآمَنَ وَعَمِلَ
صَالِحًا فَعَسَىٰ أَنْ يَكُونَ مِنَ
الْمُفْلِحِينَ (۶۷)

68. Thy Lord does create and choose as He pleases: no choice have they (in the matter): Glory to Allah! and far is He above the partners they ascribe (to Him)!

اور تمہارا پروردگار جو چاہتا ہے پیدا کرتا ہے اور (جسے
چاہتا ہے) برگزیدہ کرلیتا ہے ان کو اس کا اختیار نہیں
ہے۔ یہ جو شرک کرتے ہیں خدا اس سے پاک و بالاتر ہے (۶۸)

وَرَبُّكَ يَخْلُقُ مَا يَشَاءُ وَيَخْتَارُ ۗ مَا
كَانَ لَهُمُ الْخِيَرَةُ ۚ سُبْحَانَ اللَّهِ وَتَعَالَىٰ
عَمَّا يُشْرِكُونَ (۶۸)

69. And thy Lord knows all that their hearts conceal and all that they reveal.

اور ان کے سینے جو کچھ مخفی کرتے اور جو یہ ظاہر کرتے ہیں
تمہارا پروردگار اس کو جانتا ہے (۶۹)

وَرَبُّكَ يَعْلَمُ مَا تُكِنُّ صُدُورُهُمْ وَمَا
يُعْلِنُونَ (۶۹)

70. And He is Allah: there is no god but He. To Him be praise, at the first and at the last: for Him is the Command, and to Him shall ye (all) be brought back.

اور وہی خدا ہے اس کے سوا کوئی معبود نہیں دنیا اور
آخرت میں اسی کی تعریف ہے اور اسی کا حکم اور اُسی
کی طرف تم لوٹائے جاؤ گے (۷۰)

وَهُوَ اللَّهُ لَا إِلَٰهَ إِلَّا هُوَ ۖ لَهُ الْحَمْدُ
فِي الْأُولَىٰ وَالْآخِرَةِ ۖ وَلَهُ الْحُكْمُ وَ
إِلَيْهِ تُرْجَعُونَ (۷۰)

71. Say: See ye? If Allah were to make the Night perpetual over you to the Day of Judgment, what god is there other than Allah, who can give you light? Will ye not then hearken?

کہو بھلا دیکھو تو اگر خدا تم پر ہمیشہ قیامت کے دن تک
رات (کی تاریکی) کئے رہے تو خدا کے سوا کون معبود ہے
جو تم کو روشنی لا دے۔ تو کیا تم سنتے نہیں (۷۱)

قُلْ أَرَأَيْتُمْ إِنْ جَعَلَ اللَّهُ عَلَيْكُمُ اللَّيْلَ
سَرْمَدًا إِلَىٰ يَوْمِ الْقِيَامَةِ مَنْ إِلَٰهٌ غَيْرُ
اللَّهِ يَأْتِيكُمْ بِضِيَاءٍ ۖ أَفَلَا تَسْمَعُونَ (۷۱)

72. Say: See ye? If Allah were to make the Day perpetual over you to the Day of Judgment, what god is there other than Allah, who can give you a Night in which ye can rest? Will ye not then see?

کہو تو بھلا دیکھو تو اگر خدا تم پر ہمیشہ قیامت
تک دن کئے رہے تو خدا کے سوا کون معبود
ہے کہ تم کو رات لا دے جس میں تم آرام کرو۔ تو
کیا تم دیکھتے نہیں (۷۲)

قُلْ أَرَأَيْتُمْ إِنْ جَعَلَ اللَّهُ عَلَيْكُمُ
النَّهَارَ سَرْمَدًا إِلَىٰ يَوْمِ الْقِيَامَةِ مَنْ إِلَٰهٌ
غَيْرُ اللَّهِ يَأْتِيكُمْ بِلَيْلٍ تَسْكُنُونَ فِيهِ ۖ
أَفَلَا تُبْصِرُونَ (۷۲)

73. It is out of His Mercy that He has made for you Night and Day,— that ye may rest therein, and that ye may seek of His Grace;— and in order that ye may be grateful.

اور اس نے اپنی رحمت سے تمہارے لئے رات کو اور
دن کو بنایا تاکہ تم اس میں آرام کرو اور (اس میں)
اُس کا فضل تلاش کرو اور تاکہ شکر کرو (۷۳)

وَمِنْ رَحْمَتِهِ جَعَلَ لَكُمُ اللَّيْلَ وَالنَّهَارَ
لِتَسْكُنُوا فِيهِ وَلِتَبْتَغُوا مِنْ فَضْلِهِ وَ
لَعَلَّكُمْ تَشْكُرُونَ (۷۳)

74. The Day that He will call on them, He will say: "Where are My 'partners'? Whom ye imagined (to be such)?"

اور جس دن وہ اُن کو پکارے گا اور کہے گا کہ میرے وہ
شریک جن کا تمہیں دعویٰ تھا کہاں ہیں (۷۴)

وَيَوْمَ يُنَادِيهِمْ فَيَقُولُ أَيْنَ شُرَكَائِيَ
الَّذِينَ كُنْتُمْ تَزْعُمُونَ (۷۴)

75. And from each people shall We draw a witness, and We shall say: "Produce your Proof": then shall they know that the Truth is with Allah (alone), and the (lies) which they invented will leave them in the lurch.

اور ہم ہر ایک اُمت میں سے گواہ نکال لیں گے پھر کہیں گے
کہ اپنی دلیل پیش کرو تو وہ جان لیں گے کہ سچ بات خدا کی
ہے اور جو کچھ وہ افترا کیا کرتے تھے اُن سے جاتا رہیگا (۷۵)

وَنَزَعْنَا مِنْ كُلِّ أُمَّةٍ شَهِيدًا فَقُلْنَا
هَاتُوا بُرْهَانَكُمْ فَعَلِمُوا أَنَّ الْحَقَّ لِلَّهِ
وَضَلَّ عَنْهُمْ مَا كَانُوا يَفْتَرُونَ (۷۵) ع ۱۵

76. Qārûn was doubtless, of the people of Moses; but he acted

قارون موسیٰ کی قوم میں سے تھا اور اُن پر تعدی کرتا

إِنَّ قَارُونَ كَانَ مِنْ قَوْمِ مُوسَىٰ فَبَغَىٰ

insolently towards them: such were the treasures We had bestowed on him, that their very keys would have been a burden to a body of strong men. Behold, his people said to him: "Exult not, for Allah loveth not those who exult (in riches).

77. "But seek, with the (wealth) which Allah has bestowed on thee, the Home of the Hereafter, nor forget thy portion in this world: but do thou good, as Allah has been good to thee, and seek not (occasions for) mischief in the land: for Allah loves not those who do mischief."

78. He said: "This has been given to me because of a certain knowledge which I have." Did he not know that Allah had destroyed, before him, (whole) generations,—which were superior to him in strength and greater in the amount (of riches) they had collected? But the wicked are not called (immediately) to account for their sins.

79. So he went forth among his people in the (pride of his worldly) glitter. Said those whose aim is the life of this World: "Oh! that we had the like of what Qārūn has got! for he is truly a lord of mighty good fortune!"

80. But those who had been granted (true) knowledge said: "Alas for you! The reward of Allah (in the Hereafter) is best for those who believe and work righteousness: but this none shall attain, save those who steadfastly persevere (in good)."

81. Then We caused the earth to swallow up him and his house; and he had not (the least little) party to help him against Allah, nor could he defend himself.

82. And those who had envied his position the day before began to say on the morrow: "Ah! it is indeed Allah Who enlarges the provision or restricts it, to any of His servants He pleases! Had it not been that Allah was gracious to us, He could have caused the earth to swallow

تھا۔ اور ہم نے اس کو اتنے خزانے دیئے تھے کہ اُن کی کنجیاں
ایک طاقتور جماعت کو اُٹھانی مشکل ہوتیں جب اُس سے
اس کی قوم نے کہا کہ اترائیے مت۔ کہ خدا اترانے والوں
کو پسند نہیں کرتا (٧٦)
اور جو مال تم کو خدا نے عطا فرمایا ہے۔ اس سے آخرت (کی
بھلائی) طلب کیجئے اور دنیا سے اپنا حصہ نہ بھلائیے اور جیسی
خدا نے تم سے بھلائی کی ہے (ویسی) تم بھی (لوگوں سے) بھلائی کرو اور
ملک میں طالبِ فساد نہ ہو کیونکہ خدا فساد کرنیوالوں کو دوست نہیں رکھتا (٧٧)
بولا کہ یہ (مال) مجھے میری دانش (کے زور) سے ملا ہے۔
کیا اُس کو معلوم نہیں کہ خدا نے اس سے پہلے بہت سی
اُمتیں جو اس سے قوت میں بڑھ کر اور جمعیت میں بیشتر
تھیں ہلاک کر ڈالی ہیں۔ اور گنہگاروں سے اُنکے گناہوں
کے بارے میں پوچھا نہیں جائے گا (٧٨)
تو (ایک روز) قارون (بڑی) آرائش (اور ٹھاٹھ) سے
اپنی قوم کے سامنے نکلا۔ جو لوگ دنیا کی زندگی کے طالب تھے
کہنے لگے کہ جیسا (مال و متاع) قارون کو ملا ہے کاش
(ایسا ہی) ہمیں بھی ملے۔ وہ تو بڑا ہی صاحبِ نصیب ہے (٧٩)
اور جن لوگوں کو علم دیا گیا تھا وہ کہنے لگے کہ تم پر افسوس۔
مومنوں اور نیکوکاروں کیلئے (جو) ثواب خدا کے ہاں
(تیار ہے وہ) کہیں بہتر ہے۔ اور وہ صرف صبر کرنیوالوں ہی کو ملیگا (٨٠)
پس ہم نے قارون کو اور اُسکے گھر کو زمین میں دھنسا دیا۔
تو خدا کے سوا کوئی جماعت اس کی مددگار نہ ہو سکی۔ اور
نہ وہ بدلہ لے سکا (٨١)
اور وہ لوگ جو کل اُس کے رُتبے کی تمنا کرتے تھے صبح کو
کہنے لگے ہائے شامت! خدا ہی تو اپنے بندوں میں سے
جس کیلئے چاہتا ہے رزق فراخ کر دیتا ہے اور (جسکے لئے چاہتا
ہے) تنگ کر دیتا ہے۔ اگر خدا ہم پر احسان نہ کرتا تو ہمیں بھی

عَلَيْهِمْ ۖ وَآتَيْنَاهُ مِنَ الْكُنُوزِ مَا إِنَّ
مَفَاتِحَهُ لَتَنُوءُ بِالْعُصْبَةِ أُولِي الْقُوَّةِ ق
إِذْ قَالَ لَهُ قَوْمُهُ لَا تَفْرَحْ إِنَّ اللَّهَ لَا
يُحِبُّ الْفَرِحِينَ (٧٦)
وَابْتَغِ فِيمَا آتَاكَ اللَّهُ الدَّارَ الْآخِرَةَ ۖ وَلَا
تَنْسَ نَصِيبَكَ مِنَ الدُّنْيَا ۖ وَأَحْسِنْ كَمَا
أَحْسَنَ اللَّهُ إِلَيْكَ ۖ وَلَا تَبْغِ الْفَسَادَ فِي
الْأَرْضِ ۖ إِنَّ اللَّهَ لَا يُحِبُّ الْمُفْسِدِينَ (٧٧)
قَالَ إِنَّمَا أُوتِيتُهُ عَلَىٰ عِلْمٍ عِنْدِي ۚ
أَوَلَمْ يَعْلَمْ أَنَّ اللَّهَ قَدْ أَهْلَكَ مِنْ
قَبْلِهِ مِنَ الْقُرُونِ مَنْ هُوَ أَشَدُّ مِنْهُ
قُوَّةً وَأَكْثَرُ جَمْعًا ۚ وَلَا يُسْأَلُ عَنْ
ذُنُوبِهِمُ الْمُجْرِمُونَ (٧٨)
فَخَرَجَ عَلَىٰ قَوْمِهِ فِي زِينَتِهِ ۖ قَالَ الَّذِينَ
يُرِيدُونَ الْحَيَاةَ الدُّنْيَا يَا لَيْتَ لَنَا
مِثْلَ مَا أُوتِيَ قَارُونُ إِنَّهُ لَذُو حَظٍّ
عَظِيمٍ (٧٩)
وَقَالَ الَّذِينَ أُوتُوا الْعِلْمَ وَيْلَكُمْ
ثَوَابُ اللَّهِ خَيْرٌ لِمَنْ آمَنَ وَعَمِلَ صَالِحًا ۚ
وَلَا يُلَقَّاهَا إِلَّا الصَّابِرُونَ (٨٠)
فَخَسَفْنَا بِهِ وَبِدَارِهِ الْأَرْضَ فَمَا كَانَ
لَهُ مِنْ فِئَةٍ يَنْصُرُونَهُ مِنْ دُونِ اللَّهِ
وَمَا كَانَ مِنَ الْمُنْتَصِرِينَ (٨١)
وَأَصْبَحَ الَّذِينَ تَمَنَّوْا مَكَانَهُ بِالْأَمْسِ
يَقُولُونَ وَيْكَأَنَّ اللَّهَ يَبْسُطُ الرِّزْقَ
لِمَنْ يَشَاءُ مِنْ عِبَادِهِ وَيَقْدِرُ ۖ لَوْلَا
أَنْ مَنَّ اللَّهُ عَلَيْنَا لَخَسَفَ بِنَا ۖ وَيْكَأَنَّهُ

SÛRA–29
AL-'ANKABÛT
(INTRODUCTION)

This Sûra is the last of the series begun with S. 17 in which the growth of the spiritual man as an individual in considered, especially illustrated by the way in which the great apostles were prepared for their work and received their mission, and the nature of Revelation in relation to the environments in which it was promulgated. (See Introduction to S. 17). It also closes the sub-series beginning with S. 26 which is concerned with the spiritual Light, and the reactions to it at certain periods of spiritual history. (See Introduction to S. 26).

The last Sûra closed with a reference to the doctrine of the *Ma'ad,* or final Return of man to Allah. This theme is further developed here, and as it is continued in the subsequent three Sûras all bearing the Abbreviated Letters A.L.M., it forms a connecting link between the present series and those three Sûras.

In particular, emphasis is laid here on the necessity of linking actual conduct with the reception of Allah's revelation, and reference is again made to the stories of Noah, Abraham, and Lot among the apostles, and the stories of Midian, Ãd, Thamûd, and Pharaoh among the rejecters of Allah's Message. This world's life is contrasted with the real Life of the Hereafter.

Chronologically, the main Sûra belongs to the late Middle Makkan period, but the chronology has no significance except as showing how clearly the vision of the Future was revealed long before the Hijrat, to the struggling Brotherhood of Islam.

us up! Ah! those who reject Allah will assuredly never prosper."

83. That Home of the Hereafter We shall give to those who intend not high-handedness or mischief on earth: and the End is (best) for the righteous.

84. If any does good, the reward to him is better than his deed; but if any does evil, the doers of evil are only punished (to the extent) of their deeds.

85. Verily He Who ordained the Qur'an for thee, will bring thee back to the Place of Return. Say: "My Lord knows best who it is that brings true guidance, and who is in manifest error."

86. And thou hadst not expected that the Book would be sent to thee except as a Mercy from thy Lord: therefore lend not thou support in any way to those who reject (Allah's Message).

87. Let no one turn you away from Allah's revelations after they have been revealed to thee: and invite (men) to thy Lord and be not of the company of those who join gods with Allah.

88. And call not, besides Allah, on another god. There is no god but He. Everything (that exists) will perish except His Face. To Him belongs the Command, and to Him will ye (all) be brought back.

Al-'Ankabût, or the Spider

In the name of Allah, Most Gracious, Most Merciful.

1. A. L. M.
2. Do men think that they will be left alone on saying, "We believe", and that they will not be tested?
3. We did test those before them, and Allah will certainly know those who are true from those who are false.

4. Do those who practise evil think that they will outstrip Us? Evil

دھنسا دیتا۔ ہائے خرابی! کافر نجات نہیں پا سکتے ﴿۸۲﴾
وہ (جو) آخرت کا گھر (ہے) ہم نے اُسے اُن لوگوں کے لئے
(تیار) کر رکھا ہے جو ملک میں ظلم اور فساد کا ارادہ نہیں رکھتے۔
اور انجام (نیک) تو پرہیزگاروں ہی کا ہے ﴿۸۳﴾
جو شخص نیکی لے کر آئیگا اُسکے لئے اس سے بہتر (صلہ موجود)
ہے اور جو بُرائی لائیگا تو جن لوگوں نے بُرے کام کئے اُنکو بدلہ بھی
اسی طرح کا ملے گا جس طرح کے وہ کام کرتے تھے ﴿۸۴﴾
(اے پیغمبر) جس (خدا) نے تم پر قرآن (کے احکام) کو فرض کیا ہے
وہ تمہیں بازگشت کی جگہ لوٹا دیگا۔ کہدو کہ میرا پروردگار اس شخص کو بھی
خوب جانتا ہے جو ہدایت لیکر آیا اور (اسکو بھی) جو صریح گمراہی میں ہے ﴿۸۵﴾
اور تمہیں اُمید نہ تھی کہ تم پر یہ کتاب نازل کی جائے گی۔ مگر
تمہارے پروردگار کی مہربانی سے (نازل ہوئی) تو تم ہرگز
کافروں کے مددگار نہ ہونا ﴿۸۶﴾
اور وہ تمہیں خدا کی آیتوں (کی تبلیغ) سے بعد اسکے کہ وہ تم
پر نازل ہو چکی ہیں روک نہ دیں اور اپنے پروردگار کو پکارتے
رہو اور مشرکوں میں ہرگز نہ ہو جیو ﴿۸۷﴾
اور خدا کیساتھ کسی اور کو معبود (سمجھ کر) نہ پکارنا اسکے سوا کوئی معبود
نہیں۔ اس کی ذات (پاک) کے سوا ہر چیز فنا ہونیوالی ہے
اسی کا حکم ہے اور اسی کی طرف تم لوٹ کر جاؤ گے ﴿۸۸﴾

سورۂ عنکبوت مکی ہے اور اس میں انہتر آیتیں اور سات رکوع ہیں

شروع خدا کا نام لے کر جو بڑا مہربان نہایت رحم والا ہے
الٓمّٓ ﴿۱﴾ کیا لوگ یہ خیال کئے ہوئے ہیں کہ (صرف) یہ کہنے سے
کہ ہم ایمان لے آئے چھوڑ دیئے جائینگے اور اُنکی آزمائش نہیں کی جائیگی ﴿۲﴾
اور جو لوگ ان سے پہلے ہو چکے ہیں ہم نے اُن کو بھی آزمایا تھا
(اور اُن کو بھی آزمائینگے) سو خدا اُنکو ضرور معلوم کریگا جو (اپنے
ایمان میں) سچے ہیں اور اُن کو بھی جو جھوٹے ہیں ﴿۳﴾
کیا وہ لوگ جو بُرے کام کرتے ہیں یہ سمجھے ہوئے ہیں کہ یہ ہمارے

لَا يُفْلِحُ الْكٰفِرُوْنَ ﴿٨٢﴾ ع
تِلْكَ الدَّارُ الْاٰخِرَةُ نَجْعَلُهَا لِلَّذِيْنَ
لَا يُرِيْدُوْنَ عُلُوًّا فِي الْاَرْضِ وَلَا فَسَادًا
وَالْعَاقِبَةُ لِلْمُتَّقِيْنَ ﴿٨٣﴾
مَنْ جَآءَ بِالْحَسَنَةِ فَلَهٗ خَيْرٌ مِّنْهَا ج
وَمَنْ جَآءَ بِالسَّيِّئَةِ فَلَا يُجْزَى الَّذِيْنَ
عَمِلُوا السَّيِّاٰتِ اِلَّا مَا كَانُوْا يَعْمَلُوْنَ ﴿٨٤﴾
اِنَّ الَّذِيْ فَرَضَ عَلَيْكَ الْقُرْاٰنَ لَرَآدُّكَ
اِلٰى مَعَادٍ قُلْ رَّبِّيْٓ اَعْلَمُ مَنْ جَآءَ
بِالْهُدٰى وَمَنْ هُوَ فِيْ ضَلٰلٍ مُّبِيْنٍ ﴿٨٥﴾
وَمَا كُنْتَ تَرْجُوْٓا اَنْ يُّلْقٰٓى اِلَيْكَ الْكِتٰبُ
اِلَّا رَحْمَةً مِّنْ رَّبِّكَ فَلَا تَكُوْنَنَّ
ظَهِيْرًا لِّلْكٰفِرِيْنَ ﴿٨٦﴾
وَلَا يَصُدُّنَّكَ عَنْ اٰيٰتِ اللّٰهِ بَعْدَ اِذْ
اُنْزِلَتْ اِلَيْكَ وَادْعُ اِلٰى رَبِّكَ وَلَا
تَكُوْنَنَّ مِنَ الْمُشْرِكِيْنَ ﴿٨٧﴾
وَلَا تَدْعُ مَعَ اللّٰهِ اِلٰهًا اٰخَرَ لَآ اِلٰهَ
اِلَّا هُوَ كُلُّ شَيْءٍ هَالِكٌ اِلَّا وَجْهَهٗ
لَهُ الْحُكْمُ وَاِلَيْهِ تُرْجَعُوْنَ ﴿٨٨﴾

سُوْرَةُ الْعَنْكَبُوْتِ مَكِّيَّةٌ وَهِيَ تِسْعٌ وَّسِتُّوْنَ اٰيَةً وَّسَبْعُ رُكُوْعَاتٍ

بِسْمِ اللّٰهِ الرَّحْمٰنِ الرَّحِيْمِ
الٓمّٓ ﴿١﴾ اَحَسِبَ النَّاسُ اَنْ يُّتْرَكُوْٓا
اَنْ يَّقُوْلُوْٓا اٰمَنَّا وَهُمْ لَا يُفْتَنُوْنَ ﴿٢﴾
وَلَقَدْ فَتَنَّا الَّذِيْنَ مِنْ قَبْلِهِمْ
فَلَيَعْلَمَنَّ اللّٰهُ الَّذِيْنَ صَدَقُوْا وَ
لَيَعْلَمَنَّ الْكٰذِبِيْنَ ﴿٣﴾
اَمْ حَسِبَ الَّذِيْنَ يَعْمَلُوْنَ السَّيِّاٰتِ

is their judgment!

5. For those whose hopes are in the meeting with Allah, the Term (appointed) by Allah is surely coming: and He hears and knows (all things).

6. And if any strive (with might and main), they do so for their own souls: for Allah is free of all needs from all creation.

7. Those who believe and work righteous deeds,—from them shall We blot out all misdeeds that they have committed, and We shall reward them according to the best of their deeds.

8. We have enjoined on man kindness to parents: but if they (either of them) strive (to force) thee to join with Me (in worship) anything of which thou hast no knowledge, obey them not. Ye have (all) to return to Me, and I will tell you (the truth) of all that ye did.

9. And those who believe and work righteous deeds,—them shall We admit to the company of the Righteous.

10. Then there are among men such as say, "We believe in Allah"; but when they suffer affliction in (the cause of) Allah, they treat men's oppression as if it were the Wrath of Allah! And if help comes (to thee) from thy Lord, they are sure to say, "We have (always) been with you!" Does not Allah know best all that is in the hearts of all Creation!

11. And Allah most certainly knows those who believe, and as certainly those who are Hypocrites.

12. And the Unbelievers say to those who believe: "Follow our path, and we will bear (the consequences) of your faults." Never in the least will they bear their faults: in fact they are liars!

13. They will bear their own burdens, and (other) burdens along with their own, and on the Day of Judgment they will be called to account for their falsehoods.

قابو سے نکل جائینگے۔ جو خیال یہ کرتے ہیں بُرا ہے ﴿۴﴾
جو شخص خدا کی ملاقات کی امید رکھتا ہو تو خدا کا (مقرر کیا ہوا) وقت
ضرور آنیوالا ہے۔ اور وہ سُننے والا اور جاننے والا ہے ﴿۵﴾
اور جو شخص محنت کرتا ہے تو اپنے ہی فائدے کے لئے
محنت کرتا ہے۔ (اور) خدا تو سارے جہان سے
بے پروا ہے ﴿۶﴾
اور جو لوگ ایمان لائے اور نیک عمل کرتے رہے ہم اُن
کے گناہوں کو اُن سے دُور کردیں گے اور اُن کو اُن کے
اعمال کا بہت اچھا بدلہ دیں گے ﴿۷﴾
اور ہم نے انسان کو اپنے ماں باپ کے ساتھ نیک سلوک کرنیکا حکم
دیا ہے (اے مخاطب) اگر تیرے ماں باپ تیرے درپے ہوں کہ تو میرے ساتھ کسی کو
شریک بنائے جسکی حقیقت کی تجھے واقفیت نہیں۔ تو اُنکا کہنا نہ مانیو۔ تم
(سب) کو میری طرف لوٹ کر آنا ہے پھر جو کچھ تم کرتے تھے میں تمکو جتا دونگا ﴿۸﴾
اور جو لوگ ایمان لائے اور نیک عمل کرتے رہے اُن کو ہم
نیک لوگوں میں داخل کریں گے ﴿۹﴾
اور بعض لوگ ایسے ہیں جو کہتے ہیں کہ ہم خدا پر ایمان لائے۔
جب اُن کو خدا (کے رستے) میں کوئی ایذا پہنچتی ہے تو لوگوں کی ایذا
کو (یوں) سمجھتے ہیں جیسے خدا کا عذاب۔ اور اگر تمہارے پروردگار کی
طرف سے مدد پہنچے تو کہتے ہیں کہ ہم تو تمہارے ساتھ تھے۔ کیا جو
اہل عالم کے سینوں میں ہے خدا اس سے واقف نہیں؟ ﴿۱۰﴾
اور خدا اُن کو ضرور معلوم کرے گا جو (سچے) مومن ہیں اور
منافقوں کو بھی معلوم کرکے رہے گا ﴿۱۱﴾
اور جو کافر ہیں وہ مومنوں سے کہتے ہیں کہ ہمارے طریق کی
پیروی کرو ہم تمہارے گناہ اٹھا لینگے۔ حالانکہ وہ اُن کے
گناہوں کا کچھ بھی بوجھ اٹھانے والے نہیں۔ کچھ شک نہیں کہ یہ جھوٹے ہیں ﴿۱۲﴾
اور یہ اپنے بوجھ بھی اٹھائینگے اور اپنے بوجھوں کے ساتھ اور (لوگوں کے) بوجھ بھی
اور جو بہتان یہ باندھتے رہے قیامت کے دن اُنکی اُن سے ضرور پرسش ہوگی ﴿۱۳﴾

اَنْ يَّسْبِقُوْنَا ۭ سَاۗءَ مَا يَحْكُمُوْنَ ﴿۴﴾
مَنْ كَانَ يَرْجُوْا لِقَاۗءَ اللّٰهِ فَاِنَّ اَجَلَ
اللّٰهِ لَاٰتٍ ۭ وَهُوَ السَّمِيْعُ الْعَلِيْمُ ﴿۵﴾
وَمَنْ جَاهَدَ فَاِنَّمَا يُجَاهِدُ
لِنَفْسِهٖ ۭ اِنَّ اللّٰهَ لَغَنِيٌّ عَنِ
الْعٰلَمِيْنَ ﴿۶﴾
وَالَّذِيْنَ اٰمَنُوْا وَعَمِلُوا الصّٰلِحٰتِ
لَنُكَفِّرَنَّ عَنْهُمْ سَيِّاٰتِهِمْ وَلَنَجْزِيَنَّهُمْ
اَحْسَنَ الَّذِيْ كَانُوْا يَعْمَلُوْنَ ﴿۷﴾
وَوَصَّيْنَا الْاِنْسَانَ بِوَالِدَيْهِ حُسْنًا ۭ
وَاِنْ جَاهَدٰكَ لِتُشْرِكَ بِيْ مَا لَيْسَ
لَكَ بِهٖ عِلْمٌ فَلَا تُطِعْهُمَا ۭ اِلَيَّ مَرْجِعُكُمْ
فَاُنَبِّئُكُمْ بِمَا كُنْتُمْ تَعْمَلُوْنَ ﴿۸﴾
وَالَّذِيْنَ اٰمَنُوْا وَعَمِلُوا الصّٰلِحٰتِ لَنُدْخِلَنَّهُمْ
فِي الصّٰلِحِيْنَ ﴿۹﴾
وَمِنَ النَّاسِ مَنْ يَّقُوْلُ اٰمَنَّا بِاللّٰهِ فَاِذَآ
اُوْذِيَ فِي اللّٰهِ جَعَلَ فِتْنَةَ النَّاسِ
كَعَذَابِ اللّٰهِ ۭ وَلَىِٕنْ جَاۗءَ نَصْرٌ مِّنْ
رَّبِّكَ لَيَقُوْلُنَّ اِنَّا كُنَّا مَعَكُمْ ۭ اَوَلَيْسَ
اللّٰهُ بِاَعْلَمَ بِمَا فِيْ صُدُوْرِ الْعٰلَمِيْنَ ﴿۱۰﴾
وَلَيَعْلَمَنَّ اللّٰهُ الَّذِيْنَ اٰمَنُوْا وَلَيَعْلَمَنَّ
الْمُنٰفِقِيْنَ ﴿۱۱﴾
وَقَالَ الَّذِيْنَ كَفَرُوْا لِلَّذِيْنَ اٰمَنُوا اتَّبِعُوْا
سَبِيْلَنَا وَلْنَحْمِلْ خَطٰيٰكُمْ ۭ وَمَا هُمْ
بِحٰمِلِيْنَ مِنْ خَطٰيٰهُمْ مِّنْ شَيْءٍ ۭ اِنَّهُمْ لَكٰذِبُوْنَ ﴿۱۲﴾
وَلَيَحْمِلُنَّ اَثْقَالَهُمْ وَاَثْقَالًا مَّعَ اَثْقَالِهِمْ ۡ
وَلَيُسْـَٔــلُنَّ يَوْمَ الْقِيٰمَةِ عَمَّا كَانُوْا يَفْتَرُوْنَ ﴿۱۳﴾ ع ۱ ۱۳

14. We did send Noah to his people, and he tarried among them a thousand years less fifty: but the Deluge overwhelmed them while they (persisted in) sin.

15. But We saved him and the Companions of the Ark, and We made the (Ark) a Sign for all Peoples!

16. And (We also saved) Abraham: behold, he said to his people, "Serve Allah and fear Him: that will be best for you— if ye understand!

17. "For ye do worship idols besides Allah, and ye invent falsehood. The things that ye worship besides Allah have no power to give you sustenance: then seek ye sustenance from Allah, serve Him, and be grateful to Him: to Him will be your return.

18. "And if ye reject (the Message), so did generations before you: and the duty of the messenger is only to preach publicly (and clearly)."

19. See they not how Allah originates creation, then repeats it: truly that is easy for Allah.

20. Say: "Travel through the earth and see how Allah did originate creation; so will Allah produce a later creation: for Allah has power over all things.

21. "He punishes whom He pleases, and He grants mercy to whom He pleases, and towards Him are ye turned.

22. "Not on earth nor in heaven will ye be able (fleeing) to frustrate (His Plan), nor have ye, besides Allah, any protector or helper."

23. Those who reject the Signs of Allah and the Meeting with Him (in the Hereafter),— it is they who shall despair of My mercy: it is they

اور ہم نے نوح کو اُن کی قوم کی طرف بھیجا تو وہ اُن میں پچاس
برس کم ہزار برس رہے۔ پھر اُن کو طوفان (کے عذاب) نے آ
پکڑا۔ اور وہ ظالم تھے ﴿۱۴﴾
پھر ہم نے نوح کو اور کشتی والوں کو نجات دی۔ اور کشتی
کو اہلِ عالم کے لئے نشانی بنا دیا ﴿۱۵﴾
اور ابراہیم کو (یاد کرو) جب اُنہوں نے اپنی قوم سے کہا کہ خدا کی عبادت کرو
اور اس سے ڈرو۔ اگر تم سمجھ رکھتے ہو تو یہ تمہارے حق میں بہتر ہے ﴿۱۶﴾
تم تو خدا کو چھوڑ کر بتوں کو پوجتے اور طوفان باندھتے ہو
تو جن لوگوں کو تم خدا کے سوا پوجتے ہو وہ تم کو رزق
دینے کا اختیار نہیں رکھتے پس خدا ہی کے ہاں سے رزق
طلب کرو اور اسی کی عبادت کرو اور اسی کا شکر کرو
اسی کی طرف تم لوٹ کر جاؤ گے ﴿۱۷﴾
اور اگر تم (میری) تکذیب کرو تو تم سے پہلے بھی اُمتیں
(اپنے پیغمبروں کی) تکذیب کر چکی ہیں۔ اور پیغمبر کے ذمے
کھول کر سنا دینے کے سوا اور کچھ نہیں ﴿۱۸﴾
کیا اُنہوں نے نہیں دیکھا کہ خدا کس طرح خلقت کو پہلی بار پیدا کرتا پھر
(کس طرح) اسکو بار بار پیدا کرتا رہتا ہے۔ یہ خدا کو آسان ہے ﴿۱۹﴾
کہہ دو کہ ملک میں چلو پھرو اور دیکھو کہ اس نے کس طرح
خلقت کو پہلی دفعہ پیدا کیا ہے پھر خدا ہی پچھلی پیدائش
پیدا کریگا۔ بےشک خدا ہر چیز پر قادر ہے ﴿۲۰﴾
وہ جسے چاہے عذاب دے اور جس پر چاہے رحم کرے۔
اور اُسی کی طرف تم لوٹائے جاؤ گے ﴿۲۱﴾
اور تم (اُس کو) نہ زمین میں عاجز کر سکتے ہو نہ آسمان میں
اور نہ خدا کے سوا تمہارا کوئی دوست ہے اور
نہ مددگار ﴿۲۲﴾
اور جن لوگوں نے خدا کی آیتوں سے اور اس کے ملنے
سے انکار کیا وہ میری رحمت سے نا اُمید ہو گئے ہیں اور

وَلَقَدْ اَرْسَلْنَا نُوْحًا اِلٰى قَوْمِهٖ فَلَبِثَ فِيْهِمْ
اَلْفَ سَنَةٍ اِلَّا خَمْسِيْنَ عَامًا ؕ فَاَخَذَهُمُ
الطُّوْفَانُ وَهُمْ ظٰلِمُوْنَ ﴿۱۴﴾
فَاَنْجَيْنٰهُ وَاَصْحٰبَ السَّفِيْنَةِ وَجَعَلْنٰهَآ
اٰيَةً لِّلْعٰلَمِيْنَ ﴿۱۵﴾
وَاِبْرٰهِيْمَ اِذْ قَالَ لِقَوْمِهِ اعْبُدُوا اللّٰهَ وَاتَّقُوْهُ ؕ
ذٰلِكُمْ خَيْرٌ لَّكُمْ اِنْ كُنْتُمْ تَعْلَمُوْنَ ﴿۱۶﴾
اِنَّمَا تَعْبُدُوْنَ مِنْ دُوْنِ اللّٰهِ اَوْثَانًا وَّ
تَخْلُقُوْنَ اِفْكًا ؕ اِنَّ الَّذِيْنَ تَعْبُدُوْنَ
مِنْ دُوْنِ اللّٰهِ لَا يَمْلِكُوْنَ لَكُمْ رِزْقًا
فَابْتَغُوْا عِنْدَ اللّٰهِ الرِّزْقَ وَاعْبُدُوْهُ
وَاشْكُرُوْا لَهٗ ؕ اِلَيْهِ تُرْجَعُوْنَ ﴿۱۷﴾
وَاِنْ تُكَذِّبُوْا فَقَدْ كَذَّبَ اُمَمٌ مِّنْ
قَبْلِكُمْ ؕ وَمَا عَلَى الرَّسُوْلِ اِلَّا الْبَلٰغُ
الْمُبِيْنُ ﴿۱۸﴾
اَوَلَمْ يَرَوْا كَيْفَ يُبْدِئُ اللّٰهُ الْخَلْقَ ثُمَّ
يُعِيْدُهٗ ؕ اِنَّ ذٰلِكَ عَلَى اللّٰهِ يَسِيْرٌ ﴿۱۹﴾
قُلْ سِيْرُوْا فِى الْاَرْضِ فَانْظُرُوْا كَيْفَ
بَدَاَ الْخَلْقَ ثُمَّ اللّٰهُ يُنْشِئُ النَّشْاَةَ الْاٰخِرَةَ ؕ
اِنَّ اللّٰهَ عَلٰى كُلِّ شَىْءٍ قَدِيْرٌ ﴿۲۰﴾ ۚ
يُعَذِّبُ مَنْ يَّشَآءُ وَيَرْحَمُ مَنْ يَّشَآءُ ۚ
وَاِلَيْهِ تُقْلَبُوْنَ ﴿۲۱﴾
وَمَآ اَنْتُمْ بِمُعْجِزِيْنَ فِى الْاَرْضِ وَلَا فِى
السَّمَآءِ ؗ وَمَا لَكُمْ مِّنْ دُوْنِ اللّٰهِ مِنْ
وَّلِيٍّ وَّلَا نَصِيْرٍ ﴿۲۲﴾ ع
وَالَّذِيْنَ كَفَرُوْا بِاٰيٰتِ اللّٰهِ وَلِقَآئِهٖٓ
اُولٰٓئِكَ يَئِسُوْا مِنْ رَّحْمَتِىْ وَاُولٰٓئِكَ

who will (suffer) a most grievous Chastisement

24. So naught was the answer of (Abraham's) people except that they said: "Slay him or burn him." But Allah did save him from the Fire. Verily in this are Signs for people who believe.

25. And he said: "For you, ye have taken (for worship) idols besides Allah, out of mutual love and regard between yourselves in this life; but on the Day of Judgment ye shall disown each other and curse each other: and your abode will be the Fire, and ye shall have none to help."

26. But Lûṭ believed him: he said: "I will leave home for the sake of my Lord: for He is Exalted in Might, and Wise."

27. And We gave (Abraham) Isaac and Jacob, and ordained among his progeny Prophethood and Revelation, and We Granted him his reward in this life; and he will be in the Hereafter of the Righteous.

28. And (remember) Lûṭ: behold, he said to his people: "Ye do commit lewdness, such as no people in Creation (ever) committed before you.

29. "Do ye indeed approach men, and cut off the highway?— and practise wickedness (even) in your councils?" But his people gave no answer but this: they said: "Bring us the Wrath of Allah if thou tellest the truth."

30. He said: "O my Lord! help Thou me against people who do mischief!"

31. When Our Messengers came to Abraham with the good news, they said: "We are indeed going to destroy the people of this township: for truly they are wicked men."

32. He said: "But there is Lûṭ there." They said: "We know well

ان کو درد دینے والا عذاب ہوگا ﴿۲۳﴾
تو اُن کی قوم کے لوگ جواب میں بولے تو یہ بولے کہ اسے مار ڈالو
یا جلا دو۔ مگر خدا نے اُن کو آگ (کی سوزش) سے بچالیا۔ جو لوگ
ایمان رکھتے ہیں اُن کیلئے اس میں نشانیاں ہیں ﴿۲۴﴾
اور (ابراہیم نے) کہا کہ تم جو خدا کو چھوڑ کر بتوں کو لے بیٹھے ہو
تو دنیا کی زندگی میں باہم دوستی کے لئے (مگر) پھر قیامت
کے دن ایک دوسرے (کی دوستی) سے انکار کر دو گے
اور ایک دوسرے پر لعنت بھیجو گے اور تمہارا ٹھکانا دوزخ
ہوگا اور کوئی تمہارا مددگار نہ ہوگا ﴿۲۵﴾
پس اُن پر (ایک) لوط ایمان لائے اور (ابراہیم) کہنے لگے کہ میں اپنے
پروردگار کیطرف ہجرت کرنیوالا ہوں۔ بیشک وہ غالب حکمت والا ہے ﴿۲۶﴾
اور ہم نے اُن کو اسحٰق اور یعقوب بخشے اور اُن کی اولاد
میں پیغمبری اور کتاب (مقرر) کر دی اور اُن کو دنیا
میں بھی اُن کا صلہ عنایت کیا اور وہ آخرت میں بھی
نیک لوگوں میں ہوں گے ﴿۲۷﴾
اور لوط (کو یاد کرو) جب اُنہوں نے اپنی قوم سے
کہا کہ تم (عجب) بے حیائی کے مرتکب ہوتے ہو۔ تم سے
پہلے اہل عالم میں سے کسی نے ایسا کام نہیں کیا ﴿۲۸﴾
کیا تم (لذت کے ارادے سے) لونڈوں کی طرف مائل ہوتے
اور (مسافروں کی) رہزنی کرتے ہو۔ اور اپنی مجلسوں میں
ناپسندیدہ کام کرتے ہو۔ تو اُن کی قوم کے لوگ جواب میں بولے
تو یہ بولے کہ اگر تم سچے ہو تو ہم پر عذاب لے آؤ ﴿۲۹﴾
(لوط نے) کہا کہ اے میرے پروردگار اِن مفسد لوگوں کے مقابلے میں مجھے نصرت عنایت فرما ﴿۳۰﴾
اور جب ہمارے فرشتے ابراہیم کے پاس خوشی کی خبر لے کر آئے
تو کہنے لگے کہ ہم اس بستی کے لوگوں کو ہلاک کر دینے والے
ہیں کہ یہاں کے رہنے والے نافرمان ہیں ﴿۳۱﴾
(ابراہیم نے) کہا کہ اس میں تو لوط بھی ہیں۔ وہ کہنے لگے کہ جو

لَهُمْ عَذَابٌ أَلِيمٌ ﴿۲۳﴾
فَمَا كَانَ جَوَابَ قَوْمِهِ إِلَّا أَنْ قَالُوا
اقْتُلُوهُ أَوْ حَرِّقُوهُ فَأَنْجَاهُ اللَّهُ مِنَ
النَّارِ ۚ إِنَّ فِي ذَٰلِكَ لَآيَاتٍ لِقَوْمٍ يُؤْمِنُونَ ﴿۲۴﴾
وَقَالَ إِنَّمَا اتَّخَذْتُمْ مِنْ دُونِ اللَّهِ
أَوْثَانًا مَوَدَّةَ بَيْنِكُمْ فِي الْحَيَاةِ الدُّنْيَا ۖ
ثُمَّ يَوْمَ الْقِيَامَةِ يَكْفُرُ بَعْضُكُمْ بِبَعْضٍ
وَيَلْعَنُ بَعْضُكُمْ بَعْضًا وَمَأْوَاكُمُ
النَّارُ وَمَا لَكُمْ مِنْ نَاصِرِينَ ﴿۲۵﴾
فَآمَنَ لَهُ لُوطٌ ۘ وَقَالَ إِنِّي مُهَاجِرٌ إِلَىٰ (وقف لازم)
رَبِّي ۖ إِنَّهُ هُوَ الْعَزِيزُ الْحَكِيمُ ﴿۲۶﴾
وَوَهَبْنَا لَهُ إِسْحَاقَ وَيَعْقُوبَ وَجَعَلْنَا
فِي ذُرِّيَّتِهِ النُّبُوَّةَ وَالْكِتَابَ وَآتَيْنَاهُ
أَجْرَهُ فِي الدُّنْيَا ۖ وَإِنَّهُ فِي الْآخِرَةِ
لَمِنَ الصَّالِحِينَ ﴿۲۷﴾
وَلُوطًا إِذْ قَالَ لِقَوْمِهِ إِنَّكُمْ لَتَأْتُونَ
الْفَاحِشَةَ مَا سَبَقَكُمْ بِهَا مِنْ أَحَدٍ
مِنَ الْعَالَمِينَ ﴿۲۸﴾
أَئِنَّكُمْ لَتَأْتُونَ الرِّجَالَ وَتَقْطَعُونَ
السَّبِيلَ وَتَأْتُونَ فِي نَادِيكُمُ الْمُنْكَرَ ۖ فَمَا
كَانَ جَوَابَ قَوْمِهِ إِلَّا أَنْ قَالُوا ائْتِنَا بِعَذَابِ
اللَّهِ إِنْ كُنْتَ مِنَ الصَّادِقِينَ ﴿۲۹﴾
ع ۲ / ۱۵ قَالَ رَبِّ انْصُرْنِي عَلَى الْقَوْمِ الْمُفْسِدِينَ ﴿۳۰﴾
وَلَمَّا جَاءَتْ رُسُلُنَا إِبْرَاهِيمَ بِالْبُشْرَىٰ
قَالُوا إِنَّا مُهْلِكُو أَهْلِ هَٰذِهِ الْقَرْيَةِ ۖ
إِنَّ أَهْلَهَا كَانُوا ظَالِمِينَ ﴿۳۱﴾
قَالَ إِنَّ فِيهَا لُوطًا ۚ قَالُوا نَحْنُ أَعْلَمُ بِمَنْ

who is there: we will certainly save him and his following,— except his wife: she is of those who lag behind!"

33. And when Our Messengers came to Lûṭ, he was grieved on their account, and felt himself powerless (to protect) them: but they said: "Fear thou not, nor grieve: We are (here) to save thee and thy following, except thy wife: she is of those who lag behind.

34. "For we are going to bring down on the people of this township a Punishment from heaven, because they have been wickedly rebellious."

35. And We have left thereof an evident Sign, for any people who (care to) understand.

36. To the Madyan (people) (We sent) their brother Shu'aib. Then he said: "O my people! serve Allah, and fear the Last Day: nor commit evil on the earth, with intent to do mischief."

37. But they rejected him: then the mighty Blast seized them, and they lay prostrate in their homes by the morning.

38. (Remember also) the 'Ād and the Thamûd (people): clearly will appear to you from (the traces) of their buildings (their fate): Satan made their deeds alluring to them, and kept them back from the Path, though they were keen-sighted.

39. (Remember also) Qārûn, Pharaoh, and Hāmān: there came to them Moses with Clear Signs, but they behaved with insolence on the earth; yet they could not overreach (Us).

40. Each one of them We seized for his crime: of them, against some We sent a violent tornado (with showers of stones); some were caught by a (mighty) Blast; some We caused the earth to swallow up; and some We drowned (in the waters): it was not Allah Who wronged them: they wronged themselves.

لوگ یہاں رہتے ہیں ہمیں سب معلوم ہیں ہم اُن کو اور اُنکے گھر والوں
کو بچالینگے بجز اُنکی بیوی کے کہ وہ پیچھے رہنے والوں میں ہوگی ﴿۳۲﴾
اور جب ہمارے فرشتے لوط کے پاس آئے تو وہ اُن (کی وجہ) سے ناخوش
اور تنگ دل ہوئے۔ فرشتوں نے کہا کچھ خوف نہ کیجئے۔ اور نہ رنج کیجئے
ہم آپکو اور آپکے گھر والوں کو بچالینگے مگر آپ کی بیوی کہ پیچھے
رہنے والوں میں ہوگی ﴿۳۳﴾
ہم اس بستی کے رہنے والوں پر اس سبب سے
کہ یہ بدکرداری کرتے رہے ہیں آسمان سے عذاب نازل
کرنے والے ہیں ﴿۳۴﴾
اور ہم نے سمجھنے والے لوگوں کیلئے اس بستی سے ایک کھلی
نشانی چھوڑ دی ﴿۳۵﴾
اور مدین کی طرف اُنکے بھائی شعیب کو (بھیجا) تو انہوں
نے کہا اے قوم خدا کی عبادت کرو اور پچھلے دن (کے
آنے) کی اُمید رکھو اور ملک میں فساد نہ مچاؤ ﴿۳۶﴾
مگر انہوں نے اُنکو جھوٹا سمجھا سو اُنکو زلزلے (کے عذاب) نے
آپکڑا اور وہ اپنے گھروں میں اوندھے پڑے رہ گئے ﴿۳۷﴾
اور عاد اور ثمود کو بھی (ہم نے ہلاک کر دیا) چنانچہ اُنکے (ویران) گھر
تمہاری آنکھوں کے سامنے ہیں اور شیطان نے اُنکے اعمال اُنکو آراستہ کر دکھائے اور
اُنکو (سیدھے) رستے سے روک دیا۔ حالانکہ وہ دیکھنے والے (لوگ) تھے ﴿۳۸﴾
اور قارون اور فرعون اور ہامان کو بھی (ہلاک کر دیا) اور اُنکے پاس
موسیٰ کھلی نشانیاں لیکر آئے تو وہ ملک میں مغرور ہو گئے۔ اور
وہ (ہمارے) قابو سے نکل جانے والے نہ تھے ﴿۳۹﴾
تو ہم نے سب کو اُن کے گناہوں کے سبب پکڑ لیا سو اُن میں
کچھ تو ایسے تھے جن پر ہم نے پتھروں کا مینہ برسایا۔ اور کچھ ایسے
تھے جن کو چنگھاڑ نے آپکڑا اور کچھ ایسے تھے جن کو ہم نے زمین
میں دھنسا دیا۔ اور کچھ ایسے تھے جنکو غرق کر دیا اور خدا ایسا
نہ تھا کہ اُن پر ظلم کرتا لیکن وہی اپنے آپ پر ظلم کرتے تھے ﴿۴۰﴾

فِيهَا لَنُنَجِّيَنَّهُ وَأَهْلَهُ إِلَّا امْرَأَتَهُ ز
كَانَتْ مِنَ الْغٰبِرِينَ ﴿٣٢﴾
وَلَمَّا أَنْ جَاءَتْ رُسُلُنَا لُوطًا سِيءَ بِهِمْ
وَضَاقَ بِهِمْ ذَرْعًا وَقَالُوا لَا تَخَفْ
وَلَا تَحْزَنْ قف إِنَّا مُنَجُّوكَ وَأَهْلَكَ إِلَّا
امْرَأَتَكَ كَانَتْ مِنَ الْغٰبِرِينَ ﴿٣٣﴾
إِنَّا مُنْزِلُونَ عَلَىٰ أَهْلِ هٰذِهِ الْقَرْيَةِ
رِجْزًا مِنَ السَّمَاءِ بِمَا كَانُوا
يَفْسُقُونَ ﴿٣٤﴾
وَلَقَدْ تَرَكْنَا مِنْهَا آيَةً بَيِّنَةً لِقَوْمٍ
يَعْقِلُونَ ﴿٣٥﴾
وَإِلَىٰ مَدْيَنَ أَخَاهُمْ شُعَيْبًا فَقَالَ
يٰقَوْمِ اعْبُدُوا اللّٰهَ وَارْجُوا الْيَوْمَ الْآخِرَ
وَلَا تَعْثَوْا فِي الْأَرْضِ مُفْسِدِينَ ﴿٣٦﴾
فَكَذَّبُوهُ فَأَخَذَتْهُمُ الرَّجْفَةُ فَأَصْبَحُوا
فِي دَارِهِمْ جٰثِمِينَ ﴿٣٧﴾
وَعَادًا وَثَمُودَا وَقَدْ تَبَيَّنَ لَكُمْ مِنْ
مَسٰكِنِهِمْ قف وَزَيَّنَ لَهُمُ الشَّيْطٰنُ أَعْمَالَهُمْ
فَصَدَّهُمْ عَنِ السَّبِيلِ وَكَانُوا مُسْتَبْصِرِينَ ﴿٣٨﴾
وَقَارُونَ وَفِرْعَوْنَ وَهَامٰنَ قف وَلَقَدْ
جَاءَهُمْ مُوسَىٰ بِالْبَيِّنٰتِ فَاسْتَكْبَرُوا فِي
الْأَرْضِ وَمَا كَانُوا سٰبِقِينَ ﴿٣٩﴾
فَكُلًّا أَخَذْنَا بِذَنْبِهِ فَمِنْهُمْ مَنْ أَرْسَلْنَا
عَلَيْهِ حَاصِبًا وَمِنْهُمْ مَنْ أَخَذَتْهُ
الصَّيْحَةُ وَمِنْهُمْ مَنْ خَسَفْنَا بِهِ الْأَرْضَ
وَمِنْهُمْ مَنْ أَغْرَقْنَا وَمَا كَانَ اللّٰهُ لِيَظْلِمَهُمْ
وَلٰكِنْ كَانُوا أَنْفُسَهُمْ يَظْلِمُونَ ﴿٤٠﴾

41. The parable of those who take protectors other than Allah is that of the Spider, who builds (to itself) a house; but truly the flimsiest of houses is the Spider's house;— if they but knew.

42. Verily Allah doth know of (every thing) whatever that they call upon besides Him: and He is Exalted (in power), Wise.
43. And such are the Parables We set forth for mankind, but only those understand them who have Knowledge.
44. Allah created the heavens and the earth in truth: verily in that is a Sign for those who believe.

45. Recite what is sent of the Book by inspiration to thee, and establish regular Prayer: for Prayer restrains from shameful and evil deeds; and remembrance of Allah is the greatest (thing in life) without doubt. And Allah knows the (deeds) that ye do.
46. And dispute ye not with the People of the Book, except in the best way, unless it be with those of them who do wrong but say, "We believe in the Revelation which has come down to us and in that which came down to you; our God and your God is One; and it is to Him we submit (in Islām)."

47. And thus (it is) that We have sent down the Book to thee. So the People of the Book believe therein, as also do some of these (Pagan Arabs): and none but Unbelievers reject Our Signs.

48. And thou wast not (able) to recite a Book before this (Book came), nor art thou (able) to transcribe it with thy right hand: in that case, indeed, would the talkers of vanities have doubted.
49. Nay, here are Signs self-evident in the hearts of those endowed with knowledge: and

جن لوگوں نے خدا کے سوا (اوروں کو) کارساز بنا رکھا ہے
اُن کی مثال مکڑی کی سی ہے کہ وہ بھی ایک (طرح کا) گھر
بناتی ہے۔ اور کچھ شک نہیں کہ تمام گھروں سے کمزور
مکڑی کا گھر ہے کاش یہ (اس بات کو) جانتے ﴿۴۱﴾
یہ جس چیز کو خدا کے سوا پکارتے ہیں (خواہ) وہ کچھ ہی ہو خدا
اُسے جانتا ہے۔ اور وہ غالب (اور) حکمت والا ہے ﴿۴۲﴾
اور یہ مثالیں ہم لوگوں کے (سمجھانے کے) لئے بیان کرتے
ہیں اور اسے تو اہلِ دانش ہی سمجھتے ہیں ﴿۴۳﴾
خدا نے آسمانوں اور زمین کو حکمت کے ساتھ پیدا کیا ہے۔ کچھ شک
نہیں کہ ایمان والوں کے لئے اس میں نشانی ہے ﴿۴۴﴾
(اے محمدؐ) یہ کتاب جو تمہاری طرف وحی کی گئی ہے اس کو پڑھا
کرو اور نماز کے پابند رہو۔ کچھ شک نہیں کہ نماز بے حیائی
اور بری باتوں سے روکتی ہے۔ اور خدا کا ذکر بڑا (اچھا کام)
ہے۔ اور جو کچھ تم کرتے ہو خدا اسے جانتا ہے ﴿۴۵﴾
اور اہلِ کتاب سے جھگڑا نہ کرو مگر ایسے طریق سے کہ نہایت
اچھا ہو۔ ہاں جو ان میں سے بے انصافی کریں (اُن کے ساتھ
اسی طرح مجادلہ کرو) اور کہہ دو کہ جو (کتاب) ہم پر اُتری اور
جو (کتابیں) تم پر اُتریں ہم سب پر ایمان رکھتے ہیں اور ہمارا اور
تمہارا معبود ایک ہی ہے اور ہم اُسی کے فرمانبردار ہیں ﴿۴۶﴾
اور اسی طرح ہم نے تمہاری طرف کتاب اُتاری ہے۔ تو جن
لوگوں کو ہم نے کتابیں دی تھیں وہ اس پر ایمان لے آتے ہیں۔
اور بعض ان (مشرک) لوگوں میں سے بھی اس پر ایمان لے آتے ہیں۔
اور ہماری آیتوں سے وہی انکار کرتے ہیں جو کافر ازلی ہیں ﴿۴۷﴾
اور تم اس سے پہلے کوئی کتاب نہیں پڑھتے تھے اور نہ اسے
اپنے ہاتھ سے لکھ ہی سکتے تھے ایسا ہوتا تو اہلِ باطل ضرور شک کرتے ﴿۴۸﴾
بلکہ یہ روشن آیتیں ہیں۔ جن لوگوں کو علم دیا گیا ہے اُن کے
سینوں میں (محفوظ)، اور ہماری آیتوں سے وہی لوگ انکار

مَثَلُ الَّذِيْنَ اتَّخَذُوْا مِنْ دُوْنِ اللّٰهِ
اَوْلِيَآءَ كَمَثَلِ الْعَنْكَبُوْتِ ۚ اِتَّخَذَتْ بَيْتًا ۗ
وَاِنَّ اَوْهَنَ الْبُيُوْتِ لَبَيْتُ الْعَنْكَبُوْتِ ۘ
لَوْ كَانُوْا يَعْلَمُوْنَ ﴿۴۱﴾
اِنَّ اللّٰهَ يَعْلَمُ مَا يَدْعُوْنَ مِنْ دُوْنِهٖ
مِنْ شَيْءٍ ۗ وَهُوَ الْعَزِيْزُ الْحَكِيْمُ ﴿۴۲﴾
وَتِلْكَ الْاَمْثَالُ نَضْرِبُهَا لِلنَّاسِ ۚ وَمَا
يَعْقِلُهَآ اِلَّا الْعٰلِمُوْنَ ﴿۴۳﴾
خَلَقَ اللّٰهُ السَّمٰوٰتِ وَالْاَرْضَ بِالْحَقِّ ۗ
اِنَّ فِيْ ذٰلِكَ لَاٰيَةً لِّلْمُؤْمِنِيْنَ ﴿۴۴﴾
اُتْلُ مَآ اُوْحِيَ اِلَيْكَ مِنَ الْكِتٰبِ
وَاَقِمِ الصَّلٰوةَ ۗ اِنَّ الصَّلٰوةَ تَنْهٰى عَنِ
الْفَحْشَآءِ وَالْمُنْكَرِ ۗ وَلَذِكْرُ اللّٰهِ اَكْبَرُ ۗ
وَاللّٰهُ يَعْلَمُ مَا تَصْنَعُوْنَ ﴿۴۵﴾
وَلَا تُجَادِلُوْٓا اَهْلَ الْكِتٰبِ اِلَّا بِالَّتِيْ هِيَ
اَحْسَنُ ۖ اِلَّا الَّذِيْنَ ظَلَمُوْا مِنْهُمْ وَقُوْلُوْٓا
اٰمَنَّا بِالَّذِيْٓ اُنْزِلَ اِلَيْنَا وَاُنْزِلَ اِلَيْكُمْ
وَاِلٰهُنَا وَاِلٰهُكُمْ وَاحِدٌ وَّنَحْنُ لَهٗ
مُسْلِمُوْنَ ﴿۴۶﴾
وَكَذٰلِكَ اَنْزَلْنَآ اِلَيْكَ الْكِتٰبَ ۗ فَالَّذِيْنَ
اٰتَيْنٰهُمُ الْكِتٰبَ يُؤْمِنُوْنَ بِهٖ ۚ وَمِنْ هٰٓؤُلَآءِ
مَنْ يُّؤْمِنُ بِهٖ ۗ وَمَا يَجْحَدُ بِاٰيٰتِنَآ اِلَّا
الْكٰفِرُوْنَ ﴿۴۷﴾
وَمَا كُنْتَ تَتْلُوْا مِنْ قَبْلِهٖ مِنْ كِتٰبٍ وَّلَا
تَخُطُّهٗ بِيَمِيْنِكَ اِذًا لَّارْتَابَ الْمُبْطِلُوْنَ ﴿۴۸﴾
بَلْ هُوَ اٰيٰتٌۢ بَيِّنٰتٌ فِيْ صُدُوْرِ الَّذِيْنَ
اُوْتُوا الْعِلْمَ ۗ وَمَا يَجْحَدُ بِاٰيٰتِنَآ اِلَّا

none but the unjust reject Our Signs.

50. Yet they say: "Why are not Signs sent down to him from his Lord?" Say: "The Signs are indeed with Allah: and I am indeed a clear Warner."

51. And is it not enough for them that We have sent down to thee the Book which is rehearsed to them? Verily, in it is Mercy and a Reminder to those who believe.

52. Say: "Enough is Allah for a Witness between me and you: He knows what is in the heavens and on earth." And it is those who believe in vanities and reject Allah, that are the losers.

53. They ask thee to hasten on the Punishment (for them): had it not been for a term (of respite) appointed, the Punishment would certainly have come to them: and it will certainly reach them,— of a sudden, while they perceive not!

54. They ask thee to hasten on the Punishment: but, of a surety, Hell will encompass the rejecters of Faith!—

55. On the Day that the Punishment shall cover them from above them and from below them, and (a Voice) shall say: "Taste ye (the fruits) of your deeds"!

56. O My servants who believe! truly, spacious is My Earth: therefore serve ye Me— (and Me alone)!

57. Every soul shall have a taste of death: in the end to Us shall ye be brought back.

58. But those who believe and work deeds of righteousness— to them shall We give a Home in Heaven,— lofty mansions beneath which flow rivers,—to dwell therein for aye;—an excellent reward for those who do (good)!—

59. Those who persevere in patience, and put their trust in their Lord and Cherisher.

60. How many are the creatures that carry not their own sustenance?

کرتے ہیں جو بے انصاف ہیں ﴿۴۹﴾
اور (کافر) کہتے ہیں کہ اس پر اس کے پروردگار کی طرف سے
نشانیاں کیوں نازل نہیں ہوئیں کہہ دو کہ نشانیاں تو خدا ہی
کے پاس ہیں۔ اور میں تو کھلم کھلا ہدایت کرنے والا ہوں ﴿۵۰﴾
کیا ان لوگوں کیلئے یہ کافی نہیں کہ ہم نے تم پر کتاب نازل کی
جو اُن کو پڑھ کر سنائی جاتی ہے۔ کچھ شک نہیں کہ مومن لوگوں
کیلئے اس میں رحمت اور نصیحت ہے ﴿۵۱﴾
کہہ دو کہ میرے اور تمہارے درمیان خدا ہی گواہ کافی ہے
جو چیز آسمانوں میں اور زمین میں ہے وہ سب کو جانتا ہے۔ اور جن
لوگوں نے باطل کو مانا اور خدا سے انکار کیا وہی نقصان اُٹھانے والے ہیں ﴿۵۲﴾
اور یہ لوگ تم سے عذاب کیلئے جلدی کر رہے ہیں اگر ایک وقت مقرر
(نہ ہو چکا) ہوتا تو اُن پر عذاب آ بھی گیا ہوتا۔ اور وہ (کسی وقت میں)
اُن پر ضرور ناگہاں آ کر رہیگا اور اُنکو معلوم بھی نہ ہوگا ﴿۵۳﴾
یہ تم سے عذاب کیلئے جلدی کر رہے ہیں۔ اور دوزخ تو کافروں
کو گھیر لینے والی ہے ﴿۵۴﴾
جس دن عذاب اُن کو اُن کے اُوپر سے اور نیچے سے
ڈھانک لیگا اور (خدا) فرمائے گا کہ جو کام تم کیا کرتے تھے
(اب) اُن کا مزہ چکھو ﴿۵۵﴾
اے میرے بندو جو ایمان لائے ہو میری زمین فراخ ہے
تو میری ہی عبادت کرو ﴿۵۶﴾
ہر متنفس موت کا مزہ چکھنے والا ہے پھر تم ہماری ہی
طرف لوٹ کر آؤ گے ﴿۵۷﴾
اور جو لوگ ایمان لائے اور نیک عمل کرتے رہے اُن کو ہم بہشت
کے اُونچے اُونچے محلوں میں جگہ دینگے۔ جنکے نیچے نہریں بہ رہی
ہیں ہمیشہ ان میں رہیں گے۔ (نیک عمل کرنیوالوں کا (یہ) خوب بدلہ ہے) ﴿۵۸﴾
جو صبر کرتے اور اپنے پروردگار پر بھروسا رکھتے ہیں ﴿۵۹﴾
اور بہت سے جانور ہیں جو اپنا رزق اُٹھائے نہیں پھرتے خدا ہی انکو

الظّٰلِمُوْنَ ﴿٤٩﴾
وَقَالُوْا لَوْلَآ اُنْزِلَ عَلَيْهِ اٰيٰتٌ مِّنْ
رَّبِّهٖ ۭ قُلْ اِنَّمَا الْاٰيٰتُ عِنْدَ اللّٰهِ ۭ وَ
اِنَّمَآ اَنَا نَذِيْرٌ مُّبِيْنٌ ﴿٥٠﴾
اَوَلَمْ يَكْفِهِمْ اَنَّآ اَنْزَلْنَا عَلَيْكَ الْكِتٰبَ
يُتْلٰى عَلَيْهِمْ ۭ اِنَّ فِيْ ذٰلِكَ لَرَحْمَةً وَّ
ع ذِكْرٰى لِقَوْمٍ يُّؤْمِنُوْنَ ﴿٥١﴾
قُلْ كَفٰى بِاللّٰهِ بَيْنِيْ وَبَيْنَكُمْ شَهِيْدًا ۚ يَعْلَمُ
مَا فِي السَّمٰوٰتِ وَالْاَرْضِ ۭ وَالَّذِيْنَ اٰمَنُوْا
بِالْبَاطِلِ وَكَفَرُوْا بِاللّٰهِ ۙ اُولٰۗىِٕكَ هُمُ الْخٰسِرُوْنَ ﴿٥٢﴾
وَيَسْتَعْجِلُوْنَكَ بِالْعَذَابِ ۭ وَلَوْلَآ اَجَلٌ مُّسَمًّى
لَّجَاۗءَهُمُ الْعَذَابُ ۭ وَلَيَاْتِيَنَّهُمْ بَغْتَةً وَّ
هُمْ لَا يَشْعُرُوْنَ ﴿٥٣﴾
يَسْتَعْجِلُوْنَكَ بِالْعَذَابِ ۭ وَاِنَّ جَهَنَّمَ
لَمُحِيْطَةٌ بِالْكٰفِرِيْنَ ﴿٥٤﴾
يَوْمَ يَغْشٰىهُمُ الْعَذَابُ مِنْ فَوْقِهِمْ
وَمِنْ تَحْتِ اَرْجُلِهِمْ وَيَقُوْلُ ذُوْقُوْا
مَا كُنْتُمْ تَعْمَلُوْنَ ﴿٥٥﴾
يٰعِبَادِيَ الَّذِيْنَ اٰمَنُوْٓا اِنَّ اَرْضِيْ وَاسِعَةٌ
فَاِيَّايَ فَاعْبُدُوْنِ ﴿٥٦﴾
كُلُّ نَفْسٍ ذَاۗىِٕقَةُ الْمَوْتِ ۣ ثُمَّ اِلَيْنَا
تُرْجَعُوْنَ ﴿٥٧﴾
وَالَّذِيْنَ اٰمَنُوْا وَعَمِلُوا الصّٰلِحٰتِ لَنُبَوِّئَنَّهُمْ
مِّنَ الْجَنَّةِ غُرَفًا تَجْرِيْ مِنْ تَحْتِهَا الْاَنْهٰرُ
خٰلِدِيْنَ فِيْهَا ۭ نِعْمَ اَجْرُ الْعٰمِلِيْنَ ﴿٥٨﴾
الَّذِيْنَ صَبَرُوْا وَعَلٰي رَبِّهِمْ يَتَوَكَّلُوْنَ ﴿٥٩﴾
وَكَاَيِّنْ مِّنْ دَاۗبَّةٍ لَّا تَحْمِلُ رِزْقَهَا

It is Allah Who feeds (both) them and you: for He hears and knows (all things).

61. If indeed thou ask them who has created the heavens and the earth and subjected the sun and the moon (to His Law), they will certainly reply, "Allah". How are they then deluded away (from the truth)?

62. Allah enlarges the sustenance (which He gives) to whichever of His servants He pleases; and He (similarly) grants by (strict) measure, (as He pleases): for Allah has full knowledge of all things.

63. And if indeed thou ask them who it is that sends down rain from the sky, and gives life therewith to the earth after its death, they will certainly reply, "Allah!" Say, "Praise be to Allah!" But most of them understand not.

64. What is the life of this world but amusement and play? But verily the Home of the Hereafter,—that is life indeed, if they but knew.

65. Now, if they embark on a boat, they call on Allah, making their devotion sincerely (and exclusively) to Him; but when He has delivered them safely to (dry) land, behold! they give a share (of their worship to others)!—

66. Disdaining ungratefully Our gifts, and giving themselves up to (worldly) enjoyment! But soon will they know.

67. Do they not then see that We have made a Sanctuary secure, and that men are being snatched away from all around them? Then, do they believe in that which is vain, and reject the Grace of Allah?

68. And who does more wrong than he who invents a lie against Allah or rejects the Truth when it reaches him? Is there not a home in Hell for those who reject Faith?

69. And those who strive in Our (Cause),—We will certainly guide them to Our Paths: for verily Allah is with those who do right.

رزق دیتا ہے اور تم کو بھی۔ اور وہ سننے والا اور جاننے والا ہے ٦٠
اور اگر اُن سے پوچھو کہ آسمانوں اور زمین کو کس نے پیدا کیا۔
اور سُورج اور چاند کو کس نے (تمہارے) زیر فرمان کیا تو کہہ دینگے
خدا نے۔ تو پھر یہ کہاں اُلٹے جا رہے ہیں ٦١
خدا ہی اپنے بندوں میں سے جسکے لئے چاہتا ہے روزی فراخ کر دیتا
ہے اور جسکے لئے چاہتا ہے تنگ کر دیتا ہے بیشک خدا ہر چیز سے واقف ہے ٦٢
اور اگر تم اُن سے پوچھو کہ آسمان سے پانی کس نے برسایا پھر
اس سے زمین کو اسکے مرنے کے بعد (کس نے) زندہ کیا تو کہہ دینگے
کہ خدا نے۔ کہہ دو کہ خدا کا شکر ہے لیکن انمیں اکثر نہیں سمجھتے ٦٣
اور یہ دنیا کی زندگی تو صرف کھیل اور تماشا ہے اور (ہمیشہ
کی) زندگی (کا مقام) تو آخرت کا گھر ہے۔ کاش یہ
(لوگ) سمجھتے ٦٤
پھر جب یہ کشتی میں سوار ہوتے ہیں تو خدا کو پکارتے (اور) خالص
اُسی کی عبادت کرتے ہیں لیکن جب وہ اُنکو نجات دیکر خشکی
پر پہنچا دیتا ہے تو جھٹ شرک کرنے لگ جاتے ہیں ٦٥
تاکہ جو ہمنے اُنکو بخشا ہے اسکی ناشکری کریں اور فائدہ اٹھائیں (سو خیر) عنقریب اُنکو معلوم ہو جائیگا ٦٦
کیا انہوں نے نہیں دیکھا کہ ہمنے حرم کو مقام امن بنایا ہے
اور لوگ اُن کے گرد و نواح سے اُچک لئے جاتے ہیں۔ کیا یہ
لوگ باطل پر اعتقاد رکھتے ہیں اور خدا کی نعمتوں کی ناشکری کرتے ہیں؟ ٦٧
اور اس سے ظالم کون جو خدا پر جھوٹ بہتان باندھے یا
جب حق بات اُسکے پاس آئے تو اُسکی تکذیب کرے کیا
کافروں کا ٹھکانا جہنم میں نہیں ہے؟ ٦٨
اور جن لوگوں نے ہمارے لئے کوشش کی ہم اُن کو ضرور
اپنے رستے دکھا دینگے۔ اور خدا تو نیکو کاروں کے ساتھ ہے ٦٩

اللّٰهُ يَرْزُقُهَا وَإِيَّاكُمْ ۖ وَهُوَ السَّمِيعُ الْعَلِيمُ ٦٠
وَلَئِن سَأَلْتَهُم مَّنْ خَلَقَ السَّمٰوٰتِ وَ
الْأَرْضَ وَسَخَّرَ الشَّمْسَ وَالْقَمَرَ لَيَقُولُنَّ
اللّٰهُ ۖ فَأَنّٰى يُؤْفَكُونَ ٦١
اللّٰهُ يَبْسُطُ الرِّزْقَ لِمَن يَشَاءُ مِنْ
عِبَادِهِ وَيَقْدِرُ لَهُ ۚ إِنَّ اللّٰهَ بِكُلِّ شَيْءٍ عَلِيمٌ ٦٢
وَلَئِن سَأَلْتَهُم مَّن نَّزَّلَ مِنَ السَّمَاءِ مَاءً
فَأَحْيَا بِهِ الْأَرْضَ مِن بَعْدِ مَوْتِهَا لَيَقُولُنَّ اللّٰهُ ۚ
قُلِ الْحَمْدُ لِلّٰهِ ۚ بَلْ أَكْثَرُهُمْ لَا يَعْقِلُونَ ٦٣
وَمَا هٰذِهِ الْحَيٰوةُ الدُّنْيَا إِلَّا لَهْوٌ وَلَعِبٌ ۚ
وَإِنَّ الدَّارَ الْآخِرَةَ لَهِيَ الْحَيَوَانُ ۚ لَوْ
كَانُوا يَعْلَمُونَ ٦٤
فَإِذَا رَكِبُوا فِي الْفُلْكِ دَعَوُا اللّٰهَ مُخْلِصِينَ
لَهُ الدِّينَ ۚ فَلَمَّا نَجّٰىهُمْ إِلَى الْبَرِّ إِذَا هُمْ
يُشْرِكُونَ ٦٥
لِيَكْفُرُوا بِمَا آتَيْنٰهُمْ ۚ وَلِيَتَمَتَّعُوا ۖ فَسَوْفَ يَعْلَمُونَ ٦٦
أَوَلَمْ يَرَوْا أَنَّا جَعَلْنَا حَرَمًا آمِنًا وَيُتَخَطَّفُ
النَّاسُ مِنْ حَوْلِهِمْ ۚ أَفَبِالْبَاطِلِ يُؤْمِنُونَ
وَبِنِعْمَةِ اللّٰهِ يَكْفُرُونَ ٦٧
وَمَنْ أَظْلَمُ مِمَّنِ افْتَرٰى عَلَى اللّٰهِ كَذِبًا
أَوْ كَذَّبَ بِالْحَقِّ لَمَّا جَاءَهُ ۚ أَلَيْسَ فِي جَهَنَّمَ
مَثْوًى لِّلْكٰفِرِينَ ٦٨
وَالَّذِينَ جٰهَدُوا فِينَا لَنَهْدِيَنَّهُمْ سُبُلَنَا ۚ
وَإِنَّ اللّٰهَ لَمَعَ الْمُحْسِنِينَ ٦٩

SÛRA–30
AR-RÛM
(INTRODUCTION)

This Sûra, as remarked in the Introduction to the last Sûra, deals with the question of Ma'ãd or the Final End of Things, from various points of view. In the last Sûra, we saw that Revelation was linked up with Life and Conduct, and Time (looking backwards and forwards) figured forth the frailty of this Life. In this Sûra the Time theme and its mystery are brought into relation with human history in the foreground and the evolution of the world in all its aspects in the background. The corruption introduced by man is cleared away by Allah, Whose Universal Plan points to the Hereafter. We shall see that the next two Sûras (31 and 32) present the theme in other aspects. All four are introduced with the Abbreviated Letters A.L.M. which (without being dogmatic) I have suggested as symbolical of the Past, Present and Future.

The choronology of this Sûra is significant. It was revealed about the 7th or the 6th year *before* the Hijrat, corresponding to 615-16 of the Christian era, when the tide of Persian conquest over the Roman Empire was running strong. The Christian Empire of Rome had lost Jerusalem to the Persians, and Christianity had been humbled in the dust. At that time it seemed outside the bounds of human possibility, even to one intimately acquainted with the inner resources and conditions of the Persian and Roman armies and empires, that the tables would be turned and the position reversed within the space of eight or nine years. The pro-Persian Pagan Quraish rejoiced exceedingly, and redoubled their taunts and persecution against the Holy Prophet, whose Message was a renewal of the Message of Christ preached in Jerusalem. Then was this passage 30: 1-6 revealed, clearly foreshadowing the final defeat of Persia as a prelude to the destruction of the Persian Empire. There is no doubt about the probhecy and its fulfilment. For the exulting Pagans of Makka laid a heavy wager against the fulfilment of the prophecy with Ḥadhrat Abû Bakr, and they lost it on its fulfilment.

But the rise and fall even of such mighty empires as the Persian and Roman Empires were but small events on the chequer-board of Time, compared to a mightier movement that was taking birth in the promulgation of Islam. In the seventh or sixth year *before* the Hijrat, and for a year or two after the Hijrat, Islam was struggling in the world like the still small voice in the conscience of humanity. It was scarcely heeded, and when it sought to insist upon its divine claim, it was insulted, assaulted, persecuted, boycotted, and (as it seemed) suppressed. The agony of Ṭã-if (two years before the Hijrat) and the murder-plot on the eve of the Hijrat were yet to come. But the purpose of Allah is not to be thwarted. Badr (A.H. 2=A.D. 624), rightly called the critical Day of Decision, began to redress the balance of outward events in early Islam, in the same year in which Issus began to redress the balance of outward events in Perso-Roman relations. Mightier events were yet to come. A new inner World was being created through Islam. This spiritual Revolution was of infinitely greater moment in world-history. The toppling down of priestcraft and false worship, the restoration of simplicity in faith and life, the rehabilitation of this life as the first step to the understanding of the Hereafter, the displacement of superstition and hairsplitting theology by a spirit of rational inquiry and knowledge, and the recognition of the divine as covering not merely an isolated thing called "Religion" but the whole way of Life, Thought, and Feeling,—this was and is the true Message of Islam and its mission. Its struggle—its fight—continues, but it is not without effect, as may be seen in the march of centuries in world-history.

Ar-Rûm, or The Romans

In the name of Allah, Most Gracious, Most Merciful.

1. A. L. M.

2. The Romans have been defeated—

3. In a land close by: but they, (even) after (this) defeat of theirs, will soon be victorious—

4. Within a few years, with Allah is the Command in the Past and in the Future: on that Day shall the Believers rejoice—

5. With the help of Allah. He gives victory to whom He will, and He is Exalted in Might, Most Merciful.

6. (It is) the promise of Allah. Never does Allah fail from His promise: but most men know not.

7. They know but the outer (things) in the life of this world: but of the Hereafter they are heedless.

8. Do they not reflect in their own minds? Not but in truth and for a term appointed, did Allah create the heavens and the earth, and all between them: yet are there truly many among men who deny the meeting with their Lord (at the Resurrection)!

9. Do they not travel through the earth, and see what was the End of those before them? They were superior to them in strength: they tilled the soil and populated it in greater numbers than these have done: there came to them their messengers with Clear (Signs), (which they rejected, to their own destruction): it was not Allah who wronged them, but they wronged their own souls.

10. In the long run evil will be the End of those who do evil; for that they rejected the Signs of Allah, and held them up to ridicule.

11. It is Allah Who begins the creation; then repeats it; then shall ye be brought back to Him.

سورۂ روم مکی ہے اور اس میں ساٹھ آیتیں اور چھ رکوع ہیں

شروع خدا کا نام لے کر جو بڑا مہربان نہایت رحم والا ہے ○
الٓمٓ ﴿١﴾ (اہلِ) روم مغلوب ہو گئے ﴿٢﴾
نزدیک کے ملک میں۔ اور وہ مغلوب ہونے کے بعد
عنقریب غالب آجائیں گے ﴿٣﴾
چند ہی سال میں۔ پہلے بھی اور پیچھے بھی خدا ہی کا حکم ہے
اور اُس روز مومن خوش ہو جائیں گے ﴿٤﴾
(یعنی) خدا کی مدد سے۔ وہ جسے چاہتا ہے مدد دیتا ہے۔
اور وہ غالب (اور) مہربان ہے ﴿٥﴾
(یہ) خدا کا وعدہ (ہے) خدا اپنے وعدے کے خلاف نہیں کرتا
لیکن اکثر لوگ نہیں جانتے ﴿٦﴾
یہ تو دنیا کی ظاہری زندگی کو جانتے ہیں۔ اور آخرت
(کی طرف) سے غافل ہیں ﴿٧﴾
کیا انہوں نے اپنے دل میں غور نہیں کیا۔ کہ خدا نے
آسمانوں اور زمین کو اور جو کچھ ان دونوں کے درمیان
ہے ان کو حکمت سے اور ایک وقت مقرر تک کیلئے پیدا کیا ہے اور
بہت سے لوگ اپنے پروردگار سے ملنے کے قائل ہی نہیں ﴿٨﴾
کیا ان لوگوں نے ملک میں سیر نہیں کی (سیر کرتے) تو دیکھ لیتے
کہ جو لوگ ان سے پہلے تھے ان کا انجام کیسا ہوا۔ وہ ان سے زور و قوت
میں کہیں زیادہ تھے اور انہوں نے زمین کو جوتا اور اس کو اس سے
زیادہ آباد کیا تھا جو انہوں نے آباد کیا۔ اور اُن کے پاس
اُن کے پیغمبر نشانیاں لیکر آتے رہے۔ تو خدا ایسا نہ تھا
کہ اُن پر ظلم کرتا۔ بلکہ وہی اپنے آپ پر ظلم کرتے تھے ﴿٩﴾
پھر جن لوگوں نے بُرائی کی اُن کا انجام بھی بُرا ہوا اسلئے کہ خدا کی
آیتوں کو جھٹلاتے اور اُن کی ہنسی اُڑاتے رہے تھے ﴿١٠﴾
خدا ہی خلقت کو پہلی بار پیدا کرتا ہے وہی اس کو پھر
پیدا کرے گا پھر تم اسی کی طرف لوٹ جاؤ گے ﴿١١﴾

سُورَةُ الرُّومِ مَكِّيَّةٌ وَهِيَ سِتُّونَ آيَةً وَسِتُّ رُكُوعَاتٍ

بِسْمِ اللَّهِ الرَّحْمَٰنِ الرَّحِيمِ ○
الٓمٓ ﴿١﴾ غُلِبَتِ الرُّومُ ﴿٢﴾
فِي أَدْنَى الْأَرْضِ وَهُمْ مِنْ بَعْدِ غَلَبِهِمْ
سَيَغْلِبُونَ ﴿٣﴾
فِي بِضْعِ سِنِينَ ۗ لِلَّهِ الْأَمْرُ مِنْ قَبْلُ
وَمِنْ بَعْدُ ۚ وَيَوْمَئِذٍ يَفْرَحُ الْمُؤْمِنُونَ ﴿٤﴾
بِنَصْرِ اللَّهِ ۚ يَنْصُرُ مَنْ يَشَاءُ ۖ وَهُوَ الْعَزِيزُ
الرَّحِيمُ ﴿٥﴾
وَعْدَ اللَّهِ ۖ لَا يُخْلِفُ اللَّهُ وَعْدَهُ وَلَٰكِنَّ
أَكْثَرَ النَّاسِ لَا يَعْلَمُونَ ﴿٦﴾
يَعْلَمُونَ ظَاهِرًا مِنَ الْحَيَاةِ الدُّنْيَا
وَهُمْ عَنِ الْآخِرَةِ هُمْ غَافِلُونَ ﴿٧﴾
أَوَلَمْ يَتَفَكَّرُوا فِي أَنْفُسِهِمْ ۗ مَا خَلَقَ اللَّهُ
السَّمَاوَاتِ وَالْأَرْضَ وَمَا بَيْنَهُمَا إِلَّا
بِالْحَقِّ وَأَجَلٍ مُسَمًّى ۗ وَإِنَّ كَثِيرًا مِنَ
النَّاسِ بِلِقَاءِ رَبِّهِمْ لَكَافِرُونَ ﴿٨﴾
أَوَلَمْ يَسِيرُوا فِي الْأَرْضِ فَيَنْظُرُوا كَيْفَ
كَانَ عَاقِبَةُ الَّذِينَ مِنْ قَبْلِهِمْ ۚ كَانُوا
أَشَدَّ مِنْهُمْ قُوَّةً وَأَثَارُوا الْأَرْضَ وَ
عَمَرُوهَا أَكْثَرَ مِمَّا عَمَرُوهَا وَجَاءَتْهُمْ
رُسُلُهُمْ بِالْبَيِّنَاتِ ۖ فَمَا كَانَ اللَّهُ لِيَظْلِمَهُمْ
وَلَٰكِنْ كَانُوا أَنْفُسَهُمْ يَظْلِمُونَ ﴿٩﴾
ثُمَّ كَانَ عَاقِبَةَ الَّذِينَ أَسَاءُوا السُّوأَىٰ
ع أَنْ كَذَّبُوا بِآيَاتِ اللَّهِ وَكَانُوا بِهَا يَسْتَهْزِئُونَ ﴿١٠﴾
اللَّهُ يَبْدَأُ الْخَلْقَ ثُمَّ يُعِيدُهُ ثُمَّ إِلَيْهِ
تُرْجَعُونَ ﴿١١﴾

12. On the Day when the Hour will come the guilty will be struck dumb with despair.
13. No intercessor will they have among their "Partners", and they will (themselves) reject their "Partners".
14. On the Day when the Hour will come that Day shall (all men) be sorted out.
15. Then those who have believed and worked righteous deeds, shall be made happy in a Mead (of Delight).
16. And those who have rejected Faith and falsely denied Our Signs and the meeting of the Hereafter,—such shall be brought forth to Punishment.
17. So glory be to Allah, when ye reach eventide and when ye rise in the morning;
18. Yea, to Him be praise, in the heavens and on earth; and in the late afternoon and when the day begins to decline.
19. It is He Who brings out the living from the dead, and brings out the dead from the living, and Who gives life to the earth after it is dead: and thus shall ye be brought out (from the dead).
20. Among His Signs is this, that He created you from dust; and then,—behold, ye are men scattered (far and wide)!
21. And among His Signs is this, that He created for you mates from among yourselves, that ye may dwell in tranquillity with them, and He has put love and mercy between your (hearts): verily in that are Signs for those who reflect.
22. And among His Signs is the creation of the heavens and the earth, and the variations in your languages and your colours: verily in that are Signs for those who know.
23. And among His Signs is the sleep that ye take by night and by day, and the quest that ye (make for livelihood) out of His Bounty: verily in that are Signs for those who hearken.

اور جس دن قیامت برپا ہوگی گنہگار ناامید ہو جائینگے (۱۲)
اور انکے (بنائے ہوئے) شریکوں میں سے کوئی انکا سفارشی نہ ہوگا
اور وہ اپنے شریکوں سے نامعتقد ہو جائیں گے (۱۳)
اور جس دن قیامت برپا ہوگی اس روز وہ الگ الگ فرقے ہو جائینگے (۱۴)
تو جو لوگ ایمان لائے اور عمل نیک کرتے رہے وہ (بہشت کے)
باغ میں خوشحال ہوں گے (۱۵)
اور جنہوں نے کفر کیا اور ہماری آیتوں اور آخرت کے
آنے کو جھٹلایا۔ وہ عذاب میں ڈالے
جائیں گے (۱۶)
تو جس وقت تمکو شام ہو اور جس وقت صبح ہو خدا کی تسبیح کرو (یعنی نماز پڑھو) (۱۷)
اور آسمانوں اور زمین میں اُسی کی تعریف ہے اور تیسرے پہر بھی
اور جب دوپہر ہو اُس وقت بھی (نماز پڑھا کرو) (۱۸)
وہی زندے کو مُردے سے نکالتا اور (وہی) مُردے کو زندے
سے نکالتا ہے اور (وہی) زمین کو اُس کے مرنے کے بعد
زندہ کرتا ہے۔ اور اسی طرح تم (دوبارہ زمین میں سے) نکالے جاؤ گے (۱۹)
اور اُسی کے نشانات (اور تصرفات) میں سے ہے کہ اس نے
تمہیں مٹی سے پیدا کیا پھر اب تم انسان ہو کر جا بجا پھیل رہے ہو (۲۰)
اور اسی کے نشانات (اور تصرفات) میں سے ہے کہ اُس نے تمہارے
لئے تمہاری ہی جنس کی عورتیں پیدا کیں تاکہ اُنکی طرف (مائل ہوکر)
آرام حاصل کرو اور تم میں محبت اور مہربانی پیدا کر دی۔ جو لوگ غور
کرتے ہیں اُنکے لئے ان باتوں میں (بہت سی) نشانیاں ہیں (۲۱)
اور اُسی کے نشانات (اور تصرفات) میں سے ہے آسمانوں اور زمین کا
پیدا کرنا۔ اور تمہاری زبانوں اور رنگوں کا جُدا جُدا ہونا اہل دانش
کے لئے ان (باتوں) میں (بہت سی) نشانیاں ہیں (۲۲)
اور اسی کے نشانات (اور تصرفات) میں سے ہے تمہارا رات
اور دن میں سونا اور اُسکے فضل کا تلاش کرنا۔ جو لوگ
سنتے ہیں اُن کیلئے ان (باتوں) میں (بہت سی) نشانیاں ہیں (۲۳)

وَيَوْمَ تَقُومُ السَّاعَةُ يُبْلِسُ الْمُجْرِمُونَ (۱۲)
وَلَمْ يَكُن لَّهُم مِّن شُرَكَائِهِمْ شُفَعَاءُ
وَكَانُوا بِشُرَكَائِهِمْ كَافِرِينَ (۱۳)
وَيَوْمَ تَقُومُ السَّاعَةُ يَوْمَئِذٍ يَتَفَرَّقُونَ (۱۴)
فَأَمَّا الَّذِينَ آمَنُوا وَعَمِلُوا الصَّالِحَاتِ فَهُمْ
فِي رَوْضَةٍ يُحْبَرُونَ (۱۵)
وَأَمَّا الَّذِينَ كَفَرُوا وَكَذَّبُوا بِآيَاتِنَا
وَلِقَاءِ الْآخِرَةِ فَأُولَٰئِكَ فِي الْعَذَابِ
مُحْضَرُونَ (۱۶)
فَسُبْحَانَ اللَّهِ حِينَ تُمْسُونَ وَحِينَ تُصْبِحُونَ (۱۷)
وَلَهُ الْحَمْدُ فِي السَّمَاوَاتِ وَالْأَرْضِ وَ
عَشِيًّا وَحِينَ تُظْهِرُونَ (۱۸)
يُخْرِجُ الْحَيَّ مِنَ الْمَيِّتِ وَيُخْرِجُ الْمَيِّتَ
مِنَ الْحَيِّ وَيُحْيِي الْأَرْضَ بَعْدَ مَوْتِهَا وَ
ع ۲ كَذَٰلِكَ تُخْرَجُونَ (۱۹)
وَمِنْ آيَاتِهِ أَنْ خَلَقَكُم مِّن تُرَابٍ ثُمَّ
إِذَا أَنتُم بَشَرٌ تَنتَشِرُونَ (۲۰)
وَمِنْ آيَاتِهِ أَنْ خَلَقَ لَكُم مِّنْ أَنفُسِكُمْ
أَزْوَاجًا لِّتَسْكُنُوا إِلَيْهَا وَجَعَلَ بَيْنَكُم
مَّوَدَّةً وَرَحْمَةً إِنَّ فِي ذَٰلِكَ لَآيَاتٍ
لِّقَوْمٍ يَتَفَكَّرُونَ (۲۱)
وَمِنْ آيَاتِهِ خَلْقُ السَّمَاوَاتِ وَالْأَرْضِ
وَاخْتِلَافُ أَلْسِنَتِكُمْ وَأَلْوَانِكُمْ إِنَّ
فِي ذَٰلِكَ لَآيَاتٍ لِّلْعَالِمِينَ (۲۲)
وَمِنْ آيَاتِهِ مَنَامُكُم بِاللَّيْلِ وَالنَّهَارِ وَ
ابْتِغَاؤُكُم مِّن فَضْلِهِ إِنَّ فِي ذَٰلِكَ
لَآيَاتٍ لِّقَوْمٍ يَسْمَعُونَ (۲۳)

24. And among His Signs, He shows you the lightning, by way both of fear and of hope, and He sends down rain from the sky and with it gives life to the earth after it is dead: verily in that are Signs for those who are wise.

اور اُسی کے نشانات (اور تصرفات) میں سے ہے کہ تم کو خوف
اور اُمید دلانے کیلئے بجلی دکھاتا ہے اور آسمان سے مینہ برساتا ہے پھر
زمین کو اُسکے مرجانے کے بعد زندہ (وشاداب) کر دیتا ہے عقل
والوں کیلئے اِن (باتوں) میں (بہت سی) نشانیاں ہیں ﴿٢٤﴾

وَمِنْ اٰيٰتِهٖ يُرِيْكُمُ الْبَرْقَ خَوْفًا وَّطَمَعًا
وَّيُنَزِّلُ مِنَ السَّمَآءِ مَآءً فَيُحْيٖ بِهِ الْاَرْضَ
بَعْدَ مَوْتِهَا ۭ اِنَّ فِيْ ذٰلِكَ لَاٰيٰتٍ لِّقَوْمٍ
يَّعْقِلُوْنَ ﴿٢٤﴾

25. And among His Signs is this, that heaven and earth stand by His Command: then when He calls you, by a single call, from the earth, behold, ye (straightway) come forth.

اور اُسی کے نشانات (اور تصرفات) میں سے ہے کہ آسمان اور
زمین اُسکے حکم سے قائم ہیں پھر جب وہ تم کو زمین میں سے
(نکلنے کیلئے) آواز دے گا تو تم جھٹ نکل پڑو گے ﴿٢٥﴾

وَمِنْ اٰيٰتِهٖٓ اَنْ تَقُوْمَ السَّمَآءُ وَالْاَرْضُ
بِاَمْرِهٖ ۭ ثُمَّ اِذَا دَعَاكُمْ دَعْوَةً ڰ مِّنَ
الْاَرْضِ ڰ اِذَآ اَنْتُمْ تَخْرُجُوْنَ ﴿٢٥﴾

26. To Him belongs every being that is in the heavens and on earth: all are devoutly obedient to Him.

اور آسمانوں اور زمین میں جتنے (فرشتے اور انسان وغیرہ) ہیں
اُسی کے (مملوک) ہیں (اور) تمام اُسکے فرمانبردار ہیں ﴿٢٦﴾

وَلَهٗ مَنْ فِي السَّمٰوٰتِ وَالْاَرْضِ ۭ كُلٌّ
لَّهٗ قٰنِتُوْنَ ﴿٢٦﴾

27. It is He Who begins the creation; then repeats it; and for Him it is most easy. To Him belongs the loftiest similitude (we can think of) in the heavens and the earth: for He is Exalted in Might, full of wisdom.

اور وہی تو ہے جو خلقت کو پہلی دفعہ پیدا کرتا ہے پھر اُسے
دوبارہ پیدا کریگا۔ اور یہ اُس کو بہت آسان ہے۔ اور
آسمانوں اور زمین میں اُس کی شان نہایت بلند ہے۔
اور وہ غالب حکمت والا ہے ﴿٢٧﴾

وَهُوَ الَّذِيْ يَبْدَؤُا الْخَلْقَ ثُمَّ يُعِيْدُهٗ
وَهُوَ اَهْوَنُ عَلَيْهِ ۭ وَلَهُ الْمَثَلُ الْاَعْلٰى
فِي السَّمٰوٰتِ وَالْاَرْضِ ۚ وَهُوَ الْعَزِيْزُ
الْحَكِيْمُ ﴿٢٧﴾

28. He does propound to you a similitude from yourselves: do ye have partners among those whom your right hands possess, to share as equals in the wealth We have bestowed on you? Do ye fear them as ye fear each other? Thus do We explain the Signs in detail to a people that understand.

وہ تمہارے لئے تمہارے ہی حال کی ایک مثال بیان فرماتا
ہے کہ بھلا جن (لونڈی غلاموں) کے تم مالک ہو وہ اُس (مال) میں
جو ہم نے تمکو عطا فرمایا ہے تمہارے شریک ہیں؟ اور (کیا) تم اُس میں (اُنکو اپنے)
برابر (مالک) سمجھتے ہو اور کیا تم اُن سے اس طرح ڈرتے ہو جس طرح اپنوں سے ڈرتے ہو؟
اس طرح ہم عقل والوں کیلئے اپنی آیتیں کھول کھول کر بیان کرتے ہیں ﴿٢٨﴾

ضَرَبَ لَكُمْ مَّثَلًا مِّنْ اَنْفُسِكُمْ ۭ هَلْ
لَّكُمْ مِّنْ مَّا مَلَكَتْ اَيْمَانُكُمْ مِّنْ شُرَكَاۗءَ
فِيْ مَا رَزَقْنٰكُمْ فَاَنْتُمْ فِيْهِ سَوَاۗءٌ
تَخَافُوْنَهُمْ كَخِيْفَتِكُمْ اَنْفُسَكُمْ ۭ كَذٰلِكَ
نُفَصِّلُ الْاٰيٰتِ لِقَوْمٍ يَّعْقِلُوْنَ ﴿٢٨﴾

29. Nay, the wrong-doers (merely) follow their own desires being devoid of knowledge. But who will guide those whom Allah leaves astray? To them there will be no helpers.

مگر جو ظالم ہیں بے سمجھے اپنی خواہشوں کے پیچھے چلتے
ہیں تو جس کو خدا گمراہ کرے اُسے کون ہدایت دے سکتا ہے؟
اور اُن کا کوئی مددگار نہیں ﴿٢٩﴾

بَلِ اتَّبَعَ الَّذِيْنَ ظَلَمُوْٓا اَهْوَاۗءَهُمْ بِغَيْرِ
عِلْمٍ ۚ فَمَنْ يَّهْدِيْ مَنْ اَضَلَّ اللّٰهُ ۭ
وَمَا لَهُمْ مِّنْ نّٰصِرِيْنَ ﴿٢٩﴾

30. So set thou thy face truly to the religion being upright, the nature in which Allah has made mankind: no change (there is) in the work (wrought) by Allah: that is the true Religion: but most among mankind know not.

تو تم ایک طرف کے ہو کر دین (خدا کے رستے) پر سیدھا مُنہ کئے
چلے جاؤ (اور) خدا کی فطرت کو جس پر اُس نے لوگوں کو پیدا کیا ہے
(اختیار کئے رہو) خدا کی بنائی ہوئی (فطرت) میں تغیر وتبدل
نہیں ہو سکتا۔ یہی سیدھا دین ہے لیکن اکثر لوگ نہیں جانتے ﴿٣٠﴾

فَاَقِمْ وَجْهَكَ لِلدِّيْنِ حَنِيْفًا ۭ فِطْرَتَ
اللّٰهِ الَّتِيْ فَطَرَ النَّاسَ عَلَيْهَا ۭ لَا تَبْدِيْلَ
لِخَلْقِ اللّٰهِ ۭ ذٰلِكَ الدِّيْنُ الْقَيِّمُ ڎ وَلٰكِنَّ
اَكْثَرَ النَّاسِ لَا يَعْلَمُوْنَ ﴿٣٠﴾

31. Turn ye in repentance to Him, and fear Him: establish regular prayers, and be not ye among those who join gods with Allah,—

(مومنو) اُسی (خدا) کی طرف رجوع کئے رہو اور اُس سے ڈرتے رہو اور نماز
پڑھتے رہو اور مشرکوں میں نہ ہونا ﴿٣١﴾

مُنِيْبِيْنَ اِلَيْهِ وَاتَّقُوْهُ وَاَقِيْمُوا الصَّلٰوةَ
وَلَا تَكُوْنُوْا مِنَ الْمُشْرِكِيْنَ ﴿٣١﴾

32. Those who split up their Religion, and become (Mere) Sects,—each party rejoicing in that which is with itself!

(اور نہ) اُن لوگوں میں (ہونا) جنہوں نے اپنے دین کو ٹکڑے
ٹکڑے کر دیا اور (خود) فرقے فرقے ہو گئے سب فرقے اسی سے خوش ہیں جو اُن کے پاس ہے (۳۲)

مِنَ الَّذِيْنَ فَرَّقُوْا دِيْنَهُمْ وَكَانُوْا شِيَعًا
كُلُّ حِزْبٍ بِمَا لَدَيْهِمْ فَرِحُوْنَ ﴿۳۲﴾

33. When trouble touches men, they cry to their Lord turning back to Him in repentance: but when He gives them a taste of Mercy from Himself, behold, some of them pay part-worship to other gods besides their Lord,—

اور جب لوگوں کو تکلیف پہنچتی ہے تو اپنے پروردگار کو پکارتے اور اسی
کی طرف رجوع ہوتے ہیں۔ پھر جب وہ اُن کو اپنی رحمت کا مزا چکھاتا ہے
تو ایک فرقہ اُن میں سے اپنے پروردگار سے شرک کرنے لگتا ہے (۳۳)

وَاِذَا مَسَّ النَّاسَ ضُرٌّ دَعَوْا رَبَّهُمْ مُّنِيْبِيْنَ
اِلَيْهِ ثُمَّ اِذَا اَذَاقَهُمْ مِّنْهُ رَحْمَةً اِذَا
فَرِيْقٌ مِّنْهُمْ بِرَبِّهِمْ يُشْرِكُوْنَ ﴿۳۳﴾

34. (As if) to show their ingratitude for the (favours) We have bestowed on them! Then enjoy (your brief day); but soon will ye know (your folly).

تاکہ جو ہم نے اُن کو بخشا ہے اُس کی ناشکری کریں سو (خیر) فائدے
اُٹھا لو عنقریب تم کو (اس کا انجام) معلوم ہو جائے گا (۳۴)

لِيَكْفُرُوْا بِمَا اٰتَيْنٰهُمْ ۭ فَتَمَتَّعُوْا ۣ فَسَوْفَ
تَعْلَمُوْنَ ﴿۳۴﴾

35. Or have We sent down authority to them, which speaks to them the things to which the pay part-worship?

کیا ہم نے اُن پر کوئی ایسی دلیل نازل کی ہے کہ اُن کو خدا کے
ساتھ شرک کرنا بتاتی ہے (۳۵)

اَمْ اَنْزَلْنَا عَلَيْهِمْ سُلْطٰنًا فَهُوَ يَتَكَلَّمُ
بِمَا كَانُوْا بِهٖ يُشْرِكُوْنَ ﴿۳۵﴾

36. When We give men a taste of Mercy, they exult thereat: and when some evil afflicts them because of what their (own) hands have sent forth, behold, they are in despair!

اور جب ہم لوگوں کو اپنی رحمت کا مزا چکھاتے ہیں تو اُس سے
خوش ہو جاتے ہیں۔ اور اگر اُن کے عملوں کے سبب جو اُن کے ہاتھوں
نے آگے بھیجے ہیں کوئی گزند پہنچے تو ناامید ہو کر رہ جاتے ہیں (۳۶)

وَاِذَآ اَذَقْنَا النَّاسَ رَحْمَةً فَرِحُوْا بِهَا ۭ
وَاِنْ تُصِبْهُمْ سَيِّئَةٌۢ بِمَا قَدَّمَتْ
اَيْدِيْهِمْ اِذَا هُمْ يَقْنَطُوْنَ ﴿۳۶﴾

37. See they not that Allah enlarges the provision and restricts it, to whomsoever He pleases? Verily in that are Signs for those who believe.

کیا اُنہوں نے نہیں دیکھا کہ خدا ہی جس کیلئے چاہتا ہے رزق فراخ
کرتا ہے اور (جس کیلئے چاہتا ہے) تنگ کرتا ہے۔ بے شک اس میں
ایمان لانے والوں کے لئے نشانیاں ہیں (۳۷)

اَوَلَمْ يَرَوْا اَنَّ اللّٰهَ يَبْسُطُ الرِّزْقَ لِمَنْ
يَّشَاۗءُ وَيَقْدِرُ ۭ اِنَّ فِيْ ذٰلِكَ لَاٰيٰتٍ
لِّقَوْمٍ يُّؤْمِنُوْنَ ﴿۳۷﴾

38. So give what is due to kindred, the needy, and the wayfarer, that is best for those who seek the Countenance, of Allah, and it is they who will prosper.

تو اہلِ قرابت اور محتاجوں اور مسافروں کو اُن کا
حق دیتے رہو۔ جو لوگ رضائے خدا کے طالب ہیں
یہ اُن کے حق میں بہتر ہے۔ اور یہی لوگ نجات
حاصل کرنے والے ہیں (۳۸)

فَاٰتِ ذَا الْقُرْبٰى حَقَّهٗ وَالْمِسْكِيْنَ
وَابْنَ السَّبِيْلِ ۭ ذٰلِكَ خَيْرٌ لِّلَّذِيْنَ
يُرِيْدُوْنَ وَجْهَ اللّٰهِ ۡ وَاُولٰۗىِٕكَ هُمُ
الْمُفْلِحُوْنَ ﴿۳۸﴾

39. That which you give in usury for increase through the property of (other) people, will have no increase with Allah: but that which you give for charity, seeking the Countenance of Allah, (will increase): it is these who will get a recompense multiplied.

اور جو تم سود دیتے ہو کہ لوگوں کے مال میں افزائش ہو
تو خدا کے نزدیک اُس میں افزائش نہیں ہوتی اور جو تم زکوٰۃ
دیتے ہو اور اس سے خدا کی رضامندی طلب کرتے ہو تو (وہ موجب
برکت ہے اور) ایسے ہی لوگ (اپنے مال کو) دو چند سہ چند کرنے والے ہیں (۳۹)

وَمَآ اٰتَيْتُمْ مِّنْ رِّبًا لِّيَرْبُوَا فِيْٓ اَمْوَالِ
النَّاسِ فَلَا يَرْبُوْا عِنْدَ اللّٰهِ ۚ وَمَآ اٰتَيْتُمْ
مِّنْ زَكٰوةٍ تُرِيْدُوْنَ وَجْهَ اللّٰهِ فَاُولٰۗىِٕكَ
هُمُ الْمُضْعِفُوْنَ ﴿۳۹﴾

40. It is Allah Who has created you: further, He has provided for your sustenance; then He will cause you to die; and again He will give you life. Are there any of your (false) "Partners" who can do any single one of these things? Glory

خدا ہی تو ہے جس نے تم کو پیدا کیا پھر تم کو رزق دیا پھر
تمہیں مارے گا۔ پھر زندہ کرے گا۔ بھلا تمہارے (بنائے
ہوئے) شریکوں میں بھی کوئی ایسا ہے جو اِن کاموں
میں سے کچھ کر سکے۔ وہ پاک ہے اور (اس کی شان) اُن کے

اَللّٰهُ الَّذِيْ خَلَقَكُمْ ثُمَّ رَزَقَكُمْ
ثُمَّ يُمِيْتُكُمْ ثُمَّ يُحْيِيْكُمْ ۭ هَلْ مِنْ
شُرَكَاۗىِٕكُمْ مَّنْ يَّفْعَلُ مِنْ ذٰلِكُمْ
مِّنْ شَيْءٍ ۭ سُبْحٰنَهٗ وَتَعٰلٰى عَمَّا

to Him! and High is He above the partners they attribute (to Him)!

41. Mischief has appeared on land and sea because of (the meed) that the hands of men have earned, that (Allah) may give them a taste of some of their deeds: in order that they may turn back (from evil).

42. Say: "Travel through the earth and see what was the End of those before (you): most of them were idolaters.

43. But set thou thy face to the right Religion, before there come from Allah the Day which there is no chance of averting: on that Day shall men be divided (in two).

44. Those who reject Faith will suffer from that rejection: and those who work righteousness will make provision for themselves (in heaven):

45. That He may reward those who believe and work righteous deeds, out of His Bounty. For He loves not those who reject Faith.

46. Among His Signs is this, that He sends the Winds, as heralds of Glad Tidings, giving you a taste of His Mercy,— that the ships may sail by His Command and that ye may seek of His Bounty: in order that ye may be grateful.

47. We did indeed send, before thee, messengers to their (respective) peoples, and they came to them with Clear Signs: then, to those who transgressed, We meted out Retribution: and it was a duty incumbent upon Us to aid those who believed.

48. It is Allah Who sends the Winds, and they raise the Clouds: then does He spread them in the sky as He wills, and break them into fragments, until thou seest rain-drops issue from the midst thereof: then when He has made them reach such of His servants as He wills, behold, they do rejoice!—

شرکوں سے بلند ہے ﴿۴۰﴾
خشکی اور تری میں لوگوں کے اعمال کے سبب فساد پھیل
گیا ہے تاکہ خدا اُن کو اُن کے بعض اعمال کا مزہ چکھائے
عجب نہیں کہ وہ باز آجائیں ﴿۴۱﴾
کہہ دو کہ ملک میں چلو پھرو اور دیکھو کہ جو لوگ (تم سے)
پہلے ہوئے ہیں اُن کا کیسا انجام ہوا ہے۔ اُن میں
زیادہ تر مشرک ہی تھے ﴿۴۲﴾
تو اس روز سے پہلے جو خدا کی طرف سے آکر رہیگا اور
رُک نہیں سکے گا دین (کے رستے) پر سیدھا مُنہ کئے چلے
چلو اس روز (سب) لوگ منتشر ہو جائیں گے ﴿۴۳﴾
جس شخص نے کفر کیا تو اُسکے کفر کا ضرر اُسی کو ہے اور جس نے
نیک عمل کئے تو ایسے لوگ اپنے ہی لئے آرام گاہ درست کرتے ہیں ﴿۴۴﴾
جو لوگ ایمان لائے اور نیک عمل کرتے رہے اُنکو خدا اپنے فضل
سے بدلہ دیگا۔ بیشک وہ کافروں کو دوست نہیں رکھتا ﴿۴۵﴾
اور اُسی کی نشانیوں میں سے ہے کہ ہواؤں کو بھیجتا ہے کہ خوشخبری
دیتی ہیں تاکہ تم کو اپنی رحمت کے مزے چکھائے اور تاکہ اُسکے
حکم سے کشتیاں چلیں اور تاکہ تم اُسکے فضل سے (روزی)
طلب کرو عجب نہیں کہ تم شکر کرو ﴿۴۶﴾
اور ہم نے تم سے پہلے بھی پیغمبر بھیجے تو وہ اُنکے پاس
نشانیاں لے کر آئے سو جو لوگ نافرمانی کرتے تھے ہم نے
اُن سے بدلہ لے کر چھوڑا اور مومنوں کی مدد ہم پر
لازم تھی ﴿۴۷﴾
خدا ہی تو ہے جو ہواؤں کو چلاتا ہے تو وہ بادل کو اُبھارتی
ہیں۔ پھر خدا اُسکو جس طرح چاہتا ہے آسمان میں پھیلا دیتا اور
تہ بہ تہ کر دیتا ہے پھر تم دیکھتے ہو کہ اُسکے بیچ میں سے مینہ نکلنے لگتا ہے
پھر جب وہ اپنے بندوں میں سے جن پر چاہتا ہے اُسے برسا دیتا ہے
تو وہ خوش ہو جاتے ہیں ﴿۴۸﴾

يُشْرِكُونَ ﴿٤٠﴾
ظَهَرَ الْفَسَادُ فِي الْبَرِّ وَالْبَحْرِ بِمَا كَسَبَتْ
أَيْدِي النَّاسِ لِيُذِيقَهُمْ بَعْضَ الَّذِي
عَمِلُوا لَعَلَّهُمْ يَرْجِعُونَ ﴿٤١﴾
قُلْ سِيرُوا فِي الْأَرْضِ فَانْظُرُوا كَيْفَ
كَانَ عَاقِبَةُ الَّذِينَ مِنْ قَبْلُ ۚ كَانَ
أَكْثَرُهُمْ مُشْرِكِينَ ﴿٤٢﴾
فَأَقِمْ وَجْهَكَ لِلدِّينِ الْقَيِّمِ مِنْ قَبْلِ
أَنْ يَأْتِيَ يَوْمٌ لَا مَرَدَّ لَهُ مِنَ اللَّهِ ۖ
يَوْمَئِذٍ يَصَّدَّعُونَ ﴿٤٣﴾
مَنْ كَفَرَ فَعَلَيْهِ كُفْرُهُ ۖ وَمَنْ عَمِلَ
صَالِحًا فَلِأَنْفُسِهِمْ يَمْهَدُونَ ﴿٤٤﴾
لِيَجْزِيَ الَّذِينَ آمَنُوا وَعَمِلُوا الصَّالِحَاتِ
مِنْ فَضْلِهِ ۚ إِنَّهُ لَا يُحِبُّ الْكَافِرِينَ ﴿٤٥﴾
وَمِنْ آيَاتِهِ أَنْ يُرْسِلَ الرِّيَاحَ مُبَشِّرَاتٍ
وَلِيُذِيقَكُمْ مِنْ رَحْمَتِهِ وَلِتَجْرِيَ
الْفُلْكُ بِأَمْرِهِ وَلِتَبْتَغُوا مِنْ فَضْلِهِ
وَلَعَلَّكُمْ تَشْكُرُونَ ﴿٤٦﴾
وَلَقَدْ أَرْسَلْنَا مِنْ قَبْلِكَ رُسُلًا إِلَىٰ
قَوْمِهِمْ فَجَاءُوهُمْ بِالْبَيِّنَاتِ فَانْتَقَمْنَا
مِنَ الَّذِينَ أَجْرَمُوا ۖ وَكَانَ حَقًّا عَلَيْنَا
نَصْرُ الْمُؤْمِنِينَ ﴿٤٧﴾
اللَّهُ الَّذِي يُرْسِلُ الرِّيَاحَ فَتُثِيرُ سَحَابًا
فَيَبْسُطُهُ فِي السَّمَاءِ كَيْفَ يَشَاءُ وَيَجْعَلُهُ
كِسَفًا فَتَرَى الْوَدْقَ يَخْرُجُ مِنْ خِلَالِهِ ۖ
فَإِذَا أَصَابَ بِهِ مَنْ يَشَاءُ مِنْ عِبَادِهِ
إِذَا هُمْ يَسْتَبْشِرُونَ ﴿٤٨﴾

49. Even though, before they received (the rain)—just before this—they were dumb with despair!

اور پیشتر تو وہ مینہ کے اُترنے سے پہلے ناامید
ہو رہے تھے ﴿۴۹﴾

وَإِنْ كَانُوا مِنْ قَبْلِ أَنْ يُنَزَّلَ عَلَيْهِمْ
مِنْ قَبْلِهِ لَمُبْلِسِينَ ﴿٤٩﴾

50. Then behold (O man!) the tokens of Allah's Mercy!— how He gives life to the earth after its death: verily the Same will give life to the men who are dead: for He has power over all things.

تو (اے دیکھنے والے) خدا کی رحمت کی نشانیوں کی طرف دیکھ
کہ وہ کس طرح زمین کو اُس کے مرنے کے بعد زندہ کرتا ہے۔ بےشک وہ
مُردوں کو زندہ کرنے والا ہے۔ اور وہ ہر چیز پر قادر ہے ﴿۵۰﴾

فَانْظُرْ إِلَىٰ آثَارِ رَحْمَتِ اللَّهِ كَيْفَ يُحْيِي
الْأَرْضَ بَعْدَ مَوْتِهَا ۚ إِنَّ ذَٰلِكَ لَمُحْيِي
الْمَوْتَىٰ ۖ وَهُوَ عَلَىٰ كُلِّ شَيْءٍ قَدِيرٌ ﴿٥٠﴾

51. And if We (but) send a Wind from which they see (their tilth) turn yellow,—behold, they become, thereafter, ungrateful (Unbelievers)!

اور اگر ہم ایسی ہوا بھیجیں کہ وہ (اس کے سبب) کھیتی کو دیکھیں (کہ)
زرد (ہو گئی ہے) تو اس کے بعد وہ ناشکری کرنے لگ جائیں ﴿۵۱﴾

وَلَئِنْ أَرْسَلْنَا رِيحًا فَرَأَوْهُ مُصْفَرًّا
لَظَلُّوا مِنْ بَعْدِهِ يَكْفُرُونَ ﴿٥١﴾

52. So verily thou canst not make the dead to hear, nor canst thou make the deaf to hear the call, when they show their backs and turn away.

تو تم مُردوں کو (بات) نہیں سنا سکتے اور نہ بہروں کو جب وہ
پیٹھ پھیر کر پھر جائیں آواز سنا سکتے ہو ﴿۵۲﴾

فَإِنَّكَ لَا تُسْمِعُ الْمَوْتَىٰ وَلَا تُسْمِعُ الصُّمَّ
الدُّعَاءَ إِذَا وَلَّوْا مُدْبِرِينَ ﴿٥٢﴾

53. Nor canst thou lead back the blind from their straying: only those wilt thou make to hear, who believe in Our Signs and submit (their wills in Islām).

اور نہ اندھوں کو اُن کی گمراہی سے (نکال کر) راہِ راست پر
لا سکتے ہو۔ تم تو اُن ہی لوگوں کو سُنا سکتے ہو جو ہماری
آیتوں پر ایمان لاتے ہیں سو وہی فرمانبردار ہیں ﴿۵۳﴾

وَمَا أَنْتَ بِهَادِ الْعُمْيِ عَنْ ضَلَالَتِهِمْ ۖ
إِنْ تُسْمِعُ إِلَّا مَنْ يُؤْمِنُ بِآيَاتِنَا فَهُمْ
مُسْلِمُونَ ﴿٥٣﴾ ع

54. It is Allah Who created you in a state of (helpless) weakness, then gave (you) strength after weakness, then, after strength, gave (you) weakness and a hoary head: He creates whatever He wills, and it is He who has all knowledge and power.

خدا ہی تو ہے جس نے تم کو (ابتدا میں) کمزور حالت میں
پیدا کیا پھر کمزوری کے بعد طاقت عنایت کی پھر طاقت کے
بعد کمزوری اور بڑھاپا دیا۔ وہ جو چاہتا ہے پیدا کرتا ہے
اور وہ صاحب دانش (اور) صاحب قدرت ہے ﴿۵۴﴾

اللَّهُ الَّذِي خَلَقَكُمْ مِنْ ضَعْفٍ ثُمَّ
جَعَلَ مِنْ بَعْدِ ضَعْفٍ قُوَّةً ثُمَّ
جَعَلَ مِنْ بَعْدِ قُوَّةٍ ضَعْفًا وَشَيْبَةً ۚ
يَخْلُقُ مَا يَشَاءُ ۖ وَهُوَ الْعَلِيمُ الْقَدِيرُ ﴿٥٤﴾

55. On the Day that the Hour (of reckoning) will be established, the transgressors will swear that they tarried not but an hour: thus were they used to being deluded!

اور جس روز قیامت برپا ہوگی گنہگار قسمیں کھائیں گے کہ وہ (دنیا میں)
ایک گھڑی سے زیادہ نہیں رہے تھے۔ اسی طرح وہ (رستے سے) اُلٹے جاتے تھے ﴿۵۵﴾

وَيَوْمَ تَقُومُ السَّاعَةُ يُقْسِمُ الْمُجْرِمُونَ
مَا لَبِثُوا غَيْرَ سَاعَةٍ ۚ كَذَٰلِكَ كَانُوا يُؤْفَكُونَ ﴿٥٥﴾

56. But those endued with knowledge and faith will say: "Indeed ye did tarry, within Allah's Decree, to the Day of Resurrection, and this is the Day of Resurrection: but ye—ye did not know!"

اور جن لوگوں کو علم اور ایمان دیا گیا تھا وہ کہیں گے
کہ خدا کی کتاب کے مطابق تم قیامت تک رہے ہو۔
اور یہ قیامت ہی کا دن ہے لیکن تم کو اس کا یقین
ہی نہ تھا ﴿۵۶﴾

وَقَالَ الَّذِينَ أُوتُوا الْعِلْمَ وَالْإِيمَانَ
لَقَدْ لَبِثْتُمْ فِي كِتَابِ اللَّهِ إِلَىٰ يَوْمِ الْبَعْثِ ۖ
فَهَٰذَا يَوْمُ الْبَعْثِ وَلَٰكِنَّكُمْ كُنْتُمْ لَا
تَعْلَمُونَ ﴿٥٦﴾

57. So on that Day no excuse of theirs will avail the Transgressors, nor will they be allowed to make amends.

تو اس روز ظالم لوگوں کو اُن کا عذر کچھ فائدہ نہ دیگا
اور نہ اُن سے توبہ قبول کی جائے گی ﴿۵۷﴾

فَيَوْمَئِذٍ لَا يَنْفَعُ الَّذِينَ ظَلَمُوا مَعْذِرَتُهُمْ
وَلَا هُمْ يُسْتَعْتَبُونَ ﴿٥٧﴾

58. Verily We have propounded for men, in this Qur'an. Every kind of Parable: but if thou bring to them any Sign, the Unbelievers are sure to say, "Ye do nothing but talk vanities."

اور ہم نے لوگوں کے (سمجھانے کے) لئے اس قرآن میں ہر
طرح کی مثال بیان کر دی ہے اور اگر تم اُن کے سامنے کوئی نشانی
پیش کرو تو یہ کافر کہہ دیں گے کہ تم تو جھوٹے ہو ﴿۵۸﴾

وَلَقَدْ ضَرَبْنَا لِلنَّاسِ فِي هَٰذَا الْقُرْآنِ
مِنْ كُلِّ مَثَلٍ ۚ وَلَئِنْ جِئْتَهُمْ بِآيَةٍ لَيَقُولَنَّ
الَّذِينَ كَفَرُوا إِنْ أَنْتُمْ إِلَّا مُبْطِلُونَ ﴿٥٨﴾

SÛRA–31
LUQMÃN
(INTRODUCTION)

The argument of the Final End of Things is here continued from another point of view. What is Wisdom? Where shall she be found? Will she solve the mysteries of Time and Nature, and that world higher than physical Nature, which brings us nearer to Allah? "Yes," is the answer: "if, as in the advice of Luqmãn the Wise, human wisdom looks to Allah in true worship, enobles every act of life with true kindness, but avoids the false indulgence that infringes the divine law,—and in short follows the golden mean of virtue." And this is indicated by every Sign in Nature.

The chronology of the Sûra has no significance. In the main, it belongs to the late Makkan period.

كَذٰلِكَ يَطْبَعُ اللّٰهُ عَلٰى قُلُوْبِ الَّذِيْنَ لَا يَعْلَمُوْنَ ﴿۵۹﴾

اسی طرح خدا اُن لوگوں کے دلوں پر جو سمجھ نہیں رکھتے مہر لگا دیتا ہے ﴿۵۹﴾

59. Thus does Allah seal up the hearts of those who understand not.

فَاصْبِرْ اِنَّ وَعْدَ اللّٰهِ حَقٌّ وَّلَا يَسْتَخِفَّنَّكَ الَّذِيْنَ لَا يُوْقِنُوْنَ ﴿۶۰﴾ ع

پس تم صبر کرو بیشک خدا کا وعدہ سچا ہے اور (دیکھو) جو لوگ یقین نہیں رکھتے وہ تمہیں اوچھا نہ بنا دیں ﴿۶۰﴾

60. So patiently persevere: for verily the promise of Allah is true: nor let those excite thee, who have (themselves) no certainty of faith.

Luqmān (the Wise)

سُوْرَةُ لُقْمٰنَ مَكِّيَّةٌ وَّهِيَ اَرْبَعٌ وَّثَلٰثُوْنَ اٰيَةً وَّاَرْبَعُ رُكُوْعَاتٍ

سورہ لقمان مکی ہے اور اس میں چونتیس آیتیں اور چار رکوع ہیں

بِسْمِ اللّٰهِ الرَّحْمٰنِ الرَّحِيْمِ

شروع خدا کا نام لے کر جو بڑا مہربان نہایت رحم والا ہے

In the name of Allah, Most Gracious, Most Merciful.

الٓمّٓ ﴿۱﴾ تِلْكَ اٰيٰتُ الْكِتٰبِ الْحَكِيْمِ ﴿۲﴾
هُدًى وَّرَحْمَةً لِّلْمُحْسِنِيْنَ ﴿۳﴾
الَّذِيْنَ يُقِيْمُوْنَ الصَّلٰوةَ وَيُؤْتُوْنَ الزَّكٰوةَ
وَهُمْ بِالْاٰخِرَةِ هُمْ يُوْقِنُوْنَ ﴿۴﴾

الم ﴿۱﴾ یہ حکمت کی (بھری ہوئی) کتاب کی آیتیں ہیں ﴿۲﴾
نیکوکاروں کے لئے ہدایت اور رحمت ﴿۳﴾
جو نماز کی پابندی کرتے اور زکوٰۃ دیتے اور آخرت کا
یقین رکھتے ہیں ﴿۴﴾

1. **A. L. M.**
2. These are Verses of the Wise Book,—
3. A Guide and a Mercy to the Doers of Good,—
4. Those who establish regular Prayer, and give zakat and have sure faith in the Hereafter.

اُولٰٓئِكَ عَلٰى هُدًى مِّنْ رَّبِّهِمْ وَاُولٰٓئِكَ هُمُ الْمُفْلِحُوْنَ ﴿۵﴾

یہی اپنے پروردگار (کی طرف) سے ہدایت پر ہیں اور یہی نجات پانے والے ہیں ﴿۵﴾

5. These are on (true) guidance from their Lord; and these are the ones who will prosper.

وَمِنَ النَّاسِ مَنْ يَّشْتَرِيْ لَهْوَ الْحَدِيْثِ لِيُضِلَّ عَنْ سَبِيْلِ اللّٰهِ بِغَيْرِ عِلْمٍ ۖ وَّيَتَّخِذَهَا هُزُوًا ۚ اُولٰٓئِكَ لَهُمْ عَذَابٌ مُّهِيْنٌ ﴿۶﴾

اور لوگوں میں بعض ایسا ہے جو بیہودہ حکایتیں خریدتا ہے تاکہ (لوگوں کو) بے سمجھے خدا کے رستے سے گمراہ کرے اور اس سے استہزاء کرے یہی لوگ ہیں جن کو ذلیل کرنے والا عذاب ہوگا ﴿۶﴾

6. But there are, among men, those who purchase idle tales, without knowledge (or meaning), to mislead (men) from the Path of Allah and throw ridicule (on the Path): for such there will be a humiliating Chastisement.

وَاِذَا تُتْلٰى عَلَيْهِ اٰيٰتُنَا وَلّٰى مُسْتَكْبِرًا كَاَنْ لَّمْ يَسْمَعْهَا كَاَنَّ فِيْٓ اُذُنَيْهِ وَقْرًا ۚ فَبَشِّرْهُ بِعَذَابٍ اَلِيْمٍ ﴿۷﴾

اور جب اس کو ہماری آیتیں سنائی جاتی ہیں تو اکڑ کر منہ پھیر لیتا ہے گویا اُن کو سنا ہی نہیں جیسے اُنکے کانوں میں ثقل ہے تو اس کو درد دینے والے عذاب کی خوشخبری سنا دو ﴿۷﴾

7. When Our Signs are rehearsed to such a one, he turns away in arrogance, as if he heard them not, as if there were deafness in both his ears: announce to him a grievous Chastisement.

اِنَّ الَّذِيْنَ اٰمَنُوْا وَعَمِلُوا الصّٰلِحٰتِ لَهُمْ جَنّٰتُ النَّعِيْمِ ﴿۸﴾

جو لوگ ایمان لائے اور نیک کام کرتے رہے اُن کے لئے نعمت کے باغ ہیں ﴿۸﴾

8. For those who believe and work righteous deeds, there will be Gardens of Bliss,—

خٰلِدِيْنَ فِيْهَا ۚ وَعْدَ اللّٰهِ حَقًّا ۚ وَهُوَ الْعَزِيْزُ الْحَكِيْمُ ﴿۹﴾

ہمیشہ اُن میں رہیں گے. خدا کا وعدہ سچا ہے. اور وہ غالب حکمت والا ہے ﴿۹﴾

9. To dwell therein. The promise of Allah is true: and He is Exalted in power, Wise.

خَلَقَ السَّمٰوٰتِ بِغَيْرِ عَمَدٍ تَرَوْنَهَا وَاَلْقٰى فِي الْاَرْضِ رَوَاسِيَ اَنْ تَمِيْدَ بِكُمْ وَبَثَّ فِيْهَا مِنْ كُلِّ دَآبَّةٍ ۚ وَاَنْزَلْنَا مِنَ السَّمَآءِ مَآءً فَاَنْۢبَتْنَا فِيْهَا مِنْ كُلِّ

اُسی نے آسمانوں کو ستونوں کے بغیر پیدا کیا جیسا کہ تم دیکھتے ہو اور زمین پر پہاڑ (بنا کر) رکھ دیئے تاکہ تم کو ہلا نہ دے اور اسمیں ہر طرح کے جانور پھیلا دیئے. اور ہم ہی نے آسمان سے پانی نازل کیا پھر اُس سے اُسمیں

10. He created the heavens without any pillars that ye can see; He set on the earth mountains standing firm, lest it should shake with you; and He scattered through it beasts of all kinds. We send down rain from the sky, and produce on the earth every kind of noble

creature, in pairs.

11. Such is the Creation of Allah: now show Me what is there that others besides Him have created: nay, but the Transgressors are in manifest error.

12. We bestowed (in the past) wisdom on Luqmān: "Show (thy) gratitude to Allah." Any who is (so) grateful does so to the profit of his own soul: but if any is ungrateful, verily Allah is free of all wants, worthy of all praise.

13. Behold, Luqmān said to his son admonishing him "O my son! join not in worship (others) with Allah: for false worship is indeed the highest wrong-doing."

14. And We have enjoined on man (to be good) to his parents: in travail upon travail did his mother bear him. And in years twain was his weaning (hear the command), "Show gratitude to Me and to thy parents to Me is (thy final) Goal.

15. "But if they strive to make thee join in worship with Me things of which thou hast no knowledge, obey them not; yet bear them company in this life with justice (and consideration), and follow the way of those who turn to Me: in the End the return of you all is to Me, and I will tell you all that ye did.

16. "O my son!' (said Luqmān), "If there be (but) the weight of a mustard-seed and it were (hidden) in a rock, or (anywhere) in the heavens or on earth, Allah will bring it forth: for Allah is subtle and Aware.

17. "O my son! establish regular prayer, enjoin what is just, and forbid what is wrong: and bear with patient constancy whate'er betide thee; for this is firmness (of purpose) in (the conduct of) affairs.

18. "And swell not thy cheek (for pride) at men. Nor walk in insolence through the earth: for Allah loveth

ہر قسم کی نفیس چیزیں اُگائیں ﴿۱۰﴾
یہ تو خدا کی پیدائش ہے تو مجھے دکھاؤ کہ خدا کے سوا جو
لوگ ہیں اُنہوں نے کیا پیدا کیا ہے؟ حقیقت یہ ہے
کہ یہ ظالم صریح گمراہی میں ہیں ﴿۱۱﴾
اور ہم نے لقمان کو دانائی بخشی۔ کہ خدا کا شکر کرو۔ اور جو شخص شکر
کرتا ہے تو اپنے ہی فائدے کیلئے شکر کرتا ہے۔ اور جو ناشکری کرتا
ہے تو خدا بھی بے پروا (اور) سزاوار حمد (وثنا) ہے ﴿۱۲﴾
اور (اُس وقت کو یاد کرو) جب لقمان نے اپنے بیٹے کو نصیحت
کرتے ہوئے کہا کہ بیٹا خدا کے ساتھ شرک نہ کرنا۔ شرک تو
بڑا (بھاری) ظلم ہے ﴿۱۳﴾
اور ہم نے انسان کو جسے اُس کی ماں تکلیف پر تکلیف سہہ کر پیٹ میں
اٹھائے رکھتی ہے (پھر اس کو دودھ پلاتی ہے) اور (آخر کار) دو برس
میں اس کا دودھ چھڑانا ہوتا ہے (اپنے نیز) اس کے ماں باپ کے بارے میں تاکید
کی ہے کہ میرا بھی شکر کرتا رہ اور اپنے ماں باپ کا بھی (کہ تم کو) میری ہی طرف لوٹ کر آنا ہے ﴿۱۴﴾
اور اگر وہ تیرے درپے ہوں کہ تو میرے ساتھ کسی ایسی چیز کو شریک
کرے جس کا تجھے کچھ بھی علم نہیں تو ان کا کہنا نہ ماننا۔ ہاں دنیا
(کے کاموں) میں ان کا اچھی طرح ساتھ دینا اور جو شخص میری
طرف رجوع لائے اس کے رستے پر چلنا پھر تم کو میری طرف لوٹ کر آنا ہے
تو جو کام تم کرتے رہے میں سب سے تم کو آگاہ کروں گا ﴿۱۵﴾
(لقمان نے یہ بھی کہا کہ) بیٹا اگر کوئی عمل (بالفرض) رائی کے دانے کے برابر
بھی (چھوٹا) ہو اور ہو بھی کسی پتھر کے اندر یا آسمانوں میں (مخفی ہو) یا زمین میں
خدا اس کو قیامت کے دن لا موجود کریگا۔ کچھ شک نہیں کہ خدا باریک بین (اور) خبردار ہے ﴿۱۶﴾
بیٹا نماز کی پابندی رکھنا اور (لوگوں کو) اچھے کاموں کے کرنے کا امر اور
بُری باتوں سے منع کرتے رہنا اور جو مصیبت تجھ پر واقع ہو
اس پر صبر کرنا۔ بیشک یہ بڑی ہمت کے کام ہیں ﴿۱۷﴾
اور (ازراہ غرور) لوگوں سے گال نہ پھلانا اور زمین میں
اکڑ کر نہ چلنا۔ کہ خدا کسی اترانے والے خود پسند کو

زَوْجٍ كَرِيمٍ ﴿١٠﴾
هَٰذَا خَلْقُ اللَّهِ فَأَرُونِي مَاذَا خَلَقَ
الَّذِينَ مِن دُونِهِ ۚ بَلِ الظَّالِمُونَ فِي
ضَلَالٍ مُّبِينٍ ﴿١١﴾
وَلَقَدْ آتَيْنَا لُقْمَانَ الْحِكْمَةَ أَنِ اشْكُرْ
لِلَّهِ ۚ وَمَن يَشْكُرْ فَإِنَّمَا يَشْكُرُ لِنَفْسِهِ ۖ
وَمَن كَفَرَ فَإِنَّ اللَّهَ غَنِيٌّ حَمِيدٌ ﴿١٢﴾
وَإِذْ قَالَ لُقْمَانُ لِابْنِهِ وَهُوَ يَعِظُهُ
يَا بُنَيَّ لَا تُشْرِكْ بِاللَّهِ ۖ إِنَّ الشِّرْكَ لَظُلْمٌ
عَظِيمٌ ﴿١٣﴾
وَوَصَّيْنَا الْإِنسَانَ بِوَالِدَيْهِ حَمَلَتْهُ
أُمُّهُ وَهْنًا عَلَىٰ وَهْنٍ وَفِصَالُهُ فِي
عَامَيْنِ أَنِ اشْكُرْ لِي وَلِوَالِدَيْكَ
إِلَيَّ الْمَصِيرُ ﴿١٤﴾
وَإِن جَاهَدَاكَ عَلَىٰ أَن تُشْرِكَ بِي مَا
لَيْسَ لَكَ بِهِ عِلْمٌ فَلَا تُطِعْهُمَا ۖ وَ
صَاحِبْهُمَا فِي الدُّنْيَا مَعْرُوفًا ۖ وَاتَّبِعْ
سَبِيلَ مَنْ أَنَابَ إِلَيَّ ۚ ثُمَّ إِلَيَّ مَرْجِعُكُمْ
فَأُنَبِّئُكُم بِمَا كُنتُمْ تَعْمَلُونَ ﴿١٥﴾
يَا بُنَيَّ إِنَّهَا إِن تَكُ مِثْقَالَ حَبَّةٍ مِّنْ
خَرْدَلٍ فَتَكُن فِي صَخْرَةٍ أَوْ فِي السَّمَاوَاتِ أَوْ
فِي الْأَرْضِ يَأْتِ بِهَا اللَّهُ ۚ إِنَّ اللَّهَ لَطِيفٌ خَبِيرٌ ﴿١٦﴾
يَا بُنَيَّ أَقِمِ الصَّلَاةَ وَأْمُرْ بِالْمَعْرُوفِ وَانْهَ
عَنِ الْمُنكَرِ وَاصْبِرْ عَلَىٰ مَا أَصَابَكَ ۖ إِنَّ
ذَٰلِكَ مِنْ عَزْمِ الْأُمُورِ ﴿١٧﴾
وَلَا تُصَعِّرْ خَدَّكَ لِلنَّاسِ وَلَا تَمْشِ فِي
الْأَرْضِ مَرَحًا ۖ إِنَّ اللَّهَ لَا يُحِبُّ كُلَّ

not any arrogant boaster.

19. "And be moderate in thy pace, and lower thy voice; for the harshest of sounds without doubt is the braying of the ass."

20. Do ye not see that Allah has subjected to your (use) all things in the heavens and on earth, and has made His bounties flow to you in exceeding measure, (both) seen and unseen? Yet there are among men those who dispute about Allah, without knowledge and without guidance, and without a Book to enlighten them!

21. When they are told to follow the (Revelation) that Allah Has sent down, they say: "Nay, we shall follow the ways that we found our fathers (following)." What! even if it is Satan beckoning them to the Chastisement of the (Blazing) Fire?

22. Whoever submits his whole self to Allah, and is a doer of good, has grasped indeed the firmest hand-hold: and to Allah shall all things return.

23. But if any reject Faith, let not his rejection grieve thee: to Us is their Return, and We shall tell them the truth of their deeds: for Allah knows well all that is in (men's) hearts.

24. We grant them their pleasure for a little while: in the end shall We drive them to a chastisement unrelenting.

25. If thou ask them, who it is that created the heavens and the earth. They will certainly say, "Allah", say: "Praise be to Allah!" But most of them know not.

26. To Allah belong all things in heaven and earth: verily Allah is He (that is) free of all wants, worthy of all praise.

27. And if all the trees on earth were pens and the Ocean (were

پسند نہیں کرتا ﴿۱۸﴾
اور اپنی چال میں اعتدال کئے رہنا اور (بولتے وقت)
آواز نیچی رکھنا کیونکہ (اونچی آواز گدھوں کی سی ہے اور کچھ
شک نہیں کہ) سب سے بُری آواز گدھوں کی ہے ﴿۱۹﴾
کیا تم نے نہیں دیکھا کہ جو کچھ آسمانوں میں اور جو کچھ
زمین میں ہے سب کو خدا نے تمہارے قابو میں کر دیا ہے
اور تم پر اپنی ظاہری اور باطنی نعمتیں پُوری کر دی ہیں۔
اور بعض لوگ ایسے ہیں کہ خدا کے بارے میں جھگڑتے ہیں
نہ علم رکھتے ہیں اور نہ ہدایت اور نہ کتاب روشن ﴿۲۰﴾
اور جب اُن سے کہا جاتا ہے کہ جو (کتاب) خدا نے نازل
فرمائی ہے اُس کی پیروی کرو۔ تو کہتے ہیں کہ ہم تو اُسی کی
پیروی کرینگے جس پر اپنے باپ دادا کو پایا۔ بھلا اگرچہ
شیطان اُن کو دوزخ کے عذاب کی طرف بلاتا ہو (تب بھی) ﴿۲۱﴾
اور جو شخص اپنے تئیں خدا کا فرمانبردار کر دے اور نیکو کار
بھی ہو تو اُس نے مضبوط دست آویز ہاتھ میں لے لی۔
اور (سب) کاموں کا انجام خدا ہی کی طرف ہے ﴿۲۲﴾
اور جو کفر کرے تو اُس کا کفر تمہیں غمناک نہ کر دے۔ اُن کو
ہماری طرف لوٹ کر آنا ہے پھر جو کام وہ کیا کرتے تھے ہم
اُن کو جتا دینگے۔ بیشک خدا دلوں کی باتوں سے واقف ہے ﴿۲۳﴾
ہم اُن کو تھوڑا سا فائدہ پہنچائیں گے پھر عذاب شدید
کی طرف مجبُور کر کے لے جائیں گے ﴿۲۴﴾
اور اگر تم اُن سے پوچھو کہ آسمانوں اور زمین کو کس نے
پیدا کیا تو بول اُٹھیں گے کہ خدا نے۔ کہہ دو کہ خدا کا شکر ہے
لیکن ان میں اکثر سمجھ نہیں رکھتے ﴿۲۵﴾
جو کچھ آسمانوں اور زمین میں ہے (سب) خدا ہی کا ہے۔ بیشک
خدا بے پروا (اور) سزاوارِ حمد (وثنا) ہے ﴿۲۶﴾
اور اگر یُوں ہو کہ زمین میں جتنے درخت ہیں (سب کے

مُخْتَالٍ فَخُوْرٍ ﴿۱۸﴾
وَاقْصِدْ فِيْ مَشْيِكَ وَاغْضُضْ مِنْ
صَوْتِكَ ؕ اِنَّ اَنْكَرَ الْاَصْوَاتِ لَصَوْتُ
الْحَمِيْرِ ﴿۱۹﴾ ع ۲
اَلَمْ تَرَوْا اَنَّ اللّٰهَ سَخَّرَ لَكُمْ مَّا فِي السَّمٰوٰتِ
وَمَا فِي الْاَرْضِ وَاَسْبَغَ عَلَيْكُمْ نِعَمَهٗ
ظَاهِرَةً وَّبَاطِنَةً ؕ وَمِنَ النَّاسِ مَنْ
يُّجَادِلُ فِي اللّٰهِ بِغَيْرِ عِلْمٍ وَّلَا هُدًى وَّلَا
كِتٰبٍ مُّنِيْرٍ ﴿۲۰﴾
وَاِذَا قِيْلَ لَهُمُ اتَّبِعُوْا مَاۤ اَنْزَلَ اللّٰهُ قَالُوْا
بَلْ نَتَّبِعُ مَا وَجَدْنَا عَلَيْهِ اٰبَآءَنَا ؕ اَوَلَوْ
كَانَ الشَّيْطٰنُ يَدْعُوْهُمْ اِلٰى
عَذَابِ السَّعِيْرِ ﴿۲۱﴾
وَمَنْ يُّسْلِمْ وَجْهَهٗۤ اِلَى اللّٰهِ وَهُوَ مُحْسِنٌ
فَقَدِ اسْتَمْسَكَ بِالْعُرْوَةِ الْوُثْقٰى ؕ وَاِلَى
اللّٰهِ عَاقِبَةُ الْاُمُوْرِ ﴿۲۲﴾
وَمَنْ كَفَرَ فَلَا يَحْزُنْكَ كُفْرُهٗ ؕ اِلَيْنَا
مَرْجِعُهُمْ فَنُنَبِّئُهُمْ بِمَا عَمِلُوْا ؕ اِنَّ
اللّٰهَ عَلِيْمٌۢ بِذَاتِ الصُّدُوْرِ ﴿۲۳﴾
نُمَتِّعُهُمْ قَلِيْلًا ثُمَّ نَضْطَرُّهُمْ اِلٰى
عَذَابٍ غَلِيْظٍ ﴿۲۴﴾
وَلَئِنْ سَاَلْتَهُمْ مَّنْ خَلَقَ السَّمٰوٰتِ وَ
الْاَرْضَ لَيَقُوْلُنَّ اللّٰهُ ؕ قُلِ الْحَمْدُ لِلّٰهِ ؕ
بَلْ اَكْثَرُهُمْ لَا يَعْلَمُوْنَ ﴿۲۵﴾
لِلّٰهِ مَا فِي السَّمٰوٰتِ وَالْاَرْضِ ؕ اِنَّ اللّٰهَ
هُوَ الْغَنِيُّ الْحَمِيْدُ ﴿۲۶﴾
وَلَوْ اَنَّ مَا فِي الْاَرْضِ مِنْ شَجَرَةٍ اَقْلَامٌ

ink), with seven Oceans behind it to add to its (supply), yet would not the Words of Allah be exhausted (in the writing): for Allah is Exalted in power, full of Wisdom.

سب (قلم ہوں اور سمندر (کا تمام پانی، سیاہی ہو (اور)
اسکے بعد سات سمندر (اور (سیاہی ہو جائیں) تو خدا کی باتیں
(یعنی اسکی صفتیں) ختم نہ ہوں۔ بیشک خدا غالب حکمت والا ہے (۲۷)

وَّالْبَحْرُ يَمُدُّهٗ مِنْۢ بَعْدِهٖ سَبْعَةُ اَبْحُرٍ
مَّا نَفِدَتْ كَلِمٰتُ اللّٰهِ ؕ اِنَّ اللّٰهَ عَزِيْزٌ
حَكِيْمٌ (۲۷)

28. And your creation or your resurrection is in no wise but as an individual soul: for Allah is He Who hears and sees (all things).

(خدا کو) تمہارا پیدا کرنا اور جلا اٹھانا ایک شخص (کے پیدا کرنے
اور جلا اٹھانے) کی طرح ہے۔ بیشک خدا سننے والا دیکھنے والا ہے (۲۸)

مَا خَلْقُكُمْ وَلَا بَعْثُكُمْ اِلَّا كَنَفْسٍ
وَّاحِدَةٍ ؕ اِنَّ اللّٰهَ سَمِيْعٌۢ بَصِيْرٌ (۲۸)

29. Seest thou not that Allah merges Night into Day and He merges Day into Night; that He has subjected the sun and the moon (to His Law), each running its course for a term appointed; and that Allah is well acquainted with all that ye do?

کیا تم نے نہیں دیکھا کہ خدا ہی رات کو دن میں داخل
کرتا ہے اور اُسی نے سورج اور چاند کو (تمہارے) زیر فرمان
کر رکھا ہے۔ ہر ایک ایک وقتِ مقرر تک
چل رہا ہے اور یہ کہ خدا تمہارے سب اعمال
سے خبردار ہے (۲۹)

اَلَمْ تَرَ اَنَّ اللّٰهَ يُوْلِجُ الَّيْلَ فِى النَّهَارِ
وَيُوْلِجُ النَّهَارَ فِى الَّيْلِ وَسَخَّرَ
الشَّمْسَ وَالْقَمَرَ ؗ كُلٌّ يَّجْرِىْۤ اِلٰٓى
اَجَلٍ مُّسَمًّى وَّاَنَّ اللّٰهَ بِمَا تَعْمَلُوْنَ
خَبِيْرٌ (۲۹)

30. That is because Allah is the Truth and because whatever else they invoke besides Him is Falsehood; and because Allah,—He is the Most High, Most Great.

یہ اس لئے کہ خدا کی ذات برحق ہے۔ اور جن کو یہ
لوگ خدا کے سوا پکارتے ہیں وہ لغو ہیں۔ اور یہ کہ
خدا ہی عالی رتبہ (اور) گرامی قدر ہے (۳۰)

ذٰلِكَ بِاَنَّ اللّٰهَ هُوَ الْحَقُّ وَاَنَّ مَا
يَدْعُوْنَ مِنْ دُوْنِهِ الْبَاطِلُ ۙ وَاَنَّ
اللّٰهَ هُوَ الْعَلِىُّ الْكَبِيْرُ (۳۰) ع ۳ ۱۱ ۱۲

31. Seest thou not that the ships sail through the Ocean by the grace of Allah?—that He may show you of His Signs? Verily, in this are Signs for all who constantly persevere and give thanks.

کیا تم نے نہیں دیکھا کہ خدا ہی کی مہربانی سے کشتیاں دریا میں
چلتی ہیں تاکہ وہ تم کو اپنی کچھ نشانیاں دکھائے۔ بیشک اسمیں ہر صبر
کرنیوالے (اور) شکر کرنیوالے کے لئے نشانیاں ہیں (۳۱)

اَلَمْ تَرَ اَنَّ الْفُلْكَ تَجْرِىْ فِى الْبَحْرِ
بِنِعْمَتِ اللّٰهِ لِيُرِيَكُمْ مِّنْ اٰيٰتِهٖ ؕ اِنَّ
فِىْ ذٰلِكَ لَاٰيٰتٍ لِّكُلِّ صَبَّارٍ شَكُوْرٍ (۳۱)

32. When a wave covers them like the canopy (of clouds), they call upon Allah, offering Him sincere devotion. But when He has delivered them safely to land, there are among them those that falter between (right and wrong). But none reject Our Signs except only a perfidious ungrateful (wretch)!

اور جب اُن پر (دریا کی) لہریں سائبانوں کی طرح چھا جاتی ہیں تو
خدا کو پکارنے (اور) خالص اسکی عبادت کرنے لگتے ہیں۔ پھر جب وہ اُنکو
نجات دیکر خشکی پر پہنچا دیتا ہے تو بعض ہی انصاف پر قائم رہتے ہیں۔ اور
ہماری نشانیوں سے وہی انکار کرتے ہیں جو عہد شکن (اور) ناشکرے ہیں (۳۲)

وَاِذَا غَشِيَهُمْ مَّوْجٌ كَالظُّلَلِ دَعَوُا اللّٰهَ
مُخْلِصِيْنَ لَهُ الدِّيْنَ ۚ فَلَمَّا نَجّٰىهُمْ اِلَى
الْبَرِّ فَمِنْهُمْ مُّقْتَصِدٌ ؕ وَمَا يَجْحَدُ بِاٰيٰتِنَاۤ
اِلَّا كُلُّ خَتَّارٍ كَفُوْرٍ (۳۲)

33. O mankind! do your duty to your Lord and fear (the coming of) a Day when no father can avail aught for his son, nor a son avail aught for his father. Verily, the promise of Allah is true: let not then this present life deceive you, nor let the Chief Deceiver deceive you about Allah.

لوگو اپنے پروردگار سے ڈرو اور اُس دن کا خوف کرو کہ
نہ تو باپ اپنے بیٹے کے کچھ کام آئے۔ اور نہ بیٹا باپ کے
کچھ کام آسکے۔ بیشک خدا کا وعدہ سچا ہے پس دنیا کی
زندگی تم کو دھوکے میں نہ ڈال دے۔ اور نہ فریب دینے والا (شیطان)
تمہیں خدا کے بارے میں کسی طرح کا فریب دے (۳۳)

يٰۤاَيُّهَا النَّاسُ اتَّقُوْا رَبَّكُمْ وَاخْشَوْا يَوْمًا
لَّا يَجْزِىْ وَالِدٌ عَنْ وَّلَدِهٖ ۫ وَلَا مَوْلُوْدٌ
هُوَ جَازٍ عَنْ وَّالِدِهٖ شَيْـًٔا ؕ اِنَّ وَعْدَ
اللّٰهِ حَقٌّ فَلَا تَغُرَّنَّكُمُ الْحَيٰوةُ الدُّنْيَا ۥ وقفة
وَلَا يَغُرَّنَّكُمْ بِاللّٰهِ الْغَرُوْرُ (۳۳)

34. Verily the knowledge of the Hour is with Allah (alone). It is He Who sends down rain, and He Who knows what is in the wombs. Nor does anyone know what it is that he

خدا ہی کو قیامت کا علم ہے اور وہی مینہ برساتا ہے۔ اور
وہی (حاملہ کے) پیٹ کی چیزوں کو جانتا ہے (کہ نر ہے

اِنَّ اللّٰهَ عِنْدَهٗ عِلْمُ السَّاعَةِ ۚ وَيُنَزِّلُ
الْغَيْثَ ۚ وَيَعْلَمُ مَا فِى الْاَرْحَامِ ؕ وَمَا

SÛRA–32

AS-SAJDA

(INTRODUCTION)

This short Sûra closes the series of the four A.L.M. Sûras, which began with the 29th. Its theme is the mystery of Creation, the mystery of Time and the mystery of the *Ma'ād* (the Final End) as viewed through the light of Allah's revelation. The contemplation of these mysteries should lead to Faith and the adoration of Allah. In chronology it belongs to the middle Makkan period and is therefore a little earlier than the last, but its chronology has no significance.

will earn on the morrow: nor does anyone know in what land he is to die. Verily with Allah is full knowledge and He is acquainted (with all things).

As-Sajda, or Adoration

In the name of Allah, Most Gracious, Most Merciful.

1. **A. L. M.**

2. (This is) the revelation of the Book in which there is no doubt,—from the Lord of the Worlds.

3. Or do they say, "He has forged it"? Nay, it is the Truth from thy Lord that thou mayest admonish a people to whom no warner has come before thee: in order that they may be rightly guided.

4. It is Allah Who has created the heavens and the earth, and all between them, in six Days, then He established Himself on the Throne: ye have none, besides Him, to protect or intercede (for you): will ye not then receive admonition?

5. He directs the affairs from the heavens to the earth: then it ascends unto Him, on a Day the measure of which is a thousand years of your reckoning.

6. Such is He, the Knower of all things, hidden and open, the Exalted (in power), the Merciful;—

7. He Who created all things in the Best way and He began the creation of man from clay,

8. And made his progeny from a quintessence of despised fluid.

9. But He fashioned him in due proportion, and breathed into him of His spirit. And He gave you (the faculties of) hearing and sight and understanding little thanks do ye give!

10. And they say: "What! when we lie, hidden and lost, in the earth, shall we indeed be in a Creation renewed? Nay, they deny the

یا مادہ) اور کوئی شخص نہیں جانتا کہ وہ کل کیا کام کریگا۔
اور کوئی متنفس نہیں جانتا کہ کس سرزمین میں اُسے موت آئیگی
بے شک خدا ہی جاننے والا (اور) خبردار ہے ﴿۳۴﴾

سورۂ سجدہ مکی ہے اور اس میں تیس آیتیں اور تین رکوع ہیں

شروع خدا کا نام لیکر جو بڑا مہربان نہایت رحم والا ہے
الم ﴿۱﴾ اس میں کچھ شک نہیں کہ اس کتاب کا نازل کیا جانا
تمام جہان کے پروردگار کی طرف سے ہے ﴿۲﴾
کیا یہ لوگ یہ کہتے ہیں کہ پیغمبر نے اسکو از خود بنا لیا ہے (نہیں) بلکہ
وہ تمہارے پروردگار کی طرف سے برحق ہے تاکہ تم ان لوگوں کو ہدایت
کرو جنکے پاس تم سے پہلے کوئی ہدایت کرنیوالا نہیں آیا تاکہ یہ رستے پر چلیں ﴿۳﴾
خدا ہی تو ہے جس نے آسمانوں اور زمین کو اور جو چیزیں
ان دونوں میں ہیں سب کو چھ دن میں پیدا کیا پھر عرش
پر قائم ہوا۔ اسکے سوا تمہارا نہ کوئی دوست ہے اور نہ سفارش
کرنے والا۔ کیا تم نصیحت نہیں پکڑتے؟ ﴿۴﴾
وہی آسمان سے زمین تک (کے) ہر کام کا انتظام کرتا ہے۔
پھر وہ ایک روز جس کی مقدار تمہارے شمار کے مطابق ہزار
برس ہوگی۔ اُس کی طرف صعود (اور رجوع) کریگا ﴿۵﴾
یہی تو پوشیدہ اور ظاہر کا جاننے والا (اور) غالب (اور)
رحم والا (خدا) ہے ﴿۶﴾
جس نے ہر چیز کو بہت اچھی طرح بنایا (یعنی) اُسکو
پیدا کیا۔ اور انسان کی پیدائش کو مٹی سے شروع کیا ﴿۷﴾
پھر اُسکی نسل خلاصے سے (یعنی) حقیر پانی سے پیدا کی ﴿۸﴾
پھر اُس کو درست کیا پھر اس میں اپنی (طرف سے) روح پھونکی
اور تمہارے کان اور آنکھیں اور دل بنائے (مگر) تم
بہت کم شکر کرتے ہو ﴿۹﴾
اور کہنے لگے کہ جب ہم زمین میں ملیا میٹ ہو جائینگے
تو کیا از سرِ نو پیدا ہونگے۔ حقیقت یہ ہے کہ یہ لوگ اپنے

تَدْرِيْ نَفْسٌ مَّاذَا تَكْسِبُ غَدًا ط وَمَا
تَدْرِيْ نَفْسٌ بِاَيِّ اَرْضٍ تَمُوْتُ ط اِنَّ
اللّٰهَ عَلِيْمٌ خَبِيْرٌ ﴿٣٤﴾

سُوْرَةُ السَّجْدَةِ مَكِّيَّةٌ وَّهِيَ ثَلٰثُوْنَ اٰيَةً وَّثَلٰثُ رُكُوْعَاتٍ

بِسْمِ اللّٰهِ الرَّحْمٰنِ الرَّحِيْمِ
الٓمّٓ ﴿١﴾ تَنْزِيْلُ الْكِتٰبِ لَا رَيْبَ فِيْهِ
مِنْ رَّبِّ الْعٰلَمِيْنَ ﴿٢﴾
اَمْ يَقُوْلُوْنَ افْتَرٰىهُ ج بَلْ هُوَ الْحَقُّ مِنْ
رَّبِّكَ لِتُنْذِرَ قَوْمًا مَّآ اَتٰىهُمْ مِّنْ نَّذِيْرٍ
مِّنْ قَبْلِكَ لَعَلَّهُمْ يَهْتَدُوْنَ ﴿٣﴾
اَللّٰهُ الَّذِيْ خَلَقَ السَّمٰوٰتِ وَالْاَرْضَ
وَمَا بَيْنَهُمَا فِيْ سِتَّةِ اَيَّامٍ ثُمَّ اسْتَوٰى
عَلَى الْعَرْشِ ط مَا لَكُمْ مِّنْ دُوْنِهٖ مِنْ
وَّلِيٍّ وَّلَا شَفِيْعٍ ط اَفَلَا تَتَذَكَّرُوْنَ ﴿٤﴾
يُدَبِّرُ الْاَمْرَ مِنَ السَّمَآءِ اِلَى الْاَرْضِ
ثُمَّ يَعْرُجُ اِلَيْهِ فِيْ يَوْمٍ كَانَ مِقْدَارُهٗٓ
اَلْفَ سَنَةٍ مِّمَّا تَعُدُّوْنَ ﴿٥﴾
ذٰلِكَ عٰلِمُ الْغَيْبِ وَالشَّهَادَةِ الْعَزِيْزُ
الرَّحِيْمُ ﴿٦﴾
الَّذِيْٓ اَحْسَنَ كُلَّ شَيْءٍ خَلَقَهٗ وَبَدَاَ
خَلْقَ الْاِنْسَانِ مِنْ طِيْنٍ ﴿٧﴾
ثُمَّ جَعَلَ نَسْلَهٗ مِنْ سُلٰلَةٍ مِّنْ مَّآءٍ مَّهِيْنٍ ﴿٨﴾
ثُمَّ سَوّٰىهُ وَنَفَخَ فِيْهِ مِنْ رُّوْحِهٖ وَ
جَعَلَ لَكُمُ السَّمْعَ وَالْاَبْصَارَ وَالْاَفْئِدَةَ ط
قَلِيْلًا مَّا تَشْكُرُوْنَ ﴿٩﴾
وَقَالُوْٓا ءَاِذَا ضَلَلْنَا فِي الْاَرْضِ ءَاِنَّا
لَفِيْ خَلْقٍ جَدِيْدٍ ط بَلْ هُمْ بِلِقَآئِ

Meeting with their Lord!"

11. Say: "The Angel of Death, put in charge of you, will (duly) take your souls: then shall ye be brought back to your Lord."

12. If only thou couldst see when the guilty ones will bend low their heads before their Lord, (saying:) "Our Lord! We have seen and we have heard: now then send us back (to the world): we will work righteousness: for we do indeed (now) believe."

13. If We had so willed, we could certainly have brought every soul its true guidance: but the Word from Me will come true, "I will fill Hell with Jinns and men all together."

14. "Taste ye then—for ye forgot the Meeting of this Day of yours, and We too will forget you—taste ye the chastisement of Eternity for your (evil) deeds!"

15. Only those believe in Our Signs, who, when they are recited to them fall down in adoration, and celebrate the praises of their Lord, nor are they (ever) puffed up with pride.

16. They forsake their beds of sleep, the while they call on their Lord, in Fear and Hope: and they spend (in charity) out of the sustenance which We have bestowed on them.

17. Now no person knows what delights of the eye are kept hidden (in reserve) for them—as a reward for their (good) Deeds.

18. Is then the man who believes no better than the man who is rebellious and wicked? Not equal are they.

19. For those who believe and do righteous deeds, are Gardens as hospitable homes, for their (good) deeds.

20. As to those who are rebellious and wicked, their abode will be the Fire: every time they wish to get away therefrom, they will be forced thereinto, and it will be said to them: "Taste ye the Chastisement of the

پروردگار کے سامنے جانے ہی کے قائل نہیں ﴿١٠﴾
کہہ دو کہ موت کا فرشتہ جو تم پر مقرر کیا گیا ہے تمہاری رُوحیں
قبض کر لیتا ہے پھر تم اپنے پروردگار کی طرف لوٹائے جاؤ گے ﴿١١﴾
اور (تم تعجب کرو) جب دیکھو کہ گنہگار اپنے پروردگار کے سامنے
سر جھکائے ہونگے (اور کہیں گے کہ) اے ہمارے پروردگار ہمنے دیکھ لیا اور سُن لیا.
تو ہمکو (دنیا میں) واپس بھیجدے کہ نیک عمل کریں بیشک ہم یقین کرنیوالے ہیں ﴿١٢﴾
اور اگر ہم چاہتے تو ہر شخص کو ہدایت دے دیتے لیکن میری طرف سے
یہ بات قرار پا چکی ہے کہ میں دوزخ کو جنّوں اور انسانوں
سب سے بھر دُوں گا ﴿١٣﴾
سو (اب آگ کے) مزے چکھو اسلئے کہ تمنے اس دن کے آنے کو بھلا
رکھا تھا (آج) ہم بھی تمہیں بھُلا دینگے اور جو کام تم کرتے تھے
اُن کی سزا میں ہمیشہ کے عذاب کے مزے چکھتے رہو ﴿١٤﴾
ہماری آیتوں پر تو وہی لوگ ایمان لاتے ہیں کہ جب اُنکو اُن سے
نصیحت کی جاتی ہے تو سجدے میں گر پڑتے اور اپنے پروردگار
کی تعریف کے ساتھ تسبیح کرتے ہیں اور غرور نہیں کرتے ﴿١٥﴾
اُن کے پہلو بچھونوں سے الگ رہتے ہیں (اور) وہ اپنے پروردگار
کو خوف اور اُمید سے پکارتے اور جو (مال) ہمنے اُن کو دیا ہے
اُس میں سے خرچ کرتے ہیں ﴿١٦﴾
کوئی متنفس نہیں جانتا کہ اُنکے لئے کیسی آنکھوں کی ٹھنڈک
چھپا کر رکھی گئی ہے۔ یہ اُن اعمال کا صلہ ہے جو وہ کرتے تھے ﴿١٧﴾
بھلا جو مومن ہو وہ اس شخص کی طرح ہو سکتا ہے جو
نافرمان ہو؟ دونوں برابر نہیں ہو سکتے ﴿١٨﴾
جو لوگ ایمان لائے اور نیک عمل کرتے رہے اُن کے (رہنے کے)
لئے باغ ہیں۔ یہ مہمانی اُن کاموں کی جزا ہے جو وہ کرتے تھے ﴿١٩﴾
اور جنہوں نے نافرمانی کی اُن کے (رہنے کے) لئے دوزخ ہے
جب چاہیں گے کہ اس میں سے نکل جائیں تو اس میں
لوٹا دیئے جائیں گے۔ اور اُن سے کہا جائے گا کہ جس دوزخ

رَبِّهِمْ كٰفِرُوْنَ ﴿١٠﴾
قُلْ يَتَوَفّٰىكُمْ مَّلَكُ الْمَوْتِ الَّذِيْ وُكِّلَ
بِكُمْ ثُمَّ اِلٰى رَبِّكُمْ تُرْجَعُوْنَ ﴿١١﴾ ع ١١
وَلَوْ تَرٰٓى اِذِ الْمُجْرِمُوْنَ نَاكِسُوْا رُءُوْسِهِمْ
عِنْدَ رَبِّهِمْ ۭ رَبَّنَآ اَبْصَرْنَا وَسَمِعْنَا
فَارْجِعْنَا نَعْمَلْ صَالِحًا اِنَّا مُوْقِنُوْنَ ﴿١٢﴾
وَلَوْ شِئْنَا لَاٰتَيْنَا كُلَّ نَفْسٍ هُدٰىهَا وَ
لٰكِنْ حَقَّ الْقَوْلُ مِنِّيْ لَاَمْلَـَٔنَّ جَهَنَّمَ
مِنَ الْجِنَّةِ وَالنَّاسِ اَجْمَعِيْنَ ﴿١٣﴾
فَذُوْقُوْا بِمَا نَسِيْتُمْ لِقَاۗءَ يَوْمِكُمْ
هٰذَا ۚ اِنَّا نَسِيْنٰكُمْ وَذُوْقُوْا عَذَابَ
الْخُلْدِ بِمَا كُنْتُمْ تَعْمَلُوْنَ ﴿١٤﴾
اِنَّمَا يُؤْمِنُ بِاٰيٰتِنَا الَّذِيْنَ اِذَا ذُكِّرُوْا
بِهَا خَرُّوْا سُجَّدًا وَّسَبَّحُوْا بِحَمْدِ
رَبِّهِمْ وَهُمْ لَا يَسْتَكْبِرُوْنَ ۩ ﴿١٥﴾ السجدة ٩
تَتَجَافٰى جُنُوْبُهُمْ عَنِ الْمَضَاجِعِ
يَدْعُوْنَ رَبَّهُمْ خَوْفًا وَّطَمَعًا ۡ وَّ
مِمَّا رَزَقْنٰهُمْ يُنْفِقُوْنَ ﴿١٦﴾
فَلَا تَعْلَمُ نَفْسٌ مَّآ اُخْفِيَ لَهُمْ مِّنْ
قُرَّةِ اَعْيُنٍ ۚ جَزَاۗءًۢ بِمَا كَانُوْا يَعْمَلُوْنَ ﴿١٧﴾
اَفَمَنْ كَانَ مُؤْمِنًا كَمَنْ كَانَ فَاسِقًا ڼ وقف غفران
لَا يَسْتَوٗنَ ﴿١٨﴾
اَمَّا الَّذِيْنَ اٰمَنُوْا وَعَمِلُوا الصّٰلِحٰتِ فَلَهُمْ
جَنّٰتُ الْمَاْوٰى ۡ نُزُلًۢا بِمَا كَانُوْا يَعْمَلُوْنَ ﴿١٩﴾
وَاَمَّا الَّذِيْنَ فَسَقُوْا فَمَاْوٰىهُمُ النَّارُ ۭ كُلَّمَآ
اَرَادُوْٓا اَنْ يَّخْرُجُوْا مِنْهَآ اُعِيْدُوْا فِيْهَا
وَقِيْلَ لَهُمْ ذُوْقُوْا عَذَابَ النَّارِ الَّذِيْ

Fire, the which ye were wont to reject as false."

21. And indeed We will make them taste of the lighter Chastisement before the greater Chastisement in order that they may (repent and) return.

22. And who does more wrong than one to whom are recited the Signs of his Lord, and who then turns away therefrom? Verily from those who transgress We shall exact (due) Retribution.

23. We did indeed aforetime give the Book to Moses: be not then in doubt of its reaching (thee): and We made it a guide to the Children of Israel.

24. And We appointed, from among them, Leaders, giving guidance under Our command, so long as they persevered with patience and continued to have faith in Our Signs.

25. Verily thy Lord will judge between them on the Day of Judgment, in the matters wherein they differ (among themselves).

26. Does it not teach them a lesson, how many generations We destroyed before them, in whose dwellings they (now) go to and fro? Verily in that are Signs: do they not then listen?

27. And do they not see that We do drive Rain to parched soil (bare of herbage), and produce therewith crops, providing food for their cattle and themselves? Have they not the vision?

28. They say: "When will this Decision be, if ye are telling the truth?"

29. Say: "On the Day of Decision, no profit will it be to Unbelievers if they (then) believe! Nor will they be granted a respite."

30. So turn away from them, and wait: they too are waiting.

کُنْتُمْ بِهٖ تُكَذِّبُوْنَ ﴿٢٠﴾
وَلَنُذِيْقَنَّهُمْ مِّنَ الْعَذَابِ الْاَدْنٰى دُوْنَ
الْعَذَابِ الْاَكْبَرِ لَعَلَّهُمْ يَرْجِعُوْنَ ﴿٢١﴾
وَمَنْ اَظْلَمُ مِمَّنْ ذُكِّرَ بِاٰيٰتِ رَبِّهٖ
ثُمَّ اَعْرَضَ عَنْهَا ؕ اِنَّا مِنَ الْمُجْرِمِيْنَ
مُنْتَقِمُوْنَ ﴿٢٢﴾
وَلَقَدْ اٰتَيْنَا مُوْسَى الْكِتٰبَ فَلَا تَكُنْ
فِيْ مِرْيَةٍ مِّنْ لِّقَآئِهٖ وَجَعَلْنٰهُ هُدًى
لِّبَنِيْٓ اِسْرَآءِيْلَ ﴿٢٣﴾
وَجَعَلْنَا مِنْهُمْ اَئِمَّةً يَّهْدُوْنَ بِاَمْرِنَا
لَمَّا صَبَرُوْا ؕ وَكَانُوْا بِاٰيٰتِنَا
يُوْقِنُوْنَ ﴿٢٤﴾
اِنَّ رَبَّكَ هُوَ يَفْصِلُ بَيْنَهُمْ يَوْمَ
الْقِيٰمَةِ فِيْمَا كَانُوْا فِيْهِ يَخْتَلِفُوْنَ ﴿٢٥﴾
اَوَلَمْ يَهْدِ لَهُمْ كَمْ اَهْلَكْنَا مِنْ قَبْلِهِمْ
مِّنَ الْقُرُوْنِ يَمْشُوْنَ فِيْ مَسٰكِنِهِمْ ؕ
اِنَّ فِيْ ذٰلِكَ لَاٰيٰتٍ ؕ اَفَلَا يَسْمَعُوْنَ ﴿٢٦﴾
اَوَلَمْ يَرَوْا اَنَّا نَسُوْقُ الْمَآءَ اِلَى الْاَرْضِ
الْجُرُزِ فَنُخْرِجُ بِهٖ زَرْعًا تَاْكُلُ
مِنْهُ اَنْعَامُهُمْ وَاَنْفُسُهُمْ ؕ اَفَلَا
يُبْصِرُوْنَ ﴿٢٧﴾
وَيَقُوْلُوْنَ مَتٰى هٰذَا الْفَتْحُ اِنْ كُنْتُمْ
صٰدِقِيْنَ ﴿٢٨﴾
قُلْ يَوْمَ الْفَتْحِ لَا يَنْفَعُ الَّذِيْنَ كَفَرُوْٓا
اِيْمَانُهُمْ وَلَا هُمْ يُنْظَرُوْنَ ﴿٢٩﴾
فَاَعْرِضْ عَنْهُمْ وَانْتَظِرْ اِنَّهُمْ مُّنْتَظِرُوْنَ ﴿٣٠﴾

کے عذاب کو تم جھوٹ سمجھتے تھے اُس کے مزے چکھو ﴿۲۰﴾
اور ہم اُن کو (قیامت کے) بڑے عذاب کے سوا عذاب دنیا
کا بھی مزہ چکھائیں گے شاید (ہماری طرف) لوٹ آئیں ﴿۲۱﴾
اور اُس شخص سے بڑھ کر ظالم کون جس کو اُس کے پروردگار کی
آیتوں سے نصیحت کی جائے تو وہ اُن سے منہ پھیر لے ہم
گنہگاروں سے ضرور بدلہ لینے والے ہیں ﴿۲۲﴾
اور ہم نے موسیٰ کو کتاب دی تو تم اُن کے ملنے سے
شک میں نہ ہونا اور ہم نے اس (کتاب) کو (یا موسیٰ کو)
بنی اسرائیل کے لئے (ذریعۂ) ہدایت بنایا ﴿۲۳﴾
اور اُن میں سے ہم نے پیشوا بنائے تھے جو ہمارے حکم سے
ہدایت کیا کرتے تھے. جب وہ صبر کرتے تھے. اور وہ
ہماری آیتوں پر یقین رکھتے تھے ﴿۲۴﴾
بلاشبہ تمہارا پروردگار ان میں جن باتوں میں وہ
اختلاف کرتے تھے. قیامت کے روز فیصلہ کر دیگا ﴿۲۵﴾
کیا ان کو اس (امر) سے ہدایت نہ ہوئی کہ ہم نے ان سے پہلے
بہت سی امتوں کو جنکے مقامات سکونت میں یہ چلتے پھرتے
ہیں ہلاک کر دیا. بیشک اس میں نشانیاں ہیں. تو یہ سنتے کیوں نہیں ﴿۲۶﴾
کیا انہوں نے نہیں دیکھا کہ ہم بنجر زمین کی طرف پانی رواں
کرتے ہیں پھر اس سے کھیتی پیدا کرتے ہیں جس میں سے
ان کے چوپائے بھی کھاتے ہیں اور وہ بھی (کھاتے ہیں)
تو یہ دیکھتے کیوں نہیں؟ ﴿۲۷﴾
اور کہتے ہیں اگر تم سچے ہو تو یہ فیصلہ کب
ہوگا؟ ﴿۲۸﴾
کہہ دو کہ فیصلے کے دن کافروں کو اُن کا ایمان لانا کچھ
بھی فائدہ نہ دے گا اور نہ اُن کو مہلت دی جائیگی ﴿۲۹﴾
تو اُن سے منہ پھیر لو اور انتظار کرو یہ بھی انتظار کر رہے ہیں ﴿۳۰﴾

SÛRA–33
AL-AḤZĀB
(INTRODUCTION)

The series of mystic Sûras beginning with S. 26 having been closed with the last Sûra, we now come back to the hard facts of this life. Two questions are mainly considered there, viz. (1) the attempt by violence and brute force to crush the truth, and (2) the attempt, by slander or unseemly conduct, to poison the relations of women with men.

As regards the first, the story of the Aḥzāb or Confederates, who tried to surround and annihilate the Muslim community in Madinah, is full of underhand intrigues on the part of such diverse enemies as the Pagan Quraish, the Jews (Banû Nadhîr) who had been already expelled from Madinah for their treachery, the Ga afān tribe of Bedouin Arabs from the interior, and the Jewish tribe Banû Quraiẓa in Madinah. This was the unholy Confederacy against Islam. But though they caused a great deal of anxiety and suffering to the beleaguered Muslims, Islam came triumphantly out of the trial and got more firmly established than ever.

The Quraish in Makkah had tried all sorts of persecution, boycott, insult, and bodily injuries to the Muslims, leading to their partial *hijrat* to Abyssinia and their Hijrat as a body to Madinah. The first armed conflict between them and the Muslims took place at Badr in Ramadhān A.H. 2, when the Quraish were signally defeated. Next year (Shauwāl A.H. 3) they came to take revenge on Madinah. The battle was fought at Uḥud, and though the Muslims suffered severely, Madinah was saved and the Makkans had to return to Makkah with their object frustrated. Then they began to make a network of intrigues and alliances, and besieged Madinah with a force of 10,000 men in Shauwāl and Ẓul-qa'd A.H. 5. This is the siege of the Confederates referred to in 33: 9-27, which lasted over two weeks: some accounts give 27 days. It caused much suffering, from hunger, cold, an unceasing shower of arrows, and constant general or concentrated assaults. But it ended in the discomfiture of the Confederates, and established Islam firmer than ever. It was a well organised and formidable attack, but the Muslims had made preparations to meet it. One of the preparations, which took the enemy by surprise, was the Trench (*Khandaq*) dug round Madinah by the Prophet's order and under the supervision of Salmān the Persian. The siege and battle are therefore known as the Battle of the Trench or the Battle of the Confederates.

As regards the position and dignity of the ladies of the Prophet's Household and the Muslim women generally, salutary principles are laid down to safeguard their honour and protect them from slander and insult. The ladies of the Household interested themselves in social work and work of instruction for the Muslim women, and Muslim women were being trained more and more in community service. Two of them (the two Zainabs) devoted themselves to the poor. The nursing of the wounded on or by the battlefield was specially necessary in those days of warfare. The Prophet's daughter Fã ima, then aged about 19 to 20, lovingly nursed her father's wounds at Uḥud (A.H. 3); Rufaida nursed Sa'd ibn Muã'ẓ's wounds at the Siege of Madinah by the Confederates (A.H. 5) and in the Khaibar expedition (A.H. 7) Muslim women went out from Madinah for nursing service.

A portion of this Sûra sums up the lessons of the Battle of the Trench and must have been revealed sometime after that Battle (Shauwãl A.H. 5). The marriage with Zainab referred to in verse 37 also took place in the same year. Some portions (e.g. verse 27) were probably revealed in A.H. 7 after the Khaibar settlement.

Al-Aḥzāb, or The Confederates

In the name of Allah, Most Gracious, Most Merciful.

1. O Prophet! Fear Allah, and hearken not to the Unbelievers and the Hypocrites: verily Allah is full of knowledge and wisdom.

2. But follow that which comes to thee by inspiration from thy Lord: for Allah is well acquainted with (all) that ye do.

3. And put thy trust in Allah, and enough is Allah as a Disposer of affairs.

4. Allah has not made for any man two hearts in his breast: nor has He made your wives whom ye divorce by Zihār your mothers: nor has He made your adopted sons your sons. Such is (only) your (manner of) speech by your mouths. But Allah tells (you) the Truth, and He shows the (right) Way.

5. Call them by after their fathers: that is juster in the sight of Allah. But if ye know not their father's names, (then they are) your Brothers in faith, or your friends but there is no blame on you if ye make a mistake therein: (what counts is) the intention of your hearts: and Allah is Oft-Forgiving, Most Merciful.

6. The Prophet is closer to the Believers than their own selves, and his wives are their mothers. Blood-relations among each other have closer personal ties, in the Book of Allah, than (the Brotherhood of) Believers and Muhājirs: nevertheless do ye what is just to your closest friends: such is the writing in the Book (of Allah).

7. And remember We took from the Prophets their Covenant: and from thee: from Noah, Abraham, Moses, and Jesus the son of Mary: We took from them a solemn Covenant:

سورۂ احزاب مدنی ہے اور اس میں تہتر آیتیں اور نو رکوع ہیں

شروع خدا کا نام لے کر جو بڑا مہربان نہایت رحم والا ہے
اے پیغمبر خدا سے ڈرتے رہنا اور کافروں اور منافقوں کا
کہا نہ ماننا۔ بے شک خدا جاننے والا (اور) حکمت
والا ہے (۱)
اور جو (کتاب) تم کو تمہارے پروردگار کی طرف سے وحی کی جاتی ہے
اُسی کی پیروی کیے جانا بیشک خدا تمہارے سب عملوں سے خبردار ہے (۲)
اور خدا پر بھروسہ رکھنا۔ اور خدا ہی کارساز
کافی ہے (۳)
خدا نے کسی آدمی کے پہلو میں دو دل نہیں بنائے۔
اور نہ تمہاری عورتوں کو جن کو تم ماں کہہ بیٹھتے ہو
تمہاری ماں بنایا اور نہ تمہارے لے پالکوں کو تمہارے بیٹے
بنایا[۲۷۳] یہ سب تمہارے منہ کی باتیں ہیں۔ اور خدا تو سچی بات
فرماتا ہے اور وہی سیدھا رستہ دکھاتا ہے (۴)
مومنو! لے پالکوں کو اُن کے (اصلی) باپوں کے نام سے پکارا
کرو کہ خدا کے نزدیک یہی بات درست ہے۔ اگر تم کو اُن کے باپوں
کے نام معلوم نہ ہوں تو دین میں وہ تمہارے بھائی اور دوست ہیں
اور جو بات تم سے غلطی سے ہوگئی ہو اس میں تم پر کچھ گناہ نہیں لیکن
جو قصد دلی سے کرو (اس پر مواخذہ ہے) اور خدا بخشنے والا مہربان ہے (۵)
پیغمبر مومنوں پر اُن کی جانوں سے بھی زیادہ حق رکھتے ہیں
اور پیغمبر کی بیویاں اُن کی مائیں ہیں۔ اور رشتہ دار آپس میں
کتاب اللہ کے رو سے مسلمانوں اور مہاجروں سے ایک دوسرے
(کے ترکے) کے زیادہ حقدار ہیں مگر یہ کہ تم اپنے دوستوں سے
احسان کرنا چاہو۔ یہ حکم کتاب (یعنی قرآن) میں لکھ دیا گیا ہے (۶)
اور جب ہم نے پیغمبروں سے عہد لیا اور تم سے اور نوح
سے اور ابراہیم سے اور موسیٰ سے اور مریم کے بیٹے عیسیٰ
سے۔ اور عہد بھی اُن سے پکا لیا (۷)

سُورَةُ الْأَحْزَابِ مَدَنِيَّةٌ وَهِيَ ثَلٰثٌ وَّسَبْعُوْنَ اٰيَةً وَّتِسْعُ رُكُوْعَاتٍ

بِسْمِ اللّٰهِ الرَّحْمٰنِ الرَّحِيْمِ
يٰٓاَيُّهَا النَّبِيُّ اتَّقِ اللّٰهَ وَلَا تُطِعِ الْكٰفِرِيْنَ
وَالْمُنٰفِقِيْنَ ۗ اِنَّ اللّٰهَ كَانَ عَلِيْمًا
حَكِيْمًا ﴿۱﴾
وَّاتَّبِعْ مَا يُوْحٰٓى اِلَيْكَ مِنْ رَّبِّكَ ۗ
اِنَّ اللّٰهَ كَانَ بِمَا تَعْمَلُوْنَ خَبِيْرًا ﴿۲﴾
وَّتَوَكَّلْ عَلَى اللّٰهِ ۗ وَكَفٰى بِاللّٰهِ
وَكِيْلًا ﴿۳﴾
مَا جَعَلَ اللّٰهُ لِرَجُلٍ مِّنْ قَلْبَيْنِ فِيْ
جَوْفِهٖ ۚ وَمَا جَعَلَ اَزْوَاجَكُمُ الّٰٓـِٔيْ تُظٰهِرُوْنَ
مِنْهُنَّ اُمَّهٰتِكُمْ ۚ وَمَا جَعَلَ اَدْعِيَآءَكُمْ
اَبْنَآءَكُمْ ۗ ذٰلِكُمْ قَوْلُكُمْ بِاَفْوَاهِكُمْ ۗ وَاللّٰهُ
يَقُوْلُ الْحَقَّ وَهُوَ يَهْدِي السَّبِيْلَ ﴿۴﴾
اُدْعُوْهُمْ لِاٰبَآئِهِمْ هُوَ اَقْسَطُ عِنْدَ اللّٰهِ ۚ
فَاِنْ لَّمْ تَعْلَمُوْٓا اٰبَآءَهُمْ فَاِخْوَانُكُمْ
فِي الدِّيْنِ وَمَوَالِيْكُمْ ۗ وَلَيْسَ عَلَيْكُمْ
جُنَاحٌ فِيْمَآ اَخْطَاْتُمْ بِهٖ وَلٰكِنْ مَّا تَعَمَّدَتْ
قُلُوْبُكُمْ ۗ وَكَانَ اللّٰهُ غَفُوْرًا رَّحِيْمًا ﴿۵﴾
اَلنَّبِيُّ اَوْلٰى بِالْمُؤْمِنِيْنَ مِنْ اَنْفُسِهِمْ
وَاَزْوَاجُهٗٓ اُمَّهٰتُهُمْ ۗ وَاُولُوا الْاَرْحَامِ بَعْضُهُمْ
اَوْلٰى بِبَعْضٍ فِيْ كِتٰبِ اللّٰهِ مِنَ الْمُؤْمِنِيْنَ
وَالْمُهٰجِرِيْنَ اِلَّآ اَنْ تَفْعَلُوْٓا اِلٰٓى اَوْلِيٰٓئِكُمْ
مَّعْرُوْفًا ۗ كَانَ ذٰلِكَ فِي الْكِتٰبِ مَسْطُوْرًا ﴿۶﴾
وَاِذْ اَخَذْنَا مِنَ النَّبِيّٖنَ مِيْثَاقَهُمْ وَمِنْكَ
وَمِنْ نُّوْحٍ وَّاِبْرٰهِيْمَ وَمُوْسٰى وَعِيْسَى
ابْنِ مَرْيَمَ ۪ وَاَخَذْنَا مِنْهُمْ مِّيْثَاقًا غَلِيْظًا ﴿۷﴾

8. That (Allah) may question the Truthful about their truthfulness and He has prepared for the Unbelievers a grievous Chastisement.

9. O ye who believe! remember the Grace of Allah, (bestowed) on you, when there came down on you hosts (to overwhelm you): but We sent against them a hurricane and forces that ye saw not: but Allah sees (clearly) all that ye do.

10. Behold! they came on you from above you and from below you, and behold, the eyes swerved and the hearts gaped up to the throats, and ye imagined various (vain) thoughts about Allah!

11. In that situation were the Believers tried: they were shaken as by a tremendous shaking.

12. And behold! The Hypocrites and those in whose hearts is a disease say: "Allah and His Messenger promised us nothing but delusions!"

13. Behold! A party among them said: "Ye men of Ya<u>th</u>rib! Ye cannot stand (the attack)! Therefore go back!" And a band of them ask for leave of the Prophet, saying, "Truly our houses are bare and exposed," though they were not exposed: they intended nothing but to run away.

14. And if an entry had been effected to them from the sides of the (City), and they had been incited to sedition. They would certainly have brought it to pass, with none but a brief delay!

15. And yet they had already Covenanted with Allah not to turn their backs, and a covenant with Allah must (surely) be answered for.

16. Say: "Running away will not profit you if ye are running away from death or slaughter; and even if (ye do escape), no more than a brief (respite) will ye be allowed to enjoy!"

17. Say: "Who is it that can screen you from Allah if it be His wish to

تاکہ سچ کہنے والوں سے اُن کی سچائی کے بارے میں دریافت کرے اور اُس نے
کافروں کیلئے دُکھ دینے والا عذاب تیار کر رکھا ہے ﴿٨﴾
مومنو خدا کی اُس مہربانی کو یاد کرو جو (اُس نے) تم پر (اُس وقت)
کی جب فوجیں تم پر (حملہ کرنے کو) آئیں۔ تو ہم نے اُن پر ہوا
بھیجی اور ایسے لشکر (نازل کئے) جن کو تم دیکھ نہیں سکتے تھے
اور جو کام تم کرتے ہو خدا اُن کو دیکھ رہا ہے ﴿٩﴾
جب وہ تمہارے اُوپر اور نیچے کی طرف سے تم پر (چڑھ) آئے اور جب
آنکھیں پھر گئیں اور دل (مارے دہشت کے) گلوں تک پہنچ
گئے اور تم خدا کی نسبت طرح طرح کے گمان کرنے لگے ﴿١٠﴾
وہاں مومن آزمائے گئے اور سخت طور پر ہلائے
گئے ﴿١١﴾
اور جب منافق اور وہ لوگ جن کے دلوں میں بیماری
ہے کہنے لگے کہ خدا اور اُسکے رسُول نے تو ہم سے
محض دھوکے کا وعدہ کیا تھا ﴿١٢﴾
اور جب اُن میں سے ایک جماعت کہتی تھی کہ اے اہل مدینہ
(یہاں) تمہارے (ٹھہرنے کا) مقام نہیں تو لوٹ چلو اور
ایک گروہ اُن میں سے پیغمبر سے اجازت مانگنے اور کہنے لگا کہ ہمارے گھر
کھلے پڑے ہیں حالانکہ وہ کھلے نہیں تھے۔ وہ تو صرف بھاگنا چاہتے تھے ﴿١٣﴾
اور اگر (فوجیں) اطرافِ مدینہ سے اُن پر آ داخل ہوں پھر اُن
سے خانہ جنگی کے لئے کہا جائے تو (فوراً) کرنے لگیں اور
اس کے لئے بہت کم توقف کریں ﴿١٤﴾
حالانکہ پہلے خدا سے اقرار کر چکے تھے کہ پیٹھ نہیں پھیریں گے اور
خدا سے (جو) اقرار کیا جاتا ہے اُس کی ضرور پرسش ہوگی ﴿١٥﴾
کہہ دو کہ اگر تم مرنے یا مارے جانے سے بھاگتے ہو تو بھاگنا
تم کو فائدہ نہیں دے گا اور اس وقت تم بہت ہی کم
فائدہ اٹھاؤ گے ﴿١٦﴾
کہہ دو کہ اگر خدا تمہارے ساتھ بُرائی کا ارادہ کرے تو کون تم کو اُس سے

لِّيَسْـَٔلَ الصّٰدِقِيْنَ عَنْ صِدْقِهِمْ ۚ وَاَعَدَّ
لِلْكٰفِرِيْنَ عَذَابًا اَلِيْمًا ﴿٨﴾
يٰۤاَيُّهَا الَّذِيْنَ اٰمَنُوا اذْكُرُوْا نِعْمَةَ اللّٰهِ
عَلَيْكُمْ اِذْ جَآءَتْكُمْ جُنُوْدٌ فَاَرْسَلْنَا
عَلَيْهِمْ رِيْحًا وَّجُنُوْدًا لَّمْ تَرَوْهَا ۚ
وَكَانَ اللّٰهُ بِمَا تَعْمَلُوْنَ بَصِيْرًا ﴿٩﴾
اِذْ جَآءُوْكُمْ مِّنْ فَوْقِكُمْ وَمِنْ اَسْفَلَ
مِنْكُمْ وَاِذْ زَاغَتِ الْاَبْصَارُ وَبَلَغَتِ
الْقُلُوْبُ الْحَنَاجِرَ وَتَظُنُّوْنَ بِاللّٰهِ الظُّنُوْنَا ﴿١٠﴾
هُنَالِكَ ابْتُلِيَ الْمُؤْمِنُوْنَ وَزُلْزِلُوْا
زِلْزَالًا شَدِيْدًا ﴿١١﴾
وَاِذْ يَقُوْلُ الْمُنٰفِقُوْنَ وَالَّذِيْنَ فِيْ قُلُوْبِهِمْ
مَّرَضٌ مَّا وَعَدَنَا اللّٰهُ وَرَسُوْلُهٗۤ اِلَّا
غُرُوْرًا ﴿١٢﴾
وَاِذْ قَالَتْ طَّآئِفَةٌ مِّنْهُمْ يٰۤاَهْلَ يَثْرِبَ
لَا مُقَامَ لَكُمْ فَارْجِعُوْا ۚ وَيَسْتَاْذِنُ فَرِيْقٌ
مِّنْهُمُ النَّبِيَّ يَقُوْلُوْنَ اِنَّ بُيُوْتَنَا عَوْرَةٌ ۛ
وَمَا هِيَ بِعَوْرَةٍ ۛ اِنْ يُّرِيْدُوْنَ اِلَّا فِرَارًا ﴿١٣﴾
وَلَوْ دُخِلَتْ عَلَيْهِمْ مِّنْ اَقْطَارِهَا ثُمَّ
سُئِلُوا الْفِتْنَةَ لَاٰتَوْهَا وَمَا تَلَبَّثُوْا بِهَآ
اِلَّا يَسِيْرًا ﴿١٤﴾
وَلَقَدْ كَانُوْا عَاهَدُوا اللّٰهَ مِنْ قَبْلُ لَا
يُوَلُّوْنَ الْاَدْبَارَ ۚ وَكَانَ عَهْدُ اللّٰهِ مَسْـُٔوْلًا ﴿١٥﴾
قُلْ لَّنْ يَّنْفَعَكُمُ الْفِرَارُ اِنْ فَرَرْتُمْ مِّنَ
الْمَوْتِ اَوِ الْقَتْلِ وَاِذًا لَّا تُمَتَّعُوْنَ اِلَّا
قَلِيْلًا ﴿١٦﴾
قُلْ مَنْ ذَا الَّذِيْ يَعْصِمُكُمْ مِّنَ اللّٰهِ اِنْ

give you Punishment or to give you Mercy?" Nor will they find for themselves, besides Allah, any protector or helper.

18. Verily Allah knows those among you who keep back (men) and those who say to their brethren, "Come along to us", but come not to the fight except for just a little while,

19. Covetous over you. Then when fear comes, thou wilt see them looking to thee, their eyes revolving, like one who faints from death: but when the fear is past, they will smite you with sharp tongues, covetous of goods. Such men have no faith, and so Allah has made their deeds of none effect: and that is easy for Allah.

20. They think that the Confederates have not withdrawn; and if, the Confederates should come (again), they would wish they were in the deserts (wandering) among the Bedouins, and seeking news about you (from a safe distance); and if they were in your midst, they would fight but little.

21. Ye have indeed in the Messenger of Allah an excellent exempler for him who hopes in Allah and the Final Day, and who remember Allah much.

22. When the Believers saw the Confederate forces, they said: "This is what Allah and His Messenger had promised us, and Allah and His Messenger told us what was true." And it only added to their faith and their zeal in obedience.

23. Among the Believers are men who have been true to their covenant with Allah: of them some have died and some (still) wait: but they have never changed (their determination) in the least:

24. That Allah may reward the men of Truth for their Truth, and

بچا سکتا ہو یا اگر تم پر مہربانی کرنی چاہے تو کون اسکو ہٹا سکتا ہے؟
اور یہ لوگ خدا کے سوا کسی کو نہ اپنا دوست پائینگے اور نہ مددگار (۱۷)
خدا تم میں سے ان لوگوں کو بھی جانتا ہے جو (لوگوں کو) منع
کرتے ہیں اور اپنے بھائیوں سے کہتے ہیں کہ ہمارے پاس
چلے آؤ۔ اور لڑائی میں نہیں آتے مگر کم (۱۸)
(یہ اس لئے کہ) تمہارے بارے میں بخل کرتے ہیں۔ پھر جب
ڈر (کا وقت) آئے تو تم اُن کو دیکھو کہ تمہاری طرف دیکھ
رہے ہیں (اور) اُنکی آنکھیں (اسی طرح) پھر رہی ہیں جیسے کسی کو
موت سے غشی آرہی ہو۔ پھر جب خوف جاتا رہے تو تیز زبانوں کیساتھ تمہارے
بارے میں زبان درازی کریں اور مال میں بخل کریں۔ یہ لوگ (حقیقت میں) ایمان
لائے ہی نہ تھے تو خدا نے انکے اعمال برباد کر دیئے۔ اور یہ خدا کو آسان تھا (۱۹)
(خوف کے سبب) خیال کرتے ہیں کہ فوجیں نہیں گئیں اور
اگر لشکر آ جائیں تو تمنا کریں کہ (کاش) گنواروں میں
جا رہیں (اور) تمہاری خبر پوچھا کریں۔ اور اگر
تمہارے درمیان ہوں تو لڑائی نہ کریں
مگر کم (۲۰)
تم کو پیغمبر خدا کی پیروی (کرنی) بہتر ہے (یعنی) اس شخص کو
جسے خدا (سے ملنے) اور روز قیامت (کے آنے) کی امید ہو
اور وہ خدا کا ذکر کثرت سے کرتا ہو (۲۱)
اور جب مومنوں نے (کافروں کے) لشکر کو دیکھا تو کہنے
لگے یہ وہی ہے جس کا خدا اور اسکے پیغمبر نے ہم سے وعدہ
کیا تھا اور خدا اور اسکے پیغمبر نے سچ کہا تھا اور اس سے
اُن کا ایمان اور اطاعت اور زیادہ ہو گئی (۲۲)
مومنوں میں کتنے ہی ایسے شخص ہیں کہ جو اقرار انہوں نے خدا سے کیا تھا
اسکو سچ کر دکھایا تو ان میں بعض ایسے ہیں جو اپنی نذر سے فارغ ہو گئے اور بعض
ایسے ہیں کہ انتظار کر رہے ہیں اور انہوں نے (اپنے قول کو) ذرا بھی نہیں بدلا (۲۳)
تاکہ خدا سچوں کو اُن کی سچائی کا بدلہ دے اور

أَرَادَ بِكُمْ سُوْٓءًا أَوْ أَرَادَ بِكُمْ رَحْمَةً ط وَلَا
يَجِدُوْنَ لَهُمْ مِّنْ دُوْنِ اللّٰهِ وَلِيًّا وَّلَا نَصِيْرًا (۱۷)
قَدْ يَعْلَمُ اللّٰهُ الْمُعَوِّقِيْنَ مِنْكُمْ وَالْقَآئِلِيْنَ
لِإِخْوَانِهِمْ هَلُمَّ إِلَيْنَا ج وَلَا يَأْتُوْنَ الْبَأْسَ
إِلَّا قَلِيْلًا (۱۸)
أَشِحَّةً عَلَيْكُمْ ج فَإِذَا جَآءَ الْخَوْفُ رَأَيْتَهُمْ
يَنْظُرُوْنَ إِلَيْكَ تَدُوْرُ أَعْيُنُهُمْ كَالَّذِيْ
يُغْشٰى عَلَيْهِ مِنَ الْمَوْتِ ج فَإِذَا ذَهَبَ
الْخَوْفُ سَلَقُوْكُمْ بِأَلْسِنَةٍ حِدَادٍ أَشِحَّةً
عَلَى الْخَيْرِ ط أُولٰٓئِكَ لَمْ يُؤْمِنُوْا فَأَحْبَطَ
اللّٰهُ أَعْمَالَهُمْ ط وَكَانَ ذٰلِكَ عَلَى اللّٰهِ يَسِيْرًا (۱۹)
يَحْسَبُوْنَ الْأَحْزَابَ لَمْ يَذْهَبُوْا ج وَإِنْ
يَّأْتِ الْأَحْزَابُ يَوَدُّوْا لَوْ أَنَّهُمْ بَادُوْنَ
فِي الْأَعْرَابِ يَسْأَلُوْنَ عَنْ أَنْۢبَآئِكُمْ ط
وَلَوْ كَانُوْا فِيْكُمْ مَّا قٰتَلُوْٓا إِلَّا
قَلِيْلًا (۲۰) ع
لَقَدْ كَانَ لَكُمْ فِيْ رَسُوْلِ اللّٰهِ أُسْوَةٌ
حَسَنَةٌ لِّمَنْ كَانَ يَرْجُوا اللّٰهَ وَالْيَوْمَ
الْآخِرَ وَذَكَرَ اللّٰهَ كَثِيْرًا ط (۲۱)
وَلَمَّا رَأَ الْمُؤْمِنُوْنَ الْأَحْزَابَ لا قَالُوْا
هٰذَا مَا وَعَدَنَا اللّٰهُ وَرَسُوْلُهٗ وَصَدَقَ
اللّٰهُ وَرَسُوْلُهٗ ز وَمَا زَادَهُمْ إِلَّآ إِيْمَانًا
وَّتَسْلِيْمًا ط (۲۲)
مِنَ الْمُؤْمِنِيْنَ رِجَالٌ صَدَقُوْا مَا عَاهَدُوا
اللّٰهَ عَلَيْهِ ج فَمِنْهُمْ مَّنْ قَضٰى نَحْبَهٗ وَمِنْهُمْ
مَّنْ يَّنْتَظِرُ صلے وَمَا بَدَّلُوْا تَبْدِيْلًا (۲۳)
لِّيَجْزِيَ اللّٰهُ الصّٰدِقِيْنَ بِصِدْقِهِمْ

punish the Hypocrites if that be His Will, or turn to them in Mercy: for Allah is Oft-Forgiving, Most Merciful.

منافقوں کو چاہے تو عذاب دے یا (چاہے تو) اُن پر مہربانی کرے۔ بے شک خدا بخشنے والا مہربان ہے ﴿۲۴﴾

وَيُعَذِّبَ الْمُنٰفِقِيْنَ اِنْ شَآءَ اَوْ يَتُوْبَ عَلَيْهِمْ ۭ اِنَّ اللّٰهَ كَانَ غَفُوْرًا رَّحِيْمًا ﴿۲۴﴾

25. And Allah turned back the Unbelievers for (all) their fury: no advantage did they gain; and enough is Allah for the Believers in their fight. And Allah is full of Strength, Exalted in might.

اور جو کافر تھے اُن کو خدا نے پھیر دیا وہ اپنے غصے میں (بھرے ہوئے تھے) کچھ بھلائی حاصل نہ کر سکے۔ اور خدا مومنوں کو لڑائی کے بارے میں کافی ہوا اور خدا طاقتور (اور) زبردست ہے ﴿۲۵﴾

وَرَدَّ اللّٰهُ الَّذِيْنَ كَفَرُوْا بِغَيْظِهِمْ لَمْ يَنَالُوْا خَيْرًا ۭ وَكَفَى اللّٰهُ الْمُؤْمِنِيْنَ الْقِتَالَ ۭ وَكَانَ اللّٰهُ قَوِيًّا عَزِيْزًا ﴿۲۵﴾

26. And those of the people of the Book who aided them—Allah did take them down from their strongholds and cast terror into their hearts, (so that) some ye slew, and some ye made captives.

اور اہل کتاب میں سے جنہوں نے اُن کی مدد کی تھی اُن کو اُن کے قلعوں سے اُتار دیا اور اُن کے دلوں میں دہشت ڈال دی۔ تو کتنوں کو تم قتل کر دیتے تھے اور کتنوں کو قید کر لیتے تھے ﴿۲۶﴾

وَاَنْزَلَ الَّذِيْنَ ظَاهَرُوْهُمْ مِّنْ اَهْلِ الْكِتٰبِ مِنْ صَيَاصِيْهِمْ وَقَذَفَ فِيْ قُلُوْبِهِمُ الرُّعْبَ فَرِيْقًا تَقْتُلُوْنَ وَتَاْسِرُوْنَ فَرِيْقًا ﴿۲۶﴾

27. And He made you heirs of their lands, their houses, and their goods, and of a land which ye had not frequented (before). And Allah has power over all things.

اور اُن کی زمین اور اُن کے گھروں اور اُن کے مال کا اور اُس زمین کا جس میں تم نے پاؤں بھی نہیں رکھا تھا تم کو وارث بنا دیا اور خدا ہر چیز پر قدرت رکھتا ہے ﴿۲۷﴾

وَاَوْرَثَكُمْ اَرْضَهُمْ وَدِيَارَهُمْ وَاَمْوَالَهُمْ وَاَرْضًا لَّمْ تَطَـُٔوْهَا ۭ وَكَانَ اللّٰهُ عَلٰي كُلِّ شَيْءٍ قَدِيْرًا ﴿۲۷﴾

28. O Prophet! say to thy Consorts: "If it be that ye desire the life of this world, and its glitter,—then come! I will provide for your enjoyment and set you free in a handsome manner.

اے پیغمبر اپنی بیویوں سے کہہ دو کہ اگر تم دنیا کی زندگی اور اس کی زینت و آرائش کی خواستگار ہو تو آؤ میں تمہیں کچھ مال دوں اور اچھی طرح سے رخصت کر دوں ﴿۲۸﴾

يٰٓاَيُّهَا النَّبِيُّ قُلْ لِّاَزْوَاجِكَ اِنْ كُنْتُنَّ تُرِدْنَ الْحَيٰوةَ الدُّنْيَا وَزِيْنَتَهَا فَتَعَالَيْنَ اُمَتِّعْكُنَّ وَاُسَرِّحْكُنَّ سَرَاحًا جَمِيْلًا ﴿۲۸﴾

29. But if ye seek Allah and His Messenger, and the Home of the Hereafter, Verily Allah has prepared for the well-doers amongst you a great reward.

اور اگر تم خدا اور اُس کے پیغمبر اور عاقبت کے گھر (یعنی بہشت) کی طلبگار ہو تو تم میں جو نیکوکاری کرنے والی ہیں اُن کے لئے خدا نے اجرِ عظیم تیار کر رکھا ہے ﴿۲۹﴾

وَاِنْ كُنْتُنَّ تُرِدْنَ اللّٰهَ وَرَسُوْلَهٗ وَالدَّارَ الْاٰخِرَةَ فَاِنَّ اللّٰهَ اَعَدَّ لِلْمُحْسِنٰتِ مِنْكُنَّ اَجْرًا عَظِيْمًا ﴿۲۹﴾

30. O Consorts of the Prophet! If any of you were guilty of evident unseemly conduct, the Punishment would be doubled to her, and that is easy for Allah.

اے پیغمبر کی بیویو تم میں سے جو کوئی صریح ناشائستہ حرکت کریگی۔ اس کو دونی سزا دی جائے گی۔ اور یہ (بات) خدا کو آسان ہے ﴿۳۰﴾

يٰنِسَاۗءَ النَّبِيِّ مَنْ يَّاْتِ مِنْكُنَّ بِفَاحِشَةٍ مُّبَيِّنَةٍ يُّضٰعَفْ لَهَا الْعَذَابُ ضِعْفَيْنِ ۭ وَكَانَ ذٰلِكَ عَلَي اللّٰهِ يَسِيْرًا ﴿۳۰﴾

31. But any of you that is devout in the service of Allah and His Messenger, and works righteousness,— to her shall We grant her reward twice: and We have prepared for her a generous Sustenance.

اور جو تم میں سے خدا اور اُس کے رسول کی فرمانبردار رہے گی اور عمل نیک کرے گی۔ اُس کو ہم دونا ثواب دیں گے اور اس کے لئے ہم نے عزت کی روزی تیار کر رکھی ہے ﴿۳۱﴾

وَمَنْ يَّقْنُتْ مِنْكُنَّ لِلّٰهِ وَرَسُوْلِهٖ وَتَعْمَلْ صَالِحًا نُّؤْتِهَآ اَجْرَهَا مَرَّتَيْنِ ۙ وَاَعْتَدْنَا لَهَا رِزْقًا كَرِيْمًا ﴿۳۱﴾

الجزء الثاني والعشرون ۲۲

32. O Consorts of the Prophet! Ye are not like any of the (other) women: if ye do fear (Allah), be not too complaisant of speech, lest one in whose heart is a disease should be moved with desire: but speak ye a speech (that is) just.

اے پیغمبر کی بیویو تم اور عورتوں کی طرح نہیں ہو۔ اگر تم
پرہیزگار رہنا چاہتی ہو تو (کسی اجنبی شخص سے) نرم نرم
باتیں نہ کیا کرو تاکہ وہ شخص جس کے دل میں کسی طرح کا مرض ہے کوئی
امید (نہ) پیدا کرلے۔ اور ان سے دستور کے مطابق بات کیا کرو ﴿۳۲﴾

يٰنِسَآءَ النَّبِيِّ لَسْتُنَّ كَاَحَدٍ مِّنَ النِّسَآءِ
اِنِ اتَّقَيْتُنَّ فَلَا تَخْضَعْنَ بِالْقَوْلِ
فَيَطْمَعَ الَّذِيْ فِيْ قَلْبِهٖ مَرَضٌ وَّقُلْنَ
قَوْلًا مَّعْرُوْفًا ﴿۳۲﴾

33. And stay quietly in your houses, and make not a dazzling display, like that of the former Times of Ignorance; and establish regular Prayer, and give zakat and obey Allah and His Messenger. And Allah only wishes to remove all abomination from you, ye Members of the Family, and to make you pure and spotless.

اور اپنے گھروں میں ٹھہری رہو اور جس طرح (پہلے) جاہلیت (کے
دنوں) میں اظہار تجمل کرتی تھیں اس طرح زینت نہ دکھاؤ۔ اور نماز پڑھتی رہو
اور زکوٰۃ دیتی رہو اور خدا اور اس کے رسول کی فرمانبرداری کرتی رہو۔
اے (پیغمبر کے) اہل بیت خدا چاہتا ہے کہ تم سے ناپاکی (کا میل کچیل)
دور کردے اور تمہیں بالکل پاک صاف کردے ﴿۳۳﴾

وَقَرْنَ فِيْ بُيُوْتِكُنَّ وَلَا تَبَرَّجْنَ تَبَرُّجَ
الْجَاهِلِيَّةِ الْاُوْلٰى وَاَقِمْنَ الصَّلٰوةَ وَ
اٰتِيْنَ الزَّكٰوةَ وَاَطِعْنَ اللّٰهَ وَرَسُوْلَهٗ
اِنَّمَا يُرِيْدُ اللّٰهُ لِيُذْهِبَ عَنْكُمُ الرِّجْسَ
اَهْلَ الْبَيْتِ وَيُطَهِّرَكُمْ تَطْهِيْرًا ﴿۳۳﴾

34. And recite what is rehearsed to you in your homes, of the Signs of Allah and His Wisdom: for Allah is All-Subtle, All-Aware.

اور تمہارے گھروں میں جو خدا کی آیتیں پڑھی جاتی ہیں
اور حکمت (کی باتیں سنائی جاتی ہیں) ان کو یاد رکھو۔
بےشک خدا باریک بیں اور باخبر ہے ﴿۳۴﴾

وَاذْكُرْنَ مَا يُتْلٰى فِيْ بُيُوْتِكُنَّ مِنْ اٰيٰتِ
اللّٰهِ وَالْحِكْمَةِ اِنَّ اللّٰهَ كَانَ لَطِيْفًا
خَبِيْرًا ﴿۳۴﴾ ع

35. For Muslim men and women,—for believing men and women, for devout men and women, for true men and women, for men and women who are patient and constant, for men and women who humble themselves, for men and women who give in charity, for men and women who fast for men and women who guard their chastity, and for men and women who engage much in Allah's remembrance for them has Allah prepared forgiveness and great reward.

(جو لوگ خدا کے آگے سر اطاعت خم کرنے والے ہیں یعنی) مسلمان مرد اور
مسلمان عورتیں اور مومن مرد اور مومن عورتیں اور فرمانبردار مرد اور فرمانبردار عورتیں
اور راستباز مرد اور راستباز عورتیں اور صبر کرنے والے مرد اور صبر کرنے والی عورتیں اور فروتنی
کرنے والے مرد اور فروتنی کرنے والی عورتیں اور خیرات کرنے والے مرد اور خیرات کرنے والی عورتیں
اور روزے رکھنے والے مرد اور روزے رکھنے والی عورتیں اور اپنی شرمگاہوں کی حفاظت کرنے والے
مرد اور حفاظت کرنے والی عورتیں اور خدا کو کثرت سے یاد کرنے والے مرد اور کثرت سے یاد کرنے والی
عورتیں کچھ شک نہیں کہ ان کے لئے خدا نے بخشش اور اجر عظیم تیار کر رکھا ہے ﴿۳۵﴾

اِنَّ الْمُسْلِمِيْنَ وَالْمُسْلِمٰتِ وَالْمُؤْمِنِيْنَ
وَالْمُؤْمِنٰتِ وَالْقٰنِتِيْنَ وَالْقٰنِتٰتِ وَالصّٰدِقِيْنَ
وَالصّٰدِقٰتِ وَالصّٰبِرِيْنَ وَالصّٰبِرٰتِ وَالْخٰشِعِيْنَ
وَالْخٰشِعٰتِ وَالْمُتَصَدِّقِيْنَ وَالْمُتَصَدِّقٰتِ وَ
الصَّآئِمِيْنَ وَالصّٰٓئِمٰتِ وَالْحٰفِظِيْنَ فُرُوْجَهُمْ
وَالْحٰفِظٰتِ وَالذّٰكِرِيْنَ اللّٰهَ كَثِيْرًا وَّالذّٰكِرٰتِ
اَعَدَّ اللّٰهُ لَهُمْ مَّغْفِرَةً وَّاَجْرًا عَظِيْمًا ﴿۳۵﴾

36. It is not fitting for a Believer, man or woman, when a matter has been decided by Allah and His Messenger, to have any option about their decision: if anyone disobeys Allah and His Messenger, he is indeed on a clearly wrong Path.

اور کسی مومن مرد اور مومن عورت کو حق نہیں ہے کہ جب
خدا اور اس کا رسول کوئی امر مقرر کردیں تو وہ اس کام میں
اپنا بھی کچھ اختیار سمجھیں۔ اور جو کوئی خدا اور اس کے رسول کی
نافرمانی کرے وہ صریح گمراہ ہوگیا ﴿۳۶﴾

وَمَا كَانَ لِمُؤْمِنٍ وَّلَا مُؤْمِنَةٍ اِذَا قَضَى
اللّٰهُ وَرَسُوْلُهٗٓ اَمْرًا اَنْ يَّكُوْنَ لَهُمُ الْخِيَرَةُ
مِنْ اَمْرِهِمْ وَمَنْ يَّعْصِ اللّٰهَ وَرَسُوْلَهٗ
فَقَدْ ضَلَّ ضَلٰلًا مُّبِيْنًا ﴿۳۶﴾

37. Behold! thou didst say to one who had received the grace of Allah and thy favour: "Retain thou (in wedlock) thy wife, and fear Allah." But thou didst hide in thy heart that which Allah was about to make manifest: thou didst fear the people,

اور جب تم اس شخص سے جس پر خدا نے احسان کیا اور تم
نے بھی احسان کیا (یہ) کہتے تھے کہ اپنی بیوی کو اپنے پاس
رہنے دے اور خدا سے ڈر اور تم اپنے دل میں وہ بات پوشیدہ کرتے
تھے جس کو خدا ظاہر کرنے والا تھا اور تم لوگوں سے ڈرتے تھے حالانکہ

وَاِذْ تَقُوْلُ لِلَّذِيْٓ اَنْعَمَ اللّٰهُ عَلَيْهِ وَ
اَنْعَمْتَ عَلَيْهِ اَمْسِكْ عَلَيْكَ زَوْجَكَ
وَاتَّقِ اللّٰهَ وَتُخْفِيْ فِيْ نَفْسِكَ مَا اللّٰهُ
مُبْدِيْهِ وَتَخْشَى النَّاسَ وَاللّٰهُ اَحَقُّ

اَنْ تَخْشٰىهُ ؕ فَلَمَّا قَضٰى زَيْدٌ مِّنْهَا وَطَرًا
زَوَّجْنٰكَهَا لِكَيْ لَا يَكُوْنَ عَلَى الْمُؤْمِنِيْنَ
حَرَجٌ فِيْٓ اَزْوَاجِ اَدْعِيَآئِهِمْ اِذَا قَضَوْا
مِنْهُنَّ وَطَرًا ؕ وَكَانَ اَمْرُ اللّٰهِ
مَفْعُوْلًا ﴿۳۷﴾

خدا ہی اس کا زیادہ مستحق ہے کہ اُس سے ڈرو۔ پھر جب زید نے
اُس سے (کوئی) حاجت (متعلق) نہ رکھی (یعنی اُسکو طلاق دیدی) تو ہم نے
تم سے اُسکا نکاح کر دیا تاکہ مومنوں کیلئے اُنکے منہ بولے بیٹوں کی
بیویوں (کیساتھ نکاح کرنیکے بارے) میں جب وہ اُنسے (اپنی) حاجت (متعلق) نہ رکھیں
(یعنی طلاق دیدیں) کچھ تنگی نہ رہے۔ اور خدا کا حکم واقع ہو کر رہنے والا تھا ﴿۳۷﴾

but it is more fitting that thou shouldst. Fear Allah. Then when Zaid had dissolved (his marriage) with her We joined her in marriage to thee: in order that (in future) there may be no difficulty to the Believers in (the matter of) marriage with the wives of their adopted sons, when the latter have dissolved (their marriage) with them. And Allah's command must be fulfilled.

مَا كَانَ عَلَى النَّبِيِّ مِنْ حَرَجٍ فِيْمَا فَرَضَ
اللّٰهُ لَهٗ ؕ سُنَّةَ اللّٰهِ فِي الَّذِيْنَ خَلَوْا مِنْ
قَبْلُ ؕ وَكَانَ اَمْرُ اللّٰهِ قَدَرًا مَّقْدُوْرَا ﴿۳۸﴾

پیغمبر پر اس کام میں کچھ تنگی نہیں جو خدا نے اُن کیلئے
مقرر کر دیا۔ اور جو لوگ پہلے گزر چکے ہیں اُن میں بھی
خدا کا یہی دستور رہا ہے۔ اور خدا کا حکم ٹھہر چکا تھا ﴿۳۸﴾

38. There can be no difficulty to the Prophet in what Allah has indicated to him as a duty: It was the practice (approved) of Allah amongst those of old that have passed away. And the command of Allah is a decree determined.

الَّذِيْنَ يُبَلِّغُوْنَ رِسٰلٰتِ اللّٰهِ وَيَخْشَوْنَهٗ
وَلَا يَخْشَوْنَ اَحَدًا اِلَّا اللّٰهَ ؕ وَكَفٰى
بِاللّٰهِ حَسِيْبًا ﴿۳۹﴾

اور جو خدا کے پیغام (جوں کے توں) پہنچاتے اور
اس سے ڈرتے اور خدا کے سوا کسی سے نہیں ڈرتے تھے۔
اور خدا ہی حساب کرنے کو کافی ہے ﴿۳۹﴾

39. (It is the practice of those) who preach the Messages of Allah, and fear Him, and fear none but Allah. And enough is Allah to call (men) to account.

مَا كَانَ مُحَمَّدٌ اَبَآ اَحَدٍ مِّنْ رِّجَالِكُمْ
وَلٰكِنْ رَّسُوْلَ اللّٰهِ وَخَاتَمَ النَّبِيّٖنَ ؕ
وَكَانَ اللّٰهُ بِكُلِّ شَيْءٍ عَلِيْمًا ﴿۴۰﴾ ع

محمدؐ تمہارے مردوں میں سے کسی کے والد نہیں ہیں بلکہ خدا
کے پیغمبر اور نبیوں (کی نبوت) کی مُہر (یعنی اس کو ختم کر دینے
والے ہیں) اور خدا ہر چیز سے واقف ہے ﴿۴۰﴾

40. Muhammad is not the father of any of your men, but (he is) the Messenger of Allah, and the Seal of the Prophets: and Allah has full knowledge of all things.

يٰٓاَيُّهَا الَّذِيْنَ اٰمَنُوا اذْكُرُوا اللّٰهَ
ذِكْرًا كَثِيْرًا ﴿۴۱﴾

اے اہل ایمان خدا کا بہت ذکر کیا
کرو ﴿۴۱﴾

41. O ye who believe! remember Allah, with much remembrance;

وَّسَبِّحُوْهُ بُكْرَةً وَّاَصِيْلًا ﴿۴۲﴾

اور صبح اور شام اُس کی پاکی بیان کرتے رہو ﴿۴۲﴾

42. And glorify Him morning and evening.

هُوَ الَّذِيْ يُصَلِّيْ عَلَيْكُمْ وَمَلٰٓئِكَتُهٗ
لِيُخْرِجَكُمْ مِّنَ الظُّلُمٰتِ اِلَى النُّوْرِ ؕ
وَكَانَ بِالْمُؤْمِنِيْنَ رَحِيْمًا ﴿۴۳﴾

وہی تو ہے جو تم پر رحمت بھیجتا ہے اور اسکے فرشتے بھی تاکہ
تم کو اندھیروں سے نکال کر روشنی کی طرف لے جائے۔
اور خدا مومنوں پر مہربان ہے ﴿۴۳﴾

43. He it is Who sends bessings on you, as do His angels, that He may bring you out from the depths of Darkness into Light: and He is Full of Mercy to the Believers.

تَحِيَّتُهُمْ يَوْمَ يَلْقَوْنَهٗ سَلٰمٌ ۚۖ وَاَعَدَّ لَهُمْ
اَجْرًا كَرِيْمًا ﴿۴۴﴾

جس روز وہ اُن سے ملیں گے اُن کا تحفہ (خدا کی طرف سے)
سلام ہوگا اور اُس نے اُن کیلئے بڑا ثواب تیار کر رکھا ہے ﴿۴۴﴾

44. Their salutation on the Day they meet Him will be "Peace!"; and He has prepared for them a generous Reward.

يٰٓاَيُّهَا النَّبِيُّ اِنَّآ اَرْسَلْنٰكَ شَاهِدًا وَّمُبَشِّرًا
وَّنَذِيْرًا ﴿۴۵﴾

اے پیغمبر ہم نے تم کو گواہی دینے والا اور خوشخبری سنانے والا
اور ڈرانے والا بنا کر بھیجا ہے ﴿۴۵﴾

45. O Prophet! Truly We have sent thee as a Witness, a Bearer of Glad Tidings, and a Warner,—

وَّدَاعِيًا اِلَى اللّٰهِ بِاِذْنِهٖ وَسِرَاجًا مُّنِيْرًا ﴿۴۶﴾

اور خدا کی طرف بلانے والا اور چراغ روشن ﴿۴۶﴾

46. And as one who invites to Allah's (Grace) by His leave, and as a Lamp spreading Light.

وَبَشِّرِ الْمُؤْمِنِيْنَ بِاَنَّ لَهُمْ مِّنَ اللّٰهِ فَضْلًا
كَبِيْرًا ﴿۴۷﴾

اور مومنوں کو خوشخبری سُنا دو کہ اُن کیلئے خدا کی طرف
سے بڑا فضل ہے ﴿۴۷﴾

47. Then give the glad tidings to the Believers, that they shall have from Allah a very great Bounty.

48. And obey not (the behests) of the Unbelievers and the Hypocrites, and disregard their insolence but put thy trust in Allah. For enough is Allah as a Disposer of affairs.

49. O ye who believe! when ye marry believing women, and then divorce them before ye have touched them, no period of 'Iddat have ye to count in respect of them: so give them a present, and release them in a handsome manner.

50. O Prophet! We have made lawful to thee thy wives to whom thou hast paid their dowers; and those whom thy right hand possesses out of the captives of war whom Allah has assigned to thee; and daughters of thy paternal uncles and aunts, and daughters of thy maternal uncles and aunts, who migrated with thee; and any believing woman who gives herself to the Prophet if the Prophet wishes to wed her;—this only for thee, and not for the Believers (at large); We know what We have appointed for them as to their wives and the captives whom their right hands possess;—in order that there should be no difficulty for thee. And Allah is Oft-Forgiving, Most Merciful.

51. Thou mayest defer (the turn of) any of them that thou pleasest, and thou mayest receive any thou pleasest: and there is no blame on thee if thou invite one whose (turn) thou hadst set aside. This were nigher to the cooling of their eyes, the prevention of their grief, and their satisfaction—that of all of them—with that which thou hast to give them: and Allah knows (all) that is in your hearts: and Allah is All-Knowing, Most Forbearing.

52. It is not lawful for thee (to marry more) women after this, nor to change them for (other) wives, even though their beauty attract thee, except any thy right hand should possess (as handmaidens): and Allah doth watch over all things.

53. O ye who believe! enter not the Prophet's houses,—until leave

اور کافروں اور منافقوں کا کہا نہ ماننا اور نہ اُن کے
تکلیف دینے پر نظر کرنا اور خدا پر بھروسہ رکھنا۔ اور خدا ہی کارساز کافی ہے ﴿۴۸﴾
مومنو! جب تم مومن عورتوں سے نکاح کرکے اُن کو ہاتھ لگانے
(یعنی اُنکے پاس جانے) سے پہلے طلاق دے دو تو تم کو کچھ
اختیار نہیں کہ اُن سے عدّت پوری کراؤ۔ اُن کو کچھ فائدہ (یعنی
خرچ) دے کر اچھی طرح سے رخصت کر دو ﴿۴۹﴾
اے پیغمبر ہم نے تمہارے لئے تمہاری بیویاں جن کو تم نے
اُن کے مہر دے دیئے ہیں حلال کر دی ہیں اور تمہاری لونڈیاں
جو خدا نے تمکو (کفار سے بطور مال غنیمت) دلوائی ہیں اور تمہارے چچا کی بیٹیاں
اور تمہاری پھوپھیوں کی بیٹیاں اور تمہارے ماموؤں کی بیٹیاں اور تمہاری خالاؤں کی بیٹیاں
جو تمہارے ساتھ وطن چھوڑ کر آئی ہیں (سب حلال ہیں) اور کوئی مومن عورت اگر اپنے تئیں
پیغمبر کو بخش دے (یعنی مہر لینے کے بغیر نکاح میں آنا چاہے) بشرطیکہ پیغمبر
بھی اُس سے نکاح کرنا چاہیں (وہ بھی حلال ہے لیکن یہ اجازت)
(اے محمدؐ) خاص تم ہی کو ہے سب مسلمانوں کو نہیں۔ ہمنے اُنکی بیویوں
اور لونڈیوں کے بارے میں جو (مہر واجب الادا) مقرر کر دیا ہے ہمکو معلوم ہے (یہ)
اسلئے (کیا گیا ہے) کہ تم پر کسی طرح کی تنگی نہ رہے۔ اور خدا بخشنے والا مہربان ہے ﴿۵۰﴾
(اور تم کو یہ بھی اختیار ہے کہ) جس بیوی کو چاہو علیحدہ رکھو
اور جسے چاہو اپنے پاس رکھو۔ اور جس کو تم نے علیحدہ کر دیا ہو
اگر اُس کو پھر اپنے پاس طلب کر لو تو تم پر کچھ گناہ نہیں۔ یہ
(اجازت) اسلئے ہے کہ اُن کی آنکھیں ٹھنڈی رہیں اور وہ غمناک
نہ ہوں اور جو کچھ تم اُنکو دو اُسے لیکر سب خوش رہیں۔ اور جو کچھ تمہارے
دلوں میں ہے خدا اُسے جانتا ہے۔ اور خُدا جاننے والا (اور) بُردبار ہے ﴿۵۱﴾
(اے پیغمبر) ان کے سوا اور عورتیں تم کو جائز نہیں اور نہ یہ
کہ ان بیویوں کو چھوڑ کر اور بیویاں کر لو خواہ اُن کا حُسن
تم کو (کیسا ہی) اچھا لگے مگر وہ جو تمہارے ہاتھ کا مال ہے (یعنی
لونڈیوں کے بارے میں تمکو اختیار ہے) اور خدا ہر چیز پر نگاہ رکھتا ہے ﴿۵۲﴾
مومنو! پیغمبر کے گھروں میں نہ جایا کرو مگر اس صورت

وَلَا تُطِعِ الْكٰفِرِيْنَ وَالْمُنٰفِقِيْنَ وَدَعْ اَذٰىهُمْ
وَتَوَكَّلْ عَلَى اللّٰهِ ۭ وَكَفٰى بِاللّٰهِ وَكِيْلًا ﴿۴۸﴾
يٰۤاَيُّهَا الَّذِيْنَ اٰمَنُوْٓا اِذَا نَكَحْتُمُ الْمُؤْمِنٰتِ
ثُمَّ طَلَّقْتُمُوْهُنَّ مِنْ قَبْلِ اَنْ تَمَسُّوْهُنَّ
فَمَا لَكُمْ عَلَيْهِنَّ مِنْ عِدَّةٍ تَعْتَدُّوْنَهَا ۚ
فَمَتِّعُوْهُنَّ وَسَرِّحُوْهُنَّ سَرَاحًا جَمِيْلًا ﴿۴۹﴾
يٰۤاَيُّهَا النَّبِيُّ اِنَّآ اَحْلَلْنَا لَكَ اَزْوَاجَكَ
الّٰتِيْٓ اٰتَيْتَ اُجُوْرَهُنَّ وَمَا مَلَكَتْ يَمِيْنُكَ
مِمَّآ اَفَاۗءَ اللّٰهُ عَلَيْكَ وَبَنٰتِ عَمِّكَ وَبَنٰتِ
عَمّٰتِكَ وَبَنٰتِ خَالِكَ وَبَنٰتِ خٰلٰتِكَ الّٰتِيْ
هَاجَرْنَ مَعَكَ ۡ وَامْرَاَةً مُّؤْمِنَةً اِنْ وَّهَبَتْ
نَفْسَهَا لِلنَّبِيِّ اِنْ اَرَادَ النَّبِيُّ اَنْ يَّسْتَنْكِحَهَا ۤ
خَالِصَةً لَّكَ مِنْ دُوْنِ الْمُؤْمِنِيْنَ ۭ قَدْ
عَلِمْنَا مَا فَرَضْنَا عَلَيْهِمْ فِيْٓ اَزْوَاجِهِمْ وَمَا مَلَكَتْ
اَيْمَانُهُمْ لِكَيْلَا يَكُوْنَ عَلَيْكَ حَرَجٌ ۭ
وَكَانَ اللّٰهُ غَفُوْرًا رَّحِيْمًا ﴿۵۰﴾
تُرْجِيْ مَنْ تَشَاۗءُ مِنْهُنَّ وَتُـْٔوِيْٓ اِلَيْكَ
مَنْ تَشَاۗءُ ۭ وَمَنِ ابْتَغَيْتَ مِمَّنْ عَزَلْتَ
فَلَا جُنَاحَ عَلَيْكَ ۭ ذٰلِكَ اَدْنٰٓى اَنْ تَقَرَّ
اَعْيُنُهُنَّ وَلَا يَحْزَنَّ وَيَرْضَيْنَ بِمَآ اٰتَيْتَهُنَّ
كُلُّهُنَّ ۭ وَاللّٰهُ يَعْلَمُ مَا فِيْ قُلُوْبِكُمْ ۭ
وَكَانَ اللّٰهُ عَلِيْمًا حَلِيْمًا ﴿۵۱﴾
لَا يَحِلُّ لَكَ النِّسَاۗءُ مِنْۢ بَعْدُ وَلَآ اَنْ
تَبَدَّلَ بِهِنَّ مِنْ اَزْوَاجٍ وَّلَوْ اَعْجَبَكَ
حُسْنُهُنَّ اِلَّا مَا مَلَكَتْ يَمِيْنُكَ ۭ وَكَانَ
اللّٰهُ عَلٰي كُلِّ شَيْءٍ رَّقِيْبًا ﴿۵۲﴾ ع
يٰۤاَيُّهَا الَّذِيْنَ اٰمَنُوْا لَا تَدْخُلُوْا بُيُوْتَ

is given you,— for a meal, (and then) not (so early as) to wait for its preparation: but when ye are invited, enter; and when ye have taken your meal, disperse, without seeking familiar talk. Such (behaviour) annoys the Prophet he is shy to dismiss you, but Allah is not shy (to tell you) the truth.

And when ye ask (his ladies) for anything ye want, ask them from before a screen: that makes for greater purity for your hearts and for theirs.

Nor is it right for you that ye should annoy Allah's Messenger, or that ye should marry his widows after him at any time. Truly such a thing is in Allah's sight an enormity.

54. Whether ye reveal anything or conceal it, verily Allah has full knowledge of all things.

55. There is no blame (on those ladies if they appear) before their fathers or their sons, their brothers, or their brothers' sons, or their sisters' sons, or their women, or the (slaves) whom their right hands possess. And, (ladies), fear Allah; for Allah is Witness to all things.

56. Allah and His Angels, send blessings on the Prophet: O ye that believe! send ye blessings on him, and salute him with all respect.

57. Those who annoy Allah and His Messenger— Allah has cursed them in this world and in the Hereafter, and has prepared for them a humiliating Punishment.

58. And those who annoy believing men and women undeservedly, bear (on themselves) a calumny and a glaring sin.

59. O Prophet! tell thy wives and daughters, and the believing

ہیں کہ تم کو کھانے کے لئے اجازت دی جائے اور اُس کے
پکنے کا انتظار بھی نہ کرنا پڑے لیکن جب تمہاری دعوت
کی جائے تو جاؤ اور جب کھانا کھا چکو تو چل دو اور باتوں
میں جی لگا کر نہ بیٹھ رہو۔ یہ بات پیغمبر کو ایذا دیتی تھی۔
اور وہ تم سے شرم کرتے تھے (اور کہتے نہیں تھے) لیکن خدا
سچی بات کے کہنے سے شرم نہیں کرتا۔ اور جب پیغمبر کی بیویوں
سے کوئی سامان مانگو تو پردے کے باہر مانگو۔ یہ تمہارے اور
اُنکے دونوں کے دلوں کیلئے بہت پاکیزگی کی بات ہے۔ اور تم کو یہ شایاں نہیں
کہ پیغمبر خدا کو تکلیف دو اور نہ یہ کہ اُنکی بیویوں سے کبھی اُنکے بعد نکاح کرو
بے شک یہ خدا کے نزدیک بڑا (گناہ کا کام) ہے ﴿۵۳﴾
اگر تم کسی چیز کو ظاہر کرو یا اس کو مخفی رکھو تو (یاد رکھو کہ)
خدا ہر چیز سے باخبر ہے ﴿۵۴﴾
عورتوں پر اپنے باپوں سے (پردہ نہ کرنے میں) کچھ گناہ
نہیں اور نہ اپنے بیٹوں سے اور نہ اپنے بھائیوں سے
اور نہ اپنے بھتیجوں سے اور نہ اپنے بھانجوں سے نہ
اپنی (قسم کی) عورتوں سے اور نہ لونڈیوں سے اور (اے عورتو)
خدا سے ڈرتی رہو بے شک خدا ہر چیز سے واقف ہے ﴿۵۵﴾
خدا اور اُس کے فرشتے پیغمبر پر درود بھیجتے ہیں۔
مومنو! تم بھی پیغمبر پر درود اور سلام
بھیجا کرو ﴿۵۶﴾
جو لوگ خدا اور اُس کے پیغمبر کو رنج پہنچاتے ہیں
اُن پر خدا دنیا اور آخرت میں لعنت کرتا ہے اور
اُن کیلئے اُس نے ذلیل کرنے والا عذاب تیار کر رکھا ہے ﴿۵۷﴾
اور جو لوگ مومن مردوں اور مومن عورتوں کو ایسے کام کی
تہمت سے جو انہوں نے نہ کیا ہو ایذا دیں تو انہوں نے
بہتان اور صریح گناہ کا بوجھ اپنے سر پر رکھا ﴿۵۸﴾
اے پیغمبر اپنی بیویوں اور بیٹیوں اور مسلمانوں کی عورتوں

النبي الا ان يؤذن لكم الى طعام
غير نظرين انه ولكن اذا دعيتم
فادخلوا فاذا طعمتم فانتشروا ولا
مستانسين لحديث ان ذلكم كان
يؤذي النبي فيستحي منكم والله لا يستحي
من الحق واذا سالتموهن متاعا فسئلوهن
من وراء حجاب ذلكم اطهر لقلوبكم و
قلوبهن وما كان لكم ان تؤذوا رسول
الله ولا ان تنكحوا ازواجه من بعده
ابدا ان ذلكم كان عند الله عظيما ﴿٥٣﴾
ان تبدوا شيئا او تخفوه فان الله
كان بكل شيء عليما ﴿٥٤﴾
لا جناح عليهن في ابائهن ولا ابنائهن
ولا اخوانهن ولا ابناء اخوانهن ولا
ابناء اخوتهن ولا نسائهن ولا ما
ملكت ايمانهن واتقين الله ان
الله كان على كل شيء شهيدا ﴿٥٥﴾
ان الله وملئكته يصلون على النبي
يايها الذين امنوا صلوا عليه وسلموا
تسليما ﴿٥٦﴾
ان الذين يؤذون الله ورسوله
لعنهم الله في الدنيا والاخرة و
اعد لهم عذابا مهينا ﴿٥٧﴾
والذين يؤذون المؤمنين والمؤمنت
بغير ما اكتسبوا فقد احتملوا
بهتانا واثما مبينا ﴿٥٨﴾ ع
يايها النبي قل لازواجك

women, that they should cast their outer garments over their persons (when out of doors): that is most convenient, that they should be known (as such) and not molested. And Allah is Oft-Forgiving, Most Merciful.

سے کہہ دو کہ (باہر نکلا کریں تو) اپنے (مونہوں) پر چادر
لٹکا کر (گھونگٹ نکال) لیا کریں۔ یہ امر ان کیلئے موجب
شناخت (و امتیاز) ہوگا تو کوئی ان کو ایذا نہ دے گا۔ اور
خدا بخشنے والا مہربان ہے ﴿۵۹﴾

وَبَنٰتِكَ وَنِسَآءِ الْمُؤْمِنِيْنَ يُدْنِيْنَ
عَلَيْهِنَّ مِنْ جَلَابِيْبِهِنَّ ۭ ذٰلِكَ اَدْنٰٓى
اَنْ يُّعْرَفْنَ فَلَا يُؤْذَيْنَ ۭ وَكَانَ اللّٰهُ
غَفُوْرًا رَّحِيْمًا ﴿۵۹﴾

60. Truly, if the Hypocrites, and those in whose heart is a disease, and those who stir up sedition in the City, desist not, We shall certainly stir thee up against them: then will they not be able to stay in it as thy neighbours for any length of time:

61. They shall have a curse on them: wherever they are found, they shall be seized and slain.

اگر منافق اور وہ لوگ جن کے دلوں میں مرض ہے اور جو مدینے
(کے شہر) میں بری بری خبریں اڑایا کرتے ہیں (اپنے کردار سے)
باز نہ آئیں گے تو ہم تم کو ان کے پیچھے لگا دیں گے پھر
وہاں تمہارے پڑوس میں نہ رہ سکیں گے مگر تھوڑے دن ﴿۶۰﴾
(وہ بھی) پھٹکارے ہوئے جہاں پائے گئے پکڑے گئے۔
اور جان سے مار ڈالے گئے ﴿۶۱﴾

لَىِٕنْ لَّمْ يَنْتَهِ الْمُنٰفِقُوْنَ وَالَّذِيْنَ فِيْ
قُلُوْبِهِمْ مَّرَضٌ وَّالْمُرْجِفُوْنَ فِي الْمَدِيْنَةِ
لَنُغْرِيَنَّكَ بِهِمْ ثُمَّ لَا يُجَاوِرُوْنَكَ فِيْهَآ
اِلَّا قَلِيْلًا ﴿۶۰﴾ مع ۱۲ عند المتاخرين
مَّلْعُوْنِيْنَ ۚ اَيْنَمَا ثُقِفُوْٓا اُخِذُوْا وَقُتِّلُوْا
تَقْتِيْلًا ﴿۶۱﴾

62. (Such was) the practice (approved) of Allah among those who lived aforetime: no change wilt thou find in the practice (approved) of Allah.

جو لوگ پہلے گزر چکے ہیں ان کے بارے میں بھی خدا کی یہی
عادت رہی ہے اور تم خدا کی عادت میں تغیر و تبدل نہ پاؤ گے ﴿۶۲﴾

سُنَّةَ اللّٰهِ فِي الَّذِيْنَ خَلَوْا مِنْ قَبْلُ ۚ
وَلَنْ تَجِدَ لِسُنَّةِ اللّٰهِ تَبْدِيْلًا ﴿۶۲﴾ الربع

63. Men ask thee concerning the Hour: say, "The knowledge thereof is with Allah (alone)": and what will make thee understand?—perchance the Hour is nigh!

لوگ تم سے قیامت کی نسبت دریافت کرتے ہیں (کہ کب آئیگی)
کہہ دو کہ اس کا علم خدا ہی کو ہے۔ اور تمہیں کیا معلوم ہے
شاید قیامت قریب ہی آ گئی ہو ﴿۶۳﴾

يَسْـَٔلُكَ النَّاسُ عَنِ السَّاعَةِ ۭ قُلْ اِنَّمَا
عِلْمُهَا عِنْدَ اللّٰهِ ۭ وَمَا يُدْرِيْكَ لَعَلَّ
السَّاعَةَ تَكُوْنُ قَرِيْبًا ﴿۶۳﴾

64. Verily Allah has cursed the Unbelievers and prepared for them a Blazing Fire,—

بے شک خدا نے کافروں پر لعنت کی ہے اور ان کے
لئے (جہنم کی) آگ تیار کر رکھی ہے ﴿۶۴﴾

اِنَّ اللّٰهَ لَعَنَ الْكٰفِرِيْنَ وَاَعَدَّ لَهُمْ
سَعِيْرًا ﴿۶۴﴾

65. To dwell therein for ever: no protector will they find, nor helper.

اس میں ابدالآباد رہیں گے۔ نہ کسی کو دوست پائیں گے
اور نہ مددگار ﴿۶۵﴾

خٰلِدِيْنَ فِيْهَآ اَبَدًا ۚ لَا يَجِدُوْنَ وَلِيًّا
وَّلَا نَصِيْرًا ﴿۶۵﴾

66. The Day that their faces will be turned over in the Fire, they will say: "Woe to us! would that we had obeyed Allah and obeyed the Messenger!"

67. And they would say: "Our Lord! We obeyed our chiefs and our great ones, and they misled us as to the (right) path.

68. "Our Lord! Give Them double Chastiement and cure them with a very great Curse!"

جس دن ان کے منہ آگ میں الٹائے جائیں کہیں گے اے
کاش ہم خدا کی فرمانبرداری کرتے اور رسول (خدا) کا حکم مانتے ﴿۶۶﴾
اور کہیں گے کہ اے ہمارے پروردگار ہم نے اپنے سرداروں
اور بڑے لوگوں کا کہا مانا تو انہوں نے ہم کو رستے سے گمراہ کر دیا ﴿۶۷﴾
اے ہمارے پروردگار ان کو دگنا عذاب دے اور ان پر
بڑی لعنت کر ﴿۶۸﴾

يَوْمَ تُقَلَّبُ وُجُوْهُهُمْ فِي النَّارِ يَقُوْلُوْنَ
يٰلَيْتَنَآ اَطَعْنَا اللّٰهَ وَاَطَعْنَا الرَّسُوْلَا ﴿۶۶﴾
وَقَالُوْا رَبَّنَآ اِنَّآ اَطَعْنَا سَادَتَنَا وَكُبَرَاۗءَنَا
فَاَضَلُّوْنَا السَّبِيْلَا ﴿۶۷﴾
رَبَّنَآ اٰتِهِمْ ضِعْفَيْنِ مِنَ الْعَذَابِ
وَالْعَنْهُمْ لَعْنًا كَبِيْرًا ﴿۶۸﴾ ع ۸ ۵

69. O ye who believe! be ye not like those who hurt Moses, but Allah cleared him of the (calumnies) they had uttered: and he was

مومنو! تم ان لوگوں جیسے نہ ہونا جنہوں نے موسیٰ کو عیب
لگا کر رنج پہنچایا تو خدا نے ان کو بے عیب ثابت کیا اور

يٰٓاَيُّهَا الَّذِيْنَ اٰمَنُوْا لَا تَكُوْنُوْا كَالَّذِيْنَ
اٰذَوْا مُوْسٰى فَبَرَّاَهُ اللّٰهُ مِمَّا قَالُوْا ۭ وَ

SÛRA–34
SABÃ
(INTRODUCTION)

Now we begin a series of the Sûras, S. 34 to S. 39, which recapitulate some of the features of the spiritual world. This Sûra leads off with emphasis on Allah's Mercy and Power and Truth. Then (in S. 35) we are told how angles manifest the Power of Allah, and how different is Good from Evil and Truth from Falsehood. S. 34 is devoted to the Holy Prophet and the Qur-ãn that came through him. In S. 37 the emphasis is on the snares of the Evil One; in S. 38, on the conquest of evil by wisdom and power as in the case of David and Solomon, and by Patience and Constancy as in the case of Job: and in S. 39 on the Final Judgment, which will sort out Faith from Unfaith and give to each its due.

The chronology has here no significance. This Sûra belongs to the early Makkan period.

كَانَ عِنْدَ اللّٰهِ وَجِيْهًا ﴿٦٩﴾

وہ خدا کے نزدیک آبرو والے تھے ﴿۶۹﴾

honourable in Allah's sight.

يٰۤاَيُّهَا الَّذِيْنَ اٰمَنُوا اتَّقُوا اللّٰهَ وَقُوْلُوْا
قَوْلًا سَدِيْدًا ﴿٧٠﴾

مومنو! خدا سے ڈرا کرو اور بات سیدھی کہا
کرو ﴿۷۰﴾

70. O ye who believe! fear Allah, and make your utterance straight forward:

يُّصْلِحْ لَكُمْ اَعْمَالَكُمْ وَيَغْفِرْ لَكُمْ
ذُنُوْبَكُمْ ؕ وَمَنْ يُّطِعِ اللّٰهَ وَرَسُوْلَهٗ
فَقَدْ فَازَ فَوْزًا عَظِيْمًا ﴿٧١﴾

وہ تمہارے سب اعمال درست کر دیگا اور تمہارے گناہ بخش
دے گا۔ اور جو شخص خدا اور اسکے رسول کی فرمانبرداری
کرے گا تو بے شک بڑی مُراد پائے گا ﴿۷۱﴾

71. That He may make your conduct whole and sound and forgive you your sins: he that obeys Allah and His Messenger, has already attained the great victory.

اِنَّا عَرَضْنَا الْاَمَانَةَ عَلَى السَّمٰوٰتِ وَ
الْاَرْضِ وَالْجِبَالِ فَاَبَيْنَ اَنْ يَّحْمِلْنَهَا
وَاَشْفَقْنَ مِنْهَا وَحَمَلَهَا الْاِنْسَانُ ؕ
اِنَّهٗ كَانَ ظَلُوْمًا جَهُوْلًا ﴿٧٢﴾

ہم نے (بارِ) امانت کو آسمانوں اور زمین پر پیش کیا تو
اُنہوں نے اُس کے اُٹھانے سے انکار کیا اور اُس سے
ڈر گئے۔ اور انسان نے اس کو اُٹھا لیا۔ بے شک وہ
ظالم اور جاہل تھا ﴿۷۲﴾

72. We did indeed offer the Trust to the Heavens and the Earth and the Mountians; but they refused to undertake it, being afraid thereof: but man undertook it:— he was indeed unjust and foolish,—

لِّيُعَذِّبَ اللّٰهُ الْمُنٰفِقِيْنَ وَالْمُنٰفِقٰتِ
وَالْمُشْرِكِيْنَ وَالْمُشْرِكٰتِ وَيَتُوْبَ اللّٰهُ
عَلَى الْمُؤْمِنِيْنَ وَالْمُؤْمِنٰتِ ؕ وَكَانَ
اللّٰهُ غَفُوْرًا رَّحِيْمًا ﴿٧٣﴾

تاکہ خدا منافق مردوں اور منافق عورتوں اور مشرک
مردوں اور مشرک عورتوں کو عذاب دے اور خدا مومن
مردوں اور مومن عورتوں پر مہربانی کرے۔ اور خدا تو
بخشنے والا مہربان ہے ﴿۷۳﴾

73. (With the result) that Allah has to punish the Hypocrites, men and women, and the Unbelievers, men and women, and Allah turns in Mercy to the Believers, men and women: for Allah is Oft-Forgiving, Most merciful.

سُوْرَةُ سَبَاٍ مَّكِّيَّةٌ وَّهِيَ اَرْبَعٌ وَّخَمْسُوْنَ اٰيَةً وَّسِتُّ رُكُوْعَاتٍ

سُورۂ سبا مکی ہے اور اسمیں چون آیتیں اور چھ رکوع ہیں

Sabā, or the City of Sabā

بِسْمِ اللّٰهِ الرَّحْمٰنِ الرَّحِيْمِ

شروع خدا کا نام لے کر جو بڑا مہربان نہایت رحم والا ہے

In the name of Allah, Most Gracious, Most Merciful.

اَلْحَمْدُ لِلّٰهِ الَّذِيْ لَهٗ مَا فِي السَّمٰوٰتِ وَمَا
فِي الْاَرْضِ وَلَهُ الْحَمْدُ فِي الْاٰخِرَةِ ؕ
وَهُوَ الْحَكِيْمُ الْخَبِيْرُ ﴿١﴾

سب تعریف خدا ہی کو (سزاوار) ہے جو سب چیزوں کا مالک ہے
(یعنی) وہ کہ جو کچھ آسمانوں میں ہے اور جو کچھ زمین میں ہے سب اُسی کا ہے
اور آخرت میں بھی اسی کی تعریف ہے اور وہ حکمت والا اور خبردار ہے ﴿۱﴾

1. Praise be to Allah, to whom belong all things in the heavens and on earth: to Him be Praise in the Hereafter: and He is All-Wise, All-Aware.

يَعْلَمُ مَا يَلِجُ فِي الْاَرْضِ وَمَا يَخْرُجُ
مِنْهَا وَمَا يَنْزِلُ مِنَ السَّمَآءِ وَمَا يَعْرُجُ
فِيْهَا ؕ وَهُوَ الرَّحِيْمُ الْغَفُوْرُ ﴿٢﴾

جو کچھ زمین میں داخل ہوتا ہے اور جو اُس میں سے نکلتا ہے اور
جو آسمان سے اُترتا ہے اور جو اس پر چڑھتا ہے سب اُس کو
معلوم ہے۔ اور وہ مہربان (اور) بخشنے والا ہے ﴿۲﴾

2. He knows all that goes into the earth, and all that comes out thereof; all that comes down from the sky and all that ascends thereto and He is the Most Merciful, the Oft-Forgiving.

وَقَالَ الَّذِيْنَ كَفَرُوْا لَا تَاْتِيْنَا السَّاعَةُ ؕ
قُلْ بَلٰى وَرَبِّيْ لَتَاْتِيَنَّكُمْ ۙ عٰلِمِ الْغَيْبِ ۚ
لَا يَعْزُبُ عَنْهُ مِثْقَالُ ذَرَّةٍ فِي
السَّمٰوٰتِ وَلَا فِي الْاَرْضِ وَلَاۤ اَصْغَرُ
مِنْ ذٰلِكَ وَلَاۤ اَكْبَرُ اِلَّا فِيْ كِتٰبٍ

اور کافر کہتے ہیں کہ (قیامت کی) گھڑی ہم پر نہیں آئیگی۔
کہہ دو کیوں نہیں (آئیگی) میرے پروردگار کی قسم وہ تم پر ضرور
آکر رہیگی (وہ پروردگار) غیب کا جاننے والا (ہے) ذرہ بھر
چیز بھی اُس سے پوشیدہ نہیں (نہ) آسمانوں میں اور
نہ زمین میں اور کوئی چیز اس سے چھوٹی یا بڑی نہیں

3. The Unbelievers say, "Never to us will come the Hour": say, "Nay! but most surely, by my Lord, it will come upon you;—by Him Who knows the unseen,— from Whom is not hidden the least little atom in the Heavens or on earth: nor is there anything less than that, or

greater, but is in the Record Perspicuous:

4. That He may reward those who believe and work deeds of righteousness: for such is Forgiveness and a Sustenance Most Generous."

5. But those who strive against Our Signs, to frustrate them,—for such will be a Chastisement of painful wrath.

6. And those to whom knowledge has come see that the (Revelation) sent down to thee from thy Lord— that is the Truth, and that it guides to the Path of the Exalted (in Might), Worthy of all praise.

7. The Unbelievers say (in ridicule): "Shall we point out to you a man that will tell you, when ye are all scattered to pieces in disintegration, that ye shall (then be raised) in a New Creation?

8. "Has he invented a falsehood against Allah, or is he afflicted with madness". Nay, it is those who believe not in the Hereafter, that are in (real) Chastisement, and in farthest Error.

9. See they not what is before them and behind them, of the sky and the earth? If We wished, We could cause the earth to swallow them up, or cause a piece of the sky to fall upon them. Verily in this is a Sign for every devotee that turns to Allah (in repentance).

10. We bestowed Grace aforetime on David from Us "O ye Mountains! echo ye back the Praise of Allah with him! and ye birds (also)! And We made the iron soft for him;—

11. (Commanding), "Make thou coats of mail, balancing well the rings of chain armour, and work ye righteousness; for be sure I see (clearly) all that ye do."

12. And to Solomon (We made) the Wind (obedient): its early morning (stride) was a month's (journey), and its evening (stride) was a month's (journey); and We made a Font of molten brass to flow for him; and

مگر کتاب روشن میں (لکھی ہوئی) ہے ﴿٣﴾
اس لئے کہ جو لوگ ایمان لائے اور عمل نیک کرتے رہے اُنکو
بدلہ دے۔ یہی ہیں جن کیلئے بخشش اور عزت کی روزی ہے ﴿٤﴾
اور جنہوں نے ہماری آیتوں میں کوشش کی کہ ہمیں ہرا
دیں اُن کیلئے سخت درد دینے والے عذاب کی سزا ہے ﴿٥﴾
اور جن لوگوں کو علم دیا گیا ہے وہ جانتے ہیں کہ جو (قرآن)
تمہارے پروردگار کی طرف سے تم پر نازل ہوا ہے وہ حق ہے اور
(خدائے) غالب (اور) سزاوار تعریف کا رستہ بتاتا ہے ﴿٦﴾
اور کافر کہتے ہیں کہ بھلا ہم تمہیں ایسا آدمی بتائیں جو تمہیں
خبر دیتا ہے کہ جب تم (مرکر) بالکل پارہ پارہ ہو جاؤ گے تو
نئے سرے سے پیدا ہو گے ﴿٧﴾
یا تو اس نے خدا پر جھوٹ باندھ لیا ہے۔ یا اسے جنون ہے۔
بات یہ ہے کہ جو لوگ آخرت پر ایمان نہیں رکھتے وہ آفت
اور پرلے درجے کی گمراہی میں (مبتلا) ہیں ﴿٨﴾
کیا انہوں نے اس کو نہیں دیکھا جو اُن کے آگے اور پیچھے
ہے یعنی آسمان اور زمین۔ اگر ہم چاہیں تو اُن کو زمین میں
دھنسا دیں یا اُن پر آسمان کے ٹکڑے گرا دیں۔ اس میں ہر
بندے کے لئے جو رجوع کرنے والا ہے ایک
نشانی ہے ﴿٩﴾
اور ہم نے داؤد کو اپنی طرف سے برتری بخشی تھی۔ اے پہاڑو اُنکے ساتھ تسبیح
کرو اور پرندوں کو (اُنکا مسخر کر دیا) اور اُنکے لئے ہم نے لوہے کو نرم کر دیا ﴿١٠﴾
کہ کشادہ زرہیں بناؤ اور کڑیوں کو اندازہ سے جوڑو اور
نیک عمل کرو جو عمل تم کرتے ہو میں اُن کو دیکھنے
والا ہوں ﴿١١﴾
اور ہوا کو (ہم نے) سلیمان کا تابع کر دیا تھا اسکی صبح کی منزل
ایک مہینے کی راہ ہوتی اور شام کی منزل بھی مہینے بھر کی ہوتی اور
اُن کیلئے ہم نے تانبے کا چشمہ بہا دیا تھا اور جنوں میں سے ایسے تھے

مُّبِينٍ ﴿٣﴾
لِّيَجْزِيَ الَّذِينَ آمَنُوا وَعَمِلُوا الصَّالِحَاتِ
أُولَٰئِكَ لَهُم مَّغْفِرَةٌ وَرِزْقٌ كَرِيمٌ ﴿٤﴾
وَالَّذِينَ سَعَوْ فِي آيَاتِنَا مُعَاجِزِينَ أُولَٰئِكَ
لَهُمْ عَذَابٌ مِّن رِّجْزٍ أَلِيمٌ ﴿٥﴾
وَيَرَى الَّذِينَ أُوتُوا الْعِلْمَ الَّذِي
أُنزِلَ إِلَيْكَ مِن رَّبِّكَ هُوَ الْحَقَّ وَ
يَهْدِي إِلَىٰ صِرَاطِ الْعَزِيزِ الْحَمِيدِ ﴿٦﴾
وَقَالَ الَّذِينَ كَفَرُوا هَلْ نَدُلُّكُمْ عَلَىٰ
رَجُلٍ يُنَبِّئُكُمْ إِذَا مُزِّقْتُمْ كُلَّ مُمَزَّقٍ
إِنَّكُمْ لَفِي خَلْقٍ جَدِيدٍ ﴿٧﴾
أَفْتَرَىٰ عَلَى اللَّهِ كَذِبًا أَم بِهِ جِنَّةٌ
بَلِ الَّذِينَ لَا يُؤْمِنُونَ بِالْآخِرَةِ فِي
الْعَذَابِ وَالضَّلَالِ الْبَعِيدِ ﴿٨﴾
أَفَلَمْ يَرَوْا إِلَىٰ مَا بَيْنَ أَيْدِيهِمْ وَمَا
خَلْفَهُم مِّنَ السَّمَاءِ وَالْأَرْضِ إِن
نَّشَأْ نَخْسِفْ بِهِمُ الْأَرْضَ أَوْ نُسْقِطْ عَلَيْهِمْ
كِسَفًا مِّنَ السَّمَاءِ إِنَّ فِي ذَٰلِكَ لَآيَةً
لِّكُلِّ عَبْدٍ مُّنِيبٍ ﴿٩﴾ ع
وَلَقَدْ آتَيْنَا دَاوُودَ مِنَّا فَضْلًا يَا جِبَالُ
أَوِّبِي مَعَهُ وَالطَّيْرَ وَأَلَنَّا لَهُ الْحَدِيدَ ﴿١٠﴾
أَنِ اعْمَلْ سَابِغَاتٍ وَقَدِّرْ فِي السَّرْدِ
وَاعْمَلُوا صَالِحًا إِنِّي بِمَا تَعْمَلُونَ
بَصِيرٌ ﴿١١﴾
وَلِسُلَيْمَانَ الرِّيحَ غُدُوُّهَا شَهْرٌ وَ
رَوَاحُهَا شَهْرٌ وَأَسَلْنَا لَهُ عَيْنَ الْقِطْرِ
وَمِنَ الْجِنِّ مَن يَعْمَلُ بَيْنَ يَدَيْهِ

بِإِذْنِ رَبِّهٖ ۚ وَمَنْ يَّزِغْ مِنْهُمْ عَنْ اَمْرِنَا
نُذِقْهُ مِنْ عَذَابِ السَّعِيْرِ ⑫
يَعْمَلُوْنَ لَهٗ مَا يَشَآءُ مِنْ مَّحَارِيْبَ
وَتَمَاثِيْلَ وَجِفَانٍ كَالْجَوَابِ وَقُدُوْرٍ
رّٰسِيٰتٍ ؕ اِعْمَلُوْٓا اٰلَ دَاوٗدَ شُكْرًا ؕ وَ
قَلِيْلٌ مِّنْ عِبَادِيَ الشَّكُوْرُ ⑬
فَلَمَّا قَضَيْنَا عَلَيْهِ الْمَوْتَ مَا دَلَّهُمْ
عَلٰى مَوْتِهٖٓ اِلَّا دَآبَّةُ الْاَرْضِ تَاْكُلُ
مِنْسَاَتَهٗ ۚ فَلَمَّا خَرَّ تَبَيَّنَتِ الْجِنُّ اَنْ
لَّوْ كَانُوْا يَعْلَمُوْنَ الْغَيْبَ مَا لَبِثُوْا فِي
الْعَذَابِ الْمُهِيْنِ ⑭
لَقَدْ كَانَ لِسَبَاٍ فِيْ مَسْكَنِهِمْ اٰيَةٌ ۚ جَنَّتٰنِ
عَنْ يَّمِيْنٍ وَّشِمَالٍ ؕ كُلُوْا مِنْ رِّزْقِ
رَبِّكُمْ وَاشْكُرُوْا لَهٗ ؕ بَلْدَةٌ طَيِّبَةٌ
وَّرَبٌّ غَفُوْرٌ ⑮
فَاَعْرَضُوْا فَاَرْسَلْنَا عَلَيْهِمْ سَيْلَ الْعَرِمِ
وَبَدَّلْنٰهُمْ بِجَنَّتَيْهِمْ جَنَّتَيْنِ ذَوَاتَيْ
اُكُلٍ خَمْطٍ وَّاَثْلٍ وَّشَيْءٍ مِّنْ
سِدْرٍ قَلِيْلٍ ⑯
ذٰلِكَ جَزَيْنٰهُمْ بِمَا كَفَرُوْا ؕ وَهَلْ نُجٰزِيْٓ اِلَّا الْكَفُوْرَ ⑰
وَجَعَلْنَا بَيْنَهُمْ وَبَيْنَ الْقُرَى الَّتِيْ
بٰرَكْنَا فِيْهَا قُرًى ظَاهِرَةً وَّقَدَّرْنَا فِيْهَا
السَّيْرَ ؕ سِيْرُوْا فِيْهَا لَيَالِيَ وَاَيَّامًا اٰمِنِيْنَ ⑱
فَقَالُوْا رَبَّنَا بٰعِدْ بَيْنَ اَسْفَارِنَا وَ
ظَلَمُوْٓا اَنْفُسَهُمْ فَجَعَلْنٰهُمْ اَحَادِيْثَ
وَمَزَّقْنٰهُمْ كُلَّ مُمَزَّقٍ ؕ اِنَّ فِيْ ذٰلِكَ
لَاٰيٰتٍ لِّكُلِّ صَبَّارٍ شَكُوْرٍ ⑲

جو اُنکے پروردگار کے حکم سے اُنکے آگے کام کرتے تھے۔ اور جو کوئی اُن میں سے
ہمارے حکم سے پھریگا اسکو ہم (جہنم کی) آگ کا مزہ چکھائینگے (۱۲)
وہ جو چاہتے یہ اُن کے لئے بناتے یعنی قلعے اور مجسمے ۲۷۶
اور (بڑے بڑے) لگن جیسے تالاب اور دیگیں جو ایک
ہی جگہ رکھی رہیں۔ اے داؤد کی اولاد (میرا) شکر کرو اور
میرے بندوں میں شکر گزار تھوڑے ہیں (۱۳)
پھر جب ہم نے اُن کے لئے موت کا حکم صادر کیا تو کسی
چیز سے اُن کا مرنا معلوم نہ ہوا مگر گھن کے کیڑے سے
جو اُن کے عصا کو کھاتا رہا جب عصا گر پڑا تب جنوں
کو معلوم ہوا اور کہنے لگے کہ اگر وہ غیب جانتے ہوتے
تو ذلت کی تکلیف میں نہ رہتے (۱۴)
(اہل) سبا کے لئے اُن کے مقام بود و باش میں ایک نشانی
تھی (یعنی) دو باغ (ایک) داہنی طرف اور (ایک)
بائیں طرف۔ اپنے پروردگار کا رزق کھاؤ اور اُسکا شکر کرو۔
(یہاں تمہارے رہنے کو یہ) پاکیزہ شہر ہے اور (وہاں) بخشنے کو خدائے غفار (۱۵)
تو اُنہوں نے (شکر گزاری سے) منہ پھیر لیا پس ہم نے اُن پر
زور کا سیلاب چھوڑ دیا اور اُنہیں اُن کے باغوں کے بدلے
دو ایسے باغ دیئے جن کے میوے بدمزہ تھے اور جن میں
کچھ تو جھاؤ تھا اور تھوڑی سی بیریاں (۱۶)
یہ ہم نے اُنکی ناشکری کی اُنکو سزا دی۔ اور ہم سزا ناشکرے ہی کو دیا کرتے ہیں (۱۷)
اور ہم نے اُنکے اور (شام میں) اُنکی بستیوں کے درمیان جنہیں ہم نے برکت دی
تھی (ایک دوسرے کے متصل) دیہات بنائے تھے جو سامنے نظر آتے تھے اور
اُنمیں آمد و رفت کا اندازہ مقرر کر دیا تھا کہ رات دن بیخوف و خطر چلتے رہو (۱۸)
تو اُنہوں نے دعا کی کہ اے پروردگار ہماری مسافتوں میں بُعد (اور طول)
پیدا کر دے اور (اس سے) اُنہوں نے اپنے حق میں ظلم کیا تو ہم نے (اُنہیں
نابود کر کے) اُنکے افسانے بنا دیئے اور اُنہیں بالکل منتشر کر دیا
اس میں ہر صابر و شاکر کے لئے نشانیاں ہیں (۱۹)

there were Jinns that worked in front of him, by the leave of his Lord, and if any of them turned aside from Our command, We made him taste of the Chastisement of the Blazing Fire.

13. They worked for him as he desired, (making) Arches, Images, Basons as large as wells, and (cooking) Cauldrons fixed (in their places): "Exercise thanks sons of David, but few of My servants are grateful!"

14. Then, when We decreed (Solomon's) death, nothing showed them his death except a little worm of the earth, which kept (slowly) gnawing away at his staff: so when he fell down, the Jinns saw plainly that if they had known the unseen, they would not have tarried in the humiliating Chastisement (of their Task).

15. There was, for Sabā, aforetime, a Sign in their homeland—two Gardens to the right and to the left. "Eat of the Sustenance (provided) by your Lord, and be grateful to Him: a territory fair and happy, and a Lord Oft-Forgiving!

16. But they turned away (from Allah), and We sent against them the flood (released) from the Dams, and We converted their two garden (rows) into "gardens" producing bitter fruit, and tamarisks, and some few (stunted) Lote-trees.

17. That was the Requital We gave them because they ungratefully rejected Faith: and never do We give (such) requital except to such as are ungrateful rejecters.

18. Between them and the Cities on which We had poured Our blessings, We had placed Cities in prominent positions, and between them We had appointed stages of journey in due proportion: "Travel therein, secure, by night and by day."

19. But they said: "Our Lord! place longer distances between our journey-stages": but they wronged themselves (therein). At length We made them as a tale (that is told), and We dispersed them all in scattered fragments. Verily in this are Signs for every (soul that is) patiently constant and grateful.

20. And on them did Satan prove true his idea, and they followed him, all but a Party that believed.

21. But he had no authority over them,—except that We might test the man who believes in the Hereafter from him who is in doubt concerning it: and thy Lord doth watch over all things.

22. Say: "Call upon other (gods) whom ye fancy, besides Allah: they have no power,— not the weight of an atom,— in the heavens or on earth: no (sort of) share have they therein, nor is any of them a helper to Allah.

23. "No intercession can avail with Him, except for those for whom He has granted permission. So far (is this the case) that, when terror is removed from their hearts (at the Day of Judgment, then) will they say, 'What is it that your Lord commanded?' They will say, 'That which is true and just; and He is the Most High, Most Great'."

24. Say: "Who gives you sustenance, from the heavens and the earth?" Say: "It is Allah; and certain it is that either we or ye are on right guidance or in manifest error!"

25. Say: "Ye shall not be questioned as to our sins, nor shall we be questioned as to what ye do."

26. Say: "Our Lord will gather us together and will in the end decide the matter between us (and you) in truth and justice: and He is the One to decide, the One Who knows all."

27. Say: "Show me those whom ye have joined with Him as partners: by no means (can ye). Nay, He is Allah, the Exalted in Power, the Wise."

28. We have not sent thee but as a (Messenger) to all mankind, giving them Glad tidings, and warning them (against sin), but most men know not.

29. They say: "When will this promise (come to pass) if ye are telling the truth?"

30. Say: "The appointment to you is for a Day, which ye cannot put

اور شیطان نے اُنکے بارے میں اپنا خیال سچ کر دکھایا کہ مومنوں
کی ایک جماعت کے سوا وہ اُسکے پیچھے چل پڑے ﴿٢٠﴾
اور اُس کا اُن پر کچھ زور نہ تھا مگر (ہمارا) مقصود یہ تھا کہ
جو لوگ آخرت میں شک رکھتے ہیں اُنسے اُن لوگوں کو جو اس پر ایمان رکھتے
ہیں متمیز کر دیں۔ اور تمہارا پروردگار ہر چیز پر نگہبان ہے ﴿٢١﴾
کہہ دو کہ جن کو تم خدا کے سوا (معبود) خیال کرتے ہو اُن کو
بلاؤ۔ وہ آسمانوں اور زمین میں ذرّہ بھر چیز کے بھی مالک
نہیں ہیں اور نہ اُن میں ان کی شرکت ہے اور نہ اُن
میں سے کوئی خدا کا مددگار ہے ﴿٢٢﴾
اور خدا کے ہاں (کسی کیلئے) سفارش فائدہ نہ دیگی مگر اس کیلئے جس
کے بارے میں وہ اجازت بخشے۔ یہانتک کہ جب اُنکے دلوں سے اضطراب
دُور کر دیا جائیگا تو کہینگے کہ تمہارے پروردگار نے کیا فرمایا ہے۔
(فرشتے) کہینگے کہ حق (فرمایا ہے) اور وہ عالی رُتبہ (اور) گرامی قدر ہے ﴿٢٣﴾
پوچھو کہ تم کو آسمانوں اور زمین سے کون رزق دیتا ہے؟
کہو کہ خدا اور ہم یا تم (یا تو) سیدھے رستے پر ہیں یا صریح
گمراہی میں ﴿٢٤﴾
کہہ دو کہ نہ ہمارے گناہوں کی تم سے پرسش ہوگی اور نہ
تمہارے اعمال کی ہم سے پرسش ہوگی ﴿٢٥﴾
کہہ دو کہ ہمارا پروردگار ہم کو جمع کریگا پھر ہمارے درمیان انصاف
کیساتھ فیصلہ کر دیگا اور وہ خوب فیصلہ کرنیوالا (اور) صاحب علم ہے ﴿٢٦﴾
کہو کہ مجھے وہ لوگ تو دکھاؤ جن کو تم نے شریک (خدا) بناکر
اسکے ساتھ ملا رکھا ہے۔ کوئی نہیں بلکہ وہی (اکیلا) خدا غالب (اور) حکمت والا ہے ﴿٢٧﴾
اور (اے محمدؐ) ہم نے تم کو تمام لوگوں کیلئے خوشخبری سنانے والا
اور ڈرانے والا بناکر بھیجا ہے لیکن اکثر لوگ نہیں جانتے ﴿٢٨﴾
اور کہتے ہیں اگر تم سچ کہتے ہو تو یہ (قیامت کا) وعدہ
کب وقوع میں آئے گا؟ ﴿٢٩﴾
کہہ دو کہ تم سے ایک دن کا وعدہ ہے جس سے نہ ایک

وَلَقَدْ صَدَّقَ عَلَيْهِمْ إِبْلِيسُ ظَنَّهُ
فَاتَّبَعُوهُ إِلَّا فَرِيقًا مِّنَ الْمُؤْمِنِينَ ﴿٢٠﴾
وَمَا كَانَ لَهُ عَلَيْهِم مِّن سُلْطَانٍ إِلَّا لِنَعْلَمَ
مَن يُؤْمِنُ بِالْآخِرَةِ مِمَّنْ هُوَ مِنْهَا فِي
شَكٍّ ۗ وَرَبُّكَ عَلَىٰ كُلِّ شَيْءٍ حَفِيظٌ ﴿٢١﴾
قُلِ ادْعُوا الَّذِينَ زَعَمْتُم مِّن دُونِ
اللَّهِ ۖ لَا يَمْلِكُونَ مِثْقَالَ ذَرَّةٍ فِي السَّمَاوَاتِ
وَلَا فِي الْأَرْضِ وَمَا لَهُمْ فِيهِمَا مِن
شِرْكٍ وَمَا لَهُ مِنْهُم مِّن ظَهِيرٍ ﴿٢٢﴾
وَلَا تَنفَعُ الشَّفَاعَةُ عِندَهُ إِلَّا لِمَنْ أَذِنَ
لَهُ ۚ حَتَّىٰ إِذَا فُزِّعَ عَن قُلُوبِهِمْ قَالُوا مَاذَا
قَالَ رَبُّكُمْ ۖ قَالُوا الْحَقَّ ۖ وَهُوَ الْعَلِيُّ
الْكَبِيرُ ﴿٢٣﴾
قُلْ مَن يَرْزُقُكُم مِّنَ السَّمَاوَاتِ وَ
الْأَرْضِ ۖ قُلِ اللَّهُ ۖ وَإِنَّا أَوْ إِيَّاكُمْ لَعَلَىٰ
هُدًى أَوْ فِي ضَلَالٍ مُّبِينٍ ﴿٢٤﴾
قُل لَّا تُسْأَلُونَ عَمَّا أَجْرَمْنَا وَلَا نُسْأَلُ
عَمَّا تَعْمَلُونَ ﴿٢٥﴾
قُلْ يَجْمَعُ بَيْنَنَا رَبُّنَا ثُمَّ يَفْتَحُ بَيْنَنَا
بِالْحَقِّ وَهُوَ الْفَتَّاحُ الْعَلِيمُ ﴿٢٦﴾
قُلْ أَرُونِيَ الَّذِينَ أَلْحَقْتُم بِهِ شُرَكَاءَ ۖ
كَلَّا ۚ بَلْ هُوَ اللَّهُ الْعَزِيزُ الْحَكِيمُ ﴿٢٧﴾
وَمَا أَرْسَلْنَاكَ إِلَّا كَافَّةً لِّلنَّاسِ بَشِيرًا
وَنَذِيرًا وَلَٰكِنَّ أَكْثَرَ النَّاسِ لَا يَعْلَمُونَ ﴿٢٨﴾
وَيَقُولُونَ مَتَىٰ هَٰذَا الْوَعْدُ إِن كُنتُمْ
صَادِقِينَ ﴿٢٩﴾
قُل لَّكُم مِّيعَادُ يَوْمٍ لَّا تَسْتَأْخِرُونَ

back for an hour nor put forward."

گھڑی پیچھے رہو گے نہ آگے بڑھو گے (۳۰)

عَنْهُ سَاعَةً وَّلَا تَسْتَقْدِمُوْنَ ﴿٣٠﴾ ع

31. The Unbelievers say: "We shall neither believe in this scripture nor in (any) that (came) before it." Couldst thou but see when the wrong-doers will be made to stand before their Lord, throwing back the word (of blame) on one another! Those who were deemed weak will say to the arrogant ones: "Had it not been for you, we should certainly have been believers!"

اور جو کافر ہیں وہ کہتے ہیں کہ ہم نہ تو اس قرآن کو مانیں گے
اور نہ ان (کتابوں) کو جو اُن سے پہلے کی ہیں۔ اور کاش (ان)
ظالموں کو تم اُس وقت دیکھو جب یہ اپنے پروردگار کے
سامنے کھڑے ہونگے اور ایک دوسرے سے ردّ و کد کر رہے
ہونگے۔ جو لوگ کمزور سمجھے جاتے تھے وہ بڑے لوگوں سے
کہیں گے کہ اگر تم نہ ہوتے تو ہم ضرور مومن ہو جاتے (۳۱)

وَقَالَ الَّذِيْنَ كَفَرُوْا لَنْ نُّؤْمِنَ بِهٰذَا
الْقُرْاٰنِ وَلَا بِالَّذِيْ بَيْنَ يَدَيْهِ ۭ وَلَوْ
تَرٰٓى اِذِ الظّٰلِمُوْنَ مَوْقُوْفُوْنَ عِنْدَ
رَبِّهِمْ ښ يَرْجِعُ بَعْضُهُمْ اِلٰى بَعْضِ ۨ الْقَوْلَ ۚ
يَقُوْلُ الَّذِيْنَ اسْتُضْعِفُوْا لِلَّذِيْنَ
اسْتَكْبَرُوْا لَوْلَآ اَنْتُمْ لَكُنَّا مُؤْمِنِيْنَ ﴿٣١﴾

32. The arrogant ones will say to those who had been deemed weak: "Was it we who kept you back from Guidance after it reached you? Nay, rather, it was ye who transgressed."

بڑے لوگ کمزوروں سے کہیں گے کہ بھلا ہم نے تم کو
ہدایت سے جب وہ تمہارے پاس آچکی تھی روکا تھا
(نہیں) بلکہ تم ہی گنہگار تھے (۳۲)

قَالَ الَّذِيْنَ اسْتَكْبَرُوْا لِلَّذِيْنَ اسْتُضْعِفُوْٓا
اَنَحْنُ صَدَدْنٰكُمْ عَنِ الْهُدٰى بَعْدَ اِذْ
جَاۗءَكُمْ بَلْ كُنْتُمْ مُّجْرِمِيْنَ ﴿٣٢﴾

33. Those who had been deemed weak will say to the arrogant ones: "Nay! it was a plot (of yours) by day and by night: behold! ye (constantly) ordered us to be ungrateful to Allah and to attribute equals to Him!" They are filled with remorse. When they see the Chastisement: We shall put yokes on the necks of the Unbelievers: it would only be a requital for their (ill) Deeds.

اور کمزور لوگ بڑے لوگوں سے کہیں گے (نہیں) بلکہ (تمہاری)
رات دن کی چالوں نے (ہمیں روک رکھا تھا) جب تم
ہم سے کہتے تھے کہ ہم خدا سے کفر کریں اور اُس کا شریک
بنائیں۔ اور جب وہ عذاب کو دیکھیں گے تو دل میں پشیمان
ہونگے۔ اور ہم کافروں کی گردنوں میں طوق ڈال دیں گے۔
بس جو عمل وہ کرتے تھے اُنہی کا اُن کو بدلہ ملے گا (۳۳)

وَقَالَ الَّذِيْنَ اسْتُضْعِفُوْا لِلَّذِيْنَ اسْتَكْبَرُوْا
بَلْ مَكْرُ الَّيْلِ وَالنَّهَارِ اِذْ تَاْمُرُوْنَنَآ اَنْ
نَّكْفُرَ بِاللّٰهِ وَنَجْعَلَ لَهٗٓ اَنْدَادًا ۭ وَاَسَرُّوا
النَّدَامَةَ لَمَّا رَاَوُا الْعَذَابَ ۭ وَجَعَلْنَا
الْاَغْلٰلَ فِيْٓ اَعْنَاقِ الَّذِيْنَ كَفَرُوْا ۭ هَلْ
يُجْزَوْنَ اِلَّا مَا كَانُوْا يَعْمَلُوْنَ ﴿٣٣﴾

34. Never did We send a Warner to a population, but the wealthy ones among them said: "We believe not in the (Message) with which ye have been sent."

اور ہم نے کسی بستی میں کوئی ڈرانے والا نہیں بھیجا
مگر وہاں کے خوشحال لوگوں نے کہا کہ جو چیز تم دے کر بھیجے
گئے ہو ہم اُس کے قائل نہیں (۳۴)

وَمَآ اَرْسَلْنَا فِيْ قَرْيَةٍ مِّنْ نَّذِيْرٍ اِلَّا
قَالَ مُتْرَفُوْهَآ ۙ اِنَّا بِمَآ اُرْسِلْتُمْ بِهٖ
كٰفِرُوْنَ ﴿٣٤﴾

35. They said: "We have more in wealth and in sons, and we cannot be chastised".

اور (یہ بھی) کہنے لگے کہ ہم بہت سا مال اور اولاد
رکھتے ہیں اور ہم کو عذاب نہیں ہوگا (۳۵)

وَقَالُوْا نَحْنُ اَكْثَرُ اَمْوَالًا وَّاَوْلَادًا ۙ
وَّمَا نَحْنُ بِمُعَذَّبِيْنَ ﴿٣٥﴾

36. Say: "Verily my Lord enlarges and restricts the Provision to whom He pleases, but most men know not."

کہہ دو کہ میرا رب جس کے لئے چاہتا ہے روزی
فراخ کر دیتا ہے اور (جس کے لئے چاہتا ہے) تنگ
کر دیتا ہے لیکن اکثر لوگ نہیں جانتے (۳۶)

قُلْ اِنَّ رَبِّيْ يَبْسُطُ الرِّزْقَ لِمَنْ يَّشَاۗءُ
وَيَقْدِرُ وَلٰكِنَّ اَكْثَرَ النَّاسِ لَا
يَعْلَمُوْنَ ﴿٣٦﴾ ع

37. It is not your wealth nor your sons, that will bring you nearer to Us in degree: but only those who believe and work righteousness—these are the ones for whom there

اور تمہارا مال اور اولاد ایسی چیز نہیں کہ تم کو ہمارا
مقرب بنا دیں ہاں (ہمارا مقرب وہ ہے) جو ایمان لایا
اور عمل نیک کرتا رہا ایسے ہی لوگوں کو اُنکے اعمال کے سبب

وَمَآ اَمْوَالُكُمْ وَلَآ اَوْلَادُكُمْ بِالَّتِيْ تُقَرِّبُكُمْ
عِنْدَنَا زُلْفٰٓى اِلَّا مَنْ اٰمَنَ وَعَمِلَ
صَالِحًا ۡ فَاُولٰۗىِٕكَ لَهُمْ جَزَاۗءُ الضِّعْفِ

بما عملوا وهم في الغرفت امنون ﴿٣٧﴾
والذين يسعون في ايتنا معجزين
اولئك في العذاب محضرون ﴿٣٨﴾
قل ان ربي يبسط الرزق لمن يشاء
من عباده ويقدر له وما انفقتم
من شيء فهو يخلفه وهو خير
الرزقين ﴿٣٩﴾
ويوم يحشرهم جميعا ثم يقول للملئكة
اهؤلاء اياكم كانوا يعبدون ﴿٤٠﴾
قالوا سبحنك انت ولينا من دونهم
بل كانوا يعبدون الجن اكثرهم
بهم مؤمنون ﴿٤١﴾
فاليوم لا يملك بعضكم لبعض نفعا
ولا ضرا ونقول للذين ظلموا ذوقوا
عذاب النار التي كنتم بها تكذبون ﴿٤٢﴾
واذا تتلى عليهم ايتنا بينت قالوا
ما هذا الا رجل يريد ان يصدكم
عما كان يعبد اباؤكم وقالوا ما هذا
الا افك مفترى وقال الذين كفروا
للحق لما جاءهم ان هذا الا سحر مبين ﴿٤٣﴾
وما اتينهم من كتب يدرسونها وما
ارسلنا اليهم قبلك من نذير ﴿٤٤﴾
وكذب الذين من قبلهم وما بلغوا
معشار ما اتينهم فكذبوا رسلي
فكيف كان نكير ﴿٤٥﴾
قل انما اعظكم بواحدة ان تقوموا
لله مثنى وفرادى ثم تتفكروا ما

دگنا بدلہ ملیگا اور وہ خاطر جمع سے بالاخانوں میں بیٹھے ہونگے (٣٧)
جو لوگ ہماری آیتوں میں کوشش کرتے ہیں کہ ہمیں ہرا
دیں وہ عذاب میں حاضر کئے جائیں گے (٣٨)
کہہ دو کہ میرا پروردگار اپنے بندوں میں سے جس کے لئے
چاہتا ہے روزی فراخ کر دیتا ہے اور (جسکے لئے چاہتا ہے)
تنگ کر دیتا ہے اور تم جو چیز خرچ کرو گے وہ اس کا (تمہیں)
عوض دے گا۔ وہ سب سے بہتر رزق دینے والا ہے (٣٩)
اور جس دن وہ ان سب کو جمع کرے گا پھر فرشتوں سے
فرمائے گا۔ کیا یہ لوگ تم کو پوجا کرتے تھے (٤٠)
وہ کہیں گے تو پاک ہے تو ہی ہمارا دوست ہے
نہ یہ۔ بلکہ یہ جنّات کو پوجا کرتے تھے۔ اور اکثر اُن ہی
کو مانتے تھے (٤١)
تو آج تم میں سے کوئی کسی کو نفع اور نقصان پہنچانے کا
اختیار نہیں رکھتا۔ اور ہم ظالموں سے کہیں گے کہ دوزخ کے
عذاب کا جس کو تم جھوٹ سمجھتے تھے مزہ چکھو (٤٢)
اور جب اُن کو ہماری روشن آیتیں پڑھ کر سنائی جاتی ہیں
تو کہتے ہیں یہ ایک (ایسا) شخص ہے جو چاہتا ہے کہ جن چیزوں کی
تمہارے باپ دادا پرستش کیا کرتے تھے اُن سے تمکو روک دے اور (یہ بھی) کہتے
ہیں کہ یہ (قرآن) محض جھوٹ ہے جو (اپنی طرف سے) بنا لیا گیا ہے۔ اور کافروں کے
پاس جب حق آیا تو اسکے بارے میں کہنے لگے کہ یہ تو صریح جادو ہے (٤٣)
اور ہم نے نہ تو اُن (مشرکوں) کو کتابیں دیں جن کو یہ پڑھتے ہیں
اور نہ تم سے پہلے اُنکی طرف کوئی ڈرانے والا بھیجا (مگر انہوں نے تکذیب کی) (٤٤)
اور جو لوگ اُن سے پہلے تھے انہوں نے تکذیب کی تھی اور جو کچھ
ہم نے اُن کو دیا تھا یہ اسکے دسویں حصّے کو بھی نہیں پہنچے
تو انہوں نے میرے پیغمبروں کو جھٹلایا سو میرا عذاب کیسا ہوا؟ (٤٥)
کہہ دو کہ میں تمہیں صرف ایک بات کی نصیحت کرتا ہوں
کہ تم خدا کیلئے دو دو اور اکیلے اکیلے کھڑے ہو جاؤ پھر غور

is a multiplied Reward for their deeds, while secure they (reside) in the dwellings on high!

38. Those who strive against Our Signs, to frustrate them, will be given over into Chastisement.

39. Say: "Verily my Lord enlarges and restricts the Sustenance to such of His servants as He pleases: and nothing do ye spend in the least (in His Cause) but He replaces it: for He is the Best of those who grant Sustenance.

40. On the Day He will gather them all together, and say to the angels, "Was it you that these men used to worship?"

41. They will say, "Glory to Thee! Thou art our Protector —not them. Nay, but they worshipped the Jinns: most of them believed in them."

42. So on that Day no power shall they have over each other, for profit or harm: and We shall say to the wrong-doers, "Taste ye the Chastisement of the Fire,— the which ye were wont to deny!"

43. When Our Clear Signs are rehearsed to them, they say, "This is only a man who wishes to hinder you from the (worship) which your fathers practised." And they say, "This is only a falsehood invented!" And the Unbelievers say of the Truth when it comes to them, "This is nothing but evident magic!"

44. But We had not given them Books which they could study, nor sent messengers to them before thee as Warners.

45. And their predecessors rejected (the Truth); these have not received a tenth of what We had granted to those: yet when they rejected my messengers, how (terrible) was My punishment!

46. Say: "I do admonish you on one point: that ye do stand up before Allah,— (it may be) in pairs, or (it may be) singly,— and reflect

SÛRA–35

FÃṬIR

(INTRODUCTION)

See Introduction to the last Sûra.

This Sûra deals with the mystery of Creation and its maintenance, with various forces typified by the wings of Angels. Whether we look to outer nature or to man, Allah's Grace proclaims His Glory, and protects His votaries from Evil.

It is an early Makkan Sûra, but its chronology has no significance.

(within yourselves): your Companion is not possessed: he is no less than a Warner to you, in face of a terrible Chastisement".

47. Say: "Whatever reward do I ask of you: it is yours: my reward is only due from Allah: and He is Witness to all things."

48. Say: "Verily my Lord doth cast the Truth,—he that has full knowledge of (all) that is hidden."

49. Say: "The Truth has arrived, and Falsehood showeth not its face and will not return."

50. Say: "If I am astray, I only stray to the loss of my own soul: but if I receive guidance, it is because of the inspiration of my Lord to me: it is He Who hears all things, and is (ever) near."

51. If thou couldst but see when they will quake with terror; but then there will be no escape (for them), and they will be seized from a position (quite) near.

52. And they will say, "We do believe (now) in the (Truth)"; but how could they receive (Faith) from a position (so) far off,—

53. Seeing that they did reject Faith (entirely) before, and that they cast (conjectures) with regard to the unseen from a position far off?

54. And between them and their desires, is placed a barrier, as was done in the past with their partisans: for they were indeed in suspicious (disquieting) doubt.

Fã ir, or The Originator of Creation; or Malaîka, or The Angels

In the name of Allah, Most Gracious, Most Merciful.

1. Praise be to Allah, the Originator of the heavens and the earth, Who made the angels Messengers with wings,— two, or three, or four (Pairs): He adds to Creation as He pleases: for Allah has power over all things.

کرو۔ تمہارے رفیق کو مطلق سودا نہیں وہ تو تم کو عذاب
سخت (کے آنے) سے پہلے صرف ڈرانے والے ہیں ﴿۴۶﴾
کہہ دو کہ میں نے تم سے کچھ صلہ مانگا ہو تو وہ تمہارا ۔ میرا
صلہ خدا ہی کے ذمے ہے۔ اور وہ ہر چیز سے
خبردار ہے ﴿۴۷﴾
کہہ دو کہ میرا پروردگار اُوپر سے حق اتارتا ہے (اور وہ)
غیب کی باتوں کا جاننے والا ہے ﴿۴۸﴾
کہہ دو کہ حق آچکا اور (معبود) باطل نہ تو پہلی بار پیدا
کرسکتا ہے اور نہ دوبارہ پیدا کرے گا ﴿۴۹﴾
کہہ دو کہ اگر میں گمراہ ہوں تو میری گمراہی کا ضرر مجھی کو ہے۔ اور
اگر ہدایت پر ہوں تو یہ اسکی طفیل ہے جو میرا پروردگار میری
طرف وحی بھیجتا ہے۔ بیشک وہ سُننے والا (اور) نزدیک ہے ﴿۵۰﴾
اور کاش تم دیکھو جب یہ گھبرا جائیں گے تو (عذاب سے) بچ
نہیں سکینگے اور نزدیک ہی سے پکڑ لئے جائیں گے ﴿۵۱﴾
اور کہیں گے کہ ہم اس پر ایمان لے آئے اور (اب) اتنی دور
سے اُن کا ہاتھ ایمان کے لینے کو کیونکر پہنچ سکتا ہے؟ ﴿۵۲﴾
اور پہلے تو اس سے انکار کرتے رہے اور بن دیکھے دُور
ہی سے (ظن کے) تیر چلاتے رہے ﴿۵۳﴾
اور اُن میں اور اُن کی خواہش کی چیزوں میں پردہ حائل
کر دیا گیا جیسا کہ پہلے انکے ہمجنسوں سے کیا گیا وہ بھی
اُلجھن میں ڈالنے والے شک میں پڑے ہوئے تھے ﴿۵۴﴾

سُورۂ فاطر مکّی ہے اور اس میں پینتالیس آیتیں اور پانچ رکوع ہیں

شروع خدا کا نام لے کر جو بڑا مہربان نہایت رحم والا ہے
سب تعریف خدا ہی کو (سزاوار ہے) جو آسمانوں اور زمین کا
پیدا کرنے والا (اور) فرشتوں کو قاصد بنانے والا ہے
جن کے دو دو اور تین تین اور چار چار پر ہیں۔ وہ (اپنی مخلوقات
میں جو چاہتا ہے بڑھاتا ہے۔ بیشک خدا ہر چیز پر قادر ہے ﴿۱﴾

بِصَاحِبِكُم مِّن جِنَّةٍ ۚ إِنْ هُوَ إِلَّا نَذِيرٌ
لَّكُم بَيْنَ يَدَيْ عَذَابٍ شَدِيدٍ ﴿٤٦﴾
قُلْ مَا سَأَلْتُكُم مِّنْ أَجْرٍ فَهُوَ لَكُمْ ۖ
إِنْ أَجْرِيَ إِلَّا عَلَى اللَّهِ ۖ وَهُوَ عَلَىٰ كُلِّ
شَيْءٍ شَهِيدٌ ﴿٤٧﴾
قُلْ إِنَّ رَبِّي يَقْذِفُ بِالْحَقِّ عَلَّامُ
الْغُيُوبِ ﴿٤٨﴾
قُلْ جَاءَ الْحَقُّ وَمَا يُبْدِئُ الْبَاطِلُ
وَمَا يُعِيدُ ﴿٤٩﴾
قُلْ إِن ضَلَلْتُ فَإِنَّمَا أَضِلُّ عَلَىٰ
نَفْسِي ۖ وَإِنِ اهْتَدَيْتُ فَبِمَا يُوحِي إِلَيَّ
رَبِّي ۚ إِنَّهُ سَمِيعٌ قَرِيبٌ ﴿٥٠﴾
وَلَوْ تَرَىٰ إِذْ فَزِعُوا فَلَا فَوْتَ وَأُخِذُوا
مِن مَّكَانٍ قَرِيبٍ ﴿٥١﴾
وَقَالُوا آمَنَّا بِهِ وَأَنَّىٰ لَهُمُ التَّنَاوُشُ
مِن مَّكَانٍ بَعِيدٍ ﴿٥٢﴾
وَقَدْ كَفَرُوا بِهِ مِن قَبْلُ ۖ وَيَقْذِفُونَ
بِالْغَيْبِ مِن مَّكَانٍ بَعِيدٍ ﴿٥٣﴾
وَحِيلَ بَيْنَهُمْ وَبَيْنَ مَا يَشْتَهُونَ كَمَا
فُعِلَ بِأَشْيَاعِهِم مِّن قَبْلُ ۚ إِنَّهُمْ
كَانُوا فِي شَكٍّ مُّرِيبٍ ﴿٥٤﴾ ع ۶ ۱۲

سُورَةُ فَاطِرٍ مَكِّيَّةٌ وَهِيَ خَمْسٌ وَأَرْبَعُونَ آيَةً وَخَمْسُ رُكُوعَاتٍ

بِسْمِ اللَّهِ الرَّحْمَٰنِ الرَّحِيمِ
الْحَمْدُ لِلَّهِ فَاطِرِ السَّمَاوَاتِ وَالْأَرْضِ
جَاعِلِ الْمَلَائِكَةِ رُسُلًا أُولِي أَجْنِحَةٍ
مَّثْنَىٰ وَثُلَاثَ وَرُبَاعَ ۚ يَزِيدُ فِي الْخَلْقِ
مَا يَشَاءُ ۚ إِنَّ اللَّهَ عَلَىٰ كُلِّ شَيْءٍ قَدِيرٌ ﴿١﴾

2. What Allah out of His Mercy doth bestow on mankind none can withhold: what He doth withhold, none can grant, apart from Him: and He is the Exalted in Power, Full of Wisdom.

3. O men! Remember the grace of Allah unto you! Is there a Creator, other than Allah, to give you sustenance from heaven or earth? There is no god but He: how then are ye perverted?

4. And if they reject thee, so were messengers rejected before thee: to Allah all affairs are returned.

5. O men! certainly the promise of Allah is true, let not then this present life deceive you, nor let the Chief Deceiver deceive you about Allah.

6. Verily Satan is an enemy to you: so treat him as an enemy. He only invites his adherents, that they may become companions of the Blazing Fire.

7. For those who reject Allah, is a terrible Chastisement but for those who believe and work righteous deeds, is Forgiveness, and a magnificent Reward.

8. Is he, then, to whom the evil of his conduct is made alluring, so that he looks upon it as good, (equal to one who is rightly guided)? For Allah leaves to stray whom He wills, and guides whom He wills. So let not thy soul be vested in regret for them for Allah knows well all that they do!

9. It is Allah Who sends forth the Winds, so that they raise up the Clouds, and We drive them to a land that is dead, and revive the earth therewith after its death: even so (will be) the Resurrection !

10. If any do seek for glory and power,— to Allah belong all glory and power. To Him mount up (all) Words of Purity: it is He Who exalts each Deed of Righteousness. Those that lay Plots of Evil,—for them is a Chastisement terrible; and the plotting of such will be void (of result).

خدا جو اپنی رحمت (کا دروازہ) کھول دے تو کوئی اس کو بند
کرنے والا نہیں۔ اور جو بند کر دے تو اسکے بعد کوئی اس کو
کھولنے والا نہیں اور وہ غالب حکمت والا ہے (۲)
لوگو خدا کے جو تم پر احسانات ہیں انکو یاد کرو۔ کیا خدا کے سوا
کوئی اور خالق (اور رازق) ہے جو تم کو آسمان اور زمین سے رزق دے؟
اسکے سوا کوئی معبود نہیں پس تم کہاں بہکے پھرتے ہو (۳)
اور (اے پیغمبر) اگر یہ لوگ تم کو جھٹلائیں تو تم سے پہلے بھی پیغمبر
جھٹلائے گئے ہیں۔ اور (سب) کام خدا ہی کی طرف لوٹائے جائینگے (۴)
لوگو خدا کا وعدہ سچا ہے۔ تو تم کو دنیا کی زندگی دھوکے میں نہ
ڈال دے اور نہ (شیطان) فریب دینے والا تمہیں
فریب دے (۵)
شیطان تمہارا دشمن ہے تم بھی اُسے دشمن ہی سمجھو۔ وہ اپنے
(پیرووں کے) گروہ کو بلاتا ہے تاکہ وہ دوزخ والوں میں ہوں (۶)
جنہوں نے کفر کیا اُن کے لئے سخت عذاب ہے۔ اور
جو ایمان لائے اور عمل نیک کرتے رہے اُن کے لئے
بخشش اور بڑا ثواب ہے (۷)
بھلا جس شخص کو اسکے اعمال بد آراستہ کرکے دکھائے جائیں اور
وہ انکو عمدہ سمجھنے لگے تو (کیا وہ نیکوکار آدمی جیسا ہو سکتا ہے) بیشک خدا
جسکو چاہتا ہے گمراہ کرتا ہے اور جسکو چاہتا ہے ہدایت دیتا ہے۔ تو ان لوگوں پر
افسوس کر کے تمہارا دم نہ نکل جائے۔ یہ جو کچھ کرتے ہیں خدا اس سے واقف ہے (۸)
اور خدا ہی تو ہے جو ہوائیں چلاتا ہے اور وہ بادل کو اُبھارتی ہیں پھر ہم
اُسکو ایک بے جان شہر کی طرف چلاتے ہیں پھر اس سے زمین کو
اسکے مرنے کے بعد زندہ کر دیتے ہیں۔ اسی طرح مُردوں کو جی اٹھنا ہوگا (۹)
جو شخص عزت کا طلبگار ہے تو عزت تو سب خدا ہی کی ہے۔
اُسی کی طرف پاکیزہ کلمات چڑھتے ہیں اور نیک عمل انکو بلند
کرتے ہیں۔ اور جو لوگ بُرے بُرے مکر کرتے ہیں اُن کیلئے سخت
عذاب ہے۔ اور اُن کا مکر نابود ہو جائے گا (۱۰)

مَا يَفْتَحِ اللّٰهُ لِلنَّاسِ مِنْ رَّحْمَةٍ فَلَا
مُمْسِكَ لَهَا ۚ وَمَا يُمْسِكْ ۙ فَلَا مُرْسِلَ
لَهٗ مِنْ بَعْدِهٖ ۭ وَهُوَ الْعَزِيْزُ الْحَكِيْمُ (۲)
يٰٓاَيُّهَا النَّاسُ اذْكُرُوْا نِعْمَتَ اللّٰهِ عَلَيْكُمْ ۭ هَلْ
مِنْ خَالِقٍ غَيْرُ اللّٰهِ يَرْزُقُكُمْ مِّنَ السَّمَاۗءِ
وَالْاَرْضِ ۭ لَآ اِلٰهَ اِلَّا هُوَ ڮ فَاَنّٰى تُؤْفَكُوْنَ (۳)
وَاِنْ يُّكَذِّبُوْكَ فَقَدْ كُذِّبَتْ رُسُلٌ مِّنْ
قَبْلِكَ ۭ وَاِلَى اللّٰهِ تُرْجَعُ الْاُمُوْرُ (۴)
يٰٓاَيُّهَا النَّاسُ اِنَّ وَعْدَ اللّٰهِ حَقٌّ فَلَا
تَغُرَّنَّكُمُ الْحَيٰوةُ الدُّنْيَا ۪ وَلَا يَغُرَّنَّكُمْ
بِاللّٰهِ الْغَرُوْرُ (۵)
اِنَّ الشَّيْطٰنَ لَكُمْ عَدُوٌّ فَاتَّخِذُوْهُ عَدُوًّا ۭ
اِنَّمَا يَدْعُوْا حِزْبَهٗ لِيَكُوْنُوْا مِنْ اَصْحٰبِ السَّعِيْرِ (۶)
اَلَّذِيْنَ كَفَرُوْا لَهُمْ عَذَابٌ شَدِيْدٌ ڛ وَالَّذِيْنَ
اٰمَنُوْا وَعَمِلُوا الصّٰلِحٰتِ لَهُمْ مَّغْفِرَةٌ
وَّاَجْرٌ كَبِيْرٌ (۷) ع ۱۳
اَفَمَنْ زُيِّنَ لَهٗ سُوْۗءُ عَمَلِهٖ فَرَاٰهُ حَسَنًا ۭ
فَاِنَّ اللّٰهَ يُضِلُّ مَنْ يَّشَاۗءُ وَيَهْدِيْ مَنْ
يَّشَاۗءُ ڮ فَلَا تَذْهَبْ نَفْسُكَ عَلَيْهِمْ
حَسَرٰتٍ ۭ اِنَّ اللّٰهَ عَلِيْمٌۢ بِمَا يَصْنَعُوْنَ (۸)
وَاللّٰهُ الَّذِيْٓ اَرْسَلَ الرِّيٰحَ فَتُثِيْرُ
سَحَابًا فَسُقْنٰهُ اِلٰى بَلَدٍ مَّيِّتٍ فَاَحْيَيْنَا
بِهِ الْاَرْضَ بَعْدَ مَوْتِهَا ۭ كَذٰلِكَ النُّشُوْرُ (۹)
مَنْ كَانَ يُرِيْدُ الْعِزَّةَ فَلِلّٰهِ الْعِزَّةُ جَمِيْعًا ۭ
اِلَيْهِ يَصْعَدُ الْكَلِمُ الطَّيِّبُ وَالْعَمَلُ
الصَّالِحُ يَرْفَعُهٗ ۭ وَالَّذِيْنَ يَمْكُرُوْنَ السَّيِّاٰتِ
لَهُمْ عَذَابٌ شَدِيْدٌ ۭ وَمَكْرُ اُولٰۗىِٕكَ هُوَ يَبُوْرُ (۱۰)

11. And Allah did create you from dust; then from a sperm-drop; then He made you in pairs. And no female conceives, or lays down (her load), but with His knowledge. Nor is a man long-lived granted length of days, nor is a part cut off from his life, but is in a Book (ordained). All this is easy to Allah.

12. Nor are the two seas alike,—the one palatable, sweet, and pleasant to drink, and the other, salt and bitter. Yet from each (kind of water) do ye eat flesh fresh and tender, and ye extract ornaments to wear; and thou seest the ships therein that plough the waves, that ye may seek (thus) of the Bounty of Allah that ye may be grateful.

13. He merges Night into Day, and He merges Day into Night, and He has subjected the sun and the moon (to His Law): each one runs its course for a term appointed. Such is Allah your Lord: to Him belongs all Dominion. And those whom ye invoke besides Him own not a straw.

14. If ye invoke them, they will not listen to your call, and if they were to listen, they cannot answer your (prayer). On the Day of Judgment they will reject your "Partnership". And none, (O man!) can inform you like Him who is All-Aware.

15. O ye men! It is ye that have need of Allah: but Allah is the One Free of all wants, Worthy of all praise.

16. If He so pleased, He could blot you out and bring in a New Creation.

17. Nor is that (at all) difficult for Allah.

18. Nor can a bearer of burdens bear another's burden. If one heavily laden should call another to (bear) his load, not the least portion of it can be carried (by the other) even though he be nearly related. Thou canst but warn such as fear their Lord unseen and establish regular Prayer. And whoever purifies himself does so

اور خدا ہی نے تم کو مٹی سے پیدا کیا پھر نطفے سے پھر تم کو
جوڑا جوڑا بنا دیا۔ اور کوئی عورت نہ حاملہ ہوتی ہے اور نہ جنتی
ہے مگر اس کے علم سے۔ اور نہ کسی بڑی عمر والے کو عمر زیادہ دی
جاتی ہے اور نہ اس کی عمر کم کی جاتی ہے مگر (سب کچھ) کتاب
میں (لکھا ہوا) ہے بیشک یہ خدا کو آسان ہے ﴿١١﴾
اور دونوں دریا (مل کر) یکساں نہیں ہو جاتے یہ تو میٹھا ہے
پیاس بجھانے والا جس کا پانی خوشگوار ہے اور یہ کھاری ہے
کڑوا۔ اور سب سے تم تازہ گوشت کھاتے ہو اور زیور نکالتے ہو جسے
پہنتے ہو۔ اور تم دریا میں کشتیوں کو دیکھتے ہو کہ (پانی کو) پھاڑتی چلی آتی
ہیں تاکہ تم اس کے فضل سے (معاش) تلاش کرو اور تاکہ شکر کرو ﴿١٢﴾
وہی رات کو دن میں داخل کرتا اور (وہی) دن کو رات میں
داخل کرتا ہے اور اسی نے سورج اور چاند کو کام میں لگا دیا ہے
ہر ایک ایک وقت مقرر تک چل رہا ہے یہی خدا تمہارا پروردگار
ہے اسی کی بادشاہی ہے۔ اور جن لوگوں کو تم اس کے سوا پکارتے ہو
وہ کھجور کی گٹھلی کے چھلکے کے برابر بھی تو (کسی چیز کے) مالک نہیں ﴿١٣﴾
اگر تم ان کو پکارو تو وہ تمہاری پکار نہ سنیں اور اگر سن بھی لیں
تو تمہاری بات کو قبول نہ کر سکیں۔ اور قیامت کے روز تمہارے شرک سے
انکار کر دیں گے اور (خدائے) باخبر کی طرح تم کو کوئی خبر نہیں دے گا ﴿١٤﴾
لوگو! تم (سب) خدا کے محتاج ہو اور خدا بے پرواہ سزاوار
حمد (وثنا) ہے ﴿١٥﴾
اگر چاہے تو تم کو نابود کر دے اور نئی مخلوقات لا آباد کرے ﴿١٦﴾
اور یہ خدا کو کچھ مشکل نہیں ﴿١٧﴾
اور کوئی اٹھانے والا دوسرے کا بوجھ نہ اٹھائے گا۔ اور کوئی
بوجھ میں دبا ہوا اپنا بوجھ بٹانے کو کسی کو بلائے تو کوئی اس
میں سے کچھ نہ اٹھائے گا اگرچہ قرابت دار ہی ہو۔ (اے پیغمبر)
تم ان ہی لوگوں کو نصیحت کر سکتے ہو جو بن دیکھے اپنے پروردگار
سے ڈرتے اور نماز بالالتزام پڑھتے ہیں۔ اور جو شخص پاک

وَاللّٰهُ خَلَقَكُمْ مِّنْ تُرَابٍ ثُمَّ مِنْ نُّطْفَةٍ
ثُمَّ جَعَلَكُمْ اَزْوَاجًا ۭ وَمَا تَحْمِلُ مِنْ اُنْثٰى
وَلَا تَضَعُ اِلَّا بِعِلْمِهٖ ۭ وَمَا يُعَمَّرُ مِنْ مُّعَمَّرٍ
وَّلَا يُنْقَصُ مِنْ عُمُرِهٖٓ اِلَّا فِيْ كِتٰبٍ ۭ
اِنَّ ذٰلِكَ عَلَي اللّٰهِ يَسِيْرٌ ﴿١١﴾
وَمَا يَسْتَوِي الْبَحْرٰنِ ڰ هٰذَا عَذْبٌ فُرَاتٌ
سَاۗىِٕغٌ شَرَابُهٗ وَهٰذَا مِلْحٌ اُجَاجٌ ۭ وَمِنْ
كُلٍّ تَاْكُلُوْنَ لَحْمًا طَرِيًّا وَّتَسْتَخْرِجُوْنَ حِلْيَةً
تَلْبَسُوْنَهَا ۚ وَتَرَى الْفُلْكَ فِيْهِ مَوَاخِرَ
لِتَبْتَغُوْا مِنْ فَضْلِهٖ وَلَعَلَّكُمْ تَشْكُرُوْنَ ﴿١٢﴾
يُوْلِجُ الَّيْلَ فِي النَّهَارِ وَيُوْلِجُ النَّهَارَ فِي
الَّيْلِ ۙ وَسَخَّرَ الشَّمْسَ وَالْقَمَرَ ڮ كُلٌّ
يَّجْرِيْ لِاَجَلٍ مُّسَمًّى ۭ ذٰلِكُمُ اللّٰهُ رَبُّكُمْ
لَهُ الْمُلْكُ ۭ وَالَّذِيْنَ تَدْعُوْنَ مِنْ دُوْنِهٖ
مَا يَمْلِكُوْنَ مِنْ قِطْمِيْرٍ ﴿١٣﴾
اِنْ تَدْعُوْهُمْ لَا يَسْمَعُوْا دُعَاۗءَكُمْ ۚ وَلَوْ
سَمِعُوْا مَا اسْتَجَابُوْا لَكُمْ ۭ وَيَوْمَ الْقِيٰمَةِ
يَكْفُرُوْنَ بِشِرْكِكُمْ ۭ وَلَا يُنَبِّئُكَ مِثْلُ خَبِيْرٍ ﴿١٤﴾
يٰٓاَيُّهَا النَّاسُ اَنْتُمُ الْفُقَرَاۗءُ اِلَى اللّٰهِ ۚ
وَاللّٰهُ هُوَ الْغَنِيُّ الْحَمِيْدُ ﴿١٥﴾
اِنْ يَّشَاْ يُذْهِبْكُمْ وَيَاْتِ بِخَلْقٍ جَدِيْدٍ ﴿١٦﴾
وَمَا ذٰلِكَ عَلَي اللّٰهِ بِعَزِيْزٍ ﴿١٧﴾
وَلَا تَزِرُ وَازِرَةٌ وِّزْرَ اُخْرٰى ۭ وَاِنْ
تَدْعُ مُثْقَلَةٌ اِلٰى حِمْلِهَا لَا يُحْمَلْ مِنْهُ
شَيْءٌ وَّلَوْ كَانَ ذَا قُرْبٰى ۭ اِنَّمَا تُنْذِرُ
الَّذِيْنَ يَخْشَوْنَ رَبَّهُمْ بِالْغَيْبِ وَاَقَامُوا
الصَّلٰوةَ ۭ وَمَنْ تَزَكّٰى فَاِنَّمَا يَتَزَكّٰى لِنَفْسِهٖ

for the benefit of his own soul; and the destination (of all) is to Allah.

19. The blind and the seeing are not alike;

20. Nor are the depths of Darkness and the Light;

21. Nor are the (chilly) shade and the (genial) heat of the sun:

22. Nor are alike those that are living and those that are dead. Allah can make any that He wills to hear; but thou canst not make those to hear who are (burried) in graves.

23. Thou art no other than a warner.

24. Verily We have sent thee with truth, as a bearer of glad tidings, and as a warner: and there never was a people, without a warner having lived among them (in the past).

25. And if they reject thee, so did their predecessors, to whom came their messengers with Clear Signs, Scriptures and the illuminating Book.

26. In the end did I punish those who rejected Faith: and how (terrible) was My punishment.

27. Seest thou not that Allah sends down rain from the sky? With it We then bring out produce of various colours. And in the mountains are tracts white and red, of various shades of colour, and black intense in hue.

28. And so amongst men and beasts and cattle, are they of various colours. Those truly fear Allah, among His Servants Who have knowledge: for Allah is Exalted in Might, Oft-Forgiving.

29. Those who rehearse the Book of Allah, establish regular Prayer, and spend (in Charity) out of what We have provided for them, secretly and openly, hope for a Commerce that will never fail:

30. For He will pay them their meed, nay, He will give them (even)

ہوتا ہے اپنے ہی لئے پاک ہوتا ہے اور سب کو، خدا ہی کیطرف لوٹکر جانا ہے (۱۸)
اور اندھا اور آنکھ والا برابر نہیں (۱۹)
اور نہ اندھیرا اور روشنی (۲۰)
اور نہ سایہ اور دھوپ (۲۱)
اور نہ زندے اور مُردے برابر ہو سکتے ہیں۔ خدا جس کو
چاہتا ہے سُنا دیتا ہے۔ اور تم اُن کو جو قبروں میں
(مدفون) ہیں سنا نہیں سکتے (۲۲)
تم تو صرف ہدایت کرنے والے ہو (۲۳)
ہم نے تم کو حق کیساتھ خوشخبری سنانے والا اور ڈرانے والا بھیجا ہے
اور کوئی امت نہیں مگر اس میں ہدایت کرنیوالا گزر چکا ہے (۲۴)
اور اگر یہ تمہاری تکذیب کریں تو جو لوگ اُن سے پہلے
تھے وہ بھی تکذیب کر چکے ہیں اُن کے پاس اُنکے پیغمبر
نشانیاں اور صحیفے اور روشن کتابیں لے لے کر آتے رہے (۲۵)
پھر میں نے کافروں کو پکڑ لیا سو (دیکھ لو کہ) میرا عذاب
کیسا ہوا (۲۶)
کیا تم نے نہیں دیکھا کہ خدا نے آسمان سے مینہ برسایا تو
ہم نے اُس سے طرح طرح کے رنگوں کے میوے پیدا
کئے۔ اور پہاڑوں میں سفید اور سُرخ رنگوں کے قطعات
ہیں۔ اور (بعض) کالے سیاہ ہیں (۲۷)
انسانوں اور جانوروں اور چارپایوں کے بھی کئی طرح
کے رنگ ہیں۔ خدا سے تو اُس کے بندوں میں سے وہی
ڈرتے ہیں جو صاحب علم ہیں۔ بیشک خدا غالب
(اور) بخشنے والا ہے (۲۸)
جو لوگ خدا کی کتاب پڑھتے اور نماز کی پابندی کرتے ہیں
اور جو کچھ ہم نے اُن کو دیا ہے اُس میں سے پوشیدہ اور ظاہر خرچ کرتے
ہیں وہ اُس تجارت (کے فائدے) کے امیدوار ہیں جو کبھی تباہ نہیں ہوگی (۲۹)
کیونکہ خدا ان کو پورا پورا بدلہ دے گا اور اپنے فضل سے

وَإِلَى اللَّهِ الْمَصِيرُ ﴿١٨﴾
وَمَا يَسْتَوِي الْأَعْمَىٰ وَالْبَصِيرُ ﴿١٩﴾
وَلَا الظُّلُمَاتُ وَلَا النُّورُ ﴿٢٠﴾
وَلَا الظِّلُّ وَلَا الْحَرُورُ ﴿٢١﴾
وَمَا يَسْتَوِي الْأَحْيَاءُ وَلَا الْأَمْوَاتُ ۚ إِنَّ
اللَّهَ يُسْمِعُ مَنْ يَشَاءُ ۖ وَمَا أَنْتَ بِمُسْمِعٍ
مَنْ فِي الْقُبُورِ ﴿٢٢﴾
إِنْ أَنْتَ إِلَّا نَذِيرٌ ﴿٢٣﴾
إِنَّا أَرْسَلْنَاكَ بِالْحَقِّ بَشِيرًا وَنَذِيرًا ۚ
وَإِنْ مِنْ أُمَّةٍ إِلَّا خَلَا فِيهَا نَذِيرٌ ﴿٢٤﴾
وَإِنْ يُكَذِّبُوكَ فَقَدْ كَذَّبَ الَّذِينَ مِنْ
قَبْلِهِمْ جَاءَتْهُمْ رُسُلُهُمْ بِالْبَيِّنَاتِ
وَبِالزُّبُرِ وَبِالْكِتَابِ الْمُنِيرِ ﴿٢٥﴾
ثُمَّ أَخَذْتُ الَّذِينَ كَفَرُوا ۖ فَكَيْفَ كَانَ
نَكِيرِ ﴿٢٦﴾ ع
أَلَمْ تَرَ أَنَّ اللَّهَ أَنْزَلَ مِنَ السَّمَاءِ مَاءً
فَأَخْرَجْنَا بِهِ ثَمَرَاتٍ مُخْتَلِفًا أَلْوَانُهَا ۚ
وَمِنَ الْجِبَالِ جُدَدٌ بِيضٌ وَحُمْرٌ
مُخْتَلِفٌ أَلْوَانُهَا وَغَرَابِيبُ سُودٌ ﴿٢٧﴾
وَمِنَ النَّاسِ وَالدَّوَابِّ وَالْأَنْعَامِ
مُخْتَلِفٌ أَلْوَانُهُ كَذَٰلِكَ ۗ إِنَّمَا يَخْشَى اللَّهَ
مِنْ عِبَادِهِ الْعُلَمَاءُ ۗ إِنَّ اللَّهَ عَزِيزٌ
غَفُورٌ ﴿٢٨﴾
إِنَّ الَّذِينَ يَتْلُونَ كِتَابَ اللَّهِ وَأَقَامُوا
الصَّلَاةَ وَأَنْفَقُوا مِمَّا رَزَقْنَاهُمْ سِرًّا وَ
عَلَانِيَةً يَرْجُونَ تِجَارَةً لَنْ تَبُورَ ﴿٢٩﴾
لِيُوَفِّيَهُمْ أُجُورَهُمْ وَيَزِيدَهُمْ مِنْ فَضْلِهِ

more out of His Bounty: for He is Oft-Forgiving, Most Ready to appreciate (service).

31. That which We have revealed to thee of the Book is the Truth,—confirming what was (revealed) before it: for Allah is assuredly—with respect to His servants— well acquainted and fully Observant.

32. Then We have given the Book for inheritance to such of Our servants as We have chosen: but there are among them some who wrong their own souls; some who follow a middle course; and some who are, by Allah's leave, foremost in good deeds; that is the highest Grace.

33. Gardens of Eternity will they enter: therein will they be adorned with bracelets of gold and pearls; and their garments there will be of silk.

34. And they will say: "Praise be to Allah, Who has removed from us (all) sorrow: for our Lord is indeed Oft-Forgiving ready to appreciate (service):

35. "Who has, out of His Bounty, settled us in a Home that will last: no toil nor sense of weariness shall touch us therein."

36. But those who reject (Allah)—for them will be the Fire of Hell: no term shall be determined for them, so they should die, nor shall its Chastisement be lightened for them. Thus do We reward every ungrateful one!

37. Therein will they cry aloud (for assistance): "Our Lord! Bring us out: we shall work righteousness, not the (deeds) we used to do!"—"Did we not give you long enough life so that he that would should receive admonition? And (moreover) the warner came to you. So taste ye (the fruits of your deeds): for the Wrong-doers there is no helper."

38. Verily Allah knows (all) the hidden things of the heavens and the earth: verily He has full knowledge of all that is in (men's) hearts.

39. He it is that has made you inheritors in the earth: so, he who

کچھ زیادہ بھی دے گا۔ وہ تو بخشنے والا (اور) قدردان ہے ۳۰
اور یہ کتاب جو ہم نے تمہاری طرف بھیجی ہے برحق ہے اور ان (کتابوں)
کی تصدیق کرتی ہے جو اس سے پہلے کی ہیں۔ بیشک خدا اپنے بندوں
سے خبردار (اور ان کو) دیکھنے والا ہے ۳۱
پھر ہم نے ان لوگوں کو کتاب کا وارث ٹھہرایا جن کو اپنے بندوں
میں سے برگزیدہ کیا۔ تو کچھ تو ان میں سے اپنے آپ پر ظلم
کرتے ہیں۔ اور کچھ میانہ رو ہیں۔ اور کچھ خدا
کے حکم سے نیکیوں میں آگے نکل جانے والے ہیں۔
یہی بڑا فضل ہے ۳۲
(ان لوگوں کیلئے) بہشت جاودانی (ہیں) جن میں وہ داخل
ہوں گے۔ وہاں ان کو سونے کے کنگن اور موتی پہنائے
جائیں گے۔ اور ان کی پوشاک ریشمی ہوگی ۳۳
وہ کہیں گے کہ خدا کا شکر ہے جس نے ہم سے غم دور
کیا۔ بیشک ہمارا پروردگار بخشنے والا (اور) قدردان ہے ۳۴
جس نے ہم کو اپنے فضل سے ہمیشہ کے رہنے کے گھر
میں اتارا۔ یہاں نہ تو ہم کو رنج پہنچے گا اور نہ ہمیں
تکان ہی ہوگی ۳۵
اور جن لوگوں نے کفر کیا ان کیلئے دوزخ کی آگ ہے۔ نہ
انہیں موت آئیگی کہ مر جائیں اور نہ اسکا عذاب ہی ان سے
ہلکا کیا جائیگا۔ ہم ہر ایک ناشکرے کو ایسا ہی بدلہ دیا کرتے ہیں ۳۶
وہ اس میں چلائینگے کہ اے پروردگار ہم کو نکال لے (اب)
ہم نیک عمل کیا کرینگے نہ وہ جو (پہلے) کرتے تھے۔ کیا ہم نے تم کو
اتنی عمر نہیں دی تھی کہ اس میں جو سوچنا چاہتا سوچ لیتا اور
تمہارے پاس ڈرانے والا بھی آیا۔ تو اب مزے چکھو۔ ظالموں کا کوئی مددگار نہیں ۳۷
بے شک خدا ہی آسمانوں اور زمین کی پوشیدہ باتوں کا جاننے
والا ہے۔ وہ تو دل کے بھیدوں تک سے واقف ہے ۳۸
وہی تو ہے جس نے تم کو زمین میں (پہلوں کا) جانشین بنایا

إِنَّهُ غَفُورٌ شَكُورٌ ۳۰
وَالَّذِىٓ أَوْحَيْنَآ إِلَيْكَ مِنَ الْكِتٰبِ
هُوَ الْحَقُّ مُصَدِّقًا لِّمَا بَيْنَ يَدَيْهِ ط
إِنَّ اللّٰهَ بِعِبَادِهٖ لَخَبِيرٌۢ بَصِيرٌ ۳۱
ثُمَّ أَوْرَثْنَا الْكِتٰبَ الَّذِينَ اصْطَفَيْنَا
مِنْ عِبَادِنَا ۚ فَمِنْهُمْ ظَالِمٌ لِّنَفْسِهٖ ج
وَمِنْهُم مُّقْتَصِدٌ ۚ وَمِنْهُمْ سَابِقٌۢ
بِالْخَيْرٰتِ بِإِذْنِ اللّٰهِ ۚ ذٰلِكَ هُوَ الْفَضْلُ
الْكَبِيرُ ط ۳۲
جَنّٰتُ عَدْنٍ يَدْخُلُونَهَا يُحَلَّوْنَ فِيهَا
مِنْ أَسَاوِرَ مِن ذَهَبٍ وَلُؤْلُؤًا ج وَلِبَاسُهُمْ
فِيهَا حَرِيرٌ ۳۳
وَقَالُوا الْحَمْدُ لِلّٰهِ الَّذِىٓ أَذْهَبَ عَنَّا
الْحَزَنَ ۖ إِنَّ رَبَّنَا لَغَفُورٌ شَكُورٌ ۳۴
الَّذِىٓ أَحَلَّنَا دَارَ الْمُقَامَةِ مِن فَضْلِهٖ ج
لَا يَمَسُّنَا فِيهَا نَصَبٌ وَلَا يَمَسُّنَا فِيهَا
لُغُوبٌ ۳۵
وَالَّذِينَ كَفَرُوا لَهُمْ نَارُ جَهَنَّمَ ج لَا
يُقْضٰى عَلَيْهِمْ فَيَمُوتُوا وَلَا يُخَفَّفُ عَنْهُم
مِّنْ عَذَابِهَا ط كَذٰلِكَ نَجْزِى كُلَّ كَفُورٍ ۳۶
وَهُمْ يَصْطَرِخُونَ فِيهَا ج رَبَّنَآ أَخْرِجْنَا
نَعْمَلْ صٰلِحًا غَيْرَ الَّذِى كُنَّا نَعْمَلُ ط أَوَلَمْ
نُعَمِّرْكُم مَّا يَتَذَكَّرُ فِيهِ مَن تَذَكَّرَ وَجَآءَكُمُ
النَّذِيرُ ط فَذُوقُوا فَمَا لِلظّٰلِمِينَ مِن نَّصِيرٍ ۳۷
إِنَّ اللّٰهَ عٰلِمُ غَيْبِ السَّمٰوٰتِ وَالْأَرْضِ ط
إِنَّهُ عَلِيمٌۢ بِذَاتِ الصُّدُورِ ۳۸
هُوَ الَّذِى جَعَلَكُمْ خَلٰٓئِفَ فِى الْأَرْضِ ط

فَمَنْ كَفَرَ فَعَلَيْهِ كُفْرُهٗ ؕ وَلَا يَزِيْدُ الْكٰفِرِيْنَ
كُفْرُهُمْ عِنْدَ رَبِّهِمْ اِلَّا مَقْتًا ۚ وَلَا يَزِيْدُ
الْكٰفِرِيْنَ كُفْرُهُمْ اِلَّا خَسَارًا ﴿۳۹﴾

تو جس نے کفر کیا اُسکے کفر کا ضرر اسی کو ہے۔ اور کافروں
کے حق میں اُن کے کفر سے پروردگار کے ہاں ناخوشی ہی بڑھتی ہے
اور کافروں کو اُن کا کفر نقصان ہی زیادہ کرتا ہے ﴿۳۹﴾

disbelieves his disbelief be on his own self their disbelief: but adds to the odium for the Unbelievers in the sight of their Lord: their disbelief but adds to (their own) loss.

قُلْ اَرَءَيْتُمْ شُرَكَآءَكُمُ الَّذِيْنَ تَدْعُوْنَ
مِنْ دُوْنِ اللّٰهِ ؕ اَرُوْنِيْ مَاذَا خَلَقُوْا مِنَ
الْاَرْضِ اَمْ لَهُمْ شِرْكٌ فِي السَّمٰوٰتِ ۚ
اَمْ اٰتَيْنٰهُمْ كِتٰبًا فَهُمْ عَلٰى بَيِّنَتٍ مِّنْهُ ۚ
بَلْ اِنْ يَّعِدُ الظّٰلِمُوْنَ بَعْضُهُمْ بَعْضًا
اِلَّا غُرُوْرًا ﴿۴۰﴾

بھلا تم نے اپنے شریکوں کو دیکھا جن کو تم خدا کے سوا پکارتے
ہو۔ مجھے دکھاؤ کہ اُنہوں نے زمین سے کونسی چیز پیدا کی ہے
یا (بتاؤ کہ) آسمانوں میں اُن کی شرکت ہے۔ یا ہم نے اُن کو
کتاب دی ہے تو وہ اس کی سند رکھتے ہیں؟ (ان میں سے
کوئی بات بھی نہیں) بلکہ ظالم جو ایک دوسرے کو وعدہ
دیتے ہیں محض فریب ہے ﴿۴۰﴾

40. Say: "Have ye seen (these) 'Partners' of yours whom ye call upon besides Allah? Show me what it is they have created in the (wide) earth. Or have they a share in the heavens? Or have We given them a Book from which they (can derive) clear (evidence)?—Nay, the wrong-doers promise each other nothing but delusions.

اِنَّ اللّٰهَ يُمْسِكُ السَّمٰوٰتِ وَالْاَرْضَ اَنْ
تَزُوْلَا ۚ وَلَئِنْ زَالَتَآ اِنْ اَمْسَكَهُمَا مِنْ
اَحَدٍ مِّنْ بَعْدِهٖ ؕ اِنَّهٗ كَانَ حَلِيْمًا غَفُوْرًا ﴿۴۱﴾

خدا ہی آسمانوں اور زمین کو تھامے رکھتا ہے کہ ٹل
نہ جائیں۔ اگر وہ ٹل جائیں تو خدا کے سوا کوئی ایسا نہیں
جو اُن کو تھام سکے۔ بیشک وہ بردبار (اور) بخشنے والا ہے ﴿۴۱﴾

41. It is Allah Who sustains the heavens and the earth, lest they cease (to function): and if they should fail. There is none—not one— can sustain them thereafter: verily He is Most Forbearing, Oft-Forgiving.

وَاَقْسَمُوْا بِاللّٰهِ جَهْدَ اَيْمَانِهِمْ لَئِنْ
جَآءَهُمْ نَذِيْرٌ لَّيَكُوْنُنَّ اَهْدٰى مِنْ
اِحْدَى الْاُمَمِ ۚ فَلَمَّا جَآءَهُمْ نَذِيْرٌ
مَّا زَادَهُمْ اِلَّا نُفُوْرًا ﴿۴۲﴾

اور یہ خدا کی سخت سخت قسمیں کھاتے ہیں کہ اگر اُن کے پاس
کوئی ہدایت کرنے والا آئے تو یہ ہر ایک اُمت سے بڑھ کر
ہدایت پر ہوں۔ مگر جب اُن کے پاس ہدایت کرنے والا
آیا تو اُس سے اُن کو نفرت ہی بڑھی ﴿۴۲﴾

42. They swore their strongest oaths by Allah that if a warner came to them, they would be more rightly guided than anyone of the nations: but when a warner came to them, it has only increased their aversion.

اِسْتِكْبَارًا فِي الْاَرْضِ وَمَكْرَ السَّيِّئِ ؕ
وَلَا يَحِيْقُ الْمَكْرُ السَّيِّئُ اِلَّا بِاَهْلِهٖ ؕ
فَهَلْ يَنْظُرُوْنَ اِلَّا سُنَّتَ الْاَوَّلِيْنَ ۚ
فَلَنْ تَجِدَ لِسُنَّتِ اللّٰهِ تَبْدِيْلًا ۚ وَلَنْ
تَجِدَ لِسُنَّتِ اللّٰهِ تَحْوِيْلًا ﴿۴۳﴾

یعنی (اُنہوں نے) ملک میں غرور کرنا اور بُری چال چلنا
(اختیار کیا) اور بُری چال کا وبال اُسکے چلنے والے ہی پر
پڑتا ہے۔ یہ اگلے لوگوں کی روش کے سوا اور کسی چیز کے
منتظر نہیں۔ سو تم خدا کی عادت میں ہرگز تبدّل نہ پاؤ گے
اور خدا کے طریقے میں کبھی تغیر نہ دیکھو گے ﴿۴۳﴾

43. On account of their arrogance in the land and their plotting of Evil. But the plotting of Evil will hem in only the authors thereof. Now are they but looking for the way the ancients were dealt with? But no change wilt thou find in Allah's way (of dealing): no turning off wilt thou find in Allah's way (of dealing).

اَوَلَمْ يَسِيْرُوْا فِي الْاَرْضِ فَيَنْظُرُوْا كَيْفَ
كَانَ عَاقِبَةُ الَّذِيْنَ مِنْ قَبْلِهِمْ وَكَانُوْٓا
اَشَدَّ مِنْهُمْ قُوَّةً ؕ وَمَا كَانَ اللّٰهُ لِيُعْجِزَهٗ
مِنْ شَيْءٍ فِي السَّمٰوٰتِ وَلَا فِي الْاَرْضِ ؕ
اِنَّهٗ كَانَ عَلِيْمًا قَدِيْرًا ﴿۴۴﴾

کیا اُنہوں نے زمین میں سیر نہیں کی تا کہ دیکھتے کہ جو لوگ
اُن سے پہلے تھے اُن کا انجام کیا ہوا حالانکہ وہ ان
سے قوت میں بہت زیادہ تھے۔ اور خدا ایسا نہیں
کہ آسمانوں اور زمین میں کوئی چیز اس کو عاجز کر سکے۔
وہ علم والا (اور) قدرت والا ہے ﴿۴۴﴾

44. Do they not travel through the earth, and see what was the End of those before them,— though they were superior to them in strength? Nor is Allah to be frustrated by anything whatever in the heavens or on earth: for He is All-Knowing, All-Powerful.

وَلَوْ يُؤَاخِذُ اللّٰهُ النَّاسَ بِمَا كَسَبُوْا مَا

اور اگر خدا لوگوں کو اُن کے اعمال کے سبب پکڑنے لگتا تو

45. If Allah were to punish men according to what they deserve,

SÛRA–36
YÃSÎN
(INTRODUCTION)

See Introduction to S. 34. This particular Sûra is devoted to the Holy Prophet and the Revelation which he brought. The Abbreviated Letters *Yã-Sîn* are usually construed as a title of the Holy Prophet. But it is not permissible to be dogmatic about the meaning of Abbreviated Letters. This Sûra is considered to be "the heart of the Qur-ãn," as it concerns the central figure in the teaching of Islam and central doctrine of Revelation and the Hereafter. As referring to the Hereafter, it is apropriately read in solemn ceremonies after death.

In chronology it belongs to the middle or early Makkan period.

In S. 37: 130 (a cognate Sûra) occurs the word *Il-yã-sîn.*

He would not leave on the back of the (earth) a single living creature: but He gives them respite for a stated Term: when their Term expires, verily Allah has in His sight all His servants.

Yā-Sîn (being Abbreviated Letters)

In the name of Allah, Most Gracious, Most Merciful.

1. Yā-Sîn.
2. By the Qur'an, full of Wisdom,—
3. Thou art indeed one of the messengers,
4. On a Straight Way.
5. (It is a Revelation) sent down by (Him), the Exalted in Might, Most Merciful,
6. In order that thou mayest warn a people, whose fathers were not warned, and who therefore remain heedless (of the Signs of Allah).
7. The Word is proved true against the greater part of them: for they do not believe.
8. We have put yokes round their necks right up to their chins, so that they cannot bow their heads.
9. And We have put a bar in front of them and a bar behind them, and further, We have covered them up; so that they cannot see.
10. The same is to them whether thou admonish them or thou do not admonish them: they will not believe.
11. Thou canst but admonish such a one as follows the Message and fears the Most Gracious, unseen: give such a one, therefore, good tidings, of Forgiveness and a Reward most generous.
12. Verily We shall give life to the dead, and We record that which they send before and that which they leave behind, and of all things have We taken account. In a clear Book (of evidence).
13. Set forth to them, by way of a parable, the (story of) the Companions of the City. Behold, there came messengers to it.

روئے زمین پر ایک چلنے پھرنے والے کو نہ چھوڑتا لیکن وہ
اُنکو ایک وقت مقرر تک مہلت دیئے جاتا ہے سو جب اُنکا وقت
آجائیگا تو اُنکے اعمال کا بدلہ دیگا) خدا تو اپنے بندوں کو دیکھ رہا ہے ﴿٤٥﴾

سورہ یٰس مکی ہے اور اس میں تراسی آیتیں اور پانچ رکوع ہیں

شروع خدا کا نام لے کر جو بڑا مہربان نہایت رحم والا ہے
یٰس ﴿١﴾ قسم ہے قرآن کی جو حکمت سے بھرا ہوا ہے ﴿٢﴾
(اے محمدؐ) بیشک تم پیغمبروں میں سے ہو ﴿٣﴾
سیدھے رستے پر ﴿٤﴾
(یہ خدائے) غالب (اور) مہربان نے نازل کیا ہے ﴿٥﴾
تاکہ تم اُن لوگوں کو جن کے باپ دادا کو متنبہ نہیں کیا
گیا تھا متنبہ کر دو وہ غفلت میں پڑے ہوئے ہیں ﴿٦﴾
اُن میں سے اکثر پر (خدا کی) بات پوری ہو چکی ہے سو
وہ ایمان نہیں لائیں گے ﴿٧﴾
ہم نے اُن کی گردنوں میں طوق ڈال رکھے ہیں اور وہ
ٹھوڑیوں تک (پھنسے ہوئے) ہیں تو اُنکے سر اُلل رہے ہیں ﴿٨﴾
اور ہم نے اُنکے آگے بھی دیوار بنا دی اور اُنکے پیچھے بھی پھر اُن
پر پردہ ڈال دیا تو یہ دیکھ نہیں سکتے ﴿٩﴾
اور تم اُن کو نصیحت کرو یا نہ کرو اُن کے لئے برابر ہے۔
وہ ایمان نہیں لانے کے ﴿١٠﴾
تم تو صرف اُس شخص کو نصیحت کر سکتے ہو جو نصیحت کی
پیروی کرے اور خدا سے غائبانہ ڈرے سو اُسکو مغفرت
اور بڑے ثواب کی بشارت سُنا دو ﴿١١﴾
بیشک ہم مُردوں کو زندہ کرینگے اور جو کچھ وہ آگے بھیج چکے
اور (جو) اُنکے نشان پیچھے رہ گئے ہم اُنکو قلمبند کر لیتے ہیں اور
ہر چیز کو ہم نے کتاب روشن (یعنی لوح محفوظ) میں لکھ رکھا ہے ﴿١٢﴾
اور ان سے گاؤں والوں کا قصہ بیان کرو جب اُنکے
پاس پیغمبر آئے ﴿١٣﴾

تَرَكَ عَلٰى ظَهْرِهَا مِنْ دَآبَّةٍ وَّلٰكِنْ
يُّؤَخِّرُهُمْ اِلٰٓى اَجَلٍ مُّسَمًّى ۚ فَاِذَا جَآءَ
اَجَلُهُمْ فَاِنَّ اللّٰهَ كَانَ بِعِبَادِهٖ بَصِيْرًا ﴿٤٥﴾

سُوْرَةُ يٰسٓ مَكِّيَّةٌ وَّهِيَ ثَلٰثٌ وَّثَمَانُوْنَ اٰيَةً وَّخَمْسُ رُكُوْعَاتٍ

بِسْمِ اللّٰهِ الرَّحْمٰنِ الرَّحِيْمِ
يٰسٓ ﴿١﴾ وَالْقُرْاٰنِ الْحَكِيْمِ ﴿٢﴾
اِنَّكَ لَمِنَ الْمُرْسَلِيْنَ ﴿٣﴾
عَلٰى صِرَاطٍ مُّسْتَقِيْمٍ ﴿٤﴾
تَنْزِيْلَ الْعَزِيْزِ الرَّحِيْمِ ﴿٥﴾
لِتُنْذِرَ قَوْمًا مَّآ اُنْذِرَ اٰبَآؤُهُمْ فَهُمْ
غٰفِلُوْنَ ﴿٦﴾
لَقَدْ حَقَّ الْقَوْلُ عَلٰٓى اَكْثَرِهِمْ فَهُمْ لَا
يُؤْمِنُوْنَ ﴿٧﴾
اِنَّا جَعَلْنَا فِيْٓ اَعْنَاقِهِمْ اَغْلٰلًا فَهِيَ اِلَى
الْاَذْقَانِ فَهُمْ مُّقْمَحُوْنَ ﴿٨﴾
وَجَعَلْنَا مِنْ بَيْنِ اَيْدِيْهِمْ سَدًّا وَّمِنْ
خَلْفِهِمْ سَدًّا فَاَغْشَيْنٰهُمْ فَهُمْ لَا يُبْصِرُوْنَ ﴿٩﴾
وَسَوَآءٌ عَلَيْهِمْ ءَاَنْذَرْتَهُمْ اَمْ لَمْ
تُنْذِرْهُمْ لَا يُؤْمِنُوْنَ ﴿١٠﴾
اِنَّمَا تُنْذِرُ مَنِ اتَّبَعَ الذِّكْرَ وَخَشِيَ
الرَّحْمٰنَ بِالْغَيْبِ ۚ فَبَشِّرْهُ بِمَغْفِرَةٍ
وَّاَجْرٍ كَرِيْمٍ ﴿١١﴾
اِنَّا نَحْنُ نُحْيِ الْمَوْتٰى وَنَكْتُبُ مَا قَدَّمُوْا
وَاٰثَارَهُمْ ۗ وَكُلَّ شَيْءٍ اَحْصَيْنٰهُ فِيْٓ
اِمَامٍ مُّبِيْنٍ ﴿١٢﴾
وَاضْرِبْ لَهُمْ مَّثَلًا اَصْحٰبَ الْقَرْيَةِ ۘ
اِذْ جَآءَهَا الْمُرْسَلُوْنَ ﴿١٣﴾

14. When We (first) sent to them two messengers, they rejected them: but We strengthened them with a third: they said, "Truly, we have been sent on a mission to you."

15. The (people) said: "Ye are only men like ourselves; and The Most Gracious sends no sort of revelation: ye do nothing but lie."

16. They said: "Our Lord doth know that we have been sent on a mission to you:

17. "And our duty is only to deliver the clear Message."

18. The (people) said: "For us, we augur an evil omen from you: if ye desist not, we will certainly stone you, and a grievous punishment indeed will be inflicted on you by us."

19. They said: "Your evil omens are with yourselves: (Deem ye this an evil omen). If ye are admonished? Nay, but ye are a people transgressing all bounds!"

20. Then there came running, from the farthest part of the City, a man, saying, "O my People! obey the messengers:

21. "Obey those who ask no reward of you (for themselves), and who are themselves guided.

22. "Why should not I serve Him Who created me, and to Whom ye shall (all) be brought back.

23. "Shall I take (other) gods besides Him? If The Most Gracious should intend some adversity for me, of no use whatever will be their intercession for me, nor can they deliver me.

24. "I would indeed, then be in manifest Error.

25. "For me, I have faith in the Lord of you (all): listen, then, to me!"

26. It was said: "Enter thou the Garden." He said: "Ah me! Would that my People knew (what I know)!

27. "From That my Lord has granted me Forgiveness and has enrolled me among those held in honour!"

28. And We sent not down against his People, after him, any

(یعنی) جب ہم نے ان کی طرف دو (پیغمبر) بھیجے تو انہوں نے
اُن کو جھٹلایا۔ پھر ہم نے تیسرے سے تقویت دی۔ تو انہوں
نے کہا کہ ہم تمہاری طرف پیغمبر ہو کر آئے ہیں [۲۳۱] ﴿١٤﴾
وہ بولے کہ تم (اور کچھ) نہیں مگر ہماری طرح کے آدمی (ہو)۔ اور خدا
نے کوئی چیز بھی نازل نہیں کی تم محض جھوٹ بولتے ہو ﴿١٥﴾
انہوں نے کہا کہ ہمارا پروردگار جانتا ہے کہ ہم تمہاری طرف (پیغام
دے کر) بھیجے گئے ہیں ﴿١٦﴾
اور ہمارے ذمے تو صاف صاف پہنچا دینا ہے اور بس ﴿١٧﴾
وہ بولے کہ ہم تم کو نامبارک دیکھتے ہیں۔ اگر تم باز نہ آؤ گے تو ہم
تمہیں سنگسار کر دیں گے اور تم کو ہم سے دکھ دینے والا عذاب پہنچے گا ﴿١٨﴾
انہوں نے کہا کہ تمہاری نحوست تمہارے ساتھ ہے [۲۳۲]۔ کیا اس لئے کہ تم کو
نصیحت کی گئی [۲۳۳] بلکہ تم ایسے لوگ ہو جو حد سے تجاوز کر گئے ہو ﴿١٩﴾
اور شہر کے پرلے کنارے سے ایک آدمی دوڑتا ہوا آیا [۲۳۴] کہنے
لگا کہ اے میری قوم پیغمبروں کے پیچھے چلو ﴿٢٠﴾
ایسوں کے جو تم سے صلہ نہیں مانگتے اور وہ سیدھے
رستے پر ہیں ﴿٢١﴾
اور مجھے کیا ہے کہ میں اس کی پرستش نہ کروں جس نے
مجھے پیدا کیا اور اسی کی طرف تم کو لوٹ کر جانا ہے ﴿٢٢﴾
کیا میں ان کو چھوڑ کر اوروں کو معبود بناؤں؟ اگر خدا میرے
حق میں نقصان کرنا چاہے تو ان کی سفارش مجھے کچھ بھی
فائدہ نہ دے سکے۔ اور نہ وہ مجھے چھڑا ہی سکیں ﴿٢٣﴾
تب تو میں صریح گمراہی میں مبتلا ہو گیا ﴿٢٤﴾
میں تمہارے پروردگار پر ایمان لایا ہوں سو میری بات سن رکھو ﴿٢٥﴾
حکم ہوا کہ بہشت میں داخل ہو جا۔ بولا کاش! میری
قوم کو خبر ہو ﴿٢٦﴾
کہ خدا نے مجھے بخش دیا اور عزت والوں میں کیا ﴿٢٧﴾
اور ہم نے اس کے بعد اس کی قوم پر کوئی لشکر نہیں

إذ أرسلنا إليهم اثنين فكذبوهما
فعززنا بثالث فقالوا إنا إليكم
مرسلون ﴿١٤﴾
قالوا ما أنتم إلا بشر مثلنا وما أنزل
الرحمن من شيء إن أنتم إلا تكذبون ﴿١٥﴾
قالوا ربنا يعلم إنا إليكم
لمرسلون ﴿١٦﴾
وما علينا إلا البلاغ المبين ﴿١٧﴾
قالوا إنا تطيرنا بكم لئن لم تنتهوا
لنرجمنكم وليمسنكم منا عذاب أليم ﴿١٨﴾
قالوا طائركم معكم أئن ذكرتم
بل أنتم قوم مسرفون ﴿١٩﴾
وجاء من أقصا المدينة رجل يسعى
قال يقوم اتبعوا المرسلين ﴿٢٠﴾
اتبعوا من لا يسألكم أجرا وهم
مهتدون ﴿٢١﴾
وما لي لا أعبد الذي فطرني وإليه
ترجعون ﴿٢٢﴾
ءأتخذ من دونه آلهة إن يردن
الرحمن بضر لا تغن عني شفاعتهم
شيئا ولا ينقذون ﴿٢٣﴾
إني إذا لفي ضلل مبين ﴿٢٤﴾
إني آمنت بربكم فاسمعون ﴿٢٥﴾
قيل ادخل الجنة قال يليت قومي
يعلمون ﴿٢٦﴾
بما غفر لي ربي وجعلني من المكرمين ﴿٢٧﴾
وما أنزلنا على قومه من بعده من

جُندٍ مِّنَ السَّمَآءِ وَمَا كُنَّا مُنزِلِينَ ﴿٢٨﴾
إِن كَانَتْ إِلَّا صَيْحَةً وَاحِدَةً فَإِذَا
هُمْ خَامِدُونَ ﴿٢٩﴾
يَٰحَسْرَةً عَلَى الْعِبَادِ مَا يَأْتِيهِم مِّن
رَّسُولٍ إِلَّا كَانُوا بِهِ يَسْتَهْزِءُونَ ﴿٣٠﴾
أَلَمْ يَرَوْا كَمْ أَهْلَكْنَا قَبْلَهُم مِّنَ الْقُرُونِ
أَنَّهُمْ إِلَيْهِمْ لَا يَرْجِعُونَ ﴿٣١﴾
وَإِن كُلٌّ لَّمَّا جَمِيعٌ لَّدَيْنَا مُحْضَرُونَ ﴿٣٢﴾
وَآيَةٌ لَّهُمُ الْأَرْضُ الْمَيْتَةُ أَحْيَيْنَاهَا
وَأَخْرَجْنَا مِنْهَا حَبًّا فَمِنْهُ يَأْكُلُونَ ﴿٣٣﴾
وَجَعَلْنَا فِيهَا جَنَّاتٍ مِّن نَّخِيلٍ وَأَعْنَابٍ
وَفَجَّرْنَا فِيهَا مِنَ الْعُيُونِ ﴿٣٤﴾
لِيَأْكُلُوا مِن ثَمَرِهِ وَمَا عَمِلَتْهُ أَيْدِيهِمْ
أَفَلَا يَشْكُرُونَ ﴿٣٥﴾
سُبْحَانَ الَّذِي خَلَقَ الْأَزْوَاجَ كُلَّهَا
مِمَّا تُنبِتُ الْأَرْضُ وَمِنْ أَنفُسِهِمْ
وَمِمَّا لَا يَعْلَمُونَ ﴿٣٦﴾
وَآيَةٌ لَّهُمُ اللَّيْلُ نَسْلَخُ مِنْهُ النَّهَارَ
فَإِذَا هُم مُّظْلِمُونَ ﴿٣٧﴾
وَالشَّمْسُ تَجْرِي لِمُسْتَقَرٍّ لَّهَا ذَٰلِكَ
تَقْدِيرُ الْعَزِيزِ الْعَلِيمِ ﴿٣٨﴾
وَالْقَمَرَ قَدَّرْنَاهُ مَنَازِلَ حَتَّىٰ عَادَ
كَالْعُرْجُونِ الْقَدِيمِ ﴿٣٩﴾
لَا الشَّمْسُ يَنبَغِي لَهَا أَن تُدْرِكَ الْقَمَرَ
وَلَا اللَّيْلُ سَابِقُ النَّهَارِ وَكُلٌّ فِي فَلَكٍ
يَسْبَحُونَ ﴿٤٠﴾
وَآيَةٌ لَّهُمْ أَنَّا حَمَلْنَا ذُرِّيَّتَهُمْ فِي الْفُلْكِ

وقف غفران ۱۲
ع ۲

اُتارا اور نہ ہم اُتارنے والے تھے ہی ﴿۲۸﴾
وہ تو صرف ایک چنگھاڑ تھی (آتشیں) سو وہ (اس سے)
ناگہاں بجھ کر رہ گئے ﴿۲۹﴾
بندوں پر افسوس ہے کہ ان کے پاس کوئی پیغمبر نہیں آتا
مگر اس سے تمسخر کرتے ہیں ﴿۳۰﴾
کیا انہوں نے نہیں دیکھا کہ ہم نے اُن سے پہلے بہت سے لوگوں
کو ہلاک کردیا تھا اب وہ اُنکی طرف لوٹ کر نہیں آئینگے ﴿۳۱﴾
اور سب کے سب ہمارے روبرو حاضر کئے جائیں گے ﴿۳۲﴾
اور ایک نشانی اُن کیلئے زمین مردہ ہے۔ کہ ہم نے اسکو
زندہ کیا اور اس میں سے اناج اُگایا پھر یہ اسمیں سے کھاتے ہیں ﴿۳۳﴾
اور اس میں کھجوروں اور انگوروں کے باغ پیدا کئے اور
اس میں چشمے جاری کردیئے ﴿۳۴﴾
تاکہ یہ اُن کے پھل کھائیں اور اُن کے ہاتھوں نے
تو اُن کو نہیں بنایا۔ تو پھر کیا یہ شکر نہیں کرتے؟ ﴿۳۵﴾
وہ خدا پاک ہے جس نے زمین کی نباتات کے
اور خود اُن کے اور جن چیزوں کی اُن کو خبر نہیں
سب کے جوڑے بنائے ﴿۳۶﴾
اور ایک نشانی اُن کیلئے رات ہے کہ اسمیں سے ہم دن کو
کھینچ لیتے ہیں تو اُس وقت اُن پر اندھیرا چھا جاتا ہے ﴿۳۷﴾
اور سورج اپنے مقرر رستے پر چلتا رہتا ہے۔ یہ (خدائے)
غالب (اور) دانا کا (مقرر کیا ہوا) اندازہ ہے ﴿۳۸﴾
اور چاند کی بھی ہم نے منزلیں مقرر کردیں یہاں تک کہ
(گھٹتے گھٹتے) کھجور کی پرانی شاخ کی طرح ہوجاتا ہے ﴿۳۹﴾
نہ تو سورج ہی سے ہوسکتا ہے کہ چاند کو جا پکڑے اور
نہ رات ہی دن سے پہلے آسکتی ہے۔ اور سب اپنے
اپنے دائرے میں تیر رہے ہیں ﴿۴۰﴾
اور ایک نشانی اُن کے لئے یہ ہے کہ ہم نے اُن کی اولاد

hosts from heaven, nor was it needful for Us so to do.

29. It was no more than a single mighty Blast, and behold! they were (like ashes) quenched and silent.

30. Ah! alas for the servants! there comes not a messenger to them but they mock him!

31. See they not how many generations before them We destroyed? Not to them will they return:

32. But each one of them all—will be brought before Us (for judgment).

33. A Sign for them is the earth that is dead: We do give it life, and produce grain therefrom, of which ye do eat.

34. And We produce therein orchards with date-palms and vines, and We cause springs to gush forth therein:

35. That they may enjoy the fruits of this (artistry): it was not their hands that made this: will they not then give thanks?

36. Glory to Allah, Who created in pairs all things that the earth produces, as well as their own (human) kind and (other) things of which they have no knowledge.

37. And a Sign for them is the Night: We withdraw therefrom the Day, and behold they are plunged in darkness;

38. And the Sun runs unto a resting place, for him: that is the decree of (Him), the Exalted in Might, the All-Knowing.

39. And the Moon,—We have measured for her stations (to traverse) till she returns like the old (and withered) lower part of a date-stalk.

40. It is not permitted to the Sun to catch up the Moon, nor can the Night outstrip the Day: each (just) swims along in (its own) orbit (according to Law).

41. And a Sign for them is that We bore their race (through the

Flood) in the loaded Ark;

42. And We have created for them similar (vessels) on which they ride.

43. If it were Our Will, We could drown them: then would there be no helper (to hear their cry), nor could they be delivered,

44. Except by way of Mercy from Us, and by way of (worldly) convenience (to serve them) for a time.

45. When they are told, "Fear ye that which is before you and that which will be after you, in order that ye may receive Mercy," (they turn back).

46. Not a Sign comes to them from among the Signs of their Lord, but they turn away therefrom.

47. And when they are told, "Spend ye of (the bounties) with which Allah has provided you," the Unbelievers say to those who believe: "Shall we then feed those whom, if Allah had so willed, He would have fed, (Himself)?—Ye are in nothing but manifest error."

48. Further, they say, "When will this promise (come to pass), if what ye say is true?"

49. They will not (have to) wait for aught but a single Blast: it will seize them while they are yet disputing among themselves!

50. No (chance) will they then have, by will, to dispose (of their affairs), nor to return to their own people!

51. The trumpet shall be sounded, when behold! from the sepulchres (men) will rush forth to their Lord!

52. They will say: "Ah! woe unto us! Who hath raised us up from our beds of repose?"... (A voice will say:) "This is what The Most Gracious had promised. And true was the word of the messengers!"

53. It will be no more than a single Blast, when lo! they will all be brought up before Us!

54. Then, on that Day, not a soul will be wronged in the least, and ye shall but be repaid the meeds of your past Deeds.

کو بھری ہوئی کشتی میں سوار کیا ﴿٤١﴾
اور اُن کیلئے ویسی ہی اور چیزیں پیدا کیں جن پر وہ سوار ہوتے ہیں ﴿٤٢﴾
اور اگر ہم چاہیں تو اُن کو غرق کر دیں۔ پھر نہ تو اُن کا کوئی
فریادرس ہو اور نہ اُن کو رہائی ملے ﴿٤٣﴾
مگر یہ ہماری رحمت اور ایک مدت تک کے فائدے ہیں ﴿٤٤﴾
اور جب اُن سے کہا جاتا ہے کہ جو تمہارے آگے اور جو
تمہارے پیچھے ہے اُس سے ڈرو تاکہ تم پر رحم کیا جائے ﴿٤٥﴾
اور اُن کے پاس اُن کے پروردگار کی طرف سے کوئی نشانی
نہیں آتی مگر اُس سے منہ پھیر لیتے ہیں ﴿٤٦﴾
اور جب اُن سے کہا جاتا ہے کہ جو رزق خدا نے تم کو دیا
ہے اس میں سے خرچ کرو۔ تو کافر مومنوں سے کہتے
ہیں کہ بھلا ہم اُن لوگوں کو کھانا کھلائیں جن کو اگر خدا
چاہتا تو خود کھلا دیتا۔ تم تو صریح غلطی میں ہو ﴿٤٧﴾
اور کہتے ہیں اگر تم سچ کہتے ہو تو یہ وعدہ کب
(پورا) ہوگا؟ ﴿٤٨﴾
یہ تو ایک چنگھاڑ کے منتظر ہیں جو ان کو اس حال میں
کہ باہم جھگڑ رہے ہوں گے آپکڑے گی ﴿٤٩﴾
پھر نہ تو وصیت کر سکیں گے اور نہ اپنے گھر والوں
میں واپس جا سکیں گے ﴿٥٠﴾
اور جس وقت صور پھونکا جائے گا یہ قبروں سے
(نکل کر) اپنے پروردگار کی طرف دوڑ پڑیں گے ﴿٥١﴾
کہیں گے اے ہے ہمیں ہماری خوابگاہوں سے کس نے (جگا) اٹھایا؟ یہ
وہی تو ہے جس کا خدا نے وعدہ کیا تھا اور پیغمبروں نے سچ کہا تھا ﴿٥٢﴾
صرف ایک زور کی آواز کا ہونا ہوگا کہ سب کے سب
ہمارے روبرو آ حاضر ہوں گے ﴿٥٣﴾
اُس روز کسی شخص پر کچھ بھی ظلم نہیں کیا جائے گا اور
تم کو بدلہ ویسا ہی ملے گا جیسے تم کام کرتے تھے ﴿٥٤﴾

الْمَشْحُوْنِ ﴿٤١﴾
وَخَلَقْنَا لَهُمْ مِّنْ مِّثْلِهٖ مَا يَرْكَبُوْنَ ﴿٤٢﴾
وَاِنْ نَّشَاْ نُغْرِقْهُمْ فَلَا صَرِيْخَ لَهُمْ
وَلَا هُمْ يُنْقَذُوْنَ ﴿٤٣﴾
اِلَّا رَحْمَةً مِّنَّا وَمَتَاعًا اِلٰى حِيْنٍ ﴿٤٤﴾
وَاِذَا قِيْلَ لَهُمُ اتَّقُوْا مَا بَيْنَ اَيْدِيْكُمْ
وَمَا خَلْفَكُمْ لَعَلَّكُمْ تُرْحَمُوْنَ ﴿٤٥﴾
وَمَا تَاْتِيْهِمْ مِّنْ اٰيَةٍ مِّنْ اٰيٰتِ رَبِّهِمْ
اِلَّا كَانُوْا عَنْهَا مُعْرِضِيْنَ ﴿٤٦﴾
وَاِذَا قِيْلَ لَهُمْ اَنْفِقُوْا مِمَّا رَزَقَكُمُ
اللّٰهُ قَالَ الَّذِيْنَ كَفَرُوْا لِلَّذِيْنَ
اٰمَنُوْٓا اَنُطْعِمُ مَنْ لَّوْ يَشَآءُ اللّٰهُ اَطْعَمَهٗٓ
اِنْ اَنْتُمْ اِلَّا فِيْ ضَلٰلٍ مُّبِيْنٍ ﴿٤٧﴾
وَيَقُوْلُوْنَ مَتٰى هٰذَا الْوَعْدُ اِنْ كُنْتُمْ
صٰدِقِيْنَ ﴿٤٨﴾
مَا يَنْظُرُوْنَ اِلَّا صَيْحَةً وَّاحِدَةً تَاْخُذُهُمْ
وَهُمْ يَخِصِّمُوْنَ ﴿٤٩﴾
فَلَا يَسْتَطِيْعُوْنَ تَوْصِيَةً وَّلَآ اِلٰٓى اَهْلِهِمْ
يَرْجِعُوْنَ ﴿٥٠﴾
وَنُفِخَ فِي الصُّوْرِ فَاِذَا هُمْ مِّنَ الْاَجْدَاثِ
اِلٰى رَبِّهِمْ يَنْسِلُوْنَ ﴿٥١﴾
قَالُوْا يٰوَيْلَنَا مَنْۢ بَعَثَنَا مِنْ مَّرْقَدِنَا
هٰذَا مَا وَعَدَ الرَّحْمٰنُ وَصَدَقَ الْمُرْسَلُوْنَ ﴿٥٢﴾
اِنْ كَانَتْ اِلَّا صَيْحَةً وَّاحِدَةً فَاِذَا هُمْ
جَمِيْعٌ لَّدَيْنَا مُحْضَرُوْنَ ﴿٥٣﴾
فَالْيَوْمَ لَا تُظْلَمُ نَفْسٌ شَيْـًٔا وَّلَا تُجْزَوْنَ
اِلَّا مَا كُنْتُمْ تَعْمَلُوْنَ ﴿٥٤﴾

55. Verily the Companions of the Garden shall that Day have joy in all that they do;

اہلِ جنت اس روز عیش و نشاط کے مشغلے میں ہوں گے ﴿۵۵﴾

إِنَّ أَصْحٰبَ الْجَنَّةِ الْيَوْمَ فِيْ شُغُلٍ فٰكِهُوْنَ ﴿٥٥﴾

56. They and their associates will be in pleasant shade, reclining on raised couches;

وہ بھی اور اُن کی بیویاں بھی سایوں میں تختوں پر تکیے لگائے بیٹھے ہوں گے ﴿۵۶﴾

هُمْ وَأَزْوَاجُهُمْ فِيْ ظِلٰلٍ عَلَى الْأَرَآئِكِ مُتَّكِئُوْنَ ﴿٥٦﴾

57. (Every) fruit will be there for them; they shall have whatever they call for;

58. "Peace!—a Word (of salutation) from a Lord Most Merciful!

59. "And O ye in sin! Get ye apart this Day!

60. "Did I not enjoin on you, O ye children of Adam, that ye should not worship Satan; for that he was to you an enemy avowed?—.

وہاں اُن کیلئے میوے اور جو چاہیں گے (موجود ہوگا) ﴿۵۷﴾

پروردگار مہربان کی طرف سے سلام (کہا جائے گا) ﴿۵۸﴾

اور گنہگارو تم آج الگ ہو جاؤ ﴿۵۹﴾

اے آدم کی اولاد ہم نے تم سے کہہ نہیں دیا تھا کہ شیطان کو نہ پُوجنا وہ تمہارا کھلا دشمن ہے ﴿۶۰﴾

لَهُمْ فِيْهَا فَاكِهَةٌ وَّلَهُمْ مَّا يَدَّعُوْنَ ﴿٥٧﴾

سَلٰمٌ قَوْلًا مِّنْ رَّبٍّ رَّحِيْمٍ ﴿٥٨﴾

وَامْتَازُوا الْيَوْمَ أَيُّهَا الْمُجْرِمُوْنَ ﴿٥٩﴾

أَلَمْ أَعْهَدْ إِلَيْكُمْ يٰبَنِيْٓ اٰدَمَ أَنْ لَّا تَعْبُدُوا الشَّيْطٰنَ إِنَّهٗ لَكُمْ عَدُوٌّ مُّبِيْنٌ ﴿٦٠﴾

61. "And that ye should worship Me, (for that) this was the Straight Way?

62. "But he did lead astray a great multitude of you. Did ye not, then, understand?

اور یہ کہ میری ہی عبادت کرنا یہی سیدھا رستہ ہے ﴿۶۱﴾

اور اُس نے تم میں سے بہت سی خلقت کو گمراہ کر دیا تھا تو کیا تم سمجھتے نہیں تھے؟ ﴿۶۲﴾

وَّأَنِ اعْبُدُوْنِيْ هٰذَا صِرَاطٌ مُّسْتَقِيْمٌ ﴿٦١﴾ وقف غفران

وَلَقَدْ أَضَلَّ مِنْكُمْ جِبِلًّا كَثِيْرًا أَفَلَمْ تَكُوْنُوْا تَعْقِلُوْنَ ﴿٦٢﴾

63. "This is the Hell of which ye were promised

64. "Embrace ye the (Fire) this Day, for that ye (persistently) rejected (Truth)."

65. That Day shall We set a seal on their mouths. But their hands will speak to Us, and their feet bear witness, to all that they did.

66. If it had been Our Will, We could surely have blotted out their eyes; then they should have raced to the Path, but how could they have seen?

67. And if it had been Our Will, We could have transformed them in their places; then should they have been unable to move about, nor could they have returned (after error).

68. If We grant long life to any, We cause him to be reversed in nature: will they not then understand?

یہی وہ جہنم ہے جس کی تمہیں خبر دی جاتی تھی ﴿۶۳﴾

(سو) جو تم کفر کرتے رہے ہو اُسکے بدلے آج اس میں داخل ہو جاؤ ﴿۶۴﴾

آج ہم اُنکے مونہوں پر مہر لگا دینگے اور جو کچھ یہ کرتے رہے تھے اُنکے ہاتھ ہم سے بیان کر دینگے اور اُنکے پاؤں (اُسکی) گواہی دینگے ﴿۶۵﴾

اور اگر ہم چاہیں تو اُن کی آنکھوں کو مٹا کر (اندھا کر) دیں پھر یہ رستے کو دوڑیں تو کہاں دیکھ سکیں گے ﴿۶۶﴾

اور اگر ہم چاہیں تو اُن کی جگہ پر اُنکی صورتیں بدل دیں پھر وہاں سے نہ آگے جا سکیں اور نہ (پیچھے) لَوٹ سکیں ﴿۶۷﴾

اور جس کو ہم بڑی عمر دیتے ہیں تو اُسے خلقت میں اوندھا کر دیتے ہیں تو کیا یہ سمجھتے نہیں؟ ﴿۶۸﴾

هٰذِهٖ جَهَنَّمُ الَّتِيْ كُنْتُمْ تُوْعَدُوْنَ ﴿٦٣﴾

اِصْلَوْهَا الْيَوْمَ بِمَا كُنْتُمْ تَكْفُرُوْنَ ﴿٦٤﴾

اَلْيَوْمَ نَخْتِمُ عَلٰٓى أَفْوَاهِهِمْ وَتُكَلِّمُنَآ أَيْدِيْهِمْ وَتَشْهَدُ أَرْجُلُهُمْ بِمَا كَانُوْا يَكْسِبُوْنَ ﴿٦٥﴾

وَلَوْ نَشَآءُ لَطَمَسْنَا عَلٰٓى أَعْيُنِهِمْ فَاسْتَبَقُوا الصِّرَاطَ فَأَنّٰى يُبْصِرُوْنَ ﴿٦٦﴾

وَلَوْ نَشَآءُ لَمَسَخْنٰهُمْ عَلٰى مَكَانَتِهِمْ فَمَا اسْتَطَاعُوْا مُضِيًّا وَّلَا يَرْجِعُوْنَ ﴿٦٧﴾

وَمَنْ نُّعَمِّرْهُ نُنَكِّسْهُ فِي الْخَلْقِ أَفَلَا يَعْقِلُوْنَ ﴿٦٨﴾

69. We have not instructed the (Prophet) in Poetry, nor is it meet for him: this is no less than a Message and a Qur'an making things clear:

70. That it may give admonition to any (who are) alive, and that the word may be proved true against those who reject (Truth).

اور ہم نے اُن (پیغمبر) کو شعر گوئی نہیں سکھائی اور نہ وہ اُنکو شایاں ہے یہ تو محض نصیحت اور صاف صاف قرآن (پُر از حکمت) ہے ﴿۶۹﴾

تاکہ اُس شخص کو جو زندہ ہو ہدایت کا رستہ دکھائے اور کافروں پر بات پوری ہو جائے ﴿۷۰﴾

وَمَا عَلَّمْنٰهُ الشِّعْرَ وَمَا يَنْۢبَغِيْ لَهٗ إِنْ هُوَ إِلَّا ذِكْرٌ وَّقُرْاٰنٌ مُّبِيْنٌ ﴿٦٩﴾

لِّيُنْذِرَ مَنْ كَانَ حَيًّا وَّيَحِقَّ الْقَوْلُ عَلَى الْكٰفِرِيْنَ ﴿٧٠﴾

71. See they not that it is We Who have created for them—among the things which our hands have fashioned— cattle, which are under their dominion?—
72. And that We have subjected them to their (use)? Of them some do carry them and some they eat:
73. And they have (other) profits from them (besides), and they get (milk) to drink. Will they not then be grateful?
74. Yet they take (for worship) Gods other than Allah, (hoping) that they might be helped!
75. They have not the power to help them: and they are a host brought up before them.

76. Let not their speech, then, grieve thee. Verily We know what they hide as well as what they disclose.
77. Doth not man see that it is We Who created him from sperm? Yet behold! he (stands forth) as an open adversary!
78. And he makes comparisons for Us, and forgets his own (origin and) Creation: He says, "Who can give life to (dry) bones and decomposed ones (at that)?"
79. Say, "He will give them life Who created them for the first time! For He fully knows all creation.

80. "The same Who produces for you fire out of the green tree, when behold! Ye kindle therewith (your own fires)!
81. "Is not He Who created the heavens and the earth able to create the like thereof?"— Yea, indeed! For He is the Creator Supreme, of skill and knowledge (infinite)!
82. Verily, when He intends a thing, His Command is, "Be", and it is!

83. So glory to Him in Whose Hands is the dominion of all things: and to Him will ye be all brought back.

کیا انہوں نے نہیں دیکھا کہ جو چیزیں ہم نے اپنے ہاتھوں سے بنائیں انہیں سے
ہم نے اُن کیلئے چارپائے پیدا کر دیئے اور یہ اُن کے مالک ہیں ﴿٧١﴾
اور اُن کو اُن کے قابو میں کر دیا تو کوئی تو اُن میں سے اُن
کی سواری ہے اور کسی کو یہ کھاتے ہیں ﴿٧٢﴾
اور انہیں اُن سے (اور) فائدے اور پینے کی چیزیں ہیں تو کیا یہ شکر نہیں کرتے؟ ﴿٧٣﴾
اور انہوں نے خدا کے سوا اور معبود بنا لئے ہیں کہ شاید
(اُن سے) ان کو مدد پہنچے ﴿٧٤﴾
(مگر) وہ ان کی مدد کی (ہرگز) طاقت نہیں رکھتے۔ اور
وہ ان کی فوج ہو کر حاضر کئے جائیں گے ﴿٧٥﴾
تو اُن کی باتیں تمہیں غمناک نہ کر دیں۔ یہ جو کچھ چھپاتے
اور جو کچھ ظاہر کرتے ہیں ہمیں (سب) معلوم ہیں ﴿٧٦﴾
کیا انسان نے نہیں دیکھا کہ ہم نے اُس کو نطفے سے
پیدا کیا۔ پھر وہ تڑاق پڑاق جھگڑنے لگا ﴿٧٧﴾
اور ہمارے بارے میں مثالیں بیان کرنے لگا اور اپنی پیدائش کو بھول گیا
کہنے لگا کہ (جب) ہڈیاں بوسیدہ ہو جائیں گی تو اُن کو کون زندہ کرے گا؟ ﴿٧٨﴾
کہہ دو کہ اُن کو وہ زندہ کرے گا جس نے اُن کو پہلی بار پیدا
کیا تھا۔ اور وہ سب قسم کا پیدا کرنا جانتا ہے ﴿٧٩﴾
(وہی) جس نے تمہارے لئے سبز درخت سے آگ پیدا کی
پھر تم اس (کی ٹہنیوں کو رگڑ کر اُن) سے آگ نکالتے ہو ﴿٨٠﴾
بھلا جس نے آسمانوں اور زمین کو پیدا کیا کیا وہ اس
بات پر قادر نہیں کہ (اُن کو پھر) ویسے ہی پیدا کر دے۔
کیوں نہیں۔ اور وہ تو بڑا پیدا کرنے والا اور علم والا ہے ﴿٨١﴾
اس کی شان یہ ہے کہ جب وہ کسی چیز کا ارادہ کرتا ہے تو
اس سے فرما دیتا ہے کہ ہو جا تو وہ ہو جاتی ہے ﴿٨٢﴾
وہ (ذات) پاک ہے جس کے ہاتھ میں ہر چیز کی
بادشاہت ہے اور اُسی کی طرف تم کو لوٹ کر جانا ہے ﴿٨٣﴾

أَوَلَمْ يَرَوْا أَنَّا خَلَقْنَا لَهُمْ مِمَّا عَمِلَتْ
أَيْدِينَا أَنْعَامًا فَهُمْ لَهَا مَالِكُونَ ﴿٧١﴾
وَذَلَّلْنَاهَا لَهُمْ فَمِنْهَا رَكُوبُهُمْ وَمِنْهَا
يَأْكُلُونَ ﴿٧٢﴾
وَلَهُمْ فِيهَا مَنَافِعُ وَمَشَارِبُ أَفَلَا يَشْكُرُونَ ﴿٧٣﴾
وَاتَّخَذُوا مِنْ دُونِ اللَّهِ آلِهَةً لَعَلَّهُمْ
يُنْصَرُونَ ﴿٧٤﴾
لَا يَسْتَطِيعُونَ نَصْرَهُمْ وَهُمْ لَهُمْ
جُنْدٌ مُحْضَرُونَ ﴿٧٥﴾
فَلَا يَحْزُنْكَ قَوْلُهُمْ إِنَّا نَعْلَمُ مَا يُسِرُّونَ (وقف لازم)
وَمَا يُعْلِنُونَ ﴿٧٦﴾
أَوَلَمْ يَرَ الْإِنْسَانُ أَنَّا خَلَقْنَاهُ مِنْ نُطْفَةٍ
فَإِذَا هُوَ خَصِيمٌ مُبِينٌ ﴿٧٧﴾
وَضَرَبَ لَنَا مَثَلًا وَنَسِيَ خَلْقَهُ قَالَ
مَنْ يُحْيِي الْعِظَامَ وَهِيَ رَمِيمٌ ﴿٧٨﴾
قُلْ يُحْيِيهَا الَّذِي أَنْشَأَهَا أَوَّلَ مَرَّةٍ
وَهُوَ بِكُلِّ خَلْقٍ عَلِيمٌ ﴿٧٩﴾
الَّذِي جَعَلَ لَكُمْ مِنَ الشَّجَرِ الْأَخْضَرِ
نَارًا فَإِذَا أَنْتُمْ مِنْهُ تُوقِدُونَ ﴿٨٠﴾
أَوَلَيْسَ الَّذِي خَلَقَ السَّمَاوَاتِ وَالْأَرْضَ
بِقَادِرٍ عَلَىٰ أَنْ يَخْلُقَ مِثْلَهُمْ بَلَىٰ (وقف غفران)
وَهُوَ الْخَلَّاقُ الْعَلِيمُ ﴿٨١﴾
إِنَّمَا أَمْرُهُ إِذَا أَرَادَ شَيْئًا أَنْ يَقُولَ لَهُ
كُنْ فَيَكُونُ ﴿٨٢﴾
فَسُبْحَانَ الَّذِي بِيَدِهِ مَلَكُوتُ كُلِّ
شَيْءٍ وَإِلَيْهِ تُرْجَعُونَ ﴿٨٣﴾

SÛRA–37

AṢ-ṢÃFFÃT

(INTRODUCTION)

As explained in the Introduction to S. 34. this is the fourth of a series of Sûras in which the mysteries of the spiritual world are manifested in different ways, tending to the defeat and final extirpation of Evil. The defeat of Evil is throughout connected with Revelation, and here the ranged fight is illustrated by a reference to the angels in heaven and to the earlier Prophets in our earthly history, from Noah to Jonah. In chronology this Sûra belongs to the early middle Makkan period.

Aṣ-Ṣãffãt, or Those Ranged in Ranks

In the name of Allah, Most Gracious, Most Merciful.

1. By those who range themselves in ranks,

2. Those who so are strong in repelling (evil),

3. Those who thus proclaim the Message (of Allah)!

4. Verily, verily, your God is One!—

5. Lord of the heavens and of the earth, and all between them, and Lord of every point at the rising of the sun!

6. We have indeed decked the lower heaven with beauty (in) the stars,—

7. (For beauty) and for guardagainst all obstinate rebellious Satans.

8. (So) they should not listen their ears in the direction of the Exalted Assembly and they are cast away from every side,

9. Repulsed. And for them is a perpetual chastisement,

10. Except such as snatch away something by stealth, and they are pursued by a flaming Fire, of piercing brightness.

11. Just ask their opinion: are they the more difficult to create, or the (other) beings We have created? Them have We created out of a sticky clay!

12. Truly dost thou marvel, while they ridicule,

13. And, when they are admonished, pay no heed,—

14. And, when they see a Sign, turn it to mockery,

15. And say, "This is nothing but evident sorcery!

16. "What! when we die, and become dust and bones, shall we (then) be raised up (again)?

17. "And also our fathers of old?"

18. Say thou: "Yea, and ye shall then be humiliated (on account of your evil)."

19. Then it will be a single (compelling) cry; and behold, they will begin to see!

20. They will say, "Ah! woe to us! this is the Day of Judgment!"

سُورہ صافات مکّی ہے اس میں ایک سو بیاسی آیتیں اور پانچ رکوع ہیں

شروع خدا کا نام لے کر جو بڑا مہربان نہایت رحم والا ہے

قسم ہے صف باندھنے والوں کی پرا جما کر ﴿١﴾

پھر ڈانٹنے والوں کی جھڑک کر ﴿٢﴾

پھر ذکر (یعنی قرآن) پڑھنے والوں کی (غور کر کر) ﴿٣﴾

کہ تمہارا معبود ایک ہی ہے ﴿٤﴾

جو آسمانوں اور زمین اور جو چیزیں ان میں ہیں سب کا

مالک ہے اور سُورج کے طلوع ہونیکے مقامات کا بھی مالک ہے ﴿٥﴾

بے شک ہم ہی نے آسمانِ دُنیا کو ستاروں کی زینت سے مزین کیا ﴿٦﴾

اور ہر شیطان سرکش سے اس کی حفاظت کی ﴿٧﴾

کہ اُوپر کی مجلس کی طرف کان نہ لگا سکیں اور ہر طرف سے

(اُن پر انگارے) پھینکے جاتے ہیں ﴿٨﴾

(یعنی وہاں سے) نکال دینے کو اور اُن کیلئے عذاب دائمی ہے ﴿٩﴾

ہاں جو کوئی (فرشتوں کی کسی بات کو) چوری سے جھپٹ

لینا چاہتا ہے تو جلتا ہُوا انگارا اُسکے پیچھے لگتا ہے ﴿١٠﴾

تو اُن سے پوچھو کہ انکا بنانا مشکل ہے یا جتنی خلقت ہم نے

بنائی ہے اُن کا؟ انہیں ہم نے چپکتے گارے سے بنایا ہے ﴿١١﴾

ہاں تم تو تعجب کرتے ہو اور یہ تمسخر کرتے ہیں ﴿١٢﴾

اور جب اُنکو نصیحت دی جاتی ہے تو نصیحت قبول نہیں کرتے ﴿١٣﴾

اور جب کوئی نشانی دیکھتے ہیں تو ٹھٹھے کرتے ہیں ﴿١٤﴾

اور کہتے ہیں کہ یہ تو صریح جادُو ہے ﴿١٥﴾

بھلا جب ہم مر گئے اور مٹی اور ہڈیاں ہو گئے تو کیا پھر

اُٹھائے جائیں گے؟ ﴿١٦﴾

اور کیا ہمارے باپ دادا بھی (جو) پہلے (ہو گزرے ہیں)؟ ﴿١٧﴾

کہہ دو کہ ہاں۔ اور تم ذلیل ہو گے ﴿١٨﴾

وہ تو ایک زور کی آواز ہو گی اور یہ اس وقت دیکھنے لگیں گے ﴿١٩﴾

اور کہیں گے۔ ہائے شامت یہی جزا کا دن ہے ﴿٢٠﴾

سُوْرَةُ الصّٰفّٰتِ مَكِّيَّةٌ وَّهِيَ مِائَةٌ وَّاثْنَتَانِ وَّثَمَانُوْنَ اٰيَةً وَّخَمْسُ رُكُوْعَاتٍ

بِسْمِ اللّٰهِ الرَّحْمٰنِ الرَّحِيْمِ

وَالصّٰٓفّٰتِ صَفًّا ﴿١﴾

فَالزّٰجِرٰتِ زَجْرًا ﴿٢﴾

فَالتّٰلِيٰتِ ذِكْرًا ﴿٣﴾

اِنَّ اِلٰهَكُمْ لَوَاحِدٌ ﴿٤﴾

رَبُّ السَّمٰوٰتِ وَالْاَرْضِ وَمَا بَيْنَهُمَا وَ

رَبُّ الْمَشَارِقِ ﴿٥﴾

اِنَّا زَيَّنَّا السَّمَآءَ الدُّنْيَا بِزِيْنَةِ ٣الْكَوَاكِبِ ﴿٦﴾

وَحِفْظًا مِّنْ كُلِّ شَيْطٰنٍ مَّارِدٍ ﴿٧﴾

لَا يَسَّمَّعُوْنَ اِلَى الْمَلَاِ الْاَعْلٰى وَيُقْذَفُوْنَ

مِنْ كُلِّ جَانِبٍ ﴿٨﴾

دُحُوْرًا وَّلَهُمْ عَذَابٌ وَّاصِبٌ ﴿٩﴾

اِلَّا مَنْ خَطِفَ الْخَطْفَةَ فَاَتْبَعَهٗ

شِهَابٌ ثَاقِبٌ ﴿١٠﴾

فَاسْتَفْتِهِمْ اَهُمْ اَشَدُّ خَلْقًا اَمْ مَّنْ

خَلَقْنَا ؕ اِنَّا خَلَقْنٰهُمْ مِّنْ طِيْنٍ لَّازِبٍ ﴿١١﴾

بَلْ عَجِبْتَ وَيَسْخَرُوْنَ ﴿١٢﴾

وَاِذَا ذُكِّرُوْا لَا يَذْكُرُوْنَ ﴿١٣﴾

وَاِذَا رَاَوْا اٰيَةً يَّسْتَسْخِرُوْنَ ﴿١٤﴾

وَقَالُوْٓا اِنْ هٰذَآ اِلَّا سِحْرٌ مُّبِيْنٌ ﴿١٥﴾

ءَاِذَا مِتْنَا وَكُنَّا تُرَابًا وَّعِظَامًا ءَاِنَّا

لَمَبْعُوْثُوْنَ ﴿١٦﴾

اَوَاٰبَآؤُنَا الْاَوَّلُوْنَ ﴿١٧﴾

قُلْ نَعَمْ وَاَنْتُمْ دَاخِرُوْنَ ﴿١٨﴾

فَاِنَّمَا هِيَ زَجْرَةٌ وَّاحِدَةٌ فَاِذَا هُمْ يَنْظُرُوْنَ ﴿١٩﴾

وَقَالُوْا يٰوَيْلَنَا هٰذَا يَوْمُ الدِّيْنِ ﴿٢٠﴾

21. (A voice will say,) "This is the Day of Sorting Out, whose truth ye (once) denied!"

22. "Bring ye up", it shall be said, "The wrong-doers and their wives, and the things they worshipped—

23. "Besides Allah, and lead them to the Way to the (Fierce) Fire!

24 "But stop them, for they must be asked:

25. " 'What is the matter with you that ye help not each other?" '

26. Nay, but that day they shall submit (to Judgment);

27. And they will turn to one another, and question one another.

28. They will say: "It was ye who used to come to us from the right hand."

29. They will reply: "Nay, ye yourselves had no Faith!

30. "Nor had we any authority over you. Nay, it was ye who were a people in obstinate rebellion!

31. "So now has been proved true, against us, the Word of our Lord that we shall indeed (have to) taste (the punishment of our sins):

32. "We led you astray: for truly we were ourselves astray."

33. Truly, that Day, they will (all) share in the Chastisement.

34. Verily that is how We shall deal with Sinners.

35. For they, when they were told that there is no god except Allah, would puff themselves up with Pride,

36. And say: "What! Shall we give up our gods for the sake of a Poet possessed?"

37. Nay! he has come with the (very) Truth and he confirms (the Message of) the messengers (before him).

38. Ye shall indeed taste of the Grievous Chastisement;—

39. And you are requited naught save what ye did.

40. But the chosen servants of Allah,—

41. For them is a Sustenance determined,

42. Fruits; and they (shall enjoy) honour and dignity,

(کہا جائے گا کہ ہاں) فیصلے کا دن جس کو تم جھوٹ سمجھتے
تھے یہی ہے (۲۱)
جو لوگ ظلم کرتے تھے اُن کو اور اُن کے ہمجنسوں کو اور
جن کو وہ پوجا کرتے تھے (سب کو) جمع کرلو (۲۲)
(یعنی جن کو) خدا کے سوا (پوجا کرتے تھے) پھر اُنکو جہنم کے رستے پر چلا دو (۲۳)
اور اُن کو ٹھیرائے رکھو کہ اُن سے (کچھ) پُوچھنا ہے (۲۴)
تم کو کیا ہوا کہ ایک دوسرے کی مدد نہیں کرتے (۲۵)
بلکہ آج تو وہ فرمانبردار ہیں (۲۶)
اور ایک دوسرے کی طرف رُخ کرکے سوال (وجواب) کرینگے (۲۷)
کہیں گے کیا تم ہی ہمارے پاس دائیں (اور بائیں) سے آتے تھے (۲۸)
وہ کہیں گے بلکہ تم ہی ایمان لانے والے نہ تھے (۲۹)
اور ہمارا تم پر کچھ زور نہ تھا۔ بلکہ تم سرکش
لوگ تھے (۳۰)
سو ہمارے بارے میں ہمارے پروردگار کی بات پوری ہو گئی اب ہم مزے چکھیں گے (۳۱)
ہم نے تم کو بھی گمراہ کیا (اور) ہم خود بھی گمراہ تھے (۳۲)
پس وہ اُس روز عذاب میں ایک دوسرے کے شریک ہونگے (۳۳)
ہم گنہگاروں کے ساتھ ایسا ہی کیا کرتے ہیں (۳۴)
اُن کا یہ حال تھا کہ جب اُن سے کہا جاتا تھا کہ خدا کے
سوا کوئی معبود نہیں تو غرور کرتے تھے (۳۵)
اور کہتے تھے کہ بھلا ہم ایک دیوانے شاعر کے کہنے سے
کہیں اپنے معبودوں کو چھوڑ دینے والے ہیں (۳۶)
(نہیں) بلکہ وہ حق لیکر آئے ہیں اور (پہلے) پیغمبروں کو سچا کہتے ہیں (۳۷)
بیشک تم تکلیف دینے والے عذاب کا مزہ چکھنے والے ہو (۳۸)
اور تم کو بدلہ ویسا ہی ملے گا جیسے تم کام کرتے تھے (۳۹)
مگر جو خدا کے بندگان خاص ہیں (۴۰)
یہی لوگ ہیں جن کے لئے روزی مقرر ہے (۴۱)
(یعنی) میوے اور اُن کا اعزاز کیا جائے گا (۴۲)

هٰذَا يَوْمُ الْفَصْلِ الَّذِي كُنْتُمْ بِهٖ
تُكَذِّبُوْنَ ﴿۲۱﴾
اُحْشُرُوا الَّذِيْنَ ظَلَمُوْا وَاَزْوَاجَهُمْ وَمَا
كَانُوْا يَعْبُدُوْنَ ﴿۲۲﴾
مِنْ دُوْنِ اللّٰهِ فَاهْدُوْهُمْ اِلٰى صِرَاطِ الْجَحِيْمِ ﴿۲۳﴾
وَقِفُوْهُمْ اِنَّهُمْ مَّسْئُوْلُوْنَ ﴿۲۴﴾
مَا لَكُمْ لَا تَنَاصَرُوْنَ ﴿۲۵﴾
بَلْ هُمُ الْيَوْمَ مُسْتَسْلِمُوْنَ ﴿۲۶﴾
وَاَقْبَلَ بَعْضُهُمْ عَلٰى بَعْضٍ يَّتَسَآءَلُوْنَ ﴿۲۷﴾
قَالُوْٓا اِنَّكُمْ كُنْتُمْ تَاْتُوْنَنَا عَنِ الْيَمِيْنِ ﴿۲۸﴾
قَالُوْا بَلْ لَّمْ تَكُوْنُوْا مُؤْمِنِيْنَ ﴿۲۹﴾
وَمَا كَانَ لَنَا عَلَيْكُمْ مِّنْ سُلْطٰنٍ بَلْ
كُنْتُمْ قَوْمًا طٰغِيْنَ ﴿۳۰﴾
فَحَقَّ عَلَيْنَا قَوْلُ رَبِّنَآ اِنَّا لَذَآئِقُوْنَ ﴿۳۱﴾
فَاَغْوَيْنٰكُمْ اِنَّا كُنَّا غٰوِيْنَ ﴿۳۲﴾
فَاِنَّهُمْ يَوْمَئِذٍ فِي الْعَذَابِ مُشْتَرِكُوْنَ ﴿۳۳﴾
اِنَّا كَذٰلِكَ نَفْعَلُ بِالْمُجْرِمِيْنَ ﴿۳۴﴾
اِنَّهُمْ كَانُوْٓا اِذَا قِيْلَ لَهُمْ لَآ اِلٰهَ اِلَّا
اللّٰهُ يَسْتَكْبِرُوْنَ ﴿۳۵﴾
وَيَقُوْلُوْنَ اَئِنَّا لَتَارِكُوْٓا اٰلِهَتِنَا لِشَاعِرٍ
مَّجْنُوْنٍ ﴿۳۶﴾
بَلْ جَآءَ بِالْحَقِّ وَصَدَّقَ الْمُرْسَلِيْنَ ﴿۳۷﴾
اِنَّكُمْ لَذَآئِقُوا الْعَذَابِ الْاَلِيْمِ ﴿۳۸﴾
وَمَا تُجْزَوْنَ اِلَّا مَا كُنْتُمْ تَعْمَلُوْنَ ﴿۳۹﴾
اِلَّا عِبَادَ اللّٰهِ الْمُخْلَصِيْنَ ﴿۴۰﴾
اُولٰٓئِكَ لَهُمْ رِزْقٌ مَّعْلُوْمٌ ﴿۴۱﴾
فَوَاكِهُ وَهُمْ مُّكْرَمُوْنَ ﴿۴۲﴾

43. In Gardens of delight.

44. Facing each other on raised couches.

45. Round will be passed to them a Cup from a clear-flowing fountain,

46. Crystal-white, of a taste delicious to those who drink (thereof),

47. Free from headiness; nor will they suffer intoxication therefrom.

48. And besides them will be chaste women; restraining their glances, with big eyes (of wonder and beauty).

49. As if they were (delicate) eggs closely guarded.

50. Then they will turn to one another and question one another.

51. One of them will say: "I had an intimate companion (on the earth),

52. "Who used to say, do you really believe?

53. " 'When we die and become dust and bones, shall we indeed receive rewards and punishments?'"

54. He said: "Would ye like to look down?"

55. He looked down and saw him in the midst of the Fire.

56. He said: "By Allah! thou wast little short of bringing me to perdition!

57. "Had it not been for the Grace of my Lord, I should certainly have been among those brought (there)!

58. "Is it (the case) that we shall not die,

59. "Except our first death, and that we Shall not be punished?"

60. Verily this is the supreme triumph.

61. For the like of this let all strive, who wish to strive.

62. Is that the better entertainment or the Tree of Zaqqum?

63. For We have truly made it (as) a trial for the wrong-doers.

64. For it is a tree that springs out of the bottom of Hell-fire:

65. The shoots of its fruit-stalks are like the heads of devils:

66. Truly they will eat thereof and fill their bellies therewith.

نعمت کے باغوں میں (۴۳)
ایک دوسرے کے سامنے تختوں پر (بیٹھے ہونگے) (۴۴)
شراب لطیف کے جام کا اُن میں دور چل رہا ہوگا (۴۵)
جو رنگ کی سفید اور پینے والوں کیلئے (سراسر) لذت ہوگی (۴۶)
نہ اس سے درد سر ہو اور نہ وہ اُس سے متوالے ہوں (۴۷)
اور اُنکے پاس عورتیں ہونگی جو نگاہیں نیچی رکھتی ہونگی اور آنکھیں بڑی بڑی (۴۸)
گویا وہ محفوظ انڈے ہیں (۴۹)
پھر وہ ایک دوسرے کی طرف رُخ کر کے سوال (وجواب) کرینگے (۵۰)
ایک کہنے والا اُن میں سے کہے گا کہ میرا ایک ہمنشین تھا (۵۱)
(جو) کہتا تھا کہ بھلا تم بھی (ایسی باتوں کے) باور کرنیوالوں میں ہو (۵۲)
بھلا جب ہم مرگئے اور مٹی اور ہڈیاں ہوگئے تو کیا ہم کو
بدلہ ملے گا؟ (۵۳)
(پھر) کہے گا کہ بھلا تم (اُسے) جھانک کر دیکھنا چاہتے ہو (۵۴)
(اتنے میں) وہ (خود) جھانکے گا تو اُسکو وسط دوزخ میں دیکھے گا (۵۵)
کہے گا کہ خدا کی قسم تُو تو مجھے ہلاک ہی کرچکا تھا (۵۶)
اور اگر میرے پروردگار کی مہربانی نہ ہوتی تو میں بھی اُن
میں ہوتا جو (عذاب میں) حاضر کئے گئے ہیں (۵۷)
کیا یہ نہیں کہ ہم (آئندہ کبھی) مرنے کے نہیں (۵۸)
ہاں (جو) پہلی بار مرنا تھا (سو مرچکے) اور ہمیں عذاب بھی نہیں ہونے کا (۵۹)
بیشک یہ بڑی کامیابی ہے (۶۰)
ایسی ہی (نعمتوں) کیلئے عمل کرنیوالوں کو عمل کرنے چاہئیں (۶۱)
بھلا یہ مہمانی اچھی ہے یا تھوہر کا درخت (۶۲)
ہم نے اس کو ظالموں کیلئے عذاب بنا رکھا ہے (۶۳)
وہ ایک درخت ہے کہ جہنم کے اسفل میں اُگے گا (۶۴)
اُس کے خوشے ایسے ہونگے جیسے شیطانوں کے سر (۶۵)
سو وہ اُسی میں سے کھائیں گے اور اُسی سے پیٹ
بھریں گے (۶۶)

فِي جَنّٰتِ النَّعِيمِ (۴۳)
عَلٰى سُرُرٍ مُّتَقٰبِلِينَ (۴۴)
يُطَافُ عَلَيْهِمْ بِكَأْسٍ مِّنْ مَّعِينٍ (۴۵)
بَيْضَاءَ لَذَّةٍ لِّلشّٰرِبِينَ (۴۶)
لَا فِيهَا غَوْلٌ وَّلَا هُمْ عَنْهَا يُنْزَفُونَ (۴۷)
وَعِنْدَهُمْ قٰصِرٰتُ الطَّرْفِ عِينٌ (۴۸)
كَأَنَّهُنَّ بَيْضٌ مَّكْنُونٌ (۴۹)
فَأَقْبَلَ بَعْضُهُمْ عَلٰى بَعْضٍ يَّتَسَاءَلُونَ (۵۰)
قَالَ قَائِلٌ مِّنْهُمْ إِنِّي كَانَ لِي قَرِينٌ (۵۱)
يَقُولُ أَئِنَّكَ لَمِنَ الْمُصَدِّقِينَ (۵۲)
ءَإِذَا مِتْنَا وَكُنَّا تُرَابًا وَّعِظَامًا ءَإِنَّا
لَمَدِينُونَ (۵۳)
قَالَ هَلْ أَنْتُمْ مُّطَّلِعُونَ (۵۴)
فَاطَّلَعَ فَرَاٰهُ فِي سَوَاءِ الْجَحِيمِ (۵۵)
قَالَ تَاللّٰهِ إِنْ كِدْتَّ لَتُرْدِينِ (۵۶)
وَلَوْلَا نِعْمَةُ رَبِّي لَكُنْتُ مِنَ
الْمُحْضَرِينَ (۵۷)
أَفَمَا نَحْنُ بِمَيِّتِينَ (۵۸)
إِلَّا مَوْتَتَنَا الْأُولٰى وَمَا نَحْنُ بِمُعَذَّبِينَ (۵۹)
إِنَّ هٰذَا لَهُوَ الْفَوْزُ الْعَظِيمُ (۶۰)
لِمِثْلِ هٰذَا فَلْيَعْمَلِ الْعٰمِلُونَ (۶۱)
أَذٰلِكَ خَيْرٌ نُّزُلًا أَمْ شَجَرَةُ الزَّقُّومِ (۶۲)
إِنَّا جَعَلْنٰهَا فِتْنَةً لِّلظّٰلِمِينَ (۶۳)
إِنَّهَا شَجَرَةٌ تَخْرُجُ فِي أَصْلِ الْجَحِيمِ (۶۴)
طَلْعُهَا كَأَنَّهُ رُءُوسُ الشَّيٰطِينِ (۶۵)
فَإِنَّهُمْ لَاٰكِلُونَ مِنْهَا فَمَالِئُونَ مِنْهَا
الْبُطُونَ (۶۶)

67. Then on top of that they will be given a mixture made of boiling water.	پھر اس (کھانے) کے ساتھ اُن کو گرم پانی ملا کر دیا جائیگا (٦٧)	ثم ان لهم عليها لشوبا من حميم (٦٧)
68. Then shall their return be to the (Blazing) Fire.	پھر اُن کو دوزخ کی طرف لوٹایا جائے گا (٦٨)	ثم ان مرجعهم لالى الجحيم (٦٨)
69. Truly they found their fathers on the wrong Path;	اُنہوں نے اپنے باپ دادا کو گمراہ ہی پایا (٦٩)	انهم الفوا اباءهم ضالين (٦٩)
70. So they (too) were rushed down on their footsteps!	سو وہ اُنہی کے پیچھے دوڑے چلے جاتے ہیں (٧٠)	فهم على اثرهم يهرعون (٧٠)
71. And truly before them, many of the ancients went astray;—	اور اُن سے پیشتر بہت سے پہلے لوگ بھی گمراہ ہوگئے تھے (٧١)	ولقد ضل قبلهم اكثر الاولين (٧١)
72. But We sent aforetime, among them, warners.	اور ہم نے اُن میں متنبہ کرنے والے بھیجے (٧٢)	ولقد ارسلنا فيهم منذرين (٧٢)
73. Then see what was the End of those who were warned	سو دیکھ لو جن کو متنبہ کیا گیا تھا اُن کا انجام کیسا ہوا (٧٣)	فانظر كيف كان عاقبة المنذرين (٧٣)
74. Except the chosen Servants of Allah.	ہاں خدا کے بندگانِ خاص (کا انجام بہت اچھا ہوا) (٧٤)	الا عباد الله المخلصين (٧٤)
75. (In the days of old), Noah cried to Us, and We are the Best to hear prayer.	اور ہم کو نوح نے پکارا سو (دیکھ لو کہ) ہم (دعا کو کیسے) اچھے قبول کرنے والے ہیں (٧٥)	ولقد نادىنا نوح فلنعم المجيبون (٧٥)
76. And We delivered him and his people from the Great Calamity,	اور ہم نے اُن کو اور اُنکے گھر والوں کو بڑی مصیبت سے نجات دی (٧٦)	ونجينه واهله من الكرب العظيم (٧٦)
77. And made his progeny to endure (on this earth);	اور اُن کی اولاد کو ایسا کیا کہ وہی باقی رہ گئے (٧٧)	وجعلنا ذريته هم البقين (٧٧)
78. And We left (this blessing) for him among generations to come in later times:	اور پیچھے آنے والوں میں اُن کا ذکر (جمیل باقی) چھوڑ دیا (٧٨)	وتركنا عليه في الاخرين (٧٨)
79. "Peace and salutation to Noah among the nations!"	(یعنی) تمام جہان میں (کہ) نوح پر سلام (٧٩)	سلم على نوح في العلمين (٧٩)
80. Thus indeed do We reward those who do right.	نیکوکاروں کو ہم ایسا ہی بدلہ دیا کرتے ہیں (٨٠)	انا كذلك نجزي المحسنين (٨٠)
81. For he was one of Our believing Servants.	بے شک وہ ہمارے مومن بندوں میں سے تھے (٨١)	انه من عبادنا المؤمنين (٨١)
82. Then the rest We overwhelmed in the Flood.	پھر ہم نے دوسروں کو ڈبو دیا (٨٢)	ثم اغرقنا الاخرين (٨٢)
83. Verily from his party was Abraham.	اور اُنہی کے پیرووں میں ابراہیم تھے (٨٣)	وان من شيعته لابرهيم (٨٣)
84. Behold, he approached his Lord with a sound heart.	جب وہ اپنے پروردگار کے پاس (عیب سے) پاک دل لے کر آئے (٨٤)	اذ جاء ربه بقلب سليم (٨٤)
85. Behold, he said to his father and to his people, "What is that which ye worship?	جب اُنہوں نے اپنے باپ سے اور اپنی قوم سے کہا کہ تم کن چیزوں کو پوجتے ہو؟ (٨٥)	اذ قال لابيه وقومه ماذا تعبدون (٨٥)
86. "Is it a Falsehood— gods other than Allah that ye desire?	کیوں جھوٹ (بنا کر) خدا کے سوا اور معبودوں کے طالب ہو؟ (٨٦)	ائفكا الهة دون الله تريدون (٨٦)
87. "Then what is your idea about the Lord of the Worlds?"	بھلا پروردگارِ عالم کے بارے میں تمہارا کیا خیال ہے؟ (٨٧)	فما ظنكم برب العلمين (٨٧)
88. Then did he cast a glance at the Stars,	تب اُنہوں نے ستاروں کی طرف ایک نظر کی (٨٨)	فنظر نظرة في النجوم (٨٨)
89. And he said, "I am indeed sick (at heart)!"	اور کہا میں تو بیمار ہوں (٨٩)	فقال اني سقيم (٨٩)
90. So they turned away from him, and departed.	تب وہ اُن سے پیٹھ پھیر کر لوٹ گئے (٩٠)	فتولوا عنه مدبرين (٩٠)
91. Then did he turn to their gods and said, "Will ye not eat (of the offerings before you)?	پھر ابراہیم اُنکے معبودوں کی طرف متوجہ ہوئے اور کہنے لگے کہ تم کھاتے کیوں نہیں؟ (٩١)	فراغ الى الهتهم فقال الا تاكلون (٩١)
92. "What is the matter with you that ye speak not?"	تمہیں کیا ہوا ہے تم بولتے نہیں؟ (٩٢)	ما لكم لا تنطقون (٩٢)
93. Then did he turn upon them, striking (them) with the right hand.	پھر اُن کو داہنے ہاتھ سے مارنا اور توڑنا شروع کیا (٩٣)	فراغ عليهم ضربا باليمين (٩٣)

94. Then came (the worshippers with hurried steps, to him.
95. He said: "Worship ye that which ye have (yourselves) carved?
96. "But Allah has created you and your handiwork!"
97. They said, "Build him a furnace, and throw him into the blazing fire!"
98. (This failing), they then plotted against him, but We made them the ones most humiliated!
99. He said: "I will go to my Lord! He will surely guide me!
100. "O my Lord! grant me a righteous (son)!"
101. So We gave him the good news of a forbearing son.
102. Then, when (the son) reached (the age of) (serious) work with him, he said: "O my son! I have seen in a dream that I offer thee in sacrifice: now see what is thy view!" (The son) said: "O my father! Do as thou art commanded: thou will find me, if Allah so wills one of the steadfast."
103. So when they had both submitted (to Allah), and he had laid him prostrate on his forehead (for sacrifice),
104. We called out to him, "O Abraham!
105. "Thou hast already fulfilled the dream!"—thus indeed do We reward those who do right.
106. For this was a clear trial—
107. And We ransomed him with a momentous sacrifice:
108. And We left for him among generations (to come) in later times:
109. "Peace and salutation to Abraham!"
110. Thus indeed do We reward those who do right
111. For he was one of Our believing Servants.
112. And We gave him the good news of Isaac—a prophet,— one of the Righteous.
113. We blessed him and Isaac: but of their progeny are (some) that do right, and (some) that obviously do wrong, to themselves.
114. Again, (of old.) We bestowed Our favour on Moses and Aaron,
115. And We delivered them and their people from (their) Great distress.

تو وہ لوگ اُن کے پاس دوڑے ہوئے آئے ۹۴
اُنہوں نے کہا کہ تم ایسی چیزوں کو کیوں پوجتے ہو جنکو خود تراشتے ہو ۹۵
حالانکہ تم کو اور جو تم بناتے ہو اُسکو خدا ہی نے پیدا کیا ہے ۹۶
وہ کہنے لگے کہ اسکے لئے ایک عمارت بناؤ پھر اُسکو آگ کے ڈھیر میں ڈالدو ۹۷
غرض اُنہوں نے انکے ساتھ ایک چال چلنی چاہی اور ہم نے انہی کو زیر کر دیا ۹۸
اور ابراہیم بولے کہ میں اپنے پروردگار کی طرف جانیوالا ہوں وہ مجھے رستہ دکھائیگا ۹۹
اے پروردگار مجھے (اولاد) عطا فرما جو سعادتمندوں میں سے ہو ۱۰۰
تو ہم نے ان کو ایک نرم دل لڑکے کی خوشخبری دی ۱۰۱
جب وہ اُن کے ساتھ دوڑنے (کی عمر) کو پہنچا تو ابراہیم نے
کہا کہ بیٹا میں خواب میں دیکھتا ہوں کہ (گویا) تم کو ذبح کر رہا ہوں
تو تم سوچو کہ تمہارا کیا خیال ہے؟ ف۲۴۵ اُنہوں نے کہا کہ ابا جو آپکو
حکم ہوا ہے وہی کیجئے خدا نے چاہا تو آپ مجھے صابروں میں پائیے گا ۱۰۲
جب دونوں نے حکم مان لیا اور باپ نے بیٹے کو ماتھے کے بل لٹا دیا ۱۰۳
تو ہم نے اُن کو پکارا کہ اے ابراہیم ۱۰۴
تم نے خواب کو سچا کر دکھایا ہم نیکوکاروں کو ایسا ہی
بدلہ دیا کرتے ہیں ۱۰۵
بلاشبہ یہ صریح آزمائش تھی ۱۰۶
اور ہم نے ایک بڑی قربانی کو اُن کا فدیہ دیا ف۲۴۶ ۱۰۷
اور پیچھے آنے والوں میں ابراہیم کا ذکر (خیر باقی) چھوڑ دیا ۱۰۸
کہ ابراہیم پر سلام ہو ۱۰۹
نیکوکاروں کو ہم ایسا ہی بدلہ دیا کرتے ہیں ۱۱۰
بے شک وہ ہمارے مومن بندوں میں سے تھے ۱۱۱
اور ہم نے انکو اسحاق کی بشارت بھی دی کہ وہ نبی (اور) نیکوکاروں میں سے ہونگے ۱۱۲
اور ہم نے اُن پر اور اسحاق پر برکتیں نازل کی تھیں۔ اور اُن دونوں کی اولاد
میں سے نیکوکار بھی ہیں اور اپنے آپ پر صریح ظلم کرنیوالے (یعنی گنہگار) بھی ہیں ۱۱۳
اور ہم نے موسیٰ اور ہارون پر بھی احسان کئے ۱۱۴
اور اُن کو اور اُن کی قوم کو مصیبت عظیمہ سے نجات بخشی ۱۱۵

فَأَقْبَلُوٓا إِلَيْهِ يَزِفُّونَ ٩٤
قَالَ أَتَعْبُدُونَ مَا تَنْحِتُونَ ٩٥
وَٱللَّهُ خَلَقَكُمْ وَمَا تَعْمَلُونَ ٩٦
قَالُوا ٱبْنُوا لَهُۥ بُنْيَٰنًا فَأَلْقُوهُ فِى ٱلْجَحِيمِ ٩٧
فَأَرَادُوا بِهِۦ كَيْدًا فَجَعَلْنَٰهُمُ ٱلْأَسْفَلِينَ ٩٨
وَقَالَ إِنِّى ذَاهِبٌ إِلَىٰ رَبِّى سَيَهْدِينِ ٩٩
رَبِّ هَبْ لِى مِنَ ٱلصَّٰلِحِينَ ١٠٠
فَبَشَّرْنَٰهُ بِغُلَٰمٍ حَلِيمٍ ١٠١
فَلَمَّا بَلَغَ مَعَهُ ٱلسَّعْىَ قَالَ يَٰبُنَىَّ إِنِّىٓ
أَرَىٰ فِى ٱلْمَنَامِ أَنِّىٓ أَذْبَحُكَ فَٱنظُرْ
مَاذَا تَرَىٰ ۚ قَالَ يَٰٓأَبَتِ ٱفْعَلْ مَا تُؤْمَرُ ۖ
سَتَجِدُنِىٓ إِن شَآءَ ٱللَّهُ مِنَ ٱلصَّٰبِرِينَ ١٠٢
فَلَمَّآ أَسْلَمَا وَتَلَّهُۥ لِلْجَبِينِ ١٠٣
وَنَٰدَيْنَٰهُ أَن يَٰٓإِبْرَٰهِيمُ ١٠٤
قَدْ صَدَّقْتَ ٱلرُّءْيَآ ۚ إِنَّا كَذَٰلِكَ نَجْزِى
ٱلْمُحْسِنِينَ ١٠٥
إِنَّ هَٰذَا لَهُوَ ٱلْبَلَٰٓؤُا ٱلْمُبِينُ ١٠٦
وَفَدَيْنَٰهُ بِذِبْحٍ عَظِيمٍ ١٠٧
وَتَرَكْنَا عَلَيْهِ فِى ٱلْءَاخِرِينَ ١٠٨
سَلَٰمٌ عَلَىٰٓ إِبْرَٰهِيمَ ١٠٩
كَذَٰلِكَ نَجْزِى ٱلْمُحْسِنِينَ ١١٠
إِنَّهُۥ مِنْ عِبَادِنَا ٱلْمُؤْمِنِينَ ١١١
وَبَشَّرْنَٰهُ بِإِسْحَٰقَ نَبِيًّا مِّنَ ٱلصَّٰلِحِينَ ١١٢
وَبَٰرَكْنَا عَلَيْهِ وَعَلَىٰٓ إِسْحَٰقَ ۚ وَمِن ذُرِّيَّتِهِمَا
مُحْسِنٌ وَظَالِمٌ لِّنَفْسِهِۦ مُبِينٌ ١١٣
وَلَقَدْ مَنَنَّا عَلَىٰ مُوسَىٰ وَهَٰرُونَ ١١٤
وَنَجَّيْنَٰهُمَا وَقَوْمَهُمَا مِنَ ٱلْكَرْبِ ٱلْعَظِيمِ ١١٥

116. And We helped them, so they were victorious;
اور اُن کی مدد کی تو وہ غالب ہو گئے ﴿۱۱۶﴾
ونصرنهم فكانوا هم الغلبين ﴿۱۱۶﴾

117. And We gave them the Book which helps to make things clear;
اور اُن دونوں کو کتاب واضح (المطالب) عنایت کی ﴿۱۱۷﴾
واتينهما الكتب المستبين ﴿۱۱۷﴾

118. And We guided them to the Straight Way.
اور اُن کو سیدھا رستہ دکھایا ﴿۱۱۸﴾
وهدينهما الصراط المستقيم ﴿۱۱۸﴾

119. And We left for them among generations (to come) in later times:
اور پیچھے آنے والوں میں اُن کا ذکر (خیر باقی) چھوڑ دیا ﴿۱۱۹﴾
وتركنا عليهما في الاخرين ﴿۱۱۹﴾

120. "Peace and salutation to Moses and Aaron!"
کہ موسیٰ اور ہارون پر سلام ﴿۱۲۰﴾
سلم على موسى وهرون ﴿۱۲۰﴾

121. Thus indeed do We reward those who do right.
بیشک ہم نیکوکاروں کو ایسا ہی بدلہ دیا کرتے ہیں ﴿۱۲۱﴾
انا كذلك نجزي المحسنين ﴿۱۲۱﴾

122. For they were two of Our believing Servants.
وہ دونوں ہمارے مومن بندوں میں سے تھے ﴿۱۲۲﴾
انهما من عبادنا المؤمنين ﴿۱۲۲﴾

123. So also was Elias among those sent (by Us).
اور الیاس بھی پیغمبروں میں سے تھے ﴿۱۲۳﴾
وان الياس لمن المرسلين ﴿۱۲۳﴾

124. Behold, he said to his people, "Will ye not fear (Allah)?
جب انہوں نے اپنی قوم سے کہا کہ تم ڈرتے کیوں نہیں ﴿۱۲۴﴾
اذ قال لقومه الا تتقون ﴿۱۲۴﴾

125. "Will ye call upon Baal and forsake the Best of Creators,—
کیا تم بعل کو پکارتے (اور اُسے پوجتے) ہو اور سب سے بہتر پیدا کرنے والے کو چھوڑ دیتے ہو ﴿۱۲۵﴾
اتدعون بعلا وتذرون احسن الخالقين ﴿۱۲۵﴾

126. "Allah, your Lord and Cherisher and the Lord and Cherisher of your fathers of old?"
(یعنی) خدا کو جو تمہارا اور تمہارے اگلے باپ دادا کا پروردگار ہے ﴿۱۲۶﴾
الله ربكم ورب ابائكم الاولين ﴿۱۲۶﴾

127. But they rejected him, and they will certainly be called up (for punishment),
تو اُن لوگوں نے انکو جھٹلا دیا سو وہ (دوزخ میں) حاضر کئے جائینگے ﴿۱۲۷﴾
فكذبوه فانهم لمحضرون ﴿۱۲۷﴾

128. Except the chosen servants of Allah (among them).
ہاں خدا کے بندگانِ خاص (مبتلائے عذاب نہیں ہونگے) ﴿۱۲۸﴾
الا عباد الله المخلصين ﴿۱۲۸﴾

129. And We left for him among generations (to come) in later times:
اور اُن کا ذکر (خیر) پچھلوں میں (باقی) چھوڑ دیا ﴿۱۲۹﴾
وتركنا عليه في الاخرين ﴿۱۲۹﴾

130. "Peace and salutation to such as Elias!"
کہ الیاسین پر سلام ﴿۱۳۰﴾
سلم على ال ياسين ﴿۱۳۰﴾

131. Thus indeed do We reward those who do right.
ہم نیک لوگوں کو ایسا ہی بدلہ دیتے ہیں ﴿۱۳۱﴾
انا كذلك نجزي المحسنين ﴿۱۳۱﴾

132. For he was one of Our believing Servants.
بیشک وہ ہمارے مومن بندوں میں سے تھے ﴿۱۳۲﴾
انه من عبادنا المؤمنين ﴿۱۳۲﴾

133. So also was Lût among those sent (by Us).
اور لوط بھی پیغمبروں میں سے تھے ﴿۱۳۳﴾
وان لوطا لمن المرسلين ﴿۱۳۳﴾

134. Behold, We delivered him and his adherents, all
جب ہم نے انکو اور انکے گھر والوں کو سب کو (عذاب سے) نجات دی ﴿۱۳۴﴾
اذ نجينه واهله اجمعين ﴿۱۳۴﴾

135. Except an old woman who was among those who lagged behind:
مگر ایک بڑھیا کہ پیچھے رہ جانے والوں میں تھی ﴿۱۳۵﴾
الا عجوزا في الغبرين ﴿۱۳۵﴾

136. Then We destroyed the rest.
پھر ہم نے اوروں کو ہلاک کر دیا ﴿۱۳۶﴾
ثم دمرنا الاخرين ﴿۱۳۶﴾

137. Verily, ye pass by their (sites), by day—
اور تم دن کو بھی اُن (کی بستیوں) کے پاس سے گزرتے رہتے ہو ﴿۱۳۷﴾
وانكم لتمرون عليهم مصبحين ﴿۱۳۷﴾

138. And by night: will ye not understand?
اور رات کو بھی. تو کیا تم عقل نہیں رکھتے؟ ﴿۱۳۸﴾
وباليل افلا تعقلون ﴿۱۳۸﴾

139. So also was Jonah among those sent (by Us).
اور یونس بھی پیغمبروں میں سے تھے ﴿۱۳۹﴾
وان يونس لمن المرسلين ﴿۱۳۹﴾

140. When he ran away (like a slave from captivity) to the ship (fully) laden,
جب بھاگ کر بھری ہوئی کشتی میں پہنچے ﴿۱۴۰﴾
اذ ابق الى الفلك المشحون ﴿۱۴۰﴾

141. He (agreed to) cast lots, and he was of the rebutted:
اُس وقت قرعہ ڈالا تو اُنہوں نے زک اُٹھائی ﴿۱۴۱﴾
فساهم فكان من المدحضين ﴿۱۴۱﴾

142. Then the big Fish did swallow him, and he had done acts worthy of blame.
پھر مچھلی نے اُنکو نگل لیا اور وہ (قابل) ملامت (کام) کرنیوالے تھے ﴿۱۴۲﴾
فالتقمه الحوت وهو مليم ﴿۱۴۲﴾

143. Had it not been that he (repented and) glorified Allah,
144. He would certainly have remained inside the Fish till the Day of Resurrection.
145. But We cast him forth on the naked shore in a state of sickness,
146. And We caused to grow, over him, a spreading plant of the Gourd kind.
147. And We sent him (on a mission) to a hundred thousand (men) or more.
148. And they believed; so We permitted them to enjoy (their life) for a while.
149. Now ask them their opinion: is it that thy Lord has (only) daughters, and they have sons?—
150. Or that We created the angels female, and they are witnesses (thereto)?
151. Behold they say, out of their own invention,
152. "Allah has begotten children"? But they are liars!
153. Did He (then) choose daughters rather than sons?
154. What is the matter with you? How judge ye?
155. Will ye not then receive admonition?
156. Or have ye an authority manifest?
157. Then bring ye your Book (of authority) if ye be Truthful!
158. And they have invented a kinship between Him and the Jinns: but the Jinns know (Quite well) that they will be brought before Him.
159. Glory to Allah! (He is free) from the things they ascribe (to Him)!
160. Not (so do) the Servants of Allah, the chosen ones.
161. For, verily, neither ye nor those ye worship
162. Can lead (any) into temptation concerning Allah,
163. Except such as are (themselves) going to the blazing Fire!
164. (The angels) "Not one of us but has a place appointed;
165. "And we are verily ranged in ranks (for service);
166. "And we are verily those who declare (Allah's) glory!"
167. And there were those who said,

پھر اگر وہ (خدا کی) پاکی بیان نہ کرتے (١٤٣)
تو اس روز تک کہ لوگ دوبارہ زندہ کئے جائینگے اُسی کے پیٹ میں رہتے (١٤٤)
پھر ہم نے اُن کو جبکہ وہ بیمار تھے فراخ میدان میں ڈال دیا (١٤٥)
اور اُن پر کدو کا درخت اُگایا (١٤٦)
اور اُن کو لاکھ یا اس سے زیادہ (لوگوں) کی طرف (پیغمبر بنا کر) بھیجا (١٤٧)
تو وہ ایمان لے آئے سو ہم بھی اُن کو (دنیا میں) ایک وقت (مقرر) تک فائدے دیتے رہے (١٤٨)
ان سے پوچھو تو کہ بھلا تمہارے پروردگار کے لئے تو بیٹیاں اور اُن کے لئے بیٹے (١٤٩)
یا ہم نے فرشتوں کو عورتیں بنایا اور وہ (اُس وقت) موجود تھے (١٥٠)
دیکھو یہ اپنی جھوٹ بنائی ہوئی (بات) کہتے ہیں (١٥١)
کہ خدا کے اولاد ہے کچھ شک نہیں کہ یہ جھوٹے ہیں (١٥٢)
کیا اُس نے بیٹوں کی نسبت بیٹیوں کو پسند کیا ہے؟ (١٥٣)
تم کیسے لوگ ہو کس طرح کا فیصلہ کرتے ہو (١٥٤)
بھلا تم غور (کیوں) نہیں کرتے (١٥٥)
یا تمہارے پاس کوئی صریح دلیل ہے (١٥٦)
اگر تم سچے ہو تو اپنی کتاب پیش کرو (١٥٧)
اور اُنہوں نے خدا میں اور جنوں میں رشتہ مقرر کیا۔ حالانکہ جنات جانتے ہیں کہ وہ (خدا کے سامنے) حاضر کئے جائینگے (١٥٨)
یہ جو کچھ بیان کرتے ہیں خدا اس سے پاک ہے (١٥٩)
مگر خدا کے بندگانِ خالص (مبتلائے عذاب نہیں ہونگے) (١٦٠)
سو تم اور جن کو تم پوجتے ہو (١٦١)
خدا کے خلاف بہکا نہیں سکتے (١٦٢)
مگر اُس کو جو جہنم میں جانے والا ہے (١٦٣)
اور (فرشتے کہتے ہیں کہ) ہم میں سے ہر ایک کا ایک مقام مقرر ہے (١٦٤)
اور ہم صف باندھے رہتے ہیں (١٦٥)
اور (خدائے) پاک (ذات کا) ذکر کرتے رہتے ہیں (١٦٦)
اور یہ لوگ کہا کرتے تھے (١٦٧)

فَلَوْلَآ اَنَّهٗ كَانَ مِنَ الْمُسَبِّحِيْنَ (١٤٣)
لَلَبِثَ فِيْ بَطْنِهٖٓ اِلٰى يَوْمِ يُبْعَثُوْنَ (١٤٤)
فَنَبَذْنٰهُ بِالْعَرَآءِ وَهُوَ سَقِيْمٌ (١٤٥)
وَاَنْۢبَتْنَا عَلَيْهِ شَجَرَةً مِّنْ يَّقْطِيْنٍ (١٤٦)
وَاَرْسَلْنٰهُ اِلٰى مِائَةِ اَلْفٍ اَوْ يَزِيْدُوْنَ (١٤٧)
فَاٰمَنُوْا فَمَتَّعْنٰهُمْ اِلٰى حِيْنٍ (١٤٨)
فَاسْتَفْتِهِمْ اَلِرَبِّكَ الْبَنَاتُ وَلَهُمُ
الْبَنُوْنَ (١٤٩)
اَمْ خَلَقْنَا الْمَلٰٓئِكَةَ اِنَاثًا وَّهُمْ شٰهِدُوْنَ (١٥٠)
اَلَآ اِنَّهُمْ مِّنْ اِفْكِهِمْ لَيَقُوْلُوْنَ (١٥١)
وَلَدَ اللّٰهُ وَاِنَّهُمْ لَكٰذِبُوْنَ (١٥٢)
اَصْطَفَى الْبَنَاتِ عَلَى الْبَنِيْنَ (١٥٣)
مَا لَكُمْ كَيْفَ تَحْكُمُوْنَ (١٥٤)
اَفَلَا تَذَكَّرُوْنَ (١٥٥)
اَمْ لَكُمْ سُلْطٰنٌ مُّبِيْنٌ (١٥٦)
فَاْتُوْا بِكِتٰبِكُمْ اِنْ كُنْتُمْ صٰدِقِيْنَ (١٥٧)
وَجَعَلُوْا بَيْنَهٗ وَبَيْنَ الْجِنَّةِ نَسَبًا وَلَقَدْ
عَلِمَتِ الْجِنَّةُ اِنَّهُمْ لَمُحْضَرُوْنَ (١٥٨)
سُبْحٰنَ اللّٰهِ عَمَّا يَصِفُوْنَ (١٥٩)
اِلَّا عِبَادَ اللّٰهِ الْمُخْلَصِيْنَ (١٦٠)
فَاِنَّكُمْ وَمَا تَعْبُدُوْنَ (١٦١)
مَآ اَنْتُمْ عَلَيْهِ بِفٰتِنِيْنَ (١٦٢)
اِلَّا مَنْ هُوَ صَالِ الْجَحِيْمِ (١٦٣)
وَمَا مِنَّآ اِلَّا لَهٗ مَقَامٌ مَّعْلُوْمٌ (١٦٤)
وَّاِنَّا لَنَحْنُ الصَّآفُّوْنَ (١٦٥)
وَاِنَّا لَنَحْنُ الْمُسَبِّحُوْنَ (١٦٦)
وَاِنْ كَانُوْا لَيَقُوْلُوْنَ (١٦٧)

SÛRA–38
ṢĀD
(INTRODUCTION)

For the place of this Sûra in the series of six, dealing with some of the mysteries of the spiritual world, see Introduction to S. 34.

This Sûra, both in chronology and subject-matter, is cognate to S. 37, and carries forward the same argument. But here the emphasis is laid on the working of earthly power when combined with spiritual power, and it is pointed out how much more significant (and real) spiritual power is. For this reason the illustrative stories are mainly those of David and Solomon who were kings as well as prophets, and a parallel is suggested with the unfolding public life of our Holy Prophet.

168. "If only we had had before us a Message from those of old,
169. "We should certainly have been Servants of Allah, sincere (and devoted)!"
170. But (now that the Qur'an has come), they reject it: but soon will they know!
171. Already has Our Word been passed before (this) to Our Servants sent (by Us),
172. That they would certainly be assisted,
173. And that Our forces,— they surely must conquer.
174. So turn thou away from them for a little while,
175. And watch them (how they fare), and they soon shall see (how thou farest)!
176. Do they wish (indeed) to hurry on our Punishment?
177. But when it descends upon their courtyards before them, Evil will be the morning for those who were warned (and heeded not)!
178. So turn thou away from them for a little while,
179. And watch (how they fare) and they soon shall see (how thou farest)!
180. Glory to thy Lord, the Lord of Honour and Power! (He is free) from what they ascribe (to Him)!
181. And Peace on the messengers!
182. And Praise to Allah, the Lord and Cherisher of the Worlds.

کہ اگر ہمارے پاس اگلوں کی کوئی نصیحت (کی کتاب) ہوتی (۱۶۸)
تو ہم خدا کے خالص بندے ہوتے (۱۶۹)
لیکن (اب) اس سے کفر کرتے ہیں سو عنقریب انکو (اسکا نتیجہ) معلوم ہو جائیگا (۱۷۰)
اور اپنے پیغام پہنچانے والے بندوں سے ہمارا وعدہ ہو چکا ہے (۱۷۱)
کہ وہی (مظفرو) منصور ہیں (۱۷۲)
اور ہمارا لشکر غالب رہے گا (۱۷۳)
تو ایک وقت تک اُن سے اعراض کیے رہو (۱۷۴)
اور انہیں دیکھتے رہو۔ یہ بھی عنقریب (کفر کا انجام) دیکھ لینگے (۱۷۵)
کیا یہ ہمارے عذاب کے لئے جلدی کر رہے ہیں (۱۷۶)
مگر جب وہ اُن کے میدان میں آ اُترے گا تو جن کو ڈر سنایا گیا تھا اُن کے لئے بُرا دن ہوگا (۱۷۷)
اور ایک وقت تک اُن سے منہ پھیرے رہو (۱۷۸)
اور دیکھتے رہو یہ بھی عنقریب (نتیجہ) دیکھ لیں گے (۱۷۹)
یہ جو کچھ بیان کرتے ہیں تمہارا پروردگار جو صاحب عزت ہے (اس سے) پاک ہے (۱۸۰)
اور پیغمبروں پر سلام (۱۸۱)
سب طرح کی تعریف خدائے رب العالمین کو (سزاوار) ہے (۱۸۲)

لَوْ اَنَّ عِنْدَنَا ذِكْرًا مِّنَ الْاَوَّلِيْنَ ۙ (۱۶۸)
لَكُنَّا عِبَادَ اللّٰهِ الْمُخْلَصِيْنَ (۱۶۹)
فَكَفَرُوْا بِهٖ فَسَوْفَ يَعْلَمُوْنَ (۱۷۰)
وَلَقَدْ سَبَقَتْ كَلِمَتُنَا لِعِبَادِنَا الْمُرْسَلِيْنَ ۚ (۱۷۱)
اِنَّهُمْ لَهُمُ الْمَنْصُوْرُوْنَ (۱۷۲)
وَاِنَّ جُنْدَنَا لَهُمُ الْغٰلِبُوْنَ (۱۷۳)
فَتَوَلَّ عَنْهُمْ حَتّٰى حِيْنٍ ۙ (۱۷۴)
وَّاَبْصِرْهُمْ فَسَوْفَ يُبْصِرُوْنَ (۱۷۵)
اَفَبِعَذَابِنَا يَسْتَعْجِلُوْنَ (۱۷۶)
فَاِذَا نَزَلَ بِسَاحَتِهِمْ فَسَآءَ صَبَاحُ الْمُنْذَرِيْنَ (۱۷۷)
وَتَوَلَّ عَنْهُمْ حَتّٰى حِيْنٍ ۙ (۱۷۸)
وَّاَبْصِرْ فَسَوْفَ يُبْصِرُوْنَ (۱۷۹)
سُبْحٰنَ رَبِّكَ رَبِّ الْعِزَّةِ عَمَّا يَصِفُوْنَ ۚ (۱۸۰)
وَسَلٰمٌ عَلَى الْمُرْسَلِيْنَ ۚ (۱۸۱)
وَالْحَمْدُ لِلّٰهِ رَبِّ الْعٰلَمِيْنَ ع (۱۸۲)

Ṣād (being one of the Abbreviated Letters).

سورۂ ص مکی ہے اور اس میں اٹھاسی آیتیں اور پانچ رکوع ہیں

سُوْرَةُ صٓ مَكِّيَّةٌ وَهِيَ ثَمَانٌ وَّثَمَانُوْنَ اٰيَةً وَّخَمْسُ رُكُوْعَاتٍ

In the name of Allah, Most Gracious, Most Merciful.
1. Sād: by the Qur'an, full of Admonition: (this is the Truth).
2. But the Unbelievers (are steeped) in Self-glory and opposition.
3. How many generations before them did We destroy? In the end they cried (for mercy)—when there was no longer time for being saved!
4. So they wonder that a Warner has come to them from among themselves! And the Unbelievers say, "This is a scorcerer telling lies!
5. "Has he made gods (all) into one God? Truly this is a strange thing!"

شروع خدا کا نام لے کر جو بڑا مہربان نہایت رحم والا ہے
ص۔ قسم ہے قرآن کی جو نصیحت دینے والا ہے (کہ تم حق پر ہو) (۱)
مگر جو لوگ کافر ہیں وہ غرور اور مخالفت میں ہیں (۲)
ہم نے اُن سے پہلے بہت سی اُمتوں کو ہلاک کر دیا تو وہ (عذاب کے وقت) لگے فریاد کرنے اور وہ رہائی کا وقت نہیں تھا (۳)
اور اُنہوں نے تعجب کیا کہ اُن کے پاس اُن ہی میں سے ہدایت کرنے والا آیا اور کافر کہنے لگے کہ یہ تو جادوگر ہے جھوٹا (۴)
کیا اس نے اتنے معبودوں کی جگہ ایک ہی معبود بنا دیا؟ یہ تو بڑی عجیب بات ہے (۵)

بِسْمِ اللّٰهِ الرَّحْمٰنِ الرَّحِيْمِ
صٓ وَالْقُرْاٰنِ ذِي الذِّكْرِ (۱)
بَلِ الَّذِيْنَ كَفَرُوْا فِيْ عِزَّةٍ وَّشِقَاقٍ (۲)
كَمْ اَهْلَكْنَا مِنْ قَبْلِهِمْ مِّنْ قَرْنٍ
فَنَادَوْا وَّلَاتَ حِيْنَ مَنَاصٍ (۳)
وَعَجِبُوْٓا اَنْ جَآءَهُمْ مُّنْذِرٌ مِّنْهُمْ
وَقَالَ الْكٰفِرُوْنَ هٰذَا سٰحِرٌ كَذَّابٌ ۚ (۴)
اَجَعَلَ الْاٰلِهَةَ اِلٰهًا وَّاحِدًا ۚ اِنَّ
هٰذَا لَشَيْءٌ عُجَابٌ (۵)

6. And the leaders among them go away (impatiently), (saying), "Walk ye away, and remain constant to your gods! For this is truly a thing designed (against you)!
7. "We never heard (the like) of this in the last religion this is nothing but a made-up tale!"
8. "What! Has the Message been sent to him— (of all persons) among us?... But they are in doubt concerning My (own) Message! Nay, they have not yet tasted My Punishment!
9. Or have they the Treasures of the Mercy of thy Lord,—the Exalted in Power, the Grantor of Bounties without measure?
10. Or have they the dominion of the heavens and the earth and all between? If so, let them mount up with the ropes and means (to reach that end)!
11. They are but a host of confederates and they will be put to flight.
12. Before them (were many who) rejected messengers,— the People of Noah, and 'Ād, and Pharaoh the Lord of Stakes,
13. And Thamûd, and the People of Lût, and the Companions of the Wood;—such were the Confederates.
14. Not one (of them) but rejected the messengers, but My Punishment came justly and inevitably (on them).
15. These (to-day) only wait for a single mighty Blast, which (when it comes) will brook no delay.
16. They say: "Our Lord! Hasten to us our sentence (even) before the Day of Account!"
17. Have patience at what they say, and remember Our Servant David, the man of strength: for he ever turned (in repentance to Allah).
18. It was We that made the hills declare, in unison with him, our Praises, at eventide and at break of day,
19. And the birds gathered (in assemblies): all with him did turn (to Allah).
20. We strengthened his kingdom, and gave him wisdom

تو اُن میں جو معزز تھے وہ چل کھڑے ہوئے (اور بولے) کہ چلو اور اپنے معبودوں
کی پوجا پر قائم رہو۔ بیشک یہ ایسی بات ہے جس سے (تم پر شرف و فضیلت) مقصود ہے ﴿٦﴾
یہ پچھلے مذہب میں ہم نے کبھی سُنی ہی نہیں۔ یہ بالکل بنائی
ہوئی بات ہے ﴿٧﴾
کیا ہم سب میں سے اسی پر نصیحت (کی کتاب) اُتری ہے؟
(نہیں) بلکہ یہ میری نصیحت کی کتاب سے شک میں ہیں۔
بلکہ اُنہوں نے ابھی میرے عذاب کا مزہ نہیں چکھا ﴿٨﴾
کیا اُن کے پاس تمہارے پروردگار کی رحمت کے خزانے
ہیں جو غالب (اور) بہت عطا کرنے والا ہے ﴿٩﴾
یا آسمانوں اور زمین اور جو کچھ اُن میں ہے ان (سب) پر اُن ہی کی
حکومت ہے۔ تو چاہیئے کہ رسیاں تان کر (آسمانوں پر) چڑھ جائیں ﴿١٠﴾
یہاں شکست کھائے ہوئے گروہوں میں سے یہ بھی ایک لشکر ہے ﴿١١﴾
ان سے پہلے نوح کی قوم اور عاد اور میخوں والا فرعون
(اور اس کی قوم کے لوگ) بھی جھٹلا چکے ہیں ﴿١٢﴾
اور ثمود اور لوط کی قوم اور بن کے رہنے والے بھی۔
یہی وہ گروہ ہیں ﴿١٣﴾
(ان) سب نے پیغمبروں کو جھٹلایا تو میرا عذاب (ان پر) آ واقع ہوا ﴿١٤﴾
اور یہ لوگ تو صرف ایک زور کی آواز کا جس میں (شروع
ہوئے پیچھے) کچھ وقفہ نہیں ہوگا انتظار کرتے ہیں ﴿١٥﴾
اور کہتے ہیں کہ اے ہمارے پروردگار ہم کو ہمارا حصہ
حساب کے دن سے پہلے ہی دیدے ﴿١٦﴾
(اے پیغمبر) یہ جو کچھ کہتے ہیں اس پر صبر کرو۔ اور ہمارے بندے داؤد کو
یاد کرو جو صاحب قوت تھے (اور) بیشک وہ رجوع کرنے والے تھے ﴿١٧﴾
ہم نے پہاڑوں کو اُن کے زیر فرمان کر دیا تھا کہ صبح و شام
اُن کے ساتھ (خدائے) پاک (کا) ذکر کرتے تھے ﴿١٨﴾
اور پرندوں کو بھی کہ جمع رہتے تھے سب اُنکے فرمانبردار تھے ﴿١٩﴾
اور ہم نے اُن کی بادشاہی کو مستحکم کیا اور اُن کو حکمت

وَانْطَلَقَ الْمَلَاُ مِنْهُمْ اَنِ امْشُوْا وَاصْبِرُوْا
عَلٰٓى اٰلِهَتِكُمْ ۖۚ اِنَّ هٰذَا لَشَيْءٌ يُّرَادُ ۚ ﴿٦﴾
مَا سَمِعْنَا بِهٰذَا فِي الْمِلَّةِ الْاٰخِرَةِ ۚ اِنْ
هٰذَآ اِلَّا اخْتِلَاقٌ ۚ ﴿٧﴾
ءَاُنْزِلَ عَلَيْهِ الذِّكْرُ مِنْۢ بَيْنِنَا ۭ بَلْ
هُمْ فِيْ شَكٍّ مِّنْ ذِكْرِيْ ۚ بَلْ لَّمَّا
يَذُوْقُوْا عَذَابِ ۭ ﴿٨﴾
اَمْ عِنْدَهُمْ خَزَاۗىِٕنُ رَحْمَةِ رَبِّكَ
الْعَزِيْزِ الْوَهَّابِ ۚ ﴿٩﴾
اَمْ لَهُمْ مُّلْكُ السَّمٰوٰتِ وَالْاَرْضِ وَمَا
بَيْنَهُمَا ۣ فَلْيَرْتَقُوْا فِي الْاَسْبَابِ ﴿١٠﴾
جُنْدٌ مَّا هُنَالِكَ مَهْزُوْمٌ مِّنَ الْاَحْزَابِ ﴿١١﴾
كَذَّبَتْ قَبْلَهُمْ قَوْمُ نُوْحٍ وَّعَادٌ وَّ
فِرْعَوْنُ ذُو الْاَوْتَادِ ۙ ﴿١٢﴾
وَثَمُوْدُ وَقَوْمُ لُوْطٍ وَّاَصْحٰبُ لْـَٔيْكَةِ ۭ
اُولٰۗىِٕكَ الْاَحْزَابُ ﴿١٣﴾
اِنْ كُلٌّ اِلَّا كَذَّبَ الرُّسُلَ فَحَقَّ عِقَابِ ﴿١٤﴾ ع
وَمَا يَنْظُرُ هٰٓؤُلَاۗءِ اِلَّا صَيْحَةً وَّاحِدَةً
مَّا لَهَا مِنْ فَوَاقٍ ﴿١٥﴾
وَقَالُوْا رَبَّنَا عَجِّلْ لَّنَا قِطَّنَا قَبْلَ يَوْمِ
الْحِسَابِ ﴿١٦﴾
اِصْبِرْ عَلٰي مَا يَقُوْلُوْنَ وَاذْكُرْ عَبْدَنَا
دَاوٗدَ ذَا الْاَيْدِ ۚ اِنَّهٗٓ اَوَّابٌ ﴿١٧﴾
اِنَّا سَخَّرْنَا الْجِبَالَ مَعَهٗ يُسَبِّحْنَ بِالْعَشِيِّ
وَالْاِشْرَاقِ ۙ ﴿١٨﴾
وَالطَّيْرَ مَحْشُوْرَةً ۭ كُلٌّ لَّهٗٓ اَوَّابٌ ﴿١٩﴾
وَشَدَدْنَا مُلْكَهٗ وَاٰتَيْنٰهُ الْحِكْمَةَ وَفَصْلَ

and sound judgment in speech and decision.

21. Has the Story of the Disputants reached thee? Behold, they climbed over the wall of the private chamber;

22. When they entered to David, and he was terrified of them, they said: "Fear not: we are two disputants, one of whom has wronged the other: decide now between us with truth, and treat us not with injustice, but guide us to the even Path.

23. "This man is my brother: He has nine and ninety ewes, and I have (but) one: yet he says, 'Commit her to my care,' and he overcame me in the argument.

24. (David) said: "He has undoubtedly wronged thee in demanding thy (single) ewe to be added to his (flock of) ewes: truly many are the Partners (in business) who wrong each other: not so do those who believe and work deeds of righteousness, and how few are they?"... And David gathered that We had tried him: he asked forgiveness of his Lord, fell down, bowing (in prostration), and turned (to Allah in repentance).

25. So We forgave him this (lapse): he enjoyed, indeed, a Near Approach to Us, and a beautiful Place of (final) Return.

26. O David! We did indeed make thee a vicegerent on earth: so judge thou between men in truth (and justice): nor follow thou the lust (of thy heart), for it will mislead thee from the Path of Allah: for those who wander astray from the Path of Allah, is a Chastisement Grevious, for that they forget the Day of Account.

27. Not without purpose did We create heaven and earth and all between! That were the thought of Unbelievers! But woe to the Unbelivers because of the Fire (of Hell)!

عطا فرمائی اور (خصومت کی) بات کا فیصلہ (سکھایا) ﴿٢٠﴾
بھلا تمہارے پاس اُن جھگڑنے والوں کی بھی خبر آئی ہے
جب وہ دیوار پھاند کر اندر داخل ہوئے ﴿٢١﴾
جس وقت وہ داؤد کے پاس آئے تو وہ اُن سے گھبرا گئے انہوں
نے کہا کہ خوف نہ کیجئے ہم دونوں کا ایک مقدمہ ہے کہ ہم میں سے
ایک نے دوسرے پر زیادتی کی ہے تو آپ ہم میں انصاف سے
فیصلہ کر دیجئے اور بےانصافی نہ کیجئے گا اور ہم کو سیدھا رستہ دکھا دیجئے ﴿٢٢﴾
(کیفیت یہ ہے کہ) یہ میرا بھائی ہے اسکے (ہاں) ننانوے
دُنبیاں ہیں اور میرے (پاس) ایک دُنبی ہے۔ یہ کہتا ہے کہ یہ
بھی میرے حوالے کر دے اور گفتگو میں مجھ پر زبردستی کرتا ہے ﴿٢٣﴾
اُنہوں نے کہا کہ یہ جو تیری دُنبی مانگتا ہے کہ اپنی دُنبیوں
میں ملا لے بے شک تم پر ظلم کرتا ہے۔ اور اکثر شریک
ایک دوسرے پر زیادتی ہی کیا کرتے ہیں۔ ہاں جو
ایمان لائے اور عمل نیک کرتے رہے اور ایسے لوگ بہت
کم ہیں۔ اور داؤد نے خیال کیا کہ (اس واقعے سے) ہم نے انکو
آزمایا ہے تو اُنہوں نے اپنے پروردگار سے مغفرت مانگی
اور جھک کر گر پڑے اور (خدا کی طرف) رجوع کیا ﴿٢٤﴾
تو ہم نے اُن کو بخش دیا۔ اور بے شک اُن کے لئے
ہمارے ہاں قُرب اور عمدہ مقام ہے ﴿٢٥﴾
اے داؤد ہم نے تم کو زمین میں بادشاہ بنایا ہے تو لوگوں
میں انصاف کے فیصلے کیا کرو اور خواہش کی پیروی نہ کرنا
کہ وہ تمہیں خدا کے رستے سے بھٹکا دے گی۔ جو لوگ خدا کے
رستے سے بھٹکتے ہیں اُن کیلئے سخت عذاب (تیار) ہے
کہ اُنہوں نے حساب کے دن کو بُھلا دیا ﴿٢٦﴾
اور ہم نے آسمان اور زمین کو اور جو کائنات اُن میں ہے
اس کو خالی از مصلحت نہیں پیدا کیا۔ یہ اُن کا گمان ہے
جو کافر ہیں سو کافروں کے لئے دوزخ کا عذاب ہے ﴿٢٧﴾

الْخِطَابِ ﴿٢٠﴾
وَهَلْ أَتَاكَ نَبَأُ الْخَصْمِ إِذْ تَسَوَّرُوا
الْمِحْرَابَ ﴿٢١﴾
إِذْ دَخَلُوا عَلَىٰ دَاوُودَ فَفَزِعَ مِنْهُمْ قَالُوا
لَا تَخَفْ خَصْمَانِ بَغَىٰ بَعْضُنَا عَلَىٰ بَعْضٍ
فَاحْكُمْ بَيْنَنَا بِالْحَقِّ وَلَا تُشْطِطْ وَاهْدِنَا
إِلَىٰ سَوَاءِ الصِّرَاطِ ﴿٢٢﴾
إِنَّ هَٰذَا أَخِي لَهُ تِسْعٌ وَتِسْعُونَ نَعْجَةً
وَلِيَ نَعْجَةٌ وَاحِدَةٌ فَقَالَ أَكْفِلْنِيهَا
وَعَزَّنِي فِي الْخِطَابِ ﴿٢٣﴾
قَالَ لَقَدْ ظَلَمَكَ بِسُؤَالِ نَعْجَتِكَ
إِلَىٰ نِعَاجِهِ وَإِنَّ كَثِيرًا مِنَ الْخُلَطَاءِ
لَيَبْغِي بَعْضُهُمْ عَلَىٰ بَعْضٍ إِلَّا الَّذِينَ
آمَنُوا وَعَمِلُوا الصَّالِحَاتِ وَقَلِيلٌ
مَا هُمْ وَظَنَّ دَاوُودُ أَنَّمَا فَتَنَّاهُ
فَاسْتَغْفَرَ رَبَّهُ وَخَرَّ رَاكِعًا وَ
أَنَابَ ﴿٢٤﴾
فَغَفَرْنَا لَهُ ذَٰلِكَ وَإِنَّ لَهُ عِنْدَنَا
لَزُلْفَىٰ وَحُسْنَ مَآبٍ ﴿٢٥﴾
يَا دَاوُودُ إِنَّا جَعَلْنَاكَ خَلِيفَةً فِي الْأَرْضِ
فَاحْكُمْ بَيْنَ النَّاسِ بِالْحَقِّ وَلَا تَتَّبِعِ
الْهَوَىٰ فَيُضِلَّكَ عَنْ سَبِيلِ اللَّهِ إِنَّ
الَّذِينَ يَضِلُّونَ عَنْ سَبِيلِ اللَّهِ لَهُمْ
عَذَابٌ شَدِيدٌ بِمَا نَسُوا يَوْمَ الْحِسَابِ ﴿٢٦﴾
وَمَا خَلَقْنَا السَّمَاءَ وَالْأَرْضَ وَمَا بَيْنَهُمَا
بَاطِلًا ذَٰلِكَ ظَنُّ الَّذِينَ كَفَرُوا
فَوَيْلٌ لِلَّذِينَ كَفَرُوا مِنَ النَّارِ ﴿٢٧﴾

28. Shall We treat those who believe and work deeds of righteousness, the same as those who do mischief on earth? Shall We treat those who guard against evil, the same as those who trun aside from the right?

جو لوگ ایمان لائے اور عمل نیک کرتے رہے کیا اُن کو ہم
اُن کی طرح کر دیں گے جو ملک میں فساد کرتے ہیں۔ یا
پرہیزگاروں کو بدکاروں کی طرح کر دیں گے ﴿۲۸﴾

أَمْ نَجْعَلُ الَّذِينَ آمَنُوا وَعَمِلُوا الصَّالِحَاتِ
كَالْمُفْسِدِينَ فِي الْأَرْضِ أَمْ نَجْعَلُ
الْمُتَّقِينَ كَالْفُجَّارِ ﴿٢٨﴾

29. (Here is) a Book which we have sent down unto thee, full of blessings, that they may meditate on its Signs, and that men of understanding may receive admonition.

(یہ) کتاب جو ہم نے تم پر نازل کی ہے بابرکت ہے تاکہ لوگ
اس کی آیتوں میں غور کریں اور تاکہ اہلِ عقل نصیحت پکڑیں ﴿۲۹﴾

كِتَابٌ أَنزَلْنَاهُ إِلَيْكَ مُبَارَكٌ لِّيَدَّبَّرُوا
آيَاتِهِ وَلِيَتَذَكَّرَ أُولُو الْأَلْبَابِ ﴿٢٩﴾

30. To David We bestowed Solomon (for a son),— how excellent is the servant! ever did he turn (to Us in repentance)!

اور ہم نے داؤد کو سلیمان عطا کئے۔ بہت خوب بندے
(تھے اور) وہ (خدا کی طرف) رجوع کرنے والے تھے ﴿۳۰﴾

وَوَهَبْنَا لِدَاوُودَ سُلَيْمَانَ ۚ نِعْمَ الْعَبْدُ ۖ
إِنَّهُ أَوَّابٌ ﴿٣٠﴾

31. Behold, there were brought before him, at eventide, coursers of the highest breeding, and swift of foot;

جب اُن کے سامنے شام کو خاصے کے گھوڑے
پیش کئے گئے ﴿۳۱﴾

إِذْ عُرِضَ عَلَيْهِ بِالْعَشِيِّ الصَّافِنَاتُ
الْجِيَادُ ﴿٣١﴾

32. And he siad, "Truly do I prefer wealth to the remembrance of my Lord." Until (the sun) was hidden in the veil (of Night):

تو کہنے لگے کہ میں نے اپنے پروردگار کی یاد سے (غافل ہو کر)
مال کی محبت اختیار کی۔ یہاں تک کہ (آفتاب) پردے میں چھپ گیا ﴿۳۲﴾

فَقَالَ إِنِّي أَحْبَبْتُ حُبَّ الْخَيْرِ عَن
ذِكْرِ رَبِّي حَتَّىٰ تَوَارَتْ بِالْحِجَابِ ﴿٣٢﴾

33. "Bring them back to me." Then began he to pass his hand over (their) legs and their necks.

(بولے کہ) اُن کو میرے پاس واپس لاؤ۔ پھر اُن کی ٹانگوں
اور گردنوں پر ہاتھ پھیرنے لگے ﴿۳۳﴾

رُدُّوهَا عَلَيَّ ۖ فَطَفِقَ مَسْحًا بِالسُّوقِ وَ
الْأَعْنَاقِ ﴿٣٣﴾

34. And We did try Solomon: We placed on his throne a body but he did turn (to Us in true devotion):

اور ہم نے سلیمان کی آزمائش کی اور اُن کے تخت پر ایک
دھڑ ڈال دیا پھر اُنہوں نے (خدا کی طرف) رجوع کیا ﴿۳۴﴾

وَلَقَدْ فَتَنَّا سُلَيْمَانَ وَأَلْقَيْنَا عَلَىٰ كُرْسِيِّهِ
جَسَدًا ثُمَّ أَنَابَ ﴿٣٤﴾

35. He said, "O my Lord! forgive me, and grant me a Kingdom which, will not belong to another after me: for Thou art the Grantor of Bounties (without measure).

(اور) دعا کی کہ اے پروردگار مجھے مغفرت کر اور مجھ کو ایسی
بادشاہی عطا کر کہ میرے بعد کسی کو شایاں نہ ہو بیشک
تو بڑا عطا فرمانے والا ہے ﴿۳۵﴾

قَالَ رَبِّ اغْفِرْ لِي وَهَبْ لِي مُلْكًا لَّا
يَنبَغِي لِأَحَدٍ مِّن بَعْدِي ۖ إِنَّكَ أَنتَ
الْوَهَّابُ ﴿٣٥﴾

36. Then We subjected the Wind to his power, to flow gently to his order, whithersoever he willed,—

پھر ہم نے ہوا کو اُن کے زیرِ فرمان کر دیا کہ جہاں
وہ پہنچنا چاہتے اُن کے حکم سے نرم نرم چلنے لگتی ﴿۳۶﴾

فَسَخَّرْنَا لَهُ الرِّيحَ تَجْرِي بِأَمْرِهِ رُخَاءً
حَيْثُ أَصَابَ ﴿٣٦﴾

37. As also the Satans, (including) every kind of builder and diver,—

اور دیووں کو بھی (اُن کے زیرِ فرمان کیا) سب عمارتیں بنانے والے اور غوطہ مارنے والے تھے ﴿۳۷﴾

وَالشَّيَاطِينَ كُلَّ بَنَّاءٍ وَغَوَّاصٍ ﴿٣٧﴾

38. As also others bound together in fetters.

اور اوروں کو بھی جو زنجیروں میں جکڑے ہوئے تھے ﴿۳۸﴾

وَآخَرِينَ مُقَرَّنِينَ فِي الْأَصْفَادِ ﴿٣٨﴾

39. "Such are Our Bounties: whether thou bestow them (on others) or withhold them, no account will be asked."

(ہم نے کہا) یہ ہماری بخشش ہے (چاہو تو) احسان کرو یا
(چاہو تو) رکھ چھوڑو (تم سے) کچھ حساب نہیں ہے ﴿۳۹﴾

هَٰذَا عَطَاؤُنَا فَامْنُنْ أَوْ أَمْسِكْ بِغَيْرِ
حِسَابٍ ﴿٣٩﴾

40. And he enjoyed, indeed, a Near Approach to Us, and a beautiful Place of (final) Return.

اور بےشک اُن کے لئے ہمارے ہاں قرب اور عمدہ مقام ہے ﴿۴۰﴾

وَإِنَّ لَهُ عِندَنَا لَزُلْفَىٰ وَحُسْنَ مَآبٍ ﴿٤٠﴾

41. Commemorate Our Servant Job, behold he cried to his Lord: "Satan has afflicted me with distress and suffering!"

اور ہمارے بندے ایوب کو یاد کرو جب اُنہوں نے اپنے رب
کو پکارا کہ (بار الٰہا) شیطان نے مجھ کو ایذا اور تکلیف دے رکھی ہے ﴿۴۱﴾

وَاذْكُرْ عَبْدَنَا أَيُّوبَ إِذْ نَادَىٰ رَبَّهُ
أَنِّي مَسَّنِيَ الشَّيْطَانُ بِنُصْبٍ وَعَذَابٍ ﴿٤١﴾

42. "Strike with thy foot: here is (water) wherein to wash, cool and refreshing, and (water) to drink."
43. And We gave him (back) his people and doubled their number,—as a Grace from Us, and a thing for commemoration, for all who have Understanding.
44. "And take in thy hand a little grass, and strike therewith: and break not (thy oath)." Truly We found him full of patience and constancy. How excellent is the servant! Ever did he turn (to Us)!
45. And commemorate Our Servants Abraham, Isaac, and Jacob, possessors of Power and Vision.
46. Verily We did choose them for a special (purpose)— the remembrance of the Hereafter.
47. They were, in Our sight, truly, of the company of the Elect and the Good.
48. And commemorate Isma'īl, Elisha, and Zul-Kifl: each of them was of the company of the Good.
49. This is a Message (of admonition): and verily, for the Righteous, is a beautiful place of (final) Return,—
50. Gardens of Eternity, whose doors will (ever) be open to them;
51. Therein will they recline (at ease); therein can they call (at pleasure) for fruit in abundance, and (delicious) drink;
52. And beside them will be chaste women restraining their glances, (companions) of equal age.
53. Such is the Promise made to you for the Day of Account!
54. Truly such will be Our Bounty (to you); it will never fail;—
55. Yea, such! But— for the wrong-doers will be an evil place of (final) Return!—
56. Hell!— they will burn therein,—an evil bed (indeed, to lie on)!—
57. Yea, such!—Then shall they taste it,— a boiling fluid, and a fluid dark, murky, intensely cold!—
58. And other Penalties of a similar kind, to match them!
59. Here is a troop rushing headlong with you! No welcome for them! Truly, they shall burn in the Fire!
60. (The followers shall cry to the misleaders:) "Nay, ye (too)! No welcome for you! It is ye who have brought this upon us! Now evil is (this) place to stay in!"

(ہم نے کہا کہ زمین پر) لات مارو (دیکھو) یہ (چشمہ نکل آیا)
نہانے کو ٹھنڈا اور پینے کو (شیریں) (۴۲)
اور ہم نے اُن کو اہل (وعیال) اور اُنکے ساتھ اُنکے برابر اور بخشے
(یہ) ہماری طرف سے رحمت اور عقل والوں کیلئے نصیحت تھی (۴۳)
اور اپنے ہاتھ میں جھاڑو لو اور اس سے مارو اور قسم نہ توڑو بیشک ہم نے
انکو ثابت قدم پایا۔ بہت خوب بندے تھے بیشک وہ رجوع کرنیوالے تھے (۴۴)
اور ہمارے بندوں ابراہیم اور اسحاق اور یعقوب کو یاد
کرو جو قوت والے اور صاحب نظر تھے (۴۵)
ہم نے انکو ایک (صفت) خاص (آخرت کے) گھر کی یاد سے ممتاز کیا تھا (۴۶)
اور وہ ہمارے نزدیک منتخب اور نیک لوگوں میں سے تھے (۴۷)
اور اسمٰعیل اور الیسع اور ذوالکفل کو یاد کرو۔ وہ سب
نیک لوگوں میں سے تھے (۴۸)
یہ نصیحت ہے۔ اور پرہیزگاروں کیلئے تو عمدہ مقام ہے (۴۹)
ہمیشہ رہنے کے باغ جنکے دروازے اُنکے لئے کھلے ہونگے (۵۰)
اُن میں تکیے لگائے بیٹھے ہوں گے اور کھانے پینے کے
لئے بہت سے میوے اور شراب منگاتے رہیں گے (۵۱)
اور اُنکے پاس نیچی نگاہ رکھنے والی (اور) ہم عمر عورتیں ہونگی (۵۲)
یہ وہ چیزیں ہیں جن کا حساب کے دن کیلئے تم سے وعدہ کیا جاتا تھا (۵۳)
یہ ہمارا رزق ہے جو کبھی ختم نہیں ہوگا (۵۴)
یہ (نعمتیں تو فرمانبرداروں کیلئے ہیں) اور سرکشوں کیلئے برا ٹھکانا ہے (۵۵)
(یعنی) دوزخ جس میں وہ داخل ہونگے اور وہ بری آرامگاہ ہے (۵۶)
یہ کھولتا ہوا گرم پانی اور پیپ (ہے) اب اسکے مزے چکھیں (۵۷)
اور اسی طرح کے اور بہت سے (عذاب ہونگے) (۵۸)
یہ ایک فوج ہے جو تمہارے ساتھ داخل ہوگی ان کو
خوشی نہ ہو یہ دوزخ میں جانے والے ہیں (۵۹)
کہیں گے بلکہ تم ہی کو خوشی نہ ہو تم ہی تو یہ (بلا) ہمارے
سامنے لائے ہو سو (یہ) برا ٹھکانا ہے (۶۰)

اُرْكُضْ بِرِجْلِكَ هٰذَا مُغْتَسَلٌ بَارِدٌ
وَّشَرَابٌ (۴۲)
وَوَهَبْنَا لَهٗٓ اَهْلَهٗ وَمِثْلَهُمْ مَّعَهُمْ رَحْمَةً
مِّنَّا وَذِكْرٰى لِاُولِى الْاَلْبَابِ (۴۳)
وَخُذْ بِيَدِكَ ضِغْثًا فَاضْرِبْ بِّهٖ وَلَا تَحْنَثْ
اِنَّا وَجَدْنٰهُ صَابِرًا نِعْمَ الْعَبْدُ اِنَّهٗٓ اَوَّابٌ (۴۴)
وَاذْكُرْ عِبٰدَنَآ اِبْرٰهِيْمَ وَاِسْحٰقَ وَ
يَعْقُوْبَ اُولِى الْاَيْدِىْ وَالْاَبْصَارِ (۴۵)
اِنَّآ اَخْلَصْنٰهُمْ بِخَالِصَةٍ ذِكْرَى الدَّارِ (۴۶)
وَاِنَّهُمْ عِنْدَنَا لَمِنَ الْمُصْطَفَيْنَ الْاَخْيَارِ (۴۷)
وَاذْكُرْ اِسْمٰعِيْلَ وَالْيَسَعَ وَذَا الْكِفْلِ
وَكُلٌّ مِّنَ الْاَخْيَارِ (۴۸)
هٰذَا ذِكْرٌ وَاِنَّ لِلْمُتَّقِيْنَ لَحُسْنَ مَاٰبٍ (۴۹)
جَنّٰتِ عَدْنٍ مُّفَتَّحَةً لَّهُمُ الْاَبْوَابُ (۵۰)
مُتَّكِـِٕيْنَ فِيْهَا يَدْعُوْنَ فِيْهَا بِفَاكِهَةٍ
كَثِيْرَةٍ وَّشَرَابٍ (۵۱)
وَعِنْدَهُمْ قٰصِرٰتُ الطَّرْفِ اَتْرَابٌ (۵۲)
هٰذَا مَا تُوْعَدُوْنَ لِيَوْمِ الْحِسَابِ (۵۳)
اِنَّ هٰذَا لَرِزْقُنَا مَا لَهٗ مِنْ نَّفَادٍ (۵۴)
هٰذَا وَاِنَّ لِلطّٰغِيْنَ لَشَرَّ مَاٰبٍ (۵۵)
جَهَنَّمَ يَصْلَوْنَهَا فَبِئْسَ الْمِهَادُ (۵۶)
هٰذَا فَلْيَذُوْقُوْهُ حَمِيْمٌ وَّغَسَّاقٌ (۵۷)
وَّاٰخَرُ مِنْ شَكْلِهٖٓ اَزْوَاجٌ (۵۸)
هٰذَا فَوْجٌ مُّقْتَحِمٌ مَّعَكُمْ لَا مَرْحَبًا
بِهِمْ اِنَّهُمْ صَالُوا النَّارِ (۵۹)
قَالُوْا بَلْ اَنْتُمْ لَا مَرْحَبًا بِكُمْ اَنْتُمْ
قَدَّمْتُمُوْهُ لَنَا فَبِئْسَ الْقَرَارُ (۶۰)

61. They will say: "Our Lord! whoever brought this upon us,— add to him a double Chastisement in the Fire!"

وہ کہیں گے کہ اے پروردگار جو اس کو ہمارے سامنے
لایا ہے اُس کو دوزخ میں دُونا عذاب دے ﴿٦١﴾

قَالُوْا رَبَّنَا مَنْ قَدَّمَ لَنَا هٰذَا فَزِدْهُ
عَذَابًا ضِعْفًا فِي النَّارِ ﴿٦١﴾

62. And they will say: how is it with us that we see not men who we used to number among the bad ones?

اور کہیں گے کیا سبب ہے کہ (یہاں) ہم اُن شخصوں کو
نہیں دیکھتے جن کو بُروں میں شمار کرتے تھے ﴿٦٢﴾

وَقَالُوْا مَا لَنَا لَا نَرٰى رِجَالًا كُنَّا
نَعُدُّهُمْ مِّنَ الْاَشْرَارِ ﴿٦٢﴾

63. "Did we treat them (as such) in ridicule, or have (our) eyes failed to perceive them?"

کیا ہم نے اُن سے ٹھٹھا کیا ہے یا (ہماری) آنکھیں اُن
(کی طرف) سے پھر گئی ہیں؟ ﴿٦٣﴾

اَتَّخَذْنٰهُمْ سِخْرِيًّا اَمْ زَاغَتْ عَنْهُمُ
الْاَبْصَارُ ﴿٦٣﴾

64. That is true,— the mutual recriminations of the People of the Fire!

بے شک یہ اہلِ دوزخ کا جھگڑنا برحق ہے ﴿٦٤﴾

اِنَّ ذٰلِكَ لَحَقٌّ تَخَاصُمُ اَهْلِ النَّارِ ﴿٦٤﴾ ع

65. Say: "Truly am I a Warner: no god is there but Allah, the One, Supreme and Irresistible,—

کہہ دو کہ میں تو صرف ہدایت کرنیوالا ہوں۔ اور خدائے یکتا
(اور) غالب کے سوا کوئی معبود نہیں ﴿٦٥﴾

قُلْ اِنَّمَآ اَنَا مُنْذِرٌ ۖ وَّمَا مِنْ اِلٰهٍ
اِلَّا اللّٰهُ الْوَاحِدُ الْقَهَّارُ ﴿٦٥﴾

66. "The Lord of the heavens and the earth, and all between,— Exalted in Might, Ever-Forgiving.

جو آسمانوں اور زمین اور جو (مخلوق) اُن میں ہے سب کا
مالک ہے۔ غالب (اور) بخشنے والا ﴿٦٦﴾

رَبُّ السَّمٰوٰتِ وَالْاَرْضِ وَمَا بَيْنَهُمَا
الْعَزِيْزُ الْغَفَّارُ ﴿٦٦﴾

67. Say: "That is a Tremendous Tidings.

کہہ دو کہ یہ ایک بڑی (ہولناک چیز کی) خبر ہے ﴿٦٧﴾

قُلْ هُوَ نَبَؤٌا عَظِيْمٌ ﴿٦٧﴾

68. "From which ye do turn away!

جس کو تم دھیان میں نہیں لاتے ﴿٦٨﴾

اَنْتُمْ عَنْهُ مُعْرِضُوْنَ ﴿٦٨﴾

69. "No knowledge have I of the Exalted Chiefs when they discuss (matters) among themselves.

مجھ کو اُوپر کی مجلس (والوں) کا جب وہ جھگڑتے تھے
کچھ بھی علم نہ تھا ﴿٦٩﴾

مَا كَانَ لِيَ مِنْ عِلْمٍۢ بِالْمَلَاِ الْاَعْلٰٓى
اِذْ يَخْتَصِمُوْنَ ﴿٦٩﴾

70. "Only this has been revealed to me: that I am to give warning plainly and publicly."

میری طرف تو یہی وحی کی جاتی ہے کہ میں کُھلم کُھلا
ہدایت کرنے والا ہوں ﴿٧٠﴾

اِنْ يُّوْحٰٓى اِلَيَّ اِلَّآ اَنَّمَآ اَنَا نَذِيْرٌ
مُّبِيْنٌ ﴿٧٠﴾

71. Behold, thy Lord said to the angels: "I am about to create man from clay:

جب تمہارے پروردگار نے فرشتوں سے کہا کہ میں مٹّی
سے انسان بنانے والا ہوں ﴿٧١﴾

اِذْ قَالَ رَبُّكَ لِلْمَلٰٓئِكَةِ اِنِّيْ خَالِقٌۢ
بَشَرًا مِّنْ طِيْنٍ ﴿٧١﴾

72. "When I have fashioned him and breathed into him of My spirit, fall ye down in prostration unto him."

جب اس کو درست کرلوں اور اس میں اپنی رُوح پھونک
دوں تو اس کے آگے سجدے میں گر پڑنا ﴿٧٢﴾

فَاِذَا سَوَّيْتُهٗ وَنَفَخْتُ فِيْهِ مِنْ رُّوْحِيْ
فَقَعُوْا لَهٗ سٰجِدِيْنَ ﴿٧٢﴾

73. So the angels prostrated themselves, all of them together:

تو تمام فرشتوں نے سجدہ کیا ﴿٧٣﴾

فَسَجَدَ الْمَلٰٓئِكَةُ كُلُّهُمْ اَجْمَعُوْنَ ﴿٧٣﴾

74. Not so Iblīs: he was haughty, and became one of those who reject Faith.

مگر شیطان۔ اکڑ بیٹھا اور کافروں میں
ہوگیا ﴿٧٤﴾

اِلَّآ اِبْلِيْسَ ۭ اِسْتَكْبَرَ وَكَانَ مِنَ
الْكٰفِرِيْنَ ﴿٧٤﴾

75. (Allah) said: "O Iblîs! what prevents thee from prostrating thyself to one whom I have created with My hands? Art thou haughty? Or art thou one of the high (and mighty) ones?

(خدا نے) فرمایا کہ اے ابلیس جس شخص کو میں نے اپنے
ہاتھوں سے بنایا اُسکے آگے سجدہ کرنے سے تجھے کس چیز
نے منع کیا۔ کیا تو غرور میں آگیا یا اونچے درجے والوں میں تھا؟ ﴿٧٥﴾

قَالَ يٰٓاِبْلِيْسُ مَا مَنَعَكَ اَنْ تَسْجُدَ
لِمَا خَلَقْتُ بِيَدَيَّ ۭ اَسْتَكْبَرْتَ اَمْ
كُنْتَ مِنَ الْعَالِيْنَ ﴿٧٥﴾

SÛRA–39
AZ-ZUMAR
(INTRODUCTION)

This is the last of the series of six Sûras beginning with S. 34, which deal with the mysteries of the spiritual world, as leading up to the *Ma'ãd*, or the Hereafter. See Introductrion to S. 34.

Its subject-matter is how Creation in its great variety is yet sorted out in Groups or Classes, all governed by one Plan, and created and sustained by One Allah, Who will separate Good from Evil at the last Day. The word *zumar* occurs in verses 71 and 73.

Its chronology has no significance. It belongs to the late Makkan period.

76. (Iblîs) said: "I am better than he: Thou createdst me from fire, and him Thou createdst from clay."

77. (Allah) said: "Then get thee out from here: for thou art rejected, accursed.

78. "And My Curse shall be on thee till the Day of Judgment."

79. (Iblîs) said: "O my Lord! give me then respite till the Day the (dead) are raised."

80. (Allah) said: "Respite then is granted thee—

81. "Till the Day of the Time Appointed."

82. (Iblîs) said: "Then, by Thy Power, I will lead them all astray.

83. "Except Thy Servants amongst them, sincere and purified (by Thy grace)."

84. (Allah) said: "This is the Truth, and the Truth I say.

85. "That I will certainly fill Hell with thee and those that follow thee,—every one."

86. Say: "No reward do I ask of you for this (Qur'an), nor am I a pretender.

87. "This is no less than a Reminder to (all) the Worlds.

88. "And ye shall certainly know the truth of it (all) after a while."

Az-Zumar, or the Groups

In the name of Allah, Most Gracious, Most Merciful.

1. The revelation of this Book is from Allah, the Exalted in Power, Full of Wisdom.

2. Verily it is We Who have revealed the Book to thee in Truth: so serve Allah, offering Him sincere devotion.

3. Is it not to Allah that sincere devotion is due? But those who take for protectors others than Allah (say): "We only serve them in order that they may bring us nearer to Allah." Truly Allah will judge between them in that wherein they differ. But Allah guides not such as are false and ungrateful.

قَالَ اَنَا خَيْرٌ مِّنْهُ ۭ خَلَقْتَنِيْ مِنْ نَّارٍ
وَّخَلَقْتَهٗ مِنْ طِيْنٍ ﴿٧٦﴾
قَالَ فَاخْرُجْ مِنْهَا فَاِنَّكَ رَجِيْمٌ ﴿٧٧﴾
وَّاِنَّ عَلَيْكَ لَعْنَتِيْٓ اِلٰى يَوْمِ الدِّيْنِ ﴿٧٨﴾
قَالَ رَبِّ فَاَنْظِرْنِيْٓ اِلٰى يَوْمِ
يُبْعَثُوْنَ ﴿٧٩﴾
قَالَ فَاِنَّكَ مِنَ الْمُنْظَرِيْنَ ﴿٨٠﴾
اِلٰى يَوْمِ الْوَقْتِ الْمَعْلُوْمِ ﴿٨١﴾
قَالَ فَبِعِزَّتِكَ لَاُغْوِيَنَّهُمْ اَجْمَعِيْنَ ﴿٨٢﴾
اِلَّا عِبَادَكَ مِنْهُمُ الْمُخْلَصِيْنَ ﴿٨٣﴾
قَالَ فَالْحَقُّ ۡ وَالْحَقَّ اَقُوْلُ ﴿٨٤﴾
لَاَمْلَئَنَّ جَهَنَّمَ مِنْكَ وَمِمَّنْ تَبِعَكَ
مِنْهُمْ اَجْمَعِيْنَ ﴿٨٥﴾
قُلْ مَآ اَسْـَٔـلُكُمْ عَلَيْهِ مِنْ اَجْرٍ وَّمَآ
اَنَا مِنَ الْمُتَكَلِّفِيْنَ ﴿٨٦﴾
اِنْ هُوَ اِلَّا ذِكْرٌ لِّلْعٰلَمِيْنَ ﴿٨٧﴾
ع وَلَتَعْلَمُنَّ نَبَاَهٗ بَعْدَ حِيْنٍ ﴿٨٨﴾

بولا کہ میں اس سے بہتر ہوں (کہ) تو نے مجھ کو آگ سے
پیدا کیا اور اسے مٹی سے بنایا ﴿٧٦﴾
کہا یہاں سے نکل جا تو مردود ہے ﴿٧٧﴾
اور تجھ پر قیامت کے دن تک میری لعنت (پڑتی) رہے گی ﴿٧٨﴾
کہنے لگا کہ میرے پروردگار مجھے اس روز تک کہ لوگ
اٹھائے جائیں مہلت دے ﴿٧٩﴾
کہا تجھ کو مہلت دی جاتی ہے ﴿٨٠﴾
اُس روز تک جس کا وقت مقرر ہے ﴿٨١﴾
کہنے لگا کہ مجھے تیری عزت کی قسم میں اُن سب کو بہکاتا رہونگا ﴿٨٢﴾
سوا اُن کے جو تیرے خالص بندے ہیں ﴿٨٣﴾
کہا سچ (ہے) اور میں بھی سچ کہتا ہوں ﴿٨٤﴾
کہ میں تجھ سے اور جو اُن میں سے تیری پیروی کریں گے
سب سے جہنم کو بھر دوں گا ﴿٨٥﴾
(اے پیغمبر) کہہ دو کہ میں تم سے اِس کا صلہ نہیں مانگتا اور
نہ میں بناوٹ کرنے والوں میں ہوں ﴿٨٦﴾
یہ (قرآن) تو اہلِ عالم کے لئے نصیحت ہے ﴿٨٧﴾
اور تم کو اس کا حال ایک وقت کے بعد معلوم ہو جائیگا ﴿٨٨﴾

سُوْرَةُ الزُّمَرِ مَكِّيَّةٌ وَّهِيَ خَمْسٌ وَّسَبْعُوْنَ اٰيَةً وَّثَمَانُ رُكُوْعَاتٍ

سورۂ زمر مکی ہے اس میں پچھتر آیتیں اور آٹھ رُکوع ہیں

بِسْمِ اللّٰهِ الرَّحْمٰنِ الرَّحِيْمِ
تَنْزِيْلُ الْكِتٰبِ مِنَ اللّٰهِ الْعَزِيْزِ الْحَكِيْمِ ﴿١﴾
اِنَّآ اَنْزَلْنَآ اِلَيْكَ الْكِتٰبَ بِالْحَقِّ فَاعْبُدِ
اللّٰهَ مُخْلِصًا لَّهُ الدِّيْنَ ﴿٢﴾
اَلَا لِلّٰهِ الدِّيْنُ الْخَالِصُ ۭ وَالَّذِيْنَ
اتَّخَذُوْا مِنْ دُوْنِهٖٓ اَوْلِيَاۗءَ ۘ مَا نَعْبُدُهُمْ
اِلَّا لِيُقَرِّبُوْنَآ اِلَى اللّٰهِ زُلْفٰى ۭ اِنَّ اللّٰهَ
يَحْكُمُ بَيْنَهُمْ فِيْ مَا هُمْ فِيْهِ يَخْتَلِفُوْنَ ڛ
اِنَّ اللّٰهَ لَا يَهْدِيْ مَنْ هُوَ كٰذِبٌ كَفَّارٌ ﴿٣﴾

شروع خدا کا نام لے کر جو بڑا مہربان نہایت رحم والا ہے
اِس کتاب کا اتارا جانا خدائے غالب (اور) حکمت والے کی طرف سے ہے ﴿١﴾
(اے پیغمبر) ہم نے یہ کتاب تمہاری طرف سچائی کیساتھ نازل کی ہے
تو خدا کی عبادت کرو (یعنی) اسکی عبادت کو (شرک سے) خالص کر کے ﴿٢﴾
دیکھو خالص عبادت خدا ہی کیلئے (زیبا) ہے اور جن لوگوں
نے اس کے سوا اور دوست بنائے ہیں (وہ کہتے ہیں کہ) ہم انکو
اس لئے پوجتے ہیں کہ ہم کو خدا کا مقرب بنا دیں۔ تو جن
باتوں میں یہ اختلاف کرتے ہیں خدا انمیں انکا فیصلہ کر دیگا۔
بیشک خدا اس شخص کو جو جھوٹا ناشکرا ہے ہدایت نہیں دیتا ﴿٣﴾

4. Had Allah wished to take to Himself a son, He could have chosen whom He pleased out of those whom He doth create: but Glory be to Him! (He is above such things.) He is Allah, the One, the Overpowering.
5. He created the heavens and the earth in true (proportions): He makes the Night overlap the Day, and the Day overlap the Night: He has subjected the sun and the moon (to His law): each one follows a course for a time appointed. Is not He the Exalted in Power—He Who forgives again and again?
6. He created you (all) from a single Person: then created, of like nature, his mate; and He sent down for you eight head of cattle in pairs: He creates you, in the wombs of your mothers, in stages, one after another, in three veils of darkness. Such is Allah, your Lord and Cherisher: to Him belongs (all) dominion. There is no god but He: then how are ye turned away (from your true Lord)?
7. If ye reject (Allah), truly Allah hath no need of you; but He liketh not ingratitude from His servants: if ye are grateful, He is pleased with you. No bearer of burdens can bear of burden of another. In the End, to your Lord is your Return, when He will tell you the truth of all that ye did (in this life). For He knoweth well all that is in (men's) hearts.
8. When some trouble toucheth man He crieth unto his Lord, turning to Him in repentance: But when He bestoweth a favour upon him as from Himself, (man) doth forget what he cried and prayed for before, and he doth set up rivals unto Allah, thus misleading others from Allah's Path. Say, "Enjoy thy disbelief for a little while: verily thou art (one) of the Companions of the Fire!"
9. Is one who worships devoutly during the hours of the night prostrating himself or standing (in adoration), who takes heed of the Hereafter, and who Places his hope in the Mercy of his Lord—(like one who does not)? Say: "Are those

اگر خدا کسی کو اپنا بیٹا بنانا چاہتا تو اپنی مخلوق میں سے
جس کو چاہتا انتخاب کر لیتا۔ وہ پاک ہے وہی خدا یکتا
(اور) غالب ہے ﴿۴﴾
اُسی نے آسمانوں اور زمین کو تدبیر کے ساتھ پیدا کیا ہے
(اور) وہی رات کو دن پر لپیٹتا اور دن کو رات پر لپیٹتا ہے
اور اُسی نے سورج اور چاند کو بس میں کر رکھا ہے سب ایک وقت مقرر تک
چلتے رہیں گے۔ دیکھو وہی غالب (اور) بخشنے والا ہے ﴿۵﴾
اُسی نے تم کو ایک شخص سے پیدا کیا پھر اس سے اس کا
جوڑا بنایا اور اُسی نے تمہارے لئے چارپایوں میں سے
آٹھ جوڑے بنائے۔ وہی تمکو تمہاری ماؤں کے پیٹ میں (پہلے)
ایک طرح پھر دوسری طرح تین اندھیروں میں بناتا ہے۔ یہی خدا
تمہارا پروردگار ہے اُسی کی بادشاہی ہے۔ اس کے سوا
کوئی معبود نہیں۔ پھر تم کہاں پھرے جاتے ہو ﴿۶﴾
اگر ناشکری کروگے تو خدا تم سے بے پرواہ ہے۔ اور وہ
اپنے بندوں کیلئے ناشکری پسند نہیں کرتا ف۲۵ اور اگر شکر
کروگے تو وہ اس کو تمہارے لئے پسند کریگا۔ اور کوئی اٹھانیوالا
دوسرے کا بوجھ نہیں اٹھائیگا۔ پھر تمکو اپنے پروردگار کیطرف لوٹنا ہے پھر جو
کچھ تم کرتے رہے وہ تمکو بتائیگا وہ تو دلوں کی پوشیدہ باتوں تک سے آگاہ ہے ﴿۷﴾
اور جب انسان کو تکلیف پہنچتی ہے تو اپنے پروردگار کو پکارتا
(اور) اُسکی طرف دل سے رجوع کرتا ہے۔ پھر جب وہ اس کو
اپنی طرف سے کوئی نعمت دیتا ہے تو جس کام کیلئے پہلے اُس کو پکارتا
ہے اُسے بھول جاتا ہے اور خدا کا شریک بنانے لگتا ہے تاکہ
(لوگوں کو) اُسکے رستے سے گمراہ کرے۔ کہہ دو کہ (اے کافر نعمت)
اپنی ناشکری سے تھوڑا سا فائدہ اٹھالے پھر تو تُو دوزخیوں میں ہوگا ﴿۸﴾
(بھلا مشرک اچھا ہے) یا وہ جو رات کے وقتوں میں زمین پر پیشانی رکھ کر
اور کھڑے ہو کر عبادت کرتا اور آخرت سے ڈرتا اور اپنے پروردگار کی
رحمت کی امید رکھتا ہے۔ کہو بھلا جو لوگ علم رکھتے ہیں اور جو نہیں رکھتے

لَوْ أَرَادَ اللَّهُ أَنْ يَتَّخِذَ وَلَدًا لَّاصْطَفَىٰ
مِمَّا يَخْلُقُ مَا يَشَاءُ ۚ سُبْحَانَهُ ۖ هُوَ اللَّهُ
الْوَاحِدُ الْقَهَّارُ ﴿٤﴾
خَلَقَ السَّمَاوَاتِ وَالْأَرْضَ بِالْحَقِّ ۖ يُكَوِّرُ
اللَّيْلَ عَلَى النَّهَارِ وَيُكَوِّرُ النَّهَارَ عَلَى
اللَّيْلِ ۖ وَسَخَّرَ الشَّمْسَ وَالْقَمَرَ ۖ كُلٌّ يَجْرِي
لِأَجَلٍ مُّسَمًّى ۗ أَلَا هُوَ الْعَزِيزُ الْغَفَّارُ ﴿٥﴾
خَلَقَكُم مِّن نَّفْسٍ وَاحِدَةٍ ثُمَّ جَعَلَ
مِنْهَا زَوْجَهَا وَأَنزَلَ لَكُم مِّنَ الْأَنْعَامِ
ثَمَانِيَةَ أَزْوَاجٍ ۚ يَخْلُقُكُمْ فِي بُطُونِ أُمَّهَاتِكُمْ
خَلْقًا مِّن بَعْدِ خَلْقٍ فِي ظُلُمَاتٍ ثَلَاثٍ ۚ
ذَٰلِكُمُ اللَّهُ رَبُّكُمْ لَهُ الْمُلْكُ ۖ لَا إِلَٰهَ إِلَّا
هُوَ ۖ فَأَنَّىٰ تُصْرَفُونَ ﴿٦﴾
إِن تَكْفُرُوا فَإِنَّ اللَّهَ غَنِيٌّ عَنكُمْ ۖ وَلَا
يَرْضَىٰ لِعِبَادِهِ الْكُفْرَ ۖ وَإِن تَشْكُرُوا
يَرْضَهُ لَكُمْ ۗ وَلَا تَزِرُ وَازِرَةٌ وِزْرَ أُخْرَىٰ ۗ
ثُمَّ إِلَىٰ رَبِّكُم مَّرْجِعُكُمْ فَيُنَبِّئُكُم بِمَا كُنتُمْ
تَعْمَلُونَ ۚ إِنَّهُ عَلِيمٌ بِذَاتِ الصُّدُورِ ﴿٧﴾
وَإِذَا مَسَّ الْإِنسَانَ ضُرٌّ دَعَا رَبَّهُ
مُنِيبًا إِلَيْهِ ثُمَّ إِذَا خَوَّلَهُ نِعْمَةً مِّنْهُ
نَسِيَ مَا كَانَ يَدْعُو إِلَيْهِ مِن قَبْلُ وَ
جَعَلَ لِلَّهِ أَندَادًا لِّيُضِلَّ عَن سَبِيلِهِ ۚ
قُلْ تَمَتَّعْ بِكُفْرِكَ قَلِيلًا ۖ إِنَّكَ مِنْ
أَصْحَابِ النَّارِ ﴿٨﴾
أَمَّنْ هُوَ قَانِتٌ آنَاءَ اللَّيْلِ سَاجِدًا وَ
قَائِمًا يَحْذَرُ الْآخِرَةَ وَيَرْجُو رَحْمَةَ رَبِّهِ ۗ
قُلْ هَلْ يَسْتَوِي الَّذِينَ يَعْلَمُونَ وَالَّذِينَ

equal, those who know and those who do not know?" It is those who are endued with understanding that receive admonition.

10. Say: "O ye My servants who believe! fear your Lord. Good is (the reward) for those who do good in this world. Spacious is Allah's earth! Those who patiently persevere will truly receive a reward without measure!"

11. Say: "Verily, I am commanded to serve Allah with sincere devotion;

12. "And I am commanded to be the first of those who submit to Allah in Islam."

13. Say: "I would, if I disobeyed my Lord, indeed have fear of the Chastisement of a Mighty Day."

14. Say: "It is Allah I serve, with my sincere (and exclusive) devotion:

15. "Serve ye what ye will besides Him." Say: "Truly, those in loss are those who lose their own souls and their people on the Day of Judgment: ah! that is indeed the (real and) evident Loss!

16. They shall have Layers of Fire above them, and Layers (of Fire) below them: with this doth Allah warn off His servants: "O My Servants! then fear ye Me!"

17. Those who eschew Taghut and fall not into its worship,—and turn to Allah (in repentance),— for them is Good News: so announce the Good News to My Servants,—

18. Those who listen to the Word, and follow the best of it: those are the ones who Allah has guided, and those are the ones endued with understanding.

19. Is, then, one against whom the decree of Punishment is justly due (equal to one who eschews evil)? Wouldst thou, then, deliver one (who is) in the Fire?

20. But it is for those who fear their Lord, that lofty mansions, one

دونوں برابر ہوسکتے ہیں۔ (اور) نصیحت تو وہی پکڑتے ہیں جو عقلمند ہیں ﴿٩﴾
کہہ دو کہ اے میرے بندو جو ایمان لائے ہو اپنے پروردگار
سے ڈرو جنہوں نے اس دنیا میں نیکی کی اُن کے لئے بھلائی
ہے۔ اور خدا کی زمین کشادہ ہے۔ جو صبر کرنے والے ہیں اُنکو
بےشمار ثواب ملے گا ﴿١٠﴾
کہہ دو کہ مجھ سے ارشاد ہوا ہے کہ خدا کی عبادت کو خالص
کرکے اس کی بندگی کروں ﴿١١﴾
اور یہ بھی ارشاد ہوا ہے کہ میں سب سے اوّل مسلمان بنوں ﴿١٢﴾
کہہ دو کہ اگر میں اپنے پروردگار کا حکم نہ مانوں تو مجھے بڑے
دن کے عذاب سے ڈر لگتا ہے ﴿١٣﴾
کہہ دو کہ میں اپنے دین کو (شرک سے) خالص کرکے اُسکی عبادت کرتا ہوں ﴿١٤﴾
تو تم اسکے سوا جس کی چاہو پرستش کرو۔ کہہ دو کہ نقصان
اٹھانے والے وہی لوگ ہیں جنہوں نے قیامت کے دن
اپنے آپ کو اور اپنے گھر والوں کو نقصان میں ڈالا۔ دیکھو
یہی صریح نقصان ہے ﴿١٥﴾
اُن کے اُوپر تو آگ کے سائبان ہوں گے اور نیچے (اُسکے)
فرش ہوں گے[٢٥١]۔ یہ وہ (عذاب) ہے جس سے خدا اپنے بندوں کو
ڈراتا ہے۔ تو اے میرے بندو مجھ سے ڈرتے رہو ﴿١٦﴾
اور جنہوں نے اس سے اجتناب کیا کہ بتوں کو پوجیں اور
خدا کی طرف رجوع کیا اُن کے لئے بشارت ہے۔ تو میرے
بندوں کو بشارت سنا دو ﴿١٧﴾
جو بات کو سنتے اور اچھی باتوں[٢٥٢] کی پیروی کرتے ہیں۔
یہی وہ لوگ ہیں جن کو خدا نے ہدایت دی اور یہی عقل
والے ہیں ﴿١٨﴾
بھلا جس شخص پر عذاب کا حکم صادر ہو چکا۔ تو کیا تم
(ایسے) دوزخی کو مخلصی دے سکو گے؟ ﴿١٩﴾
لیکن جو لوگ اپنے پروردگار سے ڈرتے ہیں اُن کیلئے اونچے اونچے

ع ٥ ١٥ لَا يَعْلَمُونَ ۗ إِنَّمَا يَتَذَكَّرُ أُولُوا الْأَلْبَابِ ﴿٩﴾
قُلْ يَا عِبَادِ الَّذِينَ آمَنُوا اتَّقُوا رَبَّكُمْ ۚ
لِلَّذِينَ أَحْسَنُوا فِي هَٰذِهِ الدُّنْيَا حَسَنَةٌ ۗ
وَأَرْضُ اللَّهِ وَاسِعَةٌ ۗ إِنَّمَا يُوَفَّى الصَّابِرُونَ
أَجْرَهُمْ بِغَيْرِ حِسَابٍ ﴿١٠﴾
قُلْ إِنِّي أُمِرْتُ أَنْ أَعْبُدَ اللَّهَ مُخْلِصًا
لَهُ الدِّينَ ﴿١١﴾
وَأُمِرْتُ لِأَنْ أَكُونَ أَوَّلَ الْمُسْلِمِينَ ﴿١٢﴾
قُلْ إِنِّي أَخَافُ إِنْ عَصَيْتُ رَبِّي عَذَابَ
يَوْمٍ عَظِيمٍ ﴿١٣﴾
قُلِ اللَّهَ أَعْبُدُ مُخْلِصًا لَهُ دِينِي ﴿١٤﴾
فَاعْبُدُوا مَا شِئْتُمْ مِنْ دُونِهِ ۗ قُلْ
إِنَّ الْخَاسِرِينَ الَّذِينَ خَسِرُوا أَنْفُسَهُمْ
وَأَهْلِيهِمْ يَوْمَ الْقِيَامَةِ ۗ أَلَا ذَٰلِكَ هُوَ
الْخُسْرَانُ الْمُبِينُ ﴿١٥﴾
لَهُمْ مِنْ فَوْقِهِمْ ظُلَلٌ مِنَ النَّارِ وَ
مِنْ تَحْتِهِمْ ظُلَلٌ ۚ ذَٰلِكَ يُخَوِّفُ اللَّهُ
بِهِ عِبَادَهُ ۚ يَا عِبَادِ فَاتَّقُونِ ﴿١٦﴾
وَالَّذِينَ اجْتَنَبُوا الطَّاغُوتَ أَنْ
يَعْبُدُوهَا وَأَنَابُوا إِلَى اللَّهِ لَهُمُ
الْبُشْرَىٰ ۚ فَبَشِّرْ عِبَادِ ﴿١٧﴾
الَّذِينَ يَسْتَمِعُونَ الْقَوْلَ فَيَتَّبِعُونَ
أَحْسَنَهُ ۚ أُولَٰئِكَ الَّذِينَ هَدَاهُمُ اللَّهُ
وَأُولَٰئِكَ هُمْ أُولُو الْأَلْبَابِ ﴿١٨﴾
أَفَمَنْ حَقَّ عَلَيْهِ كَلِمَةُ الْعَذَابِ أَفَأَنْتَ
تُنْقِذُ مَنْ فِي النَّارِ ﴿١٩﴾
لَٰكِنِ الَّذِينَ اتَّقَوْا رَبَّهُمْ لَهُمْ غُرَفٌ

above another, have been built: beneath them flow rivers: (such is) the Promise of Allah: never doth Allah fail in (His) promise.

21. Seest thou not that Allah sends down rain from the sky, and leads it through springs in the earth? Then He causes to grow, therewith, produce of various colours: then it withers; thou wilt see it grow yellow; then He makes it dry up and crumble away. Truly, in this, is a Message of remembrance to men of understanding.

22. Is one whose heart Allah has opened to Islam, so that he has received Light from Allah, (no better than one hard-hearted)? Woe to those whose hearts are hardened against the remembrance of Allah! They are manifestly wandering (in error)!

23. Allah has revealed (from time to time) the most beautiful Message in the form of a Book, consistent with itself, (yet) repeating (its teaching in various aspects): the skins of those who fear their Lord tremble threat; then their skins and their hearts do soften to the remembrance of Allah. Such is the guidance of Allah; He guides therewith whom He pleases, but such as Allah leaves to stray, can have none to guide.

24. Is, then, one who has to ward off the brunt of the Chastisement on the Day of Judgment (and receive it) by his face, (like one guarded therefrom)? It will be said to the wrong-doers: "Taste ye (the fruits of) what ye earned!"

25. Those before them (also) rejected (revelation), and so the Punishment came to them from directions they did not perceive.

26. So Allah gave them a taste of humiliation in the present life, but greater is the Punishment of the Hereafter, if they only knew!

27. We have put forth for men, in the Qur'an every kind of Parable, in order that they may receive admonition.

28. (It is) a Qur-ān in Arabic, without any crookedness (therein):

محل ہیں جنکے اُوپر بالاخانے بنے ہوئے ہیں۔ (اور) اُنکے نیچے نہریں
بہہ رہی ہیں۔ (یہ) خدا کا وعدہ ہے خدا وعدے کے خلاف نہیں کرتا ﴿٢٠﴾
کیا تم نے نہیں دیکھا کہ خدا آسمان سے پانی نازل کرتا پھر اُس کو
زمین میں چشمے بنا کر جاری کرتا پھر اس سے کھیتی اگاتا ہے
جس کے طرح طرح کے رنگ ہوتے ہیں۔ پھر وہ خشک ہو جاتی ہے تو تم
اسکو دیکھتے ہو کہ (زرد) ہو گئی ہے پھر اُسے چورا چورا کر دیتا ہے
بیشک اس میں عقل والوں کے لئے نصیحت ہے ﴿٢١﴾
بھلا جس شخص کا سینہ خدا نے اسلام کیلئے کھول دیا ہو اور وہ
اپنے پروردگار کی طرف سے روشنی پر ہو تو کیا وہ سخت دل کافر کی
طرح ہو سکتا ہے پس اُن پر افسوس ہے جن کے دل خدا کی یاد سے
سخت ہو رہے ہیں۔ اور یہی لوگ صریح گمراہی میں ہیں ﴿٢٢﴾
خدا نے نہایت اچھی باتیں نازل فرمائی ہیں (یعنی) کتاب (جسکی آیتیں باہم)
ملتی جلتی (ہیں) اور دُہرائی جاتی (ہیں) جو لوگ اپنے پروردگار سے ڈرتے
ہیں اُنکے بدن کے (اس سے) رونگٹے کھڑے ہو جاتے ہیں پھر اُنکے بدن اور دل
نرم (ہو کر) خدا کی یاد کیطرف (متوجہ) ہو جاتے ہیں۔ یہی خدا کی ہدایت
ہے وہ اس سے جس کو چاہتا ہے ہدایت دیتا ہے۔ اور جس کو خدا
گمراہ کرے اُس کو کوئی ہدایت دینے والا نہیں ﴿٢٣﴾
بھلا جو شخص قیامت کے دن اپنے منہ سے بُرے عذاب کو
روکتا ہو (کیا وہ ویسا ہو سکتا ہے جو چین میں ہو) اور ظالموں
سے کہا جائیگا کہ جو کچھ تم کرتے رہے تھے اُسکے مزے چکھو ﴿٢٤﴾
جو لوگ ان سے پہلے تھے اُنہوں نے بھی تکذیب کی تھی
تو اُن پر عذاب ایسی جگہ سے آگیا کہ اُن کو خبر ہی نہ تھی ﴿٢٥﴾
پھر اُن کو خدا نے دنیا کی زندگی میں رسوائی کا مزہ چکھا دیا
اور آخرت کا عذاب تو بہت بڑا ہے۔ کاش یہ سمجھ رکھتے ﴿٢٦﴾
اور ہم نے لوگوں کے (سمجھانے کے) لئے اس قرآن میں ہر طرح
کی مثالیں بیان کی ہیں تاکہ وہ نصیحت پکڑیں ﴿٢٧﴾
(یہ) قرآن عربی (ہے) جس میں کوئی عیب (اور اختلاف)

من فوقها غرف مبنية تجري من تحتها
الأنهار وعد الله لا يخلف الله الميعاد ﴿٢٠﴾
ألم تر أن الله أنزل من السماء ماء
فسلكه ينابيع في الأرض ثم يخرج
به زرعا مختلفا ألوانه ثم يهيج
فتراه مصفرا ثم يجعله حطاما
إن في ذلك لذكرى لأولي الألباب ﴿٢١﴾
أفمن شرح الله صدره للإسلام
فهو على نور من ربه فويل للقاسية
قلوبهم من ذكر الله أولئك في
ضلال مبين ﴿٢٢﴾
الله نزل أحسن الحديث كتابا
متشابها مثاني تقشعر منه جلود
الذين يخشون ربهم ثم تلين
جلودهم وقلوبهم إلى ذكر الله
ذلك هدى الله يهدي به من يشاء
ومن يضلل الله فما له من هاد ﴿٢٣﴾
أفمن يتقي بوجهه سوء العذاب
يوم القيامة وقيل للظالمين ذوقوا
ما كنتم تكسبون ﴿٢٤﴾
كذب الذين من قبلهم فأتاهم
العذاب من حيث لا يشعرون ﴿٢٥﴾
فأذاقهم الله الخزي في الحياة الدنيا
ولعذاب الآخرة أكبر لو كانوا يعلمون ﴿٢٦﴾
ولقد ضربنا للناس في هذا القرآن
من كل مثل لعلهم يتذكرون ﴿٢٧﴾
قرآنا عربيا غير ذي عوج لعلهم

in order that they may guard against Evil.

نہیں تاکہ وہ ڈر مانیں ﴿۲۸﴾

يَتَّقُوْنَ ﴿٢٨﴾

29. Allah puts forth a Parable— a man belonging to many partners at variance with each other, and a man belonging entirely to one master: are those two equal in comparison? Praise be to Allah! but most of them have no knowledge.

خدا ایک مثال بیان کرتا ہے کہ ایک شخص ہے جس میں کئی
(آدمی) شریک ہیں۔ (مختلف المزاج اور) بدخو اور ایک آدمی خاص
ایک شخص کا (غلام) ہے۔ بھلا دونوں کی حالت برابر ہے؟ (نہیں) الحمدللہ
بلکہ یہ اکثر لوگ نہیں جانتے ﴿۲۹﴾

ضَرَبَ اللّٰهُ مَثَلًا رَّجُلًا فِيْهِ شُرَكَآءُ
مُتَشٰكِسُوْنَ وَرَجُلًا سَلَمًا لِّرَجُلٍ ؕ
هَلْ يَسْتَوِيٰنِ مَثَلًا ؕ اَلْحَمْدُ لِلّٰهِ ؕ بَلْ
اَكْثَرُهُمْ لَا يَعْلَمُوْنَ ﴿٢٩﴾

30. Truly thou wilt die (one day), and truly they (too) will die (one day).

(اے پیغمبر) تم بھی مرجاؤ گے اور یہ بھی مرجائیں گے ﴿۳۰﴾ ۲۵۳

اِنَّكَ مَيِّتٌ وَّاِنَّهُمْ مَّيِّتُوْنَ ﴿٣٠﴾

31. In the End will ye (all) dispute on the Day of Judgment, in the presence of your Lord.

پھر تم سب قیامت کے دن اپنے پروردگار کے سامنے
جھگڑو گے (اور جھگڑا فیصل کر دیا جائے گا) ﴿۳۱﴾

ثُمَّ اِنَّكُمْ يَوْمَ الْقِيٰمَةِ عِنْدَ رَبِّكُمْ
تَخْتَصِمُوْنَ ﴿٣١﴾

الجزء الرابع والعشرون

32. Who, then, doth more wrong than one who utters a lie concerning Allah and rejects the Truth when it comes to him! Is there not in Hell an abode for the unbelievers?

تو اس سے بڑھ کر ظالم کون جو خدا پر جھوٹ بولے اور
سچی بات جب اس کے پاس پہنچ جائے تو اسے جھٹلائے۔
کیا جہنم میں کافروں کا ٹھکانا نہیں ہے؟ ﴿۳۲﴾

فَمَنْ اَظْلَمُ مِمَّنْ كَذَبَ عَلَى
اللّٰهِ وَكَذَّبَ بِالصِّدْقِ اِذْ جَآءَهٗ ؕ
اَلَيْسَ فِيْ جَهَنَّمَ مَثْوًى لِّلْكٰفِرِيْنَ ﴿٣٢﴾

33. And he who brings the Truth and he who confirms (and supports) it—such are the men who do right.

اور جو شخص سچی بات لے کر آیا اور جس نے اس کی تصدیق
کی وہی لوگ متقی ہیں ﴿۳۳﴾

وَالَّذِيْ جَآءَ بِالصِّدْقِ وَصَدَّقَ بِهٖٓ
اُولٰٓئِكَ هُمُ الْمُتَّقُوْنَ ﴿٣٣﴾

34. They shall have all that they wish for, with their Lord: such is the reward of those who do good:

وہ جو چاہیں گے ان کیلئے ان کے پروردگار کے پاس (موجود)
ہے نیکوکاروں کا یہی بدلہ ہے ﴿۳۴﴾

لَهُمْ مَّا يَشَآءُوْنَ عِنْدَ رَبِّهِمْ ؕ ذٰلِكَ
جَزٰٓؤُا الْمُحْسِنِيْنَ ﴿٣٤﴾

35. So that Allah will remit from them (even) the worst in their deeds and give them their reward according to the best of what they have done.

تاکہ خدا ان سے برائیوں کو جو انہوں نے کیں دور کر دے
اور نیک کاموں کا جو وہ کرتے رہے ان کو
بدلہ دے ﴿۳۵﴾

لِيُكَفِّرَ اللّٰهُ عَنْهُمْ اَسْوَاَ الَّذِيْ عَمِلُوْا
وَيَجْزِيَهُمْ اَجْرَهُمْ بِاَحْسَنِ الَّذِيْ كَانُوْا
يَعْمَلُوْنَ ﴿٣٥﴾

36. Is not Allah enough for His servant? But they try to frighten thee with other (gods) besides Him! for such as Allah leaves to stray, there can be no guide.

کیا خدا اپنے بندے کو کافی نہیں؟ اور یہ تم کو ان لوگوں سے
جو اس کے سوا ہیں (یعنی غیر خدا سے) ڈراتے ہیں۔ اور
جس کو خدا گمراہ کرے اسے کوئی ہدایت دینے والا نہیں ﴿۳۶﴾

اَلَيْسَ اللّٰهُ بِكَافٍ عَبْدَهٗ ؕ وَيُخَوِّفُوْنَكَ
بِالَّذِيْنَ مِنْ دُوْنِهٖ ؕ وَمَنْ يُّضْلِلِ اللّٰهُ
فَمَا لَهٗ مِنْ هَادٍ ﴿٣٦﴾

37. And such as Allah doth guide there can be none to lead astray. Is not Allah Exalted in Power, Lord of Retribution?

اور جس کو خدا ہدایت دے اس کو کوئی گمراہ کرنے والا نہیں۔
کیا خدا غالب (اور) بدلہ لینے والا نہیں ہے؟ ﴿۳۷﴾

وَمَنْ يَّهْدِ اللّٰهُ فَمَا لَهٗ مِنْ مُّضِلٍّ ؕ
اَلَيْسَ اللّٰهُ بِعَزِيْزٍ ذِي انْتِقَامٍ ﴿٣٧﴾

38. If indeed thou ask them who it is that created the heavens and the earth, they would be sure to say, "Allah". Say: "See ye then? The things that ye invoke besides Allah,—can they, if Allah wills some affliction for me, remove His affliction or if He wills some Mercy

اور اگر تم ان سے پوچھو کہ آسمانوں اور زمین کو کس نے
پیدا کیا تو کہہ دیں کہ خدا نے۔ کہو کہ بھلا دیکھو تو جن کو
تم خدا کے سوا پکارتے ہو اگر خدا مجھ کو کوئی تکلیف پہنچانی
چاہے تو کیا وہ اس تکلیف کو دور کر سکتے ہیں یا اگر مجھ پر مہربانی

وَلَئِنْ سَاَلْتَهُمْ مَّنْ خَلَقَ السَّمٰوٰتِ
وَالْاَرْضَ لَيَقُوْلُنَّ اللّٰهُ ؕ قُلْ اَفَرَءَيْتُمْ
مَّا تَدْعُوْنَ مِنْ دُوْنِ اللّٰهِ اِنْ اَرَادَنِيَ
اللّٰهُ بِضُرٍّ هَلْ هُنَّ كٰشِفٰتُ ضُرِّهٖٓ اَوْ اَرَادَنِيْ

for me, can they keep back His Mercy" Say: "Sufficient is Allah for me! In Him trust those who put their trust."

39. Say: "O my people! do whatever ye can: I will do (my part): but soon will ye know—

40. "Who it is to whom comes a Chastisement or ignominy, and on whom Descends a Chastisement that abides."

41. Verily We have revealed the Book to thee in Truth, for (instructing) mankind. He, then, that receives guidance benefits his own soul: but he that strays injures his own soul. Nor art thou set a Custodian over them.

42. It is Allah that takes the souls (of men) at death; and those that die not (He takes) during their sleep: those on whom He has passed the decree of death, He keeps back (from returning to life), but the rest He sends (to their bodies) for a term appointed. Verily in this are Signs for those who reflect.

43. What! Do they take for intercessors others besides Allah? Say: "Even if they have no power whatever and no intelligence?"

44. Say: "To Allah belongs exclusively (the right) to grant) Intercession: to Him belongs the dominion of the heavens and the earth: in the End, it is to Him that ye shall be brought back."

45. When Allah, Alone is mentioned, the hearts of those who believe not in the Hereafter are filled with disgust; but when (gods) other than He are mentioned, behold, they are filled with joy!

46. Say: "O Allah! Creator of the heavens and the earth! Knower of all that is hidden and open ! It is Thou that wilt judge between Thy Servants in those matters about which they have differed."

47. Even if the wrong-doers had all that there is on earth, and as much more, (in vain) would they offer it for ransom from the pain of the Chastisement on the Day of

کرنا چاہے تو وہ اسکی مہربانی کو روک سکتے ہیں؟ کہہ دو کہ مجھے
خدا ہی کافی ہے۔ بھروسا رکھنے والے اُسی پر بھروسا رکھتے ہیں (۳۸)
کہہ دو کہ اے قوم تم اپنی جگہ عمل کئے جاؤ میں (اپنی جگہ)
عمل کئے جاتا ہوں۔ عنقریب تم کو معلوم ہو جائیگا (۳۹)
کہ کس پر عذاب آتا ہے جو اُسے رسوا کرے گا۔ اور کس پر
ہمیشہ کا عذاب نازل ہوتا ہے (۴۰)
ہم نے تم پر کتاب لوگوں (کی ہدایت) کیلئے سچائی کیساتھ نازل
کی ہے۔ تو جو شخص ہدایت پاتا ہے تو اپنے (بھلے کے) لئے۔ اور جو گمراہ
ہوتا ہے تو گمراہی سے اپنا ہی نقصان کرتا ہے۔ اور (اے پیغمبر) تم اُنکے ذمہ دار نہیں ہو (۴۱)
خدا لوگوں کے مرنے کے وقت انکی روحیں قبض کرلیتا ہے اور جو
مرے نہیں (اُنکی روحیں) سوتے میں (قبض کرلیتا ہے) پھر جن پر موت کا حکم
کر چکتا ہے انکو روک رکھتا ہے اور باقی روحوں کو ایک وقت مقرر تک کیلئے
چھوڑ دیتا ہے۔ جو لوگ فکر کرتے ہیں اُن کیلئے اسمیں نشانیاں ہیں (۴۲)
کیا اُنہوں نے خدا کے سوا اور سفارشی بنالئے ہیں۔ کہو کہ خواہ وہ کسی
چیز کا بھی اختیار نہ رکھتے ہوں اور نہ (کچھ) سمجھتے ہی ہوں؟ (۴۳)
کہہ دو کہ سفارش تو سب خدا ہی کے اختیار میں ہے۔ اسی کیلئے آسمانوں
اور زمین کی بادشاہت ہے۔ پھر تم اُسی کی طرف لوٹ کر جاؤ گے (۴۴)
اور جب تنہا خدا کا ذکر کیا جاتا ہے تو جو لوگ آخرت پر
ایمان نہیں رکھتے اُن کے دل منقبض ہو جاتے
ہیں۔ اور جب اس کے سوا اوروں کا ذکر کیا جاتا ہے
تو خوش ہو جاتے ہیں (۴۵)
کہو کہ اے خدا! (اے) آسمانوں اور زمین کے پیدا کرنے
والے (اور) پوشیدہ اور ظاہر کے جاننے والے تو ہی اپنے بندوں
میں ان باتوں کا جن میں وہ اختلاف کرتے رہے ہیں فیصلہ کریگا (۴۶)
اور اگر ظالموں کے پاس وہ سب (مال ومتاع) ہو جو زمین
میں ہے اور اسکے ساتھ اسی قدر اور ہو تو قیامت کے روز برے
عذاب (سے مخلصی پانے) کے بدلے میں دیدیں۔ اور اُن پر خدا

بِرَحْمَتِهِ هَلْ هُنَّ مُمْسِكَاتُ رَحْمَتِهِ ۚ قُلْ
حَسْبِيَ اللَّهُ ۖ عَلَيْهِ يَتَوَكَّلُ الْمُتَوَكِّلُونَ ﴿٣٨﴾
قُلْ يَا قَوْمِ اعْمَلُوا عَلَىٰ مَكَانَتِكُمْ إِنِّي
عَامِلٌ ۖ فَسَوْفَ تَعْلَمُونَ ﴿٣٩﴾
مَنْ يَأْتِيهِ عَذَابٌ يُخْزِيهِ وَيَحِلُّ
عَلَيْهِ عَذَابٌ مُقِيمٌ ﴿٤٠﴾
إِنَّا أَنْزَلْنَا عَلَيْكَ الْكِتَابَ لِلنَّاسِ بِالْحَقِّ ۖ
فَمَنِ اهْتَدَىٰ فَلِنَفْسِهِ ۖ وَمَنْ ضَلَّ فَإِنَّمَا
يَضِلُّ عَلَيْهَا ۖ وَمَا أَنْتَ عَلَيْهِمْ بِوَكِيلٍ ﴿٤١﴾
اللَّهُ يَتَوَفَّى الْأَنْفُسَ حِينَ مَوْتِهَا وَالَّتِي
لَمْ تَمُتْ فِي مَنَامِهَا ۖ فَيُمْسِكُ الَّتِي قَضَىٰ
عَلَيْهَا الْمَوْتَ وَيُرْسِلُ الْأُخْرَىٰ إِلَىٰ أَجَلٍ
مُسَمًّى ۚ إِنَّ فِي ذَٰلِكَ لَآيَاتٍ لِقَوْمٍ يَتَفَكَّرُونَ ﴿٤٢﴾
أَمِ اتَّخَذُوا مِنْ دُونِ اللَّهِ شُفَعَاءَ ۚ قُلْ
أَوَلَوْ كَانُوا لَا يَمْلِكُونَ شَيْئًا وَلَا يَعْقِلُونَ ﴿٤٣﴾
قُلْ لِلَّهِ الشَّفَاعَةُ جَمِيعًا ۖ لَهُ مُلْكُ
السَّمَاوَاتِ وَالْأَرْضِ ۖ ثُمَّ إِلَيْهِ تُرْجَعُونَ ﴿٤٤﴾
وَإِذَا ذُكِرَ اللَّهُ وَحْدَهُ اشْمَأَزَّتْ
قُلُوبُ الَّذِينَ لَا يُؤْمِنُونَ بِالْآخِرَةِ ۖ
وَإِذَا ذُكِرَ الَّذِينَ مِنْ دُونِهِ إِذَا
هُمْ يَسْتَبْشِرُونَ ﴿٤٥﴾
قُلِ اللَّهُمَّ فَاطِرَ السَّمَاوَاتِ وَالْأَرْضِ
عَالِمَ الْغَيْبِ وَالشَّهَادَةِ أَنْتَ تَحْكُمُ بَيْنَ
عِبَادِكَ فِي مَا كَانُوا فِيهِ يَخْتَلِفُونَ ﴿٤٦﴾
وَلَوْ أَنَّ لِلَّذِينَ ظَلَمُوا مَا فِي الْأَرْضِ
جَمِيعًا وَمِثْلَهُ مَعَهُ لَافْتَدَوْا بِهِ مِنْ
سُوءِ الْعَذَابِ يَوْمَ الْقِيَامَةِ ۚ وَبَدَا لَهُمْ

مِّنَ اللَّهِ مَا لَمْ يَكُونُوا يَحْتَسِبُونَ ﴿٤٧﴾
وَبَدَا لَهُمْ سَيِّئَاتُ مَا كَسَبُوا وَحَاقَ بِهِم
مَّا كَانُوا بِهِ يَسْتَهْزِءُونَ ﴿٤٨﴾
فَإِذَا مَسَّ الْإِنسَانَ ضُرٌّ دَعَانَا ثُمَّ
إِذَا خَوَّلْنَاهُ نِعْمَةً مِّنَّا قَالَ إِنَّمَا
أُوتِيتُهُ عَلَىٰ عِلْمٍ ۚ بَلْ هِيَ فِتْنَةٌ وَلَٰكِنَّ
أَكْثَرَهُمْ لَا يَعْلَمُونَ ﴿٤٩﴾
قَدْ قَالَهَا الَّذِينَ مِن قَبْلِهِمْ فَمَا أَغْنَىٰ
عَنْهُم مَّا كَانُوا يَكْسِبُونَ ﴿٥٠﴾
فَأَصَابَهُمْ سَيِّئَاتُ مَا كَسَبُوا ۚ وَالَّذِينَ
ظَلَمُوا مِنْ هَٰؤُلَاءِ سَيُصِيبُهُمْ سَيِّئَاتُ
مَا كَسَبُوا وَمَا هُم بِمُعْجِزِينَ ﴿٥١﴾
أَوَلَمْ يَعْلَمُوا أَنَّ اللَّهَ يَبْسُطُ الرِّزْقَ
لِمَن يَشَاءُ وَيَقْدِرُ ۚ إِنَّ فِي ذَٰلِكَ لَآيَاتٍ
لِّقَوْمٍ يُؤْمِنُونَ ﴿٥٢﴾
قُلْ يَا عِبَادِيَ الَّذِينَ أَسْرَفُوا عَلَىٰ أَنفُسِهِمْ
لَا تَقْنَطُوا مِن رَّحْمَةِ اللَّهِ ۚ إِنَّ اللَّهَ يَغْفِرُ
الذُّنُوبَ جَمِيعًا ۚ إِنَّهُ هُوَ الْغَفُورُ الرَّحِيمُ ﴿٥٣﴾
وَأَنِيبُوا إِلَىٰ رَبِّكُمْ وَأَسْلِمُوا لَهُ مِن قَبْلِ
أَن يَأْتِيَكُمُ الْعَذَابُ ثُمَّ لَا تُنصَرُونَ ﴿٥٤﴾
وَاتَّبِعُوا أَحْسَنَ مَا أُنزِلَ إِلَيْكُم مِّن
رَّبِّكُم مِّن قَبْلِ أَن يَأْتِيَكُمُ الْعَذَابُ
بَغْتَةً وَأَنتُمْ لَا تَشْعُرُونَ ﴿٥٥﴾
أَن تَقُولَ نَفْسٌ يَا حَسْرَتَىٰ عَلَىٰ مَا فَرَّطتُ
فِي جَنبِ اللَّهِ وَإِن كُنتُ لَمِنَ
السَّاخِرِينَ ﴿٥٦﴾
أَوْ تَقُولَ لَوْ أَنَّ اللَّهَ هَدَانِي لَكُنتُ

کی طرف سے وہ امر ظاہر ہو جائیگا جس کا اُن کو خیال بھی نہ تھا ﴿۴۷﴾
اور اُنکے اعمال کی بُرائیاں اُن پر ظاہر ہو جائیں گی اور جس
(عذاب) کی وہ ہنسی اُڑاتے تھے وہ اُن کو آگھیرے گا ﴿۴۸﴾
جب انسان کو تکلیف پہنچتی ہے تو ہمیں پکارنے لگتا ہے۔
پھر جب ہم اُس کو اپنی طرف سے نعمت بخشتے ہیں تو
کہتا ہے کہ یہ تو مجھے (میرے) علم (و دانش) کے سبب ملی ہے۔
(نہیں) بلکہ وہ آزمائش ہے مگر اُن میں سے اکثر نہیں جانتے ﴿۴۹﴾
جو لوگ اُن سے پہلے تھے وہ بھی یہی کہا کرتے تھے تو جو کچھ
وہ کیا کرتے تھے اُن کے کچھ کام بھی نہ آیا ﴿۵۰﴾
اُن پر اُن کے اعمال کے وبال پڑ گئے۔ اور جو لوگ اُن میں
سے ظلم کرتے رہے ہیں اُن پر اُن کے عملوں کے وبال عنقریب
پڑیں گے۔ اور وہ (خدا کو) عاجز نہیں کر سکتے ﴿۵۱﴾
کیا اُن کو معلوم نہیں کہ خدا ہی جس کیلئے چاہتا ہے رزق کو
فراخ کر دیتا ہے اور (جس کیلئے چاہتا ہے) تنگ کر دیتا ہے۔
جو لوگ ایمان لاتے ہیں اُن کیلئے اسمیں (بہت سی) نشانیاں ہیں ﴿۵۲﴾
(اے پیغمبر میری طرف سے لوگوں کو) کہہ دو کہ اے میرے بندو!
جنہوں نے اپنی جانوں پر زیادتی کی ہے خدا کی رحمت سے ناامید نہ ہونا۔
خدا تو سب گناہوں کو بخش دیتا ہے (اور) وہ تو بخشنے والا مہربان ہے ﴿۵۳﴾
اور اس سے پہلے کہ تم پر عذاب آ واقع ہو اپنے پروردگار کی طرف
رجوع کرو اور اسکے فرمانبردار ہو جاؤ۔ پھر تم کو مدد نہیں ملے گی ﴿۵۴﴾
اور اس سے پہلے کہ تم پر ناگہاں عذاب آجائے اور تم کو خبر بھی
نہ ہو اس نہایت اچھی (کتاب) کی جو تمہارے پروردگار کی
طرف سے تم پر نازل ہوئی ہے پیروی کرو ﴿۵۵﴾
کہ (مبادا) اُس وقت کوئی متنفس کہنے لگے کہ (ہائے
ہائے) اس تقصیر پر افسوس ہے جو میں نے خدا کے
حق میں کی اور میں تو ہنسی ہی کرتا رہا ﴿۵۶﴾
یا یہ کہنے لگے کہ اگر خدا مجھ کو ہدایت دیتا تو میں بھی

Judgment: but something will confront them from Allah, which they could never have counted upon!

48. For the evils of their Deeds will confront them, and they will be (completely) encircled by that which they used to mock at!

49. Now, when trouble touches man, he cries to Us: but when We bestow a favour upon him as from Us, he says, "This has been given to me because of a certain knowledge (I have)! Nay, but this is but a trial, but most of them understand not!

50. Thus did the (generations) before them say! But all that they did was of no profit to them.

51. Nay, the evil results of their deeds overtook them. And the wrong-doers of this (generation)—the evil results of their deeds will soon overtake them (too), and they shall not escape!

52. Know they not that Allah enlarges the provision or restricts it, for any He pleases? Verily, in this are Signs for those who believe!

53. Say: "O my Servants who have transgressed against their souls! despair not of the Mercy of Allah: for Allah forgives all sins: for He is Oft-Forgiving, Most Merciful.

54. "Turn ye to your Lord (in repentance) and submit to Him, before the Chastisement comes on you: after that ye shall not be helped.

55. "And follow the Best that which was revealed to you from your Lord, before the Chastisement comes on you—of a sudden, while ye perceive not!—

56. "Lest the soul should (then) say: 'Ah! woe is me!— In that I neglected (my Duty) towards Allah, and was but among those who mocked!'—

57. "Or (lest) it should say: 'If only Allah had guided me, I should

certainly have been among the righteous!'—
58. "Or (lest) it should say when it (actually) sees the Chastisement: 'If only I had another chance, I should certainly be among those who do good!'
59. "(The reply will be:) 'Nay, but there came to thee My Signs, and thou didst reject them: thou wast Haughty, and became one of those who reject Faith!"
60. On the Day of Judgment wilt thou see those who told lies against Allah;— their faces will be turned black; is there not in Hell an abode for the Haughty?

61. But Allah will deliver the righteous for they have earned salvation: no evil shall touch them, nor shall they grieve.

62. Allah is the Creator of all things, and He is the Guardian and Disposer of all affairs.
63. To Him belong the keys of the heavens and the earth: and those who reject the Signs of Allah,—it is they who will be in loss.

64. Say: "Is it some one other than Allah that ye order me to worship, O ye ignorant ones?"

65. But it has already been revealed to thee,— as it was to those before thee,— "If thou wert to join (gods with Allah), truly fruitless will be thy work (in life), and thou wilt surely be among the losers."
66. Nay, but worship Allah, and be of those who give thanks.
67. No just estimate have they made of Allah, such as is due to Him: on the Day of Judgment the whole of the earth will be but His handful, and the heavens will be rolled up in His right hand: glory to Him ! High is He above the Partners they attribute to Him!
68. The Trumpet will (just) be sounded, when all that are in the heavens and on earth will swoon, except such as it will please Allah (to exempt). Then will a second one

مِنَ الْمُتَّقِينَ ﴿٥٧﴾
أَوْ تَقُولَ حِينَ تَرَى الْعَذَابَ لَوْ أَنَّ
لِي كَرَّةً فَأَكُونَ مِنَ الْمُحْسِنِينَ ﴿٥٨﴾
بَلَىٰ قَدْ جَاءَتْكَ آيَاتِي فَكَذَّبْتَ بِهَا وَ
اسْتَكْبَرْتَ وَكُنْتَ مِنَ الْكٰفِرِينَ ﴿٥٩﴾
وَيَوْمَ الْقِيٰمَةِ تَرَى الَّذِينَ كَذَبُوا عَلَى
اللَّهِ وُجُوهُهُمْ مُسْوَدَّةٌ ؕ أَلَيْسَ فِي
جَهَنَّمَ مَثْوًى لِلْمُتَكَبِّرِينَ ﴿٦٠﴾
وَيُنَجِّي اللَّهُ الَّذِينَ اتَّقَوْا بِمَفَازَتِهِمْ
لَا يَمَسُّهُمُ السُّوءُ وَلَا هُمْ يَحْزَنُونَ ﴿٦١﴾
اللَّهُ خَالِقُ كُلِّ شَيْءٍ ۖ وَهُوَ عَلَىٰ كُلِّ
شَيْءٍ وَكِيلٌ ﴿٦٢﴾
لَهُ مَقَالِيدُ السَّمٰوٰتِ وَالْأَرْضِ ۗ وَالَّذِينَ
ع كَفَرُوا بِآيٰتِ اللَّهِ أُولٰٓئِكَ هُمُ الْخٰسِرُونَ ﴿٦٣﴾
قُلْ أَفَغَيْرَ اللَّهِ تَأْمُرُونِّي أَعْبُدُ أَيُّهَا
الْجٰهِلُونَ ﴿٦٤﴾
وَلَقَدْ أُوحِيَ إِلَيْكَ وَإِلَى الَّذِينَ مِنْ
قَبْلِكَ ۚ لَئِنْ أَشْرَكْتَ لَيَحْبَطَنَّ عَمَلُكَ
وَلَتَكُونَنَّ مِنَ الْخٰسِرِينَ ﴿٦٥﴾
بَلِ اللَّهَ فَاعْبُدْ وَكُنْ مِنَ الشّٰكِرِينَ ﴿٦٦﴾
وَمَا قَدَرُوا اللَّهَ حَقَّ قَدْرِهِ ۖ وَالْأَرْضُ
جَمِيعًا قَبْضَتُهُ يَوْمَ الْقِيٰمَةِ وَالسَّمٰوٰتُ
مَطْوِيّٰتٌ بِيَمِينِهِ ۚ سُبْحٰنَهُ وَتَعٰلَىٰ عَمَّا
يُشْرِكُونَ ﴿٦٧﴾
وَنُفِخَ فِي الصُّورِ فَصَعِقَ مَنْ فِي السَّمٰوٰتِ
وَمَنْ فِي الْأَرْضِ إِلَّا مَنْ شَاءَ اللَّهُ ؕ
ثُمَّ نُفِخَ فِيهِ أُخْرَىٰ فَإِذَا هُمْ قِيَامٌ

پرہیزگاروں میں ہوتا ﴿٥٧﴾
یا جب عذاب دیکھ لے تو کہنے لگے کہ اگر مجھے پھر ایک دفعہ
دنیا میں جانا ہو تو میں نیکوکاروں میں ہو جاؤں ﴿٥٨﴾
(خدا فرمائے گا) کیوں نہیں میری آیتیں تیرے پاس پہنچ گئی
ہیں مگر تو نے ان کو جھٹلایا اور شیخی میں آگیا اور تو کافر بن گیا ﴿٥٩﴾
اور جن لوگوں نے خدا پر جھوٹ بولا تم قیامت کے دن
دیکھو گے کہ ان کے منہ کالے ہو رہے ہوں گے۔ کیا غرور
کرنے والوں کا ٹھکانا دوزخ میں نہیں ہے؟ ﴿٦٠﴾
اور جو پرہیزگار ہیں ان کی (سعادت اور) کامیابی کے سبب ﴿٦١﴾
خدا ان کو نجات دیگا نہ تو ان کو کوئی سختی پہنچے گی اور نہ غمناک ہونگے
خدا ہی ہر چیز کا پیدا کرنے والا ہے اور وہی ہر چیز کا
نگراں ہے ﴿٦٢﴾
اسی کے پاس آسمانوں اور زمین کی کنجیاں ہیں اور جنہوں نے خدا کی
آیتوں سے کفر کیا وہی نقصان اٹھانے والے ہیں ﴿٦٣﴾
کہہ دو کہ اے نادانو! تم مجھ سے یہ کہتے ہو کہ میں غیر خدا
کی پرستش کرنے لگوں ﴿٦٤﴾
اور (اے محمدؐ) تمہاری طرف اور ان (پیغمبروں) کی طرف جو تم
سے پہلے ہو چکے ہیں یہی وحی بھیجی گئی ہے کہ اگر تم نے شرک کیا تو
تمہارے عمل برباد ہو جائینگے اور تم زیاں کاروں میں ہو جاؤ گے ﴿٦٥﴾
بلکہ خدا ہی کی عبادت کرو اور شکر گزاروں میں ہو ﴿٦٦﴾
اور انہوں نے خدا کی قدر شناسی جیسی کرنی چاہیے تھی نہیں کی
اور قیامت کے دن تمام زمین اس کی مٹھی میں ہوگی
اور آسمان اس کے داہنے ہاتھ میں لپٹے ہوں گے۔ (اور)
وہ ان لوگوں کے شرک سے پاک اور عالی شان ہے ﴿٦٧﴾
اور جب صور پھونکا جائے گا تو جو لوگ آسمان میں ہیں
اور جو زمین میں ہیں سب بیہوش ہو کر گر پڑیں گے مگر وہ
جس کو خدا چاہے پھر دوسری دفعہ پھونکا جائے گا تو

be sounded, when, behold, they will be standing and looking on!

69. And the Earth will shine with the light of its Lord: the Record (of Deeds) will be placed (open); the prophets and the witnesses will be brought forward; and a just decision pronounced between them; and they will not be wronged (in the least).

70. And to every soul will be paid in full (the fruit) of its deeds; and (Allah) knoweth best all that they do.

71. The Unbelievers will be led to Hell in groups: until, when they arrive there, its gates will be opened. And its Keepers will say, "Did not messengers come to you from among yourselves, rehearsing to you the Signs of your Lord, and warning you of the Meeting of this Day of yours?" The answer will be: "True: but the Decree of Chastisement has been proved true against the Unbelievers!"

72. (To them) will be said: "Enter ye the gates of Hell, to dwell therein: and evil is (this) abode of the arrogant!"

73. And those who feared their Lord will be led to the Garden in groups: until behold, they arrive there; its gates will be opened; and its Keepers will say: "Peace be upon you! Well have ye done! Enter ye here, to dwell therein."

74. They will say: "Praise be to Allah, Who has truly fulfilled His promise to us, and has given us (this) land in heritage: we can dwell in the Garden as we will: how excellent a reward for those who work (righteousness)!"

75. And thou wilt see the angels surrounding the Throne (Divine) on all sides, singing Glory and Praise to their Lord. The Decision between them (at Judgment) will be in (perfect) justice, and the cry (on all sides) will be, "Praise be to Allah, the Lord of the Worlds!"

فوراً سب کھڑے ہو کر دیکھنے لگیں گے ﴿۶۸﴾
اور زمین اپنے پروردگار کے نور سے چمک اٹھیگی اور (اعمال کی) کتاب
(کھول کر) رکھ دی جائیگی اور پیغمبر اور (اور) گواہ حاضر کئے جائینگے اور اُن میں
انصاف کیساتھ فیصلہ کیا جائیگا اور بے انصافی نہیں کی جائیگی ﴿۶۹﴾
اور جس شخص نے جو عمل کیا ہوگا اسکو اسکا پورا پورا بدلہ مل جائیگا
اور جو کچھ یہ کرتے ہیں اس کو سب کی خبر ہے ﴿۷۰﴾
اور کافروں کو گروہ گروہ بنا کر جہنم کی طرف لے جائیں گے
یہاں تک کہ جب وہ اُسکے پاس پہنچ جائینگے تو اُسکے دروازے
کھول دیئے جائیں گے تو اُسکے داروغہ اُن سے کہیں گے کیا تمہارے
پاس تم ہی میں سے پیغمبر نہیں آئے تھے جو تمکو تمہارے پروردگار کی آیتیں
پڑھ پڑھ کر سناتے اور اس دن کے پیش آنے سے ڈراتے تھے کہیں گے کیوں نہیں
لیکن کافروں کے حق میں عذاب کا حکم تحقیق ہو چکا تھا ﴿۷۱﴾
کہا جائے گا کہ دوزخ کے دروازوں میں داخل ہو جاؤ۔
ہمیشہ اس میں رہو گے تکبر کرنے والوں کا بُرا ٹھکانا ہے ﴿۷۲﴾
اور جو لوگ اپنے پروردگار سے ڈرتے ہیں اُنکو گروہ گروہ بنا کر
بہشت کی طرف لے جائینگے یہانتک کہ جب اُسکے پاس پہنچ
جائینگے اور اُسکے دروازے کھول دیئے جائینگے تو اُسکے داروغہ اُن سے کہینگے
کہ تم پر سلام تم بہت اچھے رہے۔ اب اسمیں ہمیشہ کیلئے داخل ہو جاؤ ﴿۷۳﴾
وہ کہیں گے کہ خدا کا شکر ہے جس نے اپنے وعدے کو ہم سے سچا
کر دیا اور ہمکو اس زمین کا وارث بنا دیا ہم بہشت میں جس مکان میں
چاہیں رہیں تو (اچھے) عمل کرنے والوں کا بدلہ بھی کیسا خوب ہے ﴿۷۴﴾
تم فرشتوں کو دیکھو گے کہ عرش کے گرد گھیرا باندھے ہوئے ہیں
(اور) اپنے پروردگار کی تعریف کے ساتھ تسبیح کر رہے ہیں اور اُن میں
انصاف کیساتھ فیصلہ کیا جائیگا اور کہا جائیگا کہ ہر طرح کی
تعریف خدا ہی کو سزاوار ہے جو سارے جہان کا مالک ہے ﴿۷۵﴾

يَنظُرُونَ ﴿٦٨﴾
وَأَشْرَقَتِ الْأَرْضُ بِنُورِ رَبِّهَا وَوُضِعَ
الْكِتَابُ وَجِيءَ بِالنَّبِيِّينَ وَالشُّهَدَاءِ
وَقُضِيَ بَيْنَهُم بِالْحَقِّ وَهُمْ لَا يُظْلَمُونَ ﴿٦٩﴾
وَوُفِّيَتْ كُلُّ نَفْسٍ مَّا عَمِلَتْ وَهُوَ
أَعْلَمُ بِمَا يَفْعَلُونَ ﴿٧٠﴾ ع
وَسِيقَ الَّذِينَ كَفَرُوا إِلَىٰ جَهَنَّمَ زُمَرًا
حَتَّىٰ إِذَا جَاءُوهَا فُتِحَتْ أَبْوَابُهَا وَ
قَالَ لَهُمْ خَزَنَتُهَا أَلَمْ يَأْتِكُمْ رُسُلٌ
مِّنكُمْ يَتْلُونَ عَلَيْكُمْ آيَاتِ رَبِّكُمْ وَ
يُنذِرُونَكُمْ لِقَاءَ يَوْمِكُمْ هَٰذَا قَالُوا بَلَىٰ
وَلَٰكِنْ حَقَّتْ كَلِمَةُ الْعَذَابِ عَلَى الْكَافِرِينَ ﴿٧١﴾
قِيلَ ادْخُلُوا أَبْوَابَ جَهَنَّمَ خَالِدِينَ فِيهَا
فَبِئْسَ مَثْوَى الْمُتَكَبِّرِينَ ﴿٧٢﴾
وَسِيقَ الَّذِينَ اتَّقَوْا رَبَّهُمْ إِلَى الْجَنَّةِ
زُمَرًا حَتَّىٰ إِذَا جَاءُوهَا وَفُتِحَتْ أَبْوَابُهَا
وَقَالَ لَهُمْ خَزَنَتُهَا سَلَامٌ عَلَيْكُمْ طِبْتُمْ
فَادْخُلُوهَا خَالِدِينَ ﴿٧٣﴾
وَقَالُوا الْحَمْدُ لِلَّهِ الَّذِي صَدَقَنَا وَعْدَهُ
وَأَوْرَثَنَا الْأَرْضَ نَتَبَوَّأُ مِنَ الْجَنَّةِ
حَيْثُ نَشَاءُ فَنِعْمَ أَجْرُ الْعَامِلِينَ ﴿٧٤﴾
وَتَرَى الْمَلَائِكَةَ حَافِّينَ مِنْ حَوْلِ
الْعَرْشِ يُسَبِّحُونَ بِحَمْدِ رَبِّهِمْ وَ
قُضِيَ بَيْنَهُم بِالْحَقِّ وَقِيلَ الْحَمْدُ لِلَّهِ
رَبِّ الْعَالَمِينَ ﴿٧٥﴾ ع

SÛRA–40

AL-MÛ-MIN

(INTRODUCTION)

This Sûra is called "The Believer" (*Mû-min*) from the story of the individual Believer among the people of Pharaoh, who declares his faith and looks to the Future (verses 28-45). It is also called <u>*Gãfir*</u> (He who forgives, see verse 3). In S. 23, called *The Believers (Mû-minûn)*, the argument was about the collective force of Faith and Virtue. Here it is about the Individual's witness to Faith and Virtue, and his triumph in the End.

We now begin a series of seven Sûras (40-46) to which are affixed the abbreviated Letters *Ḥa-Mîm*. Chronologically they all belong to the same period, the later Makkan Period, and they immediately follow the last Sûra in time. As to the precise meaning of *Ḥa-Mîm* no authoritative explanation is available. If *Mîm* here has a signification similar to *Mîm* in A.L.M. it means the End of things, the Last Day, and all these Sûras direct our special attention to that. *Ḥã*, the emphatic guttural, in contrast with the softer breathing of *Alif*, may be meant to suggest that the Beginning is only for the End, the Present for the Future, and to emphasise the eschatological element in Faith. But this is mere conjecture, and should be taken, for no more than it is worth.

The general theme of the whole series is the relation of Faith to Unfaith, Revelation to Rejection, Goodness to Evil, Truth to Falsehood. It is shown that the first in each of these pairs is the real friend, helper, and protector of man, while the second is his enemy. The very word *Ḥamîm* in that sense is used in Sûras 40 and 41 (40: 18 and 41: 34), while in the other Sûras we have words of equivalent import, e.g. *walî* or *naṣir* (42: 8 and 31); *qarîn* (43: 36, 38); *maulã* (44: 41); *auliyãa* or *nãṣirîn* (45: 19, 34); and *auliyãa* (46: 32). Is it permissible to connect the Abbreviated Letters *Ḥa-Mîm* with these ideas as expressed in the word *Ḥamîm*?

Another suggestion worthy of consideration is that *Ḥã* stands for *Ḥãiy*, and *Mîm* for *Qaiyûm*. These are two attributes of Allah, meaning, (1) the Living, and (2) the Self-Subsisting, Eternal. The one points to Life and Revelation, and the other to the Hereafter and Eternity; and both these matters are specially dealt with in the seven *Ḥa-Mîm* Sûras. The first letter of *Ḥãiy* (*Ḥã*) is appropriate for life, and the last letter of *Qaiyûm* is appropriate for the last Days, the *Ma'ãd*, the Hereafter. Again, this is mere conjecture, and should not be taken for more than it is worth.

Al-Mû-min, or The Believer

In the name of Allah, Most Gracious, Most Merciful.

1. Ḥã-Mîm.

2. The revelation of this Book is from Allah, Exalted in Power, Full of Knowledge,—

3. Who forgiveth Sin, accepteth Repentance, is Severe in Punishment, and is all-Bountiful. There is no god but He: to Him is the Final Goal.

4. None can dispute about the Signs of Allah but the Unbelievers. Let not, then their strutting about through the land deceive thee!

5. But (there were people) before them, who denied (the Signs), the People of Noah, and the Confederates after them; and every People plotted against their prophet, to seize him, and disputed by means of vanities, therewith to obliterate the Truth: but it was I that seized them! And how (terrible) was My Requital!

6. Thus was the Word of thy Lord proved true against the Unbelievers; that truly they are companions of the Fire!

7. Those who bear the Throne (of Allah) and those around it sing Glory and Praise to their Lord; believe in Him; and implore Forgiveness for those who believe: "Our Lord! Thou embracest all things, in Mercy and Knowledge. Forgive, then, those who turn in Repentance, and follow Thy Path; and preserve them from the Chastisement of the Blazing Fire!

8. "And grant, our Lord! that they enter the Gardens of Eternity, which Thou hast promised to them, and to the righteous among their fathers, their wives, and their posterity! for Thou art (He), the Exalted in Might, Full of Wisdom.

9. "And preserve them from (all) ills; and any whom Thou dost preserve from ills that Day,—on them wilt Thou have bestowed mercy indeed: and that will be truly the highest Achievement."

10. The Unbelievers will be

سورۂ مومن مکی ہے اس میں پچاسی آیتیں اور نو رکوع ہیں

شروع خدا کا نام لے کر جو بڑا مہربان نہایت رحم والا ہے
حٰم (١) اس کتاب کا اُتارا جانا خدائے غالب و دانا
کی طرف سے ہے (٢)
جو گناہ بخشنے والا اور توبہ قبول کرنے والا (اور) سخت
عذاب دینے والا (اور) صاحب کرم ہے۔ اُس کے سوا
کوئی معبود نہیں۔ اُسی کی طرف پھر جانا ہے (٣)
خدا کی آیتوں میں وہی لوگ جھگڑتے ہیں جو کافر ہیں۔
تو اُن لوگوں کا شہروں میں چلنا پھرنا تمہیں دھوکے
میں نہ ڈال دے (٤)
اُن سے پہلے نوح کی قوم اور اُن کے بعد اور اُمتوں نے بھی
(پیغمبروں کی) تکذیب کی اور ہر اُمت نے اپنے پیغمبر کے بارے میں یہی
قصد کیا کہ اُسکو پکڑ لیں اور بیہودہ (شبہات سے) جھگڑتے رہے کہ
اُس سے حق کو زائل کر دیں تو میں نے اُنکو پکڑ لیا سو (دیکھ لو) میرا عذاب کیسا ہوا (٥)
اور اسی طرح کافروں کے بارے میں بھی تمہارے پروردگار
کی بات پوری ہو چکی ہے کہ وہ اہلِ دوزخ ہیں (٦)
جو لوگ عرش کو اُٹھائے ہوئے اور جو اُسکے گرد اگرد (حلقہ باندھے ہوئے)
ہیں (یعنی فرشتے) وہ اپنے پروردگار کی تعریف کیساتھ تسبیح کرتے رہتے ہیں
اور اُسکے ساتھ ایمان رکھتے ہیں اور مومنوں کیلئے بخشش مانگتے رہتے ہیں
کہ اے ہمارے پروردگار تیری رحمت اور تیرا علم ہر چیز کو احاطہ کئے ہوئے ہے تو جن لوگوں نے
توبہ کی اور تیرے رستے پر چلے اُنکو بخش دے اور دوزخ کے عذاب سے بچا لے (٧)
اے ہمارے پروردگار اُنکو ہمیشہ رہنے کی بہشتوں میں داخل کر
جن کا تو نے اُن سے وعدہ کیا ہے اور جو اُنکے باپ دادا اور اُنکی بیویوں
اور اُنکی اولاد میں سے نیک ہوں اُنکو بھی بیشک تو غالب حکمت والا ہے (٨)
اور اُنکو عذابوں سے بچائے رکھ۔ اور جسکو تو اُس روز عذابوں سے بچا لیگا
تو بیشک اُس پر مہربانی فرمائی۔ اور یہی بڑی کامیابی ہے (٩)
جن لوگوں نے کفر کیا اُن سے پکار کر کہہ دیا جائیگا کہ جب تم (دنیا میں)

سورة المؤمن مكية وهي خمس وثمانون آية وتسع ركوعات

بِسْمِ اللَّهِ الرَّحْمَٰنِ الرَّحِيمِ
حٰمٓ ﴿١﴾ تَنْزِيلُ الْكِتَابِ مِنَ اللَّهِ
الْعَزِيزِ الْعَلِيمِ ﴿٢﴾
غَافِرِ الذَّنْبِ وَقَابِلِ التَّوْبِ شَدِيدِ
الْعِقَابِ ذِي الطَّوْلِ لَا إِلَٰهَ إِلَّا هُوَ
إِلَيْهِ الْمَصِيرُ ﴿٣﴾
مَا يُجَادِلُ فِي آيَاتِ اللَّهِ إِلَّا الَّذِينَ
كَفَرُوا فَلَا يَغْرُرْكَ تَقَلُّبُهُمْ فِي
الْبِلَادِ ﴿٤﴾
كَذَّبَتْ قَبْلَهُمْ قَوْمُ نُوحٍ وَالْأَحْزَابُ
مِنْ بَعْدِهِمْ وَهَمَّتْ كُلُّ أُمَّةٍ بِرَسُولِهِمْ
لِيَأْخُذُوهُ وَجَادَلُوا بِالْبَاطِلِ لِيُدْحِضُوا
بِهِ الْحَقَّ فَأَخَذْتُهُمْ فَكَيْفَ كَانَ عِقَابِ ﴿٥﴾
وَكَذَٰلِكَ حَقَّتْ كَلِمَتُ رَبِّكَ عَلَى الَّذِينَ
كَفَرُوا أَنَّهُمْ أَصْحَابُ النَّارِ ﴿٦﴾ وقف لازم وقف النبي صلى الله عليه وسلم
الَّذِينَ يَحْمِلُونَ الْعَرْشَ وَمَنْ حَوْلَهُ
يُسَبِّحُونَ بِحَمْدِ رَبِّهِمْ وَيُؤْمِنُونَ بِهِ وَ
يَسْتَغْفِرُونَ لِلَّذِينَ آمَنُوا رَبَّنَا وَسِعْتَ
كُلَّ شَيْءٍ رَحْمَةً وَعِلْمًا فَاغْفِرْ لِلَّذِينَ
تَابُوا وَاتَّبَعُوا سَبِيلَكَ وَقِهِمْ عَذَابَ الْجَحِيمِ ﴿٧﴾
رَبَّنَا وَأَدْخِلْهُمْ جَنَّاتِ عَدْنٍ الَّتِي
وَعَدْتَهُمْ وَمَنْ صَلَحَ مِنْ آبَائِهِمْ وَأَزْوَاجِهِمْ
وَذُرِّيَّاتِهِمْ إِنَّكَ أَنْتَ الْعَزِيزُ الْحَكِيمُ ﴿٨﴾
وَقِهِمُ السَّيِّئَاتِ وَمَنْ تَقِ السَّيِّئَاتِ يَوْمَئِذٍ
فَقَدْ رَحِمْتَهُ وَذَٰلِكَ هُوَ الْفَوْزُ الْعَظِيمُ ﴿٩﴾ ع ١
إِنَّ الَّذِينَ كَفَرُوا يُنَادَوْنَ لَمَقْتُ اللَّهِ

addressed: "Greater was the aversion of Allah to you than (is) your aversion to yourselves, seeing that ye were called to the Faith and ye used to refuse."
11. They will say: "Our Lord!twice hast Thou made us to die, and twice Hast Thou given us Life! Now have we recognised our sins: is there any way out (of this)?"
12. (The answer will be:) "This is because, when Allah was invoked as the Only (object of worship), ye did reject Faith, but when partners were joined to Him, ye believed! The Command is with Allah, Most High, Most Great!"
13. He it is Who showeth you His Signs, and sendeth down Sustenance for you from the sky: but only those receive admonition who turn (to Allah).
14. Call ye, then, upon Allah with sincere devotion to Him, even though the Unbelievers may detest it.
15. Exalted is He in His attributes. (He is) the Lord of the Throne: by His Command doth He send the spirit (of inspiration) to any of His servants He pleases, that it may warn (men) of the Day of Mutual Meeting,—
16. The Day whereon they will (all) come forth: not a single thing concerning them is hidden from Allah. Whose will be the Dominion that Day? That of Allah, the One, the Overpowering!
17. That Day will every soul be requited for what it earned; no injustice will there be that Day, for Allah is Swift in taking account.
18. Warn them of the Day that is (ever) drawing near, when the Hearts will (come) right up to the Throats to choke (them); no intimate friend nor intercessors will the wrong-doers have, who could be listened to.
19. (Allah) knows the treachery of the eyes, and all that the hearts (of men) conceal.
20. And Allah will judge with (Justice and) Truth: but those whom

ایمان کی طرف بلائے جاتے تھے اور مانتے نہیں تھے تو خدا اس سے
کہیں زیادہ بیزار ہوتا تھا جس قدر تم اپنے آپ سے بیزار ہو رہے ہو ⑩
وہ کہیں گے کہ اے ہمارے پروردگار تو نے ہم کو دو دفعہ بےجان
کیا اور دو دفعہ جان بخشی۔ ہم کو اپنے گناہوں کا اقرار ہے تو کیا
نکلنے کی کوئی سبیل ہے؟ ⑪
یہ اس لئے کہ جب تنہا خدا کو پکارا جاتا تھا تو تم انکار کر دیتے
تھے۔ اور اگر اس کے ساتھ شریک مقرر کیا جاتا تھا تو تسلیم کر لیتے تھے تو
تو حکم تو خدا ہی کا ہے جو (سب سے) اوپر اور (سب سے) بڑا ہے ⑫
وہی تو ہے جو تم کو اپنی نشانیاں دکھاتا ہے اور تم پر آسمان
سے رزق اتارتا ہے۔ اور نصیحت تو وہی پکڑتا ہے جو (اس کی)
طرف رجوع کرتا ہے ⑬
تو خدا کی عبادت کو خالص کر کر اسی کو پکارو اگرچہ کافر
برا ہی مانیں ⑭
وہ مالک درجات عالی (اور) صاحب عرش ہے۔ اپنے
بندوں میں سے جس کو چاہتا ہے اپنے حکم سے وحی بھیجتا ہے
تاکہ ملاقات کے دن سے ڈرائے ⑮
جس روز وہ نکل پڑیں گے ان کی کوئی چیز خدا سے مخفی
نہ رہے گی۔ آج کس کی بادشاہت ہے؟ خدا کی جو اکیلا
(اور) غالب ہے ⑯
آج کے دن ہر شخص کو اس کے اعمال کا بدلہ دیا جائیگا۔
آج (کسی کے حق میں) بے انصافی نہیں ہوگی۔ بیشک
خدا جلد حساب لینے والا ہے ⑰
اور ان کو قریب آنے والے دن سے ڈراؤ جب کہ دل غم
سے بھر کر گلوں تک آ رہے ہوں گے (اور) ظالموں کا کوئی
دوست نہیں ہوگا اور نہ کوئی سفارشی جس کی بات قبول کی جائے ⑱
وہ آنکھوں کی خیانت کو جانتا ہے اور جو (باتیں) سینوں میں پوشیدہ ہیں (ان کو بھی) ⑲
اور خدا سچائی کے ساتھ حکم فرماتا ہے۔ اور جن کو یہ لوگ

أَكْبَرُ مِن مَّقْتِكُمْ أَنفُسَكُمْ إِذْ تُدْعَوْنَ
إِلَى الْإِيمَانِ فَتَكْفُرُونَ ⑩
قَالُوا رَبَّنَا أَمَتَّنَا اثْنَتَيْنِ وَأَحْيَيْتَنَا
اثْنَتَيْنِ فَاعْتَرَفْنَا بِذُنُوبِنَا فَهَلْ إِلَىٰ
خُرُوجٍ مِّن سَبِيلٍ ⑪
ذَٰلِكُم بِأَنَّهُ إِذَا دُعِيَ اللَّهُ وَحْدَهُ كَفَرْتُمْ
وَإِن يُشْرَكْ بِهِ تُؤْمِنُوا فَالْحُكْمُ لِلَّهِ
الْعَلِيِّ الْكَبِيرِ ⑫
هُوَ الَّذِي يُرِيكُمْ آيَاتِهِ وَيُنَزِّلُ لَكُم
مِّنَ السَّمَاءِ رِزْقًا وَمَا يَتَذَكَّرُ إِلَّا
مَن يُنِيبُ ⑬
فَادْعُوا اللَّهَ مُخْلِصِينَ لَهُ الدِّينَ وَلَوْ
كَرِهَ الْكَافِرُونَ ⑭
رَفِيعُ الدَّرَجَاتِ ذُو الْعَرْشِ يُلْقِي
الرُّوحَ مِنْ أَمْرِهِ عَلَىٰ مَن يَشَاءُ مِنْ
عِبَادِهِ لِيُنذِرَ يَوْمَ التَّلَاقِ ⑮
يَوْمَ هُم بَارِزُونَ لَا يَخْفَىٰ عَلَى اللَّهِ
مِنْهُمْ شَيْءٌ لِّمَنِ الْمُلْكُ الْيَوْمَ لِلَّهِ
الْوَاحِدِ الْقَهَّارِ ⑯
الْيَوْمَ تُجْزَىٰ كُلُّ نَفْسٍ بِمَا كَسَبَتْ
لَا ظُلْمَ الْيَوْمَ إِنَّ اللَّهَ سَرِيعُ
الْحِسَابِ ⑰
وَأَنذِرْهُمْ يَوْمَ الْآزِفَةِ إِذِ الْقُلُوبُ
لَدَى الْحَنَاجِرِ كَاظِمِينَ مَا لِلظَّالِمِينَ
مِنْ حَمِيمٍ وَلَا شَفِيعٍ يُطَاعُ ⑱
⑲ يَعْلَمُ خَائِنَةَ الْأَعْيُنِ وَمَا تُخْفِي الصُّدُورُ
وَاللَّهُ يَقْضِي بِالْحَقِّ وَالَّذِينَ يَدْعُونَ

(men) invoke besides Him, will not (be in a position) to judge at all. Verily it is Allah (alone) Who hears and sees (all things).

21. Do they not travel through the earth and see what was the End of those before them? They were even superior to them in strength, and in the traces (they have left) in the land: but Allah did call them to account for their sins, and none had they to defend them against Allah.

22. That was because there came to them their messengers with Clear (Signs), but they rejected them: so Allah called them to account: for He is Full of Strength, Severe in Punishment.

23. Of old We sent Moses, with Our Signs and an Authority manifest,

24. To Pharaoh, Hãmãn, and Qãrûn; but they called (him) "a sorcerer telling lies!"...

25. Now, when he brought them the Truth, from Us, they said, "Slay the sons of those who believe with him, and keep alive their females," but the plots of unbelievers (end) in nothing but errors (and delusions)!...

26. Said Pharaoh: "Leave me to slay Moses; and let him call on his Lord! What I fear is lest He should change your religion, or lest he should cause mischief to appear in the land!"

27. Moses said: "I have indeed called upon my Lord and your Lord (for protection) from every arrogant one who believes not in the Day of Account!"

28. A Believer, a man from among the people of Pharaoh, who had concealed his faith, said: "Will ye slay a man because he says, 'My Lord is Allah'?—when he has indeed come to you with Clear (Signs) from your Lord? And if he be a liar, on him is (the sin of) his

پکارتے ہیں وہ کچھ بھی حکم نہیں دے سکتے۔ بیشک خدا
سننے والا (اور) دیکھنے والا ہے ﴿۲۰﴾
کیا انہوں نے زمین میں سیر نہیں کی تاکہ دیکھ لیتے کہ جو لوگ
اُن سے پہلے تھے اُن کا انجام کیسا ہوا۔ وہ اُن سے زور
اور زمین میں نشانات (بنانے) کے لحاظ سے کہیں بڑھ کر تھے
تو خدا نے اُن کو اُن کے گناہوں کے سبب پکڑ لیا۔ اور اُن کو
خدا (کے عذاب) سے کوئی بھی بچانے والا نہ تھا ﴿۲۱﴾
یہ اس لئے کہ اُن کے پاس پیغمبر کھلی دلیلیں لاتے تھے تو یہ
کفر کرتے تھے سو خدا نے اُن کو پکڑ لیا۔ بیشک وہ صاحبِ قوت
(اور) سخت عذاب دینے والا ہے ﴿۲۲﴾
اور ہم نے موسیٰ کو اپنی نشانیاں اور دلیل روشن دے کر بھیجا ﴿۲۳﴾
(یعنی) فرعون اور ہامان اور قارون کی طرف تو انہوں نے
کہا کہ یہ تو جادوگر ہے جھوٹا ﴿۲۴﴾
غرض جب وہ اُن کے پاس ہماری طرف سے حق لے کر
پہنچے تو کہنے لگے کہ جو لوگ اس کے ساتھ (خدا پر) ایمان
لائے ہیں اُن کے بیٹوں کو قتل کر دو اور بیٹیوں کو رہنے دو
اور کافروں کی تدبیریں بے ٹھکانے ہوتی ہیں ﴿۲۵﴾
اور فرعون بولا کہ مجھے چھوڑو کہ موسیٰ کو قتل کر دوں اور وہ
اپنے پروردگار کو بلائے۔ مجھے ڈر ہے کہ وہ (کہیں) تمہارے
دین کو (نہ) بدل دے یا ملک میں فساد (نہ) پیدا کر دے ﴿۲۶﴾
موسیٰ نے کہا کہ میں ہر متکبر سے جو حساب کے دن (یعنی قیامت)
پر ایمان نہیں لاتا۔ اپنے اور تمہارے پروردگار کی
پناہ لے چکا ہوں ﴿۲۷﴾
اور فرعون کے لوگوں میں سے ایک مومن شخص جو اپنے ایمان
کو پوشیدہ رکھتا تھا کہنے لگا کیا تم ایسے شخص کو قتل کرنا چاہتے ہو جو
کہتا ہے کہ میرا پروردگار خدا ہے اور وہ تمہارے پاس تمہارے پروردگار
(کی طرف) سے نشانیاں بھی لے کر آیا ہے اور اگر وہ جھوٹا ہو گا تو اس کے

مِنْ دُوْنِهٖ لَا يَقْضُوْنَ بِشَيْءٍ ۗ اِنَّ اللّٰهَ
هُوَ السَّمِيْعُ الْبَصِيْرُ ﴿۲۰﴾
اَوَلَمْ يَسِيْرُوْا فِي الْاَرْضِ فَيَنْظُرُوْا كَيْفَ
كَانَ عَاقِبَةُ الَّذِيْنَ كَانُوْا مِنْ قَبْلِهِمْ ۗ
كَانُوْا هُمْ اَشَدَّ مِنْهُمْ قُوَّةً وَّاٰثَارًا فِي
الْاَرْضِ فَاَخَذَهُمُ اللّٰهُ بِذُنُوْبِهِمْ ۗ
وَمَا كَانَ لَهُمْ مِّنَ اللّٰهِ مِنْ وَّاقٍ ﴿۲۱﴾
ذٰلِكَ بِاَنَّهُمْ كَانَتْ تَّاْتِيْهِمْ رُسُلُهُمْ
بِالْبَيِّنٰتِ فَكَفَرُوْا فَاَخَذَهُمُ اللّٰهُ ۗ اِنَّهٗ
قَوِيٌّ شَدِيْدُ الْعِقَابِ ﴿۲۲﴾
وَلَقَدْ اَرْسَلْنَا مُوْسٰى بِاٰيٰتِنَا وَسُلْطٰنٍ مُّبِيْنٍ ﴿۲۳﴾
اِلٰى فِرْعَوْنَ وَهَامٰنَ وَقَارُوْنَ فَقَالُوْا
سٰحِرٌ كَذَّابٌ ﴿۲۴﴾
فَلَمَّا جَآءَهُمْ بِالْحَقِّ مِنْ عِنْدِنَا قَالُوا
اقْتُلُوْٓا اَبْنَآءَ الَّذِيْنَ اٰمَنُوْا مَعَهٗ وَ
اسْتَحْيُوْا نِسَآءَهُمْ ۗ وَمَا كَيْدُ الْكٰفِرِيْنَ
اِلَّا فِيْ ضَلٰلٍ ﴿۲۵﴾
وَقَالَ فِرْعَوْنُ ذَرُوْنِيْٓ اَقْتُلْ مُوْسٰى
وَلْيَدْعُ رَبَّهٗ ۚ اِنِّيْٓ اَخَافُ اَنْ يُّبَدِّلَ
دِيْنَكُمْ اَوْ اَنْ يُّظْهِرَ فِي الْاَرْضِ الْفَسَادَ ﴿۲۶﴾
وَقَالَ مُوْسٰٓى اِنِّيْ عُذْتُ بِرَبِّيْ وَرَبِّكُمْ
مِّنْ كُلِّ مُتَكَبِّرٍ لَّا يُؤْمِنُ بِيَوْمِ
الْحِسَابِ ﴿۲۷﴾
وَقَالَ رَجُلٌ مُّؤْمِنٌ ۖ مِّنْ اٰلِ فِرْعَوْنَ
يَكْتُمُ اِيْمَانَهٗٓ اَتَقْتُلُوْنَ رَجُلًا اَنْ
يَّقُوْلَ رَبِّيَ اللّٰهُ وَقَدْ جَآءَكُمْ بِالْبَيِّنٰتِ
مِنْ رَّبِّكُمْ ۗ وَاِنْ يَّكُ كَاذِبًا فَعَلَيْهِ كَذِبُهٗ

lie; but, if he is telling the Truth, then will fall on you something of the (calamity) of which He warns you: truly Allah guides not one who transgresses and lies!

29. "O my People! yours is the dominion this day: Ye have the upper hand in the land: but who will help us from the Punishment of Allah, should it befall us?" Pharaoh said: "I but point out to you that which I see (myself); nor do I guide you but to the Path of Right!"

30. Then said the man who believed: "O my People! truly I do fear for you something like the Day (of disaster) of the Confederates (is sin)!—

31. "Something like the fate of the People of Noah, the 'Âd, and the Thamûd, and those who came after them: but Allah never wishes injustice to His Servants.

32. "And O my People! I fear for you a Day when there will be mutual calling (and wailing),—

33. "A Day when ye shall turn your backs and flee: no defender shall ye have from Allah: any whom Allah leaves to stray, there is none to guide...

34. "And to you there came Joseph in times gone by, with Clear Signs, but ye ceased not to doubt of the (mission) for which he had come: at length, when he died, ye said: 'No messenger will Allah send after him.' Thus doth Allah leave to stray such as transgress and live in doubt,—

35. "(Such) as dispute about the Signs of Allah, without any authority that hath reached them, very hateful (is such conduct) in the sight of Allah and of the Believers. Thus doth Allah seal up every heart—of arrogant tyrinical."

36. Pharaoh said: "O Haman! build me a lofty palace, that I may

جھوٹ کا ضرر اُسی کو ہوگا۔ اور اگر سچا ہوگا تو کوئی سا عذاب جسکا وہ تم سے وعدہ کرتا ہے
تم پر واقع ہو کر رہیگا بیشک خدا اس شخص کو ہدایت نہیں دیتا جو بے لحاظ جھوٹا ہے ﴿۲۸﴾
اے قوم آج تمہاری ہی بادشاہت ہے۔ اور تم ہی ملک
میں غالب ہو (لیکن) اگر ہم پر خدا کا عذاب آگیا تو اُسکے
دُور کرنے کے لئے ہماری مدد کون کرے گا؟ فرعون نے
کہا کہ میں تمہیں وہی بات سمجھاتا ہوں جو مجھے سوجھی ہے
اور وہی راہ بتاتا ہوں جس میں بھلائی ہے ﴿۲۹﴾
تو جو مومن تھا وہ کہنے لگا کہ اے قوم مجھے تمہاری نسبت خوف
ہے کہ (مبادا) تم پر اور اُمتوں کی طرح کے دن کا عذاب آجائے ﴿۳۰﴾
(یعنی) نوح کی قوم اور عاد اور ثمود اور جو لوگ اُن کے
پیچھے ہوئے ہیں اُن کے حال کی طرح (تمہارا حال نہ ہو جائے)
اور خدا تو بندوں پر ظلم کرنا نہیں چاہتا ﴿۳۱﴾
اور اے قوم مجھے تمہاری نسبت پکار کے دن (یعنی قیامت)
کا خوف ہے ﴿۳۲﴾
جس دن تم پیٹھ پھیر کر (قیامت کے میدان سے) بھاگو گے
(اُس دن) تم کو کوئی (عذاب) خدا سے بچانے والا نہ ہوگا
اور جس شخص کو خدا گمراہ کرے اسکو کوئی ہدایت دینے والا نہیں ﴿۳۳﴾
اور پہلے یوسف بھی تمہارے پاس نشانیاں لے کر آئے تھے
تو جو وہ لائے تھے اس سے تم ہمیشہ شک ہی میں رہے۔ یہاں تک
کہ جب وہ فوت ہو گئے تو تم کہنے لگے کہ خدا اسکے بعد کبھی کوئی
پیغمبر نہیں بھیجے گا۔ اسی طرح خدا اس شخص کو گمراہ کر دیتا ہے
جو حد سے نکل جانے والا (اور) شک کرنے والا ہو ﴿۳۴﴾
جو لوگ بغیر اس کے کہ اُن کے پاس کوئی دلیل آئی ہو خدا
کی آیتوں میں جھگڑتے ہیں۔ خدا کے نزدیک اور مومنوں کے
نزدیک جھگڑا سخت ناپسند ہے۔ اسی طرح خدا ہر متکبر سرکش
کے دل پر مہر لگا دیتا ہے ﴿۳۵﴾
اور فرعون نے کہا کہ ہامان میرے لئے ایک محل بنواؤ تاکہ

وَإِنْ يَكُ صَادِقًا يُصِبْكُمْ بَعْضُ الَّذِي يَعِدُكُمْ
إِنَّ اللَّهَ لَا يَهْدِي مَنْ هُوَ مُسْرِفٌ كَذَّابٌ ﴿٢٨﴾
يَا قَوْمِ لَكُمُ الْمُلْكُ الْيَوْمَ ظَاهِرِينَ
فِي الْأَرْضِ فَمَنْ يَنْصُرُنَا مِنْ بَأْسِ
اللَّهِ إِنْ جَاءَنَا ۚ قَالَ فِرْعَوْنُ مَا أُرِيكُمْ
إِلَّا مَا أَرَىٰ وَمَا أَهْدِيكُمْ إِلَّا
سَبِيلَ الرَّشَادِ ﴿٢٩﴾
وَقَالَ الَّذِي آمَنَ يَا قَوْمِ إِنِّي أَخَافُ
عَلَيْكُمْ مِثْلَ يَوْمِ الْأَحْزَابِ ﴿٣٠﴾
مِثْلَ دَأْبِ قَوْمِ نُوحٍ وَعَادٍ وَثَمُودَ
وَالَّذِينَ مِنْ بَعْدِهِمْ ۚ وَمَا اللَّهُ يُرِيدُ
ظُلْمًا لِلْعِبَادِ ﴿٣١﴾
وَيَا قَوْمِ إِنِّي أَخَافُ عَلَيْكُمْ يَوْمَ
التَّنَادِ ﴿٣٢﴾
يَوْمَ تُوَلُّونَ مُدْبِرِينَ مَا لَكُمْ مِنَ
اللَّهِ مِنْ عَاصِمٍ ۗ وَمَنْ يُضْلِلِ اللَّهُ
فَمَا لَهُ مِنْ هَادٍ ﴿٣٣﴾
وَلَقَدْ جَاءَكُمْ يُوسُفُ مِنْ قَبْلُ بِالْبَيِّنَاتِ
فَمَا زِلْتُمْ فِي شَكٍّ مِمَّا جَاءَكُمْ بِهِ ۖ
حَتَّىٰ إِذَا هَلَكَ قُلْتُمْ لَنْ يَبْعَثَ اللَّهُ
مِنْ بَعْدِهِ رَسُولًا ۚ كَذَٰلِكَ يُضِلُّ اللَّهُ
مَنْ هُوَ مُسْرِفٌ مُرْتَابٌ ﴿٣٤﴾
الَّذِينَ يُجَادِلُونَ فِي آيَاتِ اللَّهِ بِغَيْرِ
سُلْطَانٍ أَتَاهُمْ ۖ كَبُرَ مَقْتًا عِنْدَ اللَّهِ وَ
عِنْدَ الَّذِينَ آمَنُوا ۚ كَذَٰلِكَ يَطْبَعُ اللَّهُ
عَلَىٰ كُلِّ قَلْبِ مُتَكَبِّرٍ جَبَّارٍ ﴿٣٥﴾
وَقَالَ فِرْعَوْنُ يَا هَامَانُ ابْنِ لِي

attain the ways and means—

37. "The ways and means of (reaching) the heavens, and that I may look up to the God of Moses: but surely, I think (Moses) is a liar!" Thus was made alluring, in Pharaoh's eyes, the evil of his deeds, and he was hindered from the Path; and the plot of Pharaoh led to nothing but perdition (for him).

میں (اُس پر چڑھ کر) رستوں پر پہنچ جاؤں ﴿۳۶﴾
(یعنی) آسمانوں کے رستوں پر پھر موسیٰ کے خدا کو
دیکھ لوں اور میں تو اُسے جھوٹا سمجھتا ہوں۔ اور
اسی طرح فرعون کو اُس کے اعمالِ بد اچھے معلوم ہوتے
تھے اور وہ رستے سے روک دیا گیا تھا۔ اور فرعون
کی تدبیر تو بیکار تھی ﴿۳۷﴾

صَرْحًا لَّعَلِّيْٓ اَبْلُغُ الْاَسْبَابَ ﴿٣٦﴾
اَسْبَابَ السَّمٰوٰتِ فَاَطَّلِعَ اِلٰٓى اِلٰهِ
مُوْسٰى وَاِنِّيْ لَاَظُنُّهٗ كَاذِبًا ۭ وَكَذٰلِكَ
زُيِّنَ لِفِرْعَوْنَ سُوْۗءُ عَمَلِهٖ وَصُدَّ
عَنِ السَّبِيْلِ ۭ وَمَا كَيْدُ فِرْعَوْنَ اِلَّا
فِيْ تَبَابٍ ﴿٣٧﴾ ربع

38. The man who believed said further: "O my People! follow me: I will lead you to the Path of Right.

اور وہ شخص جو مومن تھا اُس نے کہا کہ بھائیو میرے
پیچھے چلو میں تمہیں بھلائی کا رستہ دکھاؤں گا ﴿۳۸﴾

وَقَالَ الَّذِيْٓ اٰمَنَ يٰقَوْمِ اتَّبِعُوْنِ
اَهْدِكُمْ سَبِيْلَ الرَّشَادِ ﴿٣٨﴾

39. "O my People! this life of the present is nothing but (temporary) enjoyment: it is the Hereafter that is the Home that will last.

بھائیو یہ دنیا کی زندگی (چند روز) فائدہ اُٹھانے
کی چیز ہے۔ اور جو آخرت ہے وہی ہمیشہ رہنے کا
گھر ہے ﴿۳۹﴾

يٰقَوْمِ اِنَّمَا هٰذِهِ الْحَيٰوةُ الدُّنْيَا
مَتَاعٌ ۡ وَّاِنَّ الْاٰخِرَةَ هِيَ دَارُ
الْقَرَارِ ﴿٣٩﴾

40. "He that works evil will not be requited but by the like thereof: and he that works a righteous deed—whether man or woman—and is a Believer—such will enter the Garden (of Bliss): therein will they have abundance without measure.

جو بُرے کام کرے گا اُس کو بدلہ بھی ویسا ہی ملے گا۔
اور جو نیک کام کریگا مرد ہو یا عورت اور وہ صاحبِ ایمان
بھی ہوگا تو ایسے لوگ بہشت میں داخل ہوں گے وہاں
اُن کو بے شمار رزق ملے گا ﴿۴۰﴾

مَنْ عَمِلَ سَيِّئَةً فَلَا يُجْزٰٓى اِلَّا مِثْلَهَا ۚ
وَمَنْ عَمِلَ صَالِحًا مِّنْ ذَكَرٍ اَوْ اُنْثٰى
وَهُوَ مُؤْمِنٌ فَاُولٰۗىِٕكَ يَدْخُلُوْنَ الْجَنَّةَ
يُرْزَقُوْنَ فِيْهَا بِغَيْرِ حِسَابٍ ﴿٤٠﴾

41. "And O my People! how (strange) it is for me to call you to Salvation while ye call me to the Fire!

اور اے قوم میرا کیا (حال) ہے کہ مَیں تو تم کو نجات کی
طرف بُلاتا ہوں اور تم مجھے (دوزخ کی) آگ کی طرف بُلاتے ہو ﴿۴۱﴾

وَيٰقَوْمِ مَا لِيْٓ اَدْعُوْكُمْ اِلَى النَّجٰوةِ وَ
تَدْعُوْنَنِيْٓ اِلَى النَّارِ ﴿٤١﴾ النصف

42. "Ye do call upon me to blaspheme against Allah, and to join with Him Partners of whom I have no knowledge; and I call you to the Exalted in Power, Who forgives again and again!

تم مجھے اس لئے بُلاتے ہو کہ خدا کے ساتھ کفر کروں اور اُس
چیز کو اُس کا شریک مقرر کروں جس کا مجھے کچھ بھی علم نہیں۔ اور
مَیں تم کو (خدائے) غالب (اور) بخشنے والے کی طرف بلاتا ہوں ﴿۴۲﴾

تَدْعُوْنَنِيْ لِاَكْفُرَ بِاللّٰهِ وَاُشْرِكَ بِهٖ
مَا لَيْسَ لِيْ بِهٖ عِلْمٌ ۡ وَّاَنَا اَدْعُوْكُمْ
اِلَى الْعَزِيْزِ الْغَفَّارِ ﴿٤٢﴾

43. "Without doubt ye do call me to one who has no claim to be called to, whether in this world, or in the Hereafter; our Return will be to Allah; and the Transgressors will be Companions of the Fire!

سچ تو یہ ہے کہ جس چیز کی طرف تم مجھے بلاتے ہو اُس کو دنیا
اور آخرت میں بلانے (یعنی دعا قبول کرنے) کا مقدور نہیں
اور ہم کو خدا کی طرف لوٹنا ہے اور حد سے نکل جانے والے
دوزخی ہیں ﴿۴۳﴾

لَا جَرَمَ اَنَّمَا تَدْعُوْنَنِيْٓ اِلَيْهِ لَيْسَ لَهٗ
دَعْوَةٌ فِي الدُّنْيَا وَلَا فِي الْاٰخِرَةِ وَ
اَنَّ مَرَدَّنَآ اِلَى اللّٰهِ وَاَنَّ الْمُسْرِفِيْنَ
هُمْ اَصْحٰبُ النَّارِ ﴿٤٣﴾

44. "Soon will ye remember what I say to you (now). My (own) affair I commit to Allah: for Allah (ever) watches over His Servants".

جو بات میں تم سے کہتا ہوں تم اُسے آگے چل کر یاد
کرو گے۔ اور مَیں اپنا کام خدا کے سُپرد کرتا ہوں بیشک
خدا بندوں کو دیکھنے والا ہے ﴿۴۴﴾

فَسَتَذْكُرُوْنَ مَآ اَقُوْلُ لَكُمْ ۭ وَ
اُفَوِّضُ اَمْرِيْٓ اِلَى اللّٰهِ ۭ اِنَّ اللّٰهَ
بَصِيْرٌۢ بِالْعِبَادِ ﴿٤٤﴾

45. Then Allah saved him from (every) evil that they plotted (against him), but the brunt of the Chastisement encompassed on all sides the People of Pharaoh.

46. In front of the Fire will they be brought, morning and evening: and (the Sentence will be) on the Day when the Hour comes to pass: "Cast ye the People of Pharaoh into the severest Penalty ! "

47. Behold, they will dispute with each other in the Fire! The weak ones (who followed) will say to those who had been arrogant, "We but followed you: can ye then take (on yourselves) from us some share of the Fire?"

48. Those who had been arrogant will say: "We are all in this (Fire)! Truly, Allah has judged between (His) Servants!"

49. Those in the Fire will say to the Keepers of Hell: "Pray to your Lord to lighten us the Chastisement for a Day (at least)!"

50. They will say: "Did there not come to you your messengers with Clear Signs?" They will say, "Yes". They will reply, "Then pray (as ye like)! But the Prayer of those without Faith is nothing but (futile wandering) in (mazes of) error!"

51. We will, without doubt, help Our messengers and those who believe, (both) in this world's life and on the Day when the Witnesses will stand forth,—

52. The Day when no profit will it be to Wrong-doers to present their excuses, but they will (only) have the Curse and the Home of Misery.

53. We did aforetime give Moses the Guidance, and We gave the Book in inheritance to the Children of Israel,—

54. A Guide and a Reminder to men of understanding.

55. Patiently, then, persevere: for the Promise of Allah is true: and ask forgiveness for thy fault, and celebrate the Praises of thy Lord in the evening and in the morning.

56. Those who dispute about the Signs of Allah without any authority

غرض خدا نے (موسیٰ کو) اُن لوگوں کی تدبیروں کی بُرائیوں سے
محفوظ رکھا اور فرعون والوں کو بُرے عذاب نے آگھیرا ﴿۴۵﴾
(یعنی) آتش (جہنم) کہ صبح و شام اُس کے سامنے پیش کئے
جاتے ہیں۔ اور جس روز قیامت برپا ہوگی (حکم ہوگا کہ)
فرعون والوں کو سخت عذاب میں داخل کرو ﴿۴۶﴾
اور جب وہ دوزخ میں جھگڑیں گے تو ادنیٰ درجے
کے لوگ بڑے آدمیوں سے کہیں گے کہ ہم تو تمہارے
تابع تھے تو کیا تم دوزخ (کے عذاب) کا کچھ حصہ ہم سے
دُور کر سکتے ہو؟ ﴿۴۷﴾
بڑے آدمی کہیں گے کہ تم (بھی) اور ہم (بھی) سب دوزخ
میں ہیں خدا بندوں میں فیصلہ کر چکا ہے ﴿۴۸﴾
اور جو لوگ آگ میں (جل رہے) ہوں گے وہ دوزخ کے
داروغوں سے کہیں گے کہ اپنے پروردگار سے دُعا کرو
کہ ایک روز تو ہم سے عذاب ہلکا کر دے ﴿۴۹﴾
وہ کہیں گے کہ کیا تمہارے پاس تمہارے پیغمبر نشانیاں لیکر
نہیں آئے تھے۔ وہ کہیں گے کیوں نہیں۔ تو وہ کہیں گے
کہ تم ہی دُعا کرو۔ اور کافروں کی دُعا (اُس روز) بیکار ہوگی ﴿۵۰﴾
ہم اپنے پیغمبروں کی اور جو لوگ ایمان لائے ہیں اُنکی دنیا کی زندگی
میں بھی مدد کرتے ہیں اور جس دن گواہ کھڑے ہونگے (یعنی قیامت کو بھی) ﴿۵۱﴾
جس دن ظالموں کو اُن کی معذرت کچھ فائدہ نہ دے گی
اور اُن کے لئے لعنت اور بُرا گھر ہے ﴿۵۲﴾
اور ہم نے موسیٰ کو ہدایت (کی کتاب) دی۔ اور بنی اسرائیل
کو اس کتاب کا وارث بنایا ﴿۵۳﴾
عقل والوں کے لئے ہدایت اور نصیحت ہے ﴿۵۴﴾
تو صبر کرو بے شک خدا کا وعدہ سچا ہے اور اپنے گناہوں کی
معافی مانگو اور صبح و شام اپنے پروردگار کی تعریف کے ساتھ تسبیح کرتے رہو ﴿۵۵﴾
جو لوگ بغیر کسی دلیل کے جو اُنکے پاس آئی ہو خدا کی آیتوں میں

فَوَقٰىهُ اللّٰهُ سَيِّاٰتِ مَا مَكَرُوْا وَحَاقَ
بِاٰلِ فِرْعَوْنَ سُوْٓءُ الْعَذَابِ ﴿۴۵﴾
اَلنَّارُ يُعْرَضُوْنَ عَلَيْهَا غُدُوًّا وَّعَشِيًّا ۚ
وَيَوْمَ تَقُوْمُ السَّاعَةُ ۟ اَدْخِلُوْٓا اٰلَ
فِرْعَوْنَ اَشَدَّ الْعَذَابِ ﴿۴۶﴾
وَاِذْ يَتَحَآجُّوْنَ فِي النَّارِ فَيَقُوْلُ الضُّعَفٰٓؤُا
لِلَّذِيْنَ اسْتَكْبَرُوْٓا اِنَّا كُنَّا لَكُمْ تَبَعًا
فَهَلْ اَنْتُمْ مُّغْنُوْنَ عَنَّا نَصِيْبًا مِّنَ
النَّارِ ﴿۴۷﴾
قَالَ الَّذِيْنَ اسْتَكْبَرُوْٓا اِنَّا كُلٌّ فِيْهَآ
اِنَّ اللّٰهَ قَدْ حَكَمَ بَيْنَ الْعِبَادِ ﴿۴۸﴾
وَقَالَ الَّذِيْنَ فِي النَّارِ لِخَزَنَةِ جَهَنَّمَ
ادْعُوْا رَبَّكُمْ يُخَفِّفْ عَنَّا يَوْمًا مِّنَ
الْعَذَابِ ﴿۴۹﴾
قَالُوْٓا اَوَلَمْ تَكُ تَاْتِيْكُمْ رُسُلُكُمْ بِالْبَيِّنٰتِ ؕ
قَالُوْا بَلٰى ؕ قَالُوْا فَادْعُوْا ۚ وَمَا دُعٰٓؤُا
الْكٰفِرِيْنَ اِلَّا فِيْ ضَلٰلٍ ﴿۵۰﴾ ع
اِنَّا لَنَنْصُرُ رُسُلَنَا وَالَّذِيْنَ اٰمَنُوْا فِي
الْحَيٰوةِ الدُّنْيَا وَيَوْمَ يَقُوْمُ الْاَشْهَادُ ﴿۵۱﴾
يَوْمَ لَا يَنْفَعُ الظّٰلِمِيْنَ مَعْذِرَتُهُمْ وَ
لَهُمُ اللَّعْنَةُ وَلَهُمْ سُوْٓءُ الدَّارِ ﴿۵۲﴾
وَلَقَدْ اٰتَيْنَا مُوْسَى الْهُدٰى وَاَوْرَثْنَا
بَنِيْٓ اِسْرَآءِيْلَ الْكِتٰبَ ﴿۵۳﴾
هُدًى وَّذِكْرٰى لِاُولِي الْاَلْبَابِ ﴿۵۴﴾
فَاصْبِرْ اِنَّ وَعْدَ اللّٰهِ حَقٌّ وَّاسْتَغْفِرْ لِذَنْۢبِكَ
وَسَبِّحْ بِحَمْدِ رَبِّكَ بِالْعَشِيِّ وَالْاِبْكَارِ ﴿۵۵﴾
اِنَّ الَّذِيْنَ يُجَادِلُوْنَ فِيْٓ اٰيٰتِ اللّٰهِ بِغَيْرِ

bestowed on them,—there is nothing in their breasts but (the quest of) greatness, which they shall never attain to: seek refuge, then, in Allah: it is He Who hears and sees (all things).

57. Assuredly the creation of the heavens and the earth is a greater (matter) than the creation of men: yet most men know not.

58. Not equal are the blind and those who (clearly) see: nor are (equal) those who believe and work deeds of righteousness, and those who do evil. Little do ye learn by admonition!

59. The Hour will certainly come: therein is no doubt: yet most men believe not.

60. And your Lord says: "Call on Me; I will answer your (Prayer): but those who are too arrogant to serve Me will surely enter Hell abased."

61. It is Allah Who has made the Night for you, that ye may rest therein, and the Day, to give you light. Verily Allah is Full of Grace and Bounty to men: yet most men give no thanks.

62. Such is Allah, your Lord, the Creator of all things, there is no god but He: then how ye are deluded away from the Truth!

63. Thus are deluded those who are wont to reject the Signs of Allah.

64. It is Allah Who has made for you the earth as a resting place, and the sky as a canopy, and has given you shape— and made your shapes beautiful,—and has provided for you Sustenance, of things pure and good;— such is Allah your Lord. So Glory to Allah, the Lord of the Worlds!

65. He is the Living (One): there is no god but He: call upon Him, giving Him sincere devotion. Praise

جھگڑتے ہیں اُنکے دلوں میں اور کچھ نہیں (ارادہ) عظمت ہے
اور وہ اس کو پہنچنے والے نہیں ۲۵۷ تو خدا کی پناہ مانگو۔ بیشک
وہ سننے والا (اور) دیکھنے والا ہے (٥٦)
آسمانوں اور زمین کا پیدا کرنا لوگوں کے پیدا کرنے کی نسبت
بڑا (کام) ہے لیکن اکثر لوگ نہیں جانتے (٥٧)
اور اندھا اور آنکھ والا برابر نہیں۔ اور نہ ایمان لانے
والے نیکوکار اور نہ بدکار برابر ہیں (حقیقت یہ ہے کہ)
تم بہت کم غور کرتے ہو (٥٨)
قیامت تو آنے والی ہے اس میں کچھ شک نہیں لیکن اکثر
لوگ ایمان نہیں رکھتے (٥٩)
اور تمہارے پروردگار نے کہا ہے کہ تم مجھ سے دُعا کرو میں
تمہاری (دعا) قبول کروں گا۔ جو لوگ میری عبادت سے
ازراہِ تکبر کنیاتے ہیں عنقریب جہنم میں ذلیل ہو کر داخل ہونگے (٦٠)
خدا ہی تو ہے جس نے تمہارے لئے رات بنائی کہ اس میں آرام
کرو اور دن کو روشن بنایا (کہ اس میں کام کرو) بے شک
خدا لوگوں پر فضل کرنے والا ہے۔ لیکن اکثر لوگ شکر
نہیں کرتے (٦١)
یہی خدا تمہارا پروردگار ہے جو ہر چیز کا پیدا کرنے والا ہے
اس کے سوا کوئی معبود نہیں پھر تم کہاں بھٹک رہے ہو (٦٢)
اسی طرح وہ لوگ بھٹک رہے تھے جو خدا کی آیتوں سے
انکار کرتے تھے (٦٣)
خدا ہی تو ہے جس نے زمین کو تمہارے لئے ٹھیرنے کی جگہ اور
آسمان کو چھت بنایا اور تمہاری صورتیں بنائیں اور صورتیں
بھی اچھی بنائیں اور تمہیں پاکیزہ چیزیں کھانے کو دیں۔ یہی خدا تمہارا
پروردگار ہے پس خدائے پروردگار عالم بہت ہی بابرکت ہے (٦٤)
وہ زندہ ہے (جسے موت نہیں) اسکے سوا کوئی عبادت کے
لائق نہیں تو اس کی عبادت کو خالص کر کر اسی کو پکارو۔ ہر

سُلْطٰنٍ اَتٰىهُمْ اِنْ فِيْ صُدُوْرِهِمْ اِلَّا
كِبْرٌ مَّا هُمْ بِبَالِغِيْهِ فَاسْتَعِذْ بِاللّٰهِ
اِنَّهٗ هُوَ السَّمِيْعُ الْبَصِيْرُ (٥٦)
لَخَلْقُ السَّمٰوٰتِ وَالْاَرْضِ اَكْبَرُ مِنْ خَلْقِ
النَّاسِ وَلٰكِنَّ اَكْثَرَ النَّاسِ لَا يَعْلَمُوْنَ (٥٧)
وَمَا يَسْتَوِي الْاَعْمٰى وَالْبَصِيْرُ وَالَّذِيْنَ
اٰمَنُوْا وَعَمِلُوا الصّٰلِحٰتِ وَلَا الْمُسِيْٓءُ قَلِيْلًا
مَّا تَتَذَكَّرُوْنَ (٥٨)
اِنَّ السَّاعَةَ لَاٰتِيَةٌ لَّا رَيْبَ فِيْهَا وَلٰكِنَّ
اَكْثَرَ النَّاسِ لَا يُؤْمِنُوْنَ (٥٩)
وَقَالَ رَبُّكُمُ ادْعُوْنِيْٓ اَسْتَجِبْ لَكُمْ
اِنَّ الَّذِيْنَ يَسْتَكْبِرُوْنَ عَنْ عِبَادَتِيْ
سَيَدْخُلُوْنَ جَهَنَّمَ دَاخِرِيْنَ (٦٠)
اَللّٰهُ الَّذِيْ جَعَلَ لَكُمُ الَّيْلَ لِتَسْكُنُوْا فِيْهِ
وَالنَّهَارَ مُبْصِرًا اِنَّ اللّٰهَ لَذُوْ فَضْلٍ
عَلَى النَّاسِ وَلٰكِنَّ اَكْثَرَ النَّاسِ لَا
يَشْكُرُوْنَ (٦١)
ذٰلِكُمُ اللّٰهُ رَبُّكُمْ خَالِقُ كُلِّ شَيْءٍ لَآ اِلٰهَ
اِلَّا هُوَ فَاَنّٰى تُؤْفَكُوْنَ (٦٢)
كَذٰلِكَ يُؤْفَكُ الَّذِيْنَ كَانُوْا بِاٰيٰتِ
اللّٰهِ يَجْحَدُوْنَ (٦٣)
اَللّٰهُ الَّذِيْ جَعَلَ لَكُمُ الْاَرْضَ قَرَارًا
وَّالسَّمَآءَ بِنَآءً وَّصَوَّرَكُمْ فَاَحْسَنَ صُوَرَكُمْ
وَرَزَقَكُمْ مِّنَ الطَّيِّبٰتِ ذٰلِكُمُ اللّٰهُ
رَبُّكُمْ فَتَبٰرَكَ اللّٰهُ رَبُّ الْعٰلَمِيْنَ (٦٤)
هُوَ الْحَيُّ لَآ اِلٰهَ اِلَّا هُوَ فَادْعُوْهُ
مُخْلِصِيْنَ لَهُ الدِّيْنَ اَلْحَمْدُ

be to Allah, Lord of the Worlds!

66. Say: "I have been forbidden to invoke those whom ye invoke besides Allah,—seeing that the Clear Signs have come to me from my Lord; and I have been commanded to submit (in Islam) to the Lord of the Worlds."

67. It is He Who has created you from dust, then from a sperm-drop, then from a leech-like clot; then does He get you out (into the light) as a child: then lets you (grow and) reach your age of full strength; then lets you become old,— though of you there are some who die before;— and lets you reach a Term appointed; in order that ye may understand.

68. It is He Who gives Life and Death; and when He decides upon an affair, He says to it, "Be", and it is.

69. Seest thou not those that dispute concerning the Signs of Allah? How are they turned away from Reality)?—

70. Those who reject the Book and the (revelations) with which We sent Our messengers: but soon shall they know,—

71. When the yokes (shall be) round their necks, and the chains; they shall be dragged along—

72. In the boiling fetid fluid; then in the Fire shall they be burned;

73. Then shall it be said to them: "Where are the (deities) to which ye gave part-worship—

74. "Besides Allah?" They will reply: "They have left us in the lurch: nay, we invoked not, of old, anything (that had real existence)." Thus does Allah leave the Unbelievers to stray.

75. "That was because ye were wont to rejoice on the earth in things other than the Truth, and that ye were wont to be insolent.

76. "Enter ye the gates of Hell, to dwell therein: and evil is (this) abode of the arrogant!"

طرح کی تعریف خدا ہی کو (سزاوار ہے) جو تمام جہان کا پروردگار ہے ﴿۶۵﴾
(اے محمدؐ ان سے) کہہ دو کہ مجھے اس بات کی ممانعت کی گئی ہے کہ
جنکو تم خدا کے سوا پکارتے ہو اُنکی پرستش کروں (اور میں اُنکی کیونکر
پرستش کروں) جبکہ میرے پاس میرے پروردگار کی طرف سے کھلی دلیلیں
آچکی ہیں اور مجھکو یہ حکم ہوا ہے کہ پروردگار عالم ہی کا تابع فرمان ہوں ﴿۶۶﴾
وہی تو ہے جس نے تم کو (پہلے) مٹی سے پیدا کیا۔ پھر نطفہ بنا کر
پھر لوتھڑا بنا کر پھر تم کو نکالتا ہے (کہ تم) بچے (ہوتے ہو) پھر تم
اپنی جوانی کو پہنچتے ہو پھر بوڑھے ہو جاتے ہو۔ اور کوئی تم میں
سے پہلے ہی مر جاتا ہے اور تم (موت کے) وقت مقرر تک
پہنچ جاتے ہو اور تاکہ تم سمجھو ﴿۶۷﴾
وہی تو ہے جو جلاتا اور مارتا ہے۔ پھر جب وہ کوئی کام کرنا (اور کسی کو
پیدا کرنا) چاہتا ہے تو اُس سے کہہ دیتا ہے کہ ہو جا تو وہ ہو جاتا ہے ﴿۶۸﴾
کیا تم نے اُن لوگوں کو نہیں دیکھا جو خدا کی آیتوں میں
جھگڑتے ہیں۔ یہ کہاں بھٹک رہے ہیں؟ ﴿۶۹﴾
جن لوگوں نے کتاب (خدا) کو اور جو کچھ ہم نے اپنے پیغمبروں کو
دے کر بھیجا اُس کو جھٹلایا۔ وہ عنقریب معلوم کرلیں گے ﴿۷۰﴾
جبکہ اُن کی گردنوں میں طوق اور زنجیریں ہوں گی (اور)
گھسیٹے جائیں گے ﴿۷۱﴾
(یعنی) کھولتے ہوئے پانی میں۔ پھر آگ میں جھونک دیئے جائینگے ﴿۷۲﴾
پھر اُنسے کہا جائیگا کہ وہ کہاں ہیں جنکو تم (خدا کے) شریک بناتے تھے ﴿۷۳﴾
(یعنی) غیر خدا۔ کہیں گے وہ تو ہم سے جاتے رہے بلکہ ہم تو
پہلے کسی چیز کو پکارتے ہی نہیں تھے۔ اسی طرح خدا
کافروں کو گمراہ کرتا ہے ﴿۷۴﴾
یہ اس کا بدلہ ہے کہ تم زمین میں حق کے بغیر (یعنی اسکے
خلاف) خوش ہوا کرتے تھے اور اُسکی (سزا ہے) کہ اترایا کرتے تھے ﴿۷۵﴾
(اب) جہنم کے دروازوں میں داخل ہو جاؤ ہمیشہ اسی میں
رہو گے۔ متکبروں کا کیا بُرا ٹھکانا ہے ﴿۷۶﴾

لِلّٰهِ رَبِّ الْعٰلَمِيْنَ ﴿٦٥﴾
قُلْ اِنِّیْ نُهِیْتُ اَنْ اَعْبُدَ الَّذِیْنَ
تَدْعُوْنَ مِنْ دُوْنِ اللّٰهِ لَمَّا جَآءَنِیَ
الْبَیِّنٰتُ مِنْ رَّبِّیْ ۫ وَاُمِرْتُ اَنْ اُسْلِمَ
لِرَبِّ الْعٰلَمِیْنَ ﴿٦٦﴾
هُوَ الَّذِیْ خَلَقَكُمْ مِّنْ تُرَابٍ ثُمَّ
مِنْ نُّطْفَةٍ ثُمَّ مِنْ عَلَقَةٍ ثُمَّ یُخْرِجُكُمْ
طِفْلًا ثُمَّ لِتَبْلُغُوْۤا اَشُدَّكُمْ ثُمَّ لِتَكُوْنُوْا
شُیُوْخًا ۚ وَمِنْكُمْ مَّنْ یُّتَوَفّٰی مِنْ قَبْلُ
وَلِتَبْلُغُوْۤا اَجَلًا مُّسَمًّی وَّلَعَلَّكُمْ تَعْقِلُوْنَ ﴿٦٧﴾
هُوَ الَّذِیْ یُحْیٖ وَیُمِیْتُ ۚ فَاِذَا قَضٰۤی اَمْرًا
فَاِنَّمَا یَقُوْلُ لَهٗ كُنْ فَیَكُوْنُ ﴿٦٨﴾
اَلَمْ تَرَ اِلَی الَّذِیْنَ یُجَادِلُوْنَ فِیْۤ اٰیٰتِ
اللّٰهِ ؕ اَنّٰی یُصْرَفُوْنَ ﴿٦٩﴾
الَّذِیْنَ كَذَّبُوْا بِالْكِتٰبِ وَبِمَاۤ اَرْسَلْنَا بِهٖ
رُسُلَنَا ۛ فَسَوْفَ یَعْلَمُوْنَ ﴿٧٠﴾
اِذِ الْاَغْلٰلُ فِیْۤ اَعْنَاقِهِمْ وَالسَّلٰسِلُ ؕ
یُسْحَبُوْنَ ﴿٧١﴾
فِی الْحَمِیْمِ ۙ ثُمَّ فِی النَّارِ یُسْجَرُوْنَ ﴿٧٢﴾
ثُمَّ قِیْلَ لَهُمْ اَیْنَ مَا كُنْتُمْ تُشْرِكُوْنَ ﴿٧٣﴾
مِنْ دُوْنِ اللّٰهِ ؕ قَالُوْا ضَلُّوْا عَنَّا بَلْ
لَّمْ نَكُنْ نَّدْعُوْا مِنْ قَبْلُ شَیْـًٔا ؕ كَذٰلِكَ
یُضِلُّ اللّٰهُ الْكٰفِرِیْنَ ﴿٧٤﴾
ذٰلِكُمْ بِمَا كُنْتُمْ تَفْرَحُوْنَ فِی الْاَرْضِ بِغَیْرِ
الْحَقِّ وَبِمَا كُنْتُمْ تَمْرَحُوْنَ ﴿٧٥﴾
اُدْخُلُوْۤا اَبْوَابَ جَهَنَّمَ خٰلِدِیْنَ فِیْهَا ۚ
فَبِئْسَ مَثْوَی الْمُتَكَبِّرِیْنَ ﴿٧٦﴾

فَاصْبِرْ إِنَّ وَعْدَ اللّٰهِ حَقٌّ فَإِمَّا نُرِيَنَّكَ
بَعْضَ الَّذِي نَعِدُهُمْ أَوْ نَتَوَفَّيَنَّكَ
فَإِلَيْنَا يُرْجَعُونَ ﴿۷۷﴾

تو (اے پیغمبر) صبر کرو خدا کا وعدہ سچا ہے۔ اگر ہم تم کو کچھ اس میں سے دکھا دیں
جس کا ہم تم سے وعدہ کرتے ہیں (یعنی کافروں پر عذاب نازل کریں) یا
تمہاری مدت حیات پوری کر دیں تو ان کو ہماری ہی طرف لوٹ کر آنا ہے (۷۷)

77. So persevere in patience; for the Promise of Allah is true: and whether We show thee (in this life) some part of what We promise them,—or We take thy soul (to Our Mercy) (before that),—(in any case) it is to Us that they shall (all) return.

وَلَقَدْ أَرْسَلْنَا رُسُلًا مِّنْ قَبْلِكَ مِنْهُمْ
مَّنْ قَصَصْنَا عَلَيْكَ وَمِنْهُمْ مَّنْ لَّمْ
نَقْصُصْ عَلَيْكَ وَمَا كَانَ لِرَسُولٍ
أَنْ يَأْتِيَ بِآيَةٍ إِلَّا بِإِذْنِ اللّٰهِ فَإِذَا جَاءَ
أَمْرُ اللّٰهِ قُضِيَ بِالْحَقِّ وَخَسِرَ هُنَالِكَ
الْمُبْطِلُونَ ﴿۷۸﴾ ع ۱۴

اور ہم نے تم سے پہلے (بہت سے) پیغمبر بھیجے۔ ان میں کچھ تو ایسے
ہیں جن کے حالات تم سے بیان کر دیئے ہیں اور کچھ ایسے ہیں
جن کے حالات بیان نہیں کئے۔ اور کسی پیغمبر کا مقدور نہ تھا
کہ خدا کے حکم کے بغیر کوئی نشانی لائے۔ پھر جب خدا کا حکم
آ پہنچا تو انصاف کے ساتھ فیصلہ کر دیا گیا اور اہل باطل
نقصان میں پڑ گئے (۷۸)

78. We did aforetime send Messengers before thee: of them there are some whose story We have related to thee, and some whose story We have not related to thee. It was not (possible) for any messenger to bring a Sign except by the leave of Allah: but when the Command of Allah issued, the matter was decided in truth and justice, and there perished, there and then, those who stood on Falsehoods.

اللّٰهُ الَّذِي جَعَلَ لَكُمُ الْأَنْعَامَ لِتَرْكَبُوا
مِنْهَا وَمِنْهَا تَأْكُلُونَ ﴿۷۹﴾

خدا ہی تو ہے جس نے تمہارے لئے چارپائے بنائے تاکہ
ان میں سے بعض پر سوار ہو اور بعض کو تم کھاتے ہو (۷۹)

79. It is Allah who made cattle for you, that ye may use some for riding and some for food;

وَلَكُمْ فِيهَا مَنَافِعُ وَلِتَبْلُغُوا عَلَيْهَا
حَاجَةً فِي صُدُورِكُمْ وَعَلَيْهَا وَعَلَى
الْفُلْكِ تُحْمَلُونَ ﴿۸۰﴾

اور تمہارے لئے ان میں (اور بھی) فائدے ہیں اور اس لئے
بھی کہ (کہیں جانے کی) تمہارے دلوں میں جو حاجت ہو ان پر
(چڑھ کر وہاں) پہنچ جاؤ۔ اور ان پر اور کشتیوں پر تم سوار ہوتے ہو (۸۰)

80. And there are (other) advantages in them for you (besides); that ye may through them attain to any need (there may be) in your hearts; and on them and on ships ye are carried.

وَيُرِيكُمْ آيَاتِهِ فَأَيَّ آيَاتِ اللّٰهِ
تُنْكِرُونَ ﴿۸۱﴾

اور وہ تمہیں اپنی نشانیاں دکھاتا ہے تو تم خدا کی کن کن
نشانیوں کو نہ مانو گے (۸۱)

81. And He shows you (always) His Signs: then which of the Signs of Allah will ye deny?

أَفَلَمْ يَسِيرُوا فِي الْأَرْضِ فَيَنْظُرُوا
كَيْفَ كَانَ عَاقِبَةُ الَّذِينَ مِنْ قَبْلِهِمْ
كَانُوا أَكْثَرَ مِنْهُمْ وَأَشَدَّ قُوَّةً وَّ
آثَارًا فِي الْأَرْضِ فَمَا أَغْنَىٰ عَنْهُمْ مَّا
كَانُوا يَكْسِبُونَ ﴿۸۲﴾

کیا ان لوگوں نے زمین میں سیر نہیں کی تاکہ دیکھتے
کہ جو لوگ ان سے پہلے تھے ان کا انجام کیسا ہوا۔
(حالانکہ) وہ ان سے کہیں زیادہ اور طاقتور اور زمین
میں نشانات (بنانے) کے اعتبار سے بہت بڑھ کر تھے۔
تو جو کچھ وہ کرتے تھے وہ ان کے کچھ کام نہ آیا (۸۲)

82. Do they not travel through the earth and see what was the End of those before them? They were more numerous than these and superior in strength and in the traces (they have left) in the land: yet all that they accomplished was of no profit to them.

فَلَمَّا جَاءَتْهُمْ رُسُلُهُمْ بِالْبَيِّنَاتِ فَرِحُوا
بِمَا عِنْدَهُمْ مِّنَ الْعِلْمِ وَحَاقَ بِهِمْ مَّا
كَانُوا بِهِ يَسْتَهْزِئُونَ ﴿۸۳﴾

اور جب انکے پیغمبر انکے پاس کھلی نشانیاں لیکر آئے تو جو علم
(اپنے خیال میں) ان کے پاس تھا اس پر اترانے لگے
اور جس چیز سے تمسخر کیا کرتے تھے اس نے ان کو آ گھیرا (۸۳)

83. For when their messengers came to them with Clear Signs, they exulted in such knowledge (and skill) as they had; but that very (Wrath) at which they were wont to scoff hemmed them in.

فَلَمَّا رَأَوْا بَأْسَنَا قَالُوا آمَنَّا بِاللّٰهِ وَحْدَهُ
وَكَفَرْنَا بِمَا كُنَّا بِهِ مُشْرِكِينَ ﴿۸۴﴾

پھر جب انہوں نے ہمارا عذاب دیکھ لیا تو کہنے لگے کہ ہم خدائے واحد پر
ایمان لائے اور جس چیز کو اس کیساتھ شریک بناتے تھے اس سے نامعتقد ہوئے (۸۴)

84. But when they saw Our Might, they said: "We believe in Allah,—the One God—and we reject the partners we used to join with Him."

فَلَمْ يَكُ يَنْفَعُهُمْ إِيمَانُهُمْ لَمَّا رَأَوْا

لیکن جب وہ ہمارا عذاب دیکھ چکے (اس وقت) انکے ایمان نے ان کو

85. But their professing the Faith when they (actually) saw Our Pun-

SÛRA–41
FUṢṢILAT
(INTRODUCTION)

This is the second of the series of seven Sûras bearing the Abbreviated Letters *Ḥã-Mîm*, as explained in the Introduction to S. 40. To prevent confusion with other Sûras of the *Ḥã-Mîm* series, the word *Sajda* is sometimes added to the title, making it *Ḥã-Mîm as-Sajda*, the double title being necessary as there is another Sûra called *Sajda* (S. 32). To avoid the double title it is sometimes called *Fuṣṣilat*, from the occurrence of the word in verse 3.

The meaning of *Ḥã-Mîm* has been explained in the Introduction to S. 40, where will also be found a note on the chronology and general theme of the seven *Ḥã-Mîm* Sûras.

For this particular Sûra the theme is that the basis of Faith and Revelation is Allah's Power and Goodness, and the fruit of both is man's righteousness and healing.

ishment was not going to profit them. (Such has been) Allah's way of dealing with His servants (from the most ancient times). And even thus did the rejecters of Allah lose (utterly)!

Ḥā-Mîm (Abbreviated Letters), Or Ḥa-Mîm Sajda, or Fuṣṣilat

In the name of Allah, Most Gracious, Most Merciful.

1. Ḥā-Mîm:

2. A revelation from The Most Gracious, Most Merciful;—

3. A Book, whereof the verses are explained in detail;— a Qur-ān in Arabic, for people who understand;—

4. Giving Good News and Admonition: yet most of them turn away, and so they hear not.

5. They say: "Our hearts are under veils, (concealed) from that to which thou dost invite us, and in our ears is a deafness, between us and thee is a screen: so do thou (what thou wilt); for us, we shall do (what we will!)"

6. Say thou: "I am but a man like you: it is revealed to me by inspiration, that your God is One God: so take the straight path unto Him and ask for His forgiveness." And woe to those who join gods with Allah,—

7. Those who pay not Zakat and who even deny the Hereafter.

8. For those who believe and work deeds of righteousness is a reward that will never fail.

9. Say: Is it that ye deny Him Who created the earth in two Days? And do ye join equals with Him? He is the Lord of (all) the Worlds.

10. He set on the (earth), mountains standing firm, high above it, and bestowed blessings on the earth, and measured therein its sustenance in four Days, alike for (all) who ask.

11. Then He turned to the sky, and it had been (as) smoke: He

کچھ بھی فائدہ نہ دیا۔ (یہ) خدا کی عادت (ہی) جو اُسکے بندوں (کے
بارے) میں چلی آتی ہے! اور وہاں کافر گھاٹے میں پڑ کر رہ گئے (۸۵)

سورہ حٰم السجدہ مکی ہے اس میں چوّن آیتیں اور چھ رکوع ہیں

شروع خدا کا نام لیکر جو بڑا مہربان نہایت رحم والا ہے
حٰم (۱) (یہ کتاب خدائے) رحمٰن و رحیم (کی طرف) سے اُتری ہے (۲)
(ایسی) کتاب جس کی آیتیں واضح (المعانی) ہیں (یعنی)
قرآن عربی اُن لوگوں کے لئے جو سمجھ رکھتے ہیں (۳)
جو بشارت بھی سُناتا ہے اور خوف بھی دلاتا ہے لیکن اُن میں
سے اکثروں نے مُنہ پھیر لیا اور وہ سنتے ہی نہیں (۴)
اور کہنے لگے کہ جس چیز کی طرف تم ہمیں بُلاتے ہو اس سے ہمارے دل
پردوں میں ہیں اور ہمارے کانوں میں بوجھ (یعنی بہرا پن) ہے
اور ہمارے اور تمہارے درمیان پردہ ہے تو تم (اپنا) کام کرو ہم (اپنا) کام کرتے ہیں (۵)
کہہ دو کہ میں بھی آدمی ہوں جیسے تم (ہاں) مجھ پر یہ وحی آتی
ہے کہ تمہارا معبود خدائے واحد ہے تو سیدھے اُسی
کی طرف متوجہ رہو اور اُسی سے مغفرت مانگو۔ اور مشرکوں
پر افسوس ہے (۶)
جو زکوٰۃ نہیں دیتے۔ اور آخرت کے بھی قائل
نہیں (۷)
جو لوگ ایمان لائے اور عمل نیک کرتے رہے اُن کے لئے
(ایسا) ثواب ہے جو ختم ہی نہ ہو (۸)
کہو کیا تم اُس سے انکار کرتے ہو جس نے زمین کو دو دن
میں پیدا کیا۔ اور (بتوں کو) اس کا مدمقابل بناتے ہو۔ وہی تو
سارے جہان کا مالک ہے (۹)
اور اسی نے زمین میں اُس کے اُوپر پہاڑ بنائے اور زمین
میں برکت رکھی اور اس میں سامانِ معیشت مقرر کیا (سب)
چار دن میں۔ (اور تمام) طلبگاروں کے لئے یکساں (۱۰)
پھر آسمان کی طرف متوجہ ہوا اور وہ دھواں تھا تو اُس نے

بَأْسَنَا ۖ سُنَّتَ اللّٰهِ الَّتِي قَدْ خَلَتْ
فِي عِبَادِهِ ۚ وَخَسِرَ هُنَالِكَ الْكٰفِرُونَ (۸۵) ع ۹ ۷ ۱۴

سُورَةُ حٰمٓ السَّجْدَةِ مَكِّيَّةٌ وَهِيَ أَرْبَعٌ وَخَمْسُونَ آيَةً وَسِتُّ رُكُوعَاتٍ

بِسْمِ اللّٰهِ الرَّحْمٰنِ الرَّحِيمِ
حٰمٓ (۱) تَنْزِيلٌ مِّنَ الرَّحْمٰنِ الرَّحِيمِ (۲)
كِتٰبٌ فُصِّلَتْ اٰيٰتُهُ قُرْاٰنًا عَرَبِيًّا لِّقَوْمٍ
يَّعْلَمُونَ (۳)
بَشِيرًا وَّنَذِيرًا ۚ فَأَعْرَضَ أَكْثَرُهُمْ
فَهُمْ لَا يَسْمَعُونَ (۴)
وَقَالُوا قُلُوبُنَا فِي أَكِنَّةٍ مِّمَّا تَدْعُونَا
إِلَيْهِ وَفِي اٰذَانِنَا وَقْرٌ وَّمِنْ بَيْنِنَا
وَبَيْنِكَ حِجَابٌ فَاعْمَلْ إِنَّنَا عٰمِلُونَ (۵)
قُلْ إِنَّمَا أَنَا بَشَرٌ مِّثْلُكُمْ يُوحٰى
إِلَيَّ أَنَّمَا إِلٰهُكُمْ إِلٰهٌ وَّاحِدٌ
فَاسْتَقِيمُوا إِلَيْهِ وَاسْتَغْفِرُوهُ ۗ وَوَيْلٌ
لِّلْمُشْرِكِينَ (۶)
الَّذِينَ لَا يُؤْتُونَ الزَّكٰوةَ وَهُمْ بِالْاٰخِرَةِ
هُمْ كٰفِرُونَ (۷)
إِنَّ الَّذِينَ اٰمَنُوا وَعَمِلُوا الصّٰلِحٰتِ
لَهُمْ أَجْرٌ غَيْرُ مَمْنُونٍ (۸) ع ۱ ۸ ۱۵
قُلْ أَئِنَّكُمْ لَتَكْفُرُونَ بِالَّذِي خَلَقَ
الْأَرْضَ فِي يَوْمَيْنِ وَتَجْعَلُونَ لَهٗ
أَنْدَادًا ۗ ذٰلِكَ رَبُّ الْعٰلَمِينَ (۹)
وَجَعَلَ فِيهَا رَوَاسِيَ مِنْ فَوْقِهَا وَ
بٰرَكَ فِيهَا وَقَدَّرَ فِيهَا أَقْوَاتَهَا فِي أَرْبَعَةِ
أَيَّامٍ ۗ سَوَاءً لِّلسَّائِلِينَ (۱۰)
ثُمَّ اسْتَوٰى إِلَى السَّمَاءِ وَهِيَ دُخَانٌ

said to it and to the earth: "Come ye together, willingly or unwillingly." They said: "We do come (together), in willing obedience."
12. So He completed them as seven firmaments in two Days, and He assigned to each heaven its duty and command. And We adorned the lower heaven with lights, and (provided it) with guard. Such is the Decree of (Him) the Exalted in Might, Full of knowledge.
13. But if they turn away, say thou: "I have warned you of a thunderbolt like the thunderbolt of the 'Ãd and the Thamûd!"
14. Behold, the messengers came to them, from before them and behind them, (preaching): "Serve none but Allah." They said, "If our Lord had so pleased, He would certainly have sent down angels: so we disbelieve in the Message you were sent with.
15. Now the 'Ãd behaved arrogantly through the land, against (all) truth and reason, and said: "Who is superior to us in strength?" What! did they not see that Allah, Who created them, was superior to them in strength? But they continued to reject Our Signs!

16. So We sent against them a furious Wind through days of disaster, that We might give them a taste of a Chastisement of humiliation in this Life; but the Penalty of the Hereafter will be more humiliating still: and they will find no help.
17. As to the Thamûd, We gave them guidance, but they preferred blindness (of heart) to Guidance: so the thunderbolt of the Chastisement of humiliation seized them, because of what they had earned.
18. But We delivered those who believed and practised righteousness.
19. The Day that the enemies of Allah will be gathered together to the Fire, they will be marched in ranks.

اُس سے اور زمین سے فرمایا کہ دونوں آؤ (خواہ) خوشی سے
خواہ ناخوشی سے۔ اُنہوں نے کہا کہ ہم خوشی سے آتے ہیں (11)
پھر دو دن میں سات آسمان بنائے اور ہر آسمان میں
اُس (کے کام) کا حکم بھیجا اور ہم نے آسمانِ دنیا کو چراغوں
(یعنی ستاروں) سے مزین کیا اور (شیطانوں سے) محفوظ رکھا۔ یہ
زبردست (اور) خبردار کے (مقرر کئے ہوئے) انداز ے ہیں (12)
پھر اگر یہ منہ پھیر لیں تو کہہ دو کہ میں تم کو ایسی چنگھاڑ (کے عذاب)
سے آگاہ کرتا ہوں جیسے عاد اور ثمود پر چنگھاڑ (کا عذاب آیا) تھا (13)
جب اُن کے پاس پیغمبر اُن کے آگے اور پیچھے سے آئے کہ خدا
کے سوا (کسی کی) عبادت نہ کرو۔ کہنے لگے کہ اگر ہمارا پروردگار
چاہتا تو فرشتے اُتار دیتا سو جو تم دے کر بھیجے گئے ہو ہم
اُس کو نہیں مانتے (14)
جو عاد تھے وہ ناحق ملک میں غرور کرنے لگے اور کہنے لگے کہ
ہم سے بڑھ کر قوت میں کون ہے؟ کیا اُنہوں نے نہیں
دیکھا کہ خدا جس نے اُن کو پیدا کیا وہ اُن سے قوت
میں بہت بڑھ کر ہے۔ اور وہ ہماری آیتوں سے
انکار کرتے رہے (15)
تو ہم نے بھی اُن پر نحوست کے دنوں میں زور کی ہوا
چلائی تاکہ اُن کو دنیا کی زندگی میں ذلت کے عذاب
کا مزہ چکھا دیں۔ اور آخرت کا عذاب تو بہت ہی ذلیل
کرنے والا ہے اور (اُس روز) اُن کو مدد بھی نہ ملے گی (16)
اور جو ثمود تھے اُن کو ہم نے سیدھا رستہ دکھا دیا تھا مگر
اُنہوں نے ہدایت کے مقابلے میں اندھا رہنا پسند کیا۔ تو اُن کے
اعمال کی سزا میں کڑک نے اُن کو آ پکڑا۔ اور وہ ذلت کا عذاب تھا (17)
اور جو ایمان لائے اور پرہیزگاری کرتے رہے اُن کو ہم نے بچا لیا (18)
اور جس دن خدا کے دشمن دوزخ کی طرف چلائے جائیں گے
تو ترتیب وار کر لئے جائیں گے (19)

فَقَالَ لَهَا وَلِلْأَرْضِ ائْتِيَا طَوْعًا أَوْ
كَرْهًا قَالَتَا أَتَيْنَا طَائِعِينَ (11)
فَقَضَاهُنَّ سَبْعَ سَمَاوَاتٍ فِي يَوْمَيْنِ
وَأَوْحَىٰ فِي كُلِّ سَمَاءٍ أَمْرَهَا وَزَيَّنَّا
السَّمَاءَ الدُّنْيَا بِمَصَابِيحَ وَحِفْظًا
ذَٰلِكَ تَقْدِيرُ الْعَزِيزِ الْعَلِيمِ (12)
فَإِنْ أَعْرَضُوا فَقُلْ أَنذَرْتُكُمْ صَاعِقَةً
مِّثْلَ صَاعِقَةِ عَادٍ وَثَمُودَ (13)
إِذْ جَاءَتْهُمُ الرُّسُلُ مِن بَيْنِ أَيْدِيهِمْ
وَمِنْ خَلْفِهِمْ أَلَّا تَعْبُدُوا إِلَّا اللَّهَ
قَالُوا لَوْ شَاءَ رَبُّنَا لَأَنزَلَ مَلَائِكَةً
فَإِنَّا بِمَا أُرْسِلْتُم بِهِ كَافِرُونَ (14)
فَأَمَّا عَادٌ فَاسْتَكْبَرُوا فِي الْأَرْضِ بِغَيْرِ
الْحَقِّ وَقَالُوا مَنْ أَشَدُّ مِنَّا قُوَّةً
أَوَلَمْ يَرَوْا أَنَّ اللَّهَ الَّذِي خَلَقَهُمْ
هُوَ أَشَدُّ مِنْهُمْ قُوَّةً وَكَانُوا بِآيَاتِنَا
يَجْحَدُونَ (15)
فَأَرْسَلْنَا عَلَيْهِمْ رِيحًا صَرْصَرًا فِي أَيَّامٍ
نَّحِسَاتٍ لِّنُذِيقَهُمْ عَذَابَ الْخِزْيِ
فِي الْحَيَاةِ الدُّنْيَا وَلَعَذَابُ الْآخِرَةِ
أَخْزَىٰ وَهُمْ لَا يُنصَرُونَ (16)
وَأَمَّا ثَمُودُ فَهَدَيْنَاهُمْ فَاسْتَحَبُّوا
الْعَمَىٰ عَلَى الْهُدَىٰ فَأَخَذَتْهُمْ صَاعِقَةُ
الْعَذَابِ الْهُونِ بِمَا كَانُوا يَكْسِبُونَ (17)
وَنَجَّيْنَا الَّذِينَ آمَنُوا وَكَانُوا يَتَّقُونَ (18) ع
وَيَوْمَ يُحْشَرُ أَعْدَاءُ اللَّهِ إِلَى النَّارِ فَهُمْ
يُوزَعُونَ (19)

حَتّٰىٓ اِذَا مَا جَآءُوْهَا شَهِدَ عَلَيْهِمْ
سَمْعُهُمْ وَاَبْصَارُهُمْ وَجُلُوْدُهُمْ بِمَا
كَانُوْا يَعْمَلُوْنَ ﴿٢٠﴾

یہاں تک کہ جب اُس کے پاس پہنچ جائیں گے تو اُنکے
کان اور آنکھیں اور چمڑے (یعنی دوسرے اعضا) اُنکے
خلاف اُن کے اعمال کی شہادت دیں گے ﴿۲۰﴾

20. At length, when they reach the (Fire), their hearing, their sight, and their skins will bear witness against them, as to (all) their deeds.

وَقَالُوْا لِجُلُوْدِهِمْ لِمَ شَهِدْتُّمْ عَلَيْنَا ؕ
قَالُوْٓا اَنْطَقَنَا اللّٰهُ الَّذِيْٓ اَنْطَقَ كُلَّ شَيْءٍ
وَّهُوَ خَلَقَكُمْ اَوَّلَ مَرَّةٍ وَّاِلَيْهِ تُرْجَعُوْنَ ﴿٢١﴾

اور وہ اپنے چمڑوں (یعنی اعضا) سے کہینگے کہ تم نے ہمارے خلاف کیوں شہادت
دی؟ وہ کہینگے کہ جس خدا نے سب چیزوں کو نطق بخشا اُسی نے ہم کو بھی
گویائی دی اور اُسی نے تم کو پہلی بار پیدا کیا تھا اور اُسی کی طرف تم کو لوٹ کر جانا ہے ﴿۲۱﴾

21. They will say to their skins: "Why bear ye witness against us?" They will say: "Allah hath given us speech, (He) Who giveth speech to everything: He created you for the first time, and unto Him were ye to return.

وَمَا كُنْتُمْ تَسْتَتِرُوْنَ اَنْ يَّشْهَدَ عَلَيْكُمْ
سَمْعُكُمْ وَلَآ اَبْصَارُكُمْ وَلَا جُلُوْدُكُمْ وَلٰكِنْ
ظَنَنْتُمْ اَنَّ اللّٰهَ لَا يَعْلَمُ كَثِيْرًا مِّمَّا تَعْمَلُوْنَ ﴿٢٢﴾

اور تم اس (بات کے خوف) سے تو پردہ نہیں کرتے تھے کہ تمہارے کان اور تمہاری
آنکھیں اور چمڑے تمہارے خلاف شہادت دینگے بلکہ تم یہ خیال کرتے
تھے کہ خدا کو تمہارے بہت سے عملوں کی خبر ہی نہیں ﴿۲۲﴾

22. "Ye did not seek to hide yourselves, lest your hearing, your sight, and your skins should bear witness against you! But ye did think that Allah knew not many of the things that ye used to do!

وَذٰلِكُمْ ظَنُّكُمُ الَّذِيْ ظَنَنْتُمْ بِرَبِّكُمْ
اَرْدٰىكُمْ فَاَصْبَحْتُمْ مِّنَ الْخٰسِرِيْنَ ﴿٢٣﴾

اور اسی خیال نے جو تم اپنے پروردگار کے بارے میں رکھتے تھے
تم کو ہلاک کر دیا اور تم خسارہ پانے والوں میں ہو گئے ﴿۲۳﴾

23. "But this thought of yours which ye did entertain concerning your Lord, hath brought you to destruction, and (now) have ye become of those utterly lost!"

فَاِنْ يَّصْبِرُوْا فَالنَّارُ مَثْوًى لَّهُمْ ۚ وَاِنْ
يَّسْتَعْتِبُوْا فَمَا هُمْ مِّنَ الْمُعْتَبِيْنَ ﴿٢٤﴾

اب اگر یہ صبر کریں گے تو اُن کا ٹھکانا دوزخ ہی ہے
اور اگر توبہ کریں گے تو اُن کی توبہ قبول نہیں کی جائیگی ﴿۲۴﴾

24. If, then, they have patience, the Fire will be a Home for them! And if they beg for pardon, their suit shall not be granted.

وَقَيَّضْنَا لَهُمْ قُرَنَآءَ فَزَيَّنُوْا لَهُمْ مَّا بَيْنَ
اَيْدِيْهِمْ وَمَا خَلْفَهُمْ وَحَقَّ عَلَيْهِمُ الْقَوْلُ
فِيْٓ اُمَمٍ قَدْ خَلَتْ مِنْ قَبْلِهِمْ مِّنَ الْجِنِّ
وَالْاِنْسِ ۚ اِنَّهُمْ كَانُوْا خٰسِرِيْنَ ﴿٢٥﴾

اور ہم نے (شیطانوں کو) اُنکا ہمنشین مقرر کر دیا تھا تو اُنہوں
نے اُنکے اگلے اور پچھلے اعمال اُن کو عمدہ کر دکھائے تھے اور
جنات اور انسانوں کی جماعتیں جو اُن سے پہلے گزر چکیں اُن پر بھی خدا کے
عذاب کا وعدہ پورا ہو گیا۔ بیشک یہ نقصان اُٹھانیوالے ہیں ﴿۲۵﴾

25. And We have destined forthem intimate companions (of like nature), who made alluring to them what was before them and behind them; and the word among the previous generations of Jinns and men, who have passed away, is proved against them; for they are utterly lost.

وَقَالَ الَّذِيْنَ كَفَرُوْا لَا تَسْمَعُوْا لِهٰذَا
الْقُرْاٰنِ وَالْغَوْا فِيْهِ لَعَلَّكُمْ تَغْلِبُوْنَ ﴿٢٦﴾

اور کافر کہنے لگے کہ اِس قرآن کو سُنا ہی نہ کرو اور (جب پڑھنے
لگیں تو) شور مچا دیا کرو تاکہ تم غالب رہو ﴿۲۶﴾

26. The Unbelievers say: "Listen not to this Qur'ān, but talk at random in the midst of its (reading), that ye may gain the upper hand!"

فَلَنُذِيْقَنَّ الَّذِيْنَ كَفَرُوْا عَذَابًا شَدِيْدًا
وَّلَنَجْزِيَنَّهُمْ اَسْوَاَ الَّذِيْ كَانُوْا يَعْمَلُوْنَ ﴿٢٧﴾

سو ہم بھی کافروں کو سخت عذاب کے مزے چکھائیں گے اور
اُن کے بُرے عملوں کی جو وہ کرتے تھے سزا دیں گے ﴿۲۷﴾

27. But We will certainly give the Unbelievers a taste of a severe Chastisement, and We will requite them for the worst of their deeds.

ذٰلِكَ جَزَآءُ اَعْدَآءِ اللّٰهِ النَّارُ ۚ لَهُمْ
فِيْهَا دَارُ الْخُلْدِ ؕ جَزَآءًۢ بِمَا كَانُوْا
بِاٰيٰتِنَا يَجْحَدُوْنَ ﴿٢٨﴾

یہ خدا کے دشمنوں کا بدلہ ہے (یعنی) دوزخ۔ اُن کیلئے
اسی میں ہمیشہ کا گھر ہے۔ یہ اس کی سزا ہے کہ ہماری آیتوں
سے انکار کرتے تھے ﴿۲۸﴾

28. Such is the requital of the enemies of Allah,— the Fire: therein will be for them the Eternal Home: a (fit) requital, for that they were wont to reject Our Signs.

وَقَالَ الَّذِيْنَ كَفَرُوْا رَبَّنَآ اَرِنَا الَّذَيْنِ
اَضَلّٰنَا مِنَ الْجِنِّ وَالْاِنْسِ نَجْعَلْهُمَا
تَحْتَ اَقْدَامِنَا لِيَكُوْنَا مِنَ الْاَسْفَلِيْنَ ﴿٢٩﴾

اور کافر کہیں گے کہ اے ہمارے پروردگار جنّوں اور انسانوں
میں سے جن لوگوں نے ہمکو گمراہ کیا تھا اُنکو ہمیں دکھا کہ ہم اُن کو اپنے
پاؤں کے تلے (روند) ڈالیں تاکہ وہ نہایت ذلیل ہوں ﴿۲۹﴾

29. And the Unbelievers will say: "Our Lord! Show us those, among Jinns and men, who misled us: we shall crush them beneath our feet, so that they become the vilest."

30. In the case of those who say, "Our Lord is Allah", and, further, stand straight and steadfast, the angels descend on them (from time to time): "Fear ye not!" (they suggest), "Nor grieve! But receive the Glad Tidings of the Garden (of Bliss), the which ye were promised!

31. "We are your protectors in this life and in the Hereafter: therein shall ye have all that you shall desire; therein shall ye have all that ye ask for!—

32. "A hospitable gift from One Oft-Forgiving, Most Merciful!"

33. Who is better in speech than one who calls (men) to Allah, works righteousness, and says, "I am of those who bow in Islam"?

34. Nor can Goodness and Evil be equal. Repel (Evil) with what is better: then will he between whom and thee was hatred become as it were thy friend and intimate!

35. And no one will be granted such goodness except those who exercise patience and self-restraint,—none but persons of the greatest good fortune.

36. And if (at any time) an incitement to discord is made to thee by the Satan, seek refuge in Allah. He is the One Who hears and knows all things.

37. Among His Signs are the Night and the Day, and the Sun and the Moon. Prostrate not to the sun and the moon, but prostrate to Allah, Who created them, if it is Him ye wish to serve.

38. But if the (Unbelievers) are arrogant, (no matter): for in the presence of thy Lord are those who celebrate His praises by night and by day. And they never flag (nor feel themselves above it).

39. And among His Signs is this: thou seest the earth humble; but when We send down rain to it, it is stirred to life and yields increase. Truly, He Who gives life to the (dead) earth can surely give life to

جن لوگوں نے کہا کہ ہمارا پروردگار خدا ہے پھر وہ (اس پر) قائم
رہے۔ اُن پر فرشتے اُتریں گے (اور کہیں گے) کہ نہ خوف کرو اور نہ
غمناک ہو اور بہشت کی جس کا تم سے وعدہ کیا جاتا ہے خوشی مناؤ (۳۰)
ہم دنیا کی زندگی میں بھی تمہارے دوست تھے اور آخرت میں
بھی (تمہارے رفیق ہیں) اور وہاں جس (نعمت) کو تمہارا جی چاہے گا
تم کو ملے گی اور جو چیز طلب کرو گے تمہارے لئے موجود ہوگی (۳۱)
(یہ) بخشنے والے مہربان کی طرف سے مہمانی ہے (۳۲)
اور اُس شخص سے بات کا اچھا کون ہو سکتا ہے جو خدا کی
طرف بلائے اور عمل نیک کرے اور کہے کہ میں مسلمان
ہوں (۳۳)
اور بھلائی اور بُرائی برابر نہیں ہو سکتی۔ تو (سخت کلامی کا)
ایسے طریق سے جواب دو جو بہت اچھا ہو (ایسا کرنے سے تم دیکھو گے
کہ جس میں اور تم میں دشمنی تھی گویا وہ تمہارا گرم جوش دوست ہے (۳۴)
اور یہ بات اُن ہی لوگوں کو حاصل ہوتی ہے جو برداشت کرنے والے
ہیں۔ اور اُن ہی کو نصیب ہوتی ہے جو بڑے صاحب نصیب ہیں (۳۵)
اور اگر تمہیں شیطان کی جانب سے کوئی وسوسہ پیدا ہو تو خدا کی
پناہ مانگ لیا کرو۔ بیشک وہ سنتا جانتا ہے (۳۶)
اور رات اور دن اور سورج اور چاند اُس کی نشانیوں میں سے
ہیں۔ تم لوگ نہ تو سورج کو سجدہ کرو اور نہ چاند کو۔ بلکہ خدا ہی
کو سجدہ کرو جس نے اُن چیزوں کو پیدا کیا ہے اگر تم کو اُس کی
عبادت منظور ہے (۳۷)
اگر یہ لوگ سرکشی کریں تو (خدا کو بھی اُن کی پروا نہیں) جو (فرشتے)
تمہارے پروردگار کے پاس ہیں وہ رات دن اس کی تسبیح
کرتے رہتے ہیں اور (کبھی) تھکتے ہی نہیں (۳۸)
اور (اے بندے یہ) اُسی کی قدرت کے نمونے ہیں کہ تو زمین کو دبی
ہوئی (یعنی خشک) دیکھتا ہے جب ہم اُس پر پانی برسا دیتے
ہیں تو شاداب ہو جاتی اور پھولنے لگتی ہے تو جس نے زمین کو

إِنَّ الَّذِينَ قَالُوا رَبُّنَا اللَّهُ ثُمَّ اسْتَقَامُوا
تَتَنَزَّلُ عَلَيْهِمُ الْمَلَائِكَةُ أَلَّا تَخَافُوا وَلَا
تَحْزَنُوا وَأَبْشِرُوا بِالْجَنَّةِ الَّتِي كُنتُمْ تُوعَدُونَ ﴿٣٠﴾
نَحْنُ أَوْلِيَاؤُكُمْ فِي الْحَيَاةِ الدُّنْيَا وَفِي
الْآخِرَةِ وَلَكُمْ فِيهَا مَا تَشْتَهِي أَنفُسُكُمْ
وَلَكُمْ فِيهَا مَا تَدَّعُونَ ﴿٣١﴾
نُزُلًا مِّنْ غَفُورٍ رَّحِيمٍ ﴿٣٢﴾ ع
وَمَنْ أَحْسَنُ قَوْلًا مِّمَّن دَعَا إِلَى اللَّهِ
وَعَمِلَ صَالِحًا وَقَالَ إِنَّنِي مِنَ
الْمُسْلِمِينَ ﴿٣٣﴾
وَلَا تَسْتَوِي الْحَسَنَةُ وَلَا السَّيِّئَةُ ادْفَعْ
بِالَّتِي هِيَ أَحْسَنُ فَإِذَا الَّذِي بَيْنَكَ
وَبَيْنَهُ عَدَاوَةٌ كَأَنَّهُ وَلِيٌّ حَمِيمٌ ﴿٣٤﴾
وَمَا يُلَقَّاهَا إِلَّا الَّذِينَ صَبَرُوا وَمَا
يُلَقَّاهَا إِلَّا ذُو حَظٍّ عَظِيمٍ ﴿٣٥﴾
وَإِمَّا يَنزَغَنَّكَ مِنَ الشَّيْطَانِ نَزْغٌ
فَاسْتَعِذْ بِاللَّهِ إِنَّهُ هُوَ السَّمِيعُ الْعَلِيمُ ﴿٣٦﴾
وَمِنْ آيَاتِهِ اللَّيْلُ وَالنَّهَارُ وَالشَّمْسُ
وَالْقَمَرُ لَا تَسْجُدُوا لِلشَّمْسِ وَلَا
لِلْقَمَرِ وَاسْجُدُوا لِلَّهِ الَّذِي خَلَقَهُنَّ
إِن كُنتُمْ إِيَّاهُ تَعْبُدُونَ ﴿٣٧﴾
فَإِنِ اسْتَكْبَرُوا فَالَّذِينَ عِندَ رَبِّكَ
يُسَبِّحُونَ لَهُ بِاللَّيْلِ وَالنَّهَارِ وَهُمْ لَا
يَسْأَمُونَ ﴿٣٨﴾ السجدة
وَمِنْ آيَاتِهِ أَنَّكَ تَرَى الْأَرْضَ خَاشِعَةً
فَإِذَا أَنزَلْنَا عَلَيْهَا الْمَاءَ اهْتَزَّتْ وَرَبَتْ
إِنَّ الَّذِي أَحْيَاهَا لَمُحْيِي الْمَوْتَىٰ إِنَّهُ

(men) who are dead. For He has power over all things.

زندہ کیا وہی مُردوں کو زندہ کرنیوالا ہے بیشک وہ ہر چیز پر قادر ہے ﴿٣٩﴾

عَلٰى كُلِّ شَيْءٍ قَدِيْرٌ ﴿٣٩﴾

40. Those who pervert the Truth in Our Signs are not hidden from Us. Which is better?—he that is cast into the Fire, or he that comes safe through, on the Day of Judgment? Do what ye will: verily He seeth (clearly) all that ye do.

جو لوگ ہماری آیتوں میں کجراہی کرتے ہیں [٢٥٧] وہ ہم سے
پوشیدہ نہیں ہیں۔ بھلا جو شخص دوزخ میں ڈالا جائے
وہ بہتر ہے یا وہ جو قیامت کے دن امن وامان سے
آئے؟ (تو خیر) جو چاہو سو کرلو۔ جو کچھ تم کرتے ہو وہ اس
کو دیکھ رہا ہے ﴿٤٠﴾

اِنَّ الَّذِيْنَ يُلْحِدُوْنَ فِيْٓ اٰيٰتِنَا لَا
يَخْفَوْنَ عَلَيْنَا ؕ اَفَمَنْ يُّلْقٰى فِى النَّارِ
خَيْرٌ اَمْ مَّنْ يَّاْتِيْٓ اٰمِنًا يَّوْمَ الْقِيٰمَةِ ؕ
اِعْمَلُوْا مَا شِئْتُمْ ۙ اِنَّهٗ بِمَا تَعْمَلُوْنَ
بَصِيْرٌ ﴿٤٠﴾

41. Those who reject the Message when it comes to them (are not hidden from Us). And indeed it is a Book of exalted power.

جن لوگوں نے نصیحت کو نہ مانا جب وہ اُن کے پاس
آئی۔ اور یہ تو ایک عالی رُتبہ کتاب ہے ﴿٤١﴾

اِنَّ الَّذِيْنَ كَفَرُوْا بِالذِّكْرِ لَمَّا جَآءَهُمْ ۚ
وَاِنَّهٗ لَكِتٰبٌ عَزِيْزٌ ۙ ﴿٤١﴾

42. No falsehood can approach it from before or behind it: it is sent down by One Full of Wisdom, Worthy of all Praise.

اس پر جھوٹ کا دخل نہ آگے سے ہو سکتا ہے نہ پیچھے
سے۔ (اور) دانا (اور) خوبیوں والے (خدا) کی اُتاری ہوئی ہے ﴿٤٢﴾

لَّا يَاْتِيْهِ الْبَاطِلُ مِنْۢ بَيْنِ يَدَيْهِ وَلَا
مِنْ خَلْفِهٖ ؕ تَنْزِيْلٌ مِّنْ حَكِيْمٍ حَمِيْدٍ ﴿٤٢﴾

43. Nothing is said to thee that was not said to the messengers before thee: surely thy Lord has at His command (all) Forgiveness as well as a most grievous Chastisement.

تم سے وہی باتیں کہی جاتی ہیں جو تم سے پہلے اور پیغمبروں
سے کہی گئی تھیں۔ بیشک تمہارا پروردگار بخش دینے والا
بھی ہے اور عذاب الیم دینے والا بھی ہے ﴿٤٣﴾

مَا يُقَالُ لَكَ اِلَّا مَا قَدْ قِيْلَ لِلرُّسُلِ
مِنْ قَبْلِكَ ؕ اِنَّ رَبَّكَ لَذُوْ مَغْفِرَةٍ
وَّذُوْ عِقَابٍ اَلِيْمٍ ﴿٤٣﴾

44. Had We sent this as a Qur'ān (in a language) other than Arabic, they would Have said: "Why are not its verses explained in detail? What! a foreign (tongue) and (a Messenger) an Arab?" Say: "It is a guide and a healing to those who believe; and for those who believe not, there is a deafness in their ears, and it is blindness in their (eyes): they are (as it were) being called from a place far distant!"

اور اگر ہم اس قرآن کو غیر زبان عرب میں (نازل) کرتے۔ تو
یہ لوگ کہتے کہ اس کی آیتیں (ہماری زبان میں) کیوں کھول کر
بیان نہیں کی گئیں۔ کیا (خوب کہ قرآن تو) عجمی اور (مخاطب) عربی۔ کہدو کہ جو
ایمان لاتے ہیں اُنکے لئے (یہ) ہدایت اور شفا ہے۔ اور جو ایمان نہیں لاتے اُنکے
کانوں میں گرانی (یعنی بہرا پن) ہے اور یہ اُنکے حق میں (موجب) نابینائی ہے۔
گرانی کے سبب اُنکو گویا دُور جگہ سے آواز دی جاتی ہے ﴿٤٤﴾

وَلَوْ جَعَلْنٰهُ قُرْاٰنًا اَعْجَمِيًّا لَّقَالُوْا لَوْلَا
فُصِّلَتْ اٰيٰتُهٗ ؕ ءَاَعْجَمِيٌّ وَّعَرَبِيٌّ ؕ
قُلْ هُوَ لِلَّذِيْنَ اٰمَنُوْا هُدًى وَّشِفَآءٌ ؕ
وَالَّذِيْنَ لَا يُؤْمِنُوْنَ فِيْٓ اٰذَانِهِمْ وَقْرٌ
وَّهُوَ عَلَيْهِمْ عَمًى ؕ اُولٰٓئِكَ يُنَادَوْنَ
مِنْ مَّكَانٍۢ بَعِيْدٍ ﴿٤٤﴾ ع ٥ ١٤ ١٩

45. We certainly gave Moses the Book aforetime: but disputes arose therein. Had it not been for a Word that went forth before from thy Lord, (their differences) would have been settled between them: but they remained in suspicious disquieting doubt thereon.

اور ہم نے موسیٰ کو کتاب دی تو اُس میں اختلاف کیا گیا اور
اگر تمہارے پروردگار کی طرف سے ایک بات پہلے نہ ٹھہر
چکی ہوتی تو اُن میں فیصلہ کر دیا جاتا۔ اور یہ اس (قرآن) سے
شک میں اُلجھ رہے ہیں ﴿٤٥﴾

وَلَقَدْ اٰتَيْنَا مُوْسَى الْكِتٰبَ فَاخْتُلِفَ
فِيْهِ ؕ وَلَوْلَا كَلِمَةٌ سَبَقَتْ مِنْ رَّبِّكَ
لَقُضِيَ بَيْنَهُمْ ؕ وَاِنَّهُمْ لَفِيْ شَكٍّ مِّنْهُ
مُرِيْبٍ ﴿٤٥﴾

46. Whoever works righteousness benefits his own soul; whoever works evil, it is against his own soul: nor is thy Lord ever unjust (in the least) to His servants.

جو نیک کام کریگا تو اپنے لئے۔ اور جو بُرے کریگا تو اُن کا ضرر
اُسی کو ہوگا۔ اور تمہارا پروردگار بندوں پر ظلم کرنیوالا نہیں ﴿٤٦﴾

مَنْ عَمِلَ صَالِحًا فَلِنَفْسِهٖ وَمَنْ اَسَآءَ
فَعَلَيْهَا ؕ وَمَا رَبُّكَ بِظَلَّامٍ لِّلْعَبِيْدِ ﴿٤٦﴾

47. To Him is referred the Knowledge of the Hour (of Judgment: He knows all): no fruit comes out of its sheath, nor does a female conceive (within her womb) nor bring forth (young), but by His Knowledge. The Day that (Allah) will propound to them the (question), "Where are the Partners (ye attributed) to Me?" They will say, "We do assure Thee not one of us can bear witness!"
48. The (deities) they used to invoke aforetime will leave them in the lurch, and they will perceive that they have no way of escape.
49. Man does not weary of asking for good (things), but if ill touches him, he gives up all hope (and) is lost in despair.

50. When We give him a taste of some mercy from Us, after some adversity has touched him, he is sure to say, "This is due to my (merit): I think not that the Hour (of Judgment) will (ever) be established; but if I am brought back to my Lord, I have (much) good (stored) in His sight!" But We will show the Unbelievers the truth of all that they did, and We shall give them the taste of a severe Chastisement.
51. When We bestow favours on man, he turns away, and gets himself remote on his side (instead of coming to Us); and when evil seizes him, (he comes) full of prolonged prayer!
52. Say: "See ye if the (Revelation) is (really) from Allah, and yet do ye Reject it? Who is more astray than one who is in a schism far (from any purpose)?"

53. Soon will We show them Our Signs in the (furthest) regions (of the earth), and in their own souls, until it becomes manifest to them that this is the Truth. Is it not enough that thy Lord doth witness all things?
54. Ah indeed! are they in doubt concerning the Meeting with their Lord? Ah indeed! it is He that doth encompass all things!

قیامت کے علم کا حوالہ اُسی کی طرف دیا جاتا ہے (یعنی قیامت کا
علم اُسی کو ہے) اور نہ تو پھل گابھوں سے نکلتے ہیں اور نہ کوئی مادہ
حاملہ ہوتی اور نہ جنتی ہے مگر اُس کے علم سے۔ اور جس دن وہ اُنکو پکاریگا
(اور کہیگا) کہ میرے شریک کہاں ہیں تو وہ کہیں گے کہ ہم تجھ سے عرض
کرتے ہیں کہ ہم میں سے کسی کو (اُن کی) خبر ہی نہیں (٤٧)
اور جن کو پہلے وہ (خدا کے سوا) پکارا کرتے تھے (سب) اُن سے
غائب ہو جائینگے اور وہ یقین کرلیں گے کہ اُن کیلئے مخلصی نہیں (٤٨)
انسان بھلائی کی دعائیں کرتا کرتا تو تھکتا نہیں اور اگر تکلیف پہنچ
جاتی ہے تو ناامید ہو جاتا اور آس توڑ بیٹھتا ہے (٤٩)
اور اگر تکلیف پہنچنے کے بعد ہم اُس کو اپنی رحمت کا مزہ چکھاتے
ہیں تو کہتا ہے کہ یہ تو میرا حق تھا اور میں نہیں خیال کرتا کہ
قیامت برپا ہو اور اگر (قیامت سچ مچ بھی ہو اور) میں اپنے
پروردگار کی طرف لوٹایا بھی جاؤں تو میرے لئے اسکے ہاں بھی
خوشحالی ہے پس کافر جو عمل کیا کرتے ہیں وہ ہم ضرور اُنکو جتائینگے
اور اُن کو سخت عذاب کا مزہ چکھائیں گے (٥٠)
اور جب ہم انسان پر کرم کرتے ہیں تو مُنہ موڑ لیتا اور پہلو
پھیر کر چل دیتا ہے اور جب اُس کو تکلیف پہنچتی ہے تو لمبی لمبی
دُعائیں کرنے لگتا ہے (٥١)
کہو کہ بھلا دیکھو تو اگر یہ (قرآن) خدا کی طرف سے ہو پھر تم
اس سے انکار کرو تو اس سے بڑھ کر کون گمراہ ہے جو (حق کی)
پرلے درجے کی مخالفت میں ہو (٥٢)
ہم عنقریب اُنکو اطراف (عالم) میں بھی اور خود اُنکی ذات میں بھی
اپنی نشانیاں دکھائینگے یہاں تک کہ اُن پر ظاہر ہو جائیگا کہ (قرآن)
حق ہے کیا تمکو یہ کافی نہیں کہ تمہارا پروردگار ہر چیز سے خبردار ہے (٥٣)
دیکھو یہ اپنے پروردگار کے رُوبرو حاضر ہونے سے شک میں ہیں۔
سُن رکھو کہ وہ ہر چیز پر احاطہ کئے ہوئے ہے (٥٤)

اليه يرد علم الساعة وما تخرج
من ثمرت من اكمامها وما تحمل
من انثى ولا تضع الا بعلمه ويوم
يناديهم اين شركاءي قالوا اذنك
ما منا من شهيد (٤٧)
وضل عنهم ما كانوا يدعون من
قبل وظنوا ما لهم من محيص (٤٨)
لا يسئم الانسان من دعاء الخير
وان مسه الشر فيئوس قنوط (٤٩)
ولئن اذقنه رحمة منا من بعد
ضراء مسته ليقولن هذا لي وما
اظن الساعة قائمة ولئن رجعت
الى ربي ان لي عنده للحسنى
فلننبئن الذين كفروا بما عملوا
ولنذيقنهم من عذاب غليظ (٥٠)
واذا انعمنا على الانسان اعرض
ونا بجانبه واذا مسه الشر فذو
دعاء عريض (٥١)
قل ارءيتم ان كان من عند الله ثم
كفرتم به من اضل ممن هو في
شقاق بعيد (٥٢)
سنريهم ايتنا في الافاق وفي انفسهم
حتى يتبين لهم انه الحق اولم يكف
بربك انه على كل شيء شهيد (٥٣)
الا انهم في مرية من لقاء ربهم
الا انه بكل شيء محيط (٥٤)

SÛRA–42
ASH-SHÛRA
(INTRODUCTION)

This is the third Sûra of the *Ḥã-Mîm* series of seven Sûras, for which see the Introduction to S. 40.

The theme is how evil and blasphemy can be cured by the Mercy and Guidance of Allah, which come through His Revelation. Men are asked to settle their differences in patience by mutual Consultation (42: 38), which explains the title of the Sûra.

Ash-Shûrã, or Consultation

In the name of Allah, Most Gracious Most Merciful.

1. Ḥã-Mîm;
2. 'Ain. Sîn. Qãf.
3. Thus doth (He) send inspiration to thee as (He did) to those before thee,— Allah, Exalted in Power, Full of Wisdom.
4. To Him belongs all that is in the heavens and on earth: and He is Most High, Most Great.
5. The heavens are almost rent asunder from above them (by His Glory): and the angels celebrate the Praises of their Lord, and pray for forgiveness for all beings on earth: behold! Verily Allah is He, the Oft-Forgiving, Most Merciful.
6. And those who take as protectors others besides Him,— Allah doth watch over them; and thou art not the disposer of their affairs.
7. Thus have We sent by inspiration to thee an Arabic Qur'ãn: that thou mayest warn the Mother of Cities and all around her,— and warn (them) of the Day of Assembly, of which there is no doubt: (when) some will be in the Garden, and some in the Blazing Fire.—
8. If Allah had so willed, he could have made them a single people; but He admits whom He will to His Mercy; and the wrong-doers will have no protector nor helper.
9. What! Have they taken (for worship) protectors besides Him? But it is Allah,—He is the Protector, and it is He Who gives life to the dead: it is He Who has power over all things.
10. Whatever it be wherein ye differ, the decision thereof is with Allah: such is Allah my Lord: in

سورۂ شوریٰ مکی ہے اور اس میں ترپن آیتیں اور پانچ رکوع ہیں

شروع خدا کا نام لے کر جو بڑا مہربان نہایت رحم والا ہے ○
حٰمٓ (١) عٓسٓقٓ (٢)
خدائے غالب و دانا اسی طرح تمہاری طرف (مضامین اور
براہین) بھیجتا ہے جس طرح تم سے پہلے لوگوں کی طرف وحی بھیجتا رہا ہے (٣)
جو کچھ آسمانوں میں ہے اور جو کچھ زمین میں ہے سب اُسی کا ہے۔
اور وہ عالی رُتبہ (اور) گرامی قدر ہے (٤)
قریب ہے کہ آسمان اُوپر سے پھٹ پڑیں اور فرشتے اپنے
پروردگار کی تعریف کے ساتھ اس کی تسبیح کرتے رہتے اور
جو لوگ زمین میں ہیں اُن کیلئے معافی مانگتے رہتے ہیں ٢٥٩
سُن رکھو کہ خدا بخشنے والا مہربان ہے (٥)
اور جن لوگوں نے اُس کے سوا کارساز بنا رکھے ہیں
وہ خدا کو یاد ہیں اور تم اُن پر داروغہ نہیں
ہو (٦)
اور اسی طرح تمہارے پاس قرآن عربی بھیجا ہے تاکہ تم بڑے
گاؤں (یعنی مکے) کے رہنے والوں کو اور جو لوگ اسکے اردگرد
رہتے ہیں اُنکو رستہ دکھاؤ اور انہیں قیامت کے دن کا بھی جس
میں کچھ شک نہیں خوف دلاؤ۔ اُس روز ایک فریق بہشت میں
ہوگا اور ایک فریق دوزخ میں (٧)
اور اگر خدا چاہتا تو اُن کو ایک ہی جماعت کر دیتا لیکن وہ
جس کو چاہتا ہے اپنی رحمت میں داخل کر لیتا ہے۔ اور
ظالموں کا نہ کوئی یار ہے اور نہ مددگار (٨)
کیا اُنہوں نے اس کے سوا کارساز بنائے ہیں؟ کارساز
تو خدا ہی ہے اور وہی مُردوں کو زندہ کرے گا اور وہ
ہر چیز پر قدرت رکھتا ہے (٩)
اور تم جس بات میں اختلاف کرتے ہو اُس کا فیصلہ خدا
کی طرف (سے ہوگا) یہی خدا میرا پروردگار ہے میں اُسی پر

سُوْرَةُ الشُّوْرٰى مَكِّيَّةٌ وَّهِيَ ثَلٰثٌ وَّخَمْسُوْنَ اٰيَةً وَّخَمْسُ رُكُوْعَاتٍ

بِسْمِ اللّٰهِ الرَّحْمٰنِ الرَّحِيْمِ ○
حٰمٓ (١) عٓسٓقٓ (٢)
كَذٰلِكَ يُوْحِيْٓ اِلَيْكَ وَاِلَى الَّذِيْنَ
مِنْ قَبْلِكَ ۙ اللّٰهُ الْعَزِيْزُ الْحَكِيْمُ (٣)
لَهٗ مَا فِي السَّمٰوٰتِ وَمَا فِي الْاَرْضِ ۭ وَهُوَ
الْعَلِيُّ الْعَظِيْمُ (٤)
تَكَادُ السَّمٰوٰتُ يَتَفَطَّرْنَ مِنْ فَوْقِهِنَّ
وَالْمَلٰۗىِٕكَةُ يُسَبِّحُوْنَ بِحَمْدِ رَبِّهِمْ وَ
يَسْتَغْفِرُوْنَ لِمَنْ فِي الْاَرْضِ ۭ اَلَآ اِنَّ
اللّٰهَ هُوَ الْغَفُوْرُ الرَّحِيْمُ (٥)
وَالَّذِيْنَ اتَّخَذُوْا مِنْ دُوْنِهٖٓ اَوْلِيَاۗءَ
اللّٰهُ حَفِيْظٌ عَلَيْهِمْ ڮ وَمَآ اَنْتَ عَلَيْهِمْ
بِوَكِيْلٍ (٦)
وَكَذٰلِكَ اَوْحَيْنَآ اِلَيْكَ قُرْاٰنًا عَرَبِيًّا
لِّتُنْذِرَ اُمَّ الْقُرٰى وَمَنْ حَوْلَهَا وَ
تُنْذِرَ يَوْمَ الْجَمْعِ لَا رَيْبَ فِيْهِ ۭ
فَرِيْقٌ فِي الْجَنَّةِ وَفَرِيْقٌ فِي
السَّعِيْرِ (٧)
وَلَوْ شَاۗءَ اللّٰهُ لَجَعَلَهُمْ اُمَّةً وَّاحِدَةً
وَّلٰكِنْ يُّدْخِلُ مَنْ يَّشَاۗءُ فِيْ رَحْمَتِهٖ ۭ
وَالظّٰلِمُوْنَ مَا لَهُمْ مِّنْ وَّلِيٍّ وَّلَا نَصِيْرٍ (٨)
اَمِ اتَّخَذُوْا مِنْ دُوْنِهٖٓ اَوْلِيَاۗءَ ۚ فَاللّٰهُ
هُوَ الْوَلِيُّ وَهُوَ يُحْيِ الْمَوْتٰى ۡ وَهُوَ عَلٰي
كُلِّ شَيْءٍ قَدِيْرٌ (٩) ع
وَمَا اخْتَلَفْتُمْ فِيْهِ مِنْ شَيْءٍ فَحُكْمُهٗٓ
اِلَى اللّٰهِ ۭ ذٰلِكُمُ اللّٰهُ رَبِّيْ عَلَيْهِ تَوَكَّلْتُ

Him I trust, and to Him I turn.

11. (He is) the Creator of the heavens and the earth: He has made for you pairs from among yourselves, and pairs among cattle: by this means does He multiply you: there is nothing whatever like unto Him, and He is the One that hears and sees.

12. To Him belong the keys of the heavens and the earth: he enlarges and restricts the Sustenance to whom he will: for He knows full well all things.

13. The same religion has He established for you as that which He enjoined on Noah— the which We have sent by inspiration to thee— and that which We enjoined on Abraham, Moses, and Jesus: namely, that ye should remain steadfast in Religion, and make no divisions therein: to those who worship other things than Allah, hard is the (way) to which thou callest them. Allah chooses to Himself those whom He pleases, and guides to Himself those who turn (to Him).

14. And they became divided only after knowledge reached them,— being insolent to one another. Had it not been for a Word that went forth before from thy Lord, (tending) to a Term appointed, the matter would have been settled between them: but truly those who have inherited the Book after them are in suspicious (disquieting) doubt concerning it.

15. Now then, for that (reason), call (them to the Faith), and stand steadfast as thou art commanded, nor follow thou their vain desires; but say: "I believe in whatever Book Allah has sent down; and I am commanded to judge justly between you. Allah is our Lord and your Lord! For us (is the responsibility for) our deeds, and for you for your deeds. There is no contention between us and you. Allah will bring us together, and to Him is (our) final goal."

بھروسا رکھتا ہوں۔ اور اُسی کی طرف رجوع کرتا ہوں ﴿١٠﴾
آسمانوں اور زمین کا پیدا کرنے والا (وہی ہے)۔ اُسی نے تمہارے
لئے تمہاری ہی جنس کے جوڑے بنائے اور چارپایوں کے بھی
جوڑے (بنائے اور) اسی طریق پر تم کو پھیلاتا رہتا ہے۔ اُس
جیسی کوئی چیز نہیں۔ اور وہ سُنتا دیکھتا ہے ﴿١١﴾
آسمانوں اور زمین کی کنجیاں اُسی کے ہاتھ میں ہیں۔ وہ
جس کیلئے چاہتا ہے رزق فراخ کر دیتا ہے اور جس کیلئے چاہتا
ہے تنگ کر دیتا ہے۔ بیشک وہ ہر چیز سے واقف ہے ﴿١٢﴾
اُس نے تمہارے لئے دین کا وہی رستہ مقرر کیا جس (کے
اختیار کرنے) کا نوح کو حکم دیا تھا اور جس کی (اے محمد) ہم نے
تمہاری طرف وحی بھیجی ہے اور جسکا ابراہیم اور موسیٰ اور عیسیٰ کو حکم دیا تھا
(وہ یہ) کہ دین کو قائم رکھنا اور اس میں پھوٹ نہ ڈالنا۔ جس چیز کی
طرف تم مشرکوں کو بلاتے ہو وہ اُن کو دشوار گزرتی ہے۔
اللہ جس کو چاہتا ہے اپنی بارگاہ کا برگزیدہ کر لیتا ہے اور
جو اُسکی طرف رجوع کرے اُسے اپنی طرف رستہ دکھا دیتا ہے ﴿١٣﴾
اور یہ لوگ جو الگ الگ ہوئے ہیں تو علم (حق) آ چکنے کے
بعد آپس کی ضد سے (ہوئے ہیں) اور اگر تمہارے پروردگار کی
طرف سے ایک وقت مقرر تک کیلئے بات نہ ٹھہر چکی ہوتی تو اُن میں فیصلہ
کر دیا جاتا۔ اور جو لوگ اُنکے بعد (خدا کی) کتاب کے وارث ہوئے وہ
اس (کی طرف) سے شبہہ کی اُلجھن میں (پھنسے ہوئے) ہیں ﴿١٤﴾
تو (اے محمد) اسی (دین کی) طرف (لوگوں کو) بلاتے رہنا اور جیسا
تم کو حکم ہوا ہے (اُسی پر) قائم رہنا۔ اور اُنکی خواہشوں کی پیروی
نہ کرنا۔ اور کہہ دو کہ جو کتاب خدا نے نازل فرمائی ہے میں اُس پر ایمان
رکھتا ہوں۔ اور مجھے حکم ہوا ہے کہ تم میں انصاف کروں۔ خدا
ہی ہمارا اور تمہارا پروردگار ہے ہم کو ہمارے اعمال (کا بدلہ ملیگا)
اور تم کو تمہارے اعمال (کا)۔ ہم میں اور تم میں کچھ بحث و تکرار نہیں۔
خدا ہم (سب) کو اکٹھا کریگا۔ اور اُسی کی طرف لوٹ کر جانا ہے ﴿١٥﴾

وَإِلَيْهِ أُنِيبُ ﴿١٠﴾
فَاطِرُ السَّمٰوٰتِ وَالْأَرْضِ ۚ جَعَلَ لَكُمْ
مِّنْ أَنفُسِكُمْ أَزْوَاجًا وَمِنَ الْأَنْعَامِ
أَزْوَاجًا ۖ يَذْرَؤُكُمْ فِيهِ ۚ لَيْسَ كَمِثْلِهِ
شَيْءٌ ۖ وَهُوَ السَّمِيعُ الْبَصِيرُ ﴿١١﴾
لَهُ مَقَالِيدُ السَّمٰوٰتِ وَالْأَرْضِ ۖ يَبْسُطُ
الرِّزْقَ لِمَن يَشَاءُ وَيَقْدِرُ ۚ إِنَّهُ بِكُلِّ
شَيْءٍ عَلِيمٌ ﴿١٢﴾
شَرَعَ لَكُم مِّنَ الدِّينِ مَا وَصَّىٰ
بِهِ نُوحًا وَالَّذِي أَوْحَيْنَا إِلَيْكَ
وَمَا وَصَّيْنَا بِهِ إِبْرٰهِيمَ وَمُوسَىٰ
وَعِيسَىٰ ۖ أَنْ أَقِيمُوا الدِّينَ وَلَا تَتَفَرَّقُوا
فِيهِ ۚ كَبُرَ عَلَى الْمُشْرِكِينَ مَا تَدْعُوهُمْ إِلَيْهِ ۚ
اللَّهُ يَجْتَبِي إِلَيْهِ مَن يَشَاءُ وَيَهْدِي
إِلَيْهِ مَن يُنِيبُ ﴿١٣﴾
وَمَا تَفَرَّقُوا إِلَّا مِن بَعْدِ مَا جَاءَهُمُ
الْعِلْمُ بَغْيًا بَيْنَهُمْ ۚ وَلَوْلَا كَلِمَةٌ سَبَقَتْ
مِن رَّبِّكَ إِلَىٰ أَجَلٍ مُّسَمًّى لَّقُضِيَ بَيْنَهُمْ ۚ
وَإِنَّ الَّذِينَ أُورِثُوا الْكِتٰبَ مِن بَعْدِهِمْ
لَفِي شَكٍّ مِّنْهُ مُرِيبٍ ﴿١٤﴾
فَلِذٰلِكَ فَادْعُ ۖ وَاسْتَقِمْ كَمَا أُمِرْتَ ۖ
وَلَا تَتَّبِعْ أَهْوَاءَهُمْ ۖ وَقُلْ آمَنتُ بِمَا
أَنزَلَ اللَّهُ مِن كِتٰبٍ ۖ وَأُمِرْتُ لِأَعْدِلَ
بَيْنَكُمُ ۖ اللَّهُ رَبُّنَا وَرَبُّكُمْ ۖ لَنَا أَعْمَالُنَا
وَلَكُمْ أَعْمَالُكُمْ ۖ لَا حُجَّةَ بَيْنَنَا
وَبَيْنَكُمُ ۖ اللَّهُ يَجْمَعُ بَيْنَنَا ۖ وَإِلَيْهِ
الْمَصِيرُ ﴿١٥﴾

16. But those who dispute concerning Allah after He has been accepted,— futile is their argument in the sight of their Lord: on them is Wrath, and for them will be a Chastisement terrible.

اور جو لوگ خدا کے بارے میں بعد اسکے کہ اُسے (مومنوں نے) مان لیا ہو جھگڑتے ہیں اُن کے پروردگار کے نزدیک اُن کا جھگڑا لغو ہے۔ اور اُن پر (خدا کا) غضب اور اُن کے لئے سخت عذاب ہے (۱۶)

والذين يحاجون في الله من بعد
ما استجيب له حجتهم داحضة عند
ربهم وعليهم غضب ولهم عذاب
شديد (۱۶)

17. It is Allah Who has sent down the Book in truth, and the Balance and what will make thee realise that perhaps the Hour is close at hand?

خدا ہی تو ہے جس نے سچائی کے ساتھ کتاب نازل کی اور (عدل وانصاف کی) ترازو۔ اور تم کو کیا معلوم شاید قیامت قریب ہی آ پہنچی ہو (۱۷)

الله الذي انزل الكتب بالحق
والميزان وما يدريك لعل الساعة
قريب (۱۷)

18. Only those wish to hasten it who believe not in it: those who believe hold it in awe, and know that it is the Truth. Behold, verily those that dispute concerning the Hour are far astray.

جو لوگ اس پر ایمان نہیں رکھتے وہ اس کے لئے جلدی کر رہے ہیں۔ اور جو مومن ہیں وہ اس سے ڈرتے ہیں۔ اور جانتے ہیں کہ وہ برحق ہے۔ دیکھو جو لوگ قیامت میں جھگڑتے ہیں وہ پرلے درجے کی گمراہی میں ہیں (۱۸)

يستعجل بها الذين لا يؤمنون بها
والذين امنوا مشفقون منها و
يعلمون انها الحق الا ان الذين
يمارون في الساعة لفي ضلل بعيد (۱۸)

19. Gracious is Allah to His servants: he gives Sustenance to whom He pleases: and He is the Strong, the Mighty.

خدا اپنے بندوں پر مہربان ہے وہ جس کو چاہتا ہے رزق دیتا ہے۔ اور وہ زور والا (اور) زبردست ہے (۱۹)

الله لطيف بعباده يرزق من يشاء
وهو القوي العزيز (۱۹)

20. To any that desires the tilth of the Hereafter, We give increase in his tilth; and to any that desires the tilth of this world, We grant somewhat thereof, but he has no share or lot in the Hereafter.

جو شخص آخرت کی کھیتی کا طالب ہو اُسکے لئے ہم اُسکی کھیتی میں افزائش کرینگے۔ اور جو دنیا کی کھیتی کا خواستگار ہو اُسکو ہم اُس میں سے دینگے۔ اور اُس کا آخرت میں کچھ حصہ نہ ہوگا (۲۰)

من كان يريد حرث الاخرة نزد له
في حرثه ومن كان يريد حرث الدنيا
نؤته منها وما له في الاخرة من نصيب (۲۰)

21. What! Have they partners (in godhead), who have established for them some religion without the permission of Allah? Had it not been for the Decree of Judgment, the matter would have been decided between them (at once). But verily the wrong-doers will have a grievous Chastisement.

کیا اُن کے وہ شریک ہیں جنہوں نے اُن کیلئے ایسا دین مقرر کیا ہے جس کا خدا نے حکم نہیں دیا۔ اور اگر فیصلے (کے دن) کا وعدہ نہ ہوتا تو اُن میں فیصلہ کر دیا جاتا۔ اور جو ظالم ہیں اُنکے لئے درد دینے والا عذاب ہے (۲۱)

ام لهم شركؤا شرعوا لهم من
الدين ما لم يأذن به الله ولولا
كلمة الفصل لقضي بينهم وان
الظلمين لهم عذاب اليم (۲۱)

22. Thou wilt see the wrong-doers in fear on account of what they have earned, and (the burden of) that must (necessarily) fall on them. But those who believe and work righteous deeds will be in the Meadows of the Gardens: they shall have, before their Lord, all that they wish for. That will indeed be the magnificent Bounty (of Allah).

تم دیکھو گے کہ ظالم اپنے اعمال (کے وبال) سے ڈر رہے ہونگے اور وہ اُن پر پڑ کر رہے گا۔ اور جو لوگ ایمان لائے اور نیک عمل کرتے رہے وہ بہشت کے باغوں میں ہونگے وہ جو کچھ چاہیں گے اُن کے پروردگار کے پاس (موجود) ہوگا۔ یہی بڑا فضل ہے (۲۲)

ترى الظلمين مشفقين مما كسبوا
وهو واقع بهم والذين امنوا و
عملوا الصلحت في روضت الجنت
لهم ما يشاءون عند ربهم ذلك
هو الفضل الكبير (۲۲)

23. That is (the Bounty) whereof Allah gives Glad Tidings to His Servants who believe and do righteous deeds. Say: "No reward

یہی وہ (انعام) ہے جس کی خدا اپنے اُن بندوں کو جو ایمان لاتے اور عمل نیک کرتے ہیں بشارت دیتا ہے۔ کہہ دو کہ میں اس کا

ذلك الذي يبشر الله عباده الذين
امنوا وعملوا الصلحت قل لا اسئلكم

do I ask of you for this except the love of those near of kin." And if anyone earns any good, We shall give him an increase of good in respect thereof: for Allah is Oft-Forgiving, Grateful.

24. What! Do they say, "He has forged a falsehood against Allah"? But if Allah willed, He could seal up thy heart. And Allah blots out falsehood, and proves the Truth by His Words. For He knows well the secrets of all hearts.

25. He is the One that accepts repentance from His Servants and forgives sins: and He knows all that ye do.

26. And He listens to those who believe and do deeds of righteousness, and gives them increase of His Bounty: but for the Unbelievers there is a terrible Chastisement.

27. If Allah were to enlarge the provision for His Servants, they would indeed transgress beyond all bounds through the earth; but He sends (it) down in due measure as He pleases. For He is with His Servants well-acquainted, Watchful.

28. He is the One that sends down rain (even) after (men) have given up all hope, and scatters His Mercy (far and wide). And He is the Protector, Worthy of all Praise.

29. And among His Signs is the creation of the heavens and the earth, and the living creatures that He has scattered through them: and He has power to gather them together when He wills.

30. Whatever misfortune happens to you, is because of the things your hands have wrought, and for many (a sin) He grants forgiveness.

31. Nor can ye escape through the earth; nor have ye, besides Allah, anyone to protect or to help.

32. And among His Signs are the ships, smooth-running through the ocean, (tall) as mountains.

33. If it be His Will, He can still the Wind: then would they become

تم سے صلہ نہیں مانگتا مگر (تم کو) قرابت کی محبت (تو چاہئے) ف۲۶
اور جو کوئی نیکی کرے گا ہم اس کے لئے اس میں ثواب بڑھائیں گے۔
بیشک خدا بخشنے والا قدردان ہے ﴿۲۳﴾
کیا یہ لوگ کہتے ہیں کہ پیغمبر نے خدا پر جھوٹ باندھ لیا ہے؟
اگر خدا چاہے تو (اے محمدؐ) تمہارے دل پر مہر لگا دے ف۲۶۔ اور خدا
جھوٹ کو نابود کرتا اور اپنی باتوں سے حق کو ثابت کرتا ہے۔
بیشک وہ سینے تک کی باتوں سے واقف ہے ﴿۲۴﴾
اور وہی تو ہے جو اپنے بندوں کی توبہ قبول کرتا اور (ان کے)
قصور معاف فرماتا ہے اور جو تم کرتے ہو (سب) جانتا ہے ﴿۲۵﴾
اور جو ایمان لائے اور عمل نیک کئے ان کی (دعا) قبول
فرماتا اور ان کو اپنے فضل سے بڑھاتا ہے۔ اور جو کافر ہیں
ان کے لئے سخت عذاب ہے ﴿۲۶﴾
اور اگر خدا اپنے بندوں کیلئے رزق میں فراخی کر دیتا تو زمین
میں فساد کرنے لگتے۔ لیکن وہ جس قدر چاہتا ہے اندازے کے
ساتھ نازل کرتا ہے۔ بیشک وہ اپنے بندوں کو جانتا اور دیکھتا ہے ﴿۲۷﴾
اور وہی تو ہے جو لوگوں کے ناامید ہو جانے کے بعد مینہ برساتا اور
اپنی رحمت (یعنی بارش کی برکت) کو پھیلا دیتا ہے۔ اور وہ
کارساز (اور) سزاوار تعریف ہے ﴿۲۸﴾
اور اسی کی نشانیوں میں سے ہے آسمانوں اور زمین کا پیدا
کرنا اور ان جانوروں کا جو اس نے ان میں پھیلا رکھے ہیں۔
اور وہ جب چاہے ان کے جمع کر لینے پر قادر ہے ﴿۲۹﴾
اور جو مصیبت تم پر واقع ہوتی ہے سو تمہارے اپنے فعلوں سے
اور وہ بہت سے گناہ تو معاف کر دیتا ہے ﴿۳۰﴾
اور تم زمین میں (خدا کو) عاجز نہیں کر سکتے۔ اور خدا کے سوا
نہ تمہارا کوئی دوست ہے اور نہ مددگار ﴿۳۱﴾
اور اسی کی نشانیوں میں سے سمندر کے جہاز ہیں (جو) گویا پہاڑ (ہیں) ﴿۳۲﴾
اگر خدا چاہے تو ہوا کو ٹھیرا دے۔ اور جہاز اس کی سطح پر کھڑے

عَلَيْهِ أَجْرًا إِلَّا الْمَوَدَّةَ فِي الْقُرْبَىٰ ۗ
وَمَن يَقْتَرِفْ حَسَنَةً نَّزِدْ لَهُ فِيهَا
حُسْنًا ۚ إِنَّ اللَّهَ غَفُورٌ شَكُورٌ ﴿٢٣﴾
أَمْ يَقُولُونَ افْتَرَىٰ عَلَى اللَّهِ كَذِبًا ۖ
فَإِن يَشَإِ اللَّهُ يَخْتِمْ عَلَىٰ قَلْبِكَ ۗ وَيَمْحُ
اللَّهُ الْبَاطِلَ وَيُحِقُّ الْحَقَّ بِكَلِمَاتِهِ ۚ
إِنَّهُ عَلِيمٌ بِذَاتِ الصُّدُورِ ﴿٢٤﴾
وَهُوَ الَّذِي يَقْبَلُ التَّوْبَةَ عَنْ عِبَادِهِ
وَيَعْفُو عَنِ السَّيِّئَاتِ وَيَعْلَمُ مَا تَفْعَلُونَ ﴿٢٥﴾
وَيَسْتَجِيبُ الَّذِينَ آمَنُوا وَعَمِلُوا الصَّالِحَاتِ
وَيَزِيدُهُم مِّن فَضْلِهِ ۚ وَالْكَافِرُونَ لَهُمْ
عَذَابٌ شَدِيدٌ ﴿٢٦﴾
وَلَوْ بَسَطَ اللَّهُ الرِّزْقَ لِعِبَادِهِ لَبَغَوْا
فِي الْأَرْضِ وَلَٰكِن يُنَزِّلُ بِقَدَرٍ مَّا يَشَاءُ ۚ
إِنَّهُ بِعِبَادِهِ خَبِيرٌ بَصِيرٌ ﴿٢٧﴾
وَهُوَ الَّذِي يُنَزِّلُ الْغَيْثَ مِن بَعْدِ
مَا قَنَطُوا وَيَنشُرُ رَحْمَتَهُ ۚ وَهُوَ الْوَلِيُّ
الْحَمِيدُ ﴿٢٨﴾
وَمِنْ آيَاتِهِ خَلْقُ السَّمَاوَاتِ وَالْأَرْضِ وَمَا
بَثَّ فِيهِمَا مِن دَابَّةٍ ۚ وَهُوَ عَلَىٰ جَمْعِهِمْ
إِذَا يَشَاءُ قَدِيرٌ ﴿٢٩﴾
وَمَا أَصَابَكُم مِّن مُّصِيبَةٍ فَبِمَا كَسَبَتْ
أَيْدِيكُمْ وَيَعْفُو عَن كَثِيرٍ ﴿٣٠﴾
وَمَا أَنتُم بِمُعْجِزِينَ فِي الْأَرْضِ ۖ وَمَا لَكُم
مِّن دُونِ اللَّهِ مِن وَلِيٍّ وَلَا نَصِيرٍ ﴿٣١﴾
وَمِنْ آيَاتِهِ الْجَوَارِ فِي الْبَحْرِ كَالْأَعْلَامِ ﴿٣٢﴾
إِن يَشَأْ يُسْكِنِ الرِّيحَ فَيَظْلَلْنَ رَوَاكِدَ

motionless on the back of the (ocean). Verily in this are Signs for everyone who patiently perseveres and is grateful.

34. Or He can cause them to perish because of the (evil) which (the men) have earned; but much doth He forgive.

35. But let those know, who dispute about Our Signs, that there is for them no way of escape.

36. Whatever ye are given (here) is (but) the enjoyment of this Life: but that which is with Allah is better and more lasting: (it is) for those who believe and put their trust in their Lord:

37. Those who avoid the greater sins and indecencies and, when they are angry even then forgive;

38. Those who respond to their Lord, and establish regular prayer; who (conduct) their affairs by mutual Consultation; who spend out of what We bestow on them for Sustenance;

39. And those who, when an oppressive wrong is inflicted on them, (are not cowed but) help and defend themselves.

40. The recompense for an injury is an injury equal thereto (in degree): but if a person forgives and makes reconciliation, his reward is due from Allah: for (Allah) loveth not those who do wrong.

41. But indeed if any do help and defend himself after a wrong (done) to him, against such there is no cause of blame.

42. The blame is only against those who oppress men with wrong-doing and insolently transgress beyond bounds through the land, defying right and justice: for such there will be a Chastisement grievous.

43. But indeed if any show patience and forgive, that would truly be an affair of great Resolution.

44. For any whom Allah leaves astray, there is no protector thereafter. And thou wilt see the wrong-doers, when in sight of the Chastisement, say: "Is there any

رہ جائیں۔ تمام صبر اور شکر کرنے والوں کے لئے ان
(باتوں) میں قدرتِ خدا کے نمونے ہیں (۳۳)
یا ان کے اعمال کے سبب ان کو تباہ کر دے۔ اور بہت سے قصور معاف کر دے (۳۴)
اور (انتقام اس لئے لیا جائے کہ) جو لوگ ہماری آیتوں میں جھگڑتے
ہیں وہ جان لیں کہ ان کے لئے خلاصی نہیں (۳۵)
(لوگو) جو (مال و متاع) تم کو دیا گیا ہے وہ دنیا کی زندگی کا (ناپائدار) فائدہ ہے
اور جو کچھ خدا کے ہاں ہے وہ بہتر اور قائم رہنے والا ہے (یعنی) ان لوگوں کے لئے
جو ایمان لائے اور اپنے پروردگار پر بھروسا رکھتے ہیں (۳۶)
اور جو بڑے بڑے گناہوں اور بے حیائی کے کاموں سے پرہیز
کرتے ہیں اور جب غصہ آتا ہے تو معاف کر دیتے ہیں (۳۷)
اور جو اپنے پروردگار کا فرمان قبول کرتے ہیں اور نماز پڑھتے ہیں اور اپنے کام
آپس کے مشورے سے کرتے ہیں اور جو مال ہم نے ان کو عطا فرمایا ہے اس میں سے خرچ کرتے ہیں (۳۸)
اور جو ایسے ہیں کہ جب ان پر ظلم (و تعدی) ہو تو (مناسب طریقے
سے) بدلہ لیتے ہیں (۳۹)
اور برائی کا بدلہ تو اسی طرح کی برائی ہے۔ مگر جو درگزر کرے
اور (معاملے کو) درست کر دے تو اس کا بدلہ خدا کے ذمے ہے۔ اس میں
شک نہیں کہ وہ ظلم کرنے والوں کو پسند نہیں کرتا (۴۰)
اور جس پر ظلم ہوا ہو اگر وہ اس کے بعد انتقام لے تو ایسے
لوگوں پر کچھ الزام نہیں (۴۱)
الزام تو ان لوگوں پر ہے جو لوگوں پر ظلم کرتے ہیں اور
ملک میں ناحق فساد پھیلاتے ہیں یہی لوگ ہیں جن کو تکلیف
دینے والا عذاب ہوگا (۴۲)
اور جو صبر کرے اور قصور معاف کر دے تو یہ ہمت
کے کام ہیں (۴۳)
اور جس شخص کو خدا گمراہ کرے تو اس کے بعد اس کا کوئی
دوست نہیں۔ اور تم ظالموں کو دیکھو گے کہ جب وہ
(دوزخ کا) عذاب دیکھیں گے تو کہیں گے کیا (دنیا میں)

عَلٰى ظَهْرِهٖ ۭ اِنَّ فِيْ ذٰلِكَ لَاٰيٰتٍ لِّكُلِّ
صَبَّارٍ شَكُوْرٍ ﴿۳۳﴾
اَوْ يُوْبِقْهُنَّ بِمَا كَسَبُوْا وَيَعْفُ عَنْ كَثِيْرٍ ﴿۳۴﴾
وَّيَعْلَمَ الَّذِيْنَ يُجَادِلُوْنَ فِيْٓ اٰيٰتِنَا ۭ
مَا لَهُمْ مِّنْ مَّحِيْصٍ ﴿۳۵﴾
فَمَآ اُوْتِيْتُمْ مِّنْ شَيْءٍ فَمَتَاعُ الْحَيٰوةِ
الدُّنْيَا ۚ وَمَا عِنْدَ اللّٰهِ خَيْرٌ وَّاَبْقٰى لِلَّذِيْنَ
اٰمَنُوْا وَعَلٰى رَبِّهِمْ يَتَوَكَّلُوْنَ ﴿۳۶﴾
وَالَّذِيْنَ يَجْتَنِبُوْنَ كَبٰۗىِٕرَ الْاِثْمِ وَ
الْفَوَاحِشَ وَاِذَا مَا غَضِبُوْا هُمْ يَغْفِرُوْنَ ﴿۳۷﴾
وَالَّذِيْنَ اسْتَجَابُوْا لِرَبِّهِمْ وَاَقَامُوا الصَّلٰوةَ
وَاَمْرُهُمْ شُوْرٰى بَيْنَهُمْ وَمِمَّا رَزَقْنٰهُمْ يُنْفِقُوْنَ ﴿۳۸﴾
وَالَّذِيْنَ اِذَآ اَصَابَهُمُ الْبَغْيُ هُمْ
يَنْتَصِرُوْنَ ﴿۳۹﴾
وَجَزٰۗؤُا سَيِّئَةٍ سَيِّئَةٌ مِّثْلُهَا ۚ فَمَنْ
عَفَا وَاَصْلَحَ فَاَجْرُهٗ عَلَي اللّٰهِ ۭ اِنَّهٗ لَا
يُحِبُّ الظّٰلِمِيْنَ ﴿۴۰﴾
وَلَمَنِ انْتَصَرَ بَعْدَ ظُلْمِهٖ فَاُولٰۗىِٕكَ مَا
عَلَيْهِمْ مِّنْ سَبِيْلٍ ﴿۴۱﴾
اِنَّمَا السَّبِيْلُ عَلَي الَّذِيْنَ يَظْلِمُوْنَ النَّاسَ
وَيَبْغُوْنَ فِي الْاَرْضِ بِغَيْرِ الْحَقِّ ۭ
اُولٰۗىِٕكَ لَهُمْ عَذَابٌ اَلِيْمٌ ﴿۴۲﴾
وَلَمَنْ صَبَرَ وَغَفَرَ اِنَّ ذٰلِكَ لَمِنْ
عَزْمِ الْاُمُوْرِ ﴿۴۳﴾
وَمَنْ يُّضْلِلِ اللّٰهُ فَمَا لَهٗ مِنْ وَّلِيٍّ
مِّنْ بَعْدِهٖ ۭ وَتَرَى الظّٰلِمِيْنَ لَمَّا
رَاَوُا الْعَذَابَ يَقُوْلُوْنَ هَلْ اِلٰى مَرَدٍّ

مِّنْ سَبِيلٍ ﴿٤٤﴾
وَتَرَاهُمْ يُعْرَضُونَ عَلَيْهَا خَاشِعِينَ
مِنَ الذُّلِّ يَنظُرُونَ مِن طَرْفٍ خَفِيٍّ
وَقَالَ الَّذِينَ آمَنُوا إِنَّ الْخَاسِرِينَ الَّذِينَ
خَسِرُوا أَنفُسَهُمْ وَأَهْلِيهِمْ يَوْمَ الْقِيَامَةِ أَلَا
إِنَّ الظَّالِمِينَ فِي عَذَابٍ مُّقِيمٍ ﴿٤٥﴾
وَمَا كَانَ لَهُم مِّنْ أَوْلِيَاءَ يَنصُرُونَهُم
مِّن دُونِ اللَّهِ وَمَن يُضْلِلِ اللَّهُ فَمَا لَهُ
مِن سَبِيلٍ ﴿٤٦﴾
اسْتَجِيبُوا لِرَبِّكُم مِّن قَبْلِ أَن يَأْتِيَ
يَوْمٌ لَّا مَرَدَّ لَهُ مِنَ اللَّهِ مَا لَكُم مِّن
مَّلْجَإٍ يَوْمَئِذٍ وَمَا لَكُم مِّن نَّكِيرٍ ﴿٤٧﴾
فَإِنْ أَعْرَضُوا فَمَا أَرْسَلْنَاكَ عَلَيْهِمْ
حَفِيظًا إِنْ عَلَيْكَ إِلَّا الْبَلَاغُ وَإِنَّا
إِذَا أَذَقْنَا الْإِنسَانَ مِنَّا رَحْمَةً فَرِحَ
بِهَا وَإِن تُصِبْهُمْ سَيِّئَةٌ بِمَا قَدَّمَتْ
أَيْدِيهِمْ فَإِنَّ الْإِنسَانَ كَفُورٌ ﴿٤٨﴾
لِّلَّهِ مُلْكُ السَّمَاوَاتِ وَالْأَرْضِ يَخْلُقُ
مَا يَشَاءُ يَهَبُ لِمَن يَشَاءُ إِنَاثًا وَ
يَهَبُ لِمَن يَشَاءُ الذُّكُورَ ﴿٤٩﴾
أَوْ يُزَوِّجُهُمْ ذُكْرَانًا وَإِنَاثًا وَيَجْعَلُ
مَن يَشَاءُ عَقِيمًا إِنَّهُ عَلِيمٌ
قَدِيرٌ ﴿٥٠﴾
وَمَا كَانَ لِبَشَرٍ أَن يُكَلِّمَهُ اللَّهُ
إِلَّا وَحْيًا أَوْ مِن وَرَاءِ حِجَابٍ أَوْ
يُرْسِلَ رَسُولًا فَيُوحِيَ بِإِذْنِهِ مَا يَشَاءُ
إِنَّهُ عَلِيٌّ حَكِيمٌ ﴿٥١﴾

واپس جانے کی کوئی سبیل ہے؟ ﴿٤٤﴾
اور تم اُن کو دیکھوگے کہ دوزخ کے سامنے لائے جائیں گے
ذلت سے عاجزی کرتے ہوئے چھپی (اور نیچی) نگاہ سے دیکھ رہے
ہونگے۔ اور مومن لوگ کہیں گے کہ خسارہ اُٹھانیوالے تو وہ ہیں جنہوں
نے قیامت کے دن اپنے آپکو اور اپنے گھروالوں کو خسارے میں ڈالا دیکھو
کہ بے انصاف لوگ ہمیشہ کے دُکھ میں (پڑے) رہیں گے ﴿٤٥﴾
اور خدا کے سوا اُن کے کوئی دوست نہ ہونگے کہ خدا کے سوا اُنکو
مدد دے سکیں۔ اور جس کو خدا گمراہ کرے اُس کے لئے
(ہدایت کا) کوئی رستہ نہیں ﴿٤٦﴾
(اُن سے کہہ دو کہ) قبل اسکے کہ وہ دن جو ٹلے گا نہیں خدا کی طرف سے
آموجود ہو اپنے پروردگار کا حکم قبول کرو۔ اُس دن تمہارے لئے نہ
کوئی جائے پناہ ہوگی اور نہ تم سے گناہوں کا انکار ہی بن پڑیگا ﴿٤٧﴾
پھر اگر یہ منہ پھیر لیں تو ہم نے تم کو اُن پر نگہبان بنا کر نہیں بھیجا۔
تمہارا کام تو صرف (احکام کا) پہنچا دینا ہے۔ اور جب ہم انسان
کو اپنی رحمت کا مزہ چکھاتے ہیں تو اس سے خوش ہوجاتا ہے اور
اگر انکو انہی کے اعمال کے سبب کوئی سختی پہنچتی ہے تو (سب احسانوں کو
بھول جاتا ہے) بیشک انسان بڑا ناشکرا ہے ﴿٤٨﴾
(تمام) بادشاہت خدا ہی کی ہے آسمانوں کی بھی اور زمین کی بھی۔
وہ جو چاہتا ہے پیدا کرتا ہے۔ جسے چاہتا ہے بیٹیاں عطا کرتا ہے
اور جسے چاہتا ہے بیٹے بخشتا ہے ﴿٤٩﴾
یا اُن کو بیٹے اور بیٹیاں دونوں عنایت فرماتا ہے اور جس کو
چاہتا ہے بے اولاد رکھتا ہے۔ وہ تو جاننے والا (اور)
قدرت والا ہے ﴿٥٠﴾
اور کسی آدمی کے لئے ممکن نہیں کہ خدا اُس سے بات کرے
مگر الہام (کے ذریعے) سے یا پردے کے پیچھے سے یا کوئی فرشتہ
بھیج دے تو وہ خدا کے حکم سے جو خدا چاہے القا کرے
بے شک وہ عالی رتبہ (اور) حکمت والا ہے ﴿٥١﴾

way (to effect) a return?"

45. And thou wilt see them brought forward to the (Penalty), abject in humbleness (and) looking with a stealthy glance. And the Believers will say: "Those are indeed in loss who lose themselves and their families. On the Day of Judgment. Behold! Truly the wrong-doers are in a lasting Chastisement!"

46. And no protectors have they to help them, other than Allah. And for any whom Allah leaves to stray, there is no way (to the Goal).

47. Respond ye to your Lord, before there come a Day which there will be no putting back, because of (the ordainment of) Allah! That Day there will be for you no place of refuge nor will there be for you any room for denial (of your sins)!

48. If then they turn away, We have not sent thee as a guard over them. Thy duty is but to convey (the Message). And truly, when We give man a taste of a Mercy from Us, he doth exult thereat, but when some ill happens to him, on account of the deeds which his hands have sent forth, truly then is man ungrateful!

49. To Allah belongs the dominion of the heavens and the earth. He creates what He wills. He bestows (children) male or female according to His Will,

50. Or He bestows both males and females, and He leaves barren whom He will: for He is full of Knowledge and Power.

51. It is not fitting for a man that Allah should speak to him except by inspiration, or from behind a veil, or by the sending of a Messenger to reveal, with Allah's permission, what Allah wills: for He is Most High, Most Wise.

SÛRA–43

AZ-ZUKHRUF

(INTRODUCTION)

This is the fourth Sûra of the *Ḥã-Mîm* series of seven Sûras. For their chronology and general theme see the Introduction to S. 40.

This Sûra deals with the contrasts between the real glory of Truth and Revelation and the false glitter of what people like to believe and worship. It cites tha examples of Abraham, Moses, and Jesus, as exposing the False holding up the Truth. The key-word *Zukhruf* (Gold Adornments) occurs in verse 38, but the idea occurs all through the Sûra.

52. And thus have We, by Our command, sent inspiration to thee: thou knewest not (before) what was Revelation, and what was Faith; but We have made the (Qur'ān) a Light, wherewith We guide such of Our servants as We will; and verily thou dost guide (men) to the Straight Way,—

53. The Way of Allah, to Whom belongs whatever is in the heavens and whatever is on earth. Behold (how) all affairs tend towards Allah!

Az-Zukhruf, or Gold Adornments

In the name of Allah, Most Gracious, Most Merciful.

1. Ḥā-Mīm.
2. By the Book that makes things clear,—
3. We have made it a Qur'ān in Arabic, that ye may be able to understand.
4. And verily, it is in the Mother of the Book, with Us, high (in dignity), full of wisdom.
5. Shall We then turn away the Reminder from you altogether, for that ye are a people transgressing beyond bounds?
6. But how many were the prophets We sent amongst the peoples of old?
7. And never came there a prophet to them but they mocked him.
8. So We destroyed men—stronger in power than these; and (thus) has passed on the example of the peoples of old.
9. If thou wert to question them, 'Who created the heavens and the earth?' they would be sure to reply, 'They were created by (Him), the Exalted in Power, full of Knowledge';—
10. (Yea, the same that) has made for you the earth spread out, and has made for you roads (and channels) therein, in order that ye may find guidance (on the way);
11. That sends down (from time to time) rain from the sky in due measure;— and We raise to life therewith a land that is dead; even so will ye be raised (from the dead);—
12. That has created pairs in all

اور اسی طرح ہم نے اپنے حکم سے تمہاری طرف روح القدس کے
ذریعے سے (قرآن) بھیجا ہے۔ تم نہ تو کتاب کو جانتے تھے اور
نہ ایمان کو۔ لیکن ہم نے اس کو نور بنایا ہے کہ اس سے ہم اپنے
بندوں میں سے جس کو چاہتے ہیں ہدایت کرتے ہیں۔ اور
بے شک (اے محمدؐ) تم سیدھا رستہ دکھاتے ہو ﴿۵۲﴾
(یعنی) خدا کا رستہ جو آسمانوں اور زمین کی سب چیزوں کا مالک ہے۔
دیکھو سب کام خدا کی طرف رجوع ہوں گے (اور وہی ان میں فیصلہ کریگا) ﴿۵۳﴾

سورۂ زخرف مکّی ہے اور اس میں نواسی آیتیں اور سات رکوع ہیں

شروع خدا کا نام لے کر جو بڑا مہربان نہایت رحم والا ہے
حٰمٓ ﴿۱﴾ کتاب روشن کی قسم ﴿۲﴾
کہ ہم نے اس کو قرآن عربی بنایا ہے تاکہ تم سمجھو ﴿۳﴾
اور یہ بڑی کتاب (یعنی لوح محفوظ) میں ہمارے پاس (لکھی
ہوئی اور) بڑی فضیلت (اور) حکمت والی ہے ﴿۴﴾
بھلا اس لئے کہ تم حد سے نکلے ہوئے لوگ ہو ہم تم کو نصیحت
کرنے سے باز رہیں گے ﴿۵﴾
اور ہم نے پہلے لوگوں میں بھی بہت سے پیغمبر بھیجے تھے ﴿۶﴾
اور کوئی پیغمبر اُن کے پاس نہیں آتا تھا مگر وہ اُس سے
تمسخر کرتے تھے ﴿۷﴾
تو جو اُن میں سخت زور والے تھے اُن کو ہم نے ہلاک کر دیا
اور اگلے لوگوں کی حالت گزر گئی ﴿۸﴾
اور اگر تم اُن سے پوچھو کہ آسمانوں اور زمین کو کس نے پیدا کیا ہے تو کہہ دیں گے
کہ اُن کو غالب (اور) علم والے (خدا) نے پیدا کیا ہے ﴿۹﴾
جس نے تمہارے لئے زمین کو بچھونا بنایا۔ اور اس میں تمہارے
لئے رستے بنائے تاکہ تم راہ معلوم کرو ﴿۱۰﴾
اور جس نے ایک اندازے کے ساتھ آسمان سے پانی نازل کیا۔
پھر ہم نے اس سے شہر مردہ کو زندہ کیا۔ اسی طرح تم (زمین سے) نکالے جاؤ گے ﴿۱۱﴾
اور جس نے تمام قسم کے حیوانات پیدا کئے اور تمہارے لئے

وَكَذٰلِكَ أَوْحَيْنَآ إِلَيْكَ رُوحًا مِّنْ أَمْرِنَا ۚ
مَا كُنتَ تَدْرِى مَا ٱلْكِتَـٰبُ وَلَا ٱلْإِيمَـٰنُ
وَلَـٰكِن جَعَلْنَـٰهُ نُورًا نَّهْدِى بِهِۦ مَن
نَّشَآءُ مِنْ عِبَادِنَا ۚ وَإِنَّكَ لَتَهْدِىٓ إِلَىٰ
صِرَٰطٍ مُّسْتَقِيمٍ ﴿٥٢﴾
صِرَٰطِ ٱللَّهِ ٱلَّذِى لَهُۥ مَا فِى ٱلسَّمَـٰوَٰتِ
وَمَا فِى ٱلْأَرْضِ ۗ أَلَآ إِلَى ٱللَّهِ تَصِيرُ ٱلْأُمُورُ ﴿٥٣﴾

سُورَةُ الزُّخْرُفِ مَكِّيَّةٌ وَهِيَ تِسْعٌ وَّثَمَانُوْنَ اٰيَةً وَّسَبْعُ رُكُوْعَاتٍ

بِسْمِ ٱللَّهِ ٱلرَّحْمَـٰنِ ٱلرَّحِيمِ
حمٓ ﴿١﴾ وَٱلْكِتَـٰبِ ٱلْمُبِينِ ﴿٢﴾
إِنَّا جَعَلْنَـٰهُ قُرْءَٰنًا عَرَبِيًّا لَّعَلَّكُمْ تَعْقِلُونَ ﴿٣﴾
وَإِنَّهُۥ فِىٓ أُمِّ ٱلْكِتَـٰبِ لَدَيْنَا لَعَلِىٌّ
حَكِيمٌ ﴿٤﴾
أَفَنَضْرِبُ عَنكُمُ ٱلذِّكْرَ صَفْحًا أَن
كُنتُمْ قَوْمًا مُّسْرِفِينَ ﴿٥﴾
وَكَمْ أَرْسَلْنَا مِن نَّبِىٍّ فِى ٱلْأَوَّلِينَ ﴿٦﴾
وَمَا يَأْتِيهِم مِّن نَّبِىٍّ إِلَّا كَانُوا۟ بِهِۦ
يَسْتَهْزِءُونَ ﴿٧﴾
فَأَهْلَكْنَآ أَشَدَّ مِنْهُم بَطْشًا وَمَضَىٰ
مَثَلُ ٱلْأَوَّلِينَ ﴿٨﴾
وَلَئِن سَأَلْتَهُم مَّنْ خَلَقَ ٱلسَّمَـٰوَٰتِ وَ
ٱلْأَرْضَ لَيَقُولُنَّ خَلَقَهُنَّ ٱلْعَزِيزُ ٱلْعَلِيمُ ﴿٩﴾
ٱلَّذِى جَعَلَ لَكُمُ ٱلْأَرْضَ مَهْدًا وَجَعَلَ
لَكُمْ فِيهَا سُبُلًا لَّعَلَّكُمْ تَهْتَدُونَ ﴿١٠﴾
وَٱلَّذِى نَزَّلَ مِنَ ٱلسَّمَآءِ مَآءًۢ بِقَدَرٍ
فَأَنشَرْنَا بِهِۦ بَلْدَةً مَّيْتًا ۚ كَذَٰلِكَ تُخْرَجُونَ ﴿١١﴾
وَٱلَّذِى خَلَقَ ٱلْأَزْوَٰجَ كُلَّهَا وَجَعَلَ

things, and has made for you ships and cattle on which ye ride,

13. In order that ye may sit firm and square on their backs, and when so seated, ye may remember the (kind) favour of your Lord, and say, "Glory to Him Who has subjected these to our (use), for we could never be able to do it.

14. "And to our Lord, surely, must we turn back!"

15. Yet they attribute to some of His servants a share with Him truly is man clearly unthankful.

16. What! Has He taken daughter out of what He himself creates, and granted to you sons for choice?

17. When news is brought to one of them of (the birth of) what he sets up as a likeness to (Allah) Most Gracious, his face darkens, and he is filled with inward grief!

18. Is then one brought up among trinkets, and unable to give a clear account in a dispute (to be associated with Allah)?

19. And they make into females angels who themselves serve Allah. Did they witness their creation? Their evidence will be recorded, and they will be called to account!

20. ("Ah!") they say, "If it had been the Will of The Most Gracious, we should not have worshipped such (deities)!" Of that they have no knowledge! They do nothing but lie!

21. What! have We given them a Book before this, to which they are holding fast?

22. Nay! they say: "We found our fathers following a certain religion, and we do guide ourselves by their footsteps."

23. Just in the same way, whenever We sent a Warner before thee to any people, the wealthy ones among them said: "We found our fathers following a certain

کشتیاں اور چارپائے بنائے جن پر تم سوار ہوتے ہو ﴿۱۲﴾
تاکہ تم اُنکی پیٹھ پر چڑھ بیٹھو اور جب اُس پر بیٹھ جاؤ پھر اپنے
پروردگار کے احسان کو یاد کرو اور کہو کہ وہ (ذات) پاک ہے
جس نے اس کو ہمارے زیرِ فرمان کر دیا اور ہم میں طاقت
نہ تھی کہ اُس کو بس میں کر لیتے ﴿۱۳﴾
اور ہم اپنے پروردگار کی طرف لوٹ کر جانے والے ہیں ﴿۱۴﴾
اور اُنہوں نے اس کے بندوں میں سے اُسکے لئے اولاد
مقرر کی۔ بے شک انسان صریح ناشکرا ہے ﴿۱۵﴾
کیا اُس نے اپنی مخلوقات میں سے خود تو بیٹیاں لیں
اور تم کو چُن کر بیٹے دیئے ﴿۱۶﴾
حالانکہ جب اُنمیں سے کسی کو اُس چیز کی خوشخبری دی جاتی ہے جو اُنہوں
نے خدا کیلئے بیان کی ہے تو اُس کا منہ سیاہ ہو جاتا اور وہ غم سے بھر جاتا ہے ﴿۱۷﴾
کیا وہ جو زیور میں پرورش پائے اور جھگڑے کے وقت بات
نہ کر سکے (خدا کی بیٹی ہو سکتی ہے؟) ﴿۱۸﴾
اور اُنہوں نے فرشتوں کو کہ وہ بھی خدا کے بندے ہیں (خدا کی) بیٹیاں
مقرر کیا۔ کیا یہ اُنکی پیدائش کے وقت حاضر تھے عنقریب اُنکی
شہادت لکھ لی جائیگی اور اُن سے بازپرس کی جائیگی ﴿۱۹﴾
اور کہتے ہیں اگر خدا چاہتا تو ہم اُن کو نہ پوجتے۔
اُن کو اس کا کچھ علم نہیں۔ یہ تو صرف اٹکلیں
دوڑا رہے ہیں ﴿۲۰﴾
یا ہم نے اُن کو اس سے پہلے کوئی کتاب دی تھی تو یہ
اس سے سند پکڑتے ہیں ﴿۲۱﴾
بلکہ کہنے لگے کہ ہم نے اپنے باپ دادا کو ایک رستے پر پایا ہے
اور ہم اُن ہی کے قدم بقدم چل رہے ہیں ﴿۲۲﴾
اور اسی طرح ہم نے تم سے پہلے کسی بستی میں کوئی ہدایت
کرنے والا نہیں بھیجا مگر وہاں کے خوشحال لوگوں نے کہا کہ
ہم نے اپنے باپ دادا کو ایک راہ پر پایا ہے اور ہم قدم بقدم

لَكُمْ مِّنَ الْفُلْكِ وَالْأَنْعَامِ مَا تَرْكَبُونَ ﴿١٢﴾
لِتَسْتَوُوا عَلَىٰ ظُهُورِهِ ثُمَّ تَذْكُرُوا نِعْمَةَ
رَبِّكُمْ إِذَا اسْتَوَيْتُمْ عَلَيْهِ وَتَقُولُوا
سُبْحَانَ الَّذِي سَخَّرَ لَنَا هَٰذَا وَمَا كُنَّا
لَهُ مُقْرِنِينَ ﴿١٣﴾
وَإِنَّا إِلَىٰ رَبِّنَا لَمُنقَلِبُونَ ﴿١٤﴾
وَجَعَلُوا لَهُ مِنْ عِبَادِهِ جُزْءًا ۚ إِنَّ
الْإِنسَانَ لَكَفُورٌ مُّبِينٌ ﴿١٥﴾
أَمِ اتَّخَذَ مِمَّا يَخْلُقُ بَنَاتٍ وَأَصْفَاكُم
بِالْبَنِينَ ﴿١٦﴾
وَإِذَا بُشِّرَ أَحَدُهُم بِمَا ضَرَبَ لِلرَّحْمَٰنِ
مَثَلًا ظَلَّ وَجْهُهُ مُسْوَدًّا وَهُوَ كَظِيمٌ ﴿١٧﴾
أَوَمَن يُنَشَّأُ فِي الْحِلْيَةِ وَهُوَ فِي
الْخِصَامِ غَيْرُ مُبِينٍ ﴿١٨﴾
وَجَعَلُوا الْمَلَائِكَةَ الَّذِينَ هُمْ عِبَادُ
الرَّحْمَٰنِ إِنَاثًا ۚ أَشَهِدُوا خَلْقَهُمْ ۚ سَتُكْتَبُ
شَهَادَتُهُمْ وَيُسْأَلُونَ ﴿١٩﴾
وَقَالُوا لَوْ شَاءَ الرَّحْمَٰنُ مَا عَبَدْنَاهُم ۗ
مَّا لَهُم بِذَٰلِكَ مِنْ عِلْمٍ ۖ إِنْ هُمْ إِلَّا
يَخْرُصُونَ ﴿٢٠﴾
أَمْ آتَيْنَاهُمْ كِتَابًا مِّن قَبْلِهِ فَهُم بِهِ
مُسْتَمْسِكُونَ ﴿٢١﴾
بَلْ قَالُوا إِنَّا وَجَدْنَا آبَاءَنَا عَلَىٰ أُمَّةٍ
وَإِنَّا عَلَىٰ آثَارِهِم مُّهْتَدُونَ ﴿٢٢﴾
وَكَذَٰلِكَ مَا أَرْسَلْنَا مِن قَبْلِكَ فِي
قَرْيَةٍ مِّن نَّذِيرٍ إِلَّا قَالَ مُتْرَفُوهَا
إِنَّا وَجَدْنَا آبَاءَنَا عَلَىٰ أُمَّةٍ وَإِنَّا عَلَىٰ

religion, and we will certainly follow in their footsteps."

24. He said "What! even if I brought you better guidance than that which ye found your fathers following?" They said: "For us, we deny that which ye (prophets) are sent with."

25. So We exacted retribution from them: now see what was the end of those who rejected (Truth)!

26. Behold! Abraham said to his father and his people: "I do indeed clear myself of what ye worship:

27. "(I worship) only Him Who originated me, and He will certainly guide me."

28. And he left it as a Word to endure among those who came after him, that they may turn back (to Allah).

29. Yea, I have given the good things of this life to these (men) and their fathers, until the Truth has come to them, and a Messenger making things clear.

30. But when the Truth came to them, they said: "This is sorcery, and we do reject it."

31. Also, they say: "Why is not this Qur'ān sent down to some leading man in either of the two (chief) cities?"

32. Is it they who would portion out the Mercy of thy Lord? It is We Who portion out between them their livelihood in the life of this world: and We raise some of them above others in ranks, so that some may command work from others. But the Mercy of thy Lord is better than the (wealth) which they amass.

33. And were it not that (all) men might become one community We would provide, for everyone that blasphemes against The Most Gracious, silver roofs for their houses, and (silver) stair-ways on which to go up,

34. And (silver) doors to their houses, and couches (of silver) on which they could recline,

35. And also adornments of gold. But all this was nothing but

اُن ہی کے پیچھے چلتے ہیں ﴿٢٣﴾
پیغمبر نے کہا اگرچہ میں تمہارے پاس ایسا (دین) لاؤں کہ جس
رستے پر تم نے اپنے باپ دادا کو پایا وہ اس سے کہیں سیدھا
رستہ دکھاتا ہو کہنے لگے کہ جو (دین) تم دیکر بھیجے گئے ہو ہم اسکو نہیں مانتے ﴿٢٤﴾
تو ہم نے اُن سے انتقام لیا سو دیکھ لو کہ جھٹلانے والوں کا انجام
کیسا ہوا ﴿٢٥﴾
اور جب ابراہیم نے اپنے باپ اور اپنی قوم کے لوگوں سے کہا کہ جن
چیزوں کو تم پوجتے ہو میں اُن سے بیزار ہوں ﴿٢٦﴾
ہاں جس نے مجھ کو پیدا کیا وہی مجھے سیدھا رستہ دکھائے گا ﴿٢٧﴾
اور یہی بات اپنی اولاد میں پیچھے چھوڑ گئے تاکہ وہ (خدا کی
طرف) رجوع رہیں ﴿٢٨﴾
بات یہ ہے کہ میں ان کفار کو اور اُنکے باپ دادا کو متمتع کرتا رہا یہاں تک
کہ اُن کے پاس حق اور صاف صاف بیان کرنیوالا پیغمبر آپہنچا ﴿٢٩﴾
اور جب اُن کے پاس حق (یعنی قرآن) آیا تو کہنے لگے کہ یہ
تو جادو ہے اور ہم اس کو نہیں مانتے ﴿٣٠﴾
اور (یہ بھی) کہنے لگے کہ یہ قرآن ان دونوں بستیوں (یعنی مکے
اور طائف) میں سے کسی بڑے آدمی پر کیوں نازل نہ کیا گیا؟ ﴿٣١﴾
کیا یہ لوگ تمہارے پروردگار کی رحمت کو بانٹتے ہیں؟ ہم نے
اُن میں اُن کی معیشت کو دنیا کی زندگی میں تقسیم کر دیا اور
ایک کے دوسرے پر درجے بلند کئے تاکہ ایک دوسرے سے
خدمت لے۔ اور جو کچھ یہ جمع کرتے ہیں تمہارے پروردگار کی
رحمت اس سے کہیں بہتر ہے ﴿٣٢﴾
اور اگر یہ (خیال) نہ ہوتا کہ سب لوگ ایک ہی جماعت ہو جائینگے تو
جو لوگ خدا سے انکار کرتے ہیں ہم اُنکے گھروں کی چھتیں چاندی
کی بنا دیتے اور سیڑھیاں (بھی) جن پر وہ چڑھتے ﴿٣٣﴾
اور اُنکے گھروں کے دروازے بھی اور تخت بھی جن پر تکیہ لگاتے ہیں ﴿٣٤﴾
اور (خوب) تجمل (و آرائش کر دیتے) اور یہ سب دنیا کی زندگی کا

آثَٰرِهِم مُّقْتَدُونَ ﴿٢٣﴾
قَٰلَ أَوَلَوْ جِئْتُكُم بِأَهْدَىٰ مِمَّا وَجَدتُّمْ
عَلَيْهِ ءَابَآءَكُمْ ۖ قَالُوٓا۟ إِنَّا بِمَآ أُرْسِلْتُم
بِهِۦ كَٰفِرُونَ ﴿٢٤﴾
فَٱنتَقَمْنَا مِنْهُمْ ۖ فَٱنظُرْ كَيْفَ كَانَ
عَٰقِبَةُ ٱلْمُكَذِّبِينَ ﴿٢٥﴾
وَإِذْ قَالَ إِبْرَٰهِيمُ لِأَبِيهِ وَقَوْمِهِۦٓ إِنَّنِى
بَرَآءٌ مِّمَّا تَعْبُدُونَ ﴿٢٦﴾
إِلَّا ٱلَّذِى فَطَرَنِى فَإِنَّهُۥ سَيَهْدِينِ ﴿٢٧﴾
وَجَعَلَهَا كَلِمَةًۢ بَاقِيَةً فِى عَقِبِهِۦ لَعَلَّهُمْ
يَرْجِعُونَ ﴿٢٨﴾
بَلْ مَتَّعْتُ هَٰٓؤُلَآءِ وَءَابَآءَهُمْ حَتَّىٰ
جَآءَهُمُ ٱلْحَقُّ وَرَسُولٌ مُّبِينٌ ﴿٢٩﴾
وَلَمَّا جَآءَهُمُ ٱلْحَقُّ قَالُوا۟ هَٰذَا سِحْرٌ وَ
إِنَّا بِهِۦ كَٰفِرُونَ ﴿٣٠﴾
وَقَالُوا۟ لَوْلَا نُزِّلَ هَٰذَا ٱلْقُرْءَانُ عَلَىٰ
رَجُلٍ مِّنَ ٱلْقَرْيَتَيْنِ عَظِيمٍ ﴿٣١﴾
أَهُمْ يَقْسِمُونَ رَحْمَتَ رَبِّكَ ۚ نَحْنُ قَسَمْنَا
بَيْنَهُم مَّعِيشَتَهُمْ فِى ٱلْحَيَوٰةِ ٱلدُّنْيَا ۚ وَ
رَفَعْنَا بَعْضَهُمْ فَوْقَ بَعْضٍ دَرَجَٰتٍ لِّيَتَّخِذَ
بَعْضُهُم بَعْضًا سُخْرِيًّا ۗ وَرَحْمَتُ رَبِّكَ
خَيْرٌ مِّمَّا يَجْمَعُونَ ﴿٣٢﴾
وَلَوْلَآ أَن يَكُونَ ٱلنَّاسُ أُمَّةً وَٰحِدَةً
لَّجَعَلْنَا لِمَن يَكْفُرُ بِٱلرَّحْمَٰنِ لِبُيُوتِهِمْ
سُقُفًا مِّن فِضَّةٍ وَمَعَارِجَ عَلَيْهَا يَظْهَرُونَ ﴿٣٣﴾
وَلِبُيُوتِهِمْ أَبْوَٰبًا وَسُرُرًا عَلَيْهَا يَتَّكِـُٔونَ ﴿٣٤﴾
وَزُخْرُفًا ۚ وَإِن كُلُّ ذَٰلِكَ لَمَّا مَتَٰعُ

enjoyment of the present life: the Hereafter, in the sight of thy Lord, is for the Righteous.

36. If anyone withdraws himself from remembrance of The Most Gracious, We appoint for him a Satan, to be an intimate companion to him.

37. Such (Satans) really hinder them from the Path, but they think that they are being guided aright!

38. At length, when (such a one) comes to Us, he says (to his evil companion): "Would that between me and thee were the distance of East and West!" Ah! evil is the companion (indeed)!

39. When ye have done wrong, it will avail you nothing, that day, that ye shall be partners in punishment!

40. Canst thou then make the deaf to hear, or give direction to the blind or to such as (wander) in manifest error?

41. Even if We take thee away, We shall be sure to exact retribution from them,

42. Or We shall show thee that (accomplished) which We have promised them: for verily We have power over them.

43. So hold thou fast to the Revelation sent down to thee: verily thou art on a Straight Way.

44. The (Qur'ãn) is indeed a Reminder for thee and for thy people; and soon shall ye (all) be brought to account.

45. And question thou our messengers whom We sent before thee; did We appoint any deities other than The Most Gracious, to be worshipped?

46. We did send Moses aforetime, with Our Signs, to Pharaoh and his Chiefs: he said, "I am a messenger of the Lord of the Worlds."

47. But when he came to them with Our Signs, behold, they laughed at them.

48. We showed them Sign after Sign, each greater than its fellow, and We seized them with Punishment, in order that they might turn (to Us).

تھوڑا سا سامان ہے اور آخرت تمہارے پروردگار کے ہاں
پرہیزگاروں کے لئے ہے ﴿۳۵﴾
اور جو کوئی خدا کی یاد سے آنکھیں بند کرلے (یعنی تغافل کرے)
ہم اُس پر ایک شیطان مقرر کردیتے ہیں تو وہ اُس کا ساتھی ہوجاتا ہے ﴿۳۶﴾
اور یہ (شیطان) اُن کو رستے سے روکتے رہتے ہیں اور وہ سمجھتے
ہیں کہ سیدھے رستے پر ہیں ﴿۳۷﴾
یہاں تک کہ جب ہمارے پاس آئیگا تو کہے گا کہ اے کاش
مجھ میں اور تجھ میں مشرق و مغرب کا فاصلہ ہوتا تو بُرا ساتھی ہے ﴿۳۸﴾
اور جب تم ظلم کرتے رہے تو آج تمہیں یہ بات فائدہ نہیں
دے سکتی کہ تم (سب) عذاب میں شریک ہو ﴿۳۹﴾
کیا تم بہرے کو سُنا سکتے ہو یا اندھے کو رستہ دکھا سکتے ہو
اور جو صریح گمراہی میں ہو اُسے (راہ پر لا سکتے ہو) ﴿۴۰﴾
اگر ہم تمکو (وفات دیکر) اُٹھالیں تو اِن لوگوں سے تو ہم انتقام لیکر رہینگے ﴿۴۱﴾
یا (تمہاری زندگی ہی میں) تمہیں وہ (عذاب) دکھادینگے جن کا
ہم نے اُن سے وعدہ کیا ہے ہم اُن پر قابو رکھتے ہیں ﴿۴۲﴾
پس تمہاری طرف جو وحی کی گئی ہے اُس کو مضبوط پکڑے رہو
بیشک تم سیدھے رستے پر ہو ﴿۴۳﴾
اور یہ (قرآن) تمہارے لئے اور تمہاری قوم کیلئے نصیحت ہے اور (لوگو) تم سے عنقریب پرسش ہوگی ﴿۴۴﴾
اور (اے محمدؐ) جو اپنے پیغمبر ہم نے تم سے پہلے بھیجے ہیں اُن سے
احوال دریافت کرلو کیا ہم نے (خدائے) رحمٰن کے سوا اور
معبود بنائے تھے کہ اُن کی عبادت کی جائے؟ ﴿۴۵﴾
اور ہم نے موسیٰ کو اپنی نشانیاں دیکر فرعون اور اُسکے درباریوں
کی طرف بھیجا تو اُنہوں نے کہا کہ میں اپنے پروردگار عالم کا بھیجا ہوا ہوں ﴿۴۶﴾
جب وہ اُن کے پاس ہماری نشانیاں لے کر آئے تو وہ
نشانیوں سے ہنسی کرنے لگے ﴿۴۷﴾
اور جو نشانی ہم اُن کو دکھاتے تھے وہ دوسری سے بڑی ہوتی
تھی اور ہم نے اُن کو عذاب میں پکڑ لیا تاکہ باز آئیں ﴿۴۸﴾

الْحَيٰوةِ الدُّنْيَا ۗ وَالْاٰخِرَةُ عِنْدَ رَبِّكَ
لِلْمُتَّقِيْنَ ﴿٣٥﴾
وَمَنْ يَّعْشُ عَنْ ذِكْرِ الرَّحْمٰنِ نُقَيِّضْ
لَهٗ شَيْطٰنًا فَهُوَ لَهٗ قَرِيْنٌ ﴿٣٦﴾
وَاِنَّهُمْ لَيَصُدُّوْنَهُمْ عَنِ السَّبِيْلِ وَ
يَحْسَبُوْنَ اَنَّهُمْ مُّهْتَدُوْنَ ﴿٣٧﴾
حَتّٰۤى اِذَا جَآءَنَا قَالَ يٰلَيْتَ بَيْنِيْ وَ
بَيْنَكَ بُعْدَ الْمَشْرِقَيْنِ فَبِئْسَ الْقَرِيْنُ ﴿٣٨﴾
وَلَنْ يَّنْفَعَكُمُ الْيَوْمَ اِذْ ظَّلَمْتُمْ اَنَّكُمْ
فِي الْعَذَابِ مُشْتَرِكُوْنَ ﴿٣٩﴾
اَفَاَنْتَ تُسْمِعُ الصُّمَّ اَوْ تَهْدِي الْعُمْيَ
وَمَنْ كَانَ فِيْ ضَلٰلٍ مُّبِيْنٍ ﴿٤٠﴾
فَاِمَّا نَذْهَبَنَّ بِكَ فَاِنَّا مِنْهُمْ مُّنْتَقِمُوْنَ ﴿٤١﴾
اَوْ نُرِيَنَّكَ الَّذِيْ وَعَدْنٰهُمْ فَاِنَّا عَلَيْهِمْ
مُّقْتَدِرُوْنَ ﴿٤٢﴾
فَاسْتَمْسِكْ بِالَّذِيْۤ اُوْحِيَ اِلَيْكَ ۚ اِنَّكَ
عَلٰى صِرَاطٍ مُّسْتَقِيْمٍ ﴿٤٣﴾
وَاِنَّهٗ لَذِكْرٌ لَّكَ وَلِقَوْمِكَ ۚ وَسَوْفَ تُسْـَٔلُوْنَ ﴿٤٤﴾
وَسْـَٔلْ مَنْ اَرْسَلْنَا مِنْ قَبْلِكَ مِنْ
رُّسُلِنَاۤ اَجَعَلْنَا مِنْ دُوْنِ الرَّحْمٰنِ
اٰلِهَةً يُّعْبَدُوْنَ ﴿٤٥﴾
وَلَقَدْ اَرْسَلْنَا مُوْسٰى بِاٰيٰتِنَاۤ اِلٰى فِرْعَوْنَ وَ
مَلَا۟ئِهٖ فَقَالَ اِنِّيْ رَسُوْلُ رَبِّ الْعٰلَمِيْنَ ﴿٤٦﴾
فَلَمَّا جَآءَهُمْ بِاٰيٰتِنَاۤ اِذَا هُمْ مِّنْهَا
يَضْحَكُوْنَ ﴿٤٧﴾
وَمَا نُرِيْهِمْ مِّنْ اٰيَةٍ اِلَّا هِيَ اَكْبَرُ مِنْ
اُخْتِهَا ۫ وَاَخَذْنٰهُمْ بِالْعَذَابِ لَعَلَّهُمْ يَرْجِعُوْنَ ﴿٤٨﴾

49. And they said, "O thou sorcerer! Invoke thy Lord for us according to His covenant with thee; for we shall truly accept guidance."—

50. But when We removed the Chastisement from them, behold, they broke their word.

51. And Pharaoh proclaimed among his people, saying: "O my people! Does not the dominion of Egypt belong to me, (witness) these streams flowing underneath my (palace)? What! See ye not then?

52. "Am I not better than this (Moses), who is a contemptible wretch and can scarcely express himself clearly?

53. "Then why are not gold bracelets bestowed on him, or (why) come (not) with him angels accompanying him in procession?"

54. Thus did he make fools of his people, and they obeyed him: truly were they a people rebellious (against Allah).

55. When at length they provoked Us, We exacted retribution from them, and We drowned them all.

56. And We made them (a People) of the Past and an Example to later ages.

57. When (Jesus) the son of Mary is held up as an example, behold, thy people raise a clamour thereat (in ridicule)!

58. And they say, "Are our gods best, or he?" This they set forth to thee, only by way of disputation: yea, they are a contentious people.

59. He was no more than a servant: We granted Our favour to him, and We made him an example to the Children of Israel.

60. And if it were Our Will, We could make angels from amongst you, succeeding each other on the earth.

61. And (Jesus) shall be a Sign (for the coming of) the Hour (Of Judgment): therefore have no doubt about the (Hour), but follow ye Me: this is a Straight Way.

62. Let not Satan hinder you: for he is to you an enemy avowed.

اور کہنے لگے کہ اے جادوگر اُس عہد کے مطابق جو تیرے
پروردگار نے تجھ سے کر رکھا ہے اُس سے دعا کر بیشک ہم ہدایت یاب ہوں گے ﴿۴۹﴾
سو جب ہم نے اُن سے عذاب کو دُور کر دیا تو وہ عہد شکنی
کرنے لگے ﴿۵۰﴾
اور فرعون نے اپنی قوم سے پکار کر کہا کہ اے قوم کیا مصر کی
حکومت میرے ہاتھ میں نہیں ہے۔ اور یہ نہریں جو میرے محلوں کے
نیچے بہہ رہی ہیں (میری نہیں ہیں) کیا تم دیکھتے نہیں؟ ﴿۵۱﴾
بیشک میں اُس شخص سے جو کچھ عزت نہیں رکھتا اور صاف
گفتگو بھی نہیں کر سکتا کہیں بہتر ہوں ﴿۵۲﴾
تو اس پر سونے کے کنگن کیوں نہ اُتارے گئے یا یہ ہوتا کہ
فرشتے جمع ہو کر اُس کے ساتھ آتے ﴿۵۳﴾
غرض اُس نے اپنی قوم کی عقل مار دی۔ اور اُنہوں نے اُس کی
بات مان لی بیشک وہ نافرمان لوگ تھے ﴿۵۴﴾
جب اُنہوں نے ہم کو خفا کیا تو ہم نے اُن سے انتقام لیکر اور اُن سب کو ڈبو کر چھوڑا ﴿۵۵﴾
اور اُن کو گئے گزرے کر دیا اور پچھلوں کیلئے عبرت بنا دیا ﴿۵۶﴾
اور جب مریم کے بیٹے (عیسیٰ) کا حال بیان کیا گیا تو
تمہاری قوم کے لوگ اس سے چلا اُٹھے ﴿۵۷﴾
اور کہنے لگے کہ بھلا ہمارے معبود اچھے ہیں یا وہ (عیسیٰ)؟ اُنہوں نے جو اِس (عیسیٰ)
کی مثال تم سے بیان کی ہے تو صرف جھگڑنے کو حقیقت یہ ہے کہ یہ لوگ ہیں ہی جھگڑالو ﴿۵۸﴾
وہ تو ہمارے ایسے بندے تھے جن پر ہم نے فضل کیا اور بنی اسرائیل
کے لئے اُن کو (اپنی قدرت کا) نمونہ بنا دیا ﴿۵۹﴾
اور اگر ہم چاہتے تو تم میں سے فرشتے بنا دیتے جو تمہاری جگہ
زمین میں رہتے ﴿۶۰﴾
اور وہ (عیسیٰ) قیامت کی نشانی ہیں۔ تو (کہہ دو کہ لوگو) اس میں
شک نہ کرو اور میرے پیچھے چلو۔ یہی سیدھا رستہ ہے ﴿۶۱﴾
اور (کہیں) شیطان تم کو (اس سے) روک نہ دے۔ وہ تو
تمہارا علانیہ دشمن ہے ﴿۶۲﴾

وَقَالُوْا يٰۤاَيُّهَ السّٰحِرُ ادْعُ لَنَا رَبَّكَ بِمَا عَهِدَ
عِنْدَكَ ۚ اِنَّنَا لَمُهْتَدُوْنَ ﴿۴۹﴾
فَلَمَّا كَشَفْنَا عَنْهُمُ الْعَذَابَ اِذَا هُمْ
يَنْكُثُوْنَ ﴿۵۰﴾
وَنَادٰى فِرْعَوْنُ فِيْ قَوْمِهٖ قَالَ يٰقَوْمِ
اَلَيْسَ لِيْ مُلْكُ مِصْرَ وَهٰذِهِ الْاَنْهٰرُ
تَجْرِيْ مِنْ تَحْتِيْ ۚ اَفَلَا تُبْصِرُوْنَ ﴿۵۱﴾
اَمْ اَنَا خَيْرٌ مِّنْ هٰذَا الَّذِيْ هُوَ مَهِيْنٌ ۙ
وَّلَا يَكَادُ يُبِيْنُ ﴿۵۲﴾
فَلَوْلَاۤ اُلْقِيَ عَلَيْهِ اَسْوِرَةٌ مِّنْ ذَهَبٍ
اَوْ جَآءَ مَعَهُ الْمَلٰۤئِكَةُ مُقْتَرِنِيْنَ ﴿۵۳﴾
فَاسْتَخَفَّ قَوْمَهٗ فَاَطَاعُوْهُ ؕ اِنَّهُمْ كَانُوْا
قَوْمًا فٰسِقِيْنَ ﴿۵۴﴾
فَلَمَّاۤ اٰسَفُوْنَا انْتَقَمْنَا مِنْهُمْ فَاَغْرَقْنٰهُمْ اَجْمَعِيْنَ ﴿۵۵﴾
فَجَعَلْنٰهُمْ سَلَفًا وَّمَثَلًا لِّلْاٰخِرِيْنَ ﴿۵۶﴾
وَلَمَّا ضُرِبَ ابْنُ مَرْيَمَ مَثَلًا اِذَا قَوْمُكَ
مِنْهُ يَصِدُّوْنَ ﴿۵۷﴾
وَقَالُوْۤا ءَاٰلِهَتُنَا خَيْرٌ اَمْ هُوَ ؕ مَا ضَرَبُوْهُ لَكَ
اِلَّا جَدَلًا ؕ بَلْ هُمْ قَوْمٌ خَصِمُوْنَ ﴿۵۸﴾
اِنْ هُوَ اِلَّا عَبْدٌ اَنْعَمْنَا عَلَيْهِ وَجَعَلْنٰهُ
مَثَلًا لِّبَنِيْۤ اِسْرَآءِيْلَ ﴿۵۹﴾
وَلَوْ نَشَآءُ لَجَعَلْنَا مِنْكُمْ مَّلٰۤئِكَةً فِي
الْاَرْضِ يَخْلُفُوْنَ ﴿۶۰﴾
وَاِنَّهٗ لَعِلْمٌ لِّلسَّاعَةِ فَلَا تَمْتَرُنَّ بِهَا
وَاتَّبِعُوْنِ ؕ هٰذَا صِرَاطٌ مُّسْتَقِيْمٌ ﴿۶۱﴾
وَلَا يَصُدَّنَّكُمُ الشَّيْطٰنُ ۚ اِنَّهٗ لَكُمْ
عَدُوٌّ مُّبِيْنٌ ﴿۶۲﴾

63. When Jesus came with Clear Signs, he said: "Now have I come to you with Wisdom, and in order to make clear to you some of the (points) on which ye dispute: therefore fear Allah and obey me.

64. "For Allan, He is my Lord and your Lord: so worship ye Him: this is a Straight Way."

65. But sects from among themselves fell into disagreement: then woe to the wrong-doers, from the Chastisement of a Grievous Day!

66. Do they only wait for the Hour—that it should come on them all of a sudden, while they perceive not?

67. Friends on that Day will be foes, one to another,—except the Righteous.

68. My devotees! no fear shall be on you today nor shall ye grieve,—

69. Those who have believed in Our Signs and submitted (to Us).

70. Enter ye the Garden, ye and your wives, in (beauty and) rejoicing.

71. To them will be passed round, dishes and goblets of gold: there will be there all that the souls could desire, all that the eyes could delight in: and ye shall abide therein (for aye).

72. Such will be the Garden of which ye are made heirs for your (good) deeds (in life).

73. Ye shall have therein abundance of fruit, from which ye shall eat.

74. The Sinners will be in the Punishment of Hell, to dwell therein (for aye):

75. Nowise will the (punishment) be lightened for them, and in despair will they be there overwhelmed.

76. Nowise shall We be unjust to them: but it is they who have been unjust themselves.

اور جب عیسیٰ نشانیاں لے کر آئے تو کہنے لگے کہ میں
تمہارے پاس دانائی (کی کتاب) لے کر آیا ہوں نیز اسلئے
کہ بعض باتیں جن میں تم اختلاف کرتے ہو تم کو سمجھا دوں۔
تو خدا سے ڈرو اور میرا کہا مانو (۶۳)
کچھ شک نہیں کہ خدا ہی میرا اور تمہارا پروردگار ہے پس
اُسی کی عبادت کرو۔ یہی سیدھا رستہ ہے (۶۴)
پھر کتنے فرقے اُن میں سے پھٹ گئے۔ سو جو لوگ ظالم
ہیں اُن کی درد دینے والے دن کے عذاب سے
خرابی ہے (۶۵)
یہ صرف اس بات کے منتظر ہیں کہ قیامت اُن پر ناگہاں
آموجود ہو اور اُن کو خبر تک نہ ہو (۶۶)
(جو آپس میں) دوست (ہیں) اُس روز ایک دوسرے کے
دشمن ہونگے مگر پرہیزگار (کہ باہم دوست ہی رہیں گے) (۶۷)
میرے بندو! آج تمہیں نہ کچھ خوف ہے اور نہ تم غمناک
ہوگے (۶۸)
جو لوگ ہماری آیتوں پر ایمان لائے اور فرماں بردار ہو گئے (۶۹)
(اُن سے کہا جائے گا) کہ تم اور تمہاری بیویاں عزت
(و احترام) کے ساتھ بہشت میں داخل ہو جاؤ (۷۰)
اُن پر سونے کی پرچوں اور پیالوں کا دور چلے گا اور وہاں
جو جی چاہے اور جو آنکھوں کو اچھا لگے (موجود ہوگا) اور (اے
اہل جنت) تم اس میں ہمیشہ رہو گے (۷۱)
اور یہ جنت جس کے تم مالک کر دیئے گئے ہو تمہارے اعمال کا
صلہ ہے (۷۲)
وہاں تمہارے لئے بہت سے میوے ہیں جن کو تم کھاؤ گے (۷۳)
(اور کفار) گنہگار ہمیشہ دوزخ کے عذاب میں رہیں گے (۷۴)
جو اُن سے ہلکا نہ کیا جائیگا اور وہ اسمیں نا اُمید ہو کر پڑے رہیں گے (۷۵)
اور ہم نے اُن پر ظلم نہیں کیا۔ بلکہ وہی اپنے آپ پر ظلم کرتے تھے (۷۶)

وَلَمَّا جَآءَ عِيسٰى بِالْبَيِّنٰتِ قَالَ قَدْ
جِئْتُكُمْ بِالْحِكْمَةِ وَلِأُبَيِّنَ لَكُمْ بَعْضَ
الَّذِي تَخْتَلِفُونَ فِيهِ ۚ فَاتَّقُوا اللّٰهَ
وَأَطِيعُونِ ﴿٦٣﴾
إِنَّ اللّٰهَ هُوَ رَبِّي وَرَبُّكُمْ فَاعْبُدُوهُ ۚ
هٰذَا صِرَاطٌ مُّسْتَقِيمٌ ﴿٦٤﴾
فَاخْتَلَفَ الْأَحْزَابُ مِنْ بَيْنِهِمْ ۚ
فَوَيْلٌ لِّلَّذِينَ ظَلَمُوا مِنْ عَذَابِ
يَوْمٍ أَلِيمٍ ﴿٦٥﴾
هَلْ يَنْظُرُونَ إِلَّا السَّاعَةَ أَنْ تَأْتِيَهُمْ
بَغْتَةً وَهُمْ لَا يَشْعُرُونَ ﴿٦٦﴾
الْأَخِلَّآءُ يَوْمَئِذٍ بَعْضُهُمْ لِبَعْضٍ عَدُوٌّ
إِلَّا الْمُتَّقِينَ ﴿٦٧﴾
يٰعِبَادِ لَا خَوْفٌ عَلَيْكُمُ الْيَوْمَ وَلَآ أَنْتُمْ
تَحْزَنُونَ ﴿٦٨﴾
الَّذِينَ آمَنُوا بِآيٰتِنَا وَكَانُوا مُسْلِمِينَ ﴿٦٩﴾
ادْخُلُوا الْجَنَّةَ أَنْتُمْ وَأَزْوَاجُكُمْ
تُحْبَرُونَ ﴿٧٠﴾
يُطَافُ عَلَيْهِمْ بِصِحَافٍ مِّنْ ذَهَبٍ
وَّأَكْوَابٍ ۚ وَفِيهَا مَا تَشْتَهِيهِ الْأَنْفُسُ وَتَلَذُّ
الْأَعْيُنُ ۚ وَأَنْتُمْ فِيهَا خٰلِدُونَ ﴿٧١﴾
وَتِلْكَ الْجَنَّةُ الَّتِي أُورِثْتُمُوهَا بِمَا كُنْتُمْ
تَعْمَلُونَ ﴿٧٢﴾
لَكُمْ فِيهَا فَاكِهَةٌ كَثِيرَةٌ مِّنْهَا تَأْكُلُونَ ﴿٧٣﴾
إِنَّ الْمُجْرِمِينَ فِي عَذَابِ جَهَنَّمَ خٰلِدُونَ ﴿٧٤﴾
لَا يُفَتَّرُ عَنْهُمْ وَهُمْ فِيهِ مُبْلِسُونَ ﴿٧٥﴾
وَمَا ظَلَمْنٰهُمْ وَلٰكِنْ كَانُوا هُمُ الظّٰلِمِينَ ﴿٧٦﴾

77. They will cry: "O Malik! would that thy Lord put an end to us!" He will say, "Nay, but ye shall abide!"

اور پکاریں گے کہ اے مالک تمہارا پروردگار ہمیں موت دیدے۔ وہ کہے گا کہ تم ہمیشہ (اسی حالت میں) رہو گے (۷۷)

وَنَادَوْا يٰمٰلِكُ لِيَقْضِ عَلَيْنَا رَبُّكَ قَالَ إِنَّكُمْ مّٰكِثُوْنَ (۷۷)

78. Verily We have brought the Truth to you: but most of you have a hatred for Truth.

ہم تمہارے پاس حق لے کر پہنچے لیکن تم میں سے اکثر حق سے ناخوش ہوتے رہے (۷۸)

لَقَدْ جِئْنٰكُمْ بِالْحَقِّ وَلٰكِنَّ أَكْثَرَكُمْ لِلْحَقِّ كٰرِهُوْنَ (۷۸)

79. What! Have they settled some Plan (among themselves)? But it is We Who settle things.

کیا انہوں نے کوئی بات ٹھہرا رکھی ہے تو ہم بھی کچھ ٹھہرانے والے ہیں[۲۶۳] (۷۹)

أَمْ أَبْرَمُوْا أَمْرًا فَإِنَّا مُبْرِمُوْنَ (۷۹)

80. Or do they think that We hear not their secrets and their private counsels? Indeed (We do), and Our Messengers are by them, to record.

کیا یہ لوگ خیال کرتے ہیں کہ ہم ان کی پوشیدہ باتوں اور سرگوشیوں کو سنتے نہیں؟ ہاں ہاں (سب سنتے ہیں) اور ہمارے فرشتے ان کے پاس (ان کی سب باتیں) لکھ لیتے ہیں (۸۰)

أَمْ يَحْسَبُوْنَ أَنَّا لَا نَسْمَعُ سِرَّهُمْ وَنَجْوٰىهُمْ بَلٰى وَرُسُلُنَا لَدَيْهِمْ يَكْتُبُوْنَ (۸۰)

81. Say: "If The Most Gracious had a son, I would be the first to worship."

کہہ دو کہ اگر خدا کے اولاد ہو تو میں (سب سے) پہلے (اس کی) عبادت کرنے والا ہوں (۸۱)

قُلْ إِنْ كَانَ لِلرَّحْمٰنِ وَلَدٌ فَأَنَا أَوَّلُ الْعٰبِدِيْنَ (۸۱)

82. Glory to the Lord of the heavens and the earth, the Lord of the Throne ! he is free from the things they attribute (to Him)!

یہ جو کچھ بیان کرتے ہیں۔ آسمانوں اور زمین کا مالک (اور) عرش کا مالک اس سے پاک ہے (۸۲)

سُبْحٰنَ رَبِّ السَّمٰوٰتِ وَالْأَرْضِ رَبِّ الْعَرْشِ عَمَّا يَصِفُوْنَ (۸۲)

83. So leave them to babble and play (with vanities) until they meet that Day of theirs, which they have been promised.

تو ان کو بک بک کرنے اور کھیلنے دو۔ یہاں تک کہ جس دن کا ان سے وعدہ کیا جاتا ہے اس کو دیکھ لیں (۸۳)

فَذَرْهُمْ يَخُوْضُوْا وَيَلْعَبُوْا حَتّٰى يُلٰقُوْا يَوْمَهُمُ الَّذِيْ يُوْعَدُوْنَ (۸۳)

84. It is He Who is God in heaven and God on earth; and He is Full of Wisdom and Knowledge.

اور وہی (ایک) آسمانوں میں معبود ہے اور (وہی) زمین میں معبود ہے۔ اور وہ دانا (اور) علم والا ہے (۸۴)

وَهُوَ الَّذِيْ فِي السَّمَآءِ إِلٰهٌ وَّفِي الْأَرْضِ إِلٰهٌ وَهُوَ الْحَكِيْمُ الْعَلِيْمُ (۸۴)

85. And blessed is He to Whom belongs the dominion of the heavens and the earth, and all between them: with Him is the knowledge of the Hour (of Judgment): and to Him shall ye be brought back.

اور وہ بہت بابرکت ہے جس کے لئے آسمانوں اور زمین اور جو کچھ ان دونوں میں ہے سب کی بادشاہت ہے۔ اور اسی کو قیامت کا علم ہے اور اسی کی طرف تم لوٹ کر جاؤ گے (۸۵)

وَتَبٰرَكَ الَّذِيْ لَهٗ مُلْكُ السَّمٰوٰتِ وَالْأَرْضِ وَمَا بَيْنَهُمَا وَعِنْدَهٗ عِلْمُ السَّاعَةِ وَإِلَيْهِ تُرْجَعُوْنَ (۸۵)

86. And those whom they invoke besides Allah have no power of intercession;—only he who bears witness to the Truth, and with full knowledge.

اور جن کو یہ لوگ خدا کے سوا پکارتے ہیں وہ سفارش کا کچھ اختیار نہیں رکھتے۔ ہاں جو علم ویقین کے ساتھ حق کی گواہی دیں (وہ سفارش کر سکتے ہیں)[۲۶۴] (۸۶)

وَلَا يَمْلِكُ الَّذِيْنَ يَدْعُوْنَ مِنْ دُوْنِهِ الشَّفٰعَةَ إِلَّا مَنْ شَهِدَ بِالْحَقِّ وَهُمْ يَعْلَمُوْنَ (۸۶)

87. If thou ask them, who created them, they will certainly say, Allah: how then are they deluded away (from the Truth)?

اور اگر تم ان سے پوچھو کہ ان کو کس نے پیدا کیا ہے تو کہہ دیں گے کہ خدا نے۔ تو پھر یہ کہاں بہکے پھرتے ہیں؟ (۸۷)

وَلَئِنْ سَأَلْتَهُمْ مَّنْ خَلَقَهُمْ لَيَقُوْلُنَّ اللّٰهُ فَأَنّٰى يُؤْفَكُوْنَ (۸۷)

88. (Allah has knowledge) of the (Prophet's) cry, "O my Lord! Truly these are a people who believe not!"

اور (بسا اوقات) پیغمبر کہا کرتے ہیں کہ اے پروردگار یہ ایسے لوگ ہیں کہ ایمان نہیں لاتے (۸۸)

وَقِيْلِهٖ يٰرَبِّ إِنَّ هٰٓؤُلَآءِ قَوْمٌ لَّا يُؤْمِنُوْنَ (۸۸)

89. But turn away from them, and say "Peace!" But soon shall they know!

تو ان سے منہ پھیر لو اور سلام کہہ دو۔ ان کو عنقریب (انجام) معلوم ہو جائے گا (۸۹)

فَاصْفَحْ عَنْهُمْ وَقُلْ سَلٰمٌ فَسَوْفَ يَعْلَمُوْنَ (۸۹)

SÛRA–44
AD-DUKHÃN
(INTRODUCTION)

For the chronology and the general theme of the Sûras of the *Ḥã-Mîm* series, of which this is the fifth, see the Introduction to S. 40.

The theme of this particular Sûra is how worldly pride and power are humbled in the dust if they resist spiritual forces, and how Evil and Good find their true setting in the Hereafter.

The title-word *Dukhãn* occurs in verse 10. It means smoke or mist, and may refer to a drought or famine.

Ad-Dukhān, or Smoke (or Mist)

In the name of Allah, Most Gracious, Most Merciful.

1. Ḥã Mîm.
2. By the Book that makes things clear;—
3. We sent it down during a blessed night: for We (ever) wish to warn (against Evil).
4. In that (night) is made distinct every affair of wisdom,
5. By command, from Us. For We (ever) send (revelations),
6. As a Mercy from thy Lord; for He hears and knows (all things);
7. The Lord of the heavens and the earth and all between them, if ye (but) have an assured faith.
8. There is no god but He: it is He Who gives life and gives death,— the Lord and Cherisher to you and your earliest ancestors.
9. Yet they play about in doubt.
10. Then watch thou for the Day that the sky will bring forth a kind of smoke (or mist) plainly visible.
11. Enveloping the people: this will be a Chastisement grievous.
12. (They will say:) "Our Lord! Remove the Chastisement from us, for we do really believe!"
13. How should they have the Reminder. Seeing that a Messenger explaining things clearly has (already) come to them,—
14. Yet they turn away from him and say: "Tutored (by others), a man possessed!"
15. We shall indeed remove the Chastisement for a while, (but) truly ye will revert (to your ways).
16. The day We shall seize you with a mighty onslaught: We will indeed (then) exact Retribution!
17. We did, before them, try the people of Pharaoh: there came to them a messenger most honourable,
18. Saying: "Restore to me the servants of Allah: I am to you a messenger worthy of all trust;
19. "And be not arrogant as against Allah: for I come to you

سورۂ دخان مکی ہے اس میں اُنسٹھ آیتیں اور تین رکوع ہیں

شروع خدا کا نام لے کر جو بڑا مہربان نہایت رحم والا ہے
حٰمٓ (۱) اس کتاب روشن کی قسم (۲)
کہ ہم نے اس کو مبارک رات میں نازل فرمایا ہم تو رستہ
دکھانے والے ہیں (۳)
اسی رات میں تمام حکمت کے کام فیصل کیے جاتے ہیں (۴)
(یعنی) ہمارے ہاں سے حکم ہو کر۔ بیشک ہم ہی پیغمبر کو بھیجتے ہیں (۵)
(یہ) تمہارے پروردگار کی رحمت ہے۔ وہ تو سننے والا جاننے والا ہے (۶)
آسمانوں اور زمین اور جو کچھ ان دونوں میں ہے سب کا
مالک۔ بشرطیکہ تم لوگ یقین کرنے والے ہو (۷)
اُس کے سوا کوئی معبود نہیں (وہی) جلاتا ہے اور (وہی) مارتا ہے (وہی) تمہارا
اور تمہارے پہلے باپ دادا کا پروردگار ہے (۸)
لیکن یہ لوگ شک میں کھیل رہے ہیں (۹)
تو اس دن کا انتظار کرو کہ آسمان سے صریح دھواں نکلے گا (۱۰)
جو لوگوں پر چھا جائیگا۔ یہ درد دینے والا عذاب ہے (۱۱)
اے پروردگار ہم سے اس عذاب کو دور کر ہم ایمان لاتے ہیں (۱۲)
(اس وقت) ان کو نصیحت کہاں مفید ہو گی جبکہ ان کے پاس پیغمبر
آ چکے جو کھول کھول کر بیان کر دیتے تھے (۱۳)
پھر انہوں نے ان سے منہ پھیر لیا اور کہنے لگے (یہ تو) پڑھایا ہوا (اور) دیوانہ ہے (۱۴)
ہم تو تھوڑے دنوں عذاب ٹال دیتے ہیں (مگر) تم پھر کفر کرنے لگتے ہو (۱۵)
جس دن ہم بڑی سخت پکڑ پکڑیں گے تو بے شک انتقام
لے کر چھوڑیں گے (۱۶)
اور ان سے پہلے ہم نے قوم فرعون کی آزمائش کی اور ان
کے پاس ایک عالی قدر پیغمبر آئے (۱۷)
(جنہوں نے) یہ (کہا) کہ خدا کے بندوں (یعنی بنی اسرائیل) کو
میرے حوالے کر دو میں تمہارا امانتدار پیغمبر ہوں (۱۸)
اور خدا کے سامنے سرکشی نہ کرو میں تمہارے پاس کھلی

سُوْرَةُ الدُّخَانِ مَكِّيَّةٌ وَّهِيَ تِسْعٌ وَّخَمْسُوْنَ اٰيَةً وَّثَلٰثُ رُكُوْعَاتٍ

بِسْمِ اللّٰهِ الرَّحْمٰنِ الرَّحِيْمِ
حٰمٓ ﴿١﴾ وَالْكِتٰبِ الْمُبِيْنِ ﴿٢﴾
اِنَّآ اَنْزَلْنٰهُ فِيْ لَيْلَةٍ مُّبٰرَكَةٍ اِنَّا كُنَّا
مُنْذِرِيْنَ ﴿٣﴾
فِيْهَا يُفْرَقُ كُلُّ اَمْرٍ حَكِيْمٍ ﴿٤﴾
اَمْرًا مِّنْ عِنْدِنَا ۭ اِنَّا كُنَّا مُرْسِلِيْنَ ﴿٥﴾
رَحْمَةً مِّنْ رَّبِّكَ ۭ اِنَّهٗ هُوَ السَّمِيْعُ الْعَلِيْمُ ﴿٦﴾
رَبِّ السَّمٰوٰتِ وَالْاَرْضِ وَمَا بَيْنَهُمَا ۘ اِنْ
كُنْتُمْ مُّوْقِنِيْنَ ﴿٧﴾
لَآ اِلٰهَ اِلَّا هُوَ يُحْيٖ وَيُمِيْتُ ۭ رَبُّكُمْ وَ
رَبُّ اٰبَاۗىِٕكُمُ الْاَوَّلِيْنَ ﴿٨﴾
بَلْ هُمْ فِيْ شَكٍّ يَّلْعَبُوْنَ ﴿٩﴾
فَارْتَقِبْ يَوْمَ تَاْتِي السَّمَاۗءُ بِدُخَانٍ مُّبِيْنٍ ﴿١٠﴾
يَّغْشَى النَّاسَ ۭ هٰذَا عَذَابٌ اَلِيْمٌ ﴿١١﴾
رَبَّنَا اكْشِفْ عَنَّا الْعَذَابَ اِنَّا مُؤْمِنُوْنَ ﴿١٢﴾
اَنّٰى لَهُمُ الذِّكْرٰى وَقَدْ جَاۗءَهُمْ رَسُوْلٌ
مُّبِيْنٌ ﴿١٣﴾
ثُمَّ تَوَلَّوْا عَنْهُ وَقَالُوْا مُعَلَّمٌ مَّجْنُوْنٌ ﴿١٤﴾
اِنَّا كَاشِفُوا الْعَذَابِ قَلِيْلًا اِنَّكُمْ عَاۗىِٕدُوْنَ ﴿١٥﴾
يَوْمَ نَبْطِشُ الْبَطْشَةَ الْكُبْرٰى ۚ اِنَّا
مُنْتَقِمُوْنَ ﴿١٦﴾
وَلَقَدْ فَتَنَّا قَبْلَهُمْ قَوْمَ فِرْعَوْنَ وَجَاۗءَهُمْ
رَسُوْلٌ كَرِيْمٌ ﴿١٧﴾
اَنْ اَدُّوْٓا اِلَيَّ عِبَادَ اللّٰهِ ۭ اِنِّىْ لَكُمْ رَسُوْلٌ
اَمِيْنٌ ﴿١٨﴾
وَاَنْ لَّا تَعْلُوْا عَلَى اللّٰهِ ۚ اِنِّىْٓ اٰتِيْكُمْ

وقف لازم

وقف لازم

with authority manifest.

20. "For me, I have sought safety with my Lord and your Lord, against your injuring me.
21. "If ye believe me not, at least keep yourselves away from me."
22. (But they were aggressive:) then he cried to his Lord: "These are indeed a people given to sin."
23. (The reply came:) "March forth with my servants by night: for ye are sure to be pursued.
24. "And leave the sea as a furrow (divided): for they are a host (destined) to be drowned."
25. How many were the gardens and springs they left behind,

26. And corn-fields and noble buildings,
27. And pleasant things wherein they had taken such delight!
28. Thus (was their end)! and We made other people inherit (those things)!
29. And neither heaven nor earth shed a tear over them: nor were they given a respite (again).
30. We did deliver aforetime the Children of Israel from humiliating Punishment,
31. Inflicted by Pharaoh, for he was arrogant (even) among inordinate transgressors.

32. And We chose them aforetime above the nations, knowingly,
33. And granted them Signs in which there was a manifest trial.

34. As to these (Quraish), they say forsooth:
35. "There is nothing beyond our first death, and we shall not be raised again.

36. "Then bring (back) our forefathers, if what ye say is true!"
37. What! are they better than the people of Tubba' and those who were before them? We destroyed them because they were guilty of

دلیل لے کر آیا ہوں ﴿١٩﴾
اور اس (بات) سے کہ تم مجھے سنگسار کرو اپنے اور تمہارے پروردگار کی پناہ مانگتا ہوں ﴿٢٠﴾
اور اگر مجھ پر ایمان نہیں لاتے تو مجھ سے الگ ہو جاؤ ﴿٢١﴾
تب (موسیٰ نے) اپنے پروردگار سے دعا کی کہ یہ نافرمان لوگ ہیں ﴿٢٢﴾
(خدا نے فرمایا کہ) میرے بندوں کو راتوں رات لیکر چلے جاؤ
اور (فرعونی) ضرور تمہارا تعاقب کریں گے ﴿٢٣﴾
اور دریا سے (کہ) خشک (ہو رہا ہوگا) پار ہو جاؤ (تمہارے بعد)
اُن کا تمام لشکر ڈبو دیا جائے گا ﴿٢٤﴾
وہ لوگ بہت سے باغ اور چشمے چھوڑ گئے ﴿٢٥﴾
اور کھیتیاں اور نفیس مکان ﴿٢٦﴾
اور آرام کی چیزیں جن میں عیش کیا کرتے تھے ﴿٢٧﴾
اسی طرح (ہوا) اور ہم نے دوسرے لوگوں کو اُنکا مالک بنا دیا ﴿٢٨﴾
پھر اُن پر نہ تو آسمان اور زمین کو رونا آیا اور نہ اُن کو مہلت
ہی دی گئی ﴿٢٩﴾
اور ہم نے بنی اسرائیل کو ذلت کے عذاب سے
نجات دی ﴿٣٠﴾
(یعنی) فرعون سے۔ بیشک وہ سرکش (اور) حد سے
نکلا ہوا تھا ﴿٣١﴾
اور ہم نے بنی اسرائیل کو اہل عالم سے دانستہ منتخب کیا تھا ﴿٣٢﴾
اور اُن کو ایسی نشانیاں دی تھیں جن میں صریح
آزمائش تھی ﴿٣٣﴾
یہ لوگ یہ کہتے ہیں ﴿٣٤﴾
کہ ہمیں صرف پہلی دفعہ (یعنی ایک بار) مرنا ہے اور
پھر اُٹھنا نہیں ﴿٣٥﴾
پس اگر تم سچے ہو تو ہمارے باپ دادا کو (زندہ کر) لاؤ ﴿٣٦﴾
بھلا یہ اچھے ہیں یا تُبّع کی قوم[265] اور وہ لوگ جو تم سے
پہلے ہو چکے ہیں۔ ہم نے اُن (سب) کو ہلاک کر دیا۔

بِسُلْطٰنٍ مُّبِیْنٍ ﴿١٩﴾
وَاِنِّیْ عُذْتُ بِرَبِّیْ وَرَبِّكُمْ اَنْ تَرْجُمُوْنِ ﴿٢٠﴾
وَاِنْ لَّمْ تُؤْمِنُوْا لِیْ فَاعْتَزِلُوْنِ ﴿٢١﴾
فَدَعَا رَبَّهٗٓ اَنَّ هٰٓؤُلَآءِ قَوْمٌ مُّجْرِمُوْنَ ﴿٢٢﴾
فَاَسْرِ بِعِبَادِیْ لَیْلًا اِنَّكُمْ
مُّتَّبَعُوْنَ ﴿٢٣﴾
وَاتْرُكِ الْبَحْرَ رَهْوًا ۭ اِنَّهُمْ جُنْدٌ
مُّغْرَقُوْنَ ﴿٢٤﴾
كَمْ تَرَكُوْا مِنْ جَنّٰتٍ وَّعُیُوْنٍ ﴿٢٥﴾
وَّزُرُوْعٍ وَّمَقَامٍ كَرِیْمٍ ﴿٢٦﴾
وَّنَعْمَةٍ كَانُوْا فِیْهَا فٰكِهِیْنَ ﴿٢٧﴾
كَذٰلِكَ ۣ وَاَوْرَثْنٰهَا قَوْمًا اٰخَرِیْنَ ﴿٢٨﴾
فَمَا بَكَتْ عَلَیْهِمُ السَّمَآءُ وَالْاَرْضُ وَمَا
ع كَانُوْا مُنْظَرِیْنَ ﴿٢٩﴾
وَلَقَدْ نَجَّیْنَا بَنِیْٓ اِسْرَآءِیْلَ مِنَ الْعَذَابِ
الْمُهِیْنِ ﴿٣٠﴾
مِنْ فِرْعَوْنَ ۭ اِنَّهٗ كَانَ عَالِیًا مِّنَ
الْمُسْرِفِیْنَ ﴿٣١﴾
وَلَقَدِ اخْتَرْنٰهُمْ عَلٰی عِلْمٍ عَلَی الْعٰلَمِیْنَ ﴿٣٢﴾
وَاٰتَیْنٰهُمْ مِّنَ الْاٰیٰتِ مَا فِیْهِ بَلٰٓؤٌا
مُّبِیْنٌ ﴿٣٣﴾
اِنَّ هٰٓؤُلَآءِ لَیَقُوْلُوْنَ ﴿٣٤﴾
اِنْ هِیَ اِلَّا مَوْتَتُنَا الْاُوْلٰی وَمَا نَحْنُ
بِمُنْشَرِیْنَ ﴿٣٥﴾
فَاْتُوْا بِاٰبَآىِٕنَآ اِنْ كُنْتُمْ صٰدِقِیْنَ ﴿٣٦﴾
اَهُمْ خَیْرٌ اَمْ قَوْمُ تُبَّعٍ ۙ وَّالَّذِیْنَ
مِنْ قَبْلِهِمْ ۭ اَهْلَكْنٰهُمْ ۡ اِنَّهُمْ كَانُوْا

مُجْرِمِينَ ﴿٣٧﴾
بیشک وہ گنہگار تھے ﴿٣٧﴾
sin.

وَمَا خَلَقْنَا السَّمٰوٰتِ وَالْاَرْضَ وَمَا بَيْنَهُمَا
لٰعِبِينَ ﴿٣٨﴾
اور ہم نے آسمانوں اور زمین کو اور جو کچھ ان میں ہے انکو
کھیلتے ہوئے نہیں بنایا ﴿٣٨﴾
38. We created not the heavens, the earth, and all between them, merely in (idle) sport:

مَا خَلَقْنٰهُمَآ اِلَّا بِالْحَقِّ وَلٰكِنَّ اَكْثَرَهُمْ
لَا يَعْلَمُونَ ﴿٣٩﴾
ان کو ہم نے تدبیر سے پیدا کیا ہے لیکن اکثر لوگ نہیں
جانتے ﴿٣٩﴾
39. We created them not except for just ends: but most of them do not know.

اِنَّ يَوْمَ الْفَصْلِ مِيقَاتُهُمْ اَجْمَعِينَ ﴿٤٠﴾
کچھ شک نہیں کہ فیصلے کا دن ان سب کے اٹھنے کا وقت ہے ﴿٤٠﴾
40. Verily the Day of sorting Out is the time appointed for all of them,—

يَوْمَ لَا يُغْنِي مَوْلًى عَنْ مَّوْلًى شَيْئًا وَّ
لَا هُمْ يُنْصَرُونَ ﴿٤١﴾
جس دن کوئی دوست کسی دوست کے کچھ کام نہ آئے گا
اور نہ ان کو مدد ملے گی ﴿٤١﴾
41. The Day when no protector can avail his client in aught, and no help can they receive,

اِلَّا مَنْ رَّحِمَ اللّٰهُ ۭ اِنَّهٗ هُوَ الْعَزِيزُ
الرَّحِيمُ ﴿٤٢﴾ ع ٢ ١٥
مگر جس پر خدا مہربانی کرے وہ تو غالب (اور)
مہربان ہے ﴿٤٢﴾
42. Except such as receive Allah's Mercy: for He is exalted in Might, Most Merciful.

اِنَّ شَجَرَتَ الزَّقُّومِ ﴿٤٣﴾
بلاشبہ تھوہر کا درخت ﴿٤٣﴾
43. Verily the tree of Zaqqum

طَعَامُ الْاَثِيمِ ﴿٤٤﴾ مع عند المتأخرين ١٢
گنہگار کا کھانا ہے ﴿٤٤﴾
44. Will be the food of the Sinful,—

كَالْمُهْلِ ۚ يَغْلِي فِي الْبُطُونِ ﴿٤٥﴾
جیسے پگھلا ہوا تانبا۔ پیٹوں میں (اس طرح) کھولے گا ﴿٤٥﴾
45. Like molten brass; it will boil in their insides,

كَغَلْيِ الْحَمِيمِ ﴿٤٦﴾
جس طرح گرم پانی کھولتا ہے ﴿٤٦﴾
46. Like the boiling of scalding water.

خُذُوهُ فَاعْتِلُوهُ اِلٰى سَوَآءِ الْجَحِيمِ ﴿٤٧﴾
حکم دیا جائیگا کہ اسکو پکڑ لو اور کھینچتے ہوئے دوزخ کے بیچوں بیچ لیجاؤ ﴿٤٧﴾
47. (A voice will cry:) "Seize ye him and drag him into the midst of the Blazing Fire!

ثُمَّ صُبُّوا فَوْقَ رَاْسِهٖ مِنْ عَذَابِ الْحَمِيمِ ﴿٤٨﴾
پھر اسکے سر پر کھولتا ہوا پانی انڈیل دو کہ عذاب پر) عذاب (ہو) ﴿٤٨﴾
48. "Then pour over his head the Chastisement of Boiling Water;

ذُقْ ۚ اِنَّكَ اَنْتَ الْعَزِيزُ الْكَرِيمُ ﴿٤٩﴾
(اب) مزہ چکھ تو بڑی عزت والا (اور) سردار ہے ﴿٤٩﴾
49. "Taste thou (this)! Truly thou art mighty, full of honour!

اِنَّ هٰذَا مَا كُنْتُمْ بِهٖ تَمْتَرُونَ ﴿٥٠﴾
یہ وہی (دوزخ) ہے جس میں تم لوگ شک کیا کرتے تھے ﴿٥٠﴾
50. "Truly this is what ye used to doubt!"

اِنَّ الْمُتَّقِينَ فِي مَقَامٍ اَمِينٍ ﴿٥١﴾
بے شک پرہیزگار لوگ امن کے مقام میں ہوں گے ﴿٥١﴾
51. As to the Righteous (they will be) in a position of Security,

فِي جَنّٰتٍ وَّعُيُونٍ ﴿٥٢﴾
(یعنی) باغوں اور چشموں میں ﴿٥٢﴾
52. Among Gardens and Springs;

يَّلْبَسُونَ مِنْ سُنْدُسٍ وَّاِسْتَبْرَقٍ
مُّتَقٰبِلِينَ ﴿٥٣﴾
حریر کا باریک اور دبیز لباس پہن کر ایک دوسرے کے
سامنے بیٹھے ہوں گے ﴿٥٣﴾
53. Dressed in fine silk and in rich brocade, they will face each other;

كَذٰلِكَ ۣ وَزَوَّجْنٰهُمْ بِحُورٍ
عِينٍ ﴿٥٤﴾
(وہاں) اس طرح (کا حال ہوگا) اور ہم بڑی بڑی آنکھوں
والی سفید رنگ کی عورتوں سے انکے جوڑے لگائیں گے ﴿٥٤﴾
54. So; and We shall wed them to maidens with beautiful, big, and lustrous eyes.

يَدْعُونَ فِيهَا بِكُلِّ فَاكِهَةٍ اٰمِنِينَ ﴿٥٥﴾
وہاں خاطر جمع سے ہر قسم کے میوے منگائینگے (اور کھائینگے) ﴿٥٥﴾
55. There can they call for every kind of fruit in peace and security;

لَا يَذُوقُونَ فِيهَا الْمَوْتَ اِلَّا الْمَوْتَةَ
الْاُولٰى ۚ وَوَقٰىهُمْ عَذَابَ الْجَحِيمِ ﴿٥٦﴾
(اور) پہلی دفعہ کے مرنے کے سوا (کہ مرچکے تھے) موت کا مزہ نہیں
چکھیں گے۔ اور خدا انکو دوزخ کے عذاب سے بچا لیگا ﴿٥٦﴾
56. Nor will they there taste Death, except the first death; and He will preserve them from the Chastisement of the Blazing Fire,—

SÛRA–45
AL-JÃTHIYA
(INTRODUCTION)

This is the sixth Sûra of *Ḥã-Mîm* series: for their general theme and chronology, see the Introduction to S. 40.

57. As a Bounty from thy Lord! That will be the supreme achievement!
58. Verily, We have made this (Qur'ãn) easy, in thy tongue, in order that they may give heed.
59. So wait thou and watch; for they (too) are waiting.

Al-Jã<u>th</u>iya, or Bowing the Knee

In the name of Allah, Most Gracious, Most Merciful.

1. Ḥã-Mîm.
2. The revelation of the Book is from Allah the Exalted in Power, full of Wisdom.
3. Verily in the heavens and the earth, are Signs for those who believe.
4. And in the creation of yourselves and the fact that animals are scattered (through the earth), are Signs for those of assured Faith.
5. And in the alternation of Night and Day, and the fact that Allah sends down Sustenance from the sky, and revives therewith the earth after its death, and in the change of the winds,— are Signs for those that are wise.
6. Such are the Signs of Allah, which We rehearse to thee in truth: then in what exposition will they believe after Allah and His Signs?
7. Woe to each sinful imposter.
8. He hears the Signs of Allah rehearsed to him, yet is obstinate and lofty, as if he had not heard them: then announce to him a Chastisement Grievous!
9. And when he learns something of Our Signs, He takes them in jest: for such there will be a humiliating Chastisement.
10. In front of them is Hell: and of no profit to them is anything they may have earned, nor any protectors they may have taken to themselves besides Allah: for them is a tremendous Chastisement.

یہ تمہارے پروردگار کا فضل ہے۔ یہی تو بڑی کامیابی
ہے ﴿٥٧﴾
ہمنے اس (قرآن) کو تمہاری زبان میں آسان کر دیا ہے تاکہ یہ لوگ نصیحت پکڑیں ﴿٥٨﴾
پس تم بھی انتظار کرو یہ بھی انتظار کر رہے ہیں ﴿٥٩﴾

سورۂ جاثیہ مکّی ہے اس میں سینتیس آیتیں اور چار رکوع ہیں

شروع خدا کا نام لیکر جو بڑا مہربان نہایت رحم والا ہے
حٰمٓ ﴿١﴾ اس کتاب کا اُتارا جانا خدائے غالب (اور)
دانا (کی طرف) سے ہے ﴿٢﴾
بیشک آسمانوں اور زمین میں ایمان والوں کے لئے
(خدا کی قدرت کی) نشانیاں ہیں ﴿٣﴾
اور تمہاری پیدائش میں بھی اور جانوروں میں بھی جن کو وہ
پھیلاتا ہے یقین کرنے والوں کے لئے نشانیاں ہیں ﴿٤﴾
اور رات اور دن کے آگے پیچھے آنے جانے میں اور وہ جو
خدا نے آسمان سے (ذریعہ) رزق نازل فرمایا پھر اس سے
زمین کو اُس کے مرجانے کے بعد زندہ کیا اُس میں اور ہواؤں
کے بدلنے میں عقل والوں کے لئے نشانیاں ہیں ﴿٥﴾
یہ خدا کی آیتیں ہیں جو ہم تم کو سچائی کیساتھ پڑھ کر سُناتے ہیں۔ تو یہ خدا
اور اُسکی آیتوں کے بعد کس بات پر ایمان لائیں گے ﴿٦﴾
ہر جھوٹے گنہگار پر افسوس ہے ﴿٧﴾
(کہ) خدا کی آیتیں اُسکو پڑھ کر سنائی جاتی ہیں تو اُن کو سُن تو لیتا ہے
مگر پھر غرور سے ضد کرتا ہے کہ گویا اُن کو سُنا ہی نہیں سو ایسے
شخص کو دُکھ دینے والے عذاب کی خوشخبری سُنا دو ﴿٨﴾
اور جب ہماری کچھ آیتیں اُسے معلوم ہوتی ہیں تو اُن کی ہنسی اُڑاتا ہے
ایسے لوگوں کے لئے ذلیل کرنے والا عذاب ہے ﴿٩﴾
ان کے سامنے دوزخ ہے۔ اور جو کام وہ کرتے رہے کچھ بھی اُنکے
کام نہ آئینگے۔ اور نہ وہی (کام آئینگے) جن کو اُنہوں نے خدا کے سوا
معبود بنا رکھا تھا۔ اور اُن کے لئے بڑا عذاب ہے ﴿١٠﴾

فَضْلًا مِّنْ رَّبِّكَ ۭ ذٰلِكَ هُوَ الْفَوْزُ
الْعَظِيْمُ ﴿٥٧﴾
فَاِنَّمَا يَسَّرْنٰهُ بِلِسَانِكَ لَعَلَّهُمْ يَتَذَكَّرُوْنَ ﴿٥٨﴾
فَارْتَقِبْ اِنَّهُمْ مُّرْتَقِبُوْنَ ﴿٥٩﴾ ع

سُوْرَةُ الْجَاثِيَةِ مَكِّيَّةٌ وَّهِيَ سَبْعٌ وَّثَلٰثُوْنَ اٰيَةً وَّاَرْبَعُ رُكُوْعَاتٍ

بِسْمِ اللّٰهِ الرَّحْمٰنِ الرَّحِيْمِ
حٰمٓ ﴿١﴾ تَنْزِيْلُ الْكِتٰبِ مِنَ اللّٰهِ
الْعَزِيْزِ الْحَكِيْمِ ﴿٢﴾
اِنَّ فِي السَّمٰوٰتِ وَالْاَرْضِ لَاٰيٰتٍ
لِّلْمُؤْمِنِيْنَ ﴿٣﴾
وَفِيْ خَلْقِكُمْ وَمَا يَبُثُّ مِنْ دَآبَّةٍ
اٰيٰتٌ لِّقَوْمٍ يُّوْقِنُوْنَ ﴿٤﴾
وَاخْتِلَافِ الَّيْلِ وَالنَّهَارِ وَمَآ اَنْزَلَ
اللّٰهُ مِنَ السَّمَآءِ مِنْ رِّزْقٍ فَاَحْيَا بِهِ
الْاَرْضَ بَعْدَ مَوْتِهَا وَتَصْرِيْفِ الرِّيٰحِ
اٰيٰتٌ لِّقَوْمٍ يَّعْقِلُوْنَ ﴿٥﴾
تِلْكَ اٰيٰتُ اللّٰهِ نَتْلُوْهَا عَلَيْكَ بِالْحَقِّ ۚ
فَبِاَيِّ حَدِيْثٍۢ بَعْدَ اللّٰهِ وَاٰيٰتِهٖ يُؤْمِنُوْنَ ﴿٦﴾
وَيْلٌ لِّكُلِّ اَفَّاكٍ اَثِيْمٍ ﴿٧﴾
يَّسْمَعُ اٰيٰتِ اللّٰهِ تُتْلٰى عَلَيْهِ ثُمَّ يُصِرُّ
مُسْتَكْبِرًا كَاَنْ لَّمْ يَسْمَعْهَا ۚ فَبَشِّرْهُ
بِعَذَابٍ اَلِيْمٍ ﴿٨﴾
وَاِذَا عَلِمَ مِنْ اٰيٰتِنَا شَيْـًٔا اتَّخَذَهَا
هُزُوًا ۭ اُولٰۗىِٕكَ لَهُمْ عَذَابٌ مُّهِيْنٌ ﴿٩﴾
مِنْ وَّرَاۗىِٕهِمْ جَهَنَّمُ ۚ وَلَا يُغْنِيْ عَنْهُمْ
مَّا كَسَبُوْا شَيْـًٔا وَّلَا مَا اتَّخَذُوْا مِنْ دُوْنِ
اللّٰهِ اَوْلِيَاۗءَ ۚ وَلَهُمْ عَذَابٌ عَظِيْمٌ ﴿١٠﴾

11. This is (true) Guidance: and for those who reject the Signs of their Lord, is a grievous Chastisement of abomination.

12. It is Allah Who has subjected the sea to you, that ships may sail through it by His command, that ye may seek of His Bounty, and that ye may be grateful.

13. And He has subjected to you, as from Him, all that is in the heavens and on earth: behold, in that are Signs indeed for those who reflect.

14. Tell those who believe, to forgive those who do not hope for the Days of Allah; it is for Him to recompense (for good or ill) each People according to what they have earned.

15. If any one does a righteous deed, it is to his own benefit; if he does evil, it works against (his own soul). In the end will ye (all) be brought back to your Lord.

16. We did aforetime grant to the Children of Israel the Book, the Power of Command, and Prophethood; We gave them, for Sustenance, things good and pure; and We favoured them above the nations.

17. And We granted them Clear Signs in affairs (of Religion): it was only after knowledge had been granted to them that they fell into schisms, through insolent envy among themselves. Verily thy Lord will judge between them on the Day of Judgment as to those matters in which they set up differences.

18. Then We put thee on the (right) Way of Religion: so follow thou that (Way), and follow not the desires of those who know not.

19. They will be of no use to thee in the sight of Allah: it is only wrongdoers (that stand as) protectors, one to another: but Allah is the Protector of the Righteous.

20. These are clear evidences to men, and a Guidance and Mercy to those of assured Faith.

یہ ہدایت (کی کتاب) ہے۔ اور جو لوگ اپنے پروردگار کی آیتوں سے
انکار کرتے ہیں اُن کو سخت قسم کا درد دینے والا عذاب ہوگا (۱۱)
خدا ہی تو ہے جس نے دریا کو تمہارے قابو میں کر دیا تاکہ اُس کے
حکم سے اُس میں کشتیاں چلیں اور تاکہ تم اُس کے فضل سے
(معاش) تلاش کرو اور تاکہ شکر کرو (۱۲)
اور جو کچھ آسمانوں میں ہے اور جو کچھ زمین میں ہے سب کو
اپنے (حکم) سے تمہارے کام میں لگا دیا۔ جو لوگ غور کرتے ہیں
اُن کے لئے اس میں (قدرت خدا کی) نشانیاں ہیں (۱۳)
مومنوں سے کہہ دو کہ جو لوگ خدا کے دنوں کی (جو اعمال کے بدلے کیلئے مقرر ہیں)
توقع نہیں رکھتے اُن سے درگزر کریں تاکہ وہ اُن لوگوں کو اُنکے اعمال کا بدلہ دے (۱۴)
جو کوئی عمل نیک کریگا تو اپنے لئے اور جو بُرے کام کریگا تو اُن کا
ضرر اُسی کو ہوگا پھر تم اپنے پروردگار کی طرف لوٹ کر جاؤ گے (۱۵)
اور ہم نے بنی اسرائیل کو کتاب (ہدایت) اور حکومت اور نبوت
بخشی اور پاکیزہ چیزیں عطا فرمائیں اور اہلِ عالم پر
فضیلت دی (۱۶)
اور اُن کو دین کے بارے میں دلیلیں عطا کیں۔ تو انہوں نے
جو اختلاف کیا تو علم آچکنے کے بعد آپس کی ضد سے کیا۔
بیشک تمہارا پروردگار قیامت کے دن اُن میں اُن باتوں کا
جن میں وہ اختلاف کرتے تھے فیصلہ کرے گا (۱۷)
پھر ہم نے تم کو دین کے کھلے رستے پر (قائم) کر دیا
تو اُسی (رستے) پر چلے چلو اور نادانوں کی خواہشوں
کے پیچھے نہ چلنا (۱۸)
یہ خدا کے سامنے تمہارے کسی کام نہیں آئیں گے۔ اور
ظالم لوگ ایک دوسرے کے دوست ہوتے ہیں۔ اور
خدا پرہیزگاروں کا دوست ہے (۱۹)
یہ (قرآن) لوگوں کے لئے دانائی کی باتیں ہیں۔ اور جو یقین
رکھتے ہیں اُن کے لئے ہدایت اور رحمت ہے (۲۰)

هٰذَا هُدًى ۚ وَالَّذِينَ كَفَرُوا بِآيَاتِ رَبِّهِمْ
لَهُمْ عَذَابٌ مِنْ رِجْزٍ أَلِيمٌ (١١)
اللَّهُ الَّذِي سَخَّرَ لَكُمُ الْبَحْرَ لِتَجْرِيَ الْفُلْكُ
فِيهِ بِأَمْرِهِ وَلِتَبْتَغُوا مِنْ فَضْلِهِ وَ
لَعَلَّكُمْ تَشْكُرُونَ (١٢)
وَسَخَّرَ لَكُمْ مَا فِي السَّمَاوَاتِ وَمَا فِي الْأَرْضِ
جَمِيعًا مِنْهُ ۚ إِنَّ فِي ذَٰلِكَ لَآيَاتٍ لِقَوْمٍ
يَتَفَكَّرُونَ (١٣)
قُلْ لِلَّذِينَ آمَنُوا يَغْفِرُوا لِلَّذِينَ لَا يَرْجُونَ
أَيَّامَ اللَّهِ لِيَجْزِيَ قَوْمًا بِمَا كَانُوا يَكْسِبُونَ (١٤)
مَنْ عَمِلَ صَالِحًا فَلِنَفْسِهِ ۖ وَمَنْ أَسَاءَ
فَعَلَيْهَا ۖ ثُمَّ إِلَىٰ رَبِّكُمْ تُرْجَعُونَ (١٥)
وَلَقَدْ آتَيْنَا بَنِي إِسْرَائِيلَ الْكِتَابَ وَ
الْحُكْمَ وَالنُّبُوَّةَ وَرَزَقْنَاهُمْ مِنَ الطَّيِّبَاتِ
وَفَضَّلْنَاهُمْ عَلَى الْعَالَمِينَ (١٦)
وَآتَيْنَاهُمْ بَيِّنَاتٍ مِنَ الْأَمْرِ ۖ فَمَا اخْتَلَفُوا
إِلَّا مِنْ بَعْدِ مَا جَاءَهُمُ الْعِلْمُ بَغْيًا
بَيْنَهُمْ ۚ إِنَّ رَبَّكَ يَقْضِي بَيْنَهُمْ يَوْمَ
الْقِيَامَةِ فِيمَا كَانُوا فِيهِ يَخْتَلِفُونَ (١٧)
ثُمَّ جَعَلْنَاكَ عَلَىٰ شَرِيعَةٍ مِنَ الْأَمْرِ
فَاتَّبِعْهَا وَلَا تَتَّبِعْ أَهْوَاءَ الَّذِينَ لَا
يَعْلَمُونَ (١٨)
إِنَّهُمْ لَنْ يُغْنُوا عَنْكَ مِنَ اللَّهِ شَيْئًا ۚ
وَإِنَّ الظَّالِمِينَ بَعْضُهُمْ أَوْلِيَاءُ بَعْضٍ ۖ
وَاللَّهُ وَلِيُّ الْمُتَّقِينَ (١٩)
هَٰذَا بَصَائِرُ لِلنَّاسِ وَهُدًى وَرَحْمَةٌ
لِقَوْمٍ يُوقِنُونَ (٢٠)

21. What! do those who do evil deeds think that We shall make them as equal with those who believe and do righteous deeds,—that equal will be their life and their death? Ill is the judgment that they make.

22. Allah created the heavens and the earth for just ends, and in order that each soul may find the recompense of what it has earned, and none of them shall be wronged.

23. Then seest thou such a one as takes as his god his own vain desire? Allah has, knowing (him as such), left him astray, and sealed his hearing and his heart (and understanding), and put a cover on his sight. Who, then, will guide him after Allah (has withdrawn guidance)? Will ye not then receive admonition?

24. And they say: "What is there but our life in this world? We shall die and we live, and nothing but Time can destroy us." But of that they have no knowledge: they merely conjecture:

25. And when Our Clear signs are rehearsed to them, their argument is nothing but this: they say, "Bring (back) our forefathers, if what ye say is true!"

26. Say: "It is Allah Who gives you life, then gives you death; then he will gather you together for the Day of Judgment about which there is no doubt": but most men do not know.

27. To Allah belongs the dominion of the heavens and the earth, and the Day that the Hour of Judgment is established,— that Day will the followers of Falsehood perish!

28. And thou wilt see every nation bowing the knee: every nation will be called to its Record: "This Day shall ye be recompensed for all that ye did!

29. "This Our Record speaks about you with truth: for We were wont to put on record all that ye did."

جو لوگ بُرے کام کرتے ہیں کیا وہ یہ خیال کرتے ہیں کہ ہم
اُن کو اُن لوگوں جیسا کر دیں گے جو ایمان لائے اور عمل نیک
کرتے رہے (اور) اُن کی زندگی اور موت یکساں ہوگی۔
یہ جو دعوے کرتے ہیں بُرے ہیں ﴿۲۱﴾
اور خدا نے آسمانوں اور زمین کو حکمت سے پیدا کیا ہے
اور تاکہ ہر شخص اپنے اعمال کا بدلہ پائے اور اُن پر ظلم
نہیں کیا جائے گا ﴿۲۲﴾
بھلا تم نے اُس شخص کو دیکھا جس نے اپنی خواہش کو معبود بنا رکھا
ہے اور باوجود جاننے بوجھنے کے (گمراہ ہو رہا ہے تو) خدا نے (بھی) اسکو گمراہ
کر دیا۔ اور اُسکے کانوں اور دل پر مہر لگا دی اور اُسکی آنکھوں پر پردہ ڈال دیا
اب خدا کے سوا اسکو کون راہ پر لا سکتا ہے تو کیا تم نصیحت نہیں پکڑتے؟ ﴿۲۳﴾
اور کہتے ہیں کہ ہماری زندگی تو صرف دنیا ہی کی ہے کہ (یہیں) مرتے
اور جیتے ہیں اور ہمیں تو زمانہ مار دیتا ہے۔ اور اُن کو اس کا کچھ علم
نہیں۔ صرف ظن سے کام لیتے ہیں ﴿۲۴﴾
اور جب اُن کے سامنے ہماری کھلی کھلی آیتیں پڑھی جاتی ہیں
تو اُن کی یہی حجت ہوتی ہے کہ اگر سچے ہو تو ہمارے باپ
دادا کو (زندہ کر) لاؤ ﴿۲۵﴾
کہہ دو کہ خدا ہی تمکو جان بخشتا ہے پھر (وہی) تم کو موت دیتا ہے پھر
تمکو قیامت کے روز جس (کے آنے) میں کچھ شک نہیں تم کو جمع
کرے گا لیکن بہت سے لوگ نہیں جانتے ﴿۲۶﴾
اور آسمانوں اور زمین کی بادشاہت خدا ہی کی ہے۔ اور جس روز قیامت
برپا ہوگی اُس روز اہل باطل خسارے میں پڑ جائیں گے ﴿۲۷﴾
اور تم ہر ایک فرقے کو دیکھو گے کہ گھٹنوں کے بل بیٹھا ہوگا۔
(اور) ہر ایک جماعت اپنی کتاب (اعمال) کی طرف بلائی
جائے گی۔ جو کچھ تم کرتے رہے ہو آج تمکو اُس کا بدلہ دیا جائیگا ﴿۲۸﴾
یہ ہماری کتاب تمہارے بارے میں سچ سچ بیان کر دیگی۔ جو کچھ
تم کیا کرتے تھے ہم لکھواتے جاتے تھے ﴿۲۹﴾

أَمْ حَسِبَ الَّذِينَ اجْتَرَحُوا السَّيِّئَاتِ
أَنْ نَجْعَلَهُمْ كَالَّذِينَ آمَنُوا وَعَمِلُوا
الصَّالِحَاتِ سَوَاءً مَحْيَاهُمْ وَمَمَاتُهُمْ
سَاءَ مَا يَحْكُمُونَ ﴿٢١﴾ ع ۱۸
وَخَلَقَ اللَّهُ السَّمَاوَاتِ وَالْأَرْضَ بِالْحَقِّ
وَلِتُجْزَىٰ كُلُّ نَفْسٍ بِمَا كَسَبَتْ وَهُمْ
لَا يُظْلَمُونَ ﴿٢٢﴾
أَفَرَأَيْتَ مَنِ اتَّخَذَ إِلَٰهَهُ هَوَاهُ وَ
أَضَلَّهُ اللَّهُ عَلَىٰ عِلْمٍ وَخَتَمَ عَلَىٰ سَمْعِهِ
وَقَلْبِهِ وَجَعَلَ عَلَىٰ بَصَرِهِ غِشَاوَةً فَمَنْ
يَهْدِيهِ مِنْ بَعْدِ اللَّهِ أَفَلَا تَذَكَّرُونَ ﴿٢٣﴾
وَقَالُوا مَا هِيَ إِلَّا حَيَاتُنَا الدُّنْيَا نَمُوتُ وَ
نَحْيَا وَمَا يُهْلِكُنَا إِلَّا الدَّهْرُ وَمَا لَهُمْ
بِذَٰلِكَ مِنْ عِلْمٍ إِنْ هُمْ إِلَّا يَظُنُّونَ ﴿٢٤﴾
وَإِذَا تُتْلَىٰ عَلَيْهِمْ آيَاتُنَا بَيِّنَاتٍ مَا كَانَ
حُجَّتَهُمْ إِلَّا أَنْ قَالُوا ائْتُوا بِآبَائِنَا
إِنْ كُنْتُمْ صَادِقِينَ ﴿٢٥﴾
قُلِ اللَّهُ يُحْيِيكُمْ ثُمَّ يُمِيتُكُمْ ثُمَّ
يَجْمَعُكُمْ إِلَىٰ يَوْمِ الْقِيَامَةِ لَا رَيْبَ فِيهِ
وَلَٰكِنَّ أَكْثَرَ النَّاسِ لَا يَعْلَمُونَ ﴿٢٦﴾ ع ۱۹
وَلِلَّهِ مُلْكُ السَّمَاوَاتِ وَالْأَرْضِ وَيَوْمَ
تَقُومُ السَّاعَةُ يَوْمَئِذٍ يَخْسَرُ الْمُبْطِلُونَ ﴿٢٧﴾
وَتَرَىٰ كُلَّ أُمَّةٍ جَاثِيَةً كُلُّ أُمَّةٍ
تُدْعَىٰ إِلَىٰ كِتَابِهَا الْيَوْمَ تُجْزَوْنَ مَا كُنْتُمْ
تَعْمَلُونَ ﴿٢٨﴾
هَٰذَا كِتَابُنَا يَنْطِقُ عَلَيْكُمْ بِالْحَقِّ إِنَّا
كُنَّا نَسْتَنْسِخُ مَا كُنْتُمْ تَعْمَلُونَ ﴿٢٩﴾

SÛRA–46
AL-AḤQÃF
(INTRODUCTION)

This is the seventh and last Sûra of the *Ḥã-Mîm* series. For the general theme and chronological place of these Sûras see the Introduction to S. 40.

The *Aḥqãf* (mentioned in verse 21) are the long and winding crooked tracts of sand-hills, characteristic of the country of the 'Ãd people, adjoining Ḥadhramaut and Yaman: See 7: 65. These people had, at that time, probably a fertile irrigated country, but their sins brought on the calamity, mentioned in 46: 24-25. The lesson of this Sûra is that if the Truth is challenged, the challenge will be duly answered, and Truth vindicated.

30. Then, as to those who believed and did righteous deeds, their Lord will admit them to His Mercy: that will be the manifest triumph.
31. But as to those who rejected Allah, (to them will be said): "Were not Our Signs rehearsed to you? But ye were arrogant, and were a people given to sin!
32. "And when it was said that the promise of Allah was true, and that the Hour— there was no doubt about its (coming), ye used to say, 'We know not what is the Hour: we only think it a conjecture, and we have no firm assurance.' "
33. Then will appear to them the evil (fruits) of what they did, and they will be completely encircled by that which they used to mock at!
34. It will also be said: "This Day We will forget you as ye forgot the meeting of this Day of yours! And your abode is the Fire, and no helpers have ye!
35. "This, because ye used to take the Signs of Allah in jest, and the life of the world deceived you:" (from) that Day, therefore, they shall not be taken out thence, nor can they make amends.
36. Then Praise be to Allah, Lord of the heavens and Lord of the earth, Lord and Cherisher of all the worlds!
37. And unto Him (alone) belongeth Majesty in the heavens and the earth: and He is Exalted in Power, Full of Wisdom!

تو جو لوگ ایمان لائے اور نیک کام کرتے رہے انکا پروردگار انہیں اپنی رحمت
کے باغ میں داخل کریگا۔ یہی صریح کامیابی ہے ﴿٣٠﴾
اور جنہوں نے کفر کیا (ان سے کہا جائے گا کہ) بھلا ہماری
آیتیں تم کو پڑھ کر سنائی نہیں جاتی تھیں؟ مگر تم نے تکبر کیا
اور تم نافرمان لوگ تھے ﴿٣١﴾
اور جب کہا جاتا تھا کہ خدا کا وعدہ سچا ہے اور قیامت میں
کچھ شک نہیں تو تم کہتے تھے ہم نہیں جانتے کہ قیامت
کیا ہے ہم اسکو محض ظنی خیال کرتے ہیں اور ہمیں یقین نہیں آتا ﴿٣٢﴾
اور انکے اعمال کی برائیاں ان پر ظاہر ہو جائینگی اور جس (عذاب)
کی وہ ہنسی اڑاتے تھے وہ ان کو آگھیرے گا ﴿٣٣﴾
اور کہا جائیگا کہ جسطرح تم نے اس دن کے آنے کو بھلا رکھا تھا اسیطرح آج
ہم تمہیں بھلا دینگے اور تمہارا ٹھکانا دوزخ ہے اور کوئی تمہارا مددگار نہیں ﴿٣٤﴾
یہ اسلئے کہ تم نے خدا کی آیتوں کو مذاق بنا رکھا تھا اور دنیا کی
زندگی نے تم کو دھوکے میں ڈال رکھا تھا سو آج یہ لوگ نہ
دوزخ سے نکالے جائینگے اور نہ انکی توبہ قبول کی جائیگی ﴿٣٥﴾
پس خدا ہی کو ہر طرح کی تعریف (سزاوار) ہے جو آسمانوں کا
مالک اور زمین کا مالک اور تمام جہان کا پروردگار ہے ﴿٣٦﴾
اور آسمانوں اور زمین میں اسی کے لئے بڑائی ہے۔
اور وہ غالب (اور) دانا ہے ﴿٣٧﴾

فَأَمَّا الَّذِينَ آمَنُوا وَعَمِلُوا الصّٰلِحٰتِ فَيُدْخِلُهُمْ
رَبُّهُمْ فِي رَحْمَتِهِ ۚ ذٰلِكَ هُوَ الْفَوْزُ الْمُبِينُ ﴿٣٠﴾
وَأَمَّا الَّذِينَ كَفَرُوا ۟ أَفَلَمْ تَكُنْ آيٰتِي
تُتْلٰى عَلَيْكُمْ فَاسْتَكْبَرْتُمْ وَكُنْتُمْ قَوْمًا
مُجْرِمِينَ ﴿٣١﴾
وَإِذَا قِيلَ إِنَّ وَعْدَ اللّٰهِ حَقٌّ وَالسَّاعَةُ
لَا رَيْبَ فِيهَا قُلْتُمْ مَا نَدْرِي مَا السَّاعَةُ
إِنْ نَظُنُّ إِلَّا ظَنًّا وَمَا نَحْنُ بِمُسْتَيْقِنِينَ ﴿٣٢﴾
وَبَدَا لَهُمْ سَيِّئَاتُ مَا عَمِلُوا وَحَاقَ بِهِمْ
مَا كَانُوا بِهِ يَسْتَهْزِئُونَ ﴿٣٣﴾
وَقِيلَ الْيَوْمَ نَنْسٰكُمْ كَمَا نَسِيتُمْ لِقَاءَ يَوْمِكُمْ
هٰذَا وَمَأْوٰكُمُ النَّارُ وَمَا لَكُمْ مِنْ نّٰصِرِينَ ﴿٣٤﴾
ذٰلِكُمْ بِأَنَّكُمُ اتَّخَذْتُمْ آيٰتِ اللّٰهِ هُزُوًا
وَغَرَّتْكُمُ الْحَيٰوةُ الدُّنْيَا ۚ فَالْيَوْمَ لَا
يُخْرَجُونَ مِنْهَا وَلَا هُمْ يُسْتَعْتَبُونَ ﴿٣٥﴾
فَلِلّٰهِ الْحَمْدُ رَبِّ السَّمٰوٰتِ وَرَبِّ الْأَرْضِ
رَبِّ الْعٰلَمِينَ ﴿٣٦﴾
وَلَهُ الْكِبْرِيَاءُ فِي السَّمٰوٰتِ وَالْأَرْضِ ۖ
وَهُوَ الْعَزِيزُ الْحَكِيمُ ﴿٣٧﴾ ع

Al-Aḥqāf, or Winding Sand-tracts

سورۂ احقاف مکی ہے اور اس میں پینتیس آیتیں اور چار رکوع ہیں

سُورَةُ الْأَحْقَافِ مَكِّيَّةٌ وَهِيَ خَمْسٌ وَّثَلٰثُونَ آيَةً وَّأَرْبَعُ رُكُوعَاتٍ

In the name of Allah, Most Gracious, Most Merciful.

1. Hā-Mīm.
2. The revelation of the Book is from Allah the Exalted in Power, Full of Wisdom.
3. We created not the heavens and the earth and all between them but for just ends, and for a term appointed: but those who reject Faith turn away from that whereof they are warned.

شروع خدا کا نام لے کر جو بڑا مہربان نہایت رحم والا ہے ○
حٰمٓ ﴿١﴾ (یہ) کتاب خدائے غالب (اور) حکمت والے کی
طرف سے نازل ہوئی ہے ﴿٢﴾
ہم نے آسمانوں اور زمین کو اور جو کچھ ان دونوں میں ہے
مبنی برحکمت اور ایک وقت مقرر تک کے لئے پیدا
کیا ہے۔ اور کافروں کو جس چیز کی نصیحت کی جاتی ہے
اس سے منہ پھیر لیتے ہیں ﴿٣﴾

بِسْمِ اللّٰهِ الرَّحْمٰنِ الرَّحِيمِ ○
حٰمٓ ﴿١﴾ تَنْزِيلُ الْكِتٰبِ مِنَ اللّٰهِ
الْعَزِيزِ الْحَكِيمِ ﴿٢﴾
مَا خَلَقْنَا السَّمٰوٰتِ وَالْأَرْضَ وَمَا
بَيْنَهُمَآ إِلَّا بِالْحَقِّ وَأَجَلٍ مُّسَمًّى ۚ
وَالَّذِينَ كَفَرُوا عَمَّآ أُنْذِرُوا
مُعْرِضُونَ ﴿٣﴾

4. Say: "Do ye see what it is ye invoke besides Allah? Show me what it is they have created on earth, or have they a share in the heavens? Bring me a Book (revealed) before this, or any remnant of knowledge (ye may have), if ye are telling the truth!

کہو کہ بھلا تم نے اُن چیزوں کو دیکھا ہے جن کو تم خدا کے سوا
پکارتے ہو (ذرا) مجھے بھی تو دکھاؤ کہ اُنہوں نے زمین میں
کونسی چیز پیدا کی ہے یا آسمانوں میں اُن کی شرکت ہے۔ اگر سچے ہو
تو اس سے پہلے کی کوئی کتاب میرے پاس لاؤ۔ یا علم (انبیاء میں)
سے کچھ (منقول) چلا آتا ہو تو اُسے پیش کرو ﴿۴﴾

قُلْ اَرَءَيْتُمْ مَّا تَدْعُوْنَ مِنْ دُوْنِ
اللّٰهِ اَرُوْنِيْ مَاذَا خَلَقُوْا مِنَ الْاَرْضِ
اَمْ لَهُمْ شِرْكٌ فِي السَّمٰوٰتِ ؕ اِيْتُوْنِيْ
بِكِتٰبٍ مِّنْ قَبْلِ هٰذَاۤ اَوْ اَثٰرَةٍ مِّنْ
عِلْمٍ اِنْ كُنْتُمْ صٰدِقِيْنَ ﴿۴﴾

5. And who is more astray than one who invokes, besides Allah, such as will not answer him to the Day of Judgment, and who (in fact) are unconscious of their call (to them)?

اور اس شخص سے بڑھ کر کون گمراہ ہوسکتا ہے جو ایسے کو پکارے
جو قیامت تک اُسے جواب نہ دے سکے اور اُن کو اُن کے
پکارنے ہی کی خبر نہ ہو ﴿۵﴾

وَمَنْ اَضَلُّ مِمَّنْ يَّدْعُوْا مِنْ دُوْنِ
اللّٰهِ مَنْ لَّا يَسْتَجِيْبُ لَهٗۤ اِلٰى يَوْمِ
الْقِيٰمَةِ وَهُمْ عَنْ دُعَآئِهِمْ غٰفِلُوْنَ ﴿۵﴾

6. And when mankind are gathered together (at the Resurrection), they will be hostile to them and deny that (men) had worshipped them.

اور جب لوگ جمع کئے جائیں گے تو وہ اُن کے دشمن ہونگے
اور اُن کی پرستش سے انکار کریں گے ﴿۶﴾

وَاِذَا حُشِرَ النَّاسُ كَانُوْا لَهُمْ اَعْدَآءً وَّ
كَانُوْا بِعِبَادَتِهِمْ كٰفِرِيْنَ ﴿۶﴾

7. When Our Clear Signs are rehearsed to them, the Unbelievers say, of the Truth when it comes to them: "This is evident sorcery!"

اور جب اُن کے سامنے ہماری کھلی آیتیں پڑھی جاتی ہیں
تو کافر حق کے بارے میں جب اُن کے پاس آچکا کہتے ہیں
کہ یہ تو صریح جادو ہے ﴿۷﴾

وَاِذَا تُتْلٰى عَلَيْهِمْ اٰيٰتُنَا بَيِّنٰتٍ قَالَ
الَّذِيْنَ كَفَرُوْا لِلْحَقِّ لَمَّا جَآءَهُمْ ۙ هٰذَا
سِحْرٌ مُّبِيْنٌ ؕ ﴿۷﴾

8. Or do they say, "He has forged it"? Say: "Had I forged it, then ye have no power to help me against Allah. He knows best of that whereof ye talk (so glibly)! Enough is He for a witness between me and you! And He is oft-Forgiving, Most Merciful."

کیا یہ کہتے ہیں کہ اُس نے اسکو از خود بنا لیا ہے کہہ دو کہ اگر میں نے اسکو
اپنی طرف سے بنایا ہو تو تم خدا کے سامنے میرے (بچاؤ کے) لئے کچھ اختیار نہیں رکھتے
وہ اُس گفتگو کو خوب جانتا ہے جو تم اسکے بارے میں کرتے ہو وہی میرے
اور تمہارے درمیان گواہ کافی ہے۔ اور وہ بخشنے والا مہربان ہے ﴿۸﴾

اَمْ يَقُوْلُوْنَ افْتَرٰىهُ ؕ قُلْ اِنِ افْتَرَيْتُهٗ فَلَا
تَمْلِكُوْنَ لِيْ مِنَ اللّٰهِ شَيْـًٔا ؕ هُوَ اَعْلَمُ بِمَا
تُفِيْضُوْنَ فِيْهِ ؕ كَفٰى بِهٖ شَهِيْدًۢا بَيْنِيْ وَ
بَيْنَكُمْ ؕ وَهُوَ الْغَفُوْرُ الرَّحِيْمُ ﴿۸﴾

9. Say: "I am not an innovation among the messengers, nor do I know what will be done with me or with you. I follow but that which is revealed to me by inspiration; I am but a Warner open and clear."

کہہ دو کہ میں کوئی نیا پیغمبر نہیں آیا۔ اور میں نہیں جانتا کہ میرے
ساتھ کیا سلوک کیا جائیگا اور تمہارے ساتھ کیا کیا جائیگا۔ میں تو
اُسی کی پیروی کرتا ہوں جو مجھ پر وحی آتی ہے اور میرا کام تو علانیہ ہدایت کرنا ہے ﴿۹﴾

قُلْ مَا كُنْتُ بِدْعًا مِّنَ الرُّسُلِ وَمَاۤ اَدْرِيْ
مَا يُفْعَلُ بِيْ وَلَا بِكُمْ ؕ اِنْ اَتَّبِعُ اِلَّا مَا
يُوْحٰۤى اِلَيَّ وَمَاۤ اَنَا اِلَّا نَذِيْرٌ مُّبِيْنٌ ﴿۹﴾

10. Say: "See ye? If (this teaching) be from Allah, and ye reject it, and a witness from among the Children of Israel testifies to its similarity (with earlier scripture), and has believed while ye are arrogant, (how unjust ye are!) Truly, Allah guides not a people unjust."

کہو کہ بھلا دیکھو تو اگر یہ (قرآن) خدا کی طرف سے ہو اور تم نے اُس سے
انکار کیا اور بنی اسرائیل میں سے ایک گواہ اسی طرح کی ایک (کتاب) کی
گواہی دے چکا اور ایمان لے آیا اور تم نے سرکشی کی (تو تمہارے ظالم
ہونے میں کیا شک ہے) بیشک خدا ظالم لوگوں کو ہدایت نہیں دیتا ﴿۱۰﴾

قُلْ اَرَءَيْتُمْ اِنْ كَانَ مِنْ عِنْدِ اللّٰهِ وَ
كَفَرْتُمْ بِهٖ وَشَهِدَ شَاهِدٌ مِّنْ ۢ بَنِيْۤ
اِسْرَآءِيْلَ عَلٰى مِثْلِهٖ فَاٰمَنَ وَاسْتَكْبَرْتُمْ ؕ
اِنَّ اللّٰهَ لَا يَهْدِي الْقَوْمَ الظّٰلِمِيْنَ ﴿۱۰﴾ ع

11. The Unbelievers say of those who believe: "If (this Message) were a good thing, (such men) would not have gone to it first, before us!" and seeing that they guide not themselves thereby, they will say, "This is an (old,) old falsehood!"

اور کافر مومنوں سے کہتے ہیں کہ اگر یہ (دین) کچھ بہتر ہوتا تو یہ لوگ
اُسکی طرف ہم سے پہلے نہ دوڑ پڑتے۔ اور جب وہ اسسے ہدایت یاب
نہ ہوئے تو اب کہیں گے کہ یہ پرانا جھوٹ ہے ﴿۱۱﴾

وَقَالَ الَّذِيْنَ كَفَرُوْا لِلَّذِيْنَ اٰمَنُوْا لَوْ
كَانَ خَيْرًا مَّا سَبَقُوْنَاۤ اِلَيْهِ ؕ وَاِذْ لَمْ يَهْتَدُوْا
بِهٖ فَسَيَقُوْلُوْنَ هٰذَاۤ اِفْكٌ قَدِيْمٌ ﴿۱۱﴾

12. And before this, was the Book of Moses as a guide and a mercy: and this Book confirms (it) in the Arabic tongue; to admonish the unjust, and as Glad Tidings to those who do right.

13. Verily those who say, "Our Lord is Allah", and remain firm (on that Path),— on them shall be no fear, nor shall they grieve.

14. Such shall be Companions of the Garden, dwelling therein (for aye): a recompense for their (good) deeds.

15. We have enjoined on man kindness to his parents: in pain did his mother bear him, and in pain did she give him birth. The carrying of the (child) to his weaning is (a period of) thirty months. At length, when he reaches the age of full strength and attains forty years, he says, "O my Lord! grant me that I may be grateful for Thy favour which Thou hast bestowed upon me, and upon both my parents, and that I may work righteousness such as Thou mayest approve; and be gracious to me in my issue. Truly have I turned to Thee and truly do I submit (to Thee) in Islam."

16. Such are they from whom We shall accept the best of their deeds and pass by their ill deeds: (they shall be) among the Companions of the Garden: a promise of truth, which was made to them (in this life).

17. But (there is one) who says to his parents, "Fie on you! Do ye hold out the promise to me that I shall be raised up, even though generations have passed before me (without rising again)?" And they two seek Allah's aid, (and rebuke the son): "Woe to thee! Have Faith! For the promise of Allah is true." But he says, "This is nothing but tales of the ancients!"

18. Such are they against whom the word proved true among the previous generations of Jinns and men, that have passed away; for

اور اس سے پہلے موسیٰ کی کتاب تھی (لوگوں کیلئے) رہنما اور رحمت۔ اور یہ
کتاب عربی زبان میں ہے اُسی کی تصدیق کرنے والی تاکہ ظالموں
کو ڈرائے۔ اور نیکوکاروں کو خوشخبری سنائے ﴿١٢﴾
جن لوگوں نے کہا کہ ہمارا پروردگار خدا ہے پھر وہ اس پر قائم رہے
تو ان کو نہ کچھ خوف ہوگا اور نہ وہ غمناک ہوں گے ﴿١٣﴾
یہی اہلِ جنت ہیں کہ ہمیشہ اس میں رہیں گے۔ (یہ) اس کا
بدلہ (ہے) جو وہ کیا کرتے تھے ﴿١٤﴾
اور ہم نے انسان کو اپنے والدین کے ساتھ بھلائی کرنے کا حکم دیا۔
اُس کی ماں نے اُس کو تکلیف سے پیٹ میں رکھا اور تکلیف ہی سے جنا۔
اور اُس کا پیٹ میں رہنا اور دودھ چھوڑنا ڈھائی برس میں ہوتا ہے۔
یہاں تک کہ جب خوب جوان ہوتا اور چالیس برس کو پہنچ جاتا ہے
تو کہتا ہے کہ اے میرے پروردگار مجھے توفیق دے کہ تو نے جو احسان
مجھ پر اور میرے ماں باپ پر کئے ہیں اُن کا شکرگزار ہوں اور
یہ کہ نیک عمل کروں جن کو تو پسند کرے۔ اور میرے لئے میری
اولاد میں اصلاح (وتقویٰ) دے۔ میں تیری طرف رجوع کرتا
ہوں اور میں فرمانبرداروں میں ہوں ﴿١٥﴾
یہی لوگ ہیں جن کے اعمال نیک ہم قبول کریں گے اور اُنکے
گناہوں سے درگزر فرمائیں گے (اور یہی) اہلِ جنت میں (ہونگے)۔
(یہ) سچا وعدہ (ہے) جو اُن سے کیا جاتا تھا ﴿١٦﴾
اور جس شخص نے اپنے ماں باپ سے کہا کہ اُف اُف! تم مجھے یہ بتاتے ہو
کہ میں (زمین سے) نکالا جاؤں گا حالانکہ بہت سے لوگ مجھ سے
پہلے گزر چکے ہیں۔ اور وہ دونوں خدا کی جناب میں فریاد کرتے
(ہوئے کہتے) تھے کہ کمبخت ایمان لا۔ خدا کا وعدہ سچا ہے۔ تو کہنے لگا
یہ تو پہلے لوگوں کی کہانیاں ہیں ﴿١٧﴾
یہی وہ لوگ ہیں جن کے بارے میں جنوں اور انسانوں کی
(دوسری) اُمتوں میں سے جو ان سے پہلے گزر چکیں عذاب کا
وعدہ متحقق ہوگیا۔ بے شک وہ نقصان اٹھانے

وَمِنْ قَبْلِهٖ كِتٰبُ مُوْسٰٓى اِمَامًا وَّرَحْمَةً ؕ
وَهٰذَا كِتٰبٌ مُّصَدِّقٌ لِّسَانًا عَرَبِيًّا لِّيُنْذِرَ
الَّذِيْنَ ظَلَمُوْا ۖ وَبُشْرٰى لِلْمُحْسِنِيْنَ ﴿١٢﴾
اِنَّ الَّذِيْنَ قَالُوْا رَبُّنَا اللّٰهُ ثُمَّ اسْتَقَامُوْا
فَلَا خَوْفٌ عَلَيْهِمْ وَلَا هُمْ يَحْزَنُوْنَ ﴿١٣﴾
اُولٰٓئِكَ اَصْحٰبُ الْجَنَّةِ خٰلِدِيْنَ فِيْهَا ۚ
جَزَآءًۢ بِمَا كَانُوْا يَعْمَلُوْنَ ﴿١٤﴾
وَوَصَّيْنَا الْاِنْسَانَ بِوَالِدَيْهِ اِحْسٰنًا ؕ
حَمَلَتْهُ اُمُّهٗ كُرْهًا وَّوَضَعَتْهُ كُرْهًا ؕ
وَحَمْلُهٗ وَفِصٰلُهٗ ثَلٰثُوْنَ شَهْرًا ؕ حَتّٰٓى
اِذَا بَلَغَ اَشُدَّهٗ وَبَلَغَ اَرْبَعِيْنَ سَنَةً ۙ
قَالَ رَبِّ اَوْزِعْنِيْٓ اَنْ اَشْكُرَ نِعْمَتَكَ
الَّتِيْٓ اَنْعَمْتَ عَلَيَّ وَعَلٰى وَالِدَيَّ وَاَنْ
اَعْمَلَ صَالِحًا تَرْضٰىهُ وَاَصْلِحْ لِيْ فِيْ
ذُرِّيَّتِيْ ۚ اِنِّيْ تُبْتُ اِلَيْكَ وَاِنِّيْ مِنَ
الْمُسْلِمِيْنَ ﴿١٥﴾
اُولٰٓئِكَ الَّذِيْنَ نَتَقَبَّلُ عَنْهُمْ اَحْسَنَ مَا
عَمِلُوْا وَنَتَجَاوَزُ عَنْ سَيِّاٰتِهِمْ فِيْٓ اَصْحٰبِ الْجَنَّةِ ؕ
وَعْدَ الصِّدْقِ الَّذِيْ كَانُوْا يُوْعَدُوْنَ ﴿١٦﴾
وَالَّذِيْ قَالَ لِوَالِدَيْهِ اُفٍّ لَّكُمَآ
اَتَعِدٰنِنِيْٓ اَنْ اُخْرَجَ وَقَدْ خَلَتِ
الْقُرُوْنُ مِنْ قَبْلِيْ ۚ وَهُمَا يَسْتَغِيْثٰنِ
اللّٰهَ وَيْلَكَ اٰمِنْ ۖ اِنَّ وَعْدَ اللّٰهِ حَقٌّ ۚ
فَيَقُوْلُ مَا هٰذَآ اِلَّآ اَسَاطِيْرُ الْاَوَّلِيْنَ ﴿١٧﴾
اُولٰٓئِكَ الَّذِيْنَ حَقَّ عَلَيْهِمُ الْقَوْلُ
فِيْٓ اُمَمٍ قَدْ خَلَتْ مِنْ قَبْلِهِمْ مِّنَ
الْجِنِّ وَالْاِنْسِ ؕ اِنَّهُمْ كَانُوْا

they will be (utterly) lost.

19. And to all are (assigned) degrees according to the deeds which they (have done), and in order that (Allah) may recompense their deeds; and no injustice will be done to them.

20. And on the Day that the Unbelievers will be placed before the Fire, (it will be said to them): "Ye squandered your good things in the life of the world, and ye took your pleasure out of them: but today shall ye be recompensed with a Chastisement of humiliation: for that ye were arrogant on earth without just cause, and that ye (ever) transgressed."

21. Mention (Hûd) one of 'Ād's (own) brethren: behold, he warned his people beside the winding Sand-tracts: but there have been Warners before him and after him: "Worship ye none other than Allah: truly I fear for you the Chastisement of a Mighty Day."

22. They said: "Hast thou come in order to turn us aside from our gods? Then bring upon us the (calamity) with which thou dost threaten us, if thou art telling the truth!"

23. He said: "The Knowledge (of when it will come) is only with Allah: I proclaim to you the mission on which I have been sent: but I see that ye are a people in ignorance!"...

24. Then, when they saw a cloud advancing towards their valleys, they said, "This cloud will give us rain!" "Nay, it is the (calamity) ye were asking to be hastened!— a wind wherein is a Grievous Chastisement!

25. "Everything will it destroy by the command of its Lord!" then by the morning they— nothing was to be seen but (the ruins of) their houses! Thus do We recompense those given to sin!

26. And We had firmly established them in a (prosperity and) power which We have not given to you (ye Quraish!) and We had endowed them with (faculties of) hearing,

والے تھے ﴿١٨﴾
اور لوگوں نے جیسے کام کئے ہونگے اُنکے مطابق سب کے درجے ہونگے (غرض یہ)
کہ اُنکو اُنکے اعمال کا پورا بدلہ دے اور اُن کا نقصان نہ کیا جائے ﴿١٩﴾
اور جس دن کافر دوزخ کے سامنے کئے جائیں گے (تو کہا
جائے گا کہ) تم اپنی دنیا کی زندگی میں لذتیں حاصل
کر چکے اور اُن سے متمتع ہو چکے۔ سو آج تم کو ذلت کا
عذاب ہے (یہ) اس کی سزا ہے کہ تم زمین میں
ناحق غرور کیا کرتے تھے۔ اور اس کی کہ بدکرداری
کرتے تھے ﴿٢٠﴾
اور (قوم) عاد کے بھائی (ہود) کو یاد کرو کہ جب اُنہوں نے
اپنی قوم کو سرزمین احقاف میں ہدایت کی اور اُن سے پہلے اور
پیچھے بھی ہدایت کرنے والے گزر چکے تھے کہ خدا کے سوا کسی کی
عبادت نہ کرو۔ مجھے تمہارے بارے میں بڑے دن کے عذاب کا ڈر لگتا ہے ﴿٢١﴾
کہنے لگے کیا تم ہمارے پاس اس لئے آئے ہو کہ ہم کو ہمارے
معبودوں سے پھیر دو۔ اگر سچے ہو تو جس چیز سے ہمیں ڈراتے ہو
اُسے ہم پر لے آؤ ﴿٢٢﴾
اُنہوں نے کہا کہ (اس کا) علم تو خدا ہی کو ہے۔ اور میں تو جو
(احکام) دے کر بھیجا گیا ہوں وہ تمہیں پہنچا رہا ہوں لیکن
میں دیکھتا ہوں کہ تم لوگ نادانی میں پھنس رہے ہو ﴿٢٣﴾
پھر جب اُنہوں نے اس (عذاب) کو دیکھا کہ بادل (کی صورت میں) اُنکے میدانوں
کی طرف آرہا ہے تو کہنے لگے یہ تو بادل ہے جو ہم پر برس کر رہیگا۔ (نہیں) بلکہ (یہ) وہ
چیز ہے جس کیلئے تم جلدی کرتے تھے یعنی آندھی جس میں دردینے والا عذاب بھرا ہوا ہے ﴿٢٤﴾
ہر چیز کو اپنے پروردگار کے حکم سے تباہ کئے دیتی ہے تو وہ ایسے
ہوگئے کہ اُن کے گھروں کے سوا کچھ نظر ہی نہیں آتا تھا۔
گنہگار لوگوں کو ہم اسی طرح سزا دیا کرتے ہیں ﴿٢٥﴾
اور ہم نے اُن کو ایسے مقدور دیئے تھے جو تم لوگوں کو نہیں
دیئے اور اُنہیں کان اور آنکھیں اور دل دیئے تھے۔ تو جب

خٰسِرِيْنَ ﴿١٨﴾
وَلِكُلٍّ دَرَجٰتٌ مِّمَّا عَمِلُوْا ۚ وَلِيُوَفِّيَهُمْ
اَعْمَالَهُمْ وَهُمْ لَا يُظْلَمُوْنَ ﴿١٩﴾
وَيَوْمَ يُعْرَضُ الَّذِيْنَ كَفَرُوْا عَلَى النَّارِ ؕ
اَذْهَبْتُمْ طَيِّبٰتِكُمْ فِيْ حَيَاتِكُمُ الدُّنْيَا
وَاسْتَمْتَعْتُمْ بِهَا ۚ فَالْيَوْمَ تُجْزَوْنَ عَذَابَ
الْهُوْنِ بِمَا كُنْتُمْ تَسْتَكْبِرُوْنَ فِي
الْاَرْضِ بِغَيْرِ الْحَقِّ وَبِمَا كُنْتُمْ
تَفْسُقُوْنَ ﴿٢٠﴾ ع
وَاذْكُرْ اَخَا عَادٍ ؕ اِذْ اَنْذَرَ قَوْمَهٗ بِالْاَحْقَافِ
وَقَدْ خَلَتِ النُّذُرُ مِنْۢ بَيْنِ يَدَيْهِ
وَمِنْ خَلْفِهٖۤ اَلَّا تَعْبُدُوْۤا اِلَّا اللّٰهَ ؕ اِنِّيْۤ
اَخَافُ عَلَيْكُمْ عَذَابَ يَوْمٍ عَظِيْمٍ ﴿٢١﴾
قَالُوْۤا اَجِئْتَنَا لِتَاْفِكَنَا عَنْ اٰلِهَتِنَا ۚ
فَاْتِنَا بِمَا تَعِدُنَاۤ اِنْ كُنْتَ مِنَ
الصّٰدِقِيْنَ ﴿٢٢﴾
قَالَ اِنَّمَا الْعِلْمُ عِنْدَ اللّٰهِ ۖ وَاُبَلِّغُكُمْ
مَّاۤ اُرْسِلْتُ بِهٖ وَلٰكِنِّيْۤ اَرٰىكُمْ قَوْمًا
تَجْهَلُوْنَ ﴿٢٣﴾
فَلَمَّا رَاَوْهُ عَارِضًا مُّسْتَقْبِلَ اَوْدِيَتِهِمْ ۙ
قَالُوْا هٰذَا عَارِضٌ مُّمْطِرُنَا ؕ بَلْ هُوَ مَا
اسْتَعْجَلْتُمْ بِهٖ ؕ رِيْحٌ فِيْهَا عَذَابٌ اَلِيْمٌ ﴿٢٤﴾
تُدَمِّرُ كُلَّ شَيْءٍۭ بِاَمْرِ رَبِّهَا فَاَصْبَحُوْا لَا
يُرٰۤى اِلَّا مَسٰكِنُهُمْ ؕ كَذٰلِكَ نَجْزِي
الْقَوْمَ الْمُجْرِمِيْنَ ﴿٢٥﴾
وَلَقَدْ مَكَّنّٰهُمْ فِيْمَاۤ اِنْ مَّكَّنّٰكُمْ فِيْهِ
وَجَعَلْنَا لَهُمْ سَمْعًا وَّاَبْصَارًا وَّاَفْـِٕدَةً ۖ

seeing, heart and intellect: but of no profit to them were their (faculties of) hearing, sight, and heart and intellect, when they went on rejecting the Signs of Allah: and they were (completely) encircled by that which they used to mock at!

27. We destroyed aforetime towns round about you; and We have shown the Signs in various ways, that they may turn (to Us).

28. Why then was no help forthcoming to them from those whom they worshipped as gods, besides Allah, as a means of access (to Allah)? Nay, they left them in the lurch: but that was their falsehood and their invention.

29. Behold, We turned towards thee a company of Jinns (quietly) listening to the Qur'ān: when they stood in the presence thereof, they said, "Listen in silence!" When the (reading) was finished, they returned to their people, to warn them.

30. They said, "O our people! we have heard a Book revealed after Moses, confirming what came before it: it guides to the Truth and to a Straight Path.

31. "O our people, hearken to the one who invites (you) to Allah, and believe in him: He will forgive you your faults, and deliver you from a Chastisement Grievous.

32. "If any does not hearken to the one who invites (us) to Allah, he cannot escape in the earth, and no protectors can he have besides Allah: such are in manifest error."

33. See they not that Allah, Who created the heavens and the earth, and never wearied with their creation, is able to give life to the dead? Yea, verily He has power over all things.

34. And on the Day that the Unbelievers will be placed before the Fire, (they will be asked,) "Is this

وہ خدا کی آیتوں سے انکار کرتے تھے تو نہ تو اُن کے کان
ہی اُن کے کچھ کام آسکے اور نہ آنکھیں اور نہ دل۔
اور جس چیز سے استہزاء کیا کرتے تھے اُس نے اُن کو
آگھیرا ﴿٢٦﴾
اور تمہارے اردگرد کی بستیوں کو ہم نے ہلاک کر دیا۔ اور بار بار
(اپنی) نشانیاں ظاہر کر دیں تاکہ وہ رجوع کریں ﴿٢٧﴾
تو جن کو اُن لوگوں نے تقرب (خدا) کیلئے خدا کے سوا معبود بنایا
تھا اُنہوں نے اُن کی کیوں مدد نہ کی؟ بلکہ وہ اُن (کے سامنے
سے) گم ہو گئے۔ اور یہ اُنکا جھوٹ تھا اور یہی وہ افترا کیا کرتے تھے ﴿٢٨﴾
اور جب ہم نے جنوں میں سے کئی شخص تمہاری طرف متوجہ کئے
کہ قرآن سنیں۔ تو جب وہ اُسکے پاس آئے تو آپس میں کہنے لگے کہ
خاموش رہو۔ جب (پڑھنا) تمام ہوا تو اپنی برادری کے لوگوں
میں واپس گئے کہ (اُن کو) نصیحت کریں ﴿٢٩﴾
کہنے لگے کہ اے قوم ہم نے ایک کتاب سنی ہے جو موسیٰ کے بعد
نازل ہوئی ہے۔ جو (کتابیں) اس سے پہلے (نازل ہوئی) ہیں اُنکی
تصدیق کرتی ہے (اور) سچا (دین) اور سیدھا رستہ بتاتی ہے ﴿٣٠﴾
اے قوم! خدا کی طرف بلانے والے کی بات کو قبول کرو۔ اور
اُس پر ایمان لاؤ۔ خدا تمہارے گناہ بخش دے گا اور تمہیں
دکھ دینے والے عذاب سے پناہ میں رکھے گا ﴿٣١﴾
اور جو شخص خدا کی طرف بلانے والے کی بات قبول نہ کرے گا
تو وہ زمین میں (خدا کو) عاجز نہیں کر سکے گا اور نہ اُسکے سوا
اُس کے حمایتی ہونگے۔ یہ لوگ صریح گمراہی میں ہیں ﴿٣٢﴾
کیا اُنہوں نے نہیں سمجھا کہ جس خدا نے آسمانوں اور زمین کو
پیدا کیا اور اُنکے پیدا کرنے سے تھکا نہیں۔ وہ اس (بات) پر
بھی قادر ہے کہ مُردوں کو زندہ کر دے۔ ہاں (ہاں) وہ
ہر چیز پر قادر ہے ﴿٣٣﴾
اور جس روز انکار کرنے والے آگ کے سامنے کئے جائیں گے۔ کیا یہ

فَمَآ اَغْنٰى عَنْهُمْ سَمْعُهُمْ وَلَآ اَبْصَارُهُمْ
وَلَآ اَفْـِٕدَتُهُمْ مِّنْ شَيْءٍ اِذْ كَانُوْا يَجْحَدُوْنَ
بِاٰيٰتِ اللّٰهِ وَحَاقَ بِهِمْ مَّا كَانُوْا بِهٖ
يَسْتَهْزِءُوْنَ ﴿٢٦﴾
وَلَقَدْ اَهْلَكْنَا مَا حَوْلَكُمْ مِّنَ الْقُرٰى
وَصَرَّفْنَا الْاٰيٰتِ لَعَلَّهُمْ يَرْجِعُوْنَ ﴿٢٧﴾
فَلَوْلَا نَصَرَهُمُ الَّذِيْنَ اتَّخَذُوْا مِنْ
دُوْنِ اللّٰهِ قُرْبَانًا اٰلِهَةً ۚ بَلْ ضَلُّوْا عَنْهُمْ ۚ
وَذٰلِكَ اِفْكُهُمْ وَمَا كَانُوْا يَفْتَرُوْنَ ﴿٢٨﴾
وَاِذْ صَرَفْنَآ اِلَيْكَ نَفَرًا مِّنَ الْجِنِّ
يَسْتَمِعُوْنَ الْقُرْاٰنَ ۚ فَلَمَّا حَضَرُوْهُ
قَالُوْٓا اَنْصِتُوْا ۚ فَلَمَّا قُضِيَ وَلَّوْا اِلٰى
قَوْمِهِمْ مُّنْذِرِيْنَ ﴿٢٩﴾
قَالُوْا يٰقَوْمَنَآ اِنَّا سَمِعْنَا كِتٰبًا اُنْزِلَ مِنْ
بَعْدِ مُوْسٰى مُصَدِّقًا لِّمَا بَيْنَ يَدَيْهِ
يَهْدِيْٓ اِلَى الْحَقِّ وَاِلٰى طَرِيْقٍ مُّسْتَقِيْمٍ ﴿٣٠﴾
يٰقَوْمَنَآ اَجِيْبُوْا دَاعِيَ اللّٰهِ وَاٰمِنُوْا بِهٖ
يَغْفِرْ لَكُمْ مِّنْ ذُنُوْبِكُمْ وَيُجِرْكُمْ مِّنْ
عَذَابٍ اَلِيْمٍ ﴿٣١﴾
وَمَنْ لَّا يُجِبْ دَاعِيَ اللّٰهِ فَلَيْسَ بِمُعْجِزٍ
فِي الْاَرْضِ وَلَيْسَ لَهٗ مِنْ دُوْنِهٖٓ اَوْلِيَآءُ ۚ
اُولٰٓئِكَ فِيْ ضَلٰلٍ مُّبِيْنٍ ﴿٣٢﴾
اَوَلَمْ يَرَوْا اَنَّ اللّٰهَ الَّذِيْ خَلَقَ السَّمٰوٰتِ
وَالْاَرْضَ وَلَمْ يَعْيَ بِخَلْقِهِنَّ بِقٰدِرٍ
عَلٰٓى اَنْ يُّحْيِۦَ الْمَوْتٰى ۚ بَلٰٓى اِنَّهٗ عَلٰى
كُلِّ شَيْءٍ قَدِيْرٌ ﴿٣٣﴾
وَيَوْمَ يُعْرَضُ الَّذِيْنَ كَفَرُوْا عَلَى النَّارِ ۗ

SÛRA–47
MUḤAMMAD
(INTRODUCTION)

We have examined and followed the current arrangement of the Sûras according to subject-matter and independently of Chronology, and we have found that a logical thread runs through them. We have now finished more than five-sixths of the Qur-ãn. The remaining sixth consists of short Sûras, but these are again grouped according to subject-matter.

We begin the first of such groups with a group of three Sûras (47 to 49), which deal with the organisation of the Muslim Ummat or community both for external defence and in internal relations. The present Sûra deals with the necessity of defence against external foes by courage and strenous fighting, and dates from about the first of the Hijra, when the Muslims were under threat of extinction by invasion from Makkah.

أَلَيْسَ هَٰذَا بِالْحَقِّ ۖ قَالُوا بَلَىٰ وَرَبِّنَا ۚ
قَالَ فَذُوقُوا الْعَذَابَ بِمَا كُنتُمْ تَكْفُرُونَ ﴿٣٤﴾
فَاصْبِرْ كَمَا صَبَرَ أُولُو الْعَزْمِ مِنَ الرُّسُلِ
وَلَا تَسْتَعْجِل لَّهُمْ ۚ كَأَنَّهُمْ يَوْمَ يَرَوْنَ مَا
يُوعَدُونَ لَمْ يَلْبَثُوا إِلَّا سَاعَةً مِّن نَّهَارٍ ۚ
بَلَاغٌ ۚ فَهَلْ يُهْلَكُ إِلَّا الْقَوْمُ الْفَاسِقُونَ ﴿٣٥﴾

حق نہیں ہے؟ تو کہیں گے کیوں نہیں ہمارے پروردگار کی قسم (حق ہے)
حکم ہوگا کہ تم جو (دنیا میں) انکار کیا کرتے تھے (اب) عذاب کے مزے چکھو (۳۴)
پس اے محمد جس طرح اور عالی ہمت پیغمبر صبر کرتے رہے ہیں اسی طرح تم بھی صبر کرو
اور ان کے لئے (عذاب) جلدی نہ مانگو جس دن یہ اس چیز کو دیکھیں گے جس کا ان سے
وعدہ کیا جاتا ہے تو (خیال کریں گے کہ) گویا (دنیا میں) رہے ہی نہ تھے مگر
گھڑی بھر دن۔ (یہ قرآن) پیغام ہے سو (اب) وہی ہلاک ہوں گے جو نافرمان تھے (۳۵)

not the Truth?" They will say, "Yea, by our Lord" (he will say:) "Then taste ye the Chastisement, for that ye were wont to deny (Truth)!"

35. Therefore patiently persevere, as did (all) messengers of firm resolution; and be in no haste about the (Unbelievers). On the Day that they see the (Punishment) promised them, (it will be) as if they had not tarried more than an hour in a single day. (Thine but) to deliver the Message: but shall any be destroyed except those who transgress?

سُورَةُ مُحَمَّدٍ مَدَنِيَّةٌ

سورۂ محمد مدنی ہے اور اس میں اڑتیس آیتیں اور چار رکوع ہیں

Muḥammad (the Prophet)

بِسْمِ اللَّهِ الرَّحْمَٰنِ الرَّحِيمِ

شروع خدا کا نام لے کر جو بڑا مہربان نہایت رحم والا ہے

In the name of Allah, Most Gracious Most Merciful.

الَّذِينَ كَفَرُوا وَصَدُّوا عَن سَبِيلِ اللَّهِ
أَضَلَّ أَعْمَالَهُمْ ﴿١﴾
وَالَّذِينَ آمَنُوا وَعَمِلُوا الصَّالِحَاتِ وَآمَنُوا
بِمَا نُزِّلَ عَلَىٰ مُحَمَّدٍ وَهُوَ الْحَقُّ مِن رَّبِّهِمْ ۙ
كَفَّرَ عَنْهُمْ سَيِّئَاتِهِمْ وَأَصْلَحَ بَالَهُمْ ﴿٢﴾
ذَٰلِكَ بِأَنَّ الَّذِينَ كَفَرُوا اتَّبَعُوا الْبَاطِلَ
وَأَنَّ الَّذِينَ آمَنُوا اتَّبَعُوا الْحَقَّ مِن
رَّبِّهِمْ ۚ كَذَٰلِكَ يَضْرِبُ اللَّهُ لِلنَّاسِ أَمْثَالَهُمْ ﴿٣﴾
فَإِذَا لَقِيتُمُ الَّذِينَ كَفَرُوا فَضَرْبَ الرِّقَابِ
حَتَّىٰ إِذَا أَثْخَنتُمُوهُمْ فَشُدُّوا الْوَثَاقَ
فَإِمَّا مَنًّا بَعْدُ وَإِمَّا فِدَاءً حَتَّىٰ تَضَعَ
الْحَرْبُ أَوْزَارَهَا ۚ ذَٰلِكَ ۛ وَلَوْ يَشَاءُ اللَّهُ
لَانتَصَرَ مِنْهُمْ وَلَٰكِن لِّيَبْلُوَ بَعْضَكُم
بِبَعْضٍ ۗ وَالَّذِينَ قُتِلُوا فِي سَبِيلِ اللَّهِ
فَلَن يُضِلَّ أَعْمَالَهُمْ ﴿٤﴾
سَيَهْدِيهِمْ وَيُصْلِحُ بَالَهُمْ ﴿٥﴾
وَيُدْخِلُهُمُ الْجَنَّةَ عَرَّفَهَا لَهُمْ ﴿٦﴾
يَا أَيُّهَا الَّذِينَ آمَنُوا إِن تَنصُرُوا اللَّهَ
يَنصُرْكُمْ وَيُثَبِّتْ أَقْدَامَكُمْ ﴿٧﴾

جن لوگوں نے کفر کیا اور (اوروں کو) خدا کے رستے سے روکا
خدا نے ان کے اعمال برباد کر دیئے (۱)
اور جو ایمان لائے اور نیک عمل کرتے رہے اور جو (کتاب) محمد پر نازل
ہوئی اسے مانتے رہے اور وہ ان کے پروردگار کی طرف سے برحق ہے ان سے
ان کے گناہ دور کر دیئے اور ان کی حالت سنوار دی (۲)
یہ (حبط اعمال اور اصلاح حال) اس لئے ہے کہ جن لوگوں نے کفر کیا
انہوں نے جھوٹی بات کی پیروی کی اور جو ایمان لائے وہ اپنے پروردگار
کی طرف سے (دین) حق کے پیچھے چلے اسی طرح خدا لوگوں سے ان کے حالات بیان فرماتا ہے (۳)
جب تم کافروں سے بھڑ جاؤ تو ان کی گردنیں اڑا دو۔ یہاں تک کہ
جب ان کو خوب قتل کر چکو تو (جو زندہ پکڑے جائیں ان کو) مضبوطی
سے قید کر لو۔ پھر اس کے بعد یا تو احسان رکھ کر چھوڑ دینا چاہیئے یا کچھ
مال لے کر یہاں تک کہ (فریق مقابل) لڑائی (کے) ہتھیار (ہاتھ سے) رکھ دے
یہ (حکم یاد رکھو) اور اگر خدا چاہتا تو (اور طرح) ان سے انتقام لے لیتا لیکن اس نے
چاہا کہ تمہاری آزمائش ایک (کو) دوسرے سے (لڑوا کر) کرے۔ اور جو لوگ
خدا کی راہ میں مارے گئے ان کے عملوں کو ہرگز ضائع نہ کرے گا (۴)
(بلکہ) ان کو سیدھے رستے پر چلائے گا اور ان کی حالت درست کر دے گا (۵)
اور ان کو بہشت میں جس سے ان کو شناسا کر رکھا ہے داخل کرے گا (۶)
اے اہل ایمان اگر تم خدا کی مدد کرو گے تو وہ بھی تمہاری مدد
کرے گا۔ اور تم کو ثابت قدم رکھے گا (۷)

1. Those who reject Allah and hinder (men) from the Path of Allah,—their deeds will Allah bring to naught.

2. But those who believe and work deeds of righteousness, and believe in the (Revelation) sent down to Muḥammad—for it is the Truth from their Lord,— he will remove from them their ills and improve their condition.

3. This because those who reject Allah follow falsehood. While those who believe follow the Truth from their Lord: thus does Allah set forth for men their lessons by similitudes.

4. Therefore, when ye meet the Unbelievers (in fight), smite at their necks; at length, when ye have thoroughly subdued them, bind (the captives) firmly: therefore (is the time for) either generosity or ransom: until the war lays down its burdens. Thus (are ye commanded): but if it had been Allah's Will, he could certainly have exacted retribution from them (Himself); but (He lets you fight) in order to test you, some with others. But those who are slain in the way of Allah,— he will never let their deeds be lost.

5. Soon will He guide them and improve their condition,

6. And admit them to the Garden which He has made known to them.

7. O ye who believe! if ye will help (the cause of) Allah, he will help you, and plant your feet firmly.

8. But those who reject (Allah),—for them is destruction, and (Allah) will bring their deeds to naught.
9. That is because they hate the Revelation of Allah; so He has made their deeds fruitless.

10. Do they not travel through the earth, and see what was the End of those before them (who did evil)? Allah brought utter destruction on them, and similar (fates await) those who reject Allah.
11. That is because Allah is the Protector of those who believe, but those who reject Allah have no protector.

12. Verily Allah will admit those who believe and do righteous deeds, to Gardens beneath which rivers flow; while those who reject Allah will enjoy (this world) and eat as cattle eat; and the Fire will be their abode.

13. And how many cities, with more power than thy city which has driven thee out, have We destroyed (for their sins)? And there was none to aid them.

14. Is then one who is on a clear (Path) from his Lord, no better than one to whom the evil of his conduct seems pleasing, and such as follow their own lusts?
15. (Here is) the description of the Garden which the righteous are promised: in it are rivers of water unstaling; rivers of milk of which the taste never changes; rivers of wine, a joy to those who drink; and rivers of honey pure and clear. In it there are for them all kinds of fruits; and Forgiveness from their Lord, (can those in such Bliss) be compared to such as shall dwell for ever in the Fire, and be given, to drink, boiling water, so that it cuts up their bowels (to pieces)?
16. And among them are men who listen to thee, till when they go out from thee, they say to those who have received Knowledge,

اور جو کافر ہیں اُن کے لئے ہلاکت ہے۔ اور وہ اُن کے
اعمال کو برباد کر دے گا (٨)
یہ اس لئے کہ خدا نے جو چیز نازل فرمائی اُنہوں نے اس کو
ناپسند کیا تو خدا نے اُن کے اعمال اکارت کر دیئے (٩)
کیا اُنہوں نے ملک میں سیر نہیں کی تاکہ دیکھتے کہ جو لوگ اُن سے
پہلے تھے اُن کا انجام کیسا ہوا؟ خدا نے اُن پر تباہی ڈال دی
اور اسی طرح کا عذاب اُن کافروں کو ہوگا (١٠)
یہ اس لئے کہ جو مومن ہیں اُن کا خدا کارساز ہے اور
کافروں کا کوئی کارساز نہیں (١١)
جو لوگ ایمان لائے اور عمل نیک کرتے رہے اُن کو خدا
بہشتوں میں جن کے نیچے نہریں بہ رہی ہیں داخل فرمائیگا۔
اور جو کافر ہیں وہ فائدے اُٹھاتے ہیں اور (اس طرح) کھاتے
ہیں جیسے حیوان کھاتے ہیں۔ اور اُن کا ٹھکانا دوزخ ہے (١٢)
اور بہت سی بستیاں تمہاری بستی سے جس (کے باشندوں) نے تمہیں (وہاں سے)
نکال دیا زور و قوت میں کہیں بڑھ کر تھیں۔ ہم نے اُن کا
ستیاناس کر دیا اور اُن کا کوئی مددگار نہ ہوا (١٣)
بھلا جو شخص اپنے پروردگار کی مہربانی سے کھلے رستے پر (چل رہا) ہو وہ اُنکی
طرح (ہو سکتا) ہے جنکے اعمال بد اُنہیں اچھے کر کے دکھائے جائیں اور جو اپنی خواہشوں کی پیروی کریں (١٤)
جنت جس کا پرہیزگاروں سے وعدہ کیا جاتا ہے اُسکی صفت یہ ہے کہ
اس میں پانی کی نہریں ہیں جو بُو نہیں کریگا۔ اور دودھ کی نہریں
ہیں جسکا مزہ نہیں بدلیگا۔ اور شراب کی نہریں ہیں جو پینے والوں کے لئے
(سراسر) لذت ہے اور شہد مصفا کی نہریں ہیں (جو حلاوت ہی حلاوت ہے)
اور (وہاں) اُن کیلئے ہر قسم کے میوے ہیں اور اُنکے پروردگار کی طرف سے مغفرت ہے
(کیا یہ پرہیزگار) اُنکی طرح (ہو سکتے) ہیں جو ہمیشہ دوزخ میں رہیں گے۔ اور
جن کو کھولتا ہوا پانی پلایا جائیگا تو اُنکی انتڑیوں کو کاٹ ڈالیگا (١٥)
اور اُنمیں بعض ایسے بھی ہیں جو تمہاری طرف کان لگائے رہتے ہیں یہاں تک کہ
(سب کچھ) سنتے ہیں لیکن جب تمہارے پاس سے نکل کر چلے جاتے ہیں تو جن لوگوں کو علم

والذين كفروا فتعسا لهم واضل
اعمالهم (٨)
ذلك بانهم كرهوا ما انزل الله
فاحبط اعمالهم (٩)
افلم يسيروا في الارض فينظروا كيف
كان عاقبة الذين من قبلهم دمر
الله عليهم وللكفرين امثالها (١٠)
ذلك بان الله مولى الذين امنوا و
ان الكفرين لا مولى لهم (١١)
ان الله يدخل الذين امنوا وعملوا
الصلحت جنت تجري من تحتها
الانهر والذين كفروا يتمتعون وياكلون
كما تاكل الانعام والنار مثوى لهم (١٢)
وكاين من قرية هي اشد قوة من
قريتك التي اخرجتك اهلكنهم
فلا ناصر لهم (١٣)
افمن كان على بينة من ربه كمن
زين له سوء عمله واتبعوا اهواءهم (١٤)
مثل الجنة التي وعد المتقون فيها
انهر من ماء غير اسن وانهر من
لبن لم يتغير طعمه وانهر من
خمر لذة للشربين وانهر من عسل
مصفى ولهم فيها من كل الثمرت
ومغفرة من ربهم كمن هو خالد في
النار وسقوا ماء حميما فقطع امعاءهم (١٥)
ومنهم من يستمع اليك حتى اذا خرجوا
من عندك قالوا للذين اوتوا العلم

"What is it he said just then?" Such are men whose hearts Allah has sealed, and who follow their own lusts.

17. But to those who receive guidance, He increases their Guidance, and bestows on them their Piety and Restraint (from evil).

18. Do they then only wait for the Hour,—that it should come on them of a sudden? But already have come some tokens thereof, and when it comes to them, how shall they have their Reminder?

19. Know, therefore, that there is no god but Allah, and ask forgiveness for thy fault, and for the men and women who believe: for Allah knows how ye move about and how ye dwell in your homes.

20. Those who believe say, "Why is not a Sûra sent down (for us)?" But when a Sûra of decisive meaning is revealed, and fighting is mentioned therein, thou wilt see those in whose hearts is a disease looking at thee with a look of one in swoon at the approach of death. But more fitting for them—

21. Were it to obey and say what is just, and when a matter is resolved on, it were best for them if they were true to Allah.

22. Then, is it to be expected of you, if ye were put in authority, that ye will do mischief in the land, and break your ties of kith and kin?

23. Such are the men whom Allah has cursed, for He has made them deaf and blinded their sight.

24. Do they not then earnestly seek to understand the Qur'ān, or is that there are locks upon their hearts?

25. Those who turn back as apostates after Guidance was clearly shown to them,— Satan has instigated them and buoyed them up with false hopes.

26. This, because they said to those who hate what Allah has

(دین) دیا گیا ہے اُنسے کہتے ہیں کہ (بھلا) انہوں نے ابھی کیا کہا تھا؟ یہی لوگ ہیں جن کے
دلوں پر خدا نے مُہر لگا رکھی ہے اور وہ اپنی خواہشوں کے پیچھے چل رہے ہیں ﴿۱۶﴾
اور جو لوگ ہدایت یافتہ ہیں اُن کو وہ ہدایت مزید بخشتا ہے اور
پرہیزگاری عنایت کرتا ہے ﴿۱۷﴾
اب تو یہ لوگ قیامت ہی کو دیکھتے ہیں کہ ناگہاں اُن پر آ واقع ہو
سو اُس کی نشانیاں (وقوع میں) آچکی ہیں۔ پھر جب وہ اُن پر
آنازل ہوگی اُس وقت اُنہیں نصیحت کہاں (مفید) ہوسکیگی؟ ﴿۱۸﴾
پس جان رکھو کہ خدا کے سوا کوئی معبود نہیں اور اپنے گناہوں
کی معافی مانگو اور (اور) مومن مردوں اور مومن عورتوں کیلئے
بھی۔ اور خدا تم لوگوں کے چلنے پھرنے اور ٹھیرنے سے واقف ہے ﴿۱۹﴾
اور مومن لوگ کہتے ہیں کہ (جہاد کی) کوئی سورت کیوں نازل
نہیں ہوتی؟ لیکن جب کوئی صاف معنوں کی سورت نازل
اور اس میں جہاد کا بیان ہو۔ تو جن لوگوں کے دلوں میں (نفاق کا)
مرض ہے تم اُنکو دیکھو کہ تمہاری طرف اس طرح دیکھنے لگیں جس طرح
کسی پر موت کی بیہوشی (طاری) ہو رہی ہو سو اُن کیلئے خرابی ہے ﴿۲۰﴾
(خوب کام تو) فرمانبرداری اور پسندیدہ بات کہنا ہے۔ پھر جب (جہاد کی)
بات پختہ ہو گئی تو اگر یہ لوگ خدا سے سچے رہنا چاہتے تو اُنکے لئے بہت اچھا ہوتا ﴿۲۱﴾
(اے منافقو) تم سے عجب نہیں کہ اگر تم حاکم ہو جاؤ تو ملک میں خرابی
کرنے لگو اور اپنے رشتوں کو توڑ ڈالو ﴿۲۲﴾
یہی لوگ ہیں جن پر خدا نے لعنت کی ہے اور اُن (کے کانوں)
کو بہرا اور (اُن کی) آنکھوں کو اندھا کر دیا ہے ﴿۲۳﴾
بھلا یہ لوگ قرآن میں غور نہیں کرتے یا (اُن کے) دلوں پر
قفل لگ رہے ہیں ﴿۲۴﴾
جو لوگ راہ ہدایت ظاہر ہونے کے بعد پیٹھ دے کر پھر گئے
شیطان نے (یہ کام) اُن کو مزین کر دکھایا۔ اور انہیں طول
(عمر کا وعدہ) دیا ﴿۲۵﴾
یہ اس لئے کہ جو لوگ خدا کی اُتاری ہوئی (کتاب) سے بیزار ہیں

مَاذَا قَالَ اٰنِفًا ۟ اُولٰٓئِكَ الَّذِيْنَ طَبَعَ
اللّٰهُ عَلٰى قُلُوْبِهِمْ وَاتَّبَعُوْٓا اَهْوَآءَهُمْ ﴿١٦﴾
وَالَّذِيْنَ اهْتَدَوْا زَادَهُمْ هُدًى وَّ
اٰتٰىهُمْ تَقْوٰىهُمْ ﴿١٧﴾
فَهَلْ يَنْظُرُوْنَ اِلَّا السَّاعَةَ اَنْ تَاْتِيَهُمْ
بَغْتَةً ۚ فَقَدْ جَآءَ اَشْرَاطُهَا ۚ فَاَنّٰى لَهُمْ
اِذَا جَآءَتْهُمْ ذِكْرٰىهُمْ ﴿١٨﴾
فَاعْلَمْ اَنَّهٗ لَآ اِلٰهَ اِلَّا اللّٰهُ وَاسْتَغْفِرْ
لِذَنْۢبِكَ وَلِلْمُؤْمِنِيْنَ وَالْمُؤْمِنٰتِ ۭ
ع وَاللّٰهُ يَعْلَمُ مُتَقَلَّبَكُمْ وَمَثْوٰىكُمْ ﴿١٩﴾
وَيَقُوْلُ الَّذِيْنَ اٰمَنُوْا لَوْلَا نُزِّلَتْ سُوْرَةٌ ۚ
فَاِذَآ اُنْزِلَتْ سُوْرَةٌ مُّحْكَمَةٌ وَّذُكِرَ فِيْهَا
الْقِتَالُ ۙ رَاَيْتَ الَّذِيْنَ فِيْ قُلُوْبِهِمْ مَّرَضٌ
يَّنْظُرُوْنَ اِلَيْكَ نَظَرَ الْمَغْشِيِّ عَلَيْهِ مِنَ
الْمَوْتِ ۭ فَاَوْلٰى لَهُمْ ﴿٢٠﴾
طَاعَةٌ وَّقَوْلٌ مَّعْرُوْفٌ ۣ فَاِذَا عَزَمَ الْاَمْرُ ۣ
فَلَوْ صَدَقُوا اللّٰهَ لَكَانَ خَيْرًا لَّهُمْ ﴿٢١﴾
فَهَلْ عَسَيْتُمْ اِنْ تَوَلَّيْتُمْ اَنْ تُفْسِدُوْا
فِي الْاَرْضِ وَتُقَطِّعُوْٓا اَرْحَامَكُمْ ﴿٢٢﴾
اُولٰٓئِكَ الَّذِيْنَ لَعَنَهُمُ اللّٰهُ فَاَصَمَّهُمْ وَ
اَعْمٰٓى اَبْصَارَهُمْ ﴿٢٣﴾
اَفَلَا يَتَدَبَّرُوْنَ الْقُرْاٰنَ اَمْ عَلٰى قُلُوْبٍ
اَقْفَالُهَا ﴿٢٤﴾
اِنَّ الَّذِيْنَ ارْتَدُّوْا عَلٰٓى اَدْبَارِهِمْ مِّنْۢ
بَعْدِ مَا تَبَيَّنَ لَهُمُ الْهُدَى ۙ الشَّيْطٰنُ
سَوَّلَ لَهُمْ ۭ وَاَمْلٰى لَهُمْ ﴿٢٥﴾
ذٰلِكَ بِاَنَّهُمْ قَالُوْا لِلَّذِيْنَ كَرِهُوْا مَا نَزَّلَ

revealed, "We will obey you in part of (this) matter"; but Allah knows their (inner) secrets.

27. But how (will it be) when the angels take their souls at death, and smite their faces and their backs?

28. This because they followed that which displeased Allah, and they hated Allah's good pleasure; so He made their deeds of no effect.

29. Or do those in whose hearts is a disease, think that Allah will not bring to light all their rancour?

30. Had We so willed, We could have shown them up to thee, and thou shouldst have known them by their marks: but surely thou wilt know them by the tone of their speech! And Allah knows all that ye do.

31. And We shall try you until We test those among you who strive their utmost and persevere in patience; and We shall try your reported (mettle).

32. Those who disbelieve, hinder (men) from the Path of Allah, and resist the Messenger, after Guidance has been clearly shown to them, will not harm Allah in the least, but He will make their deeds of no effect.

33. O ye who believe! obey Allah, and obey the Messenger, and make not vain your deeds!

34. Those who disbelieve, and hinder (men) from the Path of Allah, then die disbelieving,— Allah will not forgive them.

35. Be not weary and faint-hearted, crying for peace, when ye are the Uppermost: for Allah is with you, and will never put you in loss for your (good) deeds.

36. The life of this world is but play and amusement: and if ye believe and guard against evil, he will grant you your recompense, and will not ask you (to give up) your possessions.

یہ اُن سے کہتے ہیں کہ بعض کاموں میں ہم تمہاری بات بھی مانیں گے
اور خدا اُن کے پوشیدہ مشوروں سے واقف ہے ﴿۲۶﴾
تو اُس وقت (اُنکا) کیسا (حال) ہوگا جب فرشتے انکی جان
نکالیں گے اور اُنکے مونہوں اور پیٹھوں پر مارتے جائینگے ﴿۲۷﴾
یہ اسلئے کہ جس چیز سے خدا ناخوش ہے یہ اسکے پیچھے چلے اور اس کی
خوشنودی کو اچھا نہ سمجھے تو اُس نے بھی انکے عملوں کو برباد کر دیا ﴿۲۸﴾
کیا وہ لوگ جنکے دلوں میں بیماری ہے یہ خیال کئے ہوئے ہیں کہ خدا
اُن کے کینوں کو ظاہر نہیں کرے گا؟ ﴿۲۹﴾
اور اگر ہم چاہتے تو وہ لوگ تم کو دکھا بھی دیتے اور تم اُن کو
اُنکے چہروں ہی سے پہچان لیتے۔ اور تم انہیں (اُنکے) انداز گفتگو
ہی سے پہچان لوگے۔ اور خدا تمہارے اعمال سے واقف ہے ﴿۳۰﴾
اور ہم تم لوگوں کو آزمائینگے تاکہ جو تم میں لڑائی کرنیوالے اور ثابت قدم
رہنے والے ہیں انکو معلوم کریں۔ اور تمہارے حالات جانچ لیں ﴿۳۱﴾
جن لوگوں کو سیدھا رستہ معلوم ہو گیا (اور) پھر بھی انہوں نے کفر کیا
اور (لوگوں کو) خدا کی راہ سے روکا اور پیغمبر کی مخالفت کی وہ
خدا کا کچھ بھی بگاڑ نہیں سکیں گے۔ اور خدا اُن کا سب کیا
کرایا اکارت کر دے گا ﴿۳۲﴾
مومنو! خدا کا ارشاد مانو اور پیغمبر کی فرمانبرداری کرو اور اپنے
عملوں کو ضائع نہ ہونے دو ﴿۳۳﴾
جو لوگ کافر ہوئے اور خدا کے رستے سے روکتے
رہے پھر کافر ہی مر گئے خدا اُن کو ہرگز نہیں
بخشے گا ﴿۳۴﴾
تو تم ہمت نہ ہارو اور (دشمنوں کو) صلح کی طرف نہ بلاؤ۔ اور تم تو غالب ہو
اور خدا تمہارے ساتھ ہے وہ ہرگز تمہارے اعمال کو کم (اور گم) نہیں کریگا ﴿۳۵﴾
دنیا کی زندگی تو محض کھیل اور تماشا ہے۔ اور اگر تم ایمان لاؤ گے
اور پرہیزگاری کرو گے تو وہ تم کو تمہارا اجر دے گا۔ اور تم سے
تمہارا مال طلب نہیں کرے گا ﴿۳۶﴾

اللّٰهِ سَنُطِيعُكُمْ فِي بَعْضِ الْأَمْرِ ۖ وَاللّٰهُ
يَعْلَمُ إِسْرَارَهُمْ ﴿٢٦﴾
فَكَيْفَ إِذَا تَوَفَّتْهُمُ الْمَلٰٓئِكَةُ يَضْرِبُونَ
وُجُوهَهُمْ وَأَدْبَارَهُمْ ﴿٢٧﴾
ذٰلِكَ بِأَنَّهُمُ اتَّبَعُوا مَا أَسْخَطَ اللّٰهَ وَ
ع كَرِهُوا رِضْوَانَهُ فَأَحْبَطَ أَعْمَالَهُمْ ﴿٢٨﴾
أَمْ حَسِبَ الَّذِينَ فِي قُلُوبِهِمْ مَرَضٌ
أَنْ لَنْ يُخْرِجَ اللّٰهُ أَضْغَانَهُمْ ﴿٢٩﴾
وَلَوْ نَشَاءُ لَأَرَيْنٰكَهُمْ فَلَعَرَفْتَهُمْ بِسِيمٰهُمْ ۚ
وَلَتَعْرِفَنَّهُمْ فِي لَحْنِ الْقَوْلِ ۚ وَاللّٰهُ
يَعْلَمُ أَعْمَالَكُمْ ﴿٣٠﴾
وَلَنَبْلُوَنَّكُمْ حَتّٰى نَعْلَمَ الْمُجٰهِدِينَ
مِنْكُمْ وَالصّٰبِرِينَ ۙ وَنَبْلُوَا أَخْبَارَكُمْ ﴿٣١﴾
إِنَّ الَّذِينَ كَفَرُوا وَصَدُّوا عَنْ سَبِيلِ
اللّٰهِ وَشَاقُّوا الرَّسُولَ مِنْ بَعْدِ مَا تَبَيَّنَ
لَهُمُ الْهُدٰى ۙ لَنْ يَضُرُّوا اللّٰهَ شَيْئًا ۗ وَ
سَيُحْبِطُ أَعْمَالَهُمْ ﴿٣٢﴾
يٰٓأَيُّهَا الَّذِينَ آمَنُوٓا أَطِيعُوا اللّٰهَ وَأَطِيعُوا
الرَّسُولَ وَلَا تُبْطِلُوٓا أَعْمَالَكُمْ ﴿٣٣﴾
إِنَّ الَّذِينَ كَفَرُوا وَصَدُّوا عَنْ سَبِيلِ
اللّٰهِ ثُمَّ مَاتُوا وَهُمْ كُفَّارٌ فَلَنْ يَغْفِرَ
اللّٰهُ لَهُمْ ﴿٣٤﴾
فَلَا تَهِنُوا وَتَدْعُوٓا إِلَى السَّلْمِ ۖ وَأَنْتُمُ
الْأَعْلَوْنَ ۖ وَاللّٰهُ مَعَكُمْ وَلَنْ يَتِرَكُمْ أَعْمَالَكُمْ ﴿٣٥﴾
إِنَّمَا الْحَيٰوةُ الدُّنْيَا لَعِبٌ وَلَهْوٌ ۚ وَإِنْ
تُؤْمِنُوا وَتَتَّقُوا يُؤْتِكُمْ أُجُورَكُمْ وَلَا
يَسْأَلْكُمْ أَمْوَالَكُمْ ﴿٣٦﴾

SÛRA–48
AL-FAT-Ḥ
(INTRODUCTION)

1. This is the second of the group of three Madinah Sûras described in the Introduction to S. 47. Its date is fixed by the mention of the Treaty of Ḥudaibîya, Ẓul-qa'd A.H. 6=Feb. 628.

2. Ḥudaibîya is a plain, a short day's march to the north of Makkah, a little to the west of the Madinah-Makkah road, as used in the Prophet's time. Six years had passed since the Prophet had left his beloved City, and it had been in the hands of the Pagan autocracy. But Islam had grown during these six years. Its Qibla was towards the Ka'ba. The Pagans had tried to attack Islam at various times and had been foiled. By Arab custom every Arab was entitled to visit the Sacred Enclosure unarmed, and fighting of any kind was prohibited during the Sacred Months which included the month of Ẓul-qa'd. In Ẓul-qa'd A.H. 6, therefore, the Prophet desired to perform the 'Umra or lesser Pilgrimage, unarmed but accompanied with his followers. A large following joined him, to the number of fourteen to fiften hundred.

3. This was not to the liking of the Pagan autocracy at Makkah, which took alarm, and in breach of all Arab tradition and usage, prepared to prevent the peaceful party from performing the rites of Pilgrimage. They marched out to fight the unarmed party. The Prophet turned a little to the west of the road, and encamped at Ḥudaibîya, where negotiations took place. On the one hand the Prophet was unwilling to give the Quraish any pretended excuse for violence in the Sacred Territory; on the other, the Quraish had learnt, by six years' bitter experience, that their power was crumbling on all sides, and Islam was growing with its moral aud spiritual forces, which were also reflected in its powers of organisation and resistance. The enthusiasm with which the Covenant of Fealty was entered into under a tree in Ḥudaibîya (48: 18) by that great multitude united in devotion to their great leader, was evidence of the great power which he commanded even in a worldly sense if the Quraish had chosen to try conclusions with him.

4. A peaceful Treaty was therefore concluded, known as the Treaty of Ḥudaibîya. It stipulated: (1) that there was to be peace between the parties for ten years; (2) that any tribe or person was free to join either party or make an alliance with it; (3) that if a Quraish person from Makkah, under guardianship, should join the Prophet without the guardian's permission, he (or she) should be sent back to the guardian, but in the contrary case, they should not be sent back; and (4) that the Prophet and his party were not to enter Makkah that year, but that they could enter unarmed the following year.

5. Item (3), not being reciprocal was objected to in the Muslim camp, but it really was of little importance. Muslims under guardianship, sent back to Makkah, were not likely to renounce the blessings of Islam: on the other hand, Muslims going to Makkah would be centers of influence for Islam, and it was more important that they should be allowed to remain there than that they should be sent back to Madinah. It was impossible to think that there whould be apostates or renegades to Paganism! "Look on this picture, and on that!"

6. The Muslims faithfully observed the terms of the Treaty. The following year (A.H. 7) they performed the lesser Pilgrimage in great state for three days. It is true that the Makkans later on broke the Peace in the attack which one of their allied tribes (the Banû Bakr) made on the Muslim Banû Khuzã'a (who were in alliance with the Prophet), but this led to the conquest of Makkah and the sweeping away of the autocracy. Meanwhile Ḥudaibîya was a great victory, moral and social, as well as political, and its lessons are expounded in this Sûra, as the lessons of Badr were expounded in 8: 42-48, and of Uḥud in 3: 121-129, 149-180.

37. If He were to ask you for all of them, and press you, ye would covetously withhold, and He would bring out all your ill-feeling.

38. Behold, ye are those invited to spend (of your substance) in the Way of Allah: but among you are some that are niggardly. But any who are niggardly are so at the expense of their own souls. But Allah is free of all wants, and it is ye that are needy. If ye turn back (from the Path), He will substitute in your stead another people; then they would not be like you!

اگر وہ تم سے مال طلب کرے اور تمہیں تنگ کرے تو تم بخل
کرنے لگو اور وہ (بخل) تمہاری بدنیتی ظاہر کر کے رہے ﴿۳۷﴾
دیکھو تم وہ لوگ ہو کہ خدا کی راہ میں خرچ کرنے کیلئے بلائے جاتے ہو
تو تم میں ایسے شخص بھی ہیں جو بخل کرنے لگتے ہیں۔ اور جو بخل کرتا ہے
اپنے آپ سے بخل کرتا ہے اور خدا بےنیاز ہے اور تم محتاج۔ اور اگر تم
منہ پھیرو گے تو وہ تمہاری جگہ اور لوگوں کو لے آئے گا اور وہ
تمہاری طرح کے نہیں ہوں گے ﴿۳۸﴾

إِنْ يَسْأَلْكُمُوهَا فَيُحْفِكُمْ تَبْخَلُوا وَ
يُخْرِجْ أَضْغَانَكُمْ ﴿٣٧﴾
هَا أَنْتُمْ هَٰؤُلَاءِ تُدْعَوْنَ لِتُنْفِقُوا فِي
سَبِيلِ اللَّهِ فَمِنْكُمْ مَنْ يَبْخَلُ وَمَنْ
يَبْخَلْ فَإِنَّمَا يَبْخَلُ عَنْ نَفْسِهِ وَاللَّهُ
الْغَنِيُّ وَأَنْتُمُ الْفُقَرَاءُ وَإِنْ تَتَوَلَّوْا يَسْتَبْدِلْ
قَوْمًا غَيْرَكُمْ ثُمَّ لَا يَكُونُوا أَمْثَالَكُمْ ﴿٣٨﴾

Al-Fat-ḥ or Victory

سورۂ فتح مدنی ہے اس میں انتیس آیتیں اور چار رکوع ہیں

سُورَةُ الْفَتْحِ مَدَنِيَّةٌ وَهِيَ تِسْعٌ وَعِشْرُونَ آيَةً وَأَرْبَعُ رُكُوعَاتٍ

In the name of Allah, Most Gracious Most Merciful.

1. Verily We have granted thee a manifest Victory:

2. That Allah may forgive thee thy faults of the past and those to follow; fulfil His favour to thee; and guide thee on the Straight Way;

3. And that Allah may help thee with powerful help.

4. It is He Who sent down Tranquillity into the hearts of the Believers, that they may add Faith to their Faith;— for to Allah belong the Forces of the heavens and the earth; and Allah is Full of Knowledge and Wisdom;—

5. That He may admit the men and women who believe, to Gardens beneath which rivers flow, to dwell therein for aye, and remove their sins from them;—and that is, in the sight of Allah, the grand triumph,

6. And that He may punish the Hypocrites, men and women, and the Polytheists, men and women, who think an evil thought of Allah. On them is a round of Evil: the Wrath of Allah is on them: He has cursed them and got Hell ready for them: and evil is it for a destination.

شروع خدا کا نام لے کر جو بڑا مہربان نہایت رحم والا ہے
(اے محمدؐ) ہم نے تم کو فتح دی فتح بھی صریح و صاف ﴿۱﴾
تاکہ خدا تمہارے اگلے اور پچھلے گناہ بخش دے
اور تم پر اپنی نعمت پوری کر دے اور تم کو سیدھے
رستے چلائے ﴿۲﴾
اور خدا تمہاری زبردست مدد کرے ﴿۳﴾
وہی تو ہے جس نے مومنوں کے دلوں پر تسلی نازل فرمائی
تاکہ ان کے ایمان کے ساتھ اور ایمان بڑھے۔ اور آسمانوں
اور زمین کے لشکر (سب) خدا ہی کے ہیں۔ اور خدا
جاننے والا (اور) حکمت والا ہے ﴿۴﴾
(یہ) اس لئے کہ وہ مومن مردوں اور مومن عورتوں کو بہشتوں میں
جن کے نیچے نہریں بہ رہی ہیں داخل کرے وہ اُس میں ہمیشہ
رہیں گے اور ان سے ان کے گناہوں کو دور کر دے۔ اور یہ
خدا کے نزدیک بڑی کامیابی ہے ﴿۵﴾
اور (اس لئے کہ) منافق مردوں اور منافق عورتوں اور مشرک
مردوں اور مشرک عورتوں کو جو خدا کے حق میں برے برے
خیال رکھتے ہیں عذاب دے۔ انہی پر برے حادثے واقع ہوں۔
اور خدا ان پر غصے ہوا اور ان پر لعنت کی اور ان کے لئے
دوزخ تیار کی۔ اور وہ بری جگہ ہے ﴿۶﴾

بِسْمِ اللَّهِ الرَّحْمَٰنِ الرَّحِيمِ
إِنَّا فَتَحْنَا لَكَ فَتْحًا مُبِينًا ﴿١﴾
لِيَغْفِرَ لَكَ اللَّهُ مَا تَقَدَّمَ مِنْ ذَنْبِكَ
وَمَا تَأَخَّرَ وَيُتِمَّ نِعْمَتَهُ عَلَيْكَ وَ
يَهْدِيَكَ صِرَاطًا مُسْتَقِيمًا ﴿٢﴾
وَيَنْصُرَكَ اللَّهُ نَصْرًا عَزِيزًا ﴿٣﴾
هُوَ الَّذِي أَنْزَلَ السَّكِينَةَ فِي قُلُوبِ
الْمُؤْمِنِينَ لِيَزْدَادُوا إِيمَانًا مَعَ إِيمَانِهِمْ
وَلِلَّهِ جُنُودُ السَّمَاوَاتِ وَالْأَرْضِ وَكَانَ
اللَّهُ عَلِيمًا حَكِيمًا ﴿٤﴾
لِيُدْخِلَ الْمُؤْمِنِينَ وَالْمُؤْمِنَاتِ جَنَّاتٍ
تَجْرِي مِنْ تَحْتِهَا الْأَنْهَارُ خَالِدِينَ فِيهَا
وَيُكَفِّرَ عَنْهُمْ سَيِّئَاتِهِمْ وَكَانَ ذَٰلِكَ
عِنْدَ اللَّهِ فَوْزًا عَظِيمًا ﴿٥﴾
وَيُعَذِّبَ الْمُنَافِقِينَ وَالْمُنَافِقَاتِ وَ
الْمُشْرِكِينَ وَالْمُشْرِكَاتِ الظَّانِّينَ بِاللَّهِ
ظَنَّ السَّوْءِ عَلَيْهِمْ دَائِرَةُ السَّوْءِ وَ
غَضِبَ اللَّهُ عَلَيْهِمْ وَلَعَنَهُمْ وَأَعَدَّ لَهُمْ
جَهَنَّمَ وَسَاءَتْ مَصِيرًا ﴿٦﴾

7. For to Allah belong the Forces of the heavens and the earth; and Allah is exalted in Power, Full of Wisdom.

8. We have truly sent thee as a witness, as a bringer of Glad Tidings, and as a Warner:

9. In order that ye (O men) may believe in Allah and His Messenger, that ye may assist and honour him, and celebrate His praises morning and evening.

10. Verily those who plight their fealty to thee plight their fealty in truth to Allah: the Hand of Allah is over their hands: then anyone who violates his oath, does so to the harm of his own soul, and anyone who fulfils what he has covenanted with Allah,— Allah will soon grant him a great Reward.

11. The desert Arabs who lagged behind will say to thee: "We were engaged in (looking after) our flocks and herds, and our families: do thou then ask forgiveness for us." They say with their tongues what is not in their hearts. Say: "Who then has any power at all (to intervene) on your behalf with Allah, if His Will is to give you some loss or to give you some profit? But Allah is well acquainted with all that ye do.

12. 'Nay ye thought that the Messenger and the Believers would never return to their families; this seemed pleasing in your hearts, and ye conceived an evil thought, for ye are a people doomed to perish."

13. And if any believe not in Allah and His Messenger, We have prepared, for those who reject Allah, a Blazing Fire!

14. To Allah belongs the dominion of the heavens and the earth: He forgives whom He wills, and He punishes whom He wills: but Allah is Oft-Forgiving, Most Merciful.

15. Those who lagged behind (will say), when ye set forth to

اور آسمانوں اور زمین کے لشکر خدا ہی کے ہیں۔ اور خدا
غالب (اور) حکمت والا ہے (۷)
(اور) ہم نے (اے محمدؐ) تم کو حق ظاہر کرنے والا اور خوشخبری
سنانے والا اور خوف دلانے والا (بنا کر) بھیجا ہے (۸)
تاکہ (مسلمانو) تم لوگ خدا پر اور اُس کے پیغمبر پر ایمان لاؤ اور اس کی
مدد کرو اور اُس کو بزرگ سمجھو۔ اور صبح و شام اُس کی تسبیح کرتے رہو (۹)
جو لوگ تم سے بیعت کرتے ہیں وہ خدا سے بیعت کرتے ہیں۔
خدا کا ہاتھ اُن کے ہاتھوں پر ہے۔ پھر جو عہد کو توڑے تو عہد توڑنے کا
نقصان اُسی کو ہے۔ اور جو اس بات کو جس کا اُس نے خدا سے
عہد کیا ہے پورا کرے تو وہ اُسے عنقریب اجر عظیم دے گا (۱۰)
جو گنوار پیچھے رہ گئے وہ تم سے کہیں گے کہ ہم کو ہمارے مال
اور اہل و عیال نے روک رکھا آپ ہمارے لئے (خدا سے) بخشش
مانگیں۔ یہ لوگ اپنی زبان سے وہ بات کہتے ہیں جو اُن کے دل میں
نہیں ہے۔ کہہ دو کہ اگر خدا تم (لوگوں) کو نقصان پہنچانا چاہے
یا تمہیں فائدہ پہنچانے کا ارادہ فرمائے تو کون ہے جو اُس کے سامنے تمہارے
لئے کسی بات کا کچھ اختیار رکھے (کوئی نہیں) بلکہ جو کچھ تم
کرتے ہو خدا اس سے واقف ہے (۱۱)
بات یہ ہے کہ تم لوگ یہ سمجھ بیٹھے تھے کہ پیغمبر اور مومن اپنے
اہل و عیال میں کبھی لوٹ کر آنے ہی کے نہیں۔ اور یہی بات
تمہارے دلوں کو اچھی معلوم ہوئی۔ اور (اسی وجہ سے) تم نے بُرے
بُرے خیال کئے۔ اور (آخرکار) تم ہلاکت میں پڑ گئے (۱۲)
اور جو شخص خدا پر اور اُس کے پیغمبر پر ایمان نہ لائے تو ہم نے (ایسے)
کافروں کے لئے آگ تیار کر رکھی ہے (۱۳)
اور آسمانوں اور زمین کی بادشاہی خدا ہی کی ہے۔ وہ جسے
چاہے بخشے اور جسے چاہے سزا دے۔ اور خدا بخشنے والا
مہربان ہے (۱۴)
جب تم لوگ غنیمتیں لینے چلو گے تو جو لوگ پیچھے رہ گئے

وَلِلّٰهِ جُنُوْدُ السَّمٰوٰتِ وَالْاَرْضِ ۭ وَكَانَ
اللّٰهُ عَزِيْزًا حَكِيْمًا (۷)
اِنَّآ اَرْسَلْنٰكَ شَاهِدًا وَّمُبَشِّرًا وَّ
نَذِيْرًا (۸)
لِّتُؤْمِنُوْا بِاللّٰهِ وَرَسُوْلِهٖ وَتُعَزِّرُوْهُ وَ
تُوَقِّرُوْهُ ۭ وَتُسَبِّحُوْهُ بُكْرَةً وَّاَصِيْلًا (۹)
اِنَّ الَّذِيْنَ يُبَايِعُوْنَكَ اِنَّمَا يُبَايِعُوْنَ
اللّٰهَ ۭ يَدُ اللّٰهِ فَوْقَ اَيْدِيْهِمْ ۚ فَمَنْ نَّكَثَ
فَاِنَّمَا يَنْكُثُ عَلٰي نَفْسِهٖ ۚ وَمَنْ اَوْفٰى بِمَا
عٰهَدَ عَلَيْهُ اللّٰهَ فَسَيُؤْتِيْهِ اَجْرًا عَظِيْمًا (۱۰)
سَيَقُوْلُ لَكَ الْمُخَلَّفُوْنَ مِنَ الْاَعْرَابِ
شَغَلَتْنَآ اَمْوَالُنَا وَاَهْلُوْنَا فَاسْتَغْفِرْ لَنَا ۚ
يَقُوْلُوْنَ بِاَلْسِنَتِهِمْ مَّا لَيْسَ فِيْ قُلُوْبِهِمْ ۭ
قُلْ فَمَنْ يَّمْلِكُ لَكُمْ مِّنَ اللّٰهِ
شَيْـًٔا اِنْ اَرَادَ بِكُمْ ضَرًّا اَوْ اَرَادَ بِكُمْ
نَفْعًا ۭ بَلْ كَانَ اللّٰهُ بِمَا تَعْمَلُوْنَ
خَبِيْرًا (۱۱)
بَلْ ظَنَنْتُمْ اَنْ لَّنْ يَّنْقَلِبَ الرَّسُوْلُ
وَالْمُؤْمِنُوْنَ اِلٰٓى اَهْلِيْهِمْ اَبَدًا وَّزُيِّنَ
ذٰلِكَ فِيْ قُلُوْبِكُمْ وَظَنَنْتُمْ ظَنَّ السَّوْءِ ښ
وَكُنْتُمْ قَوْمًۢا بُوْرًا (۱۲)
وَمَنْ لَّمْ يُؤْمِنْ بِاللّٰهِ وَرَسُوْلِهٖ فَاِنَّآ
اَعْتَدْنَا لِلْكٰفِرِيْنَ سَعِيْرًا (۱۳)
وَلِلّٰهِ مُلْكُ السَّمٰوٰتِ وَالْاَرْضِ ۭ يَغْفِرُ
لِمَنْ يَّشَاۗءُ وَيُعَذِّبُ مَنْ يَّشَاۗءُ ۭ وَكَانَ
اللّٰهُ غَفُوْرًا رَّحِيْمًا (۱۴)
سَيَقُوْلُ الْمُخَلَّفُوْنَ اِذَا انْطَلَقْتُمْ اِلٰى

مَغَانِمَ لِتَأْخُذُوهَا ذَرُونَا نَتَّبِعْكُمْ ۚ
يُرِيدُونَ أَنْ يُبَدِّلُوا كَلَامَ اللَّهِ ۚ
قُلْ لَنْ تَتَّبِعُونَا كَذَٰلِكُمْ قَالَ اللَّهُ مِنْ
قَبْلُ ۖ فَسَيَقُولُونَ بَلْ تَحْسُدُونَنَا ۚ
بَلْ كَانُوا لَا يَفْقَهُونَ إِلَّا قَلِيلًا ﴿١٥﴾

تھے وہ کہیں گے ہمیں بھی اجازت دیجئے کہ آپ کے ساتھ
چلیں۔ یہ چاہتے ہیں کہ خدا کے قول کو بدل دیں۔ کہہ دو کہ تم
ہرگز ہمارے ساتھ نہیں چل سکتے۔ اسی طرح خدا نے پہلے سے فرما دیا
ہے۔ پھر کہیں گے (نہیں) تم تو ہم سے حسد کرتے ہو۔ بات یہ ہے
کہ یہ لوگ سمجھتے ہی نہیں مگر بہت کم ﴿١٥﴾

acquire booty (in war): "Permit us to follow you." They wish to change Allah's word: say: "Not thus will ye follow us: Allah has already declared (this) beforehand": then they will say, "But ye are jealous of us." Nay, but little do they understand (such things).

قُلْ لِلْمُخَلَّفِينَ مِنَ الْأَعْرَابِ سَتُدْعَوْنَ
إِلَىٰ قَوْمٍ أُولِي بَأْسٍ شَدِيدٍ تُقَاتِلُونَهُمْ
أَوْ يُسْلِمُونَ ۖ فَإِنْ تُطِيعُوا يُؤْتِكُمُ اللَّهُ
أَجْرًا حَسَنًا ۖ وَإِنْ تَتَوَلَّوْا كَمَا تَوَلَّيْتُمْ
مِنْ قَبْلُ يُعَذِّبْكُمْ عَذَابًا أَلِيمًا ﴿١٦﴾

جو گنوار پیچھے رہ گئے تھے اُن سے کہہ دو کہ تم جلد ایک سخت
جنگجو قوم کے (ساتھ لڑائی کے) لئے بلائے جاؤ گے۔ اُن سے
تم (یا تو) جنگ کرتے رہو گے یا وہ اسلام لے آئیں گے۔ اگر تم حکم مانو گے
تو خدا تم کو اچھا بدلہ دیگا۔ اور اگر منہ پھیر لوگے جیسے پہلی دفعہ پھیرا
تھا تو وہ تم کو بُری تکلیف کی سزا دے گا ﴿١٦﴾

16. Say to the desert Arabs who lagged behind: "Ye shall be summoned (to fight) against a people given to vehement war: then shall ye fight, or they shall submit. Then if ye show obedience, Allah will grant you a goodly reward, but if ye turn back as ye did before, He will punish you with a grievous Chastisement."

لَيْسَ عَلَى الْأَعْمَىٰ حَرَجٌ وَلَا عَلَى الْأَعْرَجِ
حَرَجٌ وَلَا عَلَى الْمَرِيضِ حَرَجٌ ۗ وَمَنْ
يُطِعِ اللَّهَ وَرَسُولَهُ يُدْخِلْهُ جَنَّاتٍ
تَجْرِي مِنْ تَحْتِهَا الْأَنْهَارُ ۖ وَمَنْ يَتَوَلَّ
ع ٢ يُعَذِّبْهُ عَذَابًا أَلِيمًا ﴿١٧﴾

نہ تو اندھے پر گناہ ہے (کہ سفر جنگ سے پیچھے رہ جائے) اور نہ
لنگڑے پر گناہ ہے اور نہ بیمار پر گناہ ہے۔ اور جو شخص خدا اور
اُس کے پیغمبر کے فرمان پر چلے گا خدا اُس کو بہشتوں میں داخل
کریگا جن کے تلے نہریں بہہ رہی ہیں۔ اور جو روگردانی کریگا
اُسے بُرے دُکھ کی سزا دے گا ﴿١٧﴾

17. No blame is there on the blind, nor is there blame on the lame, nor on one ill (if he joins not the war): but he that obeys Allah and His Messenger,—(Allah) will admit him to Gardens beneath which rivers flow; and he who turns back, (Allah) will punish him with a grievous Chastisement.

لَقَدْ رَضِيَ اللَّهُ عَنِ الْمُؤْمِنِينَ إِذْ
يُبَايِعُونَكَ تَحْتَ الشَّجَرَةِ فَعَلِمَ مَا فِي
قُلُوبِهِمْ فَأَنْزَلَ السَّكِينَةَ عَلَيْهِمْ وَ
أَثَابَهُمْ فَتْحًا قَرِيبًا ﴿١٨﴾

(اے پیغمبر) جب مومن تم سے درخت کے نیچے بیعت کر رہے تھے
تو خدا اُن سے خوش ہوا۔ اور جو (صدق و خلوص) اُن کے دلوں
میں تھا وہ اُس نے معلوم کر لیا۔ تو اُن پر تسلی نازل فرمائی اور
اُنہیں جلد فتح عنایت کی ﴿١٨﴾

18. Allah's Good Pleasure was on the Believers when they swore Fealty to thee under the Tree: He knew what was in their hearts, and He sent down Tranquillity to them; and He rewarded them with a speedy Victory;

وَمَغَانِمَ كَثِيرَةً يَأْخُذُونَهَا ۗ وَكَانَ
اللَّهُ عَزِيزًا حَكِيمًا ﴿١٩﴾

اور بہت سی غنیمتیں جو اُنہوں نے حاصل کیں۔ اور خدا
غالب حکمت والا ہے ﴿١٩﴾

19. And many gains will they acquire (besides): and Allah is Exalted in Power, Full of Wisdom.

وَعَدَكُمُ اللَّهُ مَغَانِمَ كَثِيرَةً تَأْخُذُونَهَا
فَعَجَّلَ لَكُمْ هَٰذِهِ وَكَفَّ أَيْدِيَ النَّاسِ
عَنْكُمْ ۚ وَلِتَكُونَ آيَةً لِلْمُؤْمِنِينَ وَ
يَهْدِيَكُمْ صِرَاطًا مُسْتَقِيمًا ﴿٢٠﴾

خدا نے تم سے بہت سی غنیمتوں کا وعدہ فرمایا ہے کہ تم اُن کو
حاصل کرو گے سو اُس نے غنیمت کی تمہارے لئے جلدی فرمائی
اور لوگوں کے ہاتھ تم سے روک دیئے۔ غرض یہ تھی کہ یہ مومنوں کیلئے
(خدا کی) قدرت کا نمونہ ہو اور وہ تم کو سیدھے رستے پر چلائے ﴿٢٠﴾

20. Allah has promised you many gains that ye shall acquire, and He has given you these beforehand; and He has restrained the hands of men from you; that it may be a Sign for the Believers, and that He may guide you to a Straight Path;

وَأُخْرَىٰ لَمْ تَقْدِرُوا عَلَيْهَا قَدْ أَحَاطَ
اللَّهُ بِهَا ۚ وَكَانَ اللَّهُ عَلَىٰ كُلِّ شَيْءٍ قَدِيرًا ﴿٢١﴾

اور اَور غنیمتیں دیں جن پر تم قدرت نہیں رکھتے تھے (اور)
وہ خدا ہی کی قدرت میں تھیں۔ اور خدا ہر چیز پر قادر ہے ﴿٢١﴾

21. And other gains (there are), which are not within your power, but which Allah has compassed: and Allah has power over all things.

22. If the Unbelievers should fight you, they would certainly turn their backs; then would they find neither protector nor helper.

23. (Such has been) the practice of Allah already in the past: no change wilt thou find in the practice of Allah.

24. And it is He Who has restrained their hands from you and your hands from them in the valley of Makkah, after that He gave you the victory over them. And Allah sees well all that ye do.

25. They are the ones who disbelieved and hindered you from the Sacred Mosque and the sacrificial animals, detained from reaching their place of sacrifice. Had there not been believing men and believing women whom ye did not know that ye were trampling down and on whose account a guilt would have accrued to you without (your) knowledge, (Allah would have allowed you to force your way, but He held back your hands) that He may admit to His Mercy whom He will. If they had been apart, We should certainly have punished the Unbelievers among them with a grievous Punishment.

26. While the Unbelievers got up in their hearts heat and cant—the heat and cant of Ignorance,— Allah sent down His Tranquillity to His Messenger and to the Believers, and made them stick close to the command of self-restraint; and well were they entitled to it and worthy of it. And Allah has full knowledge of all things.

27. Truly did Allah fulfil the vision for His Messenger: ye shall enter the Sacred Mosque, if Allah wills, with minds secure, heads shaved, hair cut short, and without fear. For He knew what ye knew not, and He granted, besides this, a speedy victory.

اور اگر تم سے کافر لڑتے تو پیٹھ پھیر کر بھاگ جاتے پھر کسی کو
دوست نہ پاتے اور نہ مددگار ﴿٢٢﴾
(یہی) خدا کی عادت ہے جو پہلے سے چلی آتی ہے۔ اور تم خدا کی
عادت کبھی بدلتی نہ دیکھو گے ﴿٢٣﴾
اور وہی تو ہے جس نے تم کو اُن (کافروں) پر فتحیاب کرنے کے
بعد سرحد مکہ میں اُن کے ہاتھ تم سے اور تمہارے ہاتھ اُن سے
روک دیئے۔ اور جو کچھ تم کرتے ہو خدا اُس کو
دیکھ رہا ہے ﴿٢٤﴾
یہ وہی لوگ ہیں جنہوں نے کفر کیا اور تم کو مسجد حرام سے
روک دیا اور قربانیوں کو بھی کہ اپنی جگہ پہنچنے سے رُکی رہیں۔
اور اگر ایسے مسلمان مرد اور مسلمان عورتیں نہ ہوتیں جن کو تم
جانتے نہ تھے کہ اگر تم اُن کو پامال کر دیتے تو تم کو اُن کی طرف سے
بے خبری میں نقصان پہنچ جاتا۔ (تو بھی تمہارے ہاتھ سے فتح
ہو جاتی مگر تاخیر) اس لئے (ہوئی) کہ خدا اپنی رحمت میں
جس کو چاہے داخل کر لے۔ اور اگر (دونوں فریق) الگ الگ
ہو جاتے تو جو اُن میں کافر تھے اُن کو ہم دُکھ دینے والا عذاب دیتے [ف ٢٦٩] ﴿٢٥﴾
جب کافروں نے اپنے دلوں میں ضد کی اور ضد بھی جاہلیت
کی۔ تو خدا نے اپنے پیغمبر اور مومنوں پر اپنی طرف سے تسکین
نازل فرمائی اور اُن کو پرہیزگاری کی بات پر قائم رکھا اور
وہ اسی کے مستحق اور اہل تھے۔ اور خدا ہر چیز سے
خبردار ہے ﴿٢٦﴾
بے شک خدا نے اپنے پیغمبر کو سچا (اور) صحیح خواب دکھایا۔
کہ تم خدا نے چاہا تو مسجد حرام میں اپنے سر منڈوا کر اور اپنے
بال کتروا کر امن و امان سے داخل ہو گے اور کسی طرح
کا خوف نہ کرو گے۔ جو بات تم نہیں جانتے تھے
اس کو معلوم تھی سو اُس نے اس سے پہلے ہی جلد
فتح کرا دی [ف ٢٧٠] ﴿٢٧﴾

وَلَوْ قٰتَلَكُمُ الَّذِيْنَ كَفَرُوْا لَوَلَّوُا الْاَدْبَارَ
ثُمَّ لَا يَجِدُوْنَ وَلِيًّا وَّلَا نَصِيْرًا ﴿٢٢﴾
سُنَّةَ اللّٰهِ الَّتِيْ قَدْ خَلَتْ مِنْ قَبْلُ ۚۖ
وَلَنْ تَجِدَ لِسُنَّةِ اللّٰهِ تَبْدِيْلًا ﴿٢٣﴾
وَهُوَ الَّذِيْ كَفَّ اَيْدِيَهُمْ عَنْكُمْ وَ
اَيْدِيَكُمْ عَنْهُمْ بِبَطْنِ مَكَّةَ مِنْۢ بَعْدِ
اَنْ اَظْفَرَكُمْ عَلَيْهِمْ ۭ وَكَانَ اللّٰهُ بِمَا تَعْمَلُوْنَ
بَصِيْرًا ﴿٢٤﴾
هُمُ الَّذِيْنَ كَفَرُوْا وَصَدُّوْكُمْ عَنِ
الْمَسْجِدِ الْحَرَامِ وَالْهَدْيَ مَعْكُوْفًا
اَنْ يَّبْلُغَ مَحِلَّهٗ ۭ وَلَوْلَا رِجَالٌ مُّؤْمِنُوْنَ
وَنِسَاۗءٌ مُّؤْمِنٰتٌ لَّمْ تَعْلَمُوْهُمْ اَنْ
تَطَـُٔوْهُمْ فَتُصِيْبَكُمْ مِّنْهُمْ مَّعَرَّةٌۢ بِغَيْرِ
عِلْمٍ ۚ لِيُدْخِلَ اللّٰهُ فِيْ رَحْمَتِهٖ مَنْ يَّشَاۗءُ ۚ
لَوْ تَزَيَّلُوْا لَعَذَّبْنَا الَّذِيْنَ كَفَرُوْا مِنْهُمْ
عَذَابًا اَلِيْمًا ﴿٢٥﴾
اِذْ جَعَلَ الَّذِيْنَ كَفَرُوْا فِيْ قُلُوْبِهِمُ
الْحَمِيَّةَ حَمِيَّةَ الْجَاهِلِيَّةِ فَاَنْزَلَ اللّٰهُ
سَكِيْنَتَهٗ عَلٰي رَسُوْلِهٖ وَعَلَي الْمُؤْمِنِيْنَ
وَاَلْزَمَهُمْ كَلِمَةَ التَّقْوٰى وَكَانُوْٓا اَحَقَّ
بِهَا وَاَهْلَهَا ۭ وَكَانَ اللّٰهُ بِكُلِّ شَيْءٍ عَلِيْمًا ﴿٢٦﴾ ع
لَقَدْ صَدَقَ اللّٰهُ رَسُوْلَهُ الرُّءْيَا بِالْحَقِّ ۚ
لَتَدْخُلُنَّ الْمَسْجِدَ الْحَرَامَ اِنْ شَاۗءَ
اللّٰهُ اٰمِنِيْنَ ۙ مُحَلِّقِيْنَ رُءُوْسَكُمْ وَ
مُقَصِّرِيْنَ ۙ لَا تَخَافُوْنَ ۭ فَعَلِمَ مَا لَمْ
تَعْلَمُوْا فَجَعَلَ مِنْ دُوْنِ ذٰلِكَ فَتْحًا
قَرِيْبًا ﴿٢٧﴾

SÛRA–49
AL-ḤUJURÃT
(INTRODUCTION)

This is the third of the group of three Madinah Sûras, which began with S. 47. See the Introduction to that Sûra.

Its subject-matter is the manners to be observed by the members of the rapidly-growing Muslim community, among themselves and towards its Leader. The key-word "*Ḥujurãt*" (Inner Apartments) occurs in verse 4.

Its date is referred to the Year of Deputations, A.H. 9, when a large number of deputations of all kinds visited Madinah to offer their allegiance to Islam.

28. It is He Who has sent His Messenger with Guidance and the Religion of Truth, to make it prevail over all religion: and enough is Allah for a Witness.

وہی تو ہے جس نے اپنے پیغمبر کو ہدایت (کی کتاب) اور
دین حق دے کر بھیجا۔ تاکہ اُس کو تمام دینوں پر غالب
کرے۔ اور حق ظاہر کرنے کے لئے خدا ہی کافی ہے ﴿٢٨﴾

هُوَ الَّذِيْٓ اَرْسَلَ رَسُوْلَهٗ بِالْهُدٰى وَ
دِيْنِ الْحَقِّ لِيُظْهِرَهٗ عَلَى الدِّيْنِ كُلِّهٖ ؕ
وَكَفٰى بِاللّٰهِ شَهِيْدًا ﴿٢٨﴾

29. Muḥammad is the Messenger of Allah; and those who are with him are strong against Unbelievers, (but) compassionate amongst each other. Thou wilt see them bow and prostrate themselves (in prayer), seeking Grace from Allah and (His) Good Pleasure. On their faces are their marks, (being) the traces of their prostration. This is their similitude in the Taurāt; and their similitude in the Gospel is: Like a seed which sends forth its blade, then makes it strong; it then becomes thick, and it stands on its own stem, (filling) the sowers with wonder and delight. As a result, it fills the Unbelievers with rage at them. Allah has promised those among them who believe and do righteous deeds forgiveness, and a great Reward.

محمد خدا کے پیغمبر ہیں۔ اور جو لوگ اُن کے ساتھ ہیں وہ کافروں
کے حق میں تو سخت ہیں اور آپس میں رحم دل (اے دیکھنے والے)
تو اُن کو دیکھتا ہے کہ (خدا کے آگے) جھکے ہوئے سر بسجود ہیں اور
خدا کا فضل اور اُسکی خوشنودی طلب کر رہے ہیں۔ (کثرت) سجود
کے اثر سے اُنکی پیشانیوں پر نشان پڑے ہوئے ہیں۔ اُنکے یہی اوصاف تورات
میں (مرقوم) ہیں۔ اور یہی اوصاف انجیل میں ہیں۔ (وہ) گویا ایک کھیتی ہیں
جس نے (پہلے زمین سے) اپنی سوئی نکالی۔ پھر اسکو مضبوط کیا پھر موٹی ہوئی اور پھر
اپنی نال پر سیدھی کھڑی ہوگئی اور لگی کھیتی والوں کو خوش کرنے تاکہ کافروں کا
جی جلائے۔ جو لوگ اُنمیں سے ایمان لائے اور نیک عمل کرتے رہے اُن سے خدا نے
گناہوں کی بخشش اور اجر عظیم کا وعدہ کیا ہے ﴿٢٩﴾

مُحَمَّدٌ رَّسُوْلُ اللّٰهِ ؕ وَالَّذِيْنَ مَعَهٗٓ اَشِدَّآءُ
عَلَى الْكُفَّارِ رُحَمَآءُ بَيْنَهُمْ تَرٰىهُمْ رُكَّعًا
سُجَّدًا يَّبْتَغُوْنَ فَضْلًا مِّنَ اللّٰهِ وَرِضْوَانًا ز
سِيْمَاهُمْ فِيْ وُجُوْهِهِمْ مِّنْ اَثَرِ السُّجُوْدِ ؕ
ذٰلِكَ مَثَلُهُمْ فِي التَّوْرٰىةِ ۚۛ وَمَثَلُهُمْ فِي ١٥ مع
الْاِنْجِيْلِ ۚۛ كَزَرْعٍ اَخْرَجَ شَطْـَٔهٗ فَاٰزَرَهٗ عند المتاخرين ١٢
فَاسْتَغْلَظَ فَاسْتَوٰى عَلٰى سُوْقِهٖ يُعْجِبُ
الزُّرَّاعَ لِيَغِيْظَ بِهِمُ الْكُفَّارَ ؕ وَعَدَ اللّٰهُ
الَّذِيْنَ اٰمَنُوْا وَعَمِلُوا الصّٰلِحٰتِ مِنْهُمْ
مَّغْفِرَةً وَّاَجْرًا عَظِيْمًا ﴿٢٩﴾ ع ٣ ١٢

Al-Ḥujurāt, or the Inner Apartments

سورۂ حجرات مدنی ہے اور اس میں اٹھارہ آیتیں اور دو رکوع ہیں

سُوْرَةُ الْحُجُرٰتِ مَدَنِيَّةٌ وَّهِيَ ثَمَانِيْ عَشْرَةَ اٰيَةً وَّفِيْهَا رُكُوْعَانِ

In the name of Allah, Most Gracious, Most Merciful.

شروع خدا کا نام لیکر جو بڑا مہربان نہایت رحم والا ہے

بِسْمِ اللّٰهِ الرَّحْمٰنِ الرَّحِيْمِ

1. O ye who believe! put not yourselves forward before Allah and His Messenger; but fear Allah: for Allah is He Who hears and knows all things.

مومنو! (کسی بات کے جواب میں) خدا اور اُس کے رسول سے
پہلے نہ بول اُٹھا کرو اور خدا سے ڈرتے رہو۔ بےشک خدا
سنتا جانتا ہے ﴿١﴾

يٰٓاَيُّهَا الَّذِيْنَ اٰمَنُوْا لَا تُقَدِّمُوْا بَيْنَ
يَدَيِ اللّٰهِ وَرَسُوْلِهٖ وَاتَّقُوا اللّٰهَ ؕ اِنَّ اللّٰهَ
سَمِيْعٌ عَلِيْمٌ ﴿١﴾

2. O ye who believe! raise not your voices above the voice of the Prophet, nor speak aloud to him in talk, as ye may speak aloud to one another, lest your deeds become vain and ye perceive not.

اے اہل ایمان! اپنی آوازیں پیغمبر کی آواز سے اونچی نہ کرو۔
اور جس طرح آپس میں ایک دوسرے سے زور سے بولتے ہو
(اس طرح) اُن کے روبرو زور سے نہ بولا کرو (ایسا نہ ہو) کہ
تمہارے اعمال ضائع ہوجائیں اور تم کو خبر بھی نہ ہو ﴿٢﴾

يٰٓاَيُّهَا الَّذِيْنَ اٰمَنُوْا لَا تَرْفَعُوْٓا اَصْوَاتَكُمْ
فَوْقَ صَوْتِ النَّبِيِّ وَلَا تَجْهَرُوْا لَهٗ بِالْقَوْلِ
كَجَهْرِ بَعْضِكُمْ لِبَعْضٍ اَنْ تَحْبَطَ اَعْمَالُكُمْ
وَاَنْتُمْ لَا تَشْعُرُوْنَ ﴿٢﴾

3. Those that lower their voice in the Presence of Allah's Messenger,—their hearts has Allah tested for piety: for them is Forgiveness and a great Reward.

جو لوگ پیغمبرِ خدا کے سامنے دبی آواز سے
بولتے ہیں خدا نے اُن کے دل تقوے کے
لئے آزما لئے ہیں۔ اُن کے لئے بخشش اور
اجر عظیم ہے ﴿٣﴾

اِنَّ الَّذِيْنَ يَغُضُّوْنَ اَصْوَاتَهُمْ عِنْدَ
رَسُوْلِ اللّٰهِ اُولٰٓئِكَ الَّذِيْنَ امْتَحَنَ اللّٰهُ
قُلُوْبَهُمْ لِلتَّقْوٰى ؕ لَهُمْ مَّغْفِرَةٌ وَّاَجْرٌ
عَظِيْمٌ ﴿٣﴾

4. Those who shout out to thee from without the Inner Apartments—

جو لوگ تم کو حجروں کے باہر سے آواز دیتے ہیں اُن میں

اِنَّ الَّذِيْنَ يُنَادُوْنَكَ مِنْ وَّرَآءِ الْحُجُرٰتِ

أَكْثَرُهُمْ لَا يَعْقِلُونَ (4)
وَلَوْ أَنَّهُمْ صَبَرُوا حَتّٰى تَخْرُجَ إِلَيْهِمْ
لَكَانَ خَيْرًا لَّهُمْ ۚ وَاللّٰهُ غَفُورٌ
رَّحِيمٌ (5)
يٰٓأَيُّهَا الَّذِينَ آمَنُوٓا إِنْ جَآءَكُمْ فَاسِقٌ
بِنَبَإٍ فَتَبَيَّنُوٓا أَنْ تُصِيبُوا قَوْمًا بِجَهَالَةٍ
فَتُصْبِحُوا عَلٰى مَا فَعَلْتُمْ نٰدِمِينَ (6)
وَاعْلَمُوٓا أَنَّ فِيكُمْ رَسُولَ اللّٰهِ ۚ لَوْ يُطِيعُكُمْ
فِي كَثِيرٍ مِّنَ الْأَمْرِ لَعَنِتُّمْ وَلٰكِنَّ اللّٰهَ
حَبَّبَ إِلَيْكُمُ الْإِيمَانَ وَزَيَّنَهُ فِي قُلُوبِكُمْ
وَكَرَّهَ إِلَيْكُمُ الْكُفْرَ وَالْفُسُوقَ وَالْعِصْيَانَ ۚ
أُولٰٓئِكَ هُمُ الرّٰشِدُونَ (7)
فَضْلًا مِّنَ اللّٰهِ وَنِعْمَةً ۚ وَاللّٰهُ عَلِيمٌ
حَكِيمٌ (8)
وَإِنْ طَآئِفَتَانِ مِنَ الْمُؤْمِنِينَ اقْتَتَلُوا
فَأَصْلِحُوا بَيْنَهُمَا ۖ فَإِنْ بَغَتْ إِحْدٰىهُمَا عَلَى
الْأُخْرٰى فَقٰتِلُوا الَّتِي تَبْغِي حَتّٰى تَفِيٓءَ
إِلٰىٓ أَمْرِ اللّٰهِ ۚ فَإِنْ فَآءَتْ فَأَصْلِحُوا بَيْنَهُمَا
بِالْعَدْلِ وَأَقْسِطُوا ۖ إِنَّ اللّٰهَ يُحِبُّ
الْمُقْسِطِينَ (9)
إِنَّمَا الْمُؤْمِنُونَ إِخْوَةٌ فَأَصْلِحُوا بَيْنَ
أَخَوَيْكُمْ ۚ وَاتَّقُوا اللّٰهَ لَعَلَّكُمْ تُرْحَمُونَ (10)
يٰٓأَيُّهَا الَّذِينَ آمَنُوا لَا يَسْخَرْ قَوْمٌ مِّنْ
قَوْمٍ عَسٰىٓ أَنْ يَكُونُوا خَيْرًا مِّنْهُمْ وَلَا
نِسَآءٌ مِّنْ نِّسَآءٍ عَسٰىٓ أَنْ يَكُنَّ خَيْرًا
مِّنْهُنَّ ۚ وَلَا تَلْمِزُوٓا أَنْفُسَكُمْ وَلَا تَنَابَزُوا
بِالْأَلْقَابِ ۖ بِئْسَ الِاسْمُ الْفُسُوقُ بَعْدَ

اکثر بے عقل ہیں (۴)
اور اگر وہ صبر کئے رہتے یہاں تک کہ تم خود نکل کر اُن
کے پاس آتے تو یہ اُن کے لئے بہتر تھا۔ اور خدا تو
بخشنے والا مہربان ہے (۵)
مومنو! اگر کوئی بدکردار تمہارے پاس کوئی خبر لیکر آئے تو خوب
تحقیق کر لیا کرو (مبادا) کہ کسی قوم کو نادانی سے نقصان
پہنچا دو۔ پھر تم کو اپنے کئے پر نادم ہونا پڑے (۶)
اور جان رکھو کہ تم میں خدا کے پیغمبر ہیں۔ اگر بہت سی
باتوں میں وہ تمہارا کہا مان لیا کریں تو تم مشکل میں پڑ جاؤ۔
لیکن خدا نے تم کو ایمان عزیز بنا دیا اور اُس کو تمہارے دلوں
میں سجا دیا اور کفر اور گناہ اور نافرمانی سے تم کو بیزار کر دیا۔ یہی
لوگ راہِ ہدایت پر ہیں (۷)
(یعنی) خدا کے فضل اور احسان سے۔ اور خدا جاننے والا
(اور) حکمت والا ہے (۸)
اور اگر مومنوں میں سے کوئی دو فریق آپس میں لڑ پڑیں
تو اُن میں صلح کرا دو۔ اور اگر ایک فریق دوسرے پر زیادتی
کرے تو زیادتی کرنے والے سے لڑو یہاں تک کہ وہ خدا کے
حکم کی طرف رجوع لائے۔ پس جب وہ رجوع لائے تو دونوں
فریق میں مساوات کے ساتھ صلح کرا دو اور انصاف سے کام لو
کہ خدا انصاف کرنے والوں کو پسند کرتا ہے (۹)
مومن تو آپس میں بھائی بھائی ہیں۔ تو اپنے دو بھائیوں میں
صلح کرا دیا کرو اور خدا سے ڈرتے رہو تاکہ تم پر رحمت کی جائے (۱۰)
مومنو! کوئی قوم کسی قوم سے تمسخر نہ کرے ممکن ہے کہ وہ لوگ
اُن سے بہتر ہوں اور نہ عورتیں عورتوں سے (تمسخر کریں)
ممکن ہے کہ وہ اُن سے اچھی ہوں۔ اور اپنے (مومن
بھائی) کو عیب نہ لگاؤ اور نہ ایک دوسرے کا بُرا نام رکھو
ایمان لانے کے بعد بُرا نام (رکھنا) گناہ ہے ۲۷ اور جو توبہ نہ

most of them lack understanding.

5. If only they had patience until thou couldst come out to them, it would be best for them: but Allah is Oft-Forgiving, Most Merciful.

6. O ye who believe! if a sinner comes to you with any news, ascertain the truth, lest ye harm people unwittingly, and afterwards become full of repentance for what ye have done.

7. And know that among you is Allah's Messenger: were he, in many matters, to follow your (wishes), ye would certainly suffer: but Allah has endeared the Faith to you, and has made it beautiful in your hearts, and He has made hateful to you unbelief, wrongdoing, and rebellion: such indeed are those who walk in righteousness;—

8. A grace and favour from Allah; and Allah is Full of Knowledge and Wisdom.

9. If two parties among the Believers fall into a fight, make ye peace between them: but if one of them transgresses beyond bounds against the other, then fight ye (all) against the one that transgresses until it complies with the command of Allah; but if it complies, then make peace between them with justice, and be fair: for Allah loves those who are fair (and just).

10. The Believers are but a single Brotherhood: So make peace and reconciliation between your two (contending) brothers; and fear Allah, that ye may receive Mercy.

11. O ye who believe! Let not some men among you laugh at others: it may be that the (latter) are better than the (former): nor let some women laugh at others: it may be that the (latter) are better than the (former): nor defame nor be sarcastic to each other, nor call each other by (offensive) nicknames: ill-seeming is a name connoting wickedness, (to

be used of one) after he has believed: and those who do not desist are (indeed) doing wrong.

12. O ye who believe! avoid suspicion as much (as possible): for suspicion in some cases is a sin: and spy not on each other, nor speak ill of each other behind their backs. Would any of you like to eat the flesh of his dead brother? Nay, ye would abhor it... But fear Allah: for Allah is Oft-Returning, Most Merciful.

13. O mankind! We created you from a single (pair) of a male and a female, and made you into nations and tribes, that ye may know each other (not that ye may despise (each other). Verily the most honoured of you in the sight of Allah is (he who is) the most righteous of you. And Allah has full knowledge and is well acquainted (with all things).

14. The desert Arabs say, "We believe." Say, "Ye have no faith; but ye (only) say, 'We have submitted our wills to Allah,' for not yet has Faith entered your hearts. But if ye obey Allah and His Messenger, He will not belittle aught of your deeds: for Allah is Oft-Forgiving, Most Merciful."

15. Only those are Believers who have believed in Allah and His Messenger, and have never since doubted, but have striven with their belongings and their persons in the Cause of Allah: such are the sincere ones.

16. Say: "What! Will ye tell Allah about your religion? But Allah knows all that is in the heavens and on earth: He has full knowledge of all things.

17. They impress on thee as a favour that they have embraced Islam. Say, "Count not your Islam as a favour upon me: nay, Allah has conferred a favour upon you that He has guided you to the Faith, if ye be true and sincere.

18. "Verily Allah knows the Unseen of the heavens and the

کریں وہ ظالم ہیں (١١)
اے اہل ایمان! بہت گمان کرنے سے احتراز کرو کہ
بعض گمان گناہ ہیں اور ایک دوسرے کے حال کا تجسس
نہ کیا کرو اور نہ کوئی کسی کی غیبت کرے. کیا تم میں سے
کوئی اس بات کو پسند کرے گا کہ اپنے مرے ہوئے بھائی کا گوشت
کھائے؟ اس سے تو تم ضرور نفرت کرو گے. (تو غیبت نہ کرو) اور
خدا کا ڈر رکھو. بیشک خدا توبہ قبول کرنے والا مہربان ہے (١٢)
لوگو! ہم نے تم کو ایک مرد اور ایک عورت سے پیدا کیا اور
تمہاری قومیں اور قبیلے بنائے. تاکہ ایک دوسرے کو شناخت
کرو. (اور) خدا کے نزدیک تم میں زیادہ عزت والا وہ ہے جو
زیادہ پرہیزگار ہے. بیشک خدا سب کچھ جاننے والا (اور) سب سے خبردار ہے (١٣)
دیہاتی کہتے ہیں کہ ہم ایمان لے آئے. کہہ دو کہ تم ایمان نہیں لائے
(بلکہ یوں) کہو کہ ہم اسلام لائے ہیں اور ایمان تو ہنوز تمہارے
دلوں میں داخل ہی نہیں ہوا. اور اگر تم خدا اور اسکے رسول کی
فرمانبرداری کرو گے تو خدا تمہارے اعمال میں سے کچھ کم نہیں
کرے گا. بیشک خدا بخشنے والا مہربان ہے (١٤)
مومن تو وہ ہیں جو خدا اور اس کے رسول پر ایمان
لائے پھر شک میں نہ پڑے اور خدا کی راہ میں
جان اور مال سے لڑے. یہی لوگ (ایمان کے)
سچے ہیں (١٥)
ان سے کہو کیا تم خدا کو اپنی دینداری جتلاتے ہو.
اور خدا تو آسمانوں اور زمین کی سب چیزوں سے واقف
ہے. اور خدا ہر شے کو جانتا ہے (١٦)
یہ لوگ تم پر احسان رکھتے ہیں کہ مسلمان ہو گئے ہیں. کہہ دو کہ
اپنے مسلمان ہونے کا مجھ پر احسان نہ رکھو بلکہ خدا تم پر احسان رکھتا ہے
کہ اس نے تمہیں ایمان کا رستہ دکھایا بشرطیکہ تم سچے (مسلمان) ہو (١٧)
بے شک خدا آسمانوں اور زمین کی پوشیدہ باتوں کو جانتا ہے

الْإِيمَانِ ۚ وَمَن لَّمْ يَتُبْ فَأُولَٰئِكَ هُمُ الظَّالِمُونَ (١١)
يَا أَيُّهَا الَّذِينَ آمَنُوا اجْتَنِبُوا كَثِيرًا مِّنَ
الظَّنِّ إِنَّ بَعْضَ الظَّنِّ إِثْمٌ ۖ وَلَا
تَجَسَّسُوا وَلَا يَغْتَب بَّعْضُكُم بَعْضًا ۚ
أَيُحِبُّ أَحَدُكُمْ أَن يَأْكُلَ لَحْمَ أَخِيهِ
مَيْتًا فَكَرِهْتُمُوهُ ۚ وَاتَّقُوا اللَّهَ ۚ إِنَّ اللَّهَ
تَوَّابٌ رَّحِيمٌ (١٢)
يَا أَيُّهَا النَّاسُ إِنَّا خَلَقْنَاكُم مِّن ذَكَرٍ
وَأُنثَىٰ وَجَعَلْنَاكُمْ شُعُوبًا وَقَبَائِلَ
لِتَعَارَفُوا ۚ إِنَّ أَكْرَمَكُمْ عِندَ اللَّهِ أَتْقَاكُمْ ۚ
إِنَّ اللَّهَ عَلِيمٌ خَبِيرٌ (١٣)
قَالَتِ الْأَعْرَابُ آمَنَّا ۖ قُل لَّمْ تُؤْمِنُوا
وَلَٰكِن قُولُوا أَسْلَمْنَا وَلَمَّا يَدْخُلِ الْإِيمَانُ
فِي قُلُوبِكُمْ ۖ وَإِن تُطِيعُوا اللَّهَ وَرَسُولَهُ
لَا يَلِتْكُم مِّنْ أَعْمَالِكُمْ شَيْئًا ۚ إِنَّ اللَّهَ
غَفُورٌ رَّحِيمٌ (١٤)
إِنَّمَا الْمُؤْمِنُونَ الَّذِينَ آمَنُوا بِاللَّهِ وَ
رَسُولِهِ ثُمَّ لَمْ يَرْتَابُوا وَجَاهَدُوا بِأَمْوَالِهِمْ
وَأَنفُسِهِمْ فِي سَبِيلِ اللَّهِ ۚ أُولَٰئِكَ هُمُ
الصَّادِقُونَ (١٥)
قُلْ أَتُعَلِّمُونَ اللَّهَ بِدِينِكُمْ وَاللَّهُ يَعْلَمُ
مَا فِي السَّمَاوَاتِ وَمَا فِي الْأَرْضِ ۚ وَاللَّهُ بِكُلِّ
شَيْءٍ عَلِيمٌ (١٦)
يَمُنُّونَ عَلَيْكَ أَنْ أَسْلَمُوا ۖ قُل لَّا تَمُنُّوا
عَلَيَّ إِسْلَامَكُم ۖ بَلِ اللَّهُ يَمُنُّ عَلَيْكُمْ أَنْ
هَدَاكُمْ لِلْإِيمَانِ إِن كُنتُمْ صَادِقِينَ (١٧)
إِنَّ اللَّهَ يَعْلَمُ غَيْبَ السَّمَاوَاتِ وَالْأَرْضِ ۚ

SÛRA–50
QÃF
(INTRODUCTION)

We now come to a group of seven Makkan Sûras (50-56) dealing with Allah's revelation through nature, through history, and through the mouths of the prophets, and pointing to the Hereafter. We saw that the last group of three (47-49) dealt with the external and internal relations of the Ummat when formed. In the present group our attention is more particularly directed to aspects eschatological,—the Future before us when this life is done.

This particular Sûra belongs to the early Makkan period. After an appeal to nature and to the fate of wicked peoples in history, it removes as it were the evil (verse 22) from the Future after death.

وَاللّٰهُ بَصِيۡرٌۢ بِمَا تَعۡمَلُوۡنَ ۱۸

سُوۡرَةُ قٓ مَكِّيَّةٌ وَّهِيَ خَمۡسٌ وَّاَرۡبَعُوۡنَ اٰيَةً وَّثَلٰثُ رُكُوۡعَاتٍ

بِسۡمِ اللّٰهِ الرَّحۡمٰنِ الرَّحِيۡمِ

قٓ وَالۡقُرۡاٰنِ الۡمَجِيۡدِ ۱
بَلۡ عَجِبُوۡۤا اَنۡ جَآءَهُمۡ مُّنۡذِرٌ مِّنۡهُمۡ
فَقَالَ الۡكٰفِرُوۡنَ هٰذَا شَىۡءٌ عَجِيۡبٌ ۲
ءَاِذَا مِتۡنَا وَكُنَّا تُرَابًا ۚ ذٰلِكَ رَجۡعٌ
بَعِيۡدٌ ۳
قَدۡ عَلِمۡنَا مَا تَنۡقُصُ الۡاَرۡضُ مِنۡهُمۡ ۚ وَ
عِنۡدَنَا كِتٰبٌ حَفِيۡظٌ ۴
بَلۡ كَذَّبُوۡا بِالۡحَقِّ لَمَّا جَآءَهُمۡ فَهُمۡ فِىۡۤ
اَمۡرٍ مَّرِيۡجٍ ۵
اَفَلَمۡ يَنۡظُرُوۡۤا اِلَى السَّمَآءِ فَوۡقَهُمۡ كَيۡفَ
بَنَيۡنٰهَا وَزَيَّنّٰهَا وَمَا لَهَا مِنۡ فُرُوۡجٍ ۶
وَالۡاَرۡضَ مَدَدۡنٰهَا وَاَلۡقَيۡنَا فِيۡهَا رَوَاسِىَ
وَاَنۡۢبَتۡنَا فِيۡهَا مِنۡ كُلِّ زَوۡجٍۢ بَهِيۡجٍ ۷
تَبۡصِرَةً وَّذِكۡرٰى لِكُلِّ عَبۡدٍ مُّنِيۡبٍ ۸
وَنَزَّلۡنَا مِنَ السَّمَآءِ مَآءً مُّبٰرَكًا
فَاَنۡۢبَتۡنَا بِهٖ جَنّٰتٍ وَّحَبَّ الۡحَصِيۡدِ ۹
وَالنَّخۡلَ بٰسِقٰتٍ لَّهَا طَلۡعٌ نَّضِيۡدٌ ۱۰
رِّزۡقًا لِّلۡعِبَادِ ۙ وَاَحۡيَيۡنَا بِهٖ بَلۡدَةً
مَّيۡتًا ؕ كَذٰلِكَ الۡخُرُوۡجُ ۱۱
كَذَّبَتۡ قَبۡلَهُمۡ قَوۡمُ نُوۡحٍ وَّاَصۡحٰبُ الرَّسِّ
وَثَمُوۡدُ ۱۲
وَعَادٌ وَّفِرۡعَوۡنُ وَاِخۡوَانُ لُوۡطٍ ۱۳
وَّاَصۡحٰبُ الۡاَيۡكَةِ وَقَوۡمُ تُبَّعٍ ؕ
كُلٌّ كَذَّبَ الرُّسُلَ فَحَقَّ وَعِيۡدِ ۱۴

المنزل السابع

اور جو کچھ تم کرتے ہو اُسے دیکھتا ہے ۱۸

سورۂ ق مکی ہے اور اس میں پینتالیس آیتیں اور تین رکوع ہیں

شروع خدا کا نام لے کر جو بڑا مہربان نہایت رحم والا ہے

ق۔ قرآن مجید کی قسم (کہ محمد پیغمبر خدا ہیں) ۱
لیکن ان لوگوں نے تعجب کیا کہ انہی میں سے ایک ہدایت
کرنے والا اُنکے پاس آیا تو کافر کہنے لگے کہ یہ بات تو (بڑی) عجیب ہے ۲
بھلا جب ہم مر گئے اور مٹی ہو گئے (تو پھر زندہ ہوں گے؟)
یہ زندہ ہونا (عقل سے) بعید ہے ۳
اُن کے جسموں کو زمین جتنا (کھا کھا کر) کم کرتی جاتی ہے
ہم کو معلوم ہے۔ اور ہمارے پاس تحریری یادداشت بھی ہے ۴
بلکہ (عجیب بات یہ ہے کہ) جب اُنکے پاس (دین) حق آ پہنچا تو انہوں نے
اسکو جھوٹ سمجھا سو یہ ایک اُلجھی ہوئی بات میں (پڑ رہے) ہیں ۵
کیا انہوں نے اپنے اوپر آسمان کی طرف نگاہ نہیں کی کہ ہم نے اسکو کیونکر
بنایا اور (کیونکر) سجایا اور اس میں کہیں شگاف تک نہیں ۶
اور زمین کو (دیکھو اسے) ہم نے پھیلایا اور اس میں پہاڑ رکھ دیئے
اور اس میں ہر طرح کی خوشنما چیزیں اُگائیں ۷
تاکہ رجوع لانے والے بندے ہدایت اور نصیحت حاصل کریں ۸
اور آسمان سے برکت والا پانی اُتارا اور اس سے باغ و بستان
اُگائے اور کھیتی کا اناج ۹
اور لمبی لمبی کھجوریں جن کا گابھا تہ بہ تہ ہوتا ہے ۱۰
(یہ سب کچھ) بندوں کو روزی دینے کیلئے (کیا ہے) اور اُس (پانی) سے ہم نے
شہر مردہ (یعنی زمین اُفتادہ) کو زندہ کیا۔ (بس) اسی طرح (قیامت کے روز) نکل پڑنا ہے ۱۱
اُن سے پہلے نوح کی قوم اور کنوئیں والے اور ثمود جھٹلا چکے
ہیں ۱۲
اور عاد اور فرعون اور لوط کے بھائی ۱۳
اور بن کے رہنے والے اور تبع کی قوم۔ (غرض) ان سب نے
پیغمبروں کو جھٹلایا تو ہمارا وعید بھی پورا ہو کر رہا ۱۴

earth: and Allah sees well all that ye do."

QÃF

In the name of Allah, Most Gracious, Most Merciful.

1. Qaf: By the Glorious Qur'ãn (thou art Allah's Messenger).

2. But they wonder that there has come to them a Warner from among themselves. So the Unbelievers say:" "This is a wonderful thing!"

3. "What! When we die and become dust, (shall we live again?) That is a (sort of) Return far (from our understanding)."

4. We already know how much of them the earth takes away: with Us is a Record guarding (the full account).

5. But they deny the truth when it comes to them: so they are in a confused state.

6. Do they not look at the sky above them?—How We have made it and adorned it, and there are no flaws in it?

7. And the earth—We have spread it out, and set thereon mountains standing firm, and produced therein every kind of beautiful growth (in pairs)—

8. For an insight and Reminder to every servant turning (to Allah).

9. And We send down from the sky Rain charged with blessing, and We produce therewith Gardens and Grain for harvests;

10. And tall (and stately) Palm-trees, with shoots of fruit-stalks, piled one over another;—

11. As sustenance for (Allah's) Servants;— and We give (new) life therewith to land that is dead: thus will be the Resurrection.

12. Before them was denied (the Hereafter) by the People of Noah, the Companions of the Rass, the Thamûd,

13. The 'Ãd, Pharaoh, the Brethren of Lûṭ,

14. The Companions of the Wood, and the People of Tubba'; each one (of them) rejected the messengers, and My warning was duly fulfilled (in them).

15. Were We then weary with the first Creation, that they should be in confused doubt about a new Creation?

16. It was We Who created man, and We know what suggestions his soul makes to him: for We are nearer to him than (his) jugular vein.

17. Behold, two (guardian angels) appointed to learn (his doings) learn (and note them), one sitting on the right and one on the left.

18. Not a word does he utter but there is a vigilant Guardian.

19. And the stupor of death comes in truth. "This was the thing which thou wast trying to escape!"

20. And the Trumpet shall be blown: that will be the Day whereof Warning (had been given).

21. And there will come forthevery soul: with each will be an (angel) to drive, and an (angel) to bear witness.

22. (It will be said:) "Thou wast heedless of this; now have We removed thy veil, and sharp is thy sight this Day!"

23. And his Companion will say: "Here is (his Record) ready with me!"

24. (The sentence will be:) "Throw, both of you, into Hell every contumacious Rejecter (of Allah)!—

25. "Who forbade what was good, transgressed all bounds, cast doubts and suspicions;

26. "Who set up another god beside Allah: throw him into a severe Chastisement."

27. His Companion will say: "Our Lord! I did not make him transgress, but he was (himself) far astray."

28. He will say: "Dispute not with each other in My Presence: I had already in advance sent you Warning.

29. "The Word changes not with Me, and I do not the least injustice to My Servants."

30. The Day We will ask Hell, "Art thou filled to the full?" It will say, "Are there any more (to come)?"

کیا ہم پہلی بار پیدا کر کے تھک گئے ہیں؟ (نہیں) بلکہ
یہ از سرِ نو پیدا کرنے میں شک میں (پڑے ہوئے) ہیں ﴿١٥﴾
اور ہم ہی نے انسان کو پیدا کیا ہے اور جو خیالات اُسکے دل میں گزرتے ہیں
ہم اُنکو جانتے ہیں۔ اور ہم اسکی رگِ جان سے بھی اس سے زیادہ قریب ہیں ﴿١٦﴾
جب (وہ کوئی کام کرتا ہے تو) دو لکھنے والے جو دائیں بائیں
بیٹھتے ہیں لکھ لیتے ہیں ﴿١٧﴾
کوئی بات اُس کی زبان پر نہیں آتی مگر ایک نگہبان اُسکے
پاس تیار رہتا ہے ﴿١٨﴾
اور موت کی بیہوشی حقیقت کھولنے کو طاری ہو گئی۔ (اے
انسان) یہی (وہ حالت ہے) جس سے تو بھاگتا تھا ﴿١٩﴾
اور صُور پھونکا جائے گا۔ یہی (عذاب کی) وعید کا دن ہے ﴿٢٠﴾
اور ہر شخص (ہمارے سامنے) آئیگا۔ ایک (فرشتہ) اسکے ساتھ
چلانیوالا ہوگا اور ایک (اسکے عملوں کی) گواہی دینے والا ﴿٢١﴾
(یہ وہ دن ہے کہ) اس سے تُو غافل ہو رہا تھا۔ اب ہم نے تجھ پر سے
پردہ اُٹھا دیا تو آج تیری نگاہ تیز ہے ﴿٢٢﴾
اور اس کا ہمنشین (فرشتہ) کہیگا کہ یہ (اعمال نامہ) میرے پاس حاضر ہے ﴿٢٣﴾
(حکم ہوگا کہ) ہر سرکش ناشکرے کو دوزخ میں ڈال دو ﴿٢٤﴾
جو مال میں بخل کرنیوالا حد سے بڑھنے والا شبہے نکالنے والا تھا ﴿٢٥﴾
جس نے خدا کے ساتھ اور معبود مقرر کر رکھے تھے۔ تو اُس کو
سخت عذاب میں ڈال دو ﴿٢٦﴾
اُس کا ساتھی (شیطان) کہے گا کہ اے ہمارے پروردگار میں نے
اس کو گمراہ نہیں کیا تھا بلکہ یہ آپ ہی رستے سے دُور بھٹکا ہوا تھا ﴿٢٧﴾
(خدا) کہے گا کہ ہمارے حضور میں ردّ و کد نہ کرو۔ ہم تمہارے پاس
پہلے ہی (عذاب کی) وعید بھیج چکے تھے ﴿٢٨﴾
ہمارے ہاں بات بدلا نہیں کرتی اور ہم بندوں پر ظلم نہیں کیا کرتے ﴿٢٩﴾
اُس دن ہم دوزخ سے پوچھیں گے کہ کیا تو بھر گئی؟ وہ
کہے گی کہ کچھ اور بھی ہے؟ ﴿٣٠﴾

أَفَعَيِينَا بِالْخَلْقِ الْأَوَّلِ ۚ بَلْ هُمْ فِي لَبْسٍ
مِّنْ خَلْقٍ جَدِيدٍ ﴿١٥﴾
وَلَقَدْ خَلَقْنَا الْإِنسَانَ وَنَعْلَمُ مَا تُوَسْوِسُ بِهِ
نَفْسُهُ ۖ وَنَحْنُ أَقْرَبُ إِلَيْهِ مِنْ حَبْلِ الْوَرِيدِ ﴿١٦﴾
إِذْ يَتَلَقَّى الْمُتَلَقِّيَانِ عَنِ الْيَمِينِ وَعَنِ
الشِّمَالِ قَعِيدٌ ﴿١٧﴾
مَا يَلْفِظُ مِن قَوْلٍ إِلَّا لَدَيْهِ رَقِيبٌ
عَتِيدٌ ﴿١٨﴾
وَجَاءَتْ سَكْرَةُ الْمَوْتِ بِالْحَقِّ ۖ ذَٰلِكَ
مَا كُنتَ مِنْهُ تَحِيدُ ﴿١٩﴾
وَنُفِخَ فِي الصُّورِ ۚ ذَٰلِكَ يَوْمُ الْوَعِيدِ ﴿٢٠﴾
وَجَاءَتْ كُلُّ نَفْسٍ مَّعَهَا سَائِقٌ وَ
شَهِيدٌ ﴿٢١﴾
لَّقَدْ كُنتَ فِي غَفْلَةٍ مِّنْ هَٰذَا فَكَشَفْنَا
عَنكَ غِطَاءَكَ فَبَصَرُكَ الْيَوْمَ حَدِيدٌ ﴿٢٢﴾
وَقَالَ قَرِينُهُ هَٰذَا مَا لَدَيَّ عَتِيدٌ ﴿٢٣﴾
أَلْقِيَا فِي جَهَنَّمَ كُلَّ كَفَّارٍ عَنِيدٍ ﴿٢٤﴾
مَّنَّاعٍ لِّلْخَيْرِ مُعْتَدٍ مُّرِيبٍ ﴿٢٥﴾
الَّذِي جَعَلَ مَعَ اللَّهِ إِلَٰهًا آخَرَ فَأَلْقِيَاهُ
فِي الْعَذَابِ الشَّدِيدِ ﴿٢٦﴾
قَالَ قَرِينُهُ رَبَّنَا مَا أَطْغَيْتُهُ وَلَٰكِن
كَانَ فِي ضَلَالٍ بَعِيدٍ ﴿٢٧﴾
قَالَ لَا تَخْتَصِمُوا لَدَيَّ وَقَدْ قَدَّمْتُ
إِلَيْكُم بِالْوَعِيدِ ﴿٢٨﴾
مَا يُبَدَّلُ الْقَوْلُ لَدَيَّ وَمَا أَنَا بِظَلَّامٍ لِّلْعَبِيدِ ﴿٢٩﴾
يَوْمَ نَقُولُ لِجَهَنَّمَ هَلِ امْتَلَأْتِ وَتَقُولُ
هَلْ مِن مَّزِيدٍ ﴿٣٠﴾

31. And the Garden will be brought nigh to the Righteous,—no more a thing distant.
32. (A voice will say:) "This is what was promised for you,—for every penitent heedful one,
33. "Who feared the Most Gracious unseen, and brought a heart turned in devotion (to Him):
34. "Enter ye therein in Peace and Security; this is a Day of Eternal Life!"
35. There will be for them therein all that they wish,—and there is more with us.
36. But how many generations before them did We destroy (for their sins),—stronger in power than they? Then did they wander through the land: was there any place of escape (for them)?
37. Verily in this is a Message for any that has a heart and understanding or who gives ear and is a witness.
38. We created the heavens and the earth and all between them in Six Days, nor did any sense of weariness touch Us.

39. Bear, then, with patience, all that they say, and celebrate the praises of thy Lord, before the rising of the sun and before (its) setting,
40. And during part of the night, (also,) celebrate His praises, and (so likewise) after the prostration.
41. And listen the Day when the Caller will call out from a place quite near,—
42. The Day when they will hear a (mighty) Blast in (very) truth: that will be the Day of Resurrection.

43. Verily it is We Who give Life and Death; and to Us is the Final Return—
44. The Day when the Earth will be rent asunder, letting them hurrying out: that will be a gathering together,—quite easy for Us.
45. We know best what they say; and thou art not one to compel them by force. So admonish with the Qur'ãn such as fear My Warning!

اور بہشت پرہیزگاروں کے قریب کر دی جائیگی (کہ مطلق) دور نہ ہوگی (٣١)
یہی وہ چیز ہے جسکا تم سے وعدہ کیا جاتا تھا (یعنی) ہر رجوع لانیوالے حفاظت کرنیوالے سے (٣٢)
جو خدا سے بن دیکھے ڈرتا رہا اور رجوع لانے والا دل لے کر آیا (٣٣)
اس میں سلامتی کے ساتھ داخل ہو جاؤ۔ یہ ہمیشہ رہنے کا دن ہے (٣٤)
وہاں وہ جو چاہیں گے اُنکے لئے حاضر ہے اور ہمارے ہاں اور بھی (بہت کچھ) ہے (٣٥)
اور ہم نے اُن سے پہلے کئی اُمتیں ہلاک کر ڈالیں وہ ان سے قوت میں کہیں بڑھ کر تھے وہ شہروں میں گشت کرنے لگے۔ کیا کہیں بھاگنے کی جگہ ہے؟ (٣٦)
جو شخص دل (آگاہ) رکھتا ہے یا دل سے متوجہ ہو کر سنتا ہے اس کے لئے اس میں نصیحت ہے (٣٧)
اور ہم نے آسمانوں اور زمین کو اور جو (مخلوقات) اُن میں ہے سب کو چھ دن میں بنا دیا اور ہم کو ذرا بھی تکان نہیں ہوا (٣٨)
تو جو کچھ یہ (کفار) بکتے ہیں اس پر صبر کرو اور آفتاب کے طلوع ہونے سے پہلے اور اسکے غروب ہونیسے پہلے اپنے پروردگار کی تعریف کے ساتھ تسبیح کرتے رہو (٣٩)
اور رات کے بعض اوقات میں بھی اور نماز کے بعد بھی اس (کے نام) کی تنزیہ کیا کرو (٤٠)
اور سنو جس دن پکارنے والا نزدیک کی جگہ سے پکارے گا (٤١)
جس دن لوگ چیخ یقیناً سن لیں گے۔ وہی نکل پڑنے کا دن ہے (٤٢)
ہم ہی تو زندہ کرتے ہیں اور ہم ہی مارتے ہیں اور ہمارے ہی پاس لوٹ کر آنا ہے (٤٣)
اُس دن زمین اُن پر سے پھٹ جائے گی اور وہ جھٹ پٹ نکل کھڑے ہونگے۔ یہ جمع کرنا ہمیں آسان ہے (٤٤)
یہ لوگ جو کچھ کہتے ہیں ہمیں خوب معلوم ہے اور تم اُن پر زبردستی کرنے والے نہیں ہو۔ پس جو ہمارے (عذاب کی) وعید سے ڈرے اس کو قرآن سے نصیحت کرتے رہو (٤٥)

وَأُزْلِفَتِ الْجَنَّةُ لِلْمُتَّقِينَ غَيْرَ بَعِيدٍ ﴿٣١﴾
هَٰذَا مَا تُوعَدُونَ لِكُلِّ أَوَّابٍ حَفِيظٍ ﴿٣٢﴾
مَنْ خَشِيَ الرَّحْمَٰنَ بِالْغَيْبِ وَجَاءَ
بِقَلْبٍ مُنِيبٍ ﴿٣٣﴾
ادْخُلُوهَا بِسَلَامٍ ذَٰلِكَ يَوْمُ الْخُلُودِ ﴿٣٤﴾
لَهُمْ مَا يَشَاءُونَ فِيهَا وَلَدَيْنَا مَزِيدٌ ﴿٣٥﴾
وَكَمْ أَهْلَكْنَا قَبْلَهُمْ مِنْ قَرْنٍ هُمْ
أَشَدُّ مِنْهُمْ بَطْشًا فَنَقَّبُوا فِي الْبِلَادِ
هَلْ مِنْ مَحِيصٍ ﴿٣٦﴾
إِنَّ فِي ذَٰلِكَ لَذِكْرَىٰ لِمَنْ كَانَ لَهُ
قَلْبٌ أَوْ أَلْقَى السَّمْعَ وَهُوَ شَهِيدٌ ﴿٣٧﴾
وَلَقَدْ خَلَقْنَا السَّمَاوَاتِ وَالْأَرْضَ وَمَا
بَيْنَهُمَا فِي سِتَّةِ أَيَّامٍ وَمَا مَسَّنَا مِنْ
لُغُوبٍ ﴿٣٨﴾
فَاصْبِرْ عَلَىٰ مَا يَقُولُونَ وَسَبِّحْ بِحَمْدِ رَبِّكَ
قَبْلَ طُلُوعِ الشَّمْسِ وَقَبْلَ الْغُرُوبِ ﴿٣٩﴾
وَمِنَ اللَّيْلِ فَسَبِّحْهُ وَأَدْبَارَ السُّجُودِ ﴿٤٠﴾
وَاسْتَمِعْ يَوْمَ يُنَادِ الْمُنَادِ مِنْ مَكَانٍ
قَرِيبٍ ﴿٤١﴾
يَوْمَ يَسْمَعُونَ الصَّيْحَةَ بِالْحَقِّ ذَٰلِكَ
يَوْمُ الْخُرُوجِ ﴿٤٢﴾
إِنَّا نَحْنُ نُحْيِي وَنُمِيتُ وَإِلَيْنَا الْمَصِيرُ ﴿٤٣﴾
يَوْمَ تَشَقَّقُ الْأَرْضُ عَنْهُمْ سِرَاعًا
ذَٰلِكَ حَشْرٌ عَلَيْنَا يَسِيرٌ ﴿٤٤﴾
نَحْنُ أَعْلَمُ بِمَا يَقُولُونَ وَمَا أَنْتَ
عَلَيْهِمْ بِجَبَّارٍ فَذَكِّرْ بِالْقُرْآنِ
ع مَنْ يَخَافُ وَعِيدِ ﴿٤٥﴾

SÛRA–51
AẒ-ẒÃRIYÃT
(INTRODUCTION)

This is an early Makkan Sûra, with a highly mystic meaning. It is the second of the seven Sûras forming a group dealing with Revelation and the Hereafter. See Introduction to S. 50. This Sûra deals with the varying ways in which Truth prevails irresistibly even against all human probabilities.

Aẓ-Ẓāriyāt, or the Winds That Scatter

In the name of Allah, Most Gracious, Most Merciful.

1. By the (Winds) that scatter broadcast;
2. And those that lift and bear away heavy weights;
3. And those that flow with ease and gentleness;
4. And those that distribute the affair;—
5. Verily that which ye are promised is true;
6. And verily Judgment and Justice will surely come to pass.
7. By the Sky with (its) numerous Paths,
8. Truly ye are of varying opinion.
9. Through which are deluded (away from the Truth) such as would be deluded.
10. Cursed be the conjecturers.
11. Those who (flounder) heedless in a flood of confusion:
12. They ask, "When will be the Day of Judgment and Justice?"
13. (It will be) a Day when they will be tried (and tested) over the Fire!
14. "Taste ye your trial! This is what ye used to ask to be hastened!"
15. As to the Righteous, they will be in the midst of Gardens and Springs,
16. Taking joy in the things which their Lord gives them, because, before then, they have done good deeds.
17. They were in the habit of sleeping but little by night,
18. And in the hours of early dawn, they (were found) praying for Forgiveness;
19. And in their wealth there is a due share for the beggar and the deprived.
20. On the earth are Signs for those of assured Faith,
21. As also in your own selves: will ye not then see?
22. And in heaven is your Sustenance, as (also) that which ye are promised.
23. Then, by the Lord of heaven

سُورَةُ الذّٰرِيٰتِ مَكِّيَّةٌ وَّهِيَ سِتُّوْنَ اٰيَةً وَّثَلٰثُ رُكُوْعَاتٍ

بِسْمِ اللّٰهِ الرَّحْمٰنِ الرَّحِيْمِ
وَالذّٰرِيٰتِ ذَرْوًا ﴿١﴾
فَالْحٰمِلٰتِ وِقْرًا ﴿٢﴾
فَالْجٰرِيٰتِ يُسْرًا ﴿٣﴾
فَالْمُقَسِّمٰتِ اَمْرًا ﴿٤﴾
اِنَّمَا تُوْعَدُوْنَ لَصَادِقٌ ﴿٥﴾
وَّاِنَّ الدِّيْنَ لَوَاقِعٌ ﴿٦﴾
وَالسَّمَآءِ ذَاتِ الْحُبُكِ ﴿٧﴾
اِنَّكُمْ لَفِيْ قَوْلٍ مُّخْتَلِفٍ ﴿٨﴾
يُّؤْفَكُ عَنْهُ مَنْ اُفِكَ ﴿٩﴾
قُتِلَ الْخَرّٰصُوْنَ ﴿١٠﴾
الَّذِيْنَ هُمْ فِيْ غَمْرَةٍ سَاهُوْنَ ﴿١١﴾
يَسْـَٔلُوْنَ اَيَّانَ يَوْمُ الدِّيْنِ ﴿١٢﴾
يَوْمَ هُمْ عَلَى النَّارِ يُفْتَنُوْنَ ﴿١٣﴾
ذُوْقُوْا فِتْنَتَكُمْ ؕ هٰذَا الَّذِيْ كُنْتُمْ
بِهٖ تَسْتَعْجِلُوْنَ ﴿١٤﴾
اِنَّ الْمُتَّقِيْنَ فِيْ جَنّٰتٍ وَّعُيُوْنٍ ﴿١٥﴾
اٰخِذِيْنَ مَآ اٰتٰىهُمْ رَبُّهُمْ ؕ اِنَّهُمْ كَانُوْا
قَبْلَ ذٰلِكَ مُحْسِنِيْنَ ﴿١٦﴾
كَانُوْا قَلِيْلًا مِّنَ الَّيْلِ مَا يَهْجَعُوْنَ ﴿١٧﴾
وَبِالْاَسْحَارِ هُمْ يَسْتَغْفِرُوْنَ ﴿١٨﴾
وَفِيْٓ اَمْوَالِهِمْ حَقٌّ لِّلسَّآئِلِ وَالْمَحْرُوْمِ ﴿١٩﴾
وَفِي الْاَرْضِ اٰيٰتٌ لِّلْمُوْقِنِيْنَ ﴿٢٠﴾
وَفِيْٓ اَنْفُسِكُمْ ؕ اَفَلَا تُبْصِرُوْنَ ﴿٢١﴾
وَفِي السَّمَآءِ رِزْقُكُمْ وَمَا تُوْعَدُوْنَ ﴿٢٢﴾
فَوَرَبِّ السَّمَآءِ وَالْاَرْضِ اِنَّهٗ لَحَقٌّ مِّثْلَ

سورۂ ذاریات مکی ہے اور اس میں ساٹھ آیتیں اور تین رکوع ہیں

شروع خدا کا نام لے کر جو بڑا مہربان نہایت رحم والا ہے
بکھیرنے والیوں کی قسم جو اُڑا کر بکھیر دیتی ہیں (۱)
پھر (پانی کا) بوجھ اُٹھاتی ہیں (۲)
پھر آہستہ آہستہ چلتی ہیں (۳)
پھر چیزیں تقسیم کرتی ہیں (۴)
کہ جس چیز کا تم سے وعدہ کیا جاتا ہے وہ سچا ہے (۵)
اور انصاف (کا دن) ضرور واقع ہوگا (۶)
اور آسمان کی قسم جس میں رستے ہیں (۷)
کہ (اے اہل مکہ) تم ایک متناقض بات میں (پڑے ہوئے) ہو (۸)
اس سے وہی پھرتا ہے جو (خدا کی طرف سے) پھیرا جائے (۹)
اٹکل دوڑانے والے ہلاک ہوں (۱۰)
جو بے خبری میں بھولے ہوئے ہیں (۱۱)
پوچھتے ہیں کہ جزا کا دن کب ہوگا؟ (۱۲)
اُس دن (ہوگا) جب اُن کو آگ میں عذاب دیا جائے گا (۱۳)
اب اپنی شرارت کا مزہ چکھو۔ یہ وہی ہے جس کے لئے تم
جلدی مچایا کرتے تھے (۱۴)
بیشک پرہیزگار بہشتوں اور چشموں میں (عیش کر رہے) ہونگے (۱۵)
(اور) جو جو نعمتیں اُن کا پروردگار اُنہیں دیتا ہوگا اُن کو
لے رہے ہوں گے۔ بے شک وہ اس سے پہلے نیکیاں کرتے تھے (۱۶)
رات کے تھوڑے سے حصے میں سوتے تھے (۱۷)
اور اوقاتِ سحر میں بخشش مانگا کرتے تھے (۱۸)
اور اُنکے مال میں مانگنے والے اور نہ مانگنے والے (دونوں) کا حق ہوتا تھا (۱۹)
اور یقین کرنے والوں کیلئے زمین میں (بہت سی) نشانیاں ہیں (۲۰)
اور خود تمہارے نفوس میں۔ تو کیا تم دیکھتے نہیں؟ (۲۱)
اور تمہارا رزق اور جس چیز کا تم سے وعدہ کیا جاتا ہے آسمان میں ہے (۲۲)
تو آسمانوں اور زمین کے مالک کی قسم یہ (اسی طرح) قابل یقین

and earth, this is the very Truth, as much as the fact that ye can speak intelligently to each other.

24. Has the story reached thee, of the honoured Guests of Abraham?

25. Behold, they entered His presence, and said: "Peace!" He said, "Peace!" (and thought), "These seem unknown people."

26. Then he turned quickly to his household, brought out a fatted calf,

27. And placed it before them... He said, "Will ye not Eat?"

28. (When they did not eat), he conceived a fear of them. They said, "Fear not," and they gave him glad tidings of a son endowed with knowledge.

29. But his wife came forward clamouring: she smote her forehead and said: "A barren old woman!"

30. They said, "Even so has thy Lord spoken: and He is Full of Wisdom and Knowledge."

31. (Abraham) said: "And what, O ye Messengers, is your errand (now)?

32. They said, "We have been sent to a people (deep) in sin;—

33. "To bring on, on them, (a shower of) stones of clay (brimstone),

34. "Marked as from thy Lord for those who trespass beyond bounds."

35. Then We evacuated those of the Believers who were there,

36. But We found not there any except one Muslim household:

37. And We left there a Sign for such as fear the Grievous Chastisement.

38. And in Moses (was another Sign): behold, We sent him to Pharaoh, with authority manifest.

39. But (Pharaoh) turned back on account of his might, and said, "A sorcerer, or one possessed!"

40. So We took him and his forces, and threw them into the sea: and his was the blame.

ہے جس طرح تم بات کرتے ہو ۲۳

بھلا تمہارے پاس ابراہیم کے معزز مہمانوں کی خبر پہنچی ہے؟ ۲۴

جب وہ اُن کے پاس آئے تو سلام کہا۔ اُنہوں نے بھی (جواب میں) سلام کہا (دیکھا تو) ایسے لوگ کہ نہ جان نہ پہچان ۲۵

تو اپنے گھر جا کر ایک (بھنا ہوا) موٹا بچھڑا لائے ۲۶

(اور کھانے کیلئے) اُنکے آگے رکھ دیا۔ کہنے لگے کہ آپ تناول کیوں نہیں کرتے؟ ۲۷

اور دل میں اُن سے خوف معلوم کیا۔ اُنہوں نے کہا کہ خوف نہ کیجئے اور اُن کو ایک دانشمند لڑکے کی بشارت بھی سُنائی ۲۸

تو ابراہیم کی بیوی چلاتی آئیں اور اپنا مُنہ پیٹ کر کہنے لگیں کہ (اے ہے ایک تو) بُڑھیا اور (دوسرے) بانجھ ۲۹

اُنہوں نے کہا (ہاں) تمہارے پروردگار نے یوں ہی فرمایا ہے۔ وہ بے شک صاحبِ حکمت (اور) خبردار ہے ۳۰

(ابراہیم نے) کہا کہ فرشتو! تمہارا مُدعا کیا ہے؟ ۳۱

اُنہوں نے کہا کہ ہم گنہگاروں کی طرف بھیجے گئے ہیں ۳۲

تاکہ اُن پر کھنگر برسائیں ۳۳

جن پر حد سے بڑھ جانے والوں کیلئے تمہارے پروردگار کے ہاں سے نشان کر دیئے گئے ہیں ۳۴

تو وہاں جتنے مومن تھے اُن کو ہم نے نکال لیا ۳۵

اور اُس میں ایک گھر کے سوا مسلمانوں کا کوئی گھر نہ پایا ۳۶

اور جو لوگ عذاب الیم سے ڈرتے ہیں اُن کے لئے وہاں نشانی چھوڑ دی ۳۷

اور موسیٰ (کے حال) میں (بھی نشانی ہے) جب ہم نے اُن کو فرعون کی طرف کھلا ہوا معجزہ دے کر بھیجا ۳۸

تو اُس نے اپنی قوت (کے گھمنڈ) پر مُنہ موڑ لیا اور کہنے لگا یہ تو جادوگر ہے یا دیوانہ ۳۹

تو ہم نے اُس کو اور اُس کے لشکروں کو پکڑ لیا اور اُن کو دریا میں پھینک دیا اور وہ کام ہی قابلِ ملامت کرتا تھا ۴۰

ع ١٨ مَآ أَنَّكُمْ تَنطِقُونَ ٢٣

هَلْ أَتَىٰكَ حَدِيثُ ضَيْفِ إِبْرَٰهِيمَ
ٱلْمُكْرَمِينَ ٢٤ وقف لازم
إِذْ دَخَلُوا۟ عَلَيْهِ فَقَالُوا۟ سَلَٰمًا ۖ قَالَ سَلَٰمٌ
قَوْمٌ مُّنكَرُونَ ٢٥
فَرَاغَ إِلَىٰٓ أَهْلِهِۦ فَجَآءَ بِعِجْلٍ سَمِينٍ ٢٦
فَقَرَّبَهُۥٓ إِلَيْهِمْ قَالَ أَلَا تَأْكُلُونَ ٢٧
فَأَوْجَسَ مِنْهُمْ خِيفَةً ۖ قَالُوا۟ لَا تَخَفْ ۖ
وَبَشَّرُوهُ بِغُلَٰمٍ عَلِيمٍ ٢٨
فَأَقْبَلَتِ ٱمْرَأَتُهُۥ فِى صَرَّةٍ فَصَكَّتْ
وَجْهَهَا وَقَالَتْ عَجُوزٌ عَقِيمٌ ٢٩
قَالُوا۟ كَذَٰلِكِ قَالَ رَبُّكِ ۖ إِنَّهُۥ هُوَ ٱلْحَكِيمُ
ٱلْعَلِيمُ ٣٠
قَالَ فَمَا خَطْبُكُمْ أَيُّهَا ٱلْمُرْسَلُونَ ٣١
قَالُوٓا۟ إِنَّآ أُرْسِلْنَآ إِلَىٰ قَوْمٍ مُّجْرِمِينَ ٣٢
لِنُرْسِلَ عَلَيْهِمْ حِجَارَةً مِّن طِينٍ ٣٣
مُّسَوَّمَةً عِندَ رَبِّكَ لِلْمُسْرِفِينَ ٣٤
فَأَخْرَجْنَا مَن كَانَ فِيهَا مِنَ ٱلْمُؤْمِنِينَ ٣٥
فَمَا وَجَدْنَا فِيهَا غَيْرَ بَيْتٍ مِّنَ
ٱلْمُسْلِمِينَ ٣٦
وَتَرَكْنَا فِيهَآ ءَايَةً لِّلَّذِينَ يَخَافُونَ
ٱلْعَذَابَ ٱلْأَلِيمَ ٣٧
وَفِى مُوسَىٰٓ إِذْ أَرْسَلْنَٰهُ إِلَىٰ فِرْعَوْنَ
بِسُلْطَٰنٍ مُّبِينٍ ٣٨
فَتَوَلَّىٰ بِرُكْنِهِۦ وَقَالَ سَٰحِرٌ أَوْ مَجْنُونٌ ٣٩
فَأَخَذْنَٰهُ وَجُنُودَهُۥ فَنَبَذْنَٰهُمْ فِى ٱلْيَمِّ
وَهُوَ مُلِيمٌ ٤٠

41. And in the 'Ād (people) (was another Sign): behold, We sent against them the devastating Wind:	اور عاد (کی قوم کے حال) میں بھی (نشانی ہے) جب ہم نے اُن پر نامبارک ہوا چلائی (٤١)	وَفِي عَادٍ إِذْ أَرْسَلْنَا عَلَيْهِمُ الرِّيحَ الْعَقِيمَ (٤١)
42. It left nothing whatever that it came up against, but reduced it to ruin and rottenness.	وہ جس چیز پر چلتی اُس کو ریزہ ریزہ کئے بغیر نہ چھوڑتی (٤٢)	مَا تَذَرُ مِن شَيْءٍ أَتَتْ عَلَيْهِ إِلَّا جَعَلَتْهُ كَالرَّمِيمِ (٤٢)
43. And in the Thamûd (was another Sign): behold, they were told, "Enjoy (your brief day) for a little while!"	اور (قوم) ثمود (کے حال) میں بھی (نشانی ہے) جب اُن سے کہا گیا کہ ایک وقت تک فائدہ اُٹھا لو (٤٣)	وَفِي ثَمُودَ إِذْ قِيلَ لَهُمْ تَمَتَّعُوا حَتَّىٰ حِينٍ (٤٣)
44. But they insolently defied the Command of their Lord: so the thunderbolt seized them, even while they were looking on.	تو اُنہوں نے اپنے پروردگار کے حکم سے سرکشی کی سو اُن کو کڑک نے آپکڑا اور وہ دیکھ رہے تھے (٤٤)	فَعَتَوْا عَنْ أَمْرِ رَبِّهِمْ فَأَخَذَتْهُمُ الصَّاعِقَةُ وَهُمْ يَنظُرُونَ (٤٤)
45. Then they could not even stand (on their feet), nor could they help themselves.	پھر وہ نہ تو اُٹھنے کی طاقت رکھتے تھے اور نہ مقابلہ کر سکتے تھے (٤٥)	فَمَا اسْتَطَاعُوا مِن قِيَامٍ وَمَا كَانُوا مُنتَصِرِينَ (٤٥)
46. So were the People of Noah before them: for they wickedly transgressed.	اور اس سے پہلے (ہم) نوح کی قوم کو (ہلاک کر چکے تھے) بے شک وہ نافرمان لوگ تھے (٤٦)	وَقَوْمَ نُوحٍ مِّن قَبْلُ إِنَّهُمْ كَانُوا قَوْمًا فَاسِقِينَ (٤٦)
47. We have built the Firmament with might: and We indeed have vast power.	اور آسمانوں کو ہم ہی نے ہاتھوں سے بنایا اور ہم کو سب مقدور ہے (٤٧)	وَالسَّمَاءَ بَنَيْنَاهَا بِأَيْدٍ وَإِنَّا لَمُوسِعُونَ (٤٧)
48. And We have spread out the (spacious) earth: how excellently We do spread out!	اور زمین کو ہم ہی نے بچھایا تو (دیکھو) ہم کیا خوب بچھانے والے ہیں (٤٨)	وَالْأَرْضَ فَرَشْنَاهَا فَنِعْمَ الْمَاهِدُونَ (٤٨)
49. And of every thing We have created pairs: that ye may reflect.	اور ہر چیز کی ہم نے دو قسمیں بنائیں تاکہ تم نصیحت پکڑو (٤٩)	وَمِن كُلِّ شَيْءٍ خَلَقْنَا زَوْجَيْنِ لَعَلَّكُمْ تَذَكَّرُونَ (٤٩)
50. Therefore flee unto Allah: I am from Him a Warner to you, clear and open!	تو تم لوگ خدا کی طرف بھاگ چلو میں اُس کی طرف سے تم کو صریح رستہ بتانے والا ہوں (٥٠)	فَفِرُّوا إِلَى اللَّهِ إِنِّي لَكُم مِّنْهُ نَذِيرٌ مُّبِينٌ (٥٠)
51. And make not another an object of worship with Allah: I am from Him a Warner to you, clear and open!	اور خدا کے ساتھ کسی اور کو معبود نہ بناؤ۔ میں اس کی طرف سے تم کو صریح رستہ بتانے والا ہوں (٥١)	وَلَا تَجْعَلُوا مَعَ اللَّهِ إِلَٰهًا آخَرَ إِنِّي لَكُم مِّنْهُ نَذِيرٌ مُّبِينٌ (٥١)
52. Similarly, no messenger came to the Peoples before them, but they said (of him) in like manner, "A sorcerer, or one possessed"!	اسی طرح ان سے پہلے لوگوں کے پاس جو پیغمبر آتا وہ اس کو جادوگر یا دیوانہ کہتے (٥٢)	كَذَٰلِكَ مَا أَتَى الَّذِينَ مِن قَبْلِهِم مِّن رَّسُولٍ إِلَّا قَالُوا سَاحِرٌ أَوْ مَجْنُونٌ (٥٢)
53. Is this the legacy they have transmitted, one to another? Nay, they are themselves a people transgressing beyond bounds!	کیا یہ لوگ ایک دوسرے کو اسی بات کی وصیت کرتے آئے ہیں بلکہ یہ شریر لوگ ہیں (٥٣)	أَتَوَاصَوْا بِهِ ۚ بَلْ هُمْ قَوْمٌ طَاغُونَ (٥٣)
54. So turn away from them: not thine is the blame.	تو ان سے اعراض کرو تم کو (ہماری طرف سے) ملامت نہ ہوگی (٥٤)	فَتَوَلَّ عَنْهُمْ فَمَا أَنتَ بِمَلُومٍ (٥٤)
55. But remind: for reminding benefits the Believers.	اور نصیحت کرتے رہو کہ نصیحت مومنوں کو نفع دیتی ہے (٥٥)	وَذَكِّرْ فَإِنَّ الذِّكْرَىٰ تَنفَعُ الْمُؤْمِنِينَ (٥٥)
56. I have only created Jinns and men, that they may serve Me.	اور میں نے جنوں اور انسانوں کو اس لئے پیدا کیا ہے کہ میری عبادت کریں (٥٦)	وَمَا خَلَقْتُ الْجِنَّ وَالْإِنسَ إِلَّا لِيَعْبُدُونِ (٥٦)
57. No Sustenance do I require of them, nor do I require that they	میں اُن سے طالب رزق نہیں اور نہ یہ چاہتا ہوں کہ مجھے	مَا أُرِيدُ مِنْهُم مِّن رِّزْقٍ وَمَا أُرِيدُ

SÛRA–52
AṬ-ṬÛR
(INTRODUCTION)

This is the third of the group of seven Makkan Sûras described in the Introduction to S. 50.

It is, like its predecessor, an early Makkan Sûra. The points here emphasised are: that Revelation is in accord with all Allah's Signs, including previous Revelations, and that the Hereafter is inevitable, and we must prepare for it.

should feed Me.

58. For Allah is He Who gives (all) Sustenance,— Lord of Power,— Steadfast (for ever).

59. For the wrong-doers, their portion is like unto the portion of their fellows (of earlier generations): then let them not ask Me to hasten (that portion)!

60. Woe, then, to the Unbelievers, from that Day of theirs which they have been promised!

A -Ṭûr, or the Mount

In the name of Allah, Most Gracious, Most Merciful.

1. By the Mount (of Revelation);
2. By a Book Inscribed
3. In a parchment unfolded;
4. By the much-frequented House;
5. By the Conopy Raised High;
6. And by the Ocean filled with Swell;—
7. Verily, the Chastisement of thy Lord will indeed come to pass;—
8. There is none can avert it;—
9. On the Day when the firmament will be in dreadful commotion.
10. And the mountains will move.
11. Then woe that Day to the rejecters (of Truth);—
12. That play (and paddle) in shallow trifles.
13. That Day shall they be thrust down to the Fire of Hell, irresistibly.
14. "This", it will be said, "Is the Fire,—which ye were wont to deny!
15. "Is this then a magic, or is it ye that do not see?
16. "Burn ye therein: the same is it to you whether ye bear it with patience, or not: ye but receive the recompense of your (own) deeds."
17. As to the Righteous, they will be in Gardens, and in Happiness,—
18. Enjoying the (Bliss) which their Lord hath bestowed on them, and their Lord shall deliver them from the Chastisement of the Fire.

(کھانا) کھلائیں ﴿۵۷﴾
خدا ہی تو رزق دینے والا زور آور (اور) مضبوط ہے ﴿۵۸﴾
کچھ شک نہیں کہ ان ظالموں کیلئے بھی (عذاب کی) نوبت مقرر ہے جس طرح
انکے ساتھیوں کی نوبت تھی تو انکو مجھ سے (عذاب) جلدی نہیں طلب کرنا چاہئے ﴿۵۹﴾
جس دن کا ان کافروں سے وعدہ کیا جاتا ہے اُس سے
اُن کے لئے خرابی ہے ﴿۶۰﴾

سورۂ طور مکی ہے اس میں انچاس آیتیں اور دو رکوع ہیں

شروع خدا کا نام لے کر جو بڑا مہربان نہایت رحم والا ہے
(کوہ) طور کی قسم ﴿۱﴾ اور کتاب کی جو لکھی ہوئی ہے ﴿۲﴾
کشادہ اوراق میں ﴿۳﴾
اور آباد گھر کی ﴿۴﴾
اور اونچی چھت کی ﴿۵﴾
اور اُبلتے ہوئے دریا کی ﴿۶﴾
کہ تمہارے پروردگار کا عذاب واقع ہو کر رہے گا ﴿۷﴾
(اور) اُس کو کوئی روک نہیں سکے گا ﴿۸﴾
جس دن آسمان لرزنے لگے کپکپا کر ﴿۹﴾
اور پہاڑ اڑنے لگیں اُون ہو کر ﴿۱۰﴾
اُس دن جھٹلانے والوں کے لئے خرابی ہے ﴿۱۱﴾
جو خوض (باطل) میں پڑے کھیل رہے ہیں ﴿۱۲﴾
جس دن اُنکو آتش جہنم کی طرف دھکیل دھکیل کر لے جائینگے ﴿۱۳﴾
یہی وہ جہنم ہے جس کو تم جھوٹ سمجھتے تھے ﴿۱۴﴾
تو کیا یہ جادو ہے یا تم کو نظر ہی نہیں آتا ﴿۱۵﴾
اس میں داخل ہو جاؤ اور صبر کرو یا نہ کرو تمہارے لئے یکساں ہے
جو کام تم کیا کرتے تھے (یہ) اُن ہی کا تم کو بدلا مل رہا ہے ﴿۱۶﴾
جو پرہیزگار ہیں وہ باغوں اور نعمتوں میں ہوں گے ﴿۱۷﴾
جو کچھ اُن کے پروردگار نے انکو بخشا اس (کی وجہ) سے خوشحال
اور اُن کے پروردگار نے اُن کو دوزخ کے عذاب سے بچالیا ﴿۱۸﴾

أَنْ يُّطْعِمُوْنِ ﴿٥٧﴾
إِنَّ اللّٰهَ هُوَ الرَّزَّاقُ ذُو الْقُوَّةِ الْمَتِيْنُ ﴿٥٨﴾
فَإِنَّ لِلَّذِيْنَ ظَلَمُوْا ذَنُوْبًا مِّثْلَ ذَنُوْبِ
أَصْحٰبِهِمْ فَلَا يَسْتَعْجِلُوْنِ ﴿٥٩﴾
فَوَيْلٌ لِّلَّذِيْنَ كَفَرُوْا مِنْ يَّوْمِهِمُ الَّذِيْ
يُوْعَدُوْنَ ﴿٦٠﴾

سُوْرَةُ الطُّوْرِ مَكِّيَّةٌ وَّهِيَ تِسْعٌ وَّأَرْبَعُوْنَ اٰيَةً وَّفِيْهَا رُكُوْعَانِ

بِسْمِ اللّٰهِ الرَّحْمٰنِ الرَّحِيْمِ
وَالطُّوْرِ ﴿١﴾ وَكِتٰبٍ مَّسْطُوْرٍ ﴿٢﴾
فِيْ رَقٍّ مَّنْشُوْرٍ ﴿٣﴾
وَّالْبَيْتِ الْمَعْمُوْرِ ﴿٤﴾
وَالسَّقْفِ الْمَرْفُوْعِ ﴿٥﴾
وَالْبَحْرِ الْمَسْجُوْرِ ﴿٦﴾
إِنَّ عَذَابَ رَبِّكَ لَوَاقِعٌ ﴿٧﴾
مَّا لَهٗ مِنْ دَافِعٍ ﴿٨﴾
يَّوْمَ تَمُوْرُ السَّمَآءُ مَوْرًا ﴿٩﴾
وَّتَسِيْرُ الْجِبَالُ سَيْرًا ﴿١٠﴾
فَوَيْلٌ يَّوْمَئِذٍ لِّلْمُكَذِّبِيْنَ ﴿١١﴾
الَّذِيْنَ هُمْ فِيْ خَوْضٍ يَّلْعَبُوْنَ ﴿١٢﴾
يَوْمَ يُدَعُّوْنَ إِلٰى نَارِ جَهَنَّمَ دَعًّا ﴿١٣﴾
هٰذِهِ النَّارُ الَّتِيْ كُنْتُمْ بِهَا تُكَذِّبُوْنَ ﴿١٤﴾
أَفَسِحْرٌ هٰذَا أَمْ أَنْتُمْ لَا تُبْصِرُوْنَ ﴿١٥﴾
اِصْلَوْهَا فَاصْبِرُوْا أَوْ لَا تَصْبِرُوْا سَوَآءٌ
عَلَيْكُمْ إِنَّمَا تُجْزَوْنَ مَا كُنْتُمْ تَعْمَلُوْنَ ﴿١٦﴾
إِنَّ الْمُتَّقِيْنَ فِيْ جَنّٰتٍ وَّنَعِيْمٍ ﴿١٧﴾
فٰكِهِيْنَ بِمَآ اٰتٰهُمْ رَبُّهُمْ وَوَقٰهُمْ
رَبُّهُمْ عَذَابَ الْجَحِيْمِ ﴿١٨﴾

19. (To them will be said:) "Eat and drink ye, with profit and health, because of your (good) deeds."

اپنے اعمال کے صلے میں مزے سے کھاؤ اور پیو (١٩)

كُلُوا وَاشْرَبُوا هَنِيئًا بِمَا كُنتُمْ تَعْمَلُونَ (١٩)

20. They will recline (with ease) upon couches arranged in ranks; and We shall wed them to maidens, with beautiful big and lustrous eyes.

تختوں پر جو برابر برابر بچھے ہوئے ہیں تکیہ لگائے ہوئے۔ اور بڑی بڑی آنکھوں والی حوروں کو ہم اُن کا رفیق بنا دیں گے (٢٠)

مُتَّكِئِينَ عَلَىٰ سُرُرٍ مَّصْفُوفَةٍ ۖ وَزَوَّجْنَاهُم بِحُورٍ عِينٍ (٢٠)

21. And those who believe and whose seeds follow them in Faith,—to them shall We join their families: nor shall We deprive them (of the fruit) of aught of their works: (yet) is each individual in pledge for his deeds.

اور جو لوگ ایمان لائے اور اُن کی اولاد بھی (راہ) ایمان میں اُن کے پیچھے چلی ہم اُن کی اولاد کو بھی اُن (کے درجے) تک پہنچا دیں گے اور اُن کے اعمال میں سے کچھ کم نہ کرینگے۔ ہر شخص اپنے اعمال میں پھنسا ہوا ہے (٢١)

وَالَّذِينَ آمَنُوا وَاتَّبَعَتْهُمْ ذُرِّيَّتُهُم بِإِيمَانٍ أَلْحَقْنَا بِهِمْ ذُرِّيَّتَهُمْ وَمَا أَلَتْنَاهُم مِّنْ عَمَلِهِم مِّن شَيْءٍ ۚ كُلُّ امْرِئٍ بِمَا كَسَبَ رَهِينٌ (٢١)

22. And We shall bestow on them, of fruit and meat, anything they shall desire.

اور جس طرح کے میوے اور گوشت کو اُن کا جی چاہے گا ہم اُن کو عطا کریں گے (٢٢)

وَأَمْدَدْنَاهُم بِفَاكِهَةٍ وَلَحْمٍ مِّمَّا يَشْتَهُونَ (٢٢)

23. They shall there exchange, one with another, a cup free of frivolity, free of sin.

وہاں وہ ایک دوسرے سے جام شراب جھپٹ لیا کرینگے جس (کے پینے) سے نہ ہذیان سرائی ہوگی نہ کوئی گناہ کی بات (٢٣)

يَتَنَازَعُونَ فِيهَا كَأْسًا لَّا لَغْوٌ فِيهَا وَلَا تَأْثِيمٌ (٢٣)

24. Round about them will serve, (devoted) to them, youths (handsome) as Pearls well-guarded.

اور نوجوان خدمتگار (جو ایسے ہوں گے) جیسے چھپائے ہوئے موتی اُن کے آس پاس پھریں گے (٢٤)

وَيَطُوفُ عَلَيْهِمْ غِلْمَانٌ لَّهُمْ كَأَنَّهُمْ لُؤْلُؤٌ مَّكْنُونٌ (٢٤)

25. They will advance to each other, engaging in mutual enquiry.

اور ایک دوسرے کی طرف رُخ کر کے آپس میں گفتگو کرینگے (٢٥)

وَأَقْبَلَ بَعْضُهُمْ عَلَىٰ بَعْضٍ يَتَسَاءَلُونَ (٢٥)

26. They will say: "Aforetime, we were not without fear for the sake of our people.

کہیں گے کہ اس سے پہلے ہم اپنے گھر میں (خدا سے) ڈرتے رہتے تھے (٢٦)

قَالُوا إِنَّا كُنَّا قَبْلُ فِي أَهْلِنَا مُشْفِقِينَ (٢٦)

27. "But Allah has been good to us, and has delivered us from the Chastisement of the Scorching Wind.

تو خدا نے ہم پر احسان فرمایا اور ہمیں لُو کے عذاب سے بچا لیا (٢٧)

فَمَنَّ اللَّهُ عَلَيْنَا وَوَقَانَا عَذَابَ السَّمُومِ (٢٧)

28. "Truly, we did call unto Him from of old: truly it is He, the Beneficent, the Merciful!"

اِس سے پہلے ہم اس سے دُعائیں کیا کرتے تھے۔ بیشک وہ احسان کرنے والا مہربان ہے (٢٨)

إِنَّا كُنَّا مِن قَبْلُ نَدْعُوهُ ۖ إِنَّهُ هُوَ الْبَرُّ الرَّحِيمُ (٢٨)

29. Therefore Remind for by the Grace of thy Lord, thou art no soothsayer, nor possessed.

تو (اے پیغمبر) تم نصیحت کرتے رہو تم اپنے پروردگار کے فضل سے نہ تو کاہن ہو اور نہ دیوانے (٢٩)

فَذَكِّرْ فَمَا أَنتَ بِنِعْمَتِ رَبِّكَ بِكَاهِنٍ وَلَا مَجْنُونٍ (٢٩)

30. Or do they say: "A Poet! we await for him some calamity (hatched) by Time!"

کیا کافر کہتے ہیں کہ یہ شاعر ہے (اور) ہم اس کے حق میں زمانے کے حوادث کا انتظار کر رہے ہیں (٣٠)

أَمْ يَقُولُونَ شَاعِرٌ نَّتَرَبَّصُ بِهِ رَيْبَ الْمَنُونِ (٣٠)

31. Say thou: "Await ye!— I too will wait along with you!"

کہہ دو کہ انتظار کئے جاؤ میں بھی تمہارے ساتھ انتظار کرتا ہوں (٣١)

قُلْ تَرَبَّصُوا فَإِنِّي مَعَكُم مِّنَ الْمُتَرَبِّصِينَ (٣١)

32. Is it that their intellects urges them to this, or are they but a people transgressing beyond bounds?

کیا اُن کی عقلیں اُن کو یہی سکھاتی ہیں بلکہ یہ لوگ ہیں ہی شریر (٣٢)

أَمْ تَأْمُرُهُمْ أَحْلَامُهُم بِهَٰذَا ۚ أَمْ هُمْ قَوْمٌ طَاغُونَ (٣٢)

33. Or do they say, "He fabricated the (Message)"? Nay, they have no faith!

کیا کفار کہتے ہیں کہ ان پیغمبر نے قرآن از خود بنا لیا ہے بات یہ ہے کہ یہ (خدا پر) ایمان نہیں رکھتے (٣٣)

أَمْ يَقُولُونَ تَقَوَّلَهُ ۚ بَل لَّا يُؤْمِنُونَ (٣٣)

34. Let them then produce a saying like unto it,— If (it be) they speak the Truth!

اگر یہ سچے ہیں تو ایسا کلام بنا تو لائیں (۳۴)

فَلْيَأْتُوا بِحَدِيثٍ مِّثْلِهِ إِن كَانُوا صَادِقِينَ ﴿٣٤﴾

35. Were they created of nothing, or were they themselves the creators?

کیا یہ کسی کے پیدا کئے بغیر ہی پیدا ہو گئے ہیں۔ یا یہ خود (اپنے تئیں) پیدا کرنے والے ہیں (۳۵)

أَمْ خُلِقُوا مِنْ غَيْرِ شَيْءٍ أَمْ هُمُ
الْخَالِقُونَ ﴿٣٥﴾

36. Or did they create the heavens and the earth? Nay, they have no firm belief.

یا انہوں نے آسمانوں اور زمین کو پیدا کیا ہے؟ (نہیں) بلکہ یہ یقین ہی نہیں رکھتے (۳۶)

أَمْ خَلَقُوا السَّمَاوَاتِ وَالْأَرْضَ ۚ بَل لَّا
يُوقِنُونَ ﴿٣٦﴾

37. Or are the Treasures of thy Lord with them, or have they control over them.

کیا ان کے پاس تمہارے پروردگار کے خزانے ہیں یا یہ (کہیں کے) داروغہ ہیں (۳۷)

أَمْ عِندَهُمْ خَزَائِنُ رَبِّكَ أَمْ هُمُ
الْمُصَيْطِرُونَ ﴿٣٧﴾

38. Or have they a ladder, by which they can (climb up to heaven and) listen (to its secrets)? Then let (such a) listener of theirs produce a manifest proof.

یا ان کے پاس کوئی سیڑھی ہے جس پر (چڑھ کر آسمان سے باتیں) سن آتے ہیں تو جو سن آتا ہے وہ صریح سند دکھائے (۳۸)

أَمْ لَهُمْ سُلَّمٌ يَسْتَمِعُونَ فِيهِ ۖ فَلْيَأْتِ
مُسْتَمِعُهُم بِسُلْطَانٍ مُّبِينٍ ﴿٣٨﴾

39. Or has He only daughters and ye have sons?

کیا خدا کی تو بیٹیاں اور تمہارے بیٹے (۳۹)

أَمْ لَهُ الْبَنَاتُ وَلَكُمُ الْبَنُونَ ﴿٣٩﴾

40. Or is it that thou dost ask for a reward, so that they are burdened with a load of debt?—

اے پیغمبر کیا تم ان سے صلہ مانگتے ہو کہ ان پر تاوان کا بوجھ پڑ رہا ہے (۴۰)

أَمْ تَسْأَلُهُمْ أَجْرًا فَهُم مِّن مَّغْرَمٍ
مُّثْقَلُونَ ﴿٤٠﴾

41. Or that the Unseen is in their hands, and they write it down?

یا ان کے پاس غیب (کا علم) ہے کہ وہ اسے لکھ لیتے ہیں (۴۱)

أَمْ عِندَهُمُ الْغَيْبُ فَهُمْ يَكْتُبُونَ ﴿٤١﴾

42. Or do they intend a plot (against thee)? But those who disbelieve are themselves ensnared in a Plot.

کیا یہ کوئی داؤں کرنا چاہتے ہیں تو کافر تو خود داؤں میں آنے والے ہیں (۴۲)

أَمْ يُرِيدُونَ كَيْدًا ۖ فَالَّذِينَ كَفَرُوا
هُمُ الْمَكِيدُونَ ﴿٤٢﴾

43. Or have they a god other than Allah? Exalted is Allah far above the things they associate with Him!

کیا خدا کے سوا ان کا کوئی اور معبود ہے؟ خدا ان کے شریک بنانے سے پاک ہے (۴۳)

أَمْ لَهُمْ إِلَٰهٌ غَيْرُ اللَّهِ ۚ سُبْحَانَ اللَّهِ عَمَّا
يُشْرِكُونَ ﴿٤٣﴾

44. Were they to see a piece of the sky falling (on them), they would (only) say: "Clouds gathered in heaps!"

اور اگر یہ آسمان (سے عذاب) کا کوئی ٹکڑا گرتا ہوا دیکھیں تو کہیں کہ یہ گاڑھا بادل ہے (۴۴)

وَإِن يَرَوْا كِسْفًا مِّنَ السَّمَاءِ سَاقِطًا
يَقُولُوا سَحَابٌ مَّرْكُومٌ ﴿٤٤﴾

45. So leave them alone until they encounter that Day of theirs, wherein they shall be thunderstruck.

پس ان کو چھوڑ دو یہاں تک کہ وہ روز جس میں وہ بے ہوش کر دیئے جائیں گے سامنے آ جائے (۴۵)

فَذَرْهُمْ حَتَّىٰ يُلَاقُوا يَوْمَهُمُ الَّذِي
فِيهِ يُصْعَقُونَ ﴿٤٥﴾

46. The Day when their plotting will avail them nothing and no help shall be given them.

جس دن ان کا کوئی داؤں کچھ بھی کام نہ آئے اور نہ ان کو (کہیں سے) مدد ہی ملے (۴۶)

يَوْمَ لَا يُغْنِي عَنْهُمْ كَيْدُهُمْ شَيْئًا وَلَا هُمْ
يُنصَرُونَ ﴿٤٦﴾

47. And verily, for those who do wrong, there is another punishment besides this: but most of them know not.

اور ظالموں کے لئے اس کے سوا اور عذاب بھی ہے لیکن ان میں کے اکثر نہیں جانتے (۴۷)

وَإِنَّ لِلَّذِينَ ظَلَمُوا عَذَابًا دُونَ ذَٰلِكَ
وَلَٰكِنَّ أَكْثَرَهُمْ لَا يَعْلَمُونَ ﴿٤٧﴾

48. Now await in patience the command of thy Lord: for verily thou art in Our eyes: and celebrate the praises of thy Lord the while thou standest forth,

اور تم اپنے پروردگار کے حکم کے انتظار میں صبر کئے رہو تم تو ہماری آنکھوں کے سامنے ہو اور جب اٹھا کرو تو اپنے پروردگار کی تعریف کے ساتھ تسبیح کیا کرو (۴۸)

وَاصْبِرْ لِحُكْمِ رَبِّكَ فَإِنَّكَ بِأَعْيُنِنَا ۖ وَ
سَبِّحْ بِحَمْدِ رَبِّكَ حِينَ تَقُومُ ﴿٤٨﴾

SÛRA–53
AN-NAJM
(INTRODUCTION)

This is an early Makkan Sûra, and is the fourth of the series of seven which were described in the Introduction to S. 50.

The particular theme of this Sûra is that Revelation is not an illusion: the illusion is in the minds of those who doubt and have false ideas of Allah: Allah is the source and goal of all things.

In some Sûras the consecutive arrangement is shown or suggested by a cue-word. Here the cue-word is "star," corresponding to "stars" in the last verse of the last Sûra. So in 46: 1, the words: "Exalted in Power, Full of Wisdom": are carried forward from the last verse of S. 45, and indeed the same words occur in the first verse of S. 45. So, again the words: "Most Merciful, Oft-Forgiving": in 34: 2, refer back to the words: "Oft-Forgiving, Most Merciful": in the last line of S. 33. In S. 54: 1, the nearness of Judgment recalls the same idea at the end of the previous Sûra (53: 57). Other examples will also be found.

49. And for part of the night also praise thou Him,— and at the setting of the stars!

An-Najm, or the Star

In the name of Allah, Most Gracious, Most Merciful.

1. By the Star when it goes down,—
2. Your Companion is neither astray nor being misled,
3. Nor does he say (aught) of (his own) Desire.
4. It is no less than inspiration sent down to him:
5. He was taught by one Mighty in Power,
6. Endued with Wisdom: for he appeared (in stately form)
7. While he was in the highest part of the horizon:
8. Then he approached and came closer,
9. And was at a distance of but two bow-lengths or (even) nearer;
10. So did (Allah) convey the inspiration to His Servant— (conveyed) what He (meant) to convey.
11. The (Prophet's) (mind and) heart in no way falsified that which he saw.
12. Will ye then dispute with him concerning what he saw?
13. For indeed he saw him at a second descent,
14. Near the Lote-tree of the utmost boundary.
15. Near it is the Garden of Abode.
16. Behold, the Lote-tree was shrouded with what shrouds.
17. (His) sight never swerved, nor did it go wrong!
18. For truly did he see, of the Signs of his Lord, the Greatest!
19. Have ye seen Lãt, and 'Uzzã,
20. And another, the third (goddess), Manãt?
21. What! For you the male sex, and for Him, the female?
22. Behold, such would be indeed a division most unfair!
23. These are nothing but names which ye have devised,— ye and your fathers,— for which Allah has

اور رات کے بعض اوقات میں بھی اور ستاروں کے غروب ہونے کے بعد بھی اُس کی تنزیہ کیا کرو (۴۹)

سورہ نجم مکی ہے اس میں باسٹھ آیتیں اور تین رکوع ہیں

شروع خدا کا نام لے کر جو بڑا مہربان نہایت رحم والا ہے

تارے کی قسم جب غائب ہونے لگے (۱)
کہ تمہارے رفیق (محمدؐ) نہ رستہ بھولے ہیں نہ بھٹکے ہیں (۲)
اور نہ خواہش نفس سے مُنہ سے بات نکالتے ہیں (۳)
یہ (قرآن) تو حکم خدا ہے جو (ان کی طرف) بھیجا جاتا ہے (۴)
اُن کو نہایت قوت والے نے سکھایا (۵)
(یعنی جبرائیل) طاقتور نے پھر وہ پورے نظر آئے (۶)
اور وہ (آسمان کے) اُونچے کنارے میں تھے (۷)
پھر قریب ہوئے اور آگے بڑھے (۸)
تو دو کمان کے فاصلے پر یا اس سے بھی کم (۹)
پھر خدا نے اپنے بندے کی طرف جو بھیجا سو بھیجا (۱۰)
جو کچھ اُنہوں نے دیکھا اُن کے دل نے اُس کو جھوٹ نہ جانا (۱۱)
کیا جو کچھ وہ دیکھتے ہیں تم اس میں اُن سے جھگڑتے ہو؟ (۱۲)
اور اُنہوں نے اس کو ایک اور بار بھی دیکھا ہے (۱۳)
پرلی حد کی بیری کے پاس (۱۴)
اُسی کے پاس رہنے کی بہشت ہے (۱۵)
جبکہ اس بیری پر چھا رہا تھا جو چھا رہا تھا (۱۶)
اُن کی آنکھ نہ تو اور طرف مائل ہوئی اور نہ (حد سے) آگے بڑھی (۱۷)
اُنہوں نے اپنے پروردگار (کی قدرت) کی کتنی ہی بڑی بڑی نشانیاں دیکھیں (۱۸)
بھلا تم لوگوں نے لات اور عزیٰ کو دیکھا (۱۹)
اور تیسرے منات کو (کہ یہ بت کہیں خدا ہو سکتے ہیں) (۲۰)
(مشرکو!) کیا تمہارے لئے تو بیٹے اور خدا کے لئے بیٹیاں (۲۱)
یہ تقسیم تو بہت بے انصافی کی ہے (۲۲)
وہ تو صرف نام ہی نام ہیں جو تم نے اور تمہارے باپ دادا
نے گھڑ لئے ہیں۔ خدا نے تو اُن کی کوئی سند نازل نہیں کی۔

ع وَمِنَ الَّيْلِ فَسَبِّحْهُ وَإِدْبَارَ النُّجُومِ ﴿٤٩﴾

سُوْرَةُ النَّجْمِ مَكِّيَّةٌ وَهِيَ اثْنَتَانِ وَسِتُّوْنَ اٰيَةً وَثَلٰثُ رُكُوْعَاتٍ

بِسْمِ اللّٰهِ الرَّحْمٰنِ الرَّحِيْمِ

وَالنَّجْمِ اِذَا هَوٰى ﴿١﴾
مَا ضَلَّ صَاحِبُكُمْ وَمَا غَوٰى ﴿٢﴾
وَمَا يَنْطِقُ عَنِ الْهَوٰى ﴿٣﴾
اِنْ هُوَ اِلَّا وَحْيٌ يُّوْحٰى ﴿٤﴾
عَلَّمَهٗ شَدِيْدُ الْقُوٰى ﴿٥﴾
ذُوْ مِرَّةٍ فَاسْتَوٰى ﴿٦﴾
وَهُوَ بِالْاُفُقِ الْاَعْلٰى ﴿٧﴾
ثُمَّ دَنَا فَتَدَلّٰى ﴿٨﴾
فَكَانَ قَابَ قَوْسَيْنِ اَوْ اَدْنٰى ﴿٩﴾
فَاَوْحٰى اِلٰى عَبْدِهٖ مَا اَوْحٰى ﴿١٠﴾
مَا كَذَبَ الْفُؤَادُ مَا رَاٰى ﴿١١﴾
اَفَتُمٰرُوْنَهٗ عَلٰى مَا يَرٰى ﴿١٢﴾
وَلَقَدْ رَاٰهُ نَزْلَةً اُخْرٰى ﴿١٣﴾
عِنْدَ سِدْرَةِ الْمُنْتَهٰى ﴿١٤﴾
عِنْدَهَا جَنَّةُ الْمَاْوٰى ﴿١٥﴾
اِذْ يَغْشَى السِّدْرَةَ مَا يَغْشٰى ﴿١٦﴾
مَا زَاغَ الْبَصَرُ وَمَا طَغٰى ﴿١٧﴾
لَقَدْ رَاٰى مِنْ اٰيٰتِ رَبِّهِ الْكُبْرٰى ﴿١٨﴾
اَفَرَءَيْتُمُ اللّٰتَ وَالْعُزّٰى ﴿١٩﴾
وَمَنٰوةَ الثَّالِثَةَ الْاُخْرٰى ﴿٢٠﴾
اَلَكُمُ الذَّكَرُ وَلَهُ الْاُنْثٰى ﴿٢١﴾
تِلْكَ اِذًا قِسْمَةٌ ضِيْزٰى ﴿٢٢﴾
اِنْ هِيَ اِلَّا اَسْمَاءٌ سَمَّيْتُمُوْهَا اَنْتُمْ
وَاٰبَاؤُكُمْ مَّا اَنْزَلَ اللّٰهُ بِهَا مِنْ

sent down no authority (whatever). They follow nothing but; conjecture and what the souls desire ! —even though there has already come to them Guidance from their Lord!

24. Nay, shall man have (just) anything he hankers after?

25. But to Allah belongeth the Hereafter and the Former life.

26. How many-so-ever be the angels in the heavens, their intercession will avail nothing except after Allah has given leave for whom He pleases and that he is acceptable to Him.

27. Those who believe not in the Hereafter, name the angels with female names.

28. But they have no knowledge therein. They follow nothing but conjecture; and conjecture avails nothing against Truth.

29. Therefore shun those who turn away from Our Message and desire nothing but the life of this world.

30. That is their attainment of Knowledge. Verily thy Lord knoweth best those who stray from His path, and He knoweth best those who receive guidance.

31. Yea, to Allah belongs all that is in the heavens and on earth: so that He rewards those who do evil, according to their deeds, and He rewards those who do good, with what is best.

32. Those who avoid great sins and indecent deeds, save lesser offences,— verily thy Lord is ample in forgiveness. He knows you well when He brings you out of the earth, and when ye are hidden in your mothers' wombs. Therefore hold not yourselves purified: He knows best who it is that guards against evil.

33. Seest thou one who turns back,

یہ لوگ محض ظن (فاسد) اور خواہشات نفس کے پیچھے چل
رہے ہیں حالانکہ اُن کے پروردگار کی طرف سے اُن کے
پاس ہدایت آچکی ہے ﴿٢٣﴾
کیا جس چیز کی انسان آرزو کرتا ہے وہ اُسے ضرور ملتی ہے؟ ﴿٢٤﴾
آخرت اور دُنیا تو خدا ہی کے ہاتھ میں ہے ﴿٢٥﴾
اور آسمانوں میں بہت سے فرشتے ہیں جن کی سفارش کچھ بھی
فائدہ نہیں دیتی مگر اس وقت کہ خدا جس کے لئے چاہے اجازت
بخشے اور (سفارش) پسند کرے ﴿٢٦﴾
جو لوگ آخرت پر ایمان نہیں لاتے وہ فرشتوں کو (خدا کی)
لڑکیوں کے نام سے موسوم کرتے ہیں ﴿٢٧﴾
حالانکہ اُن کو اس کی کچھ خبر نہیں۔ وہ صرف ظن پر چلتے
ہیں اور ظن یقین کے مقابلے میں کچھ کام
نہیں آتا ﴿٢٨﴾
تو جو ہماری یاد سے رُوگردانی کرے اور صرف دنیا ہی کی زندگی
کا خواہاں ہو اس سے تم بھی منہ پھیر لو ﴿٢٩﴾
اُن کے علم کی یہی انتہا ہے۔ تمہارا پروردگار اس کو بھی
خوب جانتا ہے جو اس کے رستے سے بھٹک گیا اور اس
سے بھی خوب واقف ہے جو رستے پر چلا ﴿٣٠﴾
اور جو کچھ آسمانوں میں ہے اور جو کچھ زمین میں ہے سب خدا ہی کا ہے (اور اس نے
خلقت کو) اسلئے (پیدا کیا ہے) کہ جن لوگوں نے بُرے کام کئے انکو اُن کے
اعمال کا (بُرا) بدلہ دے اور جنہوں نے نیکیاں کیں اُنکو نیک بدلہ دے ﴿٣١﴾
جو صغیرہ گناہوں کے سوا بڑے بڑے گناہوں اور بے حیائی کی
باتوں سے اجتناب کرتے ہیں۔ بیشک تمہارا پروردگار بڑی بخشش
والا ہے۔ وہ تم کو خوب جانتا ہے جب اُس نے تم کو مٹی سے پیدا
کیا اور جب تم اپنی ماؤں کے پیٹ میں بچے تھے۔ تو اپنے آپ کو پاک
صاف نہ جتاؤ۔ جو پرہیزگار ہے وہ اس سے خوب واقف ہے ﴿٣٢﴾
بھلا تم نے اس شخص کو دیکھا جس نے منہ پھیر لیا ﴿٣٣﴾

سُلْطٰنٍ اِنْ يَّتَّبِعُوْنَ اِلَّا الظَّنَّ وَمَا
تَهْوَى الْاَنْفُسُ وَلَقَدْ جَآءَهُمْ مِّنْ
رَّبِّهِمُ الْهُدٰى ﴿٢٣﴾
اَمْ لِلْاِنْسَانِ مَا تَمَنّٰى ﴿٢٤﴾
فَلِلّٰهِ الْاٰخِرَةُ وَالْاُوْلٰى ﴿٢٥﴾ ع ٥
وَكَمْ مِّنْ مَّلَكٍ فِى السَّمٰوٰتِ لَا تُغْنِىْ
شَفَاعَتُهُمْ شَيْئًا اِلَّا مِنْۢ بَعْدِ اَنْ يَّاْذَنَ
اللّٰهُ لِمَنْ يَّشَآءُ وَيَرْضٰى ﴿٢٦﴾
اِنَّ الَّذِيْنَ لَا يُؤْمِنُوْنَ بِالْاٰخِرَةِ لَيُسَمُّوْنَ
الْمَلٰٓئِكَةَ تَسْمِيَةَ الْاُنْثٰى ﴿٢٧﴾
وَمَا لَهُمْ بِهٖ مِنْ عِلْمٍ اِنْ يَّتَّبِعُوْنَ
اِلَّا الظَّنَّ وَاِنَّ الظَّنَّ لَا يُغْنِىْ مِنَ
الْحَقِّ شَيْئًا ﴿٢٨﴾
فَاَعْرِضْ عَنْ مَّنْ تَوَلّٰى عَنْ ذِكْرِنَا
وَلَمْ يُرِدْ اِلَّا الْحَيٰوةَ الدُّنْيَا ﴿٢٩﴾
ذٰلِكَ مَبْلَغُهُمْ مِّنَ الْعِلْمِ اِنَّ رَبَّكَ
هُوَ اَعْلَمُ بِمَنْ ضَلَّ عَنْ سَبِيْلِهٖ وَهُوَ
اَعْلَمُ بِمَنِ اهْتَدٰى ﴿٣٠﴾
وَلِلّٰهِ مَا فِى السَّمٰوٰتِ وَمَا فِى الْاَرْضِ
لِيَجْزِىَ الَّذِيْنَ اَسَآءُوْا بِمَا عَمِلُوْا وَ
يَجْزِىَ الَّذِيْنَ اَحْسَنُوْا بِالْحُسْنٰى ﴿٣١﴾
اَلَّذِيْنَ يَجْتَنِبُوْنَ كَبٰٓئِرَ الْاِثْمِ وَ
الْفَوَاحِشَ اِلَّا اللَّمَمَ اِنَّ رَبَّكَ وَاسِعُ
الْمَغْفِرَةِ هُوَ اَعْلَمُ بِكُمْ اِذْ اَنْشَاَكُمْ
مِّنَ الْاَرْضِ وَاِذْ اَنْتُمْ اَجِنَّةٌ فِىْ بُطُوْنِ
اُمَّهٰتِكُمْ فَلَا تُزَكُّوْٓا اَنْفُسَكُمْ هُوَ اَعْلَمُ بِمَنِ اتَّقٰى ﴿٣٢﴾ ع ٦
اَفَرَءَيْتَ الَّذِيْ تَوَلّٰى ﴿٣٣﴾

34. Gives a little, then hardens (his heart)?	اور تھوڑا سا دیا پھر ہاتھ روک لیا ۳۴	وَأَعْطَىٰ قَلِيلًا وَأَكْدَىٰ ۝٣٤
35. What! Has he knowledge of the unseen so that he can see?	کیا اُس کے پاس غیب کا علم ہے کہ وہ اُسے دیکھ رہا ہے ۳۵	أَعِندَهُ عِلْمُ الْغَيْبِ فَهُوَ يَرَىٰ ۝٣٥
36. Nay, is he not acquainted with what is in the books of Moses—	کیا جو باتیں موسیٰ کے صحیفوں میں ہیں اُنکی اس کو خبر نہیں پہنچی ۳۶	أَمْ لَمْ يُنَبَّأْ بِمَا فِي صُحُفِ مُوسَىٰ ۝٣٦
37. And of Abraham who fulfilled his (commandments)	اور ابراہیم کی جنہوں نے (حق طاعت و رسالت) پورا کیا ۳۷	وَإِبْرَاهِيمَ الَّذِي وَفَّىٰ ۝٣٧
38. Namely, that no bearer of burdens can bear the burden of another;	(وہ) یہ کہ کوئی شخص دوسرے (کے گناہ) کا بوجھ نہیں اُٹھائیگا ۳۸	أَلَّا تَزِرُ وَازِرَةٌ وِزْرَ أُخْرَىٰ ۝٣٨
39. That man can have nothing but what he strives for;	اور یہ کہ انسان کو وہی ملتا ہے جس کی وہ کوشش کرتا ہے ۳۹	وَأَن لَّيْسَ لِلْإِنسَانِ إِلَّا مَا سَعَىٰ ۝٣٩
40. That (the fruit of) his striving will soon come in sight;	اور یہ کہ اس کی کوشش دیکھی جائے گی ۴۰	وَأَنَّ سَعْيَهُ سَوْفَ يُرَىٰ ۝٤٠
41. Then will he be rewarded with a reward complete;	پھر اس کو اس کا پورا پورا بدلہ دیا جائے گا ۴۱	ثُمَّ يُجْزَاهُ الْجَزَاءَ الْأَوْفَىٰ ۝٤١
42. That to thy Lord is the final Goal;	اور یہ کہ تمہارے پروردگار ہی کے پاس پہنچنا ہے ۴۲	وَأَنَّ إِلَىٰ رَبِّكَ الْمُنتَهَىٰ ۝٤٢
43. That it is He Who granteth Laughter and Tears;	اور یہ کہ وہ ہنساتا اور رُلاتا ہے ۴۳	وَأَنَّهُ هُوَ أَضْحَكَ وَأَبْكَىٰ ۝٤٣
44. That it is He Who granteth Death and Life;	اور یہ کہ وہی مارتا اور جلاتا ہے ۴۴	وَأَنَّهُ هُوَ أَمَاتَ وَأَحْيَا ۝٤٤
45. That He did create the pairs,—male and female,	اور یہ کہ وہی نر اور مادہ دو قسم (کے حیوان) پیدا کرتا ہے ۴۵	وَأَنَّهُ خَلَقَ الزَّوْجَيْنِ الذَّكَرَ وَالْأُنثَىٰ ۝٤٥
46. From a sperm-drop when lodged (in its place);	(یعنی) نطفے سے جو رحم میں ڈالا جاتا ہے ۴۶	مِن نُّطْفَةٍ إِذَا تُمْنَىٰ ۝٤٦
47. That He hath promised a Second Creation (raising of the Dead);	اور یہ کہ (قیامت کو) اسی پر دوبارہ اٹھانا لازم ہے ۴۷	وَأَنَّ عَلَيْهِ النَّشْأَةَ الْأُخْرَىٰ ۝٤٧
48. That it is He Who giveth wealth and satisfaction;	اور یہ کہ وہی دولتمند بناتا اور مفلس کرتا ہے ۴۸	وَأَنَّهُ هُوَ أَغْنَىٰ وَأَقْنَىٰ ۝٤٨
49. That He is the Lord of Sirius (the Mighty Star);	اور یہ کہ وہی شعریٰ[۲۷۷] کا مالک ہے ۴۹	وَأَنَّهُ هُوَ رَبُّ الشِّعْرَىٰ ۝٤٩
50. And that it is He Who destroyed the (powerful) ancient 'Ād (people),	اور یہ کہ اُسی نے عاد اول[۲۷۸] کو ہلاک کر ڈالا ۵۰	وَأَنَّهُ أَهْلَكَ عَادًا الْأُولَىٰ ۝٥٠
51. And the Thamûd, He left no trace of them.	اور ثمود کو بھی غرض کسی کو باقی نہ چھوڑا ۵۱	وَثَمُودَ فَمَا أَبْقَىٰ ۝٥١
52. And before them, the people of Noah, for that they were (all) most unjust and most insolent transgressors,	اور ان سے پہلے قوم نوح کو بھی۔ کچھ شک نہیں کہ وہ لوگ بڑے ہی ظالم اور بڑے ہی سرکش تھے ۵۲	وَقَوْمَ نُوحٍ مِّن قَبْلُ ۖ إِنَّهُمْ كَانُوا هُمْ أَظْلَمَ وَأَطْغَىٰ ۝٥٢
53. And He destroyed the Overthrown Cities (of Sodom and Gomorrah),	اور اُسی نے اُلٹی ہوئی بستیوں کو دے پٹکا ۵۳	وَالْمُؤْتَفِكَةَ أَهْوَىٰ ۝٥٣
54. So that there covered it that which covered.	پھر اُن پر چھایا جو چھایا ۵۴	فَغَشَّاهَا مَا غَشَّىٰ ۝٥٤
55. Then which of the favours of thy Lord, (O man,) wilt thou dispute about?	تو (اے انسان) تو اپنے پروردگار کی کون سی نعمت پر جھگڑے گا ۵۵	فَبِأَيِّ آلَاءِ رَبِّكَ تَتَمَارَىٰ ۝٥٥
56. This is a Warner, of the (series of) Warners of old!	یہ (محمد) بھی اگلے ڈرسنانے والوں میں سے ایک ڈر سنانے والے ہیں ۵۶	هَٰذَا نَذِيرٌ مِّنَ النُّذُرِ الْأُولَىٰ ۝٥٦
57. The (Hour) ever approaching draws nigh:	آنے والی (یعنی قیامت) قریب آ پہنچی ۵۷	أَزِفَتِ الْآزِفَةُ ۝٥٧
58. No one but Allah can disclose it.	اس (دن کی تکلیفوں) کو خدا کے سوا کوئی دور نہیں کرسکیگا ۵۸	لَيْسَ لَهَا مِن دُونِ اللَّهِ كَاشِفَةٌ ۝٥٨
59. Do ye then wonder at this recital?	(اے منکرین خدا) کیا تم اس کلام سے تعجب کرتے ہو ۵۹	أَفَمِنْ هَٰذَا الْحَدِيثِ تَعْجَبُونَ ۝٥٩

SÛRA–54
AL-QAMAR
(INTRODUCTION)

This is an early Makkan Sûra, the fifth in the series dealing with Judgment, and the truth of Revelation, as explained in the Introduction to S. 50.

The theme of the Sûra is explained by the refrain: "Is there any that will receive admonition?" which occurs six times, at the end of each reference to a past story of sin and rejection of warnings and in the appeal to the simplicity of the Qur-ãn (verses 15,17, 22, 32, 40, and 51). There is an invitation to listen to the Message and turn to Truth and Righteousness.

60. And will ye laugh and not weep,—
61. Wasting your time in vanities?
62. But fall ye down in prostration to Allah and adore (Him)!

Al-Qamar, or the Moon

In the name of Allah, Most Gracious Most Merciful.

1. The Hour (of Judgment) is nigh, and the moon was cleft asunder.
2. But if they see a Sign, they turn away, and say, "This is (but) continuous magic."
3. They reject (the warning) and follow their (own) lusts but every matter has its appointed time.
4. There have already come to them such tidings as contain a deterrent,
5. A wisdom far-reaching:—but (the preaching of) Warners Profits them not.
6. Therefore, (O Prophet,) turn away from them. (And wait for) the Day that the Caller will call (them) to a terrible affair,
7. They will come forth,—their eyes humbled—from (their) graves, (torpid) like locusts scattered abroad,
8. Hastening, with eyes transfixed, towards the Caller!—"Hard is this Day!" the Unbelievers will say.
9. Before them the People of Noah rejected (their messenger): they rejected Our servant and said, "Here is one possessed!", and he was driven out.
10. Then he called on his Lord: "I am one overcome: do Thou then help (me)!"
11. So We opened the gates of heaven, with water pouring forth.
12. And We caused the earth to gush forth with springs. So the waters met (and rose) to the extent decreed.
13. But We bore him on an (Ark) made of broad planks and caulked with palm-fibre:
14. She floats under Our eyes (and care): a recompense to one who had been rejected (with scorn)!

اور ہنستے ہو اور روتے نہیں (۶۰)
اور تم غفلت میں پڑ رہے ہو (۶۱)
تو خدا کے آگے سجدہ کرو اور (اُسی کی) عبادت کرو (۶۲)

سورۂ قمر مکی ہے اس میں پچپن آیتیں اور تین رکوع ہیں

شروع خدا کا نام لے کر جو بڑا مہربان نہایت رحم والا ہے
قیامت قریب آپہنچی اور چاند شق ہو گیا (۱)
اور اگر کافر کوئی نشانی دیکھتے ہیں تو مُنہ پھیر لیتے ہیں اور
کہتے ہیں کہ یہ ایک ہمیشہ کا جادو ہے (۲)
اور اُنہوں نے جھٹلایا اور اپنی خواہشوں کی پیروی کی
اور ہر کام کا وقت مقرر ہے (۳)
اور اُن کو ایسے حالات (سابقین) پہنچ چکے ہیں جن میں عبرت ہے (۴)
اور کامل دانائی (کی کتاب بھی) لیکن ڈرانا اُن کو کچھ فائدہ نہیں دیتا (۵)
تو تم بھی اُن کی کچھ پروا نہ کرو جس دن بلانے والا اُن کو ایک
ناخوش چیز کی طرف بُلائے گا (۶)
تو آنکھیں نیچی کئے ہوئے قبروں سے نکل پڑیں گے گویا
بکھری ہوئی ٹڈیاں ہیں (۷)
اس بلانے والے کی طرف دوڑتے جاتے ہوں گے۔ کافر
کہیں گے یہ دن بڑا سخت ہے (۸)
ان سے پہلے نوح کی قوم نے بھی تکذیب کی تھی تو اُنہوں نے
ہمارے بندے کو جھٹلایا اور کہا کہ دیوانہ ہے اور اُنہیں ڈانٹا بھی (۹)
تو اُنہوں نے اپنے پروردگار سے دعا کی کہ (بار الٰہا) میں (اُن کے مقابلے میں) کمزور ہوں تو (اُن سے) بدلہ لے (۱۰)
پس ہم نے زور کے مینہ سے آسمان کے دہانے کھول دیئے (۱۱)
اور زمین میں چشمے جاری کر دیئے تو پانی ایک کام کے لئے
جو مقدر ہو چکا تھا جمع ہو گیا (۱۲)
اور ہم نے نوح کو ایک کشتی پر جو تختوں اور میخوں سے تیار کی گئی تھی سوار کر لیا (۱۳)
وہ ہماری آنکھوں کے سامنے چلتی تھی (یہ سب کچھ) اس شخص
کے انتقام کے لئے کیا گیا جس کو کافر مانتے نہ تھے (۱۴)

وَتَضْحَكُونَ وَلَا تَبْكُونَ ﴿٦٠﴾
وَأَنتُمْ سَامِدُونَ ﴿٦١﴾
فَاسْجُدُوا لِلَّهِ وَاعْبُدُوا ﴿٦٢﴾

سُورَةُ الْقَمَرِ مَكِّيَّةٌ وَهِيَ خَمْسٌ وَخَمْسُونَ آيَةً وَثَلَاثُ رُكُوعَاتٍ

بِسْمِ اللَّهِ الرَّحْمَٰنِ الرَّحِيمِ
اقْتَرَبَتِ السَّاعَةُ وَانشَقَّ الْقَمَرُ ﴿١﴾
وَإِن يَرَوْا آيَةً يُعْرِضُوا وَيَقُولُوا سِحْرٌ
مُّسْتَمِرٌّ ﴿٢﴾
وَكَذَّبُوا وَاتَّبَعُوا أَهْوَاءَهُمْ وَكُلُّ
أَمْرٍ مُّسْتَقِرٌّ ﴿٣﴾
وَلَقَدْ جَاءَهُم مِّنَ الْأَنبَاءِ مَا فِيهِ مُزْدَجَرٌ ﴿٤﴾
حِكْمَةٌ بَالِغَةٌ فَمَا تُغْنِ النُّذُرُ ﴿٥﴾
فَتَوَلَّ عَنْهُمْ يَوْمَ يَدْعُ الدَّاعِ إِلَىٰ شَيْءٍ
نُّكُرٍ ﴿٦﴾
خُشَّعًا أَبْصَارُهُمْ يَخْرُجُونَ مِنَ
الْأَجْدَاثِ كَأَنَّهُمْ جَرَادٌ مُّنتَشِرٌ ﴿٧﴾
مُّهْطِعِينَ إِلَى الدَّاعِ يَقُولُ الْكَافِرُونَ
هَٰذَا يَوْمٌ عَسِرٌ ﴿٨﴾
كَذَّبَتْ قَبْلَهُمْ قَوْمُ نُوحٍ فَكَذَّبُوا عَبْدَنَا
وَقَالُوا مَجْنُونٌ وَازْدُجِرَ ﴿٩﴾
فَدَعَا رَبَّهُ أَنِّي مَغْلُوبٌ فَانتَصِرْ ﴿١٠﴾
فَفَتَحْنَا أَبْوَابَ السَّمَاءِ بِمَاءٍ مُّنْهَمِرٍ ﴿١١﴾
وَفَجَّرْنَا الْأَرْضَ عُيُونًا فَالْتَقَى الْمَاءُ
عَلَىٰ أَمْرٍ قَدْ قُدِرَ ﴿١٢﴾
وَحَمَلْنَاهُ عَلَىٰ ذَاتِ أَلْوَاحٍ وَدُسُرٍ ﴿١٣﴾
تَجْرِي بِأَعْيُنِنَا جَزَاءً لِّمَن كَانَ
كُفِرَ ﴿١٤﴾

15 And We have left this as a Sign (for all time): then is there any that will receive admonition?	اور ہم نے اُس کو ایک عبرت بنا چھوڑا تو کوئی ہے کہ سوچے سمجھے؟ ﴿۱۵﴾	وَلَقَدْ تَّرَكْنٰهَآ اٰيَةً فَهَلْ مِنْ مُّدَّكِرٍ ﴿١٥﴾
16. But how (terrible) was My Chastisement and My Warning?	سو (دیکھ لو کہ) میرا عذاب اور ڈرانا کیسا ہوا؟ ﴿۱۶﴾	فَكَيْفَ كَانَ عَذَابِيْ وَنُذُرِ ﴿١٦﴾
17. And We have indeed made the Qur'ān easy to understand and remember: then is there any that will receive admonition?	اور ہم نے قرآن کو سمجھنے کے لئے آسان کر دیا تو کوئی ہے کہ سوچے سمجھے؟ ﴿۱۷﴾	وَلَقَدْ يَسَّرْنَا الْقُرْاٰنَ لِلذِّكْرِ فَهَلْ مِنْ مُّدَّكِرٍ ﴿١٧﴾
18. The 'Ād (people) (too) rejected (Truth): then how terrible was My Chastisement and My Warning?	عاد نے بھی تکذیب کی تھی سو (دیکھ لو کہ) میرا عذاب اور ڈرانا کیسا ہوا ﴿۱۸﴾	كَذَّبَتْ عَادٌ فَكَيْفَ كَانَ عَذَابِيْ وَنُذُرِ ﴿١٨﴾
19. For We sent against them a furious wind, on a Day of bitter ill-luck,	ہم نے اُن پر سخت منحوس دن میں آندھی چلائی ﴿۱۹﴾	اِنَّآ اَرْسَلْنَا عَلَيْهِمْ رِيْحًا صَرْصَرًا فِيْ يَوْمِ نَحْسٍ مُّسْتَمِرٍّ ﴿١٩﴾
20. Plucking out men as if they were roots of palm-trees torn up (from the ground).	وہ لوگوں کو (اس طرح) اکھیڑے ڈالتی تھی گویا اکھڑی ہوئی کھجوروں کے تنے ہیں ﴿۲۰﴾	تَنْزِعُ النَّاسَ كَاَنَّهُمْ اَعْجَازُ نَخْلٍ مُّنْقَعِرٍ ﴿٢٠﴾
21. Yea, how (terrible) was My Chastisement and My Warning!	سو (دیکھ لو کہ) میرا عذاب اور ڈرانا کیسا ہوا ﴿۲۱﴾	فَكَيْفَ كَانَ عَذَابِيْ وَنُذُرِ ﴿٢١﴾
22. But We have indeed made the Qur'an easy to understand and remember: then is there any that will receive admonition?	اور ہم نے قرآن کو سمجھنے کے لئے آسان کر دیا ہے۔ تو کوئی ہے کہ سوچے سمجھے؟ ﴿۲۲﴾	وَلَقَدْ يَسَّرْنَا الْقُرْاٰنَ لِلذِّكْرِ فَهَلْ مِنْ مُّدَّكِرٍ ﴿٢٢﴾ ع
23. The Thamûd (also) rejected (their) Warners.	ثمود نے بھی ہدایت کرنے والوں کو جھٹلایا ﴿۲۳﴾	كَذَّبَتْ ثَمُوْدُ بِالنُّذُرِ ﴿٢٣﴾
24. For they said: "What! a man! a solitary one from among ourselves! Shall we follow such a one? Truly should we then be in error and madness.	اور کہا کہ بھلا ایک آدمی جو ہم ہی میں سے ہے ہم اس کی پیروی کریں؟ یوں ہو تو ہم گمراہی اور دیوانگی میں پڑ گئے ﴿۲۴﴾	فَقَالُوْٓا اَبَشَرًا مِّنَّا وَاحِدًا نَّتَّبِعُهٗٓ ۙ اِنَّآ اِذًا لَّفِيْ ضَلٰلٍ وَّسُعُرٍ ﴿٢٤﴾
25. "Is it that the Message is sent to *him*, of all people amongst us? Nay, he is a liar, an insolent one!"	کیا ہم سب میں سے اسی پر وحی نازل ہوئی ہے؟ (نہیں) بلکہ یہ جھوٹا خود پسند ہے ﴿۲۵﴾	ءَاُلْقِيَ الذِّكْرُ عَلَيْهِ مِنْۢ بَيْنِنَا بَلْ هُوَ كَذَّابٌ اَشِرٌ ﴿٢٥﴾
26. Ah! they will know on the morrow, which is the liar the insolent one!	اُن کو کل ہی معلوم ہو جائے گا کہ کون جھوٹا خود پسند ہے ﴿۲۶﴾	سَيَعْلَمُوْنَ غَدًا مَّنِ الْكَذَّابُ الْاَشِرُ ﴿٢٦﴾
27. For We will send the she-camel by way of trial for them. So watch them, (O Ṣāliḥ), and possess thyself in patience!	(اے صالح) ہم اُن کی آزمائش کے لئے اُونٹنی بھیجنے والے ہیں تو تم اُن کو دیکھتے رہو اور صبر کرو ﴿۲۷﴾	اِنَّا مُرْسِلُوا النَّاقَةِ فِتْنَةً لَّهُمْ فَارْتَقِبْهُمْ وَاصْطَبِرْ ﴿٢٧﴾
28. And tell them that the water is to be divided between them: each one's right to drink being brought forward (by suitable turns).	اور اُن کو آگاہ کر دو کہ ان میں پانی کی باری مقرر کر دی گئی ہے۔ ہر (باری والے) کو اپنی (باری پر) آنا چاہیئے ﴿۲۸﴾	وَنَبِّئْهُمْ اَنَّ الْمَآءَ قِسْمَةٌۢ بَيْنَهُمْ ۚ كُلُّ شِرْبٍ مُّحْتَضَرٌ ﴿٢٨﴾
29. But they called to their companion, and he took a sword in hand, and hamstrung (her).	تو اُن لوگوں نے اپنے رفیق کو بلایا اور اُس نے (اونٹنی کو) پکڑ کر اس کی کونچیں کاٹ دیں ﴿۲۹﴾	فَنَادَوْا صَاحِبَهُمْ فَتَعَاطٰى فَعَقَرَ ﴿٢٩﴾
30. Ah! how (terrible) was My Chastisement and My Warning!	سو (دیکھ لو کہ) میرا عذاب اور ڈرانا کیسا ہوا ﴿۳۰﴾	فَكَيْفَ كَانَ عَذَابِيْ وَنُذُرِ ﴿٣٠﴾
31. For We sent against them a single Mighty Blast, and they became like the dry stubble used by one who pens cattle.	ہم نے اُن پر (عذاب کے لئے) ایک چیخ بھیجی تو وہ ایسے ہو گئے جیسے باڑ والے کی سوکھی اور ٹوٹی ہوئی باڑ ﴿۳۱﴾	اِنَّآ اَرْسَلْنَا عَلَيْهِمْ صَيْحَةً وَّاحِدَةً فَكَانُوْا كَهَشِيْمِ الْمُحْتَظِرِ ﴿٣١﴾
32. And We have indeed made the Qur'an easy to understand and remember: then is there any that will receive admonition?	اور ہم نے قرآن کو سمجھنے کیلئے آسان کر دیا ہے تو کوئی ہے کہ سوچے سمجھے؟ ﴿۳۲﴾	وَلَقَدْ يَسَّرْنَا الْقُرْاٰنَ لِلذِّكْرِ فَهَلْ مِنْ مُّدَّكِرٍ ﴿٣٢﴾
33. The People of Lût rejected (his) Warning.	لُوط کی قوم نے بھی ڈر سنانے والوں کو جھٹلایا تھا ﴿۳۳﴾	كَذَّبَتْ قَوْمُ لُوْطٍۭ بِالنُّذُرِ ﴿٣٣﴾

34. We sent against them a violent tornado with showers of stones, (which destroyed them), except Lût's household: them We delivered by early Dawn,—

35. As a Grace from Us: thus do We reward those who give thanks.

36. And (Lût) did warn them of Our violent Seizure but they disputed about the Warning.

37. And they even sought to snatch away his guests from him, but We blinded their eyes. (They heard:) "Now taste ye My Wrath and My Warning."

38. Early on the morrow an abiding Chastisement seized them:

39. "So taste ye My Chastisement and my Warning."

40. And We have indeed made the Qur'ãn easy to understand and remember: then is there any that will receive admonition?

41. To the People of Pharaoh, too, aforetime, came Warners (from Allah).

42. The (people) rejected all Our Signs; but We seized them with the Seizure of a Mighty, Powerful.

43. Are your Unbelievers, (O Quraish), better than they? Or have ye an immunity in the Sacred Books?

44. Or do they say: "We acting together can defend ourselves"?

45. Soon will their multitude be put to flight, and they will show their backs.

46. Nay, the Hour (of Judgment) is the time promised them (for their full recompense): and that Hour will be most grievous and most bitter.

47. Truly those in sin are the ones in error and madness.

48. The Day they will be dragged through the Fire on their faces, (they will hear:) "Taste ye the touch of Hell!"

49. Verily, all things have We created in proportion and measure.

50. And Our Command is but a single Word,— like the twinkling of an eye.

51. And (oft) in the past, have We destroyed gangs like unto you: then is there any that will receive admonition?

تو ہم نے اُن پر کنکر بھری ہوا چلائی مگر لُوط کے گھر والے
کہ ہم نے ان کو پچھلی رات ہی سے بچا لیا (۳۴)
اپنے فضل سے شکر کرنے والے کو ہم ایسا ہی بدلہ دیا
کرتے ہیں (۳۵)
اور لُوط نے ان کو ہماری پکڑ سے ڈرا بھی دیا تھا مگر انہوں نے ڈرانے میں شک کیا (۳۶)
اور اُن سے اُن کے مہمانوں کو لے لینا چاہا۔ تو ہم نے اُن کی
آنکھیں مٹا دیں سو اب میرے عذاب اور ڈرانے کے مزے چکھو (۳۷)
اور اُن پر صبح سویرے ہی اٹل عذاب آ نازل ہوا (۳۸)
تو اب میرے عذاب اور ڈرانے کے مزے چکھو (۳۹)
اور ہم نے قرآن کو سمجھنے کے لئے آسان کر دیا ہے تو کوئی
ہے کہ سوچے سمجھے؟ (۴۰)
اور قوم فرعون کے پاس بھی ڈر سنانے والے آئے (۴۱)
اُنہوں نے ہماری تمام نشانیوں کو جھٹلایا تو ہم نے اُن کو
اس طرح پکڑ لیا جس طرح ایک قوی اور غالب شخص پکڑ لیتا ہے (۴۲)
(اے اہل عرب) کیا تمہارے کافر اُن لوگوں سے بہتر ہیں یا تمہارے
لئے (پہلی) کتابوں میں کوئی فارغ خطی لکھ دی گئی ہے؟ (۴۳)
کیا یہ لوگ کہتے ہیں کہ ہماری جماعت بڑی مضبوط ہے؟ (۴۴)
عنقریب یہ جماعت شکست کھائیگی اور یہ لوگ پیٹھ پھیر پھیر کر بھاگ جائینگے (۴۵)
اُن کے وعدے کا وقت تو قیامت ہے اور قیامت بڑی
سخت اور بہت تلخ ہے (۴۶)
بے شک گنہگار لوگ گمراہی اور دیوانگی میں (مبتلا) ہیں (۴۷)
اُس روز منہ کے بل دوزخ میں گھسیٹے جائیں گے۔ اب
آگ کا مزہ چکھو (۴۸)
ہم نے ہر چیز اندازۂ مقرر کے ساتھ پیدا کی ہے (۴۹)
اور ہمارا حکم تو آنکھ کے جھپکنے کی طرح ایک بات ہوتی ہے (۵۰)
اور ہم تمہارے ہم مذہبوں کو ہلاک کر چکے ہیں تو کوئی ہے
کہ سوچے سمجھے؟ (۵۱)

إِنَّآ أَرْسَلْنَا عَلَيْهِمْ حَاصِبًا إِلَّآ ءَالَ لُوطٍ
نَّجَّيْنَٰهُم بِسَحَرٍ ٣٤
نِّعْمَةً مِّنْ عِندِنَا كَذَٰلِكَ نَجْزِى مَن
شَكَرَ ٣٥
وَلَقَدْ أَنذَرَهُم بَطْشَتَنَا فَتَمَارَوْا بِٱلنُّذُرِ ٣٦
وَلَقَدْ رَٰوَدُوهُ عَن ضَيْفِهِۦ فَطَمَسْنَآ
أَعْيُنَهُمْ فَذُوقُوا عَذَابِى وَنُذُرِ ٣٧
وَلَقَدْ صَبَّحَهُم بُكْرَةً عَذَابٌ مُّسْتَقِرٌّ ٣٨
فَذُوقُوا عَذَابِى وَنُذُرِ ٣٩
وَلَقَدْ يَسَّرْنَا ٱلْقُرْءَانَ لِلذِّكْرِ فَهَلْ مِن
مُّدَّكِرٍ ٤٠ ع
وَلَقَدْ جَآءَ ءَالَ فِرْعَوْنَ ٱلنُّذُرُ ٤١
كَذَّبُوا بِـَٔايَٰتِنَا كُلِّهَا فَأَخَذْنَٰهُمْ أَخْذَ
عَزِيزٍ مُّقْتَدِرٍ ٤٢
أَكُفَّارُكُمْ خَيْرٌ مِّنْ أُولَٰٓئِكُمْ أَمْ لَكُم
بَرَآءَةٌ فِى ٱلزُّبُرِ ٤٣
أَمْ يَقُولُونَ نَحْنُ جَمِيعٌ مُّنتَصِرٌ ٤٤
سَيُهْزَمُ ٱلْجَمْعُ وَيُوَلُّونَ ٱلدُّبُرَ ٤٥
بَلِ ٱلسَّاعَةُ مَوْعِدُهُمْ وَٱلسَّاعَةُ أَدْهَىٰ
وَأَمَرُّ ٤٦
إِنَّ ٱلْمُجْرِمِينَ فِى ضَلَٰلٍ وَسُعُرٍ ٤٧ وقف لازم
يَوْمَ يُسْحَبُونَ فِى ٱلنَّارِ عَلَىٰ وُجُوهِهِمْ
ذُوقُوا مَسَّ سَقَرَ ٤٨
إِنَّا كُلَّ شَىْءٍ خَلَقْنَٰهُ بِقَدَرٍ ٤٩
وَمَآ أَمْرُنَآ إِلَّا وَٰحِدَةٌ كَلَمْحٍۭ بِٱلْبَصَرِ ٥٠
وَلَقَدْ أَهْلَكْنَآ أَشْيَاعَكُمْ فَهَلْ مِن
مُّدَّكِرٍ ٥١

SÛRA–55
AR-RAḤMÃN
(INTRODUCTION)

The majority of Commentators consider this an early Makkan Sûra, though some consider at least a part of it as dating from Madinah. The graeater part of it is undoubtedly early Makkan.

It is highly poetical and mystical, and the refrain "Then which of the favours of your Lord will ye deny?" is interspersed 31 times among its 78 verses.

It is the sixth of the series of seven dealing with Revelation, the favours of Allah, and the Hereafter: see Introduction to S. 50.

Here the special theme is indicated by the refrain. The rhyme in most cases is in the Dual grammatical form and the Argument implies that though things are created in pairs, there is an underlying Unity, through the Creator, in the favours which He bestows, and in the goal to which they are marching.

52. All that they do is noted in (their) Books (of Deeds):

53. Every matter, small and great, is on record.

54. As to the Righteous, they will be in the midst of Gardens and Rivers,

55. In a sure abode with a Sovereign Omnipotent.

Ar-Rahmãn, or (Allah) Most Gracious

In the name of Allah, Most Gracious, Most Merciful.

1. The Most Gracious!
2. It is He Who has taught the Qur'ãn.
3. He has created man:
4. He has taught him an intelligent speech.
5. The sun and the moon follow courses (exactly) computed;
6. And the herbs and the trees—both (alike) bow in adoration.
7. And the Firmament has He raised high, and He has set up the Balance (of Justice),
8. In order that ye may not transgress (due) balance.
9. So establish weight with justice and fall not short in the balance.
10. It is He Who has spread out the earth for (His) creatures:
11. Therein is fruit and date-palms, producing spathes (enclosing dates);
12. Also corn, with (its) leaves and stalk for fodder, and sweet-smelling plants.
13. Then which of the favours of your Lord will ye deny?
14. He created man from sounding clay like unto pottery,
15. And He created Jinns from fire free of smoke:
16. Then which of the favours of your Lord will ye deny?
17. (He is) Lord of the two Easts and Lord of the two Wests:
18. Then which of the favours of your Lord will ye deny?
19. He has let free the two Seas meeting together:
20. Between them is a Barrier which they do not transgress:
21. Then which of the favours of your Lord will ye deny?
22. Out of them come Pearls and Coral:

اور جو کچھ انہوں نے کیا (ان کے) اعمال ناموں میں (مندرج) ہے (٥٢)
(یعنی) ہر چھوٹا اور بڑا کام لکھ دیا گیا ہے (٥٣)
جو پرہیزگار ہیں وہ باغوں اور نہروں میں ہونگے (٥٤)
(یعنی) پاک مقام میں ہر طرح کی قدرت رکھنے والے بادشاہ کی بارگاہ میں (٥٥)

سورۂ الرحمٰن مکی ہے اس میں اٹھتر آیتیں اور تین رکوع ہیں

شروع خدا کا نام لے کر جو بڑا مہربان نہایت رحم والا ہے

(خدا جو) نہایت مہربان (١) اسی نے قرآن کی تعلیم فرمائی (٢)
اسی نے انسان کو پیدا کیا (٣)
اسی نے اس کو بولنا سکھایا (٤)
سورج اور چاند ایک حساب مقرر سے چل رہے ہیں (٥)
اور بوٹیاں اور درخت سجدہ کر رہے ہیں (٦)
اور اسی نے آسمان کو بلند کیا اور ترازو قائم کی (٧)
کہ ترازو (سے تولنے) میں حد سے تجاوز نہ کرو (٨)
اور انصاف کے ساتھ ٹھیک تولو۔ اور تول کم مت کرو (٩)
اور اسی نے خلقت کے لئے زمین بچھائی (١٠)
اس میں میوے اور کھجور کے درخت ہیں جنکے خوشوں پر غلاف ہوتے ہیں (١١)
اور اناج جسکے ساتھ بھس ہوتا ہے اور خوشبودار پھول (١٢)
تو (اے گروہ جن وانس) تم اپنے پروردگار کی کون کونسی نعمت کو جھٹلاؤ گے؟ (١٣)
اسی نے انسان کو ٹھیکرے کی طرح کھنکھناتی مٹی سے بنایا (١٤)
اور جنات کو آگ کے شعلے سے پیدا کیا (١٥)
تو تم اپنے پروردگار کی کون کونسی نعمت کو جھٹلاؤ گے؟ (١٦)
وہی دونوں مشرقوں اور دونوں مغربوں کا مالک (ہے) (١٧)
تو تم اپنے پروردگار کی کون کونسی نعمت کو جھٹلاؤ گے؟ (١٨)
اسی نے دو دریا رواں کئے جو آپس میں ملتے ہیں (١٩)
دونوں میں ایک آڑ ہے کہ (اس سے) تجاوز نہیں کر سکتے (٢٠)
تو تم اپنے پروردگار کی کون کونسی نعمت کو جھٹلاؤ گے؟ (٢١)
دونوں دریاؤں سے موتی اور مونگے نکلتے ہیں (٢٢)

وَكُلُّ شَيْءٍ فَعَلُوْهُ فِي الزُّبُرِ (٥٢)
وَكُلُّ صَغِيْرٍ وَّكَبِيْرٍ مُّسْتَطَرٌ (٥٣)
اِنَّ الْمُتَّقِيْنَ فِيْ جَنّٰتٍ وَّنَهَرٍ (٥٤)
فِيْ مَقْعَدِ صِدْقٍ عِنْدَ مَلِيْكٍ مُّقْتَدِرٍ (٥٥)

سُوْرَةُ الرَّحْمٰنِ مَكِّيَّةٌ وَّهِيَ ثَمَانٍ وَّسَبْعُوْنَ اٰيَةً وَّثَلٰثُ رُكُوْعَاتٍ

بِسْمِ اللّٰهِ الرَّحْمٰنِ الرَّحِيْمِ

اَلرَّحْمٰنُ (١) عَلَّمَ الْقُرْاٰنَ (٢)
خَلَقَ الْاِنْسَانَ (٣)
عَلَّمَهُ الْبَيَانَ (٤)
اَلشَّمْسُ وَالْقَمَرُ بِحُسْبَانٍ (٥)
وَّالنَّجْمُ وَالشَّجَرُ يَسْجُدٰنِ (٦)
وَالسَّمَآءَ رَفَعَهَا وَوَضَعَ الْمِيْزَانَ (٧)
اَلَّا تَطْغَوْا فِي الْمِيْزَانِ (٨)
وَاَقِيْمُوا الْوَزْنَ بِالْقِسْطِ وَلَا تُخْسِرُوا الْمِيْزَانَ (٩)
وَالْاَرْضَ وَضَعَهَا لِلْاَنَامِ (١٠)
فِيْهَا فَاكِهَةٌ وَّالنَّخْلُ ذَاتُ الْاَكْمَامِ (١١)
وَالْحَبُّ ذُو الْعَصْفِ وَالرَّيْحَانُ (١٢)
فَبِاَيِّ اٰلَآءِ رَبِّكُمَا تُكَذِّبٰنِ (١٣)
خَلَقَ الْاِنْسَانَ مِنْ صَلْصَالٍ كَالْفَخَّارِ (١٤)
وَخَلَقَ الْجَآنَّ مِنْ مَّارِجٍ مِّنْ نَّارٍ (١٥)
فَبِاَيِّ اٰلَآءِ رَبِّكُمَا تُكَذِّبٰنِ (١٦)
رَبُّ الْمَشْرِقَيْنِ وَرَبُّ الْمَغْرِبَيْنِ (١٧)
فَبِاَيِّ اٰلَآءِ رَبِّكُمَا تُكَذِّبٰنِ (١٨)
مَرَجَ الْبَحْرَيْنِ يَلْتَقِيٰنِ (١٩)
بَيْنَهُمَا بَرْزَخٌ لَّا يَبْغِيٰنِ (٢٠)
فَبِاَيِّ اٰلَآءِ رَبِّكُمَا تُكَذِّبٰنِ (٢١)
يَخْرُجُ مِنْهُمَا اللُّؤْلُؤُ وَالْمَرْجَانُ (٢٢)

23. Then which of the favours of your Lord will ye deny?	تو تم اپنے پروردگار کی کون کونسی نعمت کو جھٹلاؤ گے؟ (۲۳)	فَبِاَيِّ اٰلَاۤءِ رَبِّكُمَا تُكَذِّبٰنِ ﴿٢٣﴾
24. And His are the Ships sailing smoothly through the seas, lofty as mountains:	اور جہاز بھی اسی کے ہیں جو دریا میں پہاڑوں کی طرح اونچے کھڑے ہوتے ہیں (۲۴)	وَلَهُ الْجَوَارِ الْمُنْشَـٰٔتُ فِى الْبَحْرِ كَالْاَعْلَامِ ﴿٢٤﴾
25. Then which of the favours of your Lord will ye deny?	تو تم اپنے پروردگار کی کون کونسی نعمت کو جھٹلاؤ گے؟ (۲۵)	فَبِاَيِّ اٰلَاۤءِ رَبِّكُمَا تُكَذِّبٰنِ ﴿٢٥﴾
26. All that is on earth will perish:	جو (مخلوق) زمین پر ہے سب کو فنا ہونا ہے (۲۶)	كُلُّ مَنْ عَلَيْهَا فَانٍ ﴿٢٦﴾
27. But will abide (for ever) the Face of thy Lord,— full of Majesty, Bounty and Honour.	اور تمہارے پروردگار ہی کی ذات (بابرکت) جو صاحب جلال وعظمت ہے باقی رہے گی (۲۷)	وَّيَبْقٰى وَجْهُ رَبِّكَ ذُو الْجَلٰلِ وَالْاِكْرَامِ ﴿٢٧﴾
28. Then which of the favours of your Lord will ye deny?	تو تم اپنے پروردگار کی کون کونسی نعمت کو جھٹلاؤ گے؟ (۲۸)	فَبِاَيِّ اٰلَاۤءِ رَبِّكُمَا تُكَذِّبٰنِ ﴿٢٨﴾
29. Of Him seeks (its need) every creature in the heavens and on earth: every day in (new) Splendour doth He (shine)!	آسمان اور زمین میں جتنے لوگ ہیں سب اسی سے مانگتے ہیں۔ وہ ہر روز کام میں مصروف رہتا ہے (۲۹)	يَسْـَٔلُهٗ مَنْ فِى السَّمٰوٰتِ وَالْاَرْضِ ۚ كُلَّ يَوْمٍ هُوَ فِىْ شَاْنٍ ﴿٢٩﴾
30. Then which of the favours of your Lord will ye deny?	تو تم اپنے پروردگار کی کون کونسی نعمت کو جھٹلاؤ گے؟ (۳۰)	فَبِاَيِّ اٰلَاۤءِ رَبِّكُمَا تُكَذِّبٰنِ ﴿٣٠﴾
31. Soon shall We settle your affairs, O both ye worlds!	اے دونوں جماعتو! ہم عنقریب تمہاری طرف متوجہ ہوتے ہیں (۳۱)	سَنَفْرُغُ لَكُمْ اَيُّهَ الثَّقَلٰنِ ﴿٣١﴾
32. Then which of the favours of your Lord will ye deny?	تو تم اپنے پروردگار کی کون کونسی نعمت کو جھٹلاؤ گے؟ (۳۲)	فَبِاَيِّ اٰلَاۤءِ رَبِّكُمَا تُكَذِّبٰنِ ﴿٣٢﴾
33. O ye assembly of Jinns and men! If it be ye can pass beyond the zones of the heavens and the earth, pass ye! Not without authority shall ye be able to pass!	اے گروہ جن وانس اگر تمہیں قدرت ہو کہ آسمان اور زمین کے کناروں سے نکل جاؤ تو نکل جاؤ اور زور کے سوا تو تم نکل سکنے ہی کے نہیں (۳۳)	يٰمَعْشَرَ الْجِنِّ وَالْاِنْسِ اِنِ اسْتَطَعْتُمْ اَنْ تَنْفُذُوْا مِنْ اَقْطَارِ السَّمٰوٰتِ وَالْاَرْضِ فَانْفُذُوْا ۚ لَا تَنْفُذُوْنَ اِلَّا بِسُلْطٰنٍ ﴿٣٣﴾
34. Then which of the favours of your Lord will ye deny?	تو تم اپنے پروردگار کی کون کونسی نعمت کو جھٹلاؤ گے؟ (۳۴)	فَبِاَيِّ اٰلَاۤءِ رَبِّكُمَا تُكَذِّبٰنِ ﴿٣٤﴾
35. On you will be sent (O ye evil ones twain!) a flame of fire (to burn) and a (flash of) molten brass no defence will ye have:	تم پر آگ کے شعلے اور دھواں چھوڑ دیا جائے گا تو پھر تم مقابلہ نہ کر سکو گے (۳۵)	يُرْسَلُ عَلَيْكُمَا شُوَاظٌ مِّنْ نَّارٍ ۙ وَّنُحَاسٌ فَلَا تَنْتَصِرٰنِ ﴿٣٥﴾
36. Then which of the favours of your Lord will ye deny?	تو تم اپنے پروردگار کی کون کونسی نعمت کو جھٹلاؤ گے؟ (۳۶)	فَبِاَيِّ اٰلَاۤءِ رَبِّكُمَا تُكَذِّبٰنِ ﴿٣٦﴾
37. When the sky is rent asunder, and it becomes red like ointment:	پھر جب آسمان پھٹ کر تیل کی تلچھٹ کی طرح گلابی ہو جائے گا (تو وہ کیسا ہولناک دن ہوگا) (۳۷)	فَاِذَا انْشَقَّتِ السَّمَاۤءُ فَكَانَتْ وَرْدَةً كَالدِّهَانِ ﴿٣٧﴾
38. Then which of the favours of your Lord will ye deny?	تو تم اپنے پروردگار کی کون کونسی نعمت کو جھٹلاؤ گے؟ (۳۸)	فَبِاَيِّ اٰلَاۤءِ رَبِّكُمَا تُكَذِّبٰنِ ﴿٣٨﴾
39. On that Day no question will be asked of man or Jinn as to his sin,	اس روز نہ تو کسی انسان سے اس کے گناہوں کے بارے میں پرسش کی جائے گی اور نہ کسی جن سے (۳۹)	فَيَوْمَئِذٍ لَّا يُسْـَٔلُ عَنْ ذَنْۢبِهٖۤ اِنْسٌ وَّلَا جَاۤنٌّ ﴿٣٩﴾
40. Then which of the favours of your Lord will ye deny?	تو تم اپنے پروردگار کی کون کونسی نعمت کو جھٹلاؤ گے؟ (۴۰)	فَبِاَيِّ اٰلَاۤءِ رَبِّكُمَا تُكَذِّبٰنِ ﴿٤٠﴾
41. (For) the sinners will be known by their Marks: and they will be seized by their forelocks and their feet.	گنہگار اپنے چہرے ہی سے پہچان لئے جائیں گے تو پیشانی کے بالوں اور پاؤں سے پکڑ لئے جائیں گے (۴۱)	يُعْرَفُ الْمُجْرِمُوْنَ بِسِيْمٰهُمْ فَيُؤْخَذُ بِالنَّوَاصِىْ وَالْاَقْدَامِ ﴿٤١﴾
42. Then which of the favours of your Lord will ye deny?	تو تم اپنے پروردگار کی کون کونسی نعمت کو جھٹلاؤ گے؟ (۴۲)	فَبِاَيِّ اٰلَاۤءِ رَبِّكُمَا تُكَذِّبٰنِ ﴿٤٢﴾

43. This is the Hell which the Sinners deny:
یہی وہ جہنم ہے جسے گنہگار لوگ جھٹلاتے تھے ﴿۴۳﴾
هٰذِهٖ جَهَنَّمُ الَّتِيْ يُكَذِّبُ بِهَا الْمُجْرِمُوْنَ ﴿۴۳﴾

44. In its midst and in the midst of boiling hot water will they wander round!
وہ دوزخ اور کھولتے ہوئے گرم پانی کے درمیان گھومتے پھریں گے ﴿۴۴﴾
يَطُوْفُوْنَ بَيْنَهَا وَبَيْنَ حَمِيْمٍ اٰنٍ ﴿۴۴﴾

45. Then which of the favours of your Lord will ye deny?
تو تم اپنے پروردگار کی کون کونسی نعمت کو جھٹلاؤ گے؟ ﴿۴۵﴾
فَبِاَيِّ اٰلَاۗءِ رَبِّكُمَا تُكَذِّبٰنِ ﴿۴۵﴾

46. But for such as fear the time when they will stand before (the Judgment Seat of) their Lord, there will be two Gardens—
اور جو شخص اپنے پروردگار کے سامنے کھڑے ہونے سے ڈرا اس کے لئے دو باغ ہیں ﴿۴۶﴾
وَلِمَنْ خَافَ مَقَامَ رَبِّهٖ جَنَّتٰنِ ﴿۴۶﴾

47. Then which of the favours of your Lord will ye deny?—
تو تم اپنے پروردگار کی کون کونسی نعمت کو جھٹلاؤ گے؟ ﴿۴۷﴾
فَبِاَيِّ اٰلَاۗءِ رَبِّكُمَا تُكَذِّبٰنِ ﴿۴۷﴾

48. Abounding in branches,—
ان دونوں میں بہت سی شاخیں (یعنی قسم قسم کے میووں کے درخت ہیں) ﴿۴۸﴾
ذَوَاتَآ اَفْنَانٍ ﴿۴۸﴾

49. Then which of the favours of your Lord will ye deny?—
تو تم اپنے پروردگار کی کون کونسی نعمت کو جھٹلاؤ گے؟ ﴿۴۹﴾
فَبِاَيِّ اٰلَاۗءِ رَبِّكُمَا تُكَذِّبٰنِ ﴿۴۹﴾

50. In them (each) will be two Springs flowing (free);
ان میں دو چشمے بہ رہے ہیں ﴿۵۰﴾
فِيْهِمَا عَيْنٰنِ تَجْرِيٰنِ ﴿۵۰﴾

51. Then which of the favours of your Lord will ye deny?—
تو تم اپنے پروردگار کی کون کونسی نعمت کو جھٹلاؤ گے؟ ﴿۵۱﴾
فَبِاَيِّ اٰلَاۗءِ رَبِّكُمَا تُكَذِّبٰنِ ﴿۵۱﴾

52. In them will be Fruits of every kind, two and two.
ان میں سب میوے دو دو قسم کے ہیں ﴿۵۲﴾
فِيْهِمَا مِنْ كُلِّ فَاكِهَةٍ زَوْجٰنِ ﴿۵۲﴾

53. Then which of the favours of your Lord will ye deny?
تو تم اپنے پروردگار کی کون کونسی نعمت کو جھٹلاؤ گے؟ ﴿۵۳﴾
فَبِاَيِّ اٰلَاۗءِ رَبِّكُمَا تُكَذِّبٰنِ ﴿۵۳﴾

54. They will recline on Carpets, whose inner linings will be of rich brocade: the Fruit of the Gardens will be near (and easy of reach).
(اہل جنت) ایسے بچھونوں پر جن کے استر اطلس کے ہیں تکیہ لگائے ہوئے ہونگے۔ اور دونوں باغوں کے میوے قریب (جھک رہے) ہیں ﴿۵۴﴾
مُتَّكِـِٕيْنَ عَلٰي فُرُشٍ بَطَاۗىِٕنُهَا مِنْ اِسْتَبْرَقٍ ۭ وَجَنَا الْجَنَّتَيْنِ دَانٍ ﴿۵۴﴾

55. Then which of the favours of your Lord will ye deny?
تو تم اپنے پروردگار کی کون کونسی نعمت کو جھٹلاؤ گے؟ ﴿۵۵﴾
فَبِاَيِّ اٰلَاۗءِ رَبِّكُمَا تُكَذِّبٰنِ ﴿۵۵﴾

56. In them will be (Maidens), chaste, restraining their glances, whom no man or Jinn before them has touched;—
ان میں نیچی نگاہ والی عورتیں ہیں جن کو اہل جنت سے پہلے نہ کسی انسان نے ہاتھ لگایا اور نہ کسی جن نے ﴿۵۶﴾
فِيْهِنَّ قٰصِرٰتُ الطَّرْفِ ۙ لَمْ يَطْمِثْهُنَّ اِنْسٌ قَبْلَهُمْ وَلَا جَاۗنٌّ ﴿۵۶﴾

57. Then which of the favours of your Lord will ye deny?
تو تم اپنے پروردگار کی کون کونسی نعمت کو جھٹلاؤ گے؟ ﴿۵۷﴾
فَبِاَيِّ اٰلَاۗءِ رَبِّكُمَا تُكَذِّبٰنِ ﴿۵۷﴾

58. Like unto rubies and coral.
گویا وہ یاقوت اور مرجان ہیں ﴿۵۸﴾
كَاَنَّهُنَّ الْيَاقُوْتُ وَالْمَرْجَانُ ﴿۵۸﴾

59. Then which of the favours of your Lord will ye deny?
تو تم اپنے پروردگار کی کون کونسی نعمت کو جھٹلاؤ گے؟ ﴿۵۹﴾
فَبِاَيِّ اٰلَاۗءِ رَبِّكُمَا تُكَذِّبٰنِ ﴿۵۹﴾

60. Is there any Reward for Good—other than Good?
نیکی کا بدلہ نیکی کے سوا کچھ نہیں ہے؟ ﴿۶۰﴾
هَلْ جَزَاۗءُ الْاِحْسَانِ اِلَّا الْاِحْسَانُ ﴿۶۰﴾

61. Then which of the favours of your Lord will ye deny?
تو تم اپنے پروردگار کی کون کونسی نعمت کو جھٹلاؤ گے؟ ﴿۶۱﴾
فَبِاَيِّ اٰلَاۗءِ رَبِّكُمَا تُكَذِّبٰنِ ﴿۶۱﴾

62. And besides these two, there are two other Gardens,—
اور ان باغوں کے علاوہ دو باغ اور ہیں ﴿۶۲﴾
وَمِنْ دُوْنِهِمَا جَنَّتٰنِ ﴿۶۲﴾

63. Then which of the favours of your Lord will ye deny?—
تو تم اپنے پروردگار کی کون کونسی نعمت کو جھٹلاؤ گے؟ ﴿۶۳﴾
فَبِاَيِّ اٰلَاۗءِ رَبِّكُمَا تُكَذِّبٰنِ ﴿۶۳﴾

64. Dark-green in colour (from plentiful watering).
دونوں خوب گہرے سبز ﴿۶۴﴾
مُدْهَاۗمَّتٰنِ ﴿۶۴﴾

65. Then which of the favours of your Lord will ye deny?
تو تم اپنے پروردگار کی کون کونسی نعمت کو جھٹلاؤ گے؟ ﴿۶۵﴾
فَبِاَيِّ اٰلَاۗءِ رَبِّكُمَا تُكَذِّبٰنِ ﴿۶۵﴾

66. In them (each) will be two Springs pouring forth water in continuous abundance:
ان میں دو چشمے ابل رہے ہیں ﴿۶۶﴾
فِيْهِمَا عَيْنٰنِ نَضَّاخَتٰنِ ﴿۶۶﴾

67. Then which of the favours of your Lord will ye deny?
تو تم اپنے پروردگار کی کون کونسی نعمت کو جھٹلاؤ گے؟ ﴿۶۷﴾
فَبِاَيِّ اٰلَاۗءِ رَبِّكُمَا تُكَذِّبٰنِ ﴿۶۷﴾

SÛRA–56
AL-WÃQI'A
(INTRODUCTION)

This is the seventh and last Sûra of the series devoted to Revelation and the Hereafter, as explained in the Introduction to S. 50.

It belongs to the early Makkan period, with the possible exception of one or two verses.

The theme is the certainty of the Day of Judgment and its adjustment of true Values (56: 1-56); Allah's Power, Goodness and Glory (56: 57-74); and the truth of Revelation (56: 75-96).

68. In them will be Fruits, and dates and pomegranates:
69. Then which of the favours of your Lord will ye deny?
70. In them will be fair (Maidens), good, beautiful;—
71. Then which of the favours of your Lord will ye deny?—
72. Maidens restrained (as to their glances), in (goodly) pavilions:—
73. Then which of the favours of your Lord will ye deny?—
74. Whom no man or Jinn before them has touched;—
75. Then which of the favours of your Lord will ye deny?—
76. Reclining on green Cushions and rich Carpets of beauty.
77. Then which of the favours of your Lord will ye deny?
78. Blessed be the name of thy Lord, Full of Majesty, Bounty and Honour.

Al-Wāqi'a, or The Inevitable Event

In the name of Allah, Most Gracious, Most Merciful.
1. When the Event Inevitable cometh to pass,
2. Then will no (soul) deny its coming.
3. (Many) will it bring low; (many) will it exalt;
4. When the earth shall be shaken to its depths,
5. And the mountains shall be crumbled to atoms,
6. Becoming dust scattered abroad,
7. And ye shall be sorted out into three classes.
8. Then (there will be) the Companions of the Right Hand;— what will be the Companions of the Right Hand?
9. And the Companions of the Left Hand,— what will be the Companions of the Left Hand!
10. And those Foremost (in Faith) will be foremost (in the Hereafter).
11. These will be those Nearest to Allah:
12. In Gardens of Bliss:
13. A number of people from those of old,

فِيهِمَا فَاكِهَةٌ وَنَخْلٌ وَرُمَّانٌ ﴿٦٨﴾
ان میں میوے اور کھجوریں اور انار ہیں ﴿٦٨﴾

فَبِأَيِّ آلَاءِ رَبِّكُمَا تُكَذِّبَانِ ﴿٦٩﴾
تو تم اپنے پروردگار کی کون کونسی نعمت کو جھٹلاؤ گے؟ ﴿٦٩﴾

فِيهِنَّ خَيْرَاتٌ حِسَانٌ ﴿٧٠﴾
ان میں نیک سیرت (اور) خوبصورت عورتیں ہیں ﴿٧٠﴾

فَبِأَيِّ آلَاءِ رَبِّكُمَا تُكَذِّبَانِ ﴿٧١﴾
تو تم اپنے پروردگار کی کون کونسی نعمت کو جھٹلاؤ گے؟ ﴿٧١﴾

حُورٌ مَقْصُورَاتٌ فِي الْخِيَامِ ﴿٧٢﴾
(وہ) حوریں (ہیں جو) خیموں میں مستور (ہیں) ﴿٧٢﴾

فَبِأَيِّ آلَاءِ رَبِّكُمَا تُكَذِّبَانِ ﴿٧٣﴾
تو تم اپنے پروردگار کی کون کونسی نعمت کو جھٹلاؤ گے؟ ﴿٧٣﴾

لَمْ يَطْمِثْهُنَّ إِنْسٌ قَبْلَهُمْ وَلَا جَانٌّ ﴿٧٤﴾
ان کو اہل جنت سے پہلے نہ کسی انسان نے ہاتھ لگایا اور نہ کسی جن نے ﴿٧٤﴾

فَبِأَيِّ آلَاءِ رَبِّكُمَا تُكَذِّبَانِ ﴿٧٥﴾
تو تم اپنے پروردگار کی کون کونسی نعمت کو جھٹلاؤ گے؟ ﴿٧٥﴾

مُتَّكِئِينَ عَلَىٰ رَفْرَفٍ خُضْرٍ وَعَبْقَرِيٍّ
سبز قالینوں اور نفیس مسندوں پر تکیہ لگائے بیٹھے
حِسَانٍ ﴿٧٦﴾
ہوں گے ﴿٧٦﴾

فَبِأَيِّ آلَاءِ رَبِّكُمَا تُكَذِّبَانِ ﴿٧٧﴾
تو تم اپنے پروردگار کی کون کونسی نعمت کو جھٹلاؤ گے؟ ﴿٧٧﴾

ع ٣ تَبَارَكَ اسْمُ رَبِّكَ ذِي الْجَلَالِ وَالْإِكْرَامِ ﴿٧٨﴾
(اے محمد) تمہارا پروردگار جو صاحب جلال و عظمت ہے اس کا نام بڑا بابرکت ہے ﴿٧٨﴾

سُورَةُ الْوَاقِعَةِ مَكِّيَّةٌ وَهِيَ سِتٌّ وَتِسْعُونَ آيَةً وَثَلَاثُ رُكُوعَاتٍ
سورہ واقعہ مکی ہے اس میں چھیانوے آیتیں اور تین رکوع ہیں

بِسْمِ اللَّهِ الرَّحْمَٰنِ الرَّحِيمِ
شروع خدا کا نام لے کر جو بڑا مہربان نہایت رحم والا ہے

إِذَا وَقَعَتِ الْوَاقِعَةُ ﴿١﴾
جب واقع ہونے والی واقع ہو جائے ﴿١﴾

لَيْسَ لِوَقْعَتِهَا كَاذِبَةٌ ﴿٢﴾ وقف لازم
اس کے واقع ہونے میں کچھ جھوٹ نہیں ﴿٢﴾

خَافِضَةٌ رَافِعَةٌ ﴿٣﴾
کسی کو پست کرے کسی کو بلند ﴿٣﴾

إِذَا رُجَّتِ الْأَرْضُ رَجًّا ﴿٤﴾
جب زمین بھونچال سے لرزنے لگے ﴿٤﴾

وَبُسَّتِ الْجِبَالُ بَسًّا ﴿٥﴾
اور پہاڑ ٹوٹ کر ریزہ ریزہ ہو جائیں ﴿٥﴾

فَكَانَتْ هَبَاءً مُنْبَثًّا ﴿٦﴾
پھر غبار ہو کر اڑنے لگیں ﴿٦﴾

وَكُنْتُمْ أَزْوَاجًا ثَلَاثَةً ﴿٧﴾
اور تم لوگ تین قسم ہو جاؤ ﴿٧﴾

فَأَصْحَابُ الْمَيْمَنَةِ مَا أَصْحَابُ الْمَيْمَنَةِ ﴿٨﴾
تو داہنے ہاتھ والے (سبحان اللہ) داہنے ہاتھ والے کیا (ہی چین میں) ہیں ﴿٨﴾

وَأَصْحَابُ الْمَشْأَمَةِ مَا أَصْحَابُ الْمَشْأَمَةِ ﴿٩﴾
اور بائیں ہاتھ والے (افسوس) بائیں ہاتھ والے کیا (گرفتار عذاب) ہیں ﴿٩﴾

وَالسَّابِقُونَ السَّابِقُونَ ﴿١٠﴾
اور جو آگے بڑھنے والے ہیں (ان کا کیا کہنا) وہ آگے ہی بڑھنے والے ہیں ﴿١٠﴾

أُولَٰئِكَ الْمُقَرَّبُونَ ﴿١١﴾
وہی (خدا کے) مقرب ہیں ﴿١١﴾

فِي جَنَّاتِ النَّعِيمِ ﴿١٢﴾
نعمت کی بہشتوں میں ﴿١٢﴾

ثُلَّةٌ مِنَ الْأَوَّلِينَ ﴿١٣﴾
وہ بہت سے تو اگلے لوگوں میں سے ہوں گے ﴿١٣﴾

14. And a few from those of later times.	اور تھوڑے سے پچھلوں میں سے ﴿۱۴﴾	وَقَلِيلٌ مِّنَ الْآخِرِينَ ﴿١٤﴾
15. (They will be) on couches encrusted (with gold and precious stones),	(لعل و یاقوت وغیرہ سے) جڑے ہوئے تختوں پر ﴿۱۵﴾	عَلَىٰ سُرُرٍ مَّوْضُونَةٍ ﴿١٥﴾
16. Reclining on them, facing each other.	آمنے سامنے تکیہ لگائے ہوئے ﴿۱۶﴾	مُّتَّكِئِينَ عَلَيْهَا مُتَقَابِلِينَ ﴿١٦﴾
17. Round about them will (serve) youths of perpetual (freshness),	نوجوان خدمتگزار جو ہمیشہ (ایک ہی حالت میں) رہیں گے ان کے آس پاس پھریں گے ﴿۱۷﴾	يَطُوفُ عَلَيْهِمْ وِلْدَانٌ مُّخَلَّدُونَ ﴿١٧﴾
18. With goblets, (shining) beakers, and cups (filled) out of clear-flowing fountains:	یعنی آبخورے اور آفتابے اور صاف شراب کے گلاس لے لے کر ﴿۱۸﴾	بِأَكْوَابٍ وَأَبَارِيقَ وَكَأْسٍ مِّن مَّعِينٍ ﴿١٨﴾
19. No after-ache will they receive therefrom, nor will they suffer intoxication:	اس سے نہ تو سر میں درد ہوگا اور نہ ان کی عقلیں زائل ہوں گی ﴿۱۹﴾	لَّا يُصَدَّعُونَ عَنْهَا وَلَا يُنزِفُونَ ﴿١٩﴾
20. And with fruits, any that they may select;	اور میوے جس طرح کے ان کو پسند ہوں ﴿۲۰﴾	وَفَاكِهَةٍ مِّمَّا يَتَخَيَّرُونَ ﴿٢٠﴾
21. And the flesh of fowls, any that they may desire.	اور پرندوں کا گوشت جس قسم کا ان کا جی چاہے ﴿۲۱﴾	وَلَحْمِ طَيْرٍ مِّمَّا يَشْتَهُونَ ﴿٢١﴾
22. And (there will be) Companions with beautiful, big, and lustrous eyes,—	اور بڑی بڑی آنکھوں والی حوریں ﴿۲۲﴾	وَحُورٌ عِينٌ ﴿٢٢﴾
23. Like unto Pearls well-guarded.	جیسے (حفاظت سے) تہ کئے ہوئے (آب دار) موتی ﴿۲۳﴾	كَأَمْثَالِ اللُّؤْلُؤِ الْمَكْنُونِ ﴿٢٣﴾
24. A Reward for the Deeds of their past (Life).	یہ ان کے اعمال کا بدلہ ہے جو وہ کرتے تھے ﴿۲۴﴾	جَزَاءً بِمَا كَانُوا يَعْمَلُونَ ﴿٢٤﴾
25. No frivolity will they hear therein, nor any Mischief,—	وہاں نہ بیہودہ بات سنیں گے اور نہ گالی گلوچ ﴿۲۵﴾	لَا يَسْمَعُونَ فِيهَا لَغْوًا وَلَا تَأْثِيمًا ﴿٢٥﴾
26. Only the Saying, "Peace! Peace".	ہاں ان کا کلام سلام سلام (ہوگا) ﴿۲۶﴾	إِلَّا قِيلًا سَلَامًا سَلَامًا ﴿٢٦﴾
27. The Companions of the Right Hand,— what will be the Companions of the Right Hand!	اور داہنے ہاتھ والے (سبحان اللہ) داہنے ہاتھ والے کیا (ہی عیش میں) ہیں ﴿۲۷﴾	وَأَصْحَابُ الْيَمِينِ مَا أَصْحَابُ الْيَمِينِ ﴿٢٧﴾
28. (They will be) among Lote-trees without thorns,	(یعنی) بے خار کی بیریوں ﴿۲۸﴾	فِي سِدْرٍ مَّخْضُودٍ ﴿٢٨﴾
29. Among Ṭalḥ trees with flowers (or fruits) piled one above another,—	اور تہ بہ تہ کیلوں ﴿۲۹﴾	وَطَلْحٍ مَّنضُودٍ ﴿٢٩﴾
30. In shade long-extended,	اور لمبے لمبے سایوں ﴿۳۰﴾	وَظِلٍّ مَّمْدُودٍ ﴿٣٠﴾
31. By water flowing constantly,	اور پانی کے جھرنوں ﴿۳۱﴾	وَمَاءٍ مَّسْكُوبٍ ﴿٣١﴾
32. And fruit in abundance.	اور میوہ ہائے کثیرہ (کے باغوں) میں ﴿۳۲﴾	وَفَاكِهَةٍ كَثِيرَةٍ ﴿٣٢﴾
33. Whose season is not limited, nor (supply) forbidden,	جو نہ کبھی ختم ہوں اور نہ ان سے کوئی روکے ﴿۳۳﴾	لَّا مَقْطُوعَةٍ وَلَا مَمْنُوعَةٍ ﴿٣٣﴾
34. And on couches raised high.	اور اونچے اونچے فرشوں میں ﴿۳۴﴾	وَفُرُشٍ مَّرْفُوعَةٍ ﴿٣٤﴾
35. We have created them of special creation.	ہم نے ان (حوروں) کو پیدا کیا ﴿۳۵﴾	إِنَّا أَنشَأْنَاهُنَّ إِنشَاءً ﴿٣٥﴾
36. And made them virgin-pure (and undefiled),—	تو ان کو کنواریاں بنایا ﴿۳۶﴾	فَجَعَلْنَاهُنَّ أَبْكَارًا ﴿٣٦﴾
37. Full of love (for their mates) equal in age,—	(اور شوہروں کی) پیاریاں اور ہمعمر ﴿۳۷﴾	عُرُبًا أَتْرَابًا ﴿٣٧﴾
38. For the Companions of the Right Hand.	(یعنی) داہنے ہاتھ والوں کے لئے ﴿۳۸﴾	لِّأَصْحَابِ الْيَمِينِ ﴿٣٨﴾
39. A (goodly) number from those of old,	(یہ) بہت سے تو اگلے لوگوں میں سے ہیں ﴿۳۹﴾	ثُلَّةٌ مِّنَ الْأَوَّلِينَ ﴿٣٩﴾
40. And a (goodly) number from those of later times.	اور بہت سے پچھلوں میں سے ﴿۴۰﴾	وَثُلَّةٌ مِّنَ الْآخِرِينَ ﴿٤٠﴾

41. The Companions of the Left Hand,—what will be the Companions of the Left Hand!

اور بائیں ہاتھ والے (افسوس) بائیں ہاتھ والے کیا (ہی عذاب میں) ہیں۔ ﴿۴۱﴾

وَاَصْحٰبُ الشِّمَالِ ۙ مَآ اَصْحٰبُ الشِّمَالِ ﴿۴۱﴾

42. (They will be) in the midst of a fierce Blast of Fire and in Boiling Water,

(یعنی دوزخ کی) لپٹ اور کھولتے ہوئے پانی میں ﴿۴۲﴾

فِیْ سَمُوْمٍ وَّحَمِیْمٍ ﴿۴۲﴾

43. And in the shades of Black Smoke:

اور سیاہ دھوئیں کے سائے میں ﴿۴۳﴾

وَّظِلٍّ مِّنْ یَّحْمُوْمٍ ﴿۴۳﴾

44. Neither cool nor refreshing:

(جو) نہ ٹھنڈا (ہے) نہ خوشنما ﴿۴۴﴾

لَّا بَارِدٍ وَّلَا كَرِیْمٍ ﴿۴۴﴾

45. For that they were wont to be indulged, before that, in sinful luxury,

یہ لوگ اس سے پہلے عیش نعیم میں پڑے ہوئے تھے ﴿۴۵﴾

اِنَّهُمْ كَانُوْا قَبْلَ ذٰلِكَ مُتْرَفِیْنَ ﴿۴۵﴾

46. And persisted obstinately in wickedness supreme!

اور گناہ عظیم پر اَڑے ہوئے تھے ﴿۴۶﴾

وَكَانُوْا یُصِرُّوْنَ عَلَى الْحِنْثِ الْعَظِیْمِ ﴿۴۶﴾

47. And they used to say, "What! when we die and become dust and bones, shall we then indeed be raised up again?—

اور کہا کرتے تھے کہ بھلا جب ہم مر گئے اور مٹی ہوگئے۔ اور
ہڈیاں (ہی ہڈیاں) رہ گئے، تو کیا ہمیں پھر اُٹھنا ہوگا؟ ﴿۴۷﴾

وَكَانُوْا یَقُوْلُوْنَ ۙ اَئِذَا مِتْنَا وَكُنَّا تُرَابًا
وَّعِظَامًا ءَاِنَّا لَمَبْعُوْثُوْنَ ﴿۴۷﴾

48. "(We) and our fathers of old?"

اور کیا ہمارے باپ دادا کو بھی؟ ﴿۴۸﴾

اَوَاٰبَآؤُنَا الْاَوَّلُوْنَ ﴿۴۸﴾

49. Say: "Yea, those of old and those of later times,

کہہ دو کہ بےشک پہلے اور پچھلے ﴿۴۹﴾

قُلْ اِنَّ الْاَوَّلِیْنَ وَالْاٰخِرِیْنَ ﴿۴۹﴾

50. "All will certainly be gathered together for the meeting appointed for a Day well-known.

(سب) ایک روز مقرر کے وقت پر جمع کئے جائیں گے ﴿۵۰﴾

لَمَجْمُوْعُوْنَ ۙ اِلٰى مِیْقَاتِ یَوْمٍ مَّعْلُوْمٍ ﴿۵۰﴾

51. "Then will ye truly,— O ye that go wrong, and deny (the truth);

پھر تم اے جھٹلانے والے گمراہو! ﴿۵۱﴾

ثُمَّ اِنَّكُمْ اَیُّهَا الضَّآلُّوْنَ الْمُكَذِّبُوْنَ ﴿۵۱﴾

52. "Ye will surely taste of the Tree of Zaqqûm.

تھوہر کے درخت کھاؤ گے ﴿۵۲﴾

لَاٰكِلُوْنَ مِنْ شَجَرٍ مِّنْ زَقُّوْمٍ ﴿۵۲﴾

53. "Then will ye fill your insides therewith,

اور اسی سے پیٹ بھرو گے ﴿۵۳﴾

فَمَالِـُٔوْنَ مِنْهَا الْبُطُوْنَ ﴿۵۳﴾

54. "And drink Boiling Water on top of it:

اور اس پر کھولتا ہوا پانی پیو گے ﴿۵۴﴾

فَشٰرِبُوْنَ عَلَیْهِ مِنَ الْحَمِیْمِ ﴿۵۴﴾

55. "Indeed ye shall drink Like diseased camels raging with thirst!"

اور پیو گے بھی تو اس طرح جیسے پیاسے اُونٹ پیتے ہیں ﴿۵۵﴾

فَشٰرِبُوْنَ شُرْبَ الْهِیْمِ ﴿۵۵﴾

56. Such will be their entertainment on the Day of Requital!

جزا کے دن یہ اُن کی ضیافت ہوگی ﴿۵۶﴾

هٰذَا نُزُلُهُمْ یَوْمَ الدِّیْنِ ﴿۵۶﴾

57. It is We Who have created you: why will ye not admit the Truth?

ہم نے تم کو (پہلی بار بھی تو) پیدا کیا ہے تو تم (دوبارہ اُٹھنے کو) کیوں سچ نہیں سمجھتے؟ ﴿۵۷﴾

نَحْنُ خَلَقْنٰكُمْ فَلَوْلَا تُصَدِّقُوْنَ ﴿۵۷﴾

58. Do ye then see? the (human Seed) that ye emit,—

دیکھو تو کہ جس (نطفے) کو تم (عورتوں کے رحم میں) ڈالتے ہو ﴿۵۸﴾

اَفَرَءَیْتُمْ مَّا تُمْنُوْنَ ﴿۵۸﴾

59. Is it ye who create it, or are We the Creators?

کیا تم اس (سے انسان) کو بناتے ہو یا ہم بناتے ہیں؟ ﴿۵۹﴾

ءَاَنْتُمْ تَخْلُقُوْنَهٗۤ اَمْ نَحْنُ الْخٰلِقُوْنَ ﴿۵۹﴾

60. We have decreed Death to be your common lot, and We are not to be frustrated

ہم نے تم میں مرنا ٹھہرا دیا ہے اور ہم اس (بات) سے
عاجز نہیں ﴿۶۰﴾

نَحْنُ قَدَّرْنَا بَیْنَكُمُ الْمَوْتَ وَمَا نَحْنُ
بِمَسْبُوْقِیْنَ ﴿۶۰﴾

61. From changing your Forms and creating you (again) in (Forms) that ye know not.

کہ تمہاری طرح کے اور لوگ تمہاری جگہ لے آئیں اور تم کو
ایسے جہان میں جس کو تم نہیں جانتے پیدا کر دیں ﴿۶۱﴾

عَلٰۤى اَنْ نُّبَدِّلَ اَمْثَالَكُمْ وَنُنْشِئَكُمْ
فِیْ مَا لَا تَعْلَمُوْنَ ﴿۶۱﴾

62. And ye certainly know already the first form of creation: why then do ye not take heed?

اور تم نے پہلی پیدائش تو جان ہی لی ہے۔ پھر تم سوچتے
کیوں نہیں؟ ﴿۶۲﴾

وَلَقَدْ عَلِمْتُمُ النَّشْاَةَ الْاُوْلٰى فَلَوْلَا
تَذَكَّرُوْنَ ﴿۶۲﴾

63. See ye the seed that ye sow in the ground?

بھلا دیکھو تو کہ جو کچھ تم بوتے ہو ﴿۶۳﴾

اَفَرَءَیْتُمْ مَّا تَحْرُثُوْنَ ﴿۶۳﴾

أَأَنتُمْ تَزْرَعُونَهُ أَمْ نَحْنُ الزَّارِعُونَ (٦٤)
تو کیا تم اسے اُگاتے ہو یا ہم اُگاتے ہیں؟ (۶۴)
64. Is it ye that cause it to grow, or are We the Cause?

لَوْ نَشَاءُ لَجَعَلْنَاهُ حُطَامًا فَظَلْتُمْ تَفَكَّهُونَ (٦٥)
اگر ہم چاہیں تو اسے چورا چورا کردیں اور تم باتیں بناتے رہ جاؤ (۶۵)
65. Were it Our Will, We could make it broken orts. And ye would be left in wonderment,

إِنَّا لَمُغْرَمُونَ (٦٦)
(کہ ہائے) ہم تو مفت تاوان میں پھنس گئے (۶۶)
66. (Saying), "We are indeed Left with debts (for nothing):

بَلْ نَحْنُ مَحْرُومُونَ (٦٧)
بلکہ ہم ہیں ہی بے نصیب (۶۷)
67. "Indeed we are deprived".

أَفَرَأَيْتُمُ الْمَاءَ الَّذِي تَشْرَبُونَ (٦٨)
بھلا دیکھو تو کہ جو پانی تم پیتے ہو (۶۸)
68. See ye the water which ye drink?

أَأَنتُمْ أَنزَلْتُمُوهُ مِنَ الْمُزْنِ أَمْ نَحْنُ الْمُنزِلُونَ (٦٩)
کیا تم نے اس کو بادل سے نازل کیا ہے یا ہم نازل کرتے ہیں؟ (۶۹)
69. Do ye bring it Down (in rain) from the Cloud or do We?

لَوْ نَشَاءُ جَعَلْنَاهُ أُجَاجًا فَلَوْلَا تَشْكُرُونَ (٧٠)
اگر ہم چاہیں تو ہم اسے کھاری کردیں پھر تم شکر کیوں نہیں کرتے؟ (۷۰)
70. Were it Our Will, We could make it Saltish (and unpalatable): then why do ye not give thanks?

أَفَرَأَيْتُمُ النَّارَ الَّتِي تُورُونَ (٧١)
بھلا دیکھو تو جو آگ تم درخت سے نکالتے ہو (۷۱)
71. See ye the Fire which ye kindle?

أَأَنتُمْ أَنشَأْتُمْ شَجَرَتَهَا أَمْ نَحْنُ الْمُنشِئُونَ (٧٢)
کیا تم نے اسکے درخت کو پیدا کیا ہے یا ہم پیدا کرتے ہیں؟ (۷۲)
72. Is it ye who grow the tree which feeds the fire, or do We grow it?

نَحْنُ جَعَلْنَاهَا تَذْكِرَةً وَمَتَاعًا لِّلْمُقْوِينَ (٧٣)
ہم نے اُسے یاد دلانے اور مسافروں کے برتنے کو بنایا ہے (۷۳)
73. We have made it a reminder and an article of comfort and convenience for the denizens of deserts.

فَسَبِّحْ بِاسْمِ رَبِّكَ الْعَظِيمِ (٧٤)
تو تم اپنے پروردگار بزرگ کے نام کی تسبیح کرو (۷۴)
74. Then glorify the name of thy Lord, the Supreme!

فَلَا أُقْسِمُ بِمَوَاقِعِ النُّجُومِ (٧٥)
ہمیں تاروں کی منزلوں کی قسم (۷۵)
75. Furthermore I swear by the setting of the Stars,—

وَإِنَّهُ لَقَسَمٌ لَّوْ تَعْلَمُونَ عَظِيمٌ (٧٦)
اور اگر تم سمجھو تو یہ بڑی قسم ہے (۷۶)
76. And that is indeed a mighty adjuration if ye but knew,—

إِنَّهُ لَقُرْآنٌ كَرِيمٌ (٧٧)
کہ یہ بڑے رُتبے کا قرآن ہے (۷۷)
77. That this is indeed a Qur'ān most honourable,

فِي كِتَابٍ مَّكْنُونٍ (٧٨)
(جو) کتاب محفوظ میں (لکھا ہوا ہے) (۷۸)
78. In a Book well-guarded,

لَّا يَمَسُّهُ إِلَّا الْمُطَهَّرُونَ (٧٩)
اس کو وہی ہاتھ لگاتے ہیں جو پاک ہیں (۷۹)
79. Which none shall touch but those who are clean:

تَنزِيلٌ مِّن رَّبِّ الْعَالَمِينَ (٨٠)
پروردگار عالم کی طرف سے اُتارا گیا ہے (۸۰)
80. A Revelation from the Lord of the Worlds.

أَفَبِهَٰذَا الْحَدِيثِ أَنتُم مُّدْهِنُونَ (٨١)
کیا تم اس کلام سے انکار کرتے ہو؟ (۸۱)
81. Is it such a Message that ye would hold in light esteem?

وَتَجْعَلُونَ رِزْقَكُمْ أَنَّكُمْ تُكَذِّبُونَ (٨٢)
اور اپنا وظیفہ یہ بناتے ہو کہ (اسے) جھٹلاتے ہو (۸۲)
82. And have ye made it your livelihood that ye should declare it false?

فَلَوْلَا إِذَا بَلَغَتِ الْحُلْقُومَ (٨٣)
بھلا جب رُوح گلے میں آ پہنچتی ہے (۸۳)
83. Then why do ye not (intervene) when (the soul of the dying man) reaches the throat,—

وَأَنتُمْ حِينَئِذٍ تَنظُرُونَ (٨٤)
اور تم اس وقت (کی حالت کو) دیکھا کرتے ہو (۸۴)
84. And ye the while (sit) looking on—

وَنَحْنُ أَقْرَبُ إِلَيْهِ مِنكُمْ وَلَٰكِن لَّا تُبْصِرُونَ (٨٥)
اور ہم اس (مرنے والے) سے تم سے بھی زیادہ نزدیک ہوتے ہیں لیکن تم کو نظر نہیں آتے (۸۵)
85. But We are nearer to him than ye, and yet see not,—

فَلَوْلَا إِن كُنتُمْ غَيْرَ مَدِينِينَ (٨٦)
پس اگر تم کسی کے بس میں نہیں ہو (۸۶)
86. Then why do ye not,— if you are exempt from (future) account,—

تَرْجِعُونَهَا إِن كُنتُمْ صَادِقِينَ (٨٧)
تو اگر سچے ہو تو رُوح کو پھیر کیوں نہیں لیتے (۸۷)
87. Call back the soul, if ye are true (in your claim of Independence)?

فَأَمَّا إِن كَانَ مِنَ الْمُقَرَّبِينَ (٨٨)
پھر اگر وہ (خدا کے) مقربوں میں سے ہے (۸۸)
88. Thus then, if he be of those Nearest to Allah,

SÛRA–57
AL-ḤADÎD
(INTRODUCTION)

We have now studied the contents of nearly nine-tenths of the Qur-ãn. We have found that the arrangement of the Sûras in the present Text is not haphazard, but that they follow a distinct logical order more helpful for study than the chronological order. The comprehensive scheme of building up the new *Ummat* or Brotherhood and its spiritual implications is now complete. The remaining tenth of the Qur-ãn may be roughly considered in two parts. The first contains ten Sûras (S. 57 to 66), all revealed in Madinah, and each dealing with some special point which needs emphasis in the social life of the Ummat. The second (S. 67 to S. 114) contains short Makkan lyrics, each dealing with some aspect of spiritual life, expressed in language of great mystic beauty.

The present Madinah Sûra is chiefly concerned with spiritual humility and the avoidance of arrogance, and a warning that retirement from the world may not be the best way of seeking the good pleasure of Allah. Its probable date is after the Conquest of Makkah, A.H. 8.

89. (There is for him) Rest and Satisfaction, and a Garden of Delights.
90. And if he be of the Companions of the Right Hand,
91. (For him is the salutation), "Peace be unto thee," from the Companions of the Right Hand.
92. And if he be of those who deny (the truth) who go wrong,
93. For him is Entertainment with Boiling Water,
94. And burning in Hell-Fire.
95. Verily, this is the very Truth of assured Certainty.
96. So glorify the name of thy Lord, the Supreme.

تو اسکے لئے آرام اور خوشبودار پھول اور نعمت کے باغ ہیں ﴿۸۹﴾
اور اگر وہ داہنے ہاتھ والوں میں سے ہے ﴿۹۰﴾
تو کہا جائیگا کہ تجھ پر داہنے ہاتھ والوں کی طرف سے سلام ﴿۹۱﴾
اور اگر وہ جھٹلانے والے گمراہوں میں سے ہے ﴿۹۲﴾
تو اس کے لئے کھولتے پانی کی ضیافت ہے ﴿۹۳﴾
اور جہنم میں داخل کیا جانا ﴿۹۴﴾
یہ (داخل کیا جانا) یقیناً صحیح یعنی حق الیقین ہے ﴿۹۵﴾
تو تم اپنے پروردگار بزرگ کے نام کی تسبیح کرتے رہو ﴿۹۶﴾

فَرَوْحٌ وَّرَيْحَانٌ ۙ وَّجَنَّتُ نَعِيْمٍ ﴿۸۹﴾
وَاَمَّآ اِنْ كَانَ مِنْ اَصْحٰبِ الْيَمِيْنِ ﴿۹۰﴾
فَسَلٰمٌ لَّكَ مِنْ اَصْحٰبِ الْيَمِيْنِ ﴿۹۱﴾
وَاَمَّآ اِنْ كَانَ مِنَ الْمُكَذِّبِيْنَ الضَّآلِّيْنَ ﴿۹۲﴾
فَنُزُلٌ مِّنْ حَمِيْمٍ ﴿۹۳﴾
وَّتَصْلِيَةُ جَحِيْمٍ ﴿۹۴﴾
اِنَّ هٰذَا لَهُوَ حَقُّ الْيَقِيْنِ ﴿۹۵﴾
فَسَبِّحْ بِاسْمِ رَبِّكَ الْعَظِيْمِ ﴿۹۶﴾

Al-Ḥadîd, or Iron,

سورۂ حدید مدنی ہے اس میں اُنتیس آیتیں اور چار رکوع ہیں

سُوْرَةُ الْحَدِيْدِ مَدَنِيَّةٌ وَّهِيَ تِسْعٌ وَّعِشْرُوْنَ اٰيَةً وَّاَرْبَعُ رُكُوْعَاتٍ

In the name of Allah, Most Gracious, Most Merciful.
1. Whatever is in the heavens and on earth,— declares the Praises and Glory of Allah: for He is the Exalted in Might, the Wise.
2. To Him belongs the dominion of the heavens and the earth: it is He Who gives Life and Death; and He has Power over all things.
3. He is the First and the Last, the Evident and the Hidden: and He has full knowledge of all things.
4. He it is Who created the heavens and the earth in six Days, then He established Himself on the Throne. He knows what enters within the earth and what comes forth out of it, what comes down from heaven and what mounts up to it. And He is with you wheresoever ye may be. And Allah sees well all that ye do.
5. To Him belongs the dominion of the heavens and the earth: and all affairs go back to Allah.
6. He merges Night into Day, and He merges Day into Night; and He has full knowledge of the secrets of (all) hearts.
7. Believe in Allah and His Messenger, and spend (in charity) out

شروع خدا کا نام لے کر جو بڑا مہربان نہایت رحم والا ہے
جو مخلوق آسمانوں اور زمین میں ہے خدا کی تسبیح کرتی ہے
اور وہ غالب (اور) حکمت والا ہے ﴿۱﴾
آسمانوں اور زمین کی بادشاہی اسی کی ہے (وہی) زندہ
کرتا اور مارتا ہے۔ اور وہ ہر چیز پر قادر ہے ﴿۲﴾
وہ (سب سے) پہلا اور (سب سے) پچھلا اور (اپنی قدرتوں سے سب پر)
ظاہر اور (اپنی ذات سے) پوشیدہ ہے اور وہ تمام چیزوں کو جانتا ہے ﴿۳﴾
وہی ہے جس نے آسمانوں اور زمین کو چھ دن میں پیدا
کیا پھر عرش پر جا ٹھہرا۔ جو چیز زمین میں داخل ہوتی
اور جو اُس سے نکلتی ہے اور جو آسمان سے اُترتی اور جو
اسکی طرف چڑھتی ہے سب اُسکو معلوم ہے۔ اور تم جہاں کہیں ہو
وہ تمہارے ساتھ ہے اور جو کچھ تم کرتے ہو خدا اس کو
دیکھ رہا ہے ﴿۴﴾
آسمانوں اور زمین کی بادشاہی اُسی کی ہے۔ اور سب
امور اُسی کی طرف رجوع ہوتے ہیں ﴿۵﴾
(وہی) رات کو دن میں داخل کرتا اور دن کو رات میں
داخل کرتا ہے۔ اور وہ دلوں کے بھیدوں تک سے واقف ہے ﴿۶﴾
(تو) خدا پر اور اُسکے رسول پر ایمان لاؤ اور جس (مال) میں سے اس نے

بِسْمِ اللّٰهِ الرَّحْمٰنِ الرَّحِيْمِ
سَبَّحَ لِلّٰهِ مَا فِي السَّمٰوٰتِ وَالْاَرْضِ ۚ
وَهُوَ الْعَزِيْزُ الْحَكِيْمُ ﴿۱﴾
لَهٗ مُلْكُ السَّمٰوٰتِ وَالْاَرْضِ ۚ يُحْيٖ
وَيُمِيْتُ ۚ وَهُوَ عَلٰى كُلِّ شَيْءٍ قَدِيْرٌ ﴿۲﴾
هُوَ الْاَوَّلُ وَالْاٰخِرُ وَالظَّاهِرُ وَالْبَاطِنُ ۚ
وَهُوَ بِكُلِّ شَيْءٍ عَلِيْمٌ ﴿۳﴾
هُوَ الَّذِيْ خَلَقَ السَّمٰوٰتِ وَالْاَرْضَ فِيْ
سِتَّةِ اَيَّامٍ ثُمَّ اسْتَوٰى عَلَى الْعَرْشِ ۚ
يَعْلَمُ مَا يَلِجُ فِي الْاَرْضِ وَمَا يَخْرُجُ
مِنْهَا وَمَا يَنْزِلُ مِنَ السَّمَآءِ وَمَا يَعْرُجُ
فِيْهَا ۚ وَهُوَ مَعَكُمْ اَيْنَ مَا كُنْتُمْ ۚ وَاللّٰهُ
بِمَا تَعْمَلُوْنَ بَصِيْرٌ ﴿۴﴾
لَهٗ مُلْكُ السَّمٰوٰتِ وَالْاَرْضِ ۚ وَاِلَى اللّٰهِ
تُرْجَعُ الْاُمُوْرُ ﴿۵﴾
يُوْلِجُ الَّيْلَ فِي النَّهَارِ وَيُوْلِجُ النَّهَارَ
فِي الَّيْلِ ۚ وَهُوَ عَلِيْمٌ ۢبِذَاتِ الصُّدُوْرِ ﴿۶﴾
اٰمِنُوْا بِاللّٰهِ وَرَسُوْلِهٖ وَاَنْفِقُوْا مِمَّا جَعَلَكُمْ

مُّسْتَخْلَفِينَ فِيهِ ۖ فَالَّذِينَ آمَنُوا مِنكُمْ
وَأَنفَقُوا لَهُمْ أَجْرٌ كَبِيرٌ ﴿٧﴾
وَمَا لَكُمْ لَا تُؤْمِنُونَ بِاللَّهِ ۙ وَالرَّسُولُ
يَدْعُوكُمْ لِتُؤْمِنُوا بِرَبِّكُمْ وَقَدْ أَخَذَ
مِيثَاقَكُمْ إِن كُنتُم مُّؤْمِنِينَ ﴿٨﴾
هُوَ الَّذِي يُنَزِّلُ عَلَىٰ عَبْدِهِ آيَاتٍ بَيِّنَاتٍ
لِّيُخْرِجَكُم مِّنَ الظُّلُمَاتِ إِلَى النُّورِ ۚ
وَإِنَّ اللَّهَ بِكُمْ لَرَءُوفٌ رَّحِيمٌ ﴿٩﴾
وَمَا لَكُمْ أَلَّا تُنفِقُوا فِي سَبِيلِ اللَّهِ وَلِلَّهِ
مِيرَاثُ السَّمَاوَاتِ وَالْأَرْضِ ۚ لَا يَسْتَوِي
مِنكُم مَّنْ أَنفَقَ مِن قَبْلِ الْفَتْحِ وَقَاتَلَ ۚ
أُولَٰئِكَ أَعْظَمُ دَرَجَةً مِّنَ الَّذِينَ أَنفَقُوا
مِن بَعْدُ وَقَاتَلُوا ۚ وَكُلًّا وَعَدَ اللَّهُ
ع الْحُسْنَىٰ ۚ وَاللَّهُ بِمَا تَعْمَلُونَ خَبِيرٌ ﴿١٠﴾
مَّن ذَا الَّذِي يُقْرِضُ اللَّهَ قَرْضًا حَسَنًا
فَيُضَاعِفَهُ لَهُ وَلَهُ أَجْرٌ كَرِيمٌ ﴿١١﴾
يَوْمَ تَرَى الْمُؤْمِنِينَ وَالْمُؤْمِنَاتِ يَسْعَىٰ
نُورُهُم بَيْنَ أَيْدِيهِمْ وَبِأَيْمَانِهِم بُشْرَاكُمُ
الْيَوْمَ جَنَّاتٌ تَجْرِي مِن تَحْتِهَا الْأَنْهَارُ
خَالِدِينَ فِيهَا ۚ ذَٰلِكَ هُوَ الْفَوْزُ الْعَظِيمُ ﴿١٢﴾
يَوْمَ يَقُولُ الْمُنَافِقُونَ وَالْمُنَافِقَاتُ لِلَّذِينَ
آمَنُوا انظُرُونَا نَقْتَبِسْ مِن نُّورِكُمْ
قِيلَ ارْجِعُوا وَرَاءَكُمْ فَالْتَمِسُوا نُورًا
فَضُرِبَ بَيْنَهُم بِسُورٍ لَّهُ بَابٌ بَاطِنُهُ
فِيهِ الرَّحْمَةُ وَظَاهِرُهُ مِن قِبَلِهِ
الْعَذَابُ ﴿١٣﴾
يُنَادُونَهُمْ أَلَمْ نَكُن مَّعَكُمْ ۖ قَالُوا بَلَىٰ

تم کو اپنا نائب بنایا ہے اُس میں سے خرچ کرو۔ جو لوگ تم میں سے ایمان
لائے اور (مال) خرچ کرتے رہے اُن کے لئے بڑا ثواب ہے ﴿٧﴾
اور تم کیسے لوگ ہو کہ خدا پر ایمان نہیں لاتے۔ حالانکہ اُسکے پیغمبر
تمہیں بُلا رہے ہیں کہ اپنے پروردگار پر ایمان لاؤ اور اگر تم کو
باور ہو تو وہ تم سے (اس کا) عہد بھی لے چکا ہے ﴿٨﴾
وہی تو ہے جو اپنے بندے پر واضح (المطالب) آیتیں نازل کرتا ہے
تاکہ تم کو اندھیروں میں سے نکال کر روشنی میں لائے بیشک
خدا تم پر نہایت شفقت کرنے والا (اور) مہربان ہے ﴿٩﴾
اور تم کو کیا ہوا ہے کہ خدا کے رستے میں خرچ نہیں کرتے حالانکہ
آسمانوں اور زمین کی وراثت خدا ہی کی ہے جس شخص نے تم
میں سے فتح (مکہ) سے پہلے خرچ کیا اور لڑائی کی وہ (اور جس نے یہ کام پیچھے
کئے وہ) برابر نہیں۔ اُن کا درجہ اُن لوگوں سے کہیں بڑھ کر ہے جنہوں نے
بعد میں خرچ (اموال) اور (کفار سے) جہاد و قتال کیا۔ اور خدا نے سب سے
(ثواب) نیک (کا) وعدہ تو کیا ہے۔ اور جو کام تم کرتے ہو خدا اُن سے واقف ہے ﴿١٠﴾
کون ہے جو خدا کو (نیت) نیک (اور خلوص سے) قرض دے تو وہ اُسکو
اس سے دُگنا ادا کرے اور اس کیلئے عزت کا صلہ (یعنی جنت) ہے ﴿١١﴾
جس دن تم مومن مردوں اور مومن عورتوں کو دیکھو گے کہ اُن
(کے ایمان) کا نور اُن کے آگے آگے اور داہنی طرف چل رہا ہے
(تو اُن سے کہا جائے گا کہ) تم کو بشارت ہو (کہ آج تمہارے لئے)
باغ ہیں جنکے تلے نہریں بہ رہی ہیں اُن میں ہمیشہ رہو گے یہی بڑی کامیابی ہے ﴿١٢﴾
اُس دن منافق مرد اور منافق عورتیں مومنوں سے کہیں گے کہ ہماری طرف
نظر (شفقت) کیجئے کہ ہم بھی تمہارے نُور سے روشنی حاصل کریں
تو اُن سے کہا جائے گا کہ پیچھے کو لوٹ جاؤ اور (وہاں) نور تلاش کرو۔
پھر اُنکے بیچ میں ایک دیوار کھڑی کر دی جائیگی جس میں ایک دروازہ
ہوگا۔ جو اس کی جانب اندرونی ہے اُس میں تو رحمت ہے اور جو
٢٨٤
جانب بیرونی ہے اُس طرف عذاب (و اذیت) ﴿١٣﴾
تو منافق لوگ مومنوں سے کہیں گے کیا ہم (دنیا میں) تمہارے ساتھ نہ تھے وہ

of the (substance) whereof He has made you heirs. For, those of you who believe and spend (in charity),—for them is a great Reward.

8. How is it with you that you believe not in Allah?—And the Messenger invites you to believe in your Lord and has indeed taken your Covenant, if ye are men of faith.

9. He is the One Who sends to His Servant Manifest Signs, that He may lead you from the depths of Darkness into the Light and verily, Allah is to you Most Kind and Merciful.

10. How is it with you that you spend not in the cause of Allah?—For to Allah belongs the heritage of the heavens and the earth. Not equal among you are those who spent (freely) and fought, before the Victory, (with those who did so later). Those are higher in rank than those who spent (freely) and fought afterwards. But to all has Allah promised a goodly (reward). And Allah is well acquainted with all that ye do.

11. Who is he that will loan to Allah a beautiful loan? For (Allah) will increase it manifold to his credit, and he will have (besides) a generous reward.

12. The Day shalt thou see the believing men and the believing women— how their Light runs forward before them and by their right hands: (their greeting will be): "Good News for you this Day! Gardens beneath which flow rivers! to dwell therein for aye! This is indeed the highest Triumph."

13. The Day will the Hypocrites—men and women—say to the Believers: "Wait for us! Let us borrow (a light) from your Light!" It will be said: "Turn ye back to your rear! Then seek a light (where ye can)!" So a wall will be put up betwixt them, with a gate therein. Within it will be Mercy throughout, and without it, all alongside, will be (Wrath and) Punishment!

14. (Those without) will call out, "Were we not with you?" (The

others) will reply, "True! but ye led yourselves into temptation; ye waited (to our ruin); ye doubted (Allah's Promise); and (your false) desires deceived you; until there issued the Command of Allah. And the Deceiver deceived you in respect of Allah.

15. "This Day shall no ransom be accepted of you, nor of those who rejected Allah. Your abode is the Fire: that is the proper place to claim you: and an evil refuge it is!"

16. Has not the time arrived for the Believers that their hearts in all humility should engage in the remembrance of Allah and of the Truth which has been revealed (to them), and that they should not become like those to whom was given the Book aforetime, but long ages passed over them and their hearts grew hard? For many among them are rebellious transgressors.

17. Know ye (all) that Allah giveth life to the earth after its death! Already have We shown the Signs plainly to you, that ye may understand.

18. For those who give in Charity, men and women, and loan to Allah a Beautiful Loan, it shall be increased manifold (to their credit), and they shall have (besides) a generous reward.

19. And those who believe in Allah and His messengers—they are the Truthful and the martyrs, in the eye of their Lord: they shall have their Reward and their Light. But those who reject Allah and deny Our Signs,—they are the Companions of Hell-Fire.

20. Know ye (all), that the life of this world is but play and a pastime, adornment and mutual boasting and multiplying, (in rivalry) among yourselves, riches and children. Here is a similitude: how rain and the growth which it brings forth, delight (the hearts of) the tillers; soon it withers; thou wilt see it grow yellow; then it becomes dry and crumbles away. But in the Hereafter is a Chastisement severe (for the devotees of wrong). And Forgiveness from Allah and (His) Good Pleasure (for the devotees of Allah). And what is the life of this world, but goods and chattels of deception?

کہینگے کیوں نہیں تھے لیکن تمنے خود اپنے تئیں بلا میں ڈالا اور (ہمارے حق میں حوادث کے)
منتظر رہے اور (اسلام میں) شک کیا اور (لاطائل) آرزوؤں نے تمکو دھوکا
دیا یہاں تک کہ خدا کا حکم آپہنچا اور خدا کے بارے میں تمکو (شیطان) دغاباز دغا دیتا رہا ﴿۱۴﴾
تو آج تم سے معاوضہ نہیں لیا جائیگا اور نہ (وہ) کافروں ہی سے
قبول کیا جائے گا، تم سب کا ٹھکانا دوزخ ہے (کہ) وہی
تمہارے لائق ہے. اور وہ بُری جگہ ہے ﴿۱۵﴾
کیا ابھی تک مومنوں کیلئے اسکا وقت نہیں آیا کہ خدا کی یاد
کرنے کے وقت اور (قرآن) جو (خدائے برحق (کی طرف) سے
نازل ہوا ہے اسکے سننے کے وقت انکے دل نرم ہو جائیں اور وہ اُن
لوگوں کی طرح نہ ہو جائیں جنکو (ان سے) پہلے کتابیں دی گئی تھیں پھر
اُنپر زمان طویل گزر گیا تو انکے دل سخت ہوگئے. اور اُنمیں سے اکثر نافرمان ہیں ﴿۱۶﴾
جان رکھو کہ خدا ہی زمین کو اسکے مرنیکے بعد زندہ کرتا ہے. ہم نے اپنی
نشانیاں تم سے کھول کھول کر بیان کر دی ہیں تاکہ تم سمجھو ﴿۱۷﴾
جو لوگ خیرات کرنے والے ہیں مرد بھی اور عورتیں بھی اور خدا کو
(نیت) نیک (اور خلوص سے) قرض دیتے ہیں انکو دو چند
ادا کیا جائے گا اور اُن کے لئے عزت کا صلہ ہے ﴿۱۸﴾
اور جو لوگ خدا اور اسکے پیغمبروں پر ایمان لائے یہی اپنے پروردگار
کے نزدیک صدیق اور شہید ہیں. اُنکے لئے اُن (کے اعمال) کا صلہ
ہوگا اور اُن (کے ایمان) کی روشنی. اور جن لوگوں نے کفر کیا اور
ہماری آیتوں کو جھٹلایا وہی اہل دوزخ ہیں ﴿۱۹﴾
جان رکھو کہ دنیا کی زندگی محض کھیل اور تماشا اور زینت (و آرائش)
اور تمہارے آپس میں فخر (و ستائش) اور مال و اولاد کی ایک دوسرے سے
زیادہ طلب (و خواہش) ہے[۲۵۵] (اسکی مثال ایسی ہے جیسے بارش کہ اس سے
کھیتی اگتی اور کسانوں کو کھیتی بھلی لگتی ہے پھر وہ خوب زور پر
آتی ہے پھر (اے دیکھنے والے) تو اسکو دیکھتا ہے کہ (پک کر) زرد پڑ جاتی ہے
پھر چورا چورا ہو جاتی ہے اور آخرت میں (کافروں کیلئے) عذاب شدید اور (مومنوں کیلئے)
خدا کی طرف سے بخشش اور خوشنودی ہے. اور دنیا کی زندگی تو متاع فریب ہے ﴿۲۰﴾

وَلٰكِنَّكُمْ فَتَنْتُمْ اَنْفُسَكُمْ وَتَرَبَّصْتُمْ وَ
ارْتَبْتُمْ وَغَرَّتْكُمُ الْاَمَانِيُّ حَتّٰى جَآءَ اَمْرُ
اللّٰهِ وَغَرَّكُمْ بِاللّٰهِ الْغَرُوْرُ ﴿١٤﴾
فَالْيَوْمَ لَا يُؤْخَذُ مِنْكُمْ فِدْيَةٌ وَّلَا مِنَ
الَّذِيْنَ كَفَرُوْا ۭ مَاْوٰىكُمُ النَّارُ ۭ هِيَ مَوْلٰىكُمْ ۭ
وَبِئْسَ الْمَصِيْرُ ﴿١٥﴾
اَلَمْ يَاْنِ لِلَّذِيْنَ اٰمَنُوْٓا اَنْ تَخْشَعَ قُلُوْبُهُمْ
لِذِكْرِ اللّٰهِ وَمَا نَزَلَ مِنَ الْحَقِّ ۙ وَلَا يَكُوْنُوْا
كَالَّذِيْنَ اُوْتُوا الْكِتٰبَ مِنْ قَبْلُ فَطَالَ
عَلَيْهِمُ الْاَمَدُ فَقَسَتْ قُلُوْبُهُمْ ۭ وَكَثِيْرٌ
مِّنْهُمْ فٰسِقُوْنَ ﴿١٦﴾
اِعْلَمُوْٓا اَنَّ اللّٰهَ يُحْيِ الْاَرْضَ بَعْدَ مَوْتِهَا ۭ
قَدْ بَيَّنَّا لَكُمُ الْاٰيٰتِ لَعَلَّكُمْ تَعْقِلُوْنَ ﴿١٧﴾
اِنَّ الْمُصَّدِّقِيْنَ وَالْمُصَّدِّقٰتِ وَاَقْرَضُوا
اللّٰهَ قَرْضًا حَسَنًا يُّضٰعَفُ لَهُمْ وَلَهُمْ
اَجْرٌ كَرِيْمٌ ﴿١٨﴾
وَالَّذِيْنَ اٰمَنُوْا بِاللّٰهِ وَرُسُلِهٖٓ اُولٰۗىِٕكَ هُمُ
الصِّدِّيْقُوْنَ ڰ وَالشُّهَدَاۗءُ عِنْدَ رَبِّهِمْ ۭ
لَهُمْ اَجْرُهُمْ وَنُوْرُهُمْ ۭ وَالَّذِيْنَ كَفَرُوْا
وَكَذَّبُوْا بِاٰيٰتِنَآ اُولٰۗىِٕكَ اَصْحٰبُ الْجَحِيْمِ ﴿١٩﴾ ع ١٨
اِعْلَمُوْٓا اَنَّمَا الْحَيٰوةُ الدُّنْيَا لَعِبٌ وَّلَهْوٌ
وَّزِيْنَةٌ وَّتَفَاخُرٌۢ بَيْنَكُمْ وَتَكَاثُرٌ فِي
الْاَمْوَالِ وَالْاَوْلَادِ ۭ كَمَثَلِ غَيْثٍ اَعْجَبَ
الْكُفَّارَ نَبَاتُهٗ ثُمَّ يَهِيْجُ فَتَرٰىهُ مُصْفَرًّا
ثُمَّ يَكُوْنُ حُطٰمًا ۭ وَفِي الْاٰخِرَةِ عَذَابٌ
شَدِيْدٌ ۙ وَّمَغْفِرَةٌ مِّنَ اللّٰهِ وَرِضْوَانٌ ۭ
وَمَا الْحَيٰوةُ الدُّنْيَآ اِلَّا مَتَاعُ الْغُرُوْرِ ﴿٢٠﴾

21. Be ye foremost (in seeking) Forgiveness from your Lord, and a Garden (of Bliss), the width whereof is as the width of Heaven and earth, prepared for those who believe in Allah and His messengers: that is the Grace of Allah, which He bestows on whom He pleases: and Allah is the Lord of Grace abounding.

22. No misfortune can happen on earth or in your souls but is recorded in a Book before We bring it into existence: that is truly easy for Allah:

23. In order that ye may not despair over matters that pass you by, nor exult over favours bestowed upon you. For Allah loveth not any vainglorious boaster,—

24. Such persons as are covetous and commend covetousness to men. And if any turn back (from Allah's Way), verily Allah is free of all needs, worthy of all praise.

25. We sent aforetime Our messengers with Clear Signs and sent down with them the Book and the Balance (of Right and Wrong), that men may stand forth in justice; and We sent down Iron, in which is great might, as well as many benefits for mankind, that Allah may test who it is that will help, unseen, Him and His messengers: for Allah is Full of Strength, Exalted in Might.

26. And We sent Noah and Abraham, and established in their line Prophethood and Revelation: and some of them were on right guidance, but many of them became rebellious transgressors.

27. Then, in their wake, We followed them up with (others of) Our messengers: We sent after them Jesus the son of Mary, and bestowed on him the Gospel; and We ordained in the hearts of those who followed him Compassion and Mercy. But the Monasticism which they invented for themselves, We did not prescribe for them: (we commanded) only the

(بندو) اپنے پروردگار کی بخشش کی طرف اور جنت کی (طرف) جس کا
عرض آسمان اور زمین کے عرض کا سا ہے اور جو اُن لوگوں کیلئے
تیار کی گئی ہے جو خدا پر اور اُس کے پیغمبروں پر ایمان
لائے ہیں لپکو۔ یہ خدا کا فضل ہے جسے چاہے عطا فرمائے۔
اور خدا بڑے فضل کا مالک ہے ﴿۲۱﴾
کوئی مصیبت مُلک پر اور خود تم پر نہیں پڑتی مگر پیشتر
اس کے کہ ہم اس کو پیدا کریں ایک کتاب میں (لکھی ہوئی)
ہے۔ (اور) یہ (کام) خدا کو آسان ہے ﴿۲۲﴾
تاکہ جو (مطلب) تم سے فوت ہو گیا ہو اس کا غم نہ کھایا کرو اور
جو تم کو اُس نے دیا ہو اس پر اترایا نہ کرو۔ اور خدا کسی اترانے
اور شیخی بگھارنے والے کو دوست نہیں رکھتا ﴿۲۳﴾
جو خود بھی بخل کریں اور لوگوں کو بھی بخل سکھائیں اور
جو شخص رُوگردانی کرے تو خدا بھی بے پرواہ ہے (اور) وہی
سزاوار حمد (وثنا) ہے ﴿۲۴﴾
ہم نے اپنے پیغمبروں کو کھلی نشانیاں دے کر بھیجا۔ اور اُن پر
کتابیں نازل کیں اور ترازو (یعنی قواعد عدل) تاکہ لوگ
انصاف پر قائم رہیں۔ اور لوہا پیدا کیا اس میں (اسلحۂ جنگ کے لحاظ سے)
خطرہ بھی شدید ہے۔ اور لوگوں کیلئے فائدے بھی ہیں اور اسلئے کہ جو لوگ بن دیکھے
خدا اور اُسکے پیغمبروں کی مدد کرتے ہیں خدا انکو معلوم کرے بیشک خدا قوی (اور) غالب ہے ﴿۲۵﴾
اور ہم نے نوح اور ابراہیم کو پیغمبر بنا کر بھیجا اور اُنکی اولاد میں
پیغمبری اور کتاب (کے سلسلے) کو (وقتاً فوقتاً) جاری (رکھا) تو بعض تو
اُنہیں سے ہدایت پر ہیں۔ اور اکثر اُن میں سے خارج از اطاعت ہیں ﴿۲۶﴾
پھر اُنکے پیچھے اُنہی کے قدموں پر (اور) پیغمبر بھیجے اور اُنکے پیچھے مریم کے
بیٹے عیسیٰ کو بھیجا اور اُنکو انجیل عنایت کی اور جن لوگوں نے اُنکی
پیروی کی اُنکے دلوں میں شفقت اور مہربانی ڈال دی۔ اور لذّات سے
کنارہ کشی کی تو اُنہوں نے خود ایک نئی بات نکال لی ہم نے اُنکو اس کا حکم نہیں دیا
تھا مگر (اُنہوں نے اپنے خیال میں) خدا کی خوشنودی حاصل کرنے کیلئے آپ ہی

سَابِقُوْٓا اِلٰى مَغْفِرَةٍ مِّنْ رَّبِّكُمْ وَجَنَّةٍ
عَرْضُهَا كَعَرْضِ السَّمَآءِ وَالْاَرْضِ ۙ اُعِدَّتْ
لِلَّذِيْنَ اٰمَنُوْا بِاللّٰهِ وَرُسُلِهٖ ۭ ذٰلِكَ فَضْلُ
اللّٰهِ يُؤْتِيْهِ مَنْ يَّشَآءُ ۭ وَاللّٰهُ ذُو الْفَضْلِ
الْعَظِيْمِ ﴿٢١﴾
مَآ اَصَابَ مِنْ مُّصِيْبَةٍ فِي الْاَرْضِ وَلَا
فِيْٓ اَنْفُسِكُمْ اِلَّا فِيْ كِتٰبٍ مِّنْ قَبْلِ اَنْ
نَّبْرَاَهَا ۭ اِنَّ ذٰلِكَ عَلَى اللّٰهِ يَسِيْرٌ ﴿٢٢﴾
لِّكَيْلَا تَاْسَوْا عَلٰى مَا فَاتَكُمْ وَلَا تَفْرَحُوْا
بِمَآ اٰتٰىكُمْ ۭ وَاللّٰهُ لَا يُحِبُّ كُلَّ مُخْتَالٍ
فَخُوْرِ ﴿٢٣﴾
الَّذِيْنَ يَبْخَلُوْنَ وَيَاْمُرُوْنَ النَّاسَ
بِالْبُخْلِ ۭ وَمَنْ يَّتَوَلَّ فَاِنَّ اللّٰهَ هُوَ
الْغَنِيُّ الْحَمِيْدُ ﴿٢٤﴾
لَقَدْ اَرْسَلْنَا رُسُلَنَا بِالْبَيِّنٰتِ وَاَنْزَلْنَا مَعَهُمُ
الْكِتٰبَ وَالْمِيْزَانَ لِيَقُوْمَ النَّاسُ بِالْقِسْطِ ۚ
وَاَنْزَلْنَا الْحَدِيْدَ فِيْهِ بَاْسٌ شَدِيْدٌ وَّ
مَنَافِعُ لِلنَّاسِ وَلِيَعْلَمَ اللّٰهُ مَنْ يَّنْصُرُهٗ
ع ٦ ١٩ وَرُسُلَهٗ بِالْغَيْبِ ۭ اِنَّ اللّٰهَ قَوِيٌّ عَزِيْزٌ ﴿٢٥﴾
وَلَقَدْ اَرْسَلْنَا نُوْحًا وَّاِبْرٰهِيْمَ وَجَعَلْنَا
فِيْ ذُرِّيَّتِهِمَا النُّبُوَّةَ وَالْكِتٰبَ فَمِنْهُمْ
مُّهْتَدٍ ۚ وَكَثِيْرٌ مِّنْهُمْ فٰسِقُوْنَ ﴿٢٦﴾
ثُمَّ قَفَّيْنَا عَلٰٓي اٰثَارِهِمْ بِرُسُلِنَا وَقَفَّيْنَا
بِعِيْسَى ابْنِ مَرْيَمَ وَاٰتَيْنٰهُ الْاِنْجِيْلَ ۥ وَ
جَعَلْنَا فِيْ قُلُوْبِ الَّذِيْنَ اتَّبَعُوْهُ رَاْفَةً
وَّرَحْمَةً ۭ وَرَهْبَانِيَّةَۨ ابْتَدَعُوْهَا مَا كَتَبْنٰهَا
عَلَيْهِمْ اِلَّا ابْتِغَاۗءَ رِضْوَانِ اللّٰهِ فَمَا رَعَوْهَا

SÛRA–58
AL-MUJÃDILA
(INTRODUCTION)

This is the second of the ten Madînah Sûras referred to in the Introduction to the last Sûra. Its subject-matter is the acceptance of a women's Plea on behalf of herself and her children and a condemnation of all secret counsels and intrigues in the Muslim Brotherhood.

The date is somewhat close to that of S. 33, say between A.H. 5. and A.H. 7.

seeking for the Good Pleasure of Allah; but that they did not foster as they should have done. Yet We bestowed, on those among them who believed, their (due) reward, but many of them are rebellious transgressors.

28. O ye that believe! fear Allah, and believe in His Messenger, and He will bestow on you a double portion of His Mercy: He will provide for you a Light by which ye shall walk (straight in your path), and He will forgive you (your past): for Allah is Oft-Forgiving, Most Merciful:

29. That the People of the Book may know that they have no power whatever over the Grace of Allah, that (His) Grace is (entirely) in His Hand, to bestow it on whomsoever He wills. For Allah is the Lord of Grace abounding.

Al-Mujādila, or The Woman who Pleads

In the name of Allah, Most Gracious, Most Merciful.

1. Allah has indeed heard (and accepted) the statement of the woman who pleads with thee concerning her husband and carries her complaint (in prayer) to Allah: and Allah (always) hears the arguments between both of you: for Allah hears and sees (all things).

2. If any men among you divorce their wives by *Ẕihār* (calling them mothers), they cannot be their mothers: none can be their mothers except those who gave them birth. And in fact they use words (both) iniquitous and false: but truly Allah is All-Pardoning, All-Forgiving.

3. But those who pronounce the word "*Ẕihār*" to their wives then wish to go back on the words they uttered,— (it is ordained that such a one) should free a slave before they touch each other: this are ye admonished to perform: and Allah is well-acquainted with (all) that ye do.

4. And if any has not (the means), he should fast for two months consecutively before they touch each other, but if any is unable to do so, he should feed sixty indigent ones. This, that ye may show your faith in Allah and His Messenger. Those are limits (set by) Allah. For those who

حَقَّ رِعَايَتِهَا ۚ فَآتَيْنَا الَّذِينَ آمَنُوا مِنْهُمْ
أَجْرَهُمْ ۖ وَكَثِيرٌ مِّنْهُمْ فَاسِقُونَ ﴿٢٧﴾
يَا أَيُّهَا الَّذِينَ آمَنُوا اتَّقُوا اللَّهَ وَآمِنُوا
بِرَسُولِهِ يُؤْتِكُمْ كِفْلَيْنِ مِن رَّحْمَتِهِ وَ
يَجْعَل لَّكُمْ نُورًا تَمْشُونَ بِهِ وَيَغْفِرْ لَكُمْ ۚ
وَاللَّهُ غَفُورٌ رَّحِيمٌ ﴿٢٨﴾
لِّئَلَّا يَعْلَمَ أَهْلُ الْكِتَابِ أَلَّا يَقْدِرُونَ
عَلَىٰ شَيْءٍ مِّن فَضْلِ اللَّهِ ۙ وَأَنَّ الْفَضْلَ
بِيَدِ اللَّهِ يُؤْتِيهِ مَن يَشَاءُ ۚ وَاللَّهُ
ذُو الْفَضْلِ الْعَظِيمِ ﴿٢٩﴾ ع ۴

سورة المجادلة مدنية وهي اثنتان وعشرون آية وثلاث ركوعات

بِسْمِ اللَّهِ الرَّحْمَٰنِ الرَّحِيمِ
قَدْ سَمِعَ اللَّهُ قَوْلَ الَّتِي تُجَادِلُكَ
فِي زَوْجِهَا وَتَشْتَكِي إِلَى اللَّهِ وَاللَّهُ
يَسْمَعُ تَحَاوُرَكُمَا ۚ إِنَّ اللَّهَ سَمِيعٌ بَصِيرٌ ﴿١﴾
الَّذِينَ يُظَاهِرُونَ مِنكُم مِّن نِّسَائِهِم
مَّا هُنَّ أُمَّهَاتِهِمْ ۖ إِنْ أُمَّهَاتُهُمْ إِلَّا اللَّائِي
وَلَدْنَهُمْ ۚ وَإِنَّهُمْ لَيَقُولُونَ مُنكَرًا مِّنَ
الْقَوْلِ وَزُورًا ۚ وَإِنَّ اللَّهَ لَعَفُوٌّ غَفُورٌ ﴿٢﴾
وَالَّذِينَ يُظَاهِرُونَ مِن نِّسَائِهِمْ ثُمَّ
يَعُودُونَ لِمَا قَالُوا فَتَحْرِيرُ رَقَبَةٍ مِّن
قَبْلِ أَن يَتَمَاسَّا ۚ ذَٰلِكُمْ تُوعَظُونَ بِهِ ۚ
وَاللَّهُ بِمَا تَعْمَلُونَ خَبِيرٌ ﴿٣﴾
فَمَن لَّمْ يَجِدْ فَصِيَامُ شَهْرَيْنِ مُتَتَابِعَيْنِ
مِن قَبْلِ أَن يَتَمَاسَّا ۖ فَمَن لَّمْ يَسْتَطِعْ
فَإِطْعَامُ سِتِّينَ مِسْكِينًا ۚ ذَٰلِكَ لِتُؤْمِنُوا
بِاللَّهِ وَرَسُولِهِ ۚ وَتِلْكَ حُدُودُ اللَّهِ ۗ

الجزء الثامن والعشرون ۲۸

ایسا کرلیا تھا) پھر جیسا اس کو نباہنا چاہیئے تھا نباہ بھی نہ سکے پس جو لوگ ان میں سے
ایمان لائے ان کو ہم نے ان کا اجر دیا۔ اور ان میں بہت سے نافرمان ہیں ﴿۲۷﴾
مومنو! خدا سے ڈرو اور اس کے پیغمبر پر ایمان لاؤ وہ تمہیں
اپنی رحمت سے دگنا اجر عطا فرمائے گا اور تمہارے لئے
روشنی کردے گا جس میں چلو گے اور تم کو بخش دے گا۔ اور
خدا بخشنے والا مہربان ہے ﴿۲۸﴾
(یہ باتیں) اس لئے (بیان کی گئی ہیں) کہ اہل کتاب جان لیں
کہ وہ خدا کے فضل پر کچھ بھی قدرت نہیں رکھتے۔ اور یہ کہ
فضل خدا ہی کے ہاتھ ہے جس کو چاہتا ہے دیتا ہے اور
خدا بڑے فضل کا مالک ہے ﴿۲۹﴾

سورۂ مجادلہ مدنی ہے اس میں بائیس آیتیں اور تین رکوع ہیں

شروع خدا کا نام لے کر جو بڑا مہربان نہایت رحم والا ہے
(اے پیغمبر) جو عورت تم سے اپنے شوہر کے بارے میں بحث وجدال کرتی
اور خدا سے شکایت (رنج وملال) کرتی تھی خدا نے اس کی التجا سن لی اور
خدا تم دونوں کی گفتگو سن رہا تھا۔ کچھ شک نہیں کہ خدا سنتا دیکھتا ہے ﴿۱﴾
جو لوگ تم میں سے اپنی عورتوں کو ماں کہہ دیتے ہیں وہ ان کی
مائیں نہیں (ہو جاتیں) ان کی مائیں تو وہی ہیں جن کے بطن سے
وہ پیدا ہوئے۔ بےشک وہ نامعقول اور جھوٹی بات کہتے
ہیں۔ اور خدا بڑا معاف کرنے والا (اور) بخشنے والا ہے ﴿۲﴾
اور جو لوگ اپنی بیویوں کو ماں کہہ بیٹھیں پھر اپنے قول سے
رجوع کرلیں تو (ان کو) ہم بستر ہونے سے پہلے ایک غلام
آزاد کرنا (ضرور) ہے۔ (مومنو) اس (حکم) سے تم کو نصیحت
کی جاتی ہے۔ اور جو کچھ تم کرتے ہو خدا اس سے خبردار ہے ﴿۳﴾
جس کو غلام نہ ملے وہ مجامعت سے پہلے متواتر دو مہینے
کے روزے رکھے جس کو اس کا بھی مقدور نہ ہو (اسے) ساٹھ
محتاجوں کو کھانا کھلانا (چاہیئے)۔ یہ (حکم) اس لئے (ہے) کہ
تم خدا اور رسول کے فرمانبردار ہو جاؤ۔ اور یہ خدا کی حدیں ہیں۔

وَلِلْكٰفِرِيْنَ عَذَابٌ اَلِيْمٌ ﴿٤﴾
اِنَّ الَّذِيْنَ يُحَآدُّوْنَ اللّٰهَ وَرَسُوْلَهٗ كُبِتُوْا
كَمَا كُبِتَ الَّذِيْنَ مِنْ قَبْلِهِمْ وَقَدْ اَنْزَلْنَآ
اٰيٰتٍۢ بَيِّنٰتٍ ۭ وَلِلْكٰفِرِيْنَ عَذَابٌ مُّهِيْنٌ ﴿٥﴾
يَوْمَ يَبْعَثُهُمُ اللّٰهُ جَمِيْعًا فَيُنَبِّئُهُمْ بِمَا عَمِلُوْا ۭ
اَحْصٰىهُ اللّٰهُ وَنَسُوْهُ ۭ وَاللّٰهُ عَلٰى كُلِّ شَيْءٍ
شَهِيْدٌ ﴿٦﴾ ع
اَلَمْ تَرَ اَنَّ اللّٰهَ يَعْلَمُ مَا فِي السَّمٰوٰتِ وَ
مَا فِي الْاَرْضِ ۭ مَا يَكُوْنُ مِنْ نَّجْوٰى ثَلٰثَةٍ
اِلَّا هُوَ رَابِعُهُمْ وَلَا خَمْسَةٍ اِلَّا هُوَ سَادِسُهُمْ
وَلَآ اَدْنٰى مِنْ ذٰلِكَ وَلَآ اَكْثَرَ اِلَّا هُوَ مَعَهُمْ
اَيْنَ مَا كَانُوْا ۚ ثُمَّ يُنَبِّئُهُمْ بِمَا عَمِلُوْا يَوْمَ
الْقِيٰمَةِ ۭ اِنَّ اللّٰهَ بِكُلِّ شَيْءٍ عَلِيْمٌ ﴿٧﴾
اَلَمْ تَرَ اِلَى الَّذِيْنَ نُهُوْا عَنِ النَّجْوٰى ثُمَّ
يَعُوْدُوْنَ لِمَا نُهُوْا عَنْهُ وَيَتَنٰجَوْنَ بِالْاِثْمِ
وَالْعُدْوَانِ وَمَعْصِيَتِ الرَّسُوْلِ ۡ وَاِذَا
جَآءُوْكَ حَيَّوْكَ بِمَا لَمْ يُحَيِّكَ بِهِ اللّٰهُ ۙ
وَيَقُوْلُوْنَ فِيْٓ اَنْفُسِهِمْ لَوْلَا يُعَذِّبُنَا اللّٰهُ
بِمَا نَقُوْلُ ۭ حَسْبُهُمْ جَهَنَّمُ ۚ يَصْلَوْنَهَا ۚ
فَبِئْسَ الْمَصِيْرُ ﴿٨﴾
يٰٓاَيُّهَا الَّذِيْنَ اٰمَنُوْٓا اِذَا تَنَاجَيْتُمْ فَلَا
تَتَنَاجَوْا بِالْاِثْمِ وَالْعُدْوَانِ وَمَعْصِيَتِ
الرَّسُوْلِ وَتَنَاجَوْا بِالْبِرِّ وَالتَّقْوٰى ۭ وَ
اتَّقُوا اللّٰهَ الَّذِيْٓ اِلَيْهِ تُحْشَرُوْنَ ﴿٩﴾
اِنَّمَا النَّجْوٰى مِنَ الشَّيْطٰنِ لِيَحْزُنَ
الَّذِيْنَ اٰمَنُوْا وَلَيْسَ بِضَاۗرِّهِمْ شَيْـًٔا اِلَّا
بِاِذْنِ اللّٰهِ ۭ وَعَلَى اللّٰهِ فَلْيَتَوَكَّلِ

اور نہ ماننے والوں کے لئے درد دینے والا عذاب ہے ﴿٤﴾
جو لوگ خدا اور اُس کے رسُول کی مخالفت کرتے ہیں وہ (اسی طرح)
ذلیل کئے جائینگے جسطرح اُنسے پہلے لوگ ذلیل کئے گئے تھے اور ہم نے صاف
اور صریح آیتیں نازل کر دی ہیں جو نہیں مانتے اُنکو ذلت کا عذاب ہوگا ﴿٥﴾
جس دن خدا اُن سب کو جِلا اُٹھائے گا تو جو کام وہ کرتے
رہے اُن کو جتائے گا. خدا کو وہ سب (کام) یاد ہیں اور یہ
اُن کو بھول گئے ہیں. اور خدا ہر چیز سے واقف ہے ﴿٦﴾
کیا تم کو معلوم نہیں کہ جو کچھ آسمانوں میں ہے اور جو کچھ زمین میں ہے
خدا کو سب معلوم ہے. (کسی جگہ) تین (شخصوں) کا (مجمع اور) کانوں میں
صلاح و مشورہ نہیں ہوتا مگر وہ اُنمیں چوتھا ہوتا ہے اور (کہیں) پانچ کا مگر
وہ اُنمیں چھٹا ہوتا ہے اور (اس سے) کم یا زیادہ مگر وہ اُنکے ساتھ ہوتا ہے خواہ
وہ کہیں ہوں. پھر جو جو کام یہ کرتے رہے ہیں قیامت کے دن وہ (ایک
ایک) اُن کو بتائے گا. بیشک خدا ہر چیز سے واقف ہے ﴿٧﴾
کیا تم نے اُن لوگوں کو نہیں دیکھا جن کو سرگوشیاں کرنے سے
منع کیا گیا تھا. پھر جس (کام) سے منع کیا گیا تھا وہی پھر کرنے لگے
اور یہ تو گناہ اور ظلم اور رسُولِ (خدا) کی نافرمانی کی سرگوشیاں کرتے ہیں.
اور جب تمہارے پاس آتے ہیں تو جس (کلمے) سے خدا نے تمکو دُعا نہیں دی اس سے
تمہیں دُعا دیتے ہیں. اور اپنے دلمیں کہتے ہیں کہ (اگر یہ واقعی پیغمبر ہیں تو) جو
کچھ ہم کہتے ہیں خدا ہمیں اسکی سزا کیوں نہیں دیتا. (اے پیغمبر) اُنکو
دوزخ (ہی کی سزا) کافی ہے. یہ اُسی میں داخل ہونگے اور وہ بُری جگہ ہے ﴿٨﴾
مومنو! جب تم آپس میں سرگوشیاں کرنے لگو تو گناہ اور زیادتی
اور پیغمبر کی نافرمانی کی باتیں نہ کرنا بلکہ نیکوکاری اور
پرہیزگاری کی باتیں کرنا. اور خدا سے جس کے سامنے جمع
کئے جاؤ گے ڈرتے رہنا ﴿٩﴾
(کافروں کی) سرگوشیاں تو شیطان (کی حرکات)
سے ہیں (جو) اس لئے (کی جاتی ہیں) کہ مومن (اُن سے)
غمناک ہوں مگر خدا کے حکم کے سوا اُن سے اُنہیں کچھ نقصان

reject (Him), there is a grievous Chastisement.

5. Those who oppose (the commands of) Allah and His Messenger will be humbled to dust, as were those before them: for We have already sent down Clear Signs. And the Unbelievers (will have) a humiliating Chastisement,

6. On the Day that Allah will raise them all up (again) and tell them of their deeds (which) Allah has reckoned and which they forgot, for Allah is Witness to all things.

7. Seest thou not that Allah doth know (all) that is in the heavens and on earth? There is not a secret consultation between three, but He is the fourth of them,— nor between five but he is the sixth,— nor between fewer nor more, but He is with them, wheresoever they be: in the end will He tell them what they did on the Day of Judgment. For Allah Has full knowledge of all things.

8. Seest thou not those who were forbidden secret counsels yet revert to that which they were forbidden (to do)? And they hold secret counsels among themselves for iniquity and hostility, and disobedience to the Messenger. And when they come to thee, they salute thee, not as Allah salutes thee, (but in crooked ways): and they say to themselves, "Why does not Allah punish us for our words?" Enough for them is Hell: in it will they burn, and evil is that destination!

9. O ye who believe! when ye hold secret counsel, do it not for iniquity and hostility, and disobedience to the Messenger; but do it for righteousness and self-restraint; and fear Allah, to Whom ye shall be brought back.

10. Secret counsels are only (inspired) by Satan, in order that he may cause grief to the Believers; but he cannot harm them in the least, except as Allah permits; and on Allah let the Believers put

their trust.

11. O ye who believe! when ye are told to make room in the assemblies, (spread out and) make room: (ample) room will Allah provide for you. And when ye are told to rise up, rise up: Allah will raise up, to (suitable) ranks (and degrees), those of you who believe and who have been granted Knowledge. And Allah is well-acquainted with all ye do.

12. O ye who believe ! when ye consult the Messenger in private, spend something in charity before your private consultation. That will be best for you, and most conducive to purity (of conduct). But if ye find not (the wherewithal), Allah is Oft-Forgiving, Most Merciful.

13. Is it that ye are afraid of spending sums in charity before your private consultation (with him)? If, then, ye do not so, and Allah forgives you, then (at least) establish regular prayer; give Zakat and obey Allah and His Messenger. And Allah is well-acquainted with all that ye do.

14. Seest thou not those who turn (in friendship) to such as have the Wrath of Allah upon them? They are neither of you nor of them, and they swear to falsehood knowingly.

15. Allah has prepared for them a severe Chastisement: evil indeed are their deeds.

16. They have made their oaths a screen (for their misdeeds): thus they obstruct (men) from the Path of Allah: therefore shall they have a humiliating Chastisement.

17. Of no profit whatever to them, against Allah, will be their riches nor their sons: they will be Companions of the Fire, to dwell therein (for aye)!

18. The Day will Allah raise them all up (for Judgment): then will they swear to Him as they swear to you: and they think that they have

نہیں پہنچ سکتا۔ تو مومنوں کو چاہیئے کہ خدا ہی پر بھروسا رکھیں (١٠)
مومنو! جب تم سے کہا جائے کہ مجلس میں کھُل کر
بیٹھو تو کھُل بیٹھا کرو خدا تم کو کشادگی بخشے گا۔ اور
جب کہا جائے کہ اُٹھ کھڑے ہو تو اُٹھ کھڑے ہُوا کرو
جو لوگ تم میں سے ایمان لائے ہیں اور جن کو علم عطا کیا گیا ہے
خدا اُنکے درجے بلند کریگا۔ اور خدا تمہارے سب کاموں سے واقف ہے (١١)
مومنو! جب تم پیغمبر کے کان میں کوئی بات کہو تو بات کہنے
سے پہلے (مساکین کو) کچھ خیرات دے دیا کرو۔ یہ تمہارے لئے
بہت بہتر اور پاکیزگی کی بات ہے۔ اور اگر خیرات تم کو میسّر
نہ آئے تو خدا بخشنے والا مہربان ہے (١٢)
کیا تم اس سے کہ پیغمبر کے کان میں کوئی بات کہنے سے پہلے
خیرات دیا کرو ڈر گئے؟ پھر جب تم نے (ایسا) نہ کیا اور
خدا نے تمہیں معاف کر دیا تو نماز پڑھتے اور زکوٰة دیتے رہو
اور خدا اور اُس کے رسول کی فرمانبرداری کرتے رہو۔ اور جو
کچھ تم کرتے ہو خدا اس سے خبردار ہے (١٣)
بھلا تم نے اُن لوگوں کو نہیں دیکھا جو ایسوں سے دوستی
کرتے ہیں جن پر خدا کا غضب ہُوا۔ وہ نہ تم میں ہیں نہ اُنمیں۔
اور جان بوجھ کر جھوٹی باتوں پر قسمیں کھاتے ہیں (١٤)
خدا نے اُن کے لئے سخت عذاب تیار کر رکھا ہے۔ یہ جو کچھ
کرتے ہیں یقیناً بُرا ہے (١٥)
اُنہوں نے اپنی قسموں کو ڈھال بنا لیا اور (لوگوں کو) خدا
کے رستے سے روک دیا ہے سو اُن کیلئے ذلّت کا عذاب ہے (١٦)
خدا کے (عذاب کے) سامنے نہ تو اُن کا مال ہی کچھ کام آئیگا
اور نہ اولاد ہی (کچھ فائدہ دے گی)۔ یہ لوگ اہلِ دوزخ ہیں۔
اس میں ہمیشہ (جلتے) رہیں گے (١٧)
جس دن خدا اُن سب کو جِلا اُٹھائے گا تو جس طرح تمہارے
سامنے قسمیں کھاتے ہیں (اسی طرح) خدا کے سامنے قسمیں کھائینگے اور

الْمُؤْمِنُوْنَ (١٠)
يٰٓاَيُّهَا الَّذِيْنَ اٰمَنُوْٓا اِذَا قِيْلَ لَكُمْ تَفَسَّحُوْا
فِي الْمَجٰلِسِ فَافْسَحُوْا يَفْسَحِ اللّٰهُ لَكُمْ ۚ
وَاِذَا قِيْلَ انْشُزُوْا فَانْشُزُوْا يَرْفَعِ اللّٰهُ
الَّذِيْنَ اٰمَنُوْا مِنْكُمْ ۙ وَالَّذِيْنَ اُوْتُوا الْعِلْمَ
دَرَجٰتٍ ۭ وَاللّٰهُ بِمَا تَعْمَلُوْنَ خَبِيْرٌ (١١)
يٰٓاَيُّهَا الَّذِيْنَ اٰمَنُوْٓا اِذَا نَاجَيْتُمُ الرَّسُوْلَ
فَقَدِّمُوْا بَيْنَ يَدَيْ نَجْوٰىكُمْ صَدَقَةً ۭ
ذٰلِكَ خَيْرٌ لَّكُمْ وَاَطْهَرُ ۭ فَاِنْ لَّمْ تَجِدُوْا
فَاِنَّ اللّٰهَ غَفُوْرٌ رَّحِيْمٌ (١٢)
ءَاَشْفَقْتُمْ اَنْ تُقَدِّمُوْا بَيْنَ يَدَيْ
نَجْوٰىكُمْ صَدَقٰتٍ ۭ فَاِذْ لَمْ تَفْعَلُوْا وَتَابَ
اللّٰهُ عَلَيْكُمْ فَاَقِيْمُوا الصَّلٰوةَ وَاٰتُوا الزَّكٰوةَ
وَاَطِيْعُوا اللّٰهَ وَرَسُوْلَهٗ ۭ وَاللّٰهُ خَبِيْرٌۢ بِمَا
تَعْمَلُوْنَ (١٣) ع
اَلَمْ تَرَ اِلَى الَّذِيْنَ تَوَلَّوْا قَوْمًا غَضِبَ اللّٰهُ
عَلَيْهِمْ ۭ مَا هُمْ مِّنْكُمْ وَلَا مِنْهُمْ ۙ وَيَحْلِفُوْنَ
عَلَى الْكَذِبِ وَهُمْ يَعْلَمُوْنَ (١٤)
اَعَدَّ اللّٰهُ لَهُمْ عَذَابًا شَدِيْدًا ۭ اِنَّهُمْ
سَاۗءَ مَا كَانُوْا يَعْمَلُوْنَ (١٥)
اِتَّخَذُوْٓا اَيْمَانَهُمْ جُنَّةً فَصَدُّوْا عَنْ
سَبِيْلِ اللّٰهِ فَلَهُمْ عَذَابٌ مُّهِيْنٌ (١٦)
لَنْ تُغْنِيَ عَنْهُمْ اَمْوَالُهُمْ وَلَآ اَوْلَادُهُمْ
مِّنَ اللّٰهِ شَيْـًٔا ۭ اُولٰۗىِٕكَ اَصْحٰبُ النَّارِ ۭ
هُمْ فِيْهَا خٰلِدُوْنَ (١٧)
يَوْمَ يَبْعَثُهُمُ اللّٰهُ جَمِيْعًا فَيَحْلِفُوْنَ لَهٗ
كَمَا يَحْلِفُوْنَ لَكُمْ وَيَحْسَبُوْنَ اَنَّهُمْ

SÛRA–59
AL-ḤASHR
(INTRODUCTION)

This is the third of the series of ten short Madinah Sûras, dealing each with a special point in the life of the Ummat: see Introduction to S. 57. The special theme here is how treachery to the Ummat on the part of its enemies recoils on the enemies themselves, while it strengthens the bond between the different sections of the Ummat itself, and this is illustrated by the story of the expulsion of the Jewish tribe of the Banû Nadhîr in Rabî' I A.H. 4.

This fixes the date of the Sûra.

something (to stand upon). No, indeed ! they are but liars !

19. Satan has got the better of them: so he has made them forgot the remembrance of Allah. They are the Party of Satan. Truly, it is the Party of Satan that will lose.

20. Those who oppose (the commands of) Allah and His Messenger will be among those most humiliated.

21. Allah has decreed: "It is I and My messengers who must prevail": for Allah is Strong, Mighty.

22. Thou wilt not find any people who believe in Allah and the Last Day, loving those who oppose Allah and His Messenger, even though they were their fathers or their sons, or their brothers, or their kindred. For such he has written Faith in their hearts, and strengthened them with a spirit from Himself. And He will admit them to Gardens beneath which Rivers flow, to dwell therein (for ever). Allah will be well pleased with them, and they with Him. They are the Party of Allah. Truly it is the Party of Allah that will achieve Success.

Al-Ḥashr, or The Gathering (or Banishment,)

In the name of Allah, Most Gracious, Most Merciful.

1. Whatever is in the heavens and on earth, declares the Praises and Glory of Allah: for He is the Exalted in Might, the Wise.

2. It is He Who got out the Unbelievers among the People of the Book from their homes at the first gathering (of the forces). Little did ye think that they would get out: and they thought that their fortresses would defend them from Allah! But the (Wrath of) Allah came to them from quarters from which they little expected (it), and cast terror into their hearts, so that they destroyed their dwellings by their own hands and the hands of the

عَلٰى شَيْءٍ اَلَآ اِنَّهُمْ هُمُ الْكٰذِبُوْنَ ⑱
اِسْتَحْوَذَ عَلَيْهِمُ الشَّيْطٰنُ فَاَنْسٰىهُمْ ذِكْرَ
اللّٰهِ اُولٰٓئِكَ حِزْبُ الشَّيْطٰنِ اَلَآ اِنَّ
حِزْبَ الشَّيْطٰنِ هُمُ الْخٰسِرُوْنَ ⑲
اِنَّ الَّذِيْنَ يُحَآدُّوْنَ اللّٰهَ وَرَسُوْلَهٗٓ
اُولٰٓئِكَ فِي الْاَذَلِّيْنَ ⑳
كَتَبَ اللّٰهُ لَاَغْلِبَنَّ اَنَا وَرُسُلِيْ اِنَّ اللّٰهَ
قَوِيٌّ عَزِيْزٌ ㉑
لَا تَجِدُ قَوْمًا يُّؤْمِنُوْنَ بِاللّٰهِ وَالْيَوْمِ الْاٰخِرِ
يُوَآدُّوْنَ مَنْ حَآدَّ اللّٰهَ وَرَسُوْلَهٗ وَلَوْ كَانُوْٓا
اٰبَآءَهُمْ اَوْ اَبْنَآءَهُمْ اَوْ اِخْوَانَهُمْ اَوْ عَشِيْرَتَهُمْ
اُولٰٓئِكَ كَتَبَ فِيْ قُلُوْبِهِمُ الْاِيْمَانَ وَاَيَّدَهُمْ
بِرُوْحٍ مِّنْهُ وَيُدْخِلُهُمْ جَنّٰتٍ تَجْرِيْ مِنْ
تَحْتِهَا الْاَنْهٰرُ خٰلِدِيْنَ فِيْهَا رَضِيَ اللّٰهُ
عَنْهُمْ وَرَضُوْا عَنْهُ اُولٰٓئِكَ حِزْبُ اللّٰهِ
اَلَآ اِنَّ حِزْبَ اللّٰهِ هُمُ الْمُفْلِحُوْنَ ㉒

سُوْرَةُ الْحَشْرِ مَدَنِيَّةٌ وَّهِيَ اَرْبَعٌ وَّعِشْرُوْنَ اٰيَةً وَّثَلٰثُ رُكُوْعَاتٍ

بِسْمِ اللّٰهِ الرَّحْمٰنِ الرَّحِيْمِ
سَبَّحَ لِلّٰهِ مَا فِي السَّمٰوٰتِ وَمَا فِي الْاَرْضِ
وَهُوَ الْعَزِيْزُ الْحَكِيْمُ ①
هُوَ الَّذِيْٓ اَخْرَجَ الَّذِيْنَ كَفَرُوْا مِنْ
اَهْلِ الْكِتٰبِ مِنْ دِيَارِهِمْ لِاَوَّلِ الْحَشْرِ
مَا ظَنَنْتُمْ اَنْ يَّخْرُجُوْا وَظَنُّوْٓا اَنَّهُمْ
مَّانِعَتُهُمْ حُصُوْنُهُمْ مِّنَ اللّٰهِ فَاَتٰىهُمُ اللّٰهُ
مِنْ حَيْثُ لَمْ يَحْتَسِبُوْا وَقَذَفَ فِيْ
قُلُوْبِهِمُ الرُّعْبَ يُخْرِبُوْنَ بُيُوْتَهُمْ
بِاَيْدِيْهِمْ وَاَيْدِي الْمُؤْمِنِيْنَ فَاعْتَبِرُوْا

وقف النبي صلى الله عليه وسلم

خیال کرینگے کہ (ایسا کرنے سے) کام نکلے ہیں۔ دیکھو یہ جھوٹے (اور برسرِ غلط) ہیں ⑱
شیطان نے اُن کو قابو میں کر لیا ہے اور خدا کی یاد اُن کو
بُھلا دی ہے۔ یہ (جماعت) شیطان کا لشکر ہے۔ اور
سُن رکھو کہ شیطان کا لشکر نقصان اُٹھانے والا ہے ⑲
جو لوگ خدا اور اُس کے رسُول کی مخالفت کرتے ہیں
وہ نہایت ذلیل ہوں گے ⑳
خدا کا حکم ناطق ہے کہ مَیں اور میرے پیغمبر ضرور غالب رہیں گے
بے شک خدا زورآور (اور) زبردست ہے ㉑
جو لوگ خدا پر اور روزِ قیامت پر ایمان رکھتے ہیں تم اُن کو خدا
اور اُسکے رسُول کے دشمنوں سے دوستی کرتے ہوئے نہ دیکھو گے۔
خواہ وہ اُنکے باپ یا بیٹے یا بھائی یا خاندان ہی کے لوگ ہوں۔
یہ وہ لوگ ہیں جنکے دلوں میں خدا نے ایمان (پتھر پر لکیر کی طرح)
تحریر کر دیا ہے اور فیضِ غیبی سے اُن کی مدد کی ہے۔ اور وہ اُنکو بہشتوں
میں جنکے تلے نہریں بہ رہی ہیں داخل کریگا ہمیشہ اُنمیں رہیں گے۔
خدا اُنسے خوش اور وہ خدا سے خوش۔ یہی گروہ خدا کا لشکر ہے۔
(اور) سُن رکھو کہ خدا ہی کا لشکر مُراد حاصل کرنے والا ہے ㉒

سورۂ حشر مدنی ہے اس میں چوبیس آیتیں اور تین رکوع ہیں

شروع خدا کا نام لے کر جو بڑا مہربان نہایت رحم والا ہے
جو چیزیں آسمانوں میں ہیں اور جو چیزیں زمین میں ہیں
(سب) خدا کی تسبیح کرتی ہیں اور وہ غالب حکمت والا ہے ①
وہی تو ہے جس نے کفار اہلِ کتاب کو حشرِ اوّل کے وقت
اُن کے گھروں سے نکال دیا۔ تمہارے خیال میں بھی نہ تھا کہ
وہ نکل جائیں گے اور وہ لوگ یہ سمجھے ہوئے تھے کہ اُن کے
قلعے اُن کو خدا (کے عذاب) سے بچا لیں گے مگر خدا نے اُن کو
وہاں سے آلیا جہاں سے اُن کو گمان بھی نہ تھا اور اُنکے
دلوں میں دہشت ڈال دی کہ اپنے گھروں کو خود اپنے ہاتھوں
اور مومنوں کے ہاتھوں سے اُجاڑنے لگے تو اے (بصیرت کی)

Believers. Take warning, then, O ye with eyes (to see)!

3. And had it not been that Allah had decreed banishment for them, he would certainly have punished them in this world: and in the Hereafter they shall (certainly) have the Punishment of the Fire.

4. That is because they resisted Allah and His Messenger and if anyone resists Allah, verily Allah is severe in Punishment.

5. Whatever ye cut down (O ye Muslims!) of the tender palm-trees, or ye left them standing on their roots, it was by leave of Allah, and in order that He might cover with shame the rebellious transgressors.

6. What Allah has bestowed on His Messenger (and taken away) from them—for this ye made no expedition with either cavalry or camelry: but Allah gives power to His messengers over any He pleases: and Allah has power over all things.

7. What Allah has bestowed on His Messenger (and taken away) from the people of the townships,—belongs to Allah,—to His Messenger and to kindred and orphans, the needy and the wayfarer; in order that it may not (Merely) make a circuit between the wealthy among you. So take what the Messenger gives you, and refrain from what he prohibits you. And fear Allah; for Allah is strict in Punishment.

8. (Some part is due) to the indigent Muhājirs, those who were expelled from their homes and their property, while seeking Grace from Allah and (His) Good Pleasure, and aiding Allah and His Messenger: such are indeed the truthful;—

9. And those who before them; had homes (in Madinah) and had adopted the Faith,—show their affection to such as came to them for refuge, and entertain no desire in their hearts for things given to the (latter), but give them preference over

آنکھیں رکھنے والو عبرت پکڑو[٢٨٨] ﴿٢﴾
اور اگر خدا نے اُن کے بارے میں جلاوطن کرنا نہ لکھا ہوتا
تو اُن کو دُنیا میں بھی عذاب دے دیتا۔ اور آخرت میں تو
اُن کے لئے آگ کا عذاب (تیار) ہے ﴿٣﴾
یہ اس لئے کہ اُنہوں نے خدا اور اُس کے رسُول کی مخالفت کی۔
اور جو شخص خدا کی مخالفت کرے تو خدا سخت عذاب دینے والا ہے ﴿٤﴾
(مومنو!) کھجور کے جو درخت تم نے کاٹ ڈالے یا اُنکو اپنی جڑوں
پر کھڑا رہنے دیا سو خدا کے حکم سے تھا اور مقصود یہ تھا
کہ وہ نافرمانوں کو رُسوا کرے[٢٨٩] ﴿٥﴾
اور جو (مال) خدا نے اپنے پیغمبر کو اُن لوگوں سے (لڑائی بھڑائی
کے بغیر) دلوایا ہے اس میں تمہارا کچھ حق نہیں کیونکہ اسکے لئے نہ تم
نے گھوڑے دوڑائے نہ اُونٹ لیکن خدا اپنے پیغمبروں کو جن پر
چاہتا ہے مُسلط کر دیتا ہے۔ اور خدا ہر چیز پر قادر ہے ﴿٦﴾
جو مال خدا نے اپنے پیغمبر کو دیہات والوں سے دلوایا ہے
وہ خدا کے اور پیغمبر کے اور (پیغمبر کے) قرابت والوں کے
اور یتیموں کے اور حاجتمندوں کے اور مسافروں کے لئے
ہے تاکہ جو لوگ تم میں دولتمند ہیں اُنہی کے ہاتھوں میں
نہ پھرتا رہے سو جو چیز تم کو پیغمبر دیں وہ لے لو اور جس سے
منع کریں (اُس سے) باز رہو۔ اور خدا سے ڈرتے رہو بیشک
خُدا سخت عذاب دینے والا ہے ﴿٧﴾
اور اُن مفلسان تارک الوطن کے لئے بھی جو اپنے گھروں اور
مالوں سے خارج (اور جُدا) کر دیئے گئے ہیں۔ (اور) خدا کے
فضل اور اُسکی خوشنودی کے طلبگار اور خدا اور اسکے پیغمبر
کے مددگار ہیں۔ یہی لوگ سچے (ایماندار) ہیں ﴿٨﴾
اور (اُن لوگوں کیلئے بھی) جو مہاجرین سے پہلے (ہجرت کے) گھر (یعنی مدینے)
میں مقیم اور ایمان میں (مستقل) رہے (اور) جو لوگ ہجرت کرکے اُنکے پاس آتے
ہیں اُن سے محبت کرتے ہیں اور جو کچھ اُنکو ملا اس سے اپنے دل میں کچھ خواہش (اور خلش)

يٰٓأُولِي الْأَبْصَارِ ﴿٢﴾
وَلَوْلَآ أَنْ كَتَبَ اللّٰهُ عَلَيْهِمُ الْجَلَآءَ
لَعَذَّبَهُمْ فِي الدُّنْيَا ۖ وَلَهُمْ فِي الْاٰخِرَةِ
عَذَابُ النَّارِ ﴿٣﴾
ذٰلِكَ بِأَنَّهُمْ شَآقُّوا اللّٰهَ وَرَسُولَهُ ۖ وَمَنْ
يُشَآقِّ اللّٰهَ فَإِنَّ اللّٰهَ شَدِيدُ الْعِقَابِ ﴿٤﴾
مَا قَطَعْتُمْ مِنْ لِينَةٍ أَوْ تَرَكْتُمُوهَا قَآئِمَةً
عَلٰٓى أُصُولِهَا فَبِإِذْنِ اللّٰهِ وَلِيُخْزِيَ
الْفٰسِقِينَ ﴿٥﴾
وَمَآ أَفَآءَ اللّٰهُ عَلٰى رَسُولِهِ مِنْهُمْ فَمَآ
أَوْجَفْتُمْ عَلَيْهِ مِنْ خَيْلٍ وَلَا رِكَابٍ وَ
لٰكِنَّ اللّٰهَ يُسَلِّطُ رُسُلَهُ عَلٰى مَنْ يَشَآءُ ۚ
وَاللّٰهُ عَلٰى كُلِّ شَيْءٍ قَدِيرٌ ﴿٦﴾
مَآ أَفَآءَ اللّٰهُ عَلٰى رَسُولِهِ مِنْ أَهْلِ الْقُرٰى
فَلِلّٰهِ وَلِلرَّسُولِ وَلِذِي الْقُرْبٰى وَالْيَتٰمٰى
وَالْمَسٰكِينِ وَابْنِ السَّبِيلِ كَيْ لَا يَكُونَ
دُولَةً بَيْنَ الْأَغْنِيَآءِ مِنْكُمْ ۚ وَمَآ اٰتٰىكُمُ
الرَّسُولُ فَخُذُوهُ ۚ وَمَا نَهٰىكُمْ عَنْهُ
فَانْتَهُوا ۚ وَاتَّقُوا اللّٰهَ ۖ إِنَّ اللّٰهَ شَدِيدُ
الْعِقَابِ ﴿٧﴾ وقف لازم
لِلْفُقَرَآءِ الْمُهٰجِرِينَ الَّذِينَ أُخْرِجُوا
مِنْ دِيَارِهِمْ وَأَمْوَالِهِمْ يَبْتَغُونَ فَضْلًا
مِنَ اللّٰهِ وَرِضْوَانًا وَيَنْصُرُونَ اللّٰهَ وَ
رَسُولَهُ ۚ أُولٰٓئِكَ هُمُ الصّٰدِقُونَ ﴿٨﴾
وَالَّذِينَ تَبَوَّءُو الدَّارَ وَالْإِيمَانَ مِنْ قَبْلِهِمْ
يُحِبُّونَ مَنْ هَاجَرَ إِلَيْهِمْ وَلَا يَجِدُونَ
فِي صُدُورِهِمْ حَاجَةً مِمَّآ أُوتُوا وَيُؤْثِرُونَ

themselves, even though poverty was their (own lot). And those saved from the covetousness of their own souls,—they are the ones that achieve prosperity.

10. And those who came after them say: "Our Lord ! forgive us, and our brethren who came before us into the Faith, and leave not, in our hearts, rancour (or sense of injury) against those who have believed. Our Lord ! Thou art indeed Full of Kindness, Most Merciful."

11. Hast thou not observed the Hypocrites say to their misbelieving brethren among the People of the Book?— "If ye are expelled, we too will go out with you, and we will never hearken to anyone in your affair; and if ye are attacked (in fight) we will help you". But Allah is witness that they are indeed liars.

12. If they are expelled, never will they go out with them; and if they are attacked (in fight), they will never help them; and if they do help them, they will turn their backs; so they will receive no help.

13. Of a truth ye arouse greater fear in their hearts, than Allah. This is because they are men devoid of understanding.

14. They will not fight you (even) together, except in fortified townships, or from behind walls. Strong is their fighting (spirit) amongst themselves: thou wouldst think they were united, but their hearts are divided: that is because they are a people devoid of wisdom.

15. Like those who lately preceded them, they have tasted the evil result of their conduct; and (in the Hereafter there is) for them a grievous Chastisement:—

16. (Their allies deceived them), like Satan when he says to man, "Disbelieve": but when (man) disbelieves, Satan says, "I am free of thee: I do fear Allah, the Lord of the Worlds !"

17. The end of both will be that they will go into the Fire, dwelling therein for ever. Such is the reward of the wrong-doers.

نہیں پاتے اور اُنکو اپنی جانوں سے مقدم رکھتے ہیں خواہ اُنکو خود احتیاج ہی ہو۔
اور جو شخص حرصِ نفس سے بچا لیا گیا تو ایسے ہی لوگ مُراد پانے والے ہیں ⑨
اور (اُن کیلئے بھی) جو اُن (مہاجرین) کے بعد آئے (اور) دُعا کرتے
ہیں کہ اے پروردگار ہمارے اور ہمارے بھائیوں کے جو ہم سے پہلے ایمان لائے
ہیں گناہ معاف فرما اور مومنوں کی طرف سے ہمارے دل میں کینہ (و حسد) نہ پیدا
ہونے دے اے ہمارے پروردگار تُو بڑا شفقت کرنیوالا مہربان ہے ⑩
کیا تم نے اُن منافقوں کو نہیں دیکھا جو اپنے کافر بھائیوں سے
جو اہلِ کتاب ہیں کہا کرتے ہیں کہ اگر تم جلا وطن کئے گئے تو ہم بھی
تمہارے ساتھ نکل چلیں گے اور تمہارے بارے میں کبھی کسی کا کہنا نہ
مانیں گے۔ اور اگر تم سے جنگ ہوئی تو تمہاری مدد کریں گے۔
مگر خدا ظاہر کئے دیتا ہے کہ یہ جھوٹے ہیں ⑪
اگر وہ نکالے گئے تو یہ اُنکے ساتھ نہیں نکلیں گے۔ اور اگر اُن سے جنگ
ہوئی تو اُنکی مدد نہیں کرینگے۔ اور اگر مدد کرینگے تو پیٹھ پھیر کر بھاگ
جائیں گے پھر اُن کو (کہیں سے بھی) مدد نہ ملے گی ⑫
(مسلمانو) تمہاری ہیبت اُن لوگوں کے دلوں میں خدا سے
بھی بڑھ کر ہے۔ یہ اس لئے کہ یہ سمجھ نہیں رکھتے ⑬
یہ سب جمع ہو کر بھی تم سے (بالمواجہہ) نہیں لڑ سکیں گے مگر
بستیوں کے قلعوں میں (پناہ لیکر) یا دیواروں کی اوٹ میں (مستور
ہو کر) انکا آپس میں بڑا رعب ہے تم شاید خیال کرتے ہو کہ یہ اکٹھے (اور ایک جان) ہیں
مگر اُنکے دل پھٹے ہوئے ہیں۔ یہ اسلئے کہ یہ بے عقل لوگ ہیں ⑭
اُن کا حال اُن لوگوں کا سا ہے جو اُن سے کچھ ہی پیشتر اپنے کاموں کی
سزا کا مزا چکھ چکے ہیں اور (ابھی) اُنکے لئے دکھ دینے والا عذاب (تیار) ہے ⑮
(منافقوں کی) مثال شیطان کی سی ہے کہ انسان سے کہتا رہا کہ
کافر ہو جا۔ جب وہ کافر ہو گیا تو کہنے لگا کہ مجھے تجھ سے کچھ
سروکار نہیں۔ مجھ کو تو خدائے رب العالمین سے ڈر لگتا ہے ⑯
تو دونوں کا انجام یہ ہوا کہ دونوں دوزخ میں (داخل ہوئے)
ہمیشہ اس میں رہیں گے۔ اور بے انصافوں کی یہی سزا ہے ⑰

عَلٰٓى اَنۡفُسِهِمۡ وَلَوۡ كَانَ بِهِمۡ خَصَاصَةٌ ؕ
وَمَنۡ يُّوۡقَ شُحَّ نَفۡسِهٖ فَاُولٰٓـئِكَ هُمُ الۡمُفۡلِحُوۡنَ ۚ ⑨
وَالَّذِيۡنَ جَآءُوۡ مِنۡۢ بَعۡدِهِمۡ يَقُوۡلُوۡنَ
رَبَّنَا اغۡفِرۡ لَنَا وَلِاِخۡوَانِنَا الَّذِيۡنَ سَبَقُوۡنَا
بِالۡاِيۡمَانِ وَلَا تَجۡعَلۡ فِىۡ قُلُوۡبِنَا غِلًّا لِّلَّذِيۡنَ
اٰمَنُوۡا رَبَّنَاۤ اِنَّكَ رَءُوۡفٌ رَّحِيۡمٌ ⑩
اَلَمۡ تَرَ اِلَى الَّذِيۡنَ نَافَقُوۡا يَقُوۡلُوۡنَ لِاِخۡوَانِهِمُ
الَّذِيۡنَ كَفَرُوۡا مِنۡ اَهۡلِ الۡكِتٰبِ لَئِنۡ
اُخۡرِجۡتُمۡ لَنَخۡرُجَنَّ مَعَكُمۡ وَلَا نُطِيۡعُ فِيۡكُمۡ
اَحَدًا اَبَدًا ۙ وَّاِنۡ قُوۡتِلۡتُمۡ لَنَنۡصُرَنَّكُمۡ ؕ
وَاللّٰهُ يَشۡهَدُ اِنَّهُمۡ لَكٰذِبُوۡنَ ⑪
لَئِنۡ اُخۡرِجُوۡا لَا يَخۡرُجُوۡنَ مَعَهُمۡ ۚ وَلَئِنۡ
قُوۡتِلُوۡا لَا يَنۡصُرُوۡنَهُمۡ ۚ وَلَئِنۡ نَّصَرُوۡهُمۡ
لَيُوَلُّنَّ الۡاَدۡبَارَ ثُمَّ لَا يُنۡصَرُوۡنَ ⑫
لَاَنۡتُمۡ اَشَدُّ رَهۡبَةً فِىۡ صُدُوۡرِهِمۡ مِّنَ
اللّٰهِ ؕ ذٰلِكَ بِاَنَّهُمۡ قَوۡمٌ لَّا يَفۡقَهُوۡنَ ⑬
لَا يُقَاتِلُوۡنَكُمۡ جَمِيۡعًا اِلَّا فِىۡ قُرًى مُّحَصَّنَةٍ
اَوۡ مِنۡ وَّرَآءِ جُدُرٍ ؕ بَاۡسُهُمۡ بَيۡنَهُمۡ شَدِيۡدٌ ؕ
تَحۡسَبُهُمۡ جَمِيۡعًا وَّقُلُوۡبُهُمۡ شَتّٰى ؕ ذٰلِكَ
بِاَنَّهُمۡ قَوۡمٌ لَّا يَعۡقِلُوۡنَ ⑭
كَمَثَلِ الَّذِيۡنَ مِنۡ قَبۡلِهِمۡ قَرِيۡبًا ذَاقُوۡا
وَبَالَ اَمۡرِهِمۡ ۚ وَلَهُمۡ عَذَابٌ اَلِيۡمٌ ⑮
كَمَثَلِ الشَّيۡطٰنِ اِذۡ قَالَ لِلۡاِنۡسَانِ اكۡفُرۡ ۚ
فَلَمَّا كَفَرَ قَالَ اِنِّىۡ بَرِىۡٓءٌ مِّنۡكَ اِنِّىۡۤ اَخَافُ
اللّٰهَ رَبَّ الۡعٰلَمِيۡنَ ⑯
فَكَانَ عَاقِبَتَهُمَاۤ اَنَّهُمَا فِى النَّارِ خَالِدَيۡنِ
فِيۡهَا ؕ وَذٰلِكَ جَزٰٓؤُا الظّٰلِمِيۡنَ ⑰

SÛRA–60

AL-MUMTAḤANA

(INTRODUCTION)

This is the fourth of the ten Madinah Sûras, each dealing with a special point in the life of the Ummat.

Here the point is: what social relations are possible with the Unbelievers? A distinction is made between those who persecute you for your Faith and want to destroy you and your Faith, and those who have shown no such rancour. For the latter there is hope of mercy and forgiveness. The question of women and cross-marriages is equitably dealt with.

The date is after the Pagans had broken the treaty of Ḥudaibîya, for which see Introduction to S. 47— say about A.H. 8, not long before the conquest of Makkah.

18. O ye who believe ! fear Allah and let every soul look to what (provision) he has sent forth for the morrow. Yea, fear Allah: for Allah is well-acquainted with (all) that ye do.

19. And be ye not like those who forgot Allah; and He made them forget themselves ! Such are the rebellious transgressors !

20. Not equal are the Companions of the Fire and the Companions of the Garden: it is the Companions of the Garden, that will achieve Felicity.

21. Had We sent down this Qur'ãn on a mountain, verily, thou wouldst have seen it humble itself and cleave asunder for fear of Allah. Such are the similitudes which We propound to men, that they may reflect.

22. Allah is He, than Whom there is no other god;— Who knows (all things) both secret and open; He, Most Gracious, Most Merciful.

23. Allah is He, than Whom there is no other god;— the Sovereign, the Holy One, the Source of Peace (and Perfection), the Guardian of Faith, the Preserver of Safety, the Exalted in Might, the Irresistible, the justly Proud glory to Allah ! (High is He) above the partners they attribute to Him.

24. He is Allah, the Creator the Originator, the Fashioner. To Him belong the Most Beautiful Names: whatever is in the heavens and on earth, doth declare His Praises and Glory: and He is the Exalted in Might, the Wise.

Al-Mumtahana, or the Woman to be Examined

In the name of Allah, Most Gracious, Most Merciful.

1. O ye who believe ! take not My enemies and yours as friends (or protectors),—offering them (your) love, even though they have rejected the Truth that has come to you, and have (on the contrary) driven out the Messenger and yourselves (from your homes), (simply) because ye believe in Allah your Lord ! If ye have come out to strive in My Way and to

اے ایمان والو! خدا سے ڈرتے رہو اور ہر شخص کو دیکھنا چاہیئے
کہ اُس نے کل (یعنی فردائے قیامت) کیلئے کیا سامان بھیجا ہے اور ہم
پھر کہتے ہیں کہ خدا سے ڈرتے رہو بیشک خدا تمہارے سب اعمال سے خبردار ہے ﴿۱۸﴾
اور اُن لوگوں جیسے نہ ہونا جنہوں نے خدا کو بھلا دیا تو خدا نے
انہیں ایسا کر دیا کہ خود اپنے تئیں بھول گئے۔ یہ بدکردار لوگ ہیں ﴿۱۹﴾
اہل دوزخ اور اہل بہشت برابر نہیں۔ اہل بہشت تو
کامیابی حاصل کرنے والے ہیں ﴿۲۰﴾
اگر ہم یہ قرآن کسی پہاڑ پر نازل کرتے تو تم اُس کو دیکھتے
کہ خدا کے خوف سے دبا اور پھٹا جاتا ہے۔ اور یہ باتیں
ہم لوگوں کے لئے بیان کرتے ہیں تاکہ وہ
غور کریں ﴿۲۱﴾
وہی خدا ہے جس کے سوا کوئی معبود نہیں۔ پوشیدہ اور
ظاہر کا جاننے والا۔ وہ بڑا مہربان نہایت رحم والا ہے ﴿۲۲﴾
وہی خدا ہے جس کے سوا کوئی عبادت کے لائق نہیں۔
بادشاہ (حقیقی) پاک ذات (ہر عیب سے) سلامتی امن دینے
والا نگہبان غالب زبردست بڑائی والا۔ خدا اُن لوگوں کے
شریک مقرر کرنے سے پاک ہے ﴿۲۳﴾
وہی خدا (تمام مخلوقات کا) خالق ایجاد و اختراع کرنیوالا صورتیں
بنانیوالا اُسکے سب اچھے سے اچھے نام ہیں۔ جتنی چیزیں آسمانوں اور زمین
میں ہیں سب اُسکی تسبیح کرتی ہیں۔ اور وہ غالب حکمت والا ہے ﴿۲۴﴾

سورۂ ممتحنہ مکّی ہے اس میں تیرہ آیتیں اور دو رکوع ہیں

شروع خدا کا نام لے کر جو بڑا مہربان نہایت رحم والا ہے
مومنو! اگر تم میری راہ میں لڑنے اور میری خوشنودی طلب
کرنے کے لئے (مکے سے) نکلے ہو تو میرے اور اپنے دشمنوں کو دوست
نہ بناؤ تم تو اُن کو دوستی کے پیغام بھیجتے ہو اور وہ (دین) حق
سے جو تمہارے پاس آیا ہے منکر ہیں اور اس باعث سے
کہ تم اپنے پروردگار خدائے تعالیٰ پر ایمان لائے ہو پیغمبر کو اور تم کو جلاوطن

يٰٓاَيُّهَا الَّذِيْنَ اٰمَنُوا اتَّقُوا اللّٰهَ وَلْتَنْظُرْ
نَفْسٌ مَّا قَدَّمَتْ لِغَدٍ ۚ وَاتَّقُوا اللّٰهَ ؕ اِنَّ
اللّٰهَ خَبِيْرٌۢ بِمَا تَعْمَلُوْنَ ﴿١٨﴾
وَلَا تَكُوْنُوْا كَالَّذِيْنَ نَسُوا اللّٰهَ فَاَنْسٰىهُمْ
اَنْفُسَهُمْ ؕ اُولٰٓئِكَ هُمُ الْفٰسِقُوْنَ ﴿١٩﴾
لَا يَسْتَوِيْٓ اَصْحٰبُ النَّارِ وَاَصْحٰبُ
الْجَنَّةِ ؕ اَصْحٰبُ الْجَنَّةِ هُمُ الْفَآئِزُوْنَ ﴿٢٠﴾
لَوْ اَنْزَلْنَا هٰذَا الْقُرْاٰنَ عَلٰى جَبَلٍ لَّرَاَيْتَهٗ
خَاشِعًا مُّتَصَدِّعًا مِّنْ خَشْيَةِ اللّٰهِ ؕ
وَتِلْكَ الْاَمْثَالُ نَضْرِبُهَا لِلنَّاسِ لَعَلَّهُمْ
يَتَفَكَّرُوْنَ ﴿٢١﴾
هُوَ اللّٰهُ الَّذِيْ لَآ اِلٰهَ اِلَّا هُوَ ۚ عٰلِمُ الْغَيْبِ
وَالشَّهَادَةِ ۚ هُوَ الرَّحْمٰنُ الرَّحِيْمُ ﴿٢٢﴾
هُوَ اللّٰهُ الَّذِيْ لَآ اِلٰهَ اِلَّا هُوَ ۚ اَلْمَلِكُ
الْقُدُّوْسُ السَّلٰمُ الْمُؤْمِنُ الْمُهَيْمِنُ
الْعَزِيْزُ الْجَبَّارُ الْمُتَكَبِّرُ ؕ سُبْحٰنَ اللّٰهِ
عَمَّا يُشْرِكُوْنَ ﴿٢٣﴾
هُوَ اللّٰهُ الْخَالِقُ الْبَارِئُ الْمُصَوِّرُ لَهُ
الْاَسْمَآءُ الْحُسْنٰى ؕ يُسَبِّحُ لَهٗ مَا فِي السَّمٰوٰتِ
وَالْاَرْضِ ۚ وَهُوَ الْعَزِيْزُ الْحَكِيْمُ ﴿٢٤﴾

سُوْرَةُ الْمُمْتَحِنَةِ مَدَنِيَّةٌ وَّهِيَ ثَلٰثَ عَشْرَةَ اٰيَةً وَّفِيْهَا رُكُوْعَانِ

بِسْمِ اللّٰهِ الرَّحْمٰنِ الرَّحِيْمِ
يٰٓاَيُّهَا الَّذِيْنَ اٰمَنُوْا لَا تَتَّخِذُوْا عَدُوِّيْ
وَعَدُوَّكُمْ اَوْلِيَآءَ تُلْقُوْنَ اِلَيْهِمْ بِالْمَوَدَّةِ
وَقَدْ كَفَرُوْا بِمَا جَآءَكُمْ مِّنَ الْحَقِّ ۚ يُخْرِجُوْنَ
الرَّسُوْلَ وَاِيَّاكُمْ اَنْ تُؤْمِنُوْا بِاللّٰهِ رَبِّكُمْ ؕ
اِنْ كُنْتُمْ خَرَجْتُمْ جِهَادًا فِيْ سَبِيْلِيْ وَ

seek My Good Pleasure, showing friendship unto them in secret: for I know full well all that ye conceal and all that ye reveal. And any of you that does this has strayed from the Straight Path.

2. If they overcome you they would behave to you as enemies, and stretch forth their hands and their tongues against you for evil; and they desire that ye should reject the Truth.

3. Of no profit to you will be your relatives and your children on the Day of Judgment: He will judge between you: for Allah sees well all that ye do.

4. There is for you an excellent example (to follow) in Abraham and those with him, when they said to their people: "We are clear of you and of whatever ye worship besides Allah: we have rejected you, and there has arisen, between us and you, enmity and hatred for ever,—unless ye believe in Allah and Him alone": but not when Abraham said to his father: "I will pray for forgiveness for thee, though I have no power (to get) aught on thy behalf from Allah." (They prayed): "Our Lord ! in Thee do we trust, and to Thee do we turn in repentance: to Thee is (our) final Return.

5. "Our Lord ! Make us not a (test and) trial for the Unbelievers, but forgive us, our Lord ! For Thou art the Exalted in Might, the Wise."

6. There was indeed in them an excellent example for you to follow,—for those whose hope is in Allah and in the last Day. But if any turn away, truly Allah is Free of all wants, Worthy of all Praise.

7. It may be that Allah will Establish friendship between you and those whom ye (now) hold as enemies. For Allah has power (Over all things); and Allah is Oft-Forgiving, Most Merciful.

8. Allah forbids you not, with regard to those who fight you not

کرتے ہو تم اُنکی طرف پوشیدہ پوشیدہ دوستی کے پیغام بھیجتے ہو۔ اور جو کچھ تم
مخفی طور پر اور جو علی الاعلان کرتے ہو وہ مجھے معلوم ہے۔ اور جو کوئی
تم میں سے ایسا کرے گا وہ سیدھے رستے سے بھٹک گیا (۱)
اگر یہ کافر تم پر قدرت پالیں تو تمہارے دشمن ہو جائیں اور
ایذا کے لئے تم پر ہاتھ (بھی) چلائیں اور زبانیں (بھی) اور
چاہتے ہیں کہ تم کسی طرح کافر ہو جاؤ (۲)
قیامت کے دن نہ تمہارے رشتے ناتے کام آئیں گے اور
نہ اولاد۔ اس روز وہی تم میں فیصلہ کرے گا۔ اور جو کچھ
تم کرتے ہو خدا اس کو دیکھتا ہے (۳)
تمہیں ابراہیم اور اُن کے رُفقاء کی نیک چال چلنی
(ضرور) ہے۔ جب اُنہوں نے اپنی قوم کے لوگوں سے کہا کہ
ہم تم سے اور اُن (بتوں) سے جن کو تم خدا کے سوا پوجتے ہو بے تعلق ہیں۔
(اور) تمہارے (معبودوں کے کبھی) قائل نہیں (ہو سکتے) اور جب تک تم خدائے واحد
پر ایمان نہ لاؤ ہم میں تم میں ہمیشہ کھلم کھلا عداوت اور دشمنی رہے گی ہاں ابراہیم
اپنے باپ سے یہ (ضرور) کہا کہ میں آپ کیلئے مغفرت مانگوں گا اور میں خدا کے سامنے آپ کے بارے
میں کسی چیز کا کچھ اختیار نہیں رکھتا۔ اے ہمارے پروردگار تجھی پر ہمارا بھروسہ ہے اور
تیری ہی طرف ہم رجوع کرتے ہیں اور تیرے ہی حضور میں (ہمیں) لوٹ کر آنا ہے (۴)
اے ہمارے پروردگار ہم کو کافروں کے ہاتھ سے عذاب نہ دلانا
اور اے پروردگار ہمارے ہمیں معاف فرما بے شک تو غالب
حکمت والا ہے (۵)
تم (مسلمانوں) کو یعنی جو کوئی خدا (کے سامنے جانے) اور روز آخرت
(کے آنے) کی اُمید رکھتا ہو اُسے اُن لوگوں کی نیک چال چلنی (ضرور) ہے
اور جو روگردانی کرے تو خدا بھی بے پروا اور سزاوار حمد (و ثنا) ہے (۶)
عجب نہیں کہ خدا تم میں اور اُن لوگوں میں جن سے تم دشمنی
رکھتے ہو دوستی پیدا کر دے۔ اور خدا قادر ہے۔ اور خدا
بخشنے والا مہربان ہے (۷)
جن لوگوں نے تم سے دین کے بارے میں جنگ نہیں کی

ابتغاء مرضاتي تسرون إليهم بالمودة
وأنا أعلم بما أخفيتم وما أعلنتم ومن
يفعله منكم فقد ضل سواء السبيل (١)
إن يثقفوكم يكونوا لكم أعداء ويبسطوا
إليكم أيديهم وألسنتهم بالسوء وودوا
لو تكفرون (٢)
ع لن تنفعكم أرحامكم ولا أولادكم يوم
القيامة يفصل بينكم والله بما تعملون
بصير (٣)
قد كانت لكم أسوة حسنة في إبراهيم
والذين معه إذ قالوا لقومهم إنا برآؤا
منكم ومما تعبدون من دون الله كفرنا
بكم وبدا بيننا وبينكم العداوة والبغضاء
أبدا حتى تؤمنوا بالله وحده إلا قول
إبراهيم لأبيه لأستغفرن لك وما أملك
لك من الله من شيء ربنا عليك توكلنا
وإليك أنبنا وإليك المصير (٤)
ربنا لا تجعلنا فتنة للذين كفروا
واغفر لنا ربنا إنك أنت العزيز
الحكيم (٥)
لقد كان لكم فيهم أسوة حسنة لمن كان
يرجو الله واليوم الآخر ومن يتول
ع فإن الله هو الغني الحميد (٦)
عسى الله أن يجعل بينكم وبين
الذين عاديتم منهم مودة والله قدير
والله غفور رحيم (٧)
لا ينهاكم الله عن الذين لم يقاتلوكم

for (your) Faith nor drive you out of your homes, from dealing kindly and justly with them: for Allah loveth those who are just.

9. Allah only forbids you, with regard to those who fight you for (your) Faith, and drive you out of your homes, and support (others) in driving you out, from turning to them (for friendship and protection). It is such as turn to them (in these circumstances), that do wrong.

10. O ye who believe ! when there come to you believing women refugees, examine (and test) them: Allah knows best as to their Faith: if ye ascertain that they are Believers, then send them not back to the Unbelievers. They are not lawful (wives) for the Unbelievers, nor are the (Unbelievers) lawful (husbands) for them. But pay the Unbelievers what they have spent (on their dower). And there will be no blame on you if ye marry them on payment of their dower to them. But hold not to the ties (marriage contract) of Unbelieving women: ask for what ye have spent on their dowers, and let the (Unbelievers) ask for what they have spent (on the dowers of women who come over to you). Such is the command of Allah: He judges (with justice) between you. And Allah is Full of Knowledge and Wisdom.

11. And if any of your wives deserts you to the Unbelievers, and ye have your turn (by the coming over of a woman from the other side). Then pay to those whose wives have deserted the equivalent of what they had spent (on their dower). And fear Allah, in whom ye believe.

12. O Prophet ! when believing women come to thee to take the oath of fealty to thee, that they will not associate in worship any other thing whatever with Allah, that they will not steal, that they will not commit adultery (or fornication), that they will not kill their children, that they will not utter slander, intentionally forging falsehood and

اور نہ تم کو تمہارے گھروں سے نکالا اُن کے ساتھ بھلائی
اور انصاف کا سلوک کرنے سے خدا تم کو منع نہیں کرتا۔ خدا تو
انصاف کرنے والوں کو دوست رکھتا ہے ﴿۸﴾
خدا اُنہی لوگوں کے ساتھ تم کو دوستی کرنے سے منع کرتا ہے جنہوں
نے تم سے دین کے بارے میں لڑائی کی اور تم کو تمہارے گھروں سے
نکالا اور تمہارے نکالنے میں اوروں کی مدد کی تو جو لوگ
ایسوں سے دوستی کریں گے وہی ظالم ہیں ﴿۹﴾
مومنو! جب تمہارے پاس مومن عورتیں وطن چھوڑ کر آئیں
تو اُن کی آزمائش کرلو۔ (اور) خدا تو اُن کے ایمان کو خوب
جانتا ہے۔ سو اگر تم کو معلوم ہو کہ مومن ہیں تو ان کو کفار
کے پاس واپس نہ بھیجو۔ کہ نہ یہ اُن کو حلال ہیں اور نہ
وہ اُن کو جائز۔ اور جو کچھ انہوں نے (اُن پر) خرچ
کیا ہو وہ اُن کو دے دو۔ اور تم پر کچھ گناہ نہیں کہ
اُن عورتوں کو مہر دے کر اُن سے نکاح کرلو۔
اور کافر عورتوں کی ناموس کو قبضے میں نہ رکھو (یعنی کفار کو واپس
دے دو) اور جو کچھ تم نے اُن پر خرچ کیا ہو تم اُن سے طلب کرلو اور جو کچھ
اُنہوں نے (اپنی عورتوں پر) خرچ کیا ہو وہ تم سے طلب کرلیں
یہ خدا کا حکم ہے جو تم میں فیصلہ کئے دیتا ہے اور خدا جاننے والا حکمت والا ہے ﴿۱۰﴾
اور اگر تمہاری عورتوں میں سے کوئی عورت تمہارے ہاتھ سے نکل کر
کافروں کے پاس چلی جائے (اور اُسکا مہر وصول نہ ہوا ہو) پھر تم
اُن سے جنگ کرو اور اُن سے تم کو غنیمت ہاتھ لگے تو جنکی عورتیں چلی گئی ہیں اُنکو
(اُس مال میں سے) اتنا دیدو جتنا اُنہوں نے خرچ کیا تھا اور خدا سے جس پر تم ایمان لائے ہو ڈرو ﴿۱۱﴾
اے پیغمبر جب تمہارے پاس مومن عورتیں اس بات پر بیعت کرنے کو
آئیں کہ خدا کے ساتھ نہ تو شرک کرینگی نہ چوری کرینگی نہ بدکاری کرینگی
نہ اپنی اولاد کو قتل کریں گی نہ اپنے ہاتھ پاؤں میں کوئی
بہتان باندھ لائیں گی نہ نیک کاموں میں تمہاری
نافرمانی کریں گی تو اُن سے بیعت لے لو اور اُن

فِي الدِّيْنِ وَلَمْ يُخْرِجُوْكُمْ مِّنْ دِيَارِكُمْ اَنْ
تَبَرُّوْهُمْ وَتُقْسِطُوْٓا اِلَيْهِمْ ؕ اِنَّ اللّٰهَ يُحِبُّ
الْمُقْسِطِيْنَ ﴿٨﴾
اِنَّمَا يَنْهٰىكُمُ اللّٰهُ عَنِ الَّذِيْنَ قَاتَلُوْكُمْ
فِي الدِّيْنِ وَاَخْرَجُوْكُمْ مِّنْ دِيَارِكُمْ وَ
ظٰهَرُوْا عَلٰٓى اِخْرَاجِكُمْ اَنْ تَوَلَّوْهُمْ ۚ
وَمَنْ يَّتَوَلَّهُمْ فَاُولٰٓئِكَ هُمُ الظّٰلِمُوْنَ ﴿٩﴾
يٰٓاَيُّهَا الَّذِيْنَ اٰمَنُوْٓا اِذَا جَآءَكُمُ الْمُؤْمِنٰتُ
مُهٰجِرٰتٍ فَامْتَحِنُوْهُنَّ ؕ اَللّٰهُ اَعْلَمُ بِاِيْمَانِهِنَّ ۚ
فَاِنْ عَلِمْتُمُوْهُنَّ مُؤْمِنٰتٍ فَلَا تَرْجِعُوْهُنَّ
اِلَى الْكُفَّارِ ؕ لَا هُنَّ حِلٌّ لَّهُمْ
وَلَا هُمْ يَحِلُّوْنَ لَهُنَّ ؕ وَاٰتُوْهُمْ
مَّآ اَنْفَقُوْا ؕ وَلَا جُنَاحَ عَلَيْكُمْ اَنْ
تَنْكِحُوْهُنَّ اِذَآ اٰتَيْتُمُوْهُنَّ اُجُوْرَهُنَّ ؕ
وَلَا تُمْسِكُوْا بِعِصَمِ الْكَوَافِرِ وَسْئَلُوْا مَآ
اَنْفَقْتُمْ وَلْيَسْئَلُوْا مَآ اَنْفَقُوْا ؕ ذٰلِكُمْ
حُكْمُ اللّٰهِ ؕ يَحْكُمُ بَيْنَكُمْ ؕ وَاللّٰهُ عَلِيْمٌ
حَكِيْمٌ ﴿١٠﴾
وَاِنْ فَاتَكُمْ شَيْءٌ مِّنْ اَزْوَاجِكُمْ اِلَى
الْكُفَّارِ فَعَاقَبْتُمْ فَاٰتُوا الَّذِيْنَ ذَهَبَتْ
اَزْوَاجُهُمْ مِّثْلَ مَآ اَنْفَقُوْا ؕ وَاتَّقُوا اللّٰهَ
الَّذِيْٓ اَنْتُمْ بِهٖ مُؤْمِنُوْنَ ﴿١١﴾
يٰٓاَيُّهَا النَّبِيُّ اِذَا جَآءَكَ الْمُؤْمِنٰتُ يُبَايِعْنَكَ
عَلٰٓى اَنْ لَّا يُشْرِكْنَ بِاللّٰهِ شَيْئًا وَّلَا يَسْرِقْنَ
وَلَا يَزْنِيْنَ وَلَا يَقْتُلْنَ اَوْلَادَهُنَّ وَلَا
يَاْتِيْنَ بِبُهْتَانٍ يَّفْتَرِيْنَهٗ بَيْنَ اَيْدِيْهِنَّ
وَاَرْجُلِهِنَّ وَلَا يَعْصِيْنَكَ فِيْ مَعْرُوْفٍ

SÛRA–61
AṢ-ṢAFF
(INTRODUCTION)

This is the fifth Sûra of the series of short Madinah Sûras beginning with S. 57. Its subject-matter is the need for discipline, practical work, and self-sacrifice in the cause of the Ummat. Its date is uncertain, but it was probably shortly after the battle of Uḥud, which was fought in Shawwal, A.H. 3.

any just matter,— then do thou receive their fealty, and pray to Allah for the forgiveness (of their sins): for Allah is Oft-Forgiving, Most Merciful.

13. O ye who believe ! turn not (for friendship) to people on whom is the Wrath of Allah. Of the Hereafter they are already in despair, just as the Unbelievers are in despair about those (buried) in graves.

Aṣ-Ṣaff, or Battle Array

In the name of Allah, Most Gracious, Most Merciful.

1. Whatever is in the heavens and on earth, declares the Praises and Glory of Allah: for He is the Exalted in Might, the Wise.

2. O ye who believe ! why say ye that which ye do not?

3. Grievously hateful is it in the sight of Allah that ye say that which ye do not.

4. Truly Allah loves those who fight in His Cause in battle array, as if they were a solid cemented structure.

5. And remember, Moses said to his people: "O my people ! why do ye vex and insult me, though ye know that I am the messenger of Allah (sent) to you?" Then when they went wrong, Allah let their hearts go wrong. For Allah guides not those who are rebellious transgressors.

6. And remember, Jesus, the son of Mary, said: "O Children of Israel ! I am the messenger of Allah (sent) to you, confirming the Taurat (which came) before me, and giving glad Tidings of a messenger to come after me, whose name shall be Ahmad." But when he came to them with Clear Signs they said, "This is Evident sorcery !"

7. Who doth greater wrong than one who forges falsehood against Allah, even as he is being invited to Islam? And Allah Guides not those who do wrong.

فَبَايِعْهُنَّ وَاسْتَغْفِرْ لَهُنَّ اللّٰهَ ۭ اِنَّ اللّٰهَ
غَفُوْرٌ رَّحِيْمٌ (12)
يٰٓاَيُّهَا الَّذِيْنَ اٰمَنُوْا لَا تَتَوَلَّوْا قَوْمًا
غَضِبَ اللّٰهُ عَلَيْهِمْ قَدْ يَىِٕسُوْا مِنَ الْاٰخِرَةِ
كَمَا يَىِٕسَ الْكُفَّارُ مِنْ اَصْحٰبِ
الْقُبُوْرِ (13) ع

کے لئے خدا سے بخشش مانگو۔ بے شک خدا بخشنے والا
مہربان ہے (۱۲)
مومنو! اُن لوگوں سے جن پر خدا غصے ہوا ہے دوستی
نہ کرو (کیونکہ) جس طرح کافروں کو مُردوں (کے جی اُٹھنے)
کی اُمید نہیں اسی طرح اُن لوگوں کو بھی آخرت (کے آنے)
کی اُمید نہیں (۱۳)

سُوْرَةُ الصَّفِّ مَدَنِيَّةٌ وَّهِيَ اَرْبَعَ عَشْرَةَ اٰيَةً وَّفِيْهَا رُكُوْعَانِ

سورۂ صف مدنی ہے اس میں چودہ آیتیں اور دو رکوع ہیں

بِسْمِ اللّٰهِ الرَّحْمٰنِ الرَّحِيْمِ
شروع خدا کا نام لے کر جو بڑا مہربان نہایت رحم والا ہے

سَبَّحَ لِلّٰهِ مَا فِي السَّمٰوٰتِ وَمَا فِي الْاَرْضِ ۚ
وَهُوَ الْعَزِيْزُ الْحَكِيْمُ (1)
يٰٓاَيُّهَا الَّذِيْنَ اٰمَنُوْا لِمَ تَقُوْلُوْنَ مَا لَا
تَفْعَلُوْنَ (2)
كَبُرَ مَقْتًا عِنْدَ اللّٰهِ اَنْ تَقُوْلُوْا مَا لَا تَفْعَلُوْنَ (3)
اِنَّ اللّٰهَ يُحِبُّ الَّذِيْنَ يُقَاتِلُوْنَ فِيْ
سَبِيْلِهٖ صَفًّا كَاَنَّهُمْ بُنْيَانٌ مَّرْصُوْصٌ (4)
وَاِذْ قَالَ مُوْسٰى لِقَوْمِهٖ يٰقَوْمِ لِمَ تُؤْذُوْنَنِيْ
وَقَدْ تَّعْلَمُوْنَ اَنِّيْ رَسُوْلُ اللّٰهِ اِلَيْكُمْ ۭ
فَلَمَّا زَاغُوْٓا اَزَاغَ اللّٰهُ قُلُوْبَهُمْ ۭ وَاللّٰهُ
لَا يَهْدِي الْقَوْمَ الْفٰسِقِيْنَ (5)
وَاِذْ قَالَ عِيْسَى ابْنُ مَرْيَمَ يٰبَنِيْٓ اِسْرَاۗءِيْلَ
اِنِّيْ رَسُوْلُ اللّٰهِ اِلَيْكُمْ مُّصَدِّقًا لِّمَا بَيْنَ
يَدَيَّ مِنَ التَّوْرٰىةِ وَمُبَشِّرًۢا بِرَسُوْلٍ يَّاْتِيْ
مِنْۢ بَعْدِي اسْمُهٗٓ اَحْمَدُ ۭ فَلَمَّا جَاۗءَهُمْ
بِالْبَيِّنٰتِ قَالُوْا هٰذَا سِحْرٌ مُّبِيْنٌ (6)
وَمَنْ اَظْلَمُ مِمَّنِ افْتَرٰى عَلَى اللّٰهِ
الْكَذِبَ وَهُوَ يُدْعٰٓى اِلَى الْاِسْلَامِ ۭ وَاللّٰهُ
لَا يَهْدِي الْقَوْمَ الظّٰلِمِيْنَ (7)

جو چیز آسمانوں میں ہے اور جو زمین میں ہے سب خدا کی
تنزیہ کرتی ہے۔ اور وہ غالب حکمت والا ہے (۱)
مومنو! تم ایسی باتیں کیوں کہا کرتے ہو جو کیا
نہیں کرتے (۲)
خدا اس بات سے سخت بیزار ہے کہ ایسی بات کہو جو کرو نہیں (۳)
جو لوگ خدا کی راہ میں (ایسے طور پر) پرے جما کر لڑتے ہیں کہ
گویا سیسہ پلائی ہوئی دیوار ہیں وہ بیشک محبوب کردگار ہیں (۴)
اور (وہ وقت یاد کرنے کے لائق ہے) جب موسیٰ نے اپنی قوم سے
کہا کہ بھائیو تم مجھے کیوں ایذا دیتے ہو حالانکہ تم جانتے ہو کہ میں
تمہارے پاس خدا کا بھیجا ہوا آیا ہوں۔ تو جب اُن لوگوں نے کجروی کی خدا
نے بھی اُنکے دل ٹیڑھے کر دیئے۔ اور خدا نافرمانوں کو ہدایت نہیں دیتا (۵)
اور (وہ وقت بھی یاد کرو) جب مریم کے بیٹے عیسیٰ نے کہا کہ
اے بنی اسرائیل میں تمہارے پاس خدا کا بھیجا ہوا آیا ہوں (اور)
جو (کتاب) مجھ سے پہلے آچکی ہے (یعنی) تورات اُسکی تصدیق کرتا ہوں اور
ایک پیغمبر جو میرے بعد آئینگے جنکا نام احمد ہوگا اُنکی بشارت سناتا ہوں۔ (پھر) جب
وہ اُن لوگوں کے پاس کھلی نشانیاں لیکر آئے تو کہنے لگے کہ یہ تو صریح جادو ہے (۶)
اور اس سے ظالم کون کہ بُلایا تو جائے اسلام کی طرف اور وہ
خدا پر جھوٹ بہتان باندھے۔ اور خدا ظالم لوگوں کو ہدایت
نہیں دیا کرتا (۷)

8. Their intention is to extinguish Allah's Light (by blowing) with their mouths: but Allah will complete His Light, even though the Unbelievers may detest (it).

۲۹۳
یہ چاہتے ہیں کہ خدا کے چراغ کی روشنی کو مُنہ سے (پھونک مار کر) بجھا دیں
حالانکہ خدا اپنی روشنی کو پورا کر کے رہیگا خواہ کافر ناخوش ہی ہوں ⑧

يريدون ليطفئوا نور الله بافواههم
والله متم نوره ولو كره الكفرون ⑧

9. It is He Who has sent His Messenger with Guidance and the Religion of Truth. That He make it prevail over all religion, even though the Pagans may detest (it).

وہی تو ہے جس نے اپنے پیغمبر کو ہدایت اور دین حق دے کر
بھیجا تاکہ اُسے اور سب دینوں پر غالب کرے خواہ مشرکوں
کو بُرا ہی لگے ⑨

هو الذي ارسل رسوله بالهدى و
دين الحق ليظهره على الدين
كله ولو كره المشركون ⑨ ع

10. O ye who believe ! shall I lead you to a bargain that will save you from a grievous Chastisement ?—

مومنو! میں تم کو ایسی تجارت بتاؤں جو تمہیں عذاب الیم
سے مخلصی دے ⑩

يايها الذين امنوا هل ادلكم على
تجارة تنجيكم من عذاب اليم ⑩

11. That ye believe in Allah and His Messenger, and that ye strive (your utmost) in the Cause of Allah, with your wealth and your persons: that will be best for you, if ye but knew !

(وہ یہ کہ) خدا پر اور اس کے رسول پر ایمان لاؤ اور خدا
کی راہ میں اپنے مال اور جان سے جہاد کرو. اگر سمجھو
تو یہ تمہارے حق میں بہتر ہے ⑪

تؤمنون بالله ورسوله وتجاهدون
في سبيل الله باموالكم وانفسكم
ذلكم خير لكم ان كنتم تعلمون ⑪

12. He will forgive you your sins, and admit you to Gardens beneath which rivers flow, and to beautiful Mansions in Gardens of Eternity: that is indeed the Supreme Triumph.

وہ تمہارے گناہ بخش دے گا اور تم کو باغہائے جنت
میں جن میں نہریں بہ رہی ہیں اور پاکیزہ مکانات میں جو
بہشت ہائے جاودانی میں (تیار) ہیں داخل کرے گا. یہ
بڑی کامیابی ہے ⑫

يغفر لكم ذنوبكم ويدخلكم جنت
تجري من تحتها الانهر ومسكن
طيبة في جنت عدن ذلك الفوز
العظيم ⑫

13. And another (favour will He bestow), which ye do love,—help from Allah and a speedy victory. So give the Glad Tidings to the Believers.

اور ایک اور چیز جسکو تم بہت چاہتے ہو (یعنی تمہیں) خدا کی طرف
سے مدد (نصیب ہوگی) اور فتح (عن) قریب (ہوگی) اور مومنوں (اسکی) خوشخبری سنا دو ⑬

واخرى تحبونها نصر من الله و
فتح قريب وبشر المؤمنين ⑬

14. O ye who believe ! be ye helpers of Allah: as said Jesus the son of Mary to the Disciples, "Who will be my helpers to (the work of) Allah ?" Said the Disciples, "We are Allah's helpers !" Then a portion of the Children of Israel believed, and a portion disbelieved: but We gave power to those who believed against their enemies, and they became the ones that prevailed.

مومنو! خدا کے مددگار ہو جاؤ جیسے عیسیٰ ابن مریم
نے حواریوں سے کہا کہ (بھلا) کون ہیں جو خدا
کی طرف (بلانے میں) میرے مددگار ہوں.
حواریوں نے کہا کہ ہم خدا کے مددگار ہیں. تو بنی اسرائیل میں سے
ایک گروہ تو ایمان لے آیا اور ایک گروہ کافر رہا. آخر الامر ہم نے
ایمان لانے والوں کو ان کے دشمنوں کے مقابلے میں
مدد دی اور وہ غالب ہو گئے ⑭

يايها الذين امنوا كونوا انصار
الله كما قال عيسى ابن مريم
للحوارين من انصاري الى الله
قال الحواريون نحن انصار الله فامنت
طائفة من بني اسراءيل وكفرت
طائفة فايدنا الذين امنوا على
عدوهم فاصبحوا ظاهرين ⑭ ع

SÛRA–62
AL-JUMU'A
(INTRODUCTION)

This is the sixth Sûra in the Madinah series of short Sûras which began with S. 57.

The special theme here is the need for mutual contact in the Community for worship and understanding: for the spirit of the Message is for all, ignorant and learned, in order that they may be purified and may learn wisdom.

The date has no special significance: it may be placed in the early Madinah period, say, between A.H. 2 and 5.

سُورَةُ الْجُمُعَةِ مَدَنِيَّةٌ وَّهِيَ اِحْدٰى عَشْرَةَ اٰيَةً وَّفِيْهَا رُكُوْعَانِ

بِسْمِ اللّٰهِ الرَّحْمٰنِ الرَّحِيْمِ ○
يُسَبِّحُ لِلّٰهِ مَا فِي السَّمٰوٰتِ وَمَا فِي الْاَرْضِ
الْمَلِكِ الْقُدُّوْسِ الْعَزِيْزِ الْحَكِيْمِ ①
هُوَ الَّذِيْ بَعَثَ فِي الْاُمِّيّٖنَ رَسُوْلًا
مِّنْهُمْ يَتْلُوْا عَلَيْهِمْ اٰيٰتِهٖ وَيُزَكِّيْهِمْ وَ
يُعَلِّمُهُمُ الْكِتٰبَ وَالْحِكْمَةَ ۗ وَاِنْ كَانُوْا
مِنْ قَبْلُ لَفِيْ ضَلٰلٍ مُّبِيْنٍ ②
وَّاٰخَرِيْنَ مِنْهُمْ لَمَّا يَلْحَقُوْا بِهِمْ ۭ وَهُوَ
الْعَزِيْزُ الْحَكِيْمُ ③
ذٰلِكَ فَضْلُ اللّٰهِ يُؤْتِيْهِ مَنْ يَّشَاۗءُ ۭ
وَاللّٰهُ ذُو الْفَضْلِ الْعَظِيْمِ ④
مَثَلُ الَّذِيْنَ حُمِّلُوا التَّوْرٰىةَ ثُمَّ
لَمْ يَحْمِلُوْهَا كَمَثَلِ الْحِمَارِ يَحْمِلُ
اَسْفَارًا ۭ بِئْسَ مَثَلُ الْقَوْمِ الَّذِيْنَ
كَذَّبُوْا بِاٰيٰتِ اللّٰهِ ۭ وَاللّٰهُ لَا يَهْدِي الْقَوْمَ
الظّٰلِمِيْنَ ⑤
قُلْ يٰٓاَيُّهَا الَّذِيْنَ هَادُوْٓا اِنْ زَعَمْتُمْ
اَنَّكُمْ اَوْلِيَاۗءُ لِلّٰهِ مِنْ دُوْنِ النَّاسِ
فَتَمَنَّوُا الْمَوْتَ اِنْ كُنْتُمْ صٰدِقِيْنَ ⑥
وَلَا يَتَمَنَّوْنَهٗٓ اَبَدًۢا بِمَا قَدَّمَتْ اَيْدِيْهِمْ ۭ
وَاللّٰهُ عَلِيْمٌۢ بِالظّٰلِمِيْنَ ⑦
قُلْ اِنَّ الْمَوْتَ الَّذِيْ تَفِرُّوْنَ مِنْهُ
فَاِنَّهٗ مُلٰقِيْكُمْ ثُمَّ تُرَدُّوْنَ اِلٰى عٰلِمِ
الْغَيْبِ وَالشَّهَادَةِ فَيُنَبِّئُكُمْ بِمَا كُنْتُمْ
تَعْمَلُوْنَ ⑧ ع
يٰٓاَيُّهَا الَّذِيْنَ اٰمَنُوْٓا اِذَا نُوْدِيَ لِلصَّلٰوةِ

سورۂ جمعہ مدنی ہے اس میں گیارہ آیتیں اور دو رکوع ہیں

شروع خدا کا نام لے کر جو بڑا مہربان نہایت رحم والا ہے ○
جو چیز آسمانوں میں ہے اور جو چیز زمین میں ہے سب خدا کی تسبیح کرتی
ہے جو بادشاہ حقیقی پاک ذات زبردست حکمت والا ہے ①
وہی تو ہے جس نے ان پڑھوں میں اُنہی میں سے (محمدؐ کو)
پیغمبر (بنا کر) بھیجا جو اُن کے سامنے اُس کی آیتیں پڑھتے
اور اُن کو پاک کرتے اور (خدا کی) کتاب اور دانائی سکھاتے
ہیں اور اس سے پہلے تو یہ لوگ صریح گمراہی میں تھے ②
اور اُن میں سے اور لوگوں کی طرف بھی (اُن کو بھیجا ہے) جو
ابھی اُن (مسلمانوں) سے نہیں ملے۔ اور وہ غالب حکمت والا ہے ③
یہ خدا کا فضل ہے جسے چاہتا ہے عطا کرتا ہے۔ اور خدا
بڑے فضل کا مالک ہے ④
جن لوگوں (کے سر) پر تورات لدوائی گئی پھر اُنہوں نے
اُس (کے بارِ تعمیل) کو نہ اٹھایا اُن کی مثال گدھے کی سی ہے
جس پر بڑی بڑی کتابیں لدی ہوں۔ جو لوگ خدا کی آیتوں
کی تکذیب کرتے ہیں اُن کی مثال بُری ہے۔ اور خدا ظالم
لوگوں کو ہدایت نہیں دیتا ⑤
کہہ دو کہ اے یہود اگر تم کو یہ دعویٰ ہو کہ تم ہی خدا کے دوست
ہو اور لوگ نہیں تو اگر تم سچے ہو تو (ذرا) موت کی
آرزو تو کرو ⑥
اور یہ اُن (اعمال) کے سبب جو کر چکے ہیں ہرگز اس کی آرزو
نہیں کریں گے۔ اور خدا ظالموں سے خوب واقف ہے ⑦
کہہ دو کہ موت جس سے تم گریز کرتے ہو وہ تو تمہارے سامنے
آ کر رہے گی پھر تم پوشیدہ اور ظاہر کے جاننے والے
(خدا) کی طرف لوٹائے جاؤ گے پھر جو جو کچھ تم کرتے
رہے ہو وہ تمہیں سب بتائے گا ⑧
مومنو! جب جمعے کے دن نماز کے لئے اذان دی جائے

Al-Jumu'a, or the Assembly (Friday) Prayer

In the name of Allah, Most Gracious, Most Merciful.

1. Whatever is in the heavens and on earth, doth declare the Praises and Glory of Allah,—the Sovereign, the Holy One, the Exalted in Might, the Wise.

2. It is He Who has sent amongst the Unlettered a messenger from among themselves, to rehearse to them His Signs, to purify them, and to instruct them in The Book and Wisdom,—although they had been, before, in manifest error;—

3. Alongwith others of them, who have not already joined them: and He is Exalted in Might, Wise.

4. Such is the Bounty of Allah, which He bestows on whom He will: and Allah is the Lord of the highest bounty.

5. The similitude of those who were entrusted with the (obligations of) Taurat, but who subsequently failed in those (obligations), is that of a donkey which carries huge tomes (but understands them not). Evil is the similitude of people who falsify the Signs of Allah: and Allah guides not people who do wrong.

6. Say: O ye of Jewry ! if ye think that ye are friends to Allah, to the exclusion of (other) men, then express your desire for Death, if ye are truthful !"

7. But never will they express their desire (for Death), because of the (deeds) their hands have sent on before them ! And Allah knows well those that do wrong !

8. Say: "The Death from which ye flee will truly overtake you: then will ye be sent back to the Knower of things secret and open: and He will tell you the things that ye did !"

9. O ye who believe ! when the call is proclaimed to prayer on

SÛRA–63
AL-MUNÃFÎQÛN
(INTRODUCTION)

This is the seventh of the ten short Madinah Sûras dealing with a special feature in the social life of the Brotherhood.

The special feature here dealt with is the wiles and mischief of the Hypocrite element in any community, and the need of guarding against it and against the temptation it throws in the way of the Believers.

The battle of Uḥud (Shawwãl A.H. 3) unmasked the Hypocrites in Madinah: see 3: 167. This Sûra may be referred to sometime after that event, say about 4 A.H. or possibly 5 A.H. if the words reported in verse 8 were uttered in the expedition against the Banu Muṣ aliq, A.H. 5.

Friday (the Day of Assembly), hasten earnestly to the Remembrance of Allah, and leave off business (and traffic): that is best for you if ye but knew !

10. And when the Prayer is finished, then may ye Disperse through the land, and seek of the Bounty of Allah: and remember Allah frequently that ye may prosper.

11. But when they see some bargain or some pastime, they disperse headlong to it, and leave thee standing. Say: "That which Allah has is better than any pastime or bargain ! And Allah is the Best to provide (for all needs)."

Al-Munāfiqūn, or the Hypocrites

In the name of Allah, Most Gracious, Most Merciful.

1. When the Hypocrites come to thee, they say, "We bear witness that thou art indeed the Messenger of Allah." Yea, Allah knoweth that thou art indeed His Messenger. And Allah beareth witness that the Hypocrites are indeed liars.

2. They have made their oaths a screen (for their misdeeds): thus they obstruct (men) from the Path of Allah: truly evil are their deeds.

3. That is because they believed, then they rejected Faith: so a seal was set on their hearts: therefore they understand not.

4. When thou lookest at them, their bodies please thee; and when they speak, thou listenest to their words. They are as (worthless as hollow) pieces of timber propped up, (unable to stand on their own). They think that every cry is against them. They are the enemies; so beware of them. The curse of Allah be on them ! How are they deluded (away from the Truth) !

5. And when it is said to them, "Come, the Messenger of Allah will pray for your Forgiveness", they turn aside their heads, and thou wouldst see them turning away their faces in arrogance.

مِنْ يَّوْمِ الْجُمُعَةِ فَاسْعَوْا اِلٰى ذِكْرِ اللّٰهِ
وَذَرُوا الْبَيْعَ ؕ ذٰلِكُمْ خَيْرٌ لَّكُمْ اِنْ كُنْتُمْ
تَعْلَمُوْنَ ⑨
فَاِذَا قُضِيَتِ الصَّلٰوةُ فَانْتَشِرُوْا فِي
الْاَرْضِ وَابْتَغُوْا مِنْ فَضْلِ اللّٰهِ وَاذْكُرُوا
اللّٰهَ كَثِيْرًا لَّعَلَّكُمْ تُفْلِحُوْنَ ⑩
وَاِذَا رَاَوْا تِجَارَةً اَوْ لَهْوَا ِۨانْفَضُّوْٓا اِلَيْهَا
وَتَرَكُوْكَ قَاۤىِٕمًا ؕ قُلْ مَا عِنْدَ اللّٰهِ خَيْرٌ مِّنَ
اللَّهْوِ وَمِنَ التِّجَارَةِ ؕ وَاللّٰهُ خَيْرُ الرّٰزِقِيْنَ ⑪

سُوْرَةُ الْمُنٰفِقُوْنَ مَدَنِيَّةٌ وَّهِيَ اِحْدٰى عَشْرَةَ اٰيَةً وَّفِيْهَا رُكُوْعَانِ

بِسْمِ اللّٰهِ الرَّحْمٰنِ الرَّحِيْمِ
اِذَا جَاۤءَكَ الْمُنٰفِقُوْنَ قَالُوْا نَشْهَدُ اِنَّكَ
لَرَسُوْلُ اللّٰهِ ۘ وَاللّٰهُ يَعْلَمُ اِنَّكَ لَرَسُوْلُهٗ ؕ
وَاللّٰهُ يَشْهَدُ اِنَّ الْمُنٰفِقِيْنَ
لَكٰذِبُوْنَ ①
اِتَّخَذُوْٓا اَيْمَانَهُمْ جُنَّةً فَصَدُّوْا عَنْ
سَبِيْلِ اللّٰهِ ؕ اِنَّهُمْ سَاۤءَ مَا كَانُوْا يَعْمَلُوْنَ ②
ذٰلِكَ بِاَنَّهُمْ اٰمَنُوْا ثُمَّ كَفَرُوْا فَطُبِعَ
عَلٰى قُلُوْبِهِمْ فَهُمْ لَا يَفْقَهُوْنَ ③
وَاِذَا رَاَيْتَهُمْ تُعْجِبُكَ اَجْسَامُهُمْ ؕ
وَاِنْ يَّقُوْلُوْا تَسْمَعْ لِقَوْلِهِمْ ؕ كَاَنَّهُمْ
خُشُبٌ مُّسَنَّدَةٌ ؕ يَحْسَبُوْنَ كُلَّ
صَيْحَةٍ عَلَيْهِمْ ؕ هُمُ الْعَدُوُّ فَاحْذَرْهُمْ ؕ
قٰتَلَهُمُ اللّٰهُ ۫ اَنّٰى يُؤْفَكُوْنَ ④
وَاِذَا قِيْلَ لَهُمْ تَعَالَوْا يَسْتَغْفِرْ لَكُمْ
رَسُوْلُ اللّٰهِ لَوَّوْا رُءُوْسَهُمْ وَرَاَيْتَهُمْ
يَصُدُّوْنَ وَهُمْ مُّسْتَكْبِرُوْنَ ⑤

تو خدا کی یاد (یعنی نماز) کے لئے جلدی کرو اور (خرید و
فروخت ترک کر دو۔ اگر سمجھو تو یہ تمہارے حق میں
بہتر ہے ⑨
پھر جب نماز ہو چکے تو اپنی اپنی راہ لو اور خدا کا فضل
تلاش کرو اور خدا کو بہت بہت یاد کرتے رہو تاکہ نجات
پاؤ ⑩
اور جب یہ لوگ سودا بکتا یا تماشا ہوتا دیکھتے ہیں تو ادھر بھاگ
جاتے ہیں اور تمہیں (کھڑے کا) کھڑا چھوڑ جاتے ہیں۔ کہہ دو کہ جو چیز
خدا کے ہاں ہے وہ تماشے اور سودے سے کہیں بہتر ہے اور خدا سب سے بہتر رزق دینے والا ہے ⑪

سورۂ منافقون مدنی ہے اس میں گیارہ آیتیں اور دو رکوع ہیں

شروع خدا کا نام لے کر جو بڑا مہربان نہایت رحم والا ہے
(اے محمد) جب منافق لوگ تمہارے پاس آتے ہیں تو (از راہ نفاق)
کہتے ہیں کہ ہم اقرار کرتے ہیں کہ آپ بیشک خدا کے پیغمبر ہیں
اور خدا جانتا ہے کہ درحقیقت تم اسکے پیغمبر ہو لیکن خدا ظاہر کئے
دیتا ہے کہ منافق (دل سے اعتقاد نہ رکھنے کے لحاظ سے) جھوٹے ہیں ①
انہوں نے اپنی قسموں کو ڈھال بنا رکھا ہے اور انکے ذریعے سے (لوگوں کو)
راہ خدا سے روک رہے ہیں۔ کچھ شک نہیں کہ جو کام یہ کرتے ہیں بُرے ہیں ②
یہ اس لئے کہ یہ (پہلے تو) ایمان لائے پھر کافر ہو گئے تو ان کے
دلوں پر مہر لگا دی گئی سو اب یہ سمجھتے ہی نہیں ③
اور جب تم ان (کے تناسب اعضا) کو دیکھتے ہو تو انکے جسم تمہیں (کیا ہی)
اچھے معلوم ہوتے ہیں۔ اور جب وہ گفتگو کرتے ہیں تو تم انکی تقریر کو توجہ سے
سنتے ہو گویا لکڑیاں ہیں جو دیواروں سے لگائی گئی ہیں (بزدل ایسے کہ)
ہر زور کی آواز کو سمجھیں (کہ) ان پر (بلا آئی)۔ یہ (تمہارے) دشمن ہیں ان سے
بے خوف نہ رہنا۔ خدا ان کو ہلاک کرے۔ یہ کہاں بہکے پھرتے ہیں ④
اور جب ان سے کہا جائے کہ آؤ رسول خدا تمہارے لئے
مغفرت مانگیں تو سر ہلا دیتے ہیں اور تم ان کو دیکھو کہ تکبر
کرتے ہوئے منہ پھیر لیتے ہیں ⑤

SÛRA–64
AT-TAG̱ÃBUN
(INTRODUCTION)

This is the eighth of the ten short Madinah Sûras, each dealing with a special aspect of the life of the Community.

The special aspect spoken of here is the mutual gain and loss of Good and Evil, contrasted in this life and in the Hereafter.

It is an early Madinah Sûra, of the year 1 of the Hijra or possibly even of the Makkan period just before the Hijrat.

6. It is equal to them whether thou pray for their forgiveness or not. Allah will not forgive them. Truly Allah guides not rebellious transgressors.

7. They are the ones who say, "Spend nothing on those who are with Allah's Messenger till they disperse (and quit Madinah)." But to Allah belong the treasures of the heavens and the earth; but the Hypocrites understand not.

8. They say, "If we return to Madinah, surely the more honourable (element) will expel therefrom the meaner". But honour belongs to Allah and His Messenger, and to the Believers; but the Hypocrites know not.

9. O ye who believe ! let not your riches or your children divert you from the remembrance of Allah. If any act thus, surely they are the losers.

10. And spend something (in charity) out of the substance which We have bestowed on you, before Death should come to any of you and he should say, "O my Lord ! Why didst Thou not give me respite for a little while? I should then have given (largely) in charity, and I should have been one of the doers of good".

11. But to no soul will Allah grant respite when the time appointed (for it) has come; and Allah is well acquainted with (all) that ye do.

Tagābun, or Mutual Loss and Gain

In the name of Allah, Most Gracious, Most Merciful.

1. Whatever is in the heavens and on earth, doth declare the Praises and Glory of Allah: to Him belongs dominion, and to Him belongs Praise: and He has power over all things.

2. It is He Who has Created you; and of you are some that are

تم اُن کے لئے مغفرت مانگو یا نہ مانگو اُن کے حق میں برابر ہے۔
خدا اُن کو ہرگز نہ بخشے گا۔ بے شک خدا نافرمان لوگوں کو
ہدایت نہیں دیا کرتا (٦)
یہی ہیں جو کہتے ہیں کہ جو لوگ رسول خدا کے پاس (رہتے)
ہیں اُن پر (کچھ) خرچ نہ کرو۔ یہاں تک کہ یہ (خود بخود)
بھاگ جائیں۔ حالانکہ آسمانوں اور زمین کے خزانے خدا ہی کے
ہیں لیکن منافق نہیں سمجھتے (٧)
کہتے ہیں کہ اگر ہم لوٹ کر مدینے پہنچے تو عزت والے ذلیل
لوگوں کو وہاں سے نکال باہر کریں گے۔ حالانکہ عزت
خدا کی ہے اور اُس کے رسُول کی اور مومنوں کی لیکن
منافق نہیں جانتے (٨)
مومنو! تمہارا مال اور اولاد تم کو خدا کی یاد سے غافل نہ کرے
اور جو ایسا کرے گا تو وہ لوگ خسارہ اُٹھانے
والے ہیں (٩)
اور جو (مال) ہم نے تم کو دیا ہے اس میں سے اُس
(وقت) سے پیشتر خرچ کرلو کہ تم میں سے کسی کی موت
آجائے تو (اُس وقت) کہنے لگے کہ اے میرے پروردگار
تو نے مجھے تھوڑی سی اور مہلت کیوں نہ دی تاکہ میں خیرات
کرلیتا اور نیک لوگوں میں داخل ہو جاتا (١٠)
اور جب کسی کی موت آجاتی ہے تو خدا اُس کو ہرگز مہلت نہیں
دیتا۔ اور جو کچھ تم کرتے ہو خدا اس سے خبردار ہے (١١)

سورۂ تغابن مدنی ہے اس میں اٹھارہ آیتیں اور دو رکوع ہیں

شروع خدا کا نام لے کر جو بڑا مہربان نہایت رحم والا ہے
جو چیز آسمانوں میں ہے اور جو چیز زمین میں ہے (سب)
خدا کی تسبیح کرتی ہے۔ اُسی کی سچی بادشاہی ہے اور اُسی
کی تعریف (لامتناہی) ہے اور وہ ہر چیز پر قادر ہے (١)
وہی تو ہے جس نے تم کو پیدا کیا پھر کوئی تم میں کافر ہے اور

سواء علیہم استغفرت لہم ام لم
تستغفر لہم لن یغفر اللہ لہم ط
ان اللہ لا یہدی القوم الفسقین ﴿٦﴾
ہم الذین یقولون لا تنفقوا علی
من عند رسول اللہ حتی ینفضوا ط
وللہ خزائن السموت والارض و
لکن المنفقین لا یفقہون ﴿٧﴾
یقولون لئن رجعنا الی المدینۃ
لیخرجن الاعز منہا الاذل ط وللہ
العزۃ ولرسولہ وللمؤمنین ولکن
المنفقین لا یعلمون ع ﴿٨﴾
یایہا الذین امنوا لا تلہکم اموالکم
ولا اولادکم عن ذکر اللہ ج ومن یفعل
ذلک فاولئک ہم الخسرون ﴿٩﴾
وانفقوا من ما رزقنکم من
قبل ان یاتی احدکم الموت
فیقول رب لولا اخرتنی الی اجل
قریب فاصدق واکن من
الصلحین ﴿١٠﴾
ولن یؤخر اللہ نفسا اذا جاء اجلہا ط
واللہ خبیر بما تعملون ع ﴿١١﴾

سورۃ التغابن مدنیۃ وہی ثمانی عشرۃ ایۃ وفیہا رکوعان

بسم اللہ الرحمن الرحیم
یسبح للہ ما فی السموت وما فی الارض
لہ الملک ولہ الحمد وہو علی کل
شیء قدیر ﴿١﴾
ہو الذی خلقکم فمنکم کافر ومنکم

Unbelievers, and some that are Believers: and Allah sees well all that ye do.

3. He has created the heavens and the earth with the truth, and has given you shape and made your shapes beautiful: and to Him is the final Return.

4. He knows what is in the heavens and on earth; and He knows what ye conceal and what ye reveal: yea, Allah knows well the (secrets) of (all) hearts.

5. Has not the story reached you, of those who rejected Faith aforetime? So they tasted the evil result of their conduct; and they had a grievous Chastisement.

6. That was because there came to them messengers with Clear Signs, but they said: "Shall (mere) human beings direct us?" So they rejected (the Message) and turned away. But Allah can do without (them): and Allah is free of all needs worthy of all praise.

7. The Unbelievers think that they will not be raised up (for Judgment). Say: "Yea, by my Lord, ye shall surely be raised up: then shall ye be told (the truth) of all that ye did. And that is easy for Allah."

مُّؤْمِنٌ ۚ وَاللَّهُ بِمَا تَعْمَلُونَ بَصِيرٌ ۝٢
خَلَقَ السَّمٰوٰتِ وَالْأَرْضَ بِالْحَقِّ وَصَوَّرَكُمْ
فَأَحْسَنَ صُوَرَكُمْ ۖ وَإِلَيْهِ الْمَصِيرُ ۝٣
يَعْلَمُ مَا فِي السَّمٰوٰتِ وَالْأَرْضِ وَيَعْلَمُ
مَا تُسِرُّونَ وَمَا تُعْلِنُونَ ۚ وَاللَّهُ عَلِيمٌ
بِذَاتِ الصُّدُورِ ۝٤
أَلَمْ يَأْتِكُمْ نَبَؤُا الَّذِينَ كَفَرُوا مِن قَبْلُ
فَذَاقُوا وَبَالَ أَمْرِهِمْ وَلَهُمْ عَذَابٌ أَلِيمٌ ۝٥
ذٰلِكَ بِأَنَّهُ كَانَت تَّأْتِيهِمْ رُسُلُهُم بِالْبَيِّنٰتِ
فَقَالُوا أَبَشَرٌ يَهْدُونَنَا فَكَفَرُوا وَتَوَلَّوا
وَّاسْتَغْنَى اللَّهُ ۚ وَاللَّهُ غَنِيٌّ حَمِيدٌ ۝٦
زَعَمَ الَّذِينَ كَفَرُوا أَن لَّن يُبْعَثُوا ۚ
قُلْ بَلَىٰ وَرَبِّي لَتُبْعَثُنَّ ثُمَّ لَتُنَبَّؤُنَّ
بِمَا عَمِلْتُمْ ۚ وَذٰلِكَ عَلَى اللَّهِ
يَسِيرٌ ۝٧

کوئی مومن۔ اور جو کچھ تم کرتے ہو خدا اُس کو دیکھتا ہے ۝٢
اُسی نے آسمانوں اور زمین کو مبنی برحکمت پیدا کیا اور اُسی نے تمہاری
صورتیں بنائیں اور صورتیں بھی پاکیزہ بنائیں اور اُسی کی طرف (تمہیں) لوٹ کر جانا ہے ۝٣
جو کچھ آسمانوں اور زمین میں ہے وہ سب جانتا ہے۔ اور
جو کچھ تم چھپا کر کرتے ہو اور جو کھلم کھلا کرتے ہو اُس سے بھی
آگاہ ہے۔ اور خدا دل کے بھیدوں سے واقف ہے ۝٤
کیا تم کو اُن لوگوں کے حال کی خبر نہیں پہنچی جو پہلے کافر ہوئے تھے تو اُنہوں
نے اپنے کاموں کی سزا کا مزہ چکھ لیا اور (ابھی) دُکھ دینے والا عذاب (ہونا) ہے ۝٥
یہ اس لئے کہ اُن کے پاس پیغمبر کھلی نشانیاں لے کر آتے تو یہ کہتے کہ کیا آدمی
ہمارے ہادی بنتے ہیں؟ تو اُنہوں نے (اُن کو) نہ مانا اور مُنہ پھیر لیا ۝٦
اور خدا نے بھی بے پروائی کی۔ اور خدا بے پروا (اور) سزاوارِ حمد (و ثنا) ہے
جو لوگ کافر ہیں اُن کا اعتقاد ہے کہ وہ (دوبارہ) ہرگز نہیں
اٹھائے جائیں گے۔ کہہ دو کہ ہاں ہاں میرے پروردگار کی قسم
تم ضرور اٹھائے جاؤ گے پھر جو کام تم کرتے رہے ہو وہ تمہیں
بتائے جائیں گے۔ اور یہ (بات) خدا کو آسان ہے ۝٧

8. Believe, therefore, in Allah and His Messenger, and in the Light which We have sent down. And Allah is well acquainted with all that ye do.

9. The Day that He assembles you (all) for a Day of Assembly,— that will be a day of mutual loss and gain (among you). And those who believe in Allah and work righteousness,—He will remove from them their ill, and He will admit them to gardens beneath which rivers flow, to dwell therein for ever: that will be the Supreme Triumph.

10. But those who reject Faith and treat Our Signs as falsehoods, they will be Companions of the Fire, to dwell therein for aye: and evil is that Goal.

11. No kind of calamity can occur, except by the leave of Allah: and if anyone believes in Allah, (Allah) guides his heart (aright): for Allah knows all things.

فَآمِنُوا بِاللَّهِ وَرَسُولِهِ وَالنُّورِ الَّذِي
أَنزَلْنَا ۚ وَاللَّهُ بِمَا تَعْمَلُونَ خَبِيرٌ ۝٨
يَوْمَ يَجْمَعُكُمْ لِيَوْمِ الْجَمْعِ ۖ ذٰلِكَ يَوْمُ
التَّغَابُنِ ۗ وَمَن يُؤْمِن بِاللَّهِ وَيَعْمَلْ
صَالِحًا يُكَفِّرْ عَنْهُ سَيِّئَاتِهِ وَيُدْخِلْهُ
جَنّٰتٍ تَجْرِي مِن تَحْتِهَا الْأَنْهٰرُ خٰلِدِينَ
فِيهَا أَبَدًا ۚ ذٰلِكَ الْفَوْزُ الْعَظِيمُ ۝٩
وَالَّذِينَ كَفَرُوا وَكَذَّبُوا بِآيٰتِنَا أُولٰئِكَ
أَصْحٰبُ النَّارِ خٰلِدِينَ فِيهَا ۖ وَبِئْسَ الْمَصِيرُ ۝١٠
مَا أَصَابَ مِن مُّصِيبَةٍ إِلَّا بِإِذْنِ اللَّهِ ۗ
وَمَن يُؤْمِن بِاللَّهِ يَهْدِ قَلْبَهُ ۚ وَاللَّهُ
بِكُلِّ شَيْءٍ عَلِيمٌ ۝١١

تو خدا پر اور اس کے رسول پر اور نور (قرآن) پر جو ہم نے نازل فرمایا ہے
ایمان لاؤ۔ اور خدا تمہارے سب اعمال سے خبردار ہے ۝٨
جس دن وہ تم کو اکٹھا ہونے (یعنی قیامت) کے دن اکٹھا کرے گا
وہ نقصان اٹھانے کا دن ہے۔ اور جو شخص خدا پر ایمان لائے
اور نیک عمل کرے وہ اُس سے اُس کی برائیاں دور کر دے گا
اور باغہائے بہشت میں جن کے نیچے نہریں بہہ رہی ہیں داخل
کرے گا ہمیشہ اُن میں رہیں گے۔ یہ بڑی کامیابی ہے ۝٩
اور جنہوں نے کفر کیا اور ہماری آیتوں کو جھٹلایا وہی اہلِ دوزخ
ہیں ہمیشہ اس میں رہیں گے اور وہ بُری جگہ ہے ۝١٠
کوئی مصیبت نازل نہیں ہوتی مگر خدا کے حکم سے۔ اور جو
شخص خدا پر ایمان لاتا ہے وہ اُس کے دل کو ہدایت دیتا ہے
اور خدا ہر چیز سے باخبر ہے ۝١١

SÛRA–65

AṬ-ṬALÃQ

(INTRODUCTION)

This is the ninth of the ten short Madinah Sûras dealing with the social life of the Community. The aspect dealt with here is Divorce and the necessity of precautions to guard against its abuse. The relations of the sexes are an important factor in the social life of the Community, and this and the following Sûra deal with certain aspects of it. "Of all things permitted by law," said the Prophet, "divorce is the most hateful in the sight of Allah" (Abû Dã-ûd, *Sunan,* 13: 3). While the sanctity of marriage is the essential basis of family life, the incompatibility of individuals and the weaknesses of human nature require certain outlets and safeguards if that sanctity is not to be made into a fetish at the expense of human life. That is why the question of Divorce is in the Sûra linked with the question of insolent impiety and its punishment.

The date is somewhere about A.H. 6, but the chronology has no significance.

12. So obey Allah, and obey his Messenger: but if ye turn back, the duty of Our Messenger is but to deliver (the Message) clearly and openly.

13. Allah ! There is no god but He: and on Allah, therefore, let the Believers put their trust.

14. O ye who believe ! truly, among your wives and your children are (some that are) enemies to yourselves: so beware of them ! But if ye forgive and overlook and cover up (their faults), verily Allah is Oft-Forgiving, Most Merciful.

15. Your riches and your children may be but a trial: whereas Allah, with Him is the highest Reward.

16. So fear Allah as much as ye can; listen and obey; and spend in charity for the benefit of your own souls. And those saved from the covetousness of their own souls,—they are the ones that achieve prosperity.

17. If ye loan to Allah a beautiful loan, He will double it to your (credit), and He will grant you Forgiveness: for Allah is All-Thankful Most Forbearing,—

18. Knower of what is hidden and what is open, Exalted in Might, Full of Wisdom.

Aṭ-Ṭalāq, or Divorce.

In the name of Allah, Most Gracious, Most Merciful.

1. O Prophet ! When ye do divorce women, divorce them at their prescribed periods, and count (accurately) their prescribed periods: and fear Allah your Lord: and turn them not out of their houses, nor shall they (themselves) leave, except in case they are guilty of some open lewdness, those are limits set by Allah: and any who transgresses the limits of Allah, does verily wrong his (own) soul: thou knowest not if perchance Allah will being about thereafter some new situation.

اور خدا کی اطاعت کرو اور اُس کے رسول کی اطاعت کرو
اگر تم منہ پھیر لوگے تو ہمارے پیغمبر کے ذمے تو صرف پیغام کا
کھول کھول کر پہنچا دینا ہے ﴿۱۲﴾
خدا (جو معبود برحق ہے اس) کے سوا کوئی عبادت کے
لائق نہیں۔ تو مومنوں کو چاہیئے کہ خدا ہی پر بھروسا رکھیں ﴿۱۳﴾
مومنو! تمہاری عورتوں اور اولاد میں سے بعض تمہارے
دشمن (بھی) ہیں سو اُن سے بچتے رہو اور اگر معاف کر دو
اور درگزر کرو اور بخش دو تو خدا بھی بخشنے والا
مہربان ہے ﴿۱۴﴾
تمہارا مال اور تمہاری اولاد تو آزمائش ہے۔ اور خدا کے ہاں
بڑا اجر ہے ﴿۱۵﴾
سو جہاں تک ہو سکے خدا سے ڈرو اور اُسکے احکام کو سنو اور اُسکے
فرمانبردار رہو اور (اُسکی راہ میں) خرچ کرو (یہ) تمہارے حق میں بہتر ہے
اور جو شخص طبیعت کے بخل سے بچایا گیا تو ایسے ہی لوگ راہ پانے والے ہیں ﴿۱۶﴾
اگر تم خدا کو (اخلاص اور نیت) نیک (سے) قرض دو گے تو وہ تم کو اُس کا
دو چند دیگا اور تمہارے گناہ بھی معاف کر دیگا۔ اور خدا قدر شناس اور بردبار ہے ﴿۱۷﴾
پوشیدہ اور ظاہر کا جاننے والا غالب اور حکمت والا ﴿۱۸﴾

سورۂ طلاق مدنی ہے اس میں بارہ آیتیں اور دو رکوع ہیں

شروع خدا کا نام لے کر جو بڑا مہربان نہایت رحم والا ہے
اے پیغمبر (مسلمانوں سے کہہ دو کہ) جب تم عورتوں کو طلاق دینے لگو
تو اُن کی عدت کے شروع میں طلاق دو ۲۹۶ اور عدت کا شمار رکھو
اور خدا سے جو تمہارا پروردگار ہے ڈرو۔ (نہ تو تم ہی) اُنکو (ایام عدت
میں) اُنکے گھروں سے نکالو اور نہ وہ (خود ہی) نکلیں۔ ہاں اگر
وہ صریح بے حیائی کریں (تو نکال دینا چاہیئے) اور یہ خدا کی
حدیں ہیں۔ جو خدا کی حدوں سے تجاوز کرے گا وہ اپنے آپ پر
ظلم کرے گا (اے طلاق دینے والے) تجھے کیا معلوم شاید خدا
اس کے بعد کوئی (رجعت کی) سبیل پیدا کر دے ﴿۱﴾

وَأَطِيعُوا اللَّهَ وَأَطِيعُوا الرَّسُولَ ۚ فَإِن
تَوَلَّيْتُمْ فَإِنَّمَا عَلَىٰ رَسُولِنَا الْبَلَاغُ
الْمُبِينُ ﴿١٢﴾
اللَّهُ لَا إِلَٰهَ إِلَّا هُوَ ۚ وَعَلَى اللَّهِ فَلْيَتَوَكَّلِ
الْمُؤْمِنُونَ ﴿١٣﴾
يَا أَيُّهَا الَّذِينَ آمَنُوا إِنَّ مِنْ أَزْوَاجِكُمْ
وَأَوْلَادِكُمْ عَدُوًّا لَّكُمْ فَاحْذَرُوهُمْ ۚ
وَإِن تَعْفُوا وَتَصْفَحُوا وَتَغْفِرُوا فَإِنَّ اللَّهَ
غَفُورٌ رَّحِيمٌ ﴿١٤﴾
إِنَّمَا أَمْوَالُكُمْ وَأَوْلَادُكُمْ فِتْنَةٌ ۚ وَاللَّهُ
عِندَهُ أَجْرٌ عَظِيمٌ ﴿١٥﴾
فَاتَّقُوا اللَّهَ مَا اسْتَطَعْتُمْ وَاسْمَعُوا وَأَطِيعُوا
وَأَنفِقُوا خَيْرًا لِّأَنفُسِكُمْ ۗ وَمَن يُوقَ شُحَّ
نَفْسِهِ فَأُولَٰئِكَ هُمُ الْمُفْلِحُونَ ﴿١٦﴾
إِن تُقْرِضُوا اللَّهَ قَرْضًا حَسَنًا يُضَاعِفْهُ
لَكُمْ وَيَغْفِرْ لَكُمْ ۚ وَاللَّهُ شَكُورٌ حَلِيمٌ ﴿١٧﴾
عَالِمُ الْغَيْبِ وَالشَّهَادَةِ الْعَزِيزُ الْحَكِيمُ ﴿١٨﴾ ع ٢

سُورَةُ الطَّلَاقِ مَدَنِيَّةٌ وَهِيَ اثْنَتَا عَشْرَةَ آيَةً وَفِيهَا رُكُوعَانِ

بِسْمِ اللَّهِ الرَّحْمَٰنِ الرَّحِيمِ
يَا أَيُّهَا النَّبِيُّ إِذَا طَلَّقْتُمُ النِّسَاءَ
فَطَلِّقُوهُنَّ لِعِدَّتِهِنَّ وَأَحْصُوا
الْعِدَّةَ ۖ وَاتَّقُوا اللَّهَ رَبَّكُمْ ۖ لَا تُخْرِجُوهُنَّ
مِن بُيُوتِهِنَّ وَلَا يَخْرُجْنَ إِلَّا أَن
يَأْتِينَ بِفَاحِشَةٍ مُّبَيِّنَةٍ ۚ وَتِلْكَ
حُدُودُ اللَّهِ ۚ وَمَن يَتَعَدَّ حُدُودَ اللَّهِ
فَقَدْ ظَلَمَ نَفْسَهُ ۚ لَا تَدْرِي لَعَلَّ اللَّهَ
يُحْدِثُ بَعْدَ ذَٰلِكَ أَمْرًا ﴿١﴾

2. Thus when they fulfil their term appointed, either take them back on equitable terms or part with them on equitable terms; and take for witness two persons from among you, endued with justice, and establish the evidence for the sake of Allah. Such is the admonition given to him who believes in Allah and the Last Day. And for those who fear Allah, He (ever) prepares a way out,

3. And He provides for him from (sources) he never could expect. And if anyone puts his trust in Allah, sufficient is (Allah) for him. For Allah will surely accomplish His purpose: verily, for all things has Allah appointed a due proportion.

4. Such of your women as have passed the age of monthly courses, for them the prescribed period, if ye have any doubts, is three months, and for those who have no courses (it is the same): for those who are pregnant, their period is until they deliver their burdens: and for those who fear Allah, He will make things easy for them.

5. That is the Command of Allah, which He has sent down to you: And if any one fears Allah, He will remove his evil deeds from him, and will enlarge his reward.

6. Let the women live (in *'iddat*) in the same style as ye live, according to your means: annoy them not, so as to restrict them. And if they are pregnant, then spend (your substance) on them until they deliver their burden: and if they suckle your (offspring), give them their recompense: and take mutual counsel together, according to what is just and reasonable. And if ye find yourselves in difficulties, let another woman suckle (the child) on the (father's) behalf.

7. Let the man of means spend according to his means: and the man whose resources are restricted, let him spend according to what Allah has given him. Allah puts no burden on any person beyond what He has given him. After a difficulty, Allah will soon grant relief.

8. How many populations that insolently opposed the command of their Lord and of His messengers, did We not then call to account,— to

پھر جب وہ اپنی میعاد (یعنی انقضائے عدت) کے قریب پہنچ جائیں تو یا تو انکو
اچھی طرح سے (زوجیت میں) رہنے دو یا اچھی طرح سے علیحدہ کر دو اور اپنے میں سے
دو منصف مردوں کو گواہ کر لو اور (گواہو!) خدا کیلئے درست گواہی دینا۔ ان
باتوں سے اس شخص کو نصیحت کیجاتی ہے جو خدا پر اور روز آخرت پر ایمان رکھتا ہے
اور جو کوئی خدا سے ڈریگا۔ وہ اُس کیلئے (رنج و محن سے) مخلصی کی صورت پیدا کریگا ﴿٢﴾
اور اُسکو ایسی جگہ سے رزق دیگا جہاں سے (وہم و) گمان بھی نہ ہو اور جو
خدا پر بھروسا رکھیگا تو وہ اُسکو کفایت کریگا۔ خدا اپنے کام کو (جو وہ کرنا
چاہتا ہے) پورا کر دیتا ہے خدا نے ہر چیز کا اندازہ مقرر کر رکھا ہے ﴿٣﴾
اور تمہاری (مطلقہ) عورتیں جو حیض سے ناامید ہو چکی ہوں اگر
تمکو (انکی عدت کے بارے میں) شبہ ہو تو انکی عدت تین مہینے ہے اور جنکو
ابھی حیض نہیں آنے لگا (انکی عدت بھی یہی ہے) اور حمل والی عورتوں
کی عدت وضع حمل (یعنی بچہ جننے) تک ہے۔ اور جو خدا سے
ڈریگا خدا اُسکے کام میں سہولت پیدا کر دے گا ﴿٤﴾
یہ خدا کے حکم ہیں جو خدا نے تم پر نازل کئے ہیں۔ اور جو خدا سے
ڈریگا وہ اُس سے اُسکے گناہ دور کر دیگا اور اُسے اجر عظیم بخشے گا ﴿٥﴾
(مطلقہ) عورتوں کو (ایام عدت میں) اپنے مقدور کے مطابق وہیں رکھو
جہاں خود رہتے ہو اور انکو تنگ کرنیکے لئے تکلیف نہ دو۔ اور اگر حمل سے
ہوں تو بچہ جننے تک اُن کا خرچ دیتے رہو۔ پھر اگر وہ بچے کو
تمہارے کہنے سے دودھ پلائیں تو انکو انکی اجرت دو اور (بچے کے
بارے میں) پسندیدہ طریق سے موافقت رکھو اور اگر باہم ضد (اور نااتفاقی)
کرو گے تو (بچے کو اسکے باپ کے) کہنے سے کوئی اور عورت دودھ پلائیگی ﴿٦﴾
صاحب وسعت کو اپنی وسعت کے مطابق خرچ کرنا چاہئے۔
اور جس کے رزق میں تنگی ہو وہ جتنا خدا نے اسکو دیا ہے اُس کے
موافق خرچ کرے۔ خدا کسی کو تکلیف نہیں دیتا مگر اُسی کے
مطابق جو اُسکو دیا ہے۔ اور خدا عنقریب تنگی کے بعد کشائش بخشے گا ﴿٧﴾
اور بہت سی بستیوں (کے رہنے والوں) نے اپنے پروردگار اور اُسکے
پیغمبروں کے احکام سے سرکشی کی تو ہم نے اُن کو سخت حساب

فاذا بلغن اجلهن فامسكوهن بمعروف
او فارقوهن بمعروف واشهدوا ذوي
عدل منكم واقيموا الشهادة لله ذلكم
يوعظ به من كان يؤمن بالله واليوم
الاخر ومن يتق الله يجعل له مخرجا ﴿٢﴾
ويرزقه من حيث لا يحتسب ومن
يتوكل على الله فهو حسبه ان الله بالغ
امره قد جعل الله لكل شيء قدرا ﴿٣﴾
والئي يئسن من المحيض من نسائكم
ان ارتبتم فعدتهن ثلثة اشهر والئي
لم يحضن واولات الاحمال اجلهن
ان يضعن حملهن ومن يتق الله
يجعل له من امره يسرا ﴿٤﴾
ذلك امر الله انزله اليكم ومن يتق
الله يكفر عنه سياته ويعظم له اجرا ﴿٥﴾
اسكنوهن من حيث سكنتم من وجدكم
ولا تضاروهن لتضيقوا عليهن وان
كن اولات حمل فانفقوا عليهن حتى
يضعن حملهن فان ارضعن لكم
فاتوهن اجورهن واتمروا بينكم بمعروف
وان تعاسرتم فسترضع له اخرى ﴿٦﴾
لينفق ذو سعة من سعته ومن قدر
عليه رزقه فلينفق مما اته الله
لا يكلف الله نفسا الا ما اتها
ع سيجعل الله بعد عسر يسرا ﴿٧﴾
وكاين من قرية عتت عن امر
ربها ورسله فحاسبنها حسابا شديدا

SÛRA–66
AT-TAḤRÎM
(INTRODUCTION)

This is the tenth and last of the series of ten short Madinah Sûras which began with S. 57: see Introduction to that Sûra. The point dealt with here is: how far the turning away from sex or the opposition of one sex against another or a want of harmony between the sexes may injure the higher interests of society.

The date may be taken to be somewhere about A.H. 7.

severe account?—And We chastised them with a horrible Chastisement.

9. Then did they taste the evil result of their conduct, and the End of their conduct was Perdition.

10. Allah has prepared for them a severe Punishment (in the Hereafter). Therefore fear Allah, O ye men of understanding–who have believed !—for Allah hath indeed sent down to you a Message,—

11. A Messenger, who rehearses to you the Signs of Allah containing clear explanations, that he may lead forth those who believe and do righteous deeds from the depths of Darknesss into Light. And those who believe in Allah and work righteousness, He will admit to Gardens beneath which rivers flow, to dwell therein for ever: Allah has indeed granted for them a most excellent provision.

12. Allah is He Who created seven Firmaments and of the earth a similar number through the midst of them (all) descends his Command: that ye may know that Allah has power over all things, and that Allah comprehends all things in (His) Knowledge.

At-Taḥrîm, or Holding (something) to be Forbidden

In the name of Allah, Most Gracious, Most Merciful.

1. O Prophet ! Why holdest thou to be forbidden that which Allah has made lawful to thee, thou seekest to please thy consorts? But Allah is Oft-Forgiving, Most Merciful.

2. Allah has already ordained for you, the expiation of your oaths (in some cases): and Allah is your Protector, and He is Full of Knowledge and Wisdom.

3. When the Prophet disclosed a matter in confidence to one of his consorts, and she then divulged it (to another), and Allah made it known to him, he confirmed part thereof and passed over a part. Then when he told her thereof, she said, "Who told thee this?" He said, "He told me Who is the Knower, The Aware."

میں پکڑ لیا اور اُن پر (ایسا) عذاب نازل کیا جو نہ دیکھا تھا نہ سُنا (٨)
سو انہوں نے اپنے کاموں کی سزا کا مزہ چکھ لیا اور انکا انجام نقصان ہی تو تھا (٩)
خدا نے اُن کے لئے سخت عذاب تیار کر رکھا ہے۔ تو اے اربابِ دانش
جو ایمان لائے ہو خدا سے ڈرو۔ خدا نے تمہارے پاس نصیحت
(کی کتاب) بھیجی ہے (١٠)
(اور اپنے) پیغمبر (بھی بھیجے ہیں) جو تمہارے سامنے خدا کی واضح المطالب
آیتیں پڑھتے ہیں تاکہ جو لوگ ایمان لائے اور عمل نیک کرتے
رہے ہیں اُن کو اندھیرے سے نکال کر روشنی میں لے آئیں۔
اور جو شخص ایمان لائیگا اور عمل نیک کرے گا اُنکو باغہائے بہشت
میں داخل کریگا جنکے نیچے نہریں بہہ رہی ہیں ابدالآباد اُنمیں رہیں گے۔
خدا نے اُن کو خوب رزق دیا ہے (١١)
خدا ہی تو ہے جس نے سات آسمان پیدا کئے اور ویسی ہی زمینیں۔
ان میں (خدا کے) حکم اُترتے رہتے ہیں تاکہ تم لوگ جان لو کہ خدا
ہر چیز پر قادر ہے۔ اور یہ کہ خدا اپنے علم سے ہر چیز پر
احاطہ کئے ہوئے ہے (١٢)

سورۂ تحریم مدنی ہے اس میں بارہ آیتیں اور دو رکوع ہیں

شروع خدا کا نام لے کر جو بڑا مہربان نہایت رحم والا ہے
اے پیغمبر جو چیز خدا نے تمہارے لئے جائز کی ہے تم اُس سے
کنارہ کشی کیوں کرتے ہو؟ (کیا اس سے) اپنی بیویوں کی خوشنودی
چاہتے ہو؟ ق ٢٩٧ وقف ٢٩٨ اور خدا بخشنے والا مہربان ہے (١)
خدا نے تم لوگوں کیلئے تمہاری قسموں کا کفارہ مقرر کر دیا ہے
اور خدا ہی تمہارا کارساز ہے۔ اور وہ دانا (اور) حکمت والا ہے (٢)
اور (یاد کرو) جب پیغمبر نے اپنی ایک بیوی سے ایک بھید کی بات کہی۔
تو (اُس نے دوسری کو بتا دی) جب اُس نے اسکو افشا کیا اور خدا نے اس (حال) سے
پیغمبر کو آگاہ کر دیا تو پیغمبر نے (ان بیوی کو وہ بات) کچھ تو جتائی اور کچھ نہ بتائی ٢٩٩
توجب وہ اُنکو جتائی تو پوچھنے لگیں کہ آپکو یہ کس نے بتایا؟ اُنہوں نے کہا
کہ مجھے اُس نے بتایا ہے جو جاننے والا خبردار ہے (٣)

وَّعَذَّبْنٰهَا عَذَابًا نُّكْرًا ﴿٨﴾
(٩) فَذَاقَتْ وَبَالَ اَمْرِهَا وَكَانَ عَاقِبَةُ اَمْرِهَا خُسْرًا
اَعَدَّ اللّٰهُ لَهُمْ عَذَابًا شَدِيْدًا ۙ فَاتَّقُوا
مع اللّٰهَ يٰٓاُولِي الْاَلْبَابِ ۚۖ الَّذِيْنَ اٰمَنُوْا ۚ
قَدْ اَنْزَلَ اللّٰهُ اِلَيْكُمْ ذِكْرًا ﴿١٠﴾ لا
عند المتقدمين ١٢ رَّسُوْلًا يَّتْلُوْا عَلَيْكُمْ اٰيٰتِ اللّٰهِ مُبَيِّنٰتٍ
لِّيُخْرِجَ الَّذِيْنَ اٰمَنُوْا وَعَمِلُوا الصّٰلِحٰتِ
مِنَ الظُّلُمٰتِ اِلَى النُّوْرِ ۭ وَمَنْ يُّؤْمِنْ
بِاللّٰهِ وَيَعْمَلْ صَالِحًا يُّدْخِلْهُ جَنّٰتٍ
تَجْرِيْ مِنْ تَحْتِهَا الْاَنْهٰرُ خٰلِدِيْنَ فِيْهَآ
اَبَدًا ۭ قَدْ اَحْسَنَ اللّٰهُ لَهٗ رِزْقًا ﴿١١﴾
اَللّٰهُ الَّذِيْ خَلَقَ سَبْعَ سَمٰوٰتٍ وَّمِنَ
الْاَرْضِ مِثْلَهُنَّ ۭ يَتَنَزَّلُ الْاَمْرُ بَيْنَهُنَّ
لِتَعْلَمُوْٓا اَنَّ اللّٰهَ عَلٰي كُلِّ شَيْءٍ قَدِيْرٌ ۙ
ع ٥ ١٨ وَّاَنَّ اللّٰهَ قَدْ اَحَاطَ بِكُلِّ شَيْءٍ عِلْمًا ﴿١٢﴾ ع

سُوْرَةُ التَّحْرِيْمِ مَدَنِيَّةٌ وَّهِيَ اثْنَتَا عَشْرَةَ اٰيَةً وَّفِيْهَا رُكُوْعَانِ

بِسْمِ اللّٰهِ الرَّحْمٰنِ الرَّحِيْمِ
يٰٓاَيُّهَا النَّبِيُّ لِمَ تُحَرِّمُ مَآ اَحَلَّ اللّٰهُ
لَكَ ۚ تَبْتَغِيْ مَرْضَاتَ اَزْوَاجِكَ ۭ وَاللّٰهُ
غَفُوْرٌ رَّحِيْمٌ ﴿١﴾
قَدْ فَرَضَ اللّٰهُ لَكُمْ تَحِلَّةَ اَيْمَانِكُمْ ۚ
وَاللّٰهُ مَوْلٰىكُمْ ۚ وَهُوَ الْعَلِيْمُ الْحَكِيْمُ ﴿٢﴾
وَاِذْ اَسَرَّ النَّبِيُّ اِلٰى بَعْضِ اَزْوَاجِهٖ
حَدِيْثًا ۚ فَلَمَّا نَبَّاَتْ بِهٖ وَاَظْهَرَهُ اللّٰهُ
عَلَيْهِ عَرَّفَ بَعْضَهٗ وَاَعْرَضَ عَنْۢ بَعْضٍ ۚ
فَلَمَّا نَبَّاَهَا بِهٖ قَالَتْ مَنْ اَنْۢبَاَكَ هٰذَا ۭ
قَالَ نَبَّاَنِيَ الْعَلِيْمُ الْخَبِيْرُ ﴿٣﴾

4. If ye two turn in repentance to Allah, your hearts are indeed so inclined; but if ye back up each other against him, truly Allah is his Protector, and Gabriel, and (every) righteous one among those who believe,—and furthermore, the angels—will back (him) up.

5. It may be, if he divorced you (all), that Allah will give him in exchange Consorts better than you,—who submit (their wills), who believe, who are devout; who turn to Allah in repentance, who worship (in humility), who fast,— previously married or virgins.

6. O ye who believe ! save yourselves and your families from a Fire whose fuel is Men and Stones, over which are (appointed) angels stern (and) severe who flinch not (from executing) the Commands they receive from Allah, but do (precisely) what they are commanded.

7. (It will be said) "O ye Unbelievers ! makes no excuses this Day ! Ye are being but requited for all that ye did !"

8. O ye who believe ! turn to Allah with sincere repentance: in the hope that your Lord will remove from you your evil deeds, and admit you to Gardens beneath which Rivers flow,—the Day that Allah will not permit to be humiliated the Prophet and those who believe with him. Their Light will run forward before them and by their right hands, while they say, "Our Lord ! perfect our Light for us, and grant us Forgiveness: for Thou hast power over all things."

9. O Prophet ! Strive hard against the Unbelievers and the Hypocrites, and be harsh with them. Their abode is Hell,—an evil refuge (indeed).

10. Allah sets forth, for an example to the Unbelievers, the wife of Noah and the wife of Lût: they were (respectively) under two of our righteous servants but they betrayed their (husbands), and they

اگر تم دونوں خدا کے آگے توبہ کرو (تو بہتر ہے کیونکہ) تمہارے
دل کج ہو گئے ہیں۔ اور اگر پیغمبر (کی ایذا) پر باہم اعانت کرو گی تو خدا اور
جبریل اور نیک کردار مسلمان اُن کے حامی (اور دوستدار) ہیں۔ اور
ان کے علاوہ (اور) فرشتے بھی مددگار ہیں ﴿۴﴾
اگر پیغمبر تم کو طلاق دے دیں تو عجب نہیں کہ اُن کا پروردگار
تمہارے بدلے اُن کو تم سے بہتر بیبیاں دے دے مسلمان صاحب ایمان
فرمانبردار توبہ کرنے والیاں عبادت گزار روزہ رکھنے والیاں
بن شوہر[ف ۳۰] اور کنواریاں ﴿۵﴾
مومنو! اپنے آپ کو اور اپنے اہل و عیال کو آتش (جہنم) سے
بچاؤ جس کا ایندھن آدمی اور پتھر ہیں اور جس پر تند خو اور
سخت مزاج فرشتے (مقرر) ہیں جو ارشاد خدا اُن کو فرماتا ہے
اُس کی نافرمانی نہیں کرتے اور جو حکم اُن کو ملتا ہے اُسے بجا لاتے ہیں ﴿۶﴾
کافرو! آج بہانے مت بناؤ۔ جو عمل تم کیا کرتے ہو اُنہی کا
تم کو بدلہ دیا جائے گا ﴿۷﴾
مومنو! خدا کے آگے صاف دل سے توبہ کرو۔ اُمید ہے کہ
وہ تمہارے گناہ تم سے دُور کر دے گا اور تم کو باغہائے بہشت
میں جن کے نیچے نہریں بہہ رہی ہیں داخل کرے گا اُس دن
خدا پیغمبر کو اور اُن لوگوں کو جو اُنکے ساتھ ایمان لائے ہیں رُسوا
نہیں کرے گا۔ (بلکہ) اُن کا نور (ایمان) اُن کے آگے اور
داہنی طرف (روشنی کرتا ہوا) چل رہا ہوگا۔ اور وہ خدا سے التجا
کریں گے کہ اے پروردگار ہمارا نور ہمارے لئے پورا کر اور
ہمیں معاف فرما۔ بے شک خدا ہر چیز پر قادر ہے ﴿۸﴾
اے پیغمبر کافروں اور منافقوں سے لڑو اور اُن پر سختی کرو۔
اُن کا ٹھکانا دوزخ ہے۔ اور وہ بہت بُری جگہ ہے ﴿۹﴾
خدا نے کافروں کیلئے نوح کی بیوی اور لوط کی بیوی کی
مثال بیان فرمائی ہے۔ دونوں ہمارے دو نیک بندوں کے گھر
میں تھیں اور دونوں نے اُنکی خیانت کی[ف ۳۱] تو وہ خدا کے مقابلے

إِن تَتُوبَآ إِلَى ٱللَّهِ فَقَدْ صَغَتْ قُلُوبُكُمَا ۖ
وَإِن تَظَٰهَرَا عَلَيْهِ فَإِنَّ ٱللَّهَ هُوَ مَوْلَىٰهُ
وَجِبْرِيلُ وَصَٰلِحُ ٱلْمُؤْمِنِينَ ۖ وَٱلْمَلَٰٓئِكَةُ
بَعْدَ ذَٰلِكَ ظَهِيرٌ ﴿٤﴾
عَسَىٰ رَبُّهُۥٓ إِن طَلَّقَكُنَّ أَن يُبْدِلَهُۥٓ
أَزْوَٰجًا خَيْرًا مِّنكُنَّ مُسْلِمَٰتٍ مُّؤْمِنَٰتٍ
قَٰنِتَٰتٍ تَٰٓئِبَٰتٍ عَٰبِدَٰتٍ سَٰٓئِحَٰتٍ ثَيِّبَٰتٍ
وَأَبْكَارًا ﴿٥﴾
يَٰٓأَيُّهَا ٱلَّذِينَ ءَامَنُوا۟ قُوٓا۟ أَنفُسَكُمْ وَأَهْلِيكُمْ
نَارًا وَقُودُهَا ٱلنَّاسُ وَٱلْحِجَارَةُ عَلَيْهَا
مَلَٰٓئِكَةٌ غِلَاظٌ شِدَادٌ لَّا يَعْصُونَ ٱللَّهَ
مَآ أَمَرَهُمْ وَيَفْعَلُونَ مَا يُؤْمَرُونَ ﴿٦﴾
يَٰٓأَيُّهَا ٱلَّذِينَ كَفَرُوا۟ لَا تَعْتَذِرُوا۟ ٱلْيَوْمَ ۖ
إِنَّمَا تُجْزَوْنَ مَا كُنتُمْ تَعْمَلُونَ ﴿٧﴾ ع ١
يَٰٓأَيُّهَا ٱلَّذِينَ ءَامَنُوا۟ تُوبُوٓا۟ إِلَى ٱللَّهِ تَوْبَةً
نَّصُوحًا عَسَىٰ رَبُّكُمْ أَن يُكَفِّرَ عَنكُمْ
سَيِّـَٔاتِكُمْ وَيُدْخِلَكُمْ جَنَّٰتٍ تَجْرِى مِن
تَحْتِهَا ٱلْأَنْهَٰرُ يَوْمَ لَا يُخْزِى ٱللَّهُ ٱلنَّبِىَّ
وَٱلَّذِينَ ءَامَنُوا۟ مَعَهُۥ ۖ نُورُهُمْ يَسْعَىٰ
بَيْنَ أَيْدِيهِمْ وَبِأَيْمَٰنِهِمْ يَقُولُونَ
رَبَّنَآ أَتْمِمْ لَنَا نُورَنَا وَٱغْفِرْ لَنَآ ۖ إِنَّكَ
عَلَىٰ كُلِّ شَىْءٍ قَدِيرٌ ﴿٨﴾
يَٰٓأَيُّهَا ٱلنَّبِىُّ جَٰهِدِ ٱلْكُفَّارَ وَٱلْمُنَٰفِقِينَ
وَٱغْلُظْ عَلَيْهِمْ ۚ وَمَأْوَىٰهُمْ جَهَنَّمُ ۖ وَبِئْسَ ٱلْمَصِيرُ ﴿٩﴾
ضَرَبَ ٱللَّهُ مَثَلًا لِّلَّذِينَ كَفَرُوا۟ ٱمْرَأَتَ
نُوحٍ وَٱمْرَأَتَ لُوطٍ ۖ كَانَتَا تَحْتَ عَبْدَيْنِ
مِنْ عِبَادِنَا صَٰلِحَيْنِ فَخَانَتَاهُمَا فَلَمْ

SÛRA–67
AL-MULK
(INTRODUCTION)

We have now done fourteen-fifteenths of the Qur-ãn, and have followed step by step the development of its argument establishing the *Ummat* or Brotherhood of Islam.

There is a logical break here. The remaining fifteenth consists of short spiritual Lyrics, mostly of the Makkan period, dealing mainly with the inner life of man, and in its individual aspects. They may be compared to Hymns or Psalms in other religious literature. But these short Quranic Sûras have a grandeur, a beauty, a mystic meaning, and a force of earnestness under persecution, all their own. With their sources in the sublimest regions of the Empyrean, their light penetrates into the darkest recesses of Life, into the concrete facts which are often mistaken for the whole of Reality, though they are but an insignificant portion and on the surface and fleeting. There is much symbolism in language and thought, in describing the spiritual in terms of the things we see and understand.

It is the contrast between the shadows of Reality here and the eternal Reality, between the surface world and the profound inner World, that is urged on our attention here.

This Sûra of 30 verses belongs to the middle Makkan period, just before S. 69 and S. 70. Allah is mentioned here by the name *Raḥmãn* (Most Gracious), as He is mentioned by the names of *Rabb* (Lord and Cherisher) and *Raḥmãn* (Most Gracious) in S. 19.

profited nothing before Allah on their account, but were told: "Enter ye the Fire along with (others) that enter !"

11. And Allah sets forth, as an example to those who believe the wife of Pharaoh: behold she said: "O my Lord ! build for me, in nearness to Thee, a mansion in the Garden, and save me from Pharaoh and his doings, and save me from those that do wrong";

12. And Mary the daughter of 'Imrān, who guarded her chastity and We breathed into (her body) of Our spirit; and she testified to the truth of the words of her Lord and of His Revelations, and was one of the devout (servants).

Al-Mulk, or Dominion

In the nane of Allah, Most Gracious, Most Merciful.

1. Blessed be He in Whose hands is Dominion; and He over all things hath Power;—

2. He Who created Death and Life, that He may try which of you is best in deed: and He is the Exalted in Might, Oft-Forgiving;—

3. He Who created the seven heavens one above another: no want of proportion wilt thou see in the Creation of The Most Gracious. So turn thy vision again: seest thou any flaw?

4. Again turn thy vision a second time: (thy) vision will come back to thee dull and discomfited, in a state worn out.

5. And We have, (from of old), adorned the lowest heaven with Lamps, and We have made such (Lamps) (as) missiles to drive away Satans, and have prepared for them the Chastisement of the Blazing Fire.

6. For those who reject their Lord (and Cherisher) is the Chastisement of Hell: and evil is (such) destination.

7. When they are cast therein, they will hear the (terrible) drawing

ہیں اُن عورتوں کے کچھ بھی کام نہ آئے۔ اور انکو حکم دیا گیا کہ
اور داخل ہونے والوں کیساتھ تم بھی دوزخ میں داخل ہو جاؤ ﴿١٠﴾
اور مومنوں کیلئے (ایک) مثال (تو) فرعون کی بیوی کی بیان
فرمائی۔ کہ اُس نے خدا سے التجا کی کہ اے میرے پروردگار میرے لئے
بہشت میں اپنے پاس ایک گھر بنا اور مجھے فرعون اور اُسکے اعمال
(زشت مآل) سے نجات بخش اور ظالم لوگوں کے ہاتھ سے مجھکو مخلصی عطا فرما ﴿١١﴾
اور (دوسری) عمران کی بیٹی مریم کی جنہوں نے اپنی شرمگاہ کو
محفوظ رکھا۔ تو ہمنے اسمیں اپنی رُوح پھونک دی اور وہ اپنے
پروردگار کے کلام اور اُس کی کتابوں کو برحق سمجھتی تھیں اور
فرمانبرداروں میں سے تھیں ﴿١٢﴾

سورۂ مُلک مکی ہے اس میں تیس آیتیں اور دو رکوع ہیں

شروع خدا کا نام لے کر جو بڑا مہربان نہایت رحم والا ہے
وہ (خدا) جس کے ہاتھ میں بادشاہی ہے بڑی برکت والا ہے
اور وہ ہر چیز پر قادر ہے ﴿١﴾
اُسی نے موت اور زندگی کو پیدا کیا تاکہ تمہاری آزمائش
کرے کہ تم میں کون اچھے کام کرتا ہے۔ اور وہ زبردست (اور) بخشنے والا ہے ﴿٢﴾
اُس نے سات آسمان اُوپر تلے بنائے۔ (اے دیکھنے والے) کیا تو
(خدائے) رحمٰن کی آفرینش میں کچھ نقص دیکھتا ہے؟ ذرا آنکھ
اُٹھا کر دیکھ بھلا تجھ کو (آسمان میں) کوئی شگاف نظر آتا ہے؟ ﴿٣﴾
پھر دوبارہ (سہ بارہ) نظر کر تو نظر (ہر بار) تیرے پاس ناکام
اور تھک کر لوٹ آئے گی ﴿٤﴾
اور ہم نے قریب کے آسمان کو (تاروں کے) چراغوں سے
زینت دی۔ اور اُن کو شیطان کے مارنے کا آلہ بنایا اور اُنکے
لئے دہکتی آگ کا عذاب تیار کر رکھا ہے ﴿٥﴾
اور جن لوگوں نے اپنے پروردگار سے انکار کیا اُن کے لئے
جہنم کا عذاب ہے۔ اور وہ بُرا ٹھکانا ہے ﴿٦﴾
جب وہ اُس میں ڈالے جائیں گے تو اُس کا چیخنا چلانا

يُغْنِيَا عَنْهُمَا مِنَ اللّٰهِ شَيْـًٔا وَّقِيْلَ
ادْخُلَا النَّارَ مَعَ الدّٰخِلِيْنَ ﴿١٠﴾
وَضَرَبَ اللّٰهُ مَثَلًا لِّلَّذِيْنَ اٰمَنُوا امْرَاَتَ
فِرْعَوْنَ ۘ اِذْ قَالَتْ رَبِّ ابْنِ لِيْ عِنْدَكَ (وقف لازم)
بَيْتًا فِي الْجَنَّةِ وَنَجِّنِيْ مِنْ فِرْعَوْنَ
وَعَمَلِهٖ وَنَجِّنِيْ مِنَ الْقَوْمِ الظّٰلِمِيْنَ ﴿١١﴾
وَمَرْيَمَ ابْنَتَ عِمْرٰنَ الَّتِيْٓ اَحْصَنَتْ
فَرْجَهَا فَنَفَخْنَا فِيْهِ مِنْ رُّوْحِنَا وَصَدَّقَتْ
بِكَلِمٰتِ رَبِّهَا وَكُتُبِهٖ وَكَانَتْ مِنَ
الْقٰنِتِيْنَ ﴿١٢﴾ ع ٢

سُوْرَةُ الْمُلْكِ مَكِّيَّةٌ وَهِيَ ثَلٰثُوْنَ اٰيَةً وَّفِيْهَا رُكُوْعَانِ

بِسْمِ اللّٰهِ الرَّحْمٰنِ الرَّحِيْمِ
تَبٰرَكَ الَّذِيْ بِيَدِهِ الْمُلْكُ ۡ وَهُوَ
عَلٰى كُلِّ شَيْءٍ قَدِيْرُ ﴿١﴾
الَّذِيْ خَلَقَ الْمَوْتَ وَالْحَيٰوةَ لِيَبْلُوَكُمْ
اَيُّكُمْ اَحْسَنُ عَمَلًا ۭ وَهُوَ الْعَزِيْزُ الْغَفُوْرُ ﴿٢﴾
الَّذِيْ خَلَقَ سَبْعَ سَمٰوٰتٍ طِبَاقًا ۭ مَا
تَرٰى فِيْ خَلْقِ الرَّحْمٰنِ مِنْ تَفٰوُتٍ ۭ
فَارْجِعِ الْبَصَرَ ۙ هَلْ تَرٰى مِنْ فُطُوْرٍ ﴿٣﴾
ثُمَّ ارْجِعِ الْبَصَرَ كَرَّتَيْنِ يَنْقَلِبْ اِلَيْكَ
الْبَصَرُ خَاسِئًا وَّهُوَ حَسِيْرٌ ﴿٤﴾
وَلَقَدْ زَيَّنَّا السَّمَاۗءَ الدُّنْيَا بِمَصَابِيْحَ وَ
جَعَلْنٰهَا رُجُوْمًا لِّلشَّيٰطِيْنِ وَاَعْتَدْنَا لَهُمْ
عَذَابَ السَّعِيْرِ ﴿٥﴾
وَلِلَّذِيْنَ كَفَرُوْا بِرَبِّهِمْ عَذَابُ جَهَنَّمَ ۭ
وَبِئْسَ الْمَصِيْرُ ﴿٦﴾
اِذَآ اُلْقُوْا فِيْهَا سَمِعُوْا لَهَا شَهِيْقًا وَّهِيَ

الجزء التاسع والعشرون ٢٩

in of its breath even as it blazes forth.

8. Almost bursting with fury: every time a Group will ask, is cast therein, its Keepers will ask, "Did no Warner come to you?"

9. They will say: "Yes indeed; a Warner did come to us, but we rejected him and said, 'Allah never sent down any (Message): ye are in nothing but a grave error' !"

10. They will further say: "Had we but listened or used our intelligence we should not (now) be among the Companions of the Blazing Fire!"

11. They will then confess their sins: but far from Allah's mercy are the Companions of the Blazing Fire!

12. As for those who fear their Lord unseen for them is Forgiveness and a great Reward.

13. And whether ye hide your word or make it known, He certainly has (full) knowledge, of the secrets of (all) hearts.

14. Should He not know,—He that created ? And He is the Subtle the Aware.

15. It is He Who has made the earth manageable for you, so traverse ye through its tracts and enjoy of the Sustenance which He furnishes: but unto Him is the Resurrection.

16. Do ye feel secure that He Who is in Heaven will not cause you to be swallowed up by the earth when it shakes (as in an earthquake) ?

17. Or do ye feel secure that He Who is in Heaven will not send against you a violent tornado (with showers of stones), so that ye shall know how (terrible) was My warning?

18. But indeed men before them rejected (My warning): then how (terrible) was My punishment (of them) ?

19. Do they not observe the birds above them, spreading their wings and folding them in ? None can uphold them except The Most

سُنیں گے اور وہ جوش مار رہی ہوگی ﴿۷﴾
گویا مارے جوش کے پھٹ پڑے گی جب اس میں انکی کوئی جماعت ڈالی جائیگی تو
دوزخ کے داروغہ ان سے پوچھیں گے کہ تمہارے پاس کوئی ہدایت کرنیوالا نہیں آیا تھا؟ ﴿۸﴾
وہ کہیں گے کیوں نہیں ضرور ہدایت کرنے والا آیا تھا لیکن
ہم نے اس کو جھٹلا دیا اور کہا کہ خدا نے تو کوئی چیز نازل ہی
نہیں کی تم تو بڑی غلطی میں (پڑے ہوئے) ہو ﴿۹﴾
اور کہیں گے اگر ہم سنتے یا سمجھتے ہوتے تو دوزخیوں
میں نہ ہوتے ﴿۱۰﴾
پس وہ اپنے گناہوں کا اقرار کرلیں گے سو دوزخیوں
کے لئے (رحمتِ خدا سے) دوری ہے ﴿۱۱﴾
(اور) جو لوگ بن دیکھے اپنے پروردگار سے ڈرتے ہیں ان کیلئے
بخشش اور اجرِ عظیم ہے ﴿۱۲﴾
اور تم (لوگ) بات پوشیدہ کہو یا ظاہر۔ وہ دل کے بھیدوں
تک سے واقف ہے ﴿۱۳﴾
بھلا جس نے پیدا کیا وہ بے خبر ہے؟ وہ تو پوشیدہ باتوں
کا جاننے والا اور (ہر چیز سے) آگاہ ہے ﴿۱۴﴾
وہی تو ہے جس نے تمہارے لئے زمین کو نرم کیا تو اُسکی راہوں
میں چلو پھرو اور خدا کا (دیا ہوا) رزق کھاؤ اور (تم کو)
اسی کے پاس (قبروں سے) نکل کر جانا ہے ﴿۱۵﴾
کیا تم اس سے جو آسمان میں ہے بے خوف ہو کہ تم کو زمین
میں دھنسا دے اور وہ اس وقت حرکت کرنے لگے ﴿۱۶﴾
کیا تم اس سے جو آسمان میں ہے نڈر ہو کہ تم پر کنکر بھری ہوا
چھوڑ دے سو تم عنقریب جان لوگے کہ میرا ڈرانا کیسا ہے ﴿۱۷﴾
اور جو لوگ ان سے پہلے تھے انہوں نے بھی جھٹلایا تھا
سو (دیکھ لو کہ) میرا کیسا عذاب ہوا ﴿۱۸﴾
کیا انہوں نے اپنے سروں پر اڑتے جانوروں کو نہیں دیکھا جو پَر
پھیلائے رہتے ہیں اور ان کو سکیڑ بھی لیتے ہیں۔ خدا کے سوا انہیں

تَفُورُ ﴿٧﴾
تَكَادُ تَمَيَّزُ مِنَ الْغَيْظِ ۖ كُلَّمَا أُلْقِيَ فِيهَا
فَوْجٌ سَأَلَهُمْ خَزَنَتُهَا أَلَمْ يَأْتِكُمْ نَذِيرٌ ﴿٨﴾
قَالُوا بَلَىٰ قَدْ جَاءَنَا نَذِيرٌ فَكَذَّبْنَا
وَقُلْنَا مَا نَزَّلَ اللَّهُ مِن شَيْءٍ إِنْ أَنتُمْ
إِلَّا فِي ضَلَالٍ كَبِيرٍ ﴿٩﴾
وَقَالُوا لَوْ كُنَّا نَسْمَعُ أَوْ نَعْقِلُ مَا كُنَّا
فِي أَصْحَابِ السَّعِيرِ ﴿١٠﴾
فَاعْتَرَفُوا بِذَنبِهِمْ فَسُحْقًا لِّأَصْحَابِ
السَّعِيرِ ﴿١١﴾
إِنَّ الَّذِينَ يَخْشَوْنَ رَبَّهُم بِالْغَيْبِ
لَهُم مَّغْفِرَةٌ وَأَجْرٌ كَبِيرٌ ﴿١٢﴾
وَأَسِرُّوا قَوْلَكُمْ أَوِ اجْهَرُوا بِهِ ۖ إِنَّهُ
عَلِيمٌ بِذَاتِ الصُّدُورِ ﴿١٣﴾
أَلَا يَعْلَمُ مَنْ خَلَقَ وَهُوَ اللَّطِيفُ
الْخَبِيرُ ﴿١٤﴾ ع
هُوَ الَّذِي جَعَلَ لَكُمُ الْأَرْضَ ذَلُولًا
فَامْشُوا فِي مَنَاكِبِهَا وَكُلُوا مِن رِّزْقِهِ
وَإِلَيْهِ النُّشُورُ ﴿١٥﴾
أَأَمِنتُم مَّن فِي السَّمَاءِ أَن يَخْسِفَ
بِكُمُ الْأَرْضَ فَإِذَا هِيَ تَمُورُ ﴿١٦﴾
أَمْ أَمِنتُم مَّن فِي السَّمَاءِ أَن يُرْسِلَ
عَلَيْكُمْ حَاصِبًا ۖ فَسَتَعْلَمُونَ كَيْفَ نَذِيرِ ﴿١٧﴾
وَلَقَدْ كَذَّبَ الَّذِينَ مِن قَبْلِهِمْ
فَكَيْفَ كَانَ نَكِيرِ ﴿١٨﴾
أَوَلَمْ يَرَوْا إِلَى الطَّيْرِ فَوْقَهُمْ صَافَّاتٍ
وَيَقْبِضْنَ ۚ مَا يُمْسِكُهُنَّ إِلَّا الرَّحْمَٰنُ

Gracious: truly it is He that watches over all things.

20. Nay, who is there that can help you, (even as) an army, besides The Most Merciful ? In nothing but delusion are the Unbelievers.

21. Or who is there that can provide you with Sustenance if He were to withhold His provision? Nay, they obstinately persist in insolent impiety and flight (from the Truth).

22. Is then one who walks headlong, with his face grovelling, better guided,—or one who walks evenly on a Straight Way ?

23. Say: "It is He Who has created you, and made for you the faculties of hearing, seeing, and understanding: little thanks it is ye give.

24. Say: "It is He Who has multiplied you through the earth, and to Him shall ye be gathered together."

25. They ask: When will this promise be (fulfilled)? If ye are telling the truth.

26. Say: "As to the knowledge of the time, it is with Allah alone: I am a plain warner."

27. At length, when they see it close at hand, grieved will be the faces of the Unbelievers, and it will be said (to them): "This is (the promise fulfilled) which ye were calling for !"

28. Say: "See ye ?—If Allah were to destroy me, and those with me, or if He bestows his Mercy on us,—yet who can deliver the Unbelievers from a grievous Chastisement ?

29. Say: "He is The most Gracious: we have believed in Him, and on Him have we put our trust: so, soon will ye know which (of us) it is that is in manifest error."

30. Say. "See ye ?— If your stream be some morning lost (in the underground earth), who then can supply you with clear-flowing water?"

کوئی تھام نہیں سکتا۔ بیشک وہ ہر چیز کو دیکھ رہا ہے (۱۹)
بھلا ایسا کون ہے جو تمہاری فوج ہو کر خدا
کے سوا تمہاری مدد کر سکے۔ کافر تو دھوکے
میں ہیں (۲۰)
بھلا اگر وہ اپنا رزق بند کرلے تو کون ہے جو تم کو رزق دے؟
لیکن یہ سرکشی اور نفرت میں پھنسے ہوئے ہیں (۲۱)
بھلا جو شخص چلتا ہوا منہ کے بل گر پڑتا ہے وہ سیدھے
رستے پر ہے یا وہ جو سیدھے رستے پر برابر چل رہا ہو؟ (۲۲)
وہ خدا ہی تو ہے جس نے تم کو پیدا کیا اور تمہارے کان اور
آنکھیں اور دل بنائے۔ (مگر) تم کم احسان مانتے ہو (۲۳)
کہہ دو کہ وہی ہے جس نے تم کو زمین میں پھیلایا اور اُسی کے
روبرو تم جمع کئے جاؤ گے (۲۴)
اور کافر کہتے ہیں کہ اگر تم سچے ہو تو یہ وعید کب
(پوری) ہوگی؟ (۲۵)
کہہ دو کہ اس کا علم خدا ہی کو ہے۔ اور میں تو کھول کھول کر
ڈر سنا دینے والا ہوں (۲۶)
سو جب وہ دیکھ لیں گے کہ وہ (وعدہ) قریب آگیا تو
کافروں کے منہ بُرے ہو جائیں گے۔ اور (اُن سے) کہا
جائے گا کہ یہ وہی ہے جس کے تم خواستگار تھے (۲۷)
کہو کہ بھلا دیکھو تو اگر خدا مجھ کو اور میرے ساتھیوں کو
ہلاک کردے یا ہم پر مہربانی کرے۔ تو کون ہے جو کافروں کو
دُکھ دینے والے عذاب سے پناہ دے؟ (۲۸)
کہہ دو کہ وہ (جو خدائے) رحمٰن (ہے) ہم اُسی پر ایمان لائے
اور اُسی پر بھروسا رکھتے ہیں۔ تم کو جلد معلوم ہو جائے گا کہ
صریح گمراہی میں کون پڑ رہا تھا (۲۹)
کہو کہ بھلا دیکھو تو اگر تمہارا پانی (جو تم پیتے ہو اور برتتے ہو) خشک
ہو جائے تو (خدا کے سوا) کون ہے جو تمہارے لئے شیریں پانی کا چشمہ بہا لائے؟ (۳۰)

إِنَّهُ بِكُلِّ شَيْءٍ بَصِيرٌ (۱۹)
أَمَّنْ هَٰذَا الَّذِي هُوَ جُندٌ لَّكُمْ يَنصُرُكُم
مِّن دُونِ الرَّحْمَٰنِ ۚ إِنِ الْكَافِرُونَ إِلَّا
فِي غُرُورٍ (۲۰)
أَمَّنْ هَٰذَا الَّذِي يَرْزُقُكُمْ إِنْ أَمْسَكَ
رِزْقَهُ ۚ بَل لَّجُّوا فِي عُتُوٍّ وَنُفُورٍ (۲۱)
أَفَمَن يَمْشِي مُكِبًّا عَلَىٰ وَجْهِهِ أَهْدَىٰ
أَمَّن يَمْشِي سَوِيًّا عَلَىٰ صِرَاطٍ مُّسْتَقِيمٍ (۲۲)
قُلْ هُوَ الَّذِي أَنشَأَكُمْ وَجَعَلَ لَكُمُ السَّمْعَ
وَالْأَبْصَارَ وَالْأَفْئِدَةَ ۖ قَلِيلًا مَّا تَشْكُرُونَ (۲۳)
قُلْ هُوَ الَّذِي ذَرَأَكُمْ فِي الْأَرْضِ وَ
إِلَيْهِ تُحْشَرُونَ (۲۴)
وَيَقُولُونَ مَتَىٰ هَٰذَا الْوَعْدُ إِن كُنتُمْ
صَادِقِينَ (۲۵)
قُلْ إِنَّمَا الْعِلْمُ عِندَ اللَّهِ وَإِنَّمَا أَنَا
نَذِيرٌ مُّبِينٌ (۲۶)
فَلَمَّا رَأَوْهُ زُلْفَةً سِيئَتْ وُجُوهُ الَّذِينَ
كَفَرُوا وَقِيلَ هَٰذَا الَّذِي كُنتُم بِهِ
تَدَّعُونَ (۲۷)
قُلْ أَرَأَيْتُمْ إِنْ أَهْلَكَنِيَ اللَّهُ وَمَن
مَّعِيَ أَوْ رَحِمَنَا فَمَن يُجِيرُ الْكَافِرِينَ
مِنْ عَذَابٍ أَلِيمٍ (۲۸)
قُلْ هُوَ الرَّحْمَٰنُ آمَنَّا بِهِ وَعَلَيْهِ
تَوَكَّلْنَا ۖ فَسَتَعْلَمُونَ مَنْ هُوَ فِي
ضَلَالٍ مُّبِينٍ (۲۹)
قُلْ أَرَأَيْتُمْ إِنْ أَصْبَحَ مَاؤُكُمْ غَوْرًا
فَمَن يَأْتِيكُم بِمَاءٍ مَّعِينٍ (۳۰)

SÛRA–68
AL-QALAM
(INTRODUCTION)

This is a very early Makkan revelation. The general Muslim opinion is that a great part of it was second in order of revelation, the first being S. 96. (*Iqraa*), verses 1-5: see *Itqãn,* Chapter 7.

The last Sûra having defined the true Reality in contrast with the false standards set up by men, this illustrates the theme by an actual historical example. Our Holy Prophet was the sanest and wisest of man: those who could not understand him called him mad or possessed. So, in every age, it is the habit of the world to call Truth Falsehood and Wisdom Madness, and, on the other hand, to exalt Selfishness as Planning, and Arrogance as Power. The contrast is shown up between the two kinds of men and their inner worth.

Al-Qalam, or the Pen, or Nûn

In the name of Allah, Most Gracious, Most Merciful.

1. Nûn. By the Pen and by the (Record) which (men) write,—

2. Thou art not, by the grace of thy Lord, mad or possessed.

3. Nay, verily for thee is a Reward unfailing:

4. And surely thou hast sublime morals.

5. Soon wilt thou see, and they will see,

6. Which of you is afflicted with madness.

7. Verily it is thy Lord that knoweth best, which (among men) hath strayed from His Path: and He knoweth best those who receive (true) Guidance.

8. So obey not to those who deny (the Truth).

9. Their desire is that thou shouldst be pliant: so would they be pliant.

10. Obey not every mean,—swearer

11. A slanderer, going about with calumnies,

12. (Habitually) hindering (all) good, transgressing beyond bounds, deep in sin,

13. Violent (and cruel),— with all that, of a doubtful birth,—

14. Because he possesses wealth and (numerous) sons.

15. When to him are rehearsed Our Signs, "Tales of the Ancients", he cries !

16. Soon shall We brand (the beast) on the snout!

17. Verily We have tried them as We tried the People of the Garden when they resolved to gather the fruits of the (garden) in the morning,

18. But made no reservation, ("if it be Allah's Will").

19. Then there came on the (garden) a visitation from thy Lord, (which swept away) all around, while they were asleep.

20. So the (garden) became, by the morning, like a dark and desolate spot, (whose fruit had been gathered).

21. As the morning broke, they called out, one to another,—

سورۂ قلم مکی ہے اس میں باون آیتیں اور دو رکوع ہیں

شروع خدا کا نام لے کر جو بڑا مہربان نہایت رحم والا ہے

نٓ۔ قلم کی اور جو (اہل قلم) لکھتے ہیں اُس کی قسم (۱)
کہ (اے محمدؐ) تم اپنے پروردگار کے فضل سے دیوانے نہیں ہو (۲)
اور تمہارے لئے بے انتہا اجر ہے (۳)
اور تمہارے اخلاق بڑے (عالی) ہیں (۴)
سو عنقریب تم بھی دیکھ لو گے اور یہ (کافر) بھی دیکھ لیں گے (۵)
کہ تم میں سے کون دیوانہ ہے (۶)
تمہارا پروردگار اسکو بھی خوب جانتا ہے جو اُسکے رستے سے
بھٹک گیا اور انکو بھی خوب جانتا ہے جو سیدھے رستے پر چل رہے ہیں (۷)
تو تم جھٹلانے والوں کا کہا نہ ماننا (۸)
یہ لوگ چاہتے ہیں کہ تم نرمی اختیار کرو تو یہ بھی نرم ہو جائیں (۹)
اور کسی ایسے شخص کے کہے میں نہ آ جانا جو بہت قسمیں کھانیوالا ذلیل اوقات ہو (۱۰)
طعن آمیز اشارتیں کرنیوالا چغلیاں لئے پھرنے والا (۱۱)
مال میں بخل کرنے والا حد سے بڑھا ہوا بدکار (۱۲)
سخت خو اور اس کے علاوہ بدذات ہے (۱۳)
اس سبب سے کہ مال اور بیٹے رکھتا ہے (۱۴)
جب اس کو ہماری آیتیں پڑھ کر سنائی جاتی ہیں تو کہتا ہے کہ
یہ اگلے لوگوں کے افسانے ہیں (۱۵)
ہم عنقریب اُس کی ناک پر داغ لگائیں گے (۱۶)
ہم نے ان لوگوں کی اسی طرح آزمائش کی ہے جس طرح باغ والوں کی آزمائش کی تھی۔
جب اُنہوں نے قسمیں کھا کھا کر کہا کہ صبح ہوتے ہوتے ہم اس کا میوہ توڑ لیں گے (۱۷)
اور انشاء اللہ نہ کہا (۱۸)
سو وہ ابھی سو ہی رہے تھے کہ تمہارے پروردگار کی طرف سے
(راتوں رات) اُس پر ایک آفت پھر گئی (۱۹)
تو وہ ایسا ہو گیا جیسے کٹی ہوئی کھیتی (۲۰)
جب صبح ہوئی تو وہ لوگ ایک دوسرے کو پکارنے لگے (۲۱)

سُوْرَةُ الْقَلَمِ مَكِّيَّةٌ وَّهِيَ اثْنَتَانِ وَخَمْسُوْنَ اٰيَةً وَّفِيْهَا رُكُوْعَانِ

بِسْمِ اللّٰهِ الرَّحْمٰنِ الرَّحِيْمِ

نٓ وَالْقَلَمِ وَمَا يَسْطُرُوْنَ (١)
مَآ اَنْتَ بِنِعْمَةِ رَبِّكَ بِمَجْنُوْنٍ (٢)
وَاِنَّ لَكَ لَاَجْرًا غَيْرَ مَمْنُوْنٍ (٣)
وَاِنَّكَ لَعَلٰى خُلُقٍ عَظِيْمٍ (٤)
فَسَتُبْصِرُ وَيُبْصِرُوْنَ (٥)
بِاَيِّكُمُ الْمَفْتُوْنُ (٦)
اِنَّ رَبَّكَ هُوَ اَعْلَمُ بِمَنْ ضَلَّ عَنْ
سَبِيْلِهٖ وَهُوَ اَعْلَمُ بِالْمُهْتَدِيْنَ (٧)
فَلَا تُطِعِ الْمُكَذِّبِيْنَ (٨)
وَدُّوْا لَوْ تُدْهِنُ فَيُدْهِنُوْنَ (٩)
وَلَا تُطِعْ كُلَّ حَلَّافٍ مَّهِيْنٍ (١٠)
هَمَّازٍ مَّشَّآءٍ بِنَمِيْمٍ (١١)
مَّنَّاعٍ لِّلْخَيْرِ مُعْتَدٍ اَثِيْمٍ (١٢)
عُتُلٍّ بَعْدَ ذٰلِكَ زَنِيْمٍ (١٣)
اَنْ كَانَ ذَا مَالٍ وَّبَنِيْنَ (١٤)
اِذَا تُتْلٰى عَلَيْهِ اٰيٰتُنَا قَالَ اَسَاطِيْرُ
الْاَوَّلِيْنَ (١٥)
سَنَسِمُهٗ عَلَى الْخُرْطُوْمِ (١٦)
اِنَّا بَلَوْنٰهُمْ كَمَا بَلَوْنَآ اَصْحٰبَ الْجَنَّةِ
اِذْ اَقْسَمُوْا لَيَصْرِمُنَّهَا مُصْبِحِيْنَ (١٧)
وَلَا يَسْتَثْنُوْنَ (١٨)
فَطَافَ عَلَيْهَا طَآئِفٌ مِّنْ رَّبِّكَ
وَهُمْ نَآئِمُوْنَ (١٩)
فَاَصْبَحَتْ كَالصَّرِيْمِ (٢٠)
فَتَنَادَوْا مُصْبِحِيْنَ (٢١)

22. "Go ye to your tilth (betimes) in the morning, if ye would gather the fruits."

أَنِ اغْدُوا عَلَىٰ حَرْثِكُمْ إِن كُنتُمْ صَارِمِينَ ﴿٢٢﴾

کہ اگر تم کو کاٹنا ہے تو اپنی کھیتی پر سویرے ہی جا پہنچو ﴿٢٢﴾

23. So they departed, conversing in secret low tones, (saying)—

فَانطَلَقُوا وَهُمْ يَتَخَافَتُونَ ﴿٢٣﴾

تو وہ چل پڑے اور آپس میں چپکے چپکے کہتے جاتے تھے ﴿٢٣﴾

24. "Let not a single indigent person break in upon you into the (garden) this day."

أَن لَّا يَدْخُلَنَّهَا الْيَوْمَ عَلَيْكُم مِّسْكِينٌ ﴿٢٤﴾

کہ آج یہاں تمہارے پاس کوئی فقیر نہ آنے پائے ﴿٢٤﴾

25. And they opened the morning, strong in an (unjust) resolve.

وَغَدَوْا عَلَىٰ حَرْدٍ قَادِرِينَ ﴿٢٥﴾

اور کوشش کے ساتھ سویرے ہی جا پہنچے (گویا کھیتی پر) قادر ہیں ﴿٢٥﴾

26. But when they saw the (garden), they said: "We have surely lost our way:

فَلَمَّا رَأَوْهَا قَالُوا إِنَّا لَضَالُّونَ ﴿٢٦﴾

جب باغ کو دیکھا تو (ویران) کہنے لگے کہ ہم رستہ بھول گئے ہیں ﴿٢٦﴾

27. "Indeed we are deprived (of the fruits of our labour) !"

بَلْ نَحْنُ مَحْرُومُونَ ﴿٢٧﴾

نہیں بلکہ ہم (برگشتہ بخت) بےنصیب ہیں ﴿٢٧﴾

28. Said one of them, more just (than the rest): "Did I not say to you, 'Why not glorify (Allah)?' "

قَالَ أَوْسَطُهُمْ أَلَمْ أَقُل لَّكُمْ لَوْلَا تُسَبِّحُونَ ﴿٢٨﴾

ایک جو ان میں فرزانہ تھا بولا کیا میں نے تم سے نہیں کہا تھا کہ تم تسبیح کیوں نہیں کرتے؟ ﴿٢٨﴾

29. They said: "Glory to our Lord! Verily we have been doing wrong!"

قَالُوا سُبْحَانَ رَبِّنَا إِنَّا كُنَّا ظَالِمِينَ ﴿٢٩﴾

(تب) وہ کہنے لگے کہ ہمارا پروردگار پاک ہے بیشک ہم ہی قصوروار تھے ﴿٢٩﴾

30. Then they turned, one against another, in reproach.

فَأَقْبَلَ بَعْضُهُمْ عَلَىٰ بَعْضٍ يَتَلَاوَمُونَ ﴿٣٠﴾

پھر لگے ایک دوسرے کو رُو در رُو ملامت کرنے ﴿٣٠﴾

31. They said: "Alas for us ! We have indeed transgressed !

قَالُوا يَا وَيْلَنَا إِنَّا كُنَّا طَاغِينَ ﴿٣١﴾

کہنے لگے ہائے شامت ہم ہی حد سے بڑھ گئے تھے ﴿٣١﴾

32. "It may be that our Lord will give us in exchange a better (garden) than this: for we do turn to Him (in repentance) !"

عَسَىٰ رَبُّنَا أَن يُبْدِلَنَا خَيْرًا مِّنْهَا إِنَّا إِلَىٰ رَبِّنَا رَاغِبُونَ ﴿٣٢﴾

اُمید ہے کہ ہمارا پروردگار اسکے بدلے میں ہمیں اس سے بہتر باغ عنایت کرے ہم اپنے پروردگار کی طرف رجوع لاتے ہیں ﴿٣٢﴾

33. Such is the Punishment (in this life); but greater is the Punishment in the Hereafter,— if only they knew !

كَذَٰلِكَ الْعَذَابُ ۖ وَلَعَذَابُ الْآخِرَةِ أَكْبَرُ ۚ لَوْ كَانُوا يَعْلَمُونَ ﴿٣٣﴾

(دیکھو) عذاب یوں ہوتا ہے۔ اور آخرت کا عذاب اس سے کہیں بڑھ کر ہے کاش! یہ لوگ جانتے ہوتے ﴿٣٣﴾

34. Verily, for the Righteous, are Gardens of Delight, with their Lord.

إِنَّ لِلْمُتَّقِينَ عِندَ رَبِّهِمْ جَنَّاتِ النَّعِيمِ ﴿٣٤﴾

پرہیزگاروں کیلئے اُنکے پروردگار کے ہاں نعمت کے باغ ہیں ﴿٣٤﴾

35. Shall We then treat the People of Faith like the People of Sin ?

أَفَنَجْعَلُ الْمُسْلِمِينَ كَالْمُجْرِمِينَ ﴿٣٥﴾

کیا ہم فرمانبرداروں کو نافرمانوں کی طرح (نعمتوں سے محروم) کر دینگے ﴿٣٥﴾

36. What is the matter with you ? How judge ye?

مَا لَكُمْ كَيْفَ تَحْكُمُونَ ﴿٣٦﴾

تمہیں کیا ہو گیا ہے کیسی تجویزیں کرتے ہو؟ ﴿٣٦﴾

37. Or have ye a Book through which ye learn—

أَمْ لَكُمْ كِتَابٌ فِيهِ تَدْرُسُونَ ﴿٣٧﴾

کیا تمہارے پاس کوئی کتاب ہے جس میں (یہ) پڑھتے ہو ﴿٣٧﴾

38. That ye shall have, through it whatever ye choose ?

إِنَّ لَكُمْ فِيهِ لَمَا تَخَيَّرُونَ ﴿٣٨﴾

کہ جو چیز تم پسند کرو گے وہ تم کو ضرور ملے گی ﴿٣٨﴾

39. Or have ye Covenants with Us on oath, reaching to the Day of Judgment, (providing) that ye shall have whatever ye shall demand ?

أَمْ لَكُمْ أَيْمَانٌ عَلَيْنَا بَالِغَةٌ إِلَىٰ يَوْمِ الْقِيَامَةِ ۙ إِنَّ لَكُمْ لَمَا تَحْكُمُونَ ﴿٣٩﴾

یا تم نے ہم سے قسمیں لے رکھی ہیں جو قیامت کے دن تک چلی جائیں گی کہ جس شے کا تم حکم کرو گے وہ تمہارے لئے حاضر ہوگی ﴿٣٩﴾

40. Ask thou of them, which of them will stand surety for that !

سَلْهُمْ أَيُّهُم بِذَٰلِكَ زَعِيمٌ ﴿٤٠﴾

اُن سے پوچھو کہ ان میں سے اس کا کون ذمہ لیتا ہے؟ ﴿٤٠﴾

41. Or have they some "partners" (in Godhead)? Then let them produce their "partners" if they are truthful !

أَمْ لَهُمْ شُرَكَاءُ فَلْيَأْتُوا بِشُرَكَائِهِمْ إِن كَانُوا صَادِقِينَ ﴿٤١﴾

کیا (اس قول میں) اُن کے اور بھی شریک ہیں؟ اگر یہ سچے ہیں تو اپنے شریکوں کو لا سامنے کریں ﴿٤١﴾

SÛRA–69
AL-ḤÃQQA
(INTRODUCTION)

This Sûra belongs to the early middle period of Makkan Revelation. The eschatological argument is pressed home: "the absolute Truth cannot fail; it must prevail; therefore, be not lured by false appearances in this life; it is Revelation that points to the sure and certain Reality."

42. The Day that the Shin shall be laid bare, to prostrate, but they shall not be able,—

43. Their eyes will be cast down, ignominy will cover them; seeing that they had been summoned aforetime to bow in adoration, while they were whole, (and had refused).

44. Then leave Me alone with such as reject this Message: by degrees shall We draw them on little by little from directions they perceive not.

45. A (long) respite will I grant them: truly powerful is My Plan.

46. Or is it that thou dost ask them for a reward, so that they are burdened with a load of debt?—

47. Or that the Unseen is in their hands, so that they can write it down?

48. So wait with patience for the Command of thy Lord, and be not like the Companion of the Fish,—when he cried out in agony.

49. Had not Grace from His Lord reached him, he would indeed have been cast off on the naked shore, in disgrace.

50. Thus did his Lord choose him and make him of the company of the Righteous.

51. And the Unbelievers would almost trip thee up with their eyes when they hear the Message; and they say: "Surely he is possessed!"

52. But it is nothing less than a Message to all the worlds.

Al-Ḥãqqa, or the Sure Reality

In the name of Allah, Most Gracious, Most Merciful.

1. The Sure Reality !
2. What is the Sure Reality ?
3. And what will make thee realise what the Sure Reality is ?
4. The Thamûd and the 'Ãd people disbelieved in the day of Noise and Clamour !
5. But the Thamûd,—they were destroyed by a terrible Storm of thunder and lightning !
6. And the 'Ãd,— they were destroyed by a furious Wind, exceedingly violent;
7. He made it rage against them seven nights and eight days in succession: so that thou couldst see

جس دن پنڈلی سے کپڑا اُٹھا دیا جائے گا اور کفار سجدے
کے لئے بلائے جائیں گے تو وہ سجدہ نہ کر سکیں گے (۴۲)
اُنکی آنکھیں جھکی ہوئی ہونگی اور اُن پر ذلت چھا رہی ہوگی حالانکہ
پہلے (اس وقت) سجدے کیلئے بلائے جاتے تھے جبکہ صحیح و سالم تھے (۴۳)
تو مجھ کو اس کلام کے جھٹلانے والوں سے سمجھ لینے دو۔ ہم اُنکو آہستہ
آہستہ ایسے طریق سے پکڑیں گے کہ اُن کو خبر بھی نہ ہوگی (۴۴)
اور میں اُن کو مہلت دیئے جاتا ہوں میری تدبیر قوی ہے (۴۵)
کیا تم اُنسے کچھ اجر مانگتے ہو کہ اُن پر تاوان کا بوجھ پڑ رہا ہے (۴۶)
یا اُن کے پاس غیب کی خبر ہے کہ (اُسے) لکھتے جاتے ہیں (۴۷)
تو اپنے پروردگار کے حکم کے انتظار میں صبر کئے رہو اور مچھلی (کا لقمہ ہونے)
والے (یونس) کیطرح نہ ہونا کہ اُنہوں نے (خدا کو) پکارا اور وہ غم و غصے میں بھرے ہوئے تھے (۴۸)
اگر تمہارے پروردگار کی مہربانی اُن کی یاوری نہ کرتی تو وہ چٹیل
میدان میں ڈال دیئے جاتے اور اُن کا حال ابتر ہو جاتا (۴۹)
پھر پروردگار نے اُن کو برگزیدہ کر کے نیکوکاروں میں کر لیا (۵۰)
اور کافر جب (یہ) نصیحت (کی کتاب) سنتے ہیں تو یوں لگتے ہیں
کہ تم کو اپنی نگاہوں سے پھسلا دیں گے اور کہتے ہیں کہ
یہ تو دیوانہ ہے (۵۱)
اور (لوگو) یہ (قرآن) اہلِ عالم کے لئے نصیحت ہے (۵۲)

سورۂ حاقہ مکی ہے اس میں باون آیتیں اور دو رکوع ہیں

شروع خدا کا نام لیکر جو بڑا مہربان نہایت رحم والا ہے
سچ مچ ہونے والی (۱) وہ سچ مچ ہونے والی کیا ہے؟ (۲)
اور تم کو کیا معلوم ہے کہ وہ سچ مچ ہونے والی کیا ہے (۳)
(وہی) کھڑکھڑانے والی (جس) کو ثمود اور عاد (دونوں) نے جھٹلایا (۴)
سو ثمود تو کڑک سے ہلاک کر دیئے گئے (۵)
رہے عاد اُن کا نہایت تیز آندھی سے ستیاناس کر دیا گیا (۶)
خدا نے اس کو سات رات اور آٹھ دن اُن پر چلائے رکھا تو
(اے مخاطب) تو لوگوں کو اس میں (اس طرح) ڈھئے (اور مرے)

يَوْمَ يُكْشَفُ عَنْ سَاقٍ وَّيُدْعَوْنَ إِلَى
السُّجُودِ فَلَا يَسْتَطِيعُونَ ﴿٤٢﴾
خَاشِعَةً أَبْصَارُهُمْ تَرْهَقُهُمْ ذِلَّةٌ ۖ وَقَدْ
كَانُوا يُدْعَوْنَ إِلَى السُّجُودِ وَهُمْ سَالِمُونَ ﴿٤٣﴾
فَذَرْنِي وَمَنْ يُّكَذِّبُ بِهٰذَا الْحَدِيثِ ۖ
سَنَسْتَدْرِجُهُمْ مِّنْ حَيْثُ لَا يَعْلَمُونَ ﴿٤٤﴾
وَأُمْلِي لَهُمْ ۚ إِنَّ كَيْدِي مَتِينٌ ﴿٤٥﴾
أَمْ تَسْأَلُهُمْ أَجْرًا فَهُمْ مِّنْ مَّغْرَمٍ مُّثْقَلُونَ ﴿٤٦﴾
أَمْ عِنْدَهُمُ الْغَيْبُ فَهُمْ يَكْتُبُونَ ﴿٤٧﴾
فَاصْبِرْ لِحُكْمِ رَبِّكَ وَلَا تَكُنْ كَصَاحِبِ
الْحُوتِ ۘ إِذْ نَادٰى وَهُوَ مَكْظُومٌ ﴿٤٨﴾
لَوْلَا أَنْ تَدٰرَكَهُ نِعْمَةٌ مِّنْ رَّبِّهِ لَنُبِذَ
بِالْعَرَاءِ وَهُوَ مَذْمُومٌ ﴿٤٩﴾
فَاجْتَبٰهُ رَبُّهُ فَجَعَلَهُ مِنَ الصّٰلِحِينَ ﴿٥٠﴾
وَإِنْ يَّكَادُ الَّذِينَ كَفَرُوا لَيُزْلِقُونَكَ
بِأَبْصَارِهِمْ لَمَّا سَمِعُوا الذِّكْرَ وَيَقُولُونَ
إِنَّهُ لَمَجْنُونٌ ﴿٥١﴾
وَمَا هُوَ إِلَّا ذِكْرٌ لِّلْعٰلَمِينَ ﴿٥٢﴾

سُورَةُ الْحَاقَّةِ مَكِّيَّةٌ وَهِيَ اثْنَتَانِ وَخَمْسُونَ آيَةً وَفِيهَا رُكُوعَانِ

بِسْمِ اللّٰهِ الرَّحْمٰنِ الرَّحِيمِ
الْحَاقَّةُ ﴿١﴾ مَا الْحَاقَّةُ ﴿٢﴾
وَمَا أَدْرٰكَ مَا الْحَاقَّةُ ﴿٣﴾
كَذَّبَتْ ثَمُودُ وَعَادٌ بِالْقَارِعَةِ ﴿٤﴾
فَأَمَّا ثَمُودُ فَأُهْلِكُوا بِالطَّاغِيَةِ ﴿٥﴾
وَأَمَّا عَادٌ فَأُهْلِكُوا بِرِيحٍ صَرْصَرٍ عَاتِيَةٍ ﴿٦﴾
سَخَّرَهَا عَلَيْهِمْ سَبْعَ لَيَالٍ وَّثَمٰنِيَةَ
أَيَّامٍ حُسُومًا فَتَرَى الْقَوْمَ فِيهَا صَرْعٰى

the (whole) people lying overthrown in its (path), as if they had been roots of hollow palm-trees tumbled down !

8. Then seest thou any of them left surviving?

9. And Pharaoh, and those before him, and the Cities Overthrown committed habitual Sin,

10. And disobeyed (each) the messenger of their Lord; so He punished them with an abundant Penalty.

11. We, when the water (of Noah's Flood) overflowed beyond its limits, carried you (mankind), in the floating (Ark),

12. That We might make it a Reminder unto you, and that ears (that should hear the tale and) retain its memory should bear its (lessons) in remembrance.

13. Then, when one blast is sounded on the Trumpet,

14. And the earth is moved, and its mountains, and they are crushed at one stroke,—

15. On that Day shall the (Great) Event come to pass,

16. And the sky will be rent asunder, for it will that Day be flimsy,

17. And the angels will be on its sides and eight will, that Day, bear the Throne of thy Lord above them.

18. That Day shall ye be brought to Judgment: not an act of yours that ye hide will be hidden.

19. Then he that will be given his Record in his right hand will say: "Ah here ! Read ye my Record!

20. "I did really think that my Account would (one Day) reach me!"

21. And he will be in a life of Bliss,

22. In a Garden on high,

23. The Fruits whereof (will hang in bunches) low and near.

24. "Eat ye and drink ye, with full satisfaction; because of the (good) that ye sent before you, in the days that are gone !"

25. And he that will be given his Record in his left hand, will say: "Ah ! would that my record had not been given to me !

پڑے دیکھے جیسے کھجوروں کے کھوکھلے تنے (۷)
بھلا تو اُن میں سے کسی کو بھی باقی دیکھتا ہے؟ (۸)
اور فرعون اور جو لوگ اس سے پہلے تھے اور وہ جو اُلٹی بستیوں
میں رہتے تھے سب گناہ کے کام کرتے تھے (۹)
انہوں نے اپنے پروردگار کے پیغمبر کی نافرمانی کی تو خدا نے بھی اُنکو بڑا سخت پکڑا (۱۰)
جب پانی طغیانی پر آیا تو ہم نے تم (لوگوں) کو کشتی میں سوار کر لیا (۱۱)
تاکہ اس کو تمہارے لئے یادگار بنائیں اور یاد رکھنے والے
کان اُسے یاد رکھیں (۱۲)
تو جب صُور میں ایک (بار) پھونک ماردی جائے گی (۱۳)
اور زمین اور پہاڑ دونوں اُٹھا لئے جائیں گے۔ پھر ایک بارگی
توڑ پھوڑ کر برابر کر دیئے جائیں گے (۱۴)
تو اُس روز ہو پڑنے والی (یعنی قیامت) ہو پڑے گی (۱۵)
اور آسمان پھٹ جائے گا تو وہ اُس دن کمزور ہو گا (۱۶)
اور فرشتے اُسکے کناروں پر (اُتر آئینگے) اور تمہارے پروردگار کے
عرش کو اُس روز آٹھ فرشتے اُٹھائے ہوں گے (۱۷)
اُس روز تم (سب لوگوں کے سامنے) پیش کئے جاؤ گے
اور تمہاری کوئی پوشیدہ بات چھپی نہ رہے گی (۱۸)
تو جس کا (اعمال) نامہ اُس کے داہنے ہاتھ میں دیا جائیگا
وہ (دوسروں سے) کہے گا کہ لیجئے میرا نامہ (اعمال) پڑھیے (۱۹)
مجھے یقین تھا کہ مجھ کو میرا حساب (کتاب) ضرور ملے گا (۲۰)
پس وہ (شخص) من مانے عیش میں ہوگا (۲۱)
(یعنی) اُونچے (اُونچے محلوں کے) باغ میں (۲۲)
جن کے میوے جھکے ہوئے ہوں گے (۲۳)
جو (عمل) تم ایام گذشتہ میں آگے بھیج چکے ہو اُس کے
صلے میں مزے سے کھاؤ اور پیو (۲۴)
اور جس کا نامہ (اعمال) اُس کے بائیں ہاتھ میں دیا جائیگا
وہ کہے گا اے کاش مجھ کو میرا (اعمال) نامہ نہ دیا جاتا (۲۵)

كَأَنَّهُمْ أَعْجَازُ نَخْلٍ خَاوِيَةٍ ﴿٧﴾
فَهَلْ تَرَىٰ لَهُم مِّنْ بَاقِيَةٍ ﴿٨﴾
وَجَاءَ فِرْعَوْنُ وَمَنْ قَبْلَهُ وَالْمُؤْتَفِكَتُ
بِالْخَاطِئَةِ ﴿٩﴾
فَعَصَوْا رَسُولَ رَبِّهِمْ فَأَخَذَهُمْ أَخْذَةً رَّابِيَةً ﴿١٠﴾
إِنَّا لَمَّا طَغَا الْمَاءُ حَمَلْنَٰكُمْ فِي الْجَارِيَةِ ﴿١١﴾
لِنَجْعَلَهَا لَكُمْ تَذْكِرَةً وَتَعِيَهَا
أُذُنٌ وَاعِيَةٌ ﴿١٢﴾
فَإِذَا نُفِخَ فِي الصُّورِ نَفْخَةٌ وَاحِدَةٌ ﴿١٣﴾
وَحُمِلَتِ الْأَرْضُ وَالْجِبَالُ فَدُكَّتَا
دَكَّةً وَاحِدَةً ﴿١٤﴾
فَيَوْمَئِذٍ وَقَعَتِ الْوَاقِعَةُ ﴿١٥﴾
وَانْشَقَّتِ السَّمَاءُ فَهِيَ يَوْمَئِذٍ وَاهِيَةٌ ﴿١٦﴾
وَالْمَلَكُ عَلَىٰ أَرْجَائِهَا وَيَحْمِلُ عَرْشَ
رَبِّكَ فَوْقَهُمْ يَوْمَئِذٍ ثَمَٰنِيَةٌ ﴿١٧﴾
يَوْمَئِذٍ تُعْرَضُونَ لَا تَخْفَىٰ مِنْكُمْ
خَافِيَةٌ ﴿١٨﴾
فَأَمَّا مَنْ أُوتِيَ كِتَٰبَهُ بِيَمِينِهِ فَيَقُولُ
هَاؤُمُ اقْرَءُوا كِتَٰبِيَهْ ﴿١٩﴾
إِنِّي ظَنَنْتُ أَنِّي مُلَٰقٍ حِسَابِيَهْ ﴿٢٠﴾
فَهُوَ فِي عِيشَةٍ رَّاضِيَةٍ ﴿٢١﴾
فِي جَنَّةٍ عَالِيَةٍ ﴿٢٢﴾
قُطُوفُهَا دَانِيَةٌ ﴿٢٣﴾
كُلُوا وَاشْرَبُوا هَنِيئًا بِمَا أَسْلَفْتُمْ فِي
الْأَيَّامِ الْخَالِيَةِ ﴿٢٤﴾
وَأَمَّا مَنْ أُوتِيَ كِتَٰبَهُ بِشِمَالِهِ فَيَقُولُ
يَٰلَيْتَنِي لَمْ أُوتَ كِتَٰبِيَهْ ﴿٢٥﴾

26. "And that I had never realised how my account (stood) !	اور مجھے معلوم نہ ہوتا کہ میرا حساب کیا ہے ﴿۲۶﴾	وَلَمْ اَدْرِ مَا حِسَابِيَهْ ﴿۲۶﴾
27. "Ah ! would that (Death) had made an end of me !	اے کاش موت (ابدالآباد کیلئے میرا کام) تمام کر چکی ہوتی ﴿۲۷﴾	يٰلَيْتَهَا كَانَتِ الْقَاضِيَةَ ﴿۲۷﴾
28. "Of no profit to me has been my wealth !	(آج) میرا مال میرے کچھ بھی کام نہ آیا ﴿۲۸﴾	مَآ اَغْنٰى عَنِّيْ مَالِيَهْ ﴿۲۸﴾
29. "My power has perished from me !"...	(ہائے) میری سلطنت خاک میں مل گئی ﴿۲۹﴾	هَلَكَ عَنِّيْ سُلْطٰنِيَهْ ﴿۲۹﴾
30. (The stern command will say): "Seize ye him, and bind ye him,	(حکم ہوگا کہ) اسے پکڑ لو اور طوق پہنا دو ﴿۳۰﴾	خُذُوْهُ فَغُلُّوْهُ ﴿۳۰﴾
31. "And burn ye him in the Blazing Fire.	پھر دوزخ کی آگ میں جھونک دو ﴿۳۱﴾	ثُمَّ الْجَحِيْمَ صَلُّوْهُ ﴿۳۱﴾
32. "Further, insert him in a chain, whereof the length is seventy cubits!	پھر زنجیر سے جس کی ناپ ستّر گز ہے جکڑ دو ﴿۳۲﴾	ثُمَّ فِيْ سِلْسِلَةٍ ذَرْعُهَا سَبْعُوْنَ ذِرَاعًا فَاسْلُكُوْهُ ﴿۳۲﴾
33. "This was he that would not believe in Allah Most High,	یہ نہ تو خدائے جل شانہٗ پر ایمان لاتا تھا ﴿۳۳﴾	اِنَّهٗ كَانَ لَا يُؤْمِنُ بِاللّٰهِ الْعَظِيْمِ ﴿۳۳﴾
34. "And would not encourage the feeding of the indigent !	اور نہ فقیر کے کھانا کھلانے پر آمادہ کرتا تھا ﴿۳۴﴾	وَلَا يَحُضُّ عَلٰى طَعَامِ الْمِسْكِيْنِ ﴿۳۴﴾
35. "So no friend hath he here this Day.	سو آج اس کا بھی یہاں کوئی دوستدار نہیں ﴿۳۵﴾	فَلَيْسَ لَهُ الْيَوْمَ هٰهُنَا حَمِيْمٌ ﴿۳۵﴾
36. "Nor hath he any food except the foul pus from the washing of wounds,	اور نہ پیپ کے سوا (اس کے لئے) کھانا ہے ﴿۳۶﴾	وَّلَا طَعَامٌ اِلَّا مِنْ غِسْلِيْنٍ ﴿۳۶﴾
37. "Which none do eat but those in sin."	جس کو گنہگاروں کے سوا کوئی نہیں کھائے گا ﴿۳۷﴾	لَّا يَاْكُلُهٗٓ اِلَّا الْخَاطِئُوْنَ ﴿۳۷﴾ ع
38. So I do call to witness what ye see	تو ہم کو اُن چیزوں کی قسم جو تم کو نظر آتی ہیں ﴿۳۸﴾	فَلَآ اُقْسِمُ بِمَا تُبْصِرُوْنَ ﴿۳۸﴾
39. And what ye see not,	اور اُن کی جو نظر نہیں آتیں ﴿۳۹﴾	وَمَا لَا تُبْصِرُوْنَ ﴿۳۹﴾
40. That this is verily the word of an honoured messenger;	کہ یہ (قرآن) فرشتۂ عالی مقام کی زبان کا پیغام ہے ﴿۴۰﴾	اِنَّهٗ لَقَوْلُ رَسُوْلٍ كَرِيْمٍ ﴿۴۰﴾
41. It is not the word of a poet: little it is ye believe!	اور یہ کسی شاعر کا کلام نہیں۔ مگر تم لوگ بہت ہی کم ایمان لاتے ہو ﴿۴۱﴾	وَّمَا هُوَ بِقَوْلِ شَاعِرٍ ۭ قَلِيْلًا مَّا تُؤْمِنُوْنَ ﴿۴۱﴾
42. Nor is it the word of a soothsayer: little admonition it is ye receive.	اور نہ کسی کاہن کے مزخرفات ہیں لیکن تم لوگ بہت ہی کم فکر کرتے ہو ﴿۴۲﴾	وَلَا بِقَوْلِ كَاهِنٍ ۭ قَلِيْلًا مَّا تَذَكَّرُوْنَ ﴿۴۲﴾
43. (This is) a Message sent down from the Lord of the Worlds.	(یہ تو) پروردگار عالم کا اُتارا (ہوا) ہے ﴿۴۳﴾	تَنْزِيْلٌ مِّنْ رَّبِّ الْعٰلَمِيْنَ ﴿۴۳﴾
44. And if the messenger were to invent any sayings in Our name,	اگر یہ پیغمبر ہماری نسبت کوئی بات جھوٹ بنا لاتے ﴿۴۴﴾	وَلَوْ تَقَوَّلَ عَلَيْنَا بَعْضَ الْاَقَاوِيْلِ ﴿۴۴﴾
45. We should certainly seize him by his right hand	تو ہم اُن کا داہنا ہاتھ پکڑ لیتے ﴿۴۵﴾	لَاَخَذْنَا مِنْهُ بِالْيَمِيْنِ ﴿۴۵﴾
46. And We should certainly then cut off the artery of his heart:	پھر اُن کی رگِ گردن کاٹ ڈالتے ﴿۴۶﴾	ثُمَّ لَقَطَعْنَا مِنْهُ الْوَتِيْنَ ﴿۴۶﴾
47. Nor could any of you withhold him (from Our wrath).	پھر تم میں سے کوئی (ہمیں) اس سے روکنے والا نہ ہوتا ﴿۴۷﴾	فَمَا مِنْكُمْ مِّنْ اَحَدٍ عَنْهُ حٰجِزِيْنَ ﴿۴۷﴾
48. But verily this is a Message for the God-fearing.	اور یہ (کتاب) تو پرہیزگاروں کے لئے نصیحت ہے ﴿۴۸﴾	وَاِنَّهٗ لَتَذْكِرَةٌ لِّلْمُتَّقِيْنَ ﴿۴۸﴾
49. And We certainly know that there are amongst you those that reject (it).	اور ہم جانتے ہیں کہ تم میں سے بعض اسکو جھٹلانیوالے ہیں ﴿۴۹﴾	وَاِنَّا لَنَعْلَمُ اَنَّ مِنْكُمْ مُّكَذِّبِيْنَ ﴿۴۹﴾
50. But truly (Revelation) is a cause of sorrow for the Unbelievers.	نیز یہ کافروں کے لئے (موجبِ) حسرت ہے ﴿۵۰﴾	وَاِنَّهٗ لَحَسْرَةٌ عَلَى الْكٰفِرِيْنَ ﴿۵۰﴾
51. But verily it is Truth of assured certainty.	اور کچھ شک نہیں کہ یہ برحق قابلِ یقین ہے ﴿۵۱﴾	وَاِنَّهٗ لَحَقُّ الْيَقِيْنِ ﴿۵۱﴾

SÛRA–70

AL-MA'ĀRIJ

(INTRODUCTION)

This is another eschatological Sûra closely connected in subject-matter with the last one. Patience and the mystery of Time will show the ways that climb to Heaven. Sin and Goodness must each eventually come to its own.

Chronologically it belongs to the late early or early middle Makkan period, possibly soon after S. 69.

52. So glorify the name of thy Lord Most High.	سو تم اپنے پروردگار عزوجل کے نام کی تنزیہ کرتے رہو (۵۲)	فَسَبِّحْ بِاسْمِ رَبِّكَ الْعَظِيمِ ﴿٥٢﴾
Al-Ma'ārij, or the Ways of Ascent.	سورہ معارج مکی ہے اس میں چوالیس آیتیں اور دو رکوع ہیں	سُورَةُ الْمَعَارِجِ مَكِّيَّةٌ وَهِيَ أَرْبَعٌ وَأَرْبَعُونَ آيَةً وَفِيهَا رُكُوعَانِ
In the name of Allah, Most Gracious, Most Merciful.	شروع خدا کا نام لے کر جو بڑا مہربان نہایت رحم والا ہے	بِسْمِ اللَّهِ الرَّحْمَٰنِ الرَّحِيمِ
1. A questioner asked about a Chastisement to befall—	ایک طلب کرنیوالے نے عذاب طلب کیا جو نازل ہو کر رہیگا (۱)	سَأَلَ سَائِلٌ بِعَذَابٍ وَاقِعٍ ﴿١﴾
2. The Unbelievers, the which there is none to ward off,—	(یعنی) کافروں پر (اور) کوئی اس کو ٹال نہ سکے گا (۲)	لِّلْكَافِرِينَ لَيْسَ لَهُ دَافِعٌ ﴿٢﴾
3. (A Penalty) from Allah, Lord of the Ways of Ascent.	(اور وہ) خدائے صاحب درجات کی طرف سے (نازل ہوگا) (۳)	مِّنَ اللَّهِ ذِي الْمَعَارِجِ ﴿٣﴾
4. The angels and the Spirit ascend unto Him in a Day the measure whereof is (as) fifty thousand years:	جس کی طرف روح (الامین) اور فرشتے چڑھتے ہیں (اور) اس روز (نازل ہوگا) جس کا اندازہ پچاس ہزار برس کا ہوگا (۴)	تَعْرُجُ الْمَلَائِكَةُ وَالرُّوحُ إِلَيْهِ فِي يَوْمٍ كَانَ مِقْدَارُهُ خَمْسِينَ أَلْفَ سَنَةٍ ﴿٤﴾
5. Therefore do thou hold Patience,—a Patience of beautiful (contentment).	(تو تم کافروں کی باتوں کو) حوصلے کے ساتھ برداشت کرتے رہو (۵)	فَاصْبِرْ صَبْرًا جَمِيلًا ﴿٥﴾
6. They see the (Day) indeed as a far-off (event):	وہ ان لوگوں کی نگاہ میں دور ہے (۶)	إِنَّهُمْ يَرَوْنَهُ بَعِيدًا ﴿٦﴾
7. But We see it (quite) near.	اور ہماری نظر میں قریب (۷)	وَنَرَاهُ قَرِيبًا ﴿٧﴾
8. The Day that the sky will be like molten brass,	جس دن آسمان ایسا ہو جائے گا جیسا پگھلا ہوا تانبا (۸)	يَوْمَ تَكُونُ السَّمَاءُ كَالْمُهْلِ ﴿٨﴾
9. And the mountains will be like wool,	اور پہاڑ (ایسے) جیسے (دھنکی ہوئی) رنگین اون (۹)	وَتَكُونُ الْجِبَالُ كَالْعِهْنِ ﴿٩﴾
10. And no friend will ask after a friend,	اور کوئی دوست کسی دوست کا پرساں نہ ہوگا (۱۰)	وَلَا يَسْأَلُ حَمِيمٌ حَمِيمًا ﴿١٠﴾
11. Though they will be put in sight of each other,—the sinner's desire will be: would that he could redeem himself from the Chastisement of that Day by his children,	(حالانکہ) ایک دوسرے کو سامنے دیکھ رہے ہونگے (اس روز) گنہگار خواہش کریگا کہ کسی طرح اس دن کے عذاب کے بدلے میں (سب کچھ) دیدے (یعنی) اپنے بیٹے (۱۱)	يُبَصَّرُونَهُمْ ۚ يَوَدُّ الْمُجْرِمُ لَوْ يَفْتَدِي مِنْ عَذَابِ يَوْمِئِذٍ بِبَنِيهِ ﴿١١﴾
12. His wife and his brother,	اور اپنی بیوی اور اپنے بھائی (۱۲)	وَصَاحِبَتِهِ وَأَخِيهِ ﴿١٢﴾
13. His kindred who sheltered him.	اور اپنا خاندان جس میں وہ رہتا تھا (۱۳)	وَفَصِيلَتِهِ الَّتِي تُؤْوِيهِ ﴿١٣﴾
14. And all, all that is on earth,—so it could deliver him:	اور جتنے آدمی زمین پر ہیں (غرض) سب (کچھ دیدے) اور اپنے تئیں عذاب سے چھڑا لے (۱۴)	وَمَن فِي الْأَرْضِ جَمِيعًا ثُمَّ يُنجِيهِ ﴿١٤﴾
15. By no means ! for it would be the Blazing Fire—	(لیکن) ایسا ہرگز نہیں ہوگا وہ بھڑکتی ہوئی آگ ہے (۱۵)	كَلَّا ۖ إِنَّهَا لَظَىٰ ﴿١٥﴾
16. Plucking out (his being) right to the skull !—	کھال ادھیڑ ڈالنے والی (۱۶)	نَزَّاعَةً لِّلشَّوَىٰ ﴿١٦﴾
17. Inviting (all) such as turn their backs and turn away their faces (from the Right),	ان لوگوں کو اپنی طرف بلائیگی جنہوں نے (دین حق سے) اعراض کیا اور منہ پھیر لیا (۱۷)	تَدْعُو مَنْ أَدْبَرَ وَتَوَلَّىٰ ﴿١٧﴾
18. And collect (wealth) and hide it (from use) !	اور (مال) جمع کیا اور بند کر رکھا (۱۸)	وَجَمَعَ فَأَوْعَىٰ ﴿١٨﴾
19. Truly man was created, very impatient;	کچھ شک نہیں کہ انسان کم حوصلہ پیدا ہوا ہے (۱۹)	إِنَّ الْإِنسَانَ خُلِقَ هَلُوعًا ﴿١٩﴾
20. Fretful when evil touches him;	جب اسے تکلیف پہنچتی ہے تو گھبرا اٹھتا ہے (۲۰)	إِذَا مَسَّهُ الشَّرُّ جَزُوعًا ﴿٢٠﴾
21. And niggardly when good reaches him;—	اور جب آسائش حاصل ہوتی ہے تو بخیل بن جاتا ہے (۲۱)	وَإِذَا مَسَّهُ الْخَيْرُ مَنُوعًا ﴿٢١﴾
22. Not so those devoted to Prayer:—	مگر نماز گذار (۲۲)	إِلَّا الْمُصَلِّينَ ﴿٢٢﴾

23. Those who remain steadfast to their prayer;

24. And those in whose wealth is a recognised right

25. For the (needy) who asks and him who is deprived (for some reason from asking);

26. And those who hold to the truth of the Day of Judgment;

27. And those who fear the punishment of their Lord,—

28. For their Lord's punishment is not a thing to feel secure from:—

29. And those who guard their chastity,

30. Except with their wives and the (captives) whom their right hands possess,— for (then) they are no to be blamed,

31. But those who trespass beyond this are transgressors;—

32. And those who respect their trusts and covenants;

33. And those who stand firm in their testimonies;

34. And those who (strictly) guard their worship;—

35. Such will be the honoured ones in the Gardens (of Bliss).

36. Now what is the matter with the Unbelievers that they rush madly before thee—

37. From the right and from the left, in crowds?

38. Does every man of them long to enter the Garden of Bliss ?

39. By no means ! for We have created them out of the (base matter) they know !

40. Now I do call to witness the Lord of all points in the East and the West that We can certainly—

41. Substitute for them better (men) than they; and We are not to be defeated (in Our Plan).

42. So leave them to plunge in vain talk and play about, until they encounter that Day of theirs which they have been promised !

43. The Day whereon they will issue from their sepulchres in

جو نماز کا التزام رکھتے (اور بلاناغہ پڑھتے) ہیں (٢٣)
اور جن کے مال میں حصہ مقرر ہے (٢٤)
(یعنی) مانگنے والے کا۔ اور نہ مانگنے والے کا (٢٥)
اور جو روزِ جزا کو سچ سمجھتے ہیں (٢٦)
اور جو اپنے پروردگار کے عذاب سے خوف رکھتے ہیں (٢٧)
بیشک اُنکے پروردگار کا عذاب ہے ہی ایسا کہ اس سے بےخوف نہ ہوا جائے (٢٨)
اور جو اپنی شرمگاہوں کی حفاظت کرتے ہیں (٢٩)
مگر اپنی بیویوں یا لونڈیوں سے کہ (اُن کے پاس جانے پر)
انہیں کچھ ملامت نہیں (٣٠)
اور جو لوگ ان کے سوا اور کے خواستگار ہوں وہ حد سے
نکل جانے والے ہیں (٣١)
اور جو اپنی امانتوں اور اقراروں کا پاس کرتے ہیں (٣٢)
اور جو اپنی شہادتوں پر قائم رہتے ہیں (٣٣)
اور جو اپنی نماز کی خبر رکھتے ہیں (٣٤)
یہی لوگ باغہائے بہشت میں عزت واکرام سے ہونگے (٣٥)
تو اُن کافروں کو کیا ہوا ہے کہ تمہاری طرف دوڑے چلے آتے ہیں (٣٦)
(اور) دائیں بائیں سے گروہ گروہ ہو کر (جمع ہوتے جاتے ہیں) (٣٧)
کیا اُن میں سے ہر شخص یہ توقع رکھتا ہے کہ نعمت کے باغ
میں داخل کیا جائے گا؟ (٣٨)
ہرگز نہیں۔ ہم نے انکو اس چیز سے پیدا کیا ہے جسے وہ جانتے ہیں (٣٩)
ہمیں مشرقوں اور مغربوں کے مالک کی قسم کہ ہم طاقت
رکھتے ہیں (٤٠)
(یعنی) اس بات پر (قادر ہیں) کہ اُن سے بہتر لوگ بدل
لائیں۔ اور ہم عاجز نہیں ہیں (٤١)
تو (اے پیغمبر) ان کو باطل میں پڑے رہنے اور کھیل لینے دو
یہانتک کہ جس دن کا اُنسے وعدہ کیا جاتا ہے وہ اُنکے سامنے آموجود ہو (٤٢)
اُس دن یہ قبروں سے نکل کر (اس طرح) دوڑیں گے جیسے (شکاری

الَّذِينَ هُمْ عَلَىٰ صَلَاتِهِمْ دَائِمُونَ (٢٣)
وَالَّذِينَ فِي أَمْوَالِهِمْ حَقٌّ مَّعْلُومٌ (٢٤)
لِّلسَّائِلِ وَالْمَحْرُومِ (٢٥)
وَالَّذِينَ يُصَدِّقُونَ بِيَوْمِ الدِّينِ (٢٦)
وَالَّذِينَ هُم مِّنْ عَذَابِ رَبِّهِم مُّشْفِقُونَ (٢٧)
إِنَّ عَذَابَ رَبِّهِمْ غَيْرُ مَأْمُونٍ (٢٨)
وَالَّذِينَ هُمْ لِفُرُوجِهِمْ حَافِظُونَ (٢٩)
إِلَّا عَلَىٰ أَزْوَاجِهِمْ أَوْ مَا مَلَكَتْ أَيْمَانُهُمْ
فَإِنَّهُمْ غَيْرُ مَلُومِينَ (٣٠)
فَمَنِ ابْتَغَىٰ وَرَاءَ ذَٰلِكَ فَأُولَٰئِكَ هُمُ
الْعَادُونَ (٣١)
وَالَّذِينَ هُمْ لِأَمَانَاتِهِمْ وَعَهْدِهِمْ رَاعُونَ (٣٢)
وَالَّذِينَ هُم بِشَهَادَاتِهِمْ قَائِمُونَ (٣٣)
وَالَّذِينَ هُمْ عَلَىٰ صَلَاتِهِمْ يُحَافِظُونَ (٣٤)
أُولَٰئِكَ فِي جَنَّاتٍ مُّكْرَمُونَ (٣٥)
فَمَالِ الَّذِينَ كَفَرُوا قِبَلَكَ مُهْطِعِينَ (٣٦)
عَنِ الْيَمِينِ وَعَنِ الشِّمَالِ عِزِينَ (٣٧)
أَيَطْمَعُ كُلُّ امْرِئٍ مِّنْهُمْ أَن يُدْخَلَ
جَنَّةَ نَعِيمٍ (٣٨)
كَلَّا ۖ إِنَّا خَلَقْنَاهُم مِّمَّا يَعْلَمُونَ (٣٩)
فَلَا أُقْسِمُ بِرَبِّ الْمَشَارِقِ وَالْمَغَارِبِ
إِنَّا لَقَادِرُونَ (٤٠)
عَلَىٰ أَن نُّبَدِّلَ خَيْرًا مِّنْهُمْ وَمَا نَحْنُ
بِمَسْبُوقِينَ (٤١)
فَذَرْهُمْ يَخُوضُوا وَيَلْعَبُوا حَتَّىٰ يُلَاقُوا
يَوْمَهُمُ الَّذِي يُوعَدُونَ (٤٢)
يَوْمَ يَخْرُجُونَ مِنَ الْأَجْدَاثِ سِرَاعًا

SÛRA–71

NÛḤ

(INTRODUCTION)

This is another early Makkan Sûra, of which the date has no significance. The theme is that while Good must uphold the standard of Truth and Righteousness, a stage is reached when it must definitely part company with Evil, lest Evil should spread its corruption abroad. This theme is embodied in the prayer of Noah just before the Flood. The story of Noah's agony is almost a Parable for the Holy Prophet's persection in the Makkan period.

sudden haste as if they were rushing to a goal-post (fixed for them),—

44. Their eyes lowered in dejection,— ignominy covering them (all over) ! Such is the Day the which they are promised !

Nûḥ, or Noah

In the name of Allah, Most Gracious, Most Merciful.

1. We sent Noah to his People (with the Command): "Do thou warn thy People before there comes to them a grievous Chastisement."

2. He said: "O my People ! I am to you a Warner, clear and open:

3. "That ye should worship Allah, fear Him, and obey me:

4. "So He may forgive you your sins and give you respite for a stated Term: for when the Term given by Allah is accomplished, it cannot be put forward: if ye only knew."

5. He said: "O my Lord ! I have called to my People night and day:

6. "But my call only increases (their) flight (from the Right).

7. "And every time I have called to them, that Thou mightest forgive them, they have (only) thrust their fingers into their ears, covered themselves up with their garments, grown obstinate, and given themselves up to arrogance.

8. "So I have called to them aloud;

9. "Further I have spoken to them in public and secretly in private,

10. "Saying, 'Ask forgiveness from your Lord, for He is Oft-Forgiving;

11. " 'He will send rain to you in abundance;

12. " 'Give you increase in wealth and sons; and bestow on you gardens and bestow on you rivers (of flowing water).

13. " 'What is the matter with you, that ye are not conscious of Allah's majesty,—

14. " 'Seeing that it is He that has created you in diverse stages ?

شکار کے جال کی طرف دوڑتے ہیں (۴۳)
اُن کی آنکھیں جھک رہی ہوں گی اور ذلت اُن پر چھا رہی
ہوگی۔ یہی وہ دن ہے جس کا اُن سے وعدہ کیا جاتا تھا (۴۴)

سورۂ نوح مکّی ہے اس میں اٹھائیس آیتیں اور دو رکوع ہیں

شروع خدا کا نام لے کر جو بڑا مہربان نہایت رحم والا ہے
ہم نے نوح کو اُن کی قوم کی طرف بھیجا کہ پیشتر اسکے
کہ ان پر درد دینے والا عذاب واقع ہو اپنی قوم کو
ہدایت کردو (۱)
اُنہوں نے کہا کہ بھائیو! میں تم کو کھلے طور پر نصیحت
کرتا ہوں (۲)
کہ خدا کی عبادت کرو اور اُس سے ڈرو اور میرا کہا مانو (۳)
وہ تمہارے گناہ بخش دے گا اور (موت کے) وقت مقرر تک
تم کو مہلت عطا کرے گا۔ جب خدا کا مقرر کیا ہوا وقت
آجاتا ہے تو تاخیر نہیں ہوتی۔ کاش تم جانتے ہوتے (۴)
جب لوگوں نے نہ مانا تو نوح نے خدا سے عرض کی کہ پروردگار میں اپنی قوم کو رات دن بلاتا رہا (۵)
لیکن میرے بلانے سے وہ اور زیادہ گریز کرتے رہے (۶)
جب جب میں نے اُن کو بلایا کہ (توبہ کریں اور) تو اُن کو معاف
فرمائے تو اُنہوں نے اپنے کانوں میں انگلیاں دے لیں اور
کپڑے اوڑھ لئے اور اَڑ گئے اور اکڑ بیٹھے (۷)
پھر میں اُن کو کھلے طور پر بھی بلاتا رہا (۸)
اور ظاہر اور پوشیدہ ہر طرح سمجھاتا رہا (۹)
اور کہا کہ اپنے پروردگار سے معافی مانگو کہ وہ بڑا معاف کرنے والا ہے (۱۰)
وہ تم پر آسمان سے مینہ برسائے گا (۱۱)
اور مال اور بیٹوں سے تمہاری مدد فرمائے گا اور تمہیں باغ
عطا کریگا اور اُن میں تمہارے لئے نہریں بہادے گا (۱۲)
تم کو کیا ہوا ہے کہ تم خدا کی عظمت کا اعتقاد نہیں رکھتے (۱۳)
حالانکہ اُس نے تم کو طرح طرح (کی حالتوں) کا پیدا کیا ہے (۱۴)

كَأَنَّهُمْ إِلَىٰ نُصُبٍ يُوفِضُونَ ﴿٤٣﴾
خَاشِعَةً أَبْصَارُهُمْ تَرْهَقُهُمْ ذِلَّةٌ ۚ
ذَٰلِكَ الْيَوْمُ الَّذِي كَانُوا يُوعَدُونَ ﴿٤٤﴾ ع

سُورَةُ نُوحٍ مَكِّيَّةٌ وَهِيَ ثَمَانٍ وَّعِشْرُونَ آيَةً وَّفِيهَا رُكُوعَانِ

بِسْمِ اللَّهِ الرَّحْمَٰنِ الرَّحِيمِ
إِنَّا أَرْسَلْنَا نُوحًا إِلَىٰ قَوْمِهِ أَنْ أَنذِرْ
قَوْمَكَ مِن قَبْلِ أَن يَأْتِيَهُمْ عَذَابٌ
أَلِيمٌ ﴿١﴾
قَالَ يَا قَوْمِ إِنِّي لَكُمْ نَذِيرٌ
مُّبِينٌ ﴿٢﴾
أَنِ اعْبُدُوا اللَّهَ وَاتَّقُوهُ وَأَطِيعُونِ ﴿٣﴾
يَغْفِرْ لَكُم مِّن ذُنُوبِكُمْ وَيُؤَخِّرْكُمْ إِلَىٰ
أَجَلٍ مُّسَمًّى ۚ إِنَّ أَجَلَ اللَّهِ إِذَا جَاءَ لَا
يُؤَخَّرُ ۖ لَوْ كُنتُمْ تَعْلَمُونَ ﴿٤﴾ وقف لازم
قَالَ رَبِّ إِنِّي دَعَوْتُ قَوْمِي لَيْلًا وَنَهَارًا ﴿٥﴾
فَلَمْ يَزِدْهُمْ دُعَائِي إِلَّا فِرَارًا ﴿٦﴾
وَإِنِّي كُلَّمَا دَعَوْتُهُمْ لِتَغْفِرَ لَهُمْ جَعَلُوا
أَصَابِعَهُمْ فِي آذَانِهِمْ وَاسْتَغْشَوْا ثِيَابَهُمْ
وَأَصَرُّوا وَاسْتَكْبَرُوا اسْتِكْبَارًا ﴿٧﴾
ثُمَّ إِنِّي دَعَوْتُهُمْ جِهَارًا ﴿٨﴾
ثُمَّ إِنِّي أَعْلَنتُ لَهُمْ وَأَسْرَرْتُ لَهُمْ إِسْرَارًا ﴿٩﴾
فَقُلْتُ اسْتَغْفِرُوا رَبَّكُمْ إِنَّهُ كَانَ غَفَّارًا ﴿١٠﴾
يُرْسِلِ السَّمَاءَ عَلَيْكُم مِّدْرَارًا ﴿١١﴾
وَيُمْدِدْكُم بِأَمْوَالٍ وَبَنِينَ وَيَجْعَل لَّكُمْ
جَنَّاتٍ وَيَجْعَل لَّكُمْ أَنْهَارًا ﴿١٢﴾
مَّا لَكُمْ لَا تَرْجُونَ لِلَّهِ وَقَارًا ﴿١٣﴾
وَقَدْ خَلَقَكُمْ أَطْوَارًا ﴿١٤﴾

15. " 'See ye not how Allah has created the seven heavens one above another,

کیا تم نے نہیں دیکھا کہ خدا نے سات آسمان کیسے اُوپر تلے بنائے ہیں ﴿۱۵﴾

اَلَمْ تَرَوْا كَيْفَ خَلَقَ اللّٰهُ سَبْعَ سَمٰوٰتٍ طِبَاقًا ﴿١٥﴾

16. " 'And made the moon a light in their midst, and made the sun as a (Glorious) Lamp?

اور چاند کو اُن میں (زمین کا) نور بنایا ہے اور سورج کو چراغ ٹھہرایا ہے ﴿۱۶﴾

وَّجَعَلَ الْقَمَرَ فِيْهِنَّ نُوْرًا وَّجَعَلَ الشَّمْسَ سِرَاجًا ﴿١٦﴾

17. " 'And Allah has produced you from the earth, growing (gradually),

اور خدا ہی نے تم کو زمین سے پیدا کیا ہے ﴿۱۷﴾

وَاللّٰهُ اَنْبَتَكُمْ مِّنَ الْاَرْضِ نَبَاتًا ﴿١٧﴾

18. " 'And in the End He will return you into the (earth), and raise you forth (again at the Resurrection) ?

پھر اسی میں تمہیں لوٹا دیگا اور (اُسی سے) تم کو نکال کھڑا کریگا ﴿۱۸﴾

ثُمَّ يُعِيْدُكُمْ فِيْهَا وَيُخْرِجُكُمْ اِخْرَاجًا ﴿١٨﴾

19. " 'And Allah has made the earth for you as a carpet (spread out),

اور خدا ہی نے زمین کو تمہارے لئے فرش بنایا ﴿۱۹﴾

وَاللّٰهُ جَعَلَ لَكُمُ الْاَرْضَ بِسَاطًا ﴿١٩﴾

20. " 'That ye may go about therein, in spacious roads.'

تاکہ اُسکے بڑے بڑے کشادہ رستوں میں چلو پھرو ﴿۲۰﴾

لِّتَسْلُكُوْا مِنْهَا سُبُلًا فِجَاجًا ﴿٢٠﴾

21. Noah said: "O my Lord! they have disobeyed me, but they follow (men) whose wealth and children give them no Increase but only Loss.

(اسکے بعد) نوح نے عرض کی کہ میرے پروردگار! یہ لوگ میرے کہنے پر نہیں چلے اور ایسوں کے تابع ہوئے ہیں جنکو اُنکے مال اور اولاد نے نقصان کے سوا کچھ فائدہ نہیں دیا ﴿۲۱﴾

قَالَ نُوْحٌ رَّبِّ اِنَّهُمْ عَصَوْنِيْ وَاتَّبَعُوْا مَنْ لَّمْ يَزِدْهُ مَالُهٗ وَوَلَدُهٗٓ اِلَّا خَسَارًا ﴿٢١﴾

22. "And they have devised a tremendous Plot.

اور وہ بڑی بڑی چالیں چلے ﴿۲۲﴾

وَمَكَرُوْا مَكْرًا كُبَّارًا ﴿٢٢﴾

23. "And they have said (to each other), 'Abandon not your gods: abandon neither Wadd nor Suwa', neither Yagûth nor Ya'ûq, nor Nasr';—

اور کہنے لگے کہ اپنے معبودوں کو ہرگز نہ چھوڑنا اور وَدّ اور سواع اور یغوث اور یعوق اور نسر کو کبھی ترک نہ کرنا ﴿۲۳﴾

وَقَالُوْا لَا تَذَرُنَّ اٰلِهَتَكُمْ وَلَا تَذَرُنَّ وَدًّا وَّلَا سُوَاعًا ۙ وَّلَا يَغُوْثَ وَيَعُوْقَ وَنَسْرًا ﴿٢٣﴾

24. "They have already misled many; and grant Thou no increase to the wrong-doers but in straying (from their mark)."

(پروردگار) اُنہوں نے بہت لوگوں کو گمراہ کر دیا ہے تو تُو اُن کو اور گمراہ کر دے ﴿۲۴﴾

وَقَدْ اَضَلُّوْا كَثِيْرًا ۚ وَلَا تَزِدِ الظّٰلِمِيْنَ اِلَّا ضَلٰلًا ﴿٢٤﴾

25. Because of their sins they were drowned (in the flood), and were made to enter the Fire and they found— in lieu of Allah— none to help them.

(آخر) وہ اپنے گناہوں کے سبب (پہلے) غرقاب کر دیئے گئے پھر آگ میں ڈال دیئے گئے۔ تو اُنہوں نے خدا کے سوا کسی کو اپنا مددگار نہ پایا ﴿۲۵﴾

مِمَّا خَطِيْٓـٰٔتِهِمْ اُغْرِقُوْا فَاُدْخِلُوْا نَارًا ۙ فَلَمْ يَجِدُوْا لَهُمْ مِّنْ دُوْنِ اللّٰهِ اَنْصَارًا ﴿٢٥﴾

26. And Noah said: "O my Lord ! Leave not of the Unbelievers, a single one on earth !

اور (پھر) نوح نے (یہ) دُعا کی کہ میرے پروردگار کسی کافر کو رُوئے زمین پر بستا نہ رہنے دے ﴿۲۶﴾

وَقَالَ نُوْحٌ رَّبِّ لَا تَذَرْ عَلَى الْاَرْضِ مِنَ الْكٰفِرِيْنَ دَيَّارًا ﴿٢٦﴾

27. "For, if Thou dost leave (any of) them, they will but mislead Thy devotees, and they will breed none but wicked ungrateful ones.

اگر تو اُن کو رہنے دے گا تو تیرے بندوں کو گمراہ کرینگے اور اُن سے جو اولاد ہو گی وہ بھی بدکار اور ناشکر گزار ہو گی ﴿۲۷﴾

اِنَّكَ اِنْ تَذَرْهُمْ يُضِلُّوْا عِبَادَكَ وَلَا يَلِدُوْٓا اِلَّا فَاجِرًا كَفَّارًا ﴿٢٧﴾

28. "O my Lord ! Forgive me, my parents, all who enter my house in Faith, and (all) believing men and beheving women: and to the wrong-doers grant Thou no increase but in Perdition !"

اے میرے پروردگار مجھ کو اور میرے ماں باپ کو اور جو ایمان لاکر میرے گھر میں آئے اُسکو اور تمام ایمان والے مردوں اور ایمان والی عورتوں کو معاف فرما۔ اور ظالم لوگوں کیلئے اور زیادہ تباہی بڑھا ﴿۲۸﴾

رَبِّ اغْفِرْ لِيْ وَلِوَالِدَيَّ وَلِمَنْ دَخَلَ بَيْتِيَ مُؤْمِنًا وَّلِلْمُؤْمِنِيْنَ وَالْمُؤْمِنٰتِ ۭ وَلَا تَزِدِ الظّٰلِمِيْنَ اِلَّا تَبَارًا ﴿٢٨﴾

SÛRA–72
AL-JINN
(INTRODUCTION)

This is a late Makkan Sûra, of which we can be tolerably certain of the date. It was two years before the Hijrat, when the Prophet, despised and rejected in his native city of Makkah, went to evangelise the lordly men of Ṭaif. They maltreated him and nearly killed him; what caused him even greater pain was the maltreatment of the humble and lowly men who went with him. Ṭabarî has handed down that memorable Prayer of faith and humility which he offered in the midst of his suffering. On his return journey to Makkah, a glorious vision was revealed to him, —hidden spiritual forces working for him, —people not known to him accepting his mission while his own people were still rejecting him. Within two months some strangers from Madinah had privately met him and laid the faundations of that Hijrat which was to change the fate of Arabia and the course of world history.

Al-Jinn, The Jinn

In the name of Allah, Most Gracious, Most Merciful.

1. Say: It has been revealed to me that a company of Jinns listened (to the Qur'an). They said, 'We have really heard a wonderful Recital!

2. 'It gives guidance to the Right, and we have believed therein: we shall not join (in worship) any (gods) with our Lord,

3. 'And exalted is the Majesty of our Lord: He has taken neither a wife nor a son.

4. 'There were some foolish ones among us, who used to utter extravagant lies against Allah;

5. 'But we do think that no man or jinn should say aught that is untrue against Allah.

6. 'True, there were persons among mankind who took shelter with persons among the Jinns, but they increased them into further error.

7. 'And they (came to) think as ye thought, that Allah would not raise up anyone (to Judgment).

8. 'And we pried into the (secrets of) heaven; but we found it filled with stern guards and flaming fires.

9. 'We used, indeed, to sit there in (hidden) stations, to (steal) a hearing; but any who listens now will find a flaming fire watching him in ambush.

10. 'And we understand not whether ill is intended to those on earth on whether their Lord (really) intends to guide them to right conduct.

11. 'There are among us some that are righteous, and some the contrary: we follow divergent paths.

12. 'But we think that we can by no means frustrate Allah throughout the earth, nor can we escape Him by flight.

13. 'And as for us, since we have listened to the Guidance, we have accepted it: and any who believes in his Lord has no fear, either of a

سورہ جن مکی ہے اس میں اٹھائیس آیتیں اور دو رکوع ہیں

شروع خدا کا نام لے کر جو بڑا مہربان نہایت رحم والا ہے

(اے پیغمبر لوگوں سے) کہہ دو کہ میرے پاس وحی آئی ہے کہ جنوں کی ایک جماعت
نے (اس کتاب کو) سنا تو کہنے لگے کہ ہم نے ایک عجیب قرآن سنا (۱)
جو بھلائی کا رستہ بتاتا ہے سو ہم اس پر ایمان لے آئے اور ہم اپنے
پروردگار کے ساتھ کسی کو شریک نہیں بنائیں گے (۲)
اور یہ کہ ہمارے پروردگار کی عظمت (شان) بہت بڑی ہے
وہ نہ بیوی رکھتا ہے نہ اولاد (۳)
(۴) اور یہ کہ ہم میں سے بعض بیوقوف خدا کے بارے میں جھوٹ افترا کرتا ہے
اور ہمارا (یہ) خیال تھا کہ انسان اور جن خدا کی نسبت
جھوٹ نہیں بولتے (۵)
اور یہ کہ بعض بنی آدم بعض جنات کی پناہ پکڑا کرتے تھے
(اس سے) اُن کی سرکشی اور بڑھ گئی تھی (۶)
اور یہ کہ اُن کا بھی یہی اعتقاد تھا جس طرح تمہارا تھا کہ
خدا کسی کو نہیں جلائے گا (۷)
اور یہ کہ ہم نے آسمان کو ٹٹولا تو اس کو مضبوط چوکیداروں
اور انگاروں سے بھرا ہوا پایا (۸)
اور یہ کہ پہلے ہم وہاں بہت سے مقامات میں (خبریں) سننے کیلئے
(۹) بیٹھا کرتے تھے۔ اب کوئی سننا چاہے تو اپنے لئے انگارا تیار پائے
اور یہ کہ ہمیں معلوم نہیں کہ اس سے اہلِ زمین کے حق میں بُرائی
(۱۰) مقصود ہے یا اُن کے پروردگار نے انکی بھلائی کا ارادہ فرمایا ہے
اور یہ کہ ہم میں کوئی نیک ہیں اور کوئی اور طرح کے ہمارے
کئی طرح کے مذہب ہیں (۱۱)
اور یہ کہ ہم نے یقین کر لیا ہے کہ ہم زمین میں (خواہ کہیں ہوں)
خدا کو ہرا نہیں سکتے اور نہ بھاگ کر اس کو تھکا سکتے ہیں (۱۲)
اور جب ہم نے ہدایت (کی کتاب) سُنی اُس پر ایمان لے آئے
تو جو شخص اپنے پروردگار پر ایمان لاتا ہے اسکو نہ نقصان

سُوْرَةُ الْجِنِّ مَكِّيَّةٌ (۷۲) وَهِيَ ثَمَانٍ وَّعِشْرُوْنَ اٰيَةً وَّفِيْهَا رُكُوْعَانِ

بِسْمِ اللّٰهِ الرَّحْمٰنِ الرَّحِيْمِ

قُلْ اُوْحِيَ اِلَيَّ اَنَّهُ اسْتَمَعَ نَفَرٌ مِّنَ الْجِنِّ
فَقَالُوْٓا اِنَّا سَمِعْنَا قُرْاٰنًا عَجَبًا (۱)
يَّهْدِيْٓ اِلَى الرُّشْدِ فَاٰمَنَّا بِهٖ ۭ وَلَنْ
نُّشْرِكَ بِرَبِّنَآ اَحَدًا (۲)
وَّاَنَّهٗ تَعٰلٰى جَدُّ رَبِّنَا مَا اتَّخَذَ صَاحِبَةً
وَّلَا وَلَدًا (۳)
(۴) وَّاَنَّهٗ كَانَ يَقُوْلُ سَفِيْهُنَا عَلَى اللّٰهِ شَطَطًا
وَّاَنَّا ظَنَنَّآ اَنْ لَّنْ تَقُوْلَ الْاِنْسُ وَالْجِنُّ
عَلَى اللّٰهِ كَذِبًا (۵)
وَّاَنَّهٗ كَانَ رِجَالٌ مِّنَ الْاِنْسِ يَعُوْذُوْنَ
بِرِجَالٍ مِّنَ الْجِنِّ فَزَادُوْهُمْ رَهَقًا (۶)
وَّاَنَّهُمْ ظَنُّوْا كَمَا ظَنَنْتُمْ اَنْ لَّنْ
يَّبْعَثَ اللّٰهُ اَحَدًا (۷)
وَّاَنَّا لَمَسْنَا السَّمَاۗءَ فَوَجَدْنٰهَا مُلِئَتْ
حَرَسًا شَدِيْدًا وَّشُهُبًا (۸)
وَّاَنَّا كُنَّا نَقْعُدُ مِنْهَا مَقَاعِدَ لِلسَّمْعِ ۭ
فَمَنْ يَّسْتَمِعِ الْاٰنَ يَجِدْ لَهٗ شِهَابًا رَّصَدًا (۹)
وَّاَنَّا لَا نَدْرِيْٓ اَشَرٌّ اُرِيْدَ بِمَنْ فِي الْاَرْضِ
اَمْ اَرَادَ بِهِمْ رَبُّهُمْ رَشَدًا (۱۰)
وَّاَنَّا مِنَّا الصّٰلِحُوْنَ وَمِنَّا دُوْنَ ذٰلِكَ ۭ
كُنَّا طَرَاۗىِٕقَ قِدَدًا (۱۱)
وَّاَنَّا ظَنَنَّآ اَنْ لَّنْ نُّعْجِزَ اللّٰهَ فِي الْاَرْضِ
وَلَنْ نُّعْجِزَهٗ هَرَبًا (۱۲)
وَّاَنَّا لَمَّا سَمِعْنَا الْهُدٰٓى اٰمَنَّا بِهٖ ۭ فَمَنْ
يُّؤْمِنْۢ بِرَبِّهٖ فَلَا يَخَافُ بَخْسًا وَّلَا

رَهَقًا ﴿١٣﴾
وَّ اَنَّا مِنَّا الْمُسْلِمُوْنَ وَمِنَّا الْقٰسِطُوْنَ ؕ
فَمَنْ اَسْلَمَ فَاُولٰٓئِكَ تَحَرَّوْا رَشَدًا ﴿١٤﴾
وَ اَمَّا الْقٰسِطُوْنَ فَكَانُوْا لِجَهَنَّمَ حَطَبًا ﴿١٥﴾
وَّ اَنْ لَّوِ اسْتَقَامُوْا عَلَى الطَّرِيْقَةِ لَاَسْقَيْنٰهُمْ
مَّآءً غَدَقًا ﴿١٦﴾
لِّنَفْتِنَهُمْ فِيْهِ ؕ وَمَنْ يُّعْرِضْ عَنْ ذِكْرِ
رَبِّهٖ يَسْلُكْهُ عَذَابًا صَعَدًا ﴿١٧﴾
وَّ اَنَّ الْمَسٰجِدَ لِلّٰهِ فَلَا تَدْعُوْا مَعَ اللّٰهِ
اَحَدًا ﴿١٨﴾
وَّ اَنَّهٗ لَمَّا قَامَ عَبْدُ اللّٰهِ يَدْعُوْهُ كَادُوْا
يَكُوْنُوْنَ عَلَيْهِ لِبَدًا ﴿١٩﴾ ع
قُلْ اِنَّمَآ اَدْعُوْا رَبِّيْ وَلَآ اُشْرِكُ بِهٖٓ
اَحَدًا ﴿٢٠﴾
قُلْ اِنِّيْ لَآ اَمْلِكُ لَكُمْ ضَرًّا وَّلَا رَشَدًا ﴿٢١﴾
قُلْ اِنِّيْ لَنْ يُّجِيْرَنِيْ مِنَ اللّٰهِ اَحَدٌ ۙ
وَّلَنْ اَجِدَ مِنْ دُوْنِهٖ مُلْتَحَدًا ﴿٢٢﴾
اِلَّا بَلٰغًا مِّنَ اللّٰهِ وَرِسٰلٰتِهٖ ؕ وَمَنْ يَّعْصِ
اللّٰهَ وَرَسُوْلَهٗ فَاِنَّ لَهٗ نَارَ جَهَنَّمَ خٰلِدِيْنَ
فِيْهَآ اَبَدًا ﴿٢٣﴾
حَتّٰٓى اِذَا رَاَوْا مَا يُوْعَدُوْنَ فَسَيَعْلَمُوْنَ
مَنْ اَضْعَفُ نَاصِرًا وَّاَقَلُّ عَدَدًا ﴿٢٤﴾
قُلْ اِنْ اَدْرِيْٓ اَقَرِيْبٌ مَّا تُوْعَدُوْنَ
اَمْ يَجْعَلُ لَهٗ رَبِّيْٓ اَمَدًا ﴿٢٥﴾
عٰلِمُ الْغَيْبِ فَلَا يُظْهِرُ عَلٰى غَيْبِهٖٓ
اَحَدًا ﴿٢٦﴾
اِلَّا مَنِ ارْتَضٰى مِنْ رَّسُوْلٍ فَاِنَّهٗ يَسْلُكُ

کا خوف ہے نہ ظلم کا ﴿١٣﴾
اور یہ کہ ہم میں بعض فرمانبردار ہیں۔ اور بعض (نافرمان) گنہگار
ہیں۔ تو جو فرمانبردار ہوئے وہ سیدھے رستے پر چلے ﴿١٤﴾
اور جو گنہگار ہوئے وہ دوزخ کا ایندھن بنے ﴿١٥﴾
اور (اے پیغمبر) یہ (بھی) اُن سے کہہ دو کہ اگر یہ لوگ سیدھے
رستے پر رہتے تو ہم اُن کے پینے کو بہت سا پانی دیتے ﴿١٦﴾
تاکہ اس سے اُن کی آزمائش کریں اور جو شخص اپنے پروردگار
کی یاد سے مُنہ پھیرے گا وہ اُس کو سخت عذاب میں داخل کریگا ﴿١٧﴾
اور یہ کہ مسجدیں (خاص) خدا کی ہیں تو خدا کے ساتھ کسی اور
کی عبادت نہ کرو ﴿١٨﴾
اور جب خدا کے بندے (محمدؐ) اس کی عبادت کو کھڑے
ہوئے تو کافر اُن کے گرد ہجوم کر لینے کو تھے ﴿١٩﴾
کہہ دو کہ میں تو اپنے پروردگار ہی کی عبادت کرتا ہوں اور
کسی کو اس کا شریک نہیں بناتا ﴿٢٠﴾
یہ بھی کہہ دو کہ میں تمہارے حق میں نقصان اور نفع کا کچھ اختیار نہیں رکھتا ﴿٢١﴾
یہ بھی کہہ دو کہ خدا (کے عذاب) سے مجھے کوئی پناہ نہیں
دے سکتا۔ اور میں اس کے سوا کہیں جائے پناہ نہیں دیکھتا ﴿٢٢﴾
ہاں خدا کی طرف سے (احکام کا) اور اسکے پیغاموں کا پہنچا دینا (ہی
میرے ذمے ہے) اور جو شخص خدا اور اسکے پیغمبر کی نافرمانی کریگا تو
ایسوں کیلئے جہنم کی آگ ہے ہمیشہ ہمیشہ اس میں رہیں گے ﴿٢٣﴾
یہاں تک کہ جب یہ لوگ وہ (دن) دیکھ لینگے جسکا ان سے وعدہ کیا
جاتا ہے تب انکو معلوم ہو جائیگا کہ مددگار کس کے کمزور اور شمار کن کا تھوڑا ہے ﴿٢٤﴾
کہہ دو کہ جس (دن) کا تم سے وعدہ کیا جاتا ہے میں نہیں جانتا کہ وہ
(عن) قریب (آنیوالا) ہے یا میرے پروردگار نے اسکی مدت دراز کر دی ہے ﴿٢٥﴾
(وہی) غیب (کی بات) جاننے والا ہے اور کسی پر اپنے غیب کو
ظاہر نہیں کرتا ﴿٢٦﴾
ہاں جس پیغمبر کو پسند فرمائے تو اُس (کو غیب کی باتیں بتا دیتا

short (account) or of any injustice.

14. 'Amongst us are some that submit their wills (to Allah), and some that swerve from justice. Now those who submit their wills—they have sought out (the path) of right conduct:

15. 'But those who swerve,— they are (but) fuel for Hell-fire'—

16. (And Allah's Message is): "If they (the Pagans) had (only) remained on the (right) Way, We should certainly have bestowed on them Rain in abundance.

17. "That We might try them by that (means). But if any turns away from the remembrance of his Lord, He will cause him to undergo ever-growing Chastisement.

18. "And the places of worship are for Allah (alone): so invoke not anyone along with Allah;

19. "Yet when the Devotees of Allah stood up to invoke Him, they just make round him a dense crowd."

20. Say: "I do no more than invoke my Lord, and I join not with Him any (false god)."

21. Say: "It is not in my power to cause you harm, or to bring you to right conduct."

22. Say: "No one can deliver me from Allah (if I were to disobey Him), nor should I find refuge except in Him,

23. "Unless I deliver what I receive from Allah and His Messages: for any that disobey Allah and His Messenger,—for them is Hell: they shall dwell therein for ever."

24. At length, when they see (with their own eyes) that which they are promised,— then will they know who it is that is weakest in (his) helper and least important in point of numbers.

25. Say: "I know not whether the (Punishment) which ye are promised is near, or whether my Lord will appoint for it a distant term.

26. "He (alone) knows the Unseen, nor does He make anyone acquainted with His Secrets.—

27. "Except a messenger whom He has chosen: and then He makes

SÛRA–73
AL-MUZZAMMIL
(INTRODUCTION)

This is one of the earliest Sûras to have been revealed. The first was S. 96: 1-5 (*Iqraa*), in the fortieth year of the Prophet's life, say about 12 years before the Hijra. Then there was an interruption (*Fatra*), of which the duration cannot be exactly ascertained, as there was no external history connected with it. The usual estimate puts it at about six months, but it may have been a year or two years. The years were then counted by the lunisolar calendar: The second Sûra in chronological order was probably a great portion of S. 68 *(Qalam),* which came after the *Fatra* was over. About the same time came this Sûra (say third) and S. 74, which follows (say fourth), and the remainder of 96. We may roughly put the date of this Sûra at about 11 to 10 years before the Hijra.

The subject-matter is the significance of Prayer and Humility in spiritual life and the terrible fate of those who reject Faith and Revelation.

a band of watchers march before him and behind him,

28. "That He may know that they have (truly) brought and delivered the Messages of their Lord and He encompasses all that is with them, and takes account of every single thing."

Al-Muzzammil, or Folded in Garments

In the name of Allah, Most Gracious, Most Merciful.

1. O thou folded in garments !

2. Stand (to prayer) by night, but not all night—

3. Half of it,— or a little less,

4. Or a little more; and recite the Qur'ān in slow, measured rhythmic tones.

5. Soon shall We send down to thee a weighty Word.

6. Truly the rising by night is a time when impression is more keen and speech more certain.

7. True, there is for thee by day prolonged occupation with ordinary duties:

8. But keep in remembrance the name of thy Lord, and devote thyself to Him whole-heartedly.

9. (He is) Lord of the East and the West: there is no god but He: take Him therefore for (thy) Disposer of Affairs.

10. And have patience with what they say, and leave them with noble (dignity).

11. And leave Me (alone to deal with) those in possession of the good things of life (who (yet) deny the Truth;) and bear with them for a little while.

12. With Us are Fetters (to bind them), and a Fire (to burn them),

13. And a Food that chokes and a Chastisement Grievous.

14. The Day the earth and the mountains will be in violent commotion. And the mountains will be as a heap of sand poured out and flowing down.

15. We have sent to you, (O men!) a Messenger, to be a witness concerning you even as We sent a messenger to Pharaoh.

اور اس) کے آگے اور پیچھے نگہبان مقرر کر دیتا ہے ﴿۲۷﴾
تاکہ معلوم فرمائے کہ انہوں نے اپنے پروردگار کے پیغام پہنچا دیئے
ہیں اور (یوں تو) اس نے ان کی سب چیزوں کو ہر طرف سے
قابو کر رکھا ہے اور ایک ایک چیز گن رکھی ہے ﴿۲۸﴾

سورۂ مزمل مکی ہے اس میں بیس آیتیں اور دو رکوع ہیں

شروع خدا کا نام لے کر جو بڑا مہربان نہایت رحم والا ہے
اے (محمدؐ) جو کپڑے میں لپٹ رہے ہو ﴿۱﴾
رات کو قیام کیا کرو مگر تھوڑی سی رات ﴿۲﴾
یعنی نصف رات یا اس سے کچھ کم ﴿۳﴾
یا کچھ زیادہ اور قرآن کو ٹھہر ٹھہر کر پڑھا کرو ﴿۴﴾
ہم عنقریب تم پر ایک بھاری فرمان نازل کریں گے ﴿۵﴾
کچھ شک نہیں کہ رات کا اٹھنا نفس بہیمی کو سخت پامال
کرتا ہے اور اس وقت ذکر بھی خوب درست ہوتا ہے ﴿۶﴾
دن کے وقت تو تمہیں اور بہت سے شغل ہوتے ہیں ﴿۷﴾
تو اپنے پروردگار کے نام کا ذکر کرو اور ہر طرف سے بےتعلق ہو کر اسی کی طرف متوجہ ہو جاؤ ﴿۸﴾
(وہی) مشرق اور مغرب کا مالک (ہے اور) اس کے سوا کوئی
معبود نہیں تو اسی کو اپنا کارساز بناؤ ﴿۹﴾
اور جو جو (دل آزار) باتیں یہ لوگ کہتے ہیں ان کو سہتے رہو
اور اچھے طریق سے ان سے کنارہ کش رہو ﴿۱۰﴾
اور مجھے ان جھٹلانے والوں سے جو دولتمند ہیں سمجھ لینے دو
اور ان کو تھوڑی سی مہلت دے دو ﴿۱۱﴾
کچھ شک نہیں کہ ہمارے پاس بیڑیاں ہیں اور بھڑکتی آگ ہے ﴿۱۲﴾
اور گلوگیر کھانا ہے اور درد دینے والا عذاب ہے ﴿۱۳﴾
جس دن زمین اور پہاڑ کانپنے لگیں اور پہاڑ (ایسے بھربھرے
گویا) ریت کے ٹیلے ہو جائیں ﴿۱۴﴾
(اے اہل مکہ) جس طرح ہم نے فرعون کے پاس (موسیٰ کو) پیغمبر (بنا کر) بھیجا تھا
(اسی طرح) تمہارے پاس بھی (محمدؐ) رسول بھیجے ہیں جو تمہارے مقابلے میں گواہ ہوں گے ﴿۱۵﴾

مِنۢ بَيۡنِ يَدَيۡهِ وَمِنۡ خَلۡفِهٖ رَصَدًا ﴿٢٧﴾
لِّيَعۡلَمَ اَنۡ قَدۡ اَبۡلَغُوۡا رِسٰلٰتِ رَبِّهِمۡ وَ
اَحَاطَ بِمَا لَدَيۡهِمۡ وَاَحۡصٰى كُلَّ شَىۡءٍ
عَدَدًا ﴿٢٨﴾ ع ٩ ١٢

سُوۡرَةُ الۡمُزَّمِّلِ مَكِّيَّةٌ وَهِىَ عِشۡرُوۡنَ اٰيَةً وَّفِيۡهَا رُكُوۡعَانِ

بِسۡمِ اللّٰهِ الرَّحۡمٰنِ الرَّحِيۡمِ
يٰۤاَيُّهَا الۡمُزَّمِّلُ ﴿١﴾
قُمِ الَّيۡلَ اِلَّا قَلِيۡلًا ﴿٢﴾
نِّصۡفَهٗۤ اَوِ انۡقُصۡ مِنۡهُ قَلِيۡلًا ﴿٣﴾
اَوۡ زِدۡ عَلَيۡهِ وَرَتِّلِ الۡقُرۡاٰنَ تَرۡتِيۡلًا ﴿٤﴾
اِنَّا سَنُلۡقِىۡ عَلَيۡكَ قَوۡلًا ثَقِيۡلًا ﴿٥﴾
اِنَّ نَاشِئَةَ الَّيۡلِ هِىَ اَشَدُّ وَطۡاً وَّاَقۡوَمُ
قِيۡلًا ﴿٦﴾
اِنَّ لَكَ فِى النَّهَارِ سَبۡحًا طَوِيۡلًا ﴿٧﴾
وَاذۡكُرِ اسۡمَ رَبِّكَ وَتَبَتَّلۡ اِلَيۡهِ تَبۡتِيۡلًا ﴿٨﴾
رَبُّ الۡمَشۡرِقِ وَالۡمَغۡرِبِ لَاۤ اِلٰهَ اِلَّا هُوَ
فَاتَّخِذۡهُ وَكِيۡلًا ﴿٩﴾
وَاصۡبِرۡ عَلٰى مَا يَقُوۡلُوۡنَ وَاهۡجُرۡهُمۡ هَجۡرًا
جَمِيۡلًا ﴿١٠﴾
وَذَرۡنِىۡ وَالۡمُكَذِّبِيۡنَ اُولِى النَّعۡمَةِ وَ
مَهِّلۡهُمۡ قَلِيۡلًا ﴿١١﴾
اِنَّ لَدَيۡنَاۤ اَنۡكَالًا وَّجَحِيۡمًا ﴿١٢﴾
وَّطَعَامًا ذَا غُصَّةٍ وَّعَذَابًا اَلِيۡمًا ﴿١٣﴾
يَوۡمَ تَرۡجُفُ الۡاَرۡضُ وَالۡجِبَالُ وَكَانَتِ
الۡجِبَالُ كَثِيۡبًا مَّهِيۡلًا ﴿١٤﴾
اِنَّاۤ اَرۡسَلۡنَاۤ اِلَيۡكُمۡ رَسُوۡلًا شَاهِدًا عَلَيۡكُمۡ
كَمَاۤ اَرۡسَلۡنَاۤ اِلٰى فِرۡعَوۡنَ رَسُوۡلًا ﴿١٥﴾

SÛRA–74

AL-MUDDATHTHIR

(INTRODUCTION)

This Sûra dates from about the same time as the last one. Its subject-matter is also similar: Prayer, and Praise, and the need of patience in a period of great spiritual stress; the unjust who cause sorrow and suffering now will themselves experience agony in the Hereafter.

16. But Pharaoh disobeyed the messenger; so We seized him with a heavy Punishment.

17. Then how shall ye, if ye deny (Allah), guard yourselves against a Day that will make children hoary-headed?—
18. Whereon the sky will be cleft asunder? His Promise needs must be accomplished.
19. Verily this is an Admonition: therefore, whoso will, let him take a (straight) path to his Lord!

20. Thy Lord doth know that thou standest forth (to prayer) nigh two-thirds of the night, or half the night, or a third of the night, and so doth a party of those with thee. But Allah doth appoint Night and Day in due measure. He knoweth that ye are unable to keep count thereof. So He hath turned to you (in mercy): read ye, therefore, of the Qur'ãn as much as may be easy for you. He knoweth that there may be (some) among you in ill-health; others travelling through the land, seeking of Allah's bounty; yet others fighting in Allah's Cause. Read ye, therefore, as much of the Qur'ãn as may be easy (for you); and establish regular Prayer and give zakat; and loan to Allah a Beautiful Loan. And whatever good ye send forth for yourselves, ye shall find it with Allah. Yea, better and greater, in Reward, and seek ye the Grace of Allah: for Allah is Oft-Forgiving, Most Merciful.

Al-Muddaththir, or One Wrapped Up.

In the name of Allah, Most Gracious, Most Merciful.
1. O thou wrapped up (in a mantle)!
2. Arise and deliver thy warning!
3. And thy Lord do thou magnify!
4. And thy garments keep free from stain!
5. And all abomination shun!

سو فرعون نے (ہمارے) پیغمبر کا کہنا نہ مانا تو ہم نے اُس کو
بڑے وبال میں پکڑ لیا ﴿١٦﴾
اگر تم بھی (اُن پیغمبر کو) نہ مانو گے تو اُس دن سے کیونکر بچو گے
جو بچوں کو بوڑھا کر دے گا ﴿١٧﴾
(اور) جس سے آسمان پھٹ جائیگا۔ یہ اسکا وعدہ (پورا) ہو کر رہیگا ﴿١٨﴾
یہ (قرآن) تو نصیحت ہے۔ سو جو چاہے اپنے پروردگار تک
(پہنچنے کا) راستہ اختیار کرے ﴿١٩﴾
تمہارا پروردگار خوب جانتا ہے کہ تم اور تمہارے ساتھ کے لوگ (کبھی)
دو تہائی رات کے قریب اور (کبھی) آدھی رات اور (کبھی) تہائی
رات قیام کیا کرتے ہو۔ اور خدا تو رات اور دن کا اندازہ رکھتا ہے۔
اُس نے معلوم کیا کہ تم اس کو نباہ نہ سکو گے تو اُس نے تم پر مہربانی
کی پس جتنا آسانی سے ہو سکے (اتنا) قرآن پڑھ لیا کرو۔ اُس نے
جانا کہ تم میں بعض بیمار بھی ہوتے ہیں اور بعض خدا کے فضل (یعنی
معاش) کی تلاش میں ملک میں سفر کرتے ہیں اور بعض خدا کی
راہ میں لڑتے ہیں۔ تو جتنا آسانی سے ہو سکے اتنا پڑھ لیا کرو
اور نماز پڑھتے رہو اور زکوٰۃ ادا کرتے رہو اور خدا کو
نیک (اور خلوص نیت سے) قرض دیتے رہو۔ اور جو
عمل نیک تم اپنے لئے آگے بھیجو گے اس کو خدا کے ہاں بہتر
اور صلے میں بزرگ تر پاؤ گے۔ اور خدا سے بخشش مانگتے رہو۔
بیشک خدا بخشنے والا مہربان ہے ﴿٢٠﴾

سورۂ مدثر مکی ہے اس میں چھپن آیتیں اور دو رکوع ہیں

شروع خدا کا نام لے کر جو بڑا مہربان نہایت رحم والا ہے
اے (محمدؐ) جو کپڑا لپیٹے پڑے ہو ﴿١﴾
اٹھو اور ہدایت کرو ﴿٢﴾
اور اپنے پروردگار کی بڑائی کرو ﴿٣﴾
اور اپنے کپڑوں کو پاک رکھو ﴿٤﴾
اور ناپاکی سے دور رہو ﴿٥﴾

فَعَصٰى فِرْعَوْنُ الرَّسُوْلَ فَاَخَذْنٰهُ اَخْذًا
وَّبِيْلًا ﴿١٦﴾
فَكَيْفَ تَتَّقُوْنَ اِنْ كَفَرْتُمْ يَوْمًا يَّجْعَلُ
الْوِلْدَانَ شِيْبًا ﴿١٧﴾
السَّمَآءُ مُنْفَطِرٌۢ بِهٖ ۭ كَانَ وَعْدُهٗ مَفْعُوْلًا ﴿١٨﴾
اِنَّ هٰذِهٖ تَذْكِرَةٌ ۚ فَمَنْ شَآءَ اتَّخَذَ اِلٰى
رَبِّهٖ سَبِيْلًا ﴿١٩﴾ ع
اِنَّ رَبَّكَ يَعْلَمُ اَنَّكَ تَقُوْمُ اَدْنٰى مِنْ ثُلُثَيِ
الَّيْلِ وَنِصْفَهٗ وَثُلُثَهٗ وَطَآىِٕفَةٌ مِّنَ
الَّذِيْنَ مَعَكَ ۭ وَاللّٰهُ يُقَدِّرُ الَّيْلَ وَ
النَّهَارَ ۭ عَلِمَ اَنْ لَّنْ تُحْصُوْهُ فَتَابَ عَلَيْكُمْ
فَاقْرَءُوْا مَا تَيَسَّرَ مِنَ الْقُرْاٰنِ ۭ عَلِمَ اَنْ
سَيَكُوْنُ مِنْكُمْ مَّرْضٰى ۙ وَاٰخَرُوْنَ يَضْرِبُوْنَ
فِي الْاَرْضِ يَبْتَغُوْنَ مِنْ فَضْلِ اللّٰهِ ۙ وَ
اٰخَرُوْنَ يُقَاتِلُوْنَ فِيْ سَبِيْلِ اللّٰهِ ڮ فَاقْرَءُوْا
مَا تَيَسَّرَ مِنْهُ ۙ وَاَقِيْمُوا الصَّلٰوةَ وَاٰتُوا الزَّكٰوةَ
وَاَقْرِضُوا اللّٰهَ قَرْضًا حَسَنًا ۭ وَمَا تُقَدِّمُوْا
لِاَنْفُسِكُمْ مِّنْ خَيْرٍ تَجِدُوْهُ عِنْدَ اللّٰهِ
هُوَ خَيْرًا وَّاَعْظَمَ اَجْرًا ۭ وَاسْتَغْفِرُوا
اللّٰهَ ۭ اِنَّ اللّٰهَ غَفُوْرٌ رَّحِيْمٌ ﴿٢٠﴾ ع

سُوْرَةُ الْمُدَّثِّرِ مَكِّيَّةٌ وَهِيَ سِتٌّ وَّخَمْسُوْنَ اٰيَةً وَّفِيْهَا رُكُوْعَانِ

بِسْمِ اللّٰهِ الرَّحْمٰنِ الرَّحِيْمِ
يٰٓاَيُّهَا الْمُدَّثِّرُ ﴿١﴾
قُمْ فَاَنْذِرْ ﴿٢﴾
وَرَبَّكَ فَكَبِّرْ ﴿٣﴾
وَثِيَابَكَ فَطَهِّرْ ﴿٤﴾
وَالرُّجْزَ فَاهْجُرْ ﴿٥﴾

6. Nor expect, in giving, any increase (for thyself) !
اور (اس نیت سے) احسان نہ کرو کہ اس سے زیادہ کے طالب ہو (٦)
ولا تمنن تستكثر (٦)

7. But, for thy Lord's (Cause) be patient and constant !
اور اپنے پروردگار کے لئے صبر کرو (٧)
ولربك فاصبر (٧)

8. Finally, when the Trumpet is sounded,
جب صور پھونکا جائے گا (٨)
فاذا نقر في الناقور (٨)

9. That will be—that Day— a Day of Distress—
وہ دن مشکل کا دن ہوگا (٩)
فذلك يومئذ يوم عسير (٩)

10. Far from easy for those without Faith.
(یعنی) کافروں پر آسان نہ ہوگا (١٠)
على الكفرين غير يسير (١٠)

11. Leave Me alone, (to deal) with the (creature) whom I created (bare and) alone !—
ہمیں اُس شخص سے سمجھ لینے دو جس کو ہم نے اکیلا پیدا کیا (١١)
ذرني ومن خلقت وحيدا (١١)

12. To whom I granted resources in abundance,
اور مال کثیر دیا (١٢)
وجعلت له مالا ممدودا (١٢)

13. And sons to be by his side !—
اور (ہر وقت) اسکے پاس حاضر رہنے والے بیٹے (دیئے) (١٣)
وبنين شهودا (١٣)

14. To whom I made (life) smooth and comfortable !
اور ہر طرح کے سامان میں وسعت دی (١٤)
ومهدت له تمهيدا (١٤)

15. Yet is he greedy— that I should add (yet more);
ابھی خواہش رکھتا ہے کہ اور زیادہ دیں (١٥)
ثم يطمع ان ازيد (١٥)

16. By no means ! for to Our Signs He has been refractory !
ایسا ہرگز نہیں ہوگا۔ یہ ہماری آیتوں کا دشمن رہا ہے (١٦)
كلا انه كان لايتنا عنيدا (١٦)

17. Soon will I visit him with a mount of calamities!
ہم اُسے صعود پر چڑھائیں گے (١٧)
سارهقه صعودا (١٧)

18. For he thought and he determined;—
اُس نے فکر کیا اور تجویز کی (١٨)
انه فكر وقدر (١٨)

19. And woe to him ! how he determined!—
یہ مارا جائے اُس نے کیسی تجویز کی (١٩)
فقتل كيف قدر (١٩)

20. Yea, woe to him: how he determined!—
پھر یہ مارا جائے اُس نے کیسی تجویز کی (٢٠)
ثم قتل كيف قدر (٢٠)

21. Then he reflected;
پھر تأمل کیا (٢١)
ثم نظر (٢١)

22. Then he frowned and he scowled;
پھر تیوری چڑھائی اور مُنہ بگاڑ لیا (٢٢)
ثم عبس وبسر (٢٢)

23. Then he turned back and was haughty;
پھر پُشت پھیر کر چلا اور (قبول حق سے) غرور کیا (٢٣)
ثم ادبر واستكبر (٢٣)

24. Then said he; "This is nothing but magic, derived from of old;
پھر کہنے لگا کہ یہ تو جادو ہے جو (اگلوں سے) منتقل ہوتا آیا ہے [۳۱۴] (٢٤)
فقال ان هذا الا سحر يؤثر (٢٤)

25. "This is nothing but the word of a mortal !"
(پھر بولا) یہ (خدا کا کلام نہیں بلکہ) بشر کا کلام ہے (٢٥)
ان هذا الا قول البشر (٢٥)

26. Soon will I cast him into Hell-Fire !
ہم عنقریب اُس کو سقر میں داخل کریں گے (٢٦)
ساصليه سقر (٢٦)

27. And what will explain to thee what Hell-Fire is?
اور تم کیا سمجھے کہ سقر کیا ہے؟ (٢٧)
وما ادرىك ما سقر (٢٧)

28. Naught doth it permit to endure, and naught doth it leave alone!—
(وہ آگ ہے کہ) نہ باقی رکھے گی اور نہ چھوڑے گی (٢٨)
لا تبقي ولا تذر (٢٨)

29. Darkening and changing the colour of man!
اور بدن کو جھلس کر سیاہ کر دے گی (٢٩)
لواحة للبشر (٢٩)

30. Over it are Nineteen.
اُس پر انیس داروغہ ہیں (٣٠)
عليها تسعة عشر (٣٠)

31. And We have set none but angels as guardians of the Fire; and We have fixed their number only as a trial for Unbelievers,—in order that the People of the Book may arrive
اور ہم نے دوزخ کے داروغہ فرشتے بنائے ہیں۔ اور اُن کا شمار
کافروں کی آزمائش کے لئے مقرر کیا ہے (اور) اسلئے کہ اہل کتاب
وما جعلنا اصحب النار الا ملئكة
وما جعلنا عدتهم الا فتنة للذين

at certainty, and the Believers may increase in Faith,—and that no doubts may be left for the People of the Book and the Believers, and that those in whose hearts is a disease and the Unbelievers may say, "What doth Allah intend by this?" Thus doth Allah leave to stray whom He pleaseth, and guide whom He pleaseth: and none can know the forces of thy Lord, except He, and this is no other than a Reminder to mankind.	یقین کریں اور مومنوں کا ایمان اور زیادہ ہو اور اہل کتاب اور مومن شک نہ لائیں۔ اور اس لئے کہ جن لوگوں کے دلوں میں (نفاق کا) مرض ہے اور (جو) کافر ہیں) کہیں کہ اس مثال (کے بیان کرنے) سے خدا کا مقصود کیا ہے؟ اسی طرح خدا جسکو چاہتا ہے گمراہ کرتا ہے اور جس کو چاہتا ہے ہدایت دیتا ہے۔ اور تمہارے پروردگار کے لشکروں کو اُسکے سوا کوئی نہیں جانتا۔ اور یہ تو بنی آدم کے لئے نصیحت ہے (۳۱)	كَفَرُوا لِيَسْتَيْقِنَ الَّذِينَ أُوتُوا الْكِتٰبَ وَيَزْدَادَ الَّذِينَ اٰمَنُوا إِيمَانًا وَلَا يَرْتَابَ الَّذِينَ أُوتُوا الْكِتٰبَ وَالْمُؤْمِنُونَ وَلِيَقُولَ الَّذِينَ فِي قُلُوبِهِمْ مَرَضٌ وَالْكٰفِرُونَ مَاذَا أَرَادَ اللّٰهُ بِهٰذَا مَثَلًا كَذٰلِكَ يُضِلُّ اللّٰهُ مَنْ يَشَاءُ وَيَهْدِي مَنْ يَشَاءُ وَمَا يَعْلَمُ جُنُودَ رَبِّكَ إِلَّا هُوَ وَمَا هِيَ إِلَّا ذِكْرٰى لِلْبَشَرِ (۳۱) ع ۱۵ / ۳۱
32. Nay, verily: by the Moon	ہاں (ہاں ہمیں) چاند کی قسم (۳۲)	كَلَّا وَالْقَمَرِ (۳۲)
33. And by the Night as it retreateth,	اور رات کی جب پیٹھ پھیرنے لگے (۳۳)	وَاللَّيْلِ إِذْ أَدْبَرَ (۳۳)
34. And by the Dawn as it shineth forth,—	اور صبح کی جب روشن ہو (۳۴)	وَالصُّبْحِ إِذَا أَسْفَرَ (۳۴)
35. This is but one of the mighty (Portents),	کہ وہ (آگ) ایک بہت بڑی (آفت) ہے (۳۵)	إِنَّهَا لَإِحْدَى الْكُبَرِ (۳۵)
36. A warning to mankind,—	(اور) بنی آدم کے لئے موجب خوف (۳۶)	نَذِيرًا لِلْبَشَرِ (۳۶)
37. To any of you that chooses to press forward, or to follow behind;—	جو تم میں سے آگے بڑھنا چاہے یا پیچھے رہنا چاہے (۳۷)	لِمَنْ شَاءَ مِنْكُمْ أَنْ يَتَقَدَّمَ أَوْ يَتَأَخَّرَ (۳۷)
38. Every soul will be (held) in pledge for its deeds.	ہر شخص اپنے اعمال کے بدلے گرو ہے (۳۸)	كُلُّ نَفْسٍ بِمَا كَسَبَتْ رَهِينَةٌ (۳۸)
39. Except the Companions of the Right Hand,	مگر داہنی طرف والے (نیک لوگ) (۳۹)	إِلَّا أَصْحٰبَ الْيَمِينِ (۳۹) مع
40. (They will be) in Gardens (of Delight): they will question each other,	(کہ) وہ باغہائے بہشت میں (ہونگے اور) پوچھتے ہونگے (۴۰)	فِي جَنّٰتٍ يَتَسَاءَلُونَ (۴۰)
41. And (ask) of the Sinners:	(یعنی آگ میں جلنے والے) گنہگاروں سے (۴۱)	عَنِ الْمُجْرِمِينَ (۴۱)
42. "What led you into Hell-Fire?"	کہ تم دوزخ میں کیوں پڑے؟ (۴۲)	مَا سَلَكَكُمْ فِي سَقَرَ (۴۲)
43. They will say: "We were not of those who prayed;	وہ جواب دیں گے کہ ہم نماز نہیں پڑھتے تھے (۴۳)	قَالُوا لَمْ نَكُ مِنَ الْمُصَلِّينَ (۴۳)
44. "Nor were we of those who fed the indigent;	اور نہ فقیروں کو کھانا کھلاتے تھے (۴۴)	وَلَمْ نَكُ نُطْعِمُ الْمِسْكِينَ (۴۴)
45. "But we used to talk vanities with vain talkers;	اور اہل باطل کے ساتھ مل کر (حق سے) انکار کرتے تھے (۴۵)	وَكُنَّا نَخُوضُ مَعَ الْخَائِضِينَ (۴۵)
46. "And we used to deny the Day of Judgment,	اور روزِ جزا کو جھٹلاتے تھے (۴۶)	وَكُنَّا نُكَذِّبُ بِيَوْمِ الدِّينِ (۴۶)
47. "Until there came to us (the Hour) that is certain."	یہاں تک کہ ہمیں موت آگئی (۴۷)	حَتّٰى أَتٰنَا الْيَقِينُ (۴۷)
48. Then will no intercession of (any) intercessors profit them.	تو (اس حال میں) سفارش کرنیوالوں کی سفارش اُنکے حق میں کچھ فائدہ نہ دیگی (۴۸)	فَمَا تَنْفَعُهُمْ شَفَاعَةُ الشّٰفِعِينَ (۴۸)
49. Then what is the matter with them that they turn away from admonition?—	اُن کو کیا ہوا ہے کہ نصیحت سے رُوگرداں ہو رہے ہیں (۴۹)	فَمَا لَهُمْ عَنِ التَّذْكِرَةِ مُعْرِضِينَ (۴۹)
50. As if they were affrighted asses,	گویا گدھے ہیں کہ بدک جاتے ہیں (۵۰)	كَأَنَّهُمْ حُمُرٌ مُسْتَنْفِرَةٌ (۵۰)
51. Fleeing from a lion !	(یعنی) شیر سے ڈر کر بھاگ جاتے ہیں (۵۱)	فَرَّتْ مِنْ قَسْوَرَةٍ (۵۱)

SÛRA–75
AL-QIYÃMAT
(INTRODUCTION)

This Sûra belongs to the early Makkan period, but comes chronologically a good deal later than the last two Sûras.

Its subject-matter is the Resurrection, viewed from the point of view of Man, especially unregenerate Man, as he is now, and as he will be then,—his inner and psychological history.

بَلْ يُرِيدُ كُلُّ امْرِئٍ مِّنْهُمْ أَنْ يُّؤْتٰى صُحُفًا مُّنَشَّرَةً ﴿٥٢﴾

اصل یہ ہے کہ اُن میں سے ہر شخص یہ چاہتا ہے کہ اُس کے پاس کُھلی ہوئی کتاب آئے ﴿٥٢﴾

52. Forsooth, each one of them wants to be given Scrolls (of revelation) spread out !

كَلَّا ۖ بَل لَّا يَخَافُونَ الْاٰخِرَةَ ﴿٥٣﴾

ایسا ہرگز نہیں ہوگا۔ حقیقت یہ ہے کہ انکو آخرت کا خوف ہی نہیں ﴿٥٣﴾

53. By no means ! But they fear not the Hereafter.

كَلَّا إِنَّهُ تَذْكِرَةٌ ﴿٥٤﴾

کچھ شک نہیں کہ یہ نصیحت ہے ﴿٥٤﴾

54. Nay, this surely is an admonition:

فَمَنْ شَاءَ ذَكَرَهُ ﴿٥٥﴾

تو جو چاہے اسے یاد رکھے ﴿٥٥﴾

55. Let any who will, keep it in remembrance !

وَمَا يَذْكُرُونَ إِلَّا أَن يَّشَاءَ اللّٰهُ ۚ هُوَ أَهْلُ التَّقْوٰى وَأَهْلُ الْمَغْفِرَةِ ﴿٥٦﴾

اور یاد بھی تبھی رکھیں گے جب خدا چاہے۔ وہی ڈرنے کے لائق اور بخشش کا مالک ہے ﴿٥٦﴾

56. But none will keep it in remembrance except as Allah wills: He is the Lord of Righteousness, and the Lord of Forgiveness.

Al-Qiyãmat, or the Resurrection

سُورَةُ الْقِيٰمَةِ مَكِّيَّةٌ وَّهِيَ أَرْبَعُونَ اٰيَةً وَّفِيهَا رُكُوعَانِ

سورۂ قیامہ مکی ہے اس میں چالیس آیتیں اور دو رکوع ہیں

بِسْمِ اللّٰهِ الرَّحْمٰنِ الرَّحِيمِ

شروع خدا کا نام لے کر جو بڑا مہربان نہایت رحم والا ہے

In the name of Allah, Most Gracious, Most Merciful.

لَا أُقْسِمُ بِيَوْمِ الْقِيٰمَةِ ﴿١﴾

ہم کو روزِ قیامت کی قسم ﴿١﴾

1. I do swear by the Resurrection Day;

وَلَا أُقْسِمُ بِالنَّفْسِ اللَّوَّامَةِ ﴿٢﴾

اور نفسِ لوّامہ کی (کہ سب لوگ اُٹھا کر کھڑے کئے جائیں گے) ﴿٢﴾

2. And I do swear by the self-reproaching soul.

أَيَحْسَبُ الْإِنْسَانُ أَلَّنْ نَّجْمَعَ عِظَامَهُ ﴿٣﴾

کیا انسان یہ خیال کرتا ہے کہ ہم اُسکی (بکھری ہوئی) ہڈیاں اکٹھی نہیں کرینگے؟ ﴿٣﴾

3. Does man think that We cannot assemble his bones ?

بَلٰى قٰدِرِينَ عَلٰى أَنْ نُّسَوِّيَ بَنَانَهُ ﴿٤﴾

ضرور کرینگے (اور) ہم اس بات پر قادر ہیں کہ اُسکی پور پور درست کر دیں ﴿٤﴾

4. Nay, We are able to put together in perfect order the very tips of his fingers.

بَلْ يُرِيدُ الْإِنْسَانُ لِيَفْجُرَ أَمَامَهُ ﴿٥﴾

مگر انسان چاہتا ہے کہ آگے کو خود سری کرتا جائے ﴿٥﴾

5. But man wishes to do wrong (even) in the time in front of him.

يَسْئَلُ أَيَّانَ يَوْمُ الْقِيٰمَةِ ﴿٦﴾

پُوچھتا ہے کہ قیامت کا دن کب ہوگا؟ ﴿٦﴾

6. He questions: "When is the Day of Resurrection ?"

فَإِذَا بَرِقَ الْبَصَرُ ﴿٧﴾

جب آنکھیں چُندھیا جائیں ﴿٧﴾

7. At length, when the Sight is dazed,

وَخَسَفَ الْقَمَرُ ﴿٨﴾

اور چاند گہنا جائے ﴿٨﴾

8. And the moon is buried in darkness.

وَجُمِعَ الشَّمْسُ وَالْقَمَرُ ﴿٩﴾

اور سُورج اور چاند جمع کر دیئے جائیں ﴿٩﴾

9. And the sun and moon are joined together,—

يَقُولُ الْإِنْسَانُ يَوْمَئِذٍ أَيْنَ الْمَفَرُّ ﴿١٠﴾

اُس دن انسان کہے گا کہ (اب) کہاں بھاگ جاؤں؟ ﴿١٠﴾

10. That Day will Man say: "Where is the refuge?"

كَلَّا لَا وَزَرَ ﴿١١﴾

بیشک کہیں پناہ نہیں ﴿١١﴾

11. By no means ! no place of safety !

إِلٰى رَبِّكَ يَوْمَئِذٍ الْمُسْتَقَرُّ ﴿١٢﴾

اُس روز پروردگار ہی کے پاس ٹھکانا ہے ﴿١٢﴾

12. Before thy Lord (alone), that Day will be the place of rest.

يُنَبَّؤُا الْإِنْسَانُ يَوْمَئِذٍ بِمَا قَدَّمَ وَأَخَّرَ ﴿١٣﴾

اُس دن انسان کو جو (عمل) اُس نے آگے بھیجے اور جو پیچھے چھوڑے ہونگے سب بتا دیئے جائینگے ﴿١٣﴾

13. That Day will Man be told (all) that he put forward, and all that he put back.

بَلِ الْإِنْسَانُ عَلٰى نَفْسِهِ بَصِيرَةٌ ﴿١٤﴾

بلکہ انسان آپ اپنا گواہ ہے ﴿١٤﴾

14. Nay, man will be evidence against himself,

وَّلَوْ أَلْقٰى مَعَاذِيرَهُ ﴿١٥﴾

اگرچہ عذر و معذرت کرتا رہے ﴿١٥﴾

15. Even though he were to put up his excuses.

لَا تُحَرِّكْ بِهِ لِسَانَكَ لِتَعْجَلَ بِهِ ﴿١٦﴾

اور (اے محمد) وحی کے پڑھنے کیلئے اپنی زبان نہ چلایا کرو کہ اسکو جلد یاد کرلو ﴿١٦﴾

16. Move not thy tongue concerning the (Qur-ãn) to make haste therewith.

إِنَّ عَلَيْنَا جَمْعَهُ وَقُرْاٰنَهُ ﴿١٧﴾

اس کا جمع کرنا اور پڑھانا ہمارے ذمّے ہے ﴿١٧﴾

17. It is for Us to collect it and to recite it:

فَإِذَا قَرَأْنٰهُ فَاتَّبِعْ قُرْاٰنَهُ ﴿١٨﴾

جب ہم وحی پڑھا کریں تو تم (اسکو سنا کرو اور) پھر اسی طرح پڑھا کرو ﴿١٨﴾

18. But when We have recited it, follow thou its recital (as promulgated):

SÛRA–76

AL-INSÃN OR AD-DAHR

(INTRODUCTION)

The revelation of this Sûra was probably in the early Makkan period, with the possible exception of some veres, but its date has no significance.

Its theme is the contrast between the two classes of men, those who choose good and those who choose evil, with special reference to the former.

The title of the Sûra recalls a Pagan Arab idea, which personified Time as existing spontaneously from eternity to enternity and responsible for the misery or the happiness of mankind. In 45: 24 we read: "They say,... 'nothing but Time can destroy us.'" This attitude is of course wrong. Time is a created thing: it has its mysteries, but it is no more eternal than matter. It is also relative to our conceptions and not absolute, as Einstein has proved. It is only Allah Who is Self-Subsisting, Eternal from the beginning and Eternal to the end, the absolute Existence and Reality. We must not transfer His attributes to any figments of our imagination.

This deification of Time (*Dahr*) as against a living personal Allah has given rise to the term *dahrîya,* as applied to an atheist or a materialist.

The whole of the Sûra is full of the highest symbolism, as is generally the case with Makkan Sûras, and this should always by remembered in their interpretation.

19. Nay more, it is for Us to explain it (and make it clear):
ثُمَّ إِنَّ عَلَيْنَا بَيَانَهُ ﴿١٩﴾
پھر اس (کے معانی) کا بیان بھی ہمارے ذمے ہے ﴿١٩﴾

20. Nay, (ye men !) but ye love the fleeting life,
كَلَّا بَلْ تُحِبُّونَ الْعَاجِلَةَ ﴿٢٠﴾
مگر (لوگو) تم دنیا کو دوست رکھتے ہو ﴿٢٠﴾

21. And leave alone the Hereafter.
وَتَذَرُونَ الْآخِرَةَ ﴿٢١﴾
اور آخرت کو ترک کئے دیتے ہو ﴿٢١﴾

22. Some faces, that Day, will beam (in brightnesss and beauty);—
وُجُوهٌ يَوْمَئِذٍ نَاضِرَةٌ ﴿٢٢﴾
اس روز بہت سے منہ رونق دار ہوں گے ﴿٢٢﴾

23. Looking towards their Lord;
إِلَىٰ رَبِّهَا نَاظِرَةٌ ﴿٢٣﴾
(اور) اپنے پروردگار کے محو دیدار ہوں گے ﴿٢٣﴾

24. And some faces, that Day, will be sad and dismal,
وَوُجُوهٌ يَوْمَئِذٍ بَاسِرَةٌ ﴿٢٤﴾
اور بہت سے منہ اس دن اداس ہوں گے ﴿٢٤﴾

25. In the thought that some back-breaking calamity was about to be inflicted on them;
تَظُنُّ أَنْ يُفْعَلَ بِهَا فَاقِرَةٌ ﴿٢٥﴾
خیال کریں گے کہ ان پر مصیبت واقع ہونے کو ہے ﴿٢٥﴾

26. Yea, when (the soul) reaches to the collar-bone (in its exit),
كَلَّا إِذَا بَلَغَتِ التَّرَاقِيَ ﴿٢٦﴾
دیکھو جب جان گلے تک پہنچ جائے ﴿٢٦﴾

27. And there will be a cry, "Who is an enchanter (to restore him)?
وَقِيلَ مَنْ ۜ رَاقٍ ﴿٢٧﴾
اور لوگ کہنے لگیں (اس وقت) کون جھاڑ پھونک کرنے والا ہے ﴿٢٧﴾

28. And he will think that it was (the time) of Parting;
وَظَنَّ أَنَّهُ الْفِرَاقُ ﴿٢٨﴾
اور اس (جاں بلب) نے سمجھا کہ اب سب سے جدائی ہے ﴿٢٨﴾

29. And one leg will be joined with another:
وَالْتَفَّتِ السَّاقُ بِالسَّاقِ ﴿٢٩﴾
اور پنڈلی سے پنڈلی لپٹ جائے ﴿٢٩﴾

30. That Day the Drive will be (all) to thy Lord !
إِلَىٰ رَبِّكَ يَوْمَئِذٍ الْمَسَاقُ ﴿٣٠﴾ ع
اس دن تجھ کو اپنے پروردگار کی طرف چلنا ہے ﴿٣٠﴾

31. So he gave nothing in charity, nor did he pray!—
فَلَا صَدَّقَ وَلَا صَلَّىٰ ﴿٣١﴾
تو اس (عاقبت نااندیش) نے نہ تو (کلام خدا کی) تصدیق کی نہ نماز پڑھی ﴿٣١﴾

32. But on the contrary, he rejected Truth and turned away !
وَلَٰكِنْ كَذَّبَ وَتَوَلَّىٰ ﴿٣٢﴾
بلکہ جھٹلایا اور منہ پھیر لیا ﴿٣٢﴾

33. Then did he stalk to his family in full conceit!
ثُمَّ ذَهَبَ إِلَىٰ أَهْلِهِ يَتَمَطَّىٰ ﴿٣٣﴾
پھر اپنے گھر والوں کے پاس اکڑتا ہوا چل دیا ﴿٣٣﴾

34. Woe to thee, (O man !), yea, woe !
أَوْلَىٰ لَكَ فَأَوْلَىٰ ﴿٣٤﴾
افسوس ہے تجھ پر پھر افسوس ہے ﴿٣٤﴾

35. Again, woe to thee, (O man!), yea, woe !
ثُمَّ أَوْلَىٰ لَكَ فَأَوْلَىٰ ﴿٣٥﴾
پھر افسوس ہے تجھ پر پھر افسوس ہے ﴿٣٥﴾

36. Does Man think that he will be left uncontrolled, (without purpose) ?
أَيَحْسَبُ الْإِنْسَانُ أَنْ يُتْرَكَ سُدًى ﴿٣٦﴾
کیا انسان خیال کرتا ہے کہ یونہی چھوڑ دیا جائے گا؟ ﴿٣٦﴾

37. Was he not a drop of sperm emitted (in lowly form) ?
أَلَمْ يَكُ نُطْفَةً مِنْ مَنِيٍّ يُمْنَىٰ ﴿٣٧﴾
کیا وہ منی کا جو رحم میں ڈالی جاتی ہے ایک قطرہ نہ تھا؟ ﴿٣٧﴾

38. Then did he become a leach-like clot; then did (Allah) make and fashion (him) in due proportion.
ثُمَّ كَانَ عَلَقَةً فَخَلَقَ فَسَوَّىٰ ﴿٣٨﴾
پھر لوتھڑا ہوا پھر (خدا نے) اسکو بنایا پھر اسکے اعضا کو درست کیا ﴿٣٨﴾

39. And of him He made two sexes, male and female.
فَجَعَلَ مِنْهُ الزَّوْجَيْنِ الذَّكَرَ وَالْأُنْثَىٰ ﴿٣٩﴾
پھر اس کی دو قسمیں بنائیں (ایک) مرد اور (ایک) عورت ﴿٣٩﴾

40. Has not He, (the same), the power to give life to the dead ?
أَلَيْسَ ذَٰلِكَ بِقَادِرٍ عَلَىٰ أَنْ يُحْيِيَ الْمَوْتَىٰ ﴿٤٠﴾ ع
کیا اسکو اس بات پر قدرت نہیں کہ مردوں کو جلا اٹھائے ﴿٤٠﴾

Ad-Dahr, or Time or Insãn, or Man

سُورَةُ الدَّهْرِ مَكِّيَّةٌ وَهِيَ إِحْدَى وَثَلٰثُونَ آيَةً وَفِيهَا رُكُوعَانِ

سورۂ دہر مکی ہے اس میں اکتیس آیتیں اور دو رکوع ہیں

In the name of Allah, Most Gracious, Most Merciful.
بِسْمِ اللَّهِ الرَّحْمَٰنِ الرَّحِيمِ
شروع خدا کا نام لے کر جو بڑا مہربان نہایت رحم والا ہے

1. Has there not been over Man a long period of Time, when he was nothing—(not even) mentioned—?
هَلْ أَتَىٰ عَلَى الْإِنْسَانِ حِينٌ مِنَ الدَّهْرِ لَمْ يَكُنْ شَيْئًا مَذْكُورًا ﴿١﴾
بے شک انسان پر زمانے میں ایک ایسا وقت بھی آچکا ہے کہ وہ کوئی چیز قابل ذکر نہ تھا ﴿١﴾

2. Verily We created man from a drop of mingled sperm, in order
إِنَّا خَلَقْنَا الْإِنْسَانَ مِنْ نُطْفَةٍ أَمْشَاجٍ
ہم نے انسان کو نطفۂ مخلوط سے پیدا کیا تاکہ اسے آزمائیں

to try him: so We gave him (the gifts), of Hearing and Sight.

3. We showed him the Way: whether he be grateful or ungrateful.

4. For the Rejecters We have prepared Chains, Yokes, and a Blazing Fire.

5. As to the Righteous, they shall drink of a Cup mixed with *Kāfūr*,—

6. A Fountain where the Devotees of Allah do drink, making it flow in unstinted abundance.

7. They perform (their) vows, and they fear a Day whose evil flies far and wide.

8. And they feed, for the love of Allah, the indigent, the orphan, and the captive,—

9. (Saying), "We feed you for the sake of Allah alone: no reward do we desire from you, nor thanks.

10. "We only fear a Day of frowning and distress from the side of our Lord".

11. But Allah will deliver them from the evil of that Day, and will shed over them brightness and a (blissful) Joy.

12. And because they were Patient and constant, He will reward them with a Garden and (garments of) silk.

13. Reclining in the (Garden) on raised couches, they will see there neither the sun's (excessive heat) nor excessive cold.

14. And the shades of the (Garden) will come low over them, and the bunches (of fruit), there, will hang low easy to reach.

15. And amongst them will be passed round vessels of silver and goblets of crystal,—

16. Crystal-clear, made of silver: they will determine the measure thereof (according to their wishes).

تو ہم نے اُس کو سنتا دیکھتا بنایا ﴿۲﴾
(اور) اُسے رستہ بھی دکھا دیا. (اب وہ) خواہ شکرگزار ہو
خواہ ناشکرا ﴿۳﴾
ہم نے کافروں کے لئے زنجیریں اور طوق اور دہکتی آگ
تیار کر رکھی ہے ﴿۴﴾
جو نیکوکار ہیں وہ ایسی شراب نوش جان کریں گے جس میں
کافور کی آمیزش ہوگی ﴿۵﴾
یہ ایک چشمہ ہے جس میں سے خدا کے بندے پئیں گے اور
اس میں سے (چھوٹی چھوٹی) نہریں نکال لیں گے ﴿۶﴾
یہ لوگ نذریں پوری کرتے ہیں اور اُس دن سے جس کی سختی
پھیل رہی ہوگی خوف رکھتے ہیں ﴿۷﴾
اور باوجودیکہ اُن کو خود طعام کی خواہش (اور حاجت) ہے
فقیروں اور یتیموں اور قیدیوں کو کھلاتے ہیں ﴿۸﴾
(اور کہتے ہیں کہ) ہم تم کو خالص خدا کے لئے کھلاتے ہیں نہ تم
سے عوض کے خواستگار ہیں نہ شکرگزاری کے (طلب گار) ﴿۹﴾
ہم کو اپنے پروردگار سے اس دن کا ڈر لگتا ہے جو (چہروں کو)
کریہ المنظر اور (دلوں کو) سخت (مضطر کر دینے والا) ہے ﴿۱۰﴾
تو خدا اُن کو اُس دن کی سختی سے بچالے گا. اور تازگی اور
خوش دلی عنایت فرمائے گا ﴿۱۱﴾
اور اُنکے صبر کے بدلے اُنکو بہشت (کے باغات) اور ریشم (کے ملبوسات) عطا کریگا ﴿۱۲﴾
اُن میں وہ تختوں پر تکئے لگائے بیٹھے ہونگے. وہاں نہ دُھوپ
(کی حدت) دیکھیں گے نہ سردی کی شدت ﴿۱۳﴾
اُن سے (ثمردار شاخیں اور) اُنکے سائے قریب ہوں گے. اور
میووں کے گچھے جھکے ہوئے لٹک رہے ہوں گے ﴿۱۴﴾
(خدام) چاندی کے باسن لئے ہوئے اُن کے اردگرد پھریں گے
اور شیشے کے (نہایت شفاف) گلاس ﴿۱۵﴾
اور شیشے بھی چاندی کے جو ٹھیک اندازے کے مطابق بنائے گئے ہیں ﴿۱۶﴾

نَّبْتَلِيهِ فَجَعَلْنٰهُ سَمِيعًا بَصِيرًا ﴿٢﴾
إِنَّا هَدَيْنٰهُ السَّبِيلَ إِمَّا شَاكِرًا وَإِمَّا
كَفُورًا ﴿٣﴾
إِنَّآ أَعْتَدْنَا لِلْكٰفِرِينَ سَلٰسِلَا۟ وَأَغْلٰلًا
وَسَعِيرًا ﴿٤﴾
إِنَّ الْأَبْرَارَ يَشْرَبُونَ مِن كَأْسٍ كَانَ
مِزَاجُهَا كَافُورًا ﴿٥﴾
عَيْنًا يَشْرَبُ بِهَا عِبَادُ اللّٰهِ يُفَجِّرُونَهَا
تَفْجِيرًا ﴿٦﴾
يُوفُونَ بِالنَّذْرِ وَيَخَافُونَ يَوْمًا كَانَ
شَرُّهُۥ مُسْتَطِيرًا ﴿٧﴾
وَيُطْعِمُونَ الطَّعَامَ عَلٰى حُبِّهِۦ مِسْكِينًا
وَيَتِيمًا وَأَسِيرًا ﴿٨﴾
إِنَّمَا نُطْعِمُكُمْ لِوَجْهِ اللّٰهِ لَا نُرِيدُ مِنكُمْ
جَزَآءً وَلَا شُكُورًا ﴿٩﴾
إِنَّا نَخَافُ مِن رَّبِّنَا يَوْمًا عَبُوسًا
قَمْطَرِيرًا ﴿١٠﴾
فَوَقٰىهُمُ اللّٰهُ شَرَّ ذٰلِكَ الْيَوْمِ وَلَقّٰىهُمْ
نَضْرَةً وَسُرُورًا ﴿١١﴾
وَجَزٰىهُم بِمَا صَبَرُوا جَنَّةً وَحَرِيرًا ﴿١٢﴾
مُّتَّكِـِٔينَ فِيهَا عَلَى الْأَرَآئِكِ ۚ لَا يَرَوْنَ
فِيهَا شَمْسًا وَلَا زَمْهَرِيرًا ﴿١٣﴾
وَدَانِيَةً عَلَيْهِمْ ظِلٰلُهَا وَذُلِّلَتْ قُطُوفُهَا
تَذْلِيلًا ﴿١٤﴾
وَيُطَافُ عَلَيْهِم بِـَٔانِيَةٍ مِّن فِضَّةٍ وَ
أَكْوَابٍ كَانَتْ قَوَارِيرَا۠ ﴿١٥﴾
قَوَارِيرَا۟ مِن فِضَّةٍ قَدَّرُوهَا تَقْدِيرًا ﴿١٦﴾

17. And they will be given to drink there of a Cup mixed with Zanjabîl,—

اور وہاں اُن کو ایسی شراب (بھی) پلائی جائے گی جس میں سونٹھ
کی آمیزش ہوگی ﴿١٧﴾

وَيُسْقَوْنَ فِيهَا كَأْسًا كَانَ مِزَاجُهَا
زَنْجَبِيلًا ﴿١٧﴾

18. A fountain there, called Salsabîl.

یہ بہشت میں ایک چشمہ ہے جس کا نام سلسبیل ہے ﴿١٨﴾

عَيْنًا فِيهَا تُسَمّٰى سَلْسَبِيلًا ﴿١٨﴾

19. And round about them will (serve) youths of perpetual (freshness): if thou seest them, thou wouldst think them scattered Pearls.

اور اُن کے پاس لڑکے آتے جاتے ہوں گے جو ہمیشہ ایک ہی حالت پر
رہیں گے جب تم اُن پر نگاہ ڈالو تو خیال کرو کہ بکھرے ہوئے موتی ہیں ﴿١٩﴾

وَيَطُوفُ عَلَيْهِمْ وِلْدَانٌ مُّخَلَّدُونَ إِذَا
رَأَيْتَهُمْ حَسِبْتَهُمْ لُؤْلُؤًا مَّنْثُورًا ﴿١٩﴾

20. And when thou lookest, it is there thou wilt see a Bliss and a Realm Magnificent.

اور بہشت میں (جہاں) آنکھ اٹھاؤ گے کثرت سے نعمت اور
عظیم (الشان) سلطنت دیکھو گے ﴿٢٠﴾

وَإِذَا رَأَيْتَ ثَمَّ رَأَيْتَ نَعِيمًا وَّمُلْكًا
كَبِيرًا ﴿٢٠﴾

21. Upon them will be Green Garments of fine silk and heavy brocade, and they will be adorned with Bracelets of silver; and their Lord will give to them to drink a pure drink.

اُن (کے بدنوں) پر دیبائے سبز اور اطلس کے کپڑے ہوں گے۔
اور اُنہیں چاندی کے کنگن پہنائے جائیں گے۔ اور اُن کا
پروردگار اُن کو نہایت پاکیزہ شراب پلائے گا ﴿٢١﴾

عٰلِيَهُمْ ثِيَابُ سُنْدُسٍ خُضْرٌ وَّإِسْتَبْرَقٌ
وَّحُلُّوا أَسَاوِرَ مِنْ فِضَّةٍ وَسَقٰهُمْ
رَبُّهُمْ شَرَابًا طَهُورًا ﴿٢١﴾

22. "Verily this is a Reward for you, and your Endeavour is accepted and recognised."

یہ تمہارا صلہ ہے اور تمہاری کوشش (خدا کے ہاں)
مقبول ہوئی ﴿٢٢﴾

إِنَّ هٰذَا كَانَ لَكُمْ جَزَآءً وَّكَانَ
سَعْيُكُمْ مَّشْكُورًا ﴿٢٢﴾ ع ٢٢

23. It is We Who have sent down the Qur'ãn to thee by stages.

(اے محمدؐ) ہم نے تم پر قرآن آہستہ آہستہ نازل کیا ہے ﴿٢٣﴾

إِنَّا نَحْنُ نَزَّلْنَا عَلَيْكَ الْقُرْاٰنَ تَنْزِيلًا ﴿٢٣﴾

24. Therefore be patient with constancy to the Command of thy Lord, and obey not to the sinner or the ingrate among them.

تو اپنے پروردگار کے حکم کے مطابق صبر کئے رہو۔ اور اُن لوگوں
میں سے کسی بدعمل اور ناشکرے کا کہنا نہ مانو ﴿٢٤﴾

فَاصْبِرْ لِحُكْمِ رَبِّكَ وَلَا تُطِعْ مِنْهُمْ
اٰثِمًا أَوْ كَفُورًا ﴿٢٤﴾

25. And celebrate the name of thy Lord morning and evening,

اور صبح وشام اپنے پروردگار کا نام لیتے رہو ﴿٢٥﴾

وَاذْكُرِ اسْمَ رَبِّكَ بُكْرَةً وَّأَصِيلًا ﴿٢٥﴾

26. And part of the night, prostrate thyself to Him; and glorify Him a long night through.

اور رات کو بڑی رات تک اُس کے آگے سجدے کرو اور
اُس کی پاکی بیان کرتے رہو ﴿٢٦﴾

وَمِنَ اللَّيْلِ فَاسْجُدْ لَهُ وَسَبِّحْهُ لَيْلًا
طَوِيلًا ﴿٢٦﴾

27. As to these, they love the fleeting life, and put away behind them a Day (that will be) hard.

یہ لوگ دنیا کو دوست رکھتے ہیں اور (قیامت کے) بھاری
دن کو پس پُشت چھوڑے دیتے ہیں ﴿٢٧﴾

إِنَّ هٰؤُلَآءِ يُحِبُّونَ الْعَاجِلَةَ وَيَذَرُونَ
وَرَآءَهُمْ يَوْمًا ثَقِيلًا ﴿٢٧﴾

28. It is We Who created them, and We have made their frame strong; but, when We will, We shall exchange their likes.

ہم نے اُن کو پیدا کیا اور اُن کے مفاصل کو مضبوط بنایا۔
اور اگر ہم چاہیں تو اُن کے بدلے اُنہی کی طرح اور لوگ لے آئیں ﴿٢٨﴾

نَحْنُ خَلَقْنٰهُمْ وَشَدَدْنَا أَسْرَهُمْ وَإِذَا
شِئْنَا بَدَّلْنَا أَمْثَالَهُمْ تَبْدِيلًا ﴿٢٨﴾

29. This is an admonition: whosoever will, let him take a (straight) Path to his Lord.

یہ تو نصیحت ہے۔ جو چاہے اپنے پروردگار کی طرف پہنچنے
کا رستہ اختیار کرے ﴿٢٩﴾

إِنَّ هٰذِهٖ تَذْكِرَةٌ فَمَنْ شَآءَ اتَّخَذَ
إِلٰى رَبِّهٖ سَبِيلًا ﴿٢٩﴾

30. But ye will not, except as Allah wills; for Allah is full of Knowledge and Wisdom.

اور تم کچھ بھی نہیں چاہ سکتے مگر جو خدا کو منظور ہو۔
بے شک خدا جاننے والا حکمت والا ہے ﴿٣٠﴾

وَمَا تَشَآءُونَ إِلَّآ أَنْ يَّشَآءَ اللّٰهُ إِنَّ
اللّٰهَ كَانَ عَلِيمًا حَكِيمًا ﴿٣٠﴾

31. He will admit to His Mercy Whom He will; but the wrong-

جس کو چاہتا ہے اپنی رحمت میں داخل کر لیتا ہے اور

يُدْخِلُ مَنْ يَّشَآءُ فِي رَحْمَتِهٖ وَ

SÛRA–77
AL-MURSALÃT
(INTRODUCTION)

This Sûra belongs to the early Makkan period, somewhere near to S. 75 (*Qiyãmat*). The theme is somewhat similar. It denounces the horrors of the Hereafter, for those who rejected Truth. The refrain, "Ah woe, that Day, to the Rejecters of Truth!" which occurs ten times in its fifty verses, or on an average, once in every five verses, indicates the *leitmotif.*

ع الظّٰلِمِيْنَ اَعَدَّ لَهُمْ عَذَابًا اَلِيْمًا ﴿٣١﴾

ظالموں کے لئے اس نے دکھ دینے والا عذاب تیار کر رکھا ہے ﴿٣١﴾

doers,— for them has He prepared a grievous Chastisement.

سُوْرَةُ الْمُرْسَلٰتِ مَكِّيَّةٌ وَّهِيَ خَمْسُوْنَ اٰيَةً وَّفِيْهَا رُكُوْعَانِ

سورۂ مرسلات مکی ہے اس میں پچاس آیتیں اور دو رکوع ہیں

Al-Mursalāt, or Those Sent Forth

بِسْمِ اللّٰهِ الرَّحْمٰنِ الرَّحِيْمِ

شروع خدا کا نام لے کر جو بڑا مہربان نہایت رحم والا ہے

In the name of Allah, Most Gracious, Most Merciful.

وَالْمُرْسَلٰتِ عُرْفًا ﴿١﴾

ہواؤں کی قسم جو نرم نرم چلتی ہیں ﴿١﴾

1. By the (Winds) Sent Forth one after another (to man s profit);

فَالْعٰصِفٰتِ عَصْفًا ﴿٢﴾

پھر زور پکڑ کر جھکڑ ہو جاتی ہیں ﴿٢﴾

2. Which then blow voilently in tempestuous Gusts,

وَّالنّٰشِرٰتِ نَشْرًا ﴿٣﴾

اور (بادلوں کو) پھاڑ کر پھیلا دیتی ہیں ﴿٣﴾

3. And scatter (things) far and wide;

فَالْفٰرِقٰتِ فَرْقًا ﴿٤﴾

پھر ان کو پھاڑ کر جدا جدا کر دیتی ہیں ﴿٤﴾

4. Then separate them, one from another,

فَالْمُلْقِيٰتِ ذِكْرًا ﴿٥﴾

پھر فرشتوں کی قسم جو وحی لاتے ہیں ﴿٥﴾

5. Then spread abroad a Reminder,

عُذْرًا اَوْ نُذْرًا ﴿٦﴾

تاکہ عذر (رفع) کر دیا جائے یا ڈر سنا دیا جائے ﴿٦﴾

6. Whether of Justification or of Warning;—

اِنَّمَا تُوْعَدُوْنَ لَوَاقِعٌ ﴿٧﴾

کہ جس کا تم سے وعدہ کیا جاتا ہے وہ ہو کر رہے گا ﴿٧﴾

7. Assuredly, what ye are promised must come to pass.

فَاِذَا النُّجُوْمُ طُمِسَتْ ﴿٨﴾

جب تاروں کی چمک جاتی رہے ﴿٨﴾

8. Then when the stars become dim;

وَاِذَا السَّمَآءُ فُرِجَتْ ﴿٩﴾

اور جب آسمان پھٹ جائے ﴿٩﴾

9. When the heaven is cleft asunder;

وَاِذَا الْجِبَالُ نُسِفَتْ ﴿١٠﴾

اور جب پہاڑ اڑے اڑے پھریں ﴿١٠﴾

10. When the mountains are scattered (to the winds) as dust;

وَاِذَا الرُّسُلُ اُقِّتَتْ ﴿١١﴾

اور جب پیغمبر فراہم کئے جائیں ﴿١١﴾

11. And when the messengers are (all) appointed a time (to collect);—

لِاَيِّ يَوْمٍ اُجِّلَتْ ﴿١٢﴾

بھلا (ان امور میں) تاخیر کس لئے کی گئی؟ ﴿١٢﴾

12. For what Day are these (portents) deferred?

لِيَوْمِ الْفَصْلِ ﴿١٣﴾

فیصلے کے دن کے لئے ﴿١٣﴾

13. For the Day of Sorting out.

وَمَآ اَدْرٰىكَ مَا يَوْمُ الْفَصْلِ ﴿١٤﴾

اور تمہیں کیا خبر کہ فیصلے کا دن کیا ہے ﴿١٤﴾

14. And what will explain to thee what is the Day of Sorting out ?

وَيْلٌ يَّوْمَئِذٍ لِّلْمُكَذِّبِيْنَ ﴿١٥﴾

اس دن جھٹلانے والوں کے لئے خرابی ہے ﴿١٥﴾

15. Ah woe, that Day, to the Rejecters of Truth!

اَلَمْ نُهْلِكِ الْاَوَّلِيْنَ ﴿١٦﴾

کیا ہم نے پہلے لوگوں کو ہلاک نہیں کر ڈالا؟ ﴿١٦﴾

16. Did We not destroy the men of old (for their evil) ?

ثُمَّ نُتْبِعُهُمُ الْاٰخِرِيْنَ ﴿١٧﴾

پھر ان پچھلوں کو بھی ان کے پیچھے بھیج دیتے ہیں ﴿١٧﴾

17. So shall We make later (generations) follow them.

كَذٰلِكَ نَفْعَلُ بِالْمُجْرِمِيْنَ ﴿١٨﴾

ہم گنہگاروں کے ساتھ ایسا ہی کرتے ہیں ﴿١٨﴾

18. Thus do We deal with men of sin.

وَيْلٌ يَّوْمَئِذٍ لِّلْمُكَذِّبِيْنَ ﴿١٩﴾

اس دن جھٹلانے والوں کی خرابی ہے ﴿١٩﴾

19. Ah woe, that Day to the Rejecters of Truth!

اَلَمْ نَخْلُقْكُّمْ مِّنْ مَّآءٍ مَّهِيْنٍ ﴿٢٠﴾

کیا ہم نے تم کو حقیر پانی سے نہیں پیدا کیا ﴿٢٠﴾

20. Have We not created you from a fluid (held) despicable?—

فَجَعَلْنٰهُ فِيْ قَرَارٍ مَّكِيْنٍ ﴿٢١﴾

(پہلے) اس کو ایک محفوظ جگہ میں رکھا ﴿٢١﴾

21. The which We placed in a place of rest, firmly fixed,

اِلٰى قَدَرٍ مَّعْلُوْمٍ ﴿٢٢﴾

ایک وقت معین تک ﴿٢٢﴾

22. For a period (of gestation), determined ?

فَقَدَرْنَا ۖ فَنِعْمَ الْقٰدِرُوْنَ ﴿٢٣﴾

پھر اندازہ مقرر کیا۔ اور ہم کیا ہی خوب اندازہ مقرر کرنے والے ہیں ﴿٢٣﴾

23. For We do determine for We are the Best to determine (things).

وَيْلٌ يَّوْمَئِذٍ لِّلْمُكَذِّبِيْنَ ﴿٢٤﴾

اس دن جھٹلانے والوں کی خرابی ہے ﴿٢٤﴾

24. Ah woe, that Day ! to the Rejecters of Truth!

25. Have We not made the earth (as a place) to draw together	کیا ہم نے زمین کو سمیٹنے والی نہیں بنایا ۲۵	اَلَمْ نَجْعَلِ الْاَرْضَ كِفَاتًا ۲۵
26. The living and the dead,	(یعنی) زندوں اور مُردوں کو ۲۶	اَحْيَآءً وَّاَمْوَاتًا ۲۶
27. And made therein mountains standing firm, lofty (in stature); and provided for you water sweet (and wholesome) ?	اور اُس پر اونچے اونچے پہاڑ رکھ دیئے اور تم لوگوں کو میٹھا پانی پلایا ۲۷	وَّجَعَلْنَا فِيْهَا رَوَاسِيَ شٰمِخٰتٍ وَّاَسْقَيْنٰكُمْ مَّآءً فُرَاتًا ۲۷
28. Ah woe, that Day, to the Rejecters of Truth!	اُس دن جھٹلانے والوں کی خرابی ہے ۲۸	وَيْلٌ يَّوْمَئِذٍ لِّلْمُكَذِّبِيْنَ ۲۸
29. (It will be said:) "Depart ye to that which ye used to reject as false!	جس چیز کو تم جھٹلایا کرتے تھے (اب) اُس کی طرف چلو ۲۹	اِنْطَلِقُوْٓا اِلٰى مَا كُنْتُمْ بِهٖ تُكَذِّبُوْنَ ۲۹
30. "Depart ye to a Shadow (of smoke ascending) in three columns,	(یعنی) اُس سائے کی طرف چلو جس کی تین شاخیں ہیں ۳۰	اِنْطَلِقُوْٓا اِلٰى ظِلٍّ ذِيْ ثَلٰثِ شُعَبٍ ۳۰
31. "(Which yields) no shade of coolness, and is of no use against the fierce Blaze.	نہ ٹھنڈی چھاؤں اور نہ لپٹ سے بچاؤ ۳۱	لَّا ظَلِيْلٍ وَّلَا يُغْنِيْ مِنَ اللَّهَبِ ۳۱
32. "Indeed it throws about sparks (huge) as Forts,	اس سے آگ کی (اتنی اتنی بڑی) چنگاریاں اُڑتی ہیں جیسے محل ۳۲	اِنَّهَا تَرْمِيْ بِشَرَرٍ كَالْقَصْرِ ۳۲
33. "As if there were (a string of) yellow camels (marching swiftly)."	گویا زرد رنگ کے اونٹ ہیں ۳۳	كَاَنَّهٗ جِمٰلَتٌ صُفْرٌ ۳۳
34. Ah woe, that Day, to the Rejecters of Truth!	اُس دن جھٹلانے والوں کی خرابی ہے ۳۴	وَيْلٌ يَّوْمَئِذٍ لِّلْمُكَذِّبِيْنَ ۳۴
35. That will be a Day when they shall not be able to speak,	یہ وہ دن ہے کہ (لوگ) لب تک نہ ہلا سکیں گے ۳۵	هٰذَا يَوْمُ لَا يَنْطِقُوْنَ ۳۵
36. Nor will it be open to them to put forth pleas.	اور نہ اُن کو اجازت دی جائے گی کہ عذر کرسکیں ۳۶	وَلَا يُؤْذَنُ لَهُمْ فَيَعْتَذِرُوْنَ ۳۶
37. Ah woe, that Day, to the Rejecters of Truth!	اُس دن جھٹلانے والوں کی خرابی ہے ۳۷	وَيْلٌ يَّوْمَئِذٍ لِّلْمُكَذِّبِيْنَ ۳۷
38. That will be a Day of Sorting out ! We shall gather you together and those before (you) !	یہی فیصلے کا دن ہے (جس میں) ہم نے تم کو اور پہلے لوگوں کو جمع کیا ہے ۳۸	هٰذَا يَوْمُ الْفَصْلِ ۚ جَمَعْنٰكُمْ وَالْاَوَّلِيْنَ ۳۸
39. Now, if ye have a trick (or plot), use it against Me !	اگر تم کو کوئی داؤں آتا ہو تو مجھ سے کر چلو ۳۹	فَاِنْ كَانَ لَكُمْ كَيْدٌ فَكِيْدُوْنِ ۳۹
40. Ah woe, that Day, to the Rejecters of Truth!	اُس دن جھٹلانے والوں کی خرابی ہے ۴۰	وَيْلٌ يَّوْمَئِذٍ لِّلْمُكَذِّبِيْنَ ۴۰ ع ۱ ۲۱
41. As to the Righteous, they shall be amidst (cool) shades and springs (of water).	بے شک پرہیزگار سایوں اور چشموں میں ہوں گے ۴۱	اِنَّ الْمُتَّقِيْنَ فِيْ ظِلٰلٍ وَّعُيُوْنٍ ۴۱
42. And (they shall have) fruits,— all they desire.	اور میووں میں جو اُن کو مرغوب ہوں ۴۲	وَّفَوَاكِهَ مِمَّا يَشْتَهُوْنَ ۴۲
43. "Eat ye and drink ye to your heart's content: for that ye worked (righteousness).	جو عمل تم کرتے رہے تھے اُن کے بدلے میں مزے سے کھاؤ اور پیو ۴۳	كُلُوْا وَاشْرَبُوْا هَنِيْٓــًٔا بِمَا كُنْتُمْ تَعْمَلُوْنَ ۴۳
44. Thus do We certainly reward the Doers of Good.	ہم نیکوکاروں کو ایسا ہی بدلہ دیا کرتے ہیں ۴۴	اِنَّا كَذٰلِكَ نَجْزِي الْمُحْسِنِيْنَ ۴۴
45. Ah woe, that Day, to the Rejecters of Truth!	اُس دن جھٹلانے والوں کی خرابی ہے ۴۵	وَيْلٌ يَّوْمَئِذٍ لِّلْمُكَذِّبِيْنَ ۴۵
46. (O ye Unjust !) eat ye and enjoy yourselves (but) a little while, for that ye are Sinners.	(اے جھٹلانے والو) تم کسی قدر کھا لو اور فائدے اٹھا لو تم بیشک گنہگار ہو ۴۶	كُلُوْا وَتَمَتَّعُوْا قَلِيْلًا اِنَّكُمْ مُّجْرِمُوْنَ ۴۶
47. Ah woe, that Day, to the Rejecters of Truth!	اُس دن جھٹلانے والوں کی خرابی ہے ۴۷	وَيْلٌ يَّوْمَئِذٍ لِّلْمُكَذِّبِيْنَ ۴۷
48. And when it is said to them, "Prostrate yourselves !" they do not so.	اور جب اُن سے کہا جاتا ہے کہ (خدا کے آگے) جھکو تو جھکتے نہیں ۴۸	وَاِذَا قِيْلَ لَهُمُ ارْكَعُوْا لَا يَرْكَعُوْنَ ۴۸
49. Ah woe, that Day, to the Rejecters of Truth!	اُس دن جھٹلانے والوں کی خرابی ہے ۴۹	وَيْلٌ يَّوْمَئِذٍ لِّلْمُكَذِّبِيْنَ ۴۹
50. Then what Message, after that, will they believe in ?	اب اس کے بعد یہ کونسی بات پر ایمان لائیں گے؟ ۵۰	فَبِاَيِّ حَدِيْثٍ بَعْدَهٗ يُؤْمِنُوْنَ ۵۰ ع ۲ ۱۰ ۲۲

SÛRA–78
AN-NABAA
(INTRODUCTION)

This beautiful Makkan Sûra is not quite so early as the last (S. 77), nor quite so late as S. 76, but nearer in time to the latter.

It sets forth Allah's loving care in a fine nature-passage, and deduces from it the Promise of the Future, when Evil will be destroyed and Good will come to its own; and invites all who have the will, to seek refuge with their Lord.

An-Nabaa, or The (Great) News

In the name of Allah, Most Gracious, Most Merciful.

1. Concerning what are they disputing ?
2. Concerning the Great News,
3. About which they cannot agree.
4. Verily, they shall soon (come to) know !
5. Verily, verily they shall soon (come to) know!
6. Have We not made the earth as a wide Expanse,
7. And the mountains as pegs ?
8. And (have We not) created you in pairs,
9. And made your sleep for rest,
10. And made the night as a covering,
11. And made the day as a means of subsistence?
12. And (have We not) built over you the seven firmaments,
13. And placed (therein) a blazing lamp.
14. And do We not send down from the clouds water in abundance,
15. That We may produce therewith grain and vegetables,
16. And gardens of luxurious growth ?
17. Verily the Day of Sorting Out is a thing appointed,—
18. The Day that the Trumpet shall be sounded, and ye shall come forth in crowds;
19. And the heavens shall be opened as if there were doors,
20. And the mountains shall vanish, as if they were a mirage,
21. Truly Hell is as a place of ambush
22. For the transgressors a place of destination:
23. They will dwell therein for ages.
24. Nothing cool shall they taste therein, nor any drink,
25. Save a boiling fluid and a fluid, dark, murky, intensely cold,—

سورۂ نبا مکی ہے اس میں چالیس آیتیں اور دو رکوع ہیں

شروع خدا کا نام لے کر جو بڑا مہربان نہایت رحم والا ہے

(یہ) لوگ کس چیز کی نسبت پوچھتے ہیں؟ (۱)
(کیا) بڑی خبر کی نسبت؟ (۲)
جس میں یہ اختلاف کر رہے ہیں (۳)
دیکھو یہ عنقریب جان لیں گے (۴)
پھر دیکھو یہ عنقریب جان لیں گے (۵)
کیا ہم نے زمین کو بچھونا نہیں بنایا؟ (۶)
اور پہاڑوں کو (اس کی) میخیں (نہیں ٹھہرایا)؟ (۷)
(بیشک بنایا) اور تم کو جوڑا جوڑا بھی پیدا کیا (۸)
اور نیند کو تمہارے لئے (موجب) آرام بنایا (۹)
اور رات کو پردہ مقرر کیا (۱۰)
اور دن کو معاش (کا وقت) قرار دیا (۱۱)
اور تمہارے اوپر سات مضبوط (آسمان) بنائے (۱۲)
اور (آفتاب کا) روشن چراغ بنایا (۱۳)
اور نچڑتے بادلوں سے موسلا دھار مینہ برسایا (۱۴)
تاکہ اس سے اناج اور سبزہ پیدا کریں (۱۵)
اور گھنے گھنے باغ (۱۶)
بیشک فیصلے کا دن مقرر ہے (۱۷)
جس دن صور پھونکا جائیگا تو تم لوگ غٹ کے غٹ آموجود ہوگے (۱۸)
اور آسمان کھولا جائے گا تو (اس میں) دروازے ہو جائینگے (۱۹)
اور پہاڑ چلائے جائیں گے تو وہ ریت ہو کر رہ جائیں گے (۲۰)
بے شک دوزخ گھات میں ہے (۲۱)
(یعنی) سرکشوں کا وہی ٹھکانا ہے (۲۲)
اس میں وہ مدتوں پڑے رہیں گے (۲۳)
وہاں نہ ٹھنڈک کا مزہ چکھیں گے نہ (کچھ) پینا (نصیب ہوگا) (۲۴)
مگر گرم پانی اور بہتی پیپ (۲۵)

سُورَةُ النَّبَإِ مَكِّيَّةٌ وَهِيَ أَرْبَعُونَ آيَةً وَفِيهَا رُكُوعَانِ

الجزء الثلاثون ٣٠

بِسْمِ اللّٰهِ الرَّحْمٰنِ الرَّحِيْمِ

عَمَّ يَتَسَآءَلُوْنَ ﴿١﴾
عَنِ النَّبَاِ الْعَظِيْمِ ﴿٢﴾
الَّذِيْ هُمْ فِيْهِ مُخْتَلِفُوْنَ ﴿٣﴾
كَلَّا سَيَعْلَمُوْنَ ﴿٤﴾
ثُمَّ كَلَّا سَيَعْلَمُوْنَ ﴿٥﴾
اَلَمْ نَجْعَلِ الْاَرْضَ مِهٰدًا ﴿٦﴾
وَّالْجِبَالَ اَوْتَادًا ﴿٧﴾
وَّخَلَقْنٰكُمْ اَزْوَاجًا ﴿٨﴾
وَّجَعَلْنَا نَوْمَكُمْ سُبَاتًا ﴿٩﴾
وَّجَعَلْنَا الَّيْلَ لِبَاسًا ﴿١٠﴾
وَّجَعَلْنَا النَّهَارَ مَعَاشًا ﴿١١﴾
وَّبَنَيْنَا فَوْقَكُمْ سَبْعًا شِدَادًا ﴿١٢﴾
وَّجَعَلْنَا سِرَاجًا وَّهَّاجًا ﴿١٣﴾
وَّاَنْزَلْنَا مِنَ الْمُعْصِرٰتِ مَآءً ثَجَّاجًا ﴿١٤﴾
لِّنُخْرِجَ بِهٖ حَبًّا وَّنَبَاتًا ﴿١٥﴾
وَّجَنّٰتٍ اَلْفَافًا ﴿١٦﴾
اِنَّ يَوْمَ الْفَصْلِ كَانَ مِيْقَاتًا ﴿١٧﴾
يَّوْمَ يُنْفَخُ فِي الصُّوْرِ فَتَاْتُوْنَ اَفْوَاجًا ﴿١٨﴾
وَّفُتِحَتِ السَّمَآءُ فَكَانَتْ اَبْوَابًا ﴿١٩﴾
وَّسُيِّرَتِ الْجِبَالُ فَكَانَتْ سَرَابًا ﴿٢٠﴾
اِنَّ جَهَنَّمَ كَانَتْ مِرْصَادًا ﴿٢١﴾
لِّلطّٰغِيْنَ مَاٰبًا ﴿٢٢﴾
لّٰبِثِيْنَ فِيْهَآ اَحْقَابًا ﴿٢٣﴾
لَا يَذُوْقُوْنَ فِيْهَا بَرْدًا وَّلَا شَرَابًا ﴿٢٤﴾
اِلَّا حَمِيْمًا وَّغَسَّاقًا ﴿٢٥﴾

SÛRA–79
AN-NÃZI'ÃT
(INTRODUCTION)

This is also an early Makkan Sûra, of about the same date as the last, and deals with the mystic theme of Judgment from the point of view of Pride and its Fall. The parable of Pharaoh occupies a central place in the argument: for he said, "I am your Lord Most High," and perished with his followers.

26. A fitting recompense (for them).	(یہ) بدلہ ہے پورا پورا ۲۶	جَزَآءً وِّفَاقًا ۲۶
27. For that they used not to look for any account (for their deeds),	یہ لوگ حساب (آخرت) کی امید ہی نہیں رکھتے تھے ۲۷	إِنَّهُمْ كَانُوا لَا يَرْجُونَ حِسَابًا ۲۷
28. But they (impudently) treated our Signs as false	اور ہماری آیتوں کو جھوٹ سمجھ کر جھٹلاتے رہتے تھے ۲۸	وَكَذَّبُوا بِآيَاتِنَا كِذَّابًا ۲۸
29. And all things have We preserved on record.	اور ہم نے ہر چیز کو لکھ کر ضبط کر رکھا ہے ۲۹	وَكُلَّ شَيْءٍ أَحْصَيْنَاهُ كِتَابًا ۲۹
30. "So taste ye (the fruits of your deeds); for no increase shall We grant you, except in Chastisement.	سو (اب) مزہ چکھو ہم تم پر عذاب ہی بڑھاتے جائیں گے ۳۰	ع فَذُوقُوا فَلَن نَّزِيدَكُمْ إِلَّا عَذَابًا ۳۰
31. Verily for the Righteous there will be an Achievement,	بے شک پرہیزگاروں کے لئے کامیابی ہے ۳۱	إِنَّ لِلْمُتَّقِينَ مَفَازًا ۳۱
32. Gardens enclosed, and Grape-vines;	(یعنی) باغ اور انگور ۳۲	حَدَآئِقَ وَأَعْنَابًا ۳۲
33. Maidens of Equal Age;	اور ہم عمر نوجوان عورتیں ۳۳	وَكَوَاعِبَ أَتْرَابًا ۳۳
34. And a Cup full (to the Brim).	اور شراب کے چھلکتے ہوئے گلاس ۳۴	وَكَأْسًا دِهَاقًا ۳۴
35. No Vanity shall they hear therein, nor Untruth;—	وہاں نہ بیہودہ بات سنیں گے نہ جھوٹ (خرافات) ۳۵	لَّا يَسْمَعُونَ فِيهَا لَغْوًا وَلَا كِذَّابًا ۳۵
36. Recompense from thy Lord, a Gift, (amply) sufficient,—	یہ تمہارے پروردگار کی طرف سے صلہ ہے انعام متعین ۳۶	جَزَآءً مِّن رَّبِّكَ عَطَآءً حِسَابًا ۳۶
37. (From) the Lord of the heavens and the earth, and all between,— the Most Gracious: none shall have power to argue with Him.	وہ جو آسمانوں اور زمین اور جو ان دونوں میں ہے سب کا مالک ہے بڑا مہربان کسی کو اس سے بات کرنے کا یارا نہ ہوگا ۳۷	رَّبِّ السَّمَاوَاتِ وَالْأَرْضِ وَمَا بَيْنَهُمَا الرَّحْمَٰنِ لَا يَمْلِكُونَ مِنْهُ خِطَابًا ۳۷
38. The Day that the Spirit and the angels will stand forth in ranks, none shall speak except any who is permitted by The Most Gracious, and he will say what is right.	جس دن روح (الامین) اور (اور) فرشتے صف باندھ کر کھڑے ہوں گے تو کوئی بول نہ سکے گا مگر جسکو (خدائے) رحمٰن اجازت بخشے اور اس نے بات بھی درست کہی ہو ۳۸	يَوْمَ يَقُومُ الرُّوحُ وَالْمَلَائِكَةُ صَفًّا لَّا يَتَكَلَّمُونَ إِلَّا مَنْ أَذِنَ لَهُ الرَّحْمَٰنُ وَقَالَ صَوَابًا ۳۸
39. That is the True Day: therefore, whoso will, let him take a (straight) Return to his Lord !	یہ دن برحق ہے پس جو شخص چاہے اپنے پروردگار کے پاس ٹھکانا بنالے ۳۹	ذَٰلِكَ الْيَوْمُ الْحَقُّ فَمَن شَآءَ اتَّخَذَ إِلَىٰ رَبِّهِ مَآبًا ۳۹
40. Verily, We have warned you of a Chastisement near,— the Day when man will see (the Deeds) which his hands have sent forth, and the Unbeliever will say, "Woe unto me ! Would that I were (mere) dust !"	ہم نے تم کو عذاب سے جو عنقریب آنیوالا ہے آگاہ کر دیا ہے۔ جس دن ہر شخص ان (اعمال) کو جو اس نے آگے بھیجے ہوں گے دیکھ لے گا اور کافر کہے گا کہ اے کاش میں مٹی ہوتا ۴۰	إِنَّآ أَنذَرْنَاكُمْ عَذَابًا قَرِيبًا يَوْمَ يَنظُرُ الْمَرْءُ مَا قَدَّمَتْ يَدَاهُ وَيَقُولُ الْكَافِرُ يَا لَيْتَنِي كُنتُ تُرَابًا ۴۰ ع

An-Nāzi'āt, or Those Who Tear Out

سورہ نازعات مکی ہے اس میں چھیالیس آیتیں اور دو رکوع ہیں

سُورَةُ النَّازِعَاتِ مَكِّيَّةٌ وَهِيَ سِتٌّ وَّأَرْبَعُونَ آيَةً وَّفِيهَا رُكُوعَانِ

In the name of Allah, Most Gracious, Most Merciful.	شروع خدا کا نام لے کر جو بڑا مہربان نہایت رحم والا ہے	بِسْمِ اللَّهِ الرَّحْمَٰنِ الرَّحِيمِ
1. By the (angels) who tear out (the souls of the wicked) with violence;	ان (فرشتوں) کی قسم جو ڈوب کر کھینچ لیتے ہیں ۱	وَالنَّازِعَاتِ غَرْقًا ۱
2. By those who gently draw out (the souls of the blessed);	اور ان کی جو آسانی سے کھول دیتے ہیں ۲	وَالنَّاشِطَاتِ نَشْطًا ۲
3. And by those who glide along (on errands of mercy),	اور ان کی جو تیرتے پھرتے ہیں ۳	وَالسَّابِحَاتِ سَبْحًا ۳
4. Then press forward as in a race,	پھر لپک کر آگے بڑھتے ہیں ۴	فَالسَّابِقَاتِ سَبْقًا ۴

5. Then arrange to do (the Commands of their Lord),—	پھر (دنیا کے) کاموں کا انتظام کرتے ہیں ⑤	فَالْمُدَبِّرٰتِ اَمْرًا ⑤
6. The Day everything that can be in commotion, will be in violent commotion,	(کہ وہ دن آکر رہے گا) جس دن زمین کو بھونچال آئیگا ⑥	يَوْمَ تَرْجُفُ الرَّاجِفَةُ ⑥
7. Followed by oft-repeated (commotions):	پھر اُس کے پیچھے اور (بھونچال) آئے گا ⑦	تَتْبَعُهَا الرَّادِفَةُ ⑦
8. Hearts that Day will be in agitation;	اُس دن (لوگوں کے) دل خائف ہو رہے ہونگے ⑧	قُلُوْبٌ يَّوْمَئِذٍ وَّاجِفَةٌ ⑧
9. Cast down will be (their owners') eyes.	(اور) آنکھیں جھکی ہوئی ⑨	اَبْصَارُهَا خَاشِعَةٌ ⑨
10. They say (now): "What! shall we indeed be returned to (our) former state?—	(کافر) کہتے ہیں کیا ہم اُلٹے پاؤں پھر لوٹیں گے؟ ⑩	يَقُوْلُوْنَ ءَاِنَّا لَمَرْدُوْدُوْنَ فِي الْحَافِرَةِ ⑩
11. "What!—when we shall have become rotten bones?"	بھلا جب ہم کھوکھلی ہڈیاں ہو جائینگے (تو پھر زندہ کئے جائینگے) ⑪	ءَاِذَا كُنَّا عِظَامًا نَّخِرَةً ⑪
12. They say: "It would, in that case, be a return with loss!"	کہتے ہیں کہ یہ لوٹنا تو (موجب) زیاں ہے ⑫	قَالُوْا تِلْكَ اِذًا كَرَّةٌ خَاسِرَةٌ ⑫
13. But verily, it will be but a single (compelling) Cry,	وہ تو صرف ایک ڈانٹ ہو گی ⑬	فَاِنَّمَا هِيَ زَجْرَةٌ وَّاحِدَةٌ ⑬
14. When, behold, they will be brought out to the open.	اُس وقت وہ (سب) میدانِ (حشر) میں آ جمع ہونگے ⑭	فَاِذَا هُمْ بِالسَّاهِرَةِ ⑭
15. Has the story of Moses reached thee?	بھلا تم کو موسیٰ کی حکایت پہنچی ہے ⑮	هَلْ اَتٰىكَ حَدِيْثُ مُوْسٰى ⑮
16. Behold, thy Lord did call to him in the sacred valley of Tuwā:—	جب اُنکے پروردگار نے اُنکو پاک میدان (یعنی) طویٰ میں پکارا ⑯	اِذْ نَادٰىهُ رَبُّهٗ بِالْوَادِ الْمُقَدَّسِ طُوًى ⑯
17. "Go thou to Pharaoh, for he has indeed transgressed all bounds:	(اور حکم دیا) کہ فرعون کے پاس جاؤ وہ سرکش ہو رہا ہے ⑰	اِذْهَبْ اِلٰى فِرْعَوْنَ اِنَّهٗ طَغٰى ⑰
18. "And say to him, 'Wouldst thou that thou shouldst be purified (from sin)?—	اور (اُس سے) کہو کیا تو چاہتا ہے کہ پاک ہو جائے ⑱	فَقُلْ هَلْ لَّكَ اِلٰٓى اَنْ تَزَكّٰى ⑱
19. " 'And that I guide thee to thy Lord, so thou shouldst fear Him?' "	اور میں تجھے تیرے پروردگار کا رستہ بتاؤں تاکہ تجھکو خوف (پیدا) ہو ⑲	وَاَهْدِيَكَ اِلٰى رَبِّكَ فَتَخْشٰى ⑲
20. Then did (Moses) show him the Great Sign.	غرض اُنہوں نے اُسکو بڑی نشانی دکھائی ⑳	فَاَرٰىهُ الْاٰيَةَ الْكُبْرٰى ⑳
21. But (Pharaoh) rejected it and disobeyed (guidance);	مگر اُس نے جھٹلایا اور نہ مانا ㉑	فَكَذَّبَ وَعَصٰى ㉑
22. Further, he turned his back, striving hard (against Allah).	پھر لوٹ گیا اور تدبیریں کرنے لگا ㉒	ثُمَّ اَدْبَرَ يَسْعٰى ㉒
23. Then he collected (his men) and made a proclamation,	اور (لوگوں کو) اکٹھا کیا اور پکارا ㉓	فَحَشَرَ فَنَادٰى ㉓
24. Saying, "I am your Lord, Most High".	کہنے لگا کہ تمہارا سب سے بڑا مالک میں ہوں ㉔	فَقَالَ اَنَا رَبُّكُمُ الْاَعْلٰى ㉔
25. But Allah did punish him, (and made an) example of him,—in the Hereafter, as in this life.	تو خدا نے اُسکو دنیا اور آخرت (دونوں) کے عذاب میں پکڑ لیا ㉕	فَاَخَذَهُ اللّٰهُ نَكَالَ الْاٰخِرَةِ وَالْاُوْلٰى ㉕
26. Verily in this is a lesson for whosoever feareth (Allah).	جو شخص (خدا سے) ڈر رکھتا ہے اسکے لئے اس (قصے) میں عبرت ہے ㉖	اِنَّ فِيْ ذٰلِكَ لَعِبْرَةً لِّمَنْ يَّخْشٰى ㉖
27. What! Are ye the more difficult to create or the heaven (above)? (Allah) hath constructed it:	بھلا تمہارا بنانا مشکل ہے یا آسمان کا؟ اُسی نے اسکو بنایا ㉗	ءَاَنْتُمْ اَشَدُّ خَلْقًا اَمِ السَّمَآءُ ۚ بَنٰىهَا ㉗
28. On high hath He raised its canopy, and He hath given it order and perfection.	اُس کی چھت کو اُونچا کیا پھر اُسے برابر کر دیا ㉘	رَفَعَ سَمْكَهَا فَسَوّٰىهَا ㉘
29. Its night doth He endow with darkness, and its splendour doth He bring out (with light).	اور اُسی نے رات تاریک بنائی اور (دن کو) دھوپ نکالی ㉙	وَاَغْطَشَ لَيْلَهَا وَاَخْرَجَ ضُحٰىهَا ㉙
30. And the earth, moreover, hath He extended (to a wide expanse);	اور اس کے بعد زمین کو پھیلا دیا ㉚	وَالْاَرْضَ بَعْدَ ذٰلِكَ دَحٰىهَا ㉚
31. He draweth out therefrom its water and its pasture,	اُسی نے اس میں سے اس کا پانی نکالا اور چارا اُگایا ㉛	اَخْرَجَ مِنْهَا مَآءَهَا وَمَرْعٰىهَا ㉛

SÛRA–80
'ABASA
(INTRODUCTION)

This is an early Makkan Sûra, and is connected with an incident which reflects the highest honour on the Prophet's sincerity in the Revelations that were vouchsafed to him even if they seemed to reprove him for some natural and human zeal that led him to a false step in his mission according to his own high standards.

He was once deeply and earnestly engaged in trying to explain the Holy Qur-ãn to Pagan Quraish leaders, when he was interrupted by blind man, 'Abdullah Umm Maktûm, one who was also poor, so that no one took any notice of him. He wanted to learn the Qur-ãn. The Holy Prophet naturally disliked the interruption and showed impatience. Perhaps the poor man's feelings were hurt. But he whose gentle heart ever sympathised with the poor and the afflicted got new Light from above, and without the least hesitation published this revelation, which forms part of the sacred scripture of Islam, as described in verses 13-16. And the Prophet always afterwards held the man in high honour.

The incident was only a passing incident, but after explaining the eternal principles of revelation, the Sûra recapitulates the Mercies of Allah to man, and the consequences of a good or a wicked life here, as seen in the spiritual world to come, in the Hereafter.

32. And the mountains hath He firmly fixed;—
اور اس پر پہاڑوں کا بوجھ رکھ دیا (۳۲)
والجبال ارسىها (۳۲)

33. A provision for you and your cattle.
یہ سب کچھ تمہارے اور تمہارے چارپایوں کے فائدے کیلئے کیا (۳۳)
متاعا لكم ولانعامكم (۳۳)

34. Therefore, when there comes the great, overwhelming (Event),—
تو جب بڑی آفت آئے گی (۳۴)
فاذا جاءت الطامة الكبرى (۳۴)

35. The Day when Man shall remember (all) that he strove for,
اُس دن انسان اپنے کاموں کو یاد کرے گا (۳۵)
يوم يتذكر الانسان ما سعى (۳۵)

36. And Hell-Fire shall be placed in full view for him who sees.—
اور دوزخ دیکھنے والے کے سامنے نکال کر رکھ دی جائیگی (۳۶)
وبرزت الجحيم لمن يرى (۳۶)

37. Then, for such as had transgressed all bounds,
تو جس نے سرکشی کی (۳۷)
فاما من طغى (۳۷)

38. And had preferred the life of this world,
اور دُنیا کی زندگی کو مقدم سمجھا (۳۸)
واثر الحيوة الدنيا (۳۸)

39. The Abode will be Hell-Fire;
اُس کا ٹھکانا دوزخ ہے (۳۹)
فان الجحيم هي الماوى (۳۹)

40. And for such as had entertained the fear of standing before their Lord's (tribunal) and had restrained (their) soul from lower Desires,
اور جو اپنے پروردگار کے سامنے کھڑے ہونے سے ڈرتا اور
جی کو خواہشوں سے روکتا رہا (۴۰)
واما من خاف مقام ربه ونهى
النفس عن الهوى (۴۰)

41. Their Abode will be the Garden.
اُس کا ٹھکانا بہشت ہے (۴۱)
فان الجنة هي الماوى (۴۱)

42. They ask thee about the Hour,—'When will be its appointed time ?'
(اے پیغمبر لوگ) تم سے قیامت کے بارے میں پوچھتے ہیں کہ اُسکا وقوع کب ہوگا؟ (۴۲)
يسئلونك عن الساعة ايان مرسىها (۴۲)

43. Wherein art thou (concerned) with the declaration thereof ?
سو تم اُس کے ذکر سے کس فکر میں ہو؟ (۴۳)
فيم انت من ذكرىها (۴۳)

44. With thy Lord is the final end of it.
اُس کا منتہا (یعنی واقع ہونیکا وقت) تمہارے پروردگار ہی کو (معلوم ہے) (۴۴)
الى ربك منتهىها (۴۴)

45. Thou art but a Warner for such as fear it.
جو شخص اُس سے ڈر رکھتا ہے تم تو اُسی کو ڈر سنانیوالے ہو (۴۵)
انما انت منذر من يخشىها (۴۵)

46. The Day they see it, (it will be) as if they had tarried but a single evening, or (at most till) the following morn !
جب وہ اُس کو دیکھیں گے (تو ایسا خیال کرینگے) کہ گویا (دُنیا
میں صرف) ایک شام یا صبح رہے تھے (۴۶)
كانهم يوم يرونها لم يلبثوا الا
عشية او ضحىها (۴۶) ع

'Abasa, or He Frowned

سورۃ عبس مکّی ہے اس میں بیالیس آیتیں اور ایک رکوع ہے

سورة عبس مكية وهي اثنتان واربعون اية وفيها ركوع واحد

In the name of Allah, Most Gracious, Most Merciful.
شروع خدا کا نام لے کر جو بڑا مہربان نہایت رحم والا ہے
بسم الله الرحمن الرحيم

1. (The Prophet) frowned and turned away,
(محمد مصطفیٰ) ترش رُو ہوئے اور مُنہ پھیر بیٹھے (۱)
عبس وتولى (۱)

2. Becuase there came to him the blind man (interrupting).
کہ اُن کے پاس ایک نابینا آیا (۲)
ان جاءه الاعمى (۲)

3. But what could tell thee but that perchance he might grow in purity?
اور تم کو کیا خبر شاید وہ پاکیزگی حاصل کرتا (۳)
وما يدريك لعله يزكى (۳)

4. Or that he might receive admoniton, and the Reminder might profit him?
یا سوچتا تو سمجھانا اُسے فائدہ دیتا (۴)
او يذكر فتنفعه الذكرى (۴)

5. As to one who regards himself as self-sufficient,
جو پروا نہیں کرتا (۵)
اما من استغنى (۵)

6. To him dost thou attend;
اُس کی طرف تو تم توجہ کرتے ہو (۶)
فانت له تصدى (۶)

7. Though it is no blame to thee if he grow not in purity.
حالانکہ اگر وہ نہ سنورے تو تم پر کچھ (الزام) نہیں (۷)
وما عليك الا يزكى (۷)

8. But as to him who came to thee striving earnestly,
اور جو تمہارے پاس دوڑتا ہوا آیا (۸)
واما من جاءك يسعى (۸)

9. And with fear (in his heart),

اور (خدا سے) ڈرتا ہے (٩)

وَهُوَ يَخْشَىٰ (٩)

10. Of him wast thou unmindful.

اُس سے تم بے رُخی کرتے ہو [ف ٣١٩] (١٠)

فَأَنتَ عَنْهُ تَلَهَّىٰ (١٠)

11. By no means (should it be so)! for it is indeed a Message of remembrance.

دیکھو یہ (قرآن) نصیحت ہے (١١)

كَلَّا إِنَّهَا تَذْكِرَةٌ (١١)

12. Therefore let whose will, keep it in remembrance.

پس جو چاہے اسے یاد رکھے (١٢)

فَمَن شَاءَ ذَكَرَهُ (١٢) وقف لازم

13. (It is) in Books held (greatly) in honour,

قابلِ ادب ورقوں میں (لکھا ہوا) (١٣)

فِي صُحُفٍ مُّكَرَّمَةٍ (١٣)

14. Exalted (in dignity), kept pure and holy,

جو بلند مقام پر رکھے ہوئے (اور) پاک ہیں (١٤)

مَّرْفُوعَةٍ مُّطَهَّرَةٍ (١٤)

15. (Written) by the hands of scribes—

(ایسے) لکھنے والوں کے ہاتھوں میں (١٥)

بِأَيْدِي سَفَرَةٍ (١٥)

16. Honourable and Pious and Just.

جو سردار (اور) نیکوکار ہیں (١٦)

كِرَامٍ بَرَرَةٍ (١٦)

17. Woe to man ! What hath made him reject Allah?

انسان ہلاک ہو جائے کیسا ناشکرا ہے (١٧)

قُتِلَ الْإِنسَانُ مَا أَكْفَرَهُ (١٧)

18. From what stuff hath He created him ?

اُسے (خدا نے) کس چیز سے بنایا؟ (١٨)

مِنْ أَيِّ شَيْءٍ خَلَقَهُ (١٨)

19. From a sperm-drop: He hath created him, and then mouldeth him in due Proportions;

نُطفے سے بنایا پھر اس کا اندازہ مقرر کیا (١٩)

مِن نُّطْفَةٍ خَلَقَهُ فَقَدَّرَهُ (١٩)

20. Then doth He make His path smooth for him;

پھر اس کے لئے رستہ آسان کر دیا (٢٠)

ثُمَّ السَّبِيلَ يَسَّرَهُ (٢٠)

21. Then He causeth him to die, and putteth him in his Grave;

پھر اس کو موت دی پھر قبر میں دفن کرایا (٢١)

ثُمَّ أَمَاتَهُ فَأَقْبَرَهُ (٢١)

22. Then, when it is His Will, He will raise him up (again).

پھر جب چاہے گا اُسے اُٹھا کھڑا کرے گا (٢٢)

ثُمَّ إِذَا شَاءَ أَنشَرَهُ (٢٢)

23. By no means hath he fulfilled what Allah hath commanded him.

کچھ شک نہیں کہ خدا نے اُسے جو حکم دیا اس نے اس پر عمل نہ کیا (٢٣)

كَلَّا لَمَّا يَقْضِ مَا أَمَرَهُ (٢٣)

24. Then let man look at his Food, (and how We provide it):

تو انسان کو چاہیئے کہ اپنے کھانے کی طرف نظر کرے (٢٤)

فَلْيَنظُرِ الْإِنسَانُ إِلَىٰ طَعَامِهِ (٢٤)

25. For that We pour forth water in abundance,

بے شک ہم ہی نے پانی برسایا (٢٥)

أَنَّا صَبَبْنَا الْمَاءَ صَبًّا (٢٥)

26. And We split the earth in fragments,

پھر ہم ہی نے زمین کو چیرا پھاڑا [ف ٣٢٠] (٢٦)

ثُمَّ شَقَقْنَا الْأَرْضَ شَقًّا (٢٦)

27. And produce therein grain,

پھر ہم ہی نے اس میں اناج اُگایا (٢٧)

فَأَنبَتْنَا فِيهَا حَبًّا (٢٧)

28. And Grapes and the fresh vegetation,

اور انگور اور ترکاری (٢٨)

وَعِنَبًا وَقَضْبًا (٢٨)

29. And Olives and Dates,

اور زیتون اور کھجوریں (٢٩)

وَزَيْتُونًا وَنَخْلًا (٢٩)

30. And enclosed Gardens, dense with lofty trees,

اور گھنے گھنے باغ (٣٠)

وَحَدَائِقَ غُلْبًا (٣٠)

31. And Fruits and Fodder,—

اور میوے اور چارا (٣١)

وَفَاكِهَةً وَأَبًّا (٣١)

32. A provision for you and your cattle.

(یہ سب کچھ) تمہارے اور تمہارے چارپایوں کیلئے بنایا (٣٢)

مَّتَاعًا لَّكُمْ وَلِأَنْعَامِكُمْ (٣٢)

33. At length, when there comes the Deafening Noise,—

تو جب (قیامت کا) غُل مچے گا (٣٣)

فَإِذَا جَاءَتِ الصَّاخَّةُ (٣٣)

34. That Day shall a man flee from his own brother,

اُس دن آدمی اپنے بھائی سے دُور بھاگے گا (٣٤)

يَوْمَ يَفِرُّ الْمَرْءُ مِنْ أَخِيهِ (٣٤)

35. And from his mother and his father,

اور اپنی ماں اور اپنے باپ سے (٣٥)

وَأُمِّهِ وَأَبِيهِ (٣٥)

SÛRA–81
AT-TAKWÎR
(INTRODUCTION)

This is quite an early Makkan Sûra, perhaps the sixth or seventh in chronological order. It opens with a series of highly mystical metaphors suggesting the break-up of the world as we know it (verses 1-13) and the enforcement of complete personal responsibility for each soul (verse 14). Then there is a mystical passage showing how the Quranic Revelation was true, and revealed through the angel Gabriel, and not merely a rhepsody from one possessed. Revelation is given for man's spiritual guidance (verses 14-29).

Comparable with this Sûra are the Sûras 82 and 84 which may be read with this.

36. And from his wife and his children.	اور اپنی بیوی اور اپنے بیٹے سے (۳۶)	وَصَاحِبَتِهِۦ وَبَنِيهِ ﴿٣٦﴾
37. Each one of them, that Day, will have enough concern (of his own) to make him indifferent to the others.	ہر شخص اس روز ایک فکر میں ہوگا جو اسے (مصروفیت کیلئے) بس کریگا (۳۷)	لِكُلِّ ٱمْرِئٍ مِّنْهُمْ يَوْمَئِذٍ شَأْنٌ يُغْنِيهِ ﴿٣٧﴾
38. Some Faces that Day will be beaming,	اور کتنے منہ اس روز چمک رہے ہوں گے (۳۸)	وُجُوهٌ يَوْمَئِذٍ مُّسْفِرَةٌ ﴿٣٨﴾
39. Laughing, rejoicing.	خنداں وشاداں (یہ نیکوکار ہیں) (۳۹)	ضَاحِكَةٌ مُّسْتَبْشِرَةٌ ﴿٣٩﴾
40. And other faces that Day will be dust-stained;	اور کتنے منہ ہوں گے جن پر گرد پڑ رہی ہوگی (۴۰)	وَوُجُوهٌ يَوْمَئِذٍ عَلَيْهَا غَبَرَةٌ ﴿٤٠﴾
41. Darkeness will cover them:	(اور) سیاہی چڑھ رہی ہوگی (۴۱)	تَرْهَقُهَا قَتَرَةٌ ﴿٤١﴾
42. Such will be the Rejecters of Allah the Doers of Iniquity.	یہ کفار بدکردار ہیں (۴۲)	أُو۟لَٰٓئِكَ هُمُ ٱلْكَفَرَةُ ٱلْفَجَرَةُ ﴿٤٢﴾

At-Takwîr, or the Folding Up

سورۂ تکویر مکی ہے اور اس میں انتیس آیتیں ہیں

سُورَةُ التَّكْوِيرِ مَكِّيَّةٌ وَهِيَ تِسْعٌ وَعِشْرُونَ آيَةً

In the name of Allah, Most Gracious, Most Merciful.	شروع خدا کا نام لے کر جو بڑا مہربان نہایت رحم والا ہے	بِسْمِ ٱللَّهِ ٱلرَّحْمَٰنِ ٱلرَّحِيمِ
1. When the sun (with its spacious light) is folded up;	جب سورج لپیٹ لیا جائے گا (۱)	إِذَا ٱلشَّمْسُ كُوِّرَتْ ﴿١﴾
2. When the stars fall, losing their lustre;	اور جب تارے بے نور ہو جائیں گے (۲)	وَإِذَا ٱلنُّجُومُ ٱنكَدَرَتْ ﴿٢﴾
3. When the mountains vanish (like a mirage);	اور جب پہاڑ چلائے جائیں گے (۳)	وَإِذَا ٱلْجِبَالُ سُيِّرَتْ ﴿٣﴾
4. When the she-camels, ten months with young, are left untended;	اور جب بیانے والی اونٹنیاں بیکار ہو جائیں گی (۴)	وَإِذَا ٱلْعِشَارُ عُطِّلَتْ ﴿٤﴾
5. When the wild beasts are herded together (in human habitations);	اور جب وحشی جانور جمع کئے جائیں گے (۵)	وَإِذَا ٱلْوُحُوشُ حُشِرَتْ ﴿٥﴾
6. When the oceans boil over with a swell;	اور جب دریا آگ ہو جائیں گے (۶)	وَإِذَا ٱلْبِحَارُ سُجِّرَتْ ﴿٦﴾
7. When the souls are sorted out, (being joined, like with like);	اور جب روحیں (بدنوں سے) ملا دی جائیں گی (۷)	وَإِذَا ٱلنُّفُوسُ زُوِّجَتْ ﴿٧﴾
8. When the female (infant), buried alive, is questioned—	اور جب اس لڑکی سے جو زندہ دفنا دی گئی ہو پوچھا جائیگا (۸)	وَإِذَا ٱلْمَوْءُۥدَةُ سُئِلَتْ ﴿٨﴾
9. For what crime she was killed,	کہ وہ کس گناہ پر مار دی گئی؟ (۹)	بِأَىِّ ذَنۢبٍ قُتِلَتْ ﴿٩﴾
10. When the Scrolls are laid open;	اور جب (عملوں کے) دفتر کھولے جائیں گے (۱۰)	وَإِذَا ٱلصُّحُفُ نُشِرَتْ ﴿١٠﴾
11. When the sky is unveiled;	اور جب آسمان کی کھال کھینچ لی جائے گی (۱۱)	وَإِذَا ٱلسَّمَآءُ كُشِطَتْ ﴿١١﴾
12. When the Blazing Fire is kindled to fierce heat;	اور جب دوزخ (کی آگ) بھڑکائی جائے گی (۱۲)	وَإِذَا ٱلْجَحِيمُ سُعِّرَتْ ﴿١٢﴾
13. And when the Garden is brought near;—	اور بہشت جب قریب لائی جائے گی (۱۳)	وَإِذَا ٱلْجَنَّةُ أُزْلِفَتْ ﴿١٣﴾
14. (Then) shall each soul know what it has put forward.	تب ہر شخص معلوم کرلے گا کہ وہ کیا لے کر آیا ہے (۱۴)	عَلِمَتْ نَفْسٌ مَّآ أَحْضَرَتْ ﴿١٤﴾
15. So verily I call to witness the Planets— that recede,	ہم کو ان ستاروں کی قسم جو پیچھے ہٹ جاتے ہیں (۱۵)	فَلَآ أُقْسِمُ بِٱلْخُنَّسِ ﴿١٥﴾
16. Go straight, or hide;	اور جو سیر کرتے اور غائب ہو جاتے ہیں (۱۶)	ٱلْجَوَارِ ٱلْكُنَّسِ ﴿١٦﴾
17. And the Night as it dissipates;	اور رات کی قسم جب ختم ہونے لگتی ہے (۱۷)	وَٱلَّيْلِ إِذَا عَسْعَسَ ﴿١٧﴾
18. And the Dawn as it breathes away the darkness;—	اور صبح کی قسم جب نمودار ہوتی ہے (۱۸)	وَٱلصُّبْحِ إِذَا تَنَفَّسَ ﴿١٨﴾

SÛRA–82

AL-INFÎṬÃR

(INTRODUCTION)

In subject-matter this Sûra is cognate to the last, though the best authorities consider it a good deal later in chronology in the early Makkan period.

Its argument is subject to the threefold interpretation referring (1) to the final Day of Judgment, (2) to the Lesser Judgment, on an individual's death, and (3) to the awakening of the Inner Light in the soul at any time, that being considered as Death to the Falsities of this life and a Rebirth to the true spiritual Reality.

19. Verily this is the word of a most honourable Messenger,
20. Endued with Power, held in honour by the Lord of the Throne,
21. With authority there, (and) faithful to his trust.
22. And (O people) ! your Companion is not one possessed;
23. And without doubt he saw him in the clear horizon.
24. Neither doth he withhold grudgingly a knowledge of the Unseen.
25. Nor is it the word of a Satan accursed.
26. Then whither go ye ?
27. Verily this is no less than a Message to (all) the Worlds:
28. (With profit) to whoever among you wills to go straight:
29. But ye shall not will except as Allah wills,— the Cherisher of the Worlds.

Al-Infiṭār, or The Cleaving Asunder

In the name of Allah, Most Grarious, Most Merciful.

1. When the Sky is cleft asunder;
2. When the Stars are scattered;
3. When the Oceans are suffered to burst forth;
4. And when the Graves are turned upside down;—
5. (Then) shall each soul know what it hath sent forward and (what it hath) kept back.
6. O man ! what has seduced thee from thy Lord Most Beneficent?
7. Him Who created thee, fashioned thee in due proportion, and gave thee a just bias;
8. In whatever Form He wills, does He put thee together.
9. Nay ! but ye do reject The Judgment !
10. But verily over you (are appointed angels) to protect you,—
11. Kind and honourable,— writing down (your deeds):
12. They know all that ye do.
13. As for the Righteous, they will be in Bliss;

إِنَّهُۥ لَقَوْلُ رَسُولٍ كَرِيمٍ ﴿١٩﴾
کہ بیشک یہ (قرآن) فرشتۂ عالی مقام کی زبان کا پیغام ہے ﴿١٩﴾

ذِي قُوَّةٍ عِندَ ذِي ٱلْعَرْشِ مَكِينٍ ﴿٢٠﴾
جو صاحب قوت مالک عرش کے ہاں اُونچے درجے والا ﴿٢٠﴾

مُّطَاعٍ ثَمَّ أَمِينٍ ﴿٢١﴾
سردار (اور) امانت دار ہے ﴿٢١﴾

وَمَا صَاحِبُكُم بِمَجْنُونٍ ﴿٢٢﴾
اور (مکے والو) تمہارے رفیق (یعنی محمدؐ) دیوانے نہیں ہیں ﴿٢٢﴾

وَلَقَدْ رَءَاهُ بِٱلْأُفُقِ ٱلْمُبِينِ ﴿٢٣﴾
بیشک انہوں نے اس (فرشتے) کو (آسمان کے) کھلے (یعنی شرقی) کنارے پر دیکھا ہے ﴿٢٣﴾

وَمَا هُوَ عَلَى ٱلْغَيْبِ بِضَنِينٍ ﴿٢٤﴾
اور وہ پوشیدہ باتوں (کے ظاہر کرنے) میں بخیل نہیں ﴿٢٤﴾

وَمَا هُوَ بِقَوْلِ شَيْطَٰنٍ رَّجِيمٍ ﴿٢٥﴾
اور یہ شیطان مردود کا کلام نہیں ﴿٢٥﴾

فَأَيْنَ تَذْهَبُونَ ﴿٢٦﴾
پھر تم کدھر جا رہے ہو؟ ﴿٢٦﴾

إِنْ هُوَ إِلَّا ذِكْرٌ لِّلْعَٰلَمِينَ ﴿٢٧﴾
یہ تو جہان کے لوگوں کے لئے نصیحت ہے ﴿٢٧﴾

لِمَن شَآءَ مِنكُمْ أَن يَسْتَقِيمَ ﴿٢٨﴾
(یعنی) اس کے لئے جو تم میں سے سیدھی چال چلنا چاہے ﴿٢٨﴾

وَمَا تَشَآءُونَ إِلَّآ أَن يَشَآءَ ٱللَّهُ رَبُّ ٱلْعَٰلَمِينَ ﴿٢٩﴾ ع
اور تم کچھ بھی نہیں چاہ سکتے مگر وہی جو خدائے رب العالمین چاہے ﴿٢٩﴾

سُورَةُ الْإِنْفِطَارِ مَكِّيَّةٌ وَهِيَ تِسْعَ عَشْرَةَ آيَةً

سورۂ انفطار مکی ہے اس میں اُنیس آیتیں ہیں

بِسْمِ ٱللَّهِ ٱلرَّحْمَٰنِ ٱلرَّحِيمِ
شروع خدا کا نام لے کر جو بڑا مہربان نہایت رحم والا ہے

إِذَا ٱلسَّمَآءُ ٱنفَطَرَتْ ﴿١﴾
جب آسمان پھٹ جائے گا ﴿١﴾

وَإِذَا ٱلْكَوَاكِبُ ٱنتَثَرَتْ ﴿٢﴾
اور جب تارے جھڑ پڑیں گے ﴿٢﴾

وَإِذَا ٱلْبِحَارُ فُجِّرَتْ ﴿٣﴾
اور جب دریا بہ (کر ایک دوسرے سے مل) جائیں گے ﴿٣﴾

وَإِذَا ٱلْقُبُورُ بُعْثِرَتْ ﴿٤﴾
اور جب قبریں اکھیڑ دی جائیں گی ﴿٤﴾

عَلِمَتْ نَفْسٌ مَّا قَدَّمَتْ وَأَخَّرَتْ ﴿٥﴾
تب ہر شخص معلوم کر لیگا کہ اُس نے آگے کیا بھیجا تھا اور پیچھے کیا چھوڑا تھا ﴿٥﴾

يَٰٓأَيُّهَا ٱلْإِنسَٰنُ مَا غَرَّكَ بِرَبِّكَ ٱلْكَرِيمِ ﴿٦﴾
اے انسان تجھ کو اپنے پروردگار کرم گستر کے بارے میں کس چیز نے دھوکا دیا ﴿٦﴾

ٱلَّذِي خَلَقَكَ فَسَوَّىٰكَ فَعَدَلَكَ ﴿٧﴾
(وہی تو ہے) جس نے تجھے بنایا اور (تیرے اعضاء کو) ٹھیک کیا اور (تیری قامت کو) معتدل رکھا ﴿٧﴾

فِيٓ أَيِّ صُورَةٍ مَّا شَآءَ رَكَّبَكَ ﴿٨﴾
اور جس صورت میں چاہا تجھے جوڑ دیا ﴿٨﴾

كَلَّا بَلْ تُكَذِّبُونَ بِٱلدِّينِ ﴿٩﴾
مگر ہیہات تم لوگ جزا کو جھٹلاتے ہو ﴿٩﴾

وَإِنَّ عَلَيْكُمْ لَحَٰفِظِينَ ﴿١٠﴾
حالانکہ تم پر نگہبان مقرر ہیں ﴿١٠﴾

كِرَامًا كَٰتِبِينَ ﴿١١﴾
عالی قدر (تمہاری باتوں کے) لکھنے والے ﴿١١﴾

يَعْلَمُونَ مَا تَفْعَلُونَ ﴿١٢﴾
جو تم کرتے ہو وہ اسے جانتے ہیں ﴿١٢﴾

إِنَّ ٱلْأَبْرَارَ لَفِي نَعِيمٍ ﴿١٣﴾
بے شک نیکوکار نعمتوں (کی بہشت) میں ہوں گے ﴿١٣﴾

SURA–83

AL-MUṬAFFIFEEN

(INTRODUCTION)

This Sûra is close in time to the last one and the next one.

It condemns all fraud—in daily dealings, as well as and especially in matters of Religion and the higher spiritual Life.

وَإِنَّ الْفُجَّارَ لَفِي جَحِيمٍ ﴿١٤﴾
اور بدکردار دوزخ میں ﴿۱۴﴾
14. And the Wicked—they will be in the Fire,

يَصْلَوْنَهَا يَوْمَ الدِّينِ ﴿١٥﴾
(یعنی) جزا کے دن اس میں داخل ہوں گے ﴿۱۵﴾
15. Which they will enter on the Day of Judgment,

وَمَا هُمْ عَنْهَا بِغَائِبِينَ ﴿١٦﴾
اور اُس سے چھپ نہیں سکیں گے ﴿۱۶﴾
16. And they will not be able to keep away therefrom.

وَمَا أَدْرَاكَ مَا يَوْمُ الدِّينِ ﴿١٧﴾
اور تمہیں کیا معلوم کہ جزا کا دن کیسا ہے ﴿۱۷﴾
17. And what will explain to thee what the Day of Judgment is ?

ثُمَّ مَا أَدْرَاكَ مَا يَوْمُ الدِّينِ ﴿١٨﴾
پھر تمہیں کیا معلوم کہ جزا کا دن کیسا ہے ﴿۱۸﴾
18. Again, what will explain to thee what the Day of Judgment is?

يَوْمَ لَا تَمْلِكُ نَفْسٌ لِّنَفْسٍ شَيْئًا ۖ وَالْأَمْرُ
يَوْمَئِذٍ لِّلَّهِ ﴿١٩﴾
جس روز کوئی کسی کا کچھ بھلا نہ کر سکے گا۔ اور حکم اُس روز
خدا ہی کا ہوگا ﴿۱۹﴾
19. (It will be) the Day when no soul shall have power (to do) aught for another: for the Command, that Day, will be (wholly) with Allah.

At-Taṭfîf, or Al-Muṭaffifeen or Dealing in Fraud

سُورَةُ التَّطْفِيفِ مَكِّيَّةٌ وَّهِيَ سِتٌّ وَّثَلٰثُونَ آيَةً

سورۂ تطفیف مکّی ہے اس میں چھتیس آیتیں ہیں

بِسْمِ اللَّهِ الرَّحْمَٰنِ الرَّحِيمِ
شروع خدا کا نام لے کر جو بڑا مہربان نہایت رحم والا ہے
In the name of Allah, Most Gracious, Most Merciful.

وَيْلٌ لِّلْمُطَفِّفِينَ ﴿١﴾
ناپ اور تول میں کمی کرنے والوں کے لئے خرابی ہے ﴿۱﴾
1. Woe to those that deal in fraud,—

الَّذِينَ إِذَا اكْتَالُوا عَلَى النَّاسِ يَسْتَوْفُونَ ﴿٢﴾
جو لوگوں سے ناپ کر لیں تو پورا لیں ﴿۲﴾
2. Those who, when they have to receive by measure from men, exact full measure,

وَإِذَا كَالُوهُمْ أَو وَّزَنُوهُمْ يُخْسِرُونَ ﴿٣﴾
اور جب اُن کو ناپ کر یا تول کر دیں تو کم دیں ﴿۳﴾
3. But when they have to give by measure or weight to men, give less than due.

أَلَا يَظُنُّ أُولَٰئِكَ أَنَّهُم مَّبْعُوثُونَ ﴿٤﴾
کیا یہ لوگ نہیں جانتے کہ اُٹھائے بھی جائیں گے ﴿۴﴾
4. Do they not think that they will be raised up?—

لِيَوْمٍ عَظِيمٍ ﴿٥﴾
(یعنی) ایک بڑے (سخت) دن میں ﴿۵﴾
5. On a Mighty Day,

يَوْمَ يَقُومُ النَّاسُ لِرَبِّ الْعَالَمِينَ ﴿٦﴾
جس دن (تمام) لوگ رب العالمین کے سامنے کھڑے ہوں گے ﴿۶﴾
6. A Day when (all) mankind will stand before the Lord of the Worlds?

كَلَّا إِنَّ كِتَابَ الْفُجَّارِ لَفِي سِجِّينٍ ﴿٧﴾
سُن رکھو کہ بدکاروں کے اعمال سجّین میں ہیں ﴿۷﴾
7. Nay ! Surely the Record of the Wicked is (preserved) in *Sijjîn.*

وَمَا أَدْرَاكَ مَا سِجِّينٌ ﴿٨﴾
اور تم کیا جانتے ہو کہ سجّین کیا چیز ہے ﴿۸﴾
8. And what will explain to thee what *Sijjîn* is?

كِتَابٌ مَّرْقُومٌ ﴿٩﴾
ایک دفتر ہے لکھا ہوا ﴿۹﴾
9. (There is) a Register (fully) inscribed.

وَيْلٌ يَوْمَئِذٍ لِّلْمُكَذِّبِينَ ﴿١٠﴾
اُس دن جھٹلانے والوں کی خرابی ہے ﴿۱۰﴾
10. Woe, that Day, to those that deny—

الَّذِينَ يُكَذِّبُونَ بِيَوْمِ الدِّينِ ﴿١١﴾
(یعنی) جو انصاف کے دن کو جھٹلاتے ہیں ﴿۱۱﴾
11. Those that deny the Day of Judgment.

وَمَا يُكَذِّبُ بِهِ إِلَّا كُلُّ مُعْتَدٍ أَثِيمٍ ﴿١٢﴾
اور اسکو جھٹلاتا وہی ہے جو حد سے نکل جانے والا گنہگار ہے ﴿۱۲﴾
12. And none can deny it but the Transgressor beyond bounds, the Sinner !

إِذَا تُتْلَىٰ عَلَيْهِ آيَاتُنَا قَالَ أَسَاطِيرُ
الْأَوَّلِينَ ﴿١٣﴾
جب اُس کو ہماری آیتیں سُنائی جاتی ہیں تو کہتا ہے یہ تو
اگلے لوگوں کے افسانے ہیں ﴿۱۳﴾
13. When Our Signs are rehearsed to him, he says, "Tales of the Ancients !"

كَلَّا ۖ بَلْ ۜ رَانَ عَلَىٰ قُلُوبِهِم مَّا كَانُوا
يَكْسِبُونَ ﴿١٤﴾
دیکھو یہ جو (اعمال بد) کرتے ہیں۔ اُن کا اُن کے دلوں
پر زنگ بیٹھ گیا ہے ﴿۱۴﴾
14. By no means ! But on their hearts is the stain of the (ill) which they do !

كَلَّا إِنَّهُمْ عَن رَّبِّهِمْ يَوْمَئِذٍ لَّمَحْجُوبُونَ ﴿١٥﴾
بیشک یہ لوگ اُس روز اپنے پروردگار (کے دیدار) سے اوٹ میں ہوں گے ﴿۱۵﴾
15. Verily, from (the Light of) their Lord, that Day, will they be veiled.

ثُمَّ إِنَّهُمْ لَصَالُو الْجَحِيمِ ﴿١٦﴾
پھر دوزخ میں جا داخل ہوں گے ﴿۱۶﴾
16. Further, they will enter the Fire of Hell.

SÛRA–84

AL-INSHIQÃQ

(INTRODUCTION)

Chronologically this Sûra is closely connected with the last one. In subject-matter it resembles more S. 82, and 81 with which it may be compared.

By a number of mystic metaphors it is shown that the present phenomenal order will not last, and Allah's full Judgment will certainly be established: man should therefore strive for that World of Eternity and True Values.

17. Further, it will be said to them: "This is the (reality) which ye rejected as false !"

پھر اُن سے کہا جائے گا کہ یہ وہی چیز ہے جس کو تم جھٹلاتے تھے ﴿١٧﴾

ثُمَّ يُقَالُ هٰذَا الَّذِيْ كُنْتُمْ بِهٖ تُكَذِّبُوْنَ ﴿١٧﴾

18. Nay, verily the Record of the Righteous is (preserved) in *'Illîyîn.*

(یہ بھی) سُن رکھو کہ نیکوکاروں کے اعمال علّیین میں ہیں ﴿١٨﴾

كَلَّآ اِنَّ كِتٰبَ الْاَبْرَارِ لَفِيْ عِلِّيِّيْنَ ﴿١٨﴾

19. And what will explain to thee what *'Illîyûn* is?

اور تم کو کیا معلوم کہ علّیین کیا چیز ہے ﴿١٩﴾

وَمَآ اَدْرٰىكَ مَا عِلِّيُّوْنَ ﴿١٩﴾

20. (There is) a Register (fully) inscribed,

ایک دفتر ہے لکھا ہُوا ﴿٢٠﴾

كِتٰبٌ مَّرْقُوْمٌ ﴿٢٠﴾

21. To which bear witness those Nearest (to Allah).

جس کے پاس مقرب (فرشتے) حاضر رہتے ہیں ﴿٢١﴾

يَّشْهَدُهُ الْمُقَرَّبُوْنَ ﴿٢١﴾

22. Truly the Righteous will be in Bliss:

بے شک نیک لوگ چین میں ہوں گے ﴿٢٢﴾

اِنَّ الْاَبْرَارَ لَفِيْ نَعِيْمٍ ﴿٢٢﴾

23. On raised couches will they command a sight (of all things):

تختوں پر بیٹھے ہوئے نظارے کریں گے ﴿٢٣﴾

عَلَى الْاَرَآئِكِ يَنْظُرُوْنَ ﴿٢٣﴾

24. Thou wilt recognise in their Faces the beaming brightness of Bliss.

تم اُن کے چہروں ہی سے راحت کی تازگی معلوم کر لو گے ﴿٢٤﴾

تَعْرِفُ فِيْ وُجُوْهِهِمْ نَضْرَةَ النَّعِيْمِ ﴿٢٤﴾

25. Their thirst will be slaked with Pure Wine sealed;

اُن کو شراب خالص سربمہر پلائی جائے گی ﴿٢٥﴾

يُسْقَوْنَ مِنْ رَّحِيْقٍ مَّخْتُوْمٍ ﴿٢٥﴾

26. The seal thereof will be musk: and for this let those aspire, who have aspirations:

جس کی مُہر مشک کی ہو گی. تو (نعمتوں کے) شائقین کو چاہیے
کہ اسی سے رغبت کریں ﴿٢٦﴾

خِتٰمُهٗ مِسْكٌ ۭ وَفِيْ ذٰلِكَ فَلْيَتَنَافَسِ
الْمُتَنَافِسُوْنَ ﴿٢٦﴾

27. With it will be (given) a mixture of *Tasnîm:*

اور اس میں تسنیم (کے پانی) کی آمیزش ہو گی ﴿٢٧﴾

وَمِزَاجُهٗ مِنْ تَسْنِيْمٍ ﴿٢٧﴾

28. A spring, from (the waters) whereof drink those Nearest to Allah.

وہ ایک چشمہ ہے جس میں سے (خدا کے) مقرب پئیں گے ﴿٢٨﴾

عَيْنًا يَّشْرَبُ بِهَا الْمُقَرَّبُوْنَ ﴿٢٨﴾

29. Those in sin used to laugh at those who believed,

جو گنہگار (یعنی کفار) ہیں وہ (دنیا میں) مومنوں سے ہنسی
کیا کرتے تھے ﴿٢٩﴾

اِنَّ الَّذِيْنَ اَجْرَمُوْا كَانُوْا مِنَ الَّذِيْنَ
اٰمَنُوْا يَضْحَكُوْنَ ﴿٢٩﴾

30. And whenever they passed by them, used to wink at each other (in mockery);

اور جب اُن کے پاس سے گزرتے تو حقارت سے اشارے کرتے ﴿٣٠﴾

وَاِذَا مَرُّوْا بِهِمْ يَتَغَامَزُوْنَ ﴿٣٠﴾

31. And when they returned to their own people, they would return jesting;

اور جب اپنے گھر کو لوٹتے تو اِتراتے ہوئے لوٹتے ﴿٣١﴾

وَاِذَا انْقَلَبُوْٓا اِلٰٓى اَهْلِهِمُ انْقَلَبُوْا فَكِهِيْنَ ﴿٣١﴾

32. And whenever they saw them, they would say, "Behold ! these are the people truly astray!"

اور جب اُن (مومنوں) کو دیکھتے تو کہتے کہ یہ تو گمراہ ہیں ﴿٣٢﴾

وَاِذَا رَاَوْهُمْ قَالُوْٓا اِنَّ هٰٓؤُلَاۗءِ لَضَاۗلُّوْنَ ﴿٣٢﴾

33. But they had not been sent as Keepers over them !

حالانکہ وہ اُن پر نگراں بنا کر نہیں بھیجے گئے تھے ﴿٣٣﴾

وَمَآ اُرْسِلُوْا عَلَيْهِمْ حٰفِظِيْنَ ﴿٣٣﴾

34. But on this Day the Believers will laugh at the Unbelievers:

تو آج مومن کافروں سے ہنسی کریں گے ﴿٣٤﴾

فَالْيَوْمَ الَّذِيْنَ اٰمَنُوْا مِنَ الْكُفَّارِ يَضْحَكُوْنَ ﴿٣٤﴾

35. On raised couches they will command (a sight) (of all things).

(اور) تختوں پر (بیٹھے ہوئے اُن کا حال) دیکھ رہے ہوں گے ﴿٣٥﴾

عَلَى الْاَرَآئِكِ ۙ يَنْظُرُوْنَ ﴿٣٥﴾

36. Will not the Unbelievers have been paid back for what they did?

تو کافروں کو اُن کے عملوں کا (پُورا پُورا) بدلہ مل گیا ﴿٣٦﴾

هَلْ ثُوِّبَ الْكُفَّارُ مَا كَانُوْا يَفْعَلُوْنَ ﴿٣٦﴾

Al-Inshiqâq, or The Rending Asunder

سُورۃ انشقاق مکی ہے اس میں پچیس آیتیں ہیں

سُوْرَةُ الْاِنْشِقَاقِ مَكِّيَّةٌ وَّهِيَ خَمْسٌ وَّعِشْرُوْنَ اٰيَةً

In the name of Allah, Most Gracious, Most Mercifrul.

شروع خدا کا نام لے کر جو بڑا مہربان نہایت رحم والا ہے ۝

بِسْمِ اللّٰهِ الرَّحْمٰنِ الرَّحِيْمِ ۝

1. When the Sky is rent asunder,

جب آسمان پھٹ جائے گا ﴿١﴾

اِذَا السَّمَاۗءُ انْشَقَّتْ ﴿١﴾

2. And hearkens to (the Command of) its Lord,—and it must needs (do so);—

اور اپنے پروردگار کا فرمان بجا لائے گا اور اسے واجب بھی یہی ہے ﴿٢﴾

وَاَذِنَتْ لِرَبِّهَا وَحُقَّتْ ﴿٢﴾

3. And when the Earth is flattened out,

اور جب زمین ہموار کر دی جائے گی ﴿٣﴾

وَاِذَا الْاَرْضُ مُدَّتْ ﴿٣﴾

4. And casts forth what is within it and becomes (clean) empty,	اور جو کچھ اس میں ہے اسے نکال کر باہر ڈال دیگی اور (بالکل) خالی ہو جائیگی ۴	وَأَلْقَتْ مَا فِيهَا وَتَخَلَّتْ ۝٤
5. And hearkens to (the Command of) its Lord,— and it must needs (do so); —(then will come home the full Reality).	اور اپنے پروردگار کے ارشاد کی تعمیل کریگی اور اسکو لازم بھی یہی ہے (تو قیامت قائم ہو جائیگی) ۵	وَأَذِنَتْ لِرَبِّهَا وَحُقَّتْ ۝٥
6. O thou man ! verily thou art ever toiling on towards thy Lord— painfully toiling,—but thou shalt meet Him.	اے انسان تو اپنے پروردگار کی طرف (پہنچنے میں) خوب کوشش کرتا ہے سو اس سے جا ملے گا ۶	يَا أَيُّهَا الْإِنْسَانُ إِنَّكَ كَادِحٌ إِلَىٰ رَبِّكَ كَدْحًا فَمُلَاقِيهِ ۝٦
7. Then he who is given his Record in his right hand,	تو جس کا نامہ (اعمال) اسکے داہنے ہاتھ میں دیا جائے گا ۷	فَأَمَّا مَنْ أُوتِيَ كِتَابَهُ بِيَمِينِهِ ۝٧
8. Soon will his account be taken by an easy reckoning,	اس سے حساب آسان لیا جائے گا ۸	فَسَوْفَ يُحَاسَبُ حِسَابًا يَسِيرًا ۝٨
9. And he will turn to his people, rejoicing !	اور وہ اپنے گھر والوں میں خوش خوش آئے گا ۹	وَيَنْقَلِبُ إِلَىٰ أَهْلِهِ مَسْرُورًا ۝٩
10. But he who is given his Record behind his back,—	اور جس کا نامہ (اعمال) اسکی پیٹھ کے پیچھے سے دیا جائے گا ۱۰	وَأَمَّا مَنْ أُوتِيَ كِتَابَهُ وَرَاءَ ظَهْرِهِ ۝١٠
11. Soon will he cry for Perdition,	وہ موت کو پکارے گا ۱۱	فَسَوْفَ يَدْعُو ثُبُورًا ۝١١
12. And he will enter a Blazing Fire.	اور دوزخ میں داخل ہوگا ۱۲	وَيَصْلَىٰ سَعِيرًا ۝١٢
13. Truly, did he go about among his people, rejoicing !	یہ اپنے اہل (وعیال) میں مست رہتا تھا ۱۳	إِنَّهُ كَانَ فِي أَهْلِهِ مَسْرُورًا ۝١٣
14. Truly, did he think that he would not have to return (to Us) !	اور خیال کرتا تھا کہ (خدا کی طرف) پھر کر نہ جائے گا ۱۴	إِنَّهُ ظَنَّ أَنْ لَنْ يَحُورَ ۝١٤
15. Nay, nay ! for his Lord was (ever) watchful of him !	ہاں (ہاں) اس کا پروردگار اس کو دیکھ رہا تھا ۱۵	بَلَىٰ إِنَّ رَبَّهُ كَانَ بِهِ بَصِيرًا ۝١٥
16. So I do call to witness the ruddy glow of Sunset;	ہمیں شام کی سرخی کی قسم ۱۶	فَلَا أُقْسِمُ بِالشَّفَقِ ۝١٦
17. The Night and its Homing;	اور رات کی اور جن چیزوں کو وہ اکٹھا کر لیتی ہے ان کی ۱۷	وَاللَّيْلِ وَمَا وَسَقَ ۝١٧
18. And the Moon in her Fulness:	اور چاند کی جب کامل ہو جائے ۱۸	وَالْقَمَرِ إِذَا اتَّسَقَ ۝١٨
19. Ye shall surely travel from stage to stage.	کہ تم درجہ درجہ (رتبۂ اعلیٰ پر) چڑھو گے ۱۹	لَتَرْكَبُنَّ طَبَقًا عَنْ طَبَقٍ ۝١٩
20. What then is the matter with them, that they believe not?—	تو ان لوگوں کو کیا ہوا ہے کہ ایمان نہیں لاتے ۲۰	فَمَا لَهُمْ لَا يُؤْمِنُونَ ۝٢٠
21. And when the Qur'ān is read to them, they fall not prostrate,	اور جب ان کے سامنے قرآن پڑھا جاتا ہے تو سجدہ نہیں کرتے ۲۱	وَإِذَا قُرِئَ عَلَيْهِمُ الْقُرْآنُ لَا يَسْجُدُونَ ۝٢١
22. But on the contrary the Unbelievers reject (it).	بلکہ کافر جھٹلاتے ہیں ۲۲	بَلِ الَّذِينَ كَفَرُوا يُكَذِّبُونَ ۝٢٢
23. But Allah has full Knowledge of what they secrete (in their breasts).	اور خدا ان باتوں کو جو یہ اپنے دلوں میں چھپاتے ہیں خوب جانتا ہے ۲۳	وَاللَّهُ أَعْلَمُ بِمَا يُوعُونَ ۝٢٣
24. So announce to them a Chastisement Grievous,	تو ان کو دکھ دینے والے عذاب کی خبر سنا دو ۲۴	فَبَشِّرْهُمْ بِعَذَابٍ أَلِيمٍ ۝٢٤
25. Except to those who believe and work righteous deeds: for them is a Reward that will never fail.	ہاں جو لوگ ایمان لائے اور نیک عمل کرتے رہے انکے لئے بے انتہا اجر ہے ۲۵	إِلَّا الَّذِينَ آمَنُوا وَعَمِلُوا الصَّالِحَاتِ لَهُمْ أَجْرٌ غَيْرُ مَمْنُونٍ ۝٢٥

معانقة عند المتأخرين ۱۲

السجدة ۱۲

ع ۱ ۵

SÛRA–85

AL-BURÛJ

(INTRODUCTION)

This is one of the earlier Makkan Sûras, chronologically cognate with S. 91. The subject-matter is the persecution of Allah's votaries. Allah watches over His own, and will deal with the enemies of Truth as He dealt with them in the past.

Al-Burûj, or The Zodiacal Signs

In the name of Allah, Most Gracious, Most Merciful.

1. By the Sky, with its constellations;
2. By the promised Day (of Judgment);
3. By one that witnesses, and the subject of the witness;—
4. Woe to the makers of the pit (of fire),
5. Fire supplied (abundantly) with Fuel:
6. Behold ! they sat over against the (fire),
7. And they witnessed (all) that they were doing against the Believers.
8. And they ill-treated them for no other reason than that they believed in Allah, exalted in Power, Worthy of all Praise !—
9. Him to Whom belongs the dominion of the heavens and the earth ! And Allah is Witness to all things.
10. Those who persecute the Believers, men and women, and do not turn in repentance, will have the Chastisement of Hell: they will have the Chastisement of the Burning Fire.
11. For those who believe and do righteous deeds, will be Gardens. Beneath which Rivers flow: that is the great Triumph.
12. Truly strong is the Grip of thy Lord.
13. It is He Who creates from the very beginning, and He can restore (life).
14. And He is the Oft-Forgiving, full of loving-kindness,
15. Lord of the Throne, full of all glory,
16. Doer (without let) of all that He intends.
17. Has the story reached thee, of the Forces—
18. Of Pharaoh and the Thamûd?
19. And yet the Unbelievers (persist) in rejecting (the Truth) !

سورہ بروج مکی ہے اس میں بائیس آیتیں ہیں

شروع خدا کا نام لے کر جو بڑا مہربان نہایت رحم والا ہے
آسمان کی قسم جس میں برج ہیں ﴿۱﴾ [۳۲۱]
اور اس دن کی جس کا وعدہ ہے ﴿۲﴾
اور حاضر ہونیوالے کی اور جو اسکے پاس حاضر کیا جائے اسکی ﴿۳﴾ [۳۲۲]
کہ خندقوں (کے کھودنے) والے ہلاک کر دیئے گئے ﴿۴﴾
(یعنی) آگ (کی خندقیں) جس میں ایندھن (جھونک رکھا) تھا ﴿۵﴾
جبکہ وہ اُن (کے کناروں) پر بیٹھے ہوئے تھے ﴿۶﴾
اور جو (سختیاں) اہلِ ایمان پر کر رہے تھے انکو سامنے دیکھ رہے تھے ﴿۷﴾
اُن کو مومنوں کی یہی بات بُری لگتی تھی کہ وہ خدا پر ایمان
لائے ہوئے تھے جو غالب اور قابلِ ستائش ہے ﴿۸﴾ [۳۲۳]
جس کی آسمانوں اور زمین میں بادشاہت ہے اور خدا ہر
چیز سے واقف ہے ﴿۹﴾
جن لوگوں نے مومن مردوں اور مومن عورتوں کو تکلیفیں
دیں اور توبہ نہ کی اُن کو دوزخ کا (اور) عذاب بھی ہوگا
اور جلنے کا عذاب بھی ہوگا ﴿۱۰﴾
(اور) جو لوگ ایمان لائے اور نیک کام کرتے رہے اُن
کے لئے باغات ہیں جن کے نیچے نہریں بہہ رہی ہیں۔ یہی
بڑی کامیابی ہے ﴿۱۱﴾
بے شک تمہارے پروردگار کی پکڑ بہت سخت ہے ﴿۱۲﴾
وہی پہلی دفعہ پیدا کرتا ہے اور وہی دوبارہ (زندہ) کریگا ﴿۱۳﴾
اور وہ بخشنے والا (اور) محبت کرنے والا ہے ﴿۱۴﴾
عرش کا مالک بڑی شان والا ﴿۱۵﴾
جو چاہتا ہے کر دیتا ہے ﴿۱۶﴾
بھلا تم کو لشکروں کا حال معلوم ہوا ہے ﴿۱۷﴾
(یعنی) فرعون اور ثمود کا ﴿۱۸﴾
لیکن کافر (جان بوجھ کر) تکذیب میں (گرفتار) ہیں ﴿۱۹﴾

سُوْرَةُ الْبُرُوْجِ مَكِّيَّةٌ وَّهِيَ اثْنَتَانِ وَعِشْرُوْنَ اٰيَةً

بِسْمِ اللّٰهِ الرَّحْمٰنِ الرَّحِيْمِ
وَالسَّمَآءِ ذَاتِ الْبُرُوْجِ ﴿۱﴾
وَالْيَوْمِ الْمَوْعُوْدِ ﴿۲﴾
وَشَاهِدٍ وَّمَشْهُوْدٍ ﴿۳﴾
قُتِلَ اَصْحٰبُ الْاُخْدُوْدِ ﴿۴﴾
النَّارِ ذَاتِ الْوَقُوْدِ ﴿۵﴾
اِذْ هُمْ عَلَيْهَا قُعُوْدٌ ﴿۶﴾
وَّهُمْ عَلٰى مَا يَفْعَلُوْنَ بِالْمُؤْمِنِيْنَ شُهُوْدٌ ﴿۷﴾
وَمَا نَقَمُوْا مِنْهُمْ اِلَّاۤ اَنْ يُّؤْمِنُوْا بِاللّٰهِ
الْعَزِيْزِ الْحَمِيْدِ ﴿۸﴾
الَّذِيْ لَهٗ مُلْكُ السَّمٰوٰتِ وَالْاَرْضِ ط
وَاللّٰهُ عَلٰى كُلِّ شَيْءٍ شَهِيْدٌ ﴿۹﴾
اِنَّ الَّذِيْنَ فَتَنُوا الْمُؤْمِنِيْنَ وَالْمُؤْمِنٰتِ
ثُمَّ لَمْ يَتُوْبُوْا فَلَهُمْ عَذَابُ جَهَنَّمَ
وَلَهُمْ عَذَابُ الْحَرِيْقِ ﴿۱۰﴾
اِنَّ الَّذِيْنَ اٰمَنُوْا وَعَمِلُوا الصّٰلِحٰتِ
لَهُمْ جَنّٰتٌ تَجْرِيْ مِنْ تَحْتِهَا الْاَنْهٰرُ ط
ذٰلِكَ الْفَوْزُ الْكَبِيْرُ ﴿۱۱﴾
اِنَّ بَطْشَ رَبِّكَ لَشَدِيْدٌ ﴿۱۲﴾
اِنَّهٗ هُوَ يُبْدِئُ وَيُعِيْدُ ﴿۱۳﴾
وَهُوَ الْغَفُوْرُ الْوَدُوْدُ ﴿۱۴﴾
ذُو الْعَرْشِ الْمَجِيْدُ ﴿۱۵﴾
فَعَّالٌ لِّمَا يُرِيْدُ ﴿۱۶﴾
هَلْ اَتٰىكَ حَدِيْثُ الْجُنُوْدِ ﴿۱۷﴾
فِرْعَوْنَ وَثَمُوْدَ ﴿۱۸﴾
بَلِ الَّذِيْنَ كَفَرُوْا فِيْ تَكْذِيْبٍ ﴿۱۹﴾

SÛRA–86

AṬ-ṬARIQ

(INTRODUCTION)

This Sûra also belongs to the early Makkan period, perhaps not far removed from the last Sûra.

Its subject-matter is the protection afforded to every soul in the darkest period of its spiritual hisroty. The physical nature of man may be insignificant, but the soul given to him by Allah must win a glorious Future in the end.

SÛRA–87

AL-A'LÃ

(INTRODUCTION)

This is one of the earliest of the Makkan Sûras, being usually placed eighth in chronological order, and immediately after S. 81.

The argument is that Allah has made man capable of progress by ordered steps, and by His Revelation will lead him still higher to purification and perfection.

20. But Allah doth encompass them from behind!

اور خدا (بھی) اُن کو گردا گرد سے گھیرے ہوئے ہے (٢٠)

وَّاللّٰهُ مِنْ وَّرَآئِهِمْ مُّحِيْطٌ (٢٠)

21. Nay, this is a Glorious Qur'ān,

(یہ کتاب ہزل و بطلان نہیں) بلکہ یہ قرآن عظیم الشان ہے (٢١)

بَلْ هُوَ قُرْاٰنٌ مَّجِيْدٌ (٢١)

22. (Inscribed) in a Tablet Preserved !

لوح محفوظ میں (لکھا ہوا) (٢٢)

فِيْ لَوْحٍ مَّحْفُوْظٍ (٢٢)

A -Ṭāriq, or The Night-Visitant

سورۂ طارق مکی ہے اس میں سترہ آیتیں ہیں

سُوْرَةُ الطَّارِقِ مَكِّيَّةٌ وَّهِيَ سَبْعَ عَشْرَةَ اٰيَةً

In the name of Allah, Most Gracious, Most Merciful.

شروع خدا کا نام لے کر جو بڑا مہربان نہایت رحم والا ہے

بِسْمِ اللّٰهِ الرَّحْمٰنِ الرَّحِيْمِ

1. By the Sky and the Night-Visitant (therein);

آسمان اور رات کے وقت آنے والے کی قسم (١)

وَالسَّمَآءِ وَالطَّارِقِ (١)

2. And what will explain to thee what the Night-Visitant is?—

اور تم کو کیا معلوم کہ رات کے وقت آنے والا کیا ہے (٢)

وَمَآ اَدْرٰىكَ مَا الطَّارِقُ (٢)

3. (It is) the Star of piercing brightness;—

وہ تارا ہے چمکنے والا (٣)

النَّجْمُ الثَّاقِبُ (٣)

4. There is no soul but has a protector over it.

کہ کوئی متنفس نہیں جس پر نگہبان مقرر نہیں (٤)

اِنْ كُلُّ نَفْسٍ لَّمَّا عَلَيْهَا حَافِظٌ (٤)

5. Now let man but think from what he is created !

تو انسان کو دیکھنا چاہیئے کہ وہ کاہے سے پیدا ہوا ہے (٥)

فَلْيَنْظُرِ الْاِنْسَانُ مِمَّ خُلِقَ (٥)

6. He is created from a drop emitted—

وہ اُچھلتے ہوئے پانی سے پیدا ہوا ہے (٦)

خُلِقَ مِنْ مَّآءٍ دَافِقٍ (٦)

7. Proceeding from between the backbone and the ribs:

جو پیٹھ اور سینے کے بیچ میں سے نکلتا ہے (٧)

يَّخْرُجُ مِنْۢ بَيْنِ الصُّلْبِ وَالتَّرَآئِبِ (٧)

8. Surely (Allah) is able to bring him back (to life) !

بے شک خدا اسکے اعادے (یعنی پھر پیدا کرنے) پر قادر ہے (٨)

اِنَّهٗ عَلٰى رَجْعِهٖ لَقَادِرٌ (٨)

9. The Day that (all) things secret will be tested,

جس دن دلوں کے بھید جانچے جائیں گے [٣٢٤] (٩)

يَوْمَ تُبْلَى السَّرَآئِرُ (٩)

10. (Man) will have no power, and no helper.

تو انسان کی کچھ پیش نہ چل سکے گی اور نہ کوئی اسکا مددگار ہوگا (١٠)

فَمَا لَهٗ مِنْ قُوَّةٍ وَّلَا نَاصِرٍ (١٠)

11. By the Firmament which giveth the returning rain,

آسمان کی قسم جو مینہ برساتا ہے (١١)

وَالسَّمَآءِ ذَاتِ الرَّجْعِ (١١)

12. And by the Earth which opens out (for the gushing of springs or the sprouting of vegetation),—

اور زمین کی قسم جو پھٹ جاتی ہے [٣٢٥] (١٢)

وَالْاَرْضِ ذَاتِ الصَّدْعِ (١٢)

13. Behold this is the Word that distinguishes (Good from Evil):

کہ یہ کلام (حق کو باطل سے) جُدا کرنے والا ہے (١٣)

اِنَّهٗ لَقَوْلٌ فَصْلٌ (١٣)

14. It is not a thing for amusement.

اور بیہودہ بات نہیں (١٤)

وَّمَا هُوَ بِالْهَزْلِ (١٤)

15. As for them, they are but plotting a scheme,

یہ لوگ تو اپنی تدبیروں میں لگ رہے ہیں (١٥)

اِنَّهُمْ يَكِيْدُوْنَ كَيْدًا (١٥)

16. And I am planning a scheme.

اور ہم اپنی تدبیر کر رہے ہیں (١٦)

وَّاَكِيْدُ كَيْدًا (١٦)

17. Therefore grant a delay to the Unbelievers: give respite to them gently (for awhile).

تو تم کافروں کو مہلت دو بس چند روز ہی مہلت دو (١٧)

فَمَهِّلِ الْكٰفِرِيْنَ اَمْهِلْهُمْ رُوَيْدًا (١٧)

Al-A'la, or The Most High

سورۂ اعلیٰ مکی ہے اس میں اُنیس آیتیں ہیں

سُوْرَةُ الْاَعْلٰى مَكِّيَّةٌ وَّهِيَ تِسْعَ عَشْرَةَ اٰيَةً

In the name of Allah, Most Gracious, Most Merciful.

شروع خدا کا نام لے کر جو بڑا مہربان نہایت رحم والا ہے

بِسْمِ اللّٰهِ الرَّحْمٰنِ الرَّحِيْمِ

1. Glorify the name of thy Guardian-Lord Most High,

(اے پیغمبر) اپنے پروردگار جلیل الشان کے نام کی تسبیح کرو (١)

سَبِّحِ اسْمَ رَبِّكَ الْاَعْلَى (١)

2. Who hath created, and further, given order and proportion;

جس نے (انسان کو) بنایا پھر (اسکے اعضا کو) درست کیا (٢)

الَّذِيْ خَلَقَ فَسَوّٰى (٢)

3. Who hath measured. And granted guidance;

اور جس نے (اسکا) اندازہ ٹھہرایا (پھر اس کو) رستہ بتایا (٣)

وَالَّذِيْ قَدَّرَ فَهَدٰى (٣)

SÛRA–88
AL-GÃSHIYA
(INTRODUCTION)

This is a late Sûra of the early Makkan period, perhaps close in date to S. 52. Its subject-matter is the contrast between the destinies of the Good and the Evil in the Hereafter,—on the Day when the true balance will be restored: the Signs of Allah even in this life should remind us of the Day of Account, for Allah is good and just, and His creation is for a just Purpose.

4. And Who bringeth out the (green and luscious) pasture,	اور جس نے چارہ اُگایا (۴)	وَالَّذِيْٓ اَخْرَجَ الْمَرْعٰى ۝٤
5. And then doth make it (but) swarthy stubble.	پھر اُس کو سیاہ رنگ کا کوڑا کر دیا (۵)	فَجَعَلَهٗ غُثَاۗءً اَحْوٰى ۝٥
6. By degrees shall We teach thee (the Message), so thou shalt not forget,	ہم تمہیں پڑھا دیں گے کہ تم فراموش نہ کرو گے (۶)	سَنُقْرِئُكَ فَلَا تَنْسٰٓى ۝٦
7. Except as Allah wills: for He knoweth what is manifest and what is hidden.	مگر جو خدا چاہے۔ وہ کھلی بات کو بھی جانتا ہے اور چھپی کو بھی (۷)	اِلَّا مَا شَاۗءَ اللّٰهُ ۭ اِنَّهٗ يَعْلَمُ الْجَهْرَ وَمَا يَخْفٰى ۝٧
8. And We will make it easy for thee (to follow) the simple (Path).	ہم تم کو آسان طریقے کی توفیق دیں گے (۸)	وَنُيَسِّرُكَ لِلْيُسْرٰى ۝٨
9. Therefore give admonition in case the admonition profits (the hearer).	سو جہاں تک نصیحت (کے) نافع (ہونے کی اُمید) ہو نصیحت کرتے رہو (۹)	فَذَكِّرْ اِنْ نَّفَعَتِ الذِّكْرٰى ۝٩
10. He will heed who fears:	جو خوف رکھتا ہے وہ تو نصیحت پکڑے گا (۱۰)	سَيَذَّكَّرُ مَنْ يَّخْشٰى ۝١٠
11. But it will be avoided by the most unfortunate one,	اور (بے خوف) بدبخت پہلو تہی کرے گا (۱۱)	وَيَتَجَنَّبُهَا الْاَشْقَى ۝١١
12. Who will enter the Great Fire,	جو (قیامت کو) بڑی (تیز) آگ میں داخل ہوگا (۱۲)	الَّذِيْ يَصْلَى النَّارَ الْكُبْرٰى ۝١٢
13. In which he will then neither die nor live.	پھر وہاں نہ مرے گا نہ جیے گا (۱۳)	ثُمَّ لَا يَمُوْتُ فِيْهَا وَلَا يَحْيٰى ۝١٣
14. But he will prosper who purifies himself.	بے شک وہ مراد کو پہنچ گیا جو پاک ہوا (۱۴)	قَدْ اَفْلَحَ مَنْ تَزَكّٰى ۝١٤
15. And remembers the name of his Guardian-Lord, and prays.	اور اپنے پروردگار کے نام کا ذکر کرتا رہا اور نماز پڑھتا رہا (۱۵)	وَذَكَرَ اسْمَ رَبِّهٖ فَصَلّٰى ۝١٥
16. Nay (behold), ye prefer the life of this world;	مگر تم لوگ تو دنیا کی زندگی کو اختیار کرتے ہو (۱۶)	بَلْ تُؤْثِرُوْنَ الْحَيٰوةَ الدُّنْيَا ۝١٦
17. But the Hereafter is better and more enduring.	حالانکہ آخرت بہت بہتر اور پائندہ تر ہے (۱۷)	وَالْاٰخِرَةُ خَيْرٌ وَّاَبْقٰى ۝١٧
18. And this is in the Books of the earliest (Revelations),—	یہی بات پہلے صحیفوں میں (مرقوم) ہے (۱۸)	اِنَّ هٰذَا لَفِي الصُّحُفِ الْاُوْلٰى ۝١٨
19. The Books of Abraham and Moses.	(یعنی) ابراہیم اور موسیٰ کے صحیفوں میں (۱۹)	صُحُفِ اِبْرٰهِيْمَ وَمُوْسٰى ۝١٩ ع ١٩ ١٢

Al-Gāshiya, or The Overwhelming Event

	سورۂ غاشیہ مکی ہے اس میں چھبیس آیتیں ہیں	سُوْرَةُ الْغَاشِيَةِ مَكِّيَّةٌ وَّهِيَ سِتٌّ وَّعِشْرُوْنَ اٰيَةً
In the name of Allah, Most Gracious, Most Merciful.	شروع خدا کا نام لے کر جو بڑا مہربان نہایت رحم والا ہے	بِسْمِ اللّٰهِ الرَّحْمٰنِ الرَّحِيْمِ
1. Has the story reached thee, of the Overwhelming (Event)?	بھلا تم کو ڈھانپ لینے والی (یعنی قیامت) کا حال معلوم ہوا ہے (۱)	هَلْ اَتٰىكَ حَدِيْثُ الْغَاشِيَةِ ۝١
2. Some faces, that Day, will be humiliated,	اُس روز بہت سے مُنہ (والے) ذلیل ہوں گے (۲)	وُجُوْهٌ يَّوْمَىِٕذٍ خَاشِعَةٌ ۝٢
3. Labouring (hard), weary,—	سخت محنت کرنے والے تھکے ماندے (۳)	عَامِلَةٌ نَّاصِبَةٌ ۝٣
4. The while they enter the Blazing Fire,—	دہکتی آگ میں داخل ہوں گے (۴)	تَصْلٰى نَارًا حَامِيَةً ۝٤
5. The while they are given, to drink, of a boiling hot spring,	ایک کھولتے ہوئے چشمے کا اُن کو پانی پلایا جائے گا (۵)	تُسْقٰى مِنْ عَيْنٍ اٰنِيَةٍ ۝٥
6. No food will there be for them but a bitter *Dharī*	اور خاردار جھاڑ کے سوا اُن کے لئے کوئی کھانا نہیں ہوگا (۶)	لَيْسَ لَهُمْ طَعَامٌ اِلَّا مِنْ ضَرِيْعٍ ۝٦
7. Which will neither nourish nor satisfy hunger.	جو نہ فربہی لائے نہ بھوک میں کچھ کام آئے (۷)	لَّا يُسْمِنُ وَلَا يُغْنِيْ مِنْ جُوْعٍ ۝٧
8. (Other) faces that Day will be joyful,	اور بہت سے مُنہ (والے) اُس روز شادماں ہوں گے (۸)	وُجُوْهٌ يَّوْمَىِٕذٍ نَّاعِمَةٌ ۝٨

SÛRA–89
AL-FAJR
(INTRODUCTION)

This is one of the earliest of the Sûras to be revealed,— probably within the first ten in chronologial order.

Its mystic meaning is suggested by contrasts,—contrasts in nature and in man's long history. Thus does it enforce the lesson of Faith in the Hereafter to "those who understand". Man's history and legendary lore show that greatness does not last and the proudest are brought low. For enforcing moral and spiritual truths, the strictest history is no better than legend. Indeed all artistic history is legend, for it is writen from a special point of view.

Man is easily cowed by contrasts in his own fortunes, and yet he does not learn from them the lesson of forbearance and kindness to others, and the final elevation of goodness in the Hereafter. When all the things on which his mind and heart are set on this earth shall be crushed to nothingness, he will see the real glory and power, love and beauty, of Allah, for these are the light of the Garden of Paradise.

9. Pleased with their Striving,—	اپنے اعمال (کی جزا) سے خوش دل ⑨	لِّسَعْيِهَا رَاضِيَةٌ ⑨
10. In a Garden on high,	بہشت بریں میں ⑩	فِي جَنَّةٍ عَالِيَةٍ ⑩
11. Where they shall hear no (word) of vanity:	وہاں کسی طرح کی بکواس نہیں سنیں گے ⑪	لَّا تَسْمَعُ فِيهَا لَاغِيَةً ⑪
12. Therein will be a bubbling spring:	اُس میں چشمے بہ رہے ہوں گے ⑫	فِيهَا عَيْنٌ جَارِيَةٌ ⑫
13. Therein will be couches (of dignity), raised on high,	وہاں تخت ہوں گے اُونچے بچھے ہوئے ⑬	فِيهَا سُرُرٌ مَّرْفُوعَةٌ ⑬
14. Goblets placed (ready),	اور آبخورے (قرینے سے) رکھے ہوئے ⑭	وَأَكْوَابٌ مَّوْضُوعَةٌ ⑭
15. And Cushions set in rows,	اور گاؤ تکیے قطار کی قطار لگے ہوئے ⑮	وَنَمَارِقُ مَصْفُوفَةٌ ⑮
16. And rich carpets (all) spread out.	اور نفیس مسندیں بچھی ہوئیں ⑯	وَزَرَابِيُّ مَبْثُوثَةٌ ⑯
17. Do they not look at the Camels, how they are made ?—	یہ لوگ اُونٹوں کی طرف نہیں دیکھتے کہ کیسے (عجیب) پیدا کئے گئے ہیں ⑰	أَفَلَا يَنظُرُونَ إِلَى الْإِبِلِ كَيْفَ خُلِقَتْ ⑰
18. And at the Sky, how it is raised high?—	اور آسمان کی طرف کہ کیسا بلند کیا گیا ہے ⑱	وَإِلَى السَّمَاءِ كَيْفَ رُفِعَتْ ⑱
19. And at the Mountains, how they are fixed firm?—	اور پہاڑوں کی طرف کہ کس طرح کھڑے کئے گئے ہیں ⑲	وَإِلَى الْجِبَالِ كَيْفَ نُصِبَتْ ⑲
20. And at the Earth, how it is spread out ?	اور زمین کی طرف کہ کس طرح بچھائی گئی ⑳	وَإِلَى الْأَرْضِ كَيْفَ سُطِحَتْ ⑳
21. Therefore do thou remind for thou art one to remind.	تو تم نصیحت کرتے رہو کہ تم نصیحت کرنے والے ہی ہو ㉑	فَذَكِّرْ إِنَّمَا أَنتَ مُذَكِّرٌ ㉑
22. Thou art not one to manage (their) affairs.	تم اُن پر داروغہ نہیں ہو ㉒	لَّسْتَ عَلَيْهِم بِمُصَيْطِرٍ ㉒
23. But if any turn away and disbelieve,—	ہاں جس نے مُنہ پھیرا اور نہ مانا ㉓	إِلَّا مَن تَوَلَّىٰ وَكَفَرَ ㉓
24. Allah will chastise him with a mighty Chastisement.	تو خدا اُس کو بڑا عذاب دے گا ㉔	فَيُعَذِّبُهُ اللَّهُ الْعَذَابَ الْأَكْبَرَ ㉔
25. For to Us will be their Return;	بے شک اُن کو ہمارے پاس لوٹ کر آنا ہے ㉕	إِنَّ إِلَيْنَا إِيَابَهُمْ ㉕
26. Then it will be for Us to call them to account.	پھر ہم ہی کو اُن سے حساب لینا ہے ㉖	ثُمَّ إِنَّ عَلَيْنَا حِسَابَهُم ㉖

Al-Fajr, or The Dawn

	سورۂ فجر مکی ہے اس میں تیس آیتیں ہیں	سُورَةُ الْفَجْرِ مَكِّيَّةٌ وَهِيَ ثَلٰثُونَ اٰيَةً
In the name of Allah, Most Gracious, Most Merciful.	شروع خدا کا نام لے کر جو بڑا مہربان نہایت رحم والا ہے	بِسْمِ اللَّهِ الرَّحْمَٰنِ الرَّحِيمِ
1. By the Dawn;	فجر کی قسم ①	وَالْفَجْرِ ①
2. By the ten Nights;	اور دس راتوں کی ② ٣٢٦	وَلَيَالٍ عَشْرٍ ②
3. By the Even and Odd (contrasted);	اور جفت اور طاق کی ③	وَالشَّفْعِ وَالْوَتْرِ ③
4. And by the Night when it passeth away;—	اور رات کی جب جانے لگے ④	وَاللَّيْلِ إِذَا يَسْرِ ④
5. Is there (not) in these an adjuration (or evidence) for those who understand ?	(اور) بے شک یہ چیزیں عقلمندوں کے نزدیک قسم کھانے کے لائق ہیں (کہ کافروں کو ضرور عذاب ہوگا) ⑤	هَلْ فِي ذَٰلِكَ قَسَمٌ لِّذِي حِجْرٍ ⑤
6. Seest thou not how thy Lord dealt with the 'Ād (people),—	کیا تم نے نہیں دیکھا کہ تمہارے پروردگار نے عاد کے ساتھ کیا کیا ⑥ ٣٢٧	أَلَمْ تَرَ كَيْفَ فَعَلَ رَبُّكَ بِعَادٍ ⑥
7. Of the (city of) Iram, with lofty pillars,	(جو) ارم (کہلاتے تھے اتنے) دراز قد ⑦	إِرَمَ ذَاتِ الْعِمَادِ ⑦

8. The like of which were not produced in (all) the land ?
الَّتِي لَمْ يُخْلَقْ مِثْلُهَا فِي الْبِلَادِ ﴿٨﴾
کہ تمام ملک میں ایسے پیدا نہیں ہوئے تھے (۸)

9. And with the Thamûd (people), who cut out (huge) rocks in the valley ?—
وَثَمُودَ الَّذِينَ جَابُوا الصَّخْرَ بِالْوَادِ ﴿٩﴾
اور ثمود کیساتھ کیا کیا، جو وادی (قریٰ) میں پتھر تراشتے (اور گھر بناتے) تھے (۹)

10. And with Pharaoh, lord of Stakes ?
وَفِرْعَوْنَ ذِي الْأَوْتَادِ ﴿١٠﴾
اور فرعون کے ساتھ کیا کیا، جو خیمے اور میخیں رکھتا تھا (۱۰)

11. (All) these transgressed beyond bounds in the lands.
الَّذِينَ طَغَوْا فِي الْبِلَادِ ﴿١١﴾
یہ لوگ ملکوں میں سرکش ہو رہے تھے (۱۱)

12. And heaped therein mischief (on mischief).
فَأَكْثَرُوا فِيهَا الْفَسَادَ ﴿١٢﴾
اور ان میں بہت سی خرابیاں کرتے تھے (۱۲)

13. Therefore did thy Lord pour on them a scourge of diverse chastisements:
فَصَبَّ عَلَيْهِمْ رَبُّكَ سَوْطَ عَذَابٍ ﴿١٣﴾
تو تمہارے پروردگار نے اُن پر عذاب کا کوڑا نازل کیا (۱۳)

14. For thy Lord is watchful.
إِنَّ رَبَّكَ لَبِالْمِرْصَادِ ﴿١٤﴾
بے شک تمہارا پروردگار تاک میں ہے (۱۴)

15. Now, as for man, when his Lord trieth him, giving him honour and gifts, then saith he, (puffed up), "My Lord hath honoured me."
فَأَمَّا الْإِنْسَانُ إِذَا مَا ابْتَلَاهُ رَبُّهُ فَأَكْرَمَهُ
وَنَعَّمَهُ فَيَقُولُ رَبِّي أَكْرَمَنِ ﴿١٥﴾
مگر انسان (عجیب مخلوق ہے کہ) جب اُس کا پروردگار اُس کو آزماتا ہے کہ اُسے
عزت دیتا اور نعمت بخشتا ہے تو کہتا ہے کہ (آہا) میرے پروردگار نے مجھے عزت بخشی (۱۵)

16. But when He trieth him, restricting his subsistence for him, then saith he (in despair), "My Lord hath humiliated me !"
وَأَمَّا إِذَا مَا ابْتَلَاهُ فَقَدَرَ عَلَيْهِ رِزْقَهُ
فَيَقُولُ رَبِّي أَهَانَنِ ﴿١٦﴾
اور جب (دوسری طرح) آزماتا ہے کہ اُس پر روزی تنگ کر دیتا ہے
تو کہتا ہے کہ (ہائے) میرے پروردگار نے مجھے ذلیل کیا (۱۶)

17. Nay, nay ! But ye honour not the orphans !
كَلَّا بَلْ لَا تُكْرِمُونَ الْيَتِيمَ ﴿١٧﴾
نہیں، بلکہ تم لوگ یتیم کی خاطر نہیں کرتے (۱۷)

18. Nor do ye encourage one another to feed the poor !—
وَلَا تَحَاضُّونَ عَلَىٰ طَعَامِ الْمِسْكِينِ ﴿١٨﴾
اور نہ مسکین کو کھانا کھلانے کی ترغیب دیتے ہو (۱۸)

19. And ye devour Inheritance— all with greed,
وَتَأْكُلُونَ التُّرَاثَ أَكْلًا لَمًّا ﴿١٩﴾
اور میراث کے مال کو سمیٹ کر کھا جاتے ہو (۱۹)

20. And ye love wealth with inordinate love !
وَتُحِبُّونَ الْمَالَ حُبًّا جَمًّا ﴿٢٠﴾
اور مال کو بہت ہی عزیز رکھتے ہو (۲۰)

21. Nay ! When the earth is pounded to powder,
كَلَّا إِذَا دُكَّتِ الْأَرْضُ دَكًّا دَكًّا ﴿٢١﴾
تو جب زمین کی بلندی کوٹ کوٹ کر پست کر دی جائے گی (۲۱)

22. And thy Lord cometh, and His angels, rank upon rank,
وَجَاءَ رَبُّكَ وَالْمَلَكُ صَفًّا صَفًّا ﴿٢٢﴾
اور تمہارا پروردگار (جلوہ فرما ہوگا) اور فرشتے قطار باندھ باندھ کر آ موجود ہونگے (۲۲)

23. And Hell,—that Day, is brought (face to face), on that Day will man remember, but how will that remembrance profit him ?
وَجِيءَ يَوْمَئِذٍ بِجَهَنَّمَ ۚ يَوْمَئِذٍ
يَتَذَكَّرُ الْإِنْسَانُ وَأَنَّىٰ لَهُ الذِّكْرَىٰ ﴿٢٣﴾
اور دوزخ اُس دن حاضر کی جائے گی تو انسان اُس دن متنبہ ہوگا
مگر (اب) انتباہ اسے (فائدہ) کہاں (مل سکے گا)؟ (۲۳)

24. He will say: "Ah ! would that I had sent forth (Good Deeds) for (this) my (Future) Life !"
يَقُولُ يَا لَيْتَنِي قَدَّمْتُ لِحَيَاتِي ﴿٢٤﴾
کہے گا کاش میں نے اپنی زندگی (جاودانی) کیلئے کچھ آگے بھیجا ہوتا (۲۴)

25. For, that Day, His Chastisement will be such as none (else) can inflict,
فَيَوْمَئِذٍ لَا يُعَذِّبُ عَذَابَهُ أَحَدٌ ﴿٢٥﴾
تو اُس دن نہ کوئی خدا کے عذاب کی طرح کا (کسی کو) عذاب دیگا (۲۵)

26. And His bonds will be such as none (other) can bind.
وَلَا يُوثِقُ وَثَاقَهُ أَحَدٌ ﴿٢٦﴾
اور نہ کوئی ویسا جکڑنا جکڑے گا (۲۶)

27. (To the righteous soul will be said:) "O (thou) soul, in (complete) rest and satisfaction !
يَا أَيَّتُهَا النَّفْسُ الْمُطْمَئِنَّةُ ﴿٢٧﴾
اے اطمینان پانے والی روح! (۲۷)

28. "Come back thou to thy Lord,— well pleased (thyself), and well-pleasing unto Him !
ارْجِعِي إِلَىٰ رَبِّكِ رَاضِيَةً مَرْضِيَّةً ﴿٢٨﴾
اپنے پروردگار کی طرف لوٹ چل۔ تو اُس سے راضی وہ تجھ سے راضی (۲۸)

29. "Enter thou, then, among My Devotees !
فَادْخُلِي فِي عِبَادِي ﴿٢٩﴾
تو میرے (ممتاز) بندوں میں شامل ہو جا (۲۹)

30. "Yea, enter thou My Heaven!"
وَادْخُلِي جَنَّتِي ﴿٣٠﴾
اور میری بہشت میں داخل ہو جا (۳۰)

SÛRA–90
AL-BALAD
(INTRODUCTION)

This is an early Makkan revelation, and refers to the mystic relation (by divine sanction) of the Holy Prophet with the city of Makkah. He was born in that City, which had already been sacred for ages before. He was nurtured in that City and had (to use a modern phrase) the freedom of that City, belonging, as he did, to the noble family which held the government of its sacred precincts in its hands. But he was an orphan, and orphans in his day had a poor time. But his mind was turned to things divine. He protested against the prevailing idolatry and sin, and his parent City persecuted him and cast him out. He made another City Yathrib, his own: it became the *Madinat un-Nabî,* the City of the Prophet, and it has ever since been Madinah. We can speak of Madinah as the Prophet's child. But the Prophet ever cherished in his heart the love of his parent City of Makkah, and in the fulness of time was received in triumph there. He purified it from all idols and abominations, re-established the worship of the One True Allah, overthrew the purse-proud selfish autocracy, restored the sway of the righteous (people of the Right Hand), the liberty of the slave, and the rights of the poor and downtrodden. What a wonderful career centring round a City! It becomes a symbol of the world's spiritual history.

Al-Balad, or The City

	سورۃ بلد مکی ہے اس میں بیس آیتیں ہیں	سُورَةُ الْبَلَدِ مَكِّيَّةٌ وَهِيَ عِشْرُونَ آيَةً
In the name of Allah, Most Gracious, Most Merciful.	شروع خدا کا نام لے کر جو بڑا مہربان نہایت رحم والا ہے	بِسْمِ اللّٰهِ الرَّحْمٰنِ الرَّحِيْمِ
1. Nay I do swear by this City;—	ہمیں اس شہر (مکہ) کی قسم (۱)	لَآ اُقْسِمُ بِهٰذَا الْبَلَدِ (۱)
2. And, thou art an inhabitant of this City;—	اور تم اسی شہر میں تو رہتے ہو[۳۷۹] (۲)	وَاَنْتَ حِلٌّۢ بِهٰذَا الْبَلَدِ (۲)
3. And the begetter and that he begot;—	اور باپ (یعنی آدم) اور اس کی اولاد کی قسم (۳)	وَوَالِدٍ وَّمَا وَلَدَ (۳)
4. Verily We have created man into toil and struggle.	کہ ہم نے انسان کو تکلیف (کی حالت میں رہنے والا) بنایا ہے (۴)	لَقَدْ خَلَقْنَا الْاِنْسَانَ فِيْ كَبَدٍ (۴)
5. Thinketh he, that none hath power over him?	کیا وہ خیال رکھتا ہے کہ اس پر کوئی قابو نہ پائے گا (۵)	اَيَحْسَبُ اَنْ لَّنْ يَّقْدِرَ عَلَيْهِ اَحَدٌ (۵) وقف لازم
6. He may say (boastfully): "Wealth have I squandered in abundance!"	کہتا ہے کہ میں نے بہت سا مال برباد کر دیا (۶)	يَقُوْلُ اَهْلَكْتُ مَالًا لُّبَدًا (۶)
7. Thinketh he that none beholdeth him ?	کیا اسے یہ گمان ہے کہ اس کو کسی نے دیکھا نہیں (۷)	اَيَحْسَبُ اَنْ لَّمْ يَرَهٗۤ اَحَدٌ (۷)
8. Have We not made for him a pair of eyes ?	بھلا ہم نے اس کو دو آنکھیں نہیں دیں؟ (۸)	اَلَمْ نَجْعَلْ لَّهٗ عَيْنَيْنِ (۸)
9. And a tongue, and a pair of lips ?	اور زبان اور دو ہونٹ (نہیں دیئے) (۹)	وَلِسَانًا وَّشَفَتَيْنِ (۹)
10. And shown him the two highways ?	(یہ چیزیں بھی دیں) اور اس کو (خیر و شر کے) دونوں رستے بھی دکھا دیئے (۱۰)	وَهَدَيْنٰهُ النَّجْدَيْنِ (۱۰)
11. But he hath made not haste on the path that is steep.	مگر وہ گھاٹی پر سے ہو کر نہ گزرا (۱۱)	فَلَا اقْتَحَمَ الْعَقَبَةَ (۱۱)
12. And what will explain to thee the path that is steep ?—	اور تم کیا سمجھے کہ گھاٹی کیا ہے؟ (۱۲)	وَمَاۤ اَدْرٰىكَ مَا الْعَقَبَةُ (۱۲)
13. (It is:) freeing the bondman;	کسی (کی) گردن کا چھڑانا (۱۳)	فَكُّ رَقَبَةٍ (۱۳)
14. Or the giving of food in a day of privation	یا بھوک کے دن کھانا کھلانا (۱۴)	اَوْ اِطْعٰمٌ فِيْ يَوْمٍ ذِيْ مَسْغَبَةٍ (۱۴)
15. To the orphan with claims of relationship,	یتیم رشتہ دار کو (۱۵)	يَّتِيْمًا ذَا مَقْرَبَةٍ (۱۵)
16. Or to the indigent (down) in the dust.	یا فقیر خاکسار کو (۱۶)	اَوْ مِسْكِيْنًا ذَا مَتْرَبَةٍ (۱۶)
17. Then will he be of those who believe, and enjoin patience, (constancy, and self-restraint), and enjoin deeds of kindness and compassion.	پھر ان لوگوں میں بھی (داخل) ہوا جو ایمان لائے اور صبر کی نصیحت اور (لوگوں پر) شفقت کرنے کی وصیت کرتے رہے (۱۷)	ثُمَّ كَانَ مِنَ الَّذِيْنَ اٰمَنُوْا وَتَوَاصَوْا بِالصَّبْرِ وَتَوَاصَوْا بِالْمَرْحَمَةِ (۱۷)
18. Such are the Companions of the Right Hand.	یہی لوگ صاحب سعادت ہیں (۱۸)	اُولٰٓئِكَ اَصْحٰبُ الْمَيْمَنَةِ (۱۸)
19. But those who reject Our Signs, they are the (unhappy) Companions of the Left Hand.	اور جنہوں نے ہماری آیتوں کو نہ مانا وہ بدبخت ہیں (۱۹)	وَالَّذِيْنَ كَفَرُوْا بِاٰيٰتِنَا هُمْ اَصْحٰبُ الْمَشْئَمَةِ (۱۹)
20. On them will be Fire vaulted over (all round).	یہ لوگ آگ میں بند کر دیئے جائیں گے (۲۰)	عَلَيْهِمْ نَارٌ مُّؤْصَدَةٌ (۲۰) ع ۱۵

SÛRA–91
ASH-SHAMS
(INTRODUCTION)

This is one of the early Makkan revelations. Beginning with a fine nature passage, and leading up to man's need of realising his spiritual responsibility, it ends with a warning of the terrible consequences for those who fear not the Hereafter.

SÛRA–92
AL-LAIL
(INTRODUCTION)

This was one of the first Sûras to be revealed,—within the first ten; and may be placed in date close to S. 89 and S. 93. Note that in all these Sûras the mystery and the contrast as between Night and Day are appealed to for the consolation of man in his spiritual yearning. Here we are told to strive our utmost towards Allah, and He will give us every help and satisfaction.

Ash-Shams, or The Sun

In the name of Allah, Most Gracious, Most Merciful.

1. By the Sun and his (glorious) splendour;
2. By the Moon as she follows him;
3. By the Day as it shows up (the Sun's) glory;
4. By the Night as it conceals it;
5. By the Firmament and its (wonderful) structure;
6. By the Earth and its (wide) expanse:
7. By the Soul, and the proportion and order given to it;
8. And its inspiration as to its wrong and its right;—
9. Truly he succeeds that purifies it,
10. And he fails that corrupts it !
11. The Thamûd (people) rejected (their prophet) through their inordinate wrong-doing.
12. Behold, the most wicked man among them was deputed (for impiety).
13. But the messenger of Allah said to them: "It is a She-camel of Allah ! And (bar her not from) having her drink !"
14. Then they rejected him (as a false prophet), and they hamstrung her. So their Lord, crushed them for their sin and levelled them.
15. And for Him is no fear of its consequences.

سورۂ شمس مکی ہے اس میں پندرہ آیتیں ہیں

شروع خدا کا نام لے کر جو بڑا مہربان نہایت رحم والا ہے

سورج کی قسم اور اس کی روشنی کی (۱)
اور چاند کی جب اُس کے پیچھے نکلے (۲)
اور دن کی جب اُسے چمکا دے (۳)
اور رات کی جب اُسے چھپا لے (۴)
اور آسمان کی اور اُس ذات کی جس نے اُسے بنایا (۵)
اور زمین کی اور اُس کی جس نے اُسے پھیلایا (۶)
اور انسان کی اور اُسکی جس نے اسکے اعضاء کو برابر کیا (۷)
پھر اُسکو بدکاری (سے بچنے) اور پرہیزگاری کرنے کی سمجھ دی (۸)
کہ جس نے (اپنے) نفس (یعنی روح) کو پاک رکھا وہ مراد کو پہنچا (۹)
اور جس نے اُسے خاک میں ملایا وہ خسارے میں رہا (۱۰)
(قوم) ثمود نے اپنی سرکشی کے سبب (پیغمبر کو) جھٹلایا (۱۱)
جب اُن میں سے ایک نہایت بدبخت اُٹھا (۱۲)
تو خدا کے پیغمبر (صالح) نے اُن سے کہا کہ خدا کی اُونٹنی اور اُسکے
پانی پینے کی باری سے حذر کرو (۱۳)
مگر اُنہوں نے پیغمبر کو جھٹلایا اور اُونٹنی کی کونچیں کاٹ دیں۔ تو خدا نے
انکے گناہ کے سبب اُنپر عذاب نازل کیا اور سب کو (ہلاک کر کے) برابر کر دیا (۱۴)
اور اُس کو اُن کے بدلہ لینے کا کچھ بھی ڈر نہیں (۱۵)

سُوْرَةُ الشَّمْسِ مَكِّيَّةٌ وَّهِيَ خَمْسَ عَشْرَةَ اٰيَةً

بِسْمِ اللّٰهِ الرَّحْمٰنِ الرَّحِيْمِ

وَالشَّمْسِ وَضُحٰىهَا ۝١
وَالْقَمَرِ اِذَا تَلٰىهَا ۝٢
وَالنَّهَارِ اِذَا جَلّٰىهَا ۝٣
وَالَّيْلِ اِذَا يَغْشٰىهَا ۝٤
وَالسَّمَآءِ وَمَا بَنٰىهَا ۝٥
وَالْاَرْضِ وَمَا طَحٰىهَا ۝٦
وَنَفْسٍ وَّمَا سَوّٰىهَا ۝٧
فَاَلْهَمَهَا فُجُوْرَهَا وَتَقْوٰىهَا ۝٨
قَدْ اَفْلَحَ مَنْ زَكّٰىهَا ۝٩
وَقَدْ خَابَ مَنْ دَسّٰىهَا ۝١٠
كَذَّبَتْ ثَمُوْدُ بِطَغْوٰىهَا ۝١١
اِذِ انْۢبَعَثَ اَشْقٰىهَا ۝١٢
فَقَالَ لَهُمْ رَسُوْلُ اللّٰهِ نَاقَةَ اللّٰهِ وَ
سُقْيٰهَا ۝١٣
فَكَذَّبُوْهُ فَعَقَرُوْهَا فَدَمْدَمَ عَلَيْهِمْ
رَبُّهُمْ بِذَنْۢبِهِمْ فَسَوّٰىهَا ۝١٤
وَلَا يَخَافُ عُقْبٰهَا ۝١٥

Al-Lail, or The Night

In the name of Allah, Most Gracious, Most Merciful.

1. By the Night as it conceals (the light);
2. By the Day as it appears in glory;
3. By the creation of male and female;—
4. Verily, (the ends) ye strive for are diverse.
5. So he who gives (in charity) and fears (Allah),
6. And (in all sincerity) testifies to the Best,—

سورۂ لیل مکی ہے اس میں اکیس آیتیں ہیں

شروع خدا کا نام لے کر جو بڑا مہربان نہایت رحم والا ہے

رات کی قسم جب (دن کو) چھپا لے (۱)
اور دن کی قسم جب چمک اُٹھے (۲)
اور اُس (ذات) کی قسم جس نے نر اور مادہ پیدا کئے (۳)
کہ تم لوگوں کی کوشش طرح طرح کی ہے (۴)
تو جس نے (خدا کے رستے میں مال) دیا اور پرہیزگاری کی (۵)
اور نیک بات کو سچ جانا (۶)

سُوْرَةُ الَّيْلِ مَكِّيَّةٌ وَّهِيَ اِحْدٰى وَّعِشْرُوْنَ اٰيَةً

بِسْمِ اللّٰهِ الرَّحْمٰنِ الرَّحِيْمِ

وَالَّيْلِ اِذَا يَغْشٰى ۝١
وَالنَّهَارِ اِذَا تَجَلّٰى ۝٢
وَمَا خَلَقَ الذَّكَرَ وَالْاُنْثٰٓى ۝٣
اِنَّ سَعْيَكُمْ لَشَتّٰى ۝٤
فَاَمَّا مَنْ اَعْطٰى وَاتَّقٰى ۝٥
وَصَدَّقَ بِالْحُسْنٰى ۝٦

SÛRA–93

ADH-DHUḤÃ

(INTRODUCTION)

This Sûra is close in date to Sûras 89 and 92, and the imagery drawn from the contrast of Night and Day is common to all three. In this Sûra the vicissitudes of human life are referred to, and a massage of hope and consolation is given to man's soul from Allah's past mercies, and he is bidden to pursue the path of goodness and proclaim the bounties of Allah. This is the general meaning. In particular, the Sûra seems to have been revealed in a dark period in the outer life of the Holy Prophet, when a man of less resolute will might have been discouraged. But the Prophet is told to hold the present of less account that the glorious Hereafter which awaited him like the glorious morning after a night of stillness and gloom. The Hereafter was, not only in the Future Life, but in his later life on this earth, full of victory and satisfaction.

7. We will indeed make smooth for him the path to Ease.	اُس کو ہم آسان طریقے کی توفیق دیں گے (۷)	فَسَنُيَسِّرُهُ لِلْيُسْرَىٰ (۷)
8. But he who is a greedy miser and thinks himself self-sufficient,	اور جس نے بخل کیا اور بے پروا بنا رہا (۸)	وَأَمَّا مَنْ بَخِلَ وَاسْتَغْنَىٰ (۸)
9. And gives the lie to the Best,–	اور نیک بات کو جھوٹ سمجھا (۹)	وَكَذَّبَ بِالْحُسْنَىٰ (۹)
10. We will indeed make smooth for him the Path to Misery;	اُسے سختی میں پہنچائیں گے (۱۰)	فَسَنُيَسِّرُهُ لِلْعُسْرَىٰ (۱۰)
11. Nor will his wealth profit him when he falls headlong (into the Pit).	اور جب وہ دوزخ کے گڑھے میں گریگا تو اُسکا مال اسکے کچھ بھی کام نہ آئیگا (۱۱)	وَمَا يُغْنِي عَنْهُ مَالُهُ إِذَا تَرَدَّىٰ (۱۱)
12. Verily We take upon Us to guide,	ہمیں تو راہ دکھا دینا ہے (۱۲)	إِنَّ عَلَيْنَا لَلْهُدَىٰ (۱۲)
13. And verily unto Us (belong) the End and the Beginning.	اور آخرت اور دنیا ہماری ہی چیزیں ہیں (۱۳)	وَإِنَّ لَنَا لَلْآخِرَةَ وَالْأُولَىٰ (۱۳)
14. Therefore do I warn you of a Fire blazing fiercely;	سو میں نے تم کو بھڑکتی آگ سے متنبہ کر دیا (۱۴)	فَأَنْذَرْتُكُمْ نَارًا تَلَظَّىٰ (۱۴)
15. None shall burn therein but those most unfortunate ones	اس میں وہی داخل ہوگا جو بڑا بدبخت ہے (۱۵)	لَا يَصْلَاهَا إِلَّا الْأَشْقَى (۱۵)
16. Who give the lie to Truth and turn their backs.	جس نے جھٹلایا اور مُنہ پھیرا (۱۶)	الَّذِي كَذَّبَ وَتَوَلَّىٰ (۱۶)
17. But those most devoted to Allah shall be removed far from it,–	اور جو بڑا پرہیزگار ہے وہ (اس سے) بچا لیا جائے گا (۱۷)	وَسَيُجَنَّبُهَا الْأَتْقَى (۱۷)
18. Those who spend their wealth for increase in self-purification,	جو مال دیتا ہے تاکہ پاک ہو (۱۸)	الَّذِي يُؤْتِي مَالَهُ يَتَزَكَّىٰ (۱۸)
19. And have in their minds no favour from anyone for which a reward is expected in return,	اور (اسلئے) نہیں (دیتا) کہ اُس پر کسی کا احسان (ہے) جس کا وہ بدلہ اُتارتا ہو (۱۹)	وَمَا لِأَحَدٍ عِنْدَهُ مِنْ نِعْمَةٍ تُجْزَىٰ (۱۹)
20. But only the desire to seek for the Countenance of their Lord Most High;	بلکہ اپنے خداوندِ اعلیٰ کی رضامندی حاصل کرنیکے لئے دیتا ہے (۲۰)	إِلَّا ابْتِغَاءَ وَجْهِ رَبِّهِ الْأَعْلَىٰ (۲۰)
21. And soon will they attain (complete) satisfaction.	اور وہ عنقریب خوش ہو جائے گا (۲۱)	وَلَسَوْفَ يَرْضَىٰ (۲۱)
Ad-Dhuhā, or The Glorious Morning Light	سورۂ ضحیٰ مکی ہے اور اس میں گیارہ آیتیں ہیں	سُورَةُ الضُّحَىٰ مَكِّيَّةٌ وَهِيَ إِحْدَىٰ عَشْرَةَ آيَةً
In the name of Allah, Most Gracious, Most Merciful.	شروع خدا کا نام لے کر جو بڑا مہربان نہایت رحم والا ہے	بِسْمِ اللَّهِ الرَّحْمَٰنِ الرَّحِيمِ
1. By the Glorious Morning Light,	آفتاب کی روشنی کی قسم (۱)	وَالضُّحَىٰ (۱)
2. And by the Night when it is still,—	اور رات (کی تاریکی) کی جب چھا جائے (۲)	وَاللَّيْلِ إِذَا سَجَىٰ (۲)
3. The Guardian-Lord hath not forsaken thee, nor is He displeased.	(اے محمدؐ) تمہارے پروردگار نے نہ تو تم کو چھوڑا اور نہ (تم سے) ناراض ہوا (۳)	مَا وَدَّعَكَ رَبُّكَ وَمَا قَلَىٰ (۳)
4. And verily the Hereafter will be better for thee than the present.	اور آخرت تمہارے لئے پہلی (حالت یعنی دنیا) سے کہیں بہتر ہے (۴)	وَلَلْآخِرَةُ خَيْرٌ لَكَ مِنَ الْأُولَىٰ (۴)
5. And soon will thy Guardian-Lord give thee (that wherewith) thou shalt be well-pleased.	اور تمہیں پروردگار عنقریب وہ کچھ عطا فرمائیگا کہ تم خوش ہو جاؤ گے (۵)	وَلَسَوْفَ يُعْطِيكَ رَبُّكَ فَتَرْضَىٰ (۵)
6. Did He not find thee an orphan and give thee shelter (and care) ?	بھلا اُس نے تمہیں یتیم پا کر جگہ نہیں دی (بے شک دی) (۶)	أَلَمْ يَجِدْكَ يَتِيمًا فَآوَىٰ (۶)
7. And He found thee wandering, and He gave thee guidance.	اور رستے سے ناواقف دیکھا تو سیدھا رستہ دکھایا (۷)	وَوَجَدَكَ ضَالًّا فَهَدَىٰ (۷)
8. And He found thee in need, and made thee independent.	اور تنگ دست پایا تو غنی کر دیا (۸)	وَوَجَدَكَ عَائِلًا فَأَغْنَىٰ (۸)
9. Therefore, treat not the orphan with harshness,	تو تم بھی یتیم پر ستم نہ کرنا (۹)	فَأَمَّا الْيَتِيمَ فَلَا تَقْهَرْ (۹)
10. Nor repulse him who asks;	اور مانگنے والے کو جھڑکی نہ دینا (۱۰)	وَأَمَّا السَّائِلَ فَلَا تَنْهَرْ (۱۰)

SÛRA–94
AL-SHARḪ
(INTRODUCTION)

This short Sûra gives a message of hope and encouragement in a time of darkness and difficulty. It was revealed to the Holy Prophet soon after the last Sûra *(Dhuḥã)*, whose argument it supplements.

SÛRA–95
AT-TÎN
(INTRODUCTION)

This is also a very early Sûra. It appeals to the most sacred symbols to show that Allah created man in the best of moulds, but that man is capable of the utmost degradation unless he has Faith and leads a good life. In subject-matter this Sûra closely resembles S. 103.

SÛRA–96
AL-'ALAQ
(INTRODUCTION)

Verses 1-5 of this Sûra were the first direct Revelation to the Holy Prophet.

After that there was an interval or break *(Fatra)*, extending over some months or perhaps over a year. S. 68 is usually considered to have been the next revelation in point of time. But the remainder of the Sûra (96: 6-19) came soon after the *Fatra*, and that portion is joined on to the first five verses containing the command to preach, because it explains the chief obstacle to the delivery of the message to man, viz. man's own obstinacy, vanity, and insolence.

11. But the Bounty of thy Lord— rehearse and proclaim !

اور اپنے پروردگار کی نعمتوں کا بیان کرتے رہنا ﴿۱۱﴾

ع ۱۱ ۱۸ وَأَمَّا بِنِعْمَةِ رَبِّكَ فَحَدِّثْ ﴿١١﴾

Al-Inshirāḥ, or The Expansion

سورۂ انشراح مکی ہے اور اس میں آٹھ آیتیں ہیں

سُوْرَةُ الْاِنْشِرَاحِ مَكِّيَّةٌ وَّهِيَ ثَمَانِ اٰيَاتٍ

In the name of Allah, Most Gracious, Most Merciful.

شروع خدا کا نام لے کر جو بڑا مہربان نہایت رحم والا ہے

بِسْمِ اللّٰهِ الرَّحْمٰنِ الرَّحِيْمِ

1. Have We not expanded thee thy breast ?—

(اے محمدؐ) کیا ہم نے تمہارا سینہ کھول نہیں دیا؟ (بیشک کھول دیا) ﴿۱﴾

أَلَمْ نَشْرَحْ لَكَ صَدْرَكَ ﴿١﴾

2. And removed from thee thy burden

اور تم پر سے بوجھ بھی اُتار دیا ﴿۲﴾

وَوَضَعْنَا عَنْكَ وِزْرَكَ ﴿٢﴾

3. The which did gall thy back?—

جس نے تمہاری پیٹھ توڑ رکھی تھی ﴿۳﴾

الَّذِيْٓ اَنْقَضَ ظَهْرَكَ ﴿٣﴾

4. And raised high the esteem (in which) thou (art held) ?

اور تمہارا ذکر بلند کیا ﴿۴﴾

وَرَفَعْنَا لَكَ ذِكْرَكَ ﴿٤﴾

5. So, verily, with every difficulty, there is relief.

ہاں (ہاں) مشکل کے ساتھ آسانی بھی ہے ﴿۵﴾

فَاِنَّ مَعَ الْعُسْرِ يُسْرًا ﴿٥﴾

6. Verily, with every difficulty there is relief.

(اور) بیشک مشکل کے ساتھ آسانی بھی ہے ﴿۶﴾

اِنَّ مَعَ الْعُسْرِ يُسْرًا ﴿٦﴾

7. Therefore, when thou art free (from thine immediate task), still labour hard,

توجب فارغ ہوا کرو تو (عبادت میں) محنت کیا کرو ﴿۷﴾

فَاِذَا فَرَغْتَ فَانْصَبْ ﴿٧﴾

8. And to thy Lord turn (all) thy attention.

اور اپنے پروردگار کی طرف متوجہ ہو جایا کرو ﴿۸﴾

ع ۱ ۱۹ وَاِلٰى رَبِّكَ فَارْغَبْ ﴿٨﴾

At-Tīn, or The Fig

سورۂ تین مکی ہے اور اس میں آٹھ آیتیں ہیں

سُوْرَةُ التِّيْنِ مَكِّيَّةٌ وَّهِيَ ثَمَانِ اٰيَاتٍ

In the name of Allah, Most Gracious, Most Merciful.

شروع خدا کا نام لے کر جو بڑا مہربان نہایت رحم والا ہے

بِسْمِ اللّٰهِ الرَّحْمٰنِ الرَّحِيْمِ

1. By the Fig and the Olive,

انجیر کی قسم اور زیتون کی ﴿۱﴾

وَالتِّيْنِ وَالزَّيْتُوْنِ ﴿١﴾

2. And the Mount of Sinai,

اور طور سینین کی ﴿۲﴾

وَطُوْرِ سِيْنِيْنَ ﴿٢﴾

3. And this City of Security,—

اور اس امن والے شہر کی ﴿۳﴾

وَهٰذَا الْبَلَدِ الْاَمِيْنِ ﴿٣﴾

4. We have indeed created man in the best of moulds,

کہ ہم نے انسان کو بہت اچھی صورت میں پیدا کیا ہے ﴿۴﴾

لَقَدْ خَلَقْنَا الْاِنْسَانَ فِيْٓ اَحْسَنِ تَقْوِيْمٍ ﴿٤﴾

5. Then do We abase him (to be) the lowest of the low,—

پھر (رفتہ رفتہ) اس کی حالت کو (بدل کر) پست سے پست کر دیا ﴿۵﴾

ثُمَّ رَدَدْنٰهُ اَسْفَلَ سٰفِلِيْنَ ﴿٥﴾

6. Except such as believe and do righteous deeds: for they shall have a reward unfailing.

مگر جو لوگ ایمان لائے اور نیک عمل کرتے رہے اُن کے لئے
بے انتہا اجر ہے ﴿۶﴾

اِلَّا الَّذِيْنَ اٰمَنُوْا وَعَمِلُوا الصّٰلِحٰتِ
فَلَهُمْ اَجْرٌ غَيْرُ مَمْنُوْنٍ ﴿٦﴾

7. What then, can after this make you deny the Last Judgment?

تو (اے آدم زاد) پھر تو جزا کے دن کو کیوں جھٹلاتا ہے؟ ﴿۷﴾

فَمَا يُكَذِّبُكَ بَعْدُ بِالدِّيْنِ ﴿٧﴾

8. Is not Allah the wisest of Judges ?

کیا خدا سب سے بڑا حاکم نہیں ہے؟ ﴿۸﴾

ع ۱ ۲۰ اَلَيْسَ اللّٰهُ بِاَحْكَمِ الْحٰكِمِيْنَ ﴿٨﴾

Iqraa, or Read ! or Proclaim ! Or Al-'Alaq, or The leech-like clot

سورۂ علق مکی ہے اور اس میں اُنیس آیتیں ہیں

سُوْرَةُ الْعَلَقِ مَكِّيَّةٌ وَّهِيَ تِسْعَ عَشْرَةَ اٰيَةً

In the name of Allah, Most Gracious, Most Merciful.

شروع خدا کا نام لے کر جو بڑا مہربان نہایت رحم والا ہے

بِسْمِ اللّٰهِ الرَّحْمٰنِ الرَّحِيْمِ

1. Proclaim ! (or Read !) in the name of thy Lord and Cherisher, Who created—

(اے محمدؐ) اپنے پروردگار کا نام لے کر پڑھو جس نے (عالم کو) پیدا کیا ﴿۱﴾

اِقْرَاْ بِاسْمِ رَبِّكَ الَّذِيْ خَلَقَ ﴿١﴾

2. Created man, out of a leech-like clot:

جس نے انسان کو خون کی پھٹکی سے بنایا ﴿۲﴾

خَلَقَ الْاِنْسَانَ مِنْ عَلَقٍ ﴿٢﴾

3. Proclaim ! And thy Lord is Most Bountiful,—

پڑھو اور تمہارا پروردگار بڑا کریم ہے ﴿۳﴾

اِقْرَاْ وَرَبُّكَ الْاَكْرَمُ ﴿٣﴾

SÛRA–97

AL-QADR

(INTRODUCTION)

The chronology of this Sûra has no significance. It is probably Makkan, though some hold that it was revealed in Madinah.

The subject-matter as the mystic Night of Power (or Honour), in which Revelation comes down to a benighted world,—it may be to the wonderful Cosmos of an individual—and transforms the conflict of wrong-doing into Peace and Harmony—through the agency of the angelic host, representing the spiritual powers of the Mercy of Allah.

4. He Who taught (the use of) the Pen,—

جس نے قلم کے ذریعے سے علم سکھایا ﴿۴﴾

الَّذِي عَلَّمَ بِالْقَلَمِ ﴿۴﴾

5. Taught man that which he knew not.

اور انسان کو وہ باتیں سکھائیں جس کا اُس کو علم نہ تھا ﴿۵﴾

عَلَّمَ الْإِنسَانَ مَا لَمْ يَعْلَمْ ﴿۵﴾

6. Nay, but man doth transgress all bounds,

مگر انسان سرکش ہو جاتا ہے ﴿۶﴾

كَلَّا إِنَّ الْإِنسَانَ لَيَطْغَىٰ ﴿۶﴾

7. In that he looketh upon himself as self-sufficient.

جبکہ اپنے تئیں غنی دیکھتا ہے ﴿۷﴾

أَن رَّآهُ اسْتَغْنَىٰ ﴿۷﴾

8. Verily, to thy Lord is the return (of all).

کچھ شک نہیں کہ (اسکو) تمہارے پروردگار ہی کی طرف لوٹ کر جانا ہے ﴿۸﴾

إِنَّ إِلَىٰ رَبِّكَ الرُّجْعَىٰ ﴿۸﴾

9. Seest thou one who forbids—

بھلا تم نے اُس شخص کو دیکھا جو منع کرتا ہے ﴿۹﴾

أَرَأَيْتَ الَّذِي يَنْهَىٰ ﴿۹﴾

10. A votary when he (turns) to pray ?

(یعنی) ایک بندے کو جب وہ نماز پڑھنے لگتا ہے ﴿۱۰﴾

عَبْدًا إِذَا صَلَّىٰ ﴿۱۰﴾

11. Seest thou if he is on (the road of) Guidance?—

بھلا دیکھو تو اگر یہ راہ راست پر ہو ﴿۱۱﴾

أَرَأَيْتَ إِن كَانَ عَلَى الْهُدَىٰ ﴿۱۱﴾

12. Or enjoins Righteousness ?

یا پرہیزگاری کا حکم کرے (تو منع کرنا کیسا) ﴿۱۲﴾

أَوْ أَمَرَ بِالتَّقْوَىٰ ﴿۱۲﴾

13. Seest thou if he denies (Truth) and turns away ?

اور دیکھو تو اگر اُس نے دین حق کو جھٹلایا اور اس سے منہ موڑا (تو کیا ہوا) ﴿۱۳﴾

أَرَأَيْتَ إِن كَذَّبَ وَتَوَلَّىٰ ﴿۱۳﴾

14. Knoweth he not that Allah doth see ?

کیا اس کو معلوم نہیں کہ خدا دیکھ رہا ہے ﴿۱۴﴾

أَلَمْ يَعْلَم بِأَنَّ اللَّهَ يَرَىٰ ﴿۱۴﴾

15. Let him beware ! If he desist not, We will drag him by the forelock,—

دیکھو اگر وہ باز نہ آئیگا تو ہم (اسکی) پیشانی کے بال پکڑ کر گھسیٹیں گے ﴿۱۵﴾

كَلَّا لَئِن لَّمْ يَنتَهِ لَنَسْفَعًا بِالنَّاصِيَةِ ﴿۱۵﴾

16. A lying, sinful forelock !

یعنی اس جھوٹے خطاکار کی پیشانی کے بال ﴿۱۶﴾

نَاصِيَةٍ كَاذِبَةٍ خَاطِئَةٍ ﴿۱۶﴾

17. Then, let him call (for help) to his council (of comrades):

تو وہ اپنے یاروں کی مجلس کو بلا لے ﴿۱۷﴾

فَلْيَدْعُ نَادِيَهُ ﴿۱۷﴾

18. We will call on the angels of punishment (to deal with him) !

ہم بھی اپنے موکلانِ دوزخ کو بلائیں گے ﴿۱۸﴾

سَنَدْعُ الزَّبَانِيَةَ ﴿۱۸﴾

19. Nay, heed him not: but prostrate in adoration, and bring thyself the closer (to Allah) !

دیکھو اس کا کہنا نہ ماننا اور سجدہ کرنا اور قُرب (خدا) حاصل کرتے رہنا ﴿۱۹﴾

كَلَّا لَا تُطِعْهُ وَاسْجُدْ وَاقْتَرِب ﴿۱۹﴾

Al-Qadr, or The Night of Power (or Honour)

سورۂ قدر مکی ہے اور اس میں پانچ آیتیں ہیں

سُورَةُ الْقَدْرِ مَكِّيَّةٌ وَهِيَ خَمْسُ آيَاتٍ

In the name of Allah, Most Gracious, Most Merciful.

شروع خدا کا نام لے کر جو بڑا مہربان نہایت رحم والا ہے

بِسْمِ اللَّهِ الرَّحْمَٰنِ الرَّحِيمِ

1. We have indeed revealed this (Message) in the Night of Power:

ہم نے اس (قرآن) کو شب قدر میں نازل (کرنا شروع) کیا ﴿۱﴾

إِنَّا أَنزَلْنَاهُ فِي لَيْلَةِ الْقَدْرِ ﴿۱﴾

2. And what will explain to thee what the Night of Power is ?

اور تمہیں کیا معلوم کہ شب قدر کیا ہے؟ ﴿۲﴾

وَمَا أَدْرَاكَ مَا لَيْلَةُ الْقَدْرِ ﴿۲﴾

3. The Night of Power is better than a thousand Months.

شب قدر ہزار مہینے سے بہتر ہے ﴿۳﴾

لَيْلَةُ الْقَدْرِ خَيْرٌ مِّنْ أَلْفِ شَهْرٍ ﴿۳﴾

4. Therein come down the angels and the Spirit by Allah's permission, on every errand:

اس میں رُوح (الامین) اور فرشتے ہر کام کے (انتظام کے) لئے
اپنے پروردگار کے حکم سے اُترتے ہیں ﴿۴﴾

تَنَزَّلُ الْمَلَائِكَةُ وَالرُّوحُ فِيهَا بِإِذْنِ
رَبِّهِم مِّن كُلِّ أَمْرٍ ﴿۴﴾

5. Peace ! . . .This until the rise of Morn !

یہ (رات) طلوع صبح تک (امان اور) سلامتی ہے ﴿۵﴾

سَلَامٌ هِيَ حَتَّىٰ مَطْلَعِ الْفَجْرِ ﴿۵﴾

SÛRA–98
AL-BAIYINA
(INTRODUCTION)

This Sûra was probably an early Madinah Sûra, or possibly a late Makkan Sûra.

In subject-matter it carries forward the argument of the last Sûra. The mystic night of revelation is indeed blessed: but those who reject Truth are impervious to Allah's Message, however clear may be the evidence in support of it.

SÛRA–99
AL-ZALZALAH
(INTRODUCTION)

This Sûra is close in date to the last: it is generally referred to the early Madinah period, though it may possibly be of the late Makkan period.

It refers to the tremendous convulsion and uprooting which will take place when the present order of the world is dissolved and the new spiritual world of Justice and Truth takes its place. The symbol used is that of an earthquake which will shake our present material and phenomenal world to its very foundations. The mystic words in which the earthquake is described are remarkable for both power and graphic aptness. With that shaking all hidden mysteries will be brought to light.

Al-Baiyina, or The Clear Evidence

In the name of Allah, Most Gracious, Most Merciful.

1. Those who disbelieve, among the People of the Book and among the Polytheists, were not going to depart (from their ways) until there should come to them clear Evidence,—

2. Messenger from Allah, rehearsing scriptures kept pure and holy:

3. Wherein are books right and straight.

4. Nor did the People of the Book make schisms, until after there came to them Clear Evidence.

5. And they have been commanded no more than this: to worship Allah, offering Him sincere devotion, being True (in faith); to establish regular Prayer; and to give zakat; and that is the Religion right and Straight.

6. Those who disbelieve, among the People of the Book and among the Polytheists, will be in Hell-Fire, to dwell therein (for aye). They are the worst of creatures.

7. Those who have faith and do righteous deeds,—they are the best of creatures.

8. Their reward is with Allah: Gardens of Eternity, beneath which rivers flow; they will dwell therein for ever; Allah well pleased with them, and they with Him: all this for such as fear their Lord and Cherisher.

سورۂ بیّنہ مدنی ہے اور اس میں آٹھ آیتیں ہیں

شروع خدا کا نام لے کر جو بڑا مہربان نہایت رحم والا ہے ○
جو لوگ کافر ہیں یعنی اہلِ کتاب اور مشرک وہ (کفر سے)
باز رہنے والے نہ تھے جب تک کہ ان کے پاس کھلی دلیل
(نہ) آتی (۱)
(یعنی) خدا کے پیغمبر جو پاک اوراق پڑھتے ہیں (۲)
جن میں مستحکم (آیتیں) لکھی ہوئی ہیں (۳)
اور اہلِ کتاب جو متفرق (و مختلف) ہوئے ہیں تو دلیل واضح
کے آنے کے بعد (ہوئے ہیں) (۴)
اور ان کو حکم تو یہی ہوا تھا کہ اخلاص عمل کے ساتھ خدا کی
عبادت کریں (اور) یکسو ہو کر، اور نماز پڑھیں اور زکوٰۃ دیں
اور یہی سچا دین ہے (۵)
جو لوگ کافر ہیں (یعنی) اہلِ کتاب اور مشرک وہ دوزخ کی
آگ میں (پڑیں گے اور) ہمیشہ اس میں رہیں گے۔ یہ لوگ
سب مخلوق سے بدتر ہیں (۶)
اور جو لوگ ایمان لائے اور نیک عمل کرتے رہے وہ تمام
خلقت سے بہتر ہیں (۷)
ان کا صلہ ان کے پروردگار کے ہاں ہمیشہ رہنے کے باغ
ہیں جن کے نیچے نہریں بہ رہی ہیں۔ ابدالآباد ان میں رہیں گے۔
خدا ان سے خوش اور وہ اس سے خوش۔ یہ (صلہ) اس کیلئے
ہے جو اپنے پروردگار سے ڈرتا ہے (۸)

سُورَةُ الْبَيِّنَةِ مَدَنِيَّةٌ وَهِيَ ثَمَانُ آيَاتٍ

بِسْمِ اللّٰهِ الرَّحْمٰنِ الرَّحِيْمِ ○
لَمْ يَكُنِ الَّذِيْنَ كَفَرُوْا مِنْ اَهْلِ
الْكِتٰبِ وَالْمُشْرِكِيْنَ مُنْفَكِّيْنَ حَتّٰى
تَاْتِيَهُمُ الْبَيِّنَةُ (١)
رَسُوْلٌ مِّنَ اللّٰهِ يَتْلُوْا صُحُفًا مُّطَهَّرَةً (٢)
فِيْهَا كُتُبٌ قَيِّمَةٌ (٣)
وَمَا تَفَرَّقَ الَّذِيْنَ اُوْتُوا الْكِتٰبَ اِلَّا
مِنْۢ بَعْدِ مَا جَآءَتْهُمُ الْبَيِّنَةُ (٤)
وَمَآ اُمِرُوْٓا اِلَّا لِيَعْبُدُوا اللّٰهَ مُخْلِصِيْنَ
لَهُ الدِّيْنَ ۙ حُنَفَآءَ وَيُقِيْمُوا الصَّلٰوةَ
وَيُؤْتُوا الزَّكٰوةَ وَذٰلِكَ دِيْنُ الْقَيِّمَةِ (٥)
اِنَّ الَّذِيْنَ كَفَرُوْا مِنْ اَهْلِ الْكِتٰبِ وَ
الْمُشْرِكِيْنَ فِيْ نَارِ جَهَنَّمَ خٰلِدِيْنَ فِيْهَا
اُولٰٓئِكَ هُمْ شَرُّ الْبَرِيَّةِ (٦)
اِنَّ الَّذِيْنَ اٰمَنُوْا وَعَمِلُوا الصّٰلِحٰتِ
اُولٰٓئِكَ هُمْ خَيْرُ الْبَرِيَّةِ (٧)
جَزَآؤُهُمْ عِنْدَ رَبِّهِمْ جَنّٰتُ عَدْنٍ
تَجْرِيْ مِنْ تَحْتِهَا الْاَنْهٰرُ خٰلِدِيْنَ فِيْهَآ
اَبَدًا ۗ رَضِيَ اللّٰهُ عَنْهُمْ وَرَضُوْا عَنْهُ
ع ٨/٢٢ ذٰلِكَ لِمَنْ خَشِيَ رَبَّهٗ (٨)

Al-Zilzāl, or The Convulsion

In the name of Allah, Most Gracious, Most Merciful.

1. When the Earth is shaken to her (utmost) convulsion,

2. And the Earth throws up her burdens (from within),

3. And man cries (distressed); 'What is the matter with her ?—

4. On that Day will she declare her tidings:

سورۂ زلزال مدنی ہے اور اس میں آٹھ آیتیں ہیں

شروع خدا کا نام لے کر جو بڑا مہربان نہایت رحم والا ہے ○
جب زمین بھونچال سے ہلا دی جائے گی (۱)
اور زمین اپنے (اندر کے) بوجھ نکال ڈالے گی (۲)
اور انسان کہے گا کہ اس کو کیا ہوا ہے؟ (۳)
اس روز وہ اپنے حالات بیان کر دے گی (۴)

سُوْرَةُ الزِّلْزَالِ مَدَنِيَّةٌ وَهِيَ ثَمَانُ آيَاتٍ

بِسْمِ اللّٰهِ الرَّحْمٰنِ الرَّحِيْمِ ○
اِذَا زُلْزِلَتِ الْاَرْضُ زِلْزَالَهَا (١)
وَاَخْرَجَتِ الْاَرْضُ اَثْقَالَهَا (٢)
وَقَالَ الْاِنْسَانُ مَا لَهَا (٣)
يَوْمَئِذٍ تُحَدِّثُ اَخْبَارَهَا (٤)

SÛRA–100
AL-'ÃDIYÃT
(INTRODUCTION)

This is one of the earlier Makkan Sûras. In the depth of its mystery and the rhythm and sublimity of its language and sybolism, it may be compared with S. 79. Its subject-matter is the irresistible nature of spiritual power and knowledge, contrasted with unregenerate man's ingratitude, pettiness, helplessness, and ignorance.

SÛRA–101
AL-QÃRI'A
(INTRODUCTION)

This Makkan Sûra describes the Judgment Day as the Day of Clamour, when men will be distracted and the landmarks of this world will be lost, but every deed will be weighed in a just balance, and find its real value and setting.

5. For that thy Lord will have given her inspiration.	کیونکہ تمہارے پروردگار نے اس کو حکم بھیجا (ہوگا) ۵	بِاَنَّ رَبَّكَ اَوْحٰى لَهَا ۵
6. On that Day will men proceed in groups sorted out, to be shown the Deeds that they (had done).	اس دن لوگ گروہ گروہ ہو کر آئیں گے تاکہ اُن کو اُنکے اعمال دکھا دیئے جائیں ۶	يَوْمَئِذٍ يَّصْدُرُ النَّاسُ اَشْتَاتًا ۙ لِّيُرَوْا اَعْمَالَهُمْ ۶
7. Then shall anyone who has done an atom's weight of good, see it !	تو جس نے ذرہ بھر نیکی کی ہوگی وہ اُس کو دیکھ لے گا ۷	فَمَنْ يَّعْمَلْ مِثْقَالَ ذَرَّةٍ خَيْرًا يَّرَهٗ ۷
8. And anyone who has done an atom's weight of evil, shall see it.	اور جس نے ذرہ بھر بُرائی کی ہوگی وہ اُسے دیکھ لے گا ۸	وَمَنْ يَّعْمَلْ مِثْقَالَ ذَرَّةٍ شَرًّا يَّرَهٗ ۸

Al-'Ādiyāt, or Those that run

	سورۂ عادیات مکّی ہے اور اس میں گیارہ آیتیں ہیں	سُوْرَةُ الْعٰدِيٰتِ مَكِّيَّةٌ وَّهِيَ اِحْدٰى عَشْرَةَ اٰيَةً
In the name of Allah, Most Gracious, Most Merciful.	شروع خدا کا نام لے کر جو بڑا مہربان نہایت رحم والا ہے	بِسْمِ اللّٰهِ الرَّحْمٰنِ الرَّحِيْمِ
1. By the (Steeds) that run, with panting (breath),	اُن سرپٹ دوڑنے والے گھوڑوں کی قسم جو ہانپ اُٹھتے ہیں ۱	وَالْعٰدِيٰتِ ضَبْحًا ۱
2. And strike sparks of fire,	پھر پتھروں پر (نعل) مار کر آگ نکالتے ہیں ۲	فَالْمُوْرِيٰتِ قَدْحًا ۲
3. And push home the charge in the morning,	پھر صبح کو چھاپا مارتے ہیں ۳	فَالْمُغِيْرٰتِ صُبْحًا ۳
4. And raise the dust in clouds the while,	پھر اس میں گرد اُٹھاتے ہیں ۴	فَاَثَرْنَ بِهٖ نَقْعًا ۴
5. And penetrate forthwith into the midst (of the foe) *en masse*;—	پھر اس وقت (دُشمن کی) فوج میں جا گھستے ہیں ۵	فَوَسَطْنَ بِهٖ جَمْعًا ۵
6. Truly Man is, to his Lord, ungrateful;	کہ انسان اپنے پروردگار کا احسان ناشناس (اور ناشکرا) ہے ۶	اِنَّ الْاِنْسَانَ لِرَبِّهٖ لَكَنُوْدٌ ۶
7. And to that (fact) he bears witness (by his deeds);	اور وہ اس سے آگاہ بھی ہے ۷	وَاِنَّهٗ عَلٰى ذٰلِكَ لَشَهِيْدٌ ۷
8. And violent is he in his love of wealth.	وہ تو مال کی سخت محبت کرنے والا ہے ۸	وَاِنَّهٗ لِحُبِّ الْخَيْرِ لَشَدِيْدٌ ۸
9. Does he not know,—when that which is in the graves is scattered abroad	کیا وہ اس وقت کو نہیں جانتا کہ جو (مُردے) قبروں میں ہیں وہ باہر نکال لئے جائیں گے ۹	اَفَلَا يَعْلَمُ اِذَا بُعْثِرَ مَا فِى الْقُبُوْرِ ۹
10. And that which is (locked up) in (human) breasts is made manifest—	اور جو (بھید) دلوں میں ہیں وہ ظاہر کر دیئے جائیں گے ۱۰	وَحُصِّلَ مَا فِى الصُّدُوْرِ ۱۰
11. That their Lord had been well-acquainted with them, (even to) that Day ?	بیشک اُن کا پروردگار اُس روز اُن سے خوب واقف ہوگا ۱۱	اِنَّ رَبَّهُمْ بِهِمْ يَوْمَئِذٍ لَّخَبِيْرٌ ۱۱

Al-Qāri'a, or The Day of Clamour

	سورۂ قارعہ مکّی ہے اور اس میں گیارہ آیتیں ہیں	سُوْرَةُ الْقَارِعَةِ مَكِّيَّةٌ وَّهِيَ اِحْدٰى عَشْرَةَ اٰيَةً
In the name of Allah, Most Gracious, Most Merciful.	شروع خدا کا نام لے کر جو بڑا مہربان نہایت رحم والا ہے	بِسْمِ اللّٰهِ الرَّحْمٰنِ الرَّحِيْمِ
1. The (Day) of Clamour:	کھڑکھڑانے والی ۱	اَلْقَارِعَةُ ۱
2. What is the (Day) of Clamour?	کھڑکھڑانے والی کیا ہے؟ ۲	مَا الْقَارِعَةُ ۲
3. And what will explain to thee what the (Day) of Clamour is ?	اور تم کیا جانو کہ کھڑکھڑانے والی کیا ہے؟ ۳	وَمَآ اَدْرٰىكَ مَا الْقَارِعَةُ ۳
4. (It is) a Day whereon Men will be like moths scattered about,	(وہ قیامت ہے) جس دن لوگ ایسے ہونگے جیسے بکھرے ہوئے پتنگے ۴	يَوْمَ يَكُوْنُ النَّاسُ كَالْفَرَاشِ الْمَبْثُوْثِ ۴
5. And the mountains will be like carded wool.	اور پہاڑ ایسے ہوجائینگے جیسے دُھنکی ہوئی رنگ برنگ کی اُون ۵	وَتَكُوْنُ الْجِبَالُ كَالْعِهْنِ الْمَنْفُوْشِ ۵

SÛRA–102
AT-TAKÃTHUR
(INTRODUCTION)

This probably early Makkan Sûra gives a warning against acquisitveness, i.e., the passion for piling up quantities or numbers, whether in the good things of this world, or in man-power or in other forms of megalomania, which leave no time or opportunity for pursuing the higher things of life.

SÛRA–103
AL-'AṢR
(INTRODUCTION)

This early Makkan Sûra refers to the testimony of Time through the Ages. All history shows that Evil came to an evil end. But Time is always in favour of those who have Faith, live clean and pure lives, and know how to wait, in patience and constancy. Cf. the theme of S. 95.

SÛRA–104
AL-HUMAZA
(INTRODUCTION)

This Makkan Sûra condemns all sorts of scandal, backbiting, and selfish hoarding of wealth, as destroying the hearts and affections of men.

6. Then, he whose balance (of good deeds) will be (found) heavy,
7. Will be in a Life of good pleasure and satisfaction.
8. But he whose balance (of good deeds) will be (found) light,—
9. Will have his home in a (bottomless) Pit.
10. And what will explain to thee what this is ?
11. (It is) a Fire blazing fiercely !

تو جس کے (اعمال کے) وزن بھاری نکلیں گے ﴿۶﴾
وہ دل پسند عیش میں ہوگا ﴿۷﴾
اور جس کے وزن ہلکے نکلیں گے ﴿۸﴾
اُس کا مرجع ہاویہ ہے ﴿۹﴾
اور تم کیا سمجھے کہ ہاویہ کیا چیز ہے؟ ﴿۱۰﴾
(وہ) دہکتی ہوئی آگ ہے ﴿۱۱﴾

فَأَمَّا مَنْ ثَقُلَتْ مَوَازِينُهُ ﴿٦﴾
فَهُوَ فِي عِيشَةٍ رَّاضِيَةٍ ﴿٧﴾
وَأَمَّا مَنْ خَفَّتْ مَوَازِينُهُ ﴿٨﴾
فَأُمُّهُ هَاوِيَةٌ ﴿٩﴾
وَمَا أَدْرَاكَ مَا هِيَهْ ﴿١٠﴾
نَارٌ حَامِيَةٌ ﴿١١﴾

At-Takāthur or Piling Up

سورۂ تکاثر مکی ہے اور اس میں آٹھ آیتیں ہیں

سُورَةُ التَّكَاثُرِ مَكِّيَّةٌ وَهِيَ ثَمَانُ آيَاتٍ

In the name of Allah, Most Gracious, Most Merciful.

شروع خدا کا نام لے کر جو بڑا مہربان نہایت رحم والا ہے

بِسْمِ اللَّهِ الرَّحْمَٰنِ الرَّحِيمِ

1. The mutual rivalry for piling up (the good things of this world) diverts you (from the more serious things),
2. Until ye visit the graves.
3. But nay, ye soon shall know (the reality).
4. Again, ye soon shall know !
5. Nay, were ye to know with certainty of mind, (ye would beware!)
6. Ye shall certainly see Hell-Fire !
7. Again, ye shall see it with certainty of sight!
8. Then, shall ye be questioned that Day about the joy (ye indulged in !)

(لوگو) تم کو (مال کی) بہت سی طلب نے غافل کر دیا ﴿۱﴾
یہاں تک کہ تم نے قبریں جا دیکھیں ﴿۲﴾
دیکھو تمہیں عنقریب معلوم ہو جائے گا ﴿۳﴾
پھر دیکھو تمہیں عنقریب معلوم ہو جائے گا ﴿۴﴾
دیکھو اگر تم جانتے (یعنی) علم الیقین (رکھتے) تو غفلت نہ کرتے ﴿۵﴾
تم ضرور دوزخ کو دیکھو گے ﴿۶﴾
پھر اس کو (ایسا) دیکھو گے (کہ) عین الیقین (آ جائے گا) ﴿۷﴾
پھر اس روز تم سے (شکر) نعمت کے (بارے میں) پرسش ہوگی ﴿۸﴾

أَلْهَاكُمُ التَّكَاثُرُ ﴿١﴾
حَتَّىٰ زُرْتُمُ الْمَقَابِرَ ﴿٢﴾
كَلَّا سَوْفَ تَعْلَمُونَ ﴿٣﴾
ثُمَّ كَلَّا سَوْفَ تَعْلَمُونَ ﴿٤﴾
كَلَّا لَوْ تَعْلَمُونَ عِلْمَ الْيَقِينِ ﴿٥﴾
لَتَرَوُنَّ الْجَحِيمَ ﴿٦﴾
ثُمَّ لَتَرَوُنَّهَا عَيْنَ الْيَقِينِ ﴿٧﴾
ثُمَّ لَتُسْأَلُنَّ يَوْمَئِذٍ عَنِ النَّعِيمِ ﴿٨﴾

Al-'Aṣr, or Time through the Ages

سورۂ عصر مکی ہے اور اس میں تین آیتیں ہیں

سُورَةُ الْعَصْرِ مَكِّيَّةٌ وَهِيَ ثَلٰثُ آيَاتٍ

In the name of Allah, Most Gracious, Most Merciful.

شروع خدا کا نام لے کر جو بڑا مہربان نہایت رحم والا ہے

بِسْمِ اللَّهِ الرَّحْمَٰنِ الرَّحِيمِ

1. By the time,
2. Verily Man is in loss,
3. Except such as have Faith, and do righteous deeds, and (join together) in the mutual enjoining of Truth, and of Patience and Constancy.

عصر کی قسم ﴿۱﴾ کہ انسان نقصان میں ہے ﴿۲﴾
مگر وہ لوگ جو ایمان لائے اور نیک عمل کرتے رہے اور
آپس میں حق (بات) کی تلقین اور صبر کی تاکید کرتے رہے ﴿۳﴾

وَالْعَصْرِ ﴿١﴾ إِنَّ الْإِنْسَانَ لَفِي خُسْرٍ ﴿٢﴾
إِلَّا الَّذِينَ آمَنُوا وَعَمِلُوا الصَّالِحَاتِ
وَتَوَاصَوْا بِالْحَقِّ وَتَوَاصَوْا بِالصَّبْرِ ﴿٣﴾

Al-Humaza, or the Scandal-monger

سورۂ ہمزہ مکی ہے اور اس میں نو آیتیں ہیں

سُورَةُ الْهُمَزَةِ مَكِّيَّةٌ وَهِيَ تِسْعُ آيَاتٍ

In the name of Allah, Most Gracious, Most Merciful.

شروع خدا کا نام لے کر جو بڑا مہربان نہایت رحم والا ہے

بِسْمِ اللَّهِ الرَّحْمَٰنِ الرَّحِيمِ

1. Woe to every (kind of) scandal-monger and backbiter,
2. Who pileth up wealth and layeth it by,
3. Thinking that his wealth would make him last for ever !
4. By no means ! He will be sure to be thrown into that which Breaks to Pieces.

ہر طعن آمیز اشارتیں کرنے والے چغل خور کی خرابی ہے ﴿۱﴾
جو مال جمع کرتا اور اس کو گن گن کر رکھتا ہے ﴿۲﴾
اور خیال کرتا ہے کہ اس کا مال اس کی ہمیشہ کی زندگی کا موجب ہوگا ﴿۳﴾
ہرگز نہیں وہ ضرور حطمہ میں ڈالا جائے گا ﴿۴﴾

وَيْلٌ لِّكُلِّ هُمَزَةٍ لُّمَزَةٍ ﴿١﴾
الَّذِي جَمَعَ مَالًا وَعَدَّدَهُ ﴿٢﴾
يَحْسَبُ أَنَّ مَالَهُ أَخْلَدَهُ ﴿٣﴾
كَلَّا لَيُنْبَذَنَّ فِي الْحُطَمَةِ ﴿٤﴾

SÛRA–105
AL-FÎL
(INTRODUCTION)

This early Makkan Sûra refers to an event that happened in the year of the birth of our Holy Prophet, say, about 570 A.D. Yaman was then under the rule of the Abyssinians (Christians), who had driven out the Jewish Ḥimyar rulers. Abraha Ashram was the Abyssinian governor or viceroy. Intoxicated with power and fired by religious fanaticism, he led a big expedition against Makkah, intending to destroy the Ka'ba. He had an elephant or elephants in his train. But his sacrilegious intentions were defeated by a miracle. No defence was offered by the custodians of the Ka'ba as the army was too strong for them, but it was believed that a shower of stones, thrown by flocks of birds, destroyed the invading army almost to a man. The stones produced sores and pustules on the skin, which spread like a pestilence.

SÛRA–106
QURAISH
(INTRODUCTION)

This Makkan Sûra may well be considered as a pendant to the last. If the Quraish were fond of Makkah and proud of it, if they profited, by its central position and its guaranteed security, from their caravans of trade and commerce, let them be grateful, adore the One True Allah, and accept His Message.

SÛRA–107
AL-MÃ'ÛN
(INTRODUCTION)

This Sûra—at least the first half of it—belongs to the early Makkan period. The subject-matter is the meaning of true worship, which requires Faith, the practical and helpful love of those in need, and sincerity rather than show in devotion and charity.

5. And what will explain to thee that which Breaks to Pieces ?
وَمَآ أَدْرٰىكَ مَا الْحُطَمَةُ ﴿٥﴾
اور تم کیا سمجھے کہ حطمہ کیا ہے ﴿٥﴾

6. (It is) the Fire of Allah kindled (to a blaze),
نَارُ اللّٰهِ الْمُوْقَدَةُ ﴿٦﴾
وہ خدا کی بھڑکائی ہوئی آگ ہے ﴿٦﴾

7. The which doth mount (right) to the Hearts:
الَّتِيْ تَطَّلِعُ عَلَى الْأَفْـِٕدَةِ ﴿٧﴾
جو دلوں پر جا لپٹے گی ﴿٧﴾

8. It shall be made into a vault over them,
إِنَّهَا عَلَيْهِمْ مُّؤْصَدَةٌ ﴿٨﴾
(اور) وہ اس میں بند کر دیئے جائیں گے ﴿٨﴾

9. In columns outstretched.
فِيْ عَمَدٍ مُّمَدَّدَةٍ ﴿٩﴾
یعنی (آگ کے) لمبے لمبے ستونوں میں ﴿٩﴾

Al-Fîl, or The Elephant

سُوْرَةُ الْفِيْلِ مَكِّيَّةٌ وَّهِيَ خَمْسُ اٰيَاتٍ
سورۂ فیل مکی ہے اور اس میں پانچ آیتیں ہیں

In the name of Allah, Most Gracious, Most Merciful.
بِسْمِ اللّٰهِ الرَّحْمٰنِ الرَّحِيْمِ
شروع خدا کا نام لے کر جو بڑا مہربان نہایت رحم والا ہے

1. Seest thou not how thy Lord dealt with the Companions of the Elephant ?
أَلَمْ تَرَ كَيْفَ فَعَلَ رَبُّكَ بِأَصْحٰبِ الْفِيْلِ ﴿١﴾
کیا تم نے نہیں دیکھا کہ تمہارے پروردگار نے ہاتھی والوں کے ساتھ کیا کیا ﴿١﴾

2. Did He not make their treacherous plan go astray ?
أَلَمْ يَجْعَلْ كَيْدَهُمْ فِيْ تَضْلِيْلٍ ﴿٢﴾
کیا اُن کا داؤں غلط نہیں کیا؟ (کیا) ﴿٢﴾

3. And He sent against them Flights of Birds,
وَّأَرْسَلَ عَلَيْهِمْ طَيْرًا أَبَابِيْلَ ﴿٣﴾
اور اُن پر جھلڑ کے جھلڑ جانور بھیجے ﴿٣﴾

4. Striking them with stones of baked clay.
تَرْمِيْهِمْ بِحِجَارَةٍ مِّنْ سِجِّيْلٍ ﴿٤﴾
جو اُن پر کنکر کی پتھریاں پھینکتے تھے ﴿٤﴾

5. Then did He make them like an empty field of stalks and straw, (of which the corn) has been eaten up.
فَجَعَلَهُمْ كَعَصْفٍ مَّأْكُوْلٍ ﴿٥﴾
تو اُن کو ایسا کر دیا جیسے کھایا ہوا بھس ﴿٥﴾ [٣٣٦]

Quraish or The Quraish, (Custodians of the Ka'ba)

سُوْرَةُ قُرَيْشٍ مَكِّيَّةٌ وَّهِيَ أَرْبَعُ اٰيَاتٍ
سورۂ قریش مکی ہے اور اس میں چار آیتیں ہیں

In the name of Allah, Most Gracious, Most Merciful.
بِسْمِ اللّٰهِ الرَّحْمٰنِ الرَّحِيْمِ
شروع خدا کا نام لے کر جو بڑا مہربان نہایت رحم والا ہے

1. For the familiarity of the Quraish,
لِإِيْلٰفِ قُرَيْشٍ ﴿١﴾
قریش کے مانوس کرنے کے سبب ﴿١﴾

2. Their familiarity with the journeys by winter and summer,—
إِلٰفِهِمْ رِحْلَةَ الشِّتَآءِ وَالصَّيْفِ ﴿٢﴾
(یعنی) اُن کو جاڑے اور گرمی کے سفر سے مانوس کرنے کے سبب ﴿٢﴾

3. Let them worship the Lord of this House,
فَلْيَعْبُدُوْا رَبَّ هٰذَا الْبَيْتِ ﴿٣﴾
(لوگوں کو) چاہیئے کہ (اس نعمت کے شکر میں) اس گھر کے مالک کی عبادت کریں ﴿٣﴾

4. Who provides them with food against hunger, and with security against fear (of danger).
الَّذِيْٓ أَطْعَمَهُمْ مِّنْ جُوْعٍ ۙ وَّاٰمَنَهُمْ مِّنْ خَوْفٍ ﴿٤﴾
جس نے اُن کو بھوک میں کھانا کھلایا۔ اور خوف سے امن بخشا ﴿٤﴾ [٣٣٧]

Al-Mā'ûn or Neighbourly Needs.

سُوْرَةُ الْمَاعُوْنِ مَكِّيَّةٌ وَّهِيَ سَبْعُ اٰيَاتٍ
سورۂ ماعون مکی ہے اور اس میں سات آیتیں ہیں

In the name of Allah, Most Gracious, Most Merciful.
بِسْمِ اللّٰهِ الرَّحْمٰنِ الرَّحِيْمِ
شروع خدا کا نام لے کر جو بڑا مہربان نہایت رحم والا ہے

1. Seest thou one who denies the Judgment (to come) ?
أَرَءَيْتَ الَّذِيْ يُكَذِّبُ بِالدِّيْنِ ﴿١﴾
بھلا تم نے اُس شخص کو دیکھا جو (روز) جزا کو جھٹلاتا ہے ﴿١﴾

2. Then such is the one who repulses the orphan,
فَذٰلِكَ الَّذِيْ يَدُعُّ الْيَتِيْمَ ﴿٢﴾
یہ وہی (بدبخت) ہے جو یتیم کو دھکے دیتا ہے ﴿٢﴾

3. And encourages not the feeding of the indigent.
وَلَا يَحُضُّ عَلٰى طَعَامِ الْمِسْكِيْنِ ﴿٣﴾
اور فقیر کو کھانا کھلانے کے لئے (لوگوں کو) ترغیب نہیں دیتا ﴿٣﴾

4. So woe to the worshippers
فَوَيْلٌ لِّلْمُصَلِّيْنَ ﴿٤﴾
تو ایسے نمازیوں کی خرابی ہے ﴿٤﴾

5. Who are neglectful of their Prayers,
الَّذِيْنَ هُمْ عَنْ صَلَاتِهِمْ سَاهُوْنَ ﴿٥﴾
جو نماز کی طرف سے غافل رہتے ہیں ﴿٥﴾

6. Those who (want but) to be seen,
الَّذِيْنَ هُمْ يُرَآءُوْنَ ﴿٦﴾
جو ریاکاری کرتے ہیں ﴿٦﴾

SÛRA–108
AL-KAUTHAR
(INTRODUCTION)

This very brief early Makkan Sûra sums up in the single mystic word *Kauthar* (Abundance) the doctrine of spiritual Riches through devotion and sacrifice. The converse also follows: indulgence in hatred means the cutting off of all hope of this life and the Hereafter.

SÛRA–109
AL-KÃFIRÛN
(INTRODUCTION)

This is another early Makkan Sûra. It defines the right attitude to those who reject Faith: in matters of Truth we can make no compromise, but there is no need to persecute or abuse anyone for his faith or belief.

SÛRA–110
AN-NAṢR
(INTRODUCTION)

This beautiful Sûra was the last of the Sûras to be revealed *as a whole,* though the portion of the verse v. 4, "This day have I perfected your religion for you," etc., contains probably the last *words* of the Qur-ãn to be revealed.

The date of this Sûra was only a few months before the passing away of the Holy Prophet from this world, Rabi' I, A.H. 11. The place was either the precincts of Makkah at the Farewell Pilgrimage, Ẓulḥijja, A.H. 10, or Madinah after his return from the Farewell Pilgrimage.

Victory is the crown of service, not an occasion for exultation. All victory comes from the help of Allah.

ṢÛRA–111
AL-MASAD OR AL-LAHAB
(INTRODUCTION)

This very early Makkan Sûra, though it referred in the first instance to a particular incident in a cruel and relentless persecution, carries the general lesson that cruelty ultimately ruins itself. The man who rages against holy things is burnt up in his own rage. His hands, which are the instruments of his action, perish, and he perishes him self. No boasted wealth or position will save him. The women, who are made for nobler emotions, may, if they go wrong, feed unholy rage with fiercer fuel—to their own loss. For they may twist the torturing rope round their own neck. It is a common experience that people perish by the very means by which they seek to destroy others.

7. But refuse (to supply) (even) neighbourly needs.
اور برتنے کی چیزیں عاریت نہیں دیتے (۷)
وَيَمْنَعُوْنَ الْمَاعُوْنَ (۷)

Al-Kauthar, or Abundance

سورۂ کوثر مکی ہے اور اس میں تین آیتیں ہیں
سُوْرَةُ الْكَوْثَرِ مَكِّيَّةٌ وَهِيَ ثَلٰثُ اٰيَاتٍ

In the name of Allah, Most Gracious, Most Merciful.
شروع خدا کا نام لے کر جو بڑا مہربان نہایت رحم والا ہے
بِسْمِ اللّٰهِ الرَّحْمٰنِ الرَّحِيْمِ

1. To thee have We granted the Abundance.
(اے محمدؐ) ہم نے تم کو کوثر عطا فرمائی ہے[٣٣٨] (۱)
اِنَّآ اَعْطَيْنٰكَ الْكَوْثَرَ (۱)

2. Therefore to thy Lord turn in Prayer and Sacrifice.
تو اپنے پروردگار کے لئے نماز پڑھا کرو اور قربانی کیا کرو (۲)
فَصَلِّ لِرَبِّكَ وَانْحَرْ (۲)

3. For he who hateth thee,—He will be cut off (from Future Hope).
کچھ شک نہیں کہ تمہارا دشمن ہی بے اولاد رہے گا[٣٣٩] (۳)
اِنَّ شَانِئَكَ هُوَ الْاَبْتَرُ (۳)

Al-Kãfirûn, or Those who reject Faith

سورۂ کافرون مکی ہے اور اس میں چھ آیتیں ہیں
سُوْرَةُ الْكٰفِرُوْنَ مَكِّيَّةٌ وَهِيَ سِتُّ اٰيَاتٍ

In the name of Allah, Most Gracious, Most Merciful.
شروع خدا کا نام لے کر جو بڑا مہربان نہایت رحم والا ہے
بِسْمِ اللّٰهِ الرَّحْمٰنِ الرَّحِيْمِ

1. Say: O ye that reject Faith !
(اے پیغمبر ان منکرانِ اسلام سے) کہہ دو کہ اے کافرو! (۱)
قُلْ يٰۤاَيُّهَا الْكٰفِرُوْنَ (۱)

2. I worship not that which ye worship,
جن (بتوں) کو تم پوجتے ہو ان کو میں نہیں پوجتا (۲)
لَاۤ اَعْبُدُ مَا تَعْبُدُوْنَ (۲)

3. Nor will ye worship that which I worship.
اور جس (خدا) کی میں عبادت کرتا ہوں اس کی تم عبادت نہیں کرتے (۳)
وَلَاۤ اَنْتُمْ عٰبِدُوْنَ مَاۤ اَعْبُدُ (۳)

4. And I will not worship that which ye have been wont to worship
اور (میں پھر کہتا ہوں کہ) جن کی تم پرستش کرتے ہو ان کی میں پرستش کرنے والا نہیں ہوں (۴)
وَلَاۤ اَنَا عَابِدٌ مَّا عَبَدْتُّمْ (۴)

5. Nor will ye worship that which I worship.
اور نہ تم اس کی بندگی کرنے والے (معلوم ہوتے ہو) جس کی میں بندگی کرتا ہوں (۵)
وَلَاۤ اَنْتُمْ عٰبِدُوْنَ مَاۤ اَعْبُدُ (۵)

6. To you be your Way, and to me mine.
تم اپنے دین پر میں اپنے دین پر (۶)
لَكُمْ دِيْنُكُمْ وَلِيَ دِيْنِ (۶)

An-Naṣr, or Help

سورۂ نصر مدنی ہے اور اس میں تین آیتیں ہیں
سُوْرَةُ النَّصْرِ مَدَنِيَّةٌ وَهِيَ ثَلٰثُ اٰيَاتٍ

In the name of Allah, Most Gracious, Most Merciful.
شروع خدا کا نام لے کر جو بڑا مہربان نہایت رحم والا ہے
بِسْمِ اللّٰهِ الرَّحْمٰنِ الرَّحِيْمِ

1. When comes the Help of Allah, and Victory,
جب خدا کی مدد آ پہنچی اور فتح (حاصل ہو گئی) (۱)
اِذَا جَآءَ نَصْرُ اللّٰهِ وَالْفَتْحُ (۱)

2. And thou dost see the People enter Allah's Religion in crowds,
اور تم نے دیکھ لیا کہ لوگ غول کے غول خدا کے دین میں
داخل ہو رہے ہیں (۲)
وَرَاَيْتَ النَّاسَ يَدْخُلُوْنَ فِيْ دِيْنِ
اللّٰهِ اَفْوَاجًا (۲)

3. Celebrate the Praises of thy Lord, and pray for His Forgiveness: for He is Oft-Returning (in forgiveness).
تو اپنے پروردگار کی تعریف کے ساتھ تسبیح کرو اور اس سے
مغفرت مانگو۔ بیشک وہ معاف کرنے والا ہے (۳)
فَسَبِّحْ بِحَمْدِ رَبِّكَ وَاسْتَغْفِرْهُ
اِنَّهٗ كَانَ تَوَّابًا (۳)

Al-Lahab, or Al-Masad, or The Flame

سورۂ لہب مکی ہے اور اس میں پانچ آیتیں ہیں
سُوْرَةُ اللَّهَبِ مَكِّيَّةٌ وَهِيَ خَمْسُ اٰيَاتٍ

In the name of Allah, Most Gracious, Most Merciful.
شروع خدا کا نام لے کر جو بڑا مہربان نہایت رحم والا ہے
بِسْمِ اللّٰهِ الرَّحْمٰنِ الرَّحِيْمِ

1. Perish the hands of the Father of Flame ! Perish he !
ابو لہب کے ہاتھ ٹوٹیں اور وہ ہلاک ہو (۱)
تَبَّتْ يَدَآ اَبِيْ لَهَبٍ وَّتَبَّ (۱)

2. No profit to him from all his wealth, and all his gains !
نہ تو اس کا مال ہی اس کے کچھ کام آیا اور نہ وہ جو اس نے کمایا (۲)
مَاۤ اَغْنٰى عَنْهُ مَالُهٗ وَمَا كَسَبَ (۲)

3. Burnt soon will he be in a Fire of blazing Flame !
وہ جلد بھڑکتی ہوئی آگ میں داخل ہو گا (۳)
سَيَصْلٰى نَارًا ذَاتَ لَهَبٍ (۳)

4. His wife shall carry the (crackling) wood —as fuel !—
اور اس کی جورو بھی جو ایندھن سر پر اٹھائے پھرتی ہے (۴)
وَّامْرَاَتُهٗ حَمَّالَةَ الْحَطَبِ (۴)

SÛRA–112
AL-IKHLÃṢ
(INTRODUCTION)

This early Makkan Sûra sums up in a few terse words the Unity of the Godhead—often professed, but frequently mixed up in the popular mind with debasing superstitions.

SÛRA–113
AL-FALAQ
(INTRODUCTION)

This early Makkan Sûra provides the antidote to superstition and fear by teaching us to seek refuge in Allah from every kind of ill arising from outer nature and from dark and evil plottings and envy on the part of others.

SÛRA–114
AN-NÃS
(INTRODUCTION)

This early Makkan Sûra is a pendant to the last Sûra, and concludes the Holy Qur-ãn with an appeal to us to trust in Allah, rather than man, as our sure shield and protection. It warns us specially against the secret whispers of evil within our own hearts.

5. A twisted rope of palm-leaf fibre round her (own) neck !

اُس کے گلے میں مُونج کی رسّی ہوگی ۵

فِي جِيدِهَا حَبْلٌ مِّن مَّسَدٍ ۝٥ ع ٣٦

Al-Ikhlāṣ, or Purity (of Faith)

سُورۂ اخلاص مکّی ہے اور اس میں چار آیتیں ہیں

سُورَةُ الْإِخْلَاصِ مَكِّيَّةٌ وَهِيَ أَرْبَعُ آيَاتٍ

In the name of Allah, Most Gracious, Most Merciful.

شروع خدا کا نام لے کر جو بڑا مہربان نہایت رحم والا ہے

بِسْمِ اللَّهِ الرَّحْمَٰنِ الرَّحِيمِ

1. Say: He is Allah the One;

کہو کہ وہ (ذات پاک جس کا نام) اللہ (ہے) ایک ہے ۱

قُلْ هُوَ اللَّهُ أَحَدٌ ۝١

2. Allah, the Eternal, Absolute;

(وہ) معبود برحق بے نیاز ہے ۲

اللَّهُ الصَّمَدُ ۝٢

3. He begetteth not, nor is He begotten;

نہ کسی کا باپ ہے اور نہ کسی کا بیٹا ۳

لَمْ يَلِدْ وَلَمْ يُولَدْ ۝٣

4. And there is none like unto Him.

اور کوئی اُس کا ہمسر نہیں ۴

وَلَمْ يَكُن لَّهُ كُفُوًا أَحَدٌ ۝٤ ع ٣٧

Al-Falaq, or The Dawn

سُورۂ فلق مدنی ہے اور اس میں پانچ آیتیں ہیں

سُورَةُ الْفَلَقِ مَدَنِيَّةٌ وَهِيَ خَمْسُ آيَاتٍ

In the name of Allah, Most Gracious, Most Merciful.

شروع خدا کا نام لے کر جو بڑا مہربان نہایت رحم والا ہے

بِسْمِ اللَّهِ الرَّحْمَٰنِ الرَّحِيمِ

1. Say: I seek refuge with the Lord of the Dawn,

کہو کہ مَیں صبح کے مالک کی پناہ مانگتا ہُوں ۱

قُلْ أَعُوذُ بِرَبِّ الْفَلَقِ ۝١

2. From the mischief of created things;

ہر چیز کی بُرائی سے جو اُس نے پیدا کی ۲

مِن شَرِّ مَا خَلَقَ ۝٢

3. From the mischief of Darkness as it overspreads;

اور شب تاریک کی بُرائی سے جب اُس کا اندھیرا چھا جائے ۳

وَمِن شَرِّ غَاسِقٍ إِذَا وَقَبَ ۝٣

4. From the mischief of those who blow on knots;

اور گنڈوں پر (پڑھ پڑھ کر) پھونکنے والیوں کی بُرائی سے ۴

وَمِن شَرِّ النَّفَّاثَاتِ فِي الْعُقَدِ ۝٤

5. And from the mischief of the envious one as he practises envy.

اور حسد کرنے والے کی بُرائی سے جب حسد کرنے لگے ۵

وَمِن شَرِّ حَاسِدٍ إِذَا حَسَدَ ۝٥ ع ٣٨

An-Nās, or Mankind

سُورۂ ناس مدنی ہے اور اس میں چھ آیتیں ہیں

سُورَةُ النَّاسِ مَدَنِيَّةٌ وَهِيَ سِتُّ آيَاتٍ

In the name of Allah, Most Gracious, Most Merciful.

شروع خدا کا نام لے کر جو بڑا مہربان نہایت رحم والا ہے

بِسْمِ اللَّهِ الرَّحْمَٰنِ الرَّحِيمِ

1. Say: I seek refuge with the Lord and Cherisher of Mankind,

کہو کہ مَیں لوگوں کے پروردگار کی پناہ مانگتا ہُوں ۱

قُلْ أَعُوذُ بِرَبِّ النَّاسِ ۝١

2. The King (or Ruler) of Mankind,

(یعنی) لوگوں کے حقیقی بادشاہ کی ۲

مَلِكِ النَّاسِ ۝٢

3. The God (or Judge) of Mankind,—

لوگوں کے معبُودِ برحق کی ۳

إِلَٰهِ النَّاسِ ۝٣

4. From the mischief of the Whisperer (of Evil), who withdraws (after his whisper),—

(شیطان) وسوسہ انداز کی بُرائی سے جو (خدا کا نام سُن کر) پیچھے ہٹ جاتا ہے ۴

مِن شَرِّ الْوَسْوَاسِ الْخَنَّاسِ ۝٤

5. Who whispers into the hearts of Mankind,—

جو لوگوں کے دلوں میں وسوسے ڈالتا ہے ۵

الَّذِي يُوَسْوِسُ فِي صُدُورِ النَّاسِ ۝٥

6. Among Jinns and among Men.

(خواہ وہ) جنّات سے (ہو) یا انسانوں میں سے ۶

مِنَ الْجِنَّةِ وَالنَّاسِ ۝٦ ع ٣٩

O Allah! Confer Thy grace on me through the Magnificent Qur-ān; make it for me a Book of instruction and evidence, light, guidance and mercy; Grant me the honour of reciting it day and night and make it an argument and proof for me, O Lord and Sustainer of all the worlds, through the gracious instrumentality of Muhammad, Thy Prophet, –May Allah shower blessings and peace on him!

دُعائے ماثورہ برائے ختم قرآن مجید

اے اللہ میری قبر کی وحشت کو اُنس سے بدل دے۔ مجھ پر قرآن عظیم (کی برکت) کے سبب سے رحم کر۔ اور اس کو میرا امام اور نور وہدایت اور رحمت بنا۔ اے اللہ اس میں سے جو بھول گیا ہُوں مجھے یاد دلا۔ جو نہیں جانتا سکھا اس کی تلاوت نصیب کر دن اور رات کے وقتوں میں۔ اور اُس کو میرے لئے دلیل بنا اے پالنے والے جہانوں کے

الدُّعَاءُ الْمَأْثُوْرَةُ:- اَللّٰهُمَّ ارْحَمْنِيْ بِالْقُرْاٰنِ الْعَظِيْمِ وَاجْعَلْهُ لِيْ إِمَامًا وَّنُوْرًا وَّهُدًى وَّرَحْمَةً وَارْزُقْنِيْ تِلَاوَتَهٗ اٰنَاۤءَ اللَّيْلِ وَاٰنَاۤءَ النَّهَارِ وَاجْعَلْهُ لِيْ حُجَّةً يَّارَبَّ الْعٰلَمِيْنَ بِحَقِّ نَبِيِّكَ مُحَمَّدٍ صَلَّى اللّٰهُ عَلَيْهِ وَسَلَّمَ

فوائد

۱- چونکہ حکم ہے کہ قرآن مجید خدا کا نام لے کر شروع کیا جائے اسلئے ہیں بِسْمِ اللّٰہِ کے ترجمے کے شروع میں کہو کا لفظ جو مقدر ہے لکھ دینا چاہیئے تھا مگر پھر سب جگہ ترجمے میں یہ لفظ لکھنا پڑتا اور اس میں وہ لطف نہ رہتا جو بِسْمِ اللّٰہِ الرَّحْمٰنِ الرَّحِیْمِ میں ہے اسلئے یہ لفظ مقدر ہی رہنے دیا۔

۲- یہ سورت خدا نے بندوں کی زبان میں نازل فرمائی ہے مقصود اس بات کا سکھانا ہے کہ وہ اس طرح خدا سے دعا کیا کریں۔ حدیث شریف میں آیا ہے کہ سب سے افضل ذکر لَآ اِلٰہَ اِلَّا اللّٰہُ ہے اور سب سے افضل دعا اَلْحَمْدُ لِلّٰہِ الخ۔

۳- انصاف کے دن سے مراد قیامت کا دن ہے کیونکہ دوسری جگہ ارشاد ہوا ہے۔ مَآ اَدْرٰىكَ مَا یَوْمُ الدِّیْنِ ○ یَوْمَ لَا تَمْلِكُ نَفْسٌ لِّنَفْسٍ شَیْـًٔا وَالْاَمْرُ یَوْمَىِٕذٍ لِّلّٰہِ ○ یعنی تم کو کیا معلوم ہے کہ انصاف کا دن کونسا ہے جس دن کوئی کسی کے کچھ کام نہ آئے گا اور اسدن خدا ہی کا حکم ہوگا۔ اگرچہ اور دونوں کا مالک بھی خدا ہی ہے مگر اس روز کی تخصیص اسلئے ہے کہ اس روز خدا کے سوا کسی کا حکم نہ چلے گا۔ خدا فرمائے گا لِمَنِ الْمُلْكُ الْیَوْمَ لِلّٰہِ الْوَاحِدِ الْقَهَّارِ ○

۴- یہ اور اسی طرح کے اور حروف جو قرآن مجید کی متعدد سورتوں کے شروع میں آئے ہیں اور جن کو حروف مقطعہ کہتے ہیں اسرار الٰہی میں سے ہیں ان پر بے قیل وقال ایمان لانا چاہیئے جناب رسالتمآب صلی اللہ علیہ وسلم نے ان کے کچھ معنی بیان نہیں فرمائے صرف یہی فرمایا ہے کہ الف ایک حرف ہے، اور لام ایک حرف اور میم ایک حرف۔

۵- ڈرنے والوں کا لفظ اس امر پر دلالت کرتا ہے کہ جن کے دلوں میں خدا کا خوف ہے وہی اسکی ہدایتوں کو مانتے اور وہی اس کتاب سے فائدہ حاصل کرتے ہیں اور جو ڈر نہیں رکھتے وہ ہدایت کی باتوں کی طرف توجہ ہی نہیں کرتے اور اسی لئے یہ کتاب ان کے لئے رہنما نہیں ہوسکتی۔

۶- غیب اس چیز کو کہتے ہیں جو آنکھ سے پوشیدہ ہو۔ اور اس جگہ وہ چیزیں مراد ہیں جن کی خبر جناب رسول خدا صلی اللہ علیہ وسلم نے دی ہے اور جو نظر سے مخفی ہیں، جیسے پل صراط، ترازوئے اعمال، بہشت اور دوزخ وغیرہ۔

۷- آخرت سے مراد قیامت کا دن ہے چونکہ وہ دن دنیا کے بعد آئے گا اسلئے اس کو آخرت کہتے ہیں اور یَوْمُ الْاٰخِر بھی۔

۸- اِنْذَار کے معنی ڈر کی خبر سنانے، خوف دلانے، وعظ ونصیحت اور ہدایت کرنے، راہ بتانے اور متنبہ وآگاہ کرنے کے ہیں پہلے معنی تو مشہور ہیں وعظ ونصیحت اور ہدایت کے معنی اس آیت سے ظاہر ہیں اِنَّمَآ اَنْتَ مُنْذِرٌ وَّلِكُلِّ قَوْمٍ هَادٍ یعنی اے پیغمبر تم تو صرف ہدایت کرنے والے ہو اور ہر قوم میں ہدایت کرنیوالے ہو گزرے ہیں۔ اسکا صاف مطلب ہے کہ جس طرح پہلے ہادی اور رہنما آتے رہے ہیں اور وہ ہر قوم میں آتے رہے ہیں۔ اسی طرح تم بھی ہدایت کرنے والے اور راستہ دکھانے والے ہو۔ اس مقام پر انذار کے معنی وعظ ونصیحت کے چسپاں ہیں اور وہی ترجمے میں اختیار کئے گئے ہیں۔

۹- دنیا میں اس قسم کے لوگ بھی موجود ہیں جن کے دل نصیحت سے متاثر اور نور ایمان سے منور نہیں ہوتے ایسے لوگ شقی ازلی کہلاتے ہیں۔ ایسوں ہی کے حق میں یہ ارشاد ہوا ہے کہ انکو نصیحت کرنا یا نہ کرنا برابر ہے۔ دلوں اور کانوں پر مہر لگنے اور آنکھوں پر پردہ پڑنے سے یہ مراد ہے کہ جن رستوں سے انسان ہدایت کی باتوں کو سن سکتا اور سمجھ سکتا ہے وہ بند ہیں۔

۱۰- اس آیت سے منافقوں کا حال شروع ہوتا ہے۔ منافق اسکو کہتے ہیں جو دل سے تو کافر ہو اور ظاہر میں اپنے تئیں مومن بیان کرے۔ اس طرح کے لوگ مدینے میں تھے اور کفار کی نسبت ان سے زیادہ ضرر کا احتمال تھا اسلئے خدا تعالٰی نے ان کے حال اور ان کی چال سے مسلمانوں کو آگاہ فرما دیا تاکہ ان سے بچتے رہیں اور انکے دھوکے میں نہ آئیں۔

۱۱- یہ لوگ مسلمانوں کے پاس بھی آتے تھے۔ اور کافروں کے ہاں بھی جاتے تھے تو ایسی باتیں کرتے جن سے فساد پیدا ہو۔ سو جب ان سے کہا جاتا کہ فساد کی باتیں نہ کرو تو جواب دیتے کہ ہماری غرض تو فریقین میں صلح وسازگاری پیدا کرنا ہے۔ خدا نے فرمایا کہ ان کے کام موجب فساد ہیں اور یہ یقیناً مفسد ہیں لیکن ان کو معلوم نہیں۔

۱۲- شیطانوں سے مراد ان کے سردار ہیں۔ منافق لوگ جب مسلمانوں سے ملتے تو کہتے کہ ہم تو تمہاری طرح مومن ہیں اور جب اپنے رؤسا کے پاس جاتے تو کہتے کہاں کا ایمان اور کیسی مسلمانی ہم تو مسلمانوں سے دل لگی کرتے ہیں اور اپنا ایمان ظاہر کر کے ان کو احمق بناتے ہیں۔

۱۳- اس آیت میں خدا منافقوں کی ان باتوں کے جواب میں فرماتا ہے کہ ان سے خدا ہنسی کرتا ہے۔ ہنسی سے مراد یہاں یہ ہے کہ جس طرح وہ بظاہر اظہار ایمان کرتے ہیں اور اپنے سرداروں سے مل کر یہ کہتے ہیں کہ ہم تمہارے ساتھ ہیں اسی طرح خدا دنیا میں ان کو پناہ دیتا اور انکے مال وجان کو محفوظ رکھتا ہے اور وہ سمجھے ہوتے ہیں کہ ان کے افعال انکو نقصان نہیں پہنچاتے لیکن قیامت کے دن انکو عذاب میں مبتلا کیا جائیگا۔

۱۴- منافق کئی قسم کے تھے بعض ایسے تھے کہ پہلے مسلمان ہو گئے تھے پھر منافق ہو گئے۔ اس آیت کی مثال انہیں کے حال پر صادق آتی ہے کہ انہوں نے پہلے ایمان لا کر روشنی حاصل کی۔ پھر منافق بنکر اس روشنی کو کھو دیا۔ اور نفاق کے اندھیرے میں پڑ گئے۔ یعنی انکے دل تاریک ہو گئے۔

۱۵ - یہ منافقوں کے حال کی دوسری مثال ہے اس میں دینِ اسلام کو مینہ سے تشبیہ دی گئی ہے جس طرح مینہ میں اندھیرا اور بجلی اور گرج ہوتی ہے اسی طرح اسلام کے آغاز میں خواہ کچھ زحمتیں اور صعوبتیں بھی ہوں لیکن بعد میں وہ سراسر رحمت ہوتا ہے۔ منافقوں کو اسلام سے فائدے پہنچتے تو اسکے قائل ہو جاتے اور جب کوئی ایسا حکم نازل ہوتا جسکو وہ سخت سمجھتے۔ تو خیال کرتے کہ بلا نازل ہوئی اور یوں ڈر جاتے جیسے بجلی سے ڈرا کرتے ہیں کڑک سے ڈر کر کانوں میں انگلیاں دے لینے کا مطلب یہ ہے کہ حکم کی سختی سے ہراساں ہو کر اُس پر عمل کرنے سے ہچکچاتے اور ایسی تدبیریں کرنے لگتے ہیں کہ مشکل میں نہ پھنس جائیں اور اس سے جان بچ جائے بعض نے کہا ہے کہ قرآن مجید میں جو کفر و شرک اور اسپر وعید اور سزا کا بیان اور خدا کی وحدانیت کی روشن دلیلیں ہیں جن کی مثال اندھیروں اور گرج اور برق کی ہے تو منافقوں کو ڈر پیدا ہوتا کہ انکو سنکر کہیں ایمان لانے پر آمادہ نہ ہو جائیں اور اپنا مذہب ترک نہ کر بیٹھیں جو اُنکے نزدیک بمنزلہ موت تھا اور اسی وجہ سے وہ اپنے کانوں میں انگلیاں دے لیتے کہ قرآن کو سن ہی نہ سکیں۔

۱۶ - اس آیت میں یہ بیان ہے کہ حضرت محمد مصطفےٰ صلی اللہ علیہ وسلم خدا کے پیغمبر اور قرآن مجید اس کا کلام ہے۔ اور کفار سے تحدی کی گئی ہے کہ اگر تم ان باتوں کو نہیں مانتے اور سمجھتے ہو کہ یہ کتاب خدا کی طرف سے نازل نہیں ہوئی بلکہ محمد صلعم نے اپنی طرف سے بنالی ہے تو اس جیسی ایک سورت تم بھی بنالاؤ۔ اس بارے میں اختلاف ہے کہ قرآن مجید کس لحاظ سے بے مثل اور معجز ہے کثرت سے مفسرین اس بات کے قائل ہیں کہ وہ باعتبارِ فصاحت و بلاغت کے بے مثل ہے یعنی جیسی عمدہ اور فصیح و بلیغ عبارت قرآن مجید کی ہے ایسی عبارت کسی سے نہیں بن سکتی۔ وہ یہ بھی کہتے ہیں اور اسے ان کے دعوے کی دلیل سمجھنا چاہیئے کہ جس زمانے میں جس چیز کا زیادہ چرچا ہوتا تھا اس وقت کے پیغمبر کو اسی قسم کا معجزہ دیا جاتا تھا چونکہ ایام نزولِ قرآن مجید میں عرب میں فصاحت و بلاغت کا بڑا چرچا تھا اسلیئے خدا نے حضرت خاتم النبیینؐ کو فصاحت و بلاغت قرآن کا ایسا معجزہ بخشا کہ بڑے بڑے قادر الکلام شاعر اور خطیب اسکے مقابل عاجز ہو گئے بعض نے کہا کہ قرآن اپنی حکیمانہ ہدایات کے لحاظ سے معجز ہے بعض اس کو روحانیت کے اعتبار سے معجز مانتے ہیں۔ بہر کیف اس میں آداب ہیں، اخلاق ہیں، حسنِ معاشرت ہے، تزکیۂ نفس ہے، قوانینِ سیاست ہیں، ضوابطِ انتظامِ مملکت ہیں، انصاف و معدلت ہے، کسب و تجارت ہے، حقوق ہیں، عبادات ہیں، معاملات ہیں، مواخات ہے، الفت ہے، نرمی ہے، رعایت ہے، خیر خواہی ہے، نصیحت ہے، خدا کی ہستی اور وحدانیت ہے۔ غرض اس میں علیٰ وجہ الکمال انسان کی اصلاح حالت ہے، اور کچھ شک نہیں کہ وہ کیا بلحاظ فصاحت کے اور کیا باعتبار حکیمانہ ہدایات اور روحانیت کے بے مثل و بے نظیر ہے اور کوئی شخص اس قسم کی کتاب بنانے پر قدرت نہیں رکھتا اسی بنا پر دوسری جگہ ارشاد ہوا ہے قُلْ لَّئِنِ اجْتَمَعَتِ الْاِنْسُ وَالْجِنُّ عَلٰۤی اَنْ یَّاْتُوْا بِمِثْلِ هٰذَا الْقُرْاٰنِ لَا یَاْتُوْنَ بِمِثْلِهٖ وَلَوْ كَانَ بَعْضُهُمْ لِبَعْضٍ ظَهِیْرًا ۝

۱۷ - قرآن میں مشرکوں اور ان کے معبودانِ باطل کی مثالیں بعض آیات میں اس طرح بیان ہوئی ہیں کہ جو لوگ خدا کو چھوڑ کر اوروں کو کارساز بناتے ہیں ان کی مثال مکڑی کی سی ہے کہ وہ بھی ایک (طرح کا) گھر بناتی ہے اور کچھ شک نہیں کہ تمام گھروں سے کمزور مکڑی کا گھر ہوتا ہے کاش یہ اس بات کو جانتے۔" دوسری آیت میں ہے "لوگو! ایک مثال بیان کی جاتی ہے اُسے غور سے سنو کہ جن لوگوں کو تم خدا کے سوا پکارتے ہو وہ ایک مکھی بھی نہیں بنا سکتے اگرچہ اس کام کے لئے سب مجتمع ہو جائیں اور اگر اُن سے مکھی کوئی چیز چھین لے جائے تو اسے اس سے چھڑا نہیں سکتے طالب اور مطلوب (یعنی عابد اور معبود) دونوں گئے گذرے ہیں۔" کافر لوگ یہ مثالیں سنتے تو کہتے کہ ایسی حقیر و صغیر چیزوں کی مثالیں بیان کرنا خدا کی شان سے بعید ہے خدا نے فرمایا کہ خدا مچھر یا جو چیزیں اس سے بڑی ہیں ان کی مثالیں بیان کرنے سے عار نہیں کرتا۔ ان چیزوں کو پیدا بھی تو اسی نے کیا ہے اور جب پیدا کرنے میں اسکو عار نہیں تو انکی مثال میں کیوں عار ہو۔

۱۸ - سَمَآء کا لفظ واحد اور جمع دونوں کے لئے استعمال کیا جاتا ہے یہاں یہ محل جمع مستعمل ہوا ہے اسی لئے فَسَوّٰهُنَّ فرمایا اور اسی بنا پر ترجمہ آسمانوں کیا گیا ہے۔

۱۹ - سجدہ دو طرح کا ہوتا ہے ایک عبادت کا۔ ایک تعظیم کا عبادت نہایت ذلت کو کہتے ہیں۔ اور خدا تعالیٰ نہیں چاہتا کہ انسان اسکے سوا کسی اور کے آگے ذلت اختیار کرے اس سے انسان کی رفعتِ شان ظاہر ہوتی ہے کہ خدا نے اسکا اپنے سوا کسی اور کی عبادت کرنا جائز نہیں رکھا۔ جو سجدہ خدا نے فرشتوں سے آدمؑ کو کرانا چاہا تھا وہ تعظیم اور اکرام اور احترام کا سجدہ تھا۔ جیسا یوسفؑ کے بھائیوں نے یوسفؑ کو کیا تھا۔ ایسا سجدہ پہلے مذہبوں میں جائز تھا۔ دینِ اسلام میں غیر مشروع قرار دیا گیا اب ایسا سجدہ جائز نہیں۔

۲۰ - شیطان نوعِ جنّ سے تھا بڑی عبادت کیا کرتا تھا اور بڑا علم رکھتا تھا۔ کثرتِ عبادت کے سبب سے فرشتوں کا درجہ مل گیا تھا۔ یہی سبب ہے کہ جب خدا تعالےٰ نے فرشتوں کو حکم دیا کہ آدمؑ کو سجدہ کریں تو اس خطاب میں وہ بھی داخل تھا۔ چونکہ اس کی پیدائش آگ سے ہوئی تھی اور آدم کی مٹی سے۔ اور آگ کو مٹی پر فوقیت ہے۔ اسکے علاوہ وہ عابد و عالم بھی بڑا تھا اسلیئے شیخی میں آگیا اور آدم علیہ السلام کو سجدہ نہ کیا خدا نے اس کبر و غرور اور نافرمانی کے سبب اُسے مردود کر دیا۔

۲۱ - فرعون کسی خاص شخص کا نام نہ تھا بلکہ ان وقتوں میں ہر بادشاہِ مصر کو فرعون کہتے تھے۔ جو فرعون حضرت موسیٰ علیہ السلام کے وقت میں تھا اسکا نام ولید بن مصعب ابن ریان تھا بعض نے مصعب بن ریان کہا ہے۔ کہتے ہیں کہ لوگوں نے فرعون سے یہ بات کہی تھی کہ بنی اسرائیل ایک ایسے شخص کے پیدا ہونے

کے منتظر ہیں جسکے سبب وہ فرعون کے پنجے سے رہائی پائینگے اور انکو بہت عروج حاصل ہوگا یہ سنکر فرعون نے حکم دیا کہ بنی اسرائیل میں جو لڑکا پیدا ہو وہ قتل کر دیا جائے بعض کہتے ہیں کہ فرعون نے ایک خواب دیکھا تھا کہ ایک آگ بیت المقدس سے نکل کر مصر کے گھروں کو آگئی ہے لیکن بنی اسرائیل کے گھر اس سے بچ گئے ہیں جسکی تعبیر معبروں نے یہ دی کہ بنی اسرائیل میں ایک لڑکا پیدا ہوگا جو موجب زوال سلطنت مصر ہوگا اس خوف سے فرعون نے وہ حکم دیا تھا۔ اسی اثنا میں موسیٰ علیہ السلام پیدا ہوئے اور جس عجیب طریقے سے خدا نے انکو فرعونیوں کے ہاتھ سے بچایا اسکا مفصل ذکر اور جگہ ہے آخر موسیٰ علیہ السلام فرعونیوں کی تباہی اور اسرائیلیوں کی مخلصی کا موجب ہوئے۔

۲۲- بنی اسرائیل جب موسیٰ علیہ السلام کے ہمراہ مصر سے نکلے تھے تو ان کو حکم ہوا تھا کہ ارض مقدس میں جاؤ وہ تمہارے باپ اسرائیل کی میراث ہے وہاں جو کافر عمالیق رہتے ہیں ان سے جنگ کر کے ان کو نکال دو خدا نے یہ بھی وعدہ فرمایا تھا کہ جنگ میں انکو فتح حاصل ہوگی مگر انہوں نے جنگ کرنے سے ہمت ہار دی۔ تو خدا نے انکو اس عذاب میں مبتلا کیا کہ چالیس برس جنگل میں سرگرداں پھرتے رہے۔ چالیس برس کے بعد وہ اس جنگل سے نکلے اسوقت موسیٰ علیہ السلام فوت ہو چکے تھے۔ یوشع بن نون علیہ السلام ساتھ تھے۔ اب انہوں نے عمالقہ سے جنگ کی تو خدا نے فتح دی اور حکم ہوا کہ دروازۂ شہر میں سجدہ کر کے اور حِطَّۃٌ کہہ کر داخل ہوں حِطَّۃٌ کے معنی مغفرت و استغفار کے ہیں یعنی ہمارے گناہ معاف کر۔ مگر انہوں نے حِطَّۃٌ کی جگہ حِنطۃٌ یعنی گیہوں کہا اور بجائے سجدے کے سُرین کے بل داخل ہوئے اس نافرمانی اور بے ادبی کے سبب خدا نے پھر انکو مبتلائے عذاب کیا۔

۲۳- یہود کو حکم تھا کہ ہفتے کے دن کی تعظیم کریں اور اسمیں مچھلی کا شکار نہ کریں تو وہ اس حکم کے خلاف کرتے اور ایک دن پہلے دریا کے کنارے گڑھے کھود کر ان میں پانی بھر دیتے تھے اور جب مچھلیاں ان میں جمع ہو جاتیں تو نکال لیتے اور کہتے کہ یہ شکار جمعہ کا ہے اس حیلہ کے سبب بندر بنا دیئے گئے۔

۲۴- مفسرین نے لکھا ہے کہ بنی اسرائیل میں ایک بڑا مالدار شخص تھا مگر بے اولاد اس کا وارث اسکا ایک بھتیجا تھا اُس نے مال کی طمع کے سبب اس کو قتل کر ڈالا۔ جو لوگ اس طرح قتل کیا کرتے ہیں۔ بڑی احتیاط سے کام لیا کرتے ہیں۔ اس نے بھی ایسے طریق سے اسے قتل کیا کہ قاتل کا کچھ پتہ نہیں ملتا تھا۔ لوگ اس بارے میں لڑنے جھگڑنے لگے۔ تو کسی نے کہا کہ تم میں خدا کے پیغمبر موجود ہیں ان سے رجوع کرو انہوں نے موسیٰ سے یہ کیفیت بیان کی۔ آپ نے بیل ذبح کرنے کا حکم دیا۔ عجب نہیں کہ قاتل کو اس امر کا خوف ہو گیا ہو کہ کہیں راز افشا نہ ہو جائے اس لئے قبل اسکے کہ بیل کے بارے میں جستجو کریں۔ یہ بات کہی کہ کیا آپ ہم سے ہنسی کرتے ہیں کیونکہ ہم پوچھتے ہیں کہ قاتل کون ہے آپ کہتے ہیں کہ بیل ذبح کرو اور یہ ایک بالکل بے مناسبت بات ہے موسیٰ نے فرمایا کہ میں ہنسی نہیں کرتا بلکہ درحقیقت وہ بات کہتا ہوں جس کا خدا نے ارشاد فرمایا ہے تو انہوں نے بیل کے اوصاف دریافت کرنے میں کئی طرح کی باتیں کیں۔ آخرالامر انہوں نے اسکو ذبح کیا تو حکم ہوا اسکا کوئی سا ٹکڑا مقتول کو مارو اسکے مارنے سے مقتول زندہ ہو گیا اور اس سے پوچھا گیا کہ تجھ کو کس نے مارا تھا تو اس نے قاتل کا نام لے دیا۔ اس قصّے سے یہ ظاہر کرنا مقصود ہے کہ جسطرح خدا نے اس مقتول کو تمہاری آنکھوں کے سامنے زندہ کر دیا اسی طرح قیامت کے روز تمام مردوں کو اٹھا کھڑا کرے گا اور یہ اسکو کچھ مشکل نہیں

۲۵- یہ لوگ کچھ بہت ہی نڈر تھے خدا کے کلام کے بدل دینے میں بھی باک نہیں کرتے تھے: تحریف میں اختلاف ہے کہ کس قسم کی تھی بعض کہتے ہیں کہ لفظی تھی یعنی الفاظ بدل دیتے تھے۔ بعض کہتے ہیں کہ معنوی تھی یعنی معنی بگاڑ دیتے تھے۔ امام فخرالدین رازی ؒ اسی کے قائل ہیں۔ بعض کہتے ہیں کہ لفظی اور معنوی دونوں طرح کی تھی۔ بہرکیف جمہور اہل اسلام کتب یہود و نصاریٰ کو محرف و مبدل مانتے ہیں اور ان پر اعتبار نہیں کرتے۔ مسلمانوں کو اس بات پر فخر ہے کہ ان کی کتاب آسمانی میں تحریف نہیں ہوئی اور ہو سکتی بھی نہیں کیونکہ خدا نے اسکی حفاظت اپنے ذمے لے لی ہے۔

۲۶- ان آیات میں منافقوں کا حال بیان فرمایا گیا ہے بعض منافق ایسے بھی تھے کہ حضرت پیغمبر آخرالزماں کی بعثت کی پیشینگوئی جو انکی کتابوں میں درج تھی۔ نیز جو ان پر ان کے گناہوں کے سبب پہلے عذاب نازل ہوتے رہے تھے وہ مسلمانوں سے بیان کر دیتے تھے۔ تو اور منافق ان سے کہتے کہ تم ایسی باتیں مسلمانوں کو کیوں بتایا کرتے ہو وہ انکی سند سے تم کو قیامت کے روز خدا کے سامنے الزام دینگے۔ خدا نے فرمایا کہ منافقوں کا یہ خیال غلط ہے کہ وہ انکے اپنے بتانے سے ہمارے حضور میں ملزم ہونگے بلکہ ہم تمام باتوں سے جو پوشیدہ یا کھلے طور کرتے ہیں آگاہ ہیں اور خود ہی ان سے پوچھ لینگے کہ تم ایسی نافرمانی کیوں کرتے رہے۔

۲۷- یہود کہتے تھے کہ ہم نے چالیس روز بچھڑے کی پرستش کی تھی سوا تنے ہی روز ہم کو دوزخ کا عذاب ہوگا اور کسی اور عمل کے سبب ہم زیادہ عذاب نہیں پائینگے۔ خدا نے اس قول کی تردید کی۔ اور فرمایا کہ کیا خدا نے تم سے وعدہ کیا ہے کہ تم چند روز سے زیادہ دوزخ میں نہ رہو گے، حالانکہ تمہارے عمل ایسے ہیں کہ ہمیشہ تک جہنم میں جلتے رہو۔

۲۸- یہودی کہتے تھے کہ ہمارے دل پردے میں ہیں یعنی ہم اپنے دین کے سوا کسی کی بات سمجھ ہی نہیں سکتے۔ خدا نے فرمایا کہ دل پردے میں نہیں ہیں بلکہ خدا نے ان کے کفر کے سبب اُن پر لعنت کر رکھی ہے۔ دوسری جگہ فرمایا ہے کہ بَلْ طَبَعَ اللّٰہُ عَلَیْہَا بِکُفْرِہِمْ یعنی اُنکے دلوں پر مُہر لگا دی ہے کچھ بھی ہو بات ایسی تھی کہ ایمان اُنکے دلوں میں داخل ہی نہیں ہوتا تھا اور یہ خدا کے غضب کی نشانی ہے۔

۲۹- جناب سرور کائنات کی مجلس میں یہودی بیٹھتے تو ارشاداتِ نبوی میں سے جو بات اچھی طرح نہ سُن سکتے اور چاہتے کہ پھر سنیں تو رَاعِنَا کہتے یعنی

ہماری طرف توجہ فرمائیے اور پھر ارشاد کیجیے مگر ایک تو اُنکی زبان میں اسکے معنے ہوتے احمق اور متکبر دُوسرے ذرا زبان دبا کر کہتے تو رَاعِیْنَا ہو جاتا یعنی ہمارا چرواہا۔ مسلمانوں کو ان شریروں کی بدنیتی کا حال معلوم نہ تھا۔ وہ بھی اُن سے سیکھ کر کسی وقت یہ لفظ کہہ دیتے، خدا نے فرمایا کہ رَاعِنَا کا لفظ جسکے کئی معنے ہو سکتے ہیں اور بعض معنی بُرے ہیں اسے مت استعمال کیا کرو اسکی جگہ اُنْظُرْنَا کہا کرو۔ اُنْظُرْنَا کے معنی بھی یہی ہیں کہ ہماری طرف متوجہ ہوجیئے اور پھر فرمایئے مگر اسمیں دُوسرے معنوں کا احتمال نہیں ہوسکتا۔

۳۰۔ اس آیت کے شانِ نزول میں مختلف اقوال ہیں کسی نے کہا یہ آیت اس آیت سے پہلے نازل ہوئی تھی جس میں کعبے کی طرف منہ کر کے نماز پڑھنے کا حکم ہے یعنی مشرق اور مغرب سب خدا ہی کا ہے جس طرف تم منہ کروگے خدا ہی کی طرف ہوگا بعض نے کہا کہ ان لوگوں کے حق میں اتری تھی جن کو سمت کعبہ معلوم نہ ہوئی اور انہوں نے اور طرف نماز پڑھ لی تھی خدا نے ان کو مطلع فرمایا تھا کہ خدا کسی طرف مخصوص نہیں اسلئے اُن کی نماز ہوگئی مجاہد کہتے ہیں کہ جب آیت اُدْعُوْنِیْ اَسْتَجِبْ لَکُمْ نازل ہوئی تو لوگوں نے پُوچھا کہ ہم کدھر مُنہ کر کے دُعا مانگا کریں خدا نے فرمایا کہ خدا ہر طرف ہے جس طرف چاہو مُنہ کر کے دُعا مانگا کرو۔

۳۱۔ اس میں اختلاف ہے کہ یہ آزمائش نبوت سے پہلے تھی یا بعد۔ اور کس امر میں تھی کیسی بھی ہوا اور کسی امر میں بھی ہو وہ اس امر میں پُورے نکلے اور خدا نے خوش ہو کر ان لوگوں کا پیشوا بنایا مگر یہ بھی فرما دیا کہ تمہاری اولاد میں ظالم بھی ہونگے اور جو ایسے ہونگے انکو منصبِ امامت عطا نہیں ہوگا۔ جو نیک ہونگے وہی امام بنائے جائینگے

۳۲۔ امن سے مُراد یہ ہے کہ کوئی شخص کوئی قصور کر کے وہاں آجاتا ہے تو اُس کو پناہ ملجاتی ہے اور کوئی اس سے تعرض نہیں کرتا۔

۳۳۔ جن پیغمبر کے لئے حضرت ابراہیمؑ نے دُعا کی تھی وہ محمد رسول اللہ صلی اللہ علیہ وسلم تھے۔ ایک حدیث میں آپ نے فرمایا کہ میں اپنے باپ براہیمؑ کی دُعا ہوں عیسیٰؑ کی بشارت ہوں اپنی والدہ کا خواب ہوں اس حدیث سے حالی نے اس بیت کا مضمون اخذ کیا ہے۔ بیت:۔ ہوئی پہلوئے آمنہ سے ہویدا دُعائے خلیل اور نویدِ مسیحا

۳۴۔ خدا کے رنگ سے مُراد اس کا دین اسلام ہے جو خدا کی توحید خالص سکھاتا اور اسی کو مستحقِ عبادت بتاتا ہے

۳۵۔ یہود اور نصاریٰ حضرت ابراہیمؑ اور اور پیغمبروں کو اپنے اپنے مذہب کی طرف منسوب کرتے تھے یعنی انہیں یہودی یا عیسائی کہتے تھے۔ خدا نے اُنکے اس قول کی تردید کی اور فرمایا کہ اُنکے حال سے تم زیادہ واقف ہو یا خدا۔ خدا کے علم میں تو نہ وہ یہودی تھے نہ عیسائی بلکہ اکیلے خدا کے فرمانبردار تھے اور ان کا مذہب اسلام یعنی خدا کی حکمبرداری تھا

۳۶۔ شہادت سے مراد اس بات کا علم ہے کہ محمدؐ رسولِ خدا ہیں جن کا حال انکی کتابوں میں لکھا ہوا تھا لیکن وہ دیدہ و دانستہ اس کو چھپاتے تھے اور خدا نے شہادت کے چھپانے والے کو نہایت ظالم قرار دیا ہے

۳۷۔ امت معتدل جس میں نہ افراط ہے نہ تفریط عیسائیوں نے افراط کیا کہ حضرت عیسیٰ علیہ السلام کو خدا کا بیٹا بنا دیا۔ اور یہودیوں نے تفریط کہ ان کی پیغمبری کو بھی نہ مانا۔ امتِ معتدل نے نہ اُن کو حد سے زیادہ بڑھایا نہ گھٹایا بلکہ اُن کے درجے پر رکھا۔

۳۸۔ یعنی اس غرض سے منہ پھیر پھیر کر دیکھنا کہ کب کعبے کی طرف منہ کر کے نماز پڑھنے کا حکم ہوتا ہے کیونکہ آپ دل سے چاہتے تھے کہ اپنے دادا ابراہیم علیہ السلام کے قبلے کی طرف منہ کر کے نماز پڑھا کریں۔

۳۹۔ یہود تو مسلمانوں کو یہ الزام دیتے تھے کہ ہمارے دین کو تو نہیں مانتے مگر ہمارے قبلے کی طرف پڑھتے ہیں۔ اور مُشرک یہ الزام دیتے تھے کہ دعوے تو ابراہیم کے دین پر چلنے کا ہے لیکن اُن کے قبلے کی طرف نماز نہیں پڑھتے۔ خانہ کعبہ کے قبلہ مقرر کر دینے سے یہ اعتراض رفع ہو گئے۔

۴۰۔ عمرہ بھی ایک قسم کا حج ہے اور اس میں اور حج میں یہ فرق ہے کہ حج خاص ذی الحج کے مہینے میں ہوتا ہے اور عمرہ اور مہینوں میں بھی ہو سکتا ہے دوسرے حج میں احرام باندھنا پھر عرفے کے دن عرفات میں حاضر ہونا پھر وہاں سے چل کر مشعر الحرام میں رات رہنا۔ پھر صبح عید کو منا میں پہنچکر کنکر پھینکنا اور حجامت بنوا کر احرام اُتارنا اور مکے میں جاکر طواف کعبہ کرنا۔ پھر صفا و مروہ کے درمیان (جو مکے میں دو پہاڑیاں ہیں) دوڑنا وغیرہ ہوتا ہے اور عمرے میں صرف احرام باندھنا خانہ کعبہ کا طواف کرنا۔ صفا اور مروہ کے درمیان دوڑنا ہوتا ہے۔

۴۱۔ مرے ہوئے جانوروں میں سے مچھلی اور ٹڈی بروئے حدیث نبوی حلال ہیں اور لہو میں سے جگر اور تلی حلال ہیں۔

۴۲۔ یہ ترجمہ لغوی معنوں کی بنا پر کیا گیا ہے۔ لغت میں اہلال کے معنی آواز بلند کرنے کے ہیں مفسرین جو اس لفظ کے معنوں میں ذبح کا لفظ شامل کرتے ہیں وہ شانِ نزول کے لحاظ سے کرتے ہیں کیونکہ جاہلیت میں جو جانور غیرِ خدا کے لئے مقرر کیا جاتا تھا ذبح کرنے کے وقت بھی اس پر اُسی غیر کا نام لیا جاتا تھا ورنہ حقیقت میں جو چیز غیر خدا کے لئے مقرر کی جائے خواہ وہ جانور ہو یا اور کچھ حرام ہے اسلئے کہ آیت میں حرف مَا استعمال فرمایا گیا ہے جسکے معنی ہیں جو چیز اور وہ عام ہے ذبح حیوان اور اور چیزوں کو خواہ وہ کھانے کی ہوں یا پہننے کی یا اور طرح استعمال کرنے کی سب کو شامل ہے چونکہ لغت مقدم ہے اسلئے ہم نے لغوی معنی اختیار کئے ہیں۔ حرمت و حلت میں نیت کو بڑا دخل ہے مثلاً جو جانور غیر خدا کے لئے مقرر کیا گیا ہو اُس پر ذبح کے وقت خدا کا نام لیا جائے یا غیر خدا کا حرمت کے لحاظ سے برابر ہے۔ خدا کا نام لینے سے وہ حلال نہ ہوگا۔ علمائے کرام نے لکھا ہے کہ اگر کسی مسلمان نے کوئی جانور غیر خدا کے تقرب کے لئے ذبح کیا تو وہ اسلام سے خارج ہوگیا اور وہ جانور ایسا ہوگا جیسے مرتد کا ذبح کیا ہوا بہر حال نذر کی نیت خدا ہی کے لئے کرنی چاہیئے اور ذبح کرنے کے وقت اس پر اسی وَحْدَہٗ لَا شَرِیْکَ لَہٗ کا نام لینا چاہیئے۔ کیونکہ وہ اپنے

ساتھ کسی کو شریک نہیں کرنا چاہتا۔۱۲

۴۳۔ گردنوں کے چھڑانے سے مراد غلامی وغیرہ کی قید سے آزاد کرانا ہے۔

۴۴۔ یعنی مقتول کے بدلے قاتل ہی کو قتل کیا جائے۔

۴۵۔ یعنی خون سے درگذر کیا جائے اور خون کے بدلے خون بہا قرار پائے۔

۴۶۔ یعنی جتنے روزے نہ رکھے ہوں بیماری اور سفر کے بعد اتنے قضا رکھ لے۔

۴۷۔ اس آیت میں تندرست اور طاقتور شخص پر روزہ رکھنا لازم نہیں کیا گیا تھا بلکہ رکھنے نہ رکھنے کا اختیار دیا گیا تھا۔ مگر اسکے بعد کی آیت میں یہ اختیار زائل کر دیا اور روزہ رکھنا لازم اور قطعی کر دیا گیا۔

۴۸۔ یعنی جس طرح پوشاک کا تعلق جسم سے ہوتا ہے اسی طرح مرد کا تعلق عورت سے اور عورت کا مرد سے ہوتا ہے۔

۴۹۔ اہلّہ ہلال کی جمع ہے اور ہلال پہلی تین راتوں کے چاند کو کہتے ہیں۔ چاند حقیقت میں ایک ہے، مگر چونکہ وہ گھٹتا بڑھتا رہتا ہے اسلئے گویا کئی چاند ہوتے اس وجہ سے ان کو اہلّہ کہا گیا ہے اس گھٹنے بڑھنے کا فائدہ یہ ہے کہ جو لوگ ان پڑھ ہیں انکو اس سے مہینہ اور تاریخ اور اوقات حج معلوم ہوتے ہیں اگر ایک حالت پر رہتا تو ان لوگوں کو بڑی مشکل پیش آتی کہ نہ مہینہ معلوم ہوتا نہ تاریخ۔ ہلال کو دیکھ کر ہر شخص مہینہ اور تاریخ اور حج کے اوقات اور اور کاموں کی میعادیں آسانی سے معلوم کر سکتا ہے۔

۵۰۔ اہل عرب میں دستور تھا کہ جب گھر سے نکل کر احرام باندھ لیتے اور گھر میں آنے کی ضرورت واقع ہوتی تو گھر میں دروازے سے نہ داخل ہوتے بلکہ پچھواڑے سے کود کر آتے۔ خدا نے اس فعل کو داخلِ نیکی نہ قرار دیا۔ اور گھر میں دروازے سے آنے کا حکم فرمایا۔

۵۱۔ عزت کے مہینے چار تھے ذی قعدہ، ذی الحج، محرم، رجب اور ان میں لڑائی نہیں کی جاتی تھی کافر ان مہینوں میں لڑائی کرنے لگتے تو مسلمان ان مہینوں کے ادب کی وجہ سے لڑائی سے رکتے اور حیران ہوتے کہ کیا کریں تو خدا نے فرمایا کہ اگر کافر ان مہینوں کا ادب ملحوظ رکھیں تو تم بھی رکھو اور اگر وہ ادب کو چھوڑ دیں اور تم پر ظلم کرنے لگیں تو تم بھی ان سے لڑو اور بدلہ لینے میں دریغ نہ کرو۔

۵۲۔ یعنی شوال۔ ذی قعدہ اور عشرۂ ذی الحجہ۔

۵۳۔ گنتی کے دنوں سے عید کے بعد کے تین دن مراد ہیں جن کو ایام تشریق کہتے ہیں ان تین دنوں یعنی گیارہ اور بارہ اور تیرہ تاریخ میں خدا کو یاد کرنا چاہیئے۔ اور اگر کوئی صرف دو دن رہ کر چلا جائے تو اسے اختیار ہے۔

۵۴۔ آغاز اسلام میں شراب حرام نہ تھی مسلمان اسکو بلا تامل پیتے تھے۔ جب یہ آیت نازل ہوئی کہ جن لوگوں نے خیال کیا کہ اس میں نقصان ہیں انہوں نے اسکو ترک کر دیا اور جن لوگوں نے سمجھا کہ اسمیں فائدے ہیں وہ پیتے رہے۔ پھر یہ آیت اتری کہ جب تم متوالے ہوا کرو تو نماز نہ پڑھا کرو۔ تو جو شراب پیا کرتے تھے انہوں نے نماز کے وقت اس کا پینا چھوڑ دیا۔ ان آیتوں سے شراب کی برائی تو ظاہر تھی لیکن صریح حرمت نہ تھی۔ پھر یہ آیت نازل ہوئی کہ اے ایمان والو شراب اور جوا اور بتوں کے تھان اور پانسے یہ سب ناپاک کام اعمالِ شیطان سے ہیں سو ان سے بچو تاکہ نجات پاؤ۔ اس سے شراب صاف طور پر حرام ہو گئی۔ حضرت عمرؓ جو شراب کے بارے میں صاف حکم کے نزول کے خواہشمند تھے جب انہوں نے یہ آیت سُنی کہ شیطان تو یہ چاہتا ہے کہ شراب اور جوئے کے سبب تمہارے آپس میں دشمنی اور رنجش ڈلوا دے اور تمہیں خدا کی یاد اور نماز سے روک دے۔ سو تم کو (ان سے) باز رہنا چاہیئے۔ تو بیساختہ کہنے لگے کہ ہم باز رہے باز رہے۔

۵۵۔ لفظوں کا لحاظ کیا جاتا تو ترجمہ یوں ہونا چاہیے تھا کہ تمہیں خدا سے ملنا ہے مگر جو ترجمہ یہاں کیا گیا ہے وہ محاورے کے لحاظ سے بہت لطیف ہے۔

۵۶۔ یعنی اس بات کی قسم نہ کھاؤ کہ میں فلاں شخص سے سلوک نہیں کروں گا یا فلاں نیک کام نہیں کروں گا اگر ایسی قسم کھالی ہو تو اسکو توڑ دینا چاہیئے اور اس کا کفارہ دے دینا چاہیئے۔

۵۷۔ لغو قسم وہ ہے جسکی نیت نہ ہو اور بے قصد و ارادہ کھائی جائے۔ جیسے بعض لوگ بطور تکیہ کلام کے بات بات میں واللہ باللہ کہا کرتے ہیں بعضوں نے کہا لغو قسم وہ ہے جو غصہ کی حالت میں کھائی جائے یا حلال کو حرام کر لیا جائے۔ ایسی قسم میں کفارہ نہیں ہے۔ بعضوں نے کہا جو گناہ کی بات پر کھائی جائے۔ بعض نے کہا جو معاملے کے وقت کھائی جائے۔ بیچنے والا کہے واللہ یہ چیز میں اتنے کو نہیں بیچوں گا۔ خریدنے والا کہے واللہ میں اتنے کو نہیں خریدوں گا۔ بہرحال لغو قسم پر مواخذہ نہیں ہے۔

۵۸۔ جس لفظ کا ہم نے حیض ترجمہ کیا ہے وہ قروء ہے قروء جمع قرء کی ہے جس کے معنی حیض کے بھی ہیں اور طہر کے بھی اس بارے میں اختلاف ہے کہ یہاں قروء سے مراد حیض ہے یا طہر۔ صحابہؓ کی ایک جماعت اس بات کی قائل ہے کہ قروء بمعنی طہر ہے امام مالکؒ اور شافعیؒ کا بھی یہی مذہب ہے مگر خلفائے اربعہ اور بہت سے اصحاب کبار اور تابعین کا یہ قول ہے کہ قروء سے مراد حیض ہے۔ امام ابو حنیفہؒ کا بھی یہی مذہب ہے۔ امام احمدؒ کہتے ہیں کہ اکابر صحابہ اسی کے قائل ہیں کہ قروء بمعنی حیض ہے لغۃً قروء کا لفظ مشترک المعنی ہے اور علمائے لسانِ عرب اور فقہا کو اس میں کچھ اختلاف نہیں ہے کہ قروء کے معنی حیض اور طہر دونوں ہیں جو لوگ اس بات کے قائل ہیں کہ آیت قرآنی کے قروء سے مراد حیض ہے انکی ایک دلیل یہ بھی ہے کہ جناب رسالتمآبؐ نے فاطمہؓ بنتِ جبیش سے فرمایا تھا کہ دعی الصلوٰۃ ایام اقرائک یعنی ایام حیض میں نماز ترک کر دیا کرو۔ ہم نے اسی روایت کی بنا پر قروء کا ترجمہ حیض کیا ہے۔

۵۹۔ یعنی اگر ماں دودھ پلانے کے لئے راضی نہ ہو تو اس پر جبر نہ کیا جائے اور باپ سے اسکی استطاعت سے زیادہ نفقہ نہ مانگا جائے۔

۶۰۔ طلاق کی عدت تین حیض اور سوگ کی عدت چار مہینے دس دن اس صورت میں ہے جب حمل معلوم نہ ہو اور اگر حمل معلوم ہو تو بچہ پیدا ہونے کے وقت تک ہے۔

٦١- پورے التزام کے ساتھ ادا کرنے سے مُراد یہ ہے کہ نماز کو اسکے اوقات میں پڑھتے رہو۔ بیچ کی نماز کے بارے میں مختلف اقوال ہیں کسی نے کہا ظہر کی نماز مُراد ہے۔ کسی نے کہا عشا کی کسی نے کہا عصر کی کسی نے کہا مغرب کی، کسی نے کہا فجر کی۔ مگر زیادہ صحیح یہ ہے کہ اس سے عصر کی نماز مراد ہے جیسا صحیح حدیثوں میں آیا ہے ؛

٦٢- کھلی ہوئی نشانیوں سے مُراد مُردوں کا زندہ کرنا، بیماروں کا اچھا کرنا اور مادر زاد اندھوں کی آنکھیں روشن کرنا ہے۔ روح القدس سے مُراد جبرئیل امین جو ہر جگہ عیسیٰ کے ساتھ رہا کرتے تھے ؛

٦٣- لڑنے اور جنگ و قتال کرنے سے مُراد اختلاف ہے یعنی اگر خدا چاہتا تو ان میں اختلاف نہ ہوتا مگر اُسنے ان کا مختلف رہنا چاہا اس لئے وہ متفق نہ ہوسکے ؛

٦٤- جس شخص نے حضرت ابراہیمؑ سے جھگڑا کیا وہ بابل کا بادشاہ نمرود تھا جو لوگوں سے اپنے تئیں سجدہ کراتا تھا۔ حضرت ابراہیمؑ نے سجدہ کرنے سے انکار کیا تو اُس نے سبب پوچھا اُنھوں نے کہا کہ میں تو اپنے خدا کو سجدہ کرتا ہوں اس نے کہا خدا کون ؟ اُنھوں نے کہا خدا وہ جس کے ہاتھ میں زندگی اور موت ہے یعنی جو حیات و ممات کا خالق ہے۔ کافر اس بات کو تو سمجھا نہیں بولا کہ میں بھی زندہ کرسکتا اور مار سکتا ہوں۔ چنانچہ اُسنے دو قیدیوں کو بلوایا، ایک جو واجب القتل تھا اسکو معاف کردیا یعنی جاں بخشی کردی دوسرا جو قاتل نہ تھا اسکو مروا ڈالا۔ تب حضرت ابراہیم نے یہ دیکھ کر کہ یہ بدفہم ہے اس سے کہا اگر آپ خدا ہیں تو آفتاب کو جو مشرق سے نکلا کرتا ہے حکم دیجئے کہ مغرب سے نکلے۔ اس کا جواب کافر سے کچھ نہ بن پڑا اور لاجواب ہو کر رہ گیا ؛

٦٥- حضرت علی رضی مرتضیٰ نے فرمایا کہ یہ قصہ حضرت عزیر پیغمبر کا ہے اور مشہور بھی یہی ہے ؛

٦٦- وابلؔ بڑے بڑے قطروں کے مینہ کو کہتے ہیں۔ طل شبنم کو بھی کہتے ہیں اور چھوٹی چھوٹی اور ہلکی ہلکی بوندوں کے مینہ یعنی پھوار کو بھی کہتے ہیں اور وہ بھی درختوں کے سرسبز رکھنے کے لئے کافی ہوتی ہے۔ ہم نے ترجمے میں پھوار اختیار کیا ہے ؛

٦٧- نذر کے لئے یہ شرط ہے کہ ایسے کام کی نذر مانی جائے جو بعض صورتوں میں فرض بھی ہو۔ مثلاً نماز اور روزہ اور صدقہ دینے کی۔ نماز تو ہر روز پانچوں وقتوں کی فرض ہے اور رمضان کے روزے بھی فرض ہیں اور صدقے کی جنس سے زکوٰۃ فرض ہے ایسی چیزوں کی نذر صحیح ہے اور اگر کسی ایسی چیز کی نذر مانی جائے جو کسی صورت میں فرض نہیں ہے وہ باطل ہے ؛

٦٨- ظالموں سے وہ لوگ مُراد ہیں جو خدا کی راہ میں مال خرچ نہیں کرتے، یا نذر کو پورا نہیں کرتے اور اگر خرچ کرتے ہیں تو دکھاوے کے لئے یا بُرے کاموں میں خرچ کرتے ہیں ؛

٦٩- سود عرب میں دو طرح کا مروج تھا۔ ایک قرض پر، ایک بیع پر۔ قرض پر اسطرح کہ روپیہ دینے والا کسی کو ایک مدت معین کے لئے روپیہ دیتا جب وہ مدت ختم ہو جاتی تو قرضدار سے روپیہ طلب کرتا۔ اس کے پاس روپیہ نہ ہوتا اور وہ مہلت مانگتا تو قرض پر سود بڑھا لیا جاتا اور اسکو اصل رقم میں شامل کرکے زیادہ مہلت دی جاتی اسی طرح سُود در سُود بھی ہو جاتا اور زیادہ مشہور یہی سُود تھا بیع پر اسطرح کہ کوئی شخص کسی کے پاس کوئی چیز بیچتا اور اسی قسم کی چیز خریدنے والے سے عوض میں لیتا تو زیادہ لیتا حضرت صلی اللہ علیہ وسلم نے فرمایا کہ گیہوں کو گیہوں کے عوض اور نمک کو نمک کے عوض اور جَو کو جَو کے عوض اور کھجور کو کھجور کے عوض اور چاندی کو چاندی کے عوض اور سونے کو سونے کے عوض فروخت کرو تو برابر فروخت کرو یعنی زیادہ لینا دینا داخل سود ہے اور یہ دونوں قسم کے سُود حرام ہیں۔ سود خوار کہتے تھے کہ قرض پر سُود لینا اور سوداگری کرنا ایک سی چیزیں ہیں۔ سوداگری سے بھی نفع مقصود ہوتا ہے اور سود سے بھی نفع مقصود ہے پس نفع کے لحاظ سے دونوں میں کوئی فرق نہیں مگر خدا تعالےٰ نے سُود کو حرام کیا ہے کیونکہ یہ مروت اور احسان اور سلوک کے خلاف ہے اس نے احسان اور ہمدردی اور امداد کی بہت تاکید فرمائی ہے اور قرض بلا سُود جس کو عرف میں قرض حسنہ کہتے ہیں داخل احسان ہے۔ سوداگری میں جتنا نفع بھی حاصل کیا جائے وہ حلال ہے مگر سُود کا ایک پیسہ بھی حرام ہے کیونکہ تنگدست مسلمان احسان اور سلوک کے مستحق اور اس قابل ہوتے ہیں کہ انکو قرض دے کر اُنکی مدد کی جائے نہ یہ کہ اُن سے سُود لے کر اُن کا خون پیا جائے۔ خدا فرماتا ہے کہ اگر قرضدار تنگدست ہو تو ہاتھ کشادہ ہونے تک اُسے مہلت دو اور اگر قرض بخش ہی دو تو تمہارے لئے زیادہ بہتر ہے۔ یہ حکم اعلیٰ درجے کی شفقت و رافت اور رحم و رحمت پر مبنی ہے اور خدا کو ایسی ہی مہربانیاں زیبا ہیں وہ غریبوں اور ناداروں کی امداد ہی تو ہے جس کو خدائے تعالےٰ نے صدقات کے لفظ سے تعبیر فرمایا ہے اور جس کے دینے کا حکم نازل کیا ہے۔ سُود لینا چونکہ مروت اور ہمدردی کے خلاف ہے اسلئے اسکے نزدیک وہ ایسا بُرا ہے کہ اس نے اسکو گویا خدا اور رسولؐ خدا سے جنگ کرنا قرار دیا ہے۔ خدائے تعالےٰ کا مقصود یہ ہے کہ مسلمان مسلمانوں کی اعانت و امداد کریں کسی مسلمان کو تکلیف نہ ہو اور پھر فطرت انسانی مقتضی راحت رسانی ہے نیک طبع شخص کسی کو رنج و ایذا کی حالت میں نہیں دیکھ سکتا چہ جائیکہ خود کسی کے لئے آزار و اضرار کا موجب ہو بہرکیف نفع پر قرض دینا اور قرض پر نفع لینا ممنوع ہے ہاں اگر کسی کو تجارت کے لئے روپیہ دیا جائے اور اس میں نفع کا حصہ مقرر کر لیا جائے تو وہ جائز ہے کیونکہ اس صورت میں روپیہ دینے والا اور لینے والا دونوں شریک تجارت ہیں ایک کا روپیہ ہے ایک کی محنت۔ یہ اس زمان پُر از عصیان میں سود خواری کی کہ قرض دینے کے وقت ہی سود مقرر کر لیا جاتا ہے۔ ایسی تیز اور زہریلی ہوا چلی ہے کہ اہل اسلام بھی اس سے متاثر ہوئے جاتے ہیں۔ جو دل نرم ہونے چاہئیں تھے وہ سخت ہوتے ہیں اور ہمدردی کی جگہ بیدردی سے کام لیا جاتا ہے خدا اس سے پناہ میں رکھے۔

۷۰۔ محکمات وہ آیتیں ہیں جن کے ایک معنی ہیں اور صاف اور کھلے ہوئے ہیں اور متشابہات وہ آیتیں ہیں جن میں کئی معنوں کا احتمال ہو اور مطلب کئی پہلو ہوں حقیقت میں مراد تو ایک ہی معنی ہوتے ہیں۔ مگر الفاظ اور انکی ترکیب کچھ ایسی واقع ہوتی ہے کہ دُوسرے معنوں کا بھی احتمال ہو جاتا ہے ایسی آیتوں کے معنے اپنی رائے سے نہیں کرنے چاہئیں کیونکہ آیات کے معنی اپنی رائے سے کرنے پر وعید شدید آئی ہے اور لوگ اس سے گمراہ ہوتے ہیں بعض نے کہا متشابہات وہ آیتیں ہیں جن کے معنی معلوم نہیں ہو سکتے جیسے حروف مقطعات جو سورتوں کے شروع میں آتے ہیں جیسے الٓمٓ اور حٰمٓ وغیرہ ایک حدیث میں آیا ہے کہ محکمات پر عمل کرو اور متشابہات پر ایمان رکھو۔

۷۱۔ اس آیت میں جنگِ بدر کی کیفیت بیان فرمائی ہے بدر ایک جگہ کا نام ہے جو مکے اور مدینے کے درمیان ہے اس لڑائی میں مسلمانوں کی تعداد تین سو تیرہ تھی اور کافر ان سے تگنے یعنی ہزار کے قریب تھے خدائے تعالٰی نے کافروں کے دل میں دہشت ڈالنے کے لئے انکی آنکھوں میں یہ دکھایا کہ مسلمان ان سے دوچند یعنی دو ہزار کے قریب ہیں کافروں کی تعداد مسلمانوں کی نظروں میں مسلمانوں سے دوچند دکھائی دی یعنی بجائے ایک ہزار کے چھ سو چھبیس تاکہ مسلمان کافروں کو اپنی دوچند تعداد سے زیادہ دیکھ کر ڈر نہ جائیں اور بھاگ نہ کھڑے ہوں اور دوگنی تعداد کی صورت میں بھاگنا جائز نہیں چنانچہ فرمایا ہے کہ ایک سو ثابت قدم مسلمان دو سو کفار پر غالب ہونگے۔ مگر صحیح یہی ہے کہ کافروں نے مسلمانوں کو اپنے سے دوچند دیکھا نہ یہ کہ مسلمانوں نے کافروں کو اپنے سے دوچند دیکھا۔ بہر کیف اس واقعے میں خدا کی قدرت کی نشانی تھی۔ کہ مسلمان جو تین سو تیرہ تھے وہ غالب رہے اور کافر جو ہزار کے قریب تھے اُنہوں نے شکست کھائی۔

۷۲۔ عمران سے مراد مریم علیہ السلام کے والد ہیں کیونکہ اسکے بعد انہیں کا قصہ مذکور ہے بعض کہتے ہیں کہ حضرت موسٰی علیہ السلام کے والد مراد ہیں کہ ان کا نام بھی عمران تھا مگر ظاہر پہلا قول ہے اس لئے کہ اس کے لئے قرینہ بھی ہے۔

۷۳۔ حضرت مریم کی والدہ نے یہ سمجھا تھا کہ لڑکا پیدا ہوگا اور اسی لئے نذر مانی کہ میں اسکو دُنیا کے کاموں سے آزاد کرکے خدا کی عبادت اور بیت المقدس کی خدمت کے لئے فارغ رکھوں گی۔ مگر ان کو کیا معلوم تھا کہ لڑکا ہوگا یا لڑکی جب لڑکی ہوئی تو خیال کیا کہ نذر تو پوری نہ ہوئی کیونکہ دستور یہ تھا کہ لڑکا نذر کیا جاتا تو کہنے لگیں کہ پروردگار یہ تو لڑکی ہوئی ہے اور عبادت کی قوت اور مسجد کی خدمت کے لحاظ سے لڑکی لڑکے جیسی نہیں ہوتی ہے مگر خدا نے اس لڑکی کو ہی قبول فرمایا وہ نہایت مستعدی سے خدا کی عبادت کیا کرتیں اور دین کی باتیں سیکھتیں خدا نے انکو جہان کی عورتوں میں برگزیدہ کیا اور ان کے بطن سے ایک جلیل القدر پیغمبر یعنی حضرت عیسٰی علیہ السلام بھی پیدا کئے۔

۷۴۔ یہود آنحضرت صلی اللہ علیہ وسلم سے کہتے تھے کہ آپ کو دعوٰی تو حضرت ابراہیم کے طریق پر چلنے کا ہے لیکن جو چیزیں خاندانِ یعقوبؑ میں جو حضرت ابراہیمؑ کے پوتے تھے حرام تھیں انکو آپ کھاتے ہیں۔ خدا نے اسکی تردید کی اور فرمایا کہ تورات نازل ہونے سے پہلے کھانے کی سب چیزیں یعقوب کو حلال تھیں۔ مگر وہ جو انہوں نے خود اپنے اُوپر حرام کرلی تھیں۔ اسکی کیفیت یہ ہے کہ حضرت یعقوبؑ ایک گاوں میں رہتے تھے وہاں انکو عرق النساء کا مرض ہو گیا جس کی وجہ سے انکو بہت تکلیف تھی۔ تو انہوں نے نذر مانی کہ جو چیز مجھ کو بہت محبوب و مرغوب ہے وہ ترک کردوں گا چنانچہ اونٹ کا گوشت کھانا چھوڑ دیا۔ یعقوب کے بیٹوں نے بھی ان کے اتباع سے اونٹ کا گوشت ترک کر دیا تھا۔ غرض تورات کے نازل ہونے سے پہلے کھانے کی تمام چیزیں حضرت یعقوبؑ پر حلال تھیں اور خدا نے انکو ان پر حرام نہیں کیا تھا۔ اسی بنا پر خدا نے فرمایا کہ اے پیغمبر یہود سے کہدو اگر سچے ہو تو تورات لاؤ اور دکھاؤ کہ اس میں کہاں لکھا ہے کہ ابراہیمؑ کے وقت میں اونٹ حرام تھا۔ ہاں یہودیوں کی نافرمانیوں اور گناہوں کے سبب کچھ چیزیں ان پر حرام کردی گئی تھیں اور اس سے انکو انکی شرارتوں کی سزا دینی مقصود تھی۔

۷۵۔ مقامِ ابراہیمؑ جس کا ترجمہ ابراہیم کے کھڑے ہونے کی جگہ کیا گیا ہے ایک پتھر ہے جس پر وہ کھڑے ہو کر کعبے کی دیواریں چنتے تھے۔ کہتے ہیں کہ اس پتھر پر حضرت ابراہیمؑ کے قدموں کے نشان تھے۔ مگر اب مٹ گئے ہیں۔

۷۶۔ نیکی جو لفظ خیر کا ترجمہ کیا گیا ہے اس سے مراد قرآن مجید کی پیروی ہے خدا نے اس امر کو فرض قرار دیا ہے کہ مسلمانوں میں ہر زمانے میں ایسی جماعت ہونی چاہیئے جو دعوت الی الخیر اور امر بالمعروف اور نہی عن المنکر کرے تاکہ لوگ قرآن پر چلیں اچھے کام کریں اور بُرائیوں سے کنارہ کش رہیں یہ حکم ایسا ہے کہ جس پر بہت توجہ اور کوشش سے عمل ہونا چاہیئے تاکہ لوگ مستحق فوز و فلاح ہوں مگر نہایت افسوس کا مقام ہے کہ اس زمانے میں اس حکم پر عمل نہیں ہوتا اسی وجہ سے مسلمانوں کی دینی و دُنیوی حالت اچھی نہیں رہی ان کے حالات دیکھ کر خوف ہوتا ہے کہ کہیں ایسا وقت نہ آجائے کہ دُعا کریں اور وہ خدا کے ہاں رد کردی جائے جیسا کہ ایک حدیث میں آیا ہے کہ "تم لوگوں کو چاہیئے کہ نیک کام کرنے کا حکم اور بُرے کاموں سے منع کرتے رہو۔ نہیں تو اس ذات کی قسم جس کے ہاتھ میں میری جان ہے کہ خدا تعالٰی تم پر عذاب بھیجے گا پھر تم خدا سے دُعا مانگو گے اور وہ اُسے قبول نہ کرے گا" خدا مسلمانوں کو توفیق بخشے کہ اسکے احکام پر عمل کریں تاکہ اسکی رحمت کے مورد ہوں اور اسکے عذاب سے محفوظ و مصئون رہیں۔

۷۷۔ بدر کی لڑائی میں جب کافروں کو شکست اور مومنوں کو فتح ہوئی تو کافروں نے اگلے سال فوج جمع کرکے مدینے پر چڑھائی کی اور اُحد کے قریب جو مدینے کے پاس ایک پہاڑ ہے اُترے۔ حضرت صلی اللہ علیہ وسلم نے صحابہ سے مشورہ لیا کہ شہر سے باہر نکل کر لڑنا چاہیئے یا شہر کے اندر رہ کر انہوں نے صلاح دی کہ باہر نکل کر لڑنا چاہیئے۔ مگر عبداللہ بن اُبَی نے جو منافقوں کا سردار تھا یہ مشورہ دیا

کہ شہر میں رہنا چاہیئے حضرت نے باہر نکل کر لڑنا مناسب سمجھا چنانچہ آپ نے خود زرہ پہن لی اور ایک ہزار صحابہ کو ساتھ لے کر مدینے سے باہر نکلے عبداللہ بھی شریک جنگ ہوا مگر ناخوشی سے کیونکہ اسکی صلاح نہیں مانی گئی تھی جب مقام سوط میں پہنچے تو عبداللہ لشکر کے ایک حصے کو لے کر لوٹ چلا اور اسکے بہکانے سے قبیلہ خزرج میں سے بنو سلمہ نے اور قبیلہ اوس میں سے بنو حارثہ نے جو میمنہ و میسرہ فوج پر مقرر تھے ہمت ہار دینی چاہی لیکن خدا نے انکے دلوں کو مضبوط کیا اور وہ میدان میں ثابت قدم رہے اس آیت میں انہیں دو جماعتوں یعنی بنو سلمہ اور بنو حارثہ کا ذکر ہے اور انہی کی نسبت خدا نے فرمایا کہ خدا ان کا مددگار تھا ؀

۷۸ - یہ جنگ احد کا قصہ ہے اس جنگ میں شروع شروع تو مسلمان غالب رہے مگر بعد میں حضرت کی نافرمانی کے سبب شکست ہوئی۔ نافرمانی یہ ہوئی تھی کہ حضرت نے تیراندازوں کی ایک جماعت کو ایک مورچے پر متعین فرما کر حکم دیا کہ تم یہاں کھڑے رہنا اور ہرگز نہ ٹلنا وہ لوگ تو وہاں کھڑے ہوئے اور باقی لشکر مصروف جنگ ہوا جنگ میں خدا تعالٰے نے مسلمانوں کی مدد کی اور انکو غلبہ دیا۔ حضرت ابن عباسؓ کہتے ہیں کہ حضرت کی جیسی مدد خدا تعالٰے نے احد کے دن کی ایسی کسی موقع پر نہیں کی جب مسلمانوں کو فتح ہوئی اور کفار شکست کھا کر بھاگنے لگے تو تیراندازوں نے چاہا کہ مورچہ چھوڑ کر فتح میں شریک ہوں اور مال غنیمت لیں۔ تو وہ مورچہ چھوڑ کر چل دیتے۔ عبداللہ بن جبیر نے جو ان کے افسر تھے انکو ہرچند منع کیا مگر انہوں نے ان کے کہنے پر عمل نہ کیا ادھر تو یہ کیفیت ہوئی ادھر خالد بن ولید نے جو اسوقت جماعت کفار میں تھے پیچھے سے حملہ کر دیا اور اس سے لڑائی کی صورت بدل گئی یعنی فتح پانے والوں کو شکست اور شکست کھانے والوں کو فتح ہوئی خود حضرت صلی اللہ علیہ وسلم کا چہرہ مبارک زخمی ہوا سامنے کے چار دانت شہید ہو گئے خود سر میں گھس گیا اور یہ مشہور ہو گیا کہ آپ شہید ہو گئے غرض مسلمان بھاگ کھڑے ہوئے۔ اس وقت آپ فرماتے تھے کہ اے خدا کے بندو میرے پاس آؤ۔ میں خدا کا پیغمبر ہوں۔ جو کوئی پھر کافروں پر حملہ کرے گا اسکو جنت ملے گی۔ غم پر غم پہنچانے سے یہ مراد ہے کہ ایک تو غنیمت کے مال سے محروم ہوئے۔ مقتول و مجروح ہوئے۔ دوسرے حضرت صلی اللہ علیہ وسلم کے شہید ہونا سنا اور کفار کا غلبہ دیکھا ؀

۷۹ - یعنی جو شہید نہیں ہوئے اور جنگ میں مصروف ہیں ؀

۸۰ - خدا تعالٰے نے بعض پیغمبروں کو یہ معجزہ بخشا تھا کہ ان کی امت کے لوگ جو قربانی اور نذر و نیاز خدا کے لئے کرتے تو اسکو میدان میں رکھ دیتے۔ آسمان سے آگ آتی اور اسکو جلا دیتی تو یہ سمجھا جاتا کہ قربانی خدا کی جناب میں قبول ہوئی۔ یہودی حضرت پیغمبر آخرالزمان سے کہنے لگے کہ خدا نے ہم کو یہ حکم دے رکھا ہے کہ ہم کسی پیغمبر پر ایمان نہ لائیں جب تک معجزہ نہ دیکھ لیں تو آپ بھی یہ معجزہ دکھائیں۔ خدا نے فرمایا کہ تم ان کے جواب میں کہہ دو کہ کئی پیغمبر مجھ سے پہلے کئی طرح کے معجزے لے کر آئے اور وہ معجزہ بھی جو تم کہتے تھے لیکن اگر تم سچے ہو تو ان پیغمبروں کو قتل کیوں کرتے رہے مطلب یہ کہ پیغمبروں کو جھٹلانا اور نافرمانی کرنا تمہاری عادت میں داخل ہے ؀

۸۱ - یعنی کافر جو شہروں میں تجارت کے لئے چلتے پھرتے ہیں اور بہت سا مال پیدا کرتے ہیں تم اس کا خیال نہ کرنا اور یہ نہ سمجھنا کہ یہ منفعت کثیر ہے بلکہ بہت تھوڑا فائدہ ہے کیونکہ فانی ہے اور دنیا کے تمام فوائد آخرت کے مقابل میں بہت کم ہیں۔ ان کفار تاجروں اور مالداروں کا آخرت میں ٹھکانا دوزخ ہے اور خدا نے جو مسلمانوں کے لئے تیار کر رکھا ہے وہ باغات بہشت ہیں جن کے آرام باقی ہیں اور ہمیشہ رہینگے

۸۲ - یعنی دائیاں کہ دودھ پلانے کے لحاظ سے وہ بھی تمہاری مائیں ہیں ؀

۸۳ - حدیث شریف میں پھوپھی اور بھتیجی اور خالہ اور بھانجی کا جمع کرنا بھی حرام ہے۔

۸۴ - عہد کرنے سے مراد ہے دینی بھائی بنانا ایسے لوگوں کے لئے ترکہ نہیں ہے ترکہ صرف قرابت والوں کا حق ہے دینی بھائیوں کا حصہ یہ ہے کہ ان سے محبت اور دوستی رکھی جائے اور حاجت کے وقت ان کی مدد کی جائے بعضوں نے آیت کا یہ مطلب لکھا ہے کہ اگر دینی بھائیوں کو کچھ دلانا منظور ہو تو ان کے لئے وصیت کر جاؤ پہلے جو لوگ متبنّٰی کئے جاتے تھے وہ وارث ٹھہرائے جاتے تھے مگر خدا تعالٰے نے میراث میں ان کا حصہ مقرر نہیں فرمایا۔ بلکہ ان کا حصہ وصیت میں ٹھیرایا ہے ؀

۸۵ - یہ اسوقت کا حکم ہے کہ شراب کے بارے میں حرمت کا حکم نازل نہیں ہوا تھا ؀

۸۶ - یہودی جناب رسول خدا صلی اللہ علیہ وسلم سے جب کوئی ایسی بات پوچھنی چاہتے جو سن نہ سکے ہوں تو رَاعِنَا کہتے اس کا مفصل بیان سورۂ بقرہ میں ہوا ہے اور جب جناب رسالتمآب بات فرماتے تو وہ لوگ جواب میں کہتے ہم نے سن لیا یعنی ہم نے قبول کیا لیکن آہستہ سے کہتے کہ نہیں مانا اور حضرت سے خطاب کے وقت یہ بھی کہتے کہ سنئے نہ سنوائے جاؤ۔ ظاہر میں یہ معنی نیک ہے۔ کہ تم ایسے غالب ہو کہ کوئی تم کو بری بات نہ سنا سکے مگر دل میں یہ مراد رکھتے کہ خدا کرے تم بہرے ہو جاؤ اور کچھ سن نہ سکو خدا نے فرمایا کہ اگر یہ لوگ بجائے سَمِعْنَا وَعَصَيْنَا کے سَمِعْنَا وَاَطَعْنَا اور اِسْمَعْ غَیْرَ مُسْمَعٍ کی جگہ صرف اِسْمَعْ اور رَاعِنَا کی جگہ اُنْظُرْنَا کہتے تو ان کے حق میں بہتر ہوتا ؀

۸۷ - مدینے میں ایک یہودی اور ایک منافق میں جھگڑا ہوا۔ یہودی نے کہا کہ چلو محمد صلی اللہ علیہ وسلم سے فیصلہ کرائیں منافق نے کہا کہ کعب بن اشرف کے پاس چلو یہ شخص یہود کا سردار تھا اس اختلاف کی وجہ یہ تھی کہ یہودی حق پر تھا اور جانتا تھا کہ حضرت اس مقدمے کو اسکے حق میں فیصل کرینگے تو وہ حضرت ہی کے پاس جانے پر زور دیتا تھا منافق جو ظاہر میں مسلمان اور باطن میں کافر تھا آپ کے پاس جانا نہیں چاہتا تھا۔ کہ آخر دونوں حضرت صلی اللہ علیہ وسلم کے پاس آئے اور حضرت نے مقدمہ یہودی کے حق میں فیصل کیا۔ جب باہر نکلے تو منافق نے کہا کہ حضرت عمرؓ کے پاس چلو جو وہ فیصلہ کر دیں وہ مجھے منظور ہے حضرت عمرؓ ان ایام میں جناب سرور کائنات کے حکم سے مدینے میں قضا کرتے تھے منافق نے یہ خیال کیا کہ حضرت عمرؓ ظاہری اسلام کے دھوکے میں آ کر میرا پاس کرینگے۔ جب وہاں گئے تو یہودی نے ماجرائے اول بیان

کر دیا اور کہہ دیا کہ ہم حضرتؐ کی خدمت میں ہو آئے ہیں اور اُنہوں نے میرا حق ثابت کر دیا۔ یہ سُنکر حضرت عمرؓ نے منافق کو قتل کر دیا۔ اس کے وارث حضرت صلی اللہ علیہ وسلم کے پاس گئے اور خون کا دعویٰ کیا اور قسمیں کھانے لگے کہ عمرؓ کے پاس صرف اسلئے گئے تھے کہ شاید وہ صلح کرا دیں تب یہ آیتیں نازل ہوئیں ؂

۸۸ - صدیق مبالغے کا صیغہ ہے یعنی بڑا سچا تو صدیقین بڑے سچے ہوئے یا صدیق سے وہ لوگ مراد ہیں جو اتباعِ انبیاء میں سب سے رُتبہ عالی رکھتے ہیں۔ حضرت ابوبکرؓ کو جو صدیق کہتے ہیں تو وہ ان دونوں معنوں کے مصداق تھے۔ شہید وہ جو خدا کی راہ میں مارے جائیں حضرت عمرؓ اور عثمانؓ اور علیؓ نسب شہید ہیں۔ صالحین عام نیکوکاروں ہیں سب سے اعلیٰ درجہ انبیاء کا ہے۔ پھر صدیقین کا پھر شہدا کا پھر عام صالحین کا ؂

۸۹ - یعنی تم سے اوروں کی پُرسش نہیں ہوگی کیونکہ ہر شخص اپنے فعل کا ذمہ دار ہے

۹۰ - سفر خواہ کسی غرض سے ہو اسمیں نماز کا قصر کرنا یعنی چار چار رکعتوں کی جگہ دو دو رکعتیں پڑھنا جائز ہے۔ آیت سے تو یہ پایا جاتا ہے کہ جب کفار سے ایذا کا خوف ہو تب قصر کرنا چاہیئے لیکن احادیثِ صحیحہ سے ثابت ہے کہ مسافر کو امن کی حالت میں بھی نماز کا قصر کرنا درست ہے۔ بخاری و مسلم میں ہے کہ آپ نے ظہر و عصر کی نماز منیٰ میں قصر کر کے پڑھی اور اسوقت کسی طرح کا خوف نہ تھا ترمذی میں ابنِ عباسؓ سے روایت ہے کہ ہم نے سرورِ کائنات صلی اللہ علیہ وسلم کے ساتھ مکے اور مدینے کے بیچ میں امن کی حالت میں دو دو رکعتیں پڑھیں تو سفر میں قصر کو حضرتؐ کی سنت سمجھنا چاہیئے ؂

۹۱ - ایک انصاری تھے اُن کی ایک زرہ ایک شخص طعمہ بن ابیرق نے چرا لی انصاری نے حضرت صلی اللہ علیہ وسلم کے پاس آکر فریاد کی طعمہ نے کیا چالاکی کی کہ زرہ کسی اور کے گھر میں ڈلوا دی اور یہ کیفیت اپنے کنبے والوں سے بیان کر کے کہنے لگا کہ تم حضرت صلی اللہ علیہ وسلم کے پاس جاؤ اور کہو کہ طعمہ بے گناہ ہے اُس نے زرہ نہیں چرائی بلکہ دوسرے شخص نے چرائی ہے۔ آپ طعمہ کی برات لوگوں کے سامنے بیان فرمائیں حضرت عالم الغیب تو تھے ہی نہیں خیال فرمایا کہ یہ لوگ سچ کہتے ہونگے۔ آپ نے کھڑے ہو کر اُس کی برارت کی تب خدا نے یہ آیتیں نازل فرمائیں کہ تم دغابازوں اور خائنوں کے طرفدار نہ ہو اور اُنکی طرف سے بحث نہ کرو اور خدا سے معافی مانگو۔ مسلمان وکیل جو چوروں رہزنوں، خائنوں اور ہر قسم کے مجرموں کی طرف سے مقدمات میں وکالت کرتے اور جھگڑتے ہیں اور اپنی لسانی اور مغالطہ آمیز تقریروں سے ان کو سزا سے بچا لیتے ہیں۔ انہیں ارشادِ ربانی پر عمل کرنا چاہیئے اور جن لوگوں کی نسبت روئیداد مقدمہ پر نظر کر کے اُن کا دِل کہہ دے کہ وہ فی الحقیقت مجرم ہیں اُنکی طرف سے وکالت نہیں کرنی چاہیئے ؂

۹۲ - یعنی بخل اور حرص انسان کی سرشت میں داخل ہے وہ اپنا حق تو پورا لینا چاہتا ہے اور دوسرے کے حق کی چنداں پروا نہیں کرتا۔ عورت چاہتی ہے کہ اپنا حق نفقہ و کسوت و شب باشی پورا کر لے اور مرد چاہتا ہے کہ بے حق دیئے اپنا کام نکالے لیکن اگر عورت مرد کو خوش کرنے کے لئے اپنا حق چھوڑ دے تو روا ہے ؂

۹۳ - یعنی نہ آسمان پر ہے نہ زمین پر مطلب یہ کہ نہ شوہر والی ہے کہ شوہر سے احسان کی اُمید ہو نہ آزاد ہے کہ اور شوہر کر لے ؂

۹۴ - کسی کی بُرائی بیان کرنا اور اُس کا عیب ظاہر کرنا کہ اسی کا نام غیبت ہے بہت بُرا کام ہے اور خدا کو نہایت ناپسند ہے ہاں اگر کسی پر کوئی ظلم کرے تو اس کا ظلم بیان کرنا اور مظلوم کا ظالم کو بُرا کہنا روا ہے ؂

۹۵ - جو چیزیں خدا نے اُن لوگوں پر حرام کر دی تھیں اس کا بیان سورۂ انعام آیت (۱۴۶) میں ہے ؂

۹۶ - عرب جاہلیت میں یہ کام کرتے تھے کہ تین پاسے ہوتے تھے ایک پر لکھا تھا افعل یعنی یہ کام کر دوسرے پر لاتفعل یعنی مت کر تیسرا خالی ہوتا تھا یعنی اس پر کچھ لکھا نہیں ہوتا تھا۔ جب وہ کوئی کام کرنا چاہتے تو پاسے ڈالتے اگر امر نکلتا تو اس کام کو کرتے اگر نہی نکلتی تو نہ کرتے۔ اور اگر خالی نکلتا تو پھر ڈالتے۔ صحیحین میں آیا ہے کہ جناب رسولِ خدا صلی اللہ علیہ وسلم جب کعبے میں داخل ہوئے تو وہاں ابراہیمؑ اور اسمٰعیل علیہ السلام کی تصویریں پائیں اُن کے ہاتھوں میں پاسے تھے آپ نے فرمایا کہ خدا ان لوگوں کو ہلاک کرے یہ خوب جانتے ہیں کہ ابراہیمؑ اور اسمٰعیلؑ نے کبھی اِستقسام نہیں کیا مجاہد کہتے ہیں کہ وہ پاسے جوا کھیلنے کے تھے۔ مگر اس میں کلام ہے کیونکہ خدا نے پاسوں اور جوئے میں فرق کیا ہے پاسوں کو ازلام کہا ہے۔ جوئے کو میسر ہاں یوں کہا جا سکتا ہے کہ کبھی ان کو استخارے میں اور کبھی قمار میں استعمال کرتے تھے۔ خدا نے اس کام کو گناہ کہا اور اس سے ممانعت فرمائی ؂

۹۷ - بعض مفسرین نے لکھا ہے کہ آغازِ اسلام میں ہر نماز کے لئے وضو کرنا واجب تھا مگر بعد میں اُس کا وجوب نہ رہا۔ ایک حدیث میں ہے کہ حضرت رسول اللہ صلی اللہ علیہ وسلم ہر نماز کے لئے وضو کیا کرتے تھے جب فتح مکہ کا دِن آیا تو آپ نے وضو کر کے دونوں موزوں پر مسح کیا اور ایک ہی وضو سے کئی نمازیں پڑھیں حضرت عمرؓ نے عرض کیا یا رسول اللہ آپ نے وہ کام کیا ہے جو ہمیشہ کبھی نہیں کرتے تھے۔ آپ نے فرمایا میں نے یہ کام دانستہ کیا ہے ؂

۹۸ - حضرت آدمؑ کے جن دو بیٹوں کا یہ قصہ ہے ان کا نام ہابیل اور قابیل تھا۔ یہ بات مشہور ہے کہ حضرت حوا کے بطن سے دو بچے توام پیدا ہوتے تھے ایک لڑکا ایک لڑکی۔ چونکہ ضرورت لاحق تھی اسلئے ایک بطن کے لڑکے کو دوسرے بطن کی لڑکی سے۔ اور اس بطن کی لڑکی کو اس بطن کے لڑکے سے بیاہ دیتے تھے اتفاق یہ ہوا کہ قابیل کے ساتھ جو لڑکی پیدا ہوئی وہ بہت خوبصورت تھی اور ہابیل کے ساتھ جو پیدا ہوئی وہ بدصورت تھی۔ قابیل نے چاہا کہ اسکی بہن کا عقد ہابیل سے نہ ہو بلکہ خود اسی سے ہو۔ آدمؑ نے کہا کہ تم دونوں نیاز کرو جس کی نیاز قبول ہو وہ اسکو ملے۔

ہابیل نے نیاز میں موٹی تازی بکری دی اور وہ قبول ہوئی اور قابیل نے اناج کی بالیں دیں اور وہ بھی نکمی اور خراب وہ قبول نہ ہوئی۔ ان ایام میں نیاز کے قبول ہونے کی یہ نشانی تھی کہ جو قبول ہوتی اسکو آگ آسمان سے اُتر کر جلا جاتی۔ ہابیل کی نیاز کو آگ جلا گئی اور قابیل کی اسی طرح پڑی رہی تب قابیل کو بھائی سے حسد پیدا ہوا اور اس سے کہنے لگا کہ میں تجھ کو قتل کر کے رہوں گا۔ چنانچہ اس نے اسکو قتل کر ہی دیا۔ ایک جماعت کا یہ خیال ہے کہ نیاز کا دیا جانا عورت کی وجہ سے نہ تھا۔ قرآن کے ظاہر الفاظ سے بھی یہی پایا جاتا ہے کہ نیاز کا سبب عورت نہ تھی۔ بلکہ دونوں بھائیوں نے نیاز کی تھی ایک کی قبول ہوئی اور دوسرے کی نامقبول ہوئی وَاللّٰہُ اَعْلَمُ بِالصَّوَاب ۔

۹۹- یہ آیت یہودیوں کے حق میں نازل ہوئی ہے۔ توارت میں حکم تھا کہ جو بدکاری کرے اسکو سنگسار کر دیا جائے۔ مگر انہوں نے اس حکم کو بدل کر یہ عمل جاری کیا کہ بدفعلی کرنے والے کو تازیانے مارتے اور گدھے پر سوار کرا کر فضیحت کرتے۔ جناب سرورِ کائنات کے وقت میں کئی واقعات ہوئے کہ وہ ان کو فیصلے کے لئے آپکے پاس لائے۔ ہجرت کے بعد یہ واقعہ ہوا کہ ایک یہودی نے یہودن سے منہ کالا کیا۔ یہودیوں نے آپس میں کہا چلو اس کا فیصلہ حضرت سے کرائیں اگر تازیانے لگانے اور منہ کالا کرنے کا حکم دیں تو تو مان لینا چاہیئے نہیں تو نہیں۔ ابنِ عمرؓ سے روایت ہے کہ یہود حضرت کے پاس لئے اور بیان کیا کہ ان میں سے ایک مرد عورت نے بدکاری کی ہے اس بارے میں کیا ارشاد ہے۔ آپ نے فرمایا کہ تورات میں کیا لکھا ہے۔ انہوں نے کہا کہ ہم تو کوڑے مارتے اور فضیحت کرتے ہیں۔ آپ نے فرمایا کہ تورات لاؤ۔ تورات لائی گئی اور ایک شخص پڑھنے لگا۔ جب اس آیت پر گذر ہوا جس میں بدکاری کی سزا رجم یعنی سنگسار کرنا لکھی تھی تو اس پر ہاتھ رکھ دیا اور آگے پیچھے کی آیتیں پڑھ دیں۔ عبداللہ بن سلامؓ نے جو تورات کے بڑے ماہر تھے عرض کیا کہ آپ حکم دیں کہ یہ ہاتھ اٹھائے ہاتھ اٹھایا تو اسکے نیچے رجم کی آیت تھی۔ حضرت نے رجم کا حکم صادر فرمایا۔ اور دونوں رجم کئے گئے۔ ابنِ عمرؓ کہتے ہیں کہ ان کے رجم کے وقت میں بھی موجود تھا۔ میں نے مرد کو دیکھا کہ عورت پر جھک جھک جاتا تھا اور اسکو پتھر سے بچاتا تھا ۔

۱۰۰- ان لوگوں کا عجب حال تھا کبھی خدائے تعالیٰ کو فقیر کہتے اور اپنے آپ کو غنی۔ یعنی جب مالدار تھے تو اپنے تئیں غنی کہتے تھے اور خدا کو فقیر اب جو آنحضرت صلی اللہ علیہ وسلم کی تکذیب و مخالفت کی شامت سے انکو افلاس نے آگھیرا تو یوں چلانے لگے کہ خدا بخیل ہے اور بخل کی وجہ سے ہم پر بذل و عطا سے اپنا ہاتھ روک لیا ہے۔ خدائے تعالیٰ نے ان بے ادبیوں کے سبب اُن پر لعنت کی اور فرمایا کہ ہمارے دونوں ہاتھ کھلے ہیں اور ہم جس طرح چاہتے ہیں خرچ کرتے ہیں ۔

۱۰۱- جیسے کوئی دور سے کسی شخص کو دیکھے اور کہے کہ خدا کی قسم یہ تو عبداللہ ہے مگر حقیقت میں عبداللہ نہ ہو یا جیسے بعض لوگوں کی عادت ہوتی ہے کہ بلا قصد لَا وَاللّٰہِ یا بَلٰی وَاللّٰہِ وَاللّٰہِ بِاللّٰہِ کہتے ہیں ایسی قسموں پر مواخذہ نہیں ہے ۔

۱۰۲- جیسے کوئی شخص قسم کھائے کہ میں کبھی گوشت نہیں کھاؤں گا یا نکاح نہیں کروں گا۔ عَلٰی ھٰذَا الْقِیَاس ۔

۱۰۳- یہ ترجمہ ہم نے فَھَلْ اَنْتُمْ مُّنْتَھُوْنَ کا کیا اور اس میں استفہام نہیں ہے کتب نحو عربی میں ھَلْ کو استفہام کا لفظ لکھا ہے اور اسی بنا پر تمام مترجمان قرآن نے اس آیت کا ترجمہ ایسا کیا ہے جس میں استفہام پایا جاتا ہے مگر حقیقت یہ ہے کہ سب مقامات میں ھَلْ استفہام کے معنی نہیں دیتا بلکہ بعض جگہ تو افادہ امر کرتا ہے۔ مثلاً اسی آیت میں حکم مقصود ہے اور اسی طرح سورۂ ہود اور سورۂ انبیا میں فَھَلْ اَنْتُمْ مُّسْلِمُوْنَ ہے جنکے یہ معنی ہیں کہ تم کو بھی اسلام لے آنا چاہیئے ایک اور آیت سورۂ شعراء قصۂ موسیٰ و فرعون میں ہے وَقِیْلَ لِلنَّاسِ ھَلْ اَنْتُمْ مُّجْتَمِعُوْنَ جب فرعون کا موسیٰ سے مقابلہ ٹھہرا اور دن مقرر ہو کر جادوگر جمع کئے گئے تو فرعون نے منادی کرا دی کہ سب لوگ اکٹھے ہو جائیں (اور ہمارا اور موسیٰ کا مقابلہ دیکھیں) تو ہمارے نزدیک فَھَلْ اَنْتُمْ مُّجْتَمِعُوْنَ کا یوں ترجمہ کرنا کیا تم لوگ اکٹھے ہو گئے صحیح نہیں کیونکہ فرعون کا مقصود منادی سے صلاح پوچھنی نہ تھی بلکہ اس نے حکم دیا تھا کہ سب لوگ جمع ہو جائیں اور بعض جگہ تحقیق کے معنی دیتا ہے جیسے ھَلْ اَتٰی عَلَی الْاِنْسَانِ حِیْنٌ مِّنَ الدَّھْرِ لَمْ یَکُنْ شَیْئًا مَّذْکُوْرًا یعنی تحقیق انسان پر ایسا وقت بھی آچکا ہے کہ وہ کوئی چیز قابلِ ذکر نہ تھی بعض مقامات میں نفی کے معنی دیتا ہے جیسے ھَلْ یَنْظُرُوْنَ اِلَّآ اَنْ یَّاْتِیَھُمُ اللّٰہُ فِیْ ظُلَلٍ مِّنَ الْغَمَامِ وَالْمَلٰٓئِکَۃُ وَقُضِیَ الْاَمْرُ یہ لوگ کسی بات کے منتظر نہیں مگر اسکے کہ اُن پر خدا کا عذاب (بادل کے سائبانوں میں آنازل ہو اور فرشتے بھی (انہیں ہلاک کرنے کو) اتر آئیں) اور کام تمام کر دیا جائے ۔

العرض ھَلْ کا لفظ چار مقامات میں مستعمل ہوتا ہے ایک استفہام میں ایک امر میں، ایک تحقیق میں، ایک نفی میں ۔

۱۰۴- اونٹنی جو بتوں کی نذر کی جاتی تھی اسکے کان پھاڑ کر چھوڑ دیتے تھے اور کوئی اسکا دودھ دوہ نہیں سکتا تھا ۔

۱۰۵- جانور جو بتوں کے نام پر چھوڑ دیا جاتا تھا اور اس پر بوجھ نہیں لادتے تھے ۔

۱۰۶- اونٹنی جو اول عمر میں اوپر تلے دو مادہ بچے دیتی اُسے بتوں کے نام پر چھوڑ دیتے تھے ۔

۱۰۷- اونٹ جسکی نسل سے چند بچے لے کر سواری وغیرہ کا کام لینا ترک کر دیتے تھے ۔

۱۰۸- کافروں نے بحیرہ اور سائبہ اور وصیلہ اور حام تو خود مقرر کر رکھے تھے اور کہتے یہ تھے کہ یہ شریعت ابراہیمی کے حکم ہیں اور ان سے تقرب الی اللہ حاصل ہوتا ہے خدا نے فرمایا یہ سب جھوٹ اور خدا پر بہتان ہے اس نے نہ کسی جانور کا نام بحیرہ وغیرہ رکھا نہ اُس کو مشروع کیا نہ اُسے ذریعۂ قربت قرار دیا ۔

۱۰۹- حضرت عیسیٰ کے اتباع و انصار یعنی اصحاب حواری کہلاتے تھے۔ حواری حقیقت میں دھوبی کو کہتے ہیں اور وہ لوگ بھی زیادہ تر دھوبی تھے آج کل یہ لفظ

زیادہ عام ہو گیا ہے اور لوگوں کے اعوان و انصار پر بھی اس کا اطلاق کرنے لگے ہیں ۔

۱۱۰ - یہ حواری یا تو حاجتمند تھے یا اطمینانِ قلب حاصل کرنے کے لئے اُنہوں نے نزولِ مائدہ کی درخواست کی تھی کچھ بھی ہو خدا نے اُن پر خوانِ طعام نازل فرمایا مفسرین نے لکھا ہے خوان اتوار کے دن نازل ہوا تھا۔ جو عیسائیوں کی عید ہے ممکن ہے کہ نزولِ مائدہ اتوار ہی کے دن ہوا ہو مگر اُن کی درخواست کے الفاظ سے پایا جاتا ہے کہ وہ اس کا اسطرح نازل ہونا چاہتے تھے کہ اُن کے لئے خوشی کا موجب ہو جائے یعنی اس زمانے کے لوگ بھی اس سے خوش ہو جائیں اور جو اُن کے بعد آئیں۔ وہ بھی خوش ہو جائیں ۔

۱۱۱ - یعنی جن چیزوں پر سورج نکلتا ڈوبتا ہے ۔

۱۱۲ - کیونکہ وہ کھانے پینے کی ضرورت سے پاک ہے۔ اسے اسکی حاجت ہی نہیں ۔

۱۱۳ - یعنی تمہاری بات تو وہی لوگ قبول کرتے ہیں جو سنتے بھی ہیں اور یہ کفار تو مردہ دل ہیں یہ کب سُننے لگے ان مُردوں کو تو خدا قیامت ہی کے دن اُٹھائے گا اور ان کے اعمال کا بدلہ دے گا ۔

۱۱۴ - سعد بن ابی وقاص روایت کرتے ہیں۔ کہ یہ آیت ہم چھ آدمیوں کے حق میں اُتری ہے۔ یعنی سعد اور ابن مسعود اور صہیب اور بلال اور عمار اور مقداد کے۔ ہم لوگ جنابِ رسول خدا صلی اللہ علیہ وسلم کی خدمت میں حاضر ہوتے تو قریب ہو کر بیٹھتے اور باتیں سنتے۔ کفار قریش کو یہ بات ناگوار ہوئی۔ اُنہوں نے آپ سے کہا کہ ہمارا دل آپ کی باتیں سننے کو چاہتا ہے لیکن ہمکو ان غلاموں کے ساتھ بیٹھتے ہوئے شرم آتی ہے پس جب ہم آپ کے پاس آیا کریں تو آپ انکو اُٹھا دیا کیجئے اور جب چلے جایا کریں تو پھر آپ کو اختیار ہے انکو اپنے پاس بٹھا لیا کریں۔ آپ نے اس بات کو مان لیا تو اُنہوں نے کہا کہ آپ ہمیں اس مضمون کی ایک تحریر لکھ دیجئے۔ آپ نے کاغذ منگوایا اور حضرت علیؓ کو لکھنے کے لئے بُلایا۔ اتنے میں جبرائیل یہ آیت لے کر آئے کہ گو طالبانِ خدا غریب ہیں لیکن اُن کی خاطر مقدم رکھنی چاہیئے تب سے آپ ہماری بہت خاطر کرنے لگے ۔

۱۱۵ - قرآن مجید سے تو حضرت ابراہیمؑ کے والد کا نام آزر معلوم ہوتا ہے مگر توراۃ میں ان کا نام تارخ لکھا ہے اور علمائے نسب و تاریخ کے نزدیک بھی ان کا نام یہی ہے مفسرین نے اسکے جواب میں کہا ہے شاید اُن کے دو نام ہوں گے ایک آزر اور دوسرا تارخ یا ایک نام ہو گا دوسرا لقب نیز آزر لفظ فارسی ہے اور اسکے معنی بوڑھے کے ہیں پس یہ بھی ممکن ہے کہ آیۂ آزر سے یہ مراد ہو کہ اُنہوں نے اپنے بوڑھے باپ سے کہا۔ بعض نے کہا آزر بت کا نام تھا شاید اس وجہ سے کہ حضرت ابراہیم کے والد اسکی بہت خدمت کرتے ہوں اُنکو بھی آزر کہنے لگے ہر کیف کوئی وجہ بھی ہو انہیں آزر بھی کہتے تھے ۔

۱۱۶ - یعنی ایک مدت تک دُنیا میں زندہ رکھے جاتے پھر زمین میں دفن ہو کر خدا کے سپرد کئے جاتے ہو ۔

۱۱۷ - جس طریق پر قرآن مجید میں آیتیں پھیر پھیر کر بیان کی گئی ہیں۔ ایسا نہیں ہے کہ کوئی یہ کہہ سکے کہ یہ مضامین کسی شخص سے سیکھے گئے ہیں۔ کہیں خدا کی قدرتوں کا بیان ہے کہیں اسکی ہستی اور وحدانیت کے بر زور دلائل ہیں۔ کہیں اہلِ ایمان کو بشارتیں سُنائی گئی ہیں۔ کہیں کفار کو ڈرایا گیا ہے۔ کہیں عمل نیک کرنے کے لئے حکم دیا گیا ہے۔ کہیں اعمالِ بد سے منع کیا گیا ہے کہیں نصیحتیں ہیں کہیں حکمتیں ہیں غرض طرح طرح کے بیان ہیں۔ اور اسی لئے ارشاد ہوا ہے کہ ہم اسی طرح اپنی آیتیں پھیر پھیر کر بیان کرتے ہیں تاکہ کفار یہ نہ کہیں کہ آنحضرت صلی اللہ علیہ وسلم نے یہ باتیں علمائے یہود سے یا کسی اور سے سیکھی ہیں ۔

۱۱۸ - یعنی جس جانور کے ذبح کرنے کے وقت خدا کا نام نہ لیا گیا ہو اس کا کھانا حرام ہے۔ امام شافعیؒ کہتے ہیں کہ خدا کا نام نہ لئے جانے سے یہ مُراد ہے کہ جو جانور غیر خدا کے لئے ذبح کیا جائے کیونکہ ایسے ہی جانور کا کھانا گناہ ہے اور اسکی دلیل اُنکے نزدیک اسی صورت کی آیت ۱۴۵ اَوْ فِسْقًا اُهِلَّ لِغَيْرِ اللّٰهِ بِهٖ ہے اس میں تو کچھ شک ہی نہیں کہ ذبح لغیر اللہ حرام ہے لیکن ایک جماعت صحابہ و تابعین و فقہا کا یہ مذہب ہے کہ جس جانور پر ذبح کرنے کے وقت اللہ کا نام نہ لیا گیا ہو خواہ بھُول کر خواہ دانستہ اس کا کھانا بھی حرام ہے البتہ ایک حدیث سے جو حضرت عائشہؓ سے مروی ہے پایا جاتا ہے کہ اگر کسی جانور کی نسبت یہ معلوم نہ ہو کہ ذبح کے وقت اس پر خدا کا نام لیا گیا ہے یا نہیں تو خدا کا نام لے کر اسکا کھانا جائز ہے۔ حدیث یوں ہے کہ چند اشخاص نے حضرت صلی اللہ علیہ وسلم کی خدمت میں عرض کیا کہ یا رسول اللہ بعض لوگ ہمارے پاس گوشت لاتے ہیں اور ہم نہیں جانتے کہ اس پر اللہ کا نام لیا گیا ہے یا نہیں۔ آپ نے فرمایا کہ تم اس پر اللہ کا نام لے لیا کرو اور کھا لیا کرو ۔

۱۱۹ - اس آیت میں خدا مشرکوں کی مذمت کرتا ہے کہ اُنہوں نے طرح طرح کی کفر و شرک کی رسمیں نکالی ہیں جن میں اوروں کو خدا کا شریک بنایا ہے۔ مخلوق تو خدا کی اور اسی میں سے ایک حصہ خدا کا مقرر کرتے یعنی زراعت اور پھلوں اور چارپایوں میں ایک حصہ خدا کا اور دوسرا حصہ بُتوں کا ٹھہراتے۔ اس سے بڑھ کر یہ حماقت کہ بُتوں کو خدا پر مقدم رکھتے اس طرح سے اگر بُتوں کے حصے میں سے کچھ خرچ ہو جاتا تو اتنا خدا کے حصے میں سے لے لیتے۔ اور اگر خدا کے حصے میں سے کچھ خرچ ہو جاتا تو بُتوں کے حصے میں سے نہ لیتے اور کہتے کہ خدا غنی ہے اور بُت فقیر ہیں ۔

۱۲۰ - مشرکوں نے ایک یہ بھی رسم نکال رکھی تھی کہ اگر جانور ذبح کیا جائے اور اسکے پیٹ میں سے بچہ نکلے تو اگر بچہ زندہ نکلے مردوں کو اس کا کھانا حلال۔ اور عورتوں کو حرام اور اگر مردہ نکلے تو مردوں اور عورتوں سب کے لئے حلال ۔

۱۲۱ - جن چیزوں کو خدا نے یہود پر ان کے ظلم اور شرارت و سرکشی کے سبب حرام کیا تھا جس کا اجمالی بیان سورۂ نساء کی آیت ۱۶۰ میں ہے ان کی تفصیل اس آیت میں ہے وہ ایک تو وہ جانور تھے جن کی انگلیاں پھٹی ہوئی ہوں جیسے اونٹ اور شتر مرغ اور بطخ۔ یا کُھر والے جانور جیسے گدھا یا پنجے والے پرندے۔ اور گائے اور بکری کی چربی سوا اس چربی کے جو ان کی پیٹھ پر یا اوجھڑی میں لگی ہوتی ہو۔ یا ہڈی سے ملی ہوئی ہو، جیسے ہاتھ پاؤں یا

یسلی یا آنکھ یا کان کی چیر دی کہ یہ حلال تھی ۔

۱۲۲۔ دین میں تفرقہ ڈالنا اور کئی کئی فرقے بن جانا خدا کو سخت ناپسند ہے اسی لئے فرمایا ہے کہ جن لوگوں نے دین کو ٹکڑے ٹکڑے کر دیا اور کئی کئی فرقے بن گئے (اے پیغمبر) ان سے تم کو کچھ سرو کار نہیں خدائے تعالےٰ کی مرضی تو یہ ہے کہ سب لوگ ایک دین (یعنی اسلام) پر جو دین برحق ہے چلیں اور اسکی ہدایتوں پر عمل کریں مگر کوئی کسی رستے پر چلتا ہے کوئی کسی پر کسی نے کوئی طریقہ اختیار کیا ہے کسی نے کوئی راہ ۔ اور آپس میں اتفاق کی جگہ نفرت و عداوت پیدا ہو گئی ہے ۔ کچھ شک نہیں کہ ان باتوں کا سبب یہ ہے کہ وہ قرآن کو غور سے نہیں پڑھتے اور اسکے احکام پر کاربند نہیں ہوتے ۔ اگر خدائے تعالےٰ کے مقصد کو سمجھ لیا جائے تو اختلاف و تفرقے کا نام و نشان نہ رہے ۔

۱۲۳۔ زینت اس چیز کو کہتے ہیں جس سے آرائش کی جائے جیسے لباس ۔ ابنِ عباسؓ کہتے ہیں کہ جاہلیت کے زمانے میں لوگ کعبے کا طواف ننگے کرتے تھے ۔ خدا نے اس سے منع فرمایا اور حکم دیا کہ جب طواف کو یا مسجد میں نماز کو آؤ تو لباس پہن کر آؤ ۔ ننگے نہ آؤ ۔ اس سے نماز میں پردے کی چیزوں کا ڈھکنا فرض ہو گیا ۔ اہل علم کے نزدیک ہر حالت میں ستر عورت فرض ہے خواہ آدمی تنہا ہی کیوں نہ ہو بعض نے کہا کہ آرائش سے مراد کنگھی کرنا اور خوشبو لگانا ہے مگر صحیح پہلی بات ہے اور اگر کنگھی بھی کر لی جائے اور خوشبو بھی لگا لی جائے تو آرائش پر آرائش ہے ۔ کھاؤ اور پیو کے ارشاد سے مقصود خدا کی نعمتوں سے فائدہ اٹھانا ہے یعنی پاکیزہ اور ستھری چیزوں سے جو خدا نے تمہارے ہی لئے پیدا کی ہیں متمتع ہو اور خدا کا شکر کرو ایک حدیث میں آیا ہے کہ کھاؤ اور پیو اور پہنو اور صدقہ دو لیکن نہ بیجا اڑاؤ نہ اتراؤ ۔ کیونکہ خدائے تعالےٰ کو یہ بات خوش آتی ہے کہ اپنی نعمت اپنے بندے پر دیکھے جس طرح طیبات رزق کے کھانے پینے کی اجازت ہے، اسی طرح بیجا اڑانے کی ممانعت ہے یعنی بے ضرورت کھانا یا شکم سیری کی حالت میں کھانا کہ یہ افراط داخلِ اسراف ہے، ۔ یہ آیت اسراف کرنے والوں کے حق میں ایک وعید ہے ۔

۱۲۴۔ اس آیت سے پایا جاتا ہے کہ جس طرح کھانے پینے کی چیزوں اور مال کا اڑانا حرام ہے ۔ اسی طرح ان کو ترک کر دینا اور ان سے فائدہ نہ اٹھانا بھی خدا کو ناپسند ہے اور سچ پوچھو تو یہ خدا کی نعمتوں کی ناشکری ہے اگر خدا کسی کو اعلیٰ قسم کی چیزیں کھانے پینے اور پہننے کو دے تو وہ ان کو چھوڑ کر ادنےٰ درجے کی چیزیں کیوں اختیار کرے ۔ ایسا کرنا خدا کی سنت کے خلاف ہے اسنے تمام کھانے پینے اور پہننے کی اور دیگر زینت کی چیزیں حلال کی ہیں ۔ اور جب تک کوئی مانع شرعی نہ ہو ان سے فائدہ اٹھانا چاہیئے امام فخرالدین رازیؒ کہتے ہیں کہ اس آیت میں ہر قسم کے لباس اور زیور داخل ہیں اگر مردوں کے لئے سونا اور ریشم کا پہننا حرام نہ ہوتا تو عموم آیت ان پر بھی مشتمل ہوتا ۔ غرض کھانے پینے، اور زینت کی اعلیٰ اور اچھی چیزوں کو زہد کی بنا پر ترک کرنا غلطی ہے ۔ ہاں اگر کوئی تواضع اور فروتنی کی راہ سے اچھے کپڑے نہ پہنا اور پھٹے پرانے پہننے لگے تو جائز ہے ۔

۱۲۵۔ یہ تعلیق بالمحال ہے کہ نہ اونٹ سوئی کے ناکے میں سے نکل سکے نہ کفار بہشت میں داخل ہوں ۔

۱۲۶۔ خدا تو بھولنے والا نہیں ہے مطلب یہ کہ ہم ان کے ساتھ ایسا معاملہ کریں گے جیسے کوئی کسی کو بھلا دیتا ہے ۔ یعنی وہ دوزخ میں جلتے رہینگے اور ہم ان کو پوچھیں گے بھی نہیں ۔

۱۲۷۔ اِسْتِوَاء کے معنی لغت میں بلند ہونے اور ٹھہرنے کے ہیں ۔ قرونِ ثلٰثہ اور ائمہ اربعہ اور تمام محدثین کا خدا کے بارے میں یہ مذہب ہے، کہ وہ عرش پر مستوی یعنی ٹھہرا ہوا ہے اور وہ ٹھہرنا ایسا ہے جو اسکی شان کے لائق ہے اور جس کی کیفیت معلوم نہیں ۔ خدائے تعالےٰ کی جو صفتیں ہیں اُن پر لفظ تو وہی بولے جاتے ہیں جو مخلوق کی صفات پر بولے جاتے ہیں مثلاً خدا کو بھی کہتے ہیں کہ دیکھتا ہے ۔ انسان کو بھی کہتے ہیں کہ دیکھتا ہے ۔ خدا کو بھی کہتے ہیں کہ سنتا ہے ۔ انسان کو بھی کہتے ہیں کہ سنتا ہے لیکن خدا کا دیکھنا اور سننا اور طرح کا ہے اور انسان کا دیکھنا اور سننا اور طرح کا ۔ مخلوق کی صفات کو خدا تعالےٰ کی صفات سے کوئی مشابہت اور مماثلت نہیں اور اس پر دلیل قرآن کی یہ آیت ہے کہ لَیْسَ کَمِثْلِهٖ شَیْءٌ یعنی کوئی چیز خدا کی مشابہ و مماثل نہیں پس جب کوئی چیز خدا کے مشابہ و مماثل نہیں تو خدا کو مجسم کیونکر کہہ سکتے ہیں مجسم چیز کی کیفیت معلوم ہوتی ہے اور خدا کی کسی صفت کی کیفیت معلوم نہیں کوئی شخص نہیں بتا سکتا کہ خدا کا دیکھنا سننا کس طرح کا ہے ۔ کیونکہ نہ اسکی ایسی آنکھیں ہیں جس طرح کی ہم رکھتے ہیں نہ ایسے کان ہیں جس طرح کے ہمارے ہیں پس جب اُسکا دیکھنا اور سننا ہی ایسا ہے کہ اسکی کیفیت معلوم نہیں اور وہ اسی طرح کا ہوگا جیسا اس کی شان کو زیبا ہے تو اسکے ٹھہرنے کی کیفیت بھی کسی کو معلوم نہیں اور وہ بھی اسی طرح کا ہوگا جیسا اسکی شان کو سزاوار ہے ۔ حیرت کی بات ہے کہ لوگ خدا میں دوسری صفتیں تو مانتے ہیں اور اُن سے اسکو مجسم قرار نہیں دیتے حالانکہ مخلوق میں ان صفات کے لئے جسمیت لازم ہے ۔ لیکن اِسْتِوَاء کے لئے اس کا مجسم ہونا قرار دیتے ہیں اور اس وجہ سے اسکی تاویل کرنا ضروری سمجھتے ہیں پھر باوجود اسکے سب اسکو ہر جگہ حاضر اور رگِ گردن سے زیادہ قریب بھی سمجھتے ہیں اگر خدا کو عرش پر ٹھہرنے کے سبب معاذ اللہ مجسم قرار دیا جائے تو وہ سب جگہ حاضر اور رگِ گردن سے زیادہ نزدیک کیونکر مانا جا سکتا ہے ۔ مجسم محدود ہوتا ہے اور جو ہر جگہ حاضر ہو وہ غیر محدود ہے پس محدود و غیر محدود کس طرح ہو سکتا ہے ۔ بہر کیف خدا تعالےٰ مجسم نہیں اسکی جتنی صفات ہیں اُنکی وہ کیفیت نہیں جو انسان کی صفات کی ہے اسلئے انسانی صفات کا خدا تعالےٰ کی صفات پر قیاس نہیں ہو سکتا اور اسلئے اسکو مجسم نہیں کہہ سکتے ۔ علمائے مذہب کہتے ہیں کہ جس نے خدا کو اسکی مخلوق کے مشابہ ٹھہرایا وہ کافر ہوا اور جس نے ان باتوں کا جو خدا تعالےٰ نے اپنی ذات بابرکات کی صفتیں ٹھہرائی ہیں انکار کیا وہ بھی کافر ہوا ۔ الغرض خدا نے جن باتوں کو اپنی صفات قرار دیا ہے اُنکو ماننا چاہیئے

اور اُنکی وہ کیفیت میں سمجھنی چاہیئے جو صفات مخلوق کی ہوتی ہے۔ ہم اُنکی کیفیت کو مطلق نہیں جان سکتے تو اُسکی صفات کی کیفیت کو کیونکر جان سکتے ہیں وہ تخت جسکو عرش کہتے ہیں اسکی کیفیت معلوم نہیں کہ وہ کس طرح کا ہے تو اس پر حملائے تعالےٰ کے ٹھہرنے کی کیفیت کیا معلوم ہو سکتی ہے :۔

۱۲۸۔ زمین میں اصلاح کے بعد خرابی نہ کرنے سے یہ مُراد ہے کہ جس زمین میں گناہ کے کام ہوتے تھے حرام چیزوں کو حلال کر لیا جاتا تھا۔ قتل و خونریزی ہوتی تھی۔ جب اسمیں پیغمبر آئے اور اُنہوں نے لوگوں کو خدا کی طرف بلایا تو اسکی اصلاح ہو گئی۔ اب اس زمین صالح میں ایسے کام نہ کرو جن سے یہ سمجھا جائے کہ اصلاح خرابی سے بدل گئی اور اسمیں فساد ہو رہا ہے :۔

۱۲۹۔ وہ لوگ رہزن اور غارت گر تھے۔ رستوں پر بیٹھ کر لوگوں کو ڈراتے تھے کہ اگر تم ہم کو مال نہ دوگے تو ہم تم کو قتل کر ڈالینگے۔ یا رستے سے مراد وہ رستے ہیں جو حضرت شعیب کی طرف جاتے تھے۔ وہ لوگ ان رستوں پر بیٹھ جاتے تھے اور جس شخص کو اس طرف جاتے دیکھتے تھے اسکو ڈراتے دھمکاتے تھے کہ تم شعیب کے پاس کیوں جاتے ہو۔ وہ تو جھوٹا مکار ہے خدا کا پیغمبر نہیں۔ خدا کی راہ سے روکنے سے مراد حضرت شعیب کے پاس جانے اور مومن بننے سے منع کرنا ہے :۔

۱۳۰۔ خدا نے حضرت موسیٰ علیہ السلام کو تیس راتوں کے لئے بلایا تھا۔ تاکہ ان کو تورات عنایت کی جائے۔ ابن عباسؓ کہتے ہیں کہ حضرت موسیٰؑ نے اپنی قوم سے کہا کہ خدا نے مجھے تیس رات کے لئے طلب فرمایا ہے۔ میں تم میں اپنے بھائی ہارون کو اپنی جگہ چھوڑے جاتا ہوں جب موسیٰ علیہ السلام ان میں سے تشریف لے گئے تو خدائے تعالےٰ نے دس راتیں اور بڑھا دیں۔ اس عشرہ آخری میں بنی اسرائیل بچھڑے کی پرستش کر کے گمراہ ہو گئے۔ چنانچہ سامری کے بچھڑا بنانے کا قصہ آگے آتا ہے جس طرح موسیٰ علیہ السلام نے اپنی قوم کے لوگوں سے کہا تھا کہ میں تم میں اپنے بھائی ہارون کو اپنا جانشین کرتا ہوں اسی طرح حضرت ہارون سے کہا کہ آپ میری قائم مقامی کیجئے گا۔ اور ان لوگوں کی اصلاح کرتے رہیئے گا تاکہ کوئی فساد نہ ہونے پائے :۔

۱۳۱۔ ایسا معلوم ہوتا ہے کہ موسیٰ علیہ السلام کی قوم کے لوگ عقل و دانش سے کام نہیں لیتے تھے۔ موسیٰ علیہ السلام کے کوہِ طور پر چلے جانے کے بعد ایک شخص سامری نام جو انہیں لوگوں میں سے تھا ان سے کہنے لگا کہ میں تم کو ایک خدا بنا دیتا ہوں اسکی پرستش کیا کرنا۔ انہوں نے یہ بات مان لی تو اُسنے سونے کا زیور جمع کیا اور اسکو گلا کر بچھڑا بنایا اور اسکے منہ میں حضرت جبرئیل کے گھوڑے کے پاؤں تلے کی مٹھی بھر مٹی جو اسکو مل گئی تھی ڈالدی۔ سو وہ گائے کی سی آواز کرنے لگا سامری نے کہا لو یہ خدا ہے اس کو پوجا کرو وہ اسکی پرستش کرنے لگے خدا فرماتا ہے کہ انہوں نے اتنا نہ سوچا کہ یہ کیسا معبود ہے جو نہ کلام کرنے کی طاقت رکھتا ہے۔ نہ ہدایت کر سکتا ہے۔ بھلا بچھڑا کیا اور خدا کیا۔ اور یہ جو فرمایا کہ قوم موسیٰ نے موسیٰ کے بعد اپنے زیور کا ایک بچھڑا بنا لیا۔ حالانکہ بچھڑا سامری نے بنایا تھا تو اس بنا پر ہے کہ سامری انہیں میں سے تھا اور سب اسکے اس فعل سے خوش تھے :۔

۱۳۲۔ اس آیت کی تفسیر میں جمہور اور مفسرین کو بڑی مشکل پیش آئی کہ اسکو حضرت آدم و حوا کا قصہ سمجھ کر خیال کیا کہ حضرت آدم علیہ السلام سے بھی شرک کا گناہ عظیم ہوا حالانکہ انبیاء شرک سے معصوم ہوتے ہیں تو بعض نے اس اشکال کو اس طرح رفع کیا ہے کہ یہ گناہ صرف حوا سے ہوا نہ آدم سے اور کہا ہے کہ تثنیہ کا صیغہ اس مطلب کے منافی نہیں ہے کیونکہ کلامِ عرب میں ایک شخص کے فعل کو دوسرے شخص یا ایک جماعت کی طرف منسوب کرنا بہت جگہ پایا جاتا ہے۔ جیسے نَسِیَا حُوْتَھُمَا کہ مچھلی بھولے تو یوشع تھے۔ مگر یوشع نے اس میں موسیٰ کو بھی شامل کیا حالانکہ موسیٰ نہیں بھولے تھے یا جیسے یَخْرُجُ مِنْھُمَا اللُّؤْلُؤُ وَالْمَرْجَانُ کہ اس آیت سے موتی اور مرجان کا بحر نمکین اور شیریں دونوں سے پیدا ہونا پایا جاتا ہے حالانکہ وہ صرف بحر نمکین سے پیدا ہوتے ہیں نہ شیریں سے یا جیسے یَا مَعْشَرَ الْجِنِّ وَالْاِنْسِ اَلَمْ یَاْتِکُمْ رُسُلٌ مِّنْکُمْ کہ اس سے جنوں اور انسانوں دونوں سے پیغمبروں کا مبعوث ہونا سمجھا جاتا ہے۔ حالانکہ پیغمبر صرف انسانوں میں سے ہوتے ہیں۔ مگر جہاں تک ہم سمجھتے ہیں یہ آدم کا نہیں بلکہ اولاد آدم کا حال بیان کیا گیا ہے اور اسی بنا پر ہم نے ترجمہ ایسا کیا ہے کہ کسی طرح کا اشکال نہیں پایا جاتا :۔

۱۳۳۔ یہ آیتیں جنگ بدر کے متعلق ہیں۔ بعض مورخین اور مفسرین نے اس جنگ کی یہ وجہ لکھی ہے کہ وہ قافلہ جو ابوسفیان شام سے مکے کو لے آ رہا تھا اسکی نسبت جناب رسالت مآب اور اُن کے صحابہ نے یہ خیال کر کے کہ اس قافلے میں لوگ بہت کم اور مال بہت زیادہ ہے لوٹ لینے کے ارادے سے کوچ کیا تھا۔ جب یہ خبر قریش مکہ کو پہنچی تو وہ بہت سی جمعیت لیکر قافلے کے بچانے کو نکلے آخر بمقام بدر جنگ ہوئی اور نتیجہ یہ ہوا کہ قریش کے ستر آدمی مارے گئے اور اسی قدر گرفتار ہوئے اور جو مال و اسباب وہ چھوڑ کر بھاگ گئے تھے وہ سب مسلمانوں کے ہاتھ آیا مگر آیاتِ قرآنی سے صاف معلوم ہوتا ہے کہ جناب رسولِ خدا کو قریش مکہ کا مدینے پر چڑھائی کرنے کا حال پہلے معلوم ہو چکا تھا اور اسکے بعد آپ نے اُن کے مقابلے کے لئے کوچ فرمایا تھا۔ بیشک بعض صحابہ کی رائے ہوگی کہ شام کے قافلے کو لوٹ لیا جائے اور اسی گروہ کی نسبت خدا نے فرمایا ہے کہ تم بے شان شوکت گروہ کو لینا چاہتے ہو۔ مگر خدا نے اس رائے کو منظور نہ فرمایا اور یہی چاہا کہ فوج مسلح سے جنگ کریں اور داد شجاعت دے کر فتح حاصل کریں چنانچہ ایسا ہی ہوا۔ اس جنگ کی وجہ جو نہایت قرین قیاس ہے یہ ہے کہ قریش مکہ کو مہاجرین اور انصار مدینہ کے ساتھ سخت عداوت تھی اور وہ ہمیشہ اُنکے درپے آزار رہتے تھے۔ تو جناب رسالتمآب اپنے دشمنوں کے حالات اور ارادوں سے آگاہ رہنے کے لئے کبھی کبھی اطرافِ مکہ میں آدمی روانہ فرماتے چنانچہ ایک دفعہ مقام نخلہ میں جو مکہ اور طائف کے درمیان واقع ہے آپ نے چند اشخاص روانہ فرمائے جن کے سردار آپ کے پھوپھی زاد بھائی عبداللہ بن جحش تھے نخلہ ایک نہایت خطرناک مقام تھا اور

وہاں جانے کا سخت اندیشہ تھا۔ آپ نے عبداللہ کو احتیاطاً ایک سر بمہر پرچہ دیا اور فرمایا کہ مکے کی طرف برابر چلے چلو تین روز کے بعد اس پرچے کو کھول کر پڑھنا اور جو کچھ اسمیں لکھا ہے اس پر عمل کرنا پرچے میں لکھا تھا کہ امض حتیٰ تنزل نخلۃ فترصد بھا قریشا و تعلم لنا من اخبارھم یعنی نخلے تک چلے جاؤ اور وہاں پہنچکر مخفی طور پر قریش کے حالات معلوم کرو اور ہمارے پاس انکی خبر لاؤ۔ مگر وہاں اور ہی معاملہ پیش آیا کہ ان کے نخلے میں پہنچنے کے دو دن بعد قریش کا ایک چھوٹا سا قافلہ طائف کا مالِ تجارت لئے ہوئے آپہنچا۔ عبداللہ اور انکے رفقاء کو ارشادِ نبوی اور اس پرچے کا خیال نہ رہا اور انہوں نے ان لوگوں پر حملہ کر دیا نتیجہ یہ ہوا کہ عمرو بن عبداللہ حضرمی جو سردارانِ قریش مکہ میں سے تھا تیر سے مارا گیا اور حکم بن کیسان اور عثمان بن عبداللہ مخزومی گرفتار ہو گئے ہر چند جناب رسول خدا نے ان لوگوں کو اس حرکت پر بہت ملامت کی اور قیدیوں کو چھوڑ بھی دیا اور عمرو بن عبداللہ حضرمی کا خون بہا بھی اپنے پاس سے دے دیا۔ مگر اہلِ مکہ کی آتشِ کینہ بے مشتعل ہوئے نہ رہی اور انہوں نے ساڑھے نو سو کے قریب جنگ آزمودہ جمع کئے جن میں سے تین سو کے پاس گھوڑے اور باقیوں کے پاس سواری اور باربرداری کے لئے سات سو اونٹ تھے اسکے علاوہ کسی نے یہ ہوائی اڑا دی کہ جناب رسول اللہ ابوسفیان والے قافلہ کو جو شام سے مکے کو آرہا ہے لوٹنے کا ارادہ رکھتے ہیں اس خبر سے ان کا غضب اور بھی بھڑک اٹھا اور وہ فوراً مدینے پر حملہ کرنے کے لئے نکل کھڑے ہوئے ادھر مدینے میں یہ خبر پہنچ ہی چکی تھی کہ قریش مکہ بہت زور شور سے مدینے پر چڑھائی کرنے کی تیاریاں کر رہے ہیں اس صورت میں ضرور تھا کہ جناب رسولِ خدا اپنی حفاظت کا انتظام فرماتے تو آپ نے تین سو تیرہ[۳۱۳] اشخاص کی جمعیت کے ساتھ مدینے سے کوچ فرمایا جن میں سے ایک یا دو کے پاس گھوڑے تھے اور باقیوں کے پاس صرف ستر اونٹ تھے جن پر نوبت بنوبت تین تین چار چار آدمی سوار ہوتے تھے۔ چنانچہ خود جناب سرورِ کائنات اور حضرت علی مرتضیٰ اور زید بن حارثہ ایک ہی اونٹ پر باری باری سے سوار ہوتے رہے جب بمقام بدر پہنچے تو قریش سے لڑائی ہوئی جس میں انکے ستر آدمی مارے گئے اور اتنے ہی گرفتار ہوئے اور بہت سا مال و اسباب مسلمانوں کے ہاتھ آیا۔ مقتولین میں ابوجہل اور عتبہ بن ربیعہ اور شیبہ بن ربیعہ اور ولید بن عتبہ اور حنظلہ بن ابی سفیان اور نوفل اور ابوالبختری وغیرہ چوبیس آدمی سردارانِ قریش میں سے تھے جن میں سے ابن ہشام کی روایت کے مطابق نو کو حضرت علیؑ نے تہ تیغ کیا تھا مسلمانوں میں سے صرف چودہ[۱۴] آدمی مارے گئے جن میں چھ[۶] مہاجر اور آٹھ[۸] انصار تھے قرآن کی آیتوں کو دیکھو پانچویں آیت سے معلوم ہوتا ہے کہ جناب سرورِ کائنات ابھی مدینے ہی میں تھے اور کوچ نہیں فرمایا تھا کہ صحابہ میں اختلاف واقع ہوا بعضے لڑائی کو پسند کرتے تھے اور بعضے ناپسند کرتے تھے۔ چھٹی آیت سے معلوم ہوتا ہے کہ مسلمان قریش مکہ کی اس فوج کثیر کے مقابلے سے ہچکچاتے تھے جو انہوں نے مدینے پر حملہ کرنے کی غرض سے جمع کی تھی۔ ورنہ قافلہ تجارت کو لوٹ لینے کے ارادے سے تکلیف کرنا کسی صورت میں موت کی طرف ہانکا جانا نہیں ہو سکتا۔ ساتویں آیت میں دو گروہوں کا ذکر ہے ایک جو لڑائی کا ساز و سامان نہیں رکھتا تھا اور وہ ابوسفیان کا قافلہ تجارت تھا جو شام سے آرہا تھا۔ دوسرا گروہ قریشِ مکہ یعنی ابوجہل کا لشکر تھا جس کی بہت سی جمعیت تھی اور جس کے ساتھ بہت سا سامانِ جنگ تھا۔ غرض نہتے لوگوں پر حملہ کرنا تو خدا کو منظور اور پسند نہ تھا۔ فوج مسلح کا مقابلہ کیا گیا تو اسکے وعدے کے مطابق مسلمانوں کو فتح حاصل ہوئی ؛

۱۳۴۔ چونکہ قرآن مجید کا ترجمہ بامحاورہ کرنا مقصود ہے اسلئے فَوْقَ الْاَعْنَاقِ کے لفظی معنی ہیں گردنوں کے اوپر کا حصہ اور وہ سر ہے تو اس مقام کا ترجمہ جو ہم نے کیا ہے ہمارے نزدیک اس سے بہتر بامحاورہ ترجمہ نہیں ہو سکتا۔ مترجم

۱۳۵۔ ثابت قدم رہنے والوں سے مراد بہادر اور قوی دل ہیں اور حقیقت میں جہاد کرنا کام بھی بہادروں کا ہے اور بہادری قوتِ ایمانی سے بڑھتی ہے جس قدر ایمان زیادہ ہوتا ہے اسی قدر شجاعت زیادہ ہوتی ہے۔ اسی بنا پر حضرت سرور کائنات صلی اللہ علیہ وسلم کے عہدِ مبارک کے مومنوں کے بارے میں یہ ارشاد ہوا ہے کہ اگر تم میں بیس[۲۰] بہادر ہونگے تو دو سو کافروں پر غالب رہینگے اور اسی قوتِ ایمانی کی بنا پر بعض نے خبر کو امر قرار دیا ہے یعنی اہلِ ایمان کو خدا کا حکم یہ ہے کہ اگر کافر ان سے دو چند بھی ہوں تب بھی ان کے مقابلے میں جمے رہیں اپنے سے دو چند کفار کے مقابلے میں ثابت قدم رہنے کا حکم تو اس قوت کی کمی اور کمزوری کی وجہ سے ہے چنانچہ اسی لئے بعد کی آیت میں یہ ارشاد ہوا ہے کہ اب خدا نے تم پر سے بوجھ ہلکا کر دیا اور معلوم کر لیا کہ ابھی تم میں کمزوری ہے۔ پس اگر تم میں سے ایک سو ثابت قدم رہنے والے ہونگے تو دو سو پر غالب رہینگے۔ اور اگر ایک ہزار ہونگے تو خدا کے حکم سے دو ہزار پر غالب رہینگے۔ اب اگر دو چند کافر مقابلے پر ہوں تو ہرگز بھاگنا نہیں چاہیئے یعنی کم سے کم ایک سو مومن دو سو کافروں پر بھاری ہونے چاہیئیں۔ اور ایک ہزار دو ہزار پر ؛

۱۳۶۔ اس سورت کے شروع میں بسم اللہ نہیں لکھی گئی۔ اسکے مختلف سبب بیان کئے گئے ہیں۔ حضرت علی رضی اللہ تعالےٰ عنہ، کہتے ہیں کہ بسم اللہ میں امان ہے کیونکہ اس میں خدا کا نام اس وصف کے ساتھ لیا جاتا ہے جو امان کو قائم کرنے والا ہے۔ یعنی رحمت اور یہ سورت جنگ و قتال اور رفع امان کے لئے نازل ہوئی ہے اسلئے اسمیں بسم اللہ نہیں ہے بعض نے کہا کہ عرب کی عادت تھی کہ جب ان میں اور کسی قوم میں عہد ہوتا تھا اور وہ اسکو توڑنا چاہتے تھے تو اس بارے میں جو خط وہ اس قوم کو لکھتے تھے اس پر بسم اللہ نہیں لکھتے تھے جب کفار نے وہ عہد جو مسلمانوں نے خدا کے اذن سے ان کے ساتھ کیا تھا توڑ ڈالا تو خدا نے مسلمانوں سے فرمایا کہ تمکو بھی اپنے عہد پر قائم رہنا ضرور نہیں پس چونکہ اس سورت میں عہد توڑ ڈالا گیا ہے اور اسکے نازل ہونے پر جناب رسالتمآب نے حضرت علیؑ کو مشرکوں

کے پاس بھیجا انہوں نے یہ سورت انکو سنا دی اور ان سے کہہ دیا کہ اب صلح کا عہد ٹوٹ گیا ہے چار مہینے کے بعد ہر جگہ تم لوگوں سے جنگ ہے اسلئے انکی عادت کے مطابق اسکے شروع میں بسم اللہ نہیں لکھی ان کے سوا اور بھی کئی اقوال ہیں۔ مگر زیادہ صحیح پہلا قول معلوم ہوتا ہے ؞

۱۳۷۔ حدیبیہ میں کفار کے ساتھ دس برس کا عہد ہوا تھا۔ اور اس شرط پر صلح قرار پائی تھی کہ جو لوگ مسلمانوں کی پناہ میں ہیں ان پر نہ مکے والے خود حملہ کرینگے۔ اور نہ حملہ کرنیوالوں کی مدد کرینگے اور جو لوگ مکے والوں کی پناہ میں ہیں ان پر مسلمان نہ حملہ کرینگے۔ نہ حملہ کرنیوالوں کی مدد کرینگے مگر قریش نے اپنا عہد توڑ ڈالا۔ یعنی بنو بکر نے جو مکے والوں کی پناہ میں تھے۔ خزاعہ پر جو حضرت رسول اللہ صلی اللہ علیہ وسلم کی پناہ میں تھے چڑھائی کر دی اور قریش نے انکی مدد کی۔ یہ واقعہ ظہور میں آنے پر خزاعہ میں سے ایک شخص عمرو بن سالم نام حضرت صلی اللہ علیہ وسلم کی خدمت میں حاضر ہوا اور کہا کہ مکے کے کافروں نے اپنا عہد توڑ ڈالا تب آپ نے فرمایا میں تمہاری مدد کروں گا غرض آپ کو مکے والوں سے جنگ کرنی پڑی چنانچہ آپ نے ۸ھ ہجری میں انپر چڑھائی کی اور مکہ فتح کر لیا ؞

۱۳۸۔ ان آیات میں خدا نے ان مہربانیوں کا اظہار فرمایا ہے جو مسلمانوں پر کی تھیں۔ جب مکہ فتح ہو چکا اور اہل مکہ اسلام لے آئے تو جناب رسول خدا صلی اللہ علیہ وسلم کو یہ خبر پہنچی کہ قوم ہوازن کے لوگ حنین میں آپ کے ساتھ لڑائی کو جمع ہیں۔ یہ واقعہ ۸ھ ہجری کا ہے ہوازن ایک تیرانداز قوم تھی اور حنین ایک وادی ہے جو مکہ اور طائف کے درمیان واقع ہے۔ مسلمانوں کی جمعیت گیارہ یا بارہ یا سولہ ہزار تھی یہ اپنی فوج کی کثرت پر مغرور ہو گئے کہ کافر ہیں ہی کیا انکو تو ریلوں ہی مار کر بھگا دیں گے خدا کو غرور پسند نہ تھا جب یہ دشمن کی طرف چلے تو وہ جنگل کے تنگ رستوں اور پہاڑوں کے دروں میں بڑی مستعدی سے انکی گھات میں لگے ہوئے تھے حضرت مع اصحاب کے صبح کے اندھیرے میں میدان میں اترے تھے کہ انہوں نے یکایک تیراندازی شروع کر دی۔ تلواریں کھینچ کر انہوں نے یکبارگی ایسا حملہ کیا کہ مسلمانوں کی جمعیت منتشر ہو گئی مگر حضرت صلی اللہ علیہ وسلم کہ اپنے خچر پر سوار تھے اسی طرح جمے رہے اور اسکو دشمنوں کی طرف بڑھایا۔ آپکے چچا عباس رض رکاب پکڑے ہوئے تھے اور دوسری رکاب ابوسفیان بن حرث بن عبدالمطلب کے ہاتھ میں تھی وہ خچر کو روکتے تھے کہ تیز نہ چلے حضرت اپنا نام مبارک لے کر مسلمانوں کو پکارتے تھے کہ خدا کے بندو کہاں جاتے ہو میری طرف آؤ۔ میں خدا کا رسول ہوں۔ یہ بھی فرماتے تھے کہ انا النبی لا کذب انا ابن عبد المطلب لکھا ہے کہ سو کے قریب صحابی ثابت قدم رہے باقی سب کے پاؤں اکھڑ گئے آپ نے اپنے چچا عباس رض سے کہ وہ بلند آواز تھے۔ ارشاد فرمایا کہ خوب زور سے پکاریں وہ پکارنے لگے تو لوگ حضرت کی طرف رجوع لائے جب کچھ لوگ اسطرح پر فراہم ہو گئے تو حضرت نے انکو حملہ کرنے کا حکم دیا۔ چنانچہ اس حملہ میں ہوازن کو شکست ہوئی اس جنگ میں خدا نے مسلمانوں کی مدد کے لئے فرشتوں کا لشکر بھیجا۔ جو مسلمانوں

کے لئے موجب تسلی اور تقویت تھا۔ غرض خدا نے مسلمانوں کو ان کے اترانے اور مغرور ہونے پر تنبیہ کر کے فتحیاب کیا۔ قتل اور گرفتاری کفار کے علاوہ اس لڑائی میں بہت سا مال ہاتھ آیا کہتے ہیں کہ اس سے زیادہ کوئی بڑی غنیمت ہاتھ نہیں آئی تھی ؞

۱۳۹۔ ذی قعدہ۔ ذی الحجہ۔ محرم۔ رجب۔

۱۴۰۔ بعض منافق جناب سرور کائنات کو ایذا دیتے تھے یعنی کہتے تھے کہ یہ تو نرے کان ہیں۔ جو کوئی ان سے کچھ بات کہہ دیتا ہے اسکو ہمارے حق میں سچ جان لیتے ہیں۔ اور جب ہم آکر قسم کھا لیتے ہیں تو ہمیں سچا جانتے ہیں خدا نے فرمایا کہ یہ بات نہیں کہ وہ حق و باطل میں تمیز نہیں کرتے بلکہ سچے کو جھوٹے سے خوب پہچانتے ہیں۔ لیکن عمداً درگذر کرتے ہیں اور منافق جو ایسی باتیں کر کے پیغمبر خدا صلی اللہ علیہ وسلم کو ایذا دیتے ہیں تو انکو سخت عذاب ہوگا ؞

۱۴۱۔ جناب رسول خدا صلی اللہ علیہ وسلم نے خیرات کے لئے حکم فرمایا تو مومن اپنے مقدور کے مطابق مال لانے لگے۔ کوئی تو بہت روپیہ لایا اور کوئی اناج۔ عبدالرحمن بن عوف چار ہزار درہم لائے اور کہا میرے پاس آٹھ ہزار درہم تھے۔ چار ہزار میں خدا تعالے کو قرض دینے کے لئے لے آیا ہوں اور چار ہزار عیال کے اخراجات کے لئے چھوڑ آیا ہوں۔ عاصم کے پاس روپیہ نہ تھا وہ چار سیر غلہ لائے۔ وہ بھی جو اور کہنے لگے کہ میں مزدوری کر کے آٹھ سیر جو لایا تھا۔ چار سیر خیرات کرتا ہوں اور چار سیر عیال کے کھانے کے لئے رکھے ہیں۔ یہ کیفیت دیکھ کر منافق طعنہ زنی اور تمسخر کرنے لگے۔ عبدالرحمن کو تو کہنے لگے کہ اس نے دکھاوے کیلئے اتنا مال دے دیا ہے تا کہ لوگ تحسین و آفرین کریں۔ اور عاصم کی نسبت کہنے لگے کہ ان میاں کو دیکھو نہ سونا نہ چاندی جو ہی اٹھا لائے کہ نام خیرات کرنے والوں میں ہو گا بھلا جو کیا اور خیرات کیا۔ اور خدا کو ان جوؤں کی حاجت ہی کیا ہے۔ خدا نے فرمایا کہ جس طرح یہ منافق مسلمانوں سے تمسخر کرتے ہیں خدا بھی ان کو عذاب دے کر ان کے تمسخر کا جواب دے گا ؞ ۱۲

۱۴۲۔ مدینے میں ایک مسجد تھی جو مسجد قبا کے نام سے مشہور تھی۔ حضرت سرور کائنات صلی اللہ علیہ وسلم اکثر ہفتے کے روز وہاں تشریف لے جاتے اور نماز پڑھتے منافقوں نے چاہا کہ اسکے مقابلے میں اپنی ایک الگ مسجد بنائیں اس کی بنا یہ ہوئی کہ مدینے میں آنحضرت کے تشریف لے جانے سے پیشتر ایک شخص ابو عامر نام رہتا تھا۔ جو ایام جاہلیت میں عیسائی تھا۔ نہایت کج سرشت تھا وہ آپ کے مدینے میں تشریف لے جانے پر اسلام تو کیا لاتا آپ کا کھلم کھلا دشمن ہو گیا اور وہاں سے نکل کر مکے کے کافروں سے جا ملا اور انکو آنحضرت سے لڑنے پر برانگیختہ کیا۔ چنانچہ احد کی لڑائی ہوئی اور وہ اس میں کافروں کے ساتھ گیا۔ پھر روم کے بادشاہ کے پاس چلا گیا اور اس سے آنحضرت صلی اللہ علیہ وسلم کے مقابلے کے لئے مدد کا خواستگار ہوا اس نے مدد کا وعدہ کر لیا یہ اسکے پاس ٹھہر رہا۔ اور مدینے کے کافروں کو لکھ بھیجا کہ روم سے عنقریب ایک لشکر آتا ہے جو مسلمانوں

کو تباہ کردیگا تم ایک مضبوط جگہ بنا رکھو۔ جہاں وہ شخص جو اسکے پاس سے
سے پیغام رسانی کے لئے آیا کرے قیام کیا کرے۔ تو اُن
لوگوں نے مسجد قبا کے پاس ہی ایک مسجد بنانی شروع کی۔ اس مسجد
کو مسجد ضرار کہتے ہیں۔ جب وہ تیار ہو چکی تو منافق آں حضرت
صلی اللہ علیہ وسلم کی خدمت میں حاضر ہوئے اور کہنے لگے کہ ہم نے
بیماروں اور ناتوانوں کے لئے نیز برسات کے خیال سے ایک
مسجد بنائی ہے آپ وہاں تشریف لے چلیں اور نماز پڑھیں
اور دُعائے برکت کریں تا کہ وہاں جماعت قائم ہو جائے آپ
کو اسوقت تک مطلق علم نہ تھا کہ یہ مسجد کس نیت اور کس غرض
سے بنائی گئی ہے اسلئے آپ نے فرمایا کہ اب تو ہم سفر میں جا رہے
ہیں جب واپس آئینگے تب انشاء اللہ وہاں نماز پڑھیں گے
جب آپ جنگ تبوک سے واپس آئے اور مدینے پہنچنے میں
ایک آدھ روز کا رستہ رہ گیا تو یہ آیت نازل ہوئی جس سے آپ
کو معلوم ہو گیا کہ منافقوں کا مقصود اس مسجد کی تعمیر سے مسلمانوں کو مسجد قبا
سے جس کی بنیاد تقویٰ پر رکھی گئی تھی متفرق کرنا اور ان میں تفرقہ ڈالنا
تھا۔ تب آپ نے حکم دیا کہ ہمارے پہنچنے سے پہلے وہ مسجد ڈھا دی جائے
اور جلا دی جائے۔ چنانچہ اس حکم کی تعمیل کی گئی اور مسجد ڈھا دی گئی اور
جلا دی گئی۔

۱۴۳- یہ تین شخص بھی انہی لوگوں میں ہیں جو غزوہ تبوک کے پیچھے رہ گئے تھے
اور جناب رسالتمآب کے ساتھ جنگ میں نہیں گئے تھے۔ تبوک ایک
قصبے کا نام ہے جو شام اور وادی القریٰ کے درمیان واقع ہے اس جنگ
سے پیچھے رہ جانے والے تین قسم کے لوگ تھے۔ ایک منافق یہ بے ایمان
بھلا کیوں گھر سے نکلنے لگے تھے۔ انہوں نے طرح طرح کے حیلے اور بہانے
کئے اور اسوجہ سے خدا نے اُن پر سخت لعن طعن کی دوسرے مسلمان جو
کسی عذر سے پیچھے رہ گئے تھے تیسرے یہی تین شخص جو بغیر عذر کے نہ
گئے تو جن شخصوں نے اپنے قصوروں کا اعتراف کیا انکو معاف کر دیا گیا۔
مگر ان تین شخصوں کا معاملہ تا دریافت پچاس دن تک ملتوی رکھا گیا۔ یہ تین
شخص مرارہ بن ربیع اور کعب بن مالک اور ہلال بن اُمیہ تھے ان ایام میں
ان پر ایسی سخت حالت گذری کہ اسے موت سے بھی بدتر سمجھتے تھے آخر
سچ کہنے کے سبب ان کے قصور بھی معاف کر دیئے گئے۔

۱۴۴- یعنی کوئی ایسا قرآن لاؤ جس میں بتوں کی مذمت نہ ہو۔ یا کم سے کم
یہی کر دو کہ جو آیتیں عقائد بت پرستی کے ابطال میں ہیں ان کو نکال کر
اور آیتیں انکی جگہ داخل کر دو۔ امام رازیؒ کہتے ہیں کہ کفار کا یہ کہنا یا تو ہنسی
کے طور پر تھا یا آزمائش کے لئے یعنی اگر وہ اس کو بدل دیں تو ہم جان لیں کہ وہ
سچے نبی نہیں ہیں خدا نے آپ کو حکم دیا کہ تم کہدو کہ قرآن میرا بنایا ہوا نہیں
کہ میں اس میں تغیر و تبدل کر دوں بلکہ خدا کا نازل کیا ہوا ہے۔ اور میں
اسے بدل دینے کا کچھ اختیار نہیں رکھتا۔

۱۴۵- یعنی جب اسکو اسکے اعمال کا بدلہ ملیگا تب اُسے معلوم ہو جائیگا کہ
اس نے دُنیا میں کیسے کام کئے تھے۔

۱۴۶- یعنی ان کا تمہاری طرف کان لگانا یا نظر کرنا ان کو کچھ فائدہ نہیں دیگا
کیونکہ اُن کی مثال بہروں اور اندھوں کی سی ہے کہ نہ سن سکیں نہ دیکھ سکیں خصوصاً
اس حالت میں کہ عقل اور سمجھ سے بے بہرہ ہوں۔ بہرے کو اشارے سے سمجھا
سکتے ہیں اندھے کو آواز سے بتا سکتے ہیں مگر جو عقل ہی نہ رکھے اس کو کسی
طرح کا سمجھانا نفع نہیں دیتا مطلب ہے کہ یہ لوگ نہ شوق اور توجہ سے
تمہاری باتوں کو سنتے ہیں نہ یقین رکھتے ہیں۔ اس لئے ان کا ہدایت یاب
ہونا دشوار ہے۔

۱۴۷- یہ عام لوگوں سے خطاب ہے جو اسلام نہیں لاتے تھے یعنی جب تم قرآن مجید کا یہ
اعجاز دیکھ چکے ہو کہ کوئی شخص ایسا کلام نہیں بنا سکتا تو تم کو بھی اُسے ماننا
چاہیئے کہ کلام خدا ہے اور اسلام لے آنا چاہیئے۔

۱۴۸- جو فرشتے خوشخبری لیکر آئے تھے وہ جبرائیلؑ اور میکائیلؑ اور اسرافیلؑ تھے
اور خوبصورت نوجوانوں کی شکل میں آئے تھے حضرت ابراہیمؑ نے اُن کو
معزز مہمان سمجھ کر ان کے لئے ایک موٹا تازہ بچھڑا ذبح کیا اور اسکے
کباب بنا کر ان کے پاس لائے۔ حضرت ابراہیمؑ کی بیوی سارہ نے جب
دیکھا کہ ابراہیم مہمانوں کی خاطر اور اکرام کرتے ہیں تو خود بھی اُنکی خدمت
کے لئے آ کھڑی ہوئیں۔ مہمانوں کی یہ کیفیت کہ کھانا سامنے رکھا ہے اور اُنکے
ہاتھ کھانے کی طرف جاتے ہی نہیں یہ حالت دیکھ کر حضرت ابراہیمؑ کے دل
میں خوف پیدا ہوا کہ یہ لوگ کسی بُرے ارادہ سے نہ آئے ہوں۔ کیونکہ ان
لوگوں کی عادت تھی کہ جب کوئی مہمان آتا اور میزبان کے ہاں کھانا نہ کھاتا تو وہ
یہ خیال کرتے کہ یہ نیت نیک سے نہیں آیا بلکہ کسی بُرے ارادہ سے آیا ہے
مہمانوں نے کہا خوف نہ کیجئے۔ ہم خدا کے فرشتے ہیں اور قوم لوط کے ہلاک
کرنے کے لئے بھیجے گئے ہیں۔ فرشتوں کا یہ قول سنکر بی بی سارہ ہنس پڑیں
پھر فرشتوں نے بی بی سارہ کو حضرت اسحٰقؑ اور حضرت اسحٰق کے بعد حضرت
یعقوب کے پیدا ہونے کی خوشخبری سُنائی تو وہ مارے خوشی کے بیساختہ ہنس
پڑیں۔ جب حضرت ابراہیمؑ کو فرشتوں کے آنے کا سبب معلوم ہو گیا۔ اور
انکی بی بی کو حضرت اسحٰق کی بشارت بھی مل گئی اور ان کا خوف بھی دور
ہو گیا تو وہ حضرت لوطؑ کے بارے میں فرشتوں سے گفتگو کرنے لگے جسکو
خدا نے اپنی طرف منسوب فرمایا ہے۔ وہ گفتگو یہ تھی کہ جب فرشتوں نے
کہا کہ ہم لوطؑ کے گاؤں کو تباہ کرنے کے لئے آئے ہیں تو حضرت ابراہیمؑ
نے کہا کیا تم ایسے گاؤں کو تباہ کرو گے جس میں تین سو مومن رہتے ہیں
فرشتوں نے کہا نہیں۔ پھر ابراہیم نے کہا کیا تم ایسے گاؤں کو ہلاک کرو گے
جس میں چالیس مومن ہیں۔ کہا نہیں۔ پھر انہوں نے کہا بھلا جس گاؤں میں
تیس یا بیس یا دس یا پانچ مومن ہوں کیا تم اسکو بھی ہلاک کرو گے۔ کہا نہیں
پھر انہوں نے کہا کہ اگر اس گاؤں میں ایک ہی مومن ہو تب بھی اُسے تباہ
کرو گے؟ کہا نہیں۔ تب ابراہیم نے کہا کہ اس گاؤں میں تو لوطؑ ہیں انہوں

نے کہا جو جو اس میں ہیں ہمیں معلوم ہیں۔ ہم لُوطؑ کو اُن کے گھر والوں کو تو بچالیں گے۔ مگر ان کی عورت نہیں بچے گی۔ حضرت ابراہیمؑ چونکہ نہایت نرم دل تھے اسلئے چاہتے تھے کہ ان لوگوں کو عذاب میں توقف ہوجائے تو اچھا ہو شاید وہ ایمان لے آئیں اور اپنی بدکرداریوں سے باز آجائیں فرشتوں نے ابراہیمؑ سے کہا یہ خیال ترک کر دیجئے۔ ان کے لئے عذاب کا حکم صادر ہوچکا ہے اور عذاب ہو کر رہے گا ؂

۱۴۹- یہود نے جناب رسالتمآب سے کہا کہ ہمیں ان پیغمبر کا حال بتایئے جو شام میں رہتے تھے۔ اور ان کا بیٹا مصر کی طرف نکال دیا گیا تھا وہ بیٹے کے غم میں اس قدر روتے رہے کہ بصارت جاتی رہی کہتے ہیں اسوقت مکے میں کوئی شخص اہل کتاب میں سے نہ تھا اور نہ کوئی ایسا آدمی تھا جو انبیائے سابقین کے حالات کا علم رکھتا ہو۔ اسلئے یہود نے ایک شخص مدینے سے یہ سوال کرنے کو حضرت صلی اللہ علیہ وسلم کے پاس مکے میں بھیجا۔ تب خدا نے یہ سورت نازل فرمائی۔

۱۵۰- حضرت یوسف علیہ السلام کے گیارہ بھائی تھے جن میں سے دس تو سوتیلے تھے اور ایک حقیقی ان کا نام بنیامین تھا۔ اور یہ سب میں چھوٹے تھے یہاں اسکے بھائی سے مُراد یہی بنیامین ہیں ؂

۱۵۱- جو سلوک اُن بے دردوں نے یوسف جیسے خوبصورت نیک طینت اور خوردسال بھائی کے ساتھ کیا اسکا تصور کرکے اس قدر رنج والم ہوتا ہے کہ بیان نہیں ہو سکتا۔ اس زمانے میں بھی بھائیوں کا بھائیوں کے ساتھ ایسا ہی سلوک ہے اور اسی لئے عام طور پر یہ کہا جاتا ہے کہ مصرعؔ "بھائی ہیں برادرانِ یوسف" خدا تعالٰی مومن بھائیوں کے دلوں میں رافت وشفقت ڈالے کہ ایک دوسرے سے مہربانی اور محبت کا سلوک کریں ؂

۱۵۲- کُرتے پر جھوٹ موٹ کا لہو لگا لانے تاکہ یہ سمجھا جائے کہ بھیڑیا درحقیقت کھا گیا ہے مگر یہ خیال نہ کیا کہ اگر بھیڑیا سچ مچ کھا جاتا تو بھیڑیئے کے دانتوں سے کرتا بھی پھٹ جاتا حالانکہ وہ بالکل سالم تھا۔ جب ان مکاروں نے حضرت یعقوبؑ سے آکر کہا کہ یوسف کو بھیڑیا کھا گیا۔ تو انہوں نے کرتا ہی دیکھ کر سمجھ لیا کہ یہ جھوٹ کہتے ہیں اور فرمایا کہ بھیڑیا بڑا دانشمند تھا کہ یوسف کو تو کھا گیا اور کُرتا نہ پھٹنے دیا ؂

۱۵۳- اس شخص کا نام قطفیر تھا بعض نے اطفیر کہا ہے۔ یہ مصر کے بادشاہ کا جس کا نام ریان بن ولید تھا وزیر تھا اور اس کا لقب عزیز تھا ؂

۱۵۴- زلیخا کا قصد جیسا ہوگا ظاہر ہے۔ کیونکہ وہ یوسف علیہ السلام کے حسن وجمال پر فریفتہ ہو رہی تھی مگر یوسف کا قصد ایسا نہیں ہوسکتا۔ کیونکہ وہ ایسے کام سے خدا کی پناہ مانگتے ہیں اور امانت میں خیانت کرنے کو ظلم سمجھتے ہیں اور یہی کہہ کر زلیخا کا کہا نہیں مانتے۔ پروردگار کی نشانی کے متعلق کہ وہ کیا تھی مفسرین نے بہت سے اقوال لکھے ہیں۔ جن میں زیادہ مشہور یہ ہے کہ انکو حضرت یعقوبؑ کی صورت اس حال میں کہ وہ انگلی دانتوں میں لئے ہوئے تھے نظر آئی اور وہ اس مقصد سے مانع ہوئی ایک نشانی بیان کی گئی ہے کہ جب زلیخا نے یوسف علیہ السلام سے اپنا مطلب حاصل کرنا چاہا تو گھر کے ایک کونے میں ایک بُت تھا اسکو کپڑے سے ڈھانپ دیا۔ یوسف علیہ السلام نے کہا یہ تم نے کیا کیا؟ بولی مجھے اپنے معبود سے شرم آتی ہے کہ وہ مجھ کو اس حالت میں دیکھے۔ یوسف علیہ السلام نے کہا کہ میں اس کا زیادہ مستحق ہوں کہ اپنے معبود برحق سے شرم کروں بہرکیف کوئی سبب ہوا ہو وہ اُن میں اور اُن کے قصد میں حائل ہوگیا۔ اور خدا تعالٰی نے اُنکی عصمت وعفت کو قائم رکھا ؂

۱۵۵- ندا کرنے والے نے اُنکو واقعی چور سمجھا تھا کیونکہ اسکو یہ معلوم نہ تھا کہ حضرت یوسف علیہ السلام نے یہ تدبیر کی ہے۔

۱۵۶- یعنی جسکے پاس چوری کی چیز نکلے وہ پکڑ لیا جائے اور اپنے پاس رکھ لیا جائے ؂

۱۵۷- شریعت ابراہیمی میں چور کی یہ سزا تھی کہ جس کی چوری کی ہو اسکا ایک برس تک مملوک و غلام بنا کر رکھا جائے اسکے بعد چھوڑ دیا جائے یہی سزا یوسف علیہ السلام کے بھائیوں نے بیان کی۔ اور اسی کے مطابق بنیامین کو لے لیا گیا ورنہ مصر کا قانون تو یہ تھا کہ چور کو ماریں پیٹیں اور مال مسروق سے دوچند تاوان لیں اور یہ قانون اجازت نہیں دیتا تھا کہ جسکے پاس سے چیز نکلے اسکو پکڑ لیا جائے غرض یہ کہ تدبیر حضرت یوسفؑ نے اسی لئے معلوم کی تھی کہ انکو معلوم تھا کہ یعقوب کی شریعت میں چور کی سزا اُسے گرفتار کرکے ایک سال تک غلام بنا رکھنا ہے۔ اور اسی سے وہ اپنے مقصد میں کامیاب ہوئے ؂

۱۵۸- اُسکے ایک بھائی سے اُنکی مُراد یوسفؑ تھے۔ کیونکہ بنیامین اور یوسفؑ ایک ماں سے تھے اور وہ دوسری ماؤں سے مگر یوسفؑ نے کبھی چوری نہیں کی اور یوسف جیسا شخص چوری کرسکتا ہی نہیں جس واقعے کو لوگوں نے چوری قرار دیا وہ یوں ہوا تھا کہ جب یوسفؑ پیدا ہوئے تو اُنکی پھوپھی اُن کی پرورش کرنے لگیں اور وہ اُن سے نہایت محبت رکھتی تھیں۔ جب آپ چند سال کے ہوئے تو یعقوب علیہ السلام بہن کے پاس آئے اور کہا اب یوسف کو مجھے دے دو۔ وہ انکا اپنے سے دم بھر جدا ہونا گوارا نہیں کرتی تھیں انہوں نے کہا واللہ میں اسکو اپنے سے علیحدہ نہیں کروں گی تم اسے کچھ مدت اور میرے پاس رہنے دو۔ تاکہ میں اسے دیکھ دیکھ کر دل ٹھنڈا کرتی رہوں۔ جب یعقوب علیہ السلام بہن کے پاس سے باہر چلے گئے تو اُنہوں نے یوسفؑ کو اپنے پاس رکھنے کی کیا تدبیر کی کہ حضرت اسحٰق کا ایک پٹکا اُن کے پاس تھا جو بطور میراث اس شخص کو ملتا تھا جو سب میں بڑا ہوتا تھا اور چونکہ یعقوبؑ کی یہ بہن سب سے بڑی تھیں اسلئے وہ اُنکو ملا تھا۔ تو انہوں نے وہ پٹکا یوسفؑ کی کمر سے باندھ دیا اور مشہور یہ کیا کہ وہ پٹکا گم ہوگیا ہے اور اسے تلاش کرنا شروع کیا جب تلاش سے نہ ملا۔ تو کہا گھر والوں کی جامہ تلاشی کرنی چاہیئے۔ جامہ تلاشی کی تو یوسفؑ کی کمر سے باندھا ہوا ملا تب کہا کہ اسنے میری چوری کی ہے لہٰذا میں اسے چھوڑنے کی نہیں اور اس تدبیر سے ان کو اپنے پاس رکھ لیا۔ چونکہ یوسفؑ پر چوری کا الزام تھا۔ اسلئے یعقوب علیہ السلام بھی ناچار تھے اور بیٹے کو بہن سے نہیں لے سکتے تھے۔ غرض

یوسفؑ پھوپھی کے پاس رہتے اور پرورش پاتے رہے یہاں تک کہ پھوپھی کا انتقال ہوگیا۔ بھلا یہ واقعہ چوری ہے؟ اور کوئی شخص اسے سُنکر کہہ سکتا ہے کہ حضرت یوسفؑ نے چوری کی تھی؟ مفسرین نے اسکے سوا اور بھی کئی باتیں لکھی ہیں۔ مثلاً گھر میں ایک مرغی تھی۔ وہ انہوں نے فقیر کو دے دی تھی۔ یا دسترخوان سے کھانا لے جاتے تھے۔ اور محتاجوں کو دے آتے تھے مگر یہ باتیں ایسی ہیں جن پر چوری کا اطلاق ہی نہیں ہوسکتا اور سچ تو یہ ہے کہ یوسف پر چوری کا الزام محض جھوٹ ہے۔ برادرانِ یوسفؑ کو تو جھوٹ بولنے میں باک ہی نہ تھا۔ مفسرین نے بھی ایسی لغو باتوں کو چوری قرار دینے اور انکو یوسفؑ کی طرف منسوب کرنے میں غلطی کی ہے ؎

۱۵۹۔ گیارہ ستارے جن کو یوسفؑ نے خواب میں سجدہ کرتے ہوئے دیکھا وہ یہی گیارہ بھائی تھے اور سورج اور چاند ان کے والدین ؎

۱۶۰۔ یعنی خدا کو مانتے بھی ہیں اور یہ جانتے بھی ہیں کہ زمین و آسمان اور جو کچھ اُن میں ہے ان کا پیدا کرنے والا اور مالک وہی ہے مگر ساتھ ہی بتوں کی پرستش بھی کرتے ہیں۔ یعنی اُنکو خدا کا مدِ مقابل بھی ٹھہراتے ہیں۔ یہ شرک واضح اور جلی ہے۔ اس طریق پر خدا کو ماننے والا مومن نہیں کہلاتا مشرک کہلاتا ہے اور شرک ایسا گناہ ہے جو کبھی نہیں بخشا جائے گا اَعَاذَنَا اللّٰہُ مِنْہُ۔ بعض نے اس آیت کا مصداق منافقوں کو ٹھہرایا ہے کہ ظاہر میں وہ مومن تھے اور باطن میں مشرک بعض نے کہا ہے کہ اس سے مراد اہلِ کتاب ہیں یعنی یہود و نصاریٰ۔ کہ وہ خدا کو بھی مانتے ہیں اور ساتھ ہی عزیر اور عیسیٰ علیہ السلام کو خدا کا بیٹا بھی کہتے ہیں اور یہ شرک ہے۔ کیونکہ خدا اولاد سے پاک ہے لَمْ یَلِدْ وَلَمْ یُوْلَدْ وَلَمْ یَکُنْ لَّہٗ کُفُوًا اَحَدٌ۔ بعض نے کہا ہے کہ اس سے ریاکار مراد ہیں کہ گو وہ خدا پر ایمان رکھتے ہیں لیکن چونکہ عمل خالص خدا کے لئے نہیں کرتے بلکہ دکھاوے کے لئے کرتے ہیں اور دکھاوے کے لئے عمل کرنا داخل شرک ہے اسلئے وہ مشرک ہیں۔ اسی بنا پر شیخ سعدیؒ نے کہا ہے

بیت:۔ کلیدِ درِ دوزخ ست آں نماز ؛ کہ در چشمِ مردم گذاری دراز

مترجم کہتا ہے کہ جو صفات ذاتِ خدا سے مخصوص ہیں انکی نسبت یہ اعتقاد رکھنا کہ وہ کسی اور میں بھی پائی جاتی ہیں۔ یہ بھی شرک ہے اور آج کل کے مسلمان جو خدا کے بھی قائل ہیں اور ساتھ ہی قبر پرستی پیر پرستی اور تعزیہ پرستی بھی کرتے ہیں یعنی ان میں اور اسی طرح کی اور چیزوں میں خدا کے سے تصرفات مانتے ہیں اس آیت کے مصداق ہیں۔ خدائے تعالےٰ مسلمانوں کو اس بات کی توفیق بخشے کہ وہ اسکو اس طرح مانیں اور اسطرح ایمان رکھیں کہ اسمیں شرک کی مطلق آمیزش نہ ہو۔ اُن کا ایمان بے شائبہ شرک ہو اور وہ خالص مومن ہوں ؎

۱۶۱۔ زمین کے گھٹانے سے یہ مراد ہے کہ کفر ملک سے کم ہوتا جاتا اور اسلام پھیلتا جاتا ہے کسی نے کہا کہ دیہات ویران ہوئے جاتے ہیں کسی نے کہا کہ جانیں اور پھل اور میوے ضائع ہو رہے ہیں ؎

۱۶۲۔ جس کے پاس کتاب کا علم ہے اس سے مُراد یا تو عبداللہ بن سلام ہیں جو اہلِ کتاب میں سے تھے اور اُنہوں نے حضرت کی رسالت کی شہادت دی تھی اور اسلام لے آئے تھے چنانچہ وہ اس بات کے قائل بھی تھے کہ یہ آیت انہیں کے حق میں نازل ہوئی ہے یا عام اہلِ کتاب مُراد ہیں جن کو کتبِ سابقہ سے آپ کی شہادت معلوم ہے ؎

۱۶۳۔ پاک بات سے مراد کلمۂ توحید یعنی لَآ اِلٰہَ اِلَّا اللّٰہُ ہے۔ فرمایا کہ کلمۂ توحید کی مثال اس پاکیزہ درخت کی ہے جس کی جڑ زمین میں مضبوط ہو اور اسکی شاخیں بلندی میں آسمان تک پہنچی ہوئی ہوں۔ اور ہر موسم میں پھل دیتا ہو۔ کلمۂ توحید کی جڑ بھی دلوں میں قائم و مستحکم ہوتی ہے۔ اور اسکی شاخیں یعنی عمل آسمان پر چڑھتے رہتے ہیں۔ اور ان کی برکت ہر وقت حاصل ہوتی رہتی ہے ؎

۱۶۴۔ ناپاک بات سے مُراد کلمۂ شرک ہے فرمایا کلمۂ شرک کی مثال ایسے درخت کی ہے جس کی جڑ زمین پر سے اکھڑی گئی ہو اسے ذرا قرار و ثبات نہ ہو یعنی کلمۂ شرک بالکل بے اصل ہوتا ہے نہ اسکے لئے دلیل قوی ہوتی ہے نہ شرک کے کاموں کی قبولیت ہوتی ہے نہ اسمیں خیر و برکت ہوتی ہے ؎

۱۶۵۔ ابن عباسؓ کہتے ہیں کہ دروازوں سے مُراد طبقے ہیں یعنی دوزخ کے نیچے اوپر سات طبقے اور منزلیں ہیں۔ پہلا طبقہ جہنم ہے دوسرا لَظٰی تیسرا حُطَمَہ چوتھا سَعِیْر پانچواں سَقَر چھٹا جَحِیْم ساتواں ھَاوِیَہ قتادہ نے کہا کہ یہ درجے بلحاظ اعمال ہیں۔ مگر اس کا علم خدا ہی کو ہے۔ کہ کس طرح کے عمل اور عقیدے کے لئے کونسا طبقہ ہے ؎

۱۶۶۔ حِجر کے رہنے والوں سے مُراد قوم ثمود ہے حِجر مدینے اور شام کے درمیان ایک بستی تھی۔ قوم ثمود وہاں رہتی تھی ؎

۱۶۷۔ شراب ہم نے سکر کا ترجمہ کیا ہے اہلِ لغت نے لکھا ہے کہ سکر شراب کا نام ہے۔ ابنِ عمرؓ کہتے ہیں کہ سکر بعینہٖ خمر ہے ابنِ مسعودؓ کا بھی یہی قول ہے۔ اس مقام پر یہ ظاہر کرنا ضرور ہے کہ یہ آیت تحریم شراب سے پہلے نازل ہوئی تھی۔ اور دلیل یہ ہے کہ یہ سُورت تین آیتوں کے سوا مکی ہے اور سورۂ مائدہ مدنی ہے۔ جسمیں شراب کی حرمت کا حکم ہے۔

۱۶۸۔ اُونچی اُونچی چھتریوں سے وہ چھتریاں مُراد ہیں جو انگور کی بیل چڑھانے کے لئے ڈالی جاتی ہیں ؎

۱۶۹۔ یہ معراج کی آیت ہے۔ اور علماء کا اس بات پر اجماع ہے کہ بندے سے مُراد اس آیت میں جناب رسالتمآب ہیں۔ اُمت میں سے کسی کا معراج کے بارے میں اختلاف نہیں ہے اسکا ہونا متفق ہے لیکن اس بارے میں اختلاف ہے، کہ وہ جسمانی تھا یا روحانی۔ کوئی کہتا ہے کہ بیداری میں تھا اور جسمانی تھا۔ کوئی کہتا ہے خواب میں تھا اور روحانی تھا۔ کوئی کہتا ہے۔ صرف ایک دفعہ ہوا۔ کوئی کہتا ہے ایک سے زیادہ دفعہ مگر ظاہر قرآنی الفاظ سے پایا جاتا ہے کہ بیداری میں ہوا تھا۔ مسجدِ اقصیٰ سے مُراد بیت المقدس ہے۔ اقصیٰ کے معنی ہیں بہت دُور۔ اس کا نام اقصیٰ اسلئے ہے کہ وہ مسجد الحرام

سے مسافتِ بعیدہ پر واقع ہے کہتے ہیں کہ مسجد اقصیٰ وہی مسجد ہے جو روئے زمین پر کعبے کے بعد بنائی گئی ﴿

۱۷۰- یعنی رنج و تاسف اور ناخوشی کا کلمہ منہ سے نہ نکالنا اور نہ گھڑکنا جھڑکنا اور یہ جو فرمایا کہ بڑھاپے کو پہنچ جائیں تو انکو اُف تک نہ کہنا۔ یہ اس لئے کہ بڑھاپے میں ماں باپ کی چنداں قدر اور پرواہ نہیں کی جاتی ورنہ ان کی عزت و حرمت اور ادب و احترام کرنا خواہ وہ جوان ہوں یا بوڑھے دونوں حالتوں میں فرض ہے۔ انسانیت اور سعادتمندی اسی امر کی مقتضی ہے کہ ماں باپ کو خوش و خرم رکھا جائے اور ان کا ادب کیا جائے۔ وہ شخص نہایت خوش نصیب ہے، جو ماں باپ کی خدمت کرے اور اُن کو خوش رکھے ﴿

۱۷۱- یعنی دینے کو کچھ پاس نہیں ہے اور تہیدستی کے سبب انکی طرف توجہ نہیں کرسکتے اور چاہتے یہ ہو کہ خدا دے تو اُن کو دو تو اس صورت میں انکو نرمی سے سمجھا دیا کرو کہ خدا کے فضل سے مال ہاتھ آتا ہے تو تم کو بھی دیتے ہیں

۱۷۲- تفسیروں میں لکھا ہے کہ یہ لوگ روسا ئے قوم کی اولاد تھے۔ ایک دن کہ روزِ عید تھا وہ باہر میلے میں گئے تو کیا دیکھتے ہیں کہ لوگ بتوں کو پوجتے ہیں اور انکے نام پر جانور ذبح کر رہے ہیں۔ خدا نے اُن کے دل کی آنکھیں نورِ بصیرت سے منور کی تھیں تو انہوں نے لوگوں کی بت پرستی کی حرکت کو ناپسندیدگی کی نظر سے دیکھا اور دل میں کہا کہ یہ باتیں تو خدا ہی کیلئے زیبا ہیں جو آسمان اور زمین کا پیدا کرنے والا ہے پھر یہ اپنی قوم کے لوگوں سے کنارہ کش ہونے لگے چنانچہ سب سے پہلے ان میں سے ایک شخص ایک درخت کے سائے تلے الگ جا بیٹھا دوسرا بھی وہیں آکر بیٹھ گیا پھر تیسرا بھی آن کے پاس آیا اور بیٹھ گیا۔ چوتھا آیا پھر پانچواں یہ اشخاص آپس میں ایک دوسرے سے تعارف نہیں رکھتے تھے۔ اسی وجہ سے اپنے دل کا حال ایک دوسرے سے کہتے ہوئے ڈرتے اور تامل کرتے تھے آخر ایک اُن میں سے بولا کہ صاحبو تم جو اپنے بھائی بندوں سے الگ ہو کر یہاں آ بیٹھے ہو اس کا کوئی نہ کوئی سبب ضرور ہے اور وہ ہر شخص کو سچائی کے ساتھ بیان کر دینا چاہیئے۔ دوسرے نے کہا بھائی سچ تو یہ ہے کہ میں نے یہ خیال کیا۔ کہ جو کام ہماری قوم کے لوگ کر رہے ہیں باطل ہے اور عبادت کا مستحق صرف خدائے واحد ہے جو آسمانوں اور زمین کا خالق ہے۔ تیسرے نے کہا بخدا میرے دل میں بھی یہی خیال پیدا ہوا تھا۔ چوتھے نے کہا کہ میرا بھی یہی حال ہے۔ غرض سب ہم خیال اور ہمصفیر ہو گئے اور اپنا ایک جدا معبد بنا لیا۔ اس میں خدائے واحد کی عبادت کرتے اور پرستشِ اصنام سے مطلق سروکار نہ رکھتے۔ ان کا یہ حال لوگوں کو معلوم ہوا تو انہوں نے بادشاہ سے جا چغلی کھائی۔ بادشاہ بڑا جابر و ظالم اور متعصب تھا لوگوں کو کفر و شرک پر آمادہ کرتا اور ان سے جبراً بت پرستی کراتا بادشاہ نے ان کو بلایا۔ اور دریافت حال کیا۔ انہوں نے سب ماجرا سچ سچ بیان کر دیا بادشاہ نے ان کو ڈرایا دھمکایا اور کچھ مہلت دی۔ کہ خدا پرستی سے باز آئیں مگر خدا پرستی اور توحید ایسی چیز نہیں کہ جب دل میں بیٹھ جائے تو کبھی نکل سکے انہوں نے یہ صلاح کی کہ جب ان لوگوں سے تمہیں کچھ سروکار نہیں رہا تو ان میں رہنا کیا ضرور ہے بہتر یہ ہے کہ غار میں چل رہیں آگے مفصل ذکر متن میں ہے ﴿

۱۷۳- یعنی جو خدا چاہتا ہے وہی ہوتا ہے اور خدا کی مدد کے سوا کسی کی کچھ قوت و قدرت نہیں ﴿

۱۷۴- اصل لفظ فتیٰ ہے جسکے معنی جوان کے ہیں فتیٰ سے یہاں مراد یوشع بن نون ہیں۔ چونکہ وہ موسیٰ علیہ السلام کے ساتھ رہتے اور ان سے علم حاصل کیا کرتے تھے اسلئے ہم نے جوان کی جگہ شاگرد لکھا ہے۔ بعض نے کہا وہ یوشع کے بھائی تھے بعض نے کہا کہ موسیٰ علیہ السلام کا غلام تھا ﴿

۱۷۵- کسی نے موسیٰ علیہ السلام سے پوچھا کہ سب سے زیادہ عالم کون ہے۔ انہوں نے کہا۔ کہ میں ہوں۔ خدا نے وحی کی کہ میرا ایک بندہ مجمع البحرین میں ہے وہ تم سے زیادہ علم رکھتا ہے تو موسیٰ علیہ السلام نے اُن سے ملنے اور علم حاصل کرنے کی غرض سے عزمِ سفر کیا یہ بندے جیسا کہ احادیثِ صحیحہ سے ثابت ہے خضر تھے۔ ان کا نام جیسا کہ صحیح بخاری میں ابو ہریرہؓ سے مروی ہے خضر اسلیئے ہوا کہ وہ ایک خشک گھاس پر بیٹھے تھے اور وہ اُن کے نیچے سرسبز ہو گئی ﴿

۱۷۶- لفظوں کا ترجمہ تو یہ ہے۔ کہ ایک لڑکے سے ملے مگر ایسے موقع پر اسی طرح گفتگو کرتے ہیں جس طرح ہم نے لکھا ہے ﴿

۱۷۷- یعنی چونکہ لڑکا ماں باپ کے طریقے پر نہ ہوتا اور کفر اور سرکشی کرتا اس لئے خضر کو یہ ڈر ہوا کہ جب یہ لڑکا بڑا ہو تو اسکے ماں باپ کہیں اسکی محبت میں اندھے ہو کر کفر اور خدا کی نافرمانی میں مبتلا نہ ہو جائیں اسلئے اسکو مار ڈالا۔ اور یہ مار ڈالنا خدائے تعالےٰ کے حکم سے تھا ۱۲ ﴿

۱۷۸- یعنی بالوں کی سفیدی کے سبب سر آگ کی طرح چمکنے لگا ہے

۱۷۹- میراث کے مالک ہونے سے مراد نبوت کا وارث ہونا ہے نہ مال و دولت کا کیونکہ پیغمبروں کی نظروں میں مال و دولت کچھ چیز نہیں ہوتا جس کے لئے وہ خدا سے وارث مانگیں اُن کے نزدیک جو چیز سب سے بہتر اور قابلِ وراثت ہے وہ خدا کا دین اور بندگانِ خدا کی ہدایت ہے اور پیغمبر سے ہی انہیں کاموں کے لئے خدا سے اولاد مانگنے کی توقع ہونی چاہیئے۔ نیز جیسا کہ حدیث صحیح سے ثابت ہے۔ پیغمبر کا مال خدا کی راہ میں صدقہ ہوتا ہے۔ اس کا کوئی وارث نہیں ہوتا ﴿

۱۸۰- ہارون سے یہاں وہ ہارون مراد نہیں جو حضرت موسیٰ کے بھائی تھے کیونکہ وہ حضرت مریم سے مدتوں پہلے ہو گذرے تھے یعنی بلحاظ قرابت کے وہ ہارون مراد نہیں ہیں بلکہ نیکوکاری اور پرہیزگاری میں مماثلت کے اعتبار سے مراد ہیں۔ یعنی تو ہارون جیسی نیکوکار اور پرہیزگار تھی۔ گویا اُن کی بہن تھی۔ پھر تو نے یہ کام کیا۔ علی بن ابی طلحہ اور سدی نے کہا کہ ہارون کی بہن اسلئے کہا گیا کہ وہ حضرت موسیٰ کے بھائی ہارون کی نسل سے تھیں۔ اور عرب کی عادت ہے

کہ جو شخص جس قوم اور قبیلے کا ہوتا ہے اسکو اس قوم اور قبیلے کا بھائی کہہ کر پکارتے ہیں۔ جیسے تمیمی کو یا اخا تمیم اور مضری یا اخا مضر کہتے ہیں اسی طرح یہاں بھی حضرت مریمؑ کو حضرت ہارون کی بہن کہہ کر پکارا ؁

ایک حدیث میں ہے کہ جب یہ آیت نصاریٰ نجران نے سنی تو کہا کہ ہارون مریم کے بھائی کیونکر ہو سکتے ہیں وہ تو موسیٰ کے بھائی تھے جو صدیوں پہلے ہو چکے تھے آنحضرت صلی اللہ علیہ وسلم نے یہ اعتراض سنا تو فرمایا کہ یہ ہارون برادرِ موسیٰ نہیں ہیں بلکہ اور ہیں۔ بنی اسرائیل اپنے بچوں کے نام پیغمبروں اور بزرگوں کے نام پر رکھ لیا کرتے تھے۔ اسی بنا پر بعض مفسرین نے کہا کہ یہ ہارون مریم علیہا السلام کے سوتیلے بھائی تھے جو نہایت صالح تھے ۱۲

۱۸۱- یعنی نبوت کا درجۂ عالی یا دنیا میں مرتبہ رفیع بخشا تھا یا یہ کہ آسمان کی طرف اٹھا لیا تھا ؁

۱۸۲- یہ فَلْیَمْدُدْ کا ترجمہ ہے فَلْیَمْدُدْ امر کا صیغہ ہے لیکن اس سے خبر مراد ہے اسی لئے اس کا ترجمہ مہلت دیئے جاتا ہے۔ کیا گیا۔ ۱۲

۱۸۳- جب قرآن نازل ہونا شروع ہوا تو جناب رسالتمآب کثرت سے عبادت کرتے اور بہت زحمت اٹھاتے راتوں کو نماز میں کھڑے رہتے اور قرآن شریف پڑھتے رہتے۔ اس سے ایک تو صحت میں خلل واقع ہونے کا خوف ہوتا تھا دوسرے کافروں نے آپ سے کہنا شروع کیا کہ قرآن تو آپکے لئے سخت تکلیف کا موجب ہو گیا تب آیت نازل ہوئی کہ خدا تعالٰے نے آپ کو ایسی مشقت اٹھانے سے منع فرمایا ۱۲

۱۸۴- یعنی بنی اسرائیل کو گمراہ کرنے کے سبب خدائے تعالٰے نے اسکو یہ سزا دی کہ تمام عمر سب سے الگ رہا۔ اسکی یہ کیفیت تھی کہ اگر وہ کسی کو ہاتھ لگاتا یا کوئی اسکو ہاتھ لگاتا تو دونوں کو تپ آجاتی اسلئے وہ یہی کہتا رہا کہ کوئی مجھے چھوئے نہیں۔ یہ دنیا کا عذاب تھا اور آخرت کا عذاب الگ رہا ۱۲

۱۸۵- یعنی یہ محمد پیغمبر تو ہیں نہیں تمہارے جیسے ایک آدمی ہیں اور جو یہ قرآن سناتے ہیں وہ جادو ہے جسکو سنکر آدمی اسکی طرف مائل ہو جاتا ہے تو تم دیدہ و دانستہ اسکو کیوں سنتے اور جادو میں کیوں پھنستے ہو ۱۲

۱۸۶- بَلْ هُوَ شَاعِرٌ کا ترجمہ تو یہ ہے "بلکہ یہ شاعر ہے" مگر چونکہ یہاں قرآن مجید کا ذکر ہے کہ کفار اسکو پریشان خواب یا پریشان خیالات یا اپنے دل کی بنائی ہوئی باتیں یا شعر کہتے ہیں اسلئے ترجمہ میں خطوط وحدانی کے اندر کے الفاظ زیادہ کرنے پڑے اور اگر انکو حذف کر دیا جائے تو الفاظ قرآنی کا ترجمہ باقی رہ جاتا ہے۔ یعنی "بلکہ یہ شاعر ہے" اس صورت میں مراد حضرت رسول اللہ صلی اللہ علیہ وسلم ہونگے ۱۲

۱۸۷- کافر کہتے تھے کہ جب محمد رحلت کر جائینگے تو اسلام کا زور بھی مٹ جائیگا۔ اور یہ سب ترک و احتشام جاتا رہے گا جس قدر یہ دھوم دھام ہے انہی کے دم سے ہے۔ خدا نے فرمایا کہ یہ لوگ تمہاری موت کا انتظار کرتے ہیں لیکن تم انتقال کر جاؤ گے تو یہ بھی ہمیشہ نہیں رہینگے۔ موت ان کو بھی فنا کر دے گی اور تمہارے انتقال سے اسلام کیوں نابود ہونے لگا۔ وہ تمہاری ذات سے وابستہ نہیں ہے کہ جب تک تمہاری حیات ہو تب تک اسکی ہستی ہو، وہ ہمیشہ رہے گا اور کبھی فنا نہیں ہوگا اور حقیقت میں اسلام آنحضرت کے انتقال کے بعد گھٹا نہیں بلکہ روز بروز بڑھتا گیا اور تمام عالم میں پھیل گیا اور قیامت تک قائم رہے گا ؁

۱۸۸- حضرت ابن عباس سے روایت ہے کہ حضرت داؤد علیہ السلام نے یہ فیصلہ کیا کہ بکریاں کھیتی والوں کو دلوا دیں۔ حضرت سلیمان علیہ السلام کو چرواہوں سے یہ حال معلوم ہوا تو انہوں نے کہا اگر میں تمہارا مقدمہ فیصل کرنے والا ہوتا تو کچھ اور فیصلہ کرتا۔ یہ خبر حضرت داؤد علیہ السلام کو ہوئی تو انہوں نے حضرت سلیمان کو بلا کر کہا کہ تم اس مقدمے کا کیا فیصلہ کرتے ہو۔ انہوں نے کہا کہ میرا فیصلہ یہ ہے کہ کھیتی والوں کو بکریاں دلائی جائیں۔ کہ انکے دودھ وغیرہ سے فائدہ اٹھائیں اور بکریوں کے مالک کھیتی میں تخم ریزی اور کاشت کریں۔ جب کھیتی اس حالت میں ہو جائے جس حالت میں پہلے تھی تو اسکو کھیتی والے لے لیں اور بکریاں ان کے مالکوں کو واپس کر دی جائیں ؁

۱۸۹- رجوع نہ کرنے کے دو معنی ہو سکتے ہیں۔ ایک تو یہ کہ قیامت سے پہلے دنیا کی طرف رجوع نہ کرینگے دوسرے یہ کہ خدا کی طرف رجوع یعنی توبہ نہ کرینگے ؁

۱۹۰- یہ ترجمہ ہم نے لِتَبْلُغُوْٓا اَشُدَّكُمْ کا کیا ہے اسی طرح اس آیت میں لِكَيْلَا يَعْلَمَ مِنْۢ بَعْدِ عِلْمٍ شَيْـًٔا کا یوں ترجمہ کیا ہے کہ بہت کچھ جاننے کے بعد بالکل بے علم ہو جاتے ہیں۔ کیونکہ ان آیات میں انسان کی حالت کا اظہار فرمایا ہے کہ پہلے تم بچے ہوتے ہو۔ پھر جوان ہو جاتے ہو پھر بڈھے اور بعض ایسے بڈھے ہو جاتے ہیں کہ حواس قائم نہیں رہتے اور دل و دماغ میں جو ذخیرہ معلومات ہوتا ہے سب جاتا رہتا ہے ۱۲ ؁

۱۹۱- ادب کی چیزیں جو خدا کے نام سے نامزد کی جاتی ہیں ۱۲ ؁

۱۹۲- خلاصہ سلالہ کا ترجمہ ہے سلالہ اسکو کہتے ہیں جو کسی چیز کے صاف اور خالص نے سے اس میں سے نکال لیتے ہیں اور وہی خلاصہ ہے اور اسی کو ست کہتے ہیں ؁

۱۹۳- یعنی وہ بھی بدکار یا مشرک مرد کے سوا اور سے تعلق زوجیت پیدا نہیں کرتی ۱۲

۱۹۴- آیت اِنَّ الَّذِيْنَ جَآءُوْ بِالْاِفْكِ سے لیکر یہاں تک دس آیتیں ام المومنین حضرت عائشہ رضی اللہ عنہا کی شان میں نازل ہوئی ہیں۔ ان میں خدا تعالٰے نے ان کی اس تہمت سے برارت ظاہر فرمائی ہے جو منافقوں نے انکی نسبت تراشی تھی۔ اور جسکو زیادہ تر عبداللہ بن ابی ابن سلول راس المنافقین نے مشہور کیا تھا اور جس کا تذکرہ مسلمانوں میں بھی ہوا۔ اس اجمال کی تفصیل جیسا کہ حدیثوں میں آیا ہے اور جیسا کہ خود حضرت عائشہ بیان فرماتی ہیں یہ ہے کہ جناب رسالتمآب کی عادت یہ تھی کہ جب آپ کسی سفر کو تشریف لیجانے کا ارادہ فرماتے تو اپنی بیبیوں میں قرعہ ڈالتے جس بی بی کے نام کا قرعہ نکلتا اسکو آپ اپنے ہمراہ لے جاتے۔ ایک غزوے میں میرے نام کا قرعہ نکلا اور میں آپکے ساتھ گئی۔ اور یہ سفر پردے کے حکم کے نازل ہونے کے بعد تھا میں اونٹ پر سواری کرتی اور ہودج یعنی کجاوے میں بیٹھتی تھی۔ جب آپ غزوہ سے فارغ ہو چکے۔ اور لوٹتے ہوئے مدینے کے قریب پہنچے تو ایک رات

کوچ کا اعلان کیا گیا میں اسوقت قضائے حاجت کو چلی۔ یہاں تک کہ لشکر کے آگے بڑھ گئی جب اپنی فرودگاہ کو واپس آئی تو دیکھا کہ میرا منکوں کا ہار کہیں رستے میں ٹوٹ کر گر گیا ہے۔ میں ہار کی تلاش کیلیے لوٹ گئی اور اسکو تلاش کرتے کرتے مجھے دیر ہو گئی اتنے میں وہ لوگ آگئے جو میرے ہودج کو کسا کرتے تھے اور انہوں نے میرے ہودج کو اٹھا لیا اور اسکو میرے اونٹ پر کس دیا۔ چونکہ عورتیں اس زمانے میں دبلی پتلی ہوتی تھیں اور انکے سوار ہونے سے ہودج کچھ بھاری نہیں ہو جاتا تھا اسلئے انہوں نے ہودج کے ہلکے پن کا کچھ خیال نہ کیا۔ اور یہ نہ سمجھا کہ میں اس میں نہیں ہوں غرض وہ اونٹ کو لیکر چل دیئے مجھکو اپنا ہار اسوقت دستیاب ہوا جب لشکر گزر گیا میں لشکر کی فرودگاہ میں آئی حالانکہ وہاں کوئی نہ تھا۔ پھر اپنی منزل کو جہاں اتری ہوئی تھی چلی گئی۔ اس خیال سے کہ جب لوگ مجھے گم پائینگے تو آکر لے جائینگے۔ اسی اثنا میں مجھے نیند آگئی اور میں وہیں سو گئی۔ ادھر صفوان بن معطل جو آخر شب کو لشکر کے پیچھے آرام لینے کے لئے اتر پڑا تھا صبح کے قریب چلا۔ جب میری منزل کے قریب پہنچا تو میری نسبت خیال کیا کہ کوئی آدمی سو رہا ہے۔ وہ میرے پاس آیا اور اسنے مجھے دیکھ کر پہچان لیا۔ کیونکہ پردے کے حکم سے پہلے وہ مجھ کو دیکھ چکا تھا۔ میں نے چادر سے گھونگٹ نکال لیا اور میں خدا کی قسم کھا کر کہتی ہوں کہ نہ تو اسنے مجھ سے کوئی بات کی نہ میں نے اس سے کوئی بات سنی۔ بجز اِنَّا لِلّٰہِ وَاِنَّا اِلَیْہِ رَاجِعُوْنَ کے جو اسنے سواری کے بٹھاتے وقت کہا تھا پھر اسنے سواری کا اگلا پاؤں دبایا تو میں اسپر سوار ہو گئی اور وہ میری سواری کی باگ ہاتھ میں لے کر چلا یہاں تک کہ ہم لشکر میں جا پہنچے اور اسوقت ٹھیک دوپہر تھی۔ پھر میرے بارے میں جو افترا پردازی کی گئی سو کی گئی اور جو ہلاک ہوا سو ہوا۔ اس طوفان اٹھانے میں جس نے سب سے بڑا حصہ لیا وہ عبداللہ بن ابی بن سلول تھا اسکے بعد ہم مدینے آئے اور وہاں آکر میں مہینہ بھر بیمار رہی لوگ میرے بارے میں تذکرے کرتے تھے لیکن مجھ کو کچھ خبر نہ تھی۔ البتہ مجھے ایک بات سے شک ہوتا تھا کہ جناب رسولِ خدا صلی اللہ علیہ وسلم مجھ پر وہ لطف و التفات نہیں فرماتے تھے جو پیشتر میرے ایام علالت میں فرمایا کرتے تھے۔ اب جو تشریف لاتے تو سلام کرنے کے بعد صرف اتنا پوچھتے کہ تمہارا حال کیسا ہے اس سے مجھے ایک طرح کا شبہ تو ہوتا لیکن افترا پردازوں کے بہتان و شرارت کی مطلق خبر نہ تھی اس حالت میں میں بہت نقیہ ہو گئی۔ ایک رات جو قضائے حاجت کیلئے باہر نکلی تو مسطح کی ماں میرے ساتھ تھی۔ اتفاق سے اس کا پاؤں لڑکھڑایا تو اسنے کہا تعس مسطح یعنی مسطح ہلاک ہو میں نے کہا کہ تم ایسے شخص کو بددعا دیتی ہو جو بدر میں شریک ہوا۔ اس نے کہا کیا تم نے سنا کہ اسنے کیا افترا پردازی کی ہے؛ میں نے کہا نہیں۔ تم بتاؤ کہ اسنے کیا کہا ہے تو اسنے تمام ماجرا بیان کیا۔ اسکو سنکر مجھے بہت رنج ہوا۔ ایک تو میں پہلے ہی بیمار تھی۔ یہ کیفیت سنکر رنج پر رنج ہوا۔ جب میں لوٹ کر اپنے گھر آئی تو جناب رسول خدا صلی اللہ علیہ وسلم تشریف لائے اور میرا حال پوچھا میں نے کہا اگر آپ اجازت بخشیں تو میں اپنے میکے چلی جاؤں میرا مطلب یہ تھا کہ وہاں جا کر اس خبر کی نسبت یقین حاصل کروں آپ نے اجازت دے دی اور میں اپنے والدین کے ہاں چلی گئی وہاں میں نے اپنی والدہ سے پوچھا کہ لوگ کیا تذکرہ کرتے ہیں انہوں نے کہا کہ بیٹا کوئی ایسی بڑی بات نہیں ہے تم کچھ خیال نہ کرو۔ اس جواب سے میرا دل مطمئن نہ ہوا اور میں رات بھر روتی رہی۔ ادھر جناب رسولِ خدا صلی اللہ علیہ وسلم پر وحی آنے میں بہت دیر ہو گئی۔ تو آپ نے مشورہ لینے کے لئے حضرت علی بن ابی طالب اور اسامہ بن زید رضی اللہ عنہما کو بلایا۔ اسامہ نے تو یہ کہا کہ یا رسول اللہ وہ آپکی بی بی ہیں اور ہم کو انکے بارے میں بھلائی کے سوا کچھ معلوم نہیں۔ رہے علی بن ابی طالب انہوں نے کہا یا رسول اللہ خدا نے آپ پر تنگی نہیں کی۔ عورتیں اور بہت ہیں۔ اگر آپ لونڈی یعنی بریرہ سے دریافت فرمائینگے تو وہ سچ سچ بیان کر دے گی۔ آپ نے بریرہ کو بلا کر دریافت کیا تو اسنے کہا کہ قسم ہے اس ذات کی جس نے آپ کو حق دے کر بھیجا ہے میں نے کوئی ایسی بات نہیں دیکھی کہ اسکا اسپر عیب لگاؤں وہ تو ایک سیدھی سادی اور بھولی بھالی نو عمر لڑکی ہے۔ یہ سنکر آپ اسی روز خطبہ پڑھنے کو کھڑے ہوئے اور فرمایا کہ اس شخص کے مقابلے میں جسکے سبب مجھے میرے اہل کے معاملے میں اس قدر ایذا پہنچی ہے کون میری مدد کرتا ہے تو سعد بن معاذ انصاری کھڑے ہوئے اور عرض کیا یا رسول اللہ میں آپ کی مدد کرتا ہوں اگر وہ شخص قبیلہ اوس سے ہے تو ہم اسکی گردن مار دینگے اور اگر ہمارے بھائیوں یعنی قبیلہ خزرج سے ہے تو آپ جو ارشاد فرمائینگے ہم اسکی تعمیل کرینگے۔ پھر سعد بن عبادہ کھڑے ہوئے یہ قبیلہ خزرج کے سردار تھے، تھے تو نیک آدمی۔ لیکن حمیت نے جوش مارا تو سعد بن معاذ سے کہنے لگے۔ کہ تم نے غلط کہا۔ خدا کی قسم نہ تم اسکو قتل کرو گے اور نہ اسکے قتل پر قادر ہو سکو گے۔ اگر وہ شخص تمہاری جماعت سے ہے تو میں بھی پسند نہیں کرتا کہ قتل کیا جائے تو اسید بن حضیر جو سعد بن معاذ کے چچا زاد بھائی ہیں کھڑے ہوئے اور سعد بن عبادہ سے کہنے لگے کہ تم نے جھوٹ کہا۔ خدا کی قسم ہم اسکو ضرور قتل کر ڈالینگے تم منافق ہو کر منافقوں کی طرف سے جھگڑتے ہو پھر دونوں قبیلے اوس اور خزرج مارے غصے کے کھڑے ہو گئے۔ اور قریب تھا کہ ان میں لڑائی اور ہاتھا پائی ہو جائے مگر جناب رسالتمآب نے ان کے جوش کو فرو کر دیا۔ اور لڑائی ہونے سے رہ گئی۔ ہاں تو میرے رونے کا یہ حال تھا کہ میرے والدین خیال کرتے تھے کہ رونا میرے کلیجے کو پھاڑ کر رہے گا اسی اثنا میں ایک دن جو دونوں میرے پاس بیٹھے تھے اور میں رو رہی تھی کہ انصار کی ایک عورت میرے پاس آئی اور وہ بھی بیٹھ کر میرے ساتھ رونے لگی۔ ابھی ہم رو ہی رہے تھے کہ رسولِ خدا تشریف لائے اور سلام کر کے بیٹھ گئے۔ جب سے لوگوں نے میرے بارے میں وہ کہا جو کہا آپ میرے پاس نہیں بیٹھتے تھے۔ اور آپ پر میری شان میں کچھ وحی نہیں ہوئی تھی جب آپ بیٹھ گئے تو خطبہ پڑھا اور فرمایا اے عائشہ تمہارے بارے میں ایسی بات مجھ تک پہنچی ہے اگر تم بری ہو تو عنقریب خدا تمہاری برأت ظاہر کر دے گا اور اگر تم سے گناہ ہوا ہے تو خدا سے بخشش مانگو اور اسکی طرف رجوع ہو کیونکہ بندہ جس وقت اپنے گناہ کا اقرار کر کے اور

توبہ کرلیتا ہے تو خدا بھی اس پر رجوع فرماتا اور اسکی توبہ قبول کرلیتا ہے جب آپ بات ختم کرچکے تو میرے آنسو تھم گئے یہاں تک کہ ایک قطرہ بھی آنکھ سے نہیں نکلتا تھا پھر میں نے اپنے والد سے کہا کہ آپ میری طرف سے رسول اللہ صلی اللہ علیہ وسلم کو جواب دیجئے انہوں نے کہا میں نہیں جانتا کہ رسول اللہ صلی اللہ علیہ وسلم سے کیا کہوں پھر میں نے اپنی والدہ سے کہا کہ آپ جواب دیجئے۔ انہوں نے بھی یہی کہا کہ بخدا میں نہیں جانتی کہ رسول اللہ صلی اللہ علیہ وسلم سے کیا کہوں پھر میں نے خود ہی کہا۔ حالانکہ میں ایک نو عمر لڑکی تھی اور قرآن بھی بہت سا نہیں پڑھا تھا کہ جو قصہ آپنے سُنا ہے وہ مجھے معلوم ہوگیا ہے اور یہ بھی کہ آپ اسکو باور کرچکے ہیں لیکن اگر میں کہوں کہ میں بَری ہوں اور خدا خوب جانتا ہے کہ میں بَری ہوں تو آپ اسکو سچ نہیں سمجھیں گے اور اگر اسکا اقرار کرلوں۔ حالانکہ خدا جانتا ہے کہ میں اس سے بری ہوں تو آپ اسکو مان لینگے سو خدا کی قسم میں وہی بات کہتی ہوں جو یوسفؑ کے باپ نے کہی تھی کہ فَصَبْرٌ جَمِيلٌ وَاللّٰهُ الْمُسْتَعَانُ عَلٰى مَا تَصِفُوْنَ پھر میں وہاں سے اُٹھ کر اپنے بستر پر آلیٹی۔ اور میں یقین کرتی تھی کہ چونکہ میں بری ہوں اسلیئے خدا ضرور میری برات ظاہر فرمائے گا۔ لیکن میں یہ خیال نہیں کرتی تھی کہ میری شان میں قرآن کی آیتیں نازل ہونگی۔ کیونکہ میں اپنی شان کو اس سے کمتر سمجھتی تھی کہ خدا میرے بارے میں اپنا کلام نازل فرمائے گا جو ہمیشہ پڑھا جائے گا۔ البتہ یہ امید ظاہر کرتی تھی کہ رسول اللہ صلی اللہ علیہ وسلم کوئی خواب دیکھ لینگے جس میں خدا میری برات ظاہر فرمائے گا سو خدا کی قسم ابھی رسول اللہ صلعم اس مجلس سے تشریف بھی نہیں لیجانے پائے تھے کہ خدا نے آپ پر قرآن نازل فرمایا اور نزولِ وحی کے وقت جس طرح آپ پسینہ پسینہ ہو جاتے تھے۔ اسی طرح اسوقت آپکے بدن اطہر سے موتیوں کی طرح پسینے کے قطرے ٹپکنے لگے جب وہ حالت رفع ہوگئی تو آپکا چہرہ ہشاش بشاش ہوگیا اور پہلا فقرہ جو آپ کی زبانِ مبارک سے نکلا یہ تھا کہ اے عائشہ رضہ خوش ہو جاؤ خدا نے تمہاری برات نازل فرمائی ہے۔ جب خدا نے حضرت عائشہ کی برات میں اِنَّ الَّذِيْنَ جَآءُوْ بِالْاِفْكِ عُصْبَةٌ مِّنْكُمْ سے دس آیتیں نازل کیں تو حضرت ابو بکر رضہ نے کہا کہ واللہ میں آئندہ مسطح کو کچھ خرچ نہیں دوں گا۔ مسطح حضرت ابو بکر کے عزیزوں میں تھے اور تھے غریب۔ حضرت ابو بکر رضہ خرچ سے اُنکی مدد کیا کرتے تھے لیکن اتفاق سے اس بہتان کے تذکرے میں وہ بھی شریک ہوگئے تھے۔ جب حضرت ابو بکر رضہ نے قسم کھائی کہ وہ مسطح کو خرچ نہیں دینگے تو خدا نے آیت وَلَا يَاْتَلِ اُولُوا الْفَضْلِ مِنْكُمْ نازل فرمائی اس پر حضرت ابو بکر رضہ نے بدستور خرچ دینا جاری کردیا اور کہنے لگے کہ واللہ میں اسکو خرچ دینے سے کبھی دست کشی نہ کروں گا ؛

۱۹۵- كَتَبَ الْكِتَابَ کے معنی فرج جمع کرنے کے ہیں کاتب کو کاتب بھی اسی مناسبت سے کہا جاتا ہے کہ وہ مختلف حروف کو جوڑ دیتا اور جمع کردیتا ہے۔ حضور چونکہ اُمّی تھے اسلیئے یہاں اکتتاب کے معنی لغوی اعتبار سے جمع کرنے کے کیئے گئے ہیں تاکہ آیات میں تعارض نہ رہے ۱۲ ؛

۱۹۶- یعنی خدا تم سے پناہ میں رکھے اہلِ عرب کی عادت ہے کہ جب اُن میں کسی پر کوئی سختی اور آفت و بلا نازل ہوتی ہے تو کہتے ہیں حِجْرًا مَّحْجُوْرًا جیسے ہم کہتے ہیں کہ خدا کی پناہ ۱۲ ؛

۱۹۷- یعنی آسمان کے پھٹنے کے ساتھ وہ بدلی بھی پھٹ جائے گی جو آسمان اور لوگوں کے درمیان ہے۔ بعض نے کہا آسمان پھٹ جائے گا اس حال میں کہ اس پر ابر ہوگا۔ بعض نے کہا کہ آسمان ابر کے سبب پھٹ جائے گا۔ یعنی بدلی نمودار ہوگی اور اسکی وجہ سے آسمان پھٹ جائے گا ۱۲ ؛

۱۹۸- جنابِ رسالتمآب قیامت کے روز خدا سے شکایت کرینگے کہ میرے پروردگار میری قوم نے قرآن کو چھوڑ دیا۔ چھوڑ دینے کی کئی صورتیں ہیں۔ اسکو نہ ماننا۔ اور اس پر ایمان نہ لانا بھی چھوڑ دینا ہے۔ اسمیں غور نہ کرنا اور سوچ سمجھ کر نہ پڑھنا بھی چھوڑ دینا ہے۔ اسکے اوامر کا بجا نہ لانا اور منہیات سے اجتناب نہ کرنا بھی چھوڑ دینا ہے۔ قرآن کی پروا نہ کرکے دوسری چیزوں جیسے بیہودہ ناولوں۔ دیوانوں۔ لغو باتوں کھیل تماشوں۔ راگ و رنگ میں مصروف ہونا بھی چھوڑ دینا ہے افسوس ہے کہ آج کل کے مسلمان قرآن کی طرف سے نہایت غافل ہو رہے ہیں اسکے پڑھنے سوچنے سمجھنے اور ہدایات سے مستفید ہونے کی طرف توجہ نہیں کرتے۔ اور یہ کھلم کھلا ترکِ قرآنِ مجید ہے۔ خدا تعالےٰ ان کو اسطرف راغب اور اسکی تلاوت میں شاغل ہونے کی توفیق بخشے۔ تاکہ وہ اس پر عمل کریں اور ان کو فلاح کونین حاصل ہو ۱۲ ؛

۱۹۹- یعنی کسی کا باپ کسی کا بیٹا کسی کا خسر کسی کا داماد بنا دیا ۱۲ ؛

۲۰۰- جانشین کے یہ معنی کہ وہ جاتی ہے تو یہ آتا ہے اور یہ جاتا ہے تو وہ آتی ہے ۱۲ ؛

۲۰۱- گو موسیٰ علیہ السلام کے ساتھ فرعون نے سلوک کیا اور اُنکو اچھی طرح اور ایک مدت تک پرورش کیا۔ مگر موسیٰ علیہ السلام نے اپنی نسبت اپنی قوم کا زیادہ خیال کیا جسے اس ظالم نے نہایت ذلت کی حالت میں رکھا تھا اور عالی خیال اور نیک دل لوگ اپنی ذات کی نسبت ہمیشہ اپنی قوم کی بھلائی کو مقدم سمجھا کرتے ہیں اسلیئے اُنہوں نے فرعون کا احسان سُنکر یہ جواب دیا کہ بھلا آپکا مجھ پر یہی احسان ہے کہ آپنے میری قوم کو غلام بنا رکھا اور ذلت اور مصیبت میں پھنسا رکھا ہے احسان تو تب تھا جب میری قوم کے ساتھ بھی سلوک کیا جاتا ۱۲ ؛

۲۰۲- یعنی ایک داہنی طرف سے اور دوسرا بائیں طرف سے ۱۲ ؛

۲۰۳- دوسروں سے مُراد فرعون اور اسکے اتباع ہیں ۱۲ ؛

۲۰۴- کھلا فیصلہ کردینے سے یہ مُراد ہے کہ اُن کفار پر اپنا عذاب نازل کر ۱۲ ؛

۲۰۵- یعنی اگلے لوگ بھی اسی طرح بہشت کی نعمتوں کی تعریفیں کیا کرتے تھے۔ اور دوزخ کے عذاب سے ڈرایا کرتے تھے ۱۲ ؛

۲۰۶- یعنی قیام سے رکوع میں جانے اور رکوع سے سجدے میں جانے کو بھی دیکھتا ہے ۱۲ ؛

۲۰۷- ان آیتوں میں شاعروں کی مذمت بیان فرمائی گئی ہے لیکن قابلِ مذمت وہی شاعر ہیں جو بُرے اور ناپاک شعر کہتے ہیں اور جو ایسے شعر کہیں جن میں خدا کی تعریف ہو یا جن سے اسکے دین کی مدد اور نصرت ہو وہ قابلِ تحسین اور مستحقِ ثواب ہیں ۱۲ ؛

۲۰۸ - یعنی اگر کسی نے اسکی ہجو کہی ہو۔ اور وہ بھی اس کی ہجو کہہ کر اس سے بدلہ لے تو یہ جائز ہے ۱۲ ÷

۲۰۹ - لفظوں کا ترجمہ ہے سلیمانؑ کے ساتھ مگر یہاں مُراد ہے سلیمان کے ہاتھ پر اس لئے ہم نے یہی ترجمہ کیا ہے ۱۲ ÷

۲۱۰ - حضرت صالح علیہ السلام ان لوگوں کو خدا پر ایمان لانے کے لئے کہتے تھے کہ ایمان لاؤ گے تو تمہارا بھلا ہوگا۔ ورنہ تم پر عذاب نازل ہوگا۔ وہ لوگ نہ ایمان لاتے تھے نہ بھلائی کے لئے کوشش کرتے تھے۔ بلکہ یہ کہتے تھے کہ وہ عذاب جس سے تم ہم کو ڈراتے ہو جلدی نازل کراؤ۔ صالح علیہ السلام نے کہا تم عذاب کے لئے کیوں جلدی مچاتے ہو۔ خدا سے بخشش مانگو تاکہ بجائے عذاب کے تم پر خدا کی رحمت نازل ہو ۱۲ ÷

۲۱۱ - یعنی آخرت کے بارے میں ان کا علم کچھ بھی نہیں ہے اور اسکا خاتمہ ہوگیا ہے ۱۲ ÷

۲۱۲ - کہتے ہیں کہ جس شخص کو حضرت موسیٰ نے مُکا مارا تھا وہ فرعون کا باورچی تھا۔ اور وہ حضرت موسیٰ کے ہم قوم شخص کو بیگار کے لئے مجبور کر رہا تھا۔ جب اس نے موسیٰ علیہ السلام کو دیکھا تو اُن سے مدد کا خواستگار ہوا۔ موسیٰ علیہ السلام نے اس مظلوم کو ظالم کے ہاتھ سے بچانے کی نیت سے اس قبطی کو مُکا مارا اور وہ مر کر رہ گیا۔ یہ قتل اگرچہ عمداً نہ تھا۔ بلکہ محض اتفاقی تھا تاہم موسیٰ علیہ السلام اس فعل پر نادم ہوئے اور اپنی شان کے لحاظ سے اسکو خطا تصور کر کے خدا سے مغفرت کے خواہاں ہوئے ÷

۲۱۳ - حضرت موسیٰ کی زبان میں چونکہ لکنت تھی اور ان کو خیال تھا کہ وہ لکنت کے سبب تقریر صاف نہ کر سکیں گے۔ اسلئے خدا سے التجا کی کہ میرے بھائی ہارون کو جن کی زبان صاف ہے میرے ساتھ میرا مددگار یعنی اپنا پیغمبر بنا کر بھیج۔ تاکہ ان دلائل کو جو میں زبان کی لکنت کی وجہ سے اچھی طرح بیان نہ کر سکوں۔ وہ اپنی فصاحت سے بخوبی بیان کر سکیں۔ اور ان لوگوں کے ذہن نشین کر دیں ۱۲ ÷

۲۱۴ - باتیں قول کا ترجمہ ہے اور اس سے مُراد قرآن مجید کی آیتیں ہیں جو ایک دوسرے کے بعد متواتر آتی رہیں ۱۲ ÷

۲۱۵ - یعنی جب تک حجت پوری نہ ہو جائے۔ اور وہ لوگ تکذیب کریں تب تک خدا اُن پر عذاب نازل نہیں کرتا ۱۲ ÷

۲۱۶ - لفظوں کا ترجمہ تو یہ ہے کہ اس روز اُن پر خبریں اندھی ہو جائیں گی اور چونکہ اس طرز کلام میں مبالغہ مقصود ہے اور اصل کلام فَعَمِيَتْ عَلَيْهِمُ الْأَنْبَاءُ ہے اسلئے ہم نے اُردو زبان کے محاورے کو مدِ نظر رکھ کر اصل کلام کا ترجمہ کر دیا ۱۲ ÷

۲۱۷ - یعنی دُنیا میں نیک عمل کیجئے کہ آخرت میں یہی ساتھ جائینگے ۱۲ ÷

۲۱۸ - یعنی گناہگاروں سے پوچھ کر اُنکو سزا نہیں دی جائے گی بلکہ جب اُنکو عذاب کا ہونا ضرور ہے تو نہ پوچھنے کی ضرورت ہے نہ اُنکو چون و چرا کرنے کی مقدرت ۱۲ ÷

۲۱۹ - بازگشت کی جگہ سے یا تو قیامت مُراد ہے یا بہشت ۱۲ ÷

۲۲۰ - ان آیات میں رُومیوں کے غالب ہونے کی پیشینگوئی تھی جو وقوع میں آچکی واقعہ یہ ہوا کہ رُوم اور فارس والوں میں جنگ ہوگئی اور فارس والے غالب آئے چونکہ رُومی اہلِ کتاب یعنی نصاریٰ تھے اور فارس والے مشرک اسلئے مکے کے مشرک مومنوں سے کہتے تھے کہ جس طرح فارس والے جو ہماری طرح مشرک ہیں رُومیوں پر جو تمہاری طرح اہلِ کتاب ہیں غالب ہو گئے ہیں۔ اسی طرح جب ہم میں تم میں جنگ ہوگی تو ہم بھی تم پر غالب ہوں گے کفار کی اس بات سے مومنوں کو رنج ہوا تب یہ آیتیں نازل ہوئیں۔ ان میں چند سال میں رُومیوں کے غالب ہو جانے کی خبر دی گئی تھی۔ اور وہ بالکل صحیح نکلی۔ آیت میں بِضْعِ سِنِيْنَ کا لفظ آیا ہے بِضْعِ کہتے ہیں۔ تین سے نو تک کو۔ ساتویں سال پھر رُوم اور فارس میں لڑائی ہوئی تو رُومی اہلِ فارس پر غالب آئے خدائے تعالےٰ کی قدرت کو دیکھئے کہ اِدھر تو بدر کی لڑائی میں مسلمان مکے کے کافروں پر غالب آئے اُدھر اسی روز رُومی اہلِ فارس پر غالب آئے اس سے مسلمانوں کو دوہری خوشی ہوئی۔ کیونکہ خدا کا وعدہ سچا نکلا۔ اور وہ اصدق الصادقین جو وعدہ کرتا ہے اسکو سچ کر دکھاتا ہے ۱۲ ÷

۲۲۱ - فطرت سے مُراد خدا تعالےٰ کی توحید ہے یعنی اسکو ایک ایک کر کے سمجھنا اور اسکے ساتھ کسی کو شریک نہ بنانا یہ توحید ہی خدا کا دین ہے اور اسی توحید کو خدا نے انسان کی فطرت میں داخل کیا ہے۔ اگر کسی شخص کو پیدا ہوتے ہی اسکی حالت پر چھوڑ دیا جائے اور شرک کرنے والے اسکے دل میں شرک کا نہ خیالات نہ ڈالیں تو وہ کبھی شرک نہیں کرے گا۔ وہ توحید پر پیدا ہوا ہے۔ یہودی ہوگا نہ عیسائی نہ آتش پرست نہ آفتاب پرست نہ بُت پرست بلکہ خالص موحد ہوگا اور توحید کے سوا کچھ نہ جانے گا۔ چونکہ توحید خدا کی طرف سے فطرتِ انسانی میں داخل کی گئی ہے اسلئے اسکو فطرت اللہ کے لفظ سے تعبیر فرمایا ہے اور حکم دیا ہے کہ توحید کو جو خدا تعالےٰ کا دین قیم ہے اختیار کئے رہو اس میں ہرگز تغیر و تبدل نہ ہونے پائے ۱۲ ÷

۲۲۲ - یعنی تم مُوسیٰ سے ضرور ملو گے چنانچہ آپ معراج کی رات آسمان پر حضرت موسیٰؑ سے ملے جیساکہ حدیث میں ہے ۱۲ ÷

۲۲۳ - یعنی نہ بیوی ماں کہہ دینے سے ماں ہو جاتی ہے نہ متبنےٰ اصلی بیٹے کے حکم میں ہوتا ہے ۱۲ ÷

۲۲۴ - اس آیت میں جن میاں بیوی کا ذکر ہے۔ وہ زیدؓ اور زینبؓ ہیں چنانچہ زیدؓ کا نام اگلی آیت میں صراحتاً مذکور ہے۔ دونوں آیتوں میں جس واقعہ کی طرف اشارہ ہے وہ اس طرح پر ہے کہ زینبؓ جناب رسول خدا صلی اللہ علیہ وسلم کی پھوپھی کی بیٹی تھیں اور ظاہر ہے کہ ایک اعلیٰ خاندان کی لڑکی تھیں زید بھی ایک شریف عرب تھے جو بچپن میں پکڑے گئے تھے اور جوانی کے قریب بحالت غلامی مکے میں آکر فروخت ہوئے آنحضرت نے ان کو خرید لیا اور آزاد کر کے اپنے ہاں رکھا۔ زیدؓ میں بجز اسکے کہ ان پر غلام آزاد کا لفظ بولا جاتا ہو اور کوئی بُرائی نہ تھی اور وہ آنحضرتؐ کی نگاہ میں بہت عزت رکھتے تھے یہاں تک کہ آپ نے ان کو متبنےٰ کر لیا۔ آپ جانتے تھے کہ غلام ہو کر فروخت ہونے سے اصلی شرافت میں فرق نہیں آسکتا ع
ہزار بار جو یوسف بکے غلام نہیں۔ تو آپ نے ارادہ فرمایا کہ ان کا زینب کے ساتھ نکاح کر دیں تاکہ آپ کے خاندان میں اُنکی وقعت زیادہ ہو نیز آپ کا یہ بھی مقصود تھا کہ غلام آزاد مذہب اسلام میں حقیر نہ سمجھے جائیں اور اُن کی عزت

بھی احرار کی طرح کی جائے یعنی آزاد اور غلام میں جو اہل عرب امتیاز کرتے ہیں وہ مسلمانوں میں نہ ہو۔ چنانچہ ان ہی امور کے پیش نظر رکھ کر آپ نے زیدؓ کا عقد زینبؓ سے کر دیا۔ زینبؓ آخر عورت تھیں اور خیالاتِ قدیم ان کے دل میں جاگزیں تھے۔ انہوں نے ہمیشہ اپنے تئیں زیدؓ سے افضل سمجھا اور انکو اپنے سے کمتر خیال کیا یہ باتیں ایسی تھیں کہ میاں بیوی میں موافقت پیدا نہیں ہونے دیتی تھیں آخر زیدؓ اس امر پر مجبور ہو گئے کہ زینبؓ کو طلاق دے دیں۔ یہ کیفیت دیکھ کر آنحضرت کو بہت تردد ہوا۔ آپ دل سے تو یہی بات چاہتے تھے کہ زینبؓ زیدؓ ہی کی زوجیت میں رہیں اور اس رشتے سے ایک بڑی اصلاح مقصود تھی وہ بدستور قائم رہے۔ اسی واسطے آپ زیدؓ کو سمجھاتے تھے کہ میاں خدا کا خوف کرو اور زینبؓ کو طلاق دینے سے باز رہو لیکن آپ کو یہ بھی اندیشہ تھا کہ لوگ کہینگے کیسا بے جوڑ رشتہ کرا دیا تھا جو قائم نہ رہ سکا۔ خدا نے فرمایا کہ اس معاملے میں لوگوں کے ڈرنے کی کیا ضرورت تھی۔ ڈر تو صرف ہم سے چاہیئے۔ لوگوں کا دستور ہے کہ اصلاح کے معاملات میں ہی طرح طرح کی باتیں کیا کرتے ہیں اسکے علاوہ آپکو یہ فکر دامنگیر ہوا کہ اگر ان میاں بیوی میں علیحدگی واقع ہوئی تو زینبؓ کے بارے میں بڑی مشکل پیش آئے گی کہ زیدؓ کی زوجیت میں رہ چکنے کے سبب لوگ زینبؓ کے اعزاز و احترام میں کمی کرینگے۔ اور یہ بات آپ کو منظور نہ تھی۔ اور ہو سکتی بھی نہ تھی جب آپ زیدؓ کی توقیر کرتے اور لوگوں سے کرانی چاہتے تھے تو زینبؓ کی تحقیر کیونکر گوارا کر سکتے۔ آخر الامر زیدؓ اور زینبؓ کا تعلق منقطع ہو کر رہا ÷

اس موقع پر خدا کو تین اور اصلاحیں مدِ نظر ہوئیں ایک یہ کہ اسلام میں متبنے کا وہ حق نہ سمجھا جائے جو صلبی بیٹوں کا ہے۔ اور دونوں قسم کے تعلقات میں جو فرق ہے وہ ظاہر کر دیا جائے۔ دوسرے یہ کہ منہ بولے لڑکوں کی عورتیں صلبی بیٹوں کی عورتوں کی طرح حرام نہ سمجھی جائیں چنانچہ خدا کے حکم سے آنحضرتؐ نے خود زینبؓ سے نکاح کر لیا اور خدا نے فرمایا: فَلَمَّا قَضٰى زَيْدٌ مِّنْهَا وَطَرًا زَوَّجْنٰكَهَا لِكَيْ لَا يَكُوْنَ عَلَى الْمُؤْمِنِيْنَ حَرَجٌ فِيْٓ اَزْوَاجِ اَدْعِيَاۗىِٕهِمْ اِذَا قَضَوْا مِنْهُنَّ وَطَرًا ۭ وَكَانَ اَمْرُ اللّٰهِ مَفْعُوْلًا متبنے بنانا ایک رسمِ قدیم ہے اور اسلام نے اسکو جائز رکھا ہے۔ لیکن متبنے بیٹوں کو صلبی بیٹوں کے سے حقوق نہیں دیتے اور نہ انکی عورتوں سے نکاح کرنا صلبی بیٹوں کی عورتوں کے ساتھ نکاح کرنے کے برابر سمجھا تیسرے یہ کہ غلاموں کی مطلقہ عورتوں کی حیثیت جن کو شریف اہل عرب اپنی زوجیت میں لینے سے دریغ اور مضائقہ کرتے تھے۔ وہی قرار دی جائے جو احرار کی مطلقہ عورتوں کی ہے یعنی ان سے بے پس و پیش نکاح کر لیا جائے اور یہ تینوں اصلاحیں آنحضرت ہی کی ذات بابرکات سے شروع ہوئیں صلی اللہ علیہ وسلم ÷

۲۲۵۔ امانت سے مراد خدا تعالےٰ کے احکام اور فرائض ہیں جن کے اٹھانے سے آسمان نے بھی اپنا عجز ظاہر کیا اور زمین اور پہاڑوں نے بھی۔ مگر انسان نے اپنی بساط کو تو دیکھا نہیں کہا کہ میں اس بار کو اٹھاؤں گا۔ نادانی سے اسکو اٹھا تو لیا لیکن اٹھاتے ہی حکمِ خدا کے خلاف عمل کرنے لگا۔ اور خدائے تعالےٰ کی طرف سے موردِ عتاب ہوا۔ تب سمجھا کہ میں نے بڑی نادانی کی۔ اور اپنے حق میں بڑا ظلم کیا اور لگا خدا سے معافی مانگنے۔ اس مشتِ خاک کو دیکھو اور اسکی بساط کو دیکھو۔ اور اسکی جرأت کو دیکھو۔ خدا کی امانت کو قبولا تو ظاہر ہو گیا اِنَّهٗ كَانَ ظَلُوْمًا جَهُوْلًا ÷

۲۲۶۔ حضرت سلیمان علیہ السلام کی شریعت میں مجسمے یعنی مورتیں بنانا جائز تھا یہ مورتیں انبیاء اور صلحا اور علما اور ملائکہ کی ہوتی تھیں جو مساجد و معابد میں رکھی جاتی تھیں اور مقصود اس سے یہ ہوتا تھا کہ ان کو دیکھ کر لوگوں کے دلوں میں عبادتِ خدا کا زیادہ شوق ہو اور وہ اس میں زیادہ مصروف ہوں عرب والوں نے غضب کر دیا کہ مجسموں کو پوجنے لگے یعنی ان کو معاذ اللہ خدا سمجھنے لگے۔ جو انسان کے لئے اشرف المخلوقات ہے بے انتہا ذلت اور خدائے تعالےٰ کے حق میں نہایت ظلم ہے۔ شریعتِ محمدیہ میں جاندار کی مورت بنانا ممنوع قرار دیا گیا۔ تاکہ بت پرستی کی جڑ کٹ جائے ۱۲ ÷

۲۲۷۔ یعنی جو مال اور دولت پہلے کافر رکھتے تھے اس کا دسواں حصہ بھی ان کفارِ عرب کے پاس نہیں۔ مگر ہم نے انکو بھی تباہ و برباد کر دیا اور یہ تو کچھ ایسی حقیقت نہیں رکھتے انکو نیست و نابود کر دینا کیا مشکل ہے ؛

۲۲۸۔ رفیق سے جو صاحب کا ترجمہ کیا گیا ہے حضرت محمد مصطفےٰ صلی اللہ علیہ وسلم مراد ہیں یعنی تم اکٹھے ہو کر بھی اور تنہائی میں بھی غور کرو تمہیں یہ معلوم ہو جائیگا کہ جس طرح وہ بعثت سے پہلے عاقل و دانا تھے اور انکی دانشمندی عالم میں مسلم تھی ایسے ہی دانا اور عاقل اب ہیں۔ اور ان کی کوئی بات جنون و دیوانگی کی نہیں ہے انکو امم سابقہ کے حالات معلوم ہیں کہ خدا کی نافرمانی سے عذاب آیا کرتا ہے سو وہ تم کو نافرمانی سے منع کرتے ہیں اور خدا کے عذاب سے ڈراتے ہیں اور یہ تو سراسر عقل و دانائی کی بات ہے اس میں جنون اور سودا کونسا ہے ۱۲ ؛

۲۲۹۔ یعنی خدائے تعالےٰ کے اس طریق کا جو اگلے لوگوں کے ساتھ برتا جاتا تھا انتظار کرتے ہیں اور وہ یہ ہے کہ ان کے کفر کے سبب ان پر عذاب نازل کیا جاتا تھا۔ یہ بھی عذاب ہی کے منتظر ہیں ۱۲ ÷

۲۳۰۔ ملک روم میں انطاکیہ ایک گاؤں تھا یہ وہاں کے لوگوں کا قصہ ہے ۱۲ ÷

۲۳۱۔ کہتے ہیں یہ لوگ حضرت عیسیٰ کے حواریوں میں سے تھے جن کو خدائے تعالےٰ نے حضرت عیسیٰ کے بعد پیغمبری عطا فرمائی تھی پہلے دو پیغمبروں کا نام یوحنا اور شمعون تھا اور تیسرے کا شکوم ۱۲ ÷

۲۳۲۔ یعنی نحوست جو تمہارے اعمالِ بد کی وجہ سے ہے تم جہاں بھی ہو گے وہ تمہارے ساتھ ہو گی ۱۲۔

۲۳۳۔ یعنی جو نصیحت تم کو کی گئی۔ کیا وہ تمہارے لئے موجبِ نحوست ہوتی ؟ یہ ہرگز نہیں ہے بلکہ تمہاری شامتِ اعمال تمہارے لئے موجبِ وبال ہو رہی ہے ۱۲

۲۳۴۔ یہ شخص شہر کے قریب ایک غار میں عبادت کرتا تھا۔ جب اسنے پیغمبروں کے آنے کا حال سنا تو شہر میں دوڑتا ہوا آیا۔ اور وہاں کے لوگوں کو تلقین کرنے لگا کہ پیغمبروں کی اطاعت کرو اور ان کی ہدایتوں پر چلو اس کا نام حبیب تھا ۱۲ ÷

۲۳۵۔ صور دو دفعہ پھونکا جائے گا پہلی دفعہ کے بعد سب لوگ بیہوش ہو جائیں گے اور ان پر نیند کی کیفیت طاری ہو جائے گی۔ دوسری دفعہ کے بعد سب زندہ ہو جائینگے وَنُفِخَ فِي الصُّوْرِ فَصَعِقَ مَنْ فِي السَّمٰوٰتِ وَمَنْ فِي الْاَرْضِ اِلَّا

مَنْ شَآءَ اللّٰہُ ثُمَّ نُفِخَ فِیْہِ اُخْرٰی فَاِذَا ھُمْ قِیَامٌ یَّنْظُرُوْنَ چونکہ صُورِ اوّل کے بعد اُن کی یہ حالت ہوگی کہ گویا سو رہے ہیں۔ لہٰذا صُورِ ثانی کے بعد یہ خیال کرینگے کہ نیند سے بیدار ہوئے ہیں۔ تب کہیں گے کہ ارے ہم کو کس نے جگا اُٹھایا ۱۲ ؎

۲۳۶۔ یعنی بچے سے جوان کرتے ہیں پھر جوان سے بڑھا کر دیتے ہیں ۱۲ ؎

۲۳۷۔ جو خدا انسان کی بناوٹ کو اسطرح بدل دیتا ہے وہ اسپر بھی قدرت رکھتا ہے کہ مُردوں کو جلا اُٹھائے ۱۲ ؎

۲۳۸۔ یعنی قیامت کے روز جہاں یہ بُت پرست خدا کے سامنے حاضر کئے جائینگے وہاں یہ بُت بھی جو بُت پرستوں کا لشکر ہوگا جواب دہی کے لئے حاضر کیا جائیگا بعض نے یہی معنی کئے ہیں کہ وہ یعنی بُت خود اپنی مدد تو کر سکتے ہی نہیں اور بُت پرست اُن کی حفاظت کے لئے ایک لشکر بنکر اُن کے سامنے موجود رہتے ہیں۔ ایسے بے اختیار اور بے لبس اُنکی کیا مدد کرینگے؟ ؎

۲۳۹۔ کہتے ہیں کہ بانس یا بعض اور درخت ایسے ہیں کہ ہیتے تو سبز ہیں لیکن اگر اُن کی شاخوں کو رگڑا جائے تو اُن میں سے آگ نکلتی ہے اور یہ خدا کی بہت بڑی قدرت کی دلیل ہے ۱۲ ؎

۲۴۰۔ صف باندھنے والوں سے یا تو مجاہد مُراد ہیں۔ جو میدانِ جنگ میں صف باندھ کر کھڑے ہوتے ہیں یا نمازی یا فرشتے کہ وہ بھی صف میں مل کر اور ڈٹ کے جما کر کھڑے ہوتے ہیں ۱۲ ؎

۲۴۱۔ ڈانٹنے والوں سے یا تو غازی مراد ہیں جو اپنے گھوڑوں کو دور سے ڈانٹ کر حملہ کرتے ہیں۔ یا عالمِ ربانی جو لوگوں کو گناہ کرنے پر گناہ سے روکنے کے لئے ڈانٹتے ہیں ۱۲ ؎

۲۴۲۔ قرآن پڑھنے والوں سے یا تو وہ لوگ مُراد ہیں جو جنگ سے فارغ ہو کر تلاوتِ قرآن میں مصروف ہوتے ہیں یا عام قرآن پڑھنے والے چونکہ خدائے تعالےٰ نے اِن صفات کے لوگوں کی قسمیں کھائی ہیں اسلئے سمجھنا چاہیئے کہ اسکے نزدیک اُن کی بڑی عظمت ہے "غور کر کر" کا لفظ جو ترجمے میں بڑھایا گیا ہے اس سے ایک تو عبارت منقفیٰ ہوگئی ہے۔ دُوسرے یہ ظاہر کرنا مقصُود ہے کہ قرآن کا پڑھنا اسی صورت میں مفید ہو سکتا ہے اور اسکے پڑھنے سے جو غرض ہے وہ تبھی پُوری ہو سکتی ہے جب غور و فکر اور تدبّر کر کے پڑھا جائے۔ قرآن مجید کا نازل کرنے والا فرماتا ہے:- کِتَابٌ اَنْزَلْنٰہُ اِلَیْکَ مُبٰرَکٌ لِّیَدَّبَّرُوْٓا اٰیٰتِہٖ وَلِیَتَذَکَّرَ اُولُوا الْاَلْبَابِ یعنی اے محمد یہ قرآن ایک بابرکت کتاب ہے جو ہم نے تم پر نازل کی ہے۔ مقصُود یہ ہے کہ لوگ اسکی آیتوں پر غور کریں۔ اور اہلِ عقل اس سے نصیحت پکڑیں ۱۲ ؎

۲۴۳۔ کیا وہ تم کو شرک کرنے پر پکڑے گا نہیں اور یُونہی چھوڑ دے گا ۱۲ ؎

۲۴۴۔ پھر وہ لوگ میلے میں جانے لگے تو حضرت ابراہیمؑ سے کہنے لگے کہ ہمارے ساتھ میلے میں چلیئے۔ چونکہ وہ لوگ اس بات کے معتقد تھے کہ دُنیا کا کارخانہ ستاروں کی گردش سے چل رہا ہے اسلئے حضرت ابراہیم نے ستاروں پر ایک نظر کی تاکہ وہ سمجھیں کہ جو کیفیت آپ پر گذرے وہ ستاروں کی گردش سے ہوگی۔ تو آپ نے کہا کہ میں تو بیمار ہوں۔ یہ عذر سُنکر وہ چل دیئے۔ ادھر ان کا جانا تھا اُدھر آپ نے اُن کے بتوں کی طرف توجہ کی۔ اور ان کو توڑ ڈالا ۱۲ ؎

۲۴۵۔ اس میں اختلاف ہے، کہ بیٹے سے اسمٰعیل مُراد ہیں یا اسحٰق۔ اکثر مفسّروں کے نزدیک اسمٰعیل مُراد ہیں اور یہی صحیح ہے ۱۲ ؎

۲۴۶۔ کہتے ہیں کہ حضرت ابراہیم علیہ السلام نے حضرت اسمٰعیل علیہ السلام کو ذبح کرنے کے لئے بڑی کوشش کی۔ مگر چھری نے جسکو بار بار تیز کرتے رہے کچھ کام نہ دیا۔ آخر چھری کا زور سے چلاتے چلاتے ایک دفعہ ایسی آواز آئی کہ گویا کوئی چیز کٹ گئی ہے خون بہنے لگا ہے۔ تب آپ نے اپنی آنکھوں پر سے پٹی کھول دی جو ذبح کرتے وقت اسلئے باندھ لی تھی کہ کہیں محبتِ پدری جوش میں نہ آئے۔ اور خدائے تعالےٰ کے حکم کی تعمیل میں لغزش نہ ہو جائے دیکھا تو ایک دُنبہ مذبوح پڑا ہوا ہے اور حضرت اسمٰعیل پاس صحیح سالم کھڑے ہیں اسی دُنبے کی نسبت خدا نے فرمایا کہ ایک بڑی قربانی کو ہم نے ان کا فدیہ دیا ۱۲ ؎

۲۴۷۔ حق تعالےٰ نے حضرت الیاسؑ کو عہدہ نبوّت پر فائز فرما کر بعلبک کی طرف بھیجا تھا۔ یہاں کے باشندے ایک بُت کی پرستش کرتے تھے جسکا نام بَعل تھا ۱۲

۲۴۸۔ یعنی جتنے بال بچے پہلے تھے وہ بھی دیئے اور اتنے ہی اور عطا کئے ۱۲ ؎

۲۴۹۔ کہتے ہیں کہ حضرت ایوب کی بی بی نے کوئی ایسی حرکت کی۔ یا آپ سے کوئی ایسی بات کہی جو آپ کو ناگوار ہوئی تو آپ نے قسم کھائی کہ میں تجھ کو سو چھڑیاں ماروں گا۔ تو آپ کو یہ ارشاد ہوا کہ سو سینکوں کی جھاڑو لے کر اس سے بی بی کو مارو قسم سچی ہو جائے گی ۱۲ ؎

۲۵۰۔ یعنی اس بات کو پسند نہیں کرتا کہ اسکے بندے ہو کر اس کی ناشکری کریں ۱۲ ؎

۲۵۱۔ جس لفظ کا یہ ترجمہ کیا گیا ہے وہ ظُلَلٌ ہے ظُلَلٌ ظُلّۃٌ کی جمع ہے ظُلّۃٌ اس چیز کو کہتے ہیں جو سایہ کرے جیسے بادل یا چھتری وغیرہ جب اسکا اطلاق اُوپر کی چیز پر ہوگا تو اُسے سائبان کہیں گے جیسے اسی آیت میں پہلے ظُلَلٌ کا ترجمہ سائبان کیا گیا ہے۔ لیکن چونکہ یہاں وہ نیچے کی چیز پر بولا گیا ہے اسلئے اس مقام پر ہم نے اُردو زبان کے لحاظ سے فرش ترجمہ کیا ہے۔ قرآن مجید میں جو سائبان اور فرش یعنی اُوپر اور نیچے کی دونوں چیزوں پر ظُلَلٌ کا لفظ بولا گیا ہے اس کی وجہ یہ ہے کہ اہلِ عرب ایک چیز کا نام اسکی ضد پر بھی رکھ لیتے ہیں ۱۲ ؎

۲۵۲۔ یعنی جن باتوں کے کرنے کا ان کو حکم دیا گیا ہے وہ کرتے ہیں اور جن سے منع کیا گیا ہے وہ نہیں کرتے یہ دونوں اچھی باتیں ہیں ۱۲ ؎

۲۵۳۔ کافر اس بات کے متمنی اور منتظر تھے کہ حضرت صلی اللہ علیہ وسلم کا رشتہ حیات منقطع ہو جائے۔ خدا تعالےٰ نے حضرت سے فرمایا کہ بقائے جاودانی تمہارے لئے بھی نہیں ہے اور ان لوگوں کے لئے بھی نہیں ہے۔ موت تم کو بھی آئے گی اور اُن کو بھی گورستان میں لے جائے گی۔ پھر اُن کا تمہاری موت کی تمنا اور انتظار کرنا محض حمق اور نادانی ہے۔ روایت ہے کہ جب حضرت صلی اللہ علیہ وسلم کا انتقال ہوا تو حضرت عمر کو باور نہ آیا تو اُنہوں نے کہا جو کوئی کہے گا کہ آپ

وفات پاگئے ہیں تو میں اُسکا سر تلوار سے (جو ننگی ہاتھ میں لئے ہوئے تھے) اڑا دوں گا۔ حضرت ابوبکرؓ نے یہ سُنا تو حضرت عمرؓ سے کہا کہ تلوار کو نیام میں کیجئے اور منبر پر چڑھ کر یہ آیت پڑھی تب سب کو یقین ہوا کہ آپ رحلت فرما گئے

ے وہی ایک ہے جسکو دائم بقا ہے ✣ جہاں کی وراثت اسی کو سزا ہے

سوا اسکے انجام سب کا فنا ہے ✣ نہ کوئی رہے گا نہ کوئی رہا ہے

جو پیدا ہوا اسکو مرنا ہے آخر ✣ یہاں سے اُسے کوچ کرنا ہے آخر

٢٥٤۔ یعنی یہ کفار جو خدائے تعالےٰ کی آیتوں میں بلا دلیل جھگڑتے اور ان کو جھٹلاتے ہیں تو ان کا مقصود یہ ہوتا ہے کہ وہ پیغمبرِ خدا سے بڑھ کر رہیں مگر وہ اس مقصد کو حاصل نہیں کر سکتے اور پیغمبرِ خدا صلی اللہ علیہ وسلم پر کبھی غالب نہیں ہو سکتے ۱۲

٢٥٥۔ یعنی اس بات کو سوچو کہ جس خدا نے تم کو پہلی بار پیدا کیا اور تم پر بچپن اور جوانی اور بڑھاپے کی حالتیں وارد کر کے پھر تم کو موت دی وہ اس بات پر بھی قادر ہے کہ تم کو قیامت کے روز پھر زندہ کرے اور جو لوگ ان باتوں پر غور کرتے ہیں۔ اُن کو اس بات کے ماننے میں تامل نہیں ہو سکتا کہ اسی طرح قیامت کے روز زندہ کئے جائینگے ۱۲

٢٥٦۔ یعنی اگر تمہاری زندگی میں اُن پر عذاب نازل کیا جائے تو تمہاری وفات کے بعد ان کو ہمارے ہی پاس لوٹ کر آنا ہے اسوقت خدا کا وعدہ پورا ہو جائے گا اور یہ عذابِ الیم میں مبتلا ہوں گے ۱۲ ✣

٢٥٧۔ کجراہی کرنے کے یہ معنی ہیں کہ آیتوں کا مطلب بدل دیتے ہیں جو صاف اور صحیح اور صریح معنی ہیں ان کو چھوڑ کر اور معنی کرتے ہیں اسی میں تاویل اور تحریف اور تفسیر بالرائے داخل ہے اگر لفظوں کو اس طرح بدل دیا جائے کہ فاعل کی جگہ مفعول یا مفعول کی جگہ فاعل کر دیا جائے تو یہ تحریف ہے اور صریح کجراہی ہے اپنی رائے سے تفسیر کرنی یعنی خدائے تعالےٰ کا ارشاد کچھ ہو اور مطلب کچھ اور بیان کیا جائے یہ نہایت مذموم ہے اور اس پر وعید جہنم ہے مَن فَسَّرَ الْقُرْاٰنَ بِرَاْیِہٖ فَلْیَتَبَوَّأْ مَقْعَدَہٗ مِنَ النَّارِ خدا اس سے پناہ میں رکھے ۱۲ ✣

٢٥٨۔ یہاں لفظ عریض ہے اُردو کے محاورے میں لمبی لمبی دُعائیں کہتے ہیں نہ چوڑی چوڑی اس لئے ترجمہ میں لمبی لمبی دُعائیں لکھا گیا ۱۲

٢٥٩۔ جو لوگ زمین پر ہیں اُس میں مومن اور کافر سب داخل ہیں کافروں کے حق میں فرشتے دُعا اسلئے کرتے ہیں کہ انکو امید ہوتی ہے کہ شاید وہ ایمان لے آئینگے۔ بعض نے کہا کہ بخشش کی دُعا سے رزق کی دُعا مراد ہے یعنی تمام فرشتے اہل زمین کے لئے روزی مانگتے رہتے ہیں۔ خواہ مومن ہوں خواہ کافر اگر یہی معنی مُراد لئے جائیں تو فرشتوں کی دُعا کا اثر ظاہر ہے ۱۲ ✣

٢٦٠۔ یعنی اگر تم مجھ پر ایمان نہیں لاتے تو قرابت کا پاس تو کرنا چاہیئے اور مجھے ایذا نہیں دینی چاہیئے۔ بعض نے یہ معنی کئے ہیں کہ خدا کا قرب حاصل کرنے کے لئے اس سے محبت رکھو ۱۲ ✣

٢٦١۔ تاکہ تم مضامین قرآن بیان نہ کر سکو اور کافروں کو برے کہنے کا موقع نہ ملے کہ تم خدا پر افترا کرتے ہو۔ مگر خدا کو کفار کے بکنے کی کیا پروا ہے۔ وہ اُن کے اقوال کو باطل کرتا ہے اور اپنے پیغمبر پر قرآن نازل کر کے حق ثابت کرتا ہے ۱۲ ✣

٢٦٢۔ روشن کے معنی ہیں صاف اور واضح جس میں احکام الٰہی صاف صاف بغیر کسی پیچیدگی کے مندرج ہیں ۱۲ ✣

٢٦٣۔ کافروں نے تو آنحضرت صلی اللہ علیہ وسلم کے قتل اور مکّے سے اُن کے اخراج کا منصوبہ سوچا تھا اور خدا نے یہ ارادہ فرمایا تھا کہ وہ آپ کو کفار پر غالب کرے گا۔ چنانچہ آپ مکّے سے ہجرت کر کے مدینہ تشریف لے گئے تو خدائے تعالےٰ نے آپکی نصرت فرمائی اور آپنے مکّہ فتح کر لیا اور کافر مغلوب ہو کر رہ گئے ۱۲ ✣

٢٦٤۔ یعنی بُت جن کی یہ کفّار پوجا کرتے تھے اُن کی سفارش نہیں کر سکیں گے سفارش کرنے کا حق تو خدا کے اُن نیک بندوں کو ہو گا جن کو خدا کی وحدانیت کا یقین ہے اور وہ اُسکی یکتائی اور معبود واحد ہونے کی گواہی دیتے ہیں۔ اور وہی سفارش کر سکتے ہیں ۱۲ ✣

٢٦٥۔ تبع یمن کا بادشاہ تھا کہتے ہیں کہ وہ تو صاحبِ ایمان تھا اور اسکی قوم بُت پرست تھی جو ہلاک کر دی گئی ۱۲ ✣

٢٦٦۔ فتح کے بارے میں اختلاف ہے، کہ اس سے کیا مُراد ہے اکثر کا قول یہ ہے کہ اس سے مُراد حدیبیہ کی صلح ہے کیونکہ کبھی صلح کا نام فتح بھی رکھ لیتے ہیں حضرت ابن مسعودؓ وغیرہ سے روایت ہے کہ تم تو مکّے کی فتح کو فتح خیال کرتے ہو اور ہم حدیبیہ کی صلح کو فتح سمجھتے ہیں۔ بخاری میں حضرت براء رضی اللہ تعالےٰ عنہ سے روایت ہے کہ تم لوگ فتح مکہ کو فتح شمار کرتے ہو اور ہم بیعت الرضوان کو جو حدیبیہ کے دن ہوئی فتح تصور کرتے ہیں اس صلح کے واقعات یہ ہیں کہ جناب رسول خدا صلی اللہ علیہ وسلم نے سنہ ٦ ہجری میں حدیبیہ جانے سے پیشتر خواب دیکھا کہ گویا آپ نے اور آپ کے اصحاب نے سر منڈوایا اور بال کتروائے۔ یہ خواب آپنے اصحاب کو سنایا تو یہ خیال کر کے خوش ہوئے کہ اسی سال مکّے میں داخل ہوں گے تو آپ بیت اللہ کی زیارت اور عمرے کی نیت سے مکّے کو روانہ ہوئے۔ جب عسفان میں پہنچے تو آپ کو بشیر بن سفیان نے خبر دی کہ آپ کی روانگی کا حال سُنکر قریش بڑی جمعیت سے نکلے ہیں اور انہوں نے عہد کیا ہے کہ ایسا ہرگز نہ ہونے پائے کہ آپ اُن پر غالب ہو کر مکّے میں داخل ہوں اور خالد بن ولید بھی اُن کے سواروں میں ہیں جو کراع غمیم کی طرف آگے بھیجا گیا ہے تو آپنے فرمایا کہ اب دو ہی صورتیں ہیں یا تو جہاد کر کے ظفر اور غلبہ حاصل کریں، یا جان ہی دے دیں ع

یا تن رسد بجاناں یا جاں ز تن بر آید

چنانچہ اصحاب کو حکم دیا کہ خدا کا نام لے کر چل دو۔ پھر وہاں سے روانہ ہوئے اور مرارہ کی گھاٹی میں سے ہو کر حدیبیہ کے پرلے سرے جا اترے وہاں آپکے پاس قریش کے کئی شخص یکے بعد دیگرے آتے رہے آپ اُن سے یہی فرماتے رہے کہ ہم تو صرف زیارتِ کعبہ کے لئے آئے ہیں جنگ و جدل کے لئے نہیں آئے وہ لوگ جو باتیں یہاں سُنتے تھے وہاں جا کر کہہ دیتے تھے۔ آخر آپ نے اپنی طرف سے حضرت عثمانؓ کو قریش کے پاس یہ پیغام دے کر بھیجا کہ ہم لڑنے نہیں آئے خانۂ خدا

کی زیارت کرنے کو آئے ہیں ابھی آپ واپس نہیں آئے تھے کہ یہاں یہ افواہ اُڑ گئی کہ آپ قتل کر دیئے گئے ہیں۔ یہ خبر سنکر جناب رسولِ خدا صلی اللہ علیہ وسلّم کو عزمِ جنگ کرنا پڑا اور اسی ارادے سے آپ نے مسلمانوں سے بیعت لی جس کو بیعت الرضوان کہتے ہیں۔ اُدھر کفار کو جو یہاں کے حالات معلوم ہوئے تو وہ جوش و خروش مدھم ہو گیا اور اُنہوں نے سہیل بن عمرو کو حضرتؐ کے پاس صلح کے لئے روانہ کیا۔ اور شرائطِ صلح یہ قرار دیں کہ آپ اب کے بے عمرہ کئے واپس چلے جائیں اگلے سال عمرے کو آئیں اور صرف تین دن قیام کریں اور تلواروں کے سوا کوئی ہتھیار ساتھ نہ لائیں۔ اور انکو بھی میان سے نہ نکالیں یہ شرطیں حضرتؐ نے منظور فرمالیں اور صلحنامہ مرتب ہونے لگا تو آپ نے حضرت علیؓ سے فرمایا کہ لکھو بِسْمِ اللّٰهِ الرَّحْمٰنِ الرَّحِيْمِ تو سہیل بولا ہم نہیں جانتے بِسْمِ اللّٰهِ الرَّحْمٰنِ الرَّحِيْمِ کیا ہے بِاسْمِكَ اللّٰهُمَّ لکھو پھر آپ نے فرمایا کہ لکھو مِنْ مُحَمَّدٍ رَّسُوْلِ اللّٰهِ تو کہا کہ اگر ہم اس بات کے قائل ہوتے کہ آپ خدا کے رسول ہیں تو آپ کی پیروی ہی نہ اختیار کر لیتے۔ اپنے والد کا نام لکھوایئے تو آپ نے فرمایا لکھو من محمد بن عبداللہ اور ایک شرط کفار نے یہ کی کہ جو شخص آپ کی طرف سے ہمارے پاس آئے ہم اسکو واپس نہ کرینگے اور جو ہماری طرف سے آپکے پاس جائے آپ اس کو واپس کر دیں۔ اس مصالحت میں جو مصلحت تھی اس کو تو جناب رسول خدا ہی خوب سمجھتے تھے لیکن پرجوش اصحاب کو صلح کی باتیں نہایت شاق معلوم ہوئیں اور سخت رنجیدہ ہوئے اور رؤیا پیرِ خواب کا معاملہ ان کو بیدل کئے دیتا تھا وہ یہ سمجھتے تھے کہ اسی سال عمرہ کرینگے مگر جاتے ہیں بے نیل و مرام۔ اسی اثناء میں ایک ناگوار واقعہ پیش آیا۔ کہ ابھی صلحنامہ لکھا ہی جا رہا تھا کہ ناگاہ ابوجندل بن سہیل بن عمرو پابزنجیر کفار میں سے بھاگ کر آپ کے پاس آموجود ہوئے تو سہیل نے کہا کہ جن لوگوں کے بارے میں میں آپ سے صلح کرتا ہوں ان میں یہ پہلا شخص ہے اسکو آپ میرے حوالے کر دیجئے۔ آپ نے فرمایا کہ ابھی تک صلحنامہ مکمل نہیں ہوا۔ اس نے کہا کہ معاملہ اس کے آنے سے پہلے فیصل ہو چکا ہے۔ آپ نے فرمایا ہاں یہ سچ ہے پھر سہیل نے اُٹھ کر ابوجندل کا گریبان پکڑ لیا۔ اور ابوجندل دھاڑیں مار مار کر رونے اور کہنے لگے کہ مسلمانو تم مجھے مشرکوں کے حوالے کیوں کرتے ہو یہ تو مجھے میرے دین سے منحرف کر دینگے۔ حضرتؐ نے فرمایا ابوجندل صبر کر اور خدا سے اپنے اجر کی اُمید رکھ۔ خدا تیری مشکلات کو حل کرنیوالا ہے ہم تجھ کو ہرگز واپس نہ دیتے لیکن ہم ان لوگوں سے اس بات کا عہد کر چکے ہیں اور ہم عہد شکنی نہیں کرنا چاہتے۔ ہر چند یہ امور مسلمانوں پر بہت گراں گزرے اور انہوں نے ان کو سخت آزردہ خاطر کیا۔ لیکن یہی صلح تھی جو تمام کامیابیوں کی تمہید ثابت ہوئی اسکے بعد وہی بات ہو گئی کہ شعر

جدھر رُخ کیا سلطنت زیرِ فرمان ٭ جدھر آنکھ اُٹھائی ممالک مسخر

۲۶۷۔ جب رسولِ خدا صلی اللہ علیہ وسلّم ہجرت کے چھٹے سال حدیبیہ سے لوٹ کر مدینہ منورہ تشریف لائے تو خدا نے آپ کو فتح خیبر کا وعدہ دیا اور وہاں کی غنیمتوں کے لئے اُنہی لوگوں کو مخصوص فرمایا جو حدیبیہ میں آپ کے ساتھ تھے جب آپ خیبر کی طرف تشریف لے چلے تو جو لوگ حدیبیہ میں نہیں گئے تھے۔ انہوں نے غنیمت کے لالچ سے درخواست کی کہ ہم کو بھی ساتھ لے چلئے۔ جواب ملا کہ تم ہمارے ساتھ چلو ہی مت کیونکہ غنیمت خیبر میں تم لوگوں کا کچھ حصہ نہیں اور خدا کا یہی ارشاد ہے تو وہ لوگ کہنے لگے کہ خدا نے تو ایسا نہیں کہا ہوگا۔ یوں کہو کہ تم کو ہم سے حسد ہے اور مارے حسد کے تم ہمیں شریک غنیمت نہیں کرنا چاہتے خدا نے فرمایا کہ یہ احمق لوگ ہیں ان کو ان باتوں کے سمجھنے کی عقل ہی نہیں ۱۲ ٭

۲۶۸۔ چونکہ اس بیعت کے سبب خدا مومنوں سے خوش ہوا تھا اسلیئے اس کو بیعت الرضوان کہتے ہیں۔ یہ بیعت اس بات پر لی گئی تھی کہ مسلمان قریش سے لڑائی کرینگے اور مرتے دم تک نہیں بھاگیں گے اسکے صلے میں خدا نے مومنوں کے دلوں میں تسلی پیدا کی اور جلد خیبر کی فتح نصیب کی جس میں بہت سی غنیمتیں ہاتھ آئیں بیعت کے وقت جناب رسولِ خدا صلی اللہ علیہ وسلّم بقول اکثر کیکر کے درخت اور بقول بعض بیری کے تلے تشریف رکھتے تھے چونکہ لوگ بیعت کے سبب اس درخت کی تعظیم کے لئے اسکے پاس آنے لگے تھے تو حضرت عمرؓ نے اس خیال سے کہ تعظیم حدِ پرستش تک نہ پہنچ جائے اسکو کٹوا ڈالا ۱۲

۲۶۹۔ اس آیت میں وجہِ تاخیرِ فتحِ مکہ بیان فرمائی گئی۔ وہ یہ کہ مکے میں اس طرح کی عورتیں اور مرد مسلمان بھی تھے کہ جان کے اندیشے سے اپنا ایمان کفار سے مخفی رکھتے تھے۔ اور خدا کے سوا ان کا حال کسی کو معلوم نہ تھا تو اگر خدا مسلمانوں کو مکے پر چڑھائی کا حکم دے دیتا تو جو سلوک کافروں کے ساتھ ہوتا وہی بحالت نادانستگی اُن کے ساتھ ہوتا اور خدا کو یہ منظور نہ تھا اور اگر وہ لوگ ان میں نہ ہوتے تو مکہ کی فتح میں توقف واقع نہ ہوتا ۱۲ ٭

۲۷۰۔ جنابِ رسولِ خدا صلی اللہ علیہ وسلّم ذی قعدہ ۶ھ میں حدیبیہ سے مدینے کو واپس تشریف لے گئے ذی الحجہ اور محرم وہاں ٹھہرے ماہ صفر میں خیبر پر چڑھائی کر کے اسکو فتح کیا اور پھر مدینے کو لوٹ گئے ذی قعدہ ۷ھ ہجری میں آپ اور حدیبیہ والے عمرہ کرنے کے لئے مکے کو روانہ ہوئے تو آپ نے ذوالحلیفہ سے احرام باندھا اور قربانیوں کے جانوروں کو ساتھ لیا غرض آپ مکے میں بیخوف و خطر داخل ہوئے اور جو باتیں آپ نے خواب میں دیکھی تھیں وہ اس سال پوری ہوئیں اسی خواب کے سچ ہونے کا اس آیت میں ذکر ہے ۱۲

۲۷۱۔ یعنی جب کوئی ایمان لے آئے تو اسکو یہودی یا نصرانی یا مجوسی وغیرہ کہہ کر نہیں پکارنا چاہیئے کہ ایسے ناموں سے پکارنا گناہ ہے۔ اگر کوئی یہودی تھا تو اسلام لانے سے پہلے تھا۔ اسی طرح نصرانی اور مجوسی وغیرہ یہ نام قبل از اسلام تھے۔ لیکن اسلام لانے کے بعد نہ یہودی یہودی رہا نہ نصرانی نصرانی نہ مجوسی مجوسی تو جاہلیت کے ناموں سے مسلمانوں کو کیوں پکارا جائے اور انکو رنج کیوں پہنچایا جائے یا یہ کہ ایمان لانے کے بعد فاسق کتنا برا نام (رکھنا) ہے اور برا نام رکھنا مذموم ہے۔ جو گناہ کسی سے اسلام لانے سے پہلے ہوا ہو اب جبکہ اس سے تائب ہے تو وہ اسکی طرف منسوب کیوں کیا جائے اور اسے

بُرے نام سے مطعون کیوں کیا جائے یا یہ کہ ایمان لانے کے بعد نام رکھنا یعنی (فسق سے منسوب کرنا) بُرا ہے۔ اس صورت میں اسم (یعنی نام) مبدل منہ ہوگا اور فسوق بدل۔ تمام صورتوں میں عیب لگانے طعنہ زنی کرنے بُرا نام رکھنے بُرے لقب سے پکارنے کی ممانعت ہے ۱۲ ؎

۲۷۲- تفاسیر میں ان چار آیتوں میں ایک ہی چیز بھی مراد لی گئی ہے یعنی ہوا۔ اور چار مختلف چیزیں بھی مراد لی گئی ہیں یعنی ذَارِیَاتِ ذَرْوًا سے تو ہوائیں کہ غبار وغیرہ کو اُڑا کر بکھیر دیتی ہیں اور حَامِلٰتِ وِقْرًا سے بدلیاں جو مینہ کا بوجھ اُٹھاتی ہیں۔ اور جَارِیٰتِ یُسْرًا سے کشتیاں جو دریا میں سہج سہج چلتی ہیں اور مُقَسِّمٰتِ اَمْرًا سے فرشتے جو بارش اور رزق اور قحط اور ارزانی اور اور چیزوں کو تقسیم کرتے ہیں بعض مفسرین نے ان چیزوں کے علاوہ اور اشیاء بھی مراد لی ہیں۔ مگر ان کا ذکر غیر ضروری ہے۔

۲۷۳- متناقض بے جوڑ باتیں یعنی رسولِ خدا صلعم کی شان میں کوئی تو کہتا ہے کہ شاعر ہے کوئی کہتا ہے کہ دیوانہ ہے کوئی کہتا ہے کہ کاہن ہے اور اسی طرح قرآن مجید کو شعر اور سحر اور کہانت وغیرہ کہتے ہیں بعض نے کہا اس سے یہ مراد ہے کہ کوئی قیامت کا انکار کرتا ہے کوئی اس میں شک کرتا ہے بعض نے کہا اس سے یہ مراد ہے کہ وہ خدا کا تو اقرار کرتے ہیں۔ اور بتوں کی پرستش کرتے ہیں ۱۲ ؎

۲۷۴- کتاب کے بارے میں کئی قول ہیں کسی نے کہا دوسری آسمانی کتابیں کسی نے کہا نامۂ اعمال ۱۲ ؎

۲۷۵- آباد گھر بَیْتِ الْمَعْمُوْرِ کا ترجمہ ہے۔ جو آسمان میں فرشتوں کا کعبہ ہے ۱۲۔

۲۷۶- اونچی چھت سے آسمان مراد ہے یا عرشِ عظیم ۱۲

۲۷۷- شِعْرٰی ایک ستارے کا نام ہے اور بعض گروہ عرب بعض وجوہ سے اس کی بھی پرستش کرتے تھے ۱۲ ؎

۲۷۸- یہ وہ لوگ ہیں جن کی طرف حضرت ہود بھیجے گئے ۱۲ ؎

۲۷۹- چاند کا شق ہونا منجملہ علاماتِ قیامت کے ہے۔ اور احادیثِ صحیحہ سے ثابت ہے کہ جناب رسولِ خدا صلی اللہ علیہ وسلم کے وقت میں یہ نشانی وقوع میں آچکی ہے ۱۲ ؎

۲۸۰- اس آیت میں خطاب دو جماعتوں کی طرف ہے اور ان سے مراد انسان اور جنات ہیں۔ چنانچہ اکتیسویں آیت میں ثقلان کا لفظ ہے۔ جسکے معنی ہیں دو گروہ اور ان سے جیسا کہ حدیثِ صحیح میں آیا ہے جن اور انسان مراد ہیں اور بتیسویں آیت میں تو صاف جن و انس کا نام لے کر ان سے خطاب کیا گیا ہے اسی بنا پر ہم نے اس آیت کے ترجمے میں "اے گروہ جن و انس" کے لفظ بڑھا دیئے ہیں ؎

۲۸۱- مطلب یہ ہے کہ جتنے تصرفات اس عالم میں ہو رہے ہیں۔ ان سب کا مصدر وہی رب العالمین ہے ۱۲ ؎

۲۸۲- اور زور تم میں ہے نہیں تو تم بھاگ کر نکل سکتے بھی نہیں ۱۲ ؎

۲۸۳- آبارِیق اِبْرِیْق کی جمع ہے ابریق اس ظرف کو کہتے ہیں جس میں دستہ اور ٹونٹی دونوں ہوں۔ شاہ عبدالقادر صاحبؒ نے اباریق کا ترجمہ تھیاں کیا ہے اور بہت موزوں کیا ہے مگر چونکہ یہ لفظ اہلِ پنجاب کے نزدیک غرائب اللغات میں داخل ہے اسلئے ہم نے ترجمے میں وہ لفظ اختیار کیا ہے جو شاہ رفیع الدین صاحب رح نے اختیار کیا ہے یعنی "آفتابے" ۱۲

۲۸۴- اندر کی جانب جہاں مومن ہوں گے وہاں تو خدا کی رحمت یعنی باغِ نعمت ہوگی۔ اور باہر کی جانب جدھر منافق ہوں گے جہنم اور عذاب ہوگا ۱۲ ؎

۲۸۵- حضرت رسولِ خدا صلی اللہ علیہ وسلم ایک دفعہ مسجد میں تشریف لائے تو دیکھا کہ کچھ لوگ مسجد میں ہنس رہے ہیں آپ نے فرمایا کیا تم لوگوں کو خوف نہیں رہا؟ ساتھ ہی یہ آیت پڑھی تو ان لوگوں نے پوچھا کہ اے رسولِ خدا اُس کا کفارہ کیا ہے آپ نے فرمایا ہے جتنا ہنسے ہو اُتنا ہی روؤ ۱۲۔

۲۸۶- یہ آیات خولہ بنتِ ثعلبہ کے حق میں نازل ہوئی ہیں۔ اس کا شوہر اوس بن صامت غصے کی حالت میں اس سے ظہار کر بیٹھا۔ اور یوں بھی عرب میں ظہار کا رواج تھا۔ ظہار اسکو کہتے ہیں کہ میاں اپنی بیوی سے اس طرح کے الفاظ کہہ دے تو میری ماں کی جگہ ہے یا تیری پیٹھ میری ماں کی پیٹھ کی جگہ ہے اس طرح کہہ دینا جاہلیت میں طلاق سمجھا جاتا تھا تو خولہ اس بارے میں حکم دریافت کرنے کے لئے حضرت کی خدمت میں حاضر ہوئی آپ نے فرمایا کہ تو اپنے شوہر پر حرام ہو گئی۔ اس نے کہا کہ اس نے طلاق تو نہیں دی۔ غرض آپ تو یہ فرماتے کہ تو اس پر حرام ہو چکی۔ اور وہ کہتی کہ اُسنے طلاق کا نام نہیں لیا۔ اسی گفتگو کو خدا نے مجادلہ سے تعبیر فرمایا ہے۔ پھر وہ خدا سے کہتی کہ ربّ العلمین میری بیکسی کا حال تجھ کو معلوم ہے میرے ننھے ننھے بچے ہیں۔ اگر میں انکو اپنے شوہر کے حوالے کر دوں تو اچھی طرح پرورش نہ ہونے کے سبب ضائع ہو جائینگے۔ اور اگر اپنے پاس رکھوں تو بھوکے مرینگے۔ اور آسمان کی طرف سر اٹھا کر کہتی کہ بارِ الہا میری شکایت تجھی سے ہے، خدا نے اسکی عجز و زاری کو قبول فرمایا اور ظہار کو طلاق نہیں بلکہ ایک نامعقول بات قرار دے کر اس کا کفارہ مقرر فرمایا ۱۲۔

۲۸۷- احادیث میں ہے کہ یہود حضرت کے پاس آتے تو بجائے اَلسَّلَامُ عَلَیْكَ کے اَلسَّامُ عَلَیْكَ کہتے۔ سام موت کو کہتے ہیں۔ تو وہ ظاہر میں تو دعائے نیک دیتے اور حقیقت میں موت مراد لیتے اور بددعا دیتے۔ آپ اسکے جواب میں صرف وَعَلَیْکُمْ فرماتے جس کا مطلب ہوتا کہ موت تم ہی پر واقع ہو وہ لوگ اپنے دل میں کہتے کہ اگر محمدؐ سچے پیغمبر ہوتے تو ہمارے اس کلمے کے کہنے سے ضرور ہم پر عذاب نازل ہوتا بعض نے یہ معنی کئے ہیں کہ اگر یہ نبی ہوتے تو ان کی بددعا ہمارے حق میں ضرور قبول ہوتی۔ اور ہم پر موت واقع ہو کر رہتی۔ ان باتوں کے جواب میں خدا نے فرمایا کہ ان لوگوں کو دوزخ ہی کا عذاب کافی ہے ۱۲ ؎

۲۸۸- ان آیات میں بنی نضیر کے غزوے کا بیان ہے۔ یہ لوگ یہودی تھے جو مدینے سے چار پانچ کوس کے فاصلے پر رہتے تھے اور حضرت کے خلاف مشرکوں کی مدد کیا کرتے تھے۔ بہت سا ساز و سامان اور قلعے اور زمینیں اور کھجوروں کے باغ رکھتے تھے اور ان چیزوں پر انکو بہت گھمنڈ تھا۔ مگر جب آپ نے ان کی عہد شکنی کے سبب اُن کا محاصرہ کیا تو اُن سے اسکے سوا کچھ نہ بن پڑا کہ وطن

چھوڑ جائیں چنانچہ اسی بات پر صلح قرار پائی اور وہ شام کی طرف جلاوطن کر دیئے گئے۔ حشر اول سے مراد یہی جلائے وطن ہے۔ کہتے ہیں کہ اس صلح میں یہ بات بھی ٹھہری تھی کہ جن چیزوں کو وہ اونٹوں پر لاد کر اپنے ساتھ لیجا سکیں ان کو لے جائیں تو وہ مکانات کی لکڑیوں اور ستونوں وغیرہ کو جن کو خوبصورت سمجھتے تھے۔ گھروں سے اکھیڑنے لگے۔ یوں وہ اپنے گھروں کو خراب کرتے تھے۔ باقی جو کچھ رہ جاتا تھا اسکو اس لئے خراب کر دیتے تھے کہ مسلمان اس میں رس بس نہ سکیں ۱۲۔

۲۸۹۔ حضرت ابن عباس رضی اللہ عنہ فرماتے ہیں کہ جب بنی نضیر اپنے مکانات سے نکال دیئے گئے اور انکی کھجوروں کے کاٹ ڈالنے کا حکم ہوا تو مسلمانوں نے کچھ کھجوریں تو کاٹ دیں اور کچھ رہنے دیں مگر ان کو اس بارے میں شبہ ہوا کہ آیا انکو کاٹنے پر ثواب ہوگا۔ اور نہ کاٹنے پر گناہ۔ تو انہوں نے یہ امر جناب رسول خدا صلی اللہ علیہ وسلم سے دریافت کرنے کا ارادہ کیا۔ اس پر خدا نے فرمایا کہ کھجوروں کے کاٹنے نہ کاٹنے سے مقصود یہ ہے کہ مسلمان اپنے غلبہ پانے سے خوش ہوں اور نافرمان لوگوں کو یہ دیکھ کر کہ ان کے مالوں میں مسلمان اپنی مرضی کے مطابق تصرف کر رہے ہیں۔ رنج اور ذلت حاصل ہو ۱۲۔

۲۹۰۔ لفظوں کا ترجمہ تو یہ ہے کہ ایسی بستیوں میں جن میں قلعے بنے ہوئے ہیں مگر چونکہ مراد یہ ہے کہ اُن قلعوں میں جو بستیوں میں ہیں اسلئے ترجمے میں یہ الفاظ اختیار کئے گئے ہیں کہ "بستیوں کے قلعوں میں" ۱۲۔

۲۹۱۔ یعنی جو بچہ ان کا نہ ہو اس کو اپنے خاوندوں سے منسوب و لاحق نہ کرینگی۔

۲۹۲۔ یہی مضمون اس قطعے میں ادا کیا گیا ہے۔

قطعہ
شعلہ شمع خدائی کبھی بجھتا ہے ٭ رہ گئے اپنا سا منہ لیکے بجھانے والے
نقش اسلام زاعداء کے مٹانے سے مٹا ٭ مٹ گئے آپ ہی جتنے تھے مٹانے والے

۲۹۳۔ جناب سرور کائنات جمعے کا خطبہ پڑھ رہے تھے اتنے میں شام کا قافلہ غلہ لیکر آیا۔ ان دنوں مدینے میں گرانی تھی اور لوگوں کو غلہ کی حاجت تھی۔ سامعین خطبہ کے کانوں میں جو نقارے کی آواز آئی تو آنحضرت کو خطبے میں کھڑا چھوڑ کر سب اسکے دیکھنے کو چلے گئے مسجد میں صرف بارہ مرد اور سات عورتیں رہ گئیں تب یہ آیت نازل ہوئی۔

۲۹۴۔ یعنی چونکہ یہ لوگ دل سے تمہاری رسالت کے قائل نہیں اور تمہارے روبرو صرف زبان سے اقرار کرتے ہیں۔ باطن کچھ رکھتے ہیں اور ظاہر کچھ۔ اسلئے جھوٹے ہیں اور ان کے کہنے کا اعتبار نہیں۔

۲۹۵۔ یعنی منہ سے تو یہ کہتے ہیں کہ ہم ایمان لائے مگر دل میں کفر ہے اور اسی پر جمے ہوتے ہیں یا یہ کہ مسلمانوں کے پاس آتے ہیں تو ان سے مومن ہونے کا اقرار کرتے ہیں اور جب کفار کے پاس جاتے ہیں تو اسلام سے انکار کرتے ہیں۔

۲۹۶۔ حضرت ابن عمرؓ سے روایت ہے کہ انہوں نے اپنی بیوی کو طلاق دی اور وہ اس وقت حیض سے تھیں۔ حضرت عمرؓ نے جناب رسول خدا صلی اللہ علیہ وسلم کی خدمت میں اسکا ذکر کیا تو آپ خفا ہوئے اور رجوع کر لینے کا حکم دیا۔ اور فرمایا کہ اسے رہنے دینا چاہیئے۔ یہاں تک کہ طاہر ہو پھر حائض ہو اور طاہر ہو۔ پھر اگر طلاق دینی چاہے تو ہم بستر ہونے سے پہلے طلاق دے یہ وہ عدت ہے جس کا خدا نے ارشاد فرمایا ہے کہ عورتوں کو اُن کی عدت کے شروع میں طلاق دو اور یہ آیت پڑھی یٰٓاَیُّھَا النَّبِیُّ اِذَا طَلَّقْتُمُ النِّسَآءَ فَطَلِّقُوْھُنَّ لِعِدَّتِھِنَّ۔

۲۹۷۔ کہتے ہیں آنحضرت نے اپنی بیوی اُم المومنین حضرت زینب کے پاس شہد پی لیا۔ جب آپ حضرت عائشہ اور حفصہ کے پاس آئے تو اُن دونوں نے جیسا کہ پہلے صلاح کر رکھی تھی آپ سے کہا کہ آپ کے منہ سے بُو آتی ہے۔ آپ کو بُو سے سخت نفرت تھی تو آپ نے فرمایا کہ میں آئندہ کبھی شہد نہیں پیوں گا بعض کہتے ہیں کہ حضرت حفصہ کو خوش کرنے کے لئے آپ نے ماریہ قبطیہ کو جو آپ کی حرم اور آپ کے صاحبزادے ابراہیم کی والدہ تھیں اپنے اوپر حرام کر لیا تھا تب یہ آیت اُتری ۱۲۔

۲۹۸۔ حلال چیز کو اپنے اوپر حرام کر لینا گویا بُری بات پر قسم کھا لینا ہے تو جو کفارہ قسم توڑ ڈالنے کا ہے وہی حلال چیز کو اپنے اوپر حرام کر کے پھر حلال کر لینے کا ہے اور قسم توڑنے کا کفارہ سورہ مائدہ میں مذکور ہے۔

۲۹۹۔ آنحضرت صلی اللہ علیہ وسلم نے ماریہ کو جو اپنے اوپر حرام کر لیا تو حضرت حفصہ سے فرمایا کہ یہ حال کسی سے بیان نہ کرنا۔ حفصہؓ اور عائشہؓ میں بہت موافقت تھی انہوں نے اسکو حضرت عائشہ رضہ پر ظاہر کر دیا۔ خدا تعالےٰ نے اس حال سے آنحضرت صلی اللہ علیہ وسلم کو مطلع فرمایا ۱۲

۳۰۰۔ ثیبہ اس عورت کو کہتے ہیں جو بیاہ ہو جانے کے بعد بے شوہر ہو گئی ہو۔

۳۰۱۔ خیانت سے مُراد بدکرداری نہیں ہے۔ کیونکہ کبھی کسی پیغمبر کی بیوی سے یہ حرکت صادر نہیں ہوئی۔ یہ خیانت دُوسری باتیں ہیں۔ جو اُنکے شایانِ شان نہ تھیں حضرت نوح کی بیوی کی خیانت تو یہ بیان کی گئی ہے کہ وہ لوگوں سے کہا کرتی تھی کہ نوح دیوانہ ہے۔ اور حضرت لُوط کی بیوی کی خیانت یہ ہے کہ جو مہمان اُن کے ہاں آتا وہ لوگوں کو بتا دیتی تھی۔ اور لوط علیہ السلام کو یہ بات منظور نہ تھی ۱۲۔

۳۰۲۔ پنڈلی سے کپڑا اُٹھا دینے سے مُراد صعوبتِ حال ہے اسی واسطے حضرت ابن عباسؓ کہتے ہیں کہ یہ ایک بڑی سخت ساعت ہوگی۔

۳۰۳۔ یعنی تم کو اس طرح گھور گھور کر دیکھتے ہیں کہ تم ڈر کر پھسل جاؤ۔ یا یہ مُراد ہے کہ یہ تمہیں نظر بد لگانا چاہتے ہیں۔ جس کے اثر سے خدا نے تم کو محفوظ رکھا ہے۔

۳۰۴۔ درجات سے مُراد آسمان ہیں چونکہ وہ درجہ بدرجہ اُوپر تلے ہیں اس لئے اُن کو درجات فرمایا ۱۲۔

۳۰۵۔ ترجمے میں ہم نے رُوح کا لفظ قائم رکھا ہے اور فرشتے سے مقدم کر دیا ہے۔ تقدیم کی وجہ یہ ہے کہ اگر اسکو اپنی جگہ رکھ کر یوں ترجمہ کیا جاتا کہ فرشتے اور روح (الامین) چڑھتے ہیں۔ تو (الامین) کے حذف کر دینے کی صورت میں رُوح کے مؤنث ہونے کی وجہ سے عبارت صحیح نہ تھی۔ دوسرے خود خدا نے سورۂ نبا میں روح کو مقدم کیا ہے اور فرمایا ہے یَوْمَ یَقُوْمُ الرُّوْحُ وَالْمَلٰٓئِکَۃُ صَفًّا روح کے ساتھ (الامین) کا لفظ شامل کرنے سے جبریل علیہ السلام مراد ہوں گے اور بغیر اس کے ارواح ۱۲۔

۳۰۶۔ صبر جمیل اس صبر کو کہتے ہیں جس میں جزع فزع نہ ہو۔ لب پہ حرف شکایت نہ آئے۔ اسی لئے ہم نے یہاں اس کا ترجمہ حوصلے کے ساتھ کیا ہے ۱۲۔

۳۰۷۔ دھنکی ہوئی کا لفظ اسلئے زیادہ کیا گیا ہے کہ سورۂ قارعہ میں عِھْنِ الْمَنْفُوْش فرمایا ہے ۱۲

۳۰۸۔ وَدّ اور سُوَاع اور یَغُوث اور یَعُوق اور نَسر بتوں کے نام ہیں ۱۲

۳۰۹۔ حضرت آغاز وحی میں وحی کے خوف سے کپڑے میں لپیٹ رہتے تھے۔ حدیث میں آیا ہے کہ آپ نے فرشتے کی آواز سنکر اسکی طرف نظر کی تو آپ کا بدن مبارک کانپنے لگا آپ نے گھر میں آکر اہلِ خانہ سے فرمایا کہ زَمِّلُوْنِی دَثِّرُوْنِی یعنی مجھ کو کپڑا اڑھا دو۔ چونکہ خطاب کے وقت آپ کپڑا اوڑھے ہوئے تھے۔ اس حالتِ موجودہ کے لحاظ سے خدا نے مزمل فرمایا ؛

۳۱۰۔ لفظی معنی تو یہ ہیں کہ مجھے اور ان جھٹلانے والوں کو جو دولتمند ہیں چھوڑ دو مگر ہم نے محاورہ اُردو کا لحاظ کیا ہے ۱۲ ؛

۳۱۱۔ حلق میں پھنسنے والا جو نہ اندر جائے نہ باہر آئے ۱۲ ؛

۳۱۲۔ اس آیت کے یہ معنی بھی ہیں کہ اگر تم اُس دن کو نہ مانو گے جو بچوں کو بوڑھا کر دے گا تو کیونکر بچو گے ۱۲ ؛

۳۱۳۔ یہ سُورت آغاز وحی میں نازل ہوئی تھی چونکہ حضرت بوجہ خوف وحی کپڑا اوڑھ لیتے تھے۔ اسلیئے مدثر سے خطاب فرمایا ۱۲ ؛

۳۱۴۔ یہ آیتیں ولید بن مغیرہ کے حق میں نازل ہوئی ہیں یہ شخص بڑا مالدار اور قریش میں ممتاز تھا بیٹے بھی بہت سے رکھتا تھا۔ غرض دنیا میں جو باتیں خوش قسمتی کی سمجھی جاتی ہیں سب اسکو حاصل تھیں۔ ایک دفعہ جو حضرت کے پاس آیا تو آپ نے اسکو قرآن سنایا۔ ایسا شیریں کلام سُنکر پھڑک اُٹھا اور بے ساختہ تعریف کرنے لگا۔ یہ بات ابو جہل کو معلوم ہوئی تو اس نے ولید سے آکر کہا کہ چچا تمہاری برادری کے لوگ تمہارے لئے چندہ جمع کرنا چاہتے ہیں۔ اُسنے کہا کس لئے۔ ابو جہل نے کہا کہ تم محمد کے پاس جاکر اُن کی باتیں سنتے ہو۔ اس نے کہا کہ قریش کو معلوم ہے کہ میں ان سب سے زیادہ دولتمند ہوں تو مجھے اُن کے چندے کی کیا حاجت ہے۔ ابو جہل نے کہا اچھا تو ایسی بات کہو جس سے ثابت ہو کہ تم اُن کے کلام کو پسند نہیں کرتے۔ اُس نے کہا کہ میں اُن کے حق میں کیا کہوں خدا کی قسم تم میں کوئی شخص مجھ سے زیادہ اشعار و قصائد کا عالم نہیں اور میں ان کے کلام کو ہرگز شعر نہیں کہہ سکتا۔ ابو جہل نے کہا جب تک تم اُن کے بارے میں کوئی بات لوگوں کی خواہش کے مطابق تجویز نہ کروگے وہ تم سے خوش نہیں ہونگے۔ آخر اُسنے سوچکر کہا کہ یہ سحر ہے۔ صعود دوزخ میں ایک پہاڑ ہے جس پر کافر کو چڑھا کر نیچے گرا دیا کرینگے۔ بعض نے کہا کہ صعود دوزخ میں ایک بہت بڑا پتھر ہے جس پر کافر کو منہ کے بل گھسیٹیں گے کسی نے کہا کہ صعود جہنم میں ایک چکنا پتھر ہے جس پر کافر کو چڑھنے کے لئے مجبور کرینگے ۱۲

۳۱۵۔ انسان کا جی تین طرح کا ہے۔ ایک جو گناہوں اور بُرے کاموں کی طرف مائل رہے اس کو نفسِ اَمّارہ یا امارہ بالسُّوء کہتے ہیں دوسرا جو برائی اور قصور کے سرزد ہونے پر ملامت کرے کہ تو نے یہ حرکت کیوں کی اُس کو نفسِ لوّامہ کہتے ہیں۔ تیسرا جو نیکیوں کی طرف راغب اور برائیوں سے متنفر ہو ایسا جی بڑے چین میں رہتا ہے اور اسکو نفسِ مطمئنہ کہتے ہیں۔ یہاں خدا نے نفسِ لوّامہ کی قسم کھائی ہے ۱۲

۳۱۶۔ چونکہ مرد اور عورت دونوں کے نطفوں کے ملنے سے بچہ بنتا ہے اسلیئے نطفۂ مخلوط فرمایا ۱۲

۳۱۷۔ کاس ساغرِ شراب کو بھی کہتے ہیں۔ اور کاس کا اطلاق نفسِ شراب پر بھی ہوتا ہے اسی لئے یہاں ہم نے اس کا ترجمہ شراب کیا ۱۲ ؛

۳۱۸۔ جن چیزوں کی یہ صفات بیان کی گئی ہیں ان کی نسبت جمہور کا قول ہے کہ وہ فرشتے ہیں اسی لئے ہم نے ترجمے میں فرشتوں کا لفظ بڑھا دیا ہے ڈوب کر کھینچنے سے مراد نزع ارواح ہے کسی کی روح کو مشکل سے نکالتے ہیں اور کسی کی روح کو آسانی سے گویا بند کھول دیتے ہیں ۱۲ ؛

۳۱۹۔ حضرت ابن عباسؓ کہتے ہیں کہ جناب رسولِ خدا صلی اللہ علیہ وسلم عتبہ بن ابی ربیعہ اور ابو جہل بن ہشام اور عباس بن عبد المطلب سے بڑی توجہ سے باتیں کر رہے تھے کیونکہ آپ دل سے چاہتے تھے کہ وہ اسلام لے آئیں اتنے میں عبد اللہ بن اُمّ مکتوم جو آنکھوں سے معذور تھے آئے اور حضرت سے کہنے لگے کہ مجھ کو قرآن سُنایئے اور جو کچھ خدا نے آپ کو سکھایا ہے وہ مجھے سکھایئے۔ آپ نے اس حالت میں اُنکی بات کو پسند نہ فرمایا اور چیں بجبیں ہو کر اس کی طرف سے منہ پھیر لیا اس پر یہ آیات نازل ہوئیں ۱۲ ؛

۳۲۰۔ یعنی پانی کو زمین میں داخل کیا۔ پھر اناج کے اجزا میں شامل کر کے زمین سے اُسے اُگایا ۱۲ ؛

۳۲۱۔ بُرجوں سے مُراد کواکب یا اُن کی منازل ہیں۔ بُرج عرب میں محل کو کہتے ہیں تاروں کی منزلوں کا نام برج اسلیئے رکھا گیا کہ وہ گویا اُنکے گھر ہیں ؛

۳۲۲۔ شاہد اور مشہود کے معنوں میں مفسرین کے بہت سے اقوال ہیں بعض نے کہا کہ شاہد سے مُراد لوگ ہیں جو قیامت کو حاضر ہونگے اور مشہود سے حالات قیامت ہیں جو مشاہدہ کئے جائینگے۔ بعض نے کہا کہ شاہد روز جمعہ ہے اور مشہود یوم عرفہ کیونکہ جمعہ کا دن سب جگہ آموجود ہوتا ہے۔ اور عرفے کے دن حج میں سب لوگ حاضر ہوتے ہیں۔ کسی نے کہا کہ شاہد عرفے کا دن ہے اور مشہود قربانی کا دن۔ کسی نے کہا کہ شاہد سے مراد خدا ہے اور مشہود سے بندے کہ وہ اُن کے اعمال و افعال کا گواہ ہوگا۔ بعض نے کہا کہ شاہد پیغمبر ہیں اور مشہود اُن کی اُمتیں۔ بعض نے کہا کہ مشہود بنی آدم ہیں اور شاہد اُن کے اعضاء کہ یہ اُن کے عملوں کی شہادت دینگے۔ بعض نے کہا کہ شاہد ملائکہ حفظہ و کاتب اعمال ہیں اور مشہود ابنائے آدم۔ غرض اس قسم کے بہت سے اقوال ہیں مگر راجح یہ ہے کہ شاہد جمعے کا دِن ہے اور مشہود عرفے کا ۱۲ ؛

۳۲۳۔ کہتے ہیں اگلے زمانے میں جبکہ دین میں بہت سی خرابیاں پڑگئیں۔ اور لوگوں میں فتنے اور فساد برپا ہوگئے۔ تو ایک دیندار اور خدا پرست قوم نے الگ ایک گاؤں آباد کیا اور اسمیں رہنے سہنے اور خدا کی عبادت کرنے لگے یہاں تک کہ اس ملک کے کافر ظالم بادشاہ کو اس حال سے اطلاع ہوئی تو اُسنے ان لوگوں کو کہلا بھیجا کہ جن بتوں کو ہم پوجتے ہیں تم بھی انہی کو پوجو انہوں نے انکار کیا اور کہا کہ ہم خدا کے سوا کسی کی عبادت نہ کرینگے۔ کیونکہ وہی ہمارا معبود ہے۔ بادشاہ نے دھمکی دی کہ اگر ہمارے معبودوں کو نہیں پوجو گے تو ہم تم کو قتل

کرا دوں گا اس کا کچھ اثر ان کے دل پر نہ ہوا۔ تب اس نے خندقیں کھدوا کر ان میں آگ جلوا دی اور خود ان کے کنارے پر کھڑے ہو کر ان سے کہنے لگا کہ یا تو ہمارے دین کو قبول کرو یا اس آگ کو اختیار کرو۔ مگر انہوں نے بتوں کو پوجنا منظور نہ کیا اور آگ میں پڑنا منظور کیا۔ یہ حال دیکھ کر عورتیں اور بچے چلا اٹھے۔ دیندار شوہر اور باپ جو خدا پر پورا ایمان رکھتے تھے انہوں نے تسلی دی کہ اسکو آگ نہ سمجھو یہ تمہارے لئے نجات ہے چنانچہ سب کے سب اس میں کود پڑے۔ کہتے ہیں کہ آگ کے شعلے ابھی انکے جسموں تک پہنچنے نہ پائے تھے کہ خدا نے ان کی روحیں قبض کر لیں اور آگ بھڑک کر بادشاہ اور اسکے اراکین میں جو کنارے پر کھڑے تھے جا لگی اور سب کو جلا کر خاک کر دیا ۱۲۔

۳۲۴۔ دلوں کے بھید جاننے سے یہ مراد ہے کہ تعلقات اور خیالات ظاہر کر دیئے جائینگے اور اچھے برے ممیز ہو جائینگے ۱۲۔

۳۲۵۔ یعنی اسمیں سے اناج اور درخت وغیرہ پھوٹ نکلتے ہیں ۱۲۔

۳۲۶۔ دس راتوں کی تعیین میں مختلف اقوال ہیں بعض کہتے ہیں کہ ان سے عشرہ ذی الحجہ مراد ہے بعض کا قول ہے کہ عشرۂ اول رمضان مراد ہے مگر کوئی دلیل اس پر نہیں کہ اس آیت سے یہی عشرات مراد ہیں ۱۲۔

۳۲۷۔ عاد دو تھے۔ عاد اولیٰ جن کو ارم کہتے ہیں دوسرا عاد ثمود۔ عاد ارم حضرت ہودؑ کی امت کے لوگ تھے۔ ارم اسکے قبیلے کا نام تھا ۱۲۔

۳۲۸۔ ثمود حضرت صالح علیہ السلام کی قوم کا نام ہے یہ لوگ ایسے کاریگر تھے کہ پہاڑوں میں پتھر تراش تراش کر گھر بناتے تھے۔ اور ان میں رہتے سہتے تھے ۱۲۔

۳۲۹۔ مفسرین نے حِلٌّ کے معنی حلال بھی کئے ہیں اور لکھا ہے کہ خدا نے اس شہر میں مقاتلہ ہمیشہ کیلئے حرام کیا ہے مگر جناب رسول خدا صلی اللہ علیہ وسلم کے لئے اس میں فتح مکہ کے دن قتال کرنا جائز کیا تھا۔ اس بناء پر آیت یوں ہونا چاہیئے کہ تم کو اس شہر میں قتال حلال ہونے والا ہے۔ مگر ہمارے نزدیک زیادہ مناسب یہ ہے کہ حِلٌّ کے معنی حال یعنی ساکن و نازل لئے جائیں اور اسی وجہ سے ہم نے یہ ترجمہ کیا ہے کہ تم اسی شہر میں تو رہتے ہو اس صورت میں مکہ معظمہ کی دوسری فضیلتوں میں سے ایک یہ فضیلت بھی اس کی قسم کھانے کا موجب ہو گی کہ وہ حضرت خاتم النبیینؐ کا مسکن تھا ۱۲۔

۳۳۰۔ خدا نے حضرت صالح کو ایک اونٹنی معجزے کے طور پر دی تھی۔ جو ایک بڑے بھاری پتھر میں سے نکالی گئی تھی صالح علیہ السلام نے ان لوگوں سے کہا کہ یہ اونٹنی خدا کی ہے۔ اس کو بری طرح ہاتھ نہ لگانا۔ اور جو دن اسکے پانی پینے کا ہو۔ اس میں تعرض نہ کرنا۔ انہوں نے یہ بات نہ مانی اور ایک نہایت بدبخت شخص نے جس کا نام قدار بن سالف تھا۔ اونٹنی کے پاؤں کاٹ دیئے۔ اس وجہ سے ان سب پر عذاب نازل ہوا ۱۲۔

۳۳۱۔ حضرت پر چند روز وحی کے آنے میں توقف ہو گیا تو آپ پریشان خاطر رہتے۔ کافروں نے کہنا شروع کیا کہ محمد کا رب اس سے ناراض ہو گیا ہے اور اسکو چھوڑ دیا ہے اس پر یہ سورت نازل ہوئی۔ اس میں پہلے تو کافروں کی بات کی تردید کی ہے۔ پھر اظہار احسانات کیا ہے پھر نصیحتیں فرمائی ہیں آپ ابھی بطنِ مادری ہی میں تھے کہ والد کا انتقال ہو گیا چھ برس کے ہوئے کہ والدہ بھی فوت ہو گئیں۔ پہلے آپکے دادا عبد المطلب پرورش کرتے رہے ان کے مرنے کے بعد آپ کے چچا ابو طالب متکفل ہوئے۔ وہ آپ کی ہمیشہ مدد و حمایت اور عزت و حرمت کرتے رہے۔ یہاں تک کہ خدا نے آپ کو پیغمبر کیا۔ رستے سے مراد یہی دین حق کا رستہ ہے جو آپ کو معلوم نہ تھا۔ وہ پیغمبر بنا کر دکھا دیا۔ اور حضرت خدیجہ جو بڑی مالدار تھیں۔ ان سے نکاح کرا کر افلاس دور کر دیا ۱۲۔

۳۳۲۔ حضرت صلعم پر جو وحی سب سے پہلے نازل ہوئی وہ اسی صورت کی یہی پہلی پانچ آیتیں ہیں۔ یہ آیتیں غار حرا میں نازل ہوئیں۔ جہاں آپ تشریف لے جا کر تنہائی میں عبادت کیا کرتے تھے۔ آپ فرماتے ہیں کہ جب فرشتے نے آ کر مجھ سے کہا کہ پڑھو تو میں نے کہا کہ میں پڑھا ہوا نہیں ہوں تو اس نے مجھے پکڑ کر دبایا یہاں تک کہ میں تھک گیا پھر چھوڑ دیا اور کہا کہ پڑھو میں نے کہا کہ مجھے پڑھنا نہیں آتا پھر دوبارہ مجھ کو دبایا یہاں تک کہ میں تھک گیا۔ پھر چھوڑ دیا۔ اور کہا کہ پڑھو میں نے کہا کہ میں پڑھنا نہیں جانتا پھر تیسری بار دبایا یہاں تک کہ میں تھک کر چور ہو گیا پھر چھوڑ دیا اور کہا اِقْرَأْ بِاسْمِ رَبِّكَ الَّذِي خَلَقَ سے اور مَا لَمْ يَعْلَمْ تک پہنچا۔ اسکے بعد آپ خوف کے سبب کانپتے کانپتے حضرت خدیجہ کے پاس آئے اور کہا کہ مجھے لحاف اڑھا دو جب خوف دور ہوا تو آپ نے اپنا حال بیان فرمایا۔ خدیجہ نے آپ کو تسلی دی اور ورقہ بن نوفل (اپنے چچازاد بھائی) کے پاس لے گئیں۔ یہ بوڑھے شخص دور جاہلیت میں عیسائی ہو گئے تھے۔ انہوں نے آپ سے یہ ماجرا سنا کر کہا کہ یہ وہی ناموس ہے جو عیسیٰ پر اترا تھا اور خدا نے آپ کو پیغمبر کیا ہے اور یہ بھی کہا کاش میں جوان ہوتا اور جس وقت آپ کی قوم آپ کو وطن سے نکالتی اس وقت تک زندہ رہتا۔ آپ نے پوچھا کیا وہ مجھ کو نکال دیں گے۔ اس نے کہا ہاں۔ جو شخص ایسی چیز لایا کرتا ہے جو آپ لائے ہیں لوگ اس کے دشمن ہو جایا کرتے ہیں اگر میں اس وقت تک جیتا رہوں گا تو تمہاری بہت نصرت و حمایت کروں گا۔ مگر اس کے تھوڑے ہی عرصے کے بعد وہ فوت ہو گئے اور جی کی آرزو جی ہی میں لے گئے ۱۲۔

۳۳۳۔ یہ معنی بھی ہو سکتے ہیں کہ اگر یہ منع کرنے والا شخص راہ راست پر ہوتا اور پرہیزگاری کی باتیں سکھاتا تو کیا اچھا ہوتا مفسرین نے لکھا ہے کہ منع کرنے والے شخص سے مراد ابو جہل ہے جو نماز پڑھتے وقت آپ کو دیکھتا تو چڑاتا۔ خدا نے فرمایا کہ کیا یہ نہیں جانتا کہ خدا اسکے افعال کو دیکھ رہا ہے اور اگر یہ ایسی گستاخیوں سے باز نہ آئے گا تو ہم اس کو گھسیٹ کر جہنم میں داخل کر دیں گے کہتے ہیں کہ دنیا میں بھی اس کو یہ سزا ملی کہ بدر کی لڑائی میں مارا گیا اور گھسیٹ کر گڑھے میں ڈال دیا گیا ۱۲

۳۳۴۔ قرآن مجید ایک ہی دفعہ نازل نہیں ہوا بلکہ پارہ پارہ نازل ہوا ہے۔

پہلے پہل اس کا نزول شبِ قدر میں ہوا اس آیت سے معلوم ہوتا ہے کہ شبِ قدر ماہِ رمضان میں ہے جیسا کہ دوسری جگہ فرمایا ہے ۔۔۔ شَهْرُ رَمَضَانَ الَّذِيْٓ اُنْزِلَ فِيْهِ الْقُرْاٰنُ یہ معلوم نہیں ہوا کہ یہ رات کس تاریخ کو ہوتی ہے ۔ لیکن احادیثِ صحیحہ سے اتنا ثابت ہے کہ حضرت رمضان کے آخری عشرے میں اعتکاف فرمایا کرتے تھے ۔ اور جتنا اہتمام اس عشرے میں فرماتے اور میں نہ فرماتے اکثر مفسرین کا یہ قول ہے کہ اس رات کا عمل ہزار مہینے کے عمل سے افضل ہے ۱۲ ÷

٣٣٥ ۔ یہاں بھی ترجمے میں روح کو فرشتے سے مقدم کیا گیا ہے اسکی وجہ وہی ہے جو سورۂ معارج کی چوتھی آیت کے فائدے میں بیان کی گئی ہے ۔ ۱۲ ÷

٣٣٦ ۔ یمن کا ایک بادشاہ تھا ابرہہ وہ خانۂ کعبہ کو لوگوں کا مرجع دیکھ کر آتشِ حسد میں جلتا تھا اُسنے کعبے کو بے رونق کرنے کی یہ تدبیر نکالی کہ ایک بتخانہ تعمیر کیا اور ایک عام حکم جاری کر دیا کہ سب لوگ وہاں پرستش کیلئے آئیں مگر وہ اسکی طرف مطلق متوجہ نہ ہوئے ۔ ناچار اُس نے خانۂ کعبہ کے ڈھا دینے کا قصد کیا کہ نہ یہ رہے نہ وہاں لوگ عبادت کے لئے جمع ہوں لشکر لے کر چڑھا تو بہت سے ہاتھی بھی ساتھ لایا جب یہ لوگ کعبے کے قریب پہنچے تو عبد المطلب نے ان سے جاکر کہا کہ یہ خدا کا گھر ہے ۔ اس پر کوئی شخص قدرت نہ پاسکے گا اور نہ اسکو ڈھا سکے گا ۔ انہوں نے کہا جب تک ہم اس کو ڈھا نہ لینگے یہاں سے ٹلنے کے نہیں ۔ خدا کی قدرت دیکھو کہ پرندوں کے جھنڈ کے جھنڈ چونچوں اور پنجوں میں کنکر لئے ہوئے وہاں آموجود ہوئے اور ان لوگوں پر کنکر برسانے شروع کئے جس پر کنکر لگتا کیا ہاتھی اور کیا سوار ہلاک ہو کر رہ جاتا غرض تمام لشکر ہاتھیوں سمیت برباد ہو گیا اور خدا نے خانۂ کعبہ کو بچا لیا ۔ اس سورت میں اس واقعے کا ذکر ہے ۱۲

٣٣٧ ۔ حضرت کی بارہویں پشت میں ایک شخص نضر بن کنانہ تھا ۔ اسکی اولاد قریش ہیں ۔ یہ بیت اللہ کے خادم تھے اور لوگ ان کا بہت ادب اور احترام کرتے تھے ۔ اس سورت میں خدا قریش پر اپنا احسان جتاتا ہے کہ وہ جاڑے اور گرمی میں تجارت کے لئے سفر کرتے ہیں اور کوئی ان کو لوٹتا نہیں چین سے کھاتے پیتے اور امن سے رہتے سہتے ہیں تو ان کو چاہیے کہ توحید اختیار کریں اور بتوں کی پرستش کو چھوڑ کر اس گھر کے مالک یعنی خدائے واحد کی عبادت کریں ۔ بعض مفسرین نے لکھا ہے کہ یہ سورت پہلی سورت سے متعلق ہے اور ان کے نزدیک اسکے یہ معنی ہیں کہ ہم نے جو مکے سے ہاتھیوں اور ہاتھی والوں کو روک کر ہلاک کیا تو اس لئے کہ قریش جاڑے اور گرمی کے سفر سے مانوس ہو کر اپنے شہر میں امن و امان سے رہیں ۱۲

٣٣٨ ۔ بہت سی حدیثیں ہیں جن سے ثابت ہوتا ہے کہ کوثر بہشت کی ایک نہر کا نام ہے جو حضرت کو عطا ہوئی ہے ۔ حضرت انس رض سے روایت ہے کہ آنحضرت کو اونگھ آگئی پھر سر اٹھا کر تبسم فرمایا اور تبسم کی یہ وجہ بیان فرمائی کہ ابھی مجھ پر ایک سورت نازل ہوئی ہے اور پھر یہ سورت پڑھی اور فرمایا کہ تم جانتے ہو کہ کوثر کیا چیز ہے ۔ صحابہ رض نے عرض کیا کہ خدا اور رسول ہی جانیں فرمایا وہ ایک نہر ہے جو خدا نے مجھ کو بہشت میں دی ہے ۔ اس میں خیرِ کثیر ہے ۔ لغت میں کوثر خیرِ کثیر کو کہتے ہیں چونکہ شرعی معنی لغوی معنوں پر مقدم ہوتے ہیں اس لئے ہم نے کوثر کے لغوی معنی ترجمے میں اختیار نہیں کئے ۱۲

٣٣٩ ۔ ابتر اسکو کہتے ہیں جس کی اولادِ ذکور میں سے کوئی نہ رہے جب حضرت کے بیٹوں کا انتقال ہو گیا تو بعض کافر کہنے لگے کہ محمد ابتر ہو گیا اسکے بعد کوئی اس کا نام لینے والا نہ رہے گا ۔ خدا نے آپ سے فرمایا کہ تمہارا بد اندیش ہی مقطوع النسل رہے گا اور آپ کا نام آپ کی اُمت کے ذریعے سے ہمیشہ کے لئے باقی رکھا ۱۲

٣٤٠ ۔ ابولہب رشتے میں حضرت کا چچا تھا ۔ مگر بڑا کافر اور آپ کا دشمنِ جانی اس کا نام تو عبد العزیٰ بن عبد المطلب تھا مگر مشہور اسی کنیت سے تھا کیونکہ نہایت حسین و جمیل تھا اور حُسن و جمال کی وجہ سے اس کا چہرہ آگ کی طرح چمکتا تھا جب آپ کو حکم ہوا کہ اپنے قبائل کو متنبہ کردو تو آپ نے قریش کو جمع کر کے فرمایا کہ بھلا اگر میں تم کو خبر دوں کہ دشمن کی فوج صبح یا شام تم پر حملہ کرنے والی ہے ۔ تو تم اس بات کو باور کرو گے ۔ اُنھوں نے کہا ضرور باور کرینگے ۔ آپ نے فرمایا کہ میں تم کو ایک سخت عذاب سے آگاہ کرتا ہوں جو تم پر نازل ہونے والا ہے ۔ تو ابولہب نے کہا کہ تمہارے ہاتھ ٹوٹیں (یعنی تم ہلاک ہو) تم نے ہم کو اسی لئے جمع کیا تھا ؟ اس کے جواب میں یہ آیت نازل ہوئی ۔ ابولہب کی جورو جس کا نام اُمِ جمیل تھا اس کو بھی آپ سے بڑی عداوت تھی ۔ اس لئے یہ شیوہ اختیار کر رکھا تھا کہ رات کو آپ کے رستے میں خاردار لکڑیاں ڈال جاتی تھی اسی لئے اسکو حَمَّالَةَ الْحَطَبِ فرمایا ۔
بعض نے کہا کہ اس سے مراد چغلخور ہے کہ وہ چغلخوری کیا کرتی تھی ۔ گلے کی رسی سے یہ مراد ہے کہ وہ قیامت کے روز جہنم کا ایندھن اٹھا اٹھا کر اپنے شوہر پر ڈالے گی تا کہ اس کا عذاب زیادہ ہوتا رہے گویا اس کام کے لئے تیار ہے اور اسی لئے اپنے گلے میں مونج کی رسی ڈالے رہتی ہے کسی نے کہا کہ اس سے مراد دوزخ کی رسی ہے جو اس کے گلے میں ڈالی جائے گی ۔ وَاللّٰهُ اَعْلَمُ بِالصَّوَابِ